Health and Safety

Redgrave Fife & Machin

Health and Safety

Second edition

John Hendy LLB, LLM, QC
of Gray's Inn

Michael Ford LLB, MA
of the Middle Temple, barrister

Consultant editor for Scotland
Douglas Brodie LLB, PhD
Lecturer in Law, University of Edinburgh

Butterworths
London, Dublin, Edinburgh
1993

United Kingdom	Butterworth & Co (Publishers) Ltd, 88 Kingsway, LONDON WC2B 6AB and 4 Hill Street, EDINBURGH EH2 3JZ
Australia	Butterworths, SYDNEY, MELBOURNE, BRISBANE, ADELAIDE, PERTH, CANBERRA and HOBART
Belgium	Butterworth & Co (Publishers) Ltd, BRUSSELS
Canada	Butterworths Canada Ltd, TORONTO and VANCOUVER
Ireland	Butterworth (Ireland) Ltd, DUBLIN
Malaysia	Malayan Law Journal Sdn Bhd, KUALA LUMPUR
New Zealand	Butterworths of New Zealand Ltd, WELLINGTON and AUCKLAND
Puerto Rico	Butterworth of Puerto Rico, Inc, SAN JUAN
Singapore	Butterworths Asia, SINGAPORE
USA	Butterworth Legal Publishers, CARLSBAD, California; and SALEM, New Hampshire

A CIP Catalogue record for this book is available from the British Library.

First edition 1990
Reprinted 1991 and 1992

ISBN 0 406 02278 X

Typeset by Thomson Litho Ltd, East Kilbride, Scotland
Printed by Clays Ltd, Bungay, Suffolk

PREFACE

This is, in effect, the 25th edition of *Redgrave's Health and Safety in Factories* (first published in 1878) and the 3rd edition of *Redgrave's Health and Safety* (first published in 1980). These two books were amalgamated in the 1990 edition of *Redgrave, Fife and Machin: Health and Safety*. That volume contained within it most of the health, safety and welfare legislation covering the major fields of employment with the principal exclusions of mines and quarries and the offshore oil and gas industry. It was a major achievement and *Redgrave* (or "Bluegrave" as the colour of its cover led it to be affectionately called) was the universal bible for inspectors, barristers, solicitors, engineers, managers, union officials and everyone else concerned with safety in British industry. We approach our task with great diffidence in the shadow of our predecessors' achievement.

The current edition takes forward the aims of Anthony Machin and the late Ian Fife to present in one volume all the statutory and subsidiary legislation on health and safety at work. We have been able to include the offshore legislation with the changes following the Piper Alpha disaster and the Cullen Report (Cmd. 1310 of 1990). We had hoped that the mines and quarries legislation could also be brought in but even with the increase in size and pages that proved not possible. Lack of space is the reason why health and safety legislation in respect of merchant shipping, aviation, and explosives remains outside *Redgrave*, at least for this edition. We have been able to include one longstanding omission: the Employers' Liability (Defective Equipment) Act 1969 but not the Occupiers' Liability Act 1957 or the Consumer Protection Act 1987 which protect workers as well as the general public.

The expanded size and length of this edition of *Redgrave* has been caused principally by the need to accommodate the numerous progeny of the European economic union.

The current edition marks a revolution as great if not greater than the Health and Safety at Work etc. Act 1974. The European Directives have landed. They have changed the face of British health and safety law. The principal Regulations to implement the Directives became law on 1 January 1993 and much of our old legislation has gone in consequence. There is a period of grace until 1 January 1996 for workplaces in existence on 31 December 1992 during which time much of the old law remains applicable. The period of grace for work equipment in existence on 31 December 1992 is until 1 January 1997.

The new law is based on concepts relatively novel in our law, in particular "risk assessment". The emphasis is very heavily on suppression of dangers before they arise wherever that can be achieved rather than guarding against risks which have been allowed to occur. At the same time the former approach, of piece-meal legislation directed towards particular kinds of workplace or work processes, is progressively to be replaced by legislation of general application.

The British Regulations giving effect to the European Directives differ from them to some extent. It remains to be seen whether this will lead to legal challenge. We have included the principal Directives as well as the implementing Regulations for this reason and because the Directives will be the guide to construction of the Regulations. Furthermore, the Directives will have direct effect in relation to employers which constitute emanations of the State. Space has not permitted the inclusion of the Approved Codes of Practice ("ACOPS") and Guidance Notes which accompany the Regulations.

The new emphasis in the legislation which directs its application to the nature of the risk rather than to the nature of the workplace or the process, has caused us to reorder the material in this edition. We hope this will provide easier access to it. In particular, as well as a new section for the principal European Directives, we have created new sections to group together statutory material dealing with equipment and substances where the applicable legislation applies to all workplaces. We have returned to the section on factories those Regulations which apply principally to factory premises. As developments in this area of the law can be rapid, it is our intention to produce annual supplements.

Like our predecessors we are grateful for the co-operation of the HSE and the help and meticulous hard work of Butterworths staff. We would also like to thank Douglas Brodie of the University of Edinburgh for his great assistance and authoritative work in fortifying this edition with Scottish material. We, of course, take responsibility for any errors.

15 Old Square	John Hendy
Lincoln's Inn	Michael Ford
London WC2A 3UH	1 December 1993

Stop press
After the text had been sent to press, two omitted items came to our attention: on page 2119, s. 25 (application to Scotland) of the Agriculture (Safety, Health and Welfare Provisions) Act 1956, as amended by S.I. 1975 No. 46 and S.I. 1977 No. 746; and on page 2378 the Certificate of Exemption No. DOW/2/88 attached to the Diving Operations at Work Regulations 1981. These items will be included in the 1994 supplement.

CONTENTS

CONTENTS

TABLE OF STATUTES

References in this Table to *Statutes* are to Halsbury's Statutes of England (Fourth Edition) showing the volume and page at which the annotated text of the Act will be found. Page references printed in **bold** type indicate where the Act is set out in part or in full.

ALPHABETICAL TABLE OF ORDERS AND REGULATIONS

References in **bold** type indicate where the Order or Regulations are set out in part or in full.

CHRONOLOGICAL TABLE OF ORDERS AND REGULATIONS

References in **bold** type indicate where the Order or Regulations are set out in part or in full.

TABLE OF EUROPEAN COMMUNITIES LEGISLATION

References in **bold** type indicate where the Directive is set out in part or in full.

TABLE OF CASES

Y

HISTORICAL INTRODUCTION

Legislative beginnings

The common law completely failed to develop any health and safety protection for employees. Doubtless in feudal times it was customary for a master to make an ex gratia payment to an injured servant but there appears to be no precedent for an action for damages based on breach of a duty of care (in contract or tort) until *Priestley v Fowler* (1837) 3 M & W 1 (see below).

The first Act of Parliament intended to protect the welfare of people at work was passed 35 years earlier. Towards the end of the eighteenth century the increasing pace of industrial revolution and its concentration of labour in factories and mills utilising powered technology had brought with it growing publicity about the conditions of those (particularly children) employed in such establishments. Largely in consequence of the revelations of the abuse of children in the textile mills, Sir Robert Peel introduced a Bill in 1802, passed the same year with little or no opposition.

The "Act for the preservation of the Health and Morals of Apprentices and others employed in Cotton and other Mills, and Cotton and other Factories" (Geo. 3, c. 73) was directed to the due cleansing of such premises by two washings with quicklime yearly, to the admission of fresh air by means of a sufficient number of windows, and to the yearly supply to every apprentice of sufficient and suitable clothing and sleeping accommodation (not more than two to a bed). The pauper apprentices were prohibited from night work, and their labour limited to 12 hours in the day. The Act provided that the apprentices should be instructed in reading, writing, arithmetic and the principles of the Christian religion and that those who were members of the Church of England should be examined annually by a clergyman, and be prepared at the proper age for confirmation. The Magistrates were to appoint two inspectors from amongst themselves (one being a clergyman) to visit the factories and mills annually and such premises in the locality were to be registered with the Clerk to the Justices.

Legislation in 1819, 1825 and 1831 was intended to fortify the 1802 Act, which was widely evaded. The 1831 Act imposed a maximum 12 hour day for all young people in cotton mills. It too was evaded. Pressure from the "Ten Hours Movement" resulted in the Factory Act 1833 which, though maintaining a 12 hour maximum day for young persons, was extended in scope to woollen and linen mills. Most significantly, in order to prevent further evasion, it provided for enforcement by Government appointed inspectors.

Four inspectors were initially appointed. The Act gave them powers of entry, power to make regulations, and the enforcement powers of the Magistrates.

The case of *Priestley v Fowler* (1837) 3 M & W 1 appeared to establish, for the first time, that an employer owed, in common law, a duty of care to his employee which was actionable by the employee if breach resulted in injury. *Priestley v Fowler* and *Bartonshill Coal Co v Reid* (1858) 3 Macq 266 and 300 also established the existence of the doctrine of common employment. Under this common law principle if the cause of the injury to the plaintiff employee was the negligence of a fellow employee, the employer was not to be held vicariously liable unless the plaintiff employee could prove that the fellow worker was incompetent and that the employer had thereby been negligent in engaging him.

li

Even in large scale factory or other industrial undertakings where the employer had no personal role at all and all functions were delegated to subordinates (who, from the managing director downwards, were in common employment), the doctrine held sway (*Wilson v Merry & Cunningham* (1868) LR 1 Sc & Div 326, HL). The dead hand of the doctrine of common employment meant that civil law as a means of regulating unsafe or unhealthy working conditions was gravely limited.

Safety legislation
In 1842 the first Report (on mines) of the Children's Employment Commission was published. Its descriptions of the sufferings of women and children working underground led to the Coal Mines Act 1842 which simply prohibited women and children from underground work. The radical nature of this measure undoubtedly eased the way for the milder Factories Act of 1844. The first Mines Inspector was appointed in 1843.

It may be said that the first safety statutes, as opposed to health and welfare legislation, were the Factories Act 1844 (which required safeguarding of mill gearing and prohibited the cleaning of machinery in motion) and the Coal Mines Inspection Act 1850.

These two Acts were also significant in giving the Home Secretary power to award part of any fine imposed on an employer to a worker injured by the criminal breach. This form of compensation was not used extensively and fell into virtual disuse by the end of the century, being finally abolished in 1959.

Between 1844 and 1856 a succession of seven factory statutes and subordinate regulations provided for the safety of children, young persons, and women, including provision for the fencing of machinery, hours, mealtimes and holidays. Under pressure from factory owners the 1856 Act relaxed some of the requirements of the 1844 Act and the judges undermined the Ten Hours Act of 1857 by legitimating children and women working in relays (*Ryder v Mills* (1850) 3 Exch 853). However the pressure for protection proved the more powerful as subsequent history demonstrated.

In 1864 and 1867 specified non-textile factories (including pottery, match-making, foundries, blastfurnaces, copper mills and all manufacturing processes employing more than 50 people) and workshops were subjected to some of the statutory requirements. In 1875 the Explosives Act introduced a system for the licensing and regulation of factories for the production of gunpowder and other explosives.

The inadequacy of the common law in health and safety had been yet further underlined. In *Clarke v Holmes* (1862) 7 H & N 937 established that an employer must provide and maintain safe machinery but *Wilson v Merry & Cunningham* (above), followed by *Allen v New Gas Co* (1876) 1 Ex D 251, established that the employer could, under the doctrine of common employment, avoid the liability for defective machinery by simply delegating to a subordinate the responsibility for making and keeping it safe. It was not until the Employers' Liability Act 1880 that the doctrine of common employment was tempered by some statutory limitations on the device of delegation.

By 1875 the law relating to factories and workshops had come to be contained in a patchwork of ad hoc statutes and regulations, each designed to meet the need (or accommodate the pressure) of the moment without regard to any general pattern of development. In these circumstances, the law was reviewed by a Royal Commission, whose report, published in 1876, led to the passing of the Factory and Workshop Act 1878. This Act may be said to be the first attempt at comprehensive factory legislation.

However, hardly was it upon the statute book than further extensions of the law were found necessary. Additional factory statutes were passed piecemeal, in 1883, 1889, 1891, 1895 and 1897. Soon the former chaos was restored.

In 1876 the first legislative provision against "coffin ships" gave some protection to merchant seamen. The first legislative steps directed towards safety in agriculture had been taken with the passing of the Threshing Machines Act 1878, and the Chaff-Cutting Machines (Accidents) Act 1897. Thereafter, despite the increasing mechanisation of the industry, workers in agriculture enjoyed no statutory protection save in the limited area covered by those Acts, since the Factories Acts did not apply (*per* Somervell LJ in *Hendon Corpn v Stanger* [1948] 1 KB 571, CA). From 1886 the working hours of shop workers had been regulated and in 1900 the first legislation to protect railway workers was enacted.

In 1898 the landmark decision of *Groves v Lord Wimborne* [1898] 2 QB 402, CA established that an injured employee could found a claim in damages for breach of statutory duty, in that case in respect of unfenced machinery. Damages claims henceforth became a prominent feature of health and safety law. Claims for breach of statutory duty rapidly overtook in significance common law claims which remained crippled by the doctrine of common employment despite the decision, seven years before the *Groves* case, of *Smith v Baker & Sons* [1891] AC 325, HL. The latter case effectively limited the doctrine of consent (see below) which had been used in tandem with common employment to defeat employees' claims.

One year before *Groves*, in 1897, the first of the Workman's Compensation Acts introduced scale payments by employers to employees in certain industries who suffered injury "arising out of and in the course of employment", one of the most litigated phrases in the English language.

Consolidation in the twentieth century
A fresh attempt at the rationalisation of factory legislation was made by the enactment of the Factory and Workshop Act 1901. It was followed by a series of detailed Regulations, many still in force. This Act remained the principal statute for the regulation of factories until its repeal by the Factories Act 1937, and during its life it was many times extended and amended.

In 1911 a comprehensive Mines Act had been passed, following earlier comprehensive legislation in 1872 and 1888. The 1911 Act provided a novel means of enforcement, the workmen's inspectors, the forerunners of which may be found in the shape of the checkweighmen recognised in the 1872 Coal Mines Regulation Act. Employees' safety representatives had no statutory existence in other workplaces until 1977. The 1872 Act had also provided for imprisonment as a penal sanction, a means of enforcement continued in the subsequent mines statutes, but not extended for a hundred years to other legislation which relied on fines as the penal sanction.

The Factories Act 1937 had repealed and replaced the Factory and Workshops Act 1901 to 1929, and other cognate enactments, but the subordinate legislation made thereunder, including, most importantly, the regulations for dangerous trades was continued in force as if made under the Factories Act 1937. This Act provided, for the first time, a comprehensive code for safety, health and welfare applicable to all factories alike irrespective of whether they were textile or non-textile factories and whether mechanical power was used or not. The many new requirements under this Act included such important safety provisions as those relating to lifting tackle and cranes, floors and stairs, means of access and places of work and steam and air receivers. Electrical stations, ships under repair in harbour or wet-dock and works of engineering construction were also brought within the scope of the legislation. The Factories Act 1937 contained a power to make regulations governing dangerous processes or plant, although owing to the wide range of such regulations made under the similar powers of the Act of 1901, it was not found necessary to make extensive use of this power, save for bringing older regulations up to date and for regulating new kinds of industry.

The Factories Act 1937 was in turn amended by the Factories Acts of 1948 and 1959. These statutes, together with the Lead Paint (Protection against Poisoning) Act 1926, the Employment of Women and Young Persons Act 1936, and s. 7 of the Slaughter-houses Act 1958, were repealed and replaced by the Factories Act 1961, a consolidating measure, which came into operation on 1 April 1962, and which still stands unrepealed. The Factories Act 1961, like its predecessors, contained power to make regulations governing dangerous processes and plant.

The Workman's Compensation Acts were replaced in 1946 by the National Insurance (Industrial Injuries) Act, with scaled benefits provided by the state and funded by contributions paid by employer and employee. Special provision was made for pneumoconiosis by the Pneumoconiosis (Workers' Compensation) Act 1979. Industrial injury (but not disablement) benefit was substituted by sickness benefit (but without the normal contribution requirements for that benefit) by the Social Security and Housing Benefit Act 1982.

By the early twentieth century the doctrine of common employment had become an embarrassment to the common law. *Wilsons and Clyde Coal v English* [1938] AC 57, HL is the most important of several cases in the 1930s and 40s which limited the doctrine of common employment by imposing on employers a personal, non-delegable duty to provide a safe system of work. These cases also concluded the line of authority which began with *Smith v Baker* (above) by holding that employees were not to be taken to have consented by virtue of an implied term in the contract of employment to the risk of the employer's negligent performance of it. *Wheeler v New Merton Board Mills* [1933] 2 KB 669, CA confirmed that *volenti non fit injuria* was no defence to breach of an employer's personal duty of care (though it still remains as a — rare — defence to an employer's vicarious liability for breach of a statutory duty delegated to another employee of similar status, e.g. *ICI Ltd v Shatwell* [1965] AC 656, HL). In 1948 the Law Reform (Personal Injuries) Act finally put an end to the doctrine of common employment.

Three years earlier the Law Reform (Contributory Negligence) Act 1945 disarmed contributory negligence as a complete defence to a damages claim against an employer, thus redressing the House of Lords' decision in *Caswell v Powell Duffryn Associated Collieries Ltd* [1940] AC 152 which held that proof of contributory negligence was a complete defence to a damages claim for breach of statutory duty just as for negligence. From 1945 proof of contributory negligence was relevant only to a reduction of the plaintiff's damages.

These developments re-established actions in negligence as a means parallel to actions for breach of statutory duty in compensating employees for injury. In particular, *Wilsons and Clyde Coal* further extended the common law by establishing that the employer's duty (in negligence) was not only to provide a competent staff of men but also adequate material, a proper system of work, and effective supervision.

The Gowers Committee of Enquiry on Health, Welfare and Safety in Non-Industrial Employment, reporting in 1949 (Cmd. 7664), recommended that safety, health and welfare legislation should be extended over a wide field of non-industrial employment, including agriculture. The Agriculture (Poisonous Substances) Act 1952 and the Agriculture (Safety, Health and Welfare Provisions) Act 1956 were two of the results.

Two years earlier the comprehensive provisions of the Mines and Quarries Act 1954 had been enacted, imposing the most extensive safety regime in any industry. It involved not only regulation in relation to equipment, places, access, egress, processes, specific hazards and methods of working but also laid statutory duties on mine managers, required pit deputies to make inspections, gave workmen's inspectors powers of inspection, and extended the functions of the Inspectors of Mines.

Although shopworkers' hours had been regulated since 1886 and local authorities had powers to limit the opening hours of shops since 1904, no other statutory protection extended to shop workers and none at all to office workers. The Gowers Committee had in 1949 recommended extension and in 1960 a private members' bill had become the Offices Act 1960. In 1963 it was repealed and replaced by the Offices, Shops and Railway Premises Act 1963. That Act gave statutory protection to the largest remaining group of unprotected workers.

Other sectors of the workforce have subsequently been brought in as, for example, offshore workers under the Mineral Workings (Offshore Installations) Act 1971. In the wake of the Cullen Report (1990, Cmd. 1310) into the Piper Alpha oilrig disaster, the offshore industry is now subject to the Offshore Safety Act 1992 and the Offshore Safety (Protection against Unfair Dismissal) Act 1992.

From the Explosives Act 1875 (itself superseded by the Explosives Act 1923), onwards particular industrial hazards to the public as well as the workforce have been the subject of statutory regulation. Examples are: the Alkali etc. Works Regulation Act 1906, the Petroleum (Consolidation) Act 1928, the Radioactive Substances Act 1960 and the Nuclear Installations Acts 1959, 1965 and 1969.

One hazard of very general risk is fire. The Fire Precautions Act 1971 brought together provisions in a number of unrelated pieces of legislation dealing with particular classes of premises and particular activities and was extended to all factory, office, shop and railway premises by the Fire Precautions (Factories, Offices, Shop and Railway Premises) Order 1989, S.I. 1989 No 76.

In 1969 two important statutes were passed. The Employers' Liability (Compulsory Insurance) Act required that all employers carry insurance to cover potential liability to employees, and the Employers' Liability (Defective Equipment) Act provided that the employer is liable in negligence for injury caused by defective equipment notwithstanding that the fault was that of a third party manufacturer or supplier.

There is no doubt that a variety of factors led to the introduction of the century and a half of legislation outlined above. Public outrage at the gross exploitation of employees, particularly women and children, public horror at major industrial disasters, public distaste at a particular lacuna in the law exhibited in a widely publicised case, trade union pressure on behalf of the employees, the response of the large (unregulated) farm-owning aristocracy to the rising power of the industrialists, parliamentary responses to the electorate and pure humanitarian instincts, all played a part. One factor, particularly in the nineteenth century, was incontestably influential. It was the pressure from large manufacturers, sensitive to public demand for safer conditions and often able to accommodate it by their investment in more productive technology, who were determined that their smaller competitors would not undercut the formers' production costs by working excessive hours or refusing to introduce safety measures.

Rationalisation in the 1970s

In 1974 the legislative approach to health and safety was transformed. The Robens Report (1992 Cmd. 5034) was the product of the first comprehensive review of "the safety and health of persons in the course of their employment (other than transport workers ...)". The Report quoted from Sidney Webb's 1919 preface to Hutchins and Harrison's *A History of Factory Legislation*:

> "This century of experiment in factory legislation affords a typical example of English practical empiricism ... Each successive statute aimed at remedying a single ascertained evil. It was in vain the objectors urged that other evils, no more defensible existed in other trades, or amongst other classes, or with persons of ages other than those to which a particular Bill applied ..."

In consequence the Report recommended that in place of what the Report described as the "haphazard and mass of ill assorted and intricate detail" of the existing legislation, there should be:

> "a comprehensive and orderly set of revised provisions under a new enabling Act. The new Act should contain a clear statement of the basic principles of safety responsibility. It should be supported by regulations and by non-statutory codes of practice, with emphasis on the latter. A determined effort should be made to revise, harmonise and update the existing large body of detailed statutory regulations, to simplify their style and to reduce their number ... The scope of the new legislation should extend to all employers and employees ... [and] to the self employed ..."

Thus was the Health and Safety at Work Act 1974 born. Work towards the objective of an orderly and universal set of revised provisions has continued. Many new and more general Regulations have been passed and much outmoded subsidiary legislation has been swept away. Codes of Practice (s. 16 and s. 17) have moved to the forefront of the regulatory regime. But the principal Acts regulating factories, offices, shops, railway premises, mines, quarries and agriculture remain.

One objective, the fulfilment of which may be doubted, was expressed by the Robens Report as "the most fundamental conclusion to which our investigations have led us". It was that "we need a more effectively self regulating system". Whether the Health and Safety at Work Act achieved that goal or not, it may be that from the 1990s the emphasis of the European Directives on employers' obligations to make risk assessments will go a long way to attaining this.

The provisions of the 1974 Act relating to health, safety and welfare in connection with work are principally contained in Part I (ss. 1–54). Part II (ss. 55–60) concerns the Employment Medical Advisory Service, which had been constituted under the Employment Medical Advisory Service Act 1972, the provisions of which have been repealed save to the extent that they amended existing legislation. Part III (ss. 61–76) modifies the law relating to building regulations under ss. 61 and 62 of the Public Health Act 1936; it is not reproduced in this book. Part IV (ss. 77–85) contains miscellaneous and general provisions and includes (s. 80(1)) a sweeping power to repeal or modify, by regulation, any provision of the 1974 Act if it appears expedient to do so in consequence of or in connection with any provision made by or under Part I of the 1974 Act.

The 1974 Act applies to employment generally, and not to specific categories of employment only. The duties of an employer towards his employee are statutorily prescribed in general terms (s. 2(1), (2)). Those duties are very much a recitation of the employers' duties at common law. An employer is obliged to provide a statement of health and safety policy in the employment (s. 2(3)). There is a duty to consult with employees' representatives (s. 2(6)). General duties with regard to the safety of persons other than employees are also imposed upon employers and the self-employed (s. 3) and on persons having control of non-domestic premises (s. 4). There is a duty to prevent the emission of harmful substances into the atmosphere (s. 5) and manufacturers and suppliers of articles for use at work are placed under specific duties in relation to the safety of such articles (s. 6). Employees are required to take reasonable care for the health and safety of themselves and others (ss. 7, 8).

The primary duties on employers and employees set out in ss. 2–8 are all qualified by the phrase "so far as is reasonably practicable". Breach of these duties is expressly not actionable in civil proceedings: s. 47(1). This statutory exclusion does not affect common law liability. Thus though, as noted above, those statutory duties by and large restate the common law position, the right of action to claim damages for injury and loss is only available at common law in respect of breach of its parallel duties. The s. 47(1) exclusion does not apply to duties arising from Regulations made under the Act, breach of which is therefore actionable unless the Regulations provide otherwise (s. 47(2)).

The Act fulfilled another Robens recommendation: that there be a unified national health and safety authority and a unified inspectorate. The Health and Safety Commission and Health and Safety Executive were created (s. 10). Under the ultimate control of the Secretary of State (s. 12) the Commission must (by s. 11) do such things and make such arrangements as it considers appropriate for the general purposes of Part I. The general functions of the Commission are specified in ss. 11, 13, 14 and 16. In particular, it is to be noted that the Commission is empowered to approve and issue the Codes of Practice (referred to above) for the purpose of providing practical guidance with respect to the requirements of any statutory provision in relation to health and safety at work (s. 12).

The Executive, which is under the general control of the Commission (s. 11(4)), is the body principally responsible for enforcing the 1974 Act (s. 18) and for exercising, on behalf of the Commission, such of the Commission's functions as it is directed to exercise (s. 11(4)).

The 1974 Act empowers every enforcing authority to appoint inspectors (s. 19) whose powers are widely defined (ss. 20–25). Particularly to be noted are the powers to issue improvement and prohibition notices (ss. 21–23), requiring the remedying of a contravention of statutory provisions or directing the cessation of activities giving rise to risk of serious personal injury, and the power to deal with a cause of imminent danger of serious personal injury due to the presence of articles in premises which an inspector has power to enter (s. 25). The functions of the factory and other inspectorates have now been transferred to the health and safety inspectorate.

The making of Regulations (s. 15, s. 80 and Sch. 3) to repeal, modify, replace, or add to the existing body of statutes and statutory instruments is the primary means by which the objectives of the Act (to secure the health, safety and welfare of persons at work etc.) are to be achieved (s. 1). These Regulations and the Codes of Practice (s. 16 and s. 17) to support them are required to be "designed to maintain or improve the standards of health, safety and welfare established by or under [the existing legislation]" (s. 1(2)).

Regulations have repealed and modified not only subsidiary legislation but also parts of the principal Acts of 1954, 1956, 1961 and 1963.

The European revolution
The transformation of statutory provision for health and safety at work brought about by the Robens Report and the Health and Safety at Work Act 1974 occurred shortly after Britain joined the "common market" by enacting the European Communities Act 1972. Few can then have detected the movement in air currents in Brussels which were to strengthen twenty years later to a wind of change for health and safety at work law far more radical in substantive terms than was the 1974 legislation.

The post-war movement towards European integration first found form in the Treaty establishing the European Coal and Steel Community in 1951. To this was added the Treaty setting up the European Atomic Energy Community and the Treaty establishing the European Economic Community both signed in Rome in 1957. The United Kingdom joined with effect from 1 January 1973 and implemented the obligations contained within the Treaties by enacting in the UK the European Communities Act 1972. This established the deference of UK law to Community law and its law-making and judicial institutions, a prerequisite of each State's membership of the European Community: *Algemene Transport-en Expeditie Onderneming Van Gend & Loos v Nederlands Administratie der Belastingen* [1963] ECR 1, ECJ.

In 1986 member states signed the Single European Act which came into effect in 1987. This Act amended the Treaty of Rome by inserting a new Article 118A to the Treaty of Rome (see below, under "Legal Principles") which permitted the Community to introduce minimum standards for the health and safety of workers by a "qualified majority" vote (rather than unanimity) of member states. The means of standard setting was by use of Directives. The latter bind each member state but leaves to each the means of implementing each Directive into its own law. It was the introduction of this Article which has enabled the European revolution in health and safety legislation.

Prior to 1987 only six Directives exclusively on health and safety at work had emerged from the European Commission. Each was implemented by Regulations in the UK. They were: the Safety Signs Directive 77/576, implemented by the Safety Signs Regulations (S.I. 1980 No. 1471 soon to be overtaken by the Safety Signs Directive 92/58 in respect of which UK Regulations are in draft); the Vinyl Chloride Monomer Directive 78/610; the Chemical, Physical and Biological Agents at Work Directive 80/1107 (subsequently amended a number of times, for example by the Carcinogens Directive 90/394 and Biological Agents Directive 90/679) implemented by the Control of Substances Hazardous to Health Regulations (S.I. 1988 No. 1657, amended by S.I. 1990 No. 2026, S.I. 1991 No. 2431, S.I. 1992 No. 2382, S.I. 1992 No. 2966); the Lead and Ionic Compounds Directive 82/605 substantially covered by the Control of Lead at Work Regulations (S.I. 1980 No. 1248); the Asbestos Directive 83/477 (amended by the Asbestos Directive 91/382) implemented originally by the Asbestos (Prohibitions) Regulations (S.I. 1985 No. 910, amended by S.I. 1988 No. 711), now the Asbestos (Prohibitions) Regulations (S.I. 1992 No. 3067), and the Control of Asbestos at Work Regulations (S.I. 1987 No. 2115 and S.I.

1992 No. 3068); the Noise at Work Directive 86/188 implemented by the Noise at Work Regulations (S.I. 1989 No. 1790).

These Directives were issued under Article 100 of the Treaty of Rome which required unanimity. That Article was also the basis for other Directives where the protection of workers was incidental to their principal purpose. Such Directives included: the Classification, Labelling and Notification of Dangerous Substances Directive 67/548, which has undergone 17 amendments (the latest of which is Directive 92/69 which came into force on 30 October 1993) implemented in the UK by (what is now) the Classification, Packaging and Labelling of Dangerous Substances Regulations (S.I. 1984 No. 1244, amended by S.I. 1986 No. 1922, 1988 No. 766, 1989 No. 2208 and 1990 No. 1255); and the Major Accidents Hazards Directive 82/501 implemented by the Control of Industrial Major Accident Hazards Regulations (S.I. 1984 No. 1902, amended by S.I. 1985 No. 2023, 1986 No. 294, 1988 No. 1462 and 1990 No. 2325).

In addition to Directives based on Article 100 of the Treaty of Rome there were also, prior to 1987, Directives derived from Articles 30 and 31 of the European Atomic Energy Community Treaty such as the Ionising Radiations Directive 80/836 implemented by the Ionising Radiations Regulations (S.I. 1985 No. 1333).

In 1987 the Single European Act established the means of implementing new health and safety at work Directives through the new Article 118A of the Treaty of Rome. That amendment reflected a turn of European policy, the intent of which was to develop the "Social Dimension" of the internal market alongside the economic and political aspects which were to culminate in the "single market" in 1992. The Social Dimension was also reflected in the Social Charter and Action Programme of 1989 in which health and safety at work was particularly prominent.

In parallel with the nineteenth century British history noted above, the factors behind the development of the Social Dimension and particularly its emphasis on health and safety, were the diverse ones of humanitarianism, union pressure, political forces and, significantly, large employers and governments determined to create "a level playing field" without "social dumping" (i.e. undercutting by competitors).

To give effect to its initiative in the health and safety at work sector of the Social Dimension, the European Commission proposed what was its Third Programme on the subject (the first two pre-dated 1987 and were not a conspicuous success, having issued only the Directives referred to above). The Third Programme included 15 new health and safety Directives. These were approved by the Council of Ministers in December 1987. More were added under the impetus of the 1989 Social Charter and Action Programme. From these initiatives came the principal Directives which have culminated in the new Regulations in the UK which came into force on 1 January 1993.

The first and most important of the Directives is the Framework Directive 89/391 which requires an employer to take preventative and protective measures on the basis of: avoiding risks, evaluating risks which cannot be avoided, combating risks at source, adapting the work to the individual, adapting to technical progress, replacing the dangerous by the non-dangerous or the less dangerous, developing a coherent overall prevention policy, giving collective protective measures priority over individual measures, and giving appropriate instructions to workers. The employer must also evaluate the risk to safety and health and ensure that the subsequent preventative measures and working and production methods assure an improvement in protection and are integrated into all the activities of the undertaking. New technology must be the subject of consultation with the workers and/or their representatives. One or more workers must be designated to carry out safety duties and given time to do so and if a sufficient level of expertise is not available in-house, then outside experts may be engaged. Workers must receive sufficient information, they must be consulted upon all health and safety questions, and they must be trained adequately in relation to workstations used and jobs performed, both on recruitment and on transfer to new work, new equipment or new technology. Arrangements must be made for first aid, fire precautions and emergency procedures.

The Framework Directive was followed by six numbered "daughter" Directives, all of which (including the Framework Directive) had to be implemented by 1 January 1993.

In response the UK has implemented Regulations supplemented by Approved Codes of Practice ("ACOPS"). This edition of *Redgrave* does not include the ACOPS but does include the Framework and six daughter Directives together with the implementing Regulations. They are:

— Framework Directive 89/391: Management of Health and Safety at Work Regulations (S.I. 1992 No. 2051);
— Workplace (the First) Directive 89/654: Workplace (Health, Safety and Welfare) Regulations (S.I. 1992 No. 3004);
— Work Equipment (the Second) Directive 89/655: Provision and Use of Work Equipment Regulations (S.I. 1992 No. 2932);
— Personal Protective Equipment (the Third) Directive 89/656: Personal Protective Equipment at Work Regulations (S.I. 1992 No. 2966);
— Manual Handling of Heavy Loads (the Fourth) Directive 90/269: Manual Handling Operations Regulations (S.I. 1992 No. 2793);
— Display Screen Equipment (the Fifth) Directive 90/270: Health and Safety (Display Screen Equipment) Regulations (S.I. 1992 No. 2792);
— Carcinogens (the Sixth) Directive 90/394: Control of Substances Hazardous to Health (Amendment) Regulations (S.I. 1992 No. 2382 and S.I. 1992 No. 2966), Control of Asbestos at Work Regulations (S.I. 1992 No. 3068).

The six specific daughter Directives to be implemented by 1 January 1993 have been followed by further Directives with later implementation dates. UK consequential Regulations are proposed but have not been implemented at the time of writing (and thus have not been included in this edition, nor have the originating Directives). The 7th to 12th daughter Directives with the latest dates of implementation of each are:

Biological Agents 90/679:   1 January 1994
Construction 92/57:   31 December 1993
Safety Signs 92/58:   24 June 1994
Pregnant Women 92/85:   19 October 1994
Drilling 92/91:   3 November 1994
Mining 92/104:   3 December 1994.

An amending Directive on Biological Agents is currently before the European Commission. Despite the implementation date for the Construction Directive of 31 December 1993, the UK implementing Regulations are not expected to be laid before Parliament until July 1994 to be implemented on 1 October 1994. A consultation document is expected from the HSE on implementation of the health and safety aspects of the Pregnancy Directive, another containing proposed Regulations and ACOPS arising from the Drilling Directive, and another containing proposed Regulations and ACOPS arising from the Mining Directive, all in January 1994. Draft Fire Precautions (Places of Work) Regulations are intended to be implemented on 1 April 1994 so as to put into effect (15 months late) the fire safety aspects of the Framework and Workplace Directives (89/391 and 89/654).

There are, in addition, other Directives on health and safety at work, some of which have been referred to above as amending earlier Directives (with their implementing Regulations). Other Directives which have implementing Regulations in force, not so far mentioned, are: the Metrication Directive 89/671 implemented by the Health and Safety (Miscellaneous Provisions) (Metrication) Regulations (S.I. 1992 No. 1181) (not included in this edition), and the Temporary Workers Directive 91/383 primarily implemented by the Management of Health and Safety at Work Regulations (S.I. 1992 No. 2051) (both included in this edition). That Directive extends equivalent health and safety protection to temporary workers and to those on fixed term contracts. Given the increasing numbers of workers in these categories, the Directive is likely to gain in significance.

The above-mentioned Directives were brought into being under Article 118A on health and safety at work. In addition, three Directives have emanated from Article 100A of the Treaty of Rome which is directed to harmonisation of laws to facilitate the establishment and functioning of the internal European market. These Directives together with their implementing Regulations (all reproduced in this edition) are:

— Contained use of Genetically Modified Organisms Directive 90/219: Genetically Modified Organisms (Contained Use) Regulations (S.I. 1992 No. 3217);
— Machinery Directive 89/392 amended by 91/368: Supply of Machinery (Safety) Regulations (S.I. 1992 No. 3073);
— Approximation of Personal Protective Equipment Laws Directive 89/686: Personal Protective Equipment (EC Directive) Regulations (S.I. 1992 No. 3139).

Finally, it is to be noted that a wealth of yet further Directives on health and safety at work (many of them under the umbrella of the Social Charter Action Programme) are proposed and are at various stages of process before implementation. There are also Directives and European "Regulations" (automatically binding as law in each member state without requiring implementation by the state) proposed and passed dealing with issues that go wider than health and safety at work but which nonetheless will have impact on this area of the law. Even to list them is beyond the scope of this edition.

The breadth and depth of the innovations to UK health and safety law since the last edition of *Redgrave* in 1990 is apparent. The HSC Annual Report (1991–92) rightly remarks that European and international developments "continue to set the agenda for developments in health and safety law and standards".

Directives under Article 118A on health and safety emanate from a department of the European Commission known as DG Vd after consultation with the Advisory Committee on Safety, Hygiene and Health Protection at Work (which consists of representatives of governments, unions and employers' associations). From the Commission the draft Directive goes for consultation to the European Parliament ("first reading") and to the Economic and Social Committee, thence to the Council of Ministers. If the latter reach "common position" (i.e. a qualified majority, at least 54 out of 76 votes), the proposal goes back to the European Parliament which can propose amendments. The Commission considers (and may reject) any amendments and submits the draft as amended to the Council of Ministers for final decision.

With the Social Policy Protocol ("the Social Chapter") accompanying the Maastricht Treaty (ratified in 1993) an alternative to Article 118A will open up by which health and safety Directives could be made. Such a route would (because of the UK opt-out from the Social Chapter) exclude the UK from Directives made under it (and from voting or debating such Directives in draft). The European Commission have made clear that without ruling out the Maastricht route, the intention is that health and safety laws will continue to be promoted under Article 118A.

Having fulfilled the object of draft Directives on all the matters set by its Third Health and Safety Action Programme and the health and safety aspects of the Social Charter Action Programme, the Commission will not be proposing a fourth action programme but will, in effect, act to consolidate by focussing on: implementation of existing Directives by member states, achieving a high level of workplace health and safety, and improving social dialogue between employers and worker representatives, particularly through safety committees. The Commission's pursuit of the draft Directive on working time shows that it continues to take a wide view of the matters that fall within the scope of health and safety.

In the UK it is the HSE which drafts the regulatory response (and ACOPS where appropriate) for approval by the HSC and submission to Parliament.

"In bringing its influence to bear on [European] Commission proposals at the draft stage, HSE has argued consistently that Directives should be expressed as general principles, leaving detail to be decided nationally, and for better prioritisation of the proposals, proper cost justification and more thorough preparation before they were advanced to Council [of Ministers] level discussion" (HSC Annual Report 1991–92).

Both the HSC and the Government have further pressed the European Commission to take into account the familiar UK limitation on employers' statutory duties: "so far as is reasonably practicable".

The European Commission have not accepted these arguments and the HSE and HSC have by and large honoured the detail of the Directives in the implementing Regulations and ACOPS. They have, however, inserted the "reasonably practicable" limitation into many of the Regulations and ACOPS. The Regulations and ACOPS have been introduced under s. 15 and s. 16 respectively of the Health and Safety at Work etc. Act 1974 since the Framework and Daughter Directives are largely compatible with the scheme of the 1974 Act. It appears that the HSE have recognised that in some respects the UK Regulations do not go as far as the Directives. There is some doubt in legal circles as to whether the Directives are sufficiently implemented in the UK and, if not, what the consequences may be. These matters are dealt with in more detail under "Legal Principles", below.

The transformation of health and safety law has come as a shock to practitioners of every kind and particularly to employers. In consequence the HSE enforcement policy recognises that:

"employers will need time to take sensible action when requirements are completely new. Formal enforcement measures are not likely unless the risks to health and safety are evident and immediate, or what needs to be done is not new, or employers appear deliberately unwilling to recognise their responsibilities" (HSC Annual Report 1991–92).

The range of sanctions available after the European intervention remains as broad as before. It is a principle of community law to leave enforcement to the member states so long as they provide effective measures. Without any European stimulus the maximum fines under the 1974 Act were significantly increased in 1992. To the extent that breach of an ACOP will not be subject, of itself, to either criminal or civil sanction, there is some doubt as to whether effective means of enforcement consistent with the requirements of European law will have been provided where implementation of a provision of a Directive is by way of a provision in an ACOP rather than a Regulation (this too is referred to below under "Legal Principles"). So far as the civil law is concerned it is assumed that the principle established by *Groves v Lord Wimborne* (above) will apply to permit an action for damages for breach of Regulations brought into effect to implement the European Directives, and an action for breach of a Directive itself where such an action can be maintained, i.e. against an emanation of the state. Any judicial decisions to the contrary would doubtless fall foul of the European Court of Justice which was held in *Rewe Handelsgesellschaft Nord mbH v Hauptzollamt Kiel* [1981] ECR 1805 (and subsequent cases) that:

"it must be possible for every type of action provided by national law to be available before the national Courts for the purpose of ensuring observance of Community provisions having direct effect..."

Regulation 15 of the Management of Health and Safety at Work Regulations (S.I. 1992 No. 2051) excludes civil liability for breach and it may be that this provision will be challenged in the European Court of Justice (to the extent that the other Regulations do not implement fully the Framework Directive 89/391 so leaving a provision of the latter unimplemented by a Regulation enforceable in civil law).

It has been suggested also that where a Directive cannot be enforced directly only because the employer is not an emanation of the state, nonetheless, the standards therein contained will come to be regarded by the courts as establishing the standard of care of a reasonable employer when determining liability in negligence (perhaps by parallel reasoning with *Butt v Inner London Education Authority* (1968) 66 LGR 379, CA).

Some commentators have suggested that the new law may stimulate claims for injunctions which, though theoretically available since *Groves*, have rarely if ever been used as a preventative tool.

Conclusion
The history of health and safety legislation has by no means reached an end. It has however entered a new and different stage. The European revolution is characterised by universality of application and a focus on the nature of the risk (rather than on the nature of the workplace or the work process). Millions of workers previously outside the scope of the legislation will receive statutory health and safety protection and employers will be stimulated to assess and act upon the risks of all their operations. The duty to carry out risk assessment will become a prominent feature of foreseeability in negligence actions. Diminution in the scale of the horror of injury, ill health or death at work is to be anticipated.

LEGAL PRINCIPLES

The purpose of this section is to consider certain general principles relating to the application of safety, health and welfare legislation and, in particular, the founding upon it of civil actions for breach of statutory duty.

Most of the general principles evolved in relation to the application of the health and safety legislation derive from judicial consideration of the Factories Acts. The principles are for the most part equally applicable to the other Acts and Regulations. Additional considerations apply, however, to the construction of Regulations passed in order to give effect to European Directives.

Statutes *in pari materia*

Where different statutes, albeit made at different times and not referring to each other, have objects of a similar or analogous nature they are said to be *in pari materia* and, as a general principle of construction, they are to be taken and construed together as one system and as explanatory of each other (*R v Loxdale* (1758) 1 Burr 445; *Goldsmith's Co v Wyatt* [1907] 1 KB 95, CA).

The Factories Acts were passed for the protection of workmen from the risks inherent in their work and it is submitted that the Health and Safety at Work etc. Act 1974, the Offices, Shops and Railway Premises Act 1963, and the agricultural safety legislation are *in pari materia* with the Factories Acts and with each other, so that, unless the context otherwise requires, expressions which have been given authoritative judicial interpretation when used in one Act ought to be given a similar interpretation when used in another of those Acts (*Webb v Outrim* [1907] AC 81, 89, PC; *Barras v Aberdeen Steam Trawling and Fishing Co Ltd* [1933] AC 402, HL). It is submitted that the principle applies equally to Regulations made under those Acts and to Regulations intended to implement European Directives.

This principle of construction is founded upon the presumed intention of Parliament to repeat, by using an expression which has received judicial interpretation, the effect of that interpretation, so that where an expression used in an earlier Act has been the subject of conflicting judicial decision or where the earlier decision is shown in fact to be erroneous there is no rule of law to prevent a different construction being placed upon the later Act (*Royal Crown Derby Porcelain Co Ltd v Russell* [1949] 2 KB 417, CA). As to the interpretation of statutes *in pari materia* generally, see 44 Halsbury's Laws (4th Edn.) paras. 885 *et seq.*

This principle is less relevant to the interpretation of Regulations implementing EEC Directives, for those should be construed to achieve, so far as is possible, the result envisaged by the Directive (see below). To that extent decisions on what particular terms have been held to mean in other areas of domestic legislation can be a misleading guide.

Interpretation

The statutes and subordinate legislation contained in this book impose penalties for infringement of their provisions, and must, therefore, be strictly construed (*Franklin v Gramophone Co Ltd* [1948] 1 KB 542, CA, *per* Somervell LJ at 557; see also, *London and North Eastern Rail Co v Berriman* [1946] AC 278, HL, a case under the Railway Employment (Prevention of Accidents) Act 1900).

Since, however, such legislation is also a remedial measure passed for the protection of those in employment, it must be read so as to effect its object so far as the wording fairly and reasonably permits (*Harrison v National Coal Board* [1951] 1 All ER 1102, *per* Lord Porter at 1107). See, further, *Thurogood v Van den Berghs and Jurgens Ltd* [1951] 2 KB 537 at 548, [1951] 1 All ER 682 at 687, 688; *McCarthy v Coldair Ltd* [1951] 2 TLR 1226, CA, and *Norris v Syndic Manufacturing Co Ltd* [1952] 2 QB 135 at 142, [1952] 1 All ER 935 at 939. Again, this principle is less relevant to Regulations implementing EEC Directives, to which special rules apply.

Many of the regulations or other instruments contain specific definitions of terms used therein. Where an Act confers power to make subordinate legislation, expressions used in that legislation have, unless the contrary intention appears, the meaning which they bear in the Act (Interpretation Act 1978, s. 11), and in construing terms which are defined neither in the instrument nor in the enabling Act it must be presumed that terms used in a like context are intended to bear the same meaning in both the instrument and the Act (*Potts (or Riddell) v Reid* [1943] AC 1, HL). Where subordinate legislation is kept in force by a repealing statute as if made thereunder it should receive the same interpretation after the repeal as it received before (*Garcia v Harland and Wolff Ltd* [1943] 1 KB 731; *Canadian Pacific SS Ltd v Bryers* [1958] AC 485, HL).

Where legislation is ambiguous or obscure or the literal meaning leads to an absurdity the court may have regard to what was said in the parliamentary debates or proceedings as an aid to construction (*Pepper (Inspector of Taxes) v Hart* [1993] 1 All ER 42, HL). That power is subject to the caveat that parliamentary material is only admissible if it clearly discloses what was the legislative intention or mischief at which the legislation was aimed; and that is unlikely to be established unless the statement is that of a minister or other promoter of the Bill. Quite how extensive this doctrine will prove to be is as yet unresolved.

Interpretation in the light of the European Directives
A regulation or statute intended to implement a European Directive must be construed "purposively" so as to give effect to the result envisaged by that Directive: *Von Colson v Land Nordrhein-Westfalen* [1984] ECR 1891 at 1909 and 1910–1, ECJ; *Pickstone v Freemans plc* [1988] ICR 697 at 722–3, 725, HL; *Litster v Forth Dry Dock and Engineering Co Ltd* [1989] ICR 341 at 350, 353, 354, 357–8, 370. This "teleological" approach to construction derives from the ECJ's approach to the construction of Directives. The court must consider the purpose of the provision in question and the context and framework within which it appears. Regard must thus be had to the text of the Treaty under which the Directive was made as well as to the preamble to the Directive and its structure. The Regulation must be construed in the light of the purpose thus discovered.

In *Litster* words were, in effect, written into a statutory provision by the House of Lords. However, in *Webb v EMO Air Cargo (UK) Ltd* [1993] ICR 175 at 186–7, HL, and *Duke v GEC Reliance Systems Ltd* [1988] ICR 339 at 352, the House of Lords indicated that, before it can be subjected to "purposive" interpretation, the relevant legislation must be reasonably capable of being construed so as to conform to the Directive or Treaty obligation. Lord Keith indicated, first, that the result envisaged by the Directive must be clear; and, second, that it must be possible to construe the national legislation to accord with the terms of the Directive. It would follow from this circumspect policy that if the relevant UK legislation is not reasonably capable of being interpreted to give effect to the Directive and a valuable right is thereby lost, an action may be brought against the UK Government for failure to implement the Directive, see *Francovich v Italian Republic* [1992] IRLR 84 (below).

Where there is at issue directly applicable provisions of European Community law which have direct effect without the need for implementing legislation by the member state (e.g. provisions of the Treaties themselves or "Regulations" of the European Community), mere purposive interpretation of domestic legislation is not enough: in *Amministrazione Delle Finanze dello Stato v Simmenthal SpA* [1978] ECR 629 the ECJ held that the Treaty and such directly applicable European law:

> "by their entry into force render automatically inapplicable any conflicting provision of current national law..."

In the UK this proposition is also supported by s. 2(4) of the European Communities Act 1972 which provides that "... any enactment passed or to be passed ... shall be construed and have effect subject to [obligations and rights] under or by virtue of the Treaties".

The ECJ will also go further than merely requiring a purposive interpretation of domestic law where at issue is a European Directive which conflicts with domestic law and a citizen seeks to enforce the Directive against the state or its emanations. Here, though the Directive requires implementation into domestic law to be enforceable against citizens, it is directly enforceable against the state and its emanations. In such an action against the state or its emanations the ECJ have held (in *European Commission v Belgium* [1985] 3 CMLR 624 at para 25) that member states must:

> "fulfil their obligations under Community Directives and may not plead provisions, practices or circumstances existing in their internal legal systems, in order to justify a failure to comply with those obligations."

So in *R v Transport Secretary, ex p Factortame (No. 2) Ltd* [1991] 1 AC 603 at 644B–D, the ECJ held that a provision of UK law (no injunctions against the Crown) which precluded the grant of interim relief should be set aside so as to permit enforcement against the state in compliance with community law. The House of Lords accordingly made the interim relief order. And in *Emmott v Minister for Social Welfare* [1993] ICR 8, a procedural time limit in Irish law was struck down so that a citizen could take the benefit of a Directive against the state.

The principle of purposive construction has been taken further by *Marleasing SA v La Commercial Internacional de Alimentation SA* [1992] 1 CMLR 305 where the ECJ held (in a dispute between companies neither of which were part of the state) that:

> "in applying the national law, whether the provisions in question were adopted before or after the Directive, the national Court called upon to interpret it is required to do so, as far as possible, in the light of the wording and the purpose of the Directive in order to achieve the result pursued by the latter and thereby comply with Article 189 of the Treaty".

The ECJ's approach in that case appears consistent with its decision in *Verholen v Sociale Verzekeringsbank Amsterdam* [1992] IRLR 38.

It is clear that purposive construction may only be applied to a provision of national law where such provision is open to divergent interpretations: para. 8 of the Opinion of van Gerven, Advocate-General, in *Marleasing*, and emphasised in *Porter v Cannon Hygiene Ltd* [1993] IRLR 329, NI CA, at paras. 13, 16–18, and see *Webb v EMO Air Cargo (UK) Ltd* [1993] ICR 175.

Where purposive construction of law predating the Directive is relied on against a citizen (as opposed to the state), it is arguable that the defendant can raise the doctrine of legitimate expectation in support of a pre-existing interpretation, see *Officer Van Justitie v Kolpinghuis Nijmegen BV* [1989] 2 CMLR 18; though this may be an argument confined to criminal proceedings.

The problem of avoiding "distortion" of the language of the statute by a "purposive" interpretation disappears of course where there is a lacuna in the UK statutory provision and hence no statutory provision to be construed in accordance with a Directive directly in point. This situation would arise where the state failed to implement a Directive or failed to do so fully. It may be that in such a situation there was no applicable national law at all (e.g. in *R v British Coal Corpn, ex p Vardy* [1993] IRLR 104 it was held that s. 188 of the Trade Union and Labour Relations Act 1992 did not fully conform to the Collective Redundancies Directive 75/129, so to the extent of the shortfall there was no underlying national law requiring consultation, other than by private agreement). However, in the field of health and safety at work, certainly as between employee and employer, any gap in implementing legislation would not expose a total absence of national law on the subject, it would merely reveal the common law as the extant law. It is submitted that, in such a situation, the effect of the ECJ authorities cited would be that any relevant common law principle capable of such construction would therefore have to be so "construed" as to provide conformity and give effect to the Directive. It seems unlikely that the ECJ would concur in a UK court refusing to so "construe" the principles of the common law so as to give effect to the Directive.

A UK court could in most if not all cases, reach the same result by treating the duties imposed by the common law an equivalent to those imposed by a Directive. So in negligence the court could take the view that the reasonable employer would regard himself as bound by duties of care equivalent to those of the Directive. There is some precedent for this kind of analogy. In *Butt v Inner London Education Authority* (1986) 66 LGR 379, CA, the duty of care owed to a student operating an unfenced printing machine at a technical school was held to be analogous to that under the Factories Act. In *Hewett v Alf Brown's Transport Ltd* [1991] ICR 471, affirmed [1992] ICR 530, CA, the standard of the common law duty of care was held to be set by the Control of Lead at Work Regulations (S.I. 1980 No. 1248). Thus an employer who fails to carry out the risk assessment required by the Framework Directive might well find his failure treated as a failure (or, at least, as evidence of a failure) to provide a safe system of work notwithstanding that the implementing Management of Health and Safety at Work Regulations 1992 are expressly not actionable in civil law (reg. 15). In contract (see *Matthews v Kuwait Bechtel Corpn* [1959] 2 QB 57, CA) duties equivalent to those of a Directive might be implied into the contract of employment, though there might be difficulties in implying a term that the duty of care altered in accordance with the coming into force of Directives not implemented into UK law at the outset of the contract.

Thus, it is submitted, the entirety of UK civil health and safety law, statutory or common law, must be construed (so far as it is capable of such construction) so as to be consistent with the relevant European Directives. It is submitted that, in contrast, nothing but the letter of the UK Regulations could be enforced by way of criminal prosecution. Thus, it is suggested, a prosecution would fail where the defendant could show compliance with the UK Regulations, even though the prosecution might be able to demonstrate non-compliance with the terms of the Directive in conformity with which it was argued the Regulations should be construed. Just as the state cannot be permitted to rely on its own failure to implement a Directive so as to defend itself from civil proceedings, so, it is submitted, it cannot be permitted to argue its own failure of implementation in order to secure a criminal conviction. Likewise the state could not be permitted to remedy its own failure of implementation by seeking to rely on a wide construction beyond the ordinary and natural meaning of the Regulations. Certainty is essential in the application of criminal law. See also *Officer Van Justitie v Kolpinghuis Nijmegen BV* [1989] 2 CMLR 18.

The Regulations made to implement the European Directives have all been made under s. 15 of the Health and Safety at Work etc. Act 1974. Section 80 of that Act allows Regulations to repeal or modify pre-existing statutory provisions where necessary. Section 1(2) of the Act provides that the Regulations made under the Act shall have effect in particular with a view to enabling the old legislation to be progressively replaced by a system of Regulations and ACOPS

> "designed to maintain or improve the standards of health, safety and welfare established by or under"

the old legislation. It is arguable that any demonstrable diminution of standard by the repeal and replacement of pre-existing legislation by subsequent Regulation might therefore be ultra vires. The Management and Administration of Safety and Health at Mines Regulations 1993 has been challenged by judicial review on this ground.

Whether or not that argument is sustainable in the UK courts, there is a parallel argument that no diminution of pre-existing national standard is permissible by the introduction of national law intended to implement a European health and safety Directive made under Article 118A of the Treaty of Rome. This is because Article 118A provides:

> "Member States shall pay particular attention to encouraging improvements, especially in the working environment, as regards the health and safety of workers and shall set as their objective the harmonisation of conditions in this area, while maintaining the improvements made."

That Article also provides that the standards which the Directives adopt are:

> "minimum requirements ... having regard to the conditions and technical rules obtaining in each of the Member States".

The preamble to the Framework Directive states explicitly that:

> "this Directive does not justify any reduction in levels of protection already achieved in individual Member States".

Although these words are not found in the daughter Directives, the fact that each of the latter are made in pursuance of the Framework Directive necessarily imports that principle, it is submitted.

Thus, in construing the UK statutory provisions it is submitted that courts should seek to place on them a construction which improves, or at the least, maintains pre-existing standards and which regards Directives as setting minimum, not optional, standards. Hence both the provisions of national law, under the ultra vires doctrine, and the rules of construction derived from the EEC lean heavily against the down-grading of existing standards. It follows that the circumstances in which a national court will find itself obliged to give effect to Regulations that do permit such a lowering of standards of protection are virtually inconceivable.

Finally, it is to be observed that the HSC advanced the argument to the European Commission that the Directives (then in draft) should not impose absolute duties because the UK courts construed statutory language strictly whereas European states' courts were more flexible, employing doctrines of "proportionality". As is evident, the European Commission did not accede to this argument. There is therefore no apparent reason why the UK courts should not continue to apply the same strict canons of construction to the language of the Regulations and Directives as apply to all statutes, subject only to the "purposive" approach established in *Litster* and developed above.

Direct application of European Directives

The ECJ decision in *Marleasing* (above) imposes an obligation on the courts of member states to construe national legislation, so far as is possible, to achieve the same result envisaged by a Directive. Where the Regulations cannot be so construed, a plaintiff may nonetheless rely on a Directive "vertically", that is, against an emanation of the state. Earlier cases such as *Marshall No. 1* (above) and *Officer Van Justitie v Kolpinghuis Nijmegen BV* (above) remain good law to the effect that a Directive (as opposed to an Article of a Treaty) has no "horizontal" effect, i.e. no direct application between citizens of a state, but only "vertical" effect, i.e. as against the state itself.

It may be better to regard the distinction as between a European cause of action, and a national cause of action. A European cause of action, suing on the Directive or Treaty, can be brought in the national courts but only against the state. There is some analogy with estoppel here: the state is, as it were, estopped from relying on its own failure properly to implement the Directive or comply with the treaty. A national cause of action, suing on national law, can be brought against anyone. The national law in the latter case, however, must now be modified (to the extent described above) so that the national law is consistent with the relevant European law.

What is beyond doubt in both the ECJ and UK courts is that, from the date on which they are to be implemented by the member states, Directives do apply directly to and can be enforced by citizens against each member state and its "emanations" in the event of non- or partial implementation (see *Suffritti v Istituto Nazionale della Previdenza Sociale* [1993] IRLR 289). This is because Article 5 of the Treaty of Rome (reflected in s. 2 of the European Communities Act 1972) provides that:

> "Member States shall take all appropriate measures whether general or particular, to ensure fulfilment of the obligations arising out of this Treaty . . ."

Thus health and safety Directives may be directly enforced by employees against state employers. This includes not only the Crown and the Civil Service but all government agencies, local government bodies (*Fratelli Costanzo v Comune di Milano* [1990] 3 CMLR 239), health authorities (*Marshall v South West Hampshire Health Authority* [1986] QB 401, ECJ), police authorities (*Johnstone v Chief Constable of the Royal Ulster Constabulary* [1986] ECR 1651), and nationalised corporations (*Foster v British Gas Corpn* [1991] ICR 84, ECJ; apld [1991] ICR 463, HL), *R v British Coal Corpn, ex p Vardy* [1993] IRLR 104, DC), but not, according to the Court of Appeal, a private corporation wholly owned by the state (*Rolls-Royce plc v Doughty* [1987] ICR 932).

To qualify as an emanation of the state the entity should provide a public service, should be under the control of the state, and should have powers in excess of those which result from the normal rules applicable in relations between individuals: *Foster v British Gas Corpn* (above). It is interesting to note that, though this is a question of European law rather than national law, in the UK such a body is akin to those bodies susceptible to judicial review, a wider and expanding category: see *CCSU v Minister for the Civil Service* [1985] AC 374 at 409, *R v Panel on Take-overs and Mergers, ex p Datafin plc* [1987] QB 815, CA.

It is arguable that not all of the three elements identified must be present in order for a Directive to be directly enforceable against an entity as an emanation of the state. It has been suggested that, because of the terms of Article 5, the most important element is that of state control especially in so far as it can be shown that it lay within the direct and immediate power of the state to require the entity to observe the obligations in the Directive. Before the ECJ this element may not be sufficient in itself, certainly it will not be enough by itself in the UK courts; *Doughty* (above). It is likely that the categories of state "emanation" will be construed widely rather than narrowly by the ECJ.

For a provision in a Directive to be capable of "direct effect" it must be clear, precise and unconditional (see *Van Duyn v Home Office* [1974] ECR 1337, [1975] 1 CMLR 1). The ECJ has stated that Directives will consequently not have direct effect where their terms are too imprecise, or in circumstances where the terms are conditional or leave a discretion to member states as to implementation: *Van Duyn* (above). In applying the test, each article relied on in each Directive must be considered individually. Plainly, almost all the provisions contained in Directives on health and safety will be directly enforceable.

Reliance on a Directive against a state employer will only become relevant where some lacuna or shortfall is found in the implementing Regulation(s) which cannot be made good by a purposive construction of the latter. In such circumstances the provision of the Directive will become paramount in civil and administrative (but not, for the reason set out earlier, in criminal) enforcement of the legislation. Therefore the opportunities for direct enforcement of the health and safety Directives will be limited. There are, however, a number of such potential situations and litigation, both civil and criminal, will doubtless reveal others (and see Smith, Goddard and Randall *Health and Safety: the New Legal Framework*, Butterworths, 1993, for a helpful commentary on the divergence of the Regulations and Directives). It is not within the scope of this book to draw attention to every arguable divergence between Directive and Regulation. However, some general points can be made and both Directives and the Regulations are included in this edition for those who need to rely directly on the Directives, and those who need to refer to them for a purposive construction of the Regulations.

One point of divergence requiring direct enforcement of a Directive against a state employer may occur where a duty imposed by a Directive is qualified in the implementing Regulation by words importing a lower standard of care (such as "so far as is reasonably practicable"). The UK Government, as noted above, failed to convince the European Commission that Directives should be drafted in general terms on the ground that the UK courts construe language strictly and not flexibly. So there now appears no justification for construing a Directive imposing an absolute duty "flexibly" so as to justify a limitation on that duty. Hence so far as possible a national court should ignore such words of limitation. By Article 118A of the Treaty, the Directives had to have regard to National "conditions and technical rules" when drafted. Thus it may be said that the strict approach to statutory construction of the UK courts was taken into account and no exception or words of guidance to construction were presumably thought to be required.

Indeed, the only limitation of employers' liability permitted by the Framework Directive (and hence incorporated into each daughter Directive) is that in Article 5(4), which permits national Regulation to exclude or limit employers' liability where occurrences are due to circumstances which are unusual, unforeseeable and beyond the employers' control, or exceptional and unavoidable despite all due care. This cannot, it is submitted, justify a Regulation permitting a defence of "not reasonably practicable".

A correlative situation may arise where the implementing Regulation fulfils the standards set by the Directive yet imposes a lower standard than the pre-existing and repealed provisions of UK law. For the reasons given earlier, such a lowering of standards appears impermissible under European law and probably under UK law. Again, it is submitted, the preamble to the Framework Directive may be relied upon against a state employer so that the court may disregard any words which would otherwise lower the previous standards.

Direct enforcement against a state employer may also be appropriate where an implementing Regulation is more limited in its scope than the Directive. Thus, for example, recording of the employers' risk assessment is required by both the Framework Directive (Article 9(1)) and the Management of Health and Safety at Work Regulations 1992; but the latter (by regs. 3(4) and 4(2)) imposes the obligation only on employers of more than five employees, a limitation not found in the Directive. Another example is found in the various provisions of the Directives which require consultation with employee representatives. This obligation is restricted by the UK Regulations to consultation with representatives of trade unions "recognised" by the employer. Since recognition and derecognition of a trade union is entirely at the discretion of the employer in the UK (*Wilson v Associated Newspapers* [1993] IRLR 336, CA) the Regulations thus would permit the unqualified duty of consultation in the Directives to be inapplicable to employment in which the employer did not (or had ceased to) recognise a union. Infraction proceedings are being brought by the European Commission against the UK Government on this very point in relation to similar consultation obligations (on matters unrelated to health and safety) arising from the Collective Redundancies Directive 75/129 (see Case C-383/92, 92/C 316/14; the same point arises from the Acquired Rights Directive 77/187). The Commission is believed to be considering its position in relation to the consultation provisions of the Framework Directive. It is submitted that the obligation to consult worker representatives, whether or not the union is recognised, is binding directly on and enforceable against state employers.

A further example of implementing legislation not extending as far as the Directives and one which demonstrates another principle of European law is found in reg. 15 of the Management of Health and Safety at Work Regulations 1992 and in the ACOPS which accompany all the implementing Regulations. Regulation 15 of the Management of Health and Safety at Work Regulations 1992 provides that breach of a duty imposed by those regulations shall not confer a right of action in any civil proceedings. This provision is not found in the other implementing Regulations (though it is being considered at the time of writing in the forthcoming Construction (Design and Management) Regulations). The 1974 Act, under which all the implementing Regulations have been introduced, provides that breach of the ACOP is not an offence although it may be taken as proof of breach of the relevant Regulation unless some other manner of compliance can be shown. There is no explicit mention of admissibility (or relevance) in civil proceedings. Therefore to the extent that any provision of the Directives is not fully implemented and enforceable in both civil and criminal proceedings by other Regulations, any provision of the Directives apparently implemented only by the Management of Health and Safety at Work Regulations or by provision in ACOPS, will be, respectively, unenforceable in civil law or unenforceable in both civil and criminal law. Against a state employer, it is submitted any such deficiency could be made good by direct enforcement of the Directive. Although the Directives do not provide for any enforcement regime to be adopted by member states, European law requires national law to provide remedies giving "effective legal protection" for those who are the beneficiaries of a Directive: *Von Colson v Land Nordrhein-Westfalen* [1984] ECR 1891. In that case the ECJ held that though the choice of remedy was a matter for the state, any "sanction must be such as to guarantee real and effective judicial protection" and "measures must be sufficiently effective to achieve the objective of the Directive".

The ECJ has held that national rules of procedure must not make "it impossible in practice to exercise rights which the national courts have a duty to enforce" (*Comet v Produktschap voor Siergewassen* [1976] ECR 2043), the so-called *principle of effectiveness.*

The ECJ held in *Rewe Handelsgesellschaft Nord mbH v Hauptzollamt Kiel* [1981] ECR 1805, that:

> "it must be possible for every type of action provided by national law to be available before the national courts for the purpose of ensuring observance of Community provisions having direct effect, on the same conditions concerning enforceability and procedure as would apply were it a question of ensuring observance of national law".

This is the so-called *principle of non-discrimination.*

In *Aministrazione delle Finanze dello Stato v San Giorgio SpA* [1983] ECR 3595 the ECJ held (at 3612 para. 12) that:

> "conditions both as to substance and form laid down by the various national laws . . . may not be less favourable than those relating to similar claims regarding national charges and they may not be so framed as to render virtually impossible the exercise of rights conferred by community law".

It is submitted that the exclusion of civil enforcement against a state employer of any sufficiently precise provision of a health and safety Directive would on its face deny the right to any effective remedy to the workers intended to be protected.

In relation to the exclusion of damages claims, it is suggested that even the existence of a criminal sanction is an insufficient means of enforcement both because prosecution does not (under s. 38 of the Health and Safety at Work etc. Act 1974) lie in the hands of the employee, and because successful prosecution would not provide the compensation which would have been available for breach of equivalent national law. Furthermore, the House of Lords held in *Garden Cottage Foods Ltd v Milk Marketing Board* [1984] AC 130, that breach of a directly (and horizontally) enforceable community provision (where there was no implementing legislation specifying any form of remedy or sanction) was actionable in damages by analogy with an action for breach of statutory duty (as in *Groves v Lord Wimborne* [1898] 2 QB 402, CA). In the situation of an injured employee seeking to enforce a provision in a Directive against a state employer who seeks to argue non-enforceability by reason that the provision finds form only in the Management of Health and Safety at Work Regulations 1992 or in an ACOP, it is submitted that the UK and European courts would follow this authority rather than the distinguishable case of *Bourgoine SA v Ministry of Agriculture, Fisheries and Food* [1986] QB 716, CA (doubted in *Kirklees Metropolitan Borough Council v Wickes Building Supplies* [1993] AC 227, HL). After all the ECJ has itself made clear in *Francovich v Italian Republic* [1992] IRLR 84 that damages are an appropriate remedy against a state for the failure to implement a Directive (see below).

The level of damages for breach of a Directive must be no less favourable than that in respect of a similar right of action in domestic law: *Amministrazione delle Finanze delle Stato v San Giorgio* [1983] ECR 3595. In *Marshall v Southampton and South West Hampshire Area Health Authority (No. 2)* [1993] IRLR 445 the ECJ set aside a statutory provision limiting compensation for unlawful discrimination holding that where compensation is appropriate it must be sufficient to enable the loss and damage actually sustained to be made good in accordance with applicable national rules. In the case of a damages claim for personal injury, loss and damage, it is submitted that the ordinary rules relating to damages calculations in the UK will therefore apply.

So far as exclusion of injunctive relief is concerned, *R v Secretary of State for Transport, ex p Factortame Ltd (No. 2)* [1991] 1 AC 603, ECJ confirmed that injunctions are available for the enforcement of rights in European law notwithstanding any pre-existing national law to the contrary. That case held that an injunction was permissible against the Crown in European law. In *Garden Cottage Foods Ltd v Milk Marketing Board* [1984] AC 130, HL, and *Cutsforth v Mansfield Inns* [1986] 1 WLR 558, HC, interlocutory injunctions were granted to restrain breach of articles of the Treaty of Rome. Where the implementing legislation purports to exclude injunctive relief, it is submitted that the ECJ would be likely to hold the exclusion impermissible since the employee would otherwise be denied any effective remedy. Even if a criminal sanction was provided that would not, it is submitted, provide an equivalent degree of protection (especially in contrast to an interlocutory injunction).

Where both civil and criminal sanctions are excluded then, a fortiori, an effective remedy is denied. In *EC Commission v Greece* [1989] ECR 2965, ECJ, followed in *Anklagemyndigheden v Hansen & Son* [1992] ICR 277, ECJ, the ECJ held that each member state in order to comply with Article 5 of the Treaty, had to:

> "ensure that infringements of community law were punished according to substantive and procedural rules analogous to those applicable to infringements of national law of a similar nature and gravity and which, in any event, ensured that the sanction was effective, proportionate and dissuasive".

The court specifically had in mind the situation (as here postulated) "where a Community Regulation did not contain any specific provision providing for a penalty in the case of infringement".

Thus, though the situations where a Directive can be directly enforced are likely to be limited, they may occur. It may be that if they do occur in relation to the health and safety Directives the problem will be avoided by the simple expedient of the court adopting the Directive's standards as those of the reasonable employer and enforcing any breach in negligence (see the analogous *Butt v Inner London Education Authority* (1968) 66 LGR 379, CA).

Finally, it should be observed that *Francovich v Italian Republic* [1992] IRLR 84, ECJ, has established that in the event of any demonstrable failure by a state to implement the standards of the Directives and provide effective means of enforcement, individuals may in appropriate and limited circumstances sue the state (in the person of the Secretary of State for Employment: *Kirklees Metropolitan Borough Council v Wickes Building Supplies Ltd* [1993] AC 227, HL) for damages for any loss sustained thereby. An employee of a private employer may, therefore, bring an action against the UK Government if the rules of construction referred to above do not give him or her the same level of protection or remedy as would be available under the relevant Directive. For such an action to lie, three conditions must be met: the objectives of the Directive must include the creation of individual rights; the Directive must make clear what is the content of those rights; and the breach of duty on the part of the state must cause the loss to the individual. In the context of health and safety law, it is probable that the last requirement will be interpreted to mean only that the individual did not, or would not, recover the proper level or any compensation because of the failure of the state correctly to implement a Directive. Time will not run against such a plaintiff prior to legislation remedying any shortfall in implementation: *Emott v Minister for Social Welfare* [1993] ICR 8.

Civil liability for breach of statutory duty

It is well settled that in certain circumstances a breach of statutory duty which results in injury to a person of a class which the statute was designed to protect gives the injured person a civil cause of action (see *Lonrho Ltd v Shell Petroleum Ltd (No. 2)* [1982] AC 173). The requirements which have to be satisfied before such a cause of action arises are, first, that the statutory provision, properly construed, was intended to protect an ascertainable class of persons of whom the plaintiff was one; secondly, that the provision has been broken; thirdly, that the plaintiff has suffered damage of a kind against which the provision was designed to give protection and, lastly, that the damage was caused by the breach. The general principles relating to this type of liability are discussed in 20 Halsbury's Laws (4th Edn.) para. 552, and an illuminating discussion of the decided cases is to be found in the judgments delivered in *Solomons v R. Gertzenstein Ltd* [1954] 2 QB 243, [1954] 2 All ER 625, CA. The purpose of the present section of this introduction is not to set out such general principles as may be said to exist in this branch of the law, but to discuss the narrower question, how far the legislation dealt with in this book may give a right of action to a person injured by a breach of its provisions.

In the case of the general provisions of that legislation and cognate provisions of subordinate legislation, it is beyond doubt that a breach gives rise to a civil right of action (see, for example, *Groves v Lord Wimborne* [1898] 2 QB 402, CA), and the courts clearly lean in favour of conferring on workers a right to claim damages for breaches of statutory duty imposed on their employers or on the occupiers of factories in which they work (*per* Somervell LJ in *Solomons v R. Gertzenstein Ltd*, above, at 631). It is not so clear, however, to what extent provisions other than safety provisions, such as "health" and "welfare" provisions will be similarly interpreted.

The cases in which these matters have arisen for decision are principally cases upon the provisions of the Factories Act 1937; but they are valid for the provisions of statutes *in pari materia* with the Factories Act, e.g. *Reid v Galbraiths Stores* 1970 SLT (Notes) 83 (the Offices, Shops and Railway Premises Act 1963 does not protect customers but only employees); *Westwood v Post Office* [1974] AC 1, HL (even if the employee goes to a place to which he is not supposed to go).

With regard to the health provisions, in *Ebbs v James Whitson & Co Ltd* [1952] 2 QB 877, CA, where the plaintiff claimed under s. 4(1) of the Factories Act 1937 (now s. 4(1) of the 1961 Act), Denning LJ (at p. 195) expressly reserved the question whether the provisions of s. 4 and of the other sections of Part I of the Act give rise to a civil action, and he pointed out that the enforcement of Part I was expressly provided for in ss. 8 and 9. It is, however, to be noted that *McCarthy v Daily Mirror Newspapers Ltd* [1949] 1 All ER 801, in which the Court of Appeal accepted without discussion that an action lay for breach of s. 43(1)—a welfare provision—of the 1937 Act (now s. 59(1) of the 1961 Act), was not cited to the court in *Ebbs v James Whitson & Co Ltd*, above. Despite the reservation of Denning LJ in the latter case, there have since been several decisions in favour of granting a right of action for breach of a health provision, although in one case alone (*Carroll v North British Locomotive Co Ltd* 1957 SLT (Sh Ct) 2) was the question expressly discussed. Thus, in *Nicholson v Atlas Steel Foundry and Engineering Co Ltd* [1957] 1 All ER 776, HL, an action was brought for, *inter alia*, breach of s. 4(1) of the 1937 Act (now s. 4(1) of the 1961 Act). The House of Lords held that the respondents were liable to the appellant for breach of this section, although no mention of the problem appears in the argument or the speeches. Section 4(1) of the Factories Act 1937 was also the subject of *Clarkson v Modern Foundries Ltd* [1958] 1 All ER 33, in which Donovan J appears to have awarded damages for a breach of the section. It seems from the report at [1957] 1 WLR 1210, 1212 that *Nicholson v Atlas Steel Foundry and Engineering Co* was cited to the court; but this is the only indication that the point under discussion was made patent. In the case of s. 5(1) of the Factories Act 1961 ("Lighting") it must now be regarded as authoritatively decided that a right of civil action is conferred (*Lane v Gloucester Engineering Co Ltd* [1967] 2 All ER 293, CA; *Thornton v Fisher & Ludlow Ltd* [1968] 2 All ER 241, CA). Finally, in *Carroll v North British Locomotive Co Ltd*, above, an action for breach (*inter alia*) of s. 1(b) of the 1937 Act (now s. 1(2)(b) of the 1961 Act) Sheriff-Substitute Walker, after full consideration, doubted the correctness of the reservation of Denning LJ in *Ebbs v James Whitson & Co Ltd*, above, and held, on a preliminary plea-in-law, that s. 1(b) gave rise to a claim in damages. The preponderance of authority is thus now strongly in favour of allowing a civil right of action for breach of a health provision.

In considering the welfare provisions of the Factories Act 1961 it is not safe to assume that all the sections which fall under the rubric "Welfare (General Provisions)" (ss. 57 to 62 of the 1961 Act) should receive a similar interpretation so far as civil rights of action are concerned. Thus, in *Reid v Westfield Paper Co Ltd* 1957 SC 218, the First Division of the Court of Session considered the effect of s. 42(1) of the 1937 Act (now s. 58(1) of the 1961 Act) and Lord President Clyde said (at p. 225):

> "Some of the welfare provisions, such as s. 44, which deals with facilities for sitting, seem to have a purely welfare outlook; others, such as s. 45, which deals with first aid, seem to impinge substantially on matters of health or safety. In the present case I find it unnecessary to decide whether a purely welfare provision could, if breached, involve a claim for damages by a person injured by its breach. In my opinion, s. 42(1), although primarily directed to protecting welfare, does also involve considerations of health and safety, which this Act is mainly devoted to protecting. If so, its breach could involve civil liability..."

Lord Sorn at p. 228, referring to ss. 41 and 45 (now ss. 57 and 61 of the 1961 Act), said that they seemed to demonstrate that the heading "Welfare" was not used in an exclusive and restricted sense, and that it was capable of covering provisions in which the element of protection of health was present, whilst s. 42 disclosed a purpose beyond that of promoting welfare in the narrow sense. Accordingly, the court held that s. 42(1) (now s. 58(1) of the 1961 Act) gave a civil right of action. It is therefore incorrect to generalise upon the welfare provisions. The only other decisions upon them are *McCarthy v Daily Mirror Newspapers Ltd*, above, in which the Court of Appeal accepted without discussion that an action lay for breach of s. 43(1) of the 1937 Act (now s. 59(1) of the 1961 Act) and *Barr v Cruickshank & Co Ltd* 1958 74 Sh Ct Rep 218, in which Sheriff-Substitute Murray held expressly that a breach of s. 43(1) of the 1937

Act gave rise to a cause of action. It is thus possible to say that of the welfare sections of the 1961 Act, which are for this purpose ss. 57 to 61, ss. 58(1) and 59(1), give rise to civil liability, whilst the interpretation of the remaining provisions is uncertain. When subordinate legislation contains like provisions these must in this respect, it is submitted, be interpreted in the same sense as those of the Act itself.

In recent years the role of ergonomics in safety has been recognised to a much greater extent. In consequence provisions that may have once been regarded as welfare may now be viewed as safety provisions.

It is to be wondered whether the courts might not be more amenable to enforcement of purely welfare provisions by way of an injunction rather than damages. In the light of the new Directives it is submitted that welfare provisions are more likely to be treated as founding civil liability at the suit of the employee whether the claim is for damages or injunctive relief.

The Health and Safety at Work etc. Act 1974 expressly provides, by s. 47, that no action will lie for breach of the "general duties" sections of the Act (ss. 2–8) but that breach of a duty imposed by health and safety regulations made under the Act is, so far as it causes damage, actionable except in so far as the regulations provide otherwise.

The same section further provides that the Act does not affect the extent, if any, to which breach of a duty imposed by any of the existing statutory provisions (which include the Factories Act 1961, the agricultural safety legislation and the Offices, Shops and Railway Premises Act 1963 and subordinate legislation made under those Acts) is actionable.

In effect, therefore, with regard to all the safety, health and welfare legislation contained in this book, with the exception of the 1974 Act itself and regulations made under it, the question, whether an action will lie, remains to be determined in accordance with the principles set out above. (See "Direct Application of European Directives", above, for a discussion on the principles applicable to the Directives.)

Causation

It has already been said that in a civil action for breach of statutory duty the plaintiff must prove that the damage of which he complains was caused by the breach: *Caswell v Powell Duffryn Associated Collieries Ltd* [1940] AC 152, HL. This general proposition is equally apposite to an action founded on breach of a Directive or implementing Regulation. The proposition, however, must yield to the words of the statutory provision if that provision in terms places the onus of disproving the causal connection upon the person on whom the duty lies. Apart, however, from cases where the onus is expressly so placed the plaintiff must prove his case by the ordinary standard of proof in civil actions: he must show at least that on a balance of probabilities the breach of duty caused or materially contributed to his injury (*Bonnington Castings Ltd v Wardlaw* [1956] AC 613, [1956] 1 All ER 613, HL; *Wilsher v Essex Area Health Authority* [1988] AC 1074, HL). One practical approach is to demonstrate that the breach was a material factor in causing the type of injury suffered by the plaintiff and then to discount other potential causes in respect of this particular individual (see *McPherson v Alexander Stephens & Sons Ltd* (1991) HSIB 175, p. 15). The application of this principle has given rise to difficulty in cases where the plaintiff's claim is based upon a failure to provide a protective device. In *Cummings* (or *McWilliams*) *v Sir William Arrol & Co Ltd* [1962] 1 All ER 623, HL, the widow of a steel erector who had been killed by a fall at a shipbuilding yard, sued, *inter alia*, the occupiers of the yard alleging a breach of s. 26(2) of the Factories Act 1937, in that the occupiers had failed to provide the deceased with a safety belt. The occupiers admitted that no belt had been provided, but contended that, since there was evidence that the deceased would not have worn a safety belt had one been provided, their failure to provide the belt did not cause the death. This contention was upheld by the House of Lords. The Lord Chancellor, Lord Kilmuir, stated that there were four steps of causation: (1) a duty to supply a safety belt; (2) a breach; (3) that if there had been a safety belt the deceased would have used it; and (4) that if there had been a safety belt the deceased would not have been killed. If the irresistible inference was that the deceased would not have worn a safety belt had it been provided, the chain of causation was broken. This case was followed in *Wigley v British Vinegars Ltd* [1964] AC 307, HL, but was distinguished in *Ross v Associated Portland Cement Manufacturers Ltd* [1964] 2 All ER 452, HL, where the evidence led to no such inference. In *Corn v Weir's Glass (Hanley) Ltd* [1960] 2 All ER 300, the Court of Appeal held that a plaintiff who, in suing for breach of reg. 27(1) of the Building (Safety, Health and Welfare) Regulations 1948, alleged a failure to provide a hand-rail on a flight of stairs, failed if he could not prove that the presence of a hand-rail would in fact have protected him from injury. In this case Devlin LJ (at p. 306) considered the position which arose when there were two or more ways in which the occupier might comply with his statutory duty, one of which would, and the others of which would not, have protected the plaintiff. In those circumstances, he said, the occupier could not rely upon a method which he was unlikely to have used simply because it was within the letter of the regulation. On the other hand, if it could not be said that any one way was more likely to have been chosen than the others, then the plaintiff as a matter of probability failed.

The question of causation is not to be decided by any logical or scientific theory, but by applying common sense to the facts of the particular case (*Stapley v Gypsum Mines Ltd* [1953] AC 663, HL, *per* Lord Reid at 681), and the onus resting upon the plaintiff to prove the necessary causal connection is not discharged merely because there was a breach of duty and it is shown to be possible that his injury may have been caused by it (*Bonnington Castings v Wardlaw*, above, *per* Lord Reid at 681). When, however, a breach of duty is proved, that has been said to constitute some *prima facie* evidence of causal connection between the breach and the subsequent damage (*Cummings* (or *McWilliams*) *v Sir William Arrol & Co Ltd*, above, *per* Viscount Simonds, *sed quaere*).

Proof by a plaintiff that the defendant's breach materially increased the risk of injury to him is not to be equated with proof that it made a material contribution to that injury, nor does the fact that the defendant's breach created a risk within the area in which the injury to the plaintiff occurred suffice to reverse the burden of proof so that it is then for the defendant to prove that his breach was not causative (*Wilshire v Essex Area Health Authority*, above, disapproving of dicta to the contrary in *McGhee v National Coal Board* [1972] 3 All ER 1008, HL, and holding that that decision laid down no new principle of law).

Breach of statutory duty and negligence

The cause of action for breach of statutory duty is distinct from that for negligence (*Caswell v Powell Duffryn Associated Collieries* [1940] AC 152, HL; *per* Lord Wright at 177) and, since the imposition of a statutory duty does not of itself relieve an employer of his ordinary duty of care in relation to the same subject matter (*Franklin v Gramophone Co Ltd* [1948] 1 KB 542, CA; *Bux v Slough Metals Ltd* [1974] 1 All ER 262, CA), it will frequently occur that an injured person will bring his action on the ground both of breach of statutory duty and negligence. Negligence, however, cannot be considered in dissociation from the statutory provision (*Roberts v Dorman Long & Co Ltd* [1953] 2 All ER 428 at 436 *per* Hodson LJ) and in very many cases, it would be difficult, if not impossible, to maintain that an employer who had complied with regulations had been negligent at common law (*Franklin v Gramophone Co Ltd*, above, *per* Somervell LJ at 558; compliance with the relevant regulations may well be of evidential value, *per* Lord Keith of Avonholm in *Qualcast (Wolverhampton) Ltd v Haynes* [1959] AC 743 at 756). On the other hand, in some cases the very existence of the statutory provision may be relied on by the plaintiff as showing that a reasonable man would have foreseen a particular risk, which the statutory provision is designed to eliminate, and may, therefore, be relied on to help establish negligence on the part of the employer (*ibid.*, *per* Somervell LJ at 558; *National Coal Board v England* [1954] AC 403, HL). However, where the circumstances of the case, although they nearly approach those to which the statutory provision applies, are in fact outside them, the question of common law negligence must be considered without regard to the statutory provision (*Chipchase v British Titan Products Co Ltd* [1956] 1 QB 545, CA). Thus, in *Bux v Slough Metals Ltd*, above, the defendants, in whose foundry the plaintiff was employed, supplied him with goggles but failed to instruct him to wear them. The Court of Appeal held that while there had been no breach of reg. 13(1) of the Non-Ferrous Metals (Melting and Founding) Regulations 1962, which required the provision of suitable goggles or other suitable eye protection in the circumstances, nevertheless that did not absolve the defendants from their duty at common law to take reasonable care to see that the goggles were worn. By contrast, a statutory provision may of course establish a more stringent duty than that at common law. Foreseeability of injury, for example, may be irrelevant to an action for breach of statutory duty: see *Larner v British Steel* [1993] IRLR 278. There is some authority that, in appropriate circumstances, the standard of care established by statute may be taken as the standard in negligence. In *Butt v Inner London Education Authority* (1968) 66 LGR 379, CA the duty of care owed to a student operating an unfenced printing machine at a technical school was held to be analogous to that under the Factories Act. In *Hewett v Alf Brown's Transport Ltd* ([1991] ICR 471, affirmed [1992] ICR 530, CA, the standard of the common law duty of care was determined by reference to the Control of Lead at Work Regulations (S.I. 1980 No. 1248) without argument. These cases may be better understood on the basis that the relevant statutory provisions make clear what risks and injuries are reasonably foreseeable.

Persons protected by safety legislation

Subject to the construction of any particular section, the general provisions of the Factories Act apply to protect all persons working in the factory, whether employed by the occupier or not (*Summers (John) & Sons Ltd v Frost* [1955] AC 740, HL; *Wigley v British Vinegars Ltd* [1964] AC 307, HL), and this is so whether they are at the material time engaged upon the work they are employed to do or upon concerns of their own (*Westwood v Post Office* [1974] AC 1, HL; *Uddin v Associated Portland Cement Manufacturers Ltd* [1965] 2 QB 582, CA; *Allen v Aeroplane and Motor Aluminium Castings Ltd* [1965] 3 All ER 377, CA); or whether they are working in an area that the occupier could not foresee they would use (*Dexter v Tenby Electrical Accessories* [1991] Crim LR 839). Such persons may, therefore, in accordance with the principles already discussed, found a civil action for damages upon injury caused by a breach of the statute. The tendency of Regulations passed pursuant to Directives is to extend the classes of person protected in keeping with the broad purpose (see e.g. Management of Health and Safety at Work Regulations (S.I. 1992 No. 2051) regs. 10 and 13).

Under the Offshore Installations (Operational Safety, Health and Welfare) Regulations (S.I. 1976 No. 1019), it has been held that the purpose of the regulations is to protect employees not only while they are working but also at all times when they are at or near the installation; hence the employer was vicariously liable for a foreman who endangered the safety of a fellow employee and it was irrelevant that the foreman was acting outside the scope of his employment (*Macmillan v Wimpey Offshore Engineers and Constructors Ltd* 1991 SLT 515).

In the case of much safety legislation, the persons protected are expressly specified; for example, "every person working in those premises" in s. 17(1) of the Offices, Shops and Railway Premises Act 1963. Where the persons protected are designated with less certainty (as, for example, by the phrase "persons employed") decisions under the Factories Acts will, it is submitted, afford guidance in accordance with the principle of construction of statutes *in pari materia*.

The provisions of the Offices, Shops and Railway Premises Act 1963, although they protect employed persons, have been held not to protect a customer in a shop (*Reid v Galbraith's Stores* 1970 SLT (Notes) 83).

Dangers protected against by safety legislation
The rule that to succeed in an action for breach of statutory duty, the damage sustained must be of the kind against which the statute was intended to protect (the rule in *Gorris v Scott* (1874) LR 9 Exch 125), has been applied to the Factories Act, most notably in *Nicholls v Austin (Leyton) Ltd* ([1946] AC 493) and *Carroll v Andrew Barclay & Sons Ltd* ([1948] AC 477), where the duty to fence machinery was held not to protect against materials being thrown out of the machine or against the breaking of a transmission belt. The rule as applied to safety legislation has been much criticised and avoided in subsequent cases, e.g. *Grant v National Coal Board* ([1956] AC 649, HL), *Donaghey v Boulton & Paul Ltd* ([1968] AC 1, HL), *Millard v Serck Tubes Ltd* ([1969] 1 All ER 598, CA), *Callow (Engineers) Ltd v Johnson* ([1971] AC 335, see Lord Hailsham LC at 341), *McGovern v British Steel Corpn* ([1986] ICR 608, CA). With the advent of the much broader Regulations which implement the European Directives, it is submitted that the rule in *Gorris v Scott* will have less application. For example, reg. 12 of the Provision and Use of Work Equipment Regulations (S.I. 1992 No. 2932) requires fencing against any article or substance being ejected from the machine and against rupture or disintegration of parts of the work equipment (amongst other things).

Delegation of statutory duty
Where an employer delegates the performance of a duty laid upon him by the Act or subordinate legislation he remains civilly liable to a person injured by breach of that duty (*Lochgelly Iron and Coal Co Ltd v M'Mullan* [1934] AC 1, HL), but where the person injured is himself the person to whom the duty was delegated he may, where there has been a definite delegation, be disentitled to recover (*Smith v A Baveystock & Co Ltd* [1945] 1 All ER 531, CA; *Vyner v Waldenberg Bros Ltd* [1946] KB 50, CA). However, whether the breach by the

injured person is of a duty delegated to him by his employer or of a duty imposed upon him by the Act or regulations, "the important and fundamental question ... is not whether there was a delegation, but simply the usual question: Whose fault was it? ... If the answer to that question is that in substance and reality the accident was solely due to the fault of the plaintiff, so that he was the sole author of his own wrong, he is disentitled to recover. But that has to be applied to the particular case and it is not necessarily conclusive for the employer to show that it was a wrongful act of the employee plaintiff which caused the accident ... One has to inquire whether the fault of the employer under the statutory regulations consists of, and is co-extensive with, the wrongful act of the employee. If there is some fault on the part of the employer which goes beyond or is independent of the wrongful act of the employee, and was a cause of the accident, the employer has some liability" (*per* Pearson J in *Ginty v Belmont Building Supplies Ltd* [1959] 1 All ER 414). This statement of the law was approved and applied by the Court of Appeal in *McMath v Rimmer Bros (Liverpool) Ltd* [1961] 3 All ER 1154, CA and was regarded by the Court of Appeal in *Quinn v J W Green (Painters) Ltd* [1966] 1 QB 509, as having been approved by the House of Lords in *Ross v Associated Portland Cement Manufacturers Ltd* [1964] 2 All ER 452, [1964] 1 WLR 768, HL, where, in distinguishing *Ginty's* case on the facts, Lord Reid said that, in the context of the question "Whose fault was it?", fault is not necessarily equivalent to blame-worthiness. The latter case and *Boyle v Kodak Ltd* ([1969] 2 All ER 439, HL), show that the employer may only avoid liability if the breach occurred *solely* through the plaintiff's conduct without any breach by or on behalf of the employer. These cases show that a plaintiff need do no more than prove a breach of an enactment making the factory occupier absolutely liable, and that the breach caused the accident. The onus is then upon the factory occupier to prove that he was not in any way at fault but that the plaintiff was alone to blame. To discharge this onus, the factory occupier must establish that he took all reasonable steps to avoid the breach including, in appropriate cases, steps to acquaint the plaintiff with the provisions of the breached enactment even though on the facts of the particular case a failure to take such steps would not constitute negligence at common law (*Boyle v Kodak Ltd* [1969] 2 All ER 439, HL). Nevertheless, there may be cases in which an injury suffered by a plaintiff may be held to have been entirely caused by his own fault although there has been a breach of statutory duty on the part of his employer and although the *Ginty* situation of co-terminous and co-extensive fault does not exist (see *Horne v Lec Refrigeration Ltd* [1965] 2 All ER 898; *Leach v Standard Telephones and Cables Ltd* [1966] 2 All ER 523; and *Jayes v IMI (Kynoch) Ltd* [1985] ICR 155, CA).

Note that the extent of the duty owed may involve having regard to the particular characteristics of the employee concerned. In *Baker v T Clarke (Leeds) Ltd* ([1992] PIQR P262), the Court of Appeal held that there was no breach of the Construction (Working Places) Regulations 1961 when a skilled employee fell from a scaffold tower he had failed to lock. In the circumstances the court considered that no duty lay on the employer constantly to remind skilled workers of things they should not do unless dangers were insidious or there is some evidence that proper precautions are not being observed. It is submitted that the decision should be narrowly confined, in keeping with the purpose of the Acts and Regulations, and should extend only to obvious dangers of which employees are well aware and which inadvertance is unlikely to cause them to overlook.

The advent of the Regulations implementing the European Directives will not alter these principles, although the obligation on employers to take into account each employee's "capabilities as regards health and safety" (reg. 11 of the Management of Health and Safety at Work Regulations (S.I. 1992 No. 2051)) may become relevant as to whether it was negligent to delegate a safety obligation to a particular employee. In fact the Regulations impose duties on employees beyond those in ss. 7 and 8 of the Health and Safety at Work etc. Act 1974: see e.g. reg. 19 of the Personal Protective Equipment at Work Regulations (S.I. 1992 No. 2966) and reg. 5 of the Manual Handling Operations Regulations (S.I. 1992 No. 2793). Regulation 12 of the Management of Health and Safety at Work Regulations (above) imposes duties on employees but reg. 15 provides that breach of these Regulations "shall not confer a right of action in any civil proceedings" (though breach can be prosecuted as a criminal offence). The wording of this exclusion of civil liability would not, it is submitted, preclude an employer from relying on the employee's breach of such a duty in order to mount a *Ginty* defence to an action brought by the employee. The submission would be yet more forceful where the employee was seeking to avoid the exclusion in his action against the employer by arguing that it was incompatible with the Directive (see above). Furthermore, breach of the employee's duties under the Regulations would be, it is submitted, admissible as evidence of contributory negligence (see above).

INTRODUCTORY NOTES

General

1. Amendments. Where the statutes or other instruments contained in this book have been amended, they are printed as so amended.

2. Definitions. Words and expressions defined in the interpretation section or elsewhere in a statute are appropriately noted; words and expressions given a defined meaning in regulations or other subordinate legislation are, at appropriate intervals, printed in *italics*.

3. References to enactments. References to enactments which have been superseded by later enactments are followed by a reference to the later enactments in square brackets.

Interpretation

Construction of common expressions

4. United Kingdom; Great Britain; England and Wales. "United Kingdom" means Great Britain and Northern Ireland (Interpretation Act 1978, Sch. 1); Great Britain comprises England, Scotland and Wales (Union with Scotland Act 1706; Wales and Berwick Act 1746); "England" means, subject to any alteration of boundaries under Part IV of the Local Government Act 1972, the area consisting of the counties established by s. 1 of the Act, Greater London and the Isles of Scilly (Interpretation Act 1978, Sch. 1): "Wales" means, subject to any alteration of boundaries under Part IV of the Local Government Act 1972, the area consisting of the counties established by s. 20 of that Act (Interpretation Act 1978, Sch. 1).

5. Reasonably practicable; practicable. "Reasonably practicable" is a narrower term than "physically possible" and implies that a computation must be made in which the *quantum* of risk is placed in one scale and the sacrifice, whether in money, time or trouble, involved in the measures necesssary to avert the risk is placed in the other; and that, if it be shown that there is a gross disproportion between them, the risk being insignificant in relation to the sacrifice, the person upon whom the duty is laid discharges the burden of proving that compliance was not reasonably practicable. This computation falls to be made at a point of time anterior to the happening of the incident complained of (*Edwards v National Coal Board* [1949] 1 KB 704 at 712, [1949] 1 All ER 743 at 747, CA, *per* Asquith LJ; *McCarthy v Coldair Ltd* [1951] 2 TLR 1226, CA; *Marshall v Gotham Co Ltd* [1954] AC 360 at 373, [1954] 1 All ER 937 at 942, *per* Lord Reid and, it seems, at 370 and at 939, *per* Lord Oaksey). It follows that reliance upon the advice or expertise of others, even if reasonable, is largely irrelevant to the issue of compliance (see *Lockhart v Kevin Oliphant* 1993 SLT 179, High Court).

Where an obligation is qualified solely by the word "practicable" a stricter standard is imposed. What this term connotes, however, is not an easy matter to decide (*Cartwright v GKN Sankey Ltd* (1973) 14 KIR 349 at 363, CA). Measures may be practicable which are not reasonably practicable (*Marshall v Gotham Co Ltd*, above, at 372, 942, *per* Lord Reid) but, nonetheless, "practicable" means something other than physically possible. The measures must be possible in the light of current knowledge and invention (*Adsett v K and L Steelfounders and Engineers Ltd* [1953] 1 All ER 97n at 98, [1953] 1 WLR 137 at 141, 142, *per* Parker J; affd. [1953] 2 All ER 320, [1953] 1 WLR 773, CA; *McLeod v Rolls Royce Ltd* 1956 Sh Ct Rep 214. See also *Moorcroft v Thomas Powles & Sons Ltd* [1962] 3 All ER 741). Thus, it is impracticable to take precautions against a danger which cannot be known to be in existence or to take precautions which have not yet been invented, so that the concept of practicability introduces at all events some degree of reason and involves at all events some regard for practice (*Jayne v National Coal Board* [1963] 2 All ER 220). If a precaution can be taken without practical difficulty, then it is a practicable precaution, notwithstanding that it may occasion some risk to those who take it and even though that risk far outweighs the benefits to be achieved (*Boyton v Willment Bros Ltd* [1971] 3 All ER 624, CA).

In civil proceedings the burden of pleading and proving that compliance with an obligation was not reasonably practicable or practicable, as the case may be, lies upon the person upon whom the obligation is placed (*Nimmo v Alexander Cowan & Sons Ltd* [1968] AC 107, HL; *Jenkins v Allied Ironfounders Ltd* [1969] 3 All ER 1609, HL; *Bowes v Sedgefield District Council* [1981] ICR 234, CA; *Larner v British Steel plc* [1993] ICR 551, CA).

In criminal proceedings the onus lies upon the defendant (Health and Safety at Work etc. Act 1974, s. 40; *Lockhart v Kevin Oliphant* 1993 SLT 179, High Court) although proof upon the balance of probabilities is sufficient (*R v Carr-Briant* [1943] KB 607, CCA; *R v Dunbar* [1958] 1 QB 1, CCA). See also INTRODUCTORY NOTE 7 on the problem of prosecuting companies.

The standard of reasonable practicability is not found in the Directives, though it occurs in places in the implementing Regulations. Where the use of that standard (in implementing or pre-existing legislation) would diminish the standard of care required by the Directives in an identical situation, the lower standard is open to challenge (see above). The preamble to the Framework Directive specifically provides that health and safety at work "is an objective which should not be subordinated to purely economic considerations", a principle which is inconsistent with the element of cost present in the assessment of what is "reasonably practicable".

6. Connivance. There is no direct authority on the construction of this term as used in the context of safety legislation. It is submitted that it connotes a specific mental state not amounting to actual consent to the commission of the offence in question, concomitant with a failure to take any step to prevent or discourage the commission of that offence. Such a mental state has been termed "wilful blindness"; that is to say, an intentional shutting of the eyes to something of which the percipient would, in his own interests, prefer to remain unaware. This construction accords both with the etymology of the word (Latin: *conivere*, to wink) and with the use of it made by the courts in expounding the common law aspects of the concept of *mens rea* (see *Roper v Taylor's Central Garages (Exeter) Ltd* [1951] 2 TLR 284). It accords also with the construction given to the word in connection with the old matrimonial offences (see *Gipps v Gipps and Hume* (1864) 11 HL Cas 1 at 14, *per* Lord Westbury; *Manning v Manning* [1950] 1 All ER 602, CA).

7. Due diligence. Where it is a defence for a person charged with a contravention of a statutory provision to prove that he used all due diligence to secure compliance with that provision, whether he did so or not is a question of fact, but on a case stated the High Court will interfere if there was no evidence to support a finding of fact upon the question (*R C Hammett Ltd v Crabb* (1931) 145 LT 638). Where the person charged is a limited company, a failure to exercise due diligence on its part will only occur where the failure is that of a director or senior manager in actual control of the company's operations who can be identified with the controlling mind and will of the company; the default of a subordinate manager who cannot be so identified will not be the default of the company but of a person other than the company (*Tesco Supermarkets Ltd v Nattrass* [1972] AC 153, HL).

8. Wilfully. In the words of Lord Russell of Killowen CJ in *R v Senior* [1899] 1 QB 283 at 290, 291, wilfully "means that the act is done deliberately and intentionally, not by accident or inadvertence, but so that the mind of the person who does the act goes with it"; see also *R v Walker* (1934) 24 Cr App Rep 117, CCA; *Eaton v Cobb* [1950] 1 All ER 1016 and *Arrowsmith v Jenkins* [1963] 2 QB 561, [1963] 2 All ER 210.

9. Provide. Where there is a duty to provide an article for the protection of a person at work, that duty is not fulfilled unless the article is so placed that it comes easily and obviously to the hand of the person for whom it is to be provided or, at the very least, unless he is given clear directions where he is to obtain it; *Finch v Telegraph Construction and Maintenance Co Ltd* [1949] 1 All ER 452; *Ginty v Belmont Building Supplies Ltd* [1959] 1 All ER 414; *Brown v Bonnington Castings Ltd* 1969 SLT (Notes) 24. Until the Personal Protective Equipment at Work Regulations (S.I. 1992 No. 2966), the duty "to provide" did not extend to taking steps to ensure that the article provided was used, once provided: *Norris v Syndic Manufacturing Co Ltd* [1952] 2 QB 135, CA (provision of goggles). Under reg. 10(1) of the Personal Protective Equipment at Work Regulations (above), the employer is under a duty to "take all reasonable steps to ensure that any personal protective equipment provided to his employees by virtue of Regulation 4(1) is properly used". Under reg. 10(2) the employee is under a duty to use the personal protective equipment provided, so that the law is likely to remain unchanged that an employee not provided with protective equipment may fail in an action if it is shown that he would not have used it anyway (*Nolan v Dental Manufacturing Co Ltd* [1958] 2 All ER 449). The burden on proving the latter will be, it is submitted, on the employer and a heavy one in the light of reg. 10(1) and will be stricter, no doubt, than the common law duty to ensure that employees use protective equipment (see e.g. *Bux v Slough Metals* [1974] 1 All ER 262, CA).

10. Properly maintained. In *Galashiels Gas Co Ltd v O'Donnell (or Millar)* [1949] AC 275, HL, it was held that the obligation imposed by the Factories Act 1937, s. 22(1) that "every hoist or lift shall be ... properly maintained" imposed an absolute obligation to maintain such appliances in an efficient state, in efficient working order and in good repair and described a result to be achieved rather than the means of achieving it. Although this decision was based upon the definition of "maintained" in s. 152(1) of the Factories Act 1937 (s. 176(1) of the Factories Act 1961), it is submitted that a similar obligation in other safety legislation should be similarly construed, despite the absence of such a definition.

11. Of good mechanical construction, sound material and adequate strength. These or similar phrases with minor variations in wording define the obligations of many provisions of the safety legislation and where the obligation is unqualified by such words as "so far as reasonably practicable" the obligation is an absolute one (*Whitehead v James Stott & Co* [1949] 1 KB 358, CA). Such an obligation imposes not only a duty to ensure that the plant or equipment is initially of good construction, sound material and adequate strength, but also a continuing duty to consider whether it has reached or passed the limit of its safe working life, although it is overstating the absolute nature of the obligation to say that breakage in use is conclusive of a breach (*Reilly v William Beardmore & Co Ltd* 1947 SC 275, Ct. of Session). The words "of good construction" have no reference to suitability for any purpose, and there is no breach of the requirement merely because an accident results from the use of plant or equipment which is not strong enough to serve a particular purpose for which it was never intended (*Beardsley v United Steel Cos Ltd* [1951] 1 KB 408, CA). The expression "good construction" imports considerations of lay-out and design (*Smith v A Davies & Co (Shopfitters) Ltd* (1968) 5 KIR 320, decided upon the predecessor to the Construction (Working Places) Regulations 1966, reg. 9(1), which contains an express reference to the purpose for which a scaffold is used). In considering whether plant or equipment is of good construction regard must be had, it is submitted, both to the stress which is likely to be imposed upon it when used for its intended purpose and to such further stress as may be imposed in circumstances which may foreseeably occur.

Having regard to the absolute nature of the duty, "sound material" means material which is in fact sound and not material which merely appears to be sound (*Whitehead v James Stott & Co* [1949] 1 KB 358, CA).

Whether plant or equipment is of "adequate strength" is to be judged by reference to the use to which it is being put at the relevant time. In exercising this judgment, provisions which prescribe safe working loads are to be regarded as supplementary to, and not exegetic of, the primary requirement of adequate strength (*Milne v C F Wilson & Co (1932) Ltd* 1960 SLT 162; *Ball v Richard Thomas & Baldwins Ltd* [1968] 1 All ER 389, CA; and see *Gledhill v Liverpool Abattoir Utility Co Ltd* [1957] 3 All ER 117, CA). There is no breach of this obligation where plant or equipment is unwieldy or otherwise unsuitable because its strength is greater than necessary (*Gledhill v Liverpool Abattoir Utility Co Ltd*, above).

12. Suitable and sufficient, effective and suitable. These phrases are to be found in the regulations which implement the European Directives and are often taken from the latter. They have some precedent in safety legislation and doubtless will acquire greater definition in the course of litigation on the Regulations. "Suitable goggles or effective screens" were required by the now repealed s. 65 of the Factories Act 1961. For goggles to be "suitable" they must be suitable both for the work for which they were intended to be used and for the worker using them; for a screen to be "effective" for its purpose it need not stop everything but if a large quantity of particle can get round or over it, so as to enter a worker's eye, it is open to the court to hold that it was not effective: *Lloyd v F Evans & Sons Ltd* [1951] WN 306, CA. Goggles are suitable if they are well adapted for the process and the wearer even if, in the event, they fail to ensure protection: *Daniels v Ford Motor Co Ltd* [1955] 1 All ER 218, CA followed in *Rodgers v George Blair & Co Ltd* (1971) 11 KIR 391, CA. "Suitable employment" under (the repealed) s. 9(33) of the Workmen's Compensation Act 1925 and under (what is now) s. 82(5)(b) of the Employment Protection (Consolidation) Act 1978 means suitable not for anybody but for the employee in question: *Hoe & Co v Dirs* [1941] 1 KB 34; *Taylor v Kent County Council* [1969] 2

QB 560. In *Baxter v Carron Co* 1965 SLT (Notes) 89 the question of suitability was said to be one of degree and that if the goggles were "... so badly fitting that they tend to slip and naturally increase the danger against which they are to be a protection, they cannot be 'suitable'".

Under s. 29 of the Factories Act 1961 (now repealed), it was held that whether or not a workplace or means of access is "safe" is a strict test, to be determined without reference to the foreseeability of injury: *Larner v British Steel plc* [1993] ICR 551. The matter is a question of fact; *per* Peter Gibson J in *Larner*. There appears no reason, it is submitted, why the question of suitability should not be equally strict.

"Effective provision" must be made for securing and maintaining sufficient and suitable lighting by s. 5(1) of the Factories Act. The duty requires that the factory occupier turns on the lights when natural lighting is insufficient or provides reasonably accessible light switches; the duty would be breached if a light bulb failed shortly before an accident even if there was a reasonably efficient system for effecting repairs; "'effective' means lighting which is functioning effectively, and lighting which may be admirable in construction and in the provision of proper bulbs and so on, is not effective when it is not turned on": *Thornton v Fisher & Ludlow Ltd* [1968] 2 All ER 241 at 243, *per* Danckwerts LJ.

13. Obstruction. An obstruction is something which has no business to be there and ought not reasonably to be there (*Churchill v Louis Marx & Co Ltd* (1964) 108 Sol Jo 334, CA); an obstruction is something the presence of which serves no useful purpose and which might cause an accident (*Jenkins v Allied Ironfounders Ltd* [1969] 3 All ER 1609 at 1611, [1970] 1 WLR 304 at 307, HL, *per* Lord Reid). The fact that the presence of the object creating the obstruction is highly improbable, or that it is unwittingly there, does not prevent it constituting an obstruction (*Bennett v Rylands Whitecross Ltd* [1978] ICR 1031). A small screw on a floor may be an obstruction if it satisfies the above test (*Gillies v Glynwed Foundries Ltd* 1977 SLT 97; *Paterson v Lothian Regional Council* 26 February 1992, Ct. of Session). However, the proper storage of things on the floor is not an obstruction on the floor (*Pengelly v Bell Punch Co Ltd* [1964] 2 All ER 945, CA), the reasonable presence of a loaded trolley in a gangway in the ordinary course of work is not an obstruction of the gangway (*Marshall v Ericsson Telephones Ltd* [1964] 3 All ER 609, CA) and part of a machine fixed to the floor is not an obstruction on the floor (*Drummond v Harland Engineering Co Ltd* 1963 SC 162). An electrical socket about 4″ high rising out of carpet tiles and used for connecting office machines to a power supply is not an obstruction within s. 16 of the Offices, Shops and Railway Premises Act 1963 (*Sommerville v Rowntree Mackintosh Ltd* (1984) unreported, CA).

14. Person aggrieved by an order. In construing this expression, it is plain that "person" includes a body of persons, corporate or unincorporate (Interpretation Act 1978, s. 5, Sch. 1) and it has been held that a local authority (see *R v Surrey Quarter Sessions, ex p Lilley* [1951] 2 KB 749, DC) or the Crown (see *A-G of the Gambia v N'Jie* [1961] AC 617, PC) may be such a person.

Whether a person is "aggrieved" by a decision may vary according to the context but, in general, it is not enough that he is dissatisfied with the decision or that his interests may be adversely affected by it (*Buxton v Minister of Housing and Local Government* [1961] 1 QB 278) but he will be such a person if he has been deprived of something to which he is legally entitled (*Re Sidebotham, ex p Sidebotham* (1880) 14 Ch D 458, CA; *Re Reed, Bowen and Co, ex p Official Receiver*

(1887) 19 QBD 174, CA) or if a legal burden has been placed upon him (*Re Hurle-Hobb's Decision* [1944] 2 All ER 261, CA; *R v Nottingham Quarter Sessions, ex p Harlow* [1952] 2 QB 601, DC) or if an order for costs has been made against him (*Jennings v Kelly* [1940] AC 206, HL; *R v Surrey Quarter Sessions, ex p Lilley*, above).

See, further, 1 Halsbury's Laws (4th Edn.) para. 49.

Regulations and Orders

15. Validity. In each of the regulations and orders printed in this book, the power under which it was made is specified. Those made under the Factory and Workshop Act 1901 and the Police, Factories, etc. (Miscellaneous Provisions) Act 1916, were continued in force by the Factories Act 1937, s. 159, and together with those made under the latter Act, the Lead Paint (Protection against Poisoning) Act 1926, the Factories Act 1948, and the Factories Act 1959, were continued in force by virtue of the Factories Act 1961, s. 183 and Sch. 6. However, the power to make welfare regulations (s. 62) and special regulations for safety and health (s. 76) under the Factories Act 1961 have been repealed by the Factories Act 1961, etc. (Repeals and Modifications) Regulations 1974, but by reg. 7(3) regulations, rules and orders made or having effect under any provision repealed by the regulations and in force immediately before the coming into operation of the regulations (1 January 1975) continue in force notwithstanding the repeal of that provision.

Similarly, the power to make regulations under the Agriculture (Safety, Health and Welfare Provisions) Act 1956, s. 1 has been repealed by the Agriculture (Safety, Health and Welfare Provisions) Act 1956 (Repeals and Modifications) Regulations (S.I. 1975 No. 46), but by reg. 5(3) regulations so made are continued in force.

For powers to make health and safety regulations and to approve and issue codes of practice, see the Health and Safety at Work, etc. Act 1974, ss. 15, 16. The Regulations and Approved Codes of Practice which implement the European Directives are all made under these powers. Codes of Practice are not printed in this book.

16. Short titles. Instruments made without provision for a short title have been given an abbreviated heading for convenience of reference. In such cases the date on which the instrument was made has been included in the heading.

17. Amendments. Where instruments have been amended they are printed as amended. Where the effect of an instrument has been modified the modifying instrument is printed in full or its purport is noted.

18. References to statutes. In the instrument which follows, references to section or schedules of superseded enactments are followed by the relevant section or schedule of the Factories Act 1961, in square brackets.

19. References to inspector of factories, etc. By S.I. 1974 No. 1941, reg. 6, references in any provision of an enactment, instrument or other document to:

(a) an inspector appointed under the Factories Act 1961;
(b) the inspector for the district, the superintending inspector for the division or the chief inspector;
(c) an employment medical adviser appointed under the Employment Advisory Service Act 1972; and
(d) the chief employment medical adviser or a deputy chief employment medical adviser,

are, except where the context otherwise requires or where the reference is otherwise expressly amended, to be construed as references respectively to:

 (i) an inspector appointed by the Health and Safety Executive under s. 19 of the Health and Safety at Work etc. Act 1974;

 (ii) an inspector so appointed who is authorised to act for the purposes of the provision in question;

 (iii) an employment medical adviser appointed under s. 56 of the Health and Safety at Work etc. Act 1974; and

 (iv) an employment medical adviser so appointed who is authorised to act for the purposes of the provision in question.

20. *Official forms.* In the instruments which follow, references to registers, notices, reports, etc., which are issued as official forms are followed by the appropriate form number in square brackets. The annotation "*Placard: Form...*" below the title or heading of an instrument refers to the placard copy of the instrument or the prescribed abstract thereof which may be used in order to comply with s. 139 of the Factories Act 1961.

PART 1
EUROPEAN DIRECTIVES

SUMMARY

THE NOISE AT WORK DIRECTIVE

General note. This Directive was implemented in the UK by the Noise at Work Regulations 1989 (S.I. 1989 No. 1790, amended by S.I. 1992 No. 2966), see page 1205.

COUNCIL DIRECTIVE

of 12 May 1986

on the protection of workers from the risks related to exposure to noise at work

(86/188/EEC)

THE COUNCIL OF THE EUROPEAN COMMUNITIES,

Having regard to the Treaty establishing the European Economic Community, and in particular Article 100 thereof,

Having regard to the proposal from the Commission, drawn up after consulting the Advisory Committee on Safety, Hygiene and Health Protection at Work,

Having regard to the opinion of the European Parliament,

Having regard to the opinion of the Economic and Social Committee,

Whereas the Council resolutions of 29 June 1978 and 27 February 1984 on action programmes of the European Communities on safety and health at work provide for the implementation of specific harmonised procedures for the protection of workers exposed to noise; whereas the measures adopted in this field vary from State to State and it is recognised that they urgently need to be approximated and improved;

Whereas exposure to high noise levels is encountered in a large number of situations and therefore many workers are exposed to a potential safety and health hazard;

Whereas a reduction of exposure to noise reduces the risk of hearing impairment caused by noise;

Whereas, where the noise level at the workplace involves a risk for the health and safety of workers, limiting exposure to noise reduces that risk without prejudice to the applicable provisions on the limitation of noise emission;

Whereas the most effective way of reducing noise levels at work is to incorporate noise prevention measures into the design of installations and to choose materials, procedures and working methods which produce less noise; whereas the priority aim must be to achieve the said reduction at source;

Whereas the provision and use of personal ear protectors is a necessary complementary measure to the reduction of noise at source, where exposure cannot reasonably be avoided by other means;

Whereas noise is an agent to which Council Directive 80/1107/EEC of 27 November 1980 on the protection of workers from the risks related to exposure to chemical, physical and biological agents at work applies; whereas Articles 3 and 4 of the said Directive provide for the possibility of laying down limit values and other special measures in respect of the agents being considered;

Whereas certain technical aspects must be defined and may be reviewed in the light of experience and progress made in the technical and scientific field;

Whereas the current situation in the Member States does not make it possible to fix a noise-exposure value below which there is no longer any risk to workers' hearing;

Whereas current scientific knowledge about the effects that exposure to noise may have on health, other than on hearing, does not enable precise safety levels to be set; whereas, however, reduction of noise will lower the risk of illnesses unrelated to auditory complaints; whereas this Directive contains provisions which will be reviewed in the light of experience and developments in scientific and technical knowledge in this field,

HAS ADOPTED THIS DIRECTIVE:

Article 1

1.   This Directive, which is the third individual Directive within the meaning of Directive 80/1107/EEC, has as its aim the protection of workers against risks to their hearing and, in so far as this Directive expressly so provides, to their health and safety, including the prevention of such risks arising or likely to arise from exposure to noise at work.

2.   This Directive shall apply to all workers, including those exposed to radiation covered by the scope of the EAEC Treaty, with the exception of workers engaged in sea transport and in air transport.

For the purpose of this Directive, the expression "workers engaged in sea transport and in air transport" shall refer to personnel on board.

On a proposal from the Commission the Council shall examine, before 1 January 1990, the possibility of applying this Directive to workers engaged in sea transport and in air transport.

3.   This Directive shall not prejudice the right of Member States to apply or introduce, subject to compliance with the Treaty, laws, regulations or administrative provisions ensuring, where possible, greater protection for workers and/or intended to reduce the level of noise experienced at work by taking action at source, particularly in order to achieve exposure values which prevent unnecessary nuisance.

Article 2

For the purposes of this Directive, the following terms shall have the meaning hereby assigned to them:

1. *Daily personal noise exposure of a worker $L_{EP,d}$*

    The daily personal noise exposure of a worker is expressed in dB(A) using the formula:

    $$L_{EP,\,d} = L_{Aeq,\,Te} + 10\log_{10}\frac{T_e}{T_o}$$

    where:

    $$L_{Aeq,\,Te} = 10\log_{10}\left\{\frac{1}{T_e}\int_o^{T_e}\left[\frac{p_A(t)}{p_o}\right]^2 dt\right\}$$

    T_e = daily duration of a worker's personal exposure to noise,

    T_o = 8 h = 28 800 s,

    p_o = 20 μPa,

    p_A = "A"-weighted instantaneous sound pressure in pascals to which is exposed, in air at atmospheric pressure, a person who might or might not move from one place to another while at work; it is determined from measurements made at the position occupied by the person's ears during work, preferably in the person's absence, using a technique which minimises the effect on the sound field.

    If the microphone has to be located very close to the person's body, appropriate adjustments should be made to determine an equivalent undisturbed field pressure.

    The daily personal noise exposure does not take account of the effect of any personal ear protector used.

2. *Weekly average of the daily values $L_{EP,w}$*

    The weekly average of the daily values is found using the following formula:

    $$L_{EP,\,w} = 10\log_{10}\left[\frac{1}{5}\sum_{k=1}^{m}10^{0,1}\,(L_{EP,\,d})\,k\right]$$

    where $(L_{EP,d})_k$ are the values of $L_{EP,d}$ for each of the m working days in the week being considered.

Article 3

1. Noise experienced at work shall be assessed and, when necessary, measured in order to identify the workers and workplaces referred to in this Directive and to determine the conditions under which the specific provisions of this Directive shall apply.

2. The assessment and measurement mentioned in paragraph 1 shall be competently planned and carried out at suitable intervals under the responsibility of the employers.

Any sampling must be representative of the daily personal exposure of a worker to noise.

The methods and apparatus used must be adapted to the prevailing conditions in the light, particularly, of the characteristics of the noise to be measured, the length of exposure, ambient factors and the characteristics of the measuring apparatus.

These methods and this apparatus shall make it possible to determine the parameters defined in Article 2 and to decide whether, in a given case, the values fixed in this Directive have been exceeded.

3.   Member States may lay down that personal exposure to noise shall be replaced by noise recorded at the workplace. In that event the criterion of personal exposure to noise shall be replaced, for the purposes of Articles 4 to 10, by that of noise exposure during the daily work period, such period being at least eight hours, at the places where the workers are situated.

Member States may also lay down that, when the noise is measured, special consideration shall be given to impulse noise.

4.   The workers and/or their representatives in the undertaking or establish-ment shall be associated, according to national law and practice, with the assessment and measurement provided for in paragraph 1. These shall be revised where there is reason to believe that they are incorrect or that a material change has taken place in the work.

5.   The recording and preservation of the data obtained pursuant to this Article shall be carried out in a suitable form, in accordance with national law and practice.

The doctor and/or the authority responsible and the workers and/or their representatives in the undertaking shall have access to these data, in accord-ance with national law and practice.

Article 4

1.   Where the daily personal exposure of a worker to noise is likely to exceed 85 dB(A) or the maximum value of the unweighted instantaneous sound pressure is likely to be greater than 200 Pa, appropriate measures shall be taken to ensure that:

(a)   workers and/or their representatives in the undertaking or establishment receive adequate information and, when relevant, training concerning:
   — potential risks to their hearing arising from noise exposure,
   — the measures taken in pursuance of this Directive,
   — the obligation to comply with protective and preventive measures, in accordance with national legislation,
   — the wearing of personal ear protectors and the role of checks on hearing in accordance with Article 7;

(b)   workers and/or their representatives in the undertaking or establishment have access to the results of noise assessments and measurements made pursuant to Article 3 and can be given explanations of the significance of those results.

2.   At workplaces where the daily personal noise exposure of a worker is likely to exceed 85 dB(A), appropriate information must be provided to workers as to where and when Article 6 applies.

At workplaces where the daily personal noise exposure of a worker is likely to exceed 90 dB(A) or where the maximum value of the unweighted instan-taneous sound pressure is likely to exceed 200 Pa, the information provided for in the first subparagraph must, where reasonably practicable, take the form of appropriate signs. The areas in question must also be delimited and access to them must be restricted, where the risk of exposure so justifies and where these measures are reasonably practicable.

Article 5

1. The risks resulting from exposure to noise must be reduced to the lowest level reasonably practicable, taking account of technical progress and the availability of measures to control the noise, in particular at source.

2. Where the daily personal noise exposure of a worker exceeds 90 dB(A), or the maximum value of the unweighted instantaneous sound pressure is greater than 200 Pa:

(a) the reasons for the excess level shall be identified and the employer shall draw up and apply a programme of measures of a technical nature and/or of organisation of work with a view to reducing as far as reasonably practicable the exposure of workers to noise;
(b) workers and their representatives in the undertaking or establishment shall receive adequate information on the excess level and on the measures taken pursuant to subparagraph (a).

Article 6

1. Without prejudice to Article 5, where the daily personal noise exposure of a worker exceeds 90 dB (A) or the maximum value of the unweighted instantaneous sound pressure is greater than 200 Pa, personal ear protectors must be used.

2. Where the exposure referred to in paragraph 1 is likely to exceed 85 dB(A), personal ear protectors must be made available to workers.

3. Personal ear protectors must be supplied in sufficient numbers by the employer, the models being chosen in association, according to national law and practice, with the workers concerned.

The ear protectors must be adapted to the individual worker and to his working conditions, taking account of his safety and health. They are deemed, for the purposes of this Directive, suitable and adequate if, when properly worn, the risk to hearing can reasonably be expected to be kept below the risk arising from the exposure referred to in paragraph 1.

4. Where application of this Article involves a risk of accident, such risk must be reduced as far as is reasonably practicable by means of appropriate measures.

Article 7

1. Where it is not reasonably practicable to reduce the daily personal noise exposure of a worker to below 85 dB(A), the worker exposed shall be able to have his hearing checked by a doctor or on the responsibility of the doctor and, if judged necessary by the doctor, by a specialist.

The [way] in which this check is carried out shall be established by the Member States in accordance with national law and practice.

2.   The purpose of the check shall be the diagnosis of any hearing impairment by noise and the preservation of hearing.

3.   The results of checks on workers' hearing shall be kept in accordance with national law and practice.

Workers shall have access to the results which apply to them in so far as national law and practice allow.

4.   Member States shall take the necessary measures with a view to the doctor and/or the authority responsible giving, as part of the check, appropriate indications on any individual protective or preventive measures to be taken.

Article 8

1.   Member States shall take appropriate measures to ensure that:

(a)   the design, building and/or construction of new plant (new factories, plant or machinery, substantial extensions or modifications to existing factories or plant and replacement of plant or machinery) comply with Article 5(1);

(b)   where a new article (tool, machine, apparatus, etc.) which is intended for use at work is likely to cause, for a worker who uses it properly for a conventional eight-hour period, a daily personal noise exposure equal to or greater than 85 dB(A) or an unweighted instantaneous sound pressure the maximum value of which is equal to or greater than 200 Pa, adequate information is made available about the noise produced in conditions of use to be specified.

2.   The Council shall establish, on a proposal from the Commission, requirements according to which, so far as is reasonably practicable, the articles referred to in paragraph 1(b), when properly used, do not produce noise likely to constitute a risk to hearing.

Article 9

1.   In the case of workplaces where the noise exposure of a worker varies markedly from one working day to the next, Member States may, for workers performing special operations, exceptionally grant derogations from Article 5(2), Article 6(1) and Article 7(1), but only on condition that the average weekly noise exposure of a worker, as shown by adequate monitoring, complies with the value laid down in these provisions.

2.   (a)   In exceptional situations where it is not reasonably practicable, by technical measures or organisation of work, to reduce daily personal noise exposure to below 90 dB(A) or to ensure that the personal ear protectors provided for in Article 6 of this Directive are suitable and adequate within the meaning of the second subparagraph of Article 6(3), the Member States may grant derogations from this provision for limited periods, such derogations being renewable.

In such a case, however, personal ear protectors affording the highest degree of protection which is reasonably practicable must be used.

(b) In addition, for workers performing special operations, Member States may exceptionally grant derogations from Article 6(1) if its application involves an increase in the overall risk to the health and/or safety of the workers concerned and if it is not reasonably practicable to reduce this risk by any other means.

(c) The derogations referred to in (a) and (b) shall be subject to conditions which, in view of the individual circumstances, ensure that the risks resulting from such derogations are reduced to a minimum. The derogations shall be reviewed periodically and be revoked as soon as is reasonably practicable.

(d) Member States shall forward to the Commission every two years an adequate overall account of the derogations referred to in (a) and (b). The Commission shall inform the Member States thereof in an appropriate manner.

Article 10

The Council, acting on a proposal from the Commission, shall re-examine this Directive before 1 January 1994, taking into account in particular progress made in scientific knowledge and technology as well as experience gained in the application of this Directive, with a view to reducing the risks arising from exposure to noise.

In the context of this re-examination, the Council, acting on a proposal from the Commission, shall endeavour to lay down indications for measuring noise which are more precise than those given in Annex I.

Article 11

Member States shall see to it that workers' and employers' organisations are consulted before the provisions for the implementation of the measures referred to in this Directive are adopted, and that where workers' representatives exist in the undertaking or establishment they can check that such provisions are applied or can be involved in their application.

Article 12

1. For the measurement of noise and checking workers' hearing, any methods may be used which at least satisfy the provisions contained in Articles 3 and 7.

2. Indications for measuring noise and for checking workers' hearing are given in Annexes I and II.

Annexes I and II shall be adapted to technical progress in accordance with Directive 80/1107/EEC and under the procedure set out in Article 10 thereof.

Article 13

1.   Member States shall bring into force the laws, regulations and administrative provisions necessary to comply with this Directive by 1 January 1990. They shall forthwith inform the Commission thereof.

However, in the case of the Hellenic Republic and the Portuguese Republic the relevant date shall be 1 January 1991.

2.   Member States shall communicate to the Commission the provisions of national law which they adopt in the field covered by this Directive. The Commission shall inform the other Member States thereof.

Article 14

This Directive is addressed to the Member States.

Done at Brussels, 12 May 1986.

For the Council
The President
W. F. van EEKELEN

ANNEX I

INDICATIONS FOR MEASURING NOISE

A.   1.   **General**

The quantities defined in Article 2 can be either:

(i)   measured directly by integrating sonometers, or
(ii)   calculated from measurements of sound pressure and exposure duration.

Measurements may be made at the workplace(s) occupied by workers, or by using instruments attached to the person.

The location and duration of the measurements must be sufficient to ensure that exposure to noise during the working day can be recorded.

2.   **Instrumentation**

2.1.   If integrating averaging sonometers are used, they shall comply with IEC standard 804.

If sonometers are used, they shall comply with IEC standard 651. Instruments incorporating an overload indication are preferred.

If data are stored on tape as an intermediate step of the measurement procedure, potential errors caused by the process of sorting and replay shall be taken into account when analysing the data.

2.2. An instrument used to measure directly the maximum (peak) value of the unweighted instantaneous sound pressure shall have an onset time constant not exceeding 100 μs.

2.3. All equipment shall be calibrated in a laboratory at suitable intervals.

3. Measurement

3.1. An on-site check shall be made at the beginning and end of each day of measurement.

3.2. Measurement of workplace sound pressure should preferably be made in the undisturbed sound field in the workplace (i.e. with the person concerned being absent) and with the microphone located at the position(s) normally occupied by the ear exposed to the highest value of exposure.

If it is necessary for the person to be present, either:

(i) the microphone should be located at a distance from the person's head which will reduce, as far as possible, the effects of diffraction and distance on the measured value (a suitable distance is 0.10 m), or

(ii) if the microphone must be located very close to the person's body, appropriate adjustments should be made to determine an equivalent undisturbed pressure field.

3.3. Generally, time weightings "S" and "F" are valid as long as the measurement time interval is long compared with the time constant of the weighting chosen, but they are not suitable for determining L_{Aeq, T_e} when the noise level fluctuates very rapidly.

3.4. *Indirect measurement of exposure*

The result of the direct measurement of L_{Aeq, T_e} can be approximated with a knowledge of the exposure time and the measurement of clearly distinguishable sound-pressure-level ranges; a sampling method and a statistical distribution may be useful.

4. Accuracy of measuring noise and determining the exposure

The type of the instrument and the standard deviation of the results influence the accuracy of measurement. For comparison with a noise limit, the measuring accuracy determines the range of readings where no decision can be made as to whether the value is exceeded; if no decision can be taken, the measurement must be repeated with a higher accuracy.

Measurements of the highest accuracy enable a decision to be taken in all cases.

B.   Short-term measurements with ordinary sonometers are quite satisfactory for workers performing, at a fixed location, repetitive activities which generate roughly the same levels of broad-band noise
throughout the day. But when the sound pressure to which a worker
is exposed shows fluctuations spread over a wide range of levels
and/or of irregular time characteristics, determining the daily personal noise exposure of a worker becomes increasingly complex; the
most accurate method of measurement is therefore to monitor
exposure throughout the entire shift, using an integrating averaging
sonometer.

When an integrating averaging sonometer conforming to IEC standard 804 (which is well suited for measurement of the equivalent
continuous sound pressure level of impulse noise) complies at least
with the specifications of type 1 and has recently been fully calibrated
in a laboratory, and the microphone is properly located (see 3.2
above), the results make it possible, with certain exceptions, to
determine whether a given exposure has been exceeded (see 4) even
in complex situations; that method is thus generally applicable, and
is well suited for reference purposes.

ANNEX II

INDICATIONS FOR CHECKING WORKERS' HEARING

In the framework of checking workers' hearing the following points are taken
into consideration:

1. The check should be carried out in accordance with occupational medical
    practice and should comprise:
    — where appropriate, an initial examination, to be carried out before or at
      the beginning of exposure to noise,
    — regular examinations at intervals which are commensurate with the
      seriousness of the risk and are determined by the doctor.

2. Each examination should consist of at least an otoscopy combined with an
    audiometric test including pure-tone airconduction threshold audiometry
    in accordance with 6 below.

3. The initial examination should include a medical history; the initial otos-
    copy and the audiometric test should be repeated within a period of 12
    months.

4. The regular examination should be carried out at least every five years
    where the worker's daily personal noise exposure remains less than 90 dB
    (A).

5. The examinations should be carried out by suitably qualified persons in
    accordance with national law and practice and may be organised in success-
    ive stages (screening, specialist examination).

6. The audiometric test should comply with the specifications of ISO standard 6189-1983, supplemented as follows:

    Audiometry also covers the frequency of 8 000 Hz; the ambient sound level enables a hearing-threshold level equal to 0 dB in relation to ISO standard 389-1975 to be measured.

    However, other methods may be used if they give comparable results.

    ———————————

THE FRAMEWORK DIRECTIVE

General note. This is the principal Directive and was implemented in the UK by the Management of Health and Safety at Work Regulations 1992 (S.I. 1992 No. 2051), see page 433.

COUNCIL DIRECTIVE

of 12 June 1989

on the introduction of measures to encourage improvements in the safety and health of workers at work

(89/391/EEC)

THE COUNCIL OF THE EUROPEAN COMMUNITIES,

Having regard to the Treaty establishing the European Economic Community, and in particular Article 118a thereof,

Having regard to the proposal from the Commission, drawn up after consultation with the Advisory Committee on Safety, Hygiene and Health Protection at Work,

In cooperation with the European Parliament,

Having regard to the opinion of the Economic and Social Committee,

Whereas Article 118a of the Treaty provides that the Council shall adopt, by means of Directives, minimum requirements for encouraging improvements, especially in the working environment, to guarantee a better level of protection of the safety and health of workers;

Whereas this Directive does not justify any reduction in levels of protection already achieved in individual Member States, the Member State being committed, under the Treaty, to encouraging improvements in conditions in this area and to harmonising conditions while maintaining the improvements made;

Whereas it is known that workers can be exposed to the effects of dangerous environmental factors at the work place during the course of their working life;

Whereas, pursuant to Article 118a of the Treaty, such Directives must avoid imposing administrative, financial and legal constraints which would hold back the creation and development of small and medium-sized undertakings;

Whereas the communication from the Commission on its programme concerning safety, hygiene and health at work provides for the adoption of Directives designed to guarantee the safety and health of workers;

Whereas the Council, in its resolution of 21 December 1987 on safety, hygiene and health at work, took note of the Commission's intention to submit to the

Council in the near future a Directive on the organisation of the safety and health of workers at the workplace;

Whereas in February 1988 the European Parliament adopted four resolutions following the debate on the internal market and worker protection; whereas these resolutions specifically invited the Commission to draw up a framework Directive to serve as a basis for more specific Directives covering all the risks connected with safety and health at the workplace;

Whereas Member States have a responsibility to encourage improvements in the safety and health of workers on their territory; whereas taking measures to protect the health and safety of workers at work also helps, in certain cases, to preserve the health and possibly the safety of persons residing with them;

Whereas Member States' legislative systems covering safety and health at the workplace differ widely and need to be improved; whereas national provisions on the subject, which often include technical specifications and/or self-regulatory standards, may result in different levels of safety and health protection and allow competition at the expense of safety and health;

Whereas the incident of accidents at work and occupational diseases is still too high; whereas preventive measures must be introduced or improved without delay in order to safeguard the safety and health of workers and ensure a higher degree of protection;

Whereas, in order to ensure an improved degree of protection, workers and/or their representatives must be informed of the risks to their safety and health and of the measures required to reduce or eliminate these risks; whereas they must also be in a position to contribute, by means of balanced participation in accordance with national laws and/or practices, to seeing that the necessary protective measures are taken;

Whereas information, dialogue and balanced participation on safety and health at work must be developed between employers and workers and/or their representatives by means of appropriate procedures and instruments, in accordance with national laws and/or practices;

Whereas the improvement of workers' safety, hygiene and health at work is an objective which should not be subordinated to purely economic considerations;

Whereas employers shall be obliged to keep themselves informed of the latest advances in technology and scientific findings concerning workplace design, account being taken of the inherent dangers in their undertaking, and to inform accordingly the workers' representatives exercising participation rights under this Directive, so as to be able to guarantee a better level of protection of workers' health and safety;

Whereas the provisions of this Directive apply, without prejudice to more stringent present or future Community provisions, to all risks, and in particular to those arising from the use at work of chemical, physical and biological agents covered by Directive 80/1107/EEC, as last amended by Directive 88/642/EEC;

Whereas, pursuant to Decision 74/325/EEC, the Advisory Committee on Safety, Hygiene and Health Protection at Work is consulted by the Commission on the drafting of proposals in this field;

Whereas a Committee composed of members nominated by the Member States needs to be set up to assist the Commission in making the technical adaptations to the individual Directives provided for in this Directive,

HAS ADOPTED THIS DIRECTIVE:

SECTION I
GENERAL PROVISIONS

Article 1
Object

1.   The object of this Directive is to introduce measures to encourage improvements in the safety and health of workers at work.

2.   To that end it contains general principles concerning the prevention of occupational risks, the protection of safety and health, the elimination of risk and accident factors, the informing, consultation, balanced participation in accordance with national laws and/or practices and training of workers and their representatives, as well as general guidelines for the implementation of the said principles.

3.   This Directive shall be without prejudice to existing or future national and Community provisions which are more favourable to protection of the safety and health of workers at work.

Article 2
Scope

1.   This Directive shall apply to all sectors of activity, both public and private (industrial, agricultural, commercial, administrative, service, educational, cultural, leisure, etc.).

2.   This Directive shall not be applicable where characteristics peculiar to certain specific public service activities, such as the armed forces or the police, or to certain specific activities in the civil protection services inevitably conflict with it.

In that event, the safety and health of workers must be ensured as far as possible in the light of the objectives of this Directive.

Article 3
Definitions

For the purposes of this Directive, the following terms shall have the following meanings:

(a) worker: any person employed by an employer, including trainee and apprentices but excluding domestic servants;
(b) employer: any natural or legal person who has an employment relationship with the worker and has responsibility for the undertaking and/or establishment;
(c) workers' representative with specific responsibility for the safety and health of workers: any person elected, chosen or designated in accordance with national laws and/or practices to represent workers where problems arise relating to the safety and health protection of workers at work;
(d) prevention: all the steps or measures taken or planned at all stages of work in the undertaking to prevent or reduce occupational risks.

Article 4

1.   Member States shall take the necessary steps to ensure that employers, workers and workers' representatives are subject to the legal provisions necessary for the implementation of this Directive.

2.   In particular, Member States shall ensure adequate control and supervision.

SECTION II
EMPLOYERS' OBLIGATIONS

Article 5

General provision

1.   The employer shall have a duty to ensure the safety and health of workers in every aspect related to the work.

2.   Where, pursuant to Article 7(3), an employer enlists competent external services or persons, this shall not discharge him from his responsibilities in this area.

3.   The workers' obligations in the field of safety and health at work shall not affect the principle of the responsibility of the employer.

4.   This Directive shall not restrict the option of Member States to provide for the exclusion or the limitation of employers' responsibility where occurrences are due to unusual and unforeseeable circumstances, beyond the employers' control, or to exceptional events, the consequences of which could not have been avoided despite the exercise of all due care.

Member States need not exercise the option referred to in the first subparagraph.

Article 6

General obligations on employers

1.   Within the context of his responsibilities, the employer shall take the measures necessary for the safety and health protection of workers, including

prevention of occupational risks and provision of information and training, as well as provision of the necessary organisation and means.

The employer shall be alert to the need to adjust these measures to take account of changing circumstances and aim to improve existing situations.

2.   The employer shall implement the measures referred to in the first sub-paragraph of paragraph 1 on the basis of the following general principles of prevention:

(a) avoiding risks;
(b) evaluating the risks which cannot be avoided;
(c) combating the risks at source;
(d) adapting the work to the individual, especially as regards the design of workplaces, the choice of work equipment and the choice of working and production methods, with a view, in particular, to alleviating monotonous work and work at a predetermined work-rate and to reducing their effect on health;
(e) adapting to technical progress;
(f) replacing the dangerous by the non-dangerous or the less dangerous;
(g) developing a coherent overall prevention policy which covers technology, organisation of work, working conditions, social relationships and the influence of factors related to the working environment;
(h) giving collective protective measures priority over individual protective measures;
(i) giving appropriate instructions to the workers.

3.   Without prejudice to the other provisions of this Directive, the employer shall, taking into account the nature of the activities of the enterprise and/or establishment:

(a) evaluate the risks to the safety and health of workers, *inter alia* in the choice of work equipment, the chemical substances or preparations used, and the fitting-out of workplaces.

Subsequent to this evaluation and as necessary, the preventive measures and the working and production methods implemented by the employer must:

— assure an improvement in the level of protection afforded to workers with regard to safety and health,
— be integrated into all the activities of the undertaking and/or establishment and at all hierarchical levels;

(b) where he entrusts tasks to a worker, take into consideration the worker's capabilities as regards health and safety;
(c) ensure that the planning and introduction of new technologies are the subject of consultation with the workers and/or their representatives, as regards the consequences of the choice of equipment, the working conditions and the working environment for the safety and health of workers;
(d) take appropriate steps to ensure that only workers who have received adequate instructions may have access to areas where there is serious and specific danger.

4.   Without prejudice to the other provisions of this Directive, where several undertakings share a workplace, the employers shall cooperate in implement-

ing the safety, health and occupational hygiene provisions and, taking into account the nature of the activities, shall coordinate their actions in matters of the protection and prevention of occupational risks, and shall inform one another and their respective workers and/or workers' representatives of these risks.

5.   Measures related to safety, hygiene and health at work may in no circumstances involve the workers in financial cost.

Article 7
Protective and preventive services

1.   Without prejudice to the obligations referred to in Articles 5 and 6, the employer shall designate one or more workers to carry out activities related to the protection and prevention of occupational risks for the undertaking and/or establishment.

2.   Designated workers may not be placed at any disadvantage because of their activities related to the protection and prevention of occupational risks.

Designated workers shall be allowed adequate time to enable them to fulfil their obligations arising from this Directive.

3.   If such protective and preventive measures cannot be organised for lack of competent personnel in the undertaking and/or establishment, the employer shall enlist competent external services or persons.

4.   Where the employer enlists such services or persons, he shall inform them of the factors known to affect, or suspected of affecting, the safety and health of the workers and they must have access to the information referred to in Article 10(2).

5.   In all cases:
— the workers designated must have the necessary capabilities and the necessary means,
— the external services or persons consulted must have the necessary aptitudes and the necessary personal and professional means, and
— the workers designated and the external services or persons consulted must be sufficient in number,

to deal with the organisation of protective and preventive measures, taking into account the size of the undertaking and/or establishment and/or the hazards to which the workers are exposed and their distribution throughout the entire undertaking and/or establishment.

6.   The protection from, and prevention of, the health and safety risks which form the subject of this Article shall be the responsibility of one or more workers, of one service or of separate services whether from inside or outside the undertaking and/or establishment.

The worker(s) and/or agency(ies) must work together whenever necessary.

7.   Member States may define, in the light of the nature of the activities and size of the undertakings, the categories of undertakings in which the employer, provided he is competent, may himself take responsibility for the measures referred to in paragraph 1.

8.   Member States shall define the necessary capabilities and aptitudes referred to in paragraph 5.

They may determine the sufficient number referred to in paragraph 5.

Article 8
First aid, fire-fighting and evacuation of workers, serious and imminent danger

1.   The employer shall:
— take the necessary measures for first aid, fire-fighting and evacuation of workers, adapted to the nature of the activities and the size of the undertaking and/or establishment and taking into account other persons present,
— arrange any necessary contacts with external services, particularly as regards first aid, emergency medical care, rescue work and fire-fighting.

2.   Pursuant to paragraph 1, the employer shall, *inter alia*, for first aid, fire-fighting and the evacuation of workers, designate the workers required to implement such measures.

The number of such workers, their training and the equipment available to them shall be adequate, taking account of the size and/or specific hazards of the undertaking and/or establishment.

3.   The employer shall:
(a)   as soon as possible, inform all workers who are, or may be, exposed to serious and imminent danger of the risk involved and of the steps taken or to be taken as regards protection;
(b)   take action and give instructions to enable workers in the event of serious, imminent and unavoidable danger to stop work and/or immediately to leave the workplace and proceed to a place of safety;
(c)   save in exceptional cases for reasons duly substantiated, refrain from asking workers to resume work in a working situation where there is still a serious and imminent danger.

4.   Workers who, in the event of serious, imminent and unavoidable danger, leave their workstation and/or a dangerous area may not be placed at any disadvantage because of their action and must be protected against any harmful and unjustified consequences, in accordance with national laws and/or practices.

5.   The employer shall ensure that all workers are able, in the event of serious and imminent danger to their own safety and/or that of other persons, and where the immediate superior responsible cannot be contacted, to take the appropriate steps in the light of their knowledge and the technical means at their disposal, to avoid the consequences of such danger.

Their actions shall not place them at any disadvantage, unless they acted carelessly or there was negligence on their part.

Article 9

Various obligations on employers

1.   The employer shall:

(a)   be in possession of an assessment of the risks to safety and health at work, including those facing groups of workers exposed to particular risks;
(b)   decide on the protective measures to be taken and, if necessary, the protective equipment to be used;
(c)   keep a list of occupational accidents resulting in a worker being unfit for work for more than three working days;
(d)   draw up, for the responsible authorities and in accordance with national laws and/or practices, reports on occupational accidents suffered by his workers.

2.   Member States shall define, in the light of the nature of the activities and size of the undertakings, the obligations to be met by the different categories of undertakings in respect of the drawing-up of the documents provided for in paragraph 1(a) and (b) and when preparing the documents provided for in paragraph 1(c) and (d).

Article 10

Worker information

1.   The employer shall take appropriate measures so that workers and/or their representatives in the undertaking and/or establishment receive, in accordance with national laws and/or practices which may take account, *inter alia*, of the size of the undertaking and/or establishment, all the necessary information concerning:

(a)   the safety and health risks and protective and preventive measures and activities in respect of both the undertaking and/or establishment in general and each type of workstation and/or job;
(b)   the measures taken pursuant to Article 8(2).

2.   The employer shall take appropriate measures so that employers of workers from any outside undertakings and/or establishments engaged in work in his undertaking and/or establishment receive, in accordance with national laws and/or practices, adequate information concerning the points referred to in paragraph 1(a) and (b) which is to be provided to the workers in question.

3.   The employer shall take appropriate measures so that workers with specific functions in protecting the safety and health of workers, or workers' representatives with specific responsibility for the safety and health of workers shall have access, to carry out their functions and in accordance with national laws and/or practices, to:

(a)   the risk assessment and protective measures referred to in Article 9(1)(a) and (b);

(b)   the list and reports referred to in Article 9(1)(c) and (d);
(c)   the information yielded by protective and preventive measures, inspection agencies and bodies responsible for safety and health.

Article 11
Consultation and participation of workers

1.   Employers shall consult workers and/or their representatives and allow them to take part in discussions on all questions relating to safety and health at work.

This presupposes:

— the consultation of workers,
— the right of workers and/or their representatives to make proposals,
— balanced participation in accordance with national laws and/or practices.

2.   Workers or workers' representatives with specific responsibility for the safety and health of workers shall take part in a balanced way, in accordance with national laws and/or practices, or shall be consulted in advance and in good time by the employer with regard to:

(a)   any measure which may substantially affect safety and health;
(b)   the designation of workers referred to in Articles 7(1) and 8(2) and the activities referred to in Article 7(1);
(c)   the information referred to in Articles 9(1) and 10;
(d)   the enlistment, where appropriate, of the competent services or persons outside the undertaking and/or establishment, as referred to in Article 7(3);
(e)   the planning and organisation of the training referred to in Article 12.

3.   Workers' representatives with specific responsibility for the safety and health of workers shall have the right to ask the employer to take appropriate measures and to submit proposals to him to that end to mitigate hazards for workers and/or to remove sources of danger.

4.   The workers referred to in paragraph 2 and the workers' representatives referred to in paragraphs 2 and 3 may not be placed at a disadvantage because of their respective activities referred to in paragraphs 2 and 3.

5.   Employers must allow workers' representatives with specific responsibility for the safety and health of workers adequate time off work, without loss of pay, and provide them with the necessary means to enable such representatives to exercise their rights and functions deriving from this Directive.

6.   Workers and/or their representatives are entitled to appeal, in accordance with national law and/or practice, to the authority responsible for safety and health protection at work if they consider that the measures taken and the means employed by the employer are inadequate for the purposes of ensuring safety and health at work.

Workers' representatives must be given the opportunity to submit their observations during inspection visits by the competent authority.

Article 12

Training of workers

1.   The employer shall ensure that each worker receives adequate safety and health training, in particular in the form of information and instructions specific to his workstation or job:

— on recruitment,
— in the event of a transfer or a change of job,
— in the event of the introduction of new work equipment or a change in equipment,
— in the event of the introduction of any new technology.

The training shall be:

— adapted to take account of new or changed risks, and
— repeated periodically if necessary.

2.   The employer shall ensure that workers from outside undertakings and/or establishments engaged in work in his undertaking and/or establishment have in fact received appropriate instructions regarding health and safety risks during their activities in his undertaking and/or establishment.

3.   Workers' representatives with a specific role in protecting the safety and health of workers shall be entitled to appropriate training.

4.   The training referred to in paragraphs 1 and 3 may not be at the workers' expense or at that of the workers' representatives.

The training referred to in paragraph 1 must take place during working hours.

The training referred to in paragraph 3 must take place during working hours or in accordance with national practice either within or outside the undertaking and/or the establishment.

SECTION III

WORKERS' OBLIGATIONS

Article 13

1.   It shall be the responsibility of each worker to take care as far as possible of his own safety and health and that of other persons affected by his acts or Commissions at work in accordance with his training and the instructions given by his employer.

2.   To this end, workers must in particular, in accordance with their training and the instructions given by their employer:

(a) make correct use of machinery, apparatus, tools, dangerous substances, transport equipment and other means of production;
(b) make correct use of the personal protective equipment supplied to them and, after use, return it to its proper place;

(c) refrain from disconnecting, changing or removing arbitrarily safety devices fitted, e.g. to machinery, apparatus, tools, plant and buildings, and use such safety devices correctly;

(d) immediately inform the employer and/or the workers with specific responsibility for the safety and health of workers of any work situation they have reasonable grounds for considering represents a serious and immediate danger to safety and health and of any shortcomings in the protection arrangements;

(e) cooperate, in accordance with national practice, with the employer and/or workers with specific responsibility for the safety and health of workers, for as long as may be necessary to enable any tasks or requirements imposed by the competent authority to protect the safety and health of workers at work to be carried out;

(f) cooperate, in accordance with national practice, with the employer and/or workers with specific responsibility for the safety and health of workers, for as long as may be necessary to enable the employer to ensure that the working environment and working conditions are safe and pose no risk to safety and health within their field of activity.

SECTION IV

MISCELLANEOUS PROVISIONS

Article 14

Health surveillance

1.   To ensure that workers receive health surveillance appropriate to the health and safety risks they incur at work, measures shall be introduced in accordance with national law and/or practices.

2.   The measures referred to in paragraph 1 shall be such that each worker, if he so wishes, may receive health surveillance at regular intervals.

3.   Health surveillance may be provided as part of a national health system.

Article 15

Risk groups

Particularly sensitive risk groups must be protected against the dangers which specifically affect them.

Article 16

Individual Directives—Amendments—General scope of this Directive

1.   The Council, acting on a proposal from the Commission based on Article 118a of the Treaty, shall adopt individual Directives, *inter alia*, in the areas listed in the Annex.

2.   This Directive and, without prejudice to the procedure referred to in Article 17 concerning technical adjustments, the individual Directives may be

amended in accordance with the procedure provided for in Article 118a of the Treaty.

3.   The provisions of this Directive shall apply in full to all the areas covered by the individual Directives, without prejudice to more stringent and/or specific provisions contained in these individual Directives.

Article 17

Committee

1.   For the purely technical adjustments to the individual Directives provided for in Article 16(1) to take account of:

— the adoption of Directives in the field of technical harmonisation and standardisation, and/or
— technical progress, changes in international regulations or specifications, and new findings,

the Commission shall be assisted by a committee composed of the representatives of the Member States and chaired by the representative of the Commission.

2.   The representative of the Commission shall submit to the committee a draft of the measures to be taken.

The committee shall deliver its opinion on the draft within a time limit which the chairman may lay down according to the urgency of the matter.

The opinion shall be delivered by the majority laid down in Article 148(2) of the Treaty in the case of decisions which the Council is required to adopt on a proposal from the Commission.

The votes of the representatives of the Member States within the committee shall be weighted in the manner set out in that Article. The chairman shall not vote.

3.   The Commission shall adopt the measures envisaged if they are in accordance with the opinion of the committee.

If the measures envisaged are not in accordance with the opinion of the committee, or if no opinion is delivered, the Commission shall, without delay, submit to the Council a proposal relating to the measures to be taken. The Council shall act by a qualified majority.

If, on the expiry of three months from the date of the referral to the Council, the Council has not acted, the proposed measures shall be adopted by the Commission.

Article 18

Final provisions

1.   Member States shall bring into force the laws, regulations and administrative provisions necessary to comply with this Directive by 31 December 1992.

They shall forthwith inform the Commission thereof.

2.   Member States shall communicate to the Commission the texts of the provisions of national law which they have already adopted or adopt in the field covered by this Directive.

3.   Member States shall report to the Commission every five years on the practical implementation of the provisions of this Directive, indicating the points of view of employers and workers.

The Commission shall inform the European Parliament, the Council, the Economic and Social Committee and the Advisory Committee on Safety, Hygiene and Health Protection at Work.

4.   The Commission shall submit periodically to the European Parliament, the Council and the Economic and Social Committee a report on the implementation of this Directive, taking into account paragraphs 1 to 3.

Article 19

This Directive is addressed to the Member States.

Done at Luxembourg, 12 June 1989.

For the Council
The President
M. CHAVES GONZALES

ANNEX

List of areas referred to in Article 16(1)

— Workplaces
— Work equipment
— Personal protective equipment
— Work with visual display units
— Handling of heavy loads involving risk of back injury
— Temporary or mobile work sites
— Fisheries and agiculture

THE MACHINERY DIRECTIVE

General note. This Directive was implemented in the UK by the Supply of Machinery (Safety) Regulations 1992 (S.I. 1992 No. 3073), see page 734.

COUNCIL DIRECTIVE

of 14 June 1989

on the approximation of the laws of the Member States relating to machinery

(89/392/EEC, as amended by 91/368/EEC)

THE COUNCIL OF THE EUROPEAN COMMUNITIES,

Having regard to the Treaty establishing the European Economic Community, and in particular Article 100a thereof,

Having regard to the proposal from the Commission,

In cooperation with the European Parliament,

Having regard to the opinion of the Economic and Social Committee,

Whereas Member States are responsible for ensuring the health and safety on their territory of their people and, where appropriate, of domestic animals and goods and, in particular, of workers notably in relation to the risks arising out of the use of machinery;

Whereas, in the Member States, the legislative systems regarding accident prevention are very different; whereas the relevant compulsory provisions, frequently supplemented by *de facto* mandatory technical specifications and/or voluntary standards, do not necessarily lead to different levels of health and safety, but nevertheless, owing to their disparities, constitute barriers to trade within the Community; whereas, furthermore, conformity certification and national certification systems for machinery differ considerably;

Whereas the maintenance or improvement of the level of safety attained by the Member States constitutes one of the essential aims of this Directive and of the principle of safety as defined by the essential requirements;

Whereas existing national health and safety provisions providing protection against the risks caused by machinery must be approximated to ensure free movement of machinery without lowering existing justified levels of protection in the Member States; whereas the provisions of this Directive concerning the design and construction of machinery, essential for a safer working environment shall be accompanied by specific provisions concerning the prevention of certain risks to which workers can be exposed at work, as well as by provisions based on the organisation of safety of workers in the working environment;

29

Whereas the machinery sector is an important part of the engineering industry and is one of the industrial mainstays of the Community economy;

Whereas paragraphs 65 and 68 of the White Paper on the completion of the internal market, approved by the European Council in June 1985, provide for a new approach to legislative harmonisation;

Whereas the social cost of the large number of accidents caused directly by the use of machinery can be reduced by inherently safe design and construction of machinery and by proper installations and maintenance;

Whereas the field of application of this Directive must be based on a general definition of the term "machinery" so as to allow the technical development of products; whereas the development of "complex installations" and the risks they involve are of an equivalent nature and their express inclusion in the Directive is therefore justified;

Whereas specific Directives containing design and construction provisions for certain categories of machinery are now envisaged; whereas the very broad scope of this Directive must be limited in relation to these Directives and also existing Directives where they contain design and construction provisions;

Whereas Community law, in its present form, provides—by way of derogation from one of the fundamental rules of the Community, namely the free movement of goods—that obstacle to movement within the Community resulting from disparities in national legislation relating to the marketing of products must be accepted in so far as the provisions concerned can be recognised as being necessary to satisfy imperative requirements; whereas, therefore, the harmonisation of laws in this case must be limited only to those requirements necessary to satisfy the imperative and essential health and safety requirements relating to machinery; whereas these requirements must replace the relevant national provisions because they are essential;

Whereas the essential health and safety requirements must be observed in order to ensure that machinery is safe; whereas these requirements must be applied with discernment to take account of the state of the art at the time of construction and of technical and economic requirements;

Whereas the putting into service of machinery within the meaning of this Directive can relate only to the use of the machinery itself as intended by the manufacturer; whereas this does not preclude the laying-down of conditions of use external to the machinery, provided that it is not thereby modified in a way not specified in this Directive;

Whereas, for trade fairs, exhibitions, etc., it must be possible to exhibit machinery which does not conform to this Directive; whereas, however, interested parties should be properly informed that the machinery does not conform and cannot be purchased in that condition;

Whereas, therefore, this Directive defines only the essential health and safety requirements of general application, supplemented by a number of more specific requirements for certain categories of machinery; whereas, in order to help manufacturers to prove conformity to these essential requirements and in order to allow inspection for conformity to the essential requirements, it is desirable to have standards harmonised at European level for the prevention of risks arising out of the design and construction of machinery; whereas these standards harmonised at European level are drawn up by private-law bodies and must retain their non-binding status; whereas for this purpose the European Committee for Standardisation (CEN) and the European Committee for Electrotechnical Standardisation (Cenelec) are the bodies recognised as competent to adopt harmonised standards in accordance with the general guidelines for cooperation between the Commission and these two bodies signed on 13 November 1984; whereas, within the meaning of this Directive, a harmonised standard is a technical specification (European standard or harmonisation document) adopted by either or both of these bodies, on the basis of a remit from the Commission in accordance with the provisions of Council Directive 83/189/EEC of 28 March 1983 laying down a procedure for the provision of information in the field of technical standards and regulations, as last amended by Directive 88/182/EEC, and on the basis of general guidelines referred to above;

Whereas the legislative framework needs to be improved in order to ensure an effective and appropriate contribution by employers and employees to the standardisation process; whereas such improvement should be completed at the latest by the time this Directive is implemented;

Whereas, as is currently the practice in Member States, manufacturers should retain the responsibility for certifying the conformity of their machinery to the relevant essential requirements; whereas conformity to harmonised standards creates a presumption of conformity to the relevant essential requirements; whereas it is left to the sole discretion of the manufacturer, where he feels the need, to have his products examined and certified by a third party;

Whereas, for certain types of machinery having a higher risk factor, a stricter certification procedure is desirable; whereas the EC type-examination procedure adopted may result in an EC declaration being given by the manufacturer without any stricter requirement such as a guarantee of quality, EC verification or EC supervision;

Whereas it is essential that, before issuing an EC declaration of conformity, the manufacturer or his authorised representative established in the Community should provide a technical construction file; whereas it is not, however, essential that all documentation be permanently available in a material manner but it must be made available on demand; whereas it need not include detailed plans of the sub-assemblies used in manufacturing the machines, unless knowledge of these is indispensable in order to ascertain conformity with essential safety requirements;

Whereas it is necessary not only to ensure the free movement and putting into service of machinery bearing the EC mark and having an EC conformity certificate but also to ensure free movement of machinery not bearing the EC mark where it is to be incorporated into other machinery or assembled with other machinery to form a complex installation;

Whereas the Member States' responsibility for safety, health and the other aspects covered by the essential requirements on their territory must be recognised in a safeguard clause providing for adequate Community protection procedures;

Whereas the addressees of any decision taken under this Directive must be informed on the reasons for such a decision and the legal remedies open to them;

Whereas the measures aimed at the gradual establishment of the internal market must be adopted by 31 December 1992; whereas the internal market consists of an area without internal frontiers within which the free movement of goods, persons, services and capital is guaranteed,

HAS ADOPTED THIS DIRECTIVE:

CHAPTER I

SCOPE, PLACING ON THE MARKET AND FREEDOM OF MOVEMENT

Article 1

1.   This Directive applies to machinery and lays down the essential health and safety requirements therefor, as defined in Annex I.

2.   For the purposes of this Directive, "machinery" means an assembly of linked parts or components, at least one of which moves, with the appropriate actuators, control and power circuits, etc., joined together for a specific application, in particular for the processing, treatment, moving or packaging of a material.

The term "machinery" also covers an assembly of machines which, in order to achieve the same end, are arranged and controlled so that they function as an integral whole.

["Machinery" also means interchangeable equipment modifying the function of a machine, which is placed on the market for the purpose of being assembled with a machine or a series of different machines or with a tractor by the operator himself in so far as this equipment is not a spare part or a tool.]

3.   The following are excluded from the scope of this Directive:

...

[— lifting equipment designed and constructed for raising and/or moving persons with or without loads, except for industrial trucks with elavating operator position.]
  — machinery whose only power source is directly applied manual effort,
  — machinery for medical use used in direct contact with patients [unless it is a machine used for lifting or lowering loads,],
  — special equipment for use in fairgrounds and/or amusement parks,
  — steam boilers, tanks and pressure vessels,
  — machinery specially designed or put into service for nuclear purposes which, in the event of failure, may result in an emission of radioactivity,

— radioactive sources forming part of a machine,
— firearms,
— storage tanks and pipelines for petrol, diesel fuel, inflammable liquids and dangerous substances,
[— means of transport, i.e. vehicles and their trailers intended solely for transporting passengers by air or on road, rail or water networks, as well as means of transport in so far as such means are designed for transporting goods by air, on public road or rail networks or on water. Vehicles used in the mineral extraction industry shall not be excluded,
— seagoing vessels and mobile offshore units together with equipment on board such vessels or units,
— cableways for the public or private transportation of persons,
— agricultural and forestry tractors, as defined in Article 1(1) of Council Directive 74/150/EEC of 4 March 1974 on the approximation of the laws of the Member States relating to the type-approval of wheeled agricultural or forestry tractors, as last amended by Directive 88/297/EEC,
— machines specially designed and constructed for military or police purposes.]

4. Where, for machinery, the risks referred to in this Directive are wholly or partly covered by specific Community Directives, this Directive shall not apply, or shall cease to apply, in the case of such machinery and of such risks on the entry into force of these specific Directives.

5. Where, for machinery, the risks are mainly of electrical origin, such machinery shall be covered exclusively by Council Directive 73/23/EEC of 19 February 1973 on the harmonisation of the laws of the Member States relating to electrical equipment designed for use within certain voltage limits.

Article 2

1. Member States shall take all appropriate measures to ensure that machinery covered by this Directive may be placed on the market and put into service only if it does not endanger the health or safety of persons and, where appropriate, domestic animals or property, when properly installed and maintained and used for its intended purpose.

2. The provisions of this Directive shall not affect Member States' entitlement to lay down, in due observance of the Treaty, such requirements as they may deem necessary to ensure that persons and in particular workers are protected when using the machines in question, provided that this does not mean that the machinery is modified in a way not specified in the Directive.

3. At trade fairs, exhibitions, demonstrations, etc., Member States shall not prevent the showing of machinery which does not conform to the [Community provisions in force], provided that a visible sign clearly indicates that such

machinery does not conform and that it is not for sale until it has been brought into conformity by the manufacturer or his authorised representative established in the Community. During demonstrations, adequate safety measures shall be taken to ensure the protection of persons.

Article 3

Machinery covered by this Directive shall satisfy the essential health and safety requirements set out in Annex I.

Article 4

1.   Member States shall not prohibit, restrict or impede the placing on the market and putting into service in their territory of machinery which complies with the provisions of this Directive.

2.   Member States shall not prohibit, restrict or impede the placing on the market of machinery where the manufacturer or his authorised representative established in the Community declares in accordance with Annex II.B that it is intended to be incorporated into machinery or assembled with other machinery or constitute machinery covered by this Directive except where it can function independently.

["Interchangeable equipment", within the meaning of the third subparagraph of Article 1(2), shall be regarded as machinery and accordingly must in all cases bear the EC mark and be accompanied by the EC declaration of conformity referred to in Annex II(A).]

Article 5

1.   Member States shall regard machinery bearing the EC mark and accompanied by the EC declaration of conformity referred to in Annex II as conforming to the essential health and safety requirements referred to in Article 3.

In the absence of harmonised standards, Member States shall take any steps they deem necessary to bring to the attention of the parties concerned the existing national technical standards and specifications which are regarded as important or relevant to the proper implementation of the essential safety and health requirements in Annex I.

2.   Where a national standard transposing a harmonised standard, the reference for which has been published in the *Official Journal of the European Communities,* covers one or more of the essential safety requirements, machinery constructed in accordance with this standard shall be presumed to comply with the relevant essential requirements.

Member States shall publish the references of national standards transposing harmonised standards.

3.   Member States shall ensure that appropriate measures are taken to enable the social partners to have an influence at national level on the process of preparing and monitoring the harmonised standards.

Article 6

1. Where a Member State or the Commission considers that the harmonised standards referred to in Article 5(2) do not entirely satisfy the essential requirements referred to in Article 3, the Commission or the Member State concerned shall bring the matter before the Committee set up under Directive 83/189/EEC, giving the reasons therefor. The Committee shall deliver an opinion without delay.

Upon receipt of the Committee's opinion, the Commission shall inform the Member States whether or not it is necessary to withdraw those standards from the published information referred to in Article 5(2).

2. A standing committee shall be set up, consisting of representatives appointed by the Member States and chaired by a representative of the Commission.

The standing committee shall draw up its own rules of procedure.

Any matter relating to the implementation and practical application of this Directive may be brought before the standing committee, in accordance with the following procedure:

The representative of the Commission shall submit to the committee a draft of the measures to be taken. The committee shall deliver its opinion on the draft, within a time limit which the chairman may lay down according to the urgency of the matter, if necessary by taking a vote.

The opinion shall be recorded in the minutes; in addition, each Member State shall have the right to ask to have its position recorded in the minutes.

The Commission shall take the utmost account of the opinion delivered by the committee. It shall inform the committee of the manner in which its opinion has been taken into account.

Article 7

1. Where a Member State ascertains that machinery bearing the EC mark and used in accordance with its intended purpose is liable to endanger the safety of persons, and, where appropriate, domestic animals or property, it shall take all appropriate measures to withdraw such machinery from the market, to prohibit the placing on the market, putting into service or use thereof, or to restrict free movement thereof.

The Member State shall immediately inform the Commission of any such measure, indicating the reasons for its decision and, in particular, whether non-conformity is due to:

(a) failure to satisfy the essential requirements referred to in Article 3;
(b) incorrect application of the standards referred to in Article 5(2);
(c) shortcomings in the standards referred to in Article 5(2) themselves.

2. The Commission shall enter into consultation with the parties concerned without delay. Where the Commission considers, after this consultation, that

the measure is justified, it shall immediately so inform the Member State which took the initiative and the other Member States. Where the Commission considers, after this consultation, that the action is unjustified, it shall immediately so inform the Member State which took the initiative and the manufacturer or his authorised representative established within the Community. Where the decision referred to in paragraph 1 is based on a shortcoming in the standards, and where the Member State at the origin of the decision maintains its position, the Commission shall immediately inform the Committee in order to initiate the procedures referred to in Article 6(1).

3.   Where machinery which does not comply bears the EC mark, the competent Member State shall take appropriate action against whomsoever has affixed the mark and shall so inform the Commission and the other Member States.

4.   The Commission shall ensure that the Member States are kept informed of the progress and outcome of this procedure.

CHAPTER II
CERTIFICATION PROCEDURE

Article 8

1.   The manufacturer, or his authorised representative established in the Community, shall, in order to certify the conformity of machinery with the provisions of this Directive, draw up an EC declaration of conformity based on the model given in Annex II for each machine manufactured and shall affix to the machinery the EC mark referred to in Article 10.

2.   Before placing on the market, the manufacturer, or his authorised representative established in the Community, shall:

(a) if the machinery is not referred to in Annex IV, draw up the file provided for in Annex V;

(b) if the machinery is referred to in Annex IV and its manufacturer does not comply, or only partly complies, with the standards referred to in Article 5(2) or if there are no such standards, submit an example of the machinery for the EC type-examination referred to in Annex VI;

(c) if the machinery is referred to in Annex IV and is manufactured in accordance with the standards referred to in Article 5(2):

— either draw up the file referred to in Annex VI and forward it to a notified body, which will acknowledge receipt of the file as soon as possible and keep it,

— submit the file referred to in Annex VI to the notified body, which will simply verify that the standards referred to in Article 5(2) have been correctly applied and will draw up a certificate of adequacy for the file,

— or submit the example of the machinery for the EC type-examination referred to in Annex VI.

3.   Where the first indent of paragraph 2(c) applies, the provisions of the first sentence of paragraph 5 and paragraph 7 of Annex VI shall also apply.

Where the second indent of 2(c) applies, the provisions of paragraphs 5, 6 and 7 of Annex VI shall also apply.

4.   Where paragraph 2(a) and the first and second indents of paragraph 2(c) apply, the EC declaration of conformity shall solely state conformity with the essential requirements of the Directive.

Where paragraph 2(b) and (c) apply, the EC declaration of conformity shall state conformity with the example that underwent EC type-examination.

5.   Where the machinery is subject to other Community Directives concerning other aspects, the EC mark referred to in Article 10 shall indicate in these cases that the machinery also fulfils the requirements of the other Directives.

6.   Where neither the manufacturer nor his authorised representative established in the Community fulfils the obligations of the preceding paragraphs, these obligations shall fall to any person placing the machinery on the market in the Community. The same obligations shall apply to any person assembling machinery or parts thereof of various origins or constructing machinery for his own use.

[7.   The obligations laid down in paragraphs shall not apply to persons who assemble with a machine or tractor interchangeable equipment as provided for in Article 1, provided that the parts are compatible and each of the constituent parts of the assembled machine bears the EC mark and is accompanied by the EC declaration of conformity.]

Article 9

1.   Each Member State shall notify the Commission and the other Member States of the approved bodies responsible for carrying out the certification procedures referred to in Article 8(2)(b) and (c). The Commission shall pubish a list of these bodies in the *Official Journal of the European Communities* for information and shall ensure that the list is kept up to date.

2.   Member States shall apply the criteria laid down in Annex VII in assessing the bodies to be indicated in such notification. Bodies meeting the assessment criteria laid down in the relevant harmonised standards shall be presumed to fulfil those criteria.

3.   A Member State which has approved a body must withdraw its notification if it finds that the body no longer meets the criteria referred to in Annex VII. It shall immediately inform the Commission and the other Member States accordingly.

CHAPTER III

EC MARK

Article 10

1.   The "EC" mark shall consist of the EC symbol followed by the last two digits of the year in which the mark was affixed.

Annex III shows the model to be used.

2.   The EC mark shall be affixed to machinery distinctly and visibly in accordance with point 1.7.3 of Annex I.

3.   Marks or inscriptions liable to be confused with the EC mark shall not be put on machinery.

CHAPTER IV

FINAL PROVISIONS

Article 11

Any decision taken pursuant to this Directive which restricts the marketing and putting into service of machinery shall state the exact grounds on which it is based. Such a decision shall be notified as soon as possible to the party concerned, who shall at the same time be informed of the legal remedies available to him under the laws in force in the Member State concerned and of the time limits to which such remedies are subject.

Article 12

The Commission will take the necessary steps to have information on all the relevant decisions relating to the management of this Directive made available.

Article 13

[1.   Before 1 January 1992 Member States shall adopt and publish the laws, regulations and administrative provisions necessary in order to comply with this Directive. They shall forthwith inform the Commission thereof.

When Member States adopt these measures, they shall contain a reference to this Directive or shall be accompanied by such reference on the occasion of their official publication. The methods of making such a reference shall be laid down by the Member States.

The Member States shall apply the measures in question with effect from 1 January 1993, except as regards the equipment referred to in Directives 86/295/EEC, 86/296/EEC and 86/663/EEC, for which these measures shall apply from 1 July 1995.

2.   Furthermore, Member States shall allow, for the period until 31 December 1994, except as regards the equipment referred to in Directives 86/295/EEC, 86/296/EEC and 86/663/EEC, for which this period shall end on 31 December 1995, the placing on the market and putting into service of machinery in conformity with the national regulations in force in their territory on 31 December 1992.

Directives 86/295/EEC, 86/296/EEC and 86/663/EEC shall not impede implementation of paragraph 1 as from 1 July 1995.

3.   Member States shall communicate to the Commission the texts of the provisions of national law which they adopt in the field governed by this Directive.

4.   The Commission shall, before 1 January 1994, examine the progress made in the standardisation work relating to this Directive and propose and appropriate measures.]

Article 14

This Directive is addressed to the Member States.

Done at Luxembourg, 14 June 1989.

For the Council
The President
P. SOLBES

ANNEX 1

ESSENTIAL HEALTH AND SAFETY REQUIREMENTS RELATING TO THE DESIGN AND CONSTRUCTION OF MACHINERY

PRELIMINARY OBSERVATIONS

1.   The obligations laid down by the essential health and safety requirements apply only when the corresponding hazard exists for the machinery in question when it is used under the conditions foreseen by the manufacturer. In any event, requirements 1.1.2, 1.7.3 and 1.7.4 apply to all machinery covered by this Directive.

2.   The essential health and safety requirements laid down in this Directive are mandatory. However, taking into account the state of the art, it may not be possible to meet the objectives set by them. In this case, the machinery must as far as possible be designed and constructed with the purpose of approaching those objectives.

1.   ESSENTIAL HEALTH AND SAFETY REQUIREMENTS

1.1.   **General remarks**

1.1.1. *Definitions*

        For the purpose of this Directive

        1. "danger zone" means any zone within and/or around machinery in which an exposed person is subject to a risk to his health or safety;

2. "exposed person" means any person wholly or partially in a danger zone;
3. "operator" means the person or persons given the task of installing, operating, adjusting, maintaining, cleaning, repairing or transporting machinery.

1.1.2.   *Principles of safety integration*

(a) Machinery must be so constructed that it is fitted for its function, and can be adjusted and maintained without putting persons at risk when these operations are carried out under the conditions foreseen by the manufacturer.
The aim of measures taken must be to eliminate any risk of accident throughout the foreseeable lifetime of the machinery, including the phases of assembly and dismantling, even where risks of accident arise from foreseeable abnormal situations.

(b) In selecting the most appropriate methods, the manufacturer must apply the following principles, in the order given:
— eliminate or reduce risks as far as possible (inherently safe machinery design and construction),
— take the necessary protection measures in relation to risks that cannot be eliminated,
— inform users of the residual risks due to any shortcomings of the protection measures adopted, indicate whether any particular training is required and specify any need to provide personal protection equipment.

(c) When designing and constructing machinery, and when drafting the instructions, the manufacturer must envisage not only the normal use of the machinery but also uses which could reasonably be expected.
The machinery must be designed to prevent abnormal use if such use would engender a risk. In other cases the instructions must draw the user's attention to ways—which experience has shown might occur—in which the machinery should not be used.

(d) Under the intended conditions of use, the discomfort, fatigue and psychological stress faced by the operator must be reduced to the minimum possible taking ergonomic principles into account.

(e) When designing and constructing machinery, the manufacturer must take account of the constraints to which the operator is subject as a result of the necessary or foreseeable use of personal protection equipment (such as footwear, gloves, etc.).

(f) Machinery must be supplied with all the essential special equipment and accessories to enable it to be adjusted, maintained and used without risk.

1.1.3.   *Materials and products*

The materials used to construct machinery or products used and created during its use must not endanger exposed persons' safety or health.

In particular, where fluids are used, machinery must be designed and constructed for use without risks due to filling, use, recovery or draining.

1.1.4. *Lighting*

The manufacturer must supply integral lighting suitable for the operations concerned where its lack is likely to cause a risk despite ambient lighting of normal intensity.

The manufacturer must ensure that there is no area of shadow likely to cause nuisance, that there is no irritating dazzle and that there are no dangerous stroboscopic effects due to the lighting provided by the manufacturer.

Internal parts requiring frequent inspection, and adjustment and maintenance areas, must be provided with appropriate lighting.

1.1.5. *Design of machinery to facilitate its handling*

Machinery or each component part thereof must:

— be capable of being handled safely,
— be packaged or designed so that it can be stored safely and without damage (e.g. adequate stability, special supports, etc.).

Where the weight, size or shape of machinery or its various component parts prevents them from being moved by hand, the machinery or each component part must:

— either be fitted with attachments for lifting gear, or
— be designed so that it can be fitted with such attachments (e.g. threaded holes), or
— be shaped in such a way that standard lifting gear can easily be attached.

Where machinery or one of its component parts is to be moved by hand, it must:

— either be easily moveable, or
— be equipped for picking up (e.g. hand-grips, etc.) and moving in complete safety.

Special arrangements must be made for the handling of tools and/or machinery parts, even if lightweight, which could be dangerous (shape, material, etc.).

1.2. **Controls**

1.2.1. *Safety and reliability of control systems*

Control system must be designed and constructed so that they are safe and reliable, in a way that will prevent a dangerous situation arising. Above all they must be designed and constructed in such a way that:

— they can withstand the rigours of normal use and external factors,
— errors in logic do not lead to dangerous situations.

1.2.2.   *Control devices*

Control devices must be:

— clearly visible and identifiable and appropriately marked where necessary,
— positioned for safe operation without hesitation or loss of time, and without ambiguity,
— designed so that the movement of the control is consistent with its effect,
— located outside the danger zones, except for certain controls where necessary, such as emergency stop, console for training of robots,
— positioned so that their operation cannot cause additional risk,
— designed or protected so that the desired effect, where a risk is involved, cannot occur without an intentional operation,
— made so as to withstand foreseeable strain; particular attention must be paid to emergency stop devices liable to be subjected to considerable strain.

Where a control is designed and constructed to perform several different actions, namely where there is no one-to-one correspondence (e.g. keyboards, etc.), the action to be performed must be clearly displayed and subject to confirmation where necessary.

Controls must be so arranged that their layout, travel and resistance to operation are compatible with the action to be performed, taking account of ergonomic principles, Constraints due to the necessary or foreseeable use of personal protection equipment (such as footwear, gloves, etc.) must be taken into account.

Machinery must be fitted with indicators (dials, signals, etc.) as required for safe operation. The operator must be able to read them from the control position.

From the main control position the operator must be able to ensure that there are no exposed persons in the danger zones.

If this is impossible, the control system must be designed and constructed so that an acoustic and/or visual warning signal is given whenever the machinery is about to start. The exposed person must have the time and the means to take rapid action to prevent the machinery starting up.

1.2.3.   *Starting*

It must be possible to start machinery only by voluntary actuation of a control provided for the purpose.

The same requirement applies:

— when restarting the machinery after a stoppage, whatever the cause,

— when effecting a significant change in the operating conditions (e.g. speed, pressure, etc.),

unless such restarting or change in operating conditions is without risk to exposed persons.

This essential requirement does not apply to the restarting of the machinery or to the change in operating conditions resulting from the normal sequence of an automatic cycle.

Where machinery has several starting controls and the operators can therefore put each other in danger, additional devices (e.g. enabling devices or selectors allowing only one part of the starting mechanism to be actuated at any one time) must be fitted to rule out such risks.

It must be possible for automated plant functioning in automatic mode to be restarted easily after a stoppage once the safety conditions have been fulfilled.

1.2.4.   *Stopping device*

Normal Stopping

Each machine must be fitted with a control whereby the machine can be brought safely to a complete stop.

Each workstation must be fitted with a control to stop some or all of the moving parts of the machinery, depending on the type of hazard, so that the machinery is rendered safe. The machinery's stop control must have priority over the start controls.

Once the machinery or its dangerous parts have stopped, the energy supply to the actuators concerned must be cut off.

Emergency stop

Each machine must be fitted with one or more emergency stop devices to enable actual or impending danger to be averted. The following exceptions apply:

— machines in which an emergency stop device would not lessen the risk, either because it would not reduce the stopping time or because it would not enable the special measures required to deal with the risk to be taken,
— hand-held portable machines and hand-guided machines.

This device must:

— have clearly identifiable, clearly visible and quickly accessible controls,
— stop the dangerous process as quickly as possible, without creating additional hazards,
— where necessary, trigger or permit the triggering of certain safe-guard movements.

The emergency stop control must remain engaged; it must be poss-ible to disengage it only by an appropriate operation; disengaging the control must not restart the machinery, but only permit restarting;

the stop control must not trigger the stopping function before being in the engaged position.

Complex installations

In the case of machinery or parts of machinery designed to work together, the manufacturer must so design and construct the machinery that the stop controls, including the emergency stop, can stop not only the machinery itself but also all equipment upstream and/or downstream if its continued operation can be dangerous.

1.2.5.   *Mode selection*

The control mode selected must override all other control systems with the exception of the emergency stop.

If machinery has been designed and built to allow for its use in several control or operating modes presenting different safety levels (e.g. to allow for adjustment, maintenance, inspection, etc.), it must be fitted with a mode selector which can be locked in each position. Each position of the selector must correspond to a single operating or control mode.

The selector may be replaced by another selection method which restricts the use of certain functions of the machinery to certain categories of operator (e.g. access codes for certain numerically controlled functions, etc.).

If, for certain operations, the machinery must be able to operate with its protection devices neutralised, the mode selector must simultaneously:

— disable the automatic control mode,
— permit movements only by controls requiring sustained action,
— permit the operation of dangerous moving parts only in enhanced safety conditions (e.g. reduced speed, reduced power, step-by-step, or other adequate provision) while preventing hazards from linked sequences,
— prevent any movement liable to pose a danger by acting voluntarily or involuntarily on the machine's internal sensors.

In addition, the operator must be able to control operation of the parts he is working on at the adjustment point.

1.2.6.   *Failure of the power supply*

The interruption, re-establishment after an interruption or fluctuation in whatever manner of the power supply to the machinery must not lead to a dangerous situation.

In particular:

— the machinery must not start unexpectedly,
— the machinery must not be prevented from stopping if the command has already been given,

— no moving part of the machinery or piece held by the machinery must fall or be ejected,
— automatic or manual stopping of the moving parts whatever they may be must be unimpeded,
— the protection devices must remain fully effective.

1.2.7. *Failure of the control circuit*

A fault in the control circuit logic, or failure of or damage to the control circuit must not lead to dangerous situations.

In particular:

— the machinery must not start unexpectedly,
— the machinery must not be prevented from stopping if the command has already been given,
— no moving part of the machinery or piece held by the machinery must fall or be ejected,
— automatic or manual stopping of the moving parts whatever they may be must be unimpeded,
— the protection devices must remain fully effective.

1.2.8. *Software*

Interactive software between the operator and the command or control system of a machine must be user-friendly.

1.3. **Protection against mechanical hazards**

1.3.1. *Stability*

Machinery, components and fittings thereof must be so designed and constructed that they are stable enough, under the foreseen operating conditions (if necessary taking climatic conditions into account) for use without risk of overturning, falling or unexpected movement.

If the shape of the machinery itself or its intended installation does not offer sufficient stability, appropriate means of anchorage must be incorporated and indicated in the instructions.

1.3.2. *Risk of break-up during operation*

The various parts of machinery and their linkages must be able to withstand the stresses to which they are subject when used as foreseen by the manufacturer.

The durability of the materials used must be adequate for the nature of the work place foreseen by the manufacturer, in particular as regards the phenomena of fatigue, ageing, corrosion and abrasion.

The manufacturer must indicate in the instructions the type and frequency of inspection and maintenance required for safety reasons. He must, where appropriate, indicate the parts subject to wear and the criteria for replacement.

Where a risk of rupture or disintegration remains despite the measures taken (e.g. as with grinding wheels) the moving parts must be mounted and positioned in such a way that in case of rupture their fragments will be contained.

Both rigid and flexible pipes carrying fluids, particularly those under high pressure, must be able to withstand the foreseen internal and external stresses and must be firmly attached and/or protected against all manner of external stresses and strains; precautions must be taken to ensure that no risk is posed by a rupture (sudden movement, high-pressure jets, etc.).

Where the material to be processed is fed to the tool automatically, the following conditions must be fulfilled to avoid risks to the persons exposed (e.g. tool breakage):

— when the workpiece comes into contact with the tool the latter must have attained its normal working conditions,
— when the tool starts and/or stops (intentionally or accidentally) the feed movement and the tool movement must be coordinated.

1.3.3.   *Risks due to falling or ejected objects*

Precautions must be taken to prevent risks from falling or ejected objects (e.g. workpieces, tools, cuttings, fragments, waste, etc.).

1.3.4.   *Risks due to surfaces, edges or angles*

In so far as their purpose allows, accessible parts of the machinery must have no sharp edges, no sharp angles, and no rough surfaces likely to cause injury.

1.3.5.   *Risks related to combined machinery*

Where the machinery is intended to carry out several different operations with the manual removal of the piece between each operation (combined machinery), it must be designed and constructed in such a way as to enable each element to be used separately without the other elements constituting a danger or risk for the exposed person.

For this purpose, it must be possible to start and stop separately any elements that are not protected.

1.3.6.   *Risks relating to variations in the rotational speed of tools*

When the machine is designed to perform operations under different conditions of use (e.g. different speeds or energy supply), it must be designed and constructed in such a way that selection and adjustment of these conditions can be carried out safely and reliably.

1.3.7.   *Prevention of risks related to moving parts*

The moving parts of machinery must be designed, built and laid out to avoid hazards or, where hazards persist, fixed with guards or protective devices in such a way as to prevent all risk of contact which could lead to accidents.

[All necessary steps must be taken to prevent accidental blockage of moving parts involved in the work. In cases where, despite the precautions taken, a blockage is likely to occur, specific protection devices or tools, the instruction handbook and possibly a sign on the machinery should be provided by the manufacturer to enable the equipment to be safely unblocked.]

1.3.8.   *Choice of protection against risks related to moving parts*

Guards or protection devices used to protect against the risks related to moving parts must be selected on the basis of the type of risk. The following guidelines must be used to help make the choice.

A. Moving transmission parts

Guards designed to protect exposed persons against the risks associated with moving transmission parts (such as pulleys, belts, gears, rack and pinions, shafts, etc.) must be:
— either fixed, complying with requirements 1.4.1 and 1.4.2.1, or
— moveable, complying with requirements 1.4.1 and 1.4.2.2.A.

Moveable guards should be used where frequent access is foreseen.

B. Moving parts directly involved in the process

Guards or protection devices designed to protect exposed persons against the risks associated with moving parts contributing to the work (such as cutting tools, moving parts of presses, cylinders, parts in the process of being machined, etc.) must be:
— wherever possible fixed guards complying with requirements 1.4.1 and 1.4.2.1,
— otherwise, moveable guards complying with requirements 1.4.1 and 1.4.2.2.B or protection devices such as sensing devices (e.g. non-material barriers, sensor mats), remote-hold protection devices (e.g. two-hand controls), or protection devices intended automatically to prevent all or part of the operator's body from encroaching on the danger zone in accordance with requirements 1.4.1 and 1.4.3.

However, when certain moving parts directly involved in the process cannot be made completely or partially inaccessible during operation owing to operations requiring nearby operator intervention, where technically possible such parts must be fitted with:
— fixed guards, complying with requirements 1.4.1 and 1.4.2.1 preventing access to those sections of the parts that are not used in the work,

— adjustable guards, complying with requirements 1.4.1 and 1.4.2.3 restricting access to those sections of the moving parts that are strictly for the work.

1.4. Required characteristics of guards and protection devices

1.4.1. *General requirement*

Guards and protection devices must:

— be of robust construction,
— not give rise to any additional risk,
— not be easy to by-pass or render non-operational,
— be located at an adequate distance from the danger zone,
— cause minimum obstruction to the view of the production process,
— enable essential work to be carried out on installation and/or replacement of tools and also for maintenance by restricting access only to the area where the work has to be done, if possible without the guard or protection device having to be dismantled.

1.4.2. *Special requirements for guards*

1.4.2.1. Fixed guards

Fixed guards must be securely held in place.

They must be fixed by systems that can be opened only with tools.

Where possible, guards must be unable to remain in place without their fixings.

1.4.2.2. Moveable guards

A. Type A moveable guards must:

— as far as possible remain fixed to the machinery when open,
— be associated with a locking device to prevent moving parts starting up as long as these parts can be accessed and to give a stop command whenever they are no longer closed.

B. Type B moveable guards must be designed and incorporated into the control system so that:

— moving parts cannot start up while they are within the operator's reach,
— the exposed person cannot reach moving parts once they have started up,
— they can be adjusted only by means of an intentional action, such as the use of a tool, key, etc.,
— the absence or failure of one of their components prevents starting or stops the moving parts,
— protection against any risk of ejection is proved by means of an appropriate barrier.

1.4.2.3.   Adjustable guards restricting access

Adjustable guards restricting access to those areas of the moving parts strictly necessary for the work must:

— be adjustable manually or automatically according to the type of work involved,
— be readily adjustable without the use of tools,
— reduce as far as possible the risk of ejection.

1.4.3.   *Special requirements for protection devices*

Protection devices must be designed and incorporated into the control system so that:

— moving parts cannot start up while they are within the operator's reach,
— the exposed person cannot reach moving parts once they have started up,
— they can be adjusted only be means of an intentional action, such as the use of a tool, key, etc.,
— the absence or failure of one of their components starting or stops the moving parts.

1.5.   **Protection against other hazards**

1.5.1.   *Electricity supply*

Where machinery has an electricity supply it must be designed, constructed and equipped so that all hazards of an electrical nature are or can be prevented.

The specific rules in force relating to electrical equipment designed for use within certain voltage limits must apply to machinery which is subject to those limits.

1.5.2.   *Static electricity*

Machinery must be so designed and constructed as to prevent or limit the build-up of potentially dangerous electrostatic charges and/or be fitted with a discharging system.

1.5.3.   *Energy supply other than electricity*

Where machinery is powered by an energy other than electricity (e.g. hydraulic, pneumatic or thermal energy, etc.), it must be so designed, constructed and equipped as to avoid all potential hazards associated with those types of energy.

1.5.4.   *Errors of fitting*

Errors likely to be made when fitting or refitting certain parts which could be a source of risk must be made impossible by the design of such parts or, failing this, by information given on the parts themselves and/or the housings. The same information must be given on moving parts and/or their housings where the direction of movement must be known to avoid a risk. Any further information that may be necessary must be given in the instructions.

Where a faulty connection can be the source of risk, incorrect fluid connections, including electrical conductors, must be made impossible by the design or, failing this, by information given on the pipes, cables, etc. and/or connector blocks.

1.5.5.   *Extreme temperatures*

Steps must be taken to eliminate any risk of injury caused by contact with or proximity to machinery parts or materials at high or very low temperatures.

The risk of hot or very cold material being ejected should be assessed. Where this risk exists, the necessary steps must be taken to prevent it or, if this is not technically possible, to render it non-dangerous.

1.5.6.   *Fire*

Machinery must be designed and constructed to avoid all risk of fire or overheating posed by the machinery itself or by gases, liquids, dusts, vapours or other substances produced or used by the machinery.

1.5.7.   *Explosion*

Machinery must be designed and constructed to avoid any risk of explosion posed by the machinery itself or by gases, liquids, dusts, vapours or other substances produced or used by the machinery.

To that end the manufacturer must take steps to:

— avoid a dangerous concentration of products,
— prevent combustion of the potentially explosive atmosphere,
— minimise any explosion which may occur so that it does not endanger the surroundings.

The same precautions must be taken if the manufacturer foresees the use of the machinery in a potentially explosive atmosphere.

Electrical equipment forming part of the machinery must conform, as far as the risk from explosion is concerned, to the provision of the specific Directives in force.

1.5.8. *Noise*

Machinery must be so designed and constructed that risks resulting from the emission of airborne noise are reduced to the lowest level taking account of technical progress and the availability of means of reducing noise, in particular at source.

1.5.9. *Vibration*

Machinery must be so designed and constructed that risks resulting from vibrations produced by the machinery are reduced to the lowest level, taking account of technical progress and the availability of means of reducing vibration, in particular at source.

1.5.10 *Radiation*

Machinery must be so designed and constructed that any emission of radiation is limited to the extent necessary for its operation and that the effects on exposed persons are non-existent or reduced to non-dangerous proportions.

1.5.11. *External radiation*

Machinery must be so designed and constructed that external radiation does not interfere with its operation.

1.5.12. *Laser equipment*

Where laser equipment is used, the following provisions should be taken into account:

— laser equipment on machinery must be designed and constructed so as to prevent any accidental radiation,
— laser equipment on machinery must be protected so that effective radiation, radiation produced by reflection or diffusion and secondary radiation do not damage health,
— optical equipment for the observation or adjustment of laser equipment on machinery must be such that no health risk is created by the laser rays.

1.5.13. *Emissions of dust, gases, etc.*

Machinery must be so designed, constructed and/or equipped that risks due to gases, liquids, dust, vapours and other waste materials which it produces can be avoided.

Where a hazard exists, the machinery must be so equipped that the said substances can be contained and/or evacuated.

Where machinery is not enclosed during normal operation, the devices for containment and/or evacuation must be situated as close as possible to the source emission.

1.6.   Maintenance

1.6.1.   *Machinery maintenance*

Adjustment, lubrication and maintenance points must be located outside danger zones. It must be possible to carry out adjustment, maintenance, repair, cleaning and servicing operations while machinery is at a standstill.

If one or more of the above conditions cannot be satisfied for technical reasons, these operations must be possible without risk (see 1.2.5).

In the case of automated machinery and, where necessary, other machinery, the manufacturer must make provision for a connecting device for mounting diagnostic fault-finding equipment.

Automated machine components which have to be changed frequently, in particular for a change in manufacture or where they are liable to wear or likely to deteriorate following an accident, must be capable of being removed and replaced easily and in safety. Access to the components must enable these tasks to be carried out with the necessary technical means (tools, measuring instruments, etc.) in accordance with an operating method specified by the manufacturer.

1.6.2.   *Access to operating position and servicing points*

The manufacturer must provide means of access (stairs, ladders, catwalks, etc.) to allow access in safety to all areas used for production, adjustment and maintenance operations.

Parts of the machinery where persons are liable to move about or stand must be designed and constructed to avoid falls.

1.6.3.   *Isolation of energy sources*

All machinery must be fitted with means to isolate it from all energy sources. Such isolators must be clearly identified. They must be capable of being locked if reconnection could endanger exposed persons. In the case of machinery supplied with electricity through a plug capable of being plugged into a circuit, separation of the plug is sufficient.

The isolator must be capable of being locked also where an operator is unable, from any of the points to which he has access, to check that the energy is still cut off.

After the energy is cut off, it must be possible to dissipate normally any energy remaining or stored in the circuits of the machinery without risk to exposed persons.

As an exception to the above requirements, certain circuits may remain connected to their energy sources in order, for example, to hold parts, protect information, light interior, etc. In this case, special steps must be taken to ensure operator safety.

1.6.4.   *Operator intervention*

Machinery must be so designed, constructed and equipped that the need for operator intervention is limited.

If operator intervention cannot be avoided, it must be possible to carry it out easily and in safety.

[1.6.5.   *Cleaning of internal parts*

The machinery must be designed and constructed in such a way that it is possible to clean internal parts which have contained dangerous substances or preparations without entering them; any necessary unblocking must also be possible from the outside. If it is absolutely impossible to avoid entering the machinery, the manufacturer must take steps during its construction to allow cleaning to take place with the minimum of danger.]

1.7.   **Indicators**

1.7.0.   *Information devices*

The information needed to control machinery must be unambiguous and easily understood.

It must not be excessive to the extent of overloading the operator.

[Where the health and safety of exposed persons may be endangered by a fault in the operation of unsupervised machinery, the machinery must be equipped to give an appropriate acoustic or light signal as a warning.]

1.7.1.   *Warning devices*

Where machinery is equipped with warning devices (such as signals, etc.), these must be unambiguous and easily perceived.

The operator must have facilities to check the operation of such warning devices at all times.

The requirements of the specific Directives concerning colours and safety signals must be complied with.

1.7.2.   *Warning of residual risks*

Where risks remain despite all the measures adopted or in the case of potential risks which are not evident (e.g. electrical cabinets, radio-active sources, bleeding of a hydraulic circuit, hazard in an unseen area, etc.), the manufacturer must provide warnings.

Such warnings should preferably use readily understandable picto-grams and/or be drawn up in one of the languages of the country in which the machinery is to be used, accompanied, on request, by the languages understood by the operators.

1.7.3.   *Marking*

All machinery must be marked legibly and indelibly with the following minimum particulars:

— name and address of the manufacturer,
— EC mark, which includes the year of construction (see Annex III),
— designation of series or type,
— serial number, if any.

Furthermore, where the manufacturer constructs machinery intended for use in a potentially explosive atmosphere, this must be indicated on the machinery.

Machinery must also bear full information relevant to its type and essential to its safe use (e.g. maximum speed of certain rotating parts, maximum diameter of tools to be fitted, mass, etc.).

[Where a machine part must be handled during use with lifting equipment, its mass must be indicated legibly, indelibly and unambiguously.

The interchangeable equipment referred to in Article 1(2), third subparagraph must bear the same information.]

1.7.4.   *Instructions*
(a) All machinery must be accompanied by instructions including at least the following:

— a repeat of the information with which the machinery is marked (see 1.7.3.), together with any appropriate additional information to facilitate maintenance (e.g. addresses of the importer, repairers, etc.),
— foreseen use of the machinery within the meaning of 1.1.2(c),
— workstation(s) likely to be occupied by operators,
— instructions for safe:
   — putting into service,
   — use,
   — handling, giving the mass of the machinery and its various parts where they are regularly to be transported separately,
   — assembly, dismantling,
   — adjustment,
   — maintenance (servicing and repair),
   — where necessary, training instructions.
   [— where necessary, the essential characteristics of tools which may be fitted to the machinery.]
Where necessary, the instructions should draw attention to ways in which the machinery should not be used.
(b) The instructions must be drawn up by the manufacturer or his authorised representative established in the Community in one of the languages of the country in which the machinery is to be used and should preferably be accompanied by the same instructions drawn up in another Community language, such as that of

the country in which the manufacturer or his authorised representative is established. By way of derogation from this requirement, the maintenance instructions for use by the specialised personnel frequently employed by the manufacturer or his authorised representative may be drawn up in only one of the official Community languages.

(c) The instructions must contain the drawings and diagrams necessary for putting into service, maintenance, inspection, checking of correct operation and, where appropriate, repair of the machinery, and all useful instructions in particular with regard to safety.

(d) Any sales literature describing the machinery must not contradict the instructions as regards safety aspects; it must give information regarding the airborne noise emissions referred to in (f) and, in the case of hand-held and/or hand-guided machinery, information regarding vibration as referred to in 2.2.

(e) Where necessary, the instructions must give the requirements relating to installation and assembly for reducing noise or vibration (e.g. use of dampers, type and mass of foundation block, etc.).

(f) The instructions must give the following information concerning airborne noise emissions by the machinery, either the actual value or a value established on the basis of measurements made on identical machinery:

— equivalent continuous A-weighted sound pressure level at workstations, where this exceeds 70 dB(A); where this level does not exceed 70 dB(A), this fact must be indicated,

— peak C-weighted instantaneous sound pressure value at workstations, where this exceeds 63 Pa (130 dB(A) in relation to 20 μPa),

— sound power level emitted by the machinery where the equivalent continuous A-weighted sound pressure level at workstations exceeds 85 dB(A).

[Where the harmonised standards are not applied, sound levels must be measured using the most appropriate method for the machinery.]

In the case of very large machinery, instead of the sound power level, the equivalent continuous sound pressure levels at specified positions around the machinery may be indicated.

Sound levels must be measured using the most appropriate method for the machinery.

The manufacturer must indicate the operating conditions of the machinery during measurement and what methods have been used for the measurement.

Where the workstation(s) are undefined or cannot be defined, sound pressure levels must be measured at a distance of 1 metre from the surface of the machinery and at height of 1,60 metres from the floor or access platform. The position and value of the maximum sound pressure must be indicated.

    (g) If the manufacturer foresees that the machinery will be used in a potentially explosive atmosphere, the instructions must give all the necessary information.

    (h) In the case of machinery which may also be intended for use by non-professional operators, the wording and layout of the instructions for use, whilst respecting the other essential requirements mentioned above, must take into account the level of general education and acumen that can reasonably be expected from such operators.

2.   ADDITIONAL ESSENTIAL HEALTH AND SAFETY REQUIREMENTS FOR CERTAIN CATEGORIES OF MACHINERY

2.1.   **Agri-foodstuffs machinery**

In addition to the essential health and safety requirements set out in 1 above, where machinery is intended to prepare and process foodstuffs (e.g. cooking, refrigeration, thawing, washing, handling, packaging, storage, transport or distribution), it must be so designed and constructed as to avoid any risk of infection, sickness or contagion and the following hygiene rules must be observed:

    (a) materials in contact, or intended to come into contact, with the foodstuffs must satisfy the conditions set down in the relevant Directives. The machinery must be so designed and constructed that these materials can be clean before each use;

    (b) all surfaces including their joinings must be smooth, and must have neither ridges nor crevices which could harbour organic materials;

    (c) assemblies must be designed in such a way as to reduce projections, edges and recesses to a minimum. They should preferably be made by welding or continuous bonding. Screws, screwheads and rivets may not be used except where technically unavoidable;

    (d) all surfaces in contact with the foodstuffs must be easily cleaned and disinfected, where possible after removing easily dismantled parts. The inside surfaces must have curves of a radius sufficient to allow thorough cleaning;

    (e) liquid deriving from foodstuffs as well as cleaning, disinfecting and rinsing fluids should be able to be discharged from the machine without impediment (possibly in a "clean" position);

    (f) machinery must be so designed and constructed as to prevent any liquids or living creatures, in particular insects, entering, or any organic matter accumulating in areas that cannot be cleaned (e.g. for machinery not mounted on feet or casters, by placing a seal between the machinery and its base, by the use of sealed units, etc.);

    (g) machinery must be so designed and constructed that no ancillary substances (e.g. lubricants, etc.) can come into contact with foodstuffs. Where necessary, machinery must be designed and

constructed so that continuing compliance with this requirement can be checked.

Instructions

In addition to the information required in section 1, the instructions
must indicate recommended products and methods for cleaning,
disinfecting and rinsing (not only for easily accessible areas but also
where areas to which access is impossible or unadvisable, such as
piping, have to be cleaned *in situ*).

2.2.   **Portable hand-held and/or hand-guided machinery**

In addition to the essential health and safety requirements set out in 1
above, portable hand-held and/or hand-guided machinery must conform to the following essential health and safety requirements:

— according to the type of machinery, it must have a supporting
  surface of sufficient size and have a sufficient number of handles
  and supports of an appropriate size and arranged to ensure the
  stability of the machinery under the operating conditions foreseen by the manufacturer,
— except where technically impossible or where there is an independent control, in the case of handles which cannot be released on
  complete safety, it must be fitted with start and stop controls
  arranged in such a way that the operator can operate them without releasing the handles,
— it must be designed, constructed or equipped to eliminate the
  risks of accidental starting and/or continued operation after the
  operator has released the handles. Equivalent steps must be taken
  if this requirement is not technically feasible,
— portable hand-held machinery must be designed and constructed
  to allow, where necessary, a visual check of the contact of the tool
  with the material being processed.

Instructions

The instructions must give the following information concerning
vibrations transmitted by hand-held and hand-guided machinery:

— the weighted root mean square acceleration value to which the
  arms are subjected, if it exceeds $2,5 \text{ m/s}^2$ as determined by the
  appropriate test code. Where the acceleration does not exceed
  $2,5 \text{ m/s}^2$, this must be mentioned.

If there is no applicable test code, the manufacturer must indicate the
measurement methods and conditions under which measurements
were made.

2.3.   **Machinery for working wood and analogous materials**

In addition to the essential health and safety requirements set out in 1
above, machinery for working wood and machinery for working

materials with physical and technological characteristics similar to those of wood, such as cork, bone, hardened rubber, hardened plastic material and other similar stiff material must conform to the following essential health and safety requirements:

(a) the machinery must be designed, constructed or equipped so that the piece being machined can be placed and guided in safety; where the piece is hand-held on a work-bench the latter must be sufficiently stable during the work and must not impede the movement of the piece;

(b) where the machinery is likely to be used in conditions involving the risk of ejection of pieces of wood, it must be designed, constructed or equipped to eliminate this ejection, or, if this is not the case, so that the ejection does not engender risks for the operator and/or exposed persons;

(c) the machinery must be equipped with an automatic brake that stops the tool in a sufficiently short time if there is a risk of contact with the tool whilst it runs down;

(d) where the tool is incorporated into a non-fully automated machine, the latter must be so designed and constructed as to eliminate or reduce the risk of serious accidental injury, for example by using cylindrical cutter blocks, restricting depth of cut, etc.

[3.   ESSENTIAL HEALTH AND SAFETY REQUIREMENTS TO OFFSET THE PARTICULAR HAZARDS DUE TO THE MOBILITY OF MACHINERY

In addition to the essential health and safety requirements given in sections 1 and 2, machinery presenting hazards due to mobility must be designed and constructed to meet the requirements below.

Risks due to mobility always exist in the case of machinery which is self-propelled, towed or pushed or carried by other machinery or tractors, is operated in working areas and whose operation requires either mobility while working, be it continuous or semi-continuous movement, between a succession of fixed working positions.

Risks due to mobility may also exist in the case of machinery operated without being moved, but equipped in such a way as to enable it to be moved more easily from one place to another (machinery fitted with wheels, rollers, runners, etc. or placed on gantries, trolleys, etc.).

In order to verify that rotary cultivators and power harrows do not present unacceptable risks to the exposed persons, the manufacturer or his authorised representative established within the Community must, for each type of machinery concerned, perform the appropriate tests or have such tests performed.

3.1. General

3.1.1 *Definition*

"Driver" means an operator responsible for the movement of machinery. The driver may be transported by the machinery or may be on foot, accompanying the machinery, or may be guiding the machinery by remote control (cables, radio, etc.),

3.1.2. *Lighting*

If intended by the manufacturer to be used in dark places, self-propelled machinery must be fitted with a lighting device appropriate to the work to be carried out, without prejudice to any other regulations applicable (road traffic regulations, navigation rules, etc.).

3.1.3. *Design of machinery to facilitate its handling*

During the handling of the machine and/or its parts, there must be no possibility of sudden movements or of hazards due to instability as long as the machine and/or its parts are handled in accordance with the manufacturer's instructions.

3.2. Work stations

3.2.1. *Driving position*

The driving position must be designed with due regard to ergonomic principles. There may be two or more driving positions and, in such cases, each driving position must be provided with all the requisite controls. Where there is more than one driving position, the machinery must be designed so that the use of one of them precludes the use of the others, except in emergency stops. Visibility from the driving position must be such that the driver can in complete safety for himself and the exposed persons, operate the machinery and its tools in their intended conditions of use. Where necessary, appropriate devices must be provided to remedy hazards due to inadequate direct vision.

Machinery must be so designed and constructed that, from the driving position, there can be no risk to the driver and operators on board from inadvertent contact with the wheels or tracks.

The driving position must be designed and constructed so as to avoid any health risk due to exhaust gases and/or lack of oxygen.

The driving position of ride-on drivers must be so designed and constructed that a driver's cab may be fitted as long as there is room. In that case, the cab must incorporate a place for the instructions needed for the driver and/or operators. The driving position must be fitted with an adequate cab where there is a hazard due to a dangerous environment.

Where the machinery is fitted with a cab, this must be designed, constructed and/or equipped to ensure that the driver has good operating conditions and is protected against any hazards that might exist (for instance: inadequate heating and ventilation, inadequate visibility, excessive noise and vibration, falling objects, penetration by objects, rolling over, etc.). The exit must allow rapid evacuation. Moreover, an emergency exit must be provided in a direction which is different from the usual exit.

The materials used for the cab and its fittings must be fire-resistant.

3.2.2.   *Seating*

The driving seat of any machinery must enable the driver to maintain a stable position and be designed with due regard to ergonomic principles.

The seat must be designed to reduce vibrations transmitted to the driver to the lowest level that can be reasonably achieved. The seat mountings must withstand all stresses to which they can be subjected, notably in the event of rollover. Where there is no floor beneath the driver's feet, the driver must have footrests covered with a slip-resistant material.

Where machinery is fitted with provision for a rollover protection structure, the seat must be equipped with a safety belt or equivalent device which keeps the driver in his seat without restricting any movements necessary for driving or any movements caused by the suspension.

3.2.3.   *Other places*

If the conditions of use provide that operators other than the driver are occasionally or regularly transported by the machinery, or work on it, appropriate places must be provided which enable them to be transported or to work on it without risk, particularly the risk of falling.

Where the working conditions so permit, these work places must be equipped with seats.

Should the driving position have to be fitted with a cab, the other places must also be protected against the hazards which justified the protection of the driving position.

3.3.   **Controls**

3.3.1.   *Control devices*

The driver must be able to actuate all control devices required to operate the machinery from the driving position, except for functions which can be safely activated only by using control devices located away from the driving position. This refers in particular to working positions other than the driving position, for which operators other than the driver are responsible or for which the driver has to leave his driving position in order to carry out the manoeuvre in safety.

Where there are pedals they must be so designed, constructed and fitted to allow operation by the driver in safety with the minimum risk of confusion; they must have a slip-resistant surface and be easy to clean.

Where their operation can lead to hazards, notably dangerous movements, the machinery's controls, except for those with preset positions, most return to the neutral position as soon as they are released by the operator.

In the case of wheeled machinery, the steering system must be designed and constructed to reduce the force of sudden movements of the steering wheel or steering lever caused by shocks to the guide wheels.

Any control that locks the differential must be so designed and arranged that it allows the differential to be unlocked when the machinery is moving.

The last sentence of secton 1.2.2 does not apply to the mobility function.

3.2.3.   *Starting/moving*

Self-propelled machinery with a ride-on driver must be so equipped as to deter unauthorised persons from starting the engine.

Travel movements of self-propelled machinery with a ride-on driver must be possible only if the driver is at the controls.

Where, for operating purposes, machinery must be fitted with devices which exceed its normal clearance zone (e.g. stabilisers, jib, etc.), the driver must be provided with the means of checking easily, before moving the machinery, that such devices are in a particular position which allows safe movement.

This also applies to all other parts which, to allow safe movement, have to be in particular positions, locked if necessary.

Where it is technically and economically feasible, movement of the machinery must depend on safe positioning of the aforementioned parts.

It must not be possible for movement of the machinery to occur while the engine is being started.

3.3.3.   *Travelling function*

Without prejudice to the provisions of road traffic regulations, self-propelled machinery and its trailers must meet the requirements for slowing down, stopping, braking and immobilisation so as to ensure safety under all the operating, loading, speed, ground and gradient conditions allowed for by the manufacturer and corresponding to conditions encountered in normal use.

The driver must be able to slow down and stop self-propelled machinery by means of a main device. Where safety so requires in the event of a failure of the main device, or in the absence of the energy supply to actuate the main device, an emergency device with fully independent and easily accessible controls must be provided for slowing down and stopping.

Where safety so requires, a parking device must be provided to render stationary machinery immobile. This device may be combined with one of the devices referred to in the second paragraph, provided that it is purely mechanical.

Remote-controlled machinery must be designed and constructed to stop automatically if the driver loses control.

Section 1.2.4 does not apply to the travelling function.

3.3.4.   *Movement of pedestrian-controlled machinery*

Movement of pedestrian-controlled self-propelled machinery must be possible only through sustained action on the relevant control by the driver. In particular, it must not be possible for movement to occur while the engine is being started.

The control systems for pedestrian-controlled machinery must be designed to minimise the hazards arising from inadvertent movement of the machine towards the driver. In particular:

(a) crushing;
(b) injury from rotating tools.

Also, the speed of normal travel of the machine must be compatible with the pace of a driver on foot.

In the case of machinery on which a rotary tool may be fitted, it must not be possible to actuate that tool when the reversing control is engaged, except where movement of the machinery results from movement of the tool. In the latter case, the reversing speed must be such that it does not endanger the driver.

3.3.5.   *Control circuit failure*

A failure in the power supply to the power-assisted steering, where fitted, must not prevent machinery from being steered during the time required to stop it.

3.4.   **Protection against mechanical hazards**

3.4.1.   *Uncontrolled movements*

When a part of a machine has been stopped, any drift away from the stopping position, for whatever reason other than action at the controls, must be such that it is not a hazard to exposed persons.

Machinery must be so designed, constructed and where appropriate placed on its mobile support as to ensure that when moved the uncontrolled oscillations of its centre of gravity do not affect its stability or exert excessive strain on its structure.

3.4.2. *Risk of break-up during operation*

Parts of machinery rotating at high speed which, despite the measures taken, may break up or disintegrate, must be mounted and guarded in such a way that, in case of breakage, their fragments will be contained or, if that is not possible, cannot be projected towards the driving and/or operation positions.

3.4.3. *Rollover*

Where, in the case of self-propelled machinery with a ride-on driver and possibly ride-on operators, there is a risk of rolling over, the machinery must be designed for and be fitted with anchorage points allowing it to be equipped with a rollover protective structure (ROPS).

This structure must be such that in case of rolling over if affords the ride-on driver and where appropriate the ride-on operators an adequate deflection-limiting volume (DLV).

In order to verify that the structure complies with the requirement laid down in the second paragraph, the manufacturer or his authorised representative established within the Community must, for each type of structure concerned, perform appropriate tests or have such tests performed.

In addition, the earth-moving machinery listed below with a capacity exceeding 15 kW must be fitted with a rollover protective structure:

— crawler loaders or wheel loaders,
— backhoe loaders,
— crawler tractors or wheel tractors,
— scrapers, self-loading or not,
— graders,
— articulated steer dumpers.

3.4.4. *Falling objects*

Where, in the case of machinery with a ride-on driver and possibly ride-on operators, there is a risk due to falling objects or material, the machinery should be designed for, and fitted with, if its size allows, anchorage points allowing it to be equipped with a falling-object protective structure (FOPS).

This structure must be such that in the case of falling objects or material, it guarantees the ride-on operators an adequate deflection-limiting volume (DLV).

In order to verify that the structure complies with the requirement laid down in the second paragraph, the manufacturer or his authorised representative established within the Community must, for each type of structure concerned, perform appropriate tests or have such tests performed.

3.4.5.   *Means of access*

Handholds and steps must be designed, constructed and arranged in such a way that the operators use them instinctively and do not use the controls for that purpose.

3.4.6.   *Towing devices*

All machinery used to tow or to be towed must be fitted with towing or coupling devices designed, constructed and arranged to ensure easy and safe connection and disconnection, and to prevent accidental disconnection during use.

In so far as the towbar load requires, such machinery must be equipped with a support with a bearing surface suited to the load and the ground.

3.4.7.   *Transmission of power between self-propelled machinery (or tractor) and recipient machinery*

Transmission shafts with universal joints linking self-propelled machinery (or tractor) to the first fixed bearing of recipient machinery must be guarded on the self-propelled machinery side and the recipient machinery side over the whole length of the shaft and associated universal joints.

On the side of the self-propelled machinery (or tractor), the power take-off to which the transmission shaft is attached must be guarded either by a screen fixed to the self-propelled machinery (or tractor) or by any other device offering equivalent protection.

On the towed machinery side, the input shaft must be enclosed in a protective casing fixed to the machinery.

Torque limiters or freewheels may be fitted to universal joint transmissions only on the side adjoining the driven machine. The universal-joint transmission shaft must be marked accordingly.

All towed machinery whose operation requires a transmission shaft to connect it to self-propelled machinery or a tractor must have a system for attaching the transmission shaft so that when the machinery is uncoupled the transmission shaft and its guard are not damaged by contact with the ground or part of the machinery.

The outside parts of the guard must be so designed, constructed and arranged that they cannot turn with the transmission shaft. The guard must cover the transmission shaft to the ends of the inner jaws in the case of simple universal joints and at least to the centre of the outer joint or joints in the case of "wide-angle" universal joints.

Manufacturers providing means of access to working positions near to the universal joint transmission shaft must ensure that shaft guards as described in the sixth paragraph cannot be used as steps unless designed and constructed for that purpose.

3.4.8. *Moving transmission parts*

By way of derogation from section 1.3.8.A, in the case of internal combustion engines, removable guards preventing access to the moving parts in the engine compartment need not have locking devices if they have to be opened either by the use of a tool or key or by a control located in the driving position if the latter is in a fully enclosed cab with a lock to prevent unauthorised access.

3.5. **Protection against other hazards**

3.5.1. *Batteries*

The battery housing must be constructed and located and the battery installed so as to avoid as far as possible the chance of electrolyte being ejected on to the operator in the event of rollover and/or to avoid the accumulation of vapours in places occupied by operators.

Machinery must be so designed and constructed that the battery can be disconnected with the aid of an easily accessible device provided for that purpose.

3.5.2. *Fire*

Depending on the hazards anticipated by the manufacturer when in use, machinery must, where its size permits:

— either allow easily accessible fire extinguishers to be fitted,
— or be provided with built-in extinguisher systems.

3.5.3. *Emissions of dust, gases, etc.*

Where such hazards exist, the containment equipment provided for in section 1.5.13 may be replaced by other means, for example precipitation by water spraying.

The second and third paragraphs of section 1.5.13 do not apply where the main function of the machinery is the spraying of products.

3.6. **Indications**

3.6.1. *Signs and warning*

Machinery must have means of signalling and/or instruction plates concerning use, adjustment and maintenance, wherever necessary, to ensure the health and safety of exposed persons. They must be chosen, designed and constructed in such a way as to be clearly visible and indelible.

Without prejudice to the requirements to be observed for travelling on the public highway, machinery with a ride-on driver must have the following equipment:

— an acoustic warning device to alert exposed persons,
— a system of light signals relevant to the intended conditions of use such as stop lamps, reversing lamps and rotating beacons. The latter requirement does not apply to machinery intended solely for underground working and having no electrical power.

Remote-controlled machinery which under normal conditions of use exposes persons to the hazards of impact or crushing must be fitted with appropriate means to signal its movements or with means to protect exposed persons against such hazards. The same applies to machinery which involves, when in use, the constant repetition of a forward and backward movement on a single axis where the back of the machine is not directly visible to the driver.

Machinery must be so constructed that the warning and signalling devices cannot all be disabled unintentionally. Where this is essential for safety, such devices must be provided with the means to check that they are in good working order and their failure must be made apparent to the operator.

Where the movement of machinery or its tools is particularly hazardous, signs on the machinery must be provided to warn against approaching the machinery while it is working; the signs must be legible at a sufficient distance to ensure the safety of persons who have to be in the vicinity.

3.6.2.   *Marking*

The minimum requirements set out in 1.7.3 must be supplemented by the following:

— nominal power expressed in kW,
— mass in kg of the most usual configuration and, where appropriate:
  — maximum drawbar pull provided for by the manufacturer at the coupling hook, in N,
  — maximum vertical load provided for by the manufacturer on the coupling hook, in N.

3.6.3.   *Instruction handbook*

Apart from the minimum requirements set out in 1.7.4, the instruction handbook must contain the following information:

(a) regarding the vibrations emitted by the machinery, either the actual value or a figure calculated from measurements performed on identical machinery:

— the weighted root mean square acceleration value to which the arms are subjected, if it exceeds $2,5 \text{ m/s}^2$; should it not exceed $2,5 \text{ m/s}^2$, this must be mentioned,
— the weighted root mean square acceleration value to which the body (feet or posterior) is subjected, if it exceeds $0,5 \text{ m/s}^2$; should it not exceed $0,5 \text{ m/s}^2$, this must be mentioned.

Where the harmonised standards are not applied, the vibration must be measured using the most appropriate method for the machinery concerned.

The manufacturer must indicate the operating conditions of the machinery during measurement and which methods were used for taking the measurements;

(b) in the case of machinery allowing several uses depending on the equipment used, manufacturers of basic machinery to which interchangeable equipment may be attached and manufacturers of the interchangeable equipment must provide the necessary information to enable the equipment to be fitted and used safely.

4.   ESSENTIAL HEALTH AND SAFETY REQUIREMENTS TO OFFSET THE PARTICULAR HAZARDS DUE TO A LIFTING OPERATION

In addition to the essential health and safety requirements given in sections 1, 2 and 3, machinery presenting hazards due to lifting operations—mainly hazards of load falls and collisions or hazards of tipping caused by a lifting operation—must be designed and constructed to meet the requirements below.

Risks due to a lifting operation exist particularly in the case of machinery designed to move a unit load involving a change in level during the movement. The load may consist of objects, materials or goods.

4.1.   General remarks

4.1.1.   *Definitions*

(a) lifting accessories:
"lifting accessories" means components or equipment not attached to the machine and placed between the machinery and the load or on the load in order to attach it;
(b) separate lifting accessories:
"separate lifting accessories" means accessories which help to make up or use a slinging device, such as eyehooks, shackles, rings, eyebolts, etc.;

(c)   guided load:

"guided load" means the load where the total movement is made along rigid or flexible guides, whose position is determined by fixed points;

(d)   working coefficient:

"working coefficient" means the arithmetic ratio between the load guaranteed by the manufacturer up to which a piece of equipment, an accessory or machinery is able to hold it and the maximum working load marked on the equipment, accessory or machinery respectively;

(e)   test coefficient:

"test coefficient" means the arithmetic ratio between the load used to carry out the static or dynamic tests on a piece of equipment, an accessory or machinery and the maximum working load marked on the piece of equipment, accessory or machinery;

(f)   static test:

"static test" means the test during which the machinery or the lifting accessory is first inspected and then subjected to a force corresponding to the maximum working load multiplied by the appropriate static test coefficient and then re-inspected once the said load has been released to ensure no damage has occurred;

(g)   dynamic test:

"dynamic test" means the test during which the machinery is operated in all its possible configurations at maximum working load with account being taken of the dynamic behaviour of the machinery in order to check that the machinery and safety features are functioning properly.

4.1.2.   *Protection against mechanical hazards*

4.1.2.1.   Risks due to lack of stability

Machinery must be so designed and constructed that the stability required in 1.3.1 is maintained both in service and out of service, including all stages of transportation, assembly and dismantling, during foreseeable component failures and also during the tests carried out in accordance with the instruction handbook.

To that end, the manufacturer or his authorised representative established within the Community must use the appropriate verification methods; in particular, for self-propelled industrial trucks with lift exceeding 1,80 m, the manufacturer or his authorised representative established within the Community must, for each type of industrial truck concerned, perform a platform stability test or similar test, or have such tests performed.

4.1.2.2.   Guide rails and rail tracks

Machinery must be provided with devices which act on the guide rails or tracks to prevent derailment.

However, if derailment occurs despite such devices, or if there is a failure of a rail or of a running component, devices must be provided which prevent the equipment, component or load from falling or the machine overturning.

4.1.2.3. Mechanical strength

Machinery, lifting accessories and removeable components must be capable of withstanding the stresses to which they are subjected, both in and, where applicable, out of use, under the installation and operating conditions provided for by the manufacturer, and in all relevant configurations, with due regard, where appropriate, to the effects of atmospheric factors and forces exerted by persons. This requirement must also be satisfied during transport, assembly and dismantling.

Machinery and lifting accessories must be designed and constructed so as to prevent failure from fatigue or wear, taking due account of their intended use.

The materials used must be chosen on the basis of the working environments provided for by the manufacturer, with special reference to corrosion, abrasion, impacts, cold brittleness and ageing.

The machinery and the lifting accessories must be designed and constructed to withstand the overload in the static tests without permanent deformation or patent defect. The calculation must take account of the values of the static test coefficient chosen to guarantee an adequate level of safety: that coefficient has, as a general rule, the following values:

(a) manually-operated machinery and lifting accessories: 1,5;
(b) other machinery: 1,25.

Machinery must be designed and constructed to undergo, without failure, the dynamic tests carried out using the maximum working load multiplied by the dynamic test coefficient. This dynamic test coefficient is chosen so as to guarantee an adequate level of safety: the coefficient is, as a general rule, equal to 1,1.

The dynamic tests must be performed on machinery ready to be put into service under normal conditions of use. As a general rule, the tests will be performed at the nominal speeds laid down by the manufacturer. Should the control circuit of the machinery allow for a number of simultaneous movements (for example, rotation and displacement of the load), the tests must be carried out under the least favourable conditions, i.e. as a general rule, by combining the movements concerned.

4.1.2.4. Pulleys, drums, chains or ropes

Pulleys, drums and wheels must have a diameter commensurate with the size of rope or chains with which they can be fitted.

Drums and wheels must be so designed, constructed and installed that the ropes or chains with which they are equipped can wind round without falling off.

Ropes used directly for lifting or supporting the load must not include any splicing other than at their ends (splicings are tolerated in installations which are intended from their design to be modified regularly according to needs for use). Complete ropes and their endings have a working coefficient chosen so as to guarantee an adequate level of safety; as a general rule, this coefficient is equal to five.

Lifting chains have a working coefficient chosen so as to guarantee an adequate level of safety; as a general rule, this coefficient is equal to four.

In order to verify that an adequate working coefficient has been attained, the manufacturer or his authorised representative established within the Community must, for each type of chain and rope used directly for lifting the load, and for the rope ends, perform the appropriate tests or have such tests performed.

4.1.2.5.   Separate lifting accessories

Lifting accessories must be sized with due regard to fatigue and ageing processes for a number of operating cycles consistent with their expected life-span as specified in the operating conditions for a given application.

Moreover:

(a) the working coefficient of the metallic rope/rope-end combination is chosen so as to guarantee an adequate level of safety; this coefficient is, as a general rule, equal to five. Ropes must not comprise any splices or loops other than at their ends;

(b) where chains with welded links are used, they must be of the short-link type. The working coefficient of chains of any type is chosen so as to guarantee an adequate level of safety; this coefficient is, as a general rule, equal to four;

(c) the working coefficient for textile ropes or slings is dependent on the material, method of manufacture, dimensions and use. This coefficient is chosen so as to guarantee an adequate level of safety; it is, as a general rule, equal to seven, provided the materials used are shown to be of very good quality and the method of manufacture is appropriate to the intended use. Should this not be the case, the coefficient is, as a general rule, set at a highter level in order to secure an equivalent level of safety.

Textile ropes and slings must not include any knots, connections or splicing other than at the ends of the sling, except in the case of an endless sling;

(d) all metallic components making up, or used with, a sling must have a working coefficient chosen so as to guarantee an adequate level of safety; this coefficient is, as a general rule, equal to four;

(e) the maximum working capacity of a multi-legged sling is determined on the basis of the safety coefficient of the weakest leg, the number of legs and a reduction factor which depends on the slinging configuration;

(f) in order to verify that an adequate working coefficient has been attained, the manufacturer or his authorised representative established within the Community must, for each type of component referred to in (a), (b), (c) and (d) perform the appropriate tests or have such tests performed.

4.1.2.6. Control of movements

Devices for controlling movements must act in such a way that the machinery on which they are installed is kept safe:

(a) machinery must be so designed or fitted with devices that the amplitude or movement of its components is kept within the specified limits. The operation of such devices must, where appropriate, be preceded by a warning;

(b) where several fixed or rail-mounted machines can be manoeuvred simultaneously in the same place, with risks of collision, such machines must be so designed and constructed as to make it possible to fit systems enabling these risks to be avoided;

(c) the mechanisms of machinery must be so designed and constructed that the loads cannot creep dangerously or fall freely and unexpectedly, even in the event of partial or total failure of the power supply or when the operator stops operating the machine;

(d) it must not be possible, under normal operating conditions, to lower the load solely by friction brake, except in the case of machinery, whose function requires it to operate in that way;

(e) holding devices must be so designed and constructed that inadvertent dropping of the loads is avoided.

4.1.2.7. Handling of loads

The driving position of machinery must be located in such a way as to ensure that widest possible view of trajectories of the moving parts, in order to avoid possible collisions with persons or equipment or other machinery which might be manoeuvring at the same time and liable to constitute a hazard.

Machinery with guided loads fixed in one place must be designed and constructed so as to prevent exposed persons from being hit by the load or the counter-weights.

4.1.2.8. Lightning

Machinery in need of protection against the effects of lightning while being used must be fitted with a system for conducting the resultant electrical charges to earth.

4.2. **Special requirements for machinery whose power source is other than manual effort**

4.2.1. *Controls*

4.2.1.1. Driving position

The requirements laid down in section 3.2.1 also apply to non-mobile machinery.

4.2.1.2.   Seating

The requirements laid down in section 3.2.2, first and second paragraphs, and those laid down in section 3.2.3 also apply to non-mobile machinery.

4.2.1.3.   Control devices

The devices controlling movements of the machinery or its equipment must return to their neutral position as soon as they are released by the operator. However, for partial or complete movements in which there is no risk of the load or the machinery colliding, the said devices may be replaced by controls authorising automatic stops at preselected levels without holding a hold-to-run control device.

4.2.1.4.   Loading control

Machinery with a maximum working load of not less than 1 000 kilograms or an overturning moment of not less than 40 000 Nm must be fitted with devices to warn the driver and prevent dangerous movements of the load in the event of:

— overloading the machinery,
   — either as a result of maximum working loads being exceeded,
   or
   — as a result of the moments due to the loads being exceeded,
— the moments conducive to overturning being exceeded as a result of the load being lifted.

4.2.2.   *Installation guided by cables*

Cable carriers, tractors or tractor carriers must be held by counterweights or by a device allowing permanent control of the tension.

4.2.3.   *Risks to exposed persons. Means of access to driving position and intervention points*

Machinery with guided loads and machinery whose load supports follow a clearly defined path must be equipped with devices to prevent any risks to exposed persons.

4.2.4.   *Fitness for purpose*

When machinery is placed on the market or is first put into service, the manufacturer or his authorised representative established within the Community must ensure, by taking appropriate measures or having them taken, that lifting accessories and machinery which are ready for use—whether manually or power-operated—can fulfil their specified functions safely. The said measures must take into account the static and dynamic aspects of the machinery.

Where the machinery cannot be assembled in the manufacturer's premises, or in the premises of his authorised representative established within the Community, appropriate measures must be taken at the place of use. Otherwise, the measures may be taken either in the manufacturer's premises or at the place of use.

4.3. **Marking**

4.3.1. *Chains and ropes*

Each length of lifting chain, rope or webbing not forming part of an assembly must bear a mark or, where this is not possible, a plate or irremovable ring bearing the name and address of the manufacturer or his authorised representative established in the Community and the identifying reference of the relevant certificate.

The certificate should show the information required by the harmonised standards or, should those not exist, at least the following information:

— the name of the manufacturer or his authorised representative established within the Community,
— the address within the Community of the manufacturer or his authorised representative, as appropriate,
— a description of the chain or rope which includes:
  — its nominal size,
  — its construction,
  — the material from which it is made, and
— any special metallurgical treatment applied to the material,
— if tested, the standard used,
— a maximum load to which the chain or rope should be subjected in service. A range of values may be given for specified applications.

4.3.2. *Lifting accessories*

All lifting accessories must show the following particulars:

— identification of the manufacturer,
— identification of the material (e.g. international classification) where this information is needed for dimensional compatability,
— identification of the maximum working load,
— EC mark.

In the case of accessories including components such as cables or ropes, on which marking is physically impossible, the particulars referred to in the first paragraph must be displayed on a plate or by some other means and securely affixed to the accessory.

The particulars must be legible and located in a place where they are not liable to disappear as a result of machining, wear, etc., or jeopardise the strength of the accessory.

4.3.3.   *Machinery*

> In addition to the minimum information provided for in 1.7.3, each machine must bear, legibly and indelibly, information concerning the nominal load:
>
> (i) displayed in uncoded form and prominently on the equipment in the case of machinery which has only one possible value;
> (ii) where the nominal load depends on the configuration of the machine, each driving position must be provided with a load plate indicating, preferably in diagrammatic form or by means of tables, the nominal loads for each configuration.
>
> Machinery equipped with a load support which allows access to persons and involves a risk of falling must bear a clear and indelible warning prohibiting the lifting of persons. This warning must be visible at each place where access is possible.

4.4.   **Instruction handbook**

4.4.1.   *Lifting accessories*

> Each lifting accessory or each commercially indivisible batch of lifting accessories must be accompanied with an instruction handbook setting out at least the following particulars:
>
> — normal conditions of use,
> — instructions for use, assembly and maintenance,
> — the limits of use (particularly for the accessories which cannot comply with 4.1.2.6(e)).

4.4.2.   *Machinery*

> In addition to section 1.7.4, the instruction handbook must include the following information:
>
> (a) the technical characteristics of the machinery, and in particular:
>
>> — where appropriate, a copy of the load table described in section 4.3.3(ii),
>> — the reactions at the supports or anchors and characteristics of the tracks,
>> — where appropriate, the definition and the means of installation of the ballast;
>
> (b) the contents of the logbook, if the latter is not supplied with the machinery;
> (c) advice for use, particularly to offset the lack of direct sight of the load by the operator;
> (d) the necessary instructions for performing the test before first putting into service machinery which is not assembled on the manufacturer's premises in the form in which it is to be used.

5.   ESSENTIAL SAFETY AND HEALTH REQUIREMENTS FOR
      MACHINERY INTENDED SOLELY FOR UNDERGROUND WORK

In addition to the essential safety and health requirements provided
for in sections 1, 2, 3 and 4, machinery intended solely for underground work must be designed and constructed to meet the requirements below.

5.1.   **Risks due to lack of stability**

Powered roof supports must be so designed and constructed as to
maintain a given direction when moving and not slip before and while
they come under load and after the load has been removed. They
must be equipped with anchorages for the top plates of the individual
hydraulic props.

5.2.   **Movement**

Powered roof supports must allow for unhindered movement of
exposed persons.

5.3.   **Lighting**

The requirements laid down in the third paragraph of section 1.1.4
do not apply.

5.4.   **Control devices**

The accelerator and brake controls for the movement of machinery
running on rails must be manual. The deadman's control may be
foot-operated, however.

The control devices of powered roof supports must be designed and
laid out so that, during displacement operations, operators are shel-
tered by a support in place. The control devices must be protected
against any accidental release.

5.5.   **Stopping**

Self-propelled machinery running on rails for use in underground
work must be equipped with a deadman's control acting on the circuit
controlling the movement of the machinery.

5.6.   **Fire**

The second indent of 3.5.2 is mandatory in respect of machinery
which comprises highly flammable parts.

The braking system of machinery meant for use in underground working must be designed and constructed so as not to produce sparks or cause fires.

Machinery with heat engines for use in underground working must be fitted only with internal combustion engines using fuel with a low vaporising pressure and which exclude any spark of electrical origin.

5.7.   **Emissions of dust, gases etc.**

Exhaust gases from internal combustion engines must not be discharged upwards.]

ANNEX II

A.   **Contents of the EC declaration of conformity**

The EC declaration of conformity must contain the following particulars:

— name and address of the manufacturer or his authorised representative established in the Community,
— description of the machinery,
— all relevant provisions complied with by the machinery,
— where appropriate, name and address of the notified body and number of the EC type-examination certificate,
— where appropriate, the name and address of the notified body to which the fill has been forwarded in accordance with the first indent of Article 8(2)(c),
— where appropriate, the name and address of the notified body which has carried out the verification referred to in the second indent of Article 8(2)(c),
— where appropriate, a reference to the harmonised standards,
— where appropriate, the national technical standards and specifications used,
— identification of the person empowered to sign on behalf of the manufacturer or his authorised representatives.

B.   **Contents of the declaration by the manufacturer or his authorised representatives established in the Community (Article 4(2))**

The manufacturer's declaration referred to in Article 4(2) must contain the following particulars:

— name and address of the manufacturer or the authorised representative,
[— where appropriate, the name and address of the notified body and the number of the EC type-examination certificate,
— where appropriate, the name and address of the notified body to which the file has been forwarded in accordance with the first indent of Article 8(2)(c),
— where appropriate, the name and address of the notified body which has carried out the verification referred to in the second indent of Article 8(2)(c),

— where appropriate, a reference to the harmonised standards.]
— description of the machinery or machinery parts,
— a statement that the machinery must not be put into service until the
machinery into which it is to be incorporated has been declared in
conformity with the provisions of the Directive,
— identification of the person signing.

ANNEX III

EC MARK

The EC mark consists of the symbol shown below and the last two figures of the
year in which the mark was affixed.

The different elements of the EC mark should have materially the same vertical
dimensions, which should not be less than 5 mm.

ANNEX IV

**TYPES OF MACHINES FOR WHICH THE PROCEDURE REFERRED TO IN
ARTICLE 8(2)(b) AND (c) MUST BE APPLIED**

1.   Circular saws (single- or multi-blade) for working with wood and meat.

1.1   Sawing machines with fixed tool during operation, having a fixed bed
with manual feed of the workpiece or with a demountable power feed.

1.2   Sawing machines with fixed tool during operation, having a manually
operated reciprocating saw-bench or carriage.

1.3   Sawing machines with fixed tool during operation, having a built-in
mechanical feed device for the workpieces, with manual loading and/or
unloading.

1.4   Sawing machines with moveable tool during operation, with a mechanical feed device and manual loading and/or unloading.

2.   Hand-fed surface planing machines for woodworking.

3.   Thicknessers for one-side dressing with manual loading and/or unloading for woodworking.

4.   Band-saws with a mobile bed or carriage and manual loading and/or unloading for working with wood and meat.

5.   Combined machines of the types referred to in 1 to 4 and 7 for woodworking.

6.   Hand-fed tenoning machines with several tool holders for woodworking.

7.   Hand-fed vertical spindle moulding machines.

8.   Portable chain saws for woodworking.

9.   Presses, including press-brakes, for the cold working of metals, with manual loading and/or unloading, whose moveable working parts may have a travel exceeding 6 mm and a speed exceeding 30 mm/s.

10.   Injection or compression plastics-moulding machines with manual loading or unloading.

11.   Injection or compression rubber-moulding machines with manual loading or unloading.

[12.   Machinery for underground working of the following types:

— machinery on rails: locomotives and brake-vans,
— hydraulic-powered roof supports,
— internal combustion engines to be fitted to machinery for underground working.

13.   Manually-loaded trucks for the collection of household refuse incorporating a compression mechanism.

14.   Guards and detachable transmission shafts with universal joints as described in section 3.4.7.

15.   Vehicles servicing lifts.]

ANNEX V

EC DECLARATION OF CONFORMITY

1.   The EC declaration of conformity is the procedure by which the manufacturer, or his authorised representative established in the Community declares that the machinery being placed on the market complies with all the essential health and safety requirements applying to it.

2.   Signature of the EC declaration of conformity authorises the manufacturer, or his authorised representative in the Community, to affix the EC mark to the machinery.

3.   Before drawing up the EC declaration of conformity, the manufacturer, or his authorised representative in the Community, shall have ensured and be

able to guarantee that the documentation listed below is and will remain available on his premises for any inspection purposes:

(a) a technical construction file comprising:
  — an overall drawing of the machinery together with drawings of the control circuits,
  — full detailed drawings, accompanied by any calculation notes, test results, etc., required to check the conformity of the machinery with the essential health and safety requirements,
  — a list of:
    — the essential requirements of this Directive,
    — standards, and
    — other technical specifications, which were used when the machinery was designed,
  — a description of methods adopted to eliminate hazards presented by the machinery,
  — if he so desires, any technical report or certificate obtained from a competent body or laboratory,
  — if he declares conformity with a harmonised standard which provides therefor, any technical report giving the results of tests carried out at his choice either by himself or by a competent body or laboratory,
  — a copy of the instructions for the machinery;
(b) for series manufacture, the internal measures that will be implemented to ensure that the machinery remains in conformity with the provisions of the Directive.

The manufacturer must carry out necessary research or tests on components, fittings or the completed machine to determine whether by its design or construction, the machine is capable of being erected and put into service safely.

Failure to present the documentation in response to a duly substantiated request by the competent national authorities may constitute sufficient grounds for doubting the presumption of conformity with the requirements of the Directive.

4. (a) The documentation referred to in 3 above need not permanently exist in a material manner but it must be possible to assemble it and make it available within a period of time commensurate with its importance. It does not have to include detailed plans or any other specific information as regards the sub-assemblies used for the manufacture of the machinery unless a knowledge of them is essential for verification of conformity with the basic safety requirements.
  (b) The documentation referred to in 3 above shall be retained and kept available for the competent national authorities for at least 10 years following the date of manufacture of the machinery or of the last unit produced, in the case of series manufacture.
  (c) The documentation referred to in 3 above shall be drawn up in one of the official languages of the Communities, with the exception of the instructions for the machinery.

ANNEX VI

EC TYPE-EXAMINATION

1. EC type-examination is the procedure by which a notified body ascertains and certifies that an example of machinery satisfies the provisions of this Directive which apply to it.

2. The application for EC type-examination shall be lodged by the manufacturer or by his authorised representative established in the Community, with a single notified body in respect of an example of the machinery.

    The application shall include:
    — the name and address of the manufacturer or his authorised representative established in the Community and the place of manufacture of the machinery,
    — a technical file comprising at least:
        — an overall drawing of the machinery together with drawings of the control circuits,
        — full detailed drawings, accompanied by any calculation notes, test results, etc., required to check the conformity of the machinery with the essential health and safety requirements,
        — a description of methods adopted to eliminate hazards presented by the machinery and a list of standards used,
        — a copy of the instructions for the machinery,
        — for series manufacture, the internal measures that will be implemented to ensure that the machinery remains in conformity with the provisions of the Directive.

    It shall be accompanied by a machine representative of the production planned or, where appropriate, a statement of where the machine may be examined.

    The documentation referred to above does not have to include detailed plans or any other specific information as regards the sub-assemblies used for the manufacture of the machinery unless a knowledge of them is essential for verification of conformity with the basic safety requirements.

3. The notified body shall carry out the EC type-examination in the manner described below:
    — it shall examine the technical construction file to verify its appropriateness and the machine supplied or made available to it.
    — during the examination of the machine, the body shall:
        (a) ensure that it has been manufactured in conformity which the technical construction file and may safely be used under its intended working conditions;
        (b) check that standards, if used, have been properly applied;
        (c) perform appropriate examinations and tests to check that the machine complies with the essential health and safety requirements applicable to it.

4. If the example complies with the provisions applicable to it the body shall draw up an EC type-examination certificate which shall be forwarded to the

applicant. That certificate shall state the conclusions of the examination, indicate any conditions to which its issue may be subject and be accompanied by the descriptions and drawings necessary for identification of the approved example.

The Commission, the Member States and the other approved bodies may obtain a copy of the certificate and, on a reasoned request, a copy of the technical construction file and of the reports on the examinations and tests carried out.

5. The manufacturer or his authorised representative established in the Community shall inform the notified body of any modifications, even of a minor nature, which he has made or plans to make to the machine to which the example relates. The notified body shall examine those modifications and inform the manufacturer or his authorised representative established in the Community whether the EC type-examination certificate remains valid.

6. A body which refuses to issue an EC type-examination certificate shall so inform the other notified bodies. A body which withdraws an EC type-examination certificate shall so inform the Member State which notified it. The latter shall inform the other Member States and the Commission thereof, giving the reasons for the decision.

7. The files and correspondence referring to the EC type-examination procedures shall be drawn up in an official language of the Member State where the notified body is established or in a language acceptable to it.

ANNEX VII

MINIMUM CRITERIA TO BE TAKEN INTO ACCOUNT BY MEMBER STATES FOR THE NOTIFICATION OF BODIES

1. The body, its director and the staff responsible for carrying out the verification tests shall not be the designer, manufacturer, supplier or installer of machinery which they inspect, nor the authorised representative of any of these parties. They shall not become either involved directly or as authorised representatives in the design, construction, marketing or maintenance of the machinery. This does not preclude the possibility of exchanges of technical information between the manufacturer and the body.

2. The body and its staff shall carry out the verification tests with the highest degree of professional integrity and technical competence and shall be free from all pressures and inducements, particularly financial, which might influence their judgement or the results of the inspection, especially from persons or groups of persons with an interest in the result of verifications.

3. The body shall have at its disposal the necessary staff and possess the necessary facilities to enable it to perform properly the administrative and technical task connected with verification; it shall also have access to the equipment required for special verification.

4. The staff responsible for inspection shall have:
    — sound technical and professional training,
    — satisfactory knowledge of the requirements of the tests they carry out and adequate experience of such tests,
    — the ability to draw up the certificates, records and reports required to authenticate the performance of the tests.

5. The impartiality of inspection shall be guaranteed. Their remuneration shall not depend on the number of tests carried out or on the results of such tests.

6. The body shall take out liability insurance unless its liability is assumed by the State in accordance with national law, or the Member State itself is directly responsible for the tests.

7. The staff of the body shall be bound to observe professional secrecy with regard to all information gained in carrying out its tasks (except *vis-à-vis* the competent administrative authorities of the State in which its activities are carried out) under this Directive of any provision of national law giving effect to it.

THE WORKPLACE DIRECTIVE

General note. This is the first daughter Directive and was implemented in the UK by the Workplace (Health, Safety and Welfare) Regulations 1992 (S.I. 1992 No. 3004), see page 443.

COUNCIL DIRECTIVE

of 30 November 1989

concerning the minimum safety and health requirements for the workplace (first individual Directive within the meaning of Article 16(1) of Directive 89/391/EEC)

(89/654/EEC)

THE COUNCIL OF THE EUROPEAN COMMUNITIES,

Having regard to the Treaty establishing the European Economic Community, and in particular Article 118a thereof,

Having regard to the proposal from the Commission, submitted after consulting the Advisory Committee on Safety, Hygiene and Health Protection at Work,

In cooperation with the European Parliament,

Having regard to the opinion of the Economic and Social Committee,

Whereas Article 118a of the Treaty provides that the Council shall adopt, by means of Directives, minimum requirements for encouraging improvements, especially in the working environment, to ensure a better level of protection of the safety and health of workers;

Whereas, under the terms of that Article, those Directives are to avoid imposing administrative, financial and legal constraints in a way which would hold back the creation and development of small and medium-sized undertakings;

Whereas the communication from the Commission on its programme concerning safety, hygiene and health at work provides for the adoption of a Directive designed to guarantee the safety and health of workers at the workplace;

Whereas, in its resolution of 21 December 1987 on safety, hygiene and health at work, the Council took note of the Commission's intention of submitting to the Council in the near future minimum requirements concerning the arrangement of the place of work;

Whereas compliance with the minimum requirements designed to guarantee a better standard of safety and health at work is essential to ensure the safety and health of workers;

Whereas this Directive is an individual Directive within the meaning of Article 16(1) of Council Directive 89/391/EEC of 12 June 1989 on the introduction of measures to encourage improvements in the safety and health of workers at work; whereas the provisions of the latter are therefore fully applicable to the workplace without prejudice to more stringent and/or specific provisions contained in the present Directive;

Whereas this Directive is a practical contribution towards creating the social dimension of the internal market;

Whereas, pursuant to Decision 74/325/EEC, as last amended by the 1985 Act of Accession, the Advisory Committee on Safety, Hygiene and Health Protection at Work is consulted by the Commission on the drafting of proposals in this field,

HAS ADOPTED THIS DIRECTIVE:

SECTION I
GENERAL PROVISIONS

Article 1
Subject

1.   This Directive, which is the first individual Directive within the meaning of Article 16(1) of Directive 89/391/EEC, lays down minimum requirements for safety and health at the workplace, as defined in Article 2.

2.   This Directive shall not apply to:

(a)   means of transport used outside the undertaking and/or the establishment, or workplaces inside means of transport;
(b)   temporary or mobile work sites;
(c)   extractive industries;
(d)   fishing boats;
(e)   fields, woods and other land forming part of an agricultural or forestry undertaking but situated away from the undertaking's buildings.

3.   The provisions of Directive 89/391/EEC are fully applicable to the whole scope referred to in paragraph 1, without prejudice to more stringent and/or specific provisions contained in this Directive.

Article 2
Definition

For the purposes of this Directive, "workplace" means the place intended to house workstations on the premises of the undertaking and/or establishment and any other place within the area of the undertaking and/or establishment to which the worker has access in the course of his employment.

SECTION II
EMPLOYERS' OBLIGATIONS

Article 3

Workplaces used for the first time

Workplaces used for the first time after 31 December 1992 must satisfy the minimum safety and health requirements laid down in Annex I.

Article 4

Workplaces already in use

Workplaces already in use before 1 January 1993 must satisfy the minimum safety and health requirements laid down in Annex II at the latest three years after that date.

However, as regards the Portuguese Republic, workplaces used before 1 January 1993 must satisfy, at the latest four years after that date, the minimum safety and health requirements appearing in Annex II.

Article 5

Modifications to workplaces

When workplaces undergo modifications, extensions and/or conversions after 31 December 1992, the employer shall take the measures necessary to ensure that those modifications, extensions and/or conversions are in compliance with the corresponding minimum requirements laid down in Annex I.

Article 6

General requirements

To safeguard the safety and health of workers, the employer shall see to it that:

— traffic routes to emergency exits and the exits themselves are kept clear at all times,
— technical maintenance of the workplace and of the equipment and devices, and in particular those referred to in Annexes I and II, is carried out and any faults found which are liable to affect the safety and health of workers are rectified as quickly as possible,
— the workplace and the equipment and devices, and in particular those referred to in Annex I, point 6, and Annex II, point 6, are regularly cleaned to an adequate level of hygiene,
— safety equipment and devices intended to prevent or eliminate hazards, and in particular those referred to in Annexes I and II, are regularly maintained and checked.

Article 7

Information of workers

Without prejudice to Article 10 of Directive 89/391/EEC, workers and/or their representatives shall be informed of all measures to be taken concerning safety and health at the workplace.

Article 8

Consultation of workers and workers' participation

Consultation and participation of workers and/or of their representatives shall take place in accordance with Article 11 of Directive 89/391/EEC on the matters covered by this Directive, including the Annexes thereto.

SECTION III

MISCELLANEOUS PROVISIONS

Article 9

Amendments to the Annexes

Strictly technical amendments to the Annexes as a result of:

— the adoption of Directives on technical harmonisation and standardisation of the design, manufacture or construction of parts of workplaces, and/or
— technical progress, changes in international regulations or specifications and knowledge with regard to workplaces,

shall be adopted in accordance with the procedure laid down in Article 17 of Directive 89/391/EEC.

Article 10

Final provisions

1.   Member States shall bring into force the laws, regulations and administrative provisions necessary to comply with this Directive by 31 December 1992. They shall forthwith inform the Commission thereof.

However, the date applicable for the Hellenic Republic shall be 31 December 1994.

2.   Member States shall communicate to the Commission the texts of the provisions of national law which they have already adopted or adopt in the field governed by this Directive.

3.   Member States shall report to the Commission every five years on the practical implementation of the provisions of this Directive, indicating the points of view of employers and workers.

The Commission shall inform the European Parliament, the Council, the Economic and Social Committee and the Advisory Council on Safety, Hygiene and Health Protection at Work.

4.   The Commission shall submit periodically to the European Parliament, the Council and the Economic and Social Committee a report on the implementation of this Directive, taking into account paragraphs 1 to 3.

Article 11

This Directive is addressed to the Member States.

Done at Brussels, 30 November 1989.

For the Council
The President
J. P. SOISSON

ANNEX I

MINIMUM SAFETY AND HEALTH REQUIREMENTS FOR WORKPLACES USED FOR THE FIRST TIME, AS REFERRED TO IN ARTICLE 3 OF THE DIRECTIVE

1.   **Preliminary note**

The obligations laid down in this Annex apply whenever required by the features of the workplace, the activity, the circumstances or a hazard.

2.   **Stability and solidity**

Buildings which house workplaces must have a structure and solidity appropriate to the nature of their use.

3.   **Electrical installations**

Electrical installations must be designed and constructed so as not to present a fire or explosion hazard; persons must be adequately protected against the risk of accidents caused by direct or indirect contact.

The design, construction and choice of material and protection devices must be appropriate to the voltage, external conditions and the competence of persons with access to parts of the installation.

4.   **Emergency routes and exits**

4.1.   Emergency routes and exits must remain clear and lead as directly as possible to the open air or to a safe area.

4.2.   In the event of danger, it must be possible for workers to evacuate all workstations quickly and as safely as possible.

4.3.   The number, distribution and dimensions of the emergency routes and exits depend on the use, equipment and dimensions of the workplaces and the maximum number of persons that may be present.

4.4.   Emergency doors must open outwards.

Sliding or revolving doors are not permitted if they are specifically intended as emergency exits.

Emergency doors should not be so locked or fastened that they cannot be easily and immediately opened by any person who may require to use them in an emergency.

4.5.   Specific emergency routes and exits must be indicated by signs in accordance with the national regulations transposing Directive 77/576/EEC into law.

Such signs must be placed at appropriate points and be made to last.

4.6.   Emergency doors must not be locked.

The emergency routes and exits, and the traffic routes and doors giving access to them, must be free from obstruction so that they can be used at any time without hindrance.

4.7.   Emergency routes and exits requiring illumination must be provided with emergency lighting of adequate intensity in case the lighting fails.

5.   **Fire detection and fire fighting**

5.1.   Depending on the dimensions and use of the buildings, the equipment they contain, the physical and chemical properties of the substances present and the maximum potential number of people present, workplaces must be equipped with appropriate fire-fighting equipment and, as necessary, with fire detectors and alarm systems.

5.2.   Non-automatic fire-fighting equipment must be easily accessible and simple to use.

The equipment must be indicated by signs in accordance with the national regulations transposing Directive 77/576/EEC into law.

Such signs must be placed at appropriate points and be made to last.

6.   **Ventilation of enclosed workplaces**

6.1.   Steps shall be taken to see to it that there is sufficient fresh air in enclosed workplaces, having regard to the working methods used and the physical demands placed on the workers.

If a forced ventilation system is used, it shall be maintained in working order.

Any breakdown must be indicated by a control system where this is necessary for workers' health.

6.2. If air-conditioning or mechanical ventilation installations are used, they must operate in such a way that workers are not exposed to draughts which cause discomfort.

Any deposit or dirt likely to create an immediate danger to the health of workers by polluting the atmosphere must be removed without delay.

7. Room temperature

7.1. During working hours, the temperature in rooms containing workstations must be adequate for human beings, having regard to the working methods being used and the physical demands placed on the workers.

7.2. The temperature in rest areas, rooms for duty staff, sanitary facilities, canteens and first aid rooms must be appropriate to the particular purpose of such areas.

7.3. Windows, skylights and glass partitions should allow excessive effects of sunlight in workplaces to be avoided, having regard to the nature of the work and of the workplace.

8. Natural and artificial room lighting

8.1. Workplaces must as far as possible receive sufficient natural light and be equipped with artificial lighting adequate for the protection of workers' safety and health.

8.2. Lighting installations in rooms containing workstations and in passageways must be placed in such a way that there is no risk of accident to workers as a result of the type of lighting fitted.

8.3. Workplaces in which workers are especially exposed to risks in the event of failure of artificial lighting must be provided with emergency lighting of adequate intensity.

9. Floors, walls, ceilings and roofs of rooms

9.1. The floors of rooms must have no dangerous bumps, holes or slopes and must be fixed, stable and not slippery.

Workplaces containing workstations must be adequately thermally insulated, bearing in mind the type of undertaking involved and the physical activity of the workers.

9.2.　　The surfaces of floors, walls and ceilings in rooms must be such that they can be cleaned or refurbished to an appropriate standard of hygiene.

9.3.　　Transparent or translucent walls, in particular all-glass partitions, in rooms or in the vicinity of workstations and traffic routes must be clearly indicated and made of safety material or be shielded from such places or traffic routes to prevent workers from coming into contact with walls or being injured should the walls shatter.

9.4.　　Access to roofs made of materials of insufficient strength must not be permitted unless equipment is provided to ensure that the work can be carried out in a safe manner.

10.　　Windows and skylights

10.1.　　It must be possible for workers to open, close, adjust or secure windows, skylights and ventilators in a safe manner. When open, they must not be positioned so as to constitute a hazard to workers.

10.2.　　Windows and skylights must be designed in conjunction with equipment or otherwise fitted with devices allowing them to be cleaned without risk to the workers carrying out this work or to workers present in and around the building.

11.　　Doors and gates

11.1.　　The position, number and dimensions of doors and gates, and the materials used in their construction, are determined by the nature and use of the rooms or areas.

11.2.　　Transparent doors must be appropriately marked at a conspicuous level.

11.3.　　Swing doors and gates must be transparent or have see-through panels.

11.4.　　If transparent or translucent surfaces in doors and gates are not made of safety material and if there is a danger that workers may be injured if a door or gate should shatter, the surfaces must be protected against breakage.

11.5.　　Sliding doors must be fitted with a safety device to prevent them from being derailed and falling over.

11.6.　　Doors and gates opening upwards must be fitted with a mechanism to secure them against falling back.

11.7.   Doors along escape routes must be appropriately marked.

It must be possible to open them from the inside at any time without special assistance.

It must be possible to open the doors when the workplaces are occupied.

11.8.   Doors for pedestrians must be provided in the immediate vicinity of any gates intended essentially for vehicle traffic, unless it is safe for pedestrians to pass through; such doors must be clearly marked and left permanently unobstructed.

11.9.   Mechanical doors and gates must function in such a way that there is no risk of accident to workers.

They must be fitted with easily identifiable and accessible emergency shut-down devices and, unless they open automatically in the event of a power failure, it must also be possible to open them manually.

12.   **Traffic routes—danger areas**

12.1.   Traffic routes, including stairs, fixed ladders and loading bays and ramps, must be located and dimensioned to ensure easy, safe and appropriate access for pedestrians or vehicles in such a way as not to endanger workers employed in the vicinity of these traffic routes.

12.2.   Routes used for pedestrian traffic and/or goods traffic must be dimensioned in accordance with the number of potential users and the type of undertaking.

If means of transport are used on traffic routes, a sufficient safety clearance must be provided for pedestrians.

12.3.   Sufficient clearance must be allowed between vehicle traffic routes and doors, gates, passages for pedestrians, corridors and staircases.

12.4.   Where the use and equipment of rooms so requires for the protection of workers, traffic routes must be clearly identified.

12.5.   If the workplaces contain danger areas in which, owing to the nature of the work, there is a risk of the worker or objects falling, the places must be equipped, as far as possible, with devices preventing unauthorised workers from entering those areas.

Appropriate measures must be taken to protect workers authorised to enter danger areas.

Danger areas must be clearly indicated.

13.   **Specific measures for escalators and travelators**

Escalators and travelators must function safely.

They must be equipped with any necessary safety devices.

They must be fitted with easily identifiable and accessible emergency shut-down devices.

14.   **Loading bays and ramps**

14.1.   Loading bays and ramps must be suitable for the dimensions of the loads to be transported.

14.2.   Loading bays must have at least one exit point.

Where technically feasible, bays over a certain length must have an exit point at each end.

14.3.   Loading ramps must as far as possible be safe enought to prevent workers from falling off.

15.   **Room dimensions and air space in rooms—freedom of movement at the workstation**

15.1.   Workrooms must have sufficient surface area, height and air space to allow workers to perform their work without risk to their safety, health or well-being.

15.2.   The dimensions of the free unoccupied area at the workstation must be calculated to allow workers sufficient freedom of movement to perform their work.

If this is not possible for reasons specific to the workstation, the worker must be provided with sufficient freedom of movement near his workstation.

16.   **Rest rooms**

16.1.   Where the safety or health of workers, in particular because of the type of activity carried out or the presence of more than a certain number of employees, so require, workers must be provided with an easily accessible rest room.

This provision does not apply if the workers are employed in offices or similar workrooms providing equivalent relaxation during breaks.

16.2.   Rest rooms must be large enough and equipped with an adequate number of tables and seats with backs for the number of workers.

16.3.   In rest rooms appropriate measures must be introduced for the protection of non-smokers against discomfort caused by tobacco smoke.

16.4.   If working hours are regularly and frequently interrupted and there is no rest room, other rooms must be provided in which workers can stay during such interruptions, wherever this is required for the safety or health of workers.

    Appropriate measures should be taken for the protection of non-smokers against discomfort caused by tobacco smoke.

17.   **Pregnant women and nursing mothers**

    Pregnant women and nursing mothers must be able to lie down to rest in appropriate conditions.

18.   **Sanitary equipment**

18.1.   *Changing rooms and lockers*

18.1.1.   Appropriate changing rooms must be provided for workers if they have to wear special work clothes and where, for reasons of health or propriety, they cannot be expected to change in another room.

    Changing rooms must be easily accessible, be of sufficient capacity and be provided with seating.

18.1.2.   Changing rooms must be sufficiently large and have facilities to enable each worker to lock away his clothes during working hours.

    If circumstances so require (e.g. dangerous substances, humidity, dirt), lockers for work clothes must be separate from those for ordinary clothes.

18.1.3.   Provision must be made for separate changing rooms or separate use of changing rooms for men and women.

18.1.4.   If changing rooms are not required under 18.1.1, each worker must be provided with a place to store his clothes.

18.2.   *Showers and washbasins*

18.2.1.   Adequate and suitable showers must be provided for workers if required by the nature of the work or for health reasons.

    Provision must be made for separate shower rooms or separate use of shower rooms for men and women.

18.2.2.   The shower rooms must be sufficiently large to permit each worker to wash without hindrance in conditions of an appropriate standard of hygiene.

    The showers must be equipped with hot and cold running water.

18.2.3.   Where showers are not required under the first subparagraph of 18.2.1, adequate and suitable washbasins with running water (hot water if necessary) must be provided in the vicinity of the workstations and the changing rooms.

Such washbasins must be separate for, or used separately by, men and women when so required for reasons of propriety.

18.2.4.   Where the rooms housing the showers or washbasins are separate from the changing rooms, there must be easy communication between the two.

18.3.   *Lavatories and washbasins*

Separate facilities must be provided in the vicinity of workstations, rest rooms, changing rooms and rooms housing showers or washbasins, with an adequate number of lavatories and washbasins.

Provision must be made for separate lavatories or separate use of lavatories for men and women.

19.   First aid rooms

19.1.   One or more first aid rooms must be provided where the size of the premises, type of activity being carried out and frequency of accidents so dictate.

19.2.   First aid rooms must be fitted with essential first aid installations and equipment and be easily accessible to stretchers.

They must be signposted in accordance with the national regulations transposing Directive 77/576/EEC into law.

19.3.   In addition, first aid equipment must be available in all places where working conditions require it.

This equipment must be suitably marked and easily accessible.

20.   Handicapped workers

Workplaces must be organised to take account of handicapped workers, if necessary.

This provision applies in particular to the doors, passageways, staircases, showers, washbasins, lavatories and workstations used or occupied directly by handicapped persons.

21.   Outdoor workplaces (special provisions)

21.1.   Workstations, traffic routes and other areas or installations outdoors which are used or occupied by the workers in the course of their activity must be organised in such a way that pedestrians and vehicles can circulate safely.

Sections 12, 13 and 14 also apply to main traffic routes on the site of the undertaking (traffic routes leading to fixed workstations), to traffic routes used for the regular maintenance and supervision of the undertaking's installations and to loading bays.

Section 12 is also applicable to outdoor workplaces.

21.2.   Workplaces outdoors must be adequately lit by artificial lighting if daylight is not adequate.

21.3.   When workers are employed at workstations outdoors, such workstations must as far as possible be arranged so that workers:

(a) are protected against inclement weather conditions and if necessary against falling objects;

(b) are not exposed to harmful noise levels nor to harmful outdoor influences such as gases, vapours or dust;

(c) are able to leave their workstations swiftly in the event of danger or are able to be rapidly assisted;

(d) cannot slip or fall.

ANNEX II

MINIMUM HEALTH AND SAFETY REQUIREMENTS FOR WORKPLACES ALREADY IN USE, AS REFERRED TO IN ARTICLE 4 OF THE DIRECTIVE

1.   **Preliminary note**

The obligations laid down in this Annex apply wherever required by the features of the workplace, the activity, the circumstances or a hazard.

2.   **Stability and solidity**

Buildings which have workplaces must have a structure and solidity appropriate to the nature of their use.

3.   **Electrical installations**

Electrical installations must be designed and constructed so as not to present a fire or explosion hazard; persons must be adequately protected against the risk of accidents caused by direct or indirect contact.

Electrical installations and protection devices must be appropriate to the voltage, external conditions and the competence of persons with access to parts of the installation.

4.   **Emergency routes and exits**

4.1.   Emergency routes and exits must remain clear and lead as directly as possible to the open air or to a safe area.

4.2.   In the event of danger, it must be possible for workers to evacuate all workstations quickly and as safely as possible.

4.3.   There must be an adequate number of escape routes and emergency exits.

4.4.   Emergency exit doors must open outwards.

Sliding or revolving doors are not permitted if they are specifically intended as emergency exits.

Emergency doors should not be so locked or fastened that they cannot be easily and immediately opened by any person who may require to use them in an emergency.

4.5.   Specific emergency routes and exits must be indicated by signs in accordance with the national regulations transposing Directive 77/576/EEC into law.

Such signs must be placed at appropriate points and be made to last.

4.6.   Emergency doors must not be locked.

The emergency routes and exits, and the traffic routes and doors giving access to them, must be free from obstruction so that they can be used at any time without hindrance.

4.7.   Emergency routes and exits requiring illumination must be provided with emergency lighting of adequate intensity in case the lighting fails.

5.   Fire detection and fire fighting

5.1.   Depending on the dimensions and use of the buildings, the equipment they contain, the physical and chemical characteristics of the substances present and the maximum potential number of people present, workplaces must be equipped with appropriate fire-fighting equipment, and, as necessary, fire detectors and an alarm system.

5.2.   Non-automatic fire-fighting equipment must be easily accessible and simple to use.

It must be indicated by signs in accordance with the national regulations transposing Directive 77/576/EEC into law.

Such signs must be placed at appropriate points and be made to last.

6.   Ventilation of enclosed workplaces

Steps shall be taken to see to it that there is sufficient fresh air in enclosed workplaces, having regard to the working methods used and the physical demands placed on the workers.

If a forced ventilation system is used, it shall be maintained in working order.

Any breakdown must be indicated by a control system where this is necessary for the workers' health.

7. Room temperature

7.1. During working hours, the temperature in rooms containing workplaces must be adequate for human beings, having regard to the working methods being used and the physical demands placed on the workers.

7.2. The temperature in rest areas, rooms for duty staff, sanitary facilities, canteens and first aid rooms must be appropriate to the particular purpose of such areas.

8. Natural and artificial room lighting

8.1. Workplaces must as far as possible receive sufficient natural light and be equipped with artificial lighting adequate for workers' safety and health.

8.2. Workplaces in which workers are especially exposed to risks in the event of failure of artificial lighting must be provided with emergency lighting of adequate intensity.

9. Doors and gates

9.1. Transparent doors must be appropriately marked at a conspicuous level.

9.2. Swing doors and gates must be transparent or have see-through panels.

10. Danger areas

If the workplaces contain danger areas in which, owing to the nature of the work, there is a risk of the worker or objects falling, the places must be equipped, as far as possible, with devices preventing unauthorised workers from entering those areas.

Appropriate measures must be taken to protect workers authorised to enter danger areas.

Danger areas must be clearly indicated.

11. Rest rooms and rest areas

11.1. Where the safety or health of workers, in particular because of the type of activity carried out or the presence of more than a certain number of employees, so require, workers must be provided with an easily accessible rest room or appropriate rest area.

This provision does not apply if the workers are employed in offices or similar workrooms providing equivalent relaxation during breaks.

11.2.   Rest rooms and rest areas must be equipped with tables and seats with backs.

11.3.   In rest rooms and rest areas appropriate measures must be introduced for the protection of non-smokers against discomfort caused by tobacco smoke.

12.   Pregnant women and nursing mothers

Pregnant women and nursing mothers must be able to lie down to rest in appropriate conditions.

13.   Sanitary equipment

13.1.   *Changing rooms and lockers*

13.1.1.   Appropriate changing rooms must be provided for workers if they have to wear special work clothes and where, for reasons of health or propriety, they cannot be expected to change in another room.

Changing rooms must be easily accessible and of sufficient capacity.

13.1.2.   Changing rooms must have facilities to enable each worker to lock away his clothes during working hours.

If circumstances so require (e.g. dangerous substances, humidity, dirt), lockers for work clothes must be separate from those for ordinary clothes.

13.1.3.   Provision must be made for separate changing rooms or separate use of changing rooms for men and women.

13.2.   *Showers, lavatories and washbasins*

13.2.1.   Workplaces must be fitted out in such a way that workers have in the vicinity:

— showers, if required by the nature of their work,
— special facilities equipped with an adequate number of lavatories and washbasins.

13.2.2.   The showers and washbasins must be equipped with running water (hot water if necessary).

13.2.3.   Provision must be made for separate showers or separate use of showers for men and women.

Provision must be made for separate lavatories or separate use of lavatories for men and women.

14. **First aid equipment**

Workplaces must be fitted with first aid equipment.

The equipment must be suitably marked and easily accessible.

15. **Handicapped workers**

Workplaces must be organised to take account of handicapped workers, if necessary.

This provision applies in particular to the doors, passageways, staircases, showers, washbasins, lavatories and workstations used or occupied directly by handicapped persons.

16. **Movement of pedestrians and vehicles**

Outdoor and indoor workplaces must be organised in such a way that pedestrians and vehicles can circulate in a safe manner.

17. **Outdoor workplaces (special provisions)**

When workers are employed at workstations outdoors, such workstations must as far as possible be organised so that workers:

(a) are protected against inclement weather conditions and if necessary against falling objects;
(b) are not exposed to harmful noise levels nor to harmful external influences such as gases, vapours or dust;
(c) are able to leave their workstations swiftly in the event of danger or are able to be rapidly assisted;
(d) cannot slip or fall.

THE WORK EQUIPMENT DIRECTIVE

General note. This was the second daughter Directive and was implemented in the UK by the Provision and Use of Work Equipment Regulations 1992 (S.I. 1992 No. 2932), see page 707.

COUNCIL DIRECTIVE

of 30 November 1989

concerning the minimum safety and health requirements for the use of work equipment by workers at work (second individual Directive within the meaning of Article 16(1) of Directive 89/391/EEC)

(89/655/EEC)

THE COUNCIL OF THE EUROPEAN COMMUNITIES,

Having regard to the Treaty establishing the European Economic Community, and in particular Article 118a thereof,

Having regard to the proposal from the Commission, submitted after consulting the Advisory Committee on Safety, Hygiene and Health Protection at Work,

In cooperation with the European Parliament,

Having regard to the opinion of the Economic and Social Committee,

Whereas Article 118a of the Treaty provides that the Council shall adopt, by means of Directives, minimum requirements for encouraging improvements, especially in the working environment, to guarantee a better level of protection of the safety and health of workers;

Whereas, pursuant to the said Article, such Directives must avoid imposing administrative, financial and legal constraints in a way which would hold back the creation and development of small and medium-sized undertakings;

Whereas the communication from the Commission on its programme concerning safety, hygiene and health at work provides for the adoption of a Directive on the use of work equipment at work;

Whereas, in its resolution of 21 December 1987 on safety, hygiene and health at work, the Council took note of the Commission's intention of submitting to the Council in the near future minimum requirements concerning the organisation of safety and health at work;

Whereas compliance with the minimum requirements designed to guarantee a better standard of safety and health in the use of work equipment is essential to ensure the safety and health of workers;

Whereas this Directive is an individual Directive within the meaning of Article 16(1) of Council Directive 89/391/EEC of 12 June 1989 on the introduction of measures to encourage improvements in the safety and health of workers at work; whereas, therefore, the provisions of the said Directive are fully applicable to the scope of the use of work equipment by workers at work without prejudice to more restrictive and/or specific provisions contained in this Directive;

Whereas this Directive constitutes a practical aspect of the realisation of the social dimension of the internal market;

Whereas, pursuant to Decision 83/189/EEC, Member States are required to notify the Commission of any draft technical regulations relating to machines, equipment and installations;

Whereas, pursuant to Decision 74/325/EEC, as last amended by the 1985 Act of Accession, the Advisory Committee on Safety, Hygiene and Health Protection at Work is consulted by the Commission on the drafting of proposals in this field,

HAS ADOPTED THIS DIRECTIVE:

SECTION I
GENERAL PROVISIONS

Article 1
Subject

1.   This Directive, which is the second individual Directive within the meaning of Article 16(1) of Directive 89/391/EEC, lays down minimum safety and health requirements for the use of work equipment by workers at work, as defined in Article 2.

2.   The provisions of Directive 89/391/EEC are fully applicable to the whole scope referred to in paragraph 1, without prejudice to more restrictive and/or specific provisions contained in this Directive.

Article 2
Definitions

For the purposes of this Directive, the following terms shall have the following meanings:

(a)   "work equipment": any machine, apparatus, tool or installation used at work;

(b)   "use of work equipment": any activity involving work equipment such as starting or stopping the equipment, its use, transport, repair, modification, maintenance and servicing, including, in particular, cleaning;

(c)   "danger zone": any zone within and/or around work equipment in which an exposed worker is subject to a risk to his health or safety;

(d) "exposed worker": any worker wholly or partially in a danger zone;
(e) "operator": the worker or workers given the task of using work equipment.

SECTION II
EMPLOYERS' OBLIGATIONS

Article 3

General obligations

1. The employer shall take the measures necessary to ensure that the work equipment made available to workers in the undertaking and/or establishment is suitable for the work to be carried out or properly adapted for that purpose and may be used by workers without impairment to their safety or health.

In selecting the work equipment which he proposes to use, the employer shall pay attention to the specific working conditions and characteristics and to the hazards which exist in the undertaking and/or establishment, in particular at the workplace, for the safety and health of the workers, and/or any *additional hazards posed by the use of work equipment in question.*

2. Where it is not possible fully so to ensure that work equipment can be used by workers without risk to their safety or health, the employer shall take appropriate measures to minimise the risks.

Article 4

Rules concerning work equipment

1. Without prejudice to Article 3, the employer must obtain and/or use:
(a) work equipment which, if provided to workers in the undertaking and/or establishment for the first time after 31 December 1992, complies with:
  (i) the provisions of any relevant Community Directive which is applicable;
  (ii) the minimum requirements laid down in the Annex, to the extent that no other Community Directive is applicable or is so only partially;
(b) work equipment which, if already provided to workers in the undertaking and/or establishment by 31 December 1992, complies with the minimum requirements laid down in the Annex no later than four years after that date.

2. The employer shall take the measures necessary to ensure that, throughout its working life, work equipment is kept, by means of adequate maintenance, at a level such that it complies with the provisions of paragraph (1)(a) or (b) as applicable.

Article 5

Work equipment involving specific risks

When the use of work equipment is likely to involve a specific risk to the safety or health of workers, the employer shall take the measures necessary to ensure that:

— the use of work equipment is restricted to those persons given the task of using it;
— in the case of repairs, modifications, maintenance or servicing, the workers concerned are specifically designated to carry out such work.

Article 6

Informing workers

1.   Without prejudice to Article 10 of Directive 89/391/EEC, the employer shall take the measures necessary to ensure that workers have at their disposal adequate information and, where appropriate, written instructions on the work equipment used at work.

2.   The information and the written instructions must contain at least adequate safety and health information concerning:

— the conditions of use of work equipment,
— foreseeable abnormal situations,
— the conclusions to be drawn from experience, where appropriate, in using work equipment.

3.   The information and the written instructions must be comprehensible to the workers concerned.

Article 7

Training of workers

Without prejudice to Article 12 of Directive 89/391/EEC, the employer shall take the measures necessary to ensure that:

— workers given the task of using work equipment receive adequate training, including training on any risks which such use may entail,
— workers referred to in the second indent of Article 5 receive adequate specific training.

Article 8

Consultation of workers and workers' participation

Consultation and participation of workers and/or of their representatives shall take place in accordance with Article 11 of Directive 89/391/EEC on the matters covered by this Directive, including the Annexes thereto.

SECTION III

MISCELLANEOUS PROVISIONS

Article 9

Amendment to the Annex

1.   Addition to the Annex of the supplementary minimum requirements applicable to specific work equipment referred to in point 3 thereof shall be

adopted by the Council in accordance with the procedure laid down in Article 118a of the Treaty.

2. Strictly technical adaptations of the Annex as a result of:

— the adoption of Directives on technical harmonisation and standardisation of work equipment, and/or
— technical progress, changes in international regulations or specifications or knowledge in the field of work equipment,

shall be adopted in accordance with the procedure laid down in Article 17 of Directive 89/391/EEC.

Article 10
Final provisions

1. Member States shall bring into force the laws, regulations and administrative provisions necessary to comply with this Directive by 31 December 1992. They shall forthwith inform the Commission thereof.

2. Member States shall communicate to the Commission the texts of the provisions of national law which they have already adopted or adopt in the field governed by this Directive.

3. Member States shall report to the Commission every five years on the practical implementation of the provisions of this Directive, indicating the points of view of employers and workers.

The Commission shall accordingly inform the European Parliament, the Council, the Economic and Social Committee, and the Advisory Council on Safety, Hygiene and Health Protection at Work.

4. The Commission shall submit periodically to the European Parliament, the Council and the Economic and Social Committee a report on the implementation of this Directive, taking into account paragraphs 1 to 3.

Article 11

This Directive is addressed to the Member States.

Done at Brussels, 30 November 1989.

For the Council
The President
J. P. SOISSON

ANNEX

MINIMUM REQUIREMENTS REFERRED TO IN
ARTICLE 4(1)(a)(ii) AND (b)

1. **General comment**

The obligations laid down in this Annex apply having regard to the provisions of the Directive and where the corresponding risk exists for the work equipment in question.

2. **General minimum requirements applicable to work equipment**

2.1. Work equipment control devices which affect safety must be clearly visible and identifiable and appropriately marked where necessary.

Except where necessary for certain devices, control devices must be located outside danger zones and in such a way that their operation cannot cause additional hazard. They must not give rise to any hazard as a result of any unintentional operation.

If necessary, from the main control position, the operator must be able to ensure that no person is present in the danger zones. If this is impossible, a safe system such as an audible and/or visible warning signal must be given automatically whenever the machinery is about to start. An exposed worker must have the time and/or the means quickly to avoid hazards caused by the starting and/or stopping of the work equipment.

Control systems must be safe. A breakdown in, or damage to, control systems must not result in a dangerous situation.

2.2. It must be possible to start work equipment only by deliberate action on a control provided for the purpose.

The same shall apply:

— to restart it after a stoppage for whatever reason,
— for the control of a significant change in the operating conditions (e.g. speed, pressure, etc.),

unless such a restart or change does not subject exposed workers to any hazard.

This requirement does not apply to restarting or a change in operating conditions as a result of the normal operating cycle of an automatic device.

2.3. All work equipment must be fitted with a control to stop it completely and safely.

Each work station must be fitted with a control to stop some or all of the work equipment, depending on the type of hazard, so that the equipment is in a safe state. The equipment's stop control must have priority over the start controls. When the work equipment or the dangerous parts of it have stopped, the energy supply of the actuators concerned must be switched off.

2.4. Where appropriate, and depending on the hazards the equipment presents and its normal stopping time, work equipment must be fitted with an emergency stop device.

2.5.   Work equipment presenting risk due to falling obects or projections must be fitted with appropriate safety devices corresponding to the risk.

Work equipment presenting hazards due to emissions of gas, vapour, liquid or dust must be fitted with appropriate containment and/or extraction devices near the sources of the hazard.

2.6.   Work equipment and parts of such equipment must, where necessary for the safety and health of workers, be stabilised by clamping or some other means.

2.7.   Where there is a risk of rupture or disintegration of parts of the work equipment, likely to pose significant danger to the safety and health of workers, appropriate protection measures must be taken.

2.8.   Where there is a risk of mechanical contact with moving parts of work equipment which could lead to accidents, those parts must be provided with guards or devices to prevent access to danger zones or to halt movements of dangerous parts before the danger zones are reached.

The guards and protection devices must:
— be of robust construction,
— not give rise to any additional hazard,
— not be easily removed or rendered inoperative,
— be situated at a sufficient distance from the danger zone,
— not restrict more than necessary the view of the operating cycle of the equipment,
— allow operations necessary to fit or replace parts and for maintenance work, restricting access only to the area where the work is to be carried out and, if possible, without removal of the guard or protection device.

2.9.   Areas and points for working on, or maintenance of, work equipment must be suitably lit in line with the operation to be carried out.

2.10.   Work equipment parts at high or very low temperature must, where appropriate, be protected to avoid the risk of workers coming into contact or coming too close.

2.11.   Warning devices on work equipment must be unambiguous and easily perceived and understood.

2.12.   Work equipment may be used only for operations and under conditions for which it is appropriate.

2.13.   It must be possible to carry out maintenance operations when the equipment is shut down. If this is not possible, it must be possible to take appropriate protection measures for the carrying out of such operations or for such operations to be carried out outside the danger zones.

If any machine has a maintenance log, it must be kept up to date.

2.14.   All work equipment must be fitted with clearly identifiable means to isolate it from all energy sources.

Reconnection must be presumed to pose no risk to the workers concerned.

2.15.   Work equipment must bear the warnings and markings essential to ensure the safety of workers.

2.16.   Workers must have safe means of access to, and be able to remain safely in, all the areas necessary for production, adjustment and maintenance operations.

2.17.   All work equipment must be appropriate for protecting workers against the risk of the work equipment catching fire or overheating, or of discharges of gas, dust, liquid, vapour or other substances produced, used or stored in the work equipment.

2.18.   All work equipment must be appropriate for preventing the risk of explosion of the work equipment of substances produced, used or stored in the work equipment.

2.19.   All work equipment must be appropriate for protecting exposed workers against the risk of direct or indirect contact with electricity.

3.   **Minimum additional requirements applicable to specific work equipment,**

As referred to in Article 9(1) of the Directive.

THE PERSONAL PROTECTIVE EQUIPMENT DIRECTIVE

General note. This was the third daughter Directive and was implemented in the UK by the Personal Protective Equipment at Work Regulations 1992 (S.I. 1992 No. 2966), see page 722.

COUNCIL DIRECTIVE
of 30 November 1989

on the minimum health and safety requirements for the use by workers of personal protective equipment at the workplace (third individual directive within the meaning of Article 16(1) of Directive 89/391/EEC)

(89/656/EEC)

THE COUNCIL OF THE EUROPEAN COMMUNITIES,

Having regard to the Treaty establishing the European Economic Community, and in particular Article 118a thereof,

Having regard to the Commission proposal, submitted after consultation with the Advisory Committee on Safety, Hygiene and Health Protection at Work,

In cooperation with the European Parliament,

Having regard to the opinion of the Economic and Social Committee,

Whereas Article 118a of the Treaty provides that the Council shall adopt, by means of Directives, minimum requirements designed to encourage improvements, especially in the working environment, to guarantee greater protection of the health and safety of workers;

Whereas, under the said Article, such Directives shall avoid imposing administrative, financial and legal constraints in a way which would hold back the creation and development of small and medium-sized undertakings;

Whereas the Commission communication on its programme concerning safety, hygiene and health at work provides for the adoption of a Directive on the use of personal protective equipment at work;

Whereas the Council, in its resolution of 21 December 1987 concerning safety, hygiene and health at work, noted the Commission's intention of submitting to it in the near future minimum requirements concerning the organisation of the safety and health of workers at work;

Whereas compliance with the minimum requirements designed to guarantee greater health and safety for the user of personal protective equipment is essential to ensure the safety and health of workers;

Whereas this Directive is an individual Directive within the meaning of Article 16(1) of Council Directive 89/391/EEC of 12 June 1989 on the introduction of measures to encourage improvements in the safety and health of workers at work; whereas, consequently, the provisions of the said Directive apply fully to the use by workers of personal protective equipment at the workplace, without prejudice to more stringent and/or specific provisions contained in this Directive;

Whereas this Directive constitutes a practical step towards the achievement of the social dimension of the internal market;

Whereas collective means of protection shall be accorded priority over individual protective equipment; whereas the employer shall be required to provide safety equipment and take safety measures;

Whereas the requirements laid down in this Directive should not entail alterations to personal protective equipment whose design and manufacture complied with Community Directives relating to safety and health at work;

Whereas provision should be made for descriptions which Member States may use when laying down general rules for the use of individual protective equipment;

Whereas, pursuant to Decision 74/325/EEC, as last amended by the 1985 Act of Accession, the Advisory Committee on Safety, Hygiene and Health Protection at Work is consulted by the Commission with a view to drawing up proposals in this field,

HAS ADOPTED THIS DIRECTIVE:

SECTION I
GENERAL PROVISIONS

Article 1
Subject

1.   This Directive, which is the third individual Directive within the meaning of Article 16(1) of Directive 89/391/EEC, lays down minimum requirements for personal protective equipment used by workers at work.

2.   The provisions of Directive 89/391/EEC are fully applicable to the whole scope referred to in paragraph 1, without prejudice to more restrictive and/or specific provisions contained in this Directive.

Article 2
Definition

1.   For the purposes of this Directive, personal protective equipment shall mean all equipment designed to be worn or held by the worker to protect him

against one or more hazards likely to endanger his safety and health at work, and any addition or accessory designed to meet this objective.

2.   The definition in paragraph 1 excludes:

(a)   ordinary working clothes and uniforms not specifically designed to protect the safety and health of the worker;
(b)   equipment used by emergency and rescue services;
(c)   personal protective equipment worn or used by the military, the police and other public order agencies;
(d)   personal protective equipment for means of road transport;
(e)   sports equipment;
(f)   self-defence or deterrent equipment;
(g)   portable devices for detecting and signalling risks and nuisances.

Article 3
General rule

Personal protective equipment shall be used when the risks cannot be avoided or sufficiently limited by technical means of collective protection or by measures, methods or procedures of work organisation.

SECTION II
EMPLOYERS' OBLIGATIONS

Article 4
General provisions

1.   Personal protective equipment must comply with the relevant Community provisions on design and manufacture with respect to safety and health.

All personal protective equipment must:

(a)   be appropriate for the risks involved, without itself leading to any increased risk;
(b)   correspond to existing conditions at the workplace;
(c)   take account of ergonomic requirements and the worker's state of health;
(d)   fit the wearer correctly after any necessary adjustment.

2.   Where the presence of more than one risk makes it necessary for a worker to wear simultaneously more than one item of personal protective equipment, such equipment must be compatible and continue to be effective against the risk or risks in question.

3.   The conditions of use of personal protective equipment, in particular the period for which it is worn, shall be determined on the basis of the seriousness of the risk, the frequency of exposure to the risk, the characteristics of the workstation of each worker and the performance of the personal protective equipment.

4.   Personal protective equipment is, in principle, intended for personal use.

If the circumstances require personal protective equipment to be worn by more than one person, appropriate measures shall be taken to ensure that such use does not create any health or hygiene problem for the different users.

5. Adequate information on each item of personal protective equipment, required under paragraphs 1 and 2, shall be provided and made available within the undertaking and/or establishment.

6. Personal protective equipment shall be provided free of charge by the employer, who shall ensure its good working order and satisfactory hygienic condition by means of the necessary maintenance, repair and replacements.

However, Member States may provide, in accordance with their national practice, that the worker be asked to contribute towards the cost of certain personal protective equipment in circumstances where use of the equipment is not exclusive to the workplace.

7. The employer shall first inform the worker of the risks against which the wearing of the personal protective equipment protects him.

8. The employer shall arrange for training and shall, if appropriate, organise demonstrations in the wearing of personal protective equipment.

9. Personal protective equipment may be used only for the purposes specified, except in specific and exceptional circumstances.

It must be used in accordance with instructions.

Such instructions must be understandable to the workers.

Article 5

Assessment of personal protective equipment

1. Before choosing personal protective equipment, the employer is required to assess whether the personal protective equipment he intends to use satisfies the requirements of Article 4(1) and (2).

This assessment shall involve:

(a) an analysis and assessment of risks which cannot be avoided by other means;
(b) the definition of the characteristics which personal protective equipment must have in order to be effective against the risks referred to in (a), taking into account any risks which this equipment itself may create;
(c) comparison of the characteristics of the personal protective equipment available with the characteristics referred to in (b).

2. The assessment provided for in paragraph 1 shall be reviewed if any changes are made to any of its elements.

Article 6

Rules for use

1. Without prejudice to Articles 3, 4 and 5, Member States shall ensure that general rules are established for the use of personal protective equipment

and/or rules covering cases and situations where the employer must provide the personal protective equipment, taking account of Community legislation on the free movement of such equipment.

These rules shall indicate in particular the circumstances or the risk situations in which, without prejudice to the priority to be given to collective means of protection, the use of personal protective equipment is necessary.

Annexes I, II and III, which constitute a guide, contain useful information for establishing such rules.

2.   When Member States adapt the rules referred to in paragraph 1, they shall take account of any significant changes to the risk, collective means of protection and personal protective equipment brought about by technological developments.

3.   Member States shall consult the employers' and workers' organisation on the rules referred to in paragraphs 1 and 2.

Article 7

Information for workers

Without prejudice to Article 10 of Directive 89/391/EEC, workers and/or their representatives shall be informed of all measures to be taken with regard to the health and safety of workers when personal protective equipment is used by workers at work.

Article 8

Consultation of workers and workers' participation

Consultation and participation of workers and/or of their representatives shall take place in accordance with Article 11 of Directive 89/391/EEC on the matters covered by this Directive, including the Annexes thereto.

SECTION III

MISCELLANEOUS PROVISIONS

Article 9

Adjustment of the Annexes

Alterations of a strictly technical nature to Annexes I, II and III resulting from:

— the adoption of technical harmonisation and standardisation Directives relating to personal protective equipment, and/or
— technical progress and changes in international regulations and specifications or knowledge in the field of personal protective equipment,

shall be adopted in accordance with the procedure provided for in Article 17 of Directive 89/391/EEC.

Article 10

Final provisions

1.   Member States shall bring into force the laws, regulations and adminstrative provisions necessary to comply with this Directive not later than 31 December 1992. They shall immediately inform the Commission thereof.

2.   Member States shall communicate to the Commission the text of the provisions of national law which they adopt, as well as those already adopted, in the field covered by this Directive.

3.   Member States shall report to the Commission every five years on the practical implementation of the provisions of this Directive, indicating the points of view of employers and workers.

The Commission shall inform the European Parliament, the Council, the Economic and Social Committee, and the Advisory Committee on Safety, Hygiene and Health Protection at Work.

4.   The Commission shall report periodically to the European Parliament, the Council and the Economic and Social Committee on the implementation of the Directive in the light of paragraphs 1, 2 and 3.

Article 11

This Directive is addressed to the Member States.

Done at Brussels, 30 November 1989.

For the Council
The President
J. P. SOISSON

ANNEX I

SPECIMEN RISK SURVEY TABLE FOR THE USE OF PERSONAL PROTECTIVE EQUIPMENT

ANNEX II

NON-EXHAUSTIVE GUIDE LIST OF ITEMS OF PERSONAL PROTECTIVE EQUIPMENT

HEAD PROTECTION

— Protective helmets for use in industry (mines, building sites, other industrial uses).

— Scalp protection (caps, bonnets, hairnets—with or without eye shade).
— Protective headgear (bonnets, caps, sou'westers, etc. in fabric with proofing, etc.).

HEARING PROTECTION

— Earplugs and similar devices.
— Full acoustic helmets.
— Earmuffs which can be fitted to industrial helmets.
— Ear defenders with receiver for LF induction loop.
— Ear protection with intercom equipment.

EYE AND FACE PROTECTION

— Spectacles.
— Goggles.
— X-ray goggles, laser-beam goggles, ultra-violet, infra-red, visible radiation goggles.
— Face shields.
— Arc-welding masks and helmets (hand masks, headband masks or masks which can be fitted to protective helmets).

RESPIRATORY PROTECTION

— Dust filters, gas filters and radioactive dust filters.
— Insulating appliances with an air supply.
— Respiratory devices including a removable welding mask.
— Diving equipment.
— Diving suits.

HAND AND ARM PROTECTION

— Gloves to provide protection:
    — from machinery (piercing, cuts, vibrations, etc.),
    — from chemicals,
    — for electricians and from heat.
— Mittens.
— Finger stalls.
— Oversleeves.
— Wrist protection for heavy work.
— Fingerless gloves.
— Protective gloves.

FOOT AND LEG PROTECTION

— Low shoes, ankle boots, calf-length boots, safety boots.
— Shoes which can be unlaced or unhooked rapidly.

— Shoes with additional protective toe-cap.
— Shoes and overshoes with heat-resistant soles.
— Heat-resistant shoes, boots and overboots.
— Thermal shoes, boots and overboots.
— Vibration-resistant shoes, boots and overboots.
— Anti-static shoes, boots and overboots.
— Insulating shoes, boots and overboots.
— Protective boots for chain saw operators.
— Clogs.
— Kneepads.
— Removable instep protectors.
— Gaiters.
— Removable soles (heat-proof, pierce-proof or sweat-proof).
— Removable spikes for ice, snow or slippery flooring.

SKIN PROTECTION

— Barrier creams/ointments.

TRUNK AND ABDOMEN PROTECTION

— Protective waistcoats, jackets and aprons to provide protection from machinery (piercing, cutting, molten metal splashes, etc.).
— Protective waistcoats, jackets and aprons to provide protection from chemicals.
— Heated waistcoats.
— Life jackets.
— Protective X-ray aprons.
— Body belts.

WHOLE BODY PROTECTION

— **Equipment designed to prevent falls**

    — Fall-prevention equipment (full equipment with all necessary accessories).
    — Braking equipment to absorb kinetic energy (full equipment with all necessary acessories).
    — Body-holding devices (safety harness).

— **Protective clothing**

    — "Safety" working clothing (two-piece and overalls).
    — Clothing to provide protection from machinery (piercing, cutting, etc.).
    — Clothing to provide protection from chemicals.
    — Clothing to provide protection from molten splashes and infra-red radiation.
    — Heat-resistant clothing.
    — Thermal clothing.
    — Clothing to provide protection from radioactive contamination.
    — Dust-proof clothing.

— Gas-proof clothing.
— Fluorescent signalling, retro-reflecting clothing and accessories (arm-bands, gloves, etc.).
— Protective coverings.

ANNEX III

NON-EXHAUSTIVE GUIDE LIST OF ACTIVITIES AND SECTORS OF ACTIVITY WHICH MAY REQUIRE THE PROVISION OF PERSONAL PROTECTIVE EQUIPMENT

1. HEAD PROTECTION (SKULL PROTECTION)

Protective helmets

— Building work, particularly work on, underneath or in the vicinity of scaffolding and elevated workplaces, erection and stripping of form-work, assembly and installation work, work on scaffolding and demo-lition work.
— Work on steel bridges, steel building construction, masts, towers, steel hydraulic structures, blast furnaces, steel works and rolling mills, large containers, large pipelines, boiler plants and power stations.
— Work in pits, trenches, shafts and tunnels.
— Earth and rock works.
— Work in underground workings, quarries, open diggings, coal stock removal.
— Work with bolt-driving tools.
— Blasting work.
— Work in the vicinity of lifts, lifting gear, cranes and conveyors.
— Work with blast furnaces, direct reduction plants, steelworks, rolling mills, metalworks, forging, drop forging and casting.
— Work with industrial furnaces, containers, machinery, silos, bunkers and pipelines.
— Shipbuilding.
— Railway shunting work.
— Slaughterhouses.

2. FOOT PROTECTION

Safety shoes with puncture-proof soles

— Carcase work, foundation work and roadworks.
— Scaffolding work.
— The demolition of carcase work.
— Work with concrete and prefabricated parts involving formwork erection and stripping.
— Work in contractors' yards and warehouses.
— Roof work.

Safety shoes without pierce-proof soles

— Work on steel bridges, steel building construction, masts, towers, lifts, steel hydraulic structures, blast furnaces, steelworks and rolling mills,

large containers, large pipelines, cranes, boiler plants and power stations.
— Furnace construction, heating and ventilation installation and metal assembly work.
— Conversion and maintenance work.
— Work with blast furnaces, direct reduction plants, steelworks, rolling mills, metalworks, forging, drop forging, hot pressing and drawing plants.
— Work in quarries and open diggings, coal stock removal.
— Working and processing of rock.
— Flat glass products and container glassware manufacture, working and processing.
— Work with moulds in the ceramics industry.
— Lining of kilns in the ceramics industry.
— Moulding work in the ceramic ware and building materials industry.
— Transport and storage.
— Work with frozen meat blocks and preserved foods packaging.
— Shipbuilding.
— Railway shunting work.

Safety shoes with heels or wedges and pierce-proof soles

— Roof work.

Protective shoes with insulated soles

— Work with and on very hot or very cold materials.

Safety shoes which can easily be removed

— Where there is a risk of penetration by molten substances.

3. EYE OR FACE PROTECTION

Protective goggles, face shields or screens
— Welding, grinding and separating work.
— Caulking and chiselling.
— Rock working and processing.
— Work with bolt-driving tools.
— Work on stock removing machines for small chippings.
— Drop forging.
— The removal and breaking up of fragments.
— Spraying of abrasive substances.
— Work with acids and caustic solutions, disinfectants and corrosive cleaning products.
— Work with liquid sprays.
— Work with and in the vicinity of molten substances.
— Work with radiant heat.
— Work with lasers.

4. RESPIRATORY PROTECTION

    Respirators/breathing apparatus

    — Work in containers, restricted areas and gas-fired industrial furnaces where there may be gas or insufficient oxygen.
    — Work in the vicinity of the blast furnace charge.
    — Work in the vicinity of gas converters and blast furnace gas pipes.
    — Work in the vicinity of blast furnace taps where there may be heavy metal fumes.
    — Work on the lining of furnaces and ladles where there may be dust.
    — Spray painting where dedusting is inadequate.
    — Work in shafts, sewers and other underground areas connected with sewage.
    — Work in refrigeration plants where there is a danger that the refrigerant may escape.

5. HEARING PROTECTION

    Ear protectors

    — Work with metal presses.
    — Work with pneumatic drills.
    — The work of ground staff at airports.
    — Pile-driving work.
    — Wood and textile working.

6. BODY, ARM AND HAND PROTECTION

    Protective clothing

    — Work with acids and caustic solutions, disinfectants and corrosive cleaning substances.
    — Work with or in the vicinity of hot materials and where the effects of heat are felt.
    — Work on flat glass products.
    — Shot blasting.
    — Work in deep-freeze rooms.

    Fire-resistant protective clothing

    — Welding in restricted areas.

    Pierce-proof aprons

    — Boning and cutting work.
    — Work with hand knives involving drawing the knife towards the body.

    Leather aprons

    — Welding.
    — Forging.
    — Casting.

    Forearm protection

    — Boning and cutting.

Gloves

— Welding.
— Handling of sharp-edged objects, other than machines where there is a danger of the gloves being caught.
— Unprotected work with acids and caustic solutions.

Metal mesh gloves

— Boning and cutting.
— Regular cutting using a hand knife for production and slaughtering.
— Changing the knives of cutting machines.

7. WEATHERPROOF CLOTHING

— Work in the open air in rain and cold weather.

8. REFLECTIVE CLOTHING

— Work where the workers must be clearly visible.

9. SAFETY HARNESSES

— Work on scaffolding.
— Assembly of prefabricated parts.
— Work on masts.

10. SAFETY ROPES

— Work in high crane cabs.
— Work in high cabs of warehouse stacking and retrieval equipment.
— Work in high sections of drilling towers.
— Work in shafts and sewers.

11. SKIN PROTECTION

— Processing of coating materials.
— Tanning.

THE APPROXIMATION OF PERSONAL PROTECTIVE EQUIPMENT LAWS DIRECTIVE

General note. This was implemented in the UK by the Personal Protective Equipment (EC Directive) Regulations 1992 (S.I. 1992 No. 3139), see page 793. The Directive is set out in full as the Schedule to the Regulations and hence is not printed here.

THE MANUAL HANDLING DIRECTIVE

General note. This was the fourth daughter Directive and was implemented in the UK by the Manual Handling Operations Regulations 1992 (S.I. 1992 No. 2793), see page 584.

COUNCIL DIRECTIVE

of 29 May 1990

on the minimum health and safety requirements for the manual handling of loads where there is a risk particularly of back injury to workers (fourth individual Directive within the meaning of Article 16 (1) of Directive 89/391/ EEC)

(90/269/EEC)

THE COUNCIL OF THE EUROPEAN COMMUNITIES,

Having regard to the Treaty establishing the European Economic Community, and in particular Article 118a thereof,

Having regard to the Commission proposal submitted after consultation with the Advisory Committee on Safety, Hygiene and Health Protection at Work,

In cooperation with the European Parliament,

Having regard to the opinion of the Economic and Social Committee,

Whereas Article 118a of the Treaty provides that the Council shall adopt, by means of Directives, minimum requirements for encouraging improvements, especially in the working environment, to guarantee a better level of protection of the health and safety of workers;

Whereas, pursuant to that Article, such Directives must avoid imposing administrative, financial and legal constraints in a way which would hold back the creation and development of small and medium-sized undertakings;

Whereas the Commission communication on its programme concerning safety, hygiene and health at work, provides for the adoption of Directives designed to guarantee the health and safety of workers at the workplace;

Whereas the Council, in its resolution of 21 December 1987 on safety, hygiene and health at work, took note of the Commission's intention of submitting to the Council in the near future a Directive on protection against the risks resulting from the manual handling of heavy loads;

Whereas compliance with the minimum requirements designed to guarantee a better standard of health and safety at the workplace is essential to ensure the health and safety of workers;

Whereas this Directive is an individual Directive within the meaning of Article 16(1) of Council Directive 89/391/EEC of 12 June 1989 on the introduction of measures to encourage improvements in the health and safety of workers at work; whereas therefore the provisions of the said Directive are fully applicable to the field of the manual handling of loads where there is a risk particularly of back injury to workers, without prejudice to more stringent and/or specific provisions set out in this Directive;

Whereas this Directive constitutes a practical step towards the achievement of the social dimensions of the internal market;

Whereas, pursuant to Decision 74/325/EEC, the Advisory Committee on Safety, Hygiene and Health Protection at Work shall be consulted by the Commission with a view to drawing up proposals in this field,

HAS ADOPTED THIS DIRECTIVE:

SECTION I

GENERAL PROVISIONS

Article 1

Subject

1. This Directive, which is the fourth individual Directive within the meaning of Article 16(1) of Directive 89/391/EEC, lays down minimum health and safety requirements for the manual handling of loads where there is a risk particularly of back injury to workers.

2. The provisions of Directive 89/391/EEC shall be fully applicable to the whole sphere referred to in paragraph 1, without prejudice to more restrictive and/or specific provisions contained in this Directive.

Article 2

Definition

For the purposes of this Directive, "manual handling of loads" means any transporting or supporting of a load, by one or more workers, including lifting, putting down, pushing, pulling, carrying or moving of a load, which, by reason of its characteristics or of unfavourable ergonomic conditions, involves a risk particularly of back injury to workers.

SECTION II

EMPLOYERS' OBLIGATIONS

Article 3

General provision

1. The employer shall take appropriate organisational measures, or shall use the appropriate means, in particular mechanical equipment, in order to avoid the need for the manual handling of loads by workers.

2.   Where the need for the manual handling of loads by workers cannot be avoided, the employer shall take the appropriate organisational measures, use the appropriate means or provide workers with such means in order to reduce the risk involved in the manual handling of such loads, having regard to Annex I.

Article 4

Organisation of workstations

Wherever the need for manual handling of loads by workers cannot be avoided, the employer shall organise workstations in such a way as to make such handling as safe and healthy as possible and:

(a)   assess, in advance if possible, the health and safety conditions of the type of work involved, and in particular examine the characteristics of loads, taking account of Annex I;

(b)   take care to avoid or reduce the risk particularly of back injury to workers, by taking appropriate measures, considering in particular the characteristics of the working environment and the requirements of the activity, taking account of Annex I.

Article 5

Reference to Annex II

For the implementation of Article 6(3)(b) and Articles 14 and 15 of Directive 89/391/EEC, account should be taken of Annex II.

Article 6

Information for, and training of, workers

1.   Without prejudice to Article 10 of Directive 89/391/EEC, workers and/or their representatives shall be informed of all measures to be implemented, pursuant to this Directive, with regard to the protection of safety and of health.

Employers must ensure that workers and/or their representatives receive general indications and, where possible, precise information on:

— the weight of a load,
— the centre of gravity of the heaviest side when a package is eccentrically loaded.

2.   Without prejudice to Article 12 of Directive 89/391/EEC, employers must ensure that workers receive in addition proper training and information on

how to handle loads correctly and the risks they might be open to particularly if these tasks are not performed correctly, having regard to Annexes I and II.

Article 7

Consultation of workers and workers' participation

Consultation and participation of workers and/or of their representatives shall take place in accordance with Article 11 of Directive 89/391/EEC on matters covered by this Directive, including the Annexes thereto.

SECTION III

MISCELLANEOUS PROVISIONS

Article 8

Adjustment of the Annexes

Alterations of a strictly technical nature to Annexes I and II resulting from technical progress and changes in international regulations and specifications or knowledge in the field of the manual handling of loads shall be adopted in accordance with the procedure provided for in Article 17 of Directive 89/391/ EEC.

Article 9

Final provisions

1.   Member States shall bring into force the laws, regulations and administrative provisions needed to comply with this Directive not later than 31 December 1992.

They shall forthwith inform the Commission thereof.

2.   Member States shall communicate to the Commission the text of the provisions of national law which they adopt, or have adopted, in the field covered by this Directive.

3.   Member States shall report to the Commission every four years on the practical implementation of the provisions of this Directive, indicating the points of view of employers and workers.

The Commission shall inform the European Parliament, the Council, the Economic and Social Committee and the Advisory Committee on Safety, Hygiene and Health Protection at Work thereof.

4.   The Commission shall report periodically to the European Parliament, the Council and the Economic and Social Committee on the implementation of the Directive in the light of paragraphs 1, 2 and 3.

Article 10

This Directive is addressed to the Member States.

Done at Brussels, 29 May 1990.

For the Council
The President
B. AHERN

ANNEX I

REFERENCE FACTORS

(Article 3(2), Article 4(a) and (b) and Article 6(2))

1. **Characteristics of the load**

    The manual handling of a load may present a risk particularly of back injury
    if it is:

    — too heavy or too large,
    — unwieldy or difficult to grasp,
    — unstable or has contents likely to shift,
    — positioned in a manner requiring it to be held or manipulated at a
       distance from the trunk, or with a bending or twisting of the trunk,
    — likely, because of its contours and/or consistency, to result in injury to
       workers, particularly in the event of a collision.

2. **Physical effort required**

    A physical effort may present a risk particularly of back injury if it is:

    — too strenuous,
    — only achieved by a twisting movement of the trunk,
    — likely to result in a sudden movement of the load,
    — made with the body in an unstable posture.

3. **Characteristics of the working environment**

    The characteristics of the work environment may increase a risk particu-
    larly of back injury if:

    — there is not enough room, in particular vertically, to carry out the
       activity,
    — the floor is uneven, thus presenting tripping hazards, or is slippery in
       relation to the worker's footwear,
    — the place of work or the working environment prevents the handling of
       loads at a safe height or with good posture by the worker,

— there are variations in the level of the floor or the working surface, requiring the load to be manipulated on different levels,
— the floor or foot rest is unstable,
— the temperature, humidity or ventilation is unsuitable.

4. **Requirements of the activity**

The activity may present a risk particularly of back injury if it entails one or more of the following requirements:

— over-frequent or over-prolonged physical effort involving in particular the spine,
— an insufficient bodily rest or recovery period,
— excessive lifting, lowering or carrying distances,
— a rate of work imposed by a process which cannot be altered by the worker.

ANNEX II

INDIVIDUAL RISK FACTORS

(Articles 5 and 6(2))

The worker may be at risk if he/she:

— is physically unsuited to carry out the task in question,
— is wearing unsuitable clothing, footwear or other personal effects,
— does not have adequate or appropriate knowledge or training.

THE DISPLAY SCREEN EQUIPMENT DIRECTIVE

General note. This was the fifth daughter Directive and was implemented in the UK by the Health and Safety (Display Screen Equipment) Regulations 1992 (S.I. 1992 No. 2792), see page 931.

COUNCIL DIRECTIVE

of 29 May 1990

on the minimum safety and health requirements for work with display screen equipment (fifth individual Directive within the meaning of Article 16(1) of Directive 87/391/EEC)

(90/270/EEC)

THE COUNCIL OF THE EUROPEAN COMMUNITIES,

Having regard to the Treaty establishing the European Economic Community, and in particular Article 118a thereof,

Having regard to the Commission proposal drawn up after consultation with the Advisory Committee on Safety, Hygiene and Health Protection at Work,

In cooperation with the European Parliament,

Having regard to the opinion of the Economic and Social Committee,

Whereas Article 118a of the Treaty provides that the Council shall adopt, by means of Directives, minimum requirements designed to encourage improvements, especially in the working environment, to ensure a better level of protection of workers' safety and health;

Whereas, under the terms of that Article, those Directives shall avoid imposing administrative, financial and legal constraints, in a way which would hold back the creation and development of small and medium-sized undertakings;

Whereas the communication from the Commission on its programme concerning safety, hygiene and health at work provides for the adoption of measures in respect of new technologies; whereas the Council has taken note thereof in its resolution of 21 December 1987 on safety, hygiene and health at work;

Whereas compliance with the minimum requirements for ensuring a better level of safety at workstations with display screens is essential for ensuring the safety and health of workers:

Whereas this Directive is an individual Directive within the meaning of Article 16(1) of Council Directive 89/391/EEC of 12 June 1989 on the introduction of measures to encourage improvements in the safety and health of workers at work; whereas the provisions of the latter are therefore fully applicable to the use by workers of display screen equipment, without prejudice to more stringent and/or specific provisions contained in the present Directive;

Whereas employers are obliged to keep themselves informed of the latest advances in technology and scientific findings concerning workstation design so that they can make any changes necessary so as to be able to guarantee a better level of protection of workers' safety and health;

Whereas the ergonomic aspects are of particular importance for a workstation with display screen equipment;

Whereas this Directive is a practical contribution towards creating the social dimension of the internal market;

Whereas, pursuant to Decision 74/325/EEC, the Advisory Committee on Safety, Hygiene and Health Protection at Work shall be consulted by the Commission on the drawing-up of proposals in this field,

HAS ADOPTED THIS DIRECTIVE:

SECTION I
GENERAL PROVISIONS

Article 1
Subject

1.   This Directive, which is the fifth individual Directive within the meaning of Article 16(1) of Directive 89/391/EEC, lays down minimum safety and health requirements for work with display screen equipment as defined in Article 2.

2.   The provisions of Directive 89/391/EEC are fully applicable to the whole field referred to in paragraph 1, without prejudice to more stringent and/or specific provisions contained in the present Directive.

3.   This Directive shall not apply to:

(a) drivers' cabs or control cabs for vehicles or machinery;
(b) computer systems on board a means of transport;
(c) computer systems mainly intended for public use;
(d) "portable" systems not in prolonged use at a workstation;
(e) calculators, cash registers and any equipment having a small data or measurement display required for direct use of the equipment;
(f) typewriters of traditional design, of the type known as "typewriter with window".

Article 2

Definitions

For the purpose of this Directive, the following terms shall have the following meanings:

(a) *display screen equipment*: an alphanumeric or graphic display screen, regard-
    less of the display process employed;
(b) *workstation*: an assembly comprising display screen equipment, which may
    be provided with a keyboard or imput device and/or software determining
    the operator/machine interface, optional accessories, peripherals includ-
    ing the diskette drive, telephone, modem, printer, document holder, work
    chair and work desk or work surface, and the immediate work environ-
    ment;
(c) *worker*: any worker as defined in Article 3(a) of Directive 89/391/EEC who
    habitually uses display screen equipment as a significant part of his normal
    work.

SECTION II

EMPLOYERS' OBLIGATIONS

Article 3

Analysis of workstations

1.   Employers shall be obliged to perform an analysis of workstations in order
to evaluate the safety and health conditions to which they give rise for their
workers, particularly as regards possible risks to eyesight, physical problems and
problems of mental stress.

2.   Employers shall take appropriate measures to remedy the risks found, on
the basis of the evaluation referred to in paragraph 1, taking account of the
additional and/or combined effects of the risks so found.

Article 4

Workstations put into service for the first time

Employers must take the appropriate steps to ensure that workstations first put
into service after 31 December 1992 meet the minimum requirements laid
down in the Annex.

Article 5

Workstations already put into service

Employers must take the appropriate steps to ensure that workstations already
put into service on or before 31 December 1992 are adapted to comply with the
minimum requirements laid down in the Annex not later than four years after
that date.

Article 6

Information for, and training of, workers

1.   Without prejudice to Article 10 of Directive 89/391/EEC, workers shall
receive information on all aspects of safety and health relating to their work-

station, in particular information on such measures applicable to workstations as are implemented under Articles 3, 7 and 9.

In all cases, workers or their representatives shall be informed of any health and safety measure taken in compliance with this Directive.

2. Without prejudice to Article 12 of Directive 89/391/EEC, every worker shall also receive training in use of the workstation before commencing this type of work and whenever the organisation of the workstation is substantially modified.

Article 7

Daily work routine

The employer must plan the worker's activities in such a way that daily work on a display screen is periodically interrupted by breaks or changes of activity reducing the workload at the display screen.

Article 8

Worker consultation and participation

Consultation and participation of workers and/or their representatives shall take place in accordance with Article 11 of Directive 89/391/EEC on the matters covered by this Directive, including its Annex.

Article 9

Protection of workers' eyes and eyesight

1. Workers shall be entitled to an appropriate eye and eyesight test carried out by a person with the necessary capabilities:

— before commencing display screen work,
— at regular intervals thereafter, and
— if they experience visual difficulties which may be due to display screen work.

2. Workers shall be entitled to an ophthalmological examination if the results of the test referred to in paragraph 1 show that this is necessary.

3. If the result of the test referred to in paragraph 1 or of the examination referred to in paragraph 2 show that it is necessary and if normal corrective

appliances cannot be used, workers must be provided with special corrective appliances appropriate for the work concerned.

4. Measures taken pursuant to this Article may in no circumstances involve workers in additional financial cost.

5. Protection of workers' eyes and eyesight may be provided as part of a national health system.

SECTION III

MISCELLANEOUS PROVISIONS

Article 10

Adaptations to the Annex

The strictly technical adaptations to the Annex to take account of technical progress, developments in international regulations and specifications and knowledge in the field of display screen equipment shall be adopted in accordance with the procedure laid down in Article 17 of Directive 89/391/EEC.

Article 11

Final provisions

1. Member States shall bring into force the laws, regulations and administrative provisions necessary to comply with this Directive by 31 December 1992.

They shall forthwith inform the Commission thereof.

2. Member States shall communicate to the Commission the texts of the provisions of national law which they adopt, or have already adopted, in the field covered by this Directive.

3. Member States shall report to the Commission every four years on the practical implementation of the provisions of this Directive, indicating the points of view of employers and workers.

The Commission shall inform the European Parliament, the Council, the Economic and Social Committee and the Advisory Committee on Safety, Hygiene and Health Protection at Work.

4. The Commission shall submit a report on the implementation of this Directive at regular intervals to the European Parliament, the Council and the Economic and Social Committee, taking into account paragraphs 1, 2 and 3.

Article 12

This Directive is addressed to the Member States.

Done at Brussels, 29 May 1990.

For the Council
The President
B. AHERN

_____

ANNEX

MINIMUM REQUIREMENTS

(Articles 4 and 5)

PRELIMINARY REMARK

The obligations laid down in this Annex shall apply in order to achieve the objectives of this Directive and to the extent that, firstly, the components concerned are present at the workstation, and secondly, the inherent requirements or characteristics of the task do not preclude it.

1. EQUIPMENT

    (a) **General comment**

    The use as such of the equipment must not be a source of risk for workers.

    (b) **Display screen**

    The characters on the screen shall be well-defined and clearly formed, of adequate size and with adequate spacing between the characters and lines.

    The image on the screen should be stable, with no flickering or other forms of instability.

    The brightness and/or the contrast between the characters and the background shall be easily adjustable by the operator, and also be easily adjustable to ambient conditions.

    The screen must swivel and tilt easily and freely to suit the needs of the operator.

    It shall be possible to use a separate base for the screen or an adjustable table.

    The screen shall be free of reflective glare and reflections liable to cause discomfort to the user.

(c) **Keyboard**

The keyboard shall be tiltable and separate from the screen so as to allow the worker to find a comfortable working position avoiding fatigue in the arms or hands.

The space in front of the keyboard shall be sufficient to provide support for the hands and arms of the operator.

The keyboard shall have a matt surface to avoid reflective glare.

The arrangement of the keyboard and the characteristics of the keys shall be such as to facilitate the use of the keyboard.

The symbols on the keys shall be adequately contrasted and legible from the design working position.

(d) **Work desk or work surface**

The work desk or work surface shall have a sufficiently large, low-reflectance surface and allow a flexible arrangement of the screen, keyboard, documents and related equipment.

The document holder shall be stable and adjustable and shall be positioned so as to minimise the need for uncomfortable head and eye movements.

There shall be adequate space for workers to find a comfortable position.

(e) **Work chair**

The work chair shall be stable and allow the operator easy freedom of movement and a comfortable position.

The seat shall be adjustable in height.

The seat back shall be adjustable in both height and tilt.

A footrest shall be made available to any one who wishes for one.

2. ENVIRONMENT

(a) **Space requirements**

The workstation shall be dimensioned and designed so as to provide sufficient space for the user to change position and vary movements.

(b) **Lighting**

Room lighting and/or spot lighting (work lamps) shall ensure satisfactory lighting conditions and an appropriate contrast between the screen and the background environment, taking into account the type of work and the user's vision requirements.

Possible disturbing glare and reflections on the screen or other equipment shall be prevented by coordinating workplace and workstation layout with the positioning and technical characteristics of the artificial light sources.

(c) Reflections and glare

Workstations shall be so designed that sources of light, such as windows and other openings, transparent or translucid walls, and brightly coloured fixtures or walls cause no direct glare and [no distracting]* reflections on the screen.

Windows shall be fitted with a suitable system of adjustable covering to attenuate the daylight that falls on the workstation.

(d) Noise

Noise emitted by equipment belonging to workstation(s) shall be taken into account when a workstation is being equipped, in particular so as not to distract attention or disturb speech.

(e) Heat

Equipment belonging to workstation(s) shall not produce excess heat which could cause discomfort to workers.

(f) Radiation

All radiation with the exception of the visible part of the electromagnetic spectrum shall be reduced to negligible levels from the point of view of the protection of workers' safety and health.

(g) Humidity

An adequate level of humidity shall be established and maintained.

3. OPERATOR/COMPUTER INTERFACE

In designing, selecting, commissioning and modifying software, and in designing tasks using display screen equipment, the employer shall take into account the following principles:

(a) software must be suitable for the task;
(b) software must be easy to use and, where appropriate, adaptable to the operator's level of knowledge or experience; no quantitative or qualitative checking facility may be used without the knowledge of the workers;
(c) systems must provide feedback to workers on their performance;
(d) systems must display information in a format and at a pace which are adapted to operators;

(e) the principles of software ergonomics must be applied, in particular to human data processing.

* Correction indicated here taken from Official Journal, L 171/30.

THE CARCINOGENS AT WORK DIRECTIVE

General note. This was the sixth daughter Directive and was implemented in the UK by the Control of Substances Hazardous to Health (Amendment) Regulations 1992 (S.I. 1992 No. 2382 and S.I. 1992 No. 2966), see page 1005 and the Control of Asbestos at Work (Amendment) Regulations 1992 (S.I. 1992 No. 3068), see page 1042.

COUNCIL DIRECTIVE

of 28 June 1990

on the protection of workers from the risks related to exposure to carcinogens at work (sixth individual Directive within the meaning of Article 16(1) of Directive 89/391/EEC)

(90/394/EEC)

THE COUNCIL OF THE EUROPEAN COMMUNITIES,

Having regard to the Treaty establishing the European Economic Community, and in particular Article 118a thereof,

Having regard to the proposal from the Commission, drawn up following consultation with the Advisory Committee on Safety, Hygiene and Health Protection at Work,

In cooperation with the European Parliament,

Having regard to the opinion of the Economic and Social Committee,

Whereas Article 118a of the Treaty provides that the Council is to adopt, by means of Directives, minimum requirements in order to encourage improvements, especially in the working environment, so as to guarantee better protection of the health and safety of workers;

Whereas, according to that Article, such Directives must avoid imposing administrative, financial and legal constraint in a way which would hold back the creation and development of small and medium-sized undertakings;

Whereas the Council resolution of 27 February 1984 on a second action programme of the European Communities on safety and health at work provides for the development of protective measures for workers exposed to carcinogens;

Whereas the Commission communication on its programme concerning safety, hygiene and health at work provides for the adoption of Directives to guarantee the health and safety of workers;

Whereas compliance with the minimum requirements designed to guarantee a better standard of health and safety as regards the protection of workers from the risks related to exposure to carcinogens at work is essential to ensure the health and safety of workers;

Whereas this Directive is an individual Directive within the meaning of Article 16(1) of Council Directive 89/391/EEC of 12 June 1989 on the introduction of measures to encourage improvements in the health and safety of workers at work; whereas therefore the provisions of that Directive are fully applicable to the exposure of workers to carcinogens, without prejudice to more stringent and/or specific provisions contained in this Directive;

Whereas Council Directive 67/548/EEC of 27 June 1967 on the approximation of laws, regulations and administrative provisions relating to the classification, packaging and labelling of dangerous substances, as last amended by Directive 88/490/EEC, contains a list of dangerous substances, together with particulars on the classification and labelling procedures in respect of each substance;

Whereas Council Directive 88/379/EEC of 7 June 1988 on the approximation of the laws, regulations and administrative provisions relating to the classification, packaging and labelling of dangerous preparations, as last amended by Directive 89/178/EEC, contains particulars on the classification and labelling procedures in respect of such preparations;

Whereas the plan of action 1987 to 1989 adopted under the "Europe against cancer" programme provides for support for European studies on the possible cancer risks of certain chemical substances;

Whereas, although current scientific knowledge is not such that a level can be established below which risks to health cease to exist, a reduction in exposure to carcinogens will nonetheless reduce those risks;

Whereas nevertheless, in order to contribute to a reduction in these risks, limit values and other directly related provisions should be established for all those carcinogens for which the available information, including scientific and technical data, make this possible;

Whereas preventive measures must be taken for the protection of the health and safety of workers exposed to carcinogens;

Whereas this Directive lays down particular requirements specific to exposure to carcinogens;

Whereas this Directive constitutes a practical aspect of the realisation of the social dimension of the internal market;

Whereas, pursuant to Decision 74/325/EEC, as last amended by the 1985 Act of Accession, the Advisory Committee on Safety, Hygiene and Health Protection at Work is to be consulted by the Commission with a view to drawing up proposals in this field,

HAS ADOPTED THIS DIRECTIVE:

SECTION I

GENERAL PROVISIONS

Article 1

Objective

1.   This Directive, which is the sixth individual Directive within the meaning of Article 16(1) of Directive 89/391/EEC, has as its aim the protection of workers against risks to their health and safety, including the prevention of such risks, arising or likely to arise from exposure to carcinogens at work.

It lays down particular minimum requirements in this area, including limit values.

2.   This Directive shall not apply to workers exposed only to radiation covered by the Treaty establishing the European Atomic Energy Community.

3.   Directive 89/391/EEC shall apply fully to the whole area referred to in paragraph 1, without prejudice to more stringent and/or specific provisions contained in this Directive.

Article 2

Definition

For the purposes of this Directive, "carcinogen" means:

(a)   a substance to which, in Annex I to Directive 67/548/EEC, the risk-phrase R45 "may cause cancer" is applied;
(b)   a preparation which, under Article 3(5) (j) of Directive 88/379/EEC, must be labelled as R45 "may cause cancer";
(c)   a substance, a preparation or a process referred to in Annex I as well as a substance or preparation released by a process referred to in Annex I.

Article 3

Scope—determination and assessment of risks

1.   This Directive shall apply to activities in which workers are or are likely to be exposed to carcinogens as a result of their work.

2.   In the case of any activity likely to involve a risk of exposure to carcinogens, the nature, degree and duration of workers' exposure must be determined in order to make it possible to assess any risk to the workers' health or safety and to lay down the measures to be taken.

The assessment must be renewed regularly and in any event when any change occurs in the conditions which may affect workers' exposure to carcinogens.

The employer must supply the authorities responsible at their request with the information used for making the assessment.

3.   Furthermore, when assessing the risk, account shall be taken of all other cases of major exposure, such as those with harmful effects on the skin.

4.   When the assessment referred to in paragraph 2 is carried out, employers shall give particular attention to any effects concerning the health or safety of workers at particular risk and shall, *inter alia,* take account of the desirability of not employing such workers in areas where they may come into contact with carcinogens.

SECTION II
EMPLOYERS' OBLIGATIONS

Article 4
Reduction and replacement

1.   The employer shall reduce the use of a carcinogen at the place of work, in particular by replacing it, in so far as is technically possible, by a substance, preparation or process which, under its conditions of use, is not dangerous or is less dangerous to workers' health or safety, as the case may be.

2.   The employer shall, upon request, submit the findings of his investigations to the relevant authorities.

Article 5
Prevention and reduction of exposure

1.   Where the results of the assessment referred to in Article 3(2) reveal a risk to workers' health or safety, workers' exposure must be prevented.

2.   Where it is not technically possible to replace the carcinogen by a substance, preparation or process which, under its conditions of use, is not dangerous or is less dangerous to health or safety, the employer shall ensure that the carcinogen is, in so far as is technically possible, manufactured and used in a closed system.

3.   Where a closed system is not technically possible, the employer shall ensure that the level of exposure of workers is reduced to as low a level as is technically possible.

4.   Wherever a carcinogen is used, the employer shall apply all the following measures:
(a)   limitation of the quantities of a carcinogen at the place of work;
(b)   keeping as low as possible the number of workers exposed or likely to be exposed;
(c)   design of work processes and engineering control measures so as to avoid or minimise the release of carcinogens into the place of work;
(d)   evacuation of carcinogens at source, local extraction system or general ventilation, all such methods to be appropriate and compatible with the need to protect public health and the environment;
(e)   use of existing appropriate procedures for the measurement of carcinogens, in particular for the early detection of abnormal exposures resulting from an unforeseeable event or an accident;

(f) application of suitable working procedures and methods;
(g) collective protection measures and/or, where exposure cannot be avoided by other means, individual protection measures;
(h) hygiene measures, in particular regular cleaning of floors, walls and other surfaces;
(i) information for workers;
(j) demarcation of risk areas and use of adequate warning and safety signs including "no smoking" signs in areas where workers are exposed or likely to be exposed to carcinogens;
(k) drawing up plans to deal with emergencies likely to result in abnormally high exposure;
(l) means for safe storage, handling and transportation, in particular by using sealed and clearly and visibly labelled containers;
(m) means for safe collection, storage and disposal of waste by workers, including the use of sealed and clearly and visibly labelled containers.

Article 6
Information for the competent authority

Where the results of the assessment referred to in Article 3(2) reveal a risk to workers' health or safety, employers shall, when requested, make available to the competent authority appropriate information on:

(a) the activities and/or industrial processes carried out, including the reasons for which carcinogens are used;
(b) the quantities of substances or preparations manufactured or used which contain carcinogens;
(c) the number of workers exposed;
(d) the preventive measures taken;
(e) the type of protective equipment used;
(f) the nature and degree of exposure;
(g) the cases of replacement.

Article 7
Unforeseen exposure

1. In the event of an unforeseeable event or an accident which is likely to result in an abnormal exposure of workers, the employer shall inform the workers thereof.

2. Until the situation has been restored to normal and the causes of the abnormal exposure have been eliminated:

(a) only those workers who are essential to the carrying out of repairs and other necessary work shall be permitted to work in the affected area;

(b) the workers concerned shall be provided with protective clothing and individual respiratory protection equipment which they must wear; the exposure may not be permanent and shall be kept to the strict minimum of time necessary for each worker;

(c) unprotected workers shall not be allowed to work in the affected area.

Article 8
Foreseeable exposure

1. For certain activities such as maintenance, in respect of which it is foreseeable that there is the potential for a significant increase in exposure of workers, and in respect of which all scope for further technical preventive measures for limiting workers' exposure has already been exhausted, the employer shall determine, after consultation of the workers and/or their representatives in the undertaking or establishment, without prejudice to the employer's responsibility, the measures necessary to reduce the duration of workers' exposure to the minimum possible and to ensure protection of workers while they are engaged in such activities.

Pursuant to the first subparagraph, the workers concerned shall be provided with protective clothing and individual respiratory protection equipment which they must wear as long as the abnormal exposure persists; that exposure may not be permanent and shall be kept to the strict minimum of time necessary for each worker.

2. Appropriate measures shall be taken to ensure that the areas in which the activities referred to in the first subparagraph of paragraph 1 take place are clearly demarcated and indicated or that unauthorised persons are prevented by other means from having access to such areas.

Article 9
Access to risk areas

Appropriate measures shall be taken by employers to ensure that access to areas in which the activities in respect of which the results of the assessment referred to in Article 3(2) reveal a risk to workers' safety or health take place are accessible solely to workers who, by reason of their work or duties, are required to enter them.

Article 10
Hygiene and individual protection

1. Employers shall be obliged, in the case of all activities for which there is a risk of contamination by carcinogens, to take appropriate measures to ensure that:

(a) workers to not eat, drink or smoke in working areas where there is a risk of contamination by carcinogens;

(b) workers are provided with appropriate protective clothing or other appropriate special clothing;
separate storage places are provided for working or protective clothing and for street clothes;

(c) workers are provided with appropriate and adequate washing and toilet facilities;

(d) protective equipment is properly stored in a well-defined place; it is checked and cleaned if possible before, and in any case after, each use; defective equipment is repaired or replaced before further use.

2. Workers may not be charged for the cost of these measures.

Article 11

Information and training of workers

1. Appropriate measures shall be taken by the employer to ensure that workers and/or workers' representatives in the undertaking or establishment receive sufficient and appropriate training, on the basis of all available information, in particular in the form of information and instructions, concerning:

(a) potential risks to health, including the additional risks due to tobacco consumption;

(b) precautions to be taken to prevent exposure;

(c) hygiene requirements;

(d) wearing and use of protective equipment and clothing;

(e) steps to be taken by workers, including rescue workers, in the case of incidents and to prevent incidents.

The training shall be:

— adapted to take account of new or changed risk, and

— repeated periodically if necessary.

2. Employers shall inform workers of installations and related containers containing carcinogens, ensure that all containers, packages and installations containing carcinogens are labelled clearly and legibly, and display clearly visible warning and hazard signs.

Article 12

Information for workers

Appropriate measures shall be taken to ensure that:

(a) workers and/or any workers' representatives in the undertaking or establishment can check that this Directive is applied or can be involved in its application, in particular with regard to:

   (i) the consequences for workers' safety and health of the selection, wearing and use of protective clothing and equipment, without prejudice to the employer's responsibility for determining the effectiveness of protective clothing and equipment;

   (ii) the measures determined by the employer which are referred to in the first subparagraph of Article 8(1), without prejudice to the employer's responsibility for determining such measures;

(b) workers and/or any workers' representatives in the undertaking or establishment are informed as quickly as possible of abnormal exposures, including those referred to in Article 8, of the causes thereof and of the measures taken or to be taken to rectify the situation;

(c) the employer keeps an up-to-date list of the workers engaged in the activities in respect of which the results of the assessment referred to in Article 3(2) reveal a risk to workers' health or safety, indicating, if the information is available, the exposure to which they have been subjected;

(d) the doctor and/or the competent authority as well as all other persons who have responsibility for health and safety at work have access to the list referred to in subparagraph (c);

(e) each worker has access to the information on the list which relates to him personally;

(f) workers and/or any workers' representatives in the undertaking or establishment have access to anonymous collective information.

Article 13

Consultation and participation of workers

Consultation and participation of workers and/or their representatives in connection with matters covered by this Directive, including the Annexes hereto, shall take place in accordance with Article 11 of Directive 89/391/EEC.

SECTION III

MISCELLANEOUS PROVISIONS

Article 14

Health surveillance

1. The Member States shall establish, in accordance with national laws and/or practice, arrangements for carrying out relevant health surveillance of workers for whom the results of the assessment referred to in Article 3(2) reveal a risk to health or safety.

2. The arrangements referred to in paragraph 1 shall be such that each worker shall be able to undergo, if appropriate, relevant health surveillance:

— prior to exposure;
— at regular intervals thereafter.

Those arrangements shall be such that it is directly possible to implement individual and occupational hygiene measures.

3. If a worker is found to be suffering from an abnormality which is suspected to be the result of exposure to carcinogens, the doctor or authority responsible for the health surveillance of workers may require other workers who have been similarly exposed to undergo health surveillance.

In that event, a reassessment of the risk of exposure shall be carried out in accordance with Article 3(2).

4. In cases where health surveillance is carried out, an individual medical record shall be kept and the doctor or authority responsible for health surveillance shall propose any protective or preventive measures to be taken in respect of any individual workers.

5.   Information and advice must be given to workers regarding any health surveillance which they may undergo following the end of exposure.

6.   In accordance with national laws and/or practice:
— workers shall have access to the results of the health surveillance which concern them, and
— the workers concerned or the employer may request a review of the results of the health surveillance.

7.   Practical recommendations for the health surveillance of workers are given in Annex II.

8.   All cases of cancer identified in accordance with national laws and/or practice as resulting from occupational exposure to a carcinogen shall be notified to the competent authority.

Article 15

Record-keeping

1.   The list referred to in Article 12(c) and the medical record referred to in Article 14(4) shall be kept for at least 40 years following the end of exposure, in accordance with national laws and/or practice.

2.   Those documents shall be made available to the responsible authority in cases where the undertaking ceases activity, in accordance with national laws and/or practice.

Article 16

Limit values

1.   The Council shall, in accordance with the procedure laid down in Article 118a of the Treaty, set out limit values in Directives on the basis of the available information, including scientific and technical data, in respect of all those carcinogens for which this is possible, and, where necessary, other directly related provisions.

2.   Limit values and other directly related provisions shall be set out in Annex III.

Article 17

Annexes

1.   Annexes I and III may be amended in accordance only with the procedure laid down in Article 118a of the Treaty.

2.   Purely technical adjustments to Annex II in the light of technical progress, changes in international regulations or specifications and new findings in the field of carcinogens shall be adopted in accordance with the procedure laid down in Article 17 of Directive 89/391/EEC.

Article 18

Use of data

The Commission shall have access to the use made by the competent national authorities of the information referred to in Article 14(8).

Article 19

Final provisions

1.   Member States shall bring into force the laws, regulations and administrative provisions necessary to comply with this Directive not later than 31 December 1992.

Should Directives 67/548/EEC or 88/379/EEC be amended by amending Directives after notification of this Directive with respect to the substances and preparations referred to in Article 2(a) and (b), Member States shall bring into force the laws, regulations and administrative provisions necessary to introduce the amendments in question into the provisions referred to in the first subparagraph by the deadlines laid down for implementation of such amending Directives.

Member States shall forthwith inform the Commission that the provisions referred to in this paragraph have been brought into force.

2.   Member States shall communicate to the Commission the provisions of national law already adopted or which they adopt in the future in the field governed by this Directive.

Article 20

This Directive is addressed to the Member States.

Done at Luxembourg, 28 June 1990.

For the Council
The President
M. GEOGHEGAN-QUINN

———————————

ANNEX I

LIST OF SUBSTANCES, PREPARATIONS AND PROCESSES

(Article 2(c))

1.   Manufacture of auramine.

2.   Work involving exposure to aromatic polycyclic hydrocarbons present in coal soots, tar, pitch, fumes or dust.

3. Work involving exposure to dusts, fumes and sprays produced during the roasting and electro-refining of cupro-nickel mattes.

4. Strong acid process in the manufacture of isopropyl alcohol.

ANNEX II

PRACTICAL RECOMMENDATIONS FOR THE HEALTH SURVEILLANCE OF WORKERS

(Article 14(7))

1. The doctor and/or authority responsible for the health monitoring of workers exposed to carcinogens must be familiar with the exposure conditions or circumstances of each worker.

2. Health monitoring of workers must be carried out in accordance with the principles and practices of occupational medicine; it must include at least the following measures:
    — keeping records of a worker's medical and occupational history,
    — a personal interview,
    — where appropriate, biological monitoring, as well as detection of early and reversible effects.

    Further tests may be decided upon for each worker when he is the subject of health monitoring, in the light of the most recent knowledge available to occupational medicine.

ANNEX III

LIMIT VALUES AND OTHER DIRECTLY RELATED PROVISIONS

(Article 16)

A. Limit values
    p.m.

B. Other directly related provisions
    p.m.

THE ASBESTOS DIRECTIVE

General note. The original Directive 83/477, see page 202, was amended by the Asbestos at Work Directive 91/382. The original Directive was implemented in the UK by the Asbestos (Prohibitions) Regulations 1985 (S.I. 1985 No. 910 amended by S.I. 1988 No. 711), now by the Asbestos (Prohibitions) Regulations 1992 (S.I. 1992 No. 3067), see page 1057, and the Control of Asbestos at Work Regulations 1987 (S.I. 1987 No. 2115 and S.I. 1992 No. 3068), see page 1042.

COUNCIL DIRECTIVE

of 25 June 1991

amending Directive 83/477/EEC on the protection of workers from the risks related to exposure to asbestos at work (second individual Directive within the meaning of Article 8 of Directive 80/1107/EEC)

(91/382/EEC)

THE COUNCIL OF THE EUROPEAN COMMUNITIES,

Having regard to the Treaty establishing the European Economic Community, and in particular Article 118a thereof,

Having regard to the proposal from the Commission drawn up following consultation with the Advisory Committee on Safety, Hygiene and Health Protection at Work,

In cooperation with the European Parliament,

Having regard to the opinion of the Economic and Social Committee,

Whereas Article 118a of the Treaty provides that the Council shall adopt, by means of Directives, minimum requirements for encouraging improvements, especially in the working environment, to ensure a better level of protection of the safety and health of workers;

Whereas, under the terms of that Article, such Directives are to avoid imposing administrative, financial and legal constraints in a way which would hold back the creation and development of small and medium-size undertakings;

Whereas the communication from the Commission on its programme concerning safety, hygiene and health at work provides for the adoption of Directives designed to guarantee the safety and health of workers;

Whereas the Council, in its resolution of 21 December 1987 on safety, hygiene and health at work, took note of the Commission's intention of submitting to the Council in the near future minimum requirements at Community level concerning protection against the risks resulting from dangerous substances, including carcinogenic substances; whereas it considered that in this connection the principle of substitution using a recognised non-dangerous or less dangerous substance should be taken as a basis;

Whereas asbestos is a particularly hazardous agent which can cause serious illness and which is found in various forms in a large number of circumstances at work;

Whereas, in view of the progress made in scientific knowledge and technology and in the light of experience gained in applying Council Directive 83/447/EEC of 19 September 1983 on the protection of workers from the risks related to exposure to asbestos at work (second individual Directive within the meaning of Article 8 of Directive 80/1107/EEC), the protection of workers should be improved and the action levels and limit values laid down in Directive 83/477/EEC should be reduced;

Whereas the prohibition of the application of asbestos by means of the spraying process is not sufficient to prevent asbestos fibres being released into the atmosphere; whereas other working procedures that involve the use of certain materials containing asbestos must also be prohibited;

Whereas a decision cannot yet be taken establishing a single method for measurement of asbestos-in-air concentrations at Community level;

Whereas this Directive should be reviewed by 31 December 1995, taking account, in particular, of progress made in scientific knowledge and technology and of experience gained in applying this Directive;

Whereas Decision 74/325/EEC, as last amended by the 1985 Act of Accession, provides that the Advisory Committee on Safety, Hygiene and Health Protection at Work is to be consulted by the Commission for the purpose of drafting proposals in this field,

HAS ADOPTED THIS DIRECTIVE:

Article 1

Directive 83/477/EEC is hereby amended as follows:

1.   Article 3(3) shall be replaced by the following:

"3.   If the assessment referred to in paragraph 2 shows that the concentration of asbestos fibres in the air at the place of work in the absence of any personal protective equipment is, at the option of the Member States, at a level as measured or calculated:

(a) for chrysotile

— lower than 0,20 fibres per cm^3 in relation to an eight-hour reference period, and/or
— lower than a cumulative dose of 12,00 fibre-days per cm^3 over a three-month period;

(b) for all other forms of asbestos either alone or in mixtures, including mixtures containing chrysotile:

　　— lower than 0,10 fibres per cm³ in relation to an eight-hour reference period, and/or
　　— lower than a cumulative dose of 6,00 fibre-days per cm³ over a three-month period,

Articles 4, 7, 13, 14(2), 15 and 16 shall not apply".

2.　Article 5 shall be replaced by the following:

"*Article 5*

The application of asbestos by means of the spraying process and working procedures that involve using low-density (less than 1g/cm³) insulating or soundproofing materials which contain asbestos shall be prohibited".

3.　In point (1) of Article 7, the third paragraph shall be replaced by the following:

"In accordance with Article 118a of the Treaty and taking account in particular of progress made in scientific knowledge and technology and of experience gained in applying this Directive, the Council shall review the provisions of the first sentence of the first paragraph by 31 December 1995, with a view to establishing a single method for measurement of asbestos-in-air concentrations at Community level;".

4.　Article 8 shall be replaced by the following:

"*Article 8*

The following limit values shall be applied:

(a)　concentration of chrysotile fibres in the air at the place of work:

　　0,60 fibres per cm³ measured or calculated in relation to an eight-hour reference period;

(b)　concentration in the air at the place of work of all other forms of asbestos fibres, either alone or in mixtures, including mixtures containing chrysotile:

　　0,30 fibres per cm³ measured or calculated in relation to an eight-hour reference period".

5.　Article 9 shall be replaced by the following:

"*Article 9*

1.　Without prejudice to the third paragraph of point 1 of Article 7, in accordance with Article 118a of the Treaty and taking account in particular of progress made in scientific knowledge and technology and of experience gained in applying this Directive, the Council shall review the provisions of this Directive by 31 December 1995.

2.　The amendments required to adapt the Annexes to this Directive to take account of technical progress shall be made in accordance with the procedure described in Articles 9 and 10 of Council Directive 80/1107/EEC of 27 November 1980 on the protection of workers from the risks related to exposure to chemical, physical and biological agents at work".

6.   Article 12 is hereby amended as follows:

   (a) the following subparagraph shall be added to paragraph 2:

   "At the request of the competent authorities, the plan shall include information on the following:

   — the nature and probable duration of the work,
   — the place where the work is carried out,
   — the methods applied where the work involves the handling of asbestos or of materials containing asbestos,
   — the characteristics of the equipment used for:
      — protection and decontamination of those carrying out the work,
      — protection of other persons present on or near the worksite".

   (b) the following paragraph shall be added:

   "3.   At the request of the competent authorities, the plan referred to in paragraph 1 must be notified to them before the start of the projected work".

Article 2

1.   Member States shall bring into force the laws, regulations and administrative provisions necessary to comply with this Directive not later than 1 January 1993.

They shall forthwith inform the Commission thereof.

When Member States adopt these measures, they shall contain a reference to this Directive or shall be accompanied by such reference on the occasion of their official publication. The methods of making such a reference shall be laid down by the Member States.

The date 1 January 1993 shall, however, be replaced by 1 January 1996 in the case of asbestos-mining activities.

However, as regards the Hellenic Republic:

— the date referred to in the first subparagraph shall be 1 January 1996,
— the date referred to in the fourth subparagraph shall be 1 January 1999.

2.   Member States shall communicate to the Commission the provisions of national law which they adopt in the field governed by this Directive.

Article 3

This Directive is addressed to the Member States.

Done at Luxembourg, 25 June 1991.

For the Council
The President
J.-C. JUNCKER

THE TEMPORARY WORKERS DIRECTIVE

General note. This Directive was implemented in the UK by the Management of Health and Safety at Work Regulations 1992 (S.I. 1992 No. 2051), see page 433, and provisions in other Regulations. Its importance consists in extending health and safety protection to workers who are technically employed by employment agencies, and to those who work under "fixed-duration contracts". This second category may be broad enough to encompass many workers who are deemed to be independent contractors under English law: such an interpretation would appear to be consistent with the aims of the Directive.

COUNCIL DIRECTIVE

of 25 June 1991

supplementing the measures to encourage improvements in the safety and health at work of workers with a fixed-duration employment relationship or a temporary employment relationship

(91/383/EEC)

THE COUNCIL OF THE EUROPEAN COMMUNITIES,

Having regard to the Treaty establishing the European Economic Community, and in particular Article 118a thereof,

Having regard to the proposal from the Commission,

In cooperation with the European Parliament,

Having regard to the opinion of the Economic and Social Committee,

Whereas Article 118a of the Treaty provides that the Council shall adopt, by means of Directives, minimum requirements for encouraging improvements, especially in the working environment, to guarantee a better level of protection of the safety and health of workers;

Whereas, pursuant to the said Article, Directives must avoid imposing administrative, financial and legal constraints which would hold back the creation and development of small and medium-sized undertakings;

Whereas recourse to forms of employment such as fixed-duration employment and temporary employment has increased considerably;

Whereas research has shown that in general workers with a fixed-duration employment relationship or temporary employment relationship are, in certain sectors, more exposed to the risk of accidents at work and occupational diseases than other workers;

Whereas these additional risks in certain sectors are in part linked to certain particular modes of integrating new workers into the undertaking; whereas

179

these risks can be reduced through adequate provision of information and training from the beginning of employment;

Whereas the Directives on health and safety at work, notably Council Directive 89/391/EEC of 12 June 1989 on the introduction of measures to encourage improvements in the safety and health of workers at work, contain provisions intended to improve the safety and health of workers in general;

Whereas the specific situation of workers with a fixed-duration employment relationship or a temporary employment relationship and the special nature of the risks they face in certain sectors calls for special additional rules, particularly as regards the provision of information, the training and the medical surveillance of the workers concerned;

Whereas this Directive constitutes a practical step within the framework of the attainment of the social dimension of the internal market,

HAS ADOPTED THIS DIRECTIVE:

SECTION I
SCOPE AND OBJECT

Article 1
Scope

This Directive shall apply to:

1. employment relationships governed by a fixed-duration contract of employment concluded directly between the employer and the worker, where the end of the contract is established by objective conditions such as: reaching a specific date, completing a specific task or the occurence of a specific event;

2. temporary employment relationships between a temporary employment business which is the employer and the worker, where the latter is assigned to work for and under the control of an undertaking and/or establishment making use of his services.

Article 2
Object

1. The purpose of this Directive is to ensure that workers with an employment relationship as referred to in Article 1 are afforded, as regards safety and health at work, the same level of protection as that of other workers in the user undertaking and/or establishment.

2. The existence of an employment relationship as referred to in Article 1 shall not justify different treatment with respect to working conditions inasmuch as the protection of safety and health at work are involved, especially as regards access to personal protective equipment.

3.   Directive 89/391/EEC and the individual Directives within the meaning of Article 16(1) thereof shall apply in full to workers with an employment relationship as referred to in Article 1, without prejudice to more binding and/or more specific provisions set out in this Directive.

SECTION II
GENERAL PROVISIONS

Article 3
Provision of information to workers

Without prejudice to Article 10 of Directive 89/391/EEC, Member States shall take the necessary steps to ensure that:

1.   before a worker with an employment relationship as referred to in Article 1 takes up any activity, he is informed by the undertaking and/or establishment making use of his services of the risks which he faces;

2.   such information:
   — covers, in particular, any special occupational qualifications or skills or special medical surveillance required, as defined in national legislation, and
   — states clearly any increased specific risks, as defined in national legislation, that the job may entail.

Article 4
Workers' training

Without prejudice to Article 12 of Directive 89/391/EEC, Member States shall take the necessary measures to ensure that, in the cases referred to in Article 3, each worker receives sufficient training appropriate to the particular characteristics of the job, account being taken of his qualifications and experience.

Article 5
Use of workers' services and medical surveillance of workers

1.   Member States shall have the option of prohibiting workers with an employment relationship as referred to in Article 1 from being used for certain work as defined in national legislation, which would be particularly dangerous to their safety or health, and in particular for certain work which requires special medical surveillance, as defined in national legislation.

2.   Where Member States do not avail themselves of the option referred to in paragraph 1, they shall, without prejudice to Article 14 of Directive 89/391/EEC, take the necessary measures to ensure that workers with an employment relationship as referred to in Article 1 who are used for work which requires special medical surveillance, as defined in national legislation, are provided with appropriate special medical surveillance.

3.   It shall be open to Member States to provide that the appropriate special medical surveillance referred to in paragraph 2 shall extend beyond the end of the employment relationship of the worker concerned.

Article 6

Protection and prevention services

Member States shall take the necessary measures to ensure that workers, services or persons designated, in accordance with Article 7 of Directive 89/391/EEC, to carry out activities related to protection from and the prevention of occupational risks are informed of the assignment of workers with an employment relationship as referred to in Article 1, to the extent necessary for the workers, services or persons designated to be able to carry out adequately their protection and prevention activities for all the workers in the undertaking and/or establishment.

SECTION III

SPECIAL PROVISIONS

Article 7

Temporary employment relationships: information

Without prejudice to Article 3, Member States shall take the necessary steps to ensure that:

1.   before workers with an employment relationship as referred to in Article 1(2) are supplied, a user undertaking and/or establishment shall specify to the temporary employment business, *inter alia*, the occupational qualifications required and the specific features of the job to be filled;

2.   the temporary employment business shall bring all these facts to the attention of the workers concerned.

Member States may provide that the details to be given by the user undertaking and/or establishment to the temporary employment business in accordance with point 1 of the first subparagraph shall appear in a contract of assignment.

Article 8

Temporary employment relationships: responsibility

Member States shall take the necessary steps to ensure that:

1.   without prejudice to the responsibility of the temporary employment business as laid down in national legislation, the user undertaking and/or establishment is/are responsible, for the duration of the assignment, for the conditions governing performance of the work;

2.   for the application of point 1, the conditions governing the performance of the work shall be limited to those connected with safety, hygiene and health at work.

SECTION IV
MISCELLANEOUS PROVISIONS

Article 9

More favourable provisions

This Directive shall be without prejudice to existing or future national or Community provisions which are more favourable to the safety and health protection of workers with an employment relationship as referred to in Article 1.

Article 10

Final provisions

1.   Member States shall bring into force the laws, regulations and administrative provisions necessary to comply with this Directive by 31 December 1992 at the latest. They shall forthwith inform the Commission thereof.

When Member States adopt these measures, the latter shall contain a reference to this Directive or shall be accompanied by such reference on the occasion of their official publication. The methods of making such a reference shall be laid down by the Member States.

2.   Member States shall forward to the Commission the texts of the provisions of national law which they have already adopted or adopt in the field covered by this Directive.

3.   Member States shall report to the Commission every five years on the practical implementation of this Directive, setting out the points of view of workers and employers.

The Commission shall bring the report to the attention of the European Parliament, the Council, the Economic and Social Committee and the Advisory Committee on Safety, Hygiene and Health Protection at Work.

4.   The Commission shall submit to the European Parliament, the Council and the Economic and Social Committee a regular report on the implementation of this Directive, due account being taken of paragraphs 1, 2 and 3.

Article 11

This Directive is addressed to the Member States.

Done at Luxembourg, 25 June 1991

For the Council
The President
J.-C. JUNCKER

THE CONTAINED USE OF GENETICALLY MODIFIED ORGANISMS DIRECTIVE

General note. This Directive was implemented in the UK by the Genetically Modified Organisms (Contained Use) Regulations (S.I. 1992 No. 3217), see page 1072.

COUNCIL DIRECTIVE

of 23 April 1990

on the contained use of genetically modified micro-organisms

(90/219/EEC)

THE COUNCIL OF THE EUROPEAN COMMUNITIES,

Having regard to the Treaty establishing the European Economic Community, and in particular Article 130s thereof,

Having regard to the proposal from the Commission,

Having regard to the opinion of the European Parliament,

Having regard to the opinion of the Economic and Social Committee,

Whereas, under the Treaty, action by the Community relating to the environment shall be based on the principle that preventive action shall be taken and shall have as its objective to preserve, protect and improve the environment and to protect human health;

Whereas the Council Resolution of 19 October 1987 concerning the Fourth Environmental Action Programme of the European Communities declares that measures concerning the evaluation and best use of biotechnology with regard to the environment are a priority area on which Community action should concentrate;

Whereas the development of biotechnology is such as to contribute to the economic expansion of the Member States; whereas this implies that genetically modified micro-organisms will be used in operations of various types and scale;

Whereas the contained use of genetically modified micro-organisms should be carried out in such way as to limit their possible negative consequences for human health and the environment, due attention being given to the prevention of accidents and the control of wastes;

Whereas micro-organisms, if released in the environment in one Member State in the course of their contained use, may reproduce and spread, crossing national frontiers and thereby affecting other Member States;

Whereas, in order to bring about the safe development of biotechnology throughout the Community, it is necessary to establish common measures for the evaluation and reduction of the potential risks arising in the course of all operations involving the contained use of genetically modified micro-organisms and to set appropriate conditions of use;

Whereas the precise nature and scale of risks associated with genetically modified micro-organisms are not yet fully known and the risk involved must be assessed case by case; whereas, to evaluate risk for human health and the environment, it is necessary to lay down requirements for risk assessment;

Whereas genetically modified micro-organisms should be classified in relation to the risks they present; whereas criteria should be provided for this purpose; whereas particular attention should be given to operations using the more hazardous genetically modified micro-organisms;

Whereas appropriate containment measures should be applied at the various stages of an operation to control emissions and to prevent accidents;

Whereas any person, before undertaking for the first time the contained use of a genetically modified micro-organism in a particular installation, should forward to the competent authority a notification so that the authority may satisfy itself that the proposed installation is appropriate to carry out the activity in a manner that does not present a hazard to human health and the environment;

Whereas it is also necessary to establish appropriate procedures for the case-by-case notification of specific operations involving the contained use of genetically modified micro-organisms, taking account of the degree of risk involved;

Whereas, in the case of operations involving high risk, the consent of the competent authority should be given;

Whereas it may be considered appropriate to consult the public on the contained use of genetically modified micro-organisms;

Whereas appropriate measures should be taken to inform any person liable to be affected by an accident on all matters relating to safety;

Whereas emergency plans should be established to deal effectively with accidents;

Whereas, if an accident occurs, the user should immediately inform the competent authority and communicate the information necessary for assessing the impact of that accident and for taking the appropriate action;

Whereas it is appropriate for the Commission, in consultation with the Member States, to establish a procedure for the exchange of information on accidents and for the Commission to set up a register of such accidents;

Whereas the contained use of genetically modified micro-organisms throughout the Community should be monitored and to this end Member States should supply certain information to the Commission;

Whereas a committee should be set up to assist the Commission on matters relating to the implementation of this Directive and to its adaptation to technical progress,

HAS ADOPTED THIS DIRECTIVE:

Article 1

This Directive lays down common measures for the contained use of genetically modified micro-organisms with a view to protecting human health and the environment.

Article 2

For the purposes of this Directive:

(a) "micro-organism" shall mean any microbiological entity, cellular or non-cellular, capable of replication or of transferring genetic material;
(b) "genetically modified micro-organism" shall mean a micro-organism in which the genetic material has been altered in a way that does not occur naturally by mating and/or natural recombination.

Within the terms of this definition:

(i) genetic modification occurs at least through the use of the techniques listed in Annex IA, Part 1;
(ii) the techniques listed in Annex IA, Part 2, are not considered to result in genetic modification;

(c) "contained use" shall mean any operation in which micro-organisms are genetically modified or in which such genetically modified micro-organisms are cultured, stored, used, transported, destroyed or disposed of and for which physical barriers, or a combination of physical barriers together with chemical and/or biological barriers, are used to limit their contact with the general population and the environment;
(d) Type A operation shall mean any operation used for teaching, research, development, or non-industrial or non-commercial purposes and which is of a small scale (e.g. 10 litres culture volume or less);
(e) Type B operation shall mean any operation other than a Type A operation;
(f) "accident" shall mean any incident involving a significant and unintended release of genetically modified micro-organisms in the course of their contained use which could present an immediate or delayed hazard to human health or the environment;
(g) "user" shall mean any natural or legal person responsible for the contained used of genetically modified micro-organisms;
(h) "notification" shall mean the presentation of documents containing the requisite information to the competent authorities of a Member State.

Article 3

This Directive shall not apply where genetic modification is obtained through the use of the techniques listed in Annex IB.

Article 4

1.   For the purposes of this Directive, genetically modified micro-organisms shall be classified as follows:

Group I: those satisfying the criteria of Annex II;
Group II: those other than in Group I.

2.   For Type A operations, some of the criteria in Annex II may not be applicable in determining the classification of a particular genetically modified micro-organism. In such a case, the classification shall be provisional and the competent authority shall ensure that relevant criteria are used with the aim of obtaining equivalence as far as possible.

3.   Before this Directive is implemented, the Commission shall draw up guidelines for classification under the procedures of Article 21.

Article 5

Articles 7 to 12 shall not apply to the transport of genetically modified micro-organisms by road, rail, inland waterway, sea or air. This Directive shall not apply to the storage, transport, destruction or disposal of genetically modified micro-organisms which have been placed on the market under Community legislation, which includes a specific risk assessment similar to that provided in this Directive.

Article 6

1.   Member States shall ensure that all appropriate measures are taken to avoid adverse effects on human health and the environment which might arise from the contained use of genetically modified micro-organisms.

2.   To this end, the user shall carry out a prior assessment of the contained uses as regards the risks to human health and the environment that they may incur.

3.   In making such an assessment the user shall, in particular, take due account of the parameters set out in Annex III, as far as they are relevant, for any genetically modified micro-organisms he is proposing to use.

4.   A record of this assessment shall be kept by the user and made available in summary form to the competent authority as part of the notification under Articles 8, 9 and 10 or upon request.

Article 7

1.   For genetically modified micro-organisms in Group I, principles of good microbiological practice, and the following principles of good occupational safety and hygiene, shall apply:

  (i) to keep workplace and environmental exposure to any physical, chemical or biological agent to the lowest practicable level;
 (ii) to exercise engineering control measures at source and to supplement these with appropriate personal protective clothing and equipment when necessary;
(iii) to test adequately and maintain control measures and equipment;
 (iv) to test, when necessary, for the presence of viable process organisms outside the primary physical containment;
  (v) to provide training of personnel;
 (vi) to establish biological safety committees or subcommittees as required;
(vii) to formulate and implement local codes of practice for the safety of personnel.

2.   In addition to these principles, the containment measures set out in Annex IV shall be applied, as appropriate, to contained uses of genetically modified micro-organisms in Group II so as to ensure a high level of safety.

3.   The containment measures applied shall be periodically reviewed by the user to take into account new scientific or technical knowledge relative to risk management and treatment and disposal of wastes.

Article 8

When a particular installation is to be used for the first time for operations involving the contained use of genetically modified micro-organisms, the user shall be required to submit to the competent authorities, before commencing such use, a notification containing at least the information listed in Annex VA.

A separate notification shall be made for first use of genetically modified micro-organisms in Group I and Group II respectively.

Article 9

1.   Users of genetically modified micro-organisms classified in Group I in Type A operations shall be required to keep records of the work carried out which shall be made available to the competent authority on request.

2.   Users of genetically modified micro-organisms classified in Group I in Type B operations shall, before commencing the contained use, be required to submit to the competent authorities a notification containing the information listed in Annex VB.

Article 10

1.   Users of genetically modified micro-organisms classified in Group II in Type A operations shall, before commencing the contained use, be required to submit to the competent authorities a notification containing the information listed in Annex VC.

2.   Users of genetically modified micro-organisms classified in Group II in Type B operations shall, before commencing the contained use, be required to submit to the competent authorities a notification containing:

— information on the genetically modified micro-organism(s),
— information on personnel and training,
— information on the installation,
— information on waste management,
— information on accident prevention and emergency response plans,
— the assessment of the risks to human health and the environment referred
  to in Article 6,

the details of which are listed in Annex VD.

Article 11

1.   Member States shall designate the authority or authorities competent to implement the measures which they adopt in application of this Directive and to receive and acknowledge the notifications referred to in Article 8, Article 9(2) and Article 10.

2.   The competent authorities shall examine the conformity of the notifications with the requirements of this Directive, the accuracy and completeness of the information given, the correctness of the classification and, where appropriate, the adequacy of the waste management, safety, and emergency response measures.

3.   If necessary, the competent authority may:

(a)   ask the user to provide further information or to modify the conditions of the proposed contained use. In this case the proposed contained use cannot proceed until the competent authority has given its approval on the basis of the further information obtained or of the modified conditions of the contained use;
(b)   limit the time for which the contained use should be permitted or subject it to certain specific conditions.

4.   In the case of first-time use in an installation as referred to in Article 8:

— where such use involves genetically modified micro-organisms in Group I, the contained use may, in the absence of any indication to the contrary from the competent authority, proceed 90 days after submission of the notification, or earlier with the agreement of the competent authority;
— where such use involves genetically modified micro-organisms in Group II, the contained use may not proceed without the consent of the competent authority. The competent authority shall communicate its decision in writing at the latest 90 days after submission of the notification.

5.   (a)   Operations notified under Article 9(2) and Article 10(1), may, in the absence of any indication to the contrary from the competent authority, proceed 60 days after submission of the notification, or earlier with the agreement of the competent authority.
     (b)   Operations notified under Article 10(2) may not proceed without the consent of the competent authority. The competent authority shall communicate its decision in writing at the latest 90 days after submission of the notification.

6.   For the purpose of calculating the periods referred to in paragraphs 4 and 5, any periods of time during which the competent authority:

— is awaiting any further information which it may have requested from the notifier in accordance with paragraph 3(a), or
— is carrying out a public inquiry or consultation in accordance with Article 13,

shall not be taken into account.

Article 12

1. If the user becomes aware of relevant new information or modifies the contained use in a way which could have significant consequences for the risks posed by the contained use, or if the category of genetically modified micro-organisms used is changed, the competent authority shall be informed as soon as possible and the notification under Article 8, 9 and 10 modified.

2. If information becomes available subsequently to the competent authority which could have significant consequences for the risks posed by the contained use, the competent authority may require the user to modify the conditions of, suspend or terminate the contained use.

Article 13

Where a Member State considers it appropriate, it may provide that groups or the public shall be consulted on any aspect of the proposed contained use.

Article 14

The competent authorities shall ensure that, where necessary, before an operation commences:

(a) an emergency plan is drawn up for the protection of human health and the environment outside the installation in the event of an accident and the emergency services are aware of the hazards and informed thereof in writing;
(b) information on safety measures and on the correct behaviour to adopt in the case of an accident is supplied in an appropriate manner, and without their having to request it, to persons liable to be affected by the accident. The information shall be repeated and updated at appropriate intervals. It shall also be made publicly available.

The Member States concerned shall at the same time make available to other Member States concerned, as a basis for all necessary consultation within the framework of their bilateral relations, the same information as that which is disseminated to their nationals.

Article 15

1. Member States shall take the necessary measures to ensure that, in the event of an accident, the user shall be required immediately to inform the competent authority specified in Article 11 and provide the following information:

— the circumstances of the accident,

— the identity and quantities of the genetically modified micro-organisms released,
— any information necessary to assess the effects of the accident on the health of the general population and the environment,
— the emergency measures taken.

2.   Where information is given under paragraph 1, the Member States shall be required to:

— ensure that any emergency, medium and long-term measures necessary are taken, and immediately alert any Member State which could be affected by the accident;
— collect, where possible, the information necessary for a full analysis of the accident and, where appropriate, make recommendations to avoid similar accidents in the future and to limit the effects thereof.

Article 16

1.   Member States shall be required to:

(a) consult with other Member States liable to be affected in the event of an accident in the drawing up and implementation of emergency plans;
(b) inform the Commission as soon as possible of any accident within the scope of this Directive, giving details of the circumstances of the accident, the identity and quantities of the genetically modified micro-organisms released, the emergency response measures employed and their effectiveness, and an analysis of the accident including recommendations to limit its effects and avoid similar accidents in the future.

2.   The Commission, in consultation with the Member States, shall establish a procedure for the exchange of information under paragraph 1. It shall also set up and keep at the disposal of the Member States a register of accidents within the scope of this Directive which have occurred, including an analysis of the causes of the accidents, experience gained and measures taken to avoid similar accidents in the future.

Article 17

Member States shall ensure that the competent authority organises inspections and other control measures to ensure user compliance with this Directive.

Article 18

1.   Member States shall send to the Commission, at the end of each year, a summary report on the contained uses notified under Article 10(2) including the description, proposed uses and risks of the genetically modified micro-organisms.

2.   Every three years, Member States shall send the Commission a summary report on their experience with this Directive, the first time being on 1 September 1992.

3.   Every three years, the Commission shall publish a summary based on the reports referred to in paragraph 2, the first time being in 1993.

4. The Commission may publish general statistical information on the implementation of this Directive and related matters, as long as it contains no information likely to cause harm to the competitive position of a user.

Article 19

1. The Commission and the competent authorities shall not divulge to third parties any confidential information notified or otherwise provided under this Directive and shall protect intellectual property rights relating to the data received.

2. The notifier may indicate the information in the notifications submitted under this Directive, the disclosure of which might harm his competitive position, that should be treated as confidential. Verifiable justification must be given in such cases.

3. The competent authority shall decide, after consultation with the notifier, which information will be kept confidential and shall inform the notifier of its decision.

4. In no case may the following information, when submitted according to Articles 8, 9 or 10, be kept confidential:

— description of the genetically modified micro-organisms, name and address of the notifier, purpose of the contained use, and location of use;
— methods and plans for monitoring of the genetically modified micro-organisms and for emergency response;
— the evaluation of foreseeable effects, in particular any pathogenic and/or ecologically disruptive effects.

5. If, for whatever reasons, the notifier withdraws the notification, the competent authority must respect the confidentiality of the information supplied.

Article 20

Amendments necessary to adapt Annexes II to V to technical progress shall be decided in accordance with the procedure defined in Article 21.

Article 21

1. The Commission shall be assisted by a committee composed of the representatives of the Member States and chaired by the representative of the Commission.

2. The representative of the Commission shall submit to the committee a draft of the measures to be taken. The committee shall deliver its opinion on the draft within a time limit which the chairman may lay down according to the urgency of the matter. The opinion shall be delivered by the majority laid down in Article 148(2) of the Treaty in the case of decisions which the Council is required to adopt on a proposal from the Commission. The votes of the representatives of the Member States within the committee shall be weighted in the manner set out in that Article. The chairman shall not vote.

3. (a) The Commission shall adopt the measures envisaged if they are in accordance with the opinion of the committee.
    (b) If the measures envisaged are not in accordance with the opinion of the committee, or if no opinion is delivered, the Commission shall, without delay, submit to the Council a proposal relating to the measures to be taken. The Council shall act by a qualified majority.

    If, on the expiry of a period of three months from the date of referral to the Council, the Council has not acted, the proposed measures shall be adopted by the Commission, save where the Council has decided against the said measures by a simple majority.

Article 22

Member States shall bring into force the laws, regulations and administrative provisions necessary to comply with this Directive not later than 23 October 1991. They shall forthwith inform the Commission thereof.

Article 23

This Directive is addressed to the Member States.

Done at Luxembourg, 23 April 1990.

For the Council
The President
A. REYNOLDS

ANNEX IA

PART 1

Techniques of genetic modification referred to in Article 2(b)(i) are, *inter alia*:

 (i) recombinant DNA techniques using vector systems as previously covered by Recommendation 82/472/EEC;
 (ii) techniques involving the direct introduction into a micro-organism of heritable material prepared outside the micro-organism including micro-injection, macro-injection and micro-encapsulation;
(iii) cell fusion or hybridisation techniques where live cells with new combinations of heritable genetic material are formed through the fusion of two or more cells by means of methods that do not occur naturally.

PART 2

Techniques referred to in Article 2(b)(ii) which are not considered to result in genetic modification, on condition they they do not involve the use of recombinant-DNA molecules or genetically modified organisms:

(1) *in vitro* fertilisation;

(2) conjugation, transduction, transformation or any other natural process;
(3) polyploidy induction.

ANNEX IB

Techniques of genetic modifications to be excluded from the Directive, on condition that they do not involve the use of genetically modified micro-organisms as recipient or parental organisms:

(1) mutagenesis;
(2) the construction and use of somatic animal hybridoma cells (e.g. for the production of monoclonal antibodies);
(3) cell fusion (including protoplast fusion) of cells from plants which can be produced by traditional breeding methods;
(4) self-cloning of non-pathogenic naturally occurring micro-organisms which fulfil the criteria of Group I for recipient micro-organisms.

ANNEX II

CRITERIA FOR CLASSIFYING GENETICALLY MODIFIED MICRO-ORGANISMS IN GROUP I

A. **Recipient or parental organism**

— non-pathogenic;
— no adventitious agents;
— proven and extended history of safe use or built-in biological barriers, which, without interfering with optimal growth in the reactor or fermentor, confer limited survivability and replicability, without adverse consequences in the environment.

B. **Vector/Insert**

— well characterised and free from known harmful sequences;
— limited in size as much as possible to the genetic sequences required to perform the intended function;
— should not increase the stability of the construct in the environment (unless that is a requirement of intended function);
— should be poorly mobilisable;
— should not transfer any resistance markers to micro-organisms not known to acquire them naturally (if such acquisition could compromise use of drugs to control disease agents).

C. **Genetically modified micro-organisms**

— non-pathogenic;
— as safe in the reactor or fermentor as recipient or parental organism, but with limited survivability and/or replicability without adverse consequences in the environment.

D. **Other genetically modified micro-organisms that could be included in Group I if they meet the conditions in C above**

—   those constructed entirely from a single prokaryotic recipient (including its indigenous plasmids and viruses) or from a signel eykaryotic recipient (including its chloroplasts, mitochondria, plasmids, but excluding viruses);
—   those that consist entirely of genetic sequences from different species that exchange these sequences by known physiological processes.

ANNEX III

SAFETY ASSESSMENT PARAMETERS TO BE TAKEN INTO ACCOUNT, AS FAR AS THEY ARE RELEVANT, IN ACCORDANCE WITH ARTICLE 6(3)

A. Characteristics of the donor, recipient or (where appropriate) parental organism(s)

B. Characteristics of the modified micro-organism

C. Health considerations

D. Environmental considerations

A. **Characteristics of the donor, recipient or (where appropriate) parental organism(s)**

—   names and designation;
—   degree of relatedness;
—   sources of the organism(s);
—   information on reproductive cycles (sexual/asexual) of the parental organism(s) or, where applicable, of the recipient micro-organism;
—   history of prior genetic manipulations;
—   stability of parental or of recipient organism in terms of relevant genetic traits;
—   nature of pathogenicity and virulence, infectivity, toxicity and vectors of disease transmission;
—   nature of indigenous vectors:
    sequence,
    frequency of mobilisation,
    specificity,
    presence of genes which confer resistance;
—   host range;
—   other potentially significant physiological traits;
—   stability of these traits;
—   natural habitat and geographical distribution. Climatic characteristics of original habitats;
—   significant involvement in environmental processes (such as nitrogen fixation or pH regulation);
—   interaction with, and effects on, other organisms in the environment (including likely competitive or symbiotic properties);
—   ability to form survival structures (such as spores or sclerotia).

B. **Characteristics of the modified micro-organism**

— the description of the modification including the method for introducing the vector-insert into the recipient organism or the method used for achieving the genetic modification involved;
— the function of the genetic manipulation and/or of the new nucleic acid;
— nature and source of the vector;
— structure and amount of any vector and/or donor nucleic acid remaining in the final construction of the modified micro-organism;
— stability of the micro-organism in terms of genetic traits;
— frequency of mobilisation of inserted vector and/or genetic transfer capability;
— rate and level of expression of the new genetic material. Method and sensitivity of measurement;
— activity of the expressed protein.

C. **Health considerations**

— toxic or allergenic effects of non-viable organisms and/or their metabolic products;
— product hazards;
— comparison of the modified micro-organism to the donor, recipient or (where appropriate) parental organism regarding pathogenicity;
— capacity for colonisation;
— if the micro-organism is pathogenic to humans who are immunocompetent:
  (a) diseases caused and mechanism of pathogenicity including invasiveness and virulence;
  (b) communicability;
  (c) infective dose;
  (d) host range, possibility of alteration;
  (e) possibility of survival outside of human host;
  (f) presence of vectors or means of dissemination;
  (g) biological stability;
  (h) antibiotic-resistance patterns;
  (i) allergenicity;
  (j) availability of appropriate therapies.

D. **Environmental considerations**

— factors affecting survival, multiplication and dissemination of the modified micro-organism in the environment;
— available techniques for detection, identification and monitoring of the modified micro-organism;
— available techniques for detecting transfer of the new genetic material to other organisms;
— known and predicted habitats of the modified micro-organism;
— description of ecosystems to which the micro-organism could be accidentally disseminated;

— anticipated mechanism and result of interaction between the modified micro-organism and the organisms or micro-organisms which might be exposed in case of release into the environment;
— known or predicted effects on plants and animals such as pathogenicity, infectivity, toxicity, virulence, vector of pathogen, allergenicity, colonisation;
— known or predicted involvement in biogeochemical processes;
— availability of methods for decontamination of the area in case of release to the environment.

ANNEX IV

CONTAINMENT MEASURES FOR MICRO-ORGANISMS IN GROUP II

The containment measures for micro-organisms from Group II shall be chosen by the user from the categories below as appropriate to the micro-organism and the operation in question in order to ensure the protection of the public health of the general population and the environment.

Type B operations shall be considered in terms of their unit operations. The characteristics of each operation will dictate the physical containment to be used at that stage. This will allow selection and design of process, plant and operating procedures best fitted to assure adequate and safe containment. Two important factors to be considered when selecting the equipment needed to implement the containment are the risk of, and the effects consequent on, equipment failure. Engineering practice may require increasingly stringent standards to reduce the risk of failure as the consequence of that failure becomes less tolerable.

Specific containment measures for Type A operations shall be established taking into account the containment categories below and bearing in mind the specific circumstances of such operations.

Specifications	Containment Categories		
	1	2	3
1. Viable micro-organisms should be contained in a system which physically separates the process from the environment (closed system)	Yes	Yes	Yes
2. Exhaust gases from the closed system should be treated so as to:	Minimise release	Prevent release	Prevent release
3. Sample collection, addition of materials to a closed system and transfer of viable micro-organisms to another closed system, should be performed so as to:	Minimise release	Prevent release	Prevent release
4. Bulk culture fluids should not be removed from the closed system unless the viable micro-organisms have been:	Inactivated by validated means	Inactivated by validated chemical or physical means	Inactivated by validated chemical or physical means

Specifications	Containment Categories		
	1	2	3
5. Seals should be designed so as to:	Minimise release	Prevent release	Prevent release
6. Closed systems should be located within a controlled area	Optional	Optional	Yes, and purpose-built
(a) Biohazard signs should be posted	Optional	Yes	Yes
(b) Access should be restricted to nominated personnel only	Optional	Yes	Yes, via airlock
(c) Personnel should wear protective clothing	Yes, work clothing	Yes	A complete change
(d) Decontamination and washing facilities should be provided for personnel	Yes	Yes	Yes
(e) Personnel should shower before leaving the controlled area	No	Optional	Yes
(f) Effluent from sinks and showers should be collected and inactivated before release	No	Optional	Yes
(g) The controlled area should be adequately ventilated to minimise air contamination	Optional	Optional	Yes
(h) The controlled areas should be maintained at an air pressure negative to atmosphere	No	Optional	Yes
(i) Input air and extract air to the controlled area should be HEPA filtered	No	Optional	Yes
(j) The controlled area should be designed to contain spillage of the entire contents of the closed system	Optional	Yes	Yes
(k) The controlled area should be sealable to permit fumigation	No	Optional	Yes
7. Effluent treatment before final discharge	Inactivated by validated means	Inactivated by validated chemical or physical means	Inactivated by validated chemical means

ANNEX V

PART A

Information required for the notification referred to in Article 8:

— name of person(s) responsible for carrying out the contained use including those responsible for supervision, monitoring and safety and information on their training and qualifications;
— address of installation and grid reference; description of the sections of the installation;

— a description of the nature of the work which will be undertaken and in particular the classification of the micro-organism(s) to be used (Group I or Group II) and the likely scale of the operation;
— a summary of the risk assessment referred to in Article 6(2).

PART B

Information required for the notification referred to in Article 9(2):

— the date of submission of the notification referred to in Article 8;
— the parental micro-organism(s) used or, where applicable, the host-vector system(s) used;
— the source(s) and the intended function(s) of the genetic material(s) involved in the manipulation(s);
— identity and characteristics of the genetically modified micro-organism;
— the purpose of the contained use including the expected results;
— the culture volumes to be used;
— a summary of the risk assessment referred to in Article 6(2).

PART C

Information required for the notification referred to in Article 10(1):

— the information required in Part B;
— description of the sections of the installation and the methods for handling the micro-organisms;
— description of the predominant meteorological conditions and of the potential sources of danger arising from the location of the installation;
— description of the protective and supervisory measures to be applied throughout the duration of the contained use;
— the containment category allocated specifying waste treatment provisions and the safety precautions to be adopted.

PART D

Information required for the notification referred to in Article 10(2):

If it is not technically possible, or if it does not appear necessary to give the information specified below, the reasons shall be stated. The level of detail in response of each subset of considerations is likely to vary according to the nature and the scale of the proposed contained use. In the case of information already submitted to the competent authority under the requirements of this Directive, reference can be made to this information by the user:

(a) the date of submission of the notification in Article 8 and the name of the responsible person(s);
(b) information about the genetically modified micro-organism(s):

  — the identity and characteristics of the genetically modified micro-organism(s),
  — the purpose of the contained use or the nature of the product,
  — the host-vector system to be used (where applicable),
  — the culture volumes to be used,
  — behaviour and characteristics of the micro-organism(s) in the case of changes in the conditions of containment or of release to the environment,

— overview of the potential hazards associated with the release of the
micro-organism(s) to the environment,
— substances which are or may be produced in the course of the use of the
micro-organism(s) other than the intended product;

(c) information about personnel:

— the maximum number of persons working in the installation and the
number of persons who work directly with the micro-organism(s);

(d) information about the installation:

— the activity in which the micro-organism(s) is to be used,
— the technological processes used,
— a description of the sections of the installation,
— the predominant meteorological conditions, and specific hazards arising from the location of the installation;

(e) information about waste management:

— types, quantities, and potential hazards of wastes arising from the use of
the micro-organism(s),
— waste management techniques used, including recovery of liquid or
solid wastes and inactivation methods,
— ultimate form and destination of inactivated wastes;

(f) information about accident prevention and emergency response plans:

— the sources of hazards and conditions under which accidents might
occur,
— the preventive measures applied such as safety equipment, alarm
systems, containment methods and procedures and available
resources,
— a description of information provided to workers,
— the information necessary for the competent authority to enable them
to draw up or establish the necessary emergency response plans for use
outside the installation in accordance with Article 14;

(g) a comprehensive assessment (referred to in Article 6(2)) of the risks to
human health and the environment which might arise from the proposed
contained use;

(h) all other information required under Parts B and C if it is not already
specified above.

THE ASBESTOS DIRECTIVE

COUNCIL DIRECTIVE

of 19 September 1983

on the protection of workers from the risks related to exposure to asbestos at work (second individual Directive within the meaning of Article 8 of Directive 80/1107/EEC)

(83/477/EEC)

THE COUNCIL OF THE EUROPEAN COMMUNITIES,

Having regard to the Treaty establishing the European Economic Community, and in particular Article 100 thereof,

Having regard to the proposal from the Commission,

Having regard to the opinion of the European Parliament,

Having regard to the opinion of the Economic and Social Committee,

Whereas the Council resolution of 29 June 1978 on an action programme of the European Communities on safety and health at work provides for the establishment of specific harmonised procedures regarding the protection of workers with respect to asbestos;

Whereas Council Directive 80/1107/EEC of 27 November 1980 on the protection of workers from the risks related to exposure to chemical, physical and biological agents at work laid down certain provisions which have to be taken into account for this protection; whereas that Directive provides for the laying down in individual Directives of limit values and specific requirements for those agents listed in Annex I, which include asbestos;

Whereas asbestos is a harmful agent found in a large number of circumstances at work; whereas many workers are therefore exposed to a potential health risk; whereas crocidolite is considered to be a particularly dangerous type of asbestos;

Whereas, although current scientific knowledge is not such that a level can be established below which risks to health cease to exist, a reduction in exposure to asbestos will nonetheless reduce the risk of developing asbestos-related disease; whereas this Directive includes minimum requirements which will be reviewed on the basis of experience acquired and of developments in technology in this area;

Whereas optical microscopy, although it does not allow a counting of the smallest fibres detrimental to health, is the most currently used method for the regular measuring of asbestos;

Whereas, therefore, preventive measures for the protection of the health of workers exposed to asbestos and the commitment envisaged for Member States with regard to the surveillance of their health are important,

HAS ADOPTED THIS DIRECTIVE:

Article 1

1.   This Directive, which is the second individual Directive within the meaning of Article 8 of Directive 80/1107/EEC, has as its aim the protection of workers against risks to their health, including the prevention of such risks, arising or likely to arise from exposure to asbestos at work. It lays down limit values and other specific requirements.

2.   This Decision shall not apply to:

— sea transport,
— air transport.

3.   This Directive shall not prejudice the right of Member States to apply or introduce laws, regulations or administrative provisions ensuring greater protection for workers, in particular as regards the replacement of asbestos by less-dangerous substitutes.

Article 2

For the purposes of this Directive, 'asbestos' means the following fibrous silicates:

— Actinolite, CAS No 77536–66–4,
— Asbestos grünerite (amosite) CAS No 12172–73–5,
— Anthophyllite, CAS No 77536–67–5,
— Chrysotile, CAS No 12001–29–5,
— Crocidolite, CAS No 12001–28–4,
— Tremolite, CAS No 77536–68–6.

Article 3

1.   This Directive shall apply to activities in which workers are or may be exposed in the course of their work to dust arising from asbestos or materials containing asbestos.

2.   In the case of any activity likely to involve a risk of exposure to dust arising from asbestos or materials containing asbestos, this risk must be assessed in such a way as to determine the nature and degree of the workers' exposure to dust arising from asbestos or materials containing asbestos.

3.   If the assessment referred to in paragraph 2 shows that the concentration of asbestos fibres in the air at the place of work in the absence of any individual protective equipment is, at the option of the Member States, at a level as measured or calculated in relation to an eight-hour reference period,

— lower than 0,25 fibre per cm^3 and/or
— lower than a cumulative dose of 15,00 fibre-days per cm^3 over three months,

Articles 4, 7, 13, 14(2), 15 and 16 shall not apply.

4.   The assessment provided for in paragraph 2 shall be the subject of consultation with the workers and/or their representatives within the undertaking or establishment and shall be revised where there is reason to believe that it is incorrect or there is a material change in the work.

Article 4

Subject to Article 3(3), the following measures shall be taken:

1.   The activities referred to in Article 3(1) must be covered by a notification system administered by the responsible authority of the Member State.

2.   The notification must be submitted by the employer to the responsible authority of the Member State, in accordance with national laws, regulations and administrative provisions. This notification must include at least a brief description of:
— the types and quantities of asbestos used,
— the activities and processes involved,
— the products manufactured.

3.   Workers and/or their representatives in undertakings or establishments shall have access to the documents which are the subject of notification concerning their own undertaking or establishment in accordance with national laws.

4.   Each time an important change occurs in the use of asbestos or of materials containing asbestos, a new notification must be submitted.

Article 5

The application of asbestos by means of the spraying process must be prohibited.

Article 6

For all activities referred to in Article 3(1), the exposure of workers to dust arising from asbestos or materials containing asbestos at the place of work must be reduced to as low a level as is reasonably practicable and in any case below the limit values laid down in Article 8, in particular through the following measures if appropriate:

1.   The quantity of asbestos used in each case must be limited to the minimum quantity which is reasonably practicable.

2.   The number of workers exposed or likely to be exposed to dust arising from asbestos or materials containing asbestos must be limited to the lowest possible figure.

3.   Work processes must, in principle, be so designed as to avoid the release of asbestos dust into the air.

If this is not reasonably practicable, the dust should be eliminated as near as possible to the point where it is released.

4.   All buildings and/or plant and equipment involved in the processing or treatment of asbestos must be capable of being regularly and effectively cleaned and maintained.

5.   Asbestos as a raw material must be stored and transported in suitable sealed packing.

6. Waste must be collected and removed from the place of work as soon as possible in suitable sealed packing with labels indicating that it contains asbestos. This measure shall not apply to mining activities.

The waste referred to in the preceding paragraph shall then be dealt with in accordance with Council Directive 78/319/EEC of 20 March 1978 on toxic and dangerous waste.

Article 7

Subject to Article 3(3), the following measures shall be taken:

1.   In order to ensure compliance with the limit values laid down in Article 8, the measurement of asbestos in the air at the place of work shall be carried out in accordance with the reference method described in Annex I or any other method giving equivalent results. Such measurement must be planned and carried out regularly, with sampling being representative of the personal exposure of the worker to dust arising from asbestos or materials containing asbestos.

For the purposes of measuring asbestos in the air, as referred to in the preceding paragraph, only fibres with a length of more than five micrometres and a length/breadth ratio greater than 3:1 shall be taken into consideration.

The Council, acting on a proposal from the Commission, and taking account in particular of progress made in scientific knowledge and technology and of experience gained in the application of this Directive, shall re-examine the provisions of the first sentence of paragraph 1 within five years following the adoption of this Directive, with a view to establishing a single method for measurement of asbestos-in-air concentrations at Community level.

2.   Sampling shall be carried out after consulting the workers and/or their representatives in undertakings or establishments.

3.   Sampling shall be carried out by suitably qualified personnel. The samples taken shall be subsequently analysed in laboratories equipped to analyse them and qualified to apply the necessary identification techniques.

4.   The amount of asbestos in the air shall be measured as a general rule at least every three months and, in any case, whenever a technical change is

introduced. The frequency of measurements may, however, be reduced in the circumstances specified in paragraph 5.

5.   The frequency of measurements may be reduced to once a year where:
— there is no substantial change in conditions at the place of work, and
— the results of the two preceding measurements have not exeeded half the limit values fixed in Article 8.

Where groups of workers are performing identical or similar tasks at the same place and are thus being exposed to the same health risk, sampling may be carried out on a group basis.

6.   The duration of sampling must be such that representative exposure can be established for an eight-hour reference period (one shift) by means of measurements or time-weighted calculations. The duration of the various sampling processes shall be determined also on the basis of point 6 of Annex I.

Article 8

The following limit values shall be applied:

(a)   concentration of asbestos fibres other than crocidolite in the air at the place of work:
1,00 fibres per cm³ measured or calculated in relation to an eight-hour reference period;
(b)   concentration of crocidolite fibres in the air at the place of work:
0,50 fibres per cm³ measured or calculated in relation to an eight-hour reference period;
(c)   concentration of asbestos fibres in the air at the place of work in the case of mixtures of crocidolite and other asbestos fibres:
the limit value is at a level calculated on the basis of the limit values laid down in (a) and (b), taking into account the proportions of crocidolite and other asbestos types in the mixture.

Article 9

The Council, acting on a proposal from the Commission, shall, taking into account, in particular, progress made in scientific knowledge and technology and in the light of experience gained in applying this Directive, review the provisions laid down in Article 3(3) and in Article 8 before 1 January 1990.

Article 10

1.   Where the limit values laid down in Article 8 are exceeded, the reasons for the limits being exceeded must be identified and appropriate measures to remedy the situation must be taken as soon as possible.

Work may not be continued in the affected area until adequate measures have been taken for the protection of the workers concerned.

2.   In order to check the effectiveness of the measures mentioned in the first subparagraph of paragraph 1, a further determination of the asbestos-in-air concentrations shall be carried out immediately.

3.   Where exposure cannot reasonably be reduced by other means and where the wearing of individual respiratory protective equipment proves necessary, this may not be permanent and shall be kept to the strict minimum necessary for each worker.

Article 11

1.   In the case of certain activities in respect of which it is foreseeable that the limit values laid down in Article 8 will be exceeded and in respect of which technical preventive measures for limiting asbestos-in-air concentrations are not reasonably practicable, the employer shall determine the measures intended to ensure protection of the workers while they are engaged in such activities, in particular the following:

(a)   workers shall be issued with suitable respiratory equipment and other personal protective equipment, which must be worn; and
(b)   warning signs shall be put up indicating that it is foreseeable that the limit values laid down in Article 8 will be exceeded.

2.   The workers and/or their representatives in the undertaking or establishment shall be consulted on these measures before the activities concerned are carried out.

Article 12

1.   A plan of work shall be drawn up before demolition work or work on removing asbestos and/or asbestos-containing products from buildings, structures, plant or installations or from ships is started.

2.   The plan referred to in paragraph 1 must prescribe the measures necessary to ensure the safety and health of workers at the place of work.

The plan must in particular specify that:

— as far as is reasonably practicable, asbestos and/or asbestos-containing products are removed before demolition techniques are applied,
— the personal protective equipment referred to in Article 11(1)(a) is provided, where necessary.

Article 13

1.   In the case of all activities referred to in Article 3(1), and subject to Article 3(3), appropriate measures shall be taken to ensure that:

(a)   the places in which the above activities take place shall:
      (i)   be clearly demarcated and indicated by warning signs;
      (ii) not be accessible to workers other than those who by reason of their work or duties are required to enter them;

    (iii) constitute areas where there should be no smoking;
(b) areas are set aside where workers can eat and drink without risking contamination by asbestos dust;
(c)   (i) workers are provided with appropriate working or protective clothing;
    (ii) this working or protective clothing remains within the undertaking. It may, however, be laundered in establishments outside the undertaking which are equipped for this sort of work if the undertaking does not carry out the cleaning itself; in that event the clothing shall be transported in closed containers;
   (iii) separate storage places are provided for working or protective clothing and for street clothes;
   (iv) workers are provided with appropriate and adequate washing and toilet facilities, including showers in the case of dusty operations;
    (v) protective equipment shall be placed in a well-defined place and shall be checked and cleaned after each use; appropriate measures shall be taken to repair or replace defective equipment before further use.

2.   Workers may not be charged with the cost of measures taken pursuant to paragraph 1.

Article 14

1.   In the case of all activities referred to in Article 3(1), appropriate measures shall be taken to ensure that workers and their representatives in the undertaking or establishment receive adequate information concerning:

— the potential risks to health from exposure to dust arising from asbestos or materials containing asbestos,
— the existence of statutory limit values and the need for the atmosphere to be monitored,
— hygiene requirements, including the need to refrain from smoking,
— the precautions to be taken as regards the wearing and use of protective equipment and clothing,
— special precautions designed to minimise exposure to asbestos.

2.   In addition to the measures referred to in paragraph 1, and subject to Article 3(3), appropriate measures shall be taken to ensure that:

(a) workers and/or their representatives in the undertaking or establishment have access to the results of asbestos-in-air concentration measurements and can be given explanations of the significance of those results;
(b) if the results exceed the limit values laid down in Article 8 the workers concerned and their representatives in the undertaking or establishment are informed as quickly as possible of the fact and the reason for it and the workers and/or their representatives in the undertaking or establishment are consulted on the measures to be taken or, in an emergency, are informed of the measures which have been taken.

Article 15

Subject to Article 3(3) the following measures shall be taken:

1. An assessment of each worker's state of health must be available prior to the beginning of exposure to dust arising from asbestos or materials containing asbestos at the place of work.

This assessment must include a specific examination of the chest. Annex II gives practical recommendations to which the Member States may refer for the clinical surveillance of workers; these recommendations shall be adapted to technical progress in accordance with the procedure set out in Article 10 of Directive 80/1107/EEC.

A new assessment must be available at least once every three years for as long as exposure continues.

An individual health record shall be established in accordance with national laws and practices for each worker referred to in the first subparagraph.

2. Following the clinical surveillance referred to in point 1, the doctor or authority responsible for the medical surveillance of the workers should, in accordance with national laws, advise on or determine any individual protective or preventive measures to be taken; these may include, where appropriate, the withdrawal of the worker concerned from all exposure to asbestos.

3. Information and advice must be given to workers regarding any assessment of their health which they may undergo following the end of exposure.

4. The worker concerned or the employer may request a review of the assessments referred to in point 2, in accordance with national laws.

Article 16

Subject to Article 3(3) the following measures shall be taken:

1. The employer must enter the workers responsible for carrying out the activities referred to in Article 3(1) in a register, indicating the nature and duration of the activity and the exposure to which they have been subjected. The doctor and/or the authority responsible for medical surveillance shall have access to this register. Each worker shall have access to the results in the register which relate to him personally. The workers and/or their representatives shall have access to anonymous, collective information in the register.

2. The register referred to in point 1 and the medical records referred to in point 1 of Article 15 shall be kept for at least 30 years following the end of exposure, in accordance with national laws.

Article 17

Member States shall keep a register of recognised cases of asbestosis and mesothelioma.

Article 18

1.   Member States shall adopt the laws, regulations and administrative provisions necessary to comply with this Directive before 1 January 1987. They shall forthwith inform the Commission thereof. The date 1 January 1987 is, however, postponed until 1 January 1990 in the case of asbestos-mining activities.

2.   Member States shall communicate to the Commission the provisions of national law which they adopt in the field covered by this Directive.

Article 19

This Directive is addressed to the Member States.

Done at Brussels, 19 September 1983.

For the Council
The President
G. VARFIS

_____

ANNEX I

REFERENCE METHOD REFERRED TO IN ARTICLE 7(1) FOR THE MEASUREMENT OF ASBESTOS IN AIR AT THE PLACE OF WORK

1.   Samples shall be taken within the individual worker's breathing zone: i.e. within a hemisphere of 300 mm radius extending in front of the face and measured from the mid-point of a line joining the ears.

2.   Membrane filters (mixed esters of cellulose or cellulose nitrate) of pore size 0,8 to 1,2 micrometres with printed squares and a diameter of 25 mm shall be used.

3.   An open-faced filter holder fitted with a cylindrical cowl extending between 33 and 44 mm in front of the filter exposing a circular area of at least 20 mm in diameter shall be used. In use, the cowl shall point downwards.

4.   A portable battery-operated pump carried on the worker's belt or in a pocket shall be used. The flow shall be smooth and the rate initially set at 1,0 litres per minute ± 5%. The flow rate shall be maintained within ± 10% of the initial rate during the sampling period.

5.   The sampling time shall be measured to within a tolerance of 2%.

6.   The optimal fibre-loading on filters shall be within the range 100 to 400 fibres/mm^2.

7.   In order of preference, the whole filter, or a section of the filter, shall be placed on a microscope slide, made transparent using the acetone-triacetin method, and covered with a glass coverslip.

8. A binocular microscope shall be used for counting and shall have the following features:

— Koehler illumination,
— its substage assembly shall incorporate an Abbe or achromatic phase-contrast condenser in a centring focusing mount. The phase-contrast centring adjustment shall be independent of the condenser centring mechanism,
— a 40 times bar-focal positive phase-contrast achromatic objective with a numerical aperture of 0,65 to 0,70 and phase ring absorption within the range 65 to 85%,
— 12,5 times compensating eyepieces; at least one eyepiece must permit the insertion of a graticule and be of the focusing type,
— a Walton-Beckett circular eyepiece graticule with an apparent diameter in the object plane of 100 micrometres ± 2 micrometres, when using the specified objective and eyepiece, checked against a stage micrometer.

9. The microscope shall be set up according to the manufacturer's instructions, and the detection limit checked using a 'phase-contrast test slide'. Up to code 5 on the AIA test slides or up to block 5 on the HSE/NPL mark 2 test slide must be visible when used in the way specified by the manufacturer. This procedure shall be carried out at the beginning of the day of use.

10. Samples shall be counted in accordance with the following rules:

— a countable fibre is any fibre referred to in the second subparagraph of point 1 of Article 7 which does not touch a particle with a maximum diameter greater than three micrometers,
— any countable fibre with both ends within the graticule area shall be counted as one fibre; any fibre with only one end within the area shall count as half,
— graticule areas for counting shall be chosen at random within the exposed area of the filter,
— an agglomerate of fibres which at one or more points on its length appears solid and undivided but at other points is divided into separate strands (a split fibre) is counted as a single fibre if it conforms with the description in the second subparagraph of point 1 of Article 7 and indent 1 of this paragraph, the diameter measured being that of the undivided part, not that of the split part,
— in any other agglomerate of fibres in which individual fibres touch or cross each other (a bundle), the fibres shall be counted individually if they can be distinguished sufficiently to determine that they conform with the description in the second subparagraph of point 1 of Article 7 and indent 1 of this paragraph. If no individual fibres meeting the definition can be distinguished, the bundle is considered to be a countable fibre if, taken as a whole, it conforms with the description in the second subparagraph of point 1 of Article 7 and indent 1 of this paragraph,
— if more than one-eighth of a graticule area is covered by an agglomerate of fibres and/or particles, the graticule area must be rejected and another counted,
— 100 fibres shall be counted, which will enable a minimum of 20 graticule areas to be examined, or 100 graticule areas shall be examined.

11. The mean number of fibres per graticule is calculated by dividing the number of fibres counted by the number of graticule areas examined. The

effect on the count of marks on the filter and contamination shall be kept below three fibres/100 graticule areas and shall be assessed using blank filters.

Concentration in air = (number per graticule area × exposed area of filter)/ (graticule area × volume of air collected).

ANNEX II

PRACTICAL RECOMMENDATIONS FOR THE CLINICAL ASSESSMENT OF WORKERS, AS REFERRED TO IN ARTICLE 15(1)

1.   Current knowledge indicates that exposure to free asbestos fibres can give rise to the following diseases:

— asbestosis,
— mesothelioma,
— bronchial carcinoma,
— gastro-intestinal carcinoma.

2.   The doctor and/or authority responsible for the medical surveillance of workers exposed to asbestos must be familiar with the exposure conditions or circumstances of each worker.

3.   Clinical surveillance of workers should be carried out in accordance with the principles and practices of occupational medicine; it should include at least the following measures:

— keeping records of a worker's medical and occupational history,
— a personal interview,
— a clinical examination of the chest,
— a respiratory function examination.

Further examinations, including a standard format radiograph of the chest and laboratory tests such as a sputum cytology test, are desirable. These examinations should be decided upon for each worker when he is the subject of medical surveillance, in the light of the most recent knowledge available to occupational medicine.

THE PRINCIPAL LEGISLATION

SUMMARY

INTRODUCTION TO THE HEALTH AND SAFETY AT WORK ETC. ACT 1974

This Act is largely based upon the Report of the Robens Committee on Safety and Health at Work (1972 Cmnd. 5034). Part III (ss. 61–76—Building Regulations and Amendment of the Building (Scotland) Act 1959) is not printed in this book. The expressed objects of Part I of the Act are (s. 1) to secure the health, safety and welfare of persons at work; to protect persons other than persons at work against risks to health or safety arising out of or in connection with the activities of persons at work; to control the keeping and use of explosive or highly flammable or otherwise dangerous substances and generally to prevent the unlawful acquisition, possession and use of such substances; and to control the emission into the atmosphere of noxious or offensive substances from prescribed premises. These objects are to be accomplished by the progressive replacement of existing statutory provisions, the multiplicity of which was criticised by the Robens Committee, by a system of regulations and approved codes of practice operating in combination with the other provisions of Part I of the Act and designed to maintain or improve the standards of health, safety and welfare established under the existing legislation. A fuller description of the Act and the Robens Report will be found in the HISTORICAL INTRODUCTION.

HEALTH AND SAFETY AT WORK ETC. ACT 1974

(1974 c. 37)

ARRANGEMENT OF SECTIONS

PART I

HEALTH, SAFETY AND WELFARE IN CONNECTION WITH WORK, AND CONTROL OF
DANGEROUS SUBSTANCES AND CERTAIN EMISSIONS INTO THE ATMOSPHERE

PART II
THE EMPLOYMENT MEDICAL ADVISORY SERVICE

PART III
BUILDING REGULATIONS AND AMENDMENT OF
BUILDING (SCOTLAND) ACT 1959
61–76. [*not printed in this book*].

PART IV
MISCELLANEOUS AND GENERAL

SCHEDULES

An Act to make further provision for securing the health, safety and welfare of persons at work, for protecting others against risks to health or safety in connection with the activities of persons at work, for controlling the keeping and use and preventing the unlawful acquisition, possession and use of dangerous substances, and for controlling certain emissions into the atmosphere; to make further provision with respect to the employment medical advisory service; to amend the law relating to building regulations, and the Building (Scotland) Act 1959; and for connected purposes.

[31st July 1974]

BE IT ENACTED by the Queen's most Excellent Majesty, by and with the advice and consent of the Lords, Spiritual and Temporal, and Commons, in this present Parliament assembled, and by the authority of the same, as follows:

PART I

HEALTH, SAFETY AND WELFARE IN CONNECTION WITH WORK, AND CONTROL OF
DANGEROUS SUBSTANCES AND CERTAIN EMISSIONS INTO THE ATMOSPHERE

Preliminary

1.—(1)   The provisions of this Part *(a)* shall have effect with a view to—

(a)   securing the health, safety and welfare of persons at work *(b)*;

(b)   protecting persons other than persons at work against risk to health or safety arising out of or in connection with the activities of persons at work *(c)*;

(c)   controlling the keeping and use of explosive or highly flammable or otherwise dangerous substances *(d)*, and generally preventing the unlawful acquisition, possession and use of such substances; and

(d)   controlling the emission into the atmostphere of noxious or offensive substances from premises *(e)* of any class prescribed *(f)* for the purposes of this paragraph.

(2)   The provisions of this Part *(a)* relating to the making of health and safety regulations *(g)* and the preparation and approval of codes of practice *(h)* shall in particular have effect with a view to enabling the enactments specified in the third column of Schedule 1 and the regulations, orders and other instruments in force under those enactments to be progressively replaced by a system of regulations and approved codes of practice operating in combination with the other provisions of this Part and designed to maintain or improve the standards of health, safety and welfare established by or under those enactments.

(3)   For the purposes of this Part *(a)* risks arising out of or in connection with the activities of persons at work shall be treated as including risks attributable to the manner of conducting an undertaking, *(i)* the plant or substances used for the purposes of an undertaking and the condition of premises so used or any part of them.

(4)   References in this Part *(a)* to the general purposes of this Part are references to the purposes mentioned in subsection (1) above.

General note.   Subsection (1)(d) and the word "and" preceding it are repealed by the Environmental Protection Act 1990, s. 162(2), Sch. 16, Pt. I, as from a date to be appointed.

(a)   **This Part.**   The reference is to Part I of the Act (ss. 1–54); see s. 82(1)(d). The provisions of Parts I, II and IV may be extended to persons, premises, work, articles, substances and other matters outside Great Britain by Order in Council; see s. 84(3), (4) and the Health and Safety at Work etc. Act 1974 (Application outside Great Britain) Order 1989 (set out after the notes to s. 84). For the application of Part I to the Crown, see s. 48.

(b)   **At work.**   For definition, see s. 52(1), (2).

(c)   **Risks . . . work.**   See sub-s. (3).

(d)   **Substance.**   For definition, see s. 53(1).

(e)   **Premises.**   For definition, see s. 53(1).

(f)   **Prescribed.**   For definition, see s. 53(1). See the Health and Safety (Emissions into the Atmosphere) Regulations 1983, S.I. 1983 No. 943.

(g)   **Health and safety regulations.**   See s. 15.

(h) **Codes of Practice.** See s. 16.

(i) **Undertaking.** See note *(c)* to 5.3.

General duties

2.   General duties of employers to their employees.—(1) It shall be the duty *(a)* of every employer *(b)* to ensure, so far as is reasonably practicable *(c)*, the health, safety and welfare at work *(d)* of all his employees *(e)*.

(2) Without prejudice to the generality of an employer's duty under the preceding subsection, the matters to which that duty extends include in particular—

(a)   the provision and maintenance of plant *(f)* and systems of work *(g)* that are, so far as is reasonably practicable *(c)*, safe and without risks to health;

(b)   arrangements for ensuring, so far as is reasonably practicable, safety and absence of risks to health in connection with the use, handling, storage and transport of articles and substances *(h)*;

(c)   the provision of such information, instruction, training and supervision as is necessary to ensure, so far as is reasonably practicable, the health and safety at work of his employees;

(d)   so far as is reasonably practicable as regards any place of work under the employer's control, the maintenance of it in a condition that is safe and without risks to health and the provision and maintenance of means of access to and egress from it that are safe and without such risks;

(e)   the provision and maintenance of a working environment for his employees that is, so far as is reasonably practicable, safe, without risks to health, and adequate as regards facilities and arrangements for their welfare at work.

(3) Except in such cases as may be prescribed *(i)*, it shall be the duty of every employer to prepare and as often as may be appropriate revise a written statement of his general policy with respect to the health and safety at work of his employees and the organisation and arrangements for the time being in force for carrying out that policy, and to bring the statement and any revision of it to the notice of all of his employees.

(4) Regulations *(j)* made by the Secretary of State *(k)* may provide for the appointment in prescribed cases by recognised trade unions (within the meaning of the regulations) of safety representatives from amongst the employees *(l)*, and those representatives shall represent the employees in consultations with the employers under subsection (6) below and shall have such other functions as may be prescribed.

(5) [*repealed*].

(6) It shall be the duty of every employer to consult any such representatives with a view to the making and maintenance of arrangements which will enable him and his employees to co-operate effectively in promoting and developing measures to ensure the health and safety at work of the employees, and in checking the effectiveness of such measures.

(7) In such cases as may be prescribed *(m)* it shall be the duty of every employer, if requested to do so by the safety representatives mentioned in

subsection (4) above, to establish, in accordance with regulations *(j)* made by the Secretary of State, a safety committee having the function of keeping under review the measures taken to ensure the health and safety at work of his employees and such other functions as may be prescribed.

General note. This section confers no right of action in civil proceedings (s. 47(1)(a)). In *Briggs Amasco Ltd v Smith* 1981 SCCR 274 a summary complaint simply alleged a contravention of s. 2(1) without alleging breaches of any of the obligations in s. 2(2)– (7), and this appears to have passed unchallenged (and see *Cardle v David Carlaw Engineering (Glasgow) Ltd* 1991 SCCR 807).

(a) Duty. For enforcement, see s. 18; for offences, see s. 33(1)(c). As to codes of practice generally, see s. 16; as to their use in criminal proceedings, see s. 17. Where the complaint is that the employer has failed to provide protective clothing this should be brought under s. 2(2)(a) and not under s. 2(2)(e): *Cardle v David Carlaw Engineering (Glasgow) Ltd* 1991 SCCR 807.

(b) Employer. For definition, see s. 53(1).

(c) Reasonably practicable. See INTRODUCTORY NOTE 5.

(d) At work. For definition, see s. 52(1), (2). Note that the section is breached if an employer makes available unsafe plant and systems of work, even if that plant or system has not yet been used: see *Bolton Metropolitan Council v Malrod Insulations Ltd* [1993] ICR 358, [1993] IRLR 374.

(e) Employee. For definition, see s. 53(1).

(f) Plant. For definition, see s. 53(1).

(g) System of work. Where the provision of a safe system of work for his own employees requires that the employees of another should be given information and instruction as to potential dangers, the employer is under a duty to provide such information and instruction: *R v Swan Hunter Shipbuilders Ltd* [1982] 1 All ER 264, CA. And also see s. 3 as to the duties of employers to persons other than their employees. Note that if a system of work leaves it to an individual employee to decide whether or not to obtain help for particular tasks, it may be unsafe unless the employee is instructed to seek assistance and that help is readily available whenever wanted (see *Mearns v Lothian Regional Council* 1991 SLT 338, a case on a similar provision in the Merchant Shipping (Health and Safety: General Duties) Regulations 1984, in which the absence of a system instructing employees what to do when lifting heavy weights led to liability).

(h) Substance. For definition, see s. 53(1).

(i) Prescribed. For definition, see s. 53(1). The Employers' Health and Safety Policy Statements (Exception) Regulations 1975, S.I. 1975 No. 1584, have been made for the purposes of sub-s. (3); they except from the provisions of s. 2(3) any employer who carries on an undertaking in which for the time being he employs less than five employees (reg. 2). To determine whether an employer comes within this exception, regard must be had only to employees present on the premises at the same time: *Osborne v Bill Taylor of Huyton Ltd* [1982] ICR 168, [1982] IRLR 17, DC.

(j) Regulations. See the Safety Representatives and Safety Committees Regulations 1977, set out below. The following codes of practice have been approved under s. 16 with regard to the requirements of these Regulations: "Safety Representatives and Safety Committees" and "Time off for the training of Safety Representatives". As to the use of codes of practice in criminal proceedings, see s. 17.

(k) Secretary of State. The Secretary of State responsible for the administration of the Act is the Secretary of State for Employment; for his style and title, see the Secretary of State for Trade and Industry Order 1970, S.I. 1970 No. 1537, art. 3(1).

(l) **From ... employees.** For a modification of this requirement, see reg. 8 of the Regulations referred to in note *(j)*.

(m) **In such cases ...** See reg. 9(1) of the Regulations referred to in note *(j)*.

THE SAFETY REPRESENTATIVES AND SAFETY COMMITTEES REGULATIONS 1977
(S.I. 1977 No. 500, as amended by S.I. 1992 No. 2051)

General note. These Regulations are to be compared with the Offshore Installations (Safety Representatives and Safety Committees) Regulations 1989 (S.I. 1989 No. 971 amended by S.I. 1992 No. 2885). One significant difference is that under the "onshore" Regulations safety representatives are appointed by recognised unions (there is no provision for safety representatives or committees if the union is not recognised). The offshore Regulations, however, provide for safety representatives to be elected by the workforce irrespective of unions, recognised or not. (See also the general note to reg. 4A.)

Citation and commencement
1. These Regulations may be cited as the Safety Representatives and Safety Committees Regulations 1977 and shall come into operation on 1st October 1978.

Interpretation
2.—(1) In these Regulations, unless the context otherwise requires—
  "the 1974 Act" means the Health and Safety at Work etc. Act 1974 as amended by *the 1975 Act*;
  "the 1975 Act" means the Employment Protection Act 1975;
  "employee" has the meaning assigned by section 53(1) of the 1974 Act and "employer" shall be construed accordingly;
  "recognised trade union" *(a)* means an independent trade union as defined in section 30(1) of the Trade Union and Labour Relations Act 1974 which the *employer* concerned recognises for the purpose of negotiations relating to or connected with one or more of the matters specified in section 29(1) of that Act in relation to persons employed by him or as to which the Advisory, Conciliation and Arbitration Service has made a recommendation for recognition under *the 1975 Act* which is operative within the meaning of section 15 of that Act;
  "safety representative" means a person appointed under Regulation 3(3) of these Regulations to be a safety representative;
  "welfare at work" means those aspects of welfare at work which are the subject of health and safety regulations or of any of the existing statutory provisions within the meaning of section 53(1) of *the 1974 Act*;
  "workplace" in relation to a *safety representative* means any place or places where the group or groups of *employees* he is appointed to represent are likely to work or which they are likely to frequent in the course of their employment or incidentially to it.
  (2) The Interpretation Act 1889 *(b)* shall apply to the interpretation of these Regulations as it applies to the interpretation of an Act of Parliament.
  (3) These Regulations shall not be construed as giving any person a right to inspect any place, article, substance or document which is the subject of restrictions on the grounds of national security unless he satisfies any test or requirement imposed on those grounds by or on behalf of the Crown.

(a) **Recognised trade union.** Section 30(1) of the Trade Union and Labour Relations Act 1974 is now s. 5 of the Trade Union and Labour Relations (Consolidation) Act 1992. Section 29(1) of the former is now s. 178(2) of the latter. "Recognised" is to be defined by reference to what is now s. 178(3) of the latter Act: *Cleveland County Council v Springett*

[1985] IRLR 131. The procedure for imposing recognition on an employer, contained in s. 15 of the Employment Protection Act 1975, was repealed by the Employment Act 1980, s. 19(b). Hence now recognition is entirely a matter of choice for the employer.

(b) **The Interpretation Act 1889.** See now the Interpretation Act 1978.

Appointment of safety representatives
    3.—(1) For the purposes of section 2(4) of *the 1974 Act, a recognised trade union* may appoint *safety representatives* from amongst the *employees* in all cases where one or more *employees* are employed by an *employer* by whom it is recognised, except in the case of *employees* employed in a mine within the meaning of section 180 of the Mines and Quarries Act 1954 which is a coal mine.
    (2) Where the *employer* has been notified in writing by or on behalf of a trade union of the names of the persons appointed as *safety representatives* under this Regulation and the group or groups of *employees* they represent, each such *safety representative* shall have the functions set out in Regulation 4 below.
    (3) A person shall cease to be a *safety representative* for the purposes of these Regulations when—
    (a) the trade union which appointed him notifies the *employer* in writing that his appointment has been terminated; or
    (b) he ceases to be employed at the *workplace* but if he was appointed to represent employees at more than one workplace he shall not cease by virtue of this sub-paragraph to be a *safety representative* so long as he continues to be employed at any one of them; or
    (c) he resigns.
    (4) A person appointed under paragraph (1) above as a *safety representative* shall so far as is reasonably practicable either have been employed by his *employer* throughout the preceding two years or have had at least two years experience in similar employment.

Functions of safety representatives
    4.—(1) In addition to his function under section 2(4) of *the 1974 Act* to represent the *employees* in consultations with the *employer* under section 2(6) of *the 1974 Act* (which requires every *employer* to consult safety representatives with a view to the making and maintenance of arrangements which will enable him and his *employees* to cooperate effectively in promoting and developing measures to ensure the health and safety at work of the *employees* and in checking the effectiveness of such measures), each *safety representative* shall have the following functions—
    (a) to investigate potential hazards and dangerous occurrences at the *workplace* (whether or not they are drawn to his attention by the *employees* he represents) and to examine the causes of accidents at the *workplace*;
    (b) to investigate complaints by any *employee* he represents relating to that *employee's* health, safety or *welfare at work*;
    (c) to make representations to the *employer* on matters arising out of sub-paragraphs (a) and (b) above;
    (d) to make representations to the *employer* on general matters affecting the health, safety or *welfare at work* of the *employees* at the *workplace*;
    (e) to carry out inspections in accordance with Regulations 5, 6 and 7 below;
    (f) to represent the *employees* he was appointed to represent in consultations at the *workplace* with inspectors of the Health and Safety Executive and of any other enforcing authority;
    (g) to receive information from inspectors in accordance with section 28(2) of *the 1974 Act*; and
    (h) to attend meetings of safety committees *(a)* where he attends in his capacity as a *safety representative* in connection with any of the above functions;
but, without prejudice to sections 7 and 8 *the 1974 Act*, no function given to a *safety representative* by this paragraph shall be construed as imposing any duty on him.
    (2) An *employer* shall permit a *safety representative* to take such time off with pay during the *employee's* working hours as shall be necessary for the purposes of—

(a) performing his functions under section 2(4) of *the 1974 Act* and paragraph (1)(a) to (h) above;
(b) undergoing such training in aspects of those functions as may be reasonable in all the circumstances *(b)* having regard to any relevant provisions of a code of practice relating to time off for training approved for the time being by the Health and Safety Commission under section 16 of *the 1974 Act.*

In this paragraph "with pay" means with pay in accordance with the Schedule to these Regulations.

(a) Safety committees. See reg. 9.

(b) Reasonable in all the circumstances. In *White v Pressed Steel Fisher* [1980] IRLR 176 it was held that, while a course run by an employer was not necessarily inadequate because it was not approved by the union, on the other hand the trade union or representational aspect was an important element of such a course. Consequently if those elements were absent the employee could be entitled to additional time off to be trained in those functions elsewhere (see, too, the similar duty in Art. 11(5) of the Framework Directive 89/391).

4A. Employer's duty to consult and provide facilities and assistance.—(1) Without prejudice to the generality of section 2(6) of the Health and Safety at Work etc. Act 1974, every *employer* shall consult *safety representatives* in good time with regard to—
(a) the introduction of any measure at the *workplace* which may substantially affect the health and safety of the *employees* the safety representatives concerned represent;
(b) his arrangements for appointing or, as the case may be, nominating persons in accordance with regulations 6(1) and 7(1)(b) of the Management of Health and Safety at Work Regulations 1992;
(c) any health and safety information he is required to provide to the *employees* the *safety representatives* concerned represent by or under the relevant statutory provisions;
(d) the planning and organisation of any health and safety training he is required to provide to the *employees* the *safety representatives* concerned represent by or under the relevant statutory provisions; and
(e) the health and safety consequences for the *employees* the *safety representatives* concerned represent of the introduction (including the planning thereof) of new technologies into the *workplace.*

(2) Without prejudice to regulations 5 and 6 of these Regulations, every *employer* shall provide such facilities and assistance as *safety representatives* may reasonably require for the purpose of carrying out their functions under section 2(4) of *the 1974 Act* and under these Regulations.

General note. This regulation was added by a Schedule to the Management of Health and Safety at Work Regulations, S.I. 1992 No. 2051, and was intended to implement the requirements of Art. 11 of the Framework Directive 89/391. Since that Article does not appear to contemplate exclusion or qualification of the right of representatives to consultation, it is arguable that reg. 4A does not properly implement the Directive because under these Regulations the right to consultation depends on "recognition" (see note *(a)* to reg. 2 above) by the employer. In the UK recognition may be refused or terminated at will by the employer and is unenforceable (*Wilson v Associated Newspapers Ltd* [1993] IRLR 336, CA). Hence, it can be said, this implementing regulation fails to provide for the enforceable right required by the Directive. In addition, the obligation under the Directive is to consult on "all questions relating to safety and health at work" (Art. 11(1); see too Art. 11(2), which requires consultation with representatives on "any measure which may substantially affect safety and health"). Regulation 4A(a) does not, it seems, fully implement these duties. In particular, the Directive is not confined to measures affecting only those employees whom the safety representative represents.

The Directive is no doubt enforceable directly against a state employer, but as against a private employer it is unclear whether a "purposive" construction of the Regulations requires that the precondition of recognition be omitted and that the consultation duties be given a wide scope. (See also "Interpretation in the Light of the European Directives" and "Direct Application of the European Directives" under LEGAL PRINCIPLES in the introductory section.)

Inspections of the workplace

5.—(1) *Safety representatives* shall be entitled to inspect the *workplace* or a part of it if they have given the *employer* or his representative reasonable notice in writing of their intention to do so and have not inspected it, or that part of it, as the case may be, in the previous three months; and may carry out more frequent inspections by agreement with the *employer.*

(2) Where there has been a substantial change in the conditions of work (whether because of the introduction of new machinery or otherwise) or new information has been published by the Health and Safety Commission or the Health and Safety Executive relevant to the hazards of the *workplace* since the last inspection under this Regulation, the *safety representative* after consultation with the *employer* shall be entitled to carry out a further inspection of the part of the *workplace* concerned notwithstanding that three months have not elapsed since the last inspection.

(3) The *employer* shall provide such facilities and assistance as the *safety representative* may reasonably require (including facilities for independent investigation by them and private discussion with the *employees*) for the purpose of carrying out an inspection under this Regulation, but nothing in this paragraph shall preclude the *employer* or his representative from being present in the *workplace* during the inspection.

(4) An inspection carried out under section 123 of the Mines and Quarries Act 1954 shall count as an inspection under this Regulation.

Inspections following notifiable accidents, occurrences and diseases

6.—(1) Where there has been a notifiable accident or dangerous occurrence in a *workplace* or a notifiable disease *(a)* has been contracted there and—

(a)   it is safe for an inspection to be carried out; and
(b)   the interests of *employees* in the group or groups which *safety representatives* are appointed to represent might be involved,

those *safety representatives* may carry out an inspection of the part of the *workplace* concerned and so far as is necessary for the purpose of determining the cause they may inspect any other part of the *workplace*; where it is reasonably practicable to do so they shall notify the *employer* or his representative of their intention to carry out the inspection.

(2) The *employer* shall provide such facilities and assistance as the *safety representative* may reasonably require (including facilities for independent investigation by them and private discussion with the *employees*) for the purpose of carrying out an inspection under this Regulation; but nothing in this paragraph shall preclude the *employer* or his representative from being present in the *workplace* during the inspection.

(3) In this Regulation "notifiable accident or dangerous occurrence" and "notifiable disease" means any accident, dangerous occurrence or disease, as the case may be, notice *(b)* of which is required to be given by virtue of any of the relevant statutory provisions within the meaning of section 53(1) of *the 1974 Act.*

(a) **Notifiable . . . disease.** See para. (3).

(b) **Notice.** As to the circumstances in which such notice is required, see 20 Halsbury's Laws (4th edn.) paras. 512 *et seq.*

Inspection of documents and provision of information

7.—(1) *Safety representatives* shall for the performance of their functions under section 2(4) of *the 1974 Act* and under these Regulations, if they have given the *employer* reasonable notice, be entitled to inspect and take copies of any document relevant to the *workplace* or to the *employees* the *safety representatives* represent which the *employer* is required to keep by virtue of any relevant statutory provision within the meaning of section 53(1) of *the 1974 Act* except a document consisting of or relating to any health record of an identifiable individual.

(2) An *employer* shall make available to *safety representatives* the information, within the *employer's* knowledge, necessary to enable them to fulfil their functions except—
   (a) any information the disclosure of which would be against the interests of national security; or
   (b) any information which he could not disclose without contravening a prohibition imposed by or under an enactment; or
   (c) any information relating specifically to an individual, unless he has consented to its being disclosed; or
   (d) any information the disclosure of which would, for reasons other than its effect on health, safety or *welfare at work*, cause substantial injury to the *employer's* undertaking or, where the information was supplied to him by some other person, to the undertaking of that other person; or
   (e) any information obtained by the *employer* for the purpose of bringing, prosecuting or defending any legal proceedings.
(3) Paragraph (2) above does not require an *employer* to produce or allow inspection of any document or part of a document which is not related to health, safety or welfare.

General note. This regulation should be compared with the obligation on the employer in Art. 10 of the Framework Directive 89/391. To the extent that reg. 7 falls short of Art. 10, a purposive construction may ensure it has the same results (see "Interpretation in the light of European Directives" in LEGAL PRINCIPLES in the introductory section).

Cases where safety representatives need not be employees
   8.—(1) In the cases mentioned in paragraph (2) below *safety representatives* appointed under Regulation 3(1) of these Regulations need not be *employees* of the *employer* concerned; and section 2(4) of *the 1974 Act* shall be modified accordingly.
   (2) The said cases are those in which the *employees* in the group or groups the *safety representatives* are appointed to represent are members of the British Actors' Equity Association or of the Musicians' Union.
   (3) Regulations 3(3)(b) and (4) and 4(2) of these Regulations shall not apply to *safety representatives* appointed by virtue of this Regulation and in the case of *safety representatives* to be so appointed. Regulation 3(1) shall have effect as if the words "from amongst the employees" were omittted.

Safety committees
   9.—(1) For the purposes of section 2(7) of *the 1974 Act* (which requires an *employer* in prescribed cases to establish a safety committee if requested to do so by *safety representatives*) the prescribed cases shall be any cases in which at least two *safety representatives* request the *employer* in writing to establish a safety committee.
   (2) Where an *employer* is requested to establish a safety committee in a case prescribed in paragraph (1) above, he shall establish it in accordance with the following provisions—
   (a) he shall consult with the *safety representatives* who made the request and with the representatives of *recognised trade unions* whose members work in any *workplace* in respect of which he proposes that the committee should function;
   (b) the *employer* shall post a notice stating the composition of the committee and the *workplace* or *workplaces* to be covered by it in a place where it may be easily read by the *employees*;
   (c) the committee shall be established not later than three months after the request for it.

Power of Health and Safety Commission to grant exemptions
   10.   The Health and Safety Commission may grant exemptions from any requirement imposed by these Regulations and any such exemption may be unconditional or subject to such conditions as the Commission may impose and may be with or without a limit of time.

Provisions as to industiral tribunals
   11.—(1) A *safety representative* may, in accordance with the jurisdiction conferred on industrial tribunals by paragraph 16(2) of Schedule 1 to the Trade Union and Labour Relations Act 1974, now s. 128 of the Employment Protection (Consolidation) Act 1978, present a complaint to an industrial tribunal that—

(a) the *employer* has failed to permit him to take time off in accordance with Regulation 4(2) of these Regulations; or

(b) the *employer* has failed to pay him in accordance with Regulation 4(2) of and the Schedule to these Regulations.

(2) An industrial tribunal shall not consider a complaint under paragraph (1) above unless it is presented within three months of the date when the failure occurred or within such further period as the tribunal considers reasonable in a case where it is satisfied that it was not reasonably practicable for the complaint to be presented within the period of three months.

(3) Where an industrial tribunal finds a complaint under paragraph (1)(a) above well-founded the tribunal shall make a declaration to that effect and may make an award of compensation to be paid by the *employer* to the *employee* which shall be of such amount as the tribunal considers just and equitable in all the circumstances having regard to the *employer's* default in failing to permit time off to be taken by the *employee* and to any loss sustained by the *employee* which is attributable to the matters complained of.

(4) Where on a complaint under paragraph (1)(b) above an industrial tribunal finds that the *employer* has failed to pay the *employee* the whole or part of the amount required to be paid under paragraph (1)(b), the tribunal shall order the *employer* to pay the *employee* the amount which it finds due to him.

(5) Paragraph 16 of Schedule 1 to the Trade Union and Labour Relations Act 1974, now s. 128 of the Employment Protection (Consolidation) Act 1978, (jurisdiction of industrial tribunals) shall be modified by adding the following sub-paragraph—

"(2) An industrial tribunal shall have jurisdiction to determine complaints relating to time off with pay for safety representatives appointed under regulations made under the Health and Safety at Work etc. Act 1974."

SCHEDULE

Regulation 4(2)

PAY FOR TIME OFF ALLOWED TO SAFETY REPRESENTATIVES

1. Subject to paragraph 3 below, where a *safety representative* is permitted to take time off in accordance with Regulation 4(2) of these Regulations, his *employer* shall pay him—

(a) where the *safety representative's* remuneration for the work he would ordinarily have been doing *(a)* during that time does not vary with the amount of work done, as if he had worked at that work for the whole of that time;

(b) where the *safety representative's* remuneration for that work varies with the amount of work done, an amount calculated by reference to the average hourly earnings for that work (ascertained in accordance with paragraph 2 below).

2. The average hourly earnings referred to in paragraph 1(b) above are the average hourly earnings of the *safety representative* concerned or, if no fair estimate can be made of those earnings, the average hourly earnings for work of that description of persons in comparable employment with the same *employer* or, if there are no such persons, a figure of average hourly earnings which is reasonable in the circumstances.

3. Any payment to a *safety representative* by an *employer* in respect of a period of time off—

(a) if it is a payment which discharges any liability which the *employer* may have under section 57 of *the 1975 Act*, now ss. 168–9 of the Trade Union and Labour Relations (Consolidation) Act 1992, in respect of that period, shall also discharge his liability in respect of the same period under Regulation 4(2) of these Regulations;

(b) if it is a payment under any contractual obligation, shall go towards discharging the *employer's* liability in respect of the same period under Regulation 4(2) of these Regulations;

(c) if it is a payment under Regulation 4(2) of these Regulations, shall go towards discharging any liability of the *employer* to pay contractual remuneration in respect of the same period.

(a) **Work he would ordinarily have been doing.** A safety representative was entitled to be paid as if he was doing his ordinary work, even though at the time he attended a training course he had been laid off: *Diamond v Courtaulds Hosiery Ltd* [1979] IRLR 449. The Industrial Tribunal emphasised that the objectives of the Regulations would be met by

ensuring that the representative was paid for what he would ordinarily have earnt rather than for what he in fact lost.

EMPLOYMENT PROTECTION (CONSOLIDATION) ACT 1978
(1978 c 44)

PART II
RIGHTS ARISING IN COURSE OF EMPLOYMENT

Right not to suffer detriment in health and safety cases

22A. Right not to suffer detriment in health and safety cases.—(1) An employee has the right not to be subjected to any detriment by any act, or any deliberate failure to act, by his employer done on the ground that—

(a) having been designated by the employer to carry out activities in connection with preventing or reducing risks to health and safety at work, he carried out, or proposed to carry out, any such activities,

(b) being a representative of workers on matters of health and safety at work, or a member of a safety committee—
   (i) in accordance with arrangements established under or by virtue of any enactment, or
   (ii) by reason of being acknowledged as such by the employer,
   he performed, or proposed to perform, any functions as such a representative or a member of such a committee,

(c) being an employee at a place where—
   (i) there was no such representative or safety committee, or
   (ii) there was such a representative or safety committee but it was not reasonably practicable for the employee to raise the matter by those means,
   he brought to his employer's attention, by reasonable means, circumstances connected with his work which he reasonably believed were harmful or potentially harmful to health or safety,

(d) in circumstances of danger which he reasonably believed to be serious and imminent and which he could not reasonably have been expected to avert, he left, or proposed to leave, or (while the danger persisted) refused to return to, his place of work or any dangerous part of his place of work, or

(e) in circumstances of danger which he reasonably believed to be serious and imminent, he took, or proposed to take, appropriate steps to protect himself or other persons from the danger.

(2) For the purposes of subsection (1)(e) whether steps which an employee took, or proposed to take, were appropriate shall be judged by reference to all the circumstances including, in particular, his knowledge and the facilities and advice available to him at the time.

(3) An employee shall not be regarded as having been subjected to any detriment on the ground specified in subsection (1)(e) if the employer shows that it was, or would have been, so negligent for the employee to take the steps which he took, or proposed to take, that a reasonable employer might have treated him as the employer did.

(4) Except where an employee is dismissed in circumstances in which, by virtue of section 142, section 54 does not apply to the dismissal, this section shall not apply where the detriment in question amounts to dismissal.

General note. This section is inserted, in relation to any detriment to which the employee was subjected on or after 30 August 1993, by the Trade Union Reform and Employment Rights Act 1993, s. 28, Sch. 5, para. 1.

22B. Proceedings for contravention of section 22A.—(1) An employee may present a complaint to an industrial tribunal on the ground that he has been subjected to a detriment in contravention of section 22A.

(2) On such a complaint it shall be for the employer to show the ground on which any act, or deliberate failure to act, was done.

(3) An industrial tribunal shall not consider a complaint under this section unless it is presented—

(a) before the end of the period of three months beginning with the date of the act or failure to act to which the complaint relates or, where that act or failure is part of a series of similar acts or failures, the last of them, or

(b) where the tribunal is satisfied that it was not reasonably practicable for the complaint to be presented before the end of that period, within such further period as it considers reasonable.

(4) For the purposes of subsection (3)—

(a) where an act extends over a period, the "date of the act" means the last day of that period, and

(b) a deliberate failure to act shall be treated as done when it was decided on,

and in the absence of evidence establishing the contrary, an employer shall be taken to decide on a failure to act when he does an act inconsistent with doing the failed act or, if he has done no such inconsistent act, when the period expires within which he might reasonably have been expected to do the failed act if it was to be done.

General note. This section is inserted, in relation to any detriment to which the employee was subjected on or after 30 August 1993, by the Trade Union Reform and Employment Rights Act 1993, s. 28, Sch. 5, para. 1.

22C.   Remedies.—(1) Where the industrial tribunal finds that a complaint under section 22B is well-founded, it shall make a declaration to that effect and may make an award of compensation to be paid to the complainant in respect of the act or failure to act complained of.

(2) The amount of the compensation awarded shall be such as the tribunal considers just and equitable in all the circumstances having regard to the infringement complained of and to any loss which is attributable to the act or failure which infringed his right.

(3) The loss shall be taken to include—

(a) any expenses reasonably incurred by the complainant in consequence of the act or failure complained of, and

(b) loss of any benefit which he might reasonably be expected to have had but for that act or failure.

(4) In ascertaining the loss, the tribunal shall apply the same rule concerning the duty of a person to mitigate his loss as applies to damages recoverable under the common law of England and Wales or Scotland.

(5) Where the tribunal finds that the act or failure complained of was to any extent caused or contributed to by action of the complainant, it shall reduce the amount of the compensation by such proportion as it considers just and equitable having regard to that finding.

General note. This section is inserted, in relation to any detriment to which the employee was subjected on or after 30 August 1993, by the Trade Union Reform and Employment Rights Act 1993, s. 28, Sch. 5, para. 1.

PART V
UNFAIR DISMISSAL

Meaning of unfair dismissal

57A.   Dismissal in health and safety cases.—(1) The dismissal of an employee by an employer shall be regarded for the purposes of this Part as having been unfair if the reason for it (or, if more than one, the principal reason) was that the employee—

    (a) having been designated by the employer to carry out activities in connection with preventing or reducing risks to health and safety at work, carried out, or proposed to carry out, any such activities,

    (b) being a representative of workers on matters of health and safety at work, or a member of a safety committee—

        (i) in accordance with arrangements established under or by virtue of any enactment, or

        (ii) by reason of being acknowledged as such by the employer,

      performed, or proposed to perform, any functions as such a representative or a member of such a committee,

    (c) being an employee at a place where—

        (i) there was no such representative or safety committee, or

        (ii) there was such a representative or safety committee but it was not reasonably practicable for the employee to raise the matter by those means,

      brought to his employer's attention, by reasonable means, circumstances connected with his work which he reasonably believed were harmful or potentially harmful to health or safety,

    (d) in circumstances of danger which he reasonably believed to be serious and imminent and which he could not reasonably have been expected to avert, left, or proposed to leave, or (while the danger persisted) refused to return to, his place of work or any dangerous part of his place of work, or

    (e) in circumstances of danger which he reasonably believed to be serious and imminent, took, or proposed to take, appropriate steps to protect himself or other persons from the danger.

    (2) For the purposes of subsection (1)(e) whether steps which an employee took, or proposed to take, were appropriate shall be judged by reference to all the circumstances including, in particular, his knowledge and the facilities and advice available to him at the time.

    (3) Where the reason (or, if more than one, the principal reason) for the dismissal of an employee was that specified in subsection (1)(e), the dismissal shall not be regarded as having been unfair if the employer shows that it was, or would have been, so negligent for the employee to take the steps which he took, or proposed to take, that a reasonable employer might have dismissed him for taking, or proposing to take, them.

General note. This section is inserted in relation to any dismissal where the effective date of termination (as defined in this Act) in relation to that dismissal falls on or after 30 August 1993 by the Trade Union Reform and Employment Rights Act 1993, s. 28, Sch. 5, para. 3.

Sections 71–79 of the 1978 Act are also amended to provide similar remedies (including interim relief) for safety representatives etc. as for those dismissed for trade union membership etc. Similar protection is also given in relation to selection for dismissal for redundancy (s. 59(2) of the 1978 Act as amended), and there is no minimum qualifying period for unfair dismissal protection for those dismissed by reason of being safety representatives ec. (s. 64(4) of the 1978 Act as amended).

Comparison may be made with the provisions for offshore safety representatives and committees under the Offshore Installations (Safety Representatives and Safety Committees) Regulations 1989, S.I. 1989 No. 971 amended by S.I. 1992 No. 2885.

---

3.   General duties of employers and self-employed to persons other than their employees.—(1) It shall be the duty *(a)* of every employer *(b)* to conduct his undertaking *(c)* in such a way as to ensure, so far as is reasonably practicable *(d)*, that persons not in his employment *(e)* who may be affected thereby are not thereby exposed to risks *(f)* to their health or safety.

(2) It shall be the duty of every self-employed person *(g)* to conduct his undertaking in such a way as to ensure, so far as is reasonably practicable, that he and other persons (not being his employees *(h)*) who may be affected thereby are not thereby exposed to risks to their health or safety.

(3) In such cases as may be prescribed *(i)*, it shall be the duty of every employer and every self-employed person, in the prescribed circumstances and in the prescribed manner, to give to persons (not being his employees) who may be affected by the way in which he conducts his undertaking the prescribed information about such aspects of the way in which he conducts his undertaking as might affect their health or safety.

General note. This section confers no right of action in civil proceedings (s. 47(1)(a)). The general duty under sub-s. (1) is not limited by the specific provisions of sub-s. (3): *R v Swan Hunter Shipbuilders Ltd* [1982] 1 All ER 264, CA; *Carmichael v Rosehall Engineering Works Ltd* 1984 SLT 40n. The purpose of the provisions is to protect the relevant persons, including the general public: see *R v Lightwater Valley* 1990 12 Cr App Rep (S) 328.

(a) Duty. Note that there is a breach of the section if there is a risk of exposure, so that proof of harm is unnecessary: see *R v Board of Trustees of the Science Museum* [1993] 3 All ER 853, [1993] 1 WLR 1171, CA. For enforcement, see s. 18; for offences, see s. 33(1)(a). Where work involving asbestos-based thermal and acoustic insulation and sprayed coatings is done at premises or in work situations where the Control of Asbestos at Work Regulations 1987, S.I. 1987 No. 2115 and S.I. 1992 No. 3068, do not apply, the Approved Code of Practice "Work with asbestos insulation and asbestos coating" provides practical guidance with regard to the requirements of sub-ss. (1) and (2). As to Codes of Practice generally, see s. 16; as to their use in criminal proceedings, see s. 17. In *Tudhope v City of Glasgow District Council* 1986 SCCR 168 the Code had not been followed but there was held to be no breach of duty given the facts that there had been an emergency situation and that the employers had acted on specialist advice.

(b) Employer. For definition, see s. 53(1).

(c) Undertaking. An undertaking includes one for the provision of services, and is "conducted" by the employer even when shut down for maintenance purposes (*R v Mara* [1987] 1 All ER 478, [1987] ICR 165, CA). In *Sterling-Winthrop Group Ltd v Allan* 1987 SCCR 25 it was stated that the conduct of the undertaking was not limited to the carrying on of industrial processes but would also cover trading and supplying or selling to customers.

(d) Reasonably practicable. See INTRODUCTORY NOTE 5.

(e) Employment. For definition, see s. 53(1). If machinery is left by the employer on his premises for contractors to use, thereby exposing the contractor's employees to risk, such employees are persons who may be affected thereby (*R v Mara, above*). In *Sterling-Winthrop Group Ltd v Allan* (above) it was held that s. 3(1) could encompass people outside of the place where the employer conducted his undertaking; the example given was where passers-by were endangered by escaping fumes.

(f) Risks. This term was widely interpreted in *R v Board of Trustees of the Science Museum* (above). Thus, the possibility of danger was sufficient and there was no need for the prosecution to show that there was an actual danger.

(g) Self-employed person. For definition, see s. 53(1). Section 3(2) is modified by the Genetically Modified Organisms (Contained Use) Regulations 1992, S.I. 1992 No. 3217, reg. 4, in relation to any activity involving genetic manipulation, and, by the Health and

Safety (Dangerous Pathogens) Regulations 1981, S.I. 1981 No. 1011, in relation to any person who keeps or handles a listed pathogen, so that "self-employed person" includes a reference to any person who is not an employer or an employed person in relation to that activity or that keeping of handling. The latter regulations are set out in Part 4 of this book.

(h) **Employee.** For definition, see s. 53(1).

(i) **Prescribed.** For definition, see s. 53(1). No regulations have yet been made under this provision.

---

4.   General duties of persons concerned with premises to persons other than their employees.—(1) This section has effect for imposing on persons duties in relation to those who—

(a)   are not their employees *(a)*; but
(b)   use non-domestic premises *(b)* made available to them as a place of work
      (c) or as a place where they may use plant *(d)* or substances *(e)* provided
      for their use there,

and applies to premises so made available and other non-domestic premises used in connection with them.

(2)   It shall be the duty *(f)* of each person *(g)* who has, to any extent, control *(h)* of premises to which this section applies or of the means of access thereto or egress therefrom or of any plant or substance in such premises to take such measures as it is reasonable for a person in his position to take *(i)* to ensure, so far as is reasonably practicable *(j)* that the premises, all means of access thereto or egress therefrom available for use by persons using the premises, and any plant or substance in the premises or, as the case may be, provided for use there, is or are safe and without risks to health *(k)*.

(3)   Where a person has, by virtue of any contract a tenancy, an obligation of any extent in relation to—

(a)   the maintenance or repair of any premises to which this section applies
      or any means of access thereto or egress therefrom; or
(b)   the safety of or the absence of risks to health arising from plant or
      substances in any such premises;

that person shall be treated, for the purposes of subsection (2) above, as being a person who has control of the matters to which his obligation extends.

(4)   Any reference in this section to a person having control of any premises or matter is a reference to a person having control of the premises or matter in connection with the carrying on by him of a trade, business or other undertaking (whether for profit or not).

General note. This section confers no right of action in civil proceedings (s. 47(1)(a)). Whereas ss. 2 and 3 impose duties in relation to safety on a single person, who is in a position to exercise complete control over the matters to which the duties extend, s. 4 recognises that more than one person may have a degree of control over the relevant premises and hence be under a duty in relation thereto (*Austin Rover Group Ltd v HM Inspector of Factories* [1990] AC 619, sub nom *Mailer v Austin Rover Group plc* [1989] 2 All ER 1087, HL). In *Aitchison v Howard Doris Ltd* 1979 SLT (Notes) 22 it was stated that "although s. 3 is general in its terms, it covers the conduct of an undertaking and prima facie that covers all systems of work. Section 4 relates to the control of premises". The court went on to add, that where there is a complaint based upon defective access, "the liability for defective access is primarily upon the party who directly controls that access as defined in s. 4".

(a) Employee. For definition, see s. 53(1).

(b) Non-domestic premises. For definition, see s. 53(1). Premises which are not in the exclusive occupation of the occupants of a private dwelling, such as lifts and electrical installations serving the common parts of a block of flats, are "non-domestic premises" and are made available as a place of work or as a place where plant is provided for the use of persons who come to repair and maintain the premises (*Westminster City Council v Select Management Ltd* [1984] 1 All ER 994, [1984] 1 WLR 1058).

(c) Work. For definition, see s. 53(1), (2).

(d) Plant. For definition, see s. 53(1).

(e) Substance. For definition, see s. 53(1).

(f) Duty. For enforcement, see s. 18; for offences, see s. 33(1)(a). Where work involving asbestos-based thermal and acoustic insulation and sprayed coatings is done at premises or in work situations where the Control of Asbestos at Work Regulations 1987, S.I. 1987 No. 2115 do not apply, the approved Code of Practice "Work with asbestos insulation and asbestos coating" provides practical guidance with regard to the requirements of sub-ss. (1) and (2). As to Codes of Practice generally, see s. 16; as to their use in criminal proceedings, see s. 17.

(g) Person. This includes any body of persons corporate or unincorporate (Interpretation Act 1978, s. 5 and Sch. 1).

(h) Control. See sub-ss. (3), (4).

(i) Such measures as it is reasonable . . . to take. These words require consideration to be given not only to the extent to which the individual in question has control of the premises, but also to his knowledge and reasonable foresight at all material times; for example, if he makes the premises available for use by another, the reasonableness of the measures which he is required to take to ensure the safety of those premises must be determined in the light of his knowledge of the anticipated use for which they have been made available and of the extent of his control and knowledge, if any, of the actual use thereafter. If premises are not a reasonably foreseeable cause of danger to anyone acting in a way in which a human being may be reasonably expected to act in circumstances which may be reasonably expected to occur during the carrying out of the work or the use of the plant or substance for the purpose of which the premises were made available it would not be reasonable to require an individual to take further measures against unknown and unexpected events towards their safety (*Austin Rover Group Ltd v HM Inspector of Factories*, above).

(j) Reasonably practicable. See INTRODUCTORY NOTE 5.

(k) Safe and without risks to health. The point of time at which the matter of safety falls to be decided is the time when the risk arises, and not the time when the premises were first made available for non-employees to work in (*Austin Rover Group Ltd v HM Inspector of Factories*, above).

---

5.   General duty of persons in control of certain premises in relation to harmful emissions into atmosphere.—(1) Subject to subsection (5) below, it shall be the duty *(a)* of the person *(b)* having control *(c)* of any premises *(d)* of a class prescribed *(e)* for the purposes of section 1(1)(d) to use the best practicable *(f)* means *(g)* for preventing the emission into the atmosphere from the premises of noxious or offensive substances *(h)* and for rendering harmless and inoffensive such substances as may be so emitted.

(2) The reference in subsection (1) above to the means to be used for the purposes there mentioned includes a reference to the manner in which the plant *(i)* provided for those purposes is used and to the supervision of any operation involving the emission of the substances to which that subsection applies.

(3) Any substance or a substance of any description prescribed *(e)* for the purposes of subsection (1) above as noxious or offensive shall be a noxious or, as the case may be, an offensive substance for those purposes whether or not it would be so apart from this subsection.

(4) Any reference in this section to a person having control of any premises is a reference to a person having control of the premises in connection with the carrying on by him of a trade, business or other undertaking (whether for profit or not) and any duty imposed on any such person by this section shall extend only to matters within his control.

(5) The foregoing provisions of this section shall not apply in relation to any process which is a prescribed process as from the date which is the determination date for that process.

(6) For the purposes of subsection (6) above, the "determination date" for a prescribed process is—

(a)   in the case of a process for which an authorisation is granted, the date on which the enforcing authority grants it, whether in pursuance of the application or, on an appeal, of a direction to grant it;

(b)   in the case of a process for which an authorisation is refused, the date of the refusal or, on an appeal, of the affirmation of the refusal.

(7) In subsection (5) and (6) above "authorisation", "enforcing authority" and "prescribed process" have the meaning given in section 1 of the Environmental Protection Act 1990 and the reference to an appeal is a reference to an appeal under section 15 of that Act.

General note. This section is amended by the Environmental Protection Act 1990, s. 162(1), Sch. 15. para. 14, and is prospectively repealed by s. 162(2) of, and Sch. 16, Pt. I to that Act, as from a day to be appointed.

This section confers no right of action in civil proceedings (s. 47(1)(a)). Responsibility for the enforcement of this section is transferred to the Secretary of State by the Control of Industrial Air Pollution (Transfer of Powers of Enforcement) Regulations 1987, S.I. 1987 No. 180.

(a) Duty. For enforcement, see s. 18; for offences, see s. 33(1)(a).

(b) Person. See note (g) to s. 4.

(c) Control. See sub-s. (4).

(d) Premises. For definition, see s. 53(1).

(e) Prescribed. For definition, see s. 53(1). The Health and Safety (Emissions into the Atmosphere) Regulations 1983, S.I. 1983 No. 943, prescribe those classes of premises from which emissions into the atmosphere may be controlled under this Act, and the substances which are to be treated as noxious or offensive for the purposes of s. 5(1). The regulations are set out after the notes to this section.

(f) **Practicable.** See INTRODUCTORY NOTE 5.

(g) **Means.** See sub-s. (2).

(h) **Substances.** For definition, see s. 53(1). See also sub-s. (3) of this section.

(i) **Plant.** For definition, see s. 53(1).

HEALTH AND SAFETY (EMISSIONS INTO THE ATMOSPHERE) REGULATIONS 1983
(S.I. 1983 No. 943, as amended by S.I. 1989 No. 319)

Whereas the Health and Safety Commission has submitted to the Secretary of State under section 11(2)(d) of the Health and Safety at Work etc. Act 1974 ("the 1974 Act") proposals for making Regulations after the carrying out by the said Commission of consultations in accordance with section 50(3) of the 1974 Act;

And whereas, under section 80(1) of the 1974 Act it appears to the Secretary of State that the repeal of section 11(2) of the Clean Air Act 1968 and of section 78(3) of the Control of Pollution Act 1974, and the modification of section 92(2) of the Public Health Act 1936 which are made by Regulation 7 of these Regulations and the revocation of the Alkali &c. Works Orders 1966 and 1971 by Regulation 8 of these Regulations are expedient in connection with the other provisions of these Regulations and whereas in accordance with section 80(4) of the 1974 Act he has consulted such bodies as appear to him to be appropriate;

Now, therefore, the Secretary of State in exercise of the powers conferred on him by sections 1(1)(d), 5(3), 15(1) and (3)(a), 49(1), (2) and (4) and 80(1), (2)(a) and (b) and (4) of the Health and Safety at Work etc. Act 1974 and of all other powers enabling him in that behalf and so as to give effect without modification to the said proposals of the Commission and to the said repeals, modification and revocations of enactments hereby makes the following Regulations:

1. Citation and commencement. These Regulations may be cited as the Health and Safety (Emissions into the Atmosphere) Regulations 1983 and shall come into operation on 5 August 1983.

2. Interpretation. (1) In these Regulations—
"the 1906 Act" means the Alkali &c. Works Regulation Act 1906;
"the 1974 Act" means the Health and Safety at Work etc. Act 1974;
(2) Notwithstanding the definition of premises in section 53(1) of *the 1974 Act*, in these Regulations premises does not include any vehicle, vessel, aircraft or hovercraft.
(3) In these Regulations, any reference to works includes a reference to the materials used in and the products of those works in so far as they are treated, handled or stored by methods which cause noxious or offensive substances to be evolved from those works.

3. Prescribed classes of premises for the purposes of section 1(1)(d) of *the 1974 Act*. The prescribed classes of premises for the purposes of section 1(1)(d) of *the 1974 Act* shall be the following classes, namely, those parts of any premises on which any of the works specified in Schedule 1 to these Regulations are carried on and any reference in that Schedule to a noxious or offensive gas shall include a reference to any substance mentioned in Schedule 2 to these Regulations.

4. Substances deemed to be noxious or offensive for the purposes of section 5(1) of *the 1974 Act*. Substances which are prescribed as noxious or offensive for the purpose of section 5(1) of *the 1974 Act* shall comprise the substances specified in Schedule 2 to these Regulations.

5. Amendment of the 1906 Act. *The 1906 Act* shall be amended as follows:—
(a) for "muriatic" whenever it appears in the Act, substitute "hydrochloric";

(b) in section 9(1), for "a scheduled work" substitute "or any works specified in Schedule 1 to the Health and Safety (Emissions into the Atmosphere) Regulations 1983";

(c) in section 9(5)—
   (i) for "an alkali or scheduled work" substitute "an alkali work or any works specified in Schedule 1 to the Health and Safety (Emissions into the Atmosphere) Regulations 1983"; and
   (ii) after the words "requirements of this Act" insert the words "or of Part I of the Health and Safety at Work etc. Act 1974";

(d) in section 27(1), for the definition of "The expression 'noxious or offensive gas'" substitute the following definition:—
   "The expression 'noxious or offensive gas' includes any substances set out in Schedule 2 to the Health and Safety (Emissions into the Atmosphere) Regulations 1983".

6. Amendments to *the 1906 Act* to substitute metric quantities for imperial quantities. The provisions of *the 1906 Act* specified in Schedule 3 in column 1 shall be amended by substituting for the quantities set out opposite thereto in column 3 the quantities set out in the corresponding entry in column 4.

7. Repeals and modification. (1) The following enactments are hereby repealed—
   (a) sections 6 and 7 of, and Schedule 1 to, *the 1906 Act*;
   (b) section 11(2) of the Clean Air Act 1968;
   (c) section 78(3) of the Control of Pollution Act 1974.

(2) At the end of section 92(2) of the Public Health Act 1936 there shall be added the words, "or for a failure to discharge the duty under section 5 of the Health and Safety at Work etc. Act 1974".

8. Revocations. The following Orders are hereby revoked:—
   (a) The Alkali &c. Works Order 1966;
   (b) The Alkali &c. Works Order 1971;
   (c) The Alkali &c. Works (Scotland) Order 1972.

SCHEDULE 1

Regulation 3

List of Works

Acetylene works
Works in which acetylene is made and used in any chemical manufacturing process.

Acrylates works
Works in which acrylates are—
   (a) made or purified; or
   (b) made and polymerised; or
   (c) purified and polymerised; or
   (d) stored and handled in fixed tanks with an aggregate capacity exceeding 20 tonnes.

Aldehyde works
Works in which formaldehyde, acetaldehyde or acrolein or the methyl, ethyl or propyl derivatives of acrolein are made.

Aluminium works
Works in which—
   (a) oxide of aluminium is extracted from any ore; or
   (b) aluminium is extracted from any compound containing aluminium by a process evolving any noxious or offensive gases; or

(c) aluminium swarf is degreased by the application of heat; or

(d) aluminium or aluminium alloys are recovered from aluminium or aluminium alloy scrap fabricated metal, swarf, skimmings, or other residues by melting under flux cover; or

(e) aluminium is recovered from slag or drosses; or

(f) molten aluminium or aluminium alloys are treated by chlorine or its compounds; or

(g) materials used in the above processes or the products thereof are treated or handled by methods which cause noxious or offensive gases to be evolved.

Amines works
Works in which—

(a) any methylamine or any ethylamine is made; or

(b) any methylamine or any ethylamine is used in any chemical process.

Ammonia works
Works in which ammonia is—

(a) made or recovered; or

(b) used in the ammonia-soda process; or

(c) used in the manufacture of carbonate, hydroxide, nitrate or phosphate of ammonia, or urea or nitriles; or

(d) stored and handled in anhydrous form in fixed tanks with an aggregate capacity exceeding 100 tonnes.

Anhydride works
Works in which acetic, maleic or phthalic anhydrides or the corresponding acids are made or recovered.

Arsenic works
Works for the preparation of arsenious acid, or where nitric acid or a nitrate is used in the manufacture of arsenic acid or an arsenate and works in which any volatile compound of arsenic is evolved in any manufacturing process and works in which arsenic is made.

Asbestos works
Works in which—

(a) raw asbestos ore is produced but excluding any process directly associated with the mining of the ore; or

(b) asbestos is used in the manufacture and industrial finishing of—

    (i) asbestos cement,

   (ii) asbestos cement products,

   (iii) asbestos fillers,

   (iv) asbestos filters,

   (v) asbestos floor coverings,

   (vi) asbestos friction products,

   (vii) asbestos insulating board,

  (viii) asbestos jointing, packaging and reinforcement materials,

   (ix) asbestos packing,

   (x) asbestos paper and card, or

   (xi) asbestos textiles; or

(c) crocidolite is stripped from railway vehicles other than as part of repair or maintenance or during vehicle recovery after an accident; or

(d) railway vehicles containing crocidolite are destroyed by burning at purpose built installations.

For the purposes of this paragraph, "asbestos" means any of the following fibrous silicates:
actinolite, amosite, anthophyllite, chrysotile, crocidolite or tremolite.

Benzene works
Works (not being tar works or bitumen works as defined in this Schedule) in which—
(a) any wash oil used for the scrubbing of coal gas is distilled; or
(b) any crude benzol is distilled; or
(c) benzene is distilled or recovered.

Beryllium works
Works in which—
(a) any ore or concentrate or any material containing beryllium or its compounds is treated for the production of beryllium or its alloys or its compounds; or
(b) any material containing beryllium or its alloys or its compounds is treated, processed or fabricated in any manner giving rise to dust or fume.

Bisulphite works
(a) Works in which sulphurous acid is used in the manufacture of acid sulphites of the alkalis or alkaline earths; or
(b) works, not defined elsewhere in this Schedule, in which oxides of sulphur are—
  (i) made; or
  (ii) used or evolved in any chemical manufacturing operation; or
  (iii) used in the production of sulphurous acid.

Bromine works
Works in which bromine is made or is used in any manufacturing operation.

Cadmium works
Works in which—
(a) metallic cadmium is recovered; or
(b) cadmium alloys are made or recovered; or
(c) any compound of cadmium is made by methods giving rise to dust or fume.

Carbon disulphide works
Works for the manufacture, use or recovery of carbon disulphide.

Carbonyl works
Works in which metal carbonyls are manufactured or used in any chemical or metallurgical manufacturing process.

Caustic soda works
Works in which black liquor produced in the manufacture of paper is calcined in the recovery of caustic soda.

Cement works
Works in which—
(a) argillaceous and calcareous materials are used in the production of cement clinker; or
(b) cement clinker is handled and ground.

Ceramic works
Works in which—
(a) heavy clay or refractory goods are fired by coal or oil in any kiln in which a reducing atmosphere is essential; or
(b) salt glazing of any earthenware or clay material is carried on.

Chemical fertiliser works
Works in which the manufacture of chemical fertiliser is carried on, and works in which any mineral phosphate is subjected to treatment involving chemical change through the

application or use of any acid and works for the granulating of chemical fertilisers involving the evolution of any noxious or offensive gas.

Chlorine works
Works in which chlorine is made or used in any manufacturing process.

Chromium works
Works in which—
  (a) any chrome ore or concentrate is treated for the production therefrom of chromium compounds; or
  (b) chromium metal is made by methods giving rise to dust or fume.

Copper works
Works in which—
  (a) by the application of heat
      (i) copper is extracted from any ore or concentrate or from any material containing copper or its compounds; or
      (ii) molten copper is refined; or
      (iii) copper or copper alloy swarf is degreased; or
      (iv) copper alloys are recovered from scrap fabricated metal, swarf or residues by processes designed to reduce the zinc content; or
      (v) copper alloys are recovered from scrap fabricated metal, swarf or residues; or
  (b) copper or copper alloy is melted and cast.
but in sub-paragraphs (a)(v) and (b) of this paragraph excluding works in which the aggregate casting capacity does not exceed 10 tonnes per day.

Di-isocyanate works
Works in which—
  (a) di-isocyanates or partly polymerised di-isocyanates are made; or
  (b) di-isocyanates or partly polymerised di-isocyanates are used in the manufacture of flexible or rigid polyurethane foams or elastomers; or
  (c) polyurethane foams are subjected to hot-wire cutting or flame-bonding.

Electricity works
Works in which solid liquid or gaseous fuel is burned—
  (a) for the generation of electricity solely for distribution to the general public or for purposes of public transport, but excluding compression ignition engines burning distillate fuel with a sulphur content of less than 1%; or
  (b) for the generation of electricity for any purpose where the net rated thermal input of the works is 50 megawatts or more, other than those mentioned in sub-paragraph (a) of this paragraph.

Fibre works
Works in which glass fibre or mineral fibre (other than asbestos fibre) is made.

Fluorine works
Works in which fluorine or its compounds with other halogens are made or used in the manufacture of any product, or works for the manufacture of fluorides, borofluorides or silicofluorides.

Gas liquor works
Works (not being sulphate of ammonia works and chloride of ammonia works as defined in this Schedule) in which hydrogen sulphide or any other noxious or offensive

gas is evolved by the use of ammoniacal liquor in any manufacturing process, and works in which any such liquor is desulphurised by the application of heat in any process connected with the purification of gas.

Gas and coke works
Works (not being producer gas works as defined in this Schedule) in which—
  (a) coal, oil, or mixtures of coal or oil with other carbonaceous materials or products of petroleum refining or natural gas or methane from coal mines or gas derived from fermentation of carbonaceous materials are handled or prepared for carbonisation or gasification or reforming and in which these materials are subsequently carbonised or gasified or reformed; or
  (b) water gas is produced or purified; or
  (c) coke or semi-coke or other solid smokeless fuel is produced and quenched, cut, crushed or graded; or
  (d) gases derived from any process mentioned in sub-paragraph (a) of this paragraph are subjected to purification processes.

Hydrochloric acid works
  (a) hydrochloric acid works or works (not being alkali works as defined in section 27(1) of the 1906 Act) where hydrogen chloride is evolved either during the preparation of liquid hydrochloric acid or for use in any manufacturing process or as the result of the use of chorides in a chemical process;
  (b) tinplate flux works that is to say works in which any residue or flux from tinplate works is calcined for the utilisation of such residue or flux, and in which hydrogen choride is evolved; and
  (c) salt works that is to say works (not being works in which salt is produced by refining rock salt, otherwise than by the dissolution of rock salt at the place of deposit) in which the extraction of salt from brine is carried on, and in which hydrogen chloride is evolved.

Hydrofluoric acid works
Works in which—
  (a) hydrogen fluoride is evolved either in the manufacture of liquid hydrofluoric acid or its compounds, or as the result of the use of fluorides in a chemical process; or
  (b) mineral phosphates are treated with acid other than in fertiliser manufacture; or
  (c) mineral phosphates are defluorinated; or
  (d) anhydrous hydrogen fluoride is stored and handled in fixed tanks with an aggregate capacity exceeding 1 tonne.

Hydrogen cyanide works
Works in which hydrogen cyanide is made or is used in any chemical manufacturing process.

Incineration works
Works for the destruction by burning of—
  (a) waste produced from chemical manufacturing processes; or
  (b) chemical waste containing combined bromine, cadmium, chlorine, fluorine, iodine, lead, mercury, nitrogen, phosphorus, sulphur or zinc; or
  (c) waste produced in the manufacture of plastics; or
  (d) other waste, where the works are capable of incinerating 1 tonne or more of waste per hour.

Iron works and steel works
Works in which—
  (a) iron ores or iron ores and other materials for the production of iron are handled, stored or prepared, but excluding the winning of iron ores; or
  (b) iron ores for the production of iron are calcined, sintered or pelletised; or

(c)　iron or ferro-alloys are produced in a blast furnace or by direct reduction; or

(d)　iron or steel is melted in
  (i)　electric arc furnaces; or
  (ii)　cupolas employing a heated air blast; or

(e)　steel is produced, melted or refined in Tropenas, open hearth or electric arc furnaces; or

(f)　air or oxygen or air enriched with oxygen is used for the refining of iron or for the production, shaping or finishing of steel; or

(g)　ferro-alloys are made by methods giving rise to dust or fume; or

(h)　iron or ferro-alloys produced in any process described in sub-paragraphs (c), (d) or (g) of this paragraph are desulphurised by methods giving rise to dust or fume.

Large combustion works
Works (other than those mentioned elsewhere in this Schedule) in which solid, liquid or gaseous fuel is burned in boilers or furnaces with a net rated thermal input of 50 megawatts or more.

Large glass works
Works capable of producing 5,000 tonnes or more of glass (other than glass fibre) per year.

Large paper pulp works
Works capable of producing 25,000 tonnes or more of paper pulp by chemical methods per year.

Lead works
(a)　works (not being works defined elsewhere in this Schedule) in which by the application of heat
  (i)　lead is extracted or recovered from any material containing lead or its compounds; or
  (ii)　lead is refined; or
  (iii)　lead is applied as a surface coating to other metals by spraying; or

(b)　works (not being works defined elsewhere in this Schedule) in which compounds of lead are manufactured, extracted, recovered or used in processes which give rise to dust or fume, but excluding the manufacture of electric accumulators and the application of glazes or vitreous enamels; or

(c)　works in which organic lead compounds are made.

Lime works
Works in which—
(a)　calcium carbonate or calcium-magnesium carbonate is burnt through the agency of solid, liquid or gaseous fuels; or

(b)　lime is slaked on premises where any process described in sub-paragraph (a) of this paragraph is carried out.

Magnesium works
Works in which magnesium or its alloys or any compound of magnesium is made by methods giving rise to dust or fume.

Manganese works
Works in which manganese or its alloys or any compound of manganese is made by methods giving rise to dust or fume.

Metal recovery works
Works in which metal is recovered from scrap cable by burning in a furnace.

Mineral works
Works in which—
(a)　metallurgical slags; or

(b) pulverised fuel ash; or

(c) minerals, other than moulding sand in foundries or coal,

are subjected to any size reduction, grading or heating by processes giving rise to dust, not being works described elsewhere in this Schedule.

Nitrate and chloride of iron works
Works in which nitric acid or a nitrate is used in the manufacture of nitrate or chloride of iron.

Nitric acid works
Works in which the manufacture of nitric acid is carried on and works in which nitric acid is recovered from oxides of nitrogen and works where in the manufacture of any product any acid-forming oxide of nitrogen is evolved.

Paraffin oil works
Works in which crude shale oil is produced or refined, and works in which—
  (a) any product of the refining of crude shale oil is treated so as to cause the evolution of any noxious or offensive gases; or
  (b) any such product as aforesaid is used in any subsequent chemical manufacturing process except as a solvent.

Petrochemical works
Works in which—
  (a) any hydrocarbons are used for the production of ethylene or propylene or other olefines; or
  (b) (i) ethylene or propylene or other olefines or mixtures thereof are used in any chemical manufacturing process, not being a chemical manufacturing process defined in any other paragraph of this Schedule; or
      (ii) any product of the processes to which sub-paragraph (b)(i) of this paragraph applies is used, except as a solvent, in any subsequent chemical manufacturing process, not being a chemical manufacturing process defined in any other paragraph of this Schedule; or
  (c) ethylene or propylene or other olefines or products of processes defined at sub-paragraphs (b)(i) and (ii) of this paragraph or mixtures thereof are polymerised.

Petroleum works
Works in which—
  (a) crude or stabilised crude petroleum or associated gas, or condensate is
      (i) handled or stored; or
      (ii) refined; or
  (b) any product of such refining is subjected to further refining or to conversion; or
  (c) natural gas is refined or odorised; or
  (d) any product of any of the foregoing operations is used, except as a solvent, in any subsequent chemical manufacturing process, provided that the process is not described elsewhere in this Schedule; or
  (e) used lubricating oil is prepared for re-use by any thermal process.

Phosphorus works
Works in which—
  (a) phosphorus is made; or
  (b) yellow phosphorus is used in any chemical or metallurgical process.

Picric acid works
Works in which nitric acid or a nitrate is used in the manufacture of picric acid.

Producer gas works
Works in which producer gas is made from coal and in which raw producer gas is transmitted or used.

Pyridine works
Works in which pyridines or picolines or lutidines are recovered or made.

Selenium works
Works in which—
    (a) any ore or concentrate or any material containing selenium or its compounds is treated for the production of selenium or its alloys or its compounds; or
    (b) any material containing selenium or its alloys or its compounds other than as colouring matter is treated, processed or fabricated in any manner giving rise to dust or fume.

Smelting works
Works in which sulphides or sulphide ores, including regulus or mattes are calcined or smelted.

Sulphate of ammonia works, and chloride of ammonia works
Works in which the manufacture of sulphate of ammonia or of chloride of ammonia is carried on.

Sulphide works
Works in which—
    (a) hydrogen sulphide is evolved by the decomposition of metallic sulphides; or
    (b) hydrogen sulphide is used in the production of such sulphides; or
    (c) hydrogen sulphide or mercaptains are—
        (i) made, or
       (ii) used in any chemical process, or
      (iii) evolved as part of any chemical process.

Sulphuric acid (Class I) works
Works in which the manufacture of sulphuric acid is carried on by the lead chamber process, namely, the process by which sulphurous acid is converted into sulphuric acid by the agency of oxides of nitrogen and by the use of a lead chamber or by any other process involving the use of oxides of nitrogen.

Sulphuric acid (Class II) works
Works in which the manufacture of sulphuric acid is carred on by any process other than the lead chamber process, and works for the concentration or distillation of sulphuric acid.

Tar works and bitumen works
    (a) works (not being works described elsewhere in this Schedule) in which gas tar or coal tar or bitumen is distilled or is heated in any manufacturing process, and any product of the distillation of gas tar or coal tar or bitumen is distilled or heated in any process involving the evolution of any noxious or offensive gas; or
    (b) works in which heated materials produced from gas tar or coal tar or bitumen are applied in coating or wrapping of iron or steel pipes or fittings.

Uranium works
Works (not being works licensed under the Nuclear Installations Acts 1965 and 1969 and not being nuclear reactors or works involving the processing of irradiated fuel there-from for the purpose of removing fission products) in which—
    (a) any ore or concentrate or any material containing uranium or its compounds is treated for the production of uranium or its alloys or its compounds; or
    (b) any volatile compounds of uranium are manufactured or used; or
    (c) uranium or its compounds are manufactured, fashioned or fabricated by methods giving rise to dust or fume.

Vinyl chloride works
Works in which vinyl chloride is made or polymerised or used or stored and handled in fixed tanks with an aggregate capacity exceeding 20 tonnes.

Zinc works
Works in which by the application of heat, zinc is extracted from the ore, or from any residue containing that metal, and works in which compounds of zinc are made by methods giving rise to dust or fume.

SCHEDULE 2

Regulation 4

Noxious or offensive substances
Acetic acid or its anhydride;
Acetylene;
Acrylates;
Acrylic acid;
Aldehydes;
Amines;
Ammonia or its compounds;
Arsenic or its compounds;
Asbestos;
Bromine or its compounds;
Carbon dioxide;
Carbon disulphide;
Carbon monoxide;
Chlorine or its compounds;
Cyanogen or its compounds;
Di-isocyanates;
Ethylene and higher olefines;
Fluorine or its compounds;
Fumaric acid;
Fumes or dust containing aluminium, antimony, arsenic, beryllium, cadmium, calcium, chlorine, chomium, copper, gallum, iron, lead, magnesium, manganese, mercury, molybdenum, nickel, phosphorus, platinum, potassium, selenium, silicon, silver, sodium, sulphur, tellurium, thallium, tin, titanium, tungsten, uranium, vanadium, zinc or their compounds;
Fumes or vapours from benzene works, paraffin oil works, petrochemical works, petroleum works, or tar works and bitumen works;
Glass fibres;
Hydrocarbons;
Hydrogen chloride;
Hydrogen sulphide;
Iodine or its compounds;
Isocyanates;
Lead or its compounds;
Maleic acid or its anhydride;
Mercury or its compounds;
Metal carbonyls;
Mineral fibres;
Nitric acid or oxides of nitrogen;
Nitriles;
Phenols;
Phosphorus or its compounds;
Phthalic acid or its anhydride;
Products containing hydrogen from the partial oxidation of hydrocarbons;
Pyridine or its homologues;
Smoke, grit and dust;
Styrene;
Sulphuric acid or sulphur trioxide;

Sulphurous acid or sulphur dioxide;
Vinyl chloride;
Volatile organic sulphur compounds.

SCHEDULE 3

Regulation 6

Amendments to the 1906 Act

1 Provision to be amended	2 Subject matter of provision	3 Present quantity	4 Quantity to be substituted
Section 1(1)	Maximum concentration of hydrochloric acid gas which may escape from alkali works	(a) Cubic foot (b) One-fifth part of a grain	(a) Cubic metre (b) 0.46 gram
Section 2(1)	Maximum concentration of hydrochloric acid gas which may be discharged from alkali works	Cubic foot	Cubic metre
Section 16	Measurement of air, smoke or gases for calculation of acids	(a) Cubic foot (b) Sixty degrees of Fahrenheit's thermometer (c) Thirty inches	(a) Cubic metre (b) 15 degrees Celsius (c) One bar

6. General duties of manufacturers etc. as regards articles and substances for use at work.—(1) It shall be the duty *(a)* of any person *(b)* who designs, manufactures, imports or supplies *(c)* any article for use at work *(d)* or any article of fairground equipment *(e)*—

    (a) to ensure, so far as is reasonably practicable *(f)*, that the article is so designed and constructed that it will be safe and without risks to health *(g)* at all times when it is being set, used, cleaned or maintained by a person at work;

    (b) to carry out or arrange for the carrying out of such testing and examination as may be necessary for the performance of the duty imposed on him by the preceding paragraph;

    (c) to take such steps as are necessary to secure that persons supplied by that person with the article are provided with adequate information about the use for which the article is designed or has been tested and about any conditions necessary to ensure that it will be safe and without risks to health at all such times as are mentioned in paragraph (a) above and when it is being dismantled or disposed of; and

    (d) to take such steps as are necessary to secure, so far as is reasonably practicable, that persons so supplied are provided with all such revisions of information provided to them by virtue of the preceeding paragraph as are necessary by reason of its becoming known that anything gives rise to a serious risk to health or safety.

(1A) It shall be the duty of any person who designs, manufactures, imports or supplies any article of fairground equipment—

(a) to ensure, so far as is reasonably practicable, that the article is so designed and constructed that it will be safe and without risks to health at all times when it is being used for or in connection with the entertainment of members of the public;

(b) to carry out or arrange for the carrying out of such testing and examination as may be necessary for the performance of the duty imposed on him by the preceding paragraph;

(c) to take such steps as are necessary to secure that persons supplied by that person with the article are provided with adequate information about the use for which the article is designed or has been tested and about any conditions necessary to ensure that it will be safe and without risks to health at all times when it is being used for or in connection with the entertainment of members of the public; and

(d) to take such steps as are necessary to secure, so far as is reasonably practicable, that persons so supplied are provided with all such revisions of information provided to them by virtue of the preceding paragraph as are necessary by reason of its becoming known that anything gives rise to a serious risk to health or safety.

(2) It shall be the duty of any person who undertakes the design or manufacture of any article for use at work or of any article of fairground equipment to carry out or arrange for the carrying out of any necessary research with a view to the discovery and, so far as is reasonably practicable, the elimination or minimisation of any risks to health or safety to which the design or article may give rise.

(3) It shall be the duty of any person who erects or installs any article for use at work in any premises *(h)* where that article is to be used by persons at work or who erects or installs any article of fairground equipment to ensure, so far as is reasonably practicable, that nothing about the way in which the article is erected or installed makes it unsafe or a risk to health at any such time as is mentioned in paragraph (a) of subsection (1) or, as the case may be, in paragraph (a) of subsection (1) or (1A) above.

(4) It shall be the duty of any person who manufactures, imports or supplies any substance *(i)*—

(a) to ensure, so far as is reasonably practicable, that the substance will be safe and without risks to health at all times when it is being used, handled, processed, stored or transported by a person at work or in premises to which section 4 above applies;

(b) to carry out or arrange for the carrying out of such testing and examination as may be necessary for the performance of the duty imposed on him by the preceding paragraph;

(c) to take such steps as are necessary to secure that persons supplied by that person with the substance are provided with adequate information about any risks to health or safety to which the inherent properties of the substance may give rise, about the results of any relevant tests which have been carried out on or in connection with the substance and about any conditions necessary to ensure that the substance will be safe and without risks to health at all such times as are mentioned in paragraph (a) above and when the substance is being disposed of; and

(d) to take such steps as are necessary to secure, so far as is reasonably practicable, that persons so supplied are provided with all such revisions of information provided to them by virtue of the preceding paragraph as are necessary by reason of its becoming known that anything gives rise to a serious risk to health or safety.

(5) It shall be the duty of any person who undertakes the manufacture of any substance to carry out or arrange for the carrying out of any necessary research with a view to the discovery and, so far as is reasonably practicable, the elimination or minimisation of any risks to health or safety to which the substance may give rise at all such times as are mentioned in paragraph (a) of subsection (4) above.

(6) Nothing in the preceding provisions of this section shall be taken to require a person to repeat any testing, examination or research which has been carried out otherwise than by him or at his instance, in so far as it is reasonable for him to rely on the results thereof for the purposes of those provisions.

(7) Any duty imposed on any person by any of the preceding provisions of this section shall extend only to things done in the course of a trade, business or other undertaking carried on by him (whether for profit or not) and to matters within his control.

(8) Where a person designs, manufactures, imports or supplies an article for use at work or an article of fairground equipment and does so for or to another on the basis of a written undertaking by that other to take specified steps sufficient to ensure so far as is reasonable that the article will be safe and without risks to health at all such times as are mentioned in paragraph (a) of subsection (1) or, as the case may be, in paragraph (a) of subsection (1) or (1A) above the undertaking shall have the effect of relieving the first mentioned person from the duty imposed by virtue of that paragraph to such extent as is reasonable having regard to the terms of the undertaking.

(8A) Nothing in subsection (7) or (8) above shall relieve any person who imports any article or substance from any duty in respect of anything which—

(a) in the case of an article designed outside the United Kingdom, was done by and in the course of any trade, profession or other undertaking carried on by, or was within the control of, the person who designed the article; or

(b) in the case of an article or substance manufactured outside the United Kingdom, was done by and in the course of any trade, profession or other undertaking carried on by, or was within the control of, the person who manufactured the article or substance.

(9) Where a person ("the ostensible supplier") supplies any article or substance to another ("the customer") under a hire-purchase agreement (*j*), conditional sale agreement (*k*) or credit-sale agreement (*l*), and the ostensible supplier—

(a) carries on the business of financing the acquisition of goods by others by means of such agreements; and

(b) in the course of that business acquired his interest in the article or substance supplied to the customer as a means of financing its acquisition by the customer from a third person ("the effective supplier"),

the effective supplier and not the ostensible supplier shall be treated for the purposes of this section as supplying the article or substance to the customer, and any duty imposed by the preceding provisions of this section on suppliers shall accordingly fall on the effective supplier and not on the ostensible supplier.

(10) For the purposes of this section an absence of safety or a risk to health shall be disregarded in so far as the case in or in relation to which it would arise is shown to be one the occurrence of which could not reasonably be foreseen; and in determining whether any duty imposed by virtue of paragraph (a) of subsection (1), (1A) or (4) above has been performed regard shall be had to any relevant information or advice which has been provided to any person by the person by whom the article has been designed, manufactured, imported or supplied or, as the case may be, by the person by whom the substance has been manufactured, imported or supplied.

General note. Subsections (1), (4) and (10) were substituted, sub-ss. (2), (3), (5), (8) and (9) were amended, and new sub-ss. (1A) and (8A) were added by the Consumer Protection Act 1987, s. 36, Sch. 3. This section confers no right of action in civil proceedings (s. 47(1)(a)). This section is modified in relation to the supply of an article under a lease by the Health and Safety (Leasing Arrangements) Regulations 1992, S.I. 1992 No. 1524, set out below.

Subsection (1) is modified by the Noise at Work Regulations 1989, S.I. 1989 No. 1790, reg. 12, set out in Part 5.

*(a) **Duty.*** For enforcement, see s. 18; for offences, see s. 33(1)(a). Where work involving asbestos-based thermal and acoustic insulation and sprayed coatings is done at premises or in work situations where the Control of Asbestos at Work Regulations 1987, S.I. 1987 No. 2115 and S.I. 1992 No. 3068 do not apply, the approved Code of Practice "Work with asbestos insulation and asbestos coating" provides practical guidance with regard to the requirements of s. 7. As to Codes of Practice generally, see s. 16; as to their use in criminal proceedings, see s. 17.

*(b) **Person.*** See note (g) to s. 4.

*(c) **Supplies.*** For definition, see s. 53(1). As to the supply of an article under a hire-purchase or similar agreement, see sub-s. (9); as to the supply of an article under a lease, see the general note.

*(d) **Article for use at work.*** For definition, see s. 53(1). In *McKay v Unwin Pyrotechnics Ltd* [1991] Crim LR 547 it was held that the section was restricted to articles to be used in the workplace and consequently did not apply to a defective dummy explosive mine.

*(e) **Article of fairground equipment.*** For definition, see s. 53(1).

*(f) **Reasonably practicable.*** See INTRODUCTORY NOTE 5.

*(g) **Safe and without risks to health.*** See sub-s. (10).

*(h) **Premises.*** For definition, see s. 53(1).

*(i) **Substance.*** For definition, see s. 53(1).

*(j) **Hire-purchase agreement.*** For definition, see s. 53(1).

*(k) **Conditional sale agreement.*** For definition, see s. 53(1).

*(l) **Credit-sale agreement.*** For definition, see s. 53(1).

THE HEALTH AND SAFETY (LEASING ARRANGEMENTS)
REGULATIONS 1992
(S.I. 1992 No. 1524)

1. Citation and commencement. These Regulations may be cited as the Health and Safety (Leasing Arrangements) Regulations 1992 and shall come into force on 3 August 1992.

2. Interpretation. In these Regulations, unless the context otherwise requires—
"the 1974 Act" means the Health and Safety at Work etc. Act 1974;
"lease" means any kind of agreement or arrangement under which payments are, or are to be, made for the supply of an article for use at work or an article of fairground equipment except a conditional sale agreement, a credit-sale agreement, a hire-purchase agreement or a contract of sale.

3. Modification of section 6 of *the 1974 Act* in the case of a first *lease*. Where a person ("the ostensible supplier") supplies an article for use at work or an article of fairground equipment to another ("the customer") under a *lease*, and the ostensible supplier—

(a) has not previously granted any *lease* to the customer in respect of that article, and

(b) carries on the business of financing by means of *leases* the use of goods by others, and

(c) in the course of that business acquired his interest in the article for the purpose of financing its provision to the customer by a third person ("the effective supplier"), and

(d) he or his agent either—

　　(i) has not had physical possession of the article, or

　　(ii) has not had physical possession of the article only for the purpose of passing it to the customer, and

(e) he or his agent has modified, overhauled, repaired or restored the article,

then section 6 of *the 1974 Act* shall be modified in relation to that class of case so that the effective supplier and not the ostensible supplier shall be treated for the purposes of that section as supplying the article to the customer; and accordingly the duties imposed by subsection (1) and (1A) of that section in respect of the supply of the article shall fall on the effective supplier and not on the ostensible supplier.

4. Modification of section 6 of *the 1974 Act* where a further *lease* is granted in continuation of a lease to which regulation 3 applies. Where—

(a) regulation 3 of these Regulations has applied in respect of a *lease*, and

(b) the ostensible supplier grants a further *lease* of the article to the same customer, and

(c) the article has remained in the physical possession of the customer since he took possession of it under the first *lease*, and

(d) the article has not at any time been modified, overhauled, repaired or restored by or on behalf of the ostensible supplier, then section 6(1) and (1A) of *the 1974 Act* shall be modified in relation to that class of case so that no duty is imposed on the ostensible supplier in relation to the supply by way of that further *lease*.

5. Revocation. The Health and Safety (Leasing Arrangements) Regulations 1980 are hereby revoked.

---

7. General duties of employees at work. It shall be the duty *(a)* of every employee *(b)* while at work *(c)*—

(a) to take reasonable care for the health and safety of himself and of other persons who may be affected by his acts or omissions at work; and

(b) as regards any duty or requirement imposed on his employer *(d)* or any other person by or under any of the relevant statutory provisions *(e)*, to co-operate with him so far as is necessary to enable that duty or requirement to be performed or complied with.

General note. This section confers no right of action in civil proceedings (s. 47(1)(a)). But see under "Delegation of statutory duty" in LEGAL PRINCIPLES in the introductory section.

(a) **Duty.** For enforcement, see s. 18; for offences, see s. 33(1)(a).

(b) **Employee.** For definition, see s. 53(1).

(c) **At work.** For definition, see s. 52(1), (2).

(d) **Employer.** For definition, see s. 53(1).

(e) **The relevant statutory provisions.** For definition, see s. 53(1).

---

8. Duty not to interfere with or misuse things provided pursuant to certain provisions. No person *(a)* shall intentionally or recklessly interfere with or misuse anything provided in the interests of health, safety or welfare in pursuance of any of the relevant statutory provisions *(b)*.

General note. This section confers no right of action in civil proceedings (s. 47(1)(a)). It is an offence to contravene this section (s. 33(1)(b)). And see General Note to s. 7.

(a) **Person.** See note *(g)* to s. 4.

(b) **The relevant statutory provisions.** For definition, see s. 53(1).

---

9. Duty not to charge employees for things done or provided pursuant to certain specific requirements. No employer *(a)* shall levy or permit to be levied on any employee *(b)* of his any charge in respect of anything done or provided in pursuance of any specific requirement of the relevant statutory provisions *(c)*.

General note. It is an offence to contravene this section (s. 33(1)(b)).

(a) **Employer.** For definition, see s. 53(1).

(b) **Employee.** For definition, see s. 53(1).

(c) **The relevant statutory provisions.** For definition, see s. 53(1).

The Health and Safety Commission and the Health and Safety Executive

10. Establishment of the Commission and the Executive.—(1) There shall be two bodies corporate to be called the Health and Safety Commission *(a)* and the Health and Safety Executive *(b)* which shall be constituted in accordance with the following provisions of this section.

(2) The Health and Safety Commission (hereafter in this Act referred to as "the Commission") shall consist of a chairman appointed by the Secretary of State *(c)* and not less than six nor more than nine other members appointed by the Secretary of State in accordance with subsection (3) below.

(3) Before appointing the members of the Commission (other than the chairman) the Secretary of State shall—

(a) as to three of them, consult such organisations representing employers *(d)* as he considers appropriate;

(b) as to three others, consult such organisations, representing employees *(e)* as he considers appropriate; and

(c) as to any other members he may appoint, consult such organisations representing local authorities *(f)* and such other organisations, including professional bodies, the activities of whose members are concerned with matters relating to any of the general purposes of this Part *(g)*, as he considers appropriate.

(4) The Secretary of State may appoint one of the members to be deputy chairman of the Commission.

(5) The Health and Safety Executive (hereafter in this Act referred to as "the Executive") shall consist of three persons of whom one shall be appointed by the Commission with the approval of the Secretary of State to be the director of the Executive and the others shall be appointed by the Commission with the like approval after consultation with the said director.

(6) The provisions of Schedule 2 shall have effect with respect to the Commission and the Executive.

(7) The functions of the Commission and of the Executive, and of their officers and servants, shall be performed on behalf of the Crown.

(8) For the purpose of any civil proceedings arising out of those functions, the Crown Proceedings Act 1947 and the Crown Suits (Scotland) Act 1857 shall apply to the Commission and the Executive as if they were government departments within the meaning of the said Act of 1947 or, as the case may be, public departments within the meaning of the said Act of 1857.

General note. For the general functions of the Commission and the Executive, see s. 11; for the control of the Commission by the Secretary of State, see s. 12, and for other powers of the Commission, see ss. 13 and 14.

(a) The Health and Safety Commission. This is referred to in the Act as "the Commission" (sub-s. (2)).

(b) The Health and Safety Executive. This is referred to in the Act as "the Executive" (sub-s. (5)).

(c) The Secretary of State. See note *(k)* to s. 2.

(d) Employer. For definition, see s. 53(1).

(e) Employee. For definition, see s. 53(1).

(f) Local authorities. For definition, see s. 53(1).

(g) The general purposes of this Part. See s. 1(4).

11. General functions of the Commission and the Executive.—(1) In addition to the other functions conferred on the Commission by virtue of this Act, but subject to subsection (3) below, it shall be the general duty of the Commission to do such things and make such arrangements as it considers appropriate for the general purposes of this Part *(a)*.

(2) It shall be the duty of the Commission—

(a) to assist and encourage persons concerned with matters relevant to any of the general purposes of this Part to further those purposes;

(b) to make such arrangements as it considers appropriate for the carrying out of research, the publication of the results of research and the provision of training and information in connection with those purposes, and to encourage research and the provision of training and information in that connection by others;

(c) to make such arrangements as it considers appropriate for securing that government departments, employers *(b)*, employees *(c)*, organisations representing employers and employees respectively, and other persons concerned with matters relevant to any of those purposes are provided with an information and advisory service and are kept informed of, and adequately advised on, such matters;

(d) to submit from time to time to the authority having power to make regulations under any of the relevant statutory provisions *(d)* such proposals as the Commission considers appropriate for the making of regulations under that power.

(3) It shall be the duty of the Commission—

(a) to submit to the Secretary of State *(e)* from time to time particulars of what it proposes *(f)* to do for the purpose of performing its functions; and

(b) subject to the following paragraph, to ensure that its activities are in accordance with proposals approved by the Secretary of State; and

(c) to give effect to any directions given to it by the Secretary of State.

(4) In addition to any other functions conferred on the Executive by virtue of this Part, it shall be the duty of the Executive—

(a) to exercise on behalf of the Commission such of the Commission's functions as the Commission directs it to exercise; and

(b) to give effect to any directions given to it by the Commission otherwise than in pursuance of paragraph (a) above;

but, except for the purpose of giving effect to directions given to the Commission by the Secretary of State, the Commission shall not give to the Executive any directions as to the enforcement of any of the relevant statutory provisions in a particular case.

(5) Without prejudice to subsection (2) above, it shall be the duty of the Executive, if so requested by a Minister of the Crown—

(a) to provide him with information about the activities of the Executive in connection with any matter with which he is concerned; and

(b) to provide him with advice on any matter with which he is concerned on which relevant expert advice is obtainable from any of the officers or servants of the Executive but which is not relevant to any of the general purposes of this Part.

(6) The Commission and the Executive shall, subject to any directions given to it in pursuance of this Part, have power to do anything (except borrow money) which is calculated to facilitate, or is conducive or incidental to, the performance of any function of the Commission or, as the case may be, the Executive (including a function conferred on it by virtue of this subsection).

(a) *The general purposes of this Part.* See s. 1(4).

(b) *Employer.* For definition, see s. 53(1).

(c) *Employee.* For definition, see s. 53(1).

(d) *The relevant statutory provisions.* For definition, see s. 53(1).

(e) *The Secretary of State.* See note (k) to s. 2.

(f) *Proposes.* As to the approval of proposals, see s. 12(a).

---

12. Control of the Commission by the Secretary of State.   The Secretary of State (a) may—

(a) approve, with or without modifications (b), any proposals submitted to him in pursuance of section 11(3)(a);

(b) give to the Commission at any time such directions as he thinks fit with respect to its functions (including directions modifying its functions, but not directions conferring on it functions other than any of which it was deprived by previous directions given by virtue of this paragraph), and any directions which it appears to him requisite or expedient to give in the interests of the safety of the State.

(a) *The Secretary of State.* See note (k) to s. 2.

(b) *Modifications.* For definition, see s. 82(1)(c).

---

13. Other powers of the Commission.—(1) The Commission shall have power—

(a) to make agreements (a) with any government department or other person for that department or person to perform on behalf of the Commission or the Executive (with or without payment) any of the functions of the Commission or, as the case may be, of the Executive;

(b) subject to subsection (2) below, to make agreements with any Minister of the Crown, government department or other public authority for the Commission to perform on behalf of that Minister, department or authority (with or without payment) functions exercisable by the Minister, department or authority (including, in the case of a Minister, functions not conferred by an enactment), being functions which in the opinion of the Secretary of State *(b)* can appropriately be performed by the Commission in connection with any of the Commission's functions;

(c) to provide (with or without payment) services or facilities required otherwise than for the general purposes of this Part *(c)* in so far as they are required by any government department or other public authority in connection with the exercise by that department or authority of any of its functions;

(d) to appoint persons or committees of persons to provide the Commission with advice in connection with any of its functions and (without prejudice to the generality of the following paragraph) to pay to persons so appointed such remuneration as the Secretary of State may with the approval of the Minister for the Civil Service determine;

(e) in connection with any of the functions of the Commission, to pay to any person such travelling and subsistence allowances and such compensation for loss of remunerative time as the Secretary of State may with the approval of the Minister for the Civil Service determine;

(f) to carry out or arrange for or make payments in respect of research into any matter connected with any of the Commission's functions, and to disseminate or arrange for or make payments in respect of the dissemination of information derived from such research;

(g) to include, in any arrangements made by the Commission for the provision of facilities or services by it or on its behalf, provision for the making of payments to the Commission or any person acting on its behalf by other parties to the arrangements and by persons who use those facilities or services.

(2) Nothing in subsection (1)(b) shall authorise the Commission to perform any function of a Minister, department or authority which consists of a power to make regulations or other instruments of a legislative character.

(a) Agreements. See s. 18(7).

(b) The Secretary of State. See note *(k)* to s. 2.

(c) The general purposes of this Part. See s. 1(4).

---

14. Power of the Commission to direct investigations and inquiries.— (1) This section applies to the following matters, that is to say any accident, occurrence, situation or other matter whatsoever which the Commission thinks it necessary or expedient to investigate for any of the general purposes of this Part *(a)* or with a view to the making of regulations for those purposes; and for the purposes of this subsection it is immaterial whether the Executive is or is not responsible for securing the enforcement *(b)* of such (if any) of the relevant statutory provisions *(c)* as relate to the matter in question.

(2) The Commission may at any time—

(a) direct the Executive or authorise any other person to investigate and make a special report on any matter to which this section applies; or

(b) with the consent of the Secretary of State *(d)* direct an inquiry to be held into any such matter.

(3) Any inquiry held by virtue of subsection (2)(b) above shall be held in accordance with regulations *(e)* made for the purposes of this subsection by the Secretary of State, and shall be held in public except where or to the extent that the regulations provide otherwise.

(4) Regulations made for the purposes of subsection (3) above may in particular include provision—

(a)   conferring on the person holding any such inquiry, and any person assisting him in the inquiry, powers of entry and inspection *(f)*;

(b)   conferring on any such person powers of summoning witnesses to give evidence or produce documents and power to take evidence on oath and administer oaths or require the making of declarations;

(c)   requiring any such inquiry to be held otherwise than in public where or to the extent that a Minister of the Crown so directs.

(5) In the case of a special report made by virtue of subsection (2)(a) above or a report made by the person holding an inquiry held by virtue of subsection (2)(b) above, the Commission may cause the report, or so much of it as the Commission thinks fit, to be made public at such time and in such manner as the Commission thinks fit.

(6) The Commission—

(a)   in the case of an investigation and special report made by virtue of subsection (2)(a) above (otherwise than by an officer or servant of the Executive), may pay to the person making it such remuneration and expenses as the Secretary of State may, with the approval of the Minister for the Civil Service, determine;

(b)   in the case of an inquiry held by virtue of subsection (2)(b) above, may pay to the person holding it and to any assessor appointed to assist him such remuneration and expenses, and to persons attending the inquiry as witnesses such expenses, as the Secretary of State may, with the like approval, determine; and

(c)   may, to such extent as the Secretary of State may determine, defray the other costs, if any, of any such investigation and special report or inquiry.

(7) Where an inquiry is directed to be held by virtue of subsection (2)(b) above into any matter to which this section applies arising in Scotland, being a matter which causes the death of any person, no inquiry with regard to that death shall, unless the Lord Advocate otherwise directs, be held in pursuance of the Sudden Deaths Inquiry (Scotland) Act 1976.

(a) The general purposes of this Part. See s. 1(4).

(b) Enforcement. See s. 18.

(c) The relevant statutory provisions. For definition, see s. 53(1).

(d) The Secretary of State. See note *(k)* to s. 2.

(e) Regulations. See the Health and Safety Inquiries (Procedure) Regulations 1975, S.I. 1975 No. 335 (set out below). It is an offence to contravene any requirement imposed by or under such regulations or intentionally to obstruct any person in the exercise of his powers under s. 14 (s. 33(1)(d)).

(f) Entry and inspection. As to the disclosure of information obtained by the exercise of this power, see s. 28(7).

THE HEALTH AND SAFETY INQUIRIES (PROCEDURE)
REGULATIONS 1975
(S.I. 1975 No. 335, as amended by S.I. 1976 No. 1246)

The Secretary of State in exercise of the powers conferred on him by sections 14(3) and (4) and 82(3)(a) of the Health and Safety at Work etc. Act 1974 and of all other powers enabling him in that behalf, and after consultation with the Health and Safety Commission and such other bodies as appeared to him to be appropriate, hereby makes the following Regulations—

Citation and commencement
1. These Regulations may be cited as the Health and Safety Inquiries (Procedure) Regulations 1975 and shall come into operation on 1 May 1975.

Interpretation
2.—(1) In these Regulations—
"the 1974 Act" means the Health and Safety at Work etc. Act 1974;
"appointed person" means a person appointed by *the Commission* to hold an inquiry;
"the Commission" means the Health and Safety Commission;
"enforcing authority" means an enforcing authority as defined in section 18(7) of *the 1974 Act*;
"the Executive" means the Health and Safety Executive;
"inquiry" means an inquiry to which these Regulations apply;
"trade union" and "employers' association" have the meanings assigned by section 28 of the Trade Union and Labour Relations Act 1974 *(a)*.
(2) The Interpretation Act 1889 [Interpretation Act 1978] shall apply to the interpretation of these Regulations as it applies to the interpretation of an Act of Parliament.

(a) **Trade Union.** Now see s. 1 of the Trade Union and Labour Relations (Consolidation) Act 1992, and, for "employers' association", s. 122 of that Act.

Application of Regulations
3.—(1) These Regulations shall have effect with respect to the proceedings at or in connection with inquiries held under section 14(2)(b) of the *1974 Act*.

Notification of inquiry
4.—(1) A date, time and place for the holding of the *inquiry* shall be fixed and may be varied by *the Commission*, who shall give not less than 28 days' notice in writing of such date, time and place to every person entitled to appear at the *inquiry* whose name and address are known to *the Commission*;
Provided that—
  (i) with the consent of all such persons, *the Commission* may give such lesser period of notice as shall be agreed with those persons; and
  (ii) where it becomes necessary or advisable to vary the time or place fixed for the *inquiry*, *the Commission* shall give such notice of the variation as may appear to it to be reasonable in the circumstances.
(2) The notice given under paragraph (1) of this Regulation shall state the name of the *appointed person* and the names of any assessors appointed to assist him in the *inquiry*.
(3) Without prejudice to the foregoing provisions of this Regulation *the Commission* shall also for the purpose of notifying persons who may be concerned of the holding of the *inquiry*, take one or more of the following steps, namely—
  (a) publish notice of the *inquiry* in one or more newspapers, including, where appropriate, newspapers circulating in the locality in which the subject matter of the *inquiry* arose; and
  (b) give such other notice of the *inquiry* as appears to *the Commission* to be appropriate,

and the requirements as to the period of notice contained in paragraph (1) of this Regulation shall not apply to any such notices.

Appearances at inquiry

5.—(1) The persons entitled to appear at the *inquiry* shall be—

(a) *the Commission*;

(b) any *enforcing authority* concerned;

(c) where the *inquiry* relates to any matter arising in Scotland, the Procurator Fiscal;

(d) any *employers' association* or *trade union* representing respectively employers or employees who are concerned;

(e) any person who was injured or suffered damage as a result of the accident, occurrence, situation, or other matter the subject of the *inquiry* or his personal representatives;

(f) the owner or occupier of any premises in which there occurred or arose the accident, occurrence, situation or other matter the subject of the *inquiry*;

(g) any person carrying on activities giving rise to the accident, occurrence, situation or other matter the subject of the *inquiry*.

(2) Any other person may appear at the discretion of the *appointed person*.

Representation

6.—(1) A body corporate may appear by its clerk or secretary or by any other officer appointed for the purpose, or by counsel or solicitor, and also, in the case of *the Commission*, by an officer of *the Executive* so appointed.

(2) A government department, an *employers' association* or a *trade union* may appear by counsel or solicitor or by any other person appointed for the purpose.

(3) Any other person may appear on his own behalf or be represented by counsel or solicitor or any other person.

(4) Where there are two or more persons having a similar interest in the matter under *inquiry*, the appointed person may allow one or more persons to appear for the benefit of some or all persons so interested.

Power to require attendance of witnesses and production of documents

7.—(1) The *appointed person* may, either of his own motion or on the application of any person entitled or permitted to appear, cause to be served on any person appearing to him to be likely to be able to give material evidence or to produce any document likely to be material evidence, a notice requiring that person to attend at the *inquiry* at the time and place specified in the notice to give evidence or produce the document.

(2) A person on whom a notice is served under paragraph (1) of this Regulation may apply to the *appointed person* either at or before the *inquiry* to vary or set aside the requirement, and where he does so before the *inquiry* he shall give notice of his application to the person, if any, who applied for the notice under paragraph (1) to be served.

(3) A notice containing a requirement under paragraph (1) of this Regulation shall contain a reference to the fact that under section 33(2) of *the 1974 Act* a person who contravenes such a requirement is liable on summary conviction to a fine not exceeding £400.

(4) No person shall be required under this Regulation to attend to give evidence or produce any document, unless the necessary expenses of his attendance are paid or tendered to him.

Procedure at inquiry

8.—(1) Except as otherwise provided in these Regulations, the procedure at and in connection with an *inquiry* shall be in the discretion of the *appointed person* who shall state at the commencement of the hearing the procedure which, subject to consideration of any submission by the persons appearing at the *inquiry*, he proposes to adopt and shall inform those persons what he proposes as regards any site inspection arising out of the hearing.

(2) Except as provided in paragraph (3) of this Regulation, the inquiry shall be held in public.

(3) The *appointed person*—

(a) shall, to the extent to which he has been so directed in writing by a Minister of the Crown, hold the inquiry otherwise than in public for the purpose of hearing evidence relating to matters specified in the direction, being matters of such a nature that it would, in the opinion of the Minister, be against the interests of national security to allow the evidence to be given in public; and

(b) may, on application made to him in that behalf, hold the inquiry otherwise than in public to such extent as he considers necessary for the purpose of hearing evidence, the giving of which is in his opinion likely to disclose information relating to a trade secret,

and information disclosed to any person by the hearing of evidence in the circumstances mentioned in sub-paragraphs (a) or (b) above shall not be disclosed by him except for the purposes of the *inquiry*:

Provided—

(i) that a member of the Council on Tribunals or of its Scottish Committee in his capacity as such shall be entitled to attend the hearing in any case; and

(ii) that a representative of any such *employers' association* or *trade union* as is mentioned in Regulation 5(1)(d) in his capacity as such shall be entitled to attend the hearing in a case falling within sub-paragraph (b) above.

(4) Persons entitled or permitted to appear shall be heard in such order as the *appointed person* may determine.

(5) Persons entitled to appear shall be entitled to make an opening statement, to call evidence and to cross-examine persons giving evidence, but any other person appearing at the inquiry may do so only to the extent permitted by the *appointed person*.

(6) Where the *appointed person* so requires, witnesses shall give evidence on oath, and for that purpose the *appointed person* may administer an oath in due form.

(7) Any evidence may be admitted at the discretion of the *appointed person*, who may direct that documents to be tendered in evidence may be inspected by any person entitled or permitted to appear at the inquiry and that facilities be afforded him to take or obtain copies thereof.

(8) The *appointed person* shall be entitled (subject to disclosure thereof at the inquiry and making available copies thereof to the persons appearing at the inquiry) to take into account any written representations or statement received by him before the *inquiry* from any person.

(9) The *appointed person* may from time to time adjourn the *inquiry*, and where he does so shall give reasonable notice to every person entitled or permitted to appear at the *inquiry* of the date, time and place of the adjourned inquiry, provided that where the date, time and place of the adjourned inquiry are announced at the inquiry, no further notice shall be required.

Site inspections

9. The *appointed person* and any person appointed to assist him in the *inquiry* may, where necessary for the purpose of the *inquiry*, at any reasonable time enter and make an inspection of any premises to which the *inquiry* relates and anything in them.

Procedure after inquiry

10.—(1) The *appointed person* shall after the close of the *inquiry* make a report in writing to *the Commission*, which shall include the *appointed person's* findings of fact and his recommendations if any or his reason for not making any recommendation.

(2) Except where the said report is to be published, in whole or in part, in pursuance of section 14(5) of *the 1974 Act*, the *Commission* shall send to any person who appeared at the *inquiry* a copy of the report or so much of it as *the Commission* thinks fit.

Notices

11.   The provisions of section 46 of *the 1974 Act* shall apply in relation to the services of notices required or authorised to be served or given by these Regulations as they apply to notices required or authorised to be served or given by *the 1974 Act.*

Health and safety regulations and approved codes of practice

15.   Health and safety regulations.—(1) Subject to the provisions of section 50, the Secretary of State *(a)*, the Minister of Agriculture, Fisheries and Food or the Secretary of State and that Minister acting jointly shall have power to make regulations *(b)* under this section for any of the general purposes of this Part *(c)* (and regulations so made are in this Part referred to as "health and safety regulations").

(2) Without prejudice to the generality of the preceding subsection, health and safety regulations may for any of the general purposes of this Part make provision for any of the purposes mentioned in Schedule 3.

(3) Health and safety regulations—

(a)   may repeal or modify *(d)* any of the existing statutory provisions *(e)*;

(b)   may exclude or modify in relation to any specified *(f)* class of case any of the provisions of sections 2 to 9 or any of the existing statutory provisions;

(c)   may make a specified authority or class of authorities responsible, to such extent as may be specified, for the enforcement *(g)* of any of the relevant statutory provisions.

(4) Health and safety regulations—

(a)   may impose requirements by reference to the approval of the Commission or any other specified body or person *(h)*;

(b)   may provide for reference in the regulations to any specified document to operate as references to that document as revised or re-issued from time to time.

(5) Health and safety regulations—

(a)   may provide (either unconditionally or subject to conditions, and with or without limit of time) for exemptions from any requirement or prohibition imposed by or under any of the relevant statutory provisions *(i)*;

(b)   may enable exemptions from any requirement or prohibition imposed by or under any of the relevant statutory provisions to be granted (either unconditionally or subject to conditions, and with or without limit of time) by any specified person or by any person authorised in that behalf by a specified authority.

(6) Health and safety regulations—

(a)   may specify the persons or classes of persons who, in the event of a contravention of a requirement or prohibition imposed by or under the regulations, are to be guilty of an offence *(j)*, whether in addition to or to the exclusion of other persons or classes of persons;

(b) may provide for any specified defence *(k)* to be available in proceedings for any offence under the relevant statutory provision either generally or in specified circumstances;

(c) may exclude proceedings on indictment in relation to offences consisting of a contravention of a requirement or prohibition imposed by or under any of the existing statutory provisions, sections 2 to 9 or health and safety regulations;

(d) may restrict the punishments (other than the maximum fine on conviction on indictment) which can be imposed in respect of any such offence as is mentioned in paragraph (c) above.

(e) in the case of regulations made for any purpose mentioned in section 1(1) of the Offshore Safety Act 1992, may provide that any offence consisting of a contravention of the regulations, or of any requirement or prohibition imposed by or under them, shall be punishable on conviction on indictment by imprisonment for a term not exceeding two years, or a fine, or both *(l)*.

(7) Without prejudice to section 35, health and safety regulations may make provision for enabling offences under any of the relevant statutory provisions to be treated as having been committed at any specified place for the purpose of bringing any such offence within the field of responsibility *(m)* of any enforcing authority *(n)* or conferring jurisdiction on any court to entertain proceedings for any such offence.

(8) Health and safety regulations may take the form of regulations applying to particular circumstances only or to a particular case only (for example, regulations applying to particular premises only).

(9) If an Order in Council is made under section 84(3) providing that this section shall apply to or in relation to persons, premises or work outside Great Britain *(o)* then, notwithstanding the Order, health and safety regulations shall not apply to or in relation to aircraft in flight, vessels, hovercraft or offshore installations *(p)* outside Great Britain or persons at work outside Great Britain in connection with submarine cables or submarine pipelines except in so far as the regulations expressly so provide.

(10) In this section "specified" means specified in health and safety regulations.

General note. Subsection (6)(e) is added by the Offshore Safety Act 1992, s. 4(1), (6), but this amendment does not affect the punishment of an offence committed before 6 March 1992.

If it appears to the Secretary of State to be necessary or expedient in connection with any provision made by health and safety regulations under this section, he may by order under the Fire Precautions Act 1971, s. 28A, amend the special provision for factory, office, railway and shop premises in Sch. 2 to the Act; see s. 28A(2) of that Act, as inserted by the Fire Safety and Safety of Places of Sport Act 1987, s. 16(1). By s. 49(2) of, and Sch. 5, para. 2 to, the 1987 Act, a fire certificate issued or deemed to be issued under regulations made under this Act is deemed to be a fire certificate within the meaning of the Fire Precautions Act 1971 and may be amended, replaced or revoked in accordance with the provisions of that Act. The Regulations implementing the European Directives which came into effect on 1 January 1993 were made under this section.

(a) **The Secretary of State.** See note *(k)* to s. 2. For his power to make regulations under the relevant statutory provisions (which include the Factories Act 1961), see s. 50.

(b) **Regulations.** Numerous Regulations have been made under this section, many of which are included in this book. They are not set out here for the sake of brevity.

(c) The general purposes of this Part. See s. 1(4).

(d) Modify. For definition, see s. 82(1)(c).

(e) The existing statutory provisions. For definition, see s. 53(1).

(f) Specified. This means specified in health and safety regulations: sub-s. (10).

(g) Enforcement. See s. 18 and, in particular, s. 18(3).

(h) Person. See note *(g)* to s. 4.

(i) The relevant statutory provisions. For definition, see s. 53(1).

(j) Offence. See s. 33(1)(c).

(k) Defence. As to civil proceedings, see s. 47(3).

(l) Field of responsibility. See s. 18(7)(b).

(m) Enforcing authority. For definition, see s. 18(7)(a).

(n) Great Britain. See INTRODUCTORY NOTE 4.

(o) Offshore installation. For definition, see s. 53(1).

---

16.   Approval of codes of practice by the Commission.—(1) For the purpose of providing practical guidance with respect to the requirements of any provision of sections 2 to 7 or of health and safety regulations *(a)* or of any of the existing statutory provisions *(b)*, the Commission may, subject to the following subsection—

(a) approve *(c)* and issue such codes of practice *(d)* (whether prepared by it or not) as in its opinion are suitable for that purpose;

(b) approve such codes of practice issued or proposed to be issued otherwise than by the Commission as in its opinion are suitable for that purpose.

(2) The Commission shall not approve a code of practice under subsection (1) above without the consent of the Secretary of State *(e)*, and shall, before seeking his consent, consult—

(a) any government department or other body that appears to the Commission to be appropriate (and, in particular, in the case of a code relating to electro-magnetic radiations, the National Radiological Protection Board *(f)*); and

(b) such government departments and other bodies, if any, as in relation to any matter dealt with in the code, the Commission is required to consult under this section by virtue of directions given to it by the Secretary of State.

(3) Where a code of practice is approved by the Commission under subsection (1) above, the Commission shall issue a notice in writing—

(a) identifying the code in question and stating the date on which its approval by the Commission is to take effect; and

(b) specifying for which of the provisions mentioned in subsection (1) above the code is approved.

(4) The Commission may—

(a) from time to time revise the whole or any part of any code of practice prepared by it in pursuance of this section;

(b) approve any revision or proposed revision of the whole or any part of any code of practice for the time being approved under this section,

and the provisions of subsections (2) and (3) above shall, with the necessary modifications, apply in relation to the approval of any revision under this subsection as they apply in relation to the approval of a code of practice under subsection (1) above.

(5) The Commission may at any time with the consent of the Secretary of State withdraw its approval from any code of practice approved under this section, but before seeking his consent shall consult the same government departments and other bodies as it would be required to consult under subsection (2) above if it were proposing to approve the code.

(6) Where under the preceding subsection the Commission withdraws its approval from a code of practice approved under this section, the Commission shall issue a notice in writing identifying the code in question, and stating the date on which its approval of it is to cease to have effect.

(7) Reference in this Part to an approved code of practice are references to that code as it has effect for the time being by virtue of any revision of the whole or any part of it approved under this section.

(8) The power of the Commission under subsection (1)(b) above to approve a code of practice issued or proposed to be issued otherwise than by the Commission shall include power to approve a part of such a code of practice; and accordingly in this Part "code of practice" may be read as including a part of such a code of practice.

General note. For the effect in civil or criminal proceedings of a failure to observe a provision of an approved code of practice, see s. 17.

As to the right to remuneration for suspension on medical grounds in consequence of any recommendation in a provision of a code of practice relating to specified matters, see the Employment Protection (Consolidation) Act 1978, ss. 19, 20 and Sch. 1.

(a) *Health and safety regulations.* For definition, see s. 53(1).

(b) *The existing statutory provisions.* For definition, see s. 53(1).

(c) *Approve.* As to approval of part of a code of practice, see sub-s. (8).

(d) *Code of practice.* This includes a standard, a specification and any other documentary form of practical guidance (s. 53(1)).

The following approved Codes of Practice relating to the subject matter of this book have been issued under this section. They are not printed in this book.

"Safety Representatives and Safety Committees" / "Time off for the Training of Safety Representatives" (in support of the Safety Representatives and Safety Committees Regulations 1977, S.I. 1977 No. 500);

"Control of Lead at Work" (in support of the Control of Lead at Work Regulations 1980, S.I. 1980 No. 1248); (June 1985 revision) "Work with Asbestos Insulation and Asbestos Coating" (in support of the Asbestos Regulations 1969, S.I. 1969 No. 690); "Control of asbestos at work: the Control of Asbestos at Work Regulations 1987" (in support of S.I. 1987 No. 2115); "First Aid" (in support of the Health and Safety (First Aid) Regulations 1981, S.I. 1981 No. 917); "Operational Provisions of the Dangerous Substances (Conveyance by Road in Road Tankers and Tank Containers) Regulations 1987"; "Notice of Approval of the Code of Practice for the operational provisions of the Road Traffic (Carriage of Dangerous Substances in Packages etc.) Regulations 1986" (in support of S.I. 1992 Nos. 742, 744 and 1213); "The protection of persons against ionising radiation arising from any work activity" (in support of the Ionising Radiations Regulations 1985, S.I. 1985, No. 1333); "Part 3: Exposure to radon. The Ionising Radiations Regulations 1985" (S.I. 1985 No. 1333); "Preventing accidents to children in agriculture"; "Safety in Docks—Docks Regulations 1988 and Guidance" (in support of S.I. 1988 No. 1655); "Control of Carcinogenic Substances—Control of Substances Hazardous to Health" (in support of S.I. 1988 No. 1657); "Control of Vinyl Chloride at Work—Control of Substances Hazardous to Health" (in support of S.I. 1988 No. 1657); "Control of Substances hazardous to health in fumigation operations—Control of Substances Hazardous to Health" (in support of S.I. 1988 No. 1657); "The use of electricity at quarries—Electricity at Work Regulations 1989" (in support of S.I. 1989, No. 635); "First aid on offshore installations and pipeline works" (in support of S.I. 1989 No. 1671); "Management of health and safety at work" (in support of the Management of Health and Safety at Work Regulations, S.I. 1992 No. 2051); "Workplace health, safety and welfare" (in support of the Workplace (Health, Safety and Welfare) Regulations, S.I. 1992 No. 3004).

The following British Standards have been approved as codes of practice for the purposes of s. 16:

BS 697: 1977 and 1986—Specification for Rubber Gloves for Electrical Purposes;
BS 1870 Part 1: 1979—Specification for Safety Footwear other than all-rubber and all-plastic moulded types;
BS 5426: 1976—Specification for Workwear;
BS 5169: 1975—Specification for fusion-welded steel air receivers;
BS 1870 Part 2: 1976—Specification for Lined Rubber Safety Boots;
BS 1870 Part 3: 1981—Specification for Polyvinyl Chloride Moulded Safety Footwear.

These British Standards are not included in this book.

(e) **The Secretary of State.** See note (k) to s. 2.

(f) **The National Radiological Protection Board.** See the Radiological Protection Act 1970, s. 1, as amended by the Health and Safety at Work etc. Act 1974, s. 77.

---

17. Use of approved codes of practice in criminal proceedings.—(1) A failure on the part of any person (a) to observe any provision of an approved code of practice (b) shall not of itself render him liable to any civil or criminal proceedings; but where in any criminal proceedings a party is alleged to have committed an offence by reason of a contravention (c) of any requirement or prohibition imposed by or under any such provision as is mentioned in section 16(1) being a provision for which there was an approved code of practice at the time of the alleged contravention, the following subsection shall have effect with respect to that code in relation to those proceedings.

(2) Any provision of the code of practice which appears to the court to be relevant to the requirement or prohibition alleged to have been contravened shall be admissible in evidence in the proceedings; and if it is proved that there was at any material time a failure to observe any provision of the code which appears to the court to be relevant to any matter which it is necessary for the prosecution to prove in order to establish a contravention of that requirement or prohibition, that matter shall be taken as proved unless the court is satisfied that the requirement or prohibition was in respect of that matter complied with otherwise than by way of observance of that provision of the code.

(3) In any criminal proceedings—

(a) a document purporting to be a notice issued by the Commission under section 16 shall be taken to be such a notice unless the contrary is proved; and

(b) a code of practice which appears to the court to be the subject of such a notice shall be taken to be the subject of that notice unless the contrary is proved.

General note. A code of practice cannot be used to impose upon a party a duty which is not specified in the Act or regulations. Even if there is a breach of a code of practice it is always open to a person to show that the statutory requirement was met otherwise than by way of an observance of the code, but if he does not show this, then the provisions of the code become good and complete evidence of the offence (*West Cumberland By Products Ltd v DPP* [1988] RTR 391, DC).

(a) *Person.* See note *(g)* to s. 4.

(b) *Code of practice.* See s. 16.

(c) *Contravention.* For definition, see s. 82(1)(b).

Enforcement

18. Authorities responsible for enforcement of the relevant statutory provisions.—(1) It shall be the duty of the Executive to make adequate arrangements for the enforcement of the relevant statutory provisions *(a)* except to the extent that some other authority or class of authorities is by any of those provisions or by regulations *(b)* under subsection (2) below made responsible for their enforcement.

(2) The Secretary of State may by regulations *(b)*—

(a) make local authorities *(c)* responsible for the enforcement of the relevant statutory provisions to such extent as may be prescribed *(d)*;

(b) make provision for enabling responsibility for enforcing any of the relevant statutory provisions to be, to such extent as may be determined under the regulations—

(i) transferred from the Executive to local authorities or from local authorities to the Executive; or

(ii) assigned to the Executive or to local authorities for the purpose of removing any uncertainty as to what are by virtue of this subsection their respective responsibilities for the enforcement of those provisions,

and any regulations made in pursuance of paragraph (b) above shall include provision for securing that any transfer or assignment effected under the regulations is brought to the notice of persons affected by it.

(3) Any provision made by regulations under the preceding subsection shall have effect subject to any provision made by health and safety regulations *(e)* in pursuance of section 15(3)(c).

(4) It shall be the duty of every local authority—

(a) to make adequate arrangements for the enforcement within their area of the relevant statutory provisions to the extent that they are by any of those provisions or by regulations under subsection (2) above made responsible for their enforcement; and

(b) to perform the duty imposed on them by the preceding paragraph and any other functions conferred on them by any of the relevant statutory provisions in accordance with such guidance as the Commission may give them.

(5) Where any authority other than the Executive or a local authority is by any of the relevant statutory provisions or by regulations under subsection (2) above made responsible for the enforcement of any of those provisions to any extent, it shall be the duty of that authority—

(a) to make adequate arrangements for the enforcement of those provisions to that extent; and

(b) to perform the duty imposed on the authority by the preceding paragraph and any other functions conferred on the authority by any of the relevant statutory provisions in accordance with such guidance as the Commission may give to the authority.

(6) Nothing in the provisions of this Act or of any regulations made thereunder charging any person in Scotland with the enforcement of any of the relevant statutory provisions shall be construed as authorising that person to institute proceedings for any offence.

(7) In this Part—

(a) "enforcing authority" means the Executive or any other authority which is by way of the relevant statutory provisions or by regulations under subsection (2) above made responsible for the enforcement of any of those provisions to any extent; and

(b) any reference to an enforcing authority's field of responsibility is a reference to the field over which that authority's responsibility for the enforcement of those provisions extend for the time being,

but where by virtue of paragraph (a) of section 13(1) the performance of any function of the Commission or the Executive is delegated to a government department or person, references to the Commission or the Executive (or to an enforcing authority where that authority is the Executive) in any provision of this Part which relates to that function shall, so far as may be necessary to give effect to any agreement under that paragraph, be construed as references to that department or person; and accordingly any reference to the field of responsibility of an enforcing authority shall be construed as a reference to the field over which that department or person for the time being performs such a function.

General note. The restriction on the disclosure of information contained in the Fire Precautions Act 1971, s. 21(1), does not apply to the disclosure of information to an enforcing authority in order to enable that authority to discharge any function falling within its field of responsibility and sub-s. (7) of this section applies for the purposes of that section as it applies for the purposes of Pt. I of this Act; see the Fire Precautions Act 1971, s. 21(2), (3) as inserted by the Fire Safety and Safety of Places of Sport Act 1987, s. 11.

(a) *The relevant statutory provisions.* For definition, see s. 53(1).

(b) *Regulations.* The Health and Safety (Enforcing Authority) Regulations 1989, S.I. 1989 No. 1903, set out below, have been made under this section.

(c) **Local authority.** For definition, see s. 53(1). As to default powers, see s. 45.

(d) **Prescribed.** For definition, see s. 53(1).

(e) **Health and safety regulations.** See s. 15.

HEALTH AND SAFETY (ENFORCING AUTHORITY) REGULATIONS 1989
(S.I. 1989 No. 1903)

1. Citation and commencement. These Regulations may be cited as the Health and Safety (Enforcing Authority) Regulations 1989 and shall come into force on 1 April 1990.

2. Interpretation.—(1) In these Regulations, unless the context otherwise requires—
"the 1974 Act" means the Health and Safety at Work etc. Act 1974;
"agricultural activities" includes horticulture, fruit growing, seed growing, dairy farming, *livestock* breeding and keeping, including the management of *livestock* up to the point of slaughter or export from Great Britain, forestry, the use of land as grazing land, market gardens and nursery grounds and the preparation of land for agricultural use; and for this purpose "*livestock* breeding and keeping" does not include activities the main purpose of which is entertainment or the breeding or keeping of *livestock* at a shop;
"the Commission" means the Health and Safety Commission;
"common parts" means those parts of premises used in common by, or for providing common services to or common facilities for, the occupiers of the premises;
"construction work" means a "building operation" or a "work of engineering construction" within the meanings assigned to those expressions by section 176(1) of the Factories Act 1961;
"contractor" means a self-employed person, or an employer of persons, carrying out *construction work*, except that in the case of a self-employed person who contracts to provide his labour only to another person, it shall mean that other person;
"dangerous substance" has the meaning assigned to it by regulation 2(1) of the Classification, Packaging and Labelling of Dangerous Substances Regulations 1984;
"dock premises" has the meaning assigned to it by regulation 2(1) of the Docks Regulations 1988;
"electricity system" does not include the consumer's installation within the meaning of regulation 3(1) of the Electricity Supply Regulations 1988;
"the Executive" means the Health and Safety Executive;
"fairground" means any part of premises which is for the time being used wholly or mainly for the operation of any fairground equipment, other than a coin-operated ride, non-powered children's playground equipment or a swimming pool slide;
"gas" has the meaning assigned to it by section 48 of the Gas Act 1986;
"gas fitting" has the meaning assigned to it by section 48 of the Gas Act 1986;
"gas system" does not include a portable or mobile appliance supplied with gas from a cylinder, or the cylinder, pipes and other fittings used for supplying gas to that appliance;
"ionising radiation" has the meaning assigned to it by regulation 2(1) of the Ionising Radiations Regulations 1985;
"livestock" means any creature kept for the production of food, wool, skins or fur or for the purpose of any *agricultural activity*;
"local authority" means—
  (a) in relation to England and Wales, a district council, a London borough council, the Common council of the City of London, the Sub-Treasurer of the Inner

Temple, the Under-Treasurer of the Middle Temple or the Council of the Isles of Scilly;

(b) in relation to Scotland, an islands or district council:

"mine" has the meaning assigned to it by section 180 of the Mines and Quarries Act 1954;

"office activities" includes any activity for the purposes of administration, clerical work, handling money, telephone and telegraph operating and the production of computer software by the use of computers; and for this purpose "clerical work" includes writing, book-keeping, sorting papers, filing, typing, duplicating, machine calculating, drawing and the editorial preparation of matter for publication except where that preparation is on the premises where newspapers, magazines, periodicals or books are printed;

"pleasure craft" has the meaning assigned to it by regulation 2(1) of the Docks Regulations 1988;

"quarry" has the meaning assigned to it by section 180 of the Mines and Quarries Act 1954;

"railway" means a railway or tramway with (in either case) a gauge of 350 millimetres or more;

"theatre" does not include a cinema;

"transport undertaking" means an undertaking primarily engaged in the transport of passengers or goods;

"veterinary surgery" has the meaning assigned to it by section 27 of the Veterinary Surgeons Act 1966;

"work" in relation to a *gas fitting* has the meaning assigned to it by regulation 2(1) of the Gas Safety (Installation and Use) Regulations 1984;

"zoo" has the meaning assigned to it by section 1(2) of the Zoo Licensing Act 1981.

(2) In these Regulations (except regulation 4(8)), unless the context otherwise requires, any reference to the enforcing authority for premises or parts of premises is a reference to the enforcing authority for the relevant statutory provisions in relation to those premises or parts, as the case may be, and to any activity carried on in them.

(3) In these Regulations, unless the context otherwise requires, any reference to—

(a) a numbered regulation or Schedule is a reference to the regulation of or Schedule to these Regulations so numbered; and

(b) a numbered paragraph is a reference to the paragraph so numbered in the regulation or Schedule in which that reference appears.

3. Local authorities to be enforcing authorities in certain cases.—(1) Where the main activity carried on in non-domestic premises is specified in Schedule 1, the *local authority* for the area in which those premises are situated shall be the enforcing authority for them, and *the Executive* shall be the enforcing authority in any other case.

(2) Where such premises are occupied by more than one occupier each part separately occupied shall be regarded as being separate premises for the purposes of paragraph (1).

(3) Where paragraph (2) applies, the *local authority* shall be the enforcing authority for the *common parts*, except that if *the Executive* is the enforcing authority for—

(a) all other parts of the premises, *the Executive* shall be the enforcing authority for the *common parts*;

(b) any other part of the premises and the occupier of that part has any obligations under the relevant statutory provisions for any matters appertaining to the *common parts, the Executive* shall be the enforcing authority for those provisions in respect of such matters.

(4) Paragraph (2) shall not apply to—

(a) any land within the perimeter of an airport;

(b) the tunnel system within the meaning of section 1(7) of the Channel Tunnel Act 1987;

(c) an offshore installation within the meaning of section 1(4) of the Mineral Workings (Offshore Installations) Act 1971;

(d) a building or construction site, that is to say, premises where the only activities being undertaken are *construction work* and activities for the purpose of or in connection with such work;

(e) the campus of a university, polytechnic, college, school or similar educational establishment;

(f) a hospital,

and *the Executive* shall be the enforcing authority for the whole of any such premises.

(5) In relation to a *railway* operated by the British Railways Board, London Regional Transport or a subsidiary of that body, Tyne and Wear Passenger Transport Executive or Strathclyde Passenger Transport Executive, notwithstanding paragraph (3), the Executive shall be the enforcing authority for the *common parts* in a *railway* station or in a goods yard served by the *railway*.

(6) Where any part of premises at or adjacent to a *railway* track or *railway* station is occupied by a *railway* undertaking not mentioned in paragraph (5), then notwithstanding paragraph (2), *the Executive* shall be the enforcing authority for the whole premises.

(7) This regulation shall have effect subject to regulations 4, 5 and 6.

4. Exceptions.—(1) *The Executive* shall be the enforcing authority for—

(a) the enforcement of any of the relevant statutory provisions against a body specified in paragraph (3) or the officers or servants of such a body;

(b) any part of premises occupied by such a body.

(2) Where premises are mainly occupied by a body specified in paragraph (3) and are partly occupied by another person for the purpose of providing services at the premises for that body, *the Executive* shall be the enforcing authority for the part of the premises occupied by that other person.

(3) The bodies referred to in paragraphs (1) and (2) are—

(a) a *local authority* as defined in regulation 2;

(b) Parish Councils in England and Community Councils in Wales and Scotland;

(c) any other *local authority* within the meaning of section 53(1) of *the 1974 Act*;

(d) a police authority or the Receiver for the Metropolitan Police District;

(e) a fire authority within the meaning of section 43(1) of the Fire Precautions Act 1971;

(f) a headquarters or an organisation designated for the purposes of the International Headquarters and Defence Organisation Act 1964; or a service authority of a visiting force within the meaning of section 12 of the Visiting Forces Act 1952;

(g) the United Kingdom Atomic Energy Authority;

(h) the Crown, but regulation 3 shall apply to any part of premises occupied by the Executive and to any activity carried on there.

(4) *The Executive* shall be the enforcing authority for premises if the main activity carried on there is indoor sports and any body referred to in paragraph (3)(a) to (c) has any duty under section 4 of *the 1974 Act* in respect of those premises or any plant therein.

(5) *The Executive* shall be the enforcing authority for—

(a) section 6 of *the 1974 Act*;

(b) the other relevant statutory provisions in respect of any activity specified in Schedule 2 (whether or not it is the main activity carried on in premises).

(6) Regulation 3 and the preceding provisions of this regulation shall have effect subject to any provisions made for enforcement responsibility by other regulations made under *the 1974 Act* or by any of the existing statutory provisions.

(7) The preceding provisions of this regulation shall have effect subject to regulations 5 and 6.

(8) Notwithstanding regulation 3 and the preceding provisions of this regulation, an authority empowered to grant a licence for a factory, magazine or store or to register premises under the 1875 Act shall be the enforcing authority for the 1875 Act in relation to such factory, magazine, store or premises, as the case may be; and in this paragraph "the 1875 Act" means such provisions of the Explosives Act 1875 and such Orders in Council, Orders, Byelaws, Regulations and Rules made thereunder as are relevant statutory provisions.

5. Arrangements enabling responsibility for enforcement to be transferred.—
(1) The responsibility for enforcing any of the relevant statutory provisions in respect of any particular premises, part of premises, or any activity carried on there may be transferred from *the Executive* to the *local authority* or from the *local authority* to *the Executive*.

(2) A transfer may be made only by agreement between the enforcing authority which has the current responsibility and the authority to which it proposed to transfer it, or by *the Commission*.

(3) Where a transfer has been made, the authority to which responsibility has been transferred shall cause notice of the transfer to be given to persons affected by it, and where a transfer has been made by *the Commission the Commission* shall cause notice of it to be given to both enforcing authorities concerned.

(4) The preceding provisions of this regulation shall not apply to any part of premises occupied by the Crown or to any activity carried on there but responsibility for enforcing any of the relevant statutory provisions in respect of *office activites* and the premises used for them may be transferred by an agreement between *the Executive*, the *local authority* concerned and the Government Department or other public body concerned.

General note. As to the Commission's duties under the earlier parallel provisions, see *R v Health and Safety Commission, ex p Spelthorne Borough Council* (1983) Times, 18 July.

6. Arrangements enabling responsibility for enforcement to be assigned in cases of uncertainty.—(1) The responsibility for enforcing any of the relevant statutory provisions in respect of any particular premises, part of premises or any activity carried on there may be assigned to *the Executive* or to the *local authority*; and an assignment under this paragraph may be made only by *the Executive* and the *local authority* jointly and only where they agree—

(a) that there is uncertainty in the particular case as to what are their respective responsibilities by virtue of regulations made under section 18(2) of *the 1974 Act*; and

(b) which authority is more appropriate to be responsible for enforcement in that case,

and where such an assignment is made the authority to which responsibility has been assigned shall cause notice of assignment to be given to persons affected by it.

(2) For the purpose of removing uncertainty in any particular case as to what are their respective responsibilites by virtue of regulations made under section 18(2) of *the 1974 Act* either *the Executive* or the *local authority* may apply to *the Commission* and where *the Commission* considers that there is uncertainty it shall, after considering the circumstances and any views which may have been expressed to them by either enforcing authority or by persons affected, assign responsibility to whichever authority it considers appropriate; and where such an assignment is made *the Commission* shall cause notice of the assignment to be given to both enforcing authorities concerned and to persons affected by it.

7. Repeals and revocations.—(1) Sections 52(5) and 83(5) of the Offices, Shops and Railway Premises Act 1963 are hereby repealed.

(2) The following regulations are hereby revoked—

(a) The Health and Safety (Enforcing Authority) Regulations 1977;

(b) The Health and Safety (Enforcing Authority) (Amendment) Regulations 1980;

(c) The Health and Safety (Enforcing Authority) Regulations 1985.

SCHEDULE 1

Main activities which determine whether local authorities will be enforcing authorities

1.   The sale or storage of goods for retail or wholesale distribution except—
   (a)   where it is part of the business of a *transport undertaking*;
   (b)   at container depots where the main activity is the storage of goods in the course of transit to or from *dock premises*, an airport or a *railway*;
   (c)   where the main activity is the safe or storage for wholesale distribution of any *dangerous substance*;
   (d)   where the main activity is the sale or storage of water or sewage or their by-products or natural or town *gas*,
and for the purposes of this paragraph where the main activity carried on in premises is the sale and fitting of motor car tyres, exhausts, windscreens or sunroofs the main activity shall be deemed to be the sale of goods.

2.   The display or demonstration of goods at an exhibition for the purposes of offer or advertisement for sale.

3.   *Office activities.*

4.   Catering services.

5.   The provision of permanent or temporary residential accommodation including the provision of a site for caravans or campers.

6.   Consumer services provided in a shop except dry cleaning or radio and television repairs, and in this paragraph "consumer services" means services of a type ordinarily supplied to persons who receive them otherwise than in the course of a trade, business or other undertaking carried on by them (whether for profit or not).

7.   Cleaning (wet or dry) in coin operated units in lauderettes and similar premises.

8.   The use of a bath, sauna or solarium, massaging, hair transplanting, skin piercing, manicuring or other cosmetic services and therapeutic treatments, except where they are carried out under the supervision or control of a registered medical practitioner, a dentist registered under the Dentists Act 1984, a physiotherapist, an osteopath or a chiropractor.

9.   The practice or presentation of the arts, sports, games, entertainment or other cultural or recreational activities except where carried on in a museum, art gallery or *theatre* or where the main activity is the exhibition of a cave to the public.

10.   The hiring out of *pleasure craft* for use on inland waters.

11.   The care, treatment, accommodation or exhibition of animals, birds or other creatures, except where the main activity is horse breeding or horse training at a stable, or is an *agricultural activity* or *veterinary surgery*.

12. The activities of an undertaker, except where the main activity is embalming or the making of coffins.

13. Church worship or religious meetings.

SCHEDULE 2

Regulation 4(5)(b)

Activities in respect of which the Health and Safety Executive is the enforcing authority

1. Any activity in a *mine* or *quarry* other than a *quarry* in respect of which notice of abandonment has been given under section 139(2) of the Mines and Quarries Act 1954.

2. Any activity in a *fairground*.

3. Any activity in premises occupied by a radio, television or film undertaking in which the activity of broadcasting, recording or filming is carried on, and the activity of broadcasting, recording or filming wherever carried on, and for this purpose "film" includes video.

4. The following activities carried on at any premises by persons who do not normally work in the premises—
  (a) *construction work* if—
    (i) section 127(6) of the Factories Act 1961 (which requires certain work to be notified to an inspector) applies to such work; or
    (ii) the whole or part of the work contracted to be undertaken by the *contractor* at the premises is to the external fabric or other external part of a building or structure; or
    (iii) it is carried out in a physically segregated area of the premises, the activities normally carried out in that area have been suspended for the purpose of enabling the *construction work* to be carried out, the *contractor* has authority to exclude from that area persons who are not attending in connection with the carrying out of the work and the work is not the maintenance of insulation of pipes, boilers or other parts of heating or water systems or its removal from them;
  (b) the installation, maintenance or repair of any *gas system*, or any work in relation to a *gas fitting*;
  (c) the installation, maintenance or repair of *electricity systems*;
  (d) work with *ionising radiations* except work in one or more of the categories set out in Schedule 3 to the Ionising Radiations Regulations 1985.

5. The use of *ionising radiations* for medical exposure (within the meaning of regulation 2(1) of the Ionising Radiations Regulations 1985).

6. Any activity in premises occupied by a radiography undertaking in which there is carried on any work with *ionising radiations*.

7. *Agricultural activities*, and any activity at an agricultural show which involves the handling of *livestock* or the working of agricultural equipment.

8. Any activity on board a sea-going ship.

9. Any activity in relation to a ski slope, ski lift, ski tow or cable car.

10. Fish, maggot and game breeding except in a *zoo*.

---

19. Appointment of inspectors.—(1) Every enforcing authority *(a)* may appoint as inspectors (under whatever title it may from time to time determine) such persons having suitable qualifications as it thinks necessary for carrying into effect the relevant statutory provisions *(b)* within its field of responsibility *(c)* and may terminate any appointment made under this section.

(2) Every appointment of a person as an inspector under this section shall be made by an instrument in writing *(d)* specifying which of the powers conferred on inspectors by the relevant statutory provisions are to be exercisable by the person appointed; and an inspector shall in right of his appointment under this section—

(a) be entitled to exercise only such of those powers as are so specified; and
(b) be entitled to exercise the powers so specified only within the field of responsibility of the authority which appointed him.

(3) So much of an inspector's instrument of appointment as specifies the powers which he is entitled to exercise may be varied by the enforcing authority which appointed him.

(4) An inspector shall, if so required when exercising or seeking to exercise any power conferred on him by any of the relevant statutory provisions, produce his instrument of appointment or a duly authenticated copy thereof.

(*a*) **Enforcing authority.** For definition, see s. 18(7)(a).

(*b*) **The relevant statutory provisions.** For definition, see s. 53(1).

(*c*) **Field of responsibility.** See s. 18(7)(b).

(*d*) **Instrument in writing.** An inspector is competent to bring proceedings under the Act without being specifically empowered so to do in his certificate of appointment, and such appointment is *prima facie* proved by an inspector stating that he is an inspector and producing his certificate (*Campbell v Wallsend Slipway and Engineering Co Ltd* [1978] ICR 1015, DC).

---

20. Powers of inspectors.—(1) Subject to the provisions of section 19 and this section, an inspector *(a)* may, for the purpose of carrying into effect any of the relevant statutory provisions *(b)* within the field of responsibility *(c)* of the enforcing authority *(d)* which appointed him, exercise the powers *(e)* set out in subsection (2) below.

(2) The powers of an inspector referred to in the preceding subsection are the following, namely—

(a) at any reasonable time (or, in a situation which in his opinion is or may be dangerous, at any time) to enter any premises *(f)* which he has reason to believe it is necessary for him to enter for the purpose mentioned in subsection (1) above;
(b) to take with him a constable if he has reasonable cause to apprehend any serious obstruction *(g)* in the execution of his duty;
(c) without prejudice to the preceding paragraph, on entering any premises by virtue of paragraph (a) above to take with him—
  (i) any other person duly authorised by his (the inspector's) enforcing authority; and

      (ii) any equipment or materials required for any purpose for which the power of entry is being exercised;

(d)   to make such examination and investigation as may in any circumstances be necessary for the purpose mentioned in subsection (1) above;

(e)   as regards any premises which he has power to enter, to direct that those premises or any part of them, or anything therein, shall be left undisturbed (whether generally or in particular respects) for so long as is reasonably necessary for the purpose of any examination or investigation under paragraph (d) above;

(f)   to take such measurements and photographs and make such recordings as he considers necessary for the purpose of any examination or investigation under paragraph (d) above;

(g)   to take samples *(h)* of any articles or substances *(i)* found in any premises which he has power to enter, and of the atmosphere in or in the vicinity of any such premises;

(h)   in the case of any article or substance found in any premises which he has power to enter, being an article or substance which appears to him to have caused or to be likely to cause danger to health or safety, to cause it to be dismantled or subjected to any process or test *(j)* (but not so as to damage or destroy it unless this is in the circumstances necessary for the purpose mentioned in subsection (1) above);

(i)   in the case of any such article or substance as is mentioned in the preceding paragraph, to take possession *(h)* of it and detain *(j)* it for so long as is necessary for all or any of the following purposes, namely—

    (i) to examine it and do to it anything which he has power to do under that paragraph;

   (ii) to ensure that it is not tampered with before his examination of it is completed;

  (iii) to ensure that it is available for use as evidence in any proceedings for an offence under any of the relevant statutory provisions or any proceedings relating to a notice under section 21 or 22;

(j)   to require *(k)* any person whom he has reasonable cause to believe to be able to give any information relevant to any examination or investigation under paragraph (d) above to answer (in the absence of persons other than a person nominated by him to be present and any person whom the inspector may allow to be present) such questions as the inspector thinks fit to ask and to sign a declaration of the truth of his answers;

(k)   to require the production of, inspect, and take copies of or of any entry in—

    (i) any books or documents which by virtue of any of the relevant statutory provisions are required to be kept; and

   (ii) any other book or documents which it is necessary for him to see for the purposes of any examination or investigation under paragraph (d) above;

(l)   to require any person to afford him such facilities and assistance with respect to any matters to things within that person's control or in relation to which that person has responsibilities as are necessary to enable the inspector to exercise any of the powers conferred on him by this section;

(m) any other power which is necessary for the purpose mentioned in subsection (l) above.

(3) The Secretary of State *(l)* may by regulations *(m)* make provisions as to the procedure to be followed in connection with the taking of samples under subsection (2)(g) above (including provision as to the way in which samples that have been so taken are to be dealt with).

(4) Where an inspector proposes to exercise the power conferrred by subsection (2)(h) above in the case of an article or substance found in any premises, he shall, if so requested by a person who at the time is present in and has responsibilities in relation to those premises, cause anything which is to be done by virtue of that power to be done in the presence of that person unless the inspector considers that its being done in that person's presence would be prejudicial to the safety of the State.

(5) Before exercising the power conferred by subsection (2)(h) above in the case of any article or substance, an inspector shall consult such persons as appear to him appropriate for the purpose of ascertaining what dangers, if any, there may be in doing anything which he proposes to do under that power.

(6) Where under the power conferred by subsection (2)(i) above an inspector takes possession of any article or substance found in any premises, he shall leave there, either with a responsible person or, if that is impracticable, fixed in a conspicuous position, a notice giving particulars of that article or substance sufficient to identify it and stating that he has taken possession of it under that power; and before taking possession of any such substance under that power an inspector shall, if it is practicable for him to do so, take a sample thereof and give to a responsible person at the premises a portion of the sample marked in a manner sufficient to identify it.

(7) No answer given by a person in pursuance of a requirement imposed under subsection (2)(j) above shall be admissible in evidence against that person or the husband or wife of that person in any proceedings.

(8) Nothing in this section shall be taken to compel the production by any person of a document of which he would on grounds of legal professional privilege be entitled to withhold production on an order for discovery in an action in the High Court or, as the case may be, on an order for the production of documents in an action in the Court of Session.

(a) **Inspector.** That is to say, an inspector appointed under s. 19 (s. 53(1)). As to the indemnification of inspectors by enforcing authorities, see s. 26. For the offence of falsely pretending to be an inspector, see s. 33(1)(n).

(b) **The relevant statutory provisions.** For definition, see s. 53(1).

(c) **Field of responsibility.** See s. 18(7)(d).

(d) **Enforcing authority.** For definition, see s. 18(7)(a).

(e) **Powers.** For restrictions upon the disclosure of information obtained by the exercise of these powers, see s. 28(7). For powers in relation to the prosecution of offences, see s. 39.

(f) **Premises.** For definition, see s. 53(1).

(g) **Obstruction.** It is an offence intentionally to obstruct an inspector in the exercise or performance of his powers or duties (s. 33(1)(h)).

(h) **Take samples; take possession.** The subsumption of paragraph (g) is that only samples will have been taken and the remainder of the article or substance left on the premises; the subsumption of paragraph (i) is that the whole of the article or substance may have been removed. Therefore, if the inspector acts under paragraph (g) he need not comply with sub-s. (6); if he acts under paragraph (i) he must do so (*Laws v Keane* [1982] IRLR 500). In *Skinner v John G McGregor (Contractors) Ltd* [1977] SLT (Sh Ct) 83 an inspector failed to comply with the conditions of s. 20(6) and the evidence so obtained was held to be inadmissible. Skinner was subsequently disapproved on other grounds in *Laws v Keane* (above).

(i) **Substance.** For definition, see s. 53(1). See also sub-s. (3).

(j) **Dismantled ... test.** See also sub-ss. (4), (5).

(k) **Require.** It is an offence to contravene such a requirement (s. 33(1)(e)), and it is an offence to prevent or attempt to prevent any other person from appearing before an inspector or from answering any question to which an inspector may by virtue of s. 20(2) require an answer (s. 33(1)(f)).

(l) **The Secretary of State.** See note *(k)* to s. 2.

(m) **Regulations.** No such regulations have yet been made.

---

21.   Improvement notices.   If an inspector *(a)* is of the opinion that a person *(b)*—

    (a)   is contravening *(c)* one or more of the relevant statutory provisions *(d)*; or

    (b)   has contravened one or more of those provisions in circumstances that make it likely that the contravention will continue or be repeated,

he may serve *(e)* on him a notice *(f)* (in this Part referred to as "an improvement notice") stating that he is of that opinion, specifying the provision or provisions as to which he is of that opinion, giving particulars of the reasons why he is of that opinion, and requiring that person to remedy the contravention or, as the case may be, the matters occasioning it within such period (ending not earlier than the period within which an appeal against the notice can be brought under section 24) as may be specified in the notice.

General note. For supplementary provisions as to improvement notices, see s. 23; for appeals, see s. 24; for powers to deal with a cause of imminent danger, see s. 25.

(a) **Inspector.** For definition, see s. 53(1); and see the general note to s. 19.

(b) **Person.** See note *(g)* to s. 4.

(c) **Contravening.** For definition, see s. 82(1)(b).

(d) **The relevant statutory provisions.** For definition, see s. 53(1).

(e) **Serve.** For provisions as to service, see s. 46.

(f) **Notice.** It is not necessary for the notice to state in what capacity the person upon whom it is served is alleged to be in contravention of any of the provisions (*R v Carter, ex p Lipson* (1984) Times, 1 December). It is an offence to contravene any requirement imposed by such a notice, including any such notice as modified on appeal (s. 33(1)(g)).

---

22.   Prohibition notices.—(1) This section applies to any activities which are being or are likely to be carried on by or under the control of any person *(a)*, being activities to or in relation to which any of the relevant statutory provisions *(b)* apply or will, if the activities are so carried on, apply.

(2) If as regards any activities to which this section applies an inspector *(c)* is of the opinion that, as carried on or likely to be carried on by or under the control of the person in question, the activities involve or, as the case may be, will involve a risk of serious personal injury *(d)*, the inspector may serve *(e)* on that person a notice *(f)* (in this Part referred to as "a prohibition notice").

(3) A prohibition notice shall—

(a) state that the inspector is of the said opinion;
(b) specify the matters which in his opinion give or, as the case may be, will give rise to the said risks;
(c) where in his opinion any of those matters involves or, as the case may be, will involve a contravention *(g)* of any of the relevant statutory provisions, state that he is of that opinion, specify the provision or provisions as to which he is of that opinion, and give particulars of the reasons why he is of that opinion; and
(d) direct that the activities to which the notice relates shall not be carried on by or under the control of the person on whom the notice is served unless the matters specified in the notice in pursuance of paragraph (b) above and any associated contraventions of provisions so specified in pursuance of paragraph (c) above have been remedied.

(4) A direction contained in a prohibition notice in pursuance of subsection (3)(d) above shall take effect—

(a) at the end of the period specified *(h)* in the notice; or
(b) if the notice so declares, immediately.

General note. Subsections (1) and (2) were amended and sub-s. (4) is substituted by the Consumer Protection Act 1987, s. 36, Sch. 3. For supplementary provisions as to prohibition notices, see s. 23; for appeals, see s. 24; for powers to deal with a cause of imminent danger, see s. 25.

(a) Person. See note *(g)* to s. 4.

(b) The relevant statutory provisions. For definition, see s. 53(1).

(c) Inspector. For definition, see s. 53(1); and see the general note to s. 19.

(d) Risk of serious personal injury. For a notice to be issued the risk need not be imminent: *Tesco v Kippax* (COIT No. 7605, HSIB 180 p. 8). For definition of "personal injury", see s. 53(1).

(e) Serve. For provisions as to service, see s. 46.

(f) Notice. It is an offence to contravene any prohibition imposed by such a notice, including any such notice as modified on appeal (s. 33(1)(g)).

(g) Contravention. For definition, see s. 82(1)(b).

(h) Period specified. In specifying the period at the end of which a direction is to take effect, the time taken to perform the safety operation should be taken into account: *Otterburn Mill Ltd v Bulman* [1975] IRLR 223.

---

23. Provisions supplementary to ss. 21 and 22.—(1) In this section "notice" means an improvement notice or a prohibition notice.

(2) A notice *(a)* may (but need not) include directions as to the measures to be taken to remedy any contravention *(b)* or matter to which the notice relates; and any such directions—

(a) may be framed to any extent by reference to any approved code of practice *(c)*; and

(b) may be framed so as to afford the person *(d)* on whom the notice is served *(e)* a choice between different ways of remedying the contravention or matter.

(3) Where any of the relevant statutory provisions *(f)* applies to a building or any matter connected with a building and an inspector proposes to serve an improvement notice relating to a contravention of that provision in connection with that building or matter, the notice shall not direct any measures to be taken to remedy the contravention of that provision which are more onerous than those necessary to secure conformity with the requirements of any building regulations *(g)* for the time being in force to which that building or matter would be required to conform if the relevant building were being newly erected unless the provision in question imposes specific requirements more onerous than the requirements of any such building regulations to which the building or matter would be required to conform as aforesaid.

In this subsection "the relevant building", in the case of a building, means that building, and, in the case of a matter connected with a building, means the building with which the matter is connected.

(4) Before an inspector serves in connection with any premises *(h)* used or about to be used as a place of work *(i)* a notice requiring or likely to lead to the taking of measures affecting the means of escape in case of fire *(j)* with which the premises are or ought to be provided, he shall consult the fire authority.

In this subsection "fire authority" has the meaning assigned by section 43(1) of the Fire Precautions Act 1971.

(5) Where an improvement notice or a prohibition notice which is not to take immediate effect has been served—

(a) the notice may be withdrawn by an inspector at any time before the end of the period specified therein in pursuance of section 21 or section 22(4) as the case may be; and

(b) the period so specified may be extended or further extended by an inspector at any time when an appeal against the notice is not pending.

(6) In the application of this section to Scotland—

(a) in subsection (3) for the words from "with the requirements" to "aforesaid" there shall be substituted the words—

"(a) to any provisions of the building standards regulations to which that building or matter would be required to conform if the relevant building were being newly erected; or

(b) where the sheriff, on an appeal to him under section 16 of the Building (Scotland) Act 1959—

(i) against an order under section 10 of that Act requiring the execution of operations necessary to make the building or matter conform to the building standards regulations, or

(ii) against an order under section 11 of that Act requiring the building or matter to conform to a provision of such regulations, has varied the order, to any provision of the building standards regulations referred to in paragraph (a) above as affected by the order as so varied,

unless the relevant statutory provison imposes specific requirements more onerous than the requirements of any provisions of building standards regulations as aforesaid or, as the case may be, than the requirements of the order as varied by the sheriff'';

(b) after subsection (5) there shall be inserted the following subsection—

"(5A) In subsection (3) above 'building standards regulations' has the same meaning as in section 3 of the Building (Scotland) Act 1959''.

(a) Notice. See sub-s. (1) and ss. 21, 22.

(b) Contravention. For definition, see s. 82(1)(b).

(c) Approved code of practice. See s. 16.

(d) Person. See note *(g)* to s. 4.

(e) Served. For provisions as to service, see s. 46.

(f) The relevant statutory provisions. For definition, see s. 53(1).

(g) Building regulations. See the Building Act 1984, s. 1, which replaces the Public Health Act 1936, s. 61(1) (repealed).

(h) Premises. For definition, see s. 53(1).

(i) Work. For definition, see s. 52(1), (2).

(j) Means of escape in case of fire. See Part 3 of this book.

---

24. Appeal against improvement or prohibition notice.—(1) In this section "a notice" means an improvement notice or a prohibition notice.

(2) A person on whom a notice *(a)* is served *(b)* may within such period from the date of its service as may be prescribed *(c)* appeal to an industrial tribunal; and on such an appeal *(d)* the tribunal may either cancel or affirm the notice and, if it affirms it, may do so either in its original form or with such modifications *(e)* as the tribunal may in the circumstances think fit *(f)*.

(3) Where an appeal under this section is brought against a notice within the period allowed under the preceding subsection, then—

(a) in the case of an improvement notice, the bringing of the appeal shall have the effect of suspending the operation of the notice until the appeal is finally disposed of or, if the appeal is withdrawn, until the withdrawal of the appeal;

(b) in the case of a prohibition notice, the bringing of the appeal shall have the like effect if, but only if, on the application of the appellant the tribunal so directs (and then only from the giving of the directions).

(4) One or more assessors may be appointed for the purposes of any proceedings brought before an industrial tribunal under this section.

(a) Notice. See sub-s. (1) and ss. 21, 22.

(b) Served. For provisions as to service, see s. 46.

(c) Prescribed. For definition, see s. 53(1). The prescribed period is one of 21 days (Industrial Tribunals (Improvement and Prohibition Notices Appeals) Regulations 1974, Schedule, para. 2, printed below).

(d) Appeal. The rules of procedure of industrial tribunals in relation to such an appeal are set out in the Industrial Tribunals (Improvement and Prohibition Notices Appeals) Regulations 1974 (set out below).

(e) Modification. For definition, see s. 82(1)(c).

(f) The Tribunal . . . fit. An industrial tribunal should not give a preliminary decision upon the validity of an improvement notice without investigating the facts; if the tribunal finds such a notice to be vague or imprecise it has jurisdiction to re-draft it (*Chrysler (UK) Ltd v McCarthy* [1978] ICR 939, DC).

It has been held by an industrial tribunal that such a tribunal has no power to amend an improvement notice so as to enable the inspector to rely upon a provision of the Act not specified in the original notice (*British Airways Board v Henderson* [1979] ICR 77). It has further been held by an industrial tribunal that the financial position of the person against whom an improvement notice has been issued is irrelevant in determining whether or not it should be affirmed (*TC Harrison (Newcastle-under-Lyme) Ltd v Ramsey* [1976] IRLR 135). A failure to include the statutory proviso of reasonable practicability in respect of the measures to be taken to remedy a contravention does not render a notice invalid so as to deprive the tribunal of jurisdiction to consider the factual basis of the notice under s. 24(2) (see *Kitching v Gateway Foodmarkets Ltd.* Queen's Bench Division, CO/766/86, 24 October 1988). An undertaking by the manager of a company to take additional precautions was insufficient for a prohibition notice to be suspended in *Grovehurst Energy Ltd v Strawson* (COIT No. 5035, HSIB 180 p. 9).

THE INDUSTRIAL TRIBUNALS (IMPROVEMENT AND
PROHIBITION NOTICES APPEALS) REGULATIONS 1974
(S.I. 1974 No. 1925)

Citation and commencement
1.   These Regulations may be cited as the Industrial Tribunals (Improvement and Prohibition Notices Appeals) Regulations 1974 and shall come into operation on 1 January 1975.

Interpretation
2.—(1) The Interpretation Act 1889 [Interpretation Act 1978] shall apply to the interpretation of these Regulations as it applies to the interpretation of an Act of Parliament.
(2) In the regulations, unless the context otherwise requires, the following expressions have the meanings hereby assigned to them respectively, that is to say—
   "appellant" means a person who has appealed to a *tribunal* under section 24 of *the principal Act*;
   "the clerk to the tribunal" means the person appointed by *the Secretary of the Tribunals* or *an Assistance Secretary* to act in that capacity at one or more *hearings*;
   "decision" in relation to a *tribunal* includes a direction under Rule 4 and any other order which is not an interlocutory order;
   "hearing" means a sitting of a *tribunal* duly constituted for the purpose of receiving evidence, hearing addresses and witnesses or doing anything lawfully requisite to enable the *tribunal* to reach a decision on any question;
   "improvement notice" means a notice under section 21 of *the principal Act*;
   "inspector" means a person appointed under section 19(1) of *the principal Act*;
   "nominated chairman" means a member of the panel of chairmen for the time being nominated by *the President*;
   "the Office of the Tribunals" means the Central Office of the Industrial Tribunals (England and Wales);
   "the panel of chairmen" means the panel of persons, being barristers or solicitors of not less than seven years' standing, appointed by the Lord Chancellor in pursuance

of Regulation 5(2) of the Industrial Tribunals (England and Wales) Regulations 1965, as amended;

"party" means the appellant and the respondent;

"the President" means the President of the Industrial Tribunals (England and Wales) or the person nominated by the Lord Chancellor to discharge for the time being the functions of the *President*;

"the principal Act" means the Health and Safety at Work etc. Act 1974;

"prohibition notice" means a notice under section 22 of *the principal Act*;

"Regional Office of the Industrial Tribunals" means a regional office which has been established under the *Office of the Tribunals* for an area specified by *the President*;

"Register" means the Register kept in pursuance of the Industrial Tribunals (Labour Relations) Regulations 1974;

"respondent" means the *inspector* who issued the *improvement notice* or *prohibition notice* which is the subject of the appeal;

"Rule" means a Rule of Procedure contained in the Schedule to these Regulations;

"the Secretary of the Tribunals" and "an Assistant Secretary of the Tribunals" means respectively the persons for the time being acting as the Secretary of the *Office of the Tribunals* and as the Assistant Secretary of a Regional Office of the Industrial Tribunals;

"tribunal" means an industrial tribunal (England and Wales) established in pursuance of the Industrial Tribunals (England and Wales) Regulations 1965, as amended, and in relation to any proceedings means the tribunal to which the proceedings have been referred by *the President* or by a *nominated chairman*.

Proceedings of tribunals

3. The Rules of Procedure contained in the Schedule to these Regulations shall have effect in relation to appeals to a *tribunal* under section 24 of *the principal Act* against *improvement notices* or *prohibition notices* relating to matters arising in England or Wales *(a)*.

(a) **England or Wales.** See INTRODUCTORY NOTE 4.

Proof of decisions of tribunals

4. The production in any proceedings in any court of a document purporting to be certified by *the Secretary of the Tribunals* to be a true copy of an entry of a decision in the *Register* shall, unless the contrary is proved, be sufficient evidence of the document and of the facts stated therein.

SCHEDULE

Regulation 3

Rules of Procedure

Notice of Appeal

1. An appeal shall be commenced by the *appellant* sending to *the Secretary of the Tribunals* a notice of appeal which shall be in writing and shall set out—

(a) the name of the *appellant* and his address for the service of documents;

(b) the date of the *improvement notice* or *prohibition notice* appeal against and the address of the premises or place concerned;

(c) the name and address of the *respondent*;

(d) particulars of the requirements or directions appealed against; and

(e) the grounds of the appeal.

Time limit for bringing appeal

2.—(1) Subject to paragraph (2) of this Rule, the notice of appeal shall be sent to *the Secretary of the Tribunals* within 21 days from the date of the service on the *appellant* of the notice appealed against.

(2) A *tribunal* may extend the time mentioned above where it is satisfied on an application made in writing to *the Secretary of the Tribunals* either before or after the

expiration of that time that it is not or was not reasonably practicable for an appeal to be brought within that time.

Action upon receipt of notice of appeal
    3.   Upon receiving a notice of appeal *the Secretary of the Tribunals* shall enter particulars of it in the *Register* and shall forthwith send a copy of it to the *respondent* and inform *the parties* in writing of the case number of the appeal entered in the *Register* (which shall thereafter constitute the title of the proceedings) and of the address to which notices and other communications to *the Secretary of the Tribunals* shall be sent.

Application for direction suspending the operation of a prohibition notice
    4.—(1) Where an appeal has been brought against a *prohibition notice* and an application is made to the *tribunal* by the *appellant* in pursuance of section 24(3)(b) of *the principal Act* for a direction suspending the operation of the notice until the appeal is finally disposed of or withdrawn, the application shall be sent in writing to *the Secretary of the Tribunals* and shall set out—
    (a) the case number of the appeal if known to the *appellant* or particulars sufficient to identify the appeal; and
    (b) the grounds on which the application is made.
    (2) Upon receiving the application, *the Secretary of the Tribunals* shall enter particulars of it against the entry in the *Register* relating to the appeal and shall forthwith send a copy of it to the *respondent*.

Power to require attendance of witnesses and production of documents etc.
    5.—(1) A *tribunal* may on the application of a *party* made either by notice to *the Secretary of the Tribunals* or at the *hearing*—
    (a) require a *party* to furnish in writing to another *party* further particulars of the grounds on which he relies and of any facts and contentions relevant thereto;
    (b) grant to a *party* such discovery or inspection of documents as might be granted by a county court; and
    (c) require the attendance of any person as a witness or require the production of any document relating to the matter to be determined,
and may appoint the time at or within which or the place at which any act required in pursuance of this Rule is to be done.
    (2) The *tribunal* shall not under paragraph (1) of this Rule require the production of any document certified by the Secretary of State as being a document of which the production would be against the interests of national security.
    (3) A person on whom a requirement has been made under paragraph (1) of this Rule may apply to the *tribunal* either by notice to *the Secretary of the Tribunals* or at the *hearing* to vary or set aside the requirement.
    (4) No such application to vary or set aside shall be entertained in a case where a time has been appointed under paragraph (1) of this Rule in relation to the requirement unless it is made before the time or, as the case may be, expiration of the time so appointed.
    (5) Every document containing a requirement under paragraph (1)(b) or (c) of this Rule shall contain a reference to the fact that under paragraph 21(6) of Schedule 1 to the Trade Union and Labour Relations Act 1974, now paragraph 1 of Schedule 9 to the Employment Protection (Consolidation) Act 1978, any person who without reasonable excuse fails to comply with any such requirement shall be liable on summary conviction to a fine not exceeding £100.

Time and place of hearing and appointment of assessor
    6.—(1) *The President* or a *nominated chairman* shall fix the date, time and place of the *hearing* of the appeal and of any application under Rule 4, and *the Secretary of the Tribunals* shall not less than 14 days (or such shorter time as may be agreed by him with the *parties*)

before the date so fixed send to each *party* a notice of the *hearing* which shall include information and guidance as to attendance at the *hearing*, witnesses and the bringing of documents (if any), representation by another person and written representations.

(2) Where *the President* or a *nominated chairman* so directs, *the Secretary of the Tribunals* shall also send notice of the *hearing* to such persons as may be directed, but the requirement as to the period of notice contained in the foregoing paragraph of this Rule shall not apply to any such notices.

(3) *The President* or a *nominated chairman* may, if he thinks fit, appoint in pursuance of section 24(4) of *the principal Act* a person or persons having special knowledge or experience in relation to the subject matter of the appeal to sit with the *tribunal* as assessor or assessors.

The hearing

7.—(1) Any *hearing* of or in connection with an appeal shall take place in public unless the *tribunal* on the application of a *party* decides that a private *hearing* is appropriate for the purpose of hearing evidence which relates to matters of such a nature that it would be against the interests of national security to allow the evidence to be given in public or hearing evidence from any person which in the opinion of the *tribunal* is likely to consist of information the disclosure of which would be seriously prejudicial to the interests of the undertaking of the *appellant* or of any undertaking in which he works for reasons other than its effect on negotiations with respect to any of the matters mentioned in section 29(1) of the Trade Union and Labour Relations Act 1974, see now section 244 of the Trade Union and Labour Relations (Consolidation) Act 1992.

(2) In cases to which the foregoing provisions of this Rule apply, a member of the Council on Tribunals in his capacity as such shall be entitled to attend the *hearing*.

Written representations

8. If a *party* shall desire to submit representations in writing for consideration by a *tribunal* at the *hearing* of the appeal, that *party* shall send such representations to *the Secretary of the Tribunals* not less than 7 days before the *hearing* and shall at the same time send a copy of it to the other *party*.

Right of appearance

9. At any *hearing* of or in connection with an appeal a *party* may appear before the *tribunal* in person or may be represented by counsel or by a solicitor or by any other person whom he desires to represent him, including in the case of the *appellant* a representative of a trade union or an employers' association.

Procedure at hearing

10.—(1) At any *hearing* of or in connection with an appeal a *party* shall be entitled to make an opening statement, to give evidence on his own behalf, to call witnesses, to cross-examine any witnesses called by the other *party* and to address the *tribunal*.

(2) If a *party* shall fail to appear or to be represented at the time and place fixed for the *hearing* of an appeal, the *tribunal* may dispose of the appeal in the absence of that *party* or may adjourn the *hearing* to a later date: Provided that before disposing of an appeal in the absence of a *party* the *tribunal* shall consider any written representations submitted by that *party* in pursuance of Rule 8.

(3) A *tribunal* may require any witness to give evidence on oath or affirmation and for that purpose there may be administered an oath or affirmation in due form.

Decision of appeal

11.—(1) A *decision* of a *tribunal* may be taken by a majority thereof and, if the *tribunal* shall be constituted of two members only, the chairman shall have a second or casting vote.

(2) The *decision* of a *tribunal* shall be recorded in a document signed by the chairman which shall contain the reasons for the *decision*.

(3) *The clerk to the tribunal* shall transmit the document signed by the chairman to *the Secretary of the Tribunals* who shall as soon as may be enter it in the *Register* and shall send a copy of the entry to each of the *parties*.

(4) The specification of the reasons for the decision shall be omitted from the *Register* in any case in which evidence has been heard in private and the *tribunal* so directs and in that event a specification of the reasons shall be sent to the *parties* and to any superior court in any proceedings relating to such *decision* together with the copy of the entry.

(5) The *Register* shall be kept at *the Office of the Tribunals* and shall be open to the inspection of any person without charge at all reasonable hours.

(6) The chairman of a *tribunal* shall have power by certificate under his hand to correct in documents recording the *tribunals' decisions* clerical mistakes or errors arising therein from any accidental slip or omission.

(7) *The clerk to the tribunal* shall send a copy of any document so corrected and the certificate of the chairman to *the Secretary of the Tribunal* who shall as soon as may be make such correction as may be necessary in the *Register* and shall send a copy of the corrected entry or of the corrected specification of the reasons, as the case may be, to each of the *parties.*

(8) If any decision is—
(a) corrected under paragraph (6) of this Rule; or
(b) reviewed, revoked or varied under Rule 12; or
(c) altered in any way by order of a superior court,
the *Secretary of the Tribunals* shall alter the entry in the *Register* to conform with any such certificate or order and shall send a copy of the new entry to each of the *parties.*

Review of tribunal's decision
12.—(1) A *tribunal* shall have power on the application of a *party* to review and to revoke or vary by certificate under the chairman's hand any of its *decisions* in a case in which a county court has power to order a new trial on the grounds that—
(a) the *decision* was wrongly made as a result of an error on the part of the *tribunal* staff; or
(b) a *party* did not receive notice of the proceedings leading to the *decision*; or
(c) the *decision* was made in the absence of a *party*; or
(d) new evidence has become available since the making of the *decision* provided that its existence could not have been reasonably known of or foreseen; or
(e) the interests of justice require such a review.

(2) An application for the purposes of paragraph (1) of this Rule may be made at the *hearing.* If the application is not made at the *hearing,* such application shall be made to *the Secretary of the Tribunals* within 14 days from the date of the entry of a decision in the *Register* and must be in writing stating the grounds in full.

(3) An application for the purposes of paragraph (1) of this Rule may be refused by the chairman of the tribunal which decided the case, by *the President* or by a *nominated chairman* if in his opinion it has no reasonable prospect of success and he shall state the reasons for his opinion.

(4) If such an application is not refused under paragraph (3) of this Rule, it shall be heard by the *tribunal* and if it is granted the *tribunal* shall either vary its *decision* or revoke its *decision* and order a re-hearing.

(5) *The clerk to the tribunal* shall send to *the Secretary of the Tribunals* the certificate of the chairman as to any revocation or variation of the *tribunal's* decision under this Rule. *The Secretary of the Tribunals* shall as soon as may be make such correction as may be necessary in the *Register* and shall send a copy of the entry to each of the *parties.*

Costs
13.—(1) A *tribunal* may make an order that a *party* shall pay to another *party* either a specified sum in respect of the costs of or in connection with an appeal incurred by that other *party* or, in default of agreement, the taxed amount on those costs.

(2) Any costs required by an order under this Rule to be taxed may be taxed in the county court according to such of the scales prescribed by the county court rules for proceedings in the county court as shall be directed by the order.

Miscellaneous powers of tribunal

14.—(1) Subject to the provisions of these Rules, a *tribunal* may regulate its own procedure.

(2) A *tribunal* may, if it thinks fit—

(a) postpone the day or time fixed for, or adjourn, any *hearing*;

(b) before granting an application under Rule 5 or 12 require the *party* making the application to give notice thereof to the other *party*;

(c) either on the application of any person or of its own motion, direct any other person to be joined as a *party* to the appeal (giving such consequential directions as it considers necessary), but may do so only after having given to the person proposed to be joined a reasonable opportunity of making written or oral objection;

(d) make any necessary amendments to the description of a *party* in the *Register* and in other documents relating to the appeal;

(e) if the appellant shall at any time give notice of the abandonment of his appeal, dismiss the appeal;

(f) if the *parties* agree in writing upon the terms of a *decision* to be made by the tribunal, decide accordingly.

(3) Any act, other than the *hearing* of an appeal or of an application for the purposes of Rule 4 or 12(1) or the granting of an extension of time under Rule 2(2), required or authorised by these Rules to be done by a *tribunal* may be done by, or on the direction of, *the President*, the chairman of the tribunal or a *nominated chairman*.

(4) Rule 13 shall apply to an order dismissing proceedings under paragraph (2) of this Rule.

(5) Where *the President* so directs, any functions of *the Secretary of the Tribunals* may be performed by *an Assistant Secretary of the Tribunals* and a notice of appeal under Rule 1, an application under Rule 4, and any other notice or other document required by these Rules to be sent to *the Secretary of the Tribunals* may be sent either to *the Secretary of the Tribunals* or to *an Assistant Secretary of the Tribunals* in accordance with such direction.

Notices, etc.

15.—(1) Any notice given under these Rules shall be in writing and all notices and documents required or authorised by these Rules to be sent or given to any person hereinafter mentioned may be sent by post (subject to paragraphs (3) and (4) of this rule) or delivered to or at—

(a) in the case of a document directed to *the Secretary of the Tribunals*, the Office of the Tribunals or such other office as may be notified by *the Secretary of the Tribunals* to the *parties*;

(b) in the case of a document directed to a *party*, his address for service specified in the notice of appeal or in a notice under paragraph (2) of this Rule or (if no address for service is so specified), his last known address or place of business in the United Kingdom or, if the party is a corporation, the corporation's registered or principal office;

(c) in the case of a document directed to any person (other than a person specified in the foregoing provisions of this paragraph), his address or place of business in the United Kingdom, or if such a person is a corporation, the corporation's registered or principal office;

and if sent or given to the authorised representative of a *party* shall be deemed to have been sent or given to that *party*.

(2) A *party* may at any time by notice to *the Secretary of the Tribunals* and to the other *party* change his address for service under these Rules.

(3) Where a notice of appeal is not delivered, it shall be sent by the recorded delivery service.

(4) Where for any sufficient reason service of any document or notice cannot be effected in the manner prescribed under this Rule, *the President* or a *nominated chairman* may make an order for substituted service in such manner as he may deem fit and such service shall have the same effect as service in the manner prescribed under this Rule.

(5) In the case of an appeal to which the *respondent* is an *inspector* appointed otherwise than by the Health and Safety Executive, *the Secretary of the Tribunals* shall send to that Executive copies of the notice of appeal and the document recording the *decision* of the *tribunal* on the appeal.

---

25.   Power to deal with cause of imminent danger.—(1) Where, in the case of any article or substance *(a)* found by him in any premises *(b)* which he has power to enter *(c)*, an inspector *(d)* has reasonable cause to believe that, in the circumstances in which he finds it, the article or substance is a cause of imminent danger of serious personal injury *(e)*, he may seize it and cause it to be rendered harmless (whether by destruction or otherwise).

(2) Before there is rendered harmless under this section—

(a) any article that forms part of a batch of similar articles; or
(b) any substance,

the inspector shall, if it is practicable for him to do so, take a sample thereof and give to a responsible person at the premises where the article or substance was found by him a portion of the sample marked in a manner sufficient to identify it.

(3) As soon as may be after any article or substance has been seized and rendered harmless under this section, the inspector shall prepare and sign a written report giving particulars of the circumstances in which the article or substance was seized and so dealt with by him, and shall—

(a) give *(f)* a signed copy of the report to a responsible person at the premises where the article or substance was found by him; and
(b) unless that person is the owner of the article or substance, also serve *(g)* a signed copy of the report on the owner,

and if, where paragraph (b) above applies, the inspector cannot after reasonable enquiry ascertain the name or address of the owner, the copy may be served on him by giving it to the person to whom a copy was given under the preceding paragraph.

(a) *Substance.* For definition, see s. 53(1).

(b) *Premises.* For definition, see s. 53(1).

(c) *Power to enter.* See s. 20(2).

(d) *Inspector.* For definition, see s. 53(1); and see the general note to s. 19. It is an offence to contravene any requirement imposed by an inspector under s. 25 (s. 33(1) (e)). As to obstruction of an inspector, see s. 33(1)(h).

(e) *Personal injury.* For definition, see s. 53(1).

(f) *Give.* For provisions relating to the giving of documents, see s. 46(8).

(g) *Serve.* For provisions as to service, see s. 46.

25A.   Power of customs officer to detain articles and substances. (1) A

customs officer *(a)* may, for the purpose of facilitating the exercise or performance by any enforcing authority *(b)* or inspector *(c)* of any of the powers or duties
of the authority or inspector under any of the relevant statutory provisions *(d)*,
seize any imported article or imported substance *(e)* and detain it for not more
than two working days.

(2) Anything seized and detained under this section shall be dealt with
during the period of its detention in such manner as the Commissioners of
Customs and Excise may direct.

(3) In subsection (1) above the reference to two working days is a reference
to a period of forty-eight hours calculated from the time when the goods in
question are seized but disregarding so much of any period as falls on a
Saturday or Sunday or on Christmas Day, Good Friday or a day which is a bank
holiday under the Banking and Financial Dealings Act 1971 in the part of Great
Britain where the goods are seized.

General note. This section was added by the Consumer Protection Act 1987, s. 36,
Sch. 3.

(a) *Customs officer.* For definition, see s. 53(1).

(b) *Enforcing authority.* For definition, see s. 18(7)(a).

(c) *Inspector.* For definition, see s. 53(1); and see the general note to s. 19.

(d) *The relevant statutory provisions.* For definition, see s. 53(1).

(e) *Substance.* For definition, see s. 53(1).

---

26. Power of enforcing authorities to indemnify their inspectors. Where an
action has been brought against an inspector *(a)* in respect of an act done in the
execution or purported execution of any of the relevant statutory provisions *(b)*
and the circumstances are such that he is not legally entitled to require the
enforcing authority *(c)* which appointed him to indemnify him, that authority
may, nevertheless, indemnify him against the whole or part of any damages and
costs or expenses which he may have been ordered to pay or may have incurred,
if the authority is satisfied that he honestly believed that the act complained of
was within his powers *(d)* and that his duty as an inspector required or entitled
him to do it.

(a) *Inspector.* For definition, see s. 53(1); and see the general note to s. 19.

(b) *The relevant statutory provisions.* For definition, see s. 53(1).

(c) *Enforcing authority.* For definition, see s. 18(7)(a).

(d) *Powers.* As to the powers of inspectors, see in particular, ss. 20–23, 25.

Obtaining and disclosure of information

**27. Obtaining of information by the Commission, the Executive, enforcing
authorities, etc.**—(1) For the purpose of obtaining—

(a) any information which the Commission needs for the discharge of its functions;

(b) any information which an enforcing authority *(a)* needs for the discharge of the authority's functions,

the Commission may, with the consent of the Secretary of State *(b)*, serve *(c)* on any person *(d)* a notice *(e)* requiring that person to furnish to the Commission or, as the case may be, to the enforcing authority in question such information about such matters as may be specified in the notice, and to do so in such form and manner and within such time as may be so specified.

In this subsection "consent" includes a general consent extending to cases of any stated description.

(2) Nothing in section 9 of the Statistics of Trade Act 1947 (which restricts the disclosure of information obtained under that Act) shall prevent or penalise—

(a) the disclosure of a Minister of the Crown to the Commission or the Executive of information obtained under that Act about any undertaking *(f)* within the meaning of that Act, being information consisting of the names and addresses of the persons carrying on the undertaking, the nature of the undertaking's activities, the numbers of persons of different descriptions who work in the undertaking, the addresses or places where activities of the undertaking are or were carried on, the nature of the activities carried on there, or the numbers of persons of different descriptions who work or worked in the undertaking there;

(b) [*repealed*].

(3) In the preceding subsection any reference to a Minister of the Crown, the Commission or the Executive includes respectively a reference to an officer of his or of that body and also, in the case of a reference to the Commission, includes a reference to—

(a) a person performing any functions of the Commission or the Executive on its behalf by virtue of section 13(1)(a);

(b) an officer of a body which is so performing any such functions; and

(c) an adviser appointed in pursuance of section 13(1)(d).

(4) A person to whom information is disclosed in pursuance of subsection (2) above shall not use the information for a purpose other than a purpose of the Commission or, as the case may be, of the Executive.

General note. Subsection (2) was amended by the Employment Act 1988, s. 33(1), Sch. 3, Pt. II, para. 7.

Subsections (2), (3) were amended by the Employment Act 1989, s. 29(3), (4), Sch. 6, para. 10, Sch. 7, Pt. I.

See s. 28 as to restrictions on the disclosure of information obtained under this section.

(a) Enforcing authority. For definition, see s. 18(7)(a).

(b) The Secretary of State. See note *(k)* to s. 2.

(c) Serve. For provisions as to service, see s. 46.

(d) Person. See note *(g)* to s. 4.

(e) Notice. It is an offence to contravene any requirement imposed by such a notice (s. 33(1)(i)).

(f) **Undertaking.** For definition, see the Statistics of Trade Act 1947, s. 17.

27A. Information communicated by the Commissioners of Customs and Excise.—(1) If they think it appropriate to do so for the purpose of facilitating the exercise or performance by any person to whom subsection (2) below applies of any of that person's powers or duties under any of the relevant statutory provisions (a), the Commissioners of Customs and Excise may authorise the disclosure to that person of any information obtained for the purposes of the exercise by the Commissioners of their functions in relation to imports.

(2) This subsection applies to an enforcing authority (b) and to an inspector (c).

(3) A disclosure of information made to any person under subsection (1) above shall be made in such manner as may be directed by the Commissioners of Customs and Excise and may be made through such persons acting on behalf of that person as may be so directed.

(4) Information may be disclosed to a person under subsection (1) above whether or not the disclosure of the information has been requested by or on behalf of that person.

General note. This section was added by the Consumer Protection Act 1987, s. 36, Sch. 3.

(a) **The relevant statutory provisions.** For definition, see s. 53(1).

(b) **Enforcing authority.** For definition, see s. 18(7)(a).

(c) **Inspector.** For definition, see s. 53(1); and see the general note to s. 19.

---

28. Restrictions on disclosure of information.—(1) In this and the two following subsections—

(a) "relevant information" means information obtained by a person (a) under section 27(1) or furnished to any person under section 27A above or in pursuance of a requirement imposed by any of the relevant statutory provisions (b); and

(b) "the recipient", in relation to any relevant information, means the person by whom that information was so obtained or to whom that information was so furnished, as the case may be.

(2) Subject to the following subsection, no relevant information (c) shall be disclosed (d) without the consent of the person (a) by whom it was furnished.

(3) The preceding subsection shall not apply to—

(a) disclosure of information to the Commission, the Executive, a government department or any enforcing authority (e);

(b) without prejudice to paragraph (a) above, disclosure by the recipient of information to any person (a) for the purpose of any function conferred on the recipient by or under any of the relevant statutory provisions;

(c) without prejudice to paragraph (a) above, disclosure by the recipient of information to—
   (i) an officer of a local authority (f) who is authorised by that authority to receive it,
   (ii) an officer of a water authority or water development board who is authorised by that authority or board to receive it,
   (iii) an officer of a river purification board who is authorised by that board to receive it, or
   (iv) a constable authorised by a chief officer of police to receive it;
(d) disclosure by the recipient of information in a form calculated to prevent it from being identified as relating to a particular person or case;
(e) disclosure of information for the purposes of any legal proceedings or any investigation or inquiry held by virtue of section 14(2), or for the purposes of a report of any such proceedings or inquiry or of a special report made by virtue of section 14(2).

(4) In the preceeding subsection any reference to the Commission, the Executive, a government department or an enforcing authority includes respectively a reference to an officer of that body or authority (including, in the case of an enforcing authority, any inspector appointed by it), and also, in the case of a reference to the Commission, includes a reference to—

(a) a person (a) performing any functions of the Commission or the Executive on its behalf by virtue of section 13(1)(a);
(b) an officer of a body which is so performing any such functions; and
(c) an adviser appointed in pursuance of section 13(1)(d).

(5) A person (a) to whom information is disclosed in pursuance of sub-section (3) above shall not use the information for a purpose other than—

(a) in a case falling within paragraph (a) of that subsection, a purpose of the Commission or of the Executive or of the government department in question, or the purposes of the enforcing authority provisions, as the case may be;
(b) in the case of information given to an officer of a local authority or of a water authority or of a river purification board or water development board, the purposes of the authority or board in connection with the relevant statutory provisions or any enactment whatsoever relating to public health, public safety or the protection of the environment;
(c) in the case of information given to a constable, the purposes of the police in connection with the relevant statutory provisions or any enactment whatsoever relating to public health, public safety or the safety of the State.

(6) References in subsections (3) and (5) above to a local authority include the Inner London Education Authority and a joint authority established by Part IV of the Local Government Act 1985.

(7) A person (a) shall not disclose any information obtained by him as a result of the exercise of any power conferred by section 14(4)(a) or 20 (includ-ing, in particular, any information with respect to any trade secret obtained by him in any premises (g) entered by him by virtue of any such power) except—

(a) for the purposes of his functions; or
(b) for the purposes of any legal proceedings or any investigation or inquiry held by virtue of section 14(2) or for the purposes of a report of any such

proceedings or inquiry or of a special report made by virtue of section
14(2); or

(c) with the relevant consent.

In this subsection "the relevant consent" means, in the case of information
furnished in pursuance of a requirement imposed under section 20, the
consent of the person who furnished it, and, in any other case, the consent of a
person having responsibilities in relation to the premises where the information was obtained.

(8) Notwithstanding anything in the preceding subsection an inspector *(h)*
shall, in circumstances in which it is necessary to do so for the purpose of
assisting in keeping persons *(a)* (or the representatives of persons) employed at
any premises adequately informed about matters affecting their health, safety
and welfare, give to such persons or their representatives the following descriptions of information, that is to say—

(a) factual information obtained by him as mentioned in that subsection
     which relates to those premises or anything which was or is therein or
     was or is being done therein; and
(b) information with respect to any action which he has taken or proposes to
     take in or in connection with those premises in the performance of his
     functions,

and, where an inspector does as aforesaid, he shall give the like information to
the employer *(i)* of the first-mentioned persons.

(9) Notwithstanding anything in subsection (7) above, a person *(a)* who has
obtained such information as is referred to in that subsection may furnish to a
person who appears to him to be likely to be a party to any civil proceedings
arising out of any accident, occurrence, situation or other matter, a written
statement of relevant facts observed by him in the course of exercising any of
the powers referred to in that subsection.

General note. Subsection (1)(a) was amended by the Consumer Protection Act 1987,
s. 36, Sch. 3.

(a) **Person.** See note *(g)* to s. 4.

(b) **The relevant statutory provisions.** For definition, see s. 53(1).

(c) **Relevant information.** See sub-s. (1).

(d) **Disclosed.** It is an offence to disclose any information in contravention of s. 28
(s. 33(1)(j)); but see sub-s. (3).

(e) **Enforcing authority.** For definition, see s. 18(7)(a).

(f) **Local authority.** For definition, see s. 53(1).

(g) **Premises.** For definition, see s. 53(1).

(h) **Inspector.** For definition, see s. 53(1).

(i) **Employer.** For definition, see s. 53(1).

Special provisions relating to agriculture

29.–32.—[*repealed*].

Provisions as to offences

33.   Offences.—(1) It is an offence *(a)* for a person *(b)*—

(a)   to fail to discharge a duty to which he is subject by virtue of sections 2 to 7;

(b)   to contravene *(c)* section 8 or 9;

(c)   to contravene any health and safety regulations *(d)* or any requirement or prohibition imposed under any such regulations (including any requirement or prohibition to which he is subject by virtue of the terms of or any condition or restriction attached to any licence, approval, exemption or other authority issued, given or granted under the regulations);

(d)   to contravene any requirement imposed by or under regulations under section 14 or intentionally to obstruct any person in the exercise of his powers under that section;

(e)   to contravene any requirement imposed by an inspector under section 20 or 25;

(f)   to prevent or attempt to prevent any other person from appearing before an inspector or from answering any question to which an inspector may by virtue of section 20(2) require an answer;

(g)   to contravene any requirement or prohibition imposed by an improvement notice *(e)* or a prohibition notice *(f)* (including any such notice as modified on appeal) *(g)*;

(h)   intentionally to obstruct an inspector *(h)* or to obstruct a customs officer in the exercise of his powers under section 25A in the exercise or performance of his powers or duties;

(i)   to contravene any requirement imposed by a notice under section 27(1);

(j)   to use or disclose any information in contravention of section 27(4) or 28;

(k)   to make a statement which he knows to be false or recklessly to make a statement which is false where the statement is made—

(i)   in purported compliance with a requirement to furnish any information imposed by or under any of the relevant statutory provisions *(i)*; or

(ii)   for the purpose of obtaining the issue of a document under any of the relevant statutory provisions to himself or another person;

(l)   intentionally to make a false entry in any register, book, notice or other document required by or under any of the relevant statutory provisions to be kept, served or given or, with intent to deceive, to make use of any such entry which he knows to be false;

(m) with intent to deceive, to use a document issued or authorised to be issued under any of the relevant statutory provisions or required for any purpose thereunder or to make or have in his possession a document so closely resembling any such document as to be calculated to deceive;

(n) falsely to pretend to be an inspector;

(o) to fail to comply with an order made by a court under section 42.

(1A) Subject to any provision made by virtue of section 15(6)(d), a person guilty of an offence under subsection (1)(a) above consisting of failing to discharge a duty to which he is subject by virtue of sections 2 to 6 shall be liable—

(a) on summary conviction, to a fine not exceeding £20,000;

(b) on conviction on indictment, to a fine.

(2) A person guilty of an offence under paragraph (d), (f), (h) or (n) of subsection (1) above, or of an offence under paragraph (e) of that subsection consisting of contravening a requirement imposed by an inspector under section 20, shall be liable on summary conviction to a fine not exceeding level 5 on the standard scale (*j*).

(2A) A person guilty of an offence under subsection (1)(g) or (o) above shall be liable—

(a) on summary conviction, to imprisonment for a term not exceeding six months, or a fine not exceeding £20,000, or both;

(b) on conviction on indictment, to imprisonment for a term not exceeding two years, or a fine, or both.

(3) Subject to any provision made by virtue of section 15(6)(d) or (e) or by virtue of paragraph 2(2) of Schedule 3, a person guilty of an offence under subsection (1) above not falling within subsection (1A), (2) or (2A), or of an offence under any of the existing statutory provisions, being an offence for which no other penalty is specified, shall be liable—

(a) on summary conviction, to a fine not exceeding £2,000 (*k*) above;

(b) on conviction on indictment—

(i) if the offence is one to which this sub-paragraph applies, to imprisonment for a term not exceeding two years, or a fine, or both;

(ii) if the offence is not one to which the preceding sub-paragraph applies, to a fine.

(4) Subsection (3)(b)(i) above applies to the following offences—

(a) an offence consisting of contravening any of the relevant statutory provisions by doing otherwise than under the authority of a licence issued by the Executive something for the doing of which such a licence is necessary under the relevant statutory provisions;

(b) an offence consisting of contravening a term of or a condition or restriction attached to any such licence as is mentioned in the preceding paragraph;

(c) an offence consisting of acquiring or attempting to acquire, possessing or using an explosive article or substance (*l*) (within the meaning of any of the relevant statutory provisions) in contravention of any of the relevant statutory provisions;

(d) [*repealed*];

(e) an offence under subsection (1)(j) above.

(5) [*repealed*].

(6) ...

General note. Subsections (1A), (2A) were added, sub-s. (3) was amended, and sub-ss. (4)(d), (5) were repealed by the Offshore Safety Act 1992, ss. 4(2)–(6), 7(2), Sch. 2; but this amendment does not affect the punishment of an offence committed before 6 March 1992. Section 33(1)(h) was amended by the Consumer Protection Act 1987, s. 36, Sch. 3.

In s. 33(2) a reference to level 5 on the standard scale is substituted for the maximum fine by virtue of the Criminal Justice Act 1982, s. 46.

The maximum fine under s. 33(3)(a) is increased from £2,000 to £5,000 for offences committed on or after 1 October 1992 by virtue of the Criminal Justice Act 1991, s. 17.

By the Criminal Law Act 1977, ss. 15, 30 and Sch. 1, offences under sub-s. (5) are triable only summarily and the sub-section is amended; sub-s. (5) is printed as so amended. Any offence falling within the provisions of s. 33(3) is an offence triable either summarily or on indictment, and is hence an "indictable offence" (Interpretation Act 1978, s. 5 and Sch. 1). As such, no time limit applies to it (Magistrates' Courts Act 1980, s. 127(2)) and proceedings may be commenced at any time, whatever the mode of trial (*Kemp v Liebherr-GB Ltd* [1987] 1 All ER 885, [1987] 1 WLR 607, DC).

(a) Offence. For penalties, see sub-ss. (2)–(4); for offences due to the fault of another person, see s. 36; for offences by bodies corporate, see s. 37; and for restrictions on the institution of prosecutions, see s. 38. A failure on the part of the employer to know of the circumstances giving rise to an offence may not amount to mitigation: see *Kvaerner Govan v HM Advocate* 1992 SCCR 10. Nor does the fact that the risk to employees may only arise if they are inadvertent, since the purpose of the Act and Regulations passed under it is, in part, to protect employees from their own inadvertence (*R v Sanyo Electrical Manufacturing (UK) Ltd* (1992) 156 JP 863, CA). An employer is not criminally liable under s. 2 for the acts of an independent contracter: *British Gas plc v Riley* (Queen's Bench Division, Co/1585/88).

(b) Person. See note *(g)* to s. 4.

(c) Contravene. For definition, see s. 82(1)(b).

(d) Health and safety regulations. See s. 15.

(e) Improvement notice. See s. 21.

(f) Prohibition notice. See s. 22.

(g) Improvement or prohibition notice. It is not a defence to a prosecution for failure to comply with an improvement notice under s. 33(1)(g) to plead compliance so far as was reasonably practicable. The provisions of s. 40 do not apply to that paragraph; *Deary v Mansion Hide Upholstery Ltd* [1983] ICR 610, [1983] IRLR 195, DC.

(h) Inspector. For definition, see s. 53(1).

(i) The relevant statutory provisions. For definition, see s. 53(1).

(j) Fine ... the standard scale. See the general note.

(k) Fine ... £2,000. See the general note.

(l) Substance. For definition, see s. 53(1). For the power of the Court to order forfeiture of explosive articles or substances, see s. 42(4).

---

34. Extension of time for bringing summary proceedings.—(1) Where—

(a) a special report on any matter to which section 14 of this Act applies is made by virtue of subsection (2) (a) of that section; or

(b) a report is made by the person holding an inquiry into any such matter by virtue of subsection (2) (b) of that section; or

(c) a coroner's inquest is held touching the death of any person whose death may have been caused by an accident which happened while he was at work *(a)* or by a disease which he contracted or probably contracted at work or by any accident, act or omission which occurred in connection with the work *(b)* of any person whatsoever; or

(d) a public inquiry into any death that may have been so caused is held under the Sudden Deaths Inquiry (Scotland) Act 1976,

and it appears from the report or, in a case falling within paragraph (c) or (d) above, from the proceedings at the inquest or inquiry, that any of the relevant statutory provisions *(c)* was contravened *(d)* at a time which is material in relation to the subject-matter of the report, inquest or inquiry, summary proceedings against any person liable to be proceeded against in respect of the contravention may be commenced at any time within three months *(e)* of the making of the report or, in a case falling within paragraph (c) or (d) above, within three months of the conclusion of the inquest or inquiry.

(2) Where an offence under any of the relevant statutory provisions *(c)* is committed by reason of a failure to do something at or within a time fixed by or under any of those provisions, the offence shall be deemed to continue until that thing is done.

(3) Summary proceedings for an offence to which this subsection applies *(f)* may be commenced at any time within six months from the date on which there comes to the knowledge of a responsible enforcing authority *(g)* evidence sufficient in the opinion of that authority to justify a prosecution for that offence; and for the purposes of this subsection—

(a) a certificate of an enforcing authority *(h)* stating that such evidence came to its knowledge on a specified date shall be conclusive evidence of that fact; and

(b) a document purporting to be such a certificate and to be signed by or on behalf of the enforcing authority in question shall be presumed to be such a certificate unless the contrary is proved.

(4) The preceding subsection applies to any offence under any of the relevant statutory provisions *(c)* which a person commits by virtue of any provision or requirement to which he is subject as the designer, manufacturer, importer or supplier of any thing; and in that subsection "responsible enforcing authority" means an enforcing authority within whose field of responsibility *(i)* the offence in question lies, whether by virtue of section 35 or otherwise.

(5) In the application of subsection (3) above to Scotland—

(a) for the words from "there comes" to "that offence" there shall be substituted the words "evidence, sufficient in the opinion of the enforcing authority to justify a report to the Lord Advocate with a view to consideration of the question of prosecution, comes to the knowledge of the authority";

(b) at the end of paragraph (b) there shall be added the words "and (c) section 331 (3) of the Criminal Procedure (Scotland) Act 1975 (date of commencement of proceedings) shall have effect as it has effect for the purposes of that section".

General note. In s. 34(5) the reference to s. 331(3) of the Criminal Procedure (Scotland) Act 1975 is substituted by virtue of Sch. 9, para. 51.

(a) *At work.* For definition, see s. 52(1), (2).

(b) *Work.* For definition, see s. 52(1), (2).

(c) *The relevant statutory provisions.* For definition, see s. 53(1).

(d) *Contravened.* For definition, see s. 82(1)(b).

(e) *Three months.* To this extent the provisions of the Magistrates' Courts Act 1980, s. 127 (information to be laid within six months from the time of commission of an offence), are abrogated.

(f) *Applies.* See sub-s. (4).

(g) *Responsible enforcing authority.* See sub-s. (4).

(h) *Enforcing authority.* For definition, see s. 18(7)(a).

(i) *Field of responsibility.* See s. 18(7)(b).

---

35.   Venue. An offence under any of the relevant statutory provisions (a) committed in connection with any plant (b) or substance (c) may, if necessary for the purpose of bringing the offence within the field of responsibility (d) of any enforcing authority (e) or conferring jurisdiction on any court to entertain proceedings for the offence, be treated as having been committed at the place where that plant or substance is for the time being.

(a) *The relevant statutory provisions.* For definition, see s. 53(1).

(b) *Plant.* For definition, see s. 53(1).

(c) *Substance.* For definition, see s. 53(1).

(d) *Field of responsibility.* See s. 18(7)(b).

(e) *Enforcing authority.* For definition, see s. 18(7)(a).

---

36.   Offences due to fault of other person.—(1) Where the commission by any person of an offence under any of the relevant statutory provisions (a) is due to (b) the act or default (c) of some other person (d), that other person shall be guilty of the offence, and a person may be charged with and convicted of the offence, by virtue of this subsection whether or not proceedings are taken against the first-mentioned person.

(2) Where there would be or have been the commission of an offence under section 33 by the Crown but for the circumstance that that section does not bind the Crown (e), and that fact is due to the act or default of a person other than the Crown, that person shall be guilty of the offence which, but for that circum-

stance, the Crown would be committing or would have committed and may be charged with and convicted of that offence accordingly.

(3) The preceding provisions of this section are subject to any provision made by virtue of section 15(6).

General note. Note that the provisions of this section are subject to what may be specified in health and safety regulations; see sub-s. (3). The offence to be charged on the wording of the section, and of which the defendant may be convicted under that section, is the offence under s. 33, although it must at the same time be made clear to the defendant that the prosecution is being brought under s. 36 (*West Cumberland By Products Ltd v DPP* [1988] RTR 391, DC).

(a) *The relevant statutory provisions.* For definition, see s. 53(1).

(b) *Due to.* There must be a causal connection between the act or default and the offence committed: *Tarleton Engineering Co Ltd v Nattrass* [1973] 3 All ER 699, [1973] 1 WLR 1261.

(c) *Act or default.* This means wrongful act or default: *Noss Farm Products Ltd v Lilico* [1945] 2 All ER 609; *Lamb v Sunderland and District Creamery Ltd* [1951] 1 All ER 923. Accordingly, the fact that what the other person did became subsequently unlawful is not enough: *Noss Farm Products Ltd v Lilico,* above. *Mens rea* or negligence need not, however, be proved if the original offence is constituted without proof of *mens rea* or negligence, as the case may be: *Lindley v George W Horner & Co Ltd* [1950] 1 All ER 234; *Lamb v Sunderland and District Creamery Ltd,* above; *Lester v Balfour Williamson Merchant Shippers Ltd* [1953] 2 QB 168, [1953] 1 All ER 1146; *Fisher v Barrett and Pomeroy (Bakers) Ltd* [1954] 1 All ER 249, [1954] 1 WLR 351.

(d) *Person.* See note (g) to s. 4 and *Tesco Supermarkets Ltd v Nattrass* [1972] AC 153, [1971] 2 All ER 127, HL.

(e) *Does not bind the Crown.* See s. 48(1); but by s. 48(2), s. 33 applies to persons in the public service of the Crown as it applies to other persons.

---

37. Offences by bodies corporate.—(1) Where an offence under any of the relevant statutory provisions *(a)* committed by a body corporate is proved to have been committed with the consent or connivance *(b)* of, or to have been attributable to *(c)* any neglect *(d)* on the part of, any director, manager *(e)*, secretary or other similar officer *(f)* of the body corporate or a person who was purporting to act in any such capacity, he as well as the body corporate shall be guilty of that offence and shall be liable to be proceeded against and punished accordingly.

(2) Where the affairs of a body corporate are managed by its members, the preceding subsection shall apply in relation to the acts and defaults of a member in connection with his functions of management as if he were a director of the body corporate.

(a) *The relevant statutory provisions.* For definition, see s. 53(1).

(b) *Connivance.* See INTRODUCTORY NOTE 6.

(c) *Attributable to.* In *Wotherspoon v HM Advocate* 1978 JC 74, 78 it was held that "any degree of attributability will suffice and in that sense it is evident that the commission of a relevant offence by a body corporate may well be found to be attributable to failure on the part of each of a number of directors, managers or other officers to take certain steps which he could and should have taken in the discharge of the particular functions of his particular office".

(d) **Neglect.** In *Wotherspoon v HM Advocate* 1978 JC 74, 78 it was said that neglect "in its natural meaning pre-supposes the existence of some obligataion or duty on the part of the person charged with neglect". Moreover, "in considering in a given case whether there has been neglect within the meaning of s. 37(1) on the part of a particular director or other particular officer charged, the search must be to discover whether the accused has failed to take some steps to prevent the commission of an offence by the corporation to which he belongs if the taking of those steps either expressly falls on or should be held to fall within the scope of the functions of the office which he holds".

(e) **Manager.** See *R v Boal (Francis)* [1992] QB 591, [1992] 3 All ER 177, CA, a case on the almost identical wording of s. 23(1) of the Fire Precautions Act 1971, in which it was held that only those responsible for deciding corporate policy and strategy were "managers".

(f) **Similar officer.** The Director of Roads of a Regional Council is such an officer: *Armour v Skeen* [1977] IRLR 310.

---

38.   Restrictions on institution of proceedings in England and Wales. Proceedings for an offence under any of the relevant statutory provisions *(a)* shall not, in England and Wales *(b)*, be instituted except by an inspector *(c)* or by or with the consent of the Director of Public Prosecutions.

(a) **The relevant statutory provisions.** For definition, see s. 53(1).

(b) **England and Wales.** See INTRODUCTORY NOTE 4.

(c) **Inspector.** For definition, see s. 53(1). See also *Campbell v Wallsend Slipway and Engineering Co Ltd* [1978] ICR 1015, cited in note *(d)* to s. 19.

---

39.   Prosecution by inspectors.—(1) An inspector *(a)*, if authorised in that behalf by the enforcing authority *(b)* which appointed him, may, although not of counsel or a solicitor, prosecute before a magistrates' court proceedings for an offence under any of the relevant statutory provisions *(c)*.

(2) This section shall not apply to Scotland.

(a) **Inspector.** For definition, see s. 53(1).

(b) **Enforcing authority.** For definition, see s. 18(7)(a).

(c) **The relevant statutory provisions.** For definition, see s. 53(1).

---

40.   Onus of proving limits of what is practicable etc. In any proceedings for an offence under any of the relevant statutory provisions *(a)* consisting of a failure to comply with a duty or requirement to do something so far as is practicable *(b)* or so far as is reasonably practicable *(c)*, or to use the best practicable means to do something, it shall be for the accused to prove *(d)* (as the case may be) that it was not practicable or not reasonably practicable to do more than was in fact done to satisfy the duty or requirement, or that there was no better practicable means than was in fact used to satisfy the duty or requirement.

(*a*) *The relevant statutory provisions.* For definition, see s. 53(1).

(*b*) *Practicable.* See INTRODUCTORY NOTE 5.

(*c*) *Reasonably practicable.* See INTRODUCTORY NOTE 5.

(*d*) *Prove.* The burden of proof laid on the defendant is less onerous than that resting on the prosecutor as regards proving the offence, and may be discharged by satisfying the court of the probability of what the defendant is called on to prove: see *R v Carr-Briant* [1943] KB 607, [1943] 2 All ER 156, CCA and *R v Dunbar* [1958] 1 QB 1, [1957] 2 All ER 737, CCA. In *Lockhart v Kevin Oliphant* 1992 SCCR 774 the High Court of Justiciary stressed that once there is a *prima facie* case against the accused in that he has not ensured the health, safety and welfare at work of his employees then the onus under s. 40 is on the accused. Thus the Crown does not have to prove that it was reasonably practicable to comply with the Act.

---

41. Evidence.—(1) Where an entry is required by any of the relevant statutory provisions *(a)* to be made in any register or other record, the entry, if made, shall, as against the person *(b)* by or on whose behalf it was made, be admissible as evidence or in Scotland sufficient evidence of the facts stated therein.

(2) Where an entry which is so required to be so made with respect to the observance of any of the relevant statutory provisions has not been made, that fact shall be admissible as evidence or in Scotland sufficient that that provision has not been observed.

General note. As to the reception in evidence of documents sealed by the Commission, see Sch. 2, para. 18.

(*a*) *The relevant statutory provisions.* For definition, see s. 53(1).

(*b*) *Person.* See note *(g)* to s. 4.

---

42. Power of court to order cause of offence to be remedied or, in certain cases, forfeiture.—(1) Where a person *(a)* is convicted of an offence under any of the relevant statutory provisions *(b)* in respect of any matters which appear to the court to be matters which it is in his power to remedy, the court may, in addition to or instead of imposing any punishment, order *(c)* him, within such time as may be fixed by the order, to take such steps as may be specified in the order for remedying the said matters.

(2) The time fixed by an order under subsection (1) above may be extended or further extended by order of the court on an application made before the end of that time as originally fixed or as extended under this subsection, as the case may be.

(3) Where a person is ordered under subsection (1) above to remedy any matters, that person shall not be liable under any of the relevant statutory provisions in respect of those matters in so far as they continue during the time fixed by the order or any further time allowed under subsection (2) above.

(4) Subject to the following subsection, the court by or before which a person is convicted of an offence such as is mentioned in section 33(4)(c) in respect of any such explosive article or substance *(d)* as is there mentioned may order *(c)* the article or substance in question to be forfeited and either destroyed or dealt with in such other manner as the court may order.

(5) The court shall not order anything to be forfeited under the preceding subsection where a person claiming to be the owner of or otherwise interested in it applies to be heard by the court, unless an opportunity has been given to him to show cause why the order should not be made.

(a) *Person.* See note *(g)* to s. 4.

(b) *The relevant statutory provisions.* For definition, see s. 53(1).

(c) *Order.* It is an offence to fail to comply with such an order (s. 33(1)(o)).

(d) *Substance.* For definition, see s. 53(1).

Financial provisions

43. Financial provisions.—(1) It shall be the duty of the Secretary of State *(a)* to pay to the Commission such sums as are approved by the Treasury and as he considers appropriate for the purpose of enabling the Commission to perform its functions; and it shall be the duty of the Commission to pay to the Executive such sums as the Commission considers appropriate for the purpose of enabling the Executive to perform its functions.

(2) Regulations *(b)* may provide for such fees as may be fixed by or determined under the regulations to be payable for or in connection with the performance by or on behalf of any authority to which this subsection applies of any function conferred on that authority by or under any of the relevant statutory provisions *(c)*.

(3) Subsection (2) above applies to the following authorities, namely the Commission, the Executive, the Secretary of State, every enforcing authority *(d)*, and any other person *(e)* on whom any function is conferred by or under any of the relevant statutory provisions.

(4) Regulations *(b)* under this section may specify the person by whom any fee payable under the regulation is to be paid; but no such fee shall be made payable by a person in any of the following capacities, namely an employee *(f)*, a person seeking employment, a person training for employment *(g)*, and a person seeking training for employment *(h)*.

(5) Without prejudice to section 82(3), regulations *(b)* under this section may fix or provide for the determination of different fees in relation to different functions, or in relation to the same function in different circumstances.

(6) The power to make regulations *(b)* under this section shall be exercisable by the Secretary of State, the Minister of Agriculture, Fisheries and Food or the Secretary of State and that Minister acting jointly.

(7) [*repealed*].

(8) In subsection (4) above the references to a person training for employment and a person seeking training for employment shall include respectively a person attending an industrial rehabilitation course provided by virtue of the Employment and Training Act 1973 and a person seeking to attend such a course.

(9) For the purposes of this section the performance by an inspector *(i)* of his functions shall be treated as the performance by the enforcing authority which appointed him of functions conferred on that authority by or under any of the relevant statutory provisions.

    General note. For the payment of expenses out of money provided by Parliament, and the payment of receipts into the Consolidated Fund, see s. 81.

    (a) The Secretary of State. See note *(k)* to s. 2.

    (b) Regulations. The Health and Safety (Fees) Regulations 1992, S.I. 1992 No. 1752, have been made under this section; they provide that specified fees are payable to the Health and Safety Executive by employers for medical examinations conducted by an employment medical adviser under specified safety, health and welfare regulations.

    (c) The relevant statutory provisions. For definition, see s. 53(1).

    (d) Enforcing authority. For definition, see s. 18(7)(a).

    (e) Person. See note *(g)* to s. 4.

    (f) Employee. For definition, see s. 53(1).

    (g) Person training for employment. See sub-s. (8).

    (h) Person seeking training for employment. See sub-s. (8).

    (i) Inspector. For definition, see s. 53(1).

Miscellaneous and supplementary

44. Appeals in connection with licensing provisions in the relevant statutory provisions.—(1) Any person *(a)* who is aggrieved *(b)* by a decision of an authority having power to issue licences *(c)* (other than nuclear site licences *(d)*) under any of the relevant statutory provisions *(e)*—

    (a) refusing to issue a licence, to renew a licence held by him, or to transfer to him a licence held by another;

    (b) issuing him a licence on or subject to any term, condition or restriction whereby he is aggrieved;

    (c) varying or refusing to vary any term, condition or restriction on or subject to which a licence is held by him; or

    (d) revoking a licence held by him,

may appeal to the Secretary of State *(f)*.

    (2) The Secretary of State may, in such cases as he considers it appropriate to do so, having regard to the nature of the questions which appear to him to arise, direct that an appeal *(g)* under this section shall be determined on his behalf by a person appointed by him for that purpose.

(3) Before the determination of an appeal the Secretary of State shall ask the appellant and the authority against whose decision the appeal is brought whether they wish to appear and be heard on the appeal and—

(a) the appeal may be determined without a hearing of the parties if both of them express a wish not to appear and be heard as aforesaid;

(b) the Secretary of State shall, if either of the parties express a wish to appear and be heard, afford to both of them an opportunity of so doing.

(4) The Tribunals and Inquiries Act 1992 shall apply to a hearing held by a person appointed in pursuance of subsection (2) above to determine an appeal as it applies to a statutory inquiry held by the Secretary of State, but as if in section 10(1) of that Act (statement of reasons for decisions) the reference to any decision taken by the Secretary of State included a reference to a decision taken on his behalf by that person.

(5) A person who determines an appeal under this section on behalf of the Secretary of State and the Secretary of State, if he determines such an appeal, may give such directions as he considers appropriate to give effect to his determination.

(6) The Secretary of State may pay to any person appointed to hear or determine an appeal under this section on his behalf such remuneration and allowances as the Secretary of State may with the approval of the Minister for the Civil Service determine.

(7) In this section—

(a) "licence" means a licence under any of the relevant statutory provisions other than a nuclear site licence;

(b) "nuclear site licence" means a licence to use a site for the purpose of installing or operating a nuclear installation within the meaning of the following subsection.

(8) For the purposes of the preceding subsection "nuclear installation" means—

(a) a nuclear reactor (other than such a reactor comprised in a means of transport, whether by land, water or air); or

(b) any other installation of such class or description as may be prescribed *(h)* for the purposes of this paragraph or section 1(1)(b) of the Nuclear Installations Act 1965, being an installation designed or adapted for—

(i) the production or use of atomic energy; or

(ii) the carrying out of any process which is preparatory or ancillary to the production or use of atomic energy and which involves or is capable of causing the emission of ionising radiations; or

(iii) the storage, processing or disposal of nuclear fuel or of bulk quantities of other radioactive matter, being matter which has been produced or irradiated in the course of the production or use of nuclear fuel;

and in this subsection—

"atomic energy" has the meaning assigned by the Atomic Energy Act 1946;

"nuclear reactor" means any plant (including any machinery, equipment or appliance, whether affixed to land or not) designed or adapted for the production of atomic energy by a fission process in which a controlled chain reaction can be maintained without an additional source of neutrons.

General note. Subsection (4) was amended by the Tribunals and Inquiries Act 1992, s. 18(1), Sch. 3, para. 9.

(a) **Person.** See note (g) to s. 4.

(b) **Aggrieved.** See INTRODUCTORY NOTE 13.

(c) **Licences.** For definition, see sub-s. 7(a), and see, for example, licences issued under ss. 15(2) and 30(4) and Sch. 3, para. 4.

(d) **Nuclear site licences.** For definition, see sub-ss. (7)(b), (8).

(e) **The relevant statutory provisions.** For definition, see s. 53(1).

(f) **The Secretary of State.** See note (k) to s. 2.

(g) **Appeal.** See sub-ss. (4)–(6), and the Health and Safety Licensing Appeals (Hearings Procedure) Rules 1974, S.I. 1974 No. 2040, set out below. The procedure for the hearing of such appeals in Scotland is governed by the Health and Safety Licensing Appeals (Hearings Procedure) (Scotland) Rules 1974, S.I. 1974 No. 2068.

(h) **Prescribed.** For definition, see s. 53(1). Certain installations are prescribed for the purposes of the Nuclear Installations Act 1965, s. 1(1)(b) (see the Nuclear Installations Regulations 1971, S.I. 1971 No. 381, reg. 3).

THE HEALTH AND SAFETY LICENSING APPEALS (HEARINGS PROCEDURE) RULES 1974
(S.I. 1974 No. 2040)

Citation and commencement
   1.   These Rules may be cited as the Health and Safety Licensing Appeals (Hearings Procedure) Rules 1974 and shall come into operation on 1 January 1975.

Interpretation
   2.—(1) In these Rules—
   "the 1974 Act" means the Health and Safety at Work etc. Act 1974;
   "appeal" means an appeal under section 44(1) of *the 1974 Act*;
   "appellant" means a person who has brought an *appeal*;
   "appointed person" means the person appointed by the Secretary of State to hold the *hearing* and, when so directed by the Secretary of State, to determine the *appeal*;
   "hearing" means a hearing to which these Rules apply;
   "licensing authority" means the authority against whose decision the *appeal* is brought;
   "the parties" means the *appellant* and the *licensing authority*;
   "the site" means the site to which the licence which is the subject of the *appeal* relates or would, if issued, relate.
   (2) The Interpretation Act 1889 [Interpretation Act 1978] shall apply to the interpretation of these Rules as it applies to the interpretation of an Act of Parliament.

Application of Rules
   3.   These Rules apply to *hearings* held in England and Wales in pursuance of section 44(3) of *the 1974 Act* on *appeals* brought under that section.

Notification of hearing
   4.—(1) A date, time and place for the holding of the *hearing* shall be fixed and may be varied by the Secretary of State, who shall given not less than 42 days' notice in writing of such date, time and place to *the parties*.

Provided that—
  (i) with the consent of *the parties*, the Secretary of State may give such lesser period of notice as shall be agreed with *the parties* and in that event he may specify a date for service of the statement referred to in rule 5(1) later than the date therein prescribed;
  (ii) where it becomes necessary or advisable to vary the time or place fixed for the *hearing*, the Secretary of State shall give such notice of the variation as may appear to him to be reasonable in the circumstances.

(2) The notice given under paragraph (1) of this rule shall state the name of the *appointed person* and whether or not he is to determine the *appeal* on behalf of the Secretary of State.

(3) Without prejudice to the foregoing provisions of this rule, the Secretary of State may require the *licensing authority* to take one or more of the following steps, namely—
  (a) to publish in one or more newspapers circulating in the locality in which the site is situated such notice of the *hearing* and in such form as he may direct;
  (b) to serve such notice of the *hearing*, in such form and on such persons or classes of persons as he may direct;
  (c) to give such other notice of the *hearing* and in such form as he may direct,
and the requirements as to the period of notice contained in paragraph (1) of this rule shall not apply to any such notices.

Statements to be served before hearing
5.—(1) Not later than 28 days before the date of the *hearing* (or such later date as the Secretary of State may specify under proviso (i) to rule 4(1)), the *licensing authority* shall serve on the *appellant* a written statement of any submission which the *licensing authority* proposes to put forward at the *hearing* and shall supply a copy of the statement to the Secretary of State for transmission to the *appointed person*.

(2) Where a government department has expressed in writing to the *licensing authority* a view in support of the decision of the *licensing authority* and the *licensing authority* proposes to rely on such expression of view in their submissions at the *hearing*, they shall include it in their statement and shall supply a copy of the statement to the government department concerned.

(3) Where the *licensing authority* intend to refer to or put in evidence at the *hearing*, documents (including photographs, maps and plans), the authority's statement shall be accompanied by a list of such documents, together with a notice stating the times and place at which the documents may be inspected by the *appellant*; and the *licensing authority* shall afford the *appellant* a reasonable opportunity to inspect and, where practicable, to take copies of the documents.

(4) The *appellant* shall, if so required by the Secretary of State—
  (a) serve on the *licensing authority* and on the Secretary of State for transmission to the *appointed person*, within such time before the *hearing* as the Secretary of State may specify, a written statement of the submissions which he proposes to put forward at the *hearing*; and such statement shall be accompanied by a list of any docments (including photographs, maps and plans) which the *appellant* intends to refer to or put in evidence at the *hearing*; and
  (b) afford the *licensing authority* a reasonable opportunity to inspect and, where practicable, to take copies of such documents as are referred to in the foregoing provision.

Appearances at hearing
6.—(1) *The parties* shall be entitled to appear at the *hearing*.

(2) Any other person may appear at the discretion of the *appointed person* provided that he has, not later than 7 days before the date of the *hearing*, served on the *licensing authority* a statement of his proposed submissions; and the *licensing authority* shall send a copy of any such statement duly served on it to the *appointed person* and to the *appellant*.

(3) A body corporate may appear by its clerk or secretary or by any other officer appointed for the purpose by that body, or by counsel or solicitor; and any other person

may appear on his own behalf or be represented by counsel, solicitor or any other person.

(4) Where there are two or more persons having a similar interest in the subject matter of the *hearing*, the *appointed person* may allow one or more persons to appear for the benefit of some or all persons so interested.

Representatives of government departments at hearing

7.—(1) Where a government department has expressed in writing to the *licensing authority* a view in support of the decision of the *licensing authority* and the *licensing authority* have included this view in the statement referred to in rule 5(1), the *appellant* may, not later than 14 days before the date of the *hearing*, apply in writing to the Secretary of State for a representative of the government department concerned to be made available at the *hearing*.

(2) The Secretary of State shall transmit any application made to him under the last foregoing paragraph to the government department concerned, who shall make a representative of the department available to attend the *hearing*.

(3) A representative of a government department who, in pursuance of this rule, attends a *hearing* shall be called as a witness by the *licensing authority* and shall state the reasons for the view expressed by his department and included in the authority's statement under rule 5(1) and shall give evidence and be subject to cross-examination to the same extent as any other witness.

(4) Nothing in the last foregoing paragraph shall require a representative of a government department to answer any question which in the opinion of the *appointed person* is directed to the merits of government policy or to matters which affect the safety of the State and the *appointed person* shall disallow any such question.

Procedure at hearing

8.—(1) Except as otherwise provided in these Rules, the procedure at the *hearing* shall be such as the *appointed person* shall in his discretion determine and the *appointed person* shall state at the commencement of the *hearing* the procedure which, subject to consideration of any submission by *the parties*, he proposes to adopt, and shall inform *the parties*, what he proposes as regards any *site* inspection arising out of the *hearing*.

(2) Unless in any particular case the *appointed person* with the consent of the *appellant* otherwise determines, the *appellant* shall begin and shall have the right of final reply.

(3) *The parties* shall be entitled to make an opening statement, to call evidence and to cross-examine persons giving evidence, but any other person appearing at the *hearing* may do so only to the extent permitted by the *appointed person*.

(4) The *appointed person* shall not require or permit the giving or production of any evidence, whether written or oral, which would be contrary to the public interest; but, save as aforesaid, any evidence may be admitted at the discretion of the *appointed person*, who may direct that documents tendered in evidence may be inspected by any person entitled or permitted to appear at the *hearing* and that facilities be afforded him to take or obtain copies thereof.

(5) The *appointed person* may allow the *licensing authority* or the *appellant*, or both of them, to alter or add to the submissions contained in any statement served under rule 5(1) or (4), or to any list of documents which accompanied such statement, so far as may be necessary for the purpose of determining the questions in controversy between *the parties*, but shall (if necessary by adjouring the *hearing*) give the *appellant* or the *licensing authority*, as the case may be, an adequate opportunity of considering any such fresh submission or document.

(6) If any person entitled to appear at the *hearing* fails to appear, the *appointed person* may proceed with the *hearing* at his discretion.

(7) The *appointed person* shall be entitled (subject to disclosure thereof at the *hearing*) to take into account any written representations or statements received by him before the *hearing* from any person.

(8) The *appointed person* may from time to time adjourn the *hearing*, and where he does so, shall give reasonable notice to every person entitled or permitted to appear at the *hearing* of the date, time and place of the adjourned *hearing*, provided that where the

date, time and place of the adjourned *hearing* are announced at the *hearing*, no further notice shall be required.

Site inspections

9.—(1) The *appointed person* may make an inspection of the *site* before or during the *hearing* after having given notice to *the parties* of the date and time at which he proposes to do so.

(2) The *appointed person* may, and shall if so requested by any party before or during the *hearing*, inspect the premises after the close of the *hearing* and shall, in all cases where he intends to make such an inspection, announce during the *hearing* the date and time at which he proposes to do so.

(3) *The parties* shall be entitled to accompany the *appointed person* on any inspection under this rule; but the *appointed person* shall not be bound to defer his inspection if any person entitled to accompany him is not present at the time appointed.

Procedure after hearing where the appointed person is to determine the appeal

10.—(1) Where the *appointed person* has been directed to determine the *appeal* on behalf of the Secretary of State and, after the close of the *hearing*, proposes to take into consideration any new evidence (including expert opinion on a matter of fact) or any new issue of fact (not being a matter of government policy or a matter affecting the safety of the State) which was not raised at the *hearing* and which he considers to be material to his decision, he shall not come to a decision without first notifying *the parties* of the substance of the new evidence or of the new issue of fact and affording them an opportunity of making representations thereon in writing within 21 days or of asking within that time for the re-opening of the *hearing*.

(2) The *appointed person* may in any case, if he thinks fit, cause the *hearing* to be re-opened and shall cause it to be re-opened if asked to do so in accordance with the foregoing paragraph; and if the *hearing* is re-opened, rule 4(1) and (3) shall apply as it applied to the original *hearing* with the substitution for references to the Secretary of State, wherever they occur, of references to the *appointed person*.

Procedure after hearing where the appointed person is to report to the Secretary of State

11.—(1) After the close of the *hearing*, unless the Secretary of State has directed the *appointed person* to determine the *appeal* on his behalf—

(a) the *appointed person* shall prepare the first part of his report comprising a summary of the evidence given at the *hearing* together with his findings of fact, and—

    (i) shall provide a copy of the first part of his report to *the parties* and to any person who appeared at the *hearing*, if so required by any of them;

    (ii) shall consider any comments received by him from either party or from any such person within 14 days from the furnishing of the first part of his report;

    (iii) may, after consulting the other party or persons, amend the first part of his report, so however that he shall not, except with the consent of both *parties* and all such persons, introduce into his report any matter that had not been raised at the *hearing*;

(b) the *appointed person* shall thereafter prepare the second part of his report and shall include therein his recommendations if any or his reason for not making any recommendation; and

(c) the *appointed person* shall then send his report to the Secretary of State.

(2) Where the Secretary of State on receipt of the *appointed person's* report made under paragraph (1) of this rule—

(a) differs from the *appointed person* on a finding of fact; or

(b) after the close of the *hearing* takes into consideration any new evidence (including expert opinion on a matter of fact) or any new issue of fact (not being a matter of government policy or a matter affecting the safety of the State) which was not raised at the *hearing*,

and by reason thereof is disposed to disagree with a recommendation made by the *appointed person*, he shall not come to a decision which is at variance with any such recommendation without first notifying *the parties* of the terms of the recommendation, of his disagreement with it and of the reasons (other than reasons of which the disclosure might in his opinion affect the safety of the State) for his disagreement with it and affording them an opportunity of making representations in writing with 21 days or (if the Secretary of State has taken into consideration any new evidence or any new issue of fact, not being a matter of government policy or a matter affecting the safety of the State) of asking within 21 days for the re-opening of the *hearing.*

(3) The Secretary of State may in any case, if he thinks fit, cause the *hearing* to be re-opened, and shall cause it to be re-opened if asked to do so in accordance with the last foregoing paragraph; and, if the *hearing* is re-opened, rule 4(1) and (3) shall apply as it applied to the original *hearing* with the substitution in paragraph (1) of "28" for "42".

Notification of decision

12.—(1) The Secretary of State or the *appointed person* (if the Secretary of State has directed the *appointed person* to determine the *appeal* on his behalf) shall notify the decision on the *appeal*, and the reasons therefor, in writing to *the parties* and to any person who, having appeared at the *hearing*, has asked to be notified of the decision.

(2) Where a report has been made by the *appointed person* under rule 11(1) and a copy of that report is not sent with the notification of the decision, the notification shall be accompanied by a summary of the *appointed person's* conclusions and recommendations.

(3) Where a report has been made by the *appointed person* under rule 11(1) and any person entitled to be notified of the decision on the *appeal* under paragraph (1) of this rule has not received a copy of that report, he shall be supplied with a copy thereof on written application made to the Secretary of State within one month from the date of such decision.

(4) For the purposes of this rule "report" does not include documents, photographs or plans appended to the report.

Service of notices by post

13. Notices or documents required or authorised to be served or sent under the provisions of any of the foregoing rules may be sent by post.

---

45. Default powers.—(1) Where, in the case of a local authority *(a)* who are an enforcing authority *(b)*, the Commission is of the opinion that an investigation should be made as to whether that local authority have failed to perform any of their enforcement functions *(c)*, the Commission may make a report to the Secretary of State *(d)*.

(2) The Secretary of State may, after considering a report submitted to him under the preceding subsection, cause a local inquiry to be held; and the provisions of subsections (2) to (5) of section 250 of the Local Government Act 1972 as to local inquiries shall, without prejudice to the generality of subsection (1) of that section, apply to a local inquiry so held as they apply to a local inquiry held in pursuance of that section.

(3) If the Secretary of State is satisified, after having caused a local inquiry to be held into the matter, that a local authority have failed to perform any of their enforcement functions, he may make an order declaring the authority to be in default.

(4) An order made by virtue of the preceding subsection which declares an authority to be in default may, for the purpose of remedying the default, direct the authority (hereafter in this section referred to as "the defaulting authority") to perform such of their enforcement functions as are specified in the order in such manner as may be so specified and may specify the time or times within which those functions are to be performed by the authority.

(5) If the defaulting authority fail to comply with any direction contained in such an order the Secretary of State may, instead of enforcing the order by mandamus *(e)*, make an order *(f)* transferring to the Executive such of the enforcement functions of the defaulting authority as he thinks fit.

(6) Where any enforcement functions of the defaulting authority are transferred in pursuance of the preceding subsection, the amount of any expenses which the Executive certifies were incurred by it in performing those functions shall on demand be paid to it by the defaulting authority.

(7) Any expenses which in pursuance of the preceding subsection are required to be paid by the defaulting authority in respect of any enforcement functions transferred in pursuance of this section shall be defrayed by the authority in the like manner, and shall be debited to the like account, as if the enforcement functions had not been transferred and the expenses had been incurred by the authority in performing them.

(8) Where the defaulting authority are required to defray any such expenses the authority shall have the like powers for the purpose of raising the money for defraying those expenses as they would have had for the purpose of raising money required for defraying expenses incurred for the purpose of the enforcement functions in question.

(9) An order transferring any enforcement functions of the defaulting authority in pursuance of subsection (5) above may provide for the transfer to the Executive of such of the rights, liabilities and obligations of the authority as the Secretary of State considers appropriate; and where such an order is revoked the Secretary of State may, by the revoking order or a subsequent order, make such provision as he considers appropriate with respect to any rights, liabilities and obligations held by the Executive for the purposes of the transferred enforcement functions.

(10) The Secretary of State may by order vary or revoke any order previously made by him in pursuance of this section.

(11) In this section "enforcement functions", in relation to a local authority, means the functions of the authority as an enforcing authority.

(12) In the application of this section to Scotland—

(a) in subsection (2) for the words "subsections (2) to (5) of section 250 of the Local Government Act 1972" there shall be substituted the words "subsections (2) to (8) of section 210 of the Local Government (Scotland) Act 1973", except that before 16 May 1975 for the said words there shall be substituted the words "subsections (2) to (9) of section 355 of the Local Government (Scotland) Act 1947";
(b) in subsection (5) the words "instead of enforcing the order by mandamus" shall be omitted.

(a) Local authority. For definition, see s. 53(1).

(b) Enforcing authority. For definition, see s. 18(7)(a).

(c) Enforcement functions. For definition, see sub-s. (11).

(d) The Secretary of State. See note *(k)* to s. 2.

(e) Mandamus. For orders of mandamus, see 1 Halsbury's Laws (4th edn.) para. 104.

(f) **Order.** See also sub-ss. (9), (10).

---

46.   Service of notices.—(1) Any notice required or authorised by any of the relevant statutory provisions *(a)* to be served on or given to an inspector *(b)* may be served or given by delivering it to him or by leaving it at, or send it by post *(c)* to, his office.

(2) Any such notice required or authorised to be served on or given to a person *(d)* other than an inspector may be served or given by delivering it to him, or by leaving it at his proper address, or by sending it by post to him at that address.

(3) Any such notice may—

(a) in the case of a body corporate, be served on or given to the secretary or clerk of that body;
(b) in the case of a partnership, be served on or given to a partner or a person having the control or management of the partnership business or, in Scotland, the firm.

(4) For the purposes of this section and of section 26 of the Interpretation Act 1889 *(e)* (service of documents by post) in its application to this section, the proper address of any person on or to whom any such notice is to be served or given shall be his last known address, except that—

(a) in the case of a body corporate or their secretary or clerk, it shall be the address of the registered *(f)* or principal office of that body;
(b) in the case of a partnership or a person having the control or the management of the partnership business, it shall be the principal office of the partnership;

and for the purposes of this subsection the principal office of a company registered outside the United Kingdom *(g)* or of a partnership carrying on business outside the United Kingdom shall be their principal office within the United Kingdom.

(5) If the person to be served with or given any such notice has specified an address within the United Kingdom other than his proper address within the meaning of subsection (4) above as the one at which he or someone on his behalf will accept notices of the same description as that notice, that address shall also be treated for the purposes of this section and section 26 of the Interpretation Act 1889 *(e)* as his proper address.

(6) Without prejudice to any other provision of this section, any such notice required or authorised to be served on or given to the owner or occupier of any premises *(h)* (whether a body corporate or not) may be served or given by sending it by post to him at those premises, or by addressing it by name to the person on or to whom it is to be served or given and delivering it to some responsible person who is or appears to be resident or employed *(i)* in the premises.

(7) If the name or the address of any owner or occupier of premises on or to whom any such notice as aforesaid is to be served or given cannot after reasonable inquiry be ascertained, the notice may be served or given by

addressing it to the person on or to whom it is to be served or given by the description of "owner" or "occupier" of the premises (describing them) to which the notice relates, and by delivering it to some responsible person who is or appears to be resident or employed in the premises, or, if there is no such person to whom it can be delivered, by affixing it or a copy of it to some conspicuous part of the premises.

(8) The preceding provisions of this section shall apply to the sending or giving of a document as they apply to the giving of a notice.

(a) *The relevant statutory provisions.* For definition, see s. 53(1).

(b) *Inspector.* For definition, see s. 53(1).

(c) *Post.* See the Interpretation Act 1978, s. 7.

(d) *Person.* See note (g) to s. 4.

(e) *Interpretation Act 1889.* Now the Interpretation Act 1978, s. 7.

(f) *Registered office.* See the Companies Act 1985, s. 287.

(g) *United Kingdom.* See INTRODUCTORY NOTE 4.

(h) *Premises.* For definition, see s. 53(1).

(i) *Employed.* For definition, see s. 53(1).

---

47.   Civil liability.—(1) Nothing in this Part (a) shall be construed—

(a) as conferring a right of action in any civil proceedings in respect of any failure to comply with any duty imposed by sections 2 to 7 or any contravention (b) of section 8; or

(b) as affecting the extent (if any) to which breach of a duty imposed by any of the existing statutory provisions (c) is actionable; or

(c) as affecting the operation of section 12 of the Nuclear Installations Act 1965 (right to compensation by virtue of certain provisions of that Act).

(2) Breach of a duty imposed by health and safety regulations (d) shall, so far as it causes damage (e), be actionable except in so far as the regulations provide otherwise.

(3) No provision made by virtue of section 15(6)(b) shall afford a defence in any civil proceedings, whether brought by virtue of subsection (2) above or not; but as regards any duty imposed as mentioned in subsection (2) above health and safety regulations may provide for any defence specified in the regulations to be available in any action for breach of that duty.

(4) Subsections (1)(a) and (2) above are without prejudice to any right of action which exists apart from the provisions of this Act, and subsection (3) above is without prejudice to any defence which may be available apart from the provisions of the regulations there mentioned.

(5) Any term of an agreement which purports to exclude or restrict the operation of subsection (2) above, or any liability arising by virtue of that subsection shall be void, except in so far as health and safety regulations provide otherwise.

(6) In this section "damage" includes the death of, or injury to, any person (including any disease and any impairment of a person's physical or mental condition).

General note. As to civil liability for breach of statutory duty generally, see the LEGAL PRINCIPLES in the Introductory Section of this book.

(a) *This Part.* The reference is to Part I of the Act (ss. 1–54); see s. 82(1)(d).

(b) *Contravention.* For definition, see s. 82(1)(b).

(c) *The existing statutory provisions.* For definition, see s. 53(1).

(d) *Health and safety regulations.* For definition, see s. 53(1).

(e) *Damage.* For definition, see sub-s. (6). It is to be observed that "damage" here is wider than "personal injury".

The use of the present tense ("so far as it causes damage") would not, it is submitted, preclude the launch of civil proceedings for an injunction to restrain an existing breach which, though it is not at that moment causing damage, is likely to cause damage in the future. It is submitted that it would be logically irrelevant (except as a matter of evidence) whether the breach had caused damage already or not. Furthermore in relation to Regulations intended to implement European Directives, it is submitted that the requirement to provide an effective remedy would necessarily mean that the remedy of injunction should not be excluded: see "Direct Application of European Directives" in LEGAL PRINCIPLES in the introductory section. It is significant that the use of injunctions has been rare in the field of health and safety at work, even in negligence where there can be no question but that the remedy is available.

---

48. Application to Crown.—(1) Subject to the provisions of this section, the provisions of this Part (a), except sections 21 to 25 and 33 to 42 (b), and of regulations made under this Part shall bind the Crown.

(2) Although they do not bind the Crown, sections 33 to 42 shall apply to persons in the public service of the Crown as they apply to other persons.

(3) For the purposes of this Part and regulations made thereunder persons in the service of the Crown shall be treated as employees (c) of the Crown whether or not they would be so treated apart from this subsection.

(4) Without prejudice to section 15(5), the Secretary of State (d) may, to the extent that it appears to him requisite or expedient to do so in the interests of the safety of the State or the safe custody of persons lawfully detained, by order exempt the Crown either generally or in particular respects from all or any of the provisions of this Part which would, by virtue of subsection (1) above, bind the Crown.

(5) The power to make orders under this section shall be exercisable by statutory instrument (e), and any such order may be varied or revoked by a subsequent order.

(6) Nothing in this section shall authorise proceedings to be brought against Her Majesty in her private capacity, and this subsection shall be construed as if section 38(3) of the Crown Proceedings Act 1947 (interpretation of references in that Act to Her Majesty in her private capacity) were contained in this Act.

General note. Civil proceedings against the Crown are governed by the Crown Proceedings Act 1947; see 8 Halsbury's Laws (4th edn.) para. 968 *et seq.*

(a) *This Part.* The reference is to Part I of the Act (ss. 1–54); see s. 82(1)(d).

(b) *Sections 33 to 42.* In relation to s. 33, see s. 36(2).

(c) *Employee.* For definition, see s. 53(1).

(d) *The Secretary of State.* See note (k) to s. 2.

(e) *Statutory instrument.* See the Statutory Instruments Act 1946 and 44 Halsbury's Laws (4th edn.) para. 981 *et seq.*

---

49. Adaptation of enactments to metric units or appropriate metric units.—
(1) Regulations (a) made under this subsection may amend—

(a) any of the relevant statutory provisions (b); or

(b) any provision of an enactment which relates to any matter relevant to any of the general purposes of this Part (c) but is not among the relevant statutory provisions; or

(c) any provision of an instrument made or having effect under any such enactment as is mentioned in the preceding paragraph,

by substituting an amount expressed in metric units for an amount or quantity not so expressed or by substituting an amount or quantity expressed in metric units of a description specified in the regulations for an amount or quantity expressed in metric units of a different description.

(2) The amendments shall be such as to preserve the effect of the provisions mentioned except to such extent as in the opinion of the authority making the regulations is necessary to obtain amounts expressed in convenient and suitable terms.

(3) Regulations (a) made under this subsection may, in the case of a provision which falls within any of paragraphs (a) to (c) of subsection (1) above and contains words which refer to units other than metric units, repeal those words if the authority making the regulations is of the opinion that those words could be omitted without altering the effect of that provision.

(4) The power to make regulations (a) under this section shall be exercisable by the Secretary of State, the Minister of Agriculture, Fisheries and Food or the Secretary of State and that Minister acting jointly.

(a) *Regulations.* The following regulations relating to the subject matter of this book have been made under this section:
The Gasholders and Steam Boilers Regulations (Metrication) Regulations 1981, S.I. 1981 No. 687;
The Kiers Regulations 1938 (Metrication) Regulations 1981, S.I. 1981 No. 1152;
The Locomotives etc. Regulations 1906 (Metrication) Regulations 1981, S.I. 1981 No. 1327;
The Health and Safety (Foundries etc.) (Metrication) Regulations 1981, S.I. 1981 No. 1332;
The Pottery (Health etc.) (Metrication) Regulations 1982, S.I. 1982 No. 877;
The Docks, Shipbuilding etc. (Metrication) Regulations 1983, S.I. 1983 No. 644,
The Health and Safety (Emissions into the Atmosphere) Regulations 1983, S.I. 1983 No. 943;

The Dry Cleaning (Metrication) Regulations 1983, S.I. 1983 No. 977;

The Factories Act 1961 etc. (Metrication) Regulations 1983, S.I. 1983 No. 978;

The Factories (Testing of Aircraft Engines and Accessories) (Metrication) Regulations 1983, S.I. 1983 No. 979;

The Hoists and Lifts (Metrication) Regulations 1983, S.I. 1983 No. 1579;

The Construction (Metrication) Regulations 1984, S.I. 1984 No. 1593;

The Health and Safety (Miscellaneous Provisions) (Metrication etc.) Regulations 1992, S.I. 1992 No. 1811.

The regulations set out in this book to which the above regulations relate are printed as so amended.

(b) **The relevant statutory provisions.** For definition, see s. 53(1).

(c) **The general purposes of this Part.** See s. 1(4).

---

50. Regulations under the relevant statutory provisions.—(1) Where any power to make regulations under any of the relevant statutory provisions *(a)* is exercisable by the Secretary of State *(b)*, the Minister of Agriculture, Fisheries and Food or both of them acting jointly that power may be exercised either so as to give effect (with or without modifications *(c)*) to proposals *(d)* submitted by the Commission under section 11(2)(d) or independently of any such proposals; but the authority who is to exercise the power shall not exercise it independently of proposals from the Commission unless he has consulted the Commission and such other bodies as appear to him to be appropriate.

(2) Where the authority who is to exercise any such power as is mentioned in subsection (1) above proposes to exercise that power so as to give effect to any such proposals as are there mentioned with modifications, he shall, before making the regulations, consult the Commission.

(3) Where the Commission proposes to submit under section 11(2)(d) any such proposals as are mentioned in subsection (1) above except proposals for the making of regulations under section 43(2), it shall, before so submitting them, consult—

(a) any government department or other body that appears to the Commission to be appropriate (and, in particular, in the case of proposals for the making of regulations under section 18(2), any body representing local authorities *(e)* that so appears, and, in the case of proposals for the making of regulations relating to electro-magnetic radiations, the National Radiological Protection Board *(f)*);

(b) such government departments and other bodies, if any, as, in relation to any matter dealt with in the proposals, the Commission is required to consult under the subsection by virtue of directions given to it by the Secretary of State.

(4)–(5) [*repealed*].

(a) **The relevant statutory provisions.** For definition, see s. 53(1).

(b) **The Secretary of State.** See note *(k)* to s. 2.

(c) **Modification.** For definition, see s. 82(1)(c).

(d) **Proposals.** See sub-s. (3).

(*e*) **Local authority.** For definition, see s. 53(1).

(*f*) **The National Radiological Protection Board.** See note (*f*) to s. 16.

---

51.   Exclusion of application to domestic employment. Nothing in this Part (*a*) shall apply in relation to a person by reason only that he employs (*b*) another, or is himself employed as a domestic servant in a private household.

(*a*) **This Part.** The reference is to Part I of the Act (ss. 1–54); see s. 82(1)(d).

(*b*) **Employ.** For definition, see s. 53(1).

---

52.   Meaning of work and at work.—(1) For the purposes of this Part (*a*)—

(a)   "work" (*b*) means as an employee (*c*) or as a self-employed person (*d*);
(b)   an employee is at work throughout the time when he is in the course of his employment (*e*), but not otherwise; and
(c)   a self-employed person is at work throughout such time as he devotes to work as a self-employed person,

and, subject to the following subsection, the expressions "work" and "at work", in whatever context, shall be construed accordingly.

(2) Regulations (*f*) made under this subsection may—

(a)   extend the meaning of "work" and "at work" for the purposes of this Part (*a*); and
(b)   in that connection provide for any of the relevant statutory provisions (*g*) to have effect subject to such adaptations as may be specified in the regulations.

(3) The power to make regulations under subsection (2) above shall be exercisable by the Secretary of State, the Minister of Agriculture, Fisheries and Food or the Secretary of State and that Minister acting jointly.

(*a*) **This Part.** The reference is to Part I of the Act (ss. 1–54); see s. 82(1)(d).

(*b*) **"Work".** By the Genetically Modified Organisms (Contained Use) Regulations 1992, S.I. 1992 No. 3217, reg. 4, "work" is extended to include any activity involving genetic manipulation and, by the Health and Safety (Dangerous Pathogens) Regulations 1981, S.I. 1981 No. 1011, reg. 9, "work" is extended to include any activity involving the keeping or handling of a listed pathogen, and in each case, the meaning of "at work" is extended accordingly. By the Health and Safety (Training for Employment) Regulations 1990, S.I. 1990 No. 1380 (set out in Part 6, below), "work" is extended to include relevant training within the meaning of the Regulations, and the meaning of "at work" is extended accordingly. A provision protecting employees "at work" extends to protecting those not engaged in the particular process for which the relevant plant was designed (see *Bolton Metropolitan Borough Council v Malrod Insulation* [1993] ICR 358).

(*c*) **Employee.** For definition, see s. 53(1).

(*d*) **Self-employed person.** For definition, see s. 53(1).

(e) **Course of his employment.** In *Coult v Szuba* [1982] ICR 380, the court discussed the meaning of the phrase "in the course of his employment" as it occurs in s. 52(1)(b), but the actual decision was merely that as a matter of law there was material upon which the justices could have reached the conclusion they did.

(f) **Regulations.** The Regulations mentioned in note *(b)* were made under this and other sections. Both these regulations are set out in Part 4 of this book.

(g) **The relevant statutory provisions.** For definition, see s. 53(1).

---

53. General interpretation of Part I.—(1) In this Part *(a)* unless the context otherwise requires—

"article for use at work" means—

(a) any plant *(b)* designed for use or operation (whether exclusively or not) by persons at work *(c)*, and
(b) any article designed for use as a component in any such plant;

"article of fairground equipment" means any fairground equipment *(a)* or any article designed for use as a component in any such equipment;
"code of practice" (without prejudice to section 16(8)) includes a standard, a specification and any other documentary form of practical guidance;
"the Commission" has the meaning assigned by section 10(2);
"conditional sale agreement" means an agreement for the sale of goods under which the purchase price or part of it is payable by instalments, and the property in the goods is to remain in the seller (notwithstanding that the buyer is to be in possession of the goods) until such conditions as to the payment of instalments or otherwise as may be specified in the agreement are fulfilled;
"contract of employment" means a contract of employment *(e)* or apprenticeship (whether express or implied and, if express, whether oral or in writing);
"credit-sale agreement" means an agreement for the sale of goods, under which the purchase price of it is payable by instalments, but which is not a conditional sale agreement;
"customs officer" means an officer within the meaning of the Customs and Excise Management Act 1979;
"domestic premises" means premises *(f)* occupied as a private dwelling (including any garden, yard, garage, outhouse or other appurtenance of such premises which is not used in common by the occupants of more than one such dwelling), and "non-domestic premises" shall be construed accordingly;
"employee" means an individual who works under a contract of employment, and related expressions shall be construed accordingly *(g)*;
"enforcing authority" has the meaning assigned by section 18(7);
"the Executive" has the meaning assigned by section 10(5);
"the existing statutory provisions" means the following provisions while and to the extent that they remain in force, namely the provisions of the Acts

mentioned in Schedule 1 which are specified in the third column of that Schedule and of the regulations, orders or other instruments of legislative character made or having effect under any provision so specified;

"fairground equipment" means any fairground ride, any similar plant which is designed to be in motion for entertainment purposes with members of the public on or inside it or any plant which is designed to be used by members of the public for entertainment purposes either as a slide or for bouncing upon, and in this definition the reference to plant which is designed to be in motion with members of the public on or inside it includes a reference to swings, dodgems and other plant which is designed to be in motion wholly or partly under the control of, or to be put in motion by, a member of the public;

"the general purposes of this Part" has the meaning assigned by section 1;

"health and safety regulations" has the meaning assigned by section 15(1);

"hire-purchase agreement" means an agreement other than a conditional sale agreement, under which—

(a) goods are bailed or (in Scotland) hired in return for periodical payments by the person to whom they are bailed or hired; and

(b) the property in the goods will pass to that person if the terms of the agreement are complied with and one or more of the following occurs:

  (i) the exercise of an option to purchase by that person;
  (ii) the doing of any other specified act by any party to the agreement;
  (iii) the happening of any other event; and hire-purchase shall be construed accordingly;

"improvement notice" means a notice under section 21;

"inspector" means an inspector appointed under section 19;

"local authority" means—

(a) in relation to England and Wales, a county council, a district council, a London borough council, the Common Council of the City of London, the Sub-Treasurer of the Inner Temple or the Under-Treasurer of the Middle Temple,

(b) in relation to Scotland, a regional, islands or district council except that before 16th May 1975 it means a town council or county council;

"micro-organism" includes any microscopic biological entity which is capable of replication;

"offshore installation" means any installation which is intended for under-water exploitation of mineral resources or exploration with a view to such exploitation;

"personal injury" includes any disease and any impairment of a person's physical or mental condition;

"plant" includes any machinery, equipment or appliance;

"premises" includes any place and, in particular, includes—

(a) any vehicle, vessel, aircraft or hovercraft,

(b) any installation on land (including the foreshore and other land intermittently covered by water), any offshore installation, and any other installation (whether floating, or resting on the seabed or the subsoil thereof, or resting on other land covered with water or the subsoil thereof), and

(c) any tent or movable structure;

"prescribed" means prescribed by regulations made by the Secretary of State;

"prohibition notice" means a notice under section 22;

"the relevant statutory provisions" means—

(a) the provisions of this Part and of any health and safety regulations *(h)* and

(b) the existing statutory provisions *(i)*;

"self-employed person" means an individual who works for gain or reward otherwise than under a contract of employment *(j)*, whether or not he himself employs others;

"substance" means any natural or artificial substance (including micro-organisms), whether in solid or liquid form or in the form of a gas or vapour;

"supply", where the reference is to supplying articles or substances *(k)*, means supplying them by way of sale, lease, hire or hire-purchase, whether as principal or agent for another.

(2)–(6) [*repealed*].

General note. In sub-s. (1), definitions of "article of fairground equipment", "customs officer", "fairground equipment" and "micro-organism" are inserted, and the definition of "substance" is amended by the Consumer Protection Act 1987, s. 36, Sch. 3.

(a) **This Part.** The reference is to Part I (ss. 1–54) of the Act; see s. 82(1)(d).

(b) **Plant.** For definition, see this subsection.

(c) **Designed for use ... at work.** See *McKay v Unwin Pyrotechnics Ltd* [1991] Crim LR 547, in which a dummy mine being used in trials was held not to be designed or manufactured for use by persons at work; instead, the trials were to establish whether it could be used at work. For definition of "at work" see s. 52(1), (2).

(d) **Fairground equipment.** For definition, see this subsection.

(e) **Employment.** For definition, see this subsection.

(f) **Premises.** For definition, see this subsection. A common foyer is "premises" but not "domestic premises", since the foyer cannot be a private dwelling (*Westminster City Council v Select Management Ltd* [1984] 1 All ER 994, [1984] 1 WLR 1058).

(g) **Employee.** By the Health and Safety (Training for Employment) Regulations 1990, S.I. 1990 No. 1380, a person provided with relevant training, within the meaning of those Regulations, is treated as being the employee of the person whose undertaking (whether carried on by him for profit or not) is for the time being the immediate provider to that person of the training, and the meaning of "employee", "worker" and "employer" is construed accordingly.

(h) **Health and safety regulations.** For definition, see this subsection. For a power to review discriminatory provisions in the health and safety legislation, see the Sex Discrimination Act 1975.

(i) **The existing statutory provisions.** For definition, see this subsection.

(j) **Employment.** For definition, see this subsection.

(k) **Substance.** For definition, see this subsection.

---

54. Application of Part I to Isles of Scilly. This Part *(a)*, in its application to the Isles of Scilly, shall apply as if those Isles were a local government area and the Council of those Isles were a local authority *(b)*.

   (a) **This Part.** The reference is to Part I (ss. 1–54) of the Act; see s. 82(1)(d).

   (b) **Local authority.** For definition, see s. 53(1).

PART II
THE EMPLOYMENT MEDICAL ADVISORY SERVICE

55. Functions of and responsibility for maintaining employment medical advisory service.—(1) There shall continue to be an employment medical advisory service, which shall be maintained for the following purposes, that is to say—

   (a) securing that the Secretary of State *(a)*, the Health and Safety Commission and others *(b)* concerned with the health of employed persons or of persons seeking or training for employment *(c)* can be kept informed of, and adequately advised on, matters of which they ought respectively to take cognisance concerning the safeguarding and improvement of the health of those persons;

   (b) giving to employed persons and persons seeking or training for employment information and advice on health in relation to employment and training for employment;

   (c) other purposes of the Secretary of State's functions relating to the employment.

   (2) The authority responsible for maintaining the said service shall be the Secretary of State; but if arrangements are made by the Secretary of State for that responsibility to be discharged on his behalf by the Health and Safety Commission or some other body, then, while those arrangements operate, the body so discharging that responsibility (and not the Secretary of State) shall be the authority responsible for maintaining that service.

   (3) The authority for the time being responsible for maintaining the said service may also for the purposes mentioned in subsection (1) above, and for the purpose of assisting employment medical advisers *(d)* in the performance of their functions, investigate or assist in, arrange for or make payments in respect of the investigation of problems arising in connection with any such matters as are so mentioned or otherwise in connection with the functions of employment medical advisers, and for the purpose of investigating or assisting in the investigation of such problems may provide and maintain such laboratories and other services as appear to the authority to be requisite.

   (4) Any arrangements made by the Secretary of State in pursuance of subsection (2) above may be terminated by him at any time, but without

prejudice to the making of other arrangements at any time in pursuance of that subsection (including arrangements which are to operate from the time when any previous arrangements so made cease to operate).

(5) Without prejudice to sections 11(4)(a) and 12(b), it shall be the duty of the Health and Safety Commission, if so directed by the Secretary of State, to enter into arrangements with him for the Commission to be responsible for maintaining the said service.

(6) In subsection (1) above—

(a) the reference to persons training for employment shall include persons attending industrial rehabilitation courses provided by virtue of the Employment and Training Act 1973; and

(b) the reference to persons (other than the Secretary of State and the Health and Safety Commission concerned with the health of employed persons or of persons seeking or training for employment shall be taken to include organisations representing employers, employees and occupational health practitioners respectively.

General note. Subsection (1)(a) was amended by the Employment Act 1988, s. 33(1), Sch. 3, Pt. II, para. 7(a).

Subsections (1)(a), (6)(b) were amended by the Employment Act 1989, s. 29(3), (4), Sch. 6, para. 11, Sch. 7, Pt. I.

The Employment Medical Advisory Service Act 1972 established an employment medical advisory service for the purpose of securing that the Secretary of State and others concerned with the health of employed persons, and of persons training for employment, should be informed of and advised of matters concerning the safeguarding and improvement of the health of such persons. Part II (ss. 55–60) of the Health and Safety at Work etc. Act 1974 re-enacts with amendments certain provisions of the 1972 Act, which had been partly repealed by the 1974 Act (ss. 60(5), 83(2) and Sch. 10) and by the Factories Act 1961 etc. (Repeals and Modifications) Regulations 1974, S.I. 1974 No. 1941. Those provisions of the Employment Medical Advisory Service Act 1972 which remain in force are provisions which amend the Factories Act 1961.

The provisions of ss. 55–60 may be extended so as to operate outside Great Britain (s. 84(3), (4)).

(a) **The Secretary of State.** See note (k) to s. 2.

(b) **Others.** See sub-s. (6)(b).

(c) **Persons training for employment.** See sub-s. (6)(a).

(d) **Employment medical adviser.** See s. 56.

---

56. Functions of authority responsible for maintaining the service.—(1) The authority for the time being responsible for maintaining the employment medical advisory service shall for the purpose of discharging that responsibility appoint persons to be employment medical advisers, and may for that purpose appoint such other officers and servants as it may determine, subject however to the requisite approval as to numbers, that is to say—

(a) where the authority is the Secretary of State (a), the approval of the Minister for the Civil Service;

(b) otherwise, the approval of the Secretary of State given with the consent of that Minister.

(2) A person shall not be qualified to be appointed, or to be, an employment medical adviser unless he is a fully registered medical practitioner.

(3) The authority for the time being responsible for maintaining the said service may determine the cases and circumstances in which the employment medical advisers or any of them are to perform the duties or exercise the powers conferred on employment medical advisers by or under this Act or otherwise.

(4) Where as a result of arrangements made in pursuance of section 55(2) the authority responsible for maintaining the said service changes, the change shall not invalidate any appointment previously made under subsection (1) above, and any such appointment subsisting when the change occurs shall thereafter have effect as if made by the new authority.

(a) *The Secretary of State.* See note (k) to s. 2.

---

57. Fees.—(1) The Secretary of State (a) may by regulations provide for such fees as may be fixed by or determined under the regulations to be payable for or in connection with the performance by the authority responsible for maintaining the employment medical advisory service of any function conferred for the purposes of that service on that authority by virtue of this Part or otherwise.

(2) For the purposes of this section, the performance by an employment medical adviser (b) of his functions shall be treated as the performance by the authority responsible for maintaining the said service of functions conferred on that authority as mentioned in the preceding subsection.

(3) The provisions of subsections (4), (5) and (8) of section 43 shall apply in relation to regulations under this section with the modification that references to subsection (2) of that section shall be read as references to subsection (1) of this section.

(4) Where an authority other than the Secretary of State is responsible for maintaining the said service, the Secretary of State shall consult that authority before making any regulations under this section.

(a) *The Secretary of State.* See note (k) to s. 2.

(b) *Employment medical adviser.* See s. 56.

---

58. Other financial provisions.—(1) The authority for the time being responsible for maintaining the employment medical advisory service may pay—

(a) to employment medical advisers (a) such salaries or such fees and travelling or other allowances; and

(b) to other persons called upon to give advice in connection with the execution of the authority's functions under this Part such travelling or other allowances or compensation for loss of remunerative time; and

(c) to persons attending for medical examinations conducted by, or in accordance with arrangements made by, employment medical advisers (including pathological, physiological and radiological tests and similar investigations so conducted) such travelling or subsistence allowances or such compensation for loss of earnings,

as the authority may, with the requisite approval, determine.

(2) For the purposes of the preceding subsection the requisite approval is—

(a) where the said authority is the Secretary of State *(b)*, the approval of the Minister for the Civil Service;
(b) otherwise, the approval of the Secretary of State given with the consent of that Minister.

(3) Where an authority other than the Secretary of State is responsible for maintaining the said service, it shall be the duty of the Secretary of State to pay to that authority such sums as are approved by the Treasury and as he considers appropriate for the purpose of enabling the authority to discharge that responsibility.

(a) **Employment medical adviser.** See s. 56.

(b) **The Secretary of State.** See note *(k)* to s. 2.

---

59. Duty of responsible authority to keep accounts and to report.—(1) It shall be the duty of the authority for the time being responsible for maintaining the employment medical advisory service—

(a) to keep, in relation to the maintenance of that service, proper accounts and proper records in relation to the accounts;
(b) to prepare in respect of each accounting year *(a)* a statement of accounts relating to the maintenance of that service in such form as the Secretary of State *(b)* may direct with the approval of the Treasury; and
(c) to send copies of the statement to the Secretary of State and the Comptroller and Auditor General before the end of the month of November next following the accounting year to which the statement relates.

(2) The Comptroller and Auditor General shall examine, certify and report on each statement received by him in pursuance of subsection (1) above and shall lay copies of each statement and of his report before each House of Parliament.

(3) It shall also be the duty of the authority responsible for maintaining the employment medical advisory service to make to the Secretary of State, as soon as possible after the end of each accounting year, a report on the discharge of its responsibilities in relation to that service during that year; and the Secretary of State shall lay before each House of Parliament a copy of each report made to him in pursuance of this subsection.

(4) Where as a result of arrangements made in pursuance of section 55(2) the authority responsible for maintaining the employment medical advisory

service changes, the change shall not affect any duty imposed by this section on the body which was responsible for maintaining that service before the change.

(5) No duty imposed on the authority for the time being responsible for maintaining the employment medical advisory service by subsection (1) or (3) above shall fall on the Commission (which is subject to corresponding duties under Schedule 2) or on the Secretary of State.

(6) In this section "accounting year" means, except so far as the Secretary of State otherwise directs, the period of twelve months ending with 31st March in any year.

(a) *Accounting year.* For definition, see sub-s. (6).

(b) *The Secretary of State.* See note (k) to s. 2.

---

60. Supplementary.—(1) It shall be the duty of the Secretary of State (a) to secure that each Area Health Authority (b) and each District Health Authority (c) arranges for one of its officers who is a fully registered medical practitioner to furnish, on the application of an employment medical adviser (d) such particulars of the school medical record of a person who has not attained the age of eighteen and such other information relating to his medical history as the adviser may reasonably require for the efficient performance of his functions; but no particulars or information about any person which may be furnished to an adviser in pursuance of this subsection shall (without the consent of that person) be disclosed by the adviser otherwise than for the efficient performance of his functions.

(2) In its application to Scotland the preceding subsection shall have effect with the substitution of the words "every Health Board arrange for one of their" for the words from "each" to "its".

(3) [*repealed*].

(4) References to the chief employment medical adviser or a deputy chief employment medical adviser in any provision of an enactment or instrument made under an enactment shall be read as references to a person appointed for the purposes of that provision by the authority responsible for maintaining the employment medical advisory service.

(5) The following provisions of the Employment Medical Advisory Service Act 1972 (which are superseded by the preceding provisions of this Part or rendered unnecessary by provisions contained in Part I), namely sections 1 and 6 and Schedule 1, shall cease to have effect; but—

(a) in so far as anything done under or by virtue of the said section 1 or Schedule 1 could have been done under or by virtue of a corresponding provision of Part I or this Part, it shall not be invalidated by the repeal of that section and Schedule by this Act but shall have effect as if done under or by virtue of that corresponding provision; and

(b) any order made under the said section 6 which is in force immediately before the repeal of that section by this Act shall remain in force notwithstanding that repeal, but may be revoked or varied by regulations under section 43(2) or 57, as if it were an instrument containing regulations made under section 43(2) or 57, as the case may require.

(6) Where any Act (whether passed before, or in the same Session as, this Act) or any document refers, either expressly or by implication, to or to any enactment contained in any of the provisions of the said Act of 1972 which are mentioned in the preceding subsection, the reference shall, except where the context otherwise requires, be construed as, or as including, a reference to the corresponding provisions of this Act.

(7) Nothing in subsection (5) or (6) above shall be taken as prejudicing the operation of section 38 of the Interpretation Act 1889 *(f)* (which relates to the effect of repeals).

(a) **The Secretary of State.** See note *(k)* to s. 2.

(b) **Area Health Authority.** See the Health Services Act 1980, s. 115.

(c) **District Health Authority.** See the Health Services Act 1980, s. 115.

(d) **Employment medical adviser.** See s. 56.

(e) **Statutory instrument.** See note *(e)* to s. 48.

(f) **Interpretation Act 1889.** Now the Interpretation Act 1978, ss. 16(1), 17(2).

Part III

Sections 61–74 and 76 are repealed and consolidated in the Building Act 1984. Section 75 has not been repealed, but is outside the scope of this book.

Part IV
Miscellaneous and General

77. Amendment of Radiological Protection Act 1970.—(1) Section 1 of the Radiological Protection Act 1970 (establishment and functions of the National Radiological Protection Board) shall be amended in accordance with the following provisions of this subsection—

(a) after subsection (6) there shall be inserted as subsection (6A)—

"(6A) In carrying out such of their functions as relate to matters to which the functions of the Health and Safety Commission relate, the Board *(a)* shall (without prejudice to subsection (7) below) act in consultation with the Commission and have regard to the Commission's policies with respect to such matters";

(b) after subsection (7) there shall be inserted as subsections (7A) and (7B)—

"(7A) Without prejudice to subsection (6) or (7) above, it shall be the duty of the Board, if so directed by the Health Ministers *(b)*, to enter into an agreement with the Health and Safety Commission for the Board to carry out on behalf of the Commission such of the Commission's functions relating to ionising or other radiations (including those which are not electro-magnetic) as may be determined by or in accordance with the direction; and the Board shall have power to carry out any agreement entered into in pursuance of a direction under this subsection.

(7B) The requirement as to consultation in subsection (7) above shall not apply to a direction under subsection (7A).'';

(c) in subsection (8), after the words "subsection (7)" there shall be inserted the words "or (7A)".

(2) In section 2(6) of the Radiological Protection Act 1970 (persons by whom, as regards premises occupied by the said Board, sections 1 to 51 of the Offices, Shops and Railway Premises Act 1963 and regulations thereunder are enforceable) for the words from "inspectors appointed" to the end of the subsection there shall be substituted the words "inspectors appointed by the Health and Safety Executive under section 19 of the Health and Safety at Work etc. Act 1974."

General note. The amendments made by this section to the Radiological Protection Act 1970 co-ordinate the activities of the National Radiological Protection Board, established under that Act, with those of the Health and Safety Commission.

(a) The Board. That is, the National Radiological Protection Board (established by the Radiological Protection Act 1970, s. 1(1)).

(b) The Health Ministers. See the Radiological Protection Act 1970, s. 1(4).

---

78. Amendment of Fire Precautions Act 1971.—(1) The Fire Precautions Act 1971 shall be amended in accordance with the following provisions of this section.

(2) In section 1(2) (power to designate uses of premises for which fire certificate is compulsory) at the end there shall be inserted as paragraph (f)—
   "(f) use as a place of work *(a).*"

(3) In section 2 (premises exempt from section 1), paragraphs (a) to (c) (which exempt certain premises covered by the Offices, Shops and Railway Premises Act 1963, the Factories Act 1961 or the Mines and Quarries Act 1954) shall cease to have effect.

(4) [*repealed*].

(5) In section 12(1) (power to make regulations about fire precautions as regards certain premises), at the end there shall be added the words "and nothing in this section shall confer on the Secretary of State *(b)* power to make provision with respect to the taking or observance of special precautions in connection with the carrying on of any manufacturing process."

(6) In section 17 (duty of fire authorities to consult other authorities before requiring alterations to buildings)—

(a) in subsection (1), the word "and" shall be omitted where last occurring in paragraph (i) and shall be added at the end of paragraph (ii), and after paragraph (ii) their shall be added as paragraph (iii)—

"(iii) if the premises are used as a place of work and are within the field of responsibility *(c)* of one or more enforcing authorities *(d)* within the meaning of Part I of the Health and Safety at Work etc. Act 1974, consult that authority or each of those authorities.";

(b) in subsection (2) (clarification of references in section 9 to persons aggrieved), for the words "or buildings authority" there shall be substituted the words "buildings authority or other authority";

(c) after subsection (2) there shall be added as subsection (3)—

"(3) Subsection 18(7) of the Health and Safety at Work etc. Act 1974 (meaning in Part I of that Act of 'enforcing authority' and of such an authority's 'field of responsibility') shall apply for the purposes of this section as it applies for the purposes of that Part.".

(7) In section 18 (enforcement of Act)—

(a) for the word "it" there shall be substituted the words "(1) Subject to subsection (2) below, it";

(b) for the word "section" there shall be substituted the word "subsection"; and

(c) after the word "offence" there shall be added as subsection (2)—

"(2) A fire authority shall have power to arrange with the Health and Safety Commission for such of the authority's functions under this Act as may be specified in the arrangement to be performed on their behalf by the Health and Safety Executive (with or without payment) in relation to any particular premises so specified which are used as a place of work.".

(8) In section 40 (application to Crown etc.)—

(a) in subsection (1)(a) (provisions which apply to premises occupied by the Crown), after the word "6" there shall be inserted the words, "9A (except subsection (4))";

(b) in subsection (1)(b) (provisions which apply to premises owned, but not occupied by, the Crown), after the word "8" there shall be inserted the word "9A";

(c) in subsection (10) (application of Act to hospital premises in Scotland), for the words from "Regional" to "hospitals" there shall be substituted the words "Health Board";

(d) after subsection (10) there shall be inserted the following subsection—

"(10A) This Act shall apply to premises in England occupied by a Board of Governors of a teaching hospital (being a body for the time being specified in an order under section 15(1) of the National Health Service Reorganisation Act 1973) as if they were premises occupied by the Crown.".

(9) In section 43(1) (interpretation) there shall be added at the end the following definition—

"work" has the same meaning as it has for the purpose of Part I of the Health and Safety at Work etc. Act 1974".

(10) Schedule 8 (transitional provisions with respect to fire certificates under the Factories Act 1961 or the Offices, Shops and Railway Premises Act 1963) shall have effect.

General note. As to fire precautions generally, see Part 3 of this book.

The amendments made by this section to the Fire Precautions Act 1971 enable the fire authority to designate office, shop and railway premises, factory premises, and mines and quarries as premises requiring a fire certificate. Section 78(4) was repealed by the Fire Safety and Safety of Places of Sport Act 1987, s. 49(1) and Sch. 4.

(a) *Work.* For definition, see sub-s. (9) and s. 52(1), (2).

(b) *The Secretary of State.* The Secretary of State responsible for the administration of the Fire Precautions Act 1971 is the Home Secretary.

(c) *Field of responsibility.* See s. 18(7)(b).

(d) *Enforcing authority.* See s. 18(7)(a).

---

79. [*spent*].

---

80.   General power to repeal or modify Acts and instruments.—(1) Regulations *(a)* made under this subsection may repeal or modify any provision to which this subsection applies if it appears to the authority making the regulations that the repeal or, as the case may be, the modification *(b)* of that provision is expedient in consequence of or in connection with any provision made by or under Part I.

(2) Subsection (1) above applies to any provision, not being among the relevant statutory provisions *(c)*, which—

(a) is contained in this Act or in any other Act passed before or in the same Session as this Act; or

(b) is contained in any regulations, order or other instrument of a legislative character which was made under an Act before the passing of this Act; or

(c) applies, excludes or for any other purpose refers to any of the relevant statutory provisions and is contained in any Act not falling within paragraph (a) above or in any regulations, order or other instrument of a legislative character which is made under an Act but does not fall within paragraph (b) above.

(2A) Subsection (1) above shall apply to provisions in the Employment Protection (Consolidation) Act 1978 which re-enact provisions previously contained in the Redundancy Payments Act 1965, the Contracts of Employment Act 1972 or the Trade Union and Labour Relations Act 1974 as it applies to provisions contained in Acts passed before or in the same Session as this Act.

(3) Without prejudice to the generality of subsection (1) above, the modifications which may be made by regulations thereunder include modifications relating to the enforcement of provisions to which this section applies (including the appointment of persons for the purpose of such enforcement, and the powers of persons so appointed).

(4) The power to make regulations under subsection (1) above shall be exercisable by the Secretary of State, the Minister of Agriculture, Fisheries and Food or the Secretary of State and that Minister acting jointly; but the authority who is to exercise the power shall, before exercising it, consult such bodies as appear to him to be appropriate.

(5) In this section "the relevant statutory provisions" has the same meaning as in Part I.

General note. By the Local Government (Miscellaneous Provisions) Act 1976, s. 12(3), this section has effect as if the provisions to which sub-s. (1) applies included s. 12(1) of that Act and byelaws in force thereunder. Section 12(3) of the 1976 Act is concerned with building regulations and is therefore outside the scope of this book. Section 80(1) also applies to: the Greater London Council (General Powers) Act 1981, ss. 4 and 5 (see s. 6); the Civic Government (Scotland) Act 1982, Part VIII and to any byelaws made under that Part (see s. 109).

(a) **Regulations.** The following regulations relating to the subject matter of this book have been made (in whole or in part) under this section:
the Factories Act 1961 (Enforcement of Section 135) Regulations 1974, S.I. 1974 No. 1776;
the Docks and Harbours Act 1966 (Modification) Regulations 1974, S.I. 1974 No. 1820;
the Fire Certificates (Special Premises) Regulations 1976, S.I. 1976 No. 2003;
the Safety Representatives and Safety Committees Regulations 1977, S.I. 1977 No. 500;
the Diving Operations at Work Regulations 1981, S.I. 1981 No. 399;
the Health and Safety (Emissions into the Atmosphere) Regulations 1983, S.I. 1983 No. 943;
the Ionising Radiations Regulations 1985, S.I. 1985 No. 1333;
the Manual Handling Operations Regulations 1992, S.I. 1992 No. 2793.

(b) **Modification.** For definition, see s. 82(1)(c).

(c) **The relevant statutory provisions.** For definition, see s. 53(1).

---

81. Expenses and receipts. There shall be paid out of money provided by Parliament—

(a) any expenses by a Minister of the Crown or government department for the purposes of this Act; and
(b) any increase attributable to the provisions of this Act in the sums payable under any other Act *(a)* out of money so provided,

and any sums received by a Minister of the Crown or government department by virtue of this Act shall be paid into the Consolidated Fund *(b)*.

(a) **Act.** For definition, see s. 81(1)(a).

(b) **The Consolidated Fund.** See 8 Halsbury's Laws (4th edn.) para. 1369 *et seq.*

---

82. General provisions as to interpretation and regulations.—(1) In this Act—

(a) "Act" includes a provisional order confirmed by an Act;
(b) "contravention" includes failure to comply, and "contravene" has a corresponding meaning;

(c) "modifications" includes additions, omissions and amendments, and related expressions shall be construed accordingly;

(d) any reference to a Part, section or Schedule not otherwise identified is a reference to that Part or section of, or Schedule to, this Act.

(2) Except in so far as the context otherwise requires, any reference in this Act to an enactment is a reference to it as amended, and includes a reference to it as applied, by or under any other enactment, including this Act.

(3) Any power conferred by Part I or II or this Part to make regulations—

(a) includes power to make different provision by the regulations for different circumstances or cases and to include in the regulations such incidental, supplemental and transitional provisions as the authority making the regulations considers appropriate in connection with the regulations; and

(b) shall be exercisable by statutory instrument *(a)*; which shall be subject to annulment in pursuance of a resolution of either House of Parliament.

(a) **Statutory instrument.** See note *(e)* to s. 48.

---

83. Minor and consequential amendments, and repeals.—(1) The enactments mentioned in Schedule 9 shall have effect subject to the amendments specified in that Schedule (being minor amendments or amendments consequential upon the provisions of this Act).

(2) The enactments mentioned in Schedule 10 are hereby repealed to the extent specified in the third column of that Schedule.

---

84. Extent, and application of Act.—(1) This Act, except—

(a) Part I *(a)* and this Part *(b)* so far as may be necessary to enable regulations under section 15 to be made and operate for the purpose mentioned in paragraph 2 of Schedule 3; and

(b) paragraph 3 of Schedule 9,

does not extend to Northern Ireland *(bb)*.

(2) Part III *(c)*, except section 75 and Schedule 7, does not extend to Scotland.

(3) Her Majesty may by Order in Council *(cc)* provide that the provisions of Parts I and II *(d)* and this Part shall, to such extent and for such purposes as may be specified in the Order, apply (with or without modification *(e)*) to or in relation to persons *(f)*, premises *(g)*, work *(h)*, articles, substances *(i)* and other matters (of whatever kind) outside Great Britain *(j)* as those provisions apply within Great Britain or within a part of Great Britain so specified.

For the purposes of this subsection "premises", "work" and "substance" have the same meaning as they have for the purposes of Part I.

(4) An order in Council under subsection (3) above—

(a) may make different provision for different circumstances or cases;

(b)   may (notwithstanding that this may affect individuals or bodies corporate outside the United Kingdom *(k)*) provide for any of the provisions mentioned in that subsection, as applied by such an Order, to apply to individuals whether or not they are British subjects and to bodies corporate whether or not they are incorporated under the law of any part of the United Kingdom;

(c)   may make provision for conferring jurisdiction on any court or class of courts specified in the Order with respect to offences under Part I committed outside Great Britain or with respect to causes of action arising by virtue of section 47(2) in respect of acts or omissions taking place outside Great Britain, and for the determination, in accordance with the law in force in such part of Great Britain as may be specified in the Order, of questions arising out of such acts or omissions;

(d)   may exclude from the operation of section 3 of the Territorial Waters Jurisdiction Act 1878 (consents required for prosecutions) proceedings for offences under any provision of Part I committed outside Great Britain;

(e)   may be varied or revoked by a subsequent Order in Council under this section,

and any such Order shall be subject to annulment in pursuance of a resolution of either House of Parliament.

(5)   [*repealed*].

(6)   Any jurisdiction conferred on any court under this section shall be without prejudice to any jurisdiction exercisable apart from this section by that or any other court.

(a) **Part I.** The reference is to ss. 1–54 (s. 82(1)(d)).

(b) **This Part.** The reference is to ss. 77–85 (s. 82(1)(d)).

(bb) **Northern Ireland.** For similar provisions, relating to Northern Ireland, to the safety provisions of the Act, see the Health and Safety at Work (Northern Ireland) Order 1978, S.I. 1978 No. 1039 (N.I. 9).

(c) **Part III.** The reference is to ss. 61–76 (s. 82(1)(d)).

(cc) **Order in Council.** The Health and Safety at Work etc. Act 1974 (Application outside Great Britain) Order 1989, S.I. 1989 No. 840 (set out below) applies certain provisions of Parts I, II and IV of this Act, with appropriate exceptions, to offshore installations and pipelines within territorial waters and areas designated under the Continental Shelf Act 1964, and to certain work activities in connection with those installations and pipelines. The Order also applies those provisions to construction works, diving operations and certain other activities within territorial waters and to mines extending under the sea.

(d) **Part II.** The reference is to ss. 55–60 (s. 82(1)(d)).

(e) **Modification.** For definition, see s. 82(1)(c).

(f) **Person.** See note *(g)* to s. 4.

(g) **Premises.** For definition, see s. 53(1) (s. 84(3)).

(h) **Work.** For definition, see s. 52(1), (2) (s. 84(3)).

(i) **Substance.** For definition, see s. 53(1) (s. 84(3)).

(j) **Great Britain.** See INTRODUCTORY NOTE 4.

(k) **United Kingdom.** See INTRODUCTORY NOTE 4.

THE HEALTH AND SAFETY AT WORK ETC. ACT 1974
(APPLICATION OUTSIDE GREAT BRITAIN) ORDER 1989
(S.I. 1989 No. 840)

Citation, commencement and revocations

1.—(1) This Order may be cited as the Health and Safety at Work etc. Act 1974 (Application outside Great Britain) Order 1989 and shall come into force on 28th May 1989.

(2) The Health and Safety at Work etc. Act 1974 (Application outside Great Britain) Order 1977 and the Health and Safety at Work etc. Act 1974 (Application outside Great Britain) (Variation) Order 1989 are hereby revoked.

Interpretation

2.—(1) In this Order, unless the context otherwise requires—

"the 1974 Act" means the Health and Safety at Work etc. Act 1974;

"designated area" means any area designated by order under section 1(7) of the Continental Shelf Act 1964 and "within a designated area" includes over and under it;

"the prescribed provision of the 1974 Act" means sections 1 to 59 and 80 to 82 of the 1974 Act;

"territorial waters" means United Kingdom *(a)* territorial waters adjacent to Great Britain, and "within territorial waters" includes on, over and under them;

"vessel" includes a hovercraft and any floating structure which is capable of being manned.

(2) For the purposes of this Order, a person shall be deemed to be engaged in diving operations throughout any period from the time when he commences to prepare for diving until the time when—

(a) he is no longer subjected to raised pressure;

(b) he has normal inert gas partial pressure in his tissues; and

(c) if he entered the water, he has left it,

and diving operations include the activity of any person in connection with the health and safety of a person who is, or is deemed to be, engaged in diving operations.

(a) **United Kingdom, Great Britain.** See INTRODUCTORY NOTE 4.

Application of the 1974 Act outside Great Britain

3.—(1) *The prescribed provisions of the 1974 Act* shall, to the extent specified in the following articles of this Order, apply to and in relation to the premises and activities outside Great Britain *(a)* which are so specified as those provisions apply within Great Britain *(a)*.

(2) The reference in paragraph (1) of this article to premises and activities includes a reference to any person, article or substance on those premises or engaged in or, as the case may be, used or for use in connection with any such activity, but does not include a reference to an aircraft which is airborne.

(a) **Great Britain.** See INTRODUCTORY NOTE 4.

Offshore installations

4.—(1) *The prescribed provisions of the 1974 Act* shall apply outside Great Britain *(a)* to and in relation to—

(a) any offshore installation and any activity on it;

(b) any of the following activities in connection with an offshore installation, whether carried on from the installation itself, on or from a *vessel* or in any other manner, that is to say, inspection, testing, loading, unloading, fuelling, provisioning, construction, reconstruction, alteration, repair, maintenance, cleaning, demolition, dismantling and diving operations and any activity which is immediately preparatory to any of the said activities;

(c) the survey and preparation of the sea bed for an offshore installation.

(2) In this article, "offshore installation" means—

(a) the fixed structures consisting of six towers referred to in the Schedule to this Order as NSR M-1 and NSR R-1, NSR R-2, NSR R-3, NSR R-4 and NSR R-5 and settled on the sea bed at the locations specified in the Schedule and the related cables between each of those towers at sea bed level and the related cables which lie or extend outside the said locations; and

(b) an offshore installation within the meaning of section 1 of the Mineral Workings (Offshore Installations) Act 1971 which is within *territorial waters* or a *designated area*.

(a) Great Britain. See INTRODUCTORY NOTE 4.

Pipelines

5.—(1) *The prescribed provisions of the 1974 Act* shall apply within *territorial waters* or a *designated area* to and in relation to—

(a) any pipeline works;

(b) the following activities in connection with pipeline works—

  (i) the loading, unloading, fuelling or provisioning of a *vessel,*

  (ii) the loading, unloading, fuelling, repair and maintenance of an aircraft on a *vessel,*

being in either case a *vessel* which is engaged in pipeline works.

(2) "Pipeline" means a pipe or system of pipes for the conveyance of any thing, together with—

(a) any apparatus for inducing or facilitating the flow of any thing through, or through a part of, the pipe or system;

(b) any apparatus for treating or cooling any thing which is to flow through, or through part of, the pipe or system;

(c) valves, valve chambers and similar works which are annexed to, or incorporated in the course of, the pipe or system;

(d) apparatus for supplying energy for the operation of any such apparatus or works as are mentioned in the preceding paragraphs;

(e) apparatus for the transmission of information for the operation of the pipe or system;

(f) apparatus for the cathodic protection of the pipe or system; and

(g) a structure used or to be used solely for the support of a part of the pipe or system, but not including—

  (i) a pipeline of which no initial or terminal point is situated in the United Kingdom or within *territorial waters* or *a designated area*; or

  (ii) any part of a pipeline which is an offshore installation within the meaning of Article 4(2) of this Order;

"pipeline works" means—

(a) assembling or placing a pipeline or length of pipeline including the provision of internal or external protection for it, and any processes incidental to any of those activities;

(b) inspecting, testing, maintaining, adjusting, repairing, altering or renewing a pipeline or length of pipeline;

(c) changing the position of or dismantling or removing a pipeline or length of pipeline;

(d) opening the bed of the sea for the purposes of the works mentioned in sub-paragraphs (a) to (c) of this definition, tunnelling or boring for those purposes and other works needed for or incidental to those purposes;

(e) diving operations in connection with any of the works mentioned in sub-paragraphs (a) to (d) of this definition or for the purpose of determining whether a place is suitable as part of the site of a proposed pipeline and the carrying out of surveying operations for settling the route of a proposed pipeline.

Mines

6.—(1) *The prescribed provisions of the 1974 Act* shall apply to and in relation to the working of a mine, and to work for the purpose of or in connection with the working of any part of a mine, within *territorial waters* or extending beyond them.

(2) In this article "mine" and "working of a mine" have the same meaning as in the Mines and Quarries Act 1954.

Other activities within territorial waters

7.   *The prescribed provisions of the 1974 Act* shall apply within *territorial waters* to and in relation to—

(a) the construction, reconstruction, alteration, repair, maintenance, cleaning, demolition and dismantling of any building or other structure not being a *vessel*, or any preparation for any such activity;

(b) the loading, unloading, fuelling or provisioning of a *vessel*;

(c) diving operations;

(d) the construction, reconstruction, finishing, refitting, repair, maintenance, cleaning or breaking up of a *vessel* except when carried out by the master or any officer or member of the crew of that *vessel*,

except that this article shall not apply in any case where at the relevant time article 4, 5, or 6 of this Order applies, or to *vessels* which are registered outside the United Kingdom *(a)* and are on passage through *territorial waters*.

(a) **United Kingdom.** See INTRODUCTORY NOTE 4.

Legal proceedings

8.—(1) Proceedings for any offence under section 33 of *the 1974 Act*, being an offence to which that section applies by virtue of this Order, may be taken, and the offence may for all incidental purposes be treated as having been committed, in any place in Great Britain *(a)*.

(2) Section 3 of the Territorial Waters Jurisdiction Act 1878 (which requires certain consents for the institution of proceedings) shall not apply to proceedings for any offence to which paragraph (1) of this article relates.

(a) **Great Britain.** See INTRODUCTORY NOTE 4.

Miscellaneous provisions

9.   *The prescribed provisions of the 1974 Act* shall apply in accordance with this Order to individuals whether or not they are British subjects, and to bodies corporate whether or not they are incorporated under the law of any part of the United Kingdom *(a)*.

(a) **United Kingdom.** See INTRODUCTORY NOTE 4.

10.   Nothing in this Order except Article 8(2) shall be taken to limit or prejudice the operation which any Act or legislative instrument may, apart from this Order, have in territorial waters or elsewhere.

SCHEDULE

Article 4(2)(a)

LOCATION OF TOWERS

Title		Degrees	Minutes	Seconds	
MASTER 1	LATITUDE	53	44	45	N
NSR M-1	LONGITUDE	02	33	30	E
REMOTE 1	LATITUDE	53	56	00	N
NSR R-1	LONGITUDE	02	24	00	E
REMOTE 2	LATITUDE	53	55	45	N
NSR R-2	LONGITUDE	02	51	00	E
REMOTE 3	LATITUDE	53	38	30	N
NSR R-3	LONGITUDE	02	56	56	E
REMOTE 4	LATITUDE	53	29	57	N
NSR R-4	LONGITUDE	02	30	50	E
REMOTE 5	LATITUDE	53	42	00	N
NSR R-5	LONGITUDE	02	08	30	E

---

85. Short title and commencement.—(1) This Act may be cited as the Health and Safety at Work etc. Act 1974.

(2) This Act shall come into operation on such day as the Secretary of State *(a)* may by order *(b)* made by statutory instrument *(c)* appoint, and different days may be appointed under this subsection for different purposes.

(3) An order under this section may contain such transitional provisions and savings as appear to the Secretary of State to be necessary or expedient in connection with the provisions thereby brought into force, including such adaptations of those provisions or any provision of this Act then in force as appear to him to be necessary or expedient in consequence of the partial operation of this Act (whether before or after the day appointed by the order).

(a) *The Secretary of State.* See note *(k)* to s. 2.

(b) *Order.* See the Health and Safety at Work etc. Act 1974 (Commencement No. 1) Order 1974, S.I. 1974 No. 1439; the Health and Safety at Work etc. Act 1974 (Commencement No. 2) Order 1975, S.I. 1975 No. 344 (spent); the Health and Safety at Work etc. Act 1974 (Commencement No. 3) Order 1975, S.I. 1975 No. 1364; the Health and Safety at Work etc. Act 1974 (Commencement No. 4) Order 1977, S.I. 1977 No. 294 (spent); the Health and Safety at Work etc. Act 1974 (Commencement No. 5) Order 1980, S.I. 1980 No. 208 (spent) and the Health and Safety at Work etc. Act 1974 (Commencement No. 6) Order 1980, S.I. 1980 No. 269 (spent). These orders are not printed in this book.

(c) *Statutory instrument.* See note *(e)* to s. 48.

SCHEDULES

SCHEDULE 1

EXISTING ENACTMENTS WHICH ARE RELEVANT
STATUTORY PROVISIONS

Chapter	Short title	Provisions which are relevant statutory provisions
1875 c. 17.	The Explosives Act 1875.	The whole Act except sections 30 to 32, 80 and 116 to 121.
1906 c. 14.	The Alkali, &c. Works Regulations Act 1906.	The whole Act.
1920 c. 65.	The Employment of Women, Young Persons and Children Act 1920.	The whole Act.
1922 c. 35.	The Celluloid and Cinematograph Film Act 1922.	The whole Act.
1923 c. 17.	The Explosives Act 1923.	The whole Act.
1928 c. 32.	The Petroleum (Consolidation) Act 1928.	The whole Act.
1936 c. 22.	The Hours of Employment (Conventions) Act 1936.	The whole Act except section 5.
1936 c. 27.	The Petroleum (Transfer of Licences) Act 1936.	The whole Act.
1937 c. 45.	The Hydrogen Cyanide (Fumigation) Act 1937.	The whole Act.
1951 c. 58.	The Fireworks Act 1951.	Sections 4 and 7.
1952 c. 60.	The Agriculture (Poisonous Substances) Act 1952.	The whole Act.
1953 c. 47.	The Emergency Laws (Miscellaneous Provisions) Act 1953.	Section 3.
1954 c. 70.	The Mines and Quarries Act 1954.	The whole Act except section 151.
1956 c. 49.	The Agriculture (Safety, Health and Welfare Provisions) Act 1956.	The whole Act.
1961 c. 34.	The Factories Act 1961.	The whole Act except section 135.
1961 c. 64.	The Public Health Act 1961.	Section 73.
1962 c. 58.	The Pipe-lines Act 1962.	Sections 20 to 26, 33, 34 and 42, Schedule 5.
1963 c. 41.	The Offices, Shops and Railway Premises Act 1963.	The whole Act.
1965 c. 57.	The Nuclear Installations Act 1965.	Sections 1, 3 to 6, 22 and 24A, Schedule 2.
1969 c. 10.	The Mines and Quarries (Tips) Act 1969.	Sections 1 to 10.
1971 c. 20.	The Mines Management Act 1971.	The whole Act.
1972 c. 28.	The Employment Medical Advisory Service Act 1972.	The whole Act except sections 1 and 6 and Schedule 1.

General note. The entry relating to the Nuclear Installations Act 1965 was amended by the Atomic Energy Act 1989, s. 6(3).

SCHEDULE 2

ADDITIONAL PROVISIONS RELATING TO CONSTITUTION ETC. OF THE
COMMISSION AND EXECUTIVE

Tenure of office

1.   Subject to paragraphs 2 to 4 below, a person shall hold and vacate office as a member or as chairman or deputy chairman in accordance with the terms of the instrument appointing him to that office.

2.   A person may at any time resign his office as a member or as chairman or deputy chairman by giving the Secretary of State *(a)* a notice in writing signed by that person and stating that he resigns that office.

3.—(1) If a member becomes or ceases to be the chairman or deputy chairman, the Secretary of State may vary the terms of the instrument appointing him to be a member so as to alter the date on which he is to vacate office as a member.

(2) If the chairman or deputy chairman ceases to be a member he shall cease to be chairman or deputy chairman, as the case may be.

4.—(1) If the Secretary of State is satisfied that a member—

(a) has been absent from meetings of the Commission for a period longer than six consecutive months without the permission of the Commission; or

(b) has become bankrupt or made an arrangement with his creditors; or

(c) is incapacitated by physical or mental illness; or

(d) is otherwise unable or unfit to discharge the functions of a member,

the Secretary of State may declare his office as a member to be vacant and shall notify the declaration in such manner as the Secertary of State thinks fit; and thereupon the office shall become vacant.

(2) In the application of the preceding sub-paragraph to Scotland for the references in paragraph (b) to a member's having become bankrupt and to a member's having made an arrangement with his creditors there shall be substituted respectively references to sequestration of a member's estate having been awarded and to a member's having made a trust deed for behoof of his creditors or a composition contract.

Remuneration etc. of members

5.   The Commission may pay to each member such remuneration and allowance as the Secretary of State may determine.

6.   The Commission may pay or make provision for paying, to or in respect of any member, such sums by way of pension, superannuation allowances and gratuities as the Secretary of State may determine.

7.   Where a person ceases to be a member otherwise than on the expiry of his term of office and it appears to the Secretary of State that there are special circumstances which make it right for him to receive compensation, the Commission may make to him a payment of such amount as the Secretary of State may determine.

Proceedings

8.   The quorum of the Commission and the arrangements relating to meetings of the Commission shall be such as the Commission may determine.

9.   The validity of any proceedings of the Commission shall not be affected by any vacancy among the members or by any defect in the appointment of a member.

Staff
   10.   It shall be the duty of the Executive to provide for the Commission such officers and servants as are requisite for the proper discharge of the Commission's functions; and any reference in this Act to an officer or servant of the Commission is a reference to an officer or servant provided for the Commission in pursuance of this paragraph.

   11.   The Executive may appoint such officers and servants as it may determine with the consent of the Secretary of State as to numbers and terms and conditions of service.

   12.   The Commission shall pay to the Minister for the Civil Service, at such times in each accounting year *(b)* as may be determined by that Minister subject to any directions of the Treasury, sums of such amounts as he may so determine for the purposes of this paragraph as being equivalent to the increase during that year of such liabilities of his as are attributable to the provision of pensions, allowances or gratuities to or in respect of persons who are or have been in the service of the Executive in so far as that increase results from the service of those persons during that accounting year and to the expense to be incurred in administering those pensions, allowances or gratuities.

Performance of functions
   13.   The Commission may authorise any member of the Commission or any officer or servant of the Commission or of the Executive to perform on behalf of the Commission such of the Commission's functions (including the function conferred on the Commission by this paragraph) as are specified in the authorisation.

Accounts and reports
   14.—(1) It shall be the duty of the Commission—
   (a)   to keep proper accounts and proper records in relation to the accounts;
   (b)   to prepare in respect of each accounting year a statement of accounts in such form as the Secretary of State may direct with the approval of the Treasury; and
   (c)   to send copies of the statement to the Secretary of State and the Comptroller and Auditor General before the end of the month of November next following the accounting year to which the statement relates.
   (2) The Comptroller and Auditor General shall examine, certify and report on each statement received by him in pursuance of this Schedule and shall lay copies of each statement and of his report before each House of Parliament.

   15.   It shall be the duty of the Commission to make to the Secretary of State, as soon as possible after the end of each accounting year, a report on the performance of its functions during that year; and the Secretary of State shall lay before each House of Parliament a copy of each report made to him in pursuance of this paragraph.

Supplemental
   16.   The Secretary of State shall not make a determination or give his consent in pursuance of paragraph 5, 6, 7 or 11 of this Schedule except with the approval of the Minister for the Civil Service.

   17.   The fixing of the common seal of the Commission shall be authenticated by the signature of the secretary of the Commission or some other person authorised by the Commission to act for that purpose.

   18.   A document purporting to be duly executed under the seal of the Commission shall be received in evidence and shall, unless the contrary is proved, be deemed to be so executed.

   19.   In the preceding provisions of this Schedule—
   (a)   "accounting year" means the period of twelve months ending with 31st March in any year except that the first accounting year of the Commission shall, if the Secretary of State so directs, be such period shorter or longer than twelve months (but not longer than two years) as is specified in the direction; and

(b) "the chairman", "a deputy chairman" and "a member" mean respectively the chairman, a deputy chairman and a member of the Commission.

20.—(1) The preceding provisions of this Schedule (except paragraphs 10 to 12 and 15) shall have effect in relation to the Executive as if—
  (a) for any reference to the Commission there were substituted a reference to the Executive;
  (b) for any reference to the Secretary of State in paragraphs 2 to 4 and 19 and the first such reference in paragraph 7 there were substituted a reference to the Commission;
  (c) for any reference to the Secretary of State in paragraphs 5 to 7 (except the first such reference in paragraph 7) there were substituted a reference to the Commission acting with the consent of the Secretary of State;
  (d) for any reference to the chairman there were substituted a reference to the director, and any reference to the deputy chairman were omitted;
  (e) in paragraph 14(1)(c) for the words from "Secretary" to "following" there were substituted the words "Commission by such date as the Commission may direct after the end of".

(2) It shall be the duty of the Commission to include in or send with the copies of the statement sent by it as required by paragraph 14(1)(c) of this Schedule copies of the statement sent to it by the Executive in pursuance of the said paragraph 14(1)(c) as adapted by the preceding sub-paragraph.

(3) The terms of an instrument appointing a person to be a member of the Executive shall be such as the Commisison may determine with the approval of the Secretary of State and the Minister for the Civil Service.

(*a*) **The Secretary of State.** See note (*k*) to s. 2; but note para 20(1) of this Schedule.

(*b*) **Accounting year.** For definition, see para. 19(a).

SCHEDULE 3

SUBJECT-MATTER OF HEALTH AND SAFETY REGULATIONS

1.—(1) Regulating or prohibiting—
  (a) the manufacture, supply or use of any plant (*a*);
  (b) the manufacture, supply, keeping or use of any substance (*b*);
  (c) the carrying on of any process or the carrying out of any operation.

(2) Imposing requirements with respect to the design, construction, guarding, siting, installation, commissioning, examination, repair, maintenance, alteration, adjustment, dismantling, testing or inspection of any plant.

(3) Imposing requirements with respect to the marking of any plant or of any articles used or designed for use as components in any plant, and in that connection regulating or restricting the use of specified markings.

(4) Imposing requirements with respect to the testing, labelling or examination of any substance.

(5) Imposing requirements with respect to the carrying out of research in connection with any activity mentioned in sub-paragraphs (1) to (4) above.

2.—(1) Prohibiting the importation into the United Kingdom (*c*) or the landing or unloading there of articles or substances of any specified (*d*) description, whether absolutely or unless conditions imposed by or under the regulations are complied with.

(2) Specifying, in a case where an act or omission in relation to such an importation, landing or unloading as is mentioned in the preceding sub-paragraph constitutes an offence under a provision of this Act and of the Customs and Excise Acts 1979, the Act under which the offence is to be punished.

3.—(1) Prohibiting or regulating the transport of articles or substances of any specified *(d)* description.

(2) Imposing requirements with respect to the manner and means of transporting articles or substances of any description, including requirements with respect to the construction, testing and marking of containers and means of transport and the packaging and labelling of articles or substances in connection with their transport.

4.—(1) Prohibiting the carrying on of any specified activity or the doing of any specified thing except under the authority and in accordance with the terms and conditions of a licence, or except with the consent or approval of a specified authority.

(2) Providing for the grant, renewal, variation, transfer and revocation of licences (including the variation and revocation of conditions attached to licences).

5.   Requiring any person *(e)*, premises *(f)* or thing to be registered in any specified circumstances or as a condition of the carrying on of any specified activity or the doing of any specified thing.

6.—(1) Requiring, in specified circumstances, the appointment (whether in a specified capacity or not) of persons (or persons with specified qualifications or experience, or both) to perform specified functions, and imposing duties or conferring powers on persons appointed (whether in pursuance of the regulations or not) to perform specified functions.

(2) Restricting the performance of specified functions to persons possessing specified qualifications or experience.

7.   Regulating or prohibiting the employment *(g)* in specified circumstances of all persons or any class of persons.

8.—(1) Requiring the making of arrangements for securing the health of persons at work *(h)* or other persons, including arrangements for medical examinations and health surveys.

(2) Requiring the making of arrangements for monitoring the atmospheric or other conditions in which persons work *(i)*.

9.   Imposing requirements with respect to any matter affecting the conditions in which persons work, including in particular such matters as the structural condition and stability of premises, the means of access to and egress from premises, cleanliness, temperature, lighting, ventilation, overcrowding, noise, vibrations, ionising and other radiations, dust and fumes.

10.   Securing the provisions of specified welfare facilities for persons at work, including in particular such things as an adequate water supply, sanitary conveniences, washing and bathing facilities, ambulance and first-aid arrangements, cloakroom accommodation, sitting facilities and refreshment facilities.

11.   Imposing requirements with respect to the provision and use in specified circumstances of protective clothing or equipment, including clothing affording protection against the weather.

12.   Requiring in specific circumstances the taking of specified precautions in connection with the risk of fire.

13.—(1) Prohibiting or imposing requirements in connection with the emission into the atmosphere of any specified gas, smoke or dust or any other specified substance whatsoever.

(2) Prohibiting or imposing requirements in connection with the emission of noise, vibrations or any ionising or other radiations.

(3) Imposing requirements with respect to the monitoring of any such emission as is mentioned in the preceding sub-paragraphs.

14. Imposing requirements with respect to the instruction, training and supervision of persons at work.

15.—(1) Requiring, in specified circumstances, specified matters to be notified in a specified manner to specified persons.

(2) Empowering inspectors *(j)* in specified circumstances to require persons to submit written particulars of measures proposed to be taken to achieve compliance with any of the relevant statutory provisions *(k)*.

16. Imposing requirements with respect to the keeping and preservation of records and other documents, including plans and maps.

17. Imposing requirements with respect to the management of animals.

18. The following purposes as regards premises of any specified description where persons work, namely—

(a) requiring precautions to be taken against dangers to which the premises or persons therein are or may be exposed by reason of conditions (including natural conditions) existing in the vicinity;

(b) securing that persons in the premises leave them in specified circumstances.

19. Conferring, in specified circumstances involving a risk of fire or explosion, power to search a person or any article which a person has with him for the purpose of ascertaining whether he has in his possession any article of a specified kind likely in those circumstances to cause a fire or explosion, and power to seize and dispose of any article of that kind found on such a search.

20. Restricting, prohibiting or requiring the doing of any specified thing where any accident or other occurrence of a specified kind has occurred.

21. As regard cases of any specified class, being a class such that the variety in the circumstances of particular cases within it calls for the making of special provision for particular cases, any of the following purposes, namely—

(a) conferring on employers *(l)* or other persons power to make rules or give directions with respect to matters affecting health or safety;

(b) requiring employers or other persons to make rules with respect to any such matters;

(c) empowering specified persons to require employers or other persons either to make rules with respect to any such matters or to modify any such rules previously made by virtue of this paragraph; and

(d) making admissible in evidence without further proof, in such circumstances and subject to such conditions as may be specified, documents which purport to be copies of rules or rules of any specified class made under this paragraph.

22. Conferring on any local *(m)* or public authority power to make byelaws with respect to any specified matter, specifying the authority or person by whom any byelaws made in the exercise of that power need to be confirmed, and generally providing for the procedure to be followed in connection with the making of any such byelaws.

Interpretation

23.—(1) In this Schedule "specified" means specified in health and safety regulations *(n)*.

(2) It is hereby declared that the mention in this Schedule of a purpose that falls within any more general purpose mentioned therein is without prejudice to the generality of the more general purpose.

General note. In para. 2(2) the words "the Customs and Excise Acts 1979" are substituted for "the Customs and Excise Act 1952" by the Customs and Excise Management Act 1979, s. 177(1), Sch. 4.

(a) **Plant.** For definition, see s. 53(1).

(b) **Substance.** For definition, see s. 53(1).

(c) **United Kingdom.** See the INTRODUCTORY NOTE 4.

(d) **Specified.** That is, specified in health and safety regulations (para. 23(1)).

(e) **Person.** See note (g) to s. 4.

(f) **Premises.** For definition, see s. 53(1).

(g) **Employment.** For definition, see s. 53(1).

(h) **At work.** For definition, see s. 52(1), (2).

(i) **Work.** For definition, see s. 52(1), (2).

(j) **Inspector.** For definition, see s. 53(1).

(k) **The relevant statutory provisions.** For definition, see s. 53(1).

(l) **Employer.** For definition, see s. 53(1).

(m) **Local authority.** For definition, see s. 53(1).

(n) **Health and safety regulations.** For definition, see s. 53(1).

SCHEDULES 4–7

Schedule 4 was repealed by the Employment Protection Act 1975, ss. 116, 125(3), Sch. 15, para. 21, Sch. 18. Schedules 5 and 6 are repealed and consolidated in the Building Act 1984. Schedule 7 has not been repealed, but is outside the scope of this book.

SCHEDULE 8

TRANSITIONAL PROVISIONS WITH RESPECT TO FIRE CERTIFICATES UNDER FACTORIES ACT 1961 OR OFFICES, SHOPS AND RAILWAY PREMISES ACT 1963

1. In this Schedule—
"the 1971 Act" means the Fire Precautions Act 1971;
"1971 Act certificate" means a fire certificate within the meaning of the 1971 Act;
"Factories Act certificate" means a certificate under section 40 of the Factories Act 1961 (means of escape in case of fire-certification by fire authority);
"Offices Act certificate" means a fire certificate under section 29 of the Offices, Shops and Railway Premises Act 1963.

2.—(1) Where by virtue of an order under section 1 of the 1971 Act a 1971 Act certificate becomes required in respect of any premises at a time when there is in force in respect of those premises a Factories Act certificate or an Offices Act certificate ("the existing certificate"), the following provisions of this paragraph shall apply.

(2) The existing certificate shall continue in force (irrespective of whether the section under which it was issued remains in force) and—
   (a) shall as from the said time be deemed to be a 1971 Act certificate validly issued with respect to the premises with respect to which it was issued and to cover the use or uses to which those premises were being put at that time; and
   (b) may (in particular) be amended, replaced or revoked in accordance with the 1971 Act accordingly.

(3) Without prejudice to sub-paragraph (2)(b) above, the existing certificate, as it has effect by virtue of sub-paragraph (2) above, shall as from the said time be treated as imposing in relation to the premises the like requirements as were previously imposed in relation thereto by the following provisions, that is to say—

    (a) if the existing certificate is a Factories Act certificate, the following provisions of the Factories Act 1961, namely sections 41(1), 48 (except subsections (5), (8) and (9)), 49(1), 51(1) and 52(1) and (4) and, so far as it relates to a proposed increase in the number of persons employed in any premises, section 41(3);

    (b) if the existing certificate is an Offices Act certificate the following provisions of the Offices, Shops and Railway Premises Act 1963, namely sections 30(1), 33, 34(1) and (2), 36(1) and 38(1) and, so far as it relates to a proposed increase in the number of persons employed to work in any premises at any one time, section 30(3).

3. Any application for a Factories Act certificate or an Offices Act certificate with respect to any premises which is pending at the time when by virtue of an order under section 1 of the 1971 Act a 1971 Act certificate becomes required in respect of those premises shall be deemed to be an application for a 1971 Act certificate in respect of them duly made in accordance with the 1971 Act and may be proceeded with accordingly; but (without prejudice to section 5(2) of the 1971 Act) the fire authority may, as a condition of proceeding with such an application, require the applicant to specify any matter or give them any information which would ordinarily have been required by section 5(1) of that Act.

SCHEDULE 9

MINOR AND CONSEQUENTIAL AMENDMENTS

The Coroners (Amendment) Act 1926
   1. [*repealed*].

The House of Commons Disqualification Act 1957
   2. [*repealed*].

The Parliamentary Commissioner Act 1967
   3. [*repealed*].

SCHEDULE 10

REPEALS

Chapter	Short title	Extent of repeal
4 & 5 Eliz. c. 52.	The Clean Air Act 1956.	Section 24.
1971 c. 40.	The Fire Precautions Act 1971.	In Section 2, paragraphs (a) to (c). Section 11. In Section 17(1)(i), the word "and" where last occurring. In section 43(1), the definition of "building regulations".
1972 c. 28.	The Employment Medical Advisory Service Act 1972.	Sections 1 and 6. Schedule 1.
1972 c. 58.	The National Health Service (Scotland) Act 1972.	In Schedule 6, paragraph 157.
1973 c. 32.	The National Health Service Reorganisation Act 1973.	In Schedule 4, paragraph 137.
1973 c. 50.	The Employment and Training Act 1973.	In Schedule 3, paragraph 14.
1973 c. 64.	The Maplin Development Act 1973.	In Schedule 2, in paragraph 2(1), the words from "and section 71" to "regulations)".

THE MANAGEMENT OF HEALTH AND SAFETY AT WORK REGULATIONS 1992

(S.I. 1992 No. 2051)

General note. These Regulations are primarily intended to implement the Framework Directive 89/391 (see page 16). The Regulations also partially implement the Temporary Workers Directive 91/383 (see page 179).

The central feature of the Regulations, and one which marks a fundamental change of emphasis from preceding law, is the duty imposed on employers to make a suitable and sufficient assessment of the risks to the health and safety of their employees and of non-employees affected by their work. The Regulations also provide that there must be effective planning and review of protective measures, health surveillance, emergency procedures, information and training.

The Regulations came into effect on 1 January 1993 and are supplemented by the "Management of Health and Safety at Work" Approved Code of Practice (not included in this book), made under s. 16(1) of the Health and Safety at Work etc. Act 1974, and which came into effect on the same date.

To the extent that the Regulations fail to give full effect to the Directives they are intended to implement, recourse, by way of aid to construction, or in some cases by way of direct enforcement, may be had to the relevant Directive (see "Interpretation in the Light of the European Directives" and "Direct Application of the European Directives" under LEGAL PRINCIPLES in the introductory section). Some possible areas of shortfall in implementation have been noted by commentators.

Thus, for example, reg. 15 provides that breach of a duty imposed by the Regulations does not confer a civil right of action and this limitation may be argued to amount to deficient implementation of the Directive, and Art. 4 in particular. Similarly, Art. 6 refers to an employer taking "measures necessary for the safety and health protection of workers", an obligation which it is not clear is met by the Regulations (see, for example, reg. 4). Likewise to the extent that obligations under the Directive are embodied in the (unenforceable) ACOP rather than an enforceable Regulation, that may amount to inadequate implementation. An example of this has been suggested to arise from the implementation of Art. 6(2) of the Framework Directive which provides a detailed set of principles for the implementation of safety measures beginning with risk avoidance and including obligations such as that to adapt the work to the individual. This set of principles is not reflected in the Regulations (c.f. reg. 4) but is only found in the ACOP (cl. 27). Another arguable deficiency in implementation relates to recording of the employers' risk assessment which is required by both the Framework Directive (Art. 9(1)) and the Management of Health and Safety at Work Regulations 1992. However the latter (by regs. 3(4) and 4(2)) imposes the obligation only on employers of five or more employees, a limitation not found in the Directive.

Further examples arise in relation to implementation of the Temporary Workers Directive 91/383. It is not clear that the user employer is made responsible for matters "connected with safety, hygiene and health at work" (Art. 8): the duties in reg. 11, for example, to take into account individual capabilities and to provide training appears to be imposed only on the employment agency (see, similarly, reg. 5). Yet more fundamentally, the definition of "fixed term contract of employment" (reg. 1) may not correspond with that of the Directive.

There is a requirement to consult workplace representatives specified in the Framework Directive. The obligation to consult representatives of the workforce finds form in the amendment to the Safety Representatives and Safety Committees Regulations 1977 (S.I. 1977 No. 500) contained in the Schedule to the Management of Health and Safety at Work Regulations 1992 (S.I. 1992 No. 2051). That obligation only arises where the employer cares to recognise a union. This deficiency in implementation of the Framework Directive has already been referred to: see the General note to reg. 4A of the Safety Representatives & Safety Committees Regulations 1977 and "Direct application of the European Directives" under LEGAL PRINCIPLES in the introductory section.

––––––––––

The Secretary of State, in exercise of the powers conferred upon her by sections 15(1), (2), (5) and (9), 47(2) and 52(2) and (3) of, and paragraphs 6(1), 7, 8(1), 14, 15(1) and 16 of Schedule 3 to, the Health and Safety at Work etc. Act 1974, and of all other powers enabling her in that behalf and for the purpose of giving effect without modifications to proposals submitted to her by the Health and Safety Commission under section 11(2)(d) of the said Act after the carrying out by the said Commission of consultations in accordance with section 50(3) of that Act, hereby makes the following Regulations:

1.   Citation, commencement and interpretation.—(1) These Regulations may be cited as the Management of Health and Safety at Work Regulations 1992 and shall come into force on 1st January 1993.

(2) In these Regulations—

"the assessment" means, in the case of an employer, the assessment made by him in accordance with regulation 3(1) and changed by him where necessary in accordance with regulation 3(3); and, in the case of a self-employed person, the assessment made by him in accordance with regulation 3(2) and changed by him where necessary in accordance with regulation 3(3);

"employment business" means a business (whether or not carried on with a view to profit and whether or not carried on in conjunction with any other business) which supplies persons (other than seafarers) who are employed in it to work for and under the control of other persons in any capacity;

"fixed-term contract of employment" means a contract of employment for a specific term which is fixed in advance or which can be ascertained in advance by reference to some relevant circumstance; and

"the preventive and protective measures" means the measures which have been identified by the employer or by the self-employed person in consequence of *the assessment* as the measures he needs to take to comply with the requirements and prohibitions imposed upon him by or under the relevant statutory provisions.

(3) Any reference in these Regulations to—

(a) a numbered regulation is a reference to the regulation in these Regulations so numbered; or

(b) a numbered paragraph is a reference to the paragraph so numbered in the regulation in which the reference appears.

––––––––––

2.   Disapplication of these Regulations. These Regulations shall not apply to or in relation to the master or crew of a seagoing ship or to the employer of such persons in respect of the normal ship-board activities of a ship's crew under the direction of the master.

---

3.   Risk assessment.—(1) Every employer shall make a suitable and sufficient
(a) assessment of—

   (a) the risks to the health and safety of his employees to which they are exposed whilst they are at work; and

   (b) the risks to the health and safety of persons not in his employment arising out of or in connection with the conduct by him of his undertaking,

for the purpose of identifying the measures he needs to take to comply with the requirements and prohibitions imposed upon him by or under the relevant statutory provisions.

(2) Every self-employed person shall make a suitable and sufficient *(a)* assessment of—

   (a) the risks to his own health and safety to which he is exposed whilst he is at work; and

   (b) the risks to the health and safety of persons not in his employment arising out of or in connection with the conduct by him of his undertaking,

for the purpose of identifying the measures he needs to take to comply with the requirements and prohibitions imposed upon him by or under the relevant statutory provisions.

(3) Any assessment such as is referred to in paragraph (1) or (2) shall be reviewed by the employer or self-employed person who made it if—

   (a) there is reason to suspect that it is no longer valid; or

   (b) there has been a significant change in the matters to which it relates,

and where as a result of any such review changes to an assessment are required, the employer or self-employed person concerned shall make them.

(4) Where the employer employs five or more employees, he shall record—

   (a) the significant findings of *the assessment*; and

   (b) any group of his employees identified by it as being especially at risk.

  *(a) **Suitable and sufficient.*** See INTRODUCTORY NOTE 12.

---

4.   Health and safety arrangements.—(1) Every employer shall make and give effect to such arrangements as are appropriate, having regard to the nature of his activities and the size of his undertaking, for the effective planning, organisation, control, monitoring and review of *the preventive and protective measures*.

(2) Where the employer employs five or more employees, he shall record the arrangements referred to in paragraph (1).

---

5.   Health surveillance. Every employer shall ensure that his employees are provided with such health surveillance as is appropriate having regard to the risks to their health and safety which are identified by *the assessment.*

---

6.   Health and safety assistance.—(1) Every employer shall, subject to paragraphs (6) and (7), appoint one or more competent persons to assist him in undertaking the measures he needs to take to comply with the requirements and prohibitions imposed upon him by or under the relevant statutory provisions.

(2) Where an employer appoints persons in accordance with paragraph (1), he shall make arrangements for ensuring adequate co-operation between them.

(3) The employer shall ensure that the number of persons appointed under paragraph (1), the time available for them to fulfil their functions and the means at their disposal are adequate having regard to the size of his undertaking, the risks to which his employees are exposed and the distribution of those risks throughout the undertaking.

(4) The employer shall ensure that—

  (a) any person appointed by him in accordance with paragraph (1) who is not in his employment—
    (i) is informed of the factors known by him to affect, or suspected by him of affecting, the health and safety of any other person who may be affected by the conduct of his undertaking, and
    (ii) has access to the information referred to in regulation 8; and
  (b) any person appointed by him in accordance with paragraph (1) is given such information about any person working in his undertaking who is—
    (i) employed by him under a *fixed-term contract of employment*, or
    (ii) employed in an *employment business,*
  as is necessary to enable that person properly to carry out the function specified in that paragraph.

(5) A person shall be regarded as competent for the purposes of paragraph (1) where he has sufficient training and experience or knowledge and other qualities to enable him properly to assist in undertaking the measures referred to in that paragraph.

(6) Paragraph (1) shall not apply to a self-employed employer who is not in partnership with any other person where he has sufficient training and experience or knowledge and other qualities properly to undertake the measures referred to in that paragraph himself.

(7) Paragraph (1) shall not apply to individuals who are employers and who are together carrying on business in partnership where at least one of the individuals concerned has sufficient training and experience or knowledge and other qualities—

(a) properly to undertake the measures he needs to take to comply with the requirements and prohibitions imposed upon him by or under the relevant statutory provisions; and

(b) properly to assist his fellow partners in undertaking the measures they need to take to comply with the requirements and prohibitions imposed upon them by or under the relevant statutory provisions.

---

7. Procedures for serious and imminent danger and for danger areas.—
(1) Every employer shall—

(a) establish and where necessary give effect to appropriate procedures to be followed in the event of serious and imminent danger to persons at work in his undertaking;

(b) nominate a sufficient number of competent persons to implement those procedures insofar as they relate to the evacuation from premises of persons at work in his undertaking; and

(c) ensure that none of his employees has access to any area occupied by him to which it is necessary to restrict access on grounds of health and safety unless the employee concerned has received adequate health and safety instruction.

(2) Without prejudice to the generality of paragraph (1) (a), the procedures referred to in that sub-paragraph shall—

(a) so far as is practicable *(a)*, require any persons at work who are exposed to serious and imminent danger to be informed of the nature of the hazard and of the steps taken or to be taken to protect them from it;

(b) enable the persons concerned (if necessary by taking appropriate steps in the absence of guidance or instruction and in the light of their knowledge and the technical means at their disposal) to stop work and immediately proceed to a place of safety in the event of their being exposed to serious, imminent and unavoidable danger; and

(c) save in exceptional cases for reasons duly substantiated (which cases and reasons shall be specified in those procedures), require the persons concerned to be prevented from resuming work in any situation where there is still a serious and imminent danger.

(3) A person shall be regarded as competent for the purposes of paragraph (1) (b) where he has sufficient training and experience or knowledge and other qualities to enable him properly to implement the evacuation procedures referred to in that sub-paragraph.

(a) Practicable. See INTRODUCTORY NOTE 5.

---

8. Information for employees. Every employer shall provide his employees with comprehensible and relevant information on—

(a) the risks to their health and safety identified by *the assessment*;

(b)   *the preventive and protective measures*;
(c)   the procedures referred to in regulation 7(1)(a);
(d)   the identity of those persons nominated by him in accordance with regulation 7(1)(b); and
(e)   the risks notified to him in accordance with regulation 9(1)(c).

---

9.   Co-operation and co-ordination.—(1) Where two or more employers share a workplace (whether on a temporary or a permanent basis) each such employer shall—

(a)   co-operate with the other employers concerned so far as is necessary to enable them to comply with the requirements and prohibitions imposed upon them by or under the relevant statutory provisions;
(b)   (taking into account the nature of his activities) take all reasonable steps to co-ordinate the measures he takes to comply with the requirements and prohibitions imposed upon him by or under the relevant statutory provisions with the measures the other employers concerned are taking to comply with the requirements and prohibitions imposed upon them by or under the relevant statutory provisions; and
(c)   take all reasonable steps to inform the other employers concerned of the risks to their employees' health and safety arising out of or in connection with the conduct by him of his undertaking.

(2) Paragraph (1) shall apply to employers sharing a workplace with self-employed persons and to self-employed persons sharing a workplace with other self-employed persons as it applies to employers sharing a workplace with other employers; and the references in that paragraph to employers and the reference in the said paragraph to their employees shall be construed accordingly.

---

10.   Persons working in host employers' or self-employed persons' undertakings.—(1) Every employer and every self-employed person shall ensure that the employer of any employees from an outside undertaking who are working in his undertaking is provided with comprehensible information on—

(a)   the risks to those employees' health and safety arising out of or in connection with the conduct by that first-mentioned employer or by that self-employed person of his undertaking; and
(b)   the measures taken by that first-mentioned employer or by that self-employed person in compliance with the requirements and prohibitions imposed upon him by or under the relevant statutory provisions insofar as the said requirements and prohibitions relate to those employees.

(2) Paragraph (1) shall apply to a self-employed person who is working in the undertaking of an employer or a self-employed person as it applies to employees from an outside undertaking who are working therein; and the reference in that paragraph to the employer of any employees from an outside undertaking who are working in the undertaking of an employer or a self-

employed person and the references in the said paragraph to employees from an outside undertaking who are working in the undertaking of an employer or a self-employed person shall be construed accordingly.

(3) Every employer shall ensure that any person working in his undertaking who is not his employee and every self-employed person (not being an employer) shall ensure that any person working in his undertaking is provided with appropriate instructions and comprehensible information regarding any risks to that person's health and safety which arise out of the conduct by that employer or self-employed person of his undertaking.

(4) Every employer shall—

(a) ensure that the employer of any employees from an outside undertaking who are working in his undertaking is provided with sufficient information to enable that second-mentioned employer to identify any person nominated by that first-mentioned employer in accordance with regulation 7(1)(b) to implement evacuation procedures as far as those employees are concerned; and

(b) take all reasonable steps to ensure that any employees from an outside undertaking who are working in his undertaking receive sufficient information to enable them to identify any person nominated by him in accordance with regulation 7(1)(b) to implement evacuation procedures as far as they are concerned.

(5) Paragraph (4) shall apply to a self-employed person who is working in an employer's undertaking as it applies to employees from an outside undertaking who are working therein; and the reference in that paragraph to the employer of any employees from an outside undertaking who are working in an employer's undertaking and the references in the said paragraph to employees from an outside undertaking who are working in an employer's undertaking shall be construed accordingly.

---

11. Capabilities and training.—(1) Every employer shall, in entrusting tasks to his employees, take into account their capabilities as regards health and safety.

(2) Every employer shall ensure that his employees are provided with adequate health and safety training—

(a) on their being recruited into the employer's undertaking; and
(b) on their being exposed to new or increased risks because of—
   (i) their being transferred or given a change of responsibilities within the employer's undertaking,
   (ii) the introduction of new work equipment into or a change respecting work equipment already in use within the employer's undertaking,
   (iii) the introduction of new technology into the employer's undertaking, or
   (iv) the introduction of a new system of work into or a change respecting a system of work already in use within the employer's undertaking.

(3) The training referred to in paragraph (2) shall—

(a) be repeated periodically where appropriate;
(b) be adapted to take account of any new or changed risks to the health and safety of the employees concerned; and
(c) take place during working hours.

---

12.   Employees' duties.—(1) Every employee shall use any machinery, equipment, dangerous substance, transport equipment, means of production or safety device provided to him by his employer in accordance both with any training in the use of the equipment concerned which has been received by him and the instructions respecting that use which have been provided to him by the said employer in compliance with the requirements and prohibitions imposed upon that employer by or under the relevant statutory provisions.

(2) Every employee shall inform his employer or any other employee of that employer with specific responsibility for the health and safety of his fellow employees—

(a) of any work situation which a person with the first-mentioned employee's training and instruction would reasonably consider represented a serious and immediate danger to health and safety; and
(b) of any matter which a person with the first-mentioned employee's training and instruction would reasonably consider represented a shortcoming in the employer's protection arrangements for health and safety,

insofar as that situation or matter either affects the health and safety of that first-mentioned employee or arises out of or in connection with his own activities at work, and has not previously been reported to his employer or to any other employee of that employer in accordance with this paragraph.

---

13.   Temporary workers.—(1) Every employer shall provide any person whom he has employed under a *fixed-term contract of employment* with comprehensible information on—

(a) any special occupational qualifications or skills required to be held by that employee if he is to carry out his work safely; and
(b) any health surveillance required to be provided to that employee by or under any of the relevant statutory provisions,

and shall provide the said information before the employee concerned commences his duties.

(2) Every employer and every self-employed person shall provide any person employed in an *employment business* who is to carry out work in his undertaking with comprehensible information on—

(a) any special occupational qualifications or skills required to be held by that employee if he is to carry out his work safely; and

(b)   any health surveillance required to be provided to that employee by or under any of the relevant statutory provisions.

(3) Every employer and every self-employed person shall ensure that every person carrying on an *employment business* whose employees are to carry out work in his undertaking is provided with comprehensible information on—

(a)   any special occupational qualifications or skills required to be held by those employees if they are to carry out their work safely; and
(b)   the specific features of the jobs to be filled by those employees (insofar as those features are likely to affect their health and safety),

and the person carrying on the *employment business* concerned shall ensure that the information so provided is given to the said employees.

---

14.   Exemption certificates.—(1) The Secretary of State for Defence may, in the interests of national security, by a certificate in writing exempt—

(a)   any of the home forces, any visiting force or any headquarters from those requirements of these Regulations which impose obligations on employers; or
(b)   any member of the home forces, any member of a visiting force or any member of a headquarters from the requirements imposed by regulation 12,

and any exemption such as is specified in sub-paragraph (a) or (b) of this paragraph may be granted subject to conditions and to a limit of time and may be revoked by the said Secretary of State by a further certificate in writing at any time.

(2)   In this regulation—

(a)   "the home forces" has the same meaning as in section 12(1) of the Visiting Forces Act 1952;
(b)   "headquarters" has the same meaning as in article 3(2) of the Visiting Forces and International Headquarters (Application of Law) Order 1965;
(c)   "member of a headquarters" has the same meaning as in paragraph 1(1) of the Schedule to the International Headquarters and Defence Organisations Act 1964; and
(d)   "visiting force" has the same meaning as it does for the purposes of any provision of Part I of the Visiting Forces Act 1952.

---

15.   Exclusion of civil liability. Breach of a duty imposed by these Regulations shall not confer a right of action in any civil proceedings.

---

16.   Extension outside Great Britain.—(1) These Regulations shall, subject to regulation 2, apply to and in relation to the premises and activities outside Great Britain to which sections 1 to 59 and 80 to 82 of the Health and Safety at Work etc. Act 1974 apply by virtue of the Health and Safety at Work etc. Act 1974 (Application outside Great Britain) Order 1989 as they apply within Great Britain.

(2) For the purposes of Part I of the 1974 Act, the meaning of "at work" shall be extended so that an employee or a self-employed person shall be treated as being at work throughout the time that he is present at the premises to and in relation to which these Regulations apply by virtue of paragraph (1); and, in that connection, these Regulations shall have effect subject to the extension effected by this paragraph.

---

17.   Modification of instrument. The Safety Representatives and Safety Committees Regulations 1977 shall be modified to the extent specified in the Schedule to these Regulations.

THE SCHEDULE

[See Safety Representatives and Safety Committees Regulations 1977, reg. 4A to be found in this book under s. 5 of the Health and Safety at Work etc. Act 1974.]

THE WORKPLACE (HEALTH, SAFETY AND WELFARE) REGULATIONS 1992

(S.I. 1992 No. 3004)

General note. These Regulations are intended to implement the Workplace Directive 89/654 (see page 83). They also apply to protect temporary workers so as to implement the Temporary Workers Directive 91/383 so far as workplaces and the like are concerned.

The Regulations are supplemented by the "Workplace Health, Safety and Welfare" Approved Code of Practice (not included in this book) made under s. 16(1) of the Health and Safety at Work etc. Act 1974 which came into effect on the same date.

The Regulations deal with "workplaces", excluding means of transport, construction sites, sites of mineral exploration and extraction, and fishing boats. The Regulations deal with the structure and layout of the building as it affects workers, and facilities for workers. They deal with: ventilation; temperature; lighting; cleaning; "suitability" (rather than safety) of workstations, floors and "traffic routes"; protection against falls or falling objects; doors, walls, windows and partitions; layout of traffic routes; escalators and travolators; sanitary conveniences; washing facilities; drinking water; clothing accommodation and changing facilities; seating for work; and rest facilities. The Regulations replace extensive and familiar parts of the Factories Act and equivalent legislation.

The Regulations came into effect on 1 January 1993 save for workplaces in existence on 31 December 1992. The Regulations will come into effect for such workplaces on 1 January 1996. The repeals to the Factories and other Acts likewise come into effect on 1 January 1992 save for workplaces in existence on 31 December 1992, in which case they come into effect on 1 January 1996. The repeals and Regulations will apply to modifications, extensions, and conversions to pre-31 December 1992 workplaces as those modifications, extensions and conversions come into use. Thus not only will the two legislative regimes co-exist until 1996, if a modification is carried to part of a pre-1993 establishment, the old law may apply to one part, and the new law to another part. It is to be noted that reg. 17(2) (provision of suitable traffic routes) will apply forthwith to pre-1993 workplaces, so far as is reasonably practicable.

The Regulations employ substantially different language to the legislation they replace. It would be speculative at this stage to attempt to anticipate how the courts will approach the Regulations, and whether much reliance will be placed on the authorities decided under the old law.

As noted earlier, to the extent that the Regulations fail to give full effect to the Directives they are intended to implement recourse, by way of aid to construction, or in some cases by way of direct enforcement, may be had to the relevant Directive (see "Interpretation in the light of the European Directives" and "Direct application of the European Directives" in LEGAL PRINCIPLES in the introductory section). Some possible areas of arguable shortfall in implementation have been noted by commentators. Amongst these are the following: the workplaces excluded by Art. 1.2 do not correspond exactly with those which fall outside the Regulations by virtue of reg. 3; an Annex (1 at 6.2) imposes obligations in respect of air conditioning and pollutants not expressly included in the Regulations (see regs. 6 and 7); an Annex to the Directive (1 at 17) requires that pregnant women and nursing mothers should have facilities to lie down, whereas reg. 25 requires merely that there should be facilities to rest; the Annex (1 at 20) also makes specific mention of handicapped workers, yet these are not specified in the Regulations or ACOP; an Annex (2 at 10) to the Directive requires the provision of devices to prevent unauthorised workers entering danger areas, which is not found specifically in the Regulations or the ACOP.

There is a requirement to consult workplace representatives specified in the Framework Directive and in this Directive (see Art. 8). These Regulations contain no reflection of that obligation. However, the obligation to consult representatives of the workforce finds form in the amendment to the Safety Representatives and Safety Committees Regulations 1977 (S.I. 1977 No. 500) contained in the Schedule to the Management of Health and Safety at Work Regulations 1992 (S.I. 1992 No. 2051). That obligation only arises where the employer cares to recognise a union. This deficiency in implementation of the Framework Directive has already been referred to: see the General note to reg. 4A of the Safety Representatives and Safety Committees Regulations and "Direct application of the European Directives" in LEGAL PRINCIPLES in the introductory section.

The Secretary of State, in exercise of the powers conferred on her by sections 15(1), (2), (3) (a) and (5) (b), and 82(3) (a) of, and paragraphs 1 (2), 9 and 10 of Schedule 3 to, the Health and Safety at Work etc. Act 1974 ("the 1974 Act") and of all other powers enabling her in that behalf and for the purpose of giving effect without modifications to proposals submitted to her by the Health and Safety Commission under section 11 (2) (d) of *the 1974 Act* after the carrying out by the said Commission of consultations in accordance with section 50(3) of that Act, hereby makes the following Regulations:

1.   Citation and commencement.—(1) These Regulations may be cited as the Workplace (Health, Safety and Welfare) Regulations 1992.

(2) Subject to paragraph (3), these Regulations shall come into force on 1st January 1993.

(3) Regulations 5 to 27 and the Schedules shall come into force on 1st January 1996 with respect to any *workplace* or part of a *workplace* which is not

    (a) a *new workplace*; or
    (b) a modification, an extension or a conversion.

---

2.   Interpretation.—(1) In these Regulations, unless the context otherwise requires—

"new workplace" means a *workplace* used for the first time as a *workplace* after 31st December 1992;

"public road" means (in England and Wales) a highway maintainable at public expense within the meaning of section 329 of the Highways Act 1980 and (in Scotland) a public road within the meaning assigned to that term by section 151 of the Roads (Scotland) Act 1984;

"traffic route" means a route for pedestrian traffic, vehicles or both and includes any stairs, staircase, fixed ladder, doorway, gateway, loading bay or ramp;

"workplace" *(a)* means, subject to paragraph (2), any premises or part of premises which are not domestic premises and are made available to any person as a place of work, and includes

(a) any place within the premises to which such person has access while at work; and

(b) any room, lobby, corridor, staircase, road or other place used as a means of access to *(b)* or egress from that place of work or where facilities are provided for use in connection with the place of work other than a *public road*,

but shall not include a modification, an extension or a conversion of any of the above until such modification, extension or conversion is completed.

(2) Any reference in these Regulations, except in paragraph (1), to a modification, an extension or a conversion is a reference, as the case may be, to a modification, an extension or a conversion of a *workplace* started after 31st December 1992.

(3) Any requirement that anything done or provided in pursuance of these Regulations shall be suitable shall be construed to include a requirement that it is suitable for any person in respect of whom such thing is so done or provided.

(4) Any reference in these Regulations to—

(a) a numbered regulation or Schedule is a reference to the regulation in or Schedule to these Regulations so numbered, and

(b) a numbered paragraph is a reference to the paragraph so numbered in the regulation in which the reference appears.

(a) **Workplace.** The definition of "workplace" is wider than that contained in s. 29 of the Factories Act 1961. In particular, the words "are made available to any person" do not imply that a worker must necessarily be under any compulsion to work there (c.f. s. 29 and see note *(c)*); but the authorities on a "place" within s. 29 may give some guidance on how "workplace" will be interpreted in these regulations (see note *(d)* on "a place" in s. 29 of the Factories Act 1961). The expression has a wide definition in Art. 2 of the Directive and includes any place "within the area of the undertaking and/or establishment to which the worker has access in the course of his employment"; but the Directive does not apply to "workplaces inside means of transport" (Art. 1(2); and see reg. 3(3)).

(b) **Means of access to.** The nice distinction between place of work and means of access as used in s. 29 of the Factories Act (see the General note to s. 29) will not be relevant to the Regulations, since "workplace" includes the means of access.

---

3. Application of these Regulations.—(1) These Regulations apply to every *workplace* but shall not apply to—

(a) a *workplace* which is or is in or on a ship within the meaning assigned to that word by regulation 2(1) of the Docks Regulations 1988;

(b) a *workplace* where the only activities being undertaken are building operations or works of engineering construction within, in either case, section 176 of the Factories Act 1961 and activities for the purpose of or in connection with the first-mentioned activities;

(c) a *workplace* where the only activities being undertaken are the exploration for or extraction of mineral resources; or

(d) a *workplace* which is situated in the immediate vicinity of another *work-*

place or intended *workplace* where exploration for or extraction of mineral resources is being or will be undertaken, and where the only activities being undertaken are activities preparatory to, for the purposes of, or in connection with such exploration for or extraction of mineral resources at that other *workplace*.

(2) In their application to temporary work sites, any requirement to ensure a *workplace* complies with any of regulations 20 to 25 shall have effect as a requirement to so ensure so far as is reasonably practicable.

(3) As respects any *workplace* which is or is in or on an aircraft, locomotive or rolling stock, trailer or semi-trailer used as a means of transport or a vehicle for which a licence is in force under the Vehicles (Excise) Act 1971 or a vehicle exempted from duty under that Act—

(a) regulations 5 to 12 and 14 to 25 shall not apply to any such *workplace*; and
(b) regulation 13 shall apply to any such *workplace* only when the aircraft, locomotive or rolling stock, trailer or semi-trailer or vehicle is stationary inside a *workplace* and, in the case of a vehicle for which a licence is in force under the Vehicles (Excise) Act 1971, is not on a *public road*.

(4) As respects any *workplace* which is in fields, woods or other land forming part of an agricultural or forestry undertaking but which is not inside a building and is situated away from the undertaking's main buildings—

(a) regulations 5 to 19 and 23 to 25 shall not apply to any such *workplace*; and
(b) any requirement to ensure that any such *workplace* complies with any of regulations 20 to 22 shall have effect as a requirement to so ensure so far as is reasonably practicable.

4.   Requirements under these Regulations.—(1) Every employer shall ensure that every *workplace*, modification, extension or conversion *(a)* which is under his control and where any of his employees works complies with any requirement of these Regulations which—

(a) applies to that *workplace* or, as the case may be, to the *workplace* which contains that modification, extension or conversion; and
(b) is in force in respect of the *workplace*, modification, extension or conversion.

(2) Subject to paragraph (4), every person who has, to any extent, control of a *workplace*, modification, extension or conversion shall ensure that such *workplace*, modification, extension or conversion complies with any requirement of these Regulations which—

(a) applies to that *workplace* or, as the case may be, to the *workplace* which contains that modification, extension or conversion;
(b) is in force in respect of the *workplace*, modification, extension, or conversion; and
(c) relates to matters within that person's control.

(3) Any reference in this regulation to a person having control of any *workplace*, modification, extension or conversion is a reference to a person having control of the *workplace*, modification, extension or conversion in connection with the carrying on by him of a trade, business or other undertaking (whether for profit or not).

(4) Paragraph (2) shall not impose any requirement upon a self-employed person in respect of his own work or the work of any partner of his in the undertaking.

(5) Every person who is deemed to be the occupier of a factory by virtue of section 175(5) of the Factories Act 1961 shall ensure that the premises which are so deemed to be a factory comply with these Regulations.

(a) *Modification, extension or conversion.* See reg. 2(2).

---

5. Maintenance of *workplace,* **and of equipment, devices and systems.**— (1) The *workplace* and the equipment, devices and systems to which this regulation applies shall be maintained (including cleaned as appropriate) in an efficient (a) state, in efficient (a) working order and in good repair.

(2) Where appropriate, the equipment, devices and systems to which this regulation applies shall be subject to a suitable system of maintenance.

(3) The equipment, devices and systems to which this regulation applies are—

(a) equipment and devices a fault in which is liable to result in a failure to comply with any of these Regulations; and
(b) mechanical ventilation systems provided pursuant to regulation 6 (whether or not they include equipment or devices within sub-paragraph (a) of this paragraph).

(a) *Efficient.* Clause 20 of the ACOP makes clear that efficient in this context means efficient from the view point of health, safety and welfare, not productivity or economy. See also INTRODUCTORY NOTE 12.

---

6. Ventilation.—(1) Effective and suitable (a) provision shall be made to ensure that every enclosed *workplace* is ventilated by a sufficient quantity of fresh or purified air (b).

(2) Any plant used for the purpose of complying with paragraph (1) shall include an effective device to give visible or audible warning of any failure of the plant where necessary for reasons of health or safety.

(3) This regulation shall not apply to any enclosed *workplace* or part of a *workplace* which is subject to the provisions of—

(a) section 30 of the Factories Act 1961;

(b) regulations 49 to 52 of the Shipbuilding and Ship-Repairing Regulations 1960;

(c) regulation 21 of the Construction (General Provisions) Regulations 1961;

(d) regulation 18 of the Docks Regulations 1988.

(a) Effective and suitable. See reg. 2(3) and INTRODUCTORY NOTE 12.

---

7.   Temperature in indoor *workplaces*.—(1) During working hours, the temperature in all *workplaces* inside buildings shall be reasonable *(a)*.

(2) A method of heating or cooling shall not be used which results in the escape into a *workplace* of fumes, gas or vapour of such character and to such extent that they are likely to be injurious or offensive to any person.

(3) A sufficient number of thermometers shall be provided to enable persons at work to determine the temperature in any *workplace* inside a building.

(a) Reasonable. Clause 43 of the ACOP states that the temperature should be at least 16 degrees celsius unless much of the work involves severe physical effort, in which case it should be at least 13 degrees. No maximum figures are stated.

---

8.   Lighting.—(1) Every *workplace* shall have suitable and sufficient *(a)* lighting.

(2) The lighting mentioned in paragraph (1) shall, so far as is reasonably practicable, be by natural light.

(3) Without prejudice to the generality of paragraph (1), suitable and sufficient *(a)* emergency lighting shall be provided in any room in circumstances in which persons at work are specially exposed to danger in the event of failure of artificial lighting.

(a) Suitable and sufficient. See reg. 2(3) and INTRODUCTORY NOTE 12. For the interpretation of that phrase in the context of lighting under the Factories Act 1961, see note *(a)* to s. 5 of that Act.

---

9.   Cleanliness and waste materials.—(1) Every *workplace* and the furniture, furnishings and fittings therein shall be kept sufficiently clean.

(2) The surfaces of the floors, walls and ceilings of all *workplaces* inside buildings shall be capable of being kept sufficiently clean.

(3) So far as is reasonably practicable, waste materials shall not be allowed to accumulate in a *workplace* except in suitable receptacles.

---

10. Room dimensions and space.—(1) Every room where persons work shall have sufficient floor area, height and unoccupied space for purposes of health, safety and welfare.

(2) It shall be sufficient compliance with this regulation in a *workplace* which is not a *new workplace*, a modification, an extension or a conversion *(a)* and which, immediately before this regulation came into force in respect of it, was subject to the provisions of the Factories Act 1961, if the *workplace* does not contravene the provisions of Part I of Schedule 1.

(a) Modification, extension or conversion. See reg. 2(2).

---

11. Workstations and seating.—(1) Every workstation *(a)* shall be so arranged that it is suitable *(b)* both for any person at work in the *workplace* who is likely to work at that workstation and for any work of the undertaking which is likely to be done there.

(2) Without prejudice to the generality of paragraph (1), every workstation outdoors shall be so arranged that—

(a) so far as is reasonably practicable, it provides protection from adverse weather;

(b) it enables any person at the workstation to leave it swiftly or, as appropriate, to be assisted in the event of an emergency; and

(c) it ensures that any person at the workstation is not likely to slip or fall.

(3) A suitable seat shall be provided for each person at work in the *workplace* whose work includes operations of a kind that the work (or a substantial part of it) can or must be done sitting.

(4) A seat shall not be suitable for the purpose of paragraph (3) unless—

(a) it is suitable for the person for whom it is provided as well as for the operations to be performed; and

(b) a suitable footrest is also provided where necessary.

(a) Workstation. This word is not defined but it is broad enough, it is submitted to overcome the narrowness of the "place at which any person has at any time to work" in the to be repealed s. 29 of the Factories Act 1961 (see *Dexter v Tenby Electrical Accessories* [1991] Crim LR 839), especially when coupled with the phrase "made available" in the definition of workplace in reg. 2(1).

(b) Suitable. See INTRODUCTORY NOTE 12. It is probable that a workstation may not be suitable owing to exposure to matters which arise from the atmosphere or nature of the place in which the employee works and not merely the fabric of the workplace, particularly in light of the words "so arranged" (and see para 21.3 to Annex I of the Directive: see, by way of analogy, *Baxter v Harland & Wolff plc* [1990] IRLR 516, Northern Ireland CA (excess noise in workplace causing deafness). Whilst under the to be repealed s. 29 of the Factories Act a place was unsafe only where the danger came from something that made the place itself dangerous, but not where it merely posed a risk to

an individual employee (see e.g. *Bowman v Harland & Wolf plc* [1992] IRLR 349: calking hammer causing injury and operated by individual employee did not make place unsafe), the standard of "suitability" should protect against a wider category of risks: see reg. 2(3).

---

12.   Condition of floors and *traffic routes*.—(1) Every floor in a *workplace* and the surface of every *traffic route (a)* in a *workplace* shall be of a construction such that the floor or surface *(b)* of the *traffic route* is suitable *(c)* for the purpose for which it is used.

(2) Without prejudice to the generality of paragraph (1), the requirements in that paragraph shall include requirements that—

(a)   the floor, or surface of the *traffic route*, shall have no hole or slope, or be uneven or slippery so as, in each case, to expose any person to a risk to his health or safety; and

(b)   every such floor shall have effective means of drainage where necessary.

(3) So far as is reasonably practicable *(d)*, every floor in a *workplace* and the surface of every *traffic route* in a *workplace* shall be kept free from obstructions *(e)* and from any article or substance which may cause a person to slip *(f)*, trip or fall.

(4) In considering whether for the purposes of paragraph (2)(a) a hole or slope exposes any person to a risk to his health or safety—

(a)   no account shall be taken of a hole where adequate measures have been taken to prevent a person falling; and

(b)   account shall be taken of any handrail provided in connection with any slope.

(5) Suitable and sufficient handrails and, if appropriate, guards shall be provided on all *traffic routes* which are staircases except in circumstances in which a handrail can not be provided without obstructing the *traffic route*.

(a) Traffic route. For definition, see reg. 2. Unlike s. 29 of the Factories Act 1961 which imposed the obligation to provide safe means of access, provision is no part of the definition in the Regulation; but it is unlikely that a traffic route which the employer has not provided (in the sense of not permitted for use), will be required to be suitable (in the sense of safe) just as under s. 29: *Smith v British Aerospace* [1982] ICR 98, CA (although in *Kirkpatrick v Scott Lithgow Ltd* 1987 SCLR 567 it was held that where a safe route is available but the employee is injured using another one then the employer will be liable if it was reasonably forseeable that the employee would use that route). Perhaps the requirement of suitability is flexible enough to deal with this situation so that an unauthorised route need not be suitable for normal traffic.

There appears now to be no significant distinction between the duties applicable to workplaces and to access and egress therefrom, a distinction which bedevilled ss. 28 and 29 of the Factories Act 1961. Thus, for example, so long as the route taken is a traffic route there is no need to show it led to the employee's place of work. Stairs as well as staircases are now included, so disposing of another distinction under s. 28 of the Factories Act.

In *Carragher v Singer Manufacturing Co Ltd* 1974 SLT (Notes) 28 it was held that a breach of the to be repealed s. 29(1) of the Factories Act 1961 could arise where occupational deafness was caused by exposure to the noise of machinery; Lord Maxwell holding that "in relation to the 'safe means of access' provisions, a breach can arise by reasons of the 'condition' of the means of access though it be structurally sound and safe in itself and that the unsafe conditions can arise by reason of the proximity of the means of access to or presence in the means of access of things which cause danger, though not themselves forming part of the means of access". See also *Canning v Kings & Co Ltd* 1986 SLT 107n and *Baxter v Harland & Wolff plc* [1990] IRLR 516, Northern Ireland CA (but c.f. *Harkins v McCluskey* 1987 SLT 289). It is unclear whether a similar obligation arises by virtue of reg. 12 owing to the reference to "construction" in reg. 12(1). Certainly, the width of the duties in reg. 12(2) and, particularly, reg. 12(3) would seem to contemplate that the Regulations apply to the condition, in a wide sense, of traffic routes.

(b) *Floor or surface.* This is likely to be more broadly interpreted than the corresponding "floor" in the to be repealed s. 28 of the Factories Act 1961. In holding that a dry dock was not an "opening in a floor" within the meaning of s. 28(4) of the 1961 Act, Somervell, LJ, in *Bath v British Transport Commission* [1954] 2 All ER 542, [1954] 1 WLR 1013, CA, said "Where words are . . . perfectly familiar all one can do is to say whether or not one regards them as apt to cover or describe the circumstances in question in any particular case", and in *Johnston v Colvilles Ltd* 1966 SLT 30, Ct of Sess, it was held that "floor" meant the ordinary floor of a factory which was used by those employed in the ordinary course of their employment. See the following cases: *Hosking v De Havilland Aircraft Co Ltd* [1949] 1 All ER 540 (plank across duct held to be a gangway; plainly now a "traffic route"); *Morris v Port of London Authority* (1950) 84 Ll L Rep 564 (floor of a gantry held to be a "floor"); *Taylor v R & H Green and Silley Weir Ltd* (1950) 84 Ll L Rep 570 (affirmed by the CA [1951] 1 Lloyd's Rep 345) (sill round inside of dry dock held to be a floor); *Harrison v Metropolitan-Vickers Electrical Co Ltd* [1954] 1 All ER 404, [1954] 1 WLR 324, CA (sand bed of foundry held to be a floor and an excavation in it an "opening in a floor"; now a "hole" under the Regulations). It is submitted that the following cases would no longer be treated as authoritative given the breadth of the phrase "floor or surface of the traffic route": *Tate v Swan, Hunter and Wigham Richardson Ltd* [1958] 1 All ER 150, [1958] 1 WLR 39, CA (planks laid across steelwork of crane gantry held not to be a floor); *Newberry v Joseph Westwood & Co Ltd* [1960] 2 Lloyd's Rep 37 ("mother earth" held not to be a floor, passage or gangway); *Sullivan v Hall, Russell & Co Ltd* 1964 SLT 192 (unmade earthen surface of a woodyard held not to be a floor); *Thornton v Fisher and Ludlow Ltd* [1968] 2 All ER 241, [1968] 1 WLR 655, CA (30 ft. wide roadway in the open not a floor, passage or gangway); *Devine v Costain Concrete Co Ltd* 1979 SLT (Notes) 97 (bottom of duct in factory floor, upon which men worked, held to be a floor). In *Allen v Avon Rubber Co Ltd* [1986] ICR 695, CA, a typical loading bay at the end of factory floor was held not to be an opening in a floor. It is submitted it would not amount to a "hole" in these Regulations.

(c) *Suitable.* See INTRODUCTORY NOTE 12 and reg. 2(3). The wording of this part of the Regulation, it is submitted, removes the distinction made under the to be repealed s. 29 of the Factories Act 1961 where the obligation was held to be that of maintaining the means of access in a structurally sound condition rather than to maintain the safety of the means of access by eliminating transient and exceptional conditions: *Levesley v Thomas Firth and John Brown Ltd* [1953] 2 All ER 866, [1953] 1 WLR 1206, CA. That case also decided that transient obstructions were outside the scope of the section but, it is submitted, they would not be outside reg. 12(3) which specifically refers to "obstruction" (but see Annex I to the Directive 89/654 at para. 12).

The duty is absolute and unqualified by matters of reasonable practicability, and is doubtless a continuing duty as under the old s. 29: *Geddes v United Wires Ltd* 1974 SLT 170.

(d) *Reasonably practicable.* See INTRODUCTORY NOTE 5 on the meaning of this phrase. The phrase is not found in the Directive (see, especially, para. 12 of Annex I) and there is doubt therefore whether it will be enforceable. See "Interpretation in the light of the European Directives" and "Direct application of the European Directives" under LEGAL PRINCIPLES in the introductory section. In relation to spillages from cups of tea, it was held (in a case decided under s. 16 of the Factories Act) to be insufficient for an employer merely to entreat employees to be more careful (*Bell v Department of Health and Social Security* (1989) Times, 13 June).

(*e*) **Obstruction.** See INTRODUCTORY NOTE 13.

(*f*) **Substance which may cause a person to slip.** Note that the Regulations apply to obstructions etc. which *may* cause someone to slip, and not which are *likely* so to do (c.f. s. 28 of the Factories Act 1961). It was held under s. 28 that once it is proved that there is a slippery substance on a factory floor on which the plaintiff has slipped it is then for the defendants to show that they have taken all reasonably practicable precautions, first, to prevent that substance being on the floor at all and then, secondly, to clear it off the floor (*Johnston v Caddies Wainwright Ltd* [1983] ICR 407, CA). In *Taylor v Gestetner Ltd* (1967) 2 KIR 133, it was held that water might be such a substance. In *Dorman Long (Steel) Ltd v Bell* [1964] 1 All ER 617, [1964] 1 WLR 333, HL, it was held that where metal plates placed temporarily on the floor became slippery when slag dust collected on them there had been a breach of this subsection, notwithstanding that the slippery substance was not itself in contact with the floor.

---

13.   Falls or falling objects.—(1) So far as is reasonably practicable (*a*), suitable and effective (*b*) measures shall be taken to prevent any event specified in paragraph (3).

(2) So far as is reasonably practicable (*a*), the measures required by paragraph (1) shall be measures other than the provision of personal protective equipment, information, instruction, training or supervision.

(3) The events specified in this paragraph are:—

(a) any person falling a distance likely to cause personal injury;

(b) any person being struck by a falling object likely to cause personal injury.

(4) Any area where there is a risk to health or safety from any event mentioned in paragraph (3) shall be clearly indicated where appropriate.

(5) So far as is practicable (*a*), every tank, pit or structure where there is a risk of a person in the *workplace* falling into a dangerous substance in the tank, pit or structure, shall be securely covered or fenced.

(6) Every *traffic route* over, across or in an uncovered tank, pit or structure such as is mentioned in paragraph (5) shall be securely fenced.

(7) In this regulation, "dangerous substance" means—

(a) any substance likely to scald or burn;

(b) any poisonous substance;

(c) any corrosive substance;

(d) any fume, gas or vapour likely to overcome a person; or

(e) any granular or free-flowing solid substance, or any viscous substance which, in any case, is of a nature or quantity which is likely to cause danger to any person.

(*a*) **Reasonably practicable.** See INTRODUCTORY NOTE 5.

(*b*) **Suitable and effective.** See INTRODUCTORY NOTE 12 and reg. 2(3). The addition of the term "effective" plainly makes the obligation closer to a strict one.

---

14.   Windows, and transparent or translucent doors, gates and walls.—(1) Every window or other transparent or translucent surface in a wall or partition and every transparent or translucent surface in a door or gate shall, where necessary for reasons of health or safety—

    (a) be of safety material or be protected against breakage of the transparent or translucent material; and

    (b) be appropriately marked or incorporate features so as, in either case, to make it apparent.

---

15. Windows, skylights and ventilators.—(1) No window, skylight or ventilator which is capable of being opened shall be likely to be opened, closed or adjusted in a manner which exposes any person performing such operation to a risk to his health or safety.

(2) No window, skylight or ventilator shall be in a position when open which is likely to expose any person in the *workplace* to a risk to his health or safety.

---

16. Ability to clean windows etc. safely.—(1) All windows and skylights in a *workplace* shall be of a design or be so constructed that they may be cleaned safely.

(2) In considering whether a window or skylight is of a design or so constructed as to comply with paragraph (1), account may be taken of equipment used in conjunction with the window or skylight or of devices fitted to the building.

---

17. Organisation etc. of *traffic routes*.—(1) Every *workplace* shall be organised in such a way that pedestrians and vehicles can circulate in a safe manner.

(2) *Traffic routes* in a *workplace* shall be suitable *(a)* for the persons or vehicles using them, sufficient in number, in suitable *(a)* positions and of sufficient size.

(3) Without prejudice to the generality of paragraph (2), *traffic routes* shall not satisfy the requirements of that paragraph unless suitable *(a)* measures are taken to ensure that—

    (a) pedestrians or, as the case may be, vehicles may use a *traffic route* without causing danger to the health or safety of persons at work near it;

    (b) there is sufficient separation of any *traffic route* for vehicles from doors or gates or from *traffic routes* for pedestrians which lead onto it; and

    (c) where vehicles and pedestrians use the same *traffic route*, there is sufficient separation between them.

(4) All *traffic routes* shall be suitably indicated where necessary for reasons of health or safety.

(5) Paragraph (2) shall apply so far as is reasonably practicable *(b)*, to a *workplace* which is not a *new workplace*, a modification, an extension or a conversion *(c)*.

  *(a) **Suitable.*** See INTRODUCTORY NOTE 12 and reg. 2(3).

  *(b) **Reasonably practicable.*** See INTRODUCTORY NOTE 5. The phrase is not found in the Directive and there is doubt therefore whether it will be enforceable. See "Interpret-

ation in the light of the European Directives" and "Direct application of the European Directives" under LEGAL PRINCIPLES in the introductory section of this book.

   (c) Modification, extension or conversion. See reg. 2(2).

---

18.   Doors and gates.—(1) Doors and gates shall be suitably constructed (including being fitted with any necessary safety devices).

   (2) Without prejudice to the generality of paragraph (1), doors and gates shall not comply with that paragraph unless—

   (a)   any sliding door or gate has a device to prevent it coming off its track during use;
   (b)   any upward opening door or gate has a device to prevent it falling back;
   (c)   any powered door or gate has suitable and effective features to prevent it causing injury by trapping any person;
   (d)   where necessary for reasons of health or safety, any powered door or gate can be operated manually unless it opens automatically if the power fails; and
   (e)   any door or gate which is capable of opening by being pushed from either side is of such a construction as to provide, when closed, a clear view of the space close to both sides.

---

19.   Escalators and moving walkways. Escalators and moving walkways shall:—

   (a)   function safely;
   (b)   be equipped with any necessary safety devices;
   (c)   be fitted with one or more emergency stop controls which are easily identifiable and readily accessible.

---

20.   Sanitary conveniences.—(1) Suitable and sufficient *(a)* sanitary conveniences shall be provided at readily accessible places.

   (2) Without prejudice to the generality of paragraph (1), sanitary conveniences shall not be suitable unless—

   (a)   the rooms containing them are adequately ventilated and lit;
   (b)   they and the rooms containing them are kept in a clean and orderly condition; and
   (c)   separate rooms containing conveniences are provided for men and women except where and so far as each convenience is in a separate room the door of which is capable of being secured from inside.

   (3) It shall be sufficient compliance with the requirement in paragraph (1) to provide sufficient sanitary conveniences in a *workplace* which is not a *new workplace*, a modification, an extension or a conversion *(b)* and which, immediately before this regulation came into force in respect of it, was subject to the provisions of the Factories Act 1961, if sanitary conveniences are provided in accordance with the provisions of Part II of Schedule 1.

(a) Suitable and sufficient. See INTRODUCTORY NOTE 12.

(b) Modification, extension or conversion. See reg. 2(2).

---

21. Washing facilities.—(1) Suitable and sufficient *(a)* washing facilities, including showers if required by the nature of the work or for health reasons, shall be provided at readily accessible places.

(2) Without prejudice to the generality of paragraph (1), washing facilities shall not be suitable *(a)* unless—

(a) they are provided in the immediate vicinity of every sanitary convenience, whether or not provided elsewhere as well;

(b) they are provided in the vicinity of any changing rooms required by these Regulations, whether or not provided elsewhere as well;

(c) they include a supply of clean hot and cold, or warm, water (which shall be running water so far as is practicable);

(d) they include soap or other suitable means of cleaning;

(e) they include towels or other suitable means of drying;

(f) the rooms containing them are sufficiently ventilated and lit:

(g) they and the rooms containing them are kept in a clean and orderly condition; and

(h) separate facilities are provided for men and women, except where and so far as they are provided in a room the door of which is capable of being secured from inside and the facilities in each such room are intended to be used by only one person at a time.

(3) Paragraph (2)(h) shall not apply to facilities which are provided for washing hands, forearms and face only.

(a) Suitable and sufficient. See INTRODUCTORY NOTE 12 and reg. 2(3). It is likely that suitability will impose no less a standard than the duty to provide and maintain adequate and suitable washing facilities under s. 58 of the Factories Act 1961. Under this section in *South Surbiton Co-operative Society v D B Wilcox* [1975] IRLR 292 a cracked wash-basin was held not to be properly maintained.

---

22. Drinking water.—(1) An adequate supply of wholesome drinking water shall be provided for all persons at work in the *workplace.*

(2) Every supply of drinking water required by paragraph (1) shall—

(a) be readily accessible at suitable *(a)* places; and

(b) be conspicuously marked by an appropriate sign where necessary for reasons of health or safety.

(3) Where a supply of drinking water is required by paragraph (1), there shall also be provided a sufficient number of suitable cups or other drinking vessels unless the supply of drinking water is in a jet from which persons can drink easily.

(a) Suitable. See INTRODUCTORY NOTE 12 and reg. 2(3).

---

23.   Accommodation for clothing.—(1) Suitable and sufficient *(a)* accommodation shall be provided—

   (a) for the clothing of any person at work which is not worn during working hours; and

   (b) for special clothing which is worn by any person at work but which is not taken home.

(2) Without prejudice to the generality of paragraph (1), the accommodation mentioned in that paragraph shall not be suitable unless—

   (a) where facilities to change clothing are required by regulation 24, it provides suitable security for the clothing mentioned in paragraph (1)(a);

   (b) where necessary to avoid risks to health or damage to the clothing, it includes separate accommodation for clothing worn at work and for other clothing;

   (c) so far as is reasonably practicable, it allows or includes facilities for drying clothing; and

   (d) it is in a suitable location.

   (a) Suitable and sufficient. See INTRODUCTORY NOTE 12 and reg. 2(3). In relation to the same phrase contained in s. 59 of the Factories Act 1961 (which applies to accommodation for clothing), it was held that the risk of theft was an element which an employer should take into consideration: see *McCarthy v Daily Mirror Newspapers Ltd* [1949] 1 All ER 801, CA, followed in *Barr v Cruikshank & Co Ltd* 1959 SLT (Sh Ct) 9. That obligation is now expressly set out in reg. 23(2)(a).

---

24.   Facilities for changing clothing.—(1) Suitable and sufficient *(a)* facilities shall be provided for any person at work in the *workplace* to change clothing in all cases where—

   (a) the person has to wear special clothing for the purpose of work; and

   (b) the person can not, for reasons of health or propriety, be expected to change in another room.

(2) Without prejudice to the generality of paragraph (1), the facilities mentioned in that paragraph shall not be suitable unless they include separate facilities for, or separate use of facilities by, men and women where necessary for reasons of propriety.

   (a) Suitable and sufficient. See INTRODUCTORY NOTE 12 and reg. 2(3).

---

25.   Facilities for rest and to eat meals.—(1) Suitable and sufficient *(a)* rest facilities shall be provided at readily accessible places.

(2) Rest facilities provided by virtue of paragraph (1) shall—

   (a) where necessary for reasons of health or safety include, in the case of a *new workplace*, an extension or a conversion, rest facilities provided in one or more rest rooms, or, in other cases, in rest rooms or rest areas;

   (b) include suitable *(a)* facilities to eat meals where food eaten in the *workplace* would otherwise be likely to become contaminated.

(3) Rest rooms and rest areas shall include suitable *(a)* arrangements to protect non-smokers from discomfort caused by tobacco smoke.

(4) Suitable *(a)* facilities shall be provided for any person at work who is a pregnant woman or nursing mother to rest.

(5) Suitable and sufficient *(a)* facilities shall be provided for persons at work to eat meals where meals are regularly eaten in the *workplace*.

(a) Suitable and sufficient. See INTRODUCTORY NOTE 12 and reg. 2(3).

---

26. Exemption certificates.—(1) The Secretary of State for Defence may, in the interests of national security, by a certificate in writing exempt any of the home forces, any visiting force or any headquarters from the requirements of these Regulations and any exemption may be granted subject to conditions and to a limit of time and may be revoked by the said Secretary of State by a further certificate in writing at any time.

(2) In this regulation—

(a) "the home forces" has the same meaning as in section 12(1) of the Visiting Forces Act 1952;

(b) "headquarters" has the same meaning as in article 3(2) of the Visiting Forces and International Headquarters (Application of Law) Order 1965;

(c) "visiting force" has the same meaning as it does for the purposes of any provision of Part I of the Visiting Forces Act 1952.

---

27. Repeals, saving and revocations.—(1) The enactments mentioned in column 2 of Part I of Schedule 2 are repealed to the extent specified in column 3 of that Part.

(2) Nothing in this regulation shall affect the operation of any provision of the Offices, Shops and Railway Premises Act 1963 as that provision has effect by virtue of section 90(4) of that Act.

(3) The instruments mentioned in column 1 of Part II of Schedule 2 are revoked to the extent specified in column 3 of that Part.

SCHEDULE 1
PROVISIONS APPLICABLE TO FACTORIES WHICH ARE NOT NEW
WORKPLACES, MODIFICATIONS, EXTENSIONS OR CONVERSIONS
Regulations 10 and 20

PART I
SPACE

1. No room in the *workplace* shall be so overcrowded as to cause risk to the health or safety of persons at work in it.

2. Without prejudice to the generality of paragraph 1, the number of persons employed at a time in any workroom shall not be such that the amount of cubic space allowed for each is less than 11 cubic metres.

3. In calculating for the purposes of this Part of this Schedule the amount of cubic space in any room no space more than 4.2 metres from the floor shall be taken into account and, where a room contains a gallery, the gallery shall be treated for the purposes of this Schedule as if it were partitioned off from the remainder of the room and formed a separate room.

PART II
NUMBER OF SANITARY CONVENIENCES

4. In *workplaces* where females work, there shall be at least one suitable water closet for use by females only for every 25 females.

5. In *workplaces* where males work, there shall be at least one suitable water closet for use by males only for every 25 males.

6. In calculating the number of males or females who work in any *workplace* for the purposes of this Part of this Schedule, any number not itself divisible by 25 without fraction or remainder shall be treated as the next number higher than it which is so divisible.

SCHEDULE 2
REPEALS AND REVOCATIONS

Regulation 27

PART I
REPEALS

1	2	3
Chapter	*Short title*	*Extent of repeal*
1961 c 34	The Factories Act 1961	Sections 1 to 7, 18, 28, 29, 57 to 60 and 69
1963 c 41	The Offices, Shops and Railway Premises Act 1963	Sections 4 to 16
1956 c 49	The Agriculture (Safety, Health and Welfare Provisions) Act 1956	Sections 3 and 5 and, in section 25, sub-ss. (3) and (6)

PART II
REVOCATIONS

(1) *Title*	(2) *Reference*	(3) *Extent of revocation*
The Flax and Tow Spinning and Weaving Regulations 1906	S.R. & O. 1906/177 amended by S.I. 1988/1657	Regulations 3, 8, 10, 11 and 14
The Hemp Spinning and Weaving Regulations 1907	S.R. & O. 1907/660, amended by S.I. 1988/1657	Regulations 3 to 5 and 8
Order dated 5 October 1917 (the Tin or Terne Plates Manufacture Welfare Order 1917)	S.R. & O. 1917/1035	The whole Order
Order dated 15 May 1918 (the Glass Bottle, etc. Manufacture Welfare Order 1918)	S.R. & O. 1918/558	The whole Order
Order dated 15 August 1919 (the Fruit Preserving Welfare Order 1919)	S.R. & O. 1919/1136, amended by S.I. 1988/1657	The whole Order
Order dated 23 April 1920 (the Laundries Welfare Order 1920)	S.R. & O. 1920/654	The whole Order
Order dated 28 July 1920 (the Gut Scraping, Tripe Dressing, etc. Welfare Order 1920)	S.R. & O. 1920/1437	The whole Order
Order dated 9 September 1920 (the Herring Curing (Norfolk and Suffolk) Welfare Order 1920)	S.R. & O. 1920/1662	The whole Order
Order dated 3 March 1921 (the Glass Bevelling Welfare Order 1921)	S.R. & O. 1921/288	The whole Order
The Herring Curing (Scotland) Welfare Order 1926	S.R. & O. 1926/535 (s. 24)	The whole Order
The Herring Curing Welfare Order 1927	S.R. & O. 1927/813, amended by S.I. 1960/1690 and 917	The whole Order
The Sacks (Cleaning and Repairing) Welfare Order 1927	S.R. & O. 1927/860	The whole Order
The Horizontal Milling Machines Regulations 1928	S.R. & O. 1928/548	The whole Regulations
The Cotton Cloth Factories Regulations 1929	S.I. 1929/300	Regulations 5 to 10, 11 and 12

(1)	(2)	(3)
Title	Reference	Extent of revocation
The Oil Cake Welfare Order 1929	S.R. & O. 1929/534	Articles 3 to 6
The Cement Works Welfare Order 1930	S.R. & O. 1930/94	The whole Order
The Tanning Welfare Order 1930	S.R. & O. 1930/312	The whole Order
The Kiers Regulations 1938	S.R. & O. 1938/106 amended by S.I. 1981/1152	Regulations 12 to 15
The Sanitary Accommodation Regulations 1938	S.R. & O. 1938/611, amended by S.I. 1974/426	The whole Regulations
The Clay Works (Welfare) Special Regulations 1948	S.I. 1948/1547	Regulations 3, 4, 6, 8 and 9
The Jute (Safety, Health and Welfare) Regulations 1948	S.I. 1948/1696, amended by S.I. 1988/1657	Regulations 11, 13, 14 to 16 and 19 to 26
The Pottery (Health and Welfare) Special Regulations 1950	S.I. 1950/65, amended by S.I. 1963/879, 1973/36, 1980/1248, 1982/877, 1988/1657, 1989/2311 and 1990/305	Regulation 15
The Iron and Steel Foundries Regulations 1953	S.I. 1953/1464, amended by S.I. 1974/1681 and 1981/1332	The whole Regulations
The Washing Facilities (Running Water) Exemption Regulations 1960	S.I. 1960/1029	The whole Regulations
The Washing Facilities (Miscellaneous Industries) Regulations 1960	S.I. 1960/1214	The whole Regulations
The Factories (Cleanliness of Walls and Ceilings) Order 1960	S.I. 1960/1794, amended by S.I. 1974/427	The whole Order
The Non-ferrous Metals (Melting and Founding) Regulations 1962	S.I. 1962/1667, amended by S.I. 1974/1681, 1981/1332 and 1988/165	Regulations 5, 6 to 10, 14 to 17 and 20
The Offices, Shops and Railway Premises Act 1963 (Exemption No. 1) Order 1964	S.I. 1964/964	The whole Order
The Washing Facilities Regulations 1964	S.I. 1964/965	The whole Regulations

(1)	(2)	(3)
Title	*Reference*	*Extent of revocation*
The Sanitary Conveniences Regulations 1964	S.I. 1964/966, amended by S.I. 1982/827	The whole Regulations
The Offices, Shops and Railway Premises Act 1963 (Exemption No. 7) Order 1968	S.I. 1968/1947, amended by S.I. 1982/827	The whole Order
The Abrasive Wheels Regulations 1970	S.I. 1970/535	Regulation 17
The Sanitary Accommodation (Amendment) Regulations 1974	S.I. 1974/426	The whole Regulations
The Factories (Cleanliness of Walls and Ceilings) (Amendment) Regulations 1974	S.I. 1974/427	The whole Regulations
The Woodworking Machines Regulations 1974	S.I. 1974/903, amended by S.I. 1978/1126	Regulations 10 to 12
The Offices, Shops and Railway Premises Act 1963 etc. (Metrication) Regulations 1982	S.I. 1982/827	The whole Regulations

PART 3
LEGISLATION OF GENERAL APPLICATION

SUMMARY

EMPLOYERS' LIABILITY (COMPULSORY INSURANCE) ACT 1969

(1969 c. 57)

An Act to require employers to insure against their liability for personal injury to their employees; and for purposes connected with the matter aforesaid

[22 October 1969]

1. Insurance against liability for employees.—(1) Except as otherwise provided by this Act, every employer carrying on any business in Great Britain shall insure, and maintain insurance, under one or more approved policies with an authorised insurer or insurers against liability for bodily injury or disease sustained by his employees, and arising out of and in the course of their employment in Great Britain in that business, but except in so far as regulations otherwise provide not including injury or disease suffered or contracted outside Great Britain.

(2) Regulations may provide that the amount for which an employer is required by this Act to insure and maintain insurance shall, either generally or in such cases or classes of case as may be prescribed by the regulations, be limited in such manner as may be so prescribed.

(3) For the purposes of this Act—

(a) "approved policy" means a policy of insurance not subject to any conditions or exceptions prohibited for those purposes by regulations;

(b) "authorised insurer" means a person or body of persons lawfully carrying on in the United Kingdom insurance business of a class specified in Schedule 1 or 2 to the Insurance Companies Act 1982, or, being an insurance company the head office of which is in a member State, lawfully carrying on in a member State other than the United Kingdom insurance business of a corresponding class, and issuing the policy or policies in the course thereof;

(c) "business" includes a trade or profession, and includes any activity carried on by a body of persons, whether corporate or unincorporate;

(d) except as otherwise provided by regulations, an employer not having a place of business in Great Britain shall be deemed not to carry on business there.

General note. Subsection (3) was amended by the Insurance Companies Act 1981, s. 36, Sch. 4, Pt. II, para. 19, the Insurance Companies Act 1982, s. 99(2), Sch. 5, para. 8, and by S.I. 1992 No. 2890, reg. 11(1). If an employee is exposed to a special risk of which he is ignorant, there is no contractual duty at common law on the employer to advise him or her to obtain insurance: see *Reid v Rush & Tompkins Group plc* [1990] ICR 61.

2. Employees to be covered.—(1) For the purposes of this Act the term "employee" means an individual who has entered into or works under a contract of service or apprenticeship with an employer whether by way of manual labour, clerical work or otherwise, whether such contract is expressed or implied, oral or in writing.

(2) This Act shall not require an employer to insure—

(a) in respect of an employee of whom the employer is the husband, wife, father, mother, grandfather, grandmother, step-father, son, daughter, grandson, granddaughter, stepson, stepdaughter, brother, sister, half-brother or half-sister; or

(b) except as otherwise provided by regulations, in respect of employees not ordinarily resident in Great Britain.

---

3. Employers exempted from insurance.—(1) This Act shall not require any insurance to be effected by—

(a) any such authority as is mentioned in subsection (2) below; or

(b) any body corporate established by or under any enactment for the carrying on of any industry or part of an industry, or of any undertaking, under national ownership or control; or

(c) in relation to any such cases as may be specified in the regulations, any employer exempted by regulations.

(2) The authorities referred to in subsection (1)(a) above are

(a) a health service body, as defined in section 60(7) of the National Health Service and Community Care Act 1990, and a National Health Service trust established under Part I of that Act or the National Health Service (Scotland) Act 1978; and

(b) the Common Council of the City of London, ..., the council of a London borough, the council of a county, ... or county district in England or Wales, the Broads Authority, a regional islands or district in Scotland, any joint board or joint committee in England and Wales or joint committee in Scotland which is so constituted as to include among its members representatives of any such council ..., any joint authority established by Part IV of the Local Government Act 1985, and any police authority.

General note. Subsection (2) is amended by the National Health Service and Community Care Act 1990, s. 60, Sch. 8, Pt. I, para. 1, the Norfolk and Suffolk Broads Act 1988, s. 21, Sch. 6, para. 7, the Local Government (Scotland) Act 1973, s. 159 and the Local Government Act 1985, s. 84, Sch. 14, para. 46; and repealed in part by the Local Government Act 1985, s. 102, Sch. 17, the Local Government Act 1972, s. 272(1), Sch. 30 and by the Education Reform Act 1988, s. 237, Sch. 13, Pt I.

Modified by the Waste Regulation and Disposal (Authorities) Order 1985, S.I. 1985 No. 1884, Art. 10, Sch. 3.

---

4. Certificates of insurance.—(1) Provision may be made by regulations for securing that certificates of insurance in such form and containing such particulars as may be prescribed by the regulations, are issued by insurers to employers entering into contracts of insurance in accordance with the requirements of this Act and for the surrender in such circumstances as may be so prescribed of certificates so issued.

(2) Where a certificate of insurance is required to be issued to an employer in accordance with regulations under subsection (1) above, the employer (subject to any provision made by the regulations as to the surrender of the certificate) shall during the currency of the insurance and such further period (if any) as may be provided by regulations—

(a) comply with any regulations requiring him to display copies of the certificate of insurance for the information of his employees;

(b) produce the certificate of insurance or a copy thereof on demand to any inspector duly authorised by the Secretary of State for the purposes of this Act and produce or send the certificate or a copy thereof to such other persons, at such place and in such circumstances as may be prescribed by regulations;

(c) permit the policy of insurance or a copy thereof to be inspected by such persons and in such circumstances as may be so prescribed.

(3) A person who fails to comply with a requirement imposed by or under this section shall be liable on summary conviction to a fine not exceeding level 3 on the standard scale.

------

5. Penalty for failure to insure. An employer who on any day is not insured in accordance with this Act when required to be so shall be guilty of an offence and shall be liable on summary conviction to a fine not exceeding level 4 on the standard scale; and where an offence under this section committed by a corporation has been committed with the consent or connivance of, or facilitated by any neglect on the part of, any director, manager, secretary or other officer of the corporation, he, as well as the corporation shall be deemed to be guilty of that offence and shall be liable to be proceeded against and punished accordingly.

General note. It is arguable that s. 5 should give rise to civil liability (see *Cameron v Fraser* 1990 SLT 652), which would enable a claim to be made against officers of a company in person if the company had insufficient assets to pay compensation.

------

6. Regulations.—(1) The Secretary of State may by statutory instrument make regulations for any purpose for which regulations are authorised to be made by this Act, but any such statutory instrument shall be subject to annulment in pursuance of a resolution of either House of Parliament.

(2) Any regulations under this Act may make different provision for different cases or classes of case, and may contain such incidental and supplementary

provisions as appear to the Secretary of State to be necessary or expedient for the purposes of the regulations.

———————————————

7.   Short title, extent and commencement.—(1) This Act may be cited as the Employers' Liability (Compulsory Insurance) Act 1969.

(2) This Act shall not extend to Northern Ireland.

(3) This Act shall come into force for any purpose on such date as the Secretary of State may by order contained in a statutory instrument appoint, and the purposes for which this Act is to come into force at any time may be defined by reference to the nature of an employer's business, or to that of an employee's work, or in any other way.

———————————————

THE CONTROL OF INDUSTRIAL MAJOR ACCIDENT HAZARDS REGULATIONS 1984

(S.I. 1984 No. 1902 as amended by S.I. 1985 No. 2023, S.I. 1986 No. 294,
S.I. 1988 No. 1462 and S.I. 1990 No. 2325)

ARRANGEMENT OF REGULATIONS

The Secretary of State, being the designated Minister for the purposes of section 2(2) of the European Communities Act 1972 in relation to measures relating to the prevention and limitation of the effects of accidents arising from industrial activities involving dangerous substances, in exercise of the powers conferred on him by the said section 2 and by sections 15(1), (2), (3)(c), (5)(b) and (6)(b), 43(2), (4), (5) and (6) and 82(3)(a) of, and paragraphs 1(1)(b) and (c) and (2), 15(1) and 20 of Schedule 3 to, the Health and Safety at Work etc. Act 1974 ("the 1974 Act") and of all other powers enabling him in that behalf and for the purpose of giving effect with modifications to proposals submitted to him by the Health and Safety Commission under section 11(2)(d) of the 1974 Act after the carrying out by the said Commission of consultations in accordance with section 50(3) of that Act and after consulting the said Commission in accordance with section 50(2) thereof, hereby makes the following Regulations—

1. Citation, commencement and powers.—(1) These Regulations may be cited as the Control of Industrial Major Accident Hazards Regulations 1984 and shall come into operation—

    (a) for the purposes of Regulations 6 to 10, on 8 January 1985;

    (b) for all other purposes, on 1 April 1985.

(2) To the extent that any provision of these Regulations is within the scope of powers contained in the Health and Safety at Work etc. Act 1974, it is made solely under those powers.

2. Interpretation.—(1) In these Regulations, unless the context otherwise requires—

"the 1974 Act" means the Health and Safety at Work etc. Act 1974;

"dangerous substance" means—

    (a) any substance which satisfies any of the criteria laid down in Schedule 1 (which sets out the provisions of Annex IV to the Directive);

    (b) any substance listed in column 1 of Part I of Schedule 2 (which sets out the provisions of Annex II to the Directive) and any substance or *preparation* falling within any of the categories set out in column 1 of Part II of that Schedule; and

    (c) any substance listed in column 1 of Schedule 3 (which sets out the provisions of Annex III to the Directive);

"the Directive" means Council Directive No. 82/501/EEC "on the major-accident hazards of certain industrial activities";

"the Executive" means the Health and Safety Executive;

"further relevant information", for the purpose of Schedule 8, means information necessary for the assessment of the potential effects of a *major accident* and which in the circumstance of the case—

    (a) is reasonably required by the enquirer to assess the risks to his health and safety created by such an accident and to know and understand what action he should take in the event of an accident; and

    (b) where the information is to be disclosed by the *manufacturer*, it is reasonable for him to disclose it having regard to the requirements of law and his commercial interests;

"industrial activity" means—

    (a) an operation carried out in an industrial installation referred to in Schedule 4 (which sets out the provisions of Annex 1 to the Directive) involving, or liable to involve, one or more *dangerous substances* which—

        (i) satisfy any of the criteria laid down in Schedule 1,

       (ii) are listed in column 1 of Schedule 3, or

     (iii) both satisfy any of the criteria and are so listed as above,

        and includes on-site storage and on-site transport which is associated with that operation, unless the operation is incapable of producing a major accident hazard;

(b) any storage to which Schedule 2 applies;

"local authority" means—

    (a) for the purposes of Regulations 11 and 15—
        (i) in relation to England and Wales, a county council, [the London Fire and Civil Defence Authority, a metropolitan county fire and civil defence authority], or the Council of the Isles of Scilly, or
        (ii) in relation to Scotland, an islands or district council; and
    (b) for the purposes of Regulation 12—
        (i) in relation to England and Wales, a district council, a London borough council, the Common Council of the City of London, the sub-Treasurer of the Inner Temple, or the Under-Treasurer of the Middle Temple, or the Council of the Isles of Scilly, or
        (ii) in relation to Scotland, an islands or district council; and
    (c) for the purposes of Regulation 13, any local authority mentioned in sub-paragraph (a) or (b) above;

"major accident" means an occurrence (including in particular, a major emission, fire or explosion) resulting from uncontrolled developments in the course of an *industrial activity*, leading to a serious danger to persons, whether immediate or delayed, inside or outside an installation, or to the environment, and involving one or more *dangerous substances*;

"manufacturer" means a person having control of an industrial activity;

"preparation" means a mixture or solution of two or more substances;

"site" means—

    (a) the whole of an area of land under the control of a manufacturer and includes a pier, jetty or similar structure, whether floating or not, or
    (b) a structure, whether floating or not, which is within the inland waters of Great Britain and which is under the control of a manufacturer.

(2) In these Regulations, unless the context otherwise requires any reference to—

    (a) a numbered Regulation or Schedule is a reference to the Regulation or Schedule in these Regulations so numbered; and
    (b) a numbered paragraph is a reference to the paragraph so numbered in the Regulation or Schedule in which that reference appears.

3. Application of these Regulations.—(1) These Regulations shall apply to any *industrial activity* except an *industrial activity* which is carried on at—

    (a) a nuclear installation within the meaning of section 44(8) of the *1974 Act*;
    (b) an installation which is under the control of—
        (i) the Secretary of State for the purposes of the Ministry of Defence, or
        (ii) a headquarters or organisation designated for the purposes of the International Headquarters and Defence Organisations Act 1964 or of the service authorities of a visiting force within the meaning of any of the provisions of Part I of the Visiting Forces Act 1952;
    (c) a factory, magazine or store licensed under the Explosives Act 1875;
    (d) a mine or a quarry within the meaning of section 180 of the Mines and Quarries Act 1954;

(e)　a *site* operated by a disposal authority in accordance with section 11(2) of the Control of Pollution Act 1974 or for which a licence issued in pursuance of section 5 of that Act is in force.

(2)　These regulations shall not apply to Northern Ireland.

4.　Demonstration of safe operation.—(1)　This Regulation shall apply to—

(a)　an *industrial activity* to which sub-paragraph (a) of the definition of *industrial activity* in Regulation 2(1) applies and in which a substance which satisfies any of the criteria laid down in Schedule 1 is involved or is liable to be involved; and

(b)　an *industrial activity* to which sub-paragraph (b) of that definition applies and in which there is involved, or liable to be involved—

　　(i)　for a substance specified in column 1 of Part I of Schedule 2, a quantity of that substance which is equal to or more than the quantity specified in the entry for that substance in column 2 of that Part;

　　(ii)　for substances and *preparations* falling within a category or categories specified in an entry in column 1 of Part II of Schedule 2, a total quantity of such substances and *preparations* in the category or categories in that entry which is equal to or more than the quantity for that entry specified in column 2 of that Part.

(2)　A *manufacturer* who has control of an *industrial activity* to which this Regulation applies shall at any time provide evidence including documents to show that he has—

(a)　identified the *major accident* hazards; and

(b)　taken adequate steps to—

　　(i)　prevent such *major accidents* and to limit their consequences to persons and the environment, and

　　(ii)　provide persons working on the site with the information, training and equipment necessary to ensure their safety.

5.　Notification of major accidents.—(1)　Where a *major accident* occurs on a *site*, the *manufacturer* shall forthwith notify the *Executive* of that accident and the *Executive* shall obtain from the *manufacturer* who made that notification—

(a)　the following information relating to the accident as soon as it becomes available—

　　(i)　the circumstances of the accident,

　　(ii)　the *dangerous substances* involved,

　　(iii)　the data available for assessing the effects of the accident on persons and the environment,

　　(iv)　the emergency measures taken; and

(b)　a statement of the steps envisaged—

　　(i)　to alleviate medium or long term effects of the accident, if any, and

　　(ii)　to prevent the recurrence of such an accident.

(2)　In such a case, the *Executive* shall—

(a)　collect, where possible, the information necessary for a full analysis of the *major accident*; and

(b) send to the European Commission the information specified in Schedule 5 (which sets out the provisions of Annex VI to the Directive).

(3) Where a *manufacturer* has notified a *major accident* to the Executive in accordance with the requirements of the Reporting of Injuries, Diseases and Dangerous Occurrences Regulations 1985, he shall be deemed to have complied with the requirement to notify that accident under paragraph (1) of this Regulation.

6. *Industrial activities* to which Regulations 7 to 12 apply.—(1) Regulations 7 to 12 shall apply to—

(a) an *industrial activity* to which sub-paragraph (a) of the definition of *industrial activity* in Regulation 2(1) applies and in which there is involved, or liable to be involved, a substance listed in column 1 of Schedule 3 in a quantity which is equal to or more than the quantity specified in the entry for that substance in column 2 of that Schedule; and

(b) an *industrial activity* to which sub-paragraph (b) of that definition applies and in which there is involved, or liable to be involved—

   (i) for a substance specified in column 1 of Part I of Schedule 2, a quantity of that substance which is equal to or more than the quantity specified in the entry for that substance in column 3 of that Part;

   (ii) for substances and *preparations* falling within a category or categories specified in an entry in column 1 of Part II of Schedule 2, a total quantity of such substances and *preparations* in the category or categories in that entry which is equal to or more than the quantity for that entry specified in column 3 of that Part.

(2) For the purposes of Regulations 7 to 11—

(a) a "new industrial activity" means an *industrial activity* which—

   (i) was commenced after the date of the coming into operation of this Regulation *(a)*, or

   (ii) if commenced before that date, is an *industrial activity* in which there has been since that date a modification which would be likely to have important implications for major accident hazards, and that activity shall be deemed to have been commenced on the date on which the change was made;

(b) an "existing industrial activity" means an *industrial activity* which is not a new *industrial activity*.

*(a) **Coming into operation of this Regulation.*** By the Control of Industrial Major Accident Hazards (Amendment) Regulations 1990, S.I. 1990 No. 2325, reg. 4, Sch. 6, para. 1, where an industrial activity becomes subject to regs. 7 to 11 of these Regulations in consequence of an amendment made by S.I. 1990 No. 2325, reg. 3, reference in reg. 6(2) to the coming into force of this regulation is construed as a reference to the coming into force of S.I. 1990 No. 2325.

7. Reports on industrial activities.—(1) Subject to the following paragraphs of this Regulation, a *manufacturer* shall not undertake any *industrial activity* to which this Regulation applies, unless he has prepared a written report containing the information specified in Schedule 6 and has sent a copy of that report to the *Executive* at least 3 months before commencing that activity or before such shorter time as the *Executive* may agree in writing.

(2) In the case of a new *industrial activity* which a *manufacturer* commences, or by virtue of Regulation 6(2)(a)(ii) is deemed to commence, within 6 months after the date of the coming into operation of these Regulations, it shall be a sufficient compliance with paragraph (1) if the *manufacturer* sends to the *Executive* a copy of the report required in accordance with that paragraph within 3 months after the coming into operation of the Regulations *(a)* or within such longer time as the *Executive* may agree in writing.

(3) In the case of an existing *industrial activity*, until 8 July 1989 [1 June 1994] it shall be a sufficient compliance with paragraph (1) if the *manufacturer* on or before 1 April 1985 [31 March 1991] sends to the *Executive* the information specified in Schedule 7 relating to that activity, except that nothing in this paragraph shall require a *manufacturer* to provide information which he has already provided by a notification made in accordance with the Notification of Installations Handling Hazardous Substances Regulations 1982.

(4) Where paragraph (3) applies, the *Executive* may, by a certificate in writing (which it may revoke in writing at any time), exempt, either unconditionally or subject to conditions, any *manufacturer* or class of manufacturers from the requirement in paragraph (1) to send to the *Executive* a copy of the report required under that paragraph.

(a) Coming into operation of the Regulation. By the Control of Industrial Major Accident Hazards (Amendments) Regulations 1990, S.I. 1990 No. 2325, reg. 4, Sch. 6, paras. 1 and 2, where an industrial activity becomes subject to regs. 7 to 11 of these Regulations in consequence of an amendment made by S.I. 1990 No. 2325, reg. 3, reference in reg. 7(2) to the coming into force of these Regulations shall be construed as a reference to the coming into force of S.I. 1990 No. 2325, and the words "or within such longer time as the Executive may agree in writing" shall not apply, and in reg. 7(3) the dates in square brackets shall be substituted for the existing dates.

8. Updating of reports under Regulation 7.—(1) Where a *manufacturer* has made a report in accordance with Regulation 7(1), he shall not make any modification to the *industrial activity* to which that report relates which could materially affect the particulars in that report, unless he has made a further report to take account of those changes and has sent a copy of that report to the *Executive* at least 3 months before making those changes or before such shorter time as the *Executive* may agree in writing.

(2) Where a *manufacturer* has made a report in accordance with Regulation 7(1), paragraph (1) of this Regulation or this paragraph, and that *industrial activity* is continuing, the *manufacturer* shall within three years of the date of the last such report, make a further report which shall have regard in particular to

new technical knowledge which materially affects the particulars in the previous report relating to safety and developments in the knowledge of hazard assessment, and shall within one month, or in such longer time as the *Executive* may agree, send a copy of the report to the *Executive.*

(3) A certificate of exemption issued under Regulation 7(4), shall apply to reports or declarations made under this Regulation as it applies to reports made under Regulation 7(1).

9. Requirement for further information to be sent to the *Executive.*— (1) Where, in accordance with Regulation 7(1), a *manufacturer* has sent a report relating to an *industrial activity* to the *Executive*, the *Executive* may, by a notice served on the *manufacturer*, require him to provide such additional information as is specified in the notice and the *manufacturer* shall send that information to the *Executive* within such time as is specified in the notice or within such longer time as the *Executive* may subsequently agree.

(2) The *Executive* shall not serve a notice under paragraph (1) unless, having regard to all the circumstances of the particular case, the information is reasonably required for the evaluation of the major accident hazards created by the activity.

(3) It shall be a defence in proceedings against any person for an offence consisting of a contravention of paragraph (1), for that person to prove that, at the time the proceedings were commenced—

(a) an improvement notice under section 21 of the 1974 Act relating to the contravention had not been served on him; or
(b) if such a notice has been served on him—
   (i) the period for compliance had not expired, or
   (ii) he had appealed against the notice and that appeal had not been dismissed or withdrawn.

10. Preparation of on-site emergency plan by the *manufacturer.*—(1) A *manufacturer* who has control of *industrial activity* to which this Regulation applies shall, after consulting such persons as appear to him to be appropriate, prepare and keep up to date an adequate on-site emergency plan detailing how major accidents will be dealt with on the site on which the industrial activity is carried on and that plan shall include the name of the person who is responsible for safety on the site and the names of those who are authorised to take action in accordance with the plan in the case of an emergency.

(2) The *manufacturer* shall ensure that the emergency plan prepared in accordance with paragraph (1) takes into account any material changes made in the *industrial activity* and that every person on the site who is affected by the plan is informed of its relevant provisions.

(3) The *manufacturer* shall prepare the emergency plan required under paragraph (1)—

(a) in the case of a new *industrial activity*, before that activity is commenced, except that, in the case of a new *industrial activity* which is commenced or is deemed to have been commenced before a date 3 months after the coming into operation of the Regulations *(a)*, by that date; or

(b) in the case of an existing *industrial activity* by 1 April 1985 [31 March 1991].

(a) **Coming into operation of the Regulations.** By the Control of Industrial Major Accident Hazards (Amendments) Regulations 1990, S.I. 1990 No. 2325, reg. 4, Sch. 6, paras. 1 and 3, where an industrial activity becomes subject to regs. 7 to 11 of these Regulations in consequence of an amendment made by S.I. 1990 No. 2325, reg. 3, reference in reg. 10(3) to the coming into force of these Regulations shall be construed as a reference to the coming into force of S.I. 1990 No. 2325, and in reg. 10(3)(b) the date in square brackets shall be substituted for the existing date.

11.   Preparation of off-site emergency plan by the *local authority.*—(1) It shall be the duty of the *local authority*, in whose area there is a *site* on which a *manufacturer* carries on an *industrial activity* to which this Regulation applies, to prepare and keep up to date an adequate off-site emergency plan detailing how emergencies relating to a possible major accident on that site will be dealt with and in preparing that plan the authority shall consult the *manufacturer*, the *Executive* and such other persons as appear to the authority to be appropriate.

(2) For the purpose of enabling the *local authority* to prepare the emergency plan required under paragraph (1), the *manufacturer* shall provide the authority with such information relating to the *industrial activity* under his control as the authority may reasonably require, including the nature, extent and likely effects off-site of possible *major accidents* and the authority shall provide the *manufacturer* with any information from the off-site emergency plan which relates to his duties under Regulation 10 or this paragraph.

(3) The *local authority* shall prepare its emergency plan for any *industrial activity* before that activity is commenced, except that in the case of an existing *industrial activity* or a new *industrial activity* commenced or deemed to have been commenced before 1 October 1985 [30 September 1991], it shall be a sufficient compliance with this Regulation if the *local authority* prepares its emergency plan by that date *(a)* or in any case within six months of its being notified by the *Executive* or the *industrial activity*, whichever is the later.

(a) **That date.** By the Control of Industrial Major Accident Hazards (Amendment) Regulations 1990, S.I. 1990 No. 2325, reg. 4, Sch. 6, para. 3, where an industrial activity becomes subject to regs. 7 to 11 of these Regulations in consequence of an amendment made by S.I. 1990 No. 2325, reg. 3, in reg. 11(3) the date in square brackets shall be substituted for the existing date.

12.   Information to the public.—(1) It shall be the duty of a *manufacturer* who has control of an *industrial activity* to which this Regulation applies to—

(a)   ensure that persons outside the *site* who are likely to be in an area in which, in the opinion of the *Executive*, they are liable to be affected by a *major accident* occurring at the *site* are supplied, in an appropriate manner, without their having to request it, with at least the information specified in Schedule 8 (which sets out the provisions of Annex VII to *the Directive*); and

(b)   make that information publicly available.

(2) In preparing the information required to be supplied in accordance with paragraph (1), the *manufacturer* shall consult the *local authority* in whose area the *industrial activity* is situated and such other persons who seem to him to be appropriate, but the *manufacturer* shall remain responsible for the accuracy, completeness and form of the information so supplied.

(3) Without prejudice to his duty under paragraph (1), the *manufacturer* shall endeavour to enter into an agreement with the *local authority* in whose area the *industrial activity* is situated for that *local authority* to disseminate the information required to be supplied in accordance with that paragraph to the persons mentioned in it.

(4) The *manufacturer* shall ensure that the information supplied in accordance with paragraph (1) is updated and supplied again in accordance with that paragraph at appropriate intervals and made publicly available.

(5) The *manufacturer* shall take the steps necessary to comply with paragraphs (1) to (3) before the *industrial activity* is commenced, except that, in the case of an *industrial activity* commenced before 31 December 1991, it shall be a sufficient compliance with those paragraphs if the *manufacturer* takes the necessary steps by that date.

13. Disclosure of information notified under these Regulations.—(1) Subject to Regulation 5(2)(b) and paragraph (2) of this Regulation, in so far as any provision of Regulations 5 and 7 to 12 is made under section 2(2) of the European Communities Act 1972, information notified to the *Executive* or a *local authority* under that provision shall be treated as relevant information for the purposes of section 28 of the *1974 Act* (which imposes restrictions on the disclosure of information).

(2) Where for the purpose of evaluating information notified under Regulation 5 or Regulations 7 to 12, the *Executive* or a *local authority* discloses that information to some other person, that other person shall not use that information for any purpose except a purpose of the *Executive* or the *local authority* disclosing it, as the case may be, and before disclosing that information the *Executive* or the *local authority*, as the case may be, shall inform that other person of his obligations under this paragraph.

14. Enforcement.—(1) In so far as any provision of these Regulations is made under section 2(2) of the European Communities Act 1972, that provision shall be enforced as if it were a health and safety regulation made under section 15 of the *1974 Act*, and the provisions of the *1974 Act* (including the provisions relating to the approval of codes of practice and the use of approved codes of practice in criminal proceedings) and any health and safety regulation made under it, shall apply to that provision as they apply to health and safety regulations.

(2) Notwithstanding Regulation 3 of the Health and Safety (Enforcing Authority) Regulations 1989 (S.I. 1989 No. 1903) and Regulation 2(1) and (3) of the Petroleum (Consolidation) Act 1928 (Enforcement) Regulations 1979, the enforcing authority for the relevant statutory provisions in relation to any industrial activity to which Regulations 7 to 12 of these Regulations apply shall be the *Executive*.

15.   Charge by the local authority for off-site emergency plan.—(1) A *local authority* which prepares or keeps up to date an off-site emergency plan in pursuance of the duty imposed on it by Regulation 11(1) may charge a fee, determined in accordance with paragraphs (2) to (4), to any *manufacturer* having control of a site to which the plan relates.

(2) The fee shall not exceed the sum of the costs reasonably incurred by the *local authority* in preparing or keeping up to date the off-site emergency plan and, where the plan covers *sites* under the control of different manufacturers, the fee charged to each manufacturer shall not exceed the proportion of such sum attributable to the part or parts of the plan relating to the *site* or *sites* under his control.

(3) In determining the fee no account shall be taken of costs other than the costs of preparing or keeping up to date those parts of the plan which relate to the protection of the health or safety of persons and which were costs incurred after the coming into operation of Regulation 11(1).

(4) The *local authority* may determine the cost of employing a graded officer for any period on work appropriate to his grade by reference to the average cost to it of employing officers of his grade for that period.

(5) When requiring payment the *local authority* shall send or give to the *manufacturer* a detailed statement of the work done and costs incurred including the dates of any *site* visits and the period to which the statement relates; and the fee, which shall be recoverable only as a civil debt, shall become payable one month after the statement has been sent or given.

SCHEDULE 1

Regulations 2(1) and 4(1)

(WHICH SETS OUT THE PROVISIONS OF ANNEX IV TO THE DIRECTIVE)

INDICATIVE CRITERIA

(a) Very toxic substances:

    — substances which correspond to the first line of the table below,

    — substances which correspond to the second line of the table below and which, owing to their physical and chemical properties, are capable of producing *major accident* hazards similar to those caused by the substance mentioned in the first line:

	LD50 (oral)[1] mg/kg body weight	LD50 (cutaneous)[2] mg/kg body weight	LC50[3] mg/1 (inhalation)
1	LD50≤5	LD50≤10	LC50≤0·1
2	5<LD50≤25	10<LD50≤50	0·1<LC50≤0·5

[1] LD50 oral in rats.
[2] LD50 cutaneous in rats or rabbits.
[3] LC50 inhalation (four hours) in rats.

(b) Other toxic substances:

    The substances showing the following values of acute toxicity and having physical and chemical properties capable of producing *major accident* hazards:

LD50 (oral) [1] mg/kg body weight	LD50 (cutaneous) [2] mg/kg body weight	LC50 [3] mg/1 (inhalation)
25<LD50≤200	50<LD50≤400	0·5<LC50≤2

[1] LD50 oral in rats.
[2] LD50 cutaneous in rats or rabbits.
[3] LC50 by inhalation (four hours) in rats.

(c) Flammable substances:

    (i) flammable gases:
        substances which in the gaseous state at normal pressure and mixed with air become flammable and the boiling point of which at normal pressure is 20°C or below;
    (ii) highly flammable liquids:
        substances which have a flash point lower than 21°C and the boiling point of which at normal pressure is above 20°C;
    (iii) flammable liquids:
        substances which have a flash point lower than 55°C and which remain liquid under pressure, where particular processing conditions, such as high pressure and high temperature, may create major accident hazards.

(d) Explosive substances:
substances which may explode under the effect of flame or which are more sensitive to shocks or friction than dinitrobenzene.

(e) Oxidizing substances:
substances which give rise to highly exothermic reaction when in contact with other substances, particularly flammable substances.

SCHEDULE 2
Regulations 2(1), 4(1) and 6(1)

(WHICH SETS OUT THE PROVISIONS OF ANNEX II TO THE DIRECTIVE)

STORAGE OTHER THAN OF SUBSTANCES LISTED IN SCHEDULE 3 ASSOCIATED WITH AN INSTALLATION REFERRED TO IN SCHEDULE 4

This Schedule applies to storage of *dangerous substances* and/or *preparations* at any place, installation, premises, building, or area of land, isolated or within an establishment, being a *site* used for the purpose of storage, except where that storage is associated with an installation covered by Schedule 4 and where the substances in question appear in Schedule 3.

The quantities set out below in Parts I and II relate to each store or group of stores belonging to the same *manufacturer* where the distance between the stores is not sufficient to avoid, in foreseeable circumstances, any aggravation of *major accident* hazards. These quantities apply in any case to each group of stores belonging to the same *manufacturer* where the distance between the stores is less than 500 metres.

The quantities to be considered are the maximum quantities which are, or are liable to be, in storage at any one time.

PART I
NAMED SUBSTANCES

Where a substance (or a group of substances) listed in Part I also falls within a category of Part II the quantities set out in Part I shall be used.

Substances or groups of substances (Column 1)	Quantities (tonnes)	
	For application of Regulation 4 (Column 2)	For application of Regulations 7 to 12 (Column 3)
Acetylene	5	50
Acrolein (2-propenal)	20	200
Acrylonitrile	20	200
Ammonia	50	500
Ammonium nitrate *(a)*	350	2,500
Ammonium nitrate in the form of fertilisers *(b)*	1,250	10,000
Bromine	50	500
Carbon disulphide	20	200
Chlorine	10	75
Diphenyl methane di-isocyanate (MDI)	20	200
Ethylene dibromide (1,2 Dibromoethane)	5	50
Ethylene oxide	5	50
Formaldehyde (concentration $\geqslant$90%)	5	50
Hydrogen	5	50
Hydrogen chloride (liquefied gas)	25	250
Hydrogen cyanide	5	20
Hydrogen fluoride	5	50
Hydrogen sulphide	5	50
Methyl bromide (Bromomethane)	20	200
Methyl isocyanate	0.15 (150 kilograms)	0.15 (150 kilograms)
Oxygen	200	2,000
Phosgene (Carbonyl chloride)	0.75 (750 kilograms)	0.75 (750 kilograms)
Propylene oxide	5	50
Sodium chlorate	25	250
Sulphur dioxide	25	250
Sulphur trioxide	15	100
Tetraethyl lead or tetramethyl lead	5	50
Toluene di-isocyanate (TDI)	10	100

(a) This applies to ammonium nitrate and mixtures of ammonium nitrate where the nitrogen content derived from the ammonium nitrate is >28% by weight and to aqueous solutions of ammonium nitrate where the concentration of ammonium nitrate is >90% by weight.

(b) This applies to straight ammonium nitrate fertilisers which comply with Council Directive 80/876/EEC "on the approximation of laws of the Member States relating to straight ammonium nitrate fertilisers of high nitrogen content" and to compound fertilisers where the nitrogen content derived from the ammonium nitrate is >28% by weight (a compound fertiliser contains ammonium nitrate together with phospahte and/or potash).

PART II

CATEGORIES OF SUBSTANCES AND *PREPARATIONS* NOT SPECIFICALLY NAMED IN PART I

The quantities of different substances and *preparations* of the same category are cumulative. Where there is more than one category specified in the same entry, the quantities of all substances and *preparations* of the specified categories in that entry shall be summed up.

Categories of substances and preparations (Column 1)	Quantities (tonnes)	
	For application of Regulation 4 (Column 2)	For application of Regulations 7 to 12 (Column 3)
1. Substances and *preparations* that are classified as "very toxic"	5	20
2. Substances and *preparations* that are classified as "very toxic", "toxic" *(a)*, "oxidising" or "explosive"	10	200
3. Gaseous substances and *preparations* including those in liquefied form, which are gaseous at normal pressure and which are classified as "highly flammable" *(b)*	50	200
4. Substances and *preparations* (excluding gaseous substances and *preparations* covered under item 3 above) which are classified as "highly flammable" or "extremely flammable" *(c)*	5,000	50,000

Substances and *preparations* shall be assigned categories in accordance with the classification provided for by regulation 5 of the Classification, Packaging and Labelling of Dangerous Substances Regulations 1984 (S.I. 1984/1244, amended by S.I. 1986/1922, 1988/766, 1989/2208 and 1990/1255) whether or not the substance or *preparation* is required to be classified for the purposes of those Regulations, or, in the case of a pesticide approved under the Food and Environment Protection Act 1985 (c. 48), in accordance with the classification assigned to it by that approval.

(a) Where the substances and *preparations* are in a state which gives them properties capable of producing a *major accident* hazard.

(b) This includes flammable gases as defined in paragraph (c)(i) of Schedule 1.

(c) This includes highly flammable liquids as defined in paragraph (c)(ii) of Schedule 1.

SCHEDULE 3

Regulations 2(1) and 6(1)

(WHICH SETS OUT THE PROVISIONS OF ANNEX III TO THE DIRECTIVE)

LIST OF SUBSTANCES FOR THE APPLICATION OF REGULATIONS 7 TO 12

The quantities set out below relate to each installation or group of installations belonging to the same *manufacturer* where the distance between the installations is not sufficient to avoid, in foreseeable circumstances, any aggravation of *major accident* hazards. These quantities apply in any case to each group of installations belonging to the same *manufacturer* where the distance between the installations is less than 500 metres.

Substance (Column 1)	Quantity (for application of Regulations 7–12) (Column 2)	CAS Number (Column 3)	EEC Number (Column 4)
Group 1—Toxic substances *(quantity ⩽ 1 tonne)*			
Aldicarb	100 kilograms	116-06-3	006-017-00-X
4-Aminodiphenyl	1 kilogram	92-67-1	
Amiton	1 kilogram	78-53-5	
Anabasine	100 kilograms	494-52-0	
Arsenic pentoxide, Arsenic (V) acid and salts	500 kilograms		
Arsenic trioxide, Arsenious (III) acid and salts	100 kilograms		
Arsine (Arsenic hydride)	10 kilograms	7784-42-1	
Azinphos-ethyl	100 kilograms	2642-71-9	051-056-00-1
Azinphos-methyl	100 kilograms	86-50-0	015-039-00-9
Benzidine	1 kilogram	92-87-5	612-042-00-2
Benzidine salts	1 kilogram		
Beryllium (powders, compounds)	10 kilograms		
Bis(2-chloroethyl) sulphide	1 kilogram	505-60-2	
Bis(chloromethyl) ether	1 kilogram	542-88-1	603-046-00-5
Carbofuran	100 kilograms	1563-66-2	006-026-00-9
Carbophenothion	100 kilograms	786-19-6	015-044-00-6
Chlorfenvinphos	100 kilograms	470-90-6	015-071-00-3
4-(Chloroformyl) morpholine	1 kilogram	15159-40-7	
Chloromethyl methyl ether	1 kilogram	107-30-2	
Cobalt metal, oxide, carbonates, sulphides, as powders	1 tonne		
Crimidine	100 kilograms	535-89-7	613-004-00-8
Cyanthoate	100 kilograms	3734-95-0	015-070-00-8
Cycloheximide	100 kilograms	66-81-9	
Demeton	100 kilograms	8065-48-3	
Dialifos	100 kilograms	10311-84-9	015-088-00-6
OO-Diethyl *S*-ethyl-sulphinylmethyl phosphorothioate	100 kilograms	2588-05-8	
OO-Diethyl *S*-ethyl-sylphonylmethyl phosphorothioate	100 kilograms	2588-06-9	
OO-Diethyl *S*-ethyl-thiomethyl phosphorothioate	100 kilograms	2600-69-3	
OO-Diethyl *S*-iso-propylthiomethyl phosphorodithioate	100 kilograms	78-52-4	
OO-Diethyl *S*-pro-pylthiomethyl phosphorodithioate	100 kilograms	3309-68-0	
Dimefox	100 kilograms	115-26-4	015-061-00-9
Dimethylcarbamoyl chloride	1 kilogram	79-44-7	
Dimethylnitrosamine	1 kilogram	62-75-9	
Dimethyl phospho-ramidocyanidic acid	1 tonne	63917-41-9	

Substance (Column 1)	Quantity (for application of Regulations 7–12) (Column 2)	CAS Number (Column 3)	EEC Number (Column 4)
Diphacinone	100 kilograms	82-66-6	
Disulfoton	100 kilograms	298-04-4	015-060-00-3
EPN	100 kilograms	2104-64-5	015-036-00-2
Ethion	100 kilograms	563-12-2	015-047-00-2
Fensulfothion	100 kilograms	115-90-2	015-090-00-7
Fluenetil	100 kilograms	4301-50-2	607-078-00-0
Fluoroacetic acid	1 kilogram	144-49-0	607-081-00-7
Fluoroacetic acid, salts	1 kilogram		
Fluoroacetic acid, esters	1 kilogram		
Fluoroacetic acid, amides	1 kilogram		
4-Fluorobutyric acid	1 kilogram	462-23-7	
4-Fluorobutyric acid, salts	1 kilogram		
4-Fluorobutyric acid, esters	1 kilogram		
4-Fluorobutyric acid, amides	1 kilogram		
4-Fluorocrotonitic acid	1 kilogram	37759-72-1	
4-Fluorocrotonitic acid, salts	1 kilogram		
4-Fluorocrotonitic acid, esters	1 kilogram		
4-Fluorocrotonitic acid, amides	1 kilogram		
4-Fluoro-2-hydroxybutyric acid	1 kilogram		
4-Fluoro-2-hydroxybutyric acid, salts	1 kilogram		
4-Fluoro-2-hydroxybutyric acid, esters	1 kilogram		
4-Fluoro-2-hydroxybutyric acid, amides	1 kilogram		
Glycolonitrile (Hydroxyacetonitrile)	100 kilograms	107-16-4	
1,2,3,7,8,9-Hexachlorodibenzo-*p*-dioxin	100 kilograms	19408-74-3	
Hexamethylphosphoramide	1 kilogram	680-31-9	
Hydrogen selenide	10 kilograms	7783-07-5	
Isobenzan	100 kilograms	297-78-9	602-053-00-0
Isodrin	100 kilograms	465-73-6	'602-050-00-4
Juglone (5-Hydroxynaphthalene-1,4-dione)	100 kilograms	481-39-0	
4,4'-Methylenebis(2-chloroaniline)	10 kilograms	101-14-4	
Methylisocyanate	150 kilograms	624-83-9	615-001-00-7
Mevinphos	100 kilograms	7786-34-7	015-020-00-5
2-Naphthylamine	1 kilogram	91-59-8	612-022-00-3
Nickel metal, oxides, carbonates, sulphides, as powders	1 tonne		
Nickel tetracarbonyl	10 kilograms	13463-39-3	028-001-00-1
Oxydisulfoton	100 kilograms	2497-07-6	015-096-00-X
Oxygen difluoride	10 kilograms	7783-41-7	
Paraoxon (Diethyl 4-nitrophenyl phosphate)	100 kilograms	311-45-5	

Substance (Column 1)	Quantity (for application of Regulations 7–12) (Column 2)	CAS Number (Column 3)	EEC Number (Column 4)
Parathion	100 kilograms	56-38-2	015-034-00-1
Parathion-methyl	100 kilograms	298-00-0	015-035-00-7
Pentaborane	100 kilograms	19624-22-7	
Phorate	100 kilograms	298-02-2	015-033-00-6
Phosacetim	100 kilograms	4104-14-7	015-092-00-8
Phosgene (Carbonyl chloride)	750 kilograms	75-44-5	006-002-00-8
Phosphamidon	100 kilograms	13171-21-6	015-022-00-6
Phosphine (Hydrogen phosphide)	100 kilograms	7803-51-2	
Promurit (1-(3,4-Dichloro-phenyl)-3-triazen-ethiocarboxamide)	100 kilograms	5836-73-7	
1,3-Propanesultone	1 kilogram	1120-71-4	
1-Propen-2-chloro-1,3-diol diacetate	10 kilograms	10118-72-6	
Pyrazoxon	100 kilograms	108-34-9	015-23-00-1
Selenium hexafluoride	10 kilograms	7783-79-1	
Sodium selenite	100 kilograms	10102-18-8	034-002-00-8
Stibine (Antimony hydride)	100 kilograms	7803-52-3	
Sulfotep	100 kilograms	3689-24-5	015-027-00-3
Sulphur dichloride	1 tonne	10545-99-0	016-013-00-X
Tellurium hexafluoride	100 kilograms	7783-80-4	
TEPP	100 kilograms	107-49-3	015-025-00-2
2,3,7,8-Tetrachlorodibenzo-*p*-dioxin (TCDD)	1 kilogram	1746-01-6	
Tetramethylene-disulphotetramine	1 kilogram	80-12-6	
Thionazin	100 kilograms	297-97-2	
Tirpate (2,4-Dimethyl-1-3-dithiolane-2-carboxaldehyde *O*-methyl-carbamoyloxime)	100 kilograms	26419-73-8	
Trichloromethanesulphenyl-chloride	100 kilograms	594-42-3	
1-Tri(cyclohexyl)stannyl-1*H*-1,2,4-triazole	100 kilograms	41083-11-8	
Triethylenemelamine	10 kilograms	51-18-3	
Warfarin	100 kilograms	81-81-2	607-056-00-0
Group 2—Toxic substances (quantity > 1 tonne)			
Acetone cyanohydrin (2-Cyanopropan-2-ol)	200 tonnes	75-86-5	608-004-00-X
Acrolein (2-Propenal)	200 tonnes	107-02-8	605-008-00-3
Acrylonitrile	200 tonnes	107-13-1	608-003-00-4
Allyl alcohol (2-Propen-1-01)	200 tonnes	107-18-6	603-015-00-6
Allylamine	200 tonnes	107-11-9	612-046-00-4
Ammonia	500 tonnes	7664-41-7	007-001-00-5
Bromine	500 tonnes	7726-95-6	035-001-00-5

Substance (Column 1)	Quantity (for application of Regulations 7–12) (Column 2)	CAS Number (Column 3)	EEC Number (Column 4)
Carbon disulphide	200 tonnes	75-15-0	006-033-00-3
Chlorine	25 tonnes	7782-50-5	017-001-00-7
Ethylene dibromide (1,2-Dibromoethane)	50 tonnes	106-93-4	602-010-00-6
Ethyleneimine	50 tonnes	151-56-4	613-001-00-1
Formaldehyde (concentration ≥90%)	50 tonnes	50-00-0	605-001-01-2
Hydrogen chloride (liquefied gas)	250 tonnes	7647-01-0	017-002-00-2
Hydrogen cyanide	20 tonnes	74-90-8	006-006-00-X
Hydrogen fluoride	50 tonnes	7664-39-3	009-002-00-6
Hydrogen sulphide	50 tonnes	7783-06-4	016-001-00-4
Methyl bromide (Bromomethane)	200 tonnes	74-83-9	602-002-00-3
Nitrogen oxides	50 tonnes	11104-93-1	
Propyleneimine	50 tonnes	75-55-8	
Sulphur dioxide	250 tonnes	7446-09-5	016-011-00-9
Sulphur trioxide	75 tonnes	7446-11-9	
Tetraethyl lead	50 tonnes	78-00-2	
Tetramethyl lead	50 tonnes	75-74-1	

Group 3—Highly reactive substances

Substance (Column 1)	Quantity (for application of Regulations 7–12) (Column 2)	CAS Number (Column 3)	EEC Number (Column 4)
Acetylene (Ethyne)	50 tonnes	74-86-2	601-015-00-0
Ammonium nitrate **(a)**	2,500 tonnes	6484-52-2	
Ammonium nitrate in the form of fertilisers *(b)*	5,000 tonnes		
2,2Bis(*tert*-butylperoxy)butane (concentration ≥70%)	50 tonnes	2167-23-9	
1,1-Bis(*tert*-butyl peroxy) cyclohexane (concentration ≥80%)	50 tonnes	3006-86-8	
tert-Butyl peroxyacetate (concentration ≥70%)	50 tonnes	107-71-1	
tert-Butyl peroxyisobutyrate (concentration ≥80%)	50 tonnes	109-13-7	
tert-Butyl peroxy isopropyl carbonate (concentration ≥80%)	50 tonnes	2372-21-6	
tert-Butyl peroxymaleate (concentration ≥80%)	50 tonnes	1931-62-0	
tert-Butyl peroxypivalate (concentration ≥77%)	50 tonnes	927-07-1	
Dibenzyl peroxycarbonate (concentration ≥90%)	50 tonnes	2144-45-8	
Di-*sec*-butyl peroxydicarbonate (concentration ≥80%)	50 tonnes	19910-65-7	
Diethyl peroxydicarbonate (concentration ≥30%)	50 tonnes	14666-78-5	

Substance (Column 1)	Quantity (for application of Regulations 7–12) (Column 2)	CAS Number (Column 3)	EEC Number (Column 4)
2,2-Dihydroperoxypropane (concentration ≥30%)	50 tonnes	2614-76-8	
Di-isobutyryl peroxide (concentration ≥50%)	50 tonnes	3437-84-1	
Di-*n*-propyl peroxydicarbonate (concentration ≥80%)	50 tonnes	16066-38-9	
Ethylene oxide	50 tonnes	75-21-8	603-023-00-X
Ethyl nitrate	50 tonnes	625-58-1	007-007-00-8
3,3,6,6,9,9-Hexamethyl-1,2,4,5-tetroxacyclononane (concentration ≥75%)	50 tonnes	22397-33-7	
Hydrogen	50 tonnes	1333-74-0	001-001-00-9
Liquid oxygen	2,000 tonnes	7782-44-7	008-001-00-8
Methyl ethyl ketone peroxide (concentration ≥60%)	50 tonnes	1338-23-4	
Methyl isobutyl ketone peroxide (concentration ≥60%)	50 tonnes	37206-20-5	
Peracetic acid (concentration ≥60%)	50 tonnes	79-21-0	607-094-00-8
Propylene oxide	50 tonnes	75-56-9	603-055-00-4
Sodium chlorate	250 tonnes	7775-09-9	017-005-00-9
Group 4—Explosive substances			
Barium azide	50 tonnes	18810-58-7	
Bis(2,4,6-trinitrophenyl)-amine	50 tonnes	131-73-7	612-018-00-1
Chloronitrobenzene	50 tonnes	28260-61-9	610-004-00-X
Cellulose nitrate (containing >12.6% nitrogen)	100 tonnes	9004-70-0	603-037-00-6
Cyclotetramethylenetetranitramine	50 tonnes	2691-41-0	
Cyclotrimethylenetrinitramine	50 tonnes	121-82-4	
Diazodinitrophenol	10 tonnes	7008-81-3	
Diethylene glycol dinitrate	10 tonnes	693-21-0	603-033-00-4
Dinitrophenol, salts	50 tonnes		609-017-00-3
Ethylene glycol dinitrate	10 tonnes	628-96-6	603-032-00-9
1-Guanyl-4-nitrosaminoguanyl-1-tetrazene	10 tonnes	109-27-3	
2,2',4,4',6,6'/Hexanitrostilbene	50 tonnes	20062-22-0	
Hydrazine nitrate	50 tonnes	13464-97-6	
Lead azide	50 tonnes	13424-46-9	082-003-00-7
Lead styphnate (Lead 2,4,6-trinitroresorcinoxide)	50 tonnes	15245-44-0	609-019-00-4
Mercury fulminate	10 tonnes	20820-45-5 628-86-4	080-005-00-2

Substance (Column 1)	Quantity (for application of Regulations 7–12) (Column 2)	CAS Number (Column 3)	EEC Number (Column 4)
N-Methyl-N,2,4,6-tetranitroaniline	50 tonnes	479-45-8	612-017-00-6
Nitroglycerine	10 tonnes	55-63-0	603-034-00-X
Pentaerythritol tetranitrate	50 tonnes	78-11-5	603-035-00-5
Picric acid (2,4,6-Trinitrophenol)	50 tonnes	88-89-1	609-009-00-X
Sodium picramate	50 tonnes	831-52-7	
Styphnic acid (2,4,6-Trinitroresorcinol)	50 tonnes	82-71-3	609-018-00-9
1,3,5-Triamino-2,4,6-trinitrobenzene	50 tonnes	3058-38-6	
Trinitroaniline	50 tonnes	26952-42-1	
2,4,6-Trinitroanisole	50 tonnes	606-35-9	609-011-00-0
Trinitrobenzene	50 tonnes	25377-32-6	609-005-00-8
Trinitrobenzoic acid	50 tonnes	34860-50-9 129-66-8	
Trinitrocresol	50 tonnes	28905-71-7	609-012-00-6
2,4,6-Trinitrophenetole	50 tonnes	4732-14-3	
2,4,6-Trinitrotoluene	50 tonnes	118-86-7	609-008-00-4
Group 5—Flammable substances			
Flammable substances as defined in Schedule 1, paragraph (c)(i)	200 tonnes		
Flammable substances as defined in Schedule 1, paragraph (c)(ii)	50,000 tonnes		
Flammable substances as defined in Schedule 1, paragraph (c)(iii)	200 tonnes		

(a) This applies to ammonium nitrate and mixtures of ammonium nitrate where the nitrogen content derived from the ammonium nitrate is >28% by weight and aqueous solutions of ammonium nitrate where the concentration of ammonium nitrate is >90% by weight.

(b) This applies to straight ammonium nitrate fertilisers which comply with Council Directive 80/876/EEC "on the approximation of the laws of the Member States relating to straight ammonium nitrate fertilisers of high nitrogen content" and to compound fertilisers where the nitrogen content derived from the ammonium nitrate is >28% by weight (a compound fertiliser contains ammonium nitrate together with phosphate and/or potash).

Note (This note does not form part of Annex III to the Directive).
1. CAS Number (Chemical Abstracts Number) means the number assigned to the substance by the Chemical Abstracts Service, details of which can be obtained from the United Kingdom Chemical Information Service, University of Nottingham, Nottingham.
2. EEC Number means the number assigned to the substance by the Commission of the European Communities, details of which can be obtained from its office at 20 Kensington Palace Gardens, London W8 4QQ.

SCHEDULE 4

Regulation 2(1)

(WHICH SETS OUT THE PROVISIONS OF ANNEX I TO THE DIRECTIVE)

INDUSTRIAL INSTALLATIONS WITHIN THE MEANING OF
REGULATION 2(1)

1. Installations for the production, processing, or treatment of organic or inorganic chemicals using for this purpose, amongst others:

—alkylation
—amination by ammonolysis
—carbonylation
—condensation
—dehydrogenation
—esterification
—halogenation and manufacture of halogens
—hydrogenation
—hydrolysis
—oxidation
—polymerisation
—sulphonation
—desulphurisation, manufacture and transformation of sulphur-containing compounds
—nitration and manufacture of nitrogen-containing compounds
—manufacture of phosphorus-containing compounds
—formulation of pesticides and of pharmaceutical products
—distillation
—extraction
—solvation
—mixing.

2. Installations for distillation, refining or other processing of petroleum or petroleum products.
3. Installations for the total or partial disposal of solid or liquid substances by incineration or chemical decomposition.
4. Installations for the production, processing or treatment of energy gases, for example, LPG, LNG, SNG.
5. Installations for the dry distillation of coal or lignite.
6. Installations for the production of metals or non-metals by a wet process or by means of electrical energy.

SCHEDULE 5

Regulation 5(2)

(WHICH SETS OUT THE PROVISIONS OF ANNEX VI TO THE DIRECTIVE)

INFORMATION TO BE SUPPLIED TO THE COMMISSION OF THE
EUROPEAN COMMUNITIES BY THE MEMBER STATES PURSUANT TO
REGULATION 5(2)

Report of major accident
Member State:
Authority responsible for report:
Address:

1. General data
   Date and time of the major accident:
   Country, administrative region, etc.:
   Address:
   Type of industrial activity:
2. Type of major accident
   Explosion ☐   Fire ☐   Emission of dangerous substance ☐
   Substance(s) emitted:
3. Description of the circumstances of the major accident
4. Emergency measures taken
5. Cause(s) of major accident
   Known: ☐
   (to be specified)   ☐
   Not known: ☐
   Information will be supplied as soon as possible   ☐
6. Nature and extent of damage
   (a) Within the establishment
       —casualties   .... killed
                                                      ....injured
                                                      ....poisoned
       —persons exposed to the major accident   ....

       —material damage   ☐
       —the danger is still present   ☐
       —the danger no longer exists   ☐
   (b) Outside the establishment
       —casualties   ....killed
                                                      ....injured
                                                      ....poisoned
       —persons exposed to the major accident   ....

       —material damage   ☐
       —damage to the environment   ☐
       —the danger is still present   ☐
       —the danger no longer exists   ☐
7. Medium and long-term measures, particularly those aimed at preventing the recurrence of similar major accidents (to be submitted as the information becomes available).

SCHEDULE 6

Regulation 7(1)

INFORMATION TO BE INCLUDED IN A REPORT UNDER REGULATION 7(1)

1. The report required under Regulation 7(1) shall contain the following information.

2. Information relating to every *dangerous substance* involved in the activity in a relevant quantity as listed in Schedule 2, column 3 or Schedule 3, namely—
   (a) the name of the *dangerous substance* as given in Schedule 2 or 3, or, for a *dangerous substance* included in either of those Schedules under a general designation, the name corresponding to the chemical formula of the *dangerous substance*;
   (b) a general description of the analytical methods available to the *manufacturer* for determining the presence of the *dangerous substance*, or reference to such methods in the scientific literature;

(c) a brief description of the hazards which may be created by the *dangerous substance*;

(d) the degree of purity of the *dangerous substance*, and the names of the main impurities and their percentages.

3. Information relating to the installation, namely—

(a) a map of the *site* and its surrounding area to a scale large enough to show any features that may be significant in the assessment of the hazard or risk associated with the *site*;

(b) a scale plan of the *site* showing the locations and quantities of all significant inventories of the *dangerous substance*;

(c) a description of the process or storage involving the *dangerous substance* and an indication of the conditions under which it is normally held;

(d) the maximum number of persons likely to be present on *site*;

(e) information about the nature of the land use and the size and distribution of the population in the vicinity of the industrial activity to which the report relates.

4. Information relating to the management system for controlling the industrial activity, namely—

(a) the staffing arrangements for controlling the industrial activity with the name of the person responsible for safety on the *site* and the names of those who are authorised to set emergency procedures in motion and to inform outside authorities;

(b) the arrangements made to ensure that the means provided for the safe operation of the industrial activity are properly designed, constructed, tested, operated, inspected and maintained;

(c) the arrangements for training of persons working on the *site*.

5. Information relating to the potential *major accidents*, namely—

(a) a description of the potential sources of a *major accident* and the conditions or events which could be significant in bringing one about;

(b) a diagram of any plant in which the industrial activity is carried on, sufficient to show the features which are significant as regards the potential for a *major accident or its prevention or control*;

(c) a description of the measures taken to prevent, control or minimise the consequences of any *major accident*;

(d) information about the emergency procedures laid down for dealing with a *major accident* occurring at the *site*;

(e) information about prevailing meteorological conditions in the vicinity of the *site*;

(f) an estimate of the number of people on *site* who may be exposed to the hazards considered in the report.

6. In the case of the storage of substances and *preparations* to which Part II of Schedule 2 applies, paragraphs 2(a), (b) and (d) and 5(b) of this Schedule shall apply so far as is appropriate.

SCHEDULE 7

Regulation 7(3)

PRELIMINARY INFORMATION TO BE SENT TO THE EXECUTIVE UNDER REGULATION 7(3)

1. The name and address of the person supplying the information.

2. The full postal address of the *site* where the industrial activity is being carried on and its ordinance survey grid reference.

3. The area of the *site*, and of any adjacent *site* which is required to be taken into account by virtue of Schedule 2 or 3.

4. A statement to the effect that the industrial activity had already commenced *(a)* on or before 7 January 1985 [30 December 1990].

5. A general description of the *industrial activity* carried on at the *site* or *sites*.

6. The name and address of the planning authority in whose area the industrial activity is being carried on.

7. The name and maximum quantity liable to be on the *site* or *sites* of each *dangerous substance* involved in the industrial activity concerning which information is being supplied.

(a) **Commenced.** By the Control of Industrial Major Accident Hazards (Amendment) Regulations 1990, S.I. 1990 No. 2325, reg. 4, Sch. 6, para. 3, where an industrial activity becomes subject to regs. 7 to 11 of these Regulations in consequence of an amendment made by S.I. 1990 No. 2325, reg. 3, in Sch. 7, para. 4 the date in square brackets shall be substituted for the existing date.

SCHEDULE 8

Regulations 2(1) and 12(1)

(WHICH SETS OUT THE PROVISIONS OF ANNEX VII TO THE DIRECTIVE)

ITEMS OF INFORMATION TO BE COMMUNICATED TO THE PUBLIC IN THE APPLICATION OF
REGULATION 12

(a)   Name of *manufacturer* and address of *site*.

(b)   Identification, by position held, of person giving the information.

(c)   Confirmation that the *site* is subject to these Regulations and that the report referred to in Regulation 7(1) or at least the information required by Regulation 7(3) has been submitted to *the Executive*.

(d)   An explanation in simple terms of the activity undertaken on the site.

(e)   The common names, or in the case of storage covered by Part II of Schedule 2, the generic names or the general danger classification, of the substances and *preparations* involved on *site* which could give rise to a *major accident*, with an indication of their principal dangerous characteristics.

(f)   General information relating to the nature of the *major accident* hazards, including their potential effects on the population and the environment.

(g)   Adequate information on how the population concerned will be warned and kept informed in the event of an accident.

(h)   Adequate information on the actions the population concerned should take and on the behaviour they should adopt in the event of an accident.

(i)   Confirmation that the *manufacturer* is required to make adequate arrangements on site, including liaison with the emergency services, to deal with accidents and to minimise their effects.

(j)   A reference to the off-site emergency plan drawn up to cope with any off-site effects from an accident. This shall include advice to co-operate with any instructions or requests from the emergency services at the time of an accident.

(k)   Details of where further relevant information can be obtained, subject to the requirements of confidentiality laid down in national legislation.

THE HEALTH AND SAFETY (FIRST-AID) REGULATIONS 1981

(S.I. 1981 No. 917)

ARRANGEMENT OF REGULATIONS

1. Citation and commencement.
2. Interpretation.
3. Duty of employer to make provision for first-aid.
4. Duty of employer to inform his employees of the arrangements made in connection with first-aid.
5. Duty of self-employed person to provide first-aid equipment.
6. Power to grant exemptions.
7. Cases where these Regulations do not apply.
8. Application to miscellaneous mines.
9. Application offshore.
10. Repeals, revocations and modification.
Schedule 1. Repeals.
Schedule 2. Revocations.

The Secretary of State, in exercise of the powers conferred on him by sections 15(1), (2), (3)(a), (4)(a), (5)(b) and (9) and 49(1) and (4) of, and paragraphs 10 and 14 of Schedule 3 to, the Health and Safety at Work etc. Act 1974 ("the 1974 Act") and of all other powers enabling him in that behalf and for the purpose of giving effect without modifications to proposals submitted to him by the Health and Safety Commission under section 11(2)(d) of the 1974 Act after the carrying out by the said Commission of consultations in accordance with section 50(3) of that Act, hereby makes the following Regulations:—

1. Citation and commencement. These Regulations may be cited as the Health and Safety (First-Aid) Regulations 1981 and shall come into operation on 1 July 1982.

General note. An Approved Code of Practice has been issued in support of these Regulations. The Regulations and Code are supplemented by a Guidance Note published by the Health and Safety Executive (Booklet (HS (R) 11). The Guidance Note gives advice on such matters as equipment and training.

2. Interpretation.—(1) In these Regulations, unless the context otherwise requires—
"first-aid" means—

(a) in cases where a person will need help from a medical practitioner or nurse, treatment for the purpose of preserving life and minimising the consequences of injury and illness until such help is obtained, and
(b) treatment of minor injuries which would otherwise receive no treatment or which do not need treatment by a medical practitioner or nurse;

532

"mine" means a mine within the meaning of section 180 of the Mines and Quarries Act 1954.

(2) In these Regulations, unless the context otherwise requires, any reference to—

(a) a numbered Regulation or Schedule is a reference to the Regulation of, or Schedule to, these Regulations bearing that number;

(b) a numbered paragraph is a reference to the paragraph bearing that number in the Regulation in which the reference appears.

3. Duty of employer to make provision for first-aid.—(1) An employer shall provide, or ensure that there are provided, such equipment and facilities as are adequate and appropriate in the circumstances for enabling *first-aid* to be rendered to his employees *(a)* if they are injured or become ill at work *(b)*.

(2) Subject to paragraphs (3) and (4), an employer shall provide, or ensure that there is provided, such number of suitable persons as is adequate and appropriate in the circumstances for rendering *first-aid* to his employees *(a)* if they are injured or become ill at work *(b)*; and for this purpose a person shall not be suitable unless he has undergone—

(a) such training and has such qualifications as the Health and Safety Executive may approve for the time being in respect of that case or class of case, and

(b) such additional training, if any, as may be appropriate in the circumstances of that case.

(3) Where a person provided under paragraph (2) is absent in temporary and exceptional circumstances it shall be sufficient compliance with that paragraph if the employer appoints a person, or ensures that a person is appointed, to take charge of—

(a) the situation relating to an injured or ill employee *(a)* who will need help from a medical practitioner or nurse, and

(b) the equipment and facilities provided under paragraph (1),

throughout the period of any such absence.

(4) Where having regard to—

(a) the nature of the undertaking, and
(b) the number of employees *(a)* at work, and
(c) the location of the establishment,

it would be adequate and appropriate if instead of a person for rendering *first-aid* there was a person appointed to take charge as in paragraph (3)(a) and (b), then instead of complying with paragraph (2) the employer may appoint such a person, or ensure that such a person is appointed.

(a) **Employee.** For definition, see the Health and Safety at Work etc. Act 1974, s. 53(1) and the Interpretation Act 1978, s. 11.

(b) **At work.** For definition, see the Health and Safety at Work etc. Act 1974, s. 52(1) and the Interpretation Act 1978, s. 11.

4.   Duty of employer to inform his employees of the arrangements made in connection with first-aid. An employer shall inform his employees *(a)* of the arrangements that have been made in connection with the provision of *first-aid*, including the location of equipment, facilities and personnel.

   (a) Employee. For definition, see note *(a)* to reg. 3.

5.   Duty of self-employed person to provide first-aid equipment. A self-employed person *(a)* shall provide *(b)*, or ensure that there is provided, such equipment, if any, as is adequate and appropriate in the circumstances to enable him to render *first-aid* to himself while he is at work *(c)*.

   (a) Self-employed person. For definition, see the Health and Safety at Work etc. Act 1974, s. 53(1) and the Interpretation Act 1978, s. 11.

   (b) Provide. See INTRODUCTORY NOTE 9.

   (c) At work. See note *(b)* to reg. 3.

6.   Power to grant exemptions.—(1) Subject to paragraph (2), the Health and Safety Executive may, by a certificate in writing, exempt any person or class of persons from any of the requirements imposed by these Regulations, and any such exemption may be granted subject to conditions and to a limit of time and may be revoked at any time.

   (2) The Executive shall not grant any such exemption unless, having regard to the circumstances of the case, and in particular to—

   (a) the conditions, if any, which it proposes to attach to the exemption, and
   (b) any other requirements imposed by or under any enactment which apply to the case,

it is satisfied that the health, safety and welfare of employees and self-employed persons and the health and safety of other persons who are likely to be affected by the exemption will not be prejudiced in consequence of it.

7.   Cases where these Regulations do not apply. These Regulations shall not apply—

   (a) where the Diving Operations at Work Regulations 1981 apply;
   (b) where the Merchant Shipping (Medical Scales) (Fishing Vessels) Regulations 1974 apply;
   (c) where the Merchant Shipping (Medical Scales) Regulations 1974 apply;
   (d) on vessels which are registered outside the United Kingdom *(a)*;
   (e) to a *mine* of coal, stratified ironstone, shale or fireclay;
   (f) in respect of the armed forces of the Crown and any force to which any provision of the Visiting Forces Act 1952 applies.

   (a) United Kingdom. For definition, see INTRODUCTORY NOTE 4.

8.   Application to miscellaneous mines. In their application to *mines* not excluded from these Regulations by Regulation 7(e), Regulations 3 and 4 shall have effect as if the manager for the time being of any such *mine* were an employer and as if the persons employed were his employees *(a)*.

  (a) Employee. For definition, see note *(a)* to reg. 3.

9.   Application offshore. Subject to Regulation 7, these Regulations shall apply to and in relation to any premises or activity to or in relation to which sections 1 to 59 of the Health and Safety at Work etc. Act 1974 apply by virtue of Articles 6 and 7(a), (b) and (d) of the Health and Safety at Work etc. Act 1974 (Application outside Great Britain) Order 1977 *(a)* (which relate respectively to *mines* extending beyond Great Britain and to certain activities concerning vessels and construction works in territorial waters).

  (a) Health and Safety at Work etc. Act 1974 (Application outside Great Britain) Order 1977. The Order has now been replaced by the Health and Safety at Work etc Act 1974 (Application outside Great Britain) Order 1989, which is set out following s. 84 of the 1974 Act.

10.   Repeals, revocations and modification.—(1) The enactments mentioned in column (1) of Schedule 1 are hereby repealed to the extent specified opposite thereto in column (3) of that Schedule.

  (2)   The Orders and Regulations mentioned in column (1) of Schedule 2 are hereby revoked to the extent specified opposite thereto in column (3) of that Schedule.

  (3)   Section 91(1) of the Mines and Quarries Act 1954 shall be modified by after the words "every mine" inserting the words "of coal, stratified ironstone, shale or fireclay".

[*The Schedules, which provide for repeals and revocations, are not printed here.*]

THE HEALTH AND SAFETY INFORMATION FOR EMPLOYEES REGULATIONS 1989

(S.I. 1989 No. 682)

ARRANGEMENT OF REGULATIONS

1. Citation and commencement.
2. Interpretation and application.
3. Meaning of and revisions to the approved poster and leaflet.
4. Provision of poster or leaflet.
5. Provision of further information.
6. Exemption certificates.
7. Defence.
8. Repeals, revocations and modifications.

The Schedule—Repeals, revocations and modifications.
<blockquote>
Part I —Repeals.
Part II —Revocations.
Part III—Modifications.
</blockquote>

The Secretary of State, in exercise of the powers conferred on him by sections 15(1), (2), (3)(a), (4)(a), (5)(b) and (6)(b) of, and paragraph 15(1) of Schedule 3 to, the Health and Safety at Work etc. Act 1974 ("the 1974 Act") and of all other powers enabling him in that behalf and for the purpose of giving effect without modifications to proposals submitted to him by the Health and Safety Commission under section 11(2)(d) of the 1974 Act after the carrying out by the said Commission of consultations in accordance with section 50(3) of that Act, hereby makes the following Regulations:

1. Citation and commencement. These Regulations may be cited as the Health and Safety Information for Employees Regulations 1989 and shall come into force on 18 October 1989.

2. Interpretation and application.—(1) In these Regulations, unless the context otherwise requires—

"the 1974 Act" means the Health and Safety at Work etc. Act 1974;

"the approved poster" and "the approved leaflet" have the meanings assigned by regulation 3;

"employment medical advisory service" means the employment medical advisory service referred to in section 55 of the 1974 Act;

"ship" has the meaning assigned to it by section 742 of the Merchant Shipping Act 1894.

(2) Any reference in these Regulations to the enforcing authority for premises is a reference to the enforcing authority which has responsibility for the

536

enforcement of section 2 of the 1974 Act in relation to the main activity carried on in those premises.

(3) Any reference in these Regulations to—

(a) a numbered regulation is a reference to the regulation so numbered in these Regulations;

(b) a numbered paragraph is a reference to the paragraph so numbered in the regulation in which the reference appears.

(4) These Regulations shall have effect for the purpose of providing information to employees relating to health, safety and welfare but they shall not apply in relation to the master and crew of a sea going ship.

3.   Meaning of and revisions to the approved poster and leaflet.—(1) In these Regulations "*the approved poster*" or "*the approved leaflet*" means, respectively, a poster or leaflet in the form approved and published for the purposes of these Regulations by the Health and Safety Executive, as revised from time to time in accordance with paragraph (2).

(2) The Health and Safety Executive may approve a revision (in whole or in part) to the form of poster or leaflet; and where it does so it shall publish the revised form of poster or leaflet and issue a notice in writing specifying the date the revision was approved.

(3) Such a revision shall not take effect until nine months after the date of its approval, but during that time the employer may use the approved poster or the approved leaflet incorporating that revision for the purposes of regulation 4(1).

4.   Provision of poster or leaflet.—(1) An employer shall, in relation to each of his employees—

(a) ensure that *the approved poster* is kept displayed in a readable condition—
   (i) at a place which is reasonably accessible to the employee while he is at work, and
   (ii) in such a position in that place as to be easily seen and read by that employee; or

(b) give to the employee *the approved leaflet.*

(2) An employer shall be treated as having complied with paragraph (1)(b) from the date these Regulations come into force or the date the employee commences employment with him (if later) if he gives to the employer *the approved leaflet* as soon as is reasonably practicable *(a)* after that date.

(3) Where the form of poster or leaflet is revised pursuant to regulation 3(2), then on or before the date the revision takes effect—

(a) an employer relying on compliance with paragraph (1)(a) shall ensure that *the approved poster* displayed is the one as revised;

(b) an employer relying on compliance with paragraph (1)(b) shall either give to the employees concerned fresh *approved leaflets* (as so revised) or being the revision to their notice in writing.

(a) **Reasonably practicable.** See INTRODUCTORY NOTE 5.

5. Provision of further information.—(1) An employer relying on compliance with regulation 4(1)(a) shall, subject to paragraph (2), ensure that the following information is clearly and indelibly written on the poster in the appropriate space—

   (a) the name of the enforcing authority for the premises where the poster is displayed and the address of the office of that authority for the area in which those premises are situated; and

   (b) the address of the office of the *employment medical advisory service* for the area in which those premises are situated.

(2) Where there is a change in any of the matters referred to in paragraph (1) it shall be sufficient compliance with that paragraph for the corresponding amendment to the poster to be made within six months from the date thereof.

(3) An employer who gives to his employee a leaflet pursuant to regulation 4(1)(b) shall give with the leaflet a written notice containing—

   (a) the name of the enforcing authority for the premises where the employee works, and the address of the office of that authority for the area in which those premises are situated; and

   (b) the address of the office of the *employment medical advisory service* for the area in which those premises are situated.

(4) Where the employee works in more than one location he shall, for the purpose of paragraph (3), be treated as working at the premises from which his work is administered, and if his work is administered from two or more premises, the employer may choose any one of them for the purpose of complying with that paragraph.

(5) Where an employer relies on compliance with regulation 4(1)(b) and there is a change in any of the matters referred to in paragraph (3) the employer shall within six months of the date thereof give to the employee a written notice specifying the change.

6. Exemption certificates.—(1) Subject to paragraph (2) the Health and Safety Executive may, by a certificate in writing, exempt any person or class of persons from all or any of the requirements imposed by these Regulations and any such exemption may be granted subject to conditions and to a limit of time and may be revoked in writing at any time.

(2) The Executive shall not grant any such exemption unless, having regard to the circumstances of the case, and in particular to—

   (a) the conditions if any, which it proposes to attach to the exemption; and

   (b) any other requirements imposed by or order any enactment which apply to the case,

it is satisfied that the health, safety and welfare of persons who are likely to be affected by the exemption will not be prejudiced in consequence of it.

7. Defence. In any proceedings for an offence for a contravention of these Regulations it shall be a defence for the accused to prove that he took all reasonable precautions and exercised all due diligence *(a)* to avoid the commission of that offence.

(a) *All due diligence.* See INTRODUCTORY NOTE 7.

8. Repeals, revocations and modifications.—(1) The enactments specified in column 1 of Part I of the Schedule to these Regulations are hereby repealed to the extent specified in the corresponding entries in column 2 thereof.

(2) The instruments specified in column 1 of part II of the Schedule to these Regulations are hereby revoked to the extent specified in the corresponding entries in column 3 thereof.

(3) The instrument specified in column 1 of Part III of the Schedule to these Regulations is hereby modified to the extent specified in the corresponding entry in column 3 thereof.

THE SCHEDULE

Regulation 8

REPEALS, REVOCATIONS AND MODIFICATIONS

PART I. REPEALS

Column 1 *Enactments*	Column 2 *Repeals*
Factories Act 1961	In section 125(2)(j) the words "the abstract of this Act and". In section 127(2)(j), the words "the abstract of this Act and". In section 127(5), the words "the prescribed abstract of this Act and of" and the words "of the abstract of this Act and". In section 138(1), paragraphs (a), (b) and (c). In section 153(1), paragraph (b).
Employment Medical Advisory Service Act 1972	Schedule 2, in so far as it relates to the amendment of section 138(1) of the Factories Act 1961.

PART II. REVOCATIONS

Column 1 *Title of instrument*	Column 2 *Reference*	Column 3 *Extent of revocation*
The Information for Employees Regulations 1965.	S.I. 1965/307 amended by S.I. 1982/827.	The whole Regulations.
The Abstract of Factories Act Order 1973.	S.I. 1973/7 amended by S.I. 1983/978.	The whole Order.
The Offices, Shops and Railway Premises Act 1963 etc. (Metrication) Regulations 1982.	S.I. 1982/827.	The Schedule in so far as it relates to the amendment of the Information for Employees Regulations 1965.
The Factories Act 1961 etc. (Metrication) Regulations 1983.	S.I. 1983/978.	Regulation 5 and Schedule 3.

PART III. MODIFICATIONS

Column 1 *Title of instrument*	Column 2 *Reference*	Column 3 *Extent of modification*
The Construction (General Provisions) Regulations 1961.	S.I. 1961/1580 to which there are amendments not relevant to these Regulations.	For regulation 5(2) substitute—"The name of every person so appointed shall be entered by the contractor or employer appointing him on the copy or abstract of these Regulations required to be posted up in accordance with sections 139 and 127 of the Factories Act 1961."

THE REPORTING OF INJURIES, DISEASES AND DANGEROUS OCCURRENCES REGULATIONS 1985

(S.I. 1985 No. 2023, as amended by S.I. 1988 No. 1729, by virtue of the Employment Act 1988, s. 24(3), S.I. 1989 No. 1457 and S.I. 1992 No. 743)

ARRANGEMENT OF REGULATIONS

The Secretary of State, in exercise of the powers conferred on him by section 15(1), (2), (3)(a), (4), (6)(a) and (b) and (9) of, and paragraphs 15(1), 16 and 20 of Schedule 3 to, the Health and Safety at Work etc. Act 1974 ("the 1974 Act") and of all other powers enabling him in that behalf and for the purpose of giving effect without modifications to proposals submitted to him by the Health and Safety Commission under section 11(2)(d) of the 1974 Act after the carrying out by the said Commission of consultations in accordance with section 50(3) of that Act, hereby makes the following Regulations:—

1. Citation and commencement. These Regulations may be cited as the Reporting of Injuries, Diseases and Dangerous Occurrences Regulations 1985 and shall come into operation on 1 April 1986.

2. Interpretation.—(1) In these Regulations, unless the context otherwise requires—

"approved" means approved for the time being for the purposes of these Regulations by the Health and Safety Executive;

"dangerous occurrence" means an occurrence which arises out of or in connection with work and is of a class specified in—

(a) Part I of Schedule 1;
(b) Part II of Schedule 1 and takes place at a mine;
(c) Part III of Schedule 1 and takes place at a quarry;
(d) Part IV of Schedule 1 and takes place on a railway;

"mine" or "quarry" means a mine or, as the case may be, a quarry within the meaning of section 180 of the Mines and Quarries Act 1954 and for the purposes of these Regulations includes a closed tip within the meaning of section 2(2)(b) of the Mines and Quarries (Tips) Act 1969 which is associated with that mine or that quarry.

"operator" means in relation to a vehicle to which paragraph 13 or 14 of Schedule 1, Part I applies—

(a) a person who holds, or is required by section 60 of the Transport Act 1968 to hold, an operator's licence for the use of that vehicle for the carriage of goods on a road; or
(b) where no such licence is required, the keeper of the vehicle;

"railway" means a railway having a gauge of 350 millimetres or more used for the purposes of public transport, whether passenger, goods, or other traffic and includes—

(a) a tramway;
(b) a railway laid on a beach or pier; and
(c) a railway providing communication between the top and bottom of a cliff;

"responsible person" means—

(a) in the case of—
   (i) a mine, the manager of that mine;
   (ii) a quarry, the owner of that quarry;
   (iii) a closed tip, the owner of the mine or quarry with which that tip is associated;
   (iv) a pipeline within the meaning of section 65 of the Pipelines Act 1962, the owner of that pipeline;
   (v) a vehicle to which paragraph 13 or 14 of Schedule 1, Part I applies, the operator of the vehicle;
(b) where sub-paragraph (a) above does not apply, in the case of any event (other than a dangerous occurrence) reportable under Regulation 3, or any case of disease reportable under Regulation 5, involving—
   (i) an employee at work (including any person who is to be treated as an employee by virtue of any relevant statutory provision), his employer;
   (ii) a person (excluding one who is to be treated as an employee by virtue of any relevant statutory provision) undergoing training for employment, the person whose undertaking makes the immediate provision of that training;

(c) in any other case, the person for the time being having control of the premises in connection with the carrying on by him of any trade, business or other undertaking (whether for profit or not) at which, or in connection with the work at which, the accident or dangerous occurrence reportable under Regulation 3, or case of disease reportable under Regulation 5, happened;

"training" includes work experience received as part of a training programme; it does not include training on a course at a university, polytechnic, college, school or similar educational or technical institute where that body is the immediate provider of the training; but it does include training at a skillcentre, training centre or other training establishment run by the Training Commission;

"work" means work as an employee, as a self-employed person or as a person undergoing training for employment (whether or not under any scheme administered by the Training Commission).

(2) In these Regulations, unless the context otherwise requires, any reference to—

(a) a numbered Regulation or Schedule is a reference to the Regulation or Schedule in these Regulations so numbered;
(b) a numbered paragraph is a reference to the paragraph so numbered in the Regulations or Schedule in which that reference appears; and
(c) an accident or a dangerous occurrence which arises out of or in connection with work shall include a reference to an accident, or as the case may be, a dangerous occurrence attributable to the manner of conducting an undertaking, the plant or substances used for the purposes of an undertaking and the condition of the premises so used or any part of them.

3. Notification and reporting of injuries and dangerous occurrences.—
(1) Subject to Regulation 10, where any person as a result of an accident arising out of or in connection with *work (a)*, dies or suffers any of the injuries or conditions specified in paragraph (2) or where there is a *dangerous occurrence,* the *responsible person* shall—

(a) forthwith notify the enforcing authority *(b)* thereof by the quickest practicable means; and
(b) within 7 days send a report thereof to the enforcing authority on a form approved for the purposes of this Regulation.

(2) The injuries and conditions referred to in paragraph (1) are—

(a) fracture of the skull, spine or pelvis;
(b) fracture of any bone—
    (i) in the arm or wrist, but not a bone in the hand; or
    (ii) in the leg or ankle, but not a bone in the foot;
(c) amputation of—
    (i) a hand or foot; or
    (ii) a finger, thumb or toe, or any part thereof if the joint or bone is completely severed;
(d) the loss of sight of an eye, a penetrating injury to an eye, or a chemical or hot metal burn to an eye;

(e) either injury (including burns) requiring immediate medical treatment, or loss of consciousness, resulting in either case from an electric shock from any electrical circuit or equipment, whether or not due to direct contact;

(f) loss of consciousness resulting from lack of oxygen;

(g) decompression sickness (unless suffered during an operation to which the Diving Operations at Work Regulations 1981 apply) requiring immediate medical treatment;

(h) either acute illness requiring medical treatment, or loss of consciousness, resulting in either case from the absorption of any substance by inhalation, ingestion or through the skin;

(i) acute illness requiring medical treatment where there is reason to believe that this resulted from exposure to a pathogen or infected material;

(j) any other injury which results in the person injured being admitted immediately into hospital for more than 24 hours.

(3) Subject to Regulation 10, where a person at *work* is incapacitated for work of a kind which he might reasonably be expected to do, either under his contract of employment, or, if there is no such contract, in the normal course of his *work*, for more than 3 consecutive days (excluding the day of the accident but including any days which would not have been working days) because of an injury (other than one specified in paragraph (2)) resulting from an accident at *work* the *responsible person* shall within 7 days of the accident send a report thereof to the enforcing authority on a form approved for the purposes of this Regulation.

(a) *Accident ... work.* See reg. 2(2)(c).

(b) *Enforcing authority.* See the Health and Safety at Work etc. Act 1974, s. 18 and the Health and Safety (Enforcing Authority) Regulations 1989, S.I. 1989 No. 1903.

4. Reporting of the death of an employee. Subject to Regulation 10, where an employee, as a result of an accident at *work*, has suffered an injury or condition reportable under Regulation 3 which is a cause of his death within one year of the date of that accident, the employer shall inform the enforcing authority (a) in writing of the death as soon as it comes to his knowledge, whether or not the accident has been reported under Regulation 3.

(a) *Enforcing authority.* See note (b) to reg. 3.

5. Reporting of cases of disease.—(1) Subject to paragraphs (2) and (3) and to Regulation 10, where a person at *work* suffers from one of the diseases specified in column 1 of Schedule 2 and his *work* involves one of the activities specified in the corresponding entry in column 2 of that Schedule, the *responsible person* shall forthwith send a report thereof to the enforcing authority (a) on a form approved for the purposes of this Regulation.

(2) Paragraph (1) shall apply only if—

(a) in the case of an employee or a person undergoing *training*, the *responsible person* has received a written statement prepared by a registered medical practitioner diagnosing the disease as one of those specified in column 1 of Schedule 2; or

(b) in the case of a self-employed person, that person has been informed by a registered medical practitioner that he is suffering from a disease so specified.

(3) In the case of a self-employed person, it shall be a sufficient compliance with paragraph (1) if that person makes arrangements for the report to be sent to the enforcing authority by some other person.

(a) Enforcing authority. See note *(b)* to reg. 3.

6. Reporting of gas incidents.—(1) Whenever a supplier of flammable gas through a fixed pipe distribution system, or a filler, importer or supplier (other than by means of retail trade) of a refillable container containing liquefied petroleum gas receives notification of any death, or any injury or condition specified in Regulation 3(2) which has arisen out of or in connection with the gas supplied, filled or imported, as the case may be, by that person, he shall forthwith notify the Executive of the incident, and shall within 14 days send a report of it to the Executive on a Form approved for the purposes of this Regulation.

(2) Whenever a supplier of flammable gas through a fixed pipe distribution system has in his possession sufficient information for it to be reasonable for him to decide that a gas fitting as defined by section 48(1) of the Gas Act 1972 of any flue or ventilation used in connection with that fitting, by reason of its design, construction, manner of installation, modification or servicing, is or has been likely to cause death, or any injury or condition specified in Regulation 3(2) by reason of—

(a) accidental leakage of gas;

(b) inadequate combustion of gas; or

(c) inadequate removal of the products of combustion of gas,

he shall within 14 days send a report of it to the Executive on a form approved for the purposes of this Regulation, unless he has previously reported such information.

(3) Nothing which is notifiable or reportable elsewhere in these Regulations shall be reportable under this Regulation.

(4) In this Regulation "liquefied petroleum gas" means commercial butane (that is, a hydrocarbon mixture consisting predominantly of butane, butylene or any mixture thereof) or commercial propane (that is, a hydrocarbon mixture consisting predominantly of propane, propylene or any mixture thereof) or any mixture of commercial butane and commercial propane.

7. Records.—(1) The *responsible person* shall keep a record of—

(a) any event which is required to be reported under Regulation 3, which shall contain the particulars specified in Part I of Schedule 3; and

(b) any case of disease required to be reported under Regulation 5, which shall contain the particulars specified in Part II of that Schedule.

(2) Any person sending a form to the Executive under Regulation 6 shall keep a record of the information provided on that form.

(3) Any record of deaths or injuries at *work* which an employer is required to keep by virtue of any other enactment shall, if it covers the injuries recordable under these Regulations and includes the particulars specified in Schedule 3, be sufficient for the requirements of paragraph (1)(a).

(4) The records referred to in paragraph (1) shall be kept at the place where the *work* to which they relate is carried on or, if this is not reasonably practicable, at the usual place of business of the *responsible person* and an entry in either of such records shall be kept for at least 3 years from the date on which it was made.

(5) The *responsible person* shall send to the enforcing authority *(a)* such extracts from the records required to be kept under paragraph (1) as the enforcing authority may from time to time require.

(a) *Enforcing authority.* See note *(b)* to reg. 3.

8.   Additional provisions relating to *mines* and *quarries*.   The provisions of Schedule 4 (which contains additional provisions relating to *mines* and *quarries*) shall have effect.

9.   Requirement for further information.   The Executive may, with the approval of the Commission, by notice in writing served on any person who has furnished a report under Regulation 3 or 5, require that person to give to the Executive in an approved form such of the information specified in Schedule 5 as may be specified in the notice within such time as may be specified in that notice.

10.   Restrictions to the application of Regulations 3, 4 and 5.—(1) The requirements of Regulation 3 relating to any death, injury or condition shall not apply to a patient when undergoing treatment in a hospital or in the surgery of a doctor or a dentist.

(2) The requirements of Regulations 3 and 4 relating to the death, injury or condition of a person as a result of an accident, shall apply to an accident arising out of or in connection with the movement of a vehicle on a road (within the meaning of section 192(1) of the Road Traffic Act 1988) only if that person—

(a) was killed or suffered an injury or condition as a result of exposure to a substance being conveyed by the vehicle; or
(b) was either himself engaged in, or was killed or suffered an injury or condition as a result of the activities of another person who was at the time of the accident engaged in, *work* connected with the loading or unloading of any article or substance onto or off the vehicle; or
(c) was either himself engaged in, or was killed or suffered an injury or condition as a result of the activities of another person who was at the time of the accident engaged in *work* on or alongside a road, being *work*

concerned with the construction, demolition, alteration, repair or maintenance of—

   (i) the road or the markings or equipment thereon;
  (ii) the verges, fences, hedges or other boundaries of the road;
 (iii) pipes or cables on, under, over or adjacent to the road; or
  (iv) building or structures adjacent to or over the road.

(3) The requirements of Regulations 3, 4 and 5 relating to any death, injury or condition, or case of disease, shall not apply to a member of the armed forces of the Crown or visiting forces who was on duty at the relevant time.

(4) Regulations 3, 4 and 5 shall not apply to anything which is required to be notified under any of the enactments or instruments specified in Schedule 6.

(5) Regulation 3(1)(a) shall not apply to a self-employed person who is injured at premises of which he is the owner or occupier, but Regulation 3(1)(b) shall apply to such a self-employed person (other than in the case of death) and it shall be sufficient compliance with that sub-paragraph if that self-employed person makes arrangements for the report to be sent to the enforcing authority by some other person.

11. Defence in proceedings for an offence contravening these Regulations. It shall be a defence in proceedings against any person for an offence under these Regulations for that person to prove that he was not aware of the event requiring him to notify or send a report to the enforcing authority and that he had taken all reasonable steps to have all such events brought to his notice.

12. Extension outside Great Britain. These Regulations shall apply to any activity to which sections 1 to 59 and 80 to 82 of the Health and Safety at Work etc. Act 1974 apply by virtue of articles 6 and 7 of the Health and Safety at Work etc. Act 1974 (Application outside Great Britain) Order 1977 as they apply to any such activity in Great Britain *(a)*.

(a) This Order has now been replaced by the Health and Safety at Work etc. Act 1974 (Application outside Great Britain) Order 1989.

13. Repeals, revocations, modifications and savings.—(1) The enactment specified in Part I of Schedule 7 in column 1 is hereby repealed to the extent specified in the corresponding entries in column 3.

(2) The instruments specified in Part II of Schedule 7 in column 1 are hereby revoked to the extent specified in the corresponding entries in column 3.

(3) The enactments and instruments specified in Part III of Schedule 7 shall be modified to the extent specified in that Part.

(4) Any record or register required to be kept under any enactment or instrument repealed or, as the case may be, revoked by these Regulations, shall be kept in the same manner and for the same period as if these Regulations had not been made.

SCHEDULE 1

Regulation 2(1)

Dangerous Occurrences

Part I. General

Lifting machinery etc.

1. The collapse of, the overturning of, or the failure of any load bearing part of—

(a) any lift, hoist, crane, derrick or mobile powered access platform, but not any winch, teagle, pulley block, gin wheel, transporter or runway;

(b) any excavator; or

(c) any pile driving frame or rig having an overall height, when operating, of more than 7 metres.

Passenger carrying amusement device

2. The following incidents at a fun fair (whether or not a travelling fun fair) while the relevant device is in use or under test—

(a) the collapse of, or the failure of any load bearing part of, any amusement device provided as part of the fun fair which is designed to allow passengers to move or ride on it or inside it; or

(b) the failure of any safety arrangement connected with such a device, which is designed to restrain or support passengers.

Pressure vessels

3. Explosion, collapse or bursting of any closed vessel, including a boiler or boiler tube, in which the internal pressure was above or below atmospheric pressure, which might have been liable to cause the death of, or any of the injuries or conditions covered by Regulation 3(2) to, any person, or which resulted in the stoppage of the plant involved for more than 24 hours.

Electrical short circuit

4. Electrical short circuit or overload attended by fire or explosion which resulted in the stoppage of the plant involved for more than 24 hours and which, taking into account the circumstances of the occurrence, might have been liable to cause the death of, or any of the injuries or conditions covered by Regultion 3(2) to, any person.

Explosion or fire

5. An explosion or fire occurring in any plant or place which resulted in the stoppage of that plant or suspension of normal work in that place for more than 24 hours, where such explosion or fire was due to the ignition of process materials, their by-products (including waste) or finished products.

Escape of flammable substances

6. The sudden, uncontrolled release of one tonne or more of highly flammable liquid, within the meaning of Regulation 2(2) of the Highly Flammable Liquids and Liquefied Petroleum Gases Regulations 1972, flammable gas or flammable liquid above its boiling point from any system or plant or pipeline.

Collapse of scaffolding

7. A collapse or partial collapse of any scaffold which is more than 5 metres high which results in a substantial part of the scaffold falling or over-turning; and where the scaffold is slung or suspended, a collapse or partial collapse of the suspension arrangements (including any outrigger) which causes a working platform or cradle to fall more than 5 metres.

Collapse of building or structure
   8.   Any unintended collapse or partial collapse of—
   (a) any building or structure under construction, reconstruction, alteration or demolition, or of any false-work, involving a fall of more than 5 tonnes of material; or
   (b) any floor or wall of any building being used as a place of work, not being a building under construction, reconstruction, alteration or demolition.

Escape of a substance or pathogen
   9.   The uncontrolled or accidental release or the escape of any substance or pathogen from any apparatus, equipment, pipework, pipeline, process plant, storage vessel, tank, in-works conveyance tanker, land-fill site, or exploratory land drilling site, which having regard to the nature of the substance or pathogen and the extent and location of the release or escape, might have been liable to cause the death of, any of the injuries or conditions covered by Regulation 3(2) to, or other damage to the health of, any person.

Explosives
   10.   Any ignition or explosion of explosives, where the ignition or explosion was not intentional.

Freight containers
   11.   Failure of any freight container or failure of any load bearing part thereof while it is being raised, lowered or suspended and in this paragraph "freight" means a container within the meaning of Regulation 2(1) of The Freight Containers (Safety Convention) Regulations 1984.

Pipelines
   12.   Either of the following incidents in relation to a pipeline as defined by section 65 of the Pipe-lines Act 1962—
   (a) the bursting, explosion or collapse of a pipeline or any part thereof; or
   (b) the unintentional ignition of anything in a pipeline, or of anything which immediately before it was ignited was in a pipeline.

Conveyance of dangerous substances by road
   13.—(1) Any incident—
   (a) in which a road tanker or tank container used for the carriage of a dangerous substance—
      (i) overturns; or
      (ii) suffers serious damage to the tank in which the dangerous substance is being carried; or
   (b) in which there is, in relation to such a road tanker or tank container—
      (i) an uncontrolled release or escape of the dangerous substance being carried; or
      (ii) a fire which involves the dangerous substance being carried.
   (2) In this paragraph, "carriage", "road tanker", "tank container" and "dangerous substance" has in each case the meaning assigned to it by Regulation 2(1) of the Road Traffic (Carriage of Dangerous Substances in Road Tankers and Tank Containers) Regulations 1992.

   14.—(1) Any incident involving a vehicle conveying a dangerous substance by road, other than a vehicle to which paragraph 13 applies, where there is—
   (a) an uncontrolled release or escape from any package or container of the dangerous substance being conveyed; or
   (b) a fire which involves the dangerous substance being conveyed.

(2) In this paragraph "dangerous substance" means a substance which is dangerous for conveyance as defined in Regulation 2(1) of the Classification, Packaging and Labelling of Dangerous Substances Regulations 1984.

Breathing apparatus

15. Any incident where breathing apparatus, while being used to enable the wearer to breathe independently of the surrounding environment, malfunctions in such a way as to be likely either to deprive the wearer of oxygen or, in the case of use in a contaminated atmosphere, to expose the wearer to the contaminant, to the extent in either case of posing a danger to his health, except that this paragraph shall not apply to such apparatus while it is being—

(a) used in a *mine*; or

(b) maintained or tested.

Overhead electric lines

16. Any incident in which plant or equipment either comes into contact with an uninsulated overhead electric line in which the voltage exceeds 200 volts, or causes an electrical discharge from such an electric line by coming into close proximity to it, unless in either case the incident was intentional.

Locomotives

17. Any case of an accidental collision between a locomotive or a train and any other vehicle at a factory or at dock premises which might have been liable to cause the death of, or any of the injuries or conditions covered by Regulation 3(2) to, any person.

PART II. DANGEROUS OCCURRENCES WHICH ARE REPORTABLE IN RELATION TO *MINES*

Fire or ignition of gas

1. The ignition, below ground, of any gas (other than gas in a safety lamp) or of any dust.

2. The accidental ignition of any gas in part of a firedamp drainage system on the surface or in an exhauster house.

3. The outbreak of any fire below ground.

4. An incident where any person in consequence of any smoke or any other indication that a fire may have broken out below ground has been caused to leave any place pursuant to either regulation 11(1) of the Coal and Other Mines (Fire and Rescue) Regulations 1956 or section 79 of the Mines and Quarries Act 1954.

5. The outbreak of any fire on the surface endangering the operation of any winding or haulage apparatus installed at a shaft or unwalkable outlet or of any mechanically operated apparatus for producing ventilation below ground.

Escape of gas

6. Any violent outburst of gas together with coal or other solid matter into the *mine* workings except when such outburst is caused intentionally.

Failure of plant or equipment

7. The breakage of any rope, chain, coupling, balance rope, guide rope, suspension gear or other gear used for or in connection with the carrying of persons through any shaft or staple shaft.

8. The breakage or unintentional uncoupling of any rope, chain, coupling, rope tensioning system or other gear used for or in connection with the transport of persons below ground, or breakage, while men are being carried, of any belt, rope or other gear used for or in connection with a belt conveyor designated by the *mine* manager as a man-riding conveyor.

9.   An incident where any conveyance being used for the carriage of persons is overwound; or any conveyance not being so used is overwound and becomes detached from its winding rope; or any conveyance operated by means of the friction of a rope on a winding sheave is brought to rest by the apparatus provided in the headframe of the shaft or in the part of the shaft below the lowest landing for the time being in use, being apparatus provided for bringing the conveyance to rest in the event of its being overwound.

10.   The stoppage of any ventilating apparatus (other than an auxiliary fan) causing a substantial reduction in ventilation of the mine lasting for a period exceeding 30 minutes, except when for the purpose of planned maintenance.

11.   The collapse of any headframe, winding engine house, fan house or storage bunker.

Breathing apparatus
  12.   At any *mine* an incident where—
  (a)   breathing apparatus or a smoke helmet or other apparatus serving the same purpose or a self rescuer, while being used, fails to function safely or develops a defect likely to affect its safe working; or
  (b)   immediately after using and arising out of the use of breathing apparatus or a smoke helmet or other apparatus serving the same purpose or a self-rescuer, any person receives first-aid or medical treatment by reason of his unfitness or suspected unfitness at the mine.

Injury by explosion of blasting material etc.
  13.   An incident in which any person suffers an injury (not being an injury covered by Regulation 3(2) or one reportable under Regulation 3(3)) resulting from an explosion or discharge of any blasting material or device within the meaning of section 69(4) of the Mines and Quarries Act 1954 for which he receives first-aid or medical treatment at the mine.

Use of emergency escape apparatus
  14.   An incident where any apparatus is used (other than for the purpose of *training* and practice) which has been provided at the mine in accordance with regulation 4 of the Mines (Safety of Exit) Regulations 1988 or where persons leave the *mine* when apparatus and equipment normally used by persons to leave the *mine* is unavailable.

  General note.   This paragraph is amended by S.I. 1988 No. 1729 as from (i) 1 April 1989 in respect of all mines (within the meaning of the Mines and Quarries Act 1954, s. 180) other than existing miscellaneous mines (i.e. mines other than mines of coal, stratified ironstone, shale or fireclay which is in existence or under construction on 1 April 1989); and (ii) 1 April 1994 in respect of existing miscellaneous mines.

Inrush of gas or water
  15.   Any inrush of noxious or flammable gas from old workings.

  16.   Any inrush of water or material which flows when wet from any source.

Insecure tip
  17.   Any movement of material or any fire or any other event which indicates that a tip to which Part I of the Mines and Quarries (Tips) Act 1969 applies, or is likely to become, insecure.

Locomotives
  18.   Any incident where an underground locomotive when not used for shunting or testing purposes is brought to rest by means other than its safety circuit protective devices or normal service brakes.

PART III. DANGEROUS OCCURRENCES WHICH ARE REPORTABLE IN RELATION TO *QUARRIES*

1.   The collapse of any storage bunker.

2.   The sinking or overturning of any waterborne craft or hovercraft.

3.   An incident in which any person suffers an injury (not being an injury covered by Regulation 3(2) or one reportable under Regulation 3(3)) resulting from an explosion or discharge of any blasting material or device within the meaning of section 69(4) of the Mines and Quarries Act 1954 for which he receives first-aid or medical treatment at the *quarry*.

4.   An occurrence in which any substance is ascertained to have been projected beyond a *quarry* boundary as a result of blasting operations in circumstances in which any person was, or might have been, endangered.

5.   Any movement of material or any fire or any other event which indicates that a tip to which Part I of the Mines and Quarries (Tips) Act 1969 applies is, or is likely to become, insecure.

PART IV. DANGEROUS OCCURRENCES WHICH ARE REPORTABLE IN RELATION TO *RAILWAYS*

1.—(1) Any of the following incidents which, taking into account the circumstances, might have been liable to cause the death of, or any of the injuries or conditions covered by Regulation 3(2) to, any person—
  (a) failure of—
      (i) a locomotive;
      (ii) a *railway* vehicle; or
      (iii) a rope haulage system used in working an inclined *railway*, or any part thereof;
  (b) failure of a structure or part of the permanent way or formation, including any tunnel or cutting; or
  (c) any train or *railway* vehicle striking an obstruction on the line.
  (2) Any case of collision, derailment, or a train unintentionally becoming divided, except one occurring on a siding or during shunting operations when there were no passengers on the train or other vehicles involved.
  (3) Failure of the equipment of any level crossing or a train running onto a level crossing when not authorised to do so.

SCHEDULE 2

Regulation 5(1) and
(2) and Schedule 3.

REPORTABLE DISEASES

Column 1	Column 2

Poisonings

1. Poisonings by any of the following:	Any activity.
(a) Acrylimide monomer;	
(b) Arsenic or one of its compounds;	
(c) Benzene or a homologue of benzene;	
(d) Beryllium or one of its compounds;	
(e) Cadmium or one of its compounds;	
(f) Carbon disulphide;	

Column 1   Column 2

(g) Diethylene dioxide (dioxan);
(h) Ethylene oxide;
(i) Lead or one of its compounds;
(j) Manganese or one of its compounds;
(k) Mercury or one of its compounds;
(l) Methyl bromide;
(m) Nitrochlorobenzene, or a nitro- or amino-
    or chloro-derivative of benzene or of a
    homologue of benzene;
(n) Oxides of nitrogen;
(o) Phosphorus or one of its compounds.

Skin diseases

2. Chrome ulceration of: *Work* involving exposure to chromic
   (a) the nose or throat; or   acid or to any other chromium com-
   (b) the skin of the hands or forearm.   pound.

3. Folliculitis.   *Work* involving exposure to mineral
                                            oil, tar, pitch or arsenic.

4. Acne

5. Skin cancer.

6. Inflammation, ulceration or malignant dis-   *Work* with ionising radiation.
   ease of the skin.

Lung diseases

7. Occupational asthma.   *Work* involving exposure to any of the
                                            following agents—
                                            (a) isocyanates;
                                            (b) platinum salts;
                                            (c) fumes or dusts arising from the
                                                manufacture, transport or use of
                                                hardening agents (including
                                                epoxy resin curing agents) based
                                                on phthalic anhydride, tetra-
                                                chlorophthalic anhydride, tri-
                                                mellitic anhydride or tri-ethyl-
                                                enetetramine;
                                            (d) fumes arising from the use of
                                                rosin as a soldering flux;
                                            (e) proteolytic enzymes;
                                            (f) animals or insects used for the
                                                purposes of research or edu-
                                                cation or in laboratories;
                                            (g) dusts arising from the sowing,
                                                cultivation, harvesting, drying,
                                                handling, milling, transport or
                                                storage of barley, oats, rye, wheat
                                                or maize, or the handling, mill-
                                                ing, transport or storage of meal
                                                or flour made therefrom.

8. Extrinsic alveolitis (including Farmer's   Exposure to moulds or fungal spores
   lung).   or heterologous proteins during *work*
                                              in—

Column 1	Column 2
	(a) agriculture, horticulture, forestry, cultivation of edible fungi or malt-working; or (b) loading or unloading or handling in storage mouldy vegetable matter of edible fungi; or (c) caring for or handling birds; or (d) handling bagasse.
9. Pneumoconiosis (excluding asbestosis).	1. (a) The mining, quarrying or working of silica rock or the working of dried quartzose sand or any dry deposit or dry residue of silica or any dry admixture containing such materials (including any activity in which any of the aforesaid operations are carried out incidentally to the mining or quarrying of other minerals or to the manufacture of articles containing crushed or ground silica rock); (b) the handling of any of the materials specified in the foregoing sub-paragraph in or incidental to any of the operations mentioned therein, or substantial exposure to the dust arising from such operations. 2. The breaking, crushing or grinding of flint or the working or handling of broken, crushed or ground flint or materials containing such flint, or substantial exposure to the dust arising from any of such operations. 3. Sand blasting by means of compressed air with the use of quartzosesand or crushed silica rock or flint, or substantial exposure to the dust arising from such sand blasting. 4. *Work* in a foundry or the performance of, or substantial exposure to the dust arising from, any of the following operations: (a) the freeing of steel castings from adherent siliceous substance; (b) the freeing of metal castings from adherent siliceous substance:

Column 1	Column 2

(i) by blasting with an abrasive propelled by compressed air, by steam or by a wheel; or

(ii) by the use of power-driven tools.

5. The manufacture of china or earthenware (including sanitary earthenware, electrical earthenware and earthenware tiles), and any activity involving substantial exposure to the dust arising therefrom.

6. The grinding of mineral graphite, or substantial exposure to the dust arising from such grinding.

7. The dressing of granite or any igneous rock by masons or the crushing of such materials, or substantial exposure to the dust arising from such operations.

8. The use, or preparation for use, of a grind-stone, or substantial exposure to the dust arising therefrom.

9. (a) *Work* underground in any *mine* in which one of the objects of the mining operations is the getting of any mineral;

(b) the working or handling above ground at any coal or tin mine of any minerals extracted therefrom, or any operation incidental thereto;

(c) the trimming of coal in any ship, barge, or lighter, or in any dock or harbour or at any wharf or quay;

(d) the sawing, splitting or dressing of slate, or any operation incidental thereto.

10. The manufacture, or *work* incidental to the manufacture, of carbon electrodes by an industrial undertaking for use in the electrolytic extraction of aluminium from aluminium oxide, and any activity involving substantial exposure to the dust arising therefrom.

Column 1	Column 2
	11. Boiler scaling or substantial exposure to the dust arising therefrom.
10. Byssinosis.	*Work* in any room where any process up to and including the weaving process is performed in a factory in which the spinning or manipulation of raw or waste cotton or of flax, or the weaving of cotton or flax, is carried on.
11. Mesothelioma.	(a) The working or handling or asbestos or any admixture of asbestos;
12. Lung cancer.	(b) The manufacture or repair of asbestos textiles or other articles containing or composed of asbestos;
13. Asbestosis.	(c) the cleaning of any machinery or plant used in any of the foregoing operations and of any chambers, fixtures and appliances for the collection of asbestos dust;
	(d) substantial exposure to the dust arising from any of the foregoing operations.
14. Cancer of a bronchus or lung.	*Work* in a factory where nickel is produced by decomposition of a gaseous nickel compound which necessitates working in or about a building or buildings where that process or any other industrial process ancillary or incidental thereto is carried on.
Infections	
15. Leptospirosis.	Handling animals, or work in places which are or may be infested by rats.
16. Hepatitis.	*Work* involving exposure to human blood products or body secretions and excretions.
17. Tuberculosis.	*Work* with persons or animals or with human or animal remains or with any other material which might be a source of infection.
18. Any illness caused by a pathogen referred to in column 2, opposite.	*Work* involving a pathogen which presents a hazard to human health.
19. Anthrax.	Any activity.
Other conditions	
20. Malignant disease of the bones.	*Work* with ionising radiation.
21. Blood dyscrasia.	

Column 1	Column 2

22. Cataract.

Work involving exposure to electro-magnetic radiation (including radiant heat).

23. Decompression sickness.
24. Barotrauma.

Breathing gases at increased pressure.

25. Cancer of the nasal cavity or associated air sinuses.

1. (a) *Work* in or about a building where wooden furniture is manufactured;
   (b) *work* in a building used for the manufacture of footwear or components of footwear made wholly or partly of leather or fibre board; or
   (c) *work* at a place used wholly or mainly for the repair of footwear made wholly or partly of leather or fibre board.

2. *Work* in a factory where nickel is produced by decomposition of a gaseous nickel compound which necessitates working in or about a building or buildings where that process or any other industrial process ancillary or incidental thereto is carried on.

26. Angiosarcoma of the liver.

(a) *Work* in or about machinery or apparatus used for the polymerisation of vinyl chloride monomer, a process which, for the purposes of this provision, comprises all operations up to and including the drying of the slurry produced by the polymerisation and the packaging of the dried product; or
(b) *work* in a building or structure in which any part of that process takes place.

27. Cancer of the urinary tract.

Work involving exposure to any of the following substances—
(a) alpha-naphthylamine, betanaphthylamine or methylene-bisorthochloroaniline;
(b) diphenyl substituted by at least one nitro or primary amino group or by at least one nitro and primary amino group (including benzidine);

Column 1   Column 2

	(c) any of the substances mentioned in sub-paragraph (b) above if further ring substituted by halo-geno, methyl or methoxy groups, but not by other groups;
	(d) the salts of any of the substances mentioned in sub-paragraphs (a) to (c) above;
	(e) auramine or magenta.
28. Vibration white finger.	(a) The use of hand-held chain saws in forestry; or
	(b) the use of hand-held rotary tools in grinding or in the sanding or polishing of metal, or the holding of material being ground, or metal being sanded or polished, by rotary tools; or
	(c) the use of hand-held percussive metal-working tools, or the holding of metal being worked upon by percussive tools, in riveting, caulking, chipping, hammering, fettling or swaging; or
	(d) the use of hand-held powered percussive drills or hand-held powered percussive hammers in mining, quarrying, demolition, or on roads or footpaths, including road construction; or
	(e) the holding of material being worked upon by pounding machines in shoe manufacture.

SCHEDULE 3

Regulation 7

RECORDS

PART I. PARTICULARS TO BE KEPT IN RECORDS OF ANY EVENT WHICH IS REPORTABLE UNDER REGULATION 3

1. Date and time of accident or dangerous occurrence.

2. The following particulars of the person affected:—
    (a) full name;
    (b) occupation;
    (c) nature of injury or condition.

3. Place where the accident or dangerous occurrence happened.

4. A brief description of the circumstances.

PART II. PARTICULARS TO BE KEPT IN RECORDS OF INSTANCES OF ANY OF THE DISEASES SPECIFIED IN SCHEDULE 2 AND REPORTABLE UNDER REGULATION 5

1. Date of diagnosis of the disease.

2. Occupation of the person affected.

3. Name or nature of the disease.

SCHEDULE 4

Regulation 8

ADDITIONAL PROVISIONS RELATING TO MINES AND QUARRIES

1. In this Schedule, unless the context otherwise requires—
"appropriate person" means—
(a) in the case of a coal mine, the *responsible person* or any official superior to a person appointed as a deputy;
(b) in the case of any other *mine*, the *responsible person*;
(c) in the case of a *quarry*—
    (i) the *responsible person*, or
    (ii) (where there is a sole manager) that manager, or
    (iii) (where there are two or more managers) the manager of the part of the quarry where the accident or *dangerous occurrence* happened, or
    (iv) any person who is for the time being treated for the purposes of the Mines and Quarries Act 1954 as such a manager;
"nominated person" means the person (if any) who is for the time being nominated—
(a) in a case where there is an association or body representative of a majority of the total number of persons employed at a *mine* or *quarry*, by that association or body;
(b) in any other case, jointly by associations or bodies which are together representative of such a majority,
to receive on behalf of the persons so employed notices under this Schedule.

2. Where at a *mine* or a *quarry* any person, as a result of an accident arising out of or in connection with *work*, dies or suffers any of the injuries or conditions specified by Regulation 3(2), or where there is a *dangerous occurrence*, the responsible person shall—
(a) forthwith notify the nominated person thereof by the quickest practicable means; and
(b) within 7 days send a report thereof to the nominated person on a form approved for the purposes of Regulation 3.

3. Where there is a non-fatal injury to any person at a *mine* or *quarry* which is reported in accordance with paragraph 2, after which that person dies and his death is as a result of the accident, then as soon as it comes to his knowledge the *responsible person* shall give notice of the death to the nominated person.

4.—(1) Where there is an accident or *dangerous occurrence* in relation to which paragraph 2 applies no person shall disturb the place where it happened or tamper with anything at that place before—
(a) the expiration of 3 clear days after the matter to which paragraph 2 applies has been notified in accordance with these Regulations; or

(b) the place has been visited by an inspector and by workmen's inspectors exercising the powers conferred on them by Section 123 of the Mines and Quarries Act 1954,

whichever is the sooner.

(2) The requirements of sub-paragraph (1) shall not apply to an accident or to a *dangerous occurrence* if an appropriate person—

(a) has taken adequate steps to ascertain that disturbing the site—

   (i) is unlikely to prejudice any investigation by an inspector into the circumstances of the accident or *dangerous occurrence*, and

   (ii) is necessary to secure the safety of any person at the *mine* or *quarry* or to avoid disrupting the normal working thereof; and

(b) (except in the case of non-fatal accident or a *dangerous occurrence*, where the nominated person or any person designated by that nominated person pursuant to this sub-paragraph cannot be contacted within a reasonable time) has notified the nominated person, or any person designated in writing by the nominated person to receive any such notification, of the proposed disturbance, and gives such a person a reasonable opportunity to visit the site before it is disturbed; and

(c) has taken adequate steps to ensure that there is obtained such information as will enable a full and accurate plan to be prepared forthwith, which plan shall show the position of any equipment or other item relevant to the accident or *dangerous occurrence* immediately after it happened; and

(d) ensures that any equipment or other item relevant to the accident or *dangerous occurrence* is kept as it was immediately after the incident until an inspector agrees that it may be disposed of.

(3) The person who has taken the steps referred to in sub-paragraph (2)(c) of this paragraph shall ensure that the plan referred to in that sub-paragraph is signed by the person who prepared it and bears the date on which it was prepared, and that a copy of that plan is supplied on request to any inspector or to the nominated person.

(4) It shall be a defence in proceedings against any person for contravening sub-paragraph (1) of this paragraph in any case which consists of the doing of any act, for that person to prove that the doing of that act was necessary for securing the safety of the *mine* and *quarry* or of any person.

5. The record kept under Regulation 7, excluding any health record of an identifiable individual, shall be available for inspection by—

(a) the nominated person;

(b) workmen's inspectors exercising the powers conferred on them by section 123 of the Mines and Quarries Act 1954.

SCHEDULE 5

Regulation 9

MATTERS WHICH THE EXECUTIVE WITH THE APPROVAL OF THE COMMISSION MAY REQUIRE TO BE NOTIFIED

1. Further details of the circumstances leading up to the reported incident.

2. Further details about the nature or design or both of any plant involved in the reported incident.

3. Safety systems and procedures for the control of the plant or substance involved in the reported incident.

4. Qualifications, experience and training of staff having use or control of any plant or substance or concerned with safety systems or procedures.

5. Design and operation documentation.

6. Arrangements for the protection of personnel from any plant or substance connected with the reported incident.

7. Details of any examination of, or tests carried out on, any plant or installation involved in the reported incident.

8. Any available information about levels of exposure of persons at the workplace to airborne substances.

SCHEDULE 6

Regulation 10(4)

PROVISIONS REQUIRING THE NOTIFICATION OF EVENTS WHICH ARE NOT
REQUIRED TO BE NOTIFIED OR REPORTED UNDER THESE REGULATIONS

1 Title of instrument	2 Reference
The Regulation of Railways Act 1871 and Orders or Regulations made or to be made thereunder.	1871 c. 78.
The Explosives Act 1875.	1875 c. 17
The Merchant Shipping Acts 1894 to 1979 and Orders and Regulations made or to be made thereunder.	The relevant enactments are— 1894 c. 60. 1970 c. 36. 1979 c. 39.
The Railway Employment (Prevention of Accidents) Act 1900.	1900 c. 27.
The Nuclear Installations Act 1965 and Orders and Regulations made or to be made thereunder.	1965 c. 57.
The Civil Aviation (Investigation of Accidents) Regulations 1969.	S.I. 1969/833.
The Air Navigation (Investigation of Combined Military and Civil Air Accidents) Regulations 1969.	S.I. 1969/1437.
The Poisonous Substances in Agriculture Regulations 1984.	S.I. 1984/1114.
The Ionising Radiations Regulations 1985.	S.I. 1985/1333.

SCHEDULE 7

Regulation 13

PART I. REPEALS

Column 1 Short title	Column 2 Chapter	Column 3 Extent of Repeal
The Factories Act 1961	1961 c. 34	Section 82 Section 140(1)(c)

PART II. REVOCATIONS

1 Title or short title of instrument	2 Reference	3 Extent of Revocation
Order dated 27 November 1915 applying s. 73 of the Factory and Workshop Act 1901 to cases of Toxic Jaundice.	S.R. & O. 1915/1170.	The whole Order.
Order dated 28 November 1919 applying s. 73 of the Factory and Workshop Act 1901 to certain diseases.	S.R. & O. 1919/1775.	The whole Order.
The Factory and Workshop (Notification of Diseases) Order 1924.	S.R. & O. 1924/1505.	The whole Order.
The Factory and Workshop (Notification of Diseases) Order 1936.	S.R. & O. 1936/686.	The whole Order.
The Factories (Notification of Diseases) Regulations 1938.	S.R. & O. 1938/1386.	The whole Regulations.
The Factories (Notification of Diseases) Regulations 1942.	S.R. & O. 1942/196.	The whole Regulations.
The Railway Running Sheds: (No. 1) Regulations 1961.	S.I. 1961/1251.	Paragraphs 1, 2, 6, 7, 12, 16 and 18 of the Schedule.
The Factories (Notification of Diseases) Regulations 1966.	S.I. 1966/1400.	The whole Regulations.
The Notice of Industrial Diseases Order 1973.	S.I. 1973/6.	The whole Order.
The Notification of Accidents and Dangerous Occurrences Regulations 1980.	S.I. 1980/804.	The whole Regulations.
The Dangerous Substances (Conveyance by Road in Road Tankers and Tank Containers) Regulations 1981.	S.I. 1981/1059.	Regulations 25(4).
Abstract of Factories Act Order 1973.	S.I. 1973/7.	Paragraph 14 of Schedule 1. Paragraph 16 of Schedule 2. Paragraph 10 of Schedule 3. Paragraph 10 of Schedule 4.
The Factories Act General Register Order 1973.	S.I. 1973/8.	Part 4 of Schedule 1. Part 4 of Schedule 2. Part 4 of Schedule 3.

PART III. MODIFICATIONS

1. The Mines and Quarries Act 1954 shall be modified as follows:—
(a) in section 22(2)(b) (which relates to the giving of notice to the nominated person that a shaft or outlet is unavailable) for "the Notification of Accidents and Dangerous Occurrences Regulations 1980" substitute "the Reporting of Injuries, Diseases and Dangerous Occurrences Regulations 1985";
(b) in section 123(3) (which relates to the giving of notice of an accident or dangerous occurrence) for "the Notification of Accidents and Dangerous Occurrences Regulations 1980" substitute "the Reporting of Injuries, Diseases and Dangerous Occurrences Regulations 1985".

2. Regulation 11(2) of the Coal and Other Mines (Fire and Rescue) Regulations 1956 (relating to precautions in case of outbreak or suspected outbreak of fire) shall be modified as follows, for the words from "responsibility for the notification" to "Regulations 1980" substitute the words "under the Reporting of Injuries, Diseases and Dangerous Occurrences Regulations 1985".

3. Section 1(4) of the Mines Management Act 1971 (which relates to the responsibilities of managers' assistants) shall be modified as follows, in paragraph (b) for "the Notification of Accidents and Dangerous Occurrences Regulations 1980" substitute "the Reporting of Injuries, Diseases and Dangerous Occurrences Regulations 1985".

4. Regulation 5(3) of the Control of Industrial Major Accident Hazards Regulations 1984 (which relates to the notification of major accidents) shall be modified as follows, for the "Notification of Accidents and Dangerous Occurrences Regulations 1980" substitute "the Reporting of Injuries, Diseases and Dangerous Occurrences Regulations 1985".

THE SAFETY SIGNS REGULATIONS 1980

(S.I. 1980 No. 1471)

The Secretary of State, in exercise of the powers conferred on him by sections 15(1), (2) and (6)(a) and 82(3)(a) of, and paragraph 1(1)(c) and (3) of Schedule 3 to, the Health and Safety at Work etc. Act 1974 ("the 1974 Act") and of all other powers enabling him in that behalf and for the purpose of giving effect without modifications to proposals submitted to him by the Health and Safety Commission under section 11(2)(d) of the 1974 Act after the carrying out by the said Commission of consultations in accordance with section 50(3) of that Act, hereby makes the following Regulations:—

1. Citation and commencement. These Regulations may be cited as the Safety Signs Regulations 1980 and shall come into operation on 1 January 1981 for the purposes of new signs and colours and on 1 January 1986 for all other purposes; in this Regulation "new signs and colours" means any sign or colour erected or placed on or after 1 January 1981.

General note. A Guidance Note relating to these Regulations (Booklet HS (R) 7) has been published by the Health and Safety Executive.

2. Interpretation.—(1) In these Regulations, unless the context otherwise requires—

"the 1974 Act" means the Health and Safety at Work etc. Act 1974;

"mine" and "quarry" means a mine or a quarry, as the case may be, within the meaning of section 180 of the Mines and Quarries Act 1954;

"Part I of BS 5378" means Standard number BS 5378: Part I: 1980 entitled "Safety signs and colours. Part I. Specification for colour and design" issued by the British Standards Institution, as published on 31 July 1980;

"safety sign" means a sign combining geometrical shape, colour and pictorial symbol to provide specific health or safety information or instruction (whether or not any text is also included);

"vessel" means a craft which is capable of travelling in or on water.

(2) Any reference in these Regulations to a numbered paragraph is a reference to the paragraph bearing that number in the Regulation in which the reference appears.

3. Safety signs and colours.—(1) Subject to paragraph (4), a *safety sign* (including any colour on it) giving health or safety information or instruction to persons at work *(a)* shall comply with *Part I of BS 5378*; but nothing in this paragraph shall be construed as requiring compliance with other standards referred to in that Part or with any other Part of BS 5378.

(2) Subject to paragraph (4), where a place at which there is a danger to the health or safety of persons at work *(a)* is identified by a strip of alternate colours,

those colours (including the proportion of each colour) shall comply with *Part I of BS 5378*.

(3) Subject to paragraph (4), a sign specified in Appendix A of *Part I of BS 5378* shall not be used at—

(a) any place of work; or
(b) any premises to which section 4 of *the 1974 Act* applies (which section relates to non-domestic premises *(b)* made available to persons as a place of work or as a place where they may use plant or substances *(c)* provided for their use there),

except to provide the health or safety information or instruction specified beside it in the said Appendix.

(4) The preceding paragraphs of this Regulation shall not apply to—

(a) any sign or colour—
  (i) for regulating rail, road, inland waterway, marine or air traffic (including pedestrians in relation to such traffic), or
  (ii) which is in such proximity to such traffic that it might be confused with a sign or colour to which head (i) above applies, or
  (iii) relating to any load carried by such traffic, or
  (iv) on an aircraft or hovercraft, or
  (v) on a *vessel*;
(b) any sign or colour at a *mine* which is a coal mine or at any premises on which there is a tip to which Part I of the Mines and Quarries (Tips) Act 1969 applies and which is associated with a coal mine;
(c) any sign or colour relating to fire fighting or rescue equipment or emergency exits;
(d) any label or marking on a package or container;
(e) any label or marking on an explosive article;
(f) any sign, colour, label or marking, as the case may be, used in simulating for training purposes any circumstances in which any of the preceding sub-paragraphs of this paragraph apply;
(g) any use of an emblem or design authorised for the time being under section 6 of the Geneva Conventions Act 1957.

(a) At work. For definition, see the Health and Safety at Work etc. Act 1974, s. 52(1) and the Interpretation Act 1978, s. 11.

(b) Non-domestic premises. For definition, see the Health and Safety at Work etc. Act 1974, s. 53(1) and the Interpretation Act 1978, s. 11.

(c) Plant; substance. For definition, see the Health and Safety at Work etc. Act 1974, s. 53(1) and the Interpretation Act 1978, s. 11.

4. Internal works traffic.—(1) Subject to paragraph (2), where at a place of work or at any premises *(a)* to which section 4 of *the 1974 Act* applies a sign is used for regulating traffic on land (including pedestrians in relation to such traffic) in circumstances in which the Road Traffic Regulation Act 1984 does not apply, then, if there is an appropriate traffic sign prescribed under that Act, that sign shall be used; in this paragraph "traffic" does not include rail traffic.

(2) This Regulation shall not apply at a *mine* which is a coal mine or at any premises on which there is a tip to which Part I of the Mines and Quarries (Tips) Act 1969 applies and which is associated with a coal mine.

    (a) *Premises.* For definition, see note *(b)* to reg. 3.

5.   Duty to ensure that these Regulations are complied with.—(1) Subject to paragraph (2), the employer *(a)* or self-employed *(b)* person, as the case may be, shall ensure that these Regulations are complied with, except that where signs or colours to which these Regulations apply are at a place of work or at premises *(c)* over which that employer or self-employed person has no control, the person having control of that place of work or those premises shall ensure that these Regulations are complied with.

    (2) In the case of a *mine* or *quarry*, the manager shall ensure that these Regulations are complied with.

    (a) *Employer.* For definition, see the Health and Safety at Work etc. Act 1974, s. 52(1) and the Interpretation Act 1978, s. 11.

    (b) *Self-employed person.* For definition, see the Health and Safety at Work etc. Act 1974, s. 52(1) and the Interpretation Act 1978, s. 11.

    (c) *Premises.* For definition, see note *(b)* to reg. 3.

THE HEALTH AND SAFETY (TRAINING FOR EMPLOYMENT) REGULATIONS 1990

(S.I. 1990 No. 1380)

1. Citation and commencement. These Regulations may be cited as the Health and Safety (Training for Employment) Regulations 1990, and shall come into force on 8 August 1990.

2. Interpretation. In these Regulations, unless the context otherwise requires—

"the 1974 Act" means the Health and Safety at Work etc. Act 1974;

"education establishment" means a university, polytechnic, college, school or similar educational or technical institute;

"relevant training" means work experience provided pursuant to a training course or programme, or training for employment, or both, except if—

(a) the immediate provider of the work experience or training for employment is an *educational establishment* and it is provided on a course run by the establishment; or

(b) received under a contract of employment.

3. Meaning of "work" and "at work". For the purposes of Part I of *the 1974 Act*—

(a) the meaning of the word "work" shall be extended to include *relevant training*;

(b) a person provided with *relevant training* is at work throughout the time when he would be in the course of his employment if he were receiving such training under a contract of employment, but not otherwise, and the meaning of "at work" shall be extended;

and in that connection in the other relevant statutory provisions, "work" and "at work" shall be construed accordingly.

4. Meaning of "employee", "employer" etc. For the purposes of the relevant statutory provisions a person provided with *relevant training* shall be treated as being the employee of the person whose undertaking (whether carried on by him for profit or not) is for the time being the immediate provider to that person of the training; and "employee", "worker", "employer" and related expressions in those provisions shall be construed accordingly.

5. Revocation. The Health and Safety (Training for Employment) Regulations 1988 and the Health and Safety (Training for Employment) (Amendment) Regulations 1989 are hereby revoked.

THE HEALTH AND SAFETY (FEES) REGULATIONS 1992

(S.I. 1992 No. 1752)

1. Citation, commencement and interpretation.—(1) These Regulations may be cited as the Health and Safety (Fees) Regulations 1992 and (except for regulations 10(2) and 11 and Part II of Schedule 9 and regulation 14, so far as it revokes regulations 10(2) and 11 and Part II of Schedule 9 and regulation 14, so far as it revokes regulations 10(2) and 11 of and Part II of Schedule 9 to the Health and Safety (Fees) Regulations 1991 which shall come into force on 2 November 1992) shall come into force on 20 August 1992.

(2) In these Regulations, unless the context otherwise requires—

"approval" includes the amendment of an approval, and "amendment of an approval" includes the issue of a new approval replacing the original incorporating an amendment;

"employment medical adviser" means an employment medical adviser appointed under section 56(1) of the 1974 Act;

"the mines and quarries provisions" means such of the relevant statutory provisions as relate exclusively to—

(a) mines and quarries within the meaning of section 180 of the Mines and Quarries Act 1954;

(b) tips within the meaning of section 2(1) of the Mines and Quarries (Tips) Act 1969,

and includes regulations, rules and orders relating to a particular mine (whether they are continued in force by regulation 7(3) of the Mines and Quarries Acts 1954 to 1971 (Repeals and Modifications) Regulations 1974 or are health and safety regulations);

"original approval" and "original authority" do not include an amendment of an approval or an amendment of an authority;

"renewal of approval" or "renewal of licence" means respectively the granting of an *approval* or licence to follow a previous *approval* or licence without any amendment or gap in time;

"respiratory protective equipment" includes any respirator and any breathing apparatus.

(3) Unless the context otherwise requires, any reference in these Regulations to—

(a) a numbered regulation or Schedule is a reference to the regulation or Schedule in these Regulations so numbered;

(b) a numbered paragraph is a reference to the paragraph so numbered in the regulation in which the reference appears.

2. Fees payable under *the mines and quarries provisions*.—(1) A fee shall be payable by the applicant to the Health and Safety Executive for an *original* *approval*, an *amendment of approval* or a *renewal of approval* under any of the mines and quarries provisions.

(2) The fee payable under paragraph (1) for each description of plant, apparatus, substance and in any other case set out in column 1 of Part I of Schedule 1 shall be respectively that specified in the corresponding entry in column 2, 3 or 4 of that Part and shall be payable on making the application for *approval*, or, where any such entry specifies a fee as an amount per hour worked, the fee so calculated shall be payable prior to the notification of the result of the application.

(3) Where the Executive requires testing to be carried out by its staff to decide whether *approval* can be granted, a fee shall be payable to the Executive by the applicant on the issue by the Executive of its determination in respect of the application for the *approval* as described below—

(a) in the case of explosives and detonators, for each text specified in column 1 of Part II of Schedule 1, the fee shall be that specified in the corresponding entry in column 2 of that Part;

(b) in any other case, the fee shall be determined under Part III of Schedule 1.

3. Fees for *approval* of *respiratory protective equipment*.—(1) A fee shall be payable by the applicant to the Health and Safety Executive on each application for *approval* of *respiratory protective equipment*—

(a) under the Factories Act 1961, or any regulations made or having effect as if made under that Act;

(b) under the Control of Lead at Work Regulations 1980;

(c) under the Ionising Radiations Regulations 1985; and

(d) under the Control of Asbestos at Work Regulations 1987; and

(e) under the Control of Substances Hazardous to Health Regulations 1988.

(2) The fee payable for *approval* of each item of the subject matter described in column 1 of Schedule 2 shall be that specified in column 2 of the Schedule and the fee so calculated shall be payable prior to the notification result of the application for *approval*.

(3) For the purposes of Schedule 2, the number of hours worked shall include time spent by the Executive's staff carrying out any testing to determine whether approval can be granted.

4. Fees under the Agriculture (Tractor Cabs) Regulations 1974.—(1) A fee shall be payable by the applicant to the Health and Safety Executive on each application for *approval* of plant and equipment under the Agriculture (Tractor Cabs) Regulations 1974.

(2) The fee payable for the *approval* of each subject matter described in column 1 of Schedule 3 shall be that specified in the corresponding entry in column 2 of that Schedule.

5. Fee payable under the Freight Containers (Safety Convention) Regulations 1984.—(1) A fee shall be payable by the applicant to the Health and Safety

Executive on each application for *approval* of a scheme or programme for examination of freight containers under the Freight Containers (Safety Convention) Regulations 1984.

(2) The fee payable for the *approval* described in column 1 of Schedule 4 shall be that specified in column 2 of that Schedule.

6.   Fee for a licence under the Asbestos (Licensing) Regulations 1983.—(1) A fee shall be payable by the applicant to the Health and Safety Executive on each application for a licence under the Asbestos (Licensing) Regulations 1983.

(2) The fee payable on application for a licence described in column 1 of Schedule 5 shall be that specified in column 2 of that Schedule.

7.   Fees for examination or surveillance by an *employment medical adviser*.— (1) A fee shall be payable to the Health and Safety Executive by an employer in respect of a medical examination or medical surveillance of each of his employees by an employment medical adviser for the purposes of any provision specified in column 1 of Schedule 6.

(2) The fee payable under paragraph (1) shall be a basic fee for each examination or on each occasion when surveillance is carried out together with additional fees for X-rays and laboratory tests where these are taken or carried out in connection with the examination; and for each provision specified in column 1 of Schedule 6—

(a)   the basic fee shall be the amount specified in column 3 of that Schedule for that provision;

(b)   the additional fee for X-rays shall be the amount specified in column 4 of that Schedule for that provision and shall cover all X-rays taken in connection with any one examination;

(c)   the additional fee for laboratory tests shall be the amount specified in column 5 of that Schedule for that provision and shall cover all such tests carried out in connection with any one examination.

(3) Where an *employment medical adviser* carries out a medical examination of a self-employed person for the purposes of the Control of Asbestos at Work Regulations 1987, that self-employed person shall pay to the Executive fees ascertained in accordance with paragraph (2).

8.   Fees for medical surveillance by an *employment medical adviser* under the Control of Lead at Work Regulations 1980.—(1) A fee shall be payable to the Health and Safety Executive by an employer in respect of medical surveillance of any of his employees by an *employment medical adviser* for the purposes of the Control of Lead at Work Regulations 1980.

(2) The fee payable for each item described in column 1 of Schedule 7 shall be that specified in the corresponding entry in column 2 of that Schedule.

9.   Fees for *approval* or reassessment of *approval* of dosimetry services and for type *approval* of radiation generators or apparatus containing radioactive substances under the Ionising Radiations Regulations 1985.—(1) A fee shall be payable by the applicant to the Health and Safety Executive on each application for an *approval* of dosimetry services or for the reassessment of an *approval* of dosimetry services previously granted for the purposes of the Ionising Radiations Regulations 1985.

(2) A fee shall be payable by the applicant to the Executive on each application for the type approval of a radiation generator or an apparatus containing a radioactive substance.

(3) The fee payable for *approval* or reassessment or type *approval* in respect of each matter described in column 1 of Schedule 8 shall be that specified in the corresponding entry in column 2 of that Schedule, together with any fee determined under paragraph (4), where applicable.

(4) Where the Executive requires an inspection to be carried out to determine whether an *approval* mentioned in paragraph (1) should be granted and it is necessary for any member of the Executive's staff to travel outside Great Britain for the purpose of the inspection, a fee shall be payable by the applicant to the Executive of an amount equal to the reasonable cost of travelling and subsistence of the member of the Executive's staff in connection with the inspection.

10.   Fees payable under the Explosives Act 1875 and instruments made thereunder, under the Petroleum (Consolidation) Act 1928, the Petroleum (Transfer of Licences) Act 1936 and the Classification and Labelling of Explosives Regulations 1983.—(1) Where any application in relation to a provision specified in column 1 of Part 1 of Schedule 9 is made for a purpose specified in column 2 of that Part, the fee specified in the corresponding entry in column 3 of that Part shall be payable by the applicant to the Health and Safety Executive.

(2) The fee or maximum fee payable under each provision specified in column 1 of Part II of Schedule 9 for the purpose described in the corresponding entry in column 2 shall be that specified in the corresponding entry in column 3 of that Part.

(3) A fee shall be payable by the applicant to the Executive on each application being made for each purpose specified in column 1 of each of Parts II, IV and V of Schedule 9, and the fee for each such purpose shall be that specified in the corresponding entry in column 2 in the respective Part.

(4) A fee shall be payable to the Executive where the Executive requires any work to be carried out by its specialist inspectors in connection with the grant of an ammonium nitrate mixtures licence as specified in column 1 of Part V of Schedule 9, and the fee for work in connection with each such purpose shall be that specified in the corresponding entry in column 3 of that Part for each hour or part of an hour worked and such fee shall be payable prior to notification of the result of the application.

(5) A fee shall be payable to the Executive where the Executive requires any testing to be carried out in connection with any purpose specified in column 1 of Part VI of Schedule 9, and the fee for testing in connection with each such purpose shall be that specified in the corresponding entry in column 2 of that

Part for each hour or part of an hour worked in respect of such testing and such fee shall be payable prior to notification of the result of the application.

11. Date from which fees are payable under the Petroleum (Consolidation) Act 1928 and the Petroleum (Transfer of Licences) Act 1936.—Notwithstanding the provisions of section 4 of the Petroleum (Consolidation) Act 1928 or section 1(4) of the Petroleum (Transfer of Licences) Act 1936 the fees for petroleum licences prescribed by these Regulations shall be payable for any licence first having effect or any transfer or *renewal of a licence* first taking effect on or after 2nd November 1992 irrespective of the date of the application for that licence, transfer or renewal.

12. Fees for explosive licences under Part IX of the Dangerous Substances in Harbour Areas Regulations 1987.—(1) A fee shall be payable by the applicant to the Health and Safety Executive on each application for an explosives licence or for any alteration in the terms of an existing licence under Part IX of the Dangerous Substances in Harbour Areas Regulations 1987.

(2) The fee on application for each purpose specified in column 1 of Schedule 10 shall be that specified in column 2 of that Schedule and where the fee is determined as an amount per hour, the fee so calculated shall be payable prior to notification of the result of the application.

13. Calculation of hours worked. In calculating the number of hours worked for the purpose of determining the amount of a fee payable under regulation 2(2), 3(2) or 10(5) no account shall be taken of any typing, messenger or ancillary work (for which no further charge shall be payable).

14. Revocations. The Health and Safety (Fees) Regulations 1991 are hereby revoked.

15. Northern Ireland. These Regulations shall not apply to Northern Ireland.

SCHEDULE 1

Regulation 2

PART I
FEES FOR *APPROVAL* OF PLANT, APPARATUS OR SUBSTANCE UNDER THE
MINES AND QUARRIES PROVISIONS

(1) Subject matter of approval	(2) Fee for an original approval	(3) Fee for amendment of approval	(4) Fee for renewal of approval
(a) *Approval* of breathing apparatus	£1,030	£515	£55
(b) *Approval* of dust respirators	£57 per hour worked	£57 per hour worked	£57 per hour worked
(c) *Approval* of explosives	£188	£130	£55
(d) *Approval* of locomotive or other vehicle	£2,027	£533	£55
(e) *Approval* of electrical equipment for use in potentially gassy zones	£632	£412	£55
(f) *Approval* of methanometers	£303	£193	£55
(g) Approval of electric safety lamps	£303	£193	£55
(h) *Approval* of other types of apparatus essential for safety	£154	£154	£55

PART II
FEES FOR TESTING EXPLOSIVES AND DETONATORS UNDER THE
MINES AND QUARRIES PROVISIONS

(1) Test	(2) Fee for test
(a) Ballistic pendulum shot	£41
(b) Break test shot	£51
(c) Deflagration shot	£35
(d) Detonator test (per 100 shots)	£380
(e) Detonator delay time test (per 100 shots)	£232
(f) Gallery shot	£82
(g) Mortar shot	£39
(h) Velocity of detonation test (per 3 shots)	£72

PART III
FEES FOR OTHER TESTING

The fee for any testing not fixed by Part II of this Schedule shall be £57 for each man-hour of work done in the testing, excluding any typing, messenger or other ancillary work (for which no further charge shall be payable).

SCHEDULE 2

Regulation 3

FEES FOR *APPROVAL* OF *RESPIRATORY PROTECTIVE EQUIPMENT*

(1) *Subject matter of approval*	(2) *Fee*
Approval of *respiratory protective equipment*	£57 per hour worked

SCHEDULE 3

Regulation 4

FEES FOR *APPROVAL* UNDER THE AGRICULTURE (TRACTOR CABS) REGULATIONS 1974

(1) *Subject matter of approval*	(2) *Fee*
(a)　*Original approval* of tractor cab	£209
(b)　Revision of an existing approval of a tractor cab	£99

SCHEDULE 4

Regulation 5

FEES FOR *APPROVAL* UNDER THE FREIGHT CONTAINERS (SAFETY CONVENTION) REGULATIONS 1984

(1) *Subject matter of approval*	(2) *Fee*
Approval of scheme or programme for examination of freight containers	£75

SCHEDULE 5

Regulation 6

LICENCE UNDER THE ASBESTOS (LICENSING) REGULATIONS 1983

(1) *Subject matter of licence*	(2) *Fee*
(a)　Licence for work with asbestos insulation or asbestos coating or renewal of original licence	£450

SCHEDULE 6

Regulation 7

FEES FOR EXAMINATION OR SURVEILLANCE BY AN EMPLOYMENT MEDICAL ADVISER

(1) *Provision*	(2) *Reference*	(3) *Basic Fee*	(4) *Additional fees where appropriate*	(5)
			Fee for X-Rays	*Fee for Laboratory tests*
(a) The Work in Compressed Air Special Regulations 1958	S.I. 1958/61 (relevant amending instrument is S.I. 1973/36)	£40	£37.40	£19.50
(b) The Ionising Radiations Regulations 1985	S.I. 1985/1333	£17 where surveillance is confined to examination of, and making entries in records £39 in other cases	£37.40	£19.50
(c) The Control of Asbestos at Work Regulations 1987	S.I. 1987/2115	£43	£34.10	£17.50
(d) The Control of Substances Hazardous to Health Regulations 1988	S.I. 1988/1657	£40	£37.40	£19.50

SCHEDULE 7

Regulation 8

FEES FOR MEDICAL SURVEILLANCE BY AN EMPLOYMENT MEDICAL ADVISER UNDER THE CONTROL OF LEAD AT WORK REGULATIONS 1980

(1) *Item*	(2) *Fee*
(a) On the first assessment of an employee (including any clinical medical examination and laboratory tests in connection with the assessment)	£40.50
(b) On each subsequent assessment of an employee—	
(i) for laboratory tests where these are carried out	£40.50
(ii) for a clinical medical examination where this is carried out	£18.50

SCHEDULE 8

Regulation 9

FEES FOR *APPROVAL* OR REASSESSMENT OF *APPROVAL* OF DOSIMETRY SERVICES AND FOR TYPE *APPROVAL* OF RADIATION GENERATORS OR APPARATUS CONTAINING RADIOACTIVE SUBSTANCES UNDER THE IONISING RADIATION REGULATIONS 1985

(1) *Description*	(2) *Fee*
Approval or reassessment of *approval* of Dosimetry Services granted under regulation 15 of the Ionising Radiations Regulations 1985	
Group I **Dose record keeping**	
(a) Where the application is solely in respect of Group 1 functions	£429
(b) Where the application for Group 1 functions is linked to an application in respect of functions in another group	£183
Group II **External dosimetry**	£500 for one sub-group and £215 for each additional sub-group
(a) Whole body (beta, gamma, thermal neutrons) film	
(b) Whole body (beta, gamma, thermal neutrons) thermoluminscent dosimeter (TLD)	
(c) Whole body (neutron), other than sub-groups (a) or (b)	
(d) Whole body, other than sub-groups (a), (b), or (c)	
(e) Extremity monitoring	
(f) Accident dosimetry, other than in the previous sub-groups	
Group III **Internal Dosimetry**	
(a) Bio-assay, in-vivo monitoring or air sampling	£439
(b) Any two or all three of the above techniques	£621
Type *approval* of a radiation generator or an apparatus containing a radioactive substance under sub-paragraph (f) or (g) respectively of Schedule 3 to the Ionising Radiations Regulations 1985 (which excepts such type-approved radiation generators or apparatus containing radioactive substances from the notification requirements of regulation 5 of those Regulations)	£87

SCHEDULE 9

Regulation 10

FEES PAYABLE UNDER THE EXPLOSIVES ACT 1875 AND INSTRUMENTS MADE THEREUNDER, UNDER THE PETROLEUM (CONSOLIDATION) ACT 1928 AND THE PETROLEUM (TRANSFER OF LICENCES) ACT 1936

PART I
APPLICATIONS FOR FACTORY LICENCES, MAGAZINE LICENCES AND IMPORTATION LICENCES AND AMENDING LICENCES UNDER SECTIONS 6, 12 AND 40(9) OF THE EXPLOSIVES ACT AND REPLACEMENT OF SUCH LICENCES

(1) *Provision under which a licence is granted*	(2) *Purpose of application*	(3) *Fee*
Explosives Act 1875 c. 17		
Section 6 (as applied to explosives other than gunpowder by sections 39 and 40)	Factory Licence	£850 plus £45 additional fee for each building or other place in which explosives are to be made or kept
	Magazine licence	£656 plus £45 additional fee for each building or other place in which explosives are to be kept
	Replacement of one of the above licences if lost	£23
Section 12 (as applied to explosives other than gunpowder by sections 39 and 40)	Factory amending licence	£308 plus £11 additional fee for each building or other place to be specified in the amending licence and in which explosives are to be made or kept
	Magazine amending licence	£53 plus £11 additional fee for each building or other place to be specified in the amending licence and in which explosives are to be kept
	Replacement of one of the above licences if lost	£23
Section 40(9)	Licence for importation of explosives	£46
	Replacement of the above licence if lost	£23

(1) Provision under which a licence is granted	(2) Purpose of application	(3) Fee
	Amendment to an existing licence	£16
Section 40(9) as applied to compressed acetylene by The Compressed Acetylene (Importation) Regulations 1978	Licence for importation of compressed acetylene	£49.50
	Replacement of the above licence if lost	£23
	Amendment to an existing licence	£16

PART II

FEE OR MAXIMUM FEE PAYABLE IN RESPECT OF GRANTING AND RENEWAL OF AN EXPLOSIVES STORE LICENCE, THE REGISTRATION OR RENEWAL OF REGISTRATION OF PREMISES USED FOR KEEPING EXPLOSIVES AND THE GRANTING AND TRANSFER OF PETROLEUM-SPIRIT LICENCES

(1) Provision under which a fee or maximum fee is payable	(2) Purpose of application	(3) Fee or maximum fee
Explosives Act 1875 c. 17		
Section 15 (see note 1)	A store licence	£56.50
Section 18 (see note 1)	Renewal of store licence	£56.50
Section 21 (see note 1)	Registration and renewal of registration of premises for the keeping of explosives with a local authority	£10
Petroleum (Consolidation) Act 1928 c. 32		
Section 4 (see notes 2 and 3)	Licence to keep petroleum spirit of a quantity—	
	not exceeding 2,500 litres	£27 for each year of licence
	exceeding 2,500 litres but not exceeding 50,000 litres	£40 for each year of licence
	exceeding 50,000 litres	£78 for each year of licence
Petroleum (Transfer of Licences) Act 1936 c. 27		
Section 1(4)	Transfer of petroleum spirit licence	£7

Note:

1. *Part I of the Explosives Act 1875 (which includes sections 15, 18 and 21) is applied to explosives other than gunpoweder by sections 39 and 40 of that Act.*

2. *In the case of a solid substance for which by virtue of an Order in Council made under section 19 of the Petroleum (Consolidation) Act 1928 a licence is required, the fee payable under this Schedule shall be calculated as if one kilogram of the substance were equivalent to one litre.*

3. *The fee payable for a licence of more or less than one year's duration shall be the fee set out above increased or decreased, as the case may be, proportionately according to the duration of the period for which the licence is granted or renewed.*

PART III

APPLICATIONS UNDER PARAGRAPH (1) OF THE PROVISO TO ORDER IN COUNCIL (NO. 30) OF 2 FEBRUARY 1937 FOR *APPROVALS* OF PREMISES AND APPARATUS IN WHICH ACETYLENE IS TO BE MANUFACTURED OR KEPT

(1) *Purpose of application*	(2) *Fee*
(a) *Original approval* of premises in which acetylene is to be manufactured or kept	£488
(b) Amendment of an *approval* of premises in which acetylene is to be manufactured or kept	£216
(c) *Approval* of apparatus in which acetylene is to be manufactured or kept	£26.40

PART IV

APPLICATIONS FOR COMPARISONS AND *APPROVALS* IN RESPECT OF CONDITIONS (1) AND (8) IN THE ORDER OF THE SECRETARY OF STATE (NO. 9) OF 23 JUNE 1919

(1) *Purpose of application*	(2) *Fee*
(a) Comparison of a porous substance with a sample porous substance	£26.40
(b) Original approval of premises in which acetylene is compressed	£488
(c) Amendment of an approval of premises in which acetylene is compresssed	£33

PART V
MISCELLANEOUS APPLICATIONS

(1) Purpose of application	(2) Fee	(3) Fee for work by specialist inspector
(a) Classification of an explosive under the Classification and Labelling of Explosives Regulations 1983, or authorisation of an explosive to be manufactured or to be imported, with or without a licence	£133	
(b) Grant of an ammonium nitrate mixtures licence under article 3 of the Ammonium Nitrate Mixtures Exemption Order 1967	£139	£34 per hour worked

PART VI
FURTHER FEES PAYABLE IN RESPECT OF CERTAIN TESTING REQUIRED BY THE HEALTH AND SAFETY EXECUTIVE

(1) Purpose of application	(2) Fee
(a) Application for a licence to be granted under or in pursuance of section 40(9) of the Explosives Act 1875 for the importation of explosives which are not at the time of application authorised to be manufactured for general sale or imported for general sale	£57 per hour worked
(b) Approval of apparatus in which acetylene is to be manufactured or kept (Part III above)	£57 per hour worked
(c) Comparison of a porous substance with a sample porous substance (Part IV above)	£57 per hour worked
(d) Classification of an explosive under the Classification and Labelling of Explosives Regulations 1983 or authorisation of an explosive to be manufactured for general sale or to be imported for general sale, with or without a licence (Part V above)	£57 per hour worked
(e) Application for a licence to manufacture in pursuance of the Ammonium Nitrate Mixtures Exemption Order 1967 (Part V above)	£57 per hour worked

SCHEDULE 10

Regulation 12

FEES FOR GRANT OR ALTERATION OF THE TERMS OF AN EXPLOSIVES LICENCE UNDER PART
IX OF THE DANGEROUS SUBSTANCES IN HARBOUR AREA REGULATIONS 1987

(1) *Purpose of application*	(2) Fee
Grant of an explosives licence or alteration of the terms of an existing explosives licence	£251 plus £43 per hour worked

THE MANUAL HANDLING
OPERATIONS REGULATIONS 1992

(S.I. 1992 No. 2793)

General note. These Regulations are intended to implement the Manual Handling Directive 90/269 (see page 148). The Regulations do not apply to protect temporary workers and so fail to implement the Temporary Workers Directive 91/383 so far as handling of loads is concerned.

The regulations came into effect on 1 January 1993 as did the repeals to which they gave effect. There is no period of grace as for other Regulations giving effect to European Directives.

These Regulations are not supplemented by any Approved Code of Practice but there is an extensive Guidance Note called "Manual Handling" (not included in this book) which has no statutory admissibility in civil or criminal proceedings, though doubtless a court might consider its recommendations relevant.

The Regulations deal with "manual handling operations" which means transporting, supporting, lifting, putting down, pushing, pulling, carrying or moving a load by hand or bodily force. The Regulations apply to all employment except seagoing ships although they apply to work on ships in territorial waters and loading and unloading ships. They apply to offshore oil and gas installations and associated vessels. The employer's duty is to avoid, so far as is reasonably practicable, manual handling with a risk of injury. If that is not reasonably practicable a risk assessment must be carried out and steps taken to reduce the risk to the lowest level reasonably practicable. Employees are under a duty to use any system of work provided. The Regulations do not specify maximum weights and the risk of injury does not include toxic or corrosive substances on or from the load.

As noted earlier, to the extent that Regulations fail to give full effect to the Directives they are intended to implement, recourse, by way of an aid to construction, or in some cases by way of direct enforcement, may be had to the relevant Directive (see "Interpretation in the Light of the European Directives" and "Direct Application of the European Directives" under LEGAL PRINCIPLES in the introductory section). Some possible areas of arguable shortfall in implementation of the Directive these Regulations are intended to implement have been noted by commentators. Amongst these are the following. Annex II of the Directive requires the employer to take into account that the worker may be at risk if physically unsuited to the task in question. Schedule 1, factor 4 of the Regulations directs the employer only to consider the pregnant worker or one with a health problem, or whether the task requires unusual strength or height. Yet a task requiring only normal strength may pose a risk to a weak or small worker who has no health problem. This shortfall is not remedied wholly by the requirement to have regard to the capacity of the individual worker contained in reg. 11 of the Management of Health and Safety at Work Regulations (S.I. 1992 No. 2051) since the latter is unenforceable in a civil action.

Another apparent deficit is that Art. 6(2) of the Directive requires that employers must ensure that workers receive proper training and information on handling loads. The Regulations contain no such requirement, although it is conceivable that a purposive construction of the requirement under reg. 4(1)(b)(ii) "to take appropriate steps to reduce the risk of injury . . ." might be held to stretch to this, the employer also being required to consider whether "special information or training" is required (Sch. 1, factor 4) (and see Guidance Note, para. 156).

Both Directive (Art. 3(1)) and Regulation (reg. 4(1)(a)) impose a hierarchy of measures the employer must take, beginning with the obligation to take steps to avoid manual handling. The Regulation introduces the qualification "so far as is reasonably practicable" (see INTRODUCTORY NOTE 5) to each step, a qualification not found in the Directive. This appears to be a failure properly to implement the Directive, and there is doubt therefore whether that limitation on the duty will be sustainable: see "Interpretation in the Light of the European Directives" and "Direct Application of the European Directives" under LEGAL PRINCIPLES in the introductory section.

There is a requirement to consult workplace representatives specified in the Framework Directive and in this Directive. These Regulations contain no reflection of that obligation. However, the obligation to consult representatives of the workforce finds form in the amendment to the Safety Representatives and Safety Committees Regulations 1977 (S.I. 1977 No. 500) contained in the Schedule to the Management of Health and Safety at Work Regulations 1992 (S.I. 1992 No. 2051). That obligation only arises where the employer cares to recognise a union. This deficiency in implementation of the Framework Directive has already been referred to, see the General Note to reg. 4A of the Safety Representatives and Safety Committee Regulations 1977.

As noted above there is a failure to implement the requirements of the Temporary Workers Directive by reason of the fact that reg. 4 only applies as between employer and employee.

The Secretary of State, in exercise of the powers conferred on her by sections 15(1), (2), (3)(a), (5)(a) and (9) and 80(1), (2)(a) and (4) of, and paragraphs 1(1)(a) and (c) and 8 of Schedule 3 to, the Health and Safety at Work etc. Act 1974 ("the 1974 Act") and of all other powers enabling her in that behalf and—

(a) for the purpose of giving effect without modifications to proposals submitted to her by the Health and Safety Commission under section 11(2)(d) of *the 1974 Act* after the carrying out by the said Commission of consultations in accordance with section 50(3) of that Act; and

(b) it appearing to her that the repeal of section 18(1)(f) of the Children and Young Persons Act 1933 and section 28(1)(f) of the Children and Young Persons (Scotland) Act 1937 except insofar as those provisions apply to such employment as is permitted under section 1(2) of the Employment of Women, Young Persons, and Children Act 1920 is expedient in consequence of the Regulations referred to below after the carrying out by her of consultations in accordance with section 80(4) of *the 1974 Act*, hereby makes the following Regulations:

1. Citation and commencement. These Regulations may be cited as the Manual Handling Operations Regulations 1992 and shall come into force on 1 January 1993.

2. Interpretation.—(1) In these Regulations, unless the context otherwise requires—

"injury" does not include injury caused by any toxic or corrosive substance which—

(a) has leaked or spilled from a *load*;
(b) is present on the surface of a *load* but has not leaked or spilled from it; or
(c) is a constituent part of a *load*,

and "injured" shall be construed accordingly;

"load" includes any person and any animal;

"manual handling operations" means any transporting or supporting of a *load* (including the lifting, putting down, pushing, pulling, carrying or moving thereof) by hand or by bodily force.

(2) Any duty imposed by these Regulations on an employer in respect of his employees shall also be imposed on a self-employed person in respect of himself.

3.   Disapplication of Regulations.   These Regulations shall not apply to or in relation to the master or crew of a seagoing ship or to the employer of such persons in respect of the normal ship-board activities of a ship's crew under the direction of the master.

4.   Duties of employers.—(1) Each employer shall—

(a)   so far as is reasonably practicable *(a)*, avoid the need for his employees to undertake any *manual handling operations* at work which involve a risk of their being *injured*; or

(b)   where it is not reasonably practicable *(a)* to avoid the need for his employees to undertake any *manual handling operations* at work which involve a risk of their being *injured*—

    (i)   make a suitable and sufficient *(b)* assessment *(c)* of all such *manual handling operations* to be undertaken by them, having regard to the factors which are specified in column 1 of Schedule 1 to these Regulations and considering the questions which are specified in the corresponding entry in column 2 of that Schedule,

    (ii)   take appropriate steps to reduce the risk of *injury* to those employees arising out of their undertaking any such *manual handling operations* to the lowest level reasonably practicable *(a)*, and

    (iii)   take appropriate steps to provide any of those employees who are undertaking any such *manual handling operations* with general indications and, where it is reasonably practicable *(a)* to do so, precise information on—

        (aa)   the weight of each *load*, and

        (bb)   the heaviest side of any *load* whose centre of gravity is not positioned centrally.

(2) Any assessment *(c)* such as is referred to in paragraph (1)(b)(i) of this regulation shall be reviewed by the employer who made it if—

(a)   there is reason to suspect that it is no longer valid; or

(b)   there has been a significant change in the *manual handling operations* to which it relates,

and where as a result of any such review changes to an assessment are required, the relevant employer shall make them.

General note. Under the repealed s. 72 of the Factories Act 1961 where a person was employed to do work which involved the moving of an object which, to the employer's knowledge, was too heavy for him to move unaided, the employers were in breach of s. 72 where they did not instruct him not to move the object without assistance; it was immaterial that the employee could have obtained assistance had he asked for it (*Brown v Allied Ironfounders Ltd* [1974] 2 All ER 135, [1974] 1 WLR 527, HL; and see *Peat v*

W J Muschamp & Co Ltd (1969) 7 KIR 469, CA). But if the system involves the employee being instructed to obtain help when necessary, that help must as a matter of fact be readily available when needed (see, for example, *Mearns v Lothian Regional Council* 1991 SLT 338). *Brown v Allied Ironfounders Ltd,* (above), was applied in *Bailey v Rolls Royce (1971) Ltd* [1984] ICR 688, CA: employer only liable under s. 72(1) if the employee was employed to lift the particular load and, in doing so, it was likely that he personally would have been injured. Note that under the Factories Act s. 72 the words "to him" meant that the employer could be liable if because of the sex, build, physique or other obvious characteristic of the employee, the employer knew or ought to have known that the particular person would be likely to be caused injury (but see *Whitfield v H & R Johnson (Tiles) Ltd* [1991] ICR 109, CA: no liability for employee who had a congenital weakness of the spine which was unknown to the employer; *Bailey v Rolls Royce,* above distinguished). Although the Regulations refer to employees in general, it is submitted that a similar approach to individual weaknesses should be followed.

(a) **Reasonably practicable.** See General Note at the beginning of these Regulations and compare Art. 3 and Art. 4 of the Directive.

(b) **Suitable and sufficient.** See INTRODUCTORY NOTE 12.

(c) **Assessment.** See Regulation 3 of the Management of Health and Safety at Work Regulations (S.I. 1992 No. 2051).

5. Duty of employees. Each employee while at work shall make full and proper use of any system of work provided for his use by his employer in compliance with regulation 4(1)(b)(ii) of these Regulations.

6. Exemption certificates.—(1) The Secretary of State for Defence may, in the interests of national security, by a certificate in writing exempt—

(a) any of the home forces, any visiting force or any headquarters from any requirement imposed by regulation 4 of these Regulations; or

(b) any member of the home forces, any member of a visiting force or any member of a headquarters from the requirement imposed by regulation 5 of these Regulations,

and any exemption such as is specified in sub-paragraph (a) or (b) of this paragraph may be granted subject to conditions and to a limit of time and may be revoked by the said Secretary of State by a further certificate in writing at any time.

(2) In this regulation—

(a) "the home forces" has the same meaning as in section 12(1) of the Visiting Forces Act 1952;

(b) "headquarters" has the same meaning as in article 3(2) of the Visiting Forces and International Headquarters (Application of Law) Order 1965;

(c) "member of a headquarters" has the same meaning as in paragraph 1(1) of the Schedule to the International Headquarters and Defence Organisations Act 1964; and

(d) "visiting force" has the same meaning as it does for the purposes of any provision of Part I of the Visiting Forces Act 1952.

7. Extension outside Great Britain. These Regulations shall, subject to regulation 3 hereof, apply to and in relation to the premises and activities outside

Great Britain to which sections 1 to 59 and 80 to 82 of the Health and Safety at Work etc. Act 1974 apply by virtue of the Health and Safety at Work etc. Act 1974 (Application Outside Great Britain) Order 1989 as they apply within Great Britain.

8.   Repeals and revocations.—(1) The enactments mentioned in column 1 of Part I of Schedule 2 to these Regulations are repealed to the extent specified in the corresponding entry in column 3 of that Part.

(2) The Regulations mentioned in column 1 of Part II of Schedule 2 to these Regulations are revoked to the extent specified in the corresponding entry in column 3 of that Part.

SCHEDULE 1

Regulation 4(1)(b)(i)

FACTORS TO WHICH THE EMPLOYER MUST HAVE REGARD AND QUESTIONS HE MUST CONSIDER WHEN MAKING AN ASSESSMENT OF *MANUAL HANDLING OPERATIONS*

Column 1 *Factors*	Column 2 *Questions*

1 The tasks	**Do they involve:**
	—holding or manipulating *loads* at distance from trunk?
	—unsatisfactory bodily movement or posture, especially:
	  —twisting the trunk?
	  —stooping?
	  —reaching upwards?
	  —excessive movement of *loads*, especially:
	  —excessive lifting or lowering distances?
	  —excessive carrying distances?
	—excessive pushing or pulling of *loads*?
	—risk of sudden movement of *loads*?
	—frequent or prolonged physical effort?
	—insufficient rest or recovery periods?
	—a rate of work imposed by a process?

2 The *loads*	**Are they:** —heavy? —bulky or unwieldy? —difficult to grasp? —unstable, or with contents likely to shift? —sharp, hot or otherwise potentially damaging?
3 The working environment	**Are there:** —space constraints preventing good posture? —uneven, slippery or unstable floors? —variations in level of floors or work surfaces? —extremes of temperature or humidity? —conditions causing ventilation problems or gusts of wind? —poor lighting conditions?

Column 1 *Factors*	Column 2 *Questions*
4 *Individual capability*	**Does the job:** —require unusual strength, height, etc? —create a hazard to those who might reasonably be considered to be pregnant or to have a health problem? —require special information or training for its safe performance?
5 Other factors	**Is movement or posture hindered by personal protective equipment or by clothing?**

SCHEDULE 2

Regulation 8

REPEALS AND REVOCATIONS

PART I
REPEALS

Column 1 *Short title of enactment*	Column 2 *Reference*	Column 3 *Extent of repeal*
The Children and Young Persons Act 1933.	1933 c. 12.	Section 18(1)(f) except insofar as that paragraph applies to such employment as is permitted under section 1(2) of the Employment of Women, Young Persons, and Children Act 1920 (1920 c. 65).
The Children and Young Persons (Scotland) Act 1937.	1937 c. 37.	Section 28(1)(f) except insofar as that paragraph applies to such employment as is permitted under section 1(2) of the Employment of Women, Young Persons, and Children Act 1920.
The Mines and Quarries Act 1954.	1954 c. 70.	Section 93; in section 115 the word "ninety-three".
The Agriculture (Safety, Health and Welfare Provisions) Act 1956.	1956 c. 49.	Section 2.
The Factories Act 1961.	1961 c. 34.	Section 72.

Column 1 *Short title of enactment*	Column 2 *Reference*	Column 3 *Extent of repeal*
The Offices, Shops and Railway Premises Act 1963.	1963 c. 41.	Section 23 except insofar as the prohibition contained in that section applies to any person specified in section 90(4) of the same Act. In section 83(1) the number "23".

PART II
REVOCATIONS

Column 1 *Title of instrument*	Column 2 *Reference*	Column 3 *Extent of revocation*
The Agriculture (Lifting of Heavy Weights) Regulations 1959.	S.I. 1959/2120.	The whole Regulations.
The Construction (General Provisions) Regulations 1961.	S.I. 1961/1580.	In regulation 3(1)(a) the phrase "and 55"; regulation 55.

PART 4
EQUIPMENT ETC.

SUMMARY

EMPLOYER'S LIABILITY (DEFECTIVE EQUIPMENT) ACT 1969

(1969 c. 37)

General note. The Act does not confer a new cause of action (see *Clarkson v William Jackson & Sons Ltd* (1984) Times, 21 November, CA) but merely redresses the unsatisfactory common law position established by *Davie v New Merton Board Mills Ltd* [1959] AC 604, HL, under which an employee would have no remedy for injury caused by defective equipment supplied by the employer if the latter had purchased the article from a reputable source and the defect was a latent one which he had no means of discovering. The effect of the Statute is to remove this defence without more: foreseeability, for example, continues to be relevant as at common law (*Deegan v North Bedford Health Authority*, Queen's Bench Division, 2 October 1990).

An Act to make further provision with respect to the liability of an employer for injury to his employee which is attributable to any defect in equipment provided by the employer for the purposes of the employer's business; and for purposes connected with the matter aforesaid
[25 July 1969]

1. Extension of employer's liability for defective equipment.—(1) Where after the commencement of this Act—

    (a) an employee suffers personal injury in the course of his employment in consequence of a defect in equipment provided by his employer for the purposes of the employer's business; and

    (b) the defect is attributable wholly or partly to the fault of a third party (whether identified or not),

the injury shall be deemed to be also attributable to negligence on the part of the employer (whether or not he is liable in respect of the injury apart from this subsection), but without prejudice to the law relating to contributory negligence and to any remedy by way of contribution or in contract or otherwise which is available to the employer in respect of the injury.

(2) In so far as any agreement purports to exclude or limit any liability of an employer arising under subsection (1) of this section, the agreement shall be void.

(3) In this section—

"business" includes the activities carried on by any public body;

"employee" means a person who is employed by another person under a contract of service or apprenticeship and is so employed for the purposes of a business carried on by that other person, and "employer" shall be construed accordingly;

"equipment" *(a)* includes any plant and machinery, vehicle, aircraft and clothing;

"fault" means negligence, breach of statutory duty or other act or omission which gives rise to liability in tort in England and Wales or which is wrongful and gives rise to liability in damages in Scotland; and

"personal injury" includes loss of life, any impairment of a person's physical or mental condition and any disease.

(4) This section binds the Crown, and persons in the service of the Crown shall accordingly be treated for the purposes of this section as employees of the Crown if they would not be so treated apart from this subsection.

(a) **Equipment.** The term was given a wide reading in *Coltman v Bibby Tankers Ltd* [1988] AC 276, so that a ship (and not merely the machinery and the like on board) fell within the definition. Consequently, the estate of a plaintiff was able to recover under the Act when he died following the sinking of a vessel caused by its unseaworthy design and construction. In the course of his judgment, Lord Oliver (with whom all the other Lords agreed) said: "The purpose of the Act was manifestly to saddle the employer with liability for defective plant of every sort with which the employee is compelled to work in the course of his employment and I can see no ground for excluding particular types of chattel merely on the ground of their size or the element upon which they are designed to operate" (at p. 301). In *Knowles v Liverpool City Council* [1993] ICR 21, [1993] IRLR 6, CA, the employee sustained injury when the flagstone he was handling in the course of paving broke. The Court of Appeal held that the flagstone was "equipment" within the meaning of s. 1(3). Leave to appeal has been granted to the House of Lords.

2. Short title, commencement and extent.—(1) This Act may be cited as the Employer's Liability (Defective Equipment) Act 1969.

(2) This Act shall come into force on the expiration of the period of three months beginning with the date on which it is passed.

(3) ...

(4) This Act ... does not extend to Northern Ireland.

General note. Words omitted from sub-ss. (3), (4) repealed by the Northern Ireland Constitution Act 1973, s. 41, Sch. 6, Pt. 1.

THE PROVISION AND USE OF WORK EQUIPMENT REGULATIONS 1992

(S.I. 1992 No. 2932)

General note. These Regulations are intended to implement the Work Equipment Directive 89/655 (see page 100). The Regulations will generally apply to temporary workers since the obligation under them falls on any person in control of the premises (reg. 4(2)(b)) and implement the Temporary Workers Directive 91/383 so far as work equipment is concerned.

The Regulations impose duties: to provide and maintain suitable work equipment which conforms to standards specified in other legislation implementing European Directives (listed in Sch. 1); to provide adequate training, information and consultation; to restrict, to trained employees only, equipment likely to carry a risk; to provide adequate information, instructions and training; to protect against dangerous parts and other hazards; to protect against high or very low temperatures; to provide visible controls to start, control, stop and emergency stop the equipment; to provide isolation from energy sources; stabilise equipment; to light it; to protect against risks while maintaining it; and to include safety markings and warning devices.

The Regulations came into effect on 1 January 1993, as did extensive repeals of the former legislation such as s. 14 of the Factories Act and the parallel s. 17 of the Offices, Shops and Railway Premises Act. There is a period of grace until 1 January 1997 in respect of equipment provided for use before 1 January 1993 so that regs. 11 to 24 and 27 (dangerous parts, specified hazards, high and low temperature, controls, isolation from energy sources, stability, lighting, maintenance operations, markings, and warnings) and the repeals of existing legislation will not affect that equipment until the end of that period (see reg. 1(3)).

These Regulations are not supplemented by any Approved Code of Practice but there is an extensive Guidance Note called "Work Equipment" (not included in this book) which has no statutory admissibility in civil or criminal proceedings, though doubtless a court might consider its recommendations relevant.

The Regulations apply not only to employers, but also to the self-employed, to occupiers of factories as defined by the Factories Act 1961 and to any person who has any degree of control of non-domestic premises made available to persons as a place of work, (reg. 4). Although sea-going ships are not covered (reg. 3), the loading and unloading of ships is caught and they apply to offshore oil and gas installations and associated vessels. Thus, they apply to many workers who may not strictly be employees, and extend detailed regulation to workplaces not previously caught by the Factories Act 1961 or the Offices, Shops and Railway Premises Act 1963.

As noted earlier, to the extent that Regulations fail to give full effect to the Directives they are intended to implement, recourse, by way of aid to construction, or in some cases by way of direct enforcement, may be had to the relevant Directive (see "Interpretation in the Light of the European Directives" and "Direct Application of the European Directives" under LEGAL PRINCIPLES in the introductory section). Some possible areas of arguable shortfall in implementation of the Directive these Regulations are intended to implement have been noted by commentators. Amongst these are the following: reg. 11 provides for protection from dangerous parts. It imposes a standard of "practicability" which (in factory, office and railway premises at least) diminishes the absolute standard of s. 14 of the Factories Act and s. 17 of the Offices, Shops and Railway Premises Act. It is submitted that diminution of existing standard is inconsistent with the Directives: see

"Direct Application of the European Directives" under LEGAL PRINCIPLES in the introductory section. Furthermore, para. 2.8 of the Annex to the Directive imposes an absolute standard to provide guards or devices to prevent access to danger "where there is a risk of mechanical contact with moving parts . . . which could lead to accidents". It is submitted that the curious use of this adjective must, in context, cover all manner of means by which the body or anything attached to, held or worn by it, could come into contact with the machine. This would equate to the absolute standard of the "old" legislation so that imposition of a standard of "practicability" in the Regulations amounts to a failure fully to implement the Directive.

Regulation 6 requires that equipment be maintained in an efficient state, whereas Art. 4(2) requires that equipment is kept in a condition so as to comply with the Directive and oher Directives. To the extent that these standards are not identical, it is submitted that a purposive construction of the Regulations will result in uniformity.

There is a requirement to consult workplace representatives specified in the Framework Directive and in this Directive. These Regulations contain no reflection of that obligation. However, the obligation to consult representatives of the workforce finds form in the amendment to the Safety Representatives and Safety Committees Regulations 1977 (S.I. 1977 No. 500) contained in the Schedule to the Management of Health and Safety at Work Regulations 1992 (S.I. 1992 No. 2051). That obligation only arises where the employer cares to recognise a union. This deficiency in implementation of the Framework Directive has already been referred to, see the General Note to reg. 4A of the Safety Representatives and Safety Committees Regulations 1977 and "Direct Application of the European Directives" under LEGAL PRINCIPLES in the introductory section."

The Secretary of State, in the exercise of the powers conferred on her by sections 15(1), (2), (3)(a), (5)(b) and (9), and 82(3)(a) of, and paragraphs 1(1), (2) and (3), 13(1) and 14 of Schedule 3 to, the Health and Safety at Work etc. Act 1974 ("the 1974 Act") and of all other powers enabling her in that behalf and for the purpose of giving effect without modifications to proposals submitted to her by the Health and Safety Commission under section 11(2)(d) of *the 1974 Act*, after the carrying out by the said Commission of consultations in accordance with section 50(3) of that Act, hereby makes the following Regulations:

1.   Citation and commencement.—(1) These Regulations may be cited as the Provision and Use of Work Equipment Regulations 1992.

(2) Subject to paragraph (3), these Regulations shall come into force on 1 January 1993.

(3) Regulations 11 to 24 and 27 and Schedule 2 in so far as they apply to *work equipment* first provided for use in the premises or undertaking before 1 January 1993 shall come into force on 1 January 1997.

2.   Interpretation.—(1) In these Regulations, unless the context otherwise requires—

"use" in relation to *work equipment* means any activity involving *work equipment* and includes starting, stopping, programming, setting, transporting, repairing, modifying, maintaining, servicing and cleaning, and related expressions shall be construed accordingly;

"work equipment" *(a)* means any machinery, appliance, apparatus or tool and any assembly of components which, in order to achieve a common end, are arranged and controlled so that they function as a whole.

(2) Any reference in these Regulations to—

(a) a numbered regulation or Schedule is a reference to the regulation or Schedule in these Regulations so numbered; and

(b) a numbered paragraph is a reference to the paragraph so numbered in the regulation in which the reference appears.

(a) Equipment. It is not clear to what extent the word "equipment" in this context is synonymous with the same word under the Employers' Liability (Defective Equipment) Act 1969. It is submitted that a ship would be included as in *Coltman v Bibby Tankers Ltd* [1988] AC 276 but it appears less likely that a flagstone being laid would be, as in *Knowles v Liverpool City Council* [1993] ICR 21, [1993] IRLR 6, CA. See the definitions of "work equipment" in Art. 2 of the Directive.

3. Disapplication of these Regulations. These Regulations shall not apply to or in relation to the master or crew of a seagoing ship or to the employer of such persons, in respect of the normal ship-board activities of a ship's crew under the direction of the master.

4. Application of requirements under these Regulations.—(1) The requirements imposed by these Regulations on an employer shall apply in respect of *work equipment* provided for *use* or *used* by any of his employees who is at work or who is on an offshore installation within the meaning assigned to that term by section 1(4) of the Offshore Safety Act 1992.

(2) The requirements imposed by these Regulations on an employer shall also apply—

(a) to a self-employed person, in respect of *work equipment* he *uses* at work;

(b) to any person who has control, to any extent, of non-domestic premises made available to persons as a place of work, in respect of *work equipment* *used* in such premises by such persons and to the extent of his control; and

(c) to any person to whom the provisions of the Factories Act 1961 apply by virtue of section 175(5) of that Act as if he were the occupier of a factory, in respect of *work equipment used* in the premises deemed to be a factory by that section.

(3) Any reference in paragraph (2)(b) to a person having control of any premises or matter is a reference to the person having control of the premises or matter in connection with the carrying on by him of a trade, business or other undertaking (whether for profit or not).

5. Suitability of *work equipment.*—(1) Every employer shall ensure that *work equipment* is so constructed or adapted as to be suitable *(a)* for the purpose for which it is *used* or provided.

(2) In selecting *work equipment,* every employer shall have regard to the working conditions and to the risks to the health and safety of persons which exist in the premises or undertaking in which that *work equipment* is to be *used* and any additional risk posed by the *use* of that *work equipment.*

(3) Every employer shall ensure that *work equipment* is *used* only for operations for which, and under conditions for which, it is suitable.

(4) In this regulation "suitable" (*a*) means suitable in any respect which it is reasonably foreseeable will affect the health or safety of any person.

(*a*) **Suitable.** See INTRODUCTORY NOTE 12. There is no requirement of reasonable foreseeability in the Directive (see Art. 3), unlike reg. 5(4).

6.   Maintenance.—(1) Every employer shall ensure that *work equipment* is maintained in an efficient state, in efficient working order and in good repair.

(2) Every employer shall ensure that where any machinery has a maintenance log, the log is kept up to date.

7.   Specific risks.—(1) Where the *use* of *work equipment* is likely to involve a specific risk to health or safety, every employer shall ensure that—

(a) the *use* of that *work equipment* is restricted to those persons given the task of using it; and

(b) repairs, modifications, maintenance or servicing of that *work equipment* is restricted to those persons who have been specifically designated to perform operations of that description (whether or not also authorised to perform other operations).

(2) The employer shall ensure that the persons designated for the purposes of sub-paragraph (b) of paragraph (1) have received adequate training related to any operations in respect of which they have been so designated.

8.   Information and instructions.—(1) Every employer shall ensure that all persons who *use work equipment* have available to them adequate health and safety information and, where appropriate, written instructions pertaining to the *use* of the *work equipment*.

(2) Every employer shall ensure that any of his employees who supervises or manages the *use* of *work equipment* has available to him adequate health and safety information and, where appropriate, written instructions pertaining to the *use* of the *work equipment*.

(3) Without prejudice to the generality of paragraphs (1) or (2), the information and instructions required by either of those paragraphs shall include information and, where appropriate, written instructions on—

(a) the conditions in which and the methods by which the *work equipment* may be *used*;

(b) foreseeable abnormal situations and the action to be taken if such a situation were to occur; and

(c) any conclusions to be drawn from experience in using the *work equipment*.

(4) Information and instructions required by this regulation shall be readily comprehensible to those concerned.

9.   Training.—(1) Every employer shall ensure that all persons who *use work equipment* have received adequate training for purposes of health and safety, including training in the methods which may be adopted when using the *work equipment*, any risks which such *use* may entail and precautions to be taken.

(2) Every employer shall ensure that any of his employees who supervises or manages the *use* of *work equipment* has received adequate training for purposes of health and safety, including training in the methods which may be adopted when using the *work equipment*, any risks which such *use* may entail and precautions to be taken.

10. Conformity with Community requirements.—(1) Every employer shall ensure that any item of *work equipment* provided for *use* in the premises or undertaking of the employer complies with any enactment (whether in an Act or instrument) which implements in Great Britain any of the relevant Community Directives listed in Schedule 1 which is applicable to that item of *work equipment*.

(2) Where it is shown that an item of *work equipment* complies with an enactment (whether in an Act or instrument) to which it is subject by virtue of paragraph (1), the requirements of regulations 11 to 24 shall apply in respect of that item of *work equipment* only to the extent that the relevant Community Directive implemented by that enactment is not applicable to that item of *work equipment*.

(3) This regulation applies to items of *work equipment* provided for *use* in the premises or undertaking of the employer for the first time after 31 December 1992.

11. Dangerous parts of machinery.—(1) Every employer shall ensure that measures are taken in accordance with paragraph (2) which are effective—

   (a) to prevent access to any dangerous part *(a)* of machinery or to any rotating stock-bar; or

   (b) to stop the movement of any dangerous part of machinery or rotating stock-bar before any part of a person enters a danger zone.

(2) The measures required by paragraph (1) shall consist of

   (a) the provision of fixed guards enclosing every dangerous part or rotating stock-bar where and to the extent that it is practicable *(b)* to do so, but where or to the extent that it is not, then

   (b) the provision of other guards or protection devices where and to the extent that it is practicable *(b)* to do so, but where or to the extent that it is not, then

   (c) the provision of jigs, holders, push-sticks or similar protection appliances *used* in conjunction with the machinery where and to the extent that it is practicable *(b)* to do so, but where or to the extent that it is not, then

   (d) the provision of information, instruction, training and supervision.

(3) All guards and protection devices provided under sub-paragraphs (a) or (b) of paragraph (2) shall—

   (a) be suitable for the purpose for which they are provided;

   (b) be of good construction, sound material and adequate strength;

   (c) be maintained in an efficient state, in efficient working order and in good repair;

   (d) not give rise to any increased risk to health or safety;

   (e) not be easily bypassed or disabled;

   (f) be situated at sufficient distance from the danger zone;

   (g) not unduly restrict the view of the operating cycle of the machinery, where such a view is necessary;

   (h) be so constructed or adapted that they allow operations necessary to fit or replace parts and for maintenance work, restricting access so that it is allowed only to the area where the work is to be carried out and, if possible, without having to dismantle the guard or protection device.

(4) All protection appliances provided under sub-paragraph (c) of paragraph (2) shall comply with sub-paragraphs (a) to (d) and (g) of paragraph (3).

(5) In this regulation—
   "danger zone" means any zone in or around machinery in which a person is exposed to a risk to health or safety from contact with a dangerous part of machinery or a rotating stock-bar;
   "stock-bar" means any part of a stock-bar which projects beyond the head-stock of a lathe.

   (a) Dangerous part. For the interpretation of "dangerous part" of a machine under the Factories Act 1961, s. 14, see the Introductory Note to ss. 12 to 16 of that Act; and compare para. 2.8 of the Annex to the Directive.

   (b) Practicable. See General Note to these Regulations.

12. Protection against specified hazards.—(1) Every employer shall take measures to ensure that the exposure of a person using *work equipment* to any risk to his health or safety from any hazard specified in paragraph (3) is either prevented, or, where that is not reasonably practicable *(a)*, adequately controlled.

(2) The measures required by paragraph (1) shall—

   (a) be measures other than the provision of personal protective equipment or of information, instruction, training and supervision, so far as is reasonably practicable *(a)*; and

   (b) include, where appropriate, measures to minimise the effects of the hazard as well as to reduce the likelihood of the hazard occurring.

(3) The hazards referred to in paragraph (1) are—

   (a) any article or substance falling or being ejected from *work equipment*;

   (b) rupture or disintegration of parts of *work equipment*;

   (c) *work equipment* catching fire or overheating;

   (d) the unintended or premature discharge of any article or of any gas, dust, liquid, vapour or other substance which, in each case, is produced, *used* or stored in the *work equipment*;

   (e) the unintended or premature explosion of the *work equipment* or any article or substance produced, *used* or stored in it.

(4) For the purposes of this regulation "adequate" means adequate having regard only to the nature of the hazard and the nature and degree of exposure to the risk, and "adequately" shall be construed accordingly.

(5) This regulation shall not apply where any of the following Regulations apply in respect of any risk to a person's health or safety for which such Regulations require measures to be taken to prevent or control such risk, namely—

(a) the Control of Lead at Work Regulations 1980;
(b) the Ionising Radiations Regulations 1985;
(c) the Control of Asbestos at Work Regulations 1987;
(d) the Control of Substances Hazardous to Health Regulations 1988;
(e) the Noise at Work Regulations 1989;
(f) the Construction (Head Protection) Regulations 1989.

(a) **Reasonably practicable.** See INTRODUCTORY NOTE 5. The phrase is not found in the Directive (see Art. 3 and the Annex) and there is doubt therefore whether it will be enforceable. See "Interpretation in the Light of the European Directives" and "Direct Application of the European Directives" under LEGAL PRINCIPLES in the introductory section of this book.

13. High or very low temperature. Every employer shall ensure that *work equipment*, parts of *work equipment* and any article or substance produced, *used* or stored in *work equipment* which, in each case, is at a high or very low temperature shall have protection where appropriate so as to prevent injury to any person by burn, scald or sear.

14. Controls for starting or making a significant change in operating conditions.—(1) Every employer shall ensure that, where appropriate, *work equipment* is provided with one or more controls for the purposes of—

(a) starting the *work equipment* (including re-starting after a stoppage for any reason); or
(b) controlling any change in the speed, pressure or other operating conditions of the *work equipment* where such conditions after the change result in risk to health and safety which is greater than or of a different nature from such risks before the change.

(2) Subject to paragraph (3), every employer shall ensure that where a control is required by paragraph (1), it shall not be possible to perform any operation mentioned in sub-paragraph (a) or (b) of that paragraph except by a deliberate action on such control.

(3) Paragraph (1) shall not apply to re-starting or changing operating conditions as a result of the normal operating cycle of an automatic device.

15. Stop controls.—(1) Every employer shall ensure that, where appropriate, *work equipment* is provided with one or more readily accessible controls the operation of which will bring the *work equipment* to a safe condition in a safe manner.

(2) Any control required by paragraph (1) shall bring the *work equipment* to a complete stop where necessary for reasons of health and safety.

(3) Any control required by paragraph (1) shall, if necessary for reasons of health and safety, switch off all sources of energy after stopping the functioning of the *work equipment.*

(4) Any control required by paragraph (1) shall operate in priority to any control which starts or changes the operating conditions of the *work equipment.*

16.   Emergency stop controls.—(1) Every employer shall ensure that, where appropriate, *work equipment* is provided with one or more readily accessible emergency stop controls unless it is not necessary by reason of the nature of the hazards and the time taken for the *work equipment* to come to a complete stop as a result of the action of any control provided by virtue of regulation 15(1).

(2) Any control required by paragraph (1) shall operate in priority to any control required by regulation 15(1).

17.   Controls.—(1) Every employer shall ensure that all controls for *work equipment* shall be clearly visible and identifiable, including by appropriate marking where necessary.

(2) Except where necessary, the employer shall ensure that no control for *work equipment* is in a position where any person operating the control is exposed to a risk to his health or safety.

(3) Every employer shall ensure where appropriate—

(a) that, so far as is reasonably practicable *(a)*, the operator of any control is able to ensure from the position of that control that no person is in a place where he would be exposed to any risk to his health or safety as a result of the operation of that control, but where or to the extent that it is not reasonably practicable *(a)*;

(b) that, so far as is reasonably practicable *(a)*, systems of work are effective to ensure that, when *work equipment* is about to start, no person is in a place where he would be exposed to a risk to his health or safety as a result of the *work equipment* starting, but where neither of these is reasonably practicable *(a)*;

(c) that an audible, visible or other suitable warning is given by virtue of regulation 24 whenever *work equipment* is about to start.

(4) Every employer shall take appropriate measures to ensure that any person who is in a place where he would be exposed to a risk to his health or safety as a result of the starting or stopping of *work equipment* has sufficient time and suitable *(b)* means to avoid that risk.

(a) **Reasonably practicable.** See INTRODUCTORY NOTE 5. The phrase is not found in the Directive (see para. 2.1 of the Annex) and there is doubt therefore whether it will be enforceable. See "Interpretation in the Light of the European Directives" and "Direct Application of the European Directives" under LEGAL PRINCIPLES in the Introductory section of this book.

(b) **Suitable.** See reg. 5(4).

18.   Control systems.—(1) Every employer shall ensure, so far as is reasonably practicable *(a)*, that all control systems of *work equipment* are safe.

(2) Without prejudice to the generality of paragraph (1), a control system shall not be safe unless—

(a) its operation does not create any increased risk to health or safety;

(b) it ensures, so far as is reasonably practicable *(a)*, that any fault in or damage to any part of the control system or the loss of supply of any source of energy *used* by the *work equipment* cannot result in additional or increased risk to health or safety;

(c) it does not impede the operation of any control required by regulation 15 or 16.

(a) **Reasonably practicable.** See INTRODUCTORY NOTE 5. The phrase is not found in the Directive (and see para. 2.1 of the Annex) and there is doubt therefore whether it will be enforceable. See "Interpretation in the Light of the European Directives" and "Direct Application of the European Directives" under LEGAL PRINCIPLES in the introductory section of this book.

19. Isolation from sources of energy.—(1) Every employer shall ensure that where appropriate *work equipment* is provided with suitable *(a)* means to isolate it from all its sources of energy.

(2) Without prejudice to the generality of paragraph (1), the means mentioned in that paragraph shall not be suitable unless they are clearly identifiable and readily accessible.

(3) Every employer shall take appropriate measures to ensure that re-connection of any energy source to *work equipment* does not expose any person using the *work equipment* to any risk to his health or safety.

(a) **Suitable.** See reg. 5(4).

20. Stability. Every employer shall ensure that *work equipment* or any part of *work equipment* is stabilised by clamping or otherwise where necessary for purposes of health or safety.

21. Lighting. Every employer shall ensure that suitable and sufficient *(a)* lighting, which takes account of the operations to be carried out, is provided at any place where a person *uses work equipment.*

(a) **Suitable and sufficient.** See INTRODUCTORY NOTE 12, reg. 5(4) and Note *(a)* to s. 5 of the Factories Act 1961, on the interpretation of that phrase in relation to lighting under that Act.

22. Maintenance operations. Every employer shall take appropriate measures to ensure that *work equipment* is so constructed or adapted that, so far as is reasonably practicable *(a)*, maintenance operations which involve a risk to health or safety can be carried out while the *work equipment* is shut down or, in other cases—

(a) maintenance operations can be carried out without exposing the person carrying them out to a risk to his health or safety; or

(b) appropriate measures can be taken for the protection of any person carrying out maintenance operations which involve a risk to his health or safety.

(a) Reasonably practicable. See INTRODUCTORY NOTE 5. The phrase is not found in the Directive and there is doubt therefore whether it will be enforceable (see para. 2.13 of the Annex to the Directive). See, too, "Interpretation in the Light of the European Directives" and "Direct Application of the European Directives" under LEGAL PRINCIPLES in the Introductory section of this book.

23.   Markings. Every employer shall ensure that *work equipment* is marked in a clearly visible manner with any marking appropriate for reasons of health and safety.

24.   Warnings.—(1) Every employer shall ensure that *work equipment* incorporates any warnings or warning devices which are appropriate for reasons of health and safety.

(2) Without prejudice to the generality of paragraph (1), warnings given by warning devices on *work equipment* shall not be appropriate unless they are unambiguous, easily perceived and easily understood.

25.   Exemption certificates.—(1) The Secretary of State for Defence may, in the interests of national security, by a certificate in writing exempt any of the home forces, any visiting force or any headquarters from any of the requirements of these Regulations and any such exemption may be granted subject to conditions and to a limit of time and may be revoked by the said Secretary of State by a further certificate in writing at any time.

(2) In this regulation—

(a) "the home forces" has the same meaning as in section 12(1) of the Visiting Forces Act 1952;
(b) "headquarters" has the same meaning as in article 3(2) of the Visiting Forces and International Headquarters (Application of Law) Order 1965;
(c) "visiting force" has the same meaning as it does for the purposes of any provision of Part I of the Visiting Forces Act 1952.

26.   Extension outside Great Britain. These Regulations shall, subject to regulation 3, apply to and in relation to the premises and activities outside Great Britain to which sections 1 to 59 and 80 to 82 of *the 1974 Act* apply by virtue of the Health and Safety at Work etc. Act 1974 (Application outside Great Britain) Order 1989 as they apply within Great Britain.

27.   Repeals, saving and revocations.—(1) Subject to paragraph (2), the enactments mentioned in Part I of Schedule 2 are repealed to the extent specified in column 3 of that Part.

(2) Nothing in this regulation shall affect the operation of any provision of the Offices, Shops and Railway Premises Act 1963 as that provision has effect by virtue of section 90(4) of that Act.

(3) The instruments mentioned in Part II of Schedule 2 are revoked to the extent specified in column 3 of that Part.

SCHEDULE 1

Regulation 10

RELEVANT COMMUNITY DIRECTIVES

1. Council Directive 73/23/EEC on the harmonization of the laws of Member States relating to electrical equipment designed for use within certain voltage limits (OJ No. L77, 26.3.1973, p. 29).

2. Council Directive 79/113/EEC on the approximation of the laws of the Member States relating to the determination of the noise emission of construction plant and equipment (OJ No. L33, 8.2.1979, p. 15).

3. Council Directive 81/1051/EEC amending Directive 79/113/EEC on the approximation of the laws of the Member States relating to the determination of the noise emission of construction plant and equipment (OJ No. L376, 30.12.1981, p. 49).

4 Council Directive 84/532/EEC on the approximation of the laws of the Member States relating to common provisions for construction plant and equipment (OJ No. L300, 19.11.1984, p. 111).

5. Council Directive 84/533/EEC on the approximation of the laws of the Member States relating to the permissible sound power level of compressors (OJ No. L300, 19.11.1984, p. 123).

6. Council Directive 84/534/EEC on the approximation of the laws of the Member States relating to the permissible sound power level of tower cranes (OJ No. L300, 19.11.1984, p. 130).

7. Council Directive 84/535/EEC on the approximation of the laws of the Member States relating to the permissible sound power level of welding generators (OJ No. L300, 19.11.1984, p. 142).

8. Council Directive 84/536/EEC on the approximation of the laws of the Member States relating to the permissible sound power level of power generators (OJ No. L300, 19.11.1984, p. 149).

9. Council Directive 84/537/EEC on the approximation of the laws of the Member States relating to the permissible sound power level of powered hand-held concrete-breakers and picks (OJ No. L300, 19.11.1984, p. 156).

10. Council Directive 84/538/EEC on the approximation of the laws of the Member States relating to the permissible sound power level of lawn mowers (OJ No. L300, 19.11.1984, p. 171).

11. Commission Directive 85/405/EEC adapting to technical progress, Council Directive 79/113/EEC on the approximation of the laws of the Member States relating to the determination of the noise emission of construction plant and equipment (OJ No. L233, 30.8.1985, p. 9).

12. Commission Directive 85/406/EEC adapting to technical progress, Council Directive 84/533/EEC on the approximation of the laws of the Member States relating to the permissible sound power level of compressors (OJ No. L233, 30.8.1985, p. 11).

13. Commission Directive 85/407/EEC adapting to technical progress, Council Directive 84/535/EEC on the approximation of the laws of the Member States relating to the permissible sound power level of welding generators (OJ No. L233, 30.8.1985, p. 16).

14. Commission Directive 85/408/EEC adapting to technical progress, Council Directive 84/536/EEC on the approximation of the laws of the Member States relating to the permissible sound power level of power generators (OJ No. L233, 30.8.1985, p. 18).

15. Commission Directive 85/409/EEC adapting to technical progress, Council Directive 84/537/EEC on the approximation of the laws of the Member States relating to the permissible sound power level of powered hand-held concrete-breakers and picks (OJ No. L233, 30.8.1985, p. 20).

16. Commission Directive 87/252/EEC adapting to technical progress, Council Directive 84/538/EEC on the approximation of the laws of the Member States relating to the permissible sound power level of lawn-mowers (OJ No. L117, 5.5.1987, p. 22 with corrigenda at OJ No. L158, 18.6.1987, p. 31).

17. Council Directive 87/405/EEC amending Council Directive 84/534/EEC on the approximation of the laws of the Member States relating to the permissible sound power level of tower cranes (OJ No. L220, 8.8.1987, p. 60).

18. Council Directive 88/180/EEC amending Council Directive 84/538/EEC on the approximation of the laws of the Member States relating to the permissible sound power level of lawn-mowers (OJ No. L81, 26.3.1988, p. 69).

19. Council Directive 88/181/EEC amending Council Directive 84/538/EEC on the approximation of the laws of the Member States relating to the permissible sound power level of lawn-mowers (OJ No. L81, 26.3.1988, p. 71).

20. Council Directive 84/539/EEC on the approximation of the laws of the Member States relating to electro-medical equipment used in human or veterinary medicine (OJ No. L300, 19.11.1984, p. 179).

21. Council Directive 86/295/EEC on the approximation of the laws of the Member States relating to roll-over protective structures (ROPS) for certain construction plant (OJ No. L186, 8.7.1986, p. 1).

22. Council Directive 86/296/EEC on the approximation of the laws of the Member States relating to falling-object protective structures (FOPS) for certain construction plant (OJ No. L186, 8.7.1986, p. 10).

23. Council Directive 86/662/EEC on the limitation of noise emitted by hydraulic excavators, rope-operated excavators, dozers, loaders and excavator-loaders (OJ No. L384, 31.12.1986, p. 1).

24. Council Directive 86/663/EEC on the approximation of the laws of the Member States relating to self-propelled industrial trucks (OJ No. L384, 31.12.1986, p. 12).

25. Council Directive 87/404/EEC on the harmonization of the laws of the Member States relating to simple pressure vessels (OJ No. L220, 8.8.1987, p. 48).

26. Council Directive 89/106/EEC on the approximation of laws, regulations and administrative provisions of the Member States relating to construction products (OJ No. L40, 11.2.1989, p. 12).

27. Commission Directive 89/240/EEC adapting to technical progress Council Directive 86/663/EEC on the approximation of the laws of the Member States relating to self-propelled industrial trucks (OJ No. L100, 12.4.1989, p. 1).

28. Council Directive 89/336/EEC on the approximation of the laws of the Member States relating to electromagnetic compatibility (OJ No. L139, 23.5.1989, p. 19).

29. Council Directive 89/392/EEC on the approximation of the laws of the Member States relating to machinery (OJ No. L183, 29.6.1989, p. 9).

30. Commission Directive 89/514/EEC adapting to technical progress Council Directive 86/662/EEC on the limitation of noise emitted by hydraulic excavators, rope-operated excavators, dozers, loaders and excavator-loaders (OJ No. L253, 30.8.1989, p. 35).

31. Council Directive 89/686/EEC on the approximation of the laws of the Member States relating to personal protective equipment (OJ No. L399, 30.12.1989, p. 18).

32. Council Directive 90/385/EEC on the approximation of the laws of the Member States relating to active implantable medical devices (OJ No. L189, 20.7.1990, p. 17).

33. Council Directive 90/396/EEC on the approximation of the laws of the Member States relating to appliances burning gaseous fuels (OJ No. L196, 26.7.1990, p. 15).

34. Council Directive 91/368/EEC amending Directive 89/392/EEC on the approximation of the laws of the Member States relating to machinery (OJ No. L198, 22.7.1991, p. 16).

35. Council Directive 92/31/EEC amending Directive 89/336/EEC on the approximation of the laws of the Member States relating to electromagnetic compatibility (OJ No. L126, 12.5.92, p. 11).

SCHEDULE 2

Regulation 27

PART I
REPEALS

(1)	(2)	(3)
Chapter	*Short title*	*Extent of repeal*
1954 c.70.	The Mines and Quarries Act 1954.	Sections 81(1) and 82.
1961 c.34.	The Factories Act 1961.	Sections 12 to 16, 17 and 19.
1963 c.41.	The Offices, Shops and Railway Premises Act 1963.	Section 17.

PART II
REVOCATIONS

(1)	(2)	(3)
Title	*Reference*	*Extent of revocation*
Regulations dated 17 October 1905 (The Spinning by Self-Acting Mules Regulations 1905).	S.R. & O. 1905/1103, amended by the Employment Act 1989 (c.38), section 29(5), Schedule 8.	The whole Regulations.
The Aerated Water Regulations 1921.	S.R. & O. 1921/1932, amended by S.I. 1981/686.	Regulations 1, 2 and 8.
The Horizontal Milling Machines Regulations 1928.	S.R. & O. 1928/548, amended by S.R. & O. 1934/207.	The exemptions and regulations 2 to 7.
The Operations at Unfenced Machinery Regulations 1938.	S.R. & O. 1938/641, amended by S.R. & O. 1946/156 and S.I. 1976/955.	The whole Regulations.

(1) Title	(2) Reference	(3) Extent of revocation
The Jute (Safety, Health and Welfare) Regulations 1948.	S.I. 1948/1696, to which there are amendments not relevant to these Regulations.	Regulations 15, 27 and 28 and the First Schedule.
The Iron and Steel Foundries Regulations 1953.	S.I. 1953/1464, amended by S.I. 1974/1681 and S.I. 1981/1332.	Regulation 5.
The Agriculture (Power Take-Off) Regulations 1957.	S.I. 1957/1386, amended by S.I. 1976/1247, S.I. 1981/1414 and S.I. 1991/1913.	The whole Regulations.
The Agriculture (Circular Saws) Regulations 1959.	S.I. 1959/427, amended by S.I. 1981/1414.	(i) In regulation 1, in sub-paragraph (b), from the beginning to "and" where it first occurs; and sub-paragraph (c); (ii) regulations 3 and 4; (iii) in regulation 5(1), the words from "unless" to "or"; and (iv) Schedule 1.
The Agriculture (Stationary Machinery) Regulations 1959.	S.I. 1959/1216, amended by S.I. 1976/1247 and S.I. 1981/1414.	The whole Regulations.
The Agriculture (Threshers and Balers) Regulations 1960.	S.I. 1960/1199, amended by S.I. 1976/1247 and S.I. 1981/1414.	In the Schedule, paragraphs 2, 3, 6, 7, 8, 9, 10, 11, 12, 16 and 17.
The Shipbuilding and Ship-Repairing Regulations 1960.	S.I. 1960/1932, to which there are amendments not relevant to these Regulations.	Regulation 67.
The Construction (General Provisions) Regulations 1961.	S.I. 1961/1580, to which there are amendments not relevant to these Regulations.	Regulations 42, 43 and 57.
The Agriculture (Field Machinery) Regulations 1962.	S.I. 1962/1472, amended by S.I. 1976/1247 and S.I. 1981/1414.	In the Schedule, paragraphs 2 to 6 and 15 to 19.
The Abrasive Wheels Regulations 1970.	S.I. 1970/535.	In regulation 3, paragraphs (2), (3) and (4); and regulations 4, 6 to 8, 10 to 16, 18 and 19.

(1)	(2)	(3)
Title	*Reference*	*Extent of revocation*
The Woodworking Machines Regulations 1974.	S.I. 1974/903, amended by S.I. 1978/1126.	In regulation 1, paragraphs (2) and (3); in regulation 2, the definitions of "cutters", "machine table", "narrow band sawing machine", "sawmill" and "squared stock"; in regulation 3, paragraph (2); regulations 5 to 9, 14 to 19, 21 to 38, and 40 to 43.
The Offshore Installations (Operational Safety, Health and Welfare) Regulations 1976.	S.I. 1976/1019, which has effect as an existing statutory provision under *the 1974 Act* by virtue of section 1(1) of the Offshore Safety Act 1992 (c.15).	Regulations 10 and 12.
The Agriculture (Power Take-off) (Amendment) Regulations 1991.	S.I. 1991/1913.	The whole Regulations.

THE PERSONAL PROTECTIVE EQUIPMENT AT WORK REGULATIONS 1992

(S.I. 1992 No. 2966)

General note. These Regulations are intended to implement the Personal Protective Equipment Directive 89/656 (see page 108). They also take account of the Approximation of Personal Protection Equipment Laws Directive 89/686 which is implemented in the UK by the Personal Protective Equipment (EC Directive) Regulations (S.I. 1992 No. 3139). The Regulations under consideration do not apply so as to require the user of temporary workers to provide personal protective equipment and so fail to implement the Temporary Workers Directive 91/383 in this regard.

The Regulations came into effect on 1 January 1993 as did the repeals and amendments to other Regulations to which these Regulations gave effect. There is no period of grace as for other Regulations implementing European Directives. Where other listed (and amended) Regulations make specific and comprehensive provision to similar or better effect, the Personal Protective Equipment Regulations are disapplied (see Reg. 3(3)).

These Regulations are not supplemented by any Approved Code of Practice but there is an extensive Guidance Note called "Personal Protective Equipment at Work" (not included in this book) which has no statutory admissibility in civil or criminal proceedings, though doubtless a court might consider its recommendations relevant.

The Regulations apply to all employment except sea-going ships. The Regulations define "personal protective equipment" very broadly excluding, in essence, only ordinary working clothes, uniforms, road vehicle safety (seat belts, crash helmets etc.), and sports equipment. The duty is on employers (and the self-employed) to provide suitable personal protective equipment to employees who may be exposed to risk except to the extent that the risk has been controlled by other effective means. The employer must carry out an assessment of the risks not avoided by other means, defining the characteristics needed from any personal protective equipment, and comparing the personal protective equipment available with those characteristics. The assessment must be kept under review. The personal protective equipment provided must be appropriate and adequate, fit the wearer, take account of ergonomic design and the state of health of the wearer, comply with the EEC standards in Directive 89/686 (see above) implemented by the relevant Regulations, be compatible and effective where worn with other protective equipment used against other risks, be maintained, cleaned and replaced to keep it efficient, and be provided with appropriate accommodation when not in use. Employees must be given adequate instruction and training and they must use the equipment and report any loss or damage. Employers must take reasonable steps to ensure the equipment is properly used.

As noted earlier, to the extent that Regulations fail to give full effect to the Directives they are intended to implement, recourse, by way of aid to construction, or in some cases by way of direct enforcement, may be had to the relevant Directive (see "Interpretation in the Light of the European Directives" and "Direct Application of the European Directives" under LEGAL PRINCIPLES in the introductory section). One possible shortfall is the absence in the Regulations of a duty to ensure that equipment used by more than one person does not create health or hygiene problems (Art. 4.4).

722

There is a requirement to consult workplace representatives specified in the Framework Directive and in this Directive (see Art. 8). These Regulations contain no reflection of that obligation. However, the obligation to consult representatives of the workforce finds form in the amendment to the Safety Representatives and Safety Committees Regulations 1977 (S.I. 1977 No. 500) contained in the Schedule to the Management of Health and Safety at Work Regulations 1992 (S.I. 1992 No. 2051). That obligation only arises where the employer cares to recognise a union. This deficiency in implementation of the Framework Directive has already been referred to: see the General Note to the 1977 Regulations and "Direct Application of the European Directives" under LEGAL PRINCIPLES in the introductory section.

As noted above, there is a deficiency in implementation of the requirements of the Temporary Workers Directive 91/383 by reason of the fact that the Regulations only apply as between employer and employee (and to the self-employed). Therefore temporary workers can only look to their employing agency and not to the user of their services for the provision of personal protective equipment. This appears to be a clear failure to implement Art. 2(1) and 2(2) of the Temporary Workers Directive.

The Secretary of State, in exercise of the powers conferred upon her by sections 15(1), (2), (3)(a) and (b), (5)(b) and (9) of, and paragraphs 11 and 14 of Schedule 3 to the Health and Safety at Work etc. Act 1974, and of all other powers enabling her in that behalf and for the purpose of giving effect without modifications to proposals submitted to her by the Health and Safety Commission under section 11(2)(d) of the said Act after the carrying out by the said Commission of consultations in accordance with section 50(3) of that Act, hereby makes the following Regulations:

1. Citation and commencement. These Regulations may be cited as the Personal Protective Equipment at Work Regulations 1992 and shall come into force on 1 January 1993.

2. Interpretation.—(1) In these Regulations, unless the context otherwise requires, "personal protective equipment" means all equipment (including clothing affording protection against the weather) which is intended to be worn or held by a person at work and which protects him against one or more risks to his health or safety, and any addition or accessory designed to meet that objective.

(2) Any reference in these Regulations to—

(a) a numbered regulation or Schedule is a reference to the regulation or Schedule in these Regulations so numbered; and

(b) a numbered paragraph is a reference to the paragraph so numbered in the regulation in which the reference appears.

3. Disapplication of these Regulations.—(1) These Regulations shall not apply to or in relation to the master or crew of a sea-going ship or to the employer of such persons in respect of the normal ship-board activities of a ship's crew under the direction of the master.

(2) Regulations 4 to 12 shall not apply in respect of *personal protective equipment* which is—

(a) ordinary working clothes and uniforms which do not specifically protect the health and safety of the wearer;

(b)   an offensive weapon within the meaning of section 1(4) of the Prevention of Crime Act 1953 used as self-defence or as deterrent equipment;

(c)   portable devices for detecting and signalling risks and nuisances;

(d)   *personal protective equipment* used for protection while travelling on a road within the meaning (in England and Wales) of section 192(1) of the Road Traffic Act 1988, and (in Scotland) of section 151 of the Roads (Scotland) Act 1984;

(e)   equipment used during the playing of competitive sports.

(3)   Regulations 4 and 6 to 12 shall not apply where any of the following Regulations apply and in respect of any risk to a person's health or safety for which any of them require the provision or use of *personal protective equipment*, namely—

(a)   the Control of Lead at Work Regulations 1980;

(b)   the Ionising Radiations Regulations 1985;

(c)   the Control of Asbestos at Work Regulations 1987;

(d)   the Control of Substances Hazardous to Health Regulations 1988;

(e)   the Noise at Work Regulations 1989;

(f)   the Construction (Head Protection) Regulations 1989.

4.   Provision of *personal protective equipment*.—(1) Every employer shall ensure that suitable *personal protective equipment* is provided to his employees *(a)* who may be exposed to a risk to their health or safety while at work except where and to the extent that such risk has been adequately controlled by other means which are equally or more effective.

(2)   Every self-employed person shall ensure that he is provided with suitable *personal protective equipment* where he may be exposed to a risk to his health or safety while at work except where and to the extent that such risk has been adequately controlled by other means which are equally or more effective.

(3)   Without prejudice to the generality of paragraphs (1) and (2), *personal protective equipment* shall not be suitable unless—

(a)   it is appropriate for the risk or risks involved and the conditions at the place where exposure to the risk may occur;

(b)   it takes account of ergonomic requirements and the state of health of the person or persons who may wear it;

(c)   it is capable of fitting the wearer correctly, if necessary, after adjustments within the range for which it is designed;

(d)   so far as is practicable, it is effective to prevent or adequately control the risk or risks involved without increasing overall risk;

(e)   it complies with any enactment (whether in an Act or instrument) which implements in Great Britain any provision on design or manufacture with respect to health or safety in any relevant Community Directive listed in Schedule 1 which is applicable to that item of *personal protective equipment*.

(a) **Employer.** For definition, see s. 53(1) of the Health and Safety at Work Act 1974.

5.   Compatibility of *personal protective equipment*.—(1) Every employer shall ensure that where the presence of more than one risk to health or safety makes it necessary for his employee to wear or use simultaneously more than one item of *personal protective equipment*, such equipment is compatible and continues to be effective against the risk or risks in question.

(2) Every self-employed person shall ensure that where the presence of more than one risk to health or safety makes it necessary for him to wear or use simultaneously more than one item of *personal protective equipment*, such equipment is compatible and continues to be effective against the risk or risks in question.

6.   Assessment of *personal protective equipment*.—(1) Before choosing any *personal protective equipment* which by virtue of regulation 4 he is required to ensure is provided, an employer or self-employed person shall ensure that an assessment is made to determine whether the *personal protective equipment* he intends will be provided is suitable *(a)*.

(2) The assessment *(b)* required by paragraph (1) shall include—

(a)   an assessment of any risk or risks to health or safety which have not been avoided by other means;
(b)   the definition of the characteristics which *personal protective equipment* must have in order to be effective against the risks referred to in sub-paragraph (a) of this paragraph, taking into account any risks which the equipment itself may create;
(c)   comparison of the characteristics of the *personal protective equipment* available with the characteristics referred to in sub-paragraph (b) of this paragraph.

(3) Every employer or self-employed person who is required by paragraph (1) to ensure that any assessment is made shall ensure that any such assessment is reviewed if—

(a)   there is reason to suspect that it is no longer valid; or
(b)   there has been a significant change in the matters to which it relates,

and where as a result of any such review changes in the assessment are required, the relevant employer or self-employed person shall ensure that they are made.

*(a) **Suitable.*** See reg. 4(3) and INTRODUCTORY NOTE 12.

*(b) **Assessment.*** See also reg. 3 of the Management of Health and Safety at Work Regulations 1992 (S.I. 1992 No. 2051).

7.   Maintenance and replacement of *personal protective equipment*.—(1) Every employer shall ensure that any *personal protective equipment* provided to his employees is maintained (including replaced or cleaned as appropriate) in an efficient *(a)* state, in efficient working order and in good repair.

(2) Every self-employed person shall ensure that any *personal protective equipment* provided to him is maintained (including replaced or cleaned as appropriate) in an efficient state, in efficient working order and in good repair.

*(a) **Efficient.*** See INTRODUCTORY NOTE 12.

8.   Accommodation for *personal protective equipment*. Where an employer or self-employed person is required, by virtue of regulation 4, to ensure *personal* *protective equipment* is provided, he shall also ensure that appropriate accommodation is provided for that *personal protective equipment* when it is not being used.

9.   Information, instruction and training.—(1) Where an employer is required to ensure that *personal protective equipment* is provided to an employee, the employer shall also ensure that the employee is provided with such information, instruction and training as is adequate and appropriate to enable the employee to know—

(a)   the risk or risks which the *personal protective equipment* will avoid or limit;

(b)   the purpose for which and the manner in which *personal protective equipment* is to be used; and

(c)   any action to be taken by the employee to ensure that the *personal protective equipment* remains in an efficient state, in efficient working order and in good repair as required by regulation 7(1).

(2)   Without prejudice to the generality of paragraph (1), the information and instruction provided by virtue of that paragraph shall not be adequate and appropriate unless it is comprehensible to the persons to whom it is provided.

**10.   Use of *personal protective equipment.*—(1) Every employer shall take all reasonable steps to ensure that any *personal protective equipment* provided to his employees by virtue of regulation 4(1) is properly used.

(2)   Every employee shall use any *personal protective equipment* provided to him by virtue of these Regulations in accordance both with any training in the use of the *personal protective equipment* concerned which has been received by him and the instructions respecting that use which have been provided to him by virtue of regulation 9.

(3)   Every self-employed person shall make full and proper use of any *personal protective equipment* provided to him by virtue of regulation 4(2).

(4)   Every employee and self-employed person who has been provided with *personal protective equipment* by virtue of regulation 4 shall take all reasonable steps to ensure that it is returned to the accommodation provided for it after use.

General note. Regulation 10(1) imposes a higher standard than some pre-existing legislation and is arguably higher than the standard of duty of care in negligence. See, for example, *Bux v Slough Metals Ltd* [1974] 1 All ER 262, [1973] 1 WLR 1358, CA, where it was held that a failure to instruct an employee to use suitable protective goggles was not a breach of reg. 13(1) of the Non Ferrous Metal Regulations 1962 (S.I. 1962 No. 1667, as amended) (although it did amount to negligence at common law, albeit with a reduction for contributing negligence).

11.   Reporting loss or defect. Every employee who has been provided with *personal protective equipment* by virtue of regulation 4(1) shall forthwith report to his employer any loss of or obvious defect in that *personal protective equipment*.

12.   Exemption certificates.—(1) The Secretary of State for Defence may, in the interests of national security, by a certificate in writing exempt—

(a) any of the home forces, any visiting force or any headquarters from those requirements of these Regulations which impose obligations on employers; or

(b) any member of the home forces, any member of a visiting force or any member of a headquarters from the requirements imposed by regulation 10 or 11,

and any exemption such as is specified in sub-paragraph (a) or (b) of this paragraph may be granted subject to conditions and to a limit of time and may be revoked by the said Secretary of State by a further certificate in writing at any time.

(2) In this regulation—

(a) "the home forces" has the same meaning as in section 12(1) of the Visiting Forces Act 1952;

(b) "headquarters" has the same meaning as in article 3(2) of the Visiting Forces and International Headquarters (Application of Law) Order 1965;

(c) "member of a headquarters" has the same meaning as in paragraph 1(1) of the Schedule to the International Headquarters and Defence Organisations Act 1964; and

(d) "visiting force" has the same meaning as it does for the purposes of any provision of Part I of the Visiting Forces Act 1952.

13. Extension outside Great Britain. These Regulations shall apply to and in relation to the premises and activities outside Great Britain to which sections 1 to 59 and 80 to 82 of the Health and Safety at Work etc. Act 1974 apply by virtue of the Health and Safety at Work etc. Act 1974 (Application Outside Great Britain) Order 1989 as they apply within Great Britain.

14. Modifications, repeal and revocations.—(1) The Act and Regulations specified in Schedule 2 shall be modified to the extent specified in the corresponding Part of that Schedule.

(2) Section 65 of the Factories Act 1961 is repealed.

(3) The instruments specified in column 1 of Schedule 3 are revoked to the extent specified in column 3 of that Schedule.

SCHEDULE 1

Regulation 4(3)(e)

RELEVANT COMMUNITY DIRECTIVE

Council Directive of 21 December 1989 on the approximation of the laws of the Member States relating to *personal protective equipment* (89/686/EEC).

SCHEDULE 2

Regulation 14(1)

MODIFICATIONS

PART I

THE FACTORIES ACT 1961

1. In section 30(6), for "breathing apparatus of a type approved by the chief inspector", substitute "suitable breathing apparatus".

PART II

THE COAL AND OTHER MINES (FIRE AND RESCUE) ORDER 1956

2. In Schedule 1, in regulation 23(a), for "breathing apparatus of a type approved by the Minister", substitute "suitable breathing apparatus".

3. In Schedule 1, in regulation 23(b), for "smoke helmets or other apparatus serving the same purpose, being helmets or apparatus of a type approved by the Minister,", substitute "suitable smoke helmets or other suitable apparatus serving the same purpose".

4. In Schedule 1, in regulation 24(a), for "smoke helmet or other apparatus serving the same purpose, being a helmet or other apparatus of a type approved by the Minister,", substitute "suitable smoke helmet or other suitable apparatus serving the same purpose".

PART III

THE SHIPBUILDING AND SHIP-REPAIRING REGULATIONS 1960

5. In each of regulations 50, 51(1) and 60(1), for "breathing apparatus of a type approved for the purpose of this Regulation", substitute "suitable breathing apparatus".

PART IV

THE COAL MINES (RESPIRABLE DUST) REGULATIONS 1975

6. In regulation 10(a), for "dust respirators of a type approved by the Executive for the purpose of this Regulation", substitute "suitable dust respirators".

PART V

THE CONTROL OF LEAD AT WORK REGULATIONS 1980

7. In regulation 7—
(a) after "respiratory protective equipment", insert "which complies with regulation 8A or, where the requirements of that regulation do not apply, which is"; and
(b) after "as will", insert ", in either case,".

8. In regulation 8, for "adequate protective clothing", substitute "protective clothing which complies with regulation 8A or, where no requirement is imposed by virtue of that regulation, is adequate".

9. After regulation 8, insert the following new regulations—

"Compliance with relevant Community Directives

8A. Any respiratory protective equipment or protective clothing shall comply with any enactment (whether in an Act or instrument) which implements any provision on design or manufacture with respect to health or safety in any relevant Community Directive listed in Schedule 1 to the Personal Protective Equipment at Work Regulations 1992 which is applicable to that item of respiratory protective equipment or protective clothing.

Assessment of respiratory protective equipment or protective clothing

8B.—(1) Before choosing respiratory protective equipment or protective clothing, an employer shall make an assessment to determine whether it will satisfy regulation 7 or 8, as appropriate.

(2) The assessment required by paragraph (1) shall involve—
(a) the definition of the characteristics necessary to comply with regulation 7 or, as the case may be, 8, and
(b) comparison of the characteristics of respiratory protective equipment or protective clothing available with the characteristics referred to in sub-paragraph (a) of this paragraph.

(3) The assessment required by paragraph (1) shall be revised if—
(a) there is reason to suspect that it is no longer valid; or
(b) there has been a significant change in the work to which it relates,

and, where, as a result of the review, changes in the assessment are required, the employer shall make them.".

10. In regulation 9, for sub-paragraph (b), substitute the following sub-paragraph—
"(b) where he is required under regulations 7 or 8 to provide respiratory protective equipment or protective clothing, adequate changing facilities and adequate facilities for the storage of—
(i) the respiratory protective equipment or protective clothing, and
(ii) personal clothing not worn during working hours.".

11. At the end of regulation 13, add the following new paragraph—
"(3) Every employee shall take all reasonable steps to ensure that any respiratory protective equipment provided to him pursuant to regulation 7 and protective clothing provided to him pursuant to regulation 8 is returned to the accommodation provided for it after use.".

12. In regulation 18(2), omit the full stop and add "and that any provision imposed by the European Communities in respect of the encouragement of improvements in the safety and health of workers at work will be satisfied.".

PART VI
THE IONISING RADIATIONS REGULATIONS 1985

13. In regulation 23(1), after "that respiratory protective equipment", insert "complies with paragraph (1A) or, where no requirement is imposed by that paragraph,".

14. After regulation 23(1), insert the following paragraphs—
"(1A) For the purposes of paragraph (1), *personal protective equipment* complies with this paragraph if it complies with any enactment (whether in an Act or instrument) which implements in Great Britain any provision on design or manufacture with respect to health or safety in any relevant Community Directive listed in Schedule 1 to the Personal Protective Equipment at Work Regulations 1992 which is applicable to that item of *personal protective equipment.*

(1B) Before choosing *personal protective equipment*, an employer shall make an assessment to determine whether it will satisfy regulation 6(3).

(1C) The assessment required by paragraph (1B) shall involve—

(a) definition of the characteristics necessary to comply with regulation 6(3), and

(b) comparison of the characteristics of available *personal protective equipment* with the characteristics referred to in sub-paragraph (a) of this paragraph.

(1D) The assessment required by paragraph (1B) shall be reviewed if—

(a) there is reason to suspect that it is no longer valid; or

(b) there has been a significant change in the work to which it relates,

and where, as a result of the review, changes in the assessment are required, the employer shall make them.".

15. Add at the end of regulation 23 the following additional paragraphs—

"(2A) Every employer shall ensure that appropriate accommodation is provided for *personal protective equipment* when it is not being worn.

(2B) Every employee shall take all reasonable steps to ensure that *personal protective equipment* provided to him is returned to the accommodation provided for it after use.".

PART VII
THE CONTROL OF ASBESTOS AT WORK REGULATIONS 1987

16. In regulation 8(3), after "shall" the first time that word appears, insert "comply with paragraph (3A) or, where no requirement is imposed by that paragraph, shall".

17. Insert the following new paragraph after regulation 8(3)—

"(3A) Any respiratory protective equipment provided in pursuance of paragraph (2) or protective clothing provided in pursuance of regulation 11(1) shall comply with this paragraph if it complies with any enactment (whether in an Act or instrument) which implements in Great Britain any provision on design or manufacture with respect to health or safety in any relevant Community Directive listed in Schedule 1 to the Personal Protective Equipment at Work Regulations 1992 which is applicable to that item of respiratory protective equipment or protective clothing.".

18. In regulation 20(2), omit the fullstop and add "and that any provision imposed by the European Communities in respect of the encouragement of improvements in the safety and health of workers at work will be satisfied.".

PART VIII
THE CONTROL OF SUBSTANCES HAZARDOUS TO HEALTH REGULATIONS 1988

19. In regulation 7, after paragraph (3), insert the following new paragraph—

"(3A) Any *personal protective equipment* provided by an employer in pursuance of this regulation shall comply with any enactment (whether in an Act or instrument) which implements in Great Britain any provision on design or manufacture with respect to health or safety in any relevant Community Directive listed in Schedule 1 to the Personal Protective Equipment at Work Regulations 1992 which is applicable to that item of *personal protective equipment*.".

20. In regulation 7, in paragraph (6)(b), insert at the beginning "complies with paragraph (3A) or, where no requirement is imposed by virtue of that paragraph,".

21. In regulation 8(2), after "these regulations", insert "and shall take all reasonable steps to ensure it is returned after use to any accommodation provided for it".

PART IX
THE NOISE AT WORK REGULATIONS 1989

22. Add the following new paragraph at the end of regulation 8—

"(3) Any personal ear protectors provided by virtue of this regulation shall comply with any enactment (whether in an Act or instrument) which implements in Great Britain any provision on design or manufacture with respect to health or safety in any relevant Community Directive listed in Schedule 1 to the Personal Protective Equipment at Work Regulations 1992 which is applicable to those ear protectors.".

PART X
THE CONSTRUCTION (HEAD PROTECTION) REGULATIONS 1989

23. Add the following paragraphs at the end of regulation 3—

"(3) Any head protection provided by virtue of this regulation shall comply with any enactment (whether in an Act or instrument) which implements any provision on design or manufacture with respect to health or safety in any relevant Community Directive listed in Schedule 1 to the Personal Protective Equipment at Work Regulations 1992 which is applicable to that head protection.

(4) Before choosing head protection, an employer or self-employed person shall make an assessment to determine whether it is suitable.

(5) The assessment required by paragraph (4) of this regulation shall involve—

(a) the definition of the characteristics which head protection must have in order to be suitable;

(b) comparison of the characteristics of the protection available with the characteristics referred to in sub-paragraph (a) of this paragraph.

(6) The assessment required by paragraph (4) shall be reviewed if—

(a) there is reason to suspect that it is no longer valid; or

(b) there has been a significant change in the work to which it relates,

and where as a result of the review changes in the assessment are required, the relevant employer or self-employed person shall make them.

(7) Every employer and every self-employed person shall ensure that appropriate accommodation is available for head protection provided by virtue of these Regulations when it is not being used.".

24. For regulation 6(4), substitute the following paragraph—

"(4) Every employee or self-employed person who is required to wear suitable head protection by or under these Regulations shall—

(a) make full and proper use of it; and

(b) take all reasonable steps to return it to the accommodation provided for it after use.".

25. In regulation 9(2), omit the full stop and add "and that any provision imposed by the European Communities in respect of the encouragement of improvements in the safety and health of workers at work will be satisfied.".

SCHEDULE 3

Regulation 14(3)

REVOCATIONS

(1) Title	(2) Reference	(3) Extent of Revocation
Regulations dated 26th February 1906 in respect of the processes of spinning and weaving of flax and tow and the processes incidental thereto (the Flax and Tow-Spinning and Weaving Regulations 1906).	S.R. & O. 1906/177, amended by S.I. 1988/1657.	In regulation 9, the words "unless waterproof skirts, and bibs of suitable material, are provided by the occupier and worn by the workers". Regulation 13.
Order dated 5th October 1917 (the Tin or Terne Plates Manufacture Welfare Order 1917).	S.R. & O. 1917/1035.	Paragraph 1.
Order dated 15th August 1919 (the Fruit Preserving Welfare Order 1919).	S.R. & O. 1919/1136, amended by S.I. 1988/1657.	Paragraph 1.
Order dated 23rd April 1920 (the Laundries Welfare Order 1920).	S.R. & O. 1920/654.	Paragraph 1.
Order dated 28th July 1920 (the Gut-Scraping, Tripe Dressing, etc Welfare Order 1920).	S.R. & O. 1920/1437.	Paragraph 1.
Order dated 3rd March 1921 (the Glass Bevelling Welfare Order 1921).	S.R. & O. 1921/288.	Paragraph 1.
The Aerated Water Regulations 1921.	S.R. & O. 1921/1932; amended by S.I. 1981/686.	The whole Regulations.
The Sacks (Cleaning and Repairing) Welfare Order 1927.	S.R. & O. 1927/860.	Paragraph 1.
The Oil Cake Welfare Order 1929.	S.R. & O. 1929/534.	Paragraph 1.
The Cement Works Welfare Order 1930.	S.R. & O. 1930/94.	Paragraph 1.
The Tanning Welfare Order 1930.	S.R. & O. 1930/312.	Paragraph 1 and the Schedule.
The Magnesium (Grinding of Castings and Other Articles) Special Regulations 1946.	S.R. & O. 1946/2107.	Regulation 12.

(1) *Title*	(2) *Reference*	(3) *Extent of Revocation*
The Clay Works (Welfare) Special Regulations 1948.	S.I. 1948/1547.	Regulation 5.
The Iron and Steel Foundries Regulations 1953.	S.I. 1953/1464; amended by S.I. 1974/1681 and S.I. 1981/1332.	Regulation 8.
The Shipbuilding and Ship-Repairing Regulations 1960.	S.I. 1960/1932; amended by S.I. 1974/1681.	Regulations 73 and 74.
The Non-Ferrous Metals (Melting and Founding) Regulations 1962.	S.I. 1962/1667; amended by S.I. 1974/1681.	Regulation 13.
The Abstract of Special Regulations (Aerated Water) Order 1963.	S.I. 1963/2058.	The whole Order.
The Construction (Health and Welfare) Regulations 1966.	S.I. 1966/95; to which there are amendments not relevant to these regulations.	Regulation 15.
The Foundries (Protective Footwear and Gaiters) Regulations 1971.	S.I. 1971/476.	The whole Regulations.
The Protection of Eyes Regulations 1974.	S.I. 1974/1681; amended by S.I. 1975/303.	The whole Regulations.
The Aerated Water Regulations (Metrication) Regulations 1981.	S.I. 1981/686.	The whole Regulations.

THE SUPPLY OF MACHINERY (SAFETY) REGULATIONS 1992

(S.I. 1992 No. 3073)

General note. These Regulations are intended to implement Machinery Directive 89/392 amended by 91/368.

The Secretary of State, being a Minister designated for the purposes of section 2(2) of the European Communities Act 1972 in relation to measures relating to the design and construction of, and to the placing on the market and putting into service of, *machinery*, in exercise of the powers conferred on him by that section and of all his other enabling powers, hereby makes the following Regulations:

PART I

PRELIMINARY

1. Citation, commencement and revocation.—(1) These Regulations may be cited as the Supply of Machinery (Safety) Regulations 1992 and shall come into force on 1 January 1993.

(2) The Regulations specified in the first column of Schedule 1 hereto are hereby revoked with effect from the date specified in the second column of that Schedule provided that each of the Regulations so specified shall continue to apply in respect of the *machinery* to which they respectively apply and which was *supplied* for the first time in *the Community* in accordance with the applicable Regulations on or before 31 December 1995.

2. Interpretation.—(1) In these Regulations, the "Machinery Directive" means Council Directive 89/392/EEC on the approximation of the laws of the Member States relating to *machinery* as amended by Council Directive 91/368/EEC.

(2) In these Regulations, unless the context otherwise requires—
  "approved body" shall be construed in accordance with regulation 17 below;
  "business" includes a profession and an undertaking, and a *supply* in the course of a business includes any *supply* by a business;
  "certificate of adequacy" shall be construed in accordance with regulation 20(1) below;
  "the Commission" means the Commission of the European Communities;
  "the Community" means the European Economic Community;
  "declaration of incorporation" shall be construed in accordance with regulation 23(2) below;

"EC declaration of conformity" shall be construed in accordance with regulation 22 below;

"EC mark" means a mark consisting of the symbol "CE" set out in the form shown in Schedule 2 hereto, followed by the last two figures of the year in which it is affixed;

"EC type-examination" shall be construed in accordance with regulation 21(1) below;

"EC type-examination certificate" means a certificate issued by an approved body certifying that an example of *relevant machinery* satisfies those provisions of the *Machinery Directive* which apply to it;

"enforcement authority" means—

(a) in Great Britain, the Health and Safety Executive established under section 10 of the Health and Safety at Work etc. Act 1974;
(b) in Northern Ireland, subject to paragraph 2(1) of Schedule 6 hereto, the Department of Economic Development and the Department of Agriculture; and
(c) save in paragraph 3(b) of Schedule 6 hereto, each of the authorities referred to in the said paragraph 3(b);

"essential health and safety requirements" means the requirements in Annex I of the *Machinery Directive* which is set out in Schedule 3 hereto;

"harmonised standard" means a *technical specification* adopted by the European Committee for Standardisation or the European Committee for Electrotechnical Standardisation or both, upon a mandate from *the Commission* in accordance with Council Directive 83/189/EEC of 28th March 1983 laying down a procedure for the provision of information in the field of technical standards and regulations, and of which the reference number is published in the Official Journal of the European Communities;

"interchangeable equipment" shall be construed in accordance with regulation 4(c) below;

"machinery" has the meaning given by regulation 4 below;

"relevant essential health and safety requirements" in relation to *relevant machinery* means those provisions of the *essential health and safety requirements* which are applicable to that particular *relevant machinery* for the purposes of establishing that it satisfies the *essential health and safety requirements* of the *Machinery Directive.*

Provided that, subject to regulation 10(1)(a) below, in so far as such provisions relate to risks which are covered by other Community Directives and to the extent that any enactment implementing any such Directive applies to that *machinery* those provisions shall not be *relevant essential health and safety requirements* for the purposes of these Regulations;

"relevant machinery" shall be construed in accordance with regulation 3(2) below;

"responsible person" means, in relation to *relevant machinery,*
(a) the manufacturer of that *machinery*;
(b) the manufacturer's authorised representative established in *the Community*; or
(c) where the manufacturer is not established in *the Community* and either—
   (i) he has not appointed an authorised representative established in *the Community*; or

(ii) his authorised representative established in *the Community* is not the
supplier of that *machinery*,
the person who first supplies the *relevant machinery* in *the Community*;
and, in this definition and in regulation 11(2)(a) below, "the manufacturer"
includes any person who assembles *machinery* or parts thereof to form *relevant
machinery*;

"safe" in relation to *relevant machinery* means that, when the *machinery* is
properly installed and maintained and used for the purposes for which it is
intended, there is no risk (apart from one reduced to a minimum) of its
being the cause or occasion of death or injury to persons or, where appropriate, to domestic animals or damage to property, and cognate expressions
shall be construed accordingly:

For the purposes of this definition, when considering whether or not a risk
has been reduced to a minimum, regard shall be had to the practicability of
so reducing that risk at the time of the construction of the *relevant machinery*;

"Schedule 4 machinery" means *machinery* posing special hazards which is
specified in Annex IV of the *Machinery Directive* and listed in Schedule 4
hereto;

"series manufacture" means the manufacture of more than one item of
relevant machinery of the same type in accordance with a common design;

"standard" means a *technical specification* approved by a recognised stan-
dardising body for repeated or continuous application, with which compliance is not compulsory;

"supply" is to be read in accordance with section 46 of the Consumer
Protection Act 1987 and includes offering to supply, agreeing to supply,
exposing for supply and possessing for supply, and cognate expressions shall
be construed accordingly:

Provided that "supply" does not include exhibitions at trade fairs and
exhibitions of *relevant machinery* in respect of which the provisions of these
Regulations are not satisfied if a notice is displayed in relation to the *machinery* in question to the effect—

(a) that it does not satisfy those provisions; and
(b) that it may not lawfully be *supplied* until the *responsible person* has ensured
that those provisions are satisfied;

"technical file" shall be construed, in respect of *relevant machinery* other
than *Schedule 4 machinery*, in accordance with regulation 13(1) below and, in
respect of *relevant machinery* which is *Schedule 4 machinery*, in accordance with
regulation 14(2) below;

"technical specification" means a specification contained in a document
which lays down the characteristics required of *relevant machinery* such as
levels of quality, performance, *safety* or dimensions, including the requirements applicable to the *relevant machinery* as regards terminology, symbols,
testing and test methods, packaging, marking or labelling; and

"transposed harmonised standard" means a national *standard* of a member State—

(a) which transposes a *harmonised standard*; and
(b) the reference number of which has been published by that member
State in adoption thereof pursuant to Article 5.2 of the *Machinery
Directive*.

PART II
APPLICATION

3. *Relevant machinery*.—(1) These Regulations apply to *relevant machinery*.

(2) *Relevant machinery* is all *machinery* within the meaning of regulation 4 below other than *machinery* which is excluded from the scope of these Regulations pursuant to regulations 5 to 10 below.

4. Definition of "*machinery*". For the purposes of these Regulations, machinery is—

(a) an assembly of linked parts or components, at least one of which moves including, without prejudice to the generality of the foregoing, the appropriate actuators, control and power circuits, joined together for a specific application, in particular for the processing, treatment, moving or packaging of a material;

(b) an assembly of machines, that is to say, an assembly of items of machinery as referred to in paragraph (a) above which, in order to achieve the same end, are arranged and controlled so that they function as an integral whole notwithstanding that the items of machinery may themselves be *relevant machinery* and accordingly severally required to comply with these Regulations; or

(c) *interchangeable equipment* modifying the function of a machine which is *supplied* for the purpose of being assembled with an item of machinery as referred to in paragraph (a) above or with a series of different items of machinery or with a tractor by the operator himself save for any such equipment which is a spare part or tool.

General exclusions

5. Excluded *machinery*. These Regulations do not apply to *machinery* specified in Schedule 5 hereto.

6. *Machinery* for export to a third country.—(1) These Regulations do not apply to *machinery* which the *supplier* believes (with reasonable cause) will not be put into service either in the United Kingdom or in another member State.

(2) Paragraph (1) above shall not apply if the *EC mark*, or any inscription liable to be confused therewith, is affixed to the *machinery*.

Transitional exclusions

7. *Machinery* first *supplied* or put into service before 1st January 1993. These Regulations do not apply to *machinery* first *supplied* or put into service in *the Community* before 1st January 1993.

8. Exclusion until 31st December 1994 of *machinery* which complies with health and safety provisions in force in a member State on 31st December 1992.—(1) Subject to paragraph (2) below, these Regulations do not apply to *machinery* first *supplied* or put into service in *the Community* on or before 31st December 1994 which—

(a) complies with any health and safety provisions with which it would have been required to comply for it to be lawfully *supplied* in the United Kingdom on 31st December 1992; or

(b) in the case of *machinery supplied* in the United Kingdom which the supplier believes (with reasonable cause) will be put into service in another member State, complies with the health and safety provisions in relation to the *supply* and putting into service of that *machinery* in force in that member State on 31st December 1992.

(2) The exceptions provided in paragraph (1) above do not apply in the case of *machinery* which—

(a) in the case of *machinery* which is not required to bear the *EC mark* pursuant to any other Community obligation, bears the *EC mark* or an inscription liable to be confused therewith; or

(b) bears or is accompanied by any other indication, howsoever expressed, that it complies with the *Machinery Directive.*

(3) In this regulation, "health and safety provisions" means any requirement imposed by an enactment which has the same, or substantially the same, effect as any of the *essential health and safety requirements* which would, but for the provisions of this regulation, be applicable to that *machinery* for the purposes of complying with these Regulations.

Exclusion of machinery covered by other Directives

9. Exclusion of specific *machinery.*—(1) These Regulations do not apply to—

(a) roll-over protective structures as referred to in Article 1 of Council Directive 86/295/EEC on the approximation of the laws of the member States relating to roll-over protective structures (ROPS) for certain construction plant;

(b) falling-object protective structures as referred to in Article 1 of Council Directive 86/296/EEC on the approximation of the laws of the member States relating to falling-object protective structures (FOPS) for certain construction plant; or

(c) industrial trucks as referred to in Article 1 of Council Directive 86/663/EEC on the approximation of the laws of the member States relating to self-propelled industrial trucks,

which are *supplied* or put into service for the first time in *the Community* before 1st July 1995.

(2) On and after 1st July 1995, in respect of *machinery* mentioned in paragraph (1) above which is *supplied* or put into service for the first time in *the Community* on or before 31st December 1995, a supplier may comply with—

(a) the requirements of these Regulations; or

(b) the requirements of—
  (i) in the case of roll-over protective structures, the Roll-Over Protective Structures for Construction Plant (EEC Requirements) Regulations 1988;
  (ii) in the case of falling-object protective structures, the Falling-Object Protective Structures for Construction Plant (EEC Requirements) Regulations 1988; or
  (iii) in the case of industrial trucks, in Great Britain, the Self-Propelled Industrial Trucks (EEC Requirements) Regulations 1988 as amended by the Self-Propelled Industrial Trucks (EEC Requirements) (Amendment) Regulations 1989, and in Northern Ireland, the Self-Propelled Industrial Trucks (EEC Requirements) Regulations (Northern Ireland) 1990.

10. *Machinery* where risks are wholly covered by other Directives.—(1) These Regulations do not apply to—

(a) *machinery* where all the *essential health and safety requirements* which would have applied to it, but for the provisions of this sub-paragraph, relate to risks wholly covered by Community Directives other than the *Machinery Directive* to the extent that any enactment implementing any such Directive is applicable to that *machinery*; or
(b) *machinery* which is electrical equipment in so far as the risks as to the safety of such equipment are mainly of electrical origin.

(2) In paragraph (1)(b) above, "electrical equipment" has the meaning given by Article 1 of Council Directive 73/23/EEC on the harmonization of the laws of member States relating to electrical equipment designed for use within certain voltage limits.

PART III
GENERAL REQUIREMENTS

11. General duty.—(1) Subject to paragraph (3) below, no person shall *supply relevant machinery* unless the requirements of regulation 12 below are complied with in relation thereto.

(2) Where a person—

(a) being the manufacturer of *relevant machinery*, himself puts that *relevant machinery* into service in the course of a *business*; or
(b) having imported *relevant machinery* from a country or territory outside *the Community*, himself puts that *relevant machinery* into service in the course of a *business*,

for the purposes of these Regulations that person shall be deemed to have *supplied* that *relevant machinery* to himself.

(3) The requirements of paragraph (1) above do not apply in relation to *supply* by any person of *relevant machinery* which has previously been put into service in *the Community*.

12. Requirements for *supply* of *relevant machinery*.—(1) The requirements of this regulation are that—

(a) the *relevant machinery* satisfies the *relevant essential health and safety require-ments*;

(b) the appropriate conformity assessment procedure in respect of the *relevant machinery* has been carried out by the *responsible person* in accord-ance with one of the procedures described in regulations 13, 14 and 15 below;

(c) the *responsible person*, at his election, has issued either—

(i) an *EC declaration of conformity* in accordance with regulation 22 below; or

(ii) in the case of *relevant machinery* to which regulation 23 below applies, a *declaration of incorporation* in accordance with that regu-lation,

in respect of the *relevant machinery*;

(d) except in the case of *relevant machinery* to which regulation 23 below applies, the *EC mark* has been properly affixed by the *responsible person* to the *relevant machinery* in accordance with regulation 25 below; and

(e) the *relevant machinery* is in fact *safe*.

(2) It is the responsibility of the manufacturer of *relevant machinery* to carry out the necessary research or tests on components, fittings or the completed machine to determine whether by its design or construction the machine is capable of being erected and put into service safely.

Conformity assessment procedures

13.   *Relevant machinery* other than *Schedule 4 machinery*.—(1) In the case of *relevant machinery* which is not *Schedule 4 machinery* the *responsible person* must draw up a *technical file* which comprises—

(a) an overall drawing of the *machinery* together with drawings of the control circuits;

(b) full detailed drawings, accompanied by any calculation notes, test results and such other data as may be required to check the conformity of the *machinery* with the *essential health and safety requirements*;

(c) a list of:

(i) the *essential health and safety requirements*;

(ii) *transposed harmonised standards*;

(iii) standards; and

(iv) other *technical specifications*,

which were used when the *machinery* was designed;

(d) a description of methods adopted to eliminate hazards presented by the *machinery*;

(e) if he so desires, any technical report or certificate obtained from a competent body or laboratory;

(f) if he declares conformity with a *transposed harmonised standard* which provides therefor, any technical report giving the results of tests carried out at his choice either by himself or by a competent body or laboratory; and

(g) a copy of the instructions for the *machinery* drawn up in accordance with paragraph 1.7.4 of Schedule 3 hereto.

(2) For *series manufacture*, the *responsible person* must also have available documentation in respect of the internal measures that will be implemented to

ensure that all the items of *machinery* so produced are in conformity with the provisions of the *Machinery Directive*.

(3) Where the file referred to in paragraph (1) above is drawn up in the United Kingdom it shall be in English always provided that the instructions for the *machinery* referred to in sub-paragraph (g) thereof shall be in such languages as are specified in paragraph 1.7.4(b) of Schedule 3 hereto.

14. *Schedule 4 machinery* **manufactured in accordance with** *transposed harmonised standards.*—(1) In the case of *relevant machinery* which is *Schedule 4 machinery* manufactured in accordance with *transposed harmonised standards* the *responsible person* must, at his election—

(a) draw up and forward to an *approved body* for retention by that body a *technical file*;

(b) submit the *technical file* referred to in paragraph (a) above to an *approved body* requesting—

   (i) verification by that body that the *transposed harmonised standards* have been correctly applied; and

   (ii) that the body draw up a *certificate of adequacy* for the file submitted in accordance with regulation 20 below; or

(c) submit the *technical file* referred to in paragraph (a) above to an *approved body* together with an example of the *relevant machinery* for *EC type-examination* or, where appropriate, a statement as to where such an example might be examined, in accordance with regulation 21 below.

(2) The *technical file* referred to in this regulation and regulation 15 below must include—

(a) an overall drawing of the *machinery* together with drawings of the control circuits;

(b) full detailed drawings, accompanied by any calculation notes, test results and such other data as may be required to check the conformity of the *machinery* with the *essential health and safety requirements*;

(c) a description of methods adopted to eliminate hazards presented by the *machinery*, a list of *transposed harmonised standards* used and, in the case of *relevant machinery* to which regulation 15 below applies, a list of standards used;

(d) a copy of the instructions for the *machinery* drawn up in accordance with paragraph 1.7.4 of Schedule 3 hereto; and

(e) for *series manufacture*, the internal measures that will be implemented to ensure that all the items of *machinery* so produced are in conformity with the provisions of the *Machinery Directive*.

(3) The *technical file* referred to in this regulation and regulations 15 and 21(2) below must be drawn up in an official language of the member State in which the *approved body* is established (in the United Kingdom, English) or in such other language as is acceptable to the *approved body*, always provided that the instructions for the *machinery* referred to in paragraph 2(d) above shall be in such languages as are specified in paragraph 1.7.4(b) of Schedule 3 hereto.

15. *Schedule 4 machinery* **not manufactured in accordance with** *transposed harmonised standards.* In the case of *relevant machinery* which is *Schedule 4 machinery* and—

(a) which is not manufactured in accordance with *transposed harmonised standards*;

(b) which is only partly manufactured in accordance with *transposed harmonised standards*; or

(c) in respect of which there are no *transposed harmonised standards*,

the *responsible person* must submit a *technical file*, as described in regulation 14(2) above, to an *approved body* together with an example of the *machinery* for *EC type-examination* or, where appropriate, a statement as to where such an example might be examined, in accordance with regulation 21 below.

16.   Modifications to *relevant machinery*. Where the *responsible person* complies with one of the conformity assessment procedures referred to in regulation 14 or 15 above he must inform the *approved body* of any modifications, even of a minor nature, which he or, where the *responsible person* is not the manufacturer, the manufacturer has made or plans to make to the *relevant machinery* to which the *technical file* relates.

17.   *Approved bodies*. For the purposes of these Regulations, an *approved body* is a body responsible for carrying out functions relating to the conformity assessment procedures set out in Article 8 of the *Machinery Directive* and described in regulations 14 and 15 above which has been—

(a) appointed as a United Kingdom *approved body* pursuant to regulation 18 below; or

(b) appointed by a member State other than the United Kingdom,

and in the case of either (a) or (b) above has been notified by the member State concerned to *the Commission* and the other member States pursuant to Article 9(1) of the *Machinery Directive*.

18.   United Kingdom *approved bodies*.—(1) The Secretary of State may from time to time appoint such qualified persons as he thinks fit to be United Kingdom *approved bodies* for the purposes of these Regulations.

(2) An appointment—

(a) may relate to all descriptions of *Schedule 4 machinery* or such descriptions (which may be framed by reference to any circumstances whatsoever) of *Schedule 4 machinery* as the Secretary of State may from time to time determine;

(b) may be made subject to such conditions as the Secretary of State may from time to time determine, and such conditions may include conditions which are to apply upon or following termination of the appointment;

(c) shall, without prejudice to the generality of sub-paragraph (b) above, require that body, subject to paragraph (4) below—

(i) to acknowledge receipt of *technical file* submitted to it for retention pursuant to regulation 14(1)(a) above;

(ii) to carry out the required procedures in respect of the provision of *certificates of adequacy* at the request of *responsible persons* in accordance with regulation 20 below; and

    (iii) to carry out *EC type-examinations* of examples of *Schedule 4 machinery* submitted to it or, where appropriate, made available for examination, in accordance with regulation 21 below;

  (d) shall be terminated—

    (i) if it appears to the Secretary of State that the *approved body* is no longer a qualified person; or

    (ii) upon 90 days' notice in writing to the Secretary of State, at the request of the *approved body*; and

  (e) may be terminated if it appears to the Secretary of State that any of the conditions of the appointment are not complied with.

(3) Subject to paragraph (2)(d) and (e) above, an appointment under this regulation may be for the time being or for such period as may be specified in the appointment.

(4) A United Kingdom *approved body* shall not be required to carry out the functions referred to in paragraph (2)(c) above where—

  (a) the documents submitted to it (other than the instructions for the *machinery*) in relation to carrying out such functions are not in English or another language acceptable to that body;

  (b) the *responsible person* has not submitted with its application the amount of the fee which the body requires to be submitted with the application pursuant to regulation 19 below; or

  (c) the body reasonably believes that, having regard to the number of applications made to it in relation to its appointment under these Regulations which are outstanding, it will be unable to carry out the required work within 3 months of receiving the application.

(5) If for any reason the appointment of an *approved body* is terminated under this regulation, the Secretary of State may authorise another United Kingdom *approved body* to take over its functions in respect of such cases as he may specify.

(6) In this regulation—

"qualified person" means a person (which may include the Secretary of State) who meets the minimum criteria; and

"minimum criteria" means the criteria set out in Annex VII of the *Machinery Directive* (minimum criteria to be taken into account by member States for the notification of bodies).

19. Fees.—(1) Without prejudice to the power of the Secretary of State, where he is a United Kingdom *approved body*, to charge fees pursuant to regulations made under section 56 of the Finance Act 1973 and subject to paragraph (2) below, a United Kingdom *approved body* other than the Secretary of State may charge such fees in connection with, or incidental to, carrying out its duties in relation to the functions referred to in regulation 18(2)(c) above as it may determine; provided that such fees shall not exceed the sum of the following—

  (a) the costs incurred or to be incurred by the *approved body* in performing the relevant function; and

  (b) an amount on account of profit which is reasonable in the circumstances having regard to—

    (i) the character and extent of the work done or to be done by the body on behalf of the *responsible person*; and

    (ii) the commercial rate normally charged on account of profit for that work or similar work.

(2) The power in paragraph (1) above includes the power to require the payment of fees or a reasonable estimate thereof in advance of carrying out the work requested by the *responsible person*.

20. **Certificate of adequacy.**—(1) A *certificate of adequacy* is a document drawn up by an *approved body* to which a *technical file* as described in regulation 14(2) above has been submitted in which that body certifies that—

(a) the *transposed harmonised standards* have been correctly applied in respect of the design and construction of the *relevant machinery* to which the file relates; and

(b) the file contains all the necessary information.

(2) A United Kingdom *approved body* to which such a file has been submitted by a *responsible person* as described in regulation 14(1)(b) above shall, if satisfied in respect of the matters referred to in paragraph (1)(a) and (b) above, draw up a *certificate of adequacy* in respect of the file, and send a copy thereof to the *responsible person*.

(3) If the United Kingdom *approved body* is not so satisfied, it shall—

(a) give the *responsible person* the opportunity, within a reasonable period, of making representations as to why it should not refuse to draw up a *certificate of adequacy* for the file; and

(b) if, after considering any representations made pursuant to sub-paragraph (a) above, it remains unsatisfied in respect of the matters referred to in paragraph (1)(a) and (b) above, it shall—

    (i) refuse to draw up a *certificate of adequacy* for the file;

    (ii) notify its decision in writing to the *responsible person* who submitted the file stating the grounds on which such refusal is based; and

    (iii) at the same time inform all other *approved bodies* of such decision.

(4) Where the United Kingdom *approved body* which has drawn up a *certificate of adequacy* for a *technical file* is notified, pursuant to regulation 16 above, by the *responsible person* who submitted the file of a modification which he or, where the *responsible person* is not the manufacturer, the manufacturer has made, or plans to make, to the *relevant machinery* to which the file relates, the United Kingdom *approved body* shall examine such modification and—

(a) if it is satisfied that the requirements of paragraph (1)(a) and (b) above are or, as the case may be, would be met in respect of the *relevant machinery* so modified, it shall notify the *responsible person* in writing that the *certificate of adequacy* remains valid; or

(b) if it is not so satisfied it shall notify the *responsible person* in writing that the *certificate of adequacy* for the file does not or would not, as the case may be, remain valid in respect of the *relevant machinery* as modified stating the grounds on which such decision was based.

21. **EC type-examination.**—(1) *EC type-examination* is the procedure whereby an *approved body* ascertains and certifies that an example of *relevant machinery* satisfies those provisions of the *Machinery Directive* which apply to it.

(2) An application for *EC type-examination* by a *responsible person* (in this regulation referred to as the applicant) to a United Kingdom *approved body* shall—

(a) specify—
    (i) the name and address of the applicant; and
    (ii) the place of manufacture of the *machinery* to which the application relates; and
(b) be accompanied by—
    (i) a *technical file* for the *machinery* as described in regulation 14(2) above; and
    (ii) an example of the *machinery* or, where appropriate, a statement as to where such an example might be examined.

(3) The United Kingdom *approved body* to which such application is made shall satisfy itself that the *technical file* contains all the necessary information.

(4) The United Kingdom *approved body* shall also—

(a) examine and perform such tests as it considers appropriate on the example; and
(b) if satisfied that—
    (i) the example has been manufactured in conformity with the *technical file* and may safely be used under its intended working conditions;
    (ii) the standards or *transposed harmonised standards*, as the case may be, if used, have been properly applied; and
    (iii) the example complies with the *relevant essential health and safety requirements*,
draw up and forward to the applicant an *EC type-examination certificate* which shall state the conclusions of the *EC type-examination*, indicate any conditions to which the issue of the certificate is subject and shall be accompanied by the descriptions and drawings necessary to identify the example to which the certificate relates.

(5) The United Kingdom *approved body* shall, if so requested, taking the necessary measures to guarantee confidentiality, *supply* to the Secretary of State a copy of the *EC type-examination certificate*, a copy of the *technical file* and copies of the reports on the examinations and tests that it has carried out in relation to that application.

(6) If the United Kingdom *approved body* is not satisfied that the requirements of paragraphs (3) and (4)(b) above are met and is minded to refuse to issue an *EC type-examination certificate*, it shall—

(a) inform the applicant in writing of the reasons why it proposes to refuse to issue an *EC type-examination certificate*;
(b) give the applicant the opportunity, within a reasonable period, of making representations as to why it should not be refused; and
(c) if, after considering any representations made pursuant to sub-paragraph (b) above, it remains unsatisfied in respect of the requirements of paragraphs (3) and (4)(b) above, it shall—

(i) notify its decision in writing to the applicant stating the grounds on which the refusal is based; and

(ii) at the same time inform all other *approved bodies* of such decision.

(7) Where the United Kingdom *approved body* which has issued an *EC type-examination certificate* in respect of an example of *relevant machinery* to an applicant is notified, pursuant to regulation 16 above, by that person of a modification which he or, where that person is not the manufacturer, the manufacturer has made, or plans to make, to the *relevant machinery* to which that example relates, the United Kingdom *approved body* shall examine such modification and—

(a) if it is satisfied that the *relevant machinery* as modified does, or would, as the case may be, conform sufficiently with the example as to the matters referred to in paragraph (4)(b) above, it shall notify the applicant in writing that the *EC type-examination certificate* is or would be, as the case may be, valid in respect of the *relevant machinery* as modified for the purposes of issuing *EC declarations of conformity* in accordance with regulation 22(5) below; or

(b) if it is not so satisfied it shall notify the applicant in writing that the *EC type-examination certificate* is not, or would not be, as the case may be, a valid certificate in respect of the *relevant machinery* as modified for the above-mentioned purposes stating the grounds on which such decision was based.

Declaration and marking procedures

22. *EC declaration of conformity.*—(1) Drawing up an *EC declaration of conformity* is the procedure whereby the *responsible person* declares in respect of each item of *relevant machinery* which he supplies in *the Community* that that particular item of *relevant machinery* complies with all the *essential health and safety requirements* applying to it.

(2) An *EC declaration of conformity* must—

(a) state the *business* name and full address of—

(i) the *responsible person*; and

(ii) where that person is not the manufacturer, of the manufacturer;

(b) contain a description of the *machinery* to which the declaration relates which, without prejudice to the generality of the foregoing, includes, in particular—

(i) its make;

(ii) type; and

(iii) serial number;

(c) indicate all relevant provisions with which the *machinery* complies;

(d) state in the case of *relevant machinery* in relation to which an *EC type-examination certificate* has been issued the name and address of the *approved body* which issued the certificate and the number of such certificate;

(e) state in the case of *relevant machinery* in respect of which a *technical file* as described in regulation 14(2) above has been drawn up the name and address of the *approved body* to which the file has been sent or which has drawn up a *certificate of adequacy* for the file, as the case may be;

(f) specify (as appropriate) the *transposed harmonised standards* used;

(g) specify (as appropriate) the national standards and any *technical specifications* used; and

(h) identify the person authorised to sign the declaration on behalf of the *responsible person.*

(3) An *EEC declaration of conformity* must be—

(a) drawn up in the same language as the instructions for the *machinery* are drawn up as specified in paragraph 1.7.4(b) of Schedule 3 hereto; and

(b) typed or written by hand in block capitals.

(4) In the case of *relevant machinery* in respect of which the *responsible person* has carried out one of the conformity assessment procedures described in regulations 13, 14(1)(a) or 14(1)(b) above, the *responsible person* must state in the *EC declaration of conformity* that the item of *machinery* to which the declaration relates complies with the *relevant essential health and safety requirements.*

(5) In the case of *relevant machinery* in respect of which the *responsible person* has carried out the conformity assessment procedure described in regulation 14(1)(c) or 15 above and an *EC type-examination certificate* has been issued in respect of an example of that *machinery*, and such certificate remains valid, the *responsible person* must state that the item of *machinery* in respect of which the declaration is made conforms with the example to which that certificate relates.

(6) For the purposes of these Regulations, the requirement in paragraph (2)(c) above shall be satisfied where the *EC declaration of conformity* specifies the *Machinery Directive* and any other Community Directives with which the *relevant machinery* complies.

23. Declaration of incorporation.—(1) This regulation applies in the case of *relevant machinery* which—

(a) is intended for—
   (i) incorporation into other *machinery*; or
   (ii) assembly with other *machinery*,
   to constitute *relevant machinery*;

(b) cannot function independently; and

(c) is not *interchangeable equipment.*

(2) A *declaration of incorporation* is a document whereby a *responsible person* declares the matters referred to in paragraph (1)(a) above and which includes the particulars set out in paragraph (3) below.

(3) A *declaration of incorporation* must—

(a) state the name and address of the *responsible person*;

(b) contain a description of the *machinery* or *machinery* parts;

(c) state in the case of *relevant machinery* in respect of which an *EC type-examination certificate* has been issued the name and address of the *approved body* which issued the certificate and the number of such certificate;

(d) state in the case of *relevant machinery* in respect of which a *technical file* as described in regulation 14(2) above has been drawn up the name and address of the *approved body* to which the file has been sent or which has drawn up a *certificate of adequacy* for the file, as the case may be;

(e)   specify the *transposed harmonised standards* (if any) used;

(f)   state that the *machinery* (to which the *declaration of incorporation* relates) must not be put into service until the *relevant machinery* into which it is to be incorporated has been declared in conformity with the provisions of the *Machinery Directive*; and

(g)   identify the person signing the *declaration of incorporation*.

24.   Retention of documentation.—(1) A *responsible person* who issues *EC declarations of conformity* or declarations of incorporation, as the case may be, in the United Kingdom shall retain on his premises the *technical file* or a copy of the *technical file* submitted to an *approved body*, as the case may be, which relates to the *relevant machinery* in respect of which such declarations are made so that such file is available to the enforcement authorities for a period of 10 years beginning with the date on which the last unit of *relevant machinery* to which the file relates is produced.

(2) Nothing in paragraph (1) above shall require the *responsible person* to keep the documents comprising a *technical file* available as a permanent file provided that all the required documents are individually available and can be assembled into a *technical file*.

(3) For the avoidance of doubt, it is hereby declared that for the purposes of enforcing these Regulations a *technical file* is a document or record and shall be construed accordingly in any of the statutory provisions applied to these Regulations pursuant to Schedule 6 hereto.

25.   The *EC mark*.—(1) For the purposes of these Regulations, the *EC mark* shall be regarded as properly affixed to *relevant machinery* if—

(a)   the *responsible person* who affixes the *EC mark* to the *relevant machinery* has issued an *EC declaration of conformity* in respect thereof;

(b)   the *EC mark* is affixed to the *relevant machinery* in a distinct, visible, legible and indelible manner; and

(c)   in the case of *relevant machinery* which is the subject of Community Directives other than the *Machinery Directive*, the requirements of those other Directives have also been complied with in respect of the *relevant machinery*.

(2) No person shall affix the *EC mark* to any *relevant machinery* unless that *machinery*—

(a)   satisfies the *relevant essential health and safety requirements*; and

(b)   is *safe*.

(3) No mark or inscription which is capable of being confused with the *EC mark* shall be affixed to *relevant machinery*.

(4) A person who supplies *relevant machinery* which does not bear the *EC mark* shall, at the request of an *enforcement authority*, or of an officer of such an authority, give any information which he has, or which is available to him, concerning the date when the *relevant machinery* was first *supplied* in *the Community* and explain (so far as he is able) why the *machinery* does not bear that mark.

Supplementary provisions

26. Conditions for *relevant machinery* being taken to comply with the *relevant essential health and safety requirements*.—(1) Subject to paragraph (2) below, *relevant machinery* which is accompanied by an *EC declaration of conformity* and to which the *EC mark* is affixed shall be taken to comply with the *relevant essential health and safety requirements*, unless there are reasonable grounds for suspecting that it does not so comply.

(2) Paragraph (1) above does not apply—

(a) in relation to an *enforcement authority* where the *responsible person* fails or refuses to make available to the *enforcement authority* the *technical file* or a copy thereof pursuant to regulation 24(1) above; or

(b) in the case of *relevant machinery*—

    (i) which is re*supplied* in the circumstances described in regulation 11(3) above; and

    (ii) to which the *EC mark* is indelibly affixed.

27. Judicial review of decisions of *approved bodies*.—(1) A person aggrieved by a decision of an *approved body* under regulation 20(3)(b), 20(4)(b), 21(6)(c) or 21(7)(b) shall, at the same time as he is notified of the decision, be given information about the judicial remedies available to him.

(2) That information shall include—

(a) a brief statement of the procedure by which judicial review may be applied for in accordance with Rules of Court (or, in Northern Ireland, with Rules of Court made, or having effect as if made, under section 55 of the Judicature (Northern Ireland) Act 1978); and

(b) the information that in England and Wales or in Northern Ireland, an application for leave to apply to the Court for judicial review shall be made promptly and in any event within three months from the date when grounds for the application first arose unless the court considers that there is good reason for extending the period within which the application shall be made.

PART IV
ENFORCEMENT

28. Application of Schedule 6. Schedule 6 shall have effect for the purposes of providing for the enforcement of these Regulations and for matters incidental thereto.

29.   Offences. Any person who—

(a) contravenes or fails to comply with regulation 11 above;

(b) affixes the *EC mark* to any *relevant machinery* in contravention of regulation 25(2) above;

(c) affixes a mark or inscription to *relevant machinery* in contravention of regulation 25(3) above;

(d) contravenes the requirements of regulation 24 above; or

(e) fails or refuses to give information or an explanation as required by regulation 25(4) above, shall be guilty of an offence.

30.   Penalties.—(1) A person guilty of an offence under regulation 29(a) or (b) above shall be liable on summary conviction—

(a) to imprisonment for a term not exceeding 3 months; or

(b) to a fine not exceeding—

  (i) in Great Britain, level 5 on the *standard* scale; or

  (ii) in Northern Ireland, £2,000,

or to both.

(2) A person guilty of an offence under regulation 29(c), (d) or (e) above shall be liable on summary conviction to a fine not exceeding—

  (i) in Great Britain, level 5 on the *standard* scale; or

  (ii) in Northern Ireland, £2,000.

31.   Defence of due diligence.—(1) Subject to the following provisions of this regulation, in proceedings against any person for an offence under regulation 29 above it shall be a defence for that person to show that he took all reasonable steps and exercised all due diligence to avoid committing the offence.

(2) Where in any proceedings against any person for such an offence the defence provided by paragraph (1) above involves an allegation that the Commission of the offence was due—

(a) to the act or default of another; or

(b) to reliance on information given by another,

that person shall not, without the leave of the court, be entitled to rely on the defence unless, not less than seven clear days before the hearing of the proceedings (or, in Scotland, the trial diet), he has served a notice under paragraph (3) below on the person bringing the proceedings.

(3) A notice under this paragraph shall give such information identifying or assisting in the identification of the person who committed the act or default or gave the information as is in the possession of the person serving the notice at the time he serves it.

(4) It is hereby declared that a person shall not be entitled to rely on the defence provided by paragraph (1) above by reason of his reliance on information *supplied* by another, unless he shows that it was reasonable in all the circumstances for him to have relied on the information, having regard in particular—

(a) to the steps which he took, and those which might reasonably have been taken, for the purpose of verifying the information; and

(b) to whether he had any reason to disbelieve the information.

32. Liability of persons other than the principal offender.—(1) Where the Commission by any person of an offence under regulation 29 above is due to the act or default committed by some other person in the course of any *business* of his, the other person shall be guilty of the offence and may be proceeded against and punished by virtue of this paragraph whether or not proceedings are taken against the first-mentioned person.

(2) Where a body corporate is guilty of an offence under these Regulations (including where it is so guilty by virtue of paragraph (1) above) in respect of any act or default which is shown to have been committed with the consent or connivance of, or to be attributable to any neglect on the part of, any director, manager, secretary or other similar officer of the body corporate or any person who was purporting to act in any such capacity he, as well as the body corporate, shall be guilty of that offence and shall be liable to be proceeded against and punished accordingly.

(3) Where the affairs of a body corporate are managed by its members, paragraph (2) above shall apply in relation to the acts and defaults of a member in connection with his functions of management as if he were a director of the body corporate.

(4) In this regulation, references to a "body corporate" include references to a partnership in Scotland and, in relation to such partnership, any reference to a director, manager, secretary or other similar officer of a body corporate is a reference to a partner.

33. Consequential disapplication of United Kingdom law.—(1) Subject to paragraph (3) below, any requirement which—

(a) is imposed by or under any of the enactments (relating in various respects to the safety of *machinery*) specified in paragraph (2) below; and

(b) but for the provisions of this paragraph, would have to be satisfied by or in respect of *relevant machinery* if it is to be lawfully *supplied,*

is hereby disapplied.

(2) The enactments referred to in paragraph (1) above are—

(a) in the Factories Act 1961—
   (i) subsection (1) of section 26 but only to the extent that it imposes requirements in respect of the *supply* of chains, ropes and lifting tackle to be put into service for raising or lowering goods or materials; and
   (ii) subsections (1) and (6) of section 27;

(b) in the Factories Act (Northern Ireland) 1965—
   (i) subsection (1) of section 27 but only to the extent that it imposes requirements in respect of the *supply* of chains, ropes and lifting tackle to be put into service for raising or lowering goods or materials; and
   (ii) subsections (1) and (6) of section 28;

(c) in the Construction (General Provisions) Regulations 1961 (having effect as if made under the Factories Act 1961) and in the Construction

(General Provisions) Regulations (Northern Ireland) 1963 (having effect as if made under the Factories Act (Northern Ireland) 1965) respectively, regulation 26, paragraphs (1) and (2) of regulation 29 and regulation 31(1);

(d) in the Construction (Lifting Operations) Regulations 1961 (having effect as if made under the Factories Act 1961), and in the Construction (Lifting Operations) Regulations (Northern Ireland) 1963 (having effect as if made under the Factories Act (Northern Ireland) 1965) respectively, regulations 10(1)(a), 11(3), 13(1), 13(2), 14(1), 14(4), 15, 16, 20(2), 21, 22, 24, 30(1), the first sentence of 30(2) and 34(1);

(e) in the Shipbuilding & Ship-repairing Regulations 1960 (having effect as if made under the Factories Act 1961), regulations 33, 34(1), 35 and 36(1);

(f) in the Shipbuilding & Ship-repairing Regulations (Northern Ireland) 1971 (made under the Factories Act (Northern Ireland) 1965), regulations 32, 33(1), 34 and 35(1);

(g) in the Mines and Quarries Act 1954 and the Mines Act (Northern Ireland) 1969 respectively, sections 83 and 85(1);

(h) in the Coal and Other Mines (Locomotives) Regulations 1956 (having effect as if made under the Mines and Quarries Act 1954), paragraphs (1), (2)(a) to (c) and (3) of regulation 3, regulation 4 and paragraphs (1)(a) to (g), (2) and (3) of regulation 5;

(i) in the Coal and Other Mines (Support) Regulations 1966 (made under the Mines and Quarries Act 1954), regulation 16(2);

(j) in the Miscellaneous Mines (General) Regulations 1956 (having effect as if made under the Mines and Quarries Act 1954), regulation 52;

(k) in the Quarries (General) Regulations 1956 (having effect as if made under the Mines and Quarries Act 1954), regulation 14;

(l) in the Quarry Vehicles Regulations 1970 (made under the Mines and Quarries Act 1954), regulations 3(1) and 4(1);

(m) in the Agriculture (Threshers and Balers) Regulations 1960 (made under the Agriculture (Safety, Health and Welfare Provisions) Act 1956) paragraph 7 of Part II of the Schedule thereto;

(n) in the Coal Mines (Firedamp Drainage) Regulations 1960 (made under the Mines and Quarries Act 1954), regulation 11.

(o) in the Docks Regulations 1988 (made under the Health and Safety at Work etc. Act 1974) and in the Docks Regulations (Northern Ireland) 1989 (made under the Health and Safety at Work (Northern Ireland) Order 1978) respectively, regulation 13(1)(a), (b), and (c), the words "or assembled" in regulation 13(1)(d), regulations 13(2)(b), (c) and (d), 14(1)(a) and 16(7);

(p) in the Electricity at Work Regulations 1989 (made under the Health and Safety at Work etc. Act 1974) and in the Electricity at Work Regulations (Northern Ireland) 1991 (made under the Health and Safety at Work (Northern Ireland) Order 1978) respectively, regulation 26; and

(q) in the Regulations specified in the first column of Schedule 7 hereto, the regulations respectively specified in the third column of that Schedule.

(3) For the avoidance of doubt, it is hereby declared that nothing in paragraph (2) above affects the application of the enactments so listed to the use in service of *relevant machinery*.

34. *Relevant machinery* **which is electrical equipment.**—(1) The Low Voltage Electrical Equipment (Safety) Regulations 1989 are hereby disapplied in respect of *relevant machinery* which is electrical equipment in so far as the risks as to the safety of such equipment are not mainly of electrical origin.

(2) In this regulation, "electrical equipment" has the meaning given by Article 1 of Council Directive 73/23 EEC on the harmonisation of the laws of member States relating to electrical equipment designed for use within certain voltage limits.

(3) For the avoidance of doubt, it is hereby declared that paragraph (1) above does not affect the applicability of the above-mentioned Regulations to *machinery* which is electrical equipment for the purposes of regulation 8(1)(a) above.

SCHEDULE 1

Regulation 1(2)

REVOCATION OF REGULATIONS

The Roll-Over Protective Structures for Construction Plant (EEC Requirements) Regulations 1988	1 January 1996
The Falling-Object Protective Structures for Construction Plant (EEC Requirements) Regulations 1988	1 January 1996
The Self-Propelled Industrial Trucks (EEC Requirements) Regulations 1988	1 January 1996
The Self-Propelled Industrial Trucks (EEC Requirements) (Amendment) Regulations 1989	1 January 1996
The Self-Propelled Industrial Trucks (EEC Requirements) Regulations (Northern Ireland) 1990	1 January 1996

SCHEDULE 2

Regulations 2(2) and 25

THE *EC MARK*

(Annex III of the *Machinery Directive*)

The *EC mark* consists of the symbol shown below and the last two figures of the year in which the mark is affixed.
   [(Please see illustration in original.)]
   The different elements of the *EC mark* should have materially the same vertical dimensions, which should not be less than 5mm.

SCHEDULE 3

Regulation 2(2)

ESSENTIAL HEALTH AND SAFETY REQUIREMENTS RELATING TO THE DESIGN AND CONSTRUC-
TION OF MACHINERY

(Annex I of the *Machinery Directive*)

General note. The full text of the Machinery Directive is at page 29; Annex I, which is reproduced in the Regulations but not in this section of the book, is at page 39.

SCHEDULE 4

Regulation 2(2)

MACHINERY POSING SPECIAL HAZARDS

(Annex IV of the *Machinery Directive*)

General note. Annex IV to the Machinery Directive is set out at page 77 in this book.

SCHEDULE 5

Regulation 5

EXCLUDED MACHINERY

Lifting equipment designed and constructed for raising and/or moving persons with or without loads, except for industrial trucks with elevating operator position.

Machinery whose only power source is directly applied manual effort unless it is a machine used for lifting or lowering loads.

Machinery for medical use used in direct contact with patients.

Special equipment for use in fairgrounds and/or amusement parks.

Steam boilers, tanks and pressure vessels.

Machinery specially designed or put into service for nuclear purposes which, in the event of failure, may result in an emission of radioactivity.

Radioactive sources forming part of a machine.

Firearms.

Storage tanks and pipelines for petrol, diesel fuel, inflammable liquids and dangerous substances.

Means of transport, that is vehicles and their trailers intended solely for transporting passengers by air or on road, rail or water networks, as well as means of transport in so far as such means are designed for transporting goods by air, on public road or rail networks or on water. Vehicles used in the mineral extraction industry shall not be excluded.

Sea-going vessels and mobile offshore units together with equipment on board such vessels or units.

Cableways for the public or private transportation of persons.

Agricultural and forestry tractors, as defined in Article 1(1) of Council Directive 74/150/EEC of 4 March 1974 on the approximation of the laws of the member States relating to the type-approval of wheeled agricultural or forestry tractors, as last amended by Directive 88/297/EEC.

Machines specially designed and constructed for military or police purposes.

SCHEDULE 6

ENFORCEMENT

1. Enforcement in Great Britain in relation to *relevant machinery for use at work.* In Great Britain, in relation to *relevant machinery for use at work*—
  (a) it shall be the duty of *the Executive* to make adequate arrangements for the enforcement of these Regulations, and accordingly a reference in the provisions applied to these Regulations by sub-paragraph (b) below to an "enforcing authority" shall be construed as a reference to *the Executive*;
  (b) sections 19 to 28, 33 to 35, 38, 39, 41 and 42 of *the 1974 Act* shall apply for the purposes of providing for the enforcement of these Regulations and in respect of proceedings for contravention thereof as if—
    (i) references to relevant statutory provisions were references to those sections as applied by this paragraph and to these Regulations;
    (ii) references to articles, substances, articles and substances, or plant, were references to *relevant machinery*;
    (iii) references to the field of responsibility of an enforcing authority, however expressed, were omitted;
    (iv) in section 20, subsection (3) were omitted;
    (v) in section 23, subsections (3), (4) and (6) were omitted;
    (vi) in section 3—
      (aa) in subsection (1) the whole of paragraphs (a) to (d) were omitted;
      (bb) subsection (1A) were omitted;
      (cc) in subsection (2), the reference to paragraph (d) of subsection (1) were omitted;
      (dd) subsection (2A) were omitted;
      (ee) for subsection (3) there were substituted the following:—

"(3) A person guilty of an offence under any paragraph of subsection (1) above not mentioned in subsection (2) above or of an offence under subsection (1)(e) above not falling within that subsection shall be liable—
  (a) on summary conviction, to a fine not exceeding level 5 on the *standard* scale; or
  (b) on conviction on indictment—
    (i) in the case of an offence under subsection (1)(g) or of an offence under subsection (1)(j), to imprisonment for a term not exceeding two years, or a fine, or both; or
    (ii) in all other cases, to a fine."; and
      (ff) subsection (4) were omitted;
    (vii) in section 34—
      (aa) paragraphs (a) and (b) were omitted from subsection (1); and
      (bb) in subsection (3) for "six months" there were substituted "twelve months"; and
    (viii) in section 42, subsections (4) and (5) were omitted; and
  (c) sections 36(1) and (2) and 37 shall apply in relation to offences under section 33 as applied to these Regulations and as modified by sub-paragraph (b)(vi) above.

2. Enforcement in Northern Ireland in relation to *relevant machinery for use at work.*—
(1) In Northern Ireland—
  (a) subject to head (b) below, it shall be the duty of the Department of Economic Development to make adequate arrangements for the enforcement of these Regulations in relation to *relevant machinery for use at work*; and
  (b) it shall be the duty of the Department of Agriculture to make adequate arrangements for the enforcement of these Regulations in relation to *relevant machinery* for use at work which is wholly or mainly *agricultural,*

and a reference in the provisions applied to these Regulations by sub-paragraph (2) below to an "enforcing authority" or to its "field of responsibility" (however expressed) or to "the Department concerned" shall be construed accordingly.

(2)

(a) For the purposes of providing for the enforcement of these Regulations and in respect of proceedings for contravention thereof, Articles 21 to 33, 35, 36, 38 and 39 of *the Order* shall apply as if—

    (i) references to relevant statutory provisions were references to those Articles as applied by this paragraph and to these Regulations;

    (ii) references to articles, substances, articles and substances, or plant, were references to *relevant machinery*;

    (iii) in Article 22, paragraph (3) were omitted;

    (iv) in Article 25, paragraphs (3), (4) and (5) were omitted;

    (v) in Article 31—

        (aa) in paragraph (1), the whole of sub-paragraphs (a) to (d) were omitted;

        (bb) paragraph (1A) were omitted;

        (cc) in paragraph (2), the reference to sub-paragraph (d) of paragraph (1) were omitted;

        (dd) paragraph (2A) were omitted;

        (ee) paragraph (3) were omitted;

        (ff) for paragraph (4) there were substituted the following—

"(4) A person guilty of an offence under any sub-paragraph of paragraph (1) not mentioned in paragraph (2) or of an offence under paragraph (1)(e) not falling within paragraph (2) shall be liable—

(a) on summary conviction, to a fine not exceeding £2000; or

(b) on conviction on indictment—

    (i) in the case of an offence under paragraph (1)(g) or of an offence under paragraph (1)(j), to imprisonment for a term not exceeding two years, or a fine, or both; or

    (ii) in all other cases, to a fine."; and

        (gg) paragraph (5) were omitted;

    (vi) in Article 32—

        (aa) sub-paragraphs (a) and (b) were omitted from paragraph (1); and

        (bb) in paragraph (3), for "six months" there were substituted "twelve months"; and

    (vii) in Article 39, paragraphs (4) and (5) were omitted; and

(b) Articles 34(1) and (2) shall apply in relation to offences under Article 31 as applied to these Regulations and as modified by sub-paragraph (2)(a)(v) above.

3. Enforcement in relation to *relevant machinery* as goods for private use or consumption. In relation to *relevant machinery* as goods for private use or consumption—

(a) it shall be the duty of—

    (i) every weights and measures authority in Great Britain; and

    (ii) every district council in Northern Ireland,

to enforce these Regulations within their area;

(b) a reference in the provisions applied to these Regulations by sub-paragraph (c) below to an *"enforcement authority"* shall be construed as a reference to each of the following authorities—

    (i) the bodies mentioned in sub-paragraph (a) above; and

    (ii) the Secretary of State;

(c) sections 14, 15, 28 to 35, 37, 38, 44 and 47 of *the 1987 Act* shall apply for the purposes of providing for the enforcement of these Regulations and in respect of proceedings for contravention thereof as if—

    (i) references to safety provisions were references to these Regulations;

    (ii) references to goods were references to *relevant machinery* or items of *relevant machinery* as the context may require;

      (iii) in section 14, in subsection (6), for "six months" there were substituted "three months";

      (iv) in sections 28, 29, 30, 33, 34 and 35, the words "or any provision made by or under Part III of this Act", on each occasion that they occur, were omitted;

      (v) in section 28, subsections (3), (4) and (5) were omitted;

      (vi) in section 29, subsection (4) were omitted;

      (vii) in section 30, subsections (7) and (8) were omitted; and

      (viii) in section 38(1), paragraphs (a) to (c) were omitted;

  (d) sections 39 and 40 shall apply to offences under section 32 as it is applied to these Regulations by sub-paragraph (c) above; and

  (e) in relation to proceedings for an offence under these Regulations—

      (i) in Great Britain, section 34 of *the 1974 Act* shall apply as if—

        (aa) paragraphs (a) and (b) of subsection (1) were omitted;

        (bb) references to an "enforcing authority" were references to each of the authorities referred to in sub-paragraph (a)(i) and (b)(ii) of this paragraph, and "responsible enforcing authority" were construed accordingly;

        (cc) references to "relevant statutory provisions" were references to these Regulations; and

        (dd) in subsection (3), for "six months" there were substituted "twelve months"; and

      (ii) in Northern Ireland, Article 32 of *the Order* shall apply as if—

        (aa) sub-paragraphs (a) and (b) of paragraph (1) were omitted;

        (bb) references to an "enforcing authority" were references to each of the authorities referred to in sub-paragraph (a)(ii) and (b)(ii) of this paragraph, and "responsible enforcing authority" were construed accordingly;

        (cc) references to "relevant statutory provisions" were references to these Regulations; and

        (dd) in paragraph (3), for "six months" there were substituted "twelve months".

4. Forfeiture: England and Wales and Northern Ireland.—(1) An *enforcement authority* in England and Wales or Northern Ireland may apply under this paragraph for an order for the forfeiture of any *relevant machinery* on the grounds that there has been a contravention in relation thereto of regulation 11.

(2) An application under this paragraph may be made—

  (a) where proceedings have been brought in a magistrates' court in respect of an offence in relation to some or all of the *relevant machinery* under regulation 29 (a) or (b) to that court;

  (b) where an application with respect to some or all of the *relevant machinery* has been made to a magistrates' court under section 15 or 33 of the 1987 Act as applied for the purposes of the enforcement of these Regulations by paragraph 3 (c) above, to that court; and

  (c) where no application for the forfeiture of the *relevant machinery* has been made under sub-paragraph (a) or (b) above, by way of complaint to a magistrates' court.

(3) On an application under this paragraph the court shall make an order for the forfeiture of the *relevant machinery* only if it is satisfied that there has been a contravention in relation thereto of regulation 11.

(4) For the avoidance of doubt it is hereby declared that a court may infer for the purposes of this paragraph that there has been a contravention in relation to any *relevant machinery* of regulation 11 if it is satisfied that that regulation has been contravened in relation to an item of *relevant machinery* which is representative of that *relevant machinery* (whether by reason of being of the same design or part of the same consignment or batch or otherwise).

(5) Any person aggrieved by an order made under this paragraph by a magistrates' court, or by a decision of such court not to make such an order, may appeal against that order or decision—

(a) in England and Wales, to the Crown Court;

(b) in Northern Ireland, to the county court,

and an order so made may contain such provision as appears to the court to be appropriate for delaying the coming into force of an order pending the making and determination of any appeal (including any application under section 111 of the Magistrates' Courts Act 1980, or Article 146 of the Magistrates' Courts (Northern Ireland) Order 1981 (statement of case)).

(6) Subject to sub-paragraph (7) below, where any *relevant machinery* is forfeited under this paragraph it shall be destroyed in accordance with such directions as the court may give.

(7) On making an order under this paragraph a magistrates' court may, if it considers it appropriate to do so, direct that the *relevant machinery* to which the order relates shall (instead of being destroyed) be released, to such person as the court may specify, on condition that that person—

(a) does not *supply* the *relevant machinery* to any person otherwise than—

    (i) to a person who carries on a *business* of buying *relevant machinery* of the same description as the first mentioned *machinery* and repairing or reconditioning it; or

    (ii) as scrap (that is to say, for the value of materials included in the *relevant machinery* rather than for the value of the *relevant machinery* itself); and

(b) complies with any order to pay costs or expenses (including any order under section 35 of *the 1987 Act* as applied for the purposes of the enforcement of these Regulations by paragraph 3(c) above) which has been made against that person in the proceedings for the order for forfeiture.

5. Forfeiture: Scotland.—(1) In Scotland a sheriff may make an order for forfeiture of any *relevant machinery* in relation to which there has been a contravention of any provision of regulation 11—

(a) on an application by the procurator-fiscal made in the manner specified in section 310 of the Criminal Procedure (Scotland) Act 1975; or

(b) where a person is convicted of any offence in respect of any such contravention, in addition to any other penalty which the sheriff may impose.

(2) The procurator-fiscal making an application under sub-paragraph (1)(a) above shall serve on any person appearing to him to be the owner of, or otherwise to have an interest in, *relevant machinery* to which the application relates a copy of the application, together with a notice giving him the opportunity to appear at the hearing of the application to show cause why the *relevant machinery* should not be forfeited.

(3) Service under sub-paragraph (2) above shall be carried out, and such service may be proved, in the manner specified for citation of an accused in summary proceedings under the Criminal Procedure (Scotland) Act 1975.

(4) Any person upon whom a notice is served under sub-paragraph (2) above and any other person claiming to be the owner of, or otherwise to have an interest in, the *relevant machinery* to which an application under this paragraph relates shall be entitled to appear at the hearing of the application to show cause why the *relevant machinery* as the case may be should not be forfeited.

(5) The sheriff shall not make an order following an application under sub-paragraph (1)(a) above—

(a) if any person on whom notice is served under sub-paragraph (2) above does not appear, unless service of the notice on that person is proved; or

(b) if no notice under sub-paragraph (2) above has been served, unless the court is satisfied that in the circumstances it was reasonable not to serve notice on any person.

(6) The sheriff shall make an order under this paragraph only if he is satisfied that there has been a contravention in relation to the *relevant machinery* of regulation 11.

(7) For the avoidance of doubt it is declared that the sheriff may infer for the purposes of this paragraph that there has been a contravention in relation to any *relevant machinery* of regulation 11 if he is satisfied that regulation 11 has been contravened in relation to an item of *relevant machinery* which is representative of that *relevant machinery* (whether by reason of being of the same design or part of the same consignment or batch or otherwise).

(8) Where an order for the forfeiture of any *relevant machinery* is made following an application by the procurator-fiscal under sub-paragraph (1)(a) above, any person who appeared, or was entitled to appear, to show cause why it should not be forfeited may, within twenty-one days of the making of the order, appeal to the High Court by Bill of Suspension on the ground of an alleged miscarriage of justice; and section 452(4)(a) to (e) of the Criminal Procedure (Scotland) Act 1975 shall apply to an appeal under this sub-paragraph as it applies to a stated case under Part II of that Act.

(9) An order following an application under sub-paragraph (1)(a) above shall not take effect—

(a) until the end of the period of twenty-one days beginning with the day after the day on which the order is made; or

(b) if an appeal is made under sub-paragraph (8) above within that period, until the appeal is determined or abandoned.

(10) An order under sub-paragraph (1)(b) shall not take effect—

(a) until the end of the period within which an appeal against the order could be brought under the Criminal Procedure (Scotland) Act 1975; or

(b) if an appeal is made within that period, until the appeal is determined or abandoned.

(11) Subject to sub-paragraph (12) below, *relevant machinery* forfeited under this paragraph shall be destroyed in accordance with such directions as the sheriff may give.

(12) If he thinks fit, the sheriff may direct the *relevant machinery* to be released to such person as he may specify, on condition that that person does not *supply* it to any person otherwise than—

(a) to a person who carries on a *business* of buying *relevant machinery* of the same description as the first-mentioned *relevant machinery* and repairing or reconditioning it; or

(b) as scrap (that is to say, for the value of materials included in the *relevant machinery* rather than for the value of the *relevant machinery* itself).

6. Duty of *enforcement authority* to inform Secretary of State of action taken. An *enforcement authority* shall, where action has been taken by it to prohibit or restrict the *supply* or putting into service (whether under these Regulations or otherwise) of any *relevant machinery* which bears the *EC mark* forthwith inform the Secretary of State of the action taken, and the reasons for it, with a view to this information being passed by him to *the Commission.*

7. Savings. Nothing in these Regulations shall be construed as preventing the taking of any action in respect of any *relevant machinery* under the provisions of *the 1974 Act, the Order* or *the 1987 Act.*

8. Nothing in these Regulations shall authorise an *enforcement authority* to bring proceedings in Scotland for an offence.

9. Interpretation. In this Schedule—

"the 1974 Act" means the Health and Safety at Work etc. Act 1974;

"the 1987 Act" means the Consumer Protection Act 1987;

"agriculture" includes horticulture, fruit growing, seed growing, dairy farming, livestock breeding and keeping, forestry, the use of land as grazing land, meadow land, osier land, market gardens and nursery grounds and the preparation of land for agricultural use;

"the Executive" means the Health and Safety Executive established under section 10 of the 1974 Act;

"the Order" means the Health and Safety at Work (Northern Ireland) Order 1978; and"machinery for use at work" means *machinery*—

(a) designed for use or operation, whether exclusively or not, by persons at work; or

(b) designed for use or operation, otherwise than at work, in non-domestic premises made available to persons at a place where they may use the *machinery* provided for their use there, and a reference to *relevant machinery* for use at work shall be construed accordingly.

SCHEDULE 7

Regulation 33(2)(q)

MINING DISAPPLICATIONS

PART I

MADE UNDER THE MINES AND QUARRIES ACT 1954

(1) Title	(2) Reference	(3) Extent of disapplication
The Loch Aline Mine (Diesel Vehicles) Special Regulations 1958	S.I. 1958/1678	Regulations 4 to 6
The Middleton-by-Wirksworth Limestone Mine (Diesel Vehicles) Special Regulations 1959	S.I. 1959/1520	Regulations 4 to 6
The Woodside Nos. 2 and 3 Mine (Diesel Vehicles) Special Regulations 1960	S.I. 1960/1291	Regulations 4 to 6
The Grimethorpe Mine (Diesel Vehicles) Special Regulations 1961	S.I. 1961/2444	Regulations 4 to 6
The Lynemouth Mine (Diesel Vehicles and Storage Battery Vehicles) Special Regulations 1961	S.I. 1961/2445	Regulations 4 to 7
The Calverton Mine (Diesel Vehicles) Special Regulations 1962	S.I. 1962/931	Regulations 4 to 6
The Brightling Mine (Diesel Vehicles) Special Regulations 1962	S.I. 1962/1094	Regulations 5 to 7
The Easington Mine (Diesel Vehicles) Special Regulations 1962	S.I. 1962/1676	Regulations 4 to 6
The Rufford Mine (Diesel Vehicles) Special Regulations 1962	S.I. 1962/2059	Regulations 4 to 6
The Trelewis Drift Mine (Diesel Vehicles) Special Regulations 1962	S.I. 1962/2114	Regulations 4 to 6
The Wharncliffe Woodmoor 4 and 5 Mine (Diesel Vehicles) Special Regulations 1962	S.I. 1962/2193	Regulations 4 to 6
The Seaham Mine (Diesel Vehicles) Special Regulations 1962	S.I. 1962/2512	Regulations 4 to 6
The Dawdon Mine (Diesel Vehicles) Special Regulations 1963	S.I. 1963/118	Regulations 4 to 6

(1) Title	(2) Reference	(3) Extent of disapplication
The Thoresby Mine (Diesel Vehicles) Special Regulations 1963	S.I. 1963/825	Regulations 4 to 6
The Westoe Mine (Diesel Vehicles) Special Regulations 1963	S.I. 1963/1096	Regulations 4 to 6
The Silverwood Mine (Diesel Vehicles) Special Regulations 1963	S.I. 1963/1618	Regulations 4 to 6
The Prince of Wales Mine (Diesel Vehicles) Special Regulations 1964	S.I. 1964/539	Regulations 4 to 6
The Newbiggin Mine (Diesel Vehicles) Special Regulations 1964	S.I. 1964/899	Regulations 5 to 7
The Cwmgwili Mine (Diesel Vehicles) Special Regulations 1964	S.I. 1964/1225	Regulations 4 to 6
The Wearmouth Mine (Diesel Vehicles) Special Regulations 1964	S.I. 1964/1476	Regulations 4 to 6
The South Crofty Mine (Locomotives) Special Regulations 1965	S.I. 1965/759	Regulations 4 to 6
The Bevercotes Mine (Diesel Vehicles) Special Regulations 1965	S.I. 1965/1194	Regulations 4 to 6
The Sallet Hole Mine (Storage Battery Locomotives) Special Regulations 1966	S.I. 1966/1325	Regulations 4 to 8
The Ellington Mine (Diesel Vehicles and Storage Battery Vehicles) Special Regulations 1967	S.I. 1967/956	Regulations 4 to 7
The Groverake Mine (Storage Battery Locomotives) Special Regulations 1967	S.I. 1967/1545	Regulations 4 to 8
The Fauld Mine (Diesel Vehicles) Special Regulations 1968	S.I. 1968/1295	Regulations 5 to 7
The Prince of Wales Mine (Captive Rail Diesel Locomotives) Special Regulations 1969	S I. 1969/1377	Regulation 4
The Winsford Rock Salt Mine (Diesel Vehicles and Storage Battery Vehicles) Special Regulations 1971	S.I. 1971/50	Regulations 4 to 7
The Boulby Mine (Storage Battery Locomotives) Special Regulations 1972	S.I. 1972/472	Regulations 4 to 8
The Marblaegis Mine (Diesel Vehicles) Special Regulations 1972	S.I. 1972/984	Regulations 5 to 7
The Longriggs Mine (Diesel Vehicles) Special Regulations 1973	S.I. 1973/371	Regulations 5 to 7
The Elsecar Main Mine (Diesel Vehicles) Special Regulations 1974	S.I. 1974/710	Regulations 4 to 6

PART II
MADE UNDER THE MINES AND QUARRIES ACT 1954 AND THE HEALTH AND SAFETY AT WORK ETC. ACT 1974

(1)	(2)	(3)
Title	*Reference*	*Extent of disapplication*
The Rixey Park Mine (Storage Battery Locomotives) Special Regulations 1974	S.I. 1974/1866	Regulations 4 to 8

PART III
MADE UNDER THE HEALTH AND SAFETY AT WORK ETC. ACT 1974

(1)	(2)	(3)
Title	*Reference*	*Extent of disapplication*
The Markham Mine (Diesel Vehicles) Regulations 1976	S.I. 1976/1734	Regulations 4 to 6
The Bentinck Mine (Diesel Engined Stone Dusting Machine) Regulations 1976	S.I. 1976/2046	Regulations 4 to 7
The Thoresby Mine (Cable Reel Load-Haul-Dump Vehicles) Regulations 1978	S.I. 1978/119	Regulations 4 to 6
The Sallet Hole Nos. 1 and 2 Mines (Diesel Vehicles) Regulations 1978	S.I. 1978/761	Regulations 5 to 7
The Trelewis Drift Mine (Diesel Vehicles) Regulations 1978	S.I. 1978/1376	Regulations 4 to 6
The Boulby Mine (Diesel Vehicles) Regulations 1979	S.I. 1979/1532	Regulations 5 to 8
The Sallet Hole No. 2 Mine (Storage Battery Locomotives) Special Regulations 1980	S.I. 1980/1203	Regulations 4 to 9
The Harworth Mine (Cable Reel Load-Haul-Dump Vehicles) Regulations 1980	S.I. 1980/1474	Regulations 4 to 6
The Point of Ayr Mine (Diesel Vehicles) Regulations 1980	S.I. 1980/1705	Regulations 4 to 6

THE PERSONAL PROTECTIVE EQUIPMENT (EC DIRECTIVE) REGULATIONS 1992

(S.I. 1992 No. 3139)

General note. These Regulations are intended to implement the Approximation of Personal Protective Equipment Laws Directive 89/686. The Directive is set out in full as the Schedule to the Regulations.

Whereas the Secretary of State is a Minister designated *(a)* for the purposes of section 2(2) of the European Communities Act 1972 *(b)* in relation to measures relating to safety as regards personal protective equipment;

Now, therefore, the Secretary of State in the exercise of the powers conferred on him by section 2(2) of that Act hereby makes the following Regulations:

1. Citation and Commencement. These Regulations may be cited as the Personal Protective Equipment (EC Directive) Regulations 1992 and shall come into force on 1 January 1993.

2. Interpretation. In these Regulations—
"the Directive" means Council Directive 89/686/EEC on the approximation of the laws of the Member States relating to personal protective equipment *(c)*, a copy of which is printed in the Schedule to these Regulations.

3. Scope, Placing on the Market and Free Movement.—(1) The Directive shall have effect within the United Kingdom for the purpose of laying down the conditions governing the placing of products to which the Directive applies on the market and their free movement within the Community and the basic safety requirements which such products must satisfy in order to ensure the health protection and safety of users.

(2) For the purposes mentioned in paragraph (1) above—

(a) section 13 of the Consumer Protection Act 1987 *(d)* (prohibition notices and notices to warn) shall (to the extent that it does not already do so) apply in relation to products to which the Directive applies as it applies in relation to relevant goods under that section;

(b) these Regulations shall constitute safety provisions for the purposes of section 14 of that Act (suspension notices) and sections 16 and 17 of that Act (forfeiture); and

793

(c) a weights and measures authority in Great Britain or a district council in Northern Ireland shall have the same duty to enforce these Regulations as it has in relation to Part II of that Act, and Part IV of that Act shall apply accordingly.

(3) For the purposes of paragraph (2) (a) above any question as to whether products to which the Directive applies are unsafe shall be determined in accordance with the Directive.

(4) Paragraph (2) (c) above is without prejudice to the duty of the Health and Safety Executive in relation to section 6 of the Health and Safety at Work etc. Act 1974 *(e)* or, in Northern Ireland, the duties of the Department of Economic Development and the Department of Agriculture in relation to Article 7 of the Health and Safety at Work (Northern Ireland) Order 1978 *(f)* (general duties of manufacturers as regards articles and substances for use at work); and no action shall be taken by virtue of that paragraph before 1 January 1994 unless it could have been taken otherwise than by virtue of these Regulations.

(5) Nothing in any enactment or rule of law shall prevent the placing on the market of products to which the Directive applies in accordance with this Directive.

4. Certification and Monitoring Procedures. The Secretary of State shall, in accordance with the Directive, approve one or more bodies for the purposes of carrying out the certification and monitoring procedures laid down in the Directive and shall withdraw his approval from such a body if he establishes that the latter no longer satisifies the criteria set out in the Directive.

Edward Leigh
Parliamentary Under-Secretary of State,
10 December 1992   Department of Trade and Industry

SCHEDULE

COUNCIL DIRECTIVE

of 21 December 1989

on the approximation of the laws of the Member States relating to personal protective equipment

(89/686/EEC)

THE COUNCIL OF THE EUROPEAN COMMUNITIES,

Having regard to the Treaty establishing the European Economic Community, and in particular Article 100a thereof,

Having regard to the proposal from the Commission,

In co-operation with the European Parliament,

Having regard to the opinion of the Economic and Social Committee,

Whereas it is necessary to adopt measures with the aim of progressively establishing the internal market over a period expiring on 31 December 1992; whereas the internal market comprises an area without internal frontiers in which the free movement of goods, persons, services and capital is guaranteed;

Whereas various Member States have, over recent years, adopted provisions covering numerous items of personal protective equipment with a view in particular to safeguarding public health, improving safety at work and ensuring user protection;

Whereas these national provisions are often very detailed as regards the requirements relating to the design, manufacture, quality level, testing and certification of personal protective equipment with a view to the protection of individuals against injury and illness;

Whereas, in particular, the national provisions relating to safety at work make the use of personal protective equipment compulsory; whereas many requirements oblige employers to make appropriate personal protective equipment available to their staff in the absence or inadequacy of priority public protection measures;

Whereas national provisions relating to personal protective equipment differ significantly from one Member State to another; whereas they may thus constitute a barrier to trade with direct consequences for the creation and operation of the common market;

Whereas it is necessary to harmonise these different national provisions in order to ensure the free movement of these products, without in any way reducing the valid levels of protection already required in the Member States, and to provide for any necessary increase therein;

Whereas the provisions governing the design and manufacture of personal protective equipment laid down in this Directive which are fundamental, in particular, to attempts to ensure a safer working environment are without prejudice to provisions relating to the use of such equipment and the organisation of the health and safety of workers at the workplace;

Whereas this Directive defines only the basic requirements to be satisfied by personal protective equipment; whereas, in order to facilitate proof of conformity with those basic requirements, it is essential that harmonised European standards be available relating, in particular, to the design and manufacture of, and the specifications and test methods applicable to, personal protective equipment, since compliance therewith confers on these products a presumption of conformity with the abovementioned basic requirements; whereas such harmonised European standards are drawn up by private bodies and must retain the status of non-mandatory texts; whereas, to this end, the

European Committee for Standardisation (CEN) and the European Committee for Electrotechnical Standardisation (Cenelec) are the competent bodies which have been authorised to adopt harmonised standards in accordance with the general guidelines governing co-operation between the Commission and those two institutions ratified on 13 November 1984; whereas, for the purposes of this Directive, a harmonised standard is a text containing technical specifications (a European standard or a harmonisation document) which has been adopted by one or both of the abovementioned bodies at the instigation of the Commission in accordance with Council Directive 83/189/EEC of 28 March 1983 laying down a procedure for the provision of information in the field of technical standards and regulations, as amended by Directive 88/182/EEC, and pursuant to the abovementioned general guidelines;

Whereas, pending the adoption of harmonised standards, which will be very numerous because of the broad scope of application and the preparation of which within the deadline set for the creation of the internal market will involve a great deal of work, it would be advisable to maintain, on a transitional basis and subject to the requirements of the Treaty, the status quo as regards conformity with existing national standards for personal protective equipment not covered by a harmonised standard at the date of adoption of this Directive;

Whereas, given the general and horizontal nature of the role played by the Standing Committee set up pursuant to Article 5 of Directive 83/189/EEC in Community standardisation policy and, more particularly, its part in the preparation of standardisation applications and the operation of the existing European standardisation agreements, this Standing Committee is especially suited to the task of assisting the Commission in monitoring the conformity of harmonised standards throughout the Community;

Whereas compliance with these technical requirements must be monitored in order to ensure adequate user and third-party protection; whereas existing monitoring procedures may differ appreciably from one Member State to another; whereas, in order to avoid numerous checks which merely impede the free movement of personal protective equipment, provision should be made for the mutual recognition of inspections conducted by the Member States; whereas, in order to facilitate such recognition, it is necessary, in particular, to lay down harmonised Community procedures and to harmonise the criteria to be taken into account in selecting the bodies responsible for examination, monitoring and verfication;

Whereas the legislative framework should be improved so that both sides of industry will make an effective and appropriate contribution to the process of standardisation,

HAS ADOPTED THIS DIRECTIVE:

CHAPTER I

SCOPE, PLACING ON THE MARKET AND FREE MOVEMENT

Article 1

1.   This Directive applies to personal protective equipment, hereinafter referred to as "PPE".

It lays down the conditions governing its placing on the market and free movement within the Community and the basic safety requirements which PPE must satisfy in order to ensure the health protection and safety of users.

2.   For the purposes of this Directive, PPE shall mean any device or appliance designed to be worn or held by an individual for protection against one or more health and safety hazards.

PPE shall also cover:

(a)   a unit constituted by several devices or appliances which have been integrally combined by the manufacturer for the protection of an individual against one or more potentially simultaneous risks;
(b)   a protective device or appliance combined, separably or inseparably, with personal non-protective equipment worn or held by an individual for the execution of a specific activity;
(c)   interchangeable PPE components which are essential to its satisfactory functioning and used exclusively for such equipment.

3.   Any system placed on the market in conjunction with PPE for its connection to another external, additional device shall be regarded as an integral part of that equipment even if the system is not intended to be worn or held permanently by the user for the entire period of risk exposure.

4.   This Directive does not apply to:
— PPE covered by another Directive designed to achieve the same objectives as this Directive with regard to placing on the market, free movement of goods and safety,
— the PPE classes specified in the list of excluded products in Annex I, independently of the reason for exclusion mentioned in the first indent.

Article 2

1.   Member States shall take all appropriate measures to ensure that the PPE referred to in Article 1 may be placed on the market and brought into service only if it preserves the health and ensures the safety of users without prejudice to the health or safety of other individuals, domestic animals or goods, when properly maintained and used for its intended purpose.

2.   This Directive shall be without prejudice to the right of Member States to lay down—in conformity with the Treaty—any requirements which they consider necessary to ensure user protection, provided that this does not give rise to modifications to PPE which could result in its non-conformity with the provisions of this Directive.

3.   Member States shall not prevent the presentation at trade fairs, exhibitions and the like of PPE which is not in conformity with the provisions of this Directive, provided that an appropriate notice is displayed drawing attention to this fact and the prohibition on its acquisition and/or use for any purpose whatsoever until it has been brought into conformity by the manufacturer or his representatives established in the Community.

Article 3

The PPE referred to in Article 1 must satisfy the basic health and safety requirements laid down in Annex II.

Article 4

1.   Member States shall not prohibit, restrict or hinder the placing on the market of PPE or PPE components which satisfy the provisions of this Directive and which bear the EC mark.

2.   Member States shall not prohibit, restrict or impede the placing on the market of PPE components which do not bear the EC mark, and which are intended to be incorporated in PPE, provided that they are not essential to its satisfactory functioning.

Article 5

1.   Member States shall regard as in conformity with the basic requirements referred to in Article 3 the PPE referred to in Article 8(3) bearing the EC mark with respect to which the manufacturer is able to produce, on demand, the declaration of conformity referred to in Article 12.

2.   Member States shall presume that the PPE referred to in Article 8(2) satisfies the basic requirements referred to in Article 3 if it bears the EC mark with respect to which the manufacturer is able to produce, on demand, not only the declaration referred to in Article 12 but also the certificate issued by the body of which notification has been given in accordance with Article 9 attesting to their conformity to the relevant national standards, transposing the harmonised standards, assessed at the EC type examination level in accordance with the first indent of Article 10(4)(a) and (b).

Where a manufacturer has not applied or has only partly applied the harmonised standards or where there are no such standards the certificate issued by the body of which notification has been given must state the conformity to the basic requirements in accordance with the second indent of Article 10(4)(a) and (b).

3.   The PPE referred to in Article 8(2) for which harmonised standards are not available may continue on a transitional basis, until 31 December 1992 at the latest, to be subject to national arrangements already in force on the date of adoption of this Directive, provided that such arrangements are compatible with the provisions of the Treaty.

4.   The Commission shall publish the references of the harmonised standards in the *Official Journal of the European Communities*.

Member States shall publish the references of the national standards transposing the harmonised standards.

5.   Member States shall ensure that by 30 June 1991 appropriate steps are taken to enable both sides of industry to have an influence at national level on the process of formulating the harmonised standards and keeping them under review.

Article 6

1.   Should a Member State or the Commission consider that the harmonised standards referred to in Article 5 do not completely satisfy the relevant basic requirements referred to in Article 3, the Commission or the Member State concerned shall refer the matter to the committee created pursuant to Directive 83/189/EEC, setting out it reasons. The committee shall deliver an opinion without delay.

In the light of the committee's opinion, the Commission shall notify Member States of whether or not it is necessary to withdraw the standards concerned from publications made pursuant to Article 5.

2.   The Standing Committee set up by Article 6(2) of Directive 89/392/EEC may be apprised, in accordance with the procedure described below, of any matter to which the implementation and practical application of this Directive give rise.

The representative of the Commission shall submit to the committee a draft of the measures to be taken. The committee shall deliver its opinion on the draft, within a time limit which the chairman may lay down according to the urgency of the matter, if necessary by taking a vote.

The opinion shall be recorded in the minutes; in addition, each Member State shall have the right to ask to have its position recorded in the minutes.

The Commission shall take the utmost account of the opinion delivered by the committee. It shall inform the committee of the manner in which its opinion has been taken into account.

Article 7

1.   If a Member State discovers that PPE bearing the EC mark and used in accordance with its intended purpose could compromise the safety of individuals, domestic animals or property, it shall take all necessary measures to remove that equipment from the market and prohibit the marketing or free movement thereof.

The Member State concerned shall immediately inform the Commission of such action, indicating the reasons for its decision and, in particular, stating whether non-conformity is due to:

(a) failure to comply with the basic requirements referred to in Article 3;
(b) the unsatisfactory application of the standards referred to in Article 5;
(c) a shortcoming in the standards referred to in Article 5.

2.   The Commission shall initiate discussions with the parties concerned as soon as possible. If, after such consultation, the Commission decides that the action taken was justified, it shall immediately inform the Member State concerned and all the other Member States to that effect. If, after such consultation, the commission decides that the action taken was not justified, it shall immediately inform the Member State concerned and the manufacturer or his authorised representative established in the Community to that effect. If the decision referred to in paragraph 1 is in response to a shortcoming in the standards, the Commission shall refer the matter to the Committee referred to in Article 6(1) if the Member State concerned intends to adhere to its decision and shall initiate the procedure referred to in Article 6(2).

3.   If PPE which is not in conformity with the relevant requirements bears the EC mark, the Member State concerned shall take the appropriate measures with regard to those responsible for affixing the mark and shall inform the Commission and the other Member States accordingly.

4.   The Commission shall ensure that the Member States are kept informed of the progess and results of the procedure provided for in this Article.

CHAPTER II
CERTIFICATION PROCEDURES

Article 8

1.   Before placing a PPE model on the market, the manufacturer or his authorised representative established in the Community shall assemble the technical documentation referred to in Annex III so that this can, if necessary, be submitted to the competent authorities.

2.   Prior to the series production of PPE other than those referred to in paragraph 3, the manufacturer or his authorised representative established in the Community shall submit a model for EC type-examination as referred to in Article 10.

3.   EC type-examination shall not be required in the case of PPE models of simple design where the designer assumes the user can himself assess the level of protection provided against the minimal risks concerned the effects of which, when they are gradual, can be safely identified by the user in good time.

This category shall cover exclusively PPE intended to protect the wearer against:
— mechanical action whose effects are superficial (gardening gloves, thimbles, etc.),
— cleaning materials of weak action and easily reversible effects (gloves affording protection against diluted detergent solutions, etc.),
— risks encountered in the handling of hot components which do not expose the user to a temperature exceeding 50°C or to dangerous impacts (gloves, aprons for professional use, etc.),

— atmospheric agents of a neither exceptional nor extreme nature (headgear, seasonal clothing, footwear, etc.),
— minor impacts and vibrations which do not affect vital areas of the body and whose effects cannot cause irreversible lesions (light anti-scalping helmets, gloves, light footwear, etc.),
— sunlight (sunglasses).

4. Production of PPE shall be subject:

(a) according to the manufacturer's choice, to one of the two procedures referred to in Article 11 in the case of PPE of complex design intended to protect against mortal danger or against dangers that may seriously and irreversibly harm the health, the immediate effects of which the designer assumes the user cannot identify in sufficient time. This category shall cover exclusively:
— filtering respiratory devices for protection against solid and liquid aerosols or irritant, dangerous, toxic or radiotoxic gases,
— respiratory protection devices providing full insulation from the atmosphere, including those for use in diving,
— PPE providing only limited protection against chemical attack or against ionizing radiation,
— emergency equipment for use in high-temperature environments the effects of which are comparable to those of an air temperature of 100°C or more and which may or may not be characterised by the presence of infra-red radiation, flames or the projection of large amounts of molten material,
— emergency equipment for use in low-temperature environments the effects of which are comparable to those of an air temperature of –50°C or less,
— PPE to protect against falls from a height,
— PPE against electrical risks and dangerous voltages or that used as insulation in high-tension work,
— motor cycle helmets and visors;
(b) the EC declaration of conformity referred to in Article 12 for all PPE.

Article 9

1. Each Member State shall inform the Commission and the other Member States of the approved bodies responsible for the execution of the certification procedures referred to in Article 8. For information purposes, the Commission shall publish in the *Official Journal of the European Communities* and keep up to date a list giving the names of these bodies and the distinguishing numbers it has assigned to them.

2. Member States shall apply the criteria laid down in Annex V in assessing the bodies to be indicated in such notification. Bodies meeting the assessment criteria laid down in the relevant harmonised standards shall be presumed to fulfil those criteria.

3. A Member State shall withdraw its approval for such a body if it establishes that the latter no longer satisfies the criteria referred to in Annex V. It shall inform the Commission and the other Member States of its action forthwith.

EC TYPE-EXAMINATION

Article 10

1.   EC type-examination is the procedure whereby the approved inspection body establishes and certifies that the PPE model in question satisfies the relevant provisions of this Directive.

2.   Application for EC type-examination shall be made by the manufacturer or his authorised representative to a single approved inspection body in respect of the model in question. The authorised representative shall be established in the Community.

3.   The application shall comprise:
—   the name and address of the manufacturer or his authorised representative and of the PPE production plant in question,
—   the manufacturer's technical file referred to in Annex III.

It shall be accompanied by the appropriate number of specimens of the model to be approved.

4.   The inspection body of which notification has been given shall conduct the EC type-examination in accordance with the undermentioned procedures:

(a)   Examination of the manufacturer's technical file
—   It shall examine the manufacturer's technical file to establish its suit-ability with respect to the harmonised standards referred to in Article 5.
—   Where a manufacturer has not applied, or has only partly applied, the harmonised standards or where there are no such standards, the body of which notification has been given must check the suitability of the technical specifications used by the manufacturer with respect to the basic requirements before examining the manufacturer's technical file to establish its suitability with respect to these technical specifications.

(b)   Examination of the model
—   When examining the model, the inspection body shall verify that it has been produced in accordance with the manufacturer's technical file and can be used in complete safety for its intended purpose.
—   It shall conduct the necessary examinations and tests to establish the conformity of the model with the harmonised standards.
—   Where a manufacturer has not applied or has only partly applied the harmonised standards or where there are no such standards the body of which notification has been given shall conduct the necessary exam-inations and tests to establish the conformity of the model with the technical specifications used by the manufacturer, subject to their being suitable with respect to these basic requirements.

5.   If the model satisfies the relevant provisions, the inspection body shall draw up an EC type-examination certificate and shall notify the applicant to this effect. This certificate shall reproduce the findings of the examination, indicate any conditions attaching to its issue and incorporate the descriptions and drawings necessary for the identification of the approved model.

The Commission, the other approved inspection bodies and the other Member States may obtain a copy of the certificate and, in response to a reasoned request, a copy of the manufacturer's technical file and the reports of the examinations and tests conducted.

The file shall be held at the disposal of the competent authorities for 10 years following the placing of the PPE on the market.

6. Any inspection body which refuses to issue an EC type-examination certificate shall inform the other approved inspection bodies of this fact. An inspection body withdrawing an EC type-examination certificate shall inform the Member State which approved it, to this effect. That Member State shall then inform the other Member States and the Commission, setting out the reasons for the decision.

CHECKING OF PPE MANUFACTURED

Article 11

A. "EC" quality control system for the final product

1. A manufacturer shall take all steps necessary to ensure that the manufacturing process, including the final inspection of PPE and tests, ensures the homogeneity of production and the conformity of PPE with the type described in the EC-type-approval certificate and with the relevant basic requirements of this Directive.

2. A body of which notification has been given, chosen by a manufacturer, shall carry out the necessary checks. Those checks shall be carried out at random, normally at intervals of at least one year.

3. An adequate sample of PPE taken by the body of which notification has been given shall be examined and appropriate tests defined in the harmonised standards or necessary to show conformity to the basic requirements of this Directive shall be carried out to check the conformity of PPE.

4. Where a body is not the body that issued the relevant EC type-approval certificate it shall contact the body of which notification has been given in the event of difficulties in connection with the assessment of the conformity of samples.

5. The body of which notification has been given shall provide the manufacturer with a test report. If the report concludes that production is not homogeneous or that the PPE examined do not conform to the type described in the EC type-approval certificate or the relevant basic requirements, the body shall take measures appropriate to the nature of the fault or faults recorded and inform the Member State which gave notification thereof accordingly.

6. The manufacturer must be able to present, on request, the report of the body of which notification has been given.

B.   System for ensuring EC quality of production by means of monitoring

1.   *The system*

(a)   Under this procedure the manufacturer submits an application for the approval of his quality-control system to a body of which notification has been given, of his choice.

That application shall include:
— all the information relating to the category of PPE concerned, including, where appropriate, documentation relating to the model approved,
— documentation on the quality-control system,
— the undertaking to maintain the obligations arising from the quality-control system and to maintain its adequacy and efficiency.

(b)   Under the quality-control system, each PPE shall be examined and the appropriate tests referred to in Section A paragraph 3 shall be carried out to check their conformity to the relevant basic requirements of this Directive.

The documentation on the quality-control system shall in particular include an adequate description of:
— the quality objectives, the organisation chart, the responsibilities of executives and their powers in respect of product quality,
— the checks and tests which must be carried out after manufacture,
— the means to be employed to check the efficient operation of the quality-control system.

(c)   The body shall assess the quality-control system to determine whether it satisfies the provisions referred to in paragraph 1(b). It shall assume that quality-control systems applying the relevant harmonised standard satisfy those provisions.

The body carrying out audits shall make all necessary objective evaluations of the components of the quality-control system and shall check in particular whether the system ensures conformity of PPE manufactured with the approved model.

The decision shall be communicated to the manufacturer. It shall include the conclusions of the check and the reasoned assessment decision.

(d)   The manufacturer shall inform the body which approved the quality-control system of any plan to alter the quality-control system.

The body shall examine the proposed changes and decide whether the altered quality-control system satisfies the relevant provisions. It shall communicate its decision to the manufacturer. The communication shall include the conclusions of the check and the reasoned assessment decision.

2.   *Supervision*

(a)   The purpose of supervision is to ensure that a manufacturer correctly fulfils the obligations arising from the approved quality-control system.

(b)   The manufacturer shall authorise the body to have access, for purposes of inspection, to PPE inspection, testing and storage sites and shall provide the body with all requisite information, in particular:

— documentation on the quality-control system,
— technical documentation,
— quality control manuals.

(c) The body shall periodically carry out audits to ensure that the manufacturer is maintaining and applying the approved quality-control system and shall provide the manufacturer with a copy of the audit report.

(d) In addition, the body may make unnannounced visits to the manufacturer. In the course of such visits the body shall provide the manufacturer with a report of the visit and, if appropriate, with an audit report.

(e) The manufacturer must be able to present, on request, the report of the body of which notification has been given.

EC DECLARATION OF PRODUCTION CONFORMITY

Article 12

The EC declaration of conformity is the procedure whereby the manufacturer:

1. draws up a declaration using the form laid down in Annex VI certifying that the PPE placed on the market are in conformity with the provisions of this Directive with a view to its submission to the competent authorities;

2. affixes the EC mark of conformity provided for by Article 13 to each PPE.

CHAPTER III

EC MARK

Article 13

1. The EC mark consists of the letters "CE" followed by the last two figures of the year in which the mark was affixed and, in the event of the involvement of a notified body having carried out an EC examination of the type referred to in Article 10, its distinguishing number shall be added.

The form of the mark to be used is shown in Annex IV.

2. The EC mark shall be affixed to each production PPE and its packaging so as to be visible, legible and indelible throughout the foreseeable useful life of that PPE.

3. Marks or inscriptions which could be confused with the EC mark may not be affixed to PPE.

CHAPTER IV

FINAL PROVISIONS

Article 14

Any decision taken in implementation of this Directive and leading to restrictions on the marketing of PPE shall be accompanied by a detailed explanation of the grounds on which it is based. The interested party shall be notified of the decision without delay and informed of the possibilities for appeal under the legislation in force in the Member State concerned and of the deadlines for lodging such appeals.

Article 15

The Commission shall taken the necessary steps to ensure that data concerning all the relevant decisions in connection with the managemenst of this Directive are made available.

Article 16

1.   By 31 December 1991, Member States shall adopt and publish the laws, regulations and administrative provisions necessary to comply with this Directive. They shall forthwith inform the Commission thereof.

They shall apply those provisions from 1 July 1992.

2.   Member States shall communicate to the Commission the texts of the provisions of national law which they adopt in the field governed by this Directive.

Article 17

This Directive is addressed to the Member States.

Done at Brussels, 21 December 1989.

For the Council
The President
E. CRESSON

ANNEX I

EXHAUSTIVE LIST OF PPE CLASSES NOT COVERED BY THIS DIRECTIVE

1.   PPE designed and manufactured specifically for use by the armed forces or in the maintenance of law and order (helmets, shields, etc.).

2.   PPE for self-defence (aerosol canisters, personal deterrent weapons, etc.).

3.   PPE designed and manufactured for private use against:

   — adverse atmospheric conditions (headgear, seasonal clothing, footwear, umbrellas, etc.),

— damp and water (dish-washing gloves, etc.),
— heat (gloves etc.).

4. PPE intended for the protection or rescue of persons on vessels or aircraft, not worn all the time.

ANNEX II

BASIC HEALTH AND SAFETY REQUIREMENTS

1. GENERAL REQUIREMENTS APPLICABLE TO ALL PPE

PPE must provide adequate protection against all risks encountered.

1.1. Design principles

1.1.1. *Ergonomics*

PPE must be so designed and manufactured that in the foreseeable conditions of use for which it is intended the user can perform the risk-related activity normally whilst enjoying appropriate protection of the highest possible level.

1.1.2. *Levels and classes of protection*

1.1.2.1 Highest level of protection possible
The optimum level of protection to be taken into account in the design is that beyond which the constraints imposed by the wearing of the PPE would prevent its effective use during the period of exposure to the risk or normal performance of the activity.

1.1.2.2. Classes of protection appropriate to different levels of risk
Where differing foreseeable conditions of use are such that several levels of the same risk can be distinguished, appropriate classes of protection must be taken into account in the design of the PPE.

1.2. Innocuousness of PPE

1.2.1. *Absence of risks and other "inherent" nuisance factors*

PPE must be so designed and manufactured as to preclude risks and other nuisance factors under foreseeable conditions of use.

1.2.1.1. Suitable constituent materials
PPE materials and parts, including any of their decomposition products, must not adversely affect user hygiene or health.

1.2.1.2. Satisfactory surface conditions of all PPE parts in contact with the user
Any PPE part in contact or in potential contact with the user when such equipment is worn must be free of roughness, sharp edges, projections and the like which could cause excessive irritation or injuries.

1.2.1.3.   Maximum permissible user impediment
Any impediment caused by PPE to movements to be made, postures to be adopted and sensory perception must be minimised; nor must PPE cause movements which endanger the user or other persons.

1.3.   **Comfort and efficiency**

1.3.1.   *Adaptation of PPE to user morphology*

PPE must be so designed and manufactured as to facilitate correct positioning on the user and to remain in place for the foreseeable period of use, bearing in mind ambient factors, movements to be made and postures to be adopted. For this purpose, it must be possible to optimise PPE adaptation to user morphology by all appropriate means, such as adequate adjustment and attachment systems or the provision of an adequate size range.

1.3.2.   *Lightness and strength*

PPE must be as light as possible without prejudicing design strength and efficiency.

Apart from the specific additional requirements which they must satisfy in order to provide adequate protection against the risks in question (see 3), PPE must be capable of withstanding the effects of ambient phenomena inherent under the foreseeable conditions of use.

1.3.3.   *Compatibility of different classes or types of PPE designed for simultaneous use*

If the same manufacturer markets several PPE models of different classes or types in order to ensure the simultaneous protection of adjacent parts of the body against combined risks, these must be compatible.

1.4.   **Information supplied by the manufacturer**

In addition to the name and address of the manufacturer and/or his authorised representative established in the Community, the notes that must be drawn up by the former and supplied when PPE is placed on the market must contain all relevant information on:

(a)   storage, use, cleaning, maintenance, servicing and disinfection. Cleaning, maintenance or disinfectant products recommended by manufacturers must have no adverse effect on PPE or users when applied in accordance with the relevant instructions;

(b)   performance as recorded during technical tests to check the levels or classes of protection provided by the PPE in question;

(c)   suitable PPE accessories and the characteristics of appropriate spare parts;

(d)   the classes of protection appropriate to different levels of risk and the corresponding limits of use;

(e)   the obsolescence deadline or period of obsolescence of PPE or certain of its components;

(f)   the type of packaging suitable for transport;

(g)   the significance of any markings (see 2.12).

These notes, which must be precise and comprehensible, must be provided at least in the official language(s) of the Member State of destination.

2.   ADDITIONAL REQUIREMENTS COMMON TO SEVERAL CLASSES OR TYPES OF PPE

2.1.   **PPE incorporating adjustment systems**

If PPE incorporates adjustment systems, the latter must be so designed and manufactured as not to become incorrectly adjusted without the user's knowledge under the foreseeable conditions of use.

2.2.   **PPE "enclosing" the parts of the body to be protected**

As far as possible PPE "enclosing" the parts of the body to be protected must be sufficiently ventilated to limit perspiration resulting from use; if this is not the case, it must if possible be equipped with devices which absorb perspiration.

2.3.   **PPE for the face, eyes and respiratory tracts**

Any restriction of the user's field of vision or sight by PPE for the face, eyes or respiratory tract must be minimised.

The degree of optical neutrality of the vision systems of these PPE classes must be compatible with the type of relatively meticulous and/or prolonged activities of the user.

If necessary, they must be treated or provided with facilities to prevent moisture formation.

PPE models intended for users requiring sight correction must be compatible with the wearing of spectacles or contact lenses.

2.4.   **PPE subject to ageing**

If it is known that the design performances of new PPE may be significantly affected by ageing, the date of manufacture and/or, if possible, the date of obsolescence, must be indelibly inscribed on every PPE item or interchangeable component placed on the market in such a way as to preclude any misinterpretation; this information must also be indelibly inscribed on the packaging.

If a manufacturer is unable to give an undertaking with regard to the useful life of PPE, his notes must provide all the information necessary to enable the purchaser or user to establish a reasonable obsolescence date, bearing in mind the quality level of the model and the effective conditions of storage, use, cleaning, servicing and maintenance.

Where appreciable and rapid deterioration in PPE performance is likely to be caused by ageing resulting from the periodic use of a cleaning process recommended by the manufacturer, the latter must, if possible, affix a mark to each item of PPE placed on the market indicating the maximum number of cleaning operations that may be carried out before the equipment needs to be inspected or discarded; failing that, the manufacturer must give this information in his notes.

2.5.   **PPE which may be caught up during use**

Where the foreseeable conditions of use include in particular the risk of the PPE being caught up by a moving object thereby creating a danger for the user, the PPE must possess an appropriate resistance threshold above which a constituent part will break and eliminate the danger.

2.6.   **PPE for use in explosive atmospheres**

PPE intended for use in explosive atmospheres must be so designed and manufactured that it cannot be the source of an electric, electro-static or impact-induced arc or spark likely to cause an explosive mixture to ignite.

2.7.   **PPE intended for emergency use or rapid installation and/or removal**

These PPE classes must be so designed and manufactured as to mini-mise the time required for attachment and (or) removal.

Any integral systems permitting correct positioning on, or removal from, the user must be susceptible of rapid and easy operation.

2.8.   **PPE for use in very dangerous situations**

The information notes supplied by the manufacturer together with PPE for use in the very dangerous situations referred to in Article 8(4)(a) must include, in particular, data intended for the exclusive use of competent trained individuals who are qualified to interpret them and ensure their application by the user.

They must also describe the procedure to be adopted in order to verify that PPE is correctly adjusted and functional when worn by the user.

If PPE incorporates an alarm which is activated in the absence of the level of protection normally provided, this must be so designed and accommodated as to be perceived by the user in the conditions of use for which the PPE is marketed.

2.9.   **PPE incorporating components which can be adjusted or removed by the user**

Any PPE components which can be adjusted or removed by the user for the purpose of replacement must be so designed and manufactured as to facilitate adjustment, attachment and removal without tools.

2.10.   **PPE for connection to another, external complementary device**

If PPE incorporates a system permitting a connection to another, complementary, device, the attachment mechanism must be so designed and manufactured as to enable it to be mounted only on appropriate equipment.

2.11.   **PPE incorporating a fluid circulation system**

If PPE incorporates a fluid circulation system, the latter must be so chosen, or designed, and incorporated as to permit adequate fluid renewal in the vicinity of the entire part of the body to be protected, irrespective of user gestures, posture or movement under the foreseeable conditions of use.

2.12. **PPE bearing one or more identification or recognition marks directly or indirectly relating to health and safety**

The identification or recognition marks directly or indirectly relating to health and safety affixed to these types or classes of PPE must preferably take the form of harmonised pictograms or ideograms and must remain perfectly legible thoroughout the foreseeable useful life of the PPE. In addition, these marks must be complete, precise and comprehensible so as to prevent any misinterpretation; in particular, when such marks incorporate words or sentences, the latter must appear in the official language(s) of the Member State where the equipment is to be used.

If PPE (or a PPE component) is too small to allow all or part of the necessary marking to be affixed, the relevant information must be mentioned on the packing and in the manufacturer's notes.

2.13. **PPE in the form of clothing capable of signalling the user's presence visually**

PPE in the form of clothing intended for foreseeable conditions of use in which the user's presence must be visibly and individually signalled must have one (or more) judiciously positioned means of or devices for emitting direct or reflected visible radiation of appropriate luminous intensity and photometric and colorimetric properties.

2.14. **"Multi-risk" PPE**

All PPE designed to protect the user against several potentially simultaneous risks must be so designed and manufactured as to satisfy, in particular, the basic requirements specific to each of those risks (see 3).

3. ADDITIONAL REQUIREMENTS SPECIFIC TO PARTICULAR RISKS

3.1. **Protection against mechanical impact**

3.1.1. *Impact caused by falling or projecting objects and collision of parts of the body with an obstacle*

Suitable PPE for this type of risk must be sufficiently shock-absorbent to prevent injury resulting, in particular, from the crushing or penetration of the protected part, at least up to an impact-energy level above which the excessive dimensions or mass of the absorbing device would preclude effective use of the PPE for the foreseeable period of wear.

3.1.2. *Falls*

3.1.2.1 Prevention of falls due to slipping
The outsoles for footwear designed to prevent slipping must be so

designed, manufactured or equipped with added elements as to ensure satisfactory adhesion by grip and friction having regard to the nature or state of the surface.

3.1.2.2. Prevention of falls from a height

PPE designed to prevent falls from a height or their effects must incorporate a body harness and an attachment system which can be connected to a reliable anchorage point. It must be designed so that under the foreseeable conditions of use the vertical drop of the user is minimised to prevent collision with obstacles and the braking force does not, however, attain the threshold value at which physical injury or the tearing or rupture of any PPE component which might cause the user to fall can be expected to occur.

It must also ensure that after braking the user is maintained in a correct position in which he may await help if necessary.

The manufacturer's notes must specify in particular all relevant information relating to:
— the characteristics required for the reliable anchorage point and the necessary minimum clearance below the user,
— the proper way of putting on the body harness and of connecting the attachment system to the reliable anchorage point.

3.1.3.   *Mechanical vibration*

PPE designed to prevent the effects of mechanical vibrations must be capable of ensuring adequate attenuation of harmful vibration components for the part of the body at risk.

Under no circumstances must the effective value of the accelerations transmitted to the user by those vibrations exceed the limit values recommended in the light of the maximum foreseeable daily exposure of the part of the body at risk.

3.2.   **Protection against (static) compression of part of the body**

PPE designed to protect part of the body against (static) compressive stress must be sufficiently capable of attenuating its effects to prevent serious injury or chronic complaints.

3.3.   **Protection against physical injury (abrasion, perforation, cuts, bites)**

PPE constituent material and other components designed to protect all or part of the body against superficial injury caused by machinery, such as abrasion, perforation, cuts or bites, must be so chosen or designed and incorporated as to ensure that these PPE classes provide sufficient resistance to abrasion, perforation and gashing (see also 3.1) under the foreseeable conditions of use.

3.4.   **Prevention of drowning (lifejackets, armbands and lifesaving suits)**

PPE designed to prevent drowning must be capable of returning to the surface as quickly as possible, without danger to his health, a user who may be exhausted or unconscious after falling into a liquid medium, and of keeping him afloat in a position which permits breathing while awaiting help.

PPE may be wholly or partially inherently buoyant or may be inflated either by gas which can be manually or automatically released or orally.

Under the foreseeable conditions of use:
— PPE must, without prejudice to its satisfactory operation, be capable of withstanding the effects of impact with the liquid medium and the environmental factors inherent in that medium,
— inflatable PPE must be capable of inflating rapidly and fully.

Where particular foreseeable conditions of use so require, certain types of PPE must also satisfy one or more of the following additional requirements:
— it must have all the inflation devices referred to in the second subparagraph, and/or a light or sound-signalling device,
— it must have a device for hitching and attaching the body so that the user may be lifted out of the liquid medium,
— it must be suitable for prolonged use throughout the period of activity exposing the user, possibly dressed, to the risk of falling into the liquid medium or requiring his immersion in it.

3.4.1.   *Buoyancy aids*

Clothing which will ensure an effective degree of buoyancy, depending on its foreseeable use, which is safe when worn and which affords positive support in water. In foreseeable conditions of use, this PPE must not restrict the user's freedom of movement but must enable him, in particular, to swim or take action to escape from danger or rescue other persons.

3.5.   **Protection against the harmful effects of noise**

PPE designed to prevent the harmful effects of noise must be capable of attenuating the latter to such an extent that the equivalent sound levels perceived by the user do not under any circumstances exceed the daily limit values laid down by Council Directive 86/188/EEC of 12 May 1986 on the protection of workers from the risks related to exposure to noise at work.

All PPE must bear labelling indicating the noise attenuation level and the value of the comfort index provided by the PPE; should this not be possible, the labelling must be fixed to the packaging.

3.6.   **Protection against heat and/or fire**

PPE designed to protect all or part of the body against the effects of heat and/or fire must possess thermal insulation capacity and mechanical strength appropriate to foreseeable conditions of use.

3.6.1.   *PPE constituent materials and other components*

Constituent materials and other components suitable for protection against radiant and convective heat must possess an appropriate coefficient of transmission of incident heat flux and be sufficiently incombustible to preclude any risk of spontaneous ignition under the foreseeable conditions of use.

Where the outside of these materials and components must be reflective, its reflective power must be appropriate to the intensity of the heat flux due to radiation in the infra-red range.

Matrials and other components of equipment intended for brief use in high-temperature environments and of PPE which may be splashed by hot products such as large quantities of molten material must also possess sufficient thermal capacity to retain most of the stored heat until after the user has left the danger area and removed his PPE.

PPE materials and other components which may be splashed by large amounts of hot products must also possess sufficient mechanical-impact absorbency (see 3.1.).

PPE materials and other components which may accidentally come into contact with flame and those used in the manufacture of fire-fighting equipment must also possess a degree of non-flammability corresponding to the risk class associated with the foreseeable conditions of use. They must not melt when exposed to flames nor contribute to flame propagation.

3.6.2.   *Complete PPE ready for use*

Under the foreseeable conditions of use:

1.   the quantity of heat transmitted by PPE to the user must be sufficiently low to prevent the heat accumulated during wear in the part of the body at risk from attaining, under any circumstances, the pain or health impairment threshold;

2.   PPE must if necessary prevent liquid or steam penetration and must not cause burns resulting from contact between its protective integument and the user.

If PPE incorporates refrigeration devices for the absorption of incident heat by means of liquid evaporation or solid sublimation, their design must be such that any volatile substances released are discharged beyond the outer protective integument and not towards the user.

If PPE incorporates a breathing device, the latter must adequately fulfil the protective function assigned to it under the foreseeable conditions of use.

The manufacturer's notes accompanying each PPE model intended for brief use in high temperature environments must in particular provide all relevant data for the determination of the maximum permissible user exposure to the heat transmitted by the equipment when used in accordance with its intended purpose.

3.7.   **Protection against cold**

PPE designed to protect all or part of the body against the effects of cold must possess thermal insulating capacity and mechanical strength appropriate to the foreseeable conditions of use for which it is marketed.

3.7.1. *PPE constituent materials and other components*

Constituent materials and other components suitable for protection against cold must possess a coefficient of transmission of incident thermal flux as low as required under the foreseeable conditions of use. Flexible materials and other components of PPE intended for use in a low-temperature environment must retain the degree of flexibility required for the necessary gestures and postures.

PPE materials and other components which may be splashed by large amounts of cold products must also possess sufficient mechanical-impact absorbency (see 3.1).

3.7.2. *Complete PPE ready for use*

Under the foreseeable conditions of use:

1. the flux transmitted by PPE to the user must be sufficiently low to prevent the cold accumulated during wear at any point on the part of the body being protected, including the tips of fingers and toes in the case of hands or feet, from attaining, under any circumstances, the pain or health-impairment threshold;
2. PPE must as far as possible prevent the penetration of such liquids as rain water and must not cause injuries resulting from contact between its cold protective integument and the user.

If PPE incorporates a breathing device, this must adequately fulfil the protective function assigned to it under the foreseeable conditions of use.

The manufacturer's notes accompanying each PPE model intended for brief use in low-temperature environments must provide all relevant data concerning the maximum permissible user exposure to the cold transmitted by the equipment.

3.8. **Protection against electric shock**

PPE designed to protect all or part of the body against the effects of electric current must be sufficiently insulated against the voltages to which the user is likely to be exposed under the most unfavourable foreseeable conditions.

To this end, the constituent materials and other components of these PPE classes must be so chosen or designed and incorporated as to ensure that the leakage current measured through the protective integument under test conditions at voltages correlated with those likely to be encountered *in situ* is minimised and, at all events, below a maximum conventional permissible value which correlates with the tolerance threshold.

Together with their packaging, PPE types intended exclusively for use during work or activities in electrical installations which are or may be under tension must bear markings indicating, in particular, their protection class and (or) corresponding operating voltage, their serial number and their date of manufacture; a space must also be provided outside the protective integument of such PPE for the subsequent inscription of the date of entry into service and those of the periodic tests or inspections to be conducted.

The manufacturer's notes must indicate, in particular, the exclusive use for which these PPE types are intended and the nature and frequency of the dielectric tests to which they are to be subjected during their useful life.

3.9.   Radiation protection

3.9.1.   *Non-ionizing radiation*

PPE designed to prevent acute or chronic eye-damage from sources of non-ionizing radiation must be capable of absorbing or reflecting the majority of the energy radiated in the harmful wavelengths without unduly affecting the transmission of the innocuous part of the visible spectrum, the perception of contrasts and the ability to distinguish colours where required by the foreseeable conditions of use.

To this end, protective glasses must be so designed and manufactured as to possess, for each harmful wave, a spectral transmission factor such that the radiant-energy illumination density capable of reaching the user's eye through the filter is minimised and, under no circumstances, exceeds the maximum permissible exposure value.

Furthermore, the glasses must not deteriorate or lose their properties as a result of the effects of radiation emitted under the foreseeable conditions of use and all marketed specimens must bear the protection-factor number corresponding to the spectral distribution curve of their transmission factor.

Glasses suitable for radiation sources of the same type must be classified in the ascending order of their protection factors and the manufacturer's notes must indicate, in particular, the transmission curves which make it possible to select the most appropriate PPE bearing in mind such inherent factors of the effective conditions of use as distance to source and the spectral distribution of the energy radiated at that distance.

The relevant protection-factor number must be marked on all specimens of filtering glasses by the manufacturer.

3.9.2.   *Ionizing radiation*

3.9.2.1.   Protection against external radioactive contamination
PPE constituent materials and other components designed to protect all or part of the body against radioactive dust, gases, liquids or mixtures thereof must be so chosen or designed and incorporated as to ensure that this equipment effectively prevents the penetration of the contaminants under the foreseeable conditions of use.

Depending on the nature or condition of these contaminants, the necessary leak-tightness can be provided by the impermeability of the protective integument and/or by any other appropriate means, such as ventilation and pressurisation systems designed to prevent the back-scattering of these contaminants.

Any decontamination measures to which PPE is subject must not prejudice its possible re-use during the foreseeable useful life of these classes of equipment.

3.9.2.2. Limited protection against external irradiation

PPE intended to provide complete user protection against external irradiation or, failing this, adequate attenuation thereof, must be designed to counter only weak electron (e.g. beta) or weak photon (e.g. X, gamma) radiation.

The constituent materials and other components of these PPE classes must be so chosen or designed and incorporated as to provide the degree of user protection required by the foreseeable conditions of use without leading to an increase in exposure time as a result of the impedance of user gestures, posture or movement (see 1.3.2.).

PPE must bear a mark indicating the type and thickness of the constituent material(s) suitable for the foreseeable conditions of use.

3.10.   **Protection against dangerous substances and infective agents**

3.10.1. *Respiratory protection*

PPE intended for the protection of the respiratory tract must make it possible to supply the user with breathable air when the latter is exposed to a polluted atmosphere and/or an atmosphere having inadequate oxygen concentration.

The breathable air supplied to the user by the PPE must be obtained by appropriate means, for example, after filtration of the polluted air through the protective device or appliance or by a piped supply from an unpolluted source.

The constituent materials and other components of these PPE classes must be so chosen or designed and incorporated as to ensure appropriate user respiration and respiratory hygiene for the period of wear concerned under the foreseeable conditions of use.

The leak-tightness of the facepiece and the pressure drop on inspiration and, in the case of the filtering devices, purification capacity must be such as to keep contaminant penetration from a polluted atmosphere low enough not be prejudicial to the health or hygiene of the user.

The PPE must bear the manufacturer's identification mark and details of the specific characteristics of that type of equipment which, in conjunction with the instructions for use, will enable a trained and qualified user to employ the PPE correctly.

The manufacturer's notes must also in the case of filtering devices, indicate the deadline for the storage of filters as new and kept in their original packaging.

3.10.2. *Protection against cutaneous and ocular contact*

PPE intended to prevent the surface contact of all or part of the body with dangerous substances and infective agents must be capable of preventing the penetration or diffusion of such substances through the protective integument under the foreseeable conditions of use for which the PPE is placed on the market.

To this end, the constituent materials and other components of these PPE classes must be so chosen, or designed and incorporated as to ensure, as far as possible, complete leak-tightness, which will allow where necessary prolonged daily use or, failing this, limited leak-tightness necessitating a restriction of the period of wear.

Where, by virtue of their nature and the foreseeable conditions of their use, certain dangerous substances or infective agents possess high penetrative power which limits the duration of the protection provided by the PPE in question, the latter must be subjected to standard tests with a view to their classification on the basis of efficiency. PPE which is considered to be in conformity with the test specifications must bear a mark indicating, in particular, the names or, failing this, the codes of the substances used in the tests and the corresponding standard period of protection. The manufacturer's notes must also contain, in particular, an explanation of the codes (if necessary), a detailed description of the standard tests and all appropriate information for the determination of the maximum permissible period of wear under the different foreseeable conditions of use.

3.11.   Safety devices for diving equipment

1.   Breathing equipment

The breathing equipment must make it possible to supply the user with a breathable gaseous mixture, under foreseeable conditions of use and taking account in particular of the maximum depth of immersion.

2.   Where the foreseeable conditions of use so require, the equipment must comprise:

(a)   a suit which protects the user against the pressure resulting from the depth of immersion (see 3.2) and/or against cold (see 3.7);

(b)   an alarm designed to give the user prompt warning of an approaching failure in the supply of breathable gaseous mixture (see 2.8);

(c)   a life-saving suit enabling the user to return to the surface (see 3.4.1).

ANNEX III

TECHNICAL DOCUMENTATION SUPPLIED BY THE MANUFACTURER

The documentation referred to in Article 8(1) must comprise all relevant data on the means used by the manufacturer to ensure that a PPE complies with the basic requirements relating to it.

In the case of PPE models referred to in Article 8(2), the documentation must comprise in particular:

1.   the manufacturer's technical file consiting of:

(a) overall and detailed plans of the PPE accompanied, where appropriate, by calculation notes and the results of prototype tests in so far as necessary for the verification of compliance with the basic requirements;

(b) an exhaustive list of the basic safety requirements and of the harmonised standards or other technical specifications referred to in Articles 3 and 5, taken into account in the design of the model;

2. a description of the control and test facilities to be used in the manufacturer's plant to check compliance of production PPE with the harmonised standards or other technical specifications and to maintain quality level;

3. a copy of the information notice referred to in Annex II, 1.4.

ANNEX IV

EC MARK OF CONFORMITY

The EC mark of conformity consists of the symbol shown below.

The vertical dimensions of the different components of the EC mark must be perceptibly the same and not less than 5 mm.

ANNEX V

CONDITIONS TO BE FULFILLED BY THE BODIES OF WHICH NOTIFICATION HAS BEEN GIVEN

(Article 9(2))

The bodies designated by the Member States must fulfil the following minimum conditions:

1. availability of personnel and of the necessary means and equipment;

2. technical competence and professional integrity of personnel;

3. independence, in carrying out the tests, preparing the reports, issuing the certificates and performing the surveillance provided for in the Directive, of staff and technical personnel in relation to all circles, groups or persons directly or indirectly concerned with PPE;

4.   maintenance of professional secrecy by personnel;

5.   subscription of a civil liability insurance unless that liability is covered by the State under national law.

Fulfilment of the conditions under 1 and 2 shall be verified at invervals by the competent authorities of the Member States.

ANNEX IV

MODEL EC DECLARATION OF CONFORMITY

The manufacturer or his authorised representative established in the Community:

....

....

....

declares that the new PPE described hereafter

....

....

....

....

....

is in conformity with the provisions of Council Directive 89/686/EEC and, where such is the case, with the national standard transposing harmonised standard No............. (for the PPE referred to in Article 8(3))

is identical to the PPE which is the subject of EC certificate of conformity No .... issued by

....

....

is subject to the procedure set out in Article 11 point A or point B of Directive 89/686/EEC under the supervision of the notified body...........................

....

....

Done at................................, on..

....

Signature

THE PRESSURE SYSTEMS AND TRANSPORTABLE GAS CONTAINERS REGULATIONS 1989

(S.I. 1989 No. 2169, as amended by S.I. 1992 No. 743)

General note. Two Approved Codes of Practice: Safety of Pressure Systems and Safety of Transportable Gas Containers have been issued in support of these Regulations, and are supplemented by a Guidance Note published by the Health and Safety Executive (Booklet HS(R) 30).

The Secretary of State, in exercise of the powers conferred on him by sections 15(1), (2), (3)(a) and (b), (4), (5), (6)(a) and (b), and (9), 43(2) to (6), 47(3) and 82(3)(a) of, and paragraphs 1(1)(a) and (c), (2) and (3), 14, 15(1) and 16 of Schedule 3 to, the Health and Safety at Work etc. Act 1974 ("the 1974 Act") and of all other powers enabling him in that behalf and for the purpose of giving effect without modifications to proposals submitted to him by the Health and Safety Commission under section 11(2)(d) of the 1974 Act after the carrying out by the said Commission of consultations in accordance with section 50(3) of that Act, hereby makes the following Regulations—

PART I
INTRODUCTION

1. Citation and commencement. These Regulations may be cited as the Pressure Systems and Transportable Gas Containers Regulations 1989 and shall come into force in accordance with the provisions of Part I of Schedule 1.

2. Interpretation.—(1) In these Regulations, unless the context otherwise requires—

"the 1974 Act" means the Health and Safety at Work etc. Act 1974;

"approved design standard" and "approved design specification" means a *design standard* or *design specification*, as the case may be, approved under regulation 16(2)(a);

"competent persons" means a competent individual person (other than an employee) or a competent body of persons corporate or unincorporate; and accordingly any reference in these Regulations to a competent person performing a function includes a reference to his performing it through his employees;

"danger" in relation to a *pressure system*, means reasonably foreseeable danger to persons from *system failure*, but (except in the case of steam) it does not mean danger from the hazardous characteristics of the *relevant fluid* other than from its pressure;

"design specification" means a specification for the design of one type of *transportable gas container*;

821

"design standard" means a standard for the design of more than one type of *transportable gas container*;

"EEC-type cylinder" has the meaning assigned by regulation 16(2)(b);

"examination" means a careful and critical scrutiny of a *pressure system*, part of a *pressure system* or *transportable gas container*, in or out of service as appropriate, using suitable techniques, including testing where appropriate, to assess—

(a) its actual condition; and

(b) whether, for the period up to the next examination, it will not cause *danger* when properly used if normal maintenance is carried out, and for this purpose "normal maintenance" means such maintenance as it is reasonable to expect the *user* (in the case of an installed system) or owner (in the case of a *mobile system* or *transportable gas container*) to ensure is carried out independently of any advice from the *competent person* making the examination;

"the Executive" means the Health and Safety Executive;

"Framework Directive" means Council Directive 76/767/EEC concerning the approximation of the laws of the Member States relating to common provisions for pressure vessels and methods of inspecting them;

"installed system" means a *pressure system* other than a *mobile system*;

"mobile system" means a *pressure system* which can be readily moved between and used in different locations but it does not include a steam locomotive;

"owner" in relation to a *pressure system* or *transportable gas container* means the employer or self-employed person who owns the *pressure system* or *transportable gas container* or, if he does not have a place of business in Great Britain, his agent in Great Britain or, if there is no such agent, the *user*;

"pipeline" means a pipe or system of pipes used for the conveyance of *relevant fluid* across the boundaries of premises, together with any apparatus for inducing or facilitating the flow of *relevant fluid* through, or through a part of, the pipe or system, and any valves, valve chambers, pumps, compressors and similar works which are annexed to, or incorporated in the course of, the pipe or system;

"pipework" means a pipe or system of pipes together with associated valves, pumps, compressors and other pressure containing components and includes a hose or bellows but does not include a *pipeline* or any *protective devices*;

"pressure system" means—

(a) a system comprising one or more pressure vessels of rigid construction, any associated *pipework* and *protective devices*;

(b) the *pipework* with its *protective devices* to which a *transportable gas container* is, or is intended to be, connected; or

(c) a *pipeline* and its *protective devices*;

which contains or is liable to contain a *relevant fluid*, but does not include a transportable gas container;

"protective devices" means devices designed to protect the *pressure system* against *system failure* and devices designed to give warning that *system failure* might occur, and include bursting discs;

"relevant fluid" means—

(a) steam;

(b) any fluid or mixture of fluids which is at a pressure greater than 0.5 bar above atmospheric pressure, and which fluid or mixture of fluids, is—

    (i) a gas, or

    (ii) a liquid which would have a vapour pressure greater than 0.5 bar above atmospheric pressure when in equilibrium with its vapour at either the actual temperature of the liquid or 17.5 degrees Celsius; or

(c) a gas dissolved under pressure in a solvent contained in a porous substance at ambient temperature and which could be released from the solvent without the application of heat;

"safe operating limits" means the operating limits (incorporating a suitable margin of safety) beyond which *system failure* is liable to occur;

"scheme of examination" means the written scheme referred to in regulation 8;

"separate Directives" means Council Directives 84/525/EEC, 84/526/EEC and 84/527/EEC concerning the approximation of the laws of the Member States relating to seamless steel gas cylinders, seamless unalloyed aluminium and aluminium alloy gas cylinders, and welded unalloyed steel gas cylinders respectively;

system failure" means the unintentional release of stored energy (other than from a pressure relief system) from a *pressure system* or *transportable gas container*;

"transportable gas container" means a container, including any permanent fitting of such a container, which is used, or, is intended to be used, to contain a *relevant fluid* and is—

(a) designed to be transportable for the purpose of refilling and has an internal volume of at least 0.5 litres and not greater than 3,000 litres;

(b) a non-refillable container having an internal volume of at least 1.4 litres and not greater than 5 litres; or

(c) for the purposes of regulation 17(3) only, a non-refillable container;

"user" in relation to a *pressure system*, or a vessel to which Part IV applies, means the employer or self-employed person who has control of the operation of the *pressure system* or such a vessel, or in the case of a *pressure system* or such a vessel at or in a mine or any part of a quarry (both within the meaning of section 180 of the Mines and Quarries Act 1954), it means the manager for the time being of that mine or that part of the quarry.

(2) In these Regulations, unless the context otherwise requires, any reference to—

(a) a numbered regulation, Part or Schedule is a reference to the regulation, Part or a Schedule in these Regulations so numbered;

(b) a numbered paragraph is a reference to that paragraph so numbered in the regulation or Schedule in which that reference appears.

3. Application and duties.—(1) Subject to Schedule 2 (which sets out exceptions to the Regulations)—

(a) Part II shall apply to or in relation to *pressure systems* and *transportable gas containers*;

(b) Part III shall apply to or in relation to *pressure systems*;

(c) Part V shall apply to or in relation to *transportable gas containers,*

which are used or intended to be used at work.

(2) Any requirements or prohibition imposed by these Regulations on an employer in respect of the activities of his employees shall also extend to a self-employed person in respect of his own activities at work.

(3) Any requirement or prohibition imposed by these Regulations on a person—

(a) who designs, manufactures, imports or supplies any *pressure system* or *transportable gas container,* or any article which is intended to be a component part of any *pressure system* or *transportable gas container,* shall extend only to such a system, container or article designed, manufactured, imported or supplied in the course of a trade, business or other undertaking carried on by him (whether for profit or not);
(b) who designs or manufactures such a system, container or article, shall extend only to matters within his control.

(4) The provisions of Schedule 3 (which relate to the modification of duties in cases where *pressure systems* are supplied by way of lease, hire or other arrangements) shall have effect.

PART II
GENERAL

4.   Design, construction, repair, and modification.—(1) Any person who designs, manufactures, imports or supplies any *pressure system* or *transportable gas container,* or any article which is intended to be a component part of any *pressure system* or *transportable gas container,* shall ensure that paragraphs (2) to (5) are complied with.

(2) The *pressure system, transportable gas container,* or article, as the case may be, shall be properly designed and properly constructed from suitable material, so as to prevent *danger.*

(3) The *pressure system, transportable gas container* or article, as the case may be, shall be so designed and constructed that all necessary examinations for preventing *danger* can be carried out.

(4) Where the *pressure system* has any means of access to its interior, it shall be so designed and constructed as to ensure, so far as practicable, that access can be gained without *danger.*

(5) The *pressure system* and *transportable gas container* shall be provided with such *protective devices* as may be necessary for preventing *danger;* and any such device designed to release contents shall do so safely, so far as practicable.

(6) The employer of a person who modifies or repairs a *pressure system* or *transportable gas container* at work shall ensure that nothing about the way in

which it is modified or repaired gives rise to *danger* or otherwise impairs the operation of any *protective device* or inspection facility.

PART III
PRESSURE SYSTEMS

5. Provision of information and marking.—(1) Any person who—

(a) designs for another any *pressure system* or any article which is intended to be a component part thereof; or
(b) supplies (whether as manufacturer, importer or in any other capacity) any *pressure system* or any such article,

shall provide sufficient written information concerning its design, construction, examination, operation and maintenance as may reasonably foreseeably be needed to enable the provisions of these Regulations to be complied with.

(2) The employer of a person who modifies or repairs any *pressure system* shall provide sufficient written information concerning the modification or repair as may reasonably foreseeably be needed to enable the provisions of these Regulations to be complied with.

(3) The information referred to in paragraph (1) or (2) shall—

(a) in the case of paragraph (1)(a), be provided with the design;
(b) in the case of paragraph (1)(b), be provided with the *pressure system* or article when it is supplied by that person;
(c) in the case of paragraph (2), be provided to the *user* of the system immediately after the modification or repair.

(4) Any person who manufactures a pressure vessel shall ensure that before it is supplied by him the information specified in Schedule 4 is marked on the vessel, or on a plate attached to it, in a visible, legible and indelible form; and no person shall import a pressure vessel unless it is so marked.

(5) No person shall remove from a pressure vessel any mark or plate containing any of the information specified in Schedule 4.

(6) No person shall falsify any mark on a *pressure system,* or on a plate attached to it, relating to its design, construction, test or operation.

6. Installation. The employer of a person who installs a *pressure system* at work shall ensure that nothing about the way in which it is installed gives rise to danger or otherwise impairs the operation of any *protective device* or inspection facility.

7. Safe operating limits.—(1) The *user* of an *installed system* and *owner* of a *mobile system* shall not operate the system or allow it to be operated unless he has established the *safe operating limits* of that system.

(2) The owner of a *mobile system* shall, if he is not also the user of it—

(a) supply the user with a written statement specifying the *safe operating limits* of that system established pursuant to paragraph (1); or

(b) ensure that the system is legibly and durably marked with such *safe operating limits* and that the mark is clearly visible.

8.   Written scheme of examination.—(1) The *user* of an *installed system* and *owner* of a *mobile system* shall not operate the system or allow it to be operated unless he has a written scheme for the periodic *examination*, by a *competent person*, of the following parts of the system, that is to say—

(a) all *protective devices*;
(b) every pressure vessel and every *pipeline* in which (in either case) a defect may give rise to *danger*; and
(c) those parts of the *pipework* in which a defect may give rise to *danger*,

and such parts of the system shall be identified in the scheme.

(2) The said *user* or *owner* shall—

(a) ensure that the scheme has been drawn up, or certified as being suitable, by a *competent person*;
(b) ensure that—
   (i) the content of the scheme is reviewed at appropriate intervals by a *competent person* for the purpose of determining whether it is suitable in current conditions of use of the system; and
   (ii) the content of the scheme is modified in accordance with any recommendations made by that competent person arising out of that review.

(3) No person shall draw up or certify a *scheme of examination* under paragraph (2)(a) unless the scheme is suitable and—

(a) specifies the nature and frequency of *examination*;
(b) specifies any measures necessary to prepare the *pressure system* for safe *examination* other than those it would be reasonable to expect the *user* (in the case of an *installed system*) or *owner* (in the case of a *mobile system*) to take without specialist advice; and
(c) where appropriate, provides for an *examination* to be carried out before the *pressure system* is used for the first time.

(4) References in paragraphs (2) and (3) to the suitability of the scheme are references to its suitability for the purposes of preventing *danger* from those parts of the *pressure system* included in the scheme.

9.   Examination in accordance with the written scheme.—(1) Subject to paragraph (7), the *user* of an *installed system* and the *owner* of a *mobile system* shall—

(a) ensure that those parts of the *pressure system* included in the *scheme of examination* are examined by a *competent person* within the intervals specified in the scheme and, where the scheme so provides, before the system is used for the first time; and
(b) before each *examination* take all appropriate safety measures to prepare the system for *examination*, including any such measures as are specified in the *scheme of examination* pursuant to regulation 8(3)(b).

(2) Where a *competent person* undertakes an *examination* for the purposes of paragraph (1) he shall carry out that *examination* properly and in accordance with the *scheme of examination*.

(3) Where a *competent person* has carried out an *examination* for the purposes of paragraph (1) he shall, subject to paragraph (4) and regulation 13(4), make a written report of the *examination*, sign or otherwise authenticate it, date it and send it to the *user* (in the case of an *installed system*) or *owner* (in the case of a *mobile system*); and the said report shall be so sent as soon as is practicable after completing the *examination* (or, in the case of integrated *installed systems* where the *examination* is part of a series, as soon as is practicable after completing the last *examination* in that series), and in any event to arrive—

    (a) within 28 days of the completion of the *examination* (or, in the case of integrated *installed systems* where the *examination* is part of a series, within 28 days of the completion of the last *examination* in that series); or

    (b) before the date specified in the report under paragraph (5)(b), whichever is sooner.

(4) Where the *competent person* referred to in paragraph (3) is the *user* (in the case of an *installed system*) or *owner* (in the case of a *mobile system*) the requirement in that paragraph to send the report to the *user* or *owner* shall not apply, but he shall make the report by the time it would have been required to have been sent to him under that paragraph if he had not been the *competent person*.

(5) The report required by paragraph (3) shall—

    (a) state which parts of the *pressure system* have been examined, the condition of those parts and the results of the *examination*;

    (b) specify any repairs or modifications to, or changes in the established *safe operating limits* of, the parts examined which, in the opinion of the *competent person*, are necessary to prevent *danger* or to ensure the continued effective working of the *protective devices*, and specify the date by which any such repairs or modifications must be completed or any such changes to the *safe operating limits* must be made;

    (c) specify the date within the limits set by the *scheme of examination* after which the *pressure system* may not be operated without a further *examination* under the *scheme of examination*; and

    (d) state whether in the opinion of the *competent person* the *scheme of examination* is suitable (for the purpose of preventing *danger* from those parts of the *pressure system* included in it) or should be modified, and if the latter, state the reasons.

(6) The *user* of an *installed system* and the *owner* of a *mobile system* which has been examined under this regulation shall ensure that the system is not operated, and no person shall supply such a *mobile system* for operation, after (in each case)—

    (a) the date specified under paragraph (5)(b), unless the repairs or modifications specified under that paragraph have been completed, and the changes in the established *safe operating limits* so specified have been made; or

    (b) the date specified under paragraph (5)(c) (or, if that date has been postponed under paragraph (7), the postponed date) unless a further *examination* has been carried out under the *scheme of examination*.

(7) The date specified in a report under paragraph (5)(c) may be postponed to a later date by agreement in writing between the *competent person* who made the report and the *user* (in the case of an *installed system*) or *owner* (in the case of a *mobile system*) if—

   (a) such postponement does not give rise to *danger*;

   (b) only one such postponement is made for any one *examination*; and

   (c) such postponement is notified by the *user* or *owner* in writing to the enforcing authority for the premises at which the *pressure system* is situated, before the date specified in the report under paragraph (5)(c).

(8) Where the *competent person* referred to in paragraph (7) is the *user* (in the case of an *installed system*) or *owner* (in the case of a *mobile system*) the reference in that paragraph to an agreement in writing shall not apply, but there shall be included in the notification under sub-paragraph (c) of that paragraph a declaration that the postponement will not give rise to *danger*.

(9) The *owner* of a *mobile system* shall ensure that the date specified under paragraph (5)(c) is legibly and durably marked on the *mobile system* and that the mark is clearly visible.

10. Action in case of imminent danger.—(1) If the *competent person* carrying out an *examination* under the *scheme of examination* is of the opinion that the *pressure system* or part of the *pressure system* will give rise to imminent *danger* unless certain repairs or modifications have been carried out or unless suitable changes to the operating conditions have been made, then without prejudice to the requirements of regulation 9, he shall forthwith make a written report to that effect identifying the system and specifying the repairs, modifications or changes concerned and give it—

   (a) in the case of an *installed system*, to the *user*; or

   (b) in the case of a *mobile system*, to the *owner* and to the *user*, if any,

and the *competent person* shall within 14 days of the completion of the *examination* send a written report containing the same particulars to the enforcing authority for the premises at which the *pressure system* is situated.

(2) Where a report is given in accordance with paragraph (1) to—

   (a) the *user* of a *pressure system*, he shall ensure that the system (or, if the report only affects a discrete part of the system, that part) is not operated;

   (b) the owner of a *mobile system*, he shall take all reasonably practicable steps to ensure that the system (or, if the report only affects a discrete part of the system, that part) is not operated,

until the repairs, modifications or changes, as the case may be, have been carried out or made.

(3) Where the *competent person* referred to in paragraph (1) is the *user* (in the case of an *installed system*) or *owner* (in the case of a *mobile system*) the requirement in that paragraph to give the report to the *user* or *owner* shall not apply, and the reference in paragraph (2) to the giving of the report to the *user* or *owner* shall be construed as a reference to the making of the report by him.

11. Operation.—(1) The *user* of an *installed system* and the *owner* of a *mobile system* shall provide for any person operating the system adequate and suitable instructions for—

   (a) the safe operation of the system; and

(b) the action to be taken in the event of an emergency.

(2) The *user* of a *pressure system* shall ensure that it is not operated except in accordance with the instructions provided in respect of that system under paragraph (1)(a).

12. Maintenance. The *user* of an *installed system* and the *owner* of a *mobile system* shall ensure that the system is properly maintained in good repair, so as to prevent *danger*.

13. Keeping of records, etc.—(1) The *user* of an *installed system* and the *owner* of a *mobile system* shall, subject to paragraph (4), keep the following documents or copies thereof:—

(a) the last report relating to the system made by the *competent person* pursuant to regulation 9(3);

(b) any such previous reports if they contain information which will materially assist in assessing whether—
    (i) the system is safe to operate, or
    (ii) any repairs or modifications to the system can be carried out safely;

(c) any documents provided pursuant to regulation 5 which relate to those parts of the *pressure system* included in the *scheme of examination*; and

(d) any agreement made pursuant to regulation 9(7), and, in a case to which regulation 9(8) applies, a copy of the notification referred to in regulation 9(7)(c), until a further *examination* has been carried out since that agreement or notification under the *scheme of examination*.

(2) The documents required to be kept by this regulation shall be kept—

(a) in the case of an *installed system*, at the premises where the system is installed, or at other premises approved for the purposes of this sub-paragraph by the enforcing authority responsible for enforcing these Regulations at the premises where the system is installed;

(b) in the case of a *mobile system*, at the premises in Great Britain from which the deployment of the system is controlled.

(3) Where the *user* or *owner* of a *pressure system* or part thereof changes, the previous user or owner shall as soon as is practicable give to the new *user* or *owner* all documents (relating to the system or part thereof, as the case may be) kept by him under this regulation, or copies thereof.

(4) Subject to paragraph (6) it shall be sufficient compliance with regulation 9(3) if the individual making the *examination* enters his report in a computer and duly authenticates it as soon as is practicable after completing the *examination* (or, in the case of integrated installed systems where the *examination* is part of a series, as soon as is practicable after completing the last *examination* in that series), and in any event by the time referred to in regulation 9(3)(a) or (b), whichever is sooner; and in such a case it shall be sufficient compliance with sub-paragraphs (a) or (b) of paragraph (1) if the report is kept by the *user* in a computer.

(5) Where the procedure referred to in paragraph (4) is used in respect of the reports mentioned in sub-paragraph (a) or (b) of paragraph (1) and the *user* or *owner* of the *pressure system* or part thereof changes, the previous *user* or

owner shall provide in writing to the new *user* or *owner* the information contained in those reports.

(6) The procedure referred to in paragraph (4) may only be used if the report—

(a) is capable of being reproduced as a written copy when required at the premises referred to in the appropriate sub-paragraph in paragraph (2);

(b) is secure from loss or unauthorised interference; and

(c) can be authenticated only by the individual making the *examination*.

(7) In this regulation "computer" means the computer system including the software.

PART IV
PRECAUTIONS TO PREVENT PRESSURISATION OF CERTAIN VESSELS

14. Application. This Part shall apply to a vessel—

(a) which is constructed with a permanent outlet to the atmosphere or to a space where the pressure does not exceed atmospheric pressure; and

(b) which could become a pressure vessel if that outlet were obstructed.

15. Precautions to prevent pressurisation. The user of a vessel to which this Part applies shall ensure that the outlet referred to in regulation 14(a) is at all times kept open and free from obstruction when the vessel is in use.

PART V
TRANSPORTABLE GAS CONTAINERS

16. Design standards, approval and certification.—(1) No person shall—

(a) supply for the first time;

(b) import; or

(c) manufacture and use,

a *transportable gas container* unless the conditions specified in sub-paragraphs (a) or (b) of paragraph (2) have been met.

(2) The conditions referred to in paragraph (1) are—

(a) the container has been verified (either by certificate in writing or by means of stamping the container) as conforming to a *design standard* or *design specification* approved by *the Executive*—

   (i) by a person or body of persons corporate or unincorporate approved by *the Executive* for the purposes of this paragraph, or

   (ii) in accordance with a quality assurance scheme approved by *the Executive*; or

(b) the container is an *EEC-type cylinder*, that is—

   (i) there is an EEC Verification Certificate in force in respect of it issued by an inspection body which, under the law of any Member State, is authorised to grant such a Certificate for the purposes of the *Framework Directive* and the *separate Directive* relating to that type of cylinder, or, in the case of a cylinder not subject to EEC verification under any of the *separate Directives*, it conforms to the requirements of the *Framework Directive* and the *separate Directive* relating to that type of cylinder, and

    (ii) it bears all the marks and inscriptions required by the *Framework Directive* and the *separate Directive* relating to that type of cylinder.

(3) Any approval under this regulation shall be by a certificate in writing, may be made subject to conditions and may be revoked by a certificate in writing at any time.

(4) Schedule 5 shall have effect with respect to fees for approvals under this regulation.

(5) In paragraph (1)(a) the reference to supplying a *transportable gas container* for the first time is a reference to supplying an unused *transportable gas container*, that is, one from which a relevant fluid has not been used.

17.　Filling of containers.—(1) The employer of a person who is to fill a *transportable gas container* with a *relevant fluid* at work shall ensure that before it is filled that person—

  (a) checks from the marks on the cylinder that—

    (i) it appears to have undergone proper *examinations* at appropriate intervals by a *competent person* (unless the manufacturer's mark reveals that such an *examination* is not yet due), and

    (ii) it is suitable for containing that fluid; and

  (b) makes all other appropriate safety checks.

(2) The employer of a person who fills a *transportable gas container* with a *relevant fluid* at work shall ensure that that person—

  (a) checks that after filling it is within its *safe operating limits*;

  (b) checks that it is not overfilled; and

  (c) removes any excess fluid in a safe manner in the event of overfilling.

(3) An employer shall ensure that no person employed by him refills at work a non-refillable container with a *relevant fluid*.

18.　Examination of containers.—(1) The owner of a *transportable gas container* shall, for the purpose of determining whether it is safe, ensure that the container is examined at appropriate intervals by a *competent person*.

(2) Where a *competent person* undertakes an *examination* for the purposes of paragraph (1), he shall carry out that *examination* properly, and if on completing the *examination* he is satisfied that the container is safe, he shall ensure that there is affixed to the container a mark showing the date of the *examination*.

(3) No person other than the *competent person* or person authorised by him shall affix to a *transportable gas container* the mark referred to in paragraph (2) or a mark liable to be confused with it.

19.　Modifications of containers.—(1) Subject to paragraph (2),

  (a) an employer shall ensure that no person employed by him modifies at work the body of a *transportable gas container*—

      (i) of seamless construction; or

      (ii) which has contained acetylene;

(b) an employer shall ensure that no person employed by him modifies at work the body of any other type of *transportable gas container* if that modification would put the *transportable gas container* outside the scope of the *design standard* or *design specification* to which it was originally constructed;

(c) a person shall not supply any modified *transportable gas container* for use unless following such work a person or body of persons approved by *the Executive* for the purposes of regulation 16(2)(a)(i) has marked or certified it as being fit for use, or, in the case of an *EEC-type cylinder*, an inspection body referred to in regulation 16(2)(b)(i) has so marked or certified it.

(2) Paragraph (1) shall not apply to the remaking of a thread if this is done in accordance with a standard approved by *the Executive.*

20. Repair work.—(1) An employer shall ensure that no person employed by him carries out at work any major repair on the body of a *transportable gas container*—

(a) of seamless construction; or

(b) which has contained acetylene.

(2) An employer shall ensure that no person employed by him carries out at work any major repair on the body of any other type of *transportable gas container* unless he is competent to do so.

(3) No person shall supply a *transportable gas container* which has undergone a major repair unless following such work a person or body of persons approved by *the Executive* for the purposes of regulation 16(2)(a)(i) has marked or certified it as being fit for use, or, in the case of an *EEC-type cylinder,* an inspection body referred to in regulation 16(2)(b)(i) has so marked or certified it.

(4) In this regulation "major repair" means any repair involving hot work or welding on the body of a transportable gas container but (except in relation to paragraph (1)(b)) it does not mean heat treatment applied for the purpose of restoring the metallurgical properties of the container.

21. Re-rating.—(1) This regulation applies to the re-rating of a *transportable gas container,* that is the reassessment of its capability to contain compressed gas safely with a view to improving its capacity by means of an increase in the charging pressure (or in the case of liquefied gas, the filling ratio) from that originally assessed and marked on the container at the time of manufacture.

(2) An employer shall ensure that no person employed by him re-rates a *transportable gas container* at work unless he is competent to do so and does it in accordance with suitable written procedures drawn up by the *owner* of the container.

(3) No person shall supply a *transportable gas container* which has been re-rated unless following the re-rating a person or body of persons approved by *the Executive* for the purposes of regulation 16(2)(a)(i) has certified it as being safe for use.

(4) In this regulation "filling ratio" means the ratio of the volume of liquefied gas in the container to the total volume of the container.

22.   Records.—(1) The manufacturer or, if he does not have a place of business in Great Britain, his agent in Great Britain, or if he has no agent, the importer, of a *transportable gas container*—

(a)   made to an approved design specification, shall keep a copy of the said specification together with any certificate of conformity issued in accordance with regulation 16(2)(a);

(b)   made to an *approved design standard,* shall keep a copy of any certificate of conformity issued in accordance with regulation 12(2) *(a);*

(c)   which is an *EEC-type cylinder,* shall keep the EEC Verification Certificate referred to in regulation 16(2)(b)(i) where one has been issued.

(2)   The *owner* of a hired out *transportable gas container*—

(a)   made to an *approved design specification,* shall keep a copy of the said specification together with a copy of any certificate of conformity issued in accordance with regulation 16(2)(a);

(b)   made to an *approved design standard,* shall keep a copy of any certificate of conformity issued in accordance with regulation 16(2)(a);

(c)   which is an *EEC-type cylinder,* shall keep a copy of the EEC Verification Certificate referred to in regulation 16(2)(b)(i) where one has been issued,

(d)   which—
     (i)   is a refillable container,
     (ii)   is used solely for containing liquefied petroleum gas, and
     (iii)   has a water capacity up to and including 6.5 litres;
     shall keep a copy of the *design specification* for the container.

(3)   The *owner* of a *transportable gas container* for acetylene shall keep records of the tare weight of the container, including the porous substance and acetone or other solvent, the nature of the solvent and the maximum pressure allowed in the container.

PART VI
MISCELLANEOUS

23.   Defence.—(1) In any proceedings for an offence for a contravention of any of the provisions of these Regulations it shall, subject to paragraphs (2) and (3), be a defence for the person charged to prove—

(a)   that the commission of the offence was due to the act or default of another person not being one of his employees (hereinafter called "the other person"); and

(b)   that he took all reasonable precautions and exercised all due diligence to avoid the commission of the offence.

(2)   The person charged shall not, without leave of the court, be entitled to rely on the defence referred to in paragraph (1) unless, within a period ending seven clear days before the hearing, he has served on the prosecutor a notice in writing giving such information identifying or assisting in the identification of the other person as was then in his possession.

(3) For the purpose of enabling the other person to be charged with and convicted of the offence by virtue of section 36 of the 1974 Act, a person who establishes a defence under this regulation shall nevertheless be treated for the purposes of that section as having committed the offence.

24.   Power to grant exemptions.—(1) Subject to paragraph (2), *the Executive* may, by a certificate in writing, exempt—

(a) any person or class of persons;
(b) any type or class of *pressure system*; or
(c) any type or class of *transportable gas container*,

from the application of any of the requirements or prohibitions imposed by these Regulations, and any such exemption may be granted subject to conditions and to a limit of time, and may be revoked by a certificate in writing at any time.

(2) *The Executive* shall not grant any such exemption unless, having regard to the circumstances, and in particular to—

(a) the conditions, if any, which it proposes to attach to the exemption; and
(b) any other requirement imposed by or under any enactment which apply to the case,

it is satisfied that the health and safety of persons who are likely to be affected by the exemption will not be prejudiced in consequence of it.

25.   Extensions outside Great Britain.   These Regulations shall apply outside Great Britain in relation to any activity to which, sections 1 to 59 and 80 to 82 of *the 1974 Act* apply by virtue of Articles 6 and 7(a), (b) and (d) of the Health and Safety at Work etc. Act 1974 (Application outside Great Britain) Order 1989 as they apply within Great Britain.

26.   Repeals, revocations and modifications.—(1) The enactment specified in Part I of Schedule 6 in column 1 is hereby repealed to the extent specified in the corresponding entry in column 3.

(2) The enactment specified in Part II of Schedule 6 in column 1 shall be modified to the extent specified in the corresponding entry in column 3.

(3) The instruments specified in Part III of Schedule 6 in column 1 are hereby revoked to the extent specified in the corresponding entry in column 3.

(4) The instruments specified in Part IV of Schedule 6 in column 1 shall be modified to the extent specified in the corresponding entry in column 3.

27.   Transitional provisions.   The provisions of Parts II and III of Schedule 1 shall have effect.

SCHEDULE 1

COMING INTO FORCE OF THE REGULATIONS AND
TRANSITIONAL PROVISIONS

PART I
COMING INTO FORCE OF THE REGULATIONS

1.   Regulations 1 to 3, 5 to 7, 13 to 15, 23 to 25 and 27 shall come into force on 1 July 1990.

2.   Regulation 4 (in so far as it relates to *transportable gas containers*), regulations 16 to 22, and regulation 26 (in so far as it revokes the instruments marked with an asterisk in Schedule 6) shall come into force on 1 January 1991.

3.   All the other provisions of these Regulations shall come into force on 1 July 1994.

PART II
TRANSITIONAL PROVISIONS FOR PLANT:
SUBJECT TO EXISTING EXAMINATION REQUIREMENTS

1.   This Part shall apply until regulations 8 to 10 come into force.

2.   The existing *examination* requirements shall not apply to any plant during any period in which the *user* (or *owner* in the case of a *mobile system*) of the *pressure system* incorporating that plant complies with regulations 8 to 10 in respect of that system (notwithstanding that those regulations are not in force).

3.   Paragraph 2 above shall not apply unless written notice explaining the effect of paragraph 4 below has been given by the *user* (or *owner* in the case of a *mobile system*) to every other person who would have duties in relation to the *pressure system* under regulations 8 to 10 if those regulations had been in force.

4.   Where a person receives a notice under paragraph 3 above he shall, as respects the *pressure system*, comply with regulations 8 to 10 as if those regulations had been in force.

5.   In this Part "the existing *examination* requirements" are the following provisions—
   (a)   sections 33(2), (3), (4), (6) to (8), 35(6), and 36(5) of the Factories Act 1961, and sections 35(5) and 36(4) of that Act to the extent that they relate to the *examination* or testing of steam receivers (and their fittings) and of air receivers respectively;
   (b)   the Examination of Steam Boilers Regulations 1964;
   (c)   the Examination of Steam Boilers Reports (No. 1) Order 1964;
   (d)   the Shipbuilding (Air Receivers) Order 1961;
   (e)   regulation 9 of the Coal and Other Mines (Steam Boilers) Regulations 1956;
   (f)   regulations 56(2), 57 and 60(2) and (3) of the Miscellaneous Mines (General) Regulations 1956, and regulations 56(1) and 60(1) of those Regulations to the extent that they relate to the examination or testing of steam boilers (and their fittings and attachments) and of air receivers respectively;

    (g)　regulation 18(1)(*b*) and (2), 19, and 22(2) and (3) of the Quarries (General) Regulations 1956, and regulation 22(1) of those Regulations to the extent that it relates to the *examination* or testing of air receivers.

PART III
FURTHER TRANSITIONAL PROVISIONS

1.　Section 33(6) of the Factories Act 1961 shall, notwithstanding its disapplication or repeal by these Regulations, be complied with in respect of a steam boiler until a report of the *examination* of the boiler has been received under regulation 9 of these Regulations.

2.　Any record or register required to be kept under any provision disapplied, repealed or revoked, by these Regulations shall, notwithstanding that disapplication, repeal or revocation, be kept in the same manner and for the same period as if these Regulations had not been made.

SCHEDULE 2

Regulation 3(1)

EXCEPTIONS TO THE REGULATIONS

PART I
PRESSURE SYSTEMS AND TRANSPORTABLE GAS CONTAINERS
EXCEPTED FROM ALL REGULATIONS

Parts II, III and V of these Regulations shall not apply to—

1.　A *pressure system* or *transportable gas container* which forms part of the equipment of—
    (a)　any ship to which the Merchant Shipping Acts 1894 to 1984 apply or would apply if the ship was registered in Great Britain;
    (b)　any ship or other vessel in the service of the Crown;
    (c)　any spacecraft, aircraft, hovercraft or hydrofoil.

2.　A *pressure system* or *transportable gas container* which forms part of, or is intended to form part of, a weapons system.

3.　A *pressure system* which forms part of any braking, control or suspension system of a wheeled, tracked or rail mounted vehicle.

4.　That part of a system which is only a *pressure system* because it is—
    (a)　subject to a leak test (except that this sub-paragraph shall not apply to a *pipeline*);
    (b)　pressurised unintentionally, such pressurisation being not reasonably foreseeable; or
    (c)　a pipeline pressurised by a *relevant fluid* solely as part of a test or line clearance operation, but this exception shall not apply if the *pipeline*—
        (i)　is used for the conveyance of a *relevant fluid*, or
        (ii)　is pressurised beyond its *safe operating limits*.

5.　Any *pipeline* and its *protective devices* in which the pressure does not exceed 2 bar above atmospheric pressure (or 2.7 bar above atmospheric pressure if the normal pressure does not exceed 2 bar and the overpressure is caused solely by the operation of a *protective device*).

6. Any *pressure system* or part thereof, or *transportable gas container* which—
(a)   is the subject of a research experiment; or
(b)   comprises temporary apparatus being used in a research experiment,
if, in the case of regulations 4, 5, 6, 7, 11, and 13, it is not reasonably practicable to comply with them.

7. Any plant or equipment, other than a *transportable gas container*, required by regulation 5(1)(d) of the Diving Operations at Work Regulations 1981 and used or intended to be used in the course of a diving operation to which those Regulations apply.

8. A working chamber, tunnel, manlock or an airlock within which persons work in compressed air, being work to which the Work in Compressed Air (Special) Regulations 1958 apply.

9. A road tanker or tank container to which the [Road Traffic (Carriage of Dangerous Substances in Road Tankers and Tank Containers) Regulations 1992] apply.

10. Any *pressure system* or *transportable gas container* being carried in a vehicle if—
(a)   the vehicle is engaged in an international transport operation within the meaning of the Convention concerning International Carriage by Rail (COTIF) as revised or re-issued from time to time; and
(b)   such carriage conforms in every respect to the provisions of the Uniform Rules concerning the Contract for International Carriage of Goods by Rail (CIM) which forms Appendix B to that Convention and to the regulations (RID) made thereunder.

11. Any *pressure system* or *transportable gas container* being carried in a vehicle if the vehicle—
(a)   is engaged in an international transport operation within the meaning of the European Agreement concerning the international carriage of dangerous goods by road (ADR) signed in Geneva on 30 September 1957, as revised or re-issued from time to time;
(b)   complies with the conditions contained in Annexes A and B to that Agreement; and
(c)   is certified pursuant to that Agreement as complying with it,
or where by a provision of that Agreement the transport operation is subject to a special bilateral or multilateral agreement under the terms of Article 4 of the agreement to which the United Kingdom is a Contracting Party.

12. Any *pressure system* or *transportable gas container* which is carried, or stored as goods in transit, as part of an international transport operation, if it complies with the appropriate provisions of the International Maritime Dangerous Goods Code issued by the International Maritime Organisation as revised or re-issued from time to time.

13. Any *pressure system* comprising a gas propulsion or a gas fired heating, cooking, ventilating or refrigerating system fitted to a motor vehicle or trailer (both within the meaning of section 185(1) of the Road Traffic Act 1988.

14. Any water cooling system on an internal combustion engine or on any compressor.

15. A container of the type known as a two-part beer keg, one part of which is intended to contain a gas or a mixture of gases under pressure.

16. A container used for the conveyance or storage of beer or carbonated drinks, the capacity of which does not exceed 0.252 cubic metres and the maximum working pressure of which is not greater than 12 bar above atmospheric pressure.

17. Any tyre used or intended to be used on a vehicle.

18. Any vapour compression refrigeration system incorporating compressor drive motors, including standby compressor motors, having a total installed power not exceeding 25 kW.

19. A *mobile system* of the type known as a slurry tanker, and containing or intended to contain agricultural slurry, and used in agriculture.

20. Prime movers including turbines but not including steam locomotives or traction engines.

21. Any *pressure system* which is an electrical or telecommunications cable.

22. Any *pressure system* containing sulphur hexafluoride gas and forming an integral part of high voltage electrical apparatus.

23. Any *pressure system* consisting of a water filled fluid coupling and used in power transmission.

24. Any portable fire extinguisher with a working pressure below 25 bar 60°C and having a total mass not exceeding 23 kilogrammes.

25. Any part of a tool or appliance (designed to be held in the hand) which is a pressure vessel.

PART II
PRESSURE SYSTEMS AND TRANSPORTABLE GAS CONTAINERS
EXCEPTED FROM CERTAIN REGULATIONS

1. Regulations 5(4), 8 to 11 and 13 shall not apply to a *pressure system* containing a *relevant fluid* (other than steam) if the product of the pressure (in bars above atmospheric) in the pressure vessel (or in the case of a system having more than one vessel, the vessel with the largest internal volume) and internal volume (in litres) is less than 250.

2. Regulations 4, 5, 7 to 10 and 13 shall not apply to a *pressure system* comprising a tank container if—
   (a) it has been used in the conveyance of a dangerous substance to which [the Road Traffic (Carriage of Dangerous Substances in Road Tankers and Tank Containers) Regulations 1992 applied, or would have applied but for the application of sub-paragraph (d) or (e) of Schedule 2 thereto];
   (b) it has been temporarily removed from a vehicle; and
   (c) it is present solely for the purpose of unloading the substance from it.

3. Regulations 4, 5, 7 to 10 and 13 shall not apply to a *pressure system* comprising a tank container if—
   (a) it is intended to be used in the conveyance of a dangerous substance to which [the Road Traffic (Carriage of Dangerous Substances in Road Tankers and Tank Containers) Regulations 1992, or would have applied but for the application of sub-paragraph (d) or (e) of Schedule 2 thereto]; and
   (b) the tank container is present solely for the purpose of being loaded with the substance to be conveyed.

4. Regulations 16, 17(1)(a), 18 and 22(1) shall not apply to a *transportable gas container* which—
   (a) is a refillable container;
   (b) is used solely for containing liquefied petroleum gas; and
   (c) has a water capacity up to and including 6.5 litres.

5. Regulation 4(1) to (5) shall not apply to an *EEC-type cylinder*.

SCHEDULE 3

Regulation 3(4)

MODIFICATION OF DUTIES IN CASES WHERE *PRESSURE SYSTEMS*
ARE SUPPLIED BY WAY OF LEASE, HIRE, OR OTHER ARRANGEMENTS

1. (a) This paragraph applies where a person supplies an *installed system* by way of lease or hire, and agrees in writing to be responsible for discharging the duties of the *user* under all the provisions of regulations 8(1) and (2), 9(1), 11(1), 12, and 13.

  (b) During such time as the agreement is in force the supplier shall discharge the duties of the *user* under the said provisions.

  (c) It shall be a defence in any proceedings against the *user* of an *installed system*—
   (i) for an offence for a contravention of any of the said provisions; or
   (ii) in any civil proceedings for breach of a duty (mentioned in Section 47(2) of *the 1974 Act*) of any such provisions;
     for that person to prove that the supplier had agreed in writing to be responsible for discharging the *user's* duty at the relevant time.

  (d) During such time as the agreement is in force the following provisions of this paragraph shall have effect.

  (e) Where the *competent person* who is to carry out the *examination* under the *scheme of examination* is a person other than the supplier, the supplier shall notify the *competent person* that any reports required to be sent or given to the *user* under regulation 9(3) or 10(1) shall be sent or given to the supplier as well.

  (f) On being so notified under sub-paragraph (e) above, the *competent person* shall comply with regulations 9(3) and 10(1) as if the reference therein to sending or giving a report to the *user* also included a reference to sending or giving a report to the supplier.

  (g) On receipt of a report from a *competent person* under regulations 9(3) or 10(1) (or in the case where the supplier is also the *competent person*, on the making by him of that report) the supplier shall take all practicable steps to ensure that the *pressure system* will not be operated in contravention of regulations 9(6) or 10(2), as the case may be.

  (h) The references in regulation 9(7) (in both places where it appears) and 9(8) to the user shall be read as references to the supplier.

  (i) The reference in regulation 13(2)(a) to the premises where the system is installed shall be read as a reference to the premises in Great Britain where the leasing or hiring out of the system is controlled; except that this modification shall not only apply to the application of that sub-paragraph to regulation 13(6)(a) where the *competent person* is using the procedure referred to in regulation 13(4) in relation to the sending of the report to the user.

2. Where a person supplies a *pressure system* to another ("the customer") under a hire-purchase agreement, conditional sale agreement, or lease, and—

  (a) he carries on the business of financing the acquisition of goods by others by means of such agreements, or, if financing by means of leases, the use of goods by others;

  (b) in the course of that business he acquired his interest in the *pressure system* supplied to the customer as a means of financing its acquisition by that customer (or, in the case of a lease, its provision to that customer); and

  (c) in the case of a lease he or his agent either has not had physical possession of that *pressure system*, or has had physical possession of it only for the purpose of passing it on to the customer,

the customer and not the person who provided the finance shall be treated for the purposes of these Regulations as being the *owner* of the *pressure system*, and duties placed on *owners* in these Regulations shall accordingly fall on the customer and not on the person providing the finance.

3. Section 6(9) of the Health and Safety at Work etc. Act 1974 and the Health and Safety (Leasing Arrangements) Regulations 1992 shall apply to these Regulations as they apply to the remainder of section 6 of that Act.

SCHEDULE 4

Regulation 5(4), (5)

MARKING OF PRESSURE VESSELS

The information referred to in regulation 5(4) is as follows—

1.   The manufacturer's name.

2.   A serial number to identify the vessel.

3.   The date of manufacture of the vessel.

4.   The standard to which the vessel was built.

5.   The maximum design pressure of the vessel.

6.   The minimum design pressure of the vessel where it is other than atmospheric.

7.   The design temperature.

SCHEDULE 5

Regulation 16(4)

FEES ON APPLICATIONS FOR APPROVALS

1.   On the making of an application under regulation 16(2) (a) to *the Executive* for the approval of—
   (a) a quality assurance scheme;
   (b) a *design specification*; or
   (c) a person or body of persons,
there shall be payable by the applicant in connection with the performance by or on behalf of *the Executive* of its functions in relation to that application a fee or fees to be determined in accordance with the following provisions of this Schedule.

2.   On receipt of the application *the Executive* shall prepare and send to the applicant an estimate of the cost to it of the work necessary for the determination of the application; and the amount so estimated shall, subject to paragraph 4 below, be the amount of the initial fee payable and shall be paid forthwith.

3.   On determination of the application *the Executive* shall prepare and send to the applicant a detailed statement of the work carried out for the determination of the application and of the cost reasonably incurred by it in carrying out that work or in having it carried out on its behalf.

4.   If the cost so stated differs from the amount estimated in accordance with paragraph 2 above—
   (a) if it is greater, the amount of the difference shall be the amount of the final fee payable and shall be paid forthwith; and
   (b) if it is less, the initial fee shall be redetermined accordingly and the amount of the difference shall be paid forthwith to the applicant by *the Executive*.

5.   In estimating or stating the cost of carrying out any work the *Executive* may determine the cost of employing an officer for any period on work appropriate to his grade by reference to the average cost to it of employing officers of his grade for that period.

SCHEDULE 6

Regulation 26

REPEALS, REVOCATIONS AND MODIFICATIONS

PART I
REPEALS

(1) *Short title*	(2) *Chapter*	(3) *Extent of repeal*
The Factories Act 1961.	1961 c. 34.	Sections 32, 33, 35 and 36. In section 38 the words "and maximum permissible working pressure" to the end of the section. In section 122(2)(a) the words "and with respect to steam boilers, steam receivers and steam containers, and air receivers". In section 122(4) the words "steam boilers, steam receivers and steam containers, and air receivers". Sections 125(2)(a), 127(2)(c).

PART II
MODIFICATIONS OF ENACTMENTS

(1) *Short title*	(2) *Chapter*	(3) *Extent of modification*
The Factories Act 1961.	1961 c. 34.	In section 37(1) for the words "Sections thirty-two to thirty-four" substitute "Section thirty-four". In section 37(2) for the words "sections thirty-two to thirty-six" substitute "section thirty-four", and delete the words "steam receiver, steam container or air receiver".

(1) Title of instrument	(2) Reference	(3) Extent of revocation
The Locomotives and Waggons (Used on Lines and Sidings) Regulations 1906.	S.R. & O. 1906/679.	Regulation 22.
*The Order of Secretary of State (No. 9), dated 23 June 1919, relating to Compressed Acetylene Porous Substance.	S.R. & O. 1919/809.	Conditions 5, 6, 7, 10 and 12 to the said Order.
*The Gas Cylinders (Conveyance) Regulations 1931.	S.R. & O. 1931/679.	The whole Regulations.
The Factories Act (Docks, Building and Engineering Construction, etc.) Modification Regulations 1938.	S.R. & O. 1938/610.	Regulation 2.
*The Compressed Gas Cylinders (Fuel for Motor Vehicles) Regulations 1940.	S.R. & O. 1940/2009.	The whole Regulations.
*The Gas Cylinders (Conveyance) Regulations 1947.	S.R. & O. 1947/1594.	The whole Regulations.
The Coal and Other Mines (Steam Boilers) Order 1956.	S.I. 1956/1772.	The whole Order.
The Miscellaneous Mines (General) Regulations 1956.	S.I. 1956/1778.	Regulations 53, 54, 55, 56, 57, 58, 59 and 60.
The Quarries (General) Regulations 1956.	S.I. 1956/1780.	Regulations 15, 16, 17, 18, 19, 20, 21 and 22.
*The Gas Cylinders (Conveyance) Regulations 1959.	S.I. 1959/1919.	The whole Regulations.
The Shipbuilding and Shiprepairing Regulations 1960.	S.I. 1960/1932.	Regulation 68.
The Shipbuilding (Air Receivers) Order 1961.	S.I. 1961/430.	The whole Order.
The Examination of Steam Boilers Regulations 1964.	S.I. 1964/781.	The whole Regulations.
The Examination of Steam Boiler Reports (No. 1) Order 1964.	S.I. 1964/1070.	The whole Order.

(1)	(2)	(3)
Title of instrument	*Reference*	*Extent of revocation*
The Factories Act 1961 etc. (Repeals and Modifications) Regulations 1974.	S.I. 1974/1941.	Paragraph 3 of Schedule 2 to the said Regulations.
*The Petroleum (Regulation) Acts 1928 and 1936 (Repeals and Modifications) Regulations 1974.	S.I. 1974/1942.	Regulation 4(1).
*The Petroleum (Consolidation) Act 1928 (Enforcement).	S.I. 1979/427.	In the Schedule to the said Regulations the whole of each item modifying the Gas Cylinders (Conveyance) Regulations 1931 and the Compressed Gas Cylinders (Fuel for Motor Vehicles) Regulations 1940.
The Gasholders and Steam Boilers Regulations (Metriculation) Regulations 1981.	S.I. 1981/687.	Regulation 3 and the Schedule to the said Regulations.

(*See paragraph 2 of Part I of Schedule 1.)

PART IV
MODIFICATIONS OF INSTRUMENTS

(1)	(2)	(3)
Title of instrument	*Reference*	*Extent of modification*
The Visiting Forces and International Headquarters (Application of Law) Order 1965.	S.I. 1965/1536.	In Article 16(3) for the words "Sections 32 to 34 (which relate to steam boilers)" substitute the words "Section 34 (which relates to steam boilers)."
*The Highly Flammable Liquids and Liquefied Petroleum Gases Regulations 1972.	S.I. 1972/917.	For regulation 7(7) there shall be substituted the following— "In this regulation 'cylinder' means a cylinder which complies with the conditions specified in regulation 16(2)(a) or (b) of the Pressure Systems and Transportable Gas Containers Regulations 1989".

(1)	(2)	(3)
Title of instrument	*Reference*	*Extent of modification*
*The Abstract of Special Regulations (Highly Flammable Liquids and Liquefied Petroleum Gases) Order 1974.	S.I. 1974/1587.	In the Schedule to the Order for the provision which relates to regulation 7(7) of the Highly Flammable Liquids and Liquefied Petroleum Gases Regulations 1972 there shall be substituted the following— "In this regulation 'cylinder' means a cylinder which complies with the conditions specified in regulation 16(2)(a) or (b) of the Pressure Systems and Transportable Gas Containers Regulations 1989".

(*See paragraph 2 of Part I of Schedule 1.)

THE ELECTRICAL EQUIPMENT FOR EXPLOSIVE ATMOSPHERES (CERTIFICATION) REGULATIONS 1990

(S.I. 1990 No. 13 (as amended by S.I. 1990 No. 2377,
S.I. 1991 No. 2570, S.I. 1991 No. 2826))

1. Citation, commencement and extent. These Regulations, which extend to Great Britain, may be cited as the Electrical Equipment for Explosive Atmospheres (Certification) Regulations 1990 and shall come into force on 31 January 1990.

2. Interpretation.—(1) In these Regulations, unless the context otherwise requires—

"certificate of conformity" means the certificate referred to in Article 8 of *the Framework Directive* except that in relation to the *electrical equipment* designed for work underground in mines susceptible to firedamp it means the certificate referred to in Article 8 of *the Gassy Mines Directive*;

"electrical equipment" means any constituent part of an electrical installation or any other electrical device to which *the Framework Directive* or *the Gassy Mines Directive* applies;

"the First Specific Directive" means Council Directive No. 79/196/EEC concerning *electrical equipment* for use in potentially explosive atmospheres employing certain types of protection, as adapted to technical progress by Commission Directives No. 84/47/EEC and No. 88/571/EEC and as amended by Council Directive No. 90/487/EEC;

"the Framework Directive" means Council Directive No. 76/117/EEC concerning electrical equipment for use in potentially explosive atmospheres;

"the Gassy Mines Directive" means Council Directive No. 82/130/EEC concerning *electrical equipment* for use in potentially explosive atmospheres in mines susceptible to firedamp, as adapted to technical progress by Commission Directive No. 88/35/EEC;

"harmonised standards" means the standards specified in Annex 1 of *the First Specific Directive* except that in relation to the *electrical equipment* designed for work underground in mines susceptible to firedamp it means the standards specified in Annex A (amended in accordance with Annex B) to *the Gassy Mines Directive*;

"certification body" means a body appointed for the purposes of regulation 3(1);

"inspection certificate" means the certificate referred to in Article 9 of *the Framework Directive* except that in relation to the *electrical equipment* designed for work underground in mines susceptible to firedamp it means the certificate referred to in Article 9 of *the Gassy Mines Directive*.

845

(2) Unless the context otherwise requires, any reference in these Regulations to—

(a) a numbered regulation, is a regulation to the regulation so numbered in these Regulations;

(b) a numbered paragaph, is a reference to the paragraph so numbered in the regulation in which that reference appears.

3.   Appointment of *certification bodies.*—(1) The Secretary of State shall appoint a body or bodies of persons for any one or more of the following purposes, that is to say,—

(a) of assessing and testing *electrical equipment* (or such electrical equipment as may be specified in the appointment) to determine whether it conforms to the appropriate *harmonised standards* and of issuing certificates of conformity;

(b) of assessing and testing *electrical equipment* (or such *electrical equipment* as may be specified in the appointment) which differs from *harmonised standards* to determine whether it offers a degree of safety at least equivalent to those standards and of issuing *inspection certificates*;

(c) of carrying out surveillance of the manufacture of *electrical equipment* (or such *electrical equipment* as may be specified in the appointment) to ascertain whether the equipment conforms to the type of equipment in respect of which a *certificate of conformity* or, as the case may be, an *inspection certificate* has been issued;

(d) of doing such other things as may be required or permitted by or in connection with these Regulations,

on such conditions as he thinks fit for the efficient and proper functioning of such body or bodies.

(2) The said appointment may be for a fixed or indefinite time and may be revoked at any time; the Secretary of State may also vary or withdraw any or all of the conditions of appointment or impose additional conditions at any time for the efficient and proper functioning of the *certification body*.

4.   Certificates of conformity.—(1) A manufacturer of *electrical equipment* may apply to a *certification body* (which has been appointed for the purpose set out in regulation 3(1)(a) in respect of the *electrical equipment* for which the application is made) for a *certificate of conformity* attesting that the *electrical equipment* which is the subject of the application conforms to the *harmonised standards*.

(2) The application shall be in writing and shall be accompanied by such information and documents as the *certification body* may reasonably require. Samples of the equipment to which the application relates and such other information and documents as the *certification body* may reasonably require shall be provided by the manufacturer when so requested by that body.

(3) On receipt of an application for a *certificate of conformity* in relation to *electrical equipment*, the *certification body* shall, on receipt of such fee as may be agreed between the *certification body* and the manufacturer (or on receipt of the acceptance by the manufacturer of the quotation given to him by the *certification body* in respect of such fee), carry out such checks, examinations and tests as are required for it to determine whether the *electrical equipment* conforms to the *harmonised standards*.

(4) If, as a result of the checks, examinations and tests carried out in accordance with paragraph (3), the *certification body* determines that the equipment conforms to the *harmonised standards* it shall issue to the manufacturer a *certificate of conformity* attesting that the equipment conforms to the *harmonised standards* and shall draw up a report of its determination.

(5) The *certificate of conformity* may be issued subject to such conditions as the *certification body* may reasonably stipulate.

5. Inspection certificates.—(1) A manufacturer of *electrical equipment* may apply to a *certification body* (which has been appointed for the purpose set out in regulation 3(1)(b) in respect of the *electrical equipment* for which the application is made) for an *inspection certificate* attesting that the *electrical equipment* which is the subject of the application offers a degree of safety at least equivalent to that of the *harmonised standards*.

(2) The application shall be in writing and shall be accompanied by such information and documents as the *certification body* may reasonably require. Samples of the equipment to which the application relates and such other information and documents as the *certification body* may reasonably require shall be provided by the manufacturer when so requested by that body.

(3) On receipt of an application for an *inspection certificate* in relation to *electrical equipment*, the *certification body* shall, on receipt of such fee as may be agreed between the *certification body* and the manufacturer (or on receipt of the acceptance by the manufacturer of the quotation given him by the *certification body* in respect of such fee), carry out such checks, examinations and tests as are required for it to determine whether the *electrical equipment* which is the subject of the application offers a degree of safety at least equivalent to that of the *harmonised standards*.

(4) If as a result of the checks, examinations and tests carried out in accordance with paragraph (3), the *certification body* determines that the equipment offers a degree of safety at least equivalent to that of the *harmonised standards*, it shall, in the case of *electrical equipment* for use in mines draw up a report of its determination, and in every case proceed in accordance with paragraphs (5) to (7).

(5) The *certification body* shall send the specifications of the equipment, the inspection records, the draft *inspection certificate* and, in the case of *electrical equipment* for use in mines, the report of its determination to the other Member States or to their *certification bodies* or both which, within 4 months of receiving those documents, may submit comments, ask for additional inspections and where appropriate refer the matter to the Committee set up under Article 6 of *the Framework Directive* in accordance with Article 7 of that Directive or, in the case of *electrical equipment* for use in mines, to the Committee referred to in Article 6 of *the Gassy Mines Directive* in accordance with Article 7 of that Directive (in either case hereinafter referred to as "the Committee').

(6) If no Member State requests that the matter be referred to the Committee by the end of the period specified in paragraph (5), after considering the comments submitted in accordance with the procedure specified in that paragraph and if the results of any additional inspections requested are satisfactory, the *certification body* shall issue the *inspection certificate*.

(7) If a Member State requests that the matter be referred to the Committee, the *certification body* shall not issue an *inspection certificate* unless it has received a favourable opinion from the Committee.

(8) The *inspection certificate* may be issued subject to such conditions as the *certification body* may reasonably stipulate.

6.   Refusal and withdrawal of *certificates of conformity* and *inspection certificates*.—(1) Where a *certification body* decides that it cannot issue a *certificate of conformity* or an *inspection certificate* it shall forthwith send the manufacturer a notice in writing of that decision.

(2) The *certification body* which has issued the *certificate of conformity* or the *inspection certificate* may withdraw the certificate if it has reason to believe that—

(a) the certificate should not have been issued;
(b) the conditions stipulated by the *certification body* have not been complied with within a reasonable specified period; or
(c) the *electrical equipment* distributed by the manufacturer is not in conformity with the certified design.

(3) Where the *certification body* decides to withdraw a *certificate of conformity* or an *inspection certificate* it shall forthwith send the manufacturer a notice in writing of its decision.

(4) Notices under paragraphs (1) and (3) shall—

(a) state in detail the grounds on which the decision is based;
(b) inform the manufacturer of his right to a review under regulation 7 and of the time-limit for making the application for review referred to in paragraph (1) of that regulation.

7.   Review of decisions.—(1) Subject to paragraph (2), a manufacturer who is aggrieved by the decision of a *certification body*—

(a) refusing to issue a *certificate of conformity* or an *inspection certificate*;
(b) issuing him a certificate on or subject to any condition whereby he is aggrieved; or
(c) withdrawing a certificate in accordance with regulation 6(2),

may within 60 days of receiving notice of the decision apply to the Secretary of State for a review of the decision in accordance with the procedure set out in regulation 8.

(2) Paragraph (1) shall not apply to the decision of a *certification body* refusing to issue an *inspection certificate*, if the sole reason for the decision is that the Committee referred to in regulation 5(5) had not reached a favourable opinion in relation to the application.

8.   Procedure for review.—(1) An application for review shall be made in writing to the Secretary of State and shall state the grounds on which it is made and shall be accompanied by—

(a) copies of the documents which the applicant provided to the *certification body* in connection with the application; and

(b) a copy of the notice of the decision referred to in regulation 6(1), or as the case may be, in regulation 6(3).

(2) On an application for review the Secretary of State may—

(a) hold an enquiry in connection therewith; and

(b) appoint one or more assessors for the purpose of assisting with the review or any such enquiry.

(3) The Secretary of State may, in such cases as he considers it appropriate to do so, having regard to the nature of the questions which appear to him to arise, direct that an application for review under this regulation shall be heard, but not determined, on his behalf by a person appointed by him for that purpose.

(4) Where an application for review is to be heard by a person appointed in pursuance of paragraph (3), he shall hold an enquiry in connection therewith, and at the conclusion of the enquiry he shall prepare his report comprising a summary of the evidence given or submitted at the enquiry together with his findings of fact and include therein his recommendations if any or his reason for not making any recommendation. He shall then send his report (together with all the documents and papers that he took into consideration in preparing his report) to the Secretary of State. After considering the report, all the relevant documents and papers, the Secretary of State shall determine the review.

(5) On an application for review the Secretary of State shall have the power to do anything which a *certification body* is authorised or required to do under these Regulations. He shall, if he determines to find in favour of the manufacturer, grant the application, and shall require the *certification body* to issue the appropriate certificate subject to such conditions as the Secretary of State may stipulate and upon being so required the *certification body* shall issue the certificate forthwith.

(6) A copy of the determination (and, where appropriate, of the report) shall be sent to each of the parties to the review.

(7) The Secretary of State may pay to any person appointed to hear an application for review under this regulation on his behalf such remuneration and allowances as the Secretary of State may with the consent of the Treasury determine.

9. Notification to the European Commission and to Member States.— (1) The Secretary of State shall send to the European Commission and the other Member States a list of the *certification bodies* appointed by him under regulation 3(1) and shall immediately notify any change in that list.

(2) A *certification body* shall send to—

(a) the Secretary of State; and

(b) the other Member States,

a copy of the main points in any *certificate of conformity* or *inspection certificate* that it has issued within one month of issuing the certificate, and shall make available to them or any one or more of them on request copies of the reports drawn in accordance with regulation 4(4) or regulation 5(4).

(3) Where a *certification body* decides to withdraw a *certificate of conformity* or an *inspection certificate* in accordance with regulation 6(2), it shall forthwith notify

its decision to the bodies specified in sub-paragraphs (a) and (b) of paragraph (2), stating the grounds for the decision.

10.   Access to place of manufacture.—(1) The manufacturer of *electrical equipment* which is the subject of an application for a *certificate of conformity* or of an *inspection certificate* shall allow the *certification body* reasonable access to the place where the equipment is manufactured if such access is essential to assist the proper determination of the application.

(2) The manufacturer shall also allow the *certification body* reasonable access to the place where the equipment is manufactured for the purpose specified in regulation 3(1)(c).

11.   Use of the distinctive Community mark.—(1) Where a *certificate of conformity* or an *inspection certificate* relating to *electrical equipment* is in force, the manufacturer of that equipment may affix to it the appropriate distinctive Community mark that is to say,—

(a) for *electrical equipment* to which *the Framework Directive* applies, that specified in Annex II to *the First Specific Directive* and such mark shall have effect as described in paragraph 1 of Article 10 of that Directive;

(b) for *electrical equipment* to which *the Gassy Mines Directive* applies, that specified in Annex C to *the Gassy Mines Directive* and such mark shall attest in accordance with paragraph 1 of Article 11 of that Directive.

(2) Where required by the *certificate of conformity* or *inspection certificate*, the manufacturer shall ensure that when equipment is supplied, it is accompanied by instructions defining the special conditions governing its use.

(3) The manufacturer shall not affix to *electrical equipment* the appropriate distinctive Community mark unless there is in force the appropriate *certificate of conformity* or the appropriate *inspection certificate* in relation to that equipment and the equipment complies in all respects with the terms of the relevant certificate.

(4) No person shall affix to *electrical equipment* any mark which is liable to be confused with the appropriate distinctive Community mark.

(5) Paragraphs (3) and (4) shall have effect as if they were health and safety regulations made under section 15 of the Health and Safety at Work etc. Act 1974 and the provisions of that Act as regards enforcement and offences shall apply to those paragraphs.

12.   Transitional provisions.—(1) On or after 31 December 1991, a manufacturer of *electrical equipment* to which *the Gassy Mines directive* applies may apply to a *certification body* (which has been appointed for the purpose set out in regulation 3(1)(a) of the unamended Regulations in respect of the *electrical equipment* for which the application is made) for issue of a *certificate of conformity* before 1 January 1993 attesting that the equipment which is the subject of the application conforms to the *harmonised standards* prescribed in the unamended Regulations; and in that case the provisions of the unamended Regulations, as appropriate, shall apply as if the application had been made under regulation 4 of those Regulations.

(2) An application for a *certificate of conformity* made under regulation 4 or for review under regulation 7 of the unamended Regulations before 31 December 1991 shall continue to be dealt with under the unamended Regulations as if the Electrical Equipment for Explosive Atmospheres (Certification) (Amendment) (No. 2) Regulations 1991 had not been made; and subject to regulation 6, a *certificate of conformity* issued before 1 January 1993, whether before, on or after 31 December 1991, in accordance with the unamended Regulations (attesting that the *electrical equipment* to which *the Gassy Mines Directive* applies conforms to the *harmonised standards* prescribed in the unamended Regulations) or by virtue of paragraph (1) shall remain valid until the end of 31 December 2009.

(3) In this regulation "the unamended Regulations" means these Regulations as in force immediately before 31 December 1991.

THE ELECTRICALLY, HYDRAULICALLY AND OIL-ELECTRICALLY OPERATED LIFTS (COMPONENTS) (EEC REQUIREMENTS) REGULATIONS 1991

(S.I. 1991 No. 2748)

The Secretary of State, being a Minister designated for the purposes of section 2(2) of the European Communities Act 1972 in relation to technical requirements relating to electrically operated lifts and their components and to hydraulically and oil-electrically operated lifts and their components, in exercise of the powers conferred on him by that section and of all his other enabling powers, hereby makes the following Regulations:—

1. Citation, commencement and revocation.—(1) These Regulations may be cited as the Electrically, Hydraulically and Oil-Electrically Operated Lifts (Components) (EEC Requirements) Regulations 1991, and shall come into force on 1 January 1992.

(2) The Electrically Operated Lifts (EEC Requirements) Regulations 1986 ("the 1986 Regulations") are hereby revoked provided that—

(a) any application made for an *EEC type-examination certificate*;

(b) any undertaking provided with or in respect of any such application;

(c) any *EEC type-examination certificate* issued (together with any conditions attached to such certificate);

(d) any certificate of conformity issued in respect of a component and EEC mark placed on a component, pursuant to such a certificate; or

(e) any other thing done,

under the 1986 Regulations (even if the form specified in the 1986 Regulations is different from that specified for the purposes of these Regulations) shall be deemed to have been made, provided, issued, placed or done under these Regulations and accordingly the provisions of these Regulations shall apply thereto.

2. Interpretation.—(1) In these Regulations, unless the context otherwise requires, the following expressions have the following meanings—

"approved body" means a body approved by the Secretary of State under Regulation 3;

"approved other body" means a body charged by a Member State other than the United Kingdom to carry out functions similar to those authorised to be carried out by an *approved body* under these Regulations;

"component" means—
  (i) landing-door locking devices;
 (ii) overspeed governors (car and counterweight);
(iii) safety gears (car and counterweight);
(iv) buffers (energy accumulation type with buffered return movement and energy dissipation buffers),
designed for use with a *lift*;

"the Directives" means Council Directive 84/528/EEC on the approximation of the laws of the Member States relating to common provisions for lifting and mechanical handling appliances and Council Directive 84/529/EEC on the approximation of the laws of the Member States relating to electrically operated *lifts* as adapted to technical progress by Commission Directive 86/312/EEC and as extended to hydraulically and oil-electrically operated *lifts* by Council Directive 90/486/EEC;

"EEC inspection" means the procedure by which an *approved body* or an *approved other body* checks—

(a) whether *components* conform with the type of component in respect of which an *EEC type-examination certificate* has been issued or *extended*;
(b) whether adequate manufacturing control facilities are provided and adequate manufacturing control records are kept by or on behalf of the manufacturer;
(c) whether the manufacturer actually carries out adequate checks to verify whether *components* manufactured by him conform with the type of *component* in respect of which an *EEC type-examination certificate* has been issued or *extended*; and
(d) whether the EEC mark is being used correctly;

"EEC type-examination certificate" means a certificate that a type of components conforms with the *EEC type-examination requirements*;

"EEC type-examination requirements" means the technical requirements referred to in *the Directives* as set out in Schedule 1;

"extend" or "extended" in relation to an *EEC type-examination certificate* means extend or extended pursuant to Regulation 4(5);

"holder" means the manufacturer, or the authorised representative established in the Community, to whom an *EEC type-examination certificate* has been issued pursuant to an application under Regulation 4(1); and

"lift" means any permanently installed electrically, hydraulically or oil-electrically operated hoisting appliance serving specific levels, having a car designed for the transport of persons or of persons and goods, suspended by ropes or chains or supported by one or more rams and moving at least partially between guides which are vertical or inclined at an angle of less than 150 to the vertical, but excluding—

  (i) lifts specially designed for military or research purposes, or those used as equipment on ships, on offshore prospecting and drilling rigs, in mines, or for the handling of radioactive materials;
 (ii) lifts intended exclusively for the transport of goods; and
(iii) any of the following hoisting appliances: paternosters, rack-and-pinion elevators, screw-driven elevators, theatre elevators, loading appliances, skips, lifts and goods hoists on building or public works sites, construction or maintenance equipment and lifts specially constructed for transporting the handicapped.

(2) Any reference in these Regulations to a numbered regulation or Schedule is a reference to the regulation or Schedule so numbered in these Regulations.

3.   *Approved bodies.*—(1) The Secretary of State may approve a body—

  (a)   to carry out examinations of *components* to ascertain whether or not they conform with the *EEC type-examination requirements*;
  (b)   to issue and extend *EEC type-examination certificates*;
  (c)   to carry out *EEC inspection*; and
  (d)   to do such other things as may be required or permitted under or in connection with these Regulations.

(2) Any approval of a body as an *approved body* by the Secretary of State, for the purposes of paragraph (1) of this regulation, may be given for an unlimited period or a specified period and may be given subject to terms and conditions and the Secretary of State may withdraw any such approval if the body ceases to comply with any such term or condition.

4.   *EEC type-examination certificates.*—(1) An application for an *EEC type-examination certificate* may be made to an *approved body* by a manufacturer, or his authorised representative established in the Community; such application shall be in writing, shall contain the information and documents set out in Schedule 2, and shall be accompanied by—

  (a)   an undertaking by the manufacturer in the form set out in Schedule 3; and
  (b)   where the application is made by his authorised representative, an undertaking by that authorised representative in the form set out in Schedule 3A;

and, if required by the *approved body*—

  (c)   an example of the type of *component* in respect of which the application is made; or
  (d)   the presribed fee in advance; or
  (e)   both (c) and (d) above.

(2) Where an application is made to an *approved body* in respect of a type of *component* and the *approved body* is aware, on receipt of that application, that another application has been made to another *approved body* or to an *approved other body* in respect of a *component* of that type manufactured by the same manufacturer, the *approved body* shall reject the application made to it and shall return any prescribed fee accompanying that application.

(3) Where the *approved body* is satisfied, on application made to it and after examination of an example of the type of *component* in respect of which the application was made, that the examined component conforms with the *EEC type-examination requirements* and after payment of the prescribed fee (if so required), unless such prescribed fee has been paid in advance under paragraph (1) of this regulation, it shall issue an *EEC type-examination certificate* in the form set out in Schedule 4 in respect of that type of *component* which shall be valid for a period of 10 years.

(4) Where the *approved body* is satisfied, on application made to it and after examination of an example of the type of *component* in respect of which the

application was made, that the examined *component* does not conform with the *EEC type-examination requirements* and after payment of the prescribed fee (if so required), unless such prescribed fee has been paid in advance under paragraph (1) of this regulation, it shall issue a test failure report which states the reasons for the issue of such report and informs the applicant of his right to apply for review of the decision of the *approved body* under regulation 9.

(5) On application made to the *approved body* by the manufacturer, or his authorised representative established in the Community, in writing and accompanied, if required by the *approved body*, by the prescribed fee, the *approved body* shall *extend* by a period of ten years the validity of an *EEC type-examination certificate* issued or *extended* by it under these Regulations and which has not been suspended or withdrawn.

(6) An *approved body* shall issue an *EEC type-examination certificate* or *extend* such a certificate subject to the conditions set out in the form of undertaking specified in Schedule 3 and, where the applicant is an authorised representative, specified in Schedule 3A.

5. Certificate of conformity and EEC mark of conformity. The manufacturer of a *component* which conforms with a type of component in respect of which an *EEC type-examination certificate* issued or *extended* under these Regulations, or under the law of a Member State other than the United Kingdom, is in force may issue a certificate of conformity in the form set out in Schedule 5 that such *component* conforms with that type, and may place on such *component* the EEC mark of conformity in the form set out in Schedule 6.

6. *EEC inspection.*—(1) An *approved body* shall either carry out or ensure that another *approved body* or an *approved other body* carries out at its request and on its behalf *EEC inspection* in respect of *components* of the same type as that for which it has issued or *extended* an *EEC type-examination certificate* under these Regulations and during the period for which such certificate remains in force.

(2) An *approved body* may carry out *EEC inspection* in respect of components of the type for which an *EEC type-examination certificate* has been issued or *extended* by another *approved body* or an *approved other body* if requested to do so by and on behalf of that other body, and shall send a report in writing following such inspection to that other body.

(3) Following an *EEC inspection* under paragraph (1) of this regulation, the approved body shall issue a report in writing to the *holder* of the *EEC type-examination certificate* and may require the *holder* of such certificate to pay to the *approved body* the prescribed fee.

7. Prescribed fee. The prescribed fee mentioned in regulation 4(1), (3), (4) and (5) and in regulation 6(3) in each case shall not exceed the sum of—

    (a) the costs of the *approved body* of and in connection with the work done or to be done by it or on its behalf under these Regulations; and

    (b) an amount on account of profit which is reasonable in the circumstances having regard to—

        (i) the character and the extent of the work done or to be done by the *approved body* under these Regulations, and

(ii) the commercial rate normally charged on account of profit for that work or similar work.

8.   Suspension and withdrawal of *EEC type-examination certificate*.—(1) If an *approved body*, after checking a *component* or after receipt of a report from another *approved body* or an *approved other body* made at the request of the *approved body*, is satisfied that a *component* of the same type as that in respect of which it has issued or *extended* an *EEC type-examination certificate* under these Regulations and which certificate remains in force has not been manufactured to conform with the *EEC type-examination requirements* in respect of such *component*, the *approved body* shall give notice to the *holder* or such certificate.

(2) If it appears to an *approved body* which has issued or *extended* an *EEC type-examination certificate* and which certificate remains in force that any condition subject to which it was issued or *extended* has not been fulfilled, the *approved body* may give notice to the *holder* of such certificate.

(3) Any notice given under paragraph (1) or (2) of this regulation shall specify—

(a) the respects in which the *component* does not so conform or the condition appears not to have been fulfilled; and

(b) that, unless the *approved body* is satisfied by the *holder* of the certificate within a specified period that *components* of the same type manufactured by the same manufacturer do so conform or that the condition is fulfilled, the certificate will be suspended or withdrawn; or

(c) if the *approved body* thinks fit, that the certificate is suspended with immediate effect.

(4) If, after the period specified under paragraph (3)(b) of this regulation, the *approved body* decides to suspend or withdraw an *EEC type-examination certificate* the *approved body* shall immediately give notice of the decision to the *holder* of the certificate and shall specify that the suspension or withdrawal is of immediate effect or the date on which the suspension or withdrawal is to take effect.

(5) A notice given under this regulation in respect of a decision to suspend or withdraw an *EEC type-examination certificate* shall specify the grounds for the decision, the conditions for revoking any suspension and shall inform the *holder* of the certificate of his right to apply for a review of the decision under regulation 9.

(6) If the *approved body* decides to suspend or withdraw an *EEC type-examination certificate* under this regulation it shall immediately give notice of the decision to the Secretary of State.

(7) The suspension or withdrawal of an *EEC type-examination certificate* shall not affect the validity of any certificate of conformity or EEC mark of conformity issued or placed on a *component* under regulation 5 prior to that suspension or withdrawal.

9.   Review.—(1) A person who is aggrieved by a decision given by an *approved body* under regulation 4(4), or under regulation 8(1), (2) or (4) may, in accordance with paragraphs (2) and (3) of this regulation, apply to the Sec-

retary of State to review that decision and on such application the Secretary of
State—

(a)   shall have the like powers as an *approved body*;

(b)   may hold an inquiry in connection therewith; and

(c)   may appoint an assessor for the purpose of assisting him with his review
or any such inquiry.

(2)   An application under paragraph (1) of this regulation shall be made by
notice to the Secretary of State, and shall be lodged with him not later than
twenty eight days from the date of receipt of the test failure report issued under
regulation 4(4) or of the notice issued under regulation 8 containing the
decision in respect of which the application for review is made.

(3)   A notice of application for review under this regulation shall state the
grounds on which the application is made and shall be accompanied by copies
of the information, documents, and the undertaking or undertakings which, in
accordance with regulation 4(1), were contained in or accompanied the application under that regulation for the *EEC type-examination certificate* in question,
and

(a)   where the application is for review of a decision under regulation 4(4), a
copy of the test failure report; or

(b)   where the application for review relates to the suspension or withdrawal
of an *EEC type-examination certificate*, a copy of that certificate and of any
notice issued under regulation 8.

(4)   On completion of the review the Secretary of State shall inform the
aggrieved person and the approved body concerned of the outcome of such
review.

SCHEDULE 1

Regulation 2(1)

EEC TYPE-EXAMINATION REQUIREMENTS

The *EEC type-examination requirements* referred to in regulation 2(1), with which *components* must comply, are the following standards adopted by the European Committee for
Standardisation (CEN):

EN81-1 (edition: December 1985). Safety rules for the construction and installation of
lifts and service *lifts*. Part 1: electric *lifts*, for electrically operated *lifts*, and

EN82-2 (edition: November 1987). Safety rules for the construction and installation
of *lifts* and services *lifts*. Part 2: hydraulic *lifts*, for hydraulically and oil-electrically
operated *lifts*.

These standards shall apply, subject to the following modifications required by *the
Directives*:

Section 13.1.1.4

Replace by the following:

"The electrical installations for *lifts* must:

(a)   comply with the requirements stated in the Cenelec harmonised documents
accepted by the national electrotechnical committees of the EEC Member States;

(b)   where no harmonised documents on electrical installations as referred to in (a)
exist, comply with the requirements of the national rules of the country in which
the *lift* is installed."

Section 13.1.2
    Replace by the following:
    "In the machine and pulley rooms, protection against direct contact by means of
casings providing a degree of protection of at least 1P 2X is necessary."

Section F.O. 1.6
    Add the following:
    "... in accordance with Article 13(2) of Directive 84/528/EEC."

SCHEDULE 2

Regulation 4(1)

INFORMATION AND DOCUMENTS TO BE PROVIDED BY THE APPLICANT FOR
EEC TYPE-EXAMINATION

The following information and documents shall be given in English:
  — the name and address of the manufacturer, and of his authorised representative
    established in the Community if the latter is the applicant.
  — the category of *component*.
  — its intended use and any prohibited use.
  — its trade name, if any, or type.
  — the technical characteristics of the *component*.
  — the position on the component where the EEC mark of conformity is to be affixed.
  — a statement certifying that no other application for EEC type-examination has
    been submitted for the same type of *component* to another *approved body* or an
    approved other body.
Two copies are to be provided of all required documents.

SCHEDULE 3

Regulation 4(1)

FORM OF UNDERTAKING BY MANUFACTURER

Category, type and make or trade name of *component*: ....
....
....
....

    I/We undertake as a condition of issue of an *EEC type-examination certificate* and the use
of the EEC mark of conformity, to comply with the following conditions:

1. To inform the *approved body* granting the *EEC type-examination certificate* of—
  (a) the places where the *components* of the same type as that in respect of which the
       application is made are manufactured and/or warehoused, as requested by the
       approved body; and
  (b) the date on which manufacture commences,
and to provide such other information as the *approved body* may reasonably require.

2. To allow representatives of the *approved body*, or of another *approved body* or of an
approved other body as defined in the Regulations, if requested to do so by the *approved
body*—
  (a) access for the purpose of *EEC inspection* to the places of manufacture and/or
       warehousing by me/us or on my/our behalf;
  (b) to take samples of components for *EEC inspection* purposes; and
  (c) access to manufacturing control records kept by me/us.

3. To carry out adequate manufacturing control and inspection including keeping
adequate records.

4. To have at my/our disposal the necessary equipment for monitoring the conformity of *components* manufactured with the type of component in respect of which the *EEC type-examination certificate* is granted.

5. To ensure that *components* do not bear any sign or inscription liable to be confused with the EEC mark.

6. To pay the prescribed fee under the Regulations if so required by the *approved body* (unless already paid by my/our authorised representative established in the Community).

Signed .... Position ....

On behalf of .... Date ....

SCHEDULE 3A

Regulation 4(1)

FORM OF UNDERTAKING BY THE AUTHORISED REPRESENTATIVE WHERE THAT
AUTHORISED REPRESENTATIVE IS THE APPLICANT FOR AN
EEC TYPE-EXAMINATION CERTIFICATE

Category, type and make or trade name of *component*: ....

....

I/We undertake as a condition of issue of an *EEC type-examination certificate* and the use of the EEC mark of conformity, to comply with the following conditions:

1. To inform the *approved body* granting the *EEC type-examination certificate* of the places where the *components* of the same type as that in respect of which the application is made are warehoused, as requested by the *approved body*, and to provide such other information as the *approved body* may reasonably require.

2. To allow representatives of the *approved body*, or of another *approved body* or of an *approved other body* as defined in the Regulations, if requested to do so by the *approved body*—

    (a) access for the purpose of *EEC inspection* to the places of warehousing by me/us or on my/our behalf;

    (b) to take samples of *components* for *EEC inspection* purposes; and

    (c) access to manufacturing control records kept by me/us.

3. To ensure that *components* do not bear any sign or inscription liable to be confused with the EEC mark.

4. To pay the prescribed fee under the Regulations if so required by the *approved body* (unless already paid by the manufacturer).

Signed .... Position ....

On behalf of .... Date ....

SCHEDULE 4

Regulation 4(3)

EEC TYPE-EXAMINATION CERTIFICATE

Name of the *approved body* ....

....

....

EEC type-examination certificate ....
....
....

EEC type-examination No. ....
  1 Category, type and make or trade name ....
  2 Manufacturer's name and address ....
  3 Name and address of certificate *holder* (if different from above) ....
....
....

  4 Date of submission for type-examination ....
  5 Certificate issued on the basis of the following requirements:
Compliance with the undertakings dated given by the manufacturer and, where relevant, by his authorised representative.
Other conditions ....
  6 Test laboratory ....
  7 Date and number of laboratory report ....
  8 Date of EEC type-examination ....
  9 The following documents, bearing the EEC type-examination number shown above,
are annexed to this certificate ....
....
....

10 Any additional information ....
....
....

Place .... Date ....
.... (Signature)

SCHEDULE 5

Regulation 5

EEC CERTIFICATE OF CONFORMITY

I, the undersigned, ...
(surname and first names)
hereby certify that the *lift component* which this certificate accompanies, as described
below:
  1 Category ....
  2 Manufactured by ....
  3 Type ....
  4 Serial No. ....
  5 Year of manufacture ....
  is in conformity with the *component* which was EEC type-examined as shown below

| | Directives | Type-examination certificate | | |
| | | No. | Date | approved body |

84/529/EEC*
90/486/EEC
*as amended by 86/312/EEC

Done at .... Date ....
(Signature)
....
(Position)

SCHEDULE 6

EEC Mark of Conformity

the year EEC type-examination
certificate granted

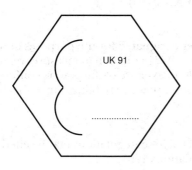

the certificate number

Note:
1   Letters and digits must be at least 5 mm high.
2   The mark must be visibly, legibly and indelibly fixed to each component.
3   The figure 91 is for purposes of illustration and refers to an EEC type-examination
    in 1991.

THE SIMPLE PRESSURE VESSELS (SAFETY) REGULATIONS 1991

(S.I. 1991 No. 2749)

The Secretary of State, being a Minister designated for the purposes of section 2(2) of the European Communities Act 1972 in relation to measures relating to safety as regards simple pressure vessels, in exercise of the powers conferred on him by the said section 2(2) and of all other powers enabling him in that behalf, hereby makes the following Regulations:—

1. Citation and commencement.—(1) These Regulations may be cited as the Simple Pressure Vessels (Safety) Regulations 1991.

(2) These Regulations shall come into force on 31 December 1991.

2. Interpretation.—(1) In these Regulations, "vessel" means a simple pressure vessel being a welded vessel intended to contain air or nitrogen at a gauge pressure greater than 0.5 bar, not intended for exposure to flame, and having the following characteristics—

(a) the components and assemblies contributing to the strength of the vessel under pressure are made either of non-alloy quality steel, or of non-alloy aluminium, or of non-age hardening aluminium alloy;

(b) the vessel consists either—
  (i) of a cylindrical component with circular cross-section, closed at each end, each end being either outwardly dished or flat and being also coaxial with the cylindrical component; or
  (ii) of two co-axial outwardly dished ends;

(c) the maximum working pressure (PS) is not more than 30 bar, and PS. V (being the product of PS and the vessel's capacity expressed in litres) is not more than 10,000 bar. litres;

(d) the minimum working temperature is not lower than minus 50°C, and the maximum working temperature is not higher than—

300°C in the case of steel vessels; and
100°C in the case of aluminium or aluminium alloy vessels,

and in this paragraph—

  (i) "maximum working pressure" means the maximum gauge pressure which may be exerted under normal conditions of use;
  (ii) "minimum working temperature" means the lowest stabilised temperature in the wall of the vessel under normal conditions of use; and
  (iii) "maximum working temperature" means the highest stabilised temperature in the wall of the vessel under normal conditions of use.

(2) The categories of vessels relevant for the purposes of these Regulations are—

Category A — vessels whose PS.V is more than 50 bar. litres, this category being subdivided into—
Category A.1 — vessels whose PS.V is more than 3,000 bar. litres;
Category A.2 — vessels whose PS.V is more than 200 but not more than 3,000 bar. litres; and
Category A.3 — vessels whose PS.V is more than 50 but not more than 200 bar. litres;
Category B — vessels whose PS.V is 50 bar. litres or less.

(3) In these Regulations—

"the Community" means the European Economic Community;
"the Commission" means the Commission of the European Communities;
"the Directive" means Council Directive 87/404/EEC on the harmonisation of the laws of the Member States relating to simple pressure vessels, as amended by Council Directive 90/488/EEC;
"EC mark" means the EC mark of conformity consisting of the symbol "CE" of which a form is shown for the purpose of illustration in Schedule 2;
"enforcement authority" has the meaning given by paragraph 9 of Schedule 5;
"manufacturer's instructions" means instructions—

(a) issued by or on behalf of the manufacturer; and
(b) complying with the requirements of regulation 4(5) below;

"property" includes domestic animals;
"relevant assembly" means any assembly incorporating a *vessel*;
"safe" has the meaning given by regulation 4(4) below;
"safety clearance" shall be construed in accordance with regulation 4(2) below; and
"supply" is to be read in accordance with section 46 of the Consumer Protection Act 1987, and includes offering or agreeing to supply, and exposing or possessing for supply, and "supplied" and "supplier" have the corresponding meanings.

(4) There is series manufacture within the meaning of these Regulations if more than one *vessel* of the same type is manufactured during a given period by the same continuous manufacturing processes, in accordance with a common design.

(5) Where these Regulations refer to a relevant national standard, the reference is to a standard of which a member State has, in compliance with Article 5.1 of *the Directive*, published the reference number.

3. Application.—(1) Subject to paragraph (2) of this regulation, and regulation 6 below, these Regulations apply only to *vessels* manufactured in series.

(2) These Regulations do not apply to—

(a) *vessels* designed specifically for nuclear use, where *vessel* failure might or would result in an emission of radioactivity;
(b) *vessels* intended specifically for installation in, or for use as part of the propulsive system of, a ship or aircraft; or
(c) fire-extinguishers,

and in this paragraph "ship" has the meaning given by section 742 of the Merchant Shipping Act 1894.

4.   Safety requirements.—(1) A vessel in Category A complies with this Regulation if—

(a) it meets the essential safety requirements specified in Schedule 1;

(b) it has *safety clearance*;

(c) it bears the *EC mark* accompanied by the other inscriptions specified in Schedule 2, such mark and such other inscriptions being properly affixed in accordance with that Schedule;

(d) in the case of a *vessel* or *relevant assembly supplied* in the United Kingdom, it is accompanied by the *manufacturer's instructions*;

(e) in the case where a person—

(i) being the manufacturer of a *vessel*, himself takes that *vessel* or a *relevant assembly* incorporating that *vessel* into service; or

(ii) having imported a *vessel* or *relevant assembly* into the United Kingdom, himself takes that *vessel* or a *relevant assembly* incorporating that *vessel* on the first mentioned *relevant assembly* into service,

that person ensures that, at the time of taking into service, the *manufacturer's instructions* are made available to all persons as are concerned with the *vessel's* installation and operation; and

(f) it is in fact *safe*.

(2) A *vessel* has *safety clearance* if an approved body has issued in respect of it an EC verification certificate or an EC certificate of conformity pursuant to the procedures described in regulations 9 to 13 below, and in these Regulations, "*safety clearance*" shall be construed accordingly.

(3) A vessel in Category B complies with this Regulation if—

(a) it is manufactured in accordance with engineering practice recognised as sound in a member State;

(b) it bears the inscriptions, other than the *EC mark*, specified in Schedule 2, such inscriptions being properly affixed in accordance with that Schedule; and

(c) it is in fact *safe*.

(4) "Safe", in relation to a *vessel*, means that, when the *vessel* is properly installed and maintained and used for the purposes for which it is intended, there is no risk (apart from one reduced to a minimum) of its being the cause or occasion of death or injury to persons, or damage to *property*.

(5) For the purpose of compliance with these Regulations, the *manufacturer's instructions* must provide for the following information—

(a) the manufacturer's name or mark;

(b) *vessel* type, batch identification or other particulars identifying the *vessel* to which the instructions relate;

(c) particulars of maximum working pressure expressed in bar, maximum and minimum working temperatures expressed in °C, and capacity of the *vessel* expressed in litres;

(d) the intended use of the *vessel*; and

(e) maintenance and installation requirements for *vessel* safety.

The instructions must be in the official language of the Member State where the *vessel* is to be first taken into service.

5. Obligations of manufacturers, suppliers and importers.—(1) Subject to the transitional and other exceptions in regulation 6 below, no person shall in the United Kingdom *supply* a *vessel* unless it complies with regulation 4 above or a *relevant assembly* unless the *vessel* incorporated therein so complies.

(2) Subject to the same exceptions, no person shall in the United Kingdom, being the manufacturer of a *vessel*, himself take that *vessel* or a *relevant assembly* incorporating that *vessel* into service, unless that *vessel* complies with regulation 4 above.

(3) Subject to the same exceptions, no person shall, having imported a *vessel* or a *relevant assembly* into the United Kingdom, himself take that *vessel* or a *relevant assembly* incorporating that *vessel* or the first mentioned *relevant assembly* into service in the United Kingdom, unless that *vessel*, or the *vessel* incorporated in the *relevant assembly*, as the case may be, complies with regulation 4 above.

6. Transitional and other exceptions.—(1) These Regulations do not apply—

(a) in the case of a *vessel* first *supplied* or taken into service within *the Community* before 1 July 1992 which conforms with safety requirements having effect in the United Kingdom apart from these Regulations; or
(b) in the case of a *relevant assembly* either—
  (i) first *supplied* or taken into service within *the Community* before 1 July 1992; or
  (ii) first *supplied* or taken into service within *the Community* on or after 1 July 1992, where the *vessel* incorporated in it was first *supplied* or taken into service within *the Community* before that date,
  where the *vessel* incorporated in it conforms with safety requirements having effect in the United Kingdom apart from these Regulations.

(2) These Regulations also do not apply in the case of a *vessel* or a *relevant assembly supplied* in the United Kingdom if the *supplier* believes (with reasonable cause) that it will not be taken into service either in the United Kingdom or in another Member State.

(3) These Regulations also do not apply—

(a) in the case of a *vessel* first *supplied* or taken into service within *the Community* before 1 July 1992 where—
  (i) the *supplier* believes (with reasonable cause) the *vessel* will not be taken into service in the United Kingdom; and
  (ii) the *vessel* conforms with safety requirements having effect in a Member State other than the United Kingdom in which the *supplier* believes (with reasonable cause) the *vessel* will be taken into service; or
(b) in the case of a *relevant assembly*—
  (i) first *supplied* or taken into service within *the Community* before 1 July 1992; or
  (ii) first *supplied* or taken into service within *the Community* on or after 1 July 1992, where the *vessel* incorporated in it was first *supplied* or taken into service within *the Community* before that date;

where—
   (aa) the *supplier* believes (with reasonable cause) that
         the *relevant assembly* will not be taken into service in the United
         Kingdom; and
   (bb) the *vessel* incorporated in the *relevant assembly*
         conforms with safety requirements having effect in a member
         State other than the United Kingdom in which the *supplier*
         believes (with reasonable cause) the *relevant assembly* will be
         taken into service.

(4) The exceptions provided above in this regulation do not apply in the
case of a *vessel* or *relevant assembly* where the *vessel*, or the *vessel* incorporated in
the *relevant assembly*, as the case may be, bears the *EC mark* or any other
inscription which is likely to be confused with the *EC mark*.

7.   Approved bodies.—(1) In accordance with *the Directive*, approved bodies
are charged by the Member States with functions relating to the safety of *vessels
supplied* or taken into service in *the Community*, and in particular that of providing *safety clearance*.

(2) The Secretary of State may from time to time designate such qualified
persons as he thinks fit to be United Kingdom approved bodies for the purposes
of these Regulations. Such a designation remains in force either for a period
specified by the Secretary of State, or for an indeterminate period.

(3) A designation—

(a) may relate to all descriptions of *vessels* or such descriptions (which may
     be framed by reference to any circumstances whatsoever) of *vessels* as the
     Secretary of State may from time to time determine;
(b) may be made subject to such conditions as the Secretary of State may
     from time to time determine, and such conditions may include
     conditions which are to apply upon or following withdrawal of the
     designation;
(c) shall be withdrawn—
     (i) if it appears to the Secretary of State that the approved body is no
          longer a qualified person; or
     (ii) upon 90 days' notice in writing to the Secretary of State, at the
          request of the approved body; and
(d) may be withdrawn if it appears to the Secretary of State that any of the
     conditions is not complied with.

(4) If for any reason an approved body ceases to be designated under this
regulation, the Secretary of State may authorise another United Kingdom
approved body to take over its functions in respect of such cases as he may
specify.

(5) In this regulation—

"minimum criteria" means the criteria listed in Annex III of *the Directive*
(minimum criteria to be taken into account by Member States when appointing
inspection bodies); and

"qualified person" means a person, which may include the Secretary of State, who meets the minimum criteria.

8.   Fees.—(1) Subject to paragraphs (2) and (3) below, a United Kingdom approved body may charge such fees in respect of—

(a)   the provision of *safety clearance*;
(b)   application of the *EC mark* to a *vessel* covered by an EC verification certificate pursuant to regulation 14(1) below; and
(c)   performing EC surveillance pursuant to regulation 17 below,
      as it may determine; provided that such fees shall not exceed the sum of the following—
   (i)   the costs incurred or to be incurred by the approved body in performing the relevant function; and
   (ii)   an amount on account of profit which is reasonable in the circumstances having regard to—
      (aa)   the character and extent of the work done or to be done by the body on behalf of the applicant or manufacturer as the case may be; and
      (bb)   the commercial rate normally charged on account of profit for that work or similar work.

(2)   The power in paragraph (1) above includes power—

(a)   in sub-paragraphs (a) and (b), to require the payment of fees or a reasonable estimate thereof with the application; and
(b)   in sub-paragraph (c), in a case where the fees remain unpaid 28 days after either the work has been completed or payment of the fees has been requested in writing, whichever is the later, to suspend the EC certificate of conformity by 14 days' notice in writing that, unless the fees are paid before the expiry of the notice, the certificate will be suspended until payment of the fees has been received.

(3)   Nothing in this regulation shall apply where the United Kingdom approved body is a Government department, and in this paragraph, "Government department" has the meaning given by section 56(5) of the Finance Act 1973.

9.   Safety clearance.—(1)   This and the following four regulations specify the means whereby *safety clearance* is obtained.

(2)   A person who, whether in the United Kingdom or elsewhere, proposes to manufacture *vessels* in Category A which are to be *supplied* or taken into service in *the Community* must, before commencing series manufacture, apply (either himself or through his authorised representative established in *the Community*) for and obtain for the *vessels* either—

(a)   an EC certificate of adequacy; or
(b)   an EC type-examination certificate.

(3)   If the *vessels* are to be so manufactured as to conform with a relevant national standard, it is for the manufacturer or his authorised representative to choose whether to apply for a certificate of adequacy or a type-examination certificate. In any other case, a type-examination certificate is required.

(4) Following compliance with paragraph (2) above—

(a) in the case of *vessels* in Category A.1, following commencement of series manufacture there must be applied for and obtained an EC verification certificate; and
(b) in the case of *vessels* in Category A.2 or A.3, either—
    (i) following commencement of series manufacture there must be applied for and obtained a verification certificate; or
    (ii) before commencement of series manufacture there must be carried out the alternative procedure (described in regulation 13 below) by which a manufacturer obtains an EC certificate of conformity.

(5) Application for any of the certificates above-mentioned except the certificate of conformity is made in writing by the manufacturer or his authorised representative to one or other of the approved bodies.

(6) Application for a certificate of conformity is made in writing by the manufacturer to the approved body which issued the certificate of adequacy or the type-examination certificate, as the case may be.

(7) All applications to an approved body, and documents accompanying any application, are to be in the official language of the member State in which that body is established (in the United Kingdom, English), or in another language acceptable to it.

10. EC certificate of adequacy.—(1) Application for an EC certificate of adequacy must be accompanied by the design and manufacturing schedule conforming with Schedule 3.

(2) A United Kingdom approved body to which such application is made shall, if satisfied—

(a) that the schedule contains all the required information; and
(b) that *vessels* manufactured in accordance with the schedule would conform with a relevant national standard,

issue a certificate of adequacy accordingly.

(3) If the United Kingdom approved body is not so satisfied and refuses to issue a certificate of adequacy, it shall make known in writing to the applicant the reasons for the refusal.

11. EC type-examination certificate.—(1) EC type-examination is the procedure whereby an approved body ascertains, and certifies by means of an EC type-examination certificate, that a prototype representative of the production envisaged satisfies the requirements of *the Directive*.

(2) Application for a type-examination certificate must—

(a) specify the name and address of the applicant;
(b) specify the proposed place of manufacture of the vessels to which the application relates; and
(c) be accompanied by the prototype and the design and manufacturing schedule conforming with Schedule 3.

The prototype may be representative of a family of *vessels*. Schedule 4 describes what is to be regarded as a family for this purpose.

(3) A United Kingdom approved body to which such application is made shall satisfy itself that the design and manufacturing schedule contains all the required information.

(4) The United Kingdom approved body shall also—

(a) examine, and perform such tests as it considers appropriate on, the prototype; and

(b) if satisfied that the prototype is manufactured in conformity with the schedule, and (whether or not conforming with a relevant national standard) meets the essential safety requirements specified in Schedule 1, and is safe,

issue a type-examination certificate recording its conclusions arrived at under this paragraph.

(5) There shall be specified in the type-examination certificate any conditions subject to which it is to have effect; and it shall be accompanied by the descriptions and drawings necessary for the identification of the prototype.

(6) A United Kingdom approved body which has issued a type-examination certificate shall—

(a) if so requested, supply copies of the certificate to the Secretary of State, *the Commission*, any other approved body or any other Member State;

(b) on receipt of a reasoned request from any of the above, supply copies of the relevant schedule and of its reports concerning the examination and tests carried out.

(7) If the United Kingdom approved body is not satisfied that the requirements of paragraphs (3) and (4)(b) above are met and refuses to issue a type-examination certificate, it shall make known in writing to the applicant and to the other approved bodies the reasons for the refusal.

12. EC verification certificate.—(1) EC verification is the procedure whereby an approved body checks, and certifies by means of an EC verification certificate, that *vessels* conform with a relevant national standard or with the prototype by reference to which an EC type-examination certificate was issued.

(2) Verification is carried out on batches of *vessels* made available to the approved body by either the manufacturer or his authorised representative established in the Community. A "batch" for this purpose is up to 3,000 *vessels* of the same series.

(3) Application for a verification certificate must be accompanied by—

(a) a copy of the relevant EC certificate of adequacy or type-examination certificate, as the case may be; and

(b) the design and manufacturing schedule conforming with Schedule 3.

(4) A United Kingdom approved body to which such application is made shall satisfy itself—

(a) that the schedule contains all the required information; and

(b) that the *vessels* in the batch have been manufactured and checked in accordance with the schedule.

(5) The United Kingdom approved body shall also perform the following tests—

(a) *test of the vessel itself*: a hydrostatic test, or a pneumatic test of equivalent effect, on each *vessel*, at a pressure equal to 1.5 times the *vessel's* design pressure (which is the gauge pressure chosen by the manufacturer and used to determine the thickness of the pressurised components); and

(b) *test of weld quality*: tests on longitudinal welds and, where different welding techniques are used for longitudinal and circular welds, equivalent tests repeated on the latter.

Pneumatic test under sub-paragraph (a) must be in accordance with safety procedures accepted in the country where they are carried out. Tests of weld quality under subparagraph (b) must be carried out on pieces taken, at the manufacturer's option, from a representative production test piece or a *vessel* in the batch submitted.

(6) The following applies in the case where a *vessel's* wall-thickness is determined by the experimental method, that is to say so as to enable the *vessel* to resist at ambient temperature a pressure equal to at least 5 times the maximum working pressure (as defined in regulation 2(1) above), with a maximum permanent circumferential deformation factor of 1 per cent. In that case the tests referred to in paragraph (5)(b) of this regulation are to be replaced by a hydrostatic test on 5 *vessels* taken at random from each batch submitted, in order to check that the maximum is not exceeded.

(7) If satisfied that the *vessels* conform with a relevant national standard or (as the case may be) with the relevant prototype, the United Kingdom approved body shall issue a verification certificate.

(8) If the United Kingdom approved body is not so satisfied and refuses to issue a verification certificate, it shall make known in writing to the applicant the reasons for the refusal.

13.   EC certificate of conformity.—(1) In cases where the manufacturer of *vessels* in Category A.2 or A.3 elects not to apply for EC verification, he may instead by means of the following procedure obtain an EC certificate of conformity.

(2) Application for a certificate of conformity must, before commencement of series manufacture, be made to the approved body which issued the relevant EC certificate of adequacy or EC type-examination certificate (as the case may be) and be accompanied by a document in which are described—

(a) the processes by which the *vessels* are to be manufactured; and

(b) all the measures which are to be taken to ensure that the *vessels* when manufactured conform with a relevant national standard or (as the case may be) with the relevant prototype.

(3) The document must—

(a) specify the address of any place where the *vessels* (or *relevant assemblies* incorporating the *vessels*) are to be manufactured or stored by or on behalf of the manufacturer of the *vessels*, and the proposed date of commencement of manufacture;

(b) be accompanied by the design and manufacturing schedule conforming with Schedule 3 including so much as has become available of any information required to be comprised in that schedule;

(c) specify the tests which are to be carried out in the course of manufacture, and the procedures by which and the frequency with which they are to be performed; and

(d) include undertakings as follows—

   (i) that those tests will be carried out as specified;

   (ii) that there will be carried out on each *vessel* a hydrostatic test (or a pneumatic test of equivalent effect in accordance with safety procedures accepted in the country where it is carried out) at a pressure equal to 1.5 times the vessel's design pressure (which is the gauge pressure chosen by the manufacturer and used to determine the thickness of the pressurised components); and

   (iii) that all the tests referred to above will be carried out by or under the responsibility of appropriately qualified personnel (who must be sufficiently independent from production personnel), and will be the subject of written reports by those personnel.

(4) A United Kingdom approved body to which such application is made shall, if satisfied—

(a) that the document and the schedule contain all the required information; and

(b) that *vessels* manufactured in accordance with the document and schedule will conform with a relevant national standard or, if not, then with the essential safety requirements specified in Schedule 1,

issue a certificate of conformity accordingly, covering the *vessels* proposed to be manufactured.

(5) If the United Kingdom approved body is not so satisfied and refuses to issue a certificate of conformity, it shall make known in writing to the manufacturer the reasons for the refusal.

14. The *EC mark*.—(1) A United Kingdom approved body which has issued an EC verification certificate shall apply, or oversee the application of, the *EC mark* to every *vessel* covered by the certificate.

(2) A manufacturer who has obtained an EC certificate of conformity may commence series manufacture and apply the *EC mark* to any *vessels* covered by the certificate, where he executes an EC declaration of conformity that they conform with a relevant national standard, or, as the case may be, with the relevant prototype.

(3) No person shall in the United Kingdom—

(a) *supply* a *vessel*, or a *relevant assembly*;

(b) being the manufacturer of a *vessel*, himself take into service that *vessel*, or a *relevant assembly* incorporating that *vessel*; or

(c) having imported a *vessel* or *relevant assembly* into the United Kingdom, himself take into service that *vessel* or a *relevant assembly* incorporating that *vessel*, or the first mentioned *relevant assembly*,

where the *vessel*, or the *vessel* incorporated in the *relevant assembly*, as the case may be, contravenes paragraph (4) below.

(4) A *vessel*, or a *vessel* incorporated in a *relevant assembly*, contravenes this paragraph—

(a) in the case of a *vessel* in Category A, though not complying with regulation 4(1) above, it bears the *EC mark* or any other inscription liable to be confused with the *EC mark*; or

(b) in the case of a *vessel* in Category B, it bears the *EC mark* or any inscription liable to be confused with the *EC mark*.

(5) A person who *supplies* or takes into service a *vessel* which does not bear the *EC mark* shall, at the request of an *enforcement authority*, or of an officer of such an authority, give any information which he has, or which is available to him, concerning the date when the *vessel* was first *supplied* or taken into service in *the Community*, and explain (so far as he is able) how it comes about that the *vessel* does not bear that mark.

15. Retention of documentation.—(1) In the United Kingdom, a manufacturer of *vessels* must retain, for a period of at least 10 years from the date on which the last *vessel* in the series is manufactured—

(a) copies of all documentation submitted by him or by his authorised representative established in *the Community* to an approved body for the purpose of obtaining any of the EC certificates referred to above in these Regulations;

(b) any certificates issued by an approved body to him or his authorised representative under these Regulations or corresponding provisions having effect elsewhere in the Community;

(c) any documents accompanying any such certificate so issued;

(d) in a case where the manufacturer has complied with regulation 13(2) and (3) above, so much of any particular information required to be comprised in the design and manufacturing schedule as has become available only subsequently to compliance with those provisions;

(e) any EC declarations of conformity executed by him under regulation 14(2) above; and

(f) any reports made by qualified personnel pursuant to regulation 13(3)(d)(iii) above.

16. Special provisions applying to *vessels* in Category A.2.—(1) In accordance with *the Directive*, a manufacturer of *vessels* in Category A.2 who has executed an EC declaration of conformity becomes thereby subject to EC surveillance in respect of *vessels* in that Category covered by that declaration.

(2) In the United Kingdom, a manufacturer to whom paragraph (1) above applies shall—

(a) authorise access at any reasonable time by or on behalf of the approved body which issued the EC certificate of conformity, to any place where *vessels* covered thereby (or *relevant assemblies* into which he has incorporated such *vessels*) are manufactured or stored by or on behalf of the manufacturer, for the purpose of inspecting the manufacturing processes and the *vessels* so covered;

(b) allow inspectors acting on the approved body's behalf to select random samples of *vessels* covered by the certificate (or *relevant assemblies* incorporating such *vessels*) for inspection;

(c) if so required by the inspectors, provide the following—

(i) copies of any reports made by qualified personnel pursuant to regulation 13(3)(d)(iii) above;

(ii) in a case where the manufacturer has complied with regulation 13(2) and (3) above, so much of any particular information required to be comprised in the design and manufacturing schedule as has become available only subsequent to compliance with those provisions; and

(d) comply with any reasonable request made by the approved body or on its behalf for additional information regarding any aspect of manufacture or any matter particularly relating to safety of the *vessels* covered by the certificate.

17. Functions of approved bodies in course of EC surveillance.—(1) In accordance with *the Directive* approved bodies are charged by the Member States with the function, in relation to a manufacturer of *vessels* in Category A.2 who is subject to EC surveillance—

(a) of ascertaining whether undertakings with regard to tests to be carried out in the course of manufacture given by him pursuant to regulation 13(3)(d) above are actually carried out; and

(b) of taking random samples of *vessels* (or *relevant assemblies*) at any place where *vessels* covered by an EC certificate of conformity (or *relevant assemblies* incorporating such *vessels*) are manufactured or stored by or on behalf of the manufacturer for the purposes of inspection.

(2) A United Kingdom approved body shall perform that function in relation to manufacturers in the United Kingdom or elsewhere, in cases where it has issued an EC certificate of conformity in respect of *vessels* in Category A.2.

(3) The United Kingdom approved body shall in respect of each such manufacturer from time to time compile written reports of the activities carried out by it in the course of surveillance and, if so requested, supply copies of any such report to the Secretary of State, *the Commission*, any other approved body or any other Member State.

18. Report by United Kingdom approved body concerning contraventions.— (1) If it is established to the satisfaction of a United Kingdom approved body carrying out EC surveillance that the *EC mark* has been wrongly applied to a *vessel* because—

(a) it does not conform with the prototype by reference to which an EC type–examination certificate was issued; or

(b) it conforms with the prototype, but the prototype does not meet the essential safety requirements specified in Schedule 1; or

(c) it does not conform with a relevant national standard by reference to which an EC certificate of adequacy was issued; or

(d) it is not in fact *safe*,

the body shall make a report of the circumstances to the Secretary of State.

(2) The same applies if the manufacturer has failed to carry out undertakings given pursuant to regulation 13(3)(d) above, or has failed to comply with any of the requirements of regulation 16(2) above or to provide corresponding facilities elsewhere than in the United Kingdom.

(3) In the circumstances mentioned above in this regulation, the United Kingdom aproved body shall, if it considers such action appropriate, withdraw the relevant certificate of adequacy, type-examination certificate or EC certificate of conformity.

(4) Where a United Kingdom approved body withdraws a type-examination certificate, it shall so inform the Secretary of State, giving its reasons, with a view to this information being passed by him to *the Commission* and the other Member States.

19.   Enforcement.   Schedule 5 shall have effect for the purposes of providing for the enforcement of these Regulations and for matters incidental thereto.

20.   Offences.—(1) A person who contravenes regulation 5 above is guilty of an offence and liable on summary conviction to—

(a) imprisonment for a term not exceeding three months; or
(b) to a fine not exceeding—
   (i) in Great Britain, level 5 on the standard scale; or
   (ii) in Northern Ireland, £2,000,
   or to both.

(2) A person who—

(a) contravenes any of the provisions of regulation 14(3) or regulation 15 above;
(b) fails or refuses to give information or explanation required by regulation 14(5) above; or
(c) fails to comply with a court order under regulation 21 below, is guilty of an offence and liable on summary conviction to a fine not exceeding—
   (i) in Great Britain, level 5 on the standard scale; or
   (ii) in Northern Ireland, £2,000.

21.   Power of the court to require matter to be remedied.—(1) Where a person is convicted of an offence under regulation 20 above in respect of any matters which appear to the court to be matters which it is in his power to remedy, the court may, in addition to or instead of imposing any punishment, order him, within such time as may be fixed by the order, to take such steps as may be specified in the order for remedying the said matters.

(2) The time fixed by an order under paragraph (1) above may be extended or further extended by order of the court on an application made before the end of that time as originally fixed or as extended under this paragraph, as the case may be.

(3) Where a person is ordered under paragraph (1) above to remedy any matters, that person shall not be guilty of an offence under regulation 20 above in respect of those matters in so far as they continue during the time fixed by the order or any further time allowed under paragraph (2) above.

22.   Defence of due diligence.—(1) Subject to the following provisions of this regulation, in proceedings against any person for an offence under regulation

20 above it shall be a defence for that person to show that he took all reasonable steps and exercised all due diligence to avoid committing the offence.

(2) Where in any proceedings against any person for such an offence the defence provided by paragraph (1) above involves an allegation that the commission of the offence was due—

(a) to the act or default of another; or
(b) to reliance on information given by another,

that person shall not, without the leave of the court, be entitled to rely on the defence unless, not less than seven clear days before the hearing of the proceedings, he has served a notice under paragraph (3) below on the person bringing the proceedings.

(3) A notice under this paragraph shall give such information identifying or assisting in the identification of the person who committed the act or default or gave the information as is in the possession of the person serving the notice at the time he serves it.

(4) It is hereby declared that a person shall not be entitled to rely on the defence provided by paragraph (1) above by reason of his reliance on information supplied by another, unless he shows that it was reasonable in all the circumstances for him to have relied on the information, having regard in particular—

(a) to the steps which he took, and those which might reasonably have been taken, for the purpose of verifying the information; and
(b) to whether he had any reason to disbelieve the information.

23. Liability of persons other than the principal offender.—(1) Where the commission by any person of an offence under regulation 20 above is due to the act or default committed by some other person in the course of any business of his, the other person shall be guilty of the offence and may be proceeded against and punished by virtue of this paragraph whether or not proceedings are taken against the first-mentioned person.

(2) Where a body corporate is guilty of an offence under these Regulations (including where it is so guilty by virtue of paragraph (1) above) in respect of any act or default which is shown to have been committed with the consent or connivance of, or to be attributable to any neglect on the part of, any director, manager, secretary or other similar officer of the body corporate or any person who was purporting to act in any such capacity he, as well as the body corporate, shall be guilty of that offence and shall be liable to be proceeded against and punished accordingly.

(3) Where the affairs of a body corporate are managed by its members, paragraph (2) above shall apply in relation to the acts and defaults of a member in connection with his functions of management as if he were a director of the body corporate.

(4) In this regulation, reference to a "body corporate" include references to a partnership in Scotland and, in relation to such partnership, any reference to a director, manager, secretary of other similar officer of a body corporate is a reference to a partner.

24.   Consequential amendment of United Kingdom law.—(1) Any requirement imposed by any of the enactments (relating in various respects to the safety of air receivers and pressure systems) specified in paragraph (2) of this regulation which has to be satisfied by or in respect of a *vessel* (including a *vessel* incorporated in a *relevant assembly*) if, in the United Kingdom, it (or the *relevant assembly* into which it is incorporated) is to be lawfully—

(a) *supplied*; or
(b) in the circumstances referred to in regulation 5(2) or (3) above, taken into service,

in conformity with these Regulations, is, subject to paragraph (3) of this regulation, hereby disapplied, except in relation to a *vessel* (including a *vessel* incorporated in a *relevant assembly*) excepted from the operation of these Regulations by regulation 6(1) above.

(2) The enactment referred to in paragraph (1) of this regulation are—

(a) in the Factories Act 1961, subsections (1) to (3) of section 36;
(b) in the Pressure Systems and Transportable Gas Containers Regulations 1989 (made under the Health and Safety at Work etc. Act 1974), paragraphs (1) to (4) of regulation 4 and paragraphs (1), (3) and (4) of regulation 5;
(c) in the Miscellaneous Mines (General) Regulations 1956 (having effect as if made under the Mines and Quarries Act 1954), paragraphs (1) and (2) of regulation 59;
(d) in the Quarries (General) Regulations 1956 (having effect as if made under the Mines and Quarries Act 1954), paragraphs (1) and (2) of regulation 21;
(e) in the Factories Act (Northern Ireland) 1965, subsections (1) to (3) of section 37;
(f) in the Pressure Systems and Transportable Gas Containers Regulations (Northern Ireland) 1991 (made under the Health and Safety at Work (Northern Ireland) Order 1978), paragraphs (1) to (4) of regulation 4 and paragraphs (1), (3) and (4) of regulation 5;
(g) in the Miscellaneous Mines (General) Regulations (Northern Ireland) 1970 (having effect as if made under the Mines Act (Northern Ireland) 1969), paragraphs (1) and (2) of regulation 60; and
(h) in the Quarries (Safety, Health and Equipment and Explosives) Rules (Northern Ireland) 1962 (made under the Quarries Act (Northern Ireland) 1927), regulations 42 and 43.

(3) Nothing in this regulation affects the application of the enactments specified in paragraph (2) above to *relevant assemblies* in so far as they comprise apparatus other than *vessels* subject to these Regulations.

SCHEDULE 1

Regulation 4

ESSENTIAL SAFETY REQUIREMENTS

PART 1
MATERIALS

1. Materials must be selected according to the intended use of the *vessels* and in accordance with the following provisions of this Part.

2. Pressurised components. The non-alloy quality steel, non-alloy aluminium or non-age hardening aluminium alloy used to manufacture the pressurised components must:
—be capable of being welded;
—be ductile and tough, so that a rupture at the minimum working temperature does not give rise to either fragmentation or brittle-type fracture; and
—not be adversely affected by ageing.
For steel *vessels*, the materials must in addition meet the requirements set out in paragraph 3 below and, for aluminium or aluminium alloy *vessels*, those set out in paragraph 4 below. They must be accompanied by an *inspection slip*.

3. Steel *vessels*. Non-alloy quality *steels* must meet the following requirements:
(a) they must be non-effervescent and be supplied after normalisation treatment, or in an equivalent state;
(b) the content per product of carbon must be less than 0.25% and that of sulphur and phosphorus must each be less than 0.05%; and
(c) they must have the following mechanical properties per product:
    —the maximum tensile strength must be less than 580 Newtons per square millimetre (N/mm^2);
    —the elongation after rupture must be:
      —if the test piece is taken parallel to the direction of rolling:
        thickness > 3 mm: $A > 22\%$
        thickness < 3 mm: $A_{80mm} > 17\%$
      —if the test piece is taken perpendicular to the direction of rolling:
        thickness > 3 mm: $A > 20\%$
        thickness < 3 mm: $A_{80mm} > 15\%$; and
    —the average rupture energy for three longitudinal test pieces at the *minimum working temperature* must not be less than 35 Joules per square centimetre (J/cms). Not more than one of the three figures may be less than 35 J/cms, with a minimum of 25 J/cms.
In the case of steels used to manufacture *vessels* whose *minimum working temperature* is lower than minus 10°C and whose wall thickness exceeds 5 millimetres, the average rupture energy must be checked.

4. Aluminium *vessels*. Non-alloy aluminium must have an aluminium content of at least 99.5% and non-age hardening aluminium alloys must display adequate resistance to intercrystalline corrosion at the *maximum working temperature*. Moreover these materials must meet the following requirements:
(a) they must be supplied in an annealed state; and
(b) they must have the following mechanical properties per product:
    —the maximum tensile strength must be no more than 350 N/mms; and
    —the elongation after rupture must be:
      —$A > 16\%$ if the test piece is taken parallel to the direction of rolling
      —$A > 14\%$ if the test piece is taken perpendicular to the direction of rolling.

5. Welding materials. The welding materials used to make the welds on or of the *vessel* must be appropriate to and compatible with the materials to be welded.

6. Accessories contributing to the strength of the *vessel*. These accessories (bolts, nuts, etc.) must be made either of a material specified in paragraphs 2 to 4 above or of another kind of steel, aluminium or aluminium alloy which:

—is appropriate to and compatible with the materials used to manufacture the pressurised components; and

—at the *minimum working temperature* has an appropriate elongation after rupture and toughness.

7. Non-pressurised components. All welded non-pressurised components must be of a material which is compatible with that of the parts to which they are welded.

PART 2
VESSEL DESIGN

8. The manufacturer must, when designing the *vessel*, define the use to which it will be put, and select:

—the *minimum working temperature*;

—the *maximum working temperature*; and

—the *maximum working pressure*.

However, should a *minimum working temperature* higher than minus 10°C be selected, the properties required of the materials must be satisfied at minus 10°C.

The manufacturer must also take account of the following requirements:

—it must be possible to inspect the inside of the *vessels*;

—it must be possible to drain the *vessels*;

—the mechanical qualities must be maintained throughout the period of use of the *vessel* for its intended purpose;

—the *vessels* must, bearing in mind their envisaged use, be adequately protected against corrosion,

and of the fact that under the conditions of use envisaged:

—the *vessels* will not be subjected to stresses likely to impair their safety in use; and

—the internal pressure will not permanently exceed the *maximum working pressure*; however, it may momentarily do so by up to 10%.

Circular and longitudinal seams must be made using full penetration welds or welds of equivalent effectiveness. Dished ends other than hemispherical ones must have a cylindrical edge.

9. Wall thickness. In the case of *vessels* of Category A.2 or A.3 whose *maximum working temperature* does not exceed 100°C, the manufacturer must select either the calculation method or the experimental method, as defined below, for determining *vessel* wall thickness.

In the case of *vessels* in Category A.1 or *vessels* in Category A.2 or A.3 whose *maximum working temperature* exceeds 100°C, the calculation method must be used.

However, the actual wall thickness of the cylindrical component and ends must in any case be not less than 2 millimetres in the case of steel *vessels*, and not less than 3 millimetres in the case of aluminium or aluminium alloy *vessels*.

Calculation method

The minimum thickness of the pressurised components must be calculated having regard to the intensity of the stresses and to the following requirements:

—the calculation pressure to be taken into account must not be less than the *maximum working pressure*; and

—the permissible general membrane stress must not exceed 0.6 times the yield strength at the maximum working temperature (R_{ET}) or 0.3 times the tensile strength (R_m) whichever value is the lower. The manufacturer must use the minimum values of R_{ET} and R_m guaranteed by the producer of the materials in order to determine the permissible stress.

However, where the cylindrical component of the *vessel* has one or more longitudinal welds made using a non-automatic welding technique, the thickness calculated as above must be multiplied by the coefficient 1.15.

Experimental method

Wall thickness must be so determined as to enable the *vessel* to resist at ambient temperature a pressure equal to at least 5 times the *maximum working pressure* with a maximum permanent circumferential deformation factor of 1%.

PART 3
MANUFACTURING PROCESSES

10. *Vessels* must be constructed and checked in accordance with the design and manufacturing schedule referred to in Schedule 3.

11. Preparation of the component parts. The preparation of the component parts (eg forming and chamfering) must not give rise to surface defects, cracks or changes in the mechanical properties of those parts likely to be detrimental to the safety of the *vessels.*

12. Welds on pressurised components. The characteristics of welds and adjacent zones must be similar to those of the welded materials and must be free of any surface or internal defects detrimental to the safety of the *vessels.*

Welds must be made by appropriately qualified welders or operators in accordance with approved welding techniques. "Qualified" means qualified by means of tests carried out by an approved body; and "approved" means approved by such a body.

The manufacturer must also, during manufacture, ensure consistent weld quality by conducting appropriate tests using adequate procedures. These tests must be the subject of a written report.

PART 4
DEFINITIONS AND SYMBOLS

13. Definitions. In this Schedule—
(a) "minimum working temperature" means the lowest stabilised temperature in the wall of the *vessel* under normal conditions of use;
(b) "inspection slip" means the document by which the producer of the materials certifies that the materials delivered to the manufacturer meet the requirements set by the manufacturer, and in which the producer sets out the results of the routine inspection tests carried out during the production of those materials (or of materials produced by the same process but not being the materials delivered to the manufacturer) in particular as to their chemical composition and mechanical properties;
(c) "maximum working temperature" means the highest stabilised temperature in the wall of the *vessel* under normal conditions of use;
(d) "maximum working pressure" means the maximum gauge pressure which may be exerted under the normal conditions of use; and
(e) "yield strength at the maximum working temperature" means:
   —the upper yield point for a material with both a lower and an upper yield point; or
   —the proof stress at 0.2%; or
   —the proof stress at 1.0% in the case of non-alloy aluminium.

14. Symbols. In this Schedule—
(a) "A" means the percentage elongation after rupture ($L_o = 5.65$ "$/S_o$) where L_o is

the gauge length expressed in millimetres and S_o is the cross-sectional area of the test section expressed in square millimetres; and
(b) "A_{80mm}" means the percentage elongation after rupture (L_o=80 mm).

SCHEDULE 2

Regulations 2, 4 and 14

EC MARK AND INSCRIPTIONS

1.   The *EC mark*, and the other inscriptions specified below, must be affixed in a visible, easily legible and indelible form, either to the *vessel* itself or to a data plate attached to the *vessel* in such a way that it cannot be removed.

2.   The other inscriptions required are—
maximum working pressure in bar
maximum working temperature in °C
minimum working temperature in °C
capacity of the *vessel* in litres
name or mark of the manufacturer
type and serial or batch identification of the *vessel*.

3.   If a data plate is used, it must be so designed that it cannot be reused, and must include a vacant space to enable other information to be provided.

4.   The *EC mark* on a *vessel* of any series consists of the symbol "CE" of which a form is shown for the purposes of illustration below, the last two digits of the year in which the mark is affixed, and (where applicable) the distinguishing number assigned, under Article 9.1 of *the Directive* to the approved body responsible for EC verification or EC surveillance in the case of *vessels* of that series.

SCHEDULE 3

Regulation 10

DESIGN AND MANUFACTURING

1.   The design and manufacturing schedule must contain a description of the techniques and operations employed in order to meet a relevant national standard or the essential safety requirements specified in Schedule 1.

2.   In particular it must comprise—
(a) a detailed manufacturing drawing of the *vessel* type;
(b) the manufacturer's instructions;
(c) a document describing—
    (i) the materials selected;
    (ii) the welding techniques selected;

    (iii) the checks selected; and
    (iv) any pertinent details as to the *vessel* design.

3. In the case of a schedule relating to two or more *vessels* of the same family, variations in length of the cylindrical component resulting in modifications of apertures or penetrations must be shown in the drawing for each variant.

4. In the case of a schedule provided pursuant to regulation 12(3)(b) or regulation 13(3)(b), it must also comprise—
  (a) evidence of approval by an approved body of the welding techniques employed and of the welders' and operators' qualifications;
  (b) the inspection slip, as defined in paragraph 13(b) of Schedule 1, for the materials used in the manufacture of components and assemblies contributing to the strength of the *vessel*; and
  (c) a report on the examinations and tests performed, or a description of the proposed checks.

SCHEDULE 4

Regulation 11

FAMILIES OF *VESSELS*

Vessels form part of the same family if they differ from the prototype only—
  (a) in diameter (provided always that they meet the requirements of paragraph 9 of Schedule 1 as to wall thickness);
  (b) in the length of the cylindrical component, provided that—
    (i) where the prototype has one or more shell rings in addition to the ends, they all have at least one shell ring; or
    (ii) where the prototype consists of two outwardly dished ends, none of them has any shell ring; or
  (c) in both (a) and (b).

SCHEDULE 5

Regulation 19

ENFORCEMENT

1. **Enforcement in Great Britain in relation to *vessels for use at work.*** In Great Britain, in relation to *vessels* and *relevant assemblies for use at work*—
  (a) it shall be the duty of *the Executive* to make adequate arrangements for the enforcement of these Regulations, and accordingly a reference in the provisions applied to these Regulations by sub-paragraph (b) below to an "enforcing authority" shall be construed as a reference to *the Executive*;
  (b) sections 19 to 21, 23, 24, 25A to 28, 33 to 35, 38, 39 and 41 of *the 1974 Act* shall apply for the purposes of providing for the enforcement of these Regulations and in respect of proceedings for contravention thereof as if—
    (i) references to relevant statutory provisions were references to those sections as applied by this paragraph and to these Regulations;
    (ii) references to articles, substances, articles or substances, or plant, were references to *vessels* or *relevant assemblies*;
    (iii) references to the field of responsibility of an enforcing authority, however expressed, were omitted;
    (iv) in section 20, subsection (3) were omitted;
    (v) in sections 23 and 24, the references to prohibition notices were omitted;
    (vi) in section 23, subsections (3), (4) and (6) were omitted;
    (vii) in section 24, paragraph (b) of subsection (3) were omitted;

(viii) in section 33—
    (aa) in subsection (1)—
        (A) the whole of paragraphs (a) to (d) were omitted;
        (B) in paragraph (e) the words "or 25" were omitted;
        (C) in paragraph (g) the words "or prohibition" and "or a prohibition notice" were omitted; and
        (D) paragraph (o) applied only to failure to comply with a court order under section 42(1) to (3) as applied to these Regulations by sub-paragraph (c) of this paragraph;
    (bb) in subsection (2), the reference to paragraph (d) of subsection (1) were omitted; and
    (cc) for subsection (3) there were substituted the following—
"(3) A person guilty of an offence under any paragraph of subsection (1) not mentioned in the preceding subsection shall be liable—
(a) on summary conviction, to a fine not exceeding level 5 on the standard scale; or
(b) on conviction on indictment—
    (i) in the case of an offence under subsection (1)(j) to imprisonment for a term not exceeding two years, or a fine, or both; or
    (ii) in all other cases, to a fine."; and
    (dd) subsection (4) were omitted; and
  (ix) in section 34, paragraphs (a) and (b) were omitted from subsection (1); and
(c) sections 36(1) and (2), 37 and 42(1) to (3) shall apply in relation to offences under section 33 as applied to these Regulations and as modified by sub-paragraph (b)(viii) above.

2.   Enforcement in Northern Ireland in relation to *vessels* for use at work. In Northern Ireland, in relation to *vessels* and *relevant assemblies* as articles for use at work—
(a) it shall be the duty of the Department of Economic Development to make adequate arrangements for the enforcement of these Regulations, and accordingly a reference to the provisions applied to these Regulations by sub-paragraph (b) below to an "enforcing authority" or to "the Department concerned" shall be construed as a reference to that Department.
(b) articles 21 to 23, 25, 26, 27A to 33, 35, 36, and 38 of *the Order* shall apply for the purposes of providing for the enforcement of these Regulations and in respect of proceedings for contravention thereof as if—
    (i) references to relevant statutory provisions where references to those articles as applied by this paragraph and to these Regulations;
    (ii) references to articles, substances, articles or substances, or plant, were references to *vessels* and *relevant assemblies*;
    (iii) references to the field of responsibility of an enforcing authority, however expressed, were omitted;
    (iv) in article 22, paragraph (3) were omitted;
    (v) in articles 25 and 26, the references to prohibition notices were omitted;
    (vi) in article 25, paragraphs (3), (4) and (5) were omitted;
    (vii) in article 26, sub-paragraph (b) of paragraph (2) were omitted;
    (viii) in article 31—
        (aa) in paragraph (1)—
            (A) the whole of sub-paragraphs (a) to (d) were omitted;
            (B) in sub-paragraph (e) the words "or 27" were omitted;
            (C) in sub-paragraph (g) the words "or prohibition" and "or a prohibition notice" were omitted; and
            (D) sub-paragraph (o) applied only to failure to comply with a court order under article 39(1) to (3) as applied to these Regulations by sub-paragraph (c) of this paragraph;
        (bb) in paragraph (2), the reference to sub-paragraph (d) of paragraph (1) were omitted;
        (cc) paragraph (3) were omitted;

(dd) for paragraph (4) there were substituted the following—

"(4) A person guilty of an offence under any sub-paragraph of paragraph (1) not mentioned in paragraph (2) shall be liable—

(a) on summary conviction, to a fine not exceeding £2,000; or

(b) on conviction on indictment—

(i) in the case of an offence under paragraph (1)(j), to imprisonment for a term not exceeding two years, or a fine, or both; or

(ii) in all cases, to a fine.";

and

(ee) paragraph (5) were omitted; and

(ix) in article 32, sub-paragaphs (a) and (b) were omitted from paragraph (1); and

(c) articles 34(1) and (2) and 39(1) to (3) shall apply in relation to offences under article 31 as applied to these Regulations and as modified by sub-paragraph (b)(viii) above.

3.   Enforcement in relation to *vessels* as consumer goods. In relation to *vessels* and *relevant assemblies* as consumer goods (meaning goods ordinarily intended for private use or consumption)—

(a) it shall be the duty of—

(i) every weights and measures authority in Great Britain; and

(ii) every district council in Northern Ireland,

to enforce these Regulations within their area;

(b) a reference in the provisions applied to these Regulations by sub-paragraph (c) below to an "*enforcement authority*" shall be construed as a reference to each of the following authorities—

(i) the bodies mentioned in sub-paragraph (a) above; and

(ii) the Secretary of State;

(c) sections 14, 15, 28 to 35, 37, 38, 44 and 47 of *the 1987 Act* shall apply for the purposes of providing for the enforcement of these Regulations and in respect of proceedings for contravention thereof as if—

(i) references to safety provisions were references to these Regulations;

(ii) references to goods were references to *vessels* or *relevant assemblies*;

(iii) in section 14—

(aa) in subsection (1), there were added at the end the words "or taking them into service contrary to regulation 5 of the Simple Pressure Vessels (Safety) Regulations 1991."; and

(bb) in subsection (6), for "six months" there were substituted "three months";

(iv) in sections 28, 29, 30, 33, 34 and 35, the words "or any provision by or under Part III of this Act", on each occasion that they occur, were omitted;

(v) in section 28, subsections (3), (4) and (5) were omitted;

(vi) in section 30, subsections (7) and (8) were omitted; and

(vii) in section 38(1), paragraphs (a) to (c) were omitted;

(d) sections 39 and 40 shall apply to offences under section 32 as it is applied to these Regulations by sub-paragraph (c) above; and

(e) in relation to proceedings for an offence under these Regulations—

(i) in Great Britain, section 34 of *the 1974 Act* shall apply as if—

(aa) paragraphs (a) and (b) of subsection (1) were omitted;

(bb) references to an "enforcing authority" were references to each of the authorities referred to in sub-paragraph (a)(i) and (b)(ii) of this paragraph, and "responsible enforcing authority" were construed accordingly; and

(cc) references to "relevant statutory provisions" were references to these Regulations; and

(ii) in Northern Ireland, article 32 of the Order shall apply as if—

(aa) sub-paragraphs (a) and (b) of paragraph (1) were omitted;

(bb)   references to an "enforcing authority" were references to each of the authorities referred to in sub-paragraph (a)(ii) and (b)(ii) of this paragraph, and "responsible enforcing authority" were construed accordingly; and

(cc)   reference to "relevant statutory provisions" were references to these Regulations.

4.   Forfeiture: England and Wales and Northern Ireland.—(1) An *enforcement authority* in England and Wales or Northern Ireland may apply under this paragraph for an order for the forfeiture of any *vessels* or *relevant assemblies* on the grounds that there has been a contravention in relation thereto of any provision of these Regulations.

(2) An application under this paragraph may be made—

(a)   where proceedings have been brought in a magistrates' court for an offence in respect of a contravention in relation to some or all of the *vessels* or *relevant assemblies* of any provisions of these Regulations, to that court;

(b)   where an application with respect to some or all of the *vessels* or *relevant assemblies* has been made to a magistrates' court under section 15 or 33 of *the 1987 Act* as applied for the purposes of the enforcement of these Regulations by paragraph 3(c) above, to that court; and

(c)   where no application for the forfeiture of the *vessels* or *relevant assemblies* has been made under sub-paragraph (a) or (b) above, by way of complaint to a magistrates' court.

(3) On an application under this paragraph the court shall make an order for the forfeiture of the *vessels* or *relevant assemblies* only if it is satisfied that there has been a contravention in relation thereto of any provision of these Regulations.

(4) For the avoidance of doubt it is hereby declared that a court may infer for the purposes of this paragraph that there has been a contravention in relation to any *vessels* or *relevant assemblies* of any provision of these Regulations if it is satisfied that any such provision has been contravened in relation to a *vessel* or *relevant assembly* which is representative of those *vessels* or *relevant assemblies* as the case may be (whether by reason of being of the same design or part of the same consignment or batch or otherwise).

(5) Any person aggrieved by an order made under this paragraph by a magistrates' court, or by a decision of such court not to make such an order, may appeal against that order or decision—

(a)   in England and Wales, to the Crown Court;

(b)   in Northern Ireland, to the county court,

and an order so made may contain such provision as appears to the court to be appropriate for delaying the coming into force of an order pending the making and determination of any appeal (including any application under section 111 of the Magistrates' Courts Act 1980 or article 146 of the Magistrates' Courts (Northern Ireland) Order 1981 (statement of case)).

(6) Subject to sub-paragraph (7) below, where any *vessel* or *relevant assembly* is forfeited under this paragraph it shall be destroyed in accordance with such directions as the court may give.

(7) On making an order under this paragraph a magistrates' court may, if it considers it appropriate to do so, direct that the *vessels* or *relevant assemblies* to which the order relates shall (instead of being destroyed) be released, to such person as the court may specify, on condition that that person—

(a)   does not *supply* the *vessels* or *relevant assemblies* as the case may be to any person otherwise than—

(i)   to a person who carries on a business of buying *vessels* or *relevant assemblies* of the same description as the first mentioned *vessels* or *relevant assemblies* as the case may be and repairing or reconditioning them; or

(ii)   as scrap (that is to say, for the value of materials included in the *vessels* or *relevant assemblies* rather than for the value of the *vessels* or *relevant assemblies* themselves); and

(b)   complies with any order to pay costs or expenses (including any order under section 35 of the 1987 Act as applied for the purposes of the enforcement of these Regulations by paragraph 3(c) above) which has been made against that person in the proceedings for the order for forfeiture.

5. Forfeiture: Scotland.—(1) In Scotland a sheriff may make an order for forfeiture of any *vessel* or *relevant assembly* in relation to which there has been a contravention of any provision of these Regulations—

(a) on an application by the procurator-fiscal made in the manner specified in section 310 of the Criminal Procedure (Scotland) Act 1975; or

(b) where a person is convicted of any offence in respect of any such conravention, in addition to any other penalty which the sheriff may impose.

(2) The procurator-fiscal making an application under sub-paragraph (1)(a) above shall serve on any person appearing to him to be the owner of, or otherwise to have an interest in, the *vessel* or *relevant assembly* to which the application relates a copy of the application, together with a notice giving him the opportunity to appear at the hearing of the application to show cause why the *vessel* or *relevant assembly* as the case may be should not be forfeited.

(3) Service under sub-paragraph (2) above shall be carried out, and such service may be proved, in the manner specified for citation of an accused in summary proceedings under the Criminal Procedure (Scotland) Act 1975.

(4) Any person upon whom a notice is served under sub-paragraph (2) above and any other person claiming to be the owner of or otherwise to have an interest in, the *vessel* or *relevant assembly* to which an application under this paragraph relates shall be entitled to appear at the hearing of the application to show cause why the *vessel* or *relevant assembly* as the case may be should not be forfeited.

(5) The sheriff shall not make an order following an application under sub-paragraph (1)(a) above—

(a) if any person on whom notice is served under sub-paragraph (2) above does not appear, unless service of the notice on that person is proved; or

(b) if no notice under sub-paragraph (2) above has been served, unless the court is satisfied that in the circumstances it was reasonable not to serve notice on any person.

(6) The sheriff shall make an order under this paragraph only if he is satisfied that there has been a contravention in relation to the *vessel* or *relevant assembly* of a provision of these Regulations.

(7) For the avoidance of doubt it is declared that the sheriff may infer for the purposes of this paragraph that there has been a contravention in relation to any *vessels* or *relevant assemblies* of any provision of these Regulations if he is satisfied that any such provision has been contravened in relation to a *vessel* or *relevant assembly* which is representative of those *vessels* or *relevant assemblies* as the case may be (whether by reason of being of the same design or part of the same consignment or batch or otherwise).

(8) Where an order for the forfeiture of any *vessel* or *relevant assembly* is made following an application by the procurator-fiscal under sub-paragraph (1)(a) above, any person who appeared, or was entitled to appear, to show cause why it should not be forfeited may, within twenty-one days of the making of the order, appeal to the High Court by Bill of Suspension on the ground of an alleged miscarriage of justice; and section 452(4)(a) to (e) of the Criminal Procedure (Scotland) Act 1975 shall apply to an appeal under this sub-paragraph as it applies to a stated case under Part II of that Act.

(9) An order following an application under sub-paragraph (1)(a) above shall not take effect—

(a) until the end of the period of twenty-one days beginning with the day after the day on which the order is made; or

(b) if an appeal is made under sub-paragraph (8) above within that period, until the appeal is determined or abandoned.

(10) An order under sub-paragraph (1)(b) shall not take effect—

(a) until the end of the period within which an appeal against the order could be brought under the Criminal Procedure (Scotland) Act 1975; or

(b) if an appeal is made within that period, until the appeal is determined or abandoned.

(11) Subject to sub-paragraph (12) below, a *vessel* or *relevant assembly* forfeited under this paragraph shall be destroyed in accordance with such directions as the sheriff may give.

(12) If he thinks fit, the sheriff may direct the *vessel* or *relevant assembly* to be released to such person as he may specify, on condition that that person does not supply it to any person otherwise than—

(a) to a person who carries on a business of buying *vessels* or *relevant assemblies* of the same description as it and repairing or reconditioning them; or

(b) as scrap (that is to say, for the value of materials included in the *vessel* or *relevant assembly* rather than for the value of the *vessel* or *relevant assembly* itself).

6. Duty of *enforcement authority* to inform Secretary of State of action taken. An *enforcement authority* shall, where action has been taken by it to prohibit or restrict the *supply* or taking into service (whether under these Regulations or otherwise) of any *vessel* to which these Regulations apply and which bears the *EC mark* (or a *relevant assembly* incorporating such *vessel*), forthwith inform the Secretary of State of the action taken, and the reasons for it, with a view to this information being passed by him to *the Commission*.

7. Savings. Nothing in these Regulations shall be construed as preventing the taking of any action in respect of a *vessel* or *relevant assembly* to which these Regulations apply under the provisions of *the 1974 Act, the Order* or *the 1987 Act.*

8. Nothing in these Regulations shall authorise an enforcement authority to bring proceedings in Scotland for an offence.

9. Interpretation. In this Schedule—

"the 1974 Act" means the Health and Safety at Work etc. Act 1974;

"the 1987 Act" means the Consumer Protection Act 1987;

"enforcement authority", save in paragraph 3(b) of this Schedule, means the Executive, the Department of Economic Development, and each of the authorities referred to in the said paragraph 3(b);

"the Executive" means the Health and Safety Executive established under section 10 of the 1974 Act;

"the Order" means the Health and Safety at Work (Northern Ireland) Order 1978; and

"*vessels* for use at work" means *vessels*—

(a) designed for use or operation, whether exclusively or not, by persons at work; or

(b) designed for use or operation, otherwise than at work, in non-domestic premises made available to persons as a place where they may use the *vessels* provided for their use there,

and a reference to *relevant assemblies* for use at work shall be construed accordingly.

THE LIFTING PLANT AND EQUIPMENT (RECORDS OF TEST AND EXAMINATION ETC.) REGULATIONS 1992

(S.I. 1992 No. 195)

General note. A guide to these regulations (L20) has been published by the Health and Safety Executive.

The Secretary of State, in exercise of the powers conferred on him by sections 15(1), (2) and (3)(a) and 82(3)(a) of, and paragraphs 1(2) and 16 of Schedule 3 to, the Health and Safety at Work etc. Act 1974 ("the 1974 Act") and of all other powers enabling him in that behalf and for the purpose of giving effect without modifications to proposals submitted to him by the Health and Safety Commission under section 11(2)(d) of the 1974 Act, after the carrying out by the said Commission of consultations in accordance with section 50(3) of that Act, hereby makes the following Regulations—

1. Citation, commencement and interpretation.—(1) These Regulations may be cited as the Lifting Plant and Equipment (Records of Test and Examination etc.) Regulations 1992 and shall come into force on 30 April 1992.

(2) For the purposes of these Regulations (including any enactment modified by these Regulations) a record need not be a document.

2. Contents of records etc.—(1) Where, under a provision specified in column 3 of Part I of Schedule 1 to these Regulations, a record is required to be obtained, kept or made following a test, test and examination or test and thorough examination carried out after the coming into force of these Regulations, that record shall contain the particulars specified in Part III of Schedule 1 to these Regulations.

(2) Where, under a provision specified in column 3 of Part I of Schedule 1 to these Regulations, a record is required to be kept or made following a thorough examination carried out after the coming into force of these Regulations, that record shall contain the particulars specified in Part IV of Schedule 1 to these Regulations.

(3) The record required to be kept pursuant to section 26(1)(g) of the Factories Act 1961 shall, in respect of any chains, ropes or lifting tackle subject to the provisions of that paragraph and first used after the coming into force of these Regulations, contain the particulars specified in Part V of Schedule 1 to these Regulations.

(4) Where, under a provision specified in column 3 of Part II of Schedule 1 to these Regulations, a record must be made or sent to a specified person

887

following a thorough examination carried out after the coming into force of these Regulations, that record shall contain the particulars specified in Part VI of Schedule 1 to these Regulations.

3.   Accuracy of particulars. Any particulars required by regulation 2 of these Regulations or by virtue of the Docks Regulations 1988 shall be correctly recorded.

4.   Authentication of records. Any record containing particulars required by regulation 2 of these Regulations or by virtue of the Docks Regulations 1988—

(a)   shall be authenticated by a person who is in a position to declare that the particulars contained in it are correct; and

(b)   may be authenticated by signature or other equally secure means.

5.   Modifications. The Act and instruments specified in Schedule 2 to these Regulations shall be modified to the extent specified therein.

6.   Savings provisions.—(1) Any record obtained, kept, made or sent to a specified person following a test, test and examination, test and thorough examination or thorough examination carried out under a provision specified in column 3 of Part I or II of Schedule 1 to these Regulations or of section 26(1)(g) of the Factories Act 1961 before the coming into force of these Regulations shall contain the same particulars as would have been required if these Regulations (including the revocations effected by these Regulations) had not been made.

(2) Any certificate, register or report which, immediately before the coming into force of these Regulations, satisfied the requirements of any of the provisions specified in Part I or II of Schedule 1 to these Regulations or of section 26(1)(g) of the Factories Act 1961 shall be deemed to satisfy those requirements after such coming into force.

7.   Revocations. The instruments specified in column 1 of Schedule 3 to these Regulations are hereby revoked to the extent specified in the corresponding entry in column 3 of that Schedule.

SCHEDULE 1

Regulation 2

REQUIREMENTS FOR A RECORD TO BE OBTAINED, KEPT, MADE OR OTHERWISE DEALT WITH FOLLOWING ANY TEST, TEST AND EXAMINATION, TEST AND THOROUGH EXAMINATION OR THOROUGH EXAMINATION

PART I
PROVISION REQUIRING A RECORD TO BE OBTAINED, KEPT, MADE OR OTHERWISE DEALT WITH FOLLOWING ANY TEST AND EXAMINATION, TEST AND THOROUGH EXAMINATION OR THOROUGH EXAMINATION

(1) *Short title of Act or title of instrument*	(2) *Reference*	(3) *Provision*
The Shipbuilding and Ship-repairing Regulations 1960	S.I. 1960/1932; modified by S.I. 1974/1941	Regulations 34(1) and (2), 36(1) and (2) and 37(1) and (2)
The Construction (Lifting Operations) Regulations 1961	S.I. 1961/1581; modified by S.I. 1974/1941	Regulations 19(4), 28(5) and (6), 34(1)(b), 35, 40, 46(1)(a) and (b) and 46(2)
The Factories Act 1961	1961 c. 34; modified by S.I. 1974/1941	Sections 26(1)(e) and 27(2) and (6)

PART II
PROVISIONS REQUIRING RECORDS TO BE MADE OR SENT TO A SPECIFIED PERSON FOLLOWING A THOROUGH EXAMINATION

(1) *Short title of Act or title of instrument*	(2) *Reference*	(3) *Provision*
The Factories Act 1961	1961 c. 34	Section 22(2)
The Offices, Shops and Railway Premises (Hoists and Lifts) Regulations 1968	S.I. 1968/849; modified by S.I. 1974/1943	Regulation 6(1)

PART III
PARTICULARS REQUIRED IN RECORDS REQUIRED TO BE OBTAINED ETC., UNDER ANY PROVISION SPECIFIED IN COLUMN 3 OF PART I OF THIS SCHEDULE AND FOLLOWING ANY TEST, TEST AND EXAMINATION OR TEST AND THOROUGH EXAMINATION

1. Description, date of manufacture, identification mark and location of the equipment referred to.

2. The safe working load (or loads) and (where relevant) corresponding radii, jib lengths and counterweights.

3. Details of the test, test and examination or test and thorough examination carried out.

4. Date (or dates) of completion of the test, test and examination or test and thorough examination.

5. A declaration that the information is correct and that the equipment has been tested, tested and examined or tested and thoroughly examined in accordance with the appropriate provisions and is found free from any defect likely to affect safety.

6. Name and address of the owner of the equipment referred to.

7. Name and address of the person declaring that the test, test and examination or test and thorough examination has been carried out.

8. Date the record of the test, test and examination or test and thorough examination is made.

9. A number or other means of identifying the record.

PART IV

PARTICULARS REQUIRED IN RECORDS REQUIRED TO BE OBTAINED ETC., UNDER ANY PROVISION SPECIFIED IN COLUMN 3 OF PART I OF THIS SCHEDULE AND FOLLOWING A THOROUGH EXAMINATION

1. Description, identification mark and location of the equipment referred to.

2. Date of the last thorough examination and number of the record of such thorough examination.

3. The safe working load (or loads) and (where relevant) corresponding radii.

4. The date of the most recent test and examination or test and thorough examination and the date and number or other identification of the record of it.

5. Details of any defects found and, where appropriate, a statement of the time by when each defect shall be rectified.

6. Date of completion of the thorough examination.

7. Latest date by which the next thorough examination should be carried out.

8. A declaration that the information is correct and that the equipment has been thoroughly examined in accordance with the appropriate provisions and is found free from any defect likely to affect safety other than any recorded by virtue of paragraph 4 of this Part.

9. Name and address of the owner of the equipment.

10. Name and address of the person responsible for the thorough examination.

11. Date the record of the thorough examination is made.

12. Name and address of the person who authenticates the record.

13. A number of other means of identifying the record.

PART V

PARTICULARS REQUIRED IN THE RECORD REQUIRED TO BE KEPT UNDER SECTION 26(1)(g) OF THE FACTORIES ACT 1961

1. Description, identification mark and location of the equipment referred to in section 26(1)(g) of the Factories Act 1961.

2. The safe working load or loads and (where relevant) corresponding radii of such equipment.

3. Details and date of completion of the test and examination carried out under section 26(1)(e) of the Factories Act 1961.

4. Details and date of completion of each thorough examination made under section 26(1)(d) of the Factories Act 1961.

5. Details of any defect found and, where appropriate, a statement of the time by when each defect shall be rectified.

6. Date of making of the record required to be obtained under section 26(1)(e) of the Factories Act 1961 and an identifying number.

7. Latest date by which the next thorough examination made under section 26(1)(d) of the Factories Act 1961 should be carried out.

8. Name and address of the owner of the equipment referred to.

9. Name and address of the person responsible for the test and examination made under section 26(1)(e) of the Factories Act 1961 or the examination made under section 26(1)(d) thereof.

10. Name, and address of the person who authenticates the record.

11. A number or other means of identifying the record.

PART VI

PARTICULARS REQUIRED IN RECORDS REQUIRED TO BE DEALT WITH UNDER ANY PROVISION
SPECIFIED IN COLUMN 3 OR PART II OF THIS SCHEDULE AND FOLLOWING A
THOROUGH EXAMINATION

1. Description, identification mark and location of the hoist or lift referred to.

2. Date of the last thorough examination and number of the record of such thorough examination.

3. The safe working load.

4. Details of any parts which were inaccessible.

5. Details of any defect found (especially in the following—
(a) enclosure or hoistway or liftway;
(b) landing gates and cage gate(s);
(c) interlocks on the landing gates and cage gate(s);
(d) other gate fastenings;
(e) cage or platform and fittings, cage guides, buffers, interior of the hoistway or liftway;
(f) over-running devices;
(g) suspension ropes or chains, and their attachments;
(h) safety gear, i.e. arrangements for preventing fall of platforms or cage;
(i) brakes;
(j) worm or spur gearing;
(k) other electrical equipment;
(l) other parts); and
where appropriate, a statement of the time by when each defect shall be rectified.

6. Date of completion of the thorough examination.

7. Latest date by which the next thorough examination should be carried out.

8. A declaration that the information is correct and that the equipment has been examined in accordance with the appropriate provisions and is found free from any defect likely to affect safety other than any such defect recorded by virtue of paragraph 4 of this Part.

9. Name and address of the owner of the hoist or lift referred to.

10. Name and address of the person responsible for the thorough examination.

11. Date the record of the thorough examination is made.

12. Name and address of the person who authenticates the record.

13. A number or other means of identifying the record.

SCHEDULE 2

Regulation 5

Modifications

1. The Shipbuilding and Ship-repairing Regulations 1960 shall be modified as follows—

(a) in regulation 34(1), for the second sentence, substitute—
   "A record of such test and thorough examination and of the results thereof containing the particulars required by the Lifting Plant and Equipment (Records of Test and Examination etc.) Regulations 1992 shall have been obtained and the particulars in that record shall be available for inspection.";

(b) for regulation 34(2), substitute the following paragraph—
   "(2) Subject as aforesaid, every lifting appliance shall be thoroughly examined by a competent person at least once in every period of twelve months and a record of every such examination and of the results thereof, containing the particulars required by the Lifting Plant and Equipment (Records of Test and Examination etc.) Regulations 1992, shall be kept and the particulars in that record shall be available for inspection. In the case of lifting appliances in a shipyard, the person by whom the record is authenticated shall within twenty-eight days of the completion of the examination send a copy of the particulars in the record to an inspector appointed by the Health and Safety Executive under section 19 of the Health and Safety at Work etc. Act 1974 who is authorised for the purposes of this provision in every case where the examination shows that the lifting appliance can not continue to be used with safety unless certain repairs are carried out immediately or within a specified time.";

(c) in regulation 36(1), for the words from "A certificate of test" to "shall be available for inspection", substitute—
   "A record of such test and thorough examination and of the results thereof, containing the particulars required by the Lifting Plant and Equipment (Records of Test and Examination etc.) Regulations 1992, shall have been obtained and the particulars in that record shall be available for inspection.";

(d) in regulation 36(2), for the words from "a certificate of such test" to the end, substitute—
   "a record of such test and thorough examination and of the results thereof, containing the particulars required by the Lifting Plant and Equipment (Records of Test and Examination etc.) Regulations 1992, has been obtained and the particulars in that record are available for inspection."; and

(e) In regulation 37(1) and (2), for the words "reports of the results" to the end, substitute in each case—
"records of such thorough examinations and of the results thereof, containing the particulars required by the Lifting Plant and Equipment (Records of Test and Examination etc.) Regulations 1992, shall be kept and the particulars in the records shall be available for inspection.".

2. The Construction (Lifting Operations) Regulations 1961 shall be modified as follows—

(a) in regulation 19(4), for the final sentence, substitute—
"A record of every such test and the results thereof, containing the particulars required by the Lifting Plant and Equipment (Records of Test and Examination etc.) Regulations 1992, shall be made forthwith.";

(b) in regulation 23(2), for "certificate of test and examination", substitute—
"record of the results of any test and thorough examination.";

(c) for regulation 28(5), substitute the following paragraph—
"(5) No crane, crab winch, pulley block or gin wheel shall be used unless there has been obtained a record of any test and thorough examination required by paragraphs (1) and (2) of this regulation and of the results thereof, containing the particulars required by the Lifting Plant and Equipment (Records of Test and Examination etc.) Regulations 1992.";

(d) for regulation 28(6), substitute the following paragraph—
"(6) A record of every test or thorough examination required by paragraphs (1) to (3) of this regulation, containing the particulars required by the Lifting Plant and Equipment (Records of Test and Examination etc.) Regulations 1992, shall be made within twenty-eight days:
Provided that this paragraph shall not apply to a test and thorough examination of which a record has been obtained in accordance with paragraph (5) of this regulation.";

(e) for regulation 28(7), substitute the following paragraph—
"(7) The person authenticating the record of any test or examination required paragraphs (1) or (3) of this regulation shall within twenty-eight days of the completion of the test or examination send a copy of the particulars in the record to an inspector appointed by the Health and Safety Executive under section 19 of the Health and Safety at Work etc. Act 1974 who is authorised for the purposes of this provision in every case where the test or examination shows that the plant or equipment cannot continue to be used with safety unless certain repairs are carried out immediately or within a specified time.";

(f) for regulation 34(1)(b), substitute the following sub-paragraph—
"(b) (except in the case of a wire rope used before the commencement of these Regulations or a fibre rope or fibre rope sling) it has been tested and examined by a competent person and a record of such test and examination and of the results thereof, containing the particulars required by the Lifting Plant and Equipment (Records of Test and Examination etc.) Regulations 1992, has been obtained; and";

(g) in regulation 34(2), for "report", substitute "record";

(h) in regulation 35—
(i) for the words "in the prescribed form" to "specifying the safe working load:", substitute the following—
"a record of such test and thorough examination and of the results thereof, containing the particulars required by the Lifting Plant and Equipment (Records of Test and Examination etc.) Regulations 1992:", and
(ii) for "certification", substitute "obtaining a record";

(i) in regulation 40, for the final sentence, substitute the following—
"A record of every such thorough examination and of the results thereof, containing the particulars required by the Lifting Plant and Equipment

(Records of Test and Examination etc.) Regulations 1992, shall be made forthwith.";

(j) in regulation 46(1)(a), for the words from "and there has been obtained" to the end, substitute the following—

"and a record of such test and thorough examination, containing the particulars required by the Lifting Plant and Equipment (Records of Test and Examination etc.) Regulations 1992, has been obtained;";

(k) in regulation 46(1)(b), for the words from "and a report of the results" to the end, substitute the following—

"and a record of the results of such test and thorough examination, containing the particulars required by the Lifting Plant and Equipment (Records of Test and Examination etc.) Regulations 1992, has been made; and";

(l) for regulation 46(2), substitute the following paragraph—

"(2) A record of every thorough examination required by sub-paragraph (c) of the foregoing paragraph and of the results thereof, containing the particulars required by the Lifting Plant and Equipment (Records of Test and Examination etc.) Regulations 1992, shall be made within twenty-eight days.";

(m) for regulation 46(3), substitute the following paragraph—

"The person authenticating the record of any test or examination required by paragraph (1) of this Regulation shall within twenty-eight days of the completion of the test or examination send a copy of the particulars contained in the record to an inspector appointed by the Health and Safety Executive under section 19 of the Health and Safety at Work etc. Act 1974 who is authorised for the purposes of this provision in every case where the test or examination shows that the hoist cannot continue to be used with safety unless certain repairs are carried out immediately or within a specified time.";

(n) in regulation 50(1)—

(i) after "reports" where it first occurs, add "or records",

(ii) after "kept" on the first occasion that it occurs, add "or the particulars in them shall be capable of inspection (which must include the ability to make an accurate and legible written copy)", and

(iii) after "kept" on the second occasion that it occurs, add "or the particulars contained in them shall be capable of inspection as aforesaid";

(o) in regulation 50(2)—

(i) for "document", substitute "record" on both occasions where it occurs, and

(ii) for "certificate" where it last occurs, substitute "certificate or record"; and

(p) in regulation 50(3), for "documents", substitute "records", and for "document", substitute "record".

3. The Factories Act 1961 shall be modified as follows—

(a) for section 22(2), substitute the following subsection—

"(2) Every hoist or lift shall be thoroughly examined by a competent person at least once in every period of six months and a record of every such thorough examination and of the results thereof, containing the particulars required by the Lifting Plant and Equipment (Records of Test and Examination etc.) Regulations 1992, shall be made within twenty-eight days, and any such record shall be kept and the particulars in it shall be available for inspection as if it formed part of the general register.";

(b) for section 22(3), substitute the following subsection—

"(3) Where the thorough examination shows that the hoist or lift cannot continue to be used with safety unless certain repairs are carried out immediately or within a specified time, the person who authenticates the record shall within twenty-eight days of the completion of the thorough examination send a copy of the particulars contained in the record to an inspector appointed by the Health and Safety Executive under section 19 of the Health and Safety at Work etc. Act 1974 who is authorised for the purposes of this provision.";

(c) for section 26(1)(e), substitute the following paragraph—
  "(e) no chain, rope or lifting tackle, except a fibre rope or a fibre rope sling, shall be taken into use in any factory for the first time in that factory, unless it has been tested and thoroughly examined by a competent person and a record of the test and thorough examination and of the results thereof, containing the particulars required by the Lifting Plant and Equipment (Records of Test and Examination etc.) Regulations 1992, has been obtained and the particulars in that record are kept available for inspection;";

(d) for section 26(1)(g), substitute the following paragraph—
  "(g) a record containing the particulars required by the Lifting Plant and Equipment (Records of Test and Examination etc.) Regulations 1992, shall be kept in respect of all such chains, ropes or lifting tackle, except fibre rope slings.";

(e) for section 27(2), substitute the following subsection—
  "(2) All such parts and gear shall be thoroughly examined by a competent person at least once in every period of fourteen months and a record shall be kept of every such thorough examination and of the results thereof, containing the particulars required by the Lifting Plant and Equipment (Records of Test and Examination etc.) Regulations 1992, and where the thorough examination shows that the lifting machine can not continue to be used with safety unless certain repairs are carried out immediately or within a specified time, the person who authenticates the record shall within twenty-eight days of the completion of the thorough examination send a copy of the particulars in the record to an inspector appointed by the Health and Safety Executive under section 19 of the Health and Safety at Work etc. Act 1974 who is authorised for the purposes of this provision."; and

(f) in section 27(6), for the words, "certificate of the test" to the end, substitute the following—
  "record of the test and thorough examination and of the results thereof, containing the particulars required by the Lifting Plant and Equipment (Records of Test and Examination etc.) Regulations 1992, has been obtained and the particulars in that record are kept available for inspection;".

4. The Offices, Shops and Railway Premises (Hoists and Lifts) Regulations 1968 shall be modified as follows—

(a) in regulation 6(1)—
  (i) for the words from "report of the result of every such examination" to "examination and", substitute the following—
    "record of every such thorough examination and of the results thereof, containing the particulars required by the Lifting Plant and Equipment (Records of Test and Examination etc.) Regulations 1992", and
  (ii) for "report of the result of the examination", substitute "record of the thorough examination and of the results thereof";

(b) for regulation 6(2), substitute the following paragraph—
  "(2) The record of every thorough examination and of the results thereof made in pursuance of paragraph (1) of this regulation shall be preserved and the particulars in that record shall be kept readily available for inspection by any inspector for, in each case, two years after the date when the record is signed or otherwise authenticated."; and

(c) in regulation 6(3)—
  (i) for "making the report", substitute "who authenticates the record", and
  (ii) for "copy of the report", substitute, on both occasions where it occurs, "copy of the particulars contained in the record".

5. The Docks Regulations 1988 shall be modified by substituting for the words "certificate or report" in regulation 15(1)(a)(i) and each time they occur in regulation 17, the word "record".

SCHEDULE 3

Regulation 7

REVOCATIONS

(1)	(2)	(3)
Title of instrument	*Reference*	*Extent of revocation*
The Chain Ropes and Lifting Tackle (Register) Order 1938	S.R. & O. 1938/599	The whole Order
The Shipbuilding (Reports on Chains and Lifting Gear) Order 1961	S.I. 1961/115	The whole Order
The Shipbuilding (Reports on Ropes and Rope Slings) Order 1961	S.I. 1961/116	The whole Order
The Shipbuilding (Lifting Appliances etc. Forms) Order 1961	S.I. 1961/431	Articles 3(1), (2), (3) and (4) and Parts I, II, III and IV of the Schedule
The Shipbuilding (Reports on Lifting Appliances) Order 1961	S.I. 1961/433	The whole Order
The Construction (Lifting Operations) Reports Order 1962	S.I. 1962/225	Articles 4 and 6 and Parts II and IV of the Schedule
The Construction (Lifting Operations) Prescribed Particulars Order 1962	S.I. 1962/226	Articles 3, 4, 5 and 7 and Parts I, II, III, IV and VI of the Schedule
The Construction (Lifting Operations) Certificates Order 1962	S.I. 1962/227	The whole Order
The Construction (Lifting Operations) Prescribed Particulars (Amendment) Order 1962	S.I. 1962/1747	The whole Order
The Lifting Machines (Particulars of Examinations) Order 1963	S.I. 1963/1382	The whole Order
The Hoists and Lifts (Reports of Examinations) Order 1963	S.I. 1963/2003	The whole Order
The Shipbuilding (Lifting Appliances etc. Forms) (Amendment) Order 1964	S.I. 1964/530	The whole Order
The Construction (Lifting Operations) Certificate (Amendment) Order 1964	S.I. 1964/531	The whole Order
The Docks Certificates Order 1964	S.I. 1964/532	The whole Order

(1) *Title of instrument*	(2) *Reference*	(3) *Extent of revocation*
The Docks Certificates (No. 2) Order 1964	S.I. 1964/1736	The whole Order
The Offices, Shops and Railway Premises (Hoists and Lifts) Reports Order 1968	S.I. 1968/863	The whole Order
The Docks, Shipbuilding etc. (Metrication) Regulations 1983	S.I. 1983/644	In the list in regulation and in the Schedule, the entries in respect of— —The Docks Regulations 1925, —The Docks Regulations 1934, —The Docks Certificates (No. 2) Order 1964
The Docks Regulations 1988	S.I. 1988/1655	Regulation 15(1)(a)(ii)

THE ROAD TRAFFIC (CARRIAGE OF DANGEROUS SUBSTANCES IN PACKAGES ETC.) REGULATIONS 1992

(S.I. 1992 No. 742, as amended by S.I. 1992 No. 744 and S.I. 1992 No. 1213)

The Secretary of State, in exercise of the powers conferred on him by section 15(1), (2), (4), (5)(b) and (6)(b) of, and paragraphs 1(1), (2) and (3), 3, 6(2), 12, 14, 15(1) and 16 of Schedule 3 to, the Health and Safety at Work etc. Act 1974 and of all other powers enabling him in that behalf, and for the purpose of giving effect without modifications to proposals submitted to him by the Health and Safety Commission under section 11(2)(d) of the said Act after the carrying out by the said Commission of consultations in accordance with section 50(3) of that Act, hereby makes the following Regulations:

1. Citation and commencement. These Regulations may be cited as the Road Traffic (Carriage of Dangerous Substances in Packages etc.) Regulations 1992 and shall come into force on 1 June 1992.

2. Interpretation.—(1) In these Regulations, unless the context otherwise requires—

"the 1974 Act" means the Health and Safety at Work etc. Act 1974;

"the 1983 Regulations" means the Classification and Labelling of Explosives Regulations 1983;

"the 1984 Regulations" means the Classification, Packaging and Labelling of Dangerous Substances Regulations 1984;

"the 1992 Regulations" means the Road Traffic (Carriage of Dangerous Substances in Road Tankers and Tank Containers) Regulations 1992;

"agriculture" includes horticulture, fruit growing, seed growing, dairy farming, livestock breeding and keeping, forestry, the use of land as grazing land, meadow land, osier land or nursery grounds or for market gardening and the preparation of land for agricultural purposes;

"approved list" has the same meaning as in regulation 4 of *the 1984 Regulations*;

"carriage" means carriage arising out of or in connection with work and shall be construed in accordance with regulations 2(2)(a)(ii) and 3(3); and related words shall be construed accordingly;

"carrying tank" means a *tank* which is referred to thus in *the 1992 Regulations* by virtue of the definition of "*road tanker*" contained in regulation 2(1) thereof;

"Class 1" has the same meaning as in regulation 2(1) of *the 1983 Regulations*;

"computer" means a computer system including its software;

898

"the consignor" of a *dangerous substance* shall be regarded as—

(a) the person who, having a place of business in Great Britain, consigns (whether as principal or as agent for another) that *dangerous substance* for *carriage*; or

(b) if no person satisfies the requirements of sub-paragraph (a) above, the consignee of that *dangerous substance*;

"dangerous substance" (whether or not a preparation or other mixture) means—

(a) any substance listed as dangerous for conveyance by *road* in column 1 of Part IA2 of the *approved list*, other than when the substance has been so diluted or treated that it no longer has any of the characteristic properties specified in column 1 of Part I of Schedule 2 to *the 1984 Regulations*;

(b) any substance which falls within one of the groups of substances listed as dangerous for conveyance by *road* in column 1 of Part IB of the *approved list*, other than when the substance has been so diluted or treated that it no longer has any of the characteristic properties specified in column 1 of Part I of Schedule 2 to *the 1984 Regulations*;

(c) any substance classified as a *flammable gas*, a *toxic gas* or an *organic peroxide* in accordance with regulation 6(4) of *the 1984 Regulations*;

(d) any controlled waste (as defined by section 30 of the Control of Pollution Act 1974) consisting of or containing asbestos not falling within sub-paragraph (a) of this definition which is designated as "special waste" by regulation 2(1)(a)(i) of the Control of Pollution (Special Waste) Regulations 1980; or

(e) any other substance which is classified as dangerous for conveyance in accordance with regulation 6(4) of *the 1984 Regulations* and possesses the properties relevant to the classification concerned which are specified in column 1 of Part I of the Schedule hereto;

"fire authority" has the same meaning as in section 38(1) of the Fire Services Act 1947;

"flammable gas" means a gas so classified in accordance with paragraph (2) or (4) of regulation 6 of *the 1984 Regulations*;

"flammable solid" means a solid so classified in accordance with paragraph (2) or (4) of regulation 6 of *the 1984 Regulations*;

"flash point" has the same meaning as in regulation 2(1) of *the 1984 Regulations*;

"freight container" means a container as defined in regulation 2(1) of the Freight Containers (Safety Convention) Regulations 1984;

"goods vehicle examiner" has the same meaning as in section 68(2) of the Road Traffic Act 1988;

"motor vehicle" has the same meaning as in the Table contained in regulation 3(2) of the Road Vehicles (Construction and Use) Regulations 1986;

"operator" shall be construed in accordance with regulation 4;

"organic peroxide" means a substance so classified in accordance with regulation 6(4) of *the 1984 Regulations*;

"receptacle" means—

(a) a vessel (other than a *carrying tank, tank container, freight container,* transformer or capacitor); or

(b) the innermost layer of packagings,

which is in contact with a *dangerous substance* and which is liable to be individually handled when the substance is used or disposed of;

"road" means—

(a) as respects England and Wales, a road within the meaning of section 192(1) of the Road Traffic Act 1988; and

(b) as respects Scotland, a road within the meaning of the Roads (Scotland) Act 1984;

"road tanker" has the same meaning as in regulation 2(1) of *the 1992 Regulations*;

"semi-trailer" has the same meaning as in the Table contained in regulation 3(2) of the Road Vehicles (Construction and Use) Regulations 1986;

"tank" has the same meaning as in regulation 2(1) of *the 1992 Regulations*;

"tank container" has the same meaning as in regulation 2(1) of *the 1992 Regulations*;

"toxic gas" means a gas so classified in accordance with paragraph (2) or (4) of regulation 6 of *the 1984 Regulations*;

"trailer" has the same meaning as in regulation 2(1) of the Road Traffic (Carriage of Explosives) Regulations 1989.

(2) For the purposes of these Regulations—

(a) a combination of a *motor vehicle* and one or more *trailers* or *semi-trailers* shall be deemed to be a single vehicle for so long as the constituent parts of that combination remain attached; and—

    (i) *dangerous substances* contained in different parts of such a vehicle shall accordingly be considered to be contained in the same vehicle, and

    (ii) without prejudice to the generality of regulation 3(3), a *trailer* or *semi-trailer* containing any *dangerous substance* shall not be considered to be engaged in any *carriage* to which these Regulations apply unless it forms part of such a combination;

(b) any reference to the *carriage* of a *dangerous substance* in bulk shall (unless the context otherwise requires) include a reference to the unconfined *carriage* of that substance in a *freight container*, but shall exclude a reference to the *carriage* of that substance—

    (i) in a *receptacle* (whether or not the *receptacle* is carried in a *freight container*),

    (ii) in a *road tanker*,

    (iii) in a *tank container*, or

    (iv) in a transformer or capacitor; and

(c) a vehicle will be deemed to be registered in the United Kingdom where the relevant *motor vehicle* is registered under the Vehicles (Excise) Act 1971 or any enactment repealed thereby.

(3) Unless the context otherwise requires, any reference in these Regulations to—

(a) a numbered regulation is a reference to the regulation in these Regulations so numbered;

(b) a numbered paragraph is a reference to the paragraph so numbered in the regulation in which the reference appears;

(c) the "packing group" of a *dangerous substance* shall be construed—

    (i) in the case of a *dangerous substance* listed as dangerous for conveyance by *road* in column 1 of Part IA2 of the *approved list* or which falls within one of the groups of substances listed as dangerous for conveyance by *road* in column 1 of Part IB of the *approved list,* as a reference to the packing group (if any) which is specified in the corresponding entry in column 7 of the Part in which it is listed or grouped as aforesaid,

(ii) in the case of a *dangerous substance* not listed or grouped as aforesaid but which is classified as dangerous for conveyance in accordance with regulation 6(4) of *the 1984 Regulations* and possesses the properties relevant to the classification concerned (which classification is that neither of a toxic nor a harmful substance) which are specified in column 1 of Part I of the Schedule hereto, as a reference to the packing group listed in column 2 of that Part which corresponds with the properties thus specified, or

(iii) in the case of a *dangerous substance* not listed or grouped as aforesaid but which is classified as dangerous for conveyance in accordance with regulation 6(4) of *the 1984 Regulations* and possesses the properties relevant to the classification concerned (which classification is that of a toxic or a harmful substance) which are specified in column 1 of Part I of the Schedule hereto, as a reference to the relevant packing group referred to in the properties thus specified; and

(d) the colour orange shall be construed as a reference to a shade of orange which, so far as is practicable, matches the colour No. 557 Light Orange identified in Table 1 to the British Standard BS 381C: 1988.

3. **Application of these Regulations.**—(1) Subject to paragraph (2)—

(a) regulation 15(2) shall apply to the *carriage* on a vehicle—
   (i) (in a *receptacle* with a capacity of less than 5 litres) of any *dangerous substance* such as is specified in sub-paragraph (c)(iv) to (vi) of this paragraph, or
   (ii) (in a *receptacle* with a capacity of less than 200 litres) of any *dangerous substance* such as is specified in sub-paragraph (c)(vii) of this paragraph;

(b) regulation 16 shall apply to the *carriage* in or, as the case may be, on a vehicle of any *dangerous substance* such as is specified in paragraph (1) thereof in bulk or in a *receptacle* (regardless of the capacity of that *receptacle*); and

(c) the remainder of these Regulations shall apply to or, where appropriate, in relation to the *carriage* in or, as the case may be, on a vehicle—
   (i) of any *dangerous substance* in bulk,
   (ii) (in a *receptacle,* regardless of its capacity) of any *organic peroxide* which is subject to regulation 11(2),
   (iii) (in a *receptacle,* regardless of its capacity) of any *flammable solid* which is subject to regulation 11(3),
   (iv) (in a *receptacle* with a capacity of 5 litres or more) of any *organic peroxide* (other than one which is subject to regulation 11(2)), any flammable or *toxic gas* or any other *dangerous substance* being within packing group I,

(v) (in a *receptacle* with a capacity of 5 litres or more) of any asbestos falling within sub-paragraph (a) of the definition of "*dangerous substance*" in regulation 2(1) or any substance such as is specified in sub-paragraph (d) of that definition,

(vi) (in a *receptacle* with a capacity of 5 litres or more) of any *dangerous substance* both listed in column 1 of the *approved list* as "hazardous waste" and designated as "special waste" by regulation 2(1)(a)(i) of the Control of Pollution (Special Waste) Regulations 1980,

(vii) (in a *receptacle* with a capacity of 200 litres or more) of any *dangerous substance* not specified in heads (ii) to (vi) of this sub-paragraph, or

(viii) (in a transformer or capacitor, regardless of its capacity) of any *dangerous substance* not specified in heads (ii) to (v) of this sub-paragraph.

(2) These Regulations shall not apply to the *carriage* of a *dangerous substance*—

(a) in so far as the *dangerous substance* being carried is being used solely in connection with the operation of a vehicle;

(b) where the *dangerous substance* being carried is a radioactive substance within the meaning of regulation 2(1) of the Ionising Radiations Regulations 1985;

(c) where the *dangerous substance* being carried has been classified (as defined by regulation 2(1) of *the 1983 Regulations*) in pursuance of regulation 3(2)(a) of those Regulations and assigned to *Class 1*;

(d) (other than for the purposes of regulations 7 and 8) where—

(i) the vehicle which is being used for the *carriage* of the *dangerous substance* is engaged in an international transport operation within the meaning of the Convention concerning International Carriage by Rail, as revised or reissued from time to time, and

(ii) such *carriage* conforms in every respect with the provisions of the Regulations concerning the International Carriage of Dangerous Goods by Rail which are specified in Annex I to the Uniform Rules concerning the Contract for International Carriage of Goods by Rail, which Rules form Appendix B to the above Convention;

(e) where—

(i) the vehicle which is being used for the *carriage* of the *dangerous substance* is engaged in international transport within the meaning of article 1(c) of the European Agreement concerning the International Carriage of Dangerous Goods by Road signed at Geneva on 30 September 1957, as revised or reissued from time to time ("ADR"), and

(ii) such *carriage* conforms in every respect with the provisions of ADR;

(f) where the transport of the *dangerous substance* concerned is subject to a special bilateral or multilateral agreement made under the terms of article 4.3 of ADR to which the United Kingdom is a signatory and conforms with any conditions attached to the agreement;

(g) where the vehicle which is being used for the *carriage* of the *dangerous substance* is not, for the time being, subject to the provisions of ADR by reason only that it is a vehicle belonging to or under the orders of the armed forces of a country which is a signatory to ADR;

(h) where the vehicle which is being used for the *carriage* of the *dangerous substance* is delivering that substance—

    (i) between private premises and another vehicle situated in the immediate vicinity of those premises, or

    (ii) between one part of private premises and another part of those premises situated in the immediate vicinity of that first part;

(i) where the vehicle which is being used for the *carriage* of the *dangerous substance* is passing from one part of an agricultural unit to another part of that unit and the *dangerous substance* is diluted ready for use or is otherwise in a condition ready for use; and in this head "agricultural unit" means a self-contained parcel of land which is occupied (whether or not by a single occupier) for *agriculture*;

(j) where the *dangerous substance* being carried is specified in sub-paragraphs (c) to (i) of regulation 3(1) of *the 1984 Regulations*;

(k) where the *dangerous substance* being carried is commercial butane, commercial propane or any mixture thereof in a cylinder and—

    (i) the vehicle concerned has been designed for a purpose which includes the use of any such substance and the substance concerned is being carried in connection with the operation of the vehicle, or

    (ii) the cylinder is part of equipment carried on the vehicle concerned, provided that the number of cylinders carried thus (including any spare cylinder) does not exceed two;

(l) (for the purposes of regulations 7, 10(1) and 12 only)—

    (i) where one or more *dangerous substances* which are listed in column 1 of Part IA2 of the *approved list* under the name "ammonium nitrate fertiliser" are being carried in or on a vehicle from one piece of land occupied by a single occupier for the purpose of *agriculture* to another piece of land occupied by that occupier alone for the purpose of *agriculture*,

    (ii) where—

        (aa) the vehicle carrying the ammonium nitrate fertiliser as aforesaid is exempted from excise duty under section 7(1) of the Vehicles (Excise) Act 1971 ("the 1971 Act") or is liable to excise duty as a "special machine" in accordance with section 1 of and Schedule 3 to the 1971 Act, and

        (bb) (in either case) the address specified in the vehicle registration document for the vehicle is that of the occupier of the pieces of land between which it is carrying the ammonium nitrate fertiliser as aforesaid and that address is within 12 kilometres of either of those pieces of land,

    (iii) where the total mass of the ammonium nitrate fertilisers being carried as aforesaid does not exceed 10 tonnes,

    (iv) where—

        (aa) the vehicle carrying the ammonium nitrate fertiliser as aforesaid displays a single rectangular reflectorised orange-coloured plate of 400 millimetres base and 300 millimetres high which has a black border not more than 15 millimetres wide, is affixed to the rear of the vehicle in a substantially vertical plane and is clean, clearly visible and free from obstruction (except that the plate need not be clearly visible or free from obstruction when the vehicle is being loaded or unloaded), or

   (bb) (when the ammonium nitrate fertiliser is being carried as
        aforesaid in *receptacles* only) those *receptacles* are labelled in
        accordance with regulation 13 of *the 1984 Regulations* and
        those labels are clearly visible from outside the vehicle carry-
        ing them, and
   (v) where the driver of the vehicle carrying the ammonium nitrate
        fertiliser as aforesaid has in his possession (or there is otherwise
        available on the vehicle) adequate written information about the
        nature of the hazards created by the particular ammonium nitrate
        fertiliser being carried and the action to be taken in an emergency
        concerning it.

(3) For the purposes of these Regulations, a vehicle shall be deemed to be
engaged in the *carriage* of a *dangerous substance* throughout the period—

(a) in the case of a vehicle carrying a *dangerous substance* in bulk other than in
     a *freight container*, from the commencement of loading the relevant
     vehicle with the *dangerous substance* concerned for the purpose of carry-
     ing that substance on a *road* until the vehicle has been unloaded (and
     where necessary cleaned or purged) so that any of the substance or its
     vapour which remains in the vehicle is not sufficient to create a risk to
     the health or safety of any person; or
(b) in the case of a vehicle carrying a *dangerous substance* in a *freight container*,
     receptacle, transformer or capacitor—
     (i) (if the relevant *freight container*, *receptacle*, transformer or capacitor
          has been loaded with the *dangerous substance* concerned before
          being placed on the vehicle) from the time when the *freight con-
          tainer*, *receptacle*, transformer or capacitor is placed on the vehicle for
          the purpose of carrying the *dangerous substance* on a *road*, or
     (ii) (if the relevant *freight container*, *receptacle*, transformer or capacitor
          has been placed on the vehicle before the commencement of
          loading) from the commencement of loading the *freight container*,
          receptacle, transformer or capacitor with the *dangerous substance* con-
          cerned for the purpose of carrying it by *road*,
     until either—
        (aa) the *freight container*, *receptacle*, transformer or capacitor is
              removed from the vehicle, or
        (bb) the *freight container*, *receptacle*, transformer or capacitor (and,
              where necessary, the vehicle carrying same) have been emp-
              tied (and where necessary cleaned or purged) so that any of
              the substance or its vapour which remains therein is not
              sufficient to create a risk to the health or safety of any person;
and, in either case, where or not the vehicle is on a *road* at the material time.

4. Meaning of *operator*.—(1) For the purposes of these Regulations, the
operator of a vehicle shall be—

(a) the person who holds an *operator*'s licence (granted under Part V of the
     Transport Act 1968 for the use of that vehicle for the *carriage* of goods on
     a *road*; except that where by virtue of regulation 32(1) to (3) of the
     Goods Vehicles (Operators' Licences, Qualifications and Fees) Regu-
     lations 1984 the vehicle is included in a licence held by a holding
     company and that company is not operating the vehicle at the relevant

time, the *"operator"* shall be the subsidiary company specified in the application made under the said regulation 32(1) or, if more than one subsidiary company is so specified, whichever one is operating the vehicle at the relevant time, and in this sub-paragraph "holding company" and "subsidiary company" have the same meanings as in the said Regulations of 1984; or

(b) where no such licence is held—

    (i) (in the case of a vehicle which is not registered in the United Kingdom) the driver of the vehicle, or

    (ii) (in the case of any other vehicle, but subject to paragraph (2)) the keeper of the vehicle; and, for this purpose, where the vehicle is on hire or lease to any person, that person shall be treated as its keeper.

(2) Where an employee who would otherwise be the *operator* of a vehicle in accordance with sub-paragraph (b)(ii) of paragraph (1) uses that vehicle for the *carriage* of any *dangerous substance* on behalf of his employer, that employer shall (notwithstanding that sub-paragraph) be regarded as the *operator* of the vehicle for the purposes of these Regulations.

5. Construction of vehicles and *freight containers*. The *operator* of any vehicle which is being used for the *carriage* of a *dangerous substance* shall ensure that—

(a) that vehicle and (in the case where the *dangerous substance* is contained in a *freight container* which is carried on the vehicle) that *freight container*—

    (i) are properly designed, of adequate strength, of good construction from sound and suitable materials and adequately maintained,

    (ii) are suitable for the purpose for which they are being used, having regard to—

        (aa) the nature and circumstances of the journey being undertaken, and

        (bb) the characteristic properties and quantity of both the *dangerous substance* and any other substance being carried; and

(b) (in the case where the *dangerous substance* is being carried in bulk) any parts of the vehicle or *freight container* containing the substance, and any fittings attached thereto, which are likely to come into contact with that substance are made of materials which are liable neither to be affected by the substance nor, in conjunction with it, to form any other substance which creates a hazard to the health or safety of any person.

6. Information relating to *dangerous substances* to be received by *operators*.—
(1) *The consignor* of a *dangerous substance* shall ensure that the *operator* of the vehicle which is to carry it receives such information as will enable that *operator*—

(a) to comply with his duties under these Regulations; and

(b) to be aware of the hazards created by the substance to the health or safety of any person.

(2) An *operator* shall not use a vehicle for the *carriage* of a *dangerous substance* unless he is in possession of the information referred to in paragraph (1).

(3) *The consignor* shall ensure that the information referred to in paragraph (1) is—

(a) so far as is reasonably practicable, provided in written form;

(b) accurate; and

(c) sufficient for the purposes specified in that paragraph.

(4) The *operator* shall keep the information referred to in paragraph (1) for a period of at least two weeks after the completion of the relevant journey, either in written form or in a *computer* under his control.

(5) Information may only be kept in a *computer* in accordance with paragraph (4) where the information concerned—

(a) has been entered in the relevant *computer* by a competent person;

(b) is capable of being reproduced in written form when required;

(c) is secure from unauthorised interference; and

(d) can be authenticated only by the person who entered it.

7.   Information in writing about *dangerous substances* to be given to drivers.— (1) The *operator* of any vehicle which is being used for the *carriage* of a *dangerous substance* shall ensure that the driver of the vehicle has received adequate information in writing about—

(a) the identity of the substance;

(b) the quantity to be carried; and

(c) the nature of the hazards created by the substance and the action to be taken in an emergency concerning it.

(2) The driver of any vehicle which is being used for the carriage of a *dangerous substance* shall ensure that—

(a) the information in writing relating to that substance received by him in accordance with paragraph (1) is (subject to paragraphs (4) and (5) and regulation 15(1)) both kept on the vehicle and readily available at all times while the substance is being carried; and

(b) (subject to paragraph (3)) any information in writing in his possession received by him in accordance with paragraph (1) and which relates to any *dangerous substance* which is not being carried is destroyed, removed from the vehicle, or placed in a securely closed container clearly marked to show that the information does not relate to a *dangerous substance* which is being carried.

(3) Nothing in paragraph (2)(b) shall require the destruction, removal or placing in a securely closed container of information in writing received by a driver in accordance with paragraph (1) which relates to any *dangerous substance* which is not being carried where that information in writing relates also to a *dangerous substance* which is being carried, and the nature of the hazards created by those *dangerous substances* is such that the action to be taken in an emergency concerning them is identical.

(4) Notwithstanding paragraph (2)(a), where the tractor unit of any articulated vehicle which is being used for the *carriage* of a *dangerous substance* is detached from the *trailer* of that vehicle on a road or in premises, the driver of the vehicle shall attach the information in writing relating to that substance received by him in accordance with paragraph (1) to the *trailer* in a readily visible position or (in the case where the tractor unit is detached as aforesaid in premises) give that information to the occupier of the premises; and in such a

case, the occupier shall ensure that said information is readily available at the premises.

(5) Notwithstanding paragraph (2)(a), the driver of any vehicle which is being used for the carriage of a *dangerous substance* shall, when so requested by any police constable or any member of the fire or ambulance services in an emergency, produce the information in writing relating to that substance received by him in accordance with paragraph (1) to that constable or other person.

9. Loading, stowage and unloading of *dangerous substances*. The *operator* of any vehicle which is being used for the *carriage* of a *dangerous substance* and every person engaged in that *carriage* shall take such steps as it is reasonable for them respectively to take to ensure that nothing in the manner in which the *dangerous substance* is loaded onto, stowed on or unloaded from the vehicle is liable to create a hazard to the health or safety of any person.

10. Precautions against fire or explosion.—(1) The *operator* of any vehicle which is being used for the *carriage* of a *dangerous substance* shall ensure that that vehicle also carries adequate fire-fighting equipment.

(2) Every driver of, and every person repairing, maintaining, examining, inspecting, loading, unloading or otherwise dealing with, a vehicle which is being used for the *carriage* of a *dangerous substance* shall observe all the precautions necessary for preventing fire or explosion.

11. Limitation on the *carriage* of certain *dangerous substances*.—(1) The *operator* of any vehicle which is being used for the *carriage* of a *dangerous substance* in respect of which a maximum concentration or other condition is specified in column 1 of the *approved list* shall ensure that during the whole of the *carriage* that concentration is not exceeded or, as the case may be, that condition is satisfied.

(2) Subject to paragraph (4), the *operator* and driver of any vehicle which is being used for the *carriage* of an *organic peroxide* which has a self-accelerating decomposition temperature of $50\infty C$ or below as packaged shall ensure that during the whole of the *carriage* the *organic peroxide* concerned is kept at a temperature which does not exceed its control temperature.

(3) The *operator* and driver of any vehicle which is being used for the *carriage* of a *flammable solid* which has a self-accelerating decomposition temperature of $55\infty C$ or below as packaged shall ensure that during the whole of the *carriage* the *flammable solid* concerned is kept at a temperature which does not exceed its control temperature.

(4) Nothing in paragraph (2) shall apply to any *organic peroxide* which has a self-accelerating decomposition temperature of greater than $45\infty C$ as packaged and which shows no effect or a negligible effect when heated under confinement.

(5) For the purposes of paragraphs (2) to (4), the self-accelerating decomposition temperature of an *organic peroxide* or, as the case may be, of a

flammable solid is the lowest temperature at which self-accelerating decomposition may occur in the package during *carriage.*

(6) For the purposes of paragraphs (2) and (3), the control temperature of an *organic peroxide* or, as the case may be, of a *flammable solid* is (where its self-accelerating decomposition temperature is 20∞C or less) 20∞C less than that self-accelerating decomposition temperature; (where its self-accelerating decomposition temperature is greater than 20∞C but less than or equal to 35∞C) 15∞C less than that self-accelerating decomposition temperature; and (where its self-accelerating decomposition temperature is greater than 35∞C) 10∞C less than that self-accelerating decomposition temperature.

12.   Marking of vehicles carrying *dangerous substances*.—(1) The *operator* of any vehicle which is being used for the *carriage* of at least 500 kilograms of one or more *dangerous substances* shall ensure that the vehicle displays two rectangular reflectorised orange-coloured plates of 400 millimetres base and 300 millimetres high in conformity with the conditions specified in paragraph (3).

(2) Nothing in paragraph (1) shall prevent the *operator* of any vehicle which is being used for the *carriage* of less than 500 kilograms of one or more *dangerous substances* from displaying on the vehicle the orange-coloured plates referred to in that paragraph; but where this occurs, the *operator* concerned shall ensure that the vehicle displays those plates in conformity with the conditions specified in paragraph (3).

(3) The orange-coloured plates referred to in paragraph (1) shall—

(a)   have a black border not more than 15 millimetres wide;

(b)   be affixed one at the front and the other at the rear of the vehicle in a substantially vertical plane; and

(c)   be kept clean, clearly visible and free from obstruction (except that the rear plate need not be kept clearly visible and free from obstruction when the vehicle is being loaded or unloaded).

(4) It shall be the duty of the driver of any vehicle being used for the *carriage* of a *dangerous substance* which is displaying the orange-coloured plates referred to in paragraph (1) to ensure that they are displayed in conformity with the conditions specified in sub-paragraphs (b) and (c) of paragraph (3).

(5) When any vehicle displaying the orange-coloured plates referred to in paragraph (1) is emptied of all the *dangerous substances* being carried by it, the *operator* and driver of the vehicle shall ensure that those plates are completely covered or completely removed from the vehicle.

(6) Paragraphs (1) to (5) shall not apply—

(a)   to the *carriage* of a *dangerous substance* to a port for *carriage* by sea, or from a port to which it has been carried by sea, if the vehicle or (in the case where the *dangerous substance* is contained in a *freight container* which is carried on the vehicle) the *freight container* is placarded in accordance with the appropriate provisions of the International Maritime Dangerous Goods Code issued by the International Maritime Organization as revised or re-issued from time to time; or

(b)   where the vehicle is being used solely for the *carriage* of a *dangerous substance* from—

    (i)   another *road* vehicle which has been damaged as the result of an accident on a *road* or has broken down on a *road,* or

    (ii) a rail vehicle which has been damaged or derailed or has broken down on a railway other than a siding on which it was loaded.

(7) Paragraphs (1) to (5) shall not apply to the *carriage* of a *dangerous substance* in a vehicle which is in the service of home forces (as defined by regulation 3(2) of the Road Vehicles Lighting Regulations 1989 ("the 1989 Regulations")) or of a visiting force (having the same meaning in this paragraph as it does for the purposes of any provision of Part I of the Visiting Forces Act 1952) insofar as the vehicle concerned is being used—

  (a) in connection with training—

    (i)   which has been certified in writing for the purposes of regulation 7 (1) (a) of the 1989 Regulations by a person duly authorised in that behalf to be training on a special occasion, and

    (ii) of which not less than 48 hours' notice has been given by that person to—

       (aa) the chief officer of police of every police area, and

       (bb) (as respects England and Wales) the chief officer or (as respects Scotland) the firemaster of the fire brigade maintained by the *fire authority* for any area,

in which the place selected for training is wholly or partially situated; or

  (b) on manoeuvres within such limits and during such periods as may from time to time be specified by Order in Council under the Manoeuvres Act 1958.

(8) Where a *trailer* or *semi-trailer* which is carrying at least 500 kilograms of one or more *dangerous substances* has become separated from the vehicle to which it was attached the persons who were for the purposes of these Regulations respectively regarded as the *operator* and driver of the combination of *motor vehicle* and one or more *trailers* or *semi-trailers* of which it formed part shall ensure that—

  (a) a single reflectorised orange-coloured plate of 400 millimetres base and 300 millimetres high and having a black border not more than 15 millimetres wide is affixed in a substantially vertical plane to the rear of the *trailer* or *semi-trailer* which has become separated as aforesaid; and

  (b) nothing is displayed on that *trailer* or *semi-trailer* which would be likely to confuse the emergency services when read in conjunction with that plate.

13. Prohibition on provision and display of orange-coloured plates and additional information.—(1) The *operator* and driver of any vehicle which is not being used for the *carriage* of a *dangerous substance* shall ensure that it does not at any time display the orange-coloured plates referred to in regulation 12(1).

(2) The *operator* and driver of any vehicle which is displaying the orange-coloured plates referred to in regulation 12(1) shall ensure that nothing is displayed on that vehicle which would be likely to confuse the emergency services when read in conjunction with those plates.

14. Supervision of vehicles containing *dangerous substances.* The driver of any vehicle which is being used—

(a) for any *carriage* to which this regulation applies by virtue of regulation 3(1)(c)(i), (iv), (v), (vi), (vii) or (viii) in circumstances where the total mass of *dangerous substances* being carried is at least 3 tonnes; or

(b) for any *carriage* to which this regulation applies by virtue of regulation 3(1)(c)(ii) or (iii),

shall ensure that the vehicle is parked in a safe place when it is not being driven, except—

(c) when supervised at all times by him or by a competent person over the age of 18 years; or

(d) (in circumstances where no such competent person is present) when the vehicle has been damaged or has broken down on a *road* and the driver has left the vehicle to seek assistance.

15. Information to be produced to police constables and *goods vehicle examiners*.—(1) The driver of any vehicle which is being used for the *carriage* of a *dangerous substance* shall (notwithstanding regulation 7(2)(a)) produce on request to any police constable or *goods vehicle examiner* the information in writing relating to that substance received by him in accordance with regulation 7(1).

(2) The driver of any vehicle which is being used for the *carriage* of a *dangerous substance* shall produce on request to any police constable or *goods vehicle examiner*—

(a) any information in his possession which will enable that constable or examiner to know the identity and quantity of the *dangerous substance* being carried; and

(b) any information which, pursuant to regulation 3(2)(1)(v), is in his possession or otherwise available on the vehicle.

16. Restrictions on the *carriage* of toxic or harmful substances in the same vehicle as food.—(1) The *operator* and driver of any vehicle which is being used for the *carriage* of a toxic or a harmful substance shall ensure that no food is carried in that vehicle unless the food is carried in a part of the vehicle effectively separated from that containing the substance or is otherwise adequately protected from the risk of contamination.

(2) In this regulation—

(a) "food" means food within the meaning of section 1(1) and (2) of the Food Safety Act 1990;

(b) "toxic substance" means a substance so classified in accordance with paragraph (2) or (4) of regulation 6 of *the 1984 Regulations*; and

(c) "harmful substance" means a substance so classified in accordance with paragraph (2) or (4) of regulation 6 of *the 1984 Regulations*.

17. Defence in proceedings for contravening these Regulations. In any proceedings for an offence consisting of a contravention of these Regulations, it shall be a defence for any person to prove that he took all reasonable precautions and exercised all due diligence to avoid the commission of that offence.

18. Exemption certificates.—(1) Subject to paragraph (2), the Health and Safety Executive may, by a certificate in writing, exempt any person or class of persons or any *dangerous substance* or class of *dangerous substances* from all or any of the requirements or prohibitions imposed by these Regulations and any such exemption may be granted subject to conditions and to a limit of time and may be revoked at any time by a certificate in writing.

(2) The Executive shall not grant any such exemption unless, having regard to the circumstance of the case, and in particular to—

(a) the conditions, if any, which it proposes to attach to the exemption; and
(b) any other requirements imposed by or under any enactments which apply to the case,

it is satisfied that the health and safety of persons who are likely to be affected by the exemption will not be prejudiced in consequence of it.

19. Revocations. The Road Traffic (Carriage of Dangerous Substances in Packages etc.) Regulations 1986 and the Road Traffic (Carriage of Dangerous Substances in Packages etc.) (Amendment) Regulations 1989 are hereby revoked.

SCHEDULE

Regulation 2(1)

PART I

PROPERTIES RELEVANT TO, AND PACKING GROUPS OF, SUBSTANCES WHICH HAVE BEEN CLASSIFIED AS DANGEROUS FOR CONVEYANCE IN ACCORDANCE WITH REGULATION 6(4) OF THE CLASSIFICATION, PACKAGING AND LABELLING OF DANGEROUS SUBSTANCES REGULATIONS 1984

Column 1	Column 2
Relevant properties	*Packing group*

1. The properties relevant to a substance which has been classified as a *flammable liquid* in accordance with regulation 6(4) of *the 1984 Regulations* are as follows:

(a) (in the case of a liquid containing not more than 20% of nitrocellulose and having a *flash point* not exceeding 21∞C)—

    (i) less than 3% of it shall separate out into a clear solvent layer following a suitable solvent separation test,

    (ii) the *flash point* of it shall be specified in column 1 of the table set out in Part III of this Schedule, and

    (iii) the kinematic viscosity of it shall be within the range   III specified in column 2 of the table set out in Part III of this Schedule which is opposite to the *flash point* of that liquid referred to in head (ii) of this sub-paragraph; or

(b) (in the case of any other liquid) its *flash point* shall be not greater than 55∞C and it shall have—

    (i) an initial boiling point of not greater than 35∞C,   I

    (ii) an initial boiling point above 35∞C and a *flash point* of less   II than 21∞C, or

    (iii) an initial boiling point above 35∞C and a *flash point* of   III 21∞C or above.

Column 1	Column 2
Relevant properties	*Packing group*

2. The properties relevant to a substance which has been classified as a *flammable solid* in accordance with regulation 6(4) of *the 1984 Regulations* are as follows:

it shall be readily combustible under conditions encountered in *carriage* in packages, etc., or it may cause or contribute to fire through friction and it shall—

   (a) be water-wetted and (when in a dry state) be required to be   I
        classified (as defined by regulation 2(1) of *the 1983 Regulations*) in pursuance of regulation 3(2)(a) of those Regulations;

   (b) be a self-reactive substance which, when ignited, burns very   II
        vigorously or intensely and is difficult to extinguish; or

   (c) when ignited, burn vigorously or intensely.   III

3. The properties relevant to a substance which has been classified as a *spontaneously combustible substance* in accordance with regulation 6(4) of *the 1984 Regulations* are as follows:

it shall be liable either to spontaneous heating under conditions encountered in *carriage* or to heating in contact with air (being in either case then liable to catch fire) and it shall be—

   (a) a pyrophoric substance which ignites instantly on contact with   I
        air;

   (b) liable to ignite on contact with air within a short space of time,   II
        particularly under conditions of spillage; or

   (c) any other substance which is liable to ignite on contact with   III
        air.

4. The properties relevant to a substance which has been classified as a *substance which in contact with water emits flammable gas* in accordance with regulation 6(4) of *the 1984 Regulations* are as follows:

in contact with water it shall be liable to become spontaneously combustible or to give off a *flammable gas* and it shall—

   (a) either react vigorously with water at ambient temperatures   I
        and demonstrate generally a tendency for the gas produced to ignite spontaneously or shall react readily with water at ambient temperatures so that the rate of evolution of *flammable gas* is equal to or greater than 10 litres per kilogram of substance over any period of one minute;

   (b) react readily with water at ambient temperatures so that the   II
        maximum rate of evolution of *flammable gas* is equal to or greater than 20 litres per kilogram of substance per hour; or

   (c) react slowly with water at ambient temperatures so that the   III
        maximum rate of evolution of *flammable gas* is greater than 1 litre per kilogram of substance per hour.

Column 1	Column 2
Relevant properties	*Packing group*

5. The properties relevant to a substance which has been classified as an *oxidizing substance* in accordance with regulation 6(4) of *the 1984 Regulations* are as follows:

it may (although not itself necessarily combustible), by yielding oxygen or by a similar process, cause or contribute to the combustion of other material and it shall exhibit oxidizing properties to a degree—

(a) greater than potassium bromate;	I
(b) equal to or greater than ammonium perchlorate; or	II
(c) equal to or greater than ammonium persulphate.	III

6. The properties relevant to a substance which has been classified as a *toxic substance* in accordance with regulation 6(4) of *the 1984 Regulations* are as follows:

it shall cause, or it may cause, a serious hazard to human health during *carriage*, and it shall have been allocated to packing group I or II in accordance with the criteria set out in Part II of this Schedule. —

7. The properties relevant to a substance which has been classified as a *harmful substance* in accordance with regulation 6(4) of *the 1984 Regulations* are as follows:

it shall cause, or it may cause, ill-health to people, but it shall be less likely to represent a serious hazard to health during *carriage* than does a toxic substance, and it shall have been allocated to packing group III in accordance with the criteria set out in Part II of this Schedule. —

8. The properties relevant to a substance which has been classified as a *corrosive substance* in accordance with regulation 6(4) of *the 1984 Regulations* are as follows:

it shall by chemical action—

(a) cause severe damage when in contact with living tissue; or	
(b) materially damage other freight or equipment if leakage occurs;	
and shall—	
(c) cause visible necrosis of the skin tissue at the site of contact when tested on the intact skin of an animal for a period of—	
(i) up to 3 minutes,	I
(ii) more than 3 and up to 60 minutes, or	II
(iii) more than 60 minutes and up to 4 hours, or	III
(d) cause corrosion in steel or aluminium surfaces at a rate exceeding 6.25 mm a year at a test temperature of 55∞C.	III

PART II

CRITERIA FOR ALLOCATION OF SUBSTANCES WHICH HAVE BEEN CLASSIFIED AS TOXIC OR HARMFUL SUBSTANCES IN ACCORDANCE WITH REGULATION 6(4) OF THE CLASSIFICATION, PACKAGING AND LABELLING OF DANGEROUS SUBSTANCES REGULATIONS 1984 INTO PACKING GROUPS

1.   Account should be taken of the physico-chemical properties of a substance, as well as reports of accidental poisonings in people and acute toxicity tests in animals. In the absence of adequate human experience, allocation should be based on data obtained from animal experiments. Acute toxicity testing in animals should be conducted using internationally-agreed protocols, such as the current edition of the Organisation for Economic Co-operation and Development's Guidelines for Testing of Chemicals, and in accordance with appropriate animal welfare provisions.

2.   When a substance exhibits a different order of toxicity by two or more of the following routes of administration, namely oral, dermal or inhalation, the highest degree of danger indicated by the tests shall be considered when allocating the substance.

3.   Subject to paragraphs 1 and 2 above, toxic and harmful substances shall be allocated into packing groups I, II or III in accordance with the criteria given in the table below:

Classification	Packing Group	Oral toxicity LD_{50} (mg/kg)	Dermal toxicity LD_{50} (mg/kg)	Inhalation toxicity of dust or mists LC_{50} (mg/L)	Inhalation toxicity of vapours where V is the saturated vapour concentration produced by the substance at $20\infty C$ expressed by reference to LC_{50} (ml/m³)
Toxic Substance	I	£5	£40	£0.5	$V^3 10.LC_{50}$ and LC_{50} £1000
	II	>5 to £50	>40 to £200	>0.5 to £2	$V^3 LC_{50}$ and LC_{50} £3000 but not placed in packing group I
Harmful Substance	III	solids: >50 to £200 liquids: >50 to £500	>200 to £1000	>2 to £10	$V^3 0.2LC_{50}$ and LC_{50} £5000 but not placed in either packing group I or II

The above criteria are based on LC_{50} data relating to one hour exposure and where such information is available it should be used. However, where only LC_{50} data relating to 4 hour exposures is available then:

LC_{50} (4 hr) x 4 shall be considered equivalent to LC_{50} (1 hr) for dusts or mists, and

LC_{50} (4 hr) x 2 shall be considered equivalent to LC_{50} (1 hr) for vapours.

PART III

TABLE OF *FLASH POINTS* AND KINEMATIC VISCOSITY RANGES OF SUBSTANCES WHICH HAVE
BEEN CLASSIFIED AS FLAMMABLE LIQUIDS IN ACCORDANCE WITH REGULATION 6(4) OF THE
CLASSIFICATION, PACKAGING AND LABELLING OF DANGEROUS SUBSTANCES REGULATIONS
1984, CONTAIN NOT MORE THAN 20% OF NITROCELLULOSE AND DO NOT IN ANY CASE HAVE
A *FLASH POINT* EXCEEDING 21°C

Column 1	Column 2
Flash point	*Kinematic viscosity g (extrapolated) (at near-zero shear rate) mm²/s at 23°C*
Above 17°C	*20 <gamma< £80*
Above 10°C	*80 <gamma< £135*
Above 5°C	*135 <gamma< £220*
Above − 1°C	*220 <gamma< £300*
Above − 5°C	*300 <gamma< £700*
− 5°C and below	*700 <gamma*

THE ROAD TRAFFIC (TRAINING OF DRIVERS OF VEHICLES CARRYING DANGEROUS GOODS) REGULATIONS 1992

(S.I. 1992 No. 744, as amended by S.I. 1992 No. 1312)

The Secretary of State, in exercise of the powers conferred on him by sections 15(1), (2), (3)(c), (4), (5)(b) and (6)(b), 43(2) to (6) and 82(3)(a) of, and paragraphs 3, 4, 6, 14 and 16 of Schedule 3 to, the Health and Safety at Work etc. Act 1974, and of all other powers enabling him in that behalf and for the purpose of giving effect without modifications to proposals submitted to him by the Health and Safety Commission under section 11(2)(d) of the said Act after the carrying out by the said Commission of consultations in accordance with section 50(3) of that Act, hereby makes the following Regulations:

1. Citation, commencement and interpretation.—(1) These Regulations may be cited as the Road Traffic (Training of Drivers of Vehicles Carrying Dangerous Goods) Regulations 1992 and, subject to paragraph (2), shall come into force on 1 July 1992.

(2) These Regulations shall come into force for the purposes of regulation 5 insofar as it applies to any *carriage* such as is specified in regulation 2(1)(b) or (d) on 1 January 1995.

(3) In these Regulations, unless the context otherwise requires—

"ADR" means the European Agreement concerning the International Carriage of Dangerous Goods by Road signed at Geneva on 30 September 1957, as revised or re-issued from time to time;

"agriculture" has the same meaning as in regulation 2(1) of the Road Traffic (Carriage of Dangerous Substances in Packages etc.) Regulations 1992;

"approved" means approved in writing for the purposes of these Regulations;

"approved list" has the same meaning as in regulation 4 of the Classification, Packaging and Labelling of Dangerous Substances Regulations 1984;

"attendant" means a person who accompanies the driver of a vehicle carrying *explosives* to help ensure their safety and security;

"break-down vehicle" has the same meaning as in regulation 3(1) of the Goods Vehicles (Plating and Testing) Regulations 1988;

"carriage" means carriage arising out of or in connection with work and shall be construed in accordance with regulations 1(7) and 2(3); and related words shall be construed accordingly;

"Compatibility Group" and "Compatibility Group letter" have the same meanings as in regulation 2(1) of the Classification and Labelling of Explosives Regulations 1983;

"Contracting Party" means a country which is a signatory to *ADR*;

"the Council Directive" means Council Directive 89/684/EEC on vocational training for certain drivers carrying *dangerous goods* by *road*, as revised from time to time;

"dangerous goods" means any substance, liquid or material which is specified in regulation 2(1);

"dangerous substance" (where used in or in relation to regulation 2(1) (a)) has the same meaning as in regulation 2(1) of the Road Traffic (Carriage of Dangerous Substances in Road Tankers and Tank Containers) Regulations 1992 and (where used in or in relation to regulation 2(1)(b)) has the same meaning as in regulation 2(1) of the Road Traffic (Carriage of Dangerous Substances in Packages etc.) Regulations 1992;

"Division" and "Division number" have the same meanings as in regulation 2(1) of the Classification and Labelling of Explosives Regulations 1983;

"explosives", "explosive article" and "explosive substance" have the same meanings as in regulation 2(1) of the Road Traffic (Carriage of Explosives) Regulations 1989;

"flammable gas" has the same meaning as in regulation 2(1) of the Road Traffic (Carriage of Dangerous Substances in Packages etc.) Regulations 1992;

"flash point" has the same meaning as in regulation 2(1) of the Classification, Packaging and Labelling of Dangerous Substances Regulations 1984;

"freight container" means a container as defined in regulation 2(1) of the Freight Containers (Safety Convention) Regulations 1984;

"member state" means a country (other than the United Kingdom) which is a member of the European Communities;

"military explosive" has the same meaning as in regulation 2(1) of the Classification and Labelling of Explosives Regulations 1983;

"motor vehicle" has the same meaning as in the Table contained in regulation 3(2) of the Road Vehicles (Construction and Use) Regulations 1986;

"organic peroxide" has the same meaning as in regulation 2(1) of the Road Traffic (Carriage of Dangerous Substances in Packages etc.) Regulations 1992;

"operator" shall be construed in accordance with regulation 3;

"packing group" has the same meaning as in regulation 2(3)(c) of the Road Traffic (Carriage of Dangerous Substances in Packages etc.) Regulations 1992;

"permissible maximum weight", in relation to a *road tanker* or other vehicle, has the same meaning as it does in section 108(1) of the Road Traffic Act 1988 in relation to a goods vehicle as defined by section 192(1) of that Act;

"petroleum licensing authority" has the same meaning as in regulation 25(2) of the Road Traffic (Carriage of Dangerous Substances in Road Tankers and Tank Containers) Regulations 1992;

"radioactive material" has the same meaning as in section 1(1) of the Radioactive Material (Road Transport) Act 1991;

"receptacle" has the same meaning as in regulation 2(1) of the Road Traffic (Carriage of Dangerous Substances in Packages etc.) Regulations 1992;

"road" means—

(a)   as respects England and Wales, a road within the meaning of section 192(1) of the Road Traffic Act 1988;

(b)   as respects Scotland, a road within the meaning of the Roads (Scotland) Act 1984;

"road tanker" has the same meaning as in regulation 2(1) of the Road Traffic (Carriage of Dangerous Substances in Road Tankers and Tank Containers) Regulations 1992;

"semi-trailer" has the same meaning as in the Table contained in regulation 3(2) of the Road Vehicles (Construction and Use) Regulations 1986;

"tank container" has the same meaning as in regulation 2(1) of the Road Traffic (Carriage of Dangerous Substances in Road Tankers and Tank Containers) Regulations 1992;

"toxic gas" has the same meaning as in regulation 2(1) of the Road Traffic (Carriage of Dangerous Substances in Packages etc.) Regulations 1992;

"trailer" has the same meaning as in regulation 2(1) of the Road Traffic (Carriage of Explosives) Regulations 1989.

(4) Where a vehicle which is engaged in the *carriage* of *dangerous goods* is—

(a)   being driven by a person undergoing training under the supervision of an instructor; or

(b)   being towed or otherwise moved by a break-down or recovery vehicle and the driver of the break-down or recovery vehicle is accompanied by the driver of the vehicle which is being towed or otherwise moved,

the instructor or (as the case may be) the driver of the vehicle which is being towed or otherwise moved shall be regarded as the driver of the vehicle concerned for the purposes of these Regulations.

(5) Any requirement imposed by regulations 4 to 9 on or in respect of the driver of a vehicle which is engaged in the *carriage* of *explosives* shall be taken to include a like requirement imposed on, or as the case may be, in respect of an *attendant*.

(6) A combination of a *motor vehicle* and one or more *trailers* or *semi-trailers* shall be deemed for the purposes of these Regulations to be a single vehicle for as long as the constituent parts of such a combination remain attached, and *dangerous goods* contained in different parts of such a vehicle shall accordingly be considered to be contained in the same vehicle.

(7) Without prejudice to the generality of regulation 2(3), a *trailer* or *semi-trailer* containing *dangerous goods* shall not be considered to be engaged in the *carriage* of *dangerous goods* for the purposes of these Regulations unless it forms part of a combination deemed to be a single vehicle in accordance with paragraph (6).

(8) For the purposes of these Regulations, a vehicle shall be deemed to be registered in the United Kingdom where the relevant *motor vehicle* is registered under the Vehicles (Excise) Act 1971 or any enactment repealed thereby.

(9) Any reference in these Regulations to—

(a)   a numbered regulation or Schedule is a reference to the regulation or Schedule in these Regulations so numbered;

(b)   a numbered paragraph is a reference to the paragraph so numbered in the regulation or Schedule in which the reference appears;

(c) the driver of a vehicle does not include a reference to a person whose work does not involve his driving the vehicle concerned on a *road*; or

(d) the particular substance identification number of a *dangerous substance* is a reference to the corresponding number set out in Part III of the list referred to in regulation 4(1) of the Road Traffic (Carriage of Dangerous Substances in Road Tankers and Tank Containers) Regulations 1992, as revised from time to time in accordance with regulation 4(2) thereof.

2. Application.—(1) These Regulations shall apply—

(a) to the *carriage* of any *dangerous substance* in—

    (i) a *road tanker* having (subject to paragraph (2) in the case of the application of regulation 4 to such *carriage*) a capacity greater than 3,000 litres or a *permissible maximum weight* exceeding 3.5 tonnes, or

    (ii) a *tank container* carried on a vehicle, regardless of the *permissible maximum weight* of the vehicle concerned,

    except where specified in Schedule 1 or Part I of Schedule 2;

(b) to the *carriage* in or, as the case may be, on a vehicle having (subject to paragraph (2) in the case of the application of regulation 4 to the *carriage* concerned) a *permissible maximum weight* exceeding 3.5 tonnes—

    (i) of any *dangerous substance* in bulk,

    (ii) (in a *receptacle*, regardless of its capacity), of any *organic peroxide* which is subject to regulation 11(2) of the Road Traffic (Carriage of Dangerous Substances in Packages etc.) Regulations 1992,

    (iii) (in a *receptacle*, regardless of its capacity) of any flammable solid which is subject to regulation 11(3) of the Road Traffic (Carriage of Dangerous Substances in Packages etc.) Regulations 1992,

    (iv) (in a *receptacle* with a capacity of 5 litres or more) of any *organic peroxide* (other than one which is subject to regulation 11(2) of the Road Traffic (Carriage of Dangerous Substances in Packages etc.) Regulations 1992), any flammable or *toxic gas* or any other *dangerous substance* being within *packing group* I,

    (v) (in a *receptacle* with a capacity of 5 litres or more) of any asbestos falling within sub-paragraph (a) of the definition of *dangerous substance* or any substance such as is specified in sub-paragraph (d) of that definition,

    (vi) (in a *receptacle* with a capacity of 5 litres or more) of any *dangerous substance* both listed in the *approved list* as "hazardous waste" and designated as "special waste" by regulation 2(1)(a)(i) of the Control of Pollution (Special Waste) Regulations 1980,

    (vii) (in a *receptacle* with a capacity of 200 litres or more) of any *dangerous substance* not specified in heads (ii) to (vi) of this sub-paragraph, or

    (viii) (in a transformer or capacitor, regardless of its capacity), of any *dangerous substance* not specified in heads (ii) to (v) of this sub-paragraph,

    except where specified in Schedule 1 or Part II of Schedule 2;

(c) to the *carriage* of any *explosives* in or on a vehicle not also being used to carry passengers for hire or reward (regardless of the *permissible maximum weight* of the vehicle concerned), except where specified in paragraph 1 of Schedule 1 or Part III of Schedule 2; and

(d) to the *carriage* of any *radioactive material* in or on a vehicle having (subject
to paragraph (2) in the case of the application of regulation 4 to such
carriage) a *permissible maximum weight* exceeding 3.5 tonnes, except where
specified in Schedule 1 or under the conditions set out in Schedules 1 to
4 of marginal 2704 of *ADR,*

and, unless the context otherwise requires, any reference in these Regulations
to the *carriage* of *dangerous goods* shall be construed as a reference to any *carriage*
to which these Regulations apply by virtue of this paragraph.

(2) Neither the capacity nor the *permissible maximum weight* of the *road tanker*
or other vehicle concerned shall be taken into account in ascertaining whether
or not regulation 4 applies to any *carriage* by virtue of sub-paragraph (a) (i), (b)
or (d) of paragraph (1).

(3) A vehicle shall be deemed to be engaged in—

(a) such *carriage* to which these Regulations apply by virtue of paragraph
(1) (a) (i), from the commencement of loading the *road tanker* with the
dangerous substance concerned for the purpose of carrying it on a *road*
until the carrying tank of the *road tanker* and (where appropriate) any
compartment of that carrying tank have been cleaned or purged so that
any of the *dangerous substance* or its vapour which remains therein is not
sufficient to create a risk to the health or safety of any person, regardless
of whether or not the *road tanker* is on a *road* at the material time;

(b) such *carriage* to which these Regulations apply by virtue of paragraph
(1) (a) (ii)—

(i) (in the case where the *tank container* has been loaded with the
dangerous substance concerned before being placed on the vehicle)
from the time the *tank container* is placed on the vehicle for the
purpose of carrying the *dangerous substance* on a *road,* or

(ii) (in the case where the *tank container* has been placed on the vehicle
before the commencement of loading) from the commencement
of loading the *tank container* with the *dangerous substance* concerned
for the purpose of carrying it by *road,*

until in either case—

(aa) the *tank container* is removed from the vehicle, or

(bb) the *tank container* and (where appropriate) any compartment
of the *tank container* have been cleaned or purged so that any
of the *dangerous substance* or its vapour which remains therein
is not sufficient to create a risk to the health or safety of any
person,

and, in either of the cases referred to in this sub-paragraph, regardless of
whether or not the *road tanker* or other vehicle is on a *road* at the material
time;

(c) such *carriage* to which these Regulations apply by virtue of paragraph
(1) (b)—

(i) in the case of a vehicle carrying a *dangerous substance* in bulk other
than in a *freight container,* from the commencement of loading the
relevant vehicle with the *dangerous substance* concerned for the
purpose of carrying that substance on a *road* until the vehicle has
been unloaded (and where necessary cleaned or purged) so that

any of the *dangerous substance* or its vapour which remains in the vehicle is not sufficient to create a risk to the health or safety of any person, or

(ii) in the case of a vehicle carrying a *dangerous substance* in a *freight container, receptacle,* transformer or capacitor—

    (aa) (if the relevant *freight container, receptacle,* transformer or capacitor has been loaded with the *dangerous substance* concerned before being placed on the vehicle) from the time the *freight container, receptacle,* transformer or capacitor is placed on the vehicle for the purpose of carrying the *dangerous substance* on a *road,* or

    (bb) (if the relevant *freight container, receptacle,* transformer or capacitor has been placed on the vehicle before the commencement of loading) from the commencement of loading the *freight container, receptacle,* transformer or capacitor with the *dangerous substance* concerned for the purpose of carrying it by *road,*

until—

    (aaa) the *freight container, receptacle,* transformer or capacitor is removed from the vehicle, or

    (bbb) the *freight container, receptacle,* transformer or capacitor (and, where necessary, the vehicle carrying same) have been emptied (and where necessary cleaned or purged) so that any of the *dangerous substance* or its vapour which remains therein is not sufficient to create a risk to the health or safety of any person,

and, in either of the cases referred to in this sub-paragraph, regardless of whether or not the vehicle is on a *road* at the material time;

(d) such *carriage* to which these Regulations apply by virtue of paragraph (1)(c), from the commencement of loading the vehicle with the *explosives* concerned for the purpose of carrying them on a *road* until all the *explosives* have been unloaded from the vehicle, regardless of whether or not the vehicle concerned is on a *road* at the material time; and

(e) such *carriage* to which these Regulations apply by virtue of paragraph (1)(d), from the commencement of loading the vehicle with the *radioactive material* concerned for the purpose of carrying it on a *road* until the vehicle has been unloaded and where necessary cleaned so that any of the material which remains on or in the vehicle is not sufficient to create a risk to the health or safety of any person, regardless of whether or not the vehicle is on a *road* at the material time;

(4) For the purposes of paragraph (1)(b)(i), the *carriage* in bulk of a *dangerous substance* shall, unless the context otherwise requires, include the unconfined *carriage* of such a substance in a *freight container,* but shall not include the *carriage* of such a substance—

(a) in a *receptacle* (whether or not the *receptacle* is carried in a *freight container*);
(b) in a *road tanker;*
(c) in a *tank container;* or
(d) in a transformer or capacitor.

(5) In this regulation, "carrying tank" means a tank which is referred to thus in the Road Traffic (Carriage of Dangerous Substances in Road Tankers and

Tank Containers) Regulations 1992 by virtue of the definition of "*road tanker*" contained in regulation 2(1) thereof.

3. Meaning of *operator*.—(1) The *operator* of any vehicle which is engaged in the *carriage* of *dangerous goods* shall be—

(a) the person who holds an *operator's* licence (granted under Part V of the Transport Act 1968) for the use of that vehicle for the *carriage* of goods on a *road*, except that where by virtue of regulation 32(1) to (3) of the Goods Vehicles (Operators' Licences, Qualifications and Fees) Regulations 1984 the vehicle is included in a licence held by a holding company and that company is not operating the vehicle at the relevant time, the "*operator*" shall be the subsidiary company specified in the application made under the said regulation 32(1) or, if more than one subsidiary company is so specified, whichever one is operating the vehicle at the relevant time, and in this regulation, "holding company" and "subsidiary company" have the same meanings as in the said Regulations of 1984; or

(b) where no such licence is held—

   (i) (in the case of a vehicle which is not registered in the United Kingdom) the driver of the vehicle, and

   (ii) (in the case of any other vehicle, but subject to paragraph (2)) the keeper of the vehicle; and for this purpose, where the vehicle is on hire or lease to any person, that person shall be treated as its keeper.

(2) Where an employee who would otherwise be the *operator* of a vehicle in accordance with sub-paragraph (b)(ii) of paragraph (1) uses that vehicle for the *carriage* of *dangerous goods* on behalf of his employer, that employer shall, notwithstanding that sub-paragraph, be regarded as the *operator* of the vehicle for the purposes of these Regulations.

4. Instruction and training for drivers.—(1) The *operator* of any vehicle registered in the United Kingdom which is engaged in the *carriage* of *dangerous goods* shall ensure that the driver of the vehicle has received—

(a) adequate instruction and training to enable him to understand—

   (i) the nature of the dangers to which the particular *dangerous goods* being carried may give rise and the action to be taken in an emergency concerning them, and

   (ii) his duties under the Health and Safety at Work etc. Act 1974; and

(b) (in respect of any *carriage* to which these Regulations apply by virtue of regulation 2(1)(a)) adequate instruction and training to enable him to understand his duties under the Road Traffic (Carriage of Dangerous Substances in Road Tankers and Tank Containers) Regulations 1992;

(c) (in respect of any *carriage* to which these Regulations apply by virtue of regulation 2(1)(b)) adequate instruction and training to enable him to understand his duties under the Road Traffic (Carriage of Dangerous Substances in Packages etc.) Regulations 1992; or

(d) (in respect of any *carriage* to which these Regulations apply by virtue of regulation 2(1)(c)) adequate instruction and training to enable him to understand his duties under the Road Traffic (Carriage of Explosives) Regulations 1989.

(2) Each *operator* shall keep a record of any training provided by him in accordance with paragraph (1) to the driver of a vehicle who is his employee and shall make available a copy of that record to the driver concerned.

5. Vocational training certificates.—(1) Subject to regulations 6 and 7, the *operator* of any vehicle which is engaged in the *carriage* of *dangerous goods* shall ensure that the driver of that vehicle holds a valid certificate applicable to that *carriage* (to be known as a "vocational training certificate") issued by the Secretary of State.

(2) A driver may only be issued with a vocational training certificate in accordance with paragraph (1) where—

(a) he has successfully completed such training in the *carriage* of the *dangerous goods* concerned as the Secretary of State has from time to time *approved*;

(b) he has passed an examination (the syllabus of which shall cover the training referred to in sub-paragraph (a) of this paragraph) which has been *approved* by the Secretary of State; and

(c) a fee of £2.50 has been paid to the Secretary of State.

(3) Each vocational training certificate issued in accordance with paragraph (1) shall be in a form *approved* by the Secretary of State.

(4) The training referred to in paragraph (2)(a) shall be given in the form of a theoretical course accompanied by practical exercises and shall cover at least the subjects specified in Schedule 3.

(5) Each vocational training certificate issued in accordance with paragraph (1) shall be valid for a period of 5 years from the date of issue, but its validity may be extended for periods of up to 5 years by the Secretary of State where, within the period of 12 months which precede the expiry of the original certificate or any extension of it granted in accordance with this paragraph—

(a) the holder can show to the satisfaction of the Secretary of State that he has—

(i) successfully completed a refresher course in the *carriage* of *dangerous goods* which has been *approved* by the Secretary of State, and

(ii) passed the examination referred to in paragraph (2)(b); and

(b) a fee of £2.50 has been paid to the Secretary of State.

(6) Schedule 4 shall have effect with respect to fees for applications for such approvals under this regulation as are specified in paragraph 1 of that Schedule.

(7) Any current certificate in the form set out in Appendix B.6 to *ADR* (regardless of whether or not that certificate has been extended in the manner described by Article 5.2 of *the Council Directive*) which is held by a driver and which was issued to him under national provisions giving effect to Article 1 of that Directive in a *member state* or in Northern Ireland shall be deemed to be a vocational training certificate issued in conformity with the foregoing provisions of this regulation valid for the *carriage* of those *dangerous goods* to which it is applicable.

6. Provisional vocational training certificates.—(1) It shall be sufficient compliance with regulation 5(1) insofar as it applies to any *carriage* such as is specified in regulation 2(1)(a) or (c) where the driver of the relevant vehicle holds a certificate (to be known as a "provisional vocational training certificate")—

(a) applicable to the *carriage* concerned;
(b) issued by the Secretary of State;
(c) in a form *approved* by the Secretary of State; and
(d) stating its expiry date.

(2) The Secretary of State may not issue a provisional vocational training certificate in accordance with paragraph (1) unless he—

(a) is satisfied that the driver concerned has, without having completed the training or passed the examination referred to in regulation 5(2), been working as a driver of vehicles engaged in the *carriage* to which it will be applicable for the 5 years preceding 1 July 1992; and
(b) has received a fee of £5.00.

(3) In ascertaining whether or not a driver has been working for the length of time specified in paragraph (2)(a), no account shall be taken of any seasonal lay-offs or holidays, or breaks between employment of up to 6 months in any 12-month period or totalling up to 18 months, during that time.

(4) Each provisional vocational training certificate issued in accordance with paragraph (1) shall expire on 1 January 1995.

(5) Any current certificate which is held by a driver and which was issued to him under national provisions giving effect to Article 4.2 of *the Council Directive* in Northern Ireland shall be deemed to be a provisional vocational training certificate issued in conformity with the foregoing provisions of this regulation valid for the *carriage* of those *dangerous goods* to which it is applicable.

7.   Existing training certificates. It shall be sufficient compliance with regulation 5(1) where the driver of the relevant vehicle holds a training certificate applicable to the *dangerous goods* being carried which was issued to him by the appropriate national authority before the coming into force of that provision as respects the *carriage* concerned on the basis of existing national provisions which the Commission of the European Communities has confirmed satisfy the corresponding requirements of *the Council Directive*, provided that such compliance shall cease—

(a) on 1 July 1997, insofar as the certificate concerned relates to such *carriage* as is specified in regulation 2(1)(a) or (c);
(b) on 1 January 2000, insofar as the certificate concerned relates to such *carriage* as is specified in regulation 2(1)(b) or (d); or
(c) at the end of the period of validity of the certificate concerned, where that date is earlier than the relevant date specified in sub-paragraph (a) or (b) above.

8.   Fees for issue of certificates. Nothing in regulation 5(2)(c) or (5)(b) or 6(2)(b) shall be construed as making a fee payable by a person in any of the capacities specified in section 43(4) of the Health and Safety at Work etc. Act 1974.

9.   Certificates to be available during *carriage*. The driver of any vehicle which is engaged in the *carriage* of *dangerous goods* shall ensure that the relevant certificate he holds in accordance with regulation 5, 6 or 7 is so kept by him that it is immediately available during the whole of the *carriage.*

10.   Certificates to be produced to police constables, etc.—(1) The driver of any vehicle which is engaged in the *carriage* of *dangerous goods* shall on request produce to any police constable or goods vehicle examiner the relevant certificate he holds in accordance with regulation 5, 6 or 7.

(2) The driver of any vehicle which is engaged in the *carriage* of any *radioactive material* shall on request produce to any inspector appointed in accordance with section 1(3)(a) of the Radioactive Material (Road Transport) Act 1991 the relevant certificate he holds in accordance with regulation 5, 6 or 7.

(3) In this regulation, "goods vehicle examiner" has the meaning assigned to it by section 68(2) of the Road Traffic Act 1988.

11.   Enforcement.   Notwithstanding the Health and Safety (Enforcing Authority) Regulations 1989, the enforcing authority for these Regulations shall—

(a)   insofar as they apply to the *carriage* of *explosives*, be the Health and Safety Executive; and

(b)   insofar as they apply to the *carriage* of petrol (and that *carriage* is also *carriage* which is subject to the provisions of Schedule 4 to the Road Traffic (Carriage of Dangerous Substances in Road Tankers and Tank Containers) Regulations 1992), be the relevant *petroleum licensing authority* ascertained in accordance with regulation 25(2)(a) of the said Regulations.

12.   Exemption certificates.—(1) The Health and Safety Executive may, by a certificate in writing, exempt the *operator* of a vehicle from any requirement imposed upon him by regulation 4; and any such exemption may be granted subject to conditions and to a limit of time and may in any event be revoked at any time by the Health and Safety Executive by a further certificate in writing.

(2) The Health and Safety Executive shall not grant any exemption in accordance with paragraph (1) unless, having regard to the circumstances of the case, and in particular to—

(a)   the conditions, if any, which it proposes to attach to the exemption; and

(b)   any other requirements imposed by or under any enactments which apply to the case,

it is satisfied that the health and safety of persons who are likely to be affected by the exemption will not be prejudiced in consequence of it.

(3) The Health and Safety Executive may, by a certificate in writing, issue exemptions from regulation 5(1) in accordance with the criteria laid down by Article 3 of *the Council Directive.*

(4) The Secretary of State for Defence may, in the interests of national security, by a certificate in writing exempt the *operator* of—

(a)   any home forces' vehicle; or

(b)   any vehicle in the service of a visiting force or a headquarters, from—

    (i) the requirements in paragraphs (a) and (b) respectively of regulation 4(1) insofar as they apply to the *carriage* of any *military explosive*, or

    (ii) the requirement in regulation 5(1),

and any such exemption may be granted subject to conditions and to a limit of time and may in any event be revoked at any time by the said Secretary of State by a further certificate in writing.

(5) In this regulation—

(a) "headquarters" has the same meaning as in article 3(2) of the Visiting Forces and International Headquarters (Application of Law) Order 1965;

(b) "home forces' vehicle" has the same meaning as in the Table contained in regulation 3(2) of the Road Vehicles Lighting Regulations 1989; and

(c) "visiting force" has the same meaning as it does for the purposes of any provision of Part I of the Visiting Forces Act 1952.

13. Defence. In any proceedings for an offence under regulation 4 or (where the driver of the vehicle is specified in paragraph 1(c) or (d) of Schedule 1 but the *carriage* of the *dangerous goods* concerned is not thereby excluded from the application of these Regulations) regulation 5(1), it shall be a defence for the *operator* to prove that he took all reasonable precautions and exercised all due diligence to avoid the commission of that offence.

14. Revocations. The following provisions are revoked by these Regulations—

(a) regulation 14 of the Road Traffic (Carriage of Explosives) Regulations 1989;

(b) regulation 8 of the Road Traffic (Carriage of Dangerous Substances in Packages etc.) Regulations 1992; and

(c) regulation 26 of the Road Traffic (Carriage of Dangerous Substances in Road Tankers and Tank Containers) Regulations 1992.

SCHEDULE 1

Regulation 2(1)

CASES WHERE THE CARRIAGE OF DANGEROUS SUBSTANCES, *EXPLOSIVES* AND *RADIOACTIVE MATERIAL* IS NOT *CARRIAGE* TO WHICH THESE REGULATIONS APPLY

1. These Regulations shall not apply to any such *carriage* as is specified in regulation 2(1) where—

(a) the *dangerous goods* concerned are used solely in connection with the operation of the vehicle carrying them;

(b) the vehicle concerned is being towed or otherwise moved by a break-down or recovery vehicle, and—

    (i) both vehicles are being escorted by a vehicle used for police or fire brigade purposes, and

    (ii) the vehicle being towed or otherwise moved as aforesaid is being driven to the nearest suitable safe place or depot with a view to it (or any *tank container* or other vessel which it is carrying) being repaired, cleaned or purged prior to its safe removal;

(c) the vehicle concerned is being driven for the purpose of testing the vehicle by a fitter, vehicle tester or any other similar person, and that person has received adequate instruction to enable him to understand the nature of the dangers to which the *dangerous goods* being carried may give rise and the action to be taken in an emergency concerning them;

(d) the vehicle concerned is being driven by a police constable in an emergency and that constable has received adequate instruction to enable him to understand the nature of the dangers to which the *dangerous goods* being carried may give rise and the action which it is appropriate to take to reduce the risks arising out of the emergency; or

(e) the vehicle concerned is delivering *dangerous goods*—
   (i) between private premises and another vehicle situated in the immediate vicinity of those premises, or
   (ii) between one part of private premises and another part of those premises situated in the immediate vicinity of that first part.

2. These Regulations shall not apply to any such *carriage* as is specified in regulation 2(1)(a), (b) or (d)—
(a) where—
   (i) the vehicle concerned is engaged in international transport within the meaning of Article 1(c) of *ADR*, and
   (ii) such *carriage* conforms in every respect with the provisions of *ADR*;
(b) where the transport of the *dangerous goods* concerned is subject to a special bilateral or multilateral agreement made under the terms of Article 4.3 of *ADR* to which the United Kingdom is a signatory and conforms with any conditions attached to such an agreement; or
(c) where the vehicle concerned is not, for the time being, subject to the provisions of *ADR* by reason only that it is a vehicle belonging to or under the orders of the armed forces of a *Contracting Party*.

SCHEDULE 2

Regulation 2(1)(a), (b) and (c)

PART I

CASES WHERE THE *CARRIAGE* OF *DANGEROUS SUBSTANCES* IN *ROAD TANKERS* OR *TANK CONTAINERS* CARRIED ON VEHICLES IS NOT *CARRIAGE* TO WHICH THESE REGULATIONS APPLY BY VIRTUE OF REGULATION 2(1)(a)

These Regulations shall not apply to any such *carriage* as is specified in regulation 2(1)(a)—
(a) (in the case of *carriage* in a *tank container* carried on a vehicle) where the substance being carried, other than any liquid nitrogen in the jacket of the *tank container* which is being carried exclusively for the purpose of insulating any liquid helium or liquid hydrogen which is also being carried in that *tank container*, is being used solely in connection with the operation of the *tank container* concerned;
(b) where the vehicle carrying the *dangerous substance* is a *road* construction vehicle engaged in the repair or construction of a *road*; and in this sub-paragraph—
   (i) the reference to a *road* construction vehicle does not include a reference to such a vehicle which is also a *road tanker* being used for the *carriage* of liquid tar (including *road* asphalt and oils, bitumen and cutbacks) which has the substance identification number 1999 or 7033),
   (ii) "built-in road construction machinery" means *road* construction machinery built-in as part of a *road* construction vehicle or permanently attached to it,

    (iii) "road construction machinery" means a machine or contrivance suitable for use in the repair and construction of *roads*, and

    (iv) "road construction vehicle" means a vehicle constructed or adapted for the *carriage* of built-in road construction machinery and not constructed or adapted for the *carriage* of any other load except articles and material used for the purposes of that machinery;

(c) where any petroleum-fuel is being carried in a volumetric prover and that volumetric prover—

    (i) is not moved, driven or kept on a *road* other than when it is nominally empty,

    (ii) before having been taken onto the *road* was last filled with kerosene or some other liquid with a *flash point* not lower than 32°C or was purged with nitrogen, and

    (iii) during its *carriage* has every valve (except those valves which need to be kept open to allow for liquid expansion on volumetric provers used for the measurement of liquefied petroleum gas) and opening closed,

and in this sub-paragraph "nominally empty" has the same meaning as in regulation 17(2) of the Road Traffic (Carriage of Dangerous Substances in Road Tankers and Tank Containers) Regulations 1992, and "petroleum-fuel" and "volumetric prover" have the same meanings as in regulation 2(1) of those Regulations; or

(d) where the *dangerous substance* being carried is a pesticide (other than dilute sulphuric acid or a wood preservative) and is diluted ready for use or is otherwise in a condition ready for use, and in relation to which there has been given an approval under regulation 5, and a consent under regulation 6, of the Control of Pesticides Regulations 1986; and in this sub-paragraph "pesticide" has the same meaning as in section 16(15) of the Food and Environment Protection Act 1985 and "wood preservative" means a pesticide used for preserving wood; or

(e) where the *dangerous substance* being carried is *radioactive material*.

PART II

CASES WHERE THE *CARRIAGE* OF *DANGEROUS SUBSTANCES* IN *RECEPTACLES,* ETC., IS NOT *CARRIAGE* TO WHICH THESE REGULATIONS APPLY BY VIRTUE OF REGULATION 2(1)(b)

These Regulations shall not apply to any such *carriage* such as is specified in regulation 2(1)(b)—

(a) where the *dangerous substance* being carried is *radioactive material*;

(b) where the *dangerous substance* being carried has been classified (as defined by regulation 2(1) of the Classification and Labelling of Explosives Regulations 1983) in pursuance of regulation 3(2)(a) of those Regulations and assigned to Class 1 (also as defined by the said regulation 2(1));

(c) where the *dangerous substance* being carried (in each case in a cylinder) is commercial butane, commercial propane, any mixture thereof or (for the purposes of regulation 5(1) only) acetylene, and—

    (i) the vehicle concerned has been designed for a purpose which includes the use of any such substance and the substance concerned is being carried in connection with the operation of the vehicle, or

    (ii) the cylinder is part of equipment carried on the vehicle concerned,

provided that the number of cylinders carried thus (including any spare cylinder) does not exceed two;

(d) where the vehicle which is being used for the *carriage* of a *dangerous substance* is passing from one part of an agricultural unit to another part of that unit and the *dangerous substance* is diluted ready for use or is otherwise in a condition ready for use; and in this sub-paragraph "agricultural unit" means a self-contained parcel of land which is occupied (whether or not by a single occupier) for *agriculture;* or

(e) where the *dangerous substance* being carried is specified in sub-paragraphs (c) to (i) of regulation 3(1) of the Classification, Packaging and Labelling of Dangerous Substances Regulations 1984.

Part III
Cases where the *Carriage* of *Explosives* is not *Carriage* to which these Regulations Apply by virtue of Regulation 2(1)(c)

These Regulations shall not apply to the *carriage*—

    (a) of any *explosives* specified in Part I of Schedule 1 to the Road Traffic (Carriage of Explosives) Regulations 1989 ("the 1989 Regulations")

    (b) of gunpowder or smokeless powder (or a mixture of them), where the total quantity of such *explosives* does not exceed 5 kilograms;

    (c) of any *explosives* specified in Part II of Schedule 1 to the 1989 Regulations, where the total quantity of such *explosives* does not exceed 50 kilograms (except that where *explosives* carried in accordance with this sub-paragraph are being carried in conjunction with *explosives* carried in accordance with sub-paragraph (b) of this Part, the total quantity of *explosives* so carried shall not exceed 50 kilograms); or

    (d) (for the purposes of regulation 5(1) only)—

        (i) of any *explosives* within a *Division* whose *Division number* is 1.4 and a *Compatibility Group* whose *Compatibility Group letter* is S,

        (ii) of any *explosives* within a *Division* whose *Division number* is 1.4 and a *Compatibility Group* whose *Compatibility Group letter* is B, C, D, E, F or G, where the total quantity of such *explosives* does not exceed 500 kilograms,

        (iii) of any *explosives* (consisting of *explosive articles* only) within—

            (aa) a *Division* whose *Division number* is 1.1 and a *Compatibility Group* whose *Compatibility Group letter* is B, C, D, E, F, G or J,

            (bb) a *Division* whose *Division number* is 1.2 and a *Compatibility Group* whose *Compatibility Group letter* is B, C, D, E, F, G, H or J, or

            (cc) a *Division* whose *Division number* is 1.3 and a *Compatibility Group* whose *Compatibility Group letter* is C, G, H or J,

        where the total quantity of such articles does not exceed 50 kilograms,

        (iv) of any *explosives* (consisting of *explosive substances* only) within a *Division* whose *Division number* is 1.3 and a *Compatibility Group* whose *Compatibility Group letter* is C or G, where the total quantity of such substances does not exceed 20 kilograms, or

        (v) of any *explosives* within a *Division* whose *Division number* is 1.1 and a *Compatibility Group* whose *Compatibility Group letter* is C, D or G, where the total quantity of such substances (consisting of explosives only) does not exceed 5 kilograms.

SCHEDULE 3

Regulation 5(4)

Minimum Training Requirements for Issue of Vocational Training Certificates

1. Any training *approved* by the Secretary of State in accordance with regulation 5(2)(a) must cover at least the following subjects:

    (a) general requirements concerning the *carriage* of *dangerous goods*;

    (b) main types of hazard;

    (c) information on environmental protection in the control or transfer of wastes;

    (d) preventive and safety measures appropriate to the various types of hazard;

    (e) what to do after an accident (first aid, *road* safety, basic knowledge about the use of protective equipment, etc.);

    (f) labelling and marking to indicate danger;

    (g) what a vehicle driver should and should not do during the *carriage* of *dangerous goods*;

    (h) the purpose and method of operation of technical equipment on vehicles used for the *carriage* of *dangerous goods*;

  (i)   prohibitions on mixed loading in the same vehicle or container;
  (j)   precautions to be taken during loading and unloading of *dangerous goods*;
  (k) general information concerning civil liability; and
  (l)   information on multi-modal transport operations.

2.   For drivers of vehicles carrying *dangerous goods* in packages, the training required to be *approved* must also cover handling and stowage of packages.

3.   For drivers of *road tankers* or vehicles carrying *dangerous goods* in *tank containers*, the training required to be *approved* must also cover the behaviour of such vehicles on *roads*, including the movement of the loads they are carrying.

SCHEDULE 4
Regulation 5(6)

FEES ON APPLICATIONS FOR APPROVALS

1.   On the making of an application to the Secretary of State—
  (a) for the approval of training under regulation 5(2)(a); or
  (b) for the approval of a refresher course under regulation 5(5)(a),
there shall be payable by the applicant to the Secretary of State in connection with the determination by him of that application a fee or fees to be determined in accordance with the following paragraphs of this Schedule.

2.   On receipt of the application, the Secretary of State shall prepare and send to the applicant an estimate of the cost of the work necessary for the determination of the application; and the amount so estimated shall, subject to paragraph 4, be the amount of the initial fee payable and shall be paid forthwith.

3.   On determination of the application, the Secretary of State shall prepare a detailed statement of the work carried out in relation to the determination of the application and of the cost reasonably incurred by him or any person acting on his behalf in carrying out that work.

4.   If the cost so stated differs from the amount estimated in accordance with paragraph 2—
  (a) if it is greater, the amount of the difference shall be notified by the Secretary of State to the applicant, shall be the amount of the final fee payable and shall be paid forthwith; and
  (b) if it is less, the initial fee shall be re-determined accordingly and the amount of the difference shall be paid forthwith to the applicant by the Secretary of State.

5.   In estimating or stating the cost of carrying out any work, the Secretary of State may take into account the cost to him or any person acting on his behalf of employing an officer for any period to perform the work concerned and shall determine that cost by reference to the average cost of employing an officer of the relevant grade for that period.

THE HEALTH AND SAFETY (DISPLAY SCREEN EQUIPMENT) REGULATIONS 1992

(S.I. 1992 No. 2792)

General note. These Regulations are intended to implement the Display Screen Equipment Directive 90/270 (see page 154). The Regulations appear to protect temporary workers in conformity with the Temporary Workers Directive 91/383, since the obligations under the Regulations are mainly owed by an employer to "users" and are not restricted to *his* employees (c.f. reg. 7(3); it is to be noted that some obligations remain on the temporary workers' employing agency: e.g. reg. 5).

The Regulations impose differing duties on the employer in relation to "operators" (i.e. the self-employed) and "users" (i.e. employees, whether of that employer or not). Operators and users are those who habitually use display screen equipment as a significant part of their work. This will be a question of fact. The duties apply to any "alphanumeric or graphic display screen, regardless of the display process involved" (reg. 1(2)(a)). The duties are to carry out an analysis of the workstations to be used by operators and users (but not others) and to assess risks. A workstation comprises screen and equipment, accessories, work surface, chair, and the immediate work environment. Workstations are to conform to the requirements of reg. 3 and Sch. 1 which contain detailed provisions as to screen, keyboard, work surface, chair, space, lighting, reflections, glare, noise, heat, radiation, humidity, systems and software. Risks are to be reduced to the lowest extent reasonably practicable. Periodic interruptions or changes of activity must be provided for users (but not operators). Eye and eyesight tests must be arranged and any special corrective appliance provided. Training on health and safety aspects of the workstation is required for employees, and training in the event of a substantial modification is required for users. Operators and users are to be given health and safety information about their workstations.

The Regulations came into effect on 1 January 1993. There is a period of grace for workstations in use prior to 1 January 1993 which must comply with the necessary requirements by 31 December 1996. Since these Regulations cover new ground they involve no repeals of former legislation.

The Regulations are not supplemented by any Approved Code of Practice but there is an extensive Guidance Note called "Display Screen Equipment Work" (not included in this book) which has no statutory admissibility in civil or criminal proceedings, though doubtless a court might consider its recommendations relevant.

The Regulations apply to all employment but not to: cabs for vehicles or machinery; display screen equipment on a means of transport or mainly for public operation, portables not in prolonged use, calculators and cash registers, and window typewriters.

As noted earlier, to the extent that Regulations fail to give full effect to the Directives they are intended to implement, recourse, by way of aid to construction, or in some cases by way of direct enforcement, may be had to the relevant Directive (see "Interpretation in the Light of the European Directives" and "Direct Application of the European Directives" under LEGAL PRINCIPLES in the introductory section). Some possible areas of arguable shortfall in implementation of the Directive by these Regulations have been noted by commentators.

Thus, for example, Art. 3(2) of the Directive requires that "employers shall take appropriate measures to remedy the risks found", but reg. 2(3) requires that "the

931

employer shall reduce the risks . . . to the lowest extent reasonably practicable". This appears to represent a shortfall in implementation since, whatever the distinction between the adjectival "appropriate" and "reasonably practicable", the Regulation requires only reduction of risk and not the actual remedying of the risk required by the Directive. Another possible shortfall is that the Regulations only demand that action be taken in respect of workstations used by users, whereas the Directive extends to any workstation.

There is a requirement to consult workplace representatives specified in the Framework Directive and in this Directive. These Regulations contain no reflection of that obligation. However, para. 29 of the Guidance Note recommends that safety representatives should be encouraged to play a part in the assessment of workstations. No other role is mentioned for them. The obligation to consult representatives of the workforce finds form in the amendment to the Safety Representatives and Safety Committees Regulations (S.I. 1977 No. 500) contained in the Schedule to the Management of Health and Safety at Work Regulations (S.I. 1992 No. 2051). That obligation only arises where the employer cares to recognise a union. This deficiency in implementation of the Framework Directive has already been referred to: see the General Note to reg. 4A of the Safety Representatives and Safety Committees Regulations 1977 and "Direct Application of the European Directives" under LEGAL PRINCIPLES in the introductory section.

The Secretary of State, in exercise of the powers conferred on her by sections 15(1), (2), (5)(b) and (9) and 82(3)(a) of, and paragraphs 1(1)(a) and (c) and (2), 7, 8(1), 9 and 14 of Schedule 3 to, the Health and Safety at Work etc. Act 1974 and of all other powers enabling her in that behalf and for the purpose of giving effect without modifications to proposals submitted to her by the Health and Safety Commission under section 11(2)(d) of the said Act after the carrying out by the said Commission of consultations in accordance with section 50(3) of that Act, hereby makes the following Regulations:

1. Citation, commencement, interpretation and application.—(1) These Regulations may be cited as the Health and Safety (Display Screen Equipment) Regulations 1992 and shall come into force on 1 January 1993.

(2) In these Regulations—

(a) "display screen equipment" means any alphanumeric or graphic display screen, regardless of the display process involved;

(b) "operator" means a self-employed person who habitually uses *display screen equipment* as a significant part of his normal work;

(c) "use" means use for or in connection with work;

(d) "user" means an employee who habitually uses *display screen equipment* as a significant part of his normal work; and

(e) "workstation" *(a)* means an assembly comprising—

(i) *display screen equipment* (whether provided with software determining the interface between the equipment and its *operator* or *user*, a keyboard or any other input device),

(ii) any optional accessories to the *display screen equipment*,

(iii) any disk drive, telephone, modem, printer, document holder, work chair, work desk, work surface or other item peripheral to the *display screen equipment*, and

(iv) the immediate work environment around the *display screen equipment*.

(3) Any reference in these Regulations to—

(a) a numbered regulation is a reference to the regulation in these Regulations so numbered; or

(b) a numbered paragraph is a reference to the paragraph so numbered in the regulation in which the reference appears.

(4) Nothing in these Regulations shall apply to or in relation to—

(a) drivers' cabs or control cabs for vehicles or machinery;
(b) *display screen equipment* on board a means of transport;
(c) *display screen equipment* mainly intended for public operation;
(d) portable systems not in prolonged *use*;
(e) calculators, cash registers or any equipment having a small data or measurement display required for direct *use* of the equipment; or
(f) window typewriters.

(a) Workstation. This has a more restricted meaning in these Regulations than in reg. 11 of the Workplace (Health, Safety and Welfare) Regulations 1992 (S.I. 1992 No. 3004).

2. Analysis of *workstations*.—(1) Every employer shall perform a suitable and sufficient *(a)* analysis of those workstations which—

(a) (regardless of who has provided them) are used for the purposes of his undertaking by *users*; or
(b) have been provided by him and are used for the purposes of his undertaking by *operators*,

for the purpose of assessing the health and safety risks to which those persons are exposed in consequence of that *use*.

(2) Any assessment made by an employer in pursuance of paragraph (1) shall be reviewed by him if—

(a) there is reason to suspect that it is no longer valid; or
(b) there has been a significant change in the matters to which it relates;

and where as a result of any such review changes to an assessment are required, the employer concerned shall make them.

(3) The employer shall reduce the risks identified in consequence of an assessment to the lowest extent reasonably practicable *(b)*.

(4) The reference in paragraph (3) to "an assessment" *(c)* is a reference to an assessment made by the employer concerned in pursuance of paragraph (1) and changed by him where necessary in pursuance of paragraph (2).

(a) Suitable and sufficient. See INTRODUCTORY NOTE 12.

(b) Reasonably practicable. See General Note and INTRODUCTORY NOTE 5.

(c) Assessment. See also reg. 3 of the Management of Health and Safety at Work Regulations 1992 (S.I. 1992 No. 2051).

3. Requirements for *workstations*.—(1) Every employer shall ensure that any *workstation* first put into service on or after 1 January 1993 which—

(a) (regardless of who has provided it) may be used for the purposes of his undertaking by *users*; or

(b) has been provided by him and may be used for the purposes of his undertaking by *operators,*

meets the requirements laid down in the Schedule to these Regulations to the extent specified in paragraph 1 thereof.

(2) Every employer shall ensure that any *workstation* first put into service on or before 31 December 1992 which—

(a) (regardless of who provided it) may be used for the purposes of his undertaking by *users*; or

(b) was provided by him and may be used for the purposes of his undertaking by *operators,*

meets the requirements laid down in the Schedule to these Regulations to the extent specified in paragraph 1 thereof not later than 31 December 1996.

4.   Daily work routine of *users.* Every employer shall so plan the activities of *users* at work in his undertaking that their daily work on *display screen equipment* is periodically interrupted by such breaks or changes of activity as reduce their workload at that equipment.

5.   Eyes and eyesight.—(1) Where a person—

(a) is already a *user* on the date of coming into force of these Regulations; or

(b) is an employee who does not habitually *use display screen equipment* as a significant part of his normal work but is to become a *user* in the undertaking in which he is already employed,

his employer shall ensure that he is provided at his request with an appropriate eye and eyesight test, any such test to be carried out by a competent person.

(2) Any eye and eyesight test provided in accordance with paragraph (1) shall—

(a) in any case to which sub-paragraph (a) of that paragraph applies, be carried out as soon as practicable after being requested by the *user* concerned; and

(b) in any case to which sub-paragraph (b) of that paragraph applies, be carried out before the employee concerned becomes a *user.*

(3) At regular intervals after an employee has been provided with an eye and eyesight test in accordance with paragraphs (1) and (2), his employer shall, subject to paragraph (6), ensure that he is provided with a further eye and eyesight test of an appropriate nature, any such test to be carried out by a competent person.

(4) Where a *user* experiences visual difficulties which may reasonably be considered to be caused by work on *display screen equipment*, his employer shall ensure that he is provided at his request with an appropriate eye and eyesight test, any such test to be carried out by a competent person as soon as practicable after being requested as aforesaid.

(5) Every employer shall ensure that each *user* employed by him is provided with special corrective appliances appropriate for the work being done by the *user* concerned where—

(a) normal corrective appliances cannot be used; and

(b) the result of any eye and eyesight test which the *user* has been given in accordance with this regulation shows such provision to be necessary.

(6) Nothing in paragraph (3) shall require an employer to provide any employee with an eye and eyesight test against that employee's will.

6. Provision of training.—(1) Where a person—

(a) is already a *user* on the date of coming into force of these Regulations; or

(b) is an employee who does not habitually *use display screen equipment* as a significant part of his normal work but is to become a *user* in the undertaking in which he is already employed,

his employer shall ensure that he is provided with adequate health and safety training in the *use* of any *workstation* upon which he may be required to work.

(2) Every employer shall ensure that each *user* at work in his undertaking is provided with adequate health and safety training whenever the organisation of any *workstation* in that undertaking upon which he may be required to work is substantially modified.

7. Provision of information.—(1) Every employer shall ensure that *operators* and *users* at work in his undertaking are provided with adequate information about—

(a) all aspects of health and safety relating to their *workstations*; and

(b) such measures taken by him in compliance with his duties under regulations 2 and 3 as relate to them and their work.

(2) Every employer shall ensure that *users* at work in his undertaking are provided with adequate information about such measures taken by him in compliance with his duties under regulations 4 and 6(2) as relate to them and their work.

(3) Every employer shall ensure that *users* employed by him are provided with adequate information about such measures taken by him in compliance with his duties under regulations 5 and 6(1) as relate to them and their work.

8. Exemption certificates.—(1) The Secretary of State for Defence may, in the interests of national security, exempt any of the home forces, any visiting force or any headquarters from any of the requirements imposed by these Regulations.

(2) Any exemption such as is specified in paragraph (1) may be granted subject to conditions and to a limit of time and may be revoked by the Secretary of State for Defence by a further certificate in writing at any time.

(3) In this regulation—

(a) "the home forces" has the same meaning as in section 12(1) of the Visiting Forces Act 1952;

(b) "headquarters" has the same meaning as in article 3(2) of the Visiting Forces and International Headquarters (Application of Law) Order 1965; and

(c) "visiting force" has the same meaning as it does for the purposes of any provision of Part I of the Visiting Forces Act 1952.

9. Extension outside Great Britain. These Regulations shall, subject to regulation 1(4), apply to and in relation to the premises and activities outside Great Britain to which sections 1 to 59 and 80 to 82 of the Health and Safety at Work etc. Act 1974 apply by virtue of the Health and Safety at Work etc. Act 1974 (Application Outside Great Britain) Order 1989 as they apply within Great Britain.

SCHEDULE

Regulation 3

(Which Sets Out the Minimum Requirements for *Workstations* which are Contained in the Annex to Council Directive 90/270/EEC on the Minimum Safety and Health Requirements for Work with *Display Screen Equipment*)

1. Extent to which employers must ensure that *workstations* meet the requirements laid down in this Schedule. An employer shall ensure that a *workstation* meets the requirements laid down in this Schedule to the extent that—
(a) those requirements relate to a component which is present in the *workstation* concerned;
(b) those requirements have effect with a view to securing the health, safety and welfare of persons at work; and
(c) the inherent characteristics of a given task make compliance with those requirements appropriate as respects the *workstation* concerned.

2. Equipment.
(a) *General comment*
The *use* as such of the equipment must not be a source of risk for *operators* or *users*.

(b) *Display screen*
The characters on the screen shall be well-defined and clearly formed, of adequate size and with adequate spacing between the characters and lines.

The image on the screen should be stable, with no flickering or other forms of instability. The brightness and the contrast between the characters and the background shall be easily adjustable by the *operator* or *user*, and also be easily adjustable to ambient conditions.

The screen must swivel and tilt easily and freely to suit the needs of the *operator* or *user*. it shall be possible to *use* a separate base for the screen or an adjustable table.

The screen shall be free of reflective glare and reflections liable to cause discomfort to the *operator* or *user*.

(c) *Keyboard*
The keyboard shall be tiltable and separate from the screen so as to allow the *operator* or *user* to find a comfortable working position avoiding fatigue in the arms or hands.

The space in front of the keyboard shall be sufficient to provide support for the hands and arms of the *operator* or *user*.

The keyboard shall have a matt surface to avoid reflective glare.

The arrangement of the keyboard and the characteristics of the keys shall be such as to facilitate the *use* of the keyboard.

The symbols on the keys shall be adequately contrasted and legible from the design working position.

(d) *Work desk or work surface*

The work desk or work surface shall have a sufficiently large, low-reflectance surface and allow a flexible arrangement of the screen, keyboard, documents and related equipment.

The document holder shall be stable and adjustable and shall be positioned so as to minimise the need for uncomfortable head and eye movements.

There shall be adequate space for *operators* or *users* to find a comfortable position.

(e) *Work chair*

The work chair shall be stable and allow the *operator* or *user* easy freedom of movement and a comfortable position.

The seat shall be adjustable in height.

The seat back shall be adjustable in both height and tilt.

A footrest shall be made available to any *operator* or *user* who wishes one.

3. Environment.

(a) *Space requirements*

The *workstation* shall be dimensioned and designed so as to provide sufficient space for the *operator* or *user* to change position and vary movements.

(b) *Lighting*

Any room lighting or task lighting provided shall ensure satisfactory lighting conditions and an appropriate contrast between the screen and the background environment, taking into account the type of work and the vision requirements of the *operator* or *user*.

Possible disturbing glare and reflections on the screen or other equipment shall be prevented by co-ordinating workplace and *workstation* layout with the positioning and technical characteristics of the artificial light sources.

(c) *Reflections and glare*

Workstations shall be so designed that sources of light, such as windows and other openings, transparent or translucid walls, and brightly coloured fixtures or walls cause no direct glare and no distracting reflections on the screen.

Windows shall be fitted with a suitable system of adjustable covering to attenuate the daylight that falls on the *workstation*.

(d) *Noise*

Noise emitted by equipment belonging to any *workstation* shall be taken into account when a *workstation* is being equipped, with a view in particular to ensuring that attention is not distracted and speech is not disturbed.

(e) *Heat*

Equipment belonging to any *workstation* shall not produce excess heat which could cause discomfort to *operators* or *users*.

(f) *Radiation*

All radiation with the exception of the visible part of the electromagnetic spectrum shall be reduced to negligible levels from the point of view of the protection of *operators'* or *users'* health and safety.

(g) *Humidity*

An adequate level of humidity shall be established and maintained.

4. Interface between computer and *operator/user*. In designing, selecting, commissioning and modifying software, and in designing tasks using *display screen equipment*, the employer shall take into account the following principles:

  (a) software must be suitable for the task;

  (b) software must be easy to *use* and, where appropriate, adaptable to the level of knowledge or experience of the *operator* or *user*; no quantitative or qualitative checking facility may be used without the knowledge of the *operators* or *users*;

(c) systems must provide feedback to *operators* or *users* on the performance of those systems;

(d) systems must display information in a format and at a pace which are adapted to *operators* or *users*;

(e) the principles of software ergonomics must be applied, in particular to human data processing.

PART 5

SUBSTANCES, NOISE, RADIATION AND OTHER PHENOMENA

SUMMARY

THE CONTROL OF SUBSTANCES HAZARDOUS TO HEALTH REGULATIONS 1988

(1988 No. 1657 as amended by S.I. 1990 No. 2026, S.I. 1991 No. 2431,
S.I. 1992 No. 2382, S.I. 1992 No. 2966 and S.I. 1993 No. 745)

General note. The amendments introduced by S.I. 1992 No. 2382 and S.I. 1992 No. 2966 implement the Carcinogens at Work Directive 90/394 (see page 163). The amended Regulations repeal a number of sections of the Factories Act 1961 and many Regulations. The Regulations, in earlier form, gave effect to the Vinyl Chloride Monomer Directive 78/610 (not in this book), the Chemical, Physical and Biological Agents at Work Directive 80/1107 (and amendment thereto) (not in this book), and the Biological Agents Directive 90/679 (not in this book).

ARRANGEMENT OF REGULATIONS

Schedule   6. Fumigations excepted from regulation 13.
Schedule   7. Notification of certain fumigations.
Schedule   8. Repeals.
Schedule   9. Revocations of regulations and orders.
Schedule 10. Other substances and processes to which the definition of
              "carcinogen" relates.

The Secretary of State, in the exercise of the powers conferred on him by
sections 15(1), (2), (3)(a), (4), (5)(b), (6)(b) and (9) and 82(3)(a) of, and
paragraphs 1(1) and (2), 2, 6(1), 8, 9, 11, 13(1) and (3), 14, 15(1) and 16 of
Schedule 3 to the Health and Safety at Work etc. Act 1974 ("the 1974 Act") and
of all other powers enabling him in that behalf and for the purpose of giving
effect without modifications to proposals submitted to him by the Health and
Safety Commission under section 11(2)(d) of the 1974 Act after the carrying
out by the said Commission of consultations in accordance with section 50(3)
of that Act, hereby makes the following Regulations:

1.   Citation and commencement. These Regulations may be cited as the
Control of Substances Hazardous to Health Regulations 1988 and shall come
into force on 1 October 1989.

2.   Interpretation.—(1) In these Regulations, unless the context otherwise
requires—

"the 1974 Act" means the Health and Safety at Work etc. Act 1974;
"approved" means approved for the time being in writing by the Health
and Safety Commission or the Health and Safety Executive as the case may
be;
"approved list" means the list published by the Health and Safety
Commission entitled "Information Approved for the Classification, Packaging and Labelling of Dangerous Substances (2nd edition)" as revised or
re-issued from time to time;
"carcinogen" means—

(a) any substance or preparation which if classified in accordance with the
     classification provided for by regulation 5 of the Classification, Packag-
     ing and Labelling of Dangerous Substances Regulations 1984 (S.I.
     1984/1244, amended by S.I. 1986/1922, S.I. 1988/766, S.I. 1989/2208
     and S.I. 1990/1255) would be required to be labelled with the risk
     phrase R45 (may cause cancer) or R49 (may cause cancer by inhalation),
     whether or not the *substance* or preparation is required to be classified in
     accordance with those Regulations; or
(b) any *substance* or preparation listed in Schedule 10 and any substance or
     preparation arising from a process specified in that Schedule which is a
     substance hazardous to health;

"fumigation" means an operation in which a *substance* is released into the
atmosphere so as to form a gas to control or kill pests or other undesirable
organisms and "fumigate" and "fumigant" shall be construed accordingly;
"maximum exposure limit" for a *substance hazardous to health* means the
maximum exposure limit for that substance set out in Schedule 1 in relation

to the reference period specified therein when calculated by a method approved by the Health and Safety Commission;

"micro-organism" includes any microscopic biological entity which is capable of replication;

"occupational exposure standard" for a *substance hazardous to health* means the standard approved by the Health and Safety Commission for that *substance* in relation to the specified reference period when calculated by a method *approved* by the Health and Safety Commission;

"substance" means any natural or artificial substance whether in solid or liquid form or in the form of a gas or vapour (including micro-organisms);

"substance hazardous to health" means any *substance* (including any preparation) which is—

(a) a *substance* which is listed in Part 1A of the approved list as dangerous for supply within the meaning of the Classification, Packaging and Labelling Regulations 1984 and for which the general indication of nature of risk is specified as very toxic, toxic, harmful, corrosive or irritant;

(b) a *substance* for which a maximum exposure limit is specified in Schedule 1 or for which the Health and Safety Commission has *approved* an *occupational exposure standard*;

(c) a *micro-organism* which creates a hazard to the health of any person;

(d) dust of any kind, when present at a substantial concentration in air;

(e) a *substance*, not being a substance mentioned in sub-paragraphs (a) to (d) above, which creates a hazard to the health of any person which is comparable with the hazards created by *substances* mentioned in those sub-paragraphs.

(2) In these Regulations, any reference to an employee being exposed to a *substance hazardous to health* is a reference to the exposure of that employee to a *substance hazardous to health* arising out of or in connection with work which is under the control of his employer.

(3) In these Regulations, unless the context otherwise requires—

(a) a reference to a numbered regulation or Schedule is a reference to the regulation or Schedule in these Regulations so numbered; and

(b) a reference to a numbered paragraph is a reference to the paragraph so numbered in the regulation or Schedule in which that reference appears.

3. Duties under these Regulations.—(1) Where any duty is placed by these Regulations on an employer in respect of his employees, he shall, so far as is reasonably practicable *(a)*, be under a like duty in respect of any other person, whether at work or not, who may be affected by the work carried on by the employer except that the duties of the employer—

(a) under regulation 11 (health surveillance) shall not extend to persons who are not his employees; and

(b) under regulations 10 and 12(1) and (2) (which relate respectively to monitoring and information, training etc.) shall not extend to persons who are not his employees, unless those persons are on the premises where the work is being carried on.

(2) These Regulations shall apply to a self-employed person as they apply to an employer and an employee and as if that self-employed person were both an

employer and employee, except that regulations 10 and 11 shall not apply to a self-employed person.

(3) The duties imposed by these Regulations shall not extend to the master or crew of a sea-going ship or to the employer of such persons in relation to the normal shipboard activities of a ship's crew under the direction of the master.

(a) *Reasonably practicable.* See INTRODUCTORY NOTE 5.

4. Prohibitions relating to certain substances.—(1) Those *substances* described in column 1 of Schedule 2 are prohibited to the extent set out in the corresponding entry in column 2 of that Schedule.

(2) The importation into the United Kingdom *(a)* of the following *substances* and articles is prohibited, namely—

(a) 2-naphthylamine, benzidine, 4-aminodiphenyl, 4-nitrodiphenyl, their salts and any substance containing any of those compounds in a total concentration equal to or greater than 0.1 per cent. by mass;

(b) matches made with white phosphorus,

and any contravention of this paragraph shall be punishable under the Customs and Excise Management Act 1979 and not as a contravention of a health and safety regulation.

(3) A person shall not supply during the course of or for use at work any *substance* of article specified in paragraph (2).

(4) A person shall not supply during the course of or for use at work, benzene or any substance containing benzene unless its intended use is not prohibited by item 11 of Schedule 2.

General note. Regulation 4(2) ceases to have effect insofar as it relates to the import-ation of substances and articles into the United Kingdom from any Member State.

(a) *Reasonably practicable.* See INTRODUCTORY NOTE 5.

5. Application of regulations 6 to 12.—(1) Regulations 6 to 12 shall have effect with a view to protecting persons against risks to their health, whether immediate or delayed, arising from exposure to *substances hazardous to health* except—

(a) where and to the extent that the following Regulations apply, namely—
   (i) the Control of Lead at Work Regulations 1980,
   (ii) the Control of Asbestos at Work Regulations 1987;

(b) where the *substance* is hazardous to health solely by virtue of its radio-active, explosive or flammable properties, or solely because it is at a high or low temperature or a high pressure;

(c) where the risk to health is a risk to the health of a person to whom the *substance* is administered in the course of his medical treatment;

(d) below ground in any mine within the meaning of section 180 of the Mines and Quarries Act 1954.

(2) In paragraph 1(c) "medical treatment" means medical or dental exam-ination or treatment which is conducted under the direction of a registered

medical or dental practitioner and includes any such examination, treatment or administration of any substance conducted for the purpose of research.

(3) Nothing in these Regulations shall prejudice any requirement imposed by or under any enactment relating to publish health or the protection of the environment.

6. Assessment of health risks created by work involving substances hazardous to health.—(1) Subject to regulation 17(1) (which relates to transitional provisions), an employer shall not carry on any work which is liable to expose any employees to any *substance hazardous to health* unless he has made a suitable and sufficient assessment of the risks created by that work to the health of those employees and of the steps that need to be taken to meet the requirements of these Regulations.

(2) The assessment required by paragraph (1) shall be reviewed regularly, and forthwith if—

(a) there is reason to suspect that the assessment is no longer valid; or
(b) there has been a significant change in the work to which the assessment relates,

and, where as a result of the review, changes in the assessment are required, those changes shall be made.

7. Prevention or control of exposure to substances hazardous to health.—(1) Every employer shall ensure that the exposure of his employees to *substances hazardous to health* is either prevented or, where this is not reasonably practicable *(a)*, adequately controlled.

(2) So far as is reasonably practicable *(a)*, the prevention or adequate control of exposure of employees to a *substance hazardous to health* except to a *carcinogen* shall be secured by measures other than the provision of personal protective equipment.

(2A) Without prejudice to the generality of paragraph (1), where the assessment made under regulation 6 shows that it is not reasonably practicable *(a)* to prevent exposure to a *carcinogen* by using an alternative *substance* or process, adequate control of exposure to the *carcinogen* shall be achieved by the application of all the following measures, namely—

(a) the total enclosure of the process and handling systems unless this is not reasonably practicable;
(b) plant, processes and systems of work which minimise the generation of, or suppress and contain, spills, leaks, dust, fumes and vapours of *carcinogens*;
(c) limitation of the quantities of a *carcinogen* at the place of work;
(d) keeping the number of persons who might be exposed to a *carcinogen* to a minimum;
(e) prohibiting eating, drinking and smoking in areas that may be contaminated by *carcinogens*;
(f) the provision of hygiene measures including adequate washing facilities and regular cleaning of walls and surfaces;

(g) the designation of those areas and installations which may be contami-
     nated by *carcinogens*, and the use of suitable and sufficient warning signs;
     and
(h) the safe storage, handling and disposal of *carcinogens* and use of closed
     and clearly labelled containers.

(3) Where the measures taken in accordance with paragraph (2) or (2A), as
the case may be, do not prevent, or provide adequate control of, exposure to
substances hazardous to health of employees, then, in addition to taking those
measures, the employer shall provide those employees with such suitable
personal protective equipment as will adequately control their exposure to
substances hazardous to health.

(3A) Any personal protective equipment provided by an employer in pursuance of this regulation shall comply with any enactment (whether in an Act or
instrument) which implements in Great Britain any provision on design or
manufacture with respect to health or safety in any relevant Community
directive listed in Schedule 1 to the Personal Protective Equipment at Work
Regulations 1992 which is applicable to that item of personal protective equipment.

(4) Where there is exposure to a *substance* for which a *maximum exposure limit*
is specified in Schedule 1, the control of exposure shall, so far as the inhalation
of that substance is concerned, only be treated as being adequate if the level of
exposure is reduced so far as is reasonably practicable *(a)* and in any case below
the *maximum exposure limit.*

(5) Without prejudice to the generality of paragraph (1), where there is
exposure to a *substance* for which an *occupational exposure standard* has been
approved, the control of exposure shall, so far as the inhalation of that substance is concerned, be treated as being adequate if—

(a) that *occupational exposure standard* is not exceeded; or
(b) where that *occupational exposure standard* is exceeded, the employer
     identifies the reasons for the standard being exceeded and takes appro-
     priate action to remedy the situation as soon as is reasonably practicable
     (a).

(6) Subject to regulation 17(2) (which relates to transitional provisions),
where respiratory protective equipment is provided in pursuance of this regulation, then it shall—

(a) be suitable for the purpose; and
(b) comply with paragraph (3A) or, where no requirement is imposed by
     virtue of that paragraph, be of a type *approved* or shall conform to a
     standard *approved*, in either case, by the Health and Safety Executive.

(6A) In the event of the failure of a control measure which might result in
the escape of *carcinogens* into the workplace, the employer shall ensure that—

(a) only those persons who are responsible for the carrying out of repairs
     and other necessary work are permitted in the affected area and they are

provided with appropriate respiratory protective equipment and protective clothing; and

(b) employees and other persons who may be affected are informed of the failure forthwith.

(7) In this regulation, "adequate" means adequate having regard only to the nature of the substance and the nature and degree of exposure to substances hazardous to health and "adequately" shall be construed accordingly.

(a) **Reasonably practicable.** See INTRODUCTORY NOTE 5.

8. Use of control measures etc.—(1) Every employer who provides any control measure, personal protective equipment or other thing or facility pursuant to these Regulations shall take all reasonable steps to ensure that it is properly used or applied as the case may be.

(2) Every employee shall make full and proper use of any control measure, personal protective equipment or other thing or facility provided pursuant to these Regulations and shall take all reasonable steps to ensure it is returned after use to any accommodation provided for it and, if he discovers any defect therein, he shall report it forthwith to his employer.

9. Maintenance, examination and test of control measures etc.—(1) Every employer who provides any control measure to meet the requirements of regulation 7 shall ensure that it is maintained in an efficient state, in efficient working order and in good repair.

(2) Subject to regulation 17(3) (which relates to transitional provisions), where engineering controls are provided to meet the requirements of regulation 7, the employer shall ensure that thorough examinations and tests of those engineering controls are carried out—

(a) in the case of local exhaust ventilation plant, at least once every 14 months, or for local exhaust ventilation plant used in conjunction with a process specified in column 1 of Schedule 3, at the interval specified in the corresponding entry in column 2 of that Schedule;

(b) in any other case, at suitable intervals.

(3) Where respiratory protective equipment (other than disposable respiratory protective equipment) is provided to meet the requirements of regulation 7, the employer shall ensure that at suitable intervals thorough examinations and, where appropriate, tests of that equipment are carried out.

(4) Every employer shall keep a suitable record of the examinations and tests carried out in pursuance of paragraphs (2) and (3) and of any repairs carried out as a result of those examinations and tests, and that record or a suitable summary thereof shall be kept available for at least 5 years from the date on which it was made.

10. Monitoring exposure at the workplace.—(1) In any case in which—

(a) it is requisite for ensuring the maintenance of adequate control of the exposure of employees to *substances hazardous to health*; or

(b) it is otherwise requisite for protecting the health of employees,

the employer shall ensure that the exposure of employees to *substances hazardous to health* is monitored in accordance with a suitable procedure.

(2) Where a *substance* or process is specified in column 1 of Schedule 4, monitoring shall be carried out at the frequency specified in the corresponding entry in column 2 of that Schedule.

(3) The employer shall keep a suitable record of any monitoring carried out for the purpose of this regulation and that record or a suitable summary thereof shall be kept available—

(a) where the record is representative of the personal exposures of identifiable employees, for at least 40 years;

(b) in any other case, for at least 5 years.

11. Health surveillance.—(1) Where it is appropriate for the protection of the health of his employees who are, or are liable to be, exposed to a *substance hazardous to health*, the employer shall ensure that such employees are under suitable health surveillance *(a)*.

(2) Health surveillance shall be treated as being appropriate where—

(a) the employee is exposed to one of the *substances* and is engaged in a process specified in Schedule 5, unless that exposure is not significant; or

(b) the exposure of the employee to a *substance hazardous to health* is such that an identifiable disease or adverse health effect may be related to the exposure, there is a reasonable likelihood that the disease or effect may occur under the particular conditions of his work and there are valid techniques for detecting indications of the disease or the effect.

(3) The employer shall ensure that a health record, containing particulars *approved* by the Health and Safety Executive, in respect of each of his employees to whom paragraph (1) relates is made and maintained and that that record or a copy thereof is kept in a suitable form for at least 40 years from the date of the last entry made in it.

(4) Where an employer who holds records in accordance with paragraph (3) ceases to trade, he shall forthwith notify the Health and Safety Executive thereof in writing and offer those records to the Executive.

(5) Subject to regulation 17(4) (which relates to transitional provisions), if an employee is exposed to a *substance* specified in Schedule 5 and is engaged in a process specified therein, the health surveillance required under paragraph (1) shall include medical surveillance under the supervision of an employment medical adviser or appointed doctor *(b)* at intervals of not more than 12 months or at such shorter intervals as the employment medical advisor or appointed doctor may require.

(6) Where an employee is subject to medical surveillance in accordance with paragraph (5) and an employment medical adviser or appointed doctor has certified in the health record of that employee that in his professional opinion that employee should not be engaged in work which exposes him to that *substance* or that he should only be so engaged under conditions specified in the

record, the employer shall not permit the employee to be engaged in such work except in accordance with the conditions, if any, specified in the health record, unless that entry has been cancelled by an employment medical adviser or appointed doctor.

(7) Where an employee is subject to medical surveillance in accordance with paragraph (5) and an employment medical adviser or appointed doctor has certified by an entry in his health record that medical surveillance should be continued after his exposure to that *substance* has ceased, the employer shall ensure that the medical surveillance of that employee is continued in accordance with that entry while he is employed by the employer, unless that entry has been cancelled by an employment medical adviser or appointed doctor.

(8) On reasonable notice being given, the employer shall allow any of his employees access to the health record which relates to him.

(9) An employee to whom this regulation applies shall, when required by his employer and at the cost of the employer, present himself during his working hours for such health surveillance procedures as may be required for the purposes of paragraph (1) and, in the case of an employee who is subject to medical surveillance in accordance with paragraph (5), shall furnish the employment medical adviser or appointed doctor with such information concerning his health as the employment medical adviser or appointed doctor may reasonably require.

(10) Where, for the purpose of carrying out his functions under these regulations, an employment medical adviser or appointed doctor requires to inspect any workplace or any record kept for the purposes of these Regulations, the employer shall permit him to do so.

(11) Where an employee or an employer is aggrieved by a decision recorded in the health record by an employment medical adviser or appointed doctor to suspend an employee from work which exposes him to a substance hazardous to health (or to impose conditions on such work), he may, by an application in writing to the Executive within 28 days of the date on which he was notified of the decision, apply for that decision to be reviewed in accordance with a procedure approved for the purposes of this paragraph by the Health and Safety Commission, and the result of that review shall be notified to the employee and employer and entered in the health record in accordance with the approved procedure.

(12) In this regulation—

"appointed doctor" means a fully registered medical practitioner who is appointed for the time being in writing by the Health and Safety Executive for the purposes of this regulation;

"employment medical adviser" means an employment medical adviser appointed under section 56 of the 1974 Act;

"health surveillance" includes biological monitoring.

(a) *Health surveillance.* This includes biological monitoring (para. (12)).

(b) *Employment medical adviser or appointed doctor.* For definition, see para. (12).

12. Information, instruction and training for persons who may be exposed to substances hazardous to health.—(1) An employer who undertakes work which may expose any of his employees to *substances hazardous to health* shall provide that employee with such information, instruction and training as is suitable and sufficient for him to know—

(a) the risks to health created by such exposure; and

(b) the precautions which should be taken.

(2) Without prejudice to the generality of paragraph (1), the information provided under that paragraph shall include—

(a) information on the results of any monitoring of exposure at the work-place in accordance with regulation 10 and, in particular, in the case of any *substance hazardous to health* specified in Schedule 1, the employee or his representatives shall be informed forthwith, if the results of such monitoring show that the maximum exposure limit has been exceeded; and

(b) information on the collective results of any health surveillance under-taken in accordance with regulation 11 in a form calculated to prevent it from being identified as relating to any particular person.

(3) Every employer shall ensure that any person (whether or not his employee) who carries out any work in connection with the employer's duties under these Regulations has the necessary information, instruction and training.

13.   Provisions relating to certain fumigations.—(1) This regulation shall apply to *fumigations* in which the *fumigant* used or intended to be used is hydrogen cyanide, ethylene oxide, phosphine or methyl bromide, except that this regulation shall not apply to *fumigations* using the *fumigant* specified in column 1 of Schedule 6 when the nature of the *fumigation* is that specified in the corresponding entry in column 2 of that Schedule.

(2) An employer shall not undertake any *fumigation* to which this regulation applies unless he has—

(a) notified the persons specified in Part I of Schedule 7 of his intention to undertake the *fumigation*; and

(b) provided to those persons the information specified in Part II of that Schedule,

at least 24 hours in advance, or such shorter time in advance as the persons required to be notified may agree.

(3) An employer who undertakes a *fumigation* to which this regulation applies shall ensure that, before the *fumigant* is released, suitable warning notices have been affixed at all points of reasonable access to the premises or to those parts of the premises in which the *fumigation* is to be carried out and that after the *fumigation* has been completed, and the premises are safe to enter, those warning notices are removed.

14.   Exemption certificates.—(1) Subject to paragraph (2) and to any of the provisions imposed by the European Communities in respect of the protection of workers from the risks related to exposure to chemical, physical and bio-logical agents at work, the Executive may, by a certificate in writing, exempt any person or class of persons or any substance or class of substances from all or any of the requirements or prohibitions imposed by these Regulations and any such exemption may be granted subject to conditions and to a limit of time any may be revoked by a certificate in writing at any time.

(2) The Executive shall not grant any such exemption unless having regard to the circumstances of the case and, in particular, to—

(a) the conditions, if any, which it proposes to attach to the exemption; and
(b) any other requirements imposed by or under any enactments which apply to the case,

it is satisfied that the health and safety of persons who are likely to be affected by the exemption will not be prejudiced in consequence of it.

15. Extension outside Great Britain. These Regulations shall apply to any work outside Great Britain to which sections 1 to 59 and 80 to 82 of the 1974 Act apply by virtue of Article 7 of the Health and Safety at Work etc. Act 1974 (Application outside Great Britain) Order 1977 *(a)* as they apply to work in Great Britain.

(a) Now the 1989 Order of the same name.

16. Defence in proceedings for contravention of these Regulations. In any proceedings for an offence consisting of a contravention of these Regulations it shall be a defence for any person to provide that he took all reasonable precautions and exercised all due diligence to avoid the commission of that offence.

17. Transitional provisions.—(1) Where work which is liable to expose employees to *substances hazardous to health* was commenced before 1 October 1989 or within 3 months after that date, it shall be a sufficient compliance with regulation 6(1) if the assessment required by that regulation is made before 1 January 1990.

(2) Until 1 January 1990, respiratory protective equipment required to be *approved* in accordance with regulation 7(6) need not be so *approved*, but until that date any such equipment which was required to be *approved* under any regulation revoked by these Regulations shall be *approved* in accordance with those Regulations or in accordance with the said regulation 7(6).

(3) Where, in respect of the engineering controls to which regulation 9(2) applies, immediately before 1 October 1989 local exhaust ventilation plant was required to be thoroughly examined and tested under any of the relevant statutory provisions then in force, the first thorough examination and test under regulation 9(2) shall not be required until the date on which it would have been required under the former provision had that provision not been revoked.

(4) Where, in respect of an employee to whom regulation 11(1) applies, immediately before 1 October 1989 the employee was subject to health surveillance under any of the relevant statutory provisions then in force, he shall not be required to be medically examined for the first time under regulation 11(5) until the date on which he would have next been required to be so examined under the former provision had that provision not been revoked.

18. Modifications relating to the Ministry of Defence etc.—(1) In this regulation, any reference to—

(a) "visiting forces" is a reference to visiting forces within the meaning of any provision of Part I of the Visiting Forces Act 1952; and

(b) "headquarters or organisation" is a reference to a headquarters or organisation designated for the purposes of the International Headquarters and Defence Organisations Act 1964.

(2) The Secretary of State for Defence may, in the interests of national security, by a certificate in writing exempt—

(a) Her Majesty's Forces;

(b) visiting forces;

(c) any member of a visiting force working in or attached to any headquarters or organisation; or

(d) any person engaged in work involving *substances hazardous to health*, if that person is under the direct supervision of a representative of the Secretary of State for Defence,

from all or any of the requirements or prohibitions imposed by these regulations and any such exemption may be granted subject to conditions and to a limit of time and may be revoked at any time by a certificate in writing, except that, where any such exemption is granted, suitable arrangements shall be made for the assessment of the health risks created by the work involving *substances hazardous to health* and for adequately controlling the exposure to those substances of persons to whom the exemption relates.

(3) Regulation 11(11) shall not apply in relation to—

(a) Her Majesty's Forces;

(b) visiting forces; or

(c) any member of a visiting force working in or attached to any headquarters or organisation.

19. Repeals, revocations and savings.—(1) The provisions of—

(a) the Mines and Quarries Act 1954 specified in column 1 of Part I of Schedule 8; and

(b) the Factories Act 1961 specified in column 1 of Part II of Schedule 8,

are repealed to the extent set out in the entry opposite thereto in the corresponding entry in column 2 of the respective Part.

(2) The Hydrogen Cyanide (Fumigation) Act 1937 is repealed.

(3) The regulations and orders specified in column 1 of Schedule 9 are revoked or, where expressly stated, modified to the extent set out in the entry opposite thereto in column 2 of that Schedule.

(4) Any record or register required to be kept under any regulations or orders revoked by paragraph (3) shall, notwithstanding those revocations, be kept in the same manner and for the same period as if these Regulations had not been made, except that the Health and Safety Executive may approve the keeping of records at a place or in a form other than at the place where, or in the form in which records were required to be kept under the regulations or orders so revoked.

SCHEDULE 1

Regulations 2(1), 7(4) and 12(2)

LIST OF SUBSTANCES ASSIGNED MAXIMUM EXPOSURE LIMITS

The *maximum exposure limits* of the dusts included in the list below refer to the total inhalable dust fraction, unless otherwise stated.

		Reference periods			
		Long-term maximum exposure limit (8-hour TWA reference period)		Short-term maximum exposure limit (10-minute reference period)	
Substance	Formula	ppm	mg m^{-3}	ppm	mg m^{-3}
Acrylamide	$CH_2=CHCONH_2$	—	0.3	—	—
Acrylonitrile	$CH_2=CHCH$	2	4	—	—
Arsenic and compounds except arsine (as As)	As	—	0.1	—	—
Benzene	C_6H_6	5	16	—	—
Bis(chloromethyl) ether	$ClCH_2OCH_2Cl$	0.001	0.005	—	—
Buta-1,3-diene	$CH_2=CHCH=CH_2$	10	22	—	—
2-Butoxyethanol	$C_4H_9OCH_2CH_2OH$	25	120	—	—
Cadmium and cadmium compounds, except cadmium oxide fume and cadmium sulphide pigments (as Cd)	Cd	—	0.05	—	—
Cadmium oxide fume (as Cd)	CdO	—	0.05	—	0.05
Cadmium sulphide pigments (respirable dust as Cd)	CdS	—	0.04	—	—
Carbon disulphide	CS_2	10	30	—	—
Chromium (VI) compounds (as Cr)	Cr	—	0.05	—	—
1,2-Dibromoethane (Ethylene dibromide)	$BrCH_2CH_2Br$	0.5	4	—	—
Dichloromethane	CH_2Cl_2	100	350	—	—
2,2'-Dichloro-4,4'-methylene dianiline (MbOCA)	$CH_2(C_6H_3ClNH_2)_2$	—	0.005	—	—
2-Ethoxyethanol	$C_2H_5OCH_2CH_2OH$	10	37	—	—
2-Ethoxyethyl acetate	$C_2H_5OCH_2OOCCH_3$	10	54	—	—
Ethylene oxide	CH_2CH_2O	5	10	—	—
Formaldehyde	HCHO	2	2.5	2	2.5
Grain dust		—	10	—	—
Hydrogen cyanide	HCN	—	—	10	10
Isocyanates, all (as–NCO)		—	0.02	—	0.07
*Man-made mineral fibre		—	5	—	—
2-Methoxyethanol	$CH_3OCH_2CH_2OH$	5	16	—	—
2-Methoxyethyl acetate	$CH_3COOCH_2CH_2OCH_3$	5	24	—	—
Nickel and its inorganic compounds (except nickel carbonyl):	Ni				
water-soluble nickel compounds (as Ni)		—	0.1	—	—
nickel and water-insoluble nickel compounds (as Ni)		—	0.5	—	—
Rubber process dust		—	8	—	—
†Rubber fume		—	0.6	—	—
Silica, respirable crystalline	SiO_2	—	0.4	—	—

		Reference periods			
		Long-term maximum exposure limit (8-hour TWA reference period)		*Short-term maximum exposure limit (10-minute reference period)*	
Substance	*Formula*	*ppm*	*mg m⁻³*	*ppm*	*mg m⁻³*
Styrene	$C_6H_5CH{=}CH_2$	100	420	250	1050
1.1.1-Trichloroethane	CH_3CCl_3	350	1900	450	2450
Trichloroethylene	$CCl_2{=}CHCl$	100	535	150	802
‡Vinyl chloride	$CH_2{=}CHCl$	7	—	—	—
Vinylidene chloride	$CH_2{=}CCl_2$	10	40	—	—
Wood dust (hard wood)		—	5	—	—

*In addition to the *maximum exposure limit* specified above man-made mineral fibre is also subject to a *maximum exposure limit* of 2 fibres ml^{-1}, 8-hour TWA, when measured or calculated by a method approved by the Health and Safety Commission.
†Limit relates to cyclohexane soluble material.
‡In addition to the *maximum exposure limit* specified above vinyl chloride is also subject to an overriding annual exposure limit of 3 ppm.

SCHEDULE 2

Regulation 4(1)

Prohibition of Certain Substances Hazardous to Health for Certain Purposes

Item No.	Column 1 *Description of substance*	Column 2 *Purpose for which the substance is prohibited*
1.	2-naphthylamine; benzidine; 4-aminodiphenyl; 4-nitrodiphenyl; their salts and any substance containing any of those compounds, in any other substance in a total concentration equal to or greater than 0.1 per cent. by mass.	Manufacture and use for all purposes, including any manufacturing process in which a substance described in column 1 of this item is formed.
2.	Sand or other substance containing free silica.	Use as an abrasive for blasting articles in any blasting apparatus (see note 1).
3.	A substance— (a) containing compounds of silicon calculated as silica to the extent of more than 3 per cent. by weight of dry material; or (b) composed of or containing dust or other matter deposited	Use as a parting material in connection with the making of metal castings (see notes 2 and 3).

Item No.	Column 1 *Description of substance*	Column 2 *Purpose for which the substance is prohibited*
4.	Carbon disulphide.	Use in the cold-cure process of vulcanising in the proofing of cloth with rubber.
5.	Oils other than white oil, or oil of entirely animal or vegetable origin or entirely of mixed animal and vegetable origin (see note 4).	Use for oiling the spindles of self mules.
6.	Ground or powdered flint or quartz other than natural sand.	Use in relation to the manufacture or decoration of pottery for the following purposes— (a) the placing of ware for the biscuit fire; (b) the polishing of ware; (c) as the ingredient of a wash for saggars, trucks, bats, cranks or other articles used in supporting ware during firing; and (d) as dusting or supporting powder in potters' shops.
7.	Ground or powdered flint or quartz other than— (a) natural sand; or (b) ground or powdered flint or quartz which forms part of a slop or paste.	Use in relation to the manufacture or decoration of pottery for any purpose except— (a) use in a separate room or for— (i) the manufacture of powdered flint or quartz; or (ii) the making of frits or glazes or the making of colours or coloured slips for the decoration of pottery; (b) use for the incorporation of the substance into the body of an enclosure in which no persons are employed and which is constructed and ventilated to prevent the escape of dust.
8.	Dust or powder of a refractory material containing not less than 80 per cent. of silica other than natural sand.	Use for sprinkling the moulds of silica bricks, namely bricks or other articles composed of refractory material and containing not less than 80 per cent. of silica.

Item No.	Column 1 *Description of substance*	Column 2 *Purpose for which the substance is prohibited*
9.	White phosphorus.	Use in the manufacture of matches.
10.	Hydrogen cyanide.	Use in *fumigation* except when— (a) released from an inert material in which hydrogen cyanide is absorbed; (b) generated from a gassing powder (see note 5); or (c) applied from a cylinder through suitable piping and applicators other than for *fumigations* in the open air to control or kill mammal pests.
11.	Benzene and any *substance* containing benzene in a concentration equal to or greater than 0.1 per cent. by mass, other than— (a) motor fuels covered by Council Directive 85/210/EEC (OJ No. L96, 3.4.1985, p. 25) (b) waste covered by Council Directives 75/442/EEC (OJ No. L194, 25.7.1975, p. 39) and 78/319/EEC (OJ No. L84, 31.3.78, p. 43).	Use for all purposes except use in industrial processes, and for the purposes of research, development and analysis.

Notes

1. "Blasting apparatus" means apparatus for cleaning, smoothing, roughening or removing of part of the surface of any article by the use as an abrasive of a jet of sand, metal shot or grit or other material propelled by a blast of compressed air or steam or by a wheel.

2. This prohibition shall not prevent the use as a parting material of the following substances—

natural sand;
zirconium silicate (zircon);
calcined china clay;
calcined aliminous fireclay;
sillimanite;
calcined or fused alumina;
olivine.

3. "Use as a parting material" means the application of the material to the surface or parts of the surface of a pattern or of a mould so as to facilitate the separation of the pattern from the mould or the separation of parts of the mould.

4. "White oil" means a refined mineral oil conforming to a specification approved by the Health and Safety Executive and certified by its manufacturer as so conforming.

5. "Gassing powder" means a chemical compound in powder form which reacts with atmospheric moisture to generate hydrogen cyanide.

SCHEDULE 3

Regulation 9(2)(a)

FREQUENCY OF THOROUGH EXAMINATION AND TEST OF LOCAL
EXHAUST VENTILATION PLANT USED IN CERTAIN PROCESSES

Column 1 *Process*	Column 2 *Minimum Frequency*
Processes in which blasting is carried out in or incidental to the cleaning of metal castings, in connection with their manufacture.	Every month.
Processes, other than wet processes, in which metal articles (other than of gold, platinum or iridium) are ground, abraded or polished using mechanical power, in any room for more than 12 hours in any week.	Every 6 months.
Processes giving off dust or fume in which non-ferrous metal castings are produced.	Every 6 months.
Jute cloth manufacture.	Every month.

SCHEDULE 4

Regulation 10(2)

SPECIFIC SUBSTANCES AND PROCESSES FOR WHICH MONITORING IS REQUIRED

Column 1 *Substances or Processes*	Column 2 *Minimum Frequency*
Vinyl chloride monomer.	Continuous or in accordance with a procedure approved by the Health and Safety Commission.
Vapour or spray given off from vessels at which an electrolytic chromium process is carried on, except trivalent chromium.	Every 14 days.

SCHEDULE 5

Regulation 11(2)(a) and (5)

MEDICAL SURVEILLANCE

Column 1 *Substances for which medical surveillance is appropriate*	Column 2 *Processes*
Vinyl chloride monomer (VCM)	In manufacture, production, reclamation, storage, discharge, transport, use of polymerisation.
Nitro or amino derivates of phenol and of benzene or its homologues.	In the manufacture of nitro or amino derivatives of phenol and of benzene or its homologues and the making of explosives with the use of any of these substances.

Column 1 *Substances for which medical surveillance is appropriate*	Column 2 *Processes*
Potassium or sodium chromate or dichromate.	In manufacture.
1-Naphthylamine and its salts. Orthotolidine and its salts. Dianisidine and its salts. Dichlorobenzidine and its salts.	In manufacture, formation or use of these substances.
Auramine, Magenta.	In manufacture.
Carbon disulphide. Disulphur dichloride. Benzene, including benzol. Carbon tetrachloride. Trichlorethylene.	Processes in which these substances are used, or given off as vapour, in the manufacture of indiarubber or of articles or goods made wholly or partially of indiarubber.
Pitch.	In manufacture of blocks of fuel consisting of coal, coal dust, coke or slurry with pitch as a binding substance.

SCHEDULE 6

Regulation 13(1)

FUMIGATIONS EXCEPTED FROM REGULATION 13

Column 1 *Fumigant*	Column 2 *Nature of fumigation*
Hydrogen cyanide.	*Fumigations* carried out for research. *Fumigations* in fumigation chambers. *Fumigations* in the open air to control or kill mammal pests.
Methyl bromide.	*Fumigations* carried out for research. *Fumigations* in fumigation chambers. *Fumigations* of soil outdoors under gas-proof sheeting where not more than 1000 kg is used in any period of 24 hours on the premises. *Fumigations* of soil under gas-proof sheeting in glasshouses where not more than 500 kg is used in any period of 24 hours on the premises. *Fumigations* of compost outdoors under gas-proof sheeting where not more than 10 kg of methyl bromide is used in any period of 24 hours on the premises. *Fumigations* under gas-proof sheeting inside structures other than glasshouses and mushroom houses where not more than 5 kg of methyl bromide is used in each structure during any period of 24 hours. *Fumigations* of soil or compost in mushroom houses where not more than 5 kg of methyl bromide is used in any one fumigation in any period of 24 hours. *Fumigations* of containers where not more than 5 kg of methyl bromide is used in any one fumigation in a period of 24 hours.

Column 1 *Fumigant*	Column 2 *Nature of fumigation*
Phosphine.	*Fumigations* carried out for research. *Fumigations* in fumigation chambers. *Fumigations* under gas-proof sheeting inside structures where not more than 1 kg phosphine in each structure is used in any period of 24 hours. *Fumigations* in containers where not more than 0.5 kg phosphine is used in any one fumigation in any period of 24 hours. *Fumigations* in individual impermeable packages. *Fumigations* in the open air to control or kill mammal pests.
Ethylene oxide.	*Fumigations* carried out for research. *Fumigations* in fumigation chambers.

SCHEDULE 7

Regulation 13(2)

NOTIFICATION OF CERTAIN FUMIGATIONS

Part I. Persons to whom notifications must be made

1.   In the case of a *fumigation* to be carried out within the area of a harbour authority, advance notification of *fumigation* shall, for the purposes of regulation 13(2)(a), be given to—
   (a) that authority;
   (b) an inspector appointed under section 19 of the 1974 Act, if that inspector so requires; and
   (c) where the *fumigation*—
       (i) is to be carried out on a sea-going ship, the chief fire officer of the area in which the ship is situated and the officer in charge of the office of Her Majesty's Customs and Excise at the harbour, or
       (ii) is the space *fumigation* of a building, the chief fire officer of the area in which the building is situated.

2.   In the case of a *fumigation*, other than a fumigation to which paragraph (1) applies, advance notification of fumigation shall be given to—
   (a) the police officer for the time being in charge of the police station for the police district in which the *fumigation* is carried out;
   (b) an inspector appointed under section 19 of the 1974 Act if that inspector so requires; and
   (c) where the fumigation is to be carried out on a sea-going ship or is the space fumigation of a building, the chief fire officer of the area in which the ship or building is situated.

Part II: Information to be given in advance notice of fumigations

3.   The information to be given in a notification made for the purposes of regulation 13(2) shall include the following—
   (a) the name, address and place of business of the fumigator and his telephone number;
   (b) the name of person requiring the *fumigation* to be carried out;
   (c) the address and description of premises where the *fumigation* is to be carried out;
   (d) the date on which the *fumigation* is to be carried out and the estimated time of commencement and completion;

(e) the name of the operator in charge of the *fumigation*; and

(f) the *fumigation* to be used.

SCHEDULE 8

Regulation 19(1)

REPEALS

Part I. Repeals of the provisions of the Mines and Quarries Act 1954

Column 1 *Provision*	Column 2 *Extent of repeal*
Section 112.	The whole section.

Part II. Repeals of the provisions of the Factories Act 1961

Column 1 *Provision*	Column 2 *Extent of repeal*
Section 4.	The words from "and for rendering harmless" to the end of the section.
Section 63.	The whole section.
Section 64.	The whole section.
Section 67.	The whole section.
Section 77.	The whole section.
Section 78.	The whole section.
Section 121.	Subsections (1)(d) and (3)(b).

SCHEDULE 9

Regulation 19(3)

REVOCATIONS OF REGULATIONS AND ORDERS

Column 1 *Regulations or Order*	Column 2 *Extent of Revocation*
Regulations dated 12 December 1905 for the processes of sorting, willeying, washing, combing and carding wool, goat hair and camel hair and processes incidental thereto, (The Wool, Goat-Hair and Camel-Hair Regulations 1905), S.R & O. 1905/1293, amended by S.I. 1980/1690.	The whole Regulations.
Regulations dated 26 February 1906 in respect of the processes of spinning and weaving flax and tow and processes incidental thereto, (The Flax and Tow Spinning and Weaving Regulations 1906),	Regulations 1, 2 and 12.

Column 1 *Regulations or Order*	Column 2 *Extent of Revocation*
Regulations dated 28 August 1907 for the processes of spinning and weaving hemp or jute, or hemp or jute tow and processes incidental thereto, (The Hemp Spinning and Weaving Regulations 1907), S.R. & O. 1907/660, amended by S.I. 1980/1696.	Regulations 1, 2 and 7.
Regulations dated 20 December 1907 in respect of processes involving the use of horsehair from China, Siberia or Russia, (The Horsehair Regulations 1907), S.R. & O. 1907/984, amended by S.I. 1980/1690.	The whole Regulations.
Regulations dated 18 December 1908 for the use of East Indian Wool, (The East India Wool Regulations 1908), S.R. & O. 1908/1287.	The whole Regulations.
Order dated 22 March 1918 for securing the welfare of the workers employed in factories or parts of factories in which bichromate of potassium or sodium is used in tanning by the "two-bath" process (The Tanning (Two-Bath Process) Welfare Order 1918), S.R. & O. 1918/368, amended by S.R. & O. 1930/312.	The whole Order.
Order dated 22 March 1918 for securing the welfare of the workers employed in factories or parts of factories in which bichromate of potassium or sodium is used in dyeing other than job-dyeing, (The Dyeing (Use of Bichromate of Potassium or Sodium) Welfare Order 1918), S.R. & O. 1918/369.	The whole Order.
Order dated 15 August 1919 (The Fruit Preserving Order 1919), S.R. & O. 1919/1136.	Article 6.
The Hollow-ware and Galvanising Welfare Order 1921, S.R. & O. 1921/2032.	The whole Order.
The Hides and Skins Regulations 1921, S.R. & O. 1921/2076, amended by S.I. 1980/1690.	The whole Regulations.
The Indiarubber Regulations 1922, S.R. & O. 1922/329, amended by S.I. 1973/36 and 1980/1248.	The definition— (a) "Appointed doctor"; (b) "Employment medical adviser"; (c) "Fume process".

Column 1 *Regulations or Order*	Column 2 *Extent of Revocation*
	The paragraph— "It shall be the duty of every person employed to observe Part II of these Regulations". Regulations 2 to 19.
The Chemical Works Regulations 1922, S.R. & O. 1922/731, amended by S.I. 1973/36, 1974/1681, 1981/16 and 917.	The whole Regulations.
The Grinding of Metals (Miscellaneous Industries) Regulations 1925, S.R. & O. 1925/904, amended by S.I. 1949/2225, 1950/688, 1970/535 and 1981/1486.	The whole Regulations.
The Grinding of Cutlery and Edge Tools Regulations 1925, S.R. & O. 1925/1089, amended by S.I. 1950/370, 1970/535 and 1981/1486.	The whole Regulations.
The Bakehouses Welfare Order 1927, S.R. & O. 1927/191.	The whole Order.
The Biscuit Factories Welfare Order 1927, S.R. & O. 1927/872.	The whole Order.
The Tanning Welfare Order 1930, S.R. & O. 1930/312.	Articles 6, 7 and 9.
The Refractory Materials Regulations 1931, S.R. & O. 1931/359.	The whole Regulations.
The Chromium Plating Regulations 1931, S.R. & O. 1931/455, amended by S.I. 1973/9.	The whole Regulations.
The Sugar Factories Welfare Order 1931, S.R. & O. 1931/684.	The whole Order.
The Patent Fuel Manufacture (Health and Welfare) Special Regulations 1946, S.R. & O. 1946/258, amended by S.I. 1973/36.	The whole Regulations.
The Pottery (Health) Special Regulations 1947, S.R. & O. 1947/2161.	In Regulation 2, the definitions— (a) "ground or powdered flint or quartz"; (b) "potters' shops". Regulations 5 and 6.
The Jute (Safety, Health and Welfare) Regulations 1948, S.I. 1948/1696.	Regulations 5 to 10. Regulation 12.
The Blasting (Castings and Other Articles) Special Regulations 1949, S.I. 1949/2225, amended by S.I. 1981/1332.	The whole Regulations.

Column 1 *Regulations or Order*	Column 2 *Extent of Revocation*
The Pottery (Health and Welfare) Special Regulations 1950, S.I. 1950/65, amended by S.I. 1973/36, 1980/1248 and 1982/877.	In regulation 2(2) the definitions— 　(a) "Damp fettling"; 　(b) "Fettling"; 　(c) "Flint or quartz milling"; 　(d) "Flintless stoneware"; 　(e) "Potters' shops"; 　(f) "Slip-house"; 　(g) "Suspension"; 　(h) "Wedging of clay". Regulation 61(1)(vii) to (ix) and (xi). In regulation 13(1) the words "in any potters' shop or in any place where clay dust is prepared or" and the words "flint or quartz milling or". In regulation 14(2) the words "in any potters' shop or" and the words "clay dust is prepared or where any flint or quartz milling or". Regulation 17(1)(i) to (xvi), (xxv) and (xxvii), 17(3), 17(6)(i) and (vi). Regulation 18(1) and 18(2). In regulation 18(3)(a) the words "all potters' shops, including such drying stoves as are entered by workpeople and in". Regulation 18(3)(a)(i), 18(3)(b)(i) and (ii) and 18(3)(c). In regulation 18(3)(d) the words "potters' shops, including such drying stoves as are entered by workpeople and of" and in regulation 18(3)(d)(i) the words "and also, in the case of any potters' shop having an impervious floor, by washing or mopping with water on at least one day in each week". Regulation 18(3)(e) to (g). In regulation 18(4) the words "biscuit placing or" in both places where they occur. In regulation 18(7) the reference to sub-paragraphs "(c)", "(e)" and "(f)". Regulation 18(12) and (13). Regulation 19(4). Regulation 20 to 22. Regulation 26. Regulation 28(3). Regulation 29(1) to 29(3). In the table in Schedule 2 the entries numbered (1) to (4), (7) to (22), (24) and (27).

Column 1 *Regulations or Order*	Column 2 *Extent of Revocation*
The Grinding of Cutlery and Edge Tools (Amendment) Special Regulations 1950, S.I. 1950/370.	The whole Regulations.
The Grinding of Metals (Miscellaneous Industries) (Amendment) Special Regulations 1950, S.I. 1950/688.	The whole Regulations.
The Foundries (Parting Materials) Special Regulations 1950, S.I. 1950/1700.	The whole Regulations.
The Hydrogen Cyanide (Fumigation of Buildings) Regulations 1951, S.I. 1951/1759, amended by S.I. 1982/695.	The whole Regulations.
The Hydrogen Cyanide (Fumigation of Ships) Regulations 1951, S.I. 1951/1760.	The whole Regulations.

The Iron and Steel Foundries Regulations 1953, S.I. 1953/1464, amended by S.I. 1974/1681 and 1981/1332.	In regulation 2(2) the definitions—
	  (a) "approved respirator";
	  (b) "dressing or fettling operations";
	  (c) "knock-out operations".
	The proviso to regulation 3(2).
	Regulation 7.
	Regulation 8(1)(b) and (2).
	In regulation 10(1), the number "7".

The Mule Spinning (Health) Special Regulations 1953, S.I. 1953/1545, amended by S.I. 1973/36.	The whole Regulations.
The Indiarubber Regulations 1955, S.I. 1955/1626.	The whole Regulations.
The Shipbuilding and Ship-repairing Regulations 1960, S.I. 1960/1932, amended by S.I. 1974/1681, 1980/1248 and 1983/644.	Regulation 4(1)(a) shall be modified by substituting for the words "to 77" the words "and 74". Regulation 4(8) shall be modified by substituting for the words "72 and 76(2)" the words "and 72". Regulation 53. Regulations 76 and 77.
The Construction (General Provisions) Regulations 1961, S.I. 1961/1580, amended by S.I. 1966/94 and 1974/1681.	In regulation 3(1)(a) the number "20". In the full out words at the end of regulation 3(1), the number "22". Regulation 20. Regulation 22.
The Non-ferrous Metals (Melting and Founding) Regulations 1962, S.I. 1962/1667, amended by S.I. 1974/1681 and 1981/1332.	In regulation 2(2) the definition "approved". In regulation 3(4) the words "Regulation 11(5) and". Regulations 11 and 12. Regulation 13(1)(b). Regulation 13(3). Regulation 19.

Column 1 *Regulations or Order*	Column 2 *Extent of Revocation*
The Carcinogenic Substances Regulations 1967, S.I. 1967/879, amended by S.I. 1973/36.	The whole Regulations.
The Carcinogenic Substances (Prohibition of Importation) Order 1967, S.I. 1967/1675.	The whole Order.
The Anthrax (Cautionary Notice) Order 1968, S.I. 1968/2005.	The whole Order.
The Abstract of Factories Act Order 1973, S.I. 1973/7, amended by S.I. 1983/978.	In Schedule 1— in paragraph 4 the words from "All practicable measures" to the end of that paragraph; paragraph 9; paragraph 13. In Schedule 3— in paragraph 8, the words from "Everyone who employs" to "are mixed". In Schedule 4— in paragraph 8, the words from "Everyone who employs" to "are mixed".
The Chromium Plating (Amendment) Regulations 1973, S.I. 1973/9.	The whole Regulations.
The Employment Medical Advisory Service (Factories Act Orders etc. Amendment) Order 1973, S.I. 1973/36.	In Part II of the Schedule the entries relating to— (a) The Indiarubber Regulations 1922; (b) The Chemical Works Regulations 1922; (c) The Patent Fuel Manufacture (Health and Welfare) Regulations 1946; (d) The Mule Spinning (Health) Special Regulations 1953; (e) The Carcinogenic Substances Regulations 1967.
The Abstract of Special Regulations (Pottery—Health and Welfare) Order 1973, S.I. 1973/37.	In Schedules 1 and 2 (each of which abstracts parts of the Pottery (Health and Welfare) Special Regulations 1950 (No. 65), the following paragraphs in each Schedule shall be revoked in so far as the reference applies to that Schedule— In regulation 2(2) the definitions— (a) "Damp fettling"; (b) "Fettling"; (c) "Flint or quartz milling"; (d) "Flintless stoneware"; (e) "Potters' shops"; (f) "Slip-house"; (g) "Suspension";

Column 1 *Regulations or Order*	Column 2 *Extent of Revocation*
	(h) "Wedging of clay".
	Regulation 6(1)(vii) to (ix) and (xi).
	Regulation 13(1).
	Regulation 14(2).
	Regulation 17(1)(i) to (xvi), (xxv) and (xxvii), 17(3), 17(6)(i) and (vi).
	Regulation 18(1) and 18(2).
	In regulation 18(3)(a) the words "all potters' shops, including such drying stoves as are entered by workpeople and in" and the words "subject to sub-paragraphs (b) and (c) of this paragraph,".
	Regulation 18(3)(a)(i), 18(3)(b) and 18(3)(c).
	In regulation 18(3)(d) the words "potters' shops, including such drying stoves as are entered by workpeople and of" and in regulation 18(3)(d)(i) the words "and also, in the case of any potters' shop having an impervious floor, by washing or mopping with water on at least one day in each week".
	Regulation 18(3)(e) to (g).
	In regulation 18(4) the words "biscuit placing or" in both places where they occur.
	In regulation 18(7) the references to sub-paragraphs "(c)", "(e)" and "(f)".
	Regulation 18(12) and (13).
	Regulation 19(4).
	Regulations 20 to 22.
	Regulation 26.
	Regulation 28(3).
	Regulation 29(1) to 29(3).
	In the table in the Second Schedule the entries numbered (1) to (4), (7) to (22), (24) and (27).
The Hydrogen Cyanide (Fumigation) Act 1937 (Repeals and Modifications) Regulations 1974, S.I. 1974/1840.	The whole Regulations.
The Health and Safety (Animal Products) (Metrication) Regulations 1980, S.I. 1980/1690.	The whole Regulations.
The Chemical Works (Metrication) Regulations 1981, S.I. 1981/16.	The whole Regulations.
The Health and Safety (Foundries etc.) (Metrication) Regulations 1981, S.I. 1981/1332.	In the Schedule the entries relating to— (a) The Blasting (Castings and other Articles) Special Regulations 1949.

Column 1 *Regulations or Order*	Column 2 *Extent of Revocation*
The Grinding of Metals etc. (Metrication) Regulations 1981, S.I. 1981/1486.	The whole Regulations.
The Hydrogen Cyanide (Fumigation of Buildings) (Amendment) Regulations 1982, S.I. 1982/695.	The whole Regulations.
The Poisonous Substances in Agriculture Regulations 1984, S.I. 1984/1114.	The whole Regulations.

SCHEDULE 10

Regulation 2(1)

OTHER *SUBSTANCES* AND PROCESSES TO WHICH THE DEFINITION OF
"CARGINOGEN" RELATES

Aflatoxins
Arsenic and inorganic arsenic compounds
Beryllium and beryllium compounds
Bichromate manufacture involving the roasting of chromite ore
Electrolytic chromium processes, excluding passivation, which involve hexavalent chromium compounds
Mustard gas (B,B'Dichlorodiethyl sulphide)
Calcining, sintering or smelting of nickel copper matte or acid leaching or electrorefining of roasted matte
Ortho-toluidine
Coal soots, coal tar, pitch and coal tar fumes
The following mineral oil:
    (i)   unrefined and mildly refined vacuum distillates;
    (ii) catalytically cracked petroleum oils with final boiling points above 320°C;
    (iii) used engine oils;
Auramine manufacture
Leather dust in boot and shoe manufacture, arising during preparation and finishing
Hard wood dusts
Isopropyl alcohol manufacture (strong acid process)
Rubber manufacturing and processing giving rise to rubber process dust and rubber fume
Magenta manufacture
4-Nitrobiphenyl

THE NOTIFICATION OF INSTALLATIONS HANDLING HAZARDOUS SUBSTANCES REGULATIONS 1982

(S.I. 1982 No. 1357)

The Secretary of State, in exercise of the powers conferred on him by sections 15(1), (2), (3) and (5)(b) and 82(3)(a) of, and paragraphs 1(1) and 15(1) of Schedule 3 to, the Health and Safety at Work etc. Act 1974 ("the 1974 Act"), and of all other powers enabling him in that behalf and for the purpose of giving effect without modifications to proposals submitted to him by the Health and Safety Commission under section 11(2)(d) of the 1974 Act after the carrying out by the said Commission of consultations in accordance with section 50(3) of that Act, hereby makes the following Regulations:—

1. Citation and commencement. These Regulations may be cited as the Notification of Installations Handling Hazardous Substances Regulations 1982 and shall come into operation on 1 January 1983.

General note. A Guidance Note relating to these Regulations has been published by the Health and Safety Executive (booklet HS(R) 16).

2. Interpretation.—(1) In these Regulations, unless the context otherwise requires—

"the Executive" means the Health and Safety Executive;

"installation" means a site or pipeline for which a notification is required under Regulation 3(1);

"hazardous substance" means a substance specified in column 1 of Part I of Schedule 1 to these Regulations or substances of any class specified in column 1 of Part II of that Schedule;

"notifiable quantity" means—

(a) in the case of a substance specified in column 1 of Part I of Schedule 1, the quantity of that substance specified in the corresponding entry in column 2 of that Part;

(b) in the case of substances of a class specified in column 1 of Part II of that Schedule, the total quantity of all substances of that class specified in the corresponding entry in column 2 of that Part,

and in either case the quantity shall be determined in accordance with regulation 3(2);

"site" means—

(a) the whole of an area of land under the control of a person and includes a pier, jetty or similar structure whether floating or not; or

1032

(b) a structure, whether floating or not, which is within the inland waters of Great Britain and which is under the control of a person.

(2) In these Regulations, unless the context otherwise requires, any reference to—

(a) a numbered regulation or Schedule is a reference to the regulation of or Schedule to these Regulations so numbered; and

(b) a numbered paragraph is a reference to the paragraph so numbered in the regulation or Schedule in which that reference appears.

3. Notification of installations handling hazardous substances.—(1) Subject to paragraph (3), a person shall not undertake any activity in which there is or is liable to be at any one time a *notifiable quantity* or more of a *hazardous substance* at any *site*, in any pipeline to which paragraph (4) applies, unless he has notified in writing to the Executive the particulars specified in the appropriate part of Schedule 2 at least 3 months before commencing that activity or before such shorter time as the Executive may agree and for the purposes of this paragraph an activity in which subsequently there is or is liable to be a *notifiable quantity* or more of an additional *hazardous substance* shall be deemed to be a different activity and shall be notified accordingly.

(2) For the purposes of paragraph (1), in determining whether there is a *notifiable quantity* of a *hazardous substance* at a *site* account shall be taken of any quantity of that substance which is—

(a) in that part of any pipeline under the control of the person having control of the *site*, which is within 500 metres of that *site* and connected to it;

(b) at any other *site* under the control of the same person any part of the boundary of which is within 500 metres of the said *site*; and

(c) in any vehicle, vessel, aircraft or hovercraft under the control of the same person which is used for storage purposes either at the *site* or within 500 metres of it,

but no account shall be taken of any *hazardous substance* which is in a vehicle, vessel, aircraft or hovercraft used for transporting it.

(3) Paragraph (1) shall not apply in relation to waste at any *site* which is licensed for the disposal of such waste by a licence issued in pursuance of section 5 of the Control of Pollution Act 1974.

(4) The pipelines referred to in paragraph (1) are any pipeline within the meaning of the Pipelines Act 1962 except—

(a) a pipeline which has been authorised under section 1 of that Act or notified under section 2 of that Act; or

(b) where the only *hazardous substance* that the pipeline contains is a substance of one of the following classes, namely:—

(i) a flammable gas as defined in item 1 of Part II of Schedule 1 at a pressure of less than 8 bars absolute, or

(ii) a flammable liquid as defined in item 4 of that Part.

4. Updating of the notification following changes in the notifiable activity. Where an activity has been notified in accordance with regulation

3(1) and the person having control of that activity makes a change in it (including an increase or a reduction in the maximum quantity of a *hazardous substance* which is or is liable to be at the site or in the pipeline or the cessation of the activity) which affects the particulars specified in that notification or any subsequent notification made under this regulation or regulation 5, he shall forthwith notify the Executive of that change.

5.   Re-notification where the quantity of a substance is increased to 3 times that already notified. Where an activity at a *site* has been notified to the Executive in accordance with regulation 3(1), the quantity of a substance notified under paragraph 7 of Part I of Schedule 2 shall not be increased to an amount 3 or more times that originally notified unless the activity has been re-notified under that regulation as if it were a new activity; and accordingly regulation 4 shall not apply to that increase.

6.   Exemption certificates.—(1) Subject to paragraph (2) below, the Executive may, by certificate in writing, exempt any person or class of persons, activity or class of activities to which these Regulations apply from any requirement or prohibition imposed by these Regulations and any such exemption may be granted subject to conditions and to a limit of time and may be revoked by a certificate in writing at any time.

(2)   The Executive shall not grant any such exemption unless, having regard to the circumstances of the case, and in particular to—

(a)   the conditions, if any, which it proposes to attach to the exemption; and

(b)   any other requirements imposed by or under any enactment which apply to the case,

it is satisfied that the health and safety of persons who are likely to be affected by the exemption will not be prejudiced because of it.

7.   Enforcing authority.—(1) Notwithstanding regulation 3 of the Health and Safety (Enforcing Authority) Regulations 1977 *(a)*, and regulation 2(3) of the Petroleum (Consolidation) Act 1928 (Enforcement) Regulations 1979, the enforcing authority for the relevant statutory provisions in relation to any *site* at which there is an activity required to be notified under these Regulations or which is to be taken into account by virtue of regulation 3(2), shall be the Executive.

(2)   After 1 February 1985, for cases where the quantity of any substance at a *site* on which there is an activity which is required to be notified under these Regulations is such that a licence is required under the Petroleum (Consolidation) Act 1928 for the keeping of that substance, the Executive shall be the authority empowered to grant such a licence and to enforce any conditions attached to any such licence (whether granted by it or not); and that Act shall be modified accordingly.

(a) Now replaced by the 1989 Order of the same name.

8.   Transitional provision. Where—

(a)   at the date of coming into operation of these Regulations a person is in control of an activity which is required to be notified under regulation 3(1); or

(b) within 6 months after that date a person commences any such activity,

it shall be a sufficient compliance with that regulation if he notifies to the Executive the particulars required by Schedule 2 to these Regulations within 3 months after the coming into operation of these Regulations or within such longer time as the Executive may agree in writing.

SCHEDULE 1

Regulations 2 and 3(2)

LIST OF HAZARDOUS SUBSTANCE

Part I. Named substances

1 *Substance*	2 *Notifiable quantity* *tonnes*
Liquefied petroleum gas, such as commercial propane and commercial butane, and any mixtures thereof held at a pressure greater than 1.4 bar absolute	25
Liquefied petroleum gas, such as commercial propane and commercial butane, and any mixture thereof held under refrigeration at a pressure of 1.4 bar absolute or less	50
Phosgene	2
Chlorine	10
Hydrogen fluoride	10
Sulphur trioxide	15
Acrylonitrile	20
Hydrogen cyanide	20
Carbon disulphide	20
Sulphur dioxide	20
Bromine	40
Ammonia (anhydrous or as solution containing more than 50 per cent. by weight of ammonia)	100
Hydrogen	2
Ethylene oxide	5
Propylene oxide	5
tert-Butyl peroxyacetate	5
tert-Butyl peroxyisobutyrate	5
tert-Butyl peroxymaleate	5
tert-Butyl peroxy isopropyl carbonate	5
Dibenzyl peroxydicarbonate	5
2,2-Bis(*tert*-butylperoxy)butane	5

1 *Substance*	2 *Notifiable quantity* *tonnes*
1,1-Bis(*tert*-butylperoxy)cyclohexane	5
Di-sec-butyl peroxydicarbonate	5
2,2-Dihydroperoxypropane	5
Di-*n*-propyl peroxydicarbonate	5
Methyl ethyl ketone peroxide	5
Sodium chlorate	25
Cellulose nitrate other than—(2) cellulose nitrate to which the Explosives Act 1875 applies; or (b) solutions of cellulose nitrate where the nitrogen content of the cellulose nitrate does not exceed 12.3 per cent. by weight and the solution contains not more than 55 parts of cellulose nitrate per 100 parts by weight of solution	50
Ammonium nitrate and mixtures of ammonium nitrate where the nitrogen content derived from the ammonium nitrate exceeds 28 per cent. of the mixture by weight other than— (a) mixtures to which the Explosives Act 1875 applies; or (b) ammonium nitrate based products manufactured chemically for use as fertiliser which comply with Council Directive 80/876/EEC	500
Aqueous solutions containing more than 90 parts by weight of ammonium nitrate per 100 parts by weight of solution	500
Liquid oxygen	500

Part II. Classes of substances not specifically named in Part I

1 *Class of Substance*	2 *Notifiable quantity* *tonnes*	
1. Gas or any mixture of gases which is flammable in air and is held in the installation as a gas.	15	
2. A substance or any mixture of substances which is flammable in air and is normally held in the installation above its boiling point (measured at 1 bar absolute) as a liquid or as a mixture of liquid and gas at a pressure of more than 1.4 bar absolute.	25	being the total quantity of substances above the boiling points whether held singly or in mixtures.

1 *Class of Substance*	2 *Notifiable quantity* *tonnes*
3. A liquefied gas or any mixture of liquefied gases, which is flammable in air, has a boiling point of less than 0°C (measured at 1 bar absolute) and is normally held in the installation under refrigeration or cooling at a pressure of 1.4 bar asbolute or less	50 being the total quantity of substances having boiling points below 0°C whether held singly or in mixtures.
4. A liquid or any mixture of liquids not included in items 1 to 3 above, which has a flash point of less than 21°C.	10,000

SCHEDULE 2

Regulations 3(1) and 5

Part I. Particulars to be included in a notification of a site

1. The name and address of the person making the notification.

2. The full postal address of the *site* where the notifiable activity will be carried on and its ordnance survey grid reference.

3. The area of the site covered by the notification and of any adjacent *site* which is required to be taken into account by virtue of regulation 3(2).

4. The date on which it is anticipated that the notifiable activity will commence, or if it has already commenced a statement to that effect.

5. A general description of the activities carried on or intended to be carried on there.

6. The name and address of the planning authority in whose area the notifiable activity is being or is to be carried on.

7. The name and maximum quantity liable to be on the site of each *hazardous substance* of which notification is being made.

Part II. Particulars to be included in a notification relating to a pipeline

1. The name and address of the person making the notification.

2. The full postal address of the place from which the pipeline activity is controlled, the ordnance survey grid references and addresses of the places where the pipeline starts and finishes and a map showing the pipeline route drawn to a scale of not less than 1:400,000.

3. The date on which it is anticipated that the notifiable activity will commence, or if it has already commenced a statement to that effect.

4. The names and addresses of the planning authorities in whose areas the pipeline lies.

5. The total length of the pipeline, its diameter and normal operating pressure and the name and maximum quantity liable to be in the pipeline of each *hazardous substance* for which notification is being made.

THE ASBESTOS (LICENSING) REGULATIONS 1983

(S.I. 1983 No. 1649, as amended by S.I. 1985 No. 279, S.I. 1986 No. 392 and S.I. 1987 No. 2115)

ARRANGEMENT OF REGULATIONS

1. Citation and commencement.
2. Interpretation.
3. Work with asbestos insulation or with asbestos coating not to be carried on without a licence.
4. Licences for work with asbestos insulation or asbestos coating.
5. Notification to the enforcing authority of work with asbestos insulation or asbestos coating at a person's own premises.
7. Exemption certificates.
8. Extension of these Regulations outside Great Britain.

The Secretary of State, in exercise of the powers conferred on him by sections 15(1), (2), (4)(a), (5)(b) and (9), 43(2) and (5) and 82(3)(a) of, and paragraphs 1(1)(b) and (c), 4, 8(1), 14, 15(1) and 16 of Schedule 3 to, the Health and Safety at Work etc. Act 1974 ("the 1974 Act") and of all other powers enabling him in that behalf and for the purposes of giving effect without modifications to proposals submitted to him by the Health and Safety Commission under section 11(2)(d) of the 1974 Act after the carrying out by the said Commission of consultations in accordance with section 50(3) of that Act, hereby makes the following Regulations:—

1. Citation and commencement. These Regulations may be cited as the Asbestos (Licensing) Regulations 1983 and shall come into operation on 1 August 1984.

General note. A Guidance Note relating to these Regulations has been published by the Health and Safety Executive (booklet HS(R)19) and was revised in 1989.

Fees payable on application to the Health and Safety Executive for approval under these Regulations are specified in the Health and Safety (Fees) Regulations 1992, S.I. 1992 No. 1752.

2. Interpretation.—(1) In these Regulations, unless the context otherwise requires—

"asbestos" means any of the following minerals, that is to say, crocidolite, amosite, chrysotile, fibrous actinolite, fibrous anthophylite, fibrous tremolite, and any mixture containing any of those minerals;

"asbestos cement" means a material which is predominantly a mixture of cement and *asbestos* and which when in a dry state has a density greater than 1 tonnes per cubic metre;

"asbestos coating" means a surface coating which contains *asbestos*;

"asbestos insulation" means any material containing *asbestos* and used for thermal, acoustic or other insulation purposes (including fire protection) except—

(a) *asbestos cement* or *asbestos insulating board*, or

(b) any article of bitumen, plastic, resin or rubber which contains *asbestos*, and the thermal and acoustic properties of which are incidental to its main purpose;

"asbestos insulating board" means any sheet, tile or building board consisting of a mixutre of *asbestos* and other material which mixture when in a dry state has a density greater than 500 kilograms per cubic metre;

"work with asbestos insulation or asbestos coating" means work in which *asbestos insulation* or *asbestos coating* is removed, repaired or disturbed and includes such work in any supervisory or ancillary capacity.

(2) Any reference in these Regulations to a paragraph not otherwise identified is a reference to a paragraph in the Regulation where the reference appears.

3. Work with asbestos insulation or asbestos coating not to be carried on without a licence.—(1) Subject to paragraph (2), an employer or self-employed person shall not undertake any *work with asbestos insulation or asbestos coating*, unless he hold a licence granted under Regulation 4 of these Regulations relating to such work and complies with the terms and conditions of that licence.

(2) Paragraph (1) shall not apply where—

(a) (i) any person who carries out *work with asbestos insulation or asbestos coating* does not spend more than a total of one hour on such work in any period of seven consecutive days, and

(ii) the total time spent on such work by all the persons working on that work does not exceed two hours; or

(b) the work is undertaken at premises of which the employer whose employees are carrying out the work or the self-employed person who is carrying out the work himself, as the case may be, is the occupier, and—

(i) that employer or self-employed person does not hold a valid licence to do such work granted under these Regulations, and

(ii) he has given notice of the work in accordance with regulation 5 of these Regulations; or

(c) the work consists solely of air monitoring or collecting of samples for the purpose of identification.

4. Licences for work with asbestos insulation or asbestos coating.—(1) The Health and Safety Executive may grant a licence for *work with asbestos insulation or asbestos* coating if it considers it appropriate to do so and—

(a) the person who wishes the licence to be granted to him has made application for it on a form approved for the time being for the purpose of this regulation by the Executive; and

(b) the application was made at least 28 days before the date from which the licence is to run, or such shorter period as the Executive may allow.

(2) A licence under this regulation—

(a) shall come into operation on the date specified in the licence and, subject to paragraph (3), may be with or without a limit of time; and

(b) may be granted subject to such conditions as the Executive may consider appropriate.

(3) The Executive may vary the terms of a licence if it considers it appropriate to do so and in particular may—

(a) add further conditions and vary or omit existing ones; and

(b) impose a limit of time where none had been imposed and where a limit had been imposed may vary or remove it.

(4) The Executive may revoke a licence if the licensee—

(a) has contravened any condition or restriction attached to a licence issued under these Regulations; or

(b) has been convicted of an offence of—

(i) contravening regulation 3 or 6 of these Regulations, or

(ii) failing to discharge a duty relating to *work with asbestos insulation or asbestos coating* to which he is subject by virtue of section 2, 3 4 or 5 of the Health and Safety at Work etc. Act 1974, or of any health and safety regulation (whenever made) or of the Asbestos Regulations 1969 *(a)*.

(5) A licensee shall, when required by the Executive, return a licence to the Executive for any amendment or following revocation.

(6) [*revoked.*]

(a) **Asbestos Regulations 1969.** These Regulations are revoked.

5.   Notification to the enforcing authority of work with *asbestos insulation* or *asbestos coating* at a person's own premises.—(1) The notice to which regulation 3(2)(b) refers is a notice in writing given to the enforcing authority at least 28 days before the work is commenced (or such shorter period as that authority may allow) and specifying the type of work to be carried out and the address of the premises at which it is to be carried out.

(2) Where in the case of *asbestos* containing crocidolite an employer or self-employed person has given notice under regulation 6 of the Asbestos Regulations 1969 *(a)* to an inspector appointed by the Health and Safety Executive, that notice shall be deemed to comply with paragraph (1).

(3) Every employer or self-employed person who is undertaking work with *asbestos insulation* or *asbestos coating* after having given notice in accordance with this regulation shall—

(a) provide adequate information to persons who may be in the vicinity or who may be affected by such work, in the case of an employer, instruction and training for his employees where appropriate; and

(b) shall ensure that he, his employees, other employees, and any other persons who may be in the vicinity of, or may be affected by, his or his employees' work activities, are exposed only to the lowest level of *asbestos* dust which is reasonably practicable *(b)*.

(*a*) **Asbestos Regulations 1969.** These Regulations are revoked.

(*b*) **Reasonably practicable.** See INTRODUCTORY NOTE 5.

6. [*revoked.*]

General note. Any certificate required to be kept under this regulation shall, notwithstanding its revocation by S.I 1987 No. 2115, reg. 22(2), be kept in the same manner and for the same period as if the revocation had not taken effect (*ibid.*, reg. 22(3)).

7. Exemption certificates.—(1) Subject to paragraph (2), the Health and Safety Executive may, by a certificate in writing, exempt any person, class of person, product containing *asbestos* or class of such products, from all or any of the prohibitions or requirements imposed by these Regulations and any such exemption may be granted subject to conditions and to a limit of time and may be revoked at any time by a certificate in writing.

(2) The Executive shall not grant any exemption unless having regard to the circumstances of the cases and in particular to—

(a) the conditions, if any, which it proposes to attach to the exemption; and

(b) any other requirements imposed by or under any enactments which apply to the case,

it is satisfied that the health and safety of persons who are likely to be affected by the exemption will not be prejudiced in consequence of it.

8. Extension of these Regulations outside Great Britain. These Regulations shall apply in relation to any work with *asbestos insulation* or *asbestos coating* to which, or in relation to which, sections 1 to 59 and 80 to 82 of the 1974 Act apply by virtue of the Health and Safety at Work etc. Act 1974 (Application outside Great Britain) Order 1977, (*a*) as they apply to such work in Great Britain.

(*a*) **Health & Safety at Work etc. Act 1974 (Application outside Great Britain) Order 1977.** The Regulations are revoked; see now the Health & Safety at Work etc. Act 1974 (Application outside Great Britain) Order 1989, S.I. 1989 No. 840.

THE CONTROL OF ASBESTOS AT WORK REGULATIONS 1987

(S.I. 1987 No. 2115, as amended by S.I. 1988 No. 712, S.I. 1992 No. 2966 and S.I. 1992 No. 3068)

ARRANGEMENT OF REGULATIONS

The Secretary of State in exercise of the powers conferred on him by sections 15(1), (2), (3)(a), (4)(a), (5)(b) and (9), 43(2), (4), (5) and (6) and 82(3) of, and paragraphs 1(1) to (4), 6(1), 8 to 11, 14, 15(1) and 16 of Schedule 3 to, the Health and Safety at Work etc. Act 1974 ("the 1974 Act") and of all other powers enabling him in that behalf and for the purpose of giving effect without modifications to proposals submitted to him by the Health and Safety Commission under section 11(2)(d) of the 1974 Act after the carrying out by the said Commission of consultations in accordance with section 50(3) of that Act, hereby makes the following Regulations:

1. Citation and commencement. These Regulations may be cited as the Control of Asbestos at Work Regulations 1987 and shall come into force on 1 March 1988.

2. Interpretation.—(1) In these Regulations, unless the context otherwise requires—

"action level" means one of the following cumulative exposures to *asbestos* over a continuous 12-week period when measured or calculated by a method approved by the Health and Safety Commission, namely—

(a) where the exposure is solely to chrysotile, 96 fibre-hours per millilitre of air; or

(b) where exposure is to any other form of asbestos either alone or in mixtures including mixtures of chrysotile with any other form of *asbestos*, 48 fibre-hours per millilitre of air; or

(c) where both types of exposure occur separately during the 12-week period concerned, a proportionate number of fibre-hours per millilitre of air;

"adequate" means adequate having regard only to the nature and degree of exposure to *asbestos* and "adequately" shall be construed accordingly;

"approved" means approved for the time being in writing by the Health and Safety Commission or the Health and Safety Executive as the case may be;

"asbestos" means any of the following minerals, that is to say, crocidolite, amosite, chrysotile, fibrous actinolite, fibrous anthophyllite, fibrous tremolite and any mixture containing any of those minerals;

"asbestos areas" and "respirator zone" shall be construed in accordance with Regulation 14;

"control limit" means one of the following concentrations of *asbestos* in the atmosphere when measured or calculated by a method approved by the Health and Safety Commission, namely—

(a) for chrysotile—
(i) 0.5 fibres per millilitre of air averaged over any continuous period of 4 hours,
(ii) 1.5 fibres per millilitre of air averaged over any continuous period of 10 minutes;

(b) for any other form of asbestos either alone or in mixtures including mixtures of chrysotile with any other form of asbestos—
(i) 0.2 fibres per millilitre of air averaged over any continuous period of 4 hours,
(ii) 0.6 fibres per millilitre of air averaged over any continuous period of 10 minutes;

"the Executive" means the Health and Safety Executive.

(2) For the purposes of these Regulations—

(a) any reference to an employee being exposed to *asbestos* shall be treated as a reference to the exposure of that employee to *asbestos* dust arising out of or in connection with any work with *asbestos* or with any product containing *asbestos* which is carried out by the employer; and

(b) in determining whether an employee is exposed to *asbestos* or whether the extent of such exposure exceeds the action level or any control limit, no account shall be taken of any respiratory protective equipment which, for the time being, is being worn by that employee.

(3) In these Regulations, unless the context otherwise requires—

(a) a reference to a number regulation or Schedule is a reference to the regulation or Schedule in these Regulations so numbered; and

(b) a reference to a numbered paragraph is a reference to the paragraph so numbered in the regulation or Schedule in which that reference appears.

3. Duties under these Regulations—(1) Where any duty is placed by these Regulations on an employer in respect of his employees, he shall, so far as is reasonably practicable *(a)*, be under a like duty in respect of any other person who may be affected by the work activity, whether at work or not, except that the duties of the employer—

(a) under regulation 7 (information, instruction and training) shall not extend to persons who are not his employees unless those persons are on the premises where the work is being carried out; and

(b) under regulation 16 (health records and medical surveillance) shall not extend to persons who are not his employees.

(2) These Regulations shall apply to a self-employed person as they apply to an employer and an employee and as if that self-employed person were both an employer and an employee.

(3) Nothing in these Regulations shall prejudice any requirement imposed by or under any enactment relating to public health or the protection of the environment.

(a) Reasonably practicable. See INTRODUCTORY NOTE 5.

4. Identification of the type of asbestos. An employer shall not carry out any work which exposes or is liable to expose any of his employees to *asbestos (a)* unless either—

(a) before commencing that work, he has identified, by analysis or other- wise, the type of *asbestos* involved in the work; or

(b) he has assumed that the *asbestos* is not chrysotile alone and for the purposes of these Regulations has treated it accordingly.

(a) Exposure to asbestos. See reg. 2(2)(a).

5. Assessment of work which exposes employees to asbestos.—(1) Subject to paragraph (3), an employer shall not carry out any work which exposes or is liable to expose any of his employees to *asbestos (a)* unless he has made an adequate assessment of that exposure.

(2) Without prejudice to the generality of paragraph (1), that assessment shall—

(a) subject to regulation 4, identify the type of *asbestos* to which employees are liable to be exposed;

(b) determine the nature and degree of exposure which may occur in the course of the work; and

(c) set out the steps to be taken to prevent or reduce to the lowest level reasonably practicable *(b)* that exposure.

(3) Where work which exposed or was liable to expose employees to *asbestos* had been commenced before the coming into force of these Regulations or within 28 days after that date, it shall be sufficient compliance with paragraph (1) if the employer makes the assessment required by that paragraph within 28 days after the date of coming into force of these Regulations.

(4) The assessment required by paragraph (1) shall be reviewed regularly and a new assessment substituted when—

(a) there is reason to suspect that the existing assessment is no longer valid; or

(b) there is a significant change in the work to which the assessment relates.

(a) **Exposure to asbestos.** See reg. 2(2)(a).

(b) **Reasonably practicable.** See INTRODUCTORY NOTE 5.

5A.   Plans of work.—(1) The employer shall not undertake any work with *asbestos* consisting of the removal of *asbestos* from any building, structure, plant, or installation or from a ship (including its demolition) unless he has prepared a suitable written plan of work detailing how the work is to be carried out and shall keep that plan at least until the date on which the work to which the plan relates has been completed.

(2) The plan of work made in pursuance of paragraph (1) shall include in particular details of—

(a) the nature and probable duration of the work;

(b) the location of the place where the work is to be carried out;

(c) the methods to be applied where the work involves the handling of *asbestos* or materials containing *asbestos*;

(d) the characteristics of the equipment to be used for—
 (i) protection and decontamination of those carrying out the work,
 (ii) protection of other persons on or near the worksite.

6.   Notification of work with asbestos.—(1) This regulation shall apply to any work in which an employee is or is liable to be exposed to *asbestos (a)* unless—

(a) the extent of that exposure neither exceeds nor is liable to exceed the *action level;* or

(b) the employer is licensed under regulation 3(1) of the Asbestos (Licensing) Regulations 1983 to carry out the work and is doing so in accordance with the terms and conditions of that licence or is exempted by regulation 3(2)(b) of those Regulations from those requirements.

(2) An employer shall not carry out work to which this regulation applies for the first time unless he has notified the enforcing authority *(b)* in writing to the

particulars specified in Schedule 1 at least 28 days before commencing that work or before such shorter time as the enforcing authority may agree.

(3) Where an employer has notified work in accordance with paragraph (2) and there is a material change in that work which might affect the particulars so notified (including the cessation of the work), the employer shall forthwith notify the enforcing authority of that change.

(4) Where the work with *asbestos* was commenced before the date of coming into force of these Regulations or is commenced within 56 days after that date, it shall be sufficient compliance with paragraph (2) if the employer either—

(a) notifies the enforcing authority in accordance with paragraph (2) within 28 days after the coming into force of these Regulations; or

(b) had, before the revocation of regulation 6 of the Asbestos Regulations 1969, notified the enforcing authority in accordance with that regulation.

(a) *Exposed to asbestos.* See reg. 2(2)(b).

(b) *Enforcing authority.* See the Health and Safety at Work etc. Act 1974, s. 18.

7. Information, instruction and training. Every employer shall ensure that adequate information, instruction and training is given to his employees—

(a) who are or are liable to be exposed to *asbestos (a)* so that they are aware of the risks from *asbestos* and the precautions which should be observed;

(b) who carry out any work in connection with the employer's duties under these Regulations, so that they can carry out that work effectively.

(a) *Exposure to asbestos.* See reg. 2(2)(a).

8. Prevention or reduction of exposure to asbestos.—(1) Every employer shall—

(a) prevent the exposure of his employees to *asbestos (a)*;

(b) where it is not reasonably practicable *(b)* to prevent such exposure, reduce to the lowest level reasonably practicable the exposure of his employees to *asbestos* by measures other than the use of respiratory protective equipment.

(1A) Without prejudice to the generality of paragraph (1), where employees may be exposed to *asbestos* in any manufacturing process or in the installation of any product, prevention of such exposure to *asbestos* shall be achieved, where it is practicable, by substituting for *asbestos* a substance which, under the conditions of its use, does not create a risk to the health of his employees or creates a lesser risk than that created by *asbestos*.

(2) Where, in pursuance of paragraph (1), it is not reasonably practicable *(b)* to reduce the exposure of an employee to below both the *control limits* which apply to that exposure, then, in addition to taking the measures required by that paragraph, the employer shall provide that employee with suitable respiratory protective equipment which will reduce the concentration of *asbestos* in

the air inhaled by the employee to a concentration which is below those *control limits.*

(3) Respiratory protective equipment provided in pursuance of paragraph (2) shall comply with paragraph (3A) or, where no requirement is imposed by that paragraph, shall be of a type approved or shall conform to a standard approved in either case by the Executive for the purposes of this regulation.

(3A) Any respiratory protective equipment provided in pursuance of paragraph (2) or protective clothing provided in pursuance of regulation 11(1) shall comply with this paragraph if it complies with any enactment (whether in an Act or instrument) which implements in Great Britain any provision on design or manufacture with respect to health or safety in any relevant Community Directive listed in Schedule 1 to the Personal Protective Equipment at Work Regulations 1992 which is applicable to that item of respiratory protective equipment or protective clothing.

(4) If an unforeseen event occurs which results in the escape of *asbestos* into the workplace at a concentration that is liable to exceed any applicable *control limit*, the employer shall ensure that—

(a) only those persons who are responsible for the carrying out of repairs and other necessary work are permitted in the affected area and that those persons are provided with appropriate respiratory protective equipment and protective clothing; and

(b) employees and other persons who may have been affected by the event are informed of it forthwith.

(a) **Exposure to asbestos.** See reg. 2(2)(a).

(b) **Reasonably practicable.** See INTRODUCTORY NOTE 5.

9. Use of control measures etc.—(1) Every employer who provides any control measure, personal protective equipment or other thing or facility pursuant to these Regulations shall ensure so far as is reasonably practicable *(a)* that it is properly used or applied as the case may be.

(2) Every employee shall make full and proper use of any control measure, personal protective equipment or other thing or facility provided pursuant to these Regulations and if he discovers any defect therein he shall report it forthwith to his employer.

(a) **Reasonably practicable.** See INTRODUCTORY NOTE 5.

10. Maintenance of control measures etc.—(1) Every employer who provides any control measure, personal protective equipment or other thing or facility pursuant to these Regulations shall ensure that it is maintained in a clean and efficient state, in efficient working order, and in good repair, and in the case of exhaust ventilation equipment, is also regularly examined and tested at suitable intervals by a competent person.

(2) Every employer shall make a suitable record of work carried out in accordance with paragraph (1) which shall be kept for at least five years from the date on which it was made.

11.   Provision and cleaning of protective clothing.—(1) Every employer shall provide *(a)* adequate and suitable protective clothing for such of his employees as are exposed to *asbestos*, unless no significant quantity of *asbestos* is liable to be deposited on the clothes of the employee while he is at work.

(2) The employer shall ensure that any protective clothing provided in pursuance of paragraph (1) is either disposed of as asbestos waste or adequately cleaned at suitable intervals.

(3) The cleaning required by paragraph (2) shall be carried out on the premises where the work with *asbestos* is being done or in a suitably equipped laundry and protective clothing which has been used and is to be removed from those premises (whether for cleaning, further use or disposal) shall, before being removed, be packed in a suitable container which shall be labelled in accordance with the provisions of Schedule 2 as if it were a product containing *asbestos* or, in the case of protective clothing intended for disposal as waste, in accordance with regulation 18(3).

(4) Where, as a result of the failure or improper use of the protective clothing provided in pursuance of paragraph (1), a significant quantity of asbestos is deposited on the personal clothing of an employee, then, for the purposes of paragraphs (2) and (3) that personal clothing shall be treated as if it were protective clothing.

   (a) Provide. See INTRODUCTORY NOTE 9.

12.   Duty to prevent or reduce the spread of asbestos. Every employer shall prevent, or, where this is not reasonably practicable *(a)*, reduce to the lowest level reasonably practicable, the spread of *asbestos* from any place where work with *asbestos* is carried out.

   (a) Reasonably practicable. See INTRODUCTORY NOTE 5.

13.   Cleanliness of premises and plant.—(1) Every employer who undertakes work which exposes his employees to *asbestos (a)* shall ensure that the premises or those parts of premises where that work is carried out and the plant used in connection with that work are kept in a clean state and, in particular, where work with *asbestos* has been completed the premises or those parts of the premises where the work was carried out are thoroughly cleaned.

(2) Subject to paragraph (3), where a manufacturing process which gives rise to *asbestos* dust is carried out in a building, the employer shall ensure that any part of the building in which the process is carried out is—

   (a) so designed and constructed as to facilitate cleaning; and
   (b) is equipped with an adequate and suitable vacuum cleaning system which shall, where reasonably practicable *(b)*, be a fixed system.

(3) Paragraph (2) (a) shall not apply to any building in which, immediately before the coming into force of these Regulations, there was carried out a process to which either—

(a) prior to its revocation regulation 13 of the Asbestos Regulations 1969 applied and the process was carried out in compliance with that regulation; or

(b) that regulation did not apply.

(*a*) **Exposes . . . to asbestos.** See reg. 2(2)(a).

(*b*) **Reasonably practicable.** See INTRODUCTORY NOTE 5.

14. Designated areas.—(1) Every employer shall ensure that any area in which work under his control is carried out is designated as—

(a) an *asbestos area*, where the exposure to *asbestos* of an employee who worked in that area for the whole of his working time would exceed or would be liable to exceed the *action level*;

(b) a *respirator zone*, where the concentration of *asbestos* in that area would exceed or would be liable to exceed any *control limit*.

(2) *Asbestos areas* and *respirator zones* shall be clearly and separately demarcated and identified by notices indicating—

(a) that the area is an *asbestos area* or a *respiratory zone* or both, as the case may be; and

(b) in the case of a *respiratory zone*, that the exposure of an employee who enters it is liable to exceed a control limit and, if it does, that respiratory protective equipment must be worn.

(3) The employer shall not permit any employee, other than an employee who by reason of his work is required to be in an area designated in accordance with paragraph (1) to enter or remain in any such area and only employees who are so permitted shall enter or remain in any such area.

(4) Every employer shall take suitable steps to ensure that—

(a) his employees do not eat, drink or smoke in any area designated as an *asbestos area* or a *respirator zone*; and

(b) in such a case, arrangements are made for such employees to eat or drink in some other place.

15. Air monitoring.—(1) Every employer shall take adequate steps to monitor the exposure of his employees to *asbestos* (*a*) where such monitoring is appropriate for the protection of the health of those employees.

(2) The employer shall keep a suitable record of any monitoring carried out in accordance with paragraph (1) and that record or a suitable summary thereof shall be kept—

(a) in a case where exposure is such that a health record is required to be kept under regulation 16, for at least 40 years;

(b) in any other case, for at least five years.

(*a*) **Exposure . . . to asbestos.** See reg. 2(2)(a).

16. Health records and medical surveillance.—(1) Every employer shall ensure that a health record containing particulars *approved* by the *Executive* relating to each of his employees who is exposed to *asbestos (a)* is maintained unless the exposure of that employee does not exceed the *action level* and that that record or a copy thereof is kept for at least 40 years from the date of the last entry made in it.

(2) Every employer shall ensure that each of his employees who is exposed to *asbestos* is under adequate medical surveillance by an employment medical adviser or appointed doctor *(b)* unless the exposure of that employee does not exceed the *action level*, and such medical surveillance shall include—

(a) a medical examination not more than two years before the beginning of such exposure; and

(b) periodic medical examinations at intervals of not more than two years or such shorter time as the employment medical adviser or appointed doctor may require while such exposure continues, and

each such medical examination shall include a specific examination of the chest.

(3) Where an employee has been examined in accordance with paragraph (2), the employment medical adviser or appointed doctor shall issue to the employer a certificate stating that he has been so examined and the date of the examination and the employer shall keep that certificate or a copy thereof for at least four years from the date on which it was issued and forthwith give a copy of the certificate to the employee.

(4) An employee to whom this regulation applies shall, when required by his employer and at the cost of the employer, present himself during his working hours for such examination and tests as may be required for the purposes of paragraph (2) and shall furnish the employment medical adviser or appointed doctor with such information concerning his health as may reasonably be required.

(5) Where medical surveillance is carried out on the premises of the employer, the employer shall ensure that suitable facilities are made available for the purpose.

(6) On reasonable notice being given, the employer shall allow any of his employees access to the health record which relates to that employee.

(7) Where before the coming into force of these Regulations, an employee was engaged in work in which he was exposed to *asbestos* to an extent which exceeds the *action level* and continues to be engaged in such work, it shall be a sufficient compliance with paragraph (2) if either—

(a) he is medically examined within six months after the date of coming into force of these Regulations; or

(b) in a case where—
 (i) he had been medically examined before the date of coming into force of these Regulations, and
 (ii) that examination was for the purpose of regulation 6 of the Asbestos (Licensing) Regulations 1983 or an employment medical adviser or appointed doctor has certified that it is appropriate for the examination to be deemed to be an examination for the purposes of paragraph (2)(a),

he is next examined within two years after the date of that examination or within such shorter time as the employment medical adviser or appointed doctor may require.

(9) In this regulation—

"appointed doctor" means a registered medical practitioner who is for the time being appointed in writing by the *Executive* for the purposes of this regulation;

"employment medical adviser" means an employment medical adviser appointed under section 56(1) of the Health and Safety at Work etc. Act 1974;

"medical examination", except in paragraph (8), includes any laboratory tests and X-rays that the employment medical adviser or appointed doctor may require.

General note. Fees payable to the Health and Safety Executive for approval and for medical examination under this regulation are specified in the Health and Safety (Fees) Regulations 1992, S.I. 1992 No. 1752.

(*a*) **Employment medical adviser; appointed doctor.** For definitions, see para. (9).

17. Washing and changing facilities.—(1) Every employer shall provide for any of his employees who is exposed to asbestos (*a*) adequate and suitable—

(a) washing and changing facilities;
(b) where he is required to provide protective clothing, facilities for the storage of—
 (i) that protective clothing, and
 (ii) personal clothing not worn during working hours;
(c) where he is required to provide respiratory protective equipment, facilities for the storage of that equipment.

(2) The facilities provided under paragraph (1) for the storage of personal protective clothing, of personal clothing not worn during working hours and of respiratory protective equipment shall be separate from each other.

(*a*) **Exposure to asbestos.** See reg. 2(2)(a).

18. Storage, distribution and labelling of raw asbestos and asbestos waste.—(1) Every employer who undertakes work with *asbestos* shall ensure that any raw *asbestos* or waste which contains *asbestos* is not—

(a) stored;
(b) received into or despatched from any place of work; or
(c) distributed, except in a totally enclosed distribution system, within any place of work,

unless it is in a suitable and sealed container clearly marked in accordance with paragraphs (2) and (3) showing that it contains *asbestos*.

(2) Raw *asbestos* shall be labelled in accordance with the provisions of Schedule 2.

(3) Waste containing asbestos shall be labelled—

(a) where the Classification, Packaging and Labelling of Dangerous Substances Regulations 1984 apply, in accordance with those Regulations;

(b) where the waste is conveyed by road in a road tanker or tank container in circumstances where the Dangerous Substances (Conveyance by Road in Road Tankers and Tank Containers) Regulations 1981 *(a)* apply, in accordance with those Regulations;

(c) in any other case, in accordance with the provisions of Schedule 2.

(a) Now replaced by S.I. 1992 No. 743.

19.   Supply of products containing asbestos for use at work.—(1) Subject to paragraph (2), a person shall not supply any product which contains *asbestos*, being an article or substance for use at work, unless that product is labelled in accordance with the provisions of Schedule 2.

(2) Where a product contains a component containing *asbestos* it shall be sufficient compliance with this regulation if such component is labelled in accordance with the provisions of Schedule 2 except that where the size of such a component makes it impossible for a label to be fixed to the component neither the component nor the product need be labelled.

20.   Exemption certificates.—(1) Subject to paragraph (2) of this regulation, the *Executive* may, by a certificate in writing, exempt any person or class of persons from all or any of the requirements or prohibitions imposed by these Regulations and any such exemption may be granted subject to conditions and to a limit of time and may be revoked by a certificate in writing at any time.

(2) The *Executive* shall not grant any such exemption unless having regard to the circumstances of the case and in particular to—

(a) the conditions, if any, which it proposes to attach to the exemption; and

(b) any other requirements imposed by or under any enactments which apply to the case,

it is satisfied that the health and safety of persons who are likely to be affected by the exemption will not be prejudiced in consequence of it and that any provision imposed by the European Communities in respect of the encouragement of improvements in the safety and health of workers at work will be satisfied.

21.   Extension outside Great Britain. These Regulations shall apply to any work outside Great Britain to which sections 1 to 59 and 80 to 82 of the Health and Safety at Work etc. Act 1974 apply by virtue of the Health and Safety etc. Act 1974 (Application outside Great Britain) Order 1989 as they apply to work in Great Britain.

22.   Revocations and savings.—(1) The Asbestos Regulations 1969 are revoked.

(2) Regulation 6 of the Asbestos (Licensing) Regulations 1983 is revoked.

(3) Any report required to be kept under regulation 7(4) of the Asbestos Regulations 1969 or certificate required to be kept under regulation 6 of the Asbestos (Licensing) Regulations 1983 shall, notwithstanding the revocation of those Regulations, be kept in the same manner and for the same period as if the revocations mentioned in paragraphs (2) and (3) had not taken effect.

SCHEDULE 1

Regulation 6(2)

PARTICULARS TO BE INCLUDED IN A NOTIFICATION

1. The following particulars are to be included in a notification made in accordance with regulation 6(2), namely—
(a) the name, address and telephone number of—
   (i) the notifier, and
   (ii) his usual place of business;
(b) a brief description of—
   (i) the type(s) of *asbestos* used or handled (crocidolite, amosite, chrysotile or other), and
   (ii) maximum quantity of *asbestos* held on the premises at any one time, and
   (iii) the activities or processes involved, and
   (iv) the products manufactured, (where applicable);
(c) date of commencement of the work activity where work has yet to begin.

SCHEDULE 2

Regulation 18(2) and (3) and (19)

THE LABELLING OF RAW *ASBESTOS*, *ASBESTOS* WASTE AND PRODUCTS CONTAINING *ASBESTOS*

1.—(1) Subject to sub-paragraphs (2) and (3) of this paragraph, the label to be used on—
(a) raw *asbestos* (together with the labelling required under the Classification, Packaging and Labelling of Dangerous Substances Regulations 1984);
(b) *asbestos* waste (when required to be so labelled by regulation 18(3)); and
(c) products containing *asbestos* (including used protective clothing to which regulation 11(2) applies),
shall be in the form and in the colours of the following diagram and shall comply with the specifications set out in paragraphs 2 and 3.

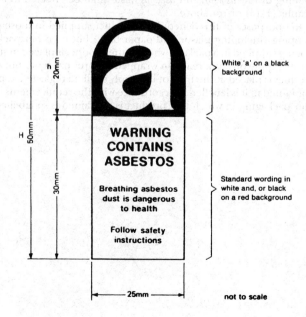

(2) In the case of any product containing crocidolite, the words "contains asbestos" shown in the diagram shall be replaced by the words "contains crocidolite/blue asbestos".

(3) Where the label is printed directly onto a product a single colour contrasting with the background colour may be used.

2. The dimensions in millimetres of the label shall be those shown on the diagram, except that larger measurements may be used, but in that case the dimension of the label indicated as h. on the diagram in paragraph 1(1) above shall be 40% of the dimension indicated as H. on that diagram.

3. The label shall be clearly and indelibly printed so that the words in the lower half of the label can be easily read, and those words shall be printed in black or white.

4.—(1) Without prejudice to the provisions of any other legislation relating to health and safety at work, where any product may undergo processing or finishing it shall bear a label containing any safety instructions appropriate to the particular product and in particular the following instructions—

"operate if possible out of doors or in a well ventilated place";

"preferably use hand tools or low speed tools equipped, if necessary, with an appropriate dust extraction facility. If high speed tools are used, they should always be so equipped";

"if possible, dampen before cutting or drilling";

"dampen dust and place it in a properly closed receptacle and dispose of it safely".

(2) Any additional safety information given on any label shall not detract from or contradict the safety information given in accordance with sub-paragraph (1) above.

5.—(1) Labelling of packaged and unpackaged products in accordance with the foregoing paragraphs shall be effected by means of—

(a) an adhesive label firmly affixed to the product or its packaging, as the case may be;

(b) a tie-on label firmly attached to the product or its packaging, as the case may be; or

(c) direct printing onto the product or its packaging, as the case may be.

(2) Where, in the case of an unpackaged product, it is not reasonably practicable to comply with the provisions of sub-paragraph (1) above the label shall be printed on a suitable sheet accompanying the product.

(3) Labelling of raw *asbestos* and *asbestos* waste shall be effected in accordance with sub-paragraphs (1)(a) or (c) above.

(4) For the purposes of this Schedule, a product supplied in loose plastic or other similar wrapping (including plastic and paper bags) but no other packaging, shall be treated as being supplied in a package whether the product is placed in such wrapping at the time of its supply or was already so wrapped before that time. But no wrapping in which a product is placed at the time of its supply shall be regarded as packaging if any product contained in it is labelled in accordance with the requirements of this Schedule or any other packaging in which that product is contained is so labelled.

THE CONTROL OF ASBESTOS IN THE AIR REGULATIONS 1990

(S.I. 1990 No. 556)

The Secretary of State for the Environment, as respects England, the Secretary of State for Wales, as respects Wales, and the Secretary of State for Scotland, as respects Scotland, in exercise of their powers (as respects Regulations 1 to 3) under sections 1(1)(b) and (d), 15(1) and (3) and 53(1) of the Health and Safety at Work etc. Act 1974, after consulting, in accordance with section 50(1) of that Act, the Health and Safety Commission and such other bodies as it appeared to them to be appropriate to consult, and (as respects regulations 1, 4 and 5) under section 2(2) of the European Communities Act 1972 being the Ministers designated for the purposes of that subsection in relation to the control of air pollution, and of all other powers enabling them in that behalf, hereby make the following Regulations:—

1. Citation, commencement and interpretation.—(1) These Regulations may be cited as the Control of Asbestos in the Air Regulations 1990 and subject to paragraph (2) shall come into force on 5 April 1990.

(2) In the case of any premises to which section 5 of the Health and Safety at Work etc. Act 1974 applied before 31 December 1988, regulations 2 and 3 shall come into force on 30 June 1991.

(3) In these Regulations "asbestos" means the following fibrous silicates— actinolite, amosite, anthophyllite, chrysotile, crocidolite or tremolite.

2. Limit value for the discharge of _asbestos_ into the air during the use of _asbestos_.—(1) Any person having control of any premises to which section 5 of the Health and Safety at Work etc. Act 1974 applies and from which _asbestos_ is emitted through discharge outlets into the air during the use of _asbestos_ shall ensure that—

    (a) the concentration of _asbestos_ so discharged, measured by the sampling and analysis procedures described in the Annex to Council Directive 87/217/EEC on the prevention and reduction of environmental pollution by _asbestos_, or any other method which gives equivalent results, does not exceed 0.1 milligram of _asbestos_ per cubic metre of air, and

    (b) the concentration of _asbestos_ so emitted is measured as mentioned in paragraph (a) at regular intervals of not more than 6 months.

(2) In this regulation—

"raw asbestos" means the product resulting from the primary crushing of asbestos ore; and

"use of asbestos" means activities which involve—

    (a) the production of raw asbestos from ore, excluding any process directly associated with the mining of the ore, or

(b) the manufacturing and industrial finishing of any of the following products using raw asbestos—

asbestos cement, asbestos cement products, asbestos fillers, asbestos filters, asbestos floor coverings, asbestos friction products, asbestos insulating board, asbestos jointing, packaging and reinforcement materials, asbestos packing, asbestos paper and card, and asbestos textiles.

3.   Enforcing authority. The Secretary of State shall be the authority responsible for enforcing regulation 2.

Control of environmental pollution by asbestos resulting from the working of products containing asbestos

4.—(1) Any person undertaking activities involving the working of products containing asbestos shall ensure that those activities do not cause significant environmental pollution by asbestos fibres or dust emitted into the air;

(2) Any person undertaking the demolition of buildings, structures and installations containing asbestos and the removal from them of asbestos or materials containing asbestos involving the release of asbestos fibres or dust into the air shall ensure that significant environmental pollution is not caused thereby.

(3) In this regulation—

"fibre" means a fibre within the meaning of Part B.II of the Annex to Council Directive 87/217/EEC; and

"the working of products containing asbestos" means activities other than the use of asbestos (within the meaning of regulation 2) which are liable to release asbestos into the environment.

5.—(1) Any person who contravenes the provisions of regulation 4 commits an offence and a person guilty of such an offence shall be liable on conviction on indictment to a fine, or on summary conviction to a fine not exceeding level 4 on the standard scale.

(2) Section 37 (offences by bodies corporate) of the Health and Safety at Work etc. Act 1974 shall apply to an offence under this regulation as it applies to an offence under any of the relevant statutory provisions of that Act.

THE ASBESTOS (PROHIBITIONS) REGULATIONS 1992

(S.I. 1992 No. 3067)

General Note. These Regulations are amongst those which implement the Asbestos Directive 83/477 amended by 91/382.

The Secretary of State in the exercise of the powers conferred on her by sections 15(1), (2), (5)(b) and (9), and 82(3)(a) of, and paragraphs 1(1) and 2 of Schedule 3 to, the Health and Safety at Work etc. Act 1974 ("the 1974 Act") and of all other powers enabling her in that behalf and for the purpose of giving effect without modification to proposals submitted to her by the Health and Safety Commission under section 11(2)(d) of *the 1974 Act* after the carrying out by the said Commission of consultations in accordance with section 50(3) of that Act, hereby makes the following Regulations:—

1. Citation and commencement. These Regulations may be cited as the Asbestos (Prohibitions) Regulations 1992 and shall come into force on 1 January 1993.

2. Interpretation and application.—(1) In these Regulations unless the context otherwise requires—

"amphibole asbestos" means any of the following minerals, namely crocidolite, amosite, fibrous actinolite, fibrous anthophyllite, fibrous tremolite and any mixture containing any of those minerals;

"asbestos" means chrysotile, and *amphibole asbestos* and any mixture containing any of those minerals;

"asbestos spraying" means the application by spraying of any material containing *asbestos* to form a continuous surface coating;

"roofing felt" means a product that is fabricated to form a waterproof covering for roofing applications, having as its base a mat of vegetable or mineral fibres or a mixture of those fibres, fixed in a matrix of bituminous materials that may contain polymers or resins.

(2) Any prohibition imposed on any person by these Regulations shall apply only to acts done in the course of a trade, business or other undertaking (whether for profit or not) carried on by him.

(3) Any prohibition imposed by these Regulations on the importation into the United Kingdom, or on the supply or use of *asbestos* shall not apply to the importation, supply or use of *asbestos* solely for the purposes of research, development or analysis.

3. Prohibition of the importation of *amphibole asbestos*. The importation into the United Kingdom of crude, fibre, flake, powder or waste *amphibole asbestos* is prohibited and any contravention of this paragraph shall be punishable under the Customs and Excise Management Act 1979 and not as a health and safety regulation.

4.   Prohibition of the supply of *amphibole asbestos*. No person shall supply *amphibole asbestos* or any product to which *amphibole asbestos* has intentionally been added.

5.   Prohibition of the use of *amphibole asbestos* and products containing it.—
(1) No person shall use *amphibole asbestos* or any product to which *amphibole asbestos* has intentionally been added in the manufacture or repair of any other product.

(2) No person shall use any product containing *amphibole asbestos*, except that this paragraph shall not apply—

(a)   in the case of products containing crocidolite or amosite, to products which were in use before 1 January 1986; or

(b)   in the case of products containing any other form of *amphibole asbestos*, but not crocidolite or amosite, to products which were in use before 1 January 1993,

or, in either case, to any activity in connection with the disposal of any such product.

6.   Prohibition of *asbestos spraying*. No person shall undertake *asbestos spraying*.

7.   Prohibition of products containing chrysotile.—(1) Subject to paragraph (2) below, the supply and use of any product containing chrysotile described in the Schedule to these Regulations is prohibited.

(2) Paragraph (1) above shall not apply to the use of—

(a)   any product which was in use before 1 January 1993 except that that paragraph shall apply to any such product the use of which was prohibited by the Asbestos (Prohibitions) Regulations 1985 as in force immediately before the coming into force of these Regulations;

(b)   any activity in connection with the disposal of any such product.

8.   Exemption certificates.—(1) Subject to paragraph (2) and to any provisions imposed by the Communities in respect of the marketing and use of dangerous substances and preparations, the Health and Safety Executive may, by a certificate in writing, exempt any person or class of persons, or any product containing *asbestos* or class of such products from all or any of the prohibitions imposed by these Regulations and any such exemption may be granted subject to conditions and to a limit of time and may be revoked by a certificate in writing at any time.

(2) The Executive shall not grant any such exemption unless, having regard to the circumstances of the case and in particular to—

(a)   the conditions, if any, that it proposes to attach to the exemption; and

(b)   any requirements imposed by or under any enactments which apply to the case,

it is satisfied that the health or safety of persons who are likely to be affected by the exemption will not be prejudiced in consequence of it.

9. Extension outside Great Britain. These Regulations shall apply to any premises and activities outside Great Britain to which sections 1 to 59 and 80 to 82 of the Health and Safety at Work etc. Act 1974 apply by virtue of the Health and Safety at Work etc. Act 1974 (Application Outside Great Britain) Order 1989 as they apply to premises and activities within Great Britain.

10. Revocations. The following Regulations are revoked—

(a) the Asbestos (Prohibitions) Regulations 1985;
(b) the Asbestos (Prohibitions) (Amendment) Regulations 1988.

SCHEDULE

Regulation 7(1)

PRODUCTS CONTAINING CHRYSOTILE WHICH ARE PROHIBITED

1. The supply or use of the products containing chrysotile described in the following paragraphs of this Schedule are prohibited.

2. Materials or preparations intended to be applied by spraying.

3. Paints or varnishes.

4. Filters for liquids, except that this prohibition shall not apply to filters for medical use until after 31 December 1994.

5. Road surfacing material where the fibre content is more than 2%.

6. Mortars, protective coatings, fillers, sealants, jointing compounds, mastics, glues and decorative products in powder form and decorative finishes.

7. Insulating or soundproofing materials which when used in their intended form have a density of less than $1g/cm^3$.

8. Air filters and filters used in the transport, distribution and utilisation of natural gas and town gas.

9. Underlays for plastic floor and wall coverings.

10. Textiles finished in the form intended to be supplied to the end user unless treated to avoid fibre release, except that this prohibition shall not apply to diaphragms for electrolysis processes until after 31 December 1998.

11. *Roofing felt* after 1 July 1993.

THE HEALTH AND SAFETY (DANGEROUS PATHOGENS) REGULATIONS 1981

(S.I. 1981 No. 1011)

ARRANGEMENT OF REGULATIONS

1. Citation and commencement.
2. Interpretation.
3. Notification of the keeping or handling of listed pathogens.
4. Provision relating to laboratories providing a diagnostic service.
5. Changes in particulars to be notified.
6. Transportation of listed pathogens.
7. Notification to the Health Ministers.
8. Defence in proceedings for contravening regulation 3.
9. Meaning of "work" and "at work".
10. Modification of section 3 (2) of the Health and Safety at Work etc. Act 1974.
11. Exemptions.

Schedule 1. List of pathogens the keeping or handling of which is to be notified.
Schedule 2. Particulars to be notified in respect of the keeping or handling of a listed pathogen.
Schedule 3. Particulars to be notified in respect of laboratories providing a diagnostic service.
Schedule 4. Particulars to be notified in respect of transportation of a listed pathogen.

In exercise of the powers conferred on me by sections 15(1), (2), 3(b), (5)(b) and 6(b) and 52(2) of, and paragraphs 1(1), 3(1) and 15(1) of Schedule 3 to the Health and Safety at Work etc. Act 1974 and of all other powers enabling me in that behalf and for the purpose of giving effect with modifications to proposals submitted by the Health and Safety Commission under Section 11(2)(d) of the said Act after the carrying out by the said Commission of consultations in accordance with section 50(3) of that Act and after consulting with the said Commission in accordance with section 50(2) of that Act, I hereby make the following Regulations:—

1. Citation and commencement. These Regulations may be cited as the Health and Safety (Dangerous Pathogens) Regulations 1981 and shall come into operation on 1 September 1981.

General note. A Guidance Note relating to these Regulations has been published by the Health and Safety Executive (booklet HS (R) 12).

2. Interpretation.—(1) In these Regulations, unless the context otherwise requires—

"listed pathogen" means—

(a) a pathogen listed in Schedule 1,
(b) a derivative of a pathogen listed in that Schedule which is capable of causing disease in humans,

but does not include any substance in respect of which there is in force a product licence granted under the Medicines Act 1968 or a clinical trial certificate or animal test certificate issued for the purposes of section 31 or 32 of that Act.

"diagnostic service" means any activity carried on with the intention of—

(a) identifying a *listed pathogen,*
(b) isolating or identifying other organisms from specimens or samples suspected of containing a *listed pathogen,*
(c) analysing specimens or samples from a patient known to be, or suspected of, harbouring a *listed pathogen* for purposes relating to the assessment of the clinical progress or assistance in the clinical management of that patient,

and "diagnosis" and "diagnostic work" shall be construed accordingly.

(2) In these Regulations, unless the context otherwise requires, any reference to—

(a) a self-employed person includes a reference to any person who keeps or handles a *listed pathogen* and who is not an employer or an employed person in relation to that keeping or handling;
(b) a numbered regulation or Schedule is a reference to the regulation of, or Schedule to, these Regulations bearing that number;
(c) a numbered paragraph is a reference to the paragraph bearing that number in the regulation in which the reference appears.

3. Notification of the keeping or handling of listed pathogens.—(1) Subject to paragraph (2), on or after 1 November 1981 an employer or self-employed person shall not keep or handle nor cause or permit the keeping or handling of a *listed pathogen* unless at least 30 days in advance he has given to the Health and Safety Executive notice in writing of the particulars set out in Schedule 2 in respect of each activity involving that pathogen.

(2) Paragraph (1) shall not apply where—

(a) the keeping or handling is soley for the purposes of transportation; or
(b) the *listed pathogen* is in a human or animal body (whether live or dead) or in any part thereof but this exception shall not apply to any specimen or sample; or
(c) the *listed pathogen* is in the bedding of an infected person or animal or in the clothing of an infected person or in any waste material kept or handled in the course of clinical treatment or post-mortem examination of such a person or animal; or
(d) the *listed pathogen* is in a specimen or sample being taken or sent for *diagnosis*; or

(e) the keeping or handling is in the course of *diagnostic work*; or
(f) the employer or self-employed person, as the case may be, does not know and could not reasonably be expected to know that a *listed pathogen* is being kept or handled.

4. Provisions relating to laboratories providing a *diagnostic service*.—(1) Subject to paragraph (2), on or after 1 November 1981 an employer or self-employed person shall not carry out a *diagnostic service* in relation to a *listed pathogen* unless at least 30 days in advance he has given to the Health and Safety Executive notice in writing of the particulars set out in Schedule 3.

(2) Paragraph (1) shall not apply where the *listed pathogen* or suspected pathogen is in a human or animal body (whether live or dead).

5. Changes in particulars to be notified. Where—

(a) there is a change in any of the particulars which have been notified in accordance with regulations 3(1) or 4(1), or
(b) the activities which have been so notified cease to be carried on,

then the employer or self-employed person, as the case may be, shall notify the Health and Safety Executive forthwith in writing of that change or cessation; but this shall not apply to the completion of a particular activity in accordance with the notification under sub-paragraph (f) of Schedule 2.

6. Transportation of listed pathogens.—(1) Subject to the following provisions of this regulation, on or after 1 November 1981 a person shall not consign a *listed pathogen* unless at least 30 days (or such lesser period as the Health and Safety Executive may allow in a particular case) before the pathogen is transported he has notified the Health and Safety Executive in writing of the particulars set out in Schedule 4.

(2) Paragraph (1) shall not apply where—

(a) the *listed pathogen* is being consigned—
    (i) for the purposes of *diagnosis*, or
    (ii) within the curtilage of any premises; or
(b) the consignor did not know and could not reasonably be expected to know that he was consigning a *listed pathogen*.

(3) In the case of a *listed pathogen* imported into Great Britain, the consignee shall give the notice required by paragraph (1), and paragraph (2)(b) shall have effect as a reference to the consignee not knowing or not reasonably being expected to know that a *listed pathogen* was being consigned to him.

(4) In this regulation "consign" includes send to any other place whether or not it is in the same ownership or control.

7. Notification to the Health Ministers.—(1) Where any notice required by regulations 3, 4, 5 or 6 is received by the Health and Safety Executive, the Executive shall forthwith give notice in writing of all the particulars included in such notice to the Health Minister or any country within which it appears, from those particulars, that a *diagnostic service* is to be, or is no longer to be, provided or that a *listed pathogen* is to be, or is no longer to be, kept or handled or is to be transported.

(2) In this regulation "Health Minister" means, in respect of England or of Wales or of Scotland, the Secretary of State concerned with health in that country.

8.   Defence in proceedings for contravening regulation 3. In any proceedings for an alleged contravention of regulation 3 it shall be a defence for the employer or self-employed person, as the case may be, to prove that on discovering that he was unintentionally keeping or handling a *listed pathogen* or causing or permitting it to be kept or handled, as the case may be, he notified the Health and Safety Executive forthwith.

9.   Meaning of "work" and "at work". For the purposes of Part I of the Health and Safety at Work etc. Act 1974 the meaning of the word "work" shall be extended to include any activity involving the keeping or handling of a *listed pathogen* and the meaning of "at work" shall be extended accordingly (*a*).

   (*a*) *At work.* See the Health and Safety at Work etc. Act 1974, s. 52(1).

10.   Modification of section 3 (2) of the Health and Safety at Work etc. Act 1974. Section 3 (2) of the Health and Safety at Work etc. Act 1974 shall be modified in relation to any person who keeps or handles a *listed pathogen* so as to have effect as if the reference to a self-employed person included a reference to any person who is not an employer or an employed person in relation to that keeping or handling.

11.   Exemptions.—(1) Subject to paragraph (2), the Health and Safety Executive may, by certificate in writing, exempt any person or class of persons, from any of the requirements of these Regulations, and any such exemption may be granted subject to conditions and to a limit of time and may be revoked at any time.

(2) The Executive shall not grant any such exemption unless, having regard to the circumstances of the case, and in particulars to—

(a) the conditions, if any, which it proposes to attach to the exemption, and
(b) any other requirements imposed by or under any enactments which apply to the case,

it is satisfied that the health and safety of persons who are likely to be affected by the exemption will not be prejudiced in consequence of it.

SCHEDULE 1

Regulation 2(1)

LIST OF PATHOGENS THE KEEPING OR HANDLING OF WHICH IS TO BE NOTIFIED

Crimean Haemorragic Fever
  virus (Congo)
Ebola virus
Junin Haemorrhagic Fever
  virus
Lassa Fever virus
Machupo Haemorrhagic Fever
  virus

Marburg virus
Rabies virus
Simian Herpes B virus
Smallpox virus
Venezuelan Equine
  Encephalitis virus

SCHEDULE 2

Regulations 3 (1) and 5

PARTICULARS TO BE NOTIFIED IN RESPECT OF THE KEEPING OR HANDLING OF A *LISTED PATHOGEN*

The particulars to be included in the notice mentioned in Regulation 3 (1) shall be—

(a) the name of the employer or self-employed person responsible for the keeping or handling of the *listed pathogen*;
(b) the address of the premises where the pathogen will be kept or handled;
(c) the location within those premises where the pathogen will be kept or handled;
(d) the name (including, where relevant, the strain) of the pathogen to be kept or handled;
(e) the name of the person from whom the pathogen will be obtained and the address of the premises from which it will be obtained;
(f) particulars of the work to be undertaken, its proposed dates of commencement and completion and whether the *listed pathogen* is likely to be propagated;
(g) the name, qualification and relevant experience of—
  (i) the individual who will be directly in charge of the work,
  (ii) any other individual who will be personally supervising the work,
  (iii) any other individual who will be directly involved in the work;
(h) whether the safety representatives, if any, appointed under the Safety Representatives and Safety Committees Regulations 1977 to represent any person who will work with the *listed pathogen* have been informed of the foregoing particulars.

SCHEDULE 3

Regulation 4(1)

PARTICULARS TO BE NOTIFIED IN RESPECT OF LABORATORIES PROVIDING A *DIAGNOSTIC SERVICE*

The particulars to be included in the notice mentioned in Regulation 4(1) shall be—

(a) the name of the employer or self-employed person responsible for carrying out the *diagnostic work*;
(b) the address of the premises where that work will be carried out;
(c) the location or locations within those premises where that work will be carried out;
(d) the *listed pathogen* in respect of which it is intended to provide a *diagnostic service*;
(e) whether the safety representatives, if any, appointed under the Safety Representatives and Safety Committees Regulations 1977 to represent any person who will be employed in the *diagnostic service* have been informed of the foregoing particulars.

SCHEDULE 4

Regulation 6(1)

Particulars to be Notified in Respect of Transport of a *Listed Pathogen*

The particulars to be included in the notice mentioned in Regulation 6(1) shall be—

   (a) the name (including where relevant, the strain), the volume of the consignment and the estimated titre of the *listed pathogen*;

   (b) the address of the premises from which it will be transported;

   (c) the address of the premises to which it will be transported;

   (d) the name of the consignor;

   (e) the name of the consignee;

   (f) the name of the carrier or other transport operator responsible for the transportation;

   (g) the name of any individual who will accompany the consignment;

   (h) the route which will be taken;

   (i) the method of transportation;

   (j) the packaging and any containment precautions which will be taken;

   (k) the proposed date of the transportation.

THE GENETIC MANIPULATION REGULATIONS 1989

(S.I. 1989 No. 1810)

1. Citation and commencement. These Regulations may be cited as the Genetic Manipulation Regulations 1989 and shall come into force on 1 November 1989.

2. Interpretation.—(1) In these Regulations, unless the context otherwise requires—

"approved" means approved for the time being in writing by the Health and Safety Executive for the purposes of these Regulations;

"genetic manipulation" means the propagation of combinations of heritable material by the insertion of that material, prepared by whatever means outside a cell or organism, into a cell or organism in which it does not occur naturally, either—

(a) directly; or

(b) into a virus, microbial plasmid or other vector system which can then be incorporated in the cell or organism;

"genetic manipulation safety committee" means a committee established under regulation 6(2);

"intentional introduction into the environment" means the intentional introduction into the environment (that is outside provision for containment) of a live cell or organism which was produced or modified by genetic manipulation, in vitro cell fusion or other in vitro technique, to form combinations of heritable material which do not occur naturally in that cell or organism;

"organism" means any biological entity capable of replication (whether microscopic or not);

"pathogen" means any of the following—

(a) an organism which falls into one of the hazard groups numbered 2, 3 and 4 in Schedule 1;

(b) an animal pathogen within the meaning of Article 3 of the Importation of Animal Pathogens Order 1980; or

(c) a plant pest within the meaning of Article 3 of the Plant Health (Great Britain) Order 1987.

(2) In these Regulations a reference to "an activity involving genetic manipulation" shall be taken as a reference to an activity involving—

(a) the construction or modification of a cell or organism by genetic manipulation;

(b) the use of a cell or organism constructed or modified by genetic manipulation; or

(c) intentional introduction into the environment,

but shall not include a reference to the supply or use of a cell or organism as a finished product for routine use if the construction or modification of that cell or organism by genetic manipulation has been notified under regulation 5.

(3) In these Regulations, references to "containment levels" and to "good large-scale practice" shall be treated as references to those terms as further described in the method of risk assessment approved for the purpose of regulation 6(1).

(4) In these Regulations, unless the context otherwise requires—

(a) a reference to a numbered regulation or Schedule is a reference to the regulation or Schedule in these Regulations so numbered; and

(b) a reference to a numbered paragraph is a reference to the paragraph so numbered in the regulation or Schedule in which that reference appears.

3. Meaning of "work" and "at work". For the purpose of these Regulations and Part I of the Health and Safety at Work etc. Act 1974 the meaning of the word "work" shall be extended to include an activity involving genetic manipulation and the meaning of "at work" shall be extended accordingly.

4. Modification of section 3(2) of the Health and Safety at Work etc. Act 1974. Section 3(2) of the Health and Safety at Work etc. Act 1974 shall be modified, in relation to an activity involving genetic manipulation, so as to have effect as if the reference to a self-employed person included a reference to any person who is not an employer or an employee in relation to that activity.

5. Notification of activities involving genetic manipulation.—(1) Subject to paragraphs (4) and (6), no person shall carry out an activity involving genetic manipulation unless, before commencing that activity, he has notified the Health and Safety Executive of his intention to do so at least—

(a) in the case of an activity involving an intentional introduction into the environment, 90 days in advance;

(b) in any other case, 30 days in advance; or

(c) in either case, such shorter time in advance as the Executive may agree.

(2) Subject to paragraph (4), the notification required by paragraph (1) shall be in an approved form and shall comprise—

(a) a notification of an intention to carry out activities involving genetic manipulation which shall contain the particulars specified in Schedule 2; and

(b) a notification of each individual activity involving genetic manipulation which shall contain the particulars specified in Schedule 3.

(3) Where a person has made a notification in accordance with paragraph 2(a) and subsequently makes a significant change in the activities to which the notification relates which would affect the particulars notified (including the cessation of those activities), he shall forthwith notify the Executive of that change.

(4) In the case of an activity involving genetic manipulation specified in paragraph (5), it shall be sufficient compliance with paragraph (1) if the person who intends to carry out the activity—

(a) notifies the Executive in accordance with paragraphs (1) and (2)(a); and

(b) as soon as is reasonably practicable after the end of each calendar year sends the Executive a list of the activities carried out during that year containing the particulars specified in Schedule 4.

(5) Paragraph (4) shall apply to an activity involving genetic manipulation (other than intentional introduction into the environment) which, when assessed for risk in accordance with regulation 6(1), is assigned to containment levels 1 or 2 or as warranting only the use of good large-scale practice, as the case may be.

(6) Paragraph (1) shall not apply where the only activities involving genetic manipulation consist of self-cloning activities (namely the application of genetic manipulation to rearrange the genome of an individual species) except where they involve a pathogen or an intentional introduction into the environment.

6.   Risk assessment.—(1) For the purpose of notifying an individual activity involving genetic manipulation under regulation 5(2)(b) or determining whether the activity is to be assessed as falling into containment levels 1 or 2 or as warranting only the use of good large-scale practice as the case may be and is therefore an activity to which regulation 5(4) applies, the person carrying out the activity shall carry out a risk assessment of the intended activity by the approved method.

(2) The person carrying out the activity shall establish a committee for the purpose of advising him in relation to any risk assessment mentioned in regulation 6(1).

7.   Application outside Great Britain. These Regulations shall apply to any work outside Great Britain to which sections 1 to 59 and 80 to 82 of the Health and Safety at Work etc. Act 1974 apply by virtue of the Health and Safety at Work etc. Act 1974 (Application outside Great Britain) Order 1989 as they apply to work within Great Britain.

8.   Exemption certificates.—(1) Subject to paragraph 2, the Health and Safety Executive may, by a certificate in writing, exempt any person or class of person or any activity or class of activities from all or any of the requirements or prohibitions imposed by these Regulations and any such exemption may be granted subject to conditions and to a limit of time and may be revoked by a certificate in writing at any time.

(2) The Executive shall not grant any such exemption unless, having regard to circumstances of the case and in particular to—

(a) the conditions, if any, which it proposes to attach to the exemption; and

(b) any other requirements imposed by or under any enactments which apply to the case,

it is satisfied that the health and safety of persons who are likely to be affected by the exemption will not be prejudiced in consequence of it.

9. Revocations and savings.—(1) The Health and Safety (Genetic Manipulation) Regulations 1978 are hereby revoked.

(2) In the case of an activity involving genetic manipulation commenced—

(a) before the date on which these Regulations come into force it shall be sufficient compliance with regulation 5(1) if the intention to carry out that activity was notified under the said Regulations of 1978;

(b) on or after the date on which these Regulations come into force it shall be sufficient compliance with regulation 5(1) (in so far as it requires a notification referred to in regulation 5(2)(a)) if the intention to carry out that activity was notified under the said Regulations of 1978.

SCHEDULE 1

Regulation 2(1)

HAZARD GROUPS FOR ORGANISMS

Group 1
An organism that is most unlikely to cause human disease.

Group 2
An organism that may cause human disease and which might be a hazard to laboratory workers but it is unlikely to spread in the community. Laboratory exposure rarely produces infection and effective prophylaxis or effective treatment is usually available.

Group 3
An organism that may cause severe human disease and present a serious hazard to laboratory workers. It may prevent a risk of spread in the community but there is usually effective prophylaxis or treatment available.

Group 4
An organism that causes severe human disease and is a serious hazard to laboratory workers. It may present a high risk of spread in the community and there is usually no effective prophylaxis or treatment.

SCHEDULE 2

Regulation 5(2)(a)

PARTICULARS TO BE GIVEN IN A NOTIFICATION OF AN INTENTION TO CARRY OUT ACTIVITIES INVOLVING GENETIC MANIPULATION

1. The name of the person who will carry out activities involving genetic manipulation.

2. The address or location of the premises or site where the work is to be carried out.

3. The name and designation of the person responsible for the work.

4. Into which of the following categories the activities fall—
   (a) the construction or modification of a cell or organism by genetic manipulation;
   (b) the use of a cell or organism constructed or modified by genetic manipulation; or
   (c) intentional introduction into the environment.

5. The arrangements for physical containment (unless the work is assigned to containment level 1 or good large-scale practice).

6. The names and capacities of members of the genetic manipulation safety committee.

7. Comments made by the genetic manipulation safety committee on the local arrangements for risk assessment.

8. The names of the biological and deputy biological safety officers concerned with the work (if any).

9. The name of the supervisory medical officer concerned with the work (if any).

10. The arrangements for health surveillance (if any).

SCHEDULE 3

Regulation 5(2)(b)

PARTICULARS TO BE GIVEN IN A NOTIFICATION OF AN ACTIVITY INVOLVING GENETIC MANIPULATION

1. In all cases—
  (a) the name of person carrying out the work;
  (b) the address of the premises or site were the work is to be carried out;
  (c) particulars of the work to be undertaken;
  (d) any variation of the particulars notified in accordance with Schedule 2;
  (e) comments by the genetic manipulation safety committee;
  (f) the proposals for physical containment (if any);
  (g) the subsequent use or distribution of nucleic acid;
  (h) the risk assessment and the categorisation date on which it is based.

2. In the case of the construction or modification of a cell or organism by genetic manipulation—
  (a) the proposed containment level of the project;
  (b) a list of staff to be involved in the project.

3. In the case of the use of a cell or organism constructed or modified by genetic manipulation—
  (a) the nature of the gene product;
  (b) the host vector system to be used;
  (c) the scale of operation proposed;
  (d) the safety precautions proposed;
  (e) the proposed process containment;
  (f) whether any part of the construction involves the use of a pathogen.

4. In the case of intentional introduction into the environment—
  (a) the objectives of the project;
  (b) the nature of the cell or organism to be released;
  (c) the procedure used to introduce the genetic modification;
  (d) the nature of any altered nucleic acid and its source, its intended function and the extent to which it has been characterised;
  (e) verification of the genetic structure of the novel organism;
  (f) the genetic stability of the novel organism;
  (g) the ability of the organism to give rise to long-term survival forms and the effect the altered nucleic acid may have on this ability;
  (h) in the case of a pest control agent, details of the target biota;
  (i) the geographical location, size and nature of the site of release;
  (j) the physical and biological proximity of the site to man and other significant biota;
  (k) details of the ecosystem into which the organism is to be released;
  (l) the method and amount of release, rate, frequency and duration of application;
  (m) monitoring capabilities and intentions;
  (n) the on-site worker safety procedures and facilities;
  (o) the contingency plans in the event of unanticipated effects of the novel organism;
  (p) an assessment of the environmental consequences of the release including—
       (i) survival and persistence of the novel organism,

(ii) susceptibility to temperature humidity, desiccation, ultra-violet light and other ecological stresses,

(iii) details of any modification of the organism designed to affect its ability to survive and to transfer genetic material,

(iv) potential for transfer of inserted polynucleotides to other organisms including methods for monitoring survival and transfer,

(v) methods to control or eliminate any superfluous organism or nucleic acid surviving in the environment or possibily in a product,

(vi) an assessment of the effects of the manipulation on the ecological behaviour of the organism in its natural habitat;

(q) detail of any local consultation undertaken;

(r) method of termination of the project.

SCHEDULE 4

Regulation 5(4)(b)

PARTICULARS TO BE GIVEN OF ACTIVITIES INVOLVING GENETIC MANIPULATION IN THE ANNUAL RETURN UNDER REGULATION 5(4)

1. The name of person carrying out activities involving genetic manipulation.

2. The address or location of the premises or site where the work was carried out.

3. Any variation in the particulars notified in accordance with Schedule 2.

4. The numbers of all projects assigned to containment levels 1 and 2 respectively.

5. The numbers of projects involving the use of a cell or organism constructed or modified by genetic manipulation warranting only the use of good large-scale practice.

THE GENETICALLY MODIFIED ORGANISMS (CONTAINED USE) REGULATIONS 1992

(S.I. 1992 No. 3217)

General note. These Regulations are intended to implement the contained use of Genetically Modified Organisms Directive 90/219.

The Secretary of State, being the designated Minister for the purpose of section 2(2) of the European Communities Act 1972 in relation to the control and regulation of *genetically modified organisms*, in the exercise of the powers conferred on her by the said section 2 and sections 15(1), (2), (3)(b) and (c), (4)(a), (5)(b) and (9), 43(2), (4), (5) and (6), 52(2) and (3) and 82(3)(a) of, and paragraphs 1(1)(b) and (c) and (5), 4(1), 6(1), 14, 15(1), 16 and 20 of Schedule 3 to, the Health and Safety at Work etc. Act 1974 ("the 1974 Act") and of all other powers enabling her in that behalf and for the purpose of giving effect without modifications to proposals submitted to her by the Health and Safety Commission under section 11(2)(d) of *the 1974 Act* after the carrying out by the said Commission of consultations in accordance with section 50(3) of that Act, hereby makes the following Regulations—

PART I

INTERPRETATION AND GENERAL

1. Citation and commencement. These Regulations may be cited as the Genetically Modified Organisms (Contained Use) Regulations 1992 and shall come into force on 1 February 1993.

2. Interpretation.—(1) In these Regulations, unless the context otherwise requires—

"the 1989 Regulations" means the Genetic Manipulation Regulations 1989;

"accident" means any incident involving a significant and unintended release of *genetically modified organisms* in the course of an *activity involving genetic modification* which presents an immediate or delayed hazard to human health or to the environment;

"approved" means approved in writing for the time being by *the Executive*;

"activity involving genetic modification" means any operation involving the *contained use* of a *genetically modified* organism;

"contained use" means any operation in which *organisms* are *genetically modified* or in which such *genetically modified organisms* are cultured, stored, used, transported, destroyed or disposed of and for which physical barriers or a combination of physical barriers with chemical or biological barriers or

1072

both, are used to limit their contact with the general population and the environment;

"the contained use Directive" means Council Directive No. 90/219/EEC on the *contained use* of *genetically modified micro-organisms*;

"the Executive" means the Health and Safety Executive;

"genetic modification" in relation to an *organism* means the altering of the genetic material in that *organism* by a way that does not occur naturally by mating or natural recombination or both and within the terms of this definition—

(a) genetic modification occurs at least through the use of the techniques listed in Part I of Schedule 1; and

(b) the techniques listed in Part II of that Schedule are not considered to result in genetic modification,

and "genetically modified" shall be construed accordingly;

"genetic modification safety committee" means the committee established in accordance with regulation 11;

"micro-organism" means a microbiological entity, cellular or non-cellular, capable of replication or of transferring genetic material including animal or plant cell cultures;

"organism" means a biological entity capable of replication or of transferring genetic material and includes a *micro-organism*;

"self-cloning" means the removal of nucleic acid from a cell or organism, followed by the re-insertion of all or part of that nucleic acid—with or without further enzymic, chemical or mechanical steps—into the same cell type (or cell-line) or into a phylogenetically closely related species which can naturally exchange genetic material with the donor species;

"Type A operation" means any activity involving *genetically modified micro-organisms* for the purposes of teaching, research, development, or for non-industrial or non-commercial purposes on a scale at which the practices and conditions of the operations relative to the culture, volume and numbers of *organisms* involved is such that—

(a) the system used to keep the *organisms* under containment reflects good microbiological practice and good occupational safety and hygiene; and

(b) it is possible easily to render the *organisms* inactive by standard laboratory decontamination techniques;

"Type B operation" means any activity involving the *genetic modification* of *micro-organisms* other than a *Type A operation*.

(2) *Genetically modified organisms* shall be classified—

(a) in the case of *micro-organisms*—

   (i) as Group I *micro-organisms* if they comply with such of the criteria set out in Part I of Schedule 2 as are applicable to the particular case, determined in accordance with the guidelines set out in Part II of that Schedule which gives effect to Commission Decision 91/448/EEC, or

   (ii) as Group II *micro-organisms* if they do not comply with the said criteria; or

(b) in the case of *genetically modified* organisms other than *micro-organisms*, in accordance with the criteria set out in Part III of Schedule 2.

(3) In these Regulations, unless the context otherwise requires—

(a)   a reference to a numbered Part, regulation or Schedule is a reference to the Part, regulation or Schedule in these Regulations so numbered; and

(b)   a reference to a numbered paragraph is a reference to the paragraph so numbered in the regulation or Schedule in which that reference occurs.

3.   Application.—(1) These Regulations shall have effect with a view to protecting persons against risks to their health, whether immediate or delayed, and for the protection of the environment, arising from activities involving *genetically modified organisms*.

(2) Regulations 8 to 12 shall not apply to the transport of *genetically modified organisms* by road, rail, inland waterway, sea or air.

(3) These Regulations shall not apply to the *genetic modification* of *organisms* solely by any of the techniques referred to in Part III of Schedule 1 or to any *organisms* so modified.

(4) Insofar as these Regulations relate to the protection of the environment, they shall only apply to *genetically modified micro-organisms*.

(5) Nothing in these Regulations shall prejudice any requirement imposed by or under any enactment which relates to public health or the protection of the environment.

(6) These Regulations shall not extend to Northern Ireland.

4.   Meaning of "work" and "at work". For the purpose of these Regulations and Part I of the Health and Safety at Work etc. Act 1974 the meaning of "work" shall be extended to include any *activity involving genetic modification* and the meaning of "at work" shall be extended accordingly.

5.   Modification of section 3(2) of the Health and Safety at Work etc. Act 1974. Section 3(2) of the Health and Safety at Work etc. Act 1974 shall be modified in relation to an *activity involving genetic modification* so as to have effect as if the reference to a self-employed person therein is a reference to any person who is not an employer or an employee and the reference in it to his undertaking includes a reference to such an activity.

PART II

NOTIFICATION OF AND CONSENT FOR ACTIVITIES INVOLVING
GENETIC MODIFICATION

6.   Prohibition of certain work with *genetically modified organisms* outside containment.—(1) Subject to paragraph (2), any operation in which *organisms* are *genetically modified* or in which such *genetically modified organisms* are cultured, stored, used, transported, destroyed or disposed of is prohibited unless it is undertaken in conditions of *contained use* in accordance with these Regulations.

(2) Paragraph (1) shall not apply to any operation in which—

(a)   *genetically modified organisms* are cultured, stored, used, transported, destroyed or disposed of, where such *organisms* are or are contained in a product marketed in pursuance of—

(i) a consent granted by the Secretary of State under section 111(1) of the Environmental Protection Act 1990, or

(ii) a written consent given by another competent authority of a member State in accordance with Article 13(4) of Council Directive 90/220/EEC on the deliberate release into the environment of *genetically modified organisms*, and

in either case, the operation is conducted in accordance with any conditions or limitations attached to that consent;

(b) *genetically modified organisms* are released or marketed in circumstances in which the consent of the Secretary of State is required under section 111(1) of the Environmental Protection Act 1990.

(3) In this regulation, "product" means a product consisting of or containing a *genetically modified organism* or a combination of *genetically modified organisms*.

7. Risk assessment.—(1) A person shall not—

(a) use any premises for activities involving *genetic modification* for the first time; or

(b) undertake any *activity involving genetic modification*,

unless he has ensured that, before commencing that use or activity, as the case may be, a suitable and sufficient assessment of the risks created thereby to human health and the environment has been made.

(2) Without prejudice to the generality of paragraph (1), the purposes of the assessment undertaken under that paragraph shall include—

(a) classifying any *genetically modified organisms* involved in the activity in accordance with the provisions of Schedule 2; and

(b) where appropriate, making decisions about the levels of containment required for the activity concerned.

(3) In making the assessment required by paragraph (1) the person undertaking that assessment shall—

(a) in particular, take due account of the parameters set out in Schedule 3 in as far as they are relevant; and

(b) in a case in which *the Executive* has *approved* a method in relation to the *activity involving genetic modification* concerned or in relation to a particular element of that assessment, undertake the assessment in accordance with that method.

(4) The assessment shall be reviewed forthwith if—

(a) there is reason to suspect that the assessment is no longer valid; or

(b) there has been a significant change in the activity to which the assessment relates.

(5) The person making the assessment shall make a record of it and of any subsequent review and shall keep that record for at least 10 years from the date on which use of the premises or the activity, as the case may be, to which the assessment related, ceased.

8. Notification of the intention to use premises for activities involving *genetic modification* for the first time.—(1) Subject to the following paragraphs of this regulation and regulation 10, no person shall undertake any *activity involving genetic modification* at any premises for the first time, unless he has notified *the Executive* of his intention to do so at least 90 days in advance or before such shorter time as *the Executive* may approve and with that notification has furnished the particulars specified in Schedule 4.

(2) In the case of activities involving the *genetic modification* of *micro-organisms*, separate notifications shall be made of an intention to use the premises for activities involving *genetically modified micro-organisms* of Group I or Group II.

(3) In the case of activities involving *genetically modified micro-organisms* of Group II, the premises shall only be used for those activities after *the Executive* has given its consent.

(4) In any other case, the use of the premises for the activity may be commenced at or after the end of the period of 90 days, or such shorter period as *the Executive* may have *approved* in pursuance of paragraph (1), unless *the Executive* objects in writing before the end of the relevant period.

(5) In any case in which a consent is required under paragraph (3), *the Executive* shall communicate its decision on the application in writing within 90 days after the application was received.

(6) Nothing in this regulation shall prevent a person from notifying under regulation 9 an individual activity which he intends to undertake in the premises at the same time as making a notification under this regulation; in such a case he shall not commence the activity except in accordance with the time periods specified in this regulation.

9. Notification of individual activities involving *genetic modification*.— (1) Subject to the following paragraphs of this regulation and regulation 10, no person shall undertake any *activity involving genetic modification* unless he has notified *the Executive* of his intention to do so at least 60 days in advance or before such shorter time as *the Executive* may approve and has furnished the particulars specified in the following paragraphs of this regulation and, except in the case of an activity to which paragraph (5) applies, the activity may be commenced after the expiry of the relevant period if by then *the Executive* has not objected in writing.

(2) In the case of an activity which is—

(a) a *Type A operation* involving only *micro-organisms* classified as Group I; or
(b) an activity involving *genetically modified organisms* other than *micro-organisms* and which satisfy the criteria set out in Part III of Schedule 2,

it shall be a sufficient compliance with paragraph (1) if the person undertaking the activity keeps a record of such activities and forthwith after the end of each calendar year notifies *the Executive*—

(i) of the total number of risk assessments under regulation 7 undertaken during that year;
(ii) where appropriate, that he is intending to continue to undertake such activities; and
(iii) that the information notified to *the Executive* in accordance with regulation 8 remains correct.

(3) In the case of an activity which is a *Type B operation* involving only *micro-organisms* classified as Group I, the specified particulars for the purposes of paragraph (1) shall be those specified in Part I of Schedule 5.

(4) In the case of an activity which is—

(a) a *Type A operation* involving *genetically modified micro-organisms* classified as Group II; or

(b) an activity involving *genetically modified* organisms other than *micro-organisms* and which do not satisfy the criteria set out in Part III of Schedule 2,

the specified particulars for the purposes of paragraph (1) shall be those specified in Parts I and II of Schedule 5.

(5) In the case of an activity which is a *Type B operation* involving *genetically modified micro-organisms* classified as Group II, the specified particulars for the purposes of paragraph (1) shall be those specified in Parts I, II and III of Schedule 5 and the activity shall only be commenced with the consent of *the Executive*.

(6) In any case in which a consent is required under paragraph (5), *the Executive* shall communicate its decision on the application in writing within 90 days after the application was received.

(7) *The Executive* may accept as a single notification a connected programme of work covering more than one *activity involving genetic modification* at one site, or a single activity carried on by the same person at more than one site.

10. Additional provisions relating to notifications and consents.—(1) Where necessary for the purpose of evaluating a notification made under regulation 8 or 9, *the Executive* may require in writing the person making the notification to give such additional information relating to the proposal as it may specify and, in such a case, the person making the notification shall not proceed with the *activity involving genetic modification*, until *the Executive* gives its approval, and the period between the time when *the Executive* requires the information and the notifier responds to the satisfaction of *the Executive* shall not be taken into account in calculating the periods of days referred to in the provisions concerned.

(2) Any consent granted by *the Executive* under regulation 8 or 9 may be granted subject to conditions or to a limit of time and may be revoked or varied at any time and in such a case the person undertaking the activity shall comply with those conditions.

(3) In so far as they relate to the protection of the environment, *the Executive* shall not grant, vary or revoke a consent under regulation 8 or 9, or give its approval under paragraph (1), without the agreement of the Secretary of State.

(4) Where a person making a notification in pursuance of regulation 8 or 9 subsequently makes a significant change in any premises or activity to which the notification relates or becomes aware of any new information which would affect the particulars previously notified, he shall forthwith notify *the Executive* thereof.

(5) If information subsequently becomes available to *the Executive* which could have significant consequences for the risks to health or the environment created by an *activity involving genetic modification* which has been notified to it, it may require the notifier to modify the conditions under which the activity is carried out, or to suspend or terminate the activity.

(6) Notifications made in pursuance of regulations 8 and 9 shall be in a form *approved* by *the Executive*.

11.   Establishment of a *genetic modification safety committee*. A person who undertakes an assessment made for the purposes of regulation 7(1) shall establish a *genetic modification safety committee* to advise him in relation to that assessment.

PART III

CONDUCT OF ACTIVITIES INVOLVING *GENETIC MODIFICATION*

12.   Standards of occupational and environmental safety and containment.—
(1) For any activity involving *genetically modified micro-organisms* of Group I, the principles of good microbiological practice and the following principles of good occupational safety and hygiene shall apply—

   (a)   to keep workplace and environmental exposure to any physical, chemical and biological agent adequately controlled;
   (b)   to exercise engineering control methods at source and to supplement these with appropriate personal protective clothing and equipment where necessary;
   (c)   to test and maintain control measures and equipment;
   (d)   to test, when necessary, for the presence of viable process *organisms* outside the primary physical containment;
   (e)   to provide training of personnel; and
   (f)   to formulate and implement local rules for the safety of personnel.

(2) For the purpose of paragraph (1) "adequate" in relation to the control of an agent means adequate having regard only to the nature of the agent and the nature and degree of exposure to such an agent and "adequately" shall be construed accordingly.

(3) For any activities involving *genetically modified micro-organisms* of Group II in *Type A operations*, in addition to the principles set out in paragraph (1) the containment measures shall be determined by a method *approved* by *the Executive*.

(4) For any activities involving *genetically modified micro-organisms* of Group II in *Type B operations*, in addition to the principles set out in paragraph (1) the containment measures set out in Schedule 6 shall be applied at an appropriate level so as to ensure a high level of health and safety and environmental protection.

(5) For any activities involving *genetically modified organisms* other than *micro-organisms*, the principles set out in paragraph (1) shall be applied in as far as they are appropriate.

13.   Emergency plans.—(1) Where the assessment made in accordance with regulation 7(1) shows that as a result of any reasonably foreseeable *accident* the health or safety of persons outside the premises in which an *activity involving genetic modification* is carried on is liable to be affected or there is a risk of damage to the environment, the person undertaking the activity shall ensure that a suitable emergency plan is prepared with a view to securing the health and safety of those persons and the protection of the environment.

(2) The person preparing the plan shall consult such persons, bodies and authorities as are appropriate and shall inform the emergency services in writing of the plan and of the hazards to which the plan relates.

(3) The person undertaking the *activity involving genetic modification* which is the subject of the emergency plan shall take appropriate measures to inform persons who are liable to be affected by an *accident* of the safety measures and the correct behaviour to adopt in the event of an *accident*.

(4) The information required to be given in pursuance of paragraph (3) shall be repeated and brought up to date at appropriate intervals and shall be made publicly available.

14. Notification of *accidents*.—(1) Where an *accident* occurs, the person undertaking the activity involving *genetically modified organisms* shall forthwith notify *the Executive* of it and shall provide the following information—

(a) the circumstances of the *accident*;
(b) the identity and quantity of *genetically modified organisms* released;
(c) any information necessary to assess the effects of the *accident* on the health of the general population and on the environment; and
(d) the emergency measures taken.

(2) Where *the Executive* receives a notification in pursuance of paragraph (1), *the Executive* shall—

(a) ensure that any emergency, medium and long term measures are taken;
(b) immediately inform any other member State that could be affected by the *accident*;
(c) collect, where possible, the information necessary for a full analysis of the *accident* and, where appropriate, make recommendations to avoid similar *accidents* in the future and to limit their effects; and
(d) send to the European Commission the information provided for under paragraph (1), together with an analysis of the *accident* and details of any recommendations made to avoid similar *accidents* in the future and to limit their effects.

PART IV
DISCLOSURE OF INFORMATION NOTIFIED AND PUBLICITY

15. Disclosure of information notified.—(1) The information notified in pursuance of regulations 8 to 10 shall not be treated as relevant information for the purposes of section 28 of the Health and Safety at Work etc. Act 1974.

(2) Where a person making a notification in pursuance of regulations 8 to 10 indicates that it contains certain information the disclosure of which might harm his competitive position and should be kept confidential, full justification for that indication shall be given and in such a case after consulting the notifier *the Executive* shall decide which information shall be kept confidential and shall inform the notifier of its decision.

(3) Nothing in paragraph (2) shall apply to the following information which shall not be kept confidential—

(a) the name and address of the notifier and the location of the *activity involving genetic modification*;
(b) the purpose of the activity;
(c) the description of the *genetically modified organism* involved;

(d) methods and plans for monitoring the *genetically modified organism* and for emergency response; and

(e) the evaluation of foreseeable effects and in particular pathogenic effects and ecologically disruptive effects.

(4) Notwithstanding paragraph (3), where *the Executive* is satisfied on the basis of detailed evidence submitted to it by the notifier and where appropriate, after consultation with the notifier, that it is necessary to withhold, for the time being, certain of the information specified in paragraph (3) in order to protect his intellectual property rights, *the Executive* shall withhold that information to the extent and for so long as it is necessary to protect those rights.

(5) Information which is kept confidential in accordance with paragraph (2) or withheld in accordance with paragraph (4) shall be disclosed only—

(a) to the Secretary of State;

(b) to the European Commission or the competent authority for Northern Ireland or another member State;

(c) for the purpose of any legal proceedings;

(d) with the consent of the notifier; or

(e) to the extent necessary to evaluate the notification.

(6) A person who receives information in accordance with sub-paragraph (e) of paragraph (5) shall not use that information except for a purpose of *the Executive* or the Secretary of State.

(7) Where the notifier has requested that certain information in the notification shall be kept confidential in accordance with paragraph (2) or withheld in accordance with paragraph (4), *the Executive* shall not disclose any of that information (except in accordance with paragraph (5)) until at least 14 days after it has reached a decision under the relevant paragraph.

(8) After consulting the notifier, *the Executive* may review any decision made under paragraph (2) or (4) and shall inform the notifier of the result of that review.

(9) Where, for whatever reason, the notifier withdraws the notification, *the Executive* shall not thereafter disclose any of the information supplied.

16. Register of notifications.—(1) *The Executive* shall maintain a register of notifications to which regulation 8(3) or 9(5) relate (for which the consent of *the Executive* is required) and that register shall be open to inspection by members of the public at any reasonable time.

(2) The register referred to in paragraph (1) shall contain in relation to each such notification—

(a) such of the information referred to in regulation 15(3) as has not been withheld in accordance with paragraph (4) of that regulation; and

(b) a statement as to whether or not the consent of *the Executive* has been granted.

(3) The information referred to in sub-paragraph (a) of paragraph (2) shall be entered in the register within 14 days of its receipt by *the Executive* and the information referred to in sub-paragraph (b) of that paragraph within 14 days of the decision whether to grant the consent or not having been made, except

that where the notifier has requested that certain information specified in regulation 15(3) be withheld in accordance with regulation 15(4), that information shall only be entered in the register not less that 14 days but not more than 28 days after *the Executive* has made a decision not to withhold that information.

(4) Copies of the register shall be maintained at—

(a) the area office of *the Executive* in whose area the notifier is situated; and

(b) Baynards House, 1, Chepstow Place, Westbourne Grove, London W2 4TF; and

(c) Magdalen House, Stanley Precinct, Bootle, Merseyside, L20 3QZ.

PART V
ADDITIONAL DUTIES PLACED ON *THE EXECUTIVE*

17. Duties on receiving notifications. *The Executive* shall examine a notification under regulation 8 or 9 for—

(a) the conformity with the requirements of these Regulations;

(b) the accuracy and completeness of the information given;

(c) the correctness of the classification of the *organisms* to which the notification relates in accordance with Schedule 2; and

(d) where appropriate, the adequacy of the waste management, safety and emergency response measures.

18. Information to be sent to the Secretary of State. Forthwith after receipt, *the Executive* shall send to the Secretary of State a copy in each case of—

(a) any notification received under regulation 8 or 9;

(b) any requirement for further information under regulation 10(1) and the response thereto; and

(c) any notification relating to an *accident* under regulation 14,

and if requested to do so by the Secretary of State shall require additional information under regulation 10(1).

19. Reports to the European Commission. *The Executive* shall send to the European Commission reports of notifications for which a consent is required under regulation 9(5) and summary reports of the application of these Regulations in accordance with Article 18 of *the contained use Directive.*

PART VI
MISCELLANEOUS AND GENERAL

20. Exemption certificates.—(1) Subject to paragraph (2) and to any provisions imposed by the Communities in respect of the control and regulation of *genetically modified organisms, the Executive* may, with the agreement of the Secretary of State in so far as the exemption relates to the environment, by a certificate in writing, exempt any person or class of persons, *genetically modified organism* or class of *genetically modified organisms* from all or any of the requirements or prohibitions imposed by these Regulations and any such exemption may be granted subject to conditions and to a limit of time and may be revoked by a certificate in writing at any time.

(2) *The Executive* shall not grant any such exemption unless, having regard to the circumstances of the case and in particular to—

(a) the conditions, if any, that it proposes to attach to the exemption; and
(b) any requirements imposed by or under any enactments which apply to the case,

it is satisfied that the health and safety of persons who are likely to be affected by the exemption or the protection of the environment will not be prejudiced in consequence of it.

21. Enforcement and civil liability.—(1) Insofar as any provision of regulations 6 to 14 is made under section 2 of the European Communities Act 1972—

(a) the provisions of the Health and Safety at Work etc. Act 1974 relating to enforcement and offences shall apply to that provision as if that provision had been made under section 15 of that Act; and
(b) in the event of a breach of duty imposed by that provision, it shall confer a right of action in civil proceedings if that breach of duty causes damage.

(2) Notwithstanding regulation 3 of the Health and Safety (Enforcing Authority) Regulations 1989, the enforcing authority for these Regulations shall be *the Executive.*

22. Fees for notifications.—(1) Fees shall be payable in accordance with paragraph (2) by a notifier to *the Executive* in relation to any matter referred to in that paragraph.

(2) The fees referred to in paragraph (1) shall be—

(a) subject to sub-paragraph (b), on each notification of the intention to use premises for activities involving *genetic modification* for the first time under regulation 8, £100;
(b) on each notification of the intention to use premises for activities involving *genetic modification* for the first time, where a consent is required under regulation 8(3), £130;
(c) subject to sub-paragraph (d), on each notification of individual activities involving *genetic modification* under regulation 9, £180;
(d) on each notification of individual activities involving *genetic modification* for which a consent is required under regulation 9(5), £270.

(3) This regulation shall not apply to any notification made for the purposes of regulation 23(1) or (3) (which relates to transitional provisions).

23. Transitional provisions.—(1) Where before 1 February 1993 a person had notified *the Executive* of his intention to undertake activities involving *genetic modification* which complied with regulation 5(1) and (2)(a) of *the 1989 Regu-*

lations as then in force, that notification shall be treated as satisfying the requirements of regulation 8 except that regulation 8(3) shall apply to that activity on or after 1 February 1994.

(2) Before 2 May 1993 it shall be a sufficient compliance with regulation 8 if the notifier commences the activity having notified his intention to do so 30 days in advance or such shorter time in advance as *the Executive* may approve and regulation 8(3) shall not apply to activities commenced before 2 May 1993 until 1 February 1994.

(3) Where before 1 February 1993 a person had notified *the Executive* of his intention to undertake activities involving *genetic modification* which complied with regulation 5(1) and (2) (b) of *the 1989 Regulations* as then in force, that notification shall be treated as satisfying the requirements of regulation 9 except that regulation 9(5) shall apply to that activity on or after 1 February 1994.

(4) Before 2 April 1993 it shall be a sufficient compliance with regulation 9 if the notifier of an *activity involving genetic modification* had notified it in accordance with that regulation 30 days in advance or such shorter time in advance as *the Executive* may approve and regulation 9(5) shall not apply to activities commenced before 2 April 1993 until 1 February 1994.

(5) Regulation 10 shall apply to any notification made on or after 1 February 1993.

24. Extension outside Great Britain. These Regulations shall apply in relation to premises and activities outside Great Britain to which sections 1 to 59 and 80 to 82 of the Health and Safety at Work etc. Act 1974 apply by virtue of the Health and Safety at Work etc. Act 1974 (Application Outside Great Britain) Order 1989 as they apply to premises and activities within Great Britain.

25. Revocation. *The 1989 Regulations* are revoked.

SCHEDULE 1

Regulations 2(1) and 3(3)

DEFINITION OF *GENETIC MODIFICATION*

PART I
EXAMPLES OF TECHNIQUES CONSTITUTING *GENETIC MODIFICATION*

1. Examples of the techniques which constitute *genetic modification* which are referred to in sub-paragraph (a) of the definition of *genetic modification* in regulation 2(1) are—
   (a) recombinant DNA techniques consisting of the formation of new combinations of genetic material by the insertion of nucleic acid molecules, produced by whatever means outside the cell, into any virus, bacterial plasmid or other vector system so as to allow their incorporation into a host *organism* in which they do not occur naturally but in which they are capable of continued propagation;
   (b) techniques involving the direct introduction into an *organism* of heritable material prepared outside the *organism* including micro-injection, macro-injection and micro-encapsulation; and

(c) cell fusion (including protoplast fusion) or hybridisation techniques where live cells with new combinations of heritable genetic material are formed through the fusion of two or more cells by means of methods that do not occur naturally.

PART II

TECHNIQUES WHICH ARE NOT CONSIDERED TO RESULT IN *GENETIC MODIFICATION*

2. The following techniques are not considered to result in *genetic modification* if they do not involve the use of recombinant-DNA molecules or *genetically modified organisms*—
(a) in vitro fertilisation;
(b) conjugation, transduction, transformation or any other natural process; and
(c) polyploidy induction.

PART III

TECHNIQUES TO WHICH THESE REGULATIONS DO NOT APPLY

3. These Regulations shall not apply to the following techniques of *genetic modification* if they do not involve the use of *genetically modified organisms* as recipient or parental *organisms*—
(a) mutagenesis;
(b) the construction and use of somatic hybridoma cells (for example, for the production of monoclonal antibodies);
(c) cell fusion (including protoplast fusion) of plant cells where the resulting *organisms* can also be produced by traditional breeding methods;
(d) *self-cloning* of non-pathogenic naturally occurring *micro-organisms* which fulfil the criteria of Group I for recipient *micro-organisms*; and
(e) *self-cloning* of non-pathogenic naturally occurring *organisms* other than *micro-organisms* which fulfil the criteria of Part III of Schedule 2.

SCHEDULE 2

Regulation 2(2)

CRITERIA FOR THE CLASSIFICATION OF *ORGANISMS*

PART I

CRITERIA AS APPLICABLE FOR CLASSIFICATION OF *MICRO-ORGANISMS* IN GROUP I

1. **Recipient or parental organism**
(a) non-pathogenic;
(b) no adventitious agents;
(c) proven and extended history of safe use or built-in biological barriers, which, without interfering with optimal growth in the reactor or fermenter, confer limited survivability and replicability, without adverse consequences in the environment.

2. **Vectors/Insert**
(a) well characterised and free from known harmful sequences;
(b) limited in size as much as possible to the genetic sequences required to perform the intended function;
(c) should not increase the stability of the construct in the environment (unless that is a requirement of intended function);
(d) should be poorly mobilisable;
(e) should not transfer any resistance markers to *micro-organisms* not known to acquire them naturally (if such acquisition could compromise use of drugs to control disease agents).

3. *Genetically modified micro-organisms*
(a) non-pathogenic;
(b) as safe in the reactor or fermenter as recipient or parental organism, but with limited survivability and/or replicability without adverse consequences in the environment.

4. Other *genetically modified micro-organisms* that could be included in Group I if they meet the conditions in paragraph 3
(a) those constructed entirely from a single prokaryotic recipient (including its indigenous plasmids and viruses) or from a single eukaryotic recipient (including its chloroplasts, mitochondria, plasmids, but excluding viruses);
(b) those that consist entirely of genetic sequences from different species that exchange these sequences by known physiological processes.

PART II
GUIDELINES AS APPLICABLE FOR CLASSIFICATION OF *MICRO-ORGANISMS* IN GROUP I

For classification into Group I the following guidelines should be used to further interpret Part I of this Schedule.

5. Characteristics of the recipient or parental organism(s)
(1) Non-pathogenic
The recipient or parental *organisms* can be classified as non-pathogenic if they satisfy the conditions of one of the following sub-paragraphs—
(a) the recipient or parental strain should have an established record of safety in the laboratory and/or industry, with no adverse effects on human health and the environment;
(b) the recipient or parental strain does not meet the conditions of sub-paragraph (a) above but it belongs to a species for which there is a long record of biological work including safety in the laboratory and/or industry, showing no adverse effects on human health and the environment;
(c) if the recipient or parental *organism* is a strain which does not satisfy the conditions of sub-paragraph (a) above and belongs to a species for which there is no record of biological work including safe use in the laboratory and/or industry, appropriate testing (including, if necessary, animals) must be carried out, in order to establish non-pathogenicity and safety in the environment;
(d) if a non-virulent strain of an acknowledged pathogenic species is used, the strain should be as deficient as possible in genetic material that determines virulence so as to ensure no reversion to pathogenicity. In the case of bacteria, special attention should be given to plasmid or phage-borne virulence determinants.
(2) No adventitious agents
The recipient or parental strain/cell line should be free of known biological contaminating agents (symbionts, mycoplasms, viruses, viroids, etc.), which are potentially harmful.
(3) The recipient or parental strain/cell line should have proven and extended history of safe use or built-in biological barriers, which, without interfering with optimal growth in the reactor or fermenter, confer limited survivability and replicability, without adverse consequences in the environment (applicable only for *Type B operations*).

6. Characteristics of the vector
(1) The vector should be well characterised.
For this purpose the following characteristics should be taken into account.
(a) Information on composition and construction
(i) the type of the vector should be defined (virus, plasmid, cosmid, phasmid, transposable element, minichromosome, etc.);

      (ii) the following information on the constituent fragments of the vector should be available—
          (aa) the origin of each fragment (progenitor genetic element, strain of *organism* in which the progenitor genetic element naturally occurred),
          (bb) if some fragments are synthetic, their functions should be known;
      (iii) the methods used for construction should be known.
   (b) Information on vector structure
      (i) the size of the vector should be known and expressed in basepairs or D;
      (ii) the function and relative positions of the following should be known—
          (aa) structural genes,
          (bb) marker genes for selection (antibiotic resistance, heavy metal resistance, phage immunity, genes coding for degradation of xenobiotics, etc.),
          (cc) regulatory elements,
          (dd) target sites (nic-sites, restriction endonuclease sites, linkers, etc.),
          (ee) transposable elements (including provirus sequences),
          (ff) genes related to transfer and mobilisation function (e.g. with respect to conjugation, transduction or chromosomal integration),
          (gg) replicon(s).
  (2) The vector should be free from harmful sequences
     The vector should not contain genes coding for potentially harmful or pathogenic traits (e.g. virulence determinants, toxins, etc.) unless for *Type A operations*, such genes constitute an essential feature of the vector without, under any conditions or circumstances, resulting in a harmful or pathogenic phenotype of the *genetically modified micro-organism.*
  (3) The vector should be limited in size as much as possible to the genetic sequences required to perform the intended function.
  (4) The vector should not increase the stability of the *genetically modified micro-organism* in the environment (unless that is a requirement of the intended function).
  (5) The vector should be poorly mobilisable
   (a) If the vector is a plasmid—
      (i) it should have a restricted host-range;
      (ii) it should be defective in transfer-mobilisation factors e.g. Tra⁻, Mob⁺, for *Type A operations* or Tra⁻, Mob⁻, for *Type B operations.*
   (b) If the vector is a virus, cosmid or phasmid—
      (i) it should have a restricted host-range;
      (ii) it should be rendered non-lysogenic when used as a cloning vector (e.g. defective in the cI-lambda repressor).
  (6) It should not transfer any resistance markers to *micro-organisms* not known to acquire them naturally (if such acquisition could compromise use of drugs to control disease agents).

7. Required characteristics of the insert.
  (1) The insert should be well characterised
     For this purpose, the following characteristics should be taken into account.
   (a) The origin of the insert should be known (genus, species, strain).
   (b) The following information on the library from which the insert originated, should be known—
      (i) the source and method for obtaining the nucleic acid of interest (cDNA, chromosomal, mitochondrial, etc.);
      (ii) the vector in which the library was constructed (e.g. lambda gt 11, pBR322, etc.) and the site in which the DNA was inserted;

      (iii) the method used for identification (colony, hybridisation, immuno-blot, etc.);

      (iv) the strain used for library construction.

  (c) If the insert is synthetic, its intended function should be identified.

  (d) The following information on the structure of the insert is required—

      (i) information on structural genes, regulatory elements;

      (ii) size of the insert;

      (iii) restriction endonuclease sites flanking the insert;

      (iv) information on transposable elements and provirus sequences.

(2) The insert should be free from harmful sequences—

  (a) the function of each genetic unit in the insert should be defined (not applicable for *Type A operations*);

  (b) the insert should not contain genes coding for potentially harmful or pathogenic traits (e.g. virulence determinants, toxins, etc.), (unless for *Type A operations*, such genes constitute an essential part of the insert without, under any circumstances, resulting in a harmful or pathogenic phenotype of the *genetically modified micro-organism*).

(3) The insert should be limited in size as much as possible to the genetic sequences required to perform the intended function.

(4) The insert should not increase the stability of the construct in the environment (unless that is a requirement of intended function).

(5) The insert should be poorly mobilisable.

      For instance, it should not contain transposing or transferable provirus sequences and other functional transposing sequences.

8. Required characteristics of the *genetically modified micro-organism*

(1) The *genetically modified micro-organism* should be non-pathogenic.

      This requirement is reasonably assured by compliance with all the requirements above.

(2) (a) The *genetically modified micro-organism* should be as safe (to man and the environment) as the recipient or parental strains (applicable only for *Type A operations*);

    (b) the *genetically modified micro-organisms* should be as safe in the reactor or fermentor as the recipient or parental strains, but with limited survivability and/or replicability outside the reactor or fermenter without adverse consequences in the environment (applicable only for *Type B operations*).

9. Other *genetically modified micro-organisms* that could be included in Group I if they meet the conditions in paragraph 8 above

(1) Those constructed entirely from a single prokaryotic recipient (including its indigenous plasmids and viruses) or from a single eukaryotic recipient (including its chloroplasts, mitochondria, plasmids, but excluding viruses).

(2) Those that consist entirely of genetic sequences from different species that exchange these sequences by known physiological processes.

PART III

CRITERIA FOR THE CLASSIFICATION OF *ORGANISMS* OTHER THAN *MICRO-ORGANISMS*

10. An *organism* which satisfies the criteria of this Part is a *genetically modified organism*—

  (a) which is not a *genetically modified micro-organism*; and

  (b) which is as safe in the containment facility as any recipient or parental organism.

SCHEDULE 3

Regulation 7(3)

PARAMETERS TO BE TAKEN INTO ACCOUNT IN RISK ASSESSMENTS, AS FAR AS THEY ARE
RELEVANT, UNDER REGULATION 7

1.   Characteristics of the donor, recipient or (where appropriate) parental organism. The following matters shall be investigated and assessed in relation to any *organism* which is or will be a donor, recipient or parental organism—
  (a)   the name, species, subspecies and strain of the organism;
  (b)   the degree of relatedness between the donor, recipient (and where appropriate the parental) *organism* in relation to which the assessment is being carried out;
  (c)   the sources of the organism;
  (d)   the reproductive cycle of the organism;
  (e)   history of prior *genetic modifications* to the organism;
  (f)   the stability of the genetic traits of the organism;
  (g)   the nature of the pathogenicity, virulence, infectivity, toxicity, and vectors of disease transmission of the organism;
  (h)   the base sequence, frequency of mobilisation and specificity of the organism's indigenous vectors;
  (i)   the presence in the *organism* of genes which confer resistance;
  (j)   the host range of an *organism* which is a parasite or pathogen;
  (k)   the organism's other potentially significant physiological traits, and the stability of those traits;
  (l)   the organism's natural habitat and geographic distribution;
  (m) the climatic characteristics of the organism's natural habitat;
  (n)   the significant involvement of the *organism* in environmental processes, including nitrogen fixation and pH regulation;
  (o)   the interaction of the *organism* with other *organisms* in the environment and its effect on those *organisms*, including its likely competitive or symbiotic properties;
  (p)   the ability of the *organism* to form survival structures, including seeds, spores or sclerotia.

2.   Characteristics of the modified organism. The following matters shall be investigated and assessed in relation to an *organism* in relation to which a risk assessment under regulation 7 is carried out—
  (a)   the description of the modification, including the technique used or proposed to be used to introduce a vector or insert into the organism;
  (b)   the nature and source of the vector introduced into the organism;
  (c)   the function of the *genetic modification* and/or of the new nucleic acid;
  (d)   the structure and amount of any vector or donor nucleic acid remaining in the final construction of the modified organism;
  (e)   the stability of the genetic traits introduced into the organism;
  (f)   the frequency of mobilisation of inserted vector or genetic transfer capability;
  (g)   the rate and level of expression of the new genetic material in the organism, and the method and sensitivity of measurement of that rate and level;
  (h)   the activity of the expressed protein.

3.   Health considerations. The following matters shall be investigated and assessed in relation to an *organism* in relation to which a risk assessment under regulation 7 is carried out—
  (a)   toxic or allergenic effects of non-viable *organisms* and/or their metabolic products;
  (b)   product hazards;
  (c)   comparison of the modified *micro-organism* to the donor, recipient or (where appropriate) parental *organism* regarding pathogenicity;

(d) capacity for colonisation;
(e) if the *organism* is pathogenic to humans who are immunocompetent—
  (i) diseases caused and mechanism of pathogenicity including invasiveness and virulence,
  (ii) communicability,
  (iii) infective dose,
  (iv) host range, possibility of alteration,
  (v) possibility of survival outside of human host,
  (vi) presence of vectors or means of dissemination,
  (vii) biological stability,
  (viii) antibiotic-resistance patterns,
  (ix) allergenicity,
  (x) availability of appropriate therapies.

4. Environmental considerations. The following matters shall also be investigated and assessed in relation to an *organism* in relation to which a risk assessment under regulation 7 is carried out—
  (a) the factors affecting survival, multiplication and dissemination of the modified *organism* in the environment;
  (b) the available techniques for detection, identification, and monitoring of the modified *organism* in the environment;
  (c) the available techniques for detecting transfer of the new genetic material to other *organisms*;
  (d) the known and predicted habitats of the modified organism;
  (e) the ecosystems to which the modified *organism* could be disseminated as a result of an escape;
  (f) the anticipated mechanism and result of interaction between the modified *organism* and the *organisms* which might be exposed in case of the escape of the *organism*;
  (g) the known or predicted effects of the *organism* on plants and animals, including pathogenicity, infectivity, toxicity, virulence, vector or pathogen allergenicity, colonisation, predation, parasitism, symbiosis and competition;
  (h) the known or predicted involvement of the *organism* in biogeochemical processes, including nitrogen fixation and pH regulation;
  (i) the availability of methods for decontamination of the area in case of release to the environment.

SCHEDULE 4

Regulation 8(1)

INFORMATION REQUIRED FOR A NOTIFICATION UNDER REGULATION 8(1)

A notification required for the purposes of regulation 8(1) shall include the following information—
  (a) the name and address of the person responsible for carrying out the activity and the names of persons responsible for supervision, monitoring and safety together with details of their training and qualifications;
  (b) address of the premises where the activity is to be carried on and its grid reference and, where appropriate, a description of the sections of the installation;
  (c) a description of the nature of the activity to be undertaken, the likely scale of the operation and in particular, in the case of *micro-organisms*, their classification (whether in Group I or Group II);
  (d) a summary of the risk assessment undertaken in accordance with regulation 7;
  (e) the names and capacities of the members of the *genetic modification safety committee*;

(f) comments made by the *genetic modification safety committee* on the local arrangements for risk assessment;

(g) the names of the biological and deputy biological safety officers concerned with the intended activities (if any);

(h) the name of the supervisory medical officer (if any);

(i) the arrangements for health surveillance (if any); and

(j) any other information *the Executive* needs for the purpose of maintaining the register referred to in regulation 16.

SCHEDULE 5

Regulation 9

INFORMATION REQUIRED FOR A NOTIFICATION UNDER REGULATION 9

PART I
INFORMATION REQUIRED UNDER REGULATION 9(3)

1. A notification required for the purposes of regulation 9(3) shall include the following information—

(a) the name and address of the person responsible for carrying out the activity;

(b) address of the premises where the activity is to be carried out;

(c) the date of the notification referred to in regulation 8(1);

(d) the parental *organism* used, or where applicable the host-vector system used;

(e) the source and the intended function of the genetic material involved in the modification;

(f) the identity and characteristics of the *genetically modified* organism;

(g) the purpose of the activity including the expected results;

(h) where appropriate the culture volumes to be used or the scale of the activity;

(i) details of waste treatment including levels of live *genetically modified micro-organisms* in the waste; and

(j) a summary of the risk assessment required in accordance with regulation 7 and of the comments of the *genetic modification safety committee* on it.

PART II
ADDITIONAL INFORMATION REQUIRED UNDER REGULATION 9(4)

2. In addition to the information required under Part I a notification made for the purposes of regulation 9(4) shall contain the following information—

(a) a description of the sections of the installation involved and the methods for handling the *organisms*;

(b) a description of the predominant meteorological conditions and the potential sources of danger arising from the location of the installation;

(c) a description of the protective and supervisory methods to be applied throughout the duration of the activity; and

(d) in the case of *micro-organisms*, the containment level to which the *micro-organism* has been allocated in accordance with the risk assessment made in accordance with regulation 7(1) and in any case the safety precautions to be observed.

PART III
ADDITIONAL INFORMATION REQUIRED UNDER REGULATION 9(5)

3. In addition to the information required under Parts I and II a notification made for the purposes of regulation 9(5) shall contain the information specified in paragraph 5.

4. If it is not technically possible, or if it does not appear necessary to give the information specified in paragraph 5, the reason shall be stated. The level of detail required in response to each subset of considerations is likely to vary according to the nature and scale of the proposed activity. In the case of information already submitted to *the Executive* by the notifier under these Regulations (or *the 1989 Regulations*) reference can be made to that information by him.

5.   The additional information required is—
(a) information about the *genetically modified micro-organisms*—
   (i)   the identity and characteristics of the *genetically modified micro-organisms,*
   (ii) the purpose of the *contained use* or the nature of the product,
   (iii) the host-vector system to be used where applicable,
   (iv) the culture volume to be used,
   (v)   behaviour and characteristics of the *micro-organisms* in the case of changes in the conditions of containment or release into the environment,
   (vi) overview of the potential hazards associated with the release of the *micro-organisms* into the environment, and
   (vii) substances which are or may be produced in the course of use of the *micro-organisms* other than the intended product;
(b) information about personnel—
   (i)   the maximum number of persons working in the installation, and
   (ii) the number of persons who will work directly with the *micro-organisms*;
(c) information about the installation—
   (i)   the activity in which the *micro-organisms* are to be used,
   (ii) the technological processes used,
   (iii) a description of the sections of the installation involved, and
   (iv) the predominant meteorological conditions and specific hazards arising from the location of the installation;
(d) information about waste management—
   (i)   types, quantities and potential hazards arising from the use of the *micro-organisms,*
   (ii) waste management techniques used including recovery of liquid or solid wastes and the inactivation techniques used, and
   (iii) ultimate form and destination of inactivated wastes;
(e) information about *accident* prevention and emergency response plans—
   (i)   the sources of hazards and conditions under which *accidents* might occur,
   (ii) the preventive measures applied such as safety equipment, alarm systems, containment methods and procedures and available resources,
   (iii) a description of information given to workers, and
   (iv) the information necessary for *the Executive* to evaluate any emergency plan prepared in accordance with regulation 13;
(f) the full risk assessment referred to in regulation 7; and
(g) any other information *the Executive* needs for the purpose of maintaining the register referred to in regulation 16.

SCHEDULE 6

Regulation 12(4)

CONTAINMENT MEASURES FOR *MICRO-ORGANISMS* OF GROUP II

1.   The containment measures for *Type B operations* using *micro-organisms* from Group II shall be chosen by the user from the levels in the Table below as appropriate to the *micro-organism* and the operation in question in order to ensure the protection of health of the general population and the environment.

2.   *Type B operations* shall be considered in terms of their unit operations. The characteristics of each operation will dictate the physical containment to be used at that stage. This will allow the selection and design of process, plant and operating pro-cedures best fitted to ensure adequate and safe containment. Two important factors to

be considered when selecting the equipment needed to implement the containment are the risk of, and the effects consequent on, equipment failure. Engineering practice may require increasingly stringent standards to reduce the risks of failure as the consequence of that failure becomes less tolerable.

		Containment levels	
SPECIFICATIONS	B2	B3	B4
1 Viable *micro-organisms* should be contained in a system which physically separates the process from the environment (closed system)	Yes	Yes	Yes
2 Exhaust gases from the closed system should be treated so as to:	Minimise release	Prevent release	Prevent release
3 Sample collection, addition of materials to a closed system and transfer of viable *micro-organisms* to another closed system, should be performed so as to:	Minimise release	Prevent release	Prevent release
4 Bulk culture fluids should not be removed from the closed system unless the viable *micro-organisms* have been:	Inactivated by validated means	Inactivated by validated chemical or physical means	Inactivated by validated chemical or physical means
5 Seals should be designed so as to:	Minimise release	Prevent release	Prevent release
6 Closed systems should be located within a controlled area	Optional	Optional	Yes, and purpose-built
(a) Biohazard signs should be posted	Optional	Yes	Yes
(b) Access should be restricted to nominated personnel only	Optional	Yes	Yes, via airlock
(c) Personnel should wear protective clothing	Yes, work clothing	Yes	Yes, A complete change
(d) Decontamination and washing facilities should be provided for personnel	Yes	Yes	Yes

	Containment levels		
SPECIFICATIONS	B2	B3	B4
(e) Personnel should shower before leaving the controlled area	No	Optional	Yes
(f) Effluent from sinks and showers should be collected and inactivated before release	No	Optional	Yes
(g) The controlled area should be adequately ventilated to minimise air contamination	Optional	Optional	Yes
(h) The controlled areas should be maintained at an air pressure negative to atmosphere	No	Optional	Yes
(i) Input air and extract air to the controlled area should be HEPA filtered	No	Optional	Yes
(j) The controlled area should be designed to contain spillage of the entire contents of the closed system	Optional	Yes	Yes
(k) The controlled area should be sealable to permit fumigation	No	Optional	Yes
7 Effluent treatment before final discharge	Inactivated by validated means	Inactivated by validated chemical or physical means	Inactivated by validated physical means

THE GENETICALLY MODIFIED ORGANISMS (CONTAINED USE) REGULATIONS 1993

(S.I. 1993 No. 15)

General note. These Regulations came into force on 1 February 1993. They require that records of risk assessment to be made pursuant to s. 108(1)(a) of the Environmental Protection Act 1990 by those importing, acquiring, releasing or marketing genetically modified organisms, be kept for 10 years. Exemption is given in respect of the importation and acquisition of certain classes of organism. They are not set out in this book.

THE ELECTRICITY AT WORK REGULATIONS 1989

(S.I. 1989 No. 635)

ARRANGEMENT OF REGULATIONS

PART IV
MISCELLANEOUS AND GENERAL

29. Defence.
30. Exemption certificates.
31. Extension outside Great Britain.
32. Disapplication of duties.
33. Revocations and modifications.

Schedule 1. Provisions applying to mines only and having effect in particular
            in relation to the use below ground in coal mines of film lighting
            circuits.
Schedule 2. Revocations and modifications.

The Secretary of State, in exercise of the powers conferred on him by sections
15(1), (2), (3)(a) and (b), (4)(a), (5)(b), (6)(b), (8) and (9) and 82(3)(a) of,
and paragraphs 1(1)(a) and (c), (2) and (3), 6(2), 9, 11, 12, 14, 15(1), 16 and
21(b) of Schedule 3 to, the Health and Safety at Work etc. Act 1974 ("the 1974
Act"), and of all other powers enabling him in that behalf and for the purpose
of giving effect without modifications to proposals submitted to him by the
Health and Safety Commission under section 11(2)(d) of the 1974 Act, after
the carrying out by the said Commission of consultations in accordance with
section 50(3) of that Act, hereby makes the following Regulations:

PART I
INTRODUCTION

1. Citation and commencement. These Regulations may be cited as the
Electricity at Work Regulations 1989 and shall come into force on 1 April 1990.

2. Interpretation.—(1) In these Regulations, unless the context otherwise
requires—

    "approved" means approved in writing for the time being by the Health
and Safety Executive for the purposes of these Regulations or conforming
with a specification approved in writing by the Health and Safety Executive
for the purposes of these Regulations;
    "circuit conductor" means any *conductor* in a system which is intended to
carry electric current in normal conditions, or to be energised in normal
conditions, and includes a combined neutral and earth conductor, but does
not include a conductor provided solely to perform a protective function by
connection to earth or other reference point;
    "conductor" means a conductor of electrical energy;
    "danger" means risk of injury;
    "electrical equipment" includes anything used, intended to be used or
installed for use, to generate, provide, transmit, transform, rectify, convert,
conduct, distribute, control, store, measure or use electrical energy;

"firedamp" means any flammable gas or any flammable mixture of gases occurring naturally in a mine;

"injury" means death or personal injury from electric shock, electric burn, electrical explosion or arcing, or from fire or explosion initiated by electrical energy, where any such death or injury is associated with the generation, provision, transmission, transformation, rectification, conversion, conduction, distribution, control, storage, measurement or use of electrical energy;

"safety-lamp mine" means—

(a) any coal mine; or
(b) any other mine in which—
   (i) there has occurred below ground an ignition of firedamp; or
   (ii) more than 0.25% by volume of firedamp is found on any occasion at any place below ground in the mine;

"system" means an electrical system in which all the *electrical equipment* is, or may be, electrically connected to a common source of electrical energy, and includes such source and such equipment.

(2) Unless the context otherwise requires, any reference in these Regulations to—

(a) a numbered regulation or Schedule is a reference to the regulation or Schedule in these Regulations so numbered;
(b) a numbered paragraph is a reference to the paragraph so numbered in the regulation or Schedule in which the reference appears.

3. Persons on whom duties are imposed by these Regulations.—(1) Except where otherwise expressly provided in these Regulations, it shall be the duty of every—

(a) employer and self-employed person to comply with the provisions of these Regulations in so far as they relate to matters which are within his control; and
(b) manager of a mine or quarry (within in either case the meaning of section 180 of the Mines and Quarries Act 1954) to ensure that all requirements or prohibitions imposed by or under these Regulations are complied with in so far as they relate to the mine or quarry or part of a quarry of which he is the manager and to matters which are within his control.

(2) It shall be the duty of every employee while at work—

(a) to co-operate with his employer so far as is necessary to enable any duty placed on that employer by the provisions of these Regulations to be complied with; and
(b) to comply with the provisions of these Regulations in so far as they relate to matters which are within his control.

PART II
GENERAL

4. Systems, work activities and protective equipment.—(1) All systems shall at all times be of such construction as to prevent, so far as is reasonably practicable *(a), danger.*

(2) As may be necessary to prevent *danger*, all *systems* shall be maintained so as to prevent, so far as is reasonably practicable *(a)*, such danger.

(3) Every work activity, including operation, use and maintenance of a *system* and work near a *system*, shall be carried out in such a manner as not to give rise, so far as is reasonably practicable *(a)*, to *danger*.

(4) Any equipment provided under these Regulations for the purpose of protecting persons at work on or near *electrical equipment* shall be suitable for the use for which it is provided, be maintained in a condition suitable for that use, and be properly used.

(a) **Reasonably practicable.** See INTRODUCTORY NOTE 5.

5.   Strength and capability of electrical equipment. No *electrical equipment* shall be put into use where its strength and capability may be exceeded in such a way as may give rise to *danger*.

6.   Adverse or hazardous environments. *Electrical equipment* which may reasonably foreseeably be exposed to—

(a) mechanical damage;
(b) the effects of the weather, natural hazards, temperature or pressure;
(c) the effects of wet, dirty, dusty or corrosive conditions; or
(d) any flammable or explosive substance, including dusts, vapours or gases,

shall be of such construction *(a)* or as necessary protected as to prevent, so far as is reasonably practicable *(b)*, danger arising from such exposure.

(a) **Reasonably practicable.** See INTRODUCTORY NOTE 5.

7.   Insulation, protection and placing of conductors. All conductors in a *system* which may give rise to *danger* shall either—

(a) be suitably covered with insulating material and as necessary protected so as to prevent, so far as is reasonably practicable *(a)*, *danger*; or
(b) have such precautions taken in respect of them (including where appropriate, their being suitably placed) as will prevent, so far as is reasonably practicable *(a)*, *danger*.

(a) **Reasonably practicable.** See INTRODUCTORY NOTE 5.

8.   Earthing or other suitable precautions. Precautions shall be taken, either by earthing or by other suitable means, to prevent *danger* arising when any conductor (other than a circuit *conductor*) which may reasonably foreseeably become charged as a result of either the use of a *system*, or a fault in a *system*, becomes so charged; and, for the purposes of ensuring compliance with this regulation, a *conductor* shall be regarded as earthed when it is connected to the general mass of earth by *conductors* of sufficient strength and current-carrying capability to discharge electrical energy to earth.

9. Integrity of referenced conductors. If a *circuit conductor* is connected to earth or to any other reference point, nothing which might reasonably be expected to give rise to *danger* by breaking the electrical continuity or introducing high impedance shall be placed in that *conductor* unless suitable precautions are taken to prevent that *danger*.

10. Connections. Where necessary to prevent *danger*, every joint and connection in a *system* shall be mechanically and electrically suitable for use.

11. Means for protecting from excess of current. Efficient means, suitably located, shall be provided for protecting from excess of current every part of a *system* as may be necessary to prevent *danger*.

12. Means for cutting off the supply and for isolation.—(1) Subject to paragraph (3), where necessary to prevent *danger*, suitable means (including, where appropriate, methods of identifying circuits) shall be available for—

(a) cutting off the supply of electrical energy to any *electrical equipment*; and

(b) the isolation of any *electrical equipment*.

(2) In paragraph (1), "isolation" means the disconnection and separation of the *electrical equipment* from every source of electrical energy in such a way that this disconnection and separation is secure.

(3) Paragraph (1) shall not apply to *electrical equipment* which is itself a source of electrical energy but, in such a case as is necessary, precautions shall be taken to prevent, so far as is reasonably practicable *(a)*, *danger*.

(a) Reasonably practicable. See INTRODUCTORY NOTE 5.

13. Precautions for work on equipment made dead. Adequate precautions shall be taken to prevent *electrical equipment*, which has been made dead in order to prevent *danger* while work is carried out on or near that equipment, from becoming electrically charged during that work if *danger* may thereby arise.

14. Work on or near live conductors. No person shall be engaged in any work activity on or near any live conductor (other than one suitably covered with insulating material so as to prevent *danger*) that *danger* may arise unless—

(a) it is unreasonable in all the circumstances for it to be dead; and

(b) it is reasonable in all the circumstances for him to be at work on or near it while it is live; and

(c) suitable precautions (including where necessary the provision of suitable protective equipment) are taken to prevent *injury*.

15. Working space, access and lighting. For the purposes of enabling *injury* to be prevented, adequate working space, adequate means of access *(a)*, and adequate lighting *(b)* shall be provided at all electrical equipment on which or near which work is being done in circumstances which may give rise to danger.

*(a) **Access.*** See generally, the notes to s. 29 of the Factories Act 1961 and, in particular, note *(e)* thereof. See also the Workplace (Health Safety and Welfare) Regulations (S.I. 1992 No. 3004).

*(b) **Adequate lighting.*** See note to s. 5 of the Factories Act 1961.

16.   Persons to be competent to prevent danger and injury. No person shall be engaged in any work activity where technical knowledge or experience is necessary to prevent *danger* or, where appropriate, injury, unless he possesses such knowledge or experience, or is under such degree of supervision as may be appropriate having regard to the nature of the work.

PART III
REGULATIONS APPLYING TO MINES ONLY

[*Not printed in this book*].

PART IV
MISCELLANEOUS AND GENERAL

29.   Defence. In any proceedings for an offence consisting of a contravention of regulations 4(4), 5, 8, 9, 10, 11, 12, 13, 14, 15, 16 or 25, it shall be a defence for any person to prove that he took all reasonable steps and exercised all due diligence *(a)* to avoid the commission of that offence.

*(a) **Due diligence.*** See INTRODUCTORY NOTE 7.

30.   Exemption certificates.—(1) Subject to paragraph (2), the Health and Safety Executive may, by a certificate in writing, exempt—

(a) any person;
(b) any premises;
(c) any *electrical equipment*;
(d) any electrical *system*;
(e) any electrical process;
(f) any activity,

or any class of the above, from any requirement or prohibition imposed by these Regulations and any such exemption may be granted subject to conditions and to a limit of time and may be revoked by a certificate in writing at any time.

(2) The Executive shall not grant any such exemption unless, having regard to the circumstances of the case, and in particular to—

(a) the conditions, if any, which it proposes to attach to the exemption; and
(b) any other requirements imposed by or under any enactment which apply to the case,

it is satisfied that the health and safety of persons who are likely to be affected by the exemption will not be prejudiced in consequence of it.

31. Extension outside Great Britain. These Regulations shall apply to and in
relation to premises and activities outside Great Britain to which sections 1 to 59
and 80 to 82 of the Health and Safety at Work etc. Act 1974 apply by virtue of
Articles 6 and 7 of the Health and Safety at Work etc. Act 1974 (Application
outside Great Britain) Order 1977 *(a)* as they apply within Great Britain.

(*a*) Now replaced by the 1989 Order of the same name.

32. Disapplication of duties. The duties imposed by these Regulations shall
not extend to—

(a) the master or crew of a sea-going ship or to the employer of such
persons, in relation to the normal ship-board activities of a ship's crew
under the direction of the master; or

(b) any person, in relation to any aircraft or hovercraft which is moving
under its own power.

33. Revocations and modifications.—(1) The instruments specified in
column 1 of Part I of Schedule 2 are revoked to the extent specified in the
corresponding entry in column 3 of that Part.

(2) The enactments and instruments specified in Part II of Schedule 2 shall
be modified to the extent specified in that Part.

(3) In the Mines and Quarries Act 1954, the Mines and Quarries (Tips) Act
1969 and the Mines Management Act 1971, and in regulations made under any
of those Acts, or in health and safety regulations, any reference to any of those
Acts shall be treated as including a reference to these Regulations.

SCHEDULE 1

Regulation 17

PROVISIONS APPLYING TO MINES ONLY AND HAVING EFFECT IN PARTICULAR IN RELATION TO
THE USE BELOW GROUND IN COAL MINES OF FILM LIGHTING CIRCUITS

[*Not printed in this book.*]

SCHEDULE 2

Regulation 33

REVOCATIONS AND MODIFICATIONS

[*Revocations and modifications applicable to regulations and orders outside the scope of this book
are not printed.*]

Part I. Revocations

Column 1 Regulations and orders revoked	Column 2 Reference	Column 3 Extent of revocation
The Electricity Regulations 1908	S.R. & O. 1980/1312	The whole Regulations.
The Cinematograph Film Stripping Regulations 1939	S.R. & O. 1939/571	Regulation 14
The Electricity (Factories Act) Special Regulations 1944	S.R. & O. 1944/739	The whole Regulations.
The Construction (General Provisions) Regulations 1961	S.I. 1961/1580	Regulation 44

Part II. Modifications

3. The Shipbuilding and Ship-repairing Regulations 1960 shall be modified as follows—
  (a) in regulation 51(3)(c) (which required the provision of lamps and torches in confined spaces in vessels) the words "of an appropriate type" shall be substituted for the words "of a safety type approved for the purpose of this Regulation";
  (b) in paragraphs (1) and (3) of regulation 59 (which impose restrictions with respect to the application etc. of naked lights, fires, lamps and heated rivets in oil-carrying vessels), the words "a lamp of an appropriate type" shall be substituted for the words "a safety lamp of a type approved for the purposes of this Regulation" where they respectively appear.

THE FIRE PRECAUTIONS ACT 1971

(1971 c. 40)

Introductory Note

A fire certificate, issued by a fire authority established under the Fire Services Act 1947, is required in respect of any premises which are put to a use designated by an order made by the Secretary of State. The classes of use which may be so designated are specified in the Fire Precautions Act 1971, s. 1 and, as that section is amended by the Health and Safety at Work etc. Act 1974, s. 78(2), include "use as a place of work".

By the Fire Precautions (Factory, Offices, Shops and Railway Premises) Order 1989, S.I. 1989 No. 76 those premises to which the Factories Act 1961 and the Offices, Shops and Railway Premises Act 1963 apply are so designated and, accordingly, the provisions of the Fire Precautions Act 1971, as amended by the Health and Safety at Work etc. Act 1974, s. 78 and as amended and modified by the Fire Safety and Safety of Places of Sport Act 1987 take the place of the provisions of both the Factories Act 1961 and the Offices, Shops and Railway Premises Act 1963 relating to fire precautions.

The Act is printed here as amended, but those sections of the Act which are outside the scope of this book are omitted.

The Fire Certificates (Special Premises) Regulations 1976, S.I. 1976 No. 2003, governing the issue of fire certificates by the Health and Safety Executive in respect of certain factory, office, shop and railway premises which are exempted from the requirement of a fire certificate under this Act, are also printed in this Part although made under the Health and Safety at Work etc. Act 1974.

The Fire Precautions (Sub-Surface Railway Stations) Regulations 1989 were made in consequence of the Kings Cross fire disaster of 1986 and the recommendations made by the Fennell Report into it (Cmd. 499 of 1988).

ARRANGEMENT OF SECTIONS

SCHEDULES

An Act to make further provision for the protection of persons from fire risks; and for purposes connected therewith.   [27 May 1971]

Be it enacted by the Queen's most Excellent Majesty, by and with the advice and consent of the Lords Spiritual and Temporal, and Commons, in this present Parliament assembled, and by the authority of the same, as follows:

Premises for which fire certificates are required

1. Uses of premises for which a fire certificate is compulsory.—(1) A certificate issued under this Act by the fire authority *(a)* (in this Act referred to as a "fire certificate" *(b)*) shall, subject to any exemption conferred by or under this Act, be required in respect of any premises *(c)* which are put to a use for the time being designated under this section (in this Act referred to as a "designated use" *(d)*).

(2) For the purposes of this section the Secretary of State *(e)* may by order *(f)* designate particular uses of premises *(c)* but shall not so designate any particular use unless it falls within at least one of the following classes of use, that is to say—

(a) use as, or for any purpose involving the provision of, sleeping accommodation;
(b) use as, or as part of, an institution providing treatment or care;
(c) use for purposes of entertainment, recreation or instruction or for purposes of any club, society or association;
(d) use for purposes of teaching, training or research;

(e) use for any purpose involving access to the premises *(c)* by members of the public, whether on payment or otherwise;

(f) use as a place of work *(g)*.

(3) An order *(f)* under this section may provide that a fire certificate *(b)* shall not by virtue of this section be required for premises *(c)* of any description specified in the order notwithstanding that they are or form part of premises which are put to a designated use *(d)*.

(3A) An order under this section may, as respects any designated use *(a)*, specify descriptions of premises *(c)* which qualify for exemption by a fire authority *(d)* under section 5A of this Act from the requirement for a fire certificate *(b)* in respect of premises *(c)* which are put to that use.

(4) For the purposes of any provision made in an order *(f)* under this section by virtue of subsection (3) or (3A) above a description of premises *(c)* may be framed by reference to the purpose for which premises are used or the frequency of their use for any purpose or their situation, construction or arrangement or by reference to any other circumstances whatsoever; and different provision may be made in pursuance of subsection (3) or (3A) above in relation to different designated uses *(d)*.

(5) An order *(f)* under this section may include such supplementary and incidental provisions as appear to the Secretary of State to be necessary or expedient for the purposes of the order.

(6) An order *(f)* under this section may be varied or revoked by a subsequent order thereunder.

(7) The power to make orders under this section shall be exercisable by statutory instrument, which shall be subject to annulment in pursuance of a resolution of either House of Parliament.

(8) Without prejudice to any exemption conferred by or under this Act, where premises *(c)* consisting of a part of a building *(h)* are put to a designated use *(d)*, any other part of the building which is occupied together with those premises in connection with that use of them shall for the purposes of this Act be treated as forming part of the premises put to that use.

General note. Premises exempted from the requirement for a fire certificate by virtue of sub-s. (3) are subject to the provisions of s. 9A.

(a) Fire authority. For definition, see s. 43(1).

(b) Fire certificate. "Fire certificate" has the meaning assigned by s. 1(1) (s. 43(1)) but by the Fire Safety and Safety of Places of Sport Act 1987, s. 49(2), Sch. 5, where immediately before a fire certificate becomes required by or under this Act in respect of any premises a fire certificate issued or deemed to be issued under regulations made under the Health and Safety at Work etc. Act 1974 ("1974 Act certificate") was in force in respect of those premises, the 1974 Act certificate continues in force and is deemed to be a fire certificate within the meaning of this Act validly issued with respect to the premises with respect to which it was issued and to cover the use or uses to which those premises were being put immediately before a fire certificate becomes required by or under this Act in respect of those premises, and without prejudice to the generality of the foregoing the 1974 Act certificate—

(a) may be amended, replaced or revoked in accordance with the provisions of this Act; and

(b) is to be treated as imposing in relation to the premises the like requirements as were previously imposed in relation thereto.

The Fire Certificates (Special Premises) Regulations 1976, S.I. 1976 No. 2003 (set out in this Part) provide for the issue of 1974 Act certificates.

(c) **Premises.** For definition, see s. 43(1).

(d) **Designated use.** For definition, see s. 43(1).

(e) **Secretary of State.** This Act is administered by the Home Office.

(f) **Order.** By the Fire Precautions (Factories, Offices, Shops and Railway Premises) Order 1989, S.I. 1989 No. 76 (set out below), the uses of premises as factory premises, offices, shop premises or railway premises are designated for the purposes of this section, but a fire certificate under s. 1(1) is not required in respect of such premises if they fall within the descriptions specified in art. 5 of the Order and the premises specified in art. 6 of the Order qualify for exemption from the requirement for a fire certificate.

(g) **Work.** For definition, see s. 43(1).

(h) **Building.** For definition, see s. 43(1).

THE FIRE PRECAUTIONS (FACTORIES, OFFICES, SHOPS AND
RAILWAY PREMISES) ORDER 1989
(S.I. 1989 No. 76)

In exercise of the powers conferred on me by section 1 of the Fire Precautions Act 1971, I hereby make the following Order:

Citation and commencement
   1.   This Order may be cited as the Fire Precautions (Factories, Offices, Shops and Railway Premises) Order 1989 and shall come into force on 1 April 1989.

Interpretation
   2.—(1) in this Order—
   "the 1971 Act" means the Fire Precautions Act 1971;
   "basement" means a floor (however described) immediately below the ground floor;
   "factory premises" means premises constituting, or forming part of, a factory within the meaning of the Factories Act 1961 and premises to which sections 123(1) and 124 of that Act (application to electrical stations and institutions) apply;
   "first floor" means the floor above the ground floor;
   "office premises", "railway premises" and "shop premises" mean (respectively, and subject to paragraphs (2) and (3) below) office premises, railway premises and shop premises within the meaning of the Offices, Shops and Railway Premises Act 1963, and premises deemed to be such premises for the purposes of that Act, other than premises consisting of a covered market place in which shop premises are aggregated.
   (2) For the purpose of the definition in paragraph (1) above of "railway premises", any reference in section 1(4) of the Offices, Shops and Railway Premises Act 1963 (which defines "railway premises" in that Act) to a building shall be construed as a reference to a building within the meaning of the 1971 Act, and accordingly the definition of "building" in section 90(1) of the Offices, Shops and Railway Premises Act 1963 shall not have effect for that purpose.
   (3) In the definition in paragraph (1) above of "shop premises" the reference to a covered market place shall be construed as limited to such a place where a market is held by virtue of a grant from the Crown or of prescription or under statutory authority.

Revocation of designation order
   3.   The Fire Precautions (Factories, Offices, Shops and Railway Premises) Order 1976 is hereby revoked.

Designation of uses of factory, office, shop and railway premises
   4.   Subject to article 7 below, the following uses of premises are hereby designated for the purposes of section 1 of the 1971 Act (which requires fire certificates for premises put to designated uses), that is to say—

    (a) use as *factory premises*;
    (b) use as *office premises*;
    (c) use as *shop premises*; and
    (d) use as *railway premises*,
being (in each case) a use of premises in which persons are employed to work.

Premises exempt from requirement for fire certificate
    5.—(1) Notwithstanding the provisions of article 4 above, a fire certificate shall not by virtue of section 1 of the 1971 Act be required for any *factory premises, office premises, shop premises or railway premises* in which—
    (a) not more than twenty persons are at work at any one time; and
    (b) not more than ten persons are at work at any one time elsewhere than on the ground floor of the building constituting or comprising the premises,
unless one or more of the conditions specified in paragraph (2) below applies to the premises.
    (2) The conditions referred to in paragraph (1) above are—
    (a) that the premises are in a building containing two or more sets of premises which are put to any of the uses designated by article 4 above and the aggregate of the persons at work at any one time in both or (as the case may be) all those sets of premises exceeds twenty;
    (b) that the premises are in a building containing two or more sets of premises which are put to any of such uses and in both or (as the case may be) all those sets of premises the aggregate of the persons at work at any one time elsewhere than on the ground floor of the building exceeds ten;
    (c) that, in the case of *factory premises*, explosive or highly flammable materials (other than materials of such a kind and in such a quantity that the fire authority have determined that they do not constitute a serious additional risk to persons in the premises in case of fire) are stored or used in or under the premises.
    (3) Any reference in this article to persons at work is a reference to any of the following persons:
    (a) an individual who works under a contract of employment or apprenticeship;
    (b) an individual who works for gain or reward otherwise than under a contract of employment or apprenticeship, whether or not he employs other persons;
    (c) a person receiving training provided pursuant to arrangements made (whether before or after the coming into force of section 25 of the Employment Act 1988) under section 2 of the Employment and Training Act 1973.

Premises qualifying for exemption by fire authorities from requirement for fire certificate
    6.—(1) As respects the uses of premises designated by article 4 above, the premises described in paragraphs (2) and (3) below in relation to such a use qualify for exemption by a fire authority under section 5A of the 1971 Act (powers for fire authority to grant exemption in particular cases) from the requirement for a fire certificate in respect of premises which are put to that use.
    (2) In the case of a use of premises as *factory premises, office premises or railway premises*, the premises referred to in paragraph (1) above are any premises consisting of or comprised in—
    (a) the ground floor of a building; or
    (b) the ground floor and *basement* of a building; or
    (c) the ground floor and first floor of a building; or
    (d) the ground floor, first floor and *basement* of a building in which the *basement* is separated from the ground floor by fire-resisting construction.
    (3) In the case of a use of premises as *shop premises*, the premises referred to in paragraph (1) above are any premises consisting of or comprised in—
    (a) the ground floor of a building; or
    (b) the ground floor and *basement* of a building in which the *basement* is separated from the ground floor by fire-resisting construction.

(4) For the purposes of paragraphs (2)(d) and (3)(b) above, construction shall be treated as fire-resisting if, and only if, it is of such a nature as to be capable of providing resistance to fire for a period of not less than thirty minutes.

Saving for premises to which regulations apply
7.   Nothing in this Order shall have effect in relation to—
   (a)   any *railway premises* to which regulations under section 12 of the 1971 Act (regulations about fire precautions) for the time being apply; or
   (b)   any premises of a description for the time being specified in any regulations made under the Health and Safety at Work etc. Act 1974 which provide for the issue of fire certificates by the Health and Safety Executive.

---

2.   Premises exempt from s. 1.   No fire certificate *(a)* shall by virtue of section 1 of this Act be required in respect of premises *(b)* consisting of or comprised in a house which is occupied as a single private dwelling.

   (a) **Fire certificate.**   For definition, see s. 43(1).

   (b) **Premises.**   For definition, see s. 43(1). Whether premises consist of a single private dwelling is a question of fact: see *West Midlands Fire Authority v Falconer* (Queen's Bench Division, 4 March 1993).

3, 4.   [*Section 3, which relates to the power of a fire authority to make a fire certificate compulsory in respect of the use of certain premises as a dwelling and s. 4, which relates to the right of appeal in respect of notices under s. 3, are not printed in this book.*]

Fire certificates

5.   Application for, and issue of, fire certificate.—(1) An application for a fire certificate *(a)* with respect to any premises *(b)* must be made to the fire authority *(c)* in the prescribed *(d)* form and—

   (a)   must specify the particular use or uses of the premises which it is desired to have covered by the certificate; and
   (b)   must give such information as may be prescribed about the premises any prescribed matter connected with them; and
   (c)   if the premises consist of part of a building *(e)* must, in so far as it is available to the applicant *(f)* give such information as may be prescribed about the rest of the building and any prescribed matter connected with it.

   (2) On receipt of an application for a fire certificate *(a)* with respect to any premises *(b)* the fire authority *(c)* shall notify the applicant of his duties under sub-section (2A) below and may require the applicant *(f)* within such time as they may specify—

   (a)   to furnish them with such plans of the premises as they may specify; and

(b) if the premises consist of part of a building *(e)* to furnish them, in so far as it is possible for him to do so, with such plans of such other part or parts of the building as they may specify;

and if the applicant fails to furnish the required plans within that time or such further time as the authority may allow, the application shall be deemed to have been withdrawn at the end of that time or further time, as the case may be.

(2A) Where an application is made for a fire certificate *(a)* with respect to any premises *(b)* it is the duty of the occupier to secure that, when the application is made and pending its disposal—

(a) the means of escape in case of fire with which the premises are provided can be safely and effectively used at all material times;

(b) the means for fighting fire with which the premises *(b)* are provided are maintained in efficient working order; and

(c) any persons employed to work in the premises *(b)* receive instruction or training in what to do in case of fire.

(3) Where an application for a fire certificate *(a)* with respect to any premises *(b)* has been duly made and all such plans (if any) as are required to be furnished under subsection (2) above in connection with it have been duly furnished, it shall be the duty of the fire authority *(c)* to consider whether or not, in the case of premises which qualify for exemption under section 5A of this Act, to grant exemption and, if they do not grant it, it shall be their duty to cause to be carried out an inspection of the relevant building *(e)* (including any part of it which consists of premises to which any exemption conferred by or under this Act applies), and if the fire authority are satisfied as regards any use of the premises which is specified in the application that—

(a) the means of escape in case of fire with which the premises are provided; and

(b) the means (other than means for fighting fire) with which the relevant building is provided for securing that the means of escape with which the premises are provided can be safely and effectively used at all material times; and

(c) the means for fighting fire (whether in the premises or affecting the means of escape) with which the relevant building is provided; and

(d) the means with which the relevant building is provided for giving to persons in the premises warning in case of fire,

are such as may reasonably be required in the circumstances of the case in connection with that use of the premises, the authority shall issue a certificate covering that use.

(4) Where the fire authority *(c)*, after causing to be carried out under subsection (3) above an inspection of the relevant building *(e)*, are, as regards any use of the premises *(b)* specified in the application, not satisfied that the means mentioned in that subsection are such as may reasonably be required in the circumstances of the case in connection with that use, they shall by notice served on the applicant—

(a) inform him of that fact and of the steps which would have to be taken (whether by way of making alterations to any part of the relevant building or of otherwise providing that building or, as the case may be, the premises with any of those means) to satisfy them as aforesaid as regards that use; and

(b) notify him that they will not issue a fire certificate *(a)* covering that use unless those steps are taken (whether by the applicant or otherwise) within a specified time,

and it at the end of that time or such further time as may be allowed by the authority or by any order made by a court on, or in proceedings arising out of, an appeal under section 9 of this Act against the notice, a certificate covering that use has not been issued, it shall be deemed to have been refused.

(5) In this Act, "escape", in relation to premises, means escape from them to some place of safety beyond the building which constitutes or comprises the premises and any area enclosed by it or enclosed with it; and accordingly, for the purposes of any provision of this Act relating to means of escape, consideration may be given to, and conditions or requirements imposed as respects, any place or thing by means of which a person escapes from premises to a place of safety.

General note. This section is modified by Sch. 2, Part II in its application to factory, office, railway and shop premises, as defined by Sch. 2, Part I, in respect of which a fire certificate is required and which are held under a lease or an agreement for a lease or under a licence and consist of a part of a building all parts of which are in the same ownership or consist of part of a building in which different parts are owned by different persons.

(a) **Fire certificate.** See note *(b)* to s. 1.

(b) **Premises.** For definition, see s. 43(1). Where the premises are factory, office, railway or shop premises as defined by Sch. 2, Part I, s. 5(2A) is modified by Sch. 2, Part II. As to "occupier", see note *(i)* to s. 6.

(c) **Fire authority.** For definition, see s. 43(1).

(d) **Prescribed.** By s. 43(1) "prescribed" means prescribed by regulations. The Fire Precautions (Application for Certificate) Regulations 1989 (set out below) have been made under s. 5(1).

(e) **Building; relevant building.** For definition, see s. 43(1).

THE FIRE PRECAUTIONS (APPLICATION FOR CERTIFICATE)
REGULATIONS 1989
(S.I. 1989 No. 77)

In exercise of the powers conferred on me by sections 5(1) and 43(1) of the Fire Precautions Act 1971, I hereby make the following Regulations:

1. These Regulations may be cited as the Fire Precautions (Application for Certificate) Regulations 1989 and shall come into force on 1 April 1989.
2. An application for a fire certificate in respect of any premises shall be in the form specified in the Schedule to these regulations or a form to the like effect.
3. The Fire Precautions (Application for Certificate) Regulations 1976 are hereby revoked.

SCHEDULE

[FIRE PRECAUTIONS ACT 1971, s. 5]
[APPLICATION FOR A FIRE CERTIFICATE]

For Official Use Only

To the Chief Executive of the Fire Authority*

In the case of Crown premises, substitute H.M. Inspector of Fire Services.

I hereby apply for a fire certificate in respect of the premises of which details are given below. I make the application as, or on behalf of, the occupier/owner of the premises.

Signature ....
Name: Mr/Mrs/Miss ....
(in block capitals)

If signing on behalf of a company or some other person, state the capacity in which signing ....
Address ....
Telephone number .... Date ....

To be completed by the Applicant:—
  1. Postal address of the premises ....
....
....

  2. Name and address of the owner of the premises
Name ....
Address ....
....
....
(In the case of premises in plural ownership the names and addresses of all owners should be given.)

  3. Details of the premises
(If the fire certificate is to cover the use of two or more sets of premises in the same building, details of each set of premises should be given on a separate sheet.)
  (a) Name of occupier ....
       (and any trading name, if different) ....
       ....
  (b) Use(s) to which premises put ....
  (c) Floor(s) in building on which premises situated (e.g. basement(s), ground floor, first floor etc.) ....
       ....
  (d) Number of persons employed to work in the premises ....
  (e) Maximum number of persons at work or it is proposed will work in the premises at any one time (including employees, self-employed persons and trainees)—
       (i) below the ground floor of the building ....
       (ii) on the ground floor of the building ....
       (iii) on the first floor of the building ....
       (iv) in the whole of the premises ....
  (f) Maximum number of persons other than persons at work likely to be in the premises at any one time ....
  (g) Number of persons (including staff, guests and other residents) for whom sleeping accommodation is provided in the premises—

    (i) below the ground floor of the building ....

    (ii) above the first floor of the building ....

    (iii) in the whole of the premises ....

4.   If the premises consist of part only of a building, the uses to which the other parts of the building are put (on a floor by floor basis):

....

....

....

5.   (a) Total number of floors (excluding basements) in the building in which the premises are situated ....

       (b) Total number of basements in that building ....

6.   Approximate date of construction of the premises ....

7.   Nature and quantity of any explosive or highly flammable materials stored or used in or under the premises

Materials	Maximum quantity stored	Method of storage	Maximum quantity liable to be exposed at any one time

(Continue on a separate sheet if necessary)

8.   Details of fire-fighting equipment available for use in the premises

Nature of equipment	Number Provided	Where installed	Is the equipment regularly maintained?
(a) Hosereels			Yes/No
(b) Portable fire extinguishers			Yes/No
(c) Others (specify types e.g. sand/water buckets, fire blanket)			Yes/No

(Continue on a separate sheet if necessary)

5A. **Powers for fire authority to grant exemption in particular case.**—(1) A fire authority *(a)* may, if they think fit as regards any premises *(b)* which appear to them to be premises qualifying for exemption under this section as respects any particular use, grant exemption from the requirement to have a fire certificate *(c)* covering that use.

(2) Exemption under this section for any premises *(b)* as respects any use of them may be granted by the fire authority *(a)*, with or without the making of an application for the purpose—

    (a) on the making of an application for a fire certificate *(c)* with respect to the premises *(b)* covering that use; or

(b)   at any time during the currency of a fire certificate with respect to the premises *(b)* which covers that use.

(3)   In deciding whether or not to grant exemption under this section for any premises *(b)* the fire authority *(a)* shall have regard to all the circumstances of the case and in particular to the degree of seriousness of the risk in case of fire to persons in the premises.

(4)   For the purpose of making that decision the fire authority may—

(a)   require the applicant or, as the case may be, the occupier of the premises *(b)* to give such information as they require about the premises and any matter connected with them; and

(b)   cause to be carried out an inspection of the relevant building *(d)*.

(5)   The fire authority *(a)* shall not grant exemption under this section for any premises *(b)* without causing an inspection to be carried out under subsection (4) above unless they have caused the premises to be inspected (under that or any other power) within the preceding twelve months.

(6)   The effect of the grant of exemption under this section as respects any particular use of premises *(b)* is that, during the currency of the exemption, no fire certificate *(c)* in respect of the premises is required to cover that use and accordingly—

(a)   where the grant is made on an application for a fire certificate *(c)*, the grant disposes of the application or of so much of it as relates to that use; and

(b)   where the grant is made during the currency of a fire certificate, the certificate shall wholly or as respects that use cease to have effect.

(7)   On granting an exemption under this section, the fire authority *(a)* shall, by notice to the applicant for the fire certificate *(c)* or the occupier of the premises *(b)*, as the case may be, inform him that they have granted exemption as respects the particular use or uses of the premises specified in the notice and of the effect of the grant.

(8)   A notice of the grant of exemption for any premises *(b)* as respects a particular use of them may include a statement specifying the greatest number of persons of a description specified in the statement for the purposes of that use who, in the opinion of the fire authority *(a)*, can safely be in the premises at any one time.

(9)   Where a notice of the grant of exemption for any premises *(b)* includes a statement under subsection (8) above, the fire authority *(a)* may, by notice served on the occupier of the premises, direct that, as from a date specified in the notice, the statement—

(a)   is cancelled; or

(b)   is to have effect as varied by the notice,

and, on such a variation the statement shall be treated, so long as the variation remains in force, as if the variation were specified in it.

General note. Premises which are exempted under this section are subject to the provisions of s. 9A.

This section is modified by Sch. 2, Part II in its application to factory, office, railway and shop premises, as defined by Sch. 2, Part I, in respect of which a fire certificate is required and which are held under a lease or an agreement for a lease or under a licence and consist of a part of a building all parts of which are in the same ownership or consist of part of a building in which different parts are owned by different persons.

(a) **Fire authority.** For definition, see s. 43(1).

(b) **Premises.** For definition, see s. 43(1).

(c) **Fire certificate.** For definition, see s. 43(1).

(d) **Building.** For definition, see s. 43(1).

5B.   Withdrawal of exemptions under s. 5A.—(1) A fire authority *(a)* who have granted an exemption under section 5A of this Act from the requirement to have a fire certificate *(b)* covering any particular use of premises *(c)* may, if they think fit, at any time, withdraw the exemption in accordance with sub-sections (2) to (4) below.

(2) In deciding whether or not to withdraw an exemption they have granted the fire authority *(a)* shall have regard to all the circumstances of the case and in particular to the degree of seriousness of the risk in case of fire to persons in the premises *(c)*.

(3) The fire authority *(a)* may withdraw an exemption they have granted as respects any particular use of premises *(c)* without exercising any of the powers of inspection or inquiry conferred by section 19 of this Act but they shall not withdraw the exemption without first giving notice to the occupier of the premises that they propose to withdraw it and the reasons for the proposal and giving him an opportunity of making representations on the matter.

(4) An exemption shall be withdrawn by serving a notice on the occupier of the premises *(c)* to which the exemption relates stating that the exemption will cease to have effect as respects the particular use or uses of the premises specified in the notice of such date as is so specified, being a date not earlier than the end of the period of fourteen days beginning with the date on which service of the notice is effected.

(5) If premises *(c)* cease to qualify for exemption under section 5A of this Act a fire authority *(a)* who have granted an exemption under that section shall notify the occupier of the premises of the fact and date of the cessation of the exemption.

General note. This section is modified by Sch. 2, Part II in its application to factory, office, railway and shop premises, as defined by Sch. 2, Part I, in respect of which a fire certificate is required and which are held under a lease or an agreement for a lease or under a licence and consist of a part of a building all parts of which are in the same ownership or consist of part of a building in which different parts are owned by different persons.

   (*a*) **Fire authority.** For definition, see s. 43(1).

   (*b*) **Fire certificate.** For definition, see s. 43(1).

   (*c*) **Premises.** For definition, see s. 43(1).

---

6.   Contents of fire certificate.—(1) Every fire certificate (*a*) issued with respect to any premises (*b*) shall specify—

   (a) the particular use or uses of the pemises which the certificate covers; and
   (b) the means of escape in case of fire with which the premises are provided; and
   (c) the means (other than means for fighting fire) with which the relevant building (*c*) is provided for securing that the means of escape with which the premises are provided can be safely and effectively used at all material times; and
   (d) the type, number and location of the means for fighting fire (whether in the premises or affecting the means of escape) with which the relevant building is provided; and
   (e) the type, number and location of the means with which the relevant building is provided for giving to persons in the premises warning in case of fire,

and may, where appropriate, do so by means of or by reference to a plan.

   (2) A fire certificate (*a*) issued with respect to any premises (*b*) may impose such requirements as the fire authority (*d*) consider appropriate in the circumstances—

   (a) for securing that the means of escape in case of fire with which the premises are provided are properly maintained (*e*) and kept free from obstruction (*f*);
   (b) for securing that the means with which the relevant building is provided as mentioned in subsection (1)(c) to (e) above are properly maintained;
   (c) for securing that persons employed to work (*g*) in the premises receive appropriate instruction or training in what to do in case of fire, and that records are kept of instruction or training given for that purpose;
   (d) for limiting the number of persons who may be in the premises at any one time; and
   (e) as to other precautions to be observed in the relevant building in relation to the risk, in case of fire, to persons in the premises.

   (3) Any requirements imposed by virtue of subsection (2) above by a fire certificate (*a*) issued with respect to any premises (*b*)—

   (a) may, in so far as they apply to the premises, be framed either so as to apply to the whole of the premises or so as to apply to one or more parts of them; and
   (b) where the premises do not constitute the whole of the relevant building (*c*) may (where appropriate) be framed either so as to apply to the whole of the rest of that building or so as to apply to one or more parts of the rest of it,

and different requirements may, in either case, be imposed in relation to different parts; and a fire certificate covering more than one use of the premises to which it relates may by virtue of subsection (2) above impose different requirements in relation to different uses of the premises or any part of the premises.

(4) For the purposes of this Act a fire certificate *(a)* issued with respect to any premises *(b)* shall be treated as requiring every matter specified in the certificate in accordance with subsection (1)(b), (c), (d) or (e) above to be kept in accordance with its specifications in the certificate; and references in this Act to requirements imposed by a fire certificate shall be construed accordingly.

(5) In so far as a requirement imposed by a fire certificate *(a)* issued with respect to any premises *(b)* requires anything to be done or not to be done to or in relation to any part of the relevant building *(c)*, the person responsible for any contravention *(h)* thereof shall (subject to any provisions included in the certificate in pursuance of this subsection) be the occupier *(i)* of that part; but if as regards any such requirement, in so far as it requires anything to be done or not to be done to or in relation to any part of the relevant building the fire authority *(d)* consider it appropriate in the circumstances to provide that some other person or persons shall be responsible for any contravention thereof instead of, or in addition to, the occupier of that part, they may so provide in the certificate and, if the certificate covers more than one use of the premises, may in pursuance of this subsection make different provision therein in relation to different uses of the premises.

(6) Subject to subsection (7) below, a fire authority *(d)*—

(a) shall not issue a fire certificate *(a)* which would have the effect of making a person responsible under or by virtue of subsection (5) above for contraventions of a requirement imposed by the certificate, or make in a fire certificate any amendment which would have that effect, unless (in either case) they have previously consulted the person in question about his proposed responsibility for contraventions *(h)* of the requirement; and,

(b) shall not amend a fire certificate so as to vary any requirement imposed by it, in a case where any person already responsible under or by virtue of subsection (5) above for contraventions of that requirement is to continue to be so responsible when the variation takes effect, unless they have previously consulted that person about the proposed variation,

but, without prejudice to any right of appeal conferred by section 9 of this Act, a fire certificate shall not be invalidated by any failure of the fire authority by whom it is issued to comply with the requirements of this subsection.

(7) Where a fire authority *(d)* propose to issue a new fire certificate *(a)* with respect to any premises *(b)* as an alternative to amending an existing fire certificate, and the new certificate would have the effect of reimposing without variation a requirement imposed by the existing certificate, and of making any person who is responsible under or by virtue of subsection (5) above for contraventions *(h)* of the existing requirement continue to be so responsible for contraventions of it as reimposed, the authority shall not be required under subsection (6) above to consult that person by reason only of that fact.

(8) A fire certificate *(a)* issued with respect to any premises *(b)* other than premises in relation to which a notice under section 3 of this Act is in force shall

be sent to the occupier of the premises and shall be kept in the premises so long as it is in force.

(9) A fire certificate *(a)* issued with respect to any premises *(b)* in relation to which a notice under section 3 of this Act is in force shall be sent to the notified person and, if that person is not the occupier of the premises, a copy of the certificate shall be sent to the occupier of the premises and so long as the certificate is in force—

    (a) the certificate shall be kept in the relevant building *(c)*; and

    (b) where a copy of the certificate is by this subsection required to be sent to the occupier of the premises, the copy shall be kept in the premises.

General note. This section is modified by Sch. 2, Part II in its application to factory, office, railway and shop premises, as defined by Sch. 2, Part I, in respect of which a fire certificate is required and which are held under a lease or an agreement for a lease or under a licence and consist of a part of a building all parts of which are in the same ownership or consist of part of a building in which different parts are owned by different persons. As it has effect in relation to factory premises, s. 6(1) is modified by Sch. 2, Part II by the insertion of the following paragraph—

    "*(f)* particulars as to any explosive or highly flammable materials which may be stored in or used in the premises".

(a) **Fire certificate.** See note *(b)* to s. 1; see also general note.

(b) **Premises.** For definition, see s. 43(1).

(c) **Relevant building; building.** For definition, see s. 43(1).

(d) **Fire authority.** For definition, see s. 43(1).

(e) **Properly maintained.** See INTRODUCTORY NOTE 10.

(f) **Obstruction.** See INTRODUCTORY NOTE 12.

(g) **Work.** For definition, see s. 43(1).

(h) **Contravention.** For definition, see s. 43(1).

(i) **Occupier.** A person may be an occupier for the purposes of the Act without being resident upon the premises (*East Sussex County Council v Brown*, (22 February 1988, unreported), DC).

---

7. Offences in relation to foregoing provisions.—(1) Subject to subsection (3) below and section 9(3) of this Act, if any premises *(a)* are at any time put to a designated use *(b)*, being premises such that, where they are put to that use, a fire certificate *(c)* is by virtue of section 1 of this Act required in respect of them, then, if no fire certificate covering that use is at that time in force in respect of the premises, the occupier of the premises shall be guilty of an offence *(e)*.

(2) Subject to subsection (3) below and section 9(3) of this Act, if any premises *(a)* are used as a dwelling at any time while section 3 of this Act applies to them and a notice under that section relating to them is in force, then, if no fire certificate *(c)* covering that use is at that time in force in respect of the premises, the notified person shall, unless he proves that at that time he no longer occupied the specified position, be guilty of an offence *(d)*.

(3) A person shall not be guilty of an offence *(d)* under subsection (1) or (2) above by reason of any premises *(a)* being put to a designated use *(b)* or used as a

dwelling at a time after an application for a fire certificate *(c)* with respect to them covering that use has been duly made and before the certificate is granted or refused.

(3A) If, pending the disposal of an application for a fire certificate *(c)* with respect to any premises *(a)* the premises are put to a designated use *(b)*, then, if any requirement imposed by section 5(2)(A) of this Act is contravened by reason of anything done or not done to or in relation to any part of the relevant building *(f)*, the occupier shall be guilty of an offence.

(4) Subject to section 9(4) and (5) of this Act, if, while a fire certificate *(c)* is in force in respect of any premises *(a)* any requirement imposed thereby is contravened by reason of anything done or not done to or in relation to any part of the relevant building *(e)*, every person who under or by virtue of section 6(5) of this Act is responsible for that contravention *(f)* shall be guilty of an offence *(d)*:

Provided that a person other than the occupier of the premises shall not be convicted of an offence under this subsection unless it is proved that his responsibility for contraventions of the requirement in question had been made known to him before the occurrence of the contravention in respect of which he is charged.

(5) A person guilty of an offence *(a)* under subsection (1), (2) or (4) above shall be liable—

(a) on summary conviction, to a fine not exceeding £2,000,
(b) on conviction on indictment, to a fine or to imprisonment for a term not exceeding two years, or both.

(5A) A person guilty of an offence under subsection (3A) above shall be liable, on summary conviction, to a fine not exceeding level 5 on the standard scale.

(6) In the event of a contravention *(f)* of subsection (8) of section 6 of this Act in the case of a fire certificate *(c)* required by that subsection to be kept in any premises *(a)* or of a contravention of subsection (9) of that section in the case of a copy of a fire certificate required by subsection (9)(b) of that section to be kept in any premises the occupier of the premises shall be guilty of an offence *(d)* and liable on summary conviction to a fine not exceeding level 3 on the standard scale.

(7) If, while there is in force a notice under section 3 of this Act relating to any premises *(a)* there occurs a contravention *(f)* of subsection (9) of section 6 of this Act in the case of a fire certificate *(c)* issued with respect to those premises and required by paragraph (a) of that subsection to be kept in the relevant building *(e)* the notified person shall, unless he proves that at the material time he no longer occupied the specified position, be guilty of an offence *(d)* and liable on summary conviction to a fine not exceeding level 3 on the standard scale.

General note. This section is modified by Sch. 2, Part II in its application to factory, office, railway and shop premises, as defined by Sch. 2, Part I, in respect of which a fire certificate is required and which are held under a lease or an agreement for a lease or under a licence and consist of a part of a building all parts of which are in the same ownership or consist of part of a building in which different parts are owned by different persons. The expressions in sub-s. (1) so modified do not include the Crown.

(a) **Premises.** For definition, see s. 43(1).

(b) **Designated use.** For definition, see s. 43(1).

(c) **Fire certificate.** See note *(b)* to s. 1, but with reference to sub-s. (6), see also the general note.

(d) **Offence.** For penalties, see sub-s. (5). As to offences generally, see ss. 22 *et seq.*

(e) **Relevant building.** For definition, see s. 43(1).

(f) **Contravention.** This includes failure to comply (s. 43(1)).

---

8.   Change of conditions affecting adequacy of certain matters specified in fire certificate, etc.—(1) So long as a fire certificate *(a)* is in force with respect to any premises *(b)*, the fire authority *(c)* may cause any part of the relevant building *(d)* to be inspected at any reasonable time for the purpose of ascertaining whether there has been a change of conditions by reason of which any of the matters mentioned in section 6(1)(b) to (e) of this Act have become inadequate in relation to any use of the premises covered by the certificate; but where a building or part of a building is used as a dwelling or consists of premises of any other description prescribed for the purposes of this subsection, an inspection of the building or, as the case may be, of such a part shall not be made under this subsection as of right unless twenty-four hours' notice has been given to the occupier of the building, or, as the case may be, of the part in question.

For the purposes of this subsection a description of premises may be framed in any of the ways mentioned in section 1(4) of this Act.

(2) If, while a fire certificate *(a)* is in force with respect to any premises *(b)*—

(a) it is proposed to make a material extension of, or material structural alteration to, the premises; or

(b) it is proposed to make a material alteration in the internal arrangement of the premises or in the furniture or equipment with which the premises are provided; or

(c) the occupier of the premises proposes to begin to keep explosive or highly flammable materials of any prescribed kind anywhere under, in or on the relevant building in a quantity or aggregate quantity greater than the quantity prescribed *(e)* for the purposes of this paragraph as the maximum in relation to materials of that kind,

the occupier shall, before the carrying out of the proposals is begun, give notice of the proposals to the fire authority *(c)*; and if the carrying out of the proposals is begun without such notice having been given, the occupier shall be guilty of an offence.

(3) If, while a fire certificate *(a)* is in force with respect to any premises *(b)* not constituting the whole of the relevant building *(d)*, any person who as occupier of any other part of that building is under section 6(5) of this Act responsible for contraventions *(g)* of any requirement imposed by the certificate proposes to begin to keep explosive or highly flammable materials of any prescribed *(e)* kind anywhere under, in or on that building in a quantity or aggregate quantity greater than the quantity prescribed for the purposes of this subsection as the maximum in relation to materials of that kind, that person shall, before the

carrying out of the proposals is begun, give notice of the proposals to the fire authority *(c)*; and if the carrying out of the proposals is begun without such notice having been given, that person shall be guilty of an offence *(f)*.

(4) If the fire authority *(c)* are satisfied, as regards any premises *(b)* with respect to which a notice under subsection (2) above has been given to them, then the carrying out of the proposals notified would result in any of the matters mentioned in section 6(1)(b) to (e) of this Act becoming inadequate in relation to any use of the premises covered by the relevant fire certificate *(a)*, they may by notice served on the occupier within two months from the receipt of the notice under subsection (2)—

(a) inform the occupier of the steps which would have to be taken in relation to the relevant building *(d)* (whether by way of making alterations to any part of the relevant building or otherwise) to prevent the matters in question from becoming in their opinion inadequate in relation to that use in the event of the proposals being carried out; and

(b) give him such directions, as the fire authority consider appropriate for securing, as regards any of the proposals which may be specified in the directions, that that proposal, or any stage of it may be so specified, is not carried out until such of those steps as may be so specified in relation to that proposal or stage have been taken (whether by him or otherwise),

and if those steps are duly taken in connection with the carrying out of the proposals, the fire authority shall amend the fire certificate or issue a new one.

(5) If the fire authority *(c)* are satisfied (whether as a result of an inspection made under subsection (1) above or otherwise) that, as regards any premises *(b)* with respect to which a fire certificate *(a)* is in force, any of the matters mentioned in section 6(1)(b) to (e) of this Act has, in consequence of a change of conditions, become inadequate in relation to any use of the premises covered by the certificate, they may by notice served on the occupier—

(a) inform him of that fact and of the steps which would have to be taken in relation to the relevant building *(d)* (whether by way of making alterations to any part of the relevant building or otherwise) to make the matter in question adequate in their opinion in relation to that use; and

(b) notify him that if those steps are not taken (whether by him or otherwise) within such period as may be specified in the notice, the fire certificate may be cancelled,

and if those steps are duly taken, the fire authority shall, if necessary, amend the fire certificate or issue a new one.

(6) If the fire authority *(c)* considers (whether as a result of an inspection made under subsection (1) above or otherwise) that, as regards any premises *(b)* with respect to which a fire certificate *(a)* is in force, it would, in consequence of a change of conditions or of the coming into force of any regulations made under section 12 of this Act, be appropriate to amend the certificate for any of the following purposes, that is to say—

(a) to vary or revoke any requirement which the certificate imposes by virtue of section 6(2) of this Act; or

(b) to add to the requirements which the certificate so imposes; or

(c) to alter the effect of the certificate as to the person or persons responsible under or by virtue of section 6(5) of this Act for contraventions *(g)* of any requirement imposed (whether by virtue of section 6(2) or otherwise) by the certificate,

the authority may, subject to section 6(6) of this Act, make such amendments in the certificate as they think appropriate for that purpose or issue a new certificate embodying those amendments.

(7) If any person contravenes *(g)* a direction given to him in pursuance of subsection (4)(b) above, he shall be guilty of an offence *(f)*; and the fire authority *(c)* may cancel the fire certificate *(a)* issued with respect to any premises *(b)* if they are satisfied that there has been such a contravention as aforesaid by the occupier, whether or not proceedings are brought in respect of the contravention.

(8) A person guilty of an offence *(f)* under subsection (2), (3) or (7) above shall be liable—

(a) on summary conviction, to a fine not exceeding £2,000;
(b) on conviction on indictment, to a fine or to imprisonment for a term not exceeding two years, or both.

(9) Where a notice has been served under subsection (5) above in connection with any premises *(b)* and the steps mentioned in it in accordance with paragraph (a) of that subsection are not taken within the period specified in the notice in accordance with paragraph (b) of that subsection or such longer period as may be allowed by the fire authority *(c)* or by any order made by a court on, or in proceedings arising out of, an appeal under section 9 of this Act against the notice, the fire authority may cancel the fire certificate *(a)* in force with respect to the premises or, if it covers two or more uses of the premises, may either cancel it or amend it so as to remove from those uses one or more of them (and in that case may make in it all such amendments as they think appropriate in connection with the removal of the use or uses in question).

(10) Where there is in force a notice under section 3*(h)* of this Act relating to any premises *(b)*, the foregoing provisions of this section shall apply to them subject to the following modifications, that it so say—

(a) in subsection (2), the first reference to the occupier shall be read as a reference to the occupier or the notified person, the second reference to the occupier shall be read as a reference to the occupier or the notified person, as the case may be, and the third reference to the occupier shall be read as a reference to the person required by that subsection to give notice of the proposals;
(b) in subsections (4) and (7), references to the occupier shall, if the notice under subsection (2) was given by the notified person, be read as references to that person; and
(c) in subsection (5), references to the occupier shall be read as references to the notified person.

(11) Where the fire authority *(c)* are satisfied, as regards any premises *(b)* with respect to which a notice under subsection (2) above has been given to them, that the carrying out of the proposals notified would not result in any of the matters mentioned in section 6(1)(b) to (e) of this Act becoming inadequate, they shall, on production of the fire certificate *(a)* in force with respect to the premises, cause to be attached to it a copy of the notice together with a written statement that they are so satisfied.

(12) Where in pursuance of this section the fire authority *(c)* amend a fire certificate *(a)* of which by virtue of section 6(9) of this Act a copy is required to be kept in the premises *(b)* to which the certificate relates, they shall cause the copy to be similarly amended; and where in pursuance of subsection (11) above the fire authority cause any document to be attached to such a fire certificate, they shall cause the like document to be attached to the copy of the certificate required to be kept in the premises to which the certificate relates.

General note. This section is modified by Sch. 2, Part II in its application to factory, office, railway and shop premises, as defined by Sch. 2, Part I, in respect of which a fire certificate is required and which are held under a lease or an agreement for a lease or under a licence and consist of a part of a building all parts of which are in the same ownership or consist of part of a building in which different parts are owned by different persons. The expressions so modified in sub-s. (7) and of the word "occupier" in the third place where it occurs in sub-s. (2) do not include the Crown. In relation to factory premises, this section is further modified by Sch. 2, Part II as follows:—
For paragraph (c) of sub-s. (2) is substituted the following paragraph—
"(c) the occupier of the premises proposes to begin to store or use explosive or highly flammable materials in the premises or materially to increase the extent of such storage or use".
In sub-s. (3) for the words from "keep explosive" to "that kind" shall be substituted the words "store or use explosive or highly flammable materials in the premises or materially to increase the extent of such storage or use".

(a) **Fire certificate.** See note *(b)* to s. 1.

(b) **Premises.** For definition, see s. 43(1).

(c) **Fire authority.** For definition, see s. 43(1).

(d) **Building; relevant building.** For definition, see s. 43(1).

(e) **Prescribed.** For definition, see s. 43(1).

(f) **Offence.** For penalties, see sub-s. (8). For offences generally, see ss. 22–27.

(g) **Contravention.** This includes failure to comply (s. 43(1)).

(h) **Notice under s. 3.** This section applies only to premises used or to be used as a dwelling and is not printed in this book.

8A.   Change of conditions affecting premises for which exemption has been granted.—(1) If, during the currency of an exemption granted under section 5A of this Act for any premises *(a)* it is intended to carry out in relation to those premises any proposals to which this section applies, the occupier shall, before the carrying out of the proposals is begun, given notice of the proposals to the fire authority *(b)*; and if the carrying out of the proposals is begun without such notice having been given, the occupier shall be guilty of an offence.

(2) This section applies to the following proposals, namely, any proposals—

(a) to make—
   (i) an extension of, or structural alteration to, the premises *(a)* which would affect the means of escape from the premises; or
   (ii) an alteration in the internal arrangement of the premises, or in the furniture or equipment with which the premises are provided, which would affect the means of escape from the premises; or

(b) on the part of the occupier, to begin to keep explosive or highly flammable materials of any prescribed kind anywhere under, in or on the building *(c)* which constitutes or comprises the premises *(a)* in a quantity or aggregate quantity greater than the quantity prescribed for the purposes of this paragraph as the maximum in relation to materials of that kind; or

(c) in a case where the notice of exemption under section 5A of this Act includes a statement under subsection (8) of that section, to make such a use of the premises *(a)* as will involve there being in the premises at any one time a greater number of persons in relation to whom the statement applies than is specified or treated as specified in the statement.

(3) A person guilty of an offence under subsection (1) above shall be liable—

(a) on summary conviction, to a fine not exceeding the statutory maximum;
(b) on conviction on indictment, to a fine or to imprisonment for a term not exceeding two years, or both.

General note. This section is modified by Sch. 2, Part II in its application to factory, office, railway and shop premises, as defined by Sch. 2, Part I, in respect of which a fire certificate is required and which are held under a lease or an agreement for a lease or under a licence and consist of a part of a building all parts of which are in the same ownership or consist of part of a building in which different parts are owned by different persons.

The modification so made of the word "occupier" in the second place where it occurs in sub-s. (1) does not include the Crown. As to the meaning of "occupier", see note *(i)* to s. 6. In relation to factory premises this section is further modified by Sch. 2, Part II as follows:—

for para. (b) of sub-s. (2) there is substituted—

"(b) on the part of the occupier of the premises to begin to store or use explosive or highly inflammable materials in the premises or materially to increase the extent of such storage or use".

(a) Premises. For definition, see s. 43(1).

(b) Fire authority. For definition, see s. 43(1).

(c) Building. For definition, see s. 43(1).

8B.   Charges for issue or amendment of fire certificates.—(1) Where a fire authority *(a)*—

(a) issue a fire certificate *(b)* under section 5 of this Act, or
(b) except in a case falling within subsection (2) below, amend a fire certificate or, as an alternative to amendment, issue a new fire certificate, under section 8 of this Act,

the applicant for the certificate or, as the case may be, the occupier of the premises *(c)* to which the amended or new certificate relates shall pay to the authority such fee as the authority determine.

(2) No fee shall be chargeable for the amendment of a fire certificate *(b)*, or issue of a new fire certificate embodying amendments, under section 8(6) of

this Act in a case where the amendment or amendments is or are made in consequence of the coming into force of regulations under section 12 of this Act.

(3) A fee charged by a fire authority *(a)* under this section in connection with the issue of a fire certificate *(b)* or the amendment of a, or issue of a new, fire certificate shall not exceed an amount which represents the cost to the authority of the work reasonably done by them for the purposes of the issue of the certificate or, as the case may be, the amendment of the certificate or issue of the new certificate, other than the cost of any inspection of the premises.

General note. This section is modified by Sch. 2, Part II in its application to factory, office, railway and shop premises, as defined by Sch. 2, Part I, in respect of which a fire certificate is required and which are held under a lease or an agreement for a lease or under a licence and consist of a part of a building all parts of which are in the same ownership or consist of part of a building in which different parts are owned by different persons.

(a) Fire authority. For definition, see s. 43(1).

(b) Fire certificate. For definition, see s. 43(1).

(c) Premises. For definition, see s. 43(1). As to "occupier", see note *(i)* to s. 6.

---

9. Right of appeal as regards matters arising out of ss. 5 to 8.—(1) A person who is aggrieved *(a)*—

(a) by anything mentioned in a notice *(b)* served under section 5(4) of this Act as a step which would have to be taken as a condition of the issue of a fire certificate *(c)* with respect to any premises *(d)*, or by the period allowed by such a notice for the taking of any steps mentioned in it; or

(b) by the refusal of the fire authority *(e)* to issue a fire certificate with respect to any premises; or

(c) by the inclusion of anything in, or the omission of anything from, a fire certificate issued with respect to any premises by the fire authority; or

(d) by the refusal of the fire authority to cancel or to amend a fire certificate issued with respect to any premises; or

(e) by any direction given in pursuance of section 8(4)(b) of this Act; or

(f) by anything mentioned in a notice served under section 8(5) of this Act with respect to any premises as a step which must be taken if the fire authority are not to become entitled to cancel the fire certificate relating to the premises, or by the period allowed by such a notice for the taking of any steps mentioned in it; or

(g) by the amendment or cancellation in pursuance of section 8(6), (7) or (9) of this Act of a fire certificate issued with respect to any premises,

may, within twenty-one days from the relevant date *(f)*, appeal to the court *(g)*; and on any such appeal the court may make such order as it thinks fit.

(2) In this section "the relevant date" means—

(a) in relation to a person aggrieved *(a)* by any such refusal, direction, cancellation or amendment as is mentioned in subsection (1) above or by any matter mentioned in paragraph (a) or (f) of that subsection, the date on which he was first served by the fire authority *(e)* with notice of the refusal, direction, cancellation, amendment or matter in question;

(b)   in relation to a person aggrieved by the inclusion of anything in, or the omission of anything from, a fire certificate *(c)* issued with respect to any premises *(d)*, the date on which the inclusion or omission was first made known to him,

and for the purposes of paragraph (b) above a person who is served with a fire certificate or a copy of, or of any part of, a fire certificate shall be taken to have had what the certificate or that part of it does and does not contain made known to him at the time of the service on him of the certificate or copy.

(3)   Where an appeal is brought under this section against the refusal of the fire authority *(e)* to issue a fire certificate *(c)* with respect to any premises *(d)* or the cancellation or amendment in pursuance of section 8(7) or (9) of this Act of a fire certificate issued with respect to any premises, a person shall not be guilty of any offence under section 7(1) or (2) of this Act by reason of the premises in question being put to a designated use *(h)* or used as a dwelling at a time between the relevant date and the final determination of the appeal.

(4)   Where an appeal is brought under this section against the inclusion in a fire certificate *(c)* of anything which has the effect of making the certificate impose a requirement, a person shall not be guilty of an offence under section 7(4) of this Act by reason of a contravention *(i)* of that requirement which occurs at a time between the relevant date and the final determination of the appeal.

(5)   Where an appeal is brought under this section against—

(a)   the inclusion in a fire certificate *(c)* in pursuance of subsection (5) of section 6 of this Act, of a provision making any person responsible for contraventions *(i)* of any requirement imposed by the certificate; or

(b)   the omission from a fire certificate of a provision which, if included in pursuance of that subsection, would prevent any person from being, as the occupier of any premises *(d)* responsible under that subsection for contraventions of any requirement imposed by the certificate,

that person shall not be guilty of an offence under section 7(4) of this Act by reason of a contravention of that requirement which occurs at a time between the relevant date and the final determination of the appeal.

General note. This section is modified by Sch. 2, Part II in its application to factory, office, railway and shop premises, as defined by Sch. 2, Part I, in respect of which a fire certificate is required and which are held under a lease or an agreement for a lease or under a licence and consist of a part of a building all parts of which are in the same ownership or consist of part of a building in which different parts are owned by different persons.

(a) Person . . . aggrieved. See INTRODUCTORY NOTE 14.

(b) Notice. For definition, see s. 43(1).

(c) Fire certificate. See note *(b)* to s. 1.

(d) Premises. For definition, see s. 43(1).

(e) Fire authority. For definition, see s. 43(1).

(f) Relevant date. See sub-s. (2).

(g) *The court.* For definition, see s. 43(1).

(h) *Designated use.* For definition, see s. 43(1).

(i) *Contravention.* For definition, see s. 43(1).

9A. Duty as to means of escape and for fighting fire.—(1) All premises (a) to which this section applies shall be provided with—

(a) such means of escape in case of fire, and
(b) such means for fighting fire,

as may reasonably be required in the circumstances of the case.

(2) The premises (a) to which this section applies are premises which are exempt from the requirement for a fire certificate (b) by virtue of—

(a) a provision made in an order under section 1 of this Act by virtue of subsection (3) of that section, or
(b) the grant of exemption by a fire authority (c) under section 5A of this Act.

(3) In the event of a contravention of the duty imposed by subsection (1) above the occupier of the premises (a) shall, except as provided in subsection (4) below, be guilty of an offence and liable on summary conviction to a fine not exceeding level 5 on the standard scale.

(4) A person is not guilty of an offence under this section in respect of any contravention of the duty imposed by subsection (1) above which is the subject of an improvement notice under section 9D of this Act.

General note. This section is modified by Sch. 2, Part II in its application to factory, office, railway and shop premises, as defined by Sch. 2, Part I, in respect of which a fire certificate is required and which are held under a lease or an agreement for a lease or under a licence and consist of a part of a building all parts of which are in the same ownership or consist of part of a building in which different parts are owned by different persons. The modifications so made to sub-s. (3) do not include the Crown.

(a) *Premises.* For definition, see s. 43(1).

(b) *Fire certificate.* For definition, see s. 43(1).

(c) *Fire authority.* For definition, see s. 43(1).

9B. Codes of practice as to means of escape and for fighting fire.—(1) The Secretary of State may from time to time, after consultation with such persons or bodies of persons as appear to him requisite—

(a) prepare and issue codes of practice for the purpose of providing practical guidance on how to comply with the duty imposed by section 9A of this Act; and
(b) revise any such code by revoking, varying, amending or adding to the provisions of the code.

(2) A code prepared in pursuance of this section and any alterations proposed to be made on a revision of such a code shall be laid before both Houses

of Parliament, and the Secretary of State shall not issue the code or revised code, as the case may be, until after the end of the period of 40 days beginning with the day on which the code or the proposed alterations were so laid.

(3) If, within the period mentioned in subsection (2) above, either House resolves that the code be not issued or the proposed alterations be not made, as the case may be, the Secretary of State shall not issue the code or revised code (but without prejudice to his power under that subsection to lay further codes or proposed alterations before Parliament).

(4) For the purposes of subsection (2) above—

    (a) where the code or proposed alterations are not laid before both Houses of Parliament on the same day, the later day shall be taken to be the day on which the code or the proposed alterations, as the case may be, were laid before both Houses, and

    (b) in reckoning any period of 40 days, no account shall be taken of any time during which Parliament is dissolved or prorogued or during which both Houses are adjourned for more than four days.

(5) In this Act references to a code of practice under this section are references to such a code as it has effect for the time being, with any revisions, under this section.

9C. Legal effect of codes of practice.—(1) A failure on the part of a person to observe any provision of a code of practice under section 9B of this Act shall not in itself render him liable to any criminal or civil proceedings.

(2) If, in any proceedings whether civil or criminal under this Act, it is alleged that there has been a contravention on the part of any person of the duty imposed by section 9A of this Act—

    (a) a failure to observe a provision of a code of practice under section 9B of this Act may be relied on as tending to establish liability, and

    (b) compliance with such a code may be relied on as tending to negative liability.

General note. For the legal effect of codes of practice, see the general note to s. 17 of the Health and Safety at Work etc. Act 1974.

9D. Improvement notices.—(1) Where a fire authority *(a)* are of the opinion that the duty imposed by section 9A of this Act has been contravened in respect of any premises *(b)* to which that section applies, they may serve on the occupier of the premises a notice (in this Act referred to as "an improvement notice") which—

    (a) states they are of that opinion;

    (b) specifies, by reference to a code of practice under section 9B of this Act if they think fit, what steps they consider are necessary to remedy that contravention; and

   (c) requires the occupier to take steps to remedy that contravention within such period (ending not earlier than the period within which an appeal against the improvement notice can be brought under section 9E of this Act) as may be specified in the notice.

(2) Where an improvement notice has been served under subsection (1) above—

   (a) the fire authority *(a)* may withdraw that notice at any time before the end of the period specified in the notice; and

   (b) if an appeal against the improvement notice is not pending, the fire authority may extend or further extend the period specified in the notice.

(3) Where any premises *(b)* are premises to which section 9A of this Act applies and—

   (a) the building *(c)* which constitutes or comprises the premises is a building to which at the time of its erection building regulations imposing requirements as to means of escape in case of fire applied; and

   (b) in connection with the erection of that building plans were, in accordance with building regulations, deposited with a local authority,

the fire authority *(a)* shall not in pursuance of subsection (1) above serve an improvement notice requiring structural or other alterations relating to the means of escape from the premises *(b)* unless the requirements of subsection (4) below are satisfied in relation to those premises.

(4) The requirements of this subsection are satisfied in relation to such premises *(b)* as are mentioned in subsection (3) above if—

   (a) regulations are in force under section 12 of this Act applying to the premises in relation to any use of them as respects which exemption under section 5A of this Act has been granted, being regulations which impose requirements as to means of escape in case of fire, and the fire authority *(a)* are satisified that alterations to the building which constitutes or comprises the premises are necessary to bring the premises into compliance with the regulations in respect of those requirements; or

   (b) the fire authority are satisfied that the means of escape in case of fire with which the premises are provided are inadequate in relation to any such use of the premises by reason of matters or circumstances of which particulars were not required by or under the building regulations to be supplied to the local authority in connection with the deposit of plans.

(5) In this section "structural or other alterations relating to means of escape from the premises", in relation to any such premises as are mentioned in this section, means structural or other alterations, directly connected with the provision of the premises *(b)* with adequate means of escape in case of fire.

(6) Subsections (3) to (5) above extend to England and Wales only.

General note. This section is modified by Sch. 2, Part II in its application to factory, office, railway and shop premises, as defined by Sch. 2, Part I, in respect of which a fire certificate is required and which are held under a lease or an agreement for a lease or under a licence and consist of a part of a building all parts of which are in the same ownership or consist of part of a building in which different parts are owned by different persons.

   (a) Fire authority. For definition, see s. 43(1).

   (b) Premises. For definition, see s. 43(1).

   (c) Building. For definition, see s. 43(1). As to the meaning of "occupier", see note *(i)* to s. 6.

9E.   Rights of appeal against improvement notices.—(1) A person on whom an improvement notice is served may, within twenty-one days from the date on which the improvement notice is served, appeal to the court.

   (2) On an appeal under this section, the court may either cancel or affirm the notice, and, if it affirms it, may do so either in its original form or with such modifications as the court may in the circumstances think fit.

   (3) Where an appeal is brought under this section against an improvement notice, the bringing of the appeal shall have the effect of suspending the operation of the notice until the appeal is finally disposed of or, if the appeal is withdrawn, until the withdrawal of the appeal.

9F.   Provisions as to offences.—(1) It is an offence for a person to contravene any requirement imposed by an improvement notice.

   (2) Any person guilty of an offence under subsection (1) above shall be liable—

     (a) on summary conviction, to a fine not exceeding the statutory maximum;

     (b) on conviction on indictment, to a fine, or imprisonment for a term not exceeding two years, or both.

Premises involving excessive risk to persons in case of fire

10.   Special procedure in case of serious risk: prohibition notices.—(1) This section applies to—

     (a) any premises *(a)* which are being or are proposed to be put to a use (whether designated or not) which falls within at least one of the classes of use mentioned in section 1(2) of this Act, other than premises of the description given in section 2 of this Act; and

     (b) any premises to which section 3 of this Act for the time being applies.

   (2) If as regards any premises *(a)* to which this section applies the fire authority *(b)* are of opinion that use of the premises involves or will involve a risk to persons on the premises in case of fire so serious that use of the premises ought to be prohibited or restricted, the authority may serve on the occupier *(c)* of the premises a notice (in this Act referred to as "a prohibition notice").

   (3) The matters relevant to the assessment by the fire authority *(b)*, for the purposes of subsection (2) above, of the risk to persons in case of fire include anything affecting their escape from the premises *(a)* in that event.

(4) A prohibition notice shall—

(a) state that the fire authority *(b)* are of the opinion referred to in subsection (2) above;

(b) specify the matters which in their opinion give or, as the case may be, will give rise to that risk; and

(c) direct that the use to which the prohibition notice *(d)* relates is prohibited or restricted to such extent as may be specified in the notice until the specified matters have been remedied.

(5) A prohibition notice *(d)* may include directions as to the steps which will have to be taken to remedy the matters specified in the notice.

(6) A prohibition or restriction contained in a prohibition notice *(d)* in pursuance of subsection (4) (c) above shall take effect immediately it is served if the authority are of the opinion, and so state in the notice, that the risk of serious personal injury is or, as the case may be, will be imminent, and in any other case shall take effect at the end of a period specified in the prohibition notice.

(7) Where a prohibition notice *(d)* has been served under subsection (2) above the fire authority may withdraw the notice at any time.

(a) Premises. For definition, see s. 43(1).

(b) Fire authority. For definition, see s. 43(1).

(c) Occupier. As to the meaning of "occupier", see note *(i)* to s. 6.

(d) Prohibition notice. For definition, see sub-s. (2).

10A.   Rights of appeal against prohibition notices.—(1) A person on whom a prohibition notice *(a)* is served may, within twenty-one days from the date on which the prohibition notice is served, appeal to the court.

(2) On an appeal under this section, the court may either cancel or affirm the notice, and, if it affirms it, may do so either in its original form or with such modifications as the court may in the circumstances think fit.

(3) Where an appeal is brought under this section against a prohibition notice *(a)*, the bringing of the appeal shall not have the effect of suspending the operation of the notice, unless, on the application of the appellant, the court so directs (and then only from the giving of the direction).

(a) Prohibition notice. For definition, see s. 43(1).

10B.   Provision as to offences.—(1) It shall be an offence for any person to contravene any prohibition or restriction imposed by a prohibition notice *(a)*.

(2) In any proceedings for an offence under subsection (1) above where the person charged is a person other than the person on whom the prohibition

notice *(a)* was served, it shall be a defence for that person to prove that he did not know and had no reason to believe the notice had been served.

(3) Any person guilty of an offence under subsection (1) above shall be liable—

(a) on summary conviction, to a fine not exceeding the statutory maximum;
(b) on conviction on indictment, to a fine, or imprisonment for a term not exceeding two years, or both.

(4) In section 43(1) of the principal Act (interpretation), after the definition of "prescribed" there shall be inserted the following definition:

"prohibition notice" has the meaning assigned to section 10(2) of this Act.

(a) **Prohibition notice.** For definition, see sub-s. (4) and s. 43(1).

Building and other regulations about fire precautions

11.   [*repealed*].

---

12.   Power of Secretary of State to make regulations about fire precautions.—
(1) In the case of any particular use of premises *(a)* which he has power to designate under section 1 of this Act the Secretary of State *(b)* may by regulations make provision as to the precautions which, as regards premises put to that use, or any specified class of such premises, are to be taken or observed in relation to the risk to persons in case of fire, but so that nothing in any regulations made under this section shall apply to premises of the description given in section 2 of this Act and nothing in this section shall confer on the Secretary of State power to make provision with respect to the taking or observation of special precautions in connection with the carrying on of any manufacturing process.

(2) The Secretary of State may by regulations make provision as to the precautions which are to be taken or observed in relation to the risk to persons in case of fire as regards premises *(a)* which, while section 3 of this Act applies to them and a notice under that section is in force in relation to them, are used as a dwelling, or any specified class of such premises.

(3) Without prejudice to the generality of the powers conferred on the Secretary of State by subsections (1) and (2) above, regulations made by him under this section may in particular, as regards any premises *(a)* to which they apply, impose requirements—

(a) as to the provision, maintenance and keeping free from obstruction of means of escape in case of fire;
(b) as to the provision and maintenance of means for securing that any means of escape can be safely and effectively used at all material times;
(c) as to the provision and maintenance of means for fighting fire and means for giving warning in case of fire;

(d) as to the internal construction of the premises and the materials used in that construction;

(e) for prohibiting altogether the presence or use in the premises of furniture *(c)* or equipment of any specified description, or prohibiting its presence or use unless specified standards or conditions are complied with;

(f) for securing that persons employed to work *(d)* in the premises receive appropriate instruction or training in what to do in case of fire;

(g) for securing that, in specified circumstances, specified numbers of attendants are stationed in specified parts of the premises, and

(h) as to the keeping of records of instruction or training given, or other things done, in pursuance of the regulations.

(4) Regulations under this section—

(a) may impose requirements on persons other than occupiers of premises *(a)* to which they apply; and

(b) may, as regards any of their provisions, make provision as to the person or persons who are to be responsible for any contravention *(e)* thereof; and

(c) may provide that if any specified provision of the regulations is contravened, the person or each of the persons who under the regulations is or are responsible for the contravention shall be guilty of an offence under this section.

(5) It shall be the duty of the Secretary of State, before making any regulations under this section, to consult with such persons or bodies of persons as appear to him requisite.

(6) A person guilty of an offence under this section by virtue of subsection (4) (c) above shall be liable—

(a) on summary conviction, to a fine not exceeding £2,000;

(b) on conviction on indictment, to a fine or to imprisonment for a term not exceeding two years, or both.

(7) While there are in force under this section any regulations applying to premises *(a)* put to a particular use, or to any specified class of such premises a fire authority *(f)*—

(a) in determining under subsection (3) of section 5 of this Act whether to issue a fire certificate *(g)* covering that use with respect to any premises to which the regulations apply, shall proceed on the footing that, as regards any matter mentioned in paragraphs (a) to (d) of that subsection about which provision is made in the regulations, no more can reasonably be required in the circumstances of the case than is required by the regulations; and

(b) shall not in any fire certificate covering that use issued with respect to any premises to which the regulations apply impose in pursuance of section 6(2) of this Act in relation to that use any requirement as to any matter about which provision is made in the regulations which is more onerous than the requirements of the regulations as to that matter.

(8) Where there are in force under this section any regulations applying to premises *(a)* put to a particular use, or to any specified class of such premises, and a fire certificate covering that use is in force with respect to any premises to which the regulations apply, then—

(a)   so long as the requirements as to any matter which are imposed by the fire certificate in relation to that use are complied with, no person shall be guilty of an offence under the regulations by reason of any contravention *(e)* of a requirement of the regulations as to that matter;

(b)   if as a result of an inspection made under section 8(1) of this Act it appears to the fire authority *(g)* that any of the matters mentioned in section 6(1)(b) to (e) of this Act is not in conformity with any provision made in the regulations about that matter, the authority shall by notice served on the occupier *(i)*—

    (i)   inform him of that fact and of the steps which would have to be taken in relation to the relevant building *(i)* (whether by way of making alterations to any part of the relevant building or otherwise) to bring the matter in question into conformity with that provision; and

    (ii)   notify him that if those steps are not taken (whether by himself or otherwise) within such period as may be specified in the notice, the fire certificate *(g)* may be cancelled,

and if those steps are duly taken, the fire authority shall, if necessary, amend the fire certificate or issue a new one.

(9)   Where there is in force a notice *(j)* under section 3 of this Act relating to any premises *(a)*, subsection 8(b) above shall apply to them subject to the modification that the first reference to the occupier shall be read as a reference to the occupier or the notified persons, and the other references to the occupier shall be read as references to the occupier or the notified person, as the case may be.

(10)   Sections 8(9) and 9 of this Act shall (with the necessary modifications) have effect in a case where a notice *(j)* is served under subsection (8)(b) above with respect to any premises *(a)* as they have effect in a case where a notice is served under section 8(5); and where in pursuance of this section the fire authority *(g)* amend a fire certificate *(i)* of which by virtue of section 6(9) of this Act a copy is required to be kept in the premises to which the certificate relates, they shall cause the copy to be similarly amended.

(11)   No regulations shall after the coming into operation of this subsection be made under section 4(2)(a) of the Cinemas Act 1985; but any regulations so made which are in force when this subsection comes into operation shall have effect as if made under this section, and may be amended or revoked accordingly.

(12)   [*repealed*].

General note. This section is modified by Sch. 2, Part II in its application to factory, office, railway and shop premises, as defined by Sch. 2, Part I, in respect of which a fire certificate is required and which are held under a lease or an agreement for a lease or under a licence and consist of a part of a building all parts of which are in the same ownership or consist of part of a building in which different parts are owned by different persons.

    (a) Premises. For definition, see s. 43(1).

    (b) Secretary of State. See note *(e)* to s. 1.

    (c) Furniture. For definition, see s. 43(1).

    (d) Work. For definition, see s. 43(1).

(e) **Contravention.** This includes failure to comply (s. 43(1)).

(f) **Fire authority.** For definition, see s. 43(1).

(g) **Fire certificate.** See note *(b)* to s. 1.

(h) **Occupier.** As to the meaning of "Occupier", see note *(i)* to s. 6.

(i) **Relevant building.** For definition, see s. 43(1).

(j) **Notice.** For definition, see s. 43(1).

---

13. Exercise of certain powers of fire authority in England or Wales where building regulations as to means of escape apply.—(1) Where an application is made for a fire certificate *(a)* with respect to any premises *(b)* and—

(a) the relevant building *(c)* is a building *(d)* to which at the time of its erection building regulations imposing requirements as to means of escape in case of fire applied; and

(b) in connection with the erection of that building plans were, in accordance with building regulations, deposited with a local authority *(e)*,

the fire authority *(f)* shall not in pursuance of section 5(4) of this Act make the issue of a certificate conditional on the making to the building of structural or other alterations relating to escape from the premises unless—

(i) there are in force under section 12 of this Act regulations applying to the premises in relation to any use of the premises specified in the application, being regulations which impose requirements as to means of escape in case of fire or means for securing that any means of escape can be safely and effectively used at all material times, and the fire authority are satisfied that alterations to the relevant building are necessary to bring the premises into compliance with the regulations in respect of those requirements; or

(ii) the fire authority are satisfied that the means of escape in case of fire with which the premises are provided or the means of the sort mentioned in section 5(3)(b) of this Act with which the relevant building is provided are inadequate in relation to any use of the premises so specified by reason of matters or circumstances of which particulars were not required by or under the building regulations to be supplied to the local authority in connection with the deposit of plans.

(2) Where an application is made for a fire certificate *(a)* with respect to any premises *(b)* in the circumstances described in subsection (1)(a) and (b) above and since the erection of the building *(d)* plans have, in accordance *(e)* in connection with any proposals relating to the building, subsection (1) above shall have effect in relation to that application as if in paragraph (ii) the reference to the deposit of plans included a reference to the deposit of plans in connection with those proposals.

(3) Where, while a fire certificate *(a)* is in force with respect to any premises *(b)*, the fire authority *(f)* receive notice *(g)* under subsection (2) of section 8 of this Act of any proposals falling within that subsection to which building regulations imposing requirements as to means of escape in case of fire apply, and in connection with those proposals plans have, in accordance with building regulations, been deposited with a local authority *(e)*, the fire authority *(f)* shall

not in pursuance of subsection (4) of that section make the carrying out of those proposals conditional on the making to the relevant building *(c)* of structural or other alterations relating to escape from the premises unless—

(a) there are in force under section 12 of this Act regulations applying to the premises in relation to any use of the premises covered by the certificate, being regulations which impose requirements such as are mentioned in subsection (1)(i) above, and the fire authority are satisfied that the carrying out of the proposals in compliance with the requirements of the building regulations will not of itself ensure that, when the proposals have been carried out, the premises will comply with the regulations under section 12 in respect of the requirements such as are mentioned in subsection (1)(i) above which the regulations under section 12 impose; or

(b) the fire authority are satisfied that, by reason of matters or circumstances of which particulars are not required by or under the building regulations to be supplied to the local authority in connection with the deposit of plans, the carrying out of the proposals in compliance with the requirements of the building regulations will not in itself ensure that, when the proposals have been carried out, the means of escape in case of fire with which the premises will then be provided and the means of the sort mentioned in section 5(3)(b) of this Act with which the relevant building will then be provided will be adequate in relation to every use of the premises covered by the certificate.

(4) In this section "structural or other alterations relating to escape from the premises", in relation to any such premises *(b)* as are mentioned in this section, means structural or other alterations directly connected with the provision of the premises with adequate means of escape in case of fire or the provision of the relevant building *(c)* with adequate means of the sort mentioned in section 5(3)(b) of this Act.

(5) [*Repealed and consolidated by the Building Act 1984, s. 133(2), Sch. 7*].

(6) This section does not extend to Scotland.

(a) *Fire certificate.* See note *(b)* to s. 1.

(b) *Premises.* For definition, see s. 43(1).

(c) *Relevant building.* For definition, see s. 43(1).

(d) *Building.* For definition, see s. 43(1).

(e) *Local authority.* For definition, see s. 43(1).

(f) *Fire authority.* For definition, see s. 43(1).

(g) *Notice.* For definition, see s. 43(1).

---

14. Exercise of certain powers of fire authority in Scotland where building standards regulations as to means of escape apply.—(1) Subject to subsection (2) below, where—

(a) building standards regulations imposing requirements as to means of escape in case of fire apply to any building *(a)*; or

(b) the sheriff, on an appeal to him under section 16 of the Building (Scotland) Act 1959—

    (i) against an order under section 10 of that Act requiring the execution of operations necessary to make a building conform to a provision of building standards regulations with respect to requirements of the means of escape in case of fire, or

    (ii) against an order under section 11 of that Act requiring the building to be made to conform to such a provision,

has varied the order by determining that such operations shall be executed as are necessary to make the building conform to a standard, or, as the case may be, that the building should conform to a different standard, and the fire authority *(b)* are satisfied that the building so conforms,

then the fire authority shall not, for the purposes of section 5, 8 or (in relation to premises to which section 9 applies) 9B(1) and (2) of this Act, specify any alterations in respect of that building to a standard higher than that of the said regulations or, as the case may be, than that determined by the sheriff.

(2) The restrictions imposed on the fire authority *(b)* by the foregoing subsection shall not apply where—

(a) there are in force under section 12 of this Act regulations applying to the building *(a)* in relation to any use of the building, being regulations which impose requirements as to means of escape from fire or means for securing that any means of escape can be safely and effectively used at all material times, and the fire authority *(b)* are satisfied that alterations to the building are necessary to bring the building into compliance with the regulations in respect of those requirements; or

(b) the fire authority are satisfied that the means of escape in case of fire with which the building is provided or the means of the sort mentioned in section 5(3)(b) of this Act with which the building is provided are inadequate in relation to any use of the building by reason of matters or circumstances of which particulars were not required by or under the building standards regulations.

(3) In this section "building standards regulations" has the same meaning as in the Building (Scotland) Act 1959.

(a) **Building.** For definition, see s. 43(1).

(b) **Fire authority.** For definition, see s. 43(1).

———————

Consultation between fire and other authorities

15.   [*Repealed and consolidated by the Building Act 1984, s. 133(2), Sch. 7*].

———————

16.–17.   [*These sections are not printed in this book*].

Enforcement

18.   Enforcement of Act.—(1) Subject to subsection (2) below, it shall be the duty of every fire authority *(a)* to enforce within their area the provisions of this Act and or regulations made under this Act, and for that purpose to appoint inspectors and cause premises to be inspected; but nothing in this subsection shall be taken to authorise a fire authority in Scotland to institute proceedings for any offence.

(2) A fire authority *(a)* shall have power to arrange with the Health and Safety Commission for such of the authority's functions under this Act as may be specified in the arrangements to be performed on their behalf by the Health and Safety Executive (with or without payment) in relation to any particular premises *(b)* so specified which are used as a place of work *(c)*.

(3) In performing the duty imposed by subsection (1) above so far as it requires premises in their areas to be inspected, fire authorities shall act in accordance with such guidance as the Secretary of State may give them.

(a) *Fire authority.* For definition, see s. 43(1).

(b) *Premises.* For definition, see s. 43(1).

(c) *Work.* For definition, see s. 43(1).

---

19.   Powers of inspectors.—(1) Subject to the provisions of this section, any of the following persons (in this section referred to as "inspectors") namely an inspector appointed under section 18 of this Act and a fire inspector *(a)* may do anything necessary for the purpose of carrying this Act and regulations thereunder into effect and, in particular, shall, so far as may be necessary for that purpose, have power do to at any reasonable time any of the following things, namely—

(a) to enter any such premises *(b)* as are mentioned in subsection (2) below, and to inspect the whole or any part thereof and anything therein;

(b) to make such inquiry as may be necessary for any of the purposes mentioned in subsection (3) below;

(c) to require the production of, and to inspect, any fire certificate *(c)* in force with respect to any premises *(b)* or any copy of any such certificate;

(d) to require any person having responsibilities in relation to any such premises as are referred to in paragraph (a) above (whether or not the owner or occupier of the premises or a person employed to work therein) to give him such facilities and assistance with respect to any matters or things to which the responsibilities of that person extend as are necessary for the purpose of enabling the inspector to exercise any of the powers conferred on him by this subsection.

(2) The premises *(b)* referred to in subsection (1)(a) above are the following, namely—

(a) any premises requiring a fire certificate *(c)* or to which any regulations made under section 12 of this Act apply;

(aa) any premises in respect of which there is in force an exemption under section 5A of this Act from the requirement for a fire certificate with respect to them;

(b) any premises such as are mentioned in section 10(1)(a) of this Act;

(c) any premises to which section 3 of this Act for the time being applies;

(d) any premises *(b)* not falling within any of the foregoing paragraphs which form part of a building *(d)* comprising any premises so falling; and

(e) any premises which the inspector has reasonable cause to believe to be premises falling within any of the foregoing paragraphs.

(3) The purposes referred to in subsection (1)(b) above are the following, namely—

(a) to ascertain, as regards any premises *(b)*, whether they fall within any of paragraphs (a) to (d) of subsection (2) above;

(b) to identify the owner or occupier of any premises *(b)*, falling within any of those paragraphs;

(c) to ascertain whether, in the case of any premises to which section 3 of this Act for the time being applies, any person has the overall management of the building constituting or comprising the premises and, if so, to identify that person;

(d) to ascertain, as regards any premises falling within any of the said paragraphs (a) to (d), whether the provisions of this Act and regulations made under section 12 thereof are complied with, and, where a fire certificate *(c)* is in force in respect of any such premises, whether the requirements imposed by the certificate are complied with.

(4) An inspector shall, if so required when visiting any premises *(b)* in the exercise of powers conferred by this section, produce to the occupier *(e)* of the premises *(b)* some duly authenticated document showing his authority.

(5) In the case of premises *(b)* used as a dwelling or premises of any other description prescribed for the purposes of this subsection, no power of entry conferred by subsection (1) above shall be exercised as of right unless twenty-four hours' notice has been given to the occupier and for the purposes of this subsection a description of premises *(b)* may be framed in any of the ways mentioned in section 1(4) of this Act.

(6) A person who—

(a) intentionally obstructs an inspector in the exercise or performance of his powers or duties under this Act; or

(b) without reasonable excuse fails to comply with any requirement imposed by an inspector under subsection (1)(d) above,

shall be guilty of an offence and liable on summary conviction to a fine not exceeding level 3 on the standard scale.

General note. Sub-s. (3)(c) is not yet in force: see the note to s. 44.

(a) Fire inspector. For definition, see s. 43(1).

(b) Premises. For definition, see s. 43(1).

(c) Fire certificate. See note *(b)* to s. 1.

(d) **Building.** For definition, see s. 43(1).

(e) **Occupier.** As to the meaning of "occupier", see note (i) to s. 6.

---

20.   Exercise on behalf of fire inspectors of their powers by officers of fire brigades.—(1) The like powers as are in relation to any premises (a) conferred by section 19 of this Act on a fire inspector (b) shall be exercisable by an officer of the fire brigade maintained by the fire authority (c) when authorised in writing by such an inspector for the purpose of reporting to him on any matter falling within his duties under this Act; and subsections (4) and (6) of that section shall, with the necessary modifications, apply accordingly.

(2) A fire inspector (b) shall not authorise an officer of a fire brigade under this section except with the consent of the fire authority (c) who maintain that brigade.

(a) **Premises.** For definition, see s. 43(1).

(b) **Fire inspector.** For definition, see s. 43(1).

(c) **Fire authority.** For definition, see s. 43(1).

---

21.   Restriction on disclosure of information.—(1) Subject to subsection (2) below if a person discloses (otherwise than in the performance of his duty or for the purposes of any legal proceedings, including an arbitration, or for the purposes of a report of any such proceedings) any information obtained by him in any premises (a) entered by him in the exercise of powers conferred by this Act, he shall be guilty of an offence (b) and liable on summary conviction to a fine not exceeding level 3 on the standard scale.

(2) Nothing in subsection (1) above prohibits the disclosure of information to an enforcing authority within the meaning of the Health and Safety at Work etc. Act 1974 in order to enable that authority to discharge any function falling within its field of responsibility.

(3) Section 18(7) of the Health and Safety at Work etc. Act 1974 (meaning in Part I of that Act of "enforcing authority" and of such an authority's "field of responsibility") shall apply for the purposes of this section as it applies for the purposes of that Part.

(a) **Premises.** For definition, see s. 43(1).

(b) **Offences.** As to offences, see ss. 22–27.

Offences, penalties and legal proceedings

22.   Falsification of documents, false statements, etc.—(1) If a person—

(a) with intent to deceive, makes or has in his possession a document so closely resembling a fire certificate as to be calculated to deceive; or

(b) for the purpose of procuring the issue of a fire certificate makes any statement or gives any information which he knows to be false in a material particular or recklessly makes any statement or gives any information which is so false; or

(c) in purported compliance with any obligation to give information to which he is subject under or by virtue of this Act, or in response to any inquiry made by virtue of section 19(1)(b) of this Act, gives any information which he knows to be false in a material particular or recklessly gives any information which is so false; or

(d) makes in any register, book, notice *(b)* or other document required by or by virtue of regulations made under this Act to be kept, served or given, an entry which he knows to be false in a material particular,

he shall be guilty of an offence and liable on summary conviction to a fine not exceeding level 5 on the standard scale.

(2) If a person with intent to deceive pretends to be—

(a) an inspector within the meaning of section 19 of this Act, or

(b) a person by whom the powers conferred by that section on a fire inspector *(c)* are exercisable by virtue of section 20 of this Act,

he shall be guilty of an offence and liable on summary conviction to a fine not exceeding level 3 on the standard scale.

(3) [*repealed*].

(a) **Fire certificate.** See note *(b)* to s. 1.

(b) **Notice.** For definition, see s. 43(1).

(c) **Fire inspector.** For definition, see s. 43(1).

---

23. Offences by bodies corporate.—(1) Where an offence under this Act committed by a body corporate is proved to have been committed with the consent or connivance *(a)* of, or to be attributable to any neglect on the part of, any director, manager, secretary or other similar officer *(b)* of the body corporate, or any person purporting to act in any such capacity, he as well as the body corporate shall be guilty of that offence, and shall be liable to be proceeded against and punished accordingly.

(2) Where the affairs of a body corporate are managed by its members, this section shall apply in relation to the acts and defaults of a member in connection with his functions of management as if he were a director of the body corporate.

(a) **Connivance.** See INTRODUCTORY NOTE 6.

(b) **Director, manager, secretary or other similar officer.** The purpose of these provisions is to fix criminal liability on those who have management of the whole affairs of the company—that is, who are responsible for deciding corporate policy and strategy (see *R v Boal (Francis)* [1992] QB 591, CA: assistant general manager in charge of day-to-day running of bookshop held not to be manager). The Director of Roads of a Regional Council is an "other similar officer": *Armour v Skeen* [1976] IRLR 310.

---

24. Offences due to fault of other person. Where the commission by any person of an offence under this Act or any regulations made thereunder is due to act or default of some other person, that other person shall be guilty of the offence, and a person may be charged with and convicted of the offence by virtue of this section whether or not proceedings are taken against the first-mentioned person.

General note. See the notes to s. 36 of the Health and Safety at Work etc. Act 1974.

---

25. Defence available to persons charged with offences. In any proceedings for an offence under this Act or under regulations made thereunder, it shall be a defence for the person charged to prove *(a)* that he took all reasonable precautions and exercised all due diligence *(b)* to avoid the commission of such an offence.

(*a*) *Prove.* See the note to s. 40 of the Health and Safety at Work etc. Act.

(*b*) *Due diligence.* See INTRODUCTORY NOTE 7.

---

26. Appeals to magistrates' courts.—(1) Where any provision of this Act provides for an appeal to a magistrates' court the procedure shall be by way of complaint for an order, and the Magistrates' Courts Act 1980 shall apply to the proceedings.

(2) For the purposes of any such provision of this Act the making of the complaint shall be deemed to be the bringing of the appeal.

---

27. Appeal from order made on complaint.—(1) A person aggrieved *(a)* by an order made by a magistrates' court on determining a complaint under this Act may appeal therefrom to the Crown Court; and for the avoidance of doubt it is hereby declared that a fire authority *(b)* or local authority *(c)* may be a person aggrieved within the meaning of this section.

(2) [*repealed*].

(*a*) *Person aggrieved.* See INTRODUCTORY NOTE 14.

(*b*) *Fire authority.* For definition, see s. 43(1).

(c) **Local authority.** For definition, see s. 43(1).

27A.　Civil and other liability.　Except in so far as this Act otherwise expressly provides, and subject to section 18 of the Interpretation Act 1978 (offences under two or more laws), the provisions of this Act shall not be construed as—

(a) conferring a right of action in any civil proceedings (other than proceedings for the recovery of a fine) in respect of any contravention of a provision of this Act, of any regulations thereunder or of any fire certificate or notice issued or served thereunder by the fire authority; or

(b) affecting any requirement or restriction imposed by or under any other enactment whether contained in a public general Act or in a local or private Act; or

(c) derogating from any right of action or other remedy (whether civil or criminal) in proceedings instituted otherwise than under this Act.

28.　Power of county court or sheriff, where notice under s. 3 is in force, to modify agreements and leases and apportion expenses.—(1) This section applies to—

(a) premises *(a)* consisting, or forming part of, a factory *(b)* within the meaning of the Factories Act 1961 and premises to which sections 123(1) and 124 of that Act (application to electrical stations and institutions, respectively) apply;

(b) premises to which section 9A of this Act applies,

in this section referred to as "the relevant premises".

(2) A person who, by reason of the terms and conditions of an agreement or lease relating to any premises *(a)* to which this section applies, is prevented from carrying out or doing with respect to the premises any structural or other alterations or other things whose carrying out or doing is requisite—

(a) as being a step mentioned in a notice *(c)* served in connection with the relevant premises *(d)* under any of the following provisions of this Act, namely sections 5(4), 8(4), 8(5) and 12(8)(b); or

(b) in order to secure compliance with a requirement imposed by a fire certificate *(e)* issued with respect to the relevant premises; or

(c) in order to secure compliance with section 9A of this Act or with a provision of regulations made under Section 12 of this Act,

may apply to the county court within whose jurisdiction the premises are situated, and the court may make such an order setting aside or modifying any of the terms and conditions of the agreement or lease as the court considers just and equitable in the circumstances of the case.

References in this subsection to the terms and conditions of an agreement or lease relating to any premises include references to the terms and conditions on or subject to which by virtue of section 3 of the Rent Act 1977 a statutory tenant retains possession of any premises.

(3) Where, in the case of any premises *(a)* to which this section applies, the carrying out or doing with respect to those premises of any structural or other

alterations or other thing whose carrying out or doing is requisite as mentioned in subsection (2) above involves a person having an interest in the premises in expense or in increased expense, and he alleges that the whole or part of the expense or, as the case may be, the increase, ought to be borne by some other person having an interest in the premises, the first-mentioned person may apply to the county court within whose jurisdiction the premises are situated, and the court may by order give such directions—

(a) with respect to the persons by whom the expenses or increase is to be borne, and the proportions in which it is to be borne by them; and

(b) if need be, for modification of the terms of any agreement or lease relating to the premises so far as concerns rent payable in respect of the premises,

as the court considers just and equitable in the circumstances of the case:

Provided that on an application under this subsection the court shall not direct the whole or any part of the expense or increase to be borne by a person other than the applicant by reason only of that other person being a statutory tenant of the premises or any part of the premises.

(4) In this section "statutory tenant" has the same meaning as in the Rent Act 1977.

(5) In the application of this section to Scotland—

(a) for references to the county court there shall be substituted references to the sheriff;

(b) in subsection (2), for the reference to section 3 of the Rent Act 1977 there shall be substituted a reference to section 12 of the Rent (Scotland) Act 1971;

(c) "statutory tenant" has the same meaning as in section 133(1) of the Rent (Scotland) Act 1971;

(d) subsection (4) shall be omitted.

General note. For modifications to this section where premises are premises for which a fire certificate is required, premises for which a fire certificate is in force, premises to which s. 9A applies or premises to which regulations under s. 12 apply and are factory, office, shop or railway premises, see Sch. 2, Part II.

(a) Premises. For definition, see s. 43(1).

(b) Factory. See the Factories Act 1961, s. 175 and the notes thereto.

(c) Notice. For definition, see s. 43(1).

(d) The relevant premises. See sub-s. (1).

(e) Fire certificate. See note *(b)* to s. 1.

28A. Special provision for factory, office, railway and shop premises.—
(1) This Act shall have effect in relation to premises of the descriptions specified in Part I of Schedule 2 to this Act subject to the modifications specified in Part II of that Schedule.

(2) The Secretary of State may by order vary the provisions of that Schedule by amending, omitting or adding to the descriptions of premises or the modifi-

cations for the time being specified in it if it appears to him to be necessary or expedient in connection with any provision made by health and safety regulations under section 15 of the Health and Safety at Work etc. Act 1974.

(3) The power to make an order under this section is exercisable by statutory instrument which shall be subject to annulment in pursuance of a resolution of either House of Parliament.

Amendments of other Acts

29.–30. [*These sections are not printed in this book*].

---

31. Suspension of terms and conditions of licences dealing with the same matters as fire certificates or regulations.—(1) Where any enactment provides for the licensing of premises *(a)* of any class or description and the authority responsible for issuing licences thereunder is required or authorised to impose terms, conditions or restrictions in connection with the issue of such licences, then, in the case of any premises of that class or description—

(a) so long as there is in force with respect to the premises a fire certificate *(b)* covering the use of the premises by reason of which a licence under that enactment is required, any term, condition or restriction imposed in connection with the issue under that enactment of any licence with respect to those premises shall be of no effect in so far as it relates to any matter in relation to which certificates are or could be imposed by that certificate; and

(b) without prejudice to paragraph (a) above, so long as there are in force under section 12 of this Act any regulations applying to the premises in respect of that use, any term, condition or restriction imposed as aforesaid shall be of no effect in so far as it relates to any matter about which provision is made in the regulations.

(2) References in this section to the issue of licences include references to their renewal, transfer or variation.

General note. This section is modified by Sch. 2, Part II as follows—where a licence issued under the Explosives Act 1875 or the Petroleum (Consolidation) Act 1928 is in force with respect to factory, office, shop or railway premises, this section shall not have effect in relation to any term, condition or restriction imposed in connection with the issue, renewal, transfer or variation of such licence.

(a) **Premises.** For definition, see s. 43(1).

(b) **Fire certificate.** For definition, see s. 43(1).

32.–34.   [*These sections are not printed in this book*].

———————————

Miscellaneous and general

35.   Power to apply Act to vessels and movable structures.   The Secretary of State *(a)* may by regulations apply any of the provisions of this Act, subject to such modifications as may be prescribed, to—

(a)   vessels remaining moored or on dry land for such periods or in such circumstances as may be prescribed; and

(b)   tents and other movable structures of any prescribed description and;

(c)   places of work in the open air of any prescribed description.

(a) Secretary of State. See note *(e)* to s. 1.

———————————

36.   Power of local authorities to make loans to meet expenditure on certain alterations to buildings occasioned by this Act.—(1) Where there is in force a notice *(a)* under section 3 of this Act relating to any premises *(b)*, any person proposing to incur expenditure in making to any part of the relevant building *(c)* any structural or other alterations the making of which is requisite as being a step mentioned in a notice served in connection with those premises under section 5(4), 8(5) or 12(8)(b) of this Act, may apply for a loan to the local authority *(d)* in whose area the premises are situated.

(2) Subject to this section, if the local authority *(d)* consider that the applicant—

(a)   can reasonably be expected to meet obligations assumed by him in pursuance of this section in respect of a loan of the amount of the expenditure to which the application relates; or

(b)   cannot reasonably be expected to meet obligations so assumed by him in respect of a loan of that obligation, but can reasonably be expected to meet obligations so assumed by him in respect of a loan of a smaller amount,

the local authority may, if they think fit, offer to enter into a contract with the applicant for a loan by the local authority to the applicant of the appropriate amount, to be secured to the local authority by a mortgage of the applicant's interest in the relevant building *(c)* or the part of it to which the application relates.

In this subsection "the appropriate amount", in a case falling within paragraph (a) above, means the amount of the expenditure to which the application relates, and in a case falling within paragraph (b) above means the smaller amount there referred to.

(3) The local authority *(d)* shall not make an offer under the foregoing provisions of this section unless they are satisfied—

(a)   that the applicant's interest in the relevant building *(c)* or the part of it to which the application relates amounts to an estate in fee simple absolute in possession or an estate for a term of years absolute which will not expire before the date for final repayment of the loan; and

(b) that, according to a valuation made on behalf of the local authority, the amount of the principal of the loan does not exceed the value which it is estimated the mortgaged security will bear when the proposed alterations have been carried out.

(4) Subject to subsection (5) of this section, every loan under this section shall bear interest at the rate which, on the date of the contract to make the loan, is the rate for the time being determined by the Treasury in accordance with section 5 of the National Loans Act 1968 in respect of local loans made on the security of local rates on that date for the same period as that loan.

In this subsection "local loans" and "made on the security of local rates" have the same meanings as in section 6(2) of the National Loans Act 1968.

(5) Where, on the date of a contract for a loan under this section, there are two or more rates of interest for the time being determined by the Treasury as mentioned in subsection (4) above, the reference in that subsection to the rate so determined shall be read as a reference to such one of those rates as may be specified in a direction given by the Treasury for the purposes of this section.

(6) The Treasury shall cause any direction given under subsection (5) above to be published in the London and Edinburgh Gazette as soon as may be after giving it.

(7) Subject to the foregoing provisions of this section, the contract offered by the local authority *(d)* under this section shall require proof of title and shall contain such other reasonable terms as the local authority may specify in their offer.

(8) The local authority's *(d)* offer may in particular include provisions—

(a) for the advance to be made by instalments from time to time as the alterations progress;

(b) for repayment either by instalments of principle or by an annuity of principal and interest combined;

(c) that in the event of any of the conditions subject to which the advance is made not being complied with, the balance for the time being unpaid shall become repayable on demand by the local authority;

(d) that the balance for the time being unpaid may be repaid on one of the usual quarter days by the person for the time being entitled to the equity of redemption after one month's written notice of intention to repay has been given to the local authority.

(9) In its application to Scotland this section shall have effect subject to the following modifications—

(a) in subsection (2), for the words "mortgage of" there shall be substituted the words "heritable security over", and at the end there shall be inserted the words "and 'heritable security' means any security capable of being constituted over any interest in land by disposition or assignation of that interest in security of any debt and of being recorded in the Register of Sasines";

(b) in subsection (3)(a), for the words from "an estate in fee simple" to "years absolute" there shall be substituted the words "ownership or a lease";

   (c) in subsection (3) (b), for the words "mortgaged security" there shall be substituted the words "security subjects";

   (d) in subsection (8) for "on one of the usual quarter days" there shall be substituted "at any term of Whitsunday or Martinmas" and for "the person for the time being entitled to the equity of redemption" there shall be substituted "the debtor".

(a) Notice. For definition, see s. 43(1).

(b) Premises. For definition, see s. 43(1).

(c) Relevant building. For definition, see s. 43(1).

(d) Local authority. For definition, see s. 43(1).

---

37.   General provisions as to regulations.—(1) Any power of the Secretary of State *(a)* to make regulations under this Act shall be exercisable by statutory instrument, which shall be subject to annulment in pursuance of a resolution of either House of Parliament.

(2) Any power conferred by this Act to make regulations includes power to make different provision in relation to different circumstances.

(3) Regulations made under this Act may grant or provide for the granting of exemptions from any of the provisions of the regulations, either unconditionally or subject to conditions.

(a) Secretary of State. See note *(e)* to s. 1.

---

38.   Service of documents.—(1) Any notice *(a)* or other document required or authorised by or by virtue of this Act to be served on any person may be served on him either by delivering it to him or by leaving it as his proper address or by sending it by post.

(2) Any notice *(a)* or other document so required or authorised to be served on a body corporate or a firm shall be duly served if it is served on the secretary or clerk of that body or a partner of that firm.

(3) For the purposes of this section, and of section 26 of the Interpretation Act 1889 *(b)* in its application to this section, the proper address of any person, in the case of the secretary or clerk of a body corporate, shall be that of the registered or principal office of that body, in the case of a partner of a firm, shall be that of the principal office of the firm, and in any other case shall be the last known address of the person to be served.

(4) If the name or the address of any owner or occupier of premises *(c)* on whom any such notice or other document as aforesaid is to be served cannot after reasonable inquiry be ascertained by the person seeking to serve it, the document may be served by addressing it to the person on whom it is to be

served by the description of "owner" or "occupier" of the premises (describing them) to which the notice relates, and by delivering it to some responsible person resident or appearing to be resident on the premises, or, if there is no such person to whom it can be delivered, by affixing it or a copy of it to some conspicuous part of the premises.

(a) **Notice.** For definition, see s. 43(1).

(b) **Interpretation Act 1889.** See now the Interpretation Act 1978, s. 7.

(c) **Premises.** For definition, see s. 43(1).

---

39. Expenses. There shall be paid out of moneys provided by Parliament any expenditure incurred by the Secretary of State (a) under or by virtue of this Act and any increase attributable to any provision of this Act in the sums payable under any other enactment out of moneys so provided.

(a) **Secretary of State.** See note (e) to s. 1.

---

40. Application to Crown, etc.—(1) Subject to the provisions of this section—

(a) the following provisions of this Act, namely sections 1, 2, 3 (except subsection (5)), 4, 5(2A), 5A, 5B, 9A (except subsections (3) and (4)), 9B and 9C and 12(1) to (3) and (4)(a) and (b), shall apply to premises (a) occupied by the Crown; and

(b) the following provisions of this Act, namely sections 1, 2, 3 (except subsection (5)), 4 to 8, 8A, 8B, 9A, 9B, 9C, 9D, 9F, 10, 10B, 12, 19 to 21 and 32, shall apply to premises owned by the Crown but not occupied by it.

(2) No fire certificate (b) shall by virtue of subsection (1) above be required in respect of premises (a) of any of the following descriptions, that it to say—

(a) any premises constituting, or forming part of, a prison within the meaning of the Prison Act 1952 or constituting, or forming part of, a remand centre or young offender institution provided by the Secretary of State under section 43 of that Act;

(b) any premises constituting, or forming part of, a prison within the meaning of the Prisons (Scotland) Act 1952 or constituting, or forming part of, a remand centre, detention centre, Borstal institution or young offenders institution provided by the Secretary of State under section 31 of that Act;

(c) [*repealed*];

(d) any premises occupied solely for purposes of the armed forces of the Crown.

(3) Any provision of this Act which, by virtue of subsection (1) above, applies to premises (a) occupied or owned by the Crown shall, in its application to any

such premises, have effect with the substitution, for any reference to the fire authority *(c)*, of a reference to a fire inspector *(d)* or any person authorised by the Secretary of State to act for the purposes of this section.

(4) As regards any premises *(a)* falling within subsection (1)(a) above, any power exercisable by virtue of subsection (3) above by a fire inspector *(d)* shall be exercisable also by an officer of the fire brigade maintained by the fire authority *(c)* if and so far as he is authorised in writing by such an inspector to exercise that power; but a fire inspector shall not authorise an officer of a fire brigade under this subsection except with the consent of the fire authority who maintain that brigade.

(5) If a person with intent to deceive pretends to be a person by whom any powers exercisable by a fire inspector *(d)* by virtue of subsection (3) above are exercisable by virtue of subsection (4) above, he shall be guilty of an offence *(e)* and liable on summary conviction to a fine not exceeding level 3 on the standard scale.

(6) In relation to any premises *(a)* falling within subsection (1)(b) above section 20(1) of this Act shall have effect as if for the reference to an officer of the fire brigade maintained by the fire authority *(c)* there were substituted a reference to any person.

(7) [*Repealed and consolidated by the Building Act 1984, s. 133(2), Sch. 7*].

(8) To such extent, if any, as they so provide, regulations under section 35 of this Act shall bind the Crown.

(9) Nothing in this Act shall be taken to authorise the entry of premises *(a)* occupied by the Crown.

(10) [*repealed*].

(10A) This Act shall apply to premises *(a)* in England occupied by a Board of Governors of a teaching hospital (being a body for the time being specified in an order under section 15(1) of the National Health Service Reorganisation Act 1973) as if they were premises occupied by the Crown.

(10B) This Act shall apply to premises *(a)* occupied by the National Radiological Protection Board as if they were occupied by the Crown.

(11) Any premises *(a)* used for the purposes of a visiting force or of a headquarters or defence organisation designated *(f)* for the purposes of the International Headquarters and Defence Organisations Act 1964 shall be exempt from the operation of this Act to the extent to which the premises would be exempt therefrom if the premises were occupied by the Crown solely for purposes of the armed forces of the Crown.

In this subsection "visiting force" means any such body, contingent or detachment of the forces of any country as is a visiting force for the purposes of any of the provisions of the Visiting Forces Act 1952.

(a) *Premises.* For definition, see s. 43(1).

(b) *Fire certificate.* See note *(b)* to s. 1.

(c) *Fire authority.* For definition, see s. 43(1).

(d) *Fire inspector.* For definition, see s. 43(1).

(e) *Offence.* As to offences, see ss. 22–27.

(f) **Designated.** See the International Headquarters and Defence Organisations (Designation and Privileges) Order 1965, S.I. 1965 No. 1535, as amended by S.I. 1987 No. 927 (not printed in this book).

---

41. Application to premises occupied by U.K. Atomic Energy Authority. Sections 17, 18, 30, 31 and 36 of this Act shall not apply to any premises *(a)* occupied by the United Kingdom Atomic Energy Authority, and in the application of other provisions of this Act to any such premises—

(a) for any reference to the fire authority *(b)* there shall be substituted a reference to a fire inspector *(c)* or any person authorised by the Secretary of State *(d)* to act for the purposes of this section; and

(b) for the reference in section 20(1) to an officer of the fire brigade maintained by the fire authority there shall be substituted a reference to any person.

(a) **Premises.** For definition, see s. 43(1).

(b) **Fire authority.** For definition, see s. 43(1).

(c) **Fire inspector.** For definition, see s. 43(1).

(d) **Secretary of State.** See note *(e)* to s. 1.

---

42. [*repealed*].

---

43. Interpretations.—(1) In this Act—
   "building" includes a temporary or movable building and also includes any permanent structure and any temporary structure other than a movable one;
   "contravention" includes failure to comply, and "contravene" has a corresponding meaning;
   "the court", except in section 28 of this Act means, in relation to premises in England or Wales, a magistrates' court acting for the petty sessions area in which they are situated and, in relation to premises in Scotland, the sheriff within whose jurisdiction they are situated;
   "designated use" has the meaning assigned by section 1(1) of this Act;
   "escape" has the meaning assigned to it by section 5(5) of this Act and "means of escape" is to be construed in accordance with that subsection;
   "fire authority", in relation to any premises or proposed premises, means the authority discharging in the area in which the premises are or are to be situated the functions of fire authority under the Fire Services Act 1947;
   "fire certificate" has the meaning assigned by section 1(1) of this Act;
   "fire inspector" means an inspector or assistant inspector appointed under section 24 of the Fire Services Act 1947;

"furniture" includes furnishings (including wall-coverings and ceiling-coverings of all sorts, as well as floor-coverings);

"local authority" means—

(a) as respects England and Wales, the council of a London borough or district, the Common Council of the City of London or the Council of the Isles of Scilly;

(b) as respects Scotland, the council of a county or the town council of a burgh;

"notice" means a notice in writing;

"the notified person" and "the specified position" have the meaning assigned by section 3(8) of this Act;

"owner" *(a)*—

(a) as respects England and Wales, means the person for the time being receiving the rackrent of the premises in connection with which the word is used, whether on his own account or as agent or trustee for another person, or who would so receive the rackrent if the premises were let at a rackrent; and

(b) as respects Scotland, means the person for the time being entitled to receive or who would, if the same were let, be entitled to receive, the rents of the premises in connection with which the word is used and includes a trustee, factor, tutor or curator, and in the case of public or municipal property, applies to the person to whom the management thereof is entrusted;

"premises" means building *(b)* or part of a building;

"prescribed" means prescribed by regulations made under this Act by the Secretary of State *(c)*;

"prohibition notice" has the meaning assigned by sections 10(2) of this Act;

"the relevant building", in relation to—

(a) any premises *(d)* in relation to which a notice under section 3 of this Act is in force; or

(b) any premises which are the subject of an application for a fire certificate *(e)*; or

(c) any premises with respect to which a fire certificate is in force,

means the building constituting or comprising the premises in question.

"work" *(f)* has the same meaning as it has for the purposes of Part I of the Health and Safety at Work etc. Act 1974.

(2) [*repealed*].

(3) Except in so far as the context otherwise requires, any reference in this Act to any enactment is a reference to it as amended, and includes a reference to it as applied, by or under any other enactment, including this Act.

(a) **Owner.** See note *(i)* to s. 176 of the Factories Act 1961.

(b) **Building.** Defined earlier in this sub-section.

(c) **Secretary of State.** See note *(e)* to s. 1.

(d) **Premises.** Defined earlier in this sub-section.

(e) **Fire certificate.** Defined earlier in this sub-section.

(*f*) **Work.** See s. 52(1) of the Health and Safety at Work etc. Act 1974.

---

44.   Short title, extent and commencement.—(1) This Act may be cited as the Fire Precautions Act 1971.

(2) This Act does not extend to Northern Ireland.

(3) This Act shall come into operation on such day as the Secretary of State may by order made by statutory instrument appoint, and different dates may be appointed under this subsection for different purposes.

General note. This Act has been largely brought into force by S.I.s 1972 No. 236, 1976 No. 2006 and 1988 Nos. 740 and 995. Those provisions not yet in force are ss. 3, 4, 12(2), (9), (11) and 16(1)(b), (2)(b), 19(3)(c), 34, 36, and 40 (part).

SCHEDULE 1

[*This Schedule modified the Rent Act 1968 and corresponding Scottish Acts and is not printed in this book.*]

SCHEDULE 2

SPECIAL PROVISIONS FOR CERTAIN PREMISES

PART I

THE PREMISES

1.   Subject to paragraph 2 below, the following are the descriptions of premises in relation to which this Act is subject to the modifications specified in relation to them in Part II—

 (a) premises constituting, or forming part of, a factory within the meaning of the Factories Act 1961 and premises to which sections 123(1) and 124 of that Act (application to electrical stations and institutions) apply (in this Schedule referred to as "factory premises");

 (b) office premises within the meaning of the Offices, Shops and Railway Premises Act 1963, or premises deemed to be such premises for the purposes of that Act (in this Schedule referred to as "office premises");

 (c) railway premises within the meaning of that Act of 1963, or premises deemed to be such premises for the purposes of that Act (in this Schedule referred to as "railway premises"); and

 (d) shop premises within the meaning of that Act of 1963, or premises deemed to be such premises for the purposes of that Act (in this Schedule referred to as "shop premises").

2.   Premises which are deemed to form part of a mine for the purposes of the Mines and Quarries Act 1954 are excluded from the descriptions of premises mentioned in sub-paragraphs (b) to (d) of paragraph 1 above.

PART II

THE MODIFICATIONS

3.—(1) This paragraph applies to premises in respect of which a fire certificate is required which are factory premises, office premises, railway premises or shop premises, and which—

  (a) are held under a lease or an agreement for a lease or under a licence and consist of part of a building all parts of which are in the same ownership; or

  (b) consist of part of a building in which different parts are owned by different persons.

(2) In relation to premises to which this paragraph applies this Act shall have effect with the following modifications.

(3) For the references to the occupier in sections 5(2A), 5A(4), 5A(6), 5A(8), 5B(3), 5B(4), 5B(5), 6(5), 7(1), 7(3A), 7(4), 8(2) (except paragraph (c) and the insertion made by sub-paragraph (5) below), 8(4), 8(5), 8(7), 8B(1), 9(5)(b), 9A(3), 9D(1) and 12(8)(b) there shall be substituted—

  (a) in the case of premises falling within sub-paragraph (1)(a) above, references to the owner of the building;

  (b) in the case of premises falling within sub-paragraph (1)(b) above, references to the persons who between them own the building.

(4) For the words "a fire certificate" where they occur in section 8(8) and where they first occur in section 7(6) there shall be substituted the words "a copy of the certificate" and in section 6(8) at the end of the subsection there shall be inserted the words "and the fire certificate shall be sent to the owner of the building or, as the case may be, the person who owns the part of the building of which the premises consist".

(5) In sections 8(2) and 8A(1) after the words "fire authority"; there shall be inserted the words "and the occupier shall, before the carrying out of the proposals is begun, furnish to the persons responsible for giving notice of the proposals to the fire authority any information in his possession which is relevant to those proposals";

(6) In section 8A(1) for the references to the occupier (except the reference inserted by sub-paragraph (5) above) there shall be substituted—

  (a) in the case of premises—
    (i) falling within paragraph (1)(a) above; and
    (ii) in relation to which it is intended to carry out proposals falling within subsection (2)(a) or (c) of that section,
    references to the owner of the building; and

  (b) in the case of premises—
    (i) falling within sub-paragraph (1)(b) above; and
    (ii) in relation to which it is intended to carry out proposals falling within subsection (2)(a) or (c) of that section,
    references to the persons who between them own the building.

(7) The expressions "owner of the building" and "the persons who between them own the building" do not include the Crown in the modifications made—

(a) by sub-paragraph (3) above of sections 7(1), 8(7), 9A(3) and of the word "occupier" in the third place where it occurs in section 8(2); and

(b) by sub-paragraph (6) above of the word "occupier" in the second place where it occurs in section 8A(1).

4. In section 6(1) as it has effect in relation to factory premises there shall be inserted after paragraph (e) the following paragraph—

"(f) particulars as to any explosive or highly flammable materials which may be stored or used in the premises,".

5. In section 8 as it has effect in relation to factory premises—

(a) for paragraph (c) of subsection (2) there shall be substituted the following paragraph—
"(c) the occupier of the premises proposes to begin to store or use explosive or highly flammable materials in the premises or materially to increase the extent of such storage or use,"; and

(b) in subsection (3) for the words from "keep explosive" to "that kind" there shall be substituted the words "store or use explosive or highly flammable materials in the premises or materially to increase the extent of such storage or use".

6. In section 8A as it has effect in relation to factory premises, for paragraph (b) of subsection (2) there shall be substituted the following paragraph—

"(b) on the part of the occupier of the premises to begin to store or use explosive or highly flammable materials in the premises or materially to increase the extent of such storage or use;".

7. Where a licence issued under the Explosives Act 1875 or the Petroleum (Consolidation) Act 1928 is in force with respect to factory premises, office premises, shop premises or railway premises, section 31 of this Act shall not have effect in relation to any term, condition or restriction imposed in connection with the issue, renewal, transfer or variation of such licence.

8. Where any premises ("the relevant premises")—

(a) are premises for which a fire certificate is required, premises for which a fire certificate is in force, premises to which section 9A of this Act applies or premises to which regulations under section 12 of this Act apply, and

(b) are factory premises, office premises, shop premises or railway premises,

section 28 shall apply to the premises or to any other premises comprised in the same building—

(i) with the substitution of the foregoing words (reading "this section" for "section 28") for subsection (1);

(ii) with the insertion, in subsection (2)(a), after "8(5)" of "9D(1)"; and

(iii) with the substitution, for subsection (2)(c) of the following—
"(c) in order to secure compliance with section 9A or a provision of regulations under section 12 of this Act;".

THE FIRE CERTIFICATES (SPECIAL PREMISES) REGULATIONS 1976

(S.I. 1976 No. 2003 as amended by S.I. 1985 No. 1333, S.I. 1987 No. 37 and S.I. 1992 No. 1811)

Whereas the Health and Safety Commission has submitted to the Secretary of State under section 11(2)(d) of the Health and Safety at Work etc. Act 1974 ("the 1974 Act") proposals for the making of Regulations after the carrying out by the said Commission of consultations in accordance with section 50(3) of the 1974 Act.

And whereas under section 80(1) of the 1974 Act it appears to the Secretary of State that the modification of local Arts contained in regulation 13 below is expedient in connection with the other provisions of these Regulations and whereas in accordance with section 80(4) of the 1974 Act he has consulted such bodies as appeared to him to be appropriate on the proposed modification.

Now therefore, the Secretary of State, in exercise of the powers conferred on him by sections 15(1), (4)(a), (5) and (6)(a) and (b), 80(1) and (4) and 82(3)(a) of, and paragraphs 4(1), 12 and 21(a) of Schedule 3 to the 1974 Act as amended by section 116 of and paragraphs 6 and 19 of Schedule 15 to the Employment Protection Act 1975 and of all other powers enabling him in that behalf and so as to give effect without modification to the said proposals of the said Commission and to the said modification of local Acts, hereby makes the following Regulations—

Citation and commencement
1. These Regulations may be cited as the Fire Certificates (Special Premises) Regulations 1976 and shall come into operation on 1 January 1977.

Interpretation
2.—(1) In these Regulations unless the context otherwise requires—

(a) "fire certificate" means a certificate issued under these Regulations by the Health and Safety Executive;
"responsible person" in relation to any premises means the person having control of those premises, whether as occupier or otherwise, in connection with the carrying on by him of a trade, business or other undertaking (whether for profit or not) except that in the case of a mine within the meaning of the Mines and Quarries Act 1954 the responsible person shall be the manager of that mine;
(b) any reference to a numbered regulation is a reference to the regulation in these Regulations bearing that number.

(2) The Interpretation Act 1889 [Interpretation Act 1978] shall apply to the interpretation of these Regulations as it applies to the interpretation of an Act of Parliament.

Premises for which a fire certificate is required
3.—(1) A *fire certificate* shall be required in respect of any premises of a description specified in Part I of Schedule 1 to these Regulations unless either—

(a) an exemption is granted in respect of them under regulation 15, or,
(b) in the case of premises to which paragraph 15 of Part I of that Schedule applies, each condition in Part II of that Schedule is satisfied.

(2) Where any premises to which paragraph (1) of this regulation applies ("specified premises") are within the close curtilage or precincts of larger premises, any part of those larger premises used for the purposes of the specified premises (including use as a means of access) shall for the purposes of these Regulations, be treated as forming part of the specified premises.

Premises for which a fire certificate is not required
3A. Notwithstanding regulation 3(1), a *fire certificate* shall not be required for any berth to which the Dangerous Substances in Harbour Areas Regulations 1987, S.I. 1987/37, apply.

Application for and issue of a fire certificate
4.—(1) An application for a *fire certificate* shall be made by the *responsible person* to the Health and Safety Executive and shall contain the particulars specified in Schedule 2 to these Regulations.

(2) On receipt of an application for a *fire certificate* the Executive may require the applicant within such time as it may specify—

(a) to furnish such plans of the premises to be covered by the certificate as it may specify; and
(b) to furnish, in so far as it is reasonably practicable for him to do so, such plans of adjoining premises as it may specify, and if the applicant fails to furnish the required plans within that time or such further time as the Executive may allow, the application shall be deemed to have been withdrawn at the end of that time or further time, as the case may be.

(3) Where an application for a *fire certificate* has been duly made and all such plans (if any) as are required to be furnished under paragraph (2) of this regulation have been duly furnished, it shall be the duty of the Executive to cause an inspection to be carried out; and if it is satisfied that—

(a) the means of escape which are provided in case of fire;
(b) the means (other than means for fighting fire) which are provided for securing that such means of escape can be safely and effectively used at all material times;
(c) the means which are provided whether on the premises or elsewhere for fighting fire; and
(d) the means which are provided whether on the premises or elsewhere for giving warnings in case of fire,

are such as may reasonably be required in the circumstances of the case in connection with the premises, the Executive shall issue a *fire certificate*.

(4) Where the Executive, after causing such an inspection to be carried out is not satisfied as aforesaid, it shall by notice served on the applicant—

(a) inform the applicant of that fact and of the steps which would have to be taken to satisfy it; and

(b) notify him that it will not issue a *fire certificate* unless those steps are taken (whether by the applicant or otherwise) within such time as may be specified in the notice,

and if at the end of that time or such further time as may be allowed by the Executive or by any order made on, or in proceedings arising out of, an appeal under Regulation 12 against the notice those steps have not been taken, the *fire certificate* shall be deemed to have been refused.

Contents of a fire certificate
5.—(1) Every *fire certificate* shall specify—

(a) the address of the premises;

(b) the name of the *responsible person*;

(c) the description of the premises by reference to the class or classes listed in Schedule 1 to these Regulations;

(d) the means of escape which are provided in case of fire;

(e) the means (other than means for fighting fire) which are provided for securing that such means of escape can be safely and effectively used at all material times;

(f) the type, number and location of the means which are provided (whether in the premises or elsewhere) for fighting fire; and

(g) the type and location of the means which are provided (whether in the premises or elsewhere) for giving warning in case of fire,

and may do so by means of or by reference to a plan or photograph.

(2) A *fire certificate* may impose such conditions as the Executive consider appropriate in the circumstances—

(a) for securing that the means of escape in case of fire which are provided are properly maintained *(a)* and kept free from obstruction;

(b) for securing that the means which are provided as mentioned in paragraph (1)(e) to (g) of this regulation are properly maintained;

(c) for securing that the means which are provided as mentioned in paragraph (1)(f) and (g) of this regulation are tested and examined at regular intervals and that records are kept of such tests and examinations;

(d) for securing that persons at work on the premises receive appropriate instruction and training in what to do in case of fire, and that records are kept of instruction and training given for that purpose;

(e) for limiting the number of persons who may be on the premises at any one time or at such times as the Executive may specify;

(f) for limiting the quantity and disposition of any substance or article which may be on the premises at any one time or at such times as the Executive may specify; and

(g) as to other precautions to be observed in relation to the risk to persons in case of fire.

(3) Any conditions imposed by virtue of paragraph (2) of this regulation may be framed so as to apply to the whole of the premises or so as to apply to one or more parts of them and different conditions may be imposed in relation to different parts.

(4) A *fire certificate* shall be sent or delivered to the *responsible person* and where he is not the occupier of the premises a copy of it shall be sent to the occupier.

(5) An occupier of premises (whether or not he is the *responsible person*) shall keep the *fire certificate*, or the copy as the case may be, on the premises and shall make it available for inspection at reasonable times by any person who might be affected by any of its provisions.

(6) Where a *fire certificate* has been issued, the occupier of the premises (whether or not he is also the *responsible person*) shall keep a notice posted at a suitable place on or about the premises to which it relates in such characters and in such a position as to be easily seen and read by any person who might be affected by any of the provisions of the certificate; the notice shall state—

(a) that a *fire certificate* has been issued;
(b) where it, or a copy of it, may be inspected, and
(c) the date of posting of the notice.

(7) Where the *responsible person* is not the occupier he shall keep the *fire certificate* and shall make it available for inspection at reasonable times by any person who might be affected by any of its provisions.

(a) **Properly maintained.** See INTRODUCTORY NOTE 10.

Changes by the responsible person affecting adequacy of matters specified in a fire certificate
6.—(1) Where the *responsible person* proposes to make any material change which will affect any of the matters specified or referred to in a *fire certificate* which is in force, he shall, before commencing to make that change, notify the Executive in writing of the proposal.

(2) The provisions of regulation 4(2)(a) and (b) shall apply to a notice under paragraph (1) of this regulation as they apply to an application for a *fire certificate*.

(3) If the Executive is satisfied that if the proposed change were made, all the matters mentioned in regulation 5(1)(d) to (g) and 5(2) would still be adequate, it shall on production of the *fire certificate* cause a copy of the notice to be attached to it together with a statement that it is so satisfied or it may vary the certificate or cancel it and issue a new one.

(4) If the Executive is satisfied that if the change were made any of the matters mentioned in regulation 5(1)(d) to (g) and 5(2) would be inadequate it shall—

(a) inform the *responsible person* of that fact and of the steps which would have to be taken to prevent their becoming inadequate in the event of the change being made;
(b) notify him that the *fire certificate* will be cancelled if the change is made without those steps being taken.

(5) Where a notice has been given under paragraph (4)(b) of this Regulation the Executive may cancel the certificate if the changes are made without the steps referred to in paragraph (4)(a) having been taken; and where the steps are taken it may vary the certificate or cancel it and issue a new one.

Changes by persons other than the responsible person affecting adequacy of matters specified in a fire certificate

7.—(1) Where the *responsible person* becomes aware that some other person proposes to make or has made any material change which affects any of the matters specified or referred to in a *fire certificate* which is in force, the *responsible person* shall notify the Executive in writing of the proposal or change as the case may be.

(2) The provisions of regulation 4(2)(a) and (b) shall apply to a notice under paragraph (1) of this regulation as they apply to an application for a *fire certificate*.

(3) If the Executive is satisfied that notwithstanding the change all of the matters mentioned in regulation 5(1)(d) to (g) and 5(2) would still be adequate, it shall on production of the *fire certificate* cause a copy of the notice to be attached to it together with a statement that it is so satisfied or it may vary the certificate or cancel it and issue a new one.

(4) If the Executive is satisfied that any of the matters mentioned in regulations 5(1)(d) to (g) and 5(2) would become inadequate if the proposed change were made, or where the change has been made it is satisfied that any of those matters have become inadequate, it shall—

(a) inform the *responsible person* of that fact and of the steps which would have to be taken to prevent their becoming or, as the case may be, remaining inadequate;

(b) notify him that the *fire certificate* will be cancelled if those steps are not taken within such time as may be specified in the notice.

(5) Where a notice has been given under paragraph (4)(b) of this regulation, the Executive may cancel the certificate if the steps are not taken within the time specified in the notice, or within such further time as may be allowed by the Executive or by any order made on, or in proceedings arising out of, an appeal under regulation 12 against the notice; and where the steps are taken it may vary the certificate or may cancel it and issue a new one.

Other cases where fire certificate becomes inadequate

8.   If the Executive considers that a *fire certificate* should be varied or cancelled because any of the matters mentioned in regulation 5(1)(d) to (g) and 5(2) is or has become inadequate it shall—

(a) inform any person to whom the certificate, or a copy of it, was given under regulation 5(4) of that fact and the steps, if any, which would have to be taken for those matters to become adequate;

(b) notify him that it will cancel the certificate unless those steps are taken within such time as may be specified in the notice; and if at the end of that time, or such further time as may be allowed by the Executive or by any order made on, or in any proceedings arising out of, an appeal under regulation 12 against the notice, those steps have been taken, the

Executive may vary the certificate accordingly and if they have not been taken may, subject to any such order, cancel it.

Applications for variation of a fire certificate
9.—(1) Where a *fire certificate* is in force, the *responsible person* may apply to the Executive for the certificate to be varied; any such application shall state the grounds on which it is made and the provision of regulation 4(2) shall apply.

(2) If the Executive is satisfied that the variation should be made it shall vary the certificate accordingly or may cancel it and issue a new one; and if it is not so satisfied it shall notify the *responsible person* that it refuses to vary the certificate.

Changes of responsible person
10. Where a *fire certificate* is in force in respect of any premises and if a person becomes the *responsible person* in respect of those premises he shall notify the Executive and the Executive shall vary the certificate accordingly.

Person not to work on specified premises unless a fire certificate is in force
11.—(1) Subject to paragraph (2) of this regulation a *responsible person* shall not work or permit any other person to work on any premises for which a *fire certificate* is required unless such a certificate is in force and the conditions attached to it are being complied with or an application has been made for a certificate and it has not been refused or withdrawn.

(2) Paragraph (1) of this regulation shall not apply where the work is solely for the purpose of—

(a) taking any steps required under regulations 4(4), 6(4), 7(4) or 8;
(b) complying with a condition imposed under regulation 5(2); or
(c) otherwise making the premises safe.

Right of appeal
12.—A person who is aggrieved *(a)* by—

(a) anything mentioned in a notice served under regulation 4(4) as a step which would have to be taken as a condition of the issue of a *fire certificate* or by the period allowed by such a notice for the taking of any steps mentioned in it;
(b) a refusal to issue a *fire certificate*;
(c) the inclusion of anything in, or the omission of anything from, a *fire certificate*;
(d) a refusal to vary a *fire certificate*;
(e) anything mentioned in a notice served under regulation 6(4), 7(4) or 8 with respect to any premises as a step which must be taken if the Executive is not to become entitled to cancel the *fire certificate* relating to the premises,

may within 21 days from the relevant date, appeal to a court in accordance with the following provisions of this regulation; and on such appeal the court may make such order as it thinks fit.

(2) In this regulation "the relevant date" means—

(a) in the case of a person who was given notice in accordance with these Regulations of the matter by which he is aggrieved, the date on which he was served with that notice (and for this purpose the date on which a certificate was issued or an application deemed to have been refused shall be treated as a date on which the applicant was served with a notice);

(b) in the case of any other person, the date on which the relevant notice, or amended notice, as the case may be, was posted under regulation 5(6).

(3) In any proceedings for an offence of contravening regulation 11 or a requirement of, or condition contained in, a *fire certificate* at any time during the period between the relevant date and the final determination of an appeal under this regulation, it shall be a defence that the appeal was brought and had not been determined.

(4) In England and Wales, an appeal under this regulation shall be brought by way of complaint to a magistrates' court for an order and the Magistrates' Courts Act 1952 *(b)* shall apply to the proceedings; and in Scotland any such appeal shall be to the sheriff within whose jurisdiction the premises are situated.

(5) The Executive and any other person aggrieved *(a)* by an order made by a magistrates' court on a complaint under this regulation may appeal therefrom to the Crown Court.

(a) **Person aggrieved.** See INTRODUCTORY NOTE 14.

(b) **Magistrates' Courts Act.** See now the Magistrates' Courts Act 1980, ss. 51–57.

Modification of local Acts
13.   Local Acts passed before or in the same session as the Health and Safety at Work etc. Act 1974 shall have effect subject to the following modification, that is to say, that a person required by or under any such local Act to do anything in relation to any premises shall not be treated as having acted in contravention of that local Act by reason of his failure to do that thing in so far as the failure is attributable to the fact that remedying it would involve a contravention of these Regulations.

Power of county court and sheriff to modify agreements and apportion expenses
14.—(1) A person who, by reason of the terms of any agreement or lease relating to any premises to which these Regulations apply is prevented from carrying out or doing any structural or other alteration or other thing whose carrying out or doing is requisite in order to secure compliance with a provision of these Regulations or with a notice served under regulation 4(4), 6(4), 7(4) or 8 or with a condition imposed under regulation 5(2) may apply to the county court within whose jurisdiction the premises are suitated and the court may make such an order setting aside or modifying any terms of the agreement or lease as it considers just and equitable in the circumstances of the case.

(2) Where the carrying out or doing on any such premises of any structural or other alterations or other thing whose carrying out or doing is requisite as mentioned in paragraph (1) of this regulation involves a person having an

interest in the premises in expense, or in increased expense, and he alleges that the whole or part of the expense or, as the case may be, the increase ought to be borne by some other person having an interest in the premises, the first-mentioned person may apply to the county within whose jurisdiction the premises are situated and the court, having regard to the terms of any agreement or lease relating to the premises may by order give such directions with respect to the persons by whom the expense or increase is to be borne and in what proportions it is to be borne by them and, if need be, for modifications of the terms of any such agreement or lease so far as concerns rent payable in respect of the premises as the court considers just and equitable in the circumstances of the case.

(3) In the application of this regulation to Scotland, for references to a county court there shall be substituted references to the sheriff.

General note. Compare the similar provisions of s. 28 of the Fire Precautions Act 1971.

Exemptions
15.—(1) Where the Executive is satisfied in respect of any particular premises or part thereof or in respect of any description of premises that any requirement of regulations 3 to 11 is inappropriate or is not reasonably practicable *(a)*, it may by certificate in writing (which it may at its discretion revoke) exempt those premises or that part of them or that description of premises from such requirement to such extent and subject to such conditions as may be specified in the certificate.

(2) An inspector shall be exempt from the requirements of section 23(4) of the Health and Safety at Work etc. Act 1974 (which requires an inspector to consult the fire authority before serving certain improvement and prohibition notices) in relation to any notice in connection with any premises in respect of which a *fire certificate* is required under these Regulations.

Reasonably practicable. See INTRODUCTORY NOTE 5.

Certain certificates under Fire Precautions Act 1971 to be deemed to have been issued under these Regulations
16. Where immediately before a *fire certificate* becomes required under these Regulations in respect of any premises a *fire certificate* issued under the Fire Precautions Act 1971 ("Fire Precautions Act certificate") was in force in respect of those premises, the Fire Precautions Act certificate shall be deemed to be a *fire certificate* issued under these Regulations and accordingly any condition attached to the Fire Precautions Act certificate shall have effect as a condition imposed under regulation 5(2) and the certificate may (in particular) be varied or cancelled in accordance with these Regulations.

Transitional provisions
17.—(1) In this regulation—

"Factories Act certificate" means a certificate under section 40 of the Factories Act 1961;

"Offices Act certificate" means a certificate under section 29 of the Offices, Shops and Railway Premises Act 1963;

"existing certificate" means a Factories Act certificate or an Offices Act certificate,

and this regulation applies where on the date of the coming into operation of these Regulations a *fire certificate* under these Regulations becomes required in respect of any premises and immediately prior to that date an existing certificate was in force in respect of those premises.

(2) The existing certificate shall continue in force (notwithstanding the repeal of the section under which it was issued) and—

(a) shall, as from the said date, be deemed to be a *fire certificate* issued under these Regulations and any condition attached to the existing certificate shall have effect as a condition imposed under regulation 5(2); and

(b) may (in particular) be varied or cancelled in accordance with these Regulations.

(3) The existing certificate, as it has effect by virtue of paragraph (2) of this regulation, shall be treated as imposing in relation to the premises the like requirements as immediately prior to the said date were imposed in relation to it by the following provisions, that is to say—

(a) if the existing certificate is a Factories Act certificate, sections 41(1) and (3), 48 (except subsections (5), (8) and (9)), 49(1), 51(1) and 52(1) and (4) of the Factories Act 1961;

(b) if the existing ertificate is an Offices Act certificate, sections 30 (1) and (3), 33, 34(1) and (2), 36(1) and 38(1) of the Offices, Shops and Railway Premises Act 1963.

(4) Any application for a Factories Act certificate or an Offices Act certificate with respect to any premises which is pending at the date of the coming into operation of these Regulations shall, in the case of premises for which a *fire certificate* is required by these Regulations, be deemed to be an application for a *fire certificate* in respect of them duly made in accordance with these Regulations and accordingly the provisions of regulation 4(2) to (4) shall apply.

(5) If any notice has been given to the appropriate authority of a proposal to undertake any of the changes of which notice is required to be given by section 41(3) of the Factories Act 1961 or section 30(3) of the Offices, Shops and Railway Premises Act 1963 such notice shall be deemed to be a notice duly given in accordance with regulation 6(1) and accordingly the provisions of regulation 6(2) to (4) shall apply.

SCHEDULE 1

Regulation 3

PART I
PREMISES FOR WHICH A FIRE CERTIFICATE IS REQUIRED

1. Any premises at which are carried on any manufacturing processes in which the total quantity of any *highly flammable liquid* under pressure greater than atmospheric pressure and above its boiling point at atmospheric pressure may exceed 50 tonnes.

2. Any premises at which is carried on the manufacture of expanded cellular plastics and at which the quantities manufactured are normally of, or in excess of, 50 tonnes per week.

3. Any premises at which there is stored, or there are facilities provided for the storage of, *liquefield petroleum gas* in quantities of, or in excess of, 100 tonnes except where the *liquefield petroleum gas* is kept for use at the premises either as a fuel, or for the production of an atmosphere for the heat-treatment of metals.

4. Any premises at which there is stored, or there are facilities provided for the storage of, liquified natural gas in quantities of, or in excess of, 100 tonnes except where the liquefied natural gas is kept solely for use at the premises as a fuel.

5. Any premises at which there is stored, or there are facilities provided for the storage of, any liquefied flammable gas consisting predominantly of methyl acetylene in quantities of, or in excess of, 100 tonnes except where the liquefied flammable gas is kept solely for use at the premises as a fuel.

6. Any premises at which oxygen is manufactured and at which there are stored, or there are facilities provided for the storage of, quantities of liquid oxygen of, or in excess of, 135 tonnes.

7. Any premises at which there are stored, or there are facilities provided for the storage of, quantities of chlorine of, or in excess of, 50 tonnes except when the chlorine is kept solely for the purpose of water purification.

8. Any premises at which artificial fertilizers are manufactured and at which there are stored, or there are facilities provided for the storage of, quantities of ammonia of, or in excess of, 250 tonnes.

9. Any premises at which there are in process, manufacture, use or storage at any one time, or there are facilities provided for such processing, manufacture, use or storage of, quantities of any of the materials listed below in, or in excess of, the quantities specified—

Phosgene	5 tonnes
Ethylene oxide	20 tonnes
Carbon disulphide	50 tonnes
Acrylonitrile	50 tonnes
Hydrogen cyanide	50 tonnes
Ethylene	100 tonnes
Propylene	100 tonnes
any *highly flammable liquid* not otherwise specified	4,000 tonnes

10. Explosives factories or magazines which are required to be licensed under the Explosives Act 1875.

11. Any building on the surface at any mine within the meaning of the Mines and Quarries Act 1954.

12. Any premises in which there is comprised—
(a) any undertaking on a site for which a licence is required in accordance with section 1 of the Nuclear Installations Act 1965 or for which a permit is required in accordance with section 2 of that Act; or
(b) any undertaking which would, except for the fact that it is carried on by the United Kingdom Atomic Energy Authority, or by, or on behalf of, the Crown, be required to have a licence or permit in accordance with the provisions mentioned in sub-paragraph (a) above.

13. Any premises containing any machine or apparatus in which charged particles can be accelerated by the equivalent of a voltage of not less than 50 megavolts except where the premises are used as a hospital.

14. Premises to which regulation 26 of the Ionising Radiations Regulations 1985 (S.I. 1985 No. 1333) applies.

15. Any building, or part of a building, which either—
(a) is constructed for temporary occupation for the purposes of building operations or works of engineering construction; or

(b) is in existence at the first commencement there of any further such operations or works,

and which is used for any process or work ancillary to any such operations or works.

Part II
Conditions to be satisfied if a Fire Certificate is not to be required for Premises specified in Paragraph 15 above

16. Not more than 20 persons are employed at any one time in the building or part of the building.

17. Not more than 10 persons are employed at any one time elsewhere than on the ground floor of the building or part of the building.

18. No explosive or highly flammable material is stored or used in or under the building or part of the building.

19. The building or part of the building is provided with such means of escape in case of fire for the persons employed there as may reasonably be required in the circumstances of the case.

20. In the building or part of the building there is provided and maintained appropriate means for fighting fire which are so placed as to be readily available for use.

21. While any person is in the building or part of the building for the purpose of employment or meals, the doors of the building or part and of any room therein in which he is, and any doors which afford a means of exit for persons employed in the building or part are not locked or fastened in such a manner that they cannot easily and immediately be opened from the inside.

22. Any doors opening on to any staircase or corridor from any room in the building or part of the building in which more than 10 persons are employed, except in the case of sliding doors, are constructed to open outwards.

23. Every window, door or other exit affording a means of escape from the building or part of the building in case of fire or giving access thereto, other than the means of exit in ordinary use, is distinctively and conspicuously marked by a notice of adequate size.

24. The contents of any room in the building or part of the building in which persons are employed are so arranged or disposed that there is a free passage way for all persons employed in the room to a means of escape in case of fire.

Part III
Definitions

25. In this Schedule—
(a) "liquefied petroleum gas" means commercial butane, commercial propane or any mixture thereof;
   "commercial butane" means a hydrocarbon mixture consisting predominantly of butane, butylene or any mixture thereof;
   "commercial propane" means a hydrocarbon mixture consisting predominantly of propane, propylene or any mixture thereof;
   "highly flammable liquid" has the same meaning as in regulation 2(2) of the Highly Flammable Liquids and Liquefied Petroleum Gases Regulations 1972 (S.I. 1972/917 as amended by S.I. 1987/209 and S.I. 1992/1811).
(b) Any reference to a provision made by an enactment or instrument shall be construed as a reference to that provision as amended by any enactment or instrument and as including reference to any provision which re-enacts or replaces it.

SCHEDULE 2

PARTICULARS TO BE INCLUDED IN AN APPLICATION FOR A FIRE CERTIFICATE

1. Address of the premises in respect of which the application is made.

2. Description of premises by reference to the list set out in Schedule 1 to these Regulations.

3. Nature of the processes carried on, or to be carried on, on the premises.

4. Nature and approximate quantities of any explosive or highly flammable substance kept, or to be kept, on the premises.

5. Maximum number of persons likely to be on the premises at any one time.

6. Maximum number of persons likely to be in any building of which the premises form part at any one time.

7. Name and address of the occupier of the premises.

8. Name and address of any other person who has control of the premises.

9. If the premises consist of part of a building, the name and postal address of the person or persons having control of the building or any part of it.

THE FIRE PRECAUTIONS (SUB-SURFACE RAILWAY STATIONS) REGULATIONS 1989

(S.I. 1989 No. 1401, as amended by S.I. 1991 No. 259)

1. Citation and commencement.—(1) These Regulations may be cited as the Fire Precautions (Sub-surface Railway Stations) Regulations 1989.

(2) These Regulations, with the exception of the provisions specified in paragraph (3) below, shall come into force on 18 September 1989.

(3) Regulations 6(3) and 7(1) and (2) shall come into force on 1 January 1990, regulations 5(4) and (5) and 6(4), (6) and (8) shall come into force on 1 January 1991 and regulation 8(3) shall come into force on 1 January 1996.

2. Interpretation. In these Regulations—

"fire brigade" means a fire brigade maintained by a fire authority;

"machine room" means a room containing any electricity generator, transformer or switchgear, or in which any machinery for operating an escalator, travolator or lift is installed;

"station manager" means the person employed to work in station premises who is for the time being in charge of the premises;

"station premises" means the premises to which these Regulations apply by virtue of regulation 3 below; and

"travolator" includes any mechanically operated moving footway other than an escalator.

3. Application of Regulations.—(1) These Regulations apply to any premises used as a railway station to which members of the public have access (whether on payment or otherwise) and in which any railway platform is an enclosed underground platform.

(2) For the purposes of paragraph (1) above a railway platform—

(a) is an enclosed platform if the platform and the permanent way to which it is adjacent (whether with or without one or more other railway platforms) are situated wholly or mainly in a tunnel or wholly or mainly within or under any building; and

(b) is an underground platform if the level of the roof or ceiling immediately above the platform and the permanent way to which it is adjacent is below the level of the surface of the ground adjacent to any exit from the railway station providing a means of escape from the station in case of fire,

and a railway platform shall be regarded as situated mainly in a tunnel or mainly within or under a building if the platform and the permanent way to which it is

1168

adjacent are covered by any part of a tunnel or building for more than half the length of the platform.

(3) In their application to the premises referred to in paragraph (1) above these Regulations apply, subject to regulation 13(4) below, to any part of the premises which is owned or occupied by the Crown.

4. Precautions relating to means of escape in case of fire.—(1) All parts of *station premises* providing means of escape from the premises in case of fire, including railway platforms, escalators, *travolators* and lifts, shall be kept free from obstruction at all times when members of the public have access to the premises and shall be so maintained as to secure that they can be safely used as such means of escape at those times.

(2) All parts of *station premises* shall be kept clear of any accumulation of combustible refuse or other combustible matter, and any combustible refuse stored in the premises pending its disposal shall be stored in an area set aside for that purpose.

(3) At all times when members of the public have access to *station premises*, and at other times when persons are at work in the premises, the door of, or barrier in, any doorway or exit through which a person might have to pass in order to leave the premises shall not be so locked or fastened that it cannot be easily and immediately opened in case of fire in the premises.

(4) Where a door in *station premises* is designed to be held open by an electromagnetic or electromechanical device to which this paragraph applies, the door and the means for holding open and closing the door shall be maintained in efficient working order and the door shall not be held open by any device or object other than the electromagnetic or electromechanical device.

(5) Paragraph (4) above applies to an electromagnetic or electromechanical device which allows a door held open by it to be operated manually at all times and to close automatically on each or any of the following occurrences, that is to say—

(a) the operation of a system for giving warning in case of fire;
(b) the manual operation of a switch for releasing the device;
(c) a failure in the supply of electricity to the device.

(6) In any passage or other area affording a means of escape from *station premises* in case of fire or giving access to such a means of escape, every door of a doorway which does not form part of, or give access to, the means of escape shall be kept locked at all times when the part of the premises to which the doorway gives access is neither in use by any person who is at work in the premises nor available for use by members of the public.

(7) Every doorway or other exit affording a means of escape from the *station premises* in case of fire or giving access to such a means of escape, including the means of exit in ordinary use by members of the public, shall be distinctively and conspicuously marked by a notice indicating that it is an ordinary means of exit or (as the case may be) an emergency exit from the premises.

(8) All parts of station premises forming part of the means of escape from the premises in case of fire shall be provided with artificial lighting capable of

providing sufficient illumination of those parts of the premises and any notice required by paragraph (7) above to enable persons in the premises to leave the premises safely in case of fire.

(9) The lighting required by paragraph (8) above shall be provided by electricity supplied from two independent sources of supply so controlled that, so far as is reasonably practicable, the requirements of that paragraph continue to be met in the event of any failure in the supply of electricity from one of the two sources of supply.

5.   Means for fighting fire.—(1) Subject to the provisions of this regulation, *station premises* shall be provided with such means for fighting fire as are appropriate and adequate in relation to the risk to persons in case of fire in the premises.

(2) The location of each fire hydrant in *station premises* shall be indicated by a distinctive and conspicuous notice in a position above or adjacent to the fire hydrant.

(3) The outlet connection of every fire hydrant in *station premises* shall be of such a type as is compatible with the type of attachment on hoses used by the *fire brigade* for the purpose of drawing water from fire hydrants.

(4) Every escalator and *travolator* in *station premises* shall be provided with a means for fighting fire comprising a water sprinkler system which is activated automatically on the operation of the means for detecting fire with which the escalator or *travolator* is provided under regulation 6(1) below.

(5) The following parts of *station premises* shall be provided with a means for fighting fire comprising a system which is activated automatically in such a part of the premises in the event of any outbreak of fire in that part of the premises, that is to say—

(a) a *machine room*, other than a *machine room* in which machinery for operating an escalator, *travolator* or lift is installed;

(b) any storage area, including an area set aside for storing refuse pending its disposal;

(c) any part of the premises used as a shop.

(6) All means for fighting fire in *station premises* shall be maintained in efficient working order and all portable equipment for fighting fire in the premises shall be so placed as to be readily available for use.

(7) When any person employed to work in *station premises* reasonably suspects that there is an outbreak of fire in the premises, immediate steps shall be taken to activate the system for giving warning in case of fire referred to in regulation 6(4) below and to call for the assistance of the *fire brigade*.

(8) A plan of the *station premises* suitable for use by members of the *fire brigade* when attending the premises for fire fighting purposes shall be kept in, or affixed to, a part of the premises where it is accessible to members of the *fire brigade* in such an event.

6.   Means for detecting fire and giving warning in case of fire.—(1) Every escalator and *travolator* in *station premises* shall be provided with a means for detecting fire comprising a linear heat detector system.

(2) Any *machine room* in *station premises* in which machinery for operating an escalator, *travolator* or lift is installed shall be provided with a means for detecting the presence of smoke in the room.

(3) The following parts of *station premises* shall be provided with a means for detecting fire which is activated automatically in case of fire in such a part of the premises, that is to say—

(a) every part of the premises required by regulation 5(5) above to be provided with the means for fighting fire referred to in that provision;
(b) any office which is not separated from other parts of the premises by fire-resisting construction within the meaning of regulation 7(6) below;
(c) any staff room for persons employed to work in the premises.

(4) The *station premises* shall be provided with an electrically operated system for giving warning in case of fire which—

(a) is designed to transmit any such warning to a place where it can be received by the *station manager* or by some other person employed by the occupier of the premises; and
(b) is capable of being activated both by manual operation at call points in the premises, including call points for use by members of the public, and by any of the means referred to in paragraph (1) to (3) above for detecting fire or the presence of smoke in the premises.

(5) Where a call point for a system for giving warning in case of fire is situated in a part of *station premises* to which members of the public have access, there shall be displayed at or near the call point a notice giving information as to how to use the call point to activate the system.

(6) The *station premises* shall be provided with a public address system for use by or on behalf of the occupier of the premises to give warning of fire to members of the public in the premises and advise them of the action to be taken by them in case of fire.

(7) All means for detecting fire and for giving warning in case of fire in *station premises* shall be maintained in efficient working order.

(8) In *station premises* arrangements shall be made to secure that in case of fire the *station manager* and any person employed to work as a member of the staff of the *station premises* who is on duty in any part of the premises can communicate with each other by personal radio or by telephone.

7. Fire-resisting construction in premises.—(1) A part of *station premises* to which this paragraph applies shall, so far as is reasonably practicable, be separated by fire-resisting construction from other parts of the premises, including any other part of the premises to which this paragraph applies.

(2) Paragraph (1) above applies to the following parts of *station premises*, that is to say a *machine room*, any storage area other than an area referred to in paragraph (3) or (4) below, and a staff room for persons employed to work in the premises.

(3) Any explosive or highly flammable materials kept in *station premises* shall be stored in an area separated from other parts of the premises by fire-resisting construction.

(4) An area set aside for storing combustible refuse in station premises pending its disposal shall be separated from other parts of the premises by fire-resisting construction.

(5) Where a door forms part of any fire-resisting construction required by this regulation, the door shall be fitted with a self-closing device and each face of the door shall have affixed to it a notice displaying the words "FIRE DOOR—KEEP SHUT".

(6) Any reference in this regulation to fire-resisting construction is a reference to construction of such a nature as to be capable of providing resistance to fire for a period of not less than one hour.

8.   Materials used in internal construction of premises.—(1) Any material which is used on or after 18 September 1989 in the construction of an internal wall or ceiling in any part of station premises to which members of the public have access shall be non-combustible or have low heat emission, and any material which is applied on or after that date to the surface of an internal wall or ceiling in such a part of the premises shall offer adequate resistance to the spread of flame over the surface of the material and shall have, if ignited, a reasonable rate of heat release.

(2) The material of which any balustrade, decking or skirting board of an escalator or *travolator in station premises* is constructed, and the material of which any display panel for advertisements or notices in an escalator shaft in the premises is constructed, shall offer adequate resistance to the spread of flame over the surface of the material and shall have, if ignited, a reasonable rate of heat release.

(3) The material of which the treads and risers in the steps of any escalator in *station premises* are constructed shall offer adequate resistance to the spread of flame over the surface of the material and shall have, if ignited, a reasonable rate of heat release.

(4) For the purposes of this regulation material shall be regarded—

(a) as non-combustible if it is material deemed non-combustible according to the test criteria specified in British Standard 476: Part 4: 1970 (as amended by amendment slips AMD 2483 and AMD 4390);

(b) as having low heat emission if it is of such a nature that if tested in accordance with British Standard 476: Part 11: 1982 it would not flame and would produce no rise in temperature on either the specimen or the furnace thermocouples;

(c) as offering adequate resistance to the spread of flame over its surface and having a reasonable rate of heat release if the material or, where it is bonded throughout to a substrate, the material combined with the substrate, is of such a nature that it would comply with the test criteria set out in relation to Class 1 in British Standard 476: Part 7: 1987 and, when tested in accordance with British Standard 476: Part 6: 1989, would have an index of performance (I) not exceeding 12 and sub-index (i)[1] not exceeding 6.

9.   Instruction and training of persons working in premises.—(1) Every person employed to work in *station premises* as a member of the staff of the *station* *premises* shall be given instruction in the fire precautions to be taken or observed there, so far as those precautions relate to his duties, including instruction as to—

(a) the means of escape from the premises in case of fire;

(b) the action to be taken by him in case of fire in the premises;

(c) the location of, and method of operating, equipment provided in the premises for fighting fire; and

(d) the location and use of the means for giving warning in case of fire in the premises,

and he shall be given such further instruction at least once in every period of seven months as is necessary to ensure that he is familiar with those matters.

(2) No person employed to work in *station premises* shall be employed as the *station manager* unless he has been given instruction in the matters specified in paragraph (1) above and, in addition, instruction—

(a) as to supervising and controlling action to be taken in case of fire in the premises by other persons employed to work there as members of the staff of the *station premises*;

(b) in arrangements for calling for the assistance of the fire brigade and securing that members of the fire brigade are directed to the source of any fire in the premises;

(c) as to taking action in case of fire in the premises to prevent the entry of members of the public to the premises;

(d) in the use of the means for advising members of the public in the premises on the action to be taken by them in case of fire in the premises; and

(e) in arrangements for securing that the means of escape from the premises can be immediately used in case of fire and for enabling persons to leave the premises by train in case of fire.

(3) A person who is employed to work in *station premises* otherwise than as a member of the staff of the *station premises* shall be given instruction in the fire precautions to be observed by him in the course of his work in the premises and the action to be taken by him in case of fire in the premises.

(4) A fire drill for persons employed to work in *station premises* as members of the staff of the *station premises* shall be held there not less than once in every period of six months for the purpose of providing those persons with training in the action to be taken in case of fire in the premises.

(5) The attendance at a fire drill of the persons referred to in paragraph (4) above shall be so organised as to secure that not less than one third of the number of those persons at work in the *station premises* at any one time have attended a fire drill in the preceding six months.

(6) Each fire drill in *station premises* shall be held at a time when members of the public have access to the premises.

10. Additional precautions to be taken.—(1) The occupier of station premises shall prepare and keep up to date an emergency plan setting out details of the action to be taken in the event of an outbreak of fire in the premises by persons employed to work in the premises and the procedure to be followed for the evacuation of members of the public from the premises in that event.

(2) All practicable steps shall be taken to prevent smoking by persons in any part of *station premises* which is a *machine room,* storage area or part of the premises used as a shop or to which members of the public have access.

(3) All practicable steps shall be taken to supervise the carrying out by persons other than members of the staff of *station premises* of any work of construction or maintenance in the premises which presents a risk to persons in case of fire.

(4) The periods of duty of the persons employed to work in *station premises* as members of the staff of the *station premises* shall be so arranged as to secure that not less than two of those persons are present on duty in the premises at all times when members of the public have access to the premises.

11.   Keeping of records of maintenance work, instruction and training.— (1) A record shall be made—

(a) of all work of maintenance done in *station premises* in pursuance of regulations 4(4), 5(6) and 6(7) above;

(b) of the occasions on which instruction is given in pursuance of regulation 9 above to each person employed to work in the premises; and

(c) of the fire drills held in the premises in pursuance of regulation 9 above and of the names of the persons attending each fire drill.

(2) A record made under paragraph (1) above in relation to *station premises* shall be kept in the premises for a period of not less than three years from the date on which it was made.

12.   Exemption from requirements.—(1) Where a fire authority are satisfied in respect of any particular *station premises* that compliance with a requirement of any of the provisions of regulations 4(1) and (3), 5(4) and (5), 6(1) and (3), 7(1), 8(2), 10(2) and (4) and 11(2) above is inappropriate, unnecessary or not reasonably practicable, they may by notice in writing to the occupier of the premises grant exemption from compliance with the requirement to such extent as is reasonable having regard to all the circumstances of the case and in particular to the risk in case of fire to persons in the premises.

(2) A fire authority may grant an exemption under paragraph (1) above subject to such conditions as may be specified in the notice granting the exemption and the authority may by notice in writing to the occupier of the premises withdraw the exemption if the occupier fails to comply with any condition subject to which the exemption was granted.

13.   Contravention of requirements.—(1) The requirements of regulations 4 to 11 above are imposed on the occupier of the *station premises* to which those regulations apply and, subject to any exemption granted (and not withdrawn) under regulation 12 above and to paragraph (2) below, the occupier of the premises shall be responsible for any contravention of the provisions of those regulations.

(2) The requirements of paragraphs (8) and (9) of regulation 4 above shall be deemed to be satisfied in *station premises* in Scotland if the premises comply

with regulation 13 of the Building Standards (Scotland) Regulations 1990, as read with specifications E2.43 and E2.44 taken together contained in the Technical Standards for Compliance with the Building Standards (Scotland) Regulations 1990 dated October 1990.

(3) If any provision of regulations 4 to 11 above is contravened the person who under this regulation is responsible for the contravention shall be guilty of an offence under section 12 of the Fire Precautions Act 1971.

(4) Paragraph (3) above shall not apply to the Crown.

THE HIGHLY FLAMMABLE LIQUIDS AND LIQUEFIED PETROLEUM GASES REGULATIONS 1972

(S.I. 1972 No. 917, as modified by S.I. 1984 No. 1244, and as amended by
S.I. 1989 No. 2169 and S.I. 1992 No. 1811)

The Secretary of State:—

   (a) by virtue of his powers under sections 50, 76 and 180(6) and (7) of the
Factories Act 1961 and of all other powers enabling him in that behalf;
and

   (b) after publishing, pursuant to Schedule 4 to the said Act of 1961, notice of
the proposal to make the Regulations and after the holding of an inquiry
under that Schedule into objections made to the draft,

hereby, makes the following special Regulations:—

1.   Citation, commencement and revocation.—(1) These Regulations may be
cited as the Highly Flammable Liquids and Liquefied Petroleum Gases Regulations 1972 and shall come into operation on 21 June 1973 with the exception
of regulation 10(4) which shall come into operation on 21 June 1974.

(2) The Regulations dated 12 August 1902 with respect to the manufacture
of felt hats are hereby revoked.

(3) The Cellulose Solutions Regulations 1934 are hereby revoked—

   (a) in the case of the second proviso to the preamble, the definitions and
regulations 3, 4 and 17 as from 21 June 1974; and

   (b) in the case of the remainder of those Regulations, as from 21 June 1973.

2.   Interpretation.—(1) The Interpretation Act 1889 [Interpretation Act
1978] shall apply to the interpretation of these Regulations as it applies to the
interpretation of an Act of Parliament, and as if these Regulations and the
Regulations hereby revoked were Acts of Parliament.

(2) In these Regulations, unless the context otherwise requires, the following expressions have the meanings hereby assigned to them respectively, that it
so say—

   "aqueous ammonia" means ammonia gas dissolved in water;

   "commercial butane" means a hydrocarbon mixture consisting predominantly of butane, butylene or any mixture thereof;

   "commercial propane" means a hydrocarbon mixture consisting predominantly of propane, propylene or any mixture thereof;

   "dangerous concentration of vapours" means a concentration greater than the
lower flammable limit of the vapours;

"factory" includes any premises and place to which these Regulations apply;

"fire resisting structure" means any of the following, that is to say, any building, part of a building, structure, cabinet and enclosure which is constructed in conformity with a specification for fire resisting structures being a specification approved for the time being for the purposes of these Regulations by certificate of the Chief Inspector;

"highly flammable liquid" means any of the following, other than *aqueous ammonia, liquefied gas* and *liquefied petroleum gas*, that is to say, any liquid, liquid solution, emulsion or suspension which, when tested in accordance with Part IV of Schedule 1 to the Classification, Packaging and Labelling of Dangerous Substances Regulations 1984 (S.I. 1984/1244) has a flash point of less than 32 degrees Celsius and when tested in the manner specified in Schedule 2 to these Regulations, supports combustion;

"liquefied gas" means any substance which at a temperature of 20 degrees Celsius and a pressure of 760 millimetres of mercury would be a flammable gas, but which is in liquid form as a result of the application of pressure or refrigeration or both;

"liquified petroleum gas" means *commercial butane, commercial propane* and any mixture thereof;

"undertaking" includes the Crown and any municipal or other public authority.

(2A) Solely for the purposes of these Regulations, for sub-paragraph (b) of paragraph 4 of Part IV of Schedule 1 to the Classification, Packaging and Labelling of Dangerous Substances Regulations 1984 there shall be substituted the following sub-paragraph—

"(b) by one of the non-equilibrium methods referred to in paragraph 6, except that when the flash point falls within the range 30°C to 34°C that flash point shall be confirmed by the use of like apparatus using the appropriate equilibrium method referred to in paragaph 5."

(3) References in these Regulations to any enactment shall be construed as references to that enactment as amended by or under any other enactment.

3. Application of Regulations.—(1) Except as provided in paragaphs (4) to (6) of this regulation and in regulations 12 and 17, these Regulations shall apply to—

(a) all *factories*; and

(b) all premises, places, processes, operations and works to which the provisions of section 50 (so far as the Secretary of State may make regulations thereunder) and of Part IV (with respect to special regulations for safety and health) of the Factories Act 1961 are applied by any of the following provisions of that Act, namely, section 123 (which relates to electrical stations), section 124 (which relates to institutions), section 125 (which relates to certain dock premises and certain warehouses), section 126 (which relates to ships) and section 127 (which relates to building operations and works of engineering construction),

where any *highly flammable liquid* is present for the purposes of, or in connection with, any *undertaking*, trade or business.

(2) Except as provided in paragraphs (4) to (6) of this regulation, regulations 1 to 4, 7 and 18 shall apply to all *factories* and all such premises, places,

processes, operations and works as are mentioned in paragraph (1) of this regulation where any *liquefied petroleum gas* is present for the purposes of, or in connection with, any *undertaking*, trade or business.

(3) Where in any *factory* there is any *highly flammable liquid* or *liquefied petroleum gas* of which the occupier is not the owner and the *highly flammable liquid* or *liquefied petroleum gas* is used by or under the direction of some person other than the occupier or a person in the employment of the occupier, that other person or (if he is in the employment of the owner) the employer of that other person shall, in relation that to *highly flammable liquid* or *liquid petroleum gas*, be deemed for the purposes of these Regulations to be the occupier of the *factory*.

(4) These Regulations shall not apply to any premises or parts of premises in respect of which a licence or a continuing certificate under the Explosives Act 1875—

(a) is in force; or

(b) would, but for the fact that the premises or parts of premises are under the control, or held for the service of the Crown, be required to be in force.

(5) Nothing in these Regulations shall apply as respects any *highly flammable liquid* in a *factory* so long as it is present in such circumstances that provisions of the Factories (Testing of Aircraft Engines and Accessories) Special Regulations 1952 apply to or in relation to it or to anything done to, with or in relation to it.

(6) Nothing in these Regulations shall apply to any *highly flammable liquid* or *liquefied petroleum gas* stored (as fuel, cargo or otherwise) in any fixed storage tanks on a ship.

(7) The provision of these Regulations shall be in addition to and not in substitution for or in diminution of other requirements imposed by or under the Factories Act 1961.

4.   Exemption certificates. The Chief Inspector *(a)* may (subject to such conditions as may be specified therein) by certificate in writing (which he may in his discretion revoke at any time) exempt from all or any of the requirements of these Regulations—

(a) any *factory* or part of any factory; or

(b) any class or description of *factories* or parts thereof; or

(c) any machine, plant, apparatus, process, operation or work, or any class or description of machines, plant, apparatus, processes, operations or works; or

(d) any *highly flammable liquid* or *liquefied petroleum gas* or any class or description of *highly flammable liquids* or *liquefied petroleum gases*,

if he is satisfied that the requirements in respect of which the exemption is granted are not necessary for the protection of persons employed.

(a)   Inspector. See INTRODUCTORY NOTE 24.

5.   Storage.—(1) Except as provided in paragraph (4) of this regulation and except in the case of *highly flammable liquids* present in any place in accordance with regulation 8(3) or being conveyed within the factory, all *highly flammable liquids* shall be stored—

(a) in suitable fixed storage tanks in safe positions; or

(b) in suitable closed vessels kept in a safe position in the open air and, where necessary, protected against direct sunlight; or

(c) in suitable closed vessels kept in a storeroom which either is in a safe position or is a *fire resisting structure;* or

(d) in the case of a workroom where the aggregate quantity of *highly flammable liquids* stored does not exceed fifty litres, in suitable closed vessels kept in a suitably placed cupboard or bin being a cupboard or bin which is a *fire-resisting structure.*

(2) Except in the case of tanks and vessels which have been emptied and made free of vapour from *highly flammable liquids,* all openings (other than those necessary for venting) in cupboards, bins, tanks and vessels which have at any time been used for storing *highly flammable liquids* (whether or not for the time being containing any *highly flammable liquid*) shall be kept closed except as necessary for the use, operation or maintenance of those cupboards, bins, tanks and vessels.

(3) Wherever *highly flammable liquids* are stored in accordance with paragraph 1(a), (b) or (c) of this regulation, all reasonably practicable *(a)* steps shall be taken to ensure that any *highly flammable liquid* which leaks, is spilt or otherwise escapes shall be contained or immediately drained off to a suitable container or to a safe place, or otherwise treated to make it safe.

(4) Nothing in this regulation shall apply to—

(a) *highly flammable liquids* (being petroleum-spirit or any substance to which provisions of section 1 of the Petroleum (Consolidation) Act 1928 were applied by the Petroleum (Mixtures) Order 1929 and the Petroleum (Liquid Methane) Order 1957 authorised to be kept by a licence in force under the said Act of 1928 or which, but for the fact that the highly flammable liquids are kept in premises occupied by the Crown, would be required to be so authorised;

(b) *highly flammable liquids* in the fuel tanks of vehicles or engines for the purposes of operating the vehicles or engines;

(c) any suitable small closed vessel containing not more than 500 cc of *highly flammable liquid.*

(a) **Reasonably practicable.** See INTRODUCTORY NOTE 5.

6. Marking of storerooms, tanks, vessels, etc.—(1) Except where it is impracticable *(a)* to do so and except as provided in paragraph (3) of this regulation, every storeroom, cupboard, bin, tank and vessel used for storing *highly flammable liquid* shall be clearly and boldly marked "Highly Flammable" or "Flashpoint below 32°C" or "Flashpoint in the range of 22°C to 32°C" or otherwise with an appropriate indication of flammability.

(2) Where it is impracticable *(a)* to mark any storeroom, cupboard, bin, tank or vessel in accordance with the foregoing paragraph of this regulation, the words "Highly Flammable Liquid" shall be clearly and boldly displayed as near to it as possible.

(3) Nothing in this regulation shall apply to—

(a) any of the following, that is to say, any cupboard, bin, tank or vessel, which contains spirits intended for human consumption;

(b) the fuel tanks of vehicles or engines which contain *highly flammable liquid* for the purpose of operating the vehicles or engines;

(c) any suitable small closed vessel containing not more than 500 cc of *highly flammable liquid*;

(d) any aerosol dispenser in which the amount of *highly flammable liquid* contained is not in excess of either 45 per cent. by weight of the total contents or 250 grammes in weight.

General note. Where a container is required to be labelled in accordance with the Classification, Packaging and Labelling of Dangerous Substances Regulations 1984, S.I. 1984 No. 1244, and is so labelled, that labelling is deemed to satisfy the requirements of these Regulations *(ibid).*

(a) *Impracticable.* See INTRODUCTORY NOTE 5.

7.   Liquefied petroleum gas—storage and marking of tanks, vessels, cylinders, etc.—(1) Except as provided in paragraphs (2), (3) and (6)(a) of this regulation, all *liquefied petroleum gas* not in use shall be stored—

(a) in suitable underground reservoirs below ground the surface of which is wholly or mainly in the open air, or in suitable fixed storage tanks or suitable fixed storage vessels being tanks or vessels in safe positions either in the open air or below ground the surface of which is wholly or mainly in the open air; or

(b) in suitable movable storage tanks or suitable movable storage vessels kept in safe positions in the open air; or

(c) in the pipelines and pumps or other appliances forming part of a totally enclosed pipeline system; or

(d) in suitable cylinders kept in safe positions in the open air, or where this is not reasonably practicable *(a)*, in a storeroom constructed of non-combustible material being a storeroom which is adequately ventilated, which either is in a safe position or is a *fire resisting structure* and which is not used for any purpose other than the storage of *liquefied petroleum gas* or acetylene cylinders.

(2) No *liquefied petroleum gas* other than in suitable cylinders or suitable pipelines shall be present in any workplace and the number of *liquefied petroleum gas* cylinders or pipelines present at any one time in any workplace shall be as small as is reasonably practicable *(a)* having regard to the processes or operations being carried on.

(3) Every *liquefied petroleum gas* cylinder shall be stored until such time before being first required for use or manipulation as is reasonable, and when its contents have been expended shall, as soon as reasonably practicable *(a)*, be removed from the workplace and stored or refilled without delay.

(4) Except where it is impracticable *(a)* to do so, and except as provided in paragraph (6) of this regulation, every tank, vessel, reservoir, cylinder and storeroom used for storing *liquefied petroleum gas* shall be clearly and boldly marked "Highly Flammable—L.P.G." or otherwise to the like effect.

(5) Where it is impracticable *(a)* to mark any tank, vessel, reservoir, cylinder or storeroom in accordance with the last foregoing paragraph of this regulation, the words "Highly Flammable—L.P.G." shall be clearly and boldly displayed as near to it as possible.

(6) (a) Nothing in this regulation shall apply to—
- (i) *liquefied petroleum gas* in the fuel tanks of vehicles or engines for the purpose of operating the vehicles or engines;
- (ii) any suitable small closed vessel containing not more than 500 cc of *liquefied petroleum gas.*

(b) Nothing in paragraphs (4) and (5) of this regulation shall apply to any aerosol dispenser in which the amount of *liquefied petroleum gas* contained is not in excess of either 45 per cent. by weight of the total contents or 250 grammes in weight.

(7) In this regulation "cylinder" means a cylinder which complies with the conditions specified in regulation 16(2) (a) or (b) of the Pressure Systems and Transportable Gas Containers Regulations 1989.

(a) **Reasonably practicable; impracticable.** See INTRODUCTORY NOTE 5.

(b) **Pressure vessel code.** The following EEC Directives are approved under reg. 7(7) as pressure vessel codes for the purposes of these Regulations by Certificate of Approval No. HFL 1986/1 (June 1986):

Council Dir. 84/525/EEC of 17 September 1984 on the approximation of the laws of the Member States relating to seamless, steel gas cylinders (OJ No. L300, 19.11.1984, p. 1);

Council Dir. 84/526/EEC of 17 September 1984 on the approximation of the laws of the Member States relating to seamless, unalloyed aluminium and aluminium alloy gas cylinders (OJ No. L 300, 19.11.1984, p. 20);

Council Dir. 84/527/EEC of 17 September 1984 on the approximation of the laws of the Member States relating to welded unalloyed steel gas cylinders (OJ No. L300, 19.11.1984, p. 48).

(c) **Inspector.** see INTRODUCTORY NOTE 24.

8. Precautions against spills and leaks.—(1) Where *highly flammable liquids* are to be conveyed within a *factory* they shall, where it is reasonably practicable *(a)* so to do, be conveyed through a totally enclosed system incorporating pipelines and pumps or similar appliances. Where conveyance of *highly flammable liquids* within a factory through such a totally enclosed system is not reasonably practicable *(a)*, they shall be conveyed in vessels which are so designed and constructed as to avoid so far as is practicable *(a)* the risk of spilling.

(2) A totally enclosed system used for such conveyance shall so far as is practicable *(a)* be so designed, constructed, installed, placed and maintained as to avoid leakage.

(3) The quantity of any *highly flammable liquid* present at any one time in any workplace in course of manufacture or for use or manipulation and in the process tanks, process vessels, pipelines, pumps, plant, equipment and apparatus in the workplace shall be as small as is reasonably practicable *(a)* having regard to the processes or operations being carried on.

(4) All reasonably practicable *(a)* steps shall be taken to ensure that tanks or vessels containing any *highly flammable liquid* do not leak. Every such tank and

vessel shall be kept closed except as necessary during the manufacture, use or manipulation of the *highly flammable liquid* therein, or for the operation or maintenance of the tank or vessel, and every such tank and vessel shall be so designed, constructed and placed as to avoid so far as reasonably practicable *(a)* the risk of spilling.

(5) Where in any process or operation any *highly flammable liquid* is liable to be spilled or to leak, all reasonably practicable *(a)* steps shall be taken to ensure that any *highly flammable liquid* which is spilt or leaks shall be contained or immediately drained off to a suitable container or to a safe place, or otherwise treated to make it safe.

(6) Any tank or vessel used to contain any *highly flammable liquid*, other than a fixed process tank, a fixed process vessel, a fixed tank or a fixed storage vessel, shall, when its contents have been expended, unless it has been made free of vapour from the liquid or is to be immediately re-used, be removed without delay to a safe place in the open air or to a suitably placed storeroom being a storeroom which is a *fire resisting structure* or be placed in a suitably placed cupboard or bin being a cupboard or bin which is a *fire resisting structure*.

(7) All such empty tanks and vessels as aforesaid which have not been made free of vapour from the liquid shall be kept in such a safe place or such a storeroom, cupboard or bin as aforesaid until next required for use or disposal, and any such tank or vessel shall be kept closed.

(a) **Reasonably practicable.** See INTRODUCTORY NOTE 5.

9.   Sources of ignition.—(1) No means likely to ignite vapour from any *highly flammable liquid* shall be present where a *dangerous concentration of vapours* from *highly flammable liquids* may reasonably be expected to be present.

(2) Where in any place a *dangerous concentration of vapours* from *highly flammable liquids* may reasonably be expected to be present, any cotton waste or other material in that place which—

(a) has been used in such a manner as to render the cotton waste or other material liable to spontaneous combustion; or

(b) is contaminated with any *highly flammable liquid*,

shall be deposited without delay in a metal container having a suitable cover or be removed without delay to a safe place.

(3) Where any cellulose nitrate is present in any *highly flammable liquid*, all practicable steps shall be taken to prevent the deposit of any solid residue resulting therefrom on any surface which is liable to attain a temperature of 120 degrees Celsius.

(4) Nothing in paragraph (2) of this regulation shall apply to lagging in position on pipework.

10.   Prevention of escape of vapours and dispersal of dangerous concentrations of vapours.—(1) Where any *highly flammable liquid* is present in any workplace, steps shall be taken to prevent so far as is reasonably practicable *(a)* the escape of vapours from any such *highly flammable liquid* into the general atmosphere of that or any other workplace.

(2) Except as provided in paragraph (5) of this regulation, where a *dangerous concentration of vapours* from highly flammable liquids may reasonably be expected to be evolved in any process or operation, the process or operation shall, where reasonably practicable *(a)*, be carried on within a cabinet or other enclosure which, in either case, is effective to prevent the escape of such vapours into the general atmosphere of the workroom or any other workroom, is adequately ventilated by mechanical means and is a *fire resisting structure.*

Provided that in the case of a batch-loaded box-type oven used to evaporate *highly flammable liquid* being an oven with a cubic capacity of less than one and a half cubic metres and having natural ventilation sufficient to prevent the occurrence of a *dangerous concentration of vapours* in the oven, the oven shall not be required to be ventilated by mechanical means.

(3) Except as provided in paragraph (5) of this regulation, where it is not reasonably practicable *(a)* to comply with the requirement of the last foregoing paragraph of this regulation where in any workroom any such *dangerous concentration of vapours* may reasonably be expected to be evolved in any process or operation, the workroom shall have exhaust ventilation provided by mechanical means, being exhaust ventilation adequate to remove such vapours from the work-room.

(4) A workroom required by the last foregoing paragraph of this regulation to have exhaust ventilation shall be a *fire resisting structure* with the exception of any following forming part of it, that is to say, any external doors, external windows and external walls, any openings provided for ventilation and any tops or ceilings of single storey buildings or of top floor rooms.

(5) Nothing in paragraphs (2) and (3) of this regulation shall apply to any room if the only work with *highly flammable liquids* which is being carried on therein is work to the room and if there is secured natural or other ventilation of the room adequate to prevent the occurrence there of a *dangerous concentration of vapour* from the liquids.

(6) Ventilation provided or secured in pursuance of this regulation shall be kept in operation or use at all necessary times.

(7) All ducts, trunks and casings used in connection with ventilation provided or secured in pursuance of this regulation shall be *fire resisting structures.*

(8) In the case of electric motors used in connection with exhaust ventilation systems provided in pursuance of this regulation which comprise ducts, being systems constructed or installed after the date of commencement of these Regulations or constructed or installed before that date and substantially reconstructed after that date, such electric motors shall not be situated in the path of vapours from any *highly flammable liquids* being exhausted by the systems.

(9) All venting devices of fixed tanks and fixed vessels containing *highly flammable liquid* shall discharge to a safe place and, where necessary, shall be provided with a suitable wire gauze effective as a flame arrestor or other suitable flame arrestor.

(a) Reasonably practicable. See INTRODUCTORY NOTE 5.

11. Explosion pressure relief of fire resisting structures.—(1) Where in accordance with provisions of regulations 5, 8 or 10 a storeroom, workroom, cabinet or enclosure is a *fire resisting structure* provision may be made in its structure for pressure relief in the case of explosion and, in the case of a storeroom, for adequate natural ventilation notwithstanding, in either case, anything contained in any specification approved for the purposes of the definition of the expression *"fire resisting structure"* contained in regulation 2.

(2) Where in pursuance of the foregoing paragraph of this regulation provision is made in a *fire resisting structure* for pressure relief in the case of explosion such provision shall be so arranged that any pressure will vent to a safe place.

12.   Means of escape in case of fire.—(1) There shall be adequate and safe means of escape in case of fire from every room in which any *highly flammable liquid* is manufactured, used or manipulated.

(2) This regulation shall not apply to *factories* other than premises and places to which provisions of the Factories Act 1961 are applied by section 125 (which relates to certain dock premises and certain warehouses) or section 127 (which relates to building operations and works of engineering construction) of that Act.

13.   Prevention and removal of solid residues.—(1) Without prejudice to regulation 9(3), whenever as a result of any process or operation involving any *highly flammable liquid* a deposit of any solid waste residue liable to give rise to a risk of fire is liable to occur on any surface—

(a)   steps shall be taken where reasonably practicable *(a)* to prevent as far as possible the occurrence of all such deposits; and

(b)   where any such deposit occurs, effective steps shall be taken, as often as necessary to prevent danger, to remove all such residues as aforesaid and put them in a safe place.

(2) No removal of any such residue containing cellulose nitrate shall be effected by use of an iron or steel implement.

(a) *Reasonably practicable.* See INTRODUCTORY NOTE 5.

14.   Smoking.—(1) No person shall smoke in any place in which any *highly flammable liquid* is present and the circumstances are such that smoking would give rise to a risk of fire.

(2) The occupier shall take all reasonably practicable *(a)* steps to ensure compliance with the foregoing paragraph of this Regulation and such steps shall include—

(a)   the display at or as near as possible to every place to which the said paragraph applies of a clear and bold notice indicating that smoking is prohibited in that place; or

(b)   the display at every entrance to the factory at which employed persons enter of a clear and bold notice indicating that smoking is prohibited throughout the factory except at those places where there is displayed a notice indicating that smoking is permitted.

(a) **Reasonably practicable.** See INTRODUCTORY NOTE 5.

15. Control of ignition and burning of highly flammable liquids.— (1) Except where the sole purpose is to dispose of it as waste by burning it and except as provided in paragraph (3) of this regulation, no *highly flammable liquid* shall be ignited except in plant or apparatus suitable for the purpose of burning that *highly flammable liquid* safely and by the proper use of that plant or apparatus.

(2) Where the sole purpose is to dispose of any *highly flammable liquid* as waste by burning it, it shall be burnt either—

(a) in plant or apparatus suitable for the purposes of burning that *highly flammable liquid* safely; or

(b) by a competent person, in a safe manner and in a safe place.

(3) The prohibition contained in paragraph (1) of this regulation shall not apply where *highly flammable liquid* is burnt in order to provide persons with training in fighting fire if—

(a) it is burnt by a competent person, in a safe manner and in a safe place; and

(b) the training is carried out under the direct and continuous supervision of a competent person.

16. Power to take samples.—(1) An inspector (a) may at any time after informing the occupier or, if the occupier is not readily available, a foreman or other responsible person, take for testing sufficient samples of any material in the *factory* which in his opinion may prove on testing to be a *highly flammable liquid.*

(2) The occupier or the foreman or other responsible person may, at any time when a sample is taken under this regulation, and on providing the necessary appliances, require the inspector (a) to divide the sample into three parts, to mark and seal up each part and—

(a) to deliver one part to the occupier, or the foreman or other responsible person;

(b) to retain one part for future comparison;

(c) to submit one part to testing,

and any test under this regulation shall, if so required, be carried out by a government department.

(3) The provisions of this regulation are without prejudice to the provisions of section 78 of the Factories Act 1961.

(a) **Inspector.** See INTRODUCTORY NOTE 24.

17. Fire fighting.—(1) There shall in every *factory* where any *highly flammable liquid* is manufactured, used or manipulated be provided and maintained appropriate means for fighting fire, which shall be so placed as to be readily available for use.

(2) This regulation shall not apply to *factories* other than premises and places to which provisions of the Factories Act 1961 are applied by section 125 (which relates to certain dock premises and certain warehouses) or section 127 (which relates to building operations and works of engineering construction) of that Act.

18. Duties of persons employed.—It shall be the duty of every person employed in a *factory* to which any of these Regulations apply to comply with such of the requirements of the Regulations as relate to the doing of or refraining from an act by him and to the use by him of any plant, equipment or appliance and to co-operate in carrying out these Regulations. If a person employed as aforesaid discovers any defect in the plant, equipment or appliances, it shall be his duty to report such defect without delay to the occupier, manager or other responsible person.

SCHEDULE 1

Regulation 2(2)

[*repealed*].

SCHEDULE 2

Regulation 2(2)

METHOD OF TEST FOR COMBUSTIBILITY

Scope
1. The method describes a procedure for determining if the product when heated under the conditions of test and exposed to an external source of flame applied in a standard manner supports combustion.

Principle of the method
2.—(1) A block of aluminium alloy, or other non-rusting metal of suitable heat conductivity, with a concave depression (called the well) is heated to the required temperature. A standard source of flame capable of being swivelled over the centre of the well and at a given distance from it is attached to the metal block.

(2) Two millimetres of product under test are transferred to the well and its combustibility characteristics are noted in relation to the standard flame.

Apparatus
3.—(1) A combustibility tester consisting of an aluminium alloy or non-rusting metal block of suitable heat conductivity fitted with a concave depression or well. The metal block has a thermometer embedded in it. A small gas jet on a swivel is attached to the metal block. The exact dimensions of the metal block, and its well, the gas jet and its positioning, and the embedded thermometer are shown on the drawing set out in the Appendix to this Schedule and are specified in Table 1 to this Schedule.

(2) A simple gauge to check height of gas jet above the top of the well.

(3) The thermometer in the metal block shall be a Celsius thermometer conforming to the dimensions and tolerances given in Table 2 to this Schedule.

(4) A hot plate fitted with a temperature controlling device or other means of heating the metal block.

(5) A stop watch or other suitable timing device.

(6) A graduated pipette or hypodermic syringe capable of delivering two millilitres to an accuracy of ±0.1 ml.

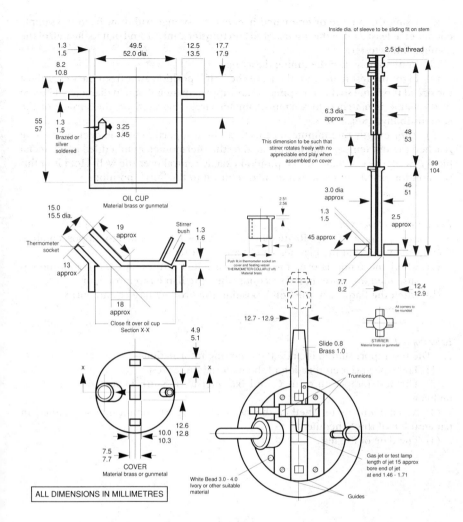

ALL DIMENSIONS IN MILLIMETRES

Sampling

4.—(1) The sample shall be representative of the material being tested and shall be kept prior to test in an airtight container.

(2) Because of the possibility of loss of volatile constituents the sample shall receive only the minimum treatment to ensure uniformity. After removing a portion for test the sample container shall be immediately closed tightly to ensure that no volatile flammable components escape.

Procedure

5.—(1) Set up the apparatus in a draught free area. Place the metal block on the hot plate fitted with a temperature controlling device or heat the metal block by other suitable means so that its temperature is maintained at 50°C (within an accuracy of −0 +5°C) or to the corrected temperature allowing for difference of barometric pressure from the standard (760 mm of mercury or 1013 millibar) by raising the test temperature for a higher or lowering the test temperature for a lower pressure at the rate of 1°C for each 30 mm of mercury (40 millibar) difference. Ensure that the top of the metal block is exactly level. Use a guage to check that the jet is 2.2 mm above the top of the well.

(2) Using the pipette or graduated hypodermic syringe withdraw from the sample container at least 2 ml of the test material and transfer 2 ml ±0.1 ml of it to the well of the combustibility tester.

(3) Immediately start the timing device.

(4) Light the test flame with the jet in the "off" position away from the well. Adjust the size of the flame so that it is spherical and approximately 4 mm in diameter. The size of the flame is matched to a 4 mm diameter circle engraved on the surface of the combustibility tester.

(5) After exactly one minute (at this time the test-portion will be deemed to have reached the test temperature as indicated by the thermometer embedded in the metal block) swing the test flame into a position exactly central over the well. Hold it in this position for exactly 15 seconds and then return it to the "off" position.

Interpretation of observation

6.   For the purpose of these Regulations a product will be deemed to support combustion if, when tested in the manner set out above, either—

  (a) when the flame is over the well the product ignites and the combustion is sustained for more than 15 seconds when the flame is removed, or

  (b) when the flame is in the "off" position the product flashes and burns.

Report of test

7.   The test report should include the following information—

  (1) The type and identification of the material under test.

  (2) The test temperature in °C and barometric pressure in mm of mercury or millibar.

  (3) A statement as to whether the products support combustion as defined in paragraph 6 of this Schedule.

  (4) The date of the test.

TABLE 1

Dimensions of Combustibility Tester

(*a*) Sample block details	Dimensions in mm	
Diameter of block	62	±0.5
Height of block	36.5	±1.5
Diameter of flange	95	±0.5
Flange thickness	3.0	approx.
Height of well "lip" above flange	0.8	±0.2
Diameter of well "lip"	41.0	approx.
Spherical radius of well	33.25	±0.25
Depth of well	6.3	±0.1
Distance from top of block to thermometer hole	16.5	±0.5
Thermometer hole diameter	7.0	approx.

(b) Test gas jet details	Dimensions in mm	
Outside diameter of jet	3.5	±0.5
Jet end tapered to	2.0	±0.3
Bore of jet	0.7	±0.1
Length of jet (from centre of axis to tip)	36.1	±0.1
Distance of axis from centre of well	38.1	±0.1
Flame gauge ring diameter	4.0	approx.
"Swing" of jet (from stop to stop)	90°	±1°
Height of jet above top of well "lip"	2.2	approx.
Note: Adjust with suitable gauge		

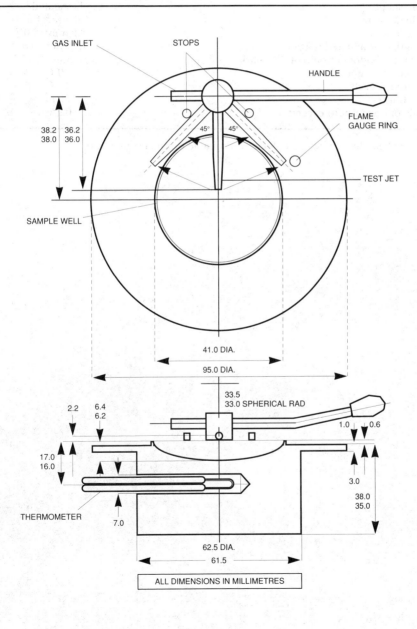

ALL DIMENSIONS IN MILLIMETRES

TABLE 2

Thermometer Specification

Type: Mercury in glass, nitrogen filled for horizontal operation

---

Range	0°C–110°C
Graduation	Each degree C
Overall length	200 mm±5
Stem diameter	6.5 mm±0.5
Bulb shape	Elongated
Bulb diameter	5.0 mm±1.0
Bulb length	12.0 mm±2.0
Length of graduated portion	125 mm±10.0
Distance, bottom of bulb of 0°C mark	50 mm±2.0
Longer lines at each	10°C
Figured at each	10°C
Top finish	Plain
Scale of error not to exceed	0.5°C

NOTE: Seal thermometer in block with suitable thermal compound.

THE LEAD SMELTING AND MANUFACTURE REGULATIONS 1911

(Dated 12 August 1911; S.R. & O. 1911 No. 752, as amended by S.I. 1973 No. 36 and S.I. 1980 No. 1248)

In pursuance of Section 79 of the Factory and Workshop Act 1901, I hereby make the following Regulations, and direct that they shall apply to all factories and workshops or parts thereof (other than laboratories), in which any of the following processes are carried on—

> the smelting of materials containing lead;
> the manufacture of red or orange lead;
> the manufacture of flaked litharge.

These Regulations shall come into force on 1 October 1911, except that so much of regulations 2 and 3 as requires the provision of *efficient exhaust draught* shall come into force on 1 May 1912.

Definitions

In these Regulations—
"*Lead material*" means—

(i) material containing not less than five per cent. of lead, including lead ore, bullion ore (lead ore rich in precious metals), red lead, orange lead, and flaked litharge; and

(ii) zinc ore, and material resulting from the treatment thereof, containing not less than two per cent. of lead,

except ores which contain lead only in the form of sulphide of lead.

"*Furnace*", "*melting pot*", "*retort*", "*condensing chamber*", mean structures as aforesaid which are used in the treatment of "*lead material*".

"*Flue*" means a flue leading from a "*furnace*".

"*Lead process*" means—

(i) manipulation, movement or other treatment of *lead material*, whether by means of any *furnace, melting pot, retort, condensing chamber, flue,* or otherwise; and

(ii) cleaning or demolition of any *furnace, melting pot, retort, condensing chamber, flue,* or part thereof or reconstruction thereof with material which has formed part of any such structure.

Duties

It shall be the duty of the occupier to observe Part I of these Regulations.

PART I
DUTIES OF OCCUPIERS

1–9. [*revoked*].

10. No person under 16 years of age, and no female, shall be employed in any *lead* process.

11–19. [*revoked*].

THE CONTROL OF LEAD AT WORK REGULATIONS 1980

(S.I. 1980 No. 1248, as amended by S.I. 1990 No. 305 and S.I. 1992 No. 2966)

ARRANGEMENT OF REGULATIONS

The Secretary of State, in exercise of the powers conferred on him by section 15(1), (2), (3)(a), (4)(a), (5)(b), (6)(a) and (9) of, and paragraphs 1(1)(b), 6(1), 7, 8, 9, 10, 11, 13(1) and (3), 14, 15(1) and 16 of Schedule 3 to, the Health and Safety at Work etc. Act 1974 ("the 1974 Act") and of all other powers enabling him in that behalf and for the purpose of giving effect without modifications to proposals submitted to him by the Health and Safety Commission under section 11(2)(d) of the 1974 Act after the carrying out by the said Commission of consultations in accordance with section 50(3) of that Act, hereby makes the following Regulations—

1. Citation and commencement. These Regulations may be cited as the Control of Lead at Work Regulations 1980 and shall come into operation on 18 August 1981.

General note. An approved Code of Practice "Control of Lead at Work" has been issued. Intermittent exposures of short duration (no more than one hour per day) to low levels of lead were said to be insignificant for the purposes of the regulations in *Hewett v Alf Brown's Transport* [1991] ICR 471, affd. [1992] ICR 530, CA; the court placed much reliance on the levels laid down in the Code of Practice. As a result, that exposure was held to give rise to no liability when the employee's wife—who was peculiarly susceptible—suffered from lead poisoning as a consequence of cleaning his overalls and boots. The case is, however, of dubious authority since the trial judge proceeded on the assumption that the regulations merely codified the common law duty in negligence (at the time of the exposure the Regulations were not in force).

Fees payable on application to the Health and Safety Executive for approval under these Regulations, and for medical surveillance by an employment medical adviser, are specified in the Health and Safety (Fees) Regulations 1992, S.I. 1992 No. 1752.

2.   Interpretation.—(1) In these Regulations unless the context otherwise requires—

"*adequate*" means adequate having regard only to the nature and degree of exposure to lead;

"*lead*" means lead (including lead alloys, any compounds of lead and lead as a constituent of any substance or material) which is liable to be inhaled, ingested or otherwise absorbed by persons except where it is given off from the exhaust system of a vehicle on a road within the meaning of section 196(1) of the Road Traffic Act 1972 *(a)*.

(2) Any reference in these Regulations to either—

(a) an employee being exposed to lead; or
(b) any place being contaminated by lead,

is a reference to exposure to or, as the case may be, contamination by lead arising out of work being carried on by the employer.

(3) In these Regulations, unless the context otherwise requires—

(a) a reference to a numbered regulation or Schedule is a reference to the regulation of or Schedule to these Regulations so numbered; and
(b) a reference to a numbered paragraph is a reference to the paragraph so numbered in the regulation in which that reference appears.

3.   Duty of employer to persons at work who are not his employees. Where any duty is placed by these Regulations on an employer in respect of his employees, he shall, so far as is reasonably practicable *(b)*, be under a like duty in respect of any other person who is at work on the premises where the work with *lead* is being carried on and who is, or is liable to be, exposed to *lead* from that work.

(a) Road Traffic Act 1972. See now the Road Traffic Act 1988.

(b) **Reasonably practicable.** See INTRODUCTORY NOTE 5.

3A.   Prohibition of certain glazes in pottery manufacture.—(1) The use of any glaze other than a leadless glaze or a low solubility glaze in the manufacture of pottery is prohibited.

(2) In this regulation—

   "glaze" does not include engobe or slip;
   "leadless glaze" means a glaze which does not contain more than one per cent. of its dry weight of a *lead* compound calculated as lead monoxide;
   "low solubility glaze" means a glaze which does not yield to dilute hydrochloric acid more than 5 per cent. of its dry weight of a soluble *lead* compound when determined in accordance with a method approved in writing for the time being by the Health and Safety Commission.

4. Assessment of work which exposes persons to lead.—(1) Where any work may expose persons to *lead*, the employer or self-employed person, as the case may be, shall assess that work to determine the nature and degree of the exposure to *lead*.

(2) The assessment required by paragraph (1) shall be made—

(a) in the case of work being carried out immediately before the date of coming into operation of these Regulations within 4 weeks of that date;
(b) in any other case, before the work is commenced.

(3) An assessment shall be revised—

(a) when there is reason to suspect that it is incorrect;
(b) when there is a material change in the work;
(c) when requested by an inspector appointed under section 19 of the Health and Safety at Work etc. Act 1974.

5. Information, instruction and training. Every employer shall ensure that *adequate* information, instruction and training is given to his employees—

(a) who are liable to be exposed to *lead* so that they are aware of the risk from *lead* and the precautions which should be observed;
(b) who carry out any work in connection with the employer's duties under regulations 4, 11, 13, 14 and 15 so that they can carry out that work effectively.

6. Control measures for materials, plant and processes. Every employer shall, so far as is reasonably practicable *(a)*, provide such control measures for materials, plant and processes as will adequately control the exposure of his employees to *lead* otherwise than by the use of respiratory protective equipment or protective clothing by those employees.

   (a) Reasonably practicable. See INTRODUCTORY NOTE 5.

7. Respiratory protective equipment. Every employer shall provide each employee who is liable to be exposed to airborne *lead* with such respiratory protective equipment which complies with regulation 8A or, where the requirements of that regulation do not apply, which is of a type approved or conforming to a standard approved, in either case, in writing by the Health and Safety Executive as will, in either case, adequately protect him against that airborne *lead* unless the control measures adopted in compliance with regulation 6 provide him with *adequate* protection.

8.   Protective clothing. Every employer shall provide each employee who is liable to be exposed to *lead* with protective clothing which complies with regulation 8A or, where no requirement is imposed by virtue of that regulation, is adequate unless the exposure to lead is not significant.

8A.   Compliance with relevant Community Directives. Any respiratory protective equipment or protective clothing shall comply with any enactment (whether in an Act or instrument) which implements any provision on design or manufacture with respect to health or safety in any relevant Community Directive listed in Schedule 1 to the Personal Protective Equipment at Work Regulations 1992 which is applicable to that item of respiratory protective equipment or protective clothing.

8B.   Assessment of respiratory protective equipment or protective clothing.— (1) Before choosing respiratory protective equipment or protective clothing, an employer shall make an assessment to determine whether it will satisfy regulation 7 or 8, as appropriate.

(2) The assessment required by paragraph (1) shall involve—

(a) definition of the characteristics necessary to comply with regulation 7 or, as the case may be, 8, and

(b) comparison of the characteristics of respiratory protective equipment or protective clothing available with the characteristics referred to in sub-paragraph (a) of this paragraph.

(3) The assessment required by paragraph (1) shall be revised if—

(a) there is reason to suspect that it is no longer valid; or

(b) there has been a significant change in the work to which it relates,

and, where, as a result of the review, changes in the assessment are required, the employer shall make them.

9.   Washing and changing facilities. Every employer shall provide for his employees who are liable to be exposed to *lead*—

(a) *adequate* washing facilities; and

(b) where he is required under regulations 7 or 8 to provide respiratory protective equipment or protective clothing, adequate changing facilities and adequate facilities for the storage of—

(i) the respiratory protective equipment or protective clothing, and

(ii) personal clothing not worn during working hours,

so however that this regulation shall not apply during the period of 12 months after the coming into operation *(a)* of these Regulations where in order to comply with this regulation it would be necessary to erect a new building or make substantial structural alterations to a building.

(a) Coming into operation. The date was 18 August 1981.

10. Eating, drinking and smoking.—(1) Every employer shall take such steps as are *adequate* to secure that—

(a) so far as is reasonably practicable *(a)*, his employees do not eat, drink or smoke in any place which is or is liable to be contaminated by *lead*;

(b) suitable arrangements are made for such employees to eat, drink or smoke in a place which is not liable to be contaminated by *lead*.

(2) An employee shall not eat, drink or smoke in any place which he has reason to believe to be contaminated by *lead*.

(3) Nothing in this regulation shall prevent the provision and use of drinking facilities which are not liable to be contaminated by *lead* where such facilities are required for the welfare of employees who are exposed to *lead*.

(a) Reasonably practicable. See INTRODUCTORY NOTE 5.

11. Cleaning. Where an employee is liable to be exposed to *lead*, the employer shall take *adequate* steps to secure the cleanliness of workplaces, premises, plant, respiratory protective equipment and protective clothing.

12. Duty to avoid spread of contamination by lead.—(1) Every employer, his employees and every self-employed person shall, so far as is reasonably practicable *(a)*, prevent the spread of contamination by *lead* from the place where work is being carried out.

(2) Nothing in paragraph (1) shall prejudice any other requirements imposed by or under any enactment which relates to preventing the spread of contamination by *lead*.

(a) Reasonably practicable. See INTRODUCTORY NOTE 5.

13. Use of control measures etc.—(1) Every employer who provides any control measure, respiratory protective equipment, protective clothing or other thing or facility pursuant to regulations 6 to 12 shall ensure, so far as is reasonably practicable *(a)*, that it is properly used or applied as the case may be.

(2) Every employee shall make full and proper use of any control measure, respiratory protective equipment, protective clothing or other thing or facility provided pursuant to regulations 6 to 12; and if he discovers any defect therein he shall report it forthwith to his employer.

(3) Every employee shall take all reasonable steps to ensure that any respiratory protective equipment provided to him pursuant to regulation 7 and protective clothing provided to him pursuant to regulation 8 is returned to the accommodation provided for it after use.

(a) Reasonably practicable. See INTRODUCTORY NOTE 5.

14. Maintenance of control measures etc. Every employer who provides any control measure, respiratory protective equipment, protective clothing or other thing or facility pursuant to regulations 6 to 12 shall ensure, so far as is practicable *(a)*, that it is maintained *(b)* in an efficient state, in efficient working order and good repair.

(a) *Practicable.* See INTRODUCTORY NOTE 5.

(b) *Maintained.* See INTRODUCTORY NOTE 10.

15.   Air monitoring.   Every employer shall—

(a) have *adequate* monitoring procedures to measure the concentrations of *lead* in air to which his employees are exposed unless the exposure is not significant;

(b) measure the concentration of *lead* in air in accordance with those procedures.

16.   Medical surveillance and biological tests.—(1) Every employer shall secure that each of his employees who is employed on work which exposes that employee to *lead* is under medical surveillance by an employment medical adviser or appointed doctor if either—

(a) the exposure of that employee to *lead* is significant; or

(b) an employment medical adviser or appointed doctor certifies that the employee should be under medical surveillance,

and where the employment medical adviser or appointed doctor has certified that in his opinion the employee should not be employed on work which exposes him to *lead* or that he should only be so employed under the conditions specified in the certificate the employer shall not expose that employee to *lead* except under the conditions, if any, specified in the certificate.

(2) Every employee who is exposed to *lead* at work shall, when required by the employer, present himself, during his normal working hours, for such medical examination or biological tests as may be required for the purposes of paragraph (1).

(3) In this Regulation—

"medical surveillance" includes biological tests;
"employment medical adviser" means an employment medical adviser appointed under section 56 of the Health and Safety at Work etc. Act 1974;
"appointed doctor" means a registered medical practitioner who is appointed in writing by the Health and Safety Executive for the purposes of this regulation.

17.   Records.—(1) Every employer shall—

(a) ensure that *adequate* records are kept of the assessments, maintenance, air monitoring, medical surveillance and biological tests required by regulations 4, 14, 15 and 16 respectively;

(b) make those records available for inspection by employees, except that this sub-paragraph shall not apply to the health record of an identifiable individual.

(2) An entry in the records shall be kept for two years from the date on which the entry was made, except in the case of an entry relating to an assessment made under Regulation 4 which shall be kept until whichever is the earlier of the following dates—

(a) two years from the date on which that assessment was revised;

(b) two years from the date on which the work to which that assessment related ceased.

18. Exemption certificates.—(1) Subject to paragraph (2) the Health and Safety Executive may, by certificate in writing, exempt any person or class of persons from all or any of the requirements or prohibitions imposed by these Regulations and any such exemption may be granted subject to conditions and to a limit of time and may be revoked at any time.

(2) The Executive shall not grant any such exemption unless having regard to the circumstances of the case and in particular to—

(a) the conditions, if any, which it proposes to attach to the exemption, and

(b) any other requirements imposed by or under any enactments which apply to the case,

it is satisfied that the health and safety of persons who are likely to be affected by the exemption will not be prejudiced in consequence of it and that any provision imposed by the European communities in respect of the encouragement of improvements in the safety and health of workers at work will be satisfied.

19. Extension outside Great Britain. These Regulations shall apply to any work outside Great Britain to which sections 1 to 59 of the Health and Safety at Work etc. Act 1974 apply by virtue of the Health and Safety at Work etc. Act 1974 (Application outside Great Britain) Order 1977 *(a)*.

(a) Health & Safety at Work etc. Act 1974 (Application outside Great Britain) Order 1977. The Regulations are revoked; see now the Health & Safety at Work etc. Act 1974 (Application outside Great Britain) Order 1989, S.I. 1989 No. 840.

20. Repeals, revocations and modifications.—(1) The provisions of the Factories Act 1961 specified in column 1 of Schedule 1 are hereby repealed to the extent set out opposite thereto in column 2 of that Schedule.

(2) The Regulations and Orders specified in column 1 of Schedule 2 are hereby revoked to the extent set out opposite thereto in column 2 of that Schedule.

(3) The Construction (Health and Welfare) Regulations 1966 shall cease to have effect in relation to *lead*.

SCHEDULE 1

Regulation 20(1)

REPEALS OF THE PROVISIONS OF THE FACTORIES ACT 1961

1 Provision	2 Extent of Repeal
Section 64(1).	The word "lead"
Section 75.	The whole section.
Section 128(a).	The words "and in processes involving the use of lead compounds".
Section 129.	The whole section.
Section 130.	The whole section.

SCHEDULE 2

Regulation 20(2)

REVOCATION OF REGULATIONS AND ORDERS

1 Regulations or Order	2 Extent of Revocation
Regulations, dated 19 June 1903, for the process of file-cutting by hand (The File-cutting by Hand Regulations 1903) S.R. & O. 1903 No. 507.	The whole Regulations.
Regulations, dated 21 January 1907, with respect to the manufacture of paints and colours (The Paints and Colours Regulations 1907) S.R. & O. 1907 No. 17; amended by S.I. 1973 No. 36.	The definitions of 　(a) "lead process"; 　(b) "appointed doctor"; 　(c) "employment medical adviser". The paragraph— "It shall be the duty of all persons employed to observe Part II of these Regulations". Regulations 1, 2 and 4 to 16.
Regulations, dated 6 August 1907, with respect to the process of the manipulation of yarn dyed by means of a lead compound (The Yarn (Dyed by Lead Compounds) Heading Regulations 1907) S.R. & O. 1907 No. 616; amended by S.I. 1973 No. 36.	The definitions of— 　(a) "appointed doctor" 　(b) "employment medical adviser". The paragraph— "It shall be the duty of all persons employed to observe Part II of these Regulations". Regulations 1 and 3 to 8.
Regulations, dated 18 December 1908, with respect to the process of vitreous enamelling of metal or glass (The Vitreous Enamelling Regulations 1908) S.R. & O. 1908 No. 1258; amended by S.I. 1973 No. 36.	The definition of— 　(a) "appointed doctor"; 　(b) "employment medical adviser";. The paragraph— "It shall be the duty of all persons employed to observe Part II of these Regulations". Regulations 1 to 6 and 8 to 15.

1 Regulations or Order	2 Extent of Revocation
Regulations, dated 30 June 1909, with respect to the coating of metal articles with a mixture of tin and lead or lead alone (The Tinning of Metal Hollow-ware Iron Drums and Harness Furniture Regulations 1909) S.R. & O. 1909 No. 720; amended by S.I. 1973 No. 36.	The definitions— (a) "mounting", "denting" and "scouring"; (b) "appointed doctor"; (c) "employment medical adviser"; (d) "efficient draught". The paragraph— "It shall be the duty of all persons employed to observe Part II of these Regulations". Regulations 1 and 3 to 13.
Regulations, dated 12 August 1911, with respect to the manufacture of lead and flaked litharge (The Lead Smelting and Manufacture Regulations 1911) S.R. & O. 1911 No. 752; amended by S.I. 1973 No. 36.	The definitions— (a) "appointed doctor"; (b) "employment medical adviser"; (c) "damp"; (d) "efficient exhaust draught". The paragraph— "It shall be the duty of every person employed to observe Part II of these Regulations". Regulations 1 to 9 and 11 to 19.
Regulations, dated 11 April 1912, with respect to bronzing with dry metallic powders in letterpress printing, lithographic printing and coating of metal sheets (The Bronzing Regulations 1912) S.R. & O. 1912 No. 361.	The whole Regulations.
Regulations, dated 23 August 1921, with respect to the manufacture of any carbonate, sulphate, nitrate or acetate of lead (The Lead Compounds Manufacture Regulations 1921) S.R. & O. 1921 No. 1443; amended by S.I. 1973 No. 36.	The whole Regulations.
Order, dated 8 November 1921, as to the meaning of the expression "lead compound" and the method of ascertaining whether any compound is a "lead compound" (The Lead Compounds (Definition) Order 1921) S.R. & O. 1921 No. 1713.	The whole Order.
Order, dated 8 November 1921, prescribing the medical examination of women and young persons employed in processes involving use of lead compounds (The Women and Young Persons (Employment in Lead Process) Medical Examinations Order 1921) S.R. & O. 1921 No. 1714; amended by S.I. 1973 No. 36.	The whole Order.

1 Regulations or Order	2 Extent of Revocation
Order, dated 8 November 1921, prescribing the cloakroom, messroom and washing accommodation to be provided in factories and workshops in which women and young persons are employed in processes involving the use of lead compounds (The Women and Young Persons Employed in Lead Process (Provision of Facilities for Clothing, Canteen and Washing Accommodation) Order 1921) S.R. & O. 1921 No. 1715.	The whole Order.

The Indiarubber Regulations 1922, S.R. & O. 1922 No. 329; amended by S.I. 1973 No. 36.	In regulation 5, the words "no lead process and".
	In regulation 8, the words, "any lead process or".
	Regulations 9 to 11.
	In regulation 12—
	  (a) in sub-paragraph (a), the words "in any lead process or";
	  (b) in sub-paragraph (c), the words "in any lead process or".
	In regulation 13, the words from "He shall further" to "one such part".
	In regulation 14, the words "in any lead process or".
	In regulation 15, the words "a lead process or".
	Regulations 16 to 18.

The Electric Accumulator Regulations 1925, S.R. & O. 1925 No. 28; amended by S.I. 1973 No. 36.	The definitions—
	  (a) "appointed doctor";
	  (b) "employment medical adviser".
	The paragraph—
	"It shall be the duty of every person employed to observe Part II of these Regulations".
	Regulations 2 to 27.

The Vehicle Painting Regulations 1926, S.R. & O. 1926 No. 299; amended by S.I. 1973 No. 36.	The whole Regulations.
Order, dated 25 December 1926, modifying the application of certain provisions of the Factory and Workshop Act 1901 in cases where persons are employed in painting buildings, S.R. & O. 1926 No. 1620; amended by S.I. 1973 No. 36.	The whole Order.
Rule, dated 24 December 1926, for ascertaining whether a paint is a lead paint, S.R. & O. 1926 No. 1621.	The whole Rule.

1	2
Regulations or Order	Extent of Revocation
The Lead Paint Regulations 1927, S.R. & O. 1927 No. 847; amended by S.I. 1973 No. 36.	The whole Regulations.
Order, dated 14 November 1927, in respect of employment of young persons in the painting trade and of women and young persons in work of decorative design, S.R. & O. 1927 No. 1094.	The whole Order.
The Pottery (Health and Welfare) Special Regulations 1950, S.I. 1950 No. 65; amended by S.I. 1973 No. 36.	In regulation 7— (a) paragraph (1); (b) paragraph (2)(a); (c) in paragraph (2) the words from "due notice" to the end of that paragraph; (d) paragraph (3). In regulation 8— (a) in paragraph (1) the words from "in a process" to "these Regulations or"; (b) paragraph (2).
The Shipbuilding and Ship-repairing Regulations 1960, S.I. 1960 No. 1932; the amending Regulations are not relevant to the subject matter of these Regulations.	In regulation 3(2) the definition of "lead paint". Regulation 78. The First Schedule.
The Lead Paint (Prescribed Leaflet) Order 1964, S.I. 1964 No. 559.	The whole Order.
The Lead Processes (Medical Examinations) Regulations 1964, S.I. 1964 No. 1728; amended by S.I. 1973 No. 36.	The whole Regulations.
The Employment Medical Advisory Service (Factories Act Orders etc. Amendment) Order 1973, S.I. 1973 No. 36.	In Part II of the Schedule the following entries relating to— (a) Regulations, dated 21 January 1907, with respect to the manufacture of paints and colours; (b) Regulations, dated 6 August 1907, with respect to the process of manipulation of yarn dyed by means of a lead compound; (c) Regulations, dated 18 December 1908, with respect to the process of vitreous enamelling metal or glass; (d) Regulations, dated 30 June 1909, with respect to coating metal articles with a mixture of tin and lead, or lead alone; (e) Regulations, dated 12 August 1911, with respect to the smelting and manufacture of lead and flaked litharge;

1 Regulations or Order	2 Extent of Revocation
	(f) Regulations, dated 23 August 1921, with respect to the manufacture of any carbonate, sulphate, nitrate or acetate of lead;
	(g) Order, dated 8 November 1921 with respect to the employment of women and young persons in certain processes involving the use of a lead compound;
	(h) The Electric Accumulator Regulations 1925;
	(i) The Vehicle Painting Regulations 1926;
	(j) Order, dated 24 December 1926, modifying the application of certain provisions of the Factory and Workshop Act 1901 in cases where persons are employed in painting buildings;
	(k) The Lead Paint Regulations 1927;
	(l) The Lead Processes (Medical Examinations) Regulations 1964.

THE NOISE AT WORK REGULATIONS 1989

(S.I. 1989 No. 1790, as amended by S.I. 1992 No. 2966)

General note. These Regulations are intended to implement the Noise at Work Directive 86/188 (see page 5).

The Secretary of State, in exercise of the powers conferred on him by section 15(1), (2), (3)(a) and (b) and (5)(b) of, and paragraphs 1(1)(a) and (2), 6, 7, 8(1), 9, 11, 13(2) and (3), 15(1) and 16 of Schedule 3 to, the Health and Safety at Work etc. Act 1974 ("the 1974 Act") and of all other powers enabling him in that behalf and for the purpose of giving effect without modifications to proposals submitted to him by the Health and Safety Commission under section 11(2)(d) of the 1974 Act after the carrying out by the said Commission of consultations in accordance with section 50(3) of that Act, hereby makes the following Regulations—

1. Citation and commencement. These Regulations may be cited as the Noise at Work Regulations 1989 and shall come into force on 1 January 1990.

2. Interpretation.—(1) In these Regulations, unless the context otherwise requires—

"daily personal noise exposure" means the level of daily personal noise exposure of an employee ascertained in accordance with Part I of the Schedule to these Regulations, but taking no account of the effect of any personal ear protector used;

"exposed" means exposed whilst at work, and "exposure" shall be construed accordingly;

"the first action level" means a *daily personal noise exposure* of 85 dB(A);

"the peak action level" means a level of peak sound pressure of 200 pascals;

"the second action level" means a *daily personal noise exposure* of 90 dB(A).

(2) In these Regulations, unless the context otherwise requires, any reference to—

(a) an employer includes a reference to a self-employed person and any duty imposed by these Regulations on an employer in respect of his employees shall extend to a self-employed person in respect of himself;

(b) an employee includes a reference to a self-employed person,

and where any duty is placed by these Regulations on an employer in respect of his employees, that employer shall, so far as is reasonably practicable, be under a like duty in respect of any other person at work who may be affected by the work carried on by him.

(3) Duties under these Regulations imposed upon an employer shall also be imposed upon the manager of a mine or a quarry (within in either case the meaning of section 180 of the Mines and Quarries Act 1954) in so far as those duties relate to the mine or quarry or part of the quarry of which he is the manager and to matters under his control.

(4) Unless the context otherwise requires, any reference in these Regulations to—

(a) a numbered regulation is a reference to the regulation in these Regulations so numbered; and
(b) a numbered paragraph is a reference to the paragraph so numbered in the regulation in which the reference appears.

3.   Disapplication of duties. The duties imposed by these Regulations shall not extend to—

(a) the master or crew of a sea-going ship or to the employer of such persons, in relation to the normal ship-board activities of a ship's crew under the direction of the master; or
(b) the crew of any aircraft or hovercraft which is moving under its own power or any other person on board any such aircraft or hovercraft who is at work in connection with its operation.

4.   Assessment of exposure.—(1) Every employer shall, when any of his employees is likely to be *exposed* to *the first action level* or above or to *the peak action level* or above, ensure that a competent person makes a noise assessment which is adequate for the purposes—

(a) of identifying which of his employees are so *exposed*; and
(b) of providing him with such information with regard to the noise to which those employees may be *exposed* as will facilitate compliance with his duties under regulations 7, 8, 9 and 11.

(2) The noise assessment required by paragraph (1) shall be reviewed when—

(a) there is reason to suspect that the assessment is no longer valid; or
(b) there has been a significant change in the work to which the assessment relates,

and, where as a result of the review changes in the assessment are required, those changes shall be made.

5.   Assessment records. Following any noise assessment made pursuant to regulation 4(1), the employer shall ensure that an adequate record of that assessment, and of any review thereof carried out pursuant to regulation 4(2), is kept until a further noise assessment is made pursuant to regulation 4(1).

6.   Reduction of risk of hearing damage. Every employer shall reduce the risk of damage to the hearing of his employees from *exposure* to noise to the lowest level reasonably practicable.

7. Reduction of noise *exposure*. Every employer shall, when any of his employees is likely to be *exposed* to *the second action level* or above or to *the peak action level* or above, reduce, so far as is reasonably practicable (other than by the provision of personal ear protectors), the *exposure* to noise of that employee.

8. Ear protection.—(1) Every employer shall ensure, so far as is practicable, that when any of his employees is likely to be *exposed* to *the first action level* or above in circumstances where the daily personal noise *exposure* of that employee is likely to be less than 90 dB(A), that employee is provided, at his request, with suitable and efficient personal ear protectors.

(2) Every employer shall ensure, so far as is practicable, that when any of his employees is likely to be *exposed* to *the second action level* or above or to *the peak action level* or above, that employee is provided with suitable personal ear protectors which, when properly worn, can reasonably be expected to keep the risk of damage to that employee's hearing to below that arising from *exposure* to *the second action level* or, as the case may be, to *the peak action level*.

(3) Any personal ear protectors provided by virtue of this regulation shall comply with any enactment (whether in an Act or instrument) which implements in Great Britain any provision on design or manufacture with respect to health or safety in any relevant Community Directive listed in Schedule 1 to the Personal Protective Equipment at Work Regulations 1992 which is applicable to those ear protectors.

9. Ear protection zones.—(1) Every employer shall, in respect of any premises under his control, ensure, so far as is reasonably practicable, that—

(a) each ear protection zone is demarcated and identified by means of the sign specified in paragraph A.3.3 of Appendix A to Part I of BS 5378, which sign shall include such text as indicates—
 (i) that it is an ear protection zone, and
 (ii) the need for his employees to wear personal ear protectors whilst in any such zone; and
(b) none of his employees enters any such zone unless that employee is wearing personal ear protectors.

(2) In this regulation, "ear protection zone" means any part of the premises referred to in paragraph (1) where any employee is likely to be *exposed* to *the second action level* or above or to *the peak action level* or above, and "Part I of BS 5378" has the same meaning as in regulation 2(1) of the Safety Signs Regulations 1980.

10. Maintenance and use of equipment.—(1) Every employer shall—

(a) ensure, so far as is practicable, that anything provided by him to or for the benefit of an employee in compliance with his duties under these Regulations (other than personal ear protectors provided pursuant to regulation 8(1)) is fully and properly used; and
(b) ensure, so far as is practicable, that anything provided by him in compliance with his duties under these Regulations is maintained in an efficient state, in efficient working order and in good repair.

(2) Every employee shall, so far as is practicable, fully and properly use personal ear protectors when they are provided by his employer pursuant to regulation 8(2) and any other protective measures provided by his employer in compliance with his duties under these Regulations; and, if the employee discovers any defect therein, he shall report it forthwith to his employer.

11.   Provision of information to employees. Every employer shall, in respect of any premises under his control, provide each of his employees who is likely to be *exposed* to *the first action level* or above or to *the peak action level* or above with adequate information, instruction and training on—

(a) the risk of damage to that employee's hearing that such *exposure* may cause;

(b) what steps that employee can take to minimise that risk;

(c) the steps that that employee must take in order to obtain the personal ear protectors referred to in regulation 8(1); and

(d) that employee's obligations under these Regulations.

12.   Modification of duties of manufacturers etc. of articles for use at work and articles of fairground equipment. In the case of articles for use at work or articles of fairground equipment, section 6 of the Health and Safety at Work etc. Act 1974 (which imposes general duties on manufacturers etc. as regards articles for use at work, substances and articles of fairground equipment) shall be modified so that any duty imposed on any person by subsection (1) of that section shall include a duty to ensure that, where any such article as is referred to therein is likely to cause any employee to be *exposed* to *the first action level* or above or to *the peak action level* or above, adequate information is provided concerning the noise likely to be generated by that article.

13.   Exemptions.—(1) Subject to paragraph (2), the Health and Safety Executive may, by a certificate in writing, exempt any employer from—

(a) the requirement in regulation 7, where the *daily personal noise exposure* of the relevant employee, averaged over a week and ascertained in accordance with Part II of the Schedule to these Regulations, is below 90 dB(A) and there are adequate arrangements for ensuring that that average will not be exceeded; or

(b) the requirement in regulation 8(2), where—

(i) the *daily personal noise exposure* of the relevant employee, averaged over a week and ascertained in accordance with Part II of the Schedule to these Regulations, is below 90 dB(A) and there are adequate arrangements for ensuring that that average will not be exceeded,

(ii) the full and proper use of the personal ear protectors referred to in that paragraph would be likely to cause risks to the health or safety of the user, or

(iii) (subject to the use of personal ear protectors affording the highest degree of personal protection which it is reasonably practicable to achieve in the circumstances) compliance with that requirement is not reasonably practicable, and any such exemption may be granted subject to conditions and to a limit of time and may be revoked at any time by a certificate in writing.

(2) The Executive shall not grant any such exemption unless, having regard to the circumstances of the case and in particular to—

(a) the conditions, if any, which it proposes to attach to the exemption; and
(b) any other requirements imposed by or under any enactments which apply to the case,

it is satisfied that the health and safety of persons who are likely to be affected by the exemption will not be prejudiced in consequence of it.

14. Modifications relating to the Ministry of Defence etc.—(1) In this regulation, any reference to—

(a) "visiting forces" is a reference to visiting forces within the meaning of any provision of Part I of the Visiting Forces Act 1952, and
(b) "headquarters or organisation" is a reference to a headquarters or organisation designated for the purposes of the International Headquarters and Defence Organisations Act 1964.

(2) The Secretary of State for Defence may, in the interests of national security, by a certificate in writing exempt—

(a) Her Majesty's Forces;
(b) visiting forces; or
(c) any member of a visiting force working in or attached to any headquarters or organisation,

from any requirement imposed by these Regulations and any such exemption may be granted subject to conditions and to a limit of time and may be revoked at any time by a certificate in writing, except that, before any such exemption is granted, the Secretary of State for Defence must be satisfied that suitable arrangements have been made for the assessment of the health risks created by the work involving *exposure* to noise and for adequately controlling the *exposure* to noise of persons to whom the exemption relates.

15. Revocation. Regulation 44 of the Woodworking Machines Regulations 1974 is hereby revoked.

SCHEDULE

Regulations 2(1), 13(1)

Part I
Daily Personal Noise Exposure of Employees

The *daily personal noise exposure* of an employee ($L_{EP,d}$) is expressed in dB(A) and is ascertained using the formula:

$$L_{EP,d} = 10 \log_{10} \left\{ \frac{1}{T_o} \int_0^{T_e} \left[\frac{p_A(t)}{p_o} \right]^2 dt \right\}$$

where—

T_e = the duration of the person's personal *exposure* to sound;
T_o = 8 hours = 28,800 seconds;
p_o = 20 μPa; and
$p_A(t)$ = the time-varying value of A—weighted instantaneous sound pressure in pascals in the undisturbed field in air at atmospheric pressure to which the person is *exposed* (in the locations occupied during the day), or the pressure of the disturbed field adjacent to the person's head adjusted to provide a notional equivalent undisturbed field pressure.

PART II
WEEKLY AVERAGE OF *DAILY PERSONAL NOISE EXPOSURE* OF EMPLOYEES

The weekly average of an employee's *daily personal noise exposure* ($L_{EP,w}$) is expressed in dB(A) and is ascertained using the formula:

$$L_{EP,\,w} = 10 \log_{10} \left[\frac{1}{5} \sum_{k=1}^{k=m} 10^{0,1 \,(L_{EP,\,d})\,k} \right]$$

where—
$(L_{EP,d})_k$ = the values of $L_{EP,d}$ for each of the m working days in the week being considered.

THE IONISING RADIATIONS REGULATIONS 1985

(S.I. 1985 No. 1333, as amended by S.I. 1992 No. 743 and S.I. 1992 No. 2966)

General note. Regard should also be had to the Nuclear Installations Acts 1965 and 1969 as amended which control the use of sites for nuclear installations, including nuclear reactors and processing and storage of nuclear material.

ARRANGEMENT OF REGULATIONS

Schedule 1. Dose limits.
Schedule 2. Quantities of radionuclides.
Schedule 3. Work not required to be notified under regulation 5(2).
Schedule 4. Particulars to be supplied in a notification under regulation 5(2).
Schedule 5. Additional particulars that the Executive may require.
Schedule 6. Designation of controlled areas.
Schedule 7. Particulars to be included in an assessment report.
Schedule 8. Further particulars that the Executive may require.
Schedule 9. Sealed sources to which regulation 26 does not apply.
Schedule 10. Revocations and modifications.

The Secretary of State, in exercise of the powers conferred on him by sections 15(1), (2), (3)(a) and (b), (4), (5), (6)(a) and (b) and (9), 43(2), (4), (5) and (6), 52(2) and (3), 80(1) and (4) and 82(3)(a) of, and paragraphs 1(1), (2) and (4), 3, 6, 7, 8, 9, 10, 11, 12, 13, 14, 15(1), 16, 20 and 21(a) and (b) of Schedule 3 to, the Health and Safety at Work etc. Act 1974 ("the 1974 Act") and of all other powers enabling him in that behalf—

(a) for the purpose of giving effect without modifications to proposals submitted to him by the Health and Safety Commission under section 11(2)(d) of the 1974 Act, after the carrying out by the said Commission of consultations in accordance with section 50(3) of that Act; and

(b) it appearing to him that the revocation of the Radioactive Substances (Road Transport Workers) (Great Britain) Regulations 1970 by virtue of section 80(1) of the 1974 Act is expedient, after the carrying out by him of consultations in accordance with subsection (4) of that section,

hereby makes the following Regulations:—

PART I

INTERPRETATION AND GENERAL

1. Citation and commencement. These Regulations may be cited as the Ionising Radiations Regulations 1985 and shall come into operation—

(a) for the purposes of regulation 10 on 1 October 1985;
(b) for all other purposes on 1 January 1986.

2. Interpretation.—(1) In these Regulations, unless the context otherwise requires—

"appointed doctor" means a registered medical practitioner who is for the time being appointed in writing by the Health and Safety Executive for the purposes of these Regulations;

"approved" means approved for the time being by the Health and Safety Executive or the Health and Safety Commission as the case may be;

"approved dosimetry service" means a dosimetry service approved in accordance with regulation 15;

"calendar year" means a period of twelve calendar months beginning with 1 January;

"classified person" means a person who has been so designated in accordance with regulation 9(1);

"contamination" means the contamination by any *radioactive substance* of any surface (including any surface of the body or clothing) or any part of absorbent objects or materials or the contamination of liquids or gases by any *radioactive substance;*

"controlled area" means an area which has been so designated by the employer in accordance with regulation 8(1) or (3);

"dose" means, in relation to *ionising radiation,* in any close quantity or sum of dose quantities mentioned in Schedule 1;

"dose limit" means, in relation to persons of a specified class, the dose limit specified in Schedule 1 in relation to a person of that class and is with respect to—

(a) the whole body, the relevant *dose limit* specified in Part I;

(b) any individual organ or tissue except the lens of the eye, the relevant *dose limit* specified in Part II;

(c) the lens of the eye, the relevant *dose limit* specified in Part III;

(d) the abdomen of a woman of reproductive capacity, the *dose limit* specified in Part IV; and

(e) the abdomen of a pregnant woman, the *dose limit* specified in Part V;

'dose rate" means, in relation to a place, the rate at which a person or part of a person would receive a *dose* of *ionising radiation* from *external radiation* if he were at that place and "instantaneous dose rate" means a *dose rate* at that place averaged over one minute and "time average dose rate" means a *dose rate* at that place averaged over any 8 hour working period;

"dose record" means, in relation to a person, the record of the *doses* received by that person as a result of his exposure to *ionising radiation,* being the record made and *maintained* on behalf of the employer by the *approved dosimetry service* in accordance with regulation 13(3)(a);

"employment medical adviser" means an employment medical adviser appointed under section 56 of the Health and Safety at Work etc. Act 1974;

"the Executive" means the Health and Safety Executive;

"external radiation" means, in relation to a person, *ionising radiation* coming from outside the body of that person;

"health record" means, in relation to an employee, the record of medical surveillance of that employee maintained by the employer in accordance with regulation 16(2);

"internal radiation" means, in relation to a person, *ionising radiation* coming from inside the body of that person;

"ionising radiation" means gamma rays, X-rays or corpuscular radiations which are capable of producing ions either directly or indirectly;

"local rules" means rules made in accordance with regulation 11(1);

"maintained", where the reference is to maintaining plant, apparatus or facilities, means maintained in an efficient state, in efficient working order and good repair *(a)*;

"medical exposure" means exposure of a person to *ionising radiation* for the purpose of his medical or dental examination or treatment which is conducted under the direction of a suitably qualified person and includes any such examination or treatment conducted for the purposes of research;

"overexposure" means any exposure of a person to *ionising radiation* to the extent that the *dose* received by that person causes a *dose limit* relevant to that person to be exceeded;

"qualified person" means a person who has been so appointed for the purposes of regulation 24(3) in accordance with regulation 10(7);

"radiation generator" means any apparatus in which charged particles are accelerated in a vacuum vessel through a potential difference of more than 5 kilovolts (whether in one or more steps) except in apparatus in which the only such generator is a cathode ray tube or visual display unit which does not cause under normal operating conditions an instantaneous *dose rate* of more than 5 μSvh⁻¹ at a distance of 50 mm from any accessible surface;

"radioactive substance" means any substance having an activity concentration of more than 100 Bqg⁻¹ and any other substance which contains one or more radionuclides whose activity cannot be disregarded for the purposes of radiation protection, and the term includes a *radioactive substance* in the form of a sealed source;

"radiation protection adviser" means a person who has been so appointed in accordance with regulation 10(1);

"sealed source" means a *radioactive substance* bonded wholly within a solid inactive material or encapsulated within an inactive receptacle of, in either case, sufficient strength to prevent any dispersion of the substance under reasonably foreseeable conditions of use and shall include the bonding or encapsulation, except that—

(a) where such bonding or encapsulation is solely for the purpose of storage, transport or disposal, the *radioactive substance* together with its bonding or encapsulation shall not be treated as a *sealed source*; and

(b) "sealed source" shall not include any *radioactive substance* inside a nuclear reactor of any nuclear fuel element;

"short-lived daughters of radon 222" means polonium 218, lead 214, bismuth 214 and polonium 214;

"supervised area" means an area which has been so designated by the employer in accordance with regulation 8(2) or (3);

"trainee" means a person aged 16 years or over (including a student) who is undergoing instruction or training which involves operations which would, in the case of an employee, be work with *ionising radiation*;

"transport" means, in relation to a *radioactive substance*, carriage of that substance on a road within the meaning of section 196(1) of the Road Traffic Act 1972 *(b)* or through another public place (whether on a conveyance or not), or by rail, inland waterway, sea or air, and in the case of transport on a conveyance, a substance shall be deemed as being transported from the time that it is loaded onto the conveyance for the purpose of transporting it until it is unloaded from that conveyance, but a substance shall not be considered as being transported if—

(a) it is transported by means of a pipeline or similar means; or

(b) it forms an integral part of a conveyance and is used in connection with the operation of that conveyance;

"woman of reproductive capacity" means a woman who is made subject to the additional *dose limit* for a *woman of reproductive capacity* specified in Part IV of Schedule 1 by an entry in her health record made by an employment medical adviser or appointed doctor;

"working with ionising radiation" means any work—

(a) involving the production, processing, handling, use, holding, storage, moving, transport or disposal of any *radioactive substance*;

(b) involving the operation or use of any *radiation generator,* or
(c) in which there is any exposure of a person to an atmosphere containing the *short-lived daughters of radon 222* at a concentration in air, averaged over any 8 hour working period, of greater than $6.25 \times 10^{-7} Jm^{-3}$ (0.03 working levels);

"working level" means the special unit of potential alpha energy concentration in air and is any combination of *short-lived daughters of radon 222* in unit volume of air such that the total potential alpha energy concentration for completion decay to lead 210 is $2.08 \times 10^{-5} Jm^{-3}$.

(2) In these Regulations, unless the context otherwise requires, any reference to—

(a) an employer includes a reference to a self-employed person and any duty imposed by these Regulations on an employer in respect of his employee shall extend to a self-employed person in respect of himself;
(b) an employee includes a reference to—
   (i) a self-employed person, and
   (ii) a trainee who but for the operation of this sub-paragraph and paragraph (4) would not be classed as an employee;
(c) exposure to *ionising radiation* is a reference to exposure to *ionising radiation* arising from work with *ionising radiation*;
(d) a person entering, remaining in or working in a controlled or *supervised* area includes a reference to any part of a person entering, remaining in or working in any such area;
(e) a numbered regulation or Schedule is a reference to the regulation or Schedule in these Regulations so numbered;
(f) a numbered paragraph is a reference to the paragraph so numbered in the regulation or Schedule in which that reference appears.

(3) Except in regulation 33, in these Regulations any reference to the exposure of a person to *ionising radiation* shall not include a reference to the *medical exposure* of that person.

(4) For the purposes of these Regulations and Part I of the Health and Safety at Work etc. Act 1974—

(a) the word "work" shall be extended to include any instruction or training which a person undergoes as a *trainee* and the meaning of "at work" shall be extended accordingly; and
(b) a *trainee* shall, while he is undergoing instruction or training be treated as the employee of the person whose undertaking (whether for profit or not) is providing that instruction or training and that person shall be treated as the employer of that *trainee* except that the duties to the *trainee* imposed upon the person providing instruction or training shall only extend to matters under the control of that person.

(5) In these Regulations, where reference is made to a quantity specified in a numbered column of Schedule 2, that quantity shall be treated as being exceeded if—

(a) where only one radionuclide is involved, the quantity of that radionuclide exceeds the quantity specified in the appropriate entry in Part I of Schedule 2; or
(b) where more than one radionuclide is involved, the quantity ratio calculated in accordance with Part II of Schedule 2 exceeds one.

(6) Where any duty is imposed by thcsc Regulations on an employer in respect of the exposure to *ionising radiation* of persons other than his employees, that duty shall only be imposed in respect of the exposure of those persons to *ionising radiation* arising from work with *ionising radiation* undertaken by that employer.

(7) Duties under these Regulations imposed upon the employer shall also be imposed upon the manager of a mine or a quarry (within in either case the meaning of section 180 of the Mines and Quarries Act 1954) in so far as those duties relate to the mine or quarry or part of the quarry of which he is the manager and to matters under his control.

(8) Duties under these Regulations imposed upon the employer shall also be imposed on the holder of a nuclear site licence under the Nuclear Installations Act 1965 in so far as those duties relate to the licensed site.

(9) Nothing in these Regulations shall be construed as preventing a person from entering or remaining in a *controlled area* or a *supervised area* where that person enters or remains in any such area—

(a) in the due exercise of a power of entry conferred on him by or under any enactment; or
(b) for the purpose of undergoing a *medical exposure.*

*(a) **Maintained.*** See INTRODUCTORY NOTE 10.

(b) **Road Traffic Act 1972.** See now the Road Traffic Act 1988.

3. Application of these Regulations in relation to the *short-lived daughters of radon 222.* These Regulations shall apply to work with *ionising radiation* in which a person is exposed to the *short-lived daughters of radon 222* as they apply to other work with *ionising radiation*, except that the following Regulations shall not apply in relation to such exposure, namely—

(a) regulation 14 (accident dosimetry);
(b) regulation 18 (sealed sources and articles containing or embodying radioactive substances);
(c) regulation 19 (accounting for radioactive substances);
(d) regulation 20 (keeping of radioactive substances);
(e) regulation 21 (transport and moving of radioactive substances);
(f) regulation 22 (washing and changing facilities);
(g) regulation 26 (special hazard assessments and reports);
(h) regulation 31 (notification of certain occurrences);
(i) regulation 33 (equipment used for medical exposure); and
(j) regulation 34 (misuse of or interference with sources of ionising radiation).

4. Co-operation between employers. Where work with *ionising radiation* undertaken by an employer is likely to give rise to the exposure to *ionising radiation* of the employee of another employer, the employers concerned shall co-operate by the exchange of information or otherwise to the extent requisite to ensure that each such employer is enabled to comply with the requirements of these Regulations in so far as his ability to comply depends upon such co-operation.

5.   Notification of certain work with ionising radiation.—(1) Subject to regulation 39(1) (which related to transitional provisions), this Regulation shall apply to any work with *ionising radiation* except—

(a)   work specified in Schedule 3; and
(b)   work carried on at a site licensed under section 1 of the Nuclear Installations Act 1965.

(2) Subject to paragraph (3) of this regulation and regulation 39(2), an employer shall not undertake for the first time work with *ionising radiation* to which this regulation applies, unless at least 28 days before commencing that work or before such shorter time as *the Executive* may agree, he has notified *the Executive* of his intention to carry out such work and has furnished it with the particulars specified in Schedule 4.

(3) Where the only work with *ionising radiation* being undertaken is work in which a person is exposed to the *short-lived daughers of radon 222*, it shall be a sufficient compliance with paragraph (2) if the employer having control of the premises where the work is carried on makes the notification required by that paragraph forthwith after the work has commenced.

(4) Where an employer has notified work in accordance with paragraph (2), *the Executive* may, by notice in writing served on him, require that employer to provide such additional particulars of that work as it may reasonably require, being any or all of the particulars specified in Schedule 5, and in such a case the employer shall furnish those particulars in such time as is specified in the notice or in such longer time as *the Executive* may subsequently agree.

(5) A notice under paragraph (4) may require the employer to notify *the Executive* or such other authority as is specified in the notice of any of the particulars specified in Schedule 5 before each occasion on which he commences work with *ionising radiation*.

(6) Where an employer has notified work in accordance with paragraph (2) and subsequently makes a material change in that work which would affect the particulars so notified, he shall forthwith notify *the Executive* of that change.

(7) Nothing in paragraph (6) shall be taken as requiring the cessation of work with *ionising radiation* to be notified in accordance with that paragraph except where—

(a)   the site or any part of the site in which the work was carried on has been or is to be vacated; and
(b)   the work involved a *radioactive substance* other than a *radioactive substance* solely in the form of a sealed source.

(8) In any proceedings against a person for an offence consisting of a contravention of paragraph (2), it shall be a defence for that person to prove that—

(a)   he neither knew nor had reasonable cause to believe that he had undertaken or might be required to undertake work with *ionising radiation*; and

(b) in a case where he discovered that he had undertaken or was under-taking work with *ionising radiation*, he had forthwith notified *the Executive* of the details specified in Schedule 4.

PART II

DOSE LIMITATION

6. Restriction of exposure.—(1) Every employer shall, in relation to any work with *ionising radiation* that he undertakes, take all necessary steps to restrict so far as reasonably practicable *(a)* the extent to which his employees and other persons are exposed to *ionising radiation*.

(2) Without prejudice to the generality of paragraph (1), every employer shall, so far as reasonably practicable *(a)*, achieve the restriction of exposure to *ionising radiation* required under that paragraph by means of engineering controls and design features which include shielding, ventilation, containment of *radioactive substances* and minimisation of contamination and in addition by the provision and use of safety features and warning devices.

(3) In addition to taking the steps required under paragraph (2), every employer shall provide such systems of work as will, so far as reasonably practicable *(a)*, restrict the exposure to *ionising radiation* of employees and other persons and, in the case of employees or other persons who enter or remain in *controlled* or *supervised areas*, provide those persons with adequate and suitable personal protective equipment (including respiratory protective equipment) unless—

(a) it is not reasonably practicable *(a)* to further restrict exposure to *ionising radiation* by such means; or

(b) the use of personal protective equipment of a particular kind is not appropriate having regard to the nature of the work or the circumstances of the particular case.

(4) An employee who is engaged in work with *ionising radiation*—

(a) shall not knowingly expose himself or any other person to *ionising radiation* to an extent greater than is reasonably necessary for the purposes of his work, and shall exercise reasonable care while carrying out such work;

(b) shall make full and proper use of any personal protective equipment provided in pursuance of paragraph (3); and

(c) shall forthwith report to his employer any defect he discovers in any personal protective equipment.

(5) The employer shall ensure that—

(a) no *radioactive substance* in the form of a *sealed source* is held in the hand or manipulated directly by hand unless the instantaneous *dose rate* to the skin of the hand does not exceed 75 μSvh^{-1}; and

(b) so far as reasonably practicable, no unsealed *radioactive substance* nor any article containing a *radioactive substance* is held in the hand or directly manipulated by hand.

(6) No employee shall eat, drink, smoke, take snuff or apply cosmetics in any area which the employer has designated as a *controlled area* by virtue of the

provisions of Part II of Schedule 6 (which related to *internal radiation*) except that an employee may drink from a drinking fountain so constructed that there is no contamination of the water.

   (a) **Reasonably practicable.** See INTRODUCTORY NOTE 5.

7.   Dose limits. Every employer shall ensure that his employees and other persons are not exposed to *ionising radiation* to an extent that any *dose limit* specified in Schedule 1 for each such employee or other person as the case may be, is exceeded.

PART III
REGULATION OF WORK WITH IONISING RADIATION

8.   Designation of controlled and supervised areas.—(1) For the purpose of designating as a *controlled area* any area in which doses of *ionising radiation* are likely to exceed three-tenths of any *dose limit* for employees aged 18 years or over, every employer shall designate as a *controlled area* any area under his control where an employee can be exposed to *ionising radiation* and which is required to be so designated by virtue of the provisions of Schedule 6.

   (2) Every employer shall designate as a *supervised area* any area under his control, not being an area designated as a *controlled area*, in which any person is likely to be exposed to *ionising radiation* to an extent which exceeds one-third of the extent to which he would be exposed in any area which is required to be designated as a *controlled area* in accordance with paragraph (1).

   (3) Notwithstanding the provisions of paragraphs (1) and (2), an employer may designate any area under his control, other than an area specified in paragraph (1), as a *controlled area* or a *supervised area* and any area so designated shall be treated for all purposes as an area designated under paragraph (1) or (2) as the case may be.

   (4) An employer shall not intentionally create in an area conditions which would require that area to be designated as a *controlled area* unless that area is for the time being under his control.

   (5) Every employer shall ensure that each *controlled area* and *supervised area* that he has designated is adequately described in *local rules* and that, in the case of any *controlled area*—

   (a)   the area is physically demarcated or, where this is not reasonably practicable, delineated by some other means; and
   (b)   access to the area is restricted by suitable means.

   (6) The employer shall not permit any employee or other person to enter or remain in a *controlled area* unless that employee or other person either—

   (a)   is a *classified person*; or
   (b)   enters or remains in the area under a written system of work such that—
     (i)   in the case of an employee aged 18 years or over, he does not receive in any *calendar year* a *dose* of *ionising radiation*, exceeding three-tenths of any relevant dose limit, or

(ii) in the case of any other person, he does not receive in any *calendar year* a dose of *ionising radiation* exceeding any relevant *dose limit.*

(7) An employer shall not permit an employee or other person to enter or remain in a *controlled area* in accordance with a written system of work under paragraph (6)(b), unless he can demonstrate, by personal *dose* assessment or other suitable measurements, that the *doses* are restricted in accordance with that paragraph.

9. Designation of classified persons.—(1) Subject to paragraph (3), the employer shall designate as *classified persons* those of his employees who are likely to receive a *dose* of *ionising radiation* which exceeds three-tenths of any relevant *dose limit* and shall forthwith inform those employees that they have been so designated.

(2) The employer shall not cease to treat an employee as a *classified person* except at the end of a *calendar year*, unless he is required to do so under regulation 16(6) by an *employment medical adviser* or *appointed doctor*, and in any case where he ceases to treat an employee as a *classified person* the employer shall forthwith inform the employee that he is no longer a *classified person.*

(3) An employer shall not designate an employee as a *classified person* unless—

(a) that employee is aged 18 years or over; and
(b) subject to regulation 39(3) (which relates to transitional provisions), an *employment medical* adviser or *appointed doctor* has certified in the *health record* that, in his professional opinion, that employee is fit to be designated as a *classified person.*

10. Appointment of *radiation protection advisers* and *qualified persons.*— (1) Subject to regulation 39(4) (which relates to transitional provisions) and paragraphs (3) and (6) of this regulation, in any case where—

(a) any employee is exposed to an instantaneous *dose rate* which exceeds 7.5 μSvh^{-1}; or
(b) the employer has designated a *controlled area* which persons enter,

the employer carrying out the work with *ionising radiation* shall appoint one or more *radiation protection advisers* for the purpose of advising him as to the observance of these Regulations and as to other health and safety matters in connection with *ionising radiation.*

(2) An employer who appoints a *radiation protection adviser* for the purposes of regulation 32(2) or in any other case where he considers it requisite in relation to the *work with ionising radiation* that he undertakes shall be deemed to have appointed that *radiation protection adviser* under paragraph (1).

(3) No employer shall appoint a person as a *radiation protection adviser* unless—

(a) that person is suitably qualified and experienced;
(b) he has notified *the Executive* in writing of the intended appointment at least 28 days in advance or, where this is not practicable, such shorter time in advance as *the Executive* may agree and that notification shall

include the name of the person that he intends to appoint and particulars of his qualifications and experience and the scope of the advice he is required to give; and

(c)   he has received from *the Executive* an acknowledgement in writing of the notification.

(4)   The employer shall forthwith notify *the Executive* of any material change in relation to a *radiation protection adviser* which would affect the particulars notified in accordance with paragraph (3)(b).

(5)   The employer shall provide any *radiation protection adviser* whom he appoints with adequate information and facilities for the performance of his functions and shall whenever appropriate consult that adviser.

(6)   Nothing in paragraph (1) shall require an employer to appoint a *radiation protection adviser* where the only work with *ionising radiation* undertaken by the employer is work specified in Schedule 3.

(7)   Paragraphs (3), (4) and (5) of this regulation shall apply to the appointment of a *qualified person* for the purposes of regulation 24(3) as they apply to the appointment of a *radiation protection adviser*, except that the notification to *the Executive* under paragraph (3)(b) shall not be required to include particulars of the advice he is required to give.

11.   Local rules, supervision and radiation protection supervisors.—
(1)   Every employer who undertakes *work with ionising radiation* shall make and set down in writing *local rules* for the purpose of enabling the *work with ionising radiation* to be carried on in compliance with the requirements of these Regulations and shall ensure that such of those rules as are relevant are brought to the attention of those employees and other persons who may be affected by them.

(2)   The employer shall ensure that the *work with ionising radiation* is supervised to the extent necessary to enable that work to be carried on in accordance with the requirements of these Regulations and shall take all reasonable steps to ensure that any *local rules* that are relevant to that work are observed.

(3)   Subject to regulation 39(5) (which relates to transitional provisions), where the *work with ionising radiation* carried on by the employer is any such work other than that specified in Schedule 3, the employer shall appoint one or more of his employees as *radiation protection supervisors* for the purpose of securing compliance with paragraph (2) and any such appointments shall be in writing and the names of persons so appointed shall be included in the *local rules*.

12.   Information, instruction and training.   Every employer shall ensure that—

(a)   subject to regulation 39(6) (which relates to transitional provisions), those of his employees who are engaged in *work with ionising radiation* receive such information, instruction and training as will enable them to conduct that work in accordance with the requirements of these Regulations;

(b) adequate information is given to other persons who are directly concerned with the *work with ionising radiation* carried on by the employer to ensure their health and safety so far as is reasonably practicable;

(c) *classified persons* and *trainees* are informed of the health hazard, if any, associated with their work, the precautions to be taken and the importance of complying with the medical and technical requirements and are given appropriate training in the field of radiation protection; and

(d) those of his employees who are engaged in work with *ionising radiation* and who are women are informed of the possible hazard arising from *ionising radiation* to the foetus in early pregnancy and of the importance of informing the employer as soon as they discover that they have become pregnant.

PART IV
DOSIMETRY AND MEDICAL SURVEILLANCE

13. Dose assessment.—(1) This Regulation shall apply in relation to—

(a) any employee who is designated as a *classified person*; and

(b) any employee who is made subject to this regulation by an approved arrangement made under regulation 17(1).

(2) Subject to regulation 39(7) (which relates to transitional provisions), every employer shall ensure that assessments are made of all significant *doses* of *ionising radiation* received by each of his employees to whom this regulation relates and for this purpose shall make suitable arrangements with an *approved dosimetry service* for the making of systematic measurements and assessments of such doses—

(a) by the use of suitable personal dosemeters which shall be worn for appropriate periods; or

(b) where the use of such dosemeters is inappropriate, by means of other suitable measurements.

(3) For the purposes of paragraph (2), the arrangements that the employer makes with the *approved dosimetry service* shall include requirements for that service—

(a) to make and maintain *dose records* relating to each employee to whom this regulation relates and to keep those *dose records* or a copy thereof for at least 50 years from when they were made;

(b) to furnish the employer at appropriate intervals with suitable summaries of the *dose records* maintained in accordance with sub-paragraph (a) above;

(c) when required by the employer to furnish him with such copies of the *dose record* relating to any of his employees as the employer may require;

(d) when required by the employer, to make a record of the information concerning the *dose* assessment relating to a person who ceases to be an employee of the employer, and to send that record to *the Executive* and a copy thereof to the employer forthwith, and a record so made is referred to in this regulation as a "termination record";

(e) within 3 months, or such longer period as *the Executive* may agree, of the end of each calendar year to send to *the Executive* summaries of all current *dose records* relating to that year;

(f) to send to *the Executive* forthwith appropriate details of any employee who has received in any calendar quarter a *dose* of *ionising radiation* greater than three-fifths of the annual *dose limit* for employees 18 years or over specified in Part I of Schedule 1 (whole body *dose limit*), and in this sub-paragraph "calendar quarter" means the three calendar months beginning with 1 January, 1 April, 1 July or 1 October;

(g) when required by *the Executive*, to furnish it with copies of any *dose record*; and

(h) to make any entry in a *dose record* in accordance with paragraphs (7) and (9).

(4) The employer shall make arrangements with the *approved dosimetry service* for that service to keep suitable summaries of any appropriate *dose records* which he holds relating to those of his employees whom he has designated, or intends to designate, as *classified persons* under these Regulations, whether or not those records were made in pursuance of a requirement imposed by or under any enactment, and the employer shall lodge those summaries with the service before 1 July 1986 or forthwith after designation whichever is the later.

(5) The employer shall—

(a) at the request of an employee and on reasonable notice being given, obtain from the *approved dosimetry service* and give to the employee a copy of the *dose record* which relates to him; and

(b) when an employee ceases to be employed by the employer, take all reasonable steps to send a copy of his termination record to that employee.

(6) The employer shall keep a copy of the summary of the *dose record* received from the *approved dosimetry service* for at least 2 years from the end of the *calendar year* to which the summary relates.

(7) In any case where a dosemeter is lost or destroyed or it is not possible to assess the *dose* received over any period by an employee to whom paragraph (1) relates, the employer shall make an investigation of the circumstances of the case with a view to estimating the *dose* received by the employee during that period and either—

(a) in a case where there is adequate information to estimate *the dose* received by the employee, shall arrange for the *approved dosimetry service* to enter that estimated *dose* in the *dose record* of the employee; or

(b) in a case where there is adequate information to estimate *the dose* received by the employee, shall arrange for *the approved dosimetry service* to enter a notional *dose* in the *dose record* of the employee which shall be the proportion of the total annual *dose limit* for the relevant period,

and in either case the employer shall arrange for the *approved dosimetry service* to identify the entry in the *dose record* as an estimated *dose* or a notional *dose* as the case may be.

(8) Where an employer has reason to believe that the *dose* received by one of his employees is much greater or much less than that shown in the *dose record*, he shall make an investigation of the circumstances of the exposure of that employee to *ionising radiation* and, if that investigation confirms his belief, he shall apply to *the Executive* for a special entry to be made in the *dose record* of that employee.

(9) Where *the Executive* has reasonable cause to believe that the *dose* received by an employee was much greater or much less than that shown in his *dose record*, it may approve a special entry in the *dose record* and in such a case the employer shall arrange for the *approved dosimetry service* to enter the special entry in that *dose record* and shall give a copy of the amended *dose record* to the employee.

(10) Any employee to whom paragraph (1) of this regulation or regulation 27(4)(b) relates shall comply with any reasonable requirements imposed on him by his employer for the purposes of making the measurements and assessment required under paragraph (2) of this regulation and regulation 14(1).

14. Accident dosimetry.—(1) Where an accident, occurrence or incident occurs which is likely to result in a person being exposed to *ionising radiation* to an extent greater than three-tenths of any relevant *dose limit*, the employer shall—

(a) in the case of an employee to whom regulation 13 relates, arrange for a *dose* assessment to be made by the *approved dosimetry service* forthwith;

(b) in the case of an employee to whom a dosemeter or other device has been issued in accordance with regulation 27(4)(b), arrange for that dosemeter or device to be examined and for the *dose* received to be assessed by the *approved dosimetry service*;

(c) in any other case, arrange for the *dose* to be assessed by an appropriate means.

(2) In such a case, the employer shall—

(a) take all reasonably practicable steps to inform each person for whom a *dose* assessment has been made of the result of that assessment; and

(b) keep a record of the assessment or a copy thereof for at least 50 years from the date of the relevant accident, occurrence or incident.

15. Approved dosimetry services. *The Executive* may by a certificate in writing, which may be made subject to conditions and may be revoked in writing at any time, approve a suitable dosimetry service for such of the purposes of regulations 13, 14 and 27 as are specified in the certificate.

General note. Fees for approval are specified in the Health and Safety (Fees) Regulations 1992, S.I. 1992 No. 1752.

16. Medical surveillance.—(1) This regulation shall apply in relation to—

(a) *classified persons* and persons whom the employer intends to classify;

(b) employees who have received an *overexposure* and are not *classified persons*;

(c) employees who are engaged in work with *ionising radiation* subject to conditions imposed by an *employment medical adviser* or *appointed doctor* under paragraph (6); and

(d) employees who are subject to this regulation by an approved arrangement made under regulation 17(1).

(2) The employer shall ensure that a health record, containing particulars approved by *the Executive*, in respect of each of his employees to whom this regulation relates is made and maintained and that that record or a copy thereof is kept for at least 50 years from the date of the last entry made in it.

(3) The employer shall ensure that each of his employees to whom this regulation relates is under adequate medical surveillance by an *employment medical adviser* or *appointed doctor.*

(4) Subject to regulation 39(8) (which relates to transitional provisions) and to paragraph (5) of this regulation, the employer shall ensure that there is a valid entry in the health record of each of his employees to whom this regulation relates (other than employees who have received an *overexposure* and who are not *classified persons*) made by an *employment medical adviser* or *appointed doctor* and an entry in the health record shall be valid—

(a) for 12 months from the date it was made; or
(b) for such shorter period as is specified in the entry by the *employment medical adviser* or *appointed doctor*; or
(c) until cancelled by an *employment medical adviser* or *appointed doctor* by a further entry in the record.

(5) Where, within the period of validity of an entry in the *health record* made under paragraph (4) (a) but not earlier than one month before the end of that period, a further entry is made as respects the same employee, the further entry shall be treated for the purpose of paragraph (4) (a) as if made at the end of the said period.

(6) Where the *employment medical adviser* or *appointed doctor* has certified in the *health record* of an employee to whom this regulation relates that in his professional opinion that employee should not be engaged in *work with ionising radiation* or that he should only be so engaged under conditions he has specified in the *health record*, the employer shall not permit that employee to be engaged in *work with ionising radiation* except in accordance with the conditions, if any, so specified.

(7) An employee to whom this regulation relates shall, when required by his employer and at the cost of the employer, present himself during his working hours for such medical examination and tests as may be required for the purpose of paragraph (3) and shall furnish the *employment medical adviser* or *appointed doctor* with such information concerning his health as the *employment medical adviser* or *appointed doctor* may reasonably require.

(8) Where, for the purpose of carrying out his functions under these Regulations, an *employment medical adviser* or *appointed doctor* requires to inspect any workplace, the employer shall permit him to do so.

(9) The employer shall make available to the *employment medical adviser* or *appointed doctor* such records kept for the purposes of these Regulations as he may reasonably require.

(10) Where an employee is aggrieved by a decision recorded in the *health record* by an *employment medical adviser* or *appointed doctor* he may, by an application in writing to *the Executive* made within three months of the date on which he was notified of the decision, apply for that decision to be reviewed in accordance with a procedure approved for the purposes of this paragraph by the Health and Safety Commission, and the result of that review shall be

notified to the employee and entered in his health record in accordance with the *approved* procedure.

General note. Fees for examination by an employment medical adviser are specified in the Health and Safety (Fees) Regulations 1992, S.I. 1992 No. 1752.

17. Approved arrangements for the protection of certain employees.— (1) Where *the Executive* has reasonable cause to believe that it is necessary for the protection of the health or safety of any employee, it may serve on his employer a notice in writing requiring that employer to make such arrangements as it may approve as respects any or all of the following, namely—

(a) the prohibiting or regulating the entry by, or presence of, the employee in any or all *controlled areas* or *supervised areas*;

(b) for the employee to be made subject to any or all of the requirements of regulation 13 (which relates to *dose* assessment); and

(c) for the employee to be made subject to any or all of the requirements of regulation 16 (which relates to medical surveillance),

and in such a case the employer shall make such arrangements as are required in the notice.

(2) Where the employer has made *approved* arrangements in respect of an employee in pursuance of a notice under paragraph (1), he shall ensure that the employee is informed of the *approved* arrangements made in respect of him and that those arrangements are complied with.

(3) Where an employer has made *approved* arrangements with respect to an employee, that employee shall comply with those arrangements.

(4) A notice served under paragraph (1) may take immediate effect, or may take effect on such a date as is specified in it, may be with or without limit of time and may be revoked at any time.

(5) *The Executive* shall not issue a notice under paragraph (1)(a) in a case where if the notice had been issued it would have related to a decision of an *employment medical adviser* or *appointed doctor* which is being or has been reviewed under regulation 16(10).

PART V

ARRANGEMENTS FOR THE CONTROL OF *RADIOACTIVE SUBSTANCES*

18. Sealed sources and articles containing or embodying radioactive substances.— (1) Where a *radioactive substance* is used as a source of *ionising radiation* in *work with ionising radiation*, the employer shall ensure that, whenever reasonably practicable, the substance is in the form of a *sealed source*.

(2) The employer shall ensure that the design, construction and maintenance of any article containing or embodying a *radioactive substance*, including its bonding, immediate container or other mechanical protection, is such as to prevent the leakage of any *radioactive substance*—

(a) as in the case of a *sealed source*, so far as is practicable *(a)*, or

(b) in the case of any other article, so far as is reasonably practicable *(a)*.

(3) Where appropriate, the employer shall ensure that suitable tests are carried out at suitable intervals, which shall in no case exceed 26 months, to detect leakage of *radioactive substances* from any article to which paragraph (2) applies and the employer shall keep a suitable record of those tests for at least three years from the date of the tests to which it refers.

(4) In any proceedings against an employer for an offence under paragraph (2) it shall be a defence for that employer to prove that—

    (a) he had received and reasonably relied on a written undertaking from the supplier of the article concerned that it complied with the requirements of that paragraph; and

    (b) he had complied with the requirements of paragraph (3).

    (a) Practicable; reasonably practicable. See INTRODUCTORY NOTE 5.

19. Accounting for *radioactive substances.* For the purpose of controlling *radioactive substances* which are involved in work with *ionising radiation* which he undertakes, every employer shall take such steps as are appropriate to account for and keep records of the quantity and location of those substances and shall keep those records or a copy thereof for at least 2 years from the date on which they were made and, in addition, for at least 2 years from the date of disposal of that *radioactive substance.*

20. Keeping of *radioactive substances.*—(1) Every employer who undertakes *work with ionising radiation* shall ensure, so far as is reasonably practicable *(a)*, that any *radioactive substance* under his control which is not for the time being in use or being moved, transported or disposed of—

    (a) is kept in a suitable receptacle; and

    (b) is kept in a suitable store.

(2) Nothing in paragraph (1) shall apply in relation to a *radioactive substance* while it is in or on the live body or corpse of a human being.

    (a) Reasonably practicable. See INTRODUCTORY NOTE 5.

21. *Transport* and moving of *radioactive substances.*—(1) Every employer who causes or permits a *radioactive substance* to be transported shall ensure, so far as is reasonably practicable *(a)*, the substance is kept in a suitable receptacle, suitably labelled, whilst it is being transported.

(2) Every employer who causes or permits a *radioactive substance* to be transported shall ensure, so far as is reasonably practicable *(a)*, that such information in writing accompanies the *radioactive substance* as will enable the person receiving it—

    (a) to know the nature and quantity of the *radioactive substance;* and

    (b) to comply with the requirements of regulations 6, 7, 8 and 18(2) and paragraph (1) of this regulation in so far as such compliance depends on that information.

(3) Every employer who causes or permits a *radioactive substance* to be moved (otherwise than by transporting it) shall ensure that, so far as is reasonably practicable *(a)*, the substance is kept in a suitable receptacle while it is being moved.

(4) In any proceedings against an employer for an offence under paragraph (1) or (2), it shall be a defence for that employer to prove that it was reasonable for him to rely upon information given to him by some other person under paragraph (2).

(2) The foregoing paragraphs of this regulation shall not apply—

(a) in relation to the *transport* of a *radioactive substance* where and to the extent that the Radioactive Substances (Carriage by Road) (Great Britain) Regulations 1974 apply in relation to that *transport*; or
(b) in relation to a *radioactive substance* while it is in or on the live body or corpse of a human being.

(a) **Reasonably practicable.** See INTRODUCTORY NOTE 5.

22. Washing and changing facilities. Subject to regulation 39(9) (which relates to transitional provisions), where an employer is required by virtue of the provisions of Part II of Schedule 6 (which related to *internal radiation*) to designate an area as a *controlled area* or a *supervised area,* he shall ensure that adequate washing and changing facilities are provided for persons who enter or leave that area and that those facilities are properly *maintained.*

23. Personal protective equipment.—(1) Every employer shall ensure that, where personal protective equipment provided in pursuance of regulation 6(3) includes respiratory protective equipment, that respiratory protective equipment complies with paragraph (1A) or, where no requirement is imposed by that paragraph, is of a type, or conforms to a standard, *approved* in either case by *the Executive,* except that this paragraph shall not apply to respiratory protective equipment supplied to the employer before 1 January 1988.

(1A) For the purposes of paragraph (1), personal protective equipment complies with this paragraph if it complies with any enactment (whether in an Act or instrument) which implements in Great Britain any provision on design or manufacture with respect to health or safety in any relevant Community Directive listed in Schedule 1 to the Personal Protective Equipment at Work Regulations 1992 which is applicable to that item of personal protective equipment.

(1B) Before choosing personal protective equipment, an employer shall make an assessment to determine whether it will satisfy regulation 6(3).

(1C) The assessment required by paragraph (1B) shall involve—

(a) definition of the characteristics necessary to comply with regulation 6(3), and
(b) comparison of the characteristics of available personal protective equipment with the characteristics referred to in sub-paragraph (a) of this paragraph.

(1D) The assessment required by paragraph (1B) shall be reviewed if—

(a) there is reason to suspect that it is no longer valid; or
(b) there has been a significant change in the work to which it relates,

and where, as a result of the review, changes in the assessment are required, the employer shall make them.

(2) Every employer shall ensure that all personal protective equipment (including respiratory protective equipment) is thoroughly examined at suitable intervals and is *properly maintained (b)* and, that, in the case of respiratory protective equipment, a suitable record of that examination is made and kept for at least two years from the date on which the examination was made and that the record includes a statement of the condition of the equipment at the time of the examination.

(2A) Every employer shall ensure that appropriate accommodation is provided for personal protective equipment when it is not being worn.

(2B) Every employee shall take all reasonable steps to ensure that personal protective equipment provided to him is returned to the accommodation provided for it after use.

General note. Fees payable for approval of respiratory protective equipment are specified by the Health and Safety (Fees) Regulations 1992, S.I. 1992 No. 1752 (not printed in this book).

(a) **Reasonably practicable.** See INTRODUCTORY NOTE 5.

(b) **Properly maintained.** See INTRODUCTORY NOTE 10.

PART VI
MONITORING OF IONISING RADIATION

24. Monitoring of levels for radiation and contamination.—(1) Every employer who undertakes work with *ionising radiation* shall take such steps are requisite, otherwise than by use of assessed *doses* of individuals, to ensure that levels of *ionising radiation* are adequately monitored for each *controlled area* or *supervised area* that he has designated, in order to ascertain the efficacy of the methods used in those areas for the restriction of exposure of persons to *ionising radiation.*

(2) The employer shall provide equipment which is suitable for carrying out the monitoring required by paragraph (1) and it shall—

(a) be properly *maintained (a)*;
(b) subject to regulation 39(10) (which related to transitional provisions), be thoroughly examined and tested at least once in every 14 months; and
(c) except in the case of equipment which was taken into use for the first time before 1 January 1988, have had its performance established by tests before it is taken into use for the first time.

(3) The examination and tests required by sub-paragraphs (b) and (c) of paragraph (2) shall be carried out by, or under the immediate supervision of, a *qualified person* appointed for the purposes of those sub-paragraphs by either—

(a) the employer who undertakes the work with *ionising radiation* in which the instruments are intended to be used; or

(b) the employer of the *qualified person* if he is not the employer mentioned in sub-paragraph (a) above.

(4) The employer shall make suitable records of the results of the monitoring carried out in accordance with paragraph (1) and of the tests which have been carried out in accordance with paragraph (2) and shall keep those records or copies thereof for at least 2 years from the respective dates on which they were made.

(*a*) **Properly maintained.** See INTRODUCTORY NOTE 10.

PART VII
ASSESSMENTS AND NOTIFICATIONS

25. Assessment of hazards.—(1) An employer shall not carry on work with *ionising radiation* unless he has made an assessment which is adequate to identify the nature and magnitude of the radiation hazard to employees or other persons which is likely to arise from that work in the event of any reasonably foreseeable accident, occurrence or incident.

(2) Where the assessment carried out for the purposes of paragraph (1) shows that a radiation hazard to employees or other persons exists, the employer shall take all reasonably practicable (*a*) steps to—

(a) prevent any such accident, occurrence or incident;

(b) limit the consequences of any such accident, occurrence or incident which does occur; and

(c) provide employees with the information, instruction and training and with the equipment necessary to restrict their exposure to *ionising radiation.*

(*a*) **Reasonably practicable.** See INTRODUCTORY NOTE 5.

26. Special hazard assessments and reports.—(1) Subject to regulation 39(11) (which relates to transitional provisions) and paragraphs (5) and (7) of this regulation, an employer shall not undertake any *work with ionising radiation* which involves—

(a) having on any site;

(b) providing facilities for there to be on any site; or

(c) transporting,

more than the quantity of any *radioactive substance* specified in column 6 of Schedule 2 or, in the case of a fissile material, the mass of that material specified in paragraph (6) of this regulation, unless he has made an assessment of the radiation hazard that could arise from that work and has sent a report of the assessment, including the particulars specified in Schedule 7, to *the Executive* at least 28 days before commencing that work or within such shorter time in advance as *the Executive* may agree.

(2) Where an assessment has been made in accordance with paragraph (1) and the employer makes a material change in the work to which that assessment

relates which could affect any of the particulars specified in Schedule 7, he shall make a further assessment to take account of that change and send a report of the further assessment to *the Executive* within 28 days of making that change or such longer time as *the Executive* may agree.

(3) Where an assessment has been made in accordance with paragraph (1) or (2) and the work to which it relates is still continuing, the employer shall within two years of the date of the last assessment report (whether made in accordance with paragraph (1) or (2) or sub-paragraph (a) below) either—

(a) make a further assessment; or
(b) if there is no change of circumstances which would affect the last such report, sign a declaration to that effect,

and shall within 28 days send to the *Executive* a copy of the latest assessment report or the declaration as the case may be.

(4) Where, for the purpose of assessing the risk to health or safety of persons who could be affected by *work with ionising radiation* to which paragraph (1) applies, *the Executive* may reasonably require a detailed assessment of any of the matters set out in Schedule 8, it may, by notice in writing served on the employer, require him to carry out such detailed assessment of such of those matters as are specified in the notice and the employer shall send a report of the assessment to *the Executive* within such time as is specified in the notice or within such longer time as *the Executive* may subsequently allow.

(5) For the purpose of paragraph (1) no account shall be taken of—

(a) any *radioactive substance* which has an activity concentration of not more than 100 Bdq^{-1};
(b) any *radioactive substance* in the form of a *sealed source* conforming to the specifications in paragraph 2 or 3 of Schedule 9; or
(c) any *radioactive substance* which is in a package which complies in every aspect with either the requirements for Type B packages or for Special Arrangements Transport Operations of, in either case, the Regulations for the Safe Transport of Radioactive Materials published by the International Atomic Energy Agency as revised or re-issued from time to time and is certified pursuant to those Regulations as complying with them.

(6) For the purpose of paragraph (1) the specified mass of fissile material shall be—

(a) plutonium as Pu 239 or Pu 241 or as a mixture of plutonium isotopes containing Pu 239 or Pu 241, 150 grams;
(b) uranium as U 233, 150 grams;
(c) uranium enriched in U 235 to more than 1% but not more than 5%, 500 grams;
(d) uranium enriched in U 235 to more than 5%, 250 grams.

(7) This Regulation shall not apply to any work with *ionising radiation* which is undertaken on a site for the time being licensed under the Nuclear Installations Act 1965.

27.   Contingency plans.—(1) Where the assessment made in accordance with regulation 25(1) shows that as a result of any reasonably foreseeable accident, occurrence or incident—

(a) employees or other persons are likely to receive a *dose of ionising radiation* which exceeds any relevant *dose limit*; or

(b) any area other than an area already designated as a *controlled area* would be required to be so designated in accordance with the requirements of Regulation 8(1) and Schedule 6 (whether or not it is for the time being under his control),

the employer shall prepare a contingency plan designated to secure so far as is reasonably practicable *(a)* the restriction of exposure to *ionising radiation* and the health and safety of persons who may be affected by the accident, occurrence or incident to which the plan relates.

(2) For the purpose of preparing the contingency plan the employer shall consult such persons, bodies and authorities as are appropriate and in a case where the emergency services form part of the plan shall give such information to those services as will enable them to perform their functions in accordance with the plan.

(3) The contingency plan shall include—

(a) arrangements for all persons (whether employees or not) who are likely to be affected as a result of an accident, occurrence or incident;

(b) the name of the person responsible for safety on the site or, in the case of a *transport* operation, of that operation;

(c) the names of persons authorised to implement the plan in the event of an accident, occurrence or incident.

(4) The employer shall ensure that—

(a) a copy of the contingency plan made in pursuance of paragraph (1) is incorporated in *local rules*;

(b) any employee under his control who may be involved with or may be affected by arrangements in the plan has been given suitable and sufficient instructions and where appropriate issued with suitable dosemeters or other devices obtained in either case from the *approved dosimetry service* with which the employer has entered into an arrangement under regulation 13(2); and

(c) where appropriate, rehearsals of the arrangements in the plan are carried out at suitable intervals.

(5) Subject to regulation 39(11) (which relates to transitional provisions), the employer shall provide *the Executive* with a copy of the contingency plan either—

(a) before a quantity of a *radioactive substance* which exceeds the quantity specified in column 6 of Schedule 2 or, in the case of fissile material, the mass of that material specified in regulation 26(6), is brought onto any site or is transported; or

(b) when *the Executive* so requires.

(6) Where the quantity of a *radioactive substance* exceeds the quantity specified in column 6 of Schedule 2 or, in the case of a fissile material, the mass of that material specified in regulation 26(6) and the employer has prepared the contingency plan specified in paragraph (1) of this regulation, *the Executive* may, by a certificate in writing which may be revoked at any time, exempt (either unconditionally or subject to conditions and with or without limit of time) the employer from the requirements of regulation 7 to the extent

necessary to give effect to the contingency plan and, in determining whether to grant an exemption in any particular case, *the Executive* shall have regard to the circumstances of that case and in particular to—

(a) the nature and extent of exposure of persons to *ionising radiation* which might result from any accident, occurrence or incident to which the contingency plan relates;

(b) the size and distribution of the population which might be affected by any such accident, occurrence or incident; and

(c) the hazard to the health or safety of persons or other detriment which might arise from the countermeasures proposed.

(a) *Reasonably practicable.* See INTRODUCTORY NOTE 5.

28.   Investigation of exposure.—(1) The employer shall ensure that an investigation is carried out forthwith when any of his employees is exposed to *ionising radiation* to an extent that three-tenths of the annual *dose limit* for employees aged 18 years or over specified in Part I of Schedule 1 (whole body *dose limit*) is exceeded for the first time in any *calendar year*, to determine whether the requirements of regulation 6(1) are being met.

(2) The employer shall keep a report of any investigation made under paragraph (1) for at least 2 years from the date on which it was made.

29.   Investigation and notification of overexposure.—(1) Where an employer who is undertaking *work with ionising radiation* suspects or has been informed that any employee or other person is likely to have received an *overexposure* as a result of that work, he shall make an immediate investigation to determine whether there are circumstances which show beyond reasonable doubt, that no *overexposure* could have occurred and, unless this is shown, the employer shall—

(a) forthwith notify the suspected *overexposure* to—
  (i) *the Executive,*
  (ii) in the case of an employee of some other employer, that other employer, and
  (iii) in the case of his own employee, an *employment medical adviser,* and, where appropriate, the *appointed doctor;* and

(b) make or arrange for a detailed investigation of the circumstances of the exposure and an assessment of the *dose* received and shall forthwith notify the results of that investigation and assessment to the person and authorities mentioned in sub-paragraph (a) above and shall—
  (i) in the case of his employee, forthwith notify that employee of the results of the investigation and assessment, or
  (ii) in the case of a person who is not his employee, where the investigation has shown that that person has received an *overexposure,* take all reasonable steps to notify him of his *overexposure.*

(2) An employer who makes any investigation in accordance with paragraph (1) shall make a report of that investigation and shall keep that report or copy thereof for at least 50 years from the date on which it was made.

(3) Where the person who received the *overexposure* is an employee who has a *dose record,* his employer shall arrange for the assessment of the *dose* received to be entered into that *dose record.*

(4) Where an employee has reasonable cause to believe that he or some other person has received an *overexposure*, he shall forthwith inform the employer of his belief.

30.   *Dose* limitation for overexposed employees.—(1) Without prejudice to the other requirements of these Regulations and in particular regulation 16(6) and Parts IV and V of Schedule 1, where an employee has been subjected to an *overexposure*, paragraph (2) of this regulation shall apply in relation to the employment of that employee on *work with ionising radiation* during the remainder of the *calendar year*, commening at the end of the personal *dose* assessment period in which he was subjected to the overexposure.

(2) The employer shall ensure that an employee to whom this regulation relates does not, in the remaining part of the *calendar year* in which he was subjected to the *overexposure*, receive a *dose* of *ionising radiation* greater than that proportion of any *dose limit* which is equal to the proportion that the remaining part of the year bears to the whole calendar year.

31.   Notification of certain occurrences.—(1) Every employer shall forthwith notify *the Executive* in any case where a quantity of a *radioactive substance* which was under his control and which exceeds the quantity specified for the substances in column 7 of Schedule 2—

(a)   has been released or is likely to have been released into the atmosphere as a gas, aerosol or dust; or
(b)   has been spilled or otherwise released in such a manner as to give rise to significant contamination,

except where such release was in a manner specified in an authorisation to dispose of radioactive waste under section 6 of the Radioactive Substances Act 1960 or, where an arrangement referred to in section 14(3) of that Act has been made, in accordance with that arrangement.

(2) Where an employer has reasonable cause to believe that a quantity of a *radioactive substance* which exceeds the quantity for that substance specified in column 2 of Schedule 2 and which was under his control is lost or has been stolen, the employer shall forthwith notify *the Executive* of that loss or theft, as the case may be.

(3) Where an employer suspects or has been informed that an occurrence mentioned in paragraph (1) or (2) may have occurred, he shall make an immediate investigation and unless that investigation shows that no such occurrence has occurred, he shall forthwith make a notification in accordance with the relevant paragraph.

(4) An employer who makes an investigation in accordance with paragraph (3) shall make a report of that investigation and shall keep that report or a copy for at least 50 years from the date on which it was made.

(5) Where an employee has reasonable cause to believe that an occurrence mentioned in paragraph (1) or (2) has occurred, he shall forthwith notify his employer of his belief.

PART VIII
SAFETY OF ARTICLES AND EQUIPMENT

32.   Duties of manufacturers etc. of articles for use in *work with ionising radiation.*—(1) In the case of articles for use at work, where that work is *work with ionising radition,* section 6 of the Health and Safety at Work etc. Act 1974 (which imposes general duties on manufacturers etc. as regards articles and substances for use at work) shall be modified so that any duty imposed on any person by subsection (1) of that section shall include a duty to ensure that any such article is so designed and constructed as to restrict so far as is reasonably practicable *(a)* the extent to which employees and other persons are or are likely to be exposed to *ionising radiation.*

(2) Where a person erects or installs an article for use at work, being *work with ionising radiation,* he shall—

(a) where appropriate, together with a *radiation protection adviser* appointed under regulation 10(1) by himself or by the employer who works with *ionising radiation,* undertake a critical examination of the way in which the article was erected or installed for the purpose of ensuring, in particular, that—
   (i) the safety features and warning devices operate correctly, and
   (ii) there is sufficient protection for persons from exposure to *ionising radiation;* and
(b) provide the employer with adequate information about proper use, testing and maintenance of the article.

*(a) **Reasonably practicable.*** See INTRODUCTORY NOTE 5.

33.   Equipment used for medical exposure.—(1) Every employer shall ensure that any equipment or apparatus under his control which is used in connection with a *medical exposure* is of such design or construction and is so installed and *maintained (a)* as to be capable of restricting so far as is *reasonably practicable (b)* the exposure to *ionising radiation* of any person who is undergoing a *medical exposure* to the extent that this is compatible with the clinical purpose or research objective in view.

(2) Where an employer who is undertaking *work with ionising radiation* suspects or has been informed that an incident may have occurred in which a person while undergoing a *medical exposure* was, as a result of a malfunction of, or defect in, radiation equipment used in that work, exposed to *ionising radiation* to an extent much greater than that intended, he shall make an immediate investigation of the suspected incident and, unless that investigation shows beyond reasonable doubt that no such incident has occurred, shall forthwith notify *the Executive* thereof and make or arrange for a detailed investigation of the circumstances of the exposure and an assessment of the *dose* received.

(3) An employer who makes any investigation in accordance with paragraph (2) shall make a report of that investigation and shall keep that report or a copy thereof for at least 50 years from the date on which it was made.

(4) Where an employee has reasonable cause to believe that an incident mentioned in paragraph (2) has occurred, he shall forthwith notify his employer of his belief.

(5) In this regulation—

"radiation equipment" means equipment which delivers *ionising radiation* to the person undergoing a *medical exposure* and equipment which directly controls the extent of the exposure.

(*a*) **Maintenance.** See INTRODUCTORY NOTE 10.

(*b*) **Reasonably practicable.** See INTRODUCTORY NOTE 5.

34. Misuse of or interference with sources of ionising radiation. No person shall intentionally or recklessly misuse or without reasonable excuse interfere with any *radioactive substance* or *radiation generator*.

PART IX
MISCELLANEOUS AND GENERAL

35. Defence on contravention of certain regulations. It shall be a defence in proceedings against any person for an offence consisting of the contravention of regulation 5(4), 17(1) or 26(4) for that person to prove that at the time proceedings were commenced—

(a) an improvement notice under section 21 of the Health and Safety at Work etc. Act 1974 relating to the contravention had not been served on him; or

(b) if such notice had been served on him—
  (i) the period for compliance had not expired, or
  (ii) he had appealed against the notice and that appeal had not been dismissed or withdrawn.

36. Exemption certificates.—(1) Subject to paragraph (2), *the Executive* may, by a certificate in writing, exempt—

(a) any person or class of person;
(b) any premises or class of premises; or
(c) any equipment, apparatus or substance or class of equipment, apparatus or substance,

from any requirement or prohibition imposed by these Regulations and any such exemption may be granted subject to conditions and to a limit of time and may be revoked at any time by a certificate in writing.

(2) *The Executive* shall not grant any such exemption unless, having regard to the circumstances of the case and in particular to—

(a) the conditions, if any, which it proposes to attach to the exemption; and

(b) any other requirements imposed by or under any enactments which apply to the case,

it is satisfied that—

(c) the health and safety of persons who are likely to be affected by the exemption will not be prejudiced in consequence of it; and
(d) compliance with the fundamental radiation protection provisions underlying regulations 6(1) and 2, 7, 8(1) and (2), 9(1), 13(2), 16(3), 24(1), 27(1) and 33(1) of these Regulations will be achieved.

37. Extension outside Great Britain. These Regulations shall apply to any work outside Great Britain to which section 1 to 59 and 80 to 82 of the Health and Safety at Work etc. Act 1974 apply by virtue of the Health and Safety at Work etc. Act 1974 (Application outside Great Britain) Order 1977 *(a)*, as they apply to work within Great Britain, except that, in any case where it is not *reasonably practicable (b)* for the employer to comply with the requirements of these Regulations in so far as they relate to functions being performed by an *employment medical adviser* or *appointed doctor* or by an *approved dosimetry service*, it shall be sufficient compliance with any such requirements if the employer makes arrangements affording an equivalent standard of protection for his employees and those arrangements are set out in *local rules.*

(a) **Application outside Great Britain.** See now S.I. 1989 No. 840.

(b) **Reasonably practicable.** See INTRODUCTORY NOTE 5.

38. Fees for medical examinations.—(1) Fees shall be payable in accordance with paragraph (2) by an employer to *the Executive* in respect of any medical surveillance of an employee made in pursuance of regulation 16(3) by an *employment medical adviser.*

(2) Where the medical surveillance includes an examination of, or interview with, the employee, the fees shall be a basic fee for each examination or interview or combination thereof of £33 together with an additional fee of £22.50 in respect of all X-rays and £15 in respect of all laboratory tests carried out in connection with any one such examination or interview or combination thereof, but where the surveillance is confined to an examination of, and making of entries in, records, the fee shall be £10.

General note. The fees payable under this provision are prescribed by the Health and Safety (Fees) Regulations 1992, S.I. 1992 No. 1752.

39. Transitional provisions.—(1) Where on 1 January 1986 a person holds a current certificate of registration under section 1 of the Radioactive Substances Act 1960 in relation to *work with ionising radiation,* that person shall be deemed to have notified that work in accordance with regulation 5(2) of these Regulations.

(2) When on or before 26 February 1986 an employer was undertaking or commences for the first time work which is required to be notified under

regulation 5(2), it shall be sufficient compliance with that regulation if the employer notifies *the Executive* and furnishes the required particulars before 29 January 1986.

(3) Where, in accordance with regulation 9, immediately before 1 January 1986 an employer would have been required to designate an employee as a *classified person* had these Regulations then applied, the employer may designate that employee as a *classified person* until 1 January 1987 unless, before that later date, an *employment medical adviser* or *appointed doctor* has certified in the *health record* of the employee that, in his professional opinion, that employee is not fit to be so designated.

(4) Until 1 January 1986 it shall be sufficient compliance with regulation 10(1) if the employer appoints the *radiation protection adviser* required under that paragraph by that date.

(5) Until 1 July 1986 it shall be a sufficient compliance with regulation 11(3) if the employer appoints the radiation protection supervisor required under that paragraph by that date.

(6) Until 1 July 1986 it shall be a sufficient compliance with regulation 12(a) if the employer ensures that those of his employees who are engaged in work with *ionising radiation* receive such information, instruction and training as will enable them to know the hazards involved in their work and the precautions to be observed.

(7) Where immediately before 1 January 1986 a laboratory had been approved under—

(a) regulation 21(2) of the Ionising Radiations (Unsealed Radioactive Substances) Regulations 1968; or
(b) regulation 18(2) of the Ionising Radiations (Sealed Sources) Regulations 1969,

that laboratory shall be treated in these Regulations as an *approved dosimetry service* for the purposes for which it has been so approved until 1 January 1987.

(8) Where—

(a) as respects an employee, his employer did not have and was not required to have a *health record* or register immediately before 1 January 1986, regulation 16(4) shall not have effect until 1 July 1986;
(b) immediately before 1 January 1986 an employee was a classified worker for the purposes of the Ionising Radiations (Unsealed Radioactive Substances) Regulations 1968, the Ionising Radiations (Sealed Sources) Regulations 1969, the Radioactive Substances (Road Transport Workers) (Great Britain) Regulations 1970 or any nuclear site licence granted under the Nuclear Installations Act 1965, regulation 16(4) shall not have effect as respects that employee until the date on which he would have been required to be medically examined under those Regulations had they then been in operation or in the case of a nuclear site licence, under that licence, or 1 March 1987, whichever is the earlier.

(9) Regulation 22 shall not apply until 1 January 1987 where in order to comply with this regulation it would be necessary to erect a new building or to make substantial alterations to an existing building.

(10) It shall be a sufficient compliance with sub-paragraph (b) of regulation 24(2) if the first examination and test required by that sub-paragraph is carried out before whichever is the later of—

(a) 1 April 1986; or
(b) within 14 months of any thorough examination and test carried out before 1 January 1986 which would have complied with the requirements of the said sub-paragraph (b) if the sub-paragraph had then been in operation.

(11) Where—

(a) on or before 1 January 1986 an employer was undertaking work to which regulation 26(1) applies; or
(b) before 1 June 1986 he commences such work,

it shall be a sufficient compliance with the requirement of Regulations 26(1) and 27(5) if he sends a copy of the assessment or contingency plan, as the case may be, to *the Executive* before 1 May 1986 or within such longer time as *the Executive* may allow.

40. Modifications relating to the Ministry of Defence etc.—(1) In this regulation, any reference to—

(a) "visiting forces" is a reference to visiting forces within the meaning of any provision of Part 1 of the Visiting Forces Act 1952; and
(b) "headquarters or organisation" is a reference to a headquarters or organisation designated for the purpose of the International Headquarters and Defence Organisations Act 1964.

(2) The Secretary of State for Defence may, in the interests of national security, by a certificate in writing exempt—

(a) Her Majesty's Forces;
(b) visiting forces;
(c) any member of a visiting force working in or attached to any headquarters or organisation; or
(d) any person engaged in work with *ionising radiation* for, or on behalf of, the Secretary of State for Defence,

from all or any of the requirements or prohibitions imposed by these Regulations and any such exemption may be granted subject to conditions and to a limit of time and may be revoked at any time by a certificate in writing, except that, where any such exemption is granted, suitable arrangements shall be made for the assessment and recording of *doses* of *ionising radiation* received by persons to whom the exemption relates.

(3) Regulation 5 shall not apply in relation to work carried out by, and on premises under the control of, the Secretary of State for Defence, visiting forces or any headquarters or organisation.

(4) The requirements in regulation 5 to notify the particulars specified in sub-paragraphs (d) and (e) of Schedule 4 or any of the particulars specified in

Schedule 5 shall not apply to an employer in relation to *work with ionising radiation* undertaken for or on behalf of the Secretary of State for Defence, visiting forces or any headquarters or organisation.

(5) Regulation 13(3)(f) shall not apply in relation to—

(a) Her Majesty's Forces;
(b) visiting forces; or
(c) any member of a visiting force working in or attached to any head-quarters or organisation.

(6) In any case in which paragraph (8) or (9) of regulation 13 relates to—

(a) Her Majesty's Forces;
(b) visiting forces; or
(c) any member of a visiting force working in or attached to any head-quarters or organisation,

that paragraph shall apply as if for "the Executive" there were substituted the "Secretary of State for Defence".

(7) Regulation 16(10) shall not apply in relation to—

(a) Her Majesty's Forces;
(b) visiting forces; or
(c) any member of a visiting force in or attached to any headquarters or organisation.

(8) The requirement in paragraphs (1) to (4) of regulation 26 to send an assessment report to *the Executive* shall not have effect in any case where the Secretary of State for Defence decides that to do so would be against the interests of national security or where suitable alternative arrangements have been agreed with *the Executive.*

(9) The requirements of paragraphs (2) to (4) of regulation 27 shall not have effect to the extent that in any particular case they would, in the opinion of the Secretary of State for Defence, be against the interests of national security.

(10) The requirement in paragraph (5) of regulation 27 to send a copy of the contingency plan to *the Executive* shall not have effect in any case where either—

(a) the Secretary of State for Defence decides that to do so would be against the interests of national security and *the Executive* has agreed the criteria to be used in preparing the plan; or
(b) suitable arrangements have been agreed by the Secretary of State for Defence with *the Executive* to view and assess the plan.

(11) In regulation 29(1) the requirement to notify *the Executive* of a suspected *overexposure* and the results of the consequent investigation and assessment shall not apply in relation to the exposure of—

(a) a member of Her Majesty's Forces;
(b) a member of a visiting force; or
(c) a member of a visiting force working in or attached to a headquarters or organisation.

(12) The requirements of regulation 31(1) shall not apply to Her Majesty's ships except where undergoing refit.

41.   Revocations, modifications and savings.—(1) The Regulations and Orders specified in Part I of Schedule 10 in column 1 are hereby revoked to the extent specified in column 3 of that Part.

(2) The Regulations specified in Part II of Schedule 10 in column 1 are hereby modified to the extent specified in column 3 of that Part.

(3) Subject to regulation 13(4) (which relates to the keeping of *dose records*), every register, certificate, or record which was required to be kept in pursuance of any regulation revoked by paragraph (1) shall, notwithstanding that paragraph, be kept in the same manner and for the same period as if these Regulations had not been made, except that *the Executive* may approve the keeping of records at a place or in a form other than where, or the form in which, records were required to be kept under the regulation so revoked.

SCHEDULE 1

Regulations 2(1), 7, 13(3)(f),
28(1) and 30(1)

DOSE LIMITS

PART I
DOSE LIMITS FOR THE WHOLE BODY

1.   The *dose limit* for the whole body resulting from exposure to the whole or part of the body, being the sum of the following *dose* quantities resulting from exposure to *ionising radiation*, namely the effective dose equivalent from *external radiataion* and the committed effective *dose* equivalent from that year's intake of radionuclides, shall in any *calendar year* be—

    (a)   for employees aged 18 years or over,   50 mSv;

    (b)   for trainees aged under 18 years,   15 mSv;

    (c)   for any other person   5 mSv.

PART II
DOSE LIMITS FOR INDIVIDUAL ORGANS AND TISSUES

2.   Without prejudice to Part I of this Schedule, the *dose limit* for individual organs or tissues, being the sum of the following *dose* quantities resulting for exposure to *ionising radiation*, namely the *dose* equivalent from *external radiation*, the dose equivalent from contamination and the committed dose equivalent from that year's intake of radionuclides averaged throughout any individual organ or tissue (other than the lens of the eye) or any body extremity or over any area of skin, shall in any *calendar year* be—

    (a)   for employees aged 18 years or over,   500 mSv;

    (b)   for trainees aged under 18 years,   150 mSv;

    (c)   for any other person,   50 mSv.

3.   In assessing the *dose* quantity to skin whether from contamination or *external radiation*, the area of skin over which the *dose* quantity is averaged shall be appropriate to the circumstances but in any event shall not exceed 100 cm^2.

PART III
DOSE LIMITS FOR THE LENS OF THE EYE

4.   The *dose limit* for the lens of the eye resulting from exposure to *ionising radiation*, being the average *dose* equivalent from external and *internal radiation* delivered between 2.5 mm and 3.5 mm behind the surface of the eye, shall in any *calendar year* be—

(a) for employees aged 18 years or over,   150 mSv;
(b) for trainees under 18 years,   45 mSv;
(c) for any other person,   15 mSv.

PART IV
DOSE LIMIT FOR THE ABDOMEN OF A WOMAN OF REPRODUCTIVE CAPACITY

5. The dose limit for the abdomen of a *woman of reproductive capacity* who is at work, being the dose equivalent for *external radiation* resulting from exposure to *ionising radiation* averaged throughout the abdomen, shall be 13 mSv in any consecutive three months interval.

PART V
DOSE LIMIT FOR THE ABDOMEN OF A PREGNANT WOMAN

6. The *dose limit* for the abdomen of a pregnant woman who is at work, being the dose equivalent from *external radiation* resulting from exposure to *ionising radiation* averaged throughout the abdomen, shall be 10 mSv during the declared term of pregnancy.

SCHEDULE 2
Regulations 2(5), 26(1), 27(5)(a) and (6)
and 31(1) and (3).

QUANTITIES OF RADIONUCLIDES

[*Not printed in this book.*]

SCHEDULE 3
Regulations 5(1)(a), 10(6) and 11(3)

WORK NOT REQUIRED TO BE NOTIFIED UNDER REGULATION 5(2)

Work with ionising radiation shall be required to be notified in accordance with regulation 5(2) when the only such work being carried out is in one or more of the following categories—
(a) no *radioactive substance* having an activity concentration of more than 100 Bqg^{-1} is involved;
(b) the quantity of *radioactive substance* does not exceed the quantity specified in column 2 of Schedule 2;
(c) timepieces and instruments containing or bearing radioluminescent paint are kept or used and effective means are taken to prevent contact with or leakage of any *radioactive substance*;
(d) articles containing or bearing radioluminscent paint are manufactured or repaired and the only liquid radioluminescent paints (if any) at the premises where the work is carried on are paints containing less than the following quantities of the following radionuclides:—
  (i) 2 GBq of tritium,
  (ii) 100 MBq of promethium 147;
(e) gas mantles containing compounds of thorium are stored or used;
(f) a *radiation generator* is operated or used which does not under normal operating conditions cause a *dose rate* of more than 1 μSvH^{-1} at a distance of 100 mm from any accessible surface and is of a type approved by *the Executive* for the purposes of this sub-paragraph;

(g) an apparatus containing a *radioactive substance* is involved which does not under normal operating conditions cause a *dose rate* of more than 1 μSvH⁻¹ at a distance of 100 mm from any accessible surface and is of a type approved by *the Executive* for the purposes of this sub-paragraph;

(h) the work involves the care of a person to whom a radioactive medicinal product (within the meaning of the Medicines (Administration of Radioactive Substances) Regulations (1978)) has been administered; or

(i) the work is carried out on a ship, aircraft, hovercraft or hydrofoil by members of its crew.

General note. The fee for type approval of a radiation generator or an apparatus containing a radioactive substance under paras. (f) and (g) above is specified by the Health and Safety (Fees) Regulations 1992, S.I. 1992 No. 1752.

SCHEDULE 4

Regulations 5(2) and (8) and 40(4)

PARTICULARS TO BE SUPPLIED IN A NOTIFICATION UNDER REGULATION 5(2)

The following particulars shall be given in a notification under regulation 5(2)—
(a) the name and address of the employer;
(b) the address of the premises where or from where the work is being carried on;
(c) the nature of the business of the employer;
(d) into which of the following categories the source or sources of *ionising radiation* fall—
  (i) *sealed source,*
  (ii) unsealed *radioactive substance,*
  (iii) *radiation generator,*
  (iv) an atmosphere containing the *short-lived daughters of radon 222*;
(e) whether or not any source is to be used at premises other than the address given at sub-paragraph (b) above; and
(f) dates of notification and commencement of work with *ionising radiation.*

SCHEDULE 5

Regulation 5(4) and (5)

ADDITIONAL PARTICULARS THAT THE EXECUTIVE MAY REQUIRE

The following additional particulars may be required under regulation 5(4)—
(a) a description of the work with *ionising radiation*;
(b) particulars of the source or sources of *ionising radiation* including the type of *radiation generator* used or operated and the nature of any *radioactive substance*;
(c) the quantities of any *radioactive substance* involved in the work;
(d) the identity of any person engaged in the work;
(e) the date of commencement and the duration of any period over which the work is carried on;
(f) the location and description of any premises at which the work is carried out on each occasion that it is so carried out;
(g) the date of termination of the work;

(h) further information on any of the particulars listed in Schedule 4.

SCHEDULE 6

Regulations 6(6), 8(1), 22 and 27(1)(b)

DESIGNATION OF CONTROLLED AREAS

PART I

DESIGNATION IN RELATION TO EXTERNAL RADIATION

1.   Subject to paragraphs 2 and 3, the employer shall designate as a *controlled* area any area in which the instantaneous *dose rate* exceeds or is likely to exceed 7.5 μSvH^{-1}.

2.   Subject to paragraph 4, the employer need not designate as a *controlled area* an area in which the instantaneous dose rate exceeds 7.5 μSvH^{-1} by reason only that a *radioactive substance* is in the area provided that—

(a)   where the *radioactive substance* is not dispersed in the live body or corpse of a human being—

(i)   in the case of an emitter of gamma rays, the product of activity and total gamma energy per disintegration does not exceed 50 MBq MeV,

(ii)   in the case of an emitter of beta particulars having a maximum energy of 0.3 MeV or more, the activity does not exceed 5 MBq;

(iii)   in the case of an emitter of beta particles having a maximum energy of less than 0.3 MeV, the activity does not exceed 50 MBq;

(b)   where the *radioactive substance* is dispersed in the live body or corpse of a human being—

(i)   the substance emits only beta particles, or

(ii)   in the case of an emitter of gamma rays, the product of activity and total gamma energy per disintegration does not exceed 150 MBq MeV.

3.   Subject to paragraphs 4 and 5, the employer need not designate as a *controlled area* any area in which the instantaneous *dose rate* exceeds 7.5 μSvH^{-1} but does not exceed 2 mSvh^{-1} and where one of the following conditions is satisfied—

(a)   the time average *dose rate* does not exceed 7.5 μSvH^{-1};

(b)   only the hands of a person can enter any area in which the instantaneous *dose rate* exceeds 7.5 μSvH^{-1} and the time average *dose rate* in that area does not exceed 75 μSvH^{-1}; or

(c)   the area is an area in which—

(i)   the time average *dose rate* does not exceed 240 μSvH^{-1},

(ii)   no one person remains for more than one hour in any working period of 8 hours, and

(iii)   no person receives a *dose* exceeding 60 μSv in any working period of 8 hours.

4.   Notwithstanding paragraph 2 or 3, the employer shall designate as a *controlled area* any area to which either of those paragraphs applies unless, following consultation with his *radiation protection adviser*—

(a)   he is satisfied and has taken suitable steps to ensure that any person entering any such area does not receive a *dose* of *ionising radiation* which exceeds three-tenths of any relevant *dose limit* as a result of entry into such areas; and

(b)   in a case where a time average *dose rate* is used, he can demonstrate that the basis on which it is calculated is sufficient to justify its use.

5.   Notwithstanding paragraph 3, the employer shall designate as a *controlled* area any area in which the instantaneous *dose* rate exceeds 7.5 μSvH^{-1} because site radiography is being carried out in that area, and in this paragraph "site radiography" means any radiography of inanimate objects other than that which is carried out in an enclosure or cabinet which restricts so far as reasonably practicable the exposure of persons to *ionising radiation*.

PART II
DESIGNATION IN RELATION TO INTERNAL RADIATION

6.   The employer shall designate as a *controlled area* any area in which either—

(a)   the air concentration of a radionuclide when averaged over any 8 hour working period exceeds or is likely to exceed the concentration for that radionuclide specified in column 3 of Schedule 2; or

(b)   the level of contamination of any surface by a radionuclide when determined by a suitable method exceeds or is likely to exceed the contamination level for that radionuclide specified in column 4 of Schedule 2 and, for the purposes of this sub-paragraph, contamination levels shall be determined by averaging—

(i)   in the case of a floor, wall or ceiling, ove an area not exceeding 1000 cm², or

(ii)   in any other case, over an area not exceeding 300 cm²,

except that an area shall not be required to be designated as a *controlled area* if the only potential or actual source of contamination in the area is a *radioactive substance* present in the area and the total activity of the radionuclide in the area does not exceed the quantity for that radionuclide specified in column 5 of Schedule 2.

PART III
DESIGNATION IN RELATION TO EXTERNAL RADIATION AND
INTERNAL RADIATION TOGETHER

7.   Where in accordance with regulation 8(2) an area is required to be designated as a *supervised area* either—

(a)   in relation to both *external* and *internal radiation*; or

(b)   in relation to *internal radiation* by reason that both the air concentration and the contamination level exceed one third of the values specified in sub-paragraphs (a) and (b) of paragraph 6 respectively,

the employer shall designate that area as a *controlled area.*

PART IV
DESIGNATION IN RELATION TO THE SHORT-LIVED DAUGHTERS OF RADON 222

8.   In the case of the *short-lived daughters of radon 222*, the employer shall designate as a *controlled area* any area in which the concentration in air of the *short-lived daughters* when averaged over any 8 hour working period exceeds $2 \times 10^{-6} Jm^{-3}$ ($\sim$.1 working levels).

SCHEDULE 7

Regulation 26(1) and (2)

PARTICULARS TO BE INCLUDED IN AN ASSESSMENT REPORT

The following particulars are required to be included in an assessment report under regulation 26(1)—

(a)   the name and address of the employer;

(b)   the postal address of the place where the *radioactive substance* will be processed, manufactured, used or stored, or where the facilities for processing, manufacture, use or storage exist or, in the case of *transport*, the postal address of the *transport* undertaking;

(c)   the date on which it is anticipated that the operation will commence or, if it has already commenced, a statement to that effect;

(d)   a general description of the premises or place except that in the case of *transport* a general description shall be given of either—

(i)   the starting and end points of the journeys, the mode of *transport* and transhipment points, or

(ii) the criteria to be used for route selection;

(e) a description of any *radioactive substance* which in any *controlled area* or other workplace is likely to exceed the quantity in column 6 of Schedule 2, which shall where practicable include details of the radionuclides present and their likely maximum quantities;

(f) except in the case of an assessment relating to *transport*, a plan of the site in question and a map of the environs to a scale large enough to enable the site and any features which could affect the general risk in an emergency to be identified;

(g) a diagram of any single plant or enclosed system containing more than the quantity of any *radioactive substance* specified in column 6 of Schedule 2 or, in the case of *transport*, the nature of the containment for the *radioactive substance*, the type of conveyance and the means of securing the load within or on the conveyance;

(h) factors which could precipitate a major release of any *radioactive substance* and the measures to be taken to prevent or control such release and information showing the maximum quantity of *radioactive substance* which, in the event of a major failure of containment, would be released to the atmosphere;

(i) factors which could precipitate a smaller but continuing release of any *radioactive substance* and the measures to be taken to prevent or control such releases;

(j) factors which could give rise to an incident involving the initiation of an intended self-sustaining nuclear chain reaction or the loss or control of an intended self-sustaining nuclear chain reaction and, in either case, the measures to be taken to prevent or control any such incident;

(k) the management system and staffing arrangements by which the substance and procedures are controlled;

(l) except in the case of an assessment relating to transport, information about the size and distribution of the population in the vicinity of premises to which the report relates.

SCHEDULE 8

Regulation 26(4)

Further Particulars that the Executive may Require

A further assessment and report may be required under regulation 26(4) in respect of the following matters—

(a) the likely consequences of any hazard, and the probability of its occurrence;

(b) the number of persons whose health or safety might be affected by the hazard;

(c) management systems and staffing arrangements by which any hazard is controlled;

(d) safety systems and procedures for the control of any hazard;

(e) the qualifications, experience and training of staff concerned;

(f) design and operating documentation;

(g) design and operation of containment and pressure systems;

(h) protection of persons from the effects of loss of containment; and

(i) procedures for reporting of and learning from accidents, occurrences and incidents.

SCHEDULE 9

Regulation 26(5)(b)

Sealed Sources to which Regulation 26 does not apply

1. Regulation 26 shall not apply to any *sealed source* which conforms to the specifications of either paragraph 2 or paragraph 3.

2.   Where the sealed source consists of a *radioactive substance* in a massive solid form, the sealed source shall—

(a)   have one dimension of at least 5 mm;

(b)   not melt, sublime or ignite below 538°C;

(c)   not break or shatter if subject to the percussion test specified in the "Regulations for the Safe Transport of Radioactive Materials" published by the International Atomic Energy Agency, as revised or re-issued from time to time;

(d)   not, during one week's immersion in water at pH6—pH8 at 20°C with a maximum conductivity of 10 microsiemens per centimetre, dissolve or convert into reaction products to the extent of more than 50 µg per gram of the material; and

(e)   not, during one week's exposure to air at 30°C, dissolve or convert into dispersible reaction products to the extent of more than 50 µg per gram of the material.

3.   Where the sealed source consists of a *radioactive substance* enclosed in a capsule, that capsule shall—

(a)   comply with the requirements of sub-paragraphs (a) to (e) of paragraph 2, except that in sub-paragraph (b) of that paragraph 800°C shall be substituted for 538°C; and

(b)   comply with the requirements of the relevant tests given in the Regulations referred to in sub-paragraph (c) of paragraph 2.

SCHEDULE 10

Regulation 41(1) and (2)

REVOCATIONS AND MODIFICATIONS

PART I
REVOCATIONS

Column 1 *Regulations and Orders revoked*	Column 2 *Reference*	Column 3 *Extent of revocation*
The Ionising Radiations (Unsealed Radioactive Substances) Regulations 1968	S.I. 1968/780	The whole Regulations.
The Ionising Radiations (Sealed Sources) Regulations 1969	S.I. 1969/808	The whole Regulations.
The Radioactive Substances (Road Transport Workers) (Great Britain) Regulations 1970	S.I. 1970/1827	The whole Regulations.
The Employment Medical Advisory Service (Factories Act Orders etc. Amendment) Order 1973	S.I. 1973/36	In Part II of the Schedule, the entries relating to the Ionising Radiations (Unsealed Radioactive Substances) Regulations 1968 and the Ionising Radiations (Sealed Sources) Regulations 1969.

PART II
MODIFICATIONS

Column 1 *Regulations modified*	Column 2 *Reference*	Column 3 *Extent of modification*
The Fire Certificates (Special Premises) Regulations 1976	S.I. 1976/2003	For paragraph 14 of Part I of Schedule 1 there shall be substituted the following paragraph—"14. Premises to which regulation 26 of the Ionising Radiations Regulations 1985 (S.I. No. 1333) applies.".
The Notification of Accidents and Dangerous Occurrences Regulations 1980	S.I. 1980/804	In Schedule 2, for the entry relating to the Ionising Radiations (Unsealed Radioactive Substances) Regulations 1968, there shall be substituted at the end of that Schedule the entry "The Ionising Radiations Regulations 1985 (S.I. No. 1333).".
The Notification of New Substances Regulations 1982	S.I. 1982/1496	In sub-paragraph (d) of regulation 3(1) for "regulation 2(2) of the Ionising Radiations (Unsealed Radioactive Substances) Regulations 1968" there shall be substituted "regulation 2(1) of the Ionising Radiations Regulations 1985 (S.I. No. 1333).".

THE PUBLIC INFORMATION FOR RADIATION EMERGENCIES REGULATIONS 1992

(S. I. 1992 No. 2997)

The Secretary of State, being the Minister designated for the purposes of section 2(2) of the European Communities Act 1972 in relation to measures relating to informing the public about health protection measures to be taken in the event of a radiological emergency, in exercise of the powers conferred on her by the said section 2 and by sections 15(1) and (2), and 82(3)(a) of, and paragraphs 13(2) of Schedule 3 to the Health and Safety at Work etc. Act 1974 ("the 1974 Act") and of all other powers enabling her in that behalf, and for the purpose of giving effect without modifications to proposals submitted to her by the Health and Safety Commission under section 11(2)(d) of *the 1974 Act* after the carrying out by the said Commission of consultations in accordance with section 50(3) of that Act, hereby makes the following Regulations:

1. Citation and commencement. These Regulations may be cited as the Public Information for Radiation Emergencies Regulations 1992 and shall come into force on 1 January 1993.

2. Interpretation. In these Regulations, unless the context otherwise requires—

"contamination" means the contamination by any radioactive substance of any surface (including any surface of the body or clothing) or any part of absorbent objects or materials or the contamination of liquids or gases by any radioactive substance;

"the Directive" means Council Directive No. 89/618/Euratom on informing the general public about health protection measures to be applied and steps to be taken in the event of a radiological emergency;

"the Executive" means the Health and Safety Executive;

"external radiation" means, in relation to a person, *ionising radiation* coming from outside the body of that person;

"first tier local authority" means—

(a) in relation to England and Wales, a county council, the London Fire and Civil Defence Authority, a metropolitan county fire and civil defence authority or the Council of the Isles of Scilly, and

(b) in relation to Scotland, a regional or islands council;

"internal radiation" means, in relation to a person, *ionising radiation* coming from inside the body of that person;

"ionising radiation" means gamma rays, X-rays or corpuscular radiations which are capable of producing ions either directly or indirectly;

1250

"member of the public" means any person not being—

(a) a person for the time being present upon premises where a *radiation emergency* is reasonably foreseeable or where a *radiation emergency* has actually occurred; or

(b) a person engaged in an activity of or associated with the response to the *radiation emergency*;

"radiation emergency" means any occurrence which is likely to result in any *member of the public* being exposed to *ionising radiation* arising from that occurrence in excess of any of the doses set out in Schedule 1 to these Regulations and for this purpose any health protection measure to be taken during the 24 hours immediately following the occurrence shall be disregarded;

"second tier local authority" means—

(a) in relation to England and Wales, a district council, a London borough council, the Common Council of the City of London, the Sub-Treasurer of the Inner Temple, or the Under-Treasurer of the Middle Temple or the Council of the Isles of Scilly, and

(b) in relation to Scotland, an islands or district council.

3. Employer or self-employed person to supply prior information.—(1) It shall be the duty of an employer or a self-employed person who conducts an undertaking from which a *radiation emergency* is reasonably foreseeable—

(a) to ensure that *members of the public* who are likely to be in an area in which, in the opinion of *the Executive* (having regard to any existing plans prepared by virtue of regulation 27 of the Ionising Radiations Regulations 1985), they are liable to be affected by a *radiation emergency* arising from the undertaking of that employer or self-employed person, are supplied, in an appropriate manner, without their having to request it, with at least the information specified in Schedule 2 to these Regulations; and

(b) to make that information publicly available.

(2) In preparing the information required to be supplied in accordance with paragraph (1) above, the employer or self-employed person shall consult each *first tier local authority* and *second tier local authority* in the area referred to in that paragraph, any authority likely to fall within paragraph 5 of Schedule 2 to these Regulations and such other persons who seem to him to be appropriate, but the employer or self-employed person shall remain responsible for the accuracy, completeness and form of the information so supplied.

(3) Without prejudice to his duty under paragraph (1) above, the employer or self-employed person shall endeavour to enter into an agreement with each *second tier local authority* in the area referred to in that paragraph for that authority to disseminate the information required to be supplied in accordance with that paragraph to the *members of the public* mentioned in it.

(4) The employer or self-employed person shall ensure that the information supplied in accordance with paragraph (1) above is updated at regular intervals but, in any case, not less than once in three years and whenever significant changes to the emergency measures, action and authorities referred to in paragraphs 3, 4 and 5 of Schedule 2 to these Regulations take place; when

information is updated under this paragraph, it shall be supplied again in accordance with paragraph (1) above and made publicly available.

(5) Where on the coming into force of these Regulations an employer or self-employed person is conducting an existing undertaking from which a *radiation emergency* is reasonably foreseeable, it shall be sufficient compliance with paragraph (1) above if that employer or self-employed person supplies the required information and makes it publicly available within six months of the coming into force of these Regulations. Arrangements for the supply of information to *members of the public* actually affected.

4.—(1) It shall be the duty of a *first tier local authority* to prepare and keep up to date arrangements to supply, in the event of a *radiation emergency*, information of and advice on the facts of the emergency, of the steps to be taken and, as appropriate, of the health protection measures applicable.

(2) The arrangements prepared and kept up to date under paragraph (1) above shall provide for the information to be supplied at regular intervals in an appropriate manner, without delay, and without their having to request it, to *members of the public* who are in that local authority's area and who are actually affected by the *radiation emergency*.

(3) In preparing those arrangements, and keeping them up to date, the *first tier local authority* shall consult any authority likely to be responsible for implementing the relevant measures referred to in Schedule 3 to these Regulations and such other persons as appear to it to be appropriate.

(4) The information and advice to be supplied in accordance with arrangements prepared and kept up to date under paragraph (1) above shall, if relevant to the type of *radiation emergency*, include that specified in Schedule 3 to these Regulations and shall in any event, mention the authority or authorities responsible for implementing the relevant measures referred to in that Schedule.

(5) For the purposes of paragraph (2) above, the *members of the public* referred to in that paragraph as actually affected are those whose cooperation is sought to put into effect any steps or health protection measures referred to in paragraph (1) above.

(6) It shall be sufficient compliance with paragraph (1) above if a *first tier local authority* prepares the required arrangements within six months of the coming into force of these Regulations.

5.   Modifications relating to the Ministry of Defence etc.   The requirements of regulation 3 shall not have effect to the extent that in any particular case they would, in the opinion of the Secretary of State for Defence, be against the interests of national security.

6.   Enforcement and offences.   In so far as any provision of regulations 3 and 4 of these Regulations is made under section 2(2) of the European Communities Act 1972, the enforcement and offences provisions of *the 1974 Act* shall apply to that provision as if that provision had been made under section 15 of *the 1974 Act*.

SCHEDULE 1

Regulation 2

DOSES OF *IONISING RADIATION* APPLICABLE TO THE DEFINITION OF *RADIATION EMERGENCY*

PART I
DOSE FOR THE WHOLE BODY

1. The dose for the whole body resulting from exposure to the whole or part of the body, being the sum of the following dose quantities resulting from exposure to *ionising radiation*, namely the effective dose equivalent from *external radiation* and the committed effective dose equivalent from that year's intake of radio-nuclides, shall in the period of one year immediately following the occurrence be 5 mSv.

PART II
DOSE FOR INDIVIDUAL ORGANS AND TISSUES

2. Without prejudice to Part I of this Schedule, the dose for individual organs or tissues, being the sum of the following dose quantities resulting from exposure to *ionising radiation*, namely the dose equivalent from *external radiation*, the dose equivalent from *contamination* and the committed dose equivalent from that year's intake of radio-nuclides averaged throughout any individual organ or tissue (other than the lens of the eye) or any body extremity or over any area of skin, shall in the period of one year immediately following the occurrence be 50 mSv.

3. In assessing the dose quantity to skin whether from *contamination* or *external radiation*, the area of skin over which the dose quantity is averaged shall be appropriate to the circumstances but in any event shall not exceed 100 cm^2.

PART III
DOSE FOR THE LENS OF THE EYE

4. The dose for the lens of the eye resulting from exposure to *ionising radiation*, being the average dose equivalent from external and *internal radiation* delivered between 2.5 mm and 3.5 mm behind the surface of the eye, shall in the period of one year immediately following the occurrence be 15 mSv.

SCHEDULE 2

Regulation 3(1)

(PARAGRAPHS 1–4 OF WHICH SET OUT THE PROVISIONS OF ANNEX 1 TO *THE DIRECTIVE*)

PRIOR INFORMATION TO BE SUPPLIED AND MADE PUBLICLY AVAILABLE

1. Basic facts about radioactivity and its effects on persons and on the environment.

2. The various types of *radiation emergency* covered and their consequences for the general public and the environment.

3. Emergency measures envisaged to alert, protect and assist the general public in the event of a *radiation emergency*.

4. Appropriate information on action to be taken by the general public in the event of a *radiation emergency*.

5. The authority or authorities responsible for implementing the emergency measures and action referred to in paragraphs 3 and 4 above.

SCHEDULE 3

Regulation 4(2)

(WHICH SETS OUT, AMONG OTHERS, THE PROVISIONS OF ANNEX II TO *THE DIRECTIVE*)

INFORMATION TO BE SUPPLIED IN THE EVENT OF A *RADIATION EMERGENCY*

1. Information on the type of emergency which has occurred, and, where possible, its characteristics, for example, its origin, extent and probable development.

2. Advice on health protection measures, which, depending on the type of emergency, might include—

    (a) any restrictions on the consumption of certain foodstuffs and water supply likely to be contaminated;

    (b) any basic rules on hygiene and decontamination;

    (c) any recommendation to stay indoors;

    (d) the distribution and use of protective substances;

    (e) any evacuation arrangements;

    (f) special warnings for certain population groups.

3. Any announcements recommending co-operation with instructions or requests by the competent authorities.

4. Where an occurrence which is likely to give rise to a release of radioactivity or *ionising radiation* has happened but no release has yet taken place, the information and advice should include the following—

    (a) an invitation to tune in to radio or television;

    (b) preparatory advice to establishments with particular collective responsibilities;

    (c) recommendations to occupational groups particularly affected.

5. If time permits, information setting out the basic facts about radioactivity and its effects on persons and on the environment.

PART 6
FACTORIES

SUMMARY

INTRODUCTION TO THE FACTORIES ACT 1961

The Factories Act 1961, a consolidating measure, came into operation on 1 April 1962 (*ibid.*, s. 185(2)), and still stands unrepealed. The Factories Act 1961, like its predecessors, contained a power (s. 76) to make regulations governing dangerous processes and plant, but by virtue of s. 183 and the Sixth Schedule all such regulations and other subordinate legislation made under the repealed statutes, or continued in force as if so made, were continued in force as if made under this Act.

By virtue of powers contained in the Health and Safety at Work etc. Act 1974, susbtantial parts of the Factories Act 1961 were replaced or modified. These changes extended to the enforcement provisions of the Act. The Secretary of State ceased, in the main, to be responsible for enforcement, and that responsibility was transferred to the new Health and Safety Executive; the functions of factory inspectors were transferred to inspectors appointed under the 1974 Act; and where powers (for example, to hold investigations and enquiries) existed under both Acts, the 1961 powers were abrogated. For similar reasons s. 136 of the 1961 Act (prohibition of deductions from wages) and s. 143 (duties of persons employed) were also repealed; see now, as to deductions, the 1974 Act, s. 9 and, as to duties of employees, ss. 7, 8.

Regulations for safety and health under the Factories Act 1961, s. 76, or welfare regulations under s. 62 are no longer made: both sections were repealed in favour of the power to make health and safety regulations continued in the 1974 Act. However, subordinate legislation made or contained in force under the Factories Act 1961 continues in force by virtue of the Factories Act 1961 etc. (Repeals and Modification) Regulations 1974, reg. 7(3).

Measurements in Imperial were converted to metric by S.I. 1983 No. 978, except in relation to premises or plant in existence before 12 August 1983, save that in the case of the Hoists Exemption Order 1962 the relevant date is 23 November 1983 (and now see the Health and Safety (Miscellaneous Provisions) (Metrication) Regulations 1992, S.I. 1992 No. 1181).

The Factories Act 1961 and many of the Regulations made under it have been much amended by the 1992 Regulations which implement the new regime introduced by the European Directives: see HISTORICAL INTRODUCTION.

THE FACTORIES ACT 1961

(9 & 10 Eliz. 2, c. 34)

ARRANGEMENT OF SECTIONS

PART III
WELFARE (GENERAL PROVISIONS)

PART IV
HEALTH, SAFETY AND WELFARE (SPECIAL PROVISIONS AND REGULATIONS)

Special provisions

Special regulations for safety and health

Supplementary provisions

PART V
NOTIFICATION AND INVESTIGATION OF ACCIDENTS AND INDUSTRIAL DISEASES

An Act to consolidate the Factories Act 1937 to 1959, and certain other enactments relating to the safety, health and welfare of employed persons.   [22 June 1961]

BE IT ENACTED by the Queen's most Excellent Majesty, by and with the advice and consent of the Lords Spiritual and Temporal, and Commons, in this present Parliament assembled, and by the authority of the same, as follows:—

PART I
HEALTH (GENERAL PROVISIONS)

1.   Cleanliness.—(1) Every factory *(a)* shall be kept in a clean state *(b)* and free from effluvia arising from any drain, sanitary convenience *(c)* or nuisance.

(2) Without prejudice to the generality of subsection (1) of this section,—

(a) accumulations of dirt and refuse shall be removed daily by a suitable method from the floors and benches of workrooms, and from the staircases and passages;

(b) the floor of every workroom shall be cleaned at least once every week by washing or, if it is effective and suitable, by sweeping or other method.

(3) Without prejudice to the generality of subsection (1) of this section but subject to subsection (4) thereof, the following provisions shall apply as respects all inside walls and partitions and all ceilings or tops of rooms, and all walls, sides and tops of passages and staircases, that is to say,—

(a) where they have a smooth impervious surface, they shall at least once in every period of fourteen months be washed with hot water and soap or other suitable detergent or cleaned by such other method as may be approved by the inspector for the district;

(b) where they are kept painted in a prescribed *(d)* manner or varnished, they shall be repainted in a prescribed manner or revarnished at such intervals of not more than seven years as may be prescribed *(d)*, and shall at least once in every period of fourteen months be washed with hot water and soap or other suitable detergent or cleaned by such other method as may be approved by the inspector for the district;

(c) in any other case they shall be kept whitewashed or colourwashed and the whitewashing or colourwashing shall be repeated at least once in every period of fourteen months.

(4) Except in a case where the inspector for the district otherwise requires, the provisions of subsection (3) of this section shall not apply to any factory *(a)* where mechanical power is not used and less than ten persons are employed.

(5) [*repealed*].

General note. This section is repealed by the Workplace (Health, Safety and Welfare) Regulations 1992, S.I. 1992 No. 3004, as from 1 January 1993, except that, in relation to any workplace or part of a workplace which is not a new workplace, or a modification, extension, or conversion started after 31 December 1992, it is repealed as from 1 January 1996.

Some Regulations made under or continued in force by the Act contain provisions as to cleanliness; see, for example, the Asbestos Regulations 1969 and the Electric Accumulator Regulations 1925.

The Order set out below, which was made under the corresponding provisions of the Factories Act 1937 and 1959, is continued in force, as if made under this section, by virtue of s. 183 and Sch. 6, and S.I. 1974 No. 1941, reg. 7(3). By the Railway Running Sheds Order 1961, S.I. 1961 No. 1250, the expression "factory" for the purposes of this Order includes railway running sheds.

(a) **Factory.** For definition, see s. 175; as to factories in which mechanical power is used, see s. 176(3); and as to "class or description of factory", see s. 176(1).

(b) **Clean state.** What is a clean state is, it is submitted, a question of fact which will depend largely upon the process carried on in the factory (*Brooks v J & P Coates (UK) Ltd* [1984] ICR 158 at 173). For a restriction as to the cleaning of certain workrooms by women and young persons, see s. 74.

In *Carroll v North British Locomotive Co Ltd* 1957 SLT (Sh Ct) 2, it was held on a preliminary plea-in-law that a breach of s. 1(b) of the Factories Act 1937 (to which this provision corresponds) gave rise to civil liability; and see LEGAL PRINCIPLES in the introductory section.

(c) **Sanitary convenience.** For definition, see s. 176(1).

(d) **Prescribed.** "Prescribed" means prescribed by the Minister (s. 176(1)). See the Factories (Cleanliness of Walls and Ceilings) Order 1960, set out below.

THE FACTORIES (CLEANLINESS OF WALLS AND CEILINGS) ORDER 1960
(S.I. 1960 No. 1794, as amended by S.I. 1974 No. 427 and S.I. 1992 No. 1811)

General note. The whole Order is revoked by the Workplace (Health, Safety and Welfare) Regulations 1992 (S.I. 1992 No. 3004), as from 1 January 1993, except that, in relation to any workplace or part of a workplace which is not a new workplace, or a modification, extension, or conversion started after 31 December 1992, it is revoked as from 1 January 1996.

The Minister of Labour by virtue of the powers conferred on him by section 1 of the Factories Act 1937, as amended by section 1 of the Factories Act 1959, and of all other powers enabling him in that behalf, hereby makes the following Order:

Citation, commencement and revocation
1.—(1) This Order may be cited as the Factories (Cleanliness of Walls and Ceilings) Order 1960, and shall come into operation on the first day of January 1961.

(2) The Factories (Cleanliness of Walls and Ceilings) Order 1938, the Factories (Cleanliness of Walls and Ceilings) (Amendment) Order 1948, and the Factories (Cleanliness of Walls and Ceilings) Order 1958, are hereby revoked.

Interpretation
2.—(1) The Interpretation Act 1889 [Interpretation Act 1978] shall apply to the interpretation of this Order as it applies to the interpretation of an Act of Parliament, and as if this Order and the Orders hereby revoked were Acts of Parliament.

(2) In this Order—
"the principal Act" means the Factories Act 1937, as amended by or under any other Act;
"to wash" means to wash with hot water and soap or other suitable detergent or to clean by such method as may be approved by the inspector for the district; and
"walls and ceilings" means all inside walls and partitions, and all ceilings or tops of rooms, and all walls, sides and tops of passages and staircases.

Manner of painting and repainting
3. For the purposes of sub-paragraph (ii) of paragraph (c) of section 1 of the principal Act [s. 1(3)(b) of the 1961 Act], the manner of painting, and of repainting, walls and ceilings shall be the application of a suitable paint in such a manner as to produce over the whole of the treated surface a compact continuous film capable of being washed with hot water and soap or other suitable detergent or of being cleaned by such other method as may be approved by the inspector for the district.

Intervals for repainting or revarnishing
4. For the purposes of the said sub-paragraph (ii)—
(a) walls and ceilings which are kept painted in a prescribed manner shall be repainted in a prescribed manner at intervals not exceeding seven years, and
(b) walls and ceilings which are kept varnished shall be revarnished at intervals not exceeding seven years,
so, however, that (without prejudice to the preceding requirements of this Article) the whole or part of the surface shall be repainted or, as the case may be, revarnished as often as may be necessary to maintain over the whole surface a compact continuous film of the kind referred to in Article 3 of this Order.

Exempted premises
5. Subject to Article 6 of this Order, paragraph (c) of section 1 of the principal Act [s. 1(3) of the 1961 Act] (which provides for the periodical washing, painting or

varnishing, or whitewashing or colourwashing of walls and ceilings) shall not apply to the factories or parts of factories specified in the Schedule to this Order:

Provided that the said paragraph (c) shall continue to apply to enginehouses, maintenance shops, messrooms, cloakrooms, lavatories and sanitary conveniences.

Cleanliness of exempted premises

6.—(1) If it appears to the inspector for the district that any part of a factory to which, by virtue of Article 5 of this Order, paragraph (c) of section 1 of the principal Act [s. 1(3) of the 1961 Act] does not apply is not being kept in a clean state, he may by written notice require the occupier to whitewash or colourwash, or to wash, or to paint in a prescribed manner or varnish, that part. In the event of the occupier failing to comply with any such requisition within two months from the date of the notice Article 5 of this Order shall ceases to apply to the part of the factory to which the notice relates unless and until the inspector for the district otherwise determines.

(2) The reference in this Article to the inspector for the district shall, in the case of any factory as respects which the provisions of paragraph (c) of section 1 of the principal Act [s. 1(3) of the 1961 Act] are enforceable by a district council, be constructed as a reference to an officer appointed for that purpose by the council.

SCHEDULE

(Exempted premises referred to in Article 5 of this Order)

1. Blast furnaces, melting shops and rolling mills and sintering, crushing and screening houses in connection with any of the foregoing.
2. Electric generating or transforming stations.
3. Saw mills including re-saw mills.
4. Brick and tile works in which unglazed bricks or tiles are made.
5. Control rooms and pump houses being rooms and houses in chemical works, in tar distillation works, in gas works or used in connection with coke ovens.
6. Retort houses of gas works and purifier houses of gas works.
7. Platers' sheds, prefabrication sheds and blacksmiths', coppersmiths', angle-smiths' and plumbers' shops being sheds and shops in shipbuilding yards.
8. Ceiling or tops of rooms in print works, bleach works or dye works being rooms in which steam is evolved in the process.
9. The following parts of factories, that is to say—
   (a) parts in which lamp black, carbon black, charcoal or graphite is manufactured or is used to a substantial extent in the form of powder for any process;
   (b) parts in which lime, limestone or chalk is crushed or ground;
   (c) parts used for storage and in which no process is regularly carried on;
   (d) parts of rooms, passages and staircases which are at least 6 metres above the floor or stair; and
   (e) parts of cement works in which dry materials are handled or manufactured.

---

2. Overcrowding.—(1) A factory *(a)* shall not, while work is carried on, be so overcrowded as to cause risk of injury to the health of the persons employed in it.

(2) Without prejudice to the generality of subsection (1) of this section but subject to subsection (3) thereof, the number of persons employed at a time in any workroom shall not be such that the amount of cubic space allowed for each is less than 11 cubic metres.

(3) If the chief inspector is satisfied that, owing to the special conditions under which the work is carried on in any workroom in which explosive

materials are manufactured or handled, the application of subsection (2) of this section to that workroom would be inappropriate or unnecessary, he may by certificate except the workroom from that subsection subject to any conditions specified in the certificate.

(4) [*repealed*].

(5) In calculating for the purposes of this section the amount of cubic space in any room on space more than 4.2 metres from the floor shall be taken into account and, where a room contains a gallery, the gallery shall be treated for the purposes of this section as if it were partitioned off from the remainder of the room and formed a separate room.

(6) Unless the inspector for the district otherwise allows, there shall be posted in the workroom a notice specifying the number of persons *(b)* who, having regard to the provisions of this section, may be employed in that room.

General note. This section is repealed by the Workplace (Health, Safety and Welfare) Regulations 1992, S.I. 1992 No. 3004, as from 1 January 1993, except that, in relation to any workplace or part of a workplace which is not a new workplace, or a modification, extension, or conversion started after 31 December 1992, it is repealed as from 1 January 1996.

Some Regulations made under or continued in force by the Act contained provisions as to air space; see, for example, the Electric Accumulator Regulations 1925.

(a) Factory. For definition, see s. 175; as to class or description of factory, see s. 176 (1).

(b) Notice specifying the number of persons. The form to be posted in the workroom is Form 46.

———————————

3. Temperature.—(1) Effective provision shall be made for securing and maintaining a reasonable temperature *(a)* in each workroom, but no method shall be employed which results in the escape into the air of any workroom of any fume *(b)* of such a character and to such extent as to be likely to be injurious or offensive to persons employed therein.

(2) In every workroom in which a substantial proportion of the work is done sitting and does not involve serious physical effort a temperature of less than 16 degrees Celsius shall not be deemed, after the first hour, to be a reasonable temperature *(a)* while work is going on, and at least one thermometer shall be provided and maintained in a suitable position in every such workroom.

(3) [*repealed*].

General note. This section is repealed by the Workplace (Health, Safety and Welfare) Regulations 1992, S.I. 1992 No. 3004, as from 1 January 1993, except that, in relation to any workplace or part of a workplace which is not a new workplace, or a modification, extension, or conversion started after 31 December 1992, it is repealed as from 1 January 1996.

The provisions of this section were formerly contained in s. 3 of the Factories Act 1937. Some Regulations made under or continued in force by the Act contain provisions as to temperature: see, for example, the Cotton Cloth Factories Regulations 1929, the Flax and Tow Spinning and Weaving Regulations 1906, the Pottery (Health and Welfare) Special Regulations 1950 and the Woodworking Machines Regulations 1974.

By the Factories Act 1961 etc. (Metrication) Regulations 1983, S.I. 1983 No. 978. Fahrenheit thermometers may continue to be used in workrooms in existence before 12 August 1983 if conversion tables to degrees Celsius are provided.

(a) **Reasonable temperature.** This is a question of fact depending, *inter alia*, upon the nature of the work carried on and upon the season of the year. In *Murray v Walnut Cabinet Works Ltd* (1954) Times, 19 October; on appeal (1955) 105 L Jo 41, CA. Cassels J held (it appears) that a breach of s. 3 of the Factories Act 1937 (to which this provision corresponds) gave rise to civil liability, but the Court of Appeal expressed no view on the matter (see 105 L Jo 41). See also LEGAL PRINCIPLES in the introductory section.

(b) **Fume.** "Fume" includes gas or vapour (s. 176(1)). See s. 4 for provisions relating to ventilation of dust.

---

4. Ventilation.—(1) Effective and suitable provision shall be made for securing and maintaining by the circulation of fresh air in each workroom (a) the adequate ventilation of the room.

(2) [*repealed*].

General note. This section is repealed by the Workplace (Health, Safety and Welfare) Regulations 1992, S.I. 1992 No. 3004, as from 1 January 1993, except that, in relation to any workplace or part of a workplace which is not a new workplace, or a modification, extension, or conversion started after 31 December 1992, it is repealed as from 1 January 1996.

Some Regulations made under or continued in force by the Act contain provisions as to general ventilation; see, for example, the Cotton Cloth Factories Regulations 1929. The provisions of this subsection relating to the rendering harmless of fumes, dust and other impurities were repealed by the Control of Substances Hazardous to Health Regulations 1988 (S.I. 1988 No. 1657).

It is established, by authorities upon the corresponding provisions of s. 4, of the Factories Act 1937, that a breach of the section gives rise to civil liability (*Nicholson v Atlas Steel Foundry and Engineering Co Ltd* [1957] 1 All ER 776, [1957] 1 WLR 613, HL; *Clarkson v Modern Foundries Ltd* [1958] 1 All ER 33, [1957] 1 WLR 1210); see also LEGAL PRINCIPLES in the introductory section.

The nature and extent of the obligations imposed by the corresponding section of the Factories Act 1937 were discussed by the Court of Appeal in *Ebbs v James Whitson & Co Ltd* [1952] 2 QB 877, [1952] 2 All ER 192. The obligation was defined as being concerned with securing effective ventilation by the circulation of fresh air. The court rejected the contention that the section imposed any obligation to render harmless, by means other than ventilation, fumes, dust or other impurities injurious to health. *Ebbs v James Whitson & Co Ltd*, above, was followed by Devlin J in *Graham v Co-operative Wholesale Society Ltd* [1957] 1 All ER 654, [1957] 1 WLR 511, in which he held that s. 4(1) of the Factories Act 1937 "refers only to adequate ventilation for ordinary purposes by the circulation of fresh air and does not include any requirement which would mean that exhaust appliances would have to be provided to remove dust from the point of egress so as to prevent it entering the air. Section 4 is dealing with the circulation of fresh air which gets rid of impurities which come into the air, whereas s. 47 (formerly s. 63 of the Factories Act 1937, now repealed) is dealing with methods of prevention, of stopping the impurities from ever getting into circulation at all". In *Ashwood v Steel Co of Scotland Ltd* 1957 SC 17, 1957 SLT 244, the 2nd Division of the Inner House of the Court of Session followed *Ebbs v James Whitson & Co Ltd*, above, and held that s. 4(1) did not require the provision of masks or respirators.

(a) **Workroom.** In *Brophy v JC Bradfield & Co Ltd* [1955] 3 All ER 286, [1955] 1 WLR 1148, CA, the deceased had died in the boiler room of the defendants' factory from inhaling carbon monoxide fumes from a coke furnace used for heating water in the boiler to provide central heating for the factory. It was held that the boiler room was not a workroom within the meaning of s. 4(1).

---

5.   Lighting.—(1) Effective provision *(a)* shall be made for securing and maintaining sufficient and suitable lighting *(b)*, whether natural or artificial, in every part of a factory *(c)* in which persons are working or passing.

(2) [*repealed*].

(3) Nothing in the foregoing provisions of this section or in any regulations *(d)* made thereunder shall be construed as enabling directions to be prescribed or otherwise given as to whether any artificial lighting is to be produced by any particular illuminant.

(4) All glazed windows and skylights used for the lighting of workrooms shall, so far as practicable, be kept clean on both the inner and outer surfaces and free from obstruction; but this subsection shall not affect the whitewashing or shading of windows and skylights for the purpose of mitigating heat or glare.

General note. This section is repealed by the Workplace (Health, Safety and Welfare) Regulations 1992, S.I. 1992 No. 3004, as from 1 January 1993, except that, in relation to any workplace or part of a workplace which is not a new workplace, or a modification, extension, or conversion started after 31 December 1992, it is repealed as from 1 January 1996.

A breach of s. 5(1) gives rise to a civil remedy (*Thornton v Fisher and Ludlow Ltd* [1968] 2 All ER 241, [1968] 1 WLR 655, CA; see also *Lane v Gloucester Engineering Co Ltd* [1967] 2 All ER 293, [1967] 1 WLR 767, CA).

(a) *Effective provision.* Such provision must be made for securing and maintaining sufficient and suitable lighting. "'Effective' means lighting which is functioning effectively, and lighting which may be admirable in construction and in the provision of proper bulbs and so on, is not effective when it is not turned on": *Thornton v Fisher & Ludlow Ltd* [1968] 2 All ER 241, per Danckwerts LJ at 243.

(b) *Suitable and sufficient lighting.* This provision requires not only that there shall be a suitable and sufficient lighting installation but also that the factory occupier must either take all practicable steps to ensure that the lights are switched on whenever the natural lighting is insufficient or provide reasonably accessible light switches (*Thornton v Fisher and Ludlow Ltd,* above). *Thornton v Fisher and Ludlow Ltd,* above, was applied in *Davies v Massey Ferguson Perkins Ltd* [1986] ICR 580, which decided that there was an absolute duty on employers to secure and maintain sufficient and suitable lighting on factory premises. That duty would be breached even if a light bulb failed shortly before an accident occurred and even if there was a reasonably efficient system in operation for effecting repairs.

(c) *Factory.* For definition, see s. 175; and as to class or description of factory, see s. 176(1).

(d) *Regulations.* The Factories (Standards of Lighting) Regulations 1941, made under s. 5(2) of the Factories Act 1937, have been revoked by S.I. 1978 No. 1126.

---

6. Drainage of floors. Where any process is carried on which renders the floor liable to be wet to such an extent that the wet is capable of being removed by drainage, effective means shall be provided and maintained for draining off the wet.

General note. This section is repealed by the Workplace (Health, Safety and Welfare) Regulations 1992, S.I. 1992 No. 3004, as from 1 January 1993, except that, in relation to any workplace or part of a workplace which is not a new workplace, or a modification, extension, or conversion started after 31 December 1992, it is repealed as from 1 January 1996.

Some regulations made under or continued in force by the Act contain provisions as to drainage; see, for example, the Flax and Tow Spinning and Weaving Regulations 1906, and the Pottery (Health and Welfare) Special Regulations 1950.

---

7. Sanitary conveniences.—(1) Sufficient and suitable sanitary conveniences *(a)* for the persons employed in the factory *(b)* shall be provided, maintained *(c)* and kept clean, and effective provision shall be made for lighting them and, where persons of both sexes are or are intended to be employed (except in the case of factories where the only persons employed are members of the same family dwelling there) the conveniences shall afford proper separate accommodation for persons of each sex.

(2) [*repealed*].

General note. This section is repealed by the Workplace (Health, Safety and Welfare) Regulations 1992, S.I. 1992 No. 3004, as from 1 January 1993, except that, in relation to any workplace or part of a workplace which is not a new workplace, or a modification, extension, or conversion started after 31 December 1992, it is repealed as from 1 January 1996.

It should be noted that the provisions of this section, but not the Regulations set out below, have been applied to building operations and works of engineering construction (s. 127). Provisions as to sanitary conveniences in such cases are to be found in the Construction (Health and Welfare) Regulations 1966.

The Regulations set out below were made under the corresponding section of the Factories Act 1937, and are continued in force by virtue of the Factories Act 1961, s. 183 and Sch. 6 and S.I. 1974 No. 1941, reg. 7(3). For the purposes of these Regulations, the expression "factory" includes railway running sheds (the Railway Running Sheds (No. 1) Regulations 1961, S.I. 1961 No. 1251) and the premises now specified in s. 175(1)(d) and (e) (the Slaughterhouses (No. 2) Regulations 1962, S.I. 1962 No. 2347).

(a) Sanitary conveniences. For definition, see s. 176(1).

(b) Factory. For definition, see s. 175; and as to class or description of factory, see s. 176(1).

(c) Maintained. For definition, see s. 176(1).

THE SANITARY ACCOMMODATION REGULATIONS 1938
(S. R. & O. 1938 No. 661, as amended by S.I. 1974 No. 426)

General note. The whole Regulations are revoked by the Workplace (Health, Safety and Welfare) Regulations 1992 (S.I. 1992 No. 3004), as from 1 January 1993, except that, in relation to any workplace or part of a workplace which is not a new workplace, or a modification, an extension or a conversion, they are revoked as from 1 January 1996.

In pursuance of section 7 of the Factories Act 1937, and of all other powers enabling me in that behalf I hereby make the following Regulations:—

1.   These Regulations shall apply to all factories as defined in section 151 of the said Act [s. 175 of the 1961 Act] and to electrical stations to which subsection (1) of section 103 of the Act [s. 123(1) of the 1961 Act] applies.

2.   In cases where females are employed there shall be at least one suitable sanitary convenience for every 25 females.

3.   In cases where males are employed there shall be at least one suitable sanitary convenience (not being a convenience suitable merely as a urinal) for every 25 males:

Provided that in the case of factories where the number of males employed exceeds 100 and sufficient urinal accomodation is also provided, it shall be sufficient if there is one such convenience as aforesaid for every 25 males up to the first 100, and one for every 40 thereafter.

Provided further that in the case of a factory where the number of males employed exceeds 500, not being a factory constructed, enlarged or converted for use as a factory after the 30 June, 1938, it shall be sufficient to provide one such convenience as aforesaid for every 60 males if sufficient urinal accommodation is also provided and if an officer appointed for that purpose by the district council issues a certificate (which shall be kept attached to the general register so long as it remains in force) that in his opinion the arrangements at the factory are such that this proviso may properly be applied to the factory. Any such certificate shall be liable at any time to be revoked by such an officer by notice in writing.

4.   In calculating the number of conveniences required by these Regulations, any odd number of persons less than 25, or 40, as the case may be, shall be reckoned as 25 or 40.

5.   Every sanitary convenience shall be sufficiently ventilated, and shall not communicate with any workroom except through the open air or through an intervening ventilated space.

Provided that in the case of workrooms in use prior to 1 January, 1903, and mechanically ventilated in such manner that air cannot be drawn into the workroom through the sanitary convenience, an intervening ventilated space shall not be required.

6.   Every sanitary convenience (other than a convenience suitable merely as a urinal) shall be under cover and so partitioned off as to secure privacy, and shall have a proper door and fastenings. Urinals shall be so placed or so screened as not to be visible from other parts of the factory where persons work or pass.

7.   The sanitary conveniences shall be so arranged as to be conveniently accessible to the persons employed at all times while they are at the factory.

8.   In the cases where persons of both sexes are employed, the sanitary conveniences for each sex shall be placed or so screened that the interior shall not be visible, even when the door of any convenience is open, from any place where persons of the other sex have to work or pass; and, if the conveniences for one sex adjoin those for the other sex, the approaches shall be separate. The conveniences for each sex shall be indicated by a suitable notice.

9.   These Regulations may be cited as the Sanitary Accommodation Regulations 1938, and shall come into force on the 1 July, 1938, and shall be without prejudice to the requirements in subsection (1) of section 7 of the Act [s 7 of the 1961 Act] that the conveniences shall be maintained and kept clean and that effective provision shall be made for lighting the conveniences.

10. As from the 1 July, 1938, the Sanitary Accommodation Order of 4 February, 1903, is hereby revoked.

8.–10. [*repealed*].

10A. Medical examinations of persons employed in factories.—(1) If an employment medical adviser is of opinion that there ought, on grounds mentioned in subsection (2) below, to be a medical examination *(a)* of a person or persons employed in a factory *(b)*, he may serve on the occupier of the factory a written notice stating that he is of that opinion and requiring that the occupier shall permit a medical examination in accordance with this section of the person or persons in question, and the examination shall be permitted accordingly.

(2) The grounds on which a medical examination of a person may be required by an employment medical adviser's notice under subsection (1) above are that (in the adviser's opinion) the person's health has been or is being injured, or it is possible that it has been, is being or will be injured, by reason of the nature of the work he is or has been called upon to do or may (to the adviser's knowledge) be called upon to do; and a notice under that subsection may be given with respect to one or more named persons or to persons of a class or description specified in the notice.

(3) A notice under subsection (1) above shall name the place where the medical examination is to be conducted and, if it is a place other than the factory, the day on which and the time at which it is to be begun; and—

(a) every person to whom the notice relates shall be informed, as soon as practicable after service thereof, of the contents thereof and of the fact that he is free to attend for the purpose of submitting to the examination; and

(b) if the notice states that the examination is to be conducted at the factory, suitable accommodation thereat shall be provided for the conduct of the examination.

(4) A medical examination conducted in pursuance of a notice under subsection (1) above shall be begun within seven days after the day on which the notice is served, and shall be conducted by, or in accordance with arrangements made by, an employment medical adviser, and take place at a reasonable time during working hours.

(5) An employment medical adviser may, by written notice served on the occupier of a factory, cancel a notice served on the occupier under subsection (1) above; and a notice which relates to two or more named persons may be cancelled either in relation to them all or in relation to any one or more of them.

(6) In this section, "medical examination" includes pathological, physiological and radiological tests and similar investigations.

General note. This section was inserted by the Employment Medical Advisory Service Act 1972, s. 3. For the employment medical advisory service, see now the Health and

Safety at Work etc. Act 1974, Part II (ss. 55–60). See also reg. 5 of the Management of Health and Safety at Work Regulations 1992, S.I. 1992 No. 2051, in relation to health surveillance.

(a) *Medical examination.* For definition, see sub-s. (6).

(b) *Factory.* For definition, see s. 175.

---

11. Power to require medical supervision.—(1) Where it appears to the Minister *(a)*—

  (a) that in any factory *(b)* or class or description of factory *(c)*—
    (i) cases of illness have occurred which he has reason to believe may be due to the nature of a process or other conditions of work; or
    (ii) by reason of changes in any process or in the substances used in any process, or by reason of the introduction of any new process or new substance for use in a process, there may be risk of injury to the health of persons employed in that process; or
    (iii) [*repealed*];
  (b) that there may be risk of injury to the health of persons employed in a factory—
    (i) from any substance or material brought to the factory to be used or handled therein; or
    (ii) from any change in the conditions of work or other conditions in the factory,

he may make special regulations *(d)* requiring such reasonable arrangements to be made for the medical supervision (not including medical treatment other than first-aid treatment and medical treatment of a preventive character) of the persons, or any class of the persons, employed at that factory or class or description of factory as may be specified in the regulations.

(2) Where the Minister *(a)* proposes to exercise his powers under this section in relation to a particular factory *(b)* and for a limited period, he may exercise those powers by order *(e)* instead of by special regulations *(e)*, and any such order shall, subject to subsection (3) of this section, cease to have effect at the expiration of such period not exceeding six months from the date when it comes into operation as may be specified in the order.

(3) The Minister *(a)* may by subsequent order or orders *(e)* extend the said period, but if the occupier of the factory *(b)* by notice in writing to him objects to any such extension, the original order shall cease to have effect as from one month after the service of the notice, without prejudice to the making of special regulations *(d)* in relation to the factory.

General note. This section is repealed by S.I. 1974 No. 1941, except in so far as it enables orders to be made otherwise than by statutory instrument (see sub-ss. (2) and (3)). Regulations and orders already made under this section continue in force, notwithstanding the repeal (S.I. 1974 No. 1941, reg. 7(3)).

Some Regulations made under or continued in force by the Act contain provisions as to medical supervision; see, for example, the Work in Compressed Air Special Regulations 1958, and the Pottery (Health and Welfare) Special Regulations 1950.

(a) *The Minister.* For definition, see s. 176(1). Sub-s. (2) has effect as if the reference to the Secretary of State ("the Minister") was a reference to the Health and Safety Executive (S.I. 1974 No. 1941, reg. 2(b), Sch. 2).

(b) **Factory.** For definition, see s. 175.

(c) **Class or description of factory.** For definition, see s. 176(1).

(d) **Special regulations.** The power to make special regulations is now repealed: see the general note.

(e) **Orders.** As to the making of orders, see s. 180. No orders under this section or the corresponding provisions of the 1937 Act have yet been made.

PART II
SAFETY (GENERAL PROVISIONS)

Introductory note to sections 12–16

These sections are to be repealed as from 1 January 1997 by the Provision and Use of Work Equipment Regulations 1992, S.I. 1992 No. 2932, by which time all work equipment first provided for use before 1 January 1993 must meet the standards established in those Regulations. For equipment provided for use after 1 January 1993, the Regulations have immediate effect and these sections of the Factories Act no longer apply.

These sections which relate to fencing have, more often than any other sections of the Act, received judicial consideration both in criminal and civil proceedings. They are clearly intended to form a single code, and should be read together (*per* Lord Hailsham of St. Marylebone LC, in *FE Callow (Engineers) Ltd v Johnson* [1971] AC 335 at 341, [1970] 3 All ER 639 at 641). In this introductory note an attempt is made both to set out those principles which can now be regarded as established and to expose certain problems which still await an authoritative solution. The references to sections apply both to the 1961 and to the 1937 Act.

1. *Machinery*

The machinery dealt with by ss. 12 to 16 is prime movers (s. 12), transmission machinery (s. 13) and any other machinery (s. 14), and includes machinery not driven by mechanical power (*Richard Thomas and Baldwins Ltd v Cummings* [1955] AC 321, [1955] 1 All ER 285, HL); "Machinery" includes any driving-belt, and "driving-belt" includes any driving strap or rope (s. 176(1)).

These sections apply only to machinery which is completely installed as part of the factory equipment; but if installation is complete the fencing provisions of the Act apply notwithstanding that the machine is not at the material time being used in the manufacturing process, provided that it is intended to be so used and capable of being so used (*Irwin v White, Tomkins and Courage Ltd* [1964] 1 All ER 545, [1964] 1 WLR 387, HL). Thus, the fencing provisions concern machinery used in the factory for or ancillary to its manufacturing processes, and not machinery within the factory which is itself a product of those manufacturing processes (*Parvin v Morton Machine Co Ltd* [1952] AC 515, [1952] 1 All ER 670, HL, in which a machine manufactured in the factory was held not to fall within the terms of s. 14(1)). It follows that cranes and lifting machinery may fall within the definition, despite their also being covered by s. 21: see *British Railways Board v Liptrot* [1969] 1 AC 136, [1967] 2 All ER 1072, HL. A fire fighting pump was held to be "machinery" in a factory although it would only fall to be used in the exceptional circumstances of an emergency: *McNeill v Roche Products Ltd* 1989 SLT 498 (applying *British Railways Board v Liptrot*, above). A machine which has been installed, but which is undergoing modification, with the intention of using it as part of the manufacturing process if the modification is successful, is machinery within s. 14(1) (*TBA Industrial Products Ltd v Lainé* [1987] ICR 75, DC). However, a temporary modification to a machine which is a product of a factory, made in order to provide warm air for the comfort of employees while testing that machine, does not make the machine subject to the provisions of s. 14 (*Ballard v Ministry of Defence* [1977] ICR 513, CA). In *Thurogood v Van Den Berghs and Jurgens Ltd* [1951] 2 KB 537, [1951] 1 All ER 682, the Court of Appeal held that an electric wall fan which had been taken from its position to an engineering shop for repair was part of the machinery of the factory, but this decision turned upon the conclusion that the engineering shop was part of the factory as a whole. Had the Court concluded that the shop was a separate factory it would have applied the principle in *Parvin v Morton Machine Co Ltd,* above, and would have dismissed the claim based upon breach of the statute (see [1951] 2 KB at 550 and [1951] 1 All ER at 689).

Mobile machinery is not by virtue only of its mobility excluded from the ambit of s. 14(1) (*British Railways Board v Liptrot,* above, overruling *Cherry v International Alloys Ltd* [1961] 1 QB 136, [1960] 3 All ER 264, CA). "Dangerous parts of machinery, not danger in movement of the whole machinery, are the considerations to which s. 14 is directed" (*per* Lord Hodson in *British Railways Board v Liptrot,* above, at 162, 1083). The machinery in question must form part of the equipment of the factory (see *Liptrot,* above) but, if it does so, it is no answer to an allegation based upon a breach of s. 14 that it may move from one place to another. Thus, the machinery of a mobile crane is within this section (*British Railways Board v Liptrot, supra*); so also is the machinery of a coke-distributing machine which travels on rails (see *Dobson v Colvilles Ltd* 1958 SLT (Notes) 30) and a portable, powered hand-tool (*Lovelidge v Anselm Odling & Sons Ltd* [1967] 2 QB 351, [1967] 1 All ER 459). In *Quintas v National Smelting Co Ltd* [1961] 1 All ER 630, [1961] 1 WLR 401, CA, the defendants operated in their factory an overhead travelling cableway supported by stanchions, so that material might be transported from one part of the factory to another. The material was placed in buckets suspended from the cable, which at one part of the route passed close to a flat roof, to which workmen might be expected to come. It was held that the cable-way, regarded as a whole, was not one piece of machinery within s. 14, and therefore that the whole of the cable-way need not be fenced. However, the decision of the majority of the Court was based, in part at least, upon *Cherry v International Alloys Ltd,* above, and its correctness has been doubted (*per* Lord Hodson in *British Railways Board v Liptrot,* above, at 163, 1083).

2. *The part required to be fenced (foreseeability of danger)*
Sections 12 and 13 specify those parts of prime movers and transmission machinery which must be fenced. Other machinery is dealt with in s. 14, which requires (subject to exceptions) the fencing of "every dangerous part of any machinery, other than prime movers and transmission machinery". It is to be noted that these sections require the fencing of "parts" of "machinery", and not the fencing of machines as such (see *British Railways Board v Liptrot* [1969] 1 AC 136, [1967] 2 All ER 1072, HL), from which it follows that there is no obligation thereunder to fence a machine if it is dangerous as a whole but has no dangerous parts which can properly be described as parts of machinery (see *per* Lord Hailsham of St. Marylebone LC in *F E Callow (Engineers) Ltd v Johnson* [1971] AC 335 at 342, [1970] 3 All ER 639 at 641). The question under s. 14(1) is not whether the part is a "part of machinery" but whether it is a part of machinery, or machinery, within s. 14(1). The reference to fencing any dangerous part, or providing a fixed guard, means that the section applies to machinery to which the concept of fencing or providing a fixed guard is apposite, If no reasonable person would contemplate fencing or providing a fixed guard to a piece of machinery it is not a part of machinery, or machinery, as that word is used in the section (*Mirza v Ford Motor Co Ltd* [1981] ICR 757, CA, holding that a crane hook, whether equipped (as in that case) with a safety device to prevent escape of the load, or whether an ordinary hook, is not a part of machinery within s. 14(1)).

The test of what is a "dangerous" part has been the subject of extended judicial decision, beginning with *Hindle v Birtwistle* [1897] 1 QB 192, and (for the present) ending with *Wearing v Pirelli Ltd* [1977] 1 All ER 339, [1977] 1 WLR 48, HL. The authoritative exposition to be found in *Close v Steel Co of Wales Ltd* [1962] AC 367, [1961] 2 All ER 953, HL, stamps the imprimatur of the House of Lords upon the proposition that the test of danger depends here (as in certain other parts of the factory legislation and the Regulations made thereunder) upon what is reasonably foreseeable. In *Close v Steel Co of Wales Ltd* [1962] AC 367, [1961] 2 All ER 953, HL, Lord Guest said (at 412, 975):

"I take the test whether a part of a machine is dangerous from the dictum of du Parcq J, in *Walker v Bletchley Flettons Ltd* [1937] 1 All ER 170 at 175, as qualified by Lord Reid in

John Summers & Sons Ltd v Frost [1955] AC 740 at 766, [1955] 1 All ER 870 at 882, whether it might be '. . . a reasonably foreseeable cause of injury to anybody acting in a way in which a human being may be reasonably expected to act in circumstances which may be reasonably expected to occur'."

This test was supported by the remaining Law Lords (see *per* Lord Denning, at 381, 955–956; *per* Lord Goddard, at 389, 960; *per* Lord Morton, at 398, 966; and *per* Lord Morris of Borth-y-Gest, at 398, 967). It is the test which is now accepted; *per* Lord Guest in *Irwin v White, Tomkins and Courage Ltd* [1964] 1 All ER 545, [1964] 1 WLR 387, HL. It follows that the facts that the machine is capable of causing injury and that injury has happened to the operator are not conclusive that the part concerned is a dangerous part (*Carr v Mercantile Produce Co Ltd* [1949] 2 KB 601, [1949] 2 All ER 531).

On the question of what is reasonably foreseeable, it is submitted that the same considerations apply as when the question of foresight is in issue in cases of common law negligence, subject to the qualification that at common law a plaintiff has to show reasonable foresight of injury to himself, whereas in an action for breach of statutory duty he has merely to show such foresight in relation to any person employed. Indeed, in *Eaves v Morris Motors Ltd* [1961] 2 QB 385, [1961] 3 All ER 233, CA, a decision upon s. 14(1), Pearson, LJ (at 401, 242) referred to the speech of Lord Porter in *Bolton v Stone* [1951] AC 850, [1951] 1 All ER 1078, HL (a negligence case) where he said:

"Nor is the remote possibility of injury occurring enough. There must be sufficient probability to lead a reasonable man to anticipate it. The existence of some risk is an ordinary incident of life, even when all due care has been, as it must be, taken."

In deciding what is reasonably foreseeable it is material to consider both the behaviour of operators or persons employed and the behaviour of the machine. The behaviour of persons which is thus material is such behaviour as is reasonably foreseeable, which is not necessarily confined to such behaviour as is reasonable behaviour. Merely because a workman does something stupid whereby he is injured upon a part of a machine it cannot be concluded that the part is not a dangerous part. Some kinds of stupid behaviour are foreseeable; other kinds of stupid behaviour are egregious and unforeseeable. Only the former kinds are relevant to the enquiry, whether the part was a dangerous part. In *Mitchell v North British Rubber Co Ltd* 1945 JC 69, the Lord Justice-Clerk, Lord Cooper, said (at 78) that a machine is dangerous if

". . . in the ordinary course of human affairs danger may reasonably be anticipated from its use unfenced, not only to the prudent, alert and skilled operative intent upon his task, but also to the careless and inattentive worker whose inadvertent or indolent conduct may expose him to risk of injury or death from the unguarded part."

This passage was approved in *John Summers & Sons Ltd v Frost* [1955] AC 740, [1955] 1 All ER 870, HL and the principle was applied in *Smithwick v National Coal Board* [1950] 2 KB 335, CA (decided upon s. 55 of the Coal Mines Act 1911), in *Woodley v Meason Freer & Co Ltd* [1963] 3 All ER 636, [1963] 1 WLR 1409 and in *Uddin v Associated Portland Cement Manufacturers Ltd* [1965] 2 QB 582, [1965] 2 All ER 213, CA. A relevant consideration may therefore be the attributes of the employees concerned if these are in any way unusual: see *Health & Safety Executive v Fortes Bakery*, 22 December 1992, Queen's Bench Division). Once, however, it has been proved that a part of a machine is dangerous, that it is unfenced, and that a workman has been injured by reason of the lack of fencing, foreseeability is no longer relevant, and so the fact that the accident occurred in an entirely unexpected way will not absolve the occupier (*Millard v Serck Tubes Ltd* [1969] 1 All ER 598, [1969] 1 WLR 211, CA, approved in *F E Callow (Engineers) Ltd v Johnson* [1971] AC 335, [1971] 3 All ER 639, HL). But in *Neil v A Cowan & Sons Ltd* 1961 SLT (Notes) 52 the question was left open whether injury was caused by the dangerous part of the machinery when in taking evasive action an employee was injured by coming into contact with another part.

On the other hand, the fact that at the time of his injury the plaintiff was acting outside the scope of his employment is irrelevant (*Westwood v Post Office* [1974] AC 1, [1973] 3 All ER 184, HL, in which the plaintiff, who was employed to work in office premises within the meaning of s. 1(2) of the Offices, Shops and Railway Premises Act 1963, recovered in respect of a breach of *ibid.*, s. 16 (soundness of floors), although he was a trespasser upon the part of the premises where he suffered injury). In *Uddin v Associated Portland Cement Manufacturers Ltd* [1965] 2 QB 582, [1965] 2 All ER 213, CA the plaintiff was injured while trying to catch a pigeon, an act which was no part of his duties. It was held that s. 14(1) applied. This decision was followed in *Allen v Aeroplane and Motor Aluminium Castings Ltd* [1965] 3 All ER 377, [1965] 1 WLR 1244, CA, in which it was held that although a plaintiff may be unable to satisfy the court precisely how the accident occurred, yet, if he shows that it occurred because of a failure to fence a dangerous part securely, it is unnecessary for him to go further and to show that he was injured in the course of his employment. However, if, at the material time, the plaintiff is not employed by the factory occupier at all, but (for example) is pursuing a hobby of his own in his own time, then the fencing provisions do not apply (*Napieralski v Curtis (Contractors) Ltd* [1959] 2 All ER 426, [1959] 1 WLR 835).

The behaviour of the machine which is material to the issue of foreseeability is its behaviour in the ordinary course of working, and not aberrant behaviour which cannot be foreseen (*Eaves v Morris Motors Ltd* [1961] 2 QB 385, [1961] 3 All ER 233, CA; *Horne v Lec Refrigeration Ltd* [1965] 2 All ER 898). It is submitted that if the machine has behaved abnormally in the past to such an extent that a reasonable man would anticipate abnormal behaviour in the future then such behaviour, even though abnormal, must be taken into account in deciding whether a part of it is a dangerous part.

Close v Steel Co of Wales Ltd, above, decided that the obligation imposed by s. 14(1) to fence securely does not require the dangerous part to be fenced for the purpose of preventing fragments of it, if shattered, from flying out of the machine. This aspect of the decision is considered later in this note. It was, however, accepted by two of their Lordships that a part of machinery was a "dangerous part" if it is likely in the ordinary course of working to throw off flying bits (see *per* Lord Denning at 382–383; 956–957, and *per* Lord Morris of Borth-y-Gest at 398–399; 967). In *Carroll v Andrew Barclay & Sons Ltd* [1948] AC 477, Lord Du Parcq (at 186–487) and, it appears, Lord Porter (at 485) took the same view, but Viscount Jowitt (at 482) and Lord Normand (at 490) expressly reserved the question. In view, however, of the *ratio* of *Close v Steel Co of Wales*, above, the point is now of academic interest only.

3. *The part required to be fenced (the character of the part)*

In order that s. 14 may apply the dangerous part must be part of "machinery". For this purpose a distinction must be drawn between material which is being worked upon in a machine, and which is dangerous when in motion, and parts of the machinery itself which are dangerous when in motion. It is only in the latter case that the obligation to fence arises (*Eaves v Morris Motors Ltd* [1961] 2 QB 385, [1961] 3 All ER 233, CA). Thus, in *Bullock v G John Power (Agencies) Ltd* [1956] 1 All ER 498, [1956] 1 WLR 171, CA, it was held that a loose end of wire which was being wound upon an electric drum was not part of the machinery; and in *Eaves v Morris Motors Ltd*, above, sharp bolts undergoing a milling operation while being held in a moving vice were similarly regarded. However, if there is an unfenced dangerous part of machinery which in fact causes injury then there is a breach of s. 14(1) in respect of which the injured employee may recover damages, even though he may not have come into contact with the dangerous part, but only with material being worked upon, or with something else which is not part of the machine (*Wearing v Pirelli Ltd* [1977] 1 All ER 339, [1977] 1 WLR 48, HL).

A more difficult problem arises where the material being worked upon is not itself dangerous, but becomes so by reason of its juxtaposition with part of the machine itself. Divergent views were expressed in *Lewis v High Duty Alloys Ltd* [1957] 1 All ER 740, [1957] 1 WLR 632; *Lenthall v Gimson & Co (Leicester) Ltd* (24 May 1956, unreported, but see [1961] 3 All ER at 238) and *Hoare v M and W Grazebrook Ltd* [1957] 1 All ER 470, [1957] 1 WLR 638; but in *Eaves v Morris Motors Ltd*, above, Holroyd Pearce LJ said (at 396, 238):

"If a moving arm of the machine does not project, and is, therefore, safe when the machine is empty, but projects dangerously when the machine is supplied with its proper material, it can obviously be labelled as dangerous machinery. And if it creates a dangerous nip when supplied with its normal material and when working normally (or in a foreseeable manner) I see no reason in principle why the court cannot consider the machinery dangerous, even if that nip is only created by the juxtaposition of material and machinery. For in that case it is not the nature of the material and it is not the material itself which causes the danger. The danger is caused by the design of the machine itself working normally with harmless material.''

The view of Holroyd Pearce LJ has now been approved by the House of Lords in *Midland and Low Moor Iron and Steel Co Ltd v Cross* [1965] AC 343, [1964] 3 All ER 752. Their Lordships there held that whether a part of machinery was a dangerous part had to be determined on consideration of the machine when in actual operation doing the work, which it was ordinarily designed to do and that if the juxtaposition of a moving part and a workpiece resulted in a dangerous nip, then the moving part was not the less a dangerous part because in the absence of the workpiece there was no danger. Their Lordships expressly reserved the question, whether a stationary part of a machine could constitute a dangerous part by reason of the fact that danger was created when a moving workpiece came close to it, as had been held or suggested in certain unreported decisions at first instance which are cited in the speech of Lord Reid; the question thus reserved has since been answered in the affirmative (*F E Callow (Engineers) Ltd v Johnson* [1971] AC 335, [1970] 3 All ER 639, HL). However, if moving material, not itself dangerous, comes close to a stationary part of a machine, not itself dangerous, the juxtaposition does not create a dangerous part of machinery (*Hindle v Joseph Porritt & Sons Ltd* [1970] 1 All ER 1142).

A tool (such as an Allen key) which is supplied for use with a machine does not become part of the machinery, so as to attract the operation of s. 14(1) (*Sarwar v Simmons and Hawker Ltd* (1971) 11 KIR 300, CA).

There is no duty to fence against a danger only arises because of the proximity of a moving part of a machine to some stationary object extraneous to the machine: *Pearce v Stanley-Bridges Ltd* [1965] 2 All ER 594, [1965] 1 WLR 931, CA, distinguishing *Irwin v White, Tomkins and Courage Ltd* [1964] 1 All ER 545, [1964] 1 WLR 387, HL, in which danger was caused by the proximity of the moving part to a stationary part of the same apparatus.

The duty to fence securely is subject to the exception, in the case of ss. 12(3), 13(1) and 14(1), (5), that fencing is not required where the part of the machine concerned is "in such a position or of such construction as to be as safe to every person employed or working on the premises as it would be if securely fenced". In s. 14(5) (which relates to a stock-bar in a lathe) the excepting phrase omits the words "or of such construction". The mere fact that unfenced machinery is inaccessible save by a ladder is not enough to bring it within the exception: *Butler v Glacier Metal Co* (23 October 1924, unreported), DC, but see [1926] 1 KB at 317; *Atkinson v London and North Eastern Rly Co* [1926] 1 KB 313; *Hodkinson v Henry Wallwork & Co Ltd* [1955] 1 WLR 1195, CA. It submitted that the words "dangerous" and "safe" in s. 14(1) are intended to be mutually exclusive, and that therefore the same test of reasonable foresight which is applied as the criterion of danger must logically be applied also, in a reverse sense, as the criterion of safety. It is further submitted that since the excepting words definitive of safety in ss. 12(3), 13(1) and 14(5) must bear the same meaning (subject to the absence of the words "or of such construction" in s. 14(5)) wherever they occur (*Carroll v Andrew Barclay & Sons Ltd* [1948] AC 477, [1948] 2 All ER 386, HL), the criterion of reasonable foresight is thereby introduced also into these subsections.

In determining whether any part of machinery is in such a position or of such construction as to be safe within the intendment of the excepting words, no account must be taken of the matters specified in paragraphs (a) and (b) of s. 15(1) (see that section and the Operations at Unfenced Machinery Regulations 1938).

4. *The dangers against which fencing is required*
The words "shall be securely fenced" appear in s. 12(1), (2) and (3), in s. 13(1), and in s. 14(1) and (5). Wherever they occur, they must be given the same meaning (*Carroll v*

Andrew Barclay & Sons Ltd [1948] AC 477, [1948] 2 All ER 386, HL; *Close v Steel Co of Wales Ltd* [1962] AC 367, [1961] 2 All ER 953, HL).

The obligation to fence securely which may arise under these sections is not unlimited in scope, but is restricted to fencing against certain hazards only. It is now settled by the House of Lords that the obligation to fence imposed by s. 14(1) requires that the dangerous part be fenced securely for the purpose of preventing the body of the operator from coming into contact with it, but that the obligation does not extend to require that the dangerous part be fenced securely for the purpose of preventing fragments of the dangerous part from flying out of the machine (*Close v Steel Co of Wales Ltd* [1962] AC 367, [1961] 2 All ER 953, so interpreting *Nicholls v Austin (Leyton) Ltd* [1946] AC 493, [1946] 2 All ER 92, HL and *Carroll v Andrew Barclay & Sons Ltd* [1948] AC 477, [1948] 2 All ER 386, HL and overruling on this point three decisions of the Court of Appeal: *Dickson v Flack* [1953] 2 QB 464, [1953] 2 All ER 840; *Newnham v Tagart Morgan and Coles Ltd* (1956) Times, 20 July, CA; and *Rutherford v R E Glanville & Sons (Bovey Tracey) Ltd* [1958] 1 All ER 532, [1958] 1 WLR 415, CA). *Carroll v Andrew Barclay & Sons Ltd*, above, placed a similar interpretation upon s. 13(1). The decision in *Close v Steel Co of Wales Ltd*, above, was a majority decision from which Lord Denning vigorously dissented and with which Lord Morris of Borth-y-Gest did not agree. Of the majority, Lord Goddard's opinion was expressed with reluctance (at 389, 961), and Lord Guest (at 409, 974) appeared to consider the decision in *Nicholls v Austin (Leyton) Ltd*, above, by which he held himself bound, to be based upon an illogical distinction. In *Eaves v Morris Motors Ltd* [1961] 2 QB 385, [1961] 3 All ER 233, CA, Holroyd Pearce LJ, having considered the effect of *Close v Steel Co of Wales*, above, expressed himself in these terms:

> "The argument (of Counsel for the Plaintiff) has shown how technical and artificial the question of protection under s. 14 has become and how illusory in certain respects the words 'Every dangerous part of any machinery . . . shall be securely fenced' have now become. One may venture, perhaps, to express regret that an important part of the protection accorded to the workman by the Factory and Workshops Act 1878 and 1891 has been destroyed by the wording of the Factories Act 1937, and the authorities based on that wording . . . There is no protection under s. 14 against a class of obvious perils caused by dangerous machinery, namely, perils which arise from a dangerous machine ejecting at the worker pieces of the material or even pieces of the machinery itself. Thus, there is not left a gap which neither logic nor common sense appears to justify."

This gap has not been closed by the Factories Act 1961 nor, indeed (in the case of offices, shops and railway premises) by the Offices, Shops and Railway Premises Act 1963, the fencing of which repeat (in s. 17) those of the Factories Act 1961 in almost identical terms. Whatever criticism, however, may be made on grounds of logic or justice of the scope of s. 14(1) as authoritatively interpreted by *Close v Steel Co of Wales Ltd*, above, the law can now be changed only by legislation. It is, however, to be noted that powers under the Act have been exercised for the purpose of making regulations which guard against ejection of parts of machinery (see the Abrasive Wheels Regulations 1970). Apart from any question of breach of statutory duty if in a factory there is a machine which it is known from experience has a tendency to throw out parts of the machine itself or of the material on which it is working, so as to be a danger to the operator, the absence of a shield to protect him may well afford him a cause of action at common law (*per* Lord Goddard in *Close v Steel Co of Wales* [1962] AC 367, [1961] 2 All ER 953, at 390, 961). For an example, see *Kilgollan v William Cooke & Co Ltd* [1956] 2 All ER 294, [1956] 1 WLR 527, CA.

Since the obligation to fence in the sections under consideration is one to fence machinery, it follows that there is no obligation to fence against articles not part of the machinery (such as materials being worked upon) being ejected (*Nicholls v Austin (Leyton) Ltd* [1946] AC 493, [1946] 2 All ER 92, HL; *Close v Steel Co of Wales Ltd* [1962] AC 367, [1961] 2 All ER 953, HL). This is so, even if the material ejected is still attached to the machine when it injures the workman (*Walker v Dick Engineering Co (Coatbridge) Ltd* 1985 SLT 465). Nor is there any obligation so to fence that a tool being held by an operator does not come into contact with the dangerous part (*Sparrow v Fairey Aviation Co Ltd* [1964] AC 1019, [1962] 3 All ER 706, HL, overruling *Johnson v J Stone & Co (Charlton) Ltd* [1961] 1 All ER 869, [1961] 1 WLR 849). In *Sparrow's* case Lord Morris of Borth-y-Gest (at 1051, 720) reserved the question, whether in particular circumstances some equipment or apparatus could be so attached to an operator that, in his capacity as an operator, such equipment or apparatus could rationally be regarded as being a part of him. It seems probable that the obligation to fence extends to preventing a workman's clothing from fouling the dangerous part; see *John Summers & Sons Ltd v Frost* [1955] AC 740, [1955] 1 All ER 870, *per* Lord Morton, at 756, 875; *Sparrow v Fairey Aviation Co Ltd, supra, per* Lord Reid (at 1033, 709), Lord MacDermott (at 1039, 713), who dissented, and Lord Morris of Borth-y-Gest (at 1051, 720) and *F E Callow (Engineers) Ltd v Johnson* [1971] AC 335, [1970] 3 All ER 639, *per* Lord Hailsham of St. Marylebone LC (at 342, 641).

5. *The absolute nature of the duty*
  The duty to fence securely is an absolute one (*John Summers & Sons Ltd v Frost* [1955] AC 740, [1955] 1 All ER 870, HL affirming *Davies v Thomas Owen & Co* [1919] 2 KB 39, a decision upon the comparable provision of s. 10 of the Factory and Workshop Act 1901). The duty is not to be qualified by such words as "so far as practicable" or "so long as it can be fenced consistently with its being used for the purpose for which it was intended", and if the result of a machine being securely fenced is that it does not remain commercially practicable or mechanically possible, that does not affect the obligation (*per* Viscount Simonds in *John Summers & Sons Ltd v Frost*, above). The courts have not shrunk from the conclusion that the absolute nature of the obligation may, in effect, prohibit the use of the machine altogether, and this result has been reached in the case of a calendering machine (*Davies v Thomas Owen & Co* [1919] 2 KB 39); a power press (*Sowter v Steel Barrel Co Ltd* (1935) 154 LT 85); a cutting machine (*Dennistoun v Charles E. Greenhill Ltd* [1944] 2 All ER 434); a drilling machine (*Mackay v Ailsa Shipbuilding Co Ltd* 1945 SC 414), and a grinding wheel (*John Summers & Sons Ltd v Frost* [1955] AC 740, [1955] 1 All ER 870). In *John Summers & Sons Ltd v Frost*, above it was pointed out that the apparent harshness of thus construing the duty to fence was mitigated, insofar as the Minister had power by what was the Factories Act 1961, s. 76(2) (now repealed) to modify by special regulations its absolute character and has, indeed, done so in the case of certain machinery (see, for example, the Abrasive Wheels Regulations 1970). This power is now exercisable under the Health and Safety at Work etc. Act 1974, s. 15(3)(a).

6. *The standard of secure fencing*
  The extent of this duty is to fence securely. "Somewhat" secure fencing is not enough (*Sowter v Steel Barrel Co Ltd* (1935) 154 LT 85, decided upon the similar provisions of s. 10 of the Factory and Workshop Act 1901; *Vowles v Armstrong-Siddley Motors Ltd* [1938] 4 All ER 796, CA, *per* Slesser, LJ). Nor is it enough that the dangerous part was provided with a means of achieving security; the sections under consideration require the result to be achieved (*Charles v S Smith & Sons (England) Ltd* [1954] 1 All ER 499, [1954] 1 WLR 451; *Foster v Flexible Metal Co Ltd* (1967) 4 KIR 49). Fencing is secure which effectively protects the workman from the danger of contact with the exposed part of the machine (*John Summers & Sons Ltd v Frost* [1955] AC 740, [1955] 1 All ER 870, *per* Viscount Simonds at 752, 873; *per* Lord Morton of Henryton at 756, 875; *per* Lord Reid at 764, 882; and *per* Lord Keith of Avonholm at 774, 888). In considering whether secure fencing has been achieved the behaviour of persons employed is material and the same criterion of reasonable foreseeability, discussed earlier in this note, must be used for this purpose as it must for the purpose of deciding whether a part of a machine is a dangerous part (*John Summers & Sons Ltd, Frost*, above; *Burns v Joseph Terry & Sons Ltd* [1951] 1 KB 454, [1950] 2 All ER 987, CA; but c.f. the Scottish case of *Simpson v Hardie & Smith Ltd* 1968 SC(J) 23).
  The fence supplied must comply with the provision of s. 16, which indicates how and when the duty imposed under ss. 12, 13 and 14 is to be carried out (*Smith v Morris Motors Ltd and Harris* [1950] 1 KB 194, [1949] 2 All ER 715). The fence need not, however, be so constructed that it cannot be climbed over, or broken down, by an employee who is determined to get at the machinery, for that would be demanding the impossible of the employers (*per* Lord Morton of Henryton in *John Summers & Sons Ltd v Frost* [1955] AC

740, [1955] 1 All ER 870, at 758, 976; and see *Carr v Mercantile Produce Co Ltd* [1949] 2 KB 601, [1949] 2 All ER 531 and *Belhaven Brewery Company Ltd v A McClean* [1975] IRLR 370).

7. *The behaviour of persons employed*

The foreseeable behaviour of persons employed, whether they are operating the machine in question or whether they are employed elsewhere in the factory, is thus relevant in the following respects:

(i) in considering whether the part of the machine is a dangerous part within s. 14(1);

(ii) in considering whether the part of the machine is securely fenced;

(iii) in considering whether the part of the machine is in such position or of such construction as to be as safe to every person employed or working on the premises as it would be if securely fenced.

The actual behaviour of a person employed who has been injured by the machine is irrelevant to the foregoing heads of enquiry, which are concerned not with actual, but with foreseeable behaviour, and which are concerned with the foreseeable behaviour not only of the person who has been injured, but of any person employed on the premises. It follows that it must not be concluded from the facts that the operator or person employed has been careless, and that his carelessness was the proximate cause of the accident, that there has been no breach of the statute (*Blenkinsop v Ogden* [1898] 1 QB 783; *Atkinson v London and North Eastern Rly Co* [1926] 1 KB 313; *Smith v Chesterfield and District Co-operative Society Ltd* [1953] 1 All ER 447, [1953] 1 WLR 370, CA; *Dunn v Birds Eye Foods Ltd* [1959] 2 QB 265, [1959] 2 All ER 403). The behaviour of the person injured may, however, be very relevant to the issue of contributory negligence in any civil proceedings he may bring upon a breach of the statute. But the court will be cautious to find that carelessness on the part of an employee does amount to contributory negligence, particularly when an employee is following an ordinary routine, since the whole purpose of s. 14 is to avoid the risk of accident through inadvertence (*McNeill v Roche Products Ltd* 1989 SLT 498: failure by employee to look where he put his hand not contributory negligence).

8. *The liability of the owner or hirer*

Where in a factory the owner or hirer of a machine moved by mechanical power is some person other than the occupier of the factory, special provisions apply in determining who is responsible for a breach of statutory duty relating to the machine (see s. 163 and the notes thereto). See, in addition, the general duties imposed, by the Health and Safety at Work etc. Act 1974, s. 6 upon designers, manufacturers, importers, suppliers and lessors of articles for use at work.

---

12.   Prime movers.—(1) Every flywheel directly connected to any prime mover *(a)* and every moving part of any prime mover, except such prime movers as are mentioned in subsection (3) of this section, shall be securely fenced *(b)*, whether the flywheel or prime mover is situated in an engine-house or not.

(2) The head and tail race of every water wheel and of every water turbine shall be securely fenced *(b)*.

(3) Every part of electric generators, motors and rotary converters, and every flywheel directly connected thereto, shall be securely fenced *(b)* unless it is in such a position or of such construction as to be as safe to every person employed or working on the premises as it would be if securely fenced *(c)*.

General note. This section is to be repealed as from 1 January 1997 by the Provision and Use of Work Equipment Regulations 1992, S.I. 1992 No. 2932, by which time all work equipment first provided for use before 1 January 1993 must meet the standards established in those Regulations. For equipment provided for use after 1 January 1993, the Regulations have immediate effect and this section of the Factories Act no longer applies. See also the Introductory note to ss. 12–16.

(*a*) *Primer mover.* For definition, see s. 176(1).

(*b*) *Securely fenced.* See the Introductory Note to ss. 12–16.

(*c*) *Unless . . . fenced.* See the Introductory Note to ss. 12–16.

---

13. Transmission machinery.—(1) Every part of the transmission machinery (*a*) shall be securely fenced (*b*) unless it is in such a position or of such construction as to be as safe to every person employed or working on the premises as it would be if securely fenced (*c*).

(2) Efficient devices (*d*) or appliances shall be provided and maintained in every room or place where work is carried on by which the power can promptly be cut off from the transmission machinery (*a*) in that room or place.

(3) No driving belt when not in use shall be allowed to rest or ride upon a revolving shaft which forms part of the transmission machinery (*a*).

(4) Suitable striking gear or other efficient mechanical appliances shall be provided and maintained and used to move driving belts to and from fast and loose pulleys which form part of the transmission machinery (*a*), and any such gear or appliances shall be so constructed, placed and maintained as to prevent the driving belt from creeping back on to the fast pulley.

(5) Where the Minister (*e*) is satisfied that owing to special circumstances the fulfilment of any of the requirements of subsections (2) to (4) of this section is unnecessary or impracticable, he may by order (*f*) direct that that requirement shall not apply in those circumstances.

General note. This section is to be repealed as from 1 January 1997 by the Provision and Use of Work Equipment Regulations 1992, S.I. 1992 No. 2932, by which time all work equipment first provided for use before 1 January 1993 must meet the standards established in those Regulations. For equipment provided for use after 1 January 1993, the Regulations have immediate effect and this section of the Factories Act no longer applies. See also the Introductory Note to ss. 12–16.

(*a*) *Transmission machinery.* For definition, see s. 176(1). The expression includes machinery which is not at the material time being driven by mechanical power (*Richard Thomas and Baldwins Ltd v Cummings* [1955] AC 321, [1955] 1 All ER 285, HL). It is, however, limited to things which move or revolve; and the words "or other device" in s. 176(1) must be read *eiusdem generis* with the words which precede them (*Weir v Andrew Barclay & Co Ltd* 1955 SLT (Notes) 56, in which Lord Guthrie held that the moving part of a hydraulic accumulator was not "transmission machinery").

(*b*) *Securely fenced.* See the Introductory Note to ss. 12–16.

(*c*) *Unless . . . fenced.* See *Butler v Glacier Metal Co Ltd* (23 October 1924, unreported), DC, but see [1926] 1 KB at 317; *Atkinson v London and North Eastern Rly Co* [1926] 1 KB 313; *Findlay v Newman, Hender & Co Ltd* [1937] 4 All ER 58; *Hodkinson v Henry Wallwork & Co Ltd* [1955] 3 All ER 236, [1955] 1 WLR 1195, CA and *Burns v Joseph Terry & Sons Ltd* [1951] 1 KB 454, [1950] 2 All ER 987, CA. The onus of coming within the proviso is placed on the employer: *Simpson v Hardie and Smith Ltd* 1968 JC 23.

(d) Efficient devices. The requirement is that the power can be promptly cut off, not that the machinery can be promptly stopped.

(e) The Minister. By S.I. 1974 No. 1941, reg. 2(b), Sch. 2 this subsection has effect as if the reference to the Secretary of State ("the Minister") was a reference to the Health and Safety Executive.

(f) Order. Sub-s. (5) is repealed except so far as it enables orders to be made otherwise than by statutory instruments (S.I. 1974 No. 1941, Sch. 1).

As to the making of orders, see s. 180. No order has yet been made under this section or the corresponding provisions of superseded enactments.

---

14.   Other machinery.—(1) Every dangerous part of any machinery *(a)*, other than prime movers and transmission machinery *(b)*, shall be securely fenced *(c)* unless it is in such a position or of such construction as to be as safe to every person employed or working on the premises *(d)* as it would be if securely fenced *(e)*.

(2) In so far as the safety of a dangerous part of any machinery *(a)* cannot by reason of the nature of the operation be secured by means of a fixed guard, the requirements of subsection (1) of this section shall be deemed to have been complied with if a device is provided which automatically prevents the operator from coming into contact with that part *(f)*.

(3)–(4) [*repealed*].

(5) Any part of a stock-bar which projects beyond the head-stock of a lathe shall be securely fenced *(c)* unless it is in such a position as to be as safe to every person employed or working on the premises *(d)* as it would be if securely fenced *(e)*.

(6) [*repealed*].

General note. This section is to be repealed as from 1 January 1997 by the Provision and Use of Work Equipment Regulations 1992, S.I. 1992 No. 2932, by which time all work equipment first provided for use before 1 January 1993 must meet the standards established in those Regulations. For equipment provided for use after 1 January 1993, the Regulations have immediate effect and this section of the Factories Act no longer applies. See also the Introductory note to ss. 12–16. The provisions of s. 14(1) do not apply in relation to any abrasive wheel (see the Abrasive Wheels Regulations 1970, reg. 3(2), set out below).

(a) Dangerous part of any machinery. See the Introductory Note to ss. 12–16.

(b) Prime movers and transmission machinery. For definition, see s. 176(1). See also s. 13.

(c) Securely fenced. See the Introductory Note to ss. 12–16.

(d) Person employed or working on the premises. See *Westwood v Post Office* [1974] AC 1, [1973] 3 All ER 184, HL; *Napieralski v Curtis (Contractors) Ltd* [1959] 2 All ER 426, [1959] 1 WLR 835; *Uddin v Associated Portland Cement Manufacturers Ltd* [1965] 2 QB 582, [1965] 2 All ER 213, CA and *Allen v Aeroplane and Motor Aluminium Castings Ltd* [1965] 3 All ER 377, [1965] 1 WLR 1244, CA, which are discussed in the Introductory Note to ss. 12–16. See also the GENERAL INTRODUCTION, "Persons protected by safety legislation".

(e) Unless . . . fenced. See note *(c)* to s. 13.

(*f*) **Automatic devices.** Efficient devices of this kind are in use upon a number of machines, for example, power presses, and guillotines for cutting paper and other material. Power presses are now the subject of regulation; see the Power Presses Regulations 1965.

---

15. Provisions as to unfenced machinery.—(1) In determining, for the purposes of the foregoing (*a*) provisions of this Part of this Act, whether any part of machinery is in such a position or of such construction as to be as safe to every person employed or working on the premises as it would be if securely fenced (*b*), the following paragraphs shall apply in a case where this section applies, that is to say—

(a) no account shall be taken of any person carrying out, while the part of machinery is in motion (*c*), an examination thereof or any lubrication or adjustment shown by the examination to be immediately necessary, if the examination, lubrication or adjustment can only be carried out while the part of machinery is in motion; and

(b) in the case of any part of transmission machinery (*d*) used in any such process as may be specified in regulations (*e*) made by the Minister (*f*), being a process where owing to the continuous nature thereof the stopping of that part would seriously interfere with the carrying on of the process, no account shall be taken of any person carrying out, by such methods and in such circumstances as may be specified in the regulations, any lubrication or any mounting or shipping of belts.

(2) This section only applies where the examination, lubrication or other operation is carried out by such persons who have attained the age of eighteen as may be specified in regulations (*e*) made by the Minister (*f*), and all such other conditions as may be so specified are complied with.

General note. This section is to be repealed as from 1 January 1997 by the Provision and Use of Work Equipment Regulations 1992, S.I. 1992 No. 2932, by which time all work equipment first provided for use before 1 January 1993 must meet the standards established in those Regulations. For equipment provided for use after 1 January 1993, the Regulations have immediate effect and this section of the Factories Act no longer applies.

(*a*) *Foregoing provisions . . . Act.* This is to say, ss. 12(3), 13(1), and 14(1), (5).

(*b*) *Position . . . fenced.* See note (*c*) to s. 13.

(*c*) *In motion.* It is submitted that these words bear the same meaning as in s. 16; see note (*c*) to that section.

(*d*) *Transmission machinery.* For definition, see s. 176(1).

(*e*) *Regulations.* As to the making of regulations, see s. 180. The Regulations set out below were made under the corresponding provisions of the Factories Act 1937, and are continued in force by virtue of s. 183 and the Sixth Schedule. For the purpose of these Regulations the expression "factory" includes railway running sheds (Railway Running Sheds (No. 1) Regulations 1961, S.I. 1961 No. 1251) and the premises now specified in s. 175(1)(d) and (c) (Slaughterhouses (No. 2) Regulations 1962, S.I. 1962 No. 2347).

In *Nash v High Duty Alloys Ltd* [1947] KB 377, [1947] 1 All ER 363 the Court of Appeal considered the Regulations set out below and held: (i) that s. 16 of the Act, and the exception provided by that section, did not apply to machinery when not in motion and did not, therefore, apply during the operation of removing and replacing dies in a stationary machine; (ii) that the operation during which the plaintiff was injured (that of pulling out a master pressing) and which required the machine to be in motion could have been performed with the guard in position, so that the dangerous parts were not "necessarily exposed" within the exception to s. 16; (iii) that even had the employers brought themselves prima facie within the exception they could not have relied upon it, since although tool-setting operations are excepted from reg. 5 they are not excepted from reg. 2, and the toolsetter and toolmaker (who were among the class of machinery attendants) were not provided with individual certificates of appointment, defining the limits of their duties, as required by reg. 2; and (iv) that the exception to s. 16 can only be relied upon if the machinery is exposed for the purposes mentioned in the section and if the Regulations are complied with.

(*f*)　*The Minister.* For definition, see s. 176(1).

THE OPERATIONS AT UNFENCED MACHINERY REGULATIONS 1938
(S.R. & O. 1938 No. 641, as amended by S.R. & O. 1946 No. 156, S.I. 1976 No. 955 and S.I. 1989 No. 1141)

Notes. The whole Regulations are revoked by S.I. 1992 No. 2932, as from 1 January 1993, except, insofar as they apply to work equipment first provided for use in the premises or undertaking before 1 January 1993, they are revoked as from 1 January 1997.

Regulation 10 (which relates to the mounting or shipping of belts) does not have effect as regards machinery used in factories in connection with the manufacture of flour from wheat (Certificate of Exemption No. 5) [Form 2322].

As to the "Chief Inspector of Factories", see the definition in s. 176(1).

PART 1 (REGULATIONS 1–7)

1.　Regulations 2 to 7 of these Regulations shall apply to the following operations namely—

   (i)　the carrying out, in pursuance of paragraph (a) of section 15 of the Act [s. 15 of the 1961 Act], of an examination of any part of machinery which is in motion and which is not securely fenced, or any lubrication or adjustment shown by such examination to be immediately necessary, being an examination, lubrication or adjustment which it is necessary to carry out while the part of machinery is in motion, and

  (ii)　the carrying out, in pursuance of Section 16 of the Act [s. 16 of the 1961 Act], of an examination or any lubrication or adjustment shown by such examination to be immediately necessary, when parts of machinery otherwise required to be fenced or safeguarded are in motion or in use but are necessarily exposed for those operations:

Provided that regulations 5 and 6 shall not apply in relation to any part of machinery which is only being moved by hand or by a barring engine or by an inching or similar device, so however that no such operation shall be carried out except by a person who has attained the age of eighteen.

Provided further that regulation 5 shall not apply to the setting up of a machine by a toolsetter or other skilled mechanic, being a person who has attained the age of eighteen and whose duty it is to set up such machine.

2.　One or more persons shall be appointed by the occupier of the factory, by signed entry in or by certificate attached to the general register, to be machinery attendants to carry out operations to which this regulation applies, and any such appointment may be made for all such operations or may be limited to such only of those operations as may be specified in the entry or certificate. The occupier shall furnish to each person so appointed a certificate of his appointment, which certificate shall indicate the limitations (if any) specified as aforesaid.

3. No person shall be appointed to be such a machinery attendant unless he is a person who has attained the age of eighteen, and has been sufficiently trained for the purposes of the work entailed by those operations which he is authorised by his appointment to carry out, and is acquainted with the dangers from moving machinery arising in connection with such operations.

4.—(1) Every such machinery attendant shall be instructed as to the requirements of these Regulations and supplied with a copy of the precautionary leaflet approved in writing for the time being for the purposes of these Regulations by the Health and Safety Commission.

(2) During the period of 2 months after the Commission has approved and published a leaflet under paragraph (1) above, it shall be a sufficient compliance with the requirement to supply such a leaflet if the attendant has been supplied with a copy of the leaflet previously so approved or in the case of the first such approval with a copy of the leaflet prescribed under the Unfenced Machinery (Prescribed Leaflet) Order 1967.

5. No operation to which this regulation applies shall be carried out—
(a) except by a machinery attendant authorised as aforesaid to carry out the operation,
(b) unless every person carrying out the operation is wearing a close-fitting single-piece overall suit in good repair which (i) is fastened by means having no exposed loose ends and (ii) has no external pockets other than a hip pocket,
(c) unless another person instructed as to the steps to be taken in case of emergency is immediately available within sight or hearing of a person carrying out the operation, and
(d) unless such steps as may be necessary, including where appropriate and reasonably practicable the erection of a barrier, are taken to prevent any person, other than a person carrying out the operation, from being in a position where he is exposed to risk of injury from the machinery.
Paragraph (a) of this regulation shall not prevent the carrying out of such an operation on a special occasion by a competent person who has attained the age of eighteen if he has been previously authorised in writing for the purposes of that occasion by the occupier or manager of the factory or other person holding a responsible position of management in the factory.

6. Without prejudice to any other obligation to fence machinery, every set-screw, bolt or key or any revolving shaft, spindle, wheel, or pinion, and all spur and other toothed or friction gearing in motion, with which a person carrying out an operation to which this regulation applies would otherwise be liable to come into contact, shall be securely fenced to prevent such contact unless it is necessarily being examined, lubricated or adjusted while in motion or is necessarily exposed for examination or for any lubrication or adjustment shown by such examination to be immediately necessary.

7. Any ladder in use for the carrying out of an operation to which this regulation applies shall be securely fixed or lashed or be firmly held by a second person.

Part II (Regulations 8–11)

8. In the case of transmission machinery used in the processes specified in the Schedule to these Regulations, paragraph (b) of section 15 of the Act [s. 15(1)(b) of the 1961 Act] shall, subject to the limitations and conditions hereinafter in these Regulations specified, apply to the following operations namely, any lubrication, or any mounting or shipping of a belt, when the circumstances are such that the lubrication, mounting or shipping cannot, without serious interference with the carrying on of the process, be deferred until the machinery is stopped.

9. Regulations 2 to 7 and regulations 10 to 11 of these Regulations shall apply to such operations:
Provided that regulations 5, 6 and 10 shall not apply in relation to any part of machinery which is only being moved by hand or by a barring engine or by an inching or

similar device, so, however, that no such operation shall be carried out except by a person who has attained the age of eighteen.

10.   A belt shall not be handled at a moving pulley for the purpose of mounting or shipping it on the pulley unless:
  (i)   the belt is less than 10 millimetres in width;
  (ii)   the belt has already been used for driving on that pulley;
  (iii)   the belt joint is either laced or flush with the belt or it is safely secured;
  (iv)   the belt, including the joint, and the pulley-rim, are in good repair;
  (v)   there is reasonable clearance between the pulley and any fixed plant or structure; and
  (vi)   secure foothold and where necessary secure handhold are afforded for the operator.

11.   All belts which are in use in the processes specified in the Schedule to these Regulations and which are liable to be handled at a moving pulley shall be inspected daily by a competent person with a view to ascertaining whether the belt requires repair or replacement; and such inspection, if made when the belt or any adjacent machinery is in motion, shall be made for a safe position. Any repair or replacement of such a belt found by such inspection to be necessary shall be carried out as soon as practicable.

PART III (REGULATIONS 12–15)

12.   Every machinery attendant or other person, when carrying out an operation to which any of these Regulations apply, shall—
  (a)   wear the overall required under paragraph (b) of regulation 5 in such a manner as to cover completely all loose ends of other clothing, and
  (b)   make proper use of any appliances provided for the safe carrying out of any such operation.

13.   If the Chief Inspector of Factories is satisfied, as respects any factory or any parts of machinery, that owing to special methods of work or other special circumstances the application of any of the requirements or conditions in regulations 5, 6, 10 and 11 of these Regulations would be unreasonable or inappropriate, he may by certificate in writing authorise such relaxation or variation of that requirement or condition and for such period as he may think fit.

14.   The Chief Inspector may at any time at his discretion revoke or vary any certificate given in pursuance of regulation 13 of these Regulations.

15.   These Regulations may be cited as the Operations at Unfenced Machinery Regulations 1938, and shall come into force on the 1 August, 1938.

SCHEDULE

  1.   All processes in the manufacture of—
  (a)   beet sugar,
  (b)   paper or paper-board,
  (c)   viscose transparent paper or film,
  (d)   flour from wheat,
  (e)   provender and compound foodstuffs for animal feeding,
  (f)   sodium carbonate by the ammonia soda or Solvay process,
  (g)   caustic soda by the ammonia soda or Solvay process, or by continuous causticising,
  (h)   sulphur dioxide,
  (i)   sodium hyposulphite ("hydrosulphite") or sodium sulphoxylate,
  (j)   inlaid linoleum.
  2.   All processes in the milling of cereals, seeds or nuts.

3.   All processes in the extraction of oil or other similar products from cereals or seeds.

4.   The filtering process in the manufacture of sulphate of ammonia.

5.   The phosphate reaction pumping process in the manufacture of concentrated fertiliser.

6.   The electrolytic process for the manufacture of metallic sodium as regards the operation of dredging the sodium cells.

7.   The electrolytic process for the manufacture of caustic soda.

8.   Any manufacturing process in which a mixture of nitric and sulphuric acids is employed and where risk of fire or explosion would arise if the transmission machinery were stopped.

9.   The reducing, volatilising and decomposing processes in the production of nickel.

10.   Any process in the manufacture of phosphorus halides directly from phosphorus involving risk of considerable rise in temperature and of evolution of toxic gases if the transmission machinery were stopped.

11.   The process of enamelling wire including re-winding after enamelling.

12.   The kier process in the manufacture of aluminium from bauxite.

---

16.   Construction and maintenance of fencing. All fencing or other safeguards provided in pursuance of the foregoing provisions *(a)* of this Part of this Act shall be of substantial construction, and constantly maintained *(b)* and kept in position while the parts required to be fenced or safeguarded are in motion or use *(c)*, except when any such parts are necessarily exposed *(d)* for examination and for any lubrication or adjustment *(e)* shown by the examination to be immediately necessary, and all such conditions as may be specified in regulations *(f)* and by the Minister *(g)* are complied with.

General note. This section is to be repealed as from 1 January 1997 by the Provision and Use of Work Equipment Regulations 1992, S.I. 1992 No. 2932, by which time all work equipment first provided for use before 1 January 1993 must meet the standards established in those Regulations. For equipment provided for use after 1 January 1993, the Regulations have immediate effect and this section of the Factories Act no longer applies.

This section operates in two ways: first, it indicates without imposing any separate and distinct obligation, how and when the duty under ss. 12–14 is to be carried out; and, secondly, it provides an exception to the obligation to fence thereunder (*Smith v Morris Motors Ltd and Harris* [1950] 1 KB 194, [1949] 2 All ER 715, DC). It is not, therefore, possible to lay any information under this section.

(a)   *Foregoing provisions.* That is to say, ss. 12–14.

(b)   *Constantly maintained.* "Maintained" means maintained in an efficient state, in efficient working order, and in good repair (s. 176(1)). It is submitted that the word "maintained" in s. 16 bears the same meaning as the word "maintained" in s. 22(1), as to which see *Galashiels Gas Co Ltd v O'Donnell* [1949] AC 275, [1949] 1 All ER 319, HL, and INTRODUCTORY NOTE 10.

(c)   *In motion or use.* The fencing and other safeguards referred to in this section have only to be constantly maintained and kept in position while the parts required to be fenced or safe-guarded are "in motion or use", and, even in such a case, those parts may be lawfully exposed if the requirements of the exception are complied with. The interpretation of the phrase, "in motion or use", has given rise to no little difficulty. It is clear that the two parts of the phrase bear different meanings. A part may be in motion but not in use; it may be in use but not in motion. A guide to the meaning of the term "in use" was given by Lord Porter in *Richard Thomas and Baldwins Ltd v Cummings* [1955] AC 321, [1955] 1 All ER 285, HL, an authority upon the corresponding phrase, "in motion or in use", in s. 16 of the Factories Act 1937. At 332, 289 he said:

> "'In use' would certainly mean running as it was meant to run and doing the work it was meant to do. But provision is required for cases where it was running as it was meant to run but not doing the work it was meant to do. In such a case it would, in my view, be in motion but not in use."

Thus, in *Knight v Leamington Spa Courier Ltd* [1961] 2 QB 253, [1961] 2 All ER 666, CA, a printing press was not being used for its ordinary commercial purpose of printing, but, during a slack period, was being slowly rotated by an inching button. It was held not to be "in use". Similar decisions were reached in *Kelly v John Dale Ltd* [1965] 1 QB 185, [1964] 2 All ER 497, another inching button case, even though the process there being carried out by the plaintiff (that of cleaning an inking cylinder on a printing machine) was one which had frequently to be performed, and in *Normille v News of the World* (1975) 119 Sol Jo 301, CA, where the plaintiff's hand was trapped in a printing press which was being inched during the removal of plates at the end of a production run. In *Conboy v King and Hutchings Ltd* (1963) 61 LGR 516, however, the inching was being carried out as part of the actual use of the press for printing, and it was held that the machine was "in motion or in use"; so also it was held in *Joy v News of the World* (1972) 13 KIR 57, where the operation being carried out was that of threading paper through the rollers of a printing machine which was running continuously at its slowest speed. In *Horne v Lec Refrigeration Ltd* [1965] 2 All ER 898, a toolsetter was setting a mould in a plastic forming machine, preparatory to its being used for its commercial purpose. It was held that the machine was not then "in use". It is clear, none the less, that a machine may be "in use" notwithstanding the fact that it is, for the time being, inert; ". . . a machine may be 'in use' notwithstanding some temporary halt in the running of it" (*per* Donovan LJ, in *Knight's case*, above, at 265, 671). Cleaning a machine may be part of the normal use of a machine (*Finnie v John Laird & Son Ltd* 1967 SLT 243).

Far more difficult problems have arisen in the interpretation of the term "in motion". It was decided in *Richard Thomas and Baldwins Ltd v Cummings*, above, that "in motion" meant more than "in movement", but it is not easy to discover what factors, other than mere movement, must be found to exist before motion can be said to be present. In *Cumming's* case their Lordships did not speak with a single voice, and the ratio is obscure (see the discussion of that case in *Irwin v White, Tomkins and Courage Ltd* [1964] 1 All ER 545, [1964] 1 WLR 387, HL). *Cumming's* case was explained by Holroyd Pearce LJ, in *Knight's* case, above, at 262, 263, 669, 670, in terms which the Court of Appeal, in *Mitchell v WS Westin Ltd* [1965] 1 All ER 657, [1965] 1 WLR 297, has accepted as authoritative. That part of the judgment of Holroyd Pearce LJ, which was thus approved was as follows:

> "The construction of the words 'in motion or in use' must be the same whether the object was repair or cleaning. In my judgment, that case [*Cumming's* case] is authority for the proposition that the words 'in motion or in use' connote the substantial movement of its normal working or, if it is not at the time achieving its normal purpose, some movement reasonably comparable to its normal working. This view is in accord with that expressed by Finnemore J in *Dodd v Ben Capper Ltd* (17 March 1961, unreported). The slow, sporadic rotation or intermittent movement of machinery intended to place it more advantageously for cleaning or repair is not normally motion or use within the section, whether it be produced by manpower or mechanical power. In some case it may be clear into which category the movement fits. In borderline cases it must be a question of fact and degree. Here the judge was right in deciding that the machinery was not in motion."

In *Mitchell v W S Westin Ltd*, Pearson LJ, while accepting as authoritative the explanation of *Cumming's* case given by Holroyd Pearce LJ, himself deduced from *Cumming's* case the following proposition (see at 307, 308, 664):

"First: in ascertaining whether machinery in fact moving is 'in motion' for the purposes of the section, regard should be had to the character of the movement more than to its purpose. If machinery is revolving rapidly in a place where a workman may come in contact with it, the guard should be kept in place on the machinery, whatever may be the purpose for which the movement is being made, whether it be production, examination, demonstration, adjustment, repairing, testing, or whatever the purpose may be. Secondly: the obvious and typical case of machinery in motion is, of course, machinery running in the usual way in its ordinary course of operation. Thirdly: there must, however, be other cases of machinery which is 'in motion', because the object of the statute is to protect the workman, and machinery may be running dangerously even though not in the ordinary course of operation or perhaps even though not running in the usual way. Fourthly: in deciding whether in a particular case the movement is or is not of such a character that the machinery is 'in motion', the factors to be taken into account include the speed of the movement, its duration, the method of starting the machinery, and probably to some extent or in some cases also the purpose for which the movement has been instituted. Then, fifthly: when the factors are rightly taken into account, it must be a question of fact and of degree whether or not the machinery is 'in motion' within the meaning of the section."

The "inching button" cases were distinguished by the Court of Appeal in *Stanbrook v Waterlow & Sons Ltd* [1964] 2 All ER 506, [1964] 1 WLR 825, in which the cylinder of a printing machine was caused to revolve at high speed for a fraction of a second only. The Court held that the fact that the motion was not intended to last for an appreciable time was immaterial, and that there was a vital distinction between a thing which is "being moved" slowly and a thing which is "in motion" at a fast pace; on the facts of the case before them the cylinder was "in motion" within s. 16. See also *Normille v News of the World*, above, and compare *Foster v Flexible Metal Co Ltd* (1967) 4 KIR 49, in which manual motion was held not to fall within s. 16; *sed quaere*; and see *Morris v Austin* (19 January 1990, Queen's Bench Division): rolls turned for purposes of cleaning task likely to last around two hours held to be in motion; *Mitchell* distinguished on facts. In *Finnie v John Laird & Son Ltd* 1967 SLT 243 at 246 the view was expressed that "*prima facie* the movements of parts to expose areas of a machine for cleaning would not readily give rise to the conception that the machine was 'in motion'. There might be cases where the movement was so fast or continuous as to amount to putting a part 'in motion'." See too *McLean v Glenrobert Wood Wool Industries Ltd* 1969 SLT (Notes) 29: machine coming to rest after being switched off held to be in motion.

In *Horne v Refrigeration Ltd* [1965] 2 All ER 898, the question arose, whether inadvertent movement of the dangerous part constituted "motion" within s. 16. In that case the dangerous part was caused to move because its operating switch was accidentally fouled by the cable of a portable electric drill held by the workman. The machine was operated by a switch provided to produce the motion which occurred; it was moving in the same manner and place as in its normal working; and it was working at the same speed and to the same extent as in its normal working. It was held that the machine was "in motion". The result might well be different, however, should a machine behave in an abnormal way, a situation envisaged by Willmer LJ, in *Eaves v Morris Motors Ltd* [1961] 2 QB 385, [1961] 3 All ER 233, CA, at 398, 239:

"But there is, I think, another and broader ground for holding that there was no breach of the statute in the present case. The provisions relating to fencing of dangerous machinery in Part II of the Act are designed, as I see it, to prevent dangers arising in the course of the normal operation of the machinery. I do not think that dangers due to the machinery breaking down or behaving in some abnormal and unexpected way are within the purview of the Act. I think that is implicit in the provisions of the Act itself. Thus it seems to me that the 'motion' referred to in s. 15, and the 'motion' and 'use' referred on in s. 16 must in their context refer to motion and use in the course of normal operation."

(d) **Necessarily exposed.** See *Nash v High Duty Alloys Ltd* [1947] KB 377, [1947] 1 All ER 363, CA, which is discussed in the notes to s. 15.

(e) **For examination . . . lubrication or adjustment.** These words do not include repair (*Richard Thomas and Baldwins Ltd v Cummings* [1955] AC 321, [1955] 1 All ER 285, HL) or cleaning (*Knight v Leamington Spa Courier* [1961] 2 QB 253, [1961] 2 All ER 666, CA).

(f) **Regulations.** As to the making of regulations, see s. 180. The Operations at Unfenced Machinery Regulations 1938, set out in the notes to s. 15, were also made under the provisions of the Factories Act 1937 which corresponded to this section.

(g) **The Minister.** For definition, see s. 176(1).

---

17.   Construction and sale of machinery.—(1) In the case of any machine *(a)* in a factory *(b)* which is a machine intended to be driven by mechanical power *(c)*—

(a)   every set-screw, bolt or key on any revolving shaft, spindle, wheel or pinion shall be so sunk, encased or otherwise effectively guarded as to prevent danger; and

(b)   all spur and other toothed or friction gearing, which does not require frequent adjustment while in motion, shall be completely encased unless it is so situated as to be as safe as it would be if completely encased.

(2) Any person who sells or lets on hire, or as agent of the seller or hirer causes or procures to be sold or let on hire, for use in a factory *(b)* in the United Kingdom any machine *(a)* intended to be driven by mechanical power *(c)* which does not comply with the requirements of this section shall be guilty of an offence.

(3)–(5) [*repealed*].

(6) Nothing in this section applies to any machine *(a)* constructed *(d)* before the thirtieth day of July, nineteen hundred and thirty-seven, and regulations under subsection (3) of this section shall not apply to any machinery *(a)* or plant constructed before the making of the Regulations.

General note. This section is to be repealed as from 1 January 1997 by the Provision and Use of Work Equipment Regulations 1992, S.I. 1992 No. 2932, by which time all work equipment first provided for use before 1 January 1993 must meet the standards established in those Regulations. For equipment provided for use after 1 January 1993, the Regulations have immediate effect and this section of the Factories Act no longer applies.

Sections 15 and 16 and the Operations at Unfenced Machinery Regulations do not apply to this section. In other respects the duties under it are, it is submitted, analogous to those under ss. 12–14 so that, in determining whether set screws, etc., are so effectively guarded "as to prevent danger", similar considerations apply as are applied to the determination of the question, whether a part is "securely fenced" under those sections, as to which see the Introductory Note to ss. 12–16. A person who sells or lets on hire to the occupier of a factory machinery which does not comply with the requirements of this section is not civilly liable for a breach of this section to a workman injured by that machinery (*Biddle v Truvox Engineering Co Ltd (Greenwood and Batley Ltd Third Party)* [1952] 1 KB 101, [1951] 2 All ER 835).

See also the provisions of the Health and Safety at Work etc. Act 1974, s. 6 which imposes duties upon the designers, manufacturers, importers, suppliers and lessors of articles for use at work (including machinery).

(a) **Machine.** The provisions of sub-s. (2) are extended to certain abrasive wheels and machines carrying such wheels (Abrasive Wheels Regulations 1970, reg. 19), to machines used in building operations and works of engineering construction (Construction (General Provisions) Regulations 1961, reg. 57), to certain machines used in the spinning and weaving of jute (Jute (Safety, Health and Welfare) Regluations 1948, reg. 28) and to certain woodworking machines (Woodworking Machines Regulations 1974, reg. 15).

(b) *Factory.* For definition, see s. 175.

(c) *Mechanical power.* This term is not defined, but see note (b) to s. 163.

(d) *Constructed.* As to the date on which machinery shall be deemed to have been constructed, see s. 176(2).

---

18. Dangerous substances.—(1) Every fixed vessel, structure, sump or pit of which the edge is less than 920 millimetres above the highest ground or platform from which a person might fall into it shall, if it contains any scalding, corrosive or poisonous liquid, either be securely covered or be securely fenced to at least 920 millimetres above that ground or platform, or where by reason of the nature of the work neither secure covering nor secure fencing to that height is practicable (a), all practicable steps shall be taken by covering, fencing or other means to prevent any person from falling into the vessel, structure, sump or pit.

(2) Where any fixed vessel, structure, sump or pit contains any scalding, corrosive or poisonous liquid but is not securely covered, no ladder, stair or gangway shall be placed above, across or inside it which is not—

(a) at least 460 millimetres wide, and
(b) securely fenced on both sides to a height of at least 920 millimetres and securely fixed.

(3) Where any such vessels, structures, sumps or pits as are mentioned in subsection (2) of this section adjoin, and the space between them, clear of any surrounding brick or other work, is less than 460 millimetres in width or is not securely fenced on both sides to a height of at least 920 millimetres secure barriers shall be so placed as to prevent passage between them.

(4) For the purpose of this section a ladder, stair or gangway shall not be deemed to be securely fenced unless it is provided either with sheet fencing or with an upper and a lower rail and toe boards.

(5)–(6) [*repealed*].

General note. This section is to be repealed as from 1 January 1996 by the Workplace (Health, Safety and Welfare) Regulations 1992, S.I. 1992 No. 3004, for workplaces in existence on 31 December 1992. Those Regulations will apply to those workplaces from the former date. Workplaces coming into use after 31 December 1992 and modifications, extensions and conversions started after 31 December 1992 to existing workplaces must conform to those Regulations as soon as they come into use.

(a) *Practicable.* See INTRODUCTORY NOTE 5.

---

19.   Self-acting machines.—(1) In any factory *(a)* or part of a factory to which this subsection applies no traversing part of any self-acting machine and no material carried thereon shall, if the space over which it runs is a space over which any person is liable to pass, whether in the course of his employment or otherwise, be allowed on its outward or inward traverse to run within a distance of 500 millimetres from any fixed structure which is not part of the machine; but nothing in this subsection shall prevent any portion of the traversing carriage of any self-acting spinning mule *(b)* being allowed to run to a point 310 millimetres distant from any part of the head stock of another such machine.

(2) Subsection (1) of this section applies—

(a)   to any factory erected *(c)* after the thirty-first day of December, eighteen hundred and ninety-five; and

(b)   to any factory or part of a factory reconstructed *(c)* after the thirtieth day of July, nineteen hundred and thirty-seven; and

(c)   to any extension of or addition *(c)* to a factory made after the said thirtieth day of July.

(3) All practicable *(d)* steps shall be taken by instructions to the person in charge of the machine and otherwise to ensure that no person employed shall be in the space between any traversing part of a self-acting spinning mule and any fixed part of the machine towards which the traversing part moves on the inward run, except when the machine is stopped with the traversing part on the outward run.

General note. This section is to be repealed as from 1 January 1997 by the Provision and Use of Work Equipment Regulations 1992, S.I. 1992 No. 2932, by which time all work equipment first provided for use before 1 January 1993 must meet the standards established in those Regulations. For equipment provided for use after 1 January 1993, the Regulations have immediate effect and this section of the Factories Act no longer applies.

(a) Factory. For definition, see s. 175.

(b) Spinning mule. See also the Spinning by Self-Acting Mules Regulations 1905.

(c) Erected, etc. As to the date upon which a factory is deemed to have been erected, reconstructed, extended or added to, see s. 176(2).

(d) Practicable. See INTRODUCTORY NOTE 5.

---

20.   Cleaning of machinery by women and young persons. A young person *(a)* shall not clean *(b)* any part of a prime mover *(c)* or of any transmission machinery *(d)* while the prime mover or transmission machinery is in motion, and shall not clean any part of any machine if the cleaning thereof would expose *(e)* the young person to risk of injury from any moving part *(f)* either of that machine or of any adjacent machinery.

(a) Young person. For definition, see s. 176(1).

(b) Clean. Whether the operation is one of cleaning is a question of fact. In *Taylor v Dawson (Mark) & Son Ltd* [1911] 1 KB 145, a child who was removing fluff from the

rollers of a moving machine, which would otherwise have become clogged, was held to be cleaning the machine although the fluff had a commercial value and was in fact sold.

(c) *Prime mover.* For definition, see s. 176(1).

(d) *Transmission machinery.* For definition, see s. 176(1).

(e) *Expose.* This word refers to the nature of the mechanism to which the employee is exposed, and if it is of a kind which may give rise to injury, even if used otherwise than in accordance with instructions, then it may be said to expose him to a risk of injury (*J H Dewhurst Ltd v Coventry Corpn* [1970] 1 QB 20, [1969] 3 All ER 1225, decided upon the cognate provisions of s. 18 (1) of the Offices, Shops and Railway Premises Act 1963).

(f) *Moving part.* Part of a machine may be a "moving part" within the meaning of this section, although it is not "in motion or use" within the meaning of s. 16 (*Kelly v John Dale Ltd* [1965] 1 QB 185, [1964] 2 All ER 497, approved in *Denyer v Charles Skipper and East Ltd* [1970] 2 All ER 382, [1970] 1 WLR 1087, CA).

---

21. Training and supervision of young persons working at dangerous machines.—(1) No young person (a) shall work at any machine (b) to which this section applies, unless he has been fully instructed as to the dangers arising in connection with it and the precautions to be observed, and—

(a) has received a sufficient training in work at the machine; or
(b) is under adequate supervision by a person who has a thorough knowledge and experience of the machine.

(2) This section applies to such machines as may be prescribed (c) by the Minister (d), being machines which in his opinion are of such a dangerous character that young persons (a) ought not to work at them unless the foregoing requirements are complied with.

General note. See *M'Cafferty v Brown* 1950 SC 300 (the section imposed no duty upon the young person and, if it did, a breach by the young person would not disentitle him from claiming damages).

(a) *Young person.* For definition, see s. 176(1).

(b) *Machine.* Sub-s. (2).

(c) *Prescribed.* The Order set out below was made under the corresponding provisions of the Factories Act 1937, and is continued in force by virtue of s. 183 and the Sixth Schedule.

(d) *The Minister.* For definition, see s. 176(1).

THE DANGEROUS MACHINES (TRAINING OF YOUNG PERSONS) ORDER, 1954
(S.I. 1954 No. 921)

The Minister of Labour and National Service (hereinafter referred to as "the Minister") by virtue of the powers conferred on him by section 21 of the Factories Act 1937, and the Transfer of Functions (Factories, &c., Acts) Order 1946, and of all other powers him enabling, hereby makes the following Order:

Citation and commencement
1.—(1) This Order may be cited as the Dangerous Machines (Training of Young Persons) Order 1954, and shall come into operation on the 1st day of August, 1954.

(2) The Interpretation Act 1889 applies to the interpretation of this Order as it applies to the interpretation of an Act of Parliament.

Revocation

2. The Dangerous Machines (Training of Young Persons) Order 1938 is hereby revoked.

Prescribed machines

3. The machines specified in the Schedule to this Order are hereby prescribed as being machines which in the opinion of the Minister are of such a dangerous character that young persons ought not to work at them unless the requirements of subsection (1) of section 21 of the Factories Act 1937 [s. 21 (1) of the 1961 Act] are complied with.

SCHEDULE

PART ONE

Machines worked with the aid of mechanical power—
1. Brick and tile presses.
2. Machines for opening or teasing in upholstery or bedding works.
3. Carding machines in use in the wood textile trades.
4. Corner staying machines.
5. Dough brakes.
6. Dough mixers.
7. Worm pressure extruding machines.
8. Gill boxes in the wool textile trades.
9. The following machines in use in laundries, that is to say—
    (a) Hydro-extractors;
    (b) Calenders;
    (c) Washing machines;
    (d) Garment presses.
10. Meat mincing machines.
11. Milling machines in use in the metal trades.
12. Pie and tart making machines.
13. Power presses, including hydraulic and pneumatic presses.
14. Loose knife punching machines.
15. Wire stitching machines.
16. Semi-automatic wood turning lathes.

PART TWO

Machines whether worked with the aid of mechanical power or not—
17. Guillotine machines.
18. Platen printing machines.

---

22. Hoists and lifts—general.—(1) Every hoist or lift *(a)* shall be of good mechanical construction, sound material and adequate strength *(b)*, and shall be properly maintained *(c)*.

(2) Every hoist or lift shall be thoroughly examined by a competent person at least once in every period of six months and a record of every such thorough examination and of the results thereof, containing the particulars required by the Lifting Plant and Equipment (Records of Test and Examination etc.)

Regulations 1992, shall be made within twenty-eight days, and any such record shall be kept and the particulars in it shall be available for inspection as if it formed part of the general register.

(3) Where the thorough examination shows that the hoist or lift cannot continue to be used with safety unless certain repairs are carried out immediately or within a specified time, the person who authenticates the record shall within twenty-eight days of the completion of the thorough examination send a copy of the particulars contained in the record to an inspector appointed by the Health and Safety Executive under section 19 of the Health and Safety at Work etc. Act 1974 who is authorised for the purposes of this provision.

(4) Every hoistway or liftway shall be efficiently protected by a substantial enclosure fitted with gates, and the enclosure shall be such as to prevent *(f)* when the gates are shut, any person falling down the way or coming into contact with any moving part of the hoist or lift.

(5) Any such gate shall, subject to subsection (6) of this section and to section twenty-five of this Act, be fitted with efficient interlocking or other devices to secure that the gate cannot be opened except when the cage or platform is at the landing and that the cage or platform cannot be moved away from the landing until the gate is closed.

(6) If in the case of a hoist or lift *(a)* constructed or reconstructed *(g)* before the thirtieth day of July, nineteen hundred and thirty-seven it is not reasonably practicable *(h)* to fit it with such devices as are mentioned in subsection (5) of this section, it shall be sufficient if the gate—

(a) is provided with such arrangements as will secure the objects of that subsection so far as is reasonably practicable *(h)*, and
(b) is kept closed and fastened except when the cage or platform is at rest at the landing.

(7) Every hoist or lift *(a)* and every such enclosure as is mentioned in subsection (4) of this section shall be so constructed as to prevent any part of any person or any goods carried in the hoist or lift from being trapped between any part of the hoist or lift and any fixed structure or between the counter-balance weight and any other moving part of the hoist or lift.

(8) There shall be marked conspicuously on every hoist or lift *(a)* the maximum working load which it can safely carry, and no load greater than that load shall be carried on any hoist or lift.

General note. In *British Railways Board v Liptrot* [1969] 1 AC 136, [1967] 2 All ER 1072, HL, the question was raised, but not decided, whether the provisions of ss. 22 to 26 of the Act (which relate to hoists, lifts, teagle openings, chains, ropes and lifting tackle) form a complete code, so as to exclude, by implication, the fencing provisions of s. 14. The decision in the case turned upon the interpretation of s. 27 (which relates to cranes and other lifting machines); it was held that the provisions of s. 14 apply to cranes and other lifting machines notwithstanding that they are specifically dealt with in s. 27. However, Lord Reid (at 156, 157, 1079) and Lord Guest (at 164, 1084) expressed the opinion that the provisions of s. 14 apply also to parts of machinery falling within ss. 22 to 26.

(a) **Hoist or lift.** As to the meaning of these words, see s. 25(1); they do not include a fork lift truck (*Oldfield v Reed and Smith Ltd* [1972] 2 All ER 104). See s. 25(2) for the exemption of continuous hoists and lifts from the requirements of sub-ss. (3) to (8); and s. 25(3) for the exemption of hoists and lifts not connected with mechanical power from the requirements of sub-ss. (5) and (6), and the application thereto of sub-ss. (2) and (4) with modifications.

(b) Of good mechanical construction, sound material and adequate strength. See INTRODUCTORY NOTE 11.

(c) Properly maintained. See INTRODUCTORY NOTE 10.

(d) Prescribed. "Prescribed" means prescribed by the Minister (s. 176(1)).

(e) General register. See s. 140.

(f) Prevent. The requirements of this subsection are absolute (*Blakely v C and H Clothing Co* [1958] 1 All ER 297, [1958] 1 WLR 378).

(g) Constructed or reconstructed. As to the date on which machinery or plant shall be deemed to have been constructed or reconstructed, see s. 176(2).

(h) Reasonably practicable. See INTRODUCTORY NOTE 5.

---

23.   Hoists and lifts used for carrying persons.—(1) The following additional requirements shall apply to hoists and lifts *(a)* used for carrying persons, whether together with goods or otherwise—

(a)   efficient automatic devices shall be provided and maintained *(b)* to prevent the cage or platform over-running;

(b)   every cage shall on each side from which access is afforded to a landing be fitted with a gate, and in connection with every such gate efficient devices shall be provided to secure that, when persons or goods are in the cage, the cage cannot be raised or lowered unless the gate is closed, and will come to rest when the gate is opened.

(2)   In the case of a hoist or lift constructed or reconstructed *(c)* before the thirtieth day of July, nineteen hundred and thirty-seven, in connection with which it is not reasonably practicable *(d)* to provide such devices as are mentioned in paragraph (b) of subsection (1) of this section it shall be sufficient if—

(a)   such arrangements are provided as will secure the objects of that paragraph so far as is reasonably practicable *(d)*; and

(b)   the gate is kept closed and fastened except when the cage is at rest or empty.

(3)   In the case of a hoist or lift used as mentioned in subsection (1) of this section which was constructed or reconstructed *(c)* after the twenty-ninth day of July, nineteen hundred and thirty-seven, where the platform or cage is suspended by rope or chain, there shall be at least two ropes or chains separately connected with the platform or cage, each rope or chain and its attachments being capable of carrying the whole weight of the platform or cage and its maximum working load, and efficient devices shall be provided and maintained *(b)* which will support the platform or cage with its maximum working load in the event of a breakage of the ropes or chains or any of their attachments.

(a) Hoist or lift. As to the meaning of these words, see s. 25(1); by s. 25(2) and (3) continuous hoists and lifts and those not connected with mechanical power are exempted from the provisions of this section. As to the application of s. 14, see the general note to s. 22.

(b) **Maintained.** For definition, see s. 176(1). See also INTRODUCTORY NOTE 10.

(c) **Constructed or reconstructed.** As to the date upon which machinery or plant shall be deemed to have been constructed or reconstructed, see s. 176(2).

(d) **Reasonably practicable.** See INTRODUCTORY NOTE 5.

---

24. Teagle openings and similar doorways.—(1) Every teagle opening or similar doorway used for hoisting or lowering goods or materials, whether by mechanical power or otherwise, shall be securely fenced *(a)* and shall be provided with a secure hand-hold on each side.

(2) The fencing shall be properly maintained *(b)* and shall, except when the hoisting or lowering of goods or materials is being carried on at the opening or doorway, be kept in position.

(a) **Securely fenced.** As to the application of s. 14, see the general note to s. 22, and as to the interpretation of "securely fenced", see the Introductory Note to ss. 12–16.

(b) **Properly maintained.** See INTRODUCTORY NOTE 10.

---

25. Exceptions and provisions supplementary to ss. 22–24.—(1) For the purposes of sections twenty-two and twenty-three of this Act, no lifting machine or appliance shall be deemed to be a hoist or lift *(a)* unless it has a platform or cage the direction of movement of which is restricted by a guide or guides.

(2) Subsections (3) to (8) of section twenty-two and section twenty-three of this Act shall not apply in the case of a continuous hoist or lift, and in such a case subsection (2) of the said section twenty-two shall have effect as if for the reference to six months there were substituted a reference to twelve months.

(3) Subsections (5) and (6) of the said section twenty-two and the said section twenty-three shall not apply in the case of a hoist or lift not connected with mechanical power; and in such a case—

(a) subsection (2) of the said section twenty-two shall have effect as if for the reference to six months there were substituted a reference to twelve months; and

(b) any gates to be fitted under subsection (4) of the said section twenty-two shall be kept closed and fastened except when the cage or platform is at rest at the landing.

(4) [*repealed*].

General note. The Order set out below was made under sub-s. (4) and is continued in force by virtue of S.I. 1974 No. 1941, reg. 7(3).

(a) **Hoist or lift.** See note *(a)* to s. 22.

THE HOISTS EXEMPTION ORDER 1962
(S.I. 1962 No. 715, as amended by S.I. 1967 No. 759 and S.I. 1983 No. 1579)

The Minister of Labour by virtue of the powers conferred on him by subsection (4) of section twenty-five of the Factories Act 1961, and of all other powers enabling him in that behalf hereby makes the following Order—

1 (1) This Order may be cited as the Hoists Exemption Order 1962, and shall come into operation on the sixteenth day of April, 1962.

(2) The Hoists Exemption Order 1938, and the Hoists Exemption (Amendment) Order 1946, are hereby revoked.

2 (1) The Interpretation Act 1889 [Interpretation Act 1978], shall apply to the interpretation of this Order as it applies to the interpretation of an Act of Parliament, and as if this Order and the Orders hereby revoked were Acts of Parliament.

(2) In this Order the expression "hoist" includes a lift and the expression "hoistway" includes a liftway.

3 As respects any class or description of hoist or hoistway specified in the first column of the Schedule to this Order, the requirements of the provisions of the Factories Act 1961, specified in the second column of the said Schedule and set opposite to that class or description shall not apply; subject however to the conditions and limitations (if any) set opposite thereto in the third column of that Schedule.

SCHEDULE

Class or description of hoist or hoistway	*Requirements of the Factories Act 1961, which shall not apply*	*Conditions or limitations (if any)*
1. Hoistways of pavement hoists, that is to say, hoists in the case of which the provision of a permanent enclosure at the top landing would obstruct a street or public place, or yard or other open space within a factory where persons are required to pass.	Subsection (4) of section twenty-two, in so far as it requires the hoistway to be protected by an enclosure and gate at or above the top landing. Except in the case of a hoist with more than one landing other than the top landing, subsections (5) and (6) of section twenty-two or subsection (3) of section twenty-five.	The hoistway shall be securely covered or securely fenced at the top landing except when and where access is required for persons, goods or materials. Every gate shall be kept closed and fastened except when the cage or platform is at the landing.
2. Mobile hoists used in various positions for the stacking of goods or materials or for loading or unloading directly to or from vehicles, which have no fixed landings above the lowest landing.	Subsections (4), (5) and (6) of section twenty-two, subsection (3) of section twenty-five and, when the maximum height of the platform above ground or floor level does not exceed 2 metres, subsection (3) of section twenty-three.	The hoist shall be so constructed that it is stable and its stability shall in all circumstances be maintained. Where the height of the platform of a hoist used for carrying persons exceeds six feet six inches above ground or floor level, the edges of the platform on which persons stand shall be protected to a height of at least 920 millimetres above the platform by suitable guard rails, lower rails

Class or description of hoist or hoistway	Requirements of the Factories Act 1961, which shall not apply	Conditions or limitations (if any)
		and toe boards of adequate strength or by other equally effective means; any gate provided shall, unless equally effective means are provided, open inwards only towards the platform and be arranged so as automatically to return to the closed and fastened position; and the button, handle or other device by which the movement of the platform is controlled shall be on the platform and be such that the platform cannot be in motion unless the control device is being held or pressed by a person on the platform.
3. Hoists which are fixed in position and which are used for stacking of goods or materials or for loading or unloading directly to or from vehicles, which have no fixed landings above the lowest landing and in the case of which the maximum height of the cage or platform above ground or floor level exceeds 2 metres.	Subsections (4), (5) and (6) of section twenty-two and subsection (3) of section twenty-five.	The hoistway shall be protected at ground or floor level by an enclosure not less than 2 metres in height and fitted with a gate or gates in connection with which subsections (5) and (6) of section twenty-two or subsection (3) of section twenty-five shall apply; and if the hoist is used for carrying persons it shall be provided with a cage.
4. Platform hoists which are fixed in position and in the case of which the maximum height of the platform above ground or floor level does not exceed 2 metres.	Subsections (4), (5) and (6) of section twenty-two, subsection (3) of section twenty-three and subsection (3) of section twenty-five.	A gate or gates or other means shall be provided to prevent any person being endangered by the underside of the platform or by any fitting attached to it.
5. Hoists used solely for lifting material directly into a machine.	Subsections (4), (5) and (6) of section twenty-two and subsection (3) of section twenty-five.	—

Class or description of hoist or hoistway	Requirements of the Factories Act 1961, which shall not apply	Conditions or limitations (if any)
6. Hoistways of hoists which are not used for carrying persons and into or from which goods or materials are not loaded or unloaded except at a height ot not less than 840 millimetres above the level of the floor or ground where loading or unloading is performed.	Subsections (5) and (6) of sections twenty-two and sub-section (3) of section twenty-five.	This exemption shall not apply to any gate unless there is a fixed enclosure not less than two feet nine inches in height below the bottom of the gate and reaching down to the level of the floor or ground; and every gate to which this exemption applies shall (i) be fitted with an efficient device to secure that the cage or platform cannot be raised or lowered unless the gate is closed, and will come to rest when the gate is opened, or (ii) where it is not reasonably practicable to fit such a device, be kept closed and fastened except when the cage or platform is at rest at the gate.
7. Hoists which are not connected with mechanical power and which are not used for carrying persons, and the enclosures of the hoistways of such hoists.	Subsection (7) of section twenty-two.	—
8. Hoists mainly used for raising materials for charging lime kilns or for charging blast furnaces in which the process of smelting iron ore is carried on.	Subsection (4) of section twenty-two, in so far as it requires a gate at the bottom landing; sub-section (5), (6) and (7) of section twenty-two; subsection (1)(b) and subsection (2) of section twenty-three; and subsection (3) of section twenty-five.	—

Class or description of hoist or hoistway	*Requirements of the Factories Act 1961, which shall not apply*	*Conditions or limitations (if any)*
9. Hoists used for raising or lowering or tipping standard-gauge or broader gauge railway rolling-stock.	Subsection (4) of section twenty-two, in so far as it requires the recognised entrances to the enclosure, being entrances through which the rolling-stock passes, to be fitted with gates; subsections (5) and (6) of section twenty-two; subsections (1)(b) and (2) of section twenty- three; and subsection (3) of section twenty-five.	So far as is reasonably practicable, means shall be provided at such entrances to the enclosure to prevent any person from falling down the hoistway or being struck by any moving part of the hoist.
10. Drop-pit hoists used for raising or lowering wheels or bogies detached from standard-gauge or broader gauge railway rolling-stock.	Subsections (4) to (8) of section twenty-two and section twenty-three.	—
11. Hoists in the case of which the doors of the hoistway are of solid construction and the interior surfaces of the said doors and of the hoistway opposite to any side of the cage in which there is an opening are, throughout the height of travel of the cage, smooth and flush with each other save for any recess designed for working purposes and not more than 13 millimetres in depth, and hand grips not exceeding 26 millimetres in depth provided for closing doors and so constructed as to prevent trapping.	Subsections (1)(b) and (2) of section twenty-three.	—

Class or description of hoist or hoistway	Requirements of the Factories Act 1961, which shall not apply	Conditions or limitations (if any)
12. Hoistways of hoists into or from which goods or materials are loaded or unloaded automatically and to the platform or cage of which there is no access for persons.	Subsection (4) of section twenty-two in so far as it requires a gate at the openings in the enclosure where goods or materials are loaded or unloaded automatically.	Means shall be provided at the loading and unloading openings in the enclosure to prevent, so far as is reasonably practicable, any person falling down the hoistway or coming into contact with any moving part of the hoist.
13. Hoistways of hoists which are not used for carrying persons and on which the goods or materials stacked on the platform or in the case are loaded or unloaded with the top layer of the stack at landing level.	Subsections (5) and (6) of section twenty-two and subsection (3) of section twenty-five.	This exemption shall not apply to any gate unless there is a fixed enclosure not less than 840 millimetres in height below the bottom of the gate and reaching down to the level of the floor or ground, and unless any such gate can only be opened or remain open when the floor of the cage or platform is at the landing level or not more than 1.5 metres below that level; and when the gate is open the cage or platform shall not be capable of being moved more than 300 millimetres at one time and at a speed not greater than 0.12 metres per second and provision shall be made to prevent any person being trapped by the top of the cage. The arrangements shall be such that when the gate is open the platform or cage cannot be in motion unless the button, handle, or other device by which the movement of the cage or platform is controlled is being held or pressed by a person close to the gate.
14. Hoists and hoistways the landing and cage entrances of which are protected by lattice gates.	Subsections (4) and (7) of section twenty-two in so far as they relate to the protection to be	The gates when shut shall extend to the full height and width of the entrance openings and, except in the case of gates installed

Class or description of hoist or hoistway	Requirements of the Factories Act 1961, which shall not apply	Conditions or limitations (if any)
	provided by the gates.	before the coming into operation of this Order, shall have no openings exceeding 65 millimetres in width. Measures shall be taken to prevent the access of feet through the cage gate or the landing gate into the hoistway, and to prevent the access of fingers through the landing gate to the inter-locking mechanism and control devices in the cage or on the platform.

---

26. Chains, ropes and lifting tackle.—(1) The following provisions shall be complied with as respects every chain, rope or lifting tackle *(a)* used *(b)* for the purpose of raising *(c)* or lowering persons, goods or materials:—

(a) no chain, rope or lifting tackle shall be used unless it is of good construction, sound material, adequate strength *(d)* and free from patent defect;

(b) subject to subsection (2) of this section, a table showing the safe working loads of every kind and size of chain, rope or lifting tackle in use, and, in the case of a multiple sling, the safe working load at different angles of the legs, shall be posted in the store in which the chains, ropes or lifting tackle are kept, and in prominent positions on the premises, and no chain, rope or lifting tackle not shown in the table shall be used;

(c) no chain, rope or lifting tackle shall be used for any load exceeding its safe working load as shown by the table mentioned in paragraph (b) of this subsection or marked as mentioned in subsection (2) of this section;

(d) all chains, ropes and lifting tackle in use shall be thoroughly examined by a competent person at least once in every period of six months or at such greater intervals as the Minister *(e)* may prescribe;

(e) no chain, rope or lifting tackle, except a fibre rope or a fibre rope sling, shall be taken into use in any factory for the first time in that factory *(f)*, unless it has been tested and thoroughly examined by a competent person and a record of the test and thorough examination and of the results thereof, containing the particulars required by the Lifting Plant and Equipment (Records of Test and Examination etc.) Regulations 1992, has been obtained and the particulars in that record are kept available for inspection;

(f) every chain and lifting tackle except a rope sling shall, unless of a class or description exempted *(g)* by certificate of the chief inspector upon the ground that it is made of such material or so constructed that it cannot be subjected to heat treatment without risk of damage or that it has been subjected to some form of heat treatment (other than annealing) approved by him, be annealed at least once in every fourteen months or, in the case of chains or slings of 13 millimetres bar or smaller, or chains used in connection with molten metal or molten slag, in every six months, except that chains and lifting tackle not in regular use need be annealed only when necessary;

(g) a record containing the particulars required by the Lifting Plant and Equipment (Records of Test and Examination etc). Regulations 1992, shall be kept in respect of all such chains, ropes or lifting tackle, except fibre rope slings.

(2) Paragraph (b) of subsection (1) of this section shall not apply in relation to any lifting tackle *(a)* if its safe working load or, in the case of a multiple sling, the safe working load at different angles of the legs is plainly marked upon it.

(3) In this section "lifting tackle" means chain slings, rope slings, rings, hooks, shackles and swivels.

General note. As to the application of s. 14, see the general note to s. 22. Similar provisions are applied to chains etc., by the Shipbuilding and Ship-repairing Regulations 1960 and the Construction (Lifting Operations) Regulations 1961.

(a) Lifting tackle. See the definition in sub-s. (3).

(b) Used. Lifting tackle is being "used" within the meaning of this section even if it has not been provided for the purpose and the person using it is knowingly misusing it (*Barry v Cleveland Bridge and Engineering Co Ltd* [1963] 1 All ER 192).

(c) Raising. A load may be "raised" although it is not a free load of calculable weight (*Ball v Richard Thomas and Baldwins Ltd* [1968] 1 All ER 389, [1968] 1 WLR 192, CA, in which the breaking away of solidified scab from a floor by means of a crane was held to involve "raising").

(d) Of good construction, sound material, adequate strength. See INTRODUCTORY NOTE 11.

(e) The Minister. For definition, see s. 176(1).

(f) Factory. For definition, see s. 175.

(g) Exemptions. By Certificate of Exemption No. 1 the following exemptions from sub-s. (1)(f) have been made:

(1) Chains made of malleable cast iron;
(2) Plate link chains;
(3) Chains, rings, hooks, shackles and swivels made of steel or of any non-ferrous metal;
(4) Pitched chains working on sprocket or pocketed wheels;
(5) Rings, hooks, shackles and swivels permanently attached to pitched chains, pulley blocks or weighing machines;
(6) Hooks and swivels having screw-threaded parts of ball-bearings or other case-hardened parts;
(7) Socket shackles secured to wire ropes by white metal capping;
(8) Bordeaux connections;
(9) Any chain or lifting tackle which has been subjected to the heat treatment known as "normalising" instead of annealing.

(Form 661, August 1938.)

---

27. Cranes and other lifting machines.—(1) All parts and working gear, whether fixed or movable, including the anchoring and fixing appliances, of every lifting machine *(a)* shall be of good construction, sound material, adequate strength and free from patent defect *(b)*, and shall be properly maintained *(c)*.

(2) All such parts and gear shall be thoroughly examined by a competent person at least once in every period of fourteen months and a record shall be kept of every such thorough examination and of the results thereof, containing the particulars required by the Lifting Plant and Equipment (Records of Test and Examination etc.) Regulations 1992, and where the thorough examination shows that the lifting machine can not continue to be used with safety unless certain repairs are carried out immediately or within a specified time, the person who authenticates the record shall within twenty-eight days of the completion of the thorough examination send a copy of the particulars in the record to an inspector *(d)* appointed by the Health and Safety Executive under section 19 of the Health and Safety at Work etc. Act 1974 who is authorised for the purpose of this provision.

(3) All rails on which a travelling crane moves and every track on which the carriage of a transporter or runway moves shall be of proper size and adequate strength *(b)* and have an even running surface; and any such rails or track shall be properly laid, adequately supported or suspended and properly maintained *(c)*.

(4) There shall be plainly marked on every lifting machine *(a)* its safe working load or loads, except that in the case of a jib crane so constructed that the safe working load may be varied by the raising or lowering of the jib, there shall be attached thereto either an automatic indicator of safe working loads or a table indicating the safe working loads at corresponding inclinations of the jib or corresponding radii of the load.

(5) No lifting machine *(a)* shall, except for the purpose of a test, be loaded beyond the safe working load as marked or indicated under subsection (4) of this section.

(6) No lifting machine *(a)* shall be taken into use in any factory for the first time in that factory *(e)* unless it has been tested and all such parts and working gear of the machine as are specified in subsection (1) of this section have been thoroughly examined by a competent person and a record of the test and thorough examination and of the results thereof, containing the particulars required by the Lifting Plant and Equipment (Records of Test and Examination etc.) Regulations 1992, has been obtained and the particulars in that record are kept available for inspection.

(7) If any person is employed or working on or near the wheeltrack of an overhead travelling crane *(f)* in any place where he would be liable to be struck by the crane, effective measures shall be taken by warning the driver of the crane or otherwise to ensure that the crane does not approach within 6 metres of that place *(g)*.

(8) If any person is employed or working otherwise than mentioned in subsection (7) of this section but in a place above floor level where he would be liable to be struck by an overhead travelling crane *(f)*, or by any load carried by such a crane, effective measures shall be taken to warn him of the approach of the crane, unless his work is so connected with or dependent on the movements of the crane as to make a warning unnecessary.

(9) In this section "lifting machine" means a crane, crab, winch, teagle, pulley block, gin wheel, transporter or runway.

General note. This section does not contain a comprehensive statement of the statutory duties applicable to cranes and lifting machines, so that, in the appropriate case, the duties imposed by s. 14 (fencing) also apply (*British Railways Board v Liptrot* [1969] 1 AC 136, [1967] 2 All ER 1072, HL, approving *Carrington v John Summers & Sons Ltd* [1957] 1 All ER 457, [1957] 1 WLR 504).

(a) **Lifting machine.** See the definition in sub-s. (9). A fork truck is not a "lifting machine" within this definition (*Walker v Andrew Mitchell & Co* 1982 SLT 266n). Electrical contactors, the function of which is to control a crane are part of a lifting machine (*Evans v Sanderson Bros and Newbould Ltd* (1968) 4 KIR 115, CA, not following dicta in *Gatehouse v John Summers & Sons Ltd* [1953] 2 All ER 117, [1953] 1 WLR 742, CA).

(b) **Of good construction, sound material, adequate strength and free from patent defect.** In *McNeil v Dickson & Mann Ltd* 1957 SC 345, it was held that it was irrelevant whether a defect was patent or latent since the words "free from patent defect" do not qualify the requirements of good construction, sound material and adequate strength, as to the meaning of which see INTRODUCTORY NOTE 11.

(c) **Properly maintained.** See INTRODUCTORY NOTE 10.

(d) **Inspector.** For definition, see s. 176(1).

(e) **Factory.** For definition, see s. 175.

(f) **Overhead travelling crane.** In *Carrington v John Summers & Sons Ltd* [1957] 1 All ER 457, [1957] 1 WLR 504, it was held that the words "overhead travelling crane" meant a crane that travelled overhead and were not applicable to a crane which ran upon rails at ground level although the crab of the crane travelled on an overhead girder.

(g) **Within six metres.** In *Lotinga v North Eastern Marine Engineering Co (1938) Ltd* [1941] 2 KB 399, [1941] 3 All ER 1, a workman was killed by movement of a large overhead crane whilst he was working near the wheel track of the crane. A notice was affixed that the crane must not approach within 20 feet (the former distance under the subsection) of men working and that men working near the track must notify the crane man of their presence before starting work. It was held that the duty to take effective measures was an absolute one and on the facts the respondents had failed in this duty.

In *Holmes v Hadfields Ltd* [1944] 1 KB 275, [1944] 1 All ER 235, CA, a workman with others was working a ratchet drill on a platform about 16 feet above the floor above which overhead cranes were employed. As one of the cranes approached the workman climbed down to a girder halfway between the platform and the floor and signalled the crane driver to proceed. The cab of the crane hit the drill which had been left in position and it fell and injured the workman. It was held that s. 24(7) (now s. 27(7) of the 1961 Act) imposed an absolute duty. The crane came within 20 feet of the place where the workman was employed and the defendants could not excuse themselves by showing that at the precise moment when the crane moved he was in a place where he was not liable to be struck by the crane. See also *Hunter v Glenfield & Kennedy* 1947 SC 536.

---

28. Floors, passages and stairs.—(1) All floors, steps, stairs, passages and gangways (*a*) shall be of sound construction (*b*) and properly maintained (*c*) and shall, so far as is reasonably practicable (*d*) be kept free from any obstruction (*e*) and from any substance likely to cause persons to slip (*f*).

(2) For every staircase (*g*) in a building or affording a means of exit from a building, a substantial hand-rail shall be provided and maintained (*h*), which, if the staircase has an open side, shall be on that side, and in the case of a staircase having two open sides or of a staircase which, owing to the nature of its construction or the condition (*i*) of the surface of the steps or other special

circumstances, is specially liable to cause accidents *(j)*, such a hand-rail shall be provided and maintained *(h)* on both sides.

(3) Any open side of a staircase shall also be guarded by the provision and maintenance *(h)* of a lower rail or other effective means.

(4) All openings in floors *(k)* shall be securely fenced *(l)*, except in so far as the nature of the work renders such fencing impracticable *(m)*.

(5) All ladders *(n)* shall be soundly constructed *(b)* and properly maintained *(c)*.

General note. This section is to be repealed as from 1 January 1996 by the Workplace (Health, Safety and Welfare) Regulations 1992, S.I. 1992 No. 3004, for workplaces in existence on 31 December 1992. Those Regulations will apply to those workplaces from the former date. Workplaces coming into use after 31 December 1992 and modifications, extensions and conversions started after 31 December 1992 to existing workplaces must conform to those Regulations as soon as they come into use. However, reg. 17(5) of those Regulations provides that reg. 17(2) (requiring the suitability of traffic routes) shall apply, so far as is reasonably practicable, to all workplaces, old and new.

(a) **Floors, steps . . . etc.** The subject matter of this section has been the subject of much controversy. In holding that a dry dock was not an "opening in a floor" within the meaning of s. 25(3) of the 1937 Act (now s. 28(4) of the 1961 Act), Somervell, LJ, in *Bath v British Transport Commission* [1954] 2 All ER 542, [1954] 1 WLR 1013, said "Where words are . . . perfectly familiar all one can do is to say whether or not one regards them as apt to cover or describe the circumstances in question in any particular case", and in *Johnston v Colvilles* 1966 SLT 30, Ct of Sess, it was held that "floor" meant the ordinary floor of a factory which was used by those employed in the ordinary course of their employment. See the following cases: *Hosking v De Havilland Aircraft Co Ltd* [1949] 1 All ER 540 (plank across duct held to be a gangway); *Morris v Port of London Authority* (1950) 84 Ll L Rep 564 (floor of a gantry held to be within the section); *Taylor v R & H Green and Silley Weir Ltd* (1950) 84 Ll L Rep 570 (affirmed by the CA [1951] 1 Lloyd's Rep 345) (sill round inside of dry dock held to be a floor); *Harrison v Metropolitan-Vickers Electrical Co Ltd* [1954] 1 All ER 404, [1954] 1 WLR 324 (sand bed of foundry held to be a floor and an excavation in it an "opening in a floor"); *Tate v Swan, Hunter and Wigham Richardson Ltd* [1958] 1 All ER 150, [1958] 1 WLR 39 (planks laid across steelwork of crane gantry held not be a floor); *Newberry v Joseph Westwood & Co Ltd* [1960] 2 Lloyd's Rep 37 ("mother earth" held not to be a floor, passage or gangway); *Sullivan v Hall, Russell & Co* 1964 SLT 192 (unmade earthern surface of a woodyard held not to be a floor); *Thornton v Fisher and Ludlow Ltd* [1968] 2 All ER 241, [1968] 1 WLR 655, CA (30 ft. wide roadway in the open not a floor, passage or gangway); *Devine v Costain Concrete Co Ltd* 1979 SLT (Notes) 97 (bottom of duct in factory floor, upon which men worked, held to be a floor); *Sanders v F H Lloyd & Co Ltd* [1982] ICR 360 (pit 30″ by 17″ by 8″ deep held to be an opening in a floor; the phrase is not to be restricted to a hole of sufficient size and depth to permit someone to fall into it, or to permit it to be railed off); *MacKay v Drybrough & Co Ltd* 1986 SLT 624n (inclines to the view that a lifted trapdoor would be an opening in a floor); *Allen v Avon Rubber Co Ltd* [1986] ICR 695, CA (typical loading bay at end of factory floor held not to be an opening in a floor; *Harper v Mander and Germain Ltd* (1992) Times, 28 December, CA (duckboard held to be floor, passage or gangway).

(b) **Of sound construction.** This requirement is, it is submitted, analogous to the requirement of good construction contained in other sections of the Act, as to which see INTRODUCTORY NOTE 11. In order to be of sound construction a floor must be of such construction as to withstand both the stress imposed upon it when used for its intended purpose and such further stress as may be imposed in circumstances which may foreseeably occur (*Mayne v Johnstone and Cumbers* [1947] 2 All ER 159).

(c) Properly maintained. In this context "properly maintained" refers to the structural conditions of floors, etc. The criterion is safety, which is a question of degree dependent upon the particular facts (*Payne v Weldless Steel Tube Co Ltd* [1956] 1 QB 196, [1955] 3 All ER 612, CA). There may be a breach of this requirement, which is absolute, where lack of safety arises from some permanent fitting or from something put upon the floor so that it may properly be regarded as part of the floor, although not incorporated in it, but there is no breach where the lack of safety arises from some transient and exceptional condition (*Latimer v AEC Ltd* [1953] AC 643, [1953] 2 All ER 449, HL). See also INTRODUCTORY NOTE 10.

(d) Reasonably practicable. See INTRODUCTORY NOTE 5.

(e) Obstruction. See INTRODUCTORY NOTE 13.

(f) Substance likely to cause persons to slip. Once it is proved that there is a slippery substance on a factory floor on which the plaintiff has slipped it is then for the defendants to show that they have taken all reasonably practicable precautions, first, to prevent that substance being on the floor at all and then, secondly, to clear it off the floor (*Johnston v Caddies Wainwright Ltd* [1983] ICR 407, CA). In *Taylor v Gestetner Ltd* (1967) 2 KIR 133, it was held that water might be such a substance. In *Dorman Long (Steel) Ltd v Bell* [1964] 1 All ER 617, [1964] 1 WLR 333, HL, it was held that where metal plates placed temporarily on the floor became slippery when slag dust collected on them there had been a breach of this subsection, notwithstanding that the slippery substances was not itself in contact with the floor.

(g) Staircase. See the general remarks on interpretation in note *(a)*, above; see also *Kimpton v Steel Co of Wales Ltd* [1960] 2 All ER 274, [1960] 1 WLR 527, CA (three steps from floor to part of a machine held not to be a staircase).

(h) Maintained. For definition, see s. 176(1). See also INTRODUCTORY NOTE 10.

(i) Condition. It is submitted that "condition" in this context includes both the structural condition, as where steps have worn smooth, and a condition arising from the frequent presence thereon of slippery substances.

(j) Special circumstances; is specially liable to cause accidents. In *Harris v Rugby Portland Cement Co Ltd* [1955] 2 All ER 500, [1955] 1 WLR 648, the Court of Appeal held that a special circumstance meant something continually repeated or so frequently repeated that permanent protection is necessary, and that "specially liable" meant more than usually liable to cause accidents, so that a long accident-free history is relevant.

(k) Openings in floors. See note *(a)*, above, and *Harrison v Metropolitan Vickers Electrical Co Ltd* there cited.

(l) Securely fenced. It is submitted that "securely fenced" in this context has the same meaning as in the context of fencing dangerous parts of machinery, as to which see the Introductory Note to ss. 12–16. Fencing includes railing off, covering or otherwise protecting the opening against the possibility of anyone falling into it (*Sanders v F H Lloyd & Co Ltd* [1982] ICR 360).

(m) Impracticable. See INTRODUCTORY NOTE 5. In the context of s. 28(1) the question is whether it is reasonably practicable to keep the floor free of obstruction, not whether it is reasonably practicable to adopt any particular preventive measures (*Gillies v Glynwed Foundries Ltd* 1977 SLT 97).

(n) Ladders. This expression includes a step-ladder (*Ross v British Steel Corpn (Colvilles) Ltd* 1973 SLT (Notes) 34). In *Cole v Blackstone & Co Ltd* [1943] KB 615, it was held that the duty imposed by sub-s. (5) is absolute and cannot be discharged by the occupier taking all practicable steps to see that a ladder is of sound construction and properly maintained.

29. Safe means of access and safe place of employment.—(1) There shall, so far as is reasonably practicable *(a)*, be provided *(b)* and maintained safe means of access to every place at which any person has *(c)* at any time to work, and every such place *(d)* shall, so far as is reasonably practicable, be made and kept safe for any person working there.

(2) Where any person has to work *(b)* at a place *(d)* from which he will be liable to fall *(e)* a distance more than two metres, then unless the place is one which affords secure foothold *(f)* and, where necessary, secure hand-hold *(f)*, means shall be provided, so far as is reasonably practicable *(a)*, by fencing or otherwise, for ensuring his safety.

General note. This section is to be repealed as from 1 January 1996 by the Workplace (Health, Safety and Welfare) Regulations 1992, S.I. 1992 No. 3004, for workplaces in existence on 31 December 1992. Those Regulations will apply to those workplaces from the former date. Workplaces coming into use after 31 December 1992 and modifications, extensions and conversions started after 31 December 1992 to existing workplaces must conform to those Regulations as soon as they come into use. However reg. 17(5) of those Regulations provides that reg. 17(2) (requiring the suitability of traffic routes) shall apply, so far as is reasonably practicable, to all workplaces, old and new. The duties imposed by this section are of general application, but are qualified by the words "so far as is reasonably practicable" (as to the meaning of which see INTRODUCTORY NOTE 5). A place in a factory may attract the operation both of s. 28 and s. 29, but if the occupier has satisfied s. 28, then it follows that he has satisfied s. 29 also (*Ashdown v Jonas Woodhead & Sons Ltd* [1975] KILR 27, CA).

Subsection (1) of the corresponding section of the 1937 Act has been the subject of much controversy, and it may be that the qualified obligation to make and keep safe the working place itself, added by s. 5 of the 1959 Act, has increased, rather than diminished, the importance of the distinction, which is discussed below, between the means of access and the place of work.

With regard to "means of access", it is first of all to be noted that the duty applies solely to the means of access "to every place at which any person has . . . to work", and that this does not include, for example, a passage leading to a canteen, whether it is being used to go to, or to return from, the canteen (*Davies v De Havilland Aircraft Co Ltd* [1951] 1 KB 50, [1950] 2 All ER 582); or the way to a lavatory (*Rose v Colville's Ltd* 1950 SLT (Notes) 72); and is to be distinguished from the place of work itself (*Dorman Long & Co Ltd v Hillier* [1951] 1 All ER 357 and *Prince v Carrier Engineering Co Ltd* [1951] 1 Lloyd's Rep 401). Such a distinction, however, may be a fine and difficult one, as in *Hopwood v Rolls Royce Ltd* (1947) 176 LT 514 and *Whitby v Burt, Boulton and Hayward Ltd* [1947] KB 918, [1947] 2 All ER 324; and any given place may be both a means of access and a place of work; see *Hopwood v Rolls Royce Ltd,* above; *Rolland v United Glass Bottle Manufacturing Co Ltd* 1959 SLT (Notes) 10; *Gardiner v Admiralty Comrs* [1964] 2 All ER 93, [1964] 1 WLR 590, HL; and *Armstrong v James Miller & Partners* 1964 SLT (Notes) 42. In such a case, said Devlin J in *Dorman Long Ltd v Hillier,* above, "it is necessary to see for which purpose it is being used, or may require to be used, at the material time". The same place cannot, however, be both the employee's place of work and the means of access to his place of work at the same time (*Taylor v Coalite Oils and Chemicals Ltd* (1967) 3 KIR 315, CA). See too *Sloan v Almond Fabrication Ltd* 1992 SLT 114n: ladder to driving cab of crane on factory premises held to be means of access (and unsafe because not equipped with protective hoops).

Secondly, it must be regarded as authoritatively decided that the obligation to maintain is, so far as is reasonably practicable, to maintain the means of access in a structurally sound condition, rather than to maintain the safety of the means of access by eliminating transient and exceptional conditions or temporary obstruction (*Levesley v Thomas Firth and John Brown Ltd* [1953] 2 All ER 866, [1953] 1 WLR 1206, CA and see *Nisbet v J W Ward Ltd* 1968 SLT (Notes) 73). In the *Levesley* case Denning LJ held that the decision of the House of Lords in *Latimer v AEC Ltd* [1953] AC 643, [1953] 2 All ER 449 as to the meaning to be given to "properly maintained" in s. 25 of the 1937 Act (s. 28 of the 1961 Act) made necessary a reconsideration of those cases under s. 26 of that Act (s. 29 of the 1961 Act) in which the duty has been equated with "maintain the safety of the access"; see, for example, *Callaghan v Fred Kidd & Son (Engineers) Ltd* [1944] 1 KB 560 and, since, *Geddes v United Wires Ltd* 1974 SLT 170, in which the duty to maintain a safe means of access was held to be a continuing duty to maintain the means of access as safe in its condition, location and structure. On this topic, see also *Thomas v Bristol Aeroplane Co Ltd* [1954] 2 All ER 1 (no duty at all times to guard against the ordinary incidents of daily life resulting from the vagaries of the weather; compare *Woodward v Renold Ltd* [1980] ICR 387, in which liability under s. 29(1) was established on the ground that the defendants had instituted no system at all to deal with icy conditions in a factory car park). Note, too, *Carragher v Singer Manufacturing Co Ltd* [1974] SLT (Notes) 28: means of access could be unsafe if excess noise caused occupational deafness. The court held that the lack of safety could arise from the proximity of the means of access to or preserve in the means of access of things that cause danger, though not themselves part of that means.

Further questions which arise under the first part of sub-s. (1) are (i) whether safe means of access have been "provided" when safe and suitable means, such as ladders, are, to the knowledge of the workman, available for his use within a reasonable distance and (ii) whether the temporary removal of a safe means of access, such as a ladder, from a platform upon which a person is at work, but only to a place from which he can conveniently recall it at need, amounts to a breach of the duty to provide and maintain. Since, on the authority of *Levesley's* case, above, it can no longer be said that there is a duty to maintain the safety of the access, it is submitted that both the above questions turn solely upon the meaning to be given to "provide", and that the decision of the Divisional Court in *Farquhar v Chance Bros Ltd* (1951) 115 JP 469, upon facts similar to question (i), and of Devlin J in *Finch v Telegraph Construction and Maintenance Co Ltd* [1949] 1 All ER 452 (a case under s. 49 of the 1937 Act), are authority for the proposition that in neither case has there been a breach of sub-s. (1); see INTRODUCTORY NOTE 9.

Where more than one means of access is provided each must, it is submitted, be safe; but if a safe means of access is provided, the fact that a workman chooses to use something else, which is unsafe, as a means of access does not make the occupier liable unless that also was provided as a means of access. These propositions receive support in principle from the reasoning in two decisions under the Docks Regulations 1934 (*Cottrell v Vianda Steamship Co Ltd* [1955] 2 Lloyd's Rep 450 and *Lowe v Scruttons Ltd* [1953] 1 Lloyd's Rep 342). But in *Kirkpatrick v Scott Lithgow Ltd* 1987 SCLR 567, it was said that where a safe route is available but the employee is injured using another one then the employer will be liable if it was reasonably foreseeable that the employee would use that (second) route.

It was suggested above that the distinction between the means of access and the place of work may be of greater importance, now that obligations have been imposed with regard to the place of work, than it was when the duty was confined to the means of access. That this is likely to be so is shown by a consideration of the respective duties— on the one hand to provide safe means of access and to maintain it in the sense of *Latimer's* and *Levesley's* cases, above, so that, for example, the presence of a film of oil is not a breach of sub-s. (1)—on the other hand to make and keep the working place safe, a duty which, it is submitted, would entail the elimination of any danger, however transitory or exceptional, within the limits of reasonable practicability. This statement of the respective duties was approved by Lloyd J in *Cox v H C B Angus Ltd* [1981] ICR 683. As to how the distinction is to be drawn, see the cases cited above and, in particular, *Dorman Long Ltd v Hillier*, above.

Whether or not a workplace or means of access is "safe" is a strict test, to be determined without reference to the reasonable foreseeability of injury (see *Larner v British Steel plc* [1993] 4 All ER 102, [1993] IRLR 278. CA: otherwise the statutory protection would be no greater than that for negligence at common law. The matter is a question of fact (see Peter Gibson J in *Larner* at p. 111). Probably a court should have regard to similar considerations as are applied to the question, whether a part of a machine is "dangerous" within the meaning of s. 14, as to which see the Introductory

Note to ss. 12–16. In particular, if a place is safe to start with, and the only thing which renders it unsafe is the temporary use of dangerous equipment, that does not involve a breach of sub-s. (1), although the operation of permanent equipment or the carrying on of permanent activities may well have their impact upon the question of whether the place has been made safe (*Evans v Sant* [1975] QB 626, [1975] 1 All ER 294, decided upon the cognate provisions of the Construction (Working Places) Regulations 1966, reg. 6). See also, *McCarthy v Coldair Ltd* [1951] 2 TLR 1226, CA and *Trott v W E Smith (Erectors) Ltd* [1957] 3 All ER 500, [1957] 1 WLR 1154, CA. A workplace may, of course, be unsafe owing to prolonged exposure to a condition (such as excessive noise) which would not be dangerous if exposure were shorter: e.g. *Baxter v Harland & Wolff plc* [1990] IRLR 516 (NI CA).

Finally, it is to be noted that the duty to provide and maintain safe means of access is owed by the occupier to any person who has to work on the premises, including an independent contractor and his servants (*Whitby v Burt, Boulton and Hayward Ltd*, above; *Lavender v Diamints Ltd* [1949] 1 KB 585, [1949] 1 All ER 532, CA; *Wigley v British Vinegars Ltd* [1964] AC 307, [1962] 3 All ER 161, HL). This is so whether or not the independent contractor is also under a similar but independent duty, for example, under the Building (Safety, Health and Welfare) Regulations 1948 (*Whincup v Joseph Woodhead & Sons (Engineers) Ltd* [1951] 1 All ER 387) although in such a case if the independent contractor's duty is broken the occupier will usually be granted contribution or an indemnity from him (see, for example, *Hosking v De Havilland Aircraft Co Ltd* [1949] 1 All ER 540). In *Flannigan v British Dyewood Co Ltd* 1970 SLT 285, however, a fireman was unable to invoke s. 29(1) after being injured whilst engaged in fighting a fire. The rationale for exclusion appears to be that "in such circumstances the occupiers have . . . no means of predicting or choosing or controlling the fireman's place of work whereas in the case of a sub-contractor on his servant, they have at least some degree of control over his movements". For provisions similar to those of sub-s. (1) see the Construction (Working Places) Regulations 1966, reg. 6 and the Shipbuilding and Ship-repairing Regulations 1960, regs. 6–13; and for provisions similar to those of sub-s. (2), see the Shipbuilding and Ship-repairing Regulations 1960, reg. 24.

*(a) **Reasonably practicable.*** The meaning of this expression is discussed in INTRODUC-TORY NOTE 5. To escape liability, the employer must plead and prove that it was not reasonably practicable to keep the workplace safe (*Larner v British Steel plc* [1993] 4 All ER 102, CA). In the context of s. 29, Diplock LJ, in *Taylor v Coalite Oils and Chemicals Ltd* (1967) 3 KIR 315 at 320, said that this expression meant "reasonably practicable for the occupier upon whom the duty to make and keep the working place safe is imposed. In so far as Lord Denning MR's dictum in *Braham v J Lyons & Co Ltd* [1962] 1 WLR 1048 at 1051 suggests that it means reasonably practicable for anyone, including an independent contractor, we think with great respect that this is wrong. Nor do the judgments of the Inner House in the Scots case of *McWilliams v Sir William Arrol & Co Ltd* 1961 SC 134, which Lord Denning MR cited as authority for his dictum, go far enough to support it. All that they decided was that lack of knowledge by the occupier of the risk caused by the operations of an independent contractor in the factory did not of itself constitute a defence. The occupier had made no attempt to acquire such knowledge. The occupier's duty is to take all measures which it is reasonably practicable for him to take to make and keep the working place safe. In so far as they are measures taken for that purpose, he may (and, if he is a corporation, he must) entrust their devising and their execution to others, and, as far as they are not properly devised or executed by those so entrusted, the occupier is liable. If measures properly devised for that purpose are executed negligently by those entrusted by the occupier with their execution, with the consequence that the working place is not made and kept safe, the occupier is liable, but that is not vicarious liability for the negligence of his servants; it is direct liability arising from the fact that the measures which it was his duty to take have not in the result been taken. If, however, the measures properly devised and executed fail to avert injury to a person working at a working place because of the act of someone other than those to whom he has entrusted their execution, which, even though foreseeable, it is not reasonably practicable to prevent or render harmless, the occupier is not liable for breach of

statutory duty. If the act which causes the measures to be ineffective to avert injury is a negligent act of a servant of the occupier, he may be vicariously liable at common law for that negligence, but that is not in itself a breach of statutory duty. This does not mean that the measures which it is the statutory duty of the occupier to take do not include all practicable precautions to prevent or render harmless acts rendering a working place unsafe which it is reasonably foreseeable may be done by any person in the factory other than those entrusted with the execution of the measures, and that is so whether the person by whom the act is done is a servant of the occupier or not". For an example of the application of the test, see *Gitsham v C H Pearce & Sons plc* [1992] PIQR P57, CA, in which the Court of Appeal thought it "perfectly correct" to approach the matter by considering, first, whether the system was proper and, second, whether it was properly carried out (the case concerned the clearing of snow and ice from walkways).

(b) *Provided.* When an employee uses a means of access other than one supplied by the employer, there is no provision of that access by the employer within s. 29(1) unless the employer has permitted that means of access to be so used by adopting it; for example, by knowingly allowing its use. It is not sufficient that the employer may reasonably anticipate that a man may, for his own purposes, use a means of access not supplied or adopted by the employer (*Smith v British Aerospace* [1982] ICR 98, CA).

(c) *Has ... to work.* Any orders or compulsion to work are clearly within this expression (see *Kendrick v Cozens and Sutcliffe* (1968) 4 KIR 469, CA and *Davies v John G Stein* 1965 JC 17); and the occupier is liable even if the order to work in a place is made by an independent contractor: see *Dexter v Tenby Electrical Accessories Ltd* [1991] Crim LR 839. Less clear is whether the phrase covers the performance of any duties that are reasonably incidental to the work of the employee (per Lloyd LJ in *Dexter*, doubting the narrower test of *Kendrick*; but c.f. *Walsh v Crown Decorative Products Ltd* [1993] PIQR P194, CA in which Bedlam LJ followed *Kendrick* and ruled that the words implied that the task needed to be done from the place at which the employee was working).

(d) *A place.* This does not simply mean the floor space within a factory; regard must also be had to the permanently installed machinery and the regular activities carried out in the factory: *Yates v Rockwell Graphic Systems Ltd* [1988] ICR 8 (lathe coolant causing dermatitis in operator). The term extends to dangers which arise from the atmosphere or nature of the place in which the employee works and not merely the fabric of the workplace: see e.g. *Baxter v Harland & Wolff plc* [1990] IRLR 516, Northern Ireland, CA (excess noise in workplace causing deafness); and *Carragher v Singer Manufacturing Co Ltd* 1974 SLT (Notes) 28. But the danger must come from something that makes the place itself dangerous, and not merely from something that poses a risk to an individual employee (see e.g. *Bowman v Harland & Wolff* [1992] IRLR 349: calking hammer causing injury and operated by individual employee did not make place unsafe; and *Harkins v McCluskey* 1987 SLT 289.) The place from which a person using a ladder is liable to fall is the ladder, so that if this, properly positioned and unlikely to slip, provides secure foothold and, where necessary, secure hand-hold there is no breach of this requirement (*Wigley v British Vinegars Ltd* [1964] AC 307, [1962] 3 All ER 161, HL). Similarly, the cab of a fire engine in which an electrician is working may be a place of work (*Cox v H C B Angus Ltd* [1981] ICR 683); but c.f. *McFaulds v Reed Corrugated Cases Ltd* 1993 SLT 670n, in which a forklift truck driven by an employee both inside and outside a factory was held to fall outside the term, being treated as a "moveable tool employed within the place" and not the place itself. The top of boxes on which a welder had been working was held to be a place of work in *Harrison v R B Tennent Ltd* 1992 SLT 1060n (the platform onto which he lowered himself in order to descend was thus a means of egress).

(e) *Liable to fall.* The question, whether a person will be liable to fall more than two metres is, it is submitted, a question of fact to be considered objectively without regard to the mental or physical condition of the person at work.

(f) *Secure foothold ... secure handhold.* The test of whether a foothold or handhold is "secure" is the test formulated by du Parcq J, in *Walker v Bletchley Flettons Ltd* [1937] 1 All ER 170 at 175, namely, is it secure to an experienced workman acting in a way in which such a person might reasonably be expected to act in circumstances which might reasonably be expected to occur? (*Wigley v British Vinegars Ltd* [1961] 3 All ER 418,

[1961] 1 WLR 1261, CA; affd [1964] AC 307, [1962] 3 All ER 161, HL). In the latter case it was also held that "handhold" meant something which a man could hold or grasp from time to time as and when he wished to do so and that the upright of a ladder afforded such a handhold. A foothold which is secure in normal circumstances is not insecure merely because the abnormal occurrence of an explosion might throw a man off it (*Tinto v Stewarts & Lloyds Ltd* 1962 SLT 314), It is for the plaintiff to prove, on a balance of probabilities, that the absence of secure foothold played some part in bringing about the accident (*Thompson v Bowaters United Kingdom Paper Co Ltd* [1975] KIR 47, CA).

---

30. Dangerous fumes and lack of oxygen.—(1) The provisions of subsections (2) to (8) of this section shall have effect where work in any factory *(a)* has to be done inside any chamber, tank, vat, pit, pipe, flue or similar confined space, in which dangerous fumes *(b)* are liable to be present to such an extent as to involve risk of persons being overcome thereby.

(2) The confined space shall, unless there is other adequate means of egress, be provided with a manhole, which may be rectangular, oval or circular in shape, and shall be not less than 460 millimetres long and 410 millimetres wide or (if circular) not less than 460 millimetres in diameter, or in the case of tank wagons and other mobile plant *(c)*, not less than 410 millimetres long and 360 millimetres wide or (if circular) not less than 410 millimetres in diameter.

(3) Subject to subsection (4) of this section, no person shall enter or remain in the confined space for any purpose unless he is wearing a suitable breathing apparatus and has been authorised to enter by a responsible person, and, where practicable *(d)*, he is wearing a belt with a rope securely attached and a person keeping watch outside and capable of pulling him out is holding the free end of the rope.

(4) Where the confined space has been certified by a responsible person as being, for a specified period, safe for entry without breathing apparatus and the period so specified has not expired, subsection (3) of this section shall not apply, but no person shall enter or remain in the space unless he has been warned when that period will expire.

(5) A confined space shall not be certified under subsection (4) of this section unless—

(a) effective steps have been taken to prevent any ingress of dangerous fumes *(b)*; and

(b) any sludge or other deposit liable to give off dangerous fumes has been removed and the space contains no other material liable to give off dangerous fumes; and

(c) the space has been adequately ventilated and tested for dangerous fumes and has a supply of air adequate for respiration,

but no account shall be taken for the purposes of paragraph (b) of this subsection of any deposit or other material liable to give off dangerous fumes in insignificant quantities only.

(6) There shall be provided and kept readily available a sufficient supply of suitable breathing apparatus, of belts and ropes, and of suitable reviving apparatus and oxygen, and the apparatus, belts and ropes shall be maintained

(e) and shall be thoroughly examined, at least once a month or at such other intervals as may be prescribed, by a competent person; and a report on every such examination, signed by the person making the examination and containing the prescribed particulars *(f)*, shall be kept available for inspection.

(7) A sufficient number of the persons employed shall be trained and practised in the use of the apparatus mentioned in subsection (6) of this section and in a method of restoring respiration.

(8) The chief inspector may by certificate grant, subject to any conditions specified in the certificate, exemption from compliance with any of the requirements of the foregoing provisions of this section in any case where he is satisfied that compliance with those requirements is unnecessary or impracticable *(d)*.

(9) No person shall enter or remain in any confined space in which the proportion of oxygen in the air is liable to have been substantially reduced unless either—

(a) he is wearing a suitable breathing apparatus; or
(b) the space has been and remains adequately ventilated and a responsible person has tested and certified it as safe for entry without breathing apparatus.

(10) No work shall be permitted in any boiler-furnace or boiler-flue until it has been sufficiently cooled by ventilation or otherwise to make work safe for the persons employed.

(a) **Factory.** For definition, see s. 175.

(b) **Fumes.** "Fume" includes gas or vapour (s. 176(1)).

(c) **Tank wagons and other mobile plant.** It is submitted that the inclusion of such vehicles means that when they are upon the factory premises the requirements of the section must be observed.

(d) **Practicable.** See INTRODUCTORY NOTE 5.

(e) **Maintained.** For definition, see s. 176(1); see also INTRODUCTORY NOTE 10.

(f) **Prescribed.** The order set out below was made under s. 27 of the Factories Act 1937, as re-enacted by s. 6 of the Factories Act 1959 and is continued in force as if made under this section by virtue of s. 183 and the Sixth Schedule.

THE BREATHING APPARATUS, ETC. (REPORT ON EXAMINATION) ORDER 1961
(S.I. 1961 No. 1345)

The Minister of Labour by virtue of the powers conferred on him by subsection (6) of section 27 of the Factories Act 1937, as re-enacted by section 6 of the Factories Act 1959, and of all other powers enabling him in that behalf, hereby makes the following Order:—

1.—(1) This Order may be cited as the Breathing Apparatus, Etc. (Report on Examination) Order 1961, and shall come into operation on the first day of August, 1961.

(2) The Breathing Apparatus, Etc. (Report on Examination) Order 1949, is hereby revoked.

2. The Interpretation Act 1889 shall apply to the interpretation of this Order as it applies to the interpretation of an Act of Parliament, and as if this Order and the Order hereby revoked were Acts of Parliament.

3. Every report on an examination of any apparatus, belts or ropes made for the purpose of subsection (6) of section 27 of the Factories Act 1937, as re-enacted by section 6 of the Factories Act 1959 [s. 30 of the 1961 Act] (which requires the provision of breathing, reviving and rescue apparatus for the protection of persons working in confined spaces in which dangerous fumes are liable to be present) shall contain the following particulars:—

   (i) the name of the occupier of the factory;

  (ii) the address of the factory;

 (iii) in the case of breathing apparatus or reviving apparatus, particulars of the type of apparatus and of the distinguishing number or mark, together with a description sufficient to identify the apparatus, and the name of the maker;

 (iv) in the case of a belt or rope, the distinguishing number or mark and a description sufficient to identify the belt or rope;

  (v) the date of the examination and by whom it was carried out;

 (vi) the condition of the apparatus, belt or rope, and particulars of any defect found at the examination;

(vii) in the case of a compressed oxygen apparatus, a compressed air apparatus or a reviving apparatus, the pressure of oxygen or of air as the case may be in the supply cylinder.

---

31. Precautions with respect to explosive or inflammable dust, gas, vapour or substance.—(1) Where, in connection with any grinding, sieving, or other process giving rise to dust, there may escape dust of such a character and to such an extent as to be liable to explode on ignition, all practicable *(a)* steps shall be taken to prevent such an explosion by enclosure of the plant used in the process, and by removal or prevention of accumulation of any dust that may escape in spite of the enclosure, and by exclusion or effective enclosure of possible sources of ignition.

(2) Where there is present in any plant used in any such process as aforesaid dust of such a character and to such an extent as to be liable to explode on ignition, then, unless the plant is so constructed as to withstand the pressure likely to be produced by any such explosion, all practicable *(a)* steps shall be taken to restrict the spread and effects of such an explosion by the provision, in connection with the plant, of chokes, baffles and vents, or other equally effective appliances.

(3) Where any part of a plant contains any explosive or inflammable gas or vapour under pressure greater than atmospheric pressure, that part shall not be opened, except in accordance with the following provisions:—

 (a) before the fastening of any joint of any pipe connected with the part of the plant or the fastening of the cover of any opening into the part is loosened, any flow of the gas or vapour into the part or into any such pipe shall be effectively stopped by a stop-valve or otherwise;

 (b) before any such fastening is removed, all practicable *(a)* steps shall be taken to reduce the pressure of the gas or vapour in the pipe or part of the plant to atmospheric pressure,

and if any such fastening has been loosened or removed, no explosive or inflammable gas or vapour shall be allowed to enter the pipe or part of the plant until the fastening has been secured or, as the case may be, securely replaced; but nothing in this subsection applies to a plant installed in the open air.

(4) No plant *(b)*, tank or vessel which contains or has contained any explosive or inflammable substance shall be subjected—

(a) to any welding, brazing or soldering operation;

(b) to any cutting operation which involves the application of heat; or

(c) to any operation involving the application of heat for the purpose of taking apart or removing the plant, tank or vessel or any part of it,

until all practicable *(a)* steps have been taken to remove the substance and any fumes *(c)* arising from it, or to render the non-explosive or non-inflammable; and if any plant, tank, or vessel has been subjected to any such operation, no explosive or inflammable substance shall be allowed to enter the plant, tank or vessel until the metal has cooled sufficiently to prevent any risk of igniting the substance.

(5) The chief inspector *(d)* may by certificate grant, subject to any conditions specified in the certificate, exemption *(e)* from compliance with any of the requirements of subsections (3) and (4) of this section any case where he is satisfied that compliance with the requirement is unnecessary or impracticable *(a)*.

General note. The dangers which sub-ss. (1) and (2) aim at preventing are most commonly experienced in the grinding of coal or carbonaceous material and the grinding of farinaceous beans or oilcake, although many other kinds of dust are explosive under certain conditions. In *Merrington v Ironbridge Metal Works Ltd* [1952] 2 All ER 1101, Hallett J expressed the view, *obiter*, that "other processes" meant a process *ejusdem generis* with grinding or sieving. See also the Shipbuilding and Ship-repairing Regulations 1960 as to precautions similar to those required by sub-s. (4).

The duties under this section are absolute; see, for example, *Williams v L B Holliday & Co Ltd* (1957) 107 L Jo 378 (decided upon s. 28(4) of the 1937 Act).

(a) Practicable, impracticable. See INTRODUCTORY NOTE 5.

(b) Plant. The meaning of "plant" in this context was extensively discussed in *Haigh v Charles W Ireland Ltd* [1973] 3 All ER 1137, [1974] 1 WLR 43, HL (old safe containing gelignite exploded when metal merchants used burning equipment to open it). It was held that "plant" denoted any part of the apparatus in a factory used in carrying on the industrial process, but that an article on the premises for the purpose of being subjected to that process was not "plant", whatever might have been the use to which it had been previously put, or might subsequently be put, elsewhere.

(c) Fumes. "Fume" includes gas or vapour (s. 176(1)).

(d) Inspector. See INTRODUCTORY NOTE 19.

(e) Exemptions. The following exemptions have been allowed from sub-s. (4) subject to the stated conditions:

Certificate of Exemption No. 3. The operations of cutting or welding steel or wrought iron gas mains and services by the application of heat.
Conditions.—

(1) The main or service,

(a) shall be situated in the open air;

(b) shall contain only town gas or gases used in the manufacture of town gas at a pressure greater than atmospheric pressure;

(c) shall not contain acetylene or any gas or mixture of gases to which acetylene has been added intentionally.

(2) The operation shall be carried out by an experienced person or persons and at least two persons (including those carrying out the operation) experienced in work on gas mains and over eighteen years of age shall be present during the operation.

(3) The site of the operation shall be free from inflammable or explosive gas or vapour.

(4) Where acetylene gas is used as the source of heat in connection with an operation, it shall be compressed and contained in a porous substance in a cylinder in accordance with the requirements of the Order of the Secretary of State (No. 9), dated 23 June, 1919 (S.R. & O. 1919 No. 809).

(5) Prior to the application of any flame to the gas main or service, this shall be pierced or drilled and the escaping gas ignited.

(Form 664, February 1939.)

Certificate of Exemption No. 5. Cutting and welding operations on wrought iron gas mains and services other than those used for the supply of town gas and the operations of cutting or welding steel or wrought iron gas mains and services by the application of heat.

Conditions.—

(1) The main or service,
  (a) shall be situated in the open air;
  (b) shall contain only the following gases, separately or mixed, at a pressure greater than atmospheric pressure, namely, town gas, coke oven gas, producer gas, blast-furnace gas, or gases, other than air, used in their manufacture;
  (c) shall not contain acetylene or any gas or mixture of gases to which acetylene has been added intentionally.

(2) The operation shall be carried out by a person or persons experienced in work on gas mains and over eighteen years of age, and at least two such persons (including those carrying out the operation) shall be present during the operation.

(3) The site of the operation shall be free from inflammable or explosive gas or vapour.

(4) Where acetylene gas is used as the source of heat in connection with an operation, it shall be compressed and contained in a porous substance in a cylinder in accordance with the requirements of the Order of the Secretary of State (No. 9), dated 23 June, 1919 (S.R. & O. 1919 No. 809).

(5) Prior to the application of any flame to the gas main or service, this shall be pierced or drilled with a small hole, and the escaping gas ignited to act as an indicator.

(Form 672, December 1939.)

Certificate of Exemption No. 36 (General). The carrying out of minor repairs:
  (1) to the outer surface of an oil-tank on board or in a vessel; or
  (2) in or to the outer surface of any compartment or space adjacent to any such oil-tank in cases where the only oil last carried was oil having a flash point of one hundred and fifty degrees Fahrenheit or above (Pensky-Martens Closed test).

In this Certificate "oil-tank" means any tank or compartment in which oil is, or has been, carried as cargo or for use as lubricating oil, as engine fuel or boiler fuel or as fuel for aircraft on board.

(Form 2052, February 1964.)

[See also the Shipbuilding and Ship-repairing Regulations 1960, reg. 66.]

---

32. Steam boilers—attachments and construction.—(1) Subject to subsection (3) of this section, every steam boiler *(a)*, whether separate or one of a range,—

  (a) shall have attached to it the devices mentioned in subsection (2) of this section;

(b) shall be provided with means for attaching a test pressure gauge; and

(c) shall, unless externally fired, be provided with a suitable fusible plug or an efficient low-water alarm device.

(2) The devices referred to in subsection (1) of this section are—

(a) a suitable safety valve *(b)*, separate from any stop-valve, which shall be so adjusted as to prevent the boiler being worked at a pressure greater than the maximum permissible working pressure *(c)* and shall be fixed directly to, or as close as practicable *(d)* to, the boiler;

(b) a suitable stop-valve connecting the boiler to the steam pipe;

(c) a correct steam pressure gauge connected to the steam space and easily visible by the boiler attendant, which shall indicate the pressure of steam in the boiler and have marked on it in a distinctive colour the maximum permissible working pressure;

(d) at least one water gauge of transparent material or other type approved *(e)* by the chief inspector *(f)* to show the water level in the boiler, together, if the gauge is of the glass tubular type and the working pressure of the boiler normally exceeds 2.75 bars, with an efficient guard provided so as not to obstruct the reading of the gauge;

(e) where the boiler is one of two or more boilers, a plate bearing a distinctive number which shall be easily visible.

(3) Paragraph (b) of subsection (2) of this section shall not apply with respect to economisers, and paragraphs (c), (d) and (e) of that subsection and paragraphs (b) and (c) of subsection (1) of this section shall not apply with respect to either economisers or superheaters.

(4) For the purposes of the foregoing provisions of this section, a lever-valve shall not be deemed a suitable safety valve unless the weight is secured on the lever in the correct position.

(5) Every part of every steam boiler *(a)* shall be of good construction, sound material and adequate strength *(g)*, and free from patent defect.

General note. This section is repealed by S.I. 1989 No. 2169, as from 1 July 1994.

The section applies to docks by virtue of s. 125, and to building operations and works of engineering construction by virtue of s. 127. By virtue of s. 37(2) many classes and types of steam boiler have been excepted from certain provisions of this section. These exceptions are set out below.

(a) Steam boiler. For definition, see s. 38.

(b) Safety valve. See also sub-s. (4).

(c) Maximum permissible working pressure. For definition, see s. 38.

(d) Practicable. See INTRODUCTORY NOTE 5.

(e) Approved. See Certificate of Approval No. 2 (General), dated 3 November 1970 [Form 2327].

(f) Inspector. For definition, see s. 176(1).

(g) Of good construction, sound material and adequate strength. See INTRODUCTORY NOTE 11.

Exceptions

Certificate of Exemptions No. 21. Economisers of the steaming type.
Excepted from sub-s. (2)(a).

Conditions.—

(1) This exception shall not apply to any such economiser which is fitted with a stop valve or other means of controlling or preventing the free flow of hot water or steam to the steam boiler connected therewith.

(2) The maximum permissible working pressure of such economiser shall not be less than that of the said steam boiler.

(3) The safety valve or safety values of the said steam boiler shall be such as to prevent either the boiler or the economiser being worked at a pressure greater than the maximum permissible working pressure of either.

(Form 685, June 1941.)

Certificate of Exception No. 32. Steam Boilers—Interconnected Steam-Water Drum and Steam Generators of the Evaporative Cooling Type.

Excepted from the provisions of section 32(1)(a) to the extent that the said provisions require steam boilers to have attached to them the devices mentioned in section 32(2)(c) and (d), the following types of evaporative cooling steam boilers associated with steel melting furnaces, that is to say:—

1. door frames,
2. burners,
3. chills,
4. burner port coolers, and
5. up-take coolers,

(but not including any steam-water drum connected to a system of interconnected steam boilers of which any of the types to which this Certificate applies forms part).

Conditions.—

(1) Any such steam-water drum as aforesaid shall be treated as if it were a separate steam boiler and as if all the provisions of the Factories Act 1961 relating to steam boilers applied to it.

(2) Any such steam-water drum as aforesaid shall be provided with an efficient low water alarm device.

(3) Where a steam boiler to which this Certificate applies forms part of a system of interconnected steam boilers, then in the event of failure of any part of that system which might result in a loss of water from that part of the system, provision shall be made so as to prevent such loss of water in consequence throughout the remainder of the system as might result in a shortage of water in any interconnected boiler sufficient to render any part thereof liable to failure by overheating.

(4) Where a steam boiler to which this Certificate applies forms part of a system of interconnected boilers and the feed and the circulation of the water through that system is obtained by any mechanical contrivance or mechanical contrivances, provisions shall be made by automatic means for the continuance of such feed and circulation in the event of failure of any such contrivance or contrivances (other than failure of the said automatic means).

(Form 2113, August 1962.)

Certificate of Exception No. 34. The type of steam boiler known as a Viscomat Closed Circuit Steam Generator, which is manufactured by Duncan Low Ltd., 57–61 Trossachs Street, Glasgow, N.W.

Excepted from the provisions of paragraphs (b) and (c) of section 32(1) and from the provisions of paragraph (a) thereof, to the extent that that paragraph requires steam boilers to have attached to them the devices mentioned in paragraphs (a) to (d) of section 32(2).

Conditions.—

(1) The steam boiler shall be fitted with a control regulator so adjusted that if the maximum permissible working pressure is exceeded the supply of electricity to the heating elements will be automatically cut off.

(2) The boiler shall be subjected to hydraulic tests to prove the adequate strength of the inner chamber and coil and the space between the inner and outer shell and inside the inner oil coil.

(Form 2137, October 1963.)

Certificate of Exemption No. 35. 1. Steam boilers in which steam is generated solely by means of steam or hot water passing through a pipe or coil contained in such boiler.

2. Steam boilers in which steam is generated by passing an alternating electric current through the water by means of electrodes.

3. Steam boilers which are heated by means of a metal coil or element fitted within the boiler and energised by an electric current.

Excepted from the provisions of paragraph (c) of section 32(1) and from the provisions of paragraph (a) thereof to the extent that that paragraph requires steam boilers to have attached to them the devices mentioned in paragraph (d) of section 32(2).

(Form 2138, November 1963.)

Certificate of Exception No. 52. The type of steam boiler which consists of a sealed tube partly filled with water and which forms part of a steam tube oven or a steam tube hotplate. Excepted from the provisions of sections 32(1) and (2) and 33(2) and (3).
Conditions.—

(1) In the case of a steam tube oven fired by gas or oil—

(a) a thermometer accurately indicating the temperature in the baking chamber and having clearly marked on it the maximum working temperature of the said chamber shall be fitted where it can be easily read by the oven attendant; in the case of an oven having more than one chamber, each chamber shall be fitted with at least one thermometer as aforesaid; and

(b) an efficient device shall be provided which shall automatically cut off the supply of fuel to the oven when the temperature of the baking chamber exceeds by 10 per cent. the maximum working temperature specified by the manufacturer or a competent person; the device shall be of a type which, after if has operated to cut off the supply of fuel, must be re-set manually before it can operate again. At an oven having more than one baking chamber a separate efficient device as aforesaid shall be provided for each chamber.

(2) In the case of a steam tube oven fired by solid fuel—

(a) a thermometer accurately indicating the temperature in the baking chamber and having clearly marked on it the maximum working temperature of the said chamber shall be fitted where it can easily be read by the oven attendant; in the case of an oven having more than one chamber, each chamber shall be fitted with at least one thermometer as aforesaid; and

(b) an efficient device shall be provided which will give audible warning to the oven attendant when the temperature of the baking chamber exceeds by 10 per cent. the maximum working temperature specified by the manufacturer or a competent person. At an oven having more than one baking chamber a separate efficient device as aforesaid shall be provided for each chamber.

(3) No steam tube oven shall be worked at a higher temperature than the maximum work temperature certified by the manufacturer or by a competent person.

(4) In the case of a steam tube hot-plate—

(a) a correct steam pressure gauge easily visible by the hotplate attendant shall be fitted to at least one of the tubes and shall be provided with an arrangement for indicating the highest pressure generated in that tube at any time; the maximum permissible working pressure shall be marked in a distinctive colour on the dial of each pressure gauge; and

(b) the hotplate shall not be worked at a higher pressure than the maximum permissible working pressure certified by the manufacturer or by a competent person.

(5) The thermometers, gauges and other devices referred to in conditions (1), (2) and (4) and the brickwork surrounding the tubes in the furnace shall be properly maintained.

(6) Accumulation of dust, soot or other deposits shall not be allowed to accumulate to such an extent as to impair the safe working of a steam tube oven or steam tube hotplate.

(7) 1. Every tube fitted for the first time to a steam tube oven or a steam tube hotplate on or after 1 July, 1970 shall before it is sealed be properly tested by hydraulic pressure. A certificate of test, specifying the pressure applied, and signed by the person making or supervising the test, shall be kept attached to the general register. Such a certificate may relate to tests of more than one tube.

2. In a case where a tube fitted to a steam tube oven or a steam tube hotplate between 31 December 1939 and 1 July, 1970 is still in use, there shall be kept attached to the general register the certificate required by Condition (5) of Certificate of Exemption No. 6 (General) dated 21 July, 1939 (which required that every tube fitted to an oven or hotplate after 31 December, 1939 should before sealing up have been properly tested by hydraulic pressure and that a certificate of such test, specifying the test pressure applied, and signed by the person making or supervising such test, should be kept attached to the general register).

(8) There shall be prominently displayed near the working place at each steam tube oven and steam tube hotplate instructions for working it which shall be obtained from the manufacturer or from a competent person.

(9) In the case of a steam tube oven or a steam tube hotplate which is constructed or in which the furnaces is rebuilt after 1 July, 1970—

(a) all tubes shall be so secured that they cannot slide towards the furnace of the oven or hotplate; and

(b) the arrangement of furnace and tubes shall be such as to enable a person to examine thoroughly the tube ends and furnace.

(10) 1. Every steam tube oven or steam tube hotplate shall be thoroughly examined by a competent person as far as the construction permits at least once in every period of 14 months.

2. The said examination shall be made firstly with the fire drawn and the oven or hotplate cooled and cleaned sufficiently to permit examination in accordance with the foregoing sub-paragraph, and secondly when the oven is at its normal operating temperature or the hotplate is at its normal steam pressure.

(11) Whenever there is carried out to any steam tube oven or any steam tube hotplate the repair of a defect, which in the opinion of a competent person, will affect its safe working, that oven or hotplate shall be examined by a competent person in such a manner as will enable that person to satisfy himself that the repair has been properly carried out.

(12) In the case of a steam tube oven which is in use at the date of the coming into force of this certificate, the requirements of paragraphs 1(b) and 2(b) shall not apply until two years after the said date.

(13) A report of the result of every examination under this certificate in the form and containing the particulars specified in the Schedules hereto shall as soon as practicable and in any case within twenty-eight days after the completion of the examination, be entered in or attached to the general register, and the report shall be signed by the person making the examination, and if that person is an inspector of a boiler-inspecting company or association, countersigned by the chief engineer of the company or association or by such other responsible officer of the company or association as may be authorised in writing in that behalf by the chief engineer.

(14) Where the report of any examination under this certificate specifies conditions for securing the safe working of a steam tube oven or a steam tube hotplate, the oven or hotplate shall not be used except in accordance with those conditions.

(15) The person making the report of an examination under this certificate or, in the case of a boiler-inspecting company or association, the chief engineer thereof, shall within twenty-eight days after the completion of the examination send to the inspector

for the district a copy of the report in every case where the examination shows that the oven or hotplate cannot continue to be used unless certain repairs are carried out immediately or within a specified time.

SCHEDULE 1

F62A

REPORT OF EXAMINATION WHEN COLD OF STEAM TUBE OVEN
OR STEAM TUBE HOTPLATE

---

1 Name of occupier

---

2 Address of factory

---

3 Description and disinctive number of oven or hotplate

---

4 Date of construction

---

5 Number of baking chambers

---

6 Type of fuel used

---

7 (a) Maximum permissible working temperature (Oven)
    (b) Maximum permissible working pressure (Hotplate)

---

8 OVEN OR HOTPLATE
   (a) Was the oven/hotplate so prepared
        as to allow the examination of the
        tube ends or loops projecting into
        the furnace?
   (b) What parts were inaccessible for
        examination?
   (c) What was the external condition of
        the tubes?
   (d) Were the flues clear?
   (e) Were the tubes properly secured?

---

9 FURNACE
   (a) Was the brickwork properly
        maintained?
   (b) Which tubes, if any, were out of use
        because of defects?

---

10 Repairs (if any) required, and period
        within which they should be
        executed, and any other conditions
        which the person making the
        examination thinks it necessary to
        specify for securing safe working.

---

11 OTHER OBSERVATIONS

I CERTIFY that on .... I thoroughly examined the oven/hotplate above described so far as its construction permitted, and the above is a true report of the result.
Signature ....   Counter-Signature ....
                                               Name of Company
Qualification ....   or Association ....
Address ....
Date ....   Date ....

F62B

REPORT OF EXAMINATION OF STEAM TUBE OVEN
AT ITS NORMAL OPERATING TEMPERATURE
OR STEAM TUBE HOTPLATE
AT ITS NORMAL STEAM PRESSURE

---

1 Name of occupier

---

2 Address of factory

---

3 Description and distinctive number of oven or hotplate

---

4 FITTINGS
OVEN
(a) Was a thermometer fitted at each
 baking chamber?
(b) Was each of the thermometers in
 proper working order?
(c) Was the maximum working
 temperature clearly marked on
 each thermometer?
(d) Was there an efficient device fitted
 for each baking chamber for
  (i) automatically cutting-off the
   supply of fuel (oven fired by
   gas or oil)
  (ii) giving audible warning (oven
   fired by solid fuel)?
(e) Was each of them in proper
 working order?
HOTPLATE
(f) Was the pressure gauge in proper
 working order?
(g) Was the maximum permissible
 working pressure marked on the
 dial in a distinctive colour?
(h) Was the pressure gauge provided
 with an arrangement to indicate
 the highest pressure generated?
(i) What pressure was shown by the
 "maximum" pointer of the
 gauge?

---

5 Repairs (if any) required, and period
 within which they should be
 executed, and any other conditions
 which the person making the
 examination thinks it necessary to
 specify for securing safe working.

---

6 OTHER OBSERVATIONS

I CERTIFY that on .... I examined the oven/hotplate above described at
its normal operating temperature/pressure and above is a true report of the result.

Signature ....   Counter-Signature ....
                                                   Name of Company
Qualification ....   or Association ....
Address ....
Date ....   Date ....
(Form 2341, in force from 1.7.70.)

Certificate of Exception No. 63.   Examination of Steam Boilers and Associated Air Receivers and Steam Receivers.

1.   In pursuance of section 37(2) and (3) of the Factories Act 1961 being satisfied that the provisions cannot reasonably be applied, I hereby except

(a) those steam boilers which are operated solely for the generation of electricity distributed through the national grid and of the type specified in Schedule 1 hereto from the provisions of section 32(1)(b) and (c) and section 33(2) and (3) of that Act; and if those boilers are of the Forced-Flow-Once-Through type, I additionally except them from the provisions of section 32(1)(a) of that Act insofar as that paragraph requires the attachment to a boiler of the devices mentioned in section 32(2)(d) of that Act;

(b) any steam receiver which forms part of the primary steam circuit associated with such steam boiler from the provisions of section 35(5) of that Act to the extent that that section refers to examination; and

(c) any air receiver associated with such steam boiler from the provision of section 36(4) of that Act.

2.   This Exception is granted subject to the conditions in Schedule 2 hereto, and additionally, in the case of Forced-Flow-Once-Through boilers, the conditions contained in Schedule 3 hereto, and subject to a report being made containing the appropriate particulars set out in Schedules 4 to 8 hereto.

3.   This Certificate shall remain in force until revoked in writing by an inspector appointed under section 19 of the Health and Safety at Work etc. Act 1974 and duly authorised in that behalf.

4.   Certificate of Exception No. 62 (which relates to the examination of steam boilers), Certificate of Exception No. 54 (which relates to the examination of steam receivers) and Certificate of Exception No. 53 (which relates to the examination of air receivers) all under the Factories Act 1961, are hereby revoked.

SCHEDULE 1
STEAM BOILERS TO WHICH THIS CERTIFICATE RELATES

1.   The steam boiler shall be a steam boiler as defined in section 38 of the Factories Act 1961 and shall be one in which the steam is generated by means of—

(a) burning fossil fuel, or

(b) operating a nuclear reactor of the Magnox or Advanced Gas Cooled types.

2.   The steam boiler shall be either—

(a) a water-tube boiler which is associated with a generating unit of a nominal capacity of not less than 500 megawatts; or

(b) any other water-tube boiler of which the drums and any headers are of fusion welded or solid forged construction and which has an evaporative capacity of not less than 50,000 pounds of steam per hour; or

(c) any other boiler in a group of water-tube boilers of which the drums and headers are of fusion welded or solid forged construction, being a group of which—

(i) each boiler has an evaporative capacity of not less than 25,000 pounds of steam per hour; and

(ii) the total evaporative capacity of all the boilers is not less than 100,000 pounds of steam per hour.

SCHEDULE 2
CONDITIONS

First two examinations
1. The steam boiler together with its fittings and attachments (referred to in this Schedule as "the boiler"), the air receiver and the steam receiver shall be thoroughly examined by a competent person in the manner specified in paragraph 4 of this Schedule before being taken into use for the first time in any factory, and examined again after such period as the person making the first examination may specify, which period may not exceed 18 months.

Subsequent examinations
2. (1) Subject to paragraph 2(2) the boiler, air receiver and steam receiver shall not thereafter be used in a factory unless is has been thoroughly examined in the manner specified in paragraph 4 of this Schedule—
(a) in the case of the outer surfaces of any part of a boiler heated by nuclear power which lies within—
　(i) a steel pressurised containment vessel, provided that not longer than 60 months have elapsed since the completion of the examination of such surfaces in the manner specified in paragraph 4 of this Schedule; and
　(ii) a steel-lined pressurised concrete containment vessel, provided that they are examined as far as is reasonably practicable whenever entry is made for any purpose;
(b) in any other case, if the boiler is of the type specified in—
　(i) paragraph 2(a) of Schedule 1 hereto, no greater period has elapsed than 38 months, or such shorter period as the person making the previous examination has specified, since the completion of the last examination; or
　(ii) paragraphs 2(b) or (c) of Schedule 1 hereto, no greater period has elapsed than 30 months, or such shorter period as the person making the previous examination has specified, since the completion of the last examination.
(2) If more than 21 years have elapsed since the boiler first came into use, and, at its last examination under a Certificate of Exception previous to this Certificate, the period specified by the examining person was less than 30 months, such period may not be increased in any subsequent examination, until it has been subjected to three examinations in the manner specified in paragraph 4 of this Schedule, with the first and last of those examinations not less than four years apart.
(3) In addition to the provisions of sub-paragraphs (1) and (2) above, the boiler shall be examined within one month of the mid-point of the period specified by the competent person, which examination shall be under normal steam pressure and shall be as thorough as the operating conditions permit.

Examination after repair
3. Whenever the boiler, air receiver or steam receiver is repaired in such a way that in the opinion of a competent person its safe working may be affected, it shall be examined by a competent person in such a manner as will enable him to satisfy himself that the repair has been properly carried out before the boiler, air receiver or steam receiver is used.

Method of examination
4. (1) The air receiver shall be thoroughly cleaned.
(2) If the boiler is fired by nuclear power, all practicable steps shall be taken to prevent entry of any dangerous substances from the nuclear reactor circuits into any place where a person may be for the purpose of examining the boiler.
(3) The boiler shall be prepared for examination by any or all of the following, as the competent person may decide—
(a) the opening out, cleaning and descaling of the boiler including the removal of doors from manholes, mudholes and handholes;
(b) the removal of fire bars;

    (c) the opening out for cleaning and inspection of fittings including the pressure parts of automatic controls;

    (d) in the case of water tube boilers, the removal of drum internal fittings; and brickwork, baffles and coverings shall be removed for the purpose of thorough examination to the extent required by the persons making the examination.

(4) The steam receiver shall have its interior and exterior prepared in a proper manner.

(5) The boiler, air receiver and steam receiver shall be thoroughly examined when cold, and in particular—

    (a) every pressure gauge and safety valve provided under sections 32(1)(a), 35(1) and 36(1) of the Factories Act 1961 shall be thoroughly examined and tested for accuracy;

    (b) every safety valve which can only be set when cold shall be set and have a seal affixed;

    (c) there are arrangements to ensure that, in the event of a failure (in relation to fault studies against which the parts were designed) of any part of that boiler within the containment vessel, the maximum accumulation of pressure cannot exceed 110% of the design pressure of the containment vessel;

    (d) the internal surfaces of those parts of a boiler fired by nuclear power which lie within the containment vessel shall be examined in a manner which is as thorough as is reasonably practicable from outside the containment vessel.

(6) In addition to paragraph (5) above, the person making the examination of the boiler, air receiver or steam receiver may—

    (a) measure the thickness of any part;

    (b) test any part for flaws;

    (c) prove clear waterways in the tubes; and

    (d) withdraw samples tubes to measure their thickness, assess their condition, and test or measure them.

(7) Any test or measurement may include the use of ultrasonic, radiographic, magnetic or electronic devices, or tube calibration gauges, steam trial or hydraulic testing, but may not include any destructive methods other than paragraph (6)(d) above.

(8) The boiler (other than any economiser or superheater) and the steam receiver shall be thoroughly examined under normal pressure and the air receiver shall be thoroughly examined under normal air pressure within 28 days of steam being raised after the examination when cold, and every boiler safety valve adjusted so as to prevent working at a pressure greater than the maximum permissible working pressure.

(9) Different parts of the examination and testing may be made by different persons.

Renewal of boilers parts

5.   Where the competent person examining the boiler states in his report that the effective life of any part of the boiler is likely to terminate through creep, fatigue or any reason, it shall be renewed by the date specified in that report.

Quality of feed water

6.   The feed water supplied to the boiler shall be of such quality as to prevent, so far as is reasonably practicable—

    (a) corrosion in any part of the boiler; and

    (b) formation of scale or sludge to an extent liable to affect the safe operation of the boiler.

Periodic checks and blowing down

7.   (1) When the boiler is in use, at least once in every shift, or every 12 hours, whichever period is less—

    (a) a check shall be made to ensure that every device specified in Schedule 3 is operating satisfactorily; and

    (b) the boiler shall be down in such a manner and at such a rate as to minimise deposits of scale and sludge.

(2) Samples of water from the boiler shall be taken at suitable intervals and analysed by a competent person in order to verify that the boiler water is free from sludge and scale, so far as is reasonably practicable, and a suitable record of these analyses shall be kept.

Report of examination
8.   (1) A report of every examination made in pursuance of paragraph 4 of this Schedule shall as soon as is practicable and in any case within 28 days after the completion of the examination be entered in or attached to the general register as defined in the Factories Act 1961, section 176, and that report shall be signed by the person or persons making the examination (and where that person is an employee of a boiler inspecting company or association, that part of the report concerning the steam boiler shall also be counter-signed by the Chief Engineer of the company or association or by such other responsible officer of the company or association as may be authorised in writing on their behalf by the Chief Engineer) and that report shall contain the appropriate particulars set out in Schedules 4 to 8 hereto.

(2) The person making an examination or part of an examination under this Certificate shall notify the occupier in writing forthwith and within 28 days after the completion of the examination and shall send to the Health and Safety Executive a copy of the report in every case where the maximum permissible working pressure is reduced or the examination shows that the boiler, air receiver or steam receiver cannot continue to be used with safety unless certain repairs are carried out immediately or within a specified time, or the person making this examination is of the opinion that a defect exists which would be liable to affect the safe working of any of them.

(3) Where the report of any examination under this Certificate specifies conditions for securing the safe working of a boiler, air receiver or steam receiver, they shall not be used except in accordance with those conditions.

SCHEDULE 3
ADDITIONAL REQUIREMENTS FOR FORCED-FLOW-ONCE-THROUGH
BOILERS

1.   There shall be provided an effective automatic device fitted to interrupt the firing or nuclear heating of the boiler in the event of imminence of shortage of water within the boiler.
2.   There shall be provided an effective automatic signalling device fitted to give audible or visual warning in the event of interruption of the supply of water to the boiler.

SCHEDULE 4
(Paragraph 8 of Schedule 2)

PART A

1. Name of occupier ....
2. Address of Factory ....
....

PART B
REPORT OF EXAMINATION WHEN COLD OF A STEAM BOILER
INCLUDING ALL FITTINGS AND ATTACHMENTS TO WHICH CERTIFICATE
OF EXCEPTION NO. 63 APPLIES

1. Description and distinctive number of boiler
....
2. Date of examination of boiler ....

3. Maximum permissible working pressure .... pounds per square inch.
4. State which type of fuel and whether the boiler is of the Forced-Flow-Once-Through Type
   ....
5. Date of construction, and brief history ..... the examiner should state whether he has seen the last previous report
   ....
   ....
   ....
6. Date of hydraulic test. Pressure applied and period pressure applied.
   Date ....
   Pressure Applied .... pounds per square inch.
7. Water Tube Boilers
   (a) *Downcomer Tubes*
   7.1 Have the downcomer tubes been checked for distortion? ....
   7.2 Have the downcomer tubes been checked for thickness? ....
   7.3 Have the downcomer tubes been checked for signs of corrosion?
   ....
   7.4 Do any need repair? ....
   7.5 Do any need replacement? ....
   (b) *Riser Tubes*
   7.6 Have the riser rubes been checked for distortion? ....
   7.7 Have the riser tubes been checked for thickness? ....
   7.8 Have the riser tubes been checked for signs of corrosion? ....
   7.9 Do any need repair? ....
   7.10 Do any need replacement? ....
   (c) *Headers*
   7.11 Have the headers been checked for thickness? ....
   7.12 Have the headers been checked for signs of corrosion? ....
   7.13 Do any need repair? ....
   7.14 Do any need replacement? ....
   (d) *Header Caps*
   7.15 Have the header caps been checked for thickness? ....
   7.16 Have the header caps been checked for signs of corrosion? ....
   7.17 Do any need repair? ....
   7.18 Do any need replacement? ....
   (e) *Drums*
   7.19 Has the exterior been checked for corrosion etc? ....
   7.20 Has the interior been checked for corrosion etc? ....
   7.21 Are any repairs needed? ....
   (f) *Condition of Parts not listed above*
8. Boiler Fittings
   8.1 Has the stop-valve been examined? ....
   8.2 Does it require repair/replacement? ....
   8.3 Has the water gauge been examined? ....
   8.4 Does it require repair/replacement? ....
   8.5 Has the low-water alarm device been examined? ....
   8.6 Does it require repair/replacement? ....
   8.7 Has the safety valve been thoroughly examined? ....
   8.8 Has it been set where necessary? ....
   8.9 Does it require repair/replacement? ....
   8.10 Has the pressure gauge been tested for accuracy? ....
   8.11 Does it require repair/replacement? ....
   8.12 Have the automatic devices provided in pursuance of Schedule 3 of the Certificate been thoroughly examined?
   ....

8.13 Have they been tested for accuracy and correct functioning? ....

8.14 Do they require repair/replacement? ....

8.15 Are the suitable arrangements if so made in accordance with Schedule 2, paragraph 4(5)(c) of the Certificate, so adjusted as to prevent the containment vessel being worked at a pressure not exceeding 110% of the design pressure of that vessel?

....

9. State any defect as a result of which:

(a) The boiler cannot continue to be used with safety unless repairs are carried out immediately, or within a specified time.

(b) The maximum permissible working pressure has been reduced.

....

....

10. I CERTIFY that the boiler above described was sufficiently descaled, prepared and (so far as its construction permits) made accessible for thorough examination, and for such tests as were necessary for thorough examination, and that on the said date I thoroughly examined the boiler including its fittings and attachments, and the above is a true report of the results. In my opinion the boiler can continue to be steamed under normal operating conditions and pressure for .... months (period to be entered in words).

Signature ....

Qualification ....

Address ....

....

Date ....

Counter-signature (Chief Engineer) ....

Name of company or association ....

Date ....

PART C

REPORT OF EXAMINATION WHEN COLD OF AN ECONOMISER
INCLUDING ALL FITTINGS AND ATTACHMENTS TO
WHICH CERTIFICATE OF EXCEPTION NO. 63 APPLIES

1. Description and distinctive number of economiser ....

....

Type ....

Number of tubes ....

2. State which type of fuel and whether the boiler with which it is associated is of the Forced-Flow-Once-Through Type

....

3. Date of examination ....

4. Date of construction and brief history. The examiner should state whether he has seen the last previous report.

....

5. Date of last hydraulic test (if any) ....

Pressure applied ....

6. Are the dampers in proper working order? ....

7. (a) What parts are inaccessible? ....

(b) State number of top caps removed for examination ....

(c) State number of bottom caps removed for examination ....

(d) What examinations and tests were made (see Schedule 2, paragraph 4 of this Certificate)

....

(e) Conditions of economiser (state any defects materially affecting the maximum permissible working pressure)
External ....
Internal ....

8. (a) Are these proper fittings and attachments? ....
    (b) Are all fittings and attachments in satisfactory condition (so far as ascertainable when not under pressure)?
....

9. Repairs (if any) required, and period within which they should be executed, and any other conditions which the person making the examination thinks it necessary to specify for securing safe working.
....

10. Maximum permissible working pressure calculated from dimensions and from the thickness, and other data ascertained by the present examination (due allowance being made for conditions of working if unusual or exceptionally severe)
....

11. Where repairs affecting the working pressure are required state the maximum permissible working pressure.
    (a) Before the expiration of the period specified in paragraph 9 above
....

    (b) After the expiration of such period if the required repairs have not been completed
....

    (c) After the completion of the required repairs
....

12. Other observations ....
....
....
....
....

13. I CERTIFY that the economiser above described was sufficiently descaled, prepared and (so far as its construction permits) made accessible for thorough examination, and for such tests as were necessary for through examination and that on the said date I thoroughly examined the economiser including its fittings and attachments, and the above is a true report of the result. In my opinion the economiser can continue to be steamed under normal operating conditions and pressure for
.... months (to be entered in words).

Signature ....
Qualification ....
Address ....
....
Date ....
Counter-signature (Chief Engineer) ....
Name of company or association ....
Date ....

PART D
REPORT OF EXAMINATION WHEN COLD OF A SUPERHEATER
INCLUDING ALL FITTINGS AND ATTACHMENTS TO
WHICH CERTIFICATE OF EXCEPTION No. 63 APPLIES

1. Description and distinctive number of superheater and type ....
....

2. State which type of fuel and whether the boiler with which it is associated belongs to the Forced-Flow-Once-Through Type
....

3. Date of construction and brief history. The examiner should state whether he has seen the last previous report.

   ....

   ....

4. Date of examination ....
5. Date of last hydraulic test (if any) ....
   Pressure applied ....
6. (a) What parts are covered by brickwork? ....

   ....

   (b) Date of last exposure of such parts for the purpose of examination

   ....

   (c) What parts (if any) other than those covered by brickwork were inaccessible?

   ....

7. Headers
   (a) Have the headers been checked for thickness? ....
   (b) Are they being affected by creep? ....
   (c) Do any need repair/replacing? ....
8. Tubes
   (a) Have the tubes been checked for distortion?

   ....

   (b) Have the tubes been checked for thickness?

   ....

   (c) Have the tubes been checked for signs of corrosion?

   ....

   (d) Do they need repair/replacement? ....
9. Safety valve(s)
   (a) Has the safety valve(s) been thoroughly examined? ....
   (b) Does it/they require repair/replacement? ....
   (c) Has it/they been set and sealed where necessary? ....
10. Fittings and attachments
    (a) Are all the necessary fittings and attachments present and in a satisfactory condition (so far as is ascertainable when not under pressure)?

    ....

11. Conditions of superheater (state any defects materially affecting the maximum permissible working pressure).
    External ....
    Internal ....
12. State the period within which repairs (if any) should be executed and any other conditions which the person making the examination thinks it necessary to secure safe working.

    ....

    ....

13. Maximum permissible working pressure calculated from dimensions and from the thickness and other data ascertained by the present examination; due allowance being made for the conditions of working if unusual or exceptionally severe.

    ....

14. Where repairs affecting the working pressure are required, state the maximum working pressure:
    (a) Before the expiration of the period specified in paragraph 12 above.

    ....

    (b) After the expiration of such period if the required repairs have not been completed.

    ....

    (c) After the completion of the required repairs.

    ....

15. Other observations ....
....
....

16. I CERTIFY that the superheater above described was sufficiently descaled, prepared and (so far as its construction permits) made accessible for thorough examination, and for such tests as were necessary for thorough examination and that on the said date I thoroughly examined the superheater including its fittings and attachments, and the above is a true report of the result. In my opinion the superheater can continue to be steamed under normal operating conditions and pressure for .... months (period to be entered in words).

Signature ....
Qualification ....
Address ....
....
Date ....
Counter-signature (Chief Engineer) ....
Name of company or association ....
....
Date ....

SCHEDULE 5
(Paragraph 8 of Schedule 2)

REPORT OF EXAMINATION UNDER NORMAL STEAM PRESSURE OF A STEAM BOILER TO WHICH CERTIFICATE OF EXCEPTION NO. 63 APPLIES

1. Name of occupier...
2. Address of factory   ....
   ....
3. Description and distinctive number of boiler ....
   ....
   State which type of fuel and whether the boiler is of the Forced-Flow-Once-Through Type
   ....
4. Date of examination   ....

Examination
5. (i) General condition (external) of the boiler including fittings and attachments.
   ....

   (ii) Fittings and attachments
   Were the following operating satisfactorily?
   (a) Pressure gauge ....
   (b) Water level gauge ....
   (c) Blow-down arrangements ....
   (d) Automatic water level control(s) ....
   (e) Automatic devices provided in pursuance of Schedule 3
   ....
   (f) Safety valves ....
6. State any defects as a result of which:
   (a) The boiler cannot continue to be used with safety unless repairs are carried out immediately or within a specified time.
   ....
   (b) The maximum permissible working pressure has been reduced.
   ....

7. Repairs (if any) required and period within which they should be executed and any other conditions which the person making the examination thinks it necessary to specify for securing safe working

    ....

    ....

8. (i) Is the safety valve so adjusted as to prevent the boiler being worked at a pressure greater than the maximum permissible working pressure specified in the last report (Schedule 4 of this Certificate) on examination when cold?

    ....

    (ii) (If a lever valve)—Is the weight secured on the lever in the correct position?

    ....

9. Any other observations ....

    ....

    ....

10. I CERTIFY that I examined the above mentioned steam boiler under normal pressure and the above is a true report of the results.

Signature ....

Qualification ....

Address ....

....

Date ....

Counter-signature (Chief Engineer) ....

Name of company or association ....

....

Date ....

*These particulars may also be used (as far as possible) for supplementary reports on economisers and superheaters.

SCHEDULE 6
(Paragraph 8 of Schedule 2)

PART A

1. Name of occupier..

2. Address of factory ....

PART B
REPORT OF AN EXAMINATION WHEN COLD OF A STEAM RECEIVER
INCLUDING ALL FITTINGS AND ATTACHMENTS TO WHICH
CERTIFICATE OF EXCEPTION NO. 63 APPLIES

1. Description and distinctive number of receiver and type:

....

2. Date of examination of steam receiver ....

3. Date of construction and brief history (the examiner should state whether he has seen the last previous report):

....

....

4. Date of last hydraulic test (if any), pressure applied and for how long maintained:

....

5. Maximum pressure of steam at source of supply to receiver (see Note A)

....

6. Receiver

    6.1 What parts (if any) were inaccessible? (see Schedule 2, paragraph 4, of this Certificate)

    ....

6.2 What examinations and tests were made?
....

6.3 Conditions of receiver (state any defects materially affecting the safe working pressure or the safe working of the receiver):
External ....
Internal ....

7. Fittings
7.1 Is the receiver so constructed as to withstand with safety the maximum pressure of steam at source of supply?
....

7.2 If not, are the required fittings and appliances provided in accordance with the Factories Act 1961, section 35(1) and (2)?
....

7.3 Are all fittings and appliances properly maintained and in good condition?
....

7.4 Has the safety valve been set correctly then sealed if necessary?
....

8. Repairs (if any) required, period within which they should be executed, and any other conditions which the person making the examination thinks it is necessary to specify for securing safe working:
....
....

9. Safe working pressure, calculated from dimensions and other data ascertained by the present examination, due allowance being made for conditions of working if unusual or exceptionally severe:
....

Where repairs affecting the working pressure are required, state the safe working pressure:
(a) Before the expiration of the period specified in (8):
....

(b) After the expiration of such period if the required repairs have not been completed:
....

(c) After the completion of the required repairs:
....

10. Other observations
....
....
....
....

I CERTIFY that on the said date I thoroughly examined the steam receiver above described (so far as construction of the receiver permits), including its fittings and appliances, and that the above is a true report of the result. In my opinion, the steam receiver can continue to be used under normal operating conditions and pressure for
.... months (period to be entered in words).
Signature ....
Qualification ....
Address ....
....
Date ....
If employed by a company or association give name and address:
....
....

Note A
Where the source of supply of steam is a boiler, the maximum pressure of steam at the source of supply should be taken to mean the maximum permissible working pressure of the boiler. In other cases (e.g. steam "passed out" from power plant) it should be taken

to mean the maximum pressure of steam which can be obtained in the pipe connecting the receiver with the source of supply. Where there is more than one source of supply, the source from which the greatest pressure can be obtained should be taken.

SCHEDULE 7
(Paragraph 8 of Schedule 2)

PART A

1. Name of factory occupier ....
2. Address of factory   ....

PART B
REPORT OF EXAMINATION OF AN AIR RECEIVER (NOT UNDER
PRESSURE) (INCLUDING ALL FITTINGS AND APPLIANCES) TO WHICH
CERTIFICATE OF EXCEPTION No. 63 APPLIES

1. Description and distinguishing mark of receiver and type: ....
....
2. Date of examination of air receiver: ....
3. Date of construction (if ascertainable) and brief history (the examiner should state whether he has seen the last previous report)
   ....
   ....
   ....
   ....
4. *Receiver*
   4.1 (a) What parts (if any) were inaccessible?
       ....
       (b) What examination and tests were made? (see Schedule 2, paragraph 4, of this Certificate)
       ....
   4.2 (a) Date of last hydraulic test ....
       (b) Pressure applied ....
   4.3 Condition of receiver
       (State cleanliness of receiver and any defects materially affecting the safe working pressure):
       External ....
       Internal ....
4. *Fittings*
   4.4 Are the required fittings and appliances provided in accordance with the Factories Act 1961, section 36(1)?
       ....
   4.5 Are all fittings and appliances properly maintained and in good condition?
       ....
   4.6 Has the safety valve been set correctly then sealed if necessary?
       ....
5. Repairs (if any) required and period within which they should be executed and any other conditions which the person making the examination thinks it necessary to specify for securing safe working:
   ....
   ....
6. Safe working pressure, calculated from dimensions and from the thickness and other data ascertained by the present examination (due allowance being made for conditions of working if unusual or exceptionally severe):
   ....

7. Where repairs affecting the working pressure are required, state the safe working pressure:
   (a) Before the expiration of the period specified in (5)
   ....
   (b) After the expiration of such period if the required repairs have not been completed
   ....
   (c) After the completion of the required repairs
   ....
8. Other observations ....
   ....
   ....
   ....

I CERTIFY that on the said date the air receiver described above was thoroughly cleaned adn (so far as its construction permits) made accessible for thorough examination and for such tests as were necessary for thorough examination and that on the said date I thoroughly examined this receiver, including its fittings, and that the above is a true report of my examination.

In my opinion the air receiver can continue to be used under normal operating conditions and pressure for

....months (period to be entered in words).

Signature ....

Qualification ....

Address ....

....

Date ....

If employed by a company or association give name and address:

....

....

....

SCHEDULE 8

(Paragraph 8 of Schedule 2)

PART A

1. Name of factory..
2. Address of factory ....

PART B

REPORT OF EXAMINATION UNDER NORMAL PRESSURE OF AN
AIR/STEAM* RECEIVER (INCLUDING ALL FITTINGS AND APPLIANCES)
TO WHICH CERTIFICATE OF EXCEPTION NO. 63 APPLIES

1. Description and distinctive number of receiver and type: ....
   ....
2. Date of examination of air/stream* receiver: ....
3. Receiver
   3.1 Condition (external) ....
   3.2 Result of examination under normal pressure ....
   ....
4. Fittings
   4.1 Are the fittings properly maintained and in good working order? ....
   ....
   4.2 Is the safety valve correctly set? ....

5. Repairs (if any) required, and period within which they should be executed.

....

6. Other observations ....

....

....

....

I CERTIFY that on the said date I examined the above-mentioned steam/air* receiver under normal pressure (including its fittings and applicances) and that the above is a true report of the result.

Signature   ....

Qualification   ....

Address   ....

....

Date ....

If employed by a company or association give name and address:

....

....

Date ....

*Delete whichever is appropriate.

(Form 2517, 23rd August 1983)

Certificate of Exception No. 64. Examination of Steam Boilers and Associated Air Receivers and Steam Receivers

1. In pursuance of section 37(2) and (3) of the Factories Act 1961 being satisfied that the provisions cannot reasonably be applied, I hereby except—
   (a) those steam boilers of the type specified in Part I of Schedule 1 hereto from the provisions of section 32(1)(b) and (c) and section 33(2) and (3) of that Act.
   (b) any steam receiver of the type specified in Part II of Schedule 1 hereto associated with such steam boiler, from the provisions of section 35(5) of that Act to the extent that that section refers to examination; and
   (c) any air receiver associated with such steam boiler, from the provision of section 36(4) of that Act.

2. This exception is granted subject to the conditions of Schedule 2 hereto and subject to a report being made containing the appropriate particulars set out in Schedules 3 to 7 hereto.

3. This Certificate shall remain in force until revoked in writing by an inspector appointed under Section 19 of the Health and Safety at Work etc. Act 1974 and duly authorised in that behalf.

SCHEDULE 1

PART I
STEAM BOILERS TO WHICH THIS CERTIFICATE APPLIES

The steam boiler shall be a steam boiler as defined in section 38 of the Factories Act 1961 which—
   (a) is an intergral part of a continuous flow installation in an ammonia methanol or hydrogen process;
   (b) is of welded or solid forged construction;
   (c) is so constructed that the drums and headers are outside the heat transfer zone;
   (d) has a maximum permissible pressure under section 33(5) of the Factories Act 1961 not exceeding 140 bar above atmospheric pressure;
   (e) is provided with an effective automatic water level control device fitted to regulate the feed water supply to the boiler which maintains the level of water in the boiler between predetermined limits;

(f)　is provided with an effective automatic signalling device which gives audible or visual warning in the event of imminence of shortage of water within the boiler; and

(g)　is so constructed that no naked flame is in contact with any part of it.

PART II

STEAM RECEIVERS TO WHICH THIS CERTIFICATE APPLIES

The steam receiver shall be of welded or solid forged construction and shall not have any pipe supplying steam to it at a pressure exceeding 140 bar above atmospheric pressure.

PART III

AIR RECEIVERS TO WHICH THIS CERTIFICATE APPLIES

The air receiver shall not be of solid drawn construction.

SCHEDULE 2

CONDITIONS

First two examinations

1. The steam boiler together with its fittings and attachements (referred to in this Schedule as "the boiler"), the air receiver and the steam receiver shall be thoroughly examined by a competent person in the manner specified in paragraph 4 of this Schedule before being taken into use for the first time in any factory, and examined again after such period as the person making the first examination may specify, which period may not exceed 18 months.

Subsequent examinations

2.—(1) The boiler, air receiver or steam receiver shall not thereafter be used in a factory unless it has been thoroughly examined in the manner specified in paragraph 4 of this Schedule, and no greater period has elapsed than 48 months, or such shorter period as the person making the previous examination has specified, since the completion of the last examination.

(2) In addition to the provisons of sub-paragraph (1) above, the boiler shall be examined within one month of the mid-point of the period specified by the competent person, which examination shall be under normal steam pressure and shall be as thorough as the operating conditions permit.

Examination after repair

3. Whenever the boiler, air receiver or steam receiver is repaired in such a way that in the opinion of the competent person its safe working may be affected it shall be examined by a competent person in such a manner as will enable him to satisfy himself that the repair has been properly carried out before the boiler, air receiver or steam receiver is used.

Method of examination

4.—(1) The air receiver shall be thoroughly cleaned.

(2) The boiler shall be prepared for examination by any or all of the following, as the competent person may decide—

(a)　the opening out, cleaning and descaling of the boiler including the removal of doors from manholes, mudholes and handholes;

(b)　the opening out for cleaning and inspection of fittings including the pressure parts of automatic controls;

(c)　in the case of water tube boilers, the removal of drum internal fittings; and brickwork, baffles and coverings shall be removed for the purpose of the thorough examination to the extent required by the person making the examination.

(3) The steam receiver shall have its interior and exterior prepared in a proper manner.

(4) The boiler and steam receiver when cold and the air receiver when not under pressure shall be thoroughly examined and in particular—

  (a) every pressure gauge and safety valve provided under sections 32(1)(a), 35(1) and 36(1) of the Factories Act 1961 shall be removed, tested for accuracy and correct functioning whilst removed, thoroughly examined and again tested for accuracy; and

  (b) every safety valve which can only be set when cold shall be set and have a seal affixed.

(5) In addition to sub-paragraph (4) above, the person making the examination of the boiler, air receiver or steam receiver may—

  (a) measure the thickness of any part;

  (b) test any part for flaws;

  (c) prove clear waterways in the tubes; and

  (d) withdraw sample tubes to measure their thickness, assess their condition and test or measure them.

(6) Any test or measurement may include the use of ultrasonic, radiographic, magnetic or electronic devices, or tube calibration gauges, steam trial or hydraulic testing, but may not include any destructive methods other than paragraph 4(5)(d) hereto.

(7) The boiler (other than any economiser or superheater) and the steam receiver shall be thoroughly examined under normal steam pressure and the air receiver shall be thoroughly examined under normal air pressure within 28 days of steam first being raised after the examination when cold, and every boiler safety valve adjusted so as to prevent working at a pressure greater than the maximum permissible working pressure.

(8) Different parts of the examination and testing may be made by different persons.

Renewal of boiler parts

5. Where the competent person examining the boiler states in his report that the effective life of any part of the boiler is likely to terminate through creep, fatigue or any other reason, it shall be renewed by the date specified in that report.

Quality of feed water

6. The feed water supplied to the boiler shall be of such quality as to prevent, so far as is reasonably practicable—

  (a) corrosion in any part of the boiler; and

  (b) formation of scale or sludge to an extent liable to affect the safe operation of the boiler.

Periodic checks and blowing down

7.—(1) When the boiler is in use, at least once in every shift, or every 12 hours, whichever period is less—

  (a) a check shall be made to ensure that every device specified in sub-paragraphs (e) and (f) of Part I of Schedule 1 hereto is operating satisfactorily; and

  (b) the boiler shall be blown down in such a manner and at such a rate as to minimise deposits of scale and sludge.

(2) Samples of water from the boiler shall be taken at suitable intervals and analysed by a competent person in order to verify that the boiler water is free from sludge and scale, so far as is reasonably practicable, and a suitable record of these analyses shall be kept.

Report of examination

8.—(1) A report of every examination made in pursuance of paragraph 4 of this Schedule shall as soon as is practicable and in any case within 28 days after the completion of the examination be entered in or attached to the general register as defined in the Factories Act 1961, section 176, and that report shall be signed by the person or persons making the examination (and where that person is an employee of a boiler inspecting company or association, that part of the report concerning the steam boiler shall also be counter-signed by the Chief Engineer of the company or association or by such other responsible officer of the company or association as may be authorised in writing on their behalf by the Chief Engineer) and that report shall contain the appropriate particulars set out in Schedules 3 to 7 hereto.

(2) The person making an examination or part of an examination under this Certificate shall notify the occupier in writing forthwith and within 28 days after the completion of the examination shall send to the Health and Safety Executive a copy of the report in every case where the maximum permissible working pressure is reduced or the examination shows that the boiler, air receiver or steam receiver cannot continue to be used with safety unless certain repairs are carried out immediately or within a specified time, or the person making this examination is of the opinion that a defect exists which would be liable to affect the safe working of any of them.

(3) Where the report of any examination under this Certificate specifies conditions for securing the safe working of a boiler, air receiver or steam receiver, they shall not be used except in accordance with these conditions.

SCHEDULE 4
(Paragraph 8)

PART A

1. Name of occupier ....
2. Address of factory ....
....

PART B
REPORT OF EXAMINATION WHEN COLD OF A STEAM BOILER
INCLUDING ALL FITTINGS AND ATTACHMENTS TO WHICH CERTIFICATE
OF EXCEPTION NO. 64 APPLIES

1. Description and distinctive number of boiler and type ....
....
2. Date of examination of boiler ....
3. Maximum permissible working pressure ....
4. Date of construction, and brief history (the examiner shall state whether he has seen the last previous report)
....
....
....
5. Date of hydraulic test. Pressure applied and period pressure applied.
   Date ....
   Pressure Applied ....
   Period pressure applied ....
6. Water Tube Boilers
   (a) *Downcomer Tubes*
   6.1 Have the downcomer tubes been checked for distortion? ....
   6.2 Have the downcomer tubes been checked for thickness? ....
   6.3 Have the downcomer tubes been checked for signs of corrosion? ....
   6.4 Do any need repair? ....
   6.5 Do any need replacement? ....
   (b) *Riser Tubes*
   6.6 Have the riser tubes been checked for distortion? ....
   6.7 Have the riser tubes been checked for thickness? ....
   6.8 Have the riser tubes been checked for signs of corrosion? ....
   6.9 Do any need repair? ....
   6.10 Do any need replacement? ....

(c) *Headers*

6.11 Have the headers been checked for thickness? ....

6.12 Have the headers been checked for signs of corrosion? ....

6.13 Do any need repair? ....

6.14 Do any need replacement? ....

(d) *Header Caps*

6.15 Have the header caps been checked for thickness? ....

6.16 Have the header caps been checked for signs of corrosion? ....

6.16 Do any need repair? ....

6.17 Do any need replacement? ....

(e) *Drums*

6.19 Has the exterior been checked for corrosion etc? ....

6.20 Has the interior been checked for corrosion etc? ....

6.21 Are any repairs needed? ....

(f) *Condition of parts not listed above* ....

....

7. Shell Boilers

(a) *Furnace Tubes*

7.1 Have the tubes been checked for thickness? ....

7.2 Have the tubes been checked for corrosion etc? ....

7.3 Do any need repair? ....

7.4 Do any need replacement? ....

(b) *Tube Plates*

7.5 Have the plates been checked for thickness? ....

7.6 Have the plates been checked for corrosion etc? ....

7.7 Do any need repair? ....

7.8 Do any need replacement? ....

(c) *Condition of parts not listed above*

....

....

....

8. Boiler Fittings

8.1 Has the stop-valve been examined? ....

8.2 Does it require repair/replacement? ....

8.3 Has the water gauge been examined? ....

8.4 Does it require repair/replacement? ....

8.5 Has the low-water alarm device been examined? ....

8.6 Does it require repair/replacement? ....

8.7 Has the safety valve been thoroughly examined? ....

8.8 Has it been set where necessary? ....

8.9 Does it require repair/replacement? ....

8.10 Has the pressure gauge been tested for accuracy? ....

8.11 Does it require repair/replacement? ....

9. State any defects as a result of which:

(a) The boiler cannot continue to be used with safety unless repairs are carried out immediately, or within a specified time.

....

(b) The maximum permissible working pressure has been reduced.

....

....

10. I CERTIFY that the boiler above described was sufficiently descaled, prepared and (so far as its construction permits) made accessible for thorough examination, and for such tests as were necessary for thorough examination, and that on the said date I thoroughly examined the boiler including its fittings and attachments, and the above is a true report of the results. In my opinion the boiler can continue to be

steamed under normal operating conditions and pressure for .... months
(period to be entered in words).
Signature ....
Qualification ....
Address ....
....
Date ....
Counter-signature (Chief Engineer) ....
Name of company or association ....
Date ....

PART C

REPORT OF AN EXAMINATION WHEN COLD OF AN ECONOMISER
INCLUDING ALL FITTINGS AND ATTACHMENTS TO WHICH CERTIFICATE
OF EXCEPTION NO. 64 APPLIES

1. Description and distinctive number of economiser ....
....
....
   Type ....
   Number of tubes ....
2. Date of examination ....
3. Date of construction and brief history (the examiner should state whether he has
   seen the last previous report)
....
....
....
4. Date of last hydraulic test (if any) ....
   Pressure applied ....
5. Are the dampers in proper working order? ....
6. (a) What parts are inaccessible? ....
   (b) State number of top caps removed for examination ....
   (c) State number of bottom caps removed for examination ....
   (d) What examinations and tests were made (see paragraph 4 of this Certificate)
....
....
   (e) External ....
....
        Internal ....
....
7. (a) Are there proper fittings and attachments? ....
   (b) Are all fittings and attachments in satisfactory condition (so far as is ascertain-
        able when not under pressure)?
....
8. Repairs (if any) required, and period within which they should be executed, and any
   other conditions which the person making the examination thinks it necessary to
   specify for securing safe working.
....
....
....
9. Maximum permissible working pressure calculated from dimensions and from the
   thickness, and other data ascertained by the present examination (due allowance
   being made for conditions of working if unusual or exceptionally severe)
....
10 Where repairs affecting the working pressure are required state the maximum
   permissible working pressure:

(a) Before the expiration of the period specified in paragraph 9 above.

....

(b) After the expiration of such period if the required repairs have not been completed

....

(c) After the completion of the required repairs

....

11. Other observations ....

....

....

....

12. I CERTIFY that the economiser above described was sufficiently descaled, prepared and (so far as its construction permits) made accessible for thorough examination, and for such tests as were necessary for thorough examination and that on the said date I thoroughly examined the economiser including its fittings and attachments, and the above is a true report of the result. In my opinion the economiser can continue to be steamed under normal operating conditions and pressure for .... months (to be entered in words).

Signature ....

Qualification ....

Address ....

....

Date ....

Counter-signature (Chief Engineer) ....

Name of company or association ....

Date ....

PART D

REPORT OF AN EXAMINATION WHEN COLD OF A SUPERHEATER
INCLUDING ALL FITTINGS AND ATTACHMENTS TO WHICH
CERTIFICATE OF EXCEPTION NO. 64 APPLIES

1. Description and distinctive number of superheater and type ....

....

2. Date of examination ....

3. Date of construction and brief history. (The examiner should state whether he has seen the last previous report)

....

....

....

4. Date of last hydraulic test (if any) ....

Pressure applied ....

5. (a) What parts are covered by brickwork? ....

....

(b) Date of last exposure of such parts for the purpose of examination

....

(c) What parts (if any) other than those covered by brickwork were inaccessible?

....

6. *Headers*

(a) Have the headers been checked for thickness? ....

(b) Are they being affected by creep? ....

(c) Do any need repair/replacing? ....

7. *Tubes*

(a) Have the tubes been checked for distortion? ....

(b) Have the tubes been checked for thickness? ....

(c) Have the tubes been checked for signs of corrosion? ....

....

    (d) Do they need repair/replacement?..
8. *Safety valve(s)*
    (a) Has the safety valve(s) been thoroughly examined? ....
    (b) Does it/they require repair/replacement? ....
    (c) Has it/they been set and sealed where necessary? ....
9. *Fittings and attachements*
    (a) Are all the necessary fittings and attachments present and in a satisfactory
        condition (so far as is ascertainable when not under pressure)? ....
        ....

10. Condition of superheater (state any defects materially affecting the maximum
    permissible working pressure).
    External ....
    Internal ....

11. State the period within which repairs (if any) should be executed and any other
    conditions which the person making the examination thinks it necessary to secure
    safe working.
    ....
    ....

12. Maximum permissible working pressure calculated from dimensions and from the
    thickness and other data ascertained by the present examination; due allowance
    being made for the conditions of working if unusual or exceptionally severe.
    ....

13. Where repairs affecting the working pressure are required, state the maximum
    working pressure:
    (a) Before the expiration of the period specified in (11) above.
        ....

    (b) After the expiration of such period if the required repairs have not been
        completed.
        ....

    (c) After the completion of the required repairs.
        ....

14. Other observations ....
    ....
    ....

15. I CERTIFY that the superheater above described was sufficiently descaled, prepared
    and (so far as its construction permits) made accessible for thorough examination,
    and for such tests as were necessary for thorough examination and that on the said
    date I thoroughly examined the superheater including its fittings and attachments,
    and the above is a true report of the result. In my opinion the superheater can
    continue to be steamed under normal operating conditions and pressure for
    .... months (to be entered in words).
    Signature ....
    Qualification ....
    Address ....
    ....
    Date ....
    Counter-signature (Chief Engineer) ....
    Name of company or association ....
    ....
    Date ....

SCHEDULE 4
(Paragraph 8)

REPORT OF EXAMINATION UNDER NORMAL STEAM PRESSURE OF A
STEAM BOILER TO WHICH CERTIFICATE OF EXCEPTION NO. 63 APPLIES*

1. Name of occupier ....
2. Address of Factory ....
   ....
3. Description and distinctive number of boiler and type ....
   ....
4. Date of examination ....

Examination

5. (i) General condition (external) of the boiler including fittings and attachments.
   ....

   (ii) Fittings and attachments
   Were the following operating satisfactorily?
   (a) pressure gauge ....
   (b) water level gauge ....
   (c) blow-down arrangements ....
   (d) automatic water level control(s) ....
   (e) safety valve(s) ....
6. State any defects as a result of which:
   (a) the boiler cannot continue to be used with safety unless repairs are carried out
        immediately or within a specified time.
        ....
   (b) the maximum permissible working pressure has been reduced.
        ....

7. Repairs (if any) required and period within which they should be executed and any
   other conditions which the person making the examination thinks it necessary to
   specify for securing safe working
   ....
   ....

8. Is the safety valve(s) so adjusted as to prevent the boiler being worked at a pressure
   greater than the maximum permissible working pressure specified in the last report
   (Schedule 3 of this Certificate) on examination when cold?
   ....

9. Any other observations ....
   ....
   ....

10. I CERTIFY that I examined the above mentioned steam boiler under normal pressure
    and the above is a true report of the result.
Signature ....
Qualification ....
Address ....
....
Date ....
Counter-signature (Chief Engineer) ....
Name of company or association ....
....
Date ....
* These forms may also be used (as far as possible) for supplementary reports on
economisers and superheaters.

SCHEDULE 5

PART A

1. Name of occupier ....
2. Address of factory ....
   ....

PART B
REPORT OF AN EXAMINATION WHEN COLD OF A STEAM RECEIVER
INCLUDING ALL FITTINGS AND ATTACHMENTS TO WHICH
CERTIFICATE OF EXCEPTION NO. 64 APPLIES:

1. Description and distinctive number of receiver and type: ....
2. Date of examination of steam receiver ....
3. Date of construction and brief history (the examiner should state whether he has
   seen the last previous report):
   ....
   ....
4. Date of last hydraulic test (if any), pressure applied and for how long maintained:
   ....
5. Maximum pressure of steam at source of supply to receiver (see Note A)
   ....
6. *Receiver*
   6.1 What parts (if any) were inaccessible?
        ....
   6.2 What examinations and tests were made?
        ....
   6.3 Condition of receiver (state any defects materially affecting the safe working
        pressure or the safe working of the receiver):
        External ....
        Internal ....
7. *Fittings*
   7.1 Is the receiver so constructed as to withstand with safety the maximum pressure
        of steam at source of supply?
        ....
   7.2 If not, are the required fittings and appliances provided in accordance with the
        Factories Act 1961, section 35(1) and (2)?
        ....
   7.3 Are all fittings and appliances properly maintained and in good condition?
        ....
   7.4 Has the safety valve been set correctly then sealed if necessary?
        ....
8. Repairs (if any) required, period within which they should be executed, and any
   other conditions which the person making the examination thinks it is necessary to
   specify for securing safe working:
   ....
   ....
9. Safe working pressure, calculated from dimensions and other data ascertained by
   the present examination, due allowance being made for conditions of working if
   unusual or exceptionally severe:
   ....

   Where repairs affecting the working pressure are required, state the safe working
   pressure:

(a) Before the expiration of the period specified in (8):
....

(b) After the expiration of such period if the required repairs have not been completed:
....

(c) After the completion of the required repairs:
....

10. Other observations
....
....
....
....

I CERTIFY that on the said date I thoroughly examined the steam receiver above described (so far as construction of the receiver permits), including its fittings and appliances, and that the above is a true report of the result. In my opinion, the steam receiver can continue to be used under normal operating conditions and pressure for
.... months (period to be entered in words).
Signature ....
Qualification ....
Address ....
....
Date ....
If employed by a company or association give name and address:
....
....

Note A: where the source of supply of steam is a boiler, the maximum pressure of steam at the source of supply should be taken to mean the maximum permissible working pressure of the boiler. In other cases (e.g. steam "passed out" from power plant) it should be taken to mean the maximum pressure of steam which can be obtained in the pipe connecting the receiver with the source of supply. Where there is more than one source of supply, the source from which the greatest pressure can be obtained should be taken.

SCHEDULE 6

PART A

1. Name of factory occupier ....
2. Address of factory ....
....

PART B
REPORT OF AN EXAMINATION OF AN AIR RECEIVER (NOT UNDER PRESSURE) (INCLUDING ALL FITTINGS AND APPLIANCES) TO WHICH CERTIFICATE OF EXCEPTION NO. 64 APPLIES

1. Description and distinguishing mark of receiver and type: ....
....
2. Date of examination of air receiver: ....
3. Date of construction (if ascertainable) and brief history (the examiner should state whether he has seen the last previous report)
....
....
....
....

4. *Receiver*

   4.1 (a) What parts (if any) were inaccessible?

   ....

      (b) What examination and tests were made?

   ....

   4.2 (a) Date of last hydraulic test ....
      (b) Pressure applied ....
   4.3 Condition of receiver
      (State cleanliness of receiver and any defects materially affecting the safe
      working pressure):
      External ....
      Internal ....

5. *Fittings*

   5.1 Are the required fittings and appliances provided in accordance with the
      Factories Act 1961, section 36(1)?

   ....

   5.2 Are all fittings and appliances maintained and in good condition?

   ....

   5.3 Has the safety value been set correctly then sealed if necessary?

   ....

6. Repairs (if any) required and period within which they should be executed and any
   other conditions which the person making the examinations thinks it necessary to
   specify for securing safe working:

   ....
   ....

7. Safe working pressure, calculated from dimensions and from the thickness and
   other data ascertained by the present examination (due allowance being made for
   conditions of working if unusual or exceptionally severe):

   ....

8. Where repairs affecting the working pressure are required, state the safe working
   pressure:
   (a) Before the expiration of the period specified in (5)

   ....

   (b) After the expiration of such period if the required repairs have not been
      completed

   ....

   (c) After the completion of the required repairs

   ....

9. Other observations ....
   ....
   ....
   ....
   ....

I CERTIFY that on the said date I examined the above-mentioned air receiver under
normal pressure (including its fittings and appliances) and that the above is a true
report of the result. In my opinion the air receiver can continue to be used under normal
operating conditions and pressure for
.... months (period to be entered in words).
Signature ....
Qualification ....
Address ....
....
Date ....
If employed by a company or association give name and address:
....
....

SCHEDULE 7

PART A

1. Name of factory ....
2. Address of factory ....

PART B

REPORT OF EXAMINATION UNDER NORMAL PRESSURE OF AN AIR/STEAM*
RECEIVER (INCLUDING ALL FITTINGS AND APPLIANCES) TO WHICH
CERTIFICATE OF EXCEPTION NO. 64 APPLIES

1. Description and distinctive number of receiver and type: ....
   ....
2. Date of examination of air/steam* receiver: ....
3. *Receiver*
   3.1 Conditions (external) ....
   3.2 Result of examination under normal pressure:
   ....
4. *Fittings*
   4.1 Are the fittings properly maintained and in good working order? ....
   ....
   4.2 Is the safety valve correctly set? ....
5. Repairs (if any) required, and period within which they should be executed.
   ....
6. Other observations ....
   ....
   ....
   ....

I CERTIFY that on the said date I examined the above-mentioned air receiver under
normal pressure (including its fittings and appliances) and that the above is a true
report of the result. In my opinion the air receiver can continue to be used under normal
operating conditions and pressure for
.... months (period to be entered in words).
Signature ....
Qualification ....
Address ....
....
If employed by a company or association give name and address:
....
Signature ....
Name and address of company or association ....
....
....
....
*Delete whichever is appropriate.

(F2518, 23 September 1983)

Certificate of Exception No. SPA/FA/1984/4 (General) Pursuant to sections 37(2)
and (3) of the Factories Act 1961, being satisfied that the provisions cannot reasonably
be applied, I hereby except from the provisions of section 32 and sections 33(1), 33(2),
33(3) and 33(5) of the said Act any steam boiler, within the meaning of section 38 of the
said Act, of the type specified in Part I of the Schedule to this Certificate subject to the
conditions specified in Part II of the Schedule to this Certificate.

This Certificate shall come into operation on 12 February 1985 and shall remain in force until revoked in writing by an Inspector appointed and authorised as hereinafter appears.

Certificate of Exemption No. 6; (Electrical Induction Heated Rieter J7/3 Vapour Trimmed Rolls) dated 17 February 1976 under the Factories Act 1961 is hereby revoked.

SCHEDULE

PART I

Any steam boiler which forms part of inductively heated vapour trimmed rolls used for the processing of synthetic fibres which is:

(a) of good construction, sound material and adequate strength, and free from patent defect;
(b) for steam boilers manufactured after the coming into operation of this Certificate, designed and manufactured to British Standard BS 5500 "Unfired fusion welded pressure vessels" Category 1, as in force at the time of manufacture;
(c) designed to take into account the rotational speed of the rolls;
(d) provided with effective automatic means to shut off the supply of electricity to the heated elements at an appropriate steam temperature which is below the saturated steam temperature corresponding to the maximum permissible working pressure of the boiler;
(e) provided with effective automatic means to lock out the supply of electricity to the heating elements when the temperature of the steam exceeds the saturated steam temperature corresponding to the maximum permissible working pressure of the steam boiler, which means requires to be manually reset before the supply of electricity can be restored; and
(f) where the steam boiler is one of two or more boilers, fitted with a plate bearing a distinctive number which is easily visible.

PART II

Initial examination, testing etc.

1. Every steam boiler to which this Certificate applies, and which is manufactured after the coming into operation of this Certificate, shall, before being taken into use for the first time, be inspected, tested and certified as required by the relevant parts of British Standards BS 5500 "Unfired fusion welded pressure vessels".

2. Every steam boiler to which this Certificate applies shall, before it is sealed, be thoroughly examined so far as its construction permits, and be properly tested by hydraulic pressure.

3. A certificate of the test carried out to comply with paragraph 2 of this Part of the Schedule, specifying the pressure applied and signed by the person carrying out or supervising the tests shall be entered in or attached to the general register required by Section 140 of the Factories Act 1961.

Subsequent examinations

4. Every steam boiler to which this Certificate applies, together with all its fittings and attachments, shall be thoroughly examined by a competent person before being taken into use for the first time and subsequently within the period of use allowed by the competent person at each thorough examination, which period shall not exceed fourteen months.

Examination after repair

5. Every steam boiler to which this Certificate applies shall, whenever the steam boiler is repaired in such a manner that in the opinion of a competent person its safe working may be affected, be thoroughly examined by a competent person before the

steam boiler is used, in such a manner as will enable that competent person to be satisfied that the repair has been properly carried out.

Method of examination

6. Every thorough examination carried out to comply with paragraphs 4 and 5 of this Part of the Schedule shall consist of at least a thorough external examination of the steam boiler and examination and testing of the fittings specified in paragraphs (d) and (e) of Part I of this Schedule, when the steam boiler is cold and under steam pressure.

7. Different parts of the examination and testing may be made by different persons.

Reports of thorough examinations etc.

8. The provisions of sections 33(4), 33(6), 33(7), 33(8), 33(9), 33(10) and 33(11) of the Factories Act 1961 shall with the substitution of the words "Under this Certificate" for the words "Under this Section" be deemed to be incorporated in this Certificate, and any prescription for the purpose of those sections shall be deemed to be a prescription for the purpose of this Certificate.

Conditions of use

9. The internal pressure in every steam boiler to which this Certificate applies shall be such that the product of internal pressure (in KiloNewtons per square metre above atmospheric pressure) and vapour space volume (in cubic metres) does not exceed 20.

10. No steam boiler to which this Certificate applies shall be supplied with any water other than de-ionising water.

11. The design stress of the shell unit shall be the summation of the stress due to the internal pressure and that stress due to the rotational forces at the normal operating rotational speed. The maximum rotational speed shall be such that the resultant stress does not exceed 110% of the design stress.

(6 February 1985)

---

33. Steam boilers—maintenance, examination and use.—(1) Every steam boiler *(a)* and all its fittings and attachments shall be properly maintained *(b)*.

(2) A steam boiler *(a)* shall not be used in any factory *(c)* unless it has been examined, together with its fittings and attachments, in such manner as the Minister *(d)* may by regulations *(e)* prescribe and no greater period than may be so prescribed has elapsed since the examination, but the regulations may provide for extending in special circumstances the time during which a boiler which has been examined as required by the regulations may be used in a factory without being again so examined.

(3) The Minister *(d)* may by regulations *(e)* prescribe the manner in which a steam boiler, together with its fittings and attachments, is to be examined after any such repairs as may be specified in the regulations; and where such repairs are carried out to a steam boiler after it has been examined under subsection (2) of this section, then, notwithstanding that the period prescribed under that subsection has not expired, the steam boiler shall not be used in any factory until the examination prescribed under this subsection has been made.

(4) A report of the result of every examination under this section in the prescribed form *(f)* and containing the prescribed particulars *(f)* (including the maximum permissible working pressure) *(g)* shall as soon as practicable and in any case within twenty-eight days, or such other period as the Minister *(d)* may by regulations *(e)* prescribe, after the completion of the examination, be entered in or attached to the general register *(h)*, and the report shall be signed

by the person making the examination, and if that person is an inspector of a boiler-inspecting company or association, countersigned by the chief engineer of the company or association or by such other responsible officer of the company or association as may be authorised in writing in that behalf by the chief engineer.

(5) No new steam boiler *(a)* shall be taken into use unless there has been obtained from the manufacturer of the boiler, or from a boiler-inspecting company or association, a certificate specifying its maximum permissible working pressure *(h)*, and stating the nature of the tests to which the boiler and fittings have been submitted, and the certificate is kept available for inspection, and the boiler is so marked as to enable it to be identified as the boiler to which the certificate relates.

(6) Where the report of any examination under this section specifies conditions for securing the safe working of a steam boiler, the boiler shall not be used except in accordance with those conditions.

(7) The person making the report of an examination under this section or, in the case of a boiler-inspecting company or association, the chief engineer thereof, shall within twenty-eight days, or such other period as the Minister *(d)* may by regulations *(e)* prescribe, after the completion of the examination send to the inspector for the district *(i)* a copy of the report in every case where the maximum permissible working pressure *(h)* is reduced, or the examination shows that the boiler cannot continue to be used with safety unless certain repairs are carried out immediately or within a specified time.

(8) If the person employed to make any such examination fails to make a thorough examination as required by this section or makes a report which is false or deficient in any material particular, or if the chief engineer of any boiler-inspecting company or association permits any such report to be made, he shall be guilty of an offence *(j)*, and if any such person or chief engineer fails to send to the inspector for the district a copy of any report as required by subsection (7) of this section, he shall be guilty of an offence *(j)*.

(9) If the chief inspector *(i)* is not satisfied as to the competency of the person employed to make the examination or as to the thoroughness of the examination, he may require the boiler to be re-examined by a person nominated by him, and the occupier *(l)* shall give the necessary facilities for the re-examination.

(10) If as a result of the re-examination it appears that the report of the examination was inadequate or inaccurate in any material particular, the cost of the re-examination shall be recoverable from the occupier *(l)*, and the report of the re-examination purporting to be signed by the person making it shall be admissible in evidence of the facts stated therein.

(11) Any sum recoverable under subsection (10) of this section shall, in England and Wales, be recoverable summarily as a civil debt.

General note. This section is repealed by S.I. 1989 No. 2169, as from 1 July 1994.

By virtue of s. 37(2), certain exceptions have been made from the provisions of this section. These exceptions are set out below. See also Certificates of Exception Nos. 63 and 64 and No. SPA/FA/1984/4 (General), which are set out following the notes to s. 32.

(a) Steam boiler. For definition, see s. 38.

(b) **Properly maintained.** See INTRODUCTORY NOTE 10.

(c) **Factory.** For definition, see s. 175.

(d) **The Minister.** For definition, see s. 176(1).

(e) **Regulations.** Regulations made under sub-ss. (2) and (3) are set out below.

(f) **Prescribed forms and particulars.** Prescribed means prescribed by the Minister (s. 176(1)). The prescribed forms for reports are as follows: Examinations of steam boiler cold—Form 55; Examination of steam boiler under normal pressure (also for economiser and superheater)—Form 55A; Examination when cold of steam boiler, heat exchanger or superheater to which Exception No. 57 applies—Form 55B; Examination under normal pressure of steam boiler to which Exception No. 57 applies—Form 55C; Examination of superheater cold—Form 57; Examination of steam tube oven (fold) or steam tube hotplate—Form 62A.

(g) **Maximum permissible working pressure.** For definition, see s. 38.

(h) **General register.** See ss. 140, 141 and 166(3).

(i) **Inspector.** For definition, see s. 176(1).

(j) **Offence.** See s. 155.

(l) **Occupier.** It is singular that there is no statutory definition of this word, which occurs so often in the Act. In *Ramsay v Mackie* (1904 7 F 106), Lord Maclaren gave the following definition (at 109): "'Occupier' plainly means the person who runs the factory . . ., who regulates and controls the work that is done there". This definition was adopted and applied by the Court of Appeal in *Cox v S Cutler & Sons Ltd and Hampton Court Gas Co* [1948] 2 All ER 665.

See also *Meigh v Wickenden* [1942] 2 KB 160, [1942] 2 All ER 68, where the receiver and manager for debenture holders was held to be the occupier. *Lord Advocate v Aero Technologies Ltd* 1991 SLT 134 shows that the company and receiver may be regarded as joint occupiers. In *Rippon v Port of London Authority and J Russell & Co* [1940] 1 KB 858, [1940] 1 All ER 637, Tucker J held that the first defendants, who were the owners of a public dry-dock which they had let out to the second defendants, were nevertheless the "occupiers" for the purposes of the Factories Act 1937, since they retained possession and control of the dry-dock.

THE EXAMINATION OF STEAM BOILERS REGULATIONS 1964
(S.I. 1964 No. 781, as amended by S.I. 1981 No. 687)

General note. The whole Regulations are revoked by S.I. 1989 No. 2169, as from 1 July 1994.

The Minister of Labour—
(a) by virtue of the powers conferred on him by section 33(2) and (3) and section 180(3) of the Factories Act 1961 and of all other powers enabling him in that behalf; and
(b) after publishing, pursuant to Schedule 4 to the said Act of 1961, notice of the proposal to make the Regulations and not having received any objection to the draft in regard to which he is required by the said Schedule to direct any inquiry to be held,
hereby makes the following special Regulations:—

Citation and commencement
1. These Regulations may be cited as the Examination of Steam Boilers Regulations 1964 and shall come into operation on 27 June 1964. Provided that as respects any steam boiler that was thoroughly examined by a competent person before the coming into operation of these Regulations they shall not apply until its first examination thereafter; so, however, that the interval between the said two examinations shall not in the case of

any boiler exceed the relevant period prescribed by regulation 4 or, in the case of a boiler as respects which an exemption order was in force immediately before the coming into operation of these Regulations, such greater period as may be specified in the exemption order.

Interpretation

2.—(1) The Interpretation Act 1889 shall apply to the interpretation of these Regulations as it applies to the interpretation of an Act of Parliament.

(2) In these Regulations, unless the context otherwise requires, the following expressions have the meanings hereby assigned to them—

"excepted boiler" means a boiler belonging to or exclusively used in the service of Her Majesty or belonging to and used by the United Kingdom Atomic Energy Authority or the boiler of any ship or of any locomotive which belongs to and is used by any railway company;

"exemption order" means an order made, or having effect as if made, under the substituted subsection (3A) of section 33 set out in paragraph 3 of Schedule 6 to the principal Act;

"factory" means a factory as defined in section 175 of the principal Act or any place to which the provisions of Part II of that Act with respect to steam boilers are applied by any of the following provisions of that Act, that is to say, section 123(1) (which relates to electrical stations), section 124 (which relates to institutions), section 125(1) and (3) (which relates to certain dock premises and certain warehouses) and section 127 (which relates to building operations and works of engineering construction);

"the principal Act" means the Factories Act 1961 as amended by or under any other Act;

"section 33" means section 33 of the principal Act;

"steam boiler" does not include any excepted boiler but save as aforesaid means any closed vessel in which for any purpose steam is generated under pressure greater than atmospheric pressure, and includes any economiser used to heat water being fed to any such vessel, and any superheater used for heating steam, and any reference to a steam boiler shall include a reference to all its fittings and attachments.

Manner of examination

3.—(1) The manner in which a steam boiler shall be examined as required by section 33(2)—

(a) before it is used in any factory; and

(b) thereafter before the expiry of each of the relevant periods prescribed by regulations 4 or 5,

shall be the manner specified in this regulation.

(2) In the first place, the boiler shall be thoroughly examined by a competent person when it is cold after the interior and exterior have been prepared in the manner described in the Schedule to these Regulations, and secondly, except in the case of an economiser or superheater, the boiler shall be thoroughly examined by a competent person when it is under normal steam pressure, and each part of the examination may be made by a different person. The examination under steam pressure shall be made on the first occasion when steam is raised after the examination of the boiler when cold, or as soon as possible thereafter, and the person making the examination shall see that the safety valve is so adjusted as to prevent the boiler being worked at a pressure greater than the maximum permissible pressure to be specified in the report of the examination pursuant to section 33(4).

(3) The examination of a boiler in the manner specified in the preceding paragraphs of this regulation may, at the discretion of the person making the examination, include all or anyone or more of the following, that is to say, hammer testing, drilling, lifting, proving a clear waterway through tubes, withdrawal of sample tubes for determination of thickness, examination, testing or measurement by means of ultrasonic, radiographic, magnetic or electronic devices or of tube calibration gauges, steam trial and hydraulic testing.

Intervals between examinations

4.—(1) For the purposes of section 33(2) (which prohibits the use in any factory, for any greater period than may be prescribed, of a steam boiler since its last examination) the prescribed period shall be as follows, that it to say—

(a) in a case where a stationary steam boiler (other than a boiler used in the course of any building operation or work of engineering construction) after being used or installed in one factory is to be used in another factory, a period which expires after it has been installed, and before it is used, in the second of those factories;

(b) in a case where a steam boiler of a kind specified in paragraph (2) of this regulation is taken into use in any factory for the first time in that factory (whether or not in the circumstances specified in the preceding sub-paragraph), a period which expires not more than 14 months after the date when it was so taken into use; and

(c) in all other cases, subject to regulation 5.

   (i) 26 months as respects a steam boiler of a kind specified in paragraph (2) of this regulation; and

   (ii) 14 months as respects any other steam boiler.

(2) Sub-paragraphs (b) and (c)(i) of the preceding paragraph apply to a steam boiler of any of the following kinds in the case of which a period of 21 years has not expired since it was first taken into use, that is to say—

(a) a water tube boiler of which the drums and any headers are of fusion welded or solid forged construction which has an evaporative capacity of not less than 6.3 kilograms of steam per second;

(b) a boiler in a group of water tube boilers of which the drums and any headers are of fusion welded or solid forged construction being a group in which—

   (i) each boiler has an evaporative capacity of not less than 3.15 kilograms of steam per second; and

   (ii) the total evaporative capacity of all the boilers is not less than 12.6 kilograms of steam per second; and

(c) a boiler which is a waste heat boiler or heat exchanger with fusion welded longitudinal and circumferential seams, or a superheater of fusion welded construction, and which is an integral part of a continuous flow installation, in a chemical or oil refinery processing plant.

Boilers previously subject to exemption order

5. In the case of any steam boiler, as respects which an exemption order was in force immediately before the coming into operation of these Regulations, being an order made on conditions by which a greater period is allowed between examinations than that specified in regulation 4, the prescribed period for the purposes of section 33(2) shall be in accordance with the provisions of that order:

Provided that this regulation shall not apply—

(a) in respect of any period after the expiration of 3 years from the coming into operation of these Regulations; or

(b) as respects any steam boiler, after the expiration of the period of 21 years since it was first taken into use.

Examinations of boilers after repair

6. Where at any time there is carried out to any steam boiler the repair of a defect which, in the opinion of a competent person, will affect its safe working, that boiler shall be examined by a competent person in such a manner as will enable that person to satisfy himself that the repair has been properly carried out.

SCHEDULE

Regulation 3(2)

THE MANNER OF PREPARING A STEAM BOILER FOR EXAMINATION WHEN IT IS COLD

(1) In addition to the steps required to be taken under paragraph (2) of this Schedule, the preparation of the interior and exterior of a boiler for its thorough examination when cold in pursuance of regulation 3(2) shall, according as the person making the examination may require, consist of all or any one or more of the following, that is to say—

    (a) the opening out, cleaning and scaling of the boiler; including the removal of doors from manholes, mudholes and handholes;

    (b) the removal of firebars;

    (c) in the case of shell type boilers, the dismantling of firebridges (if made of brick) and all furnace protective brickwork;

    (d) the opening out for cleaning and inspection of fittings including the pressure parts of automatic controls; and

    (e) in the case of water-tube boilers, the removal of drum internal fittings.

(2) All brickwork, bales and coverings must be removed for the purpose of the thorough examination to the extent required by the person making the examination, but in any case these parts must be removed to the extent necessary to expose headers, seams of shells and drums—

    (a) not less frequently than once in every six years in the case of a steam boiler situated in the open or exposed to the weather or damp; and

    (b) not less frequently than once in every ten years in the case of every other steam boiler.

THE EXAMINATION OF STEAM BOILERS REPORTS (NO. 1) ORDER 1964
(S.I. 1964 No. 1070)

General note. The whole Order is revoked by S.I. 1989 No. 2169, as from 1 July 1994.

The Minister of Labour by virtue of the powers conferred on him by sections 33(4) and 180(3) of the Factories Act 1961 and of all other powers enabling him in that behalf, hereby makes the following Order:—

1.—(1) This Order may be cited as the Examination of Steam Boilers Reports (No. 1) Order 1964 and shall come into operation on 16 July 1964.

(2) The Order made by the Secretary of State on 1 June 1938 prescribing the forms of reports of the results of examinations of steam boilers is hereby revoked.

2. The Interpretation Act 1889 shall apply to the interpretation of this Order as it applies to the interpretation of an Act of Parliament and as if this Order and the Order hereby revoked were Acts of Parliament.

3. A report of the result of every examination of a steam boiler under section 33 of the Factories Act 1961 shall in any of the following cases be in the form and contain the particulars hereinafter specified for that case, that is to say—

    (a) in the case of an examination when cold

        (i) of a steam boiler other than an economiser, a superheater, a steam tube oven and a steam tube hotplate, the form and the particulars set out in Part I of Schedule 1 to this Order,

       (ii) of an economiser, the form and the particulars set out in Part III of Schedule 1 to this Order, and

      (iii) of a superheater, the form and the particulars set out in Part III of Schedule 1 to this Order; and

(b) in the case of an examination under normal steam pressure of a steam boiler other than an economiser and a superheater, the form and the particulars set out in Schedule 2 to this Order.

SCHEDULE

Article 3(a)(i)

PART I

MINISTRY OF LABOUR

Form F.55

H.M. FACTORY INSPECTORATE
FACTORIES ACT 1961, SECTIONS 32–34 AND
EXAMINATION OF STEAM BOILERS REGULATIONS 1964
PRESCRIBED FORM FOR
REPORT OF EXAMINATION WHEN COLD OF STEAM BOILERS
OTHER THAN ECONOMISERS, SUPERHEATERS, STEAM TUBE
OVENS, AND STEAM TUBE HOTPLATES

1 Name of Occupier	
2 Address of (a) Factory. (b) Head Office of Occupier. *Note—Address* (b) *is required only in the case of a boiler used in a temporary location, e.g. on a building operation, work of engineering construction.*	
3 Description and distinctive number of boiler and type.	
4 If the boiler is one of those described in regulation 4(2), this should be stated and the appropriate sub-paragraph ((a), (b) or (c)) should be given.	
5 Date of Construction. *The history should be briefly given, and the examiner should state whether he has seen the last previous report.*	
6 Date of last hydraulic test (if any), and pressure applied.	
7 Quality and source of feed water.	
8 Is the boiler in the open or otherwise exposed to the weather or to damp?	
9 **Boiler** (a) What parts of seams, drums or headers are covered by brickwork? (b) Date of last exposure of such parts for the purpose of examination.	

(c) What parts (if any) other than parts covered by brickwork and mentioned above were inaccessible?

(d) What examination and tests were made? (If there was any removal of brickwork, particulars should be given here.)

(e) Condition of boiler. *(State any defects materially affecting the maximum permissible working pressure.)*　External:

Internal:

10 **Fittings and Attachments**

(a) Are there proper fittings and attachments?

(b) Are all fittings and attachments in satisfactory condition (so far as ascertainable when not under pressure)?

11 Repairs (if any) required, and period within which they should be executed, and any other conditions which the person making the examination thinks it necessary to specify for securing safe working.

12 Maximum permissible working pressure calculated from dimensions and from the thickness and other data ascertained by the present examination; due allowance being made for conditions of working if unusual or exceptionally severe.

13 Where repairs affecting the working pressure are required, state the maximum permissible working pressure:

(a) Before the expiration of the period specified in 11 above

(b) After the expiration of such period if the required repairs have not been completed

(c) After the completion of the required repairs

14 Other observations

Subject to the reservation (noted above) of certain points of examination under steam pressure,* I certify that on .... the boiler above described was sufficiently descaled, prepared, and (so far as its construction permits) made accessible for thorough examination and for such tests as were necessary for thorough examination, and that on the said date I thoroughly examined this boiler, including its fittings and attachments and that the above is a true report of the result.

Signature ....　Counter-Signature ....

Qualification ....

Name of Company or

Association ....

Address ....

Date ....　Date ....

* Delete if not required. Where the examiner considers this necessary, he may insert in his report on any of the items "subject to further report after examination under normal steam pressure".

Article 3(a)(iii)

PART III

MINISTRY OF LABOUR   Form F.57

H.M. FACTORY INSPECTORATE

FACTORIES ACT 1961, SECTIONS 32–34, AND THE

EXAMINATION OF STEAM BOILERS REGULATIONS 1964

PRESCRIBED FORM FOR

REPORT OF EXAMINATION OF SUPERHEATER WHEN COLD

1 Name of Occupier.	
2 Address of (a) Factory. (b) Head Office of Occupier. *Note—Address* (b) *is required only in the case of a superheater used with a boiler in a temporary location.*	
3 Description and distinctive number of superheater and type.	
4 If the boiler is one of those described in regulation 4(2), this should be stated and the appropriate sub-paragraph ((a), (b) or (c)) should be given.	
5 Date of Construction *The history should be briefly given, and the examiner should state whether he has seen the last previous report.*	
6 Date of last hydraulic test (if any), and pressure applied.	
7 **Superheater** (a) What parts are covered by brickwork? (b) Date of last exposure of such parts for the purpose of examination. (c) What parts (if any) other than parts covered by brickwork, were inaccessible? (d) What examination and tests were made? (e) Condition of superheater. *(State any defects materially affecting the maximum permissible working pressure.)* External: Internal:	
8 **Fittings and Attachments** (a) Are there proper fittings and attachments? (b) Are all fittings and attachments in satisfactory condition (so far as ascertainable when not under pressure)?	

9　Repairs (if any) required, and period within which they should be executed and any other conditions which the person making the examination thinks it necessary to specify for securing safe working.	
10　Maximum permissible working pressure calculated from dimensions and from the thickness and other data ascertained by the present examination; due allowance being made for conditions of working if unusual or exceptionally severe.	
11　Where repairs affecting the working pressure are required, state the maximum permissible working pressure: 　　(a) Before the expiration of the period specified in 9 above 　　(b) After the expiration of such period if the required repairs have not been completed 　　(c) After the completion of the required repairs	
12　Other observations	

Subject to the reservation (noted above) of certain points for examination under steam pressure,* I certify that on .... the superheater above described was sufficiently scaled, prepared, and (so far as its construction permits) made accessible for thorough examination and for such tests as were necessary for thorough examination, and that on the said date I thoroughly examined this superheater, including its fittings and attachments, and that the above is a true report of the result.

Signature ....　Counter-Signature ....

Qualification ....

　　　　　　　　　　　　　　　　　　　　Name of Company or

Address ....　Association ....

Date ....　Date ....

Delete if not required

SCHEDULE 2

Article 3(b)

MINISTRY OF LABOUR

Form F.55A

H.M. FACTORY INSPECTORATE

FACTORIES ACT 1961, SECTIONS 32–34 AND THE

EXAMINATION OF STEAM BOILERS REGULATIONS 1964

PRESCRIBED FORM OF

REPORT OF EXAMINATION OF STEAM BOILER

UNDER NORMAL STEAM PRESSURE

1　Name of Occupier.	
2　Address of 　　(a) Factory. 　　(b) Head Office or Occupier. 　*Note—Address* (b) *is required only in the case of a boiler used in a temporary location.*	
3　Description and distinctive number of boiler and type.	
4　If the boiler is one of those described in regulation 4(2), this should be stated and the appropriate sub-paragraph ((a), (b) or (c)) should be given.	

5 Condition (external).	
6 **Fittings and Attachments** (a) (i) Is the safety valve so adjusted as to prevent the boiler being worked at a pressure greater than the maximum permissible working pressure specified in the last report (F.55) on examination when cold? (ii) (If a lever safety valve.) Is the weight secured on the lever in the correct position? (b) Is the pressure gauge working correctly? (c) Is the water gauge in proper working order?	
7 Repairs (if any) required, and period within which they should be executed and any other conditions which the person making the examination thinks it necessary to specify for securing safe working.	
8 Other observations	

I certify that on .... I examined the above-mentioned boiler under normal steam pressure and that the above is a true report of the result.

Signature .... Counter-Signature ....

Qualification ....

Name of Company

or Association ....

Address ....

Date... Date ....

Exceptions

Certificate of Exception No. 57. Examination of Steam Boilers.

In pursuance of section 37(2) and (3) of the Factories Act 1961, I hereby except from the provisions of section 33(2), (3) and (4) of the said Act the classes of steam boiler specified in paragraph 1 of this Certificate, subject to the conditions contained in paragraphs 2–12 thereof.

1. This Certificate applies to steam boilers:
   (a) which are waste heat boilers, heat exchangers or superheaters as the case may be;
   (b) which are of welded or solid forged construction;
   (c) which are an integral part of a continuous flow installation in a petro-chemical or oil refinery processing plant using a hydro-carbon feed stock;
   (d) of which the drums and headers are outside the heat transfer zone; and
   (e) in the case of which—
      (i) a period of 21 years has not expired since the steam boiler was taken into use for the first time in any factory;
      (ii) the maximum permissable pressure specified in pursuance of section 33 (5) of the said Act does not exceed 660 pounds per square inch above atmospheric pressure.

2. Where in any case arrangements are provided for raising the temperature of the waste heat gases generated in the process, those arrangements shall ensure that no flame is in contact with any part of a steam boiler to which this Certificate applies.

.3. A steam boiler to which this Certificate applies shall not be used in any factory unless it has been examined, together with its fittings and attachments, in such manner as is prescribed in this Certificate, and no greater period than is so prescribed has elapsed since the examination.

4. (a) The manner of examination of a steam boiler to which this Certificate applies shall be the manner specified in this paragraph;

(b) in the first place, the boiler shall be thoroughly examined by a competent person when it is cold after the interior and exterior have been prepared in a suitable manner, and secondly, except in the case of a heat exchanger or superheater, the boiler shall be thoroughly examined by a competent person when it is under normal steam pressure, and each part of the examination may be made by a different person.

The examination under steam pressure shall be made on the first occasion steam is raised after the examination of the boiler when cold, or as soon as possible thereafter;

(c) the person making the examination of the boiler when cold shall test it for accuracy and correct functioning, and shall thoroughly examine every safety valve and pressure gauge provided in pursuance of Section 32(2)(a) and (c) of the said Act:

(i) in the condition as removed from the boiler, and

(ii) in the case of a safety valve after reassembly following the test and thorough examination required by the foregoing sub-paragraph;

(d) the person making a test and examination of a safety valve, as required by the foregoing sub-paragraph (ii) shall affix to the safety valve an effective seal which shall be removed only:

(i) when the safety valve is refitted to the boiler, and

(ii) by the person carrying out the examination of the boiler under normal steam pressure;

(e) the person making the examination under normal steam pressure shall see the safety valve is so adjusted as to prevent the boiler being worked at a pressure greater than the maximum permissible working pressure;

(f) the examination of a boiler in the manner specified in this paragraph may, at the discretion of the person making the examination, include all or any one or more of the following, that is to say, drilling, testing and thickness measurement of the material of the steam boiler by means of any recognised non-destructive testing method, proving a clear waterway through tubes, removal of sample tubes, removal from the boiler and opening out any fitting including any pressure part of parts of automatic controls, and hydraulic testing.

5. Every steam boiler to which this Certificate applies which is taken into use in any factory for the first time in that factory after the date of this Certificate shall be examined before being taken into use.

6. For the purposes of paragraph 3 of this Certificate, the prescribed period shall be as follows, that is to say:

(a) in a case where a steam boiler to which this Certificate applies is taken into use in any factory for the first time in that factory,

(i) eighteen months where the person making the thorough examination of the steam boiler when cold before it was taken into use in the said factory has certified that in his opinion the said steam boiler may continue to be used with safety for a period of eighteen months after being taken into use;

(ii) fourteen months in any other case.

(b) in all other cases—

(i) thirty-six months where the person making the last thorough examination when cold has certified that in his opinion the steam boiler may continue to be used with safety for a period of not less than thirty-six months after the examination, under pressure;

(ii) twenty-six months in any other case.

7. In addition to any examination required by paragraphs 3 and 5 of this Certificate, every steam boiler to which this Certificate applies, other than a heat exchanger or superheater, shall be examined under normal steam pressure not less than twenty and not more than twenty-six months from the date of completion of the last thorough examination made in pursuance of paragraph 3 or 5. The examination required by this paragraph shall be as thorough as the operating conditions permit.

8. (a) The feed water supplied to every steam boiler to which this Certificate applies shall be of such quality as to prevent, so far as is reasonably practicable, any corrosion in any part of the boiler and to avoid the deposit of scale and sludge to an extent liable to affect the safe operation of the boiler.

    (b) In the case of every steam boiler to which this Certificate applies, other than a heat exchanger or superheater, at least once on each shift or every twelve hours whichever period is less when the boiler is in use—

        (i) the water and steam connections of every water gauge shall be properly blown through;

        (ii) the boiler shall be blown down in such a manner and at such a rate as to reduce so far as practicable the liability of dissolved and undissolved solids in the water to cause deposits of scale and sludge; and

        (iii) a sample of water from the boiler shall be taken and analysed by a person competent for this purpose in order to verify that the boiler is being blown-down in the manner and at the rate required in sub paragraph (ii) of this paragraph and a suitable record shall be kept of these analyses.

9. A report of the result of every examination under this Certificate in the form and containing the particulars specified in the Schedules hereto shall be obtained as soon as practicable and in any case within twenty-eight days after the completion of the examination, and shall be kept available for inspection. The report shall be signed by the person making the examination, and if that person is an inspector of a boiler-inspecting company or assocation, countersigned by the chief engineer of the company or association or by such other responsible officer of the company or association as may be authorised in writing in that behalf by the chief engineer.

10. The person making an examination under this Certificate shall notify the occupier in writing forthwith, and within fourteen days after the completion of the examination shall send to the inspector for the district a copy of the report, in every case where the maximum permissible working pressure is reduced, or the examination shows that the boiler cannot continue to be used with safety unless certain repairs are carried out immediately or within a specified time, or the person making the examination is of the opinion that a defect exists which would be liable to affect the safe working of the boiler.

11. Where at any time there is carried out to any steam boiler to which this Certificate applies the repair of a defect which in the opinion of a competent person will-affect its safe working, the boiler shall be examined by a competent person in such a manner as will enable that person to satisfy himself that the repair has been properly carried out and the steam boiler shall not be used in any factory after such repairs have been carried out and before it has been so examined.

12. The provisions of section 33(6) and (8) of the said Act, with the substitution of the words—
"under this Certificate" for the words "under this section" shall be deemed to be incorporated in this Certificate.

13. This Certificate shall remain in force until revoked in writing by the Chief Inspector of Factories.

Schedule 1   F55B

Report of Examination When Cold of a Steam Boiler, Heat Exchanger or Superheater Including All Fittings and Attachments to Which Certificate of Exception No. 57 Applies

1. Name of Occupier
2. Address of Factory

3. Description and distinctive
   number of boiler/heat
   exchanger/superheater and
   type*
4. Date of examination of boiler/
   heat exchanger/superheater*
5. Maximum permissible working pressure: .... pounds per sq. inch
6. Date of construction
7. Date of hydraulic test,   Date ....
   pressure applied and   Pressure applied ....
   period pressure applied   pounds per sq. inch
                                  Period pressure applied ....

EXAMINATION

8. Condition of boiler/heat exchanger/superheater:*
   INTERNAL   EXTERNAL
9. State any defects as a result of which:
   (a) the boiler/heat exchanger/superheater*
       cannot continue to be used with safety
       unless repairs are carried out
       immediately or within a
       specified time
   (b) the maximum permissible working
       pressure has been reduced.
10. Any other observations;
11. (i) The safety valve of the boiler/heat exchanger/superheater* was tested in
        accordance with paragraph 4(c)(i) of the Certificate of Exception on ....
        (date) and lifted satisfactorily at   psi. The pressure gauge (in the case of a
        boiler) functioned correctly/incorrectly*.
    (ii) The safety valve of the boiler/heat exchanger/superheater* was tested in
        accordance with paragraph 4(c)(ii) of the Certificate of Exception on ....
        (date) and lifted satisfactorily at .... psi. The pressure gauge (in the
        case of a boiler) functioned correctly/incorrectly*.
12. I certify that the boiler/heat exchanger/superheater* above described was suf-
    ficiently descaled, prepared, and (so far as its construction permits) made accessible
    thorough examination and for such tests as were necessary for thorough examin-
    ation, and that on the said date I thoroughly examined the boiler/heat exchanger/
    superheater* including its fittings and attachments and the above is a true report of
    the result. In my opinion the boiler/heat exchanger* can continue to be steamed
    with safety under normal operating conditions and pressure for .... months
    (period to be entered in words).

Signature ....   Counter-Signature ....
                                                       (Chief Boiler Engineer)
                                                       Name of Company
Qualification ....   or Association ....
Address ....

....
                                                       Date ....
Date ....
* *Delete as appropriate*

SCHEDULE 2   F55C
REPORT OF EXAMINATION UNDER NORMAL STEAM PRESSURE OF A
STEAM BOILER TO WHICH CERTIFICATE OF EXCEPTION No. 57 APPLIES

1. Name of Occupier
2. Address of Factory

3. Description and distinctive
   number of boiler and type
4. Date of examination

EXAMINATION

5. (i) General condition (external) of
   the boiler:
   (ii) Fittings and attachments:
   Were the following operating satisfactorily?
   (a) pressure gauge ....
   (b) water level gauge ....
   (c) blow-down arrangements ....
   (d) automatic water level control(s)
   ....
6. State any defects as a result of which:
   (a) the boiler cannot continue to be
       used with safety unless repairs are
       carried out immediately or within
       a specified time;
   (b) the maximum permissible work-
       ing pressure has been reduced.
7. Any other observations:
8. I certify that I examined the above mentioned steam boiler under normal steam
   pressure and the above is a true report of the result.

   Signature ....   Counter-Signature ....
                                (Chief Boiler Engineer)
   Qualification ....   Name of Company
   Address ....   or Association
   ....
   Date ....   Date ....
   * *Delete as appropriate*   (Form 2466, March 1974)

Certificate of Exception No. 61. Examination of steam boilers.

In pursuance of section 37(2) and (3) of the Factories Act 1961, I hereby except from the
provisions of section 33(2), (3) and (4) of the said Act, classes of steam boiler specified in
paragraph 1 of this Certificate subject to the conditions contained in paragraphs 2–13
thereof.

1. This Certificate applies to any steam boiler (other than a steam boiler in which the
steam is used solely for the generation of electricity for distribution through the
National Electricity Supply System) of any of the following types where a period of
21 years has expired since it was first taken into use, that is to say:
   (a) A water tube boiler of which the drums and any headers are of fusion welded or
       solid forged construction which has an evaporative capacity of not less than
       50,000 lbs of steam per hour;
   (b) A boiler in a group of water tube boilers of which the drums and any headers are
       of fusion welded or solid forged construction, being a group in which:
       (1) Each boiler has an evaporative capacity of not less than 25,000 lbs of steam
           per hour;
       (2) The total evaporative capacity of all boilers is not less than 100,000 lbs of
           steam per hour;
   (c) A boiler which is a waste heat boiler or heat exchanger with fusion welded
       longitudinal and circumferential seams, or a superheater of fusion welded
       construction, and which is an integral part of a continuous flow installation, in a
       chemical or oil refinery processing plant.
2. A steam boiler to which this Certificate applies shall not be used in any factory
unless it has been examined together with its fittings and attachments in such a manner

as is prescribed in this Certificate, and no greater period than so prescribed has elapsed since the examination.

3.   For the purpose of paragraph 2 of this Certificate the prescribed period shall be as follows:

(a)   in the case where the steam boiler is being used for the first time in that factory, a period which expires after it has been installed and before it is used;

in all other cases:

(b)   26 months where the person making the last examination has certified that in his opinion the steam boiler may continue to be used with safety for a period of not less than 26 months after that examination; otherwise

(c)   14 months.

4.   The manner of examination of a steam boiler to which this Certificate applies shall be the manner specified in this paragraph:

(a)   Firstly the steam boiler together with its fittings and attachments shall be thoroughly examined by a competent person when it is cold after the interior and exterior have been prepared in the manner prescribed in the First Schedule to this Certificate and secondly, except in the case of an economiser or superheater or heat exchanger the steam boiler shall be thoroughly examined by a competent person when it is under normal steam pressure, and each part of the examination may be made by a different person. The examination under normal steam pressure shall be made on the first occasion when steam is raised after the examination of the steam boiler when cold or where this is not reasonably practicable, within 28 days of the date steam was so raised.

(b)   Where an economiser or superheater is an integral part of a steam boiler for the purpose of this Certificate, the date of expiration of the period of examination for such an economiser or superheater, shall be that of the steam boiler.

(c)   The person making the examination of the steam boiler when cold shall test for accuracy and correct functioning every pressure gauge and shall thoroughly examine every safety valve provided in pursuance of section 32(a) and (c) of the said Act.

(d)   In the case of a safety valve which can only be set whilst cold, the person making the examination of the safety valve as required by the foregoing sub-paragraph (c) shall set and then affix to the safety valve an effective seal which shall be removed only by the person carrying out the examination of the boiler under normal steam pressure.

(e)   The person making the examination under normal steam pressure shall see that the safety valves are so adjusted as to prevent the boiler being worked at a pressure greater than the maximum permissible working pressure.

(f)   The examination of a boiler in the manner specified in this paragraph may, at the discretion of the person making the examination, include all or any one or more of the following, that is to say drilling, testing the thickness measurement of the material by means of any effective non-destructive testing method, proving a clear water way through tubes, removal of sample tubes, removal from the boiler and opening out any fitting including any pressure part or parts of automatic controls and hydraulic testing.

5.   The competent person should require any part of the steam boiler to which this Certificate applies whose effective life is governed by creep or fatigue, or any other reason, to be renewed if in his estimation the termination of the effective life is liable to arise during the prescribed period.

6.   Where at any time there is carried out to any steam boiler to which this Certificate applies the repair of a defect which in the opinion of a competent person will affect its safe working that steam boiler shall be examined by a competent person in such a manner as will enable that person to satisfy himself that the repair has been properly carried out and the steam boiler shall not be used in any factory after the carrying out of such repairs before it has been so examined.

7.   Where the competent person has certified that a steam boiler can be used for 26 months that boiler shall in addition to any examination required by paragraph 2 of

this Certificate, be examined under normal steam pressure not less than 12 and not more than 15 months from the date of completion of the last thorough examination made in pursuance of paragraph 2. The examination required by this paragraph shall be as thorough as the operating conditions permit, and may at the discretion of the person making the examination include all or any one or more of the methods specified in paragraph 4(f).

8. (a) The feed water supplied to every steam boiler to which this Certificate applies shall be of such quality as to prevent, so far as is reasonably practicable, any corrosion in any part of the boiler, and to avoid so far as is reasonably practicable the deposit of scale and sludge to an extent liable to affect the safe operation of the boiler. Samples of water from the boiler shall be taken at appropriate intervals and analysed by a person competent for this purpose in order to verify that the required quality of the water in the boiler is maintained.

(b) When a steam boiler to which this Certificate applies is in use a check of that boiler shall be made at least once on each shift or every 12 hours, whichever period is less to ensure that every water gauge and every such other automatic device as is mentioned in Certificate of Exception No. 29 is operating satisfactorily.

(c) In the case of a steam boiler to which this Certificate applies (other than the type of steam boiler specified in Certificate of Exception No. 29) at least once on each shift or every 12 hours, whichever period is less, when the boiler is in use:

(1) The steam boiler shall be blown down in such a manner and at such a rate and frequency as to reduce, so far as is practicable, the liability of dissolved and undissolved solids in the water to cause deposits of scale and sludge;

(2) A sample of the water from the steam boiler shall be taken and analysed by a person competent for this purpose in order to verify that the boiler is being blown down in the manner and at the rate and frequency required in sub-paragraph (1) of this paragraph, and a suitable record shall be kept of these analyses.

9. A report of the result of every examination under this Certificate in the form and containing the particulars prescribed by the Second and Third Schedules hereto shall as soon after the completion of the examination as practicable and in any case within 28 days be entered in or attached to the general register kept in pursuance of section 140 of the Factories Act 1961 and the report shall be signed by the person making the examination and, if that person is an inspector of a boiler inspecting company or association, counter-signed by the chief engineer of the company or association or by such other responsible officer of the company or association as may be authorised in writing in that behalf by the chief engineer.

10. The person making an examination or part of an examination under this Certificate shall notify the occupier in writing forthwith, and within 28 days after the completion of the examination shall send to the District Inspector or Area Director as the case may be a copy of the report in every case where the maximum permissible working pressure is reduced or the examination shows that the steam boiler cannot continue to be used with safety unless certain repairs are carried out immediately or within a specified time, or the person making this examination is of the opinion that a defect exists which would be liable to affect the safe working of the steam boiler.

11. The provisions of section 33(6) and (8) of the said Act shall with the substitution of the words "Under this Certificate" for the words "Under this section" be deemed to be incorporated in this Certificate.

12. This Certificate shall remain in force until revoked in writing by the Chief Inspector of Factories.

13. Certificate of Exception No. 49 dated 7.7.69 is hereby revoked.

FIRST SCHEDULE
(Paragraph 4(a))

THE MANNER OF PREPARING A STEAM BOILER TO WHICH CERTIFICATE
OF EXCEPTION NO. 61 APPLIES FOR EXAMINATION WHEN COLD

1.   In addition to the steps required to be taken under paragraph 2 of this Schedule, the preparation of the interior and exterior of a boiler for its thorough examination when cold in pursuance of paragraph 4(a) shall, according as the person making the examination may require, consist of all or any one or more of the following, that is to say:

  (a) the opening out, cleaning and scaling of the boiler, including the removal of doors from man holes, mud holes and hand holes;
  (b) the removal of firebars;
  (c) in the case of shell type boilers, the dismantling of firebridges (if made of brick) and all furnace protective brickwork;
  (d) the opening out for cleaning and inspection of fittings, including the pressure parts of automatic controls; and
  (e) in the case of water-tube boilers, the removal of drum internal fittings.

2.   All brickwork, baffles and coverings must be removed for the purpose of the thorough examination to the extent required by the person making the examination.

SECOND SCHEDULE
(Paragraph 9)

PART A

1. Name of occupier ....
2. Address of factory ....

PART B

REPORT OF EXAMINATION WHEN COLD OF A STEAM BOILER
INCLUDING ALL FITTINGS AND ATTACHMENTS TO WHICH
CERTIFICATE OF EXCEPTION NO. 61 APPLIES

1. Description and distinctive number of boiler and type ....
2. Date of examination of boiler ....
3. Maximum permissible working pressure: .... pounds per square inch.
4. Date of construction, and brief history—the examiner shall state whether he has seen the last previous report ....
5. Date of hydraulic test. Pressure applied and period pressure applied.
   Date ....
   Pressure applied .... pounds per square inch
   Period pressure applied ....
6. **Water Tube Boilers**
   (a) *Downcomer Tubes*
   6.1 Have the downcomer tubes been checked for distortion? ....
   6.2 Have the downcomer tubes been checked for thickness? ....
   6.3 Have the downcomer tubes been checked for signs of corrosion? ....
   6.4 Do any need repair? ....
   6.5 Do any need replacement? ....
   (b) *Riser Tubes*
   6.6 Have the riser tubes been checked for distortion? ....
   6.7 Have the riser tubes been checked for thickness? ....
   6.8 Have the riser tubes been checked for signs of corrosion? ....
   6.9 Do any need repair? ....

6.10 Do any need replacement? ....

(c) *Headers*

6.11 Have the headers been checked for thickness? ....

6.12 Have the headers been checked for signs of corrosion? ....

6.13 Do any need repair? ....

6.14 Do any need replacement? ....

(d) *Header Caps*

6.15 Have the header caps been checked for thickness? ....

6.16 Have the header caps been checked for signs of corrosion? ....

6.17 Do any need repair? ....

6.18 Do any need replacement? ....

(e) *Drums*

6.19 Has the exterior been checked for corrosion, etc? ....

6.12 Has the interior been checked for corrosion, etc? ....

6.21 Are any repairs required? ....

(f) *Condition of parts not listed above* ....

7. **Shell Boilers**

(a) *Furnace and Smoke Tubes*

7.1 Have the tubes been checked for thickness? ....

7.2 Have the tubes been checked for corrosion, etc? ....

7.3 Do any need repair? ....

7.4 Do any need replacement? ....

(b) *Tube Plates*

7.5 Have the plates been checked for thickness? ....

7.6 Have the plates been checked for corrosion, etc? ....

7.7 Do any need repair? ....

7.8 Do any need replacement? ....

(c) *Condition of parts not listed above* ....

8. **Boiler Fittings**

8.1 Has the stop-valve been examined? ....

8.2 Does it require repair/replacement? ....

8.3 Has the water gauge been examined? ....

8.4 Does it require repair/replacement? ....

8.5 Has the low-water alarm device been examined? ....

8.6 Does it require repair/replacement? ....

8.7 Has the safety valve been thoroughly examined ....

8.8 Has it been set where necessary? ....

8.9 Does it require repair/replacement? ....

8.10 Has the pressure gauge been tested for accuracy? ....

8.11 Does it require repair/replacement? ....

9. State any defects as a result of which:

(a) The boiler cannot continue to be used with safety unless repairs are carried out immediately, or within a specified time.

(b) The maximum permissible working pressure has been reduced.

10. I certify that the boiler above described was sufficiently descaled, prepared and (so far as its construction permits) made accessible for thorough examination, and for such tests as were necessary for thorough examination, and that on the said date I thoroughly examined the boiler including its fittings and attachments, and the above is a true report of the result. In my opinion the boiler can continue to be steamed under normal operating conditions and pressure for .... months (period to be entered in words).

Signature ....

Qualification ....

Address ....

....

Date ....

Counter-signature (Chief Engineer) ....

Name of company or association ....

Date ....

PART C

REPORT OR EXAMINATION WHEN COLD OF A STEAM ECONOMISER
INCLUDING ALL FITTINGS AND ATTACHMENTS TO WHICH
CERTIFICATE OF EXCEPTION No. 61 APPLIES

1. Description and distinctive number of economiser ....

....

Type ....

No. of tubes ....

2. State appropriate sub-paragraph (a), (b) or (c) of paragraph 1 to which the economiser belongs ....

3. Date of construction and brief history. The examiner should state whether he has seen the last previous report ....

....

....

4. Date of last hydraulic test (if any) ....

Pressure applied .... pounds per square inch

5. Are the dampers in proper working order? ....

6. (a) What parts are inaccessible? ....

   (b) State no. of top caps removed for examination ....

   (c) State no. of bottom caps removed for examination ....

   (d) What examinations and tests were made? (see Schedule 1 and paragraph 4 of this Certificate) ....

....

....

   (e) Condition of economiser (state any defects materially affecting the maximum permissible working pressure)

   External ....

   Internal ....

7. (a) Are there proper fittings and attachments? ....

....

   (b) Are all fittings and attachments in satisfactory condition? (so far as is ascertainable when not under pressure) ....

8. Repairs (if any) required, and period within which they should be executed, and any other conditions which the person making the examination thinks it necessary to specify for securing safe working

....

....

....

9. Maximum permissible working pressure calculated from dimensions and from the thickness and other data ascertained by the present examination (due allowance being made for conditions of working if unusual or exceptionally severe)

....

10. Where repairs affecting the working pressure are required state the maximum permissible working pressure:

   (a) Before the expiration of the period specified in 8 above ....

....

   (b) After the expiration of such period if the required repairs have not been completed

....

(c) After the completion of the required repairs ....
11. Other observations ....
   ....
12. I certify that the economiser above described was sufficiently descaled, prepared
   and (so far as its construction permits) made accessible for thorough examination,
   and for such tests as were necessary for thorough examination, and that on the said
   date I thoroughly examined the economiser including its fittings and attachments,
   and the above is a true report of the result. In my opinion the economiser can
   continue to be steamed under normal operating conditions and pressure for
   ....
   months (periods to be entered in words).
   Signature ....
   Qualification ....
   Address ....
   ....
   Date ....
   Counter-signature (Chief Engineer) ....
   Name of company or association ....
   Date ....

PART D

REPORT OF EXAMINATION WHEN COLD OF A SUPERHEATER/HEAT EXCHANGER INCLUDING ALL FITTINGS AND ATTACHMENTS TO WHICH CERTIFICATE OF EXCEPTION No. 61 APPLIES

1. Description and distinctive number of superheater/heat exchanger and type .....
2. State appropriate sub-paragraph (a), (b) or (c) of paragraph 1 to which the
   superheater/heat exchanger belongs ....
3. Date of construction and brief history. The examiner should state whether he has
   seen the last previous report ....
   ....
4. Date of last hydraulic test (if any) ....
   Pressure applied .... pounds per square inch
5. (a) What parts are covered by brickwork? ....
   ....
   (b) Date of last exposure of such parts for the purpose of examination ....
   ....
   (c) What parts (if any) other than those covered by brickwork were inaccessible?
6. **Headers**
   (a) Have the headers been checked for thickness? ....
   (b) Are they being affected by creep? ....
   (c) Do they need repair/replacing? ....
7. **Tubes**
   (a) Have the tubes been checked for distortion? ....
   (b) Have the tubes been checked for thickness? ....
   (c) Have the tubes been checked for signs of corrosion? ....
   (d) Do they need repair/replacement? ....
8. **Safety Valve(s)**
   (a) Has the safety valve(s) been thoroughly examined? ....
   (b) Does it/they require/repair/replacement? ....
   (c) Has it/they been set and sealed where necessary? ....
9. **Fittings and Attachments**
   Are all the necessary fittings and attachments present and in a satisfactory condition
   (so far as is ascertainable when not under pressure)? ....
10. Condition of superheater/heat exchanger (state any defects materially affecting
   the maximum permissible working pressure)

External ....

Internal ....

11. State the period within which repairs (if any) should be executed and any other conditions which the person making the examination thinks it necessary to secure safe working ....

12. Maximum permissible working pressure calculated from dimensions and from the thickness and other data ascertained by the present examination; due allowance being made for the conditions of working if unusual or exceptionally severe ......

....

13. Where repairs affecting the working pressure are required, state the maximum working pressure:

(a) Before the expiration of the period specified in 11 above ....

....

(b) After the expiration of such period if the required repairs have not been completed

....

....

(c) After the completion of the required repairs ....

14. Other observations ....

....

15. I certify that the superheater/heat exchanger above described was sufficiently descaled, prepared and (so far as its construction permits) made accessible for thorough examination, and for such tests as were necessary for thorough examination, and that on the said date I thoroughly examined the superheater/heat exchanger including its fittings and attachments, and the above is a true report of the result.

In my opinion the superheater/heat exchanger can continue to be steamed under normal operating conditions and pressure for ....

.... months (period to be entered in words).

Signature ....

Qualification ....

Address ....

....

Date ....

Counter-signature (Chief Engineer) ....

Name of company or association ....

Date ....

THIRD SCHEDULE
(Paragraph 9)

REPORT OF EXAMINATION UNDER NORMAL STEAM PRESSURE OF A
STEAM BOILER TO WHICH CERTIFICATE OF EXCEPTION NO. 61 APPLIES

1. Name of occupier ....

2. Address of factory ....

3. Description and distinctive number of boiler and type ....

4. Date of examination ....

Examination

5. (i) General condition (external) of the boiler including fittings and attachments

(ii) Fittings and attachments:

Were the following operating satisfactorily?

(a) pressure gauge ....

(b) water level gauge ....

(c) blow-down arrangements ....

(d) automatic water level control(s) ....

(e) safety valve(s) ....

6. State any defects as a result of which:
    (a) the boiler cannot continue to be used with safety unless repairs are carried out immediately or within a specified time;
    (b) the maximum permissible working pressure has been reduced.
7. Repairs (if any) required, and period within which they should be executed and any other conditions which the person making the examination thinks it necessary to specify for securing safe working.
8. Is the safety valve(s) so adjusted as to prevent the boiler being worked at a pressure greater than the maximum permissible working pressure specified in the last report (Second Schedule) on examination when cold? (If a lever safety valve). Is the weight secured on the lever in the correct position?
9. Any other observations?
10. I certify that I examined the above mentioned steam boiler under normal steam pressure and the above is a true report of the result.
    Signature ....
    Qualification ....
    Address ....
    ....
    Date ....
    Counter-signed (Chief Engineer) ....
    Name of company or association ....
    Date ....
    *This form may also be used (as far as possible) for supplementary reports on economisers and superheaters.

---

34. Steam boilers—restrictions on entry. No person shall enter or be in any steam boiler *(a)* which is one of a range of two or more steam boilers unless—
    (a) all inlets through which steam or hot water might otherwise enter the boiler from any part of the range are disconnected from that part; or
    (b) all valves or taps controlling the entry of steam or hot water are closed and securely locked, and, where the boiler has a blow-off pipe in common with one or more other boilers or delivering into a common blow-off vessel or sump, the blow-off valve or tap on each such boiler is so constructed that it can only be opened by a key which cannot be removed until the value or tap is closed and is the only key in use for that set of blow-off valves or taps.

(a) Steam boiler. For definition, see s. 38.

---

35. Steam receivers and steam containers.—(1) Every steam receiver *(a)*, not so constructed and maintained *(b)* as to withstand with safety the maximum permissible working pressure *(c)* of the boiler *(d)* or the maximum pressure which can be obtained in the pipe connecting the receiver with any other source of supply, shall be fitted with—

    (a) a suitable reducing valve or other suitable automatic appliance to prevent the safe working pressure *(e)* being exceeded; and

(b) a suitable safety valve so adjusted as to permit the steam to escape as soon as the safe working pressure is exceeded, or a suitable appliance for cutting off automatically the supply of steam as soon as the safe working pressure is exceeded; and

(c) a correct steam pressure gauge, which must indicate the pressure of steam in the receiver; and

(d) a suitable stop valve; and

(e) except where only one steam receiver is in use, a plate bearing a distinctive number which shall be easily visible.

(2) The safety valve and pressure gauge shall be fitted either on the steam receiver *(a)* or on the supply pipe between the receiver and the reducing valve or other appliance to prevent the safe working pressure *(e)* being exceeded.

(3) Where any set of receivers is supplied with steam through a single pipe and the reducing valve or other appliance required by paragraph (a) of subsection (1) of this section is fitted on that pipe, the set shall be treated as one receiver for the purposes of paragraphs (a) to (c) of subsection (1) and for the purposes of subsection (2) of this section, and if the set forms part of a single machine, also for the purposes of paragraph (d) of the said subsection (1).

(4) Every part of every steam receiver *(a)* shall be of good construction, sound material, adequate strength *(f)* and free from patent defect *(g)*.

(5) Every steam receiver *(a)* and its fittings shall be properly maintained *(h)*, and shall be thoroughly examined by a competent person, so far as the construction of the receiver permits, at least once in every period of twenty-six months.

(6) A report of the result of every such examination containing the prescribed particulars *(i)* (including particulars of the safe working pressure *(e)*) shall be entered in or attached to the general register *(k)*.

(7) Every steam container *(l)* shall be so maintained *(b)* as to secure that the outlet is at all times kept open and free from obstruction.

(8) In this section—

"Safe working pressure" means, in the case of a new steam receiver, that specified by the maker, and in the case of a steam receiver which has been examined in accordance with the provisions of this section, that specified in the report of the last examination;

"steam receiver" means any vessel or apparatus (other than a steam boiler, steam container, a steam pipe or coil, or a part of a prime mover) used for containing steam under pressure greater than atmospheric pressure;

"steam container" means any vessel (other than a steam pipe or coil) constructed with a permanent outlet into the atmosphere or into a space where the pressure does not exceed atmospheric pressure, and through which steam is passed at atmospheric pressure or at approximately that pressure for the purpose of heating, boiling, drying, evaporating or other similar purpose.

General note. This section is repealed by S.I. 1989 No. 2169, as from 1 July 1994.

By virtue of s. 37(2) certain classes and types of steam receiver or container have been excepted from certain provisions of this section. These exceptions are set out below.

(a) ***Steam receiver.*** For definition, see sub-s. (8).

(b) **Maintained.** For definition, see s. 176(1).

(c) **Maximum permissible working pressure.** For definition, see s. 38.

(d) **Boiler.** For definition, see s. 38.

(e) **Safe working pressure.** For definition, see sub-s. (8).

(f) **Of good construction, sound material, adequate strength.** See INTRODUCTORY NOTE 11.

(g) **Free from patent defect.** See note *(b)* to s. 27.

(h) **Properly maintained.** See INTRODUCTORY NOTE 10.

(i) **Report containing prescribed particulars.** "Prescribed" means prescribed by the Minister (s. 176(1)).

(k) **General register.** See s. 140.

(l) **Steam container.** For definition, see sub-s. (8).

Certificate of Exemption No. 12. Steam heated rolls, the body of which is formed from a single piece of cast-iron, steel, or semi-steel, and which has a thickness of metal at any cross-section of not less than one-fifth of the bore at that cross-section, subject to the condition that every such steam receiver shall be properly maintained.
Excepted from sub-ss (1)(e), (5) and (6).

(Form 676, November 1939)

Certificate of Exemption No. 13. Any steam receiver connected with a steam boiler and having a safe working pressure of not less than nine-tenths of the maximum permissible working pressure of such steam boiler.
Excepted from sub-s. (1)(a).
Conditions.—
(1) That such steam receiver and the pipes and fittings connecting it to such steam boiler are so constructed and arranged as to prevent the pressure of the steam in the receiver exceeding the safe working pressure thereof. For the purpose of this condition, no account shall be taken of any regulation of the pressure in the receiver by means of any valve (including a safety valve) or cock, or of any other special fitting provided for controlling the flow of steam into or out of such receiver.
(2) The application of this exception to such steam receiver shall be noted in the report on every examination made in pursuance of subsection (5) of section 35.
(3) This exception shall not otherwise affect the application of section 35 to such steam receiver.

(Form 677, November 1939)

----

36. Air receivers.—(1) Every air receiver *(a)—*

(a) shall have marked on it so as to be plainly visible the safe working pressure; and

(b) if it is connected with an air compressing plant, shall either be so constructed as to withstand with safety the maximum pressure that can be obtained in the compressor, or be fitted with a suitable reducing valve or other suitable appliance to prevent the safe working pressure of the receiver being exceeded; and

(c) shall be fitted with a suitable safety valve so adjusted as to permit the air to escape as soon as the safe working pressure is exceeded; and

(d) shall be fitted with a correct pressure gauge indicating the pressure in the receiver; and

- (e) shall be fitted with a suitable appliance for draining the receiver; and
- (f) shall be provided with a suitable manhole, handhole, or other means which will allow the interior to be thoroughly cleaned; and
- (g) in a case where more than one receiver is in use in the factory, shall bear a distinguishing mark which shall be easily visible.

(2) For the purposes of the provisions of subsection (1) of this section relating to safety valves and pressure gauges, any set of air receivers supplied with air through a single pipe may be treated as one receiver but, where a suitable reducing valve or other suitable appliance to prevent the safe working pressure being exceeded is required to be fitted, only if the valve or appliance is fitted on that pipe.

(3) Every air receiver *(a)* and its fittings shall be of sound construction *(b)* and properly maintained *(c)*.

(4) Every air receiver *(a)* shall be thoroughly cleaned and examined at least once in every period of twenty-six months, except that in the case of a receiver of solid drawn construction—

- (a) the person making any such examination may specify in writing a period exceeding twenty-six months but not exceeding four years within which the next examination is to be made; and
- (b) if it is so constructed that the internal surface cannot be thoroughly examined, a suitable hydraulic test of the receiver shall be carried out in lieu of internal examination.

(5) Every such examination and test shall be carried out by a competent person, and a report of the result of every such examination and test, containing the prescribed particulars *(d)* (including particulars of the safe working pressure) shall be entered in or attached to the general register *(e)*.

(6) In this section "air receiver" means—

- (a) any vessel (other than a pipe or coil, or an accessory, fitting or part of a compressor) for containing compressed air and connected with an air compressing plant; or
- (b) any fixed vessel for containing compressed air or compressed exhaust gases and used for the purpose of starting an internal combustion engine; or
- (c) any fixed or portable vessel (not being part of a spraying pistol) used for the purpose of spraying by means of compressed air any paint, varnish, lacquer or similar material; or
- (d) any vessel in which oil is stored and from which it is forced by compressed air,

but paragraph (e) of subsection (1) of this section shall not apply to any such vessel as is mentioned in paragraph (c) or paragraph (d) of this subsection.

General note. This section is repealed by S.I. 1989 No. 2169, as from 1 July 1994.

By virtue of s. 37(2) certain classes and types of air receiver have been excepted from certain provisions of this section. These exceptions are set out below.

The requirements of this section apply to building operations and works of engineering construction (s. 127). For an amendment of the requirements contained in sub-ss. (4) and (5), see the Factories Act (Docks, Buildings and Engineering Construction) Modification Regulations 1938.

See also the Shipbuilding (Air Receivers) Order 1961. This Order was made under s. 31 of the 1937 Act, superseded by this section, but for greater convenience is printed with the other Shipbuilding Regulations in Part 4 of this book.

(*a*) **Air receiver.** See sub-s. (6). In *Friel v East Kilbride Dairy Farmers Ltd* 1948 SLT (Notes) 23 it was argued that a motor tyre attached to a wheel was an air compressor. In rejecting this argument Lord Russell stated that "... it was impossible to interpret the language of the enactment as intended to bring within the definition 'air receiver' the wide range of articles in daily use which were filled with air introduced by means of a temporary connection with an air-compressing plant in a factory ...".

(*b*) **Of sound construction.** It is submitted that the obligation is absolute and the apparatus must be sound in fact and not merely give the appearance of soundness; compare "sound material" in s. 22(1).

(*c*) **Properly maintained.** See INTRODUCTORY NOTE 10.

(*d*) **Report containing prescribed particulars.** "Prescribed" means prescribed by the Minister (s. 176(1)). The prescribed forms for reports are as follows: Examination of an air receiver—Form 59: Supplementary report—Form 60.

(*e*) **General register.** See ss. 140, 141, 166(3).

Certificate of Exemption No. 22. The air receiver known as the air pressure tank used in conjunction with a fire sprinkler installation.
    Exempted from the whole section.
(Form 686, January 1942)

Certificate of Exemption No. 31. The type of air receiver specified in the first column of the Schedule to this Certificate is excepted from the requirements of section 36 specified in the second column of the Schedule subject, however, to the conditions and limitations set opposite thereto in the third column of the Schedule.

SCHEDULE

Type of Air Receiver	Requirements which shall not apply	Conditions or limitations
Air receivers made by Charles S. Madan and Company Limited, Vortex Works, Broadheath, Altrincham, Cheshire.	Paragraph (e) of sub-section (1)	The receivers shall be machined from solid forgings of steel. The internal volumetric capacity of any receiver shall not exceed two cubic feet.

(Form 2094, April 1962)

Certificate of Exception No. 46. The class of air receiver specified in the first column of the Schedule to this Certificate is excepted from the requirements of section 36 specified in the second column of the Schedule subject, however, to the conditions and limitations set opposite thereto in the third column of the Schedule.

SCHEDULE

Type of Air Receiver	Requirements which shall not apply	Conditions or limitations
Air receivers used to contain air of exceptional purity, that is, air which (1) has a water vapour content such that the dew point of the air when expanded to one atmosphere does not exceed two hundred and three degrees Kelvin; (2) contains no particle of solid matter larger than five microns; (3) contains no contaminant sufficient to be harmful to the production of liquid air by the Joule-Thompson effect.	Subsection (4)	The receivers shall be examined externally by a competent person at least once in every period of 26 months. The receivers shall be examined by a competent person using an ultrasonic method at least once in every period of 4 years.

(Form 2308, September 1968)

Certificate of Exception No. 65
1. In pursuance of section 37(2) and (3) of the Factories Act 1961 being satisfied that the provisions cannot reasonably be applied. I hereby except any air receiver of the type specified in Schedule 1 hereto from the provision of section 36(4) of that Act.
2. This exception is granted subject to the conditions in Schedule 2 hererto and subject to reports being made containing the appropriate particulars set out in Schedule 2 hereto.
3. This Certificate shall remain in force until revoked in writing by an inspector appointed under section 19 of the Health and Safety at Work etc. Act 1974 and duly authorised in that behalf.

SCHEDULE 1

AIR RECEIVERS TO WHICH THIS CERTIFICATE APPLIES

The air receiver shall be an air receiver as defined in section 36 of the Factories Act 1961, shall be used in connection with a continuous flow process plant incorporating a primary steam circuit to which steam is supplied from a steam boiler of a class specified in Certificate of Exception No. 57, but shall not be of solid drawn construction.

SCHEDULE 2

CONDITIONS

First two examinations
1. The air receiver together with its fittings and attachments (referred to in this Schedule as "the air receiver") shall be thoroughly examined by a competent person in

the manner specified in paragraph 4 of this Schedule before being taken into use for the first time in any factory, and examined again after such period as the person making the first examination may specify, which period may not exceed 18 months.

Subsequent examinations

2.—(1) The air receiver shall not thereafter be used in a factory unless it has been thoroughly examined in the manner specified in paragraph 4 of his Schedule—

(a) whenever the primary steam circuit with which it is associated is examined in accordance with section 32 of the Factories Act 1961, or with Certificate of Exception No. 57; and

(b) no greater period has elapsed than 36 months or other such shorter period as the person making the previous examination specified, since the completion of the last examination.

(2) In addition to the provision of sub-paragraph (1) above, the air receiver shall be examined not less than twenty and not more than twenty-six months from the date of completion of the last thorough examination made in pursuance of paragraphs 1 and 2(1), which examination shall be under normal pressure and shall be as thorough as the operating conditions permit.

Examination after repair

3. Whenever the air receiver is repaired in such a way that in the opinion of a competent person its safe working may be affected it shall be examined by a competent person in such a manner as will enable him to satisfy himself that the repair has been properly carried out before the air receiver is used.

Method of examination

4.—(1) The air receiver shall be thoroughly cleaned.

(2) The air receiver, when not subject to pressure, shall be thoroughly examined and in particular every pressure gauge and safety valve provided under section 36(1) of the Factories Act 1961 shall be removed, tested for accuracy and correct functioning whilst removed, thoroughly examined and again tested for accuracy.

(3) The air receiver shall be examined under normal pressure as thoroughly as the operating conditions permit.

(4) Different parts of the examination and testing may be made by different persons.

Report of examination

5.—(1) A report of every examination made in pursuance of paragraph 4 of this Schedule shall be entered in or attached to the general register as defined in section 176 of the Factories Act 1961 and shall contain the prescribed particulars referred to in section 36(5) of the Factories Act 1961.

(2) Where the report of any examination under this Certificate specifies conditions for securing the safe working of an air receiver, it shall not be used except in accordance with those conditions.

(F2519, 9 November 1983)

Certificate of Exception No. SPA/FA/1984/1 (General).—1. Pursuant to section 37(2) and (3) of the Factories Act 1961, being satisfied that the provisions cannot reasonably be applied, I hereby except from the provisions of section 36(4) of the said Act the classes of air receiver specified in Part I of the Schedule to this Certificate, subject to the conditions in Part II of that Schedule.

2. This Certificate shall come into operation on 20 June 1984 and shall remain in force until revoked by an inspector appointed and authorised as hereinafter appears.

SCHEDULE

PART I

Any air receiver which—

(a) forms part of an oil-flooded air compressor plant;

(b) contains oil which is forced from the receiver by means of compressed air;
(c) separates oil from an oil/air mixtures; and
(d) is designed and manufactured to British Standard 5169 as in force at the time of manufacture, or an equivalent standard.

PART II

1. The air compressor plant which contains any air receiver to which this Certificate applies shall be fitted with an automatic device which switches off the compressor if the temperature of the mixture in the receiver exceeds 120 degrees Celsius.

2. Every air receiver to which this Certificate applies shall be thoroughly cleaned and examined internally before being used and at least once in the period laid down in conditions 5 and 6.

3. Every such examination shall be carried out by a person who is competent to assess the condition of the air receiver and its fitness for use until the next examination.

4. Every such examination shall include a test to ensure the correct operation of the device required by Paragraph 1 of this Part of the Schedule.

5. The person carrying out every such examination shall specify the period during which the air receiver may continue to be used and shall certify in writing that, in his opinion, the air receiver is safe for use for that period.

6. The period specified by the competent person shall not be greater than 6 years.

7. A report of every such examination containing the same particulars as are prescribed under section 36(5) of the Factories Act 1961 shall be entered in or attached to the general register required by section 140 of that Act.

(F2520, 20 June 1984)

37. Exceptions as to steam boilers, steam receivers and containers, and air receivers.—(1) Sections thirty-two to thirty-four of this Act do not apply to any boiler belonging to or exclusively used in the service of Her Majesty or belonging to and used by the United Kingdom Atomic Energy Authority, or to the boiler of any ship or of any locomotive which belongs to and is used by any railway company.

(2) The chief inspector *(a)* may by certificate *(b)* except from any of the provisions of sections thirty two to thirty six of this Act any class or type of steam boiler, steam receiver, steam container or air receiver to which he is satisfied that the provision cannot reasonably be applied.

(3) Any such exception may be unqualified or may be subject to such conditions as may be contained in the certificate.

General note. In sub-s. (1), for the words "sections thirty-two to thirty-four" there are substituted the words "section thirty-four", and in sub-s. (2) for the words "sections thirty-two to thirty-six" there are substituted the words "section thirty-four", and the words "steam receiver, steam container or air receiver" are repealed by S.I. 1989 No. 2169, as from 1 July 1994.

(a) **Inspector.** For definition, see s. 176(1).

(b) **Certificate.** The certificates of exception relating to ss. 32 to 36 are set out at the end of the notes to those sections.

———————————

38. Steam boilers—supplementary provisions. In this Part of this Act "steam boiler" means any closed vessel in which for any purpose steam is generated under pressure greater than atmospheric pressure, and includes any economiser used to heat water being fed to any such vessel, and any superheater used for heating steam; and "maximum permissible working pressure", in relation to any steam boiler, means (except in subsections (4) and (5) of section thirty-three) that specified in the report of the last examination under that section.

General note. The words from "and 'maximum permissible working pressure'" to the end are repealed by S.I. 1989 No. 2169, as from 1 July 1994.

---

39. Precautions as respects water-sealed gasholders.—(1) Every gasholder *(a)* shall be of sound construction *(b)* and shall be properly maintained *(c)*.

(2) Every gasholder *(a)* shall be thoroughly examined externally by a competent person at least once in every period of two years, and a record containing the prescribed *(d)* particulars of every such examination shall be entered in or attached to the general register *(e)*.

(3) In the case of a gasholder of which any lift has been in use for more than twenty years, the internal state of the sheeting shall, at least once in every period of ten years, be examined by a competent person by cutting samples from the crown and sides of the holder or by other sufficient means, and all samples so cut and a report on every such examination signed by the person making it shall be kept available for inspection.

(4) A record signed by the occupier *(f)* of the factory *(g)* or by a responsible official authorised in that behalf showing the date of the construction, as nearly as it can be ascertained, of the oldest lift of every gasholder in the factory shall be kept available for inspection.

(5) Where there is more than one gasholder in the factory *(g)*, every gasholder shall be marked in a conspicuous position with a distinguishing number or letter.

(6) No gasholder shall be repaired or demolished *(h)* except under the direct supervision of a person who, by his training and experience and his knowledge of the necessary precautions against risks of explosion and of persons being overcome by gas, is competent to supervise such work.

(7) In this section "gasholder" means a water-sealed gasholder which has a storage capacity of not less than 140 cubic metres.

(a) Gasholder. For definition, see sub-s. (7).

(b) Of sound construction. See note *(b)* to s. 36.

(c) Properly maintained. See INTRODUCTORY NOTE 10.

(d) Prescribed. "Prescribed" means prescribed by the Minister (s. 176(1)). The Order set out below as made under the corresponding provisions of the Factories Act 1937, and is continued in force as if made under this section by virtue of the Factories Act 1961, s. 183 and Sch. 6 and S.I. 1947 No. 1941, reg. 7(3).

(e) **General Register.** See ss. 140, 141 and 166(3).

(f) **Occupier.** See note (j) to s. 33.

(g) **Factory.** For definition, see s. 175.

(h) **Demolished.** It should be noted that the demolition of a gasholder is a work of engineering construction (see s. 176(1)) to which certain parts of the Act apply by virtue of s. 127. It is submitted that both s. 39 and s. 127 will apply to the work of demolition if this takes place on premises which are subject to the Factories Act 1961.

THE GASHOLDERS (RECORD OF EXAMINATIONS) ORDER 1938
(S.R. & O. 1938 No. 598, as amended by S.I. 1981 No. 687)

1. In pursuance of subsection (2) of section 33 of the Factories Act 1937, I hereby prescribe that the record required by that subsection to be kept with respect to examinations of water sealed gasholders shall contain the following particulars:—
   (i) Name of occupier of factory.
  (ii) Address of factory.
 (iii) Distinguishing number or letter and type of gasholder.
 (iv) (a) Number of lifts.
     (b) Maximum capacity.
     (c) Pressure thrown by holder when full of gas.
  (v) Particulars as to the condition of:—
     (a) Crown.
     (b) Side sheeting, including grips and cups.
     (c) Guiding mechanism (roller carriages, rollers, pins, guides, rails or ropes).
     (d) Tank.
     (e) Other structure, if any (columns, framing and bracing).
 (vi) Particulars as to the position of the lifts at the time of examination.
(vii) Particulars as to whether the tank and lifts were found sufficiently level for safe working and if not, as to the steps taken to remedy the defect.
(viii) Date of examination and by whom it was carried out.

2. This Order may be cited as the Gasholders (Record of Examinations) Order 1938.

40–55. [*repealed*].

---

56. Application of Part II to Scotland. In the application of this Part of this Act to Scotland, for any reference to a magistrates' court there shall be substituted a reference to the sheriff, for any reference to a complaint a reference to a summary application, and subsection (3) of section fifty-four shall be omitted.

PART III
WELFARE (GENERAL PROVISIONS)

57. Supply of drinking water.—(1) There shall be provided and maintained (a) at suitable points conveniently accessible to all persons employed an adequate supply of wholesome drinking water from a public main or from some other source approved in writing by the district council *(b)*.

(2) A supply of drinking water which is not laid on shall be contained in suitable vessels, and shall be renewed at least daily, and all practicable steps shall be taken to preserve the water and vessels from contamination; and a drinking water supply (whether laid on or not) shall, in such cases as the inspector for the district may direct, be clearly marked "Drinking Water".

(3) Except where the water is delivered in an upward jet from which employed persons can conveniently drink, one or more suitable cups or drinking vessels shall be provided at each point of supply with facilities for rinsing them in drinking water.

(4) The approval required under subsection (1) of this section shall not be withheld except on the ground that the water is not wholesome.

General note. This section is to be repealed as from 1 January 1996 by the Workplace (Health, Safety and Welfare) Regulations 1992, S.I. 1992 No. 3004, for workplaces in existence on 31 December 1992. Those Regulations will apply to those workplaces from the former date. This section ceases to have effect and the Regulations apply to workplaces coming into use after 31 December 1992 and to modifications, extensions and conversions started after 31 December 1992 to existing workplaces as soon as they come into use.

(a) **Maintained.** For definition, see s. 176(1). See also INTRODUCTORY NOTE 10.

(b) **District council.** For definition, see s.176(1), (8).

---

58. Washing facilities.—(1) There shall be provided and maintained *(a)* for the use of employed persons adequate and suitable facilities for washing which shall include a supply of clean running hot and cold or warm water and, in addition, soap and clean towels or other suitable means of cleaning or drying; and the facilities shall be conveniently accessible and shall be kept in a clean and orderly condition.

(2)–(4) [*repealed*].

General note. This section is to be repealed as from 1 January 1996 by the Workplace (Health, Safety and Welfare) Regulations 1992, S.I. 1992 No. 3004, for workplaces in existence on 31 December 1992. Those Regulations will apply to those workplaces from the former date. This section ceases to have effect and the Regulations apply to workplaces coming into use after 31 December 1992 and to modifications, extensions and conversions started after 31 December 1992 to existing workplaces as soon as they come into use. In *Reid v Westfield Paper Co Ltd* 1957 SC 218, the Inner House of the Court of Session decided that a pursuer could recover damages for a breach of s. 42 of the Factories Act 1937 [s. 58 of the 1961 Act] if he proved the dermatitis from which he was suffering to be due to that breach. See also the General Introduction.

The provision of facilities for washing is required under many of the regulations and orders for safety, health and welfare set out in Part III and by the Washing Facilities (Miscellaneous Industries) Regulations 1960, S.I. 1960 No. 1214. None of those requirements is in substitution for, or in diminution of, the requirements of s. 58(1) relating to a supply of clean running hot and cold or warm water, subject to regulations made under sub-ss. (3) or (4) with regard to the requirements that the water shall be running water (see S.I. 1960 No. 1029, set out below).

(a) **Maintained.** For definition, see s. 176(1). See also INTRODUCTORY NOTE 10.

The Regulations set out below were made under s. 42(3) of the Factories Act 1937, s. 8(4) of the Factories Act 1948 and s. 18(2) of the Factories Act 1959 and are continued in force by virtue of s. 183 and Sch. 6 and S.I. 1974 No. 1941, reg. 7(3). By the Railway Running Sheds (No. 1) Regulations 1961, the expression "factory" in these Regulations includes railway running sheds.

THE WASHING FACILITIES (RUNNING WATER) EXEMPTION REGULATIONS 1960
(S.I. 1960 No. 1029)

General note. The whole Regulations are revoked by S.I. 1992 No. 3004, as from 1 January 1993 except, in relation to any workplace or part of a workplace which is not a new workplace, or a modification, an extension or a conversion, they are revoked as from 1 January 1996.

The Minister of Labour by virtue of the powers conferred on him by subsection (3) of section forty-two of the Factories Act 1937, subsection (4) of section eight of the Factories Act 1948, and subsection (2) of section eighteen of the Factories Act 1959, and of all other powers enabling him in that behalf, hereby makes the following Regulations:

1. These Regulations may be cited as the Washing Facilities (Running Water) Exemption Regulations 1960, and shall come into operation on the first day of August, 1960.

2. The Interpretation Act 1889 shall apply to the interpretation of these Regulations as it applies to the interpretation of an Act of Parliament.

3.—(1) The inspector for the district may by certificate exempt from so much of subsection (1) of section eighteen of the Factories Act 1959 [s. 58(1) of the 1961 Act], as requires the water supplied for the use of employed persons to be running water any factory as respects which he is satisfied—
  (a) that accommodation is restricted and adequate and suitable facilities for washing in clean hot and cold or warm water are otherwise conveniently available; or
  (b) that the provision of a piped water supply or of drainage facilities or of facilities for heating running water would not be reasonably practicable.
(2) An exemption granted by a certificate under this regulation shall be subject to such conditions (if any) as may be specified in the certificate and be for such period as may be so specified, without prejudice however to the granting of exemptions for further periods by further certificates. Any such certificates may be varied or revoked by the inspector for the district.

4. Factories in which the largest number of persons at work at any one time does not exceed five are hereby exempted until the expiration of the thirty-first day of July, 1961, from so much of the said subsection (1) of section eighteen of the Factories Act 1959 [s. 58(1) of the 1961 Act], as requires the water supplied to be running water.

---

59. Accommodation for clothing.—(1) There shall be provided and maintained (a) for the use of employed persons adequate and suitable (b) accommodation for clothing not worn during working hours; and such arrangements as are reasonably practicable or, when a standard is prescribed, such arrangements as are laid down thereby shall be made for drying such clothing.

(2)–(3) [*repealed*].

General note. This section is to be repealed as from 1 January 1996 by the Workplace (Health, Safety and Welfare) Regulations 1992, S.I. 1992 No. 3004, for workplaces in existence on 31 December 1992. Those Regulations will apply to those workplaces from the former date. This section ceases to have effect and the Regulations apply to workplaces coming into use after 31 December 1992 and to modifications, extensions and conversions started after 31 December 1992 to existing workplaces as soon as they come into use.

As to the civil liability for breach of this section and of other welfare provisions of the Act, see the GENERAL INTRODUCTION and *McCarthy v Daily Mirror Newspapers Ltd* [1949] 1 All ER 801, CA.

(a) **Maintained.** For definition, see s. 176(1). See also INTRODUCTORY NOTE 10.

(b) **Adequate and suitable.** There is no obligation to keep the clothing of workpeople safe, but the risk of theft is an element which should be taken into consideration in deciding whether the accommodation provided is suitable (*McCarthy v Daily Mirror Newspapers Ltd*, above, followed in *Barr v Cruikshank & Co Ltd* 1959 SLT (Sh Ct) 9).

---

60. Sitting facilities.—(1) Where any employed persons have in the course of their employment reasonable opportunities for sitting without detriment to their work, there shall be provided and maintained *(a)* for their use suitable facilities for sitting sufficient to enable them to take advantage of those opportunities.

(2) Where a substantial proportion of any work can properly be done sitting—

(a) there shall be provided and maintained *(a)* for any employed person doing that work a seat of a design, construction and dimensions suitable for him and the work, together with a foot-rest on which he can readily and comfortably support his feet if he cannot do so without a foot-rest; and

(b) the arrangements shall be such that the seat is adequately and properly supported while in use for the purpose for which it is provided.

(3) For the purposes of subsection (2) of this section the dimensions of a seat which is adjustable shall be taken to be its dimensions as for the time being adjusted.

General note. This section is to be repealed as from 1 January 1996 by the Workplace (Health, Safety and Welfare) Regulations 1992, S.I. 1992 No. 3004, for workplaces in existence on 31 December 1992. Those Regulations will apply to those workplaces from the former date. This section ceases to have effect and the Regulations apply to workplaces coming into use after 31 December 1992 and to modifications, extensions and conversions started after 31 December 1992 to existing workplaces as soon as they come into use.

The provisions relating to sitting facilities formerly contained in certain orders and regulations were revoked by the Factories (Miscellaneous Welfare Orders, etc., Amendments) Order 1951, S.I. 1951 No. 926.

(a) **Maintained.** For definition, see s. 176(1). See also INTRODUCTORY NOTE 10.

---

61.   [*repealed*].

---

62.   [*repealed*].

PART IV
HEALTH, SAFETY AND WELFARE (SPECIAL PROVISIONS AND REGULATIONS)

Special provisions

63–67.   [*repealed*].

---

68.   Humid factories.—(1) The occupier (a) of every humid factory (b) shall, on or before the first occasion on which artificial humidity is produced at that factory, give notice thereof in writing to the inspector (c) for the district.

(2) The following provisions of this section shall have effect with respect to every humid factory (b) with respect to which regulations under this Act concerning humidity are not for the time being in force (d).

(2A) In this section, unless the context otherwise requires—
  "dry bulb temperature" means the temperature measured by an accurate and properly maintained thermometer (which may form part of the hygrometer) and any reference in this section to a dry bulb thermometer, or without qualification to a thermometer, shall be taken to be a reference to such a thermometer and a reference without qualification to temperature shall be taken to be a reference to the dry bulb temperature;
  "hygrometer" means an accurate and properly maintained and calibrated instrument for the measurement of the relative humidity in the workplace;
  "wet bulb temperature" means either—

  (a) the temperature indicated by the wet bulb of a static hygrometer which relies on natural circulation of air around the thermometers; or
  (b) the temperature calculated from the dry bulb temperature and relative humidity by the method approved for the time being by the Health and Safety Executive,

and any reference in this section to the reading of the wet bulb thermometer shall be taken to be a reference to the wet bulb temperature.

(3) There shall be provided and maintained (e) in every room in which artificial humidity is produced two hygrometers (f) and a thermometer close to each hygrometer, and—

(a) one of the hygrometers shall be placed in the centre and the other at the side of the room, or in such other position as may be directed or sanctioned by an inspector, so as to be plainly visible to the persons employed;

(b) [*repealed*];

(c) the occupier *(a)* or other person authorised for the purpose shall read the hygrometers and the thermometers between ten and eleven o'clock in the morning on every day on which any persons are employed in the room in the morning and between three and four o'clock in the afternoon on every day on which any persons are employed in the room in the afternoon, and when persons are employed before six o'clock in the morning or after eight o'clock in the evening, at such other times as may be directed by the inspector *(c)* for the district, and shall enter the readings on a record;

(d) the records of the wet bulb temperature or temperature and hygrometer readings shall be kept by the occupier for at least two years from when they were made and the occupier shall give his employees immediate access to those records on request together with such information as is necessary for their interpretation.

(4) There shall be no artificial humidification in any room at any time when the reading of the wet bulb thermometer exceeds 22.5 degrees Celsius or, in the case of a room in which the spinning of cotton or the spinning of merino or cashmere by the French or dry process or the spinning or combing of wool by that process is carried on, 26.5 degrees Celsius.

(5) There shall be no artificial humidification in any room at any time when the difference between the readings of the dry and wet bulb thermometers is less than that indicated in Schedule 1 to this Act.

(6) No water which is liable to cause injury to the health of the persons employed, or to the yield effluvia, shall be used for artificial humidification, and for the purposes of this subsection any water which absorbs from acid solution of permanganate of potash in four hours at 16 degrees Celsius more than 7 milligrams of oxygen per litre of water shall be deemed to be liable to cause injury to the health of the persons employed.

(7) The chief inspector *(c)* may direct in writing, in the case of any factory or any room in a factory that only one hygrometer, and one thermometer close to it placed in such position as may be directed by an inspector, need be provided instead of two hygrometers and thermometers placed as mentioned in paragraph (a) of subsection (3) of this section.

(8) Where in respect of any room notice has been given in the prescribed manner to the inspector *(c)* for the district that it is intended that the humidity of the atmosphere should never be greater than will maintain a difference of at least 2 degrees Celsius between the readings of the dry and wet bulb thermometers, the provisions of paragraphs (c) and (d) of subsection (3) of this section shall not apply as respects that room so long as at least that difference is maintained.

General note. This section is amended by S.I. 1992 No. 1811.

(a) Occupier. See note *(j)* to s. 33.

(b) Humid factory. For definition, see s. 176(1).

(c) **Inspector.** For definition, see s. 176(1).

(d) **Regulations . . . in force.** Regulations are at present in force for spinning and weaving of jute (S.I. 1948 No. 1696), weaving of flax and tow (S.R. & O. 1906 No. 177), spinning and weaving of hemp, etc. (S.R. & O. 1907 No. 660) and for cotton cloth factories (S.R. & O. 1929 No. 300).

(e) **Maintained.** For definition, see s. 176(1). See also INTRODUCTORY NOTE 10.

(f) **Hygrometers.** The construction and maintenance of hygrometers have not been prescribed under this section or the corresponding provisions of the Factories Act 1937, but see the Hygrometers Order made under the Cotton Cloth Factories Regulations 1929, set out in Part 4 of this book.

(g) **Hygrometer records.** The record of hygrometer readings is Form 48. See s. 141 as to the keeping of records.

---

69. Underground rooms.—(1) The inspector (a) for the district may certify any underground room (b) as unsuitable for work other than work involved in the use of the room for the purpose of storage or such other purpose as the Minister may by order specify (c), and where such a certificate is in force with respect to any room no work for which it is certified as unsuitable shall be carried on in it.

(2) Where the inspector (a) certifies as unsuitable any room which is in actual use, he shall suspend the operation of the certificate for such period as he considers reasonable with a view to enabling the occupier (d) to render the room suitable or to obtain other premises.

(3) Except in the case of a room which on the first day of July, nineteen hundred and thirty-eight was part of a factory (e) (within the meaning of the Factories Act 1937, as originally enacted) and was used for work which it may be certified as unsuitable under this section, the occupier (d) of an underground room (b)—

(a) shall, before the room is used for work for which it may be certified as unsuitable under this section, give notice in the prescribed form (f) and containing the prescribed particulars to the inspector (a) for the district; and

(b) shall not use the room for any such process as may be prescribed (g), being a process of a hot, wet or dusty nature or which is liable to give off any fume (h), without the consent in writing of the inspector for the district.

(4) If the occupier (d) is aggrieved by any decision of an inspector (a) under this section, he may, within twenty-one days of the date of issue of the certificate or the refusal of the consent, as the case may be, appeal to a magistrates' court, or, in Scotland, the sheriff, and, pending the final determination of an appeal against a decision under subsection (1) of this section in the case of a room in actual use, no offence shall be deemed to be committed under that subsection in respect of the room to which the appeal relates.

(5) In this section—

"underground room" means any room which, or any part of which, is so situate that at least half its height, measured from the floor to the ceiling, is below the surface of the footway of the adjoining street or of the ground adjoining or nearest to the room; and

"unsuitable" means unsuitable as regards construction, height, light or ventilation, or on any hygienic ground, or on the ground that adequate means of escape in case of fire are not provided.

(6) Any certificate issued under this section may be withdrawn by the inspector *(a)* for the district if such alterations are made as in his opinion to render the room suitable.

General note. This section is to be repealed as from 1 January 1996 by the Workplace (Health, Safety and Welfare) Regulations 1992, S.I. 1992 No. 3004, for workplaces in existence on 31 December 1992. Those Regulations will apply to those workplaces from the former date. This section ceases to have effect and the Regulations apply to workplaces coming into use after 31 December 1992 and to modifications, extensions and conversions started after 31 December 1992 to existing workplaces as soon as they come into use.

(a) **Inspector.** For definition, see s. 176(1).

(b) **Underground room.** For definition, see sub-s. (5).

(c) **As the Minister ... may ... specify.** This section, in so far as it enables orders to be made otherwise than by statutory instrument, has effect as if the reference to the Secretary of State ("the Minister") was a reference to the Health and Safety Executive; S.I. 1974 No. 1941, reg. 2(b) Sch. 2.

(d) **Occupier.** See note *(j)* to s. 33.

(e) **Factory.** For definition, see s. 175.

(f) **Prescribed form.** "Prescribed" means prescribed by the Minister (s. 176(1)). The Work in Underground Rooms (Form of Notice) Order 1946, S.R. & O. 1946 No. 2247, made under the corresponding provisions of the Factories Act 1937, and continued in force as if made under this section by virtue of s. 183 and the Sixth Schedule, prescribed the form of notice, which is issued as Form 1229. The Order is not reproduced here.

(g) **Prescribed process.** No process has yet been prescribed under this subsection or under the corresponding provisions of the Factories Act 1937.

(h) **Fume.** "Fume" includes gas or vapour (s. 176(1)).

70.–73. [*repealed*].

---

74. Prohibition of employment of women and young persons in certain processes connected with lead manufacture.—A woman or young person *(a)* shall not be employed in any factory *(b)* in any of the following operations:—

   (a) work at a furnace where the reduction or treatment of zinc or lead ores is carried on *(c)*;

   (b) the manipulation, treatment or reduction of ashes containing lead, the desilverising of lead, or the melting of scrap lead or zinc *(c)*;

   (c) the manufacture of solder or alloys containing more than ten per cent of lead *(c)*;

(d) the manufacture of any oxide, carbonate, sulphate, chromate, acetate, nitrate, or silicate of lead;

(e) mixing or pasting in connection with the manufacture or repair of electric accumulators *(d)*;

(f) the cleaning of workrooms where any of the processes aforesaid are carried on.

General note. For other provisions for the protection of workers against contamination by lead, see the Control of Lead at Work Regulations 1980.

See s. 128 as to the extension of this section to premises which are not a factory.

The prohibitions contained in this section are in addition to those in force under the regulations referred to in notes *(c)* and *(d)*, *infra*.

(a) Woman; young person. For definition, see s. 176(1).

(b) Factory. For definition, see s. 175.

(c) Lead smelting. See the Lead Smelting and Manufacture Regulations 1911, reg. 10.

(d) Electric accumulators. See the Electric Accumulator Regulations 1925, reg. 1(ii).

---

75. [*repealed*].

Special regulations for safety and health

76. [*repealed*].

General note. This section is repealed by S.I. 1974 No. 1941, reg 2(a), Sch 1, but by reg. 7(3) regulations for safety and health made under the repealed power, or made under the cognate provisions of superseded enactments and continued in force as if so made by virtue of s. 183 and Sch. 6, are continued in force notwithstanding this repeal.

Supplementary provisions

77.–79. [*repealed*].

PART V
NOTIFICATION AND INVESTIGATION OF ACCIDENTS AND INDUSTRIAL DISEASES

80.–82. [*repealed*].

The notification of events previously prescribed by ss. 80–82 is now the subject of the Reporting of Injuries, Diseases and Dangerous Occurrences Regulations 1985, S.I. 1985 No. 2023.

---

83.   [*repealed*].

---

84.   Power to direct formal investigation of accidents and cases of disease.—
(1) The Minister *(a)* may, where he considers it expedient to do so, direct a
formal investigation to be held into any accident *(b)* occurring or case of disease
contracted or suspected to have been contracted in a factory *(c)* and of its causes
and circumstances, and the following provisions of this section shall have effect
with respect to any such investigation.

(2) The Minister *(a)* may appoint a competent person to hold the investigation, and may appoint any person possessing legal or special knowledge to act
as assessor in holding it.

(3) The person or persons so appointed (in this section referred to as "the
court") shall hold the investigation in open court in such manner and under
such conditions as the court may think most effectual for ascertaining the
causes and circumstances of the accident *(b)* or case of disease, and for enabling
the court to make the report required by this section.

(4) The court shall have for the purposes of the investigation all the powers
of a magistrates' court when trying informations for offences under this Act (or,
in Scotland, all the powers of a court of summary jurisdiction when hearing
complaints in respect of such offences) and all the powers of an inspector
under this Act, and, in addition, power—

(a)   to enter and inspect any place or building the entry or inspection of
which appears to the court requisite for the purposes of the investigation;
(b)   by summons or, in Scotland, order, signed by the court to require the
attendance of all such persons as the court thinks fit to call before it and
examine and to require answers or returns to such inquiries as it thinks
fit to make;
(c)   to require the production of all books, papers and documents which it
considers important for the purposes of the investigation;
(d)   to administer an oath and require any person examined to make and
sign a declaration of the truth of the statements made by him in his
examination.

(5) Persons attending as witnesses before the court shall be allowed such
expenses as would be allowed to witnesses attending before a court of record or,
in Scotland, to witnesses attending an inquiry under the Fatal Accidents Inquiry
(Scotland) Act 1895; and in case of dispute as to the amount to be allowed, the
dispute shall be referred by the court to a master of the Supreme Court or, in
Scotland, the auditor of the sheriff court, and the master or auditor shall, on
request signed by the court, ascertain and certify the proper amount of the
expenses.

(6) The court shall make a report to the Minister *(a)* stating the causes and
circumstances of the accident *(b)* or case of disease and its circumstances, and
adding any observations which the court thinks right to make.

(7) The court may require the expenses incurred in and about the investigation (including the remuneration of any persons appoined to act as assessors) to be paid in whole or part by any person summoned before it who appears to the court to be, by reason of any act or default on his part or on the part of any servant or agent of his, responsible in any degree for the occurrence of the accident or case of disease, but any such expenses not required to be so paid shall be deemed to be part of the expenses of the Minister *(a)* in the execution of this Act.

(8) Any person who without reasonable excuse (proof whereof shall lie on him) either fails, after having had the expenses (if any) to which he is entitled tendered to him, to comply with any summons, order or requisition of the court, or prevents or impedes the court in the execution of its duty, shall be guilty of an offence, and liable to a fine not exceeding twenty pounds, and, in the case of a failure to comply with a requisition for making any return or producing any document, if the failure in respect of which he was convicted is continued after the conviction, he shall (subject to the provisions of section one hundred and fifty-seven of this Act) be guilty of a further offence and liable to a fine not exceeding twenty pounds for every day on which the failure was so continued.

(9) The Minister *(a)* may cause the report of the court to be made public at such time and in such manner as he thinks fit.

(10) Where an investigation under subsection (1) of this section is directed to be held into an accident in Scotland which causes the death of any person, no inquiry with regard to that death shall, unless the Lord Advocate otherwise directs, be held in pursuance of the Fatal Accidents Inquiry (Scotland) Act 1895.

General note. This section is repealed, except in relation to investigations commenced before 1 January 1975 by S.I. 1974 No. 1941, reg. 2(a), Sch 1. It is therefore for practical purposes spent.

See s. 164(4) as to the initiation of proceedings where it appears from a report made by a court appointed to make a formal investigation that any of the provisions of this Act, or of Orders or Regulations made under it or under previous enactments consolidated therein, have not been complied with.

(a) The Minister. For definition, see s. 176(1).

(b) Accident. This word must be given its ordinary meaning (see *Fenton v J Thorley & Co Ltd* [1903] AC 443, HL, decided under the Workmen's Compensation Act 1897).

(c) Factory. For definition, see s. 175. This section also applies to tenement factories (s. 121), electrical stations (s. 123), docks (s. 125), ships (s. 126) and building operations and works of engineering construction (s. 127).

---

85. [*repealed*].

PART VI
EMPLOYMENT OF WOMEN AND YOUNG PERSONS

Hours and Holidays

86.–116. [*Repealed*].

Exemptions in interest of efficiency of industry or transport

117. Exemptions from provisions regulating hours of employment.—
(1) Where the Minister *(a)* is satisfied, on an application made to him in that behalf, that it is desirable in the public interest to do so for the purpose of maintaining or increasing the efficiency of industry, he may, after such consultations as he may think appropriate or as may be required under subsection (5) of this section, exempt the employment of persons (other than children) from the Hours of Employment (Conventions) Act 1936.

(2) An exemption granted under this section may extend to the employment of persons generally, of a class of persons or of particular persons, and to employment generally, or any class of employment or particular employment, and may be granted to such extent and on such conditions as may be specified in the instrument by which it is granted and, subject to subsection (4) of this section, either indefinitely or for such period as may be so specified.

(3) An exemption under this section extending only to particular persons or a particular employment or to a class of persons or employment defined by reference to particular premises or to work supervised from particular premises, and any exemption under this section for a particular day or particular days only, shall be granted by order, to be known as a special exemption order *(b)*, and any other exemption under this section shall be granted by special regulations, to be known as general exemption regulations.

(4) An exemption granted by a special exemption order shall not be for more than one year, without prejudice however to the granting of the like exemption for further period by further special exemption orders.

(5) The Minister *(a)* shall not make general exemption regulations *(e)* except—

    (a) on the application of a joint industrial council, conciliation board or other similar body constituted by organisations which appear to him to be representative respectively of workers and employers concerned; or
    (b) on the application of a wages council; or
    (c) on the joint application of an organisation which appears to him to be representative of employers concerned and of an organisation which appears to him to be representative of workers concerned; or

(d) on the application of an organisation which appears to him to be representative of employers concerned and after consulting an organisation which appears to him to be representative of workers concerned; or

(e) on the application of an organisation which appears to him to be representative of workers concerned and after consulting an organisation which appears to him to be representative of employers concerned.

(6) The Minister *(a)* shall publish in the London Gazette such particulars of special exemption orders *(b)* as he considers appropriate.

(7) In this section "organisation" includes—

(a) in relation to workers, an association of trade unions, and

(b) in relation to employers, an association of organisations of employers and also any body established by or under any enactment for the purpose of carrying on under national ownership any industry or part of an industry or undertaking,

and "trade union" includes an association of trade unions.

General note. By S.I. 1974 No. 1941, reg. 2(b), Sch. 2, this section has effect as if the reference to special regulations (see sub-s. (3)) was reference to regulations.

(a) The Minister. For definition, see s. 176(1). By S.I. 1974 No. 1941, reg. 2(b), Sch. 2, in so far as this section enables orders to be made otherwise than by statutory instrument (see sub-ss. (3), (4), (6)) references to the Secretary of State ("the Minister" have effect as if they were references to the Health and Safety Executive.

(b) Special exemption order. See, for example, the annual Baking and Sausage Making (Christmas and New Year) Order (not printed in this book).

Certificate of fitness for employment of young persons

118. [*repealed*].

---

119. Power of inspector to require certificate of fitness for work.—Where an inspector *(a)* is of opinion that the employment of a young person *(b)* in a factory *(c)* or in a particular process or kind of work in a factory is prejudicial to his health or the health of other persons, he may serve *(d)* written notice on the occupier *(e)* of the factory informing him thereof and requiring that the employment of that young person in the factory or in the process or kind of work, as the case may be, be discontinued after the period named in the notice (which shall not be less than one nor more than seven days after the service of the notice) and the occupier shall not continue after that period to employ the young person unless the appointed factory doctor or an employment medical adviser has, after the service of the notice personally examined the young person and certified that he is fit for employment in the factory or in the process or kind of work as the case may be.

(*a*) **Inspector.** For definition, see s. 176(1).

(*b*) **Young person.** For definition, see s. 176(1).

(*c*) **Factory.** For definition, see s. 175.

(*d*) **Serve.** As to the service of documents, see s. 168.

(*e*) **Occupier.** See note (*j*) to s. 33.

119A. Duty of factory occupier to give notice of employment of a young person.—(1) Where the occupier (*a*) of a factory (*b*) takes a young person (*c*) into his employment to work in the factory (or transfers to work in the factory from work elsewhere than in a factory a young person already in his employment), the occupier shall, not later than seven days after the day on which he does so, send to the local careers office a written notice stating the name of the occupier, the address of the factory (*d*) and the fact of the young person's having been so taken or transferred, and the date on which, and the work to do which, he was so taken or transferred, and giving such of the following information as is within the occupier's knowledge, namely—

(a) the young person's Christian name (or forename) and surname;
(b) the date of his birth;
(c) his usual residential address; and
(d) the name and address of the school (if any) which he last attended before he was so taken or transferred.

(2) In this section—

(a) "the local careers office" means the premises from which, under arrangements made in pursuance of subsection (1), (4) or (5) of section 8 of the Employment and Training Act 1973, the facilities provided in pursuance of the said subsection (1) are made available in the area (as determined in pursuance of the arrangements) in which the factory is situated; and
(b) "school" means a school within the meaning of the Education Act 1944 or the Education (Scotland) Act 1962.

General note. This section is repealed by the Employment Act 1989, ss. 10, 29(4), Sch. 3, Pt. II, Sch. 7, Pt. III, as from a day to be appointed.

(*a*) **Occupier.** See note (*j*) to s. 33.

(*b*) **Factory.** For definition, see s. 175.

(*c*) **Young person.** For definition, see s. 176(1).

*(d) **Address of factory.*** Where this section applies by virtue of s. 125(3)(a), s. 126(2) or s. 127(2) the notice must state as the address of the factory the place where the young person works (Employment Medical Advisory Service Act 1972, s. 8(1)(b)) (repealed by the Employment Act 1989, s. 29(4), Sch 7, Pt. III, as from a day to be appointed).

PART VII

SPECIAL APPLICATIONS AND EXTENSION

Factories occupying parts of buildings

120. [*repealed*].

121. Tenement factories—other provisions.—(1) Subject to the following provisions of this section, the owner *(a)* (whether or not he is one of the occupiers *(b)*) of a tenement factory *(c)* shall, instead of the occupier, be responsible for any contravention *(d)* of the following provisions of this Act, that is to say—

    (a) the provisions of Part I with respect to the drainage of floors *(e)*, sanitary conveniences *(f)*, cleanliness *(g)*, overcrowding *(h)*, temperature *(i)*, ventilation *(k)* and lighting *(l)*;
    (b) the provisions of Part II with respect to the provision and maintenance of fencing *(m)* and safety appliances *(n)*, the construction, maintenance, testing and examination of machinery or plant *(o)*, the construction and maintenance of floors, passages and stairs *(p)*;
    (c) the provisions of Part III *(q)*;
    (d) [*repealed*];
    (e) the provisions of Part V *(r)*;
    (f) [*repealed*]; and
    (g) the provisions of Part X as to posting of abstracts and notices *(s)*,

and for the purposes of those provisions the whole of a tenement factory shall be deemed to be one factory in the occupation of the owner.

(2) Subsection (1) of this section does not apply to any contravention *(d)* arising from the use in a tenement of any fencing, appliances, machinery or plant, if the use is a matter outside the control of the owner.

(3) Subsection (1) of this section does not apply to a contravention *(d)* in rooms occupied by only one tenant—

    (a) of the provisions of Part I with respect to cleanliness *(g)*, overcrowding *(h)*, temperature *(i)*, ventilation *(k)* and lighting *(l)*; or

(b) [*repealed*],

unless the contravention arises from a failure to carry out any necessary structural work or from any defect in any machinery, plant or fixtures belonging to the owner; and does not apply to a contravention in any such room of the provisions of Part V *(r)*.

(4) Subsection (1) of this section does not apply to a contravention *(d)* of the provisions of Part II *(q)* unless it arises from any such failure or defect as is mentioned in subsection (3) of this section.

(5) [*repealed*].

(6) The provision of this Act shall, so far as they are applicable and have not been applied by the foregoing provisions of this section, apply to any part of a tenement factory *(c)* which is not comprised with respect to persons employed by him, have effect in substitution for the corresponding notice posted by the owner.

(7) [*repealed*].

General note. See also the requirements of s. 122 as to premises where part of a building is let off as a separate factory.

(a) **Owner.** For definition, see s. 176(1).

(b) **Occupier.** See note *(j)* to s. 33.

(c) **Tenement factory.** For definition, see s. 176(1).

(d) **Contravention.** For definition, see s. 176(1).

(e) **Drainage of floors.** See s. 6.

(f) **Sanitary convenience.** See s. 7.

(g) **Cleanliness.** See s. 1.

(h) **Overcrowding.** See s. 2.

(i) **Temperature.** See s. 3.

(k) **Lighting.** See s. 5.

(m) **Provision and maintenance of fencing.** See ss. 12–16.

(n) **Safety appliances.** These are not defined in the Act. It is submitted that they would include the appliances to which reference is made in ss. 13 and 14.

(o) **Construction of machinery or plant.** See ss. 22–39.

(p) **Construction, etc., of floors, passages and stairs.** See s. 28.

(q) **Part III.** See ss. 57–62.

(r) **Part V.** See s. 84.

(s) **Abstracts and notices.** See s. 138.

---

122. Parts of buildings let off as separate factories—other provisions.—
(1) Where a part of a building is let off as a separate factory *(a)* but is not part of a tenement factory *(b)*,—

(a) the provisions of this Act specified in paragraphs (a) and (b) of subsection (2) of this section shall apply to any part of the building used for the purposes of the factory but not comprised therein;

(b) subject to subsections (4) and (5) of this section, the owner *(c)* of the building shall be responsible for any contravention *(d)* of the provisions specified in the said paragraph (a) as so applying; and

(c) subject to subsection (5) of this section, the owner of the building shall be responsible, instead of the occupier *(e)*, for any contravention as respects the factory, of the provisions specified in paragraph (c) of subsection (2) of this section.

(2) The said provisions are—

(a) the provisions of Part I with respect to cleanliness *(f)* and lighting *(g)*, and the provisions of Part II with respect to prime movers *(h)*, transmission machinery *(i)*, hoists and lifts *(k)*, chains, ropes and lifting tackle *(l)*, cranes and other lifting machines *(m)*, the construction and maintenance of floors, passages and stairs *(n)*, the keeping free from obstruction and slippery substances of floors, steps, stairs, passages and gangways *(o)*, and with respect to steam boilers *(p)*, steam receivers and steam containers *(q)*, and air receivers *(r)*;

(b) [*repealed*];

(c) the provisions of Part I with respect to sanitary conveniences *(s)* and the provisions of Part II with respect to hoists and lifts *(k)*.

(3) For the purposes of the provisions applied by the foregoing provisions of this section, lifting machines *(m)* attached to the outside of the building, and chains, ropes and lifting tackle *(l)* used in connection with those machines, shall be treated as being in the building, but any lifting machine not used for the purposes of the factory *(a)*, and any chains, ropes of lifting tackle not used in connection with a lifting machine so used, shall be disregarded.

(4) For any contravention *(d)* (whether as respects the factory *(a)* or otherwise) of the provisions of Part II with respect to chains, ropes and lifting tackle *(l)*, cranes and other lifting machines *(m)*, steam boilers *(p)*, steam receivers and steam containers *(q)*, and air receivers *(r)*—

(a) the occupier *(e)* of the factory *(a)* shall be responsible if it is a contravention with respect to any machinery or plant belonging to or supplied by him; and

(b) the owner *(c)* of the building shall be responsible in any other case,

except that the owner shall not be responsible for a contravention of those provisions in so far as they relate to matters outside his control, and for any such contravention as respects the factory the occupier shall be responsible.

(5) The owner *(c)* shall be responsible by virtue of this section—

(a) for the cleanliness of sanitary conveniences *(s)* only when used in common by several tenants; and

(b) for a contravention of the provisions relating to hoists and lifts *(k)* only so far as those provisions relate to matters within his control.

(6) [*repealed*].

(7) Any reference in the provisions applied by the foregoing provisions of this section to the general register *(t)* shall, in relation to matters in respect of

which the owner *(c)* of the building is responsible, be construed as a reference to a register to be kept by him.

General note. In sub-s. (2)(a), the words "and with respect to steam boilers, steam receivers and steam containers, and air receivers" and, in sub-s. (4), the words "steam boilers, steam receivers and steam containers, and air receivers" are repealed by S.I. 1989 No. 2169, as from 1 July 1994.

(a) Factory. For definition, see s. 175.

(b) Tenement factory. For definition, see s. 176(1).

(c) Owner. For definition, see s. 176(1).

(d) Contravention. For definition, see s. 176(1).

(e) Occupier. See note *(j)* to s. 33.

(f) Cleanliness. See s. 1.

(g) Lighting. See s. 5.

(h) Prime movers. See s. 12.

(i) Transmission machinery. See s. 13.

(k) Hoists and lifts. See ss. 22–25.

(l) Chains, ropes and lifting tackle. See s. 26.

(m) Cranes and other lifting machines. See s. 27.

(n) Construction and maintenance of floors, passages and stairs. See s. 28.

(o) Keeping free from obstruction, etc., of floors, etc. See s. 28.

(p) Steam boilers. See ss. 32–34, 37, 38.

(q) Steam receivers and steam containers. See s. 35.

(r) Air receivers. See s. 36.

(s) Sanitary conveniences. See s. 7.

(t) General register. See s. 140.

Electrical stations

123. Application of Act to electrical stations.—(1) The provisions of this Act shall apply to any premises in which persons are regularly employed in or in connection with the processes or operations of generating, transforming or converting, or of switching, controlling or otherwise regulating, electrical energy for supply by way of trade *(a)*, or for supply for the purposes of any transport undertaking or other industrial or commercial undertaking *(b)* or of any public building *(c)* or public institution *(d)*, or for supply to streets or other public places, as if the premises were a factory *(e)* and the employer of any person employed in the premises in or in connection with any such process or operation were the occupier *(f)* of a factory.

(2) Where any such process or operation is carried on or performed for such a supply as is mentioned in subsection (1) of this section but in other premises than those mentioned therein, then, if the premises are large enough to admit the entrance of a person after the machinery or plant therein is in position, the

following provisions of this Act shall apply to the premises as if they were a factory *(e)* and the employer of any person employed therein in or in connection with any such process or operation were the occupier *(f)* of the factory, that is to say,—

   (a) the provisions of sections fifty and fifty-one so far as they enable the Minister *(g)* to make regulations;

   (b) [*repealed*];

   (c) Part V *(h)*;

   (d) [*repealed*];

   (e) Part XII *(i)*;

   (f) Part XIII *(k)*;

   (g) Part XIV *(l)*.

(3) The Minister *(g)* may by special regulations *(m)* apply any of the provisions mentioned in subsection (2) of this section to any machinery or plant used—

   (a) in such processes or operations as are mentioned in subsection (1) of this section and for such a supply as is mentioned therein; but

   (b) elsewhere than in such premises as are mentioned in subsection (1) or subsection (2) of this section,

as if the machinery or plant were machinery or plant in a factory *(e)*, and the employer of any person employed in connection with any such use of the machinery or plant were the occupier *(f)* of a factory.

(4) Subsections (1) and (2) of this section shall not, except in so far as the Minister *(g)* may by special regulations *(o)* direct, apply to any premises where the said processes or operations are only carried on or performed for the immediate purpose of working an electric motor or working any apparatus which consumes electrical energy for lighting, transmitting or receiving messages or communications, or other purposes.

General note. By S.I. 1974 No. 1941, reg. 2(b), Sch. 2, references in this section to special regulations (see sub-ss. (3), (4)) are to have effect as if they were references to regulations.

Office premises within the meaning of the Offices, Shops and Railway Premises Act 1963 which are comprised in premises to which this section applies are, notwithstanding that they are so comprised, deemed not to form part of the premises for the purposes of the Factories Act 1961, except in so far as regulations made under the 1963 Act may provide; see the 1963 Act, s. 74(1).

  (a) **By way of trade.** See note *(i)* to s. 175.

  (b) **Transport undertaking or industrial or commercial undertaking.** There is no definition in the Act of these terms.

  (c) **Public building.** This is not defined in the Act.

  (d) **Public institution.** "Public institution" is not defined. A school for the sons of freemasons has been held to be a public institution (*Royal Masonic Institution for Boys v Parkes* [1912] 3 KB 212).

  (e) **Factory.** For definition, see s. 175.

  (f) **Occupier.** See note *(j)* to s. 33.

  (g) **The Minister.** For definition, see s. 176(1).

  (h) **Part V.** See s. 84.

(i) **Part XII.** See ss. 155–171.

(k) **Part XIII.** See ss. 172–174.

(l) **Part XIV.** See ss. 175–185.

(m) **Special regulations.** See the general note. For the making of regulations, see s. 180.

Institutions

124. Institutions.—(1) Where, in any premises forming part of an institution carried on for charitable or reformatory purposes *(a)*, any manual labour is exercised in or incidental to the making, altering, repairing, ornamenting, finishing, washing, cleaning or adapting for sale, of articles not intended for the use of the institution, but the premises do not constitute a factory *(b)*, the provisions of this Act shall nevertheless apply to the premises.

(2)–(3) [*repealed*].

General note. It should be noted that the breaking up or demolition of articles by manual labour is not included in sub-s. (1); compare s. 175(1)(b). In addition, the types of manual labour specified in that subsection need not be carried on by way of trade or for purposes of gain; compare s. 175(1). See also s. 175(9).

(a) **Reformatory purposes.** A prison for adult offenders is not carried on for such purposes since its primary purpose is to deprive an individual of his liberty (*Macdonald v Secretary of State for Scotland* 1979 SLT (Sh Ct) 8).

(b) **Factory.** For definition, see s. 175. In *Wood v LCC* [1941] 2 KB 232, [1941] 2 All ER 230, CA, it was held that the kitchen of a mental hospital in which an electrically driven meat mincing machine was used was not a factory within the Factories Act 1937.

Docks, wharves, quays, warehouses and ships

125. Docks, etc.—(1) The provisions of this Act specified in subsection (2) of this section shall apply to every dock *(a)*, wharf *(b)* or quay (including any warehouse *(c)* belonging to the owners, trustees or conservators of the dock, wharf or quay, and any line or siding used in connection with and for the purposes of the dock, wharf or quay and not forming part of a railway or tramway *(d)*) and every other warehouse (nor forming part of a factory *(e)*) in or for the purpose of which mechanical power is used—

(a) as if it were a factory; and

(b) as if the person having the actual use or occupation of it or of any premises within it or forming part of it, were the occupier *(f)* of a factory.

(2) The said provisions are—

(a) the provisions of Part II with respect to steam boilers *(g)*, but with the modification that the owner of the boiler shall, instead of the person deemed to be the occupier, be responsible for any contravention of those provisions;

(b)   the provisions of sections fifty and fifty-one so far as they enable the
        Minister *(h)* to make regulations;
(c)–(e) [*repealed*];
(f)   Part V *(i)*;
(g)   the provisions of Part VII with respect to premises where part of a
        building is a separate factory *(j)* subject to such modifications as may be
        made by regulations *(k)* of the Minister;
(h)   [*repealed*];
(j)   the provisions of Part X with respect to notices *(l)*, special regulations
        (m), general registers *(n)* (so far as applicable), preservation of registers
        and records *(o)*, but subject to such modifications as may be made by
        regulations *(p)* of the Minister;
(k)   [*repealed*];
(l)   Part XII *(q)*; and
(m)   Part XIV *(r)*.

(3) Subject to subsection (4) of this section,—

(a)   the provisions of this Act mentioned in paragraph (a) (subject to the
        modification mentioned in that paragraph) and in paragraphs (f), (j),
        (l) and (m) of subsection (2) of this section;
(b)   [*repealed*],

shall apply to the process of loading, unloading *(s)* or coaling of any ship *(t)* in
any dock, harbour *(u)* or canal, and to all machinery or plant used in those
processes, as if the processess were carried on in a factory *(e)* and the machinery
or plant were machinery or plant in a factory, and the person who carries on
those processes were the occupier *(f)* of a factory.

(4) Nothing in this section shall apply to any machinery or plant which is on
board a ship and is the property of the ship owner or charterer, or is rented,
leased or hired by him or his agent, or is being purchased by him or his agent
under a hire-purchase agreement or a conditional sale agreement (each within
the meaning of section 53 of the Health and Safety at Work etc. Act 1974).

(5) In subsections (3) and (4) of this section "plant" includes any gangway
or ladder used by any person employed to load or unload or coal a ship.

(6) The provisions of Part II of this Act with respect to prime movers *(v)*,
transmission machinery *(w)*, other machinery *(x)*, provisions as to unfenced
machinery *(y)*, construction and maintenance of fencing *(z)*, construction and
sale of new machinery *(aa)*, cleaning of machinery by women and young
persons *(bb)*, training and supervision of young persons working at dangerous
machines *(cc)*, hoists and lifts *(dd)*, chains, ropes and lifting tackle *(ee)*, cranes
and other lifting machines *(ff)*, construction and maintenance of floor, passages and stairs *(gg)*, shall apply to every warehouse mentioned in subsection (1)
of this section as if the warehouse were a factory *(e)* and the person having the
actual use or occupation thereof were the occupier *(f)* of a factory except that
this subsection shall not operate to apply the provisions to chains, ropes and
lifting tackle, cranes and other lifting machines, or to the construction and
maintenance of floors, passages and stairs, in warehouses which are dock
premises.

(7) The provisions of Part II of this Act, and any regulations made under that
Part, with respect to prime movers *(v)*, transmission machinery *(w)*, other
machinery *(x)*, provisions as to unfenced machinery *(y)*, construction and

maintenance of fencing, hoists and lifts *(dd)* shall apply to all dock premises *(hh)* as if the dock premises were a factory, and the person having the control of such matter were the occupier of the factory in respect of that matter.

(8) The provisions of section 173 of this Act (application to Crown) shall apply to all dock premises *(hh)* as if the dock premises were a factory, but only for the purpose of applying to the Crown such provisions of this Act as are applied to docks, wharfs, quays and dock premises by virtue of the foregoing provisions of this section.

(9) In subsections (6), (7) and (8) of this section "dock premises" means any dock, wharf, quay, jetty or other place at which ships load or unload goods or embark or disembark passengers, together with neighbouring land or water which is used or occupied, or intended to be used or occupied, for those or incidental activities, and any part of a ship when used for those or incidental activities.

General note. Subsection (2)(a) is repealed by S.I. 1989 No. 2169, as from 1 July 1994. By the Employment Medical Advisory Service Act 1972, s. 8(1), sub-ss (2) and (3)(a) of s. 125 have effect as if ss. 10A and 119A of the 1961 Act were included among the provisions of the 1961 Act mentioned therein, subject to the qualifications that neither s. 10A nor s. 119A, by virtue of their inclusion in sub-s. (3)(a), apply to a member of the crew of a ship; and, where s. 119A applies by virtue of its inclusion in sub-s. (3)(a), the notice under s. 119A must state as the address of the factory the place where the young person works. Section 8(1) of the 1972 Act, so far as relating to s. 119A of the 1961 Act, is repealed by the Employment Act 1989, s. 29(4), Sch. 7, Pt. III, as from a day to be appointed.

Office premises within the meaning of the Offices, Shops and Railway Premises Act 1963 which are comprised in premises to which this section applies are, notwithstanding that they are so comprised, deemed not to form part of the premises for the purposes of the Factories Act 1961; see the 1963 Act, s. 75(1). The reference to a warehouse in or for the purpose of which mechanical power is used, being a warehouse neither forming part of a factory nor belonging to the owners, trustees or conservators of a dock, wharf or quay, is to be construed as not including a building occupied by a wholesale dealer or merchant where goods are kept for sale wholesale or part of a building so occupied where goods are so kept; see s. 75(3) of the Offices, Shops and Railway Premises Act 1963. As to the meaning of "warehouse", see note *(c)*.

(a) **Dock.** In *Houlder Line Ltd v Griffin* [1905] AC 220, HL, it was held that the word "dock" in the 1901 Act meant the structure of the dock itself, so that a ship in the dock was not necessarily a part of a factory even when repairs were being carried out in the ship. Ships under repair in wet docks are now themselves deemed to be factories (see s. 126) but in *Gardiner v Admiralty Comrs* [1964] 2 All ER 93, [1964] 1 WLR 590, HL, it was held that a ship under repair in a dry dock was an article which was being worked on in the "factory" and that s. 26 imposed a duty to provide safe means of access to the place of work over such an article.

(b) **Wharf.** In *Haddock v Humphrey* [1900] 1 QB 609, the Court of Appeal held that a timber yard owned by a dock company and occupied by timber merchants, divided from the quay by a wall and a public road, was not a "wharf". The word "wharf" had to be construed in "its ordinary popular sense", and, so construed, "wharf" connoted a place contiguous to water over which goods pass in the process of loading and unloading. Accordingly, in *Ellis v Cory & Son Ltd* [1902] 1 KB 38, the Court of Appeal held that a structure moored in a river at some distance from, and not connected with, the shore, and used for the purpose of discharging coal from ships into barges, was a "wharf". Similarly, in *Kenny v Harrison* [1902] 2 KB 168, the Court of Appeal held that a piece of land within a system of docks, 40 yards from the actual waterside and separated from the

wharf by a dock railway, and used for stacking timber landed from the various docks and wharves of the system, was a "dock, wharf or quay", distinguishing *Haddock v Humphrey*, above.

(c) **Warehouse.** Where a warehouse does not form part of a factory, the combined effect of sub-s. (1) of the Factories Act 1961 and s. 75(3) of the Offices, Shops and Railway Premises Act 1963 is to bring within those provisions of the 1961 Act specified in *ibid.*, s. 125(2) only those warehouses:

   (i) which belong to the owners, trustees or conservators of a dock, wharf or quay; or
   (ii) in or for the purposes of which mechanical power is used and which are not occupied by a wholesale dealer or merchant for the storage of goods for sale wholesale.

A warehouse is a place used for the storage of goods, even temporarily as in a dock transit shed: *Fisher v Port of London Authority* [1962] 1 All ER 458, [1962] 1 WLR 234. It seems that a roof is a necessary element in a warehouse; *per* Collins LJ in *Haddock v Humphrey* [1900] 1 QB 609, CA. In *Green v Britten and Gilson* [1904] 1 KB 350, the Court of Appeal held that a storage place ancillary to a business wholly or substantially retail is not a warehouse, but in *Moreton v Reeve* [1907] 2 KB 401, CA it was said (*per* Gorell Barnes P, at 407) that there is no absolute rule of law that a storage place ancillary to a retail business cannot be a warehouse; the distinction between retail and wholesale is a useful, but not a conclusive, test.

A building, or part of a building, which is not a shop but which is solely or principally used for the carrying on there of retail trade or business constitutes "shop premises" within the meaning of the Offices, Shops and Railway Premises Act 1963, as does a building occupied by a wholesale dealer or merchant where goods are kept for sale wholesale and part of a building so occupied where goods are so kept (*ibid.*, s. 1(3)(a)).

(d) **Railway; tramway.** For definitions, see s. 176(1).

(e) **Factory.** For definition, see s. 175.

(f) **Occupier.** See note (j) to s. 33.

(g) **Steam boilers.** See ss. 32–34, 37, 38.

(h) **The Minister.** For definition, see s. 176(1). Sections 50 and 51 are repealed.

(i) **Part V.** See s. 84.

(j) **Separate factory.** See s. 122.

(k) **Regulations.** No regulations modifying the provisions of sub-s. (2)(g) have yet been made under this provision or the corresponding provision of the Factories Act 1937.

(l) **Notices.** See s. 138.

(m) **Special regulations.** By S.I. 1974 No. 1941, reg. 2(b), Sch. 2 the reference in this subsection to special regulations has effect as if it were a reference to regulations made before the coming into operation of S.I. 1974 No. 1941 (1 January 1975) in accordance with the provisions (now repealed) of Sch. 4 or in accordance with the provisions superseded by the provisions of that Schedule and any regulations made after that date under ss. 33, 50, 51, 117 or 123.

(n) **General registers.** See s. 140 and, for the form of register to be kept at docks etc., see note (c) there to.

(o) **Preservation of records.** See s. 141.

(p) **Regulations.** The Factories Act (Docks, Building and Engineering Construction, etc.) Modification Regulations 1938, set out below, were made under the corresponding provisions of the Factories Act 1937, and are continued in force by virtue of s. 183 and Sch. 6.

(q) **Part XII.** See ss. 155–171.

(r) Part XIV. See ss. 175–185.

(s) Loading; unloading. In *Stuart v Nixon and Bruce* [1901] AC 79, a ship in dock was being loaded by machinery. The actual loading was finished, and the men were putting in the hatchway beams. The House of Lords held that the ship was in process of loading, such process not being complete till the hatchway was secured. Similarly, the process of unloading is not complete until the hatch covers have been replaced: see *Manchester Ship Canal Co v DPP* [1930] 1 KB 547; *Hawkins v Thames Stevedore Co Ltd* [1936] 2 All ER 472.

(t) Ship. Section 176(1) defines "ship" as having the same meaning as in the Merchant Shipping Act 1894. The definition is as follows (*ibid.*, s. 742): " 'Ship' includes every description of vessel used in navigation not propelled by oars". The following cases illustrate the definition: A ship which has been dismantled and used as a coal hulk for four years is no longer a "ship" (*European and Australian Royal Mail Co Ltd v Peninsular and Oriental Steam Navigation Co* (1866) 14 LT 704, 14 WR 843). A half-decked herring coble of ten tons, 24 feet long, with two masts, but propelled by oars whenever occasion requires, is a "ship" (*Ex p Ferguson* (1871) LR 6 QB 280). A hopper barge used for dredging, and not provided with any means of propulsion, is a "ship" (*The Mac* (1882) 7 PD 126, CA, followed in *The Harlow* [1922] P 175). An electric launch used for carrying passengers round an artificial lake half a mile long, 180 yards wide and 3 feet deep is not a "ship" (*Southport Corpn v Morriss* [1893] 1 QB 359). A gas-float used as a floating beacon, shaped like a boat, 50 feet long, with no rudder or means of propulsion, but supporting a light and containing a large cylinder of gas is not a "ship" (*Wells v Gas Float Whitton (No 2)* [1897] AC 337). A spritsail barge navigating only upon the tidal waters and estuary of the Thames, but never going to sea, is a "ship" within the definition (*Corbett v Pearce* [1904] 2 KB 422).

(u) Harbour. Section 176(1) defines "harbour" as having the same meaning as in the Merchant Shipping Act 1894. The definition is as follows (*ibid.*, s. 742): " 'Harbour' includes harbours properly so called, whether natural or artificial, estuaries, navigable rivers, piers, jetties, and other works in or at which ships can obtain shelter, or ship and unship goods or passengers".

(v) Prime movers. See s. 12.

(w) Transmission machinery. See s. 13.

(x) Other machinery. See s. 14.

(y) Unfenced machinery. See s. 15.

(z) Maintenance of fencing. See s. 16.

(aa) Construction and sale of new machinery. See s. 17.

(bb) Cleaning of machinery by women and young persons. See s. 20.

(cc) Young persons working at dangerous machines. See s. 21.

(dd) Hoists and lifts. See ss. 22–25.

(ee) Chains, ropes and lifting tackle. See s. 26.

(ff) Cranes and other lifting machines. See s. 27.

(gg) Floors, passages and stairs. See s. 28.

(hh) Dock premises. For definition, see sub-s. (9).

THE FACTORIES ACT (DOCKS, BUILDING AND ENGINEERING
CONSTRUCTION, ETC.) MODIFICATION REGULATIONS 1938
(S.R. & O. 1938 No. 610, as amended by S.I. 1989 No. 2169)

In pursuance of sections 105(1)(g), 107(2) and 108(2) of the Factories Act 1937, I hereby make the following Regulations modifying and adapting certain provisions of the Act in their application to docks, wharves, quays, warehouses, building operations and works of engineering construction.

1. Subsection (1) of section 116 of the said Act [s. 140 of the 1961 Act] (which requires the occupier of every factory to keep a register, called the general register, for the factory and to enter in or attach to the register certain particulars and reports) shall, in its application to docks, wharves, quays and warehouses by virtue of section 105 of the Act, [s. 125 of the 1961 Act], or to building operations or works of engineering construction by virtue of section 107 or section 108 of the Act [s. 127 of the 1961 Act], be construed as requiring every person who by virtue of section 105, section 107 or section 108 [ss. 125, 127 of the 1961 Act] is deemed to be the occupier of a factory, to keep in relation to the persons employed by him and to those provisions of the Act for the observance of which he is responsible, a general register, in the prescribed form, in which shall be entered, or to which shall be attached, such of the particulars and reports referred to in the said subsection as may be applicable and as may be indicated in the directions given in the prescribed form.

2.   Section 29 (Steam Boilers) and 31 (Air Receivers) of the Act [ss. 33(5), 36(4) of the 1961 Act] shall, in their application to building operations or works of engineering construction by virtue of section 107 or section 108 of the Act [s. 127 of the 1961 Act], have effect subject to the following modifications, namely—

(a) subsection (9) of section 29 shall have effect as if for the words "taken into use in any factory for the first time in that factory until it has been examined" there were substituted the words, "used in any building operation or work of engineering construction to which this Act applies unless it has, within the preceding period of fourteen months, been examined";

(b) subsection (4) of section 31 shall have effect as if it required that no air receiver shall be used in any building operation or work of engineering construction unless it has been examined and reported on in accordance with the provisions of that subsection within the preceding period of twenty-six months, or such preceeding period not exceeding four years as may have been specified under proviso (a) to that subsection.

3.   These Regulations may be cited as the Factories Act (Docks, Building and Engineering Construction, etc.) Modification Regulations 1938, and shall come into force on the 1 July 1938.

General note. This regulation is revoked by S.I. 1989 No. 2169, as from 1 July 1994.

---

126.   Ships.—(1) Subject to subsection (3) of this section, the provisions of this Act specified in subsection (2) of this section shall apply to any work carried out in a harbour *(a)* or wet dock in constructing, reconstructing, repairing, refitting, painting, finishing or breaking up a ship *(b)* or in scaling, scurfing or cleaning boilers (including combustion chambers and smoke boxes) in a ship, or in cleaning oil-fuel tanks or bilges in a ship or any tank in a ship last used for oil of any description carried as cargo or any tank or hold last used for any substance so carried of a description specified in regulations *(c)* of the Minister *(d)* as being of a dangerous or injurious nature; and for the purposes of those provisions as so applying the ship shall be deemed to be a factory *(e)*, and any person undertaking the work shall be deemed to be the occupier *(f)* of a factory.

(2) The said provisions are—

(a)   the provisions of sections fifty and fifty-one so far as they enable the Minister *(d)* to make regulations;

(b)–(d) [*repealed*];
(e) Part V *(g)*;
(f)–(h) [*repealed*];
(j) the provisions of Part X with respect to general registers *(h)* (so far as applicable), preservation of registers and records *(i)*;
(k) [*repealed*];
(l) Part XII *(j)*;
(m) Part XIV *(k)*.

(3) Nothing in this Act shall apply to any such work as is mentioned in subsection (1) of this section which is done by the master or crew of a ship or done on board a ship *(b)* during a trial run.

General note. By the Employment Medical Advisory Service Act 1972, s. 8(1), sub-s. (2) of s. 126 has effect as if ss. 10A and 119A of the 1961 Act were included among the provisions of the 1961 Act mentioned therein, subject to the qualification that where s. 119A applies by virtue of its inclusion in sub-s. (2), the notice under s. 119A must state as the address of the factory the place where the young person works. Section 8(1) of the 1972 Act, so far as relating to s. 119A of the 1961 Act, is repealed by the Employment Act 1989, s. 29(4), Sch. 7, Pt. III, as from a day to be appointed. Sections 50 and 51, referred to in sub-s. (2)(a), are now repealed.

(a) Harbour. See note *(u)* to s. 125.

(b) Ship. For definition, see s. 176(1) and note *(t)* to s. 125.

(c) Regulations under s. 126(1). No regulations as to dangerous or injurious substances have been made under this subsection or the corresponding provisions of the Factories Act 1948.

(d) The Minister. For definition, see s. 176(1).

(e) Factory. For definition, see s. 175.

(f) Occupier. See note *(j)* to s. 33.

(g) Part V. See s. 84.

(h) General registers. See ss. 140, 141 and 166(3). No form has yet been prescribed for a general register under this section.

(i) Preservation of records. See s. 141.

(j) Part XII. See ss. 155–171.

(k) Part XIV. See ss. 175, 176.

Works of building and engineering construction

127. Building operations and works of engineering construction.—(1) Subject to the following provisions of this section, the provisions of this Act specified in subsection (2) of this section shall apply—

(a) to building operations *(a)*; and
(b) to works of engineering construction *(b)*,

undertaken by way of trade or business, or for the purpose of any industrial or commercial undertaking, and to any line or siding which is used in connection therewith and for the purposes thereof and is not part of a railway or tramway *(c)*.

(2) The said provisions are—

(a)   the provisions of Part I with respect to sanitary conveniences *(d)*;

(b)   the provisions of sections fifty and fifty-one so far as they enable the Minister *(e)* to make regulations;

(c)   the provisions of Part II with respect to steam boilers *(f)* and air receivers *(g)*;

(d)–(e)   [*repealed*];

(f)   Part V *(h)*;

(g)–(h)   [*repealed*];

(j)   the provisions of Part X with respect to notices *(i)*, special regulations *(j)*, general registers *(k)* (so far as applicable), preservation of registers and records *(l)*;

(k)   the provisions of Part XI with respect to duties of district councils *(m)*;

(l)   Part XII *(n)*;

(m)   Part XIII *(o)*;

(n)   Part XIV *(p)*.

(3) No special regulations *(q)* made under Part IV of this Act shall operate so as to interfere with the design of any works of engineering construction or with the adoption in the execution of those works of any method not inconsistent with the safety of the works or of the persons employed which is prescribed in the specification or in any signed plans issued, or written directions given, by the consulting engineer or the engineer in charge.

(4) The provisions of this Act in their application to building operations or to works of engineering construction shall have effect as if any place where such operations or works are carried on were a factory *(r)* and any person undertaking any such operations or works to which this Act applies were the occupier *(s)* of a factory, and with such other adaptations and modifications as may be made by regulations *(t)* made by the Minister *(e)*.

(5) The provisions of this Act requiring general registers *(k)* to be kept and copies of special regulations *(j)* or the prescribed abstract *(u)* of such regulations to be kept posted up on the premises shall be deemed to be complied with as respects building operations or works of engineering construction if the register is kept at an office of the person undertaking the operation or works and copies of the regulations or abstract thereof are kept posted up at each office, yard or shop of the person undertaking the operations or works at which persons employed by him on the operations or works attend, and in a position where they can easily be read by those persons.

(6) Subject to subsection (7) of this section, any person undertaking any building operations or works of engineering construction to which this Act applies shall, not later than seven days after the beginning thereof, serve on the inspector *(v)* for the district a written notice stating the name and postal address of that person, the place and nature of the operations or works, whether any mechanical power is used and, if so, its nature, the name of the district council within whose district the operations or works are situated and such other particulars as may be prescribed *(w)*.

(7) Subsection (6) of this section shall not apply to any operations or works which the person undertaking them has reasonable grounds for believing will

be completed in a period of less than six weeks, except in such cases as the chief inspector *(v)* may direct; and where a person undertakes any building operations *(a)* or works of engineering construction *(b)* in a place where such operations or, as the case may be, works are in progress, he shall not be required to give a notice under that subsection if such a notice was given in respect of the operations or works in progress.

(8) The application of this Act to any building operations *(a)* or works of engineering construction *(b)* by virtue of the foregoing provisions of this section shall not be excluded by reason of the fact that they are undertaken on premises to which this Act applies apart from those provisions; and nothing in this section shall be taken as prejudicing the application of this Act to those premises apart from this section.

General note. Subsection (2)(c) is repealed by S.I. 1989 No. 2169, as from 1 July 1994. By the Employment Medical Advisory Service Act 1972, s. 8(1), s. 127(2) has effect as if ss. 10A and 119A of the 1961 Act were included among the provisions of the 1961 Act mentioned therein, subject to the qualification that, where s. 119A applies by virtue of its inclusion in sub-s. (2), the notice under s. 119A must state as the address of the factory the place where the young person works. Section 8(1) of the 1972 Act, so far as relating to s. 119A of the 1961 Act, is repealed by the Employment Act 1989, s. 29(4), Sch. 7, Pt. III, as from a day to be appointed.

Provisions relating to building operations which affect public safety are contained in the Highways Act 1980, s. 168.

Prior to the coming into force of the 1948 Act different views had been entertained as to the obligations under the Act which were applicable when a building operation was being conducted in premises which were, independently of s. 107 of the 1937 Act (see now s. 127 of the 1961 Act), a factory: see the discussion in *Whitby v Burt, Boulton and Hayward Ltd* [1947] KB 918, [1947] 2 All ER 324, and in *Lavender v Diamints Ltd* [1949] 1 KB 585, [1949] 1 All ER 532.

In *Whincup v Joseph Woodhead & Sons (Engineeers) Ltd* [1951] 1 All ER 387, McNair J followed the decision of Denning J in *Whitby's* case that the factory did not cease to be a factory nor was its occupier relieved of his general duties under the Act merely because building operations were being conducted on the premises which attracted to themselves the obligations imposed by s. 107 of the 1937 Act upon the person conducting such operations. McNair J further held that the 1948 Act had made it clear that Parliament intended that the occupier of the ordinary factory should continue to be bound by his general duty under the Act and that s. 14(4) of the 1948 Act (now s. 127(8) of the 1961 Act) was declaratory of the law as laid down by Denning J in *Whitby's* case, above.

For building operations being undertaken at a mine or quarry, see the Mines and Quarries Act 1954, s. 184(5)(a) as amended by s. 174(1) of the Factories Act 1961.

See s. 175(2)(m) for the application of the Act to premises in which articles are made or prepared incidentally to the carrying on of building operations or works of engineering construction, not being premises in which such operations or works are being carried on.

The employment of children on building operations and works of engineering construction is prohibited by virtue of s. 1(1) of the Employment of Women, Young Persons and Children Act 1920.

See also the Construction (Working Places) Regulations 1966, the Construction (Health and Welfare) Regulations 1966, the Construction (General Provisions) Regulations 1961 and the Construction (Lifting Operations) Regulations 1961.

(a) **Building operations.** For definition, see s. 176(1).

(b) **Works of engineering construction.** For definition, see s. 176(1).

(c) **Railway; tramway.** For definition, see s. 176(1).

(d) Sanitary conveniences. See s. 7.

(e) The Minister. For definition, see s. 176(1). Sections 50 to 51 are now repealed.

(f) Steam boilers. See ss. 32–34, 37, 38; see also the Regulations referred to in note *(p)* to s. 125.

(g) Air receivers. See s. 36; see also the Regulations referred to in note *(f)*, above.

(h) Part V. See s. 84.

(i) Notices. See s. 138.

(j) Special regulations. By S.I. 1974 No. 1941, reg. 2(b), Sch. 2, in s. 127(2)(j), (3) and (5), the references to special regulations have effect as if they were references to regulations made before the coming into operation of S.I. 1974 No. 1941, (1 January 1975) in accordance with the provisions (now repealed) of Sch. 4 or in accordance with provisions superseded by the provision of that Schedule and (except in sub-s. (3)) any regulations made after that date under ss. 33, 50, 51, 117 or 123.

(k) General register. See s. 140, and for the form of register applicable to building operations and works of engineering construction, see note *(c)* thereto.

(l) Preservation of registers and records. See s. 141.

(m) District councils. See s. 153.

(n) Part XII. See ss. 155–171.

(o) Part XIII. See ss. 172–174.

(p) Part XIV. See ss. 175, 176.

(q) Regulations . . . under Part IV. See the Regulations referred to in the general note.

(r) Factory. For definition, see s. 175.

(s) Occupier. See note *(j)* to s. 33. As to the charging of an offence by a notional occupier within sub-s. (4), see *Davies v Camerons Industrial Services Ltd* [1980] 2 All ER 680, and s. 155 and the notes thereto.

(t) Adaptations and modifications. See the Factories Act (Docks, Building and Engineering Construction, etc.) Modification Regulations 1938 (set out following the notes to s. 125).

(u) Abstract of regulations. No abstract of the Regulations under this section has yet been prescribed.

(v) Inspector. For definition, see s. 176(1).

(w) Prescribed. Prescribed means prescribed by the Minister (s. 176(1)). The form is Form 10.

Lead processes carried on in places other than factories

128. Employment of women and young persons in places other than factories in processes connected with lead manufacture or involving the use of lead compounds.—The following provisions of this Act, that is to say—

   (a) the provisions relating to the employment of women and young persons *(a)* in certain processes connected with lead manufacture *(b)*;

   (b) the provisions requiring notification *(c)* to be sent to the chief inspector *(d)*, or to the inspector for the district, of lead poisoning contracted or occurring in factories *(e)*; and

(c)   any provision relating to offences, penalties and legal proceedings (*f*),

shall apply to employment in any such processes as aforesaid in any place other than a factory as if the place were a factory (*e*) and the employers were the occupier (*g*) of the factory, and as if the references to young persons included references to all persons who had not attained the age of eighteen.

General note. For general provisions concerning the use of lead at work see the Control of Lead at Work Regulations 1980.

(*a*) *Women and young persons.* For definition, see s. 176(1).

(*b*) *Lead manufacture.* See s. 74.

(*c*) *Notification of lead poisoning.* Such provisions were formerly contained in s. 82, now repealed.

(*d*) *Inspector.* For definition, see s. 176(1).

(*e*) *Factory.* For definition, see s. 175.

(*f*) *Offences, penalties and legal proceedings.* See ss. 155–171.

(*g*) *Occupier.* See note (*j*) to s. 33.

———————

129.–130. [*repealed*].

———————

131.   Prohibition of employment of women and young persons in painting buildings with lead paint.—(1) Subject to subsection (2) of this section a woman or young person (*a*) shall not be employed in painting any part of a building (*b*) with lead paint (*c*).

(2)   This section shall not apply to the employment of—

(a)   persons employed as apprentices in the painting trade under arrange-ments approved by an order (*d*) of the Minister (*e*) made after consul-tation with the organisations, if any, representative of the employers and workers in the trade; or

(b)   women or young persons (*a*) in such special decorative or other work (other than work of an industrial character) as may be excluded from the provisions of this section by an order of the Minister.

(*a*) *Woman or young person.* For definition, see s. 176(1).

(*b*) *Building.* In this section "building" includes fixtures (s. 132).

(*c*) *Lead paint.* For definition, see s. 132.

(*d*) *Order.* By S.I. 1974 No. 1941, reg. 2(b), Sch. 2, in so far as sub-s. (2) enables orders to be made otherwise than by statutory instrument it has effect as if the reference to the Secretary of State ("the Minister") was a reference to the Health and Safety Executive.

(*e*) *The Minister.* For definition, see s. 176(1); see also note (*b*).

———————

132. Provisions supplementary to ss. 129–131.—In sections one hundred and twenty-nine to one hundred and thirty-one of this Act "lead paint" means any paint, paste, spray, stopping, filling, or other material used in painting which, when treated in a manner prescribed by rules *(a)* made by the Minister *(b)*, yields to an aqueous solution of hydrochloric acid a quantity of soluble lead compound exceeding, when calculated as lead monoxide, five per cent. of the dry weight of the portion taken for analysis; and "building" includes fixtures.

(a) **Rules.** The Order dated 24 December 1926 (S.R. & O. 1926 No. 1621), made under s. 7 of the Lead Paint (Protection against Poisoning) Act 1926 and continued in force as if made under the Factories Act 1961 by virtue of s. 183 and Sch. 6 was revoked by the Control of Lead at Work Regulations 1980, S.I. 1980 No. 1248, reg. 22, Sch. 2.

(b) **The Minister.** For definition, see s. 176(1).

PART VIII
HOME WORK

133. Lists of outworkers to be kept in certain trades.—(1) In the case of persons employed in such classes of work as may from time to time be specified by regulations *(a)* of the Minister *(b)*, the occupier *(c)* of every factory *(d)* and every contractor employed by any such occupier in the business of the factory shall—

(a) keep in the prescribed form *(e)* and manner, and with the prescribed particulars, lists showing the names and addresses of all persons (in this section referred to as outworkers) directly employed by him, either as workmen or as contractors, in the business of the factory, outside the factory, and of the places where they are employed; and

(b) send to an inspector *(f)* such copies of or extracts from those lists as the inspector may from time to time require; and

(c) send to the district council *(g)* during the month of February and the month of August in each year copies of those lists, showing all outworkers employed by him during the preceding six months.

(2) Every district council *(g)* shall cause the lists received by the council in pursuance of this section to be examined, and shall furnish the name and place of employment of every outworker included in any such lists whose place of employment is outside the district of the council to the council in whose district his place of employment is.

(3) The lists kept by the occupier *(c)* or contractor shall be open to inspection by an inspector, and by any officer duly authorised by the district council, and the copies sent to the council and the particulars furnished by one council to another shall be open to inspection by any inspector or officer of any Government department.

(4) This section shall apply to any place from which any work is given out in connection with the business of a factory *(d)* (whether the materials for the work are supplied by the occupier *(c)* or not), and to the occupier of that place, and to every contractor employed by the occupier in connection with the said work, as if that place were a factory.

(5) In the event of a contravention of this section by the occupier *(c)* of a factory *(d)* or place, or by a contractor, the occupier or contractor shall be guilty of an offence and liable on summary conviction to a fine not exceeding level 1 on the standard scale.

General note. In s. 133 the amendment from "twenty pounds" to "level 1 on the standard scale" is by virtue of the Criminal Justice Act 1982, ss. 38, 46.

(a) **Regulations.** As to the making of regulations, see s. 180. No regulations specifying classes of work have been made under this section or under the corresponding provisions of the Factories Act 1937, but orders (known originally as "special orders") made under ss. 107 and 108 of the Factory and Workshop Act 1901 are continued in force by virtue of s. 159 of the 1937 Act and the 1961 Act, s. 183 and Sch. 6. The principal Order, set out below, specifies the classes of work to which the provisions of what are now ss. 133 and 134 of the Factories Act 1961 are to apply. The Order is printed as amended by the Home Work Orders Variation Order 1938 and as extended by S.R. & O's. 1912 No. 158, 1913 No. 91 and 1929 No. 1118.

(b) **The Minister.** For definition, see s. 176(1).

(c) **Occupier.** See note *(j)* to s. 33.

(d) **Factory.** For definition, see s. 175.

(e) **Prescribed.** Prescribed means prescribed by the Minister (s. 176(1)).

(f) **Inspector.** For definition, see s. 176(1).

(g) **District council.** See s. 153. The powers of the district council do not extend to premises belonging to or in the occupation of the Crown; see s. 173.

HOMEWORK ORDER OF THE 10 APRIL 1911
(S.R. & O. 1911 No. 394 as amended)

1. Section 107 [s. 133 of the 1961 Act] (relating to lists of outworkers) and section 108 [s. 134 of the 1961 Act *(repealed)*] (relating to employment in unwholesome premises) shall apply to the following classes of work:—
The making, cleaning, washing, altering, ornamenting, finishing and repairing of wearing apparel;
The making up, ornamenting, finishing and repairing of table linen, bed linen or other household linen (including in the term linen, articles of cotton or cotton and linen mixtures) and any processes incidental thereto;
The making, ornamenting, mending, and finishing of lace and of lace curtains and nets;
The making of curtains and furniture hangings and any processes incidental thereto;
Cabinet and furniture making and upholstery work;
The making of electro-plate;
The making of files;
The manufacture of brass and of any articles or parts of articles of brass (including in the term brass any alloy or compound of copper with zinc or tin);
Fur-pulling;
The making of iron and steel cables and chains;
The making of iron and steel anchors and grapnels;
The making of cart gear, including swivels, rings, loops, gear buckles, mullin bits, hooks, and attachments of all kinds;
The making of locks, latches, and keys;
The making or repairing of umbrellas, sunshades, parasols, or parts thereof;
The making of artificial flowers;
The making of nets other than wire nets;

The making of tents;

The making or repairing of sacks;

The covering of racquet or tennis balls;

The making of paper bags;

The making of boxes or other receptacles or parts thereof made wholly or partially of paper, cardboard, chip, or similar material;

The making of brushes;

Pea picking;

Feather sorting;

The carding, boxing, or packeting of buttons, hooks and eyes, pins, and hair pins;

The making of stuffed toys;

The making of baskets;

The manufacture of chocolates or sweetmeats, and any work incidental thereto;

The making or filling of cosaques, Christmas crackers, Christmas stockings or similar articles or parts thereof, and any work incidental thereto;

The weaving of any textile fabric, and any process incidental thereto;

And any processes incidental to the above;

The manufacture of lampshades other than lampshades made wholly of metal or glass or stone.

2. Section 110 (relating to the prohibition of homework in places where there is infectious disease) shall apply to the following classes of work:—

The making, cleaning, washing, altering, ornamenting, finishing, and repairing of wearing apparel and any work incidental thereto (as in the said section specified);

The making up, ornamenting, finishing and repairing of table linen, bed linen or other household linen (including in the term linen articles of cotton or cotton and linen mixtures) and any processes incidental thereto;

The making, ornamenting, mending, and finishing of lace and of lace curtains and nets;

The making of curtains and furniture hangings and any processes incidental thereto;

Upholstery work;

Fur-pulling;

The making or repairing of umbrellas, sunshades, parasols, or parts thereof;

The making of artificial flowers;

The making of nets other than wire nets;

The making of tents;

The making or repairing of sacks;

The covering of racquet or tennis balls;

The making of paper bags;

The making of boxes or other receptacles or parts thereof made wholly or partially of paper, cardboard, chip, or similar material;

The making of brushes;

Pea picking;

Feather sorting;

The carding, boxing, or packeting of buttons, hooks and eyes, pins, and hair pins;

The making of stuffed toys;

The making of baskets;

The manufacture of chocolates or sweetmeats;

The making or filling of cosaques, Christmas crackers, Christmas stockings or similar articles or parts thereof;

The weaving of any textile fabric;

And any processes incidental to the above.

3. The lists of out-workers required to be kept by s. 107 [s. 133 of the 1961 Act] and the copies thereof shall be kept and made in the form and manner and with the particulars shown in the Schedule hereto.

4. This Order may be referred to as the Home Work Order of the 10 April 1911.

5. The Home Work Order of the 23 May 1907 is hereby repealed.

SCHEDULE
LIST OF OUTWORKERS

A correct list of outworkers employed in the following classes of work—

(1) the making, cleaning, washing, altering, ornamenting, finishing, and repairing of wearing apparel;

(2) the making-up, ornamenting, finishing and repairing of table linen, bed linen, or other household linen (including in the term linen, articles of cotton or cotton and linen mixtures) and any processes incidental thereto;

(3) the making, ornamenting, mending, and finishing of lace and of lace curtains and nets;

(4) the making of curtains and furniture hangings and any processes incidental thereto;

(5) cabinet and furniture making and upholstery work;

(6) the making of electro-plate;

(7) the making of files;

(8) the manufacture of brass and of any article or parts of articles of brass (including in the term brass any alloy or compound of copper with zinc or tin);

(9) fur-pulling;

(10) the making of iron and steel cables and chains;

(11) the making of iron and steel anchors and grapnels;

(12) the making of cart gear, including swivels, rings, loops, gear buckles, mullin bits, hooks, and attachments of all kinds;

(13) the making of locks, latches, and keys;

(14) the making or repairing of umbrellas, sunshades, parasols or parts thereof;

(15) the making of artificial flowers;

(16) the making of nets other than wire nets;

(17) the making of tents;

(18) the making or repairing of sacks;

(19) the covering of racquet or tennis balls;

(20) the making of paper bags;

(21) the making of boxes or other receptacles or parts thereof made wholly or partially of paper, cardboard, chip, or similar material;

(22) the making of brushes;

(23) pea picking;

(24) feather sorting;

(25) the carding, boxing, or packeting of buttons, hooks and eyes, pins, and hair pins;

(26) the making of stuffed toys;

(27) the making of baskets;

(28) the manufacture of chocolates or sweetmeats;

(29) the making or filling of cosaques, Christmas crackers, Christmas stockings, or similar articles or parts thereof;

(30) the weaving of any textile fabric;

(31) the making of lampshades other than lampshades made wholly of metal or glass or stone;

And any processes incidental to the above,
must be kept in the form and with the particulars specified below in the factory or workshop or place from which the work is given out, and must be open to inspection by H.M. Inspectors and the officers of the local authority.

In order that the list may be correct, the name of any person newly taken into employment should be immediately entered, and the name of any person ceasing to be employed should be immediately struck out but this shall be without prejudice to the obligation of an occupier or contractor under section 110(1)(c) of the Act [s. 133(1)(c) of the 1961 Act] to send to the district council during the month of February and the month of August in each year a list showing all the outworkers employed by him during the preceding six months.

Factory, Workshop, or ⎤ Full Postal Address
Place from which the ⎬ Business
work is given out. ⎦ Name of Occupier

LIST OF PERSONS directly employed by [1]   [2]   in the business of, but outside the above Factory, Workshop, or Place, in the classes of work specified above.

Name in full (1)	Whether employed as Workman (W) or Contractor (C) (2)	Class of Work (Specify by means of index numbers as above) (3)	Place of Employment, *i.e.* place where the work is actually done (4)	Address [*No entry need be made in this column if the entry in column (4) is a sufficient address*] (5)

[1] Give name of employer.
[2] Say whether the occupier or a contractor employed by the occupier.

---

134.   [*repealed*].

PART IX
WAGES

135.–136.   [*repealed*].

PART X
NOTICES, RETURNS, RECORDS, DUTIES OF PERSONS EMPLOYED, AND APPLICATION OF WEIGHTS AND MEASURES ACTS

137. Notice of occupation of factory, and use of mechanical power.— (1) Subject to subsection (3) of this section, every person who begins to occupy or to use any premises as a factory *(a)* shall, not less than one month before he does so, serve on the inspector *(b)* for the district a written notice stating the name of the occupier *(c)* or the title of the firm, the postal address of the factory, the nature of the work, whether mechanical power *(d)* is to be used and, if so, its nature, the name of the district council within whose district the factory is situated and such other particulars as may be prescribed *(e)*.

(2) Subject to subsection (3) of this section, not less than one month before the date on which mechanical power is first used in a factory *(a)* the occupier *(c)*

shall serve on the inspector *(b)* for the district a written notice stating the nature of the mechanical power.

(3) A person may begin to occupy, or to use any premises as, a factory *(a)*, and mechanical power *(d)* may be first used in a factory, less than one month after the notice required by the foregoing provisions of this section has been served, if the inspector *(b)* of the district gives written permission; and a person may also begin to occupy a factory less than one month after the notice has been served or before serving the notice, if he takes over from another person without changing the nature of the work and the notice is served as soon as practicable and in any case within one month of his taking over.

(4) If a person begins to occupy, or to use any premises as, a factory *(a)* before he is entitled to do so under the foregoing provisions of this section, or if a person entitled thereunder to occupy a factory before giving notice fails to give the required notice within the time allowed, he shall be guilty of an offence.

(5) [*repealed*].

General note. The provisions of this section are not applicable to unmanned electrical stations (s. 123), docks, wharves and warehouses (s. 125), and certain work on ships in harbour or wet dock (s. 126); but see similar requirements for notification on building sites and at works of engineering construction (s. 127(6)).

(*a*) **Factory.** For definition, see s. 175.

(*b*) **Inspector.** For definition, see s. 176(1).

(*c*) **Occupier.** See note *(j)* to s. 33.

(*d*) **Mechanical power.** There is no definition in the Act, but see s. 176(3) and note *(b)* to s. 163.

(*e*) **Prescribed.** Prescribed means prescribed by the Minister (s. 176(1)). The form is Form 9. No other particulars have been prescribed under this section or under the corresponding provisions of superseded enactments.

---

138. Posting of abstract of Act and notices.—(1) Subject to subsection (2) of this section, there shall be kept posted at the principal entrances of a factory *(a)* at which employed persons enter—

(a)–(d) [*repealed*];
(e) every notice and document required by this Act to be posted in the factory.

(2) An inspector *(b)* may direct that all or any of the documents mentioned in subsection (1) of this section shall be posted in such parts of the factory, either in addition to or in substitution for the principal entrances, as he may direct.

(3) All such documents shall be posted in such characters and in such positions as to be conveniently read by the persons employed in the factory and, if a form has been prescribed *(c)* for any document, it shall be posted in that form.

(4) If any person pulls down any abstract, notice, regulations or other document posted in pursuance of this Act, he shall be guilty of an offence *(d)* and liable on summary conviction to a fine not exceeding level 1 on the standard scale.

General note. Provision is made on the abstract for the entries required by s. 138(1) (b), (c) and (d). Secondary evidence of the contents of the abstract and notices may be given without giving notice to produce, since (i) the production of the originals would be highly inconvenient, and (ii) such production would involve an offence under s. 138(4): see *Owner v Bee Hive Spinning Co Ltd* [1914] 1 KB 105 (decided upon s. 32 of the Factory and Workshop Act 1901).

In s. 138(4) reference to level 1 on the standard scale is substituted for the reference to ten pounds by virtue of the Criminal Justice Act 1982, ss. 38, 46.

(a) Factory. For definition, see s. 175.

(b) Inspector. For definition, see s. 176(1).

(c) Prescribed. Prescribed means prescribed by the Minister (s. 176(1)).

(d) Offence. See s. 155. See also the Criminal Damage Act 1971.

---

139. Provisions as to special regulations.—(1) Printed copies of all special regulations *(a)* for the time being in force in any factory *(b)* or the prescribed abstract *(c)* of such regulations shall be kept posted in the factory in such characters and in such positions as to be conveniently read by the persons employed in the factory.

(2) A printed copy of all such regulations shall be given by the occupier *(d)* to any person affected thereby on his application.

(a) Special regulations. By S.I. 1974 No. 1941, reg. 2(b), Sch. 2, in this section the references to special regulations have effect as if they were references to regulations made before the coming into operation of S.I. 1974 No. 1941 (1 January 1975) in accordance with the provisions (now repealed) of Sch. 4 to the 1961 Act or in accordance with provisions superseded by the provisions of that Schedule and any regulations made after that date under ss. 33, 50, 51, 117 or 123. Copies of regulations or a prescribed abstract thereof are printed in placard form for posting in the factory. Each placard bears a form number.

No regulations other than those referred to in this section are required to be posted in the factory.

(b) Factory. For definition, see s. 175.

(c) Prescribed abstract. Prescribed means prescribed by the Minister (s. 176(1)). See also note *(a)*.

(d) Occupier. See note *(j)* to s. 33.

---

140. General registers.—(1) There shall be kept in every factory *(a)* or in such place outside the factory as may be approved by the inspector for the district *(b)*, a register in the prescribed form, called the general register *(c)*, and there shall be entered in or attached to that register:

(a) the prescribed particulars as to the young persons *(d)* employed in the factory; and

(b) the prescribed particulars *(e)* as to the washing, whitewashing or colour washing, painting or varnishing, of the factory; and

(c), (d) [*repealed*]; and

(e) all reports and particulars *(g)* required by any other provisions of this Act to be entered in or attached to the general register; and

(f) such other matters as may be prescribed *(h)*.

(2) [*repealed*].

(3) The occupier *(f)* of a factory *(a)* shall send to an inspector *(b)* such extracts from the general register as the inspector may from time to time require for the purpose of the execution of his duties under this Act.

(a) Factory. For definition, see s. 175.

(b) Inspector for the district. For definition, see s. 176(1).

(c) Register. The prescribed form is No. 31. The general register to be kept at docks, wharves, quays and warehouses is Form 35 and in connection with building operations and works of engineering construction is Form 36 (the forms are prescribed by the Factories Act General Register Order 1973, S.I. 1973 No. 8 as amended by S.I. 1980 No. 804, S.I. 1981 No. 917, S.I. 1985 No. 2023 and S.I. 1989 No. 2311).

(d) Prescribed particulars as to young persons. The particulars are prescribed in Part 2 of the general register.

(e) Prescribed particulars as to washing, whitewashing, etc. The particulars are prescribed in Part 5 of the general register.

(f) Occupier. See note *(j)* to s. 33.

(g) Other reports and particulars. See ss. 22–25 (hoists and lifts); ss. 32–34, 37, 38 (steam boilers); s. 35 (steam receivers); s. 36 (air receivers); s. 39 (gasholders).

(h) Such other matters. See, for example, the following matters:—(i) certificate for machinery attendants under the Operations at Unfenced Machinery Regulations 1938 and 1946 (ii) certificate of examination of hygrometer thermometers by the National Physical Laboratory (Jute (Safety, Health and Welfare) Regulations 1948, set out in Part 4 of this book).

---

141. Preservation of registers and records.—The general register *(a)* and every other register *(b)* or record *(c)* kept in pursuance of this Act shall be preserved and shall be kept available for inspection by an inspector *(d)* or by an employment medical adviser *(e)* for at least two years, or such other period as may be prescribed *(f)* for any class or description of register or record, after the date of the last entry in the register or record.

(a) General register. See s. 140.

(b) Other registers. See s. 26, chains, ropes and slings; s. 27, cranes and other lifting machines.

(c) Records. See s. 39, gasholders; s. 68, humid factories.

(d) Inspector. For definition, see s. 176(1).

(e) **Employment medical adviser.** See s. 56 of the Health and Safety at Work etc. Act 1974.

(f) **Prescribed.** Prescribed means prescribed by the Minister (s. 176(1)). No period other than two years has been prescribed.

142.–144. [*repealed*].

PART XI

ADMINISTRATION

145.–152. [*repealed*].

---

153. Provisions as to county and district councils.—(1) The medical officer of health *(a)* of every district council *(b)* shall—

(a) in his annual report to the council report specifically on the administration of, and furnish the prescribed particulars with respect to, the matters under Part VIII *(c)* of this Act which are administered by the district council, and shall send a copy of his annual report or so much of it as deals with those matters to the Minister *(d)*; and

(b) [*repealed*].

(2)–(3) [*repealed*].

General note. See s. 154 as to the prohibition of disclosure of information.

The powers of a district council or a local authority do not extend to premises belonging to or in the occupation of the Crown; see s. 173(2) and the Visiting Forces Act 1952.

(a) **Medical officer of health.** The reference to the medical officer of health in s. 153(1) is to be construed in England and Wales as a reference to the "proper officer" appointed for the purpose by virtue of the Local Government Act 1972, s. 270(3), (4), Sch. 29, para. 4, and in Scotland as a reference to the "sanitary inspector" by virtue of the National Health Service (Scotland) Act 1972, Sch. 6, para. 121(a).

(b) **District council.** For definition, see s. 176(1), (8).

(c) **Part VIII.** See ss. 133, 134.

(d) **The Minister.** For definition, see s. 176(1).

---

154. Prohibition of disclosure of information.—If any person who, in pursuance of powers conferred by section one hundred and forty-eight or section one hundred and fifty-three of this Act, is admitted into any factory *(a)* or place discloses to any person any information obtained by him in the factory or place with regard to any manufacturing process or trade secret, he shall, unless the disclosure was made in the performance of his duty, be guilty of an offence.

    (a) **Factory.** For definition, see s. 175.

PART XII
OFFENCES, PENALTIES AND LEGAL PROCEEDINGS

155. Offences.—(1) In the event of any contravention *(a)* in or in connection with or in relation to a factory *(b)* of the provisions of this Act, or of any regulation or order made thereunder, the occupier *(c)* or (if the contravention is one in respect of which the owner *(d)* is by or under this Act made responsible) the owner, of the factory shall, subject to the following provisions of this Part of this Act, be guilty of an offence *(e)*.

    (2) In the event of a contravention *(a)* by any person of any regulation or order made under this Act which expressly imposes any duty upon him, that person shall be guilty of an offence *(e)* and the occupier *(c)* or owner *(d)*, as the case may be, shall not be guilty *(f)* of an offence, by reason only of the contravention of the provision imposing the said duty, as the case may be, unless it is provided that he failed to take all reasonable steps to prevent the contravention; but this subsection shall not be taken as affecting any liability of the occupier or owner in respect of the same matters by virtue of some provision other than the provisions or provision aforesaid.

    (3) If the occupier *(c)* of a factory *(b)* avails himself of any exception allowed by or under this Act and fails to comply with any of the conditions attached to the exception *(g)*, he shall be deemed to have contravened *(a)* the provisions of this Act.

    (4) If any persons are employed *(h)* in a factory *(b)* otherwise than in accordance with the provisions of this Act or of any regulation or order made thereunder, there shall be deemed to be a separate contravention *(a)* in respect of each person so employed.

    (5) [*spent*].

General note. The provisions of sub-s. (2) apply only to criminal liability, and do not affect any right of action for breach of statutory duty (*Potts (or Riddell) v Reid* [1943] AC 1, [1942] 2 All ER 161, HL). As to civil liability in like cases, see *Ginty v Belmont Building Supplies Ltd* [1959] 1 All ER 414, and the GENERAL INTRODUCTION.
    Where there is a clear and absolute liability cast on an employer in his capacity as employer of workmen (e.g. under reg. 3(1) of the Construction (Working Places) Regulations 1966), as well as a liability which may rest on him as a notional occupier (e.g. under s. 127(4)) an information should be laid under s. 155(2) and not under s. 155(1) (*Davies v Camerons Industrial Services Ltd* [1980] 2 All ER 680).
    For offences under the Health and Safety at Work etc. Act 1974, and health and safety regulations made thereunder, see s. 33 thereof.
    (a) **Contravention.** For definition, see s. 176(1). An employer is not made liable by subsection (1), as occupier of a factory, in respect of a contravention of provisions of the

Act (such as s. 143(1)) for the performance of which the sole obligation is imposed on his employee (*Wright v Ford Motor Co Ltd* [1967] 1 QB 230, [1966] 2 All ER 518).

(b) Factory. For definition, see s. 175(1).

(c) Occupier. See note *(j)* to s. 33.

(d) Owner. For definition, see s. 176(1).

(e) Offence. The Act contains third party and short-circuit procedures in relation to certain offences; see s. 161. Certain offences under the Act are triable summarily (s. 164(1)).

(f) The occupier . . . shall not be guilty. This subsection applies whether or not the occupier or owner has brought the actual offender before the court pursuant to s. 161, and the onus is on the prosecution to prove that the occupier or owner failed to take all reasonable steps to prevent the contravention (*Carr v Decca Gramophone Co Ltd* [1947] KB 728, [1947] 2 All ER 20. An owner or occupier has no defence under this subsection where the offence charged is one which he commits in another capacity, e.g. as the operator of locomotives and wagons under the Locomotives and Wagons (Used on Lines and Sidings) Regulations 1906 (*Wagon Repairs v Vosper* (1967) 3 KIR 605). Thus, when defendants were charged as employers in respect of a contravention of reg. 3(1) of the Construction (Working Places) Regulations 1966 they were liable "by virtue of some [other] provision" and could not, therefore, rely upon the defence afforded, by s. 155(2), to an occupier or owner (*Davies v Camerons Industrial Services Ltd*, above).

(g) Fails to comply with . . . conditions. For an example, see *Nash v High Duty Alloys* [1947] KB 377, [1947] 1 All ER 363, CA, *per* Cohen LJ.

(h) Persons employed. This term is not defined in the Act.

(i) Connivance. See INTRODUCTORY NOTE 6.

156.–157. [*spent*].

---

158. Fine for offence by parent. If a young person is employed in any factory in contravention of the provisions of this Act, the parent of the young person shall be guilty of an offence and liable on summary conviction to a fine not exceeding level 1 on the standard scale, unless it appears to the court that the contravention occurred without the consent, or wilful default of the parent.

---

159. [*repealed*].

---

160. [*spent*].

---

161. [*spent*].

---

162. Proceedings against persons not primarily liable. Where, under this Act, any person is substituted for another with respect to any provisions of this Act, any order, summons, notice or proceeding which for the purpose of any of those provisions is by or under this Act required or authorised to be served on or taken in relation to that other person, is hereby required or authorised (as the case may be) to be served on or taken in relation to the first-mentioned person.

---

163. Owner of machine liable in certain cases instead of occupier. Where in a factory *(a)* the owner or hirer of a machine or implement moved by mechanical power *(b)* is some person other than the occupier *(c)* of the factory the owner or hirer shall, so far as respects any offence under this Act committed in relation to a person who is employed in or about or in connection with that machine or implement, and is in the employment or pay of the owner or hirer, be deemed to be the occupier of the factory.

    General note. For the general duties of those who supply articles for use at work, see the Health and Safety at Work etc. Act 1974, s. 6.

    The effect of this section is to make the owner or hirer of a machine or implement taken into a factory for any purpose (such as repair of the premises or plant) responsible, *quoad* his own employees working with such machine or implement, for compliance with the Act: see *Whalley v Briggs Motor Bodies Ltd* [1954] 2 All ER 193, [1954] 1 WLR 840.

    (a) Factory. For definition, see s. 175.

    (b) Mechanical power. The term "mechanical power" is not defined in the Act, nor was it defined in the 1937 Act, when it appeared in its present form for the first time. In the Acts of 1878 and 1901 this term was used in the context "steam, water or other mechanical power" and the courts then held that "mechanical power" was to be construed *ejusdem generis* with steam and water power, so as to exclude the application of hand-power by means of the mechanical powers in the technical sense of that expression, i.e. the lever, wheel and axle, pulley, inclined plane, wedge and screw. See *Wrigley v Bagley and Wright* [1901] 1 KB 780, CA; *Willmott v Paton* [1902] 1 KB 237; *Turner v Courtaulds Ltd* [1937] 1 All ER 467. Whether, by omitting the words "steam, water or other" Parliament intended to alter the law on this point remains an open question. A lorry used in a factory is within the definition: see *Robinson v R Durham & Sons* (1992) Times, 10 June.

    (c) Occupier. See note *(j)* to s. 33.

---

164. Prosecution of offences and application of fines.—(1) All offences under this Act shall be triable summarily.

    (2) In any proceedings under this Act it shall be sufficient in the information or, in Scotland, complaint to allege that the factory is a factory within the meaning of this Act and to state the name of the ostensible occupier of the factory, or, where the occupier is a firm, the title of the firm.

    (3) [*repealed*].

    (4) Where, with respect to or in consequence of any accident in a factory, a report is made by the court appointed to hold a formal investigation under this

Act or under the Boiler Explosions Acts 1882 and 1890, or a coroner's inquest or a public inquiry under the Fatal Accidents Inquiry (Scotland) Act 1895, or the Fatal Accidents and Sudden Deaths Inquiry (Scotland) Act 1906, is held, and it appears from the report, or from the proceedings at the inquest or inquiry, that any of the provisions of this Act, or any order or regulations made thereunder, were not complied with at or before the time of the accident, summary proceedings against any person liable to be proceeded against in respect of the non-compliance may be commenced at any time within three months after the making of the report or the conclusion of the inquest or inquiry.

(5) Where any offence is committed under this Act by reason of a failure to make an examination, enter a report, or do any other thing, at or within a time specified by this Act or any regulation or order made thereunder, the offence shall be deemed to continue until the examination is made, or the report entered, or the other thing done, as the case may be.

(6) All fines imposed in Scotland in respect of offences under this Act shall be paid into the Exchequer.

(7) Where a proceeding is taken before a magistrates' court or other court of summary jurisdiction with respect to an offence under this Act alleged to be committed in or with reference to a factory, no person shall be qualified to act as a member of the court who is the occupier or owner of the factory, or the husband, wife, parent, son, daughter, brother, or sister of the occupier or owner of the factory, or a person engaged in, or an officer of any association of persons engaged in, the same trade or occupation as any person charged with the offence.

General note. Subsections. (1) and (2) are repealed by S.I. 1977 No. 2004, except in relation to offences committed before 1 January 1977 and offences under s. 135. By S.I. 1974 No. 1971, sub-s (4) is repealed, except in relation to investigations, inquests and inquiries commenced before 1 January 1975, and sub-ss (5) and (7) are repealed, except in relation to offences under s. 135, now repealed. The section, save from sub-s. (6), is therefore spent.

---

165. [*repealed*].

---

166. Special provisions as to evidence.—(1) If a person is found in a factory *(a)* at any time at which work is going on or the machinery *(b)* is in motion, except during the intervals for meals or rest, he shall, until the contrary is proved, be deemed for the purposes of this Act to have been then employed in the factory, unless the factory is one in which the only persons employed are members of the same family *(c)* dwelling there.

(2) Where in any proceedings under this Act with respect to a young person *(d)* it appears to the court that that young person is apparently of or below the age alleged by the informant, or, in Scotland, by the prosecutor, it shall lie on the accused to prove that the young person is not of or below that age.

(3) [*spent*].

(a) **Factory.** For definition, see s. 175.

(b) **Machinery.** For definition, see s. 176(1).

(c) **Members of the same family.** See also s. 7(1).

(d) **Young person.** For definition, see s. 176(1).

(e) **Evidence.** For provisions as to the admissibility of records, see the Civil Evidence Act 1968 and, in particular, s. 4 thereof.

---

167. Proceedings for offences in respect of the employment of children. For the purposes of any proceedings under this Act in respect of the employment of children (a) in contravention of section seventeen of the Education (Scotland) Act 1918, or section one of the Employment of Women, Young Persons, and Children Act 1920, or any other enactment prohibiting the employment of children which is incorporated with this Act, references in this Part of this Act to young persons (b) shall be construed as including references to children within the meaning of any such enactment.

(a) **Children.** For definition of "child", see s. 176(1).

(b) **References . . . to young persons.** The references are contained in ss. 158 and 166(2).

---

168. [*spent*].

---

169. Power of county court or sheriff to modify agreements. If by reason of an agreement between the owner (a) and the occupier (b) of premises the whole or any part of which has been let as a factory (c) the owner or occupier is prevented from carrying out any structural or other alterations in the premises which are necessary to enable him to comply with the provisions of this Act or of any regulation or order made under this Act or in order to conform with any standard or requirement imposed by or under this Act, he may apply to the county court (d) or, in Scotland, the sheriff, and the court or sheriff, after hearing the parties and any witnesses whom they desire to call, may make such an order setting aside or modifying the terms of the agreement as the court or sheriff considers just and equitable (e) in the circumstances of the case.

(a) **Owner.** For definition, see s. 176(1).

(b) **Occupier.** See note (j) to s. 33.

(c) **Factory.** For definition, see s. 175.

(d) **May apply to the county court.** It was decided by the Court of Appeal in *Horner v Franklin* [1905] 1 KB 479 and *Stuckey v Hooke* [1906] 2 KB 20 that the effect of s. 7(2) of the 1891 Act and of the subsections in the 1901 Act giving a remedy similar to that given by the present section was to exclude the jurisdiction of the High Court altogether.

(e) Just and equitable. The question arose under those provisions of the 1891 Act (which gave to the lessor a similar right of application to the county court) how far the county court judge, in determining what is just and equitable, is bound by the terms of the covenants in the lease or other contract between the parties. In *Monk v Arnold* [1902] 1 KB 761 the Divisional Court decided that although the county court judge ought to have regard to any covenants in the occupier's lease, yet he is not bound by them if he considers that in the particular circumstances it would be inequitable to insist upon their being strictly carried out. This case was approved by the Court of Appeal in *Horner v Franklin*, above, where it was expressly stated that the terms of the tenancy constituted one of the circumstances of the case which the county court judge was to consider; and in *Stuckey v Hooke*, above, Fletcher Moulton LJ thought that the covenant was only part of the circumstances of the case, and that the judge was not necessarily bound by it. For particular examples of the exercise of this jurisdiction, see *Goldstein v Hollingsworth* [1904] 2 KB 578 and *Morris v Beal* [1904] 2 KB 585.

---

170.   Power of county court or sheriff to apportion expenses. Where in any premises the whole or any part of which has been let as a factory *(a)* any structural or other alterations *(b)* are required in order to comply with the provisions of this Act or of any regulation or order made under this Act or in order to conform with any standard or requirement imposed by or under this Act and the owner *(c)* or occupier *(d)* as the case may be alleges that the whole or part of the expenses of the alterations ought to be borne by the occupier or owner, the owner or occupier may apply to the county court or, in Scotland, the sheriff, and the court or sheriff, after hearing the parties and any witnesses whom they may desire to call, may make such an order concerning the expenses or their apportionment as the court or sheriff considers just and equitable in the circumstances of the case, regard being had to the terms of any contract between the parties, or in the alternative the court or sheriff may at the request of the owner or occupier determine the lease.

(a) *Factory.* For definition, see s. 175.

(b) *Structural or other alterations.* See, for example, s. 121.

(c) *Owner.* For definition, see s. 176(1).

(d) *Occupier.* See note *(j)* to s. 33.

---

171.   Application of Arbitration Act 1950. The Arbitration Act 1950 shall not apply to proceedings under this Act except in so far as it may be applied by regulations *(a)* made under this Act.

(a) *Regulations.* As to the making of regulations, see s. 180. No regulations were made under this section or the corresponding provisions of superseded enactments. See, further, the Arbitration Act 1979, s. 7(1) (d).

PART XIII

APPLICATION OF ACT

172. General application. Save as in this Act otherwise expressly provided *(a)*, the provisions of this Act shall apply only to factories as defined by this Act *(b)*, but shall, except where the contrary intention appears, apply to all such factories.

General note. For provisions as to safety in installations in transit, in territorial waters or outside territorial waters, see the Mineral Workings (Offshore Installations) Act 1971, and ss. 22, 23 of the Oil and Gas (Enterprise) Act 1982.

(a) *Otherwise expressly provided.* See ss. 123 to 129.

(b) *Factory.* For definition, see s. 175.

---

173. Application to Crown.—(1) This Act applies to factories *(a)* belonging to or in the occupation of the Crown, to building operations and works of engineering construction *(b)* undertaken by or on behalf of the Crown, and to the employment by or under the Crown of persons in painting buildings; but in case of any public emergency the Minister *(c)* may, by order *(d)*, to the extent and during the period named in the order exempt from this Act any factory belonging to the Crown or any building operations or works of engineering construction undertaken by or on behalf of the Crown, or any factory in respect of work which is being done on behalf of the Crown.

(2) The duties under this Act *(e)* of a district council *(f)* or other local authority shall, in the case of a factory belonging to or in the occupation of the Crown, or building operations or works of engineering construction undertaken by or on behalf of the Crown, be exercised by an inspector *(g)* under this Act; and any notice required by this Act to be sent to a district council shall in any such case be sent to the inspector for the district.

General note. By S.I. 1974 No 1941, sub-s. (1) of this section, in so far as it enables orders to be made otherwise than by statutory instrument, has effect as if references to the Secretary of State ("the Minister") were references to the Health and Safety Executive.

This section is extended by the Atomic Energy Authority Act 1954, s. 6(4) and Sch. 3, which provides that any premises belonging to or in the occupation of the Authority and any building operation or work of engineering construction undertaken by or on behalf of the Authority shall be deemed to be premises belonging to or in the occupation of the Crown or operations and works undertaken by or on behalf of the Crown. By the Atomic Energy Authority Act 1971, s. 18, where an order is made under the Nuclear Installations Act 1965, s. 2, in relation to a body corporate to which a permit has been granted under that section, then, in relation to premises on a site in respect of which the permit is in force and in relation to building operations or works of engineering construction undertaken by or on behalf of that body corporate the Factories Act 1961 applies as it applies by virtue of Sch. 3 to the 1954 Act to premises etc. of the Authority, that is as if the premises belonged to or were in occupation of the Crown or as if the operations or works were undertaken by or on behalf of the Crown.

The section is also extended by art. 16(2) of the Visiting Forces and International Headquarters (Application of Law) Order 1965 to include factories belonging to or occupied by, and operations and works undertaken by or on behalf of, the service authorities of a visiting force or a headquarters as if they were Crown factories or operations or works undertaken by or on behalf of the Crown.

For certain purposes this section is applied to dock premises as if they were a factory (see s. 125(8)). Civil proceedings against the Crown are governed by the Crown Proceedings Act 1947.

(a) **Factory.** For definition, see s. 175.

(b) **Building operations and works of engineering construction.** For definitions, see s. 176 (1), and for the provisions of the Act applicable thereto, see s. 127.

(c) **The Minister.** For definition, see s. 176(1); see also the general note.

(d) **Order.** As to the making of orders, see s. 180.

(e) **Duties under this Act.** See ss. 133 and 153.

(f) **District council.** For definition, see s. 176(1). As respects the City of London, the common council is substituted for the district council (s. 176(8)).

(g) **Inspector.** For definition, see s. 176(1).

---

174.   Mines and quarries.—(1) In section one hundred and eighty-four of the Mine and Quarries Act 1954 (which relates to premises forming part of a mine (a) or quarry (b) which, but for that fact, would be factories or premises treated in some respect as if they were factories) the words "the Factories Act 1961" shall be substituted for the words "the Factories Acts 1937 and 1948", wherever they occur, and for the words "the Factories Act 1937" in subsection (7); and for subsection (5) there shall be substituted the following subsection—

"(5) References in subsections (1) to (4) of this section to provisions of the Factories Act 1961 shall be construed as exclusive of references to section one hundred and twenty-seven (which applies other provisions of that Act to building operations (c) and works of engineering construction (d)) and to the other provisions of that Act in so far as, by virtue of that section, they are applicable to such operations or works; but the said section shall not apply—

(a) to any building operations undertaken below ground in a mine; or
(b) to any works of engineering construction undertaken at a mine (whether above or below ground) or at a quarry.".

(2) [*repealed*].

(a) **Mine.** For definition, see s. 180 of the Mines and Quarries Act 1954.

(b) **Quarry.** For definition, see s. 180 of the Mines and Quarries Act 1954.

(c) **Building operations.** For definition, see s. 176(1).

(d) ***Works of engineering construction.*** For definition, see s. 176(1).

PART XIV

INTERPRETATION AND GENERAL

Interpretation

175. Interpretation of expression "factory".—(1) Subject to the provisions of this section, the expression "factory" means any premises in which, or within the close or curtilage or precincts *(a)* of which, persons *(b)* are employed *(c)* in manual labour *(d)* in any process *(e)* for or incidental to any of the following purposes, namely—

(a) the making of any article *(f)* or of part of any article; or

(b) the altering, repairing, ornamenting, finishing, cleaning, or washing or the break up or demolition of any article; or

(c) the adapting for sale *(g)* of any article;

(d) the slaughtering of cattle, sheep, swine, goats, horses, asses or mules *(h)*; or

(e) the confinement of such animals as aforesaid while awaiting slaughter at other premises, in a case where the place of confinement is available in connection with those other premises, is not maintained primarily for agricultural purposes within the meaning of the Agriculture Act 1947, or, as the case may be, the Agriculture (Scotland) Act 1948, and does not form part of premises used for the holding of a market in respect of such animals *(h)*,

being premises in which, or within the close or curtilage or precincts of which, the work is carried on by way of trade or for purposes of gain *(i)* and to or over which the employer of the persons employed therein has the right of access or control.

(2) The expression "factory" also includes the following premises in which persons are employed in manual labour (whether or not they are factories by virtue of subsection (1) of this section), that is to say,—

(a) any yard or dry dock (including the precincts thereof) *(j)* in which ships or vessels are constructed, reconstructed, repaired, refitted, finished or broken up;

(b) any premises in which the business of sorting any articles *(k)* is carried on as a preliminary to the work carried on in any factory or incidentally to the purposes of any factory;

(c) any premises in which the business of washing or filling bottles *(l)* or containers or packing articles is carried on incidentally to the purposes of any factory;

(d) any premises in which the business of hooking, plaiting, lapping, making-up or packing of yarn or cloth is carried on;

(e) any laundry carried on as ancillary to another business *(m)*, or incidentally to the purposes of any public institution *(n)*;

(f) except as provided in subsection (10) of this section, any premises in which the construction, reconstruction or repair *(o)* of locomotives, vehicles or other plant for use for transport purposes is carried on as ancillary to a transport undertaking or other industrial or commercial undertaking;

(g) any premises in which printing by letterpress, lithography, photo-gravure, or other similar process, or bookbinding is carried on by way of trade or for purposes of gain *(i)* or incidentally to another business so carried on;

(h) any premises in which the making, adaptation or repair of dresses, scenery or properties is carried on incidentally to the production, exhibition or presentation by way of trade or for purposes of gain of cinematograph films or theatrical performances, not being a stage or dressing-room of a theatre in which only occasional adaptations or repairs are made;

(j) any premises in which the business of making or mending nets is carried on incidentally to the fishing industry;

(k) any premises in which mechanical power *(p)* is used in connection with the making or repair of articles of metal or wood incidentally to any business carried on by way of trade or for purposes of gain;

(l) any premises in which the production of cinematograph films *(q)* is carried on by way of trade or for purposes of gain, so, however, that the employment at any such premises of theatrical performers within the meaning of the Theatrical Employers Registration Act 1925 *(r)*, and of attendants on such theatrical performers shall not be deemed to be employment in a factory;

(m) any premises in which articles are made or prepared incidentally to the carrying on of building operations or works of engineering construc-tion *(s)*, not being premises in which such operations or works are being carried on;

(n) any premises used for the storage of gas in a gasholder *(t)* having a storage capacity of not less than 140 cubic metres.

(3) Any line or siding (not being part of a railway or tramway *(u)*) which is used in connection with and for the purpose of a factory, shall be deemed to be part of the factory; and if any such line or siding is used in connection with more than one factory belonging to different occupiers, the line or siding shall be deemed to be a separate factory.

(4) A part of a factory may, with the approval in writing of the chief inspec-tor, be taken to be a separate factory and two or more factories may, with the like approval, be taken to be a single factory.

(5) Any workplace in which, with the permission of or under agreement with the owner or occupier, two or more persons carry on any work which would constitute the workplace a factory if the persons working therein were in the employment of the owner or occupier, shall be deemed to be a factory for the purposes of this Act, and, in the case of any such workplace not being a tenement factory or part of a tenement factory *(v)*, the provisions of this Act shall apply as if the owner *(w)* or occupier *(x)* of the workplace were the occupier of the factory and the persons working therein were persons employed in the factory.

(6) Where a place situate within the close, curtilage, or precincts forming a factory is solely used for some purpose other than the processes carried on in the factory *(y)*, that place shall not be deemed to form part of the factory for the purposes of this Act, but shall, if otherwise it would be a factory, be deemed to be a separate factory.

(7) Premises shall not be excluded from the definition of a factory by reason only that they are open air premises.

(8) Where the Minister *(z)* by regulations *(aa)* so directs as respects all or any purposes of this Act, different branches or departments of work carried on in the same factory shall be deemed to be different factories.

(9) Any premises belonging to or in the occupation of the Crown or any municipal or other public authority shall not be deemed not to be a factory, and building operations or works of engineering construction *(s)* undertaken by or on behalf of the Crown or any such authority shall not be excluded from the operation of this Act, by reason only that the work carried on thereat is not carried on by way of trade or for purposes of gain *(i)*.

(10) Premises used for the purpose of housing locomotives or vehicles where only cleaning, washing, running repairs or minor adjustments are carried out shall not be deemed to be a factory by reason only of paragraph (f) of subsection (2) of this section, unless they are premises used for the purposes of a railway undertaking where running repairs *(o)* to locomotives are carried out.

General note. The importance of the definition will, of course, disappear as the obligations under the Act are progressively replaced by Regulations of general application to workplaces.

The provisions of the Fire Precautions Act 1971 apply with modifications where premises, in respects of which a fire certificate under that Act is required, are premises constituting, or forming part of, a factory within the meaning of this Act or are premises to which ss. 123(1) and 124 of this Act apply, and the premises are held under a lease or an agreement for a lease or under a licence and consist of part of a building all parts of which are in the same ownership or consist of part of a building in which different parts are owned by different persons; see the Fire Precautions Act 1971, s. 28A and Sch. 2 as inserted by the Fire Safety and Safety of Places of Sport Act 1987, s. 16(1), (2), Sch. 1.

Some useful guidance as to what premises or parts of premises are not factories or not parts of factories is to be obtained from a line of cases decided under other Acts— notably the Rating and Valuation (Apportionment) Act 1928—in which Acts, the expressions "factory" and "workshops" have been defined as having the same meanings as in the Factories Acts.

Before turning to the cases referred to it is necessary first to consider whether decisions given in cases under statutes such as the Rating Acts are to be regarded as applicable and authoritative in the interpretation of the Factories Act 1961.

In *Thurogood v Van den Berghs and Jurgens Ltd* [1951] 2 KB 537, [1951] 1 All ER 682, the Court of Appeal held that since the Rating and Valuation (Apportionment) Act 1928, s. 3(2), provided that the expressions "factory" and "workshop" should have the same meaning as in the Factory and Workshops Acts 1901–20, the nature of the definition prevented a different interpretation being given under different Acts, based on the particular object of the particular Act in question. Earlier, Somervell LJ, in *Stanger v Hendon Borough Council* [1948] 1 KB 571, [1948] 1 All ER 377 at 379, had expressed the same view. It is thus clear that the guidance to be derived from decisions under the Rating Acts may be regarded as dependable and authoritative.

There is, however, this caution to be observed. In many of the cases under the Rating Acts the point at issue was not whether the premises were a factory, but whether they were such a factory as constituted an industrial hereditament. In a number of cases the decision was that though the premises were undoubtedly a factory they were not an industrial hereditament. These cases are relevant to the present purposes in so far as they show what features or attributes or activities have been held or conceded to render premises factories.

A group of cases was dealt with together by the House of Lords in a composite opinion of the House delivered by Lord Dunedin and reported at [1931] AC 446. These included:

(i) *Sedgwick v Watney Combe Reid & Co Ltd.* (The defendants had a bottling store in which beer brewed by them elsewhere was matured, carbonated, filtered and bottled, and from which, after corking and labelling, the bottled beer was distributed. It was admitted that the activities mentioned made the premises a factory, and it was held that the premises were also an industrial hereditament.)

(ii) *Grove v Lloyd's British Testing Co Ltd* (The respondent company's establishment was one licensed by the Board of Trade under the Anchors and Chain Cables Act 1899, to test chain cables made by others and to issue certificates in respect of such cables as passed the test. The test involved cutting links out of the chain cable and joining the cable at a later stage by a new link forged on the respondent's premises. It was accepted that the forging of links to join up the chain was enough to render the premises a factory. The matter which had caused a deep division of opinion below, but presented no difficulty to the House of Lords, was whether the whole process of testing and certification constituted an adapting for sale of the chain cable, so as to make the premises a factory on that account also. The House of Lords held that it did not. Lord Dunedin, at 467, said: "I think 'adapting for sale' points clearly to something being done to the article in question which, in some way, makes it in itself a little different from what it was before." It seems to follow from the decision of the House of Lords that if the respondents' test had not included any manufacturing element, but had been confined solely to testing cables manufactured by others, their premises would have been held not to be a factory.) Compare this case with *Acton Borough Council v West Middlesex Assessment Committee* [1949] 2 KB 10, below.

(iii) *Turpin v Assessment Committee for Middlesbrough Assessment Area.* (A garage and motor depot containing *inter alia* inspection pits, and a workshop with plant, machinery and power, suitable for repair work, was held to be on that account clearly a factory, but not to be an industrial hereditament because it was primarily occupied and used for the purpose of a retail shop.)

(iv) *Kaye v Burrows.* (In the premises in this case there was carried on among other activities the activity of preparing, ripping, clipping, grading, classifying, blending and sorting of rags consisting on the one hand of old garments, and on the other of tailor's new clippings. After these activities had been completed the occupier of the premises sold the rags to heavy woollen cloth manufacturers for use in their business. It was held that the aforementioned treatment of the rags constituted an adapting for sale, that the premises were a factory, and that in so far as the decision in *Paterson v Hunt* (1909) 101 LT 571 was not distinguishable on its facts it was to be regarded as wrongly decided and to be overruled.) Sorting of articles is specifically dealt with in s. 175(2)(b) of the 1961 Act as an activity which can render premises a factory which might otherwise not have been so regarded.

(v) *Hines v Eastern Counties Farmers' Co-operative Association Ltd* (In a seed merchant's warehouse, seed coming from the threshing machines in a rough, unclean and impure state was treated with the object of separating weed seeds and dusts of various sorts from the good seeds. No chemical change was effected in the seed itself. The true view of the treatment was that it effected both an alteration of substance, and an adaptation for sale in bulk making a substantially different article in bulk from that which existed before the processes were applied. The case could not be correctly decided by concentrating upon the fact that any given seed remained unchanged by the process. What the treatment had done was to alter the bulk so as to make commercially saleable what previously could not have been sold. The premises were held to be a factory.)

(vi) *Union Cold Storage Co Ltd v Bancroft* (In premises part of which did undoubtedly constitute a factory because of the activities carried on in that part the primary use to which the premises as a whole were put was the storage of goods by means of an elaborate refrigeration process involving the use of machinery. It was argued that these refrigeration processes made the premises a factory because, it was submitted, the processes by which the goods were frozen, kept frozen and defrosted both altered the article and adapted the article for sale. That argument the House of Lords rejected, holding that storage was the dominant purpose of the occupiers, that storage was the primary use to which they put their premises and that the processes of refrigeration were a mere incident of storage applied only in order to render storage possible and not otherwise.)

The last-mentioned case provides a good illustration of the necessity for caution in the use of rating cases when determining Factories Act questions. Thus it has been doubted (by Sir Raymond Evershed MR in *Cockram (Valuation Officer) v Tropical Preservation Co Ltd* [1951] 2 KB 827 at 839, [1951] 2 All ER 520 at 526) whether Lord Dunedin in that case had held that the processes of refrigeration could not amount to an adaptation of an article for sale. The Master of the Rolls suggested that his speech should be read as deciding no more than that on the facts of that case, the process of refrigeration, viewed in relation to the storage uses of the premises, was not sufficient to render the hereditament an industrial hereditament under the Rating Acts.

In *Acton Borough Council v West Middlesex Assessment Committee* [1949] 2 KB 10, [1949] 1 All ER 409 the facts were that de Havilland Propellers Ltd made propellers in premises at one place and tested them in premises at another. The question in the case related to the testing premises. In these some of the testing work was exclusively experimental, but most of the testing which was done was production testing of propellers which had been manufactured for sale and which had, under the contract, to be tested before delivery. The component parts of propellers arriving for production testing had to be assembled before test at the testing establishment and were also there fitted to aero engines mounted on test beds. Propellers showing fault on test were adjusted or modified where possible at the testing establishment but if they still failed to satisfy the test they were returned for rectification to the manufacturing establishment. The Divisional Court considered that on the whole what went on at the testing establishment made the premises there a factory. Lord Goddard CJ took the view that the testing in this case was part of the process of manufacture or incidental thereto. Finnemore J agreed with that, and suggested also that the testing was incidental to the adapting for sale of the propellers. It is submitted that this second ground is weaker than that selected by the Lord Chief Justice and that, in spite of the factual distinction which Finnemore J was able to draw between this case and that of *Grove v Lloyd's British Testing Co Ltd*, above, the activities of this testing establishment should not properly be regarding as constituting an adaptation for sale of propellers merely because some propellers might be shown by test to be defective, and of these some might be so little defective that they could be rectified at the testing establishment.

The question, how far the sorting of articles constitutes an adaptation for sale, was considered by the House of Lords in *Hudson's Bay Co v Thompson (Valuation Officer)* [1960] AC 926, [1959] 3 All ER 150. The hereditament in question was used for the sorting, grading and matching of furs and for their arrangement in matched lots of skins of uniform grade for sale. It was held that the article which was adapted for sale was not a single item (which had undergone no change); it was the whole collection of unmatched skins which arrived at the premises and were arranged in the form of bales of matched skins. There had, therefore, been an adapting for sale within the meaning of the definition of "workshop" in s. 149(1) of the Factory and Workshop Act 1901.

Stanger v Hendon Borough Council [1948] 1 KB 571, [1948] 1 All ER 377 was a case under the Town and Country Planning Act 1932, in which the expression "industrial building" was defined as "... building ... designed for use as a factory ... within the meaning of the Factory and Workshop Acts 1901 to 1929." It was common ground that for reference to the Acts of 1901 to 1929 reference to the Factories Act 1937 (now the Factories Act 1961) had to be substituted in the definition. The issue in the case accordingly resolved itself into a consideration of the activities carried on in the premises and the determination of the question whether these activities were covered by the words of s. 151 of the 1937 Act (now s. 175 of the 1961 Act). The facts were that the occupier of the premises was a consulting engineer who specialised in testing materials used in building and engineering construction, for which services he was paid fees by the builders who consulted him and to whom he reported the results of his research and gave advice as to the suitability of the materials submitted. *Inter alia* the occupier used a laboratory concrete mixer (which would have been useless to a builder) to make small concrete blocks or briquettes, and a crushing machine to discover what amount of strain the concrete would bear and at what point it would break up. The occupier employed persons in manual labour in connection with these operations. It was held that in spite of the experimental nature of the work and in spite of the fact that the article made and destroyed was not made to be used save in the course of the testing and was, save for that purpose, useless, the premises were a factory by reason of sub-paras. (a) and (b) of s. 151(1) (now s. 175(1)(a) and (b) of the 1961 Act), and that the process of making and breaking the concrete blocks was carried on "for purposes of gain" even though the concrete was not sold and the fees received by the occupier were paid for his professional advice and reports.

The question, whether an uncompleted factory building in which there was neither electric power to drive the machines nor shafting to transmit power to the plant could be a factory within the meaning of the section, was considered by Hilbery J in *Barrington v Kent Rivers Catchment Board* [1947] 2 All ER 782. The judge held that in the circumstances the incomplete building was a factory because the plaintiff and another had begun to do therein the kind of work that it was intended to do in the building when it was completed, and such work involved manual labour in a process incidental to the altering, repairing, ornamenting or cleaning of an article. Though the work being done was not being carried on by way of trade or for purposes of gain that circumstances did not matter, as the occupiers were a public authority and, accordingly, sub-s. (9) (s. 175 (9) of the 1961 Act) prevented the exclusion of the premises from the category of factory on that account.

In *Weston v LCC* [1941] 1 KB 608, Wrottesley J held that a technical institute conducted by the LCC was not a factory either within the general definition of the section or within s. 151(1)(x) (now s. 175(2)(k) of the 1961 Act). Nor did the fact that the institute was occupied by a municipal or public authority make the institute a factory by virtue of s. 151(9) (now s. 175(9)). "The subsection does not say that premises in the occupation of or belonging to a public authority shall be deemed to be a factory, but says that they are not to be excluded from the definition, if they comply with other particulars in the definition, merely because the work carried on in them is not carried on by way of trade or for the purposes of gain" (p. 613). The judge held that the premises with which he was concerned did not comply with the other particulars, principally because the pupils of the institute were not "employed" persons of whom the LCC were the "employers". "Employed" in the section does not, he held, mean "busy", "engaged" or "occupied". In *Pullen v Prison Comrs* [1957] 3 All ER 470, [1957] 1 WLR 1186, Lord Goddard CJ, holding that a prison workshop was not a "factory", followed the decision and reasoning of Wrottesley J in *Weston v LCC*, above. See also the note *(c)*, below.

In *Wood v LCC* [1941] 2 KB 232, [1941] 2 All ER 230, the Court of Appeal held that the kitchen of a mental hospital was not a factory within the definition in s. 151 (now s. 175 of the 1961 Act), and in *Chatburn v Manchester Dry Dock Co* (1950) 83 Ll L Rep 1, the Court of Appeal decided that the Act did not apply to a trawler moored to and having work done upon it at the defendants' jetty, abutting on the Manchester Ship Canal, for the trawler was not itself a factory nor was it within the precincts of a factory. Compare *Moor v Greenhithe Lighterage Co Ltd* [1961] 1 Lloyd's Rep 149, in which Elwes J held that a barge moored to a backyard of the defendants' premises, where vessels were repaired, was within the precincts of the yard, and within a factory as defined by s. 151(1) of the Factories Act 1937 (now s. 175(1) of the 1961 Act). A workshop which would otherwise fall within the definition is not excluded from it merely because it forms part of and is ancillary to hospital premises (*Bromwich v National Ear, Nose and Throat Hospital* [1980] 2 All ER 663, distinguishing *Wood v LCC*, above).

(a) **Close or curtilage or precincts.** In *Back v Dirk, Kerr & Co Ltd* [1906] AC 325, HL, it was said that a factory was something "having geographical boundaries", was "an undertaking within a physical area" and that "the walls or fences built around the factory or dock as the case may be fix the boundaries and determine the area". A close, however, need not have any boundary wall or fence: *Barry v Cleveland Bridge and Engineering Co Ltd* [1963] 1 All ER 192 (areas of quay with clearly recognisable boundaries); *Walsh v Allweather Mechanical Grouting Co Ltd* [1959] 2 QB 300, [1959] 2 All ER 588, CA (apron outside aircraft hangar). If premises consist of a building occupied with land, forming its close, curtilage or precinct, the existence of a manufacturing activity in that close or precinct will make the whole premises a factory, subject to s. 175(6): see *Hosking v De Havilland Aircraft Co Ltd* [1949] 1 All ER 540; *Newton v John Stanning & Son Ltd* [1962] 1 All ER 78, [1962] 1 WLR 30; and *Paul Popper Ltd v Grimsey* [1963] 1 QB 44, [1962] 1 All ER 864, following the dictum of Wynn Parry J in *Cox v S Cutler & Sons Ltd and Hampton Court Gas Co* [1948] 2 All ER 665 at 673, CA, which had been approved by the Court of Appeal in *Street v British Electricity Authority* [1952] 2 QB 399, [1952] 1 All ER 679.

(b) **Persons.** In *Griffith v Ferrier* 1952 SLT 248, it was decided that the mere fact that only one person is employed does not prevent the premises being a factory (see the Interpretation Act 1978, s. 6).

(c) **Employed.** "If the definition of 'factory' is to apply, there must exist (except in certain express cases, for instance, apprentices, for there is a subsection which deals with apprentices) the relationship of master and servant and employment for wages" (*Pullen v Prison Comrs* [1957] 3 All ER 470, *per* Lord Goddard LJ at 471, holding that a prison workshop was not a factory). For the same reason, a technical institute is not a factory (*Weston v LCC* [1941] 1 KB 608, [1941] 1 All ER 555). See also the general note to this section.

(d) **Manual labour.** This expression has not necessarily the same meaning here that it has in the Employers and Workmen Act 1875 (*Hoare v Robert Green Ltd* [1907] 2 KB 315; *Fullers Ltd v Square* [1901] 2 KB 209).

The many authorities which have been decided upon the interpretation of the expression were discussed and reviewed in *J and F Stone Lighting and Radio v Haygarth* [1968] AC 157, [1966] 3 All ER 539, HL. The basis of this important decision appears in the following passage from the speech of Lord Morris of Borth-y-Gest, at 179; 547:

"In legislation in relation to those employed in manual labour it would seem reasonable to suppose that the legislature was contemplating those whose work involved to a substantial extent the use of their hands. If manual labour denotes working with the hands, I can find nothing in the Act of 1961 which requires that the work must be heavy work which demands great strength. Some manual labour may require much strength; other manual labour may require but little. Similarly there may be manual labour which requires much knowledge; other manual labour may require but little. Some knowledge may be generally possessed by most people; some knowledge may be specially possessed by a few. Furthermore, that which yesterday was the special knowledge of the few may tomorrow be the commonplace knowledge of all. The Act neither prescribes nor defines any varieties of manual labour. If, therefore, someone is employed to work with his hands, so that in a realistic way it can be said that such work with his hands forms his main or predominant activity (as opposed to work with his hands which is merely incidental to or accessory to work which is not so done), then he would be employed in manual labour. He would still be so employed, even if his work required knowledge or skill or ability. The Act is not limited to unskilled manual labour. There is no exemption for skilled manual labour. Were it so, the act might cease to operate in some of the very places for which its provisions would seem to be appropriate."

A valuable summary of a number of the more important preceding authorities is to be found in the speech of Lord Pearson at 190; 555:

"There is however a principle which seems to be common to all the relevant cases under all the Acts, and it can be stated shortly in these terms. A person is not employed in 'manual labour' for the purposes of any of the Acts, if his occupation is primarily or substantially an activity of a different kind and the manual work he does is merely ancillary or accessory to that activity. There are many decided cases illustrating the application of this principle: *Morgan v London General Omnibus Co* (1884) 13 QBD 832 (bus conductor not 'engaged in manual labour'); *Cook v North Metropolitan Tramways Co* (1887) 18 QBD 683 (tram driver not 'engaged in manual labour'); *Bound v Lawrence* [1892] 1 QB 226, CA (grocer's assistant not 'engaged in manual labour'); *Fullers Ltd v Squire* [1901] 2 KB 209 ('manual labour'); *Hoare v Robert Green Ltd* [1907] 2 KB 315 (girls engaged in making wreaths, crosses and bouquets behind a florist's shop were exercising 'manual labour'); *Re Dairymen's Foremen, Re Tailors' Cutters* (1912) 107 LT 342 (held to be 'employed otherwise than in manual labour' within the National Insurance Act 1911, as they were in substance employed as managers); *Re National Insurance Act 1911, Re Lithographic Artists, Re Engravers* (1913) 108 LT 894 (held to be exercising the highest degree of artistic intelligence and artistic skill, and to be employed 'otherwise than in manual labour'); *Jacques v Steam Tug Alexandra (Owners)* [1921] 2 AC 339, HL (tug master employed 'otherwise than by way of manual labour' within s. 13 of the Workmen's Compensation Act 1906, on the facts set out in the report); *Re Gardner, Re Mascher, Re Tyrrell* [1938] 1 All ER 20 (modellers held not to be employed 'otherwise than by way of manual labour' for the purposes of the Unemployment Insurance Act 1935); *Joyce v Boots Cash Chemist (Southern) Ltd* [1950] 2 All ER 719 (dispenser at chemist's shop held not 'employed in manual labour').

There may be difficulty in applying the principle in particular cases (e.g. in the case of the dispenser at the chemist's shop, who seems to me a borderline case) but in general the principle is clear. Examples of activities which are primarily non-manual, though involving some manual work are: (i) the work of a painter, sculptor or lithographic artist; (ii) managerial or supervisory work; (iii) selling in a shop; (iv) clerical work; (v) driving a vehicle or acting as conductor of a public service vehicle. In the sphere of repairing there seems to be no decided case, but it can be suggested with at any rate, plausibility, that an artist restoring or even cleaning a picture, an expert in oriental ceramics repairing a Ming vase, or an archaeologist piecing together fragments of an Egyptian papyrus or Linear B script, would not be held to be employed in manual labour. There ought also to be examples of primarily intellectual activities involving some incidental element of manual labour. Mathematicians, scientists, inventors, actors and musicians—even authors—may have to do some incidental manual work."

In that case, the Court held, accordingly, that a radio and television engineer who diagnosed and repaired faults in television and radio sets was employed in manual labour.

(e) **In any process.** These words should be read as equivalent to "in any activity": *Joyce v Boots Cash Chemists (Southern) Ltd* [19550] 2 All ER 719 affd on another point at [1951] 1 All ER 682n, CA) *per* Slade J, following the view expressed by Lord Moncrieff in *Ward v Coltness Iron Co Ltd* 1944 SC 318 at 324. Note, however, that the word "process" may be interpreted differently in the context of regulations passed under the Act: see *Nurse v Morganite Crucible Ltd* [1989] AC 692 at 701, HL, *per* Lord Griffiths.

(f) **Article.** In *Longhurst v Guildford, Godalming and District Water Board* [1963] AC 265, [1961] 3 All ER 545, HL, the Water Board occupied a filter house and a pump house. In the pump house were engines with pumps which forced water either to a reservoir feeding the public mains or direct to the mains themselves. It was held that the word "article" in s. 151(1) of the Factories Act 1937 (s. 175(1) of the 1961 Act) was apt to comprehend the water in the filter house, and that, by reason of its treatment in the filter house, the premises were a factory. It was further held, however, that the pump house (in which the plaintiff had met with his accident) was excluded from the factory by s. 151(6) (s. 175(6) of the 1961 Act); see note *(y)*, below. Lord Reid said that the word "article" appeared to him to be capable of meaning anything corporeal, and approved the opinion of Scott LJ in *Cox v S Cutler & Sons Ltd* [1948] 2 All ER 665. It follows from this decision that an "article" need not be something which has been "made"; and Lord Guest disapproved the contrary views expressed by Darling and Phillimore JJ in *Hoare v*

Robert Green Ltd [1907] 2 KB 315 at 321, 322. No opinion was expressed on the question, whether the natural elements in their unconfined state, could be "articles". In *Granada TV Network v Kerridge (Valuation Officer)* [1961] RVR 687, the Lands Tribunal held that an electrical impulse was not an "article". A live animal is not an "article" (*per* Parker LJ in *Fatstock Marketing Corpn Ltd v Morgan* [1958] 1 All ER 646 at 654, CA), but a photographic print produced in a darkroom is (*Paul Popper Ltd v Grimsey* [1963] 1 QB 44, [1962] 1 All ER 864). A building under construction on a site is not an "article", so as to constitute the site a factory (*Findlay v Miller Construction (Northern)* 1977 SLT (Sh Ct) 8). An oil rig under construction in a construction yard is an article (*Faith v CBI Constructors Ltd* 1987 SLT 248).

(g) **Adapting for sale.** The question, whether the activities constitute an adaptation for sale, is one of degree and therefore of fact, and there are certain guiding principles which can most conveniently be found in Lord Dunedin's speech in [1931] AC 447, and in *Hudson's Bay Co v Thompson (Valuation Officer)* [1960] AC 926, [1959] 3 All ER 150, HL, which are more fully considered in the general note to this section. Some guidance as to the application of the general principles may be found in the cases cited below.

In *Henderson v Glasgow Corpn* 1900 2 F 1127, it was held that separating the saleable parts of town refuse from the unsaleable parts was an "adapting for sale", and in *Fullers Ltd v Squire* [1901] 2 KB 209, it was held that packing and arranging sweetmeats in ornamental boxes and tying them up with ornamental ribbons might be adapting for sale. In *Law v Graham* [1901] 2 KB 327, Lord Alverstone CJ thought it possible that the process of putting beer into bottles at a beer-bottling establishment might be an adapting for sale; but in *Keith Ltd v Kirkwood* 1914 SC (J) 150 the Court of Justiciary in Scotland took the opposite view. In *Hoare v Truman, Hanbury, Buxton & Co* (1902) 71 LJKB 380 it was held by the Divisional Court that where, in a beer-bottling store, the beer was taken from the cask and mixed with carbonic acid gas by mechanical power, after which it flowed into bottles by the gas pressure whenever a tap was turned, this process was an adapting for sale of beer, and that the store was a factory. The court distinguished *Law v Graham*, above. In *Hoare v Robert Green Ltd* [1907] 2 KB 315 a number of girls and women were employed in a florist's shop, partly in serving in the shop and partly in making up natural flowers into wreaths, crosses, etc. The Divisional Court held that they were employed in making or adapting an article for sale. In *Kinder v Camberwell Borough Council* [1944] 2 All ER 315, Viscount Caldecote LCJ, applying *Henderson v Glasgow Corpn*, above, held that the compressing of waste paper into bales so that it might be sold was an adapting for sale, and in *Smith v Supreme Wood Pulp Co Ltd* [1968] 3 All ER 753, it was held that cutting timber for the purpose of resale was an adapting for sale. The "sorting" cases were fully considered by the House of Lords in *Hudson's Bay Co v Thompson*, see the general note to this section.

The case of *Wiltshire County Valuation Committee v London Co-operative Society Ltd* [1950] 1 All ER 937 should be compared and contrasted with *Sedgwick's* case and *Hines'* case mentioned in the general note, above. In the *Wiltshire* case the premises were a milk-collecting depot in which, in order that the bulk milk might travel well during its 100 mile journey to London, and be fit for pasteurisation when it got there, the occupiers subjected it to cleaning and cooling processes. The Divisional Court held that this was not adapting the milk for sale. In an adaptation for sale, it was held, something is done to change an unfinished article into a finished one, or something analogous thereto is done to the article. Making the milk cleaner and cooler for its journey was not making such a change.

The ripening of bananas by artificial heat has been held to be adapting for sale (*Lanarkshire Assessor v Geest Industries Ltd* 1962 SLT 189). So also has the maturation of whisky into Scotch whisky (*Lanarkshire Assessor v Arbuckle, Smith & Co Ltd* 1968 SLT 20; *Arthur Bell & Sons Ltd v Fife Assessor* 1968 SLT 185).

In *Fatstock Marketing Corpn Ltd v Morgan* [1958] 1 All ER 646, [1958] 1 WLR 357, the Court of Appeal held, on the particular facts of the case, that the work carried on in a slaughterhouse was an adaptation of the carcasses for sale within s. 149 of the Factory and Workshop Act 1901. See now the provisions of s. 175(1) (d) of the Factories Act 1961 and note *(h)*, below. In *McLeavy v Liptons* (1959) 228 LT Jo 195, the back room of a retail grocer's shop was used for the reception and unpacking of goods in bulk and their treatment for retail sale. The plaintiff was injured by a bacon slicer used in the room. Finnemore J held that the room was factory within s. 151(1)(c) of the Factories Act 1937 (now s. 175(1)(c) of the 1961 Act). Further authorities on adaptation for sale are discussed in the general note to this section.

(h) Slaughtering. Paragraphs (d) and (e) of s. 175(1) were introduced by s. 7 of the Slaughterhouses Act 1958, now repealed.

(i) By way of trade, or for purposes of gain. See the general note to this section. These words were considered, and the earlier cases upon them discussed, by the Court of Appeal in *Stanger v Hendon Borough Council* [1948] 1 KB 571, [1948] 1 All ER 377. The effect of this decision and of the judgment of Scrutton LJ, in *Bailey (Stoke on Trent Revenue Officer) v Potteries Electric Traction Co Ltd* [1931] 1 KB 385 at 491 *et seq.,* is, it is submitted, that:

(i) the earlier cases cannot be relied upon except in so far as they embody and express the principles enunciated in *Stanger's* case and in *Bailey's* case, above;

(ii) the "gain" referred to need not be direct gain. That part of the judgment of A L Smith, MR in *Nash v Hollinshead* [1901] 1 KB 700, CA, which gave as a ground for that decision that the gain was indirect is disapproved and is not to be regarded as forming any part of the *ratio decidendi.* Cases such as *Curtis v Shinner* (1906) 95 LT 31, which proceeded on the same ground, were wrongly decided; see *Jones v Crosville Motor Services Ltd* [1956] 3 All ER 417, *per* Hallett J at 418, 419, 420;

(iii) the words "by way of trade" and the words "for purposes of gain" are separated by the disjunctive "or". If there is a trade there is no need to consider "gain". A factory will be "carried on" "for trade or gain" if its products are to be sold in trade or directly used in carrying on trade. "The fact that the products are only used to enable a trade to be carried on does not prevent the manufacture being for trade or gain" (*per* Scrutton LJ, in *Bailey (Stoke on Trent Revenue Officer) v Potteries Electric Traction Co Ltd,* above);

(iv) the true *ratio decidendi* of *Nash v Hollinshead* was that "looking at the Acts as a whole they were not intended to cover farming and could not be construed as so doing" (*per* Somervell LJ, in *Stanger's* case at 380); compare the judgment of MacKinnon LJ, in *Wood v LCC* [1941] 2 KB 232, [1941] 2 All ER 230. See also the similar decision of the Court of Appeal in Northern Ireland, based upon a consideration of the like terms of the Factories Act (Northern Ireland) 1938 (*Kerr v Mitchell* [1959] NI 21).

These cases illustrate the principle that a process will not constitute premises a factory if it appears that the general provisions of the Factories Act 1961 as a whole are clearly inapplicable to the circumstances under consideration (see *per* Lord Evershed MR, in *Fatstock Marketing Corpn Ltd v Morgan* [1958] 1 All ER 646 at 653). Safety, health and welfare in agriculture are protected by special statutory provisions, of which the principal are the Agriculture (Poisonous Substances) Act 1952, and the Agriculture (Safety, Health and Welfare Provisions) Act 1956, and subordinate legislation made thereunder (see Part 9 of this book).

As to premises in the occupation of the Crown or a public authority, see sub-s. (9).

(j) Yard or dry dock. It should be noted that wet docks are excluded from the definition; see, however, s. 125, which applies certain provisions of the Act to docks, s. 126, which applies certain provisions of the Act to specified kinds of work on a ship in a harbour or wet dock, and the Shipbuilding and Shiprepairing Regulations 1960, set out in Part 6 of this book, which apply to the construction and repair of ships in shipbuilding yards.

(k) Sorting of articles. See the general note to this section, and note *(f)*.

(l) Washing of bottles. These words overrule the decisions in *Kavanagh v Caledonian Rly Co* 1903 5 F 1128, and *Keith Ltd v Kirkwood* 1914 SC (J) 150.

(m) Ancillary to another business or public institution. Under s. 1 of the Factory and Workshop Act 1907 it has been held that a laundry used exclusively for washing the table and bed linen at a hotel, but not for visitors' linen, is carried on as ancillary to the hotel business, though the court were inclined to doubt whether such a place is a "laundry" at all (*Sadler v Roberts* (1911) 75 JP 342). This doubt was removed by the decision in *Royal Masonic Institution for Boys' Trustees v Parkes* [1912] 3 KB 212, where it was held that a place used exclusively for the inmates' washing was a "laundry" within the meaning of the section.

(n) Public institution. These words bring the laundries of hospitals, etc., within the Act. Note that the laundry need not be carried on by way of trade or for purposes of gain.
   It was held in *Hall v Derby Sanitary Authority* (1885) 16 QBD 163, that an orphanage for the children of deceased railway servants, supported mainly by public donations, but partly by subscriptions from railway servants, was a "public charity". Following that decision, the courts have held that the following places were "public institutions" within the meaning of s. 1 of the Factory and Workshop Act 1907, which, so far as material, used words identical with the words of this section: an asylum for orphan children, maintained by public subscriptions, receiving no Government grant, and not under any public control, whose premises and grounds were private, and whose inmates were elected by the subscribers, though some were admitted on payment (*Seat v British Orphan Asylum Trustees* (1911) 75 JP 152); and an institution for the children of freemasons, supported almost entirely by the subscriptions of freemasons, but receiving a grant from the Board of Education and a very small sum from the general public (*Royal Masonic Institution for Boys, Trustees v Parkes* [1912] 3 KB 212).

(o) Repairs. As to running repairs, see sub-s. (10). Repairs necessitated by a collision are not "running repairs" within sub-s. (10) (*Griffin v London Transport Executive* [1950] 1 All ER 716, followed in *Jones v Crosville Motor Services Ltd* [1956] 3 All ER 417, [1956] 1 WLR 1425).

(p) Mechanical power. See note *(b)* to s. 163.

(q) Cinematograph films. See also the Manufacture of Cinematograph Film Regulations 1928, and the Cinematograph Film Stripping Regulations 1939, set out in Part 7 of this book. During an action for personal injuries sustained at work the question arose as to whether a film studio owned by the BBC was a factory within the meaning of the Factories Act 1961, s. 175(1)(a). It was held that as films were made at the studio it was clearly a factory within the meaning of that provision (*Dunsby v BBC* (1983) Times, 25 July).

(r) Theatrical performers. By the Theatrical Employers Registration Act 1925, s. 13, (repealed by the Local Government (Miscellaneous Provisions) Act 1982) the expression "theatrical performer" includes any actor, singer, dancer, acrobat or performer of any kind employed to act, sing, dance, play or perform in any theatre, music hall or other place of public entertainment, or to rehearse with a view to so acting, singing, dancing, playing or performing, as well as any person employed to take part in the acting or representation of any play, act, event or scene being photographed or otherwise recorded as a picture or pictures or other optical effect suitable or intended for being exhibited by means of a cinematograph or other similar apparatus; and the term theatrical performer shall include all persons employed or engaged for purposes of a chorus or crowd, but shall not include stage hands and members of an orchestra".

(s) Building operations or works of engineering construction. See s. 127, and, for definitions, see s. 176(1).

(t) Gasholder. A gasholder which once held but can no longer hold gas is not included (*Cox v S Cutler & Sons Ltd* [1948] 2 All ER 665, CA).

(u) Railway; tramway. For definitions, see s. 176(1).

(v) **Tenement factory.** For definition, see s. 176(1).

(w) **Owner.** For definition, see s. 176(1).

(x) **Occupier.** The Act does not define "occupier". See note (j) to s. 33.

(y) **For some purpose other than the processes carried on in the factory.** A "place" means a defined and ascertainable place, whether or not there is a physical boundary to mark it off from the rest of the factory (*Lewis v Gilbertson & Co Ltd* (1904) 68 JP 323; *Cox v S Cutler & Sons Ltd* [1948] 2 All ER 665, CA; *Ham River Grit Co Ltd v Richmond Rating Authority* [1949] 1 All ER 286; *Walsh v Allweather Mechanical Grouting Co Ltd* [1959] 2 QB 300, [1959] 2 All ER 588, CA). In construing this subsection the following propositions are to be derived from the authorities (see *Powley v British Siddeley Engines Ltd* [1965] 3 All ER 612 [1966] 1 WLR 729, *per* Megaw J):

   (i) the subsection must be interpreted as if it read ". . . solely used for some purpose other than the processes for and incidental to the main purpose of the factory" (*Thurogood v Van Den Berghs and Jurgens Ltd* [1951] 2 KB 537 at 545; *Longhurst v Guildford, Godalming and District Water Board* [1963] AC 265, [1961] 3 All ER 545, *per* Lord Guest);

  (ii) the difficulty, inherent in the subsection, of comparing a "purpose" with a "process" must be overcome by treating the words "solely used for some purpose" as though they were "solely used for some process" (*Thurogood's* case, above);

 (iii) despite the words, "processes carried on in the factory" in this subsection the process carried on in the "place" need not be the same as a process actually carried on in the factory. It suffices to prevent "the place" from being excluded from the factory if a process carried on in "the place" is a process which is incidental to what is done in the main factory (*Thurogood's* case, above);

 (iv) the fact that the persons principally employed in "the place" are not engaged in manual labour is irrelevant to the provisions of the first part of the subsection, although it is relevant to the application of the later words "if otherwise it would be a factory";

  (v) a "process" does not necessarily connote a manufacturing process, or one incidental to such a process; a "process" in an "activity" (*Joyce v Boots Cash Chemists (Southern) Ltd* [1950] 2 All ER 719 at 721 (affirmed on another point at [1951] 1 All ER 682n, CA); and see the "canteen" cases, below).

The following decisions illustrate the foregoing principles; in applying them it must be borne in mind that each depended upon its particular facts. In *Wood v LCC* [1941] 2 KB 232, [1941] 2 All ER 230, CA, the kitchen of a mental hospital was held not to be a factory, and in *Thomas v British Thomson-Houston Co Ltd* [1953] 1 All ER 29, [1953] 1 WLR 67, Havers J, following *Wood's* case, held that a restaurant within the curtilage of a factory and used by executive and administrative employees was not part of the factory. However, in *London Co-operative Society Ltd v Southern Essex Assessment Committee* [1942] 1 KB 53, [1941] 3 All ER 252, the Divisional Court held that a laundry canteen was part of the factory, since it was a necessary and essential feature of the premises for the welfare of the workers engaged in the industrial part of the undertaking, and this decision was followed in *Luttman v Imperial Chemical Industries* [1955] 3 All ER 481, [1955] 1 WLR 980 where a canteen used for feeding and entertaining the people working in the factory was held to be part of the factory. *Thomas'* case, above, was not cited to the court in *Luttman v Imperial Chemical Industries Ltd* and the difference in result would appear to depend upon the absence, in *Thomas'* case, of any substantial benefit to the industrial workers by means of the activities of the restaurant.

In *Longhurst v Guildford, Godalming and District Water Board* [1963] AC 265, [1961] 3 All ER 545, HL, it was held that a pump house which merely sent filtered water on its way to consumers was not part of a factory; compare *Newton v John Stanning & Son Ltd* [1962] 1 All ER 78, [1962] 1 WLR 30, in which a pump-house, used to pump water under pressure into a mill in a factory, was held to be part of the factory.

In *Powley v Bristol Siddeley Engines Ltd* [1965] 3 All ER 612, [1966] 1 WLR 729, it was held that an administration block in a factory was part of it, because the activities carried on therein (such as the designing, drawing and indirect development of aircraft engines) were processes incidental to the making of such engines.

In *King v Magnatex Ltd* (1951) 44 R & IT 742, it was held that a workshop in a factory which had been cleared of machinery and benches and had been converted into a hall for a party had ceased to be part of the factory.

If part of the factory is for the time being set aside for the purpose of construction or reconstruction it is a question of fact and degree whether the part set aside falls within this subsection; but radical replacements cannot, normally speaking, be said to be incidental to the main purpose of the factory (*Cox v S Cutler & Sons Ltd and Hampton Court Gas Co* [1948] 2 All ER 665, CA; *Street v British Electricity Authority* [1952] 2 QB 399, [1952] 1 All ER 679, CA; *Walsh v Allweather Mechanical Grouting Co Ltd* [1959] 2 QB 300, [1959] 2 All ER 588, CA).

(z) **The Minister.** For definition, see s. 176(1).

(aa) **Regulations.** As to the making of regulations, see s. 180.

---

176. General interpretation.—(1) In this Act, unless the context otherwise requires, the following expressions have the meanings hereby assigned to them respectively, that is to say—

"bakehouse" means any place in which bread, biscuits or confectionery is or are baked by way of trade or for purposes of gain (a);

"bodily injury" includes injury to health;

"building operation" means the construction, structural alteration, repair or maintenance of a building (b) (including repointing, redecoration and external cleaning of the structure), the demolition of a building, and the preparation for, and laying the foundation of, an intended building, but does not include any operation which is a work of engineering construction within the meaning of this Act (c);

"calendar year" means the period of twelve months beginning with the first day of January in any year;

"child" means any person who is not for the purposes of the Education Act 1944, over compulsory school age (d) (or for the purposes of the Education (Scotland) Act 1980, over school age);

"class or description", in relation to factories, includes a group of factories described by reference to locality;

"contravention" includes, in relation to any provision, a failure to comply with that provision and the expression "contravene" shall be construed accordingly;

"cotton cloth factory" means any room, shed or workshop, or part thereof, in which the weaving of cotton cloth is carried on;

"district council" means, as respects England and Wales, the council of a district (e), and, as respects Scotland, an islands or a district council;

"driving-belt" includes any driving strap or rope;

"fume" includes gas or vapour;

"general register" means the register kept in accordance with the requirements of section one hundred and forty of this Act;

"humid factory" means a factory in which atmospheric humidity is artificially produced by steaming or other means in connection with any textile process;

"inspector" means an inspector appointed by the Health and Safety Executive under s. 19 of the Health and Safety at Work, etc. Act 1974 and references in any provision of this Act to the inspector for the district, the superintending inspector for the division or the chief inspector are references to an inspector so appointed for the purposes of that provision;

"machinery" includes any driving-belt;

"magistrates' court" has the same meaning as in the Magistrates' Courts Act 1980 *(f)*;

"maintained" means maintained in an efficient state, in efficient working order, and in good repair *(g)*;

"the Minister" means the Minister of Labour *(h)*;

"owner"—

(a) as respects England and Wales, means the person for the time receiving the rackrent of the premises in connection with which the word is used, whether on his own account or as agent or trustee for another person or who would so receive the rackrent if the premises were let at a rackrent *(i)*; and

(b) as respects Scotland, means the person for the time entitled to receive or who would, if the same were let, be entitled to receive, the rents of the premises, and includes a trustee factor, tutor or curator, and in the case of public or municipal property, applies to the persons to whom the management thereof is entrusted;

"parent" means a parent of a child or young person or any person who is not a parent of his but who has parental responsibility for him (within the meaning of the Children Act 1989);

"period of employment" means the period (inclusive of the time allowed for meals and rest) within which persons may be employed on any day;

"prescribed" means prescribed by order of the Minister;

"prime mover" means every engine, motor or other appliance which provides mechanical energy derived from steam, water, wind, electricity, the combustion of fuel or other source;

"process" includes the use of any locomotive;

"railway" means any railway used for the purposes of public traffic whether passenger, goods, or other traffic and includes any works of the railway company connected with the railway;

"railway company" includes [. . .] a company or person working a railway under lease or otherwise *(j)*;

"sanitary conveniences" includes urinals, water-closets, earthclosets, privies, ashpits, and any similar convenience;

"ship", "vessel", and "harbour" have the same meanings as in the Merchant Shipping Act 1894 *(k)*;

"tenement factory" means any premises where mechanical power from any prime mover within the close or curtilage of the premises is distributed for use in manufacturing processes to different parts of the same premises occupied by different persons in such manner that those parts constitute in law separate factories;

"tramway" means a tramway authorised by or under any Act of Parliament and used for the purpose of public traffic;

"transmission machinery" means every shaft, wheel, drum, pulley, system of fast and loose pulleys, coupling, clutch, driving-belt or other device *(l)* by which the motion of a prime mover is transmitted to or received by any machine or appliance;

"week" means the period between midnight on Saturday night and midnight on the succeeding Saturday night;

"woman" means a woman who has attained the age of eighteen;

"work of engineering construction"—means the construction of any railway line or siding otherwise than upon an existing railway, and the construction, structural alteration or repair (including repointing and repainting) or the demolition of any dock, harbour, inland navigation, tunnel, bridge, viaduct, waterworks, reservoir, pipeline, aqueduct, sewer, sewage works or gasholder, except where carried on upon a railway or tramway, and includes such other works as may be specified by regulations *(n)* of the Minister;

"young person" means a person who has ceased to be a child *(o)* but has not attained the age of eighteen.

(2) For the purposes of this Act, machinery or plant shall be deemed to have been constructed or reconstructed, and a factory *(p)* or building to have been constructed, reconstructed, extended, added to, or converted for use as a factory, before any date, if the construction, reconstruction, extension, addition, or conversion was begun before that date.

(3) For the purposes of this Act, a factory *(p)* shall not be deemed to be a factory in which mechanical power *(q)* is used by reason only that mechanical power is used for the purpose of heating, ventilating or lighting the workrooms or other parts of the factory.

(4) A woman *(r)*, young person *(s)*, or child *(o)* who works in a factory *(p)*, whether for wages or not, either in a process *(t)* or in cleaning any part of the factory used for any process, or in cleaning or oiling any part of the machinery *(u)* or plant, or in any other kind of work whatsoever incidental to or connected with the process, or connected with the article made or otherwise the subject of the process therein, shall, save as is otherwise provided by this Act, be deemed to be employed therein for the purposes of this Act or of any proceedings thereunder.

(5) A young person *(s)* who works in a factory *(p)*, whether for wages or not, in collecting, carrying or delivering goods, carrying messages or running errands shall be deemed to be employed in the factory for the purposes of this Act or of any proceedings thereunder, but the provisions of Part VI of this Act shall not apply, except as expressly provided to any such young person who is employed mainly outside the factory.

(6) For the purposes of this Act, employment shall be deemed to be continuous unless interrupted by an interval of at least half an hour.

(7) For the purposes of this Act, an apprentice shall be deemed to be a person employed.

(8) This Act shall in its application to London have effect as if for references to district councils there were substituted, as respects the City of London, references to the common council.

(9) References in this Act to any enactment shall be construed as references to that enactment as amended by any subsequent enactment, including this Act.

General note. In sub-s. (5), the words "the provisions of Part VI of this Act shall not apply, except as expressly provided" are substituted by "section 119 of this Act shall not apply" by the Employment Act 1989, s. 29(3), Sch. 6, para. 6, as from a day to be appointed.

(a) **By way of trade or for purposes of gain.** See note (i) to s. 175.

(b) **Construction, etc., of a building.** This definition has been considered in a number of cases under the regulations governing building operations, the questions for decision being (i) the meaning of "a building"; (ii) whether the installation of plant constitutes the construction of a building; and (iii) whether work which contributes to or is ancillary to the construction or the repair and maintenance of a building or to the preparation for an intended building is a building operation.

(i) The term "building" is used in a wide sense (*per* Romer LJ in *Elms v Foster Wheeler* [1954] 2 All ER 714, [1954] 1 WLR 1071). It is quite possible for a structure to be a building notwithstanding that it is not enclosed by walls and a roof, and is not one of the more ordinary forms of buildings; see *McGuire v Power Gas Corpn Ltd* [1961] 2 All ER 544n (catalytic oil plant held to be a building); *Boyle v Kodak Ltd* [1969] 2 All ER 439, [1969] 1 WLR 661, HL (oil tank 30 feet high held to be a building). See, further, *Wood v Cooper* [1894] 3 Ch 671, and *Paddington Corpn v A-G* [1906] AC 1. Each case must depend upon its own facts, bearing in mind the object of the Factories Act 1961 (see *Knight v Demolition and Construction Co Ltd* [1953] 2 All ER 508, [1953] 1 WLR 981). In that case, Parker J held that a part of the plant in a building might be a "building", notwithstanding that it could also be described as plant, and that gas retort blocks in a retort house were accordingly "buildings". On appeal ([1954] 1 All ER 711n, [1954] 1 WLR 563), the point was not dealt with. In *McCallum v Butters Bros & Co Ltd* 1954 SLT (Notes) 45, the Outer House of the Court of Session held that a crane was not a building, and in *Price v Claudgen Ltd* [1967] 1 All ER 695, [1967] 1 WLR 575, HL, it was held, on the particular facts, that a neon sign fixed to the front of a cinema was not part of a building.

(ii) No general answer is possible to the question whether the installation of plant constitutes the construction of a building. It must depend upon the circumstances of each case whether such an operation attracts the regulations in question or not (*Elms v Foster Wheeler Ltd* [1954] 2 All ER 714, [1954] 1 WLR 1071, CA). The words "the construction . . . of a building" should be read "the construction of a building or any part thereof" (*ibid., per* Romer LJ). Thus, in *Elms v Foster Wheeler Ltd*, above, itself, the defendants were under contract to manufacture, deliver and erect four steam generating plants at a power station. On the evidence, the defendants were contributing to the construction of the power station inasmuch as they were installing the essential apparatus which it was the object of the outer walls and roof to house and which was to be united with the structure. The Court of Appeal held that the defendants were taking part in the construction of a building and that therefore the Building (Safety, Health and Welfare) Regulations 1948, applied. A similar conclusion was reached by Ashworth J in *Hughes v McGoff and Vickers Ltd* [1955] 2 All ER 291, [1955] 1 WLR 416 (installation of electric conduit pipes in building under construction) and by Barry J in *Simmons v Bovis Ltd* [1956] 1 All ER 736, [1956] 1 WLR 381 (preparation of lift-shaft in building under construction). In *Hutchinson v Cocksedge & Co Ltd* [1952] 1 All ER 696n, on the other hand, Croom-Johnson J held that the erection of pulp bagging plant in a sugar beet factory was not a building operation, but was merely the provision of plant for a building; and in *Copeland v R & H Green and Silley Weir Ltd* [1954] 2 Lloyd's Rep 315, Finnemore J held that the installation of an exhaust funnel in a blacksmith's shop upon the defendant's premises to deal with exhaust fumes from forges was the provision of plant rather than the construction or structural alteration of a building. The scientific complexity of the operation being carried out is inconclusive upon, if not immaterial to, the question, whether that operation is the "construction . . . of a building"; see *Byers v Head Wrightson & Co Ltd* [1961] 2 All ER 538, [1961] 1 WLR 961 (work in sealed reactor building), in which Elwes J followed the decision of

Salmon J in *McGuire v Power Gas Corpn Ltd* [1961] 2 All ER 544n. In *Baxter v Central Electricity Generating Board* [1964] 2 All ER 815, [1965] 1 WLR 200, Ashworth J held that the installation of pulverising units and their motors in a power station involved the construction of a building.

(iii) Each case must turn on its own facts, but in general, if a workman is doing an act which can fairly be said to form part of or to be contributing to the operation of the construction of a building, he is engaged in a building operation (*Vineer v C Doidge & Sons Ltd* [1972] 2 All ER 794, [1972] 1 WLR 893, CA, *per* Roskill LJ; workman measuring up glass required for glazing the windows of a house under construction). See too *Drysdale v Kelsey Roofing Industries Ltd* 1981 SLT (Notes) 118: surveying a roof in preparation for repairs falls within the definition; and *Beech v Costain-John Brown Ltd* 1950 SLT (Notes) 34. In *Smith v Vange Scaffolding and Engineering Co Ltd* [1970] 1 All ER 249, [1970] 1 WLR 733 it was held that erecting scaffolding for the purpose of a building operation was part of the building operation in which it was used, but a contrary decision was reached on similar facts in *Ritchie v James H Russell & Co* 1966 SC 158, Ct of Sess.

It is a matter of doubt how far the erection or dismantling of scaffolding used in the repair or maintenance of a building is a building operation (*Sexton v Scaffolding (Great Britain) Ltd* [1953] 1 QB 153, [1952] 2 All ER 1085, CA) in *Campbell v City of Glasgow District Council* 1991 SLT 616 the Outer House ruled that the dismantling of a temporary structure of scaffolding was not a building operation. The operation of making a wire profile of a gutter as a pattern for a new gutter is not repair or maintenance (*Sumner v Robert L Priestley Ltd* [1955] 3 All ER 445, [1955] 1 WLR 1202, CA). Cleaning before painting is "redecoration" (*O'Brien v Udec Ltd* (1968) 5 KIR 449, CA) and a glazed roof supported by rafters and purlins is part of the structure of the building, so that cleaning it is a building operation (*Bowie v Great International Plate Glass Insurance Cleaning Co Ltd* (1981) Times, 14 May, CA). Similarly the cleaning of "windows" may amount to a building operation if, for instance, the external structure consists of "glass ... so extensive that it is impossible to say that the structure is pierced by windows" (*per* Bowsher QC in *Potter v Actual Window Cleaning Co*, Queen's Bench Division, 6 March 1987, applying *Bowie v Great International Plate Glass Insurance Cleaning Co Ltd*, (above). However, ordinary internal domestic cleaning is not a building operation (*O'Brien v Udec Ltd*, above, *per* Sachs LJ at 455). Replacement of external lighting forming part of a building is repair or maintenance (*Morter v Electrical Installations Ltd* (1969) 6 KIR 130). The words "the preparation for ... an intended building" should be read as including operations for the preparation for necessary but ancillary work in connection with the intended building (*Horsley v Collier and Catley Ltd* [1965] 2 All ER 423, [1965] 1 WLR 1359, *per* Neild J).

(c) **Work of engineering construction.** This expression is defined later in sub-s. (1).

(d) **Compulsory school age.** See the Education Act 1944, s. 35.

(e) **Council... district.** As respects the City of London the reference is to the common council (s. 176(8)). See also, as to Scotland, s. 181(3).

(f) **Magistrates' Courts Act 1980.** See, ibid., s. 148(1).

(g) **Maintained.** See INTRODUCTORY NOTE 10.

(h) **Minister of Labour.** The reference is now to the Secretary of State for Employment (S.I. 1968 No. 729 and S.I. 1970 No. 1537).

(i) **Owner.** This definition, so far as it relates to England and Wales, may be compared with that contained in s. 90(1) of the Offices, Shops and Railway Premises Act 1963, or in s. 343(1) of the Public Health Act 1936.

A "rackrent" is "a rent of the full value of the tenement or near it" (Blackstone, Comm. 43), and see *London Corpn v Cusack-Smith* [1955] AC 337, [1955] 1 All ER 302, HL. The date at which the question, whether premises are let at a rackrent, is to be investigated, is the date of the lease, and later changes of circumstances are irrelevant (*ibid.*, and see also *Borthwick-Norton v Collier* [1950] 2 KB 594, [1950] 2 All ER 204, CA).

There is no statutory definition of "rackrent" in the Factories Act 1961 (compare the Public Health Act 1936, s. 343(1)). The question, whether the tenant is paying the full, or nearly the full, economic rent of the premises is thus one of fact and degree in the circumstances of any particular case. If the lease contains covenants restricting the use of the premises, these must be taken into account (*Borthwick-Norton v Collier*, above), and the payment of premium for the lease is usually conclusive that the rent received is not a rackrent (*Ex p Connolly to Sheridan and Russell* [1900] 1 IR 1, CA). Other factors which tend to indicate that the rent is not a rackrent are, for example, the surrender by the tenant of an existing lease of the premises at less than the current rent in consideration of the grant of the lease under examination, or the existence of a covenant by the tenant to do extensive repairs immediately upon the grant of the lease.

If premises are let to a tenant at a rackrent, then the landlord is plainly the "owner" within the definition under consideration. If premises are let to a tenant at less than a rackrent, the first limb of the definition does not apply, and the person who "would so receive the rackrent if the premises . . . were let at a rackrent" is the tenant, for he alone is entitled to make a new lease at a rackrent (*London Corpn v Cusack-Smith*, above, *per* Lord Oaksey (at 348; 306), *per* Lord Reid (at 358; 313), *per* Lord Tucker (at 366; 318), and *per* Lord Keith of Avonholm (at 367; 319)). If premises are both let and sublet at rackrents, the head-landlord is undoubtedly an "owner", and, according to some of the opinions expressed in *London Corpn v Cusack-Smith*, above, the intermediate tenant may also be an "owner" (see *ibid.*, *per* Lord Porter (at 353–356; 307–310), *per* Lord Reid (at 358–359; 312–313) and *per* Lord Tucker (at 366; 318)). The opinions thus last expressed turned to some extent upon the presence of the phrase, "any owner", in s. 19(1) of the Town and Country Planning Act 1947, so that it does not necessarily follow from them that a similar construction would be placed upon the wording of the definition now under examination. If premises are let at a rackrent and sublet at less than a rackrent the head-landlord is the "owner"; if premises are let at less than a rackrent and sublet at a rackrent the intermediate tenant is the owner; and if premises and both let and sublet at less than rackrents the sub-tenant is the "owner".

(j) Railway company. The omitted words were repealed by the Transport Act 1962, s. 95 and Sch. 1.

(k) Ship. A hovercraft is not included (Hovercraft Act 1968, s. 4(3)).

(l) Other device. See note *(a)* to s. 13.

(m) Work of engineering construction. In Scotland it has been held that "pipeline" means only a water pipeline: *Griffith v Scottish Gas Board* 1963 SLT 286; but see now the Engineering Construction (Extension of Definition) (No. 2) Regulations, 1968, S.I. 1968 No. 1530, set out below. Interpreting the Statute in accordance with its purpose, in *Cullen v NEI Thompson Ltd* 1992 SLT 1105n the construction of a bridge, although not carried out *in situ*, was held to be within the definition.

(n) Regulations. As to the making of regulations, see s. 180 and the Fourth Schedule. The Regulations set out below are made under this section.

(o) Child. See the definition set out earlier in this subsection and note *(d)*, above.

(p) Factory. For definition, see s. 175.

(q) Mechanical power. See note *(b)* to s. 163.

(r) Woman. See the definition set out in sub-s. (1).

(s) Young person. See the definition set out in sub-s. (1).

(*t*) **Process.** See the definition set out in sub-s. (1).

(*u*) **Machinery.** See the definition set out in sub-s. (1).

THE ENGINEERING CONSTRUCTION (EXTENSION OF DEFINITION) REGULATIONS 1960
(S.I. 1960 No. 421)

The Minister of Labour by virtue of the powers conferred on him by subsection (1) of section one hundred and fifty-two of the Factories Act 1937, and of all other powers enabling him in that behalf, hereby makes the following Regulations:—

1.   These Regulations may be cited as the Engineering Construction (Extension of Definition) Regulations 1960, and shall come into operation on the fifteenth day of May, 1960.

2.—(1) The Interpretation Act 1889 [Interpretation Act 1978] shall apply to the interpretation of these Regulations as it applies to the interpretation of an Act of Parliament.

(2) In these Regulations the expression "the principal Act" means the Factories Act 1937, as amended by or under any other Act.

3.   The definition of the expression "work of engineering construction" in subsection (1) of section one hundred and fifty-two of the principal Act [s. 176(1) of the 1961 Act] shall be extended to include the works specified in the Schedule to these Regulations.

SCHEDULE

Regulation 3

WORKS TO BE INCLUDED IN THE DEFINITION OF THE EXPRESSION
"WORK OF ENGINEERING CONSTRUCTION"

The construction, structural alteration or repair (including re-pointing and re-painting) or the demolition of any of the following except where carried on—

(a)   in a factory as defined in section one hundred and fifty-one of the principal Act [s. 175 of the 1961 Act] or on premises to which that Act applies by virtue of subsection (1) of section one hundred and three thereof [s. 123(1) of the 1961 Act]; or

(b)   upon a railway or tramway,

that is to say, any steel or reinforced concrete structure other than a building, any road, airfield, sea defence works or river works, and any other civil or constructional engineering works of a similar nature to any of the foregoing works.

Note. These Regulations should be interpreted as extending, and not impliedly restricting, the ambit of "work or engineering construction" in the Factories Act (see *Cullen v NEI Thompson Ltd* 1992 SLT 1105n. The words "steel or reinforced concrete structure" do not include a ship (*Shepherd v Pearson Engineering Services (Dundee) Ltd* 1981 SLT 197 and 1980 SC 268) and the words "structure other than a building" are not limited to permanent works forming part of the land on which they stand; the supporting lattice-work and platform of a dockside crane which can be moved on rails is a steel structure within the meaning of the Schedule or, at any rate, an engineering work of a similar nature to such a structure, the words "the foregoing works" including "any . . . structure other than a building" as well as "any road, airfield, sea defence works or river works": *British Transport Docks Board v Williams* [1970] 1 All ER 1135, [1970] 1 WLR 652, DC. In *Park v Tractor Shovels Ltd* 1980 SLT 94 it was held that the repair and maintenance of vehicles is not encompassed by the words "works of engineering construction".

THE ENGINEERING CONSTRUCTION (EXTENSION OF
DEFINITION) (No. 2) REGULATIONS 1968
(S.I. 1968 No. 1530)

The Secretary of State by virtue of her powers under section 176(1) of the Factories Act
1961 and of all other powers enabling her in that behalf, hereby makes the following
Regulations—

1.—(1) These Regulations may be cited as the Engineering Construction (Extension
of Definition) (No. 2) Regulations 1968 and shall come into operation on 15 November
1968.

(2) The Interpretation Act 1889 [Interpretation Act 1978] shall apply to the
interpretation of these Regulations as it applies to the interpretation of an Act of
Parliament.

2. The definition of the expression "work of engineering construction" in
section 176(1) (general interpretation) of the Factories Act 1961 as extended by the
Engineering Construction (Extension of Definition) Regulations 1960 shall be further
extended to include the works specified in the Schedule to these Regulations.

SCHEDULE

Regulation 2

WORKS TO BE INCLUDED IN THE DEFINITION OF THE EXPRESSION
"WORK OF ENGINEERING CONSTRUCTION"

The construction, structural alteration or repair (including re-painting) or the demolition of any pipeline for the conveyance of any thing other than water, except where
carried on upon a railway or tramway.

General

177. [*repealed*].

---

178. Certificates of birth.—(1) Where the age of any person is required to be
ascertained or proved for the purposes of this Act, any person shall, on
presenting a written requisition in such form and containing such particulars as
the Minister of Housing and Local Government or, as respects Scotland, the
Secretary of State may by regulations prescribe *(a)* and on payment of a fee of
£1.50, be entitled to obtain a certified extract under the hand of a registrar or
superintendent registrar of births and deaths of the entry in the register under
the Births and Deaths Registration Act 1953, or the Registration of Births,
Deaths and Marriages (Scotland) Act 1965, of the birth of that person.

(2) A form of such a requisition shall on request be supplied without charge
by every superintendent registrar and registrar of births and deaths.

(a) **Prescribed form.** Forms of requisition which, pursuant to sub-s. (2), are supplied without charge are prescribed for England by S.R. & O. 1937 No. 885, and for Scotland by S.R. & O. 1938 No. 601/S. 36.

---

179. [*repealed*].

---

180. Regulations, rules and orders.—(1) Any regulations, rules or orders made under this Act shall be made by statutory instrument, except an order applicable only to particular persons, premises, boilers, employment, operations or work or to persons employed at particular premises or on work supervised from particular premises.

(2) Any statutory instrument containing regulations under this Act shall be subject to annulment in pursuance of a resolution of either House of Parliament.

(3) Any power conferred by this Act to make regulations, rules or orders shall include power to make different provisions in relation to different circumstances.

(4) Any power conferred by this Act to make an order shall include power to revoke such an order by a subsequent order and the provisions of s. 50 of the Health and Safety at Work, etc. Act 1974 shall apply to any such power which is exercisable by statutory instrument as they apply to a power to make regulations.

(5) [*repealed*].

(6) Any power conferred by this Act to prescribe standards or impose requirements shall include power to do so by reference to the approval of the chief inspector *(a)* or of the chief employment medical adviser or a deputy chief employment medical adviser.

(7)–(8) [*repealed*].

(9) Any regulations or order made by the Minister under this Act may be made for a limited period or without limit of period and may be made subject to such conditions as he thinks fit, and may contain such supplemental and consequential provisions as he considers necessary for giving full effect to the regulations or order.

(10) [*repealed*].

General note. Regulations and orders made under the Factory and Workshop Act 1901 and the Factories Acts 1937 to 1959, which were in force at the commencement of this Act, are continued in force by virtue of s. 183 and Sch. 6.

By the Statutory Instruments Act 1946, ss. 4, 5(1) and 5(2), a copy of any rules, orders or regulations is to be laid before Parliament before, in general, they come into operation, and if either House within the next 40 days resolves that the regulations shall be annulled they will be of no effect, but without prejudice to the validity of anything done in the meantime or to the making of new regulations. When the forty days have elapsed after the order has been laid before Parliament, it has the effect of a statute and its validity, if it is *intra vires*, cannot be questioned; see *Institute of Patent Agent's v Lockwood* [1894] AC 347 and *Hamilton v Fyfe* 1907 SC (J) 79. But if the order was altogether *ultra vires*, it would appear that its validity can be questioned, even after the forty days: see *Mackey v James Henry Monks (Preston) Ltd* [1918] AC 59 and also the report of the same cases in the court below in [1916] 2 IR 200. Subordinate legislation is discussed in 44 *Halsbury's Laws* (4th edn.) 981 *et seq.*

(a) **Chief inspector.** For definition, see s. 176(1), "inspector".

---

181. Substitution of corresponding provisions for certain provisions of Factory and Workshop Act 1901.—(1) The provisions contained in the Fifth Schedule to this Act (being provisions of the Factory and Workshop Act 1901, which do not apply in England, set out with the necessary modifications) shall have effect in Scotland in lieu of the corresponding provisions repealed by the Factories Act 1937.

(2) [*repealed*].

---

182.   General application to Scotland.—(1) The provisions of this section shall, in addition to any express provision *(a)* for the application to Scotland of any provision of this Act, have effect for the general application of this Act to Scotland.

(2) [*repealed*].

(3) All matters required by this Act to be published in the London Gazette shall, if they relate to Scotland, be published in the Edinburgh Gazette either in addition or in substitution, as the case may require.

(4) Any offence against this Act for which the maximum penalty that may be imposed does not exceed ten pounds may be prosecuted in any court of summary jurisdiction within the meaning of the Criminal Procedure (Scotland) Act 1975 having jurisdiction in the place where the offence was committed.

(5)–(6) [*repealed*].

(7) Every person convicted of an offence against this Act may be found liable in expenses.

(8) Section twenty-nine of the Public Health (Scotland) Act 1897 shall not apply in relation to any factory *(b)* within the meaning of this Act.

(9) Any powers exercisable by an inspector appointed by a county or town council (or, on or after 16 May, 1975, by the islands or district council) under s. 19 of the Health and Safety at Work etc. Act 1974 shall, for the purposes of their duties under the Public Health (Scotland) Act 1897, extend to factories within the meaning of that Act.

General note. In s. 182(4) a reference to the Criminal Procedure (Scotland) Act 1975 is substituted for the reference to the Summary Jurisdiction (Scotland) Act 1954 by virtue of s. 460(1)(b) of the 1975 Act.

(*a*) **Express provision.** See s. 56.

(*b*) **Factory.** For definition, see s. 175.

---

183. Transitional provisions and repeals.—(1) This Act shall have effect subject to the provisions of the Sixth Schedule to this Act.

(2) [*repealed*].

---

184. Construction of references in other enactments to factories and work-shops, etc. and exclusion of certain provisions of Public Health (London) Act 1936.—(1) Nothing in this Act shall affect the definition of the expressions "factory" and "workshop" for the purposes of the Rating and Valuation (Apportionment) Act 1928, but save as aforesaid references in any enactment to a factory or workshop within the meaning of the Factory and Workshop Acts 1901 to 1929, or any of those Acts, shall be construed as references to a factory within the meaning of this Act.

(2)–(3) [*repealed*].

---

185. Short title, commencement and extent.—(1) This Act may be cited as the Factories Act 1961.

(2) This Act shall come into force on the first day of April, nineteen hundred and sixty-two.

(3) This Act, except subsections (1) and (2) of section seventy-seven, does not extend to Northern Ireland (*a*).

(*a*) **Application of the Act.** The Act applies generally to Scotland, subject to the modifications introduced by ss. 56, 181 and 182.

For statutory provisions as to safety in off-shore and similar installations, see the general note to s. 172.

1500   *The Factories Act 1961*

FIRST SCHEDULE

Section 68

TABLE OF HUMIDITY

I Dry Bulb Temperature	II Wet Bulb Temperature
Degrees Celsius	Degrees Celsius
10	9
11	10
12	11
13	11
14	13
15	14
16	15
17	16
18	17
19	18
20	19
21	20
22	20.5
23	21
24	22
25	22.5
26	23.5
27	24
28	25
29	26
30	26.5

General note. Substituted by the Factories Act 1961 etc. (Metrication) Regulations 1983, S.I. 1983 No. 978, save in relation to premises in existence before 12 August 1983.

SECOND SCHEDULE

[*repealed*].

THIRD SCHEDULE

[*repealed*].

FOURTH SCHEDULE

[*repealed*].

FIFTH SCHEDULE

Section 181

PROVISIONS OF THE FACTORY AND WORKSHOP ACT 1901, APPLICABLE IN LONDON AND SCOTLAND ONLY AND ADMINISTERED BY DISTRICT COUNCILS

s. 61. Prohibition of employment of women after childbirth. If the occupier of a factory knowingly allows a woman or girl to be employed therein within four weeks after she has given birth to a child, he shall be liable to a fine not exceeding level 1 on the standard scale, or if the offence was committed during the night level 1 on the standard scale, for each person so employed, and in the case of a second or subsequent conviction within two years after the last conviction for the like offence not less than level 1 on the standard scale for each offence *(a)*.

s. 109. Making of wearing apparel where there is scarlet fever or smallpox. If the occupier of a factory or of any place from which any work is given out, or any contractor employed by any such occupier, causes or allows wearing apparel to be made, cleaned, or repaired, in any dwelling-house or building occupied therewith, while any inmate of the dwelling-house is suffering from scarlet fever or smallpox, then, unless he proves that he was not aware of the existence of the disease in the dwelling-house, and could not reasonably have been expected to become aware of it, he shall be guilty of an offence and liable to a fine not exceeding level 1 on the standard scale.

s. 110. Prohibition of home work in places where there is infectious disease.—(1) If any inmate of a house is suffering from an infectious disease to which this section applies, the district council of the district in which the house is situate may make an order forbidding any work to which this section applies to be given out to any person living or working in that house, or such part thereof as may be specified in the order, and any order so made may be served on the occupier of any factory, or any other place from which work is given out, or on the contractor employed by any such occupier.

(2) The order may be made notwithstanding that the person suffering from an infectious disease may have been removed from the house and the order shall be made either for a specified time or subject to the conditiion that the house or part thereof liable to be infected shall be disinfected to the satisfaction of the designated medical officer, or that other reasonable precautions shall be adopted.

(3) In any case of urgency the powers conferred on the district council by this section may be exercised by any two or more members of the council acting on the advice of the designated medical officer.

(4) If any occupier or contractor on whom an order under this section has been served contravenes the provisions of the order, he shall be guilty of an offence and liable to a fine not exceeding level 1 on the standard scale.

(5) The infectious diseases to which this section applies are the infectious diseases required to be notified under the law for the time being in force in relation to the notification of infectious diseases *(b)*, and the work to which this section applies is the making, cleaning, washing, altering, ornamenting, finishing and repairing of wearing apparel and any work incidental thereto, and such other classes of work as may be specified by order *(c)* of the Minister of Health or, as respects Scotland, the Secretary of State.

General note. This Schedule, as from 1 April 1965, has effect only in Scotland (London Government Act 1963, s. 93(1), Sch. 18).

In the Fifth Schedule a fine at level 1 on the standard scale is substituted for each of the fines mentioned by virtue of the Criminal Procedure (Scotland) Act 1975, s. 289G. Certain of these fines were previously increased by s. 289C(3), (5), (8).

(a) Employment after childbirth. The employment of women in a factory within four weeks after childbirth is prohibited by the Public Health Act 1936, s. 205.

(b) Infectious diseases. See, as to England, the Public Health (Control of Diseases) Act 1984, ss. 10, 11 and 16, and, as to Scotland, the Infectious Diseases (Notification) Act 1889, applied by s. 44 of the Public Health (Scotland) Act 1897.

(c) Classes of work specified by order. The classes of work to which this section applies were specified in the Home Work Order of 10 April, 1911 (S.R. & O. 1911 No. 394), as extended by subsequent orders.

SIXTH SCHEDULE

Section 183

TRANSITIONAL PROVISIONS

1. Any reference in any enactment or document, whether express or implied, to any enactment repealed by this Act or by any enactment so repealed or to any provision contained in any such enactment shall be construed as a reference to this Act or, as the case may be, to the corresponding provision of this Act.

2. Any order, regulation, rule, byelaw or appointment made, direction, certificate or notice given, or other thing done under any provision contained in an enactment repealed by this Act or by an enactment so repealed shall continue in force and—
  (a) if it could have been made, given or done under the corresponding provision of this Act, shall have effect as if it had been so made, given or done;
  (b) if it is an order or regulation made under a power which, under the corresponding provision of this Act, is exercisable by a different class of instrument, shall have effect as if it were an instrument of that class made under that provision.

3. [*repealed*].

4.—(1) Subject to sub-paragraph (2) of this paragraph, a factory which has been furnished with a certificate in pursuance of subsection (1) of section fourteen of the Factory and Workshop Act 1901, and a factory in respect of which a notice issued in pursuance of subsection (2) of that section has been complied with, or in respect of which an award has been made under subsection (3) of that section and has been complied with, shall be entitled to receive a certificate under section forty of this Act and, pending the receipt of the certificate, no offence shall be deemed to be committed by reason of the use of the factory while no certificate under this section is in force with respect to it.

(2) Sub-paragraph (1) of this paragraph shall only apply to any factory if and so long as the means of escape provided therein are properly maintained, and shall not apply to any factory if, since the certificate was furnished or the notice or award was complied with in pursuance of the said section fourteen, any action has been taken of which notice would, if this Act had been in force and a certificate under section forty had been granted, have been required by section forty-one of this Act to be given to the fire authority.

5. In the case of any factory constructed or coverted for use as a factory before the coming into operation of section thirty-four of the Factories Act 1937, (that is to say the first day of July, nineteen hundred and thirty-eight) which is not a factory to which paragraph 4 of this Schedule applies, no offence shall be deemed to be committed under section forty of this Act by reason of the use of the factory during any period that may elapse before the grant or refusal of a certificate under that section by the fire authority, and if the fire authority refuse to grant a certificate in respect of the factory unless alterations are made, no such offence shall be deemed to be committed while the alterations are being carried out in accordance with the requirements of the authority.

6.   Where, before the coming into operation of the First Schedule to the Factories Act 1959, (that is to say the first day of December, nineteen hundred and sixty) a certificate was issued under section thirty-four of the Factories Act 1937 with respect to such a factory as is mentioned in paragraph 1 of the Second Schedule to this Act, but—

(a)   neither the certificate nor a copy thereof was issued to the owner of the building in which the factory is comprised; or

(b)   neither the certificate nor a copy thereof or of the relevant part thereof was issued to the occupier of the factory,

the council by whom the certificate was issued shall, at his request, send him a copy thereof or, as the case may be, of the relevant part thereof; and the owner may, in the case of any such certificate, comply with the requirement as to its registration by attaching a copy thereof to the register mentioned in sub-paragraph (c) of paragraph 8 of the Second Schedule to this Act.

7.   Any order made under Regulation 59 of the Defence (General) Regulations 1939, which is in force at the commencement of this Act shall continue in force, but may be revoked by order of the Minister; and any provision made by an order continued in force by this paragraph which could have been made by special regulations under section one hundred and seventeen of this Act shall be deemed, until the order is revoked, to be contained in such regulations.

8.   The mention of particular matters in this Schedule shall be without prejudice to the general application of section thirty-eight of the Interpretation Act 1889 (which relates to the effect of repeals).

SEVENTH SCHEDULE

[*repealed*].

THE ABRASIVE WHEELS
REGULATIONS 1970

(S.I. 1970 No. 535, as amended by S.I. 1992 No. 2932 and S.I. 1992 No. 3004)

[Placard: Form 2345]

The Secretary of State:

    (a) by virtue of her powers under sections, 17(3), 76 and 180(6) and (7) of the Factories Act 1961 and of all other powers enabling her in that behalf; and

    (b) after publishing, pursuant to Schedule 4 to the said Act of 1961, notice of the proposal to make the special Regulations and after the holding of an inquiry under that Schedule into objections made to the draft,

hereby makes the following Regulations of which all, with the exception of Regulation 19, are special Regulations:—

1. Citation, commencement and revocation.—(1) These Regulations may be cited as the Abrasive Wheels Regulations 1970 and shall come into operation on 2 April 1971.

    (2) *[spent]*.

2. Interpretation.—(1) The Interpretation Act 1889 [Interpretation Act 1978] shall apply to the interpretation of these Regulations as it applies to the interpretation of an Act of Parliament and as if these Regulations and the Regulations hereby revoked were Acts of Parliament.

    (2) For the purposes of these Regulations, unless the context otherwise requires, the following expressions have the meanings hereby assigned to them respectively, that is to say:—

"*abrasive wheel*" means—

    (a) a wheel, cylinder, disc or cone which, whether or not any other material is comprised therein, consists of abrasive particles held together by mineral, metallic or organic bonds whether natural or artificial;

    (b) a *mounted wheel or point* and a wheel or disc having in either case separate segments of abrasive material;

    (c) a wheel or disc in either case of metal, wood, cloth, felt, rubber or paper and having any surface consisting wholly or partly of abrasive material; and

    (d) a wheel, disc or saw to any surface of any of which is attached a rim or segments consisting in either case of diamond abrasive particles,

and which is, or is intended to be, power driven and which is for use in any grinding or cutting operation;

"*approved*" means approved for the time being for the purposes of these Regulations by certificate of the Chief Inspector;

"*factory*" includes any place to which these Regulations apply *(a)*;

"*mounted wheel or point*" means a wheel or point consisting in either case of abrasive particles held together by mineral, metallic or organic bonds whether natural or artificial and securely and permanently mounted on the end of a mandrel or quill;

"*overhang*" means in relation to a mounted wheel or point that part of the mandrel or quill which is exposed between the collet in which the mandrel or quill is held and the part of the abrasive material nearest to the said collet;

"*principal Act*" means the Factories Act 1961 as amended by or under any other Act.

(a) Place ... apply. See reg. 3(1).

3.   Application and operation of Regulations.—(1) These Regulations, other than regulation 19, shall apply to any *abrasive wheel* used for any grinding or cutting operation in any of the following, that is to say, *factories* and any premises, places, processes, operations and works to which the provisions of Part IV of the *principal Act* with respect to special Regulations for safety and health are applied by any of the following provisions of that Act, namely, section 123 (which relates to electrical stations), section 124 (which relates to institutions), section 125 (which relates to certain dock premises and certain warehouses), section 126 (which relates to ships) and section 127 (which relates to building operations and works of engineering construction).

(2) In relation to *abrasive wheels*, the provisions of these Regulations are in substitution for the provisions of section 14(1)(a) of the *principal Act* and accordingly the provisions of that subsection shall not apply in relation to any *abrasive wheel.*

(3) Regulation 19 shall apply to any *abrasive wheel* (other than an *abrasive wheel* of any of the kinds referred to in regulation 4(1), (4) and (6), and to any machine of the kind referred to in regulation 7(1).

(4) Regulations 67(2) of the Shipbuilding and Ship-repairing Regulations 1960 and Regulation 42 of the Construction (General Provisions) Regulations 1961 shall not apply in relation to any *abrasive wheel.*

General note. Paragraphs (2)–(4) are revoked by the Provision and Use of Work Equipment Regulations 1992, S.I. 1992 No. 2932, as from 1 January 1993 except, insofar as they apply to work equipment first provided for use in the premises or undertaking before 1 January 1993, they are revoked as from 1 January 1997.

(a) Section 14(1). This provision removes, in respect of abrasive wheels, the difficulties occasioned by the decison in *John Summers & Sons Ltd v Frost* [1955] AC 740, [1955] 1 All ER 870, HL, as to which see the Introductory Note to sections 12–16 of the Factories Act 1961.

4.   Exceptions.—(1) Regulations 6, 7, 11 (a) and (b), 12 and 19 shall not apply to any *abrasive wheel* manufactured of metal, wood, cloth, felt, rubber or paper and having any surface consisting wholly or partly of abrasive material.

(2) Regulations 11(a) and (b) and 12 shall not apply to any *abrasive wheel* which consists wholly of abrasive particles held together by natural bonds.

(3) Regulation 6 shall not apply to any *abrasive wheel* having separate segments of abrasive materials.

(4) Regulations 6, 7, 10(1), 11, 12, 18 and 19 shall not apply to any *abrasive wheel* which does not exceed 235 millimetres in diameter, is manufactured of cloth, felt, rubber or paper and has any surface consisting wholly or partly of abrasive material, when that *abrasive wheel* is used, or in the case of regulation 19, is for use, in a portable machine.

(5) Regulations 7, 10(1), 11, and 12 shall not apply to any *abrasive wheel* when it is used for the grinding of glass.

(6) Regulations 6, 7, 12 and 19 shall not apply to any wheel, disc or saw being a wheel, disc or saw of a kind specified in regulation 2(2)(d).

General note. This regulation is revoked by the Provision and Use of Work Equipment Regulations 1992, S.I. 1992 No. 2932, as from 1 January 1993 except, insofar as it applies to work equipment first provided for use in the premises or undertaking before 1 January 1993, it is revoked as from 1 January 1997.

5. Exemptions. The Chief Inspector *(a)* may (subject to such conditions, if any, as may be specified therein) by certificate in writing (which he may in his discretion revoke at any time) exempt from all or any of the requirements of these Regulations—

(a) any particular *abrasive wheel* or any type of *abrasive wheel*; or
(b) any machine or part of a machine or any class or description of machines or parts of machines; or
(c) any operation or process or any class or description of operations or processes,

if he is satisfied that the said requirements in respect of which the exemption is granted are impracticable *(b)* or inappropriate or are not necessary for the protection of persons employed.

General note. The following Certificates of Exemption are in force: No. 1 (F 2353); No. 2 (F 2354); No. 3 (F 2355); No. 4 (F 2364); No. 6 (F 2365); No. 7 (F 2367) and No. 10 (F 2507); they are set out following these Regulations.

(a) Inspector. See INTRODUCTORY NOTE 24.

(b) Impracticable. See INTRODUCTORY NOTE 5.

6. Speeds of abrasive wheels.—(1) No *abrasive wheel* having a diameter of more than 55 millimetres shall be taken into use in any *factory* for the first time in that *factory* after the coming into operation of these Regulations unless the *abrasive wheel* or its washer is clearly marked with the maximum permissible speed in revolutions per minute specified by the manufacturer for that *abrasive wheel*.

(2) No *abrasive wheel* having a diameter of 55 millimetres or less shall be taken into use in any *factory* for the first time in that *factory* after the coming into operation of these Regulations unless there is kept permanently fixed in the room in which grinding is ordinarily carried out with that *abrasive wheel* a notice

[Forms 2350 and 2351] clearly stating the maximum permissible speed in revolutions per minute specified by the manufacturer for that *abrasive wheel* or for *abrasive wheels* of the class to which that *abrasive wheel* belongs and, in the case of *mounted wheels and points*, the *overhang* permissible at that speed:

Provided that when grinding with such an *abrasive wheel* is not ordinarily carried out in any one room the said notice shall be kept posted at a place and in a position where it may easily be read by persons employed in grinding with that *abrasive wheel*.

(3) No *abrasive wheel* shall be operated at a speed in excess of the maximum permissible speed in revolutions per minute specified in accordance with the foregoing provisions of this regulation for that *abrasive wheel*:

Provided that where the diameter of an *abrasive wheel* has been reduced its said maximum permissible speed may be increased to that speed which bears the same proportion to the said maximum permissible speed as the original diameter of the *abrasive wheel* bears to its reduced diameter.

General note. This regulation is revoked by the Provision and Use of Work Equipment Regulations 1992, S.I. 1992 No. 2932, as from 1 January 1993 except, insofar as it applies to work equipment first provided for use in the premises or undertaking before 1 January 1993, it is revoked as from 1 January 1997.

In certain circumstances this regulation does not apply; see reg. 4(1), (3), (4) and (6).

7. Speeds of spindles.—(1) There shall be securely affixed to every power driven machine having any spindle on which an *abrasive wheel* is, or is intended to be, mounted a notice specifying—

(a) in the case of each such spindle (other than a spindle to which sub-paragraph (b) or (c) of this paragraph applies) its maximum working speed;

(b) in the case of any such spindle for which there are provided arrangements for operating the spindle at more than one specific working speed, each such speed; and

(c) in the case of any such spindle for which there are provided arrangements for operating the spindle at any infinite number or working speeds within a specified range, the maximum and minimum working speeds of the spindle.

(2) No such spindle shall while an *abrasive wheel* is mounted on it be operated at a speed in excess of the maximum working speed specified in accordance with the foregoing provisions of this regulation for that spindle.

(3) The occupier shall, when so required by an inspector, provide him with all facilities and information as are necessary to enable him to determine the working speed of any spindle, shaft, pulley, or other appliance, which is used to operate an *abrasive wheel*.

(4) The speed of every air driven spindle on which an *abrasive wheel* is mounted shall be controlled by a governor or other device so that the speed of the spindle does not at any time exceed the maximum working speed specified for that spindle in accordance with paragraph (1) of this regulation.

(5) Every governor and other device used for controlling the speed of an air driven spindle on which an *abrasive wheel* is mounted shall be properly maintained *(a)*.

General note. This Regulation is revoked by the Provision and Use of Work Equipment Regulations 1992, S.I. 1992 No. 2932, as from 1 January 1993 except, insofar as it applies to work equipment first provided for use in the premises or undertaking before 1 January 1993, it is revoked as from 1 January 1997.

In certain circumstances this regulation does not apply; see reg. 4(1), (4), (5) and (6).

(a) *Properly maintained.* See INTRODUCTORY NOTE 10.

8.   Mounting.   Every *abrasive wheel* shall be properly mounted.

General note. This Regulation is revoked by the Provision and Use of Work Equipment Regulations 1992, S.I. 1992 No. 2932, as from 1 January 1993 except, insofar as it applies to work equipment first provided for use in the premises or undertaking before 1 January 1993, it is revoked as from 1 January 1997.

9.   Training and appointment of persons to mount abrasive wheels.—
(1) Except as provided in paragraphs (4) and (5) of this regulation, no person shall mount any *abrasive wheel* unless he—

(a) has been trained in accordance with the Schedule to these Regulations;
(b) is competent to carry out that duty; and
(c) has been appointed by the occupier of the factory to carry out that duty in respect of the class or description of *abrasive wheel* to which the *abrasive wheel* belongs; and every such appointment shall be made by a signed and dated entry in, or signed and dated certificate attached to, a register [Form 2346] kept for the purposes of this regulation.

(2) Particulars of the class or description of *abrasive wheel* to which any appointment made in accordance with paragraph (1)(c) of this regulation relates shall be set out in the entry or certificate (as the case may be) of the appointment. Every person appointed under the said paragraph (1)(c) shall be furnished by the occupier with a copy of the entry or certificate of his appointment and of any entry revoking the same.

(3) Any appointment made under paragraph (1)(e) of this regulation may be revoked by the occupier at any time by signed and dated entry in the said register.

(4) Paragraph (1) of this regulation shall not apply to a person who is undergoing training in the work of mounting *abrasive wheels* and working under the immediate supervision (a) of a competent person appointed under the said paragraph (1).

(5) Paragraph (1) of this regulation shall not apply to any person who mounts any *mounted wheel or point.*

(a) *Immediate supervision.* It is submitted that the constant presence of the supervisor is required; cf. note (a) to reg. 17 of the Construction (General Provisions) Regulations 1961.

10.   Provision of guards.—(1) Except as provided in paragraph (2) of this regulation, a guard shall be provided and kept in position at every *abrasive wheel* in motion.

(2) Paragraph (1) of this regulation shall not apply to an *abrasive wheel* where, by reason of the work being done thereat, or of the work which is ordinarily done thereat (or, in the case of a new wheel, is intended ordinarily to be done thereat), or the nature of the wheel, the use of a guard is impracticable *(a)*.

General note. This regulation is revoked by the Provision and Use of Work Equipment Regulations 1992, S.I. 1992 No. 2932, as from 1 January 1993 except, insofar as it applies to work equipment first provided for use in the premises or undertaking before 1 January 1993, it is revoked as from 1 January 1997.

In certain circumstances, para. 1 of this regulation does not apply: see reg. 4(4), (5). Further, by Certificate of Exemption No. 6 (Form 2365), para. 1 does not apply to the operation of determining the working speed of any spindle, shaft, pulley or other appliance, which is used to operate an abrasive wheel.

(a) Impracticable. See INTRODUCTORY NOTE 5.

11. Construction, maintenance, etc., of guards. Every guard provided in pursuance of these Regulations shall—

(a) so far as is reasonably practicable *(a)*, be of such a design and so constructed as to contain every part of the *abrasive wheel* in the event of any fracture of the *abrasive wheel* or of any part thereof occurring while the *abrasive wheel* is in motion;

(b) be properly maintained *(b)* and so secured as to prevent its displacement in the event of any such fracture as aforesaid; and

(c) enclose the whole of the *abrasive wheel* except such part thereof as is necessarily exposed *(c)* for the purpose of any work being done at that *abrasive wheel* or, where a guard which is not adjustable is used, for the purpose of the work which is ordinarily done thereat (or, in the case of a new *abrasive wheel*, is intended ordinarily to be done thereat).

General note. This regulation is revoked by the Provision and Use of Work Equipment Regulations 1992, S.I. 1992 No. 2932, as from 1 January 1993 except, insofar as it applies to work equipment first provided for use in the premises or undertaking before 1 January 1993, it is revoked as from 1 January 1997.

For exceptions to this regulation, see reg. 4(1), (2), (4) and (5).

(a) Reasonably practicable. See INTRODUCTORY NOTE 5.

(b) Properly maintained. See INTRODUCTORY NOTE 10.

(c) Necessarily exposed. See the notes to s. 15 of the Factories Act 1961.

12. Tapered wheels and protection flanges.—(1) Where the work which is ordinarily done (or, in the case of a new *abrasive wheel*, is intended ordinarily to be done) at any *abrasive wheel* requires that the exposed arc of the wheel shall exceed 180 degrees measured at the centre of the wheel then, where practicable *(a)*, the wheel used shall be tapered from its centre towards its periphery by at least 6 per cent. on each side and shall be mounted between suitable protection flanges.

(2) Protection flanges between which any *abrasive wheel* is mounted in accordance with this regulation shall be of substantial construction and prop-

erly maintained *(b)* and shall have the same degree of taper as the wheel and shall—

(a) in the case of a wheel of 300 millimetres or less in diameter, be of a diameter equal to at least half the diameter of the wheel;

(b) in the case of a wheel of more than 300 millimetres but not exceeding 750 millimetres in diameter, be of a diameter equal to at least the diameter of the wheel less 150 millimetres; and

(c) in the case of a wheel of more than 750 millimetres in diameter, be of a diameter equal to at least the diameter of the wheel less 200 millimetres.

General note. This regulation is revoked by the Provision and Use of Work Equipment Regulations 1992, S.I. 1992 No. 2932, as from 1 January 1993 except, insofar as it applies to work equipment first provided for use in the premises or undertaking before 1 January 1993, it is revoked as from 1 January 1997.

For exceptions to this regulation, see reg. 4(1), (2), (4), (5) and (6).

(a) Practicable. See INTRODUCTORY NOTE 5.

(b) Properly maintained. See INTRODUCTORY NOTE 10.

13.   Selection of *abrasive wheels*. All practicable *(a)* steps shall be taken to ensure that any *abrasive wheel* used is suitable for the work for which it is used to the extent necessary to reduce the risk of injury to persons employed.

General note. This regulation is revoked by the Provision and Use of Work Equipment Regulations 1992, S.I. 1992 No. 2932, as from 1 January 1993 except, insofar as it applies to work equipment first provided for use in the premises or undertaking before 1 January 1993, it is revoked as from 1 January 1997.

(a) Practicable. See INTRODUCTORY NOTE 5.

14.   Machine controls. No *abrasive wheel* shall be used in a machine unless the said machine is provided with an efficient device or efficient devices for starting, and cutting off, the power to the machine and the control or controls of the device or devices shall be in such a position and of such design and construction as to be readily and conveniently operated by the person operating the machine.

General note. This regulation is revoked by the Provision and Use of Work Equipment Regulations 1992, S.I. 1992 No. 2932, as from 1 January 1993 except, insofar as it applies to work equipment first provided for use in the premises or undertaking before 1 January 1993, it is revoked as from 1 January 1997.

15.   Rests.—(1) Where at any *abrasive wheel* there is a rest for supporting a workpiece that rest shall at all times while the wheel is in motion be—

(a) properly secured; and

(b) adjusted so as to be as close as practicable *(a)* to the exposed part of the *abrasive wheel.*

(2) Every such rest as aforesaid shall be of substantial construction and properly maintained *(b)*.

General note. This regulation is revoked by the Provision and Use of Work Equipment Regulations 1992, S.I. 1992 No. 2932, as from 1 January 1993 except, insofar as it applies to work equipment first provided for use in the premises or undertaking before 1 January 1993, it is revoked as from 1 January 1997.

(*a*) *Practicable.* See INTRODUCTORY NOTE 5.

(*b*) *Properly maintained.* See INTRODUCTORY NOTE 10.

16.   Cautionary notice. The *approved* cautionary notice [Form 2347] as to the dangers arising from the use of *abrasive wheels* and the precautions to be observed shall be affixed in every room in which grinding or cutting by means of *abrasive wheels* is ordinarily carried out, or, where such grinding or cutting is not ordinarily carried out in a room, at a place and in such a position where it may be easily ready by persons employed in grinding or cutting.

General note. This regulation is revoked by the Provision and Use of Work Equipment Regulations 1992, S.I. 1992 No. 2932, as from 1 January 1993 except, insofar as it applies to work equipment first provided for use in the premises or undertaking before 1 January 1993, it is revoked as from 1 January 1997.

17.   Condition of floors.—(1) The floor immediately surrounding every fixed machine on which an *abrasive wheel* is, or is intended to be, mounted shall be maintained in good and even condition and shall, so far as practicable (*a*), be kept clear of loose material and prevented from becoming slippery.

(2) All reasonably practicable (*a*) steps shall be taken to ensure that the floor of any room or place in which any portable machine on which an *abrasive wheel* is mounted is used is in good and even condition, is kept clear of loose material and is prevented from becoming slippery.

General note. This regulation is revoked by the Provision and Use of Work Equipment Regulations 1992, S.I. 1992 No. 3004, as from 1 January 1993 except, in relation to any workplace or part of a workplace which is not a new workplace, or a modification, an extension or a conversion, it is revoked as from 1 January 1996.

(*a*) *Practicable; reasonably practicable.* See INTRODUCTORY NOTE 5.

18.   Duties of employed persons.—(1) No employed person using an *abrasive wheel* shall wilfully misuse or remove any guard, or wilfully misuse any protection flanges or other appliance provided in pursuance of these Regulations or any rest for a workpiece.

(2) Every employed person shall make full and proper use of guards, protection flanges and other appliances provided in pursuance of these Regulations and of rests for workpieces and if he discovers any defect in the same shall forthwith report such defect to the occupier, manager or other appropriate person.

General note. This regulation is revoked by the Provision and Use of Work Equipment Regulations 1992, S.I. 1992 No. 2932, as from 1 January 1993 except, insofar as it

applies to work equipment first provided for use in the premises or undertaking before 1 January 1993, it is revoked as from 1 January 1997.

This regulation does not apply to certain abrasive wheels: see reg. 4(4).

19.   Sale or hire of machinery. The provisions of section 17(2) of the *principal Act* (which prohibits the sale or letting on hire of certain machines which do not comply with the requirements of that section) shall extend to—

(a)   any *abrasive wheel* to which this regulation applies *(a)* having a diameter of more than 55 millimetres which is for use in a *factory* and which is not marked in the manner required by regulation 6(1); and

(b)   any machine *(b)* supplied with its prime mover as a unit which is for use in a *factory* and is of a kind specified in regulation 7(1) which does not comply with the requirements of that paragraph.

General note. This regulation is revoked by the Provision and Use of Work Equipment Regulations 1992, S.I. 1992 No. 2932, as from 1 January 1993 except, insofar as it applies to work equipment first provided for use in the premises or undertaking before 1 January 1993, it is revoked as from 1 January 1997.

For exceptions to this regulation, see reg. 4(1), (4) and (6).

*(a) **Abrasive wheel . . . applies.*** See reg. 3(3).

*(b) **Machine.*** See reg. 3(3).

SCHEDULE

Regulation 9

PARTICULARS OF TRAINING REQUIRED BY PARAGRAPH (1) OF REGULATION 9

The training shall include suitable and sufficient instruction in the following matters in relation to each class or description of *abrasive wheel* in respect of which it is proposed to appoint the person being trained, that is to say—

(1)   Approved advisory literature *(a)* relating to the mounting of *abrasive wheels*;

(2)   Hazards arising from the use of *abrasive wheels* and precautions which should be observed;

(3)   Methods of marking *abrasive wheels* as to type and speed;

(4)   Methods of storing, handling and transporting *abrasive wheels*;

(5)   Methods of inspecting and testing *abrasive wheels* to check for damage;

(6)   The functions of all components used with *abrasive wheels*, including flanges, washers, bushes and nuts used in mounting and including knowledge of the correct and incorrect methods of assembling all components and correct balancing of *abrasive wheels*;

(7)   The proper method of dressing an *abrasive wheel*;

(8)   The adjustment of the rest of an *abrasive wheel*;

(9)   The requirements of these Regulations.

*(a) **Approved advisory literature.*** Guidance Note PM22 "Advice on the mounting of abrasive wheels" is approved.

CERTIFICATE OF EXEMPTION No. 1

F 2353, 28 August 1970

Whereas I am satisfied that, as respects the processes hereinafter mentioned, the requirements of regulations 9(1) and 16 of the Abrasive Wheels Regulations 1970 are inappropriate:

Now, therefore, in pursuance of the powers conferred on me by regulation 5 of the said Regulations, I hereby exempt from the requirements of regulation 9(1) the mounting of abrasive wheels for use in the manufacture of crystal glass, and I hereby exempt from the requirements of regulation 16 grinding or cutting by means of abrasive wheels in the manufacture of crystal glass.

This Certificate shall come into operation on 2 April 1971 and shall remain in force until revoked in writing by the Chief Inspector of Factories.

CERTIFICATE OF EXEMPTION No. 2
F 2354, 13 October 1970

Whereas I am satisfied that the requirements of regulation 12 of the Abrasive Wheels Regulations 1970 are inappropriate in the case of the type of abrasive wheel hereinafter specified:

Now, therefore, in pursuance of regulation 5 of the said Regulations, I hereby exempt the type of abrasive wheel specified in the Schedule to this Certificate from the requirements of the said regulation 12.

This Certificate shall remain in force until revoked in writing by the Chief Inspector of Factories.

Type of Abrasive Wheel to which this Certificate Applies

Abrasive wheels which

1. are mounted between dovetail flanges which bear on corresponding dovetail recesses in the wheels; and

2. of which the thickness, measured between points adjacent to the dovetail recesses, is not less than 100 millimetres.

CERTIFICATE OF EXEMPTION No. 3
F 2355, 13 October 1970

Whereas I am satisfied that, as respects the types of abrasive wheels specified in the Schedule to this Certificate, the requirements of regulation 9(1) of the Abrasive Wheels Regulations 1970 are not necessary for the protection of persons employed:

Now, therefore, in pursuance of the powers conferred on me by regulation 5 of the said Regulations, I hereby exempt from the requirements of regulation 9(1) the mounting of the said types of abrasive wheel.

This Certificate shall come into operation on 2 April 1971 and remain in force until revoked in writing by the Chief Inspector of Factories.

SCHEDULE

1. Wheels and discs having in either case separate segments of abrasive material;

2. Wheels and discs made in either case of metal, wood, cloth, felt, rubber or paper and having any surface consisting wholly or partly of abrasive material;

3. Wheels, discs and saws to any surface of any of which is attached a rim or segments consisting in either case of diamond abrasive particles.

CERTIFICATE OF EXEMPTION No. 4
F 2364, 18 December 1970

Whereas I am satisfied that, as respects the operation described below, the requirements of regulation 9(1)(c) of the Abrasive Wheels Regulations 1970 are not appropriate:

Now, therefore, in pursuance of the powers conferred on me by regulation 5 of the said Regulations, I hereby exempt from the requirements of regulation 9(1)(c) the mounting of an abrasive wheel by a person employed by the supplier of the wheel or by a person employed by the supplier of the grinding machine at which the wheel is to be mounted.

This Certificate shall come into operation on 2 April 1971 and remain in force until revoked in writing by the Chief Inspector of Factories.

CERTIFICATE OF EXEMPTION No. 6
F 2365, 29 March 1971

Whereas I am satisfied that, as respects the operation described below, the requirements of regulation 10(1) of the Abrasive Wheels Regulations 1970 are not appropriate:

Now, therefore, in pursuance of the powers conferred on me by regulation 5(c) of the Regulations, I hereby exempt from the requirements of the said regulation 10(1) the operation of determining the working speed of any spindle, shaft, pulley, or other appliance, which is used to operate an abrasive wheel.

This Certificate shall come into force on 2 April 1971 and remain in force until revoked in writing by the Chief Inspector of Factories.

CERTIFICATE OF EXEMPTION No. 7
F 2367, 7 July 1971

Whereas I am satisfied that, as respects the types of abrasive wheel specified in column 1 of the Schedule to this Certificate certain of the requirements of the Abrasive Wheels Regulations 1970 are not necessary for the protection of persons employed:

Now, therefore, in pursuance of the powers conferred on me by regulation 5 of the said Regulations, I hereby exempt each said type of abrasive wheel from the requirements specified for that type in column 2 of the said Schedule.

This Certificate shall remain in force until revoked in writing by the Chief Inspector of Factories.

SCHEDULE

Column 1	Column 2
Threaded-hole abrasive wheels mounted on fixed machines and used for grinding domestic pottery and sanitary ware	Regulations 6(2), 7(1), 9(1), 10(1), 11, 12 and 16
Abrasive wheels used for sorting or ginetting of domestic pottery	Regulations 6(2), 7(1), 9(1), 10(1), 11, 12 and 16
Straight-sided abrasive wheels used for grinding sanitary ware	Regulations 10(1), 11 and 12

CERTIFICATE OF EXEMPTION No. 9
F 2405, 27 November 1972

Whereas I am satisfied that, as respects the type of abrasive wheel hereinafter specified, the requirements of regulation 6(1) and 19(a) of the Abrasive Wheels Regulations 1970 are impracticable:

Now, therefore, in pursuance of the powers conferred on me by regulation 5 of the said Regulations, I hereby exempt rubber bonded abrasive wheels having a thickness of 0.5 mm or less, subject to the condition specified in the Schedule of this Certificate, from the requirements of the said regulations 6(1) and 19(a).

This Certificate shall come into operation on 28 November 1972 and shall remain in force until revoked in writing by the Chief Inspector of Factories.

Certificate of Exemption No. 8 dated 18 August 1972 is hereby revoked.

SCHEDULE

No such abrasive wheel shall be taken into use in any factory for the first time in that factory unless there is kept permanently fixed in the room in which grinding is ordinarily carried out with that abrasive wheel a notice clearly stating the maximum permissible speed in revolutions per minute specified by the manufacturer for that abrasive wheel or for abrasive wheels of the class to which that abrasive wheel belongs:

Provided that when grinding with such an abrasive wheel is not ordinarily carried out in any one room the said notice shall be kept posted at a place and in a position where it may easily be read by persons employed in grinding with that abrasive wheel.

CERTIFICATE OF EXEMPTION No. 10
F 2507, 17 January 1980

Being satisfied in respect of abrasive wheels of which the abrasive surface consists of cubic boron nitride abrasive particles that the requirements of regs. 6, 7, 9(1), 12 and 19 of the Abrasive Wheels Regulations 1970 are not necessary for the protection of persons employed, I hereby exempt all such wheels from those requirements.

This certificate shall come into operation on 18 January 1980 and shall remain in force until revoked in writing by an inspector appointed and authorised as hereinafter appears.

THE CELLULOID
REGULATIONS 1921

(Dated 20 November 1921; S.R. & O. 1921 No. 1825, as amended by S.R. & O. 1928 No. 82 and S.I. 1992 No. 1811)

[Placard: Form 980]

In pursuance of section 79 of the Factory and Workshop Act 1901, I hereby make the following Regulations and direct that they shall apply (except as otherwise provided) to all factories and workshops or parts thereof in which celluloid or any article wholly or partly made of celluloid is manufactured, manipulated or stored.

General note. So much of these Regulations as related to the manufacture of cinematograph film was revoked by the Manufacture of Cinematograph Film Regulations 1928; and the Cinematograph Film Stripping Regulations 1939, provide that these Regulations shall not be deemed to apply to the stripping and drying of cinematograph film. As to the meaning of "cinematograph film", see the appropriate Regulations.

Definitions

"Workroom" means a room which any process in the manufacture of celluloid or any manufacturing process involving the use of celluloid is carried on.

"Manufacture" of cinematograph film means the production of negative and positive pictures on a celluloid film and the operations incidental thereto, including the cutting and perforating of the film.

"Darkened" means a *"workroom"* from which ordinary light has to be excluded.

Exceptions

For the purpose of these Regulations, celluloid shall not be deemed to include any material not containing nitrated-cellulose.

Nothing in these Regulations shall apply to any factory or workshop or part thereof in which celluloid is only used in solution except as follows:—regulations, 5, 6, 8, 9, 12, 14 and 15 shall apply where celluloid in solution is applied to fabrics of a readily inflammable nature.

Where the Chief Inspector *(a)* of Factories is satisfied that by reason of the small quantity of celluloid in use in a factory or workshop at any one time or for any other reason all or any of the provisions in the Regulations are not necessary for the protection of the persons employed, he may by certificate in writing (which he may in his discretion revoke) exempt such factory or workshop from all such provisions subject to such conditions as he may prescribe.

(a) *Inspector.* See INTRODUCTORY NOTE 24.

Duties

It shall be the duty of the occupier to observe Part I of these Regulations. It shall be the duty of all persons employed to observe Part II of these Regulations.

PART I
DUTIES OF OCCUPIERS

1.—(i) Stocks of celluloid shall be kept in a suitable place, outside the *workrooms*, plainly marked "Celluloid Store".

Stocks of celluloid exceeding 50 kilograms shall only be kept in a chamber constructed of fire-resisting materials, in which no open light or fire shall be allowed and which shall not be used for any purpose other than the storage of celluloid.

Any store not complying with the provisions in the foregoing paragraph shall have a notice, "Not to contain more than 50 kilograms of celluloid" plainly marked or affixed on the outside of the door; and the occupier shall, if so required by an Inspector of Factories for the purpose of determining the amount of celluloid in any such store, cause the same to be weighed in the presence of the Inspector.

(ii) The store shall not be situated so as to endanger the means of escape from the factory or workshop or from any part thereof in the event of a fire occurring in the store.

(iii) No unauthorised person shall be allowed to have access to the store.

2. The amount of celluloid in a *workroom* at any one time shall be kept as small as is practicable without unduly interfering with the work carried on.

3.—(i) Celluloid waste created in the process carried on shall not be allowed to accumulate on the floor of the *workroom*, but shall be collected either automatically as created, or at frequent intervals, in suitable receptacles.

(ii) When work ceases for the day such waste shall be removed from the *workroom* and placed in a substantial receptacle provided with a cover and plainly marked "Celluloid Waste"; provided that para. (ii) shall not apply to a factory or workshop in which cutlery is manufactured if the waste is kept in a strong metal receptacle provided with a tight-fitting cover.

4.—(i) Finished articles made wholly or partly of celluloid shall be removed from the *workroom* without undue delay and kept in a suitable place.

(ii) [*revoked*].

5.—(i) Efficient steps shall be taken to prevent celluloid from coming into contact with open lights or fires, or except to the extent that may be necessary for the processes of the industry remaining near thereto.

(ii) [*revoked*].

6.   No person shall be allowed to smoke in any room in which celluloid is manufactured, manipulated or stored.

7.   When a saw is used for cutting celluloid the cutting edge shall wherever practicable be kept constantly wet.

8.—(i) Sealing wax shall not be used on any parcel or package containing celluloid, unless the articles are packed in tins and the sealing is done in a room in which no manufacturing process involving the use of celluloid is carried on.

(ii) If any package or case containing celluloid requires to be soldered efficient steps shall be taken to prevent the solder from coming into contact with the celluloid.

9.   Adequate means for extinguishing fire, having regard to the amount of celluloid present in the room at any one time, shall be kept constantly provided for each *workroom* and storeroom.

10.—(i) Adequate means of escape in case of fire shall be provided (a) from each floor of the factory or workshop, and (b) in each *workroom* from all parts of the room, and such means of escape shall be kept free from obstruction during working hours.

(ii) The doors of a *workroom* shall, except in the case of sliding doors, be constructed so as to open outwards.

(iii) In each *workroom* other than a "*darkroom*" a notice [Form 987] shall be affixed, in a position where it can be easily read, specifying the means of escape provided for the persons employed in the room.

Persons working in a "*darkroom*" shall be instructed as to the means of escape from such room.

11.—(i) A competent person shall be appointed in writing to exercise supervision with regard to the requirements of these Regulations and to enforce the observance of them and of any directions given by the occupier with a view to carrying out the Regulations.

(ii) A printed copy of these Regulations shall be kept posted up in legible characters in each *workroom* other than a "*darkroom*," and outside each "*darkroom*" in a position where it can be easily read by all persons in the room.

PART II
DUTIES OF PERSONS EMPLOYED

12.   No person shall smoke in any room in which celluloid is manufactured, manipulated or stored.

13.   No person shall use a saw for cutting celluloid, except in accordance with Regulation 7.

14.   No person shall use sealing wax on any parcel or package containing celluloid, except in accordance with regulation 8.

15. Every person shall observe such directions as may be given to him with a view to carrying out these Regulations.

Regulation 15 1515

15. Every person shall comply with directions may be given to him with view to facilitating out these regulations.

THE CEMENT WORKS
WELFARE ORDER 1930

(S.R. & O. 1930 No. 94, as amended by S.I. 1951 No. 926, the Employment Act 1989, ss. 9(6), 29(5), Sch. 2, Pt. 1, Sch. 8 and S.I. 1992 No. 2966)

General note. This whole Order is revoked by the Provision and Use of Work Equipment Regulations 1992, S.I. 1992 No. 3004, as from 1 January 1993 except, in relation to any workplace or part of a workplace which is not a new workplace, or a modification, an extension or a conversion, it is revoked as from 1 January 1996.

In pursuance of section 7 of the Police, Factories, etc. (Miscellaneous Provisions) Act 1916, I hereby make the following Order for all factories and workshops in which the manufacture of Portland Cement or cement of a similar character is carried on.

1. [*revoked*].

2. The occupier shall provide and maintain for the use of all persons employed in cleaning or repairing sacks, suitable accommodation for clothing put off during working hours.

The accommodation so provided shall be made secure and shall be kept clean.

3. [*revoked*].

4. The occupier shall provide and maintain for the use of all workers, except those employed in continuous processes, a suitable and adequate messroom which shall be furnished with (a) sufficient tables and chairs or benches and (b) adequate means of warming food and boiling water. The messroom shall be sufficiently warmed for use during meal intervals.

The messroom shall be placed under the charge of a responsible person, and shall be kept clean.

5. The occupier shall provide and maintain in the works for the use of all persons employed suitable washing facilities *(a)* conveniently accessible and comprising a sufficient supply of basins and clean water.

The facilities so provided shall be placed under the charge of a responsible person, and shall be kept clean.

(*a*) **Washing facilities.** See INTRODUCTORY NOTE 2.

6. This Order may be cited as the Cement Works Welfare Order 1930, and shall come into force on 1 April 1930.

General note. In *Harvey v New Zealand Shipping Co* [1955] 1 Lloyd Rep 251 it was said that the Regulations were not directed towards protection against dermatitis.

THE MANUFACTURE OF CINEMATOGRAPH FILM REGULATIONS 1928

(S.R. & O. 1928 No. 82, as amended by S.I. 1989 No. 635 and S.I. 1992 No. 1811)

In pursuance of section 79 of the Factory and Workshop Act 1901, I hereby make the following Regulations and direct that they shall apply to all factories and workshops or parts thereof in which cinematograph film (as defined below) is manufactured, repaired, manipulated, used or stored.

These Regulations, which may be cited as the Manufacture of Cinematograph Film Regulations 1928, shall come into force on the 1 March 1928, from which date so much of the Regulations dated 28 November 1921, for the manufacture, manipulation and storage of celluloid or any article wholly or partly made of celluloid, as relates to the manufacture, repair, manipulation, use or storage of such cinematograph film, shall be revoked.

Definitions

"*Cinematograph film*" means any film, including uncoated raw base, containing nitro-cellulose or other nitrated product which is intended for use in a cinematograph or other similar apparatus.

"*Manufacture of cinematograph film*" includes the production of negative and positive pictures on the film and also the operations incidental thereto, including the cutting and perforating and the projection of the pictures upon a screen for the purpose of examination.

"*Darkroom*" means a room from which ordinary light has to be excluded.

"*Fire-resisting material*" means—

(a) properly constructed brickwork not less than 100 millimetres in thickness; or
(b) concrete not less than 75 millimetres of thickness; or
(c) efficiently jointed breeze slabbing not less than 75 millimetres in thickness, or;
(d) oak or teak not less than 50 millimetres in thickness; or
(e) glass not less than 6 millimetres in thickness in the centre of which wire mesh is embedded; or
(f) other *approved* material.

"*Storeroom*" means a room or chamber of similar enclosure in which *cinematograph film* is kept or stored, other than a room in which a quantity not exceeding twenty reels or 37 kilograms in weight, whichever is the greater, is kept in accordance with the exception to No. 2 of these Regulations.

"*Approved*" means approved in writing by the Chief Inspector *(a)* of Factories.

Duties

It shall be the duty of the occupier to observe Part I of these Regulations. It shall be the duty of all persons employed to observe Part II of these Regulations.

Exception

Where the Chief Inspector *(a)* of Factories is satisfied that, by reason of the small quantity of *cinematograph film* manufactured, repaired, manipulated, used or stored in a factory or workshop or for any other reason, all or any of the provisions in these Regulations are not necessary for the protection of the persons employed, he may by certificate in writing (which he may in his discretion revoke) exempt such factory or workshop from all or any of such provisions, subject to such conditions as he may prescribe.

(a) **Inspector.** See INTRODUCTORY NOTE 24.

PART I
DUTIES OF OCCUPIERS

1.   Each reel of *cinematograph film* shall, except when required to be exposed for the purposes of the work carried on, be kept in a separate box, properly closed and constructed of metal or of other *approved* material.

2.   All *cinematograph film* not being actually used, or manipulated, or in the course of manufacture or repair, shall be kept in a room or chamber or similar enclosure satisfying the requirements of these Regulations with regard to *storerooms*, except that a quantity not exceeding twenty reels or 37 kilograms in weight, whichever is the greater, may be kept in any room provided it is contained in a properly closed receptacle constructed of metal or of other *approved* material.

3.—(a)   All waste and scrap *cinematograph film* shall be collected at frequent intervals during each day and be placed in a strong metal receptacle with self-closing lid, and clearly marked with the words "Film Waste".
   (b)   No material liable to ignite spontaneously nor anything likely to ignite or decompose *cinematograph film* shall be placed in the receptacle.
   (c)   At the end of each day's work the waste and scrap shall be either transferred to a *storeroom* or removed from the premises.

4.   *Cinematograph film* shall not be manufactured, repaired, manipulated or used in any room unless:—

   (a)   the top of the room is constructed of *fire-resisting material*: provided that this requirement shall not apply to any room on the top floor of a building nor to any room of a single-storey building;
   (b)   the room is separated from any other room or passage by walls and floor constructed of *fire-resisting material*;

(c)   all the doors of the room are constructed of *fire-resisting material*;

(d)   the fittings are, as far as practicable, constructed of *fire-resisting material*;

(e)   the furniture and apparatus are so arranged as to afford unimpeded egress for every person in the room in the event of fire; and

(f)   the room is adequately equipped with fire-extinguishing appliances.

5.—(a)   Adequate means of escape in case of fire shall be provided for every building and for every room in which *cinematograph film* is manufactured, repaired, manipulated or used, and the means of escape shall not be deemed adequate unless:—

(i)   at least two separate safe exits are provided from every such room and two safe ways of escape from the building are available for all persons employed in the factory or workshop; and

(ii)   all doors and windows provided in connection with the means of escape are so arranged as to open outward readily:

Provided that the foregoing provisions shall not apply where the factory or workshop forms part of a building from all parts of which means of escape can be required under the London Building Acts (Amendment) Act 1905, now the London Building Acts 1930–1939 or the London County Council (Celluloid, etc.) Act 1915.

(b)   Intercommunicating fire alarm signals shall be arranged for every room.

(c)   A notice shall be affixed in every room other than a *darkroom* and immediately outside each *darkroom* and in such other parts of the building as may be named in writing by the District Inspector of Factories, clearly specifying the means of escape provided for the persons employed therein.

6.   All hatchways, lifts or similar openings between any rooms, or between any rooms and other parts of the premises, shall be so fitted, constructed and arranged that fire or products of combustion or decomposition of *cinematograph film* will not be likely to pass.

7.—(a)   Every *storeroom* shall be either—

(i)   a single-storey building in an *approved* situation; or

(ii)   situated on the roof or top floor of a building; or

(iii)   situated in some other *approved* position; or

(iv)   fitted with an efficient automatic water-sprinkling system.

(b)   Every *storeroom* constructed or adapted for use as a *storeroom* on or after the 1 March 1928, shall comply with part (i), (ii), or (iii) of paragraph (a) of this regulation and shall, in addition, comply with part (iv).

8.—(a)   In every *storeroom* situated in accordance with regulation 7(a)(i) or 7(a)(ii) and in any other *storeroom* if so required by notice in writing from the Chief Inspector of Factories, there shall be a part of a wall or part of the roof constructed of ordinary sheet glass lightly fixed in position, so as to provide a gas relief space in the event of an explosion or fire occurring within the *storeroom*. The area of the gas relief space shall not be less than 200 square centimetres and not more than 260 square centimetres for every 100 kilograms of *cinematograph film* that may be stored in the storeroom.

(b)   The gas relief space shall be protected against external breakage by a stong wire mesh guard fitted on the outside of the glass.

(c) The position of the gas relief space shall be such that an outburst of flame through the space would not be likely to endanger the safety of the building or other premises.

9.—(a) Every *storeroom* shall be—
  (i) constructed entirely of *fire-resisting material* except as regards the gas relief space;
  (ii) fitted with a self-closing door or doors which shall be, as far as practicable, kept locked, except when any person is in the *storeroom*;
  (iii) clearly marked with the words "Film Store"; and
  (iv) provided with adequate ventilation.
(b) No *storeroom* shall—
  (i) be used for any purpose other than the storage or keeping of *cinematograph film* or film waste; or
  (ii) contain more than 1 tonne or five hundred and sixty reels of *cinematograph film*, whichever is the greater.

10.—(a) No open fire or light, nor any smoking materials or matches, nor anything likely to ignite or decompose *cinematograph film*, shall be allowed in any *storeroom* or in any room in which *cinematograph film* is manufactured, repaired, manipulated or used.
(b) Suitable arrangements shall be provided for the temporary reception outside such rooms of smoking materials, matches and similar articles.

11. Soldering of cases or packages containing *cinematograph film* shall not be done except in a suitable place reserved for that purpose, and all due precautions shall be taken effectively to prevent the heat generated during the process from affecting the *cinematograph film*.

12. [*revoked*].

13. A competent person shall be appointed in writing to exercise supervision with regard to the requirements of these Regulations and to enforce the observance of them and of any directions given to him in writing by the occupier with a view to carrying out the Regulations.

14. A printed copy of these Regulations shall be kept posted up in each room other than a *darkroom* and immediately outside each *darkroom* in a position where it can be easily read by all persons employed in the room.

PART II
DUTIES OF PERSONS EMPLOYED

15. No person shall take any open light or flame, or any smoking materials or matches, or anything likely to ignite or decompose *cinematograph film* into any *storeroom* or into any room in which *cinematograph film* is manufactured, repaired, manipulated or used.

16.   Every person shall observe such directions as may be given to him with a view to carrying out these Regulations.

THE CINEMATOGRAPH FILM STRIPPING REGULATIONS 1939

(S.R. & O. 1939 No. 571, as amended by S.I. 1989 No. 635 and S.I. 1992 No. 1811)

[Placard: Form 998]

In pursuance of section 60 *(a)* of the Factories Act 1937, and, as respects Part II of these Regulations, in pursuance of section 35 of the said Act, I hereby make the following Regulations and direct that they shall apply to all factories or parts thereof in which stripping or drying of cinematograph film (as defined below) is done.

These Regulations, which may be cited as the Cinematograph Film Stripping Regulations 1939, shall come into force on the 1 June 1939, from which date the Cinematograph Film Stripping Regulations 1928 shall be revoked; and notwithstanding such revocation the Regulations dated 28 November 1921, for the manufacture, manipulation and storage of celluloid or any article wholly or partly made of celluloid shall not be deemed to apply to the processes (as defined below) of stripping and drying of cinematograph film.

(a) **In pursuance of s. 60.** Parts I and III of these Regulations were made under s. 60 of the Factories Act 1937, before that section was amended by s. 12 of the Factories Act 1948. Consequently, the class of persons for whose benefit they were made is limited to persons employed "in connection with" the processes specified; see the GENERAL INTRODUCTION and *Canadian Pacific Steamships Ltd v Bryers* [1958] AC 485, [1957] 3 All ER 572, HL.

Definitions

In these Regulations, unless the context otherwise requires:—

"*Cinematograph film*" means any film containing nitro-cellulose or other nitrated product which was intended for use or has been used in a cinematograph or sound recording or other similar apparatus.

"*Stripping*" means the removal of emulsion from *cinematograph film* and includes all unpacking, sorting, unwinding, winding, decolouring, washing, grading and packing of *cinematograh film* incidental thereto.

"*Drying*" means the drying of *cinematograph film* from which the emulsion has been removed.

"*Sorting*" includes the removal of extraneous material and any other preliminary sorting of *cinematograph film* before washing, and also the preparation of reeled pieces for rewinding.

"*Grading*" means the separation of different grades of material after washing.

"*Fire-resisting material*" means

(a) properly constructed brickwork not less than 100 millimetres in thickness; or
(b) concrete not less than 75 millimetres in thickness; or
(c) efficiently jointed breeze slabbing not less than 75 millimetres in thickness; or
(d) oak or teak not less than 50 millimetres in thickness; or
(e) glass not less than 6 millimetres in thickness in the centre of which wire mesh is embedded; or
(f) other *approved* material.

"*Storeroom*" means a room or chamber or similar enclosure in which *cinematograph film* is kept or stored, and which satisfies the requirements hereinafter laid down in regard to storerooms.

"*Approved*" means approved in writing by the Chief Inspector *(a)* of Factories.

Duties

It shall be the duty of the occupier to observe Parts I and II of these Regulations. It shall be the duty of all persons employed to observe Part III of these Regulations.

Exception

Where the Chief Inspector *(a)* of Factories is satisfied that in any particular circumstances all or any of the provisions in these Regulations are not necessary for the protection of the persons employed or, in the case of factories constructed before the coming into force of these Regulations, are not reasonably practicable, he may by certificate in writing (which he may in his discretion revoke) grant an exemption from all or any of such provisions in such cases and to such extent and subject to such conditions as he may specify in the certificate.

(a) Inspector. See INTRODUCTORY NOTE 24.

PART I
DUTIES OF OCCUPIERS

1. All *cinematograph film* which is not in process of *stripping* or *drying* shall be kept in a *storeroom*.

2. The maximum quanity of *cinematograph film* in any room other than a *storeroom* shall not exceed 45 kilograms in weight or such other quantity as may be *approved*.

3.—(a) All scrap *cinematograph film* arising from *stripping* or *drying* shall be collected at frequent intervals during each day and be placed in a strong metal receptacle fitted with a self-closing lid, and clearly marked with the words "Film scrap".
(b) No material liable to ignite spontaneously nor anything likely to ignite or decompose *cinematograph film* shall be placed in the receptacle.

    (c) At the end of each day's work the scrap shall be either transferred to a *storeroom* or removed from the premises.

4.   *Stripping* or *drying* of *cinematograph film* shall not be done in any room unless—

    (a) the room is a single-storey building or part of a single-storey building;

    (b) all walls and windows of the room, including partitions by which the room is separated from any other room or passage way, but not including windows in a roof, are constructed of *fire-resisting material*;

    (c) all the doors of the room are constructed of *fire-resisting material*, and are self-closing;

    (d) the fittings are, as far as practicable, constructed of material that is not readily combustible;

    (e) the fittings and other contents of the room are so arranged or disposed as to afford unimpeded egress for every person in the room in the event of fire; and

    (f) the room is adequately equipped with fire-extinguishing appliances.

5.   In the case of every factory constructed or reconstructed or taken into use for the process of *cinematograph film stripping* after 1 December 1938—

    (a) no process other than *sorting* or rewinding for washing purposes shall be carried on in any room in which either or both of the said processes is carried on;

    (b) no process other than washing without the aid of mechanical power shall be carried on in any room in which the said process is carried on;

    (c) no process other than *drying* without the aid of mechanical power shall be carried on in any room in which the said power is carried on;

    (d) no process other than packing or *grading* shall be carried on in any room in which either or both of the said processes is carried on.

6.   No loose unwound *cinematograph film* shall be placed on the floor or ground in any room or other part of the factory.

7.   The process of sorting of cuttings shall not be carried on unless the *cinematograph film* being sorted is on a bench or in a trough.

8.   Loose unwound *cinematograph film* shall not be carried from one part of the factory to another except in a suitable tray or container.

    Cinematograph film (including reeled *cinematograph film*) carried on power trucks shall be enclosed in covered containers.

9.—(a) *Drying of cinematograph film* shall not be done except under such conditions as will prevent the *cinematograph film* from coming into contact or proximity with any source of heat or heated surface in such a manner as would render the *cinematograph film* liable to be ignited or decomposed.

    (b) Loose unwound *cinematograph film* shall not be hung up to dry whether in a room or enclosed space or in the open air.

    (c) Loose unwound *cinematograph film* shall be enclosed during *drying* in such a manner that a person in the room will be protected as far as practicable from an outburst of flame.

(d) The temperature in any part of a drying enclosure for loose unwound *cinematograph film*, shall not at any time exceed 38 degrees Celsius. A thermometer shall be kept available in every room in which such *drying* is done.

10. The following are the requirements prescribed in regard to *storerooms*:—

(a) Every *storeroom* shall be—
   (i) a single-storey building or part of a single-storey bulding in an *approved* situation, and in the case of a factory constructed or reconstructed or taken into use for the process of *cinematograph film stripping* after 1 December 1938, shall be a separate single-storey building at least 6 metres from any building in which persons are regularly present;
   (ii) constructed entirely of *fire-resisting material* except as regards the gas relief space required by regulation 11;
   (iii) fitted with a self-closing door or doors which shall be, as far as practicable, kept locked, except when any person is in the *storeroom*, and such door or doors shall be capable of being readily opened from the inside;
   (iv) clearly marked with the words "Film Store";
   (v) provided with adequate ventilation; and
   (vi) separated from any adjacent *storeroom* by a wall built up to 920 millimetres above the roof.
(b) No *storeroom* shall—
   (i) be used for any purpose other than the storage or keeping of *cinematograph film*; or
   (ii) contain more than 1 tonne of *cinematograph film*, or such other quantity as may be *approved*.

11.—(a) In every storeroom there shall be provided a gas relief space of *approved* design for the relief of pressure in the event of an explosion or fire occurring in the *storeroom*. The area of the gas relief space shall not be less than 1 square metre for every 15 cubic metres of space in the *storeroom*.
(b) The gas relief space shall be so constructed as to protect any glass from external breakage and to prevent the projection of articles from within the *storeroom*.
(c) The position of the gas relief space shall be such that an outburst of flame through the space would not be likely to endanger the safety of the building or other premises.

12. No premises shall be used for the *stripping* or *drying* of *cinematograph film*, (a) unless and until plans of the premises accompanied by particulars as to the number of persons to be employed and as to the arrangements for carrying on the processes and complying with the requirements of regulations 4 (other than paragraph (e)), 5, 7, 9(c), 10(a) and 11, have been submitted and *approved*, nor (b) otherwise than in accordance with the arrangements so *approved*; and no material addition shall be subsequently made to such premises or to the number of persons employed or alteration made in the arrangements unless such addition or alteration has been first *approved*.

13.—(a) No open fire or light, nor any smoking materials or matches nor anything likely to ignite or decompose *cinematograph film*, shall be allowed in any part of the premises.

(b) Suitable arrangements shall be provided for the temporary reception outside the premises of smoking materials, matches and similar articles.

14. [*revoked*].

15. A competent person shall be appointed in writing to exercise supervision with regard to the requirements of these Regulations and to enforce the observance of them and of any directions given to him in writing by the occupier with a view to carrying out the Regulations.

16. A printed copy of these Regulations shall be kept posted up in each room in which *stripping* or drying of *cinematograph film* is done.

PART II

17. There shall be provided adequate means of escape in case of fire from the factory and from every building and every room being a building or room in which *stripping* or *drying* of *cinematograph film* is done and from every *storeroom* and from every building of which a *storeroom* forms part; and the means of escape shall not be deemed adequate unless:—

(i) there are at least two safe ways of escape from the factory available for all persons employed in the factory;

(ii) there are at least two separate safe exits from every building and every room being a building or room in which *stripping* or *drying* of *cinematograph film* is done; and

(iii) all doors and windows provided in connection with the means of escape are so arranged as to open outwards readily:

Provided that the foregoing provisions of this regulation shall not apply where the factory forms part of a building from all parts of which means of escape can be required under the London Building Act 1930 *(a)*.

(a) **Act.** See now the London Building Acts (Amendment) Act 1939, ss. 34, 35 and 157(1)(e). For fire precautions generally, see the Fire Precautions Act 1971.

18. Regulation 17 shall be in addition to and not in substitution for or diminution of any other requirements as to the means of escape in case of fire imposed in pursuance of section 34 or section 35 of the Act.

PART III
DUTIES OF PERSONS EMPLOYED

19. No person shall take any open light or flame, or any smoking materials or matches, or anything likely to ignite or decompose *cinematograph film* into any part of any premises in which *stripping* or *drying* of *cinematograph film* is done.

20. Every person shall observe such directions as may be given to him with a view to carrying out these Regulations.

THE CLAY WORKS (WELFARE) SPECIAL REGULATIONS 1948

(S.I. 1948 No. 1547, as amended by S.I. 1981 No. 917,
S.I. 1992 No. 1811, S.I. 1992 No. 2966 and S.I. 1992 No. 3004)

[Placard: Form 1034]

Whereas under section 46 of the Factories Act 1937, Special Regulations may be made for the purpose of securing the welfare of persons employed;

And whereas the Factories Act 1937 (Extension of Section 46) Regulations 1948, made under subsection (6) of that section, extend the matters to which the section relates;

And whereas it appears to the Minister of Labour and National Service that owing to the conditions and circumstances of employment or the nature of the processes carried on in factories to which these Regulations apply, provision requires to be made for securing the welfare of persons employed in such factories;

Now, therefore, the Minister by virtue of the above powers and of the Transfer of Functions (Factories, &c., Acts) Order 1946, hereby makes the following Special Regulations:—

1. Short title, commencement, interpretation and revocation.—(1) These Regulations may be cited as the Clay Works (Welfare) Special Regulations 1948, and shall come into force on the 1st day of October 1948.

(2) The Interpretation Act 1889 [Interpretation Act 1978] applies to the interpretation of these Regulations as it applies to the interpretation of an Act of Parliament.

(3) The Clay Works Welfare Order 1932 is hereby revoked.

2. Application.—(1) Subject to the provisions of paragraph (2) hereof these Regulations apply to all factories in which clay, shale, sand, lime or similar materials are made into bricks, tiles, blocks, slabs, pipes, stilts and spurs, nozzles or similar articles.

(2) There shall be excluded from the factories (*a*) to which these Regulations apply any factory to which the Regulations made by the Secretary of State on 2 January 1913, for the Manufacture and Decoration of Pottery apply:

Provided that where the latter Regulations apply only to part of a factory this exclusion shall relate only to that part, and provided further that this exclusion shall not relate to a factory if the only obligation imposed on the occupier of the factory in relation thereto by the latter Regulations is an obligation to allow samples of materials to be taken for analysis.

(*a*) **Excluded factories.** The Regulations of 1913 have been revoked and replaced by the Pottery (Health and Welfare) Special Regulations 1950, reg. 4(1) of which excludes certain factories from the application of these Regulations.

3. Shelters. Where kiln burning is carried on, a safe and suitable shelter shall (unless the messroom or other accommodation provided in pursuance of regulation 8 is available for their use and conveniently accessible to them) be provided and maintained for the workers attending the kilns. Every such shelter shall be sufficiently ventilated and warmed and lighted and furnished with chairs or benches. Adequate means of warming food and boiling water shall be provided in or adjacent to the shelter.

General note. This regulation is revoked by the Provision and Use of Work Equipment Regulations 1992, S.I. 1992 No. 3004, as from 1 January 1993 except, in relation to any workplace or part of a workplace which is not a new workplace, or a modification, an extension or a conversion, it is revoked as from 1 January 1996.

4. Washing facilities.—(1) Without prejudice to the requirements of section 42 of the Factories Act 1937 [s. 38], the occupier shall provide and maintain for the use of the persons employed suitable facilities for washing, including a sufficient supply of clean towels, renewed daily, and of soap and nail brushes, and basins or troughs for washing the face, hands and forearms. The basins and troughs so provided and maintained shall satisfy the following requirements—

(a) basins and troughs shall have a smooth impervious upper surface;

(b) each basin shall be fitted with a waste-pipe and plug and shall have a supply of hot and cold water or of warm water laid on or made readily available at all times when employed persons for whose use the basin is reckoned as provided are in or within the precincts of the factory;

(c) each trough shall be fitted with an unplugged waste-pipe and shall have a supply (*a*) of warm water laid on at points above the trough and at intervals of not more than 600 millimetres and available at all times when employed persons for whose use the trough or part thereof is reckoned as provided are in or within the precincts of the factory;

(d) basins and troughs shall be so situated as to afford facilities for washing under cover and protected from the weather;

(e) basins and troughs shall be sufficient in number and dimensions to provide at least one unit for every 10 persons employed up to a total of 50, and at least one unit for every 20 persons employed above 50. Where the persons employed are employed in shifts, the calculation of the number employed shall be according to the largest number at work at any one time.

(2) For the purposes of this regulation—

(a) a "unit" means one basin or 600 millimetres of the length of a trough or, in the case of circular or oval troughs, 600 millimetres of the circumference of a trough;

(b) in dividing by 10 for the purpose of finding the number of units required any remainder shall be counted as 10, and in dividing by 20 for the like purpose any remainder shall be counted as 20;

(c) a unit shall not be reckoned as provided for a number of persons unless that unit is conveniently accessible to every one of that number;

(d) a basin or other receptacle shal not be reckoned as a trough unless it measures internally at least 1.2 metres over its longest or widest part.

General note. This regulation is revoked by the Provision and Use of Work Equipment Regulations 1992, S.I. 1992 No. 3004, as from 1 January 1993 except, in relation to any workplace or part of a workplace which is not a new workplace, or a modification, an extension or a conversion, it is revoked as from 1 January 1996.

(a) **Washing facilities.** See INTRODUCTORY NOTE 20.

5.   [*revoked*].

6.   Clothing accommodation. The occupier shall provide and maintain adequate and suitable accommodation for overalls and other protective clothing worn during working hours, whether provided in pursuance of regulation 5 or not, and adequate and suitable arrangements for drying such clothing.

General note. This regulation is revoked by the Provision and Use of Work Equipment Regulations 1992, S.I. 1992 No. 3004, as from 1 January 1993 except, in relation to any workplace or part of a workplace which is not a new workplace, or a modification, an extension or a conversion, it is revoked as from 1 January 1996.

7.   [*revoked*].

8.   Canteens and messrooms.—(1) In the case of factories at which more than 50 persons are employed, there shall be provided at or in the immediate vicinity of the factory, for the use of persons employed, an adequate and suitable canteen where they may purchase appropriate meals.

(2) In the case of factories at which not more than 50 persons are employed there shall be provided at or in the immediate vicinity of the factory, for the use of persons employed, an adequate and suitable messroom with adequate means of warming food and boiling water.

(3) The accommodation provided in pursuance of this regulation shall be adequately ventilated and lighted and sufficiently warmed for use at meal times, shall include sufficient tables and chairs or benches, shall be kept in a clean and orderly condition, and in a good state of repair, and shall be separate from the accommodation provided for clothing, whether clothing not worn during working hours or protective clothing worn during working hours. In the case of a canteen or messroom newly constructed or reconstructed after the date of the making of these Regulations, the floor shall be constructed of material impervious to water and with a readily washable surface.

(4) Messroom or canteen facilities shall not be treated as adequate for the purpose of this regulation if they are not sufficient for all the persons employed at the factory whom it is reasonable to regard as desirous of availing themselves of such facilities.

General note. This regulation is revoked by the Provision and Use of Work Equipment Regulations 1992, S.I. 1992 No. 3004, as from 1 January 1993 except, in relation to any workplace or part of a workplace which is not a new workplace, or a modification, an extension or a conversion, it is revoked as from 1 January 1996.

9.   Supervision. The occupier shall appoint a person or persons whose name or names shall be recorded in the general register [Form 31] to be specially charged with the duty of supervising the cleaning and maintenance of the accommodation and facilities provided in pursuance of these Regulations.

General note. This regulation is revoked by the Provision and Use of Work Equipment Regulations 1992, S.I. 1992 No. 3004, as from 1 January 1993 except, in relation to any workplace or part of a workplace which is not a new workplace, or a modification, an extension or a conversion, it is revoked as from 1 January 1996.

THE WORK IN COMPRESSED AIR SPECIAL REGULATIONS 1958

(S.I. 1958 No. 61, as amended by S.I. 1960 No. 1037, S.I. 1973 No. 36 and S.I. 1984 No. 1593)

The Minister of Labour and National Service by virtue of the powers conferred on him by sections 46 and 60 of the Factories Act 1937 (hereinafter referred to as "the principal Act"), section 8 of the Factories Act 1948, and of all other powers in that behalf, hereby makes the following Special Regulations—

1. Citation and commencement. These Regulations may be, cited as the Work in Compressed Air Special Regulations 1958, and shall come into operation on the 21st day of April 1958.

General note. Measurements in Imperial have been converted to metric by S.I. 1984 No. 1593. These amendments do not apply to premises or plant in existence before 9 November 1984.

2. Application of Regulations.—(1) These Regulations shall apply as respects work in compressed air carried out therein—

(a) to all factories; and
(b) to all premises, places, processes, operations and works to which the provisions of Part IV of the principal Act [Part IV] with respect to special regulations for safety and health are applied by sections 103 to 108 of that Act [ss. 123–128].

(2) These Regulations shall not apply to work in a gasholder where the pressure does not exceed 150 millibars.

(3) If the Chief Inspector *(a)* is satisfied that in the case of any particular class or description of plant, equipment or appliance or of any special description or method of work any requirement of these Regulations relating to safety or health is, in any class or description of circumstances, not necessary for the protection of the persons employed or not reasonably practicable, he may by certificate in writing (which he may at his discretion revoke at any time) grant an exemption *(b)* from that requirement in the case of that class or description of plant, equipment or appliance or of that special description or method of

work in such circumstances and subject to such conditions as may be specified in the certificate.

(a) **Inspector.** See INTRODUCTORY NOTE 24.

(b) **Exemption.** See Certificate of Exemption No. 1 [F 2075], set out following these Regulations.

3. Interpretation.—(1) The Interpretation Act 1889 [Interpretation Act 1978] shall apply to the interpretation of these Regulations as it applies to the interpretation of an Act of Parliament.

(2) In these Regulations unless the context otherwise requires the following expressions have the meanings hereby assigned to them respectively, that is to say—

"*appointed doctor*" means a fully registered medical practitioner appointed by written certificate of the Chief Employment Medical Adviser or of a Deputy Chief Medical Adviser for such of the purposes of these Regulations as are specified in the certificate;

"*employment medical adviser*" means an employment medical adviser appointed under the Employment Medical Advisory Service Act 1972;

"*approved*" means approved for the time being by certificate of the Chief Inspector (a) of Factories;

"*man-lock*" means any air lock or decompression chamber used for the compression or decompression of persons, but does not include an air lock which is only so used in emergency or a medical lock used solely for treatment purposes;

"*pressure*" means pressure in millibars above atmospheric pressure.

(a) **Inspector.** See INTRODUCTORY NOTE 24.

4. Obligation under Regulations.—(1) It shall be the duty of every contractor and employer of workmen who is undertaking any work to which these Regulations apply to comply with such of the requirements of regulations 5 to 21 as affect any workman employed by him; provided that the requirements of the said Regulations shall be deemed not to affect any workman if and so long as his presence in any place is not in the course of performing any work on behalf of his employer or is not expressly or impliedly authorised or permitted by his employer.

(2) It shall be the duty of every person employed to comply with the requirements of such Regulations as relate to the doing of or abstaining from an act by him and to co-operate in carrying out these Regulations and if he discovers any defect in the plant, equipment or appliances to report such defect without unreasonable delay to his employer or foreman, or to a person appointed by the employer to supervise the safe conduct of the work.

(3) No person shall be held not to have complied with a requirement of any of these Regulations by reason of any matter proved to have been due to causes over which he had no control and against the happening of which it was not reasonably practicable (a) for him to make provision, including (without

prejudice to the generality of the foregoing), physical conditions which were unknown and which could not have been reasonably forseen by a person experienced in the work or in the use of any material, appliance or equipment involved.

General note. See the similar provisions of reg. 3 of the Construction (General Provisions) Regulations 1961, and the notes thereto.

(*a*) **Reasonably practicable.** See INTRODUCTORY NOTE 5

5.   Supervision of compressed air operations. Where persons are employed in compressed air, their employer shall make arrangements to ensure that, at all times when they are actually so employed, a person competent to take charge of compressed air operations is in charge of the operations and in attendance on the site.

6.   Construction and maintenance of bulkheads, air locks, etc. Every bulkhead, air lock or other structure used in connection with work in compressed air shall be of good construction, sound material and adequate strength (*a*) and shall be properly maintained (*b*).

General note. A door to a man-lock which was ill-fitting and leaked and breached this regulation in *Ransom v Sir Robert Macalpine & Sons Ltd* (1971) 11 KIR 141.

(*a*) **Good construction, sound material and adequate strength.** See INTRODUCTORY NOTE 11.

(*b*) **Properly maintained.** See INTRODUCTORY NOTE 10.

7.   Air supply plant. The plant for the production and supply of compressed air to any working chamber or air lock shall be of suitable design, and in the case of a working chamber shall deliver a supply sufficient to provide at the *pressure* in the chamber 0.3 cubic metres of fresh air per minute per person for the time being in the chamber. The plant shall be in the immediate charge of a competent person who shall be in attendance whilst any person is in compressed air.

8.   Size and equipment of man-locks.—(1) Every *man-lock* shall be of adequate internal dimensions and capacity for the purposes for which it is used and shall be suitably equipped.

(2) Without prejudice to the generality of the preceding paragraph, there shall be provided in connection with every *man-lock*—

(a)   pressure gauges which will readily indicate (i) to the man-lock attendant the *pressure* in the *man-lock* and the *pressure* in each working chamber to which the *man-lock* affords direct or indirect access, and (ii) to persons in the *man-lock* the *pressure* in the *man-lock*;

(b)   a clock or clocks in a suitable position or suitable positions so that the *man-lock* attendant and persons in the *man-lock* can readily ascertain the time;

   (c) efficient means of verbal communication between the lock attendant, the lock and the working chamber or chambers, and means enabling the person in the lock to convey visible or other non-verbal signals to the lock attendant outside; and

   (d) efficient means enabling the lock attendant, from outside the lock, to reduce or cut off the supply of compressed air into the lock.

(3) Valves or taps for controlling the flow of air into or from the lock shall be such as to enable the flow to be controlled with sufficient accuracy to ensure compliance with paragraph (3) of Regulation 10 of these Regulations.

(4) The arrangements shall be such that persons in the lock cannot reduce the air *pressure* except under the control of the lock attendant otherwise than by special means which shall be operated only in emergency and which shall normally be kept so sealed or protected as to disclose their use:

Provided that this paragraph need not be complied with when no person in the lock has been exposed to a *pressure* exceeding 1250 millibars.

(5) An *approved* notice [Form 753] which can be easily read, indicating precautions which should be taken by persons during their compression or decompression and after decompression, shall be affixed in each *man-lock*.

General note. See *Ransom v Sir Robert Mcalpine & Sons Ltd* (1971) 11 KIR 141, in which overcrowding in a man-lock was held to breach this regulation.

9. Use of man-locks.—(1) Subject to paragraphs (2) and (3) of this regulation, a *man-lock* shall be used solely for the compression or decompression of persons and not for the passage of plant or material and shall be maintained in a reasonably clean and sufficiently warm state; so, however, that nothing in this paragraph shall prevent any person carrying with him into the *man-lock* any hand-tools or hand-instruments used for the purpose of the work.

(2) Paragraph (1) of this regulation shall not apply where it is not reasonably practicable *(a)* to provide a separate *man-lock* for persons only, but in any such case not excepted by paragraph (3) of this regulation a lock when in actual use for the compression or decompression of a person or persons shall not be put, simultaneously, to any other use and shall be in a reasonably clean and sufficiently warm state.

(3) Nothing in the two preceding paragraphs of this Regulation shall apply to a lock which does not afford direct or indirect access to a working chamber in which the *pressure* exceeds 1250 millibars and in so far as a lock affords only indirect access to such a working chamber those paragraphs shall apply only whilst persons who have worked in the chamber are in the lock.

   (a) Reasonably practicable. See INTRODUCTORY NOTE 5.

10. Lock attendants, and Rules as to compression or decompression.— (1) Every *man-lock* shall, whilst any person is in that *man-lock* or in a working chamber to which the *man-lock* affords direct or indirect access, be in charge of a competent lock attendant who shall control the maximum rate of compressions and shall perform all decompressions in the *man-lock*. Where persons are employed in compresssed air at *pressures* exceeding 1250 millibars the lock attendant shall enter in a register [Form 752] kept in such form as may be prescribed—

(a) the times at which each person enters and leaves the *man-lock*;

(b) the *pressures* at the times of his entering and leaving the working chamber;

(c) the times taken to decompress each person and such other particulars as may be prescribed as to conditions in the *man-lock* or working chamber.

(2) Subject to the overall control by the lock attendant of the admission of compressed air into the lock he may on behalf of and if so authorised by his employer, allocate to a competent person who is to be compressed in the lock a duty of regulating from inside the lock in accordance with the Rules for the compression of persons, the admission of compressed air, and a duty to signify the lock attendant (unless the lock attendant is clearly aware of it) any complaint of discomfort by a person in the lock and any report by that person that the discomfort has ceased.

(3) Compression of a person in a *man-lock* shall not be carried out otherwise than in accordance with the Rules set forth in Part I of the Schedule to these Regulations and decompression of a person in a *man-lock* after being in a working chamber shall not be carried out otherwise than in accordance with the Rules set forth in Part II of the said Schedule:

Provided:—

(i) that compression or decompression, as the case may be, may be carried out in accordance with such alternative Rules (if any) as are *approved* for the purposes of this regulation, either generally or in such circumstances and subject to such conditions as may be specified in the certificate of approval; and

(ii) that this paragraph shall not apply as respects the emergency recompression and subsequent decompression of a person on health grounds.

(4) Save in an unforseen emergency, no person shall be compressed to a *pressure* exceeding 3450 millibars unless Rules for the decompression of persons from such a *pressure* have been *approved* under the foregoing paragraph of this Regulation.

(5) Where a person who has within the immediately proceeding period of five hours been exposed to a *pressure* greater than 1250 millibars is to be compressed in a *man-lock* other than the lock in which he was last decompressed, he shall, before compression, produce to the lock-attendant written particulars [Form 750], signed by the lock-attendant of the lock where he was last decompressed, indicating his last working period as defined in Part II of the Schedule to these Regulations. The said particulars shall as soon as practicable be entered in the prescribed register [Form 752] for the lock where he is compressed, and shall as soon as practicable be communicated to the attendant at any other lock from which the person is liable to return to the open air.

General note. See *Ransom v Sir Robert Mcalpine & Sons Ltd* (1971) 11 KIR 141: inadequately trained staff breached reg. 10.

11. Egress from working chamber. Whilst any person is in a working chamber the door between such chamber and any *man-lock* providing for his egress towards a lower *pressure* and not in use shall be kept open except when this is not reasonably practicable.

12. Temperature in working chamber.—(1) No person shall be employed or allowed to remain in any part of a working chamber under *pressure* where the wet bulb temperature exceeds 12 degrees Celsius except where and when his presence is essential for work which has to be done and all reasonably practicable *(a)* steps have been and are being taken towards securing that the wet bulb temperature does not exceed that figure.

(2) A wet bulb thermometer, in good working order, shall be provided in every working chamber.

(a) **Reasonably practicable.** See INTRODUCTORY NOTE 5.

13. Employment of persons without previous experience. No person shall be employed on work in compressed air unless he has had previous experience of such work or, if he has not had such experience, is under the supervision of a person experienced in such work; and in the case of a person not previously employed in compressed air, compression shall not be carried out unless he is accompanied in the *man-lock* by a person competent to advise him as to the appropriate conduct of persons during compression.

14. Medical supervision and certification.—(1) Where persons are employed in compressed air, their employer shall make arrangements for their medical supervision by an *employment medical adviser* or an *appointed director* and for their medical examination at a suitable place or places in accordance with these Regulations.

(2) Subject to the provisions of paragraph (7) of this regulation, no person shall be employed in compressed air unless he has been examined by an *employment medical adviser* or an *appointed doctor* and certified by him, by signed entry in that person's Compressed Air Health Register [Form 751] as provided in regulation 15 of these Regulations, to be fit for such employment and either—

(a) the date of such certificate is not more than three days earlier; or
(b) the person has been so employed within the previous three months having been certified in accordance with the requirements of these Regulations to be fit for such employment and has not to the knowledge of the employer suffered since the date of that certificate from any injury, disease or illness causing an incapacity for work of more than three days' duration.

(3) Without prejudice to any other requirement of these Regulations restricting employment in compressed air, no person shall be employed where the *pressure* exceeds 1250 millibars unless he has within the previous four weeks been examined and certified as aforesaid to be fit for employment in compressed air.

(4) Without prejudice to any other requirement of these Regulations a certificate by an *employment medical adviser* or an *appointed doctor* that a person is

fit for employment in compressed air may be issued subject to conditions as to the maximum *pressure* in which that person may be employed and as to the re-examination of that person after an interval specified in the certificate; and until that certificate is varied or revoked as provided for in these Regulations that person shall not be employed in compressed air otherwise than in accordance with a condition so imposed in the certificate, but account need not be taken for this purpose of variations of *pressure* which are of a sudden and exceptional character and which do not involve excess over the maximum for more than a very short time.

(5) If, when it is proposed to employ a person in compressed air, that person is suffering from a cold in the head, a sore throat, earache or any other ailment which he has reason to believe is likely to render him unfit for such employment, he shall forthwith report the matter to his employer or to the person placed in charge of the operations for the purposes of regulation 5 or to an *employment medical adviser* or an *appointed doctor*, and thereupon (subject to the provisions of paragraph 7 of this regulation) he shall not be employed in compressed air until he has, since so reporting, been examined by an *employment medical adviser* or an *appointed doctor* and certified by him, by signed entry in that person's Compressed Air Health Register [Form 751], to be fit for such employment.

(6) An *employment medical adviser* or an *appointed doctor* may, on examining or re-examining a person who has been or is proposed to be employed in compressed air, vary or revoke, by signed entry in that person's Compressed Air Health Register [Form 751], any current certificate as to his fitness for employment in compressed air, and if such certificate is revoked that person shall not thereafter be employed in compressed air until he has, since such revocation, been certified by an *employment medical adviser* or an *appointed doctor*, by signed entry in his said Health Register, to be fit for such employment.

(7) Where work in compressed air is urgently required to be done before it is reasonably practicable, because of the inaccessibility of an *employment medical adviser* or an *appointed doctor*, to arrange for any examination or obtain any certificate required by the foregoing provisions of this regulation, any examination so required of a person proposed to be employed on such work and any certificate so required in relation to any such person may be made or given by any duly qualified medical practitioner who in that behalf shall have all the powers of an *employment medical adviser* or an *appointed doctor*. The employer shall notify a Superintending Inspector *(a)* of Factories as soon as practicable whenever any work in compressed air is carried out in reliance on the provisions of this paragraph.

General note. Fees for examination by an employment medical adviser under this regulation are specified in the Health and Safety (Fees) Regulations 1992, S.I. 1992 No 1752.

(a) Inspector. See INTRODUCTORY NOTE 24.

15. Compressed Air Registers. Every person employed in compressed air shall have a Compressed Air Health Register, in the prescribed form [Form 751], in which his employer shall enter the name and address and telephone number (if any) of an *employment medical adviser* or an *appointed doctor* with whom for the time being the employer has made arrangements for his medical supervision under regulation 14(1) and in which *employment medical advisers* or *appointed doctors* shall enter particulars as to the certificates issued by them for the purposes of these Regulations. The said Health Register shall be kept by the employer or his representative whilst the person is in his employment, except at times when it is required by that person or by an *employment medical adviser* or an *appointed doctor* for purposes of these Regulations and shall be handed to the person on the termination of such employment. When an employer proposes to employ a person in compressed air and is not already in possession of a current Health Register for that person, that person shall produce his Health Register (if any) to the employer, and if the person is unable or fails to produce such Register the employer shall supply a fresh form of Register and shall not employ the person in compressed air until a certificate of fitness for such employment is entered therein in accordance with these Regulations. The employer shall also supply a fresh form of Register when an existing Register has become full and a further entry is required.

16. Advisory leaflets. When an employer commences to employ any person in compressed air for the first time in that employer's employment, he shall supply that person with the prescribed leaflet [Form 754] *(a)* containing advice as to precautions to be taken in connection with such work.

(*a*) *Prescribed leaflet.* The terms of the leaflet are set out in the Schedule to S.I. 1967 No. 112 (not printed in this book).

17. Health facilities. There shall be provided and maintained for the use of persons employed in compressed air—

(a) adequate and suitable accommodation for clothing, with adequate and suitable facilities for changing;

(b) adequate and suitable facilities for washing, including soap and clean towels; and

(c) adequate and suitable facilities for remaining on the site after decompression.

The facilities to be provided for the purposes of paragraph (c) of this regulation shall include facilities for sitting in shelter when not required to work, and shall be available for at least one-and-a-half hours after decompression in the case of persons who, in the course of the preceding working period, were under *pressures* exceeding 2750 millibars and for at least one hour after decompression in other cases:

Provided that the requirements in paragraph (c) shall apply only in the case of persons employed under a *pressure* exceeding 1250 millibars.

18. Medical lock.—(1) Where the *pressure* in a working chamber exceeds, otherwise than on an exceptional occasion, 1250 millibars a suitably constructed medical lock shall be provided and maintained and used solely for the treatment of persons working in compressed air. It shall be situated so as to be convenient for such treatment.

(2) The medical lock shall have not less than 1.83 metres clear headroom at its highest point, shall have two compartments so that the lock can be entered

while under *pressure*, and shall be adequately ventilated, heated and lighted. The lock and its equipment shall be kept in a clean state.

The lock shall be provided with suitable equipment including a couch not less than 1.83 metres in length, blankets, dry woollen garments, food lock, efficient means of verbal communication and of giving non-verbal signals between the inside and outside of the lock and between the two compartments, and a window or windows through which persons in either compartment can be observed from outside.

(3) The medical lock shall at all times be kept for immediate use and, whilst any person is actually employed in compressed air, shall be constantly in charge of a person trained in the use of a medical lock and in first aid, and suitably instructed as to the steps to be taken in the event of any person suffering from ill-effects of compressed air.

19. Supply of labels. Where any person is employed in compressed air at a *pressure* exceeding 1250 millibars, his employer shall supply him with a suitable and durable label, to be worn next to the body, for the guidance of others should the person be taken ill after leaving work, indicating that the person has been employed in compressed air, and giving up-to-date information as to the whereabouts of the medical lock provided near his place of employment.

20. Notification to hospitals. Where persons are employed in compressed air at *pressures* exceeding 1250 millibars, their employer shall see that a convenient and suitable public hospital is acquainted with the fact that such work is being undertaken and with the whereabouts of the site and with the name, address and telephone number (if any) of an *employment medical adviser* or an *appointed doctor* with whom arrangements have been made under regulation 14(1); and the hospital shall be notified when the compressed air operations on the site are completed.

21. Supply of hot drinks. Where persons are employed in compressed air at *pressures* exceeding 1250 millibars suitable arrangements shall be made for the supply of hot drinks to such persons when leaving the *man-lock* and when at any medical lock.

22. Duty to submit to medical examination. It shall be the duty of every person employed or proposed to be employed in compressed air to submit himself for medical examination in accordance with these Regulations at the appointed times.

23. Consumption of alcohol. No person employed shall consume alcohol whilst in compressed air.

SCHEDULE

RULES AS TO COMPRESSION AND DECOMPRESSION OF PERSONS
UNDER REGULATION 10(3)

PART I
RULES AS TO COMPRESSION

1. The *pressure* shall not, in the first minute after starting compression, be increased to more than 350 millibars.

2. When that *pressure* is reached, the *pressure* shall not be further increased until after the lapse of a period sufficiently long to enable the lock attendant to discover whether or not any person in the *man-lock* complains of discomfort.

3. After the lapse of that period, the *pressure* shall not be increased at a rate faster than 700 millibars.

4. Subject to the foregoing Rules, the *pressure* shall be increased gradually so as to ensure as far as practicable that no person suffers discomfort.

5. If any person complains of discomfort and such complaint is signified to the lock attendant or to a person to whom duties have been allocated under paragraph (2) of Regulation 10, any compression then proceeding shall be immediately stopped, and unless the person who complained of discomfort quickly reports that the discomfort has ceased and such report is conveyed to the lock attendant the lock attendant shall, without further delay, gradually reduce the *pressure* in the lock until the person reports that the discomfort has ceased; and if he does not so report the *pressure* shall be reduced gradually to atmospheric *pressure* and the person released from the lock.

PART II
RULES AS TO DECOMPRESSION

A. General

6. For the purposes of this Part of these Rules:
"working period" means when used in relation to a person the period or the sum of periods during which, since last subject to ordinary atmospheric *pressure* for at least five consecutive hours, the person has been under *pressure* in a working chamber or chambers. For this purpose the expression "working chamber" includes any place other than a lock in which the person is for the purpose of compression or decompression;
"basic pressure", that is to say, the *pressure* on which, subject to Rule 9, the procedure for the decompression of a person is to be based, means the highest *pressure* to which the person has been exposed in the course of his working period:
Provided that—
   (a) sudden and exceptional variations of *pressure* not involving excess *pressure* for more than a very short time may be disregarded.
   (b) where during the whole of his working period a person about to be decompressed has been in a working chamber in which (as in tidal waters) the *pressure* has gradually varied by more than 350 millibars in the course of that period, the basic *pressure* shall be the mean of the *pressures* halfway through that period and at the end of it;
   (c) where the conditions specified in Rule 10 (as to phases decompression) are fulfilled, the basic *pressure* may be taken to be a figure ascertained in accordance with Rule 11.

7.—(1) These Rules shall not apply to the decompression of a person who has not, in the course of his working period as defined in Rule 6, been exposed to a *pressure* exceeding 1250 millibars.

(2) If, in an unforseen emergency, a person has been exposed to a *pressure* exceeding 3450 millibars these Rules shall, as nearly as may be practicable, be applied as if the Decompression Table referred to in Rule 8 had been extended by the addition of figures calculated in accordance with the same principles.

B. Normal Procedure

8. Save as provided for in Rules 12 to 14 (as to decanting), the procedure specified in this Rule shall, subject to Rule 9 and (where they apply) Rules 10 and 11 (as to phase decompression), be followed in the decompression of persons—

(1) ascertain in the case of each person to be decompressed, his "basic pressure" and his "working period";

(2) reduce the *pressure* fairly quickly at first, but do not, within the first two minutes after starting decompression, reduce it to less than the figure given in section 2 of the Decompression Table (contained in Table I annexed to this Schedule) next to the *pressure* range in section 1 of that Table within which the person's basic pressure falls;

(3) after that figure is reached, but not before the end of the first two minutes, the *pressure* may be reduced further but reduced at a rate not faster than the rate (or approximately the rate) given in Column R and reduced to atmospheric *pressure* in a time not less than that given in column T in section 3 of the said Table in the same line as the figure and *pressure* range in sections 1 and 2 and underneath the working period.

9. Where two or more persons are being decompressed in a *man-lock* at the same time then—

(1) if their basic *pressures* all fall within the same range in section 1 of the Decompression Table (contained in Table I annexed to this Schedule), but their working periods do not fall within the same range in section 3 of that Table, the procedure to be applied shall be that for the longest of their working periods;

(2) if their basic pressures do not fall within the same range, the lowest permissible pressure within the first two minutes shall be that for the person or persons with the highest basic *pressure*, and after that lowest permissible *pressure* is reached but not before the end of the first two minutes the *pressure* shall be reduced, as uniformly as may be, at a rate not faster than the rate which reduces the *pressure* to zero in a time equivalent to the longest and the respective times which would be required according to column T of the said Table for the respective persons in the lock if each of them were being separately decompressed.

C. Phase Decompression

10. If—

(1) a person employed in a working chamber under *pressure* passes through an intermediate *man-lock*, where he is partly decompressed, into a chamber intermediate between the first-mentioned chamber and the *man-lock* in which he is further decompressed to atmospheric *pressure*; and

(2) the *pressure* in the intermediate chamber when he enters it is not less than the lowest *pressure* to which he could, in accordance with these Rules, be decompressed in the intermediate *man-lock* within the first two minutes; and

(3) he remains in the intermediate chamber for a period (referred to in these Rules as "the intermediate period") of more than half-an-hour before entering a *man-lock* for further decompression,

then for the purposes of decompression to that *man-lock* in accordance with these Rules the basic *pressure* for that person may be taken to be a figure ascertained in accordance with the next following Rule.

11.—(1) Ascertain in the case of the person to be decompressed (a) his intermediate period and (b) his working period up to the commencement of his intermediate period.

(2) Ascertain from Table II annexed to this Schedule the zone (signified by a capital letter) corresponding to those two periods.

(3) Ascertain the difference (referred to in these Rules as "the *pressure* difference") between the highest *pressure* to which the person has been exposed in the first working chamber and the *pressure* in the intermediate chamber when he entered that chamber.

(4) Ascertain from Table III annexed to this Schedule the allowable deduction corresponding to the zone and *pressure* difference.

(5) Deduct the allowable deduction from the highest *pressure* to which the person has been exposed in the course of his working period. The resultant figure may be taken to be the basic pressure.

D. Decanting

12. In these Rules "decanting" means rapid decompression of persons in a *man-lock* to atsmospheric *pressure*, followed promptly by their rapid re-compression in a separate decompression chamber and subsequent more gradual decompression to atmospheric *pressure*.

13. Instead of compliance with the foregoing Rules in this Part of this Schedule as to decompression, the procedure of decanting may, subject to compliance with the conditions specified in Rule 14 hereof, be resorted to where and when—

(1) it is not reasonably practicable to provide, opening directly to air at atmospheric *pressure*, and as a means of egress to the open air from a place or places where persons are employed in compressed air, either

    (a) a separate *man-lock* used solely for the compression or decompression of persons and not for the passage of plant or material, or

    (b) a *man-lock* other than a *man-lock* of the vertical type; and

(2) compliance with the foregoing Rules of this Schedule as to rates of decompression would, in view of the numbers of workmen concerned in conjunction with the long delay which would be involved in affording them egress from the working chamber or chambers, seriously interfere with the carrying on of the work or be likely to be detrimental to their safety or health; and

(3) it is not reasonably practicable to avoid decanting by means of one or more transfer locks in which the workmen are transferred, at the same *pressure* as that in the working chamber, from a lock opening out of the working chamber to a separate decompression chamber in which the foregoing Rules in this Part of this Schedule as to decompression are complied with.

14. The following provisions shall apply in connection with decanting, namely—

(1) a separate decompression chamber or chambers shall be provided and suitably situated in sufficient numbers, to the extent of not less than one for each working chamber. Such decompression chambers shall be deemed to be *man-locks* for the purposes of the Regulations and of these Rules. The medical lock shall not be used for decanting;

(2) the Doctor appointed under paragraph (1) or paragraph (7) of regulation 14 shall have been specifically informed by the employer that decanting is to be carried out at the site in question;

(3) re-compression in the decompression chamber shall be to a *pressure* equivalent as nearly as practicable to the *pressure* in the working chamber from which the persons in the decompression chamber entered the *man-lock* in which they were decompressed. Part I of these Rules (which relates to the compression of persons) shall not apply to such re-compression. Rules 6 to 11 of this Part of these Rules shall apply to their subsequent decompression in the decompression chamber as if it were decompression in the said *man-lock*;

(4) the total time spent on (a) the primary decompression in the *man-lock*, (b) going from that *man-lock* to the decompression chamber, and (c) re-compression in that chamber shall, except when this is not reasonably practicable, not exceed five minutes.

[**Note.** *The Decompression Table and Phase Decompression Tables which conclude these Rules are not printed in this book.*]

CERTIFICATE OF EXEMPTION No. 1—TESTING OF AIRCRAFT
F 2075, 9 October 1961

THE WORK IN COMPRESSED AIR SPECIAL REGULATIONS 1958 (AS AMENDED BY THE
WORK IN COMPRESSED AIR (AMENDMENT) REGULATIONS 1960

Whereas I am satisfied that the requirements of the Work in Compressed Air Special Regulations 1958 (as amended by the Work in Compressed Air (Amendment) Regulations 1960) are not necessary for the protection of the persons employed in the case of the work hereinafter referred to, now, therefore, in pursuance of the powers conferred on me by paragraph (3) of regulation 2 of the said Regulations I hereby exempt from the requirements of the said Regulations work in compressed air at pressures not exceeding ten pounds per square inch above atmospheric pressure when undertaken in aircraft subject to test pressures.

This certificate shall come into operation on the ninth day of October 1961 and shall remain in force until revoked by H.M. Chief Inspector of Factories.

THE COTTON CLOTH FACTORIES REGULATIONS 1929

(S.R. & O. 1929 No. 300 as amended by S.I. 1992 No. 1811 and
S.I. 1992 No. 3004)

[Placard: Form 321]

In pursuance of section 1 of the Factory and Workshop (Cotton Cloth Factories) Act 1929, I hereby make the following Regulations.

These Regulations, which may be cited as the Cotton Cloth Factories Regulations 1929, shall come into force on 15 May 1929, from which date the Regulations under the Factory and Workshop (Cotton Cloth Factories) Act 1911 shall be repealed.

Definitions

For the purposes of these Regulations,—

"Weaving shed" means any room in which the weaving of cotton cloth is carried on.

"Humid shed" means any room in which the weaving of cotton cloth is carried on with the aid of *artificial humidification*.

"Artificial humidification" means humidification of the air of a room by any artificial means whatsoever, except the use of gas or oil for lighting purposes only.

"Dry bulb temperature" means the temperature measured by an accurate and properly maintained thermometer (which may form part of the *hygrometer*) and any reference in the Regulations to a dry bulb thermometer or without qualification to a thermometer shall be taken to be a reference to such a thermometer and a reference without qualification to temperature shall be taken to be a reference to the dry bulb temperature.

"Dry shed" means any room, other than a *humid shed,* in which the weaving of cotton cloth is carried on.

"Degrees" (of temperature) means degrees on the Celsius scale.

"Hygrometer" means an acccurate and properly maintained and calibrated instrument for the measurement of the relative humidity in the workplace.

"Wet bulb temperature" means either—

(a) the temperature indicated by the wet bulb of a static *hygrometer* which relies on natural circulation of air around the thermometer; or
(b) the temperature calculated from the dry bulb temperature and relative humidity by the method approved for the time being by the Health and Safety Executive.

In these Regulations references to the *dry bulb reading of the hygrometer* and the *wet bulb reading of the hygrometer* shall be taken to be references to the *dry bulb temperature* and the *wet bulb temperature* respectively.

Regulations

1.   There shall be no artificial humidification in any *weaving shed*—

  (a) at any time when the wet-bulb reading of the *hygrometer* exceeds 22.5 *degrees*, the reading to be the average of the readings of all the *hygrometers* provided in the shed in pursuance of regulation 3; or
  (b) at any time when the wet-bulb reading of the *hygrometer* is higher than that specified in the Schedule of this Order in relation to the dry-bulb reading of the *hygrometer* at that time; or, as regards a dry-bulb reading intermediate between any two dry-bulb readings indicated consecutively in the Schedule, when the dry-bulb reading does not exceed the wet-bulb reading to the extent indicated in relation to the lower of those two dry-bulb readings.

If the average wet-bulb reading of all the *hygrometers* provided in the shed in pursuance of regulation 3 exceeds 27 *degrees*, all work shall cease in the shed until the reading drops to 27 *degrees* or less, and the workers shall leave the shed.

2.   No water which is liable to cause injury to the health of the persons employed, or to yield effluvia, shall be used for *artificial humidification*, and for the purpose of this regulation any water which absorbs from acid solution of permanganate of potash in four hours at 16 *degrees* more than 7 milligrams of oxygen per litre of water, shall be deemed to be liable to cause injury to the health of the persons employed.

3.   In each *weaving shed* two *hygrometers* and a thermometer close to each *hygrometer* and one additional *hygrometer* and thermometer for every 500 or part of 500 looms in excess of 700 looms shall be provided, in such positions as may be approved by an inspector.

4.—(1) In every *weaving shed* the readings of each *hygrometer* and thermometer provided in pursuance of regulation 3 shall be observed on every day on which any workers are employed in the shed, between 15 and 30 minutes from the commencement of work, between 11 a.m. and 12 noon and (except on Saturday) between 4 and 5 p.m. and a record of those readings shall be made.

   (2) The said records shall be kept by the occupier for at least two years from when they were made and the occupier shall give his employees immediate access to those records on request together with such information as is necessary for their interpretation.

5.   In every *weaving shed* the arrangements shall be such that (1) during working hours the temperature shall not be below 10 *degrees* during the first half hour and 13 *degrees* thereafter throughout the working day, and (2) no person employed shall be exposed to a direct draught from any air inlet, or to any draught at a temperature of less than 10 *degrees*.
   In a tenement factory it shall be the duty of the owner to provide and maintain the arrangements required for the purposes of the requirement marked (1) in this regulation.

General Note. This Regulation is to be repealed as from 1 January 1996 by the Workplace (Health, Safety and Welfare) Regulations 1992, S.I. 1992 No. 3004, for

workplaces in existence on 31 December 1992. The "new" Regulations will apply to those workplaces from the former date. The "old" Regulations cease to have effect and the "new" Regulations apply: to workplaces coming into use after 31 December 1992; and to modifications, extensions and conversions started after 31 December 1992 to existing workplaces as soon as they come into use.

6. In a *weaving shed* in which steam pipes are used for the introduction of steam for the purpose of *artificial humidification* of the air—

(a) the diameter of such pipes shall not exceed 50 millimetres bore, and in the case of pipes installed after 1 April 1912; the diameter shall not exceed 25 millimetres bore;

(b) such pipes shall be as short as is reasonably practicable;

(c) such pipes shall be kept effectively covered with insulating material in good repair;

(d) all hangers supporting such pipes shall be separated from the bare pipes by an efficient insulator not less than 13 millimetres in thickness;

(e) no uncovered jet from such a pipe shall project more than 115 millimetres beyond the outer surface of such covering;

(f) the steam pressure shall be as low as practicable, and shall not exceed 4.8 bar.

General Note. This Regulation is to be repealed as from 1 January 1996 by the Workplace (Health, Safety and Welfare) Regulations 1992, S.I. 1992 No. 3004, for workplaces in existence on 31 December 1992. The "new" Regulations will apply to those workplaces from the former date. The "old" Regulations cease to have effect and the "new" Regulations apply: to workplaces coming into use after 31 December 1992; and to modifications, extensions and conversions started after 31 December 1992 to existing workplaces as soon as they come into use.

7. In every *humid shed* erected after 1 April 1912, and in every *dry shed* hereafter erected and any building (not being part of an existing cotton cloth factory) hereafter converted for use as a weaving shed—

(a) the average height of the shed shall not be less than 4.4 metres nor the height of the valley-gutters from the floor less than 3.6 metres;

(b) the lights shall face between North-East and North-North-West;

(c) the glass of the lights shall be at an angle of not more than 30 degrees to the vertical, except in the case of flat concrete or brick roofs;

(d) the boiler-house and engine-room shall be separated from the shed by an alley-way, not less than 2 metres wide and either open to the outside air or provided with louvre or roof ventilators capable of being opened in summer and of an area equal to one quarter of the floor area in the alley-way;

(e) no boiler flue shall pass under the shed, or within 2 metres horizontally from the wall of the shed.

The provisions of paragraphs (d) and (e) shall apply also to any existing *weaving shed* in which any alteration or addition is made, unless exemption is granted by the Chief Inspector *(a)* of Factories in the manner provided by these Regulations.

General Note. This Regulation is to be repealed as from 1 January 1996 by the Workplace (Health, Safety and Welfare) Regulations 1992, S.I. 1992 No. 3004, for

workplaces in existence on 31 December 1992. The "new" Regulations will apply to those workplaces from the former date. The "old" Regulations cease to have effect and the "new" Regulations apply: to workplaces coming into use after 31 December 1992; and to modifications, extensions and conversions started after 31 December 1992 to existing workplaces as soon as they come into use.

   (a) *Inspector.* See INTRODUCTORY NOTE 24.

8. In every *weaving shed* the whole of the outside of the roof (windows excepted) and the inside or outside surface of the glass of the roof-windows shall be white-washed every year before 31 May, and the white-wash shall be effectively maintained until 15 September.

   General Note. This Regulation is to be repealed as from 1 January 1996 by the Workplace (Health, Safety and Welfare) Regulations 1992, S.I. 1992 No. 3004, for workplaces in existence on 31 December 1992. The "new" Regulations will apply to those workplaces from the former date. The "old" Regulations cease to have effect and the "new" Regulations apply: to workplaces coming into use after 31 December 1992; and to modifications, extensions and conversions started after 31 December 1992 to existing workplaces as soon as they come into use.

9. In every *humid shed* and in every *dry shed* the arrangements for ventilation shall be such that at no time during working hours shall the proportion of carbon dioxide in the air in any part of the shed exceed the limit specified below for that shed, namely,—

for *humid sheds* eight
for *dry sheds* eleven

parts by volume of carbon dioxide per 10,000 parts of air in excess of the proportion in the outside air at the time.

   Provided that—
   (1) during any period in which it is necessary to use gas or oil for lighting purposes, and
   (2) before the end of the dinner-hour on any day in which gas or oil has been so used,

it shall be sufficient compliance with this regulation if means of ventilation sufficient to secure observance of the above requirement during daylight are maintained in full use and in efficient working order.

   Where roof ventilators are used, the intakes shall be at least 920 millimetres above the ridges, and where the ventilator intake is at the side of the mill, it shall be on the cool or shady side of the shed.

   If the average of the wet-bulb readings of the *hygrometers* between 11 a.m. and 12 noon shows that a reading of 22.5 *degrees* has been reached, all the available means of natural ventilation shall be kept in full operation during the whole of the mid-day meal interval, and if the average between 4 and 5 p.m. shows the same reading has been reached, all the available means of natural ventilation shall be kept in full operation for two hours at least after the time at which the period of employment ends.

   General Note. This Regulation is to be repealed as from 1 January 1996 by the Workplace (Health, Safety and Welfare) Regulations 1992, S.I. 1992 No. 3004, for

workplaces in existence on 31 December 1992. The "new" Regulations will apply to those workplaces from the former date. The "old" Regulations cease to have effect and the "new" Regulations apply: to workplaces coming into use after 31 December 1992; and to modifications, extensions and conversions started after 31 December 1992 to existing workplaces as soon as they come into use.

10.　In every *humid shed* erected after 2 February 1898, and in every *dry shed* erected after the 1 January 1928, sufficient and suitable cloak-room or cloak-rooms shall be provided for the use of all persons employed therein, and shall be ventilated and kept at a suitable temperature, provided that in any *weaving shed* erected after 1 January 1928, the accommodation shall not be regarded as sufficient unless a locker or separated space for the clothing of each worker is provided, nor as suitable unless the cloak-room is kept clean, properly warmed and ventilated, and under the supervision of a responsible person.

　In every *humid shed* and *dry shed* to which the above provision does not apply and in which a suitable and sufficient cloak-room is not provided, suitable and sufficient accommodation within the shed shall be provided for the clothing of all persons employed, within a reasonable distance of the place of employment and consisting of a sufficient number of pegs, not less than one for each person employed and not less than 460 millimetres measured in a horizontal direction apart, and of a covering of suitable non-conducting material spaced not less than 13 millimetres from the wall or pillar, and so arranged that no moisture either from above, or from the wall or pillar, can reach the clothing.

　General Note. This Regulation is to be repealed as from 1 January 1996 by the Workplace (Health, Safety and Welfare) Regulations 1992, S.I. 1992 No. 3004, for workplaces in existence on 31 December 1992. The "new" Regulations will apply to those workplaces from the former date. The "old" Regulations cease to have effect and the "new" Regulations apply: to workplaces coming into use after 31 December 1992; and to modifications, extensions and conversions started after 31 December 1992 to existing workplaces as soon as they come into use.

10A.—(1)　Subject to paragraph (2) of this regulation, the Health and Safety Executive may, by a certificate in writing, exempt any person or class of persons, from all or any of the requirments or prohibitions imposed by these Regulations and any such exemption may be granted subject to conditions and to a limit of time and may be revoked by a certificate in writing at any time.

　(2)　The Executive shall not grant any such exemption unless, having regard to the circumstances of the case and in particular to—

　　(a)　the conditions, if any, that it proposes to attach to the exemption; and
　　(b)　any requirements imposed by or under any enactments which apply to the case,

it is satisfied that the health or safety of persons who are likely to be affected by the exemption will not be prejudiced in consequence of it.

Duties of persons employed

11.　Every person employed shall (a) report to his foreman any defect in any appliance or other thing provided in pursuance of these Regulations as soon as he becomes aware of it; (b) use the appliances or other things required by the Regulations for the purpose for which they are provided.

General Note. This Regulation is to be repealed as from 1 January 1996 by the Workplace (Health, Safety and Welfare) Regulations 1992, S.I. 1992 No. 3004, for workplaces in existence on 31 December 1992. The "new" Regulations will apply to those workplaces from the former date. The "old" Regulations cease to have effect and the "new" Regulations apply: to workplaces coming into use after 31 December 1992; and to modifications, extensions and conversions started after 31 December 1992 to existing workplaces as soon as they come into use.

12. No person (unless duly authorised to do so) shall interfere with the (i) *hygrometers* and thermometers (ii) means of ventilation (iii) means of heating or (iv) means of humidification, provided in pursuance of these Regulations.

General Note. This Regulation is to be repealed as from 1 January 1996 by the Workplace (Health, Safety and Welfare) Regulations 1992, S.I. 1992 No. 3004, for workplaces in existence on 31 December 1992. The "new" Regulations will apply to those workplaces from the former date. The "old" Regulations cease to have effect and the "new" Regulations apply: to workplaces coming into use after 31 December 1992; and to modifications, extensions and conversions started after 31 December 1992 to existing workplaces as soon as they come into use.

SCHEDULE

Regulation 1(b)

Dry bulb readings	Wet bulb readings
(1)	(2)
10	9
11	10
12	11
13	12
14	13
15	14
16	15
17	16
18	17
19	18
20	19
21	20
22	20.5
23	21
24	22
25	22.5

THE FACTORIES (COTTON SHUTTLES) SPECIAL REGULATIONS 1952

(S.I. 1952 No. 1495)

The Minister of Labour and National Service, by virtue of the powers conferred upon him by section 50 of the Factories Act 1937, section 8 of the Factories Act 1948 and the Transfer of Functions (Factories, &c., Acts) Order 1946 and of all other powers enabling him hereby makes the following Special Regulations:

Short title and commencement

1. These Regulations may be cited as the Factories (Cotton Shuttles) Special Regulations 1952, and shall come into operation on the 1st day of November 1952.

Interpretation

2.—(1) The Interpretation Act 1889 [Interpretation Act 1978] applies to the interpretation of these Regulations as it applies to the interpretation of an Act of Parliament.

(2) In these Regulations, the expression "non-suction shuttle" means a shuttle which is not capable of being threaded or readily threaded by suction of the mouth.

Application

3. These Regulations apply to cotton cloth factories.

Use of non-suction shuttles

4.—(1) After the expiry of two years and six months from the making of these Regulations, it shall be an offence to take into use any shuttle (other than a non-suction shuttle) which has not previously been used.

(2) After the expiry of six years from the making of these Regulations no shuttle other than a non-suction shuttle shall be used.

(3) No person shall interfere with the threading arrangements of a non-suction shuttle in such a manner as to enable it to be threaded by suction of the mouth.

Exemptions

5.—(1) If the Chief Inspector *(a)* is satisfied in respect of any factory, or in respect of factories of any specified class or description, that, owing to the special conditions or special methods of work, or as respects a particular manufacture or process, any requirement of these Regulations is inappropriate or is not reasonably practicable, he may by certificate in writing (which he may at his discretion revoke at any time) exempt that factory or factories of that class or description or that manufacture or process from that requirement either absolutely or subject to such conditions as may be specified in the certificate.

(2) Where any certificate is issued under this regulation a legible copy thereof, showing the conditions (if any) subject to which it has been granted, shall be kept posted up in every factory to which the exemption applies in a position where it may be conveniently read by the persons employed.

*(a) **Inspector.*** See INTRODUCTORY NOTE 24.

THE DOCKS REGULATIONS 1988

(S.I. 1988 No. 1655, as amended by S.I. 1992 No. 195)

ARRANGEMENT OF REGULATIONS

1. Citation and commencement.
2. Interpretation.
3. Applications of the Regulations.
4. Persons upon whom duties are imposed.
5. Planning and execution of work.
6. Lighting.
7. Access.
8. Transport by water.
9. Rescue, life-saving and fire-fighting equipment, and means of escape.
10. Hatches, ramps and car-decks.
11. Drivers of vehicles and operators of lifting appliances.
12. Use of vehicles.
13. Use of lifting plant.
14. Testing of lifting plant.
15. Examinations of lifting plant.
16. Markings and indicators on lifting plant.
17. Certificates and reports.
18. Confined spaces.
19. Welfare amenities and protective clothing.
20. Duty to report defective plant.
21. Exemption certificates.
22. Enforcement.
23. Modifications to the Factories Act 1961.
24. Revocations and transitional provisions.

The Secretary of State, in exercise of the powers conferred on him by sections 15(1), (2), (3)(a) and (c), (4)(a), (5)(b) and 82(3)(a) of, and paragraphs 1(1)(a) and (c), (2), ((3), 9, 10, 11, 12, 14, 15(1), 16 and 18(a) of Schedule 3 to, the Health and Safety at Work etc. Act 1974 ("the 1974 Act") and of all other powers enabling him in that behalf and for the purpose of giving effect without modifications to proposals submitted to him by the Health and Safety Commission under section 11(2)(d) of the 1974 Act after carrying out by the said Commission of consultations in accordance with section 50(3) of that Act, hereby makes the following Regulations:

1. Citation and commencement. These Regulations may be cited as the Docks Regulations 1988 and shall come into force on 1 January 1989, except that regulation 14(2) shall come into force on 1 January 1993 and regulation 16(7) shall come into force on 1 September 1990.

2. Interpretation.—(1) In these Regulations, unless the context otherwise requires —

"the 1974 Act" means the Health and Safety at Work etc. Act 1974;

"access to" includes egress from;

"dock gate" means any lock gate or other gate which can close off the entrance to the dock or part of the dock from the sea or other waterway but does not include any gate on land which controls access by *vehicles* or pedestrians;

"dock operations" means—

(a) the loading or unloading *(a)* of *goods* on or from a *ship* at *dock premises*;

(b) the embarking or disembarking of passengers on or from a *ship* at *dock premises*;

(c) any activity incidental to the activities in sub-paragraphs (a) and (b) of this definition which takes place on *dock premises*, including any of the following activities specified in this sub-paragraph if they are so incidental and take place on *dock premises*—

  (i) the fuelling and provisioning of a *ship*,

  (ii) the mooring of a *ship*,

  (iii) the storing, sorting, inspecting, checking, weighing or handling of *goods*,

  (iv) the movement of *goods*, passengers or *vehicles*,

  (v) the use of *welfare amenities* in relation to the carrying out of activities referred to in sub-paragraphs (a), (b) and (c)(i) to (iv) above,

  (vi) attending *dock premises* for the purposes of the activities referred to in sub-paragraphs (a), (b) and (c)(i) to (v) above; or

(d) the embarking or disembarking on or from a *ship* of its crew at *dock premises*; but does not include—

(e) a fish loading process within the meaning of the Loading and Unloading of Fishing Vessels Regulations 1988,

(f) the loading or unloading of *goods*, or embarking or disembarking of persons, from a *pleasure craft* or any activity incidental to those activities, or

(g) beach landing operations wholly carried out by serving members of Her Majesty's Forces or visiting forces within the meaning of the provisions of Part I of the Visiting Forces Act 1952 or a combination of both;

"dock premises" means any dock, wharf, quay, jetty or other place at which *ships* load or unload *goods* or embark or disembark passengers, together with neighbouring land or water which is used or occupied, or intended to be used or occupied, for those or incidental activities, and any part of a ship when used for those or incidental activities;

"freight container" means a container as defined in regulation 2 of the Freight Containers (Safety Convention) Regulations 1984;

"goods" include—

(a) animals,

(b) pallets and *freight containers*,

(c) waste,

(d) solid ballast, and

(e) *vehicles* which are being transported as cargo;

"hatch" means a ship's hatch;

"hatch covering" includes *hatch* covers, *hatch* beams and attached fixtures and fittings;

"lifting appliance" means any stationary or mobile appliance (and every part thereof including attachments used for anchoring, fixing or supporting that appliance but not including *vehicle* coupling arrangements) which is used on *dock premises* for the purpose of suspending, raising or lowering loads or moving them from one position to another whilst suspended and includes lift trucks; it does not include—

(a) pipes, roadways or gangways, or
(b) screw, belt, bucket or other conveyors,

used for the continuous movement of goods or people, but does include the *lifting appliance* used to suspend, raise, lower or move any of those items;

"lifting gear" means any gear by means of which a load can be attached to a *lifting appliance* and which does not form an integral part of that appliance or load but does not include pallets, *one-trip slings*, *pre-slung cargo slings* and *freight containers*;

"lifting plant" means any *lifting appliance* or *lifting gear*;

"maintained" means maintained in an efficient state, in efficient working order and in good repair;

"one-trip sling" means a sling which has not previously been used for lifting any other load and is fitted to the load at the commencement of the journey and intended to be disposed of at the destination of that journey;

"pleasure craft" means any description of *vessel* when used solely for sport or recreation, other than for carrying fare paying passengers;

"pre slung cargo sling" means a sling which was in position round the *goods* before they were handled in the course of *dock operations*;

"safe working load" in relation to *lifting plant* means—

(a) the *safe working load* for that plant specified in the latest certificate or report of examination obtained pursuant to regulation 17, except that where the *safe working load* so specified is restricted to one particular operation, then for the purposes of regulation 16(1) to (5) only (which relates to markings and indicators on lifting plant), the *safe working load* shall be that appropriate to the plant under normal use; or

(b) where no certificate or report has been obtained pursuant to regulation 17 but a certificate or examination of the plant has been obtained pursuant to the Docks Regulations 1925 or the Docks Regulations 1934 which specifies the *safe working load*, the safe working load specified in the latest certificate so obtained; or

(c) where neither sub-paragraph (a) nor (b) above applies, the *safe working load* specified by the manufacturer of the plant in any written information supplied with the plant;

"ship" (except in regulation 4(4)) includes all *vessels* and hovercraft which operate on water or land and water;

"vehicle" includes all lift trucks, locomotives and rolling-stock, and trailers, and semi-trailers and other mechanical plant which moves on wheels, tracks, skids or any combination thereof;

"vessel" means any description of craft used for the transport of *goods* or passengers or the storage of *goods* or the accommodation of passengers on water, whether used in navigation or not;

"welfare amenities" means—

(a) sanitary conveniences;

(b) baths and shower baths;
(c) washing facilities (including wash basins, hot and cold running water and soap and clean towels or other suitable means of cleaning and drying);
(d) a supply of wholesome drinking water;
(e) a supply of protective clothing, that is to say, clothing suitable for the protection of the wearer in refrigerated spaces or against dirt from handling dirty *goods* or against inclement weather;
(f) accommodation and facilities for changing into clothing worn during working hours and for storing and drying clothing so worn and clothing not so worn;
(g) canteens or accommodation and facilities (including facilities for heating food and boiling water) for workers employed at *dock premises* to partake of meals provided by themselves;
(h) shelters for use during inclement weather.

(2) Unless the context otherwise requires, any reference in these Regulations to—

(a) a numbered regulation is a reference to the regulation of these Regulations so numbered;
(b) a numbered paragraph is a reference to that paragraph so numbered in the regulation in which the reference appears.

(3) Where a person supplies plant to another ("the customer") under a hire-purchase agreement, conditional sale agreement or lease and—

(a) he carries on the business of financing the acquisition of *goods* by others by means of such agreements, or, if financing by means of leases, the use of *goods* by others, and
(b) in the course of that business he acquired an interest in the plant supplied to the customer as a means of financing its acquisition by that customer (or, in the case of a lease, its provision to that customer), and
(c) in the case of a lease he or his agent either has not had physical possession of that plant, or has had physical possession of it only for the purpose of passing it on to the customer,

the customer and not the person who provided the finance shall be treated for the purposes of these Regulations as being the owner of the plant, and duties placed on owners in these Regulations shall accordingly fall on the customer and not on the person providing the finance.

(a) **Loading, unloading.** As to when loading or unloading is completed, see note (S) to s. 125 of the Factories Act 1961.

3. Application of the Regulations. These Regulations shall apply to and in relation to all *dock operations*—

(a) in Great Britain; and
(b) outside Great Britain within territorial waters to and in relation to the loading, unloading, fuelling or provisioning of a *vessel,* as sections 1 to 59 and 80 to 82 of the 1974 Act apply by virtue of Article 7 (b) of the Health and Safety at Work etc. Act 1974 (Application outside Great Britain) Order 1977 (a).

(*a*) *Health and Safety at Work etc. Act 1974 (Application outside Great Britain) Order 1977.* The Regulations are revoked; see now the Health and Safety at Work etc. Act 1974 (Application outside Great Britain) Order 1989, S.I. 1989 No. 840.

4. Persons upon whom duties are imposed.—(1) Subject to paragraphs (3) and (4), it shall be the duty of every—

(a) employer;

(b) self-employed person; and

(c) other person on whom a duty is imposed by section 4 of the *1974 Act*,

to comply with all provisions of these Regulations, but such a duty shall extend only to matters within his control.

(2) Subject to paragraphs (3) and (4), it shall be the duty of every employee to comply with such of these Regulations as relate to the performance of or the refraining from an act by him in the course of a *dock operation*.

(3) Paragraphs (1) and (2) shall not apply to regulations 8(4), 11(5), 17, 19(2) to (5), and 20, which expressly say on whom the duties are imposed.

(4) No duty imposed by these Regulations shall be placed upon—

(a) the master or crew of a ship; or

(b) any person employing the persons in sub-paragraph (a) above,

in relation to plant which remains on board the ship and any *dock operation* carried out on the ship solely by the master of the crew of the ship; and in this paragraph "master" and "ship" have the meanings assigned to them by section 742 of the Merchant Shipping Act 1894.

5. Planning and execution of work. Dock operations shall be planned and executed in such a manner as to ensure so far as is reasonably practicable that no person will be exposed to danger.

6. Lighting.—(1) Each part of *dock premises* which is being used for *dock operations* shall be suitably and adequately lighted.

(2) Every obstacle or hazard in *dock premises* which is likely to be dangerous when *vehicles, lifting appliances* or people move shall be made conspicuous by means of colouring, marking, lighting, or any combination thereof.

7. Access.—(1) Subject to paragraph (2), there shall be provided and properly *maintained* safe means of *access* to (*a*) every part of *dock premises* which any person has to visit for the purpose of *dock operations*, and in particular floors, decks, surfaces, stairs, steps, passages or gangways comprised in *dock premises* shall not be used unless they are of adequate strength for the purpose required, of sound construction (*b*) and properly *maintained* (*c*).

(2) So far as is reasonably practicable (*d*), all floors, decks, surfaces, stairs, steps, passages and gangways in *dock premises* shall be kept free from any substance or obstacle likely to cause persons to slip (*e*) or fall or *vehicles* to skid.

(3) Portable ladders shall not be used as a means of access to—

(a) *ships*;
(b) holds;
(c) *freight container* stacks on board *ships*; or
(d) a vertical stack of three or more *freight containers* on *dock premises* which are not part of a *ship*,

except where no other safer means of access is reasonably practicable *(d)*.

(4) All ladders (whether portable or not) shall be of good construction, *(e)* sound material, of adequate strength *(b)* for the purpose for which they are used, free from patent defect and properly *maintained (c)*.

(5) A ladder shall not be used unless—

(a) effective measures are taken to prevent it from slipping or falling; and
(b) it extends to at least 1 metre above the place of landing to which it provides access, or there is other adequate handhold *(f)*.

(6) There shall be secure and adequate fencing *(g)* at the following places where persons are engaged in *dock operations*, that is to say—

(a) every break, dangerous corner and other dangerous part or edge of a dock, wharf, quay or jetty;
(b) every open side of a gangway, footway over a bridge, caisson or dock gate; and
(c) any other place not being a quay or jetty where any person working or passing might fall *(h)* a distance of more than 2 metres,

except in so far as such fencing is impracticable *(c)* because of the nature of work carried out there and either the work is in progress or there is a short interruption for a meal or other purpose.

(a) **Safe means of access.** See the general note to s. 29 of the Factories Act 1961. Where a safe means of access is provided a plaintiff has no redress under this regulation if, for his own purposes, he uses another means of access which is not safe (*Lowe v Scruttons Ltd* [1953] 1 Lloyd's Rep 342).

(b) **Of sound construction; of good construction.** See INTRODUCTORY NOTE 11 and see also note *(b)* to s. 28 of the Factories Act 1961.

(c) **Properly maintained.** See INTRODUCTORY NOTE 10; see also note *(c)* to s. 28 of the Factories Act 1961.

(d) **Reasonably practicable.** See INTRODUCTORY NOTE 5.

(e) **Likely to cause persons to slip.** See note *(f)* to s. 28 of the Factories Act 1961.

(f) **Adequate handhold.** In *Wigley v British Vinegars Ltd* [1961] 3 All ER 418, [1961] 1 WLR 1261, CA; affd [1964] AC 307, [1962] 3 All ER 161, HL) it was held that "handhold" meant something which a man could hold or grasp from time to time as and when he wished to do so.

(g) **Secure . . . fencing.** See note *(l)* to s. 28 of the Factories Act 1961.

(h) **Might fall.** The question whether a person might fall a distance of more than 2 metres is, it is submitted, a question of fact to be considered objectively without regard to the mental or physical condition of the person working or passing.

(i) **Impracticable.** See INTRODUCTORY NOTE 5.

8. Transport by water.—(1) No *vessel* shall be used to transport a person at work to or from any working place unless the *vessel* is safe.

(2) Without prejudice to the generality of paragraph (1) vessels used for this purpose shall be—

(a) of a sound and suitable construction *(a)*;
(b) properly equipped;
(c) properly *maintained (b)*;
(d) in the charge of a competent person;
(e) neither overcrowded nor overloaded; and
(f) subject to paragraph (3), currently certified as suitable by a competent person in a certificate containing such particulars as are approved in writing for the time being by the Health and Safety Executive for the purposes of this regulation.

(3) Paragraph (2)(f) shall not apply to a vessel in respect of which there is in force a certificate as to a survey carried out pursuant to section 271 of the Merchant Shipping Act 1894.

(4) The current certificate referred to in paragraph (2)(f) shall be kept by the owner of the vessel.

(a) Sound . . . construction. See INTRODUCTORY NOTE 11; see also note *(b)* to s. 28 of the Factories Act 1961.

(b) Properly maintained. See INTRODUCTORY NOTE 10.

9.   Rescue, life-saving and fire-fighting equipment, and means of escape. All *dock premises* shall be provided with adequate and suitable—

(a) rescue and life-saving equipment;
(b) means to effect escape from danger; and
(c) fire-fighting equipment,

which shall be spaced at intervals that are reasonable in all the circumstances and be properly maintained *(c)*.

(a) Properly maintained. See INTRODUCTORY NOTE 10.

10.   Hatches, ramps and car-decks.—(1) A *hatch covering* shall not be used unless it is of sound construction *(a)* and material, of adequate strength for the purpose for which it is used, free from patent defect and properly *maintained (b)*.

(2) A *hatch covering* shall not be used unless—

(a) it can be removed and replaced, whether manually or with mechanical power, without endangering any person; and
(b) information showing the correct replacement position is clearly marked, except in so far as *hatch coverings* are interchangeable or incapable of being incorrectly replaced.

(3) A *hatch* shall not be used unless either the *hatch covering* has been completely removed or, if not completely removed, it is secure.

(4) A *hatch covering* shall not be replaced contrary to information showing the correct replacement position.

(5) A load shall not be placed on a *hatch covering* if it is likely to affect the safety of the *hatch covering* or endanger any person.

(6) Except in the event of an emergency endangering health or safety, no—

(a) ship's ramp or door associated with a ship's ramp;
(b) power operated *hatch covering*;
(c) retractable car-deck; or
(d) shore-based ramp,

shall be operated in the course of a *dock operation* except by a person authorised to do so by the person in control of that operation.

(a) *Sound construction.* See INTRODUCTORY NOTE 11; see also note (b) to s. 28 of the Factories Act 1961.

(b) *Properly maintained.* See INTRODUCTORY NOTE 10.

11.   Drivers of vehicles and operators of lifting appliances.—(1) Subject to paragraph (6), no powered *vehicle* shall be driven, or powered *lifting appliance* operated, by an employee in the course of *dock operations* unless he is authorised to do so by his employer.

(2) A person shall not be authorised under paragraph (1) to drive a *vehicle* or operate a *lifting appliance* unless he is fit to do so.

(3) Without prejudice to the generality of the preceding paragraph, a person shall be deemed to be unfit for the purpose specified in that paragraph if he is certified as so unfit by a registered medical practitioner.

(4) A person shall not be authorised under paragraph (1) to drive a *vehicle* or operate a *lifting appliance* unless—

(a) he is competent to do so;
(b) he has been appropriately trained; and
(c) in the case of a *lifting appliance* he is over 18 years of age or is a serving member of Her Majesty's Forces,

except where he is undergoing a suitable course of training under the proper supervision of a competent instructor.

(5) Every employer shall keep a record of the names of his employees who drive powered *vehicles* or operate powered *lifting appliances* in the course of *dock operations*, and such a record shall contain particulars of any relevant training provided by that employer.

(6) This regulation shall not apply to employees who drive *vehicles* on *dock premises* only in the course of visiting or passing through the premises or for the purpose of travelling on board a *ship* with that *vehicle*.

12.   Use of vehicles.—(1) *Vehicles* used by employees or self-employed persons in the course of *dock operations* shall be properly *maintained* (a).

(2) Danger from use and movement of all *vehicles* on *dock premises* shall so far as is reasonably practicable (b) be prevented and the means of preventing such danger shall where applicable include—

(a) safe and adequate railways, roadways, and parking facilities;
(b) adequate arrangements for traffic control which shall include proper signs and markings informing and warning drivers;
(c) safe arrangements for operating and moving *vehicles* where the driver's field of view is not sufficient to carry out the required operation or movement without risk of danger to any person;
(d) safe arrangements for refuelling *vehicles*;
(e) suitable barriers;
(f) safe arrangements for the movement and stacking of *freight containers*; and
(g) safe arrangements for coupling of *vehicles*.

(3) A *vehicle* used by an employee or a self-employed person in the course of *dock operations* shall not—

(a) carry any passenger except—
   (i) where proper passenger seating is available for and used by him, or other safe arrangements are made; and
   (ii) it is appropriate and necessary for the work being carried out;
(b) be driven in an unsafe manner; or
(c) carry any load which is insecure.

(a) Properly maintained. See INTRODUCTORY NOTE 10.

(b) Reasonably practicable. See INTRODUCTORY NOTE 5.

13. Use of lifting plant.—(1) No *lifting plant* shall be used unless it is—

(a) of good design and construction *(a)*;
(b) of adequate strength for the purpose for which it is used;
(c) of sound material and free from patent defect;
(d) properly installed or assembled; and
(e) properly *maintained (b)*.

(2) No—

(a) pallet or other similar piece of equipment for supporting loads;
(b) lifting attachment which forms an integral part of the load;
(c) *one-trip sling*; or
(d) *pre-slung cargo sling*,

shall be used unless it is of good construction (a), or adequate strength for the purpose for which it is used and free from patent defect.

(3) *Lifting plant* shall not be used other than in a safe and proper manner.

(4) Without prejudice to the generality of paragraph (3), the manner of use shall be deemed not to be safe and proper if, except for the purpose of carrying out a test under regulation 14, the *lifting plant* is loaded in excess of its *safe working load*.

(a) Good ... construction. See INTRODUCTORY NOTE 11; see also note *(b)* to s. 28 of the Factories Act 1961.

(b) Properly maintained. See INTRODUCTORY NOTE 10.

14. Testing of lifting plant.—(1) Subject to paragraph (3), no *lifting plant* shall be used—

(a) after manufacture or installation; or

(b) after any repair or modification which is likely to require an alteration to the *safe working load* or affect the *lifting plant's* strength or stability,

without first being suitably tested by a competent person except in the case of a rope sling manufactured from rope which has been tested by a competent person and spliced in a safe manner.

(2) Subject to paragraph (3), a *lifting appliance* which is on board a *ship* and is the property of the *ship* owner or is rented, leased or otherwise hired by him shall not be used unless it has been suitably tested by a competent person *(a)* within the preceding five years.

(2) This regulation shall not apply in relation to the use of *lifting plant* which is subject to the requirements of regulation 7 of the Merchant Shipping (Hatches and Lifting Plant) Regulations 1988.

*(a) **Competent person.*** A "competent person" is one who is a practical and reasonable man, who knows what to look for and how to recognise it when he sees it. (*Gibson v Skibs A/S Marina and Orkla Grobe A/B and Smith Cogging Ltd* [1966] 2 All ER 476).

15. Examination of lifting plant.—(1) Subject to paragraph (2), no *lifting plant* shall be used unless it has been thoroughly examined by a competent person—

(a) at least once in the preceding twelve months period or such shorter period as may have been specified by a competent person *(a)* in—

   (i) the latest record of examination of the plant obtained pursuant to regulation 17, or

   (ii) [*revoked*];

(b) following a test in accordance with regulation 14.

(2) This regulation shall not apply in relation to the use of *lifting plant* which is subject to the requirements of regulation 8 of the Merchant Shipping (Hatches and Lifting Plant) Regulations 1988.

*(a) **Competent person.*** See note *(a)*, reg. 14, above.

16. Markings and indicators on lifting plant.—(1) Every *lifting appliance* shall, subject to paragraph (2), be clearly and legibly marked with—

(a) its *safe working load* or *safe working loads*; and

(b) a means of identification.

(2) In the case of a *lifting appliance* having more than one *safe working load*, it shall be sufficient compliance with paragraph (1)(a) to have attached to the appliance tables setting out the *safe working loads*.

(3) Every crane whose *safe working load* varies with its operating radius shall, subject to paragraph (4), be fitted with an accurate indicator, clearly visible to the driver, showing the radius of the load lifting attachment at any time and the

safe working load corresponding to that radius; and in this paragraph the reference to the radius of the load lifting attachment is, in a case where the attachment is suspended on the end of a rope, a reference to the radius of the attachment when it is vertically below the point at which the rope is suspended from the crane.

(4) In the case of a telescopic jib mobile crane operating with a fly jib or a locked jib extension, it shall be sufficient compliance with paragraph (3) for the said indicator to show the angle of inclination of the jib at any time and the *safe working load* corresponding to that angle; and in this paragraph "fly jib" means an accessory fitted to the jib to form an extended jib, and "locked jib extension" means a part of the crane extended from the jib manually to form an extended jib.

(5) Every item of *lifting gear* shall be clearly and legibly marked with its *safe working load* or *safe working loads* and a means of identification, except where such marking is not reasonably practicable *(a)*, but in such a case the *safe working load* or loads shall be readily ascertainable to any user.

(6) Every item of *lifting gear* which weighs a significant proportion of the *safe working load* or any *lifting appliance* with which it is intended to be used shall, in addition to the requirement in paragraph (5), be clearly marked with its weight.

(7) Every mobile crane having either a fixed or a derricking jib shall, subject to paragraph (8), be fitted with an automatic safe load indicator or a type approved for the purposes of regulation 30 of the Construction (Lifting Operations) Regulations 1961, which indicator shall be–

(a) properly *maintained (b)*; and
(b) tested and inspected by a competent person *(c)* at appropriate intervals.

(8) Paragraph (7) shall not apply to any crane which—

(a) travels on a line of rails;
(b) has a *safe working load* of one tonne or less; or
(c) is fitted with a grab or magnet.

(a) **Reasonably practicable.** See INTRODUCTORY NOTE 5.

(b) **Properly maintained.** See INTRODUCTORY NOTE 10.

(c) **Competent person.** See note (a), reg. 14, above.

17. Certificates and reports.—(1) A record containing particulars approved in writing for the time being by the Health and Safety Executive for the purposes of this regulation shall be obtained from the competent person by the owner of the plant within 28 days following any test pursuant to regulation 14 or examination pursuant to regulation 15.

(2) A record of a test pursuant to regulation 14 shall be kept in a safe place by the owner until the plant is taken out of use, and a record of an examination pursuant to regulation 15 shall be kept by the owner in a safe place for a period of at least two years from receipt of the record of the next following examination.

(3) Where a test pursuant to regulation 14 or an examination pursuant to regulation 15 shows that a *lifting appliance* cannot be used with safety unless certain repairs are carried out immediately or within a specified time, a copy of

the record completed in accordance with paragraph (1) shall be supplied by the competent person to the Health and Safety Executive within 28 days of completion of the test or examination.

(4) The owner of the plant shall supply a copy of the latest record obtained under paragraph (1) to any employer or self-employed person hiring or using the plant, and any such hirer or user shall ensure that he receives it from the owner and consults it.

18.   Confined spaces. A person shall not be permitted to enter or remain in any space if he is liable to be overcome by gases or fumes or incapacitated by oxygen deficiency unless—

(a) it is necessary for him to do so; and
(b) effective steps have been taken to protect him from such danger.

19.   Welfare amenities and protective clothing.—(1) There shall be provided and maintained for the use of persons at work *welfare amenities* which are in all the circumstances adequate and suitable.

(2) If an employee is to work in a part of *dock premises* where there is a foreseeable risk of injury to the head and a suitable safety helmet would provide protection against that risk, his employer shall provide the employee with such a helmet, and the employee shall wear the helmet in a proper manner when working there.

(3) If an employee is to work on foot in an area in dock premises—

(a) where roll-on and roll-off operations are carried out,
(b) where work with straddle carriers is carried out, or
(c) which is a lorry park,

his employer shall provide the employee with a suitable high visibility garment, and the employee shall wear the garment in a proper manner when so working there; except that in the case of an area described in sub-paragraph (c) above, the garment need only be provided and worn if it is necessary for the employee's safety.

(4) In paragraph (3) (a) "roll-on and roll-off operations" means the driving of *vehicles* onto and off *ships* carried out on the shoreside approach to the *ship*, on the means of *access* to the *ship*, or on board the *ship*.

(5) Every self-employed person shall wear in a proper manner a suitable safety helmet or a suitable high visibility garment in the circumstances where an employee would be required by paragraphs (2) or (3), as the case may be, to wear such a helmet or garment provided to him under the appropriate paragraph.

20.   Duty to report defective plant. Where a self-employed person or an employee discovers any defect in any plant which he is required to use in the course of *dock operations* which he cannot rectify he shall, without unreasonable delay, report that defect to the person in control of that plant, or in the case of an employee, to his employer or the person in control of the plant.

21. Exemption certificates.—(1) Subject to paragraph (2), the Health and Safety Executive may, by certificate in writing, exempt any person or class of persons, or activity or class of activities to which these Regulations apply, from any requirement or prohibition imposed by these Regulations and any such exemption may be granted subject to conditions and to a limit of time and may be revoked by a certificate in writing at any time.

(2) The Executive shall not grant any such exemption unless, having regard to the circumstances of the case, and in particular to—

(a) the conditions, if any, which it proposes to attach to the exemption; and
(b) any other requirements imposed by or under any enactment which apply to the case,

it is satisfied that the health and safety of persons who are likely to be affected by the exemption will not be prejudiced because of it.

(3) The Secretary of State for Defence may in the interests of national security, by a certificate in writing, exempt from all or any requirements or prohibitions imposed by these Regulations—

(a) Her Majesty's Forces;
(b) visiting forces within the meaning of any of the provisions of Part I of the Visiting Forces Act 1952;
(c) any headquarters or organisation designated for the purposes of the International Headquarters and Defence Organisations Act 1964, and
(d) any person engaged in the carriage, keeping or supply of any military explosives (within the meaning of regulation 2(1) of the Classification and Labelling of Explosives Regulations 1983) if that person is under the direct supervision of the Ministry of Defence,

and any such exemption may be granted subject to conditions and to a limit of time and may be revoked by a certificate in writing at any time.

22. Enforcement.—(1) Notwithstanding the provisions of regulation 3, but without prejudice to regulation 5, of the Health and Safety (Enforcing Authority) Regulations 1977 *(a)*, the Health and Safety Executive shall, subject to paragraph (2), be responsible for the enforcement of the relevant statutory provisions in relation to any activity carried on in *dock premises.*

(2) Paragraph (1) shall not apply to the extent that some other authority or class of authorities is made responsible for such enforcement by any of the relevant statutory provisons other than the said Regulations of 1977.

(a) Now replaced by the 1989 Regulations of the same name.

23. Modifications to the Factories Act 1961. Section 125 of the Factories Act 1961 shall be modified as follows—

(a) for subsection (4), substitute:
"(4) Nothing in this section shall apply to any machinery or plant which is on board a ship and is the property of the ship owner or charterer, or is rented, leased or hired, by him or his agent, or is being purchased by him or his agent under a hire-purchase agreement or a conditional sale agreement (each within the meaning of section 53 of the Health and Safety at Work etc. Act 1974).";

(b) at the end of subsection (6), substitute a comma for the full stop and add:

> "except that this subsection shall not operate to apply the provisions to chains, ropes and lifting tackle, cranes and other lifting machines, or to the construction and maintenance of floors, passages and stairs, in warehouses which are dock premises.";

(c) after subsection (6) add the following subsections:

> "(7) The provisions of Part II of this Act, and any regulations made under that Part, with respect to prime movers, transmission machinery, other machinery, provisions as to unfenced machinery, construction and maintenance of fencing, hoists and lifts shall apply to all dock premises as if the dock premises were a factory , and the person having the control of such matter were the occupier of the factory in respect of that matter.

> (8) The provisions of section 173 of this Act (application to Crown) shall apply to all dock premises as if the dock premises were a factory, but only for the purpose of applying to the Crown such provisions of this Act as are applied to docks, wharfs, quays and dock premises by virtue of the foregoing provisions of this section.

> (9) In subsections (6), (7) and (8) of this section "dock premises" means any dock, wharf, quay, jetty or other place at which ships load or unload goods or embark or disembark passengers, together with neighbouring land or water which is used or occupied, or intended to be used or occupied, for those or incidental activities, and any part of a ship when used for those or incidental activities.".

24.   Revocations and transitional provisions.—(1) The Docks Regulations 1925 and the Docks Regulations 1934 are hereby revoked.

(2) Every certificate or register relating to a test or examination of plant carried out before the plant was taken into use, and which certificate or register was required to be kept in pursuance of any regulation revoked by these Regulations, shall, notwithstanding the revocation, continue to be kept for the same period and in the same manner as if these Regulations had not been made.

(3) Every certificate or register relating to a periodic thorough examination after the plant was taken into use, and which certificate or register was required to be kept in pursuance of any regulation revoked by these Regulations, shall, notwithstanding the revocation, continue to be kept for at least two years following the date of the examination, and shall be so kept in the same manner as if these Regulations had not been made.

THE DRY CLEANING SPECIAL REGULATIONS 1949

(S.I. 1949 No. 2224, as amended by S.I. 1983 No. 977 and S.I. 1992 No. 1811)

[Placard: Form 1036]

The Minister of Labour and National Service by virtue of the powers conferred upon him by section 60 of the Factories Act 1937, section 8 of the Factories Act 1948, and the Transfer of Functions (Factories, &c. Acts) Order 1946 and of all other powers in that behalf hereby makes the following Special Regulations:

1. Short title and commencement. These Regulations may be cited as the Dry Cleaning Special Regulations 1949, and shall come into operation on the 1st day of June 1950.

2. Interpretation.—(1) The Interpretation Act 1889 [Interpretation Act 1978] applies to the interpretation of these Regulations as it applies to the interpretation of an Act of Parliament.

(2) In these Regulations, unless the context otherwise requires, the following expressions have the meaning hereby assigned to them respectively, that is to say:

"*Dry cleaning*" means cleaning, with the aid of inflammable liquid, articles of a textile character or articles of wearing apparel, whether of a textile character or not.

"*Flash point*" means the flash point determined in accordance with Part IV of Schedule 1 to the Classification, Packaging and Labelling of Dangerous Substances Regulations 1984 (S.I. 1984/1244).

"*Spotting*" means the removal, by hand, of small stains with the aid of liquid taken from a receptacle of a capacity of not more than 570 millilitres.

(2A) Solely for the purposes of these Regulations, for sub-paragraph (b) of paragraph 4 of Schedule 1 to the Classification, Packaging and Labelling of Dangerous Substances Regulations 1984 there shall be substituted the following sub-paragraph—

"(b) by one of the non-equilibrium methods referred to in paragraph 6, except that when the flash point falls within the range 30°C to 34°C that flash point shall be confirmed by the use of like apparatus using the appropriate equilibrium method referred to in paragraph 5.".

3. Application of Regulations. Subject to the provisions of Regulation 5, these Regulations shall apply to all factories in which *dry cleaning* is carried on otherwise than by *spotting*:

Provided that these Regulations shall not apply to—

(a) factories in which no articles of a textile character and no articles of wearing apparel (other than articles made wholly or mainly of metal or articles of jewellery) are cleaned; or

(b) the cleaning in any factory of the textile parts of, or the textile equipment of, any machine or plant used in that factory.

4. Prohibition of the use of certain liquids.—(1) No liquid having a *flash point* below 32 degrees Celsius shall be used for *dry cleaning* otherwise than by *spotting*.

(2) [*Revoked*].

5. Exemptions.—(1) If the Chief Inspector *(a)* is satisfied that in any factory, or, in factories of any specified class or description, the prohibition in Regulation 4 cannot reasonably be applied to the cleaning of articles of any specified class or description, he may by certificate in writing (which he may in his discretion revoke at any time) as respects the cleaning of articles of that class or description exempt that factory or factories of that class or description from the application of these Regulations either absolutely or subject to such conditions as may be specified in the certificate.

(2) Where any certificate is issued under this regulation a legible copy thereof, showing the conditions (if any) subject to which it has been granted, shall be kept posted up in every factory to which the exemption applies in a position where it may conveniently be read by the persons employed.

(a) **Inspector.** See INTRODUCTORY NOTE 19.

THE ELECTRIC ACCUMULATOR REGULATIONS 1925

(S.R. & O. 1925 No. 28, as amended by S.I. 1973 No. 36 and
S.I. 1980 No. 1248)

In pursuance of section 79 of the Factory and Workshop Act 1901, I hereby make the following Regulations, and direct that they shall apply to all factories and workshops or parts thereof in which is carried on the manufacture or repair of electric accumulators or parts thereof:

Provided that these Regulations shall not apply to the manufacture or repair of electric accumulators or parts thereof not containing lead or any compound thereof; nor to the repair on the premises of any accumulator forming part of a stationary battery.

These Regluations, which may be cited as the Electric Accumulator Regulations 1925, shall come into force on 1 March 1925, from which date the Regulations for the Manufacture of Electric Accumulators made on 21 November 1903, under the above section shall be revoked.

Definitions

In these Regulations—

"*Lead Process*" means the melting of lead or any material containing lead, casting, pasting, lead burning, or any other work, including trimming, or any other abrading or cutting of pasted plates, involving the use, movement or manipulation of, or contact with, any oxide of lead.

"*Manipulation of raw oxide of lead*" means any *lead process* involving any manipulation or movement of raw oxide of lead other than its conveyance in a receptacle or by means of an implement from one operation to another.

Duties

It shall be the duty of the occupier to observe Part I of these Regulations.

PART I
DUTIES OF OCCUPIERS

1.—(i) No person under 18 years of age shall be employed in any *lead process*. Provided that nothing in this Regulation shall affect male young persons employed in (a) washing of formed pasted or Planté plates and subsequent brushing or racking thereof while in a wet state, or (b) casting of small accessory parts, who were so employed at the commencement of these Regulations.

(ii) No woman or young person under 18 years of age shall be employed in any room in which the *manipulation of raw oxide of lead* or pasting is carried on.

2–27. [*revoked*].

THE VITREOUS ENAMELLING REGULATIONS 1908

(dated 18 December 1908; S.R. & O. 1908 No. 1258, as amended
by S.I. 1973 No. 36, S.I. 1980 No. 1248 and
S.I. 1989 No. 2311)

[Placard: Form 952]

Whereas the process of vitreous *enamelling* of metal or glass has been certified in pursuance of section 79 of the Factory and Workshop Act 1901, to be dangerous:

I hereby, in pursuance of the powers conferred on me by that Act, make the following Regulations, and direct that they shall apply to all factories and workshops in which vitreous *enamelling* of metal or glass is carried on:

Provided that nothing in these Regulations shall apply to—

(a)   the *enamelling* of jewellery or watches; or
(b)   the manufacture of stained glass; or
(c)   *enamelling* by means of glazes or colours containing less than 1 per cent. lead.

These Regulations shall come into force on 1 April 1909.

Definitions

In these Regulations—

"*Enamelling*" means crushing, grinding, sieving, dusting or laying on, brushing or woolling off, spraying, or any other process for the purpose of vitreous covering and decoration of metal or glass;

"*Employed*" means employed in *enamelling*;

Duties

It shall be the duty of the occupier to observe Part I of these Regulations.

PART I
DUTIES OF EMPLOYERS

1.–6.   [*revoked*].

7.   No child shall be *employed* in any *enamelling* process.

8.–15.   [*revoked*].

THE LOADING AND UNLOADING OF FISHING VESSELS REGULATIONS 1988

(S.I. 1988 No. 1656)

ARRANGEMENT OF REGULATIONS

1. Citation and commencement.
2. Interpretation.
3. Application.
4. Duties.
5. Safe working place and safe access.
6. Safety of work and equipment.
7. Exemption certificates.
8. Enforcement.

The Secretary of State, in exercise of the powers conferred on him by sections 15(1), (2), (3)(c), (5)(b), and 82(3)(a) of, and paragraphs 1(1)(c), (2), 9, 12 and 18(a) of Schedule 3 to, the Health and Safety at Work etc. Act 1974 ("the 1974 Act") and of all other powers enabling him in that behalf and for the purpose of giving effect without modifications to proposals submitted to him by the Health and Safety Commission under section 11(2)(d) of the 1974 Act after carrying out by the said Commission of consultations in accordance with section 50(3) of that Act, hereby makes the following Regulations:

1. Citation and commencement. These Regulations may be cited as the Loading and Unloading of Fishing Vessels Regulations 1988, and shall come into force on 1 January 1989.

2. Interpretation. In these Regulations, unless the context otherwise requires—

"the 1974 Act" means the Health and Safety at Work etc. Act 1974;

"dock gate" means any lock gate or other gate which can close off the entrance to the dock or part of the dock from the sea or other waterway but does not include any gate on land which controls access by vehicles or pedestrians;

"fishing vessel" means any description of craft used for the transport or storage of wet fish, whether used in navigation or not, but does not include a craft when used—

(a) for the principal purpose of carrying passengers or goods other than *wet fish*; or

(b) solely for sport or recreation;

"fish loading process" means the loading, unloading, moving or handling of *wet fish* on, at, or nearby any *quay* or on any *fishing vessel* when moored at the

1575

quay or any activity incidental to those activities including the mooring, fuelling and provisioning of the *fishing vessel* at the *quay* or the transfer of *wet fish* from one *fishing vessel* to another when at least one of the *fishing vessels* is moored at the *quay*;

"handling" includes gutting of *wet fish* and loading of *wet fish* for transport, but does not include tinning, freezing solid in blocks, curing, freeze-drying or other means of *processing*;

"maintained" means *maintained* in an efficient state, in efficient working order and in good repair;

"processed" or "processing" does not include keeping fish, molluscs or crustaceans (or part of them) fresh by placing them on ice;

"quay" includes any wharf, jetty or dock;

"skipper" means the person (except a pilot) having command or charge of the *fishing vessel*;

"wet fish" includes all fish, molluscs and crustaceans whether living or dead but does not include—

(i) fishmeal, fish manure or fish guano, or

(ii) fish, molluscs or crustaceans which are, or have been, tinned, frozen solid on blocks, or otherwise processed.

3.   Application. These Regulations shall apply to and in relation to all *fish loading processes* in Great Britain *(a)*.

*(a) **Great Britain.** See* INTRODUCTORY NOTE *4.*

4.   Duties. It shall be the duty of every—

(a) employer;

(b) self-employed person;

(c) *skipper* of a *fishing vessel*; and

(d) other person on whom a duty is imposed by section 4 of the 1974 Act,

to comply with all provisions of these Regulations, but such a duty shall extend only to matters within his control.

5.   Safe working place and safe access.—(1) Subject to paragraph (2) below, there shall be provided and properly *maintained* a safe place of work for any person engaged in a *fish loading process*, and safe access to *(a)* and egress from that place of work or any other place which any person has to visit for the purpose of the *fish loading process*.

(2) So far as is reasonably practicable *(b)* all floors, decks, surfaces, stairs, steps, passages and gangways in any place described in paragraph (1) above shall be kept free from any substance likely to cause persons to slip *(c)* or fall or vehicles to skid.

(3) There shall be provided secure and adequate fencing *(d)* at the following places where persons are engaged in *fish loading processes*, that is to say—

(a) every break, dangerous corner or other dangerous part or edge of a quay;

(b) every open side of a gangway, footway over a bridge, caisson or dock gate; and

(c) any other place not being a *quay* where any person working or passing might fall *(e)* a distance of more than two metres,

except in so far as such fencing is impracticable *(b)* because of the nature of the work carried out there and either work is in progress or there is a short interruption for a meal or other purpose.

(4) Each part of a *quay* or *fishing vessel* where persons are engaged in a *fish loading process,* and every means of access to and egress from there, shall be suitably and adequately lighted (*f*).

(5) Where persons are engaged in a *fish loading process* there shall be provided adequate and suitable—

(a) rescue and life-saving equipment;

(b) means to effect escape from danger; and

(c) fire-fighting equipment,

and they shall be spaced at intervals that are reasonable in all the circumstances and properly *maintained.*

(a) *Safe access.* See the general note to s. 29 of the Factories Act 1961; see also note *(a)* to reg. 7 of the Docks Regulations 1988.

(b) *Reasonably practicable; impracticable.* See INTRODUCTORY NOTE 5.

(c) *Likely to cause persons to slip.* See note *(f)* to s. 28 of the Factories Act 1961.

(d) *Secure . . . fencing.* See, generally, the Introductory Note to ss. 12–16 of the Factories Act 1961, and in particular, paragraphs 4–6 thereof.

(e) *Might fall.* See note *(h)* to reg. 7 of the Docks Regulations 1988.

(f) *Suitably and adequately lighted.* See note *(a)* to s. 5 of the Factories Act 1961.

6. Safety of work and equipment.—(1) Every *fish loading process* shall be planned and executed in such a manner as to ensure, so far as is reasonably practicable *(a)*, that no persons will be exposed to danger.

(2) Where persons are engaged in a *fish loading process* safe plant and equipment shall, so far as is reasonably practicable *(a)*, be provided and properly *maintained.*

(a) *Reasonably practicable.* See INTRODUCTORY NOTE 5.

7. Exemption certificates.—(1) Subject to paragraph (2) below, the Health and Safety Executive may, by certificate in writing, exempt any person or class of persons, or activity or class of activities to which these Regulations apply, from any requirement imposed by these Regulations and any such exemption may be granted subject to conditions and to a limit of time and may be revoked by a certificate in writing at any time.

(2) The Executive shall not grant any such exemption unless, having regard to the circumstances of the case, and in particular to—

    (a) the conditions, if any, which it proposes to attach to the exemption; and

    (b) any other requirements imposed by or under any enactment which apply to the case,

it is satisfied that the health and safety of persons who are likely to be affected by the exemption will not be prejudiced because of it.

8.   Enforcement. Notwithstanding the provisions of regulation 3, but without prejudice to regulation 5, of the Health and Safety (Enforcing Authority) Regulations 1977 *(a)*, the authority responsible for enforcing—

    (a) these Regulations; and

    (b) sections 2 to 4 and 6 to 8 of the 1974 Act in relation to a fish loading process,

shall be the Health and Safety Executive.

    (a) Now replaced by the 1989 Regulations of the same name.

THE FLAX AND TOW SPINNING AND WEAVING REGULATIONS 1906

(Dated 26 February 1906; S.R. & O. 1906 No. 177,
as amended by S.I. 1988 No. 1657, S.I. 1992 No. 1811,
S.I. 1992 No. 2966 and S.I. 1992 No. 3004)

[*Placard: Form 943*]

Whereas the processes of spinning and weaving flax and tow and the processes incidental thereto have been certified in pursuance of section 79 of the Factory and Workshop Act 1901, to be dangerous:

I hereby in pursuance of the powers conferred on me by that Act make the following Regulations, and direct that they shall apply to all factories in which the processes named above are carried on, and to all workshops in which the processes of *roughing, sorting,* or *hand-hackling* of flax or tow are carried on.

These Regulations shall come into force on the 1st day of February 1907:

Provided that in the case of all rooms in which *roughing* or *hand-hackling* is now carried on, and in which there is respectively (a) no system of local mechanical exhaust ventilation, or (b) no artificial means of regulating the temperature, regulations 2 and 3 respectively shall not come into force until the 1st day of February 1908.

Definitions

In these Regulations—

"*Degrees*" means degrees on the Celsius scale.

"*Dry bulb temperature*" means the temperature measured by an accurate and properly maintained theremometer (which may form part of the *hygrometer*) and any reference in these Regulations to a dry bulb thermometer or without qualification to a "*thermometer*" shall be taken to be a reference to such a thermometer and a reference without qualification to temperature shall be taken to be a reference to the dry bulb temperature.

"*Hygrometer*" means an accurate and properly maintained and calibrated instrument for the measurement of the relative humidity in the work-place.

"*Roughing, sorting, hand-hackling, machine-hackling, carding* and *preparing*" means those processes in the manufacture of flax or tow.

"*Wet bulb temperature*" means either—

(a) the temperature indicated by the wet bulb of a static *hygrometer* which relies on natural circulation of the air around the thermometer; or

(b) the temperature calculated from the dry bulb temperature and relative humidity by the method approved for the time being by the Health and Safety Executive,

and any reference in these Regulations to the reading of the wet bulb thermometer shall be treated as a reference to the wet bulb temperature.

1579

It shall be the duty of the occupier to observe Part I of these Regulations.

It shall be the duty of all persons employed to observe Part II of these Regulations.

PART I
DUTIES OF OCCUPIERS

1. [*revoked*].

2. [*revoked*].

3. In every room in which *hand-hackling, roughing, sorting, machine-hackling, carding*, or *preparing* is carried on, an accurate *thermometer* shall be kept affixed; and the arrangements shall be such that the temperature of the room shall not at any time during working hours where *hand-hackling, roughing*, or *machine-hackling* is carried on, fall below 10 *degrees*, or where *sorting, carding*, or *preparing* is carried on, below 13 *degrees*; and that no person employed shall be exposed to a direct draught from any air inlet, or to any draught at a temperature of less than 10 *degrees*:

Provided that it shall be a sufficient compliance with this regulation if the heating apparatus be put into operation at the commencement of work, and if the required temperature be maintained after the expiration of one hour from the commencement of work.

General note. This regulation is revoked by the Workplace (Health, Safety and Welfare) Regulations 1992, S.I. 1992 No. 3004, as from 1 January 1993 except, in relation to any workplace or part of a workplace which is not a new workplace, or a modification, an extension or a conversion, it is revoked as from 1 January 1996.

4.—(1) In every room in which wet spinning is carried on, or in which artificial humidity is produced in aid of manufacture a *hygrometer* and a *thermometer* close to the *hygrometer* shall be positioned in the centre of the room or in such other position as may be directed by an inspector by notice in writing.

(2) The *hygrometer* and the *thermometer* shall be read between 10 and 11 a.m. on every day that any person is employed in the room and again between 3 and 4 p.m. on every day that any person is employed in the room after 1 p.m. and a record of all such readings shall be kept.

(3) The said record shall be kept by the occupier for at least two years from when it was made and the occupier shall give his employees immediate access to those records on request together with such information as is necessary for their interpretation.

5.   The humidity of the atmosphere of any room to which Regulation 4 applies shall not at any time be such that the difference between the readings of the wet and dry bulb thermometers is less than 1 *degree*.

6.   No water shall be used for producing humidity of the air, or in wet-spinning troughs, which is liable to cause injury to the health of the persons employed or to yield effluvia; and for the purpose of this regulation any water which absorbs from acid solution of permanganate of potash in four hours at 16 *degrees* more than 7 milligrams of oxygen per litre of water shall be deemed to be liable to cause injury to the health of the persons employed.

7. Efficient means shall be adopted to prevent the escape of steam from wet-spinning troughs.

8. The pipes used for the introduction of steam into any room in which the temperature exceeds 21 *degrees*, or for heating the water in any wet-spinning trough, shall, so far as they are within the room and not covered by water, be as small in diameter and as limited in length as is reasonably practicable and shall be effectively covered with non-conducting material.

General note. This regulation is revoked by the Workplace (Health, Safety and Welfare) Regulations 1992, S.I. 1992 No. 3004, as from 1 January 1993 except, in relation to any workplace or part of a workplace which is not a new workplace, or a modification, an extension or a conversion, it is revoked as from 1 January 1996.

9. Efficient splash guards shall be provided and maintained on all wet-spinning frames of 70 millimetres pitch and over, and on all other wet-spinning frames:

Provided that if the Chief Inspector is satisfied with regard to premises in use prior to 30 June 1905, that the structural conditions are such that splash guards cannot conveniently be used, he may suspend the requirement as to splash guards. Such suspension shall only be allowed by certificate in writing signed by the Chief Inspector, and shall be subject to such conditions as may be stated in the certificate.

10. The floor of every wet-spinning room shall be kept in sound condition, and drained so as to prevent retention or accumulation of water.

General note. This regulation is revoked by the Workplace (Health, Safety and Welfare) Regulations 1992, S.I. 1992 No. 3004, as from 1 January 1993 except, in relation to any workplace or part of a workplace which is not a new workplace, or a modification, an extension or a conversion, it is revoked as from 1 January 1996.

11. There shall be provided for all persons employed in any room in which wet-spinning is carried on, or in which artificial humidity of air is produced in aid of manufacture, suitable and convenient accommodation (*a*) in which to keep the clothing taken off before starting work, and in the case of a building erected after 30 June 1905, in which the difference between the readings of the *wet and dry bulb thermometers* is at any time less than 2 *degrees*, such accommodation shall be provided in cloak-rooms ventilated and kept at a suitable temperature and situated in or near the workrooms in question.

General note. This regulation is revoked by the Workplace (Health, Safety and Welfare) Regulations 1992, S.I. 1992 No. 3004, as from 1 January 1993 except, in relation to any workplace or part of a workplace which is not a new workplace, or a modification, an extension or a conversion, it is revoked as from 1 January 1996.

(a) **Suitable and convenient accommodation.** It is a question of fact in each case what is "suitable and convenient accommodation" within the meaning of this regulation. It does not necessarily mean either a wardrobe in a workroom or a separate cloakroom outside the workrooms (*Erault v Ross* [1910] 2 IR 591). See also note (*b*) to s. 59 of the Factories Act 1961.

12.—(1) Subject to paragraph (2) of this regulation, the Health and Safety Executive may, by a certificate in writing, exempt any person or class of persons, from all or any of the requirements or prohibitions imposed by these Regulations and any such exemption may be granted subject to conditions and to a limit of time and may be revoked by a certificate in writing at any time.

(2) The Executive shall not grant any such exemption unless, having regard to the circumstances of the case and in particular to—

(a) the conditions, if any, that it proposes to attach to the exemption; and

(b) any requirements imposed by or under any enactments which apply to the case,

it is satisfied that the health or safety of persons who are likely to be affected by the exemption will not be prejudiced in consequence of it.

PART II
DUTIES OF PERSONS EMPLOYED

13. [*revoked*].

14. No person shall in any way interfere, without the concurrence of the occupier or manager, with the means and appliances provided for ventilation, or for the removal of dust, or for the other purposes of these Regulations.

General note. This regulation is revoked by the Workplace (Health, Safety and Welfare) Regulations 1992, S.I. 1992 No. 3004, as from 1 January 1993 except, in relation to any workplace or part of a workplace which is not a new workplace, or a modification, an extension or a conversion, it is revoked as from 1 January 1996.

THE FREIGHT CONTAINERS (SAFETY CONVENTION) REGULATIONS 1984

(S.I. 1984 No. 1890)

ARRANGEMENT OF REGULATIONS

1. Citation and commencement.
2. Interpretation.
3. Application of Regulations.
4. Conditions of use.
5. Approval of containers—either by design type or individually.
6. Fixing of safety approval plate.
7. Examination of containers.
8. Exemptions.

Schedule—Safety approval plate

The Secretary of State, in exercise of the powers conferred on him by sections 15(1), (2), (4), (5)(b), (6)(b) and (9), 43(2) and (4), and 82(3) and paragraphs 1(1)(a) and (c), (2) and (3), 3, 4, (1), and 6(1) of Schedule 3 to, the Health and Safety at Work etc. Act 1974 and of all other powers enabling him in that behalf and for the purpose of giving effect without modifications to the proposals submitted to him by the Health and Safety Commission under section 11(2)(d) of that Act, after the carrying out by the said Commission of consultations in accordance with section 50(3) of that Act, hereby makes the following Regulations—

1. Citation and commencement. These Regulations may be cited as the Freight Containers (Safety Convention) Regulations 1984 and shall come into operation on 1 January 1985.

2. Interpretation.—(1) In these Regulations, unless the context otherwise requires—

"the Convention" means the International Convention for Safe Containers signed at Geneva on 2 December 1972 and ratified by the United Kingdom on 8 March 1978;
"container" means an article of transport equipment which is

(a) of a permanent character and accordingly strong enough for repeated use, and
(b) designed to facilitate the transport of goods by one or more modes of transport without intermediate reloading, and

1583

(c) designed to be secured or readily handled or both, having *corner fittings* for these purposes, and
(d) of a size such that the area enclosed by the outer bottom corners is either
    (i) if the container is fitted with top *corner fittings*, at least 7 square metres, or
    (ii) in any other case, at least 14 square metres,

and includes a *container* when carried on a chassis but does not include a vehicle or packaging, or any article of transport equipment designed solely for use in air transport, or a *swap body* except when it is carried by or on board a sea-going ship and is not mounted on a road vehicle or rail wagon;

"corner fittings" means an arrangement of apertures and faces at either the top or the bottom or both at the top and the bottom of the container for the purposes of handling, stacking and securing or any of those purposes;

"maintained" means maintained in an efficient state in efficient working order and in good repair *(a)*;

"safety approval plate" means a plate in the form and containing the information specified by the Schedule;

"swap body" means *container* which is specially designed for carriage by road only or by rail and road only and is without stacking capability and top lift facilities;

"use" means use for the purpose for which the container is designed but shall not include—

(a) movement to a place for remedial action provided:
    (i) so far as is reasonably practicable *(b)* the movement is without risk to the safety of any person, and
    (ii) the remedial action is carried out before the *container* is repacked with goods,
(b) if the container is not loaded with goods,
    (i) transport to a place for testing the container to obtain approval under regulation 5, or
    (ii) delivery of the container to its purchaser by the vendor or his agent.

(2) Unless the context otherwise requires, any reference in these Regulations to—

(a) a numbered regulation is a reference to the regulation of these Regulations which bears that number,
(b) a numbered paragraph is a reference to that paragraph so numbered in the regulation in which the reference appears,
(c) "the Schedule" is a reference to the Schedule to these Regulations,
(d) any document operates as a reference to that document as revised or re-issued from time to time.

(a) Maintained. See INTRODUCTORY NOTE 10.

(b) Reasonably practicable. See INTRODUCTORY NOTE 5.

3. Application of Regulations. These Regulations apply to—

(a) any container used at work, or supplied for *use* at work, and which is in Great Britain;

(b) any container so *used* or supplied and which is outside Great Britain in circumstances in which sections 1 to 59 and 80 to 82 of the Health and Safety at Work etc. Act 1974 apply by virtue of the Health and Safety at Work etc. Act 1974 (Application outside Great Britain) Order 1977 *(a)*.

(a) Health & Safety at Work etc 1974 (Application outside Great Britain) Order 1977. The Regulations are revoked; see now the Health & Safety at Work etc. Act 1974 (Application outside Great Britain) Order 1989, S.I. 1989 No. 840.

4. Conditions of use.—(1) The owner or lessee of a *container* shall not *use* or permit that *container* to be used unless—

(a) it has valid approval in accordance with regulation 5, and
(b) it has a valid safety approval plate fixed to it in accordance with regulation 6, and
(c) it is properly *maintained*, and
(d) the examination requirements in regulation 7 are met in respect of that *container*, and
(e) all markings on the *container* showing maximum gross weight are consistent with the maximum gross weight information on the *safety approval plate*, except that if construction of the *container* commenced before 1 January 1984 then compliance with this sub-paragraph is not required before 1 January 1989.

(2) Any other person using or permitting the *use* of a *container* shall, so far as is reasonably practicable, ensure that—

(a) a valid *safety approval plate* is fixed to it in accordance with regulation 6, and
(b) all markings on the *container* showing maximum gross weight are consistent with the maximum gross weight information on the *safety approval plate*, except that if construction of the *container* commenced before 1 January 1984 then compliance with this sub-paragraph is not required before 1 January 1989.

(3) Where it is an express term of a bailment of a *container* that the bailee should be responsible for ensuring that the container is *maintained* or examined, the bailee shall, in addition to any duty placed on him by paragraph (2), ensure that—

(a) it is properly *maintained*, and
(b) the examination requirements in regulation 7 are met in respect of that *container*.

(4) It shall be a defence to any proceedings for *using* or permitting to be *used* a *container* which does not have a valid approval in accordance with regulation 5 that at the time of the contravention an approval had been given by an organisation authorised for this purpose by the Health and Safety Executive before these Regulations come into operation and such an approval had not ceased to be valid for the purposes for which it was given.

(5) It shall be a defence to any proceedings for *using* or permitting a *container* to be *used* which had not been properly *maintained* or examined that at the time of the contravention a bailment or lease was in force in respect of the *container* and

(a) in the case of an owner, that it was an express term of the bailment or lease that the bailee or lessee, as the case may be, should be responsible for ensuring that the *container* was *maintained* or examined,

(b) in the case of a lessee
  (i) that it was not an express term of the lease that he should be responsible for ensuring that the *container* was *maintained* or examined, or
  (ii) that he had become a lessor under a further lease and that it was an express term of the further lease that the further lessee should be responsible for ensuring that the *container* was *maintained* or examined,

(c) in the case of a bailee that he had become a bailor under a further bailment and that it was an express term of the further bailment that the further bailee should be responsible for ensuring that the *container* was *maintained* or examined.

5.   Approval of *containers* – either by design type or individually.—(1) An approval referred to in regulation 4(1)(a) (whether relating to a design type or to an individual *container*) shall be valid only if—

(a) it has been issued:
  (i) by the Health and Safety Executive, or
  (ii) by a person or body of persons appointed for the time being by the Executive in accordance with paragraph (3), or
  (iii) by or under the authority of a Government which has ratified or accepted or approved or acceded to the Convention, and

(b) it has not ceased in accordance with paragraph (2) to be valid.

(2) If—

(a) the person or body of persons which issued the approval states in writing that it is no longer valid, or

(b) the Executive states in writing that the approval is no longer valid, whether or not it was issued by the Executive,

then that approval shall cease to be valid for the purposes of paragraph (1).

(3) The Executive shall appoint in writing such persons and bodies as it considers appropriate for the purpose of issuing approvals under paragraph (1)(a)(ii) and any such appointment may be subject to conditions and limited as to time and may be varied or revoked at any time by the Executive in writing.

6.   Fixing of safety approval plate. The *container* has a valid *safety approval plate* fixed to it if—

(a) the *safety approval plate* is marked and fixed to the *container* in accordance with the Schedule, and

(b) the information on the *safety approval plate* is correct and relates to a valid approval, and

(c) the *safety approval plate* is fixed either—
  (i) after the *container* is manufactured and before it is first *used,* or
  (ii) after the *container* is examined in accordance with regulation 7 and before it is again *used.*

7. Examination of *containers.*—(1) The examination referred to in regulation 4(1)(d) and (3)(b) shall be in accordance with an examination scheme or programme approved by the Health and Safety Executive for the purposes of this regulation.

(2) There shall be clearly marked on the *container* either on or as close as practicable to the *safety approval plate* all matters which the examination scheme or programme requires to be marked.

(3) A fee is £75 is payable by the applicant to the Executive when any application for approval of a scheme or programme under regulation 7(1) is made.

(4) Compliance with the procedure adopted by the State where the owner is permanently resident or incorporated shall be deemed to be in compliance with this regulation provided the procedure has been approved or prescribed by the Government of that State, or by any organisation authorised by such a Government to act on its behalf, for the purpose of the Convention and that Government has ratified accepted approved or acceded to the Convention.

8. Exemptions.—(1) Subject to paragraph (2) below the Health and Safety Executive may by certificate in writing exempt any *container* or class of containers, or any person or class of persons to which these Regulations apply from any requirement or prohibition imposed by these Regulations and any such exemption may be granted subject to conditions and to a limit of time and may be revoked by a certificate in writing at any time.

(2) The Health and Safety Executive shall not grant any such exemption unless, having regard to the circumstances of the case, and in particular to—

(a) the conditions, if any, which it proposes to attach to the exemption, and
(b) any other requirements imposed by or under any enactments which apply to the case,

it is satisfied that the health and safety of persons who are likely to be affected by the exemption will not be prejudiced because of it.

SCHEDULE

Regulations 2 and 6

Safety approval plate
1. The safety approval plate required by regulation 6 shall be permanently fixed to the container in a position such that it is—
(a) readily visible, and
(b) adjacent to any other officially approved plate carried on the container, and
(c) not likely to be easily damaged.
2. *The safety approval plate* shall—
(a) be in the form prescribed by figure 1 of this Schedule;
(b) consist of a permanent, non-corroding, fireproof rectangular plate measuring not less than 200mm by 100mm,
(c) be marked with:
(i) the legend "CSC Safety Approval" in letters of at least 8mm in height, and
(ii) the other legends and information prescribed by sub-paragraph (d) and by figure 1 of this Schedule in letters of at least 5mm in height,
and such markings shall be permanent, clear and legible and in at least the English or French language, but nothing in this sub-paragraph shall prevent any markings for the purposes of an examination scheme or programme being by means of a decal,

(d) contain the following information in at least the English or French language—
    (i) line 1—the country of approval and approval reference,
    (ii) line 2—the month and year of manufacture,
    (iii) line 3—the manufacturer's identification number in respect of the container, or in the case of containers for which that number is unknown the owner's identification number, or the number allotted by the Government or organisation which has granted the approval,
    (iv) line 4—the maximum gross weight in kilograms and pounds,
    (v) line 5—the allowable stacking weight for 1.8g in kilograms and pounds (that is to say, the designed maximum superimposed static stacking weight),
    (vi) line 6—the transverse racking test load value in kilograms and pounds,
    (vii) line 7—the end wall strength value as a proportion of the maximum permissible payload, which shall not be entered unless the end walls are designed to withstand a load of less or more than 0.4 times the maximum permissible payload,
    (viii) line 8—the side wall strength value as a proportion of the maximum permissible payload, which shall not be entered unless the side walls are designed to withstand a load of less or more than 0.6 times the maximum permissible payload,
    (ix) line 9—on and after 1 January 1987 (if the approved examination scheme or programme so requires)—
        (a) a legend indicating that the container is subject to a continuous examination programme, or
        (b) the date (expressed in month and year only) before which the container shall next be thoroughly examined.
        Lines 7 and 8 may be used for the above purposes (a) and (b) if they are not required to contain other information.

Figure 1

CSC SAFETY APPROVAL

1	
2	DATE MANUFACTURED
3	Identification No. ....
4	MAXIMUM GROSS WEIGHT .... Kg 1b
5	ALLOWABLE STACKING WEIGHT
	FOR 1.8g..........kg..........1b
6	RACKING TEST LOAD VALUE ....kg 1b
7	
8	
9	

THE FRUIT PRESERVING WELFARE ORDER 1919

(Dated 15 August 1919; S.R. & O. 1919 No. 1136, as amended by
S.I. 1988 No. 1657, S.I. 1992 No. 2966 and S.I. 1992 No. 3004)

General note. The whole Order is revoked by the Workplace (Health, Safety and
Welfare) Regulations 1992, S.I. 1992 No. 3004, as from 1 January 1993 except, in relation
to any workplace or part of a workplace which is not a new workplace, or a modification,
an extension or a conversion started after 31 December 1992, it is revoked as from
1 January 1996.

1. [*revoked*].

2. The occupier shall provide and maintain for the use of all persons
employed in the factory suitable accommodation for clothing put off during
working hours, with adequate arrangements for drying the clothing if wet.

The accommodation so provided shall be placed under the charge of a
responsible person and shall be kept clean.

3. The occupier shall provide and maintain for the use of all persons
employed and remaining on the premises during the meal intervals a suitable
messroom, which shall be furnished with (a) sufficient tables and chairs or
benches with back rests, (b) unless a canteen serving hot meals is provided on
the premises, adequate means for warming food and boiling water, and (c)
suitable facilities for washing, comprising a sufficient supply of clean towels,
soap and warm water *(a)*. The messroom shall be sufficiently warmed for use
during meal intervals.

The messroom shall be separate from the cloakroom, and shall be placed
under the charge of a responsible person, and shall be kept clean.

(a) **Washing facilities.** See INTRODUCTORY NOTE 20.

4. There shall be provided and maintained, for the use of all persons
employed in the processes of picking, preparing and boiling, fruit filling, and
finishing and covering filled vessels, suitable facilities for washing, comprising a
sufficient supply of clean towels, soap and warm water *(a)*, adjacent to the place
where the work is done.

(a) **Washing facilities.** See INTRODUCTORY NOTE 20.

5. [*revoked*].

6. [*revoked*].

7. [*revoked*].

THE GLASS BEVELLING WELFARE ORDER 1921

(Dated 3 March 1922; S.R. & O. 1921 No. 288, as amended by
S.I. 1992 No. 2966 and S.I. 1992 No. 3004)

General note. The whole Order is revoked by the Workplace (Health, Safety and Welfare) Provisions Regulations 1992, S.I. 1992 No. 3004, as from 1 January 1993, except, in relation to any workplace or part of a workplace which is not a new workplace, or a modification, extension, or a conversion started after 31 December 1992, it is revoked as from 1 January 1996.

1. [*revoked*].

2. The occupier shall provide and maintain, for the use of all persons employed in the process of bevelling glass or in any process incidental thereto, suitable accommodation with adequate drying arrangements for clothing put off during working hours and also for the aprons or other protective clothing worn by the workers in such processes.

The accommodation so provided, unless it consists of a proper drying closet, shall be separate from any workroom, and shall be kept clean.

3. The occupier shall provide and maintain in good and clean condition, for the use of all persons employed in the above-mentioned processes, suitable washing facilities conveniently accessible.

Such accommodation shall comprise at least one lavatory basin, sink or trough, with a smooth impervious surface, fitted with a waste pipe, for every seven persons so employed, a constant supply of cold water and a sufficient supply of hot water *(a)* always at hand, and in addition a sufficient supply of soap, nail brushes and clean towels.

(a) **Washing facilities.** See INTRODUCTORY NOTE 20.

4. This Order shall come into force on 1 May 1921.

THE GLASS BOTTLE, ETC. MANUFACTURE WELFARE ORDER 1918

(Dated 15 May 1918; S.R. & O. 1918 No. 558)

General note. This whole Order is revoked by the Workplace (Health, Safety and Welfare) Regulations 1992, S.I. 1992 No. 3004, as from 1 January 1993 except, in relation to any workplace or part of a workplace which is not a new workplace, or a modification, an extension or a conversion, it is revoked as from 1 January 1996.

In pursuance of section 7 of the Police, Factories, etc. (Miscellaneous Provisions) Act 1916, I hereby make the following Order for all factories or parts of factories in which the manufacture of (i) glass bottles or (ii) pressed glass articles is carried on.

1. The occupier shall provide and maintain for the use of all persons employed a suitable cloakroom, with sufficient accommodation for the clothing put off during working hours, and adequate arrangements for drying the clothing if wet.

The accommodation so provided shall be placed under the charge of a responsible person, and shall be kept clean.

2. The occupier shall provide and maintain for the use of all persons employed and remaining on the premises during the meal intervals a suitable messroom which shall be furnished with (a) sufficient tables and chairs or benches with back rests, (b) adequate means of warming food and boiling water, and (c) suitable facilities for washing, comprising a sufficient supply of clean towels, soap and warm water *(a)*. The messroom shall be sufficiently warmed for use during meal intervals.

The messroom shall be separate from the cloakroom, and shall be placed under the charge of a responsible person, and shall be kept clean.

(a) **Washing facilities.** See INTRODUCTORY NOTE 20.

3. The occupier shall provide and maintain at suitable points, conveniently accessible at all times to all persons employed—

(a) an adequate supply of wholesome drinking water from a public main or from some other source of supply approved in writing by the local authority of the district in which the factory is situated, which shall be either laid on, or contained in a suitable vessel;

(b) (except when the water is derived in an upward jet from which the workers can conveniently drink) at least one suitable cup or drinking vessel at each point of supply, with facilities for rinsing it in drinking water.

Each drinking water supply shall be clearly marked "Drinking Water".

All practicable steps shall be taken to preserve the water and vessels from contamination.

4.   This Order shall come into force on 1 July 1918, but Clause 1 and, subject to the condition that temporary washing facilities are provided, Clause 2 shall not take effect during the period of war.

THE GUT SCRAPING, TRIPE DRESSING, ETC. WELFARE ORDER 1920

(Dated 28 July 1920; S.R. & O. 1920 No. 1437,
as amended by S.I. 1992 No. 2966)

General note. This whole Order is revoked by the Workplace (Health, Safety and Welfare) Regulations 1992, S.I. 1992 No. 3004, as from 1 January 1993 except, in relation to any workplace or part of a workplace which is not a new workplace, or a modification, an extension or a conversion, it is revoked as from 1 January 1996.

In pursuance of section 7 of the Police, Factories, etc. (Miscellaneous Provisions) Act 1916, I hereby make the following Order for all factories *(a)* or workshops or parts thereof in which any of the following processes are carried on—

gut-scraping and gut-washing, and processes incidental thereto;
the preparing and dressing of tripe:

Provided that this Order shall not apply to any factory or workshop in which such processes are only occasionally carried on.

(a) **Factories.** See INTRODUCTORY NOTE 18.

1.　[*revoked*].

2.　The occupier shall provide and maintain for the use of all persons employed (1) suitable accommodation for clothing put off during working hours, with adequate arrangements for drying the clothing if wet, and (2) suitable and *separate* accommodation for overalls and other protective clothing.

The accommodation so provided shall be placed under the charge of a responsible person, and shall be kept clean.

3.　The occupier shall provide and maintain for the use of all persons employed and remaining on the premises during the meal intervals a suitable messroom, which shall be furnished with (a) sufficient tables and chairs or benches with back rests, and (b) unless a canteen serving hot meals is provided, adequate means of warming food and boiling water. The messroom shall be sufficiently warmed for use during meal intervals.

The messroom shall be entirely separate from the accommodation provided in pursuance of Clause 2, and shall be placed under the charge of a responsible person and shall be kept clean.

4.　The occupier shall provide and maintain for the use of all persons employed suitable facilities for washing *(a)*, comprising a sufficient supply of clean towels, soap and warm water, adjacent to the place where the work is done.

The facilities so provided shall be placed under the charge of a responsible person and shall be kept clean.

(a) *Washing facilities.* See INTRODUCTORY NOTE 20.

5.–6.   [*revoked*].

THE HEMP SPINNING AND WEAVING REGULATIONS 1907

(Dated 28 August 1907; S.R. & O. 1907 No. 660, as amended by
S.I. 1988 No. 1657, S.I. 1992 No. 1811 and S.I. 1992 No. 3004)

[Placard: Form 946]

Whereas the processes of spinning and weaving hemp or jute or hemp or jute tow, and the processes incidental thereto, have been certified in pursuance of section 79 of the Factory and Workshop Act 1901, to be dangerous:

I hereby in pursuance of the powers conferred on me by that Act make the following Regulations, and direct that they shall apply to all factories, other than scutch mills, in which any of the processes *(a)* named above are carried on.

These Regulations shall come into force of the first day of January 1908.

(a) Processes. By reg. 3 of the Jute (Safety, Health and Welfare) Regulations 1948 (set out in this Part of this book), these Regulations are not to apply to factories to which those Regulations apply, namely, any factory in which is carried on the spinning or weaving of jute or any process incidental thereto or the calendering or cropping of jute cloth.

Definitions

In these Regulations—

"Degrees" means degrees on the Celsius scale.

"Dry bulb temperature" means the temperature measured by an accurate and properly maintained thermometer (which may form part of the hygrometer) and any reference in the Regulations to a dry bulb thermometer or without qualification to a *"thermometer"* shall be taken to be a reference to such a thermometer and a reference without qualification to temperature shall be taken to be a reference to the dry bulb temperature.

"Hygrometer" means an accurate and properly maintained and calibrated instrument for the measurement of the relative humidity in the workplace.

"Opening of bales," *"batching,"* *"machine-hackling,"* *"carding"*, and *"preparing"* means those processes in the manufacture of hemp or jute, or hemp or jute tow.

"Wet bulb temperature" means either—

(a) the temperature indicated by the wet bulb of a static *hygrometer* which relies on natural circulation of air around the thermometer; or

(b) the temperature calculated from the *dry bulb temperature* and relative humidity by the method approved for the time being by the Health and Safety Executive,

and any reference in these Regulations to the reading of the wet bulb thermometer shall be treated as a reference to the wet bulb temperature.

It shall be the duty of the occupier to observe Part I of these Regulations.
It shall be the duty of all persons employed to observe Part II of these Regulations.

PART I
DUTIES OF OCCUPIERS

1.   [*revoked*].

2.   [*revoked*].

3.   In every room in which the *opening of bales, batching, machine-hackling, carding,* or *preparing* is carried on an accurate thermometer shall be kept affixed.

General note. This regulation is revoked by the Workplace (Health, Safety and Welfare) Regulations 1992, S.I. 1992 No. 3004, as from 1 January 1993 except, in relation to any workplace or part of a workplace which is not a new workplace, or a modification, an extension or a conversion, it is revoked as from 1 January 1996.

4.   The temperature of any room where *machince-hackling* is carried on shall not fall below 10 *degrees,* or where *carding* or *preparing* is carried on, below 13 *degrees*:
Provided that it shall be a sufficient compliance with this regulation if the heating apparatus be put in operation at the commencement of work, and if the required temperature be maintained after the expiration of one hour from the commencement of work.

General note. This regulation is revoked by the Workplace (Health, Safety and Welfare) Regulations 1992, S.I. 1992 No. 3004, as from 1 January 1993 except, in relation to any workplace or part of a workplace which is not a new workplace, or a modification, an extension or a conversion, it is revoked as from 1 January 1996.

5.   Where *machine-hackling, carding,* or *preparing* is carried on the arrangements shall be such that no person employed shall be exposed to a direct draught from any air inlet, or to any draught at a temperature of less than 10 *degrees*.

General note. This regulation is revoked by the Workplace (Health, Safety and Welfare) Regulations 1992, S.I. 1992 No. 3004, as from 1 January 1993 except, in relation to any workplace or part of a workplace which is not a new workplace, or a modification, an extension or a conversion, it is revoked as from 1 January 1996.

6.—(1)   In every room in which artificial humidity of air is produced in aid of manufacture, a *hygrometer* and a thermometer close to the *hygrometer* shall be positioned in the centre of the room or in such other position as may be directed by an inspector by notice in writing.

(2)   The *hygrometer* and the thermometer shall be read between 11 and 12 a.m. on every day that any person is employed in the room and again between 4

and 5 p.m. on every day that any person is employed in the room after 1 p.m. and a record of all such readings shall be kept.

(3) The said record shall be kept by the occupier for at least two years from when it was made and the occupier shall give his employees immediate access to those records on request together with such information as is necessary for their interpretation.

(4) Paragraphs (2) and (3) of this regulation shall not apply to any room in which the difference of reading between the *wet and dry bulb thermometers* is never less than 2 degrees, if notice of the intention to work on that system has been given in writing to an inspector.

7.—(1) Subject to paragraph (2) of this regulation, the Health and Safety Executive may, by a certificate in writing, exempt any person or class of persons, from all or any of the requirements or prohibitions imposed by these Regulations and any such exemption may be granted subject to conditions and to a limit of time and may be revoked by a certificate in writing at any time.

(2) The Executive shall not grant any such exemption unless, having regard to the circumstances of the case and in particular to—

(a) the conditions, if any, that it proposes to attach to the exemption; and
(b) any requirements imposed by or under any enactments which apply to the case,

it is satisfied that the health or safety of persons who are likely to be affected by the exemption will not be prejudiced in consequence of it.

PART II
DUTIES OF PERSONS EMPLOYED

8. No person shall in any way interfere, without the concurrence of the occupier or manager with the means and appliances provided for ventilation, or for the removal of dust, or for the other purposes of these Regulations.

General note. This regulation is revoked by the Health, Safety and Welfare Regulations 1992, S.I. 1992 No. 3004, as from 1 January 1993 except, in relation to any workplace or part of a workplace which is not a new workplace, or a modification, an extension or a conversion, it is revoked as from 1 January 1996.

THE HERRING CURING (NORFOLK AND SUFFOLK) WELFARE ORDER 1920

(Dated 9 September 1920; S.R. & O. 1920 No. 1662,
as amended by S.I. 1992 No. 1811)

General note. This whole Order is revoked by the Workplace (Health, Safety and Welfare) Regulations 1992, S.I. 1992 No. 3004, as from 1 January 1993 except, in relation to any workplace or part of a workplace which is not a new workplace, or a modification, an extension or a conversion, it is revoked as from 1 January 1996.

In pursuance of section 7 of the Police, Factories, etc. (Miscellaneous Provisions) Act 1916, I hereby make the following Order for all factories and workshops situated in the counties of Norfolk and Suffolk, in which the processes of Gutting, Salting and Packing of Herring are carried on.

1. The occupier shall provide and maintain for the use of all persons employed a suitable and adequate mess and rest room, which shall be furnished with (a) sufficient tables and chairs or benches with back rests, (b) unless a canteen serving hot meals is provided, adequate means of warming food and boiling water. The room shall be kept open for the use of workers during working hours, and shall be kept sufficiently warmed.

Provided that except in the case of plots situated on the South Denes of Great Yarmouth and the Denes of Lowestoft, this paragraph shall not apply to any occupier who does not employ any worker residing outside a radius of 400 metres walking distance of the factory or workshop.

2. The occupier shall provide and maintain for the use of all the persons employed suitable cloakroom accommodation and arrangements for the hanging of the workers' clothing.

3. The occupier shall provide and maintain for the use of all persons employed suitable facilities for washing *(a)* comprising a sufficient supply of clean towels, soap and warm water, easily accessible at all times during working hours.

The accommodation in paragraphs 2 and 3 shall be separate form the messroom.

    (a) **Washing facilities.** See INTRODUCTORY NOTE 20.

4. The accommodation required under the foregoing paragraphs shall be on the site of the factory or workshop or adjacent thereto; provided that where two or more occupiers combine to provide the accommodation, it shall be sufficient if such accommodation is within 250 metres of each of the factories or workshops for which it is provided.

5. The occupier or occupiers shall be responsible that the accommodation required under paragraphs 1, 2, 3 and 4 hereof shall be kept under proper and efficient superintendence, and shall be kept clean.

6.–8. [*revoked*].

THE HERRING CURING WELFARE ORDER 1927

(S.R. & O. 1927 No. 813, as amended by S.I. 1981 No. 917)

General note. This whole Order is revoked by the Workplace (Health, Safety and Welfare) Regulations 1992, S.I. 1992 No. 3004, as from 1 January 1993 except, in relation to any workplace or part of a workplace which is not a new workplace, or a modification, an extension or a conversion, it is revoked as from 1 January 1996.

In pursuance of section 7 of the Police, Factories, etc. (Miscellaneous Provisions) Act 1916, I hereby make the following Order for all factories and workshops in England and Wales (excluding the counties of Norfolk and Suffolk), in which the processes of Gutting, Salting and Packing of Herring are carried on:

Provided that where the Chief Inspector (a) of Factories is satisfied in respect of any such factory or workshop that by reason of the infrequency of the process or for other sufficient reason all or any of the requirements of this Order are not necessary for the welfare of persons employed therein, he may by certificate in writing (which he may in his discretion revoke) exempt any such factory or workshop from all or any of the provisions of the Order for such period and on such conditions as he may think fit.

(a) *Inspector.* See INTRODUCTORY NOTE 24.

1. The occupier shall at or in the immediate vicinity of the factory or workshop provide and maintain in good repair for the use of all persons employed, facilities (a) to enable them to rinse their clothing and hands in fresh water after work. Such facilities shall be kept in a cleanly condition, and adequate drainage provided for the disposal of waste water.

(a) *Washing facilities.* See INTRODUCTORY NOTE 20.

2. The occupier shall provide and maintain at suitable points an adequate supply of wholesome drinking water which shall be conveniently accessible at all times to all persons employed.

3.–4. [*revoked*].

5. This Order may be cited as the Herring Curing Welfare Order, 1927, and shall come into force on 1 October 1927.

THE HERRING CURING (SCOTLAND) WELFARE ORDER 1926

(S.R. & O. 1926 No. 535/S. 24)

General note. This whole Order is revoked by the Workplace (Health, Safety and Welfare) Regulations 1992, S.I. 1992 No. 3004, as from 1 January 1993 except, in relation to any workplace or part of a workplace which is not a new workplace, or a modification, an extension or a conversion, it is revoked as from 1 January 1996.

In pursuance of section 7 of the Police, Factories, etc. (Miscellaneous Provisions) Act 1916, I hereby make the following Order for all factories and workshops in Scotland, in which the processes of Gutting, Salting and Packing of Herring are carried on:

Provided that where the Chief Inspector *(a)* of Factories is satisfied in respect of any such factory or workshop that by reason of the infrequency of the process or for other sufficient reason all or any of the requirements of this Order are not necessary for the welfare of persons employed therein, he may by certificate in writing (which he may in his discretion revoke) exempt any such factory or workshop from all or any of the provisions of the Order for such period and on such conditions as he may think fit.

(a) **Inspector.** See INTRODUCTORY NOTE 24.

1. The occupier shall at or in the immediate vicinity of the factory or workshop provide and maintain in good repair for the use of all persons employed, facilities *(a)* to enable them to rinse their clothing and hands after work. Such facilities shall be kept in a cleanly condition, and adequate drainage provided for the disposal of waste water.

(a) **Washing facilities.** See INTRODUCTORY NOTE 20.

2.–4. [*revoked*].

5. This Order may be cited as the Herring Curing (Scotland) Welfare Order, 1926, and shall come into force on 1 October 1926.

THE HORIZONTAL MILLING MACHINES REGULATIONS 1928

(S.R. & O. 1928 No. 548, as amended by S.R. & O. 1934 No. 207, S.I. 1992 No. 1811, S.I. 1992 No. 2932 and S.I. 1992 No. 3004)

General note. These Regulations are revoked by the Workplace (Health, Safety and Welfare) Regulations 1992, S.I. 1992 No. 3004, as from 1 January 1993 except, in relation to any workplace or part of a workplace which is not a new workplace, or a modification, an extension or a conversion, they are revoked as from 1 January 1996. Note that the exemptions and regulations 2–7 are also revoked by the Provision and Use of Work Equipment Regulations 1992, S.I. 1992 No. 2932.

[*Placard: Form 999*]

In pursuance of section 79 of the Factory and Workshop Act 1901, I hereby make the following Regulations and direct that they shall apply to any factory *(a)* or part thereof in which a horizontal milling machine is used:

Provided that if the Chief Inspector *(b)* of Factories is satisfied in respect of any class of horizontal milling machine or of any class of milling cutter used on such machines that, owing to the special conditions of work or otherwise, any of the requirements of the Regulations can be suspended or relaxed without danger to the persons employed, he may be certificate in writing authorise such suspension or relaxation for such period and under such conditions as he may think fit. Any such certificate may be revoked by the Chief Inspector at any time.

These Regulations may be cited as the Horizontal Milling Machines Regulations 1928, and shall come into force on 1 September 1928.

(a) **Factory.** See INTRODUCTORY NOTE 17.

(b) **Inspector.** See INTRODUCTORY NOTE 24.

Duties

It shall be the duty of the occupier to observe Part I of these Regulations.

It shall be the duty of every person employed to observe Part II of these Regulations.

Exemptions

Nothing in regulation 3 shall apply to any milling cutter used on
   (i) a spindle which exceeds 65 millimetres in diameter, or abor which exceeds 50 millimetres in diameter at the place where the cutter is mounted;
or when used for
   (ii) making tools, jigs, or gauges for use in the factory, or similarly accurate operations where, during the actual cutting process, all those parts of the machine which control the relative position of the work and the

cutter can be manipulated by the operator at his unrestricted discretion;
  (iii) internal milling;
  (iv) end milling other than face milling;
  (v) automatic gear cutting;
  (vi) automatic hobbing;
  (vii) automatic profiling;
  (viii) thread milling:

Provided that these exemptions shall not prejudice the application of section 10 of the Factory and Workshop Act 1901 [s. 14] in regard to fencing of such machinery *(a)*.

General note. The exemptions are revoked by the Provisions and Use of Work Equipment Regulations 1992, S.I. 1992 No. 2932, as from 1 January 1993 except, insofar as it applies to work equipment first provided for use in the premises or undertaken before 1 January 1993, they are revoked as from 1 January 1997.

(a) Provided that ... machinery. The effect of this proviso is that the fencing obligations imposed by s. 14 of the Factories Act 1961 apply to a milling cutter even though its use falls within an exemption to the Regulations (*Quinn v Horsfall and Bickham Ltd* [1956] 2 All ER 467, [1956] 1 WLR 652, CA).

Where, on the other hand, no exemption to this regulation applies, then, if the Regulations are complied with, the factory occupier is relieved from the corresponding obligation imposed by s. 14 of the Factories Act 1961. If, however, the milling machine contains other dangerous parts, which are not required to be fenced under the Regulations, then the provisions of s. 14 of the Act continue to apply to those other parts (*Benn v Kamm & Co Ltd* [1962] 2 QB 127, [1952] 1 All ER 833, CA). Provisions in special regulations supersede the comprehensive obligations of the Act only when they both deal with the same subject of danger and, of course, only where the language of the particular regulations permits the conclusion that they are supersessive; the relevant principles are discussed in the GENERAL INTRODUCTION.

PART I
DUTIES OF OCCUPIERS

1. The floor immediately surrounding every horizontal milling machine shall be maintained in good and even condition and kept clear from loose material, and effective measures shall be taken to prevent it becoming slippery by the splashing of suds or otherwise.

2. Effective measures shall be taken for securing and maintaining sufficient and suitable lighting at the machines, and where artificial lighting is provided the lighting points shall be so placed or shaded as to prevent direct rays of light from impinging on the eyes of the operator while he is operating the machine.

General note. This regulation is revoked by the Provision and Use of Work Equipment Regulations 1992, S.I. 1992 No. 2932, as from 1 January 1993 except, insofar as it applies to work equipment first provided for use in the premises or undertaken before 1 January 1993, it is revoked as from 1 January 1997.

3.—(1) The cutter or cutters of every horizontal milling machine shall be fenced *(a)*, by a strong guard properly adjusted to the work, which shall enclose the whole cutting surface except such part as is necessarily exposed for the milling operations.

(ii) The guard shall either:—

(a) be provided with adequate side flanges; or
(b) extend on each side of the cutter or cutters to the end of the arbor, or to the arbor support, or to a distance of not less than half the diameter of the cutter:

Provided that paragraph (ii) of this regulation shall not apply to cutters used for face milling.

General note. This regulation is revoked by the Provision and Use of Work Equipment Regulations 1992, S.I. 1992 No. 2932, as from 1 January 1993 except, insofar as it applies to work equipment first provided for use in the premises or undertaken before 1 January 1993, it is revoked as from 1 January 1997.

(a) Shall be fenced. In *Morris Motors Ltd v Hopgood* [1957] 1 QB 30, [1956] 3 All ER 467, the Divisional Court held that reg. 3 and reg. 6 must be read together and that it was no breach of reg. 3 for the milling cutter not to be fenced when it was not in motion. Compare the similar interpretation accorded to ss. 12–16 of the Factories Act 1961, and see the Introductory Note to those sections.

4. Every horizontal milling machine shall be provided with an efficient starting and stopping appliance, and the control of this appliance shall be in such a position as to be readily and conveniently operated by the person operating the machine.

General note. This regulation is revoked by the Provision and Use of Work Equipment Regulations 1992, S.I. 1992 No. 2932, as from 1 January 1993 except, insofar as it applies to work equipment first provided for use in the premises or undertaken before 1 January 1993, it is revoked as from 1 January 1997.

5. When suds or other cutting lubricants are used on a horizontal milling machine suitable arrangements shall be made to enable the operator to apply the suds or lubricant or to adjust the supply pipe, and suitable means shall be provided for removing the swarf.

General note. This regulation is revoked by the Provision and Use of Work Equipment Regulations 1992, S.I. 1992 No. 2932, as from 1 January 1993 except, insofar as it applies to work equipment first provided for use in the premises or undertaken before 1 January 1993, it is revoked as from 1 January 1997.

6. The guards or other appliances required by these Regulations shall be maintained in an efficient state and shall be constantly kept in position while the milling cutter is in motion, except when the tool setter is setting up the machine.

General note. This regulation is revoked by the Provision and Use of Work Equipment Regulations 1992, S.I. 1992 No. 2932, as from 1 January 1993 except, insofar as it

applies to work equipment first provided for use in the premises or undertaken before 1 January 1993, it is revoked as from 1 January 1997.

PART II
DUTIES OF PERSONS EMPLOYED

7. Every person employed on a horizontal milling machine shall use and maintain in proper adjustment the guards or appliances provided in accordance with these Regulations.

General note. This regulation is revoked by the Provision and Use of Work Equipment Regulations 1992, S.I. 1992 No. 2932, as from 1 January 1993 except, insofar as it applies to work equipment first provided for use in the premises or undertaken before 1 January 1993, it is revoked as from 1 January 1997.

THE INDIARUBBER REGULATIONS 1922

(S.R. & O. 1922 No. 329, as amended by S.I. 1973 No. 36, S.I. 1980 No. 1248 and S.I. 1988 No. 1657)

[Placard: Form 983]

In pursuance of section 79 of the Factory and Workshop Act 1901, I hereby make the following Regulations, and direct that they shall apply to all factories and workshops or parts thereof in which is carried on the manufacture of indiarubber or of articles or goods made wholly or partially of indiarubber:

Provided that nothing in these Regulations shall apply to processes in the repair of any article.

Provided also that where it is proved to the satisfaction of the Chief Inspector (*a*) of Factories that by reason of the restricted use of dangerous materials or the methods of working in any factory or workshop, all or any of these Regulations are not necessary to safeguard the health of the persons employed, he may, by certificate in writing (which he may in his discretion revoke), exempt any such factory or workshop from the application of all or any of the Regulations, subject to such conditions as he may by such certificate prescribe.

These Regulations shall come into force on the 1 May 1922, and may be cited as the Indiarubber Regulations 1922.

(*a*) **Inspector.** See INTRODUCTORY NOTE 24.

Definitions

In these Regulations—

"*Lead Process*" means the weighing, manipulation or other treatment of any dry compound of lead, or of any dry mixture containing dry compound of lead, in processes preparatory to the incorporation of such compound or mixture with indiarubber at the incorporating or mixing rolls; and also includes the process of incorporation if the total weight of dry compound of lead calculated as lead monoxide contained in the mixing when determined in the manner described in the Schedule hereto or in such other manner as shall satisfy an Inspector exceeds five per cent. of the total weight of the mixing inclusive of indiarubber and all other ingredients incorporated therewith at the mixing rolls.

Duties

It shall be the duty of the occupier to observe Part I of these Regulations.

PART I
DUTIES OF OCCUPIERS

1.—(a) No person under 16 years of age, and no female under 18 years of age, shall be employed in any *lead process.*

(b) No woman and no young person shall be employed at mixing or incorporating rolls in the process of incorporating dry compound of lead with indiarubber.

SCHEDULE

MANNER OF ASCERTAINING THE PERCENTAGE OF A DRY COMPOUND OF LEAD
PRESENT IN A MIXING

The mixing as a whole shall be weighed. The dry material of the mixing which is to be incorporated in powder form with the indiarubber shall likewise be weighed; thereafter and before incorporation the said weighed dry material shall be mixed to the satisfaction of an Inspector who shall take three approximately equal samples from different parts of the mixture. The three samples shall be intimately mixed together to form the test sample. A weighed quantity of the test sample is to be continuously shaken for one hour at the common temperature, with 1,000 times its weight of an aqueous solution of hydrochloric acid containing 0.2 per cent. by weight of hydrogen chloride. This solution is thereafter to be allowed to stand for one hour and then filtered. The lead salt contained in an aliquot portion of the clear filtrate is then to be precipitated as lead sulphide and weighed as lead sulphate. The proportion of lead compound calculated as lead monoxide thus found in the test sample shall be used for the calculation of the percentage required for the purposes of the definition of *lead process.*

THE IRON AND STEEL FOUNDRIES REGULATIONS 1953

(S.I. 1953 No. 1464, as amended by S.I. 1974 No. 1681, S.I. 1981 No. 1332, S.I. 1988 No. 1657, S.I. 1992 No. 2932 and S.I. 1992 No. 2966)

[Placard: Form 953]

General note. These Regulations are to be repealed as from 1 January 1996 by the Workplace (Health, Safety and Welfare) Regulations 1992, S.I. 1992 No. 3004, for workplaces in existence on 31 December 1992. The "new" Regulations will apply to those workplaces from the former date. The "old" Regulations cease to have effect and the "new" Regulations apply: to workplaces coming into use after 31 December 1992; and to modifications, extensions and conversions started after 31 December 1992 to existing workplaces as soon as they come into use.

The Minister of Labour and National Service by virtue of the powers conferred on him by sections 46 and 60 of the Factories Act 1937, section 8 of the Factories Act 1948, and the Transfer of Functions (Factories, &c., Acts) Order 1946, and of all other powers in that behalf, hereby makes the following Special Regulations—

1. Citation and commencement. These Regulations may be cited as the Iron and Steel Foundries Regulations 1953, and save as provided in regulations 7 and 9 of these Regulations shall come into operation on 1 January 1954.

2. Interpretation.—(1) The Interpretation Act 1889 [Interpretation Act 1978] shall apply to the interpretation of these Regulations as it applies to the interpretation of an Act of Parliament.

(2) For the purposes of these Regulations, unless the context otherwise requires, the following expressions have the meanings hereby assigned to them respectively, that is to say—

"cupola or furnace" includes a receiver associated therewith;
"iron foundry" and *"steel foundry"* mean those parts of a factory in which the production of iron castings or, as the case may be, steel castings (not being the production of pig iron or the production of steel in the form of ingots and not including die-casting) is carried on by casting in moulds made of sand, loam, moulding composition or other mixture of materials, or by shell moulding or by centrifugal casting in metal moulds lined with sand, together with any part of the factory in which any of the following processes are carried on as incidental processes in connection with, and in the course of, such production, namely, the preparation and mixing of materials used in the foundry process, the preparation of moulds and cores, knockout operations and dressing or fettling operations;

"pouring aisle" means an aisle leading from the main gangway or directly from a cupola or furnace to where metal is poured into moulds;

"principal act" means the Factories Act 1937, as amended by or under any other Act;

"steel foundry" has the meaning assigned to it earlier in this paragraph.

(a) **Inspector.** See INTRODUCTORY NOTE 24.

3.   Application and operation of Regulations.—(1) These Regulations shall apply to all *iron foundries* and *steel foundries*.

(2) Subject to the provisions of this paragraph, the provisions of these Regulations shall be in addition to and not in substitution for or in dimunition of other requirements imposed by or under the *principal Act*.

4.   Arrangement and storage. For the purposes of promoting safety and cleanliness in workrooms the following requirements shall be observed—

(a)   moulding boxes, loam plates, ladles, patterns, pattern plates, frames, boards, box weights, and other heavy articles shall be so arranged and placed as to enable work to be carried on without unnecessary risk;

(b)   suitable and conveniently accessible racks, bins or other receptacles shall be provided and used for the storage of other gear and tools;

(c)   where there is bulk storage of sand, fuel, metal scrap or other materials or residues, suitable bins, bunkers or other receptacles shall be provided for the purpose of such storage.

5.   Work near *cupolas* and *furnaces*. No person (a) shall carry out any work within a distance of 4 metres from a vertical line passing through the delivery end of any spout of a *cupola or furnace*, being a spout used for delivering molten metal, or within a distance of 2.4 metres from a vertical line passing through the nearest part of any ladle which is in position at the end of such a spout, except, in either case, where it is necessary for the proper use or maintenance of a *cupola or furnace* that that work should be carried out within that distance or that is being carried out at such a time and under such conditions that there is no danger to the person carrying it out from molten metal which is being obtained from the *cupola or furnace* or is in a ladle in position at the end of the spout.

General note. This regulation is revoked by the Provision and Use of Work Equipment Regulations 1992, S.I. 1992 No. 2932, as from 1 January 1993 except, insofar as it applies to work equipment first provided for use in the premises or undertaken before 1 January 1993, it is revoked as from 1 January 1997.

Dimensions in these Regulations have been metricated by S.I. 1981 No. 1332, which provides (reg. 3) that where any premises or plant in existence or under construction before December 1981 complied with the provisions of those Regulations then in force, those premises or plant shall be deemed to comply with these Regulations as amended by the metricating Regulations.

(a) **No person.** This includes persons whose work brings them near the spout when molten metal is being drawn and collected (*Lewis v Matthew Swain Ltd* (1969) 6 KIR 481, CA).

6. Gangways and pouring aisles.—(1) In every workroom to which this regulation applies constructed, reconstructed or converted for use as such after the making of these Regulations and, so far as reasonably practicable, in every other workroom to which this regulation applies, sufficient and clearly defined main gangways shall be provided and properly maintained which—

(a) shall have an even surface of hard material and shall, in particular, not be of sand or have on them more sand than is necessary to avoid risk of flying metal from accidental spillage;

(b) shall be kept so far as reasonably practicable free from obstruction;

(c) if not used for carrying molten metal, shall be at least 920 millimetres in width;

(d) if used for carrying molten metal shall be—

    (i) where truck ladles are used exclusively, at least 600 millimetres wider than the overall width of the ladle;

    (ii) where hand shanks are carried by not more than two men, at least 920 millimetres in width;

    (iii) where hand shanks are carried by more than two men, at least 1.2 metres in width; and

    (iv) where used for simultaneous travel in both directions by men carrying hand shanks, at least 1.8 metres in width.

(2) (a) Subject to the provisions of sub-paragraph (c) of this paragraph, in every workroom to which this regulation applies constructed, reconstructed or converted for use as such after the making of these Regulations, sufficient and clearly defined *pouring aisles* shall be provided *(a)* and properly maintained which—

    (i) shall have an even surface of hard material and shall, in particular, not be of sand or have on them more sand than is necessary to avoid risk of flying metal from accidental spillage;

    (ii) shall be kept so far as reasonably practicable free from obstruction;

    (iii) shall be wide enough not to imperil the safety of persons carrying or pouring molten metal and shall in no case be less than 460 millimetres in width.

(b) Subject as aforesaid, in every other workroom to which this regulation applies, sufficient *pouring aisles* shall be provided and properly maintained which—

    (i) shall have a firm and even surface and shall be kept so far as reasonably practicable free from obstruction;

    (ii) shall be wide enough not to imperil the safety of persons carrying or pouring molten metal, and shall be not less than 460 millimetres in width.

(c) This paragraph shall not apply to any workroom or part of a workroom if, by reason of the nature of the work done therein, the floor of that workroom or, as the case may be, that part of a workroom has to be of sand.

(3) In this regulation "workroom to which this regulation applies" means a part of an *iron foundry* or *steel foundry* in which molten metal is transported or used, and a workroom to which this regulation applies shall be deemed for the purposes of this regulation to have been constructed, reconstructed or converted for use as such after the making of these Regulations if the construction, reconstruction of conversion thereof was begun after the making of these Regulations.

General note. See the general note to reg. 5.

(a) *Provided.* This requirement is not complied with by leaving to workmen, however skilled and experienced, the responsibility of leaving sufficient passageway round the moulds they happen to be filling (*Hawkins v Ian Ross (Castings) Ltd* [1970] 1 All ER 180). See also INTRODUCTORY NOTE 9.

7., 8.   [*revoked*].

9.   Bathing facilities and clothing accommodation.—(1) The occupier shall provide and maintain, for the use of persons employed in the foundry, adequate and suitable facilities (a) for taking shower or other baths, with suitable arrangements for privacy (including, in close proximity to such facilities, suitable accommodation for dressing, undressing or changing clothes, and an adequate number of lockers or other suitable arrangements for the accommodation of clothing belong to persons using the baths) and such arrangements as are reasonably practicable for drying clothing belonging to persons using the baths.

(2) The facilities provided for the purposes of paragraph (1) of this regulation shall be placed in charge of a responsible person or persons and maintained in a clean and orderly condition.

(3) This regulation shall come into operation on 1 January 1956.

(a) *Washing facilities.* See INTRODUCTORY NOTE 20.

10.   Exemptions.—(1) If the Chief Inspector (a) is satisfied in respect of any foundry, or in respect of foundries of any specified class or description, that, owing to the special conditions, or special methods of work or otherwise, any requirement of regulations 5, 6 and 9 of these Regulations can be suspended or relaxed without danger to the health or safety of the persons employed, or that the application of any such requirement is for any reason impracticable or inappropriate, he may by certificate in writing (which he may at his discretion revoke at any time) exempt the foundry or foundries of that class of description from the application of that requirement subject to such conditions as may be specified in the certificate.

(2) Where any certificate is issued under this regulation a legible copy thereof, showing the conditions (if any) subject to which it has been granted, shall be kept posted up in every foundry to which the exemption applies in a position where it may conveniently be read by the persons employed.

(a) *Inspector.* See INTRODUCTORY NOTE 24.

THE JUTE (SAFETY, HEALTH AND WELFARE) REGULATIONS 1948

(S.I. 1948 No. 1696, as amended by S.I. 1988 No. 1657, S.I. 1989 No. 1141, the Employment Act 1989, s. 9(6), Sch. 2, Pt. I, S.I. 1992 No. 1811, S.I. 1992 No. 2932 and S.I. 1992 No. 3004)

The Minister of Labour and National Service by virtue of sections 46, 56 and 60(a) of the Factories Act 1937 (thereinafter referred to as "the Act"), the Factories Act 1937 (Extension of Section 46) Regulations 1948 and the Transfer of Functions (Factories, &c., Acts) Order 1946 hereby makes as Special Regulations the Regulations set out in Parts I to VI hereof and by virtue of section 17 of the Act and the Order aforesaid makes the regulation set out in Part VII hereof.

(a) **By virtue of . . . s. 60.** These Regulations were made on 21 July 1948, so that they were made under the powers conferred by s. 60 of the Factories Act 1937, before the amendment of that section by s. 12 of the Factories Act 1948, which did not come into force until 1 October 1948. Consequently the class of persons for whose benefit they were made is limited to persons employed "in connection with" the processes specified; see the GENERAL INTRODUCTION and *Canadian Pacific Steamships Ltd v Bryers* [1958] AC 485, [1959] 3 All ER 572, HL.

PART I
INTERPRETATION AND GENERAL

1. Short title, commencement and intepretation.—(1) These Regulations may be cited as the Jute (Safety, Health and Welfare) Regulations 1948 and shall come into force on the 1st day of January, 1949.

The interpretation Act 1889 [Interpretation Act 1978] applies to the interpretation of these Regulations as it applies to the interpretation of an Act of Parliament.

1A. Interpretation.—(1) In these Regulations unless the context otherwise requires—
"*dry bulb temperature*" means the temperature measured by an accurate and properly maintained thermometer (which may form part of the hygrometer) and any reference without qualification in the Regulations to a *thermometer* shall be taken to be a reference to such a thermometer and a reference without qualification to temperature shall be taken as a reference to the dry bulb temperature;
"*hygrometer*" means an accurate and properly maintained and calibrated instrument for the measurement of the relative humidity in the workplace;
"*wet bulb temperature*" means either—

(a) the temperature indicated by the wet bulb of a static *hygrometer* which relies on natural circulation of air around the *thermometer*, or

(b) the temperature calculated from the *dry bulb temperature* and relative humidity by the method approved for the time being by the Health and Safety Executive.

(2) In these Regulations references to the dry bulb reading of the *hygrometer* and the wet bulb reading of the *hygrometer* shall be taken as references to the *dry bulb temperature* and the *wet bulb temperature* respectively.

2.   Application. These Regulations shall apply to any factory in which is carried on the spinning or weaving of jute or any process incidental thereto or the calendering or cropping of jute cloth.

3.   Revocation. The Regulations dated 28 August 1907 *(a)* made by the Secretary of State in pursuance of the powers conferred on him by the Factory and Workshop Act 1901 with respect to the processes of spinning and weaving hemp or jute, or hemp or jute tow, and processes incidental thereto shall cease to apply as respects the factories specified in regulation 2 hereof.

(a) Regulations ... 1907. See the Hemp Spinning and Weaving Regulations 1907.

3A.—(1) Subject to paragraph (2) of this regulation, the Health and Safety Executive may, by a certificate in writing, exempt any person or class of persons, from all or any of the requirements or prohibitions imposed by these Regulations and any such exemption may be granted subject to conditions and to a limit of time and may be revoked by a certificate in writing at any time.

(2) The Executive shall not grant any such exemption unless, having regard to the circumstances of the case and in particular to—

(a) the conditions, if any, that it proposes to attach to the exemption; and
(b) any requirements imposed by or under any enactment which apply to the case,

it is satisfied that the health or safety of persons who are likely to be affected by the exemption will not be prejudiced in consequence of it.

PART II

VENTILATION

4.–10.   [*revoked*].

11.   Removal of steam or vapour. Adequate arrangements shall be made for the removal of steam or vapour generated at a dressing machine so as to prevent, so far as is practicable, its escape into the general air of any workroom.

General note. This regulation is revoked by the Workplace (Health, Safety and Welfare) Regulations 1992, S.I. 1992 No. 3004, as from 1 January 1993 except, in relation to any workplace or part of a workplace which is not a new workplace, or a modification, an extension or a conversion, it is revoked as from 1 January 1996.

12. [*revoked*].

13. Scope of Part III. The requirements of this Part of these Regulations shall be without prejudice to the provisions of Sections 4 and 47 of the Act.

General note. This regulation is revoked by the Workplace (Health, Safety and Welfare) Regulations 1992, S.I. 1992 No. 3004, as from 1 January 1993 except, in relation to any workplace or part of a workplace which is not a new workplace, or a modification, an extension or a conversion, it is revoked as from 1 January 1996.

PART IV

TEMPERATURE AND HUMIDITY

14. Minimum temperatures. As respects any factory to which these Regulations apply, the provisions of Section 3 of the Act [s. 3] shall apply with the following modifications and extensions—

(a) In any workroom in which the only work done is the opening of bales or work incidental thereto or the batching or softening of jute, a temperature of less than 13 degrees Celsius shall not be deemed, after the first hour, to be a reasonable temperature while work is going on.

(b) In any workroom in which work other than the opening of bales or work incidental thereto or the batching or softening of jute is done, a temperature of less than 16 degrees Celsius shall not be deemed, after the first hour, to be a reasonable temperature while work is going on.

(c) An accurate *thermometer* shall be kept affixed as near as is practicable to the centre of every workroom.

General note. This regulation is revoked by the Workplace (Health, Safety and Welfare) Regulations 1992, S.I. 1992 No. 3004, as from 1 January 1993 except, in relation to any workplace or part of a workplace which is not a new workplace, or a modification, an extension or a conversion, it is revoked as from 1 January 1996.

15. Heat insulation at dressing machine. In any workroom, every steam pipe and steam exhaust pipe and the ends of every steam heated cylinder used in connection with a dressing machine shall be kept effectively covered with insulating material in good repair in such manner as to prevent, so far as is reasonably practicable, the escape of heat therefrom.

General note. This regulation is revoked by the Provisions and Use of Work Equipment Regulations 1992, S.I. 1992 No. 2932, as from 1 January 1993 except, insofar as it applies to work equipment first provided for use in the premises or undertaking before 1 January 1993, it is revoked as from 1 January 1997.
It is further revoked by the Workplace (Health, Safety and Welfare) Regulations 1992 (S.I. 1992 No. 3004), as from 1 January 1993 except, in relation to any workplace or part of a workplace which is not a new workplace, or a modification, an extension or a conversion, it is revoked as from 1 January 1996.

16. Separation of engine-rooms, boiler-houses and boiler-flues.—
(1) (a) Every engine-room, boiler-house and boiler-flue shall be separated

from the workrooms by an alleyway which is not less than 2 metres wide and is freely ventilated by the open air.

(b) Any boiler-flue which passes below a workroom shall be separated from the workroom by a ventilated space of at least 2 metres measured vertically.

(2) In any case in which compliance with any of the requirements of this regulation would involve the structural alteration of any part of a factory in which any of the processes specified in regulation 2 of these Regulations was being carried on before the first day of January, 1947, that requirement shall not come into force until it is reasonably practicable to comply with such requirement in connection with rebuilding or structural alterations undertaken at the factory.

General note. This regulation is revoked by the Workplace (Health, Safety and Welfare) Regulations 1992, S.I. 1992 No. 3004, as from 1 January 1993 except, in relation to any workplace or part of a workplace which is not a new workplace, or a modification, an extension or a conversion, it is revoked as from 1 January 1996.

17. Artificial humidification.—(1) This regulation applies to every room in which atmospheric humidity is artificially produced.

(2) A *hygrometer* and a *thermometer* close to it shall be kept as near as practicable to the centre of every room, and if an inspector so directs, a second *hygrometer* and *thermometer* shall be placed at the side of the room or in such other position as may be directed by an inspector.

(3), (4) [*revoked*].

(5) No water which is liable to cause injury to the health of the persons employed, or to yield effluvia, shall be used for artificial humidification, and for the purpose of this provision any water which absorbs from an acid solution of permanganate of potash in four hours at 16 degrees Celsius more than 7 milligrams of oxygen per litre of water shall be deemed to be liable to cause injury to the health of the persons employed.

18. Restriction of artificial humidification.—(1) There shall be no artificial humidification in any room at any time when—

(i) the reading of the wet-bulb thermometer in that room exceeds 22.5 degrees Celsius, or

(ii) the difference between the reading of the wet-bulb thermometer and the reading of the dry-bulb thermometer is less than 2 degrees Celsius.

(2) If, while work is going on in any room, the reading of the wet-bulb thermometer in that room exceeds 24 degrees Celsius, all available means of ventilation and of reducing the temperature shall be put into operation and maintained in operation until the reading of the wet-bulb thermometer has fallen to 22.5 degrees Celsius.

(3) For the purposes of this regulation, in the case of a room in which two *hygrometers* and two thermometers are placed in accordance with regulation 17 the readings to be recorded are the average of those of both *hygrometers* or both thermometers as the case may be.

PART V

WELFARE

19. Provision of cloakrooms.—(1) The accommodation for clothing not worn during working hours provided for the purpose of section 43 of the Act [s. 59] shall, wherever it is reasonably practicable to do so, be provided in a cloakroom or cloakrooms, that is to say in a separate room or rooms conveniently accessible to the persons for whose use the accommodation is provided.

(2) Where the accommodation is provided in a cloakroom as aforesaid, it shall include, for the separate use of each employed person, either
  (i) a suitable locker or cupboard, or
  (ii) a clothes' hook or peg and a suitable receptacle for footwear.

(3) Every cloakroom shall be placed in charge of a responsible person.

General note. This regulation is revoked by the Workplace (Health, Safety and Welfare) Regulations 1992, S.I. 1992 No. 3004, as from 1 January 1993 except, in relation to any workplace or part of a workplace which is not a new workplace, or a modification, an extension or a conversion, it is revoked as from 1 January 1996.

20. Provisions of lockers and cupboards. For the separate use of each employed person for whom accommodation is not provided in a cloakroom in accordance with regulation 19, there shall be provided as accommodation for clothing not worn during working hours a suitable locker or cupboard which shall be either in the workroom in which that person is employed or in an easily accessible position in the immediate vicinity of that workroom.

General note. This regulation is revoked by the Workplace (Health, Safety and Welfare) Regulations 1992, S.I. 1992 No. 3004, as from 1 January 1993 except, in relation to any workplace or part of a workplace which is not a new workplace, or a modification, an extension or a conversion, it is revoked as from 1 January 1996.

21. Further provisions as to clothing accommodation. The accommodation provided in pursuance of regulations 19 and 20 shall be adequately ventilated and kept clean and shall be so constructed, enclosed or protected as to reduce, so far as is reasonably practicable, the deposit of dust on the clothing; and the arrangements made for the custody of articles deposited in the accommodation shall not prevent free access to any washing facilities or sanitary conveniences.

General note. This regulation is revoked by the Workplace (Health, Safety and Welfare) Regulations 1992, S.I. 1992 No. 3004, as from 1 January 1993 except, in relation to any workplace or part of a workplace which is not a new workplace, or a modification, an extension or a conversion, it is revoked as from 1 January 1996.

22. Washing facilities. The washing facilities provided for the purpose of section 42 of the Act [s. 58]

(1) shall include basins or troughs so provided and maintained as to satisfy the following requirements—

(a) basins and troughs shall have a smooth, impervious upper surface;

(b) each basin shall be fitted with a waste-pipe and plub and each trough shall be fitted with an unplugged waste-pipe;

(c) each trough shall have a supply of warm water laid on and each basin shall have a supply *(a)* of hot and cold water or of warm water laid on or made readily available at all times when employed persons for whose use they are provided are in or within the precincts of the factory; and the supply of water to troughs shall be laid on at points above the trough at intervals of not more than 600 millimetres;

(d) basins and troughs shall be sufficient in number and dimensions to provide at least one unit for every twenty persons employed; and for the purpose of this requirement a "unit" means one basin or 600 millimetres of the length of a trough or, in the case of circular or oval troughs, 600 millimetres of the circumference of a trough;

(2) shall be placed in charge of a responsible person or persons;

(3) shall be placed, in part if practicable, near to sanitary conveniences.

General note. This regulation is revoked by the Workplace (Health, Safety and Welfare) Regulations 1992, S.I. 1992 No. 3004, as from 1 January 1993 except, in relation to any workplace or part of a workplace which is not a new workplace, or a modification, an extension or a conversion, it is revoked as from 1 January 1996.

(a) Washing facilities. See INTRODUCTORY NOTE 20.

23.   Existing washing facilities. Washing facilities provided for the purpose of section 42 of the Act [s. 58] shall not be in a workroom except in the case of fixed facilities installed in a workroom before the first day of January, 1947, which it has not been reasonably practicable to remove, and any such fixed facilities may be taken into account in ascertaining whether the provisions of the Act and these Regulations, with reference to washing facilities, have been complied with.

General note. This regulation is revoked by the Workplace (Health, Safety and Welfare) Regulations 1992, S.I. 1992 No. 3004, as from 1 January 1993 except, in relation to any workplace or part of a workplace which is not a new workplace, or a modification, an extension or a conversion, it is revoked as from 1 January 1996.

24.   Facilities for taking meals. There shall be provided, for the use of the persons employed at any factory to which these Regulations apply, adequate and suitable facilities for taking meals.

General note. This regulation is revoked by the Workplace (Health, Safety and Welfare) Regulations 1992, S.I. 1992 No. 3004, as from 1 January 1993 except, in relation to any workplace or part of a workplace which is not a new workplace, or a modification, an extension or a conversion, it is revoked as from 1 January 1996.

25.   Provision of canteen or mess rooms.—(1) In the case of a factory in which more than 250 persons are employed, a canteen where hot meals can be purchased shall be provided at or in the immediate vicinity of the factory:

Provided that, in the case of any such factory in respect of which the Chief Inspector has certified that the service of hot meals at the canteen is either not required or not reasonably practicable, there shall be provided in lieu thereof at such canteen such facilities for the purchase of light refreshments and hot drinks as may reasonably be required in the circumstances of the case.

(2) In the case of a factory in which not more than 250 persons are employed, the facilities provided shall include either—

(a) at or in the immediate vicinity of the factory, a canteen where hot meals can be purchased, or

(b) at the factory, a mess room or mess rooms equipped with adequate means of warming food and boiling water; and, if the Inspector for the district so directs, such facilities for purchasing light refreshment and hot drinks as may reasonably be required in the circumstances of the case.

General note. This regulation is revoked by the Workplace (Health, Safety and Welfare) Regulations 1992, S.I. 1992 No. 3004, as from 1 January 1993 except, in relation to any workplace or part of a workplace which is not a new workplace, or a modification, an extension or a conversion, it is revoked as from 1 January 1996.

26. Particulars regarding facilities to be provided for taking meals. A canteen or mess room provided in pursuance of regulations 24 and 25, shall be

(a) adequately ventilated and lighted and sufficiently warmed for use at meal times;

(b) provided with sufficient tables and chairs or benches with back rests;

(c) placed in charge of a responsible person;

(d) kept in a clean and orderly condition; and

(e) separate from any workroom and from the accommodation provided for clothing.

General note. This regulation is revoked by the Workplace (Health, Safety and Welfare) Regulations 1992, S.I. 1992 No. 3004, as from 1 January 1993 except, in relation to any workplace or part of a workplace which is not a new workplace, or a modification, an extension or a conversion, it is revoked as from 1 January 1996.

PART VI
CONSTRUCTION AND USE OF NEW MACHINERY

27. Construction and guarding of new machinery.—(1) This regulation applies to machines of the classes or descriptions specified in the first column of the First Schedule to these Regulations, being machines the construct of which is begun after the date on which these Regulations come into force.

(2) No machine to which this regulation applies shall be used unless it is constructed or provided with guards, fencing or other protective devices in conformity with the requirements set opposite to the class or description to which the machine belongs in the second column of the First Schedule to these Regulations.

(3) The provisions of paragraph (2) of this regulation shall be without prejudice to the requirements of subsection (1) of section 14 and subsection (1) of section 17 of the Act [ss. 14(1) and 17(1)].

General note. This regulation is revoked by the Provision and Use of Work Equipment Regulations 1992, S.I. 1992 No. 2932, as from 1 January 1993 except, insofar as it applies to work equipment first provided for use in the premises or undertaking before 1 January 1993, it is revoked as from 1 January 1997.

PART VII

SALE OF HIRE OF MACHINERY

28.   Extension of section 17 of the Act. The provisions of subsection (2) of section 17 of the Act [s. 17(2)] (which prohibits the sale or letting on hire of certain machines which do not comply with the provisions of that section) shall extend to any machine (being a machine to which regulation 27 of these Regulations applies and which is intended to be used in a factory to which these Regulations apply) that does not comply with the requirements of that regulation.

General note. This regulation is revoked by the Provision and Use of Work Equipment Regulations 1992, S.I. 1992 No. 2932, as from 1 January 1993 except, insofar as it applies to work equipment first provided for use in the premises or undertaking before 1 January 1993, it is revoked as from 1 January 1997.

FIRST SCHEDULE

Regulation 27

REQUIREMENTS AS TO CONSTRUCTION AND SAFEGUARDING OF MACHINES

First Column	Second Column
Classes or descriptions of machines	Requirements
(1) Opening Machines	(a) The minimum length of the feed table or feed band shall be 1.35 metres. The table or band shall be fitted with guards on each side extending to a height of 1.35 metres from the floor throughout a distance of 600 millimetres from the vertical plane in which the nip of the rollers lies.
	(b) An effective automatic safety stopping device shall be fitted at the end of the feed table or feed band.
(2) Softening Machines	(a) An effective safety stopping device shall be fitted, which shall provide for stopping the machine at both the feed and delivery ends.
	(b) The starting gear shall be so arranged and designed at the feed end and with the co-operation of the operator at the delivery end.
	(c) In front of the first pair of rollers there shall be provided a feed table at least 1.80 metres long, provided on each side with solid side guards extending to a height of 1.35 metres from the floor throughout a distance of at least 1.05 metres from the vertical plane in which the axis of the rollers lies.

First Column	Second Column
Classes or descriptions of machines	Requirements
	(d) The side shafts and gears shall be completely enclosed by sheet metal covers, which shall be so arranged that the covers cannot be opened whilst the machine is in motion and the machine cannot be started unless the covers are closed.
(3) Carding and Teasing Machines	(a) All side gearing shall be enclosed by a guard with panels and sliding doors of sheet metal. The distance from the floor to the under side of this guard shall not exceed 200 millimetres, and the sliding doors shall be interlocked by a device which will ensure that they cannot be opened until the machine has come to rest and the machine cannot be started unless the said doors are closed.
	(b) The in-running nip between the delivery roller and the pressing ball shall be securely fenced throughout its length, and where part of the fencing consists of the nozzle of the conductor to the delivery roller, this nozzle shall be so constructed as to prevent a person's hand from reaching the nip.
	(c) The doffing roller shall be securely fenced by an adequately strong and rigid set of bars or rods or by a solid cover. The guard shall follow the circumference of the roller and shall be securely bolted in position. Where such a guard is constructed of bars or rods, the space between such bars or rods shall not exceed 38 millimetres. The distance from the doffer pin points to the under side of the rods or bars shall be not less than 100 millimetres. The space between the drawing pressing roller and the first rod shall not exceed 50 millimetres, and the distance between the outermost bars or rods measured over the periphery of the guard shall not be less than 300 millimetres.
	(d) A hand or guard rail shall be fitted in a convenient position in front of and above the level of the drawing pressing roller and extending throughout its full width.
	(e) The underframe shall be guarded in such a manner that it is not possible for any person to obtain access under the machine until the cylinder has ceased to revolve. The lowest cross-member of the under-frame shall be not more than 200 millimetres above the floor, and all openings above this member large enough to permit access under the machine shall be covered with sheet metal or with bars or rods the space between which is not more than 150 millimetres. Any door or detachable panel which,

First Column	Second Column
Classes or descriptions of machines	Requirements

	when opened, allows of such access shall be provided with a locking device which will ensure that the door or panel cannot be opened until the cylinder has come to rest, and that the machine cannot be started unless the door or panel is closed.
(4) Drawing Frames	(a) The space between the bend rail and the bottom of the retaining roller shall be completely closed by a sheet metal guard. The guard shall be either (i) arranged so as to turn about a horizontal axis near its centre, and so that the top edge shall swing towards the gill bar when the guard is opened, or (ii) so constructed as to be as safe as if it were so arranged. The guard shall be so interlocked with the starting gear of the machine that it cannot be opened while the machine is running and the machine cannot be started unless the guard is closed.
	(b) The in-running nip between the delivery rollers shall be securely fenced throughout its length, and where part of the fencing consists of the nozzel of the conductor to the delivery roller, this nozzel shall be so constructed as to prevent a person's hand from reaching the nip.
	(c) The train of gears comprising the end gearing shall be completely enclosed. Where any hinged or moveable panels are provided in such enclosure they shall be so interlocked with the driving mechanism that they cannot be opened whilst the machine is running and the machine cannot be started unless all such panels are closed.
	(d) The cam tramper motions shall be so arranged that there is no risk of trapping between the collars of the sliding shafts of such motions and the fixed guides in which these shafts move, provided that where this is not reasonably practicable the collars shall be enclosed by guards extending beyond the limits of travel of the collars in both directions.
(5) Roving Frames	(a) Gearing shall be enclosed as specified under 4(c) above.
	(b) The starting and stopping gear shall be fitted with an effective device which shall ensure that the machine can be stopped from both sides, but, if more than one person is employed in the operation of the machine, can only be started by an operator on the delivery side and with the co-operation of an operator on the feed side.
(6) Spinning Frames	Gearing shall be completely enclosed as specified under 4(c).

First Column	Second Column
Classes or descriptions of machines	Requirements
(7) Cop Winding Machines	The spindles of Cop Winding Machines of the "cop above cone" type shall be securely fenced. Any slots provided in such fencing for pedal levers shall not exceed 25 millimetres in width, or if of greater width, shall be so guarded as to prevent access to the spindles.
(8) Dressing Machines— Cylinder and Box or Stove Type	(a) All cross and side shafts shall be completely enclosed except those portions of sliding shafts carrying the beam between the gables on Hibbert type dressing machines.
	(b) Friction drive hand wheels shall be plated.
	(c) On cylinder type machines the space between any yard guide roller and its adjacent steam cylinder shall be not less than 75 millimetres.
	(d) Secure fencing shall be provided for the nip between the yard beam pressing roller and the top weight roller on the side at which the beam is inserted and removed.
(9) Looms	Guards shall be fitted to the sleys of all looms so as to prevent, as far as practicable, shuttles from flying. Such guards shall be strongly constructed, fixed and maintained in position as low as possible, and in particular, the clearance between the guard and a shuttle when the shuttle is placed on the fell of the cloth with the loom crank shaft on the top centre shall not exceed 13 millimetres. Laterally the guard shall extend to within a distance equivalent to not more than half the shuttle's length from the entrance to the shuttle box on each side of the loom.
(10) Calendars	All in-running nips of the bowls or rollers shall be securely fenced. Wherever practicable such fencing shall consist of a fixed guard so constructed that it will prevent a worker's fingers from reaching the nip. In all other cases the nips shall be securely fenced by means of metal tubular safety rollers, which shall be as light in weight as practicable. These safety rollers shall be pivoted on their supporting brackets so that, while normally resting on the lower bowl or roller, they are free to lift in the vertical direction and make contact with the upper bowl or roller, so that when there is a maximum clearance between the safety roller and either bowl it is impossible for a worker's fingers to reach the nip.

First Column	Second Column
Classes or descriptions of machines	Requirements
(11) Cropping Machines	The spiral cutters shall be securely fenced by sheet metal guards which, if not bolted or screwed in position, shall be interlocked in such a manner that the guard cannot be opened whilst the machine is running and the machine cannot be started unless the guard is in position.
(12) Cloth Cutting Machines—Harnden "Guillotine" type	(a) The knife shall be securely fenced on the delivery side. (b) The nip of the feed roller shall be securely fenced.
(13) Lapping Machines	The side arms shall be securely fenced by solid guards.

General note. This Schedule is revoked by the Provision and Use of Work Equipment Regulations 1992, S.I. 1992 No. 2932, as from 1 January 1993 except, insofar as it applies to work equipment first provided for use in the premises or undertaking before 1 January 1993, it is revoked as from 1 January 1997.

THE KIERS REGULATIONS 1938

(S.R. & O. 1938 No. 106, as amended by S.I. 1981 No. 1152
and S.I. 1992 No. 3004)

In pursuance of section 79 of the Factory and Workshop Act 1901, I hereby make the following Regulations and direct that they shall apply to factories and workshops (being print works, bleaching and dyeing works, or works in which cotton or cotton waste is bleached) wherein kiers are used for the purpose of boiling textile material.

The Regulations may be cited as the Kiers Regulations 1938, and shall come into force on 1 May 1938, except that regulations 3, 4, 5 and 8 shall not apply until after the expiration of twelve months from the said date.

General note. Dimensions in these Regulations have been metricated by S.I. 1981 No. 1152, which provides (reg. 3) that where the dimensions of any premises or plant in existence or under construction immediately before 1 October 1981 complied with the Regulations then in force then those premises or that plant shall be deemed to comply with these Regulations as amended by the metricating regulations.

Definitions

For the purposes of these Regulations:—

"Print works" means any premises in which any persons are employed to print figures, patterns or designs upon any cotton, linen, woollen, worsted or silken yard or upon any woven or felted fabric not being paper.

"Bleaching and dyeing works" means any premises in which the processes of bleaching, beetling, dyeing, calendering, finishing, hooking, lapping and making up and packing any yarn or cloth of any material or the dressing or finishing of lace or any one or more of such processes or any process incidental thereto are or is carried on.

"Kier" means a fixed vessel used for boiling textile material, wherein boiling liquid is circulated by means of steam or mechanical power through a pipe, channel or duct, so constructed and arranged that the liquid is discharged over the textile materials and percolates through it.

"Atmospheric or open kier" means a *kier* so constructed and arranged that it cannot be worked at a pressure above atmospheric pressure.

"Kier system" means a *kier* together with its inlet and outlet and circulating pipes, and any pump, injector, steam pipe or heater used in connection with that *kier*.

"Disconnection" means the complete interruption of the flow of liquor, water, or steam through a pipe either (a) by the removal of a sufficient portion of the pipe, together with the blanking of the end of the pipe on the supple side, or (b) by a special disconnecting appliance of a type approved in writing by the Chief Inspector *(a)* of Factories.

"Disconnect" means to interrupt completely the flow of liquor, water or steam through a pipe by one of the two methods of *disconnection.*

"Hot liquor" or *"hot water"* means liquor or water at a temperature exceeding 40°C.

"Competent person" means a person who is experienced in the operation and working of *kiers* and capable of manipulating and working in accordance with these Regulations all valves, taps, pumps, *disconnecting* arrangements, or other appliances provided for the *kiers.*

"Authorised person" has the meaning assigned to it in regulation 19.

"Entry" into a *kier* shall be deemed to have been made by a person if either of his feet is within the *kier,* and *"enter"* shall have a similar meaning.

Exceptions

(i) Nothing in these Regulations shall apply to a *kier* in which the material is boiled in a container or wagon or on a movable carriage, provided that the loading and unloading of such container, wagon or carriage is carried on entirely outside the *kier.*

(ii) Regulations 3, 4, 5, 17 and 21 shall not apply in the case of a *kier* which is filled from outside without *entry* by a person into the *kier,* and which is entered only for the purpose of sheeting up the material after filling or occasionally for rectifying a fault or for repair or maintenance purposes.

(iii) If the Chief Inspector *(a)* of Factories is satisfied that by reason of exceptional circumstances in any works subject to these Regulations, or by reason of the infrequency of the process, or for any other reason, all or any of the requirements of the Regulations are not necessary for the protection of persons employed in such works, he may by certificate in writing (which he may in his discretion revoke at any time) except such works or any part of such works, or any *kier* or *kier system,* from the operation of all or any such requirements, subject to such conditions as he may prescribe in that certificate. Where such an exemption is granted, a legible copy of the certificate, showing the conditions subject to which it has been granted, shall be kept affixed in the works.

(a) **Inspector.** See INTRODUCTORY NOTE 24.

Duties

It shall be the duty of the occupier to observe Part I of these Regulations.

It shall be the duty of every person employed to observe Part II of these Regulations.

PART I
DUTIES OF OCCUPIERS

Steam Admission
1. The admission of steam into a *kier* or *kier system* shall be controlled by a screw-down wheel valve, and not merely by a tap or cock. In the case of every *kier* which is customarily entered for the purpose of plaiting down, filling, arranging, packing or emptying textile material, means shall be provided for locking the valve in the closed position or for *disconnecting* the steam supply pipe.

Hot Liquor Admission

2. *Hot liquor* shall not be prepared except in a vessel or tank separate from the *kier* in which such *hot liquor* is to be used, and *hot liquor* shall not be admitted to nor shall liquor be rendered *hot* in the *kier* until the loading has been completed.

Liquor and Water Admission Pipes

3. Every supply pipe through which liquor or water is conducted to a *kier* shall, in addition to the valve or cock controlling admission of liquor or water for the ordinary working of the *kier*, be provided with arrangements for *disconnection* of the pipe on the *kier* side of such valve or cock in such a way as it isolate the *kier* from any other *kier* or vessel, and to ensure that no liquor or water can flow from the supply side of the pipe:

Provided that in the case of a water supply pipe such arrangements for *disconnection* shall not be required if there is a non-return valve in the pipe to each *kier* on the *kier* side of the control valve or cock.

External Circulation Pipes

4. Every *kier system* in which the circulation is affected through an external pipe shall be provided with arrangements for *disconnection* of the pipe in such a way as to ensure that no liquor or water can flow into the upper part of the *kier* or escape from the ends of the pipe where it is *disconnected*.

Internal Circulation Pipes

5. Every *kier system* in which the circulation is effected through an internal pipe or puffer pipe, shall be provided with either:—

(a) arrangements for *disconnection* of the steam pipe, such arrangements to be in addition to the valve controlling the steam supply and to be placed on the *kier* side of such valve; or

(b) efficient means for closing the top of the puffer pipe.

Pumps

6. Where the circulation of liquor in a *kier system* is effected by means of a pump, efficient means shall be provided for preventing the accidental starting of the pump.

Position of Discharges

7. The open end of the pipe through which the liquor is discharged from a *kier*, and the open end of a vent, inlet or other pipe through which liquor may escape from a *kier*, shall be so placed or arranged that no person is exposed to risk of scalding.

Discharge Pipes and Channels

8. The pipe used for discharging the liquor from a *kier* shall not be connected with a discharge pipe from any other *kier* through any common pipe, channel or chamber in which the pressure can rise above atmospheric pressure.

Position of Valves and Taps

9. The control for any valve or tap shall be so placed that the person operating it is not exposed to risk of scalding.

Baynot-jointed Kier Cover

10. Where a *kier* has a bayonet-joined cover, efficient means shall be provided for preventing (a) the rise of pressure inside the *kier* above atmospheric pressure before the cover is in the fully locked position, and (b) the cover becoming moved from that position before the pressure inside the *kier* has been reduced to atmospheric pressure.

Distinguishing Marks

11. Every *kier* shall have a number or distinguishing mark clearly and legibly marked on it. The control of every valve or tap, and every *disconnecting* arrangement, used on a *kier* or *kier system* shall be clearly and legibly marked with the same number or distinguishing mark as the *kier*, except where it is otherwise clear that the valve, tap or *disconnecting* arrangement is connected with one particular *kier* and no other.

Height of Atmospheric or Open Kiers above Platforms

12.—(1) In crofts or keir houses erected or substantially reconstructed after the date on which these Regulations come into force, the height of the edge of an *atmospheric or open kier* above the working platform or standing place shall be not less than 840 millimetres.

(2) In other crofts or kier houses, if the height of the edge of an *atmospheric or open kier* above the working platform or standing place is less than 840 millimetres, the *kier* shall be securely fenced to that height.

General note. This regulation is revoked by the Workplace (Health, Safety and Welfare) Regulations 1992, S.I. 1992 No. 3004, as from 1 January 1993 except, in relation to any workplace or part of a workplace which is not a new workplace, or a modification, an extension or a conversion, it is revoked as from 1 January 1996.

Height of Hot Liquor Tanks or Hot Water Tanks above Platforms

13. Every fixed vessel or tank (other than a *kier*) used in connection with a *kier* or *kier system*, and containing *hot liquor* or *hot water* shall, if the edge of such vessel or tank is less than 920 millimetres above the level of the adjoining platform or standing place, be either—
   (i) securely fenced to a height of not less than 920 millimetres, or
   (ii) provided with an effective grid or other effective cover.

General note. This regulation is revoked by the Workplace (Health, Safety and Welfare) Regulations 1992, S.I. 1992 No. 3004, as from 1 January 1993 except, in relation to any workplace or part of a workplace which is not a new workplace, or a modification, an extension or a conversion, it is revoked as from 1 January 1996.

Ways above Kiers or Tanks containing Hot Liquor or Hot Water

14. No plank, ladder, stair or gangway shall be placed over any uncovered *kier*, tank or other fixed vessel containing *hot liquor* or *hot water* unless it is securely fixed and fenced on each side to a height of not less than 840 millimetres either by upper and lower rails or by sheet fencing.

General note. This regulation is revoked by the Workplace (Health, Safety and Welfare) Regulations 1992, S.I. 1992 No. 3004, as from 1 January 1993 except, in relation to any workplace or part of a workplace which is not a new workplace, or a modification, an extension or a conversion, it is revoked as from 1 January 1996.

Spacing of Atmospheric or Open Kiers

15.—(1) In crofts or kier houses erected or substantially reconstructed after the date on which these Regulations come into force, the distance between the edges of an *atmospheric or open kier* and of an adjacent *kier* shall be not less than 460 millimetres, and there shall be a space for passage round each *kier* which at no point shall be less than 310 millimetres wide.

(2) In other crofts or kier houses, where the edges of adjacent *kiers* are less than 230 millimetres apart, a gangway not less than 460 millimetres wide shall be provided over the space between the adjacent *kiers*. This gangway shall be of adequate length and provided with safe means of access. Both the gangway and the means of access to it shall be fenced on each side to a height of not less than 840 millimetres either by upper and lower rails or by sheet fencing.

General note. This regulation is revoked by the Workplace (Health, Safety and Welfare) Regulations 1992, S.I. 1992 No. 3004, as from 1 January 1993 except, in relation to any workplace or part of a workplace which is not a new workplace, or a modification, an extension or a conversion, it is revoked as from 1 January 1996.

Access to Interior of Kiers

16. Suitable ladders to enable persons to *enter* into and emerge from *kiers* easily shall be provided and kept available in positions near to the *kiers*.

Notice of Permission to enter Kier

17. There shall be provided for every *kier* to which regulations 3, 4 and 5 apply an appropriate notice or sign to be affixed when the *kier* may be entered in accordance with regulation 21.

Maintenance

18. Every valve or tap controlling the admission of steam, liquor or water to a *kier*, and the special safety appliances required by these Regulations, shall be kept in good repair.

Responsibility for Kier Operation

19. The occupier shall appoint a *competent person* to supervise the working of each set of *kiers* in accordance with these Regulations and to control the *entry* of persons into those *kiers*. Each person so appointed shall be known as the *authorised person* for that set of *kiers*. The occupier may appoint a second *competent person* as an *authorised person* to act as deputy in the absence of the first *authorised person*, and may also appoint a particular person to perform specified duties in connection with the completion of operation and blowing down of the *kiers*. The name of every person appointed in pursuance of this regulation shall be stated in a notice affixed near the *kiers* concerned.

PART II
DUTIES OF PERSONS EMPLOYED

Control of Appliances

20. The *authorised person* shall take all reasonable steps to secure that all valves, taps, *disconnecting* arrangement, pumps, notices, signs, and other appliances in connection with the *kiers* under his supervision, are properly manipulated and used in accordance with these Regulations.

Precautions before Entry into Kiers

21.—(1) Subject to regulation 23, the *authorised person* shall take all reasonable steps to ensure that no person shall *enter* into or remain in a *kier* to which this regulation applies unless—

(a) no *hot liquor* or *hot water* is present in the *kier* or *kier system*;

(b) either every branch steam pipe through which steam may flow into the *kier* or *kier system* is *disconnected*, or the valve controlling the supply of steam is closed and locked;

(c) the *kier* is isolated from every other vessel by the means required by regulation 3;

(d) in the case of a *kier* with an external circulating pipe, such pipe is *disconnected* by the arrangements required by regulation 4;

(e) in the case of a *kier* with an internal circulating pipe or puffer pipe, the steam pipe is *disconnected*, or the top of the puffer pipe is effectively closed, by the means required by regulation 5;

(f) in the case of a *kier* with pump circulation the pump is, by the means required by regulation 6, effectively secured against accidental starting; and

(g) the notice or sign required by regulation 17 is affixed close to the entrance to the *kier*.

(2) The *authorised person* shall not affix the said notice or sign or cause it to be affixed until he has ascertained that the foregoing conditions (a) to (f) are fulfilled. He shall not remove it or permit it to be removed until he has ascertained that no person is in the *kier*, but subject to this he shall cause its removal as soon as the purpose for which entry of the *kier* was required has been completed. So long at the notice or sign is affixed, he shall take all reasonable care to ensure that the said conditions (a) to (f) remain fulfilled.

22.   Subject to regulation 23, in the case of a *kier* which is filled by means of a mechanical piler or is customarily filled from outside without *entry* into such *kier*, the *authorised person* shall take all reasonable steps to ensure that no person shall *enter* into or remain in such *kier* except for the purpose of sheeting up the material after filing or occasionally for rectifying a fault, and then only if—

(a) no *hot liquor* or *hot water* is present in the *kier* or *kier system*;

(b) all valves or taps which control the admission of steam, liquor or *hot water* into that *kier* are closed; and

(c) the pumps, or other means by which the movement or circulation of liquor in that *kier system* is effected, are secured to prevent such circulation.

Entry into Kiers for Repairs or Maintenance

23.   In the case of *entry* by a person into a *kier* for the purpose of examination, repair, limewashing, or any similar purpose in connection with maintenance, regulations 21 and 22 shall not apply, and instead thereof the following provisions shall apply—

The foreman, or persons in charge of the persons engaged in the above-named work, shall take all reasonable care to ensure that no person shall *enter* or remain in a *kier* unless—

(a) no *hot liquor* or *hot water* is present in the *kier* or *kier system*;

(b) all valves or taps which control the admission of steam, liquor or *hot water* into the *kier* are closed, or adequate isolation is effected by *disconnection*; and

(c) the pumps, or other means by which the movement or circulation of liquor in that *kier system* is effected, are secured to prevent such circulation.

Unauthorised Entry into Kiers

24. No person shall *enter* a *kier* except—

(i) when a notice or sign provided in pursuance of regulation 17 is affixed close to the entrance to the *kier*; or

(ii) in the case of a *kier* to which regulation 22 applies, with the consent of the *authorised person*; or

(iii) in cases where regulation 23 applies, with the consent of the foreman or person in charge.

Standing or Sitting on Edge of Kiers

25. No person shall sit or stand on the edge of an open *kier* or on the fencing round it.

Interference with Appliances by Unauthorised Persons

26. No person other than an *authorised person* shall, without the knowledge and consent of the *authorised person*, interfere with, manipulate or work any valve, taps, *disconnecting* arrangements, pumps, notices, signs or other appliances used in connection with a *kier*:

Provided that this Regulation shall not preclude any other person, in a case of emergency or likelihood of serious danger or damage, from taking such action as may be necessary in the circumstances of the case to avoid such danger or damage.

THE LAUNDRIES WELFARE ORDER 1920

(Dated 23 April 1920; S.R. & O. 1920 No. 654, as amended by S.I. 1992 No. 2966 and S.I. 1992 No. 3004)

General note. This whole Order is revoked by the Workplace (Health, Safety and Welfare) Regulations 1992, S.I. 1992 No. 3004, as from 1 January 1993 except, in relation to any workplace or part of a workplace which is not a new workplace, or a modification, an extension or a conversion, it is revoked as from 1 January 1996.

In pursuance of section 7 of the Police, Factories, etc. (Miscellaneous Provisions) Act 1916, I hereby make the following Order for all factories and workshops or parts of factories and workshops which are laundries:

Provided that paragraphs 3 and 5 of the Order shall not apply to laundries in which no mechanical power is used and in which not more than five persons are employed.

1. [*revoked*].

2. The occupier shall provide and maintain for the use of all the persons employed suitable accommodation for clothing put off during working hours, with adequate arrangements for drying the clothing if wet.

The accommodation so provided shall be placed under the charge of a responsible person, and shall be kept clean.

3. The occupier shall provide and maintain for the use of all the persons employed and remaining on the premises during the meal intervals a suitable messroom, which shall be furnished with (a) sufficient tables and chairs or benches with back rests, and (b) unless a canteen serving hot meals is provided, adequate means of warming food and boiling water. The messroom shall be sufficiently warmed for use during meal intervals.

The messroom shall be separate from the cloakroom, and shall be placed under the charge of a responsible person, and shall be kept clean:

Provided that, in the case of an existing laundry where there are structural difficulties in the way of such separation, the Chief Inspector (*a*) of Factories may by written certificate (which may be revoked at any time) allow some other arrangement if satisfied that it provides suitable accommodation for the workers.

4. The occupier shall provide and maintain for the use of all the persons employed suitable facilities (*b*) for washing, comprising a sufficient supply of clean towels, soap and warm water, adjacent to where the work is done.

(*a*) **Inspector.** See INTRODUCTORY NOTE 24.

(*b*) **Washing facilities.** See INTRODUCTORY NOTE 20.

5.–6. [*revoked*].

7. The occupier shall provide and maintain at suitable points, conveniently accessible at all times to all persons employed—

(a) an adequate supply of wholesome drinking water from a public main or from some other source of supply approved in writing by the local authority of the district in which the laundry is situated, which shall be either laid on, or contained in a suitable vessel;

(b) (except where the water is delivered in an upward jet from which the works can conveniently drink) at least one suitable cup or drinking vessel at each point of supply, with facilities for rinsing it in drinking water.

Each drinking water supply shall be clearly marked "Drinking Water".

All practicable steps shall be taken to preserve the water and vessels from contamination.

THE LOCOMOTIVES AND WAGGONS (USED ON LINES AND SIDINGS) REGULATIONS 1906

(Dated 24 August 1906; S.R. & O. 1906 No. 679, as amended by
S.I. 1981 No. 1327 and S.I. 1989 No. 2169)

[*Placard: Form 944*]

Whereas the use of *locomotives, waggons,* and other rolling stock on *lines of rail* or sidings in any factory or workshop or any place to which the provisions of section 79 of the Factory and Workshop Act 1901 are applied by that Act or on *lines of rail* or sidings used in connection with any factory or workshop or any place as aforesaid, and not being part of a railway within the meaning of the Railway Employment (Prevention of Accidents) Act 1900 *(a)* (63 & 64 Vict. c. 27), has been certified in pursuance of the said section to be dangerous:

I hereby in pursuance of the powers conferred upon me by that Act make the following Regulations and direct that they shall apply to all places before mentioned.

These Regulations shall come into force on the 1st day of January, 1907, except regulations 1, 2, and 22, which shall come into force on the 1st day of January, 1908.

Subject to the exemptions below, it shall be the duty of—

(i) the occupier of any factory or workshop and any place to which any of the provisions of the Factory and Workshop Act 1901 [now the 1961 Act] are applied, and

(ii) the occupier of any *line of rails* or sidings used in connection with a factory or workshop, or with any place to which any of the provisions of the Factory and Workshop Act 1901 [now the 1961 Act] are applied,

to comply with Part I of these Regulations.

And it shall be the duty of every person *(b)* who by himself, his agents or workmen, carries on any of the operations to which these Regulations apply, and of all agents, workmen and persons employed to comply with Part II of these Regulations.

And it shall be the duty of every person who by himself, his agents or workmen, carried on any of the operations to which these Regulations apply, to comply with Part III of these Regulations.

In these Regulations—

Line of rails means a line of rails or sidings for the use of *locomotives or waggons*, except such lines as are used exclusively for (a) a gantry crane or travelling crane, or (b) any charging machine or other apparatus or vehicle used exclusively in or about any actual process of manufacture.

Waggon includes any wheeled vehicle or non-self-moving crane on a *line of rails*.

Locomotive includes any wheeled motor on a *line of rails* used for the movement of *waggons* and any self-moving crane.

Gantry means an elevated structure of wood, masonry, or metal, exceeding 2 metres in height and used for loading or unloading, which carries a *line of rails*, whereon *waggons* are worked by mechanical power.

Nothing in these Regulations shall apply to—

(a) A *line of rails* of less than 920 millimetres gauge, and *locomotives and waggons* used thereon.

(b) A *line of rails* not worked by mechanical power.

(c) A *line of rails* forming part of a mine within the meaning of the Coal Mines Regulation Act 1887 *(c)*, or of a quarry within the meaning of the Quarries Act 1894 *(c)*, not being a *line of rails* within or used solely in connection with any factory or workshop not incidental to the maintenance or working of the mine or quarry or to the carrying on of the business thereof.

(e) Pit banks of mines to which the Metalliferous Mines Regulation Act 1872 *(c)* applies, and private *lines of rails* used in connection therewith.

(f) Lines of railways used in connection with factories or workshops, so far as they are outside the factory or workshop premises, and used for running purposes only.

(g) *Waggons* not moved by mechanical power.

(h) Buildings in course of construction.

(i) Explosives factories or workshops within the meaning of the Explosives Act 1875.

(j) All lines and sidings on or used in connection with docks, wharves and quays not forming part of a factory or workshop as defined in section 149 of the Factory and Workshop Act 1901 [s. 175].

(k) *Waggon or locomotive* building or repairing shops, and all lines and sidings used in connection with such shops if such shops are in the occupation of a railway company within the meaning of the Regulation of Railways Act 1871.

(l) Depots or car-sheds being parts or tramway or light railway undertakings authorised by Parliament, and used for the storage, cleaning, inspection or repair of tramway cars or light railway cars.

General note. Dimensions in these Regulations have been metricated by S.I. 1981 No. 1327 which provides (reg. 3) that where any plant in existence or under construction immediately before 1 November 1981 complied with the requirements of these Regulations as then in force, then that plant shall be deemed to comply with these Regulations as amended by the metricating regulations.

(a) **Railway.** As defined by s. 16 of the Railway Employment (Prevention of Accidents) Act 1900, *"railway"* means any railway used for the purposes of public traffic, whether passenger, goods or other traffic, and includes any works of the railway company connected with the railway.

(b) **Person ... carries on ... operations.** An owner or occupier who is also a person who carries on operations to which these Regulations apply cannot rely upon s. 155 of the Act to absolve him from liability for a failure to comply with an operator's duty under Part II or III of these Regulations (*Wagon Repairs Ltd v Vosper* (1967) 3 KIR 605, DC).

(c) **Acts.** The Acts of 1872, 1887 and 1894 have been repealed and are replaced by the Mines and Quarries Act 1954.

PART I

1. Point rods and signal wires in such a position as to be a source of danger to persons employed shall be sufficiently covered or otherwise guarded.

2. Ground levers working points shall be so placed that men working them are clear of adjacent lines, and shall be placed in a position parallel to the adjacent lines, or in such other position, and be of such form, as to cause as little obstruction as possible to persons employed.

3. *Lines of rails* and points shall be periodically examined and kept in efficient order having regard to the nature of the traffic.

4. Every *gantry* shall be properly constructed and kept in proper repair. It shall have a properly fixed structure to act as a stop-block at any terminal point; and at every part where persons employed have to work or pass on foot there shall be a suitable footway, and if such footway is provided between a *line of rails* and the edge of the *gantry* the same shall, so far as is reasonably practicable, having regard to the traffic and working, be securely fenced at such a distance from the *line of rails* as to afford a reasonably sufficient space for such persons to pass in safety between the fence and a *locomotive, waggon* or load on the *line of rails*.

5. Coupling poles or other suitable mechanical appliances shall be provided where required for the purpose of regulation 11.

6. Proper sprags and scotches when required shall be provided for the use of persons in charge of the movement of *waggons*.

7. Where during the period between one hour after sunset and one hour before sunrise, or in foggy weather, shunting or any operations likely to cause danger to persons employed are frequently carried on, efficient lighting shall be provided either by hand lamps or stationary lights as the case may require at all points where necessary for the safety of such persons.

8. The mechanism of a capstan worked by power and used for the purpose of traction of *waggons* on a *line of rails* shall be maintained in efficient condition and if operated by a treadle such treadle shall be tested daily before use.

PART II

9. When materials are placed within 920 millimetres of a *line of rails* and persons employed are exposed to risk of injury from traffic by having to pass on foot over them or between them and the line such material shall, as far as reasonably practicable, be so placed as not to endanger such persons, and there shall be adequate recesses at intervals of not more than 20 metres where the materials exceed that length.

10. No person shall cross a *line of rails* by crawling or passing underneath a train or *waggons* thereon where there may be a risk of danger from traffic.

11. *Locomotives* or *waggons* shall wherever it is reasonably practicable without structural alterations be coupled or uncoupled only by means of a coupling pole or other suitable mechanical appliance, except where the construction of *locomotives or waggons* is such that coupling or uncoupling can be safely and conveniently performed without any part of a man's body being within the space between the ends or buffers of one *locomotive* or *waggon* and another.

12.   Sprags and scotches shall be used as and when they are required.

13.   *Waggons* shall not be moved or be allowed to be moved on a *line of rails* by means of a prop or pole, or by means of towing by a rope or chain attached to a *locomotive* or *waggon* moving on an adjacent *line of rails* when other reasonably practicable means can be adopted; provided that this shall not apply to the movement of ladles containing hot material on a *line of rails* in front of and adjacent to a furnace.

In no case shall props be used for the above purpose unless made of iron, steel or strong timber hooped with iron to prevent splitting.

14.   Where a *locomotive* pushes more than one *waggon*, and risk of injury may thereby be caused to persons employed *(a)*, a man shall, wherever it is safe and reasonably practicable, accompany or precede the front *waggon* or other efficient means *(b)* shall be taken to obviate such risk:

Provided that this regulation shall not apply to the following—

(a)   fly shunting;
(b)   movement of *waggons* used for conveyance of molten or hot material or other dangerous substance.

(a) **Persons employed.** In this context this term means any persons working at the factory, whether they are servants of the occupier or of an independent contractor; see *Stanton Ironworks Co Ltd v Skipper* [1956] 1 QB 255, [1955] 3 All ER 544, DC. In that case the Divisional Court refrained from deciding whether a duty was owed to persons employed by an independent contractor, so as to give such a person a right of action under these Regulations, but on the principles discussed in the GENERAL INTRODUCTION, and in particular the cases of *Massey-Harris-Ferguson (Manufacturing) Ltd v Piper* and *Canadian Pacific Steamships Ltd v Bryers*, there cited, it is submitted that these Regulations are for the benefit of all persons employed on work in the factory, whether servants of the occupier or not.

(b) **Other efficient means.** It is not a compliance with this regulation merely to ensure that the driver and shunter are aware of what is required (*Wagon Repairs Ltd v Vosper* (1967) 3 KIR 605, DC).

15.   No person shall be upon the buffer of a *locomotive* or *waggon* in motion unless there is a secure handhold and shall not stand thereon unless there is also a secure footplace; nor shall any person ride on a *locomotive* or *waggon* by means of a coupling pole or other like appliance.

16.   No *locomotive* or *waggon* shall be moved on a *line of rails* until warning has been given by the person in charge to persons employed whose safety is likely to be endangered:

Provided that this Regulation shall not apply to a self-moving crane within a building or to a charging machine or other vehicle so long as it is used in or about any actual process of manufacture.

17.   Where persons employed have to pass on foot or work, no *locomotive* or *waggon* shall be moved on a *line of rails* during the period between one hour after sunset and one hour before sunrise, or in foggy weather, unless the approaching end, wherever it is safe and reasonably practicable, is distinguished by a suitable light or accompanied by a man with a lamp:

Provided that this regulation shall not apply to the movement of *locomotives* or *waggons* within any area which is efficiently lighted by stationary lights.

18.   The driver in charge of a *locomotive*, or a man preceding it on foot, shall give an efficient sound signal as a warning on approaching any level crossing over a *line of rails* regularly used by persons employed, or any curve where sight is intercepted, or any other point of danger to persons employed.

19.   A danger signal shall be exhibited at or near the end of any *waggon* or train of *waggons* undergoing repair wherever persons employed are liable to be endangered by an approaching *locomotive* or *waggon*.

20.—(a) The space immediately around such a capstan as mentioned in regulation 8 shall be kept clear of all obstruction.

   (b) Such a capstan shall not be set in motion until signals have been exchanged between the man in charge of the capstan and the man working the rope or chain attached to it.
   (c) No person under 18 years of age shall work such a capstan.

21.   No person under the age of 18 shall be employed as a *locomotive* driver, and no person under the age of 16 shall be employed as a shunter.

PART III

22.   All glass tubes of water gauges on *locomotives* or stationary boilers used for the movement of *waggons* shall be adequately protected by a covering or guard.

General note. This regulation is revoked by S.I. 1989 No. 2169 as from 1 July 1994.

THE MAGNESIUM (GRINDING OF CASTINGS AND OTHER ARTICLES) SPECIAL REGULATIONS 1946

(S.R. & O. 1946 No. 2107, as amended by S.I. 1992 No. 1811 and S.I. 1992 No. 2966)

[Placard: Form 1030]

Whereas the Minister of Labour and National Service (hereinafter referred to as "the Minister") is satisfied that the grinding or polishing of castings or other articles consisting wholly or mainly of *magnesium,* or of alloys containing *magnesium,* and work incidental thereto are of such a nature as to cause risk of bodily injury to persons employed in connection therewith:

Now therefore the Minister by virtue of the powers conferred upon him by section 60(*a*) of the Factories Act 1937, and of all other powers enabling him in that behalf, hereby makes the following Special Regulations:—

(*a*) **Powers conferred ... by s. 60.** These Regulations were made under s. 60 of the Factories Act 1937, before that section was amended by s. 12 of the Factories Act 1948. Consequently, the class of persons for whose benefit they were made is limited to persons employed "in connection with" the processes specified; see the GENERAL INTRODUCTION and *Canadian Pacific Steamships Ltd v Bryers,* there cited.

1. Short title and commencement. These Regulations may be cited as the Magnesium (Grinding of Castings and Other Articles) Special Regulations 1946, and shall come into operation on 27 January 1947.

2. Interpretation. In these Regulations, unless the context otherwise requires, the following expressions have the meanings hereby assigned to them respectively, that is to say:—

"*Grinding or polishing device*" means any abrasive wheel, disc, buff, mop, brush, bob, dolly or band.

"*Magnesium*" includes any alloy containing more than 20 per cent. of magnesium.

"*The processes*" means grinding or polishing of castings or other articles consisting wholly or mainly of *magnesium* by means of any *grinding or polishing device* driven by mechanical power.

"*Racing*" means the trueing up, cutting, dressing or roughing of an abrasive wheel.

3. Application of Regulations. These Regulations shall apply to factories in which any of *the processes* is carried on, but nothing in these Regulations shall be

1639

deemed to apply to the crushing or grinding of *magnesium* in the manufacture of *magnesium* powder:

Provided that regulations 7 to 13 shall not apply in respect of the brushing of metal surfaces where the surface is thoroughly drenched during brushing by a spray of water or other suitable liquid if effective arrangements are made for the safe draining away of the liquid and to prevent or safely remove any accumulation of *magnesium* dust or of sludge containing such dust in or on the plant or the drainage arrangements.

4.   Maintenance of plant and apparatus. The occupier shall provide and maintain in efficient working order and in good repair all plant and apparatus necessary for compliance with these Regulations.

5.   Precautions against causing sparks. None of *the processes* shall be carried out by means of any *grinding or polishing device* which has been used for abrading iron or other ferrous material, nor shall any *racing*, with a tool capable of causing sparks, be done at any plant used in *the processes*.

6.   Interception and removal of dust. None of *the processes* shall be carried out without the use of adequate appliances for the interception of the dust as near as possible to the point of origin thereof, and for its safe removal.

7.   Appliances for interception and removal of dust. Applicances shall not be deemed adequate for the purposes of the foregoing regulation unless they include—

(a) a hood or casing so arranged as substantially to intercept the dust thrown off; and

(b) a duct of adequate size which (i) is so designed that the dust is carried away without lodgement therein and (ii) is kept free from obstruction and (iii) has proper means of access for inspection and cleaning; and

(c) a fan or other applicance capable of producing a draught sufficient to extract the dust; and

(d) a scrubber in which the dust-laden air is effectively drenched with water when such air has travelled, from the hood or casing referred to in sub-paragraph (a), a horizontal distance of not more than 3 metres or not more than such greater horizontal distance as may be authorised for the time being in the particular case by certificate of the Chief Inspector *(a)*, so however that no scrubbing chamber serves more than one *grinding or polishing device* and every scrubbing chamber shall be provided with a suitable explosion relief:

Provided that one scrubbing chamber may serve two such devices on a common spindle.

Provided further that where grinding or polishing is being done by means of a portable device, the use of a hood or casing shall not be required if the process is carried on in an enclosed space from which the dust is effectively and safely removed by means of appliances in accordance with sub-paragraphs (b), (c) and (d) of this regulation or is carried on under such other conditions as may be authorised for the time being by certificate of the Chief Inspector.

(a) Inspector. See INTRODUCTORY NOTE 24.

8. Automatic operation of appliances. There shall be automatic arrangement to ensure that no *grinding or polishing device* used in *the processes* is being driven by mechanical power unless the appliances serving that device in accordance with sub-paragraphs (c) and (d) of regulation 7 are in effective operation.

9. Previous operation of appliances. None of *the processes* shall be actually begun on any *grinding or polishing device* unless the appliances serving that device in accordance with sub-paragraphs (c) and (d) of regulation 7 have been in operation for the immediately preceding five minutes.

10. Further provisions as to removal of dust.—(1) All dust, sludge and scale deposited in any scrubber used in connection with *the processes* shall be removed from the scrubber at least once a week, and no tool containing iron or ferrous material shall be used for that purpose.

(2) Measures shall be taken to prevent any dust of *magnesium* which may remain outside the appliances for the interception and safe removal of the dust from accumulating in work rooms in quantities likely to prove dangerous, and dust removed for that purpose shall so far as reasonably practicable be collected and placed in metal containers with closely fitting metal covers and the metal containers shall be kept in a dry place.

11. Disposal of dust.—(1) Dust, sludge or scale removed from any scrubber used in connection with *the processes* shall be disposed of without avoidable delay either by being spread on the surface of the ground in the open air and burned at least 30 metres from any building in which persons are regularly present, or by removal from the factory:
　Provided that if the material is so wet as to prevent it burning when spread on the ground, it may be burned in an open incinerator at least 30 metres from any such building.

(2) Dust of *magnesium,* other than dust from scrubbers, shall, after collection, be removed from the factory at intervals of not more than one week or be disposed of by burning in accordance with regulation 11(1) hereof or, in so far as not so removed or disposed of within a week, kept in metal containers with closely fitting metal covers in a dry room constructed of fire-resisting material and used only for storage.

12. [*revoked*].

13. Prohibition of smoking, open lights and fires. No smoking, open light, fire or other agency capable of igniting dust of *magnesium* shall be permitted:—

　(a) at any place less than 6 metres from any of the following, that is to say,
　　(i) a *grinding or polishing device* used in *the processes,* or
　　(ii) any hood or casing or scrubber used in connection with *the processes* or any part of a duct between such hood or casing and scrubber or any outlet for a duct between the scrubber and the open air, or

(iii) any container in which *magnesium* dust is kept, unless that place is effectively separated therefrom by substantial fire resisting walls or partitions; or

(b) in any room used for keeping dust of *magnesium* in pursuance of regulation 11(2).

14.   No person shall be permitted to smoke when handling dust of *magnesium* or *magnesium* sludge or scale.

15.   Obligations in respect of regulations 5, 6, 9 and 10(1), smoking, lights, etc. No person employed in a factory to which these Regulations apply shall—

(a) wilfully do anything which is prohibited by any of the provisions of regulations 5, 6 and 9;

(b) use a tool containing iron or ferrous material for the purpose specified in regulation 10(1);

(c) smoke or use an open light, fire or other agency capable of igniting dust of *magnesium* in any of the circumstances specified in regulation 13, or

(d) smoke when handling dust of *magnesium* or *magnesium* sludge or scale.

16.   Every person engaged in any of *the processes* shall, without delay, report to the occupier or other responsible person any defect which he may find in any of the appliances or facilities provided for the purposes of his work in pursuance of these Regulations.

THE SPINNING BY SELF-ACTING MULES REGULATIONS 1905

(Dated 17 October 1905; S.R. & O. 1905 No. 1103, as amended by the Employment Act 1989, ss. 9(6), 29(5), Sch. 2, Pt. II, para. 1, Sch. 8 and S.I. 1992 No. 2932)

[*Placard: Form 941*]

General note. The whole Regulations are revoked by the Provision and Use of Work Equipment Regulations 1992, S.I. 1992 No. 2932, as from 1 January 1993 except, insofar as they apply to work equipment first provided for use in the premises or undertaken before 1 January 1993, they are revoked as from 1 January 1997.

Whereas certain machinery used in the process of spinning in textile factories, and known as self-acting mules, has been certified in pursuance of section 79 of the Factory and Workshop Act 1901, to be dangerous to life and limb:

I hereby, in pursuance of the powers conferred on me by that Act, make the following Regulations, and direct that they shall apply to all factories or parts thereof in which the process of spinning by means of self-acting mules is carried on.

1. In these Regulations the term "*Minder*" means the person in charge of a self-acting mule for the time being.

2. Save as hereinafter provided it shall be the duty of the occupier of a factory to observe Part I of these Regulations: provided that it shall be the duty of the owner (whether or not he is one of the occupiers) of a tenement factory *(a)* to observe Part I of these Regulations, except so far as relates to such parts of the machinery as are supplied by the occupier.

It shall be the duty of the persons employed to observe Part II of these Regulations, but it shall be the duty of the occupier, for the purpose of enforcing their observance, to keep a copy of the Regulations in legible characters affixed in every mule room, in a conspicuous position where they may be conveniently read.

(a) **Tenement factory.** See s. 121 of the Factories Act 1961.

PART I
DUTIES OF OCCUPIERS

3. After 1 January 1906, the following parts of every self-acting mule shall be securely fenced as far as is reasonably practicable, unless it can be shown that by their position or construction they are equally safe to every person employed as they would be if securely fenced:

(a) Back shaft scrolls and carrier pulleys and draw band pulleys.
(b) Front and back carriage wheels.
(c) Faller stops.
(d) Quadrant pinions.
(e) Back of head-stocks, including rim-pulleys and taking-in scrolls.
(f   Rim ban tightening pulleys, other than plate wheels, connected with a self-acting mule erected after 1 January 1906.

PART II
DUTIES OF PERSONS EMPLOYED

4. It shall be the duty of the *minder* of every self-acting mule to take all reasonable care to ensure:—

(a) That no child cleans any part or under any part thereof whilst the mule is in motion by the aid of mechanical power.
(b) That no child works between the fixed and traversing parts thereof whilst the mule is in motion by the aid of mechanical power.
(c) That no person is in the space between the fixed and traversing parts thereof unless the mule is stopped on the outward run.

5. No self-acting mule shall be started or restarted except by the *minder* or at his express order, nor until he has ascertained that no person is in the space between the fixed and traversing parts thereof.

THE NON-FERROUS METALS (MELTING AND FOUNDING) REGULATIONS 1962

(S.I. 1962 No. 1667, as amended by S.I. 1974 No. 1681, S.I. 1981 No. 1332, S.I. 1988 No. 1657, S.I. 1992 No. 2966 and S.I. 1992 No. 3004)

[*Placard: Form 2118*]

The Minister of Labour—

(a) by virtue of the powers conferred on him by sections 62, 76 and 180(6) and (7) of the Factories Act 1961 and of all other powers enabling him in that behalf; and

(b) after publishing, pursuant to Schedule 4 to the said Act of 1961, notice of the proposal to make the Regulations and not having received any objection to the draft in regard to which he is required by the said Schedule to direct an inquiry to be held,

hereby makes the following special Regulations—

General note. Dimensions in these Regulations have been metricated by S.I. 1981 No. 1332, which provides (reg. 3) that where premises or plant in existence or under construction immediately before 1 December 1981 complied with these Regulations as then in force, those premises or plant shall be deemed to comply with these Regulations as amended by the metricating regulations.

PART I
PROVISIONS WHICH APPLY TO ALL PREMISES COMING WITHIN THE SCOPE OF THE REGULATIONS

1. Citation, commencement and revocation.—(1) These Regulations may be cited as the Non-Ferrous Metals (Melting and Founding) Regulations 1962. These Regulations shall come into operation on 30 January 1963, with the exception of the following provisions which shall come into operation on 30 July 1964, namely, paragraph (2) of this regulation, and regulations 6, 11, 14, 15 and 16.

(2) The Regulations dated 20 June 1908, with respect to the casting of brass are hereby revoked.

2. Interpretation.—(1) The Interpretation Act 1889 [Interpretation Act 1978] shall apply to the interpretation of these Regulations as it applies to the interpretation of an Act of Parliament, and as if these Regulations and the Regulations hereby revoked were Acts of Parliament.

(2) For the purposes of these Regulations, unless the context otherwise requires, the following expressions have the meanings hereby assigned to them respectively, that is to say—

1645

"*degrees*" means degrees Celsius;

"*dressing operations*" includes fettling, stripping and other removal of adherent sand, cores, runners, risers, flash and other surplus metal from a casting and the production of a reasonably clean and smooth surface, but does not include (a) the removal of metal from a casting when performed incidentally in connection with the machining or assembling of castings after they have been dressed or (b) any operation which is a knock-out operation within the meaning of these Regulations;

"*knock-out operations*" means all methods of removing castings from moulds and the following operations when done in connection therewith, namely, stripping, coring-out and the removal of runners and risers;

"*persons employed*" means a person employed in the processes;

"*pouring aisle*" means an aisle leading from a main gangway or directly from a furnace to where metal is poured into moulds;

"*the principal Act*" means the Factories Act 1961, as amended by or under any other Act;

"*the processes*" means all or any of the operations or processes specified in regulations 3(1) or (2) being operations or processes to which these Regulations apply.

3. Application of Regulations.—(1) Subject to paragraph (3) of this regulation, the whole of these Regulations shall apply to those parts of all factories in which any of the following operations and processes are carried on, or which are used in connection with any such operations and processes, that is to say—

(a) any operation (not being an operation to which paragraph (2) of this regulation applies) in the production of non-ferrous castings by casting metal in moulds made of sand, loam, metal, moulding composition or other material or mixture of materials, or by shell moulding, diecasting (including pressure diecasting), centrifugal casting or continuous casting; and

(b) where carried on as incidental processes in connection with and in the course of production to which sub-paragraph (a) applies, the preparation and mixing of materials, the preparation of moulds and cores (but not the making of patterns or dies in a separate room not used for any of *the processes*), *knock-out operations* and *dressing operations*.

(2) Subject to paragraph (3) of this regulation, the provisions of Part I of these Regulations (and only those provisions) shall apply to those parts of all factories in which are carried on the melting and casting of non-ferrous metal for the production of ingots, billets, slabs or other similar products, or the stripping thereof; so, however, that the whole of these Regulations shall apply to any such part in which there is also carried on any of the operations or processes specified in paragraph (1) of this Regulation.

(3) Nothing in these Regulations shall apply with respect to—

(a) any process to which either of the following Regulations apply, that is to say, the Regulations *(a)* dated 12 August 1911, with respect to the smelting and manufacture of lead and the Electric Accumulator Regulations 1925; or

(b) any process for the purposes of a printing works; or

(c) any smelting process in which metal is obtained by a reducing operation or any process incidental to such operation; or

(d) any process in the course of the manufacture of solder or any process incidental to such manufacture; or

(e) the melting and casting of lead or any lead-based allow for the production of ingots, billets, slabs or other similar products, or the stripping thereof, or any process incidental to such melting, casting or stripping.

(4) Save as expressly provided in regulation 15(6), the provisions of these Regulations shall be in addition to and not in substitution for or in diminution of other requirements imposed by or under the principal Act.

(a) Regulations ... 1911. These are the Lead Smelting and Manufacture Regulations 1911, now largely revoked.

4. Exemption certificates.—(1) The Chief Inspector *(a)* may (subject to such conditions as may be specified therein) by certificate in writing (which he may in his direction revoke at any time) exempt from all or any of the requirements of these Regulations—

(a) any premises; or

(b) any class or description of premises; or

(c) any machine, plant, apparatus or process or any class or description of machines, plant, apparatus or processes; or

(d) the employment of any person or any class or description of persons, if he is satisfied that the requirements in respect of which the exemption is granted can be suspended or relaxed without danger to the health or safety of *persons employed* or are for any reason impracticable or inappropriate. Where such exemption is granted a legible copy of the certificate, showing the conditions (if any) subject to which it has been granted, shall be kept posted in a position where it may be conveniently read by the *persons employed.*

(a) Inspector. See INTRODUCTORY NOTE 24.

5. Cleanliness of floors. Effective cleaning by a suitable method shall be carried out at least once every working day of all accessible parts of the floor of every indoor workplace in which *the processes* are carried on, other than parts which are of sand; and the parts which are of sand shall be kept in good order.

General note. This regulation is revoked by the Workplace (Health, Safety and Welfare) Regulations 1992, S.I. 1992 No. 3004, as from 1 January 1993 except, in relation to any workplace or part of a workplace which is not a new workplace, or a modification, an extension or a conversion, it is revoked as from 1 January 1996.

6. Construction of floors.—(1) Floors of indoor workplaces in which *the processes* are carried on, other parts which are of sand, shall have an even surface of hard material.

(2) No part of the floor of any such indoor workplace shall be of sand except where this is necessary by reason of the work done.

(3) All parts of the surface of the floor of any such indoor workplace which are of sand shall, so far as practicable, be maintained in an even and firm condition.

General note. This regulation is revoked by the Workplace (Health, Safety and Welfare) Regulations 1992, S.I. 1992 No. 3004, as from 1 January 1993 except, in relation to any workplace or part of a workplace which is not a new workplace, or a modification, an extension or a conversion, it is revoked as from 1 January 1996.

7.   Manual operations involving molten metal.—(1) There shall be provided and properly maintained for all *persons employed* on manual operations involving molten metal with which they are liable to be splashed, a working space for that operation—

(a) which is adequate for the safe performance of the work and
(b) which, so far as reasonably practicable, is kept free from obstruction.

(2) Any operation involving the carrying by hand of a container holding molten metal shall be performed on a floor all parts of which where any person walks while engaged in the operation shall be on the same level:

Provided that, where necessary to enable the operation to be performed without undue risk, nothing in this paragraph shall prevent the occasional or exceptional use of a working space on a different level from the floor, being a space provided with a safe means of access from the floor for any person while engaged in the operation.

General note. This regulation is revoked by the Workplace (Health, Safety and Welfare) Regulations 1992, S.I. 1992 No. 3004, as from 1 January 1993 except, in relation to any workplace or part of a workplace which is not a new workplace, or a modification, an extension or a conversion, it is revoked as from 1 January 1996.

8.   Disposal of dross and skimmings. Dross and skimmings removed from molten metal or taken from a furnace shall be placed forthwith in suitable receptacles.

General note. This regulation is revoked by the Workplace (Health, Safety and Welfare) Regulations 1992, S.I. 1992 No. 3004, as from 1 January 1993 except, in relation to any workplace or part of a workplace which is not a new workplace, or a modification, an extension or a conversion, it is revoked as from 1 January 1996.

9.   Arrangement and storage.—(1) Subject to paragraph (3) of this regulation, and (in the case of parts of factories of the kind specified in regulation 3(1)) to regulation 19, all raw materials and all dies, patterns, patter plates, core boxes, core plates, grids, moulding boxes, loam plates and ladles, and all other heavy equipment, shall be so arranged and placed as to enable work to be carried on without unnecessary risk.

(2) Suitable and conveniently accessible racks, bins or other receptacles shall be provided and used for the storage of all other gear and tools.

(3) Where scrap metal, sand, fuel or other similar loose materials are stored indoors, suitable bins, bunkers or other receptacles shall be provided and used for such storage.

General note. This regulation is revoked by the Workplace (Health, Safety and Welfare) Regulations 1992, S.I. 1992 No. 3004, as from 1 January 1993 except, in relation to any workplace or part of a workplace which is not a new workplace, or a modification, an extension or a conversion, it is revoked as from 1 January 1996.

10. Gangways and pouring aisles.—(1) In every workroom to which this regulation applies, where necessary for the safe carrying of molten metal for pouring into moulds, sufficient and clearly defined *pouring aisles* shall be provided which shall be properly maintained and, so far as reasonably practicable, be kept free from obstruction and which—

(a) if molten metal is carried in hand ladles or bull ladles by not more than two men per ladle, shall be at least 460 millimetres wide, but where any moulds alongside the aisle are more than 510 millimetres above the floor of the aisle, the aisle shall be not less than 600 millimetres wide;

(b) if molten metal is carried in hand ladles or bull ladles by more than two men per ladle, shall be at least 760 millimetres wide;

(c) if molten metal is carried in crane, trolly or truck ladles, shall be of a width adequate for the safe performance of the work.

All measurements of the width of an aisle shall be taken between the extreme ends of the box handles or other projections into the aisle.

(2) In every workroom to which this regulation applies, constructed, reconstructed or converted for use as such after the making of these Regulations and, so far as reasonably practicable, in every other workroom to which this regulation applies, sufficient and clearly defined main gangways shall be provided and properly maintained which—

(a) shall be at least 920 millimetres wide;

(b) shall, so far as reasonably practicable, be kept free from obstruction; and

(c) if used for carrying molten metal shall—

   (i) where truck ladles are used, be at least 600 millimetres wider than the overall width of the ladle;

   (ii) where hand shanks are carried by more than two men per hand shank, be at least 1.2 metres wide; and

   (iii) where used for simultaneous travel in both directions by men carrying hand shanks, be at least 1.8 metres wide.

(3) In this regulation the expression "workroom to which this regulation applies" means a part of a factory in which molten metal is transported or used, and a workroom to which this regulation applies shall be deemed for the purposes of this regulation to have been constructed, reconstructed or converted for use as such after the making of these Regulations if the construction, reconstruction or conversion thereof was begun after the making of these Regulations.

General note. This regulation is revoked by the Workplace (Health, Safety and Welfare) Regulations 1992, S.I. 1992 No. 3004, as from 1 January 1993 except, in relation to any workplace or part of a workplace which is not a new workplace, or a modification, an extension or a conversion, it is revoked as from 1 January 1996.

11.–13. [*revoked*].

14. Temperature. The temperature of that part of a room where work is being carried on (other than a separate storeroom not used for any of *the processes*) shall, after the first hour, be not less than 10 *degrees*; but when the outside temperature is less than 1 *degree* it shall suffice if the temperature at that part is not less than 11 *degrees* higher than the outside temperature.

General note. This regulation is revoked by the Workplace Health, Safety and Welfare) Regulations 1992, S.I. 1992 No. 3004, as from 1 January 1993 except, in relation to any workplace or part of a workplace which is not a new workplace, or a modification, an extension or a conversion, it is revoked as from 1 January 1996.

15. Washing facilities and clothing accommodation.—(1) There shall be provided and maintained for the use of all the *persons employed* adequate and suitable facilities for washing which shall be conveniently accessible and shall include a sufficient supply of clean towels or other suitable means of drying and of soap and nail brushes, and basins or troughs with running hot and cold or warm water.

(2) The basins and troughs required to be provided and maintained by paragraph (1) of this regulation shall satisfy the following requirements—

(a) basins and troughs shall have a smooth impervious upper surface;
(b) each basin shall be fitted with a waste pipe and plug;
(c) each trough shall be fitted with suitable taps or jets at intervals of not more than 600 millimetres and with a waste pipe without plug;
(d) basins and troughs shall be sufficient in number and dimensions to provide at least one unit for every ten *persons employed* at any one time.

(3) For the purposes of this regulation—

(a) a "unit" means one basin or 600 millimetres of the length of a trough or, in the case of circular or oval troughs, 600 millimetres of the circumference of a trough;
(b) in dividing by ten for the purpose of finding the number of units required, any remainder shall be counted as ten;
(c) a basin or other receptacle shall not be reckoned as a trough unless it measures internally at least 1.2 metres over its longest or widest part.

(4) In addition there shall be provided and maintained for the use of all the *persons employed* on hot, dirty and arduous work, adequate and suitable facilities for taking a shower or other baths with suitable arrangements for privacy (including, in close proximity to such facilities, adequate and suitable accommodation for dressing, undressing or changing clothes, and an adequate number of lockers or other suitable arrangements for the accommodation of clothing belonging to persons using the baths) and such arrangements as are reasonably practicable for drying clothing belonging to persons using the baths.

(5) The facilities and accommodation provided in pursuance of this regulation shall be placed in the charge of a responsible person or persons, be maintained in a clean and orderly condition, and shall, so far as reasonably practicable, be separate from any workroom.

(6) The provisions of this regulation shall be in substitution for the provisions of section 58(1) of *the principal Act* (which relates to washing facilities).

General note. This regulation is revoked by the Workplace (Health, Safety and Welfare) Regulations 1992, S.I. 1992 No. 3004, as from 1 January 1993 except, in relation to any workplace or part of a workplace which is not a new workplace, or a modification, an extension or a conversion, it is revoked as from 1 January 1996.

16.   Facilities for meals.—(1) There shall be provided and maintained for the use of the *persons employed* adequate and suitable accommodation for taking meals which accommodation shall be properly heated and shall include sufficient tables and seats and facilities for the warming of the food of *persons employed* and for boiling water.

(2) No person shall be permitted to take a main meal in any indoor workroom in which *the processes* are carried on and it shall be the duty of every *person employed* not to take a main meal in any such indoor workroom.

General note. This regulation is revoked by the Workplace (Health, Safety and Welfare) Regulations 1992, S.I. 1992 No. 3004, as from 1 January 1993 except, in relation to any workplace or part of a workplace which is not a new workplace, or a modification, an extension or a conversion, it is revoked as from 1 January 1996.

PART II

PROVISIONS WHICH APPLY ONLY TO THE PREMISES SPECIFIED IN REGULATION 3(1)

17.   Cleanliness of indoor workplaces.—(1) All accessible parts of the walls of every indoor workplace in which *the processes* are carried on and of everything affixed to those walls shall be effectively cleaned by a suitable method to a height of not less than 4.2 metres from the floor at least once in every period of fourteen months. A record of the carrying out of every such effective cleaning in pursuance of this paragraph including the date (which shall be not less than five months nor more than nine months after the last immediately preceding washing, cleaning or other treatment in pursuance of section 1(3) of the *principal Act*) shall be entered in an approved register [Form 2093].

General note. This regulation is revoked by the Workplace (Health, Safety and Welfare) Regulations 1992, S.I. 1992 No. 3004, as from 1 January 1993 except, in relation to any workplace or part of a workplace which is not a new workplace, or a modification, an extension or a conversion, it is revoked as from 1 January 1996.

18.   Dressing operations. All *dressing operations* shall be carried out inside a weather-proof building.

19.   [*revoked*].

20.   Material and equipment left out of doors. All material and equipment left out of doors (including material and equipment so left only temporarily or occasionally) shall be so arranged and placed as to avoid unnecessary risk. There shall be safe means of access to all such material and equipment and, so far as reasonably practicable, such access shall be by roadways or pathways which shall be properly maintained. Such roadways or pathways shall have a firm and even surface and shall, so far as reasonably practicable, be kept free from obstruction.

General note. This regulation is revoked by the Workplace (Health, Safety and Welfare) Regulations 1992, S.I. 1992 No. 3004, as from 1 January 1993 except, in relation to any workplace or part of a workplace which is not a new workplace, or a modification, an extension or a conversion, it is revoked as from 1 January 1996.

THE OIL CAKE WELFARE ORDER 1929

(S.R. & O. 1929 No. 534, as amended by S.I. 1992 No. 1811,
S.I. 1992 No. 2966 and S.I. 1992 No. 3004)

In pursuance of section 7 of the Police, Factories, etc. (Miscellaneous Provisions) Act 1916, I hereby make the following Order for all factories or parts of factories in which the manufacture of oil cake, extracted meal or compound cake is carried on, including the incidental operations of refining and grease manufacture:

Provided that nothing in this Order shall apply to the loading or unloading wharves a such factories.

1., 2. [*revoked*].

3. The occupier shall provide and maintain for the use of all the persons employed suitable accommodation for clothing put off during working hours, with adequate arrangements for drying the clothing if wet.

The accommodation so provided shall be placed under the charge of a responsible person, and shall be kept clean.

> **General note.** This article is revoked by the Workplace (Health, Safety and Welfare) Regulations 1992, S.I. 1992 No. 3004, as from 1 January 1993 except, in relation to any workplace or part of a workplace which is not a new workplace, or a modification, an extension or a conversion, it is revoked as from 1 January 1996.

4. The occupier shall provide and maintain for the use of all the persons employed, and remaining on the premises during the meal intervals, a suitable and adequate messroom, which shall be furnished with (a) sufficient tables and chairs or benches with back rests, (b) unless a canteen serving hot meals is provided, adequate means of warming food and boiling water, (c) suitable facilities for washing, comprising a sufficient supply of clean towels, soap and warm water. The messroom shall be sufficiently warmed for use during meal intervals.

The messroom shall be separate from the cloakroom, and shall be placed under the charge of a responsible person, and shall be kept clean.

> **General note.** This article is revoked by the Workplace (Health, Safety and Welfare) Regulations 1992, S.I. 1992 No. 3004, as from 1 January 1993 except, in relation to any workplace or part of a workplace which is not a new workplace, or a modification, an extension or a conversion, it is revoked as from 1 January 1996.

5. The occupier shall provide and maintain in the works for the use of all persons employed suitable washing facilities *(a)* conveniently accessible and comprising a sufficient supply of clean towels, soap and warm water.

The facilities so provided shall be placed under the charge of a responsible person, and shall be kept clean.

General note. This article is revoked by the Workplace (Health, Safety and Welfare) Regulations 1992, S.I. 1992 No. 3004, as from 1 January 1993 except, in relation to any workplace or part of a workplace which is not a new workplace, or a modification, an extension or a conversion, it is revoked as from 1 January 1996.

(a) *Washing facilities.* See INTRODUCTORY NOTE 20.

6.   The occupier shall, if an application is made to him in writing, signed by not less than one-half of the persons of either sex employed in the works, asking for the provision of bath accommodation, provide at the factory shower baths in the proportion of one bath for every 50 persons of that sex employed at one time, any odd number of persons less than 50 being reckoned as 50. Provided that if on objection being taken by the occupier the Chief Inspector *(a)* of Factories is satisfied that in the particular circumstances the provision of bath accommodation as specified above is not necessary and reasonable, he may, by certificate in writing (which he may at his discretion revoke) exempt such occupier from the foregoing requirement to such extent and on such conditions as he may think fit.

Notice of the application having been made shall be sent forthwith to the District Inspector *(a)* of Factories by or on behalf of the persons making it.

The baths shall be suitably constructed and supplied with water at a temperature as near as may be of 38 degrees Celsius and a sufficient supply of clean towels and soap.

The accommodation shall be placed under the charge of a responsible person, and shall be kept clean.

General note. This article is revoked by the Workplace (Health, Safety and Welfare) Regulations 1992, S.I. 1992 No. 3004, as from 1 January 1993 except, in relation to any workplace or part of a workplace which is not a new workplace, or a modification, an extension or a conversion, it is revoked as from 1 January 1996.

(a) *Inspector.* See INTRODUCTORY NOTE 24.

7.   [*revoked*].

8.   This Order may be cited as the Oil Cake Welfare Order 1929, and shall come into force on 1 August 1929, from which date the Order for the welfare of workers in oil cake mills, dated 21 July 1919, shall be revoked.

THE PAINTS AND COLOURS MANUFACTURE REGULATIONS 1907

(Dated 21 January 1907; S.R. & O. 1907 No. 17, as amended by
S.I. 1973, No. 36, S.I. 1980 No. 1248 and S.I. 1992 No. 1811)

[Placard: Form 945]

Whereas the manufacture of paints and colours has been certified in pursuance of section 79 of the Factory and Workshop Act 1901, to be dangerous:

I hereby in pursuance of the powers conferred on me by that Act make the following Regulations, and direct that they shall apply to all factories and workshops in which dry carbonate of lead or red lead is used in the manufacture of paints and colours, or chromate of lead is produced by boiling, provided as follows—

(1) The Regulations shall not apply to factories and workshops in which paints and colours are manufactured not for sale but solely for use in the business of the occupier; or to factories or workshops in which only the manufacture of artists' colours is carried on; or to the manufacture of varnish paints.

(2) Regulation 2, and so much of regulation 3 as prevents the employment of a woman in manufacturing *lead colour,* shall not apply to the packing in parcels or kegs not exceeding 6 kilograms in weight, unless and until so required by notice in writing from the Chief Inspector of Factories.

(3) Regulations 4, 5, 6, 11, and 12 shall not apply to factories or workshops in which the grinding of *lead colour* occupies less than three hours in any week, unless and until so required by notice in writing from the Chief Inspector of Factories.

Definitions

For the purpose of these Regulations—
   "*Lead colour*" means dry carbonate of lead and red lead, and any colour into which either of these substances enters.
   It shall be the duty of the occupier to observe Part I of these Regulations.

PART I
DUTIES OF EMPLOYERS

1.–2.   [*revoked*].

3.   No woman, young person, or child shall be employed in manipulating *lead colour.*

4.–6.   [*revoked*].

THE POTTERY (HEALTH AND WELFARE) SPECIAL REGULATIONS 1950

(S.I. 1950 No. 65, as amended by S.I. 1963 No. 879, S.I. 1973 No. 36, S.I. 1980 No. 1248, S.I. 1982 No. 877, S.I. 1988 No. 1657, S.I. 1989 No. 2311, the Employment Act 1989, ss. 9(6), 29(5), Sch. 2, Pts. I, II, Sch. 8, S.I. 1990 No. 305 and S.I. 1992 No. 3004)

[Placard: Form 1048]

Whereas the Minister of Labour and National Service (hereinafter referred to as "the Minister") is satisfied that the manufacture and decoration of *pottery*, as hereinafter defined, and the following manufactures or processes, namely—

(a) the calcining, crushing, grinding or sieving of flint or quartz,

(b) the mixing of flint or quartz with clay or other material in the preparation of a *pottery* body, and

(c) the manufacture of lithographic transfers, frits or glazes for use in the manufacture or decoration of *pottery*,

are manufactures or processes of such a nature as to cause risk of bodily injury to the persons employed;

And whereas it appears to the Minister that, owing to the conditions and circumstances of employment or the nature of the processes carried on in factories to which these Regulations apply, provision requires to be made for securing the welfare of persons employed in such factories:

Now, therefore, the Minister by virtue of the powers conferred by sections 46 and 60 of the Factories Act 1937, (hereinafter referred to as "the principal Act"), the Factories Act 1948, and the Transfer of Functions (Factories, &c.,) Order 1946, and of all other powers in that behalf hereby makes the following Special Regulations—

1. Short title, commencement and revocation.—(1) These Regulations may be cited as the Pottery (Health and Welfare) Special Regulations 1950, and shall come into operation on the 2nd day of April, 1950.

(2) The Regulations made by the Secretary of State on 2 January 1913, for the Manufacture and Decoration of Pottery, and the Pottery (Silicosis) Regulations 1932, are hereby revoked.

(3) Factories to which these Regulations apply shall be excluded from the application of the Clay Works (Welfare) Special Regulations 1948, except that

1656

where, in any such factory, there is carried on the manufacture of any of the articles mentioned in paragraph (1) of Regulation 4 hereof this exclusion shall relate only to a part of the factory which is not used for the purpose of such manufacture.

General note. Measurements in Imperial have been converted to metric by S.I. 1982 No. 877. These amendments do not apply to premises or plant in existence before 1 October 1982.

2. Interpretation.—(1) The Interpretation Act 1889 [Interpretation Act 1978] applies to the interpretation of these Regulations as it applies to the interpretation of an Act of Parliament.

(2) In these Regulations, unless the context otherwise requires the following expressions have the meaning hereby assigned to them—

"*Appointed doctor*" means a fully registered medical practitioner appointed by written certificate of the Chief Employment Medical Adviser or of a Deputy Chief Employment Medical Adviser for such of the purposes of these Regulations as are specified in the certificate.

"*Employment medical adviser*" means an employment medical adviser appointed under the provisions of the Employment Medical Advisory Service Act 1972.

"*Flow material*" means any material which contains a lead compound and which is placed in saggars with a view to its entire or partial volatilisation during the glost firing of the ware.

"*Glaze*" does not include an engobe or slip.

"*Glost placing*" includes—

(i) the placing of ware coated with unfired *glaze* onto cranks or similar articles prior to their transference to saggars, trucks, ovens or kilns for glost firing;

(ii) the placing of such ware into saggars or onto trucks or onto oven-conveyors;

(iii) the placing of saggars containing such ware into ovens or kilns or onto trucks; and

(iv) the removal and carrying of saggars or cranks from the oven, kiln or truck after glost except in the case of tunnel ovens.

"*Leadless glaze*" means a *glaze* which does not contain more than one per cent. of its dry weight of a lead compound calculated as lead monoxide.

"*Leadless glaze factory*" means a factory the occupier of which has given an undertaking to the satisfaction of the Chief Inspector that none but *leadless glaze* shall be used therein and in which none but *leadless glaze* is in fact used.

"*Lithographic transfer making*" includes the wiping of colour from and the subsequent brushing of the transfer sheets.

"*Low solubility glaze*" means a *glaze* which does not yield to dilute hydrochloric acid more than five per cent. of its dry weight of a soluble lead compound calculated as lead monoxide when determined in the manner described below—

A weighted quantity of the material which has been dried at 100 degrees Celsius and thoroughly mixed is to be continuously shaken for one hour, at the common temperature, with 1,000 times its weight of an aqueous solution of hydrochloric acid containing 0.25 per cent. by weight of hydrogen chloride. This solution is thereafter to be allowed to stand for one hour and then filtered. The lead salt contained in the clear filtrate is then to be precipitated as lead sulphide and weighed as lead sulphate.

"*Pottery*" includes china, earthenware and any article made from clay or from a mixture containing clay and other materials.

"*Stopping of biscuit ware*" means the filling up of cracks in ware which had been fired but to which *glaze* has not been applied.

"*Ware cleaning*" means the removal of surplus *glaze* from ware after the application of the *glaze* but before glost firing, and includes panel-cutting.

3. Application of Regulations.—Subject to the provisions of regulations 4 and 5, these Regulations shall apply to all factories in which the manufacture or decoration of *pottery* is carried on or in which, for use in the manufacture or decoration of *pottery*, lithographic transfers, frits or *glazes* are made, or flint or quartz is ground or powdered, or ground or powdered flint or quartz is mixed with clay or other material to form the body of the ware.

4. Factories excluded from the Regulations.—(1) Nothing in these Regulations shall apply to a factory in which any of the following articles but no other *pottery* is made—

(a) unglazed or salt-glazed ware made from natural clay in the plastic state, to which no flint or quartz or other form of free silica is or has been added;

(b) bricks glazed or unglazed;

(c) architectural terra-cotta made from plastic clay and either unglazed or glazed with a *leadless glaze* only.

(2) Nothing in these Regulations shall apply to the manufacture of potters' colours in a factory in which no *pottery* is manufactured or decorated.

5. Certificate of Exemption.—(1) These Regulations, or such of them as may be specified, shall not apply to a factory or to a part or parts of a factory if a certificate in writing to that effect has been issued by the Chief Inspector.

(2) The Chief Inspector *(a)* may issue a certificate for the purpose of paragraph (1) of this regulation if he is satisfied with respect to the Regulations specified therein—

(a) that they are not necessary for the protection of the persons employed in the factory or part thereof; or

(b) that their application is impracticable in the circumstances; or

(c) that their application is inappropriate by reason of the fact that the industry carried on in the part of the factory to which the certificate relates is separate and distinct from the operations specified in regulation 3 hereof.

(3) Any such certificate as aforesaid may be issued subject to such conditions as the Chief Inspector *(a)* thinks fit and may be revoked by him at any time.

(4) Where any such certificate as aforesaid is issued a legible copy thereof showing the conditions subject to which it has been granted shall be kept

posted up in the factory to which it relates in a position where it may conveniently be read by the persons employed.

(a) *Inspector.* See INTRODUCTORY NOTE 24.

6. Prohibition of employment of women and young persons in certain processes.—(1) No woman or young person shall be employed or work in the following processes—

(i) The *stopping of biscuit ware* with material which yields to dilute hydrochloric acid more than five per cent. of its dry weight of soluble lead compound calculated as lead monoxide when determined in the manner described in the definition of *low solubility glaze*;

(ii) the weighing out, shovelling or mixing of unfritted lead compounds in the preparation or manufacture of frits, *glazes* or colours;

(iii) the preparation or weighing out of *flow material*;

(iv) the washing of saggars with a wash which yields to dilute hydrochloric acid more than five per cent. of its dry weight of a soluble lead compound calculated as lead monoxide when determined in the manner described in the definition of *low solubility glaze*;

(v) the cleaning of boards used in any place where dipping, drying after dipping, *ware-cleaning* or *glost placing* is done, except in the case of a *leadless glaze factory*;

(vi) the cleaning of mangles or any part thereof, except in a *leadless glaze factory.*

(2) [*revoked*].

(3) No young person shall be employed or work—

(i) on any process included in Part I of the First Schedule to these Regulations; or

(ii) as a wheel turner at a press for pressing tiles.

(4) No young person under sixteen years of age shall be employed or work in any process included in Part II of the First Schedule to these Regulations.

(5)–(7) [*revoked*].

7.–14. [*revoked*].

15. Ventilation.—(1) In the case of every workroom there shall be provided for the admission of fresh air into the room sufficient inlets suitably placed and so constructed or with such arrangements as to prevent a draught blowing directly from the inlet onto a worker.

(2) (a) The drying of *pottery* articles by means of heat shall, save as provided in sub-paragraphs (b) and (c) of this paragraph, be carried on only in drying stoves or in rooms set apart for that purpose.

(b) In so far as compliance with the foregoing requirement is not reasonably practicable by reason of the nature or size of the article or through lack of space, *pottery* articles may be left to be dried in a workroom, provided that in any such case (except where sub-paragraph (c) of this paragraph applies) ventilation shall so far as reasonably practicable be so arranged that there is not a flow of air towards the workers from the direction of the sources of artificial heat used for drying the articles.

(c) In the case of a workroom in which sanitary fireclay ware is dried by heat arising from the floor or from pipes near the floor, the requirements of sub-paragraph (b) of this paragraph shall not apply but the arrangements for ventilating the room shall, so far as reasonably practicable, be such as to facilitate the vertically upward movement of air from the articles being dried.

(3) Every drying stove, dryer and mangle shall be so ventilated that there is no flow of hot air from the stove, dryer or mangle into any place where any person works.

(4) In the case of vertical or tower mangles the pipes used for heating shall not be fixed below the level of the top of any opening at which workers put in or take off ware.

(5) The requirements of this regulation shall be without prejudice to the provisions of section 4 of the principal Act.

General note. This regulation is revoked by the Workplace (Health, Safety and Welfare) Regulations 1992, S.I. 1992 No. 3004, as from 1 January 1993 except, in relation to any workplace or part of a workplace which is not a new workplace, or a modification, an extension or a conversion, it is revoked as from 1 January 1996.

16. Temperature.—(1) The dry-bulb temperature in any workroom shall not, while work is going on, be above 24 degrees Celsius; provided that when the temperature in the shade in the open air exceeds 18 degrees Celsius the temperature in the workroom may exceed 24 degrees Celsius but may not exceed by more than 6 degrees the temperature in the shade in the open air.

(2) The dry-bulb temperature in any workroom in which *pottery* is made by the compression of clay dust or is fettled after being so made shall not after the first hour be less than 13 degrees Celsius while work is going on.

(3) A suitable thermometer shall be provided and maintained in a suitable position in every workroom.

(4) When any person is in an oven for the purpose of drawing, the temperature at his head-height shall not exceed 46 degrees Celsius.

(5) Upon demand being made at any time by persons employed or immediately proposed to be employed in an oven for the purpose of drawing, the temperature in the oven shall be taken by the occupier or his representative and the occupier shall provide a suitable thermometer for the purpose.

(6) The requirements of this regulation shall be without prejudice to the provisions of section 3 of the principal Act [s. 3].

17.–32. [*revoked*].

FIRST SCHEDULE

Regulations 6, 7, 8, 11, 12, 13, 14 and 28

SCHEDULED PROCESSES

PART I

(i) The making or mixing of frits or *glazes* containing lead or of colours.
(ii) The preparation or weighing out of *flow material.*
(iii) Colour blowing, or the wiping off of colour after that process.
(iv) Ground laying or colour dusting, or the wiping off of colour after either of those processes.
(v) Colour grinding.
(vi) *Lithographic transfer making.*
(vii) Any other process in which any material, other than *glaze*, which contains more than five per cent. of its dry weight of a soluble lead compound (calculated in the manner described in the definition of *low solubility glaze*) is used or handled in a dry state or in the form of spray or in *suspension* in liquid other than oil or similar medium.

PART II

The following processes when carried on in factories other than *leadless glaze factories*—

(i) Dipping or other process carried on in the dipping house.
(ii) The application of majolica or other *glaze* by blowing, painting or any other process except dipping.
(iii) Drying after the application of *glaze* by dipping, blowing or any other process.
(iv) *Ware-cleaning* after the application of *glaze* by dipping, blowing or any other process.
(v) *Glost placing.*
(vi) Any other process in which *glaze* is used or in which *pottery* articles treated with *glaze* are handled before glost firing.

THE POWER PRESSES REGULATIONS 1965

(S.I. 1965 No. 1441, as amended by S.I. 1972 No. 1512)

[Placard: Form 2258]

The Minister of Labour—

(a) by virtue of the power conferred on him by sections 76 and 180(6) and (7) of the Factories Act 1961, and of all other powers enabling him in that behalf; and

(b) after publishing, pursuant to Schedule 4 to the said Act of 1961, notice of the proposal to make the Regulations and not having received any objection to the draft in regard to which he is required by the said Schedule to direct an inquiry to be held,

hereby makes the following special Regulations—

1. Citation and commencement. These Regulations may be cited as the Power Presses Regulations 1965, and shall come into operation on 20 July 1966.

2. Interpretation.—(1) The Interpretation Act 1889 [Interpretation Act 1978] shall apply to the interpretation of these Regulations as it applies to the interpretation of an Act of Parliament.

(2) In these Regulations, unless the context otherwise requires, the following expressions have the meanings hereby assigned to them respectively, that is to say—

"*approved*" means approved for the time being by certificate of the Chief Inspector *(a)*;

"*clutch mechanism*" means in relation to a *power press* a device designed to impart when required the movement of the flywheel to any tool;

"*factory*" includes any premises to which these Regulations apply *(b)*;

"*fixed fencing*" means fencing provided for the tools of a *power press* being fencing which has no moving parts associated with or dependent upon the mechanism of a *power press* and includes that part of a closed tool which acts as a guard;

"*power press*" means a press or a press brake which in either case is used wholly or partly for the working of metal by means of tools or for the purpose of die proving, being a press or a press brake which is power driven and which embodies a flywheel and a clutch mechanism;

"*the principal Act*" means the Factories Act 1961, as amended by or under any other Act; and

"*safety device*" means the fencing and any other safeguard provided for the tools of a *power press* in pursuance of requirements imposed by *(c)* or under *the principal Act*.

(a) **Inspector.** See INTRODUCTORY NOTE 24.

(b) **Premises... apply.** See reg. 3(1).

(c) **Fencing, etc.** For the requirements as to fencing imposed by the Factories Act 1961, see *ibid.*, ss. 12–16.

3. Application and operation of Regulations.—(1) Subject to paragraph (2) of this regulation, these Regulations apply to the following premises in which *any power press* is used, that is to say, all factories *(a)* and all premises to which the provisions of *the principal Act* are applied by section 123(1) of that Act (which relates to electrical stations).

(2) Nothing in these Regulations shall apply as respects any *power press* when used for working hot metal or which is not being used for working cold metal and is intended next to be used for working hot metal.

(3) The provisions of these Regulations are in addition and not in substitution for or in diminution of other requirements imposed by or under the principal Act *(b)*.

(a) **Factory.** For definition, see s. 175 of the Factories Act 1961.

(b) **In addition... Act.** See the GENERAL INTRODUCTION.

4. Appointment of persons to prepare power presses for use.—(1) Except as provided in paragraph (4) of this regulation, no person shall set, re-set, adjust or try out the tools on a *power press* or install or adjust any *safety device* thereon, being installation or adjustment preparatory to production or die proving, or carry out an inspection and test of any *safety device* thereon required by regulation 7, unless he—

(a) has attained the age of eighteen;
(b) has been trained in accordance with the Schedule to these Regulations;
(c) is competent to carry out those duties; and
(d) has been appointed by the occupier of the *factory* to carry out those duties in respect of the class or description of *power press* or the class or description of *safety device* to which the *power press* or the *safety device* (as the case may be) belongs; and every such appointment shall be made by signed and dated entry in, or by signed and dated certificate attached to, a register kept for the purposes of this regulation [Form 2198].

(2) Any appointment made under paragraph (1)(d) of this regulation may be made in respect of all the duties specified in paragraph (1) of this regulation or may be limited to certain of those duties, and where the said appointment is so limited, particulars of the limitation shall be set out in the entry or certificate (as the case may be) of the appointment. Every person appointed under the said paragraph (1)(d) shall be furnished by the occupier with a copy of the entry or certificate of his appointment and of any entry revoking the same.

(3) Any appointment made under paragraph (1)(d) of this regulation may be revoked by the occupier at any time by signed and dated entry in the said register.

(4) Paragraph (1) of this regulation shall not apply to and shall not prevent the employment on setting, re-setting, adjusting or trying out of the tools on a

power press or on installing or adjusting as aforesaid a *safety device* thereon required by regulation 7, of a person who (whether or not he has attained the age of eighteen), is undergoing training (whether or not in accordance with the Schedule to these Regulations) for those duties or any of them and who is working under the immediate supervision of a competent person appointed under the said paragraph (1) in respect of the duties on which the first-mentioned person is employed, provided that an entry has been made in, or a certificate has been attached to, the register kept for the purposes of this regulation, specifying that the said first mentioned person is undergoing such training. Every such entry or certificate shall be signed by the said competent person and shall specify the date on which the entry was made or the certificate was given (as the case may be).

5.   Examination and testing of power presses and safety devices.—(1) No *power press* or *safety device* shall be taken into use in any *factory* for the first time in that *factory*, or in the case of a *safety device* for the first time on any *power press*, unless it has been thoroughly examined and tested, in the case of a *power press*, after installation in the *factory*, or in the case of a *safety device*, when in position on the *power press* in connection with which it is to be used, by a competent person.

(2) No *power press* shall be used unless it has been thoroughly examined and tested by a competent person—

(a) in the case of a *power press* on which the tools are fenced exclusively by means of a fixed fencing within the immediately preceding period of twelve months; or

(b) in any other case, within the immediately preceding period of six months.

(3) No *power press* shall be used unless every *safety device* (other than fixed fencing) thereon has within the immediately preceding period of six months when in position on that *power press*, been thoroughly examined and tested by a competent person.

(4) The competent person carrying out an examination and test under the foregoing provisions of this regulation shall make a report of the examination and test in the *approved* form [Form 2197] and containing the *approved* particulars and every such report shall within fourteen days of the completion of the examination and test be entered in or attached to a register [Form 2198] kept for the purposes of this regulation.

6.   Defects disclosed during a thorough examination and test.—(1) Where any defect is disclosed in any *power press* or in any *safety device* by any examination and test under regulation 5 and, in the opinion of the competent person carrying out the examination and test, either—

(a) the said defect is a cause of danger to employed persons and in consequence the *power press* or *safety device* (as the case may be) ought not to be used until the said defect has been remedied; or

(b) the said defect may become a cause of danger to employed persons and in consequence the *power press* or *safety device* (as the case may be) ought not to be used after the expiration of a specified period unless the said defect has been remedied, such defect shall, as soon as possible after the completion of the examination and test, be notified in writing by the competent person to the occupier of the *factory* and, in the case of a defect falling within sub-paragraph (b) of this paragraph, such notification shall include the period within which, in the opinion of the competent person, the defect ought to be remedied.

In every case where notification has been given under this paragraph, a copy of the report made under regulation 5(4) shall be sent by the competent person to the inspector for the district within fourteen days of the completion of the examination and test.

(2) Where any such defects is notified to the occupier in accordance with the foregoing provisions of this regulation the *power press* or *safety device* (as the case may be) having the said defect shall not be used—

(a) in the case of a defect falling within sub-paragraph (a) of paragraph (1) of this regulation until the said defect has been remedied; and

(b) in the case of a defect falling within sub-paragraph (b) of paragraph (1) of this regulation, after the expiration of the said specified period unless the said defect has been remedied.

(3) As soon as is practicable after any defect of which notification has been given under paragraph (1) of this regulation has been remedied, a record shall be made by or on behalf of the occupier stating the measures by which and the date on which the defect was remedied. The said record, where practicable, shall be made in an *approved* form on the document [Form 2197] containing the report of the examination and test under Regulation 5 during which the defect was disclosed, or, in any other case, shall be made in writing and attached as soon as is practicable to the said report.

7. Inspection and test of safety devices.—(1) No *power press* shall be used after the setting, re-setting or adjustment of the tools thereon unless a person appointed or authorised for the purpose under regulation 4 has inspected and tested every *safety device* thereon while it is in position on the said *power press* and has given a certificate in accordance with paragraph (3) of this regulation:

Provided that an inspection, test and certificate as aforesaid shall not be required where any adjustment of the tools has not caused or resulted in any alteration to or disturbance of any *safety device* on the *power press* and if, after the adjustment of the tools, the *safety devices* remain, in the opinion of such a person as aforesaid, in efficient working order.

(2) No *power press* shall be used after the expiration of the fourth hour of any working period unless between the time when the said *power press* last ceased to be used before the commencement of that period and the expiration of the said fourth hour a person appointed or authorised for the purpose under regulation 4 has inspected and tested (whether or not in pursuance of paragraph (1) of this regulation) every *safety device* thereon while it is in position on the said *power press* and has given a certificate in accordance with paragraph (3) of this regulation.

In this paragraph the expression "working period" means the daily hours worked in a *factory* or, in the case of a *factory* where a shift system is in operation, a shift.

(3) Every certificate of an inspection and test made under this regulation—

(a) shall contain sufficient particulars to identify every *safety device* inspected and tested and the *power press* on which that *safety device* was fitted at the time of the inspection and test;

(b) shall state the date and time of the inspection and test;

(c) shall be signed by the person carrying out the inspection and test; and

(d) shall state that every *safety device* on the said *power press* is in efficient working order.

(4) In determining, for the purpose of giving a certificate of an inspection and test made under this regulation or of forming an opinion for the purposes of the proviso to paragraph (1) of this regulation, whether or not any *safety device* is in efficient working order, the person carrying out the inspection and test or forming the opinion shall not treat as a defect any defect in a *safety device* which at the time of the inspection and test is the subject of a notification in writing under regulation 6(1) by virtue of which the use of the *safety device* may be continued during a specified period which has not then expired unless he is of opinion that the said defect has then become a cause of danger to employed persons.

(5) Every certificate of an inspection and test under this regulation shall be kept available at or near the *power press* to which it relates for inspection by the persons employed until the expiration of the period during which the said *power press* may be used in reliance upon that certificate and shall be preserved in the *factory* and kept available for a period of six months thereafter for inspection by any inspector.

8.   Defects disclosed during an inspection and test.—(1) Where it appears to any person as a result of any inspection and test carried out by him under regulation 7 that any necessary *safety device* is not in position or is not properly in position on a *power press* or that any *safety device* which is in position on a *power press* is not in his opinion suitable, he shall notify the occupier or his agent forthwith.

(2) Except as provided in paragraph (3) of this regulation, where any defect is disclosed in a *safety device* by any inspection and test under regulation 7, the person carrying out the inspection and test shall notify the occupier or his agent forthwith.

(3) Where any defect in a *safety device* is the subject of a notification in writing under regulation 6 by virtue of which the use of the *safety device* may be continued during a specified period without the said defect having been remedied, the requirement in paragraph (2) of this regulation shall not apply to the said defect until the said period has expired.

9.   Identification of power presses and safety devices. For the purpose of identification in the registers required to be kept by these Regulations, every *power press* and every *safety device* provided for the same shall be distinctively and plainly marked.

10.   Indication of speed and direction of flywheel. The maximum permissible flywheel speed as certified by the makers and the direction of rotation of the flywheel shall be conspicuously marked on every *power press* constructed after the coming into operation of these Regulations and where such a *power press* is in use the flywheel shall not be driven at a greater speed than that so marked, or in the direction opposite to that so marked; but nothing in this paragraph shall prevent in an emergency the reversal of the direction of rotation of the flywheel.

11.   Preservation of registers. Every register kept for the purposes of regulation 4 or 5 shall be preserved in the *factory* and kept available for inspection by an inspector for a period of two years after the date of the last entry in the register.

12.   Exemption certificates. The Chief Inspector *(a)* may (subject to such conditions as may be specified therein) by certificate in writing (which he may in his discretion revoke at any time) *(b)* exempt from all or any of the requirements of these Regulations—

(a)   any *power press* or *safety device* or any class or description of *power presses* or *safety devices*; or

(b)   any operation or process or any class or description of operations or processes,

if he is satisfied that the requirements in respect of which the exemption is granted are not necessary for the protection of persons employed or are impracticable or inappropriate. Where such exemption is granted a legible copy of the certificate, showing the conditions (if any) subject to which it has been granted, shall be kept posted in any *factory* in which the exemption applies in a position where it may be conveniently read by the persons employed.

*(a)   **Inspector.*** See INTRODUCTORY NOTE 24.

*(b)   **Certificates of Exemption.*** Certificates of Exemption are set out following these Regulations.

SCHEDULE

Regulation 4

PARTICULARS OF TRAINING REQUIRED BY PARAGRAPH (1) OF REGULATION 4

The training shall include suitable and sufficient practical instruction in the following matters in relation to each type of *power press* and *safety device* in respect of which it is proposed to appoint the person being trained, that is to say—

1. *Power press mechanisms* with particular reference to their bearing on safety. The nature and function of *clutch mechanisms*, flywheels, rakes and ancillary equipment.

2. *Safety devices.* Types of devices. Functions of each type of device. Methods of installing, inspecting and testing including detection of defects.

3. *Accident causation and prevention.* The causes and prevention of accidents with special reference to *power presses.*

4. *The work of the tool setter.* Safe methods of working. Lubrication. Co-operation with the press operator.

5. *Tool design.*—in relation to safe methods of working.

CERTIFICATE OF EXEMPTION No. 6
F2369, 13 August 1969

Whereas I am satisfied that the requirements of the Power Presses Regulations 1965 are inappropriate to the class of power presses hereinafter specified:

Now, therefore, in pursuance of regulation 12 of the said Regulations, I hereby exempt from all the requirements of the said Regulations power presses designed and used for the compacting of metal powders.

This Certificate shall remain in force until revoked in writing by the Chief Inspector of Factories.

CERTIFICATE OF EXEMPTION No. 7
F2370, 30 August 1971

Whereas I am satisfied that the requirements of the Power Presses Regulations 1965 are inappropriate to the classes of power presses specified in the Schedule to this Certificate:

Now, therefore, in pursuance of regulation 12 of the said Regulations, I hereby exempt from all the requirements of the said Regulations the classes of power presses specified in the said Schedule.

This Certificate shall remain in force until revoked in writing by the Chief Inspector of Factories.

SCHEDULE

1. Guillotines.
2. Combination punching and shearing machines, turret punch presses, and similar machines where in any case the machine is constructed and used solely for one or more of the following operations, that is to say, punching, shearing or cropping.
3. Machines, other than press brakes, designed and used solely for bending steel sections.
4. Straightening machines.
5. Upsetting machines.
6. Heading machines.
7. Riveting machines.
8. Eyeletting machines.
9. Press-stud machines.
10. Zip fastener bottom stop attaching machines.
11. Stapling machines.
12. Wire stitching machines.

CERTIFICATE OF EXEMPTION No. 8
F2382, 23 November 1971

Whereas I am satisfied that, in respect of the class of safety device specified in the First Schedule to this Certificate, compliance with the requirements of regulation 5(1) of the Power Presses Regulations 1965 is not necessary for the protection of persons employed:

Now, therefore, in pursuance of the powers conferred on me by regulation 12 of the said Regulations, I hereby exempt from the requirements of the said regulation 5(1) the class of safety device specified in the said First Schedule subject to the conditions set out in the Second Schedule hereto.

This Certificate shall remain in force until revoked in writing by the Chief Inspector of Factories.

FIRST SCHEDULE

Any fixed fencing as defined in regulation 2(2) which consists of that part of a closed tool which acts as a guard.

SECOND SCHEDULE

1. No safety device in the First Schedule shall be taken into use for the first time in a factory on any power press unless it has been thoroughly examined and tested by a competent person when in position on a power press in that factory.

2. The competent person shall comply with the requirements of regulation 5(4) as if the examination and test were an examination and test under regulation 5(1), and shall state in the report thereof that it is a report of an examination and test carried out in pursuance of the requirements of this Certificate.

3. Where the competent person considers that the device will only be effective if the length of the stroke of any press with which it is used is limited, he shall, when making his report, enter therein the maximum permissible length of stroke of any press to be used with the device. Where such entry has been made, the maximum permissible length of press stroke as specified in the entry shall be clearly marked on the tool set of which the device forms a part, and no press shall be used with that safety device if the said safety maximum permissible length of stroke is exceeded.

CERTIFICATE OF EXEMPTION No. 9
F2417, 31 October 1972

Whereas I am satisfied that the requirements of regulation 7(1) of the Power Presses Regulations 1965 (which require the inspection, testing and certification of the safety devices on a power press, after the tools have been set, re-set or adjusted and before the power press is used) are not necessary for the protection of persons employed in relation to the use of a power press for the operation of trying out the tools after the setting, re-setting or adjustment of the said tools or in the course of die proving:
 Now, therefore, in pursuance of regulation 12 of the said Regulations, I hereby exempt the said operation from the requirements of the said regulation 7(1).
 This Certificate shall remain in force until revoked in writing by the Chief Inspector of Factories.

CERTIFICATE OF EXEMPTION No. 10
F2435, 13 April 1973

Whereas I am satisfied that the provisions of regulation 7(1) of the Power Presses Regulations 1965 are inappropriate in the case of the operation hereinafter specified:
 Now, therefore, in pursuance of the powers conferred on me by regulation 12 of the said Regulations, I hereby exempt from the provisions of the said regulation 7(1) the operation specified in the Schedule to this Certificate, subject to the condition set out in the said Schedule.
 This Certificate shall remain in force until revoked in writing by the Chief Inspector of Factories.

SCHEDULE

The operation to which this Certificate applies is the use of power presses to emboss symbols on registration plates for motor vehicles, and the condition referred to above is that the setting, resetting, or adjustment of the tools for the purposes of the said operation shall not cause or result in any alteration to or disturbance of the safety devices on the said power presses.

CERTIFICATE OF EXEMPTION No. 13
F2476, 13 May 1975

Whereas I am satisfied that, in respect of the class of power presses hereinafter specified, compliance with the requirements of the Power Presses Regulations 1965 and 1972 is not necessary for the protection of persons employed:

Now, therefore, in pursuance of regulation 12 of the said Regulations, I hereby exempt from all the requirements of the said Regulations, subject to the conditions specified in the Schedule to this Certificate, power presses of which the stroke is not greater than 6 millimetres.

SCHEDULE

1. This exemption shall not apply to power presses of which the stroke is capable of being varied unless measures have been taken to prevent the stroke from exceeding 6 millimetres.

2. Where any power press of which the stroke is capable of being varied is used as in 1 above and is subsequently modified to be used with a stroke exceeding 6 millimetres, the period during which the press was used under this exemption shall be reckoned in full for the purposes of regulation 5 of the said Regulations.

EXPLANATORY NOTE
(Not part of the exemption)

The effect of this exemption is that none of the requirements of the Power Presses Regulations 1965 and 1972 will apply to power presses with a stroke not greater than 6 millimetres. Variable stroke power presses are also exempted when the stroke is restricted to 6 millimetres or less by an effective modification.

Where a variable stroke press is so modified and used within the terms of the exemption and is subsequently re-modified so that the stroke is greater than 6 millimetres the Regulations will again apply and the time during which the press was used under the exemption will be counted in full towards the period within which the press and safety devices must be thoroughly examined and tested by a competent person under regulation 5.

The Regulations require that regular examinations, tests and inspections of power presses and safety devices be carried out and records kept in approved forms. The exemption does not affect the requirements under section 14 of the Factories Act 1961 to guard the tools whenever they constitute a dangerous part of machinery.

CERTIFICATE OF EXEMPTION No. 15
F2524, 8 April 1988

Whereas I am satisfied that the requirements of the Power Presses Regulations 1965 are inappropriate to the class of power press specified in the Schedule to this Certificate:

Now, therefore, in pursuance of regulation 12 of the said Regulations, I hereby exempt from all the requirements of the said Regulations the class of power press specified in the said Schedule.

This Certificate shall remain in force until revoked in writing either wholly or in part by a duly authorised person

SCHEDULE

Platen machines, both hand and mechanically fed, of the type normally used for cutting, creasing and embossing paper and board.

THE SACKS (CLEANING AND REPAIRING) WELFARE ORDER 1927

(S.R. & O. 1927 No. 860, as amended by S.I. 1992 No. 2966
and S.I. 1992 No. 3004)

General note. This whole Order is revoked by the Workplace (Health, Safety and Welfare) Regulations 1992, S.I. 1992 No. 3004, as from 1 January 1993 except, in relation to any workplace or part of a workplace which is not a new workplace, or a modification, an extension or a conversion, it is revoked as from 1 January 1996.

In pursuance of section 7 of the Police, Factories, etc. (Miscellaneous Provisions) Act 1916, I hereby make the following Order for all factories and workshops, or parts thereof, in which the cleaning or repairing of sacks is carried on:

Provided that this Order shall not apply (i) to any factory or workshop where such processes are carried on only occasionally and are ancillary to another business, or (ii) to any factory or workshop in which the manufacture of cement is carried on.

1.–2. [*revoked*].

3. The occupier shall provide and maintain for the use of all the persons employed suitable accommodation for clothing put off during working hours.

The accommodation so provided shall be placed under the charge of a responsible person, and shall be kept clean.

4. The occupier shall provide and maintain for the use of all the persons employed, and remaining on the premises during the meal intervals, a suitable and adequate messroom, which shall be furnished with (a) sufficient tables and chairs or benches with back rests, (b) unless a canteen serving hot meals is provided, adequate means of warming food and boiling water. The messroom shall be sufficiently warmed for use during meal intervals.

The messroom shall be separate from the accommodation provided in pursuance of Clause 3 of this Order, and shall be placed under the charge of a responsible person, and shall be kept clean:

Provided that the Chief Inspector of Factories may by written certificate (which he may revoke at any time) allow some other arrangements in lieu of a messroom, if satisfied that it provides suitable accommodation for the workers.

5. The occupier shall provide and maintain in the works for the use of all persons employed suitable washing facilities *(a)* conveniently accessible and comprising a sufficient supply of clean towels, soap and warm water.

The facilities so provided shall be placed under the charge of a responsible person, and shall be kept clean.

(a) Washing facilities. See INTRODUCTORY NOTE 20.

6. This Order may be cited as the Sacks (Cleaning and Repairing) Welfare Order 1927, and shall come into force on 1 November 1927.

THE SHIPBUILDING AND SHIP-REPAIRING REGULATIONS 1960

(S.I. 1960 No. 1932, as amended by S.I. 1969 No. 690, S.I. 1974 No. 1681, S.I. 1980 No. 1248, S.I. 1981 No. 917, S.I. 1983 No. 644, S.I. 1988 No. 1657, S.I. 1989 No. 635, S.I. 1989 No. 1141, S.I. 1989 No. 2169, S.I. 1989 No. 2311, S.I. 1992 No. 195, S.I. 1992 No. 1811, S.I. 1992 No. 2932 and S.I. 1992 No. 2966)

ARRANGEMENT OF REGULATIONS

The Minister of Labour by virtue of the powers conferred on him by sections 46 and 60 of the Factories Act 1937, section 8 of the Factories Act 1948, and of all other powers enabling him in that behalf, hereby makes the following special Regulations—

PART I
INTERPRETATION AND GENERAL

1. Citation, commencement and revocation.—(1) These Regulations may be cited as the Shipbuilding and Ship-repairing Regulations 1960, and, save as provided in regulations 8, 9(2), 24 and 25 of these Regulations, shall come into operation on the 31st day of March 1961.

(2) The Shipbuilding Regulations 1931 are hereby revoked.

General note. Measurements in Imperial have been converted to metric by S.I. 1983 No. 644. These amendments do not apply to premises or plant in existence before 1 June 1983.

2. Application of Regulations.—(1) Subject to paragraph (2) of this regulation, these Regulations shall apply—

(a) as respects work carried out in any of the operations in a *shipyard* in the case of a *ship* or *vessel* whether or not the shipyard forms part of a *harbour* or wet dock;

(b) as respects work carried out in any of the operations in a *harbour* or wet dock in the case of a *ship* (but not in the case of a *vessel* other than a ship) not being work done—

   (i) by the master or crew of a *ship*, or

   (ii) on board a *ship* during a trial run, or

   (iii) for the purpose of raising or removing a *ship* which is sunk or stranded, or

   (iv) on a *ship* which is not under command, for the purpose of bringing it under command.

(2) (a) Nothing in Parts II to IX of these Regulations, except regulations 6, 31 to 67, 73 to 78 and 80 shall apply as respects the operations in a *shipyard* in which the operations are not carried on upon *vessels* with both exceed 30 metres in length measured overall and have an *overall depth* exceeding 2.9 metres;

(b) Nothing in Parts II to IX of these Regulations, except regulations 6, 31 to 67 and 73 to 78 shall apply as respects the carrying out of the operations, in a *harbour* or wet dock, upon *ships* which either do not exceed 30 metres in length measured overall or have an *overall depth* not exceeding 2.9 metres;

(c) Regulations 7, 12 to 24 and 26 to 30 of these Regulations shall not apply as respects the carrying out of the operations in a *public dry dock*, upon *vessels* which either do not exceed 30 metres in length measured overall or have an *overall depth* not exceeding 2.9 metres.

(3) The Chief Inspector may (subject to such conditions as may be specified therein) by certificate in writing (which he may at his discretion revoke at any time) exempt *(a)* from all or any of the requirements of these Regulations—

(a) any *shipyard* or any *harbour* or wet dock or any class or description of *shipyards, harbours* or wet docks;

(b) any class or description of machinery, plant, equipment or appliances;

(c) any class or description of *ships* or *vessels*; or

(d) any particular work or any class or description of work,

if he is satisfied that the requirements in respect of which the exemption is granted are not necessary for the protection of *persons employed* or not reasonably practicable. Where such exemption is granted a legible copy of the certificate, showing the conditions, if any, subject to which it has been granted, shall be kept posted in a position where it may be conveniently read by the *persons employed.*

(4) Save as expressly provided in regulations 32, 52, 53, 67 and 68 of these Regulations, the provisions of these Regulations shall be in addition to and not in substitution for or in diminution of other requirements imposed by or under *the principal Act.*

(a) **Exempt.** See the Certificate of Exemption set out following these Regulations.

3.   Interpretation.—(1) The Interpretation Act 1889 [Interpretation Act 1978] shall apply to the interpretation of these Regulations as it applies to the interpretation of an Act of Parliament, and as if these Regulations and the Regulations hereby revoked were Acts of Parliament.

(2) In these Regulations, unless the context otherwise requires, the following expressions have the meanings hereby assigned to them respectively, that is to say—

"Abel closed test" means a test carried out with Abel apparatus according to a method for that apparatus set out in Part IV of Schedule 1 to the Classification, Packaging and Labelling of Dangerous Substances Regulations 1984, S.I. 1984/ 1244.

"approved" means approved for the time being by certificate of the Chief Inspector (a);

"available for inspection" means available for inspection by any person using or proposing to use the machinery or plant and by any inspector appointed under *the principal Act;*

"certificate of entry" means a certificate which—

(a) is given by a person who is a competent analyst and who is competent to give such certificates; and

(b) certificates that he has in an adequate and suitable manner tested the atmosphere in the *oil-tank* or *oil-tanks* specified in the certificate and found that having regard to all the circumstances of the case, including the likelihood or otherwise of the atmosphere being or becoming dangerous, entry to the *oil-tank* or *oil-tanks* without wearing breathing apparatus may in his opinion be permitted;

"lifting appliance" means a crab, winch, pulley block or gin wheel used for raising or lowering and a crane, derrick, sheer-legs, tagle, transporter or runway;

"lifting gear" means a chain sling, rope sling, plate clamp, ring, link, hook, shackle, swivel or eye-bolt;

"naked light certificate" means a certificate which—

(a) is given by a person who is a competent analyst and who is competent to give such certificates; and

(b) certifies that he has in an adequate and suitable manner tested for the presence of inflammable vapour the *oil-tank*, compartment, space or other part of the *vessel* specified in the certificate and found it to be free therefrom and that having regard to all the circumstances of the case, including the likelihood or otherwise of the atmosphere becoming inflammable, the use of naked lights, fires, lamps or heated rivets may in his opinion be permitted in the oil-tank, compartment, space or other part of the vessel specified in the certificate;

"oil" means any liquid which has a flashpoint below 132 degrees Celsius (*Abel closed test* or *Pensky-Martens closed test,* whichever is appropriate) and also includes lubricating oil, liquid methane, liquid butane and liquid propane;

"oil-tank" means any tank or compartment in which oil is, or has been, carried as cargo or for use as lubricating oil, as engine fuel or boiler fuel or as fuel for aircraft on board;

"the operations" means, in relation to a *ship* or *vessel*, its construction, reconstruction, repairing *(b)*, refitting, painting and finishing, the scaling, scurfing or cleaning of its boilers (including combustion chambers or smoke boxes) and the cleaning of its bilges or oil-fuel tanks or any of its tanks last used for carrying *oil*. For the purpose of this definition the expression *"oil"* means *oil* of any description whether or not *oil* within the meaning of the foregoing definition of that expression;

"overall depth" means the vertical distance between the upper-most deck at the side of the *vessel* and the bottom of the keel, measured at the middle of the overall length;

"Pensky-Martens closed test" means a test carried out with the apparatus specified and in the manner described in British Standard 2839: 1957, as published by the British Standards Institution on 14 March 1957, including any approved revision thereof;

"person employed" means a person employed in any of *the operations*;

"the principal Act" means the Factories Act 1937;

"public dry dock" means a dry dock which is availabe for hire;

"safe working load" means the relevant safe working load specified in the latest certificate of test obtained for the purposes of regulation 34 or 36;

"ship", *"vessel"* and *"harbour"* have the same meanings as in the Merchant Shipping Act, 1894 *(c)*, except that neither the expression *"ship"* nor the expression *"vessel"* shall include a caisson, dock gate or pontoon;

"shipyard" means any yard or dry dock (including the precincts thereof) in which *ships* or *vessels* are constructed, reconstructed, repaired, refitted or finished;

"stage" means any temporary platform on or from which *persons employed* perform work in connection with *the operations*, but does not include a boatswain's chair;

"staging" includes any stage, and any upright, thwart, thwart pin, wedge, distance piece, bolt or other appliance or material, not being part of the structure of the *vessel*, which is used in connection with the support of any *stage*, and any guard-rails connected with a *stage*;

"structure" in regulations 33, 36, 37 and 38 includes a *vessel*;

"tanker" means a vessel constructed or adapted for carrying a cargo of *oil* in bulk.

(3) References in these Regulations to any enactment shall be construed as references to that enactment as amended by or under any other enactment.

(a) **Inspector.** See INTRODUCTORY NOTE 24.

(b) **Repairing.** Under the revoked Regulations of 1931 the question whether any particular operation was one of repair was of greater importance than it would seem to be under these Regulations, having regard to the comprehensive definition of "the operations". The meaning of "repair" for the purposes of the Regulations of 1931 was considered in *Day v Harland and Wolff Ltd* [1953] 2 All ER 387, [1953] 1 WLR 906; *Taylor v Ellerman's Wilson Line Ltd and Amos and Smith Ltd* [1952] 1 Lloyd's Rep 144 and *Hurley v J. Sanders Ltd* [1955] 1 All ER 833, [1955] 1 WLR 470.

(c) **Ship, vessel, harbour.** By s. 742 of the Merchant Shipping Act 1894, these terms are defined as follows: "Vessel" includes any ship or boat or any other description of vessel used in navigation; "Ship" includes every description of vessel used in navigation not propelled by oars; "Harbour" includes harbours properly so called, whether natural or artificial, estuaries, navigable rivers, piers, jetties, and other works in or at which ships can obtain shelter, or ship and unship goods or passengers. As to hovercraft, see note *(k)* to s. 176 of the Factories Act 1961.

4.   Obligations under Regulations.—(1) It shall be the duty of every employer who is undertaking any of *the operations* to comply with such of the provisions of the following regulations as relate to any work, act or operation performed by him, that is to say—

(a)   in so far as they affect any *person employed* by him—
   (i)   regulations 6, 8(2), 11(1), 13, 14(1), (2), (3) and (5), 15, 17(1), (2), (3), (4) and (6), 18, 19(1), 20 to 24, 25(2), 28(1), 48 to 51, 56(2), 60(1) and (2), 70(1) and (4), 73 and 74, 80 and 81;
   (ii)   regulations 11(2) and 16, except in so far as the person having the general management and control of a *public dry dock* is responsible under paragraph (5) of this regulation;
   (iii)   regulation 69(1), except in so far as the person having the general management and control of a *public dry dock* is responsible under paragraph (5) of this regulation or the person having the general management and control of a dock, wharf or quay is responsible under paragraph (6) of this regulation;
   (iv)   regulation 26, except in so far as the shipowner or master or officer in charge is responsible under paragraph (7) of this regulation and except in so far as the stevedore or other person carrying on any of the processes of loading, unloading or coaling the *ship* or *vessel* is responsible by virtue of the Docks Regulations 1934 *(a)*; and
   (v)   regulation 70(2) and (3), except in so far as the shipowner or master or officer in charge is responsible under paragraph (7) of this regulation.
(b)   in so far as they affect any person whether or not a *person employed* by him—
   (i)   regulations 27, 29(1) and (2), 30(1), 53, 54(1), 63 to 66, 71, 72 and 78; and
   (ii)   regulations 59 and 62, except in so far as the shipowner or master or officer in charge is responsible under paragraph (7) of this regulation.

(a) See now the Docks Regulations 1988, S.I. 1988 No. 1655.

(2) It shall be the duty of the owner of any machinery, plant, equipment or appliance to which any of the provisions of regulations 33 to 39, 67 and 68 applies to comply with those provisions; and in the case of any such machinery, plant, equipment or appliance carried on board a *ship* not registered in the United Kingdom it shall also be the duty of the master or officer in charge of the *shop* to comply with those provisions. It shall be the duty of every employer not the use any machinery, plant, equipment or appliance which does not comply with those provisions.

(3)   (a)   It shall be the duty of every person who installs or places in position any machinery, plant, equipment or appliance to which any of the provisions of regulations 42, 55(1) and (2), 56(1)(a) and 57 applies to install or place in position such machinery, plant, equipment or appliance in a manner which complies with those provisions;
   (b)   It shall be the duty of every person who works or uses any machinery, plant, equipment or appliance to which any of the provisions of regulations 40 to 47, 55(1) and (2), 56, 57(1), (2), (3) and (4), 58 and 69(4)

and (5) applies to work or use such machinery, plant, equipment or appliance in a manner which complies with those provisions.

(4) In the case of a *shipyard* other than a *public dry dock*, it shall be the duty of the person having the general management and control of the *shipyard* to comply with the provisions of regulations 7 and 8, regulation 9(2) in so far as it relates to hand-holds provided by him, regulations 17(5), 25(1) and 79 and (except in so far as the shipowner or master or officer in charge is responsible under paragraph (7) of this regulation) regulations 9(1), 10, 12, 59 and 62.

(5) In the case of a *public dry dock*—

(a) it shall be the duty of the person having the general management and control of the dock to comply as respects gangways, platforms and stairways provided by him with the provisions of regulations 7, 9(1) and 12, other than the provisions relating to use of such gangways, platform and stairways, and to comply with the provisions of regulation 8(1), regulation 9(2) in so far as it relates to hand-holds provided by him, regulation 11(2) in so far as it relates to the sound construction of scows or floating platform provided by him, regulation 16 in so far as it relates to the soundness of any material or appliance provided by him for the construction of *staging*, regulations 17(5) and 25(1), regulations 69(1) as respects lighting of approaches to the edge of the dock, and regulations 79(1) and (2); and

(b) it shall be the duty of every employer who is undertaking any of the *operations* to comply with such of the provisions of the following regulations as relate to any work, act or operation performed by him, in so far as those provisions affect any *person employed* by him, that is to say, regulations 7, 9 and 12 (except, in the case of each of these regulations, in so far as the person having the general management and control of the dock is responsible under sub-paragraph (2) of this paragraph and except, in the case of regulations 9 and 12, in so far as the shipowner or master or officer in charge is responsible under paragraph (7) of this regulation), and regulation 10.

(6) In the case of a *ship* lying in or at a dock, wharf or quay but not in a *shipyard*, it shall be the duty of the person having the general management and control of the dock, wharf or quay to comply with regulation 69(1) as respects the lighting of approaches to the edge of the dock, wharf or quay.

(7) It shall be the duty of the shipowner and of the master or officer in charge of a *ship* or *vessel*—

(a) to comply with such of the provisions of regulations 9(1), 10 and 12 as relate to any means of access provided by him, regulation 59 in so far as it relates to any work, act or operation performed by him, and regulation 62 in so far as it relates to a *naked light certificate* or a *certificate of entry* obtained by him; and

(b) where the control of the *ship* or *vessel* apart from *the operations* remains with the shipowner or master or officer in charge—

(i) to provide the protection specified in regulation 26 in so far as concerns those hatches or opening which are not required to be used for the purposes of *the operations* (but if such protection be removed by or at the request of any employer who is undertaking any of *the operations*, that employer shall be responsible for its replacement as soon as practicable), and

   (ii) to comply with the provisions of regulation 69(2) and regulation 70(2) and (3); and
  (c) not to remove any fencing provided in compliance with regulation 26 at openings used or created in the course of *the operations*, save as permitted by that regulation:

Provided that where a stevedore or other person carrying on any of the processes of loading, unloading or coaling the *ship* or *vessel*, is responsible under the Docks Regulations 1934 *(a)* for the protection of a hatch for the time being, that stevedore or other person shall be solely responsible for maintaining in position, as far as practicable, any protection provided in compliance with regulaton 26.

(8) It shall be the duty of every *person employed* to comply with such of the provisions of regulations 14(4), 19(2), 28(2), 29(3), 30(2), 46(2), 48(2), 54(2), 55(2), 56(2), 57(4)(b), 59(3), 60(3), 69(6), 70(4), and 72 as expressly impose a duty on him. It shall further be the duty of every *person employed* if he discovers any defect in any machinery, plant, equipment or appliance, to report such defect without unreasonable delay to his employer or foreman or to a person appointed by the employer under regulation 81.

(9) For the purposes of the provisions in this regulation which impose upon an employer a duty to comply with the requirements of certain specified regulations in so far as they affect any *person employed* by him, the requirements of those regulations, other than regulations 48 to 51, 59, 60, 65 and 70, shall be deemed not to affect any *person employed* if and so long as his presence in any place is not in the course of performing any work on behalf of his employer or is not expressly or impliedly authorised or permitted by his employer.

(a) See now the Docks Regulations 1988, S.I. 1988 No. 1655.

5. Publication of Regulations.—(1) Every employer who employs persons in *the operations* shall ensure that a printed copy of these Regulations or of the prescribed abstract of these Regulations is kept posted in such characters and in such positions as to be conveniently read by the *persons employed*.

(2) Every such employer as aforesaid shall give a printed copy of these Regulations to any *person employed* by him and affected thereby on his application.

PART II
MEANS OF ACCESS AND STAGING

6. Safe access in general.—(1) Without prejudice to the other provisions of these Regulations there shall, so far as is reasonably practicable *(a)*, be provided and maintained safe means of access *(b)* to every place at which any person has at any time to work in connection with *the operations*, which means of access shall be sufficient having regard to the number of *persons employed* and shall, so far as is reasonably practicable, be kept clear of substances likely to make foothold or hand-hold insecure and any obstruction *(c)*.

(a) *Reasonably practicable.* See INTRODUCTORY NOTE 5.

(b) *Safe means of access.* Compare s. 29(1) of the Factories Act 1961, and see the notes thereto.

(c) **Obstruction.** See INTRODUCTORY NOTE 12.

7.   General access to vessels in a shipyard. All main gangways *(a)* giving general access to a *vessel* in a *shipyard*, whether from the ground or from a wharf or quay, and all cross gangways leading from such a main gangway on to the *vessel*, shall—

(a)   be sufficiently wide having regard to the number of *persons employed* on or at the *vessel*; and

(b)   be securely protected on each side to a height of at least 840 millimetres by strongly constructed upper and lower hand-rails and by a secure toe-board projecting at least six inches above the floor; and

(c)   be of good construction, sound material and adequate strength *(b)*; and

(d)   be stable and, wherever practicable *(c)*, of permanent construction; and

(e)   be kept in position as long as required.

(a) **Main gangway.** a short, hinged extension linking the end of a ship's gangway to the quayside does not form part of the main gangway and is thus outside the scope of reg. 7 (*Williams v Swan Hunter Shipbuilders Ltd* (1988) Times, 24 March, CA).

(b) **Good construction, sound material and adequate strength.** See INTRODUCTORY NOTE 11.

(c) **Practicable.** See INTRODUCTORY NOTE 5.

8.   Access to dry dock.—(1) Every flight of steps giving access from ground level either to an altar or to the bottom of a dry dock shall be provided throughout on each side or in the middle with a substantial hand-rail. In the case of an open side, secure fencing to a height of at least 840 millimetres shall be provided by means of upper and lower rails, taut ropes or chains, or by other equally safe means. For the purposes of this paragraph a flight of steps which is divided into two by a chute for materials, with no space between either side of the chute and the steps, shall be deemed to be one flight of steps.

(2) Such hand-rails and fencing as aforesaid shall be kept in position save when and to the extent to which their absence is necessary (whether or not for the purposes of *the operations*) for the access of persons, or for the movement of materials or *vessels* or for traffic or working, or for repair, but hand-rails or fencing removed for any of these purposes shall be kept readily available and shall be replaced as soon as practicable *(a)*.

(3) This regulation shall come into operation at the expiration of twelve months after the making *(b)* of these Regulations.

(a) **Practicable.** See INTRODUCTORY NOTE 5.

(b) **Making.** The Regulations were made on 20 October 1960.

9.   Access to vessels at wharf or quay or in dry dock.—(1) If a *ship* is lying at a wharf or quay, or is in a dry dock for the purpose of undergoing any of *the operations* other than its construction or re-construction, there shall be provided means of access for the use of *persons employed* at such times as they have to pass to, or from, the *ship* or to the wharf, quay or dock side, as follows—

(a) where reasonably practicable *(a)* one or more ship's accommodation ladders or one or more soundly constructed gangways or similar constructions or a combination of any such ladders, gangways or constructions, being ladders, gangways and constructions not less than 560 millimetres wide, properly secured, and fenced throughout on each side to a clear height of 840 millimetres by means of upper and lower rails, taut ropes or chains or by other equally safe means, except that in the case of a ship's accommodation ladder, such fencing may be on one side only if the other side is properly protected by the ship's side;

(b) in other cases *(b)* one or more ladders of sound material *(c)* and adequate length which shall be properly secured to prevent them from slipping.

(2) Where at any dry dock there is a gangway giving access from an altar of the dock to a *vessel* which is in the dock for the purpose of undergoing any of *the operations*, and the edge of the altar is unfenced, adequate hand-holds shall be available for any length of the altar which *persons employed* commonly use when passing between the gangway and the nearest flight of steps which gives access to ground level. This paragraph shall come into operation at the expiration of twelve months after the making *(d)* of these Regulations.

(a) Reasonably practicable. See INTRODUCTORY NOTE 5.

(b) In other cases. In *Walter Wilson & Sons Ltd v Summerfield* [1956] 3 All ER 550, [1956] 1 WLR 1429, DC (a case upon the similar provisions of reg. 9 of the Docks Regulations 1934) it was held that compliance with para. (b) was no defence unless the person upon whom the duty lay could prove that it was not reasonably practicable to comply with para. (a).

(c) Sound material. See INTRODUCTORY NOTE 11.

(d) Making. The Regulations were made on 20 October 1960.

10.   Access between vessels.—(1) If a *ship* is alongside any *vessel* and *persons employed* have to pass from the one to the other, safe means of access *(a)* shall be provided for their use, unless the conditions are such that it is possible without undue risk *(b)* to pass from the one to the other without the aid of any special appliance.

(2) Where the means of access provided consists of, or includes a rope ladder, such means of access shall not be deemed to be safe unless in the case of the *vessel* with the higher free-board—

(a) the top step of the ladder is not more than 300 millimetres below the gunwale or top of the bulwark where the ladder gives immediate access to the *vessel*; and

(b) at least one adequate and secure hand-hold *(c)* is available at the position of boarding the *vessel*; and

(c) a suitable gangway or stairway is provided leading from the top of the bulwark on to the deck, the gangway or stairway being so placed as to be as nearly as practicable *(d)* opposite to the rope ladder.

(a) Safe means of access. Compare s. 29(1) of the Factories Act 1961, and see the notes thereto.

(b) Without undue risk. In *Norton v Straits Steamship Co Ltd* [1954] 2 Lloyd's Rep 635, a case under reg. 10 of the Docks Regulations 1934, it was held that the onus of showing

that it was possible without undue risk to pass from one vessel to the other without the aid of any special appliance lay upon the defendants.

(c) *Hand-hold.* See s. 29 of the Factories Act 1961 and the notes thereto.

(d) *Practicable.* See INTRODUCTORY NOTE 5.

11. Vessels used for access or as a working place.—(1) Where any *person employed* has to proceed to or from a *ship* by water, proper measures shall be taken to provide for his safe transport.

(2) Scows and floating platforms used for the purpose of *the operations* shall be of sound construction (a) and properly maintained (b) and shall not be overcrowded.

(a) *Sound construction.* See INTRODUCTORY NOTE 11.

(b) *Properly maintained.* See INTRODUCTORY NOTE 10.

12. Access to and from bulwarks. Where there is a gangway leading on to a bulwark of a *vessel,* there shall be provided—

(a) wherever practicable (a), a platform at the inboard end of the gangway with safe means of access therefrom to the deck; or

(b) where such a platform is not practicable, a second gangway or stairway leading from the bulwark on to the deck which shall either be attached to the end of the first-mentioned gangway or be placed contiguous to it, in which case means of access, securely protected by fencing, shall be provided from the one to the other.

(a) *Practicable.* See INTRODUCTORY NOTE 5.

13. Further provisions as to access.—(1) Where outside *staging* is erected in a *shipyard,* there shall be provided sufficient ladders giving direct access to the *stages* having regard to the extent of the *staging* and to work to be done.

(2) Where a *vessel* is under construction or reconstruction and *persons employed* are liable to go forward or aft or athwartship across or along uncovered deck-beams, or across or along floors, sufficient planks shall be provided on those deck-beams or on those floors for the purpose of access to or from places of work, and sufficient and suitable portable ladders shall be provided so as to give access either from the ground or outer bottom plating to the top of the floor.

(3) Without prejudice to any other provision in these Regulations requiring a greater width, no footway or passageway constructed of planks shall be less than 430 millimetres wide.

14. Ladders.—(1) Subject to paragraphs (2) and (3) of the regulation, every ladder which affords a means of access, communication or support to a *person* or *persons employed* shall—

(a) be soundly constructed *(a)* and properly maintained *(b)*; and
(b) be of adequate strength *(a)* for the purpose for which it is used; and
(c) be securely fixed either—
   (i) as near its upper resting place as possible, or
   (ii) where this is impracticable *(c)*, at its base, or where such fixing is impracticable a person shall be stationed at the base of the ladder when in use to prevent it from slipping; and
(d) unless there is other adequate hand-hold *(d)*, extend to a height of at least 760 millimetres above the place of landing or the highest rung to be reached by the feet of any person working on the ladder, as the case may be, or, if this is impracticable *(c)*, to the greatest practicable height.

(2) Requirements (c) and (d) of the preceding paragraph of this regulation shall not apply to fixed ladders of a *ship* or to rope ladders. Effective measures by means of roping off or other similar means shall be taken to prevent the use of fixed ladders of a *ship* which do not comply with requirements (a) and (b) of that paragraph.

(3) Requirement (c) of paragraph (1) of this regulation shall not apply in the case of a small portable ladder carried from place to place in the course of his work by a *person employed*.

(4) Any *person employed* who removes any ladder and sets it up in a new position shall, as regards that ladder, comply with requirement (c) of paragraph (1) of this regulation.

(5) Rope ladders shall provide adequate foothold *(d)* and, so far as reasonably practicable *(c)*, suitable provision shall be made for preventing such ladders from twisting.

(a) **Soundly constructed; adequate strength.** See INTRODUCTORY NOTE 11.

(b) **Properly maintained.** See INTRODUCTORY NOTE 10.

(c) **Practicable; reasonably practicable.** See INTRODUCTORY NOTE 5.

(d) **Hand-hold; foothold.** See s. 29 of the Factories Act 1961 and the notes thereto.

15.   Lashing of ladders.—(1) A fibre rope, or a rope made with strands consisting of wire cores covered with fibre, shall not be used to secure a ladder used for the purpose of *the operations*.

(2) A wire rope shall not be used to secure any such ladder unless its ends are ferruled, but this provision shall not apply in the case of an end which is so situated or protected that a person using the ladder is not liable to come into contact with it so as to suffer injury.

16.   Material for staging.—(1) A sufficient supply of sound and substantial material and appliances shall be available in a convenient place or places for the construction of *staging*.

(2) All planks and other materials and appliances intended to be used or re-used for *staging* shall be carefully examined before being taken into use or re-use in any *staging*. Every examination required by this paragraph shall be carried out by a person competent for the purpose.

17. *Staging,* **dry dock altars and shoring sills.**—(1) All *staging,* and every part thereof shall be of good construction, of suitable and sound material and of adequate strength *(a)* for the purpose for which it is used and shall be properly maintained *(b)*, and every upright and thwart shall be kept so fixed, secured or placed in position as to prevent, so far as is reasonably practicable *(c)*, accidental displacement.

(2) All planks forming *stages* shall be securely fastened to prevent them from slipping unless they extend 460 millimetres or more beyond the inside edge of the thwart or support on which they rest.

(3) All *staging* suspended on the inside of a *vessel,* all *staging* supported by brackets, all *staging* on the outside of a *vessel* at the fore and after ends and, where there is a gap in the *staging* caused by the inside uprights, any plank in the way of such gap, shall be erected and adjusted by *staging* gangs specially, though not necessarily exclusively employed for the purpose.

(4) All *staging* used in connection with *the operations* shall be inspected before use, and thereafter at regular and frequent intervals, by a competent person.

(5) All dry dock altars and shoring sills on or from which persons perform work in connection with *the operations* shall be of sound construction *(a)* and properly maintained *(b)*.

(6) All parts of *stages,* all parts of footways or passageways constructed of planks, and all parts of dry dock altars or shoring sills, being parts on or from which persons perform work in connection with *the operations,* shall so far as is reasonably practicable *(c)*, be kept clear of all substances likely to make foothold or hand-hold *(d)* insecure.

   (a) **Good construction; sound material; adequate strength.** See INTRODUCTORY NOTE 11.

   (b) **Properly maintained.** See INTRODUCTORY NOTE 10.

   (c) **Reasonably practicable.** See INTRODUCTORY NOTE 5.

   (d) **Foothold; hand-hold.** See s. 29 of the Factories Act 1961 and the notes thereto.

18. **Upright used for hoisting block.**—(1) If any upright forming part of *staging* is used as a fixing for a pulley block for hoisting material—

   (a) it shall be properly housed in the ground or shall otherwise be adequately secured so as to prevent it from rising; and
   (b) it shall be suitably protected against damage by the action of the chain or wire or other means of securing the pulley block to the upright.

(2) No upright forming part of *staging* shall be used as an anchorage for a lead pulley block, unless the upright is not likely to be displaced by such use.

19. **Support of** *stages* **on planks.**—(1) Planks supported on the rungs of ladders shall not be used to support *stages.*

(2) It shall be the duty of the *persons employed* to comply with the foregoing paragraph of this regulation.

20. **Suspended** *stages.*—(1) *Stages* suspended by ropes or chains shall be secured as far as possible so as to prevent them from swinging.

(2) A fibre rope, or a rope made of strands consisting of wire cores covered with fibre, shall not be used for suspending a *stage* except that fibre ropes may be used in the case of a *stage* of which the suspension ropes are reeved through blocks.

(3) Chains, ropes, blocks and other gear used for the suspension of *stages* shall be of sound material, adequate strength *(a)* and suitable quality, and in good condition.

(4) Appropriate steps shall be taken to prevent ropes or chains used for supporting a *stage* from coming into contact with sharp edges of any part of a *vessel.*

   (a) Sound material; adequate strength. See INTRODUCTORY NOTE 11.

21. Boatswains' chairs.—(1) Boatswains' chairs and chains, ropes or other gear used for their suspension shall be of sound material, adequate strength *(a)* and suitable quality and the chains, ropes or other gear shall be securely attached.

(2) Suitable measures shall be taken to prevent where possible the spinning of a boatswain's chair, to prevent the tipping of a boatswain's chair and to prevent any occupant falling therefrom.

   (a) Sound materials; adequate strength. See INTRODUCTORY NOTE 11.

22. Rising *stages.*—(1) All planks forming a rising *stage* at the bow end of a *vessel* shall be securely fastened to prevent them from slipping.

23. Width of *stages.* Without prejudice to the other provisions of these Regulations, all *stages* shall be of sufficient width as is reasonable in all the circumstances of the case to secure the safety of the persons working thereon.

24. *Stages* from which a person is liable to fall more than 2 metres or into water.—(1) The regulation applies to *stages* from which a person is liable to fall a distance of more than 2 metres or into water in which there is a risk of drowning.

(2) Every *stage* to which this regulation applies—

(a) shall so far as is reasonably practicable *(a)* be closely boarded, planked or plated;
(b) shall be so constructed or placed that a person is not liable to fall as aforesaid through a gap in the *staging* not being a gap necessary and no larger than necessary having regard to the nature of the work being carried on;
(c) shall be at least 430 millimetres wide.

(3) Every side of a *stage* to which this regulation applies shall—

(a) if it is not a side immediately adjacent to any part of a *vessel*, be fenced (subject to the provisions of paragraphs (4) to (7) of this regulation) with a guard rail or guard rails to a height of at least 920 millimetres above the *stage*, which rail or rails shall be so placed as to prevent so far as practicable *(a)* the fall of persons from the *stage* or from any raised standing place on the *stage*, or

(b) if it is a side immediately adjacent to any part of a *vessel*, be placed as near as practicable to that part having regard to the nature of the work being carried on and to the nature of the structure of the *vessel*.

(4) In the case of *stages* which are suspended by ropes or chains, and which are used solely for painting, the fencing required by sub-paragraph (a) of the preceding paragraph may be provided by means of a taut guard rope or taut guard ropes.

(5) No side of a *stage* or, as the case may be, not part of the side of a *stage* need be fenced in pursuance of paragraph (3)(a) of this regulation in cases where, and so long as, the nature of work being carried on makes the fencing of that side or, as the case may be, that part impracticable *(a)*.

(6) Guard rails provided in pursuance of paragraph (3)(a) of this regulation may be removed for the time and to the extend necessary for the access of persons or for the movement of materials; but guard rails removed for either of these purposes shall be replaced as soon as practicable *(a)*.

(7) Where it is not reasonably practicable *(a)* to comply with the provisions of paragraph (3)(a) of this regulation, the *stage* shall in cases where the limitations of space make this possible be at least 640 millimetres wide and, in other cases, as wide as those limitations permit.

(8) This Regulation shall come into operation at the expiration of twelve months after the making *(b)* of these Regulations.

(a) Reasonably practicable; practicable. See INTRODUCTORY NOTE 5.

(b) Making. The Regulations were made on 20 October 1960.

PART III
FURTHER PRECAUTIONS AGAINST FALLS OF PERSONS,
MATERIALS AND ARTICLES

25. Fencing of dry docks.—(1) Fencing shall be provided at or near the edges of a dry dock at ground level, including edges above flights of steps and chutes for materials. The height of such fencing shall at no point be less than 920 millimetres or, in the case of fencing which was placed in such position before the making *(a)* of these Regulations, 760 millimetres.

(2) Such fencing as aforesaid shall be kept in position save when and to the extent to which its absence is necessary (whether or not for the purposes of *the operations*) for the access of persons, or for the movement of materials or *vessels* or for traffic or working, or for repair, but fencing removed for any of these purposes shall be kept readily available and shall be replaced as soon as practicable *(b)*.

(3) This regulation shall come into operation at the expiration of twenty-four months after the making *(a)* of these Regulations.

(a) **Making.** The Regulations were made on 20 October 1960.

(b) **Practicable.** See INTRODUCTORY NOTE 5.

26.   Protection of openings.—(1) Every side or edge of an opening in a deck or tank top of a *vessel*, being a side or edge which may be a source of danger to *persons employed*, shall, except where and while the opening is securely covered or where the side or edge is protected to a height of not less than 760 millimetres by a coaming or other part of the *vessel*, be provided with fencing to a height of not less than 920 millimetres above the side or edge, and such fencing shall be kept in position save when and to the extent to which its absence is necessary (whether or not for the purposes of *the operations*) for the access of persons, or for the movement of materials, or for traffic or working, or for repair, but fencing removed for any of these purposes shall be kept readily available and shall be replaced as soon as practicable *(a)*.

(2) Paragraph (1) of this regulation shall not apply—

(a) to that part of an opening in a deck or tank top which is at the head of a stairway or ladder-way intended to be used while *the operations* are being carried on; or

(b) to parts of a deck or tank top which are intended to be plated, except such parts where the plating has necessarily to be delayed so that the opening may be used for the purposes of *the operations*.

(a) **Practicable.** See INTRODUCTORY NOTE 5.

27.   Fall of articles from *stages*.—(1) Where *persons employed* are at work outside a *vessel* on a *stage* adjacent to part of the structure of the *vessel* and other *persons employed* are at work directly beneath that *stage*, the planks of the *stage* shall be in such a position that no article liable to cause injury to the *persons employed* can fall between the planks, and the inside plank of the *stage* shall be placed as near as practicable *(a)* to the structure of the *vessel* having regard to the nature of the work being carried on.

(a) **Practicable.** See INTRODUCTORY NOTE 5.

28.   Boxes for rivets, etc.—(1) Boxes or other suitable receptacles for rivets, nuts, bolts and welding rods shall be provided for the use of the *persons employed*.

(2) It shall be the duty of the *persons employed* to use, so far as practicable *(a)*, the boxes or other suitable receptacles so provided.

(a) **Practicable.** See INTRODUCTORY NOTE 5.

29.   Throwing down materials and articles.—(1) Subject to the provisions of paragraph (2) of this regulation, parts of *staging*, tools and other articles and materials shall not be thrown down from a height where they are liable to cause injury to *persons employed*, but shall be properly lowered.

(2) When the work to be done necessarily involves the throwing down from a height of articles or materials, conspicuous notices shall be posted to warn persons from working or passing underneath the place from which articles or materials may fall, or the work shall be done under the direct supervision of a competent person in authority.

(3) No *person employed* shall throw down any articles or materials from a height except in accordance with the requirements of this regulation.

30.   Loose articles or materials.—(1) So far as practicable *(a)* steps shall be taken to minimise the risk from loose articles or materials being left lying in any place from which they may fall on persons working or passing underneath.

(2) It shall be the duty of the *persons employed* to comply with the foregoing paragraph of this regulation.

(a) Practicable. See INTRODUCTORY NOTE 5.

PART IV
RAISING AND LOWERING, ETC.

31.   Application of Part IV. The provisions of this Part of these Regulations shall apply in the case of any chain, rope, *lifting gear* or *lifting appliance* used in raising or lowering, and the provisions of regulation 33 shall apply in the case of any plant or gear used for anchoring or fixing a *lifting appliance.*

32.   Operation of Part IV. In the case of a *shipyard* this Part of these Regulations shall, as respects *the operations*, be in substitution for the following provisions of *the principal Act*, that it to say, section 23 [s. 26] (which relates to chains, ropes and lifting tackle) and subsections (1), (2), (4), (5), (6) and (8) of section 24 [s. 27] (which relates to cranes and other lifting machines).

33.   Construction of lifting appliances. Every *lifting appliance*, including all parts and working gear thereof, whether fixed or movable, and all plant or gear used for anchoring or fixing such an appliance, shall be of good construction, sound material, adequate strength *(a)* and free from patent defect and shall be properly maintained *(b)*:
Provided that plant or gear permanently attached to a *structure* may be used for anchoring or fixing any *lifting appliance* if that plant or gear is first thoroughly examined and appears to satisfy the requirements of this regulation.

(a) Good construction, sound material and adequate strength. See INTRODUCTORY NOTE 11.

(b) Properly maintained. See INTRODUCTORY NOTE 10.

34.   Tests, examinations and marking of lifting appliances.—(1) Subject to the provisions of paragraphs (4) and (5) of this regulation, no *lifting appliance* shall be taken into use for the first time in *the operations* or after it has undergone any substantial alteration or repair, unless it has been tested and thoroughly examined by a competent person in the manner described in the Second Schedule to these Regulations. A record of such test and thorough examination and of the results thereof containing the particulars required by the Lifting Plant and Equipment (Records of Test and Examination etc.) Regulations 1992 shall have been obtained and the particulars in that record shall be *available for inspection.*

(2) Subject as aforesaid, every *lifting appliance* shall be thoroughly examined by a competent person at least once in every period of twelve months and a record of every such examination and of the results thereof, containing the particulars required by the Lifting Plant and Equipment (Records of Test and Examination etc.) Regulations 1992, shall be kept and the particulars in that record shall be *available for inspection.* In the case of *lifting appliances* in a *shipyard*, the person by whom the record is authenticated shall within twenty-eight days of the completion of the examination send a copy of the particulars in the record to an inspector appointed by the Health and Safety Executive under section 19 of the Health and Safety at Work etc. Act 1974 who is authorised for the purposes of this provision in every case where the examination shows that the *lifting appliance* can not continue to be used with safety unless certain repairs are carried out immediately or within a specified time.

(3) Subject as aforesaid, every *lifting appliance* shall have plainly marked upon it the *safe working load.* Every crane of variable operating radius (including a crane with a derricking jib) shall—

(a) have plainly marked upon it the *safe working load* at various radii of the jib or crab and, in the case of a crane with a derricking jib, the maximum radius at which the jib may be worked; and

(b) be fitted with an accurate indicator, clearly visible to the driver, showing the radius of the jib or crab at any time and the *safe working load* corresponding to that radius.

(4) The foregoing provisions of this regulation shall not apply to sheer-legs temporarily erected for the purpose of *the operations.*

(5) This Regulation shall not apply as respects—

(a) any *lifting appliance* to which the Docks Regulations 1934 *(a)* apply and which *satisfies* the requirements of those Regulations; or

(b) any operation carried out on a *ship* not registered in the United Kingdom by means of any of the ship's engine room cranes where such cranes are used with the express authorisation and under the supervision of a competent person.

(a) **Docks Regulations 1934.** See now the Docks Regulations 1988, S.I. 1988 No. 1655.

35.   Construction of chains, ropes and *lifting gear*. Chains, ropes and *lifting gear* shall be of good construction, sound material, adequate strength *(a)* and free from patent defect.

(a) **Good construction; sound material; adequate strength.** See INTRODUCTORY NOTE 11.

36. Testing and annealing of chains, etc.—(1) No chain, rope or *lifting gear* shall be taken into use for the first time in *the operations*, or after it has undergone any substantial alteration or repair, unless it has been tested and thoroughly examined by a competent person in the manner described in the Second Schedule to these Regulations. A record of such test and thorough examination and of the results thereof, containing the particulars required by the Lifting Plant and Equipment (Records of Test and Examination etc.) Regulations 1992, shall have been obtained and the particulars in that record shall be *available for inspection.*

Provided:

(a) that this paragraph shall not apply to a fibre rope or fibre rope sling; and

(b) that a wire rope sling need not be tested and examined in accordance with this paragraph if the rope of which the sling is constructed has been so tested and examined and all joins in the sling are by splices which satisfy the requirements of regulation 39.

(2) A chain, ring, link, hook, shackle, swivel, eye-bolt or plate clamp being a chain, ring, link, hook, shackle, swivel, eye-bolt or plate clamp which has been lengthened, altered or repaired shall not be used unless, since such lengthening, alteration or repair, it has been tested and thoroughly examined by a competent person and a record of such test and thorough examination and of the results thereof, containing the particulars required by the Lifting Plant and Equipment (Records of Test and Examination etc.) Regulations 1992, has been obtained and the particulars in that record are *available for inspection.*

(3) This paragraph applies only to chains and *lifting gear* made of wrought iron. Chains and *lifting gear* to which this paragraph applies shall be annealed at least once in every fourteen months or, in the case of chains, slings, rings, links, hooks, shackles, or swivels being chains, slings, rings, links, hooks, shackles or swivels of 13 millimetres bar or smaller material, at least once in every six months, so however, that chains and *lifting gear* not in regular use need be annealed only when necessary; and the prescribed particulars of the annealing *(a)* shall be kept in an *approved* manner and shall be *available for inspection.*

(4) Nothing in this regulation shall apply to chains, ropes or *lifting gear*—

(a) to which the Docks Regulations 1934 *(b)* apply and which satisfy the requirements of those Regulations; or

(b) which are permanently attached to a structure.

(a) Annealing. For the prescribed particulars, see the Shipbuilding (Particulars of Annealing) Order 1961, set out following these Regulations.

(b) Docks Regulations 1934. See now the Docks Regulations 1988, S.I. 1988 No. 1655.

37. Periodic examination of chains, ropes, etc.—(1) Chains and *lifting gear* other than rope slings shall be thoroughly examined by a competent person at least once in every period of six months and records of such thorough examination and of the results thereof, containing the particulars required by the Lifting Plant and Equipment (Records of Test and Examination etc.) Regulations 1992, shall be kept and the particulars in the records shall be *available for inspection.*

(2) Ropes and rope slings shall have been thoroughly examined by a competent person within the immediately preceding period of three months, or, in

the case of a wire rope or wire rope sling in which such an examination has disclosed that a wire of the rope has broken, one month, and records of such thorough examination and of the results thereof, containing the particulars required by the Lifting Plant and Equipment (Records of Test and Examination etc.) Regulations 1992, shall be kept and the particulars in the records shall be *available for inspection.*

(3) Nothing in this regulation shall apply to chains, ropes or *lifting gear*—

(a) to which the Docks Regulations 1934 *(a)* apply and which satisfy the requirements of those Regulations; or

(b) which are permanently attached to a *structure.*

(a) See now the Docks Regulations 1988, S.I. 1988 No. 1655.

38. Indication of safe working loads.—(1) A table showing the safe working load of every chain, rope and article of *lifting gear* in use, and, in the case of a multiple sling, the safe working loads at different angles of the legs, shall be posted in a permanent position in the store in which the chains, ropes and articles of *lifting gear* are kept; so, however, that this regulation shall not apply to any article of *lifting gear* if the safe working load thereof, or, in the case of a multiple sling, the safe working loads at different angles of the legs, is or are plainly marked upon it.

(2) Nothing in this regulation shall apply to chains, ropes or *lifting gear*—

(a) to which the Docks Regulations 1934 *(a)* apply and which satisfy the requirements of those Regulations; or

(b) which are permanently attached to a *structure.*

(a) See now the Docks Regulations 1988, S.I. 1988 No. 1655.

39. Splices in wire ropes. A thimble or loop splice made in any wire rope shall have at least three tucks with a whole strand of the rope and two tucks with one half of the wires cut out of each strand. All tucks shall be against the lay of the rope:

Provided that this regulation shall not operate to prevent the use of another form of splice which can be shown to be as efficient as the form of splice specified in this regulation.

40. Load not to exceed safe working load. No *lifting appliance* or chain or rope or *lifting gear* shall be loaded beyond its safe working load except—

(a) for the purpose of making a test of the appliance, chain, rope or gear, and then only to such extent as is specified in the Second Schedule to these Regulations, or

(b) in the case of a crane, in exceptional circumstances to such extent and subject to such conditions as may be approved by the engineer in charge or other competent person, if on each occasion—

(i) the written permission of the owner or his responsible agent has been obtained; and

(ii) a record of the overload is kept in the prescribed form [Form 2032].

41. Secureness of loads.—(1) Loads shall be securely suspended or supported whilst being raised or lowered, and all reasonable precautions shall be taken to prevent danger from slipping or displacement.

(2) Where by reason of the nature or position of the operation a load is liable, whilst being moved by a *lifting appliance* or *lifting gear*, to come into contact with any object so that the object may become displaced, special measures shall be adopted to prevent the danger so far as reasonably practicable *(a)*.

(a) **Reasonably practicable.** See INTRODUCTORY NOTE 5.

42. Support of *lifting appliances* and *lifting gear*. Every *lifting appliance* and all *lifting gear* shall be adequately and suitably supported or suspended having regard to the purpose for which it is used.

General note. In *Forsyth's Curator Bonis v Govan Shipbuilders Ltd* 1988 SLT 321 it was argued, unsuccessfully, that the regulation did not apply to a sling when it was not actually being used for a lift.

43. Wire rope with broken wires. No wire rope shall be used if in any length of ten diameters the total number of visible broken wires exceeds five per cent. of the total number of wires, or if the rope shows signs of excessive wear or corrosion or other serious defect.

44. Knotted chains, etc.—(1) No chain or wire rope shall be used when there is a knot tied in any part thereof.

(2) No chain which is shortened or joined to another chain by means of bolts and nuts shall be used.

45. Precautions against damage to chains and ropes. Appropriate steps shall be taken to prevent, so far as practicable *(a)*, the use of chains or ropes for raising or lowering in circumstances in which they are in or liable to come into contact with sharp edges of plant, materials or loads, or with sharp edges of any part of the *vessel* on which work is being carried out.

(a) **Practicable.** See INTRODUCTORY NOTE 5.

46. Loads on *lifting appliances*.—(1) No load shall be left suspended from a *lifting appliance* other than a self-sustaining, manually operated *lifting appliance* unless there is a competent person in charge of the appliance while the load is so left.

(2) It shall be the duty of the *persons employed* to comply with the foregoing paragraph of this regulation.

47. Heavy loads. Where there is reason to believe that a load being lifted or lowered on a *lifting appliance* weighs more than 20 tonnes its weight shall be ascertained by means of an accurate weighing machine or by the estimation of a person competent for the purpose, and shall be clearly marked on the load:

Provided that this regulation shall not apply to any load lifted or lowered by crane which has either a fixed or a derricking jib and which is fitted with an *approval* type of indicator in good working order which—

(a) indicates clearly to the driver or person operating the crane when the load being carried approaches the safe working load of the crane for the radius of the jib at which the load is carried; and

(b) gives an efficient sound signal when the load moved is in excess of the safe working load of the crane at that radius.

PART V

PRECAUTIONS AGAINST ASPHYXIATION, INJURIOUS FUMES OR EXPLOSIONS

48.   Ventilation of confined spaces.—(1) All reasonably practicable *(a)* steps shall be taken to secure and maintain the adequate ventilation of any confined space in which persons are employed.

(2) Compressed oxygen shall not be used to ventilate any confined space in a vessel and no *person employed* shall use compressed oxygen for this purpose.

(a) Reasonably practicable. See INTRODUCTORY NOTE 5.

49.   Precautions against inflammable gas or vapour. Where in any confined space in any part of a *vessel* inflammable solvents are used in the application or removal of paint or there is carried on any other process liable to produce inflammable gas or vapour, effective and suitable provision shall be made by adequate ventilation or by other means to prevent the formation of an inflammable atmosphere in the confined space.

50.   Precautions against shortage of oxygen. No person shall enter or remain in any confined space in a *vessel*, being a confined space in which there is reason to apprehend that the proportion of oxygen in the air is so low as to involve risk of persons being overcome, unless either—

(a) the space has been and remains adequately ventilated and a responsible person has tested it and certified that it is safe for entry without breathing apparatus, or

(b) he is wearing a suitable breathing apparatus.

51.   Precautions against dangerous fumes.—(1) No person shall enter or remain in any confined space in any part of a *vessel*, being a confined space in which there is reason to apprehend the presence of any dangerous fumes to such extent as to involve risk or persons being overcome thereby, unless he is wearing a suitable breathing apparatus, or a responsible person has certified the space as being, for a specified period, safe for entry without breathing apparatus, and the period so specified has not expired; but no person shall enter or remain in the space without breathing apparatus unless he has been warned when the period so specified will expire.

(2) A space shall not be certified under paragraph (1) of this regulation unless—

(a) effective steps have been taken to prevent any ingress of dangerous fumes, and

(b) any sludge or other deposit liable to give off dangerous fumes has been removed and the space contains no other material liable to give off dangerous fumes, and

(c) the space has been adequately ventilated and tested for dangerous fumes and has a supply of air adequate for respiration,

but no account shall be taken for the purposes of sub-paragraph (b) of this paragraph of this regulation of any deposit or other material liable to give off dangerous fumes in insignificant quantities only.

(3) Where any person is employed in any confined space to which paragraph (1) of this regulation applies, there shall be provided and kept readily available—

(a) not less than two sets of breathing apparatus of a type *approved* for the purpose of this regulation on board the *vessel*; and

(b) no less than two additional sets of such apparatus off the *vessel*; and

(c) a lamp or torch of an appropriate type with each set of breathing apparatus; and

(d) not less than two belts and ropes suitable for the purpose of rescue.

The apparatus, belts, ropes, lamps and torches shall be maintained and shall be thoroughly examined, at least once a month or at such other intervals as may be prescribed, by a competent person; and a report *(a)* on every such examination, signed by the person making the examination and containing the prescribed particulars, shall be kept available for inspection.

(4) A sufficient number of the *persons employed* shall be trained and practised in the use of the apparatus mentioned in the preceding paragraphs of this Regulation and in a method of restoring respiration.

(a) **Report.** For the prescribed particulars, see the Shipbuilding (Reports on Breathing Apparatus, etc.) Order 1961, set out following these Regulations.

52. Application of regulations 50 and 51. In the case of a *shipyard*, the provisions of regulations 50 and 51, shall, as respects *the operations* carried out in confined spaces formed by the structure of any *ship* or *vessel*, or of part of any *ship* or *vessel*, under construction or repair, be in substitution for the provisions of section 27 [s. 30] of the *principal Act* (which relates to precautions in places where dangerous fumes are liable to be present).

53. [*revoked*].

54. Rivet fires.—(1) Rivet fires shall not be taken into or used in or remain in any confined space on board or in a *vessel* unless there is adequate ventilation to prevent the accumulation of fumes.

(2) No *person employed* shall move a rivet fire into any confined space on board or in a *vessel* unless he has been authorised by his employer to move the fire into that space.

55. Placing of gas cylinders and acetylene generators.—(1) No cylinder which contains or has contained oxygen or any inflammable gas or vapour under pressure, and no acetylene generating plant, shall be installed or placed within 5 metres of any substantial source of heat (including any boiler or furnace when alight) other than the burner or blow-pipe operated from the cylinder or plant.

(2) No such cylinder and no such plant shall be taken below the weather deck in the case of a *vessel* undergoing repair, or below the topmost completed deck in the case of a *vessel* under construction, unless it is installed or placed in a part of the *vessel* which is adequately ventilated to prevent any dangerous concentration of gas or fumes.

(3) It shall be the duty of the *persons employed* to comply with the foregoing provisions of this regulation.

56. Further provisions as to acetylene generators.—(1) The following provisions shall be observed as respects any acetylene generating plant—

(a) no such plant shall be installed or placed in any confined space unless effective and suitable provision is made for securing and maintaining the adequate ventilation of that space so as to prevent, so far as practicable *(a)*, any dangerous accumulation of gas;

(b) any person attending or operating any such plant shall have been fully instructed in its working and a copy of the maker's instructions for that type of plant shall be constantly available for his use;

(c) the charging and cleaning of such plant shall so far as practicable be done during daylight;

(d) partly spent calcium carbide shall not be recharged into an acetylene generator.

(2) No person (whether or not a *person employed*) shall smoke or strike a light or take a naked light or a lamp in or into any acetylene generator house or shed or in or into dangerous proximity to any acetylene generating plant in the open air or on board a *vessel*:

Provided that this paragraph shall not apply as respects a generator in the open air or on board a *vessel* which, since it was last charged, has been thoroughly cleansed and freed from any calcium carbide and acetylene gas.

(3) A prominent notice prohibiting smoking, naked lights and lamps shall be exhibited on or near every acetylene generating plant whilst it is charged or is being charged or is being cleaned.

(a) *Practicable.* See INTRODUCTORY NOTE 5.

57. Construction of plant for cutting, welding or heating metal.—(1) Pipes or hoses for the supply of oxygen or any inflammable gas or vapour to any apparatus for cutting, welding or heating metal shall be of good construction and sound material *(a)* and be properly maintained *(b)*.

(2) Such pipes or hoses shall be securely attached to the apparatus and other connections by means of suitable clips of other equally effective appliances.

(3) Efficient reducing and regulating valves for reducing the pressure of the gases shall be provided and maintained in connection with all cylinders con-

taining oxygen or any inflammable gas or vapour under pressure while the gases or vapours for such cylinders are being used in any process of cutting, welding or heating metal.

(4) Where acetylene gas is used for cutting, welding or heating metal—

(a) a properly constructed and efficient back-pressure valve and flame arrester shall be provided and maintained in the acetylene supply pipe between each burner or blow-pipe and the acetylene generator, cylinder or container from which it is supplied, and shall be placed as near as practicable to the burner or blow-pipe, except that these requirements shall not apply where an acetylene cylinder serves only one burner or blow-pipe; and

(b) any hydraulic valve provided in pursuance of the preceding sub-paragraph shall be inspected on each day by every person who uses the burner or blow-pipe on that day and it shall be the duty of every *person employed* who uses the burner or blow-pipe to inspect the hydraulic valve accordingly.

(5) The operative valves of burners of blow-pipes to which oxygen or any inflammable gas or vapour is supplied for the purpose of cutting, welding or heating metal shall be so constructed, or the operating mechanism shall be so protected, that the valves cannot be opened accidentally.

(a) *Good construction and sound material.* See INTRODUCTORY NOTE 11.

(b) *Properly maintained.* See INTRODUCTORY NOTE 10.

58.   Precautions after use of apparatus for cutting, welding or heating metal.—(1) In the case of apparatus on board a *vessel* and used for cutting, welding or heating metal with the aid of oxygen or any inflammable gas or vapour supplied under pressure, the precautions specified in the following paragraphs of this regulation shall be taken when such use ceases for the day or for a substantial period and the apparatus is to be left on board, but need not be taken when such use is discontinued merely during short interruptions of work. The requirements in paragraphs (3) and (4) of this regulation shall not apply during a meal interval.

(2) Supply valves of cylinders, generators and gas mains shall be securely closed.

(3) Moveable pipes or hoses used for conveying oxygen or inflammable gas or vapour shall, in the case of a *vessel* undergoing construction, be brought to the topmost completed deck or, in the case of a *vessel* undergoing repair, to a weather deck or in either case to some other place of safety which is adequately ventilated to prevent any dangerous concentration of gas or fumes:
Provided that where, owing to the nature of the work, it is impracticable to comply with the foregoing requirements of this paragraph, the pipes or hoses shall be disconnected from cylinders, generators or gas mains, as the case may be.

(4) When cylinders or acetylene generating plant have been taken below deck as permitted by paragraph (2) of regulation 55, such cylinders or acetylene generating plant shall be brought to a weather deck or, in the case of a *vessel* undergoing construction, to the topmost completed deck.

59.   Naked lights on oil-carrying *vessels.*—(1) Subject to the provisions of paragraph (2) of this regulation and to the provisions of regulation 66, and without prejudice to the provisions of regulations 64 and 65, no naked light, fire or lamp (other than a lamp of an appropriate type) and no heated rivet—

(a)   shall be permitted to be applied to, or to be in, any part of a *tanker* unless, since *oil* was last carried in that *tanker*, a *naked light certificate* has been obtained and is in force in respect of those parts of the *tanker* for which, in the opinion of a competent analyst, a *naked light certificate* is necessary: Provided that a naked light, fire, lamp or heated rivet of a kind specified in writing by a competent analyst may be applied to, or be in, any part of the *tanker* so specified;

(b)   shall be permitted—

   (i)   to be in any *oil-tank* on board or in a *vessel* in which *oil-tank* the *oil* last carried was *oil* having a flash point of less than 23 degrees Celsius *(Abel closed test)* or was liquid methane, liquid propane or liquid butane, unless a *naked light certificate* has previously been obtained on the same day and is in force in respect of that oil-tank and of any *oil-tank*, compartment or space adjacent thereto;

   (ii)   to be applied to the outer surface of any *oil-tank* on board or in a *vessel* in which *oil-tank* the *oil* last carried was such *oil* as aforesaid, unless a *naked light certificate* has previously been obtained on the same day and is in force in respect of that *oil-tank*;

   (iii)   to be applied to the outer surface of, or to be in, any compartment or space adjacent to an *oil-tank* on board or in a *vessel* in which *oil-tank* the *oil* last carried was such *oil* as aforesaid, unless a *naked light certificate* has previously been obtained on the same day and is in force in respect of that compartment or space:

   Provided that where in any such case referred to in paragraph (i), (ii), or (iii) of this sub-paragraph a competent analyst has certified that daily *naked light certificates* are unnecessary or are necessary only to a specified extent, such a daily certificate need not be obtained or, as the case may be, need only be obtained to the specified extent;

(c)   shall be permitted to be applied to the outer surface of, or to be in, any *oil-tank* on board or in a *vessel* unless, since *oil* was last carried on that *oil-tank*, a *naked light certificate* has been obtained and is in force in respect of that oil-tank;

(d)   shall be permitted to be applied to the outer surface of, or to be in, any compartment or space adjacent to an *oil-tank* on board or in a *vessel* unless, since *oil* was last carried as cargo in that *oil-tank*, a *naked light certificate* has been obtained and is in force in respect of that compartment or space.

(2) Notwithstanding anything in paragraph (1) of this regulation, heated rivets may be permitted in any place without a *naked light certificate* being in force in respect of that place if expressly so authorised by a competent analyst who certifies that after adequate and suitable testing he is satisfied having regard to all the circumstances of the case, including the likelihood or otherwise of the atmosphere becoming inflammable, that the place is sufficiently free from inflammable vapour; but such heated rivets shall, where practicable *(a)*, be passed through tubes.

(3) No person (whether or not a *person employed*) shall introduce, have or apply a naked light, fire or lamp (other than a lamp of an appropriate type), or

any heated rivet into, in or to any place where they are prohibited by this regulation.

(4) In this regulation the expression "competent analyst" means an analyst who is competent to give a *naked light certificate.*

(*a*) **Practicable.** See INTRODUCTORY NOTE 5.

60.   Entering *oil-tanks.*—(1) No person (other than an analyst entering with a view to issuing a *certificate of entry*) shall, unless he is wearing a suitable breathing apparatus, enter or remain in an *oil-tank* on board or in a *vessel* unless, since the *oil-tank* last contained *oil,* a certificate of entry has been obtained and is in force in respect of the tank.

(2) Without prejudice to paragraph (1) of this regulation, no person (other than an analyst entering as aforesaid) shall be allowed or required to enter or remain in an *oil-tank* on board or in a *vessel* in which *oil-tank* the *oil* last carried was *oil* having a flash point of less than 23 degrees Celsius *(Abel closed test)* unless, since the *oil-tank* last contained *oil,* an analyst has certified that the atmosphere is sufficiently free from inflammable mixture.

(3) It shall be the duty of the *persons employed* to comply with the foregoing provisions of this regulation.

(4) The provisions of this regulation are without prejudice to the requirements of Regulations 50 and 51.

(*a*) **Approved breathing apparatus.** See note (*a*) to reg. 50.

61.   Duration of certificates. Any *naked light certificate* or *certificate of entry* may be issued subject to a condition that it shall not remain in force after a time specified in the certificate.

62.   Posting of certificates. Every employer or shipowner for whom a *naked light certificate* or a *certificate of entry* is obtained shall ensure that the certificate or a duplicate thereof is posted as soon as may be and remains posted in a position where it may be conveniently read by all persons concerned.

63.   Cleaning of *oil-tanks.*—(1) Subject to the provisions of regulation 66, before a test for inflammable vapour is carried out with a view to the issue of a *naked light certificate* for the purposes of regulation 59 in respect of an *oil-tank* on board or in a *vessel, that oil-tank* shall, since *oil* was last introduced into the tank, be cleaned and ventilated in accordance with paragraph (2) of this regulation.

(2) The said cleaning and ventilation shall be carried out by the following methods:—

(a)   the *oil-tank* shall be treated in such manner and for such period as will ensure the vaporisation of all volatile *oil;*
(b)   all residual *oil* and any sludge or other deposit in the *oil-tank* shall be removed therefrom;

(c) after the *oil-tank* has been so cleaned—
- (i) all covers of manholes and other openings therein shall be removed and it shall be thoroughly ventilated by mechanical or other efficient means with a view to the removal of all *oil* vapour; and then
- (ii) the interior surface, if any deposit remains thereon, shall be washed or scraped down.

64. Invalidation of certificates.—(1) If during the course of work in, or to the outer surface of, any part of a *tanker* or aircraft carrier, any pipe or tank joint is opened or broken or any other event occurs so that there is a risk of *oil* vapour entering or arising in that part of the *tanker* or aircraft carrier, that work shall be suspended and thereafter any *certificate of entry* previously issued in respect of any *oil-tank* in that part and any *naked light certificate* previously issued in respect of that part shall be no longer in force.

(2) If (in the case of a *vessel* other than a *tanker* or aircraft carrier) during the course of work in any *oil-tank* or in any compartment or space adjacent thereto, any pipe or tank joint is opened or broken or any other event occurs so that there is a risk of *oil* vapour entering or arising in the *oil-tank* or in any compartment or space adjacent thereto, work in the *oil-tank* and in the compartments and spaces adjacent thereto shall be suspended and thereafter any *certificate of entry* previously issued in respect of the *oil-tank* and any *naked light certificate* previously issued in respect of the *oil-tank* or any compartment or space adjacent thereto shall be no longer in force.

65. Provisions as to work in other compartments or spaces.—(1) Without prejudice to the other provisions of these Regulations, if the presence of *oil* in such quantity and in such position as to be likely to give rise to fire or explosion is detected in any part of a *vessel*, being a part to which this regulation applies and in which repairs of the following kind are to be or are being undertaken, that is to say, repairs involving the use of a naked light, fire or lamp (other than a safety lamp of a type *approved* for the purpose of regulation 59) or of a heated rivet, such repairs shall not be started or contained until a *naked light certificate* has been issued or, as the case may be, reissued in respect of that part of the *vessel*.

(2) This regulation shall apply to bilges, shaft tunnels, pump rooms, lamp rooms, and to compartments and spaces other than those to which paragraph (1)(d) of regulation 59 applies.

66. Exceptions from regulations 59 and 63.—(1) The provisions of paragraphs (1)(c) and (1)(d) of regulation 59 as to *naked light certificates* and the provisions of regulation 63 as to the cleaning and ventilation of *oil-tanks*, shall not apply in the case of minor repairs to be carried out—

- (a) to the outer surface of an *oil-tank* on board or in a *vessel*; or
- (b) in or to the outer surface of any compartment or space adjacent to any such *oil-tank*,

in cases where the only *oil* last carried was *oil* having a flash point of 66 degrees Celsius or above *(Pensky-Martens closed test)*:

Provided that adequate areas of the interior and exterior surfaces of the *oil-tank* or, as the case may be, of the compartment or space adjacent thereto, in the immediate neighbourhood of the part to be repaired shall be freed from *oil* or sludge; so, however, that as respects repairs to be carried out to the outer surface of an *oil-tank* below the level of any *oil* in that tank the exterior surface of that *oil-tank* need be so freed.

In every case to which this paragraph applies appropriate special precautions shall be taken for preventing and extinguishing fire.

(2) The provisions of paragraphs (1)(a) and (1)(b)(iii) of regulation 59 as to *naked light certificates* shall not apply in the case of minor repairs involving the application of a naked light to the outer surface only of the hull of a *tanker* in which the only *oil* last carried as cargo was liquid methane, liquid propane or liquid butane, being liquid methane, liquid propane or liquid butane at atmospheric pressure, provided that a *naked light certificate* has previously been obtained on the same day and is in force in respect of the space between the hull and any *oil-tank* on board, and the space is adequately and continuously ventilated by mechanical means so as to ensure that an inflammable concentration of gas or vapour cannot be formed in it during the period for which the *naked light certificate* is in force.

(3) The provisions of paragraph (1)(a) of regulation 59 shall not apply to any part of a *tanker* where naked lights were allowed when the *vessel* was in service afloat;

Provided that the said paragraph (1)(a) shall apply whilst any *oil-tank* in the *tanker* is open except an *oil-tanker* in respect of which a *naked light certificate* is in force.

(4) The provisions of paragraph (1)(a) of regulation 59 shall not apply in the case of *tankers* in which the only *oil* last carried was *oil* used for the purpose of a basin trial or a trial trip.

PART VI
MISCELLANEOUS SAFETY PROVISIONS

67. Fencing of machinery.—(1) All motors, gear-wheels, chain and friction gearing and shafting, being motors, gear-wheels, chain and friction gearing and shafting on a *vessel* which are used for the purpose of *the operations* shall (unless it can be shown that by their position and construction they are equally safe to every *person employed* as they would be if securely fenced) be securely fenced *(a)* as far as is practicable *(b)* but without infringing any requirements imposed by or under the Merchant Shipping Acts 1894 to 1958, in respect of life-saving appliances.

(2) Every dangerous part *(c)* of any machinery used for the purpose of *the operations* to which the preceding paragraph of this regulation does not apply, being machinery in a place, or part of a *vessel*, to which Part II of *the principal Act* does not apply, shall be securely fenced *(a)* unless it is in such a position or of such construction as to be as safe to every *person employed* as it would be if securely fenced.

(3) Nothing in this regulation shall require any part of the machinery on a *vessel* which is used for the purpose of *the operations* to be fenced during an examination of that part or during any lubrication, adjustment or repair shown

by such examination to be immediately necessary, being an examination, lubrication, adjustment or repair which is carried out by a competent person who has attained the age of eighteen, and which it is necessary to carry out while the part of the machinery is in motion *(d)*.

(4) In the case of a *shipyard*, the provisions of paragraph (1) of this regulation shall, as respects the dangerous parts of any machinery to which that paragraph applies, be in substitution for the provisions of subsection (1) of section 14 [s. 14(1)] of *the principal Act* (which relates to the fencing of dangerous parts of machinery).

General note. This regulation is revoked by the Provisions and Use of Work Equipment Regulations 1992, S.I. 1992 No. 2932, as from 1 January 1993 except, insofar as it applies to work equipment first provided for use in the premises or undertaking before 1 January 1993, it is revoked as from 1 January 1997.

(a) Securely fenced. Compare s. 14(1) of the Factories Act 1961, and see the Introductory Note to ss. 12–16 thereof. This provision does not apply in relation to any abrasive wheel; see the Abrasive Wheels Regulations 1970, reg. 3(4).

(b) Practicable. See INTRODUCTORY NOTE 5.

(c) Dangerous part. See the Introductory Note to ss. 12–16 of the Factories Act 1961.

(d) In motion. See the note to s. 16 of the Factories Act 1961.

68. Air receivers.—(1) The provisions of section 31 [s. 36] of *the principal Act* (which relates to air receivers) shall apply *(a)* to air receivers used for the purpose of *the operations* (other than fixed air receivers permanently installed in a *ship*).

(2) In the case of a *shipyard*, the provisions of this regulation shall be in substitution for the provisions of section 31 [s. 36] of *the principal Act*.

General note. This regulation is revoked by S.I. 1989 No. 2169, as from 1 July 1994.

(a) Shall apply. The provisions of s. 36 applied by this regulation include provisions as to the examination and testing of air receivers (s. 36(5)); the form of report prescribed thereunder for air receivers to which this regulation applies is to be found in the Shipbuilding (Air Receivers) Order 1961 set out following these Regulations.

69. Lighting.—(1) All parts of a *vessel* and all other places where *the operations* are being carried on, and all approaches to such parts and to places to which a *person employed* may be required to proceed *(a)* in the course of his employment, shall be sufficiently and suitably lighted; so, however, that due regard shall be had to the safety of the *vessel* and cargo and of the navigation of other *vessels* and to any local statutory requirements as to the lighting of the *harbour* or dock.

(2) Where in a *harbour* or wet dock the control of a *ship* apart from *the operations* remains with the shipowner the ship's permanent lighting shall be maintained in operation by him to the extent that it may be required for the purpose of lighting—

(a) the *ship*; and
(b) the means of access to the *ship* where that access is provided by the shipowner:

Provided that if the shipowner has given written notice to every contractor undertaking any of *the operations* for which the ship's permanent lighting is required that for a specified period (for reasons connected with the management or working of the *ship* or the use, repair or maintenance of its equipment) the permanent lighting will not be maintained in operation by him or will be maintained in operation by him only to a specified extent, the foregoing provisions of this paragraph shall for that period not apply or, as the case may be, shall for that period apply only to the extent that the permanent lighting is maintained in operation.

In this paragraph—

"contractor" means a person who has contracted with the shipowner or his agent to carry out any of the operations; and

"shipowner" means the shipowner or master or officer in charge.

(3) No person shall be held not to have complied with the foregoing provisions of this regulation by reason only of a failure of the electricity supply, provided that in the case of such failure alternative means of lighting, which shall be sufficient and suitable in the circumstances, shall be provided as soon as practicable *(b)*.

(4) Portable lamps (including held lamps carried by *persons employed*) used for the purposes of *the operations* shall be maintained in an efficient state, in efficient working order and in good repair, and in the case of lamps in which liquid fuel is used the lamp shall have a properly fitting screw lid or stopper and be so constructed as to prevent, so far as practicable, the development of leaks.

(5) Petroleum spirit or naphtha shall not be used in lamps used for lighting and only paraffin or another liquid having a flash point over 38 degrees Celsius (*Abel closed test* or *Pensky-Martens closed test,* whichever is appropriate) shall be so used.

(6) No person (whether or not a *person employed*) shall, unless duly authorised or in case of necessity, interfere with or remove any means of lighting provided in pursuance of this regulation.

(a) **Required to proceed.** In *Wenborn v Harland and Wolff Ltd* [1952] 1 Lloyd's Rep 255, it was held that these words were not equivalent to "ordered to proceed" and that a person was required to proceed when it was necessary for him to proceed to a place for the purposes of his work. See also *Henaghan v Rederiet Forangirene* [1936] 2 All ER 1426.

(b) **Practicable.** See INTRODUCTORY NOTE 5.

70. Work on boilers, etc.—(1) No work shall be permitted in any boiler, boiler-furnace or boiler-flue until it has been sufficiently cooled to make work safe for the *persons employed.*

(2) Before any *person employed* enters any steam boiler which is one of a range of two or more steam boilers—

(a) all inlets through which steam or hot water might otherwise enter the boiler from any part of the range shall be disconnected from that part, or

(b) all valves or taps controlling such entry shall be closed and securely locked.

(3) While *persons employed* remain in any steam boiler to which paragraph (2) of this regulation applies all such inlets as are referred to in that paragraph

shall remain disconnected or all such valves or taps as are therein referred to shall remain closed and securely locked.

(4) No *person employed* shall be allowed or required to enter or remain in, and no person shall enter or remain in, any steam boiler to which paragraph (2) of this regulation applies unless the provisions of that paragraph are being complied with.

71.   Hatch beams. The hatch beams of any hatch in use for *the operations* shall, if not removed, be adequately secured to prevent their displacement.

72.   Jumped up bolts. Bolts which have been jumped-up and rescrewed shall not be used for securing plates on the sides of *vessels*, and no *person employed* shall use such bolts for this purpose.

PART VII

PROTECTIVE WEAR

73.   Hand protection. Adequate protection for the hands shall be available for all *persons employed* when using cutting or welding apparatus to which oxygen or any inflammable gas or vapour is supplied under pressure or when engaged in machine caulking or machine riveting or in transporting or stacking plates or in handling plates at machines.

74.   Protection in connection with cutting or welding.—(1) [*revoked*].

(2) There shall be provided *(a)* and maintained for the use of all *persons employed* when engaged in the process of electric welding—

    (a) [*revoked*];

    (b) suitable gauntlets to protect the hands and forearms from hot metal and from rays likely to be injurious.

(3) [*revoked*].

    *(a) **Provided.** See* INTRODUCTORY NOTE 9.

75. [*revoked*].

76. [*revoked*].

PART VIII

MISCELLANEOUS HEALTH AND WELFARE PROVISIONS

77. [*revoked*].

78. [*revoked*].

79. [*revoked*].

Part IX
Training and Supervision

80. Young persons.—(1) No person shall, until he has been employed in a *shipyard* or *shipyards* for at least six months, be employed in connection with *the operations* in a *shipyard* on a *stage* from which, or in any part of a *ship* where, he is liable to fall a distance of more than 2 metres, or into water in which there is a risk of drowning.

(2) [*revoked*].

81. Safety supervision.—(1) In the case of every *shipyard* other than a *public dry dock*, being a *shipyard* where the number of *persons employed* regularly or from time to time exceeds five hundred, a person experienced in the work of such yards shall be appointed and employed exclusively to exercise general super-ivision of the observance of these Regulations and to promote the safe conduct of the work generally.

(2) This regulation shall not be construed as preventing two or more employers from jointly appointing the same person or persons to perform some of all of the aforesaid duties for those employers.

First Schedule

[*revoked*].

Second Schedule
Regulations 34(1), 36(1) and 40

Manner of Test and Examination before taking any Chain, Wire Rope, Lifting Appliance or Lifting Gear into use

(a) Every winch, and every derrick with the whole of the gear accessory thereto, shall be tested with a proof load which shall not be less than the following—

Safe working load		*Proof load*	
under 20 tonnes	25 per cent.	in excess of
20–50 tonnes	5 tonnes	the safe
over 50 tonnes	10 per cent.	working load

In the case of a derrick with its accessory gear the proof load shall be applied as follows:—(i) where reasonably practicable by hoisting movable weights; or (ii) in other cases by maintaining the load by means of an accurate spring or hydraulic balance or similar device for a period of not less than five minutes. Where movable test weights are used the derrick shall be swung, with the load suspended, as far as possible in both directions. Where a spring or hydraulic balance or similar device is employed it shall be sufficient if the proof load is applied with the derrick swung as far as practicable first in one direction and then in the other. In each case the derrick shall be tested at the smallest angle to the horizontal at which it will operate and this angle shall be stated in the certificate of the test.

(b) Every crane, crab, sheer-legs, teagle, transporter or runway, with its accessory gear, shall be tested with a proof load which shall not be less than the following—

Safe working load		Proof load
under 20 tonnes	25 per cent.	in excess of
20–50 tonnes	5 tonnes	the safe
over 50 tonnes	10 per cent.	working load

In the case of a crane having a variable radius it shall be tested with a proof load applied at the maximum and minimum working radii. At each such radius the crane shall be swung as far as possible in both directions with the corresponding proof load suspended. In the case of hydraulic cranes where, owing to the limitation of pressure it is impossible to hoist a load 25 per cent. in excess of the safe working load, it shall be sufficient to hoist the greatest possible load.

(c) Every article of *lifting gear* (whether it is accessory to any *lifting appliance* or not) and every pulley block other than a pulley block specially constructed for use with a crane to which it is permanently attached, and every chain shall be tested with a proof load at least equal to that shown against it in the following table:—

Article of gear	Safe working load	Proof load
Chain sling		
Rope sling		
Plate clamp		
Ring		
Link..		Twice the safe
Hook (other than a ramshorn hook)		working load
Shackle		
Swivel		
Eye-bolt	Under 50 tonnes	Twice the safe working load
	50 tonnes to 100 tonnes	Safe working load plus 50 tonnes
Ramshorn hook	Over 100 tonnes	One and a half times the safe working load
Pulley blocks		
Single sheave block		Four times the safe working load
Multiple sheave block with safe working load over 20 tonnes up to and including 40 tonnes		20 tonnes in excess of the safe working load
Multiple sheave block with safe working load over 40 tonnes		One and a half times the safe working load
Chains		
(other than calibrated load chains)		Twice the safe working load
Calibrated load chains		One and half times the safe working load

(d) After being tested as aforesaid, every *lifting appliance* with the whole of the gear accessory thereto, every article of *lifting gear* and every chain shall be examined, and the sheaves and the pins of the pulley blocks shall be removed for the purpose of the examination, to see that no part is injured or permanently deformed by the test.

(e) In the case of wire ropes, a sample shall be tested to destruction.

THIRD SCHEDULE

[*revoked*].

CERTIFICATE OF EXEMPTION
MANNER OF TEST OF LIFTING GEAR BEFORE BEING
TAKEN INTO USE

F 2054, 23 January 1961

In pursuance of paragraph (3) of regulation 2 of the Shipbuilding and Ship-repairing Regulations 1960, I hereby exempt from the requirements set out in paragraph (c) of the Second Schedule to the Regulations the following classes of gear:

PULLEY BLOCKS FITTED WITH CALIBRATED LOAD CHAINS

Subject to the conditions that such gear shall have been tested by a competent person with a proof load at least equal to ONE AND A HALF times the safe working load.

This certificate shall remain in force until revoked by H.M. Chief Inspector of Factories.

CERTIFICATE OF EXEMPTION
ANNEALING

F 2507, 22 February 1961

In pursuance of paragraph (3) of regulation 2 of the Shipbuilding and Ship-repairing Regulations 1960, I hereby exempt from the requirements of paragraph (3) of regulation 36 the following chains and lifting gear made of wrought-iron:—

(1) Pitched chains working on sprocket or pocketed wheels.
(2) Rings, hooks, shackles and swivels permanently attached to pitched chains, pulley blocks or weighing machines.
(3) Socket shackles secured to wire ropes by white metal capping.

This certificate shall come into effect on 31 March 1961, and shall remain in force until revoked by H.M. Chief Inspector of Factories.

CERTIFICATE OF EXEMPTION No. 1
(GENERAL)

F 2080, 1 September 1961

Whereas I am satisfied that the requirements of paragraph (1) of regulation 8 of the Shipbuilding and Ship-repairing Regulations 1960, that every flight of steps giving access from ground level either to an altar or to the bottom of a dry dock shall be provided throughout on each side or in the middle with a substantial hand-rail and on any open side with secure fencing, are not necessary for the protection of persons employed in the case of any such flight of steps which has a chute for materials immediately adjacent with no space between the chute and the steps, now therefore, in pursuance of the powers conferred on me by paragraph (3) of regulation 2 of the said Regulations, I hereby exempt (subject to the conditions specified in the Schedule hereto) from the said requirements of paragraph (1) of regulation 8 of the said Regulations every such flight of steps which has a chute for materials immediately adjacent with no space between the chute and the steps.

This certificate shall come into operation on the 20th day of October 1961, and shall remain in force until revoked by me.

SCHEDULE

The exemption granted by this certificate is subject to the following conditions, namely:—

(1) that the flight of steps shall be provided on the side remote from the chute, or in the middle, with a substantial hand-rail;

(2) that if that side is an open side, secure fencing thereof to a height of at least two feet nine inches shall be provided by means of upper and lower rails, taut ropes, or chains, or by other equally safe means; and

(3) that where the side of the chute remote from the steps is an open side, secure fencing thereof to a height of at least two feet nine inches shall be provided by means of upper and lower rails, taut ropes or chains, or by other equally safe means.

CERTIFICATE OF EXEMPTION No. 3
(GENERAL)

F 2194, 18 October 1965

Whereas I am satisfied that the requirement of the Shipbuilding and Ship-repairing Regulations 1960 hereinafter referred to is not reasonably practicable as respects the class or description of appliances and the class or description of work hereinafter referred to: Now, therefore, in pursuance of regulation 2(3) of the said Regulations and subject to the conditions specified in Part II of the Schedule to this Certificate, I hereby exempt from the requirement of the regulations specified in Part I of the said Schedule suspended stages in the case of which all the following circumstances exist, that is to say (a) that they are being used only by persons employed in painting or red-leading, or in any hand slicing, hand scaling, hand scraping or washing down incidental thereto, (b) that they are being used in circumstances such that a person falling from the stage would not be liable to strike the ground or a solid object, and (c) that the work for which they are being used is not work in a yard or dry dock (including the precincts thereof) in which ships or vessels are constructed, reconstructed, repaired, refitted or finished.

This Certificate shall remain in force until revoked in writing by the Chief Inspector of Factories.

SCHEDULE

PART I
REQUIREMENT OF THE REGULATIONS FROM WHICH EXEMPTION IS GRANTED

The requirement of regulation 20(2) that a fibre rope shall not be used for suspending a stage except that such ropes may be used in the case of a stage of which the suspension ropes are reeved through blocks.

PART II
CONDITIONS OF EXEMPTION

1. The rope for the suspension of a stage shall be a manila of quality not less than Grade 1 of B.S. 2052: 1953 or rope of equivalent quality.
2. The rope shall be carefully examined by a competent person on every occasion immediately before use.
3. Where the rope is reeved through the eye of a length of wire rope secured to the ship, the eye shall be fitted with a thimble.

CERTIFICATE OF EXEMPTION No. 5
(GENERAL)

F 2497, 28 August 1977

STAGES

In pursuance of the powers conferred on me by regulation 2(3) of the Shipbuilding and Ship-repairing Regulations 1960, and subject to the conditions specified in the Second Schedule to this certificate, I hereby exempt from the requirements of the said regulations specified in the First Schedule to this certificate, open metalwork stages used as working platforms in the structure of catenary-hung staging known as "Swiftstage" manufactured by Reejac Ltd., 8–10 Market Street, Newcastle-upon-Tyne.

This certificate shall remain in force until revoked by the Chief Inspector of Factories.

FIRST SCHEDULE

REQUIREMENTS OF THE REGULATIONS FROM WHICH EXEMPTION IS GRANTED

The requirement of regulation 24(2)(a) that every stage from which a person is liable to fall a distance of more than six feet six inches or into water in which there is a risk of drowning, shall so far as is reasonably practicable, be closely boarded, planked or plated.

SECOND SCHEDULE

CONDITIONS OF EXEMPTION

Where persons are liable to be struck by objects falling through open metalwork stages—
(a) access to any stage beneath the work stage shall be effectively blocked and a prominent warning notice indicating that the stage is not to be used shall be affixed at or near to the point at which access is so blocked; and
(b) either
  (i) suitable protective coverings shall be erected or extended to protect persons who, at ground level, work or pass beneath or adjacent to such stages, or,
  (ii) access to any area beneath such stages shall be effectively blocked and adequate prominent warning notices prohibiting entry to that area shall be displayed.

CERTIFICATE OF EXEMPTION No. 6 (GENERAL)
TELESCOPIC JIB CRANES

F 2490, 23 December 1976

In pursuance of the powers conferred on me by regulation 2(3) of the Shipbuilding and Ship-repairing Regulations 1960 and regulation 5 of the Construction (Lifting Operations) Regulations 1961, I hereby exempt cranes with telescopic jibs from the requirements of regulation 34(3) of the said Regulations of 1960 and of regulation 29(2) of the said Regulations of 1961, subject to the conditions specified in the Schedule to this Certificate.

Expressions used in this Certificate shall have the same respective meanings as in the relevant Regulations.

I hereby revoke Certificate of Exemption No. 4 dated 12 April 1973.

This certificate shall remain in force until revoked by the Chief Inspector of Factories.

THE SCHEDULE

1. The crane shall be fitted with—
   (a) accurate indicators which show the operating radius of the jib and the inclination of the jib for the time being; and
   (b) tables prepared by the maker of the crane or by a competent person setting out:
       (i) for operations with a fly jib or locked jib extension fitted used either singly or in combination, the safe working loads at specified inclinations of the jib; and
       (ii) for other operations, the safe working loads corresponding to any combination of specified operating radii and inclination of the jib.

2.—(1) In the following cases, the said tables shall be fitted in the driver's cabin of the crane, but the said indicators may be fitted on the jib—
   (a) in the case of cranes of a maximum safe working load of 8 tons or less; and
   (b) in the case of cranes of a maximum safe working load exceeding 8 tons but not exceeding 15 tonnes and manufactured before 12 April 1973.

(2) In all other cases, both the said tables and the said indicators shall be fitted in the driver's cabin of the crane.

3. The said indicators and the said tables shall be properly maintained.

4. Without prejudice to paragraph 5 of this Schedule, the sub-divisions on the scales of the said indicators shall be as small as is practicable.

5. The markings on the said indicator scales shall at all times be clearly legible to the crane driver from his operating position in the cabin.

6. The tables provided shall have suitable and efficient entries to enable the crane driver to determine the safe working load of the crane at any position of the jib within a specified range:
   (a) of inclinations in the circumstances described in paragraph 1(b)(i) of this Schedule; or
   (b) of radii and inclinations in the circumstances described in paragraph 1(b)(ii) of this Schedule.

7. The crane shall not be used outside the limits of the range so specified.

8. In the case of cranes manufactured before 12 April 1973 which have the following arrangements—
   (a) an indicator fitted on the jib which shows the inclination of the jib for the time being; and
   (b) markings on the jib which show the amount of extension of the jib for the time being; and
   (c) tables of the kind mentioned in paragraph 1(b) of this Schedule fitted in the driver's cabin,

the requirements of paragraphs 1 to 5 of this Schedule shall not apply until 1 January 1978, provided that the said indicator, markings and tables are properly maintained.

CERTIFICATE OF APPROVAL No. COM (LO) 1990/1 (GENERAL)

1 May 1990

1. In pursuance of regulation 30 of the Construction (Lifting Operations) Regulations 1961 and regulation 47 of the Shipbuilding and Ship-repairing Regulations

1960, I hereby approve automatic safe load indicators of the electro-mechanical type which sense the load on the crane by monitoring any one or combination of the following:

(1) deflections of part or parts of the crane structure;

(2) tensions in the rope systems of the crane;

(3) pressure in the hydraulic circuits of the crane,

and conform to British Standard 7262:1990 Specification for automatic safe load indicators which came into effect on 28 February 1990.

2. This certificate shall come into force on 1 May 1990 and shall remain in force until revoked in writing by a duly authorised person.

THE SHIPBUILDING (REPORTS ON BREATHING APPARATUS, ETC.) ORDER 1961

(S.I. 1961 No. 114)

The Minister of Labour in pursuance of paragraph (3) of regulation 51 of the Shipbuilding and Ship-repairing Regulations 1960, hereby prescribes the particulars to be contained in reports on examinations under that paragraph of breathing apparatus, belts, ropes, lamps and torches.

1. This Order may be cited as the Shipbuilding (Reports on Breathing Apparatus, etc.) Order 1961, and shall come into operation on the 31st day of March 1961.

2. The Interpretation Act 1889 [Interpretation Act 1978] shall apply to the interpretation of this Order as it applies to the interpretation of an Act of Parliament.

3. Reports on the results of examination under the said paragraph (3) of regulation 51 of breathing apparatus, belts, ropes, lamps and torches shall contain the following particulars, namely—
  (i) the name and address of the employer of the worker for whose use the equipment is provided;
 (ii) the date of the examination and by whom it was carried out;
(iii) in the case of breathing apparatus, particulars of the type of apparatus, the name of the maker, and the distinguishing number or mark together with a description sufficient to identify the apparatus;
 (iv) in the case of belts, ropes, lamps and torches, the distinguishing number or mark and a description sufficient to identify each of them;
  (v) the condition of the breathing apparatus, belts, ropes, lamps and torches, particulars of any defects found at the examination, and of the steps taken to remedy such defects; and
 (vi) in the case of compressed oxygen apparatus or of a compressed air apparatus, the pressure of oxygen or of air, as the case may be, in the supply cylinder.

THE SHIPBUILDING (PARTICULARS OF ANNEALING) ORDER 1961

(S.I. 1961 No. 117)

The Minister of Labour in pursuance of paragraph (3) of regulation 36 of the Shipbuilding and Ship-repairing Regulations 1960, hereby prescribes the particulars to be kept of the annealing of chains and lifting gear made of wrought iron.

1. This Order may be cited as the Shipbuilding (Particulars of Annealing) Order 1961, and shall come into operation on the 31st day of March 1961.

2. The Interpretation Act 1889 [Interpretation Act 1978] shall apply to the interpretation of this Order as it applies to the interpretation of an Act of Parliament.

3. The particulars to be kept under the said paragraph (3) of regulation 36 of the annealing of chains and lifting gear made of wrought iron shall be as follows, namely—
  - (i) the name and address of the owner of the chain or lifting gear and, in the case of a ship not registered in the United Kingdom, of the master or officer in charge;
  - (ii) the distinguishing number or mark and a description sufficient to identify the chain or lifting gear;
  - (iii) in the case of a chain, the nominal size of the wrought iron bar from which the links are made;
  - (iv) the date of annealing;
  - (v) the temperature at which annealing was carried out;
  - (vi) the method of carrying out the annealing (that is to say, the type of furnace or oven employed, whether cooled in still air or otherwise after withdrawal from the furnace etc.);
  - (vii) any defects found after annealing;
  - (viii) the name and address of the public service, association, company, firm or person carrying out the annealing;
  - (ix) the position in the public service, association, company or form of the person who carried out the annealing or his qualification if he is working on his own account; and
  - (x) the steps taken to remedy the defects (if any) specified in (vii) hereof.

THE SHIPBUILDING (AIR RECEIVERS) ORDER 1961

(S.I. 1961 No. 430)

General note. This whole Order is revoked by S.I. 1989 No. 2169, as from 1 July 1994.

The Minister of Labour by virtue of the powers conferred on him by subsection (4) of section 31 of the Factories Act 1937, and of all other powers enabling him in that behalf, hereby makes the following Order:—

1. This Order may be cited as the Shipbuilding (Air Receivers) Order 1961, and shall come into operation on the 31st day of March 1961.

2. The Interpretation Act 1889 [Interpretation Act 1978] shall apply to the interpretation of this Order as it applies to the interpretation of an Act of Parliament.

3. A report of the result of every examination and test required to be made under the said subsection (4) of section 31 of every air receiver to which the said section 31 applies by virtue of regulation 68 of the Shipbuilding and Ship-repairing Regulations 1960, shall contain the following particulars, that is to say:—

(1) in the case of any such air receiver which is not of such solid drawn construction that it cannot be thoroughly examined internally, the particulars specified in Part I of the Schedule hereto;

(2) in the case of any such air receiver which is of the kind specified in sub-paragraph (1) and which is to be additionally examined under normal pressure, the particulars specified in Part I and Part II of the said Schedule; and

(3) in the case of any such air receiver which is of solid drawn construction and which cannot be thoroughly examined internally, the particulars specified in Part III of the said Schedule.

SCHEDULE

Article 3(1)

PART I

Particulars to be contained in a report of the result of an examination of an air receiver (other than an air receiver of solid drawn construction which cannot be thoroughly examined internally).

Name of owner.	
Address of head office of owner.	
Description and distinguishing mark of receiver and type.	

Date of construction (if ascertainable). The history should be briefly given, and the examiner should state whether he has seen the last previous report.	
1. Condition of receiver: External (State cleanliness of receiver and any defects Internal materially affecting the safe working pressure).	....
2. Fittings: (a) Are the required fittings and appliances provided in accordance with the Factories Act 1937? (b) Are all fittings and appliances properly maintained and in good condition?	....
3. Repairs (if any) required and period within which they should be executed and any other condition which the examiner thinks is necessary to specify for securing safe working.	....
4. Safe working pressure, calculated from dimensions and from the thickness and other data ascertained by the present examination; due allowance being made for conditions of working if unusual or exceptionally severe. Where repairs affecting the working pressure are required, state the safe working pressure: (a) before the expiration of the period specified in 3, (b) after the expiration of such period if such repairs have not been completed, and (c) after the completion of the required repairs.	.... (a) .... (b) .... (c) ....
5. Other observations.	

I certify that on .... the air receiver described above was made accessible for thorough examination and that on the said date I thoroughly examined this receiver, including its fittings, and that the above is a true report of the result of my examination.

If employed in the Public Service or by an Association, Company or Firm, give name and address:	Signature .... Qualification .... Address .... Date ....

PART II

Article 3(2)

Particulars to be contained in a supplementary report of an examination under normal pressure of an air receiver of the kind to which Part I relates.

Name of owner.	
Address of head office of owner.	
Description and distinguishing mark of receiver and type.	

1. Receiver:
  (a) External condition
  (b) Result of examination under pressure.
	....
	
	....

2. Fittings: Are the fittings properly maintained and in good working order?	....
3. Repairs (if any) required and period within which they should be executed.	
4. Other observations.	

I certify that on .... I examined the air receiver described above under normal pressure and that the above is a true report of the result of my examination.

If employed in the Public Service or by an Association, Company or Firm, give name and address:	Signature .... Qualification .... Address .... Date ....

PART III

Article 3(3)

Particulars to be contained in a report of the results of an examination and hydraulic test of an air receiver of solid drawn construction which cannot be thoroughly examined internally.

Name of owner.	
Address of head office of owner.	
Description and distinguishing mark of receiver and type.	
Date of construction (if ascertainable). The history should be briefly given and the examiner should state whether he has seen the last previous report.	
Date of last previous hydraulic test and pressure applied.	

1. Receiver: (a) External condition (including cleanliness). (b) Hydraulic test pressure applied, and (c) Result of hydraulic test.	
2. Fittings: (a) Are the required fittings and appliances provided in accordance with the Factories Act 1937? (b) Are all fittings and appliances properly maintained and in good condition?	
3. Repairs (if any) required and period within which they should be executed and any other condition which the examiner thinks is necessary to specify for securing safe working.	
4. Safe working pressure, calculated from dimensions and from the thickness or other data ascertained by the present examination; due allowance being made for conditions of working if unusual or exceptionally severe. Where repairs affecting the working pressure are required, state the safe working pressure: (a) before the expiration of the period specified in 3, (b) after the expiration of such period if such repairs have not been completed, and (c) after the completion of the required repairs.	(a) .... (b) .... (c) ....
5. Other observations.	

I certify that on .... I examined the air receiver described above and tested it hydraulically, and that the above is a true report of the results of my examination and test.

If employed in the Public Service or by an Association, Company or Firm, give name and address:
....
....
....
....

Signature ....
Qualification ....
Address ....
....
....
Date ....

THE SHIPBUILDING (LIFTING APPLIANCES ETC. FORMS) ORDER 1961

(S.I. 1961 No. 431, as amended by S.I. 1964 No. 530, S.I. 1983 No. 644 and S.I. 1992 No. 195)

The Minister of Labour, in pursuance of regulations 34, 36 and 40 of the Shipbuilding and Ship-repairing Regulations 1960, hereby makes the following Order:—

1. This Order may be cited as the Shipbuilding (Lifting Appliances etc. Forms) Order 1961, and shall come into operation on 31 March 1961.

General note. Measurements in Imperial have been converted to metric by S.I. 1983 No. 644. These amendments do not apply to premises or plant in existence before 1 June 1983.

2. The Interpretation Act 1889 [Interpretation Act 1978] shall apply to the interpretation of this Order as it applies to the interpretation of an Act of Parliament.

3.—(1)–(4) [*revoked*].

(5) The record of overload of a crane required under paragraph (b)(ii) of the said regulation 40 shall be in accordance with the form set out in Part V of the Schedule hereto.

SCHEDULE

Article 3(1)

PARTS I–IV [*revoked*]

PART V

Article 3(5)

RECORD OF OVERLOAD OF CRANE REQUIRED UNDER REGULATION 40(B)(II)
[FORM 2032]

(1) Name and address of Owner.	....
(2) Situation of crane.	....
(3) Description of crane and any distinguishing number or mark.	....
(4) Date when crane was last tested and thoroughly examined in accordance with regulation 34(1)	....

(5) Safe working load or, in the case of a crane having a variable radius, the safe working load at each radius at which the crane was proof loaded for the purpose of regulation 34(1).	....
(6) Date when crane was last thoroughly examined in accordance with regulation 34(2).	....
(7) (a) Load applied. (b) Radius (if applicable).	(a) .... (b) ....
(8) Date of overload.	....
(9) Exceptional circumstances in which overload necessary.	....
(10) Date or dates of previous occasions on which the crane has been overloaded. If it has not been overloaded before enter "Nil".	....

THE TANNING WELFARE ORDER 1930

(S.R. & O. 1930 No. 312, as amended by S.I. 1992 No. 2966)

General note. This whole Order is revoked by the Workplace (Health, Safety and Welfare) Regulations 1992, S.I. 1992 No. 3004, as from 1 January 1993 except, in relation to any workplace or part of a workplace which is not a new workplace, or a modification, an extension or a conversion, it is revoked as from 1 January 1996.

In pursuance of section 7 of the Police, Factories, etc. (Miscellaneous Provisions) Act 1916, I hereby make the following Order for all factories and workshops, or parts thereof, in which are carried on the processes of liming and tanning of raw hides and skins (including the re-tanning of tanned or partly tanned hides and skins) and processes incidental thereto.

1. [*revoked*].

2. [*revoked*; see INTRODUCTORY NOTE *(vi)(a)*].

3. The occupier shall provide and maintain, for the use of all the persons employed, (a) suitable accommodation for clothing put off during working hours, (b) suitable and separate accommodation for the protective clothing, and (c) adequate arrangements in both cases for drying the clothing if wet.

The accommodation so provided shall be placed under the charge of a responsible person, and shall be kept clean.

4. The occupier shall provide and maintain, for the use of all the persons employed and remaining on the premises during the meal intervals a suitable messroom, which shall be furnished with (a) sufficient tables and chairs, and benches with back-rests, and (b) adequate means of warming food and boiling water. The messroom shall be sufficiently warmed for use during the meal intervals.

The messroom shall be separate from the accommodation provided in pursuance of clause 3 and shall be placed under the charge of a responsible person, and shall be kept clean:

Provided that the Chief Inspector of Factories may by written certificate (which he may revoke at any time) allow some other arrangement in lieu of a messroom, if satisfied that it provides suitable accommodation for the workers.

5. The occupier shall provide and maintain, for the use of all the persons employed, suitable facilities *(a)* for washing, including a sufficient supply of clean towels, soap and warm water.

The facilities so provided shall be placed under the charge of a responsible person and shall be kept clean.

(a) **Washing facilities.** See INTRODUCTORY NOTE 20.

6. [*revoked*].

7. [*revoked*].

8. This Order may be cited as the Tanning Welfare Order 1930, and shall come into force on 1 July 1930.

9. [*revoked*].

SCHEDULE

[*revoked*].

THE FACTORIES (TESTING OF AIRCRAFT ENGINES AND ACCESSORIES) SPECIAL REGULATIONS 1952

(S.I. 1952 No. 1689, as amended by S.I. 1983 No. 979, S.I. 1989 No. 635 and S.I. 1992 No. 1811)

[Placard: Form 1021]

The Minister of Labour and National Service, by virtue of the powers conferred upon him by section 60 of the Factories Act 1937, section 8 of the Factories Act 1948, and the Transfer of Functions (Factories, &c., Act) Order 1946 and all other powers him enabling, hereby makes the following Special Regulations.

1. Short title and commencement. These Regulations may be cited as the Factories (Testing of Aircraft Engines and Accessories) Special Regulations 1952, and shall come into operation on the 1st day of November 1952.

2. Interpretation.—(1) The Interpretation Act 1889 [Interpretation Act 1978] applies to the interpretation of these Regulations as it applies to the interpretations of an Act of Parliament.

(2) In these Regulations, unless the context otherwise requires, the following expressions have the meanings hereby assigned to them respectively, that is to say:—

"Accessory" means any carburettor or fuel pump for aircraft.

"Aircraft engine" means any *aircraft engine* in which *petroleum-spirit* is used.

"Control room" means any room, compartment, gallery, corridor or other enclosure in which testing is controlled.

"Engine room" means any room, compartment or other enclosure in which *aircraft engines* are placed for testing.

"Fire-resisting material" means

(a) properly constructed brickwork not less than 100 millimetres in thickness; or

(b) concrete not less than 75 millimetres in thickness; or

(c) efficiently jointed breeze slabbing not less than 75 millimetres in thickness; or

(d) oak or teak not less than 44 millimetres in finished thickness; or

(e) glass not less than 6 millimetres in thickness in the centre of which wire mesh is embedded; or

(f) structural material completely and securely covered, on all sides from which there is a risk of fire, with compressed asbestos not less than 4.5 millimetres in thickness, or other protective covering approved in writing by the Chief Inspector *(a)* for any for the purposes of these Regulations; or

(g) other material approved in writing by the Chief Inspector for any of the purposes of these Regulations.

"The Minister" means the Minister of Labour and National Service.

"Petroleum-spirit" means *petroleum-spirit* as defined in section 23 of the Petroleum (Consolidation) Act 1928 (1928 c. 32 amended by S.I. 1992/1811) and any other flammable liquid or substance which when tested in accordance with Part IV of Schedule 1 to the Classification, Packaging and Labelling of Dangerous Substances Regulations 1984 (S.I. 1984/1244) has a flash point of less than 21 degrees Celsius.

"Test room" means a control room or an *engine room* or any room, compartment or other enclosure in which *testing* is carried out.

"Testing" means the various operations and processes carried out to determine the performance or condition of *aircraft engines* or *accessories* or incidental to such determination, being operations or processes in which *petroleum-spirit* is used and carried out when such *aircraft engines* or *accessories* are not mounted in aircraft.

"Testing equipment" means all apparatus, appliances, pipework and other equipment used for or incidental to *testing*.

3. Application of Regulations. Save as hereinafter provided, these Regulations shall apply to all factories in which the *testing* of *aircraft engines* or of carburettors or fuel pumps for aircraft is carried on.

4. Saving. Nothing in these Regulations shall be deemed to relieve the occupier of a factory or any person of any obligation imposed by the Electricity (Factories Act) Special Regulations 1908 and 1944.

5. Exemptions. If the Chief Inspector *(a)* is satisfied in respect of any factory to which these Regulations apply or in respect of any class or description of such factories that by reason of special circumstances in that factory or in such class or description of factories, or by reason of the small extent of the *testing* carried on therein, or for any other reason, all or any of the requirements of regulations 6 to 24 hereof are not necessary for the protection of the persons employed, he may by certificate in writing (which he may at his discretion revoke at any time) exempt such factory or any part or parts thereof or such class or description of such factories or any part or parts thereof or such class or description of such factories or any part or parts thereof from the operation of any such requirements, subject to such conditions as may be specified in the certificate, and where such exemption is granted a legible copy of the certificate showing the conditions subject to which it has been granted shall be kept posted up in any factory to which the exemption applies in a position where it may be conveniently read by the persons employed.

(a) Inspector. See INTRODUCTORY NOTE 24.

6. Construction of rooms. Every *test room* and every other room or enclosure in which *testing equipment* is installed or used shall be constructed of *fire-resisting* *materials.* All cable or pipe trenches or other apertures between one *test room* and another and between *test rooms* and other parts of the premises shall (except in the case of apertures provided for ventilation or other air-conveying purposes between a *test room* and the open air or a part of the premises other than another *test room*) be sealed so far as is practicable by such materials and in such manner as are specified in Part V and Appendix D of British Standard Specification No. 1043 of 1942, or by such materials and in such manner as may be approved in writing by the Chief Inspector *(a)* of Factories. All doors of *test rooms* and of other rooms in which *testing equipment* is installed or used shall be constructed of *fire-resisting materials* and closely fitting:

Provided that—

   (i) iron or steel may be used in the construction of any part of any such room (including a door) if the part is so situated that there is no danger of fire spreading from that part to any other building or to any highly inflammable material outside such a room;

  (ii) glass not being *fire-resisting material* may be used in the construction of windows in outside walls or roofs of such rooms if the window is so situated that there is no danger of fire spreading from the window to any other building or to any highly inflammable material outside the room;

 (iii) glass of the category known as heat-treated safety glass and not less than 6 millimetres in thickness may, notwithstanding that it may not be *fire-resisting material,* be used in the construction of windows, so, however, that in the case of windows between *engine rooms* and *control rooms* there shall be two such thicknesses of such glass with an air space between them;

 (iv) doors may be constructed of wood not less than 38 millimetres in finished thickness and completely sheathed in iron or steel not less than 0.45 millimetres in thickness or may be of such other type of fire-resisting construction as may be approved in writing by the Chief Inspector *(a)*.

(a) **Inspector.** See INTRODUCTORY NOTE 24.

7.   Separation of work. *Testing* shall not be carried out in any room or other enclosure in which work other than *testing* or work directly incidental to *testing* is being carried out.

8.   Drainage of tanks and pipework.—(1) Suitable means controlled if reasonably practicable *(a)* from a position immediately outside the *control room,* shall be provided to effect the rapid drainage of tanks and pipes from or through which *petroleum-spirit* can reach *testing equipment* by gravity so that, after the operation of such means of drainage, not more than 9 litres of *petroleum-spirit* can reach any *testing equipment* by gravity, and arrangements shall be made to ensure that when the means of drainage are brought into operation the supply of *petroleum-spirit* to such tanks or pipes shall be automatically cut off. Where the only such means as aforesaid are electrically controlled they shall be such as to be effective in the event of a failure of the electrical supply.

   (2) The requirements of paragraph (1) of this regulation shall not apply as respects *testing equipment* in connection with which the arrangements are such

that *petroleum-spirit* cannot flow into the equipment except when pumping is in operation, but in any such case means of promptly stopping the pumping shall be provided in the *control room.*

   (a) **Reasonably practicable.** See INTRODUCTORY NOTE 5.

9.   Drainage where leakage is liable to occur from testing equipment. Where leakage or escape of *petroleum-spirit* is liable to occur, whether in ordinary working or through accidental damage to the equipment, from or from the vents of a float chamber, metering tube, Venturi chamber, flowmeter or other part of the *testing equipment,* there shall be provided adequate and suitable overflow or drainage arrangements for preventing such leakage or escape or for draining away any leaking or escaping spirit as near as is reasonably practicable (a) to the point of leakage or escape, and unless such leakage or escape can be directly observed there shall be provided an easily visible indicator in such a position as to show readily when a leakage or escape is occurring.

   (a) **Reasonably practicable.** See INTRODUCTORY NOTE 5.

10.   Drainage in engine rooms and where accessories are tested. In every *test room* there shall be provided adequate drainage arrangements, in conjunction where necessary with pumping arrangements, for draining or pumping away from a point as near as is reasonably practicable (a) to the point of leakage or escape any *petroleum-spirit* leaking or escaping from an *aircraft engine* or any *accessory* or from connections thereto:

   Provided that draining or pumping away from an engine bed shall not be required where not reasonably practicable but in any such case portable receptacles of suitable design shall be provided and used to catch any leaking or escaping spirit as near as is reasonably practicable to the point of leakage or escape and to convey the spirit away.

   (a) **Reasonably practicable.** See INTRODUCTORY NOTE 5.

11.   Drains. Every drain for *petroleum-spirit* shall lead to a closed tank which shall be fitted with a contents gauge and with a suitable trap to prevent the return of vapour and shall not be situated in or under any building. Where it is impracticable (a) to comply with the last foregoing requirement, the drain may lead to a closed receptacle so fitted and situated in or under a building if it is installed within an adequately ventilated and readily accessible space. Arrangements shall be made for frequent inspection and frequent emptying of such a receptacle.

   (a) **Practicable.** See INTRODUCTORY NOTE 5.

12.   Ventilation of test rooms. Exhaust ventilation, suitably arranged having regard to the part or parts of the room where leakage or escape of *petroleum-spirit* is liable to occur, shall be maintained by mechanical means in every *test room* at all times when any *aircraft engine, accessory, testing equipment* or vessel in the room contains *petroleum-spirit* or when vapour from *petroleum-spirit* may be present:

Provided that, in the case of an *engine room*, exhaust ventilation maintained by mechanical means shall not be required if there is substantial ventilation of the room by other means and if there is installed fixed fire-extinguishing equipment suitably arranged having regard to the part or parts of the room where a fire due to leakage or escape of *petroleum-spirit* is liable to occur.

13.   Control valves.—(1) In the case of each *control room* one or more quick acting valves shall be provided by means of which there can be cut off the supply of *petroleum-spirit* to all the *testing equipment* controlled from that room and, unless the *control room* contains no *testing equipment* used for containing or carrying *petroleum-spirit* and vapour from *petroleum-spirit* is not liable to be present, arrangements shall be made so that any such valve can be operated both from within and from a position immediately outside the *control room*.

(2)   In any case where there is mechanical exhaust ventilation in a *control room* for the purposes of regulation 14, arrangements shall be made by means of a valve or valves interlocked with the control of the mechanical exhaust so that *petroleum-spirit* cannot be supplied to any *testing equipment* in the room until the ventilation is in operation, and the arrangements for cutting off supplies of *petroleum-spirit* shall not be such as to prevent such exhaust ventilation from being maintained when the supply is cut off.

19.   Use of petroleum-spirit for purposes other than test, etc. No *petroleum-spirit* shall be used and no person shall use *petroleum-spirit* in *test rooms* for any purpose except *testing* or the cleaning of *accessories* or of *testing equipment* used for containing or carrying *petroleum-spirit*.

20.   Naked flames and smoking.—(1) No naked flame shall be allowed or used, no smoking shall be allowed, and no person shall smoke in any room, department or place even in the open air where *testing* of *aircraft engines* or *accessories* is done, and no person shall strike a light or spark in or introduce a naked flame into any such room, department or place:
Provided that—

(a)   electric arc or other welding or any other process involving the use of naked flame may be carried out if all *testing equipment* used for containing *petroleum-spirit* and situated in such room, department or place has been so far as possible emptied by drainage and if adequate ventilation is maintained whilst such process is being carried out; and

(b)   the exhaust flame from a running engine shall not be deemed to be a naked flame for the purpose of this regulation.

(2)   Notices shall be kept prominently affixed, particularly in or immediately outside each *test room*, clearly stating that smoking is prohibited in such rooms, departments or places.

21.   Escape from fire. There shall be adequate means of escape in case of fire from every position in which a person is employed in a *test room* or in any room or other enclosure containing *testing equipment* used for containing or carrying *petroleum-spirit*, and such means of escape shall be kept free from obstruction at all times.

22. Fire extinguishing equipment.—(1) There shall be available for every *test room* adequate fire extinguishing equipment, being fixed or portable equipment, capable of discharging carbon dioxide gas, foam, or other suitable substance, or fixed equipment which will automatically discharge water at high pressure in the form of a fine spray.

(2) Where there is fixed fire extinguishing equipment in a *test room,* means for operating it shall be arranged both within and outside the *test room;* and where such equipment is provided with arrangements for its automatic operation means shall also be provided for putting such arrangements out of operation and substituting hand control, such means to be so designed as to prevent the equipment from being under both methods of control simultaneously; and an automatic indicator shall be installed near the entrance to the room to show whether the equipment is under automatic or under hand control. The equipment shall be under hand control at all times when persons are employed within the room:
Provided that the requirements of this paragraph shall not apply as respects fixed equipment which operates automatically and discharges only water.

(3) The means of operating fixed equipment shall be so arranged that when operated the mechanical ventilation system of the *test room* is put out of action, and so far as is practicable any ventilating apertures are closed.

(4) Not more than 50 per cent. of the total discharge capacity of the portable fire extinguishing equipment for a *test room* shall be installed within the room; the remainder shall be kept available for immediate use at a position as near as possible to but outside the room.

(5) Effective provision shall be made for giving warning to an appropriate fire control centre in the factory of an outbreak of fire in any room, department or place in which the *testing* of *aircraft engines* or *accessories* is carried out.

23. Reporting defects. Every person engaged in *testing* shall without delay report to the occupier of the factory or other responsible person any defect which he may find in any of the apparatus or appliances provided, or the arrangements made for the purposes of his work in pursuance of these Regulations.

24. Abstract to be posted. An Abstract of these Regulations in such form as may be approved [Form 1021] by the Minister shall be kept posted up in legible characters in each *control room* and *engine room* in a position where it can be easily read by all persons employed in the room.

THE TIN OR TERNE PLATES MANUFACTURE WELFARE ORDER 1917

(Dated 5 October 1917; S.R. & O. 1917 No. 1035, as amended by the
Employment Act 1989 and S.I. 1992 No. 1811)

General note. This whole Order is revoked by the Workplace (Health, Safety and
Welfare) Regulations 1992, S.I. 1992 No. 3004, as from 1 January 1993 except, in relation
to any workplace or part of a workplace which is not a new workplace, or a modification,
an extension or a conversion, it is revoked as from 1 January 1996.

In pursuance of section 7 of the Police, Factories, etc. (Miscellaneous Provisions) Act 1916, I hereby make the following Order for all factories in which
the manufacture of tin or terne plates is carried on:—

1., 2. [*revoked*].

3. The occupier shall provide and maintain for the use of all persons
employed in the factory and remaining on the premises during the meal
intervals a suitable messroom, which shall be furnished with (a) sufficient tables
and chairs or benches with back rests, (b) adequate means of warming food and
boiling water, (c) suitable facilities *(a)* for washing, comprising a sufficient
supply of clean towels, soap and warm water. The messroom shall be sufficiently
warmed for use during meal intervals.
   The messroom shall be separate from the cloakroom and shall be placed
under the charge of a responsible person, and shall be kept clean.

   (a) **Washing facilities.** See INTRODUCTORY NOTE 20.

4. This Order shall come into force on 1 December 1917.

THE TINNING OF METAL HOLLOW-WARE, IRON DRUMS, AND HARNESS FURNITURE REGULATIONS 1909

(Dated 2 July 1909; S.R. & O. 1909 No. 720, as amended by S.I. 1973 No. 36, S.I. 1980 No. 1248 and S.I. 1989 No. 2311)

[Placard: Form 955]

Whereas the coating of metal articles with a mixture of tin and lead, or lead alone, has been certified in pursuance of section 79 of the Factory and Workshop Act 1901, to be dangerous: I hereby in pursuance of the powers conferred on me by that Act make the following Regulations and direct that they shall apply to all factories and workshops where *tinning* is carried on in the manufacture of metal hollow-ware, iron drums, and harness furniture.

Provided that these Regulatons shall not apply to—

(a) Any process in silver plating.
(b) Any process in which a soldering iron is used.
(c) Any other process if and so far as it is exempted by written certificate of the Chief Inspector *(a)* of Factories, on the ground that he is satisfied that any of these Regulations are not required for the protection of the persons employed, by reason of the intermittency or infrequency of the *tinning* or other special circumstances.

    Any such certificate of exemption shall be subject to the conditions therein prescribed and may be revoked at any time.

These Regulations shall come into force on 1 October 1909, except that regulation 1 shall come into force on 1 April 1910.

(a) **Inspector.** See INTRODUCTORY NOTE 24.

Definitions

In these Regulations—

"*Tinning*" means the dipping and wiping of any metal in the process of coating it with a mixture of tin and lead or lead alone where hydrochloric acid or any salt of that acid is used.

Duties

It shall be the duty of the occupier to observe Part I of these Regulations.

PART I

Duties of Employers

1. [*revoked*].

2. No person under school-leaving age shall be employed in *tinning*.

3.–13. [*revoked*].

THE WOODWORKING MACHINES REGULATIONS 1974

(S.I. 1974 No. 903, as amended by S.I. 1978 No. 1126, S.I. 1989 No. 1790, S.I. 1992 No. 2932 and S.I. 1992 No. 3004)

ARRANGEMENT OF REGULATIONS

The Secretary of State—

(a) in exercise of powers conferred by sections 17(3), 76 and 180(6) and (7) of the Factories Act 1961 and now vested in him and of all other power enabling him in that behalf; and

(b) after publishing, pursuant to Schedule 4 to the said Act of 1961, notice of the proposal to make the Regulations and after the holding of an inquiry under the Schedule into objections made to the draft,

hereby makes the following Regulations of which all with the exception of regulation 15 are special Regulations—

PART I
APPLICATION, INTERPRETATION AND EXEMPTIONS

1. Citation, commencement, revocation and amendment.—(1) These Regulations may be cited as the Woodworking Machines Regulations 1974 and shall come into operation on 24 November 1974 with the exception of regulation 41 which shall come into operation on 24 May 1976.

(2) The Regulations specified in columns 1 and 2 of Schedule 2 to these Regulations are hereby revoked to the extent respectively specified in relation thereto in column 3 of that Schedule.

(3) Regulation 67(2) of the Shipbuilding and Ship-repairing Regulations 1960 and regulation 42 of the Construction (General Provisions) Regulations 1961 shall not apply to the parts of woodworking machines required by these Regulations to be guarded or to have other safeguards.

1732

General note. Paragraphs (2), (3) are revoked by the Provision and Use of Work Regulations 1992, S.I. 1992 No. 2932, as from 1 January 1993 except, insofar as they apply to work equipment first provided for use in the premises or undertaking before 1 January 1993, they are revoked as from 1 January 1997.

A Guidance Note (booklet HS (R) 9) to these Regulations has been published by the Health and Safety Executive.

2. Interpretation.—(1) The Interpretation Act 1889 [Interpretation Act 1978] shall apply to the interpretation of these Regulations as it applies to the interpretation of an Act of Parliament, and as if these Regulations and the Regulations hereby revoked were Acts of Parliament.

(2) In these Regulations, unless the context otherwise requires, the following expressions have the meanings hereby assigned to them respectively, that is to say—

"*approved*" means approved for the time being for the purposes of these Regulations by certificate of the Chief Inspector *(a)*;

"*circular sawing machine*" means a sawing machine comprising a saw bench (including a bench in the form of a roller table and a bench incorporating a travelling table) with a spindle situated below the machine table to which a circular saw blade can be fitted for the purpose of dividing material into separate parts, but does not include a multiple rip machine, a straight line edging machine or any sawing machine in the operation of which the blade is moved towards the material which is being cut;

"*cutters*" include saw blades, chain cutters, knives, boring tools, detachable cutters and solid cutters;

"*factory*" includes any place *(b)* to which these Regulations apply;

"*machine table*" includes, in relation to a circular sawing machine, any frame which supports the material being cut;

"*narrow band sawing machine*" means a sawing machine designed to be fitted with a blade not exceeding 50 millimetres in width in the form of a continuous band or strip the cutting portion of which runs in a vertical direction, but does not include a log band sawing machine or a band re-sawing machine;

"*planing machine*" means a machine for *surfacing* or for thicknessing or a combined machine for both those operations but does not include a multi-cutter moulding machine having two or more cutter spindles;

"*principal Act*" means the Factories Act 1961 as amended by or under any other Act;

"*sawmill*" means the premises which are used solely or mainly for the purpose of sawing logs (including square logs) into planks or boards;

"*squared stock*" means material having a rectangular (including square) cross section of which the dimensions remain substantially constant throughout the length of the material;

"*surfacing*" means the planing or smoothing of the surface of material by passing it over cutters and includes chamfering and bevelling, but does not include moulding, tenoning, rebating or recessing;

"*vertical spindle moulding machine*" includes a high-speed routing machine; and

"*woodworking machine*" means any machine (including a portable machine) of a kind specified in Schedule 1 to these Regulations for use on all or any one or more of the following, that is to say, wood, cork and fibre board and material composed partly of any of those materials.

General note. Definitions "cutters", "machine table", "narrow band sawing machine", "sawmill" and "squared stock" are revoked by the Provision and Use of Equipment at Work Regulations 1992, S.I. 1992 No. 2932, as from 1 January 1993 except, insofar as they apply to work equipment first provided for use in the premises or undertaking before 1 January 1993, they are revoked as from 1 January 1997.

(a) **Inspector.** See INTRODUCTORY NOTE 24.

(b) **Place.** See reg. 3(1).

3.   Application and operation of Regulations.—(1) These Regulations, other than regulation 15 (which relates to the sale or hire of machinery), shall apply to any of the following, in which any *woodworking machine* is used, that is to say, to *factories* and to any premises, places, processes, operations and works to which the provisions of Part IV of the *principal Act* with respect to special regulations for safety and health are applied by any of the following provisions of that Act, namely, section 123 (which relates to electrical stations), section 124 (which relates to institutions), section 125 (which relates to certain dock premises and certain warehouses), section 126 (which relates to ships) and section 127 (which relates to building operations and works of engineering construction).

(2) In relation to the parts of *woodworking machines* required by these Regulations to be guarded or to have other safeguards, the provisions of these Regulations as respects guarding and the provision of other safeguards are in substitution for the provisions of section 14(1) of the *principal Act* and accordingly the provisions of that subsection shall not apply in relation to any such parts.

(3) The provisions of regulation 12 are in substitution for section 3(1) of the *principal Act* and accordingly the provisions of that subsection shall not apply in relation to any room to which that regulation applies.

(4) Except as provided in paragraphs (2) and (3) of this regulation, the provisions of these Regulations shall be in addition to and not in substitution for the provisions of the principal Act.

General note. Paragraph (2) is revoked by the Provision and Use of Work Equipment Regulations 1992, S.I. 1992 No. 2932, as from 1 January 1993 except, insofar as it applies to work equipment first provided for use in the premises or undertaking before 1 January 1993, it is revoked as from 1 January 1997.

4.   Exemptions. The Chief Inspector (a) may (subject to such conditions, if any, as may be specified therein) by certificate (b) in writing (which he may in his discretion revoke at any time) exempt from all or any of the requirements of these Regulations—

(a)   any particular *woodworking machine* or any type of *woodworking machine*; or
(b)   any operation or process or any class or description of operations or processes; or
(c)   any *factory* or any part of any *factory* or any class or description of *factories* or parts thereof,

if he is satisfied that the requirements in respect of which the exemption is granted are not necessary for the protection of persons employed. Where such exemption is granted, a legible copy of the certificate, showing the conditions (if any) subject to which it has been granted, shall be kept posted in any *factory* in which the exemption applies in a position where it may be conveniently read by the persons employed.

(a) *Inspector.* See INTRODUCTORY NOTE 24.

(b) *Certificate.* Certificates of Exemption are set out following these Regulations.

PART II
ALL WOODWORKING MACHINES—GENERAL

5. Provision and construction of guards.—(1) Without prejudice to the other provisions of these Regulations, the *cutters* of every *woodworking machine* shall be enclosed by a guard or guards to the greatest extent that is practicable *(a)* having regard to the work being done thereat, unless the *cutters* are in such position as to be as safe to every person employed as they would be if so enclosed.

(2) All guards provided in pursuance of the foregoing paragraph of this regulation shall be of substantial construction *(b)*.

General note. This regulation is revoked by the Provision and Use of Work Equipment Regulations 1992, S.I. 1992 No. 2932, as from 1 January 1993 except, insofar as it applies to work equipment first provided for use in the premises or undertaking before 1 January 1993, it is revoked as from 1 January 1997.

(a) *Practicable.* See INTRODUCTORY NOTE 5.

(b) *Substantial construction.* See INTRODUCTORY NOTE 11.

6. Adjustment of machines and guards. No person shall, while the *cutters* are in motion—

(a) make any adjustment to any guard on a *woodworking machine* unless means are provided whereby such an adjustment can be made without danger; or

(b) make any adjustment to any part of a *woodworking machine*, except where the adjustment can be made without danger.

General note. This regulation is revoked by the Provision and Use of Work Equipment Regulations 1992, S.I. 1992 No. 2932, as from 1 January 1993 except, insofar as it applies to work equipment first provided for use in the premises or undertaking before 1 January 1993, it is revoked as from 1 January 1997.

7. Use and maintenance of guards, etc.—(1) At all times while the *cutters* are in motion, the guards and devices required by these Regulations and all such safeguards as are mentioned in regulation 8 shall be kept constantly in position and properly secured and adjusted except when, and to the extent to which, because of the nature of the work being done, the use of any such guard, device, or safeguard is rendered impracticable *(a)*:

Provided that the said exception shall not apply to the use of any guard required by regulations 18(1), 21(1) or (2), 22(1), 23, 28, 30 or 31.

(2) The said guards, devices, and safeguards, and all such applicances as are mentioned in regulation 14(1)(b) shall be properly maintained *(b)*.

General note. This regulation is revoked by the Provision and Use of Work Equipment Regulations 1992, S.I. 1992 No. 2932, as from 1 January 1993 except, insofar as it applies to work equipment first provided for use in the premises or undertaking before 1 January 1993, it is revoked as from 1 January 1997.

(a) Impracticable. See INTRODUCTORY NOTE 5.

(b) Properly maintained. See INTRODUCTORY NOTE 10.

8.   Exception from obligations to provide guards, etc. Regulations 5, 16, 21, 22, 26, 28, 30, 31 and 36 shall not apply to any machine in respect of which other safeguards are provided which render the machine as safe as it would be if the provisions of those regulations were complied with.

General note. This regulation is revoked by the Provision and Use of Work Equipment Regulations 1992, S.I. 1992 No. 2932, as from 1 January 1993 except, insofar as it applies to work equipment first provided for use in the premises or undertaking before 1 January 1993, it is revoked as from 1 January 1997.

9.   Machine controls. Every *woodworking machine* shall be provided with an efficient device or efficient devices for starting and stopping the machine and the control or controls of the device or devices shall be in such a position and of such design and construction as to be readily and conveniently operated by the person operating the machine.

General note. This regulation is revoked by the Provision and Use of Work Equipment Regulations 1992, S.I. 1992 No. 2932, as from 1 January 1993 except, insofar as it applies to work equipment first provided for use in the premises or undertaking before 1 January 1993, it is revoked as from 1 January 1997.

10.   Working space. There shall be provided around every *woodworking machine* sufficient clear and unobstructed space to enable, in so far as is thereby practicable *(a)*, the work being done at the machine to be done without risk of injury to persons employed.

General note. This regulation is revoked by the Workplace (Health, Safety and Welfare) Regulations 1992, S.I. 1992 No. 3004, as from 1 January 1993 except, in relation to any workplace or part of a workplace which is not a new workplace, or a modification, an extension or a conversion, it is revoked as from 1 January 1996.

(a) Practicable. See INTRODUCTORY NOTE 5.

11.   Floors. The floor or surface of the ground around every *woodworking machine* shall be maintained in good and level condition and, as far as reasonably practicable *(a)*, free from chips and other loose material and shall not be allowed to become slippery.

General note. This regulation is revoked by the Workplace (Health, Safety and Welfare) Regulations 1992, S.I. 1992 No. 3004, as from 1 January 1993 except, in relation to any workplace or part of a workplace which is not a new workplace, or a modification, an extension or a conversion, it is revoked as from 1 January 1996.

*(a) **Reasonably practicable.*** See INTRODUCTORY NOTE 5.

12. Temperature.—(1) Subject to the following provisions of this regulation, effective provision shall be made for securing and maintaining a reasonable temperature in every room or other place (not in the open air) in which a *woodworking machine* is being worked.

(2) In that part of any room or other place (not in the open air) in which a *woodworking machine* is being worked, a temperature of less than 13 degrees Celsius shall not be deemed at any time to be a reasonable temperature except where and in so far as the necessities of the business carried on make it impracticable *(a)* to maintain a temperature of at least 13 degrees Celsius.

(3) Where it is impracticable *(a)* for the aforesaid reasons to maintain a temperature of at least 13 degrees Celsius in any such part of a room or place as aforesaid, there shall be provided in the said part, to the extent that is reasonably practicable *(a)*, effective means of warming persons working there.

(4) There shall not be used in any such room or place as aforesaid any heating appliance other than an appliance in which the heating element or flame is so enclosed within the body of the appliance that there is no likelihood of the accidental ignition of any material in that room or place by reason of contact with or proximity to the heating element or any flame, except where the heating appliance is so positioned or protected that there is no such likelihood.

(5) Paragraphs (2) and (3) of this regulation shall in their application to parts of factories which are used as *sawmills* have effect as if for the references to 13 degrees Celsius there were substituted references to 10 degrees Celsius.

(6) No method of heating shall be employed which results in the escape into the air of any such room or place as aforesaid of any fume of such a character and to such extent as to be likely to be injurious *(b)* or offensive to persons employed therein.

General note. This regulation is revoked by Workplace (Health, Safety and Welfare) Regulations, S.I. 1992 No. 3004, as from 1 January 1993 except, in relation to any workplace or part of a workplace which is not a new workplace, or a modification, an extension or a conversion, it is revoked as from 1 January 1996.

*(a) **Practicable; reasonably practicable.*** See INTRODUCTORY NOTE 5.

*(b) **Likely to be injurious.*** In *Carmichael v Cockburn & Co* 1956 SC 487 the LJC took the view that "whether something is likely to be injurious is susceptible of ascertainment as a matter of objective fact. I cannot see what the state of knowledge of the occupier of the factory has got to do with it. The conditions are either present or absent." However, Lords Mackintosh and Birnam took the view that whether something was likely to be injurious had to be decided in the light of the employer's knowledge. See also *Boyle v Laidlaw & Fairgrieve Ltd* 1989 SLT 139n.

13.   Training.—(1) No person shall be employed on any kind of work at a *woodworking machine* unless—

    (a) he has been sufficiently trained at machines of a class to which that machine belongs in the kind of work on which he is to be employed; and

    (b) he has been sufficiently instructed in accordance with paragraph (2) of this regulation,

except where he works under the adequate supervision of a person who has a thorough knowledge and experience of the working of the machine and of the matters specified in paragraph (2) of this regulation.

(2) Every person, while being trained to work at a *woodworking machine*, shall be fully and carefully instructed as to the dangers arising in connection with such a machine, the precautions to be observed, the requirements of these Regulations which apply and, in the case of a person being trained to operate a *woodworking machine*, the method of using the guards, devices and appliances required by these Regulations.

(3) Without prejudice to the foregoing provisions of this Regulation, a person who has not attained the age of 18 years shall not operate any *circular sawing machine*, any sawing machine fitted with a circular blade, any *planing machine* for *surfacing* which is not mechanically fed, or any *vertical spindle moulding machine*, unless he has successfully completed an approved course of training in the operation of such a machine. Save that where required to do so as part of such a course of training, he may operate such a machine under the adequate supervision of a person who has a thorough knowledge and experience of the working of the machine and of the matters specified in paragraph (2) of this regulation.

14.   Duties of persons employed.—(1) Every person employed shall, while he is operating a *woodworking machine*—

    (a) use and keep in proper adjustment the guards and devices provided in accordance with these Regulations and all such safeguards as are mentioned in regulation 8; and

    (b) use the spikes, push-sticks, push-blocks, jigs, holders and back stops provided in accordance with these Regulations,

except (in cases other than those specified in the proviso in regulation 7(1)) when, because of the nature of the work being done, the use of the said guards, devices and other safeguards, or of the appliance mentioned in sub-paragraph (b) of this paragraph, is rendered impracticable *(a)*.

(2) It shall be the duty of every person, being a person employed by the occupier of a *factory* and trained in accordance with regulation 13, who discovers any defect in any *woodworking machine* in that *factory* or in any guard, device or appliance provided in accordance with these Regulations or in any such safeguard as is mentioned in regulation 8 (being a defect which may affect the safe working of a *woodworking machine*) or who discovers that the floor or surface of the ground around any *woodworking machine* in that *factory* is not in good and level condition or is slippery, to report the matter without delay to the occupier, manager or other appropriate person.

General note. This regulation is revoked by the Provision and Use of Work Equipment Regulations 1992, S.I. 1992 No. 2932, as from 1 January 1993 except, insofar as it

applies to work equipment first provided for use in the premises or undertaking before 1 January 1993, it is revoked as from 1 January 1997.

   (a) *Impracticable.* See INTRODUCTORY NOTE 5.

15.   Sale or hire of machinery. The provisions of section 17(2) of the principal Act (which prohibits the sale or letting on hire of certain machines which do not comply with the requirements of that section) shall extend to any *woodworking machine* which is for use in a *factory* and which is not provided with such guards or devices as are necessary, and is not so designed and constructed as to enable any requirement of the following regulations to be complied with, that is to say, regulations 9, 16, 17(3), 21, 22, 24, 25, 26, 27, 28, 30 and 39 in so far as the requirement applies to that *woodworking machine.*

   General note. This regulation is revoked by the Provision and Use of Work Equipment Regulations 1992, S.I. 1992 No. 2932, as from 1 January 1993 except, insofar as it applies to work equipment first provided for use in the premises or undertaking before 1 January 1993, it is revoked as from 1 January 1997.

PART III
CIRCULAR SAWING MACHINES

16.   Guarding circular sawing machines.—(1) That part of the saw blade of every *circular sawing machine* which is below the machine table shall be guarded to the greatest extent that is practicable *(a)*.

   (2) There shall be provided for every *circular sawing machine* a riving knife which shall be securely fixed by means of a suitable device situated below the machine table, be behind and in a direct line with the saw blade, have a smooth surface, be strong, rigid and easily adjustable and fulfil the following conditions:—

   (a)   the edge of the knife nearer the saw blade shall form an arc of a circle having a radius not exceeding the radius of the largest saw blade with which the saw bench is designed to be used;
   (b)   the knife shall be capable of being so adjusted and shall be kept so adjusted that it is as close as practicable to the saw blade, having regard to the nature of the work being done, and so that at the level of the machine table the distance between the edge of the knife nearer to the saw blade and the teeth of the saw blade does not exceed 12 millimetres;
   (c)   for a saw blade of a diameter of less than 600 millimetres, the knife shall extend upwards from the machine table to a height above the machine table which is not more than 25 millimetres below the highest point of the saw blade, and for a saw blade of a diameter of 600 millimetres or over, the knife shall extend upwards from the machine table to a height of at least 225 millimetres above the machine table; and
   (d)   in the case of a parallel plate saw blade the knife shall be thicker than the plate of the saw blade.

   (3) Without prejudice to the requirements of regulation 18(1), that part of the saw blade of every *circular sawing machine* which is above the machine table shall be guarded with a strong and easily adjustable guard, which shall be

capable of being so adjusted and shall be kept so adjusted that it extends from the top of the riving knife to a point above the upper surface of the material being cut which is as close as practicable *(a)* to the surface or, where *squared stock* is being fed to the saw blade by hand, to a point which is not more than 12 millimetres above the upper surface of the material being cut.

(4) The guard referred to in the last foregoing paragraph shall have a flange of adequate depth on each side of the saw blade and the said guard shall be kept so adjusted that the said flanges extend beyond the roots of the teeth of the saw blade. Where the guard is fitted with an adjustable front extention piece, that extension piece shall have along the whole of its length a flange of adequate depth on the side remote from the fence and the said extension piece shall be kept so adjusted that the flange extends beyond the roots of the teeth of the saw blade:

Provided that in the case of *circular sawing machines* manufactured before the date of the coming into operation of this regulation *(b)*, the requirements of this paragraph shall not apply until two years after the said date and in the case of such machines, until the expiration of the said period, the said guard shall have along the whole of its length a flange of adequate depth on the side remote from the fence and shall be kept so adjusted that the said flange extends beyond the roots of the teeth of the saw blade.

General note. This regulation is revoked by the Provision and Use of Work Equipment Regulations 1992, S.I. 1992 No. 2932, as from 1 January 1993 except, insofar as it applies to work equipment first provided for use in the premises or undertaking before 1 January 1993, it is revoked as from 1 January 1997.

(a) Practicable. See INTRODUCTORY NOTE 5.

(b) Coming into operation. 24 November 1974 (reg. 1(1)).

17. Sizes of circular saw blades.—(1) In the case of a *circular sawing machine* the spindle of which is not capable of being operated at more than one working speed, no saw blade shall be used thereat for dividing material into separate parts which has a diameter of less than six-tenths of the diameter of the largest saw blade with which the saw bench is designed to be used.

(2) In the case of a *circular sawing machine* which has arrangements for the spindle to operate at more than one working speed, no saw blade shall be used thereat for dividing material into separate parts which has a diameter of less than six-tenths of the diameter of the largest saw blade which can properly be used at the fastest working speed of the spindle at that saw bench.

(3) There shall be securely affixed to every *circular sawing machine* a notice specifying the diameter of the smallest saw blade which may be used in the machine in compliance with paragraph (1) or (2) (as the case may be) of this regulation.

General note. This regulation is revoked by the Provision and Use of Work Equipment Regulations 1992, S.I. 1992 No. 2932, as from 1 January 1993 except, insofar as it applies to work equipment first provided for use in the premises or undertaking before 1 January 1993, it is revoked as from 1 January 1997.

18. Limitations on the use of circular sawing machines for certain purposes.—(1) No *circular sawing machine* shall be used for cutting any rebate, tenon, mould or groove, unless that part of the saw blade or other cutter which is above the machine table is effectively guarded.

(2) No *circular sawing machine* shall be used for a ripping operation (other than any such operation involved in cutting a rebate, tenon, mould or groove) unless the teeth of the saw blade project throughout the operation through the upper surface of the material being cut.

(3) No *circular sawing machine* shall be used for cross-cutting logs or branches unless the material being cut is firmly held by a gripping device securely fixed to a travelling table.

General note. This regulation is revoked by the Provision and Use of Work Equipment Regulations 1992, S.I. 1992 No. 2932, as from 1 January 1993 except, insofar as it applies to work equipment first provided for use in the premises or undertaking before 1 January 1993, it is revoked as from 1 January 1997.

19. Provision of push-sticks.—(1) A suitable push-stick shall be provided and kept available for use at every *circular sawing machine* which is fed by hand.

(2) Except where the distance between a circular saw blade and its fence is so great or the method of feeding material to the saw blade is such that the use of a push-stick can safely be dispensed with, the push-stick so provided shall be used—

(a) to exert feeding pressure on the material between the saw blade and the fence throughout any cut of 300 millimetres or less in length;

(b) to exert feeding pressure on the material between the saw blade and the fence during the last 300 millimetres of any cut of more than 300 millimetres in length; and

(c) to remove from between the saw blade and the fence pieces of material which have been cut.

General note. This regulation is revoked by the Provision and Use of Work Equipment Regulations 1992, S.I. 1992 No. 2932, as from 1 January 1993 except, insofar as it applies to work equipment first provided for use in the premises or undertaking before 1 January 1993, it is revoked as from 1 January 1997.

20. Removal of material cut by circular sawing machines.—(1) Except as provided in paragraph (3) of this regulation, where any person (other than the operator) is employed at a *circular sawing machine* in removing while the saw blade is in motion material which has been cut, that person shall not for that purpose stand elsewhere than at the delivery end of the machine.

(2) Except as provided in paragraph (3) of this regulation, where any person (other than the operator) is employed at a *circular sawing machine* in removing while the saw blade is in motion material which has been cut, the machine table shall be constructed or shall be extended over its whole width (by the provision of rollers or otherwise) so that the distance between the delivery end of the table or of any such extension thereof and the up-running part of the saw blade is not less than 1200 millimetres:

Provided that this requirement shall not apply to moveable machines which cannot accommodate a blade having a diameter of more than 450 millimetres.

(3) The requirements of paragraphs (1) and (2) of this regulation shall not apply to a *circular sawing machine* having a saw bench in the form of a roller table or a saw bench incorporating a table which (in either case) is in motion during the cutting operation.

PART IV
MULTIPLE RIP SAWING MACHINES AND STRAIGHT LINE EDGE MACHINES

21. Multiple rip sawing machines and straight line edging machines.— (1) Every multiple rip sawing machine and straight line edging machine shall be provided on the operator's side of the infeed pressure rollers with a suitable device which shall be of such design and so constructed as to contain so far as practicable *(a)* any material accidentally ejected by the machine and every such device shall extend for not less than the full width of the said pressure rollers.

(2) Every multiple rip sawing machine and straight line edging machine on which the saw spindle is mounted above the machine table shall, in addition to the device required to be provided under paragraph (1) of this regulation, be fitted on the side remote from the fence with a suitable guard, which shall extend from the edge of the said device along a line parallel to the blade of the saw at least 300 millimetres towards the axis of the saw and shall be of such a design and so constructed as to contain as far as practicable *(b)* any material accidentally ejected from the machine.

(3) In the case of multiple rip sawing machines and straight line edging machines manufactured before the date of the coming into operation of this regulation *(b)*, the requirements of this regulation shall not apply until two years after the said date.

General note. This regulation is revoked by the Provision and Use of Work Equipment Regulations 1992, S.I. 1992 No. 2932, as from 1 January 1993 except, insofar as it applies to work equipment first provided for use in the premises or undertaking before 1 January 1993, it is revoked as from 1 January 1997.

(a) Practicable. See INTRODUCTORY NOTE 5.

(b) Coming into operation. 24 November 1974 (reg. 1(1)).

PART V
NARROW BAND SAWING MACHINES

22. Narrow band sawing machines.—(1) The saw wheels of every narrow band sawing machine and the whole of the blade of every such machine, except that part of the blade which runs downwards between the top wheel and the machine table, shall be enclosed by a guard or guards of substantial construction.

(2) The part of the blade of every such machine as aforesaid which is above the friction disc or rollers and below the top wheel shall be guarded by a frontal plate which is as close as is practicable *(a)* to the saw blade and has at least one flange at right angles to the place and extending beyond the saw blade.

(3) The friction disc or rollers of every such machine as aforesaid shall be kept so adjusted that they are as close to the surface of the machine table as is practicable *(a)* having regard to the nature of the work being done.

General note. This regulation is revoked by the Provision and Use of Work Equipment Regulations 1992, S.I. 1992 No. 2932, as from 1 January 1993 except, insofar as it applies to work equipment first provided for use in the premises or undertaking before 1 January 1993, it is revoked as from 1 January 1997.

(*a*) *Practicable.* See INTRODUCTORY NOTE 5.

PART VI
PLANING MACHINES

23. Limitation of the use of planing machines. No *planing machine* shall be used for cutting any rebate, recess, tenon or mould unless the *cutter* is effectively guarded.

General note. This regulation is revoked by the Provision and Use of Work Equipment Regulations 1992, S.I. 1992 No. 2932, as from 1 January 1993 except, insofar as it applies to work equipment first provided for use in the premises or undertaking before 1 January 1993, it is revoked as from 1 January 1997.

24. Cutter blocks for planing machines for surfacing. Every *planing machine* for *surfacing* which is not mechanically fed shall be fitted with a cylindrical *cutter* block.

General note. This regulation is revoked by the Provision and Use of Work Equipment Regulations 1992, S.I. 1992 No. 2932, as from 1 January 1993 except, insofar as it applies to work equipment first provided for use in the premises or undertaking before 1 January 1993, it is revoked as from 1 January 1997.

25. Table gap.—(1) Every *planing machine* for *surfacing* which is not mechanically fed shall be so designed and constructed as to be capable of adjustment so that the clearance between the *cutters* and the front edge of the delivery table does not exceed 6 millimetres (measured radially from the centre of the *cutter* block) and the gap between the feed table and the delivery table is as small as practicable having regard to the operation being performed, and no such *planing machine* which is not so adjusted shall be used for *surfacing*.

(2) In the case of *planing machines* manufactured before the date of the coming into operation of this regulation (*a*), the requirements of the foregoing paragraph of this regulation shall not apply until twelve months after the said date.

General note. This regulation is revoked by the Provision and Use of Work Equipment Regulations 1992, S.I. 1992 No. 2932, as from 1 January 1993 except, insofar as it applies to work equipment first provided for use in the premises or undertaking before 1 January 1993, it is revoked as from 1 January 1997.

(*a*) *Coming into operation.* 24 November 1974 (reg. 1(1)).

26. Provision of bridge guards.—(1) Every *planing machine* for *surfacing* which is not mechanically fed shall be provided with a bridge guard which shall be strong and rigid, have a length not less than the full length of the *cutter* block and a width not less than the diameter of the *cutter* block and be so constructed as to be capable of easy adjustment both in a vertical and horizontal direction.

(2) Every bridge and guard provided in pursuance of paragraph (1) of this regulation shall be mounted on the machine in a position which is approximately central over the axis of the *cutter* block and shall be so constructed as to prevent its being accidentally displaced from that position.

(3) In the case of *planing machines* manufactured before the date of the coming into operation of this regulation *(a)*, the requirements of this regulation shall not apply until twelve months after the said date, and until the expiration of the said period such machines for *surfacing* shall be provided with a bridge guard capable of covering the full length and breadth of the cutting slot in the bench and so constructed as to be easily adjusted both in a vertical and horizontal direction.

General note. This regulation is revoked by the Provision and Use of Work Equipment Regulations 1992, S.I. 1992 No. 2932, as from 1 January 1993 except, insofar as it applies to work equipment first provided for use in the premises or undertaking before 1 January 1993, it is revoked as from 1 January 1997.

(a) Coming into operation. 24 November 1974 (reg. 1(1)).

27. Adjustment of bridge guards.—(1) While a *planing machine* which is not mechanically fed is being used for *surfacing*, the bridge guard provided in pursuance of regulation 26 shall be so adjusted as to enable, so far as is thereby practicable *(a)*, the work being done at the machine to be done without risk of injury to persons employed.

(2) Except as provided in paragraph (4) of this regulation and in regulation 29, when a wider surface of *squared stock* is being planed or smoothed, the bridge guard so provided shall be adjusted so that the distance between the end of the guard and the fence does not exceed 10 millimetres and the underside of the guard is not more than 10 millimetres above the surface of the material.

(3) Except as provided in paragraph (4) of this regulation, when a narrower surface of *squared stock* is being planed or smoothed, the bridge guard so provided shall be adjusted so that the end of the guard is at a point not more than 10 millimetres from the surface of the said material which is remote from the fence and the underside of the guard is not more than 10 millimetres above the surface of the feed table.

(4) When the planing or smoothing both of a wider and of a narrower surface of *squared stock* is being carried out, one operation immediately following the other, the bridge guard so provided shall be adjusted so that when a wider surface is being planed or smoothed the underside of the guard is not more than 10 millimetres above the upper surface of the material and, when a narrower surface is being planed or smoothed, the end of the guard is at a point not more than 10 millimetres from the surface of the said material which is remote from the fence.

(5) Except as provided in paragraph (6) of this regulation, when the planing of *squared stock* of square cross section is being carried out, the bridge guard so provided shall be adjusted in a manner which complies with the requirements either of paragraph (2) or of paragraph (3) of this regulation.

(6) When the planing of two adjoining surfaces of *squared stock* of square cross section is being carried out, one operation immediately following the other, the bridge guard so provided shall be adjusted so that neither the height of the underside of the guard above the feed table nor the distance between the end of the guard and the fence exceeds the width of the material by more than 10 millimetres.

(7) When the smoothing of *squared stock* of square cross section is being carried out, the bridge guard so provided shall be adjusted in a manner which complies with the requirements either of paragraph (2) or paragraph (3) or of paragraph (6) of this regulation.

General note. This regulation is revoked by the Provision and Use of Work Equipment Regulations 1992, S.I. 1992 No. 2932, as from 1 January 1993 except, insofar as it applies to work equipment first provided for use in the premises or undertaking before 1 January 1993, it is revoked as from 1 January 1997.

(a) **Practicable.** See INTRODUCTORY NOTE 5.

28. Cutter block guards.—(1) In addition to being provided with a bridge guard as required by Regulation 26, every *planing machine* for *surfacing* which is not mechanically fed shall be provided with a strong, effective and easily adjustable guard for that part of the *cutter* block which is on the side of the fence remote from the bridge guard.

(2) In the case of *planing machines* manufactured before the date of the coming into operation of this regulation *(a)*, the requirements of the foregoing paragraph of this regulation shall not apply until twelve months after the said date.

General note. This regulation is revoked by the Provision and Use of Work Equipment Regulations 1992, S.I. 1992 No. 2932, as from 1 January 1993 except, insofar as it applies to work equipment first provided for use in the premises or undertaking before 1 January 1993, it is revoked as from 1 January 1997.

(a) **Coming into operation.** 24 November 1974 (reg. 1(1)).

29. Provision and use of push-blocks. When a wider surface of *square stock* is being planed or smoothed and by reason of the shortness of the material the work cannot be done with the bridge guard adjusted as required by regulation 27(2), a suitable push-block having suitable handholds which afford the operator a firm grip shall be provided and used.

General note. This regulation is revoked by the Provision and Use of Work Equipment Regulations 1992, S.I. 1992 No. 2932, as from 1 January 1993 except, insofar as it applies to work equipment first provided for use in the premises or undertaking before 1 January 1993, it is revoked as from 1 January 1997.

30. Combined machines used for thicknessing. That part of the *cutter* block or a combined machine which is exposed in the table gap shall when the said machine is used for thicknessing, be effectively guarded.

General note. This regulation is revoked by the Provision and Use of Work Equipment Regulations 1992, S.I. 1992 No. 2932, as from 1 January 1993 except, insofar as it applies to work equipment first provided for use in the premises or undertaking before 1 January 1993, it is revoked as from 1 January 1997.

31.   Protection against ejected material.—(1) Every *planing machine* used for thicknessing shall be provided on the operator's side of the feed roller with sectional feed rollers, or other suitable devices which shall be of such a design and so constructed as to restrain so far as practicable *(a)* any workpiece ejected by the machine.

(2) Paragraph (1) of this regulation shall not apply to any machine manu-factured before the date of coming into operation of this regulation *(b)*; provided that—

(a)   not more than one work piece at a time shall be fed to any such machine, and

(b)   there shall be securely affixed to every such machine a notice specifying that only single pieces shall be fed.

General note. This regulation is revoked by the Provision and Use of Work Equipment Regulations 1992, S.I. 1992 No. 2932, as from 1 January 1993 except, insofar as it applies to work equipment first provided for use in the premises or undertaking before 1 January 1993, it is revoked as from 1 January 1997.

(a) Practicable. See INTRODUCTORY NOTE 5.

(b) Coming into operation. 24 November 1974 (reg. 1(1)).

PART VII
VERTICAL SPINDLE MOULDING MACHINES

32.   Construction, maintenance and mounting of cutters etc. Every detach-able *cutter* for any *vertical spindle moulding machine* shall be of the correct thickness for the *cutter* block or spindle on which it is to be mounted and shall be so mounted as to prevent it, so far as practicable *(a)*, from becoming acciden-tally detached therefrom.

General note. This regulation is revoked by the Provision and Use of Work Equipment Regulations 1992, S.I. 1992 No. 2932, as from 1 January 1993 except, insofar as it applies to work equipment first provided for use in the premises or undertaking before 1 January 1993, it is revoked as from 1 January 1997.

(a) Practicable. See INTRODUCTORY NOTE 5.

33.   Provision of false fences. Where straight fences are being used for the purposes of the work being done at a *vertical spindle moulding machine*, the gap between the fences shall be reduced as far as practicable *(a)* by a false fence or otherwise.

General note. This regulation is revoked by the Provision and Use of Work Equipment Regulations 1992, S.I. 1992 No. 2932, as from 1 January 1993 except, insofar as it

applies to work equipment first provided for use in the premises or undertaking before 1 January 1993, it is revoked as from 1 January 1997.

(*a*) *Practicable.* See INTRODUCTORY NOTE 5.

34. Provision of jigs or holders. Where by reason of the work being done at a *vertical spindle moulding machine* it is impracticable (*a*) to provide in pursuance of regulation 5 a guard enclosing the *cutters* of the said machine to such an extent that they are effectively guarded, but it is practicable (*a*) to provide, in addition to the guard required to be provided by regulation 5, a jig or holder of such a design and so constructed as to hold firmly the material being machined and having suitable handholds which afford the operator a firm grip, the machine shall not be used unless such a jig or holder is provided.

General note. This regulation is revoked by the Provision and Use of Work Equipment Regulations 1992, S.I. 1992 No. 2932, as from 1 January 1993 except, insofar as it applies to work equipment first provided for use in the premises or undertaking before 1 January 1993, it is revoked as from 1 January 1997.

(*a*) *Practicable.* See INTRODUCTORY NOTE 5.

35. Design and construction of guards for protection against ejected parts. Every guard provided in pursuance of regulation 5 for the *cutters* of any *vertical spindle moulding machine* shall be of such a design and so constructed as to contain, so far as reasonably practicable (*a*), any part of the *cutters* or their fixing appliance or any part thereof in the event of their ejection.

General note. This regulation is revoked by the Provision and Use of Work Equipment Regulations 1992, S.I. 1992 No. 2932, as from 1 January 1993 except, insofar as it applies to work equipment first provided for use in the premises or undertaking before 1 January 1993, it is revoked as from 1 January 1997.

(*a*) *Reasonably practicable.* See INTRODUCTORY NOTE 5.

36. Provision and use of back stops. Where the work being done at a *vertical spindle moulding machine* is work in which the cutting of the material being machined commences otherwise than at the end of a surface of the said material and it is impracticable (*a*) to provide a jig or holder in pursuance of regulation 34, the trailing end of the said material shall if practicable (*a*) be supported by a suitable back stop where this would prevent the said material being thrown back when the *cutters* first make contact with it.

General note. This regulation is revoked by the Provision and Use of Work Equipment Regulations 1992, S.I. 1992 No. 2932, as from 1 January 1993 except, insofar as it applies to work equipment first provided for use in the premises or undertaking before 1 January 1993, it is revoked as from 1 January 1997.

(*a*) *Impracticable; practicable.* See INTRODUCTORY NOTE 5.

37. Limitation on the use of vertical spindle moulding machines. No work shall be done on a *vertical spindle moulding machine* being work in which the cutting of the material being machined commences otherwise than at the end of a surface of the said material and during the progress of the cutting the material is moved in the same direction as the movement of the *cutters*, unless a jig or holder provided in pursuance of regulation 34 is being used.

General note. This regulation is revoked by the Provision and Use of Work Equipment Regulations 1992, S.I. 1992 No. 2932, as from 1 January 1993 except, insofar as it applies to work equipment first provided for use in the premises or undertaking before 1 January 1993, it is revoked as from 1 January 1997.

38.   Provision of spikes or push-sticks. Where the nature of the work being performed at a *vertical spindle moulding machine* is such that the use of a suitable spike or push-stick would enable the work to be carried on without unnecessary risk, such a spike or push-stick shall be provided and kept available *(a)* for use.

General note. This regulation is revoked by the Provision and Use of Work Equipment Regulations 1992, S.I. 1992 No. 2932, as from 1 January 1993 except, insofar as it applies to work equipment first provided for use in the premises or undertaking before 1 January 1993, it is revoked as from 1 January 1997.

(a) **Kept available.** In *Schwalb v H Fass & Sons Ltd* (1946) 175 LT 345, it was held that the similar requirement of the superseded regulations was not complied with merely by keeping available material from which a spike or push-stick could be made.

39.   Machines driven by two speed motors.—(1) Where the motor driving a *vertical spindle moulding machine* (other than a high-speed routing machine) is designed to operate at two working speeds the device controlling the speed of the motor shall be arranged that the motor cannot run at the higher of those speeds, without first running at the lower of those speeds.

(2) In the case of machines manufactured before the coming into operation of this regulation (a), the requirements of the foregoing paragraph of this regulation shall not apply until twelve months after the said date.

(a) Coming into operation. 24 November 1974 (reg. 1(1)).

PART VIII
EXTRACTION EQUIPMENT AND MAINTENANCE

40.   Cleaning of saw blades. The blade of a sawing machine shall not be cleaned by hand while the blade is in motion.

General note. This regulation is revoked by the Provision and Use of Work Equipment Regulations 1992, S.I. 1992 No. 2932, as from 1 January 1993 except, insofar as it applies to work equipment first provided for use in the premises or undertaking before 1 January 1993, it is revoked as from 1 January 1997.

41.   Extraction of chips and other particles. Effective exhaust appliances shall be provided and maintained at every *planing machine* used for thicknessing other than a combined machine for *surfacing* and thicknessing, every *vertical spindle moulding machine*, every multi-cutter moulding machine, every tenoning machine and every automatic lathe, for collecting from a position as close to the *cutters* as practicable *(a)* and to the extent that it is practicable, the chips and other particles of material removed by the action of the *cutters* and for discharging them into a suitable receptacle or place:

Providing that this regulation shall not apply to any high-speed routing machine which incorporates means for blowing away from the *cutters* the chips or particles as they are removed or to either of the following which is not used for more than six hours in any week, that is to say, any *verticle spindle moulding machine* and any tenoning machine.

General note. This regulation is revoked by the Provision and Use of Work Equipment Regulations 1992, S.I. 1992 No. 2932, as from 1 January 1993 except, insofar as it applies to work equipment first provided for use in the premises or undertaking before 1 January 1993, it is revoked as from 1 January 1997.

(a) **Practicable.** See INTRODUCTORY NOTE 5.

42. Maintenance and fixing.—(1) Every *woodworking machine* and every part therefore, including *cutters* and *cutter* blocks, shall be of good construction, sound material *(a)* and properly maintained *(b)*.

(2) Every *woodworking machine*, other than a machine which is held in the hand, shall be securely fixed to a foundation, floor, or to a substantial part of the structure of the premises, save that where that is impracticable *(c)*, other arrangements shall be made to ensure its stability.

General note. This regulation is revoked by the Provision and Use of Work Equipment Regulations 1992, S.I. 1992 No. 2932, as from 1 January 1993 except, insofar as it applies to work equipment first provided for use in the premises or undertaking before 1 January 1993, it is revoked as from 1 January 1997.

(a) **Good construction, sound material.** See INTRODUCTORY NOTE 11.

(b) **Properly maintained.** See INTRODUCTORY NOTE 10.

(c) **Impracticable.** See INTRODUCTORY NOTE 5.

PART IX
LIGHTING

43. Lighting. In addition to the requirements of subsections (1) and (4) of section 5 in the *principal Act*, the following provisions shall have effect in respect of any work done with any *woodworking machine*—

(a) the lighting, whether natural or artificial, for every *woodworking machine* shall be sufficient and suitable for the purpose for which the machine is used;

(b) the means of artificial lighting for every *woodworking machine* shall be so placed or shaded as to prevent glare and so that direct rays of light do not impinge on the eyes of the operator while he is operating such machine.

General note. This regulation is revoked by the Provision and Use of Work Equipment Regulations 1992, S.I. 1992 No. 2932, as from 1 January 1993 except, insofar as it applies to work equipment first provided for use in the premises or undertaking before 1 January 1993, it is revoked as from 1 January 1997.

PART X

NOISE

44.   [*revoked*].

SCHEDULE 1

Regulation 2(2)

MACHINES WHICH ARE WOODWORKING MACHINES FOR THE PURPOSES OF
THESE REGULATIONS

1.   Any sawing machine designed to be fitted with one or more circular blades.
2.   Grooving machines.
3.   Any sawing machine designed to be fitted with a blade in the form of continuous band or strip.
4.   Chain sawing machines.
5.   Mortising machines.
6.   Planing machines.
7.   Vertical spindle moulding machines (including high-speed routing machines).
8.   Multi-cutter moulding machines having two or more cutter spindles.
9.   Tenoning machines.
10.   Trenching machines.
11.   Automatic and semi-automatic lathes.
12.   Boring machines.

SCHEDULE 2

Regulation 1(2)

Column 1 *Regulations revoked*	Column 2 *References*	Column 3 *Extent of Revocation*
1. The Woodworking Machinery Regulations 1922.	S.R. & O. 1922/1196 (Rev. VII, p. 458: 1922, p. 273).	The whole Regulations.
2. The Woodworking Machinery (Amendment) Regulations 1927.	S.R. & O. 1927/207 (Rev. VII, p. 462: 1927, p. 440).	The whole Regulations.
3. The Woodworking (Amendment of Scope) Special Regulations 1945.	S.R. & O. 1945/1227 (Rev. VII, p. 462: 1945 I, p. 380).	The whole Regulations.
4. The Railway Running Sheds (No. 2) Regulations 1961.	S.I. 1961/1768 (1961 II p. 3410).	In the Schedule, the items numbered 2, 5 and 9.

CERTIFICATE OF EXEMPTION NO. 1
F 2477, 12 June 1975

Whereas I am satisfied that, as respects planing machines fitted with the attachment specified in Schedule 1 to this Certificate, the requirements of those parts of regulation 23 of the Woodworking Machines Regulations 1974 relating to the cutting of any rebate or tenon are not necessary for the protection of persons employed:

Now, therefore, in pursuance of the powers conferred on me by regulation 4 of the said Regulations, I hereby exempt the said machines from the requirements of those parts of regulation 23 relating to the cutting of any rebate or tenon subject to the conditions specified in Schedule 2.

This Certificate shall remain in force until revoked in writing by the Chief Inspector of Factories.

SCHEDULE 1

The attachment to which this exemption applies is a tenoning attachment made by Multico Limited, Salfords, Redhill, Surrey, consisting of a carriage to which the material to be machined is clamped and two rails on which the carriage runs, the rails being connected together by a metal frame which is bolted to the front of the machine table.

SCHEDULE 2

1. The material to be machined shall be clamped to the carriage.
2. There shall be provided a strong and easily adjustable guard having a length not less than the working length of the cutter block and width not less than the diameter of the cutter block.
3. The guard shall be so adjusted as to enable, so far as is thereby practicable, the work being done at the machine to be done without risk of injury to persons employed.

CERTIFICATE OF EXEMPTION NO. 2
F 2478, 5 August 1975

Whereas I am satisfied that, as respects planing machines fitted with the attachment specified in Schedule 1 to this Certificate, the requirements of those parts of regulation 23 of the Woodworking Machines Regulations 1974 relating to the cutting of any rebate or tenon are not necessary for the protection of persons employed:

Now, therefore, in pursuance of the powers conferred on me by regulation 4 of the said Regulations, I hereby exempt the said machines from the requirements of those parts of regulation 23 relating to the cutting of any rebate or tenon, subject to the conditions specified in Schedule 2.

This Certificate shall remain in force until revoked in writing by the Chief Inspector of Factories.

SCHEDULE 1

The attachment to which this exemption applies is a tenoning attachment made by A. Cooksley Limited, The Causeway, Staines, consisting of a carriage to which the material to be machined is clamped, supported on slides on which the carriage runs, the slides being mounted on the front of the machine table.

SCHEDULE 2

1.   The material to be machined shall be clamped to the carriage.
2.   There shall be provided a strong and easily adjustable guard having a length not
less than the working length of the cutter block and a width not less than the diameter of
the cutter block.
3.   The guard shall be so adjusted as to enable, so far as is thereby practicable, the
work being done at the machine to be done without risk of injury to persons employed.

THE YARN (DYED BY LEAD COMPOUNDS) HEADING REGULATIONS 1907

(Dated 6 August 1907; S.R. & O. 1907 No. 616, as amended by S.I. 1973 No. 36, S.I. 1980 No. 1248 and S.I. 1989 No. 2311)

Whereas the process of *heading* of yarn dyed by means of a lead compound has been certified in pursuance of section 79 of the Factory and Workshop Act 1901, to be dangerous.

I hereby, in pursuance of the powers conferred on me by that Act, make the following Regulations, and direct that they shall apply to all factories in which the said process is carried on:

Provided that if the Chief Inspector *(a)* of Factories is satisfied, with regard to any such factory, that the *heading* of yarn dyed by means of a lead compound will not occupy more than three hours in any week, he may, by certificate, suspend regulations 2, 3, 4, 7(a), and 8(a), or any of them. Every such certificate shall be in writing, signed by the Chief Inspector *(a)* of Factories, and shall be revocable at any time by further certificate.

(a) **Inspector.** See INTRODUCTORY NOTE 24.

Definitions

"*Heading*" means the manipulation of yarn dyed by means of a lead compound over a bar or post, and includes picking, making-up, and noddling.

"*Employed*" means employed in *heading* of yarn dyed by means of a lead compound.

Duties

It shall be the duty of the occupier to observe Part I of these Regulations.

PART I
DUTIES OF EMPLOYERS

1. [*revoked*].

2. No person under school-leaving age shall be employed.

3.–8. [*revoked*].

PART 7

CONSTRUCTION

SUMMARY

THE CONSTRUCTION (GENERAL PROVISIONS) REGULATIONS 1961

(S.I. 1961 No. 1580, as amended by S.I. 1966 No. 94, S.I. 1974 No. 1681, S.I. 1984 No. 1593, S.I. 1988 No. 1657, S.I. 1989 Nos. 635 and 682, S.I. 1992 No. 2793 and S.I. 1992 No. 2932)

The Minister of Labour by virtue of the powers conferred on him by sections 17, 46 and 60 of the Factories Act 1937, section 8 of the Factories Act 1948, and of all other powers enabling him in that behalf, hereby makes the special regulations set out in Parts I to XI hereof and the regulation set out in Part XII hereof, after publishing, pursuant to the Second Schedule to the said Act of 1937, notice of the proposal to make the said special Regulations and after the holding of an inquiry under that Schedule into objections made to the draft special Regulations—

PART I
APPLICATION AND INTERPRETATION

1. Citation, commencement and revocation.—(1) These Regulations may be cited as the Construction (General Provisions) Regulations 1961, and shall come into operation on the first day of March, 1962.

(2) Regulations 5 and 75 to 79 and 85 to 98 and 100 of the Building (Safety, Health and Welfare) Regulations 1948, and the Building (Safety, Health and Welfare) Amendment Regulations 1952, are hereby revoked.

General note. In the notes which follow use has been made of such of the authorities decided upon the provisions of the Building (Safety, Health and Welfare) Regulations 1948, as appear also to govern the interpretation of the cognate provisions of these Regulations. The 1948 Regulations are now entirely revoked or spent and are no longer printed in this book.

Measurements in Imperial have been converted to metric by S.I. 1984 No. 1593. These amendments do not apply to premises or plant in existence before 9 November 1984.

2. Application of Regulations.—(1) These Regulations apply—

(a) to building operations (*a*); and
(b) to works of engineering construction (*b*),

undertaken by way of trade of business, or for the purpose of any industrial or commercial undertaking, or by or on behalf of the Crown or any municipal or other public authority, and to any line or siding which is used in connection therewith and for the purposes thereof and is not part of a railway or tramway (*c*).

1805

(2) The Chief Inspector *(d)* may (subject to such conditions, if any, as may be specified therein) by certificate in writing (which he may in his discretion revoke at any time) exempt from all or any of the requirements of these Regulations—

(a) any particular plant or equipment or any class or description of plant or equipment; or

(b) any particular work or any class or description of work,

if he is satisfied that the requirements in respect of which the exemption is granted are not necessary for the protection of persons employed or are not reasonably practicable.

(a) **Building operation.** For meaning, see s. 176(1) of the Factories Act 1961.

(b) **Works of engineering construction.** For meaning, see s. 176(1) of the Factories Act 1961.

(c) **Railway; tramway.** For meaning, see s. 176(1) of the Factories Act 1961.

(d) **Inspector.** See INTRODUCTORY NOTE 24.

3.   Obligations under Regulations.—(1) It shall be the duty *(a)* of every contractor *(b)*, and every employer of workmen, who is undertaking any of the operations of works to which these Regulations apply *(c)*

(a) to comply with such of the requirements of the following regulations as affect him *(d)* or any workman employed by him *(e)*, that is to say, regulations 8 to 11, 13, 15 to 17, 21, 23 to 25, 35, 36, 45, 46(1), 47 to 49, and 52:

Provided that the requirements of the said regulations shall be deemed not to affect any workman if and so long as his presence in any place is not in the course of performing any work on behalf of his employer and is not expressly or impliedly authorised or permitted by his employer; and

(b) to comply with such of the requirements of regulations 12, 14, 18, 19, 30, 38, 39, 40, 41, 44, 46(2), 50, 51 and 56 as relate to any work, act or operation performed or about to be performed by any such contractor or employer of workmen *(f)*,

and it shall be the duty of every contractor, and every employer of workmen, who erects, installs, works or uses *(g)* any *plant or equipment* to which any of the provisions of regulations 26 to 29, 31 to 34, 37, 42, 43 and 53 applies, to erect, install, work or use any such *plant or equipment* in a manner which complies with those provisions.

(2) It shall be the duty of every person employed *(h)* to comply with the requirements of such of these Regulations as relate to the performance of or the refraining from an act by him and to co-operate in carrying out these Regulations and if he discovers any defect in the *plant or equipment* to report such defect without unreasonable delay to his employer or foreman, or to a person appointed by the employer under Part II of these Regulations.

(a) **Duty.** Section 155(2) of the Factories Act 1961, in so far as it affords a defence to occupiers, is not to be taken as affecting any liability of the occupiers in respect of the

same matters by virtue of a provision, namely that imposing a duty on them by reg. 3(1), other than the provision (that in reg. 3(2) expressly imposing a duty on their employees (*Davies v Canerons Industrial Services Ltd* [1980] 2 All ER 680, (decided upon the similar provisions of reg. 3 of the Construction (Working Places) Regulations 1966).

(*b*) **Contractor.** A building owner employing specialist tradesmen to carry out building operations is a "contractor" but not one who is undertaking operations or works to which the Regulations apply (*Kealey v Heard* [1983] 1 All ER 973, [1983] 1 WLR 573).

(*c*) **Undertaking . . . apply.** Where a contractor hires out plant together with an operator employed by him in order that the plant shall be used for operations or works to which the Regulations apply he is a contractor or employer of workmen "undertaking" such operations or works within reg. 3(1) (*Williams v West Wales Plant Hire Co Ltd* [1984] 3 All ER 397, [1984] 1 WLR 1311, CA). Furthermore, if the evidence shows that a person is engaged in a joint venture with another (such as a builder) who is undertaking such operations or works he is on that account alone "undertaking" the operations or works within reg. 3(1) (*ibid., per* Lawton LJ, at 401–402).

(*d*) **As affect him.** In *Upton v Hipgrave Bros* [1965] 1 All ER 6, [1965] 1 WLR 208, Marshall J held that in a case where a sub-contractor's employee was injured by a breach of reg. 46(1) the main contractor was also liable since, having provided the hoist from which an article fell and being the main contractor upon whom the regulation imposed the main responsibility, the requirement under the regulation affected him. However, in *Bunker v Charles Brand & Son Ltd*, [1969] 2 QB 480, [1969] 2 All ER 59, O'Connor J, declining to follow *Upton's* case, held that the words "as affect him" were designed to close the loophole disclosed by the case of *Herbert v Harold Shaw Ltd* [1959] 2 QB 138, [1959] 2 All ER 189, CA, and to make it clear that a working man on his own who is carrying on an operation to which the Regulations apply is under a duty, albeit a duty to himself, to comply with the Regulations. The latter case was followed by Orr J in *Taylor v Sayers* [1971] 1 All ER 934 and approved by the Court of Appeal in *Smith v George Wimpey & Co Ltd* [1972] 2 QB 329, [1972] 2 All ER 723, CA. This case (which disapproved *Upton's* case, above) decides that the employee of a sub-contractor is owed by the main contractor no duty under reg. 3(1)(a); the purpose and effect of adding the words "him or" in the Regulations was to bring the self-employed person or independent contractor within their scope in order to make him responsible for his own safety and subject to penalties for breach. Equally, a sub-contractor owes no duty under reg. 3(1)(a) to an independent contractor engaged by him (*Clare v Whittaker & Son (London) Ltd* [1976] ICR 1). In *Wimpey Homes Holding Ltd v Lees* 1991 SCCR 447 there was no evidence that the employees referred to in the charge were in the region of the defective hoist/platforms. Nevertheless the employer was convicted and the court held that the test is whether any of the employer's workmen might reasonably be expected to be exposed to that risk in the course of the work which they have to do. This test was approved on appeal: 1993 SLT 564.

(*e*) **Any workman employed by him.** In *Field v Perrys (Ealing), Ltd* [1950] 2 All ER 521. Devlin J held that the corresponding words in the Building Regulations 1926 ("any workman engaged by him") were not confined to workmen engaged in some part of the building operations themselves, but included a night watchman. See too *Campbell v City of Glasgow DC* 1991 SLT 616: the words apply to any worker sent to the site where building operations are carried out (and see *Wimpey Homes Holding Ltd v Lees* 1993 SLT 564: a supervisor is a "workman"). The words, however, do not include an independent contractor engaged by the employer, and the definition of "workman" in s. 10 of the Employers and Workmen Act 1875 has no bearing on the interpretation of reg. 4; see *Herbert v Harold Shaw Ltd* [1959] 2 QB 138, [1959] 2 All ER 189, CA. It is doubtful whether the statutory provisions by virtue of which these Regulations were made empower the Minister to make regulations imposing obligations for the protection of an independent contractor (*Barry v Black-Clawson International Ltd* (1960) 2 KIR 237 CA; *Galek's Curator Bonis v Thomson* 1991 SLT 29n; cf *Smith v George Wimpey & Co Ltd* [1974] 2 QB 329, [1972] 2 All ER 723, CA).

(f) **Work ... performed by any such contractor** ... In *Donaghey v Boulton and Paul Ltd* [1968] AC 1, [1967] 2 All ER 1014, HL, it was held that where work was sub-contracted the main contractor nevertheless "performed" the work within the meaning of the similar provision of the Building (Safety, Health and Welfare) Regulations 1948 if he had not divested himself of control of the execution of the work (approving, in this respect, *Mulready v J H & W Bell Ltd* [1952] 2 All ER 633) but that the work was not "performed" by a main contractor who had divested himself of such control (disapproving the decision of the Court of Appeal on this point in the same case, [1953] 2 QB 117, [1953] 2 All ER 215).

Where, by virtue of a specific regulation, the obligation is to provide something, that is an obligation of the employer: but where the obligation is to use, the obligation is that both of the employer and the employee (*Ginty v Belmont Building Supplies Ltd* [1959] 1 All ER 414, approved and distinguished in *McMath v Rimmer Bros (Liverpool) Ltd* [1961] 3 All ER 1154, [1962] 1 WLR 1, CA). For further discussion of this principle, see the GENERAL INTRODUCTION.

(g) **Works or uses.** In *Gallagher v Wimpey & Co* 1951 SLT 377, the pursuer was injured by a mechanical digger which had, together with its operator, been hired by his employers for use in building operations. The Inner House of the Court of Session held that the employers were "using" the digger within the meaning of the similar provisions (now lapsed) of reg. 4 of the Building (Safety, Health and Welfare) Regulations 1948. In *Teague v William Baxter & Son Ltd* 1982 SLT (Sh Ct) 28 the owners of a crane hired it to the main contractor. The owners were nonetheless held to be using the crane. In *Smith v W & J R Watson Ltd* 1977 SLT 204 the High Court of Justiciary held that "uses" is intended to cover the kind of case in which it could be said that a machine was "in use" within the meaning of s. 16 of the Factories Act 1961, and that "works" means sets in motion in the sense of the words "in motion" in s. 16, so that the words "works or uses" embrace not only the commercial or industrial operation of a machine for its designed purpose but any operation thereof for whatever purpose which involves the activation of the machine itself.

Smith v W & J R Watson Ltd, was followed in *Johns v Martin Simms (Cheltenham) Ltd* [1983] 1 All ER 127, [1983] ICR 305. An excavator driver's hand was caught in the radiator fan of an excavator's engine during cleaning and adjustment operations at the end of the day. As it was to be expected that such daily inspection, checking and adjustments would be a normal part of the machine's daily use, the injury occurred while the machine was in "use" within the meaning of reg. 3(1).

(h) **Duties of persons employed.** Regulation 3(2) is not limited to the provisions in the Regulations under which particular employees are required to do particular acts (*Davison v Apex Scaffolds Ltd* [1956] 1 QB 551, [1956] 1 All ER 473, CA; *McMullen v Alexander Findley & Co Ltd* 1966 SLT 146). However, the decision in *Davison's* case is limited to the proposition that an employee must comply with regulations in so far as they relate to work which he himself has to do. Thus, merely because a workman is using equipment which does not comply with the Regulations he is not thereby in breach of reg. 3(2) (*Quinn v J W Green (Painters) Ltd* [1966] 1 QB 509, [1965] 3 All ER 785, CA). Where a regulation enjoins the use of something, an employee who fails to use it is in breach of reg. 3(2) (*Ginty v Belmont Building Supplies* [1959] 1 All ER 414) that aspect of this case which deals with the apportionment of fault is discussed in the GENERAL INTRODUCTION. It is a failure to "co-operate" within reg. 3(2) if an employee knowingly uses someone else's unsuitable material when his employers have provided him with all the material, so as to put themselves within the Regulations (*Davison v Apex Scaffolds Ltd,* above, *per* Singleton LJ; compare *Quinn v J W Green (Painters) Ltd,* above, where the employee merely used equipment in which there was a latent defect).

4. Interpretation.—(1) The Interpretation Act 1889 [Interpretation Act 1978] shall apply to the interpretation of these Regulations as it applies to the interpretation of an Act of Parliament, and as if these Regulations and the Regulations hereby revoked were Acts of Parliament.

(2) In these Regulations, unless the context otherwise requires, the following expressions have the meanings hereby assigned to them—

"locomotive" in Part IX of these Regulations means any self-propelled wheeled vehicle used on a line of rails for the movement of *trucks* or *wagons;*

"plant or equipment" includes any plant, equipment, gear, machinery, apparatus or appliance, or any part thereof;

"the Principal Act" means the Factories Act 1937, as amended by or under any other Act;

"scaffold" (a) means any temporarily provided structure on or from which persons perform work in connection with operations or works to which these Regulations apply, and any temporarily provided structure which enables persons to obtain access to or which enables materials to be taken to any place at which such work is performed, and includes any working platform (b), working stage, gangway, run, ladder or step-ladder (other than an independent ladder or step-ladder which does not form part of such a structure) together with any guard-rail, toe-board or other safeguards and all fixings, but does not include a lifting appliance or a structure used merely to support such an appliance or to support other *plant or equipment;*

"truck" or *"wagon"* in Part IX of these Regulations means, respectively, a truck or wagon used on a line of rails.

(a) **Scaffold.** See note (a) to reg. 4 of the Construction (Working Places) Regulations 1966.

(b) **Working platform.** See note (b) to reg. 4 of the Construction (Working Places) Regulations 1966.

PART II
SUPERVISION OF SAFE CONDUCT OF WORKS

5. Appointment of safety supervisors.—(1) Every contractor, and every employer of workmen, who undertakes operations or works to which these Regulations apply and who normally employs more than twenty persons thereon at any one time (whether or not all those persons are employed on the same site or are all at work at any one time) shall specifically appoint in writing one or more persons experienced in such operations or works and suitably qualified for the purpose to be specially charged with the duties—

(a) of advising the contractor or employer as to the observance of the requirements for the safety or protection of persons employed imposed by or under the Factories Act 1937 to 1959, or the Lead Paint (Protection against Poisoning) Act 1926 (a), and as to other safety matters; and

(b) of exercising a general supervision of the observance of the aforesaid requirements and of promoting the safe conduct of the work generally.

(2) The name of every person so appointed shall be entered by the contractor or employer appointing him on the copy or abstract of these Regu-

lations required to be posted up in accordance with sections 139 and 127 of the Factories Act 1961.

(a) **Lead Paint (Protection against Poisoning) Act 1926.** This Act was repealed and replaced by the cognate provisions of the Factories Act 1961 ss. 131, 132 and of the Control of Lead at Work Regulations 1980.

6.   Other duties and joint appointments of safety supervisors.—(1) The duties assigned to any person appointed under the preceding regulation by the contractor or employer appointing him, including any duties other than those mentioned in that regulation, shall not be such as to prevent that person from discharging with reasonable efficiency the duties assigned to him under that regulation.

(2) Nothing in these Regulations shall be construed as preventing the same person or persons being appointed for a group of sites or as preventing two or more contractors or employers from jointly appointing the same person or persons.

PART III
SAFETY OF WORKING PLACES AND MEANS OF ACCESS

7.   [*revoked*]

PART IV
EXCAVATIONS, SHAFTS AND TUNNELS

8.   Supply and use of timber.—(1) An adequate supply of timber of suitable quality or other suitable support shall where necessary be provided (a) and used to prevent, so far as is reasonably practicable (b) and as early as is practicable in the course of the work, danger to any person employed from a fall or dislodgement of earth, rock or other material, forming a side or the roof of or adjacent to any excavation (c), shaft, earthwork or tunnel:
Provided that this regulation shall not apply—

(a) to any excavation, shaft or earthwork where, having regard to the nature and slope of the sides of the excavation, shaft or earthwork and other circumstances, no fall or dislodgement of earth or other material so as to bury to trap a person employed or as to strike a person employed from a height of more than 1.20 metres is liable to occur; or

(b) in relation to a person actually engaged in timbering or other work which is being carried out for the purpose of compliance with this regulation, if appropriate precautions are taken to ensure his safety as far as circumstances permit.

(2) In the case of tunnelling operations on works of engineering construction (d), no person shall be held not to have complied with a requirement of the foregoing paragraph of this regulation by reason of any matter proved to have been due to physical conditions over which he had no control and against which it was not reasonably practicable (b) for him to make provision.

General note. Regulations 8–14 do not exclude other regulations so far as excavations, etc., are concerned (*Horsley v Collier and Catley Ltd* [1956] 2 All ER 423, [1965] 1 WLR

1359, decided upon the cognate, and now revoked, provisions of the Building (Safety, Health and Welfare) Regulations 1948).

(*a*) **Provided.** See INTRODUCTORY NOTE 9.

(*b*) **Reasonably practicable.** See INTRODUCTORY NOTE 5.

(*c*) **Excavation.** In *Knight v Lambrick Contractors Ltd* [1957] 1 QB 562, [1956] 3 All ER 746, the Court of Appeal held that Part IV ("Excavations") of the Building (Safety, Health and Welfare) Regulations 1948 (now revoked and replaced by Part IV of the present Regulations) applied only to excavations made by the contractor in the course of his work on the site.

(*d*) **Works of engineering construction.** For definition, see s. 176(1) of the Factories Act 1961.

9. Inspections and examinations of excavations, etc.—(1) Subject to the provision of paragraph (4) of this regulation, every part of any excavation (*a*), shaft, earthwork or tunnel where persons are employed shall be inspected by a competent person at least once on every day during which persons are employed therein; and the face of every tunnel and the working end of every trench more than 2 metres deep and the base or crown of every shaft shall be inspected by a competent person at the commencement of every shift.

(2) Subject to the provisions of paragraph (4) of this regulation no person shall be employed in any excavation (*a*), shaft, earthwork or tunnel unless a thorough examination has been carried out by a competent person—

(a) of those parts thereof, and in particular any timbering or other support, in the region of the blast since explosives have been used in or near the excavation, shaft, earthwork or tunnel in a manner likely to have affected the strength or stability of that timbering or other support or any part thereof; and

(b) of those parts thereof in the region of any timbering or other support or any part thereof that has been substantially damaged and in the region of any unexpected fall of rock or earth or other material; and

(c) of every part thereof within the immediately proceding seven days:

Provided that sub-paragraph (*c*) shall not apply to timbering or other support which has not been erected or installed for more than seven days.

(3) A report [Form 91, Part 1, Section B] of the results of every thorough examination required by paragraph (2) of this regulation, signed by the person carrying out the examination, shall be made on the day of the examination in the prescribed form and containing the prescribed particulars:

Provided that in the case of a site where the employer for whom a thorough examination as aforesaid was carried out has reasonable grounds for believing that the operations or works will be completed in a period of less than six weeks, the provisions of paragraph (3) of this regulation shall be deemed to have been satisfied if the person in charge of the operations or works carried on by that employer at such a site has himself carried out the examination and is a competent person and if within one week of the date of the examination he reports to his employer in writing the results of such examination, and the date of such examination and the results thereof together with the name of the person making the examination are entered by the employer in the prescribed form together with the prescribed particulars.

(4) This regulation shall not apply—

(a) to any excavation *(a)*, shaft or earthwork where, having regard to the nature and slope of the sides of the excavation, shaft or earthwork and other circumstances, no fall or dislodgement of earth or other material so as to bury or trap a person employed or so as to strike a person employed from a height of more than 1.20 metres is liable to occur; or

(b) in relation to persons carrying out inspections or examinations required by this regulation or actually engaged in timbering or other work for the purpose of making a place safe, if appropriate precautions are taken to ensure their safety as far as circumstances permit.

(a) Excavation. See note *(c)* to reg. 8.

10. Supervision and execution of timbering and other work.—(1) No timbering or other support for any part of an excavation *(a)*, shaft, earthwork or tunnel shall be erected or be substantially added to, altered or dismantled except under the direction of a competent person and so far as possible by competent workmen possessing adequate experience of such work. All material for any such work shall be inspected by a competent person on each occasion before being taken into use and material found defective in any respect shall not be used.

(2) Timbering or other support for any part of an excavation *(a)*, shaft, earthwork or tunnel shall be of good construction, sound material, free from patent defect and of adequate strength *(b)* for the purpose for which it is used and shall be properly maintained *(c)*.

(3) All struts and braces in any excavation *(a)*, shaft, earthwork or tunnel shall be properly and adequately secured so as to prevent their accidental displacement or fall.

(a) Excavation. See note *(c)* to reg. 8.

(b) Good construction, etc. See INTRODUCTORY NOTE 11.

(c) Properly maintained. See INTRODUCTORY NOTE 10.

11. Means of egress in case of flooding.—(1) In any excavation *(a)*, shaft or tunnel where there is reason to apprehend danger to persons employed therein from rising water or from an irruption of water or material there shall be provided, so far as practicable *(b)*, means to enable such persons to reach positions of safety.

(2) In the case of tunnelling operations on works of engineering construction *(c)*, no person shall be held not to have complied with a requirement of the foregoing paragraph of this regulation by reason of any matter proved to have been due to physical conditions over which he had no control and against which it was not reasonably practicable *(b)* for him to make provision.

(a) Excavation. See note *(c)* to reg. 8.

(b) Practicable; reasonably practicable. See INTRODUCTORY NOTE 5.

(c) **Works of engineering construction.** For definition, see s. 176(1) of the Factories Act 1961.

12. Excavations, etc., likely to reduce security of a structure.—(1) No excavation *(a)*, shaft, earthwork or tunnel which is likely to reduce, so as to endanger any person employed, the security or stability of any part of any structure, whether temporary or permanent, shall be commenced or continued unless adequate steps are taken before and during the progress of the work to prevent danger to any person employed from collapse of the structure or the fall of any part thereof.

(2) In the case of tunnelling operations on works of engineering construction *(b)*, no person shall be held not to have complied with a requirement of the foregoing paragraph of this regulation by reason of any matter proved to have been due to physical conditions over which he had no control and against which it was not reasonably practicable *(c)* for him to make provision.

(a) **Excavation.** See note *(c)* to reg. 8.

(b) **Works of engineering construction.** For definition, see s. 176(1) of the Factories Act 1961.

(c) **Reasonably practicable.** See INTRODUCTORY NOTE 5.

13. Fencing of excavations, etc.—Every accessible part of an excavation *(a)*, shaft, pit or opening in the ground near to which employed persons are working and into or down a side of which a person is liable to fall a distance of more than 2 metres shall be provided with a suitable barrier placed as close as is reasonably practicable *(b)* to the edge or shall be securely covered:
Provided that the foregoing requirement shall not apply to any part of an excavation, shaft, pit or opening while (and to the extent to which) the absence of such barrier and covering is necessary for the access of persons or for the movement of *plant or equipment* or materials or while (and to the extent to which) it has not yet been practicable *(b)* to erect such barrier or covering since the formation of that part of the excavation, shaft, pit or opening.

(a) **Excavation.** See note *(c)* to reg. 8. In calculating the 2 metres one only takes account of the depth of the excavation and it is not permissible to add in the height above the ground from which the pursuer has fallen: *Cameron v Woodhall-Duckham Construction Co Ltd* 1964 SLT (Notes) 38.

(b) **Reasonably practicable; practicable.** See INTRODUCTORY NOTE 5.

14. Safeguarding edges of excavations, etc.—(1) Material shall not be placed or stacked near the edge of any excavation *(a)*, shaft, pit or opening in the ground so as to endanger persons employed below.

(2) No load or *plant or equipment* shall be placed or moved near the edge of any excavation *(a)*, shaft, pit or opening in the ground where it is likely to cause a collapse of the side of the excavation, shaft, pit or opening and thereby endanger any person.

(a) **Excavation.** See note *(c)* to reg. 8.

PART V
COFFERDAMS AND CAISSONS

15.   Construction and maintenance. Every cofferdam or caisson and every part thereof shall be of good construction, of suitable and sound material, free from patent defect and of adequate strength *(a)* and shall be properly maintained *(b)*.

(a) *Good construction, etc.* See INTRODUCTORY NOTE 11.

(b) *Properly maintained.* See INTRODUCTORY NOTE 10.

16.   Means of egress in case of flooding.—(1) In any cofferdam or caisson there shall, so far as is reasonably practicable *(a)*, be adequate means for persons to reach places of safety in the event of an inrush of water.

(2) No person shall be held not to have complied with a requirement of the foregoing paragraph of this regulation by reason of any matter proved to have been due to physical conditions over which he had no control and against which it was not reasonably practicable *(a)* for him to make provision.

(a) *Reasonably practicable.* See INTRODUCTORY NOTE 5.

17.   Supervision of work and inspection of material.—(1) No cofferdam or caisson or part thereof shall be constructed or be placed in position or be substantially added to or altered to be dismantled except under the immediate supervision *(a)* of a competent person and so far as possible by competent workmen possessing adequate experience of such work.

(2) All material for the construction or fixing of a cofferdam or caisson shall be inspected by a competent person on each occasion before being taken into use for such a purpose and material which is unsuitable or defective in any respect shall not be so used.

(a) *Immediate supervision.* In *Moloney v A Cameron Ltd* [1961] 2 All ER 934, [1961] 1 WLR 1087, CA, Holroyd Pearce LJ, construing reg. 6, said, "... though there must be supervision, the proper extent of that supervision must be a question of degree related to the structure being built, the difficulties and dangers involved. There must be some person—not the workman himself—who is 'immediately' responsible. The word 'immediate' is, I think, devoted to this relationship rather than intended to indicate that every act must be strictly supervised. In some cases the supervision may have to be constant and relate to every act that is done—when, for instance, great danger and difficulty are involved. In other cases, where there is no risk and the men are competent, the supervision may be less intensive." This passage was approved by the Court of Appeal (construing what is now reg. 41(2)(i) of the Construction (General Provisions) Regulations 1961) in *Owen v Evans and Owen (Builders) Ltd* [1962] 3 All ER 128, [1962] 1 WLR 933.

18.   Inspections and examinations.—(1) Subject to paragraph (2) of this regulation, no person shall be employed in a cofferdam or caisson unless it has been inspected by a competent person at least once on the same or preceding day and unless it has been thoroughly examined by a competent person—

(a)   since explosives have been used in or near to the cofferdam or caisson in a manner likely to have affected the strength or stability of the cofferdam or caisson or any part thereof; and

(b)   since the cofferdam or caisson has been substantially damaged; and

(c)   in any case within the immediately preceding seven days:

Provided that sub-paragraph *(c)* shall not apply until seven days have elapsed since the cofferdam or caisson was erected or placed in its position on the site.

A report [Form 91, Part 1, Section B] of the results of every such examination, signed by the person carrying out the examination, shall be made on the day of the examination in the prescribed form and containing the prescribed particulars.

(2)   This regulation shall not apply in relation to persons actually engaged in the construction, placing, repairing or alteration of the cofferdam or caisson or carrying out inspections or examinations required by this Regulation if appropriate precautions are taken to ensure their safety as far as circumstances permit.

PART VI
EXPLOSIVES

19.   Explosives. Explosives shall not be handled or used except by or under the immediate control of a competent person with adequate knowledge of the dangers connected with their use and steps shall be taken to see that, when a charge is fired, persons employed are in positions in which, so far as can reasonably be anticipated, they are not exposed to risk of injury from the explosion or from flying material.

PART VII
DANGEROUS OR UNHEALTHY ATMOSPHERES

20.   [*revoked*].

21.   Ventilation of excavations, etc.—(1) Effective steps shall be taken to secure and maintain the adequate ventilation of every working place in any excavation, pit, hole, adit, tunnel, shaft, caisson or other enclosed or confined space and of every approach to any such working place so as—

(a)   to maintain an atmosphere which is fit for respiration; and

(b)   to render harmless, so far as is reasonably practicable *(a)*, all fumes *(b)*, dust or other impurities which may be dangerous or injurious to health and which are generated, produced or released by explosives or by any other means in such working place or approach thereto.

(2)   Where there is reason to apprehend that the atmosphere in any of the working places or approaches thereto mentioned in paragraph (1) of this regulation is poisonous or asphyxiating, then, without prejudice to the requirements of the said paragraph, no person shall be employed in or allowed to enter

such working place or approach until the atmosphere has been suitably tested by or under the immediate supervision *(c)* of a competent person and he is satisfied that the working place or approach is, for the time being, free from the danger of a person being overcome by poisoning or asphyxiation.

(3) No person shall be held not to have complied with a requirement of the foregoing paragraphs of this regulation by reason of any matter proved to have been due to physical conditions over which he had no control and against which it was not reasonably practicable *(a)* for him to make provision.

   (a) Reasonably practicable. See INTRODUCTORY NOTE 5.

   (b) Fume. For definition, see s. 176(1) of the Factories Act 1961.

   (c) Immediate supervision. See note *(a)* to reg. 17.

22.   [*revoked*].

PART VIII
WORK ON OR ADJACENT TO WATER

23.   Transport by water. When any person employed is conveyed to or from any working place by water, proper measures shall be taken to provide for his safe transport. Vessels used for this purpose shall be of suitable construction, shall be properly maintained *(a)* and shall be in the charge of a competent person and shall not be overcrowded or overloaded.

   (a) Properly maintained. See INTRODUCTORY NOTE 10.

24.   Prevention of drowning. Where, on or adjacent to the site of any operations or works to which these regulations apply *(a)*, there is water into which a person employed is, in the course of his employment, liable to fall with risk of drowning, suitable rescue equipment shall be provided and kept in an efficient state and ready for use and measures shall be taken to arrange for the prompt rescue of any such person in danger of drowning. Where there is special risk of such fall from the edge of adjacent land or of a structure adjacent to or above the water, or of a floating stage, secure fencing shall be provided near the edge to prevent such fall, so, however, that such fencing may be removed or remain unerected for the time and to the extent necessary for the access of persons or the movement of materials.

   (a) Operations or works . . . apply. See reg. 2.

PART IX
TRANSPORT

25.   Rails and rail tracks. All rails on which any *locomotive, truck* or *wagons* moves shall—

(a) have an even running surface, be sufficiently and adequately supported, and be of adequate section;
(b) be joined by fish plates or double chairs;
(c) be securely fastened to sleepers or bearers;
(d) be supported on a surface sufficiently firm to prevent undue movement of the rails;
(e) be laid in straight lines or in curves of such radii that the *locomotive, truck* or *wagon* can be moved freely and without danger of derailment;
(f) be provided with an adequate stop or buffer on each rail at each end of the track.

All rails and equipment referred to in this regulation shall be properly maintained *(a)*:

Provided that requirements (b) and (c) of this regulation shall not apply if other adequate steps are taken to ensure the proper junction of the rails, and to prevent any material variation in their gauge.

(a) **Properly maintained.** See INTRODUCTORY NOTE 10.

26. Maintenance of locomotives, etc. Every *locomotive, truck* and *wagon* in use for transport purposes and every power-driven capstan or winch used for the movement of *trucks* or *wagons* shall be of good construction, sound material, adequate strength, free from patent defect *(a)* and properly maintained *(b)*.

(a) **Good construction, etc.** See INTRODUCTORY NOTE 11.

(b) **Properly maintained.** See INTRODUCTORY NOTE 10.

27. Clearance.—(1) In connection with the erection, installation, working or use of any line of rails on which any *locomotive, truck* or *wagon* moves, there shall, except where such clearance is not reasonably practicable *(a)*, be adequate clearance so that persons are not liable to be crushed or trapped by any passing *locomotive, truck* or *wagon* or any part of a load thereon. Without prejudice to the foregoing requirement there shall, save to the extent to which such arrangements are impracticable *(a)*, be arrangements, including where appropriate the provision of suitable recesses, such that the lack of adequate clearance as aforesaid does not extend for more than twenty metres in length.

(2) In any case where there is not adequate clearance as aforesaid there shall be effective arrangements for warning any person liable to be crushed or trapped of the danger and of the approach of a *locomotive, truck* or *wagon*.

(3) Where a *locomotive* is or is to be driven, all reasonable steps shall be taken to avoid or obviate low clearances and overhead obstructions which will not afford a clearance of at least 1.10 metres above the seat of the driver when driving the *locomotive* in a normal sitting position and 2 metres above the footplate if he is driving it in a standing position; and appropriate steps shall be taken by means of suitable warning devices, warning notices or otherwise, to make the driver aware of the danger when the *locomotive* is approaching any point at which there is such a low clearance or obstruction and to warn any persons riding on the train of approaching danger to them due to lack of overhead or side clearance.

(a) **Reasonably practicable; impracticable.** See INTRODUCTORY NOTE 5.

28.   Gantries. Every gantry or elevated structure carrying rails on which a *locomotive, truck* or *wagon* moves shall, at every part along which persons employed have to pass on foot, be provided with a suitable and adequate footway. If such footway is on the outside of the rail track and any person is liable to fall more than 2 metres therefrom, the footway shall be provided with suitable guard-rails not less than 910 millimetres in height.

29.   Brakes, sprags and scotches.—(1) Every *locomotive* shall be fitted with effective brakes.

(2) Every *truck* or *wagon* shall be fitted with an effective brake or brakes unless the circumstances in which it is used render a brake unnecessary for safety.

(3) A sufficient number of suitable sprags or scotches shall be provided for the use of persons employed on the movement of *trucks* or *wagons*. Sprags or scotches shall be used whenever necessary and shall be in good condition.

30.   Replacement of derailed locomotives, etc. Suitable equipment shall be provided and used for replacing on the track any *locomotive, truck* or *wagon* which may become derailed.

31.   Warning of movement of locomotives, trucks or wagons.—(1) Every *locomotive* shall be fitted with an efficient whistle or other warning device which shall be properly maintained.

(2) Where any person may be endangered by the movement of any *locomotive, truck* or *wagon* the person in charge of the movement of the *locomotive, truck* or *wagon* shall see that adequate warning is given.

32.   Competent persons to drive locomotives, etc. A *locomotive*, power-driven capstan or haulage winch or a vehicle in which Regulation 34 applies shall be driven or operated only by a trained and competent person who has attained the age of eighteen, except that for the purpose of training it shall be permissible for a *locomotive* or any such capstan or haulage winch or any such vehicle to be driven or operated by a person under eighteen years of age who is under the direct supervision of a person qualified for that purpose.

33.   Precautions in connection with the use of capstans and haulage winches.—(1) Where any power-driven capstan or haulage winch is used for the movement of *trucks* or *wagons* the space in the immediate vicinity thereof shall be kept clear of all obstructions and shall be sufficient for safe working.

(2) No power-driven capstan or haulage winch shall be set in motion for the movement of *trucks* or *wagons* until adequate warning by means of efficient sound or visual signals has been given by the person in charge of such movement to any person who may be endangered thereby.

34. Mechanically propelled vehicles and trailers.—(1) Subject to paragraph (2) of this regulation, a mechanically propelled vehicle or a mechanically drawn trailer-vehicle if owned or used by, or hired by and operated under the control of, a contractor or employer undertaking operations or works to which these Regulations apply *(a)* and used for conveying workmen, goods or materials for the purpose of such operations or works shall, when being moved at a site where such operations or works are carried on (whether or not workmen, goods or materials are actually being conveyed on the vehicle at the time)—

(a) be in an efficient state, in efficient working order and in good repair;

(b) not be used in an improper manner;

(c) not be loaded in such a manner or to such extent as to interfere with the safe driving or operation of the vehicle.

Provided that, where all practicable precautions are taken to avoid danger to the persons affected, sub-paragraph (a) of this paragraph shall not apply to a vehicle which has broken down or been damaged on the site and—

(i) on which no workmen, goods or materials are being conveyed and which is being moved only for the purpose of its repair or disposal or so as not to cause an obstruction; or

(ii) on which no workmen are being conveyed and which is being moved only so far as is necessary to render unloading of goods or materials practicable.

(2) This regulation shall not apply to *locomotives, trucks* or *wagons.*

(a) Operations or works . . . apply. See reg. 2.

35. Riding in insecure positions on vehicles, etc. No person shall ride or be required or permitted to ride on the buffer, running board or other insecure position—

(a) on any vehicle to which Regulation 34 applies; or

(b) on any *locomotive, truck* or *wagon,*

and shall only ride at the place thereon provided for that purpose.

36. Remaining on vehicles during loading. No person shall remain or be required or permitted to remain on any vehicle to which Regulation 34 applies or on any *truck* or *wagon* during the loading of loose materials by means of a grab, excavator or similar appliance, if he is endangered by so remaining.

37. Vehicles near edge of excavation, etc. Where any vehicle is used for tipping material into any excavation or pit or over the edge of any embankment or earthwork adequate measures shall be taken where necessary so as to prevent such vehicle from over-running the edge of such excavation, pit, embankment or earthwork.

Part X
Demolition

38. Application of Part X. The requirements of this Part of these Regulations shall apply as respects the demolition of the whole or any substantial part of a building or other structure.

General note. Although Part X of the Regulations applies in terms to demolition, the application of the remainder of the regulations to demolition operations is not excluded in cases where, on their proper construction, they are intended to apply to such operations; see *Knight v Demolition and Construction Co Ltd* [1953] 2 All ER 508, [1953] 1 WLR 981 (approved by the Court of Appeal without discussion of the Regulations, [1954] 1 All ER 711n, [1954] 1 WLR 563) and *Horsley v Collier and Catley Ltd* [1965] 2 All ER 423, [1965] 1 WLR 1359.

39.   Supervision.—(1) Every contractor (other than an individual contractor) undertaking demolition operations to which this Part of these Regulations applies shall appoint a competent person experienced in such operations to supervise the work; so, however, that where more than one contractor (other than an individual contractor) takes part in such demolition operations, each such contractor shall appoint a competent person as aforesaid and either the same person shall be jointly appointed by every contractor or each contractor shall make arrangements to ensure that no operation is undertaken by his workmen except after consultation between all the persons so appointed as to the method by which and the time at which the operation is to be carried out.

(2) Where part of any demolition operations to which this Part of these Regulations applies is to be undertaken by an individual contractor—

(a)   no operation shall be undertaken by that individual contractor except after consultation with every other individual contractor undertaking the operations and with the person or persons appointed under the foregoing paragraph of this regulation; and

(b)   no operation shall be undertaken by any contractor except after consultation between the person or persons appointed under the said paragraph and every individual contractor undertaking the operations as to the method by which and the time at which the operation is to be carried out.

(3) In this regulation the expression "individual contractor" means a contractor who personally performs the demolition operations without employing any workmen thereon.

40.   Fire and flooding. Before demolition is commenced and also during the progress of the work all practicable *(a)* steps shall be taken to prevent danger to persons employed—

(a)   from risk of fire or explosion through leakage or accumulation of gas or vapour; and

(b)   from risk of flooding.

(a)   Practicable. See INTRODUCTORY NOTE 5.

41.   Precautions in connection with demolition *(a).*—(1) No part of a building or other structure shall be so overloaded with debris or materials as to render it unsafe to persons employed.

(2) The following operations shall be carried out only (i) under the immediate supervision *(b)* of a competent foreman or chargehand with adequate

experience of the particular kind of work, or (ii) by workmen experienced in the kind of work and under the direction of a competent foreman or chargehand as aforesaid, that is to say—

(a) the actual demolition of a building or part thereof or any other structure or part thereof except where there is no risk of a collapse *(c)* of any part of the building or the structure in the course or as a result of the said demolition, so as to endanger any person employed, other than a risk which could not reasonably have been foreseen *(d)*;

(b) the actual demolition of any part of a building or other structure where there is a special risk of collapse, whether of that or of any other part of the building or structure, in the course or as a result of the said demolition, so as to endanger any person employed;

(c) the cutting of reinforced concrete, steelwork or ironwork forming part of the building or other structure which is being demolished,

and before any steelwork or ironwork is cut or released, precautions shall be taken to avoid danger from any sudden twist, spring or collapse.

(3) All practicable *(e)* precautions shall be taken to avoid danger from collapse of the building or other structure when any part of the framing is removed from a frame or partly framed building or other structure.

(4) Before demolition is commenced and also during the progress of the work *(f)*, precautions shall, where necessary *(g)*, be taken by adequate shoring or otherwise *(h)* to prevent, as far as practicable *(e)*, the accidental collapse *(a)* of any part of the building or structure or of any adjoining building or structure the collapse of which may endanger any person employed *(i)*:

Provided that this requirement shall not apply in relation to any person actually engaged in erecting or placing shoring or other safe-guards for the purpose of compliance with the requirement, if appropriate precautions are taken to ensure his safety as far as circumstances permit.

(a) **Demolition.** In *Shaw v Young's Paraffin Light & Mineral Oil Co Ltd* 1962 SLT (N) 85 it was said that actual demolition "is taking place when men engaged in the demolition operations are doing something to the wall or building that is to be demolished and that is not limited to occasions when a part of the structure is actually being brought down" (decided under the Building (Safety, Health and Welfare) Regulations 1948). *Fleming v Clarmac Engineering Co Ltd* 1969 SLT (Notes) 96 decides that demolition implies destruction of an object and not merely its removal.

(b) **Immediate supervision.** See note *(a)* to reg. 17.

(c) **Collapse of any part of the building.** The word "collapse" must be given its ordinary meaning, which is the action of falling together, or a sudden shrinking together, or a giving-way through external pressure or loss of rigidity or loss of support (*Mortimer v Samuel B Allison Ltd* [1959] 1 All ER 567, [1959] 1 WLR 330, HL).

(d) **Risk . . . foreseen.** If the operation of demolition in question may be carried out in a manner that is dangerous and may cause a collapse, then the regulation applies, even though the employer may have laid down a system of work which is safe in the particular case (*Owen v Evans and Owen (Builders) Ltd* [1962] 3 All ER 128, [1962] 1 WLR 933, CA).

(e) **Practicable.** See INTRODUCTORY NOTE 5.

(f) **During the progress of the work.** See *Clay v A J Crump & Sons Ltd* [1964] 1 QB 533, [1963] 3 All ER 687, CA.

(g) **Where necessary.** This phrase must, at any rate, cover a case where, if the danger had been appreciated, any reasonable person would say that precautions were necessary

(*Knight v Demolition and Construction Co Ltd* [1953] 2 All ER 508, [1953] 1 WLR 981 (affirmed by the Court of Appeal without discussion of the Regulations, [1954] 1 All ER 711n, [1954] 1 WLR 563).

(*h*) *By adequate shoring or otherwise.* "Shoring" means support from below; the words "or otherwise" cover other physical measures to prevent collapse (*Mortimer v Samuel D Allison Ltd* [1959] 1 All ER 567, [1959] 1 WLR 330, HL).

(*i*) *Person employed.* These words comprehend, not only employees of the demolition contractor, but also employees of other contractors on the site (*Clay v A J Crump & Sons Ltd*, above, *per* Ormrod LJ).

PART XI
MISCELLANEOUS

42. Fencing of machinery. Every wheel and every moving part of any prime mover, every part of transmission machinery and every dangerous part of other machinery (*a*) (whether or not driven by mechanical power) shall be securely fenced unless it is in such a position or of such construction as to be as safe to every person employed or working on the site of the operations or works as it would be if it were securely fenced.

General note. This regulation is revoked by the Provision and Use of Work Equipment Regulations 1992, S.I. 1992 No. 2932, as from 1 January 1993 except, insofar as it applies to work equipment first provided for use in the premises or undertaking before 1 January 1993, it is revoked as from 1 January 1997.

See ss. 12–16 of the Factories Act 1961, the Introductory Note thereto and the notes of those sections. This regulation applies only to machinery which is in use, and not to machinery under examination or repair (*Baxter v Central Electricity Generating Board* [1964] 2 All ER 815, [1965] 1 WLR 200). It does not apply to abrasive wheels within the meaning of the Abrasive Wheels Regulations 1970 (see reg. 3(4) thereof).

(*a*) *Machinery.* As to the circumstances in which portable hand tools may constitute machinery, see *Lovelidge v Anselm Olding & Sons Ltd* [1967] 2 QB 351, [1967] 1 All ER 459.

43. Fencing of new machinery. Without prejudice to the provisions of regulation 42, every prime mover and other machine intended to be driven by mechanical power (being a prime mover or machine used or intended to be used in operations or works to which these Regulations apply (*a*)) shall, unless constructed before the date of commencement of these Regulations (*b*), be so constructed that the following parts of such prime mover or machine are securely fenced (*c*) or are in such a position or of such construction as to be as safe as they would be if they were securely fenced, that is to say—

all revolving shafts, flywheels, couplings, toothed gearing, friction gearing, belt and pulley drives, chain and sprocket drives and all projecting screws, bolts or keys or any revolving shaft, wheel or pinion:

Provided that where a prime mover provides energy for another machine the foregoing requirements of this regulation shall not apply to parts which transmit energy from the prime mover to that other machine unless the prime mover and that machine are constructed as a unit.

General note. This regulation is revoked by the Provision and Use of Work Equipment Regulations 1992, S.I. 1992 No. 2932, as from 1 January 1993 except, insofar as it

applies to work equipment first provided for use in the premises or undertaking before 1 January 1993, it is revoked as from 1 January 1997.

(a) **Operations or works ... apply.** See reg. 2.

(b) **Date ... Regulations.** 1 March 1962 (reg. 1(1)).

(c) **Securely fenced.** See the Introductory Note to ss. 12–16 of the Factories Act 1961.

44. [*revoked*].

45. Generation of steam, smoke and vapour. Measures shall be taken to prevent, so far as practicable, steam, smoke or other vapour generated on the site from obscuring any part of the work, scaffolding, machinery or other *plant or equipment* where any person is employed.

46. Protection from falling material.—(1) At any place on the site of the operations or works where any person is habitually employed (a) steps shall be taken to prevent any person who is working in that place from being struck by any falling materials or article.

(2) *Scaffold* materials, tools, other objects and material (including waste material) shall not be thrown, tipped or shot down from a height where they are liable to cause injury, but where practicable shall be properly lowered. In any place where proper lowering is not practicable and also where any part of a building or other structure is being demolished or broken off adequate steps shall be taken to protect persons employed from falling or flying debris.

General note. In *Begbie v Henry Bruce & Sons Ltd* 1952 SLT (Notes) 56 it was held that para. (1) protects workmen against the accidental fall of material whereas para. (2) deals with debris allowed to fall by design (decided under the 1948 Regulations).

Regulation 46 applies to excavations, notwithstanding the fact that excavations are expressly dealt with in regs. 8–14 (*Horsley v Collier and Catley Ltd* [1965] 2 All ER 423, [1965] 1 WLR 1359, decided upon the cognate, and now revoked, provisions of the Building (Safety, Health and Welfare) Regulations 1948).

(a) **Place ... where any person is habitually employed.** The test as to whether this regulation applies is not whether the person struck by falling material was habitually employed at the place but whether it was an ''habitual'' place of employment, or a contemplated place of employment, where men would work, not casually, but habitually; *per* Parker LJ in *Bailey v Ayr Engineering and Construction Co Ltd* [1959] 1 QB 183, [1958] 2 All ER 222, CA, applying *Kearns v Gee, Walker and Slater* [1937] 1 KB 187, [1956] 3 All ER 151, CA; *Byrne v Truscon Ltd* 1967 SLT 159.

47. Lighting of working places, etc. Every working place (a) and approach thereto, every place where raising or lowering operations with the use of a lifting appliance are in progress, and all openings dangerous to persons employed, shall be adequately and suitably lighted.

(a) **Working place.** In *Field v Perrys (Ealing) Ltd* [1950] 2 All ER 521, Devlin J, considering the somewhat similar wording of reg. 15 of the Building Regulations 1926 (now revoked), held that the regulation contemplated a specific working place where people are doing a specific piece of work, and that it did not extend to the case of a night-watchman who (apart, conceivably, from his hut) had no specific working place at all. Furthermore, the working place itself must be lit; it is not sufficient to provide the workman with a light to take there *(ibid.)*. This case was approved in *Gill v Donald Humberstone & Co Ltd* [1963] 3 All ER 180, [1963] 1 WLR 929, HL, in which Lord Evershed said that the term "working place" must be construed with regard to the context in which it is found so as sensibly to serve that context.

48.   Projecting nails and loose material.—(1) No timber or material with projecting nails should be used in any work in which they are a source of danger to persons employed or be allowed to remain in any place where they are a source of danger to such persons.

(2) Loose materials *(a)* where not required for use shall not be placed or left so as to restrict unduly the passage of persons upon platforms, gangways, floors or other places on the site used for such passage, but shall be removed, stacked or stored so as to leave an unobstructed passage. Materials shall not be insecurely stacked in a place where they may be dangerous to persons employed, or so stacked as to overload and render unsafe any floor, roof or other part of a building or other structure.

(a) *Loose materials.* In this context "loose" materials applies to materials required for use as such on the site, not to materials unconnected with the work (*Morter v Electrical Installations Ltd* (1969) 6 KIR 130).

49.   Construction of temporary structures. Any temporary structure erected for the purpose of operations or works to which these Regulations apply *(a)*, not being a *scaffold* or other structure to which regulation 11 of the Construction (Lifting Operations) Regulations 1961 applies, shall (having regard to the purpose for which it is used) be of good construction and adequate strength and stability and shall be of sound material, free from patent defect *(b)* and properly maintained *(c)*.

General note. In *Davies v A C D Bridge Co* 1966 SLT 339 it was held that the regulation imposes an absolute duty and applies when the structure is being moved from one place to another.

(a) *Operations or works . . . apply.* See reg. 2.

(b) *Good construction, etc.* See INTRODUCTORY NOTE 11.

(c) *Properly maintained.* In *Davies*, above, it was held that the phrase "free from patent defect" does not qualify the preceding phrases. See INTRODUCTORY NOTE 10.

50.   Avoidance of danger from collapse of structure.—(1) All practicable *(a)* precautions shall be taken by the use of temporary guys, stays, supports and fixings or otherwise where necessary to prevent danger to any person employed through the collapse *(b)* of any part of a building or other structure during any temporary state of weakness or instability of the building or structure or part thereof before the building or structure is completed *(c)*.

(2) Where any work is carried on which is likely to reduce, so as to endanger any person employed, the security or stability of any part of an existing building

or structure or of a building or structure in course of construction all practicable *(a)* precautions shall be taken by shoring or otherwise *(d)* to prevent danger to any person employed from the collapse *(b)* of the building or structure or the fall of any part thereof.

(a) **Practicable.** See INTRODUCTORY NOTE 5.

(b) **Collapse.** See note *(b)* to reg. 41.

(c) **Before . . . completed.** This regulation does not apply to demolition work (*Knight v Demolition and Construction Co Ltd* [1953] 2 All ER 508, [1953] 1 WLR 981, affirmed, but not on this point, [1954] 1 All ER 711n, [1954] 1 WLR 563, CA).

(d) **By shoring or otherwise.** See note *(g)* to reg. 41.

51. Wet paint or cement wash on ironwork or steelwork. No ironwork or steelwork which has been painted or cement washed shall be moved or manipulated on the site of the operations or works unless all the paint or wash on it (other than paint for the purpose of jointing) is dry and no person shall walk or work or be required or permitted to walk or work on erected ironwork or steelwork on which the paint (other than paint for the purpose of jointing) or cement wash is wet:

Provided that the requirement of this regulation as to moving or manipulating shall not apply to moving or manipulating in connection with the painting or cement washing of ironwork or steelwork on the site.

52. [*revoked*].

53. Helmets or crowns for pile driving. Every helmet or crown used in connection with pile driving shall be of good construction, of sound and suitable material, of adequate strength and free from patent defect *(a)*.

(a) **Good construction, etc.** See INTRODUCTORY NOTE 11.

54. [*revoked*].

55. [*revoked*].

56. Keeping of records.—(1) The reports required by regulation 9(3) and 18(1) shall be kept on the site of the operations or works and when there are no relevant operations or works shall be kept at an office of the contractor or employer for whom the examination was carried out:

Provided that in the case of a site where the contractor or employer has reasonable grounds for believing that the operations or works will be completed in a period of less than six weeks, the contractor or employer may keep the said reports at his office.

(2) All reports and other documents required for the purposes of these Regulations shall at all reasonable times be open to inspection by any of H.M.

Inspectors of Factories, and the person keeping any such report or other document shall send to any such inspector such extracts therefrom or copies thereof as the inspector may from time to time require for the purpose of the execution of his duties under the Factories Act 1937 to 1959.

PART XII

OFFENCES UNDER SECTION 17 OF THE PRINCIPAL ACT

57.   Prohibited sale or hire of machinery. The provisions of subsection (2) of section 17 of the Factories Act 1937 [s. 17(2)] (which prohibits the sale or letting on hire of certain machines which do not comply with the provisions of that section) shall extend to prime movers or machines which do not comply with the requirements of regulation 43 of these Regulations.

General note. This regulation is revoked by the Provision and Use of Work Equipment Regulations 1992, S.I. 1992 No. 2932, as from 1 January 1993 except, insofar as it applies to work equipment first provided for use in the premises or undertaking before 1 January 1993, it is revoked as from 1 January 1997.

THE CONSTRUCTION (LIFTING OPERATIONS) REGULATIONS 1961

(S.I. 1961 No. 1581, as amended by S.I. 1984 No. 1593, S.I. 1989 No. 1141 and S.I. 1992 No. 195)

ARRANGEMENT OF REGULATIONS

SCHEDULES

FIRST SCHEDULE.—Extent of exclusions under regulation 6.
SECOND SCHEDULE.—Chains and lifting gear excepted under regulation 41 (as to heat treatment).

REGULATIONS

The Minister of Labour by virtue of the powers conferred on him by sections 46 and 60 of the Factories Act 1937, section 8 of the Factories Act 1948, section 27 of the Factories Act 1959, and of all other powers enabling him in that behalf, hereby makes the following special Regulations after publishing, pursuant to the Second Schedule to the said Act of 1937, notice of the proposal to make the said Regulations and after the holding of any inquiry under that Schedule into objections made to the draft Regulations—

PART I
APPLICATION AND INTERPRETATION

1. Citation, commencement and revocation.—(1) These Regulations may be cited as the Construction (Lifting Operations) Regulations 1961, and shall come into operation on the first day of March, 1962.

(2) Regulations 34 to 74 of the Building (Safety, Health and Welfare) Regulations 1948, and the Building (Safety, Health and Welfare) (Amendment) Regulations 1958, are hereby revoked.

General note. Measurements in Imperial have been converted to metric by S.I. 1984 No. 1593. These amendments do not apply to premises or plant in existence before 9 November 1984.

A Guidance Note PM27 "Construction Hoists" is published by the Health and Safety Executive.

2.   Application of Regulations. These Regulations apply—

(a)   to building operations; and
(b)   to works of engineering construction,

undertaken by way of trade or business, or for the purpose of any industrial or commercial undertaking, or by or on behalf of the Crown or any municipal or other public authority, and to any line or siding which is used in connection therewith and for the purposes thereof and is not part of a railway or tramway.

General note. See the notes to reg. 2 of the Construction (General Provisions) Regulations 1961.

3.   Obligations under Regulations.—(1) It shall be the duty of every contractor, and every employer of workmen, who is undertaking any of the operations or works to which these Regulations apply—

(a)   to comply with such of the requirements of the following regulations as affect him or any workman employed by him, that is to say, regulation 42(1) in so far as it relates to the protection of the hoistway, and regulation 47:
    Provided that the requirements of the said Regulations shall be deemed not to affect any workman if and so long as his presence in any place is not in the course of performing any work on behalf of his employer and is not expressly or impliedly authorised or permitted by his employer; and
(b)   to comply with such of the requirements of regulations 49(1) to (6) and 50 as relate to any work, act or operation performed or about to be performed by any such contractor or employer of workmen,

and it shall be the duty of every contractor, and every employer of workmen, who erects, installs, works or uses any *plant or equipment* to which any of the provisions of regulations 8 to 46, 48 and 49(7) applies, to erect, install, work or use any such *plant or equipment* in a manner which complies with those provisions.

(2) It shall be the duty of every person employed to comply with the requirements of such regulations as relate to the doing of or refraining from an act by him and co-operate in carrying out these Regulations and if he discovers any defect in the *plant or equipment* to report such defect without unreasonable delay to his employer or foreman, or to a person appointed by the employer in writing to supervise the safe conduct of the work generally.

General note. See the notes to reg. 3 of the Construction (General Provisions) Regulations 1961.

4.   Interpretation.—(1) The Interpretation Act 1889 [Interpretation Act 1978] shall apply to the interpretation of these Regulations as it applies to the interpretation of an Act of Parliament, and as if these Regulations and the Regulations hereby revoked were Acts of Parliament.

(2) In these Regulations, unless the context otherwise requires, the following expressions have the meanings hereby assigned to them respectively, that is to say—

"approved" means approved for the time being by certificate of the Chief Inspector *(a)*;

"hoist" means a lifting machine, whether worked by mechanical power or not, with a carriage, platform or cage the movement of which is restricted by a guide or guides, but does not include a *lifting appliance* used for the movement of trucks or wagons on a line or rails;

"lifting appliance" means a crab, winch, pulley block or gin wheel used for raising or lowering and a *hoist*, crane, sheer legs, excavator, dragline, piling frame, aerial cableway, aerial ropeway or overhead runway;

"lifting gear" means a chain sling, rope sling, or similar gear and a ring, link, hook, plate clamp, shackle, swivel or eye-bolt;

"mobile crane" means a crane capable of travelling under its own power, but does not include a crane which travels on a line of rails;

"plant or equipment" includes any plant, equipment, gear, machinery, apparatus or appliance, or any part thereof;

"the principal Act" means the Factories Act 1937, as amended by or under any other Act;

"raising or lowering or as a means of suspension" where that expression occurs in regulations 34, 35, 36, 40 and 41 means raising or lowering or as a means of suspension either of a load on a *lifting appliance* or *lifting gear* or of a *scaffold* but does not include the use of a rope or chain solely as a means of lashing or securing together two or more rigid members of a *scaffold* to form a frame or as a means of making a lapped joint or the use of a rope or chain solely for the movement of a load in a horizontal direction;

"safe working load" means either the relevant safe working load required to be specified in the latest certificate of test obtained for the purposes of regulations 28, 34, 35 and 46 or where no such certificate is required the relevant safe working load required to be marked or exhibited on the *lifting appliance, lifting gear,* chain, rope or other article of *plant or equipment* by regulations 29 and 34;

"scaffold" *(b)* means any temporarily provided structure on or from which persons perform work in connection with operations or works to which these Regulations apply, and any temporarily provided structure which enables persons to obtain access to or which enables materials to be taken to any place at which such work is performed, and includes any working platform *(c)*, working stage, gangway, run, ladder or step-ladder (other than an independent ladder or step-ladder which does not form part of such a structure) together with any guard-rail, toe-board or other safeguards and all fixings, but does not include a *lifting appliance* or a structure used merely to support such an appliance or to support other *plant or equipment*;

"suspended scaffold" means a *scaffold* suspended by means of ropes or chains and capable of being raised or lowered by such means but does not include a boatswain's chair or similar appliance.

(a) **Inspector.** See INTRODUCTORY NOTE 19.

(b) *Scaffold.* See note *(a)* to reg. 4 of the Construction (Working Places) Regulations 1966.

(c) *Working platform.* See note *(b)* to reg. 4 of the Construction (Working Places) Regulations 1966.

PART II

EXEMPTIONS

5. Certificates of exemption. The Chief Inspector *(a)* may (subject to such conditions, if any, as may be specified therein) by certificate *(b)* in writing (which he may in his discretion revoke at any time) exempt from all or any of the requirements of these Regulations—

(a) any particular *plant or equipment* or any class or description of *plant or equipment*; or

(b) any particular work or any class or description of work,

if he is satisfied that the requirements in respect of which the exemption is granted are not necessary for the protection of persons employed or are not reasonably practicable.

(a) *Inspector.* See INTRODUCTORY NOTE 19.

(b) *Certificate.* See Certificate of Exemption Nos. 6 (General) (F 2490), Con (LO)/1981/1 (F2514) and Con (LO)/1981/2 (F 2513), set out following these Regulations, and Certificate of Approval No. Con (LO) 1990/1 (F 2529) set out following the Shipbuilding and Ship-repairing Regulations 1960, S.I. 1960 No. 1932.

6. Lifting machinery in factory premises and in docks etc.—(1) *Lifting appliances,* chains, ropes and *lifting gear* to which this regulation applies shall, as respects the incidental or occasional use thereof in or for the purposes of operations or works to which these Regulations apply *(a)*, be excluded from the operation of the Regulations specified in column 1 of the First Schedule hereto to the extent specified in column 2 thereof and subject to the exceptions and conditions specified in column 3 thereof.

(2) This regulation applies to any *lifting appliance,* chain, rope or *lifting gear*—

(a) which forms part of the permanent equipment of a factory or other premises to which the safety provisions in sections 23 and 24 of the *principal Act* [ss. 26 and 27] apply and which is used at that factory or those premises in raising or lowering for purposes other than the operations or works to which these Regulations apply, but is being used for such operations or works at that factory or those premises; or

(b) which is regularly and ordinarily used in the processes of loading, unloading, moving or handling goods in, on or at any dock, wharf or quay or of loading, unloading or coaling any ship in any dock, harbour or canal, but is being used for operations or works to which these Regulations apply in, on or at a dock, wharf, quay, harbour or canal.

(a) *Operations or works ... apply.* See reg. 2.

7. Delivery of loads with lifting gear attached. Where any article, material or other load intended for use in operations or works to which these Regulations apply *(a)* is delivered at, or adjacent to, the site of such operations or works with a chain, rope or *lifting gear* attached thereto and designed for use as a means of raising and lowering that class of load when removing the same from the point of delivery to a position on the site, and the chain, rope or gear is free from patent defect whether of construction or quality and is not owned or hired by any contractor or employer of workmen who is undertaken any such operations or works as aforesaid on the site, then the requirements of regulations 34, 35, 40 and 41 shall not apply in respect of the use of such chain or *lifting gear* for raising or lowering the load so long as the chain, rope or gear remains attached to the article, material or load.

(a) *Operations or works . . . apply.* See reg. 2.

8. Hoists forming part of the permanent equipment. Regulations 10, 15, 42 to 46 and 48 shall not apply to a *hoist* forming part of the permanent equipment of any structure or underground shaft and which is regularly and ordinarily used for the carriage of persons or goods, but no such *hoist* shall be used for the purposes of any operations or works to which these Regulations apply *(a)* unless the following conditions are complied with, that is to say—

(a) the *hoist* shall not be so used for carrying persons unless a maximum number of persons to be carried at any one time has been specified by the maker or by an insurer of the *hoist* or by a competent firm of lift engineers carrying out periodic examinations of the *hoist*, and a greater number is not being carried;

(b) the *hoist* shall not be so used for carrying materials, tools or other articles, other than light articles readily carried by a person who is riding in the *hoist*, unless a *safe working load* for the *hoist* has been specified by the marker or an insurer or firm as aforesaid and that *safe working load* is not being exceeded; and

(c) on any occasion when the *hoist* has been used for raising or lowering for the purposes of such operations or works the hoistway gate at a landing place shall not be left open except where it is immediately necessary for it to be open to afford access to the *hoist* for some other purpose.

(a) *Operations or works . . . apply.* See reg. 2.

9. Hoists manufactured before the commencement of the Regulations. In the case of a *hoist* manufactured before the date of commencement of these Regulations *(a)*, if it is not reasonably practicable *(b)* to comply fully with any requirement of regulation 42(2), 42(3), 44 or 48 it shall be sufficient if—

(a) the *hoist* has been brought as near as is reasonably practicable *(b)* into conformity with that requirement and a certificate that this has been done has been obtained from a competent person:
    Provided that in the case of a *hoist* which at the date of commencement of these Regulations *(a)* is used, and so long thereafter as it is continued to be used, in works of engineering construction, it shall be

sufficient if the requirements of this paragraph are complied with within three years from the said date of commencement; or
(b) there has been obtained in respect of the *hoist* a certificate under regulation 72(2) of the Building (Safety, Health and Welfare) Regulations 1948 *(c)*, which certificate shall be deemed to be a certificate obtained under this regulation.

(a) Date of commencement. 1 March 1962 (reg. 1(1)).

(b) Reasonably practicable. See INTRODUCTORY NOTE 5.

(c) Regulation 72(2). Under this regulation, now revoked, the application of cognate provisions of the 1948 Regulations was similarly relaxed.

PART III
LIFTING APPLIANCES

10. Construction, maintenance and inspection.—(1) Every *lifting appliance* and every part thereof including all working gear and all other *plant or equipment* used for anchoring or fixing such appliances shall—

(a) be of good mechanical construction, sound material, adequate strength and free from patent defect *(a)*;
(b) be properly maintained *(b)*;
(c) as far as the construction permits be inspected at least once in every week by the driver, if competent for the purpose, or other competent person. A report [Form 91, Part 1, Section C] of the results of every such inspection, signed by the person carrying out the inspection, shall be made forthwith in the prescribed form and containing the prescribed particulars.

(2) In the case of a site where the employer for whom the inspection was carried out has reasonable grounds for believing that the operations or works will be completed in a period of less than six weeks, the provision in this regulation requiring that a report [Form 91, Part 1, Section C] shall be made and signed, in so far as it relates to *lifting appliances* not worked by mechanical power and all *plant or equipment* used for anchoring or fixing such appliances, shall be deemed to have been satisfied if the person in charge of the operations or works carried on by that employer at that site has himself carried out the inspection and is a competent person, and if, within one week of the date of the inspection, he reports to his employer in writing that the *lifting appliance* and *plant or equipment* were inspected by him and that he found them in good order, or observed certain defects as the case may be, and the date of such inspection and the results thereof together with the name of the person making the inspection are entered by the employer in the prescribed form together with the prescribed particulars.

(a) Good mechanical construction, etc. See INTRODUCTORY NOTE 11.

(b) Properly maintained. See INTRODUCTORY NOTE 10.

11. Support, anchoring, fixing and erecting.—(1) Every *lifting appliance* shall be adequately and securely supported.

(2) (a) Every part of a stage, *scaffold,* framework or other structure; and

(b) every mast, beam, pole or other article of *plant or equipment,*

supporting a *lifting appliance* or any part thereof shall (having regard to the nature of the *lifting appliance,* its lifting and reaching capacity and the circumstances of its use) be of good construction and adequate strength and shall be of sound material and free from patent defect *(a).*

(3) Every part of the framework of every crab or winch (other than a jack roll) including its bearers, shall be of metal.

(4) Any anchoring or fixing arrangements provided in connection with a *lifting appliance* shall be adequate and secure.

(5) Every temporary attachment or connection of a rope, chain or other *plant or equipment,* used in the erection or dismantling of any *lifting appliance* shall be adequate and secure.

(6) In the case of a crane which is on occasion dismantled or partially dismantled, any jib or boom which is separated from the crane in dismantling shall be clearly marked so as to indicate the crane of which it was a part.

(a) Good construction, etc. See INTRODUCTORY NOTE 1.

12. Precautions where lifting appliance has travelling or slewing motion. On every stage, gantry or other place where a *lifting appliance* having a travelling or slewing motion is in use, an unobstructed passageway not less than 600 millimetres wide shall be maintained between any part of the appliance liable so to move and any guard-rails, fencing or other nearby fixture:

Provided that if at any time it is impracticable *(a)* to maintain such a passageway at any place or point all reasonable steps shall be taken to prevent the access of any person to such place or point at such time.

(a) Impracticable. See INTRODUCTORY NOTE 5.

13. Platforms for crane drivers and signallers.—(1) Where a platform is provided for the person or person driving or operating a crane, or for any signaller, it shall be—

(a) of sufficient area for the persons employed thereon;

(b) close planked or plated; and

(c) provided with safe means of access *(a),*

and every side of every such platform being a side thereof from which a person is liable to fall a distance of more than 2 metres shall be provided with a suitable guard-rail *(b)* or guard-rails of adequate strength, to a height of at least three feet above the platform and above any raised standing on the platform, and with toe-boards up to a sufficient height being in no case less than 200 millimetres and so placed as to prevent as far as possible the fall of persons, materials and tools from such platform.

(2) The space between any toe-board and the lowest guard-rail above it on any platform for the person or persons driving or operating a crane, or for any signaller, shall not exceed 700 millimetres.

(3) Guard-rails and toe-boards required by this regulation may be removed or remain unerected only for the time and to the extent necessary for the access of persons or the movement of materials.

(a) *Safe means of access.* Compare s. 29(1) of the Factories Act 1961, and reg. 6 of the Construction (Working Places) Regulations 1966, and see the notes thereto.

(b) *Guard-rail.* See note (a) to reg. 29 of the Construction (Working Places) Regulations 1966.

14.   Cabins for drivers.—(1) Subject to paragraphs (2) and (4) of this regulation, the driver of every power-driven *lifting appliance* shall be provided with a suitable cabin which shall—

(a) afford him adequate protection from the weather; and
(b) be so constructed as to afford ready access to such part of the *lifting appliance* as are within the cabin and need periodic inspection or maintenance,

so, however, that no cabin shall be provided which prevents the driver from having such clear and unrestricted view as is necessary for the safe use of the appliance.

(2) Subject to paragraph (4) of this regulation, where reasonably practicable (a) the cabin shall, before such *lifting appliance* is put into general use, be completely erected, or other adequate provision shall be made for the protection of the driver from the weather.

(3) Subject to paragraph (4) of this regulation, where reasonably practicable (a) the cabin shall when in use during the cold weather be adequately heated by suitable means.

(4) Paragraphs (1), (2) and (3) of this regulation shall not apply—

(a) in cases where the driver is indoors or otherwise adequately protected from the weather; or
(b) to a *hoist* other than a *hoist* operated only from one position alongside the winch; or
(c) to *lifting appliances* mounted on wheels and having a maximum *safe working load* of 1 tonne or less; or
(d) to any machine incorporating a *lifting appliance* where the primary purpose of that machine is not that of a *lifting appliance*; or
(e) to *lifting appliances* for occasional use or for use for only short periods.

(a) *Reasonably practicable.* See INTRODUCTORY NOTE 5.

15.   Drums and pulleys. Every drum or pulley round which the chain or wire rope of any *lifting appliance* is carried shall be of suitable diameter and construction for the chain or rope used. Every chain or rope which terminates at the winding drum of a *lifting appliance* shall be properly secured thereto and at least two turns of such chain or rope shall remain on the drum in every operating position of the appliance.

16.   Brakes, controls, safety devices, etc.—(1) Every crane, crab and winch (other than a jack roll) shall be provided with an efficient brake or brakes or other safety device which will prevent the fall of the load when suspended, and by which the load can be effectively controlled whilst being lowered.

(2) On every *lifting appliance* every lever, handle, switch or other device provided for controlling the operation of any part of the appliance being a lever, handle, switch or other device whose accidental movement or displacement is liable to cause danger, shall, where practicable (unless it is so placed or the applicance is so constructed as to prevent accidental movement or displacement) be provided with a suitable spring or other locking arrangement to prevent the accidental movement or displacement:

Provided that in the case of a *lifting appliance* which at the date of commencement *(a)* of these Regulations is used, and so long thereafter as it is continued to be used, in works of engineering construction, it shall be sufficient if the requirements of this paragraph are complied with within two years from the said date of commencement.

(3) Every lever, handle, switch or other device provided for controlling the operation of any part of a *lifting appliance* shall have upon or adjacent to it clear markings to indicate its purpose and mode of operation:

Provided that this paragraph shall not apply to rotating handles for raising or lowering the load in the case of a winch or non-derricking jib crane not operated by mechanical power.

(a) Date of commencement. 1 March 1962 (reg. 1(1)).

17. Safe means of access. Where any person engaged in the examination, repair or lubrication of any *lifting appliance* is liable to fall a distance or more than 2 metres there shall, so far as is reasonably practicable *(a)*, be provided and maintained safe means of access *(b)* to and egress from the place at which the person has to work, with (where necessary) adequate handholds and footholds *(c)*.

(a) Reasonably practicable. See INTRODUCTORY NOTE 5.

(b) Safe means of access. Compare s. 29(1) of the Factories Act 1961, and see the notes thereto.

(c) Handhold; foothold. See note *(d)* to s. 29 of the Factories Act 1961, and *Roberts v Dorman Long & Co Ltd* [1953] 2 All ER 428, [1953] 1 WLR 942, CA.

18. Poles or beams supporting pulley blocks or gin wheels. No pulley block or gin wheel suspended from or supported by a pole or beam shall be used for raising or lowering materials unless it is effectively secured to the pole or beam and the pole or beam—

(a) is of adequate strength for the purpose for which it is being used; and
(b) is adequately and properly secured so as to support the pulley block or gin wheel and the load with safety and so as to prevent undue movement of the pole or beam.

19. Stability of lifting appliances.—(1) Appropriate precautions shall be taken to ensure the stability of *lifting appliances* used on a soft or uneven surface or on a slope.

(2) No crane shall be used for raising or lowering unless, so as to ensure stability, it is either—

(a) securely anchored; or
(b) adequately weighted by suitable ballast which shall be properly placed on the crane structure and sufficiently secured to prevent its being accidentally displaced.

No part of any rails on which a crane is mounted or the sleepers supporting such rails shall be used as anchorage for this purpose.

(3) The whole of the appliances for the anchorage or ballasting of a crane shall be examined by a competent person on each occasion before the crane is erected.

(4) After each erection of a crane on a site of operations or works to which these Regulations apply *(a)*, and after each removal of a crane about or to such a site, or any adjustment to any member of a crane, being a removal or adjustment which involves changes in the arrangements for anchoring or ballasting the crane, the securing of the anchorage or the adequacy of the ballasting, as the case may be, shall, before the crane is taken into use, be tested by a competent person, by the imposition either—

(a) of a load of twenty-five per cent. above the maximum load to be lifted by the crane as erected as the positions where there is the maximum pull on each anchorage, or
(b) of a less load arranged to provide an equivalent test of the anchorage or ballasting arrangements.

A record of every such test and the results thereof, containing the particulars required by the Lifting Plant and Equipment (Records of Test and Examination etc.) Regulations 1992, shall be made forthwith.

(5) If the person making tests under paragraph (4) of this regulation considers that the maximum load which may safely be lifted by that crane as erected is less than the *safe working load* of the crane as defined in regulation 4 he shall specify that maximum among the said particulars and a loading diagram appropriate to the stability of the crane at the time of the test, taking into account, in the case of a crane mounted on wheels, the conditions of the track, and indicating a modified *safe working load* or loads shall be affixed in a position where it can readily be seen by the crane driver. Such modified *safe working load* or loads shall be deemed for the purposes of these Regulations to be the *safe working load* or loads of the crane as erected.

(6) Where the stability of a crane is secured by means of removable weights a diagram or notice indicating the position and amount of such weights shall be affixed on the crane where it can be readily seen.

(7) No crane shall be used or erected under weather conditions likely to endanger its stability. After exposure to weather conditions likely to have affected the stability of a crane, the anchorage arrangements and ballast shall be examined by a competent person as soon as practicable and before the crane is used, and any necessary steps taken to ensure the stability of the crane.

(a) Operations or works . . . apply. See reg. 2.

20.   Rail mounted cranes.—(1) All rails on which a crane moves shall—

(a) be supported on a surface sufficiently firm to prevent undue movement of the rails;

(b) have an even running surface, be sufficiently and adequately supported, and be of adequate section;

(c) be jointed by fish plates or double chairs;

(d) be securely fastened to sleepers or bearers;

(e) be laid in straight lines or in curves of such radii that the crane can be moved freely and without danger of derailment; and

(f) be provided with adequate stops or buffers on each rail at each end of the track.

All rails and equipment referred to in this paragraph shall be properly maintained *(a)*:

Provided that requirements (c) and (d) of this paragraph shall not apply in the case of cranes on bridge rails or in the case of any crane if other adequate steps are taken to ensure the proper junction of the rails and to prevent any material variation in their gauge.

(2) In the case of every crane mounted on rails either—

(a) the crane shall be provided with effective brakes for the travelling motion; or

(b) sprags, scotches or chocks shall be available, and used when necessary.

(3) Where a Scotch derrick crane is mounted on more than one bogie, trolley or wheeled carriage, the crane sleepers or land ties, and if necessary the bogies, trolleys or wheeled carriages shall be rigidly braced and properly connected together, and the rails on which each bogie, trolley or wheeled carriage moves shall be level. The crane shall be moved on the track only in a manner not liable to cause instability, racking or distortion either of the crane structure or of the supporting framework or track.

(4) Every travelling crane on rails shall be provided with guards to remove from the rails any loose material likely to cause danger.

(a) *Properly maintained.* See INTRODUCTORY NOTE 10.

21.   Mounting of cranes. Every bogie, trolley or wheeled carriage on which a crane is mounted shall, having regard to the purposes for which the crane is being used, be of good construction, adequate strength and suitable to support the crane and shall be of sound material *(a)*, free from patent defect and properly maintained *(b)*.

(a) *Good construction, etc.* See INTRODUCTORY NOTE 11.

(b) *Properly maintained.* See INTRODUCTORY NOTE 10.

22.   Cranes with derricking jibs. On every crane having a derricking jib operated through a clutch there shall be provided and properly maintained an effective interlocking arrangement between the derricking clutch and the pawl sustaining the derricking drum which shall ensure that the clutch cannot be disengaged unless the pawl is in effective engagement with the derricking drum and the pawl cannot be disengaged unless the clutch is in effective engagement with the derricking drum:

Provided that this regulation shall not apply to any crane in which—

(a) the hoisting drum and the derricking drum are independently driven; or

(b) the mechanism driving the derricking drum is self-locking.

23.   Restriction on use of cranes.—(1) Without prejudice to paragraph (2) of this regulation, the hoisting mechanism of a crane shall not be used for any purpose other than raising or lowering a load vertically unless no undue stress is imposed on any part of the crane structure or mechanism, and the stability of the crane is not thereby endangered and unless such use is supervised by a competent person.

(2) A crane with a derricking jib shall not be used with the job at a radius exceeding the maximum radius required to be specified for the jib in the record of the results of any test and thorough examination required by regulation 28.

24.   Use of cranes with timber structural member prohibited. No crane which has any timber structural member shall be used.

25.   Erection of cranes under supervision. A crane shall not be erected except under the supervision of a competent person.

26.   Competent persons to operate lifting appliances and give signals.—(1) A *lifting appliance* shall not be operated otherwise than by a person trained and competent to operate that appliance except that it shall be permissible for the appliance to be operated by a person who is under the direct supervision of a qualified person for the purpose of training.

(2) No person under eighteen years of age shall be employed (except under the direct supervision of a competent person for the purpose of training) either to give signals to the operator of any *lifting appliance* driven by mechanical power or to operate any such appliance.

(3) Subject to paragraph (4) of this regulation, if the person operating a *lifting appliance* has not a clear and unrestricted view of the load, or, where there is no load, of the point of attachment for a load, and of its vicinity, throughout the operation, except at any place where such view is not necessary for safe working, there shall be appointed and suitably stationed one or more competent persons as may be necessary to give necessary signals to the operator:

Provided that where and in so far as it is impracticable *(a)* to comply with the foregoing requirements of this paragraph effective measures shall be taken to enable the driver or operator of the *lifting appliance*—

(a) to ascertain the position of the load, or point of attachment for a load, when it is in the vicinity of a loading or unloading point or of any other place at which danger is reasonably to be anticipated; or

(b) to ensure the safe movement of the load by other means.

(4) The provisions of paragraph (3) of this regulation shall not apply

(a) in the case of a *hoist* of an aerial cableway, or of an aerial ropeway; or

(b) (in the case other than that of a *hoist*) as respects places where the appliance can raise or lower the load (or point of attachment for a load) vertically only, without any horizontal or slewing motion, if for safe working the driver or operator of the appliance needs information related to the movement, stopping or position of the load, or point of attachment for a load, when it is at or in the immediate vicinity of certain points only, and effective arrangements are made by means of a signalling system, position indicators or otherwise, for providing the driver or operator with any such information necessary for safe working.

(5) There shall be efficient signalling arrangements between the driver or operator and persons employed at a loading or unloading point of an aerial cableway or aerial ropeway.

(a) *Impracticable.* See INTRODUCTORY NOTE 5.

27. Signals.—(1) Every signal given for the movement or stopping of a *lifting appliance* shall be distinctive in character and such that the person to whom it is given is able to hear or see it easily.

(2) Devices or apparatus used for giving sound, colour or light signals for the purposes aforesaid shall be properly maintained (a), and the means of communication shall be adequately protected from accidental interference.

(a) *Properly maintained.* See INTRODUCTORY NOTE 10.

28. Testing and examination of cranes, etc.—(1) Subject to paragraph (4) of this regulation, no crane, crab or winch shall be used unless it has been tested and thoroughly examined by a competent person within the previous four years and no pulley block, gin wheel or sheer legs shall be used in the raising or lowering of any load weighing 1 tonne or more unless it has been tested and thoroughly examined by a competent person.

(2) Subject to paragraph (4) of this regulation, no crane, crab or winch shall be used after any substantial alteration or repair affecting its strength or stability until it has been tested and thoroughly examined by a competent person and no pulley block, gin wheel or sheer legs shall, after any substantial alteration or repair, be used in the raising or lowering of any load weighing 1 tonne or more until it has been tested and thoroughly examined by a competent person.

(3) Subject to paragraph (4) of this regulation, no *lifting appliance* shall be used unless it has been thoroughly examined by a competent person within the previous fourteen months and since it has undergone any substantial alteration or repair.

(4) Nothing in paragraphs (1) to (3) of this regulation shall apply to a *hoist*.

(5) No crane, crab winch, pulley block or gin wheel shall be used unless there has been obtained a record (a) of any test and thorough examination

required by paragraphs (1) and (2) of this regulation and of the results thereof, containing the particulars required by the Lifting Plant and Equipment (Records of Test and Examination etc.) Regulations 1992.

(6) A record of every test or thorough examination required by paragraphs (1) to (3) of this regulation, containing the particulars required by the Lifting Plant and Equipment (Records of Test and Examination etc.) Regulations 1992, shall be made within twenty-eight days:

Provided that this paragraph shall not apply to a test and thorough examination of which a record has been obtained in accordance with paragraph (5) of this regulation.

(7) The person authenticating the record of any test or examination required by paragraphs (1) or (3) of this regulation shall within twenty-eight days of the completion of the test or examination send a copy of the particulars in the record to an inspector appointed by the Health and Safety Executive under section 19 of the Health and Safety at Work etc. Act 1974 who is authorised for the purposes of this provision in every case where the test or examination shows that the plant or equipment cannot continue to be used with safety unless certain repairs are carried out immediately or within a specified time.

General note.   For exemptions relating to certain excavators used as cranes, see Certificate of Exemption No. CON (LO)/1981/2[F2513], set out following these Regulations.

29.   Marking of safe working loads.—(1) *The safe working load* or *safe working loads* and a means of identification shall be plainly marked—

   (a) upon every crane, crab or winch;
   (b) upon every pulley block, gin wheel, sheer legs, derrick pole, derrick mast or aerial cableway used in the raising or lowering of any load weighing 1 tonne or more.

(2) Every crane of variable operating radius (including a crane with a derricking jib) shall—

   (a) have plainly marked upon it the *safe working load* at various radii of the jib, trolley or crab, and, in the case of a crane with a derricking jib, the maximum radius at which the jib may be worked; and
   (b) be fitted with an accurate indicator, clearly visible to the driver, showing the radius of the jib, trolley or crab, at any time and the *safe working load* corresponding to that radius.

General note.   For exemptions relating to certain excavators used as cranes, see Certificate of Exemption No. CON (LO)/1981/2[F2513], and for exceptions relating to telescopic jib cranes, see Certificate of Exemption No. 6 (General) [F2490], set out following these Regulations.

30.   Indication of safe working load of jib cranes.—(1) No jib crane having either a fixed or a derricking jib (other than a *mobile crane*) shall be used unless it is fitted with an *approved* type of automatic safe load indicator which shall be properly maintained *(a)*. Every such indicator shall be tested by a competent person other than the crane driver after erection or installation of the crane for the purpose of any operations or works to which these Regulations apply *(b)* and before the crane is taken into use. The indicator shall be inspected in any case at intervals not exceeding one week, when the crane is in use, by the person carrying out the inspection required under sub-paragraph (c) of paragraph (1) of regulation 10 and the results of every such inspection shall be reported in the manner specified in that sub-paragraph.

(2) No *mobile crane* having either a fixed or a derricking jib shall be used unless it is fitted with an *approved* type of automatic safe load indicator which shall be properly maintained *(a)*. Every such indicator shall be tested by a competent person before the crane is taken into use—

(a) on each occasion after it has been wholly or partially dismantled; and
(b) after each erection, alteration or removal of the crane for the purpose of any operations or works to which these Regulations apply *(b)*, being an erection, alteration or removal likely to have affected the proper operation of the indicator.

The indicator shall be inspected in any case at intervals not exceeding one week, when the crane is in use, by the person carrying out the inspection required under sub-paragraph (c) or paragraph (1) of regulation 10 and the results of every such inspection shall be reported in the manner specified in that sub-paragraph.

(3) A report [Form 91, Part 1, Section E] of the results of every test required by this regulation, signed by the person carrying out the test, shall be made forthwith in the prescribed form and containing the prescribed particulars.

(4) This regulation does not apply—

(a) to any guy derrick crane, being a crane of which the mast is held upright solely by means of ropes with the necessary fittings and tightening screws;
(b) to any hand crane which is being used solely for erecting or dismantling another crane; or
(c) to any crane having a maximum *safe working load* of 1 tonne or less; or
(d) until the expiration of two years after the date of commmencement *(c)* of these Regulations, to any excavator adapted for use as a crane.

General note. For exemptions relating to certain excavators used as cranes, see Certificate of Exemption No. CON (LO)/1981/2 [F2513], set out following these Regulations.
 The fees payable to the Health and Safety Executive for the approvals required by reg. 30(1) and (2) are specified by the Health and Safety (Fees) Regulations 1992, S.I. 1992 No. 1752.

(a) Properly maintained. See INTRODUCTORY NOTE 10.

(b) Operations or works . . . apply. See reg. 2.

(c) Date of commencement. 1 March 1962 (reg. 1(1)).

31. Load not to exceed safe working load. None of the following appliances, nor any part of any such appliances, shall be loaded beyond the *safe working load,* that is to say, cranes, crabs, winches, pulley blocks, gin wheels, sheer legs, derrick poles, and derrick masts; so, however, that for the purpose of making tests of any such appliance the *safe working load* may be exceeded by such an amount as a competent person appointed to carry out the tests may authorise.

32.   Precautions on raising or lowering loads.—(1) Where there is lifted on a crane, crab, winch (other than a piling winch), sheer legs or aerial cableway a load which is equal to or slightly less than the relevant *safe working load* and which is not already sustained wholly by the appliance, the lifting shall be halted after the load has been raised a short distance and before the operation is proceeded with.

(2) Where more than one *lifting appliance* is required to raise or lower one load—

(a)   the *plant or equipment* used shall be so arranged and fixed that no such *lifting appliance* shall at any time be loaded beyond its *safe working load* or be rendered unstable in the raising or lowering of the load; and

(b)   a competent person shall be specially appointed to supervise the operation.

33.   Scotch and guy derrick cranes.—(1) The jib of a Scotch derrick crane shall not be erected between the back stays of the crane.

(2) No load which lies in the angle between the back stays of a Scotch derrick crane shall be moved by that crane.

(3) Appropriate measures shall be taken to prevent the foot of the king post of any Scotch derrick crane from being lifted out of its socket or support whilst in use.

(4) Where the guys of a guy derrick crane cannot be fixed at approximately equal inclinations to the mast and so that the angles between adjacent pairs of guys are approximately equal such other measures shall be taken as will ensure the stability of the crane.

PART IV
CHAINS, ROPES AND LIFTING GEAR

34.   Construction, testing, examination and safe working load.—(1) Subject to the provisions of paragraph (2) of this regulation, no chain, rope or *lifting gear* shall be used in *raising or lowering or as a means of suspension* unless—

(a)   it is of good construction, sound material, adequate strength, suitable quality, and free from patent defect *(a)*; and

(b)   (except in the case of a wire rope used before the commencement of these Regulations or a fibre rope or fibre rope sling) it has been tested and examined by a competent person and a record of such test and examination and of the results thereof, containing the particulars required by the Lifting Plant and Equipment (Records of Test and Examination etc.) Regulations 1992, has been obtained; and

(c)   it is marked in plain legible figures and letters with the *safe working load* and means of identification.

(2) A rope or rope sling need not be marked with the *safe working load* if its *safe working load* is contained in the record required by regulation 40 and the rope or sling is so marked as to enable its *safe working load* to be ascertained from the said record or if, in the case of a rope or rope sling to which sub-paragraph (b) of paragraph (1) of this regulation does not apply, its *safe working load* can be ascertained from a table of *safe working loads* posted in a prominent position on the site of the operations or works; and in the case of a rope or rope sling which is not required to have been tested and which is not marked with the *safe working load*, the *safe working load* required to be entered in the said record or required to be shown by the table, as the case may be, shall be deemed for the purpose of these Regulations to be the *safe working load* of the rope or rope sling.

(3) No wire rope shall be used in *raising or lowering or as a means of suspension* if in any length of ten diameters the total number of visible broken wires exceeds five per cent. of the total number of wires in the rope.

(4) No chain, rope or *lifting gear* shall be loaded beyond its *safe working load* except for the purpose of making tests and then only to such extent as a competent person appointed to carry out the tests may authorise.

General note. For an exemption, see reg. 7.

(a) **Good construction.** See the similar provisions of s. 26(1)(a) of the Factories Act 1961, and INTRODUCTORY NOTE 11.

35. Testing of chains, rings, etc. altered or repaired by welding. No chain, ring, link, hook, plate clamp, shackle, swivel or eye-bolt which has been lengthened, altered or repaired by welding shall be used in *raising or lowering or as a means of suspension* unless since such lengthening, alteration or repair it has been tested and thoroughly examined by a competent person and there has been obtained "a record of such test and thorough examination and of the results thereof, containing the particulars required by the Lifting Plant and Equipment (Records of Test and Examination etc.) Regulations 1992":
Provided that the requirements of this regulation as to testing and obtaining a record shall not apply to a chain attached to the bucket of either a dragline or an excavator.

36. Hooks. Every hook used for *raising or lowering or as a means of suspension* shall either—

(a) be provided with an efficient device to prevent the displacement of the sling or load from the hook; or
(b) be of such shape as to reduce as far as possible the risk of such displacement.

37. Slings.—(1) Every sling used for raising or lowering on a *lifting appliance* shall be securely attached to the appliance, and the method of attachment shall not be a method likely to result in damage to any part of the sling or to any *lifting gear* supporting it.

(2) No double or multiple sling shall be used for raising or lowering if—

(a) the upper ends of the sling legs are not connected by means of a shackle, ring or link of adequate strength; or

(b) the *safe working load* of any sling leg is exceeded as a result of the angle between the sling legs.

38. Edges of load not to come into contact with sling, etc. Adequate steps shall be taken by the use of suitable packing or otherwise to prevent the edges of the load from coming into contact with any sling, rope or chain, where this would cause danger.

39. Knotted chains, etc.—(1) A load shall not be raised, lowered or suspended on a chain or wire rope which has a knot tied in any part of the chain or rope under direct tension.

(2) No chain which is shortened or joined to another chain by means of bolts and nuts inserted through the links shall be used for raising, lowering or suspending any load.

40. Examination of chains, ropes and lifting gear. No chain, rope or *lifting gear* shall be used for *raising or lowering or as a means of suspension* unless it has been thoroughly examined by a competent person at least once within the previous six months; so, however, that chains, ropes and *lifting gear* not in regular use need only be so examined when necessary.

A record of every such thorough examination and of the results thereof, containing the particulars required by the Lifting Plant and Equipment (Records of Test and Examination etc.) Regulations 1992, shall be made forthwith.

41. Annealing of chains and lifting gear. A chain or *lifting gear* (other than a rope sling or *lifting gear* of a class or description specified in the Second Schedule to these Regulations or exempted by certificate of the Chief Inspector upon the ground that it is made of such material or so constructed that it cannot be subjected to heat treatment without risk of damage) shall not be used in *raising or lowering or as a means of suspension* unless—

(a) it has been effectively annealed or subjected to some appropriate form of heat treatment under the supervision of a competent person within the previous fourteen months or, in the case of chains or slings of 13 millimetres bar or smaller material, within the previous six months; so, however, that chains or *lifting gear* not in regular use or used solely on *lifting appliances* worked by hand need be annealed or subjected to appropriate heat treatment only when necessary; and

(b) a report [Form 91, Part 2, Section K] has been made in writing containing the prescribed particulars of every annealing or appropriate heat treatment, signed by the competent person under whose supervision the annealing or heat treatment was carried out.

PART V
SPECIAL PROVISIONS AS TO HOISTS

42. Safety of hoistways, platforms and cages.—(1) The hoistway of every *hoist* shall at all points at which access to the hoistway is provided or at which persons are liable to be struck by any moving part of the *hoist* be efficiently protected by a substantial enclosure, and the enclosure shall where access to the *hoist* is needed be fitted with gates. Such enclosure and gates shall where practicable extend to a height of at least 2 metres except where a lesser height is sufficient to prevent any person falling down the hoistway and there is no risk of any person coming into contact with any moving part of the *hoist*, but shall in no case be less than 910 millimetres. Gates so fitted shall be kept closed except at a landing place where the platform or cage is at rest and it is for the time being necessary for the gate to be open for the purpose of loading or unloading goods, plant or material, or to allow persons to enter or leave the cage; and without prejudice to the obligation of every contractor and employer of workmen under these Regulations, it shall be the duty of every person, immediately after using any gateway, to see that the gate is closed unless it is for the time being necessary for the gate to be open for any of the purposes aforesaid.

(2) In connection with every *hoist* there shall where practicable *(a)* be provided and maintained efficient devices which will support the platform or cage together with its *safe working load* in the event of failure of the hoist rope or ropes or any part of the hoisting gear.

(3) In connection with every *hoist* there shall be provided and maintained efficient automatic devices which will ensure that the platform or cage does not over-run the highest point to which it is for the time being constructed to travel.

General note. For exemption relating to rack and pinion hoists, see Certificate of Exemption CON (LO)/1981/1 [F2514], set out following these Regulations.

(a) Practicable. See INTRODUCTORY NOTE 5.

43. Operation of hoists.—(1) The construction and the installation arrangements of every *hoist* shall where practicable *(a)* be such that it can be operated at any one time only from one position and a *hoist* shall not be operated from the cage unless the requirements of regulation 48 are complied with.

(2) If a person operating a *hoist* has not a clear and unrestricted view of the platform or cage throughout its travel, except at points where such a view is not necessary for safe working, then effective arrangements shall be made for signals for operating the *hoist* to be given to him from each landing place at which the *hoist* is used and to enable him to stop the platform or cage at the appropriate level.

(a) Practicable. See INTRODUCTORY NOTE 5.

44. Winches. Where a *hoist* is operated by means of a winch, the winch shall be so constructed that the brake is applied when the control lever, handle or switch is not held in the operating position, and the winch shall not be a winch fitted with a pawl and ratchet gear on which the pawl has to be disengaged before the platform or cage can be lowered.

45. Safe working load and marking of hoists. The *safe working load* shall be plainly marked on every *hoist* platform or cage and no load greater than that load shall be carried, except that for the purpose of carrying out a test the *safe working load* may be exceeded by such amount as a competent person appointed to carry out the test may authorise. In the case of a *hoist* used for carrying persons the maximum number of persons to be carried at any one time shall also be so marked, and a greater number of persons shall not be so carried. In the case of any other *hoist* there shall be a readily legible notice on the platform or cage stating that the carriage of persons is prohibited.

46.   Test and examination of hoists.—(1) No *hoist* shall be used unless—

(a) in the case of a *hoist* manufactured or substantially altered or substantially repaired after the date of commencement *(a)* of these Regulations, it has, since such manufacture, alteration or repair, as the case may be, been tested and thoroughly examined by a competent person, and a record of such test and thorough examination, containing the particulars required by the Lifting Plant and Equipment (Records of Test and Examination etc.) Regulations 1992, has been obtained;

(b) in the case of use for carrying persons, it has, since it was last erected or the height of travel of the cage was last altered, whichever is the later, been tested and thoroughly examined by a competent person and a record of the results of such test and thorough examination, containing the particulars required by the Lifting Plant and Equipment (Records of Test and Examination etc.) Regulations 1992, has been made; and

(c) it has been thoroughly examined by a competent person at least once within the previous six months.

(2) A record of every thorough examination required by sub-paragraph *(c)* of the foregoing paragraph and of the results thereof, containing the particulars required by the Lifting Plant and Equipment (Records of Test and Examination etc.) Regulations 1992, shall be made within twenty-eight days.

(3) The person authenticating the record of any test or examination required by paragraph (1) of this regulation shall within twenty-eight days of the completion of the test or examination send a copy of the particulars contained in the record to an inspector appointed by the Health and Safety Executive under section 19 of the Health and Safety at Work etc. Act 1974 who is authorised for the purposes of this provision in every case where the test or examination shows that the hoist cannot continue to be used with safety unless certain repairs are carried out immediately or within a specified time.

(a) ***Date of commencement.*** 1 March 1962 (reg. 1(1)).

PART VI

CARRIAGE OF PERSONS AND SECURENESS OF LOADS

47.   Carrying persons by means of lifting appliances.—(1) No person shall be raised, lowered or carried by a power driven *lifting appliance* except—

(a) on the driver's platform in the case of a crane; or

(b) on a *hoist*; or

(c) on a suspended scaffold which is of good construction, sound material, adequate strength and properly maintained; or

(d) as permitted by paragraph (2) of this regulation.

(2) A person may be raised, lowered or carried by a power driven *lifting appliance* otherwise than in accordance with the provisions of paragraph (1) of this regulation only—

(a) in circumstances where the use of a *hoist* or of a suspended scaffold which complies with the requirements of paragraph (1)(c) of this regulation is not reasonably practicable *(a)* and the requirements of paragraph (3) of this regulation are complied with; or

(b) on an aerial cableway or aerial ropeway provided that the requirements of sub-paragraphs (b) to (d) of paragraph (3) of this regulation are complied with.

(3) The requirements referred to in paragraph (2) of this regulation are—

(a) that the appliance can be operated from one position only;

(b) that any winch used in connection with the appliance shall comply with the requirements of regulation 44 of these Regulations;

(c) that no person shall be carried except—
   (i) in a suitable chair or cage, or
   (ii) in a suitable skip or other receptacle at least 910 millimetres deep; and any such chair, cage, skip or other receptacle shall be of good construction *(b)*, sound material, adequate strength and properly maintained, and shall be provided with suitable means to prevent any occupant falling out and shall not contain material or tools liable to interfere with his handhold or foothold *(c)* or otherwise endanger him; and

(d) that suitable measures shall be taken to prevent the chair, cage, skip or other receptacle from spinning or tipping in a manner dangerous to any occupant.

(a) **Reasonably practicable.** See INTRODUCTORY NOTE 5.

(b) **Good construction, etc.** See INTRODUCTORY NOTE 11.

(c) **Handhold; foothold.** See note *(c)* to reg. 17.

48. Hoists carrying persons.—(1) No person shall be carried by a *hoist* unless it is provided with a cage which—

(a) is so constructed as to prevent, when the cage gate or gates are shut, any person carried from falling out or from being trapped between any part of the cage and any fixed structure or other moving part of the *hoist* or from being struck by articles or materials falling down the hoistway; and

(b) is fitted on each side from which access is provided to a landing place with a gate which, so far is reasonably practicable *(a)*, shall have efficient interlocking or other devices to secure that the gate cannot be opened except when the cage is at a landing place and that the cage cannot be moved away from any such place until the gate is closed.

(2) Every gate in the hoistway enclosure of a *hoist* used for carrying persons shall be fitted with efficient interlocking or other devices to secure that the gate cannot be opened except when the cage is at the landing place, and that the cage cannot be moved away from the landing place until the gate is closed.

(3) In connection with every *hoist* used for carrying persons there shall be provided suitable efficient automatic devices which will ensure that the cage comes to rest at a point above the lowest point to which the cage can travel.

(a) *Reasonably practicable.* See INTRODUCTORY NOTE 5.

49. Secureness of loads.—(1) Every part of a load shall be securely suspended or supported whilst being raised or lowered and shall be adequately secured to prevent danger from slipping or displacement.

(2) Where by reason of the nature or position of the operation a load is liable, whilst being moved on a *lifting appliance* or *lifting gear* to come into contact with any object so that the object may become displaced, special measures shall be adopted to prevent the danger so far as reasonably practicable (a).

(3) Every container or receptacle used for raising or lowering stone, bricks, tiles, slates or other objects shall be so enclosed, constructed or designed as to prevent the accidental fall of such objects:
Provided that this requirement shall not apply to a grab, shovel or other similar excavating receptacle if effective steps are taken to prevent any person being endangered by a fall of objects therefrom.

(4) Goods or loose material shall not be placed directly on a platform of a *hoist* unless such platform is enclosed or other effective precautions are taken where necessary to prevent the fall of any such goods or material.

(5) No truck or wheelbarrow shall be carried on a *hoist* platform unless it is efficiently scotched or secured on the platform.

(6) No loaded truck or wheelbarrow shall be carried on the open platform of a *hoist* unless the truck or wheelbarrow is so loaded that no part of the load is liable to fall off.

(7) No load shall be left suspended from a *lifting appliance* unless a competent person is actually in charge of the appliance.

(a) *Reasonably practicable.* See INTRODUCTORY NOTE 5.

PART VII
KEEPING OF RECORDS

50. Reports, certificates, etc.—(1) The reports or records required by regulations 10, 19(4) and (5), 30 and 46(1)(b) shall be kept or the particulars in them shall be capable of inspection (which must include the ability to make an accurate and legible written copy) on the site of the operations or works and when there are no relevant operations or works shall be kept or the particulars contained in them shall be capable of inspection as aforesaid at an office of the contractor or employer for whom the inspection, test by examination, as the case may be, was carried out:
Provided that in the case of a site where the contractor or employer has reasonable grounds for believing that the operation or works will be completed in a period of less than six weeks, the contractor or employer may keep the reports required by regulation 10 at his office.

(2) All other reports and every certificate or other record required for the purposes of these Regulations shall be kept either on the site of the relevant

operations or works or at an office of the contractor or employer for whom the report was made or the certificate or record was obtained or of the owner of the *plant or equipment* to which the certificate or record relates.

(3) All reports, certificates and other records required for the purposes of these Regulations shall at all reasonable times be open to inspection by any of HM Inspectors *(a)* of Factories, and the person keeping any such report, certificate or other record shall send to any such inspector such extracts therefrom or copies thereof as the inspector may from time to time require for the purpose of the execution of his duties under the Factories Act 1937 to 1959.

(a) **Inspector.** See INTRODUCTORY NOTE 24.

FIRST SCHEDULE

EXTENT OF EXCLUSIONS UNDER REGULATION 6

Regulation	Extent of exclusion	Exceptions and conditions
10	Requirement (c) of paragraph (1)	—
11	Paragraph (5)	—
12	The whole regulation	—
13	The whole regulation except requirements (a) and (c) of paragraph (1)	—
14	The whole regulation	—
16	Paragraphs (2) and (3)	—
19	Paragraphs (4) and (5)	Save that where the crane is specially erected for use in the operations or works to which these Regulations apply, the crane shall before such use be tested in accordance with paragraph (4), and a record shall be kept of the particulars of the tests and paragraph (5) shall then apply.
20	Requirement (f) of paragraph (1) and paragraph (4)	—
22	The whole regulation	—
28	The whole regulation	—
29	Requirement (b) of paragraph (2)	—
30	The whole regulation	—
34	Sub-paragraph (c) of paragraph (1)	If there are available to any person using the chain, rope or gear, means of ascertaining its *safe working load*.
36	The whole regulation	—
40	The provisions relating to the keeping of a register.	—
41	Sub-paragraph (b)............	—

SECOND SCHEDULE

CHAINS AND LIFTING GEAR EXCEPTED UNDER REGULATION 41
(AS TO HEAT TREATMENT)

(1) Chains made of malleable cast-iron.

(2) Plate link chains.

(3) The following when made of steel or of any non-ferrous metal, namely, chains, rings, links, hooks, plate clamps, shackles, swivels and eye-bolts.

(4) Pitched chains working on sprocket or pocketed wheels.

(5) The following when permanently attached to pitched chains, pulley blocks or weighing machines, namely, rings, links, hooks, shackles and swivels.

(6) The following when having screw-threaded parts or ball-bearings or other case-hardened parts, namely, hooks, eye-bolts, and swivels.

(7) Socket shackles secured to wire ropes by white metal cappings.

(8) Bordeaux connections.

CERTIFICATE OF EXEMPTION NO. 6 (GENERAL)
TELESCOPIC JIB CRANES
F 2490, 23 December 1976

In pursuance of the powers conferred on me by regulation 2(3) of the Shipbuilding and Ship-repairing Regulations 1960 and regulation 5 of the Construction (Lifting Operations) Regulations 1961, I hereby exempt cranes with telescopic jibs from the requirements of regulation 34(3) of the said Regulations of 1960 and of regulation 29(2) of the said Regulations of 1961, subject to the conditions specified in the Schedule to this Certificate.

Expressions used in this Certificate shall have the same respective meanings as in the relevant Regulations.

I hereby revoke Certificate of Exemption No. 4 dated 12 April 1973.

This certificate shall remain in force until revoked by the Chief Inspector of Factories.

SCHEDULE

1.   The crane shall be fitted with—
   (a)   accurate indicators which show the operating radius of the jib and the inclination of the jib for the time being; and
   (b)   tables prepared by the maker of the crane or by a competent person setting out:
      (i)   for operations with a fly jib or locked jib extension fitted used either singly or in combination, the safe working loads at specified inclinations of the jib; and
      (ii)   for other operations, the safe working loads corresponding to any combination of specified operating radii and inclination of the jib.

2.   (1) In the following cases, the said tables shall be fitted in the driver's cabin of the crane, but the said indicators may be fitted on the jib—
   (a)   in the case of cranes of a maximum safe working load of 8 tons or less; and
   (b)   in the case of cranes of a maximum safe working load exceeding 8 tons but not exceeding 15 tons and manufactured before 12 April 1973.
   (2) In all other cases, both the said tables and the said indicators shall be fitted in the driver's cabin of the crane.

3.   The said indicators and the said tables shall be properly maintained.

4.   Without prejudice to paragraph 5 of this Schedule, the sub-divisions on the scales of the said indicators shall be as small as is practicable.

5.   The markings on the said indicator scales shall at all times be clearly legible to the crane driver from his operating position in the cabin.

6.   The tables provided shall have suitable and sufficient entries to enable the crane driver to determine the safe working load of the crane at any position of the jib within a specified range:

(a) of inclinations in the circumstances described in paragraph 1(b)(i) of this Schedule; or

(b) of radii and inclinations in the circumstances described in paragraph 1(b)(ii) of this Schedule.

7.   The crane shall not be used outside the limits of the range so specified.

8.   In the case of cranes manufactured before 12 April 1973 which have the following arrangements—

(a) an indicator fitted on the jib which shows the inclination of the jib for the time being; and

(b) markings on the jib which show the amount of extension of the jib for the time being; and

(c) tables of the kind mentioned in paragraph 1(b) of this Schedule fitted in the driver's cabin,

the requirements of paragraphs 1 to 5 of this Schedule shall not apply until 1 January 1978, provided that the said indicator, markings and tables are properly maintained.

CERTIFICATE OF EXEMPTION No. CON (LO)/1981/1 RACK
AND PINION HOISTS
F 2514, 16 July 1981

In pursuance of the powers conferred on me by regulation 5 of the Construction (Lifting Operations) Regulations 1961 I hereby exempt from the requirements of regulation 42(2) of the said Regulations, subject to the conditions specified in the Schedule to this Certificate, the following plant in the following circumstances; that is to say hoists, as defined in regulation 4 of the said Regulations used in building operations or works of engineering construction to which the said Regulations apply, in which the cage or platform is raised and lowered by means of one or more rotating pinions driven by a prime mover or prime movers mounted upon the said cage or platform and acting upon a single rack fixed and parallel to the mast of the hoist, and in which the pinion(s) of the governor-operated safety device also engages in the same rack.

Unless the context otherwise requires, expressions used in this Certificate have the same meaning as in the said Regulations. For the purpose of this Certificate and the Schedule, "section of rack" shall mean the single length of rack spanning any mast section and "mast section" shall mean the length of mast between two successive joints.

Certificate of Exemption No. 5 and Certificate of Exemption No. 31 issued on 18 February 1976 are hereby revoked.

This Certificate shall come into operation on 17 July 1981 and shall remain in force until revoked in writing by an inspector appointed and authorised as hereinafter appears.

SCHEDULE

CONDITIONS OF EXEMPTION FROM THE REGULATIONS

1.   There shall be provided and maintained means which shall in all positions of the cage or platform positively prevent any driving or safety device pinion from becoming disengaged from the rack by any lateral movement.

2.   The maximum contract speed at which the cage or platform has been designed to travel by the manufacturer shall be stated in the specification of the hoist and shall be plainly marked inside the cage or on the platform.

3.   There shall be provided and maintained an efficient safety device which will operate to arrest and support the platform or cage with its safe working load in the event of any

failure of the hoist (other than a structural failure of the mast) which results in the maximum contract speed (see 2 above) being exceeded by an amount likely to cause danger. The speed at which the safety device is set to operate shall be known as the tripping speed.

4.   The tripping speed and the maximum stopping distance of the cage or platform to be achieved during testing of the safety device shall be plainly marked on the device. The maximum stopping distance is the distance the cage or platform will fall measured from the point of release of the stationary cage or platform to the point of arrest.

5.   For the purposes of condition 3 of this Schedule the rack and any section and fixings thereof shall not be deemed to be part of the structure of the mast.

6.   The safety device shall be so designed or suitably protected to prevent it becoming ineffective due to extraneous matter or atmospheric conditions, and no part of the safety device shall depend on an electrical circuit for its action.

7.   When the arresting device has been tripped it shall not be possible to release or reset it by movement of the cage or platform by means of the normal controls.

8.   A notice shall be clearly displayed inside the cage or on the platform setting out adequate instructions to be followed in the event of the safety device being operated in an emergency situation. The instructions shall include a warning that in such an event no attempt should be made to move the cage or platform until effective action has been taken to prevent further uncontrolled movement of the cage or platform.

9.   In addition to the tests required by regulation 46(1)(a) of the said Regulations and where applicable regulation 46(1)(b) of the said Regulations, in so far as reference is made to testing and examinations since the hoist was last erected, there shall be tests to prove the ability of the safety device to arrest (without the use of motor brakes) the descending cage or platform when carrying a load equal to the safe working load of the hoist, within the appropriate stopping distance specified in condition 4.

10.   The said tests required by condition 9 on the safety device shall be carried out at intervals not exceeding 3 months or such period as is recommended by the manufacturer whichever is the shorter period, commencing from the date of the test required by regulation 46(1) of the said Regulations.

11.   The results of all the tests required by condition 9 of this Schedule shall be recorded in the form used for the prescribed particulars of the results of thorough examinations made in pursuance of regulation 46(1)(c) of the said Regulations (Form 91 Part II Section H).

12.   No hoist shall be used unless the tests in pursuance of conditions 9 and 10 have been carried out, and the safety device operates to arrest the hoist within the distance marked in conformity with condition 4.

13.   In the case of those hoists where the rotating pinion(s) driven by the prime mover(s) can at any time engage in the same section of rack as a pinion associated with any safety device the following additional conditions will apply before any such hoist is used or within 6 months of the date of this Exemption:
  (a) A representative model of the said type of hoist shall have been subjected to consecutive drop tests (without the use of motor brakes) at least 12 in number, with the cage or platform loaded to its safe working load and allowed to accelerate to an appropriate overspeed condition.
  (b) The said drop tests shall be carried out so that during each test the pinion of the safety device required by condition 3 traverses, while arresting the hoist a section of rack which has the following defects:
    (i) sufficient screws, welds and other means used to attach the section of rack to the mast are removed so that from either end of the section of rack positive restraint does not extend over a distance greater than 12% of the total length of the section
    (ii) a tooth is removed

    (iii) the section of rack is cut through at its mid point.

(c) The said drop tests shall be carried out with the counterweight (if fitted) disconnected from the cage or platform.

(d) The said drop tests shall be immediately supervised by a competent person and the results of each test giving details of the maximum working load, the contract speed, the type of safety device, the model number, the drawing number, the year of manufacture, the dropping distance of the cage or platform before stopping and any observations as to the safety of the hoist shall be made in writing and signed by the competent person.

    (i) A copy of the report of each test shall be sent to HM Chief Inspector of Factories.

    (ii) A copy of the report shall be supplied with each hoist of the same type and it shall be attached to the report referred to in regulation 46(2) of the said Regulations (Form 91 Part II Section H).

CERTIFICATE OF EXEMPTION No. CON (LO)/1981/2 (GENERAL)
EXCAVATORS, LOADERS AND COMBINED EXCAVATOR/LOADERS
F 2513, 4 June 1981

In pursuance of the powers conferred on me by regulation 5 of the Construction (Lifting Operations) Regulations 1961, I hereby exempt from the requirements of regulations 28(1), (2) and (5), 29 and 30 of the said Regulations, subject to the conditions specified in the First Schedule forming part of this Certificate, the following machines, that is to say excavators, loaders and combined excavator/loaders, when used in connection with any excavation to which the said Regulations apply and, when so used, they are for the time being used as cranes, solely by the secure attachment of lifting gear to the bucket or part of the machine specifically designed for the purpose and solely for work immediately connected with that excavation.

For the purpose of this Certificate, "excavator" shall mean a machine which is fitted with a bucket and which is capable of excavating without depending on the travel of the machine to fill the bucket; "loader" shall mean a machine which is fitted with a bucket and which depends mainly upon the travel of the machine to fill the bucket; and "combined excavator/loader" shall mean a machine which is equipped both as a loader and as an excavator.

Unless the context otherwise requires, other expressions used in this Certificate shall have the same respective meaning as in the said Regulations.

Certificate of Exemption No. 2 (General) dated 29 April 1966 is hereby revoked.

This Certificate shall come into operation on 1 July 1981 and shall remain in force until revoked by an inspector appointed and authorised as hereinafter appears.

CONDITIONS OF EXEMPTION

FIRST SCHEDULE

1. Before an excavator, loader or a combined excavator/loader is first used as aforesaid as a crane, a competent person appointed by the owner shall specify the safe working load to be raised and lowered by the said machine when used as a crane, or, if it may be used with jibs or booms of different lengths or construction, the safe working loads relevant to those jibs or booms which it is intended to use.

When an excavator is fitted with outriggers, the competent person shall specify safe working loads for both the following positions, namely free-on-wheels or tracks and with outriggers fully extended and blocked, for each length or construction of jib or boom which it is intended to use.

The safe working load shall be the same for all radii at which the jib or boom is operated and shall not be greater than the load which the machine in its least stable configuration is designed to lift with that jib or boom.

2.   Before the machine is first used as a crane, a certificate signed by the competent person giving the particulars specified in the Second Schedule hereto shall be obtained. The requirements of regulation 50(2) of the said Regulations shall apply to the said certificate as they apply to the certificates required by the Regulations, except that the certificate, or a copy thereof, shall be kept available for inspection on the site of the operation or works.

3.   The machine, when used as a crane, shall not be loaded beyond the relevant safe working load specified in the certificate required by condition 2 of this Schedule.

4.   Means of identification shall be plainly marked on the machine.

5.   The specified safe working load or loads and the outrigger position and the length of jib or boom to which the safe working load relates, shall either be plainly marked on the machine or a copy of the table of safe working loads, specified in the Second Schedule, shall be affixed in a clearly visible position in the driver's cab.

   If, after the issue of the certificate required by condition 2 of this Schedule, the machine undergoes any substantial alteration or repair likely to affect the specified safe working loads, the said certificate shall be cancelled and a new certificate giving the particulars specified in the Second Schedule shall be required.

6.   In the case of hydraulically-operated machines this exemption shall only apply to machines fitted with check valves on the hydraulic lifting cylinders, or some other suitable device, to prevent a gravity fall of the load in the event of a hydraulic failure. This condition will not come into operation until 5 years after the date of this Certificate of Exemption.

SECOND SCHEDULE

Owner's name and address—

Description and identification no. of excavator loader or combined excavator/loader (2)	Safe working load to be lifted or lowered when adapted for use as a crane		
	Length of jib or boom (a)	*Safe working load free of wheels or tracks* (b)	*Safe working load blocked (outriggers fully extended)* (c)
	....	....	....

Signature of competent person:..
Date of signature: ....
Name of competent person: ....
(BLOCK Letters)
* Address of competent person:...
....
* Qualification of competent person: ....
Name and address of employer of competent person (if other than owner):..............
....
....
Position held by competent person if employed: ....

* To be completed only if the competent person is self-employed

THE CONSTRUCTION (WORKING PLACES) REGULATIONS 1966

(S.I. 1966 No. 94, as amended by S.I. 1984 No. 1593)

ARRANGEMENT OF REGULATIONS

The Minister of Labour—

(a) by virtue of the powers conferred on him by sections 76 and 180(7) of the Factories Act 1961, and of all other powers enabling him in that behalf; and

(b) after publishing, pursuant to Schedule 4 to the said Act of 1961, notice of the proposal to make the Regulations and after the holding of an inquiry under that Schedule into objections made to the draft,

hereby makes the following special Regulations—

PART I
APPLICATION AND INTERPRETATION

1. Citation, commencement and revocation.—(1) These Regulations may be cited as the Construction (Working Places) Regulations 1966 and shall come into operation on 1 August 1966.

(2) The following provisions are hereby revoked, that is to say,

(a) regulations 6 to 33 of the Building (Safety, Health and Welfare) Regulations 1948;

(b) in regulation 3(1) of the Construction (General Provisions) Regulations 1961, the words from "every contractor" (in the first place where those words occur after sub-paragraph (b)) to "and of"; and

(c) regulations 7 and 54 of the said Regulations of 1961.

(3) In regulation 3(1)(a) of the said Regulations of 1961 "8" shall be substituted for "7", and in regulation 3(1)(b) thereof the reference to regulation 54 shall be omitted.

General note. In the notes which follow use has been made of such of the authorities decided upon the provisions of the Building (Safety, Health and Welfare) Regulations 1948 as appear also to govern the interpretation of cognate provisions of these Regulations.

1855

Measurements in Imperial have been converted to metric by S.I. 1984 No. 1593. These amendments do not apply to premises or plant in existence before 9 November 1984.

2.   Application of Regulations.—(1) These Regulations apply—

(a) to building operations; and
(b) to works of engineering construction,

undertaken by way of trade or business, or for the purpose of any industrial or commercial undertaking, or by or on behalf of the Crown or any municipal or other public authority, and to any line or siding which is used in connection therewith and for the purposes thereof and is not part of a railway or tramway.

(2) The provisions of these Regulations shall be in addition to and not in substitution for or in diminution of other requirements imposed by or under *the principal Act.*

General note. See the notes to reg. 2 of the Construction (General Provisions) Regulations 1961.

3.   Obligations under Regulations.—(1) It shall be the duty of every contractor, and every employer of workmen, who is undertaking any of the operations or works to which these Regulations apply—

(a) to comply with such of the requirements of the following regulations as affect him or any workman employed by him, that is to say, regulations 6 to 23, 25, 30, 31, 32, 36 and 38 and, in so far as they relate to the falling or slipping of persons, Regulations 24, 26, 27, 28, 29, 33, 34 and 35: Provided that the requirements of the said Regulations shall be deemed not to affect any workman if and so long as his presence in any place is not in the course of performing any work on behalf of his employer and is not expressly or impliedly authorised or permitted by his employer; and
(b) to comply with such of the requirements of the following regulations as relate to any work, act or operation performed by any such contractor or employer of workmen, that is to say, regulations 37 and 39 and, in so far as they relate to the falling of materials and articles, regulations 24, 26, 27, 28, 29, 33, 34 and 35,

and it shall be the duty of every contractor and every employer of workmen who erects or alters *(a)* any *scaffold* to comply with such of the requirements of these Regulations as relate to the erection or alteration of *scaffolds* having regard to the purpose or purposes for which the *scaffold* is designed at the time of erection or alteration *(b)*; and of every contractor and every employer of workmen who erects, installs, works or uses any other *plant or equipment* to which any of the provisions of these Regulations applies, to erect, install, work or use any such *plant or equipment* in a manner which complies with those provisions.

(2) It shall be the duty of every person employed to comply with the requirements of such of these Regulations as relate to the performance of or the refraining from an act by him and to co-operate in carrying out these Regulations and if he discovers any defect in the *plant or equipment* to report such defect without unreasonable delay to his employer or foreman, or to a

person appointed by the employer under Part II of the Construction (General Provisions) Regulations 1961.

General note. See the notes to reg. 3 of the Construction (General Provisions) Regulations 1961. On the standard of care owed under the Regulations, see *Baker v T Clarke (Leeds) Ltd* [1992] PIQR P262 (the general application of the case is discussed in the Introduction).

(a) *Alters any scaffold.* The duty imposed by reg. 3(1) upon "every contractor and every employer of workmen who erects or alters any scaffold" rests solely upon those who erect or alter scaffolds and upon no one else (*Kearney v Eric Waller Ltd* [1967] 1 QB 29, [1965] 3 All ER 352). Such person must have regard not only to the purposes for which he himself wishes to use it, but also to the whole purpose for which the scaffold, as altered, is designed to be put, whether by himself, his employees, or by others (*Martin v Claude Hamilton (Aberdeen), Ltd* 1952 SLT (Notes) 14 (Second Division of the Court of Session)). Note, however, that if a person makes an alteration to the scaffold that will not of itself make him or her liable for other breaches of the Regulations attributable to other persons: *Galek's Curator Bonis v Thomson* 1991 SLT 29n.

(b) *Every construction . . . alteration.* These special provisions impose additional liability upon persons erecting scaffolding and do not relieve them from any obligations owed to their own workmen under reg. 3(1)(a), including those imposed by reg. 6(1) (*Smith v Vange Scaffolding and Engineering Co Ltd* [1970] 1 All ER 249, [1970] 1 WLR 733).

4. Interpretation.—(1) The Interpretation Act 1889 [Interpretation Act 1978] shall apply to the interpretation of these Regulations as it applies to the interpretation of an Act of Parliament, and as if these Regulations and the regulations hereby revoked were Acts of Parliament.

(2) In these Regulations, unless the context otherwise requires, the following expressions have the meanings hereby assigned to them respectively, that is to say—

"ladder" does not include a folding step-ladder;

"ladder scaffold" means a *scaffold* with a *working platform* which is supported directly on a *ladder* or by means of a crutch or bracket on a rung or rungs of a *ladder*;

"lifting appliance" means a crab, winch, pulley block or gin wheel used for raising or lowering, and a hoist, crane, sheer legs, excavator, dragline, piling frame, aerial cableway, aerial ropeway or overhead runway;

"lifting gear" means a chain sling, rope sling, or similar gear, and a ring, link, hook, plate clamp, shackle, swivel or eye-bolt;

"plant or equipment" includes any plant, equipment, gear, machinery, apparatus or appliance, or any part thereof;

"the principal Act" means the Factories Act 1961, as amended by or under any other Act;

"scaffold" (a) means any temporarily provided structure on or from which persons perform work in connection with operations or works to which these Regulations apply, and any temporarily provided structure which enables persons to obtain access to or which enables materials to be taken to any place at which such work is performed, and includes any *working platform*, gangway (b), run, *ladder* or step-ladder (other than an independent ladder or step-ladder which does not form part of such a structure) together with any guard-rail, toe-board or other safeguards and all fixings, but does not include a *lifting appliance* or a structure used merely to support such an appliance or to support other *plant or equipment*;

"sloping roof" has the meaning assigned to it by regulation 35;

"slung scaffold" means a *scaffold* suspended by means of lifting gear, ropes or chains or rigid members and not provided with means of raising or lowering by a *lifting appliance* or similar device;

"suspended scaffold" means a *scaffold* (not being a slung scaffold) suspended by means of ropes or chains and capable of being raised or lowered but does not include a boatswain's chair or similar appliance;

"trestle scaffold" includes a *scaffold* in which the supports for the platform are any of the following which are self-supporting, that is to say, split heads, folding-step-ladders, tripods or movable contrivances similar to any of the foregoing; and

"working platform" includes a working stage.

(a) **Scaffold.** The words "... and includes any working platform, gangway, run" include structures which are permanent as well as those which are temporary, in contrast to the earlier part of the definition; see *Curran v William Neill & Son (St Helens) Ltd* [1961] 3 All ER 108, [1961] 1 WLR 1069, CA. Thus, a structure which is part of the permanent fixed equipment of a building may be a scaffold for the purpose of the Regulations, provided it otherwise falls within the definitive words quoted above (*ibid.*). The extended meaning given to the word "scaffold" by reg. 4(2) has the consequence that many structures which would not ordinarily be termed scaffolds fall within the definition. Thus, a temporary plank bridge used to cross a depression in the ground may be a scaffold (*Byres v Head Wrightson & Co Ltd* [1961] 2 All ER 538, [1961] 1 WLR 961; *Conlan v Glasgow Corpn* 1964 SLT 134, Ct of Sess (plank with one end resting on ground and the other on the top of a flight of three steps)), and so may boards used as a working platform (*Harris v Bright's Asphalt Contractors Ltd* [1953] 1 QB 617, [1953] 1 All ER 395). In *Traves v Woodall-Duckham Construction Co* (1962) 106 Sol Jo 282, CA, corrugated iron sheets used as a dump for materials were held not to be a scaffold. In *Milliken v James Rome & Sons* 1952 SLT (Notes) 15, the Outer House of the Court of Session held that a plank placed from the ground on to the bottom step of a flight of steps to provide easier access for builders' workmen was not a scaffold within reg. 3(2); but this case was not followed in *Conlan v Glasgow Corpn*, above, in which, after a valuable review of the authorities, the Outer House of the Court of Session followed *Curran v William Neill & Son (St Helens) Ltd*, above, and held that a "gangway" was anything which in fact is used as such, as the word is normally understood in building operations. As to the words, "an operation to which these Regulations apply", in this definition, see reg. 2.

(b) **Working platform; gangway.** These words must bear their ordinary meaning as they are understood in relation to building operations. Although they include platforms and gangways of a permanent character (see note (a)) they include only such structures as are, in the normal sense of the words, working platforms and gangways. The mere fact that a structure is being used, at the material time, as a working platform or gangway will not bring it within the definition if otherwise it would fall outside it (*Curran v William Neill & Son (St Helens) Ltd* [1961] 3 All ER 108, CA; and see *Jennings v Norman Collison (Contractors) Ltd* [1970] 1 All ER 1121, CA).

PART II
EXEMPTIONS

5.   **Certificates of exemption.** The Chief Inspector (a) may (subject to such condition, if any, as may be specified therein) by certificate in writing (which he

may in his discretion revoke at any time) exempt from all or any of the requirements of these Regulations—

(a) any particular *plant or equipment* or any class or description of *plant or equipment*; or

(b) any particular work or any class or description of work,

if he is satisfied that the requirements in respect of which the exemption is granted are not necessary for the protection of persons employed or are not reasonably practicable *(b)*.

General note. See Certificates of Exemption Nos. 6[F2410] and 8[F2485], set out following these Regulations.

(a) Inspector. See INTRODUCTORY NOTE 19.

(b) Reasonably practicable. See INTRODUCTORY NOTE 5.

PART III
SAFETY OF WORKING PLACES AND ACCESS AND EGRESS

6. General.—(1) Without prejudice to the other provisions of these Regulations, there shall, so far as is reasonably practicable *(a)*, be suitable and sufficient safe access to and egress *(b)* from every place at which any person at any time works, which access and egress shall be properly maintained *(c)*.

(2) Without prejudice to the other provisions of these Regulations, every place at which any person at any time works shall, so far as is reasonably practicable *(a)*, be made and kept safe for any person working there.

General note. Although the provisions of this regulation are analogous to those of s. 29(1) of the Factories Act 1961 it should be noted that the obligation is to provide "safe access," not "safe means of access" as under that section; and that the relevant place is that at which "any person . . . works," not "has . . . to work". The words "sufficient safe means of access" were fully discussed in *Trott v W E Smith (Erectors) Ltd* [1957] 3 All ER 500, [1957] 1 WLR 1154, CA. It was there held that a means of access is not a sufficient safe means if it is a possible cause of injury to anyone acting in a way that a human being of the type who will use the means of access may reasonably be expected to act in circumstances which may reasonably be expected to occur.

Where it was foreseeable that certain weather conditions might make the means of access slippery and dangerous the employer who permitted the means of access to be used in such weather conditions was in breach of reg. 6(1): *Byrne v E H Smith (Roofing)* [1973] 1 All ER 490, CA.

In *Evans v Sant* [1975] QB 626, [1975] 1 All ER 294, it was held that where the place of work, having regard to the equipment permanently there and the activities normally carried on there, was safe the mere fact that a piece of equipment brought onto it temporarily for a particular purpose produced a danger did not render the place unsafe for the purposes of reg. 6(2). In *McGrath v Marples Ridgeway Ltd* 1972 SLT (Sh Ct) 50 it was held that that reg. 6(2) does not apply to the erecting or dismantling of scaffolding.

(a) Reasonably practicable. See INTRODUCTORY NOTE 5. It is for the defendants to plead and prove that it was not reasonably practicable to provide a safe means of access (*Bowes v Sedgefiled District Council* [1981] ICR 234, CA).

(b) Access . . . egress. A public highway within a demolition site may be an access to or an egress from a place of work (*Glasgow v City of Glasgow District Council* 1983 SLT 65). In

Manford v George Leslie Ltd 1987 SCLR 684 both a safe and unsafe means of access were provided. The employer was held not to be in breach of the Regulations when an employee was injured using the unsafe access even though he was discouraged from using the safe route. This decision would seem to be difficult to reconcile with the decision in *Kirkpatrick v Scott Lithgow Ltd* 1987 SCLR 567 on s. 29(1).

(c) ***Properly maintained.*** See INTRODUCTORY NOTE 5. It is not necessary to maintain every conceivable access or egress to and from a place of work; in general the statutory requirement is satisfied if there is a safe access or egress, even though not every access and egress is safe (*Morrow v Enterprise Sheet Metal Works (Aberdeen) Ltd* 1968 SLT 697 at 700, *per* Lord Justice-Clerk Ross).

7.　Provision of scaffolds, etc. Without prejudice to the other provisions of these Regulations, where work cannot safely be done *(a)* on or from the ground or from part of a building or other permanent structure, there shall be provided *(b)*, placed and kept in position for use and properly maintained *(c)* either *scaffolds* or where appropriate *ladders* or other means of support *(d)*, all of which shall be sufficient and suitable for the purpose.

(a) ***Cannot safely be done.*** The test here is whether, on all the facts known or which ought to have been known, the doing of the work involved foreseeable risk (*Connolly v McGee* [1961] 2 All ER 111, [1961] 1 WLR 811; *Curran v William Neill & Son (St Helens) Ltd* [1961] 3 All ER 108, [1961] 1 WLR 1069, CA and *Woods v Power Gas Corpn Ltd* (1969) 8 KIR 834, CA).

(b) ***Provided.*** See INTRODUCTORY NOTE 9.

(c) ***Properly maintained.*** See INTRODUCTORY NOTE 10.

(d) ***Other means of support.*** In *Harkness v Oxy-Acetylene Welding Co* 1963 SC 642 the majority took the view that the phrase did not include a support that is only safe when used with the assistance of another human being (decided under the Building (Safety, Health and Welfare) Regulations 1948).

8.　Supervision of work and inspection of material. No *scaffold* shall be erected or be substantially added to or altered or be dismantled except under the immediate supervision *(a)* of a competent person and so far as possible by competent workmen possessing adequate experience of such work. All material for any *scaffold* shall be inspected by a competent person on each occasion before being taken into use.

(a) ***Immediate supervision.*** See note *(a)* to reg. 17 of the Construction (General Provisions) Regulations 1961.

9.　Construction and material.—(1) Every *scaffold* and every part thereof shall be of good construction, of suitable and sound material and of adequate strength *(a)* for the purpose for which it is used.

(2) Sufficient material shall be provided for and shall be used in the construction of *scaffolds*.

(3) Timber used for *scaffolds* shall be of suitable quality, be in good condition, and have the bark completely stripped off.

(4) Timber used for *scaffolds*, trestles, *ladders*, and folding step-ladders shall not be so painted or treated that defects cannot easily be seen.

(5) Metal parts used for *scaffolds* shall be of suitable quality and be in good condition and free from corrosion or other patent defect likely to affect their strength materially.

General note. The duty imposed by this regulation is absolute, and is not one which has to be performed merely within the limits of knowledge and foresight (*Curran v William Neill & Son (St Helens) Ltd* [1961] 3 All ER 108, [1961] 1 WLR 1069, CA). As to the extent to which reg. 9 imposes duties upon a workman, see *Quinn V J W Green (Painters) Ltd* [1966] 1 QB 509, [1965] 3 All ER 785, CA, and note *(h)* to reg. 3 of the Construction (General Provisions) Regulations 1961. The reference to "parts" in the Regulations means that they apply to a partly dismantled scaffold as well as to a completed one (*Campbell v City of Glasgow District Council* 1991 SLT 616). In that case the Outer House also considered that the soundness of construction should be assessed at the time the scaffold was constructed or altered (but see *Barclay v J & W Henderson* 1980 SLT (Notes) 71: regulation did apply to scaffold temporarily not of good construction following removal of windbrace by an employee). In *Campbell* (above) it was also held that this regulation does not cover the design of the scaffold (c.f. regs. 7 and 15).

(a) *Good construction . . . adequate strength.* See INTRODUCTORY NOTE 11.

10. Defective material.—(1) No defective material or defective part shall be used for a *scaffold*.

(2) No rope or bond which is defective whether through contact with an acid or other corrosive substance or otherwise shall be used.

(3) All material and parts for *scaffolds* shall when not in use be kept under good conditions and apart from any materials or parts unsuitable for *scaffolds*.

General note. The duty imposed by this regulation is absolute, and is not one which has to be performed merely within the limits of knowledge and foresight (*Curran v William Neill & Son (St Helens) Ltd* [1961] 3 All ER 108, [1961] 1 WLR 1069, CA).

11. Maintenance of scaffolds.—Every *scaffold* shall be properly maintained *(a)*, and every part shall be kept so fixed, secured or placed in position as to prevent so far as is practicable *(b)* accidental displacement.

General note. In *Moloney v A Cameron Ltd* [1961] 2 All ER 934, [1961] 1 WLR 1087, CA, it was held that the similar provisions of reg. 9(1) of the Building Regulations 1948 applied only to completed scaffolds and not to scaffolds in course of erection. *Barclay v J & W Henderson Ltd* 1980 SLT (Notes) 71 suggests, obiter, that this is the correct approach. *Paterson v Lothian Regional Council* 1979 SLT (Sh Ct) 7 held that reg. 11 protects not only those working on a scaffold but also, for example, someone hit by a collapsing scaffold.

(a) *Properly maintained.* See INTRODUCTORY NOTE 10.

(b) *Practicable.* See INTRODUCTORY NOTE 5.

12. Partly erected or dismantled scaffolds. No *scaffold* or part of a *scaffold* shall be partly erected or dismantled and remain in such a condition that it is capable of being used *(a)* unless—

(a) the *scaffold* as so erected or dismantled complies with these Regulations; or

(b) a prominent warning notice indicating that the *scaffold* or part as the case may be, is not to be used is affixed near any point at which the *scaffold* or part, as the case may be, is liable to be approached for the purpose of use; or

(c) access to the *scaffold* or part, as the case may be, is as far as reasonably practicable *(b)* effectively blocked.

General note. As to the application of other provisions of these Regulations to the operation of dismantling a scaffold, see *Sexton v Scaffolding (Great Britain) Ltd* [1953] 1 QB 153, [1952] 2 All ER 1085, CA, decided upon the similar provisions of the Building (Safety, Welfare and Health) Regulations 1948. In *Barclay v J & W Henderson Ltd* 1980 SLT (Notes) 71 it was held that reg. 12 does not apply to the continuing operation of dismantling by scaffolders.

(a) Partly . . . used. See *Skelton v AVP Developments Ltd* (1970) 8 KIR 927, CA.

(b) Reasonably practicable. See INTRODUCTORY NOTE 5.

13.   Standards or uprights, ledgers and putlogs.—(1) Standards or uprights of *scaffolds* shall—

(a) where practicable *(a)*, be either vertical or slightly inclined towards the building or other structure *(b)*; and

(b) be fixed sufficiently close together to secure the stability of the *scaffold* having regard to all the circumstances.

(2) The foot or base of any standard or upright shall be placed on an adequate base plate in a manner to prevent slipping or sinking, or its displacement shall be prevented in some other sufficient way.

(3) Ledgers shall be as nearly as possible horizontal and shall be securely fastened to the standards or uprights by efficient means.

(4) Putlogs or other supports on which a platform rests shall be securely fastened to the ledgers or to the standards or uprights, or their movement shall be prevented by other efficient means. Where one end of a putlog is supported by a wall that end shall extend into or on to the wall sufficiently to provide a supporting surface of sufficient area.

(5) The distance between two consecutive putlogs and other supports on which a platform rests shall be fixed with due regard to the anticipated load and the nature of the platform flooring. The distance with single planking shall not as a general rule exceed 1 metre with planks of 32 millimetres in thickness, 1.50 metres with planks 38 millimetres in thickness, or 2.60 metres with planks 50 millimetres in thickness.

General note. For exemptions relating to certain external scaffolds, see Certificate of Exemption No. 8[F2485], set out following these Regulations.

(a) Practicable. See INTRODUCTORY NOTE 5.

(b) Vertical . . . structure. In *Norris v William Moss & Sons Ltd* [1954] 1 All ER 324, [1954] 1 WLR 346, the Court of Appeal discussed, without deciding, whether the principal of *Sexton v Scaffolding (Great Britain) Ltd* [1953] 1 QB 153, [152] 2 All ER 1085, CA (see the general note to reg. 12) applied to reg. 13(1)(a).

14.   Ladders used in scaffolds.—(1) *Ladders* serving as uprights or *scaffolds* shall—

(a) be of adequate strength;

(b) be placed so that the two stiles or sides of each *ladder* are evenly supported or suspended; and

(c) be secured to prevent slipping.

(2) *Ladder scaffolds* shall be used only if the work is of such a light nature and the material required for the work is such that this type of *scaffold* can be used safely.

General note. Regulation 14(1) applies not only when the scaffold is complete, but also to a scaffold in course of erection or dismantling: see *Sexton v Scaffolding (Great Britain) Ltd* [1953] 1 QB 153, [1952] 2 All ER 1085, CA, *per* Somervell LJ.

15.   Stability of scaffolds.—(1) Every *scaffold* shall be *(a)* securely supported or suspended and shall where necessary be sufficiently and properly strutted or braced to prevent collapse, and shall be rigidly connected with the building or other structure unless the *scaffold* is so designed and constructed as to ensure stability without such connection.

(2) Every structure and appliance used as a support for a *scaffold* shall be of sound construction, have a firm footing or be firmly supported, and shall where necessary be sufficiently and properly strutted or braced to prevent collapse and to ensure stability.

(3) Every *scaffold* which can be moved on wheels or skids (not being a *suspended scaffold* or *slung scaffold*) shall—

(a) be constructed with due regard to stability and, if necessary for stability, be adequately weighted at the base;

(b) be used only on a firm and even surface not so sloping as to involve risk of instability of the *scaffold* or any load thereon;

(c) be adequately secured to prevent movement when any person is working upon it or upon any *ladder* or other *plant or equipment,* being a *ladder, plant or equipment* which is supported by the *scaffold;* and

(d) be moved only by the application of force at or near the base.

(4) Loose bricks, drain pipes, chimney pots or other unsuitable material shall not be used for the construction or support of *scaffolds* save the bricks or small blocks may, if they provide a firm support, be used to support a platform not more than 600 millimetres above the ground or floor.

General note. In *Moloney v A Cameron Ltd* [1961] 2 All ER 934, [1961] 1 WLR 1087, the Court of Appeal discussed, without deciding the question, whether, having regard to the decision in *Sexton v Scaffolding (Great Britain) Ltd* [1953] 1 QB 153, [1952] 2 All ER 1085, CA, reg. 15(1) applied to scaffolds in course of erection or dismantling; but in *Campbell v City of Glasgow District Council* 1991 SLT 616 it was held that the regulation is only intended to apply to a completed scaffold, following Pearson LJ in *Moloney* (above). In *Paterson v Lothian R C* 1979 SLT (Sh Ct) 7 it was held that reg. 15 protects not only those working on a scaffold but also, for example, someone hit by a collapsing scaffold.

(a) Shall be . . . These words create an absolute obligation (*Curran v William Neill & Son (St Helens) Ltd* [1961] 3 All ER 108, [1961] 1 WLR 1069, CA).

16.   Slung scaffolds.—(1) No chain, wire rope, *lifting gear*, metal tube or other means of suspension for *slung scaffolds* shall be used unless the following requirements (in so far as they are applicable) are observed, (in addition as respects chains, ropes and *lifting gear* to satisfying the requirements of the Construction (Lifting Operations) Regulations 1961), that is to say—

(a) it is suitable and of adequate strength *(a)* for the purpose for which it is used;

(b) it is properly and securely fastened to safe anchorage points and to the *scaffold* ledgers or other main supporting members;

(c) it is so placed as to ensure stability of the *scaffold*;

(d) it is as nearly vertical as is reasonably practicable *(b)*; and

(e) it is kept taut.

(2) No rope other than a wire rope shall be used for the suspension of a *slung scaffold*.

(3) Where chains or wire ropes are used for the suspension of a *slung scaffold*, steps shall be taken to prevent such chains or wire ropes coming into contact at points of suspension with edges where this would cause danger.

(4) Every *slung scaffold* shall be secured to prevent undue horizontal movement while it is used as a *working platform*.

(a) Adequate strength. See INTRODUCTORY NOTE 11.

(b) Reasonably practicable. See INTRODUCTORY NOTE 5.

17.   Cantilever, jib, figure and bracket scaffolds.—(1) No cantilever *scaffold* or jib *scaffold* shall be used unless it is adequately supported, fixed and anchored, has outriggers of adequate length and strength and is where necessary sufficiently and properly strutted or braced to ensure rigidity and stability.

(2) No figure *scaffold* or bracket *scaffold* supported or held by dogs, spikes, or similar fixings liable to pull out of the stone-work, brickwork or other surface in which they are gripped or fixed shall be used.

18.   Support for scaffolds, etc. No part of a building or other structure shall be used as support for a *scaffold, ladder*, folding step-ladder or crawling ladder or for part of a *scaffold, ladder*, folding step-ladder or crawling ladder, unless the part of the building or other structure is of sound material and sufficiently stable and of sufficient strength to afford safe support. Gutters shall not be used as such supports unless they and their fixings are suitable and are of adequate strength *(a)* and in the case of overhanging eaves gutters shall not be so used unless in addition they have been specially designed as walkways.

(a) Adequate strength. See INTRODUCTORY NOTE 11.

19.   Suspended scaffolds (not power operated).—(1) The requirements of this regulation (in addition, as respects *lifting appliances*, chains, ropes and *lifting gear* used in connection therewith, to the requirements of the Construction (Lifting Operations) Regulations 1961), shall be observed as respects—

(a) every *suspended scaffold*; and

(b) *plant or equipment* which is permanent *plant or equipment* of a building and which, but for the fact that it is permanently provided, would be a *suspended scaffold,*

being in any case a *suspended scaffold, plant or equipment* which is not raised or lowered by a power-driven *lifting appliance* or power-driven *lifting appliances* and no such *suspended scaffold, plant or equipment* shall be used unless it complies with the requirements of this regulation.

(2) In the application of the succeeding paragraphs of this regulation, references therein to *suspended scaffolds* shall be construed as references to *suspended scaffolds* to which this regulation applies and as including references to *plant or equipment* of the kind referred to in sub-paragraph (b) of the foregoing paragraph of this regulation.

(3) Every *suspended scaffold* shall be provided with adequate and suitable chains or ropes and winches or other *lifting appliances* or similar devices and shall be suspended from suitable outriggers, joists, runways, rail tracks or other equally safe anchorage.

(4) The winches or other *lifting appliances* or similar devices of a *suspended scaffold* shall be—

(a) provided with a brake or similar device which comes into operation when the operating handle or lever is released; and

(b) adequately protected against the effects of weather, dust or material likely to cause damage.

(5) The outriggers for a *suspended scaffold* shall be of adequate length and strength *(a)* and properly installed and supported and, subject to paragraph (15) of this regulation, shall be installed horizontally and provided with adequate stops at their outer ends. The outriggers shall be properly spaced having regard to the construction of the *scaffold* and of the runway, joist or rail track on which the *scaffold* is carried.

(6) Where counterweights are used with outriggers the counter-weights shall be securely attached to the outriggers and shall be not less in weight than three times the weight which would counter-balance the weight suspended from the outrigger including the weight of the runway, joist or rail track, the *suspended scaffold* and persons and other load thereon.

(7) The points of suspension of every *suspended scaffold* shall be an adequate horizontal distance from the face of the building or other structure.

(8) Every runway, joist and rail tack supporting a *suspended scaffold* shall be of suitable and sound material, adequate strength *(a)* for the purpose for which it is used and free from patent defect, shall be provided with adequate stops at each end and shall be properly secured to the building or other structure or, where outriggers are used, to the outriggers.

(9) The suspension ropes or chains of a *suspended scaffold*—

(a) shall be securely attached to the outriggers or other supports and to the platform framework or to any *lifting appliance* or other device attached thereto, as the case may be; and

(b) shall be kept in tension.

(10) Where winches are used with *suspended scaffolds* the suspension ropes shall be of such a length that at the lowest positions at which the *scaffold* is

intended to be used there are not less than two turns of rope remaining on each winch drum and the length of each rope shall be clearly marked on its winch.

(11) Every part of a *suspended scaffold* and all *plant and equipment* used for the purposes thereof shall be of good construction, suitable and sound material, of adequate strength *(a)* for the purpose for which it is used and shall be properly maintained *(b)*, and, where constructed of metal, shall be free from corrosion and other patent defects, being corrosion and defects likely materially to affect its strength. Adequate arrangements shall be made to prevent undue tipping, tilting or swinging of a *suspension scaffold* and to secure it to prevent undue horizontal movement while it is being used as a *working platform.*

(12) No rope other than a wire rope shall be used for the raising, lowering and suspension of a *suspended scaffold*, except that the raising, lowering and suspension may be carried out by means of fibre ropes and pulley blocks in the case of work to which paragraph (15) of this regulation applies.

(13) The platform of every *suspended scaffold* shall—

(a) except to the extent necessary for drainage, be closely boarded, planked or plated; and
(b) subject to paragraph (15) of this regulation, be of adequate width to afford adequate working space at every working point and shall, in any event,
   (i) be at least 600 millimetres wide if used as a footing only and not for the deposit of any material;
   (ii) be at least 800 millimetres wide if used for the deposit of material; and
   (iii) not be used for the support of any higher *scaffold,*

and shall be so arranged or secured that at each working position the space between the face of the building or other structure and the platform is as small as reasonably practicable; so, however, that where workmen sit at the edge of the platform to work there may be a space not exceeding 300 millimetres. Where necessary, devices shall be provided and used to keep the platform a sufficient distance from the wall when persons have to work in a sitting position.

(14) If a *suspended scaffold* is carried on fibre ropes and pulley blocks the ropes shall be spaced not more than 3.20 metres apart.

(15) Where the work to be carried out from a *suspended scaffold* is of such a light nature and the material required for the work is such that a cradle or similar light-weight *suspended scaffold* can be used with safety and where such *suspended scaffold* is used, the following requirements of this regulation shall not apply, that is to say—

(a) the requirement of paragraph (5) that the outriggers shall be installed horizontally and that stops shall be provided; and
(b) the requirements of paragraph (13)(b) as to the width of the platform.

The platform of a *suspended scaffold* to which this paragraph applies shall be not less than 430 millimetres wide.

(a) Sound material; adequate strength. See INTRODUCTORY NOTE 11.

(b) Properly maintained. See INTRODUCTORY NOTE 10.

20. Boatswain's chairs, cages, skips, etc. (Not power operated).—(1) No boatswain's chair, cage, skip or similar *plant or equipment* (not being a boatswain's chair, cage, skip or similar *plant or equipment* which is raised or lowered by a power-driven *lifting appliance*) shall be used unless—

  (a) it is of good construction, suitable and sound material, adequate strength *(a)*, free from patent defect and properly maintained *(b)*;
  (b) the outriggers or other supports are of adequate strength and properly installed and supported;
  (c) the chains, ropes, *lifting gear* or other means of suspension used therewith (in addition to satisfying the requirements of the Construction (Lifting Operations) Regulations, 1961) are securely attached to the outriggers or other supports and to the chair, cage, ship or similar *plant or equipment* or to any *lifting appliance* or other device attached thereto, as the case may be;
  (d) suitable means are provided to prevent any occupant falling out;
  (e) it is free of materials or articles liable to interfere with the occupant's handhold or foothold or otherwise endanger him;
  (f) suitable measures are taken to prevent spinning or tipping in a manner dangerous to any occupant;
  (g) in the case of any skip or other receptacle it is at least 910 millimetres deep; and
  (h) its installation has been, and its use is, supervised by a competent person.

  (2) No boatswain's chair, cage, skip or similar *plant or equipment* (not being a boatswain's chair, cage, skip or similar *plant or equipment* which is raised or lowered by a power-driven *lifting appliance*) shall be used as a working place in circumstances in which a *suspended scaffold* could be used unless the work is of such short duration as to make the use of a *suspended scaffold* unreasonable or the use of a *suspended scaffold* is not reasonably practicable *(c)*.

  (a) Good construction . . . adequate strength. See INTRODUCTORY NOTE 11.

  (b) Properly maintained. See INTRODUCTORY NOTE 10.

  (c) Reasonably practicable. See INTRODUCTORY NOTE 5.

21. Trestle scaffolds.—(1) All trestles and supports used for the construction of any *trestle scaffold* shall be of good construction, suitable and sound material, adequate strength *(a)* for the purposes for which they are used and free from patent defect and shall be properly maintained *(b)*.

  (2) A *trestle scaffold* shall not be used—

  (a) if the *scaffold* is so situated that a person would be liable to fall from its working platform a distance of more than 4.50 metres; or
  (b) if constructed with more than one tier where folding supports are used.

  (3) No *trestle scaffold* shall be erected on a *scaffold* platform unless—

  (a) the width of the said platform is such as to leave sufficient clear space for the transport of materials along the platform; and

(b) the trestles or supports are firmly attached to the said platform and adequately braced to prevent displacement.

(a) **Good construction ... adequate strength.** See INTRODUCTORY NOTE 11.

(b) **Properly maintained.** See INTRODUCTORY NOTE 10.

22.   Inspection of scaffolds, boatswain's chairs, etc.—(1) Subject to the provisions of this regulation, no *scaffold (a)* (including any boatswain's chair, cage, skip or similar *plant or equipment*) and no *plant or equipment* used for the purposes of any of the foregoing shall be used unless (in addition to satisfying the requirements of the Construction (Lifting Operations) Regulations 1961)—

(a) it has been inspected by a competent person within the immediately preceding 7 days;

(b) it has been inspected by a competent person since exposure to weather conditions likely to have affected its strength or stability or to have displaced any part; and

(c) a report has been made of the results of every such inspection in the form [Form 91, Part I] set out in the Schedule to these Regulations and containing the particulars therein specified and signed by the person making the inspection:

Provided that sub-paragraph (a) shall not apply in the case of a *scaffold* no part of which has been erected for more than 7 days, and sub-paragraph (c) shall not apply to a *ladder scaffold, trestle scaffold* or a *scaffold* from no part of which a person is liable to fall a distance of more than 2 metres.

(2) Paragraph (1) of this regulation shall not require a *scaffold* to be inspected by reason only that it has been added to, altered or partly dismantled.

(3) In the case of a site where the employer for whom the inspection was carried out has reasonable grounds for believing that the operations or works will be completed in a period of less than 6 weeks, the provision in this regulation requiring that a report shall have been made and signed shall be deemed to have been satisfied if the person in charge of the operations or works carried on by that employer at that site has himself carried out the inspection and is a competent person and if, within 1 week of the date of the inspection, he reports to his employer in writing that the *scaffold*, boatswain's chair, cage, skip or similar *plant or equipment* (as the case may be) and any plant and equipment used for the purposes of any of the foregoing was inspected by him and that he found it in good order or observed certain defects, as the case may be, and the date of such inspection and the results thereof together with the name of the person making the inspection are entered by the employer in the said form together with the said particulars.

(a) **Scaffold.** The provisions as to inspection contained in reg. 22(1) apply only where scaffolding, or, perhaps, some new lift of the scaffolding, has been completed. They do not apply to a scaffold in course of construction (*Sexton v Scaffolding (Great Britain) Ltd* [1953] 1 QB 153, [1952] 2 All ER 1085, CA, *per* Somervell LJ).

23.   Scaffolds used by workmen of different employers. Where a *scaffold* or part of a *scaffold* is to be used by or on behalf of an employer other than the employer for whose workmen it was first erected, the first-mentioned employer shall, before such use, and without prejudice to any other obligations imposed upon him by these Regulations, take express steps either personally or by a competent agent, to satisfy himself that the *scaffold* or part thereof is stable *(a)*, that the materials used in its construction are sound and that the safeguards required by these Regulations are in position.

(a) Express steps ... stable. Express steps are such as are directed specifically to the question of stability. The obligation is more than that of mere inspection; it is an obligation on the employer to take "express steps" to satisfy himself that the scaffold is stable, although if no ordinary reasonable investigation could possibly have discovered the default it might be held that the plaintiff had failed to discharge the onus upon him. One way to find out the facts is to ask questions, simple and straightforward (*Clarke v ER Wright & Son* [1957] 3 All ER 486, [1957] 1 WLR 1191, CA, *per* Lord Evershed MR).

The fact that a workman, sent to do work which involves the use of a scaffold erected by another employer, asks questions as to whether the scaffold is all right is not a compliance with the obligation in the absence of a specific delegation to him of the duty to carry out an inspection (*Vineer v C Doidge & Sons Ltd* [1972] 2 All ER 794, [1972] 1 WLR 893, CA).

24. Construction of working platforms, gangways and runs.—(1) Every *working platform*, gangway *(a)* and run from any part of which a person is liable to fall a distance of more than 2 metres *(b)* shall be closely boarded, planked or plated: Provided that this requirement shall not apply to—

(a) a platform, gangway or run consisting of open metal work having interstices none of which exceeds 4,000 square millimetres in area, if there is no risk of persons below any such platform, gangway or run being struck by materials or articles falling through the platform, gangway or run; or

(b) a platform, gangway or run, the boards, planks or plates of which are so secured as to prevent their moving and so placed that the space between adjacent boards, planks or plates does not exceed 25 millimetres, if there is no risk of persons below any such platform, gangway or run being struck by materials or articles falling through the platform.

(2) No gangway or run shall be used the slope of which exceeds 1 vertical to 1½ horizontal.

(3) Where the slope of a gangway or run renders additional foothold necessary, and in every case where the slope is more than 1 vertical to 4 horizontal there shall be provided proper stepping laths which shall—

(a) be placed at suitable intervals; and

(b) be the full width of the gangway or run, except that where necessary they may be interrupted over widths of not more than 100 millimetres to facilitate the movement of barrows.

General note. In *Black v Duncan Logan (Contractors) Ltd* 1969 SLT (Notes) 19 it was stated that the mischief which the regulation "... was designed to prevent was the risk of injury resulting from gaps in a platform through which a workman might fall from a height or through which material might fall and injure those below and not the risk of a workman falling on the platform" (decided under the Building (Safety, Health and Welfare) Regulations 1948).

(a) **Gangway.** See note *(b)* to reg. 4.

(b) *More than 2 metres.* If the falling distance is less, the regulation does not apply, and liability at common law must be considered independently of the regulation (*Chipchase v British Titan Products Co Ltd* [1956] 1 QB 545, [1956] 1 All ER 613, CA).

25.   Boards and planks in working platforms, gangways and runs.—(1) Every board or plank forming part of a *working platform*, gangway *(a)* or run shall be—

(a)   of a thickness which is such as to afford adequate security having regard to the distance between the putlogs or other supports; and

(b)   not less than 200 millimetres wide, or, in the case of boards or planks exceeding 50 millimetres in thickness, not less than 150 millimetres wide.

(2) No board or plank which forms part of a *working platform*, gangway or run shall project beyond its end support to a distance exceeding four times the thickness of the board or plank unless it is effectively secured to prevent tipping, or to a distance which, having regard to the thickness and strength of the plank, renders the projecting part of the plank an unsafe support for any weight liable to be upon it.

(3) Suitable measures shall be taken by the provision of adequate bevelled pieces or otherwise to reduce to a minimum the risk of tripping and to facilitate the movement of barrows where boards or planks which form part of a *working platform*, gangway or run overlap each other or are not of reasonably uniform thickness where they meet each other or owing to warping or for some other reason do not provide an even surface.

Provided that this paragraph shall not apply to a *working platform*, gangway or run one side of which is contiguous to a curved surface of any cylindrical or spherical structure forming part of a work of engineering construction.

(4) Every board or plank which forms part of a *working platform*, gangway or run shall—

(a)   rest securely and evenly on its supports; and

(b)   rest on at least 3 supports unless, taking into account the distance between the supports and the thickness of the board or plank, the conditions are such as to prevent undue or unequal sagging.

(5) Where work has to be done at the end of a wall or working face the *working platform* at such wall or face shall, wherever practicable, extend at least 600 millimetres beyond the end of the wall or face.

General note. For exemptions relating to certain scaffolds, see Certificate of Exemption No. 8 [F2485], set out following these Regulations.

(a) *Gangway.* See note *(b)* to reg. 4.

26.   Widths of working platforms.—(1) Subject to paragraphs (2) and (4) of this Regulation, every *working platform* (other than *working platforms* of *suspended scaffolds* and *working platforms* referred to in regulation 28(6)(c) and 35) from which a person is liable to fall a distance of more than 2 metres shall—

(a)   if used as a footing only and not for the deposit of any material *(a),* be at least 600 millimetres wide;

(b) if used for the deposit of material *(a)*, be at least 800 millimetres wide and have a clear passage way between one side of the *working platform* and the deposited material adequate in width for the passage of persons being a passage way which is in any case at least 430 millimetres wide;

(c) if used for the passage of materials, afford a clear passage way which is adequate in width for the passage of the materials without removal of the guard-rails and toe-boards being a passage way which is in any case at least 600 millimetres wide;

(d) if used for the support of any higher platform, be at least 1.05 metres wide;

(e) if used to dress or roughly shape stone be at least 1.30 metres wide;

(f) if used for the support of any higher platform and is one upon which stone is dressed or roughly shaped, be at least 1.50 metres wide,

and in every case be of sufficient width to afford adequate working space at every part.

(2) Subject to paragraph (4) of this regulation, the following *working platforms* to which this regulation applies shall be at least 430 millimetres wide—

(a) a platform of a *ladder scaffold* or a platform supported directly by folding trestles or folding step-ladders or a platform under a roof used for work on or in the vicinity of the roof being a platform which is supported by or suspended from roof members or the roof, there in any such case the work thereon is of a light nature and of short duration in any one position and a platform less than 600 or 800 millimetres wide (as the case may be) can be used with safety; and

(b) a platform which is used for work in connection with cylindrical or spherical metal structures.

(3) Where work at the face of a building or other structure is done from a *working platform* to which this regulation applies the space between such face and the *working platform* shall be as small as practicable *(b)*, so, however, that where workmen sit at the edge of the platform to work, there may be a space not exceeding 300 millimetres.

(4) The provisions of paragraphs (1) and (2) of this regulation shall not apply to a *working platform* to which this regulation applies where it is impracticable *(b)* by reason of limitations of space to provide a platform of the width required by the said paragraphs; so, however, that in any such case the platform shall be as wide as is reasonably practicable *(b)*.

General note. For exemptions relating to certain external scaffolds, see Certificate of Exemption No. 8 [F2485], and for exemptions relating to work done from certain internal working platforms, see Certificate of Exemption No. 6 [F2410], set out following these Regulations.

(a) Deposit of material. In *Cork v Kirby Maclean Ltd* [1952] 1 All ER 1064, it was held that a bucket of distemper and a brush were "material" and that, as the painter placed them on the working platform from time to time, the platform was used for the deposit of material.

(b) Practicable: impracticable; reasonably practicable. See INTRODUCTORY NOTE 5.

27. Widths of gangways and runs.—(1) Subject to paragraph (2) of this regulation, every gangway *(a)* and run from any part of which a person is liable to fall a distance of more than 2 metres shall,

(a) if used for the passage of persons only, be at least 430 millimetres wide;

(b) if used for the passage of materials, be adequate in width for the passage of the materials and in any case be at least 600 millimetres wide.

(2) The foregoing provisions of this regulation shall not apply to a gangway or run where it is impracticable *(b)* by reason of limitations of space to provide a gangway or run of the width required by the said provisions; so, however, that in any such case the gangway or run shall be as is reasonably practicable *(b)*.

(a) *Gangway.* See note *(b)* to reg. 4.

(b) *Impracticable; reasonably practicable.* See INTRODUCTORY NOTE 5.

28.   Guard-rails and toe-boards at working platforms and places.—(1) Every side of a *working platform* or working place *(a)*, being a side thereof from which a person is liable to fall a distance of more than 2 metres, shall, subject to paragraphs (3) to (6) and except as provided in paragraph (7) of this regulation, be provided *(b)* with a suitable guard-rail or guard-rails of adequate strength to a height of between 910 millimetres and 1.15 metres above the platform or place and above any raised standing place on the platform, and with toe-boards or other barriers up to a sufficient height which shall in no case be less than 150 millimetres. Such guard-rails and toe-boards or other barriers shall be so placed as to prevent so far as possible the fall of persons, materials and articles from such platform or place.

(2) Without prejudice to the provisions of regulation 11, the outward movement of guard-rails and toe-boards or barriers shall (unless they are so designed and used as to prevent such movement) be prevented by placing them on the inside of the uprights or by other equally effective means.

(3) Where guard-rails are required to be provided, the distance between any toe-board or other barrier and the lowest guard-rail above it shall not exceed 765 millimetres.

(4) Guard-rails, toe-boards and barriers required by paragraph (1) of this regulation may be removed or remain unerected for the time and to the extent necessary for the access of persons or the movement of materials or other purposes of the work; but guard-rails, toe-boards and barriers removed or remaining unerected for any of those purposes shall be replaced or erected as soon as practicable.

(5) On the side of a *suspended scaffold* next to the wall or working face—

(a) guard-rails where required by this regulation need not extend to a height of more than 700 millimetres above the platform if the work is impracticable with a guard-rail at a greater height; and

(b) guard-rails and toe-boards or other barriers shall not be required if the workers sit at the edge of the platform to work and ropes or chains affording all the workers a safe and secure handhold are provided.

(6) None of the requirements of paragraphs (1) and (2) of this regulation shall apply to—

(a) the platform of a *ladder scaffold* if a secure handhold is provided along the full length of such platform;

(b) the platform of a *trestle scaffold* when the platform is supported on folding trestles, split heads or similar devices or folding step-ladders;

(c) a platform which is used only in the course of erecting any framework or prefabricated unit forming part of a building or other permanent structure for the purposes of jointing, bolting-up, riveting or welding work and which is used for such a short period as to make the provision of guard-rails and toe-boards or barriers unreasonable if—
   (i) the platform is at least 800 millimetres wide;
   (ii) there is adequate handhold; and
   (iii) the platform is not used for the deposit of materials or articles otherwise than in boxes or receptacles suitable to prevent the fall of the materials or articles from the platform;

(d) a temporary platform *(c)* passing between two adjacent glazing bars of a roof with a sloping surface if those bars or the roof framework afford secure handhold along the full length of the platform:
   Provided that toe-boards or barriers shall be provided in accordance with paragraphs (1) and (2) of this regulation except where the provision of toe-boards or barriers is impracticable *(d)* on account of the nature or circumstances of the work;

(e) a platform under a roof being a platform which is supported by or suspended from roof members or the roof and which is used only for work on or in the vicinity of the roof and of a light nature and of such short duration as to make the provision of guard-rails and toe-boards or barriers unreasonable if—
   (i) there is adequate handhold at every working position; and
   (ii) the material required for the work is such that the platform can be used with safety;

(f) a *working platform* or working place one side of which is contiguous to the conclave surface of a cylindrical or spherical structure so long as reasnably practicable *(d)* steps are being taken to prevent persons working thereon from falling a distance of more than 2 metres.

(7) Except as provided in regulation 35, the provisions of this regulation shall not apply to *working platforms* and working places being *working platforms* and working places to which that regulation applies.

General note. For exemptions relating to certain external scaffolds, see Certificate of Exemption No. 8 [F 2485], set out following these Regulations.

*(a) **Working place.*** The whole, or a part, of a flat roof may constitute a working place (*Kelly v Pierhead Ltd* [1967] 1 All ER 657, [1967] 1 WLR 65, CA, distinguishing *Gill v Donald Humberstone & Co Ltd* [1963] 3 All ER 180, [1963] 1 WLR 929, HL); and see *Regan v G and F Asphalt Ltd* (1967) 2 KIR 666; *Boyton v Willment Bros Ltd* [1971] 3 All ER 624, [1971] 1 WLR 1625, CA. The foregoing authorities establish that a necessary characteristic of a working place is that it is to be used for work for an appreciable time; a period of ten to fifteen minutes is such a time (*Ferguson v John Dawson & Patners (Contractors) Ltd* [1976] 3 All ER 817, [1976] 1 WLR 1213, CA).

*(b) **Shall ... be provided.*** Subject to the provisions of paragraphs (3) to (7) the obligation to provide a guard-rail or rails is absolute (*Westcott v Structural and Marine Engineers Ltd* [1960] 1 All ER 775, [1960] 1 WLR 349).

*(c) **Temporary platform.*** This expression points to and covers the case of a platform erected temporarily for a particular purpose, and does not apply to a fixed structure, part of the building, which is being used as a working place for the time being.

"Temporary" does not refer to the fact that the platform is used only temporarily, but that it is there only temporarily (*Westcott v Structural and Marine Engineers Ltd,* above).

(d) *Impracticable; reasonably practicable.* See INTRODUCTORY NOTE 5.

29.   Guard-rails, etc. for gangways, runs and stairs.—(1) Except for the time and to the extent necessary for the access of persons or the movement of materials, stairs shall be provided throughout their length with hand-rails (a) or other efficient means (b) to prevent the fall of persons. If necessary to prevent danger to any person the hand-rails or other means shall be continued beyond the end of the stairs.

(2) Every side of any gangway, run or stairs from which a person is liable to fall a distance of more than 2 metres shall be provided—

(a)   with a suitable (c) guard-rail (a) or guard-rails of adequate strength to a height of between 910 millimetres and 1.15 metres above the gangway, run or stairs; and

(b)   except in the case of stairs, with toe-boards or other barriers up to a sufficient height which shall in no case be less than 150 millimetres and so placed as to prevent as far as possible the fall of persons, materials and articles. The space between any such toe-board or barrier and the lowest guard-rail above it shall not exceed 765 millimetres:

Provided that the provisions of this paragraph shall not apply to a temporary gangway which is used only in the course of erecting any framework forming part of a building or other permanent structure for work of such short duration as to make the provision of a gangway with guard-rails and toe-boards or other barriers unreasonable.

(3) Guard-rails, toe-boards and barriers required by paragraph (2) of this regulation may be removed or remain unerected for the time and to the extent necessary for the access of persons or the movement of materials or other purposes of the work; but guard-rails, toe-boards and barriers removed or remaining unerected for any of those purposes shall be replaced or erected as soon as practicable (d).

(a) *Hand-rail; guard-rail.* A hand-rail is quite different from a guard-rail. A guard-rail is one of such a character as will provide a physical barrier against a person falling over the side which is guarded. A hand-rail is a rail that can be gripped by the hand; it need not necessarily act as a physical barrier; it need only be such a rail as to enable any person, by gripping it, to steady himself against falling. This regulation does not require the hand-rail prescribed to be fixed on the open side of the stairs, and it may, in suitable cases, be fixed on the wall side, or in the middle. (*Corn v Weir's Glass (Hanley) Ltd* [1960] 2 All ER 300, [1960] 1 WLR 577, CA).

(b) *Other efficient means.* 'These words must be construed *ejusdem generis* with hand-rails (*Corn v Weir's Glass (Hanley) Ltd* [1960] 2 All ER 300, [1960] 1 WLR 577, CA, *per* Wilmer LJ).

(c) **Suitable.** This word imports an element of degree and must be considered in relation to the purpose to be achieved. In the case of guard-rails the purpose to be achieved is the provision of an effective physical barrier against the risk of falling (*Astell v London Transport Board* [1966] 2 All ER 748, [1966] 1 WLR 1047, CA).

(d) **Practicable.** See INTRODUCTORY NOTE 5.

30. Platforms, gangways, runs and stairs, etc. to afford safe foothold.—(1) If a platform, gangway *(a)*, run or stair becomes slippery, appropriate steps shall as soon as can reasonably practicable *(b)* be taken by way of sanding, cleaning or otherwise to remedy the condition.

(2) Every platform, gangway *(a)*, run or stair shall be kept free from an unnecessary obstruction *(c)* and material and free from rubbish and any projecting nails.

(a) **Gangway.** See note *(b)* to reg. 4. In *Woodcock v Gilbert Ash (General Works) Ltd* 1987 SLT 678 it was argued, unsuccessfully, that reg. 30(2) did not apply to someone stepping on to a platform rather than proceeding along it.

(b) **Reasonably practicable.** See INTRODUCTORY NOTE 5.

(c) **Free from . . . obstruction.** Where an employee suffered a back injury in attempting to remove an obstruction from a walkway, that was held to amount to a breach of reg. 30(2). Because it was likely in the circumstances that someone who found an obstruction in the walkway would attempt to remove it, the plaintiff's acts did not break the chain of causation: *McGovern v British Steel Corpn* [1986] ICR 608, CA. The Court of Appeal took a broad view of the scope of the Regulations: provided that the breach caused the injury, the precise manner in which the injury was suffered was not significant. Compare the provisions of s. 28(1) of the Factories Act 1961, and see the notes thereto.

31. Construction and maintenance of ladders and folding stepladders.—(1) Every *ladder* and folding step-ladder shall be of good construction, of suitable and sound material and of adequate strength *(a)* for the purpose for which it is used and shall be properly maintained *(b)*.

(2) No *ladder* shall be used in which a rung is missing or is defective.

(3) Every rung of a *ladder* shall be properly fixed to the stiles or sides. No *ladder* shall be used in which any rung depends for its support solely on nails, spikes or other similar fixing. Where in the case of a wooden *ladder* the tenon joints are not secured by wedge, reinforcing ties shall be used. Wooden stiles or sides and wooden rungs of *ladders* shall have the grain running lengthwise:
Provided that the requirements of this paragraph shall not apply to *ladders* to which regulation 35 applies.

(a) **Good construction . . . adequate strength.** See INTRODUCTORY NOTE 11.

(b) **Properly maintained.** See INTRODUCTORY NOTE 10.

32. Use of ladders *(a)* and folding step-ladders.—(1) This regulation shall—

(a) apply to *ladders (a)* and folding step-ladders being *ladders (a)* and folding step-ladders which afford a means of access, egress, communication or support to a person or persons employed; and

(b) not apply to any ladder *(a)* lying upon a roof or to any crawling board or crawling *ladder (a)*.

(2) Subject to the provisions of paragraph (4) of this regulation, no *ladder (a)* standing on a base shall be used unless—

(a) except as provided in the next following paragraph of this regulation, it is securely fixed near to its upper resting place, or, in the case of a vertical *ladder (a)* near to its upper end:
Provided that where such fixing is impracticable *(b)* the *ladder (a)* shall be securely fixed at or near to its lower end;

(b) it has a level and firm footing and is not standing on loose bricks or other loose packing;

(c) it is secured where necessary to prevent undue swaying or sagging; and

(d) it is equally and properly supported on each stile or side.

(3) Subject to the provisions of paragraph (4) of this regulation, where it is impracticable *(b)* in the case of a *ladder (a)* standing on a base to comply with either of the requirements of sub-paragraph (a) of the last foregoing paragraph, a person shall be stationed at the foot of the *ladder (a)* when in use to prevent it slipping.

(4) Paragraphs (2) and (3) of this regulation shall not apply to a *ladder (a)* which is not more than 3 metres in length and which is not used as a means of communication, if the *ladder (a)* is securely placed so as to prevent it from slipping or falling.

(5) No *ladder (a)* shall be used unless—

(a) (i) it extends to a height of at least 1.05 metres above the place of landing or the highest rung to be reached by the feet of any person using the *ladder (a)*, as the case may be, or if this is impracticable, to the greatest practicable height; or
(ii) there is other adequate handhold *(c)*; and

(b) there is sufficient space at each rung to provide adequate foothold *(c)*.

(6) Every *ladder (a)*, other than *ladders (a)* to which paragraphs (2) and (3) of this regulation apply, shall before being used—

(a) be securely suspended;

(b) be secured where necessary to prevent undue swinging or swaying; and

(c) be equally and properly suspended by each stile or side.

(7) No folding step-ladder shall be used unless it has a level and firm footing or while it is standing on loose bricks or other loose packing.

(8) No *ladder (a)* or run of ladders rising a vertical distance of over 9 metres shall be used unless it is, if practicable *(b)*, provided with an intermediate landing place or intermediate landing places so that the vertical distance between any two successive landing places shall not exceed 9 metres. Every landing place shall be of adequate dimensions and, if a person is liable to fall therefrom a distance of more than 2 metres, shall, except in so far as it is not reasonably practicable *(b)*, be provided with sufficient and suitable guard-rails to a height of between 910 millimetres and 1.15 metres above the landing place and with toe-boards or other barriers up to a sufficient height which shall in no

case be less than 150 millimetres, so placed as to prevent as far as possible the fall of persons, materials and articles and so that the space between any toe-board or other barrier and the lowest guard-rail above it shall not exceed 765 millimetres. Where a *ladder* passes through an opening in the floor of a landing place, the opening shall be as small as is reasonably practicable.

(a) **Ladder.** In *McChlery v J W Haron Ltd* 1987 SLT 662n it was held, in a case on reg. 33(3), that a reference to a ladder does not include a reference to a step ladder. Regulation 32(1) applies where a ladder is used as a means of access or egress irrespective of whether or not it was placed there for that purpose: *Lanigan v Derek Crouch Construction Ltd* 1985 SLT 346n.

(b) **Impracticable; practicable; reasonably practicable.** See INTRODUCTORY NOTE 5.

(c) **Handhold; foothold.** See note (c) to reg. 17 of the Construction (Lifting Operations) Regulations 1961.

33. Openings, corners, breaks, edges and open jousting.—(1) Paragraphs (1) to (3) of this regulation apply to every opening, corner, break or edge being an opening, corner, break or edge which any person employed is liable to approach or near or across which any person is liable to pass—

(a) in or of a roof (a) (other than a roof to which regulation 35 applies), floor, wall or other similar part either of a building or of any other structure whether the roof, floor, wall or other similar part of the building or of the other structure is complete or only partly complete or is in course of construction, maintenance, repair or demolition; or

(b) in or of a *working platform*, gangway or run.

(2) Subject to regulation 34, in the case of any such opening, corner, break or edge through or from which any person is liable to fall a distance or more than 2 metres or to fall into any liquid or material so as to involve risk of drowning or serious injury there shall be provided either—

(a) a suitable guard-rail or guard-rails of adequate strength to a height of between 910 millimetres and 1.15 metres above the surface which persons are liable to pass together with toe-boards or other barriers up to a sufficient height which shall in no case be less than 150 millimetres, so placed as to prevent as far as possible the fall of persons, materials and articles and so that the space between any toe-board or other barrier and the lowest guard-rail above it shall not exceed 765 millimetres, or

(b) a covering so contructed as to prevent the fall of persons, materials and articles; any such covering shall be clearly and boldly marked to show its purpose or be securely fixed in position.

(3) Subject to regulation 34, in the case of any such opening, corner, break or edge (not being an opening, corner, break or edge to which the last foregoing paragraph of this Regulation applies) through or from which materials or articles are liable to fall so as to endanger persons employed, suitable precautions by way of the erection of toe-boards, secure covering or otherwise shall be taken to prevent materials and articles so falling.

(4) Subject to regulation 34, when work is done on or immediately above any open jousting through which a person is liable to fall a distance of more than 2 metres, such jousting shall be securely covered by boards or other temporary

covering to the extent necessary to afford safe access to or foothold for the work, or other effective measures shall be taken to prevent persons from falling.

(a) **Opening in a roof.** An opening must be fully surrounded or enclosed before it can be regarded as such (*Phillips v Robertson Thain Ltd* [1962] 1 All ER 527, [1962] 1 WLR 227). Note however that reg. 33 applies also to corners, breaks and edges. As to what constitutes joisting see *Buist v Dundee Corpn* 1971 SLT (Notes) 76.

34.   Exceptions from regulation 33.—(1) Guard-rails, toe-boards, barriers and coverings required by regulation 33 may be removed or remain une-rected—

   (a)   where and when this is necessary in order to proceed with any perma-nent filling in, covering or enclosure; or
   (b)   for the time and to the extent necessary for the access of persons or the movement of materials or other purposes of the work,

but guard-rails, toe-boards, barriers and covering removed or remaining un-erected for any of those purposes shall be replaced or erected as soon as practicable *(a)*.

(2) Without prejudice to regulation 28, regulation 33 shall not apply to any opening, corner, break or edge created in the course of demolition operations to which Part X of the Construction (General Provisions) Regulations 1961, applies, or to any opening, corner, break or edge created in the course of any other demolition operation, if in the course of such last mentioned demolition operation the opening, corner, break or edge is not left unattended.

(a) **Practicable.** See INTRODUCTORY NOTE 5.

35.   Sloping roofs.—(1) In this regulation "sloping roof" means a roof or part of a roof being a roof or part having a pitch of more than 10 degrees which is covered either wholly or partly and—

   (a)   which is in the course of construction, maintenance, repair or demo-lition; or
   (b)   which is used as a means of access to or egress from operations or works on a roof or part of a roof being operations or works to which these Regulations apply.

(2) Except as provided in paragraphs (6) and (7) of this regulation, where any sloping roof has—

   (a)   a pitch of more than 30 degrees; or
   (b)   a pitch of 30 degrees or less and a surface on or from which a person is by reason of the nature or condition of the surface or of the weather liable to slip or fall to such an extent that he is liable to fall from the edge of the roof *(a)*,

work thereon or therefrom shall only be carried out by workmen who are suitable for such work and the requirements of paragraph (3) and (4) of this regulation shall be complied with.

(3) Where any sloping roof is used as a means of access to or egress from operations or works on a roof or a part of a roof being operations or works to

which these Regulations apply, sufficient and suitable crawling *ladders* or crawling boards shall be provided *(b)* on that sloping roof.

(4) Where any work is done on or from any sloping roof sufficient and suitable crawling *ladders* or crawling boards shall be provided *(b)* on that sloping roof and (except where the work is not extensive) either—

(a) a barrier shall be provided at the lower edge of the sloping roof, other than the upper surface of a tank or similar structure of metal construction, of such a design and so constructed as to prevent any person falling from that edge; or

(b) the work shall be done from a securely supported *working platform* not less than 430 millimetres wide which complies with the requirements of regulation 28(1) to (4).

(5) Crawling *ladders* and crawling boards provided in pursuance of paragraph (3) or (4) of this regulation shall be—

(a) of good construction, suitable and sound material, adequate strength *(c)* for the purposes for which they are used, free from patent defect and properly maintained *(d)*;

(b) properly supported; and

(c) securely fixed or anchored to the sloping surface or over the roof ridge or securely fixed in some other effective way, so as, in every case, to prevent slipping.

(6) The provision of crawling *ladders* or crawling boards shall not be required in the case of any sloping roof where the handhold and foothold afforded by the battens or other similar members of the structure are such that the said sloping roof is as safe for every person thereon as it would be if the said provision had been made.

(7) The requirements of paragraph (4)(a) and (b) of this regulation shall apply only in the case of any sloping roof from the eaves of which a person is liable to fall a distance of more than 2 metres.

(8) Suitable and sufficient means shall be provided to prevent the fall of materials or articles from a sloping roof.

(a) Edge of the roof. This cannot comprise the sides of a hole in the roof (*Donaghey v Boulton and Paul Ltd* [1968] AC 1, [1967] 2 All ER 1014, HL). In *McInally v Frank B Price & Co (Roofings) Ltd* 1971 SLT (Notes) 43 it was held that reg. 35(4) covers not only the risk of falling off the edge of a sloping roof but also other dangers inherent in working upon or from a sloping roof.

(b) Provided. As to the meaning of "provided", see INTRODUCTORY NOTE 9, but note that sub-ss. (3) and (4) require the provision to be made "on that sloping roof".

(c) Good construction . . . adequate strength. See INTRODUCTORY NOTE 11.

(d) Properly maintained. See INTRODUCTORY NOTE 10.

36. Work on or near fragile materials.—(1) Without prejudice to the provisions of regulations 33 and 35, no person shall pass across, or work on or from, material which would be liable to fracture if his weight were to be applied to it and so situated that if it were to be so fractured he would be liable to fall a distance of more than 2 metres unless such one or more of all or any of the following, that is to say, suitable and sufficient *ladders*, crawling *ladders*, crawling boards and duck-boards (which shall in any case be securely supported and, if necessary, secured so as to prevent their slipping) as are necessary are provided *(a)* and so used that the weight of any person so passing or working is wholly or mainly supported by such *ladders* or boards unless his weight is supported by other equally safe and sufficient means.

(2) Without prejudice to the provisions of regulations 33 and 35, no person shall pass or work near material of the kind and situated as specified in paragraph (1) of this regulation unless provision is made by means of such one or more of all or any of the following, that is to say, suitable guard-rails, suitable covering and other suitable means as are necessary for preventing, so far as reasonably practicable *(b)*, any person so passing or working from falling through the said material.

(3) Where any person passes across or near or works on or near material of the kind and situated as specified in paragraph (1) of this regulation prominent warning notices shall, except where the material consists wholly of glass, be affixed at the approaches *(c)* to the place where the material is situated.

(4) References in this regulation to a person's weight shall be construed as references to the aggregate of his weight and that of anything he may for the time being be supporting by his person.

(5) All plant and equipment provided in pursuance of this regulation shall be of good construction, suitable and sound material, adequate strength *(d)* for the purpose for which it is used, free from patent defect and properly maintained *(e)*.

(a) Provided. For the meaning of "provided", see INTRODUCTORY NOTE 9, but note that this subsection requires both provision and use of the ladders, etc.

(b) Reasonably practicable. See, in general, INTRODUCTORY NOTE 5. Regulation 36(2) imposes an absolute duty to provide the suitable means referred to, and "reasonably practicable" qualifies the standard necessary to prevent a person falling through the material (*Briggs Amasco Ltd v Thurgood* (1984) Times, 30 July, DC).

(c) Approaches. "Approaches" means something of such a character that, if a notice was affixed to it, it would give a warning to a person who was about to work on or under the roof (*Harris v Bright's Asphalt Contractors Ltd* (1953) 1 QB 617, [1953] 1 All ER 395).

(d) Good construction . . . adequate strength. See INTRODUCTORY NOTE 11.

(e) Properly maintained. See INTRODUCTORY NOTE 11.

37. Loads on scaffolds.—(1) A *scaffold* shall not be overloaded and so far as practicable *(a)* the load thereon shall be evenly distributed.

(2) When any material is transferred on or to a *scaffold* it shall be moved or deposited without imposing any violent shock. Materials shall not be kept upon a *scaffold* unless needed for work within a reasonable time.

(a) Practicable. See INTRODUCTORY NOTE 5.

38. Prevention of falls and provision of safety nets and belts.—(1) Where by reason of the special nature or circumstances of any part of the work or of the access thereto or the egress therefrom it is impracticable *(a)* to comply with all or any of the requirements of the provisions of regulations 6, 7, 24 to 30, 33, 35 and 36, so far as they relate to the falls of persons, the requirements of those provisions shall be complied with so far as practicable *(a)* and in any such case, except as provided in paragraph (2) and (3) of this regulation, there shall in addition where practicable *(a)* be provided *(b)* and so erected and kept in such positions as to be effective to protect persons carrying on that part of the work using the said access or egress suitable safety nets or safety sheets of such a design and so constructed and installed as to prevent so far as practicable injury to persons falling on to them:

Provided that such safety nets or safety sheets may be removed or remain unerected for the time and to the extent necessary for the access of persons or the movement of materials or other purposes of the work, but shall be replaced or erected as soon as practicable.

(2) Where by virtue of the preceding paragraph of this regulation safety nets or safety sheets would be required to be provided *(b)* for the protection of the persons carrying on any part of the work or using the access thereto or the egress therefrom but all such persons are able to carry on that work or use the said access or egress while making use of safety belts attached continuously to a suitable and secured fixed anchorage, such safety nets or safety sheets shall not be required to be provided if there are provided and so used by those persons while carrying on that work and using the said access and egress suitable and sufficient safety belts or other suitable and sufficient equipment.

(3) In any of the following cases, that is to say—

(a) where it is impracticable *(a)* to provide *(b)* all such safety nets or safety sheets as would be required to comply with the requirements of paragraph (1) of this regulation;

(b) where it is not reasonably practicable *(a)* so to provide all such nets or sheets by reason of the frequent movement of materials or other purposes of the work; and

(c) where the work is of such short duration as to make the provision of all such nets or sheets unreasonable,

safety nets or safety sheets in accordance with the provisions of that paragraph shall be provided to the extent to which it is reasonably practicable to provide them and in any such case as aforesaid there shall also be provided (together with suitable and sufficient anchorages) suitable and sufficient safety belts or other suitable and sufficient equipment having suitable fittings and being of such a design and so constructed as to prevent serious injury in the event of a fall to persons using them.

(4) All safety nets, safety sheets, safety belts and other equipment provided in pursuance of this regulation shall be properly maintained *(c)*.

(a) **Impracticable; practicable; reasonably practicable.** See INTRODUCTORY NOTE 5. For this regulation to apply, there must first be a provision in one of the specific regulations, compliance with which is impracticable (*Montgomery v A Monk & Co Ltd* [1954] 1 All ER 252, [1954] 1 WLR 258, CA). See also, *Boyton v Willment Bros Ltd* [1971] 3 All ER 624, CA.

The regulation does not apply where compliance with the other provisions has, on the facts of a particular case, been excused or excluded (*Gardiner v Thames Water Authority* (1984) Times, 8 June).

(b) Provided. For the meaning of "provide", see INTRODUCTORY NOTE 9, but note that sub-s. (1) requires safety nets or sheets both to be provided and erected, and that sub-s. (2) requires that safety belts shall both be provided and used.

(c) Properly maintained. See INTRODUCTORY NOTE 10.

PART IV
KEEPING OF RECORDS

39.   Reports, etc.—(1) The reports required by regulation 22 shall be kept on the site of the operations or works and when there are no relevant operations or works shall be kept at an office of the contractor or employer for whom the examination was carried out:

Provided that in the case of a site where the contractor or employer has reasonable grounds for believing that the operations or works will be completed in a period of less than 6 weeks, the contractor or employer may keep the said reports at his office.

(2) All reports and other documents required for the purposes of these Regulations shall at all reasonable times be open to inspection by any inspector and the person keeping any such report or other document shall send to any such inspector such extracts therefrom or copies thereof as the inspector may from time to time require for the purpose of the execution of his duties under *the principal Act.*

SCHEDULE

Regulation 22

FACTORIES ACT 1961

CONSTRUCTION (WORKING PLACES) REGULATIONS 1966
SCAFFOLD INSPECTIONS

FORM OF REPORTS OF RESULTS OF INSPECTIONS UNDER REGULATION 22 OF SCAFFOLDS INCLUDING BOATSWAIN'S CHAIRS, CAGES, SKIPS AND SIMILAR PLANT OR EQUIPMENT (AND PLANT OR EQUIPMENT USED FOR THE PURPOSES THEREOF)

Name or title of Employer or Contractor ....
Address of Site ....
Work Commenced—Date ....

Location and Description of Scaffold, etc., and other Plant or Equipment Inspected (1)	Date of Inspection (2)	Result of Inspection. State whether in good order (3)	Signature (or, in case where signature is not legally required, name) of person who made the inspection (4)

CERTIFICATE OF EXEMPTION No. 6 (GENERAL)
F 2410, 21 September 1972

In pursuance of the powers conferred on me by regulation 5 of the Construction (Working Places) Regulations 1966, I hereby exempt from the requirements of regulation 26(1)(a), (b) and (c) (which relate to the width of working platforms) of the said Regulations, subject to the conditions specified in the Schedule below, work done from working platforms positioned on internal staircases, landings or corridors (in each case) not exceeding 1 metre in width.

This certificate shall remain in force until revoked in writing by the Chief Inspector of Factories.

Certificate of Exemption No. 2 dated 27 January 1972, Certificate of Exemption No. 4 dated 4 May 1972 and Certificate of Exemption No. 5 dated 7 June 1972 are hereby revoked.

THE SCHEDULE

1. The working platform used shall be constructed as one unit and shall not be less than 380 millimetres in width.

2. The work done from the platform shall be of a light nature and the material required for such work shall be such that a platform can be used with safety.

3. The platform shall be used only in conjunction with a suitable scaffold manufactured specifically for use on internal staircases, landings and corridors with that type of platform.

4. The scaffold shall be properly erected.

CERTIFICATE OF EXEMPTION No. 8 STEEPLEJACKS ETC., SCAFFOLDS
F 2485, 7 April 1976

In pursuance of the power conferred on me by regulation 5 of the Construction (Working Places) Regulations 1966, and subject to the conditions specified in the Second Schedule to this Certificate, I hereby exempt from the requirements of the said Regulations specified in the First Schedule to this certificate, the following plant in the following circumstances, that is to say, external scaffolds which are erected for the structural alteration, repair or maintenance (including re-pointing, re-decoration and external cleaning) or partial or total demolition of steeples, towers, chimney stacks or similar structures, and which are supported entirely from such structures.

The Certificate of Exemption No. 1 External Scaffolds on Steeples etc. issued by the Chief Inspector of Factories on 18 August 1967 pursuant to regulation 5 of the Construction (Working Places) Regulation 1966, is hereby revoked.

This certificate will remain in force until revoked by the Chief Inspector of Factories.

FIRST SCHEDULE

REQUIREMENTS OF THE REGULATIONS FROM WHICH EXEMPTION IS GRANTED

The requirements in paragraph (5) of regulation 13 that as a general rule the distance between supports on which a platform rests shall not exceed certain measurements specified in the said paragraph.

The requirements of paragraph (3) of regulation 25 (which relates to reducing the risk of tripping where scaffolding boards overlap).

The requirements of paragraph (1) of regulation 26 (which specifies minimum widths of working platforms).

The requirements of regulation 28 (which relates to guard-rails and toeboards at working platforms and places).

SECOND SCHEDULE

CONDITIONS OF EXEMPTION

1. The whole of the work for which the scaffold is used and the erection, alteration and dismantling of the scaffold, shall be carried out only by persons—
    (a) qualified by training and experience to do such work, erection, alteration and dismantling, save that one person undergoing systematic training for such work may be employed on such work, erection, alteration and dismantling under the immediate supervision of each person so qualified; and
    (b) properly instructed as to the markings used on boards and planks for the purpose of condition 8 hereof.

2. There shall be kept posted at each office, yard, or shop of every person undertaking such at which work persons employed by him on such work attend, in positions where they can easily be read by the persons so employed—
    (a) a copy of this certificate; and
    (b) a list of the names and addresses of persons qualified by training and experience for the purposes of condition 1 hereof; and
    (c) particulars of the markings used on boards and planks for the purposes of condition 8 hereof.

3. There shall be platform bearers on opposite sides of the structure which are tied and drawn together by bolts fitted with adequate washer plates and nuts.

4. The platform bearers shall be supported by adequate dogs, spikes or similar fixings to the structure and, where necessary, by struts securely bolted to the bearers and securely fixed to the structure by adequate dogs, spikes or similar fixings.

5. The dogs, spikes and similar fixings shall be so fixed that they are not liable to pull out of the structure and in the case of brickwork or masonry shall be driven into wooden plugs fitted into the brickwork or masonry.

6. All platforms, boards or planks shall be firmly secured to the bearers.

7. Adjacent boards or planks placed alongside each other so as to afford a platform shall be firmly cleated together by adequate plates and bolts.

8. Without prejudice to the requirements of regulation 9 every board and plank used in the scaffold shall have been thoroughly examined by a competent person and passed by him as satisfactory for use in scaffolds to which this exemption applies, and shall bear clear and distinctive markings indicating that it has been so examined and passed.

9. Working platforms shall, whenever practicable, be at least 17 inches wide.

10. Secure handholds shall, wherever practicable, be provided for persons on a working platform.

THE CONSTRUCTION (HEALTH AND WELFARE) REGULATIONS 1966

(S.I. 1966 No. 95, as amended by S.I. 1974 No. 209, S.I. 1981 No. 917 and S.I. 1992 No. 2966)

The Minister of Labour—

(a) by virtue of the powers conferred on him by sections 7, 62, 76 and 180(3), (6) and (7) of the Factories Act 1961, and of all other powers enabling him in that behalf; and

(b) after publishing, pursuant to Schedule 4 to the said Act of 1961, notice of the proposal to make the special Regulations and after the holding of an inquiry under that Schedule into objections made to the draft,

hereby makes the following Regulations all of which, except regulations 13 and 14, are special Regulations:—

1. Citation, commencement and revocation.—(1) These Regulations may be cited as the Construction (Health and Welfare) Regulations 1966, and shall come into operation on 1 May 1966.

(2) The Building Operations (First-Aid and Ambulance Room Equipment) Order 1948, regulations 80 to 84 of, and Schedule 2 to, the Building (Safety, Health and Welfare) Regulation 1948, and the Building Operations (First-aid Boxes) Order 1959, are hereby revoked.

2. Application of Regulations.—(1) These Regulations apply—

(a) to building operations; and

(b) to works of engineering construction,

undertaken by way of trade or business, or for the purposes of any industrial or commercial undertaking, or by or on behalf of the Crown or any municipal or other public authority, and to any line or siding which is used in connection therewith and for the purposes thereof and is not part of a railway or tramway.

(2) The Chief Inspector may (subject to such conditions, if any, as may be specified therein) by certificate in writing (which he may in his discretion revoke at any time) exempt from all or any of the requirements of these Regulations—

(a) any particular site or any class or description of sites; or

(b) any particular work or any class or description of work,

if he is satisfied that the requirements in respect of which the exemption is granted are not necessary for the protection of persons employed or are not reasonably practicable.

General note. See the notes to reg. 2 of the Construction (General Provisions) Regulations, 1961.

From 18 August 1981 these Regulations ceased to have effect in relation to lead (see the Control of Lead at Work Regulations 1980, regs. 1 and 20(3)).

3. Interpretation.—(1) The Interpretation Act 1889 [Interpretation Act 1978] shall apply to the interpretation of these Regulations as it applies to the interpretation of an Act of Parliament and as if these Regulations and the Regulations and Orders hereby revoked were Acts of Parliament.

(2) In these Regulations, unless the context otherwise requires, the following expressions have the meanings hereby assigned to them respectively, that is to say—

"approved" means approved for the time being by certificate of the Chief Inspector *(a)*;

"contractor" means a contractor or an employer of workmen who is undertaking any of the operations or works to which these Regulations apply;

"the ambulance authority" means, in relation to any site, the authority, person or body who under or by virtue of the provisions of the National Health Service Reorganisation Act 1973 provides ambulance services for the locality in which that site is situated;

"the principal Act" means the Factories Act 1961;

"site" means any place where building operations or works of engineering construction or both such operations and such works are being carried on.

(3) For the purpose of these Regulations the number of persons employed shall be determined by reference to the number at work at any one time.

(4) References in these Regulations to any enactment shall be construed as references to that enactment as amended by or under any other enactment.

*(a) **Inspector.*** See INTRODUCTORY NOTE 24.

4. Obligations under Regulations.—(1) Except as otherwise provided in this Regulation and subject to the provisions of regulation 10, it shall be the duty of every *contractor* to comply with such of the requirements of these Regulations as affect any person employed by him *(a)*.

(2) The requirements of any of the following Regulations, that is to say, regulations 11, 12 and 13 shall be deemed to be complied with by a *contractor* as regards any period during which there are in operation—

(a) effective arrangements made by him with another *contractor* on the site, being arrangements in respect of which the requirements of paragraph (3) of this regulation are fulfilled, or

(b) effective arrangements made by him with any other person, for enabling persons employed by the first-mentioned *contractor* to have adequate access to and use of facilities which are respectively of the same kind, and as adequate and suitable, as those required by any of the said provisions to be provided, being facilities which are reasonably accessible to every working position on the *site.*

(3) A *contractor* who provides facilities in accordance with any arrangement made in pursuance of paragraph (2)(a) of this regulation shall as soon as the said arrangement comes into operation—

(a)   enter in a register [Form 2202] in an *approved* form the *approved* particulars of the said arrangement; and

(b)   give to the *contractor* with whom he has made the said arrangement a certificate in an *approved* form containing the *approved* particulars.

(4)   All registers kept and certificates given in pursuance of paragraph (3) of this regulation shall be preserved either on the *site* of the relevant operations or works or at an office of the *contractor* by whom the register is kept or to whom the certificate was given, as the case may be.

(5)   All registers kept and certificates given in pursuance of paragraph (3) of this regulation shall at all reasonable times be open to inspection by any inspector. All such certificates shall at all reasonable times be open to inspection by any person employed affected thereby. The person keeping any such register or having any such certificate shall send to any such inspector such extracts therefrom or copies thereof as the inspector may from time to time require for the purpose of the execution of his duties under the principal Act.

(6)   Where by virtue of an arrangement in accordance with paragraph (2) (a) of this Regulation a *contractor* is deemed to have complied with any requirement of these Regulations, the *contractor* who has undertaken to provide facilities in accordance with that arrangement shall be responsible instead of the first-mentioned *contractor* for complying with that requirement and the persons employed by the first-mentioned *contractor* shall for the purpose of that requirement be deemed to be persons in the employment of the *contractor* who has undertaken to provide the said facilities.

(7)   Nothing in these Regulations shall be construed as preventing two or more *contractors* from jointly appointing the same person or persons to have charge of first-aid boxes or cases or of a first-aid room or to be responsible for summoning an ambulance or other means of transport in pursuance of regulation 8.

(a) **Person employed by him.** See note (e) to reg. 3 of the Construction (General Provisions) Regulations 1961.

5.–10.   [*revoked*].

11.   Shelters and accommodation for clothing and for taking meals.—
(1)   Subject to the provisions of paragraphs (2) and (3) of this regulation, there shall be provided at or in the immediate vicinity of every *site* for the use of the persons employed and conveniently accessible to them—

(a)   adequate and suitable accommodation for taking shelter during interruptions or work owing to bad weather and for depositing clothing not worn during working hours, being accommodation containing—

(i)   where more than 5 persons are employed by a *contractor* on a *site*, adequate and suitable means of enabling the persons employed to warm themselves and to dry wet clothing; or

(ii)   where 5 persons or less are employed by a *contractor* on a *site*, such arrangements as are reasonably practicable (a) for enabling persons to warm themselves and for drying wet clothing;

(b) adequate and suitable accommodation for the deposit of protective clothing used for work and kept, when not in use, at or in the immediate vicinity of the *site*, with such arrangements as are reasonably practicable *(a)* for drying such clothing if it becomes wet;

(c) adequate and suitable accommodation, affording protection from the weather and including sufficient tables and seats or benches, for taking meals, with facilities for boiling water and, where a *contractor* has more than 10 persons in his employment on a *site* and heated food is not otherwise available on the *site*, adequate facilities for heating food; and

(d) an adequate supply of wholesome drinking water at a convenient point or convenient points and clearly marked "Drinking Water" or patently intended to be used as such.

(2) For the purposes of paragraph (1)(c) of this regulation in determining whether accommodation of any kind provided in pursuance of that sub-paragraph at any time and place is adequate, regard shall be had to the number of persons who appear to be likely to use such accommodation at that time and place.

(3) For the purposes of paragraph 1(a), (b) and (c) of this regulation, in determining whether accommodation is conveniently accessible account shall be taken of any transport provided at appropriate times for the persons employed.

(4) All accommodation provided in pursuance of paragraph (1)(a) to (c) of this regulation shall be kept in a clean and orderly condition and shall not be used for the deposit or storage of materials or plant.

(a) Reasonably practicable. See INTRODUCTORY NOTE 5.

12. Washing facilities.—(1) Except in the cases provided for by paragraphs (2), (3) and (4) of this regulation, every *contractor* who has in his employment on a *site* one or more persons of whom at least one is present on the *site* on any occasion for more than four consecutive hours shall provide adequate and suitable facilities for washing.

(2) Subject to the provisions of paragraph (4), and except in the case provided for by paragraph (3), of this regulation, where a *contractor* has more than 20 persons in his employment on a *site* or there are reasonable grounds for believing that the operations or works to be undertaken by him on the *site* will not be completed within 6 weeks from their commencement, he shall provide for the persons employed suitable facilities for washing which shall include—

(a) adequate troughs, basins or buckets having in every case a smooth impervious internal surface;

(b) adequate and suitable means of cleaning and drying being soap and towels or other means, as the case may require; and

(c) a sufficient supply of hot and cold or warm water.

(3) Subject to the provisions of paragraph (4) of this regulation, where a *contractor* has more than 100 persons in his employment on a *site* and there are reasonable grounds for believing that the operations or works to be undertaken by him on the *site* will not be completed within 12 months from their commencement, he shall provide for the persons employed facilities such as are

required by paragraph 2(b) and (c) of this regulation and also wash-basins on the following scale, that is to say, 4 with the addition of one for every unit of 35 persons by which the number of persons exceeds 100 (any fraction of a unit of 35 persons being treated as one).

(4) In any case where persons are employed on a *site* in a process in which a lead compound or other poisonous substance is used facilities shall be provided in accordance with paragraph (2) or in accordance, in a case to which it applies, with paragraph (3) of this regulation and shall include nail brushes and the troughs, basins, buckets or washbasins so provided shall be on the scale of one for every 5 persons so employed.

(5) Washing facilities provided in pursuance of this regulation shall be conveniently accessible from the accommodation for taking meals provided in pursuance of regulation 11 and shall be kept in a clean and orderly condition.

(6) For the purpose of this regulation "lead compound" means any material containing lead, which, when treated in the manner prescribed by rules made under section 132 of *the principal Act* yields to an aqueous solution of hydrochloric acid a quantity of soluble lead compound exceeding, when calculated as lead monoxide, 5 per cent. of the dry weight of the portion taken for analysis.

13.   Numbers of sanitary conveniences.—(1) Subject to paragraph (2) of this regulation, a *contractor* shall provide at least one suitable sanitary convenience (not being a convenience suitable only as a urinal) for every 25 persons in his employment on a *site*.

(2) Where a *contractor* has more than 100 persons in his employment on a *site*, and sufficient urinal accommodation is also provided, it shall be sufficient if there is one such convenience as aforesaid for every 25 persons in his employment on the *site* up to the first 100 and one for every 35 persons thereafter.

(3) In calculating the number of conveniences required by this regulation any number of persons less than 25 or 35, or in excess of a multiple of 25 or 35, as the case may be, shall be reckoned as 25 or 35.

14.   Other requirements as to sanitary conveniences.—(1) Every sanitary convenience shall be sufficiently ventilated, and shall not communicate with any workroom or messroom except through the open air or through an intervening ventilated space.

(2) Every sanitary convenience (other than a convenience suitable merely as a urinal) shall be under cover and so partitioned off as to secure privacy, and shall have a proper door and fastening. Urinals shall be so placed or so screened as not to be visible from other places, whether on or off the *site*.

(3) The sanitary conveniences shall be so arranged as to be conveniently accessible to the persons employed at all times while they are at the *site*.

(4) This regulation is without prejudice to the requirements in section 7(1) of *the principal Act* that the conveniences shall be maintained and kept clean, that effective provision shall be made for lighting the conveniences and that where persons of both sexes are or are intended to be employed the conveniences shall afford proper separate accommodation for persons of each sex.

15.   [*revoked*].

16.   Safe access to places where facilities are provided. Safe means of access and egress shall so far as reasonably practicable be provided and maintained to and from every place at which any of the facilities provided in pursuance of these Regulations is situated and every such place shall, so far as reasonably practicable, be made and kept safe for persons using the said facilities.

General note. Compare the provisions of s. 29(1) of the Factories Act 1961, and see the notes thereto.

CONSTRUCTION (HEAD PROTECTION) REGULATIONS 1989

(S.I. 1989 No. 2209, as amended by S.I. 1992 No. 2966)

1. Citation, commencement and interpretation.—(1) These Regulations may be cited as the Construction (Head Protection) Regulations 1989 and shall come into force on 30 March 1990.

(2) In these Regulations, unless the context otherwise requires, "suitable head protection" means head protection which—

(a) is designed to provide protection, so far as is reasonably practicable, against foreseeable risks of injury to the head to which the wearer may be exposed;
(b) after any necessary adjustment, fits the wearer; and
(c) is suitable having regard to the work or activity in which the wearer may be engaged.

2. Application of these Regulations.—(1) Subject to paragraph (2) of this regulation, these Regulations shall apply to—

(a) building operations; and
(b) works of engineering construction,

within, in either case, the meaning of the Factories Act 1961.

(2) These Regulations shall not apply to a diving operation as construed in accordance with regulation 2(2)(a) of the Diving Operations at Work Regulations 1981.

3. Provision, maintenance and replacement of suitable head protection.— (1) Every employer shall provide each of his employees who is at work on operations or works to which these Regulations apply with *suitable head protection* and shall maintain it and replace it whenever necessary.

(2) Every self-employed person who is at work on operations or works to which these Regulations apply shall provide himself with *suitable head protection* and shall maintain it and replace it whenever necessary.

(3) Any head protection provided by virtue of this regulation shall comply with any enactment (whether in an Act or instrument) which implements any provision on design or manufacture with respect to health or safety in any relevant Community Directive listed in Schedule 1 to the Personal Protective Equipment at Work Regulations 1992 which is applicable to that head protection.

(4) Before choosing head protection, an employer or self-employed person shall make an assessment to determine whether it is suitable.

(5) The assessment required by paragraph (4) of this regulation shall involve—

(a) the definition of the characteristics which head protection must have in order to be suitable;

(b) comparison of the characteristics of the protection available with the characteristics referred to in sub-paragraph (a) of this paragraph.

(6) The assessment required by paragraph (4) shall be reviewed—

(a) there is reason to suspect that it is no longer valid; or

(b) there has been a significant change in the work to which it relates,

and where as a result of the review changes in the assessment are required, the relevant employer or self-employed person shall make them.

(7) Every employer and every self-employed person shall ensure that appropriate accommodation is available for head protection provided by virtue of these Regulations when it is not being used.

4. Ensuring *suitable head protection* is worn.—(1) Every employer shall ensure so far as is reasonably practicable that each of his employees who is at work on operations or works to which these Regulations apply wears *suitable head protection*, unless there is no foreseeable risk of injury to his head other than by his falling.

(2) Every employer, self-employed person or employee who has control over any other person who is at work on operations or works to which these Regulations apply shall ensure so far as reasonably practicable that each such other person wears *suitable head protection*, unless there is no foreseeable risk of injury to that other person's head other than by his falling.

5. Rules and directions.—(1) The person for the time being having control of a site where operations or works to which these Regulations apply are being carried out may, so far as is necessary to comply with regulation 4 of these Regulations, make rules regulating the wearing of *suitable head protection* on that site by persons at work on those operations or works.

(2) Rules made in accordance with paragraph (1) of this regulation shall be in writing and shall be brought to the notice of persons who may be affected by them.

(3) An employer may, so far as is necessary to comply with regulation 4(1) of these Regulations, give directions requiring his employees to wear *suitable head protection*.

(4) An employer, self-employed person or employee who has control over any other self-employed person may, so far as is necessary to comply with regulation 4(2) of these Regulations, give directions requiring each such other self-employed person to wear *suitable head protection*.

6. Wearing of *suitable head protection*.—(1) Every employee who has been provided with *suitable head protection* shall wear that head protection when required to do so by rules made or directions given under regulation 5 of these Regulations.

(2) Every self-employed person shall wear *suitable head protection* when required to do so by rules made or directions given under regulation 5 of these Regulations.

(3) Every self-employed person who is at work on operations or works to which these Regulations apply, but who is not under the control of another employer or self-employed person or of an employee, shall wear *suitable head protection* unless there is no foreseeable risk to injury to his head other than by his falling.

(4) Every employee or self-employed person who is required to wear *suitable head protection* by or under these Regulations shall—

    (a) make full and proper use of it; and

    (b) take all reasonable steps to return it to the accommodation provided for it after use.

7. Reporting the loss of, or defect in, *suitable head protection*. Every employee who has been provided with *suitable head protection* by his employer shall take reasonable care of it and shall forthwith report to his employer any loss of, or obvious defect in, that head protection.

8. Extension outside Great Britain. These Regulations shall apply to any activity to which sections 1 to 59 and 80 to 82 of the Health and Safety at Work etc. Act 1974 apply by virtue of article 7 of the Health and Safety at Work etc. Act 1974 (Application outside Great Britain) Order 1989 other than the activities specified in sub-paragraphs *(b)*, *(c)* and *(d)* of that article as they apply to any such activity in Great Britain.

9. Exemption certificates.—(1) Subject to paragraph (2) below, the Health and Safety Executive may, by certificate in writing, exempt any person or class of persons or any activity or class of activities from any requirement imposed by these Regulations and any such exemption may be granted subject to conditions and to a limit of time and may be revoked by a certificate in writing at any time.

(2) The Executive shall not grant any such exemption unless having regard to the circumstances of the case, and in particular to—

    (a) the conditions, if any, which it proposes to attach to the exemption; and

    (b) any other requirements imposed by or under any enactment which apply to the case,

it is satisfied that the health and safety of persons who are likely to be affected by the exemption will not be prejudiced because of it and that any provision imposed by the European Communities in respect of the encouragement of improvements in the safety and health of workers at work will be satisfied.

PART 8

OFFICES, SHOPS AND RAILWAY PREMISES

SUMMARY

INTRODUCTION TO THE OFFICES, SHOPS AND RAILWAY PREMISES ACT 1963

The 1963 Act followed the general pattern of, and adhered to much of the wording of, the Factories Act 1961. Like that Act, it empowered the appropriate Minister to appoint inspectors and to make regulations, but these powers, together with many other provisions of the Act, were repealed by the Health and Safety at Work etc. Act 1974.

This Act, like the Factories Act, has been deeply affected by the 1992 Regulations implementing the European Directives (see HISTORICAL INTRODUCTION). The Management of Health and Safety at Work Regulations 1992 (S.I. 1992 No. 2051), the Workplace (Health, Safety and Welfare) Regulations 1992 (S.I. 1992 No. 3004) and the Provision and Use of Work Equipment Regulations 1992 (S.I. 1992 No. 2932) are of particular significance. There are more likely to be VDUs in offices than elsewhere so that the Health and Safety (Display Screen Equipment) Regulations 1992 (S.I. 1992 No. 2792) are of special relevance here. Of course, all the implementing Regulations apply to offices, shops and railway premises as well as (practically) all other workplaces.

Although a breach of this Act may lead to a criminal prosecution, just like the Factories Act 1961 it also gives rise to a civil action for breach of statutory duty (at least where the provision breached is one designed to promote safety: see *Groves v Lord Wimborne* [1898] 2 QB 402, CA; *Britannic Merthyr Coal Co Ltd v David* [1910] AC 74, HL; *Black v Fife Coal Co Ltd* [1912] AC 149, HL; *Westwood v Post Office* [1974] AC 1, HL). The position is not clear in relation to provisions which appear to be designed to protect health or welfare. But the Act does not protect a shop customer: *Reid v Galbraith Stores* 1970 SLT (Notes) 83.

THE OFFICES, SHOPS AND RAILWAY PREMISES ACT 1963

(1963 c. 41)

ARRANGEMENT OF SECTIONS

An Act to make fresh provision for securing the health, safety and welfare of persons employed to work in office or shop premises and provision for securing the health, safety and welfare of persons employed to work in certain railway premises; to amend certain provisions of the Factories Act 1961; and for purposes connected with the matters aforesaid. [31 July 1963]

Scope of Act

1. Premises to which this Act applies.—(1) The premises to which this Act applies are office premises *(a)*, shop premises *(b)* and railway premises *(c)*, being (in each case) premises in the case of which persons *(d)* are employed *(e)* to work therein.

(2) In this Act—

(a) "office premises" means a building *(f)* or part of a building, being a building or part the sole or principal use of which is an office or for office purposes *(g)*;
(b) "office purposes" includes the purposes of administration, clerical work, handling money and telephone and telegraph operating; and
(c) "clerical work" includes writing, book-keeping, sorting papers, filing, typing, duplicating, machine calculating, drawing and the editorial preparation of matter for publication;

and for the purposes of this Act premises occupied together with office premises for the purposes of the activities *(h)* there carried on shall be treated as forming part of the office premises *(i)*.

(3) In this Act—

(a) "shop premises" means—
   (i) a shop *(j)*;
  (ii) a building *(f)* or part of a building, being a building or part which is not a shop but of which the sole or principal use is the carrying on there of retail or business *(k)*;
  (iii) a building occupied by a wholesale dealer or merchant where goods are kept for sale wholesale or a part of a building so occupied where goods are so kept, but not including a warehouse *(l)* belonging to the owners, trustees or conservators of a dock, wharf or quay;
  (iv) a building to which members of the public are invited to resort for the purpose of delivering there goods for repair or other treatment or of themselves there carrying out repairs to, or other treatment of, goods, or a part of a building to which members of the public are invited to resort for that purpose;
  (v) any premises (in this Act referred to as "fuel storage premises") occupied for the purpose of a trade or business which consists of, or includes, the sale of solid fuel, being premises used for the storage of such fuel intended to be sold in the course of that trade or business, but not including dock storage premises or colliery storage premises;
(b) "retail trade or business" *(k)* includes the sale to members of the public of food or drink for immediate consumption, retail sales by auction and the business of lending books or periodicals for the purpose of gain *(m)*;
(c) "solid fuel" means coal, coke and any solid fuel derived from coal or of which coal or coke is a constituent;
(d) "dock storage premises" means fuel storage premises which constitute or are comprised in premises to which certain provisions of the Factories Act 1961 apply *(n)* by virtue of section 125(1) (docks, etc.) of that Act; and
(e) "colliery storage premises" means fuel storage premises which form part of premises which, for the purposes of the Mines and Quarries Act 1954 *(o)*, form part of a mine or quarry, other than premises where

persons are regularly employed *(e)* to work by a person other than the owner (as defined by that Act) of the mine or quarry,

and for the purposes of this Act premises occupied together with a shop or with a building or part of a building falling within sub-paragraph (ii), (iii) or (iv) of paragraph (a) above for the purposes of the trade or business carried on in the shop or, as the case may be, the building or part of a building, shall be treated as forming part of the shop or, as the case may be, of the building or part of the building, and premises occupied together with fuel storage premises for the purposes of the activities there carried on (not being office premises) shall be treated as forming part of the fuel storage premises, but for the purposes of this Act office premises comprised in fuel storage premises shall be deemed not to form part of the last-mentioned premises.

(4) In this Act "railway premises" *(p)* means a building *(f)* occupied by railway undertakers *(q)* for the purposes of the railway undertaking carried on by them and situate in the immediate vicinity of the permanent way or a part (so occupied) of a building so situate, but does not include—

(a) office or shop premises *(r)*;
(b) premises used for the provision of living accommodation for persons employed *(e)* in the undertaking, or hotels; or
(c) premises wherein are carried on such processes or operations as are mentioned in section 123(1) (electrical stations) of the Factories Act 1961 *(s)* and for such supply as is therein mentioned.

(5) For the purposes of this Act premises maintained in conjunction with office, shop or railway premises for the purpose of the sale or supply for immediate consumption of food or drink wholly or mainly to persons employed *(e)* to work in the premises in conjunction with which they are maintained shall, if they neither form part of those premises nor are required by the foregoing provisions of this section to be treated as forming part of them, be treated for the purposes of this Act as premises of the class within which fall the premises in conjunction with which they are maintained.

General note. Sections 2 and 3 exclude from the application of the Act premises in which only employer's relatives or outworkers work, and premises where only 21 man-hours weekly are normally worked.

Special provisions apply with respect to buildings of which part only fall within the definition in s. 1 (see s. 42), with respect to buildings plurally owned (see s. 43) and with respect to contiguous fuel storage premises in single ownership (see s. 44).

Nothing in the Act applies to factory premises within the meaning of the Factories Act 1961 (see s. 85(1)).

With the exception of s. 75(3) (which places a limitation upon the application of the Factories Act 1961 to warehouses) nothing in the Act applies to certain premises used for the sale of fish by wholesale (see s. 85(2)).

Nothing in the Act applies to underground parts of mines within the Mines and Quarries Act 1954 (see s. 85(3)).

Special provisions apply to premises used for transitory purposes (see s. 86).

(a) **Office premises.** See sub-ss. (2) and (5).

(b) **Shop premises.** See sub-ss. (3) and (5).

(c) **Railway premises.** See sub-ss. (4) and (5).

(d) **Persons.** Since, by virtue of the Interpretation Act 1978, s. 6(c), the plural includes the singular, premises are not outside the Act merely because only one person is

employed to work therein (see *Griffith v Ferrier* 1952 JC 56, so interpreting the similar words of what is now s. 175 of the Factories Act 1961).

(*e*) **Employed.** For definition, see s. 90(1). For the exception of premises in which only employer's relatives or outworkers work, see s. 2; for the exception of premises where only 21 man-hours weekly are worked, see s. 3. As to the protection of this Act extending only to employed persons, see the Introduction to this Act.

(*f*) **Building; part of a building.** By s. 90(1) "building", except in s. 1(4) (occupation by railway undertakers), includes structure; the term is not further defined. The meaning of the term as used in other legislation has been judicially considered; for example, in relation to public health legislation (see 38 *Halsbury's Laws* (4th edn.) 453 *et seq.*) and in relation to the factory legislation (see the notes to s. 176 of the Factories Act 1961). It is thought that the principal difficulty in the interpretation of the words "building or part of a building", in s. 1(2)(a) of the present Act will arise when it becomes necessary to distinguished between a "building", on the one hand, and a "part of a building", on the other hand. It is submitted that a "building", must have its feet upon the ground, so that in the case of a multi-storey building each storey is a part of a building and not a separate building in itself. Where, however, what outwardly appears to be a single building is divided vertically by party walls, and the various divisions are occupied as separate units without intercommunication, it is thought that each such division will constitute a separate "building" for the purpose of the Act. The question is in any event one of fact and degree, to be decided upon an examination of the circumstances of each particular case.

Where a building as a whole does not qualify as office premises (as where it is a library) nevertheless a definable part of that building (such as a room) may constitute a "part of a building", and if that part is solely or principally used as an office or for office purposes it is "office premises" within s. 1(2)(a) (*Oxfordshire County Council v University of Oxford* (1980) Times, 10 December, DC).

(*g*) **Office purposes.** See sub-s. (2)(b).

(*h*) **Activities.** It is not enough that the ancillary premises are occupied for the purposes of the office premises if they are not occupied for the purposes of the activities there carried on.

(*i*) **Treated as forming part of the office premises.** This deeming provision only operates when the premises in question are neither a "building ... the sole or principal use of which is as an office or for office purposes" nor a "part of a building the sole or principal use of which is as an office or for office purposes": see s. 1(2)(a).

(*j*) **Shop.** This term is not defined in the Act (compare s. 74(1) of the Shops Act 1950, which defines "shop" for the purposes of that Act as including "any premises where any retail trade or business is carried on"; by s. 74(1) of that Act, "retail trade or business" includes "the business of a barber or hairdresser, the sale of refreshments or intoxicating liquors, the business of lending books or periodicals when carried on for purposes of gain, and retail sales by auction, but does not include the sale of programmes and catalogues and other similar sales at theatres and places of amusement"). The definition in the Shops Act 1950 cannot be applied in construing the word "shop" for the purposes of the present Act, and any attempt to make use of it for that purpose would be misleading. In view of the extended definition of "shop premises" contained in s. 1(3)(a) of the present Act, the difficulties which have arisen in interpreting the statutory definition of "shop" contained in s. 74(1) of the Shops Act 1950 seem unlikely to arise.

Since a "shop" is a species of the genus "shop premises" for the purpose of s. 1(3)(a) it seems clear that nothing can be a "shop" unless it is also "premises". Thus, it would seem that a mobile shop is not a "shop" within the Act (compare the similar interpretation accorded to s. 74(1) of the Shops Act 1950 in *Stone v Boreham* [1959] 1 QB 1, [1958]

2 All ER 715, DC, and see, also, *Cowlairs Co-operative Society v Glasgow Corpn* 1957 JC 51, *Kahn v Newberry* [1959] 2 QB 1, [1959] 2 All ER 202, DC; *Greenwood v Whelan* [1967] 1 QB 396, [1967] 1 All ER 294, DC and *Maby v Warwick Corpn* [1972] 2 QB 242, [1972] 2 All ER 1198, DC).

In deciding what is a "shop" for the purposes of the Act, it is submitted that once it is clear that there are "premises" the sole remaining question is whether what is being considered is a "shop" in the ordinary and natural sense of the word. "Where words are . . . perfectly familiar, all one can do is to say whether or not one regards them as apt to cover or describe the circumstances in question in any particular case" (*per* Somervell LJ in *Bath v British Transport Commission* [1954] 2 All ER 542 at 543). It is probably true to say, however, that the carrying on of a retail trade is the hallmark of a "shop" (see *per* Tindal, CJ in *R v Chapman and Alderman* (1843) 7 JP 132).

(k) **Retail trade or business.** "Carrying on" involves a degree of permanency (see *Golder v Thomas Johnston's (Bakers) Ltd* 1950 SLT (Sh Ct) 50, decided upon the Tenancy of Shops (Scotland) Act 1949). The definition of "retail trade or business" in s. 1(3)(b) is plainly not intended to be exhaustive (for a discussion of the meaning of the word "includes" in statutory definitions, see *Dilworth v Comrs of Stamps* [1899] AC 99, PC. It is less comprehensive than the corresponding definition in s. 74(1) of the Shops Act 1950. A retailer is one who deals with customers, as opposed to a wholesaler, who deals only with persons who buy to sell again (*per* Bacon VC in *Treacher & Co Ltd v Treacher* [1874] WN 4); and see, further, *Staincross Revenue Officer v Staincross Assessment Committee and Whitehead* (1930) 143 LT 525 at 567 and *Phillips v Parnaby* [1934] 2 KB 299. The interpretation of the words, "retail trade or business", in s. 74(1) of the Shops Act 1950 has raised the problem whether they are apt to cover the provision of services as well as the supply of goods. In *M & F Frawley Ltd v Ve-Ri-Best Manufacturing Co Ltd* [1953] 1 QB 318, [1953] 1 All ER 50, CA, Somervell LJ took the view that the word "retail" primarily suggested the selling of goods rather than the selling of services, and whilst both he and Jenkins LJ thought that the terms of the definition suggested that a business might be a retail business although it was concerned with matters other than the sale of goods, they also took the view that to satisfy the definition where there was a sale of services the services rendered must be performed in circumstances comparable with those in which a sale of goods is carried on in a retail shop. The Court of Appeal therefore held that the business in issue, which was that of a builder and decorator, fell outside the definition. The dictum of Jenkins LJ was considered in *Ilford Corpn v Betterclean (Seven Kings) Ltd* [1965] 2 QB 222, [1965] 1 All ER 900, DC, in which Parker LJ expressed the view that, within certain limits, a "retail business" in the Shops Act 1950 covered the provision of services. These dicta, however, were not followed by the High Court of Justiciary in *Boyd v A Bell & Sons Ltd* 1969 SLT 156, holding that "retail trade or business" in s. 74(1) only applied to the selling of goods and holding, accordingly, that premises used for taking in dry cleaning were not a "shop". It will be noted that the expression, "retail trade or business", in s. 74(1) of the Shops Act 1950, is used in order to define the word "shop" therein, so that the interpretation of that expression is necessarily coloured by its being linked with the word "shop" (see *M & F Frawley Ltd v Ve-Ri-Best Manufacturing Co Ltd*, above, as 323, 52). In s. 1(3)(a)(ii) of the present Act the expression, "retail trade or business", is expressly used in connection with buildings which are not shops, so that there is room for interpreting that expression in a wider sense than it is capable of bearing in the context of the Shops Act 1950.

(l) **Warehouse.** Such warehouses as are here excepted fall within the provisions of s. 125 of the Factories Act 1961, provided that mechanical power is used in or for the purposes of the warehouse; and by s. 125 thereof certain provisions of the Factories Act 1961, are applied thereto. A transit shed may be a "warehouse" (*Fisher v Port of London Authority* [1962] 1 All ER 458, [1962] 1 WLR 234).

(m) **Gain.** The ordinary meaning of "gain" is acquisition. "Gain is something obtained or acquired. It is not limited to pecuniary gain . . . and still less is it limited to commercial profits . . ." (*per* Jessel MR in *Ex p Hargrove & Co* (1875) 10 Ch App 542 at 546, 547n, construing the words "not involving the acquisition of gain by the company"

in s. 31 of the Companies Act 1862); see, further, on the construction of the word "gain" in this context, *Greenberg v Cooperstein* [1926] Ch 657. The construction of the phrase, "for purposes of gain", in what is now s. 175(1) of the Factories Act 1961, was considered by the Court of Appeal in *Stanger v Hendon Borough Council* [1948] 1 KB 571 [1948] 1 All ER 377, to include indirect as well as direct gain.

(n) *Premises to which . . . Factories Act 1961 apply.* The premises referred to in s. 125(1) are ". . . every dock, wharf or quay (including any warehouse belonging to the owners, trustees or conservators of the dock, wharf or quay, and any line or siding used in connection with and for the purposes of the dock, wharf or quay and not forming part of a railway or tramway) and every other warehouse (not forming part of a factory) in or for the purposes of which mechanical power is used."

(o) *Mines and Quarries Act 1954.* See 31 *Halsbury's Laws* (4th edn.) 409.

(p) *Railway premises.* It is to be noted that, by virtue of s. 85(1), the Act does not apply to premises which for the purposes of the Factories Act 1961, form part of a factory. By s. 175(2) of that Act the expression "factory" includes the following premises in which persons are employed in manual labour:

"(f) except as provided in subsection (10) of this section, any premises in which the construction, reconstruction or repair of locomotives, vehicles or other plant for use for transport purposes is carried on as ancillary to a transport undertaking or other industrial or commercial undertaking."

By s. 175(10) of that Act:

"Premises used for the purpose of housing locomotives or vehicles where only cleaning, washing, running repairs or minor adjustments are carried out shall not be deemed to be a factory by reason only of paragraph (f) of subsection (2) of this section, unless they are premises used for the purposes of a railway undertaking where running repairs to locomotives are carried out."

The effect of s. 175(2)(f), (10) of the Factories Act 1961 is that railway running sheds where running repairs to locomotives are carried out are subject to the provisions of that Act and (by virtue of the Railway Running Sheds Order 1961 (S.I. 1961 No. 1250) and the Railway Running Sheds (No. 1) Regulations 1961 (S.I. 1961 No. 1251)) many of the Orders and Regulations made under the Factories Act are extended so as to apply to such running sheds. It follows that such running sheds are excepted from the definition of "railway premises" contained in the present Act.

(q) *Railway undertakers.* For definition, see s. 90(1).

(r) *Office of shop premises.* See s. 1(2), (3).

(s) *Factories Act 1961.* The processes, operations and supply mentioned in s. 123(1) of that Act are "the processes or operations of generating, transforming or converting, or of switching, controlling or otherwise regulating, electrical energy for supply by way of trade, or for supply for the purposes of any transport undertaking or other industrial or commercial undertaking or of any public building or public institution, or for supply to streets or other public places . . .".

---

2. Exception for premises in which only employer's relatives or outworkers work.—(1) This Act shall not apply to any premises to which it would, apart from this subsection, apply, if none of the persons employed *(a)* to work in the premises is other than the husband, wife, parent, grand-parent, son, daughter, grandchild, brother or sister of the person by whom they are so employed.

(2) A dwelling shall not, for the purposes of this Act, be taken to constitute or comprise premises to which this Act applies by reason only that a person

dwelling there who is employed (*a*) by a person who does not so dwell does there the work that he is employed to do in compliance with a term of his contract of service that he shall do it there.

(*a*) **Employed.** For definition, see s. 90(1).

---

3. Exception for premises where only 21 man-hours weekly normally worked.—(1) This Act shall not apply to any premises to which it would, apart from this subsection, apply, if the period of time worked (*a*) there during each week (*b*) does not normally exceed twenty-one hours.

(2) For the purposes of this section the period of time worked (*a*) in any premises shall be deemed to be—

(a) as regards a week (*b*) in which one person only is employed (*c*) to work (*a*) in the premises, the period of time worked by him there;

(b) as regards a week (*b*) in which two persons or more are so employed, the sum of the periods of time for which respectively those persons work (*a*) there.

(3) [*repealed*].

(*a*) **Worked; work.** As to when persons employed by railway undertakers shall be deemed to be employed to work in premises to which the Act applies, see s. 90(3).

(*b*) **Week.** For definition, see s. 90(1).

(*c*) **Employed.** For definition, see s. 90(1)(4).

Health, safety and welfare of employees (general provisions)

4. Cleanliness.—(1) All premises to which this Act applies (*a*), and all furniture, furnishings and fittings in such premises shall be kept in a clean state.

(2) No dirt or refuse shall be allowed to accumulate in any part of premises to which this Act applies (*a*) in which work, or through which pass, any of the persons employed (*b*) to work in the premises; and the floors of, and any steps comprised in, any such part as aforesaid shall be cleaned not less than once a week (*c*) by washing or, if it is effective and suitable, by sweeping or other method.

(3) [*repealed*].

(4) Subsection (2) of this section shall not be construed as being in derogation of the general obligation imposed by subsection (1) of this section.

(5) Nothing in this section or in regulations thereunder shall apply to fuel storage premises (*d*) which are wholly in the open, and, in the case of such premises which are partly in the open, so much of them as is in the open shall, for the purposes of this section and of such regulations, be treated as not forming part of the premises.

General note. This section is to be repealed as from 1 January 1996 by the Workplace (Health, Safety and Welfare) Regulations 1992 for workplaces in existence on 31 December 1992. Those Regulations will apply to those workplaces from the former date. Workplaces coming into use afer 31 December 1992 and modifications, extensions and conversions started after 31 December 1992 to existing workplaces must conform to those Regulations as soon as they come into use.

As to whether a breach of the provisions of this section gives rise to civil liability, see the Introduction to this Act.

Accumulations of dirt or refuse may also constitute a statutory nuisance; see the Environmental Protection Act 1990, ss. 79 *et seq.*

For special provisions as to the cleanliness of the common parts of buildings, part of which consists of premises within the Act, see s. 42(1), (2), (5) and s. 43(1), (2). See also s. 8(3) (cleanliness of windows and skylights), s. 9(2) (cleanliness of sanitary conveniences) and s. 10(2) (cleanliness of washing places).

Section 1 of the Factories Act 1961 contains cognate provisions.

(*a*) **Premises to which the Act applies.** See ss. 1 to 3.

(*b*) **Employed.** For definition, see s. 90(1), (4). As to persons employed by railway undertakers, see note (*a*) to s. 3.

(*c*) **Week.** For definition, see s. 90(1).

(*d*) **Fuel storage premises.** For definition, see s. 1(3)(a)(v).

---

5.   Overcrowding.—(1) No room comprised in, or constituting, premises to which this Act applies (*a*) shall, while work (*b*) is going on therein, be so overcrowded as to cause risk to injury to the health of persons working therein; and in determining, for the purposes of this subsection, whether any such room is so overcrowded as aforesaid, regard shall be had (amongst other things) not only to the number of persons who may be expected to be working in the room at any time but also to the space in the room occupied by furniture, furnishings, fittings, machinery, plant, equipment, appliances and other things (whether similar to any of those aforesaid or not).

(2) The number of persons habitually employed at a time to work in such a room as aforesaid shall not be such that the quotient derived by dividing by that number the number which expresses in square metres the area of the surface of the floor of the room is less than 3.7 or the quotient derived by dividing by the first-mentioned number the number which expresses in cubic metres the capacity of the room is less than 11.

(3) Subsection (2) of this section—

(a)   shall not prejudice the general obligation imposed by subsection (1) thereof;
(b)   shall not apply to a room to which members of the public are invited to resort; and
(c)   shall not, in the case of a room comprised in, or constituting, premises of any class (being a room which at the passing of this Act (*c*) is comprised

in, or constitutes, premises to which this Act applies *(a)*), have effect until the expiration of the period of three years *(d)* beginning with the day on which the said subsection (1) comes into force as respects premises of that class.

General note. This section is to be repealed as from 1 January 1996 by the Workplace (Health, Safety and Welfare) Regulations 1992 for workplaces in existence on 31 December 1992. Those Regulations will apply to those workplaces from the former date. Workplaces coming into use after 31 December 1992 and modifications, extensions and conversions started after 31 December 1992 to existing workplaces must conform to those Regulations as soon as they come into use.

With respect to civil liability, see the Introduction to this Act. Overcrowding may constitute a statutory nuisance; see the General note to s. 4.

The enforcing authority has power to exempt particular premises or rooms from these provisions (s. 46(1)).

Section 2 of the Factories Act 1961 contains cognate provisions.

(a) **Premises to which this Act applies.** See ss. 1 to 3.

(b) **Work.** See note *(a)* to s. 3.

(c) **Passing of this Act.** The date is 31 July 1963.

(d) **Period of three years . . .** In calculating the period of three years, the day from which it runs (1 August 1964) must be included; see *Hare v Gocher* [1962] 2 QB 641, [1962] 2 All ER 763.

---

6. Temperature.—(1) Effective provision shall be made for securing and maintaining a reasonable temperature in every room comprised in, or constituting, premises to which this Act applies *(a)*, being a room in which persons are employed *(b)* to work *(c)* otherwise than for short periods, but no method shall be used which results in the escape into the air of any such room of any fume *(d)* of such a character and to such extent as to be likely to be injurious or offensive to persons working therein.

(2) Where a substantial proportion of the work *(c)* done in a room to which the foregoing subsection applies does not involve severe physical effort, a temperature of less than 16 degrees Celsius shall not be deemed, after the first hour, to be a reasonable temperature while work *(c)* is going on.

(3) The foregoing subsections shall not apply—

(a) to a room which comprises, or is comprised in or constitutes, office premises *(e)*, being a room to which members of the public are invited to resort, and in which the maintenance of a reasonable temperature is not reasonably practicable *(f)*; or

(b) to a room which comprises, or is comprised in or constitutes, shop *(g)* or railway premises *(h)*, being a room in which the maintenance of a reasonable temperature is not reasonably practicable *(f)* or would cause deterioration of goods,

but there shall be provided for persons who are employed *(b)* to work *(c)* in a room to which, but for the foregoing provisions of this subsection, subsection (1) of this section would apply, conveniently accessible and effective means of enabling them to warm themselves.

(4) In premises to which this Act applies *(a)* there shall, on each floor on which there is a room to which subsection (1) of this section applies, be provided in a conspicuous place and in such a position as to be easily seen by the persons employed *(b)* to work *(c)* in the premises on that floor a thermometer of a kind suitable for enabling the temperature in any such room on that floor to be readily determined; and a thermometer provided in pursuance of this subsection shall be kept available for use by those persons for that purpose.

(5) [*repealed*].

(6) It shall be the duty of the employer or persons for whom means of enabling them to warm themselves are provided in pursuance of subsection (3) of this section to afford them reasonable opportunities for using those means, and if he fails so to do he shall be guilty of an offence *(i)*.

(7) In this section "fume" includes gas or vapour.

General note. This section is to be repealed as from 1 January 1996 by the Workplace (Health, Safety and Welfare) Regulations 1992 for workplaces in existence on 31 December 1992. Those Regulations will apply to those workplaces from the former date. Workplaces coming into use after 31 December 1992 and modifications, extensions and conversions started after 31 December 1992 to existing workplaces must conform to those Regulations as soon as they come into use.

With respect to civil liability, see the Introduction to this Act, and, in particular, *Murray v Walnut Cabinet Works Ltd* (1955) 105 L Jo 41, CA, in which Cassels J held (it appears) that a breach of the corresponding provision of the Factories Act 1937 gave rise to civil liability. On appeal, the Court of Appeal expressed no view on the matter (see 105 L Jo 41).

The enforcing authority has power to exempt particular premises or rooms for these provisions (s. 46(1)). For an exception relating to office premises at building and engineering sites see the Offices, Shops and Railway Premises Act 1963 (Exemption No. 1) Order 1964 (S.I. 1964 No. 964), printed below.

Section 3 of the Factories Act 1961 contains cognate provisions.

(a) **Premises to which this Act applies.** See ss. 1 to 3.

(b) **Employed.** For definition, see s. 90(1), (4).

(c) **Work; working.** See note *(a)* to s. 3.

(d) **Fume.** See sub-s. (7).

(e) **Office premises.** See s. 1(2), (5).

(f) **Reasonably practicable.** See INTRODUCTORY NOTE 5.

(g) **Shop premises.** See s. 1(3), (5).

(h) **Railway premises.** See s. 1(4), (5).

(i) **Offence.** For offences, see ss. 63 *et seq.*, 86(1); and note sub-s. (6) of this section.

THE OFFICES SHOPS AND RAILWAY PREMISES ACT 1963
(EXEMPTION No. 1) ORDER 1964
(S.I. 1964 No. 964)

Dated 25 June 1964

General note. This whole Order is revoked by the Workplace (Health, Safety and Welfare) Regulations 1992, as from 1 January 1993 except, in relation to any workplace or part of a workplace which is not a new workplace, or a modification, an extension or a conversion, it is revoked as from 1 January 1996.

The Minister of Labour—
- (a) by virtue of the powers conferred on him by section 45 of the Offices, Shops and Railway Premises Act 1963 (hereinafter in this Order referred to as "the Act") and of all other powers enabling him in that behalf; and
- (b) after consulting, pursuant to section 45(4) of the Act, organisations appearing to him to be representative of workers concerned and employers concerned, respectively, and it appearing to him that there are no other persons concerned,

hereby makes the following Order:—

1.—(1) This Order may be cited as the Offices, Shops and Railway Premises Act 1963 (Exemption No. 1) Order 1964 and shall come into operation on 1 August 1964.

(2) The Interpretation Act 1889 [Interpretation Act 1978] shall apply to the interpretation of this Order as it applies to the interpretation of an Act of Parliament.

2. The Minister of Labour hereby exempts the following class of premises, that is to say, office premises to which the Act applies, being premises erected at, or adjacent to, a place where there are carried on operations to which section 127(1) (building operations and works of engineering construction) of the Factories Act 1961 applies or works to which that section applies, and erected for the purpose of, or in connection with, the operation or works—
- (a) from the requirements imposed by section 6 (which relates to temperature) of the Act, subject to the conditions specified in article 3 of this Order; and
- (b) from so much of section 10(1) (which relates to washing facilities) of the Act as requires water supplied to be running water.

3. The conditions referred to in article 2(a) of this Order are—
- (a) that there shall be provided for persons who are employed to work in any premises of a class to which this Order applies conveniently accessible and effective means of enabling them to warm themselves;
- (b) that the persons for whom means of enabling them to warm themselves are provided in pursuance of this Order shall be afforded reasonable opportunities for using those means; and
- (c) that no method of providing means of enabling persons to warm themselves shall be used which results in the escape into the air of any such premises as aforesaid of any fume (including gas or vapour) of such a character and to such extent as to be likely to be injurious or offensive to persons working therein.

---

7. Ventilation.—(1) Effective and suitable provision shall be made for securing and maintaining, by the circulation of adequate supplies of fresh or artificially purified air, the ventilation of every room comprised in, or constituting, premises to which this Act applies *(a)*, being a room in which persons are employed *(b)* to work *(c)*.

(2) [*repealed*].

General note. This section is to be repealed as from 1 January 1966 by the Workplace (Health, Safety and Welfare) Regulations 1992 for workplaces in existence on 31 December 1992. Those Regulations will apply to those workplaces from the former date. Workplaces coming into use after 31 December 1992 and modifications, extensions and conversions started after 31 December 1992 to existing workplaces must conform to those Regulations as soon as they come into use.

With respect to civil liability, see the Introduction to this Act. It is established that the ventilation provisions of the Factories Act 1961 give rise to such liability (*Nicholson v Atlas Steel Foundry and Engineering Co Ltd* [1957] 1 All ER 776, [1957] 1 WLR 613, HL).

Lack of ventilation may constitute a statutory nuisance; see the general note to s. 4.

See also s. 9(2) (ventilation of sanitary conveniences) and the cognate provisions of s. 4 of the Factories Act 1961.

(a) **Premises to which this Act applies.** See ss. 1 to 3.

(b) **Employed.** For definition, see s. 90(1), (4).

(c) **Work.** See note (a) to s. 3.

---

8. Lighting.—(1) Effective provision shall be made for securing and maintaining, in every part of premises to which this Act applies (a) in which persons are working (b) or passing, sufficient and suitable lighting, whether natural *or artificial.*

(2) [*repealed*].

(3) All glazed windows and skylights used for the lighting of any part of premises to which this Act applies (a), in which work (b), or through which pass, any of the persons employed (c) to work in the premises shall, so far as reasonably practicable (d), be kept clean on both the inner and outer surfaces and free from obstruction; but this subsection shall not affect the white-washing or shading of windows or skylights for the purpose of mitigating heat or glare.

(4) All apparatus installed at premises to which this Act applies (a) for producing artificial lighting thereat in parts in which the securing of lighting is required by this section to be provided for shall be properly maintained (e).

General note. This section is to be repealed as from 1 January 1996 by the Workplace (Health, Safety and Welfare) Regulations 1992 for workplaces in existence on 31 December 1992. Those Regulations will apply to those workplaces from the former date. Workplaces coming into use after 31 December 1992 and modifications, extensions and conversions started after 31 December 1992 to existing workplaces must conform to those Regulations as soon as they come into use.

A breach of s. 8(1) gives rise to a civil remedy (*Thornton v Fisher and Ludlow Ltd* [1968] 2 All ER 241, [1968] 1 WLR 655, CA; *Lane v Gloucester Engineering Co Ltd* [1967] 2 All ER 293, [1967] 1 WLR 767, CA, cases decided upon the similar provisions of s. 5(1) of the Factories Act 1961).

See also, s. 9(2) (lighting of sanitary conveniences) and s. 10(2) (lighting of washing places).

For special provisions as to the lighting of the common parts of buildings, part of which consists of premises to which this Act applies, see ss. 42(1), (3), (5) and 43(1), (2).

See the cognate provisions of s. 5 of the Factories Act 1961.

(a) **Premises to which this Act applies.** See ss. 1 to 3.

(b) **Working; work.** See note (a) to s. 3.

(c) **Employed.** For definition, see s. 90(1), (4).

(d) **Reasonably practicable.** See INTRODUCTORY NOTE 5.

(e) **Properly maintained.** See INTRODUCTORY NOTE 10.

---

9.   Sanitary conveniences.—(1) There shall, in the case of premises to which this Act applies *(a)*, be provided, at places conveniently accessible to the persons employed *(b)* to work *(c)* in the premises, suitable and sufficient sanitary conveniences for their use.

(2) Conveniences provided in pursuance of the foregoing subsection shall be kept clean and properly maintained *(d)* and effective provision shall be made for lighting and ventilating them.

(3), (4) [*repealed*].

(5) Subsection (1) of this section shall be deemed to be complied with in relation to any premises as regards any period during which there are in operation arrangements for enabling the persons employed *(b)* to work *(c)* in the premises to have the use of sanitary conveniences provided for the use of other, being conveniences whose provision would have constituted compliance with that subsection had they been provided in pursuance thereof for the first-mentioned persons and with respect to which the requirements of subsection (2) of this section are satisfied.

(6) Neither section 45 of the Public Health Act 1936 nor section 29 of the Public Health (Scotland) Act 1897 . . . (which relate to the provision and repair of sanitary conveniences for factories, &c.) shall apply to premises to which this Act applies.

General note. This section is to be repealed as from 1 January 1996 by the Workplace (Health, Safety and Welfare) Regulations 1992 for workplaces in existence on 31 December 1992. Those Regulations will apply to those workplaces from the former date. Workplaces coming into use after 31 December 1992 and modifications, extensions and conversions started after 31 December 1992 to existing workplaces must conform to those Regulations as soon as they come into use.

With respect to civil liability, see the Introduction to this Act.

The enforcing authority has power to exempt particular premises from these provisions (s. 46(1)). The Minister has exempted certain small buildings and structures used for retail sales and situated in certain public open spaces or on or near branches (see the Offices, Shops and Railway Premises Act 1963 (Exemption No. 7) Order 1968, printed below).

See the cognate provisions of s. 7 of the Factories Act 1961.

The Regulations printed below were made under the powers formerly contained in subsection (4), now repealed by S.I. 1974 No. 1943, reg. 2(a), Sch. 1, and, by reg. 4(3) thereof, are continued in force.

(a) Premises to which this Act applies. See ss. 1 to 3.

(b) Employed. For definition, see s. 90(1), (4).

(c) Work. See note *(a)* to s. 3.

(d) Properly maintained. See INTRODUCTORY NOTE 10.

THE SANITARY CONVENIENCES REGULATIONS 1964
(S.I. 1964 No. 966, as amended by S.I. 1982 No. 827)

Dated 25 June 1964

General note. The whole Regulations are revoked by the Workplace (Health, Safety and Welfare) Regulations 1992, as from 1 January 1993 except, in relation to any workplace or part of a workplace which is not a new workplace, or a modification, an extension or a conversion, they are revoked as from 1 January 1996.

The Minister of Labour by virtue of the powers conferred on him by sections 9 and 80(3) of the Offices, Shops and Railway Premises Act 1963 (hereafter in these Regulations referred to as "the Act") and of all other powers enabling him in that behalf, hereby makes the following Regulations:—

Citation, commencement and interpretation

1.—(1) These Regulations may be cited as the Sanitary Conveniences Regulations 1964 and shall come into operation on 1 January 1966.

(2) The Interpretation Act 1889 [Interpretation Act 1978] shall apply to the interpretation of these Regulations as it applies to the interpretation of an Act of Parliament.

(3) In these Regulations, unless the context otherwise requires, the following expressions have the meanings hereby assigned to them respectively, that is to say:—

"chemical closet" means a closet having a receptacle for the reception of faecal matter and its deodorisation by the use of suitable chemicals;

"drainage system" means a drainage system connected to a sewer, to a cesspool or to a settlement tank or other tank for the reception or disposal of foul matter;

"urinal" means a urinal which is connected to a *drainage system* and which has provision for flushing from a supply of clean water either by the operation of mechanism or by automatic action; and

"watercloset" means a closet which has a separate fixed receptacle connected to a *drainage system* and separate provision for flushing from a supply of clean water either by the operation of mechanism or by automatic action.

Application of Regulations

2.—(1) Subject to paragraph (2) of this regulation, these Regulations shall apply to all office premises, shop premises and railway premises to which the Act applies.

(2) Nothing in these Regulations shall apply to any premises to which the Act applies which are aggregated in a market, being either—

(a) a market held by virtue of a grant from the Crown or of prescription or under statutory authority and which is maintained or regulated by a local or other authority;

(b) any market (other than as aforesaid) held in a market place of which the sole or principal use is for and in connection with the sale of horticultural produce by wholesale; or

(c) any market (other than a market specified in sub-paragraph (a) or (b) of this paragraph) which is a covered market place to which section 51 (power to adapt Act in relation to covered markets) of the Act relates.

Provision of sanitary conveniences

3.—(1) Except as otherwise provided in these Regulations, in the case of premises to which these Regulations apply the provision of sanitary conveniences for the use of persons employed to work therein shall not be suitable and sufficient provision for the purposes of section 9(1) of the Act—

(a) unless provision is made—

(i) in the case of premises other than those to which sub-paragraph (ii) of this paragraph applies, in accordance with the appropriate provisions of Part I of the Schedule to these Regulations (which relates to the provision of *waterclosets* and *urinals*); or

(ii) where it is not reasonably practicable in the case of any premises to provide a *drainage system* for, and a supply of clean water for flushing, *waterclosets* and *urinals,* in accordance with the appropriate provisions of Part II of the said Schedule (which relates to the provision of *chemical closets*); and

(b) unless the following provisions of these Regulations are observed.

(2) Sanitary conveniences available for use by all members of the public (or all members of the public of the same sex) and provided by a county council or local authority by virtue of powers contained in any enactment shall not constitute the provision of suitable and sufficient sanitary conveniences for the purposes of section 9(1) of the Act.

(3) Subject to paragraph 4 of this regulation, in reckoning, for the purposes of regulations 4, 5 and 9 and paragraphs 1(a), 2, 4(a) and 5 of the said Schedule, a number of persons, no account shall be taken of any person whose daily hours of work in the premises do not normally exceed two.

(4) In its application to persons employed by railway undertakers, who, by virtue of section 90(3) of the Act, are deemed to be employed to work in the premises at which the general control of the doing of their work is exercised, the last foregoing paragraph shall have effect as if the expression "in the premises" were omitted.

Sanitary conveniences the use of which is shared

4.—(1) Where in the case of any premises to which these Regulations apply—

(a) there are in operation arrangements made in pursuance of section 9(5) of the Act for enabling all or any of the persons employed to work in the premises to have the use of sanitary conveniences provided for the use of others; or

(b) sanitary conveniences provided for the use of all or any of the persons employed to work in the premises are made available for regular use by other persons (not being members of the public),

then in either of such cases, in determining the number of sanitary conveniences required by these Regulations to be provided in the case of the said premises for the said employed persons, the total number of persons for whose regular use the said sanitary conveniences are made available during the periods during which persons are employed to work in the said premises shall be treated as if that were the number of persons regularly employed to work in the said premises at any one time.

(2) Where in any of the following cases, that is to say—

(a) in the case of a building to which section 42 of the Act applies containing two sets or more of premises to which the Act applies;

(b) in the case of a part in single ownership of a building to which section 43 of the Act applies containing two sets or more of premises to which the Act applies; or

(c) in the case of a parcel of land in single ownership containing two sets or more of fuel storage premises to which section 44 of the Act applies,

all or any of the persons employed to work in any two or more of any such premises have the use of the same sanitary conveniences provided in pursuance of section 9 of the Act, the total number of the persons regularly so employed at any one time for whose use the conveniences are provided shall, for the purpose of applying these Regulations, be treated as if that were a number of persons all of whom are employed to work in one set of premises to which the Act applies.

Sanitary conveniences used by the public

5.   Where in the case of any premises to which these Regulations apply in which the number of persons employed at work therein at any one time regularly exceeds ten, the sanitary conveniences provided for the use of, or used by arrangements by, all or any of such persons are also ordinarily made available for general use by members of the public resorting to the premises, the number of *waterclosets* or *chemical closets* (as the case may be) required by the other provisions of these Regulations to be provided, or to be provided separately according to their sex (as the case may be), for the use of those persons shall in every case be increased by one.

Situation of sanitary conveniences

6.—(1) No sanitary convenience provided in pursuance of these Regulations shall be situated in any room in which any person (other than a lavatory attendant) is employed to work.

(2) Except as provided in paragraph (3) of this regulation, no *watercloset* and *chemical closet*, no accommodation in which a *urinal* is provided and no accommodation containing a *watercloset* or *chemical closet* which, in either case, is not wholly enclosed shall be so situated that access to it is obtained directly from any room in which any person (other than a lavatory attendant) is employed to work.

(3) The requirements of paragraph (2) of this regulation shall not apply where—

(a) it is not reasonably practicable to comply with such requirements in the case of any *watercloset, chemical closet* or accommodation of any kind referred to in the said paragraph (as the case may be); and

(b) the *watercloset, chemical closet* or accommodation (as the same may be) was first installed or construed before the date of the making of these Regulations in a building for use therein,

and in any such case the *watercloset, chemical closet* or accommodation shall be provided with effective mechanical means of ventilation which shall discharge directly into the open air and which shall be kept in operation during the periods during which any person is employed to work in the room from which access is obtained directly to the *watercloset, chemical closet* or accommodation (as the case may be).

(4) Any enclosed space between a *watercloset, chemical closet* or accommodation where a *urinal* is provided and any room in which any person (other than a lavatory attendant) is employed to work shall be provided with effective means of ventilation.

Protection and privacy of sanitary conveniences

7.—(1) All accommodation where any *watercloset, chemical closet* or *urinal* is provided in pursuance of these Regulations shall be covered to an extent sufficient to ensure protection from the weather for persons using it.

(2) Every *watercloset* and *chemical closet* provided in pursuance of these Regulations shall be enclosed to an extent sufficient to ensure privacy and be fitted with a suitable door and door fastening.

(3) Every *urinal* provided in pursuance of these Regulations shall be so placed or so screened as not to be visible from outside the accommodation where the *urinal* is situated.

Marking of sanitary accommodation

8.   Where in accordance with these Regulations separate accommodation is provided for persons of each sex, the accommodation shall be clearly marked to show for persons of which sex it is so provided.

Disposal of sanitary dressings

9.—(1) Where in any case the total number of female persons (not being members of the public) for whose regular use sanitary conveniences are made available exceeds ten, suitable and effective means for the disposal of sanitary dressings shall be provided.

(2) All means provided for the disposal of sanitary dressings in accordance with the foregoing paragraph of this regulation shall be constantly maintained in proper condition and where the means provided consist of or include bins the contents of the bins shall be disposed of at suitable intervals.

SCHEDULE

Regulation 3

PART I

WATERCLOSETS AND URINALS TO BE PROVIDED IN ACCORDANCE WITH
SECTION 9 OF THE ACT

1. In the case of premises (whether or not persons of both sexes are employed to work therein) where—
  (a) the number of persons employed to work therein does not regularly exceed five at any one time; or
  (b) of the number of persons regularly employed to work therein there is none whose daily hours of work in the premises normally exceed two,
one *watercloset.*

2. In the case of premises other than premises to which paragraph 1 of this Schedule applies—accommodation in accordance with the following scales, which accommodation shall be provided separately for persons of each sex—
  (a) for females, and
  (b) for males (where *urinal* accommodation is not provided in accordance with the scale set out in sub-paragraph *(c)* of this paragraph)—

Number of persons of each sex regularly employed to work in the premises at any one time	*Number of waterclosets*
1 to 15	1
16 to 30	2
31 to 50	3
51 to 75	4
76 to 100	5
Exceeding 100	5, with the addition of one for every unit of 25 persons by which the number of persons exceeds 100 (any fraction of a unit of 25 persons being treated as one).

  (c) for males (where urinal accommodation is provided)—

Number of male persons regularly employed to work in the premises at any one time	*Number of waterclosets*	*Units of urinal accommodation*
1 to 15	1	—
16 to 20	1	1
21 to 30	2	1
31 to 45	2	2
46 to 60	3	2
61 to 75	3	3
76 to 90	4	3
91 to 100	4	4
Exceeding 100	4	4

with the addition of one sanitary convenience (being either a *watercloset* or a unit of *urinal* accommodation) for every unit of 25 persons by which the number of persons exceeds 100 (any fraction of a unit of 25 persons being treated as one) of which additional number of sanitary conveniences not less than three-quarters shall be *waterclosets* (any fraction being treated as one).

3. For the purposes of this Part of this Schedule, the expression "unit of urinal accommodation" means one stall of a *urinal* or, where stalls are not provided, 600 millimetres of space of a *urinal.*

PART II

CHEMICAL CLOSETS TO BE PROVIDED IN ACCORDANCE WITH
SECTION 9 OF THE ACT

4. In the case of premises (whether or not persons of both sexes are employed to work therein) where—
   (a) the number of persons employed to work therein does not regularly exceed five at any one time; or
   (b) of the number of persons regularly employed to work therein there is none whose daily hours of work in the premises normally exceed two,
one *chemical closet.*

5. In the case of premises other than premises to which paragraph 4 of this Schedule applies—accommodation in accordance with the following scales, which accommodation shall be provided separately for persons of each sex—

Number of persons of each sex regularly employed to work in the premises at any one time	*Number of chemical closets*
1 to 15	1
16 to 30	2
31 to 50	3
51 to 75	4
76 to 100	5
Exceeding 100	5, with the addition of one for every unit of 25 persons by which the number of persons exceeds 100 (any fraction of a unit of 25 persons being treated as one).

THE OFFICES, SHOPS AND RAILWAY PREMISES ACT 1963
(EXEMPTION No. 7) ORDER 1968
(S.I. 1968 No. 1947, as amended by S.I. 1982 No. 827)

Dated 6 December 1968, made by the Secretary of State under s. 45 of the Offices, Shops and Railway Premises Act 1963 and all other enabling powers.

General note. This whole Order is revoked by the Workplace (Health, Safety and Welfare) Regulations 1992, as from 1 January 1993 except, in relation to any workplace or part of a workplace which is not a new workplace, or a modification, an extension or a conversion, it is revoked as from 1 January 1996.

1.—(1) This Order may be cited as the Offices, Shops and Railway Premises Act 1963 (Exemption No. 7) Order 1968 and shall come into operation on 1 January 1969.
(1) The Offices, Shops and Railway Premises Act 1963 (Exemption No. 3) Order 1965 is hereby revoked.
(3) The Interpretation Act 1889 [Interpretation Act 1978] shall apply to the interpretation of this Order as it applies to the interpretation of an Act of Parliament, and as if this Order and the Order hereby revoked were Acts of Parliament.
(4) For the purposes of this Order "building" includes structure.

2. The Secretary of State hereby exempts the class of premises specified in article 3 of this Order from the requirements imposed by section 9 (which relates to sanitary conveniences) of the Act, subject to the conditions specified in article 4 of this Order.

3. Article 2 of this Order applies to *buildings* in the case of which all the following circumstances exist, that is to say—

(a) that they consist of one room only;

(b) that their floor area does not exceed 9 square metres;

(c) that they do not form part of a larger *building* and are unconnected with and separate from any other *building*;

(d) that members of the public are not permitted to enter therein;

(e) that they are used solely or principally for the purpose of retail sales (including the sale to members of the public of food or drink for immediate consumption);

(f) that they are situated in a public park, garden, pleasure ground, ornamental enclosure or recreation ground, or in public grounds being or containing any place of historic, architectural, artistic or similar interest, or on a heath or common, or on or immediately adjacent to any public walk or promenade by sea, river or lake, or in a public open space similar to any of the foregoing, or on or in the immediate vicinity of a beach; and

(g) that members of the public are admitted to the place where the *building* is situated for the purposes of recreation and are able to resort to the *building* without payment for admission to that place.

4. The conditions referred to in article 2 of this Order are the following, that is to say—

(a) that suitable and conveniently accessible sanitary conveniences (whether or not they are sanitary conveniences available for use by all members of the public, or all members of the public of the same sex, and whether or not provided by a county council or local authority by virtue of powers contained in any enactment) shall be available for use by persons employed to work in any premises of the class to which article 2 of this Order applies;

(b) that the said sanitary conveniences shall be kept clean and properly maintained and that effective provision shall be made for lighting and ventilating them;

(c) that the accommodation in which the said sanitary conveniences are situated shall be covered to an extent sufficient to ensure protection from the weather for persons using them;

(d) that every such sanitary convenience (other than urinals) shall be enclosed to an extent sufficent to ensure privacy and be fitted with a suitable door and door fastening;

(e) that every urinal shall be so placed or so screened as not to be visible outside the accommodation where the urinal is situated;

(f) except in the case of sanitary conveniences which are not available for general use by members of the public and are not regularly available for use by more than five persons, that there shall be separate accommodation available for persons of each sex; and

(g) that the occupier of any premises of the class to which article 2 of this Order applies shall pay or discharge on behalf of the persons employed to work in those premises or shall refund to them any charge in respect of the use of the said sanitary conveniences.

---

10. Washing facilities.—(1) There shall, in the case of premises to which this Act applies *(a)*, be provided, at places conveniently accessible to the persons employed *(b)* to work *(c)* in the premises, suitable and sufficient washing facilities, including a supply of clean, running hot water and cold or warm water and, in addition, soap and clean towels or other suitable means of cleaning or drying.

(2) Every place where facilities are provided in pursuance of this section shall be provided with effective means of lighting it and be kept clean and in orderly condition, and all apparatus therein for the purpose of washing or drying shall be kept clean and be properly maintained *(d)*.

(3), (4) [*repealed*].

(5) Subsection (1) of this section shall be deemed to be complied with in relation to any premises as regards any period during which there are in operation arrangements for enabling the persons employed *(b)* to work *(c)* in the premises to have the use of washing facilities provided for the use of others, being facilities whose provision would have constituted compliance with that subsection had they been provided in pursuance thereof for the first-mentioned persons and which are provided at a place with respect to which the requirements of subsection (2) of this section are satisfied.

General note. This section is to be repealed as from 1 January 1996 by the Workplace (Health, Safety and Welfare) Regulations 1992 for workplaces in existence on 31 December 1992. Those Regulations will apply to those workplaces from the former date. Workplaces coming into use after 31 December 1992 and modifications, extensions and conversions started after 31 December 1992 to existing workplaces must conform to those Regulations as soon as they come into use.

With respect to civil liablity, see the Introduction to this Act, and, in particular, *Reid v Westfield Paper Co Ltd* 1957 SC 218, in which the Inner House of the Court of Session decided that a plaintiff could recover damages in respect of dermatitis caused by a breach of the corresponding provisions of the Factories Act 1937.

The enforcing authority has power to exempt particular premises from the requirement to supply running water (s. 46(2)). The Minister has exempted (i) certain railway signal boxes from some of the requirements of s. 10 (see the Offices, Shops and Railway Premises Act 1963 (Exemption No. 10) Order 1972, S.I. 1972 No. 1086) and (ii) office premises at building and engineering sites from so much of s. 10(1) as requires running water to be supplied (see the Offices, Shops and Railway Premises Act 1963 (Exemption No. 1) Order 1964 (S.I. 1964 No. 964), printed after s. 6.

See the cognate provisions of s. 58 of the Factories Act 1961.

(a) *Premises to which this Act applies.* See ss. 1 to 3.

(b) *Employed.* For definition, see s. 90(1), (4).

(c) *Work.* See note *(a)* to s. 3.

(d) *Properly maintained.* See INTRODUCTORY NOTE 10.

THE WASHING FACILITIES REGULATIONS 1964
(S.I. 1964 No. 965, as amended by S.I. 1982 No. 827)

Dated 25 June 1964

General note. The whole Regulations are revoked by the Workplace (Health, Safety and Welfare) Regulations 1992, as from 1 January 1993 except, in relation to any workplace or part of a workplace which is not a new workplace, or a modification, an extension or a conversion, they are revoked as from 1 January 1996.

The Minister of Labour by virtue of the power conferred on him by sections 10 and 80(3) of the Offices, Shops and Railway Premises Act 1963 (hereafter in these Regulations referred to as "the Act") and of all other powers enabling him in that behalf, hereby makes the following Regulations:—

Citation, commencement and interpretation

1.—(1) These Regulations may be cited as the Washing Facilities Regulations 1964 and shall come into operation on 1 January 1966.

(2) The Interpretation Act 1889 [Interpretation Act 1978] shall apply to the interpretation of these Regulations as it applies to the interpretation of an Act of Parliament.

(3) In these Regulations, unless the context otherwise requires, the following expressions have the meanings hereby assigned to them respectively, that is to say:—

"trough" means a trough measuring internally at least 1.20 metres over its longest or widest part with a smooth impervious surface and fitted with an unplugged waste pipe and having a supply of warm water laid on at points above the trough and at suitable intervals of not more than 600 millimetres;

"unit of trough or washing fountain accommodation" means 600 millimetres of length of a *trough* or, in the cases of circular or oval *troughs* and *washing fountains*, 600 millimetres of the circumference of the *trough* or fountain;

"wash-basin" means a fixed basin with a smooth impervious surface, having a supply of clean running hot and cold or warm water and fitted with a waste pipe and (except where the supply of water is from a spray tap) with a plug;

"wash-bowl" includes any water container suitable for use as a washing facility; and

"washing fountain" means a washing fountain measuring internally at least 920 millimetres over its widest part, with a smooth impervious surface and fitted with an unplugged waste pipe and having a supply of running warm water.

Application of Regulations

2.—(1) Subject to paragraph (2) of this regulation, these Regulations shall apply to all office premises, shop premises and railway premises to which the Act applies.

(2) Nothing in these Regulations shall apply to any premises to which the Act applies which are aggregated in a market, being either—

(a) a market held by virtue of a grant from the Crown or of prescription or under statutory authority and which is maintained or regulated by a local or other authority;

(b) any market (other than as aforesaid) held in a market place of which the sole or principal use is for and in connection with the sale of horticultural produce by wholesale; or

(c) any market (other than a market specified in sub-paragraph (a) or (b) of this paragraph) which is a covered market place to which section 51 (power to adapt Act in relation to covered markets) of the Act relates.

Provision of washing facilities

3.—(1) Except as otherwise provided in these Regulations, in the case of premises to which these Regulations apply the provision of washing facilities for the use of persons employed to work therein shall not be suitable and sufficient provision for the purposes of section 10(1) of the Act—

(a) unless, in addition to the provision of the facilities specified in the said section 10(1), provision is made—

(i) in the case of premises other than those to which sub-paragraph (ii) of this paragraph applies, in accordance with the appropriate provisions of Part I of the Schedule to these Regulations (which relates to the provision of *wash-basins, troughs* and *washing fountains*); or

(ii) in the case of premises to which Part II of the said Schedule applies, in accordance with the appropriate provisions of that Part of the said Schedule (which relates to the provision of fixed or portable *wash-bowls*); and

(b) unless the following provisions of these Regulations are observed.

(2) The premises to which Part II of the said Schedule applies are—

(a) premises of a class which by virtue of an order of the Minister of Labour pursuant to section 45 of the Act is for the time being exempted from so much of section 10(1) of the Act as requires the water supplied to be running water; and

(b) premises which by virtue of section 46 of the Act are for the time being exempted from so much of section 10(1) of the Act as requires the water supplied to be running water.

(3) Where in the case of any premises to which these Regulations apply—

(a) the number of persons employed to work therein regularly exceeds five at any one time;

(b) persons of each sex are regularly employed to work therein; and

(c) the circumstances affecting the premises are such that it is reasonably practicable to provide washing facilities in proper separate accommodation for persons of each sex,

the provision of washing facilities shall be deemed not to be suitable for the purposes of section 10(1) of the Act unless it affords proper separate accommodation for persons of each sex.

(4) Subject to paragraph 5 of this regulation, in reckoning, for the purposes of this regulation, regulations 4 and 5 and paragraphs 1(a), 2, 3(a) and 4 of the said Schedule, a number of persons, no account shall be taken of any person whose daily hours of work in the premises do not normally exceed two.

(5) In its application to persons employed by railway undertakers, who, by virtue of section 90(3) of the Act, are deemed to be employed to work in the premises at which the general control of the doing of their work is exercised, the last foregoing paragraph shall have effect as if the expression "in the premises" were omitted.

Washing facilities the use of which is shared
   4.—(1) Where in the case of any premises to which these Regulations apply—

(a) there are in operation arrangements made in pursuance of section 10(5) of the Act for enabling all or any of the persons employed to work in the premises to have the use of washing facilities provided for the use of others; or

(b) washing facilities provided for the use of all or any of the persons employed to work in the premises are made available for regular use by other persons (not being members of the public),

then in either of such cases, in determining the number of *wash-basins, wash-bowls* or *units of trough or washing fountain accommodation* (as the case may be) required by these Regulations to be provided in the case of the said premises for the said employed persons, the total number of persons for whose regular use the said washing facilities are made available during the periods during which persons are employed to work in the said premises shall be treated as if that were the number of persons regularly employed to work in the said premises at any one time.

(2) Where in any of the following cases, that is to say—

(a) in the case of a building to which section 42 of the Act applies containing two sets or more of premises to which the Act applies;

(b) in the case of a part in single ownership of a building to which section 43 of the Act applies containing two sets or more of premises to which the Act applies; or

(c) in the case of a parcel of land in single ownership containing two sets or more of fuel storage premises to which section 44 of the Act applies,

all or any of the persons employed to work in any two sets or more of any such premises have the use of the same washing facilities provided in pursuance of section 10 of the Act, the total number of the persons regularly so employed at any one time for whose use the facilities are provided shall, for the purpose of applying these Regulations, be treated as if that were a number of persons all of whom are employed to work in one set of premises to which the Act applies.

Washing facilities used by the public
   5.   Where in the case of any premises to which these Regulations apply in which the number of persons employed to work therein at any one time regularly exceeds ten, the washing facilities provided for the use of, or used by arrangements by, all or any of such persons are also ordinarily made available for general use by members of the public resorting to the premises, the total number of *wash-basins, wash-bowls* and *units of trough and washing fountain accommodation* (as the case may be) required by the other provisions

of these Regulations to be provided, or to be provided separately according to their sex (as the case may be), for the use of those persons shall in every case be increased by one.

Protection of washing facilities
6.   All accommodation where washing facilities are provided in pursuance of section 10(1) of the Act and of these Regulations shall be covered and enclosed to an extent sufficient to ensure protection from the weather for persons using them.

Ventilation of washing accommodation
7.   Effective provision shall be made, as far as reasonably practicable, for ventilating rooms in which washing facilities are situated.

Marking of washing accommodation
8.   Where in accordance with these Regulations separate accommodation is provided for persons of each sex, the accommodation shall be clearly marked to show for persons of which sex it is so provided.

SCHEDULE

Regulation 3

PART I

WASH-BASINS; TROUGHS OR WASHING FOUNTAINS TO BE PROVIDED AS WASHING, FACILITIES IN ACCORDANCE WITH SECTION 10 OF THE ACT IN THE CASE OF PREMISES NOT EXEMPTED FROM THE REQUIREMENT TO SUPPLY RUNNING WATER

1.   In the case of premises (whether or not persons of both sexes are employed to work therein) where—
  (a) the number of persons employed to work therein does not regularly exceed five at any one time; or
  (b) of the number of persons regularly employed to work therein there is none whose daily hours of work in the premises normally exceed two,
one *wash-basin* or *trough* or *washing fountain.*
2.   In the case of premises other than premises to which paragraph 1 of this Schedule applies—*wash-basins, troughs* or *washing fountains* in accordance with the following scale—

Number of persons regularly employed to work in the premises at any one time (or, where separate accommodation for the sexes is required to be provided, number of such persons of each sex)	*Number of wash-basins or units of trough or washing fountain accommodation*
1 to 15	1
16 to 30	2
31 to 50	3
51 to 75	4
76 to 100	5
Exceeding 100	5, with the addition of one for every unit of 25 persons by which the number of persons exceeds 100 (any fraction of a unit of 25 persons being treated as one).

PART II

FIXED OR PORTABLE WASH-BOWLS TO BE PROVIDED AS WASHING FACILITIES IN ACCORDANCE WITH SECTION 10 OF THE ACT IN THE CASE OF PREMISES EXEMPTED FROM THE REQUIREMENT TO SUPPLY RUNNING WATER

3.   In the case of premises to which this Part of this Schedule applies (whether or not persons of both sexes are employed to work therein) where—

(a) the number of persons employed to work therein does not regularly exceed five at any one time; or

(b) of the number of persons regularly employed to work therein there is none whose daily hours of work in the premises normally exceed two,

one fixed or portable *wash-bowl*.

4.   In the case of premises to which this Part of this Schedule applies, other than premises to which paragraph 3 of this Schedule applies—facilities on the scale of one fixed or portable *wash-bowl* for every unit of five persons (or, where separate accommodation for the sexes is required to be provided, for every unit of five persons of each sex) regularly employed at any one time to work therein (any fraction of a unit being treated as one).

---

11. Supply of drinking water.—(1) There shall in the case of premises to which this Act applies *(a)*, be provided and maintained, at suitable places conveniently accessible to the persons employed *(b)* to work *(c)* in the premises, an adequate supply of wholesome drinking water.

(2) Where a supply of water provided at a place in pursuance of the foregoing subsection is not piped, it must be contained in suitable vessels and must be renewed at least daily; and all practicable steps *(d)* must be taken to preserve it and the vessels in which it is contained from contamination.

(3) Where a supply of water which is provided in pursuance of this section is delivered otherwise than in a jet from which persons can conveniently drink, there shall either—

(a) be provided, and be renewed so often as occasion requires, a supply of drinking vessels of a kind designed to be discarded after use; or

(b) be provided a sufficient number of drinking vessels of a kind other than as aforesaid, together with facilities for rinsing them in clean water.

(4) Subsection (1) of this section shall be deemed to be complied with in relation to any premises as regards any period during which there are in operation arrangements for enabling the persons employed *(b)* to work *(c)* in the premises to avail themselves of a supply of drinking water provided and maintained for the use of others, being a supply whose provision and maintenance would have constituted compliance with that subsection had it been provided and maintained for the use of the first-mentioned persons, and—

(a) where the supply provided is not piped, the requirements of subsection (2) of this section are satisfied as respects it and the vessels in which it is contained; and

(b) where the water supplied is delivered as mentioned in subsection (3) of this section, the requirements of that subsection are satisfied.

General note. This section is to be repealed as from 1 January 1996 by the Workplace (Health, Safety and Welfare) Regulations 1992 for workplaces in existence on 31 December 1992. Those Regulations will apply to those workplaces from the former date. Workplaces coming into use after 31 December 1992 and modifications, extensions and conversions started after 31 December 1992 to existing workplaces must conform to those Regulations as soon as they come into use.

As to civil liability, see the Introduction to this Act. See the cognate provisions of s. 57 of the Factories Act 1961.

(a) *Premises to which this Act applies.* See ss. 1 to 3.

(b) *Employed.* For definition, see s. 90(1), (4).

(c) *Work.* See note (a) to s. 3.

(d) *All practicable steps.* See INTRODUCTORY NOTE 5.

---

12.   Accommodation for clothing.—(1) There shall, in the case of premises to which this Act applies (a),—

(a) be made, at suitable places, suitable and sufficient (b) provision for enabling such of the clothing of the persons employed (c) to work (d) in the premises as is not worn by them during working hours to be hung up or otherwise accommodated; and

(b) be made, for drying that clothing, such arrangments as are reasonably practicable (e) or, if a standard of arrangements for drying that clothing is prescribed such arrangements as conform to that standard.

(2) Where persons are employed (c) to do such work (d) in premises to which this Act applies (a) as necessitates the wearing of special clothing, and they do not take that clothing home, there shall, in the case of those premises,—

(a) be made, at suitable places, suitable and sufficient provision for enabling that clothing to be hung up or otherwise accommodated; and

(b) be made, for drying that clothing, such arrangements as are reasonably practicable (e) or, if a standard of arrangements for drying that clothing is prescribed such arrangements as conform to that standard.

(3) [*repealed*].

General note. This section is to be repealed as from 1 January 1996 by the Workplace (Health, Safety and Welfare) Regulations 1992 for workplaces in existence on 31 December 1992. Those Regulations will apply to those workplaces from the former date. Workplaces coming into use after 31 December 1992 and modifications, extensions and conversions started after 31 December 1992 to existing workplaces must conform to those Regulations as soon as they come into use.

With respect to civil liability, see the Introduction to this Act. In *McCarthy v Daily Mirror Newspapers Ltd* [1949] 1 All ER 801, the Court of Appeal accepted without discussion that an action lay for a breach of the similar provisions of s. 43(1) of the Factories Act 1937 (now s. 59(1) of the Factories Act 1961), and it has been expressly so held in Scotland (*Barr v Cruickshank & Co Ltd* 1958 74 Sh Ct Rep 218).

See the cognate provisions of s. 59 of the Factories Act 1961.

(a) *Premises to which this Act applies.* See ss. 1 to 3.

(b) *Suitable and sufficient.* Whether the provision is suitable and sufficient is, it is submitted, a question of fact in the circumstances of each case. In *McCarthy v Daily Mirror Newspapers Ltd*, above, and *Barr v Cruickshank & Co Ltd*, above, it was held that the obligation under the corresponding provision of the Factories Act 1937, to provide "adequate and suitable accommodation for clothing not worn during working hours" did not include a duty to keep the clothing safe, but that nevertheless the risk of theft was an element to be taken into consideration in deciding whether the accommodation was suitable.

(c) *Employed.* For definition, see s. 90(1), (4).

(d) Work. See note *(a)* to s. 3.

(e) Reasonably practicable. See INTRODUCTORY NOTE 5.

---

13.   Sitting facilities.—(1) Where persons who are employed *(a)* to work *(b)* in office *(c)*, shop *(d)* or railway premises *(e)* have, in the course of their work, reasonable opportunities for sitting without detriment to it, there shall be provided for their use, at suitable places conveniently accessible to them, suitable facilities for sitting sufficient to enable them to take advantage of those opportunities.

(2) Where persons are employed *(a)* to work *(b)* in a room which comprises, or is comprised in or constitutes, shop premises *(d)*, being a room whereto customers are invited to resort, and have in the course of their work, reasonable opportunities for sitting without detriment to it, facilities provided for their use in pursuance of subsection (1) of this section shall be deemed not to be sufficient if the number of seats provided and the number of the persons employed are in less ratio than 1 to 3.

(3) It shall be the duty of the employer of persons for whose use facilities are provided in pursuance of the foregoing provisions of this section to permit them to use them whenever the use thereof does not interfere with their work, and if he fails so to do he shall be guilty of an offence *(f)*.

General note. This section is to be repealed as from 1 January 1996 by the Workplace (Health, Safety and Welfare) Regulations 1992 for workplaces in existence on 31 December 1992. Those Regulations will apply to those workplaces from the former date. Workplaces coming into use after 31 December 1992 and modifications, extensions and conversions started after 31 December 1992 to existing workplaces must conform to those Regulations as soon as they come into use.

Requirements as to the seating to be provided for sedentary work are contained in s. 14.

As to civil liability, see the Introduction to this Act.

See the cognate provisions of s. 60(1) of the Factories Act 1961.

(a) Employed. For definition, see s. 90(1), (4).

(b) Work. See note *(a)* to s. 3.

(c) Office premises. See s. 1(2), (5).

(d) Shop premises. See s. 1(3), (5).

(e) Railway premises. See s. 1(4), (5).

(f) Offence. For offences, see ss. 63 *et seq.*, 86(1).

---

14.   Seats for sedentary work.—(1) Without prejudice to the general obligation imposed by the last foregoing section, where any work done in any premises to which this Act applies *(a)* is of such a kind that it (or a substantial part of it) can, or must, be done sitting, there shall be provided for each person employed *(b)* to do it there a seat of a design, construction and dimensions suitable for him and it, together with a foot-rest on which he can readily and comfortably support his feet if he cannot do so without one.

(2) A seat provided in pursuance of the foregoing subsection, and a foot-rest so provided that does not form part of a seat, must be adequately and properly supported while in use for the purpose for which it is provided.

(3) For the purpose of subsection (1) of this section, the dimensions of an adjustable seat shall be taken to be its dimensions as for the time being adjusted.

General note. This section is to be repealed as from 1 January 1996 by the Workplace (Health, Safety and Welfare) Regulations 1992 for workplaces in existence on 31 December 1992. Those Regulations will apply to those workplaces from the former date. Workplaces coming into use after 31 December 1992 and modifications, extensions and conversions started after 31 December 1992 to existing workplaces must conform to those Regulations as soon as they come into use.
As to civil liability, see the Introduction to this Act.
See the cognate provisions of s. 60(2) of the Factories Act 1961.

(a) *Premises to which this Act applies.* See ss. 1 to 3.

(b) *Employed.* For definition, see s. 90(1), (4).

---

15. Eating facilities. Where persons employed *(a)* to work *(b)* in shop premises *(c)* eat meals there, suitable and sufficient facilities for eating them shall be provided.

General note. This section is to be repealed as from 1 January 1996 by the Workplace (Health, Safety and Welfare) Regulations 1992 for workplaces in existence on 31 December 1992. Those Regulations will apply to those workplaces from the former date. Workplaces coming into use after 31 December 1992 and modifications, extensions and conversions started after 31 December 1992 to existing workplaces must conform to those Regulations as soon as they come into use.
As to civil liability, see the Introduction to this Act.

(a) *Employed.* For definition, see s. 90(1), (4).

(b) *Work.* See note *(a)* to s. 3.

(c) *Shop premises.* See s. 1(3), (5).

---

16. Floors, passages and stairs.—(1) All floors *(a)*, stairs, steps, passages and gangways *(b)* comprised in premises to which this Act applies *(c)* shall be of sound construction and properly maintained *(d)* and shall, so far as is reasonably practicable *(e)*, be kept free *(f)* from obstruction *(g)* and from any substance *(h)* likely to cause persons to slip.

(2) For every staircase *(i)* comprised in such premises as aforesaid, a substantial hand-rail *(k)* or hand-hold *(l)* shall be provided and maintained, which, if the staircase has an open side, shall be on that side; and in the case of a staircase having two open sides or of a staircase which, owing to the nature of its

construction or the condition of the surface of the steps or other special circumstances *(m)*, is specially liable to cause accidents *(m)*, such a hand-rail or hand-hold shall be provided and maintained on both sides.

(3) Any open side of a staircase *(i)* to which the last foregoing subsection applies, shall also be guarded by the provision and maintenance of efficient means of preventing any person from accidentally falling through the space between the hand-rail *(k)* or hand-hold *(l)* and the steps of the staircase.

(4) All openings *(n)* in floors *(a)* comprised in premises to which this Act applies *(c)* shall be securely fenced *(o)* except in so far as the nature of the work renders such fencing impracticable *(e)*.

(5) The foregoing provisions of this section shall not apply to any such part of any fuel storage premises *(o)* as is in the open, but in relation to any such part the following provisions shall have effect, namely—

   (a)   the surface of the ground shall be kept in good repair;
   (b)   all steps and platforms shall be of sound construction and properly maintained *(d)*;
   (c)   all openings in platforms shall be securely fenced, except in so far as the nature of the work renders such fencing impracticable.

General note. This section is to be repealed as from 1 January 1996 by the Workplace (Health, Safety and Welfare) Regulations 1992 for workplaces in existence on 31 December 1992. Those Regulations will apply to those workplaces from the former date. Workplaces coming into use after 31 December 1992 and modifications, extensions and conversions started after 31 December 1992 to existing workplaces must conform to those Regulations as soon as they come into use. However, reg. 17(5) of the Regulations provides that reg. 17(2) (requiring the suitability of traffic routes) shall apply, so far as is reasonably practicable, to all workplaces, old and new.

As to civil liability, see the Introduction to this Act. This section protects employees, and not shop customers (*Reid v Galbraith's Stores* 1970 SLT (Notes) 83).

Subsections (1) to (4) of this section substantially reproduce s. 28(1) to (4) of the Factories Act 1961, the provisions of which were formerly contained in s. 25 of the Factories Act 1937 and s. 4 of the Factories Act 1959. In the notes which follow, the cases cited are, unless otherwise stated, decisions upon the provisions of those Acts. As to the interpretation of statutes *in pari materia* see the General Introduction.

(a) Floors, etc. The subject matter of this section has been the subject of much controversy. In holding that a dry dock was not an "opening in a floor" within the meaning of s. 25(3) of the 1937 Act (now s. 28(4) of the 1961 Act), Somervell LJ, in *Bath v British Transport Commission* [1954] 2 All ER 542, [1954] 1 WLR 1013, CA, said "Where words are ... perfectly familiar all one can do is to say whether or not one regards them as apt to cover or describe the circumstances in question in any particular case", and in *Johnston v Colvilles Ltd* 1966 SLT 30, Ct of Sess it was held that "floor" meant the ordinary floor of a factory which was used by those employed in the ordinary course of their employment. See the following cases: *Hosking v De Havilland Aircraft Co Ltd* [1949] 1 All ER 540 (plank across duct held to be a gangway); *Morris v Port of London Authority* (1950) 84 Ll L Rep 564 (floor of a gantry held to be within the section); *Taylor v R and H Green and Silley Weir Ltd* (1950) 84 Ll L Rep 570 (affd. by the CA [1951] 1 Lloyd's Rep 345) (sill round inside of dry dock held to be a floor); *Harrison v Metropolitan-Vickers Electrical Co Ltd* [1954] 1 All ER 404, [1954] 1 WLR 324, CA (sand bed of foundry held to be a floor and an excavation in it an "opening in a floor"); *Tate v Swan, Hunter and Wigham Richardson Ltd* [1958] 1 All ER 150, [1958] 1 WLR 39, CA (planks laid across steelwork of crane gantry held not be a floor); *Newberry v Joseph Westwood & Co Ltd* [1960] 2 Lloyd's Rep 37 ("mother earth" held not to be a floor, passage or gangway); *Sullivan v Hall, Russell & Co*

1964 SLT 192 (unmade earthen surface of a woodyard held not to be a floor); *Thornton v Fisher and Ludlow Ltd* [1968] 2 All ER 241, [1968] 1 WLR 655 (30 ft. wide roadway in the open not a floor, passage or gangway).

(*b*) **Gangway.** In *Hosking v De Havilland Aircraft Co Ltd* [1949] 1 All ER 540, a plank laid across a duct was held to be a gangway.

(*c*) **Premises to which this Act applies.** See ss. 1 to 3.

(*d*) **Of sound construction and properly maintained.** It is submitted that these words should receive the same interpretation as in s. 28(1) of the Factories Act 1961. There, it has been held that the duty flowing from the use of these words is absolute and applies primarily to the structural condition of floors, etc., but it may also apply to something put upon a floor, if it can be regarded as part of the floor although not incorporated in it (*Latimer v AEC Ltd* [1953] AC 643, [1953] 2 All ER 449, HL). Where, therefore, a floor, etc., is in some transient and exceptional condition, or there is temporarily something upon it which gives rise to danger, there has been no breach of this obligation if the floor, etc., is otherwise sound. In determining whether a floor is "of sound construction and properly maintained" regard must be had to the purpose for which it is intended to be used (*Mayne v Johnstone and Cumbers Ltd* [1947] 2 All ER 159). In each case the criterion is safety, which is a question of degree dependent upon the particular facts (*Payne v Weldless Steel Tube Co Ltd* [1956] 1 QB 196, [1956] 3 All ER 612, CA). As to "properly maintained" in other contexts, see INTRODUCTORY NOTE 10.

(*e*) **Reasonably practicable; impracticable.** See INTRODUCTORY NOTE 5 and, as to the responsibility of the occupier for the acts of his servants and independent contractors, see *Taylor v Coalite Oils and Chemicals Ltd* (1967) 3 KIR 315, CA, decided upon the provisions of s. 29 of the Factories Act 1961, and explaining *Braham v J Lyons & Co Ltd* [1962] 3 All ER 281, [1962] 1 WLR 1048, CA.

(*f*) **Kept free.** In *Hull v Fairfield Shipbuilding and Engineering Co Ltd* 1964 SLT 97, the House of Lords held that the duty to keep a floor free from obstruction and from any substance likely to cause persons to slip requires the occupier, so far as reasonably practicable, both to prevent things from getting on to the floor and to remove things which have got on to it.

(*g*) **Obstruction.** See INTRODUCTORY NOTE 13.

(*h*) **Substance.** In *Hall v Fairfield Shipbuilding and Engineering Co* 1963 SLT 37; affd. by the House of Lords, 1964 SLT 97, the Court of Session held that a short length of metal rod of unspecified dimensions which had fallen from a bench was a "substance" likely to cause persons to slip. They held, further, that the words "likely to cause persons to slip" qualify only the word "substance", and do not limit the area to be kept free. In *Dorman Long (Steel) Ltd v Bell* [1964] 1 All ER 617, HL, the plaintiff fell when walking on some metal plates which were themselves "obstructions" and he fell because of the slope of the plates and a slippery film on them. Lord Reid (at 618) expressed the opinion that the obligation was to keep the floor free from slippery substances on which anyone on the floor was likely to slip and that it was immaterial whether or not the slippery substance was entirely in contact with the floor. In *Taylor v Gestetner Ltd* (1967) 2 KIR 133, it was held that water might be a substance likely to cause persons to slip.

(*i*) **Staircase.** See the general remarks on interpretation in the note, "Floors . . . gangways", to sub-s. (1), above. See, also *Kimpton v Steel Co of Wales* [1960] 2 All ER 274, [1960] 1 WLR 527, CA (three steps from floor to part of a machine in factory held not to be a "staircase").

(*k*) **Hand-rail.** A hand-rail is a rail that can be gripped by the hand; it need not necessarily act as a physical barrier; it need only be such a rail as to enable any person, by gripping it, to steady himself against falling (*Corn v Weir's Glass (Hanley) Ltd* [1960] 2 All ER 300, [1960] 1 WLR 577, CA so interpreting reg. 27(1) of the Building (Safety, Health and Welfare) Regulations) 1948, S.I. 1948 No. 1145). Note, however, sub-s. (3) of this section.

*(l) **Hand-hold**.* A hand-hold is something which a man can hold or grab from time to time as and when he wishes to do so; see *Wigley v British Vinegars Ltd* [1961] 3 All ER 418, [1961] 1 WLR 1261, CA; affd. (without touching the point) [1964] AC 307, [1962] 3 All ER 1261, HL.

*(m) **Special circumstances; specially liable to cause accidents**.* In *Harris v Rugby Portland Cement Co Ltd* [1955] 2 All ER 500, [1955] 1 WLR 648, decided upon the cognate provisions of s. 25(2) of the Factories Act 1937, the Court of Appeal held that a special circumstance meant something continually repeated or so frequently repeated that permanent protection is necessary, and that "specially liable" meant more than usually liable to cause accidents, so that a long accident-free history is relevant.

*(n) **Openings in floors**.* See the cognate provisions of s. 28(4) of the Factories Act 1961 and note *(a)* thereto.

*(o) **Fuel storage premises**.* See s. 1(3)(a)(i), (5).

---

17. Fencing of exposed parts of machinery.—(1) Every dangerous part *(a)* of any machinery *(a)* used as, or forming part of the equipment *(a)* of premises to which this Act applies *(b)* shall be securely fenced *(a)* unless it is in such a position or of such construction as to be as safe to every person working in the premises as it would be if securely fenced *(a)*.

(2) In so far as the safety of a dangerous part of any machinery cannot, by reason of the nature of the operation effected by means of the machinery, be secured by means of a fixed guard, the requirements of the foregoing subsection shall be deemed to be complied with if a device *(c)* is provided that automatically prevents the operator from coming into contact with that part.

(3) [*repealed*].

(4) Fencing provided in pursuance of the foregoing provisions of this section shall be of substantial construction, be properly maintained *(d)* and be kept in position while the parts required to be fenced are in motion or use *(e)*.

(5) [*repealed*].

General note. This section is to be repealed as from 1 January 1997 by the Provision and Use of Work Equipment Regulations, S.I. 1992 No. 2932, by which time all work equipment first provided for use before 1 January 1993 must meet the standards established in those Regulations. For equipment provided for use after 1 January 1993, the Regulations have immediate effect and this section of the Offices, Shops and Railway Premises Act no longer applies.

For provisions relating to hoists and lifts see the Offices, Shops and Railway Premises (Hoists and Lifts) Regulations, 1968, printed after s. 20.

The provisions of s. 17 may be compared with those of ss. 14 to 16 of the Factories Act 1961; see the Introductory Note to those sections.

The wording of s. 17 of the present Act is plainly modelled upon that of ss. 14 to 16 of the Factories Act 1961, and where the phraseology is identical it should, it is submitted, bear the same interpretation as has been accorded to the cognate provisions of the 1961 Act. (As to the judicial interpretation of statutes *in pari materia* see the General Introduction and *44 Halsbury's Laws* (4th edn.) 885, *et seq.*) In accordance with this principle the case law relating to the factories legislation is authoritative upon the interpretation of s. 17 of the present Act, save where the context may indicate that a departure from the meaning of the factories legislation is intended.

(a) Dangerous part; machinery; equipment; securely fenced. See the General note, above.

(b) Premises to which this Act applies. See ss. 1 to 3.

(c) Device. Compare the cognate provisions of s. 14(2) of the Factories Act 1961.

(d) Properly maintained. Compare the cognate provisions of s. 16 of the Factories Act 1961 and see INTRODUCTORY NOTE 10.

(e) Motion or use. Compare the cognate provisions of s. 16 of the Factories Act 1961.

---

18. Avoidance of exposure of young persons to danger in cleaning machinery.—(1) No young person *(a)* employed *(b)* to work *(c)* in premises to which this Act applied *(d)* shall clean any machinery used as, or forming part of the equipment of the premises if doing so exposes him to risk of injury from a moving part of that or any adjacent machinery.

(2) In this section "young person" means a person who has not attained the age *(e)* of eighteen.

General note. As to civil liability, see the Introduction to this Act. See the cognate provisions of s. 20 of the Factories Act 1961.

(a) Young person. See sub-s. (2).

(b) Employed. For definition, see s. 90(1), (4).

(c) Work. See note *(a)* to s. 3.

(d) Premises to which this Act applies. See ss. 1 to 3.

(e) Age. A person attains a particular age expressed in years at the commencement of the relevant anniversary of the date of his birth Family Law Reform Act 1969, s. 9.

---

19. Training and supervision of persons working at dangerous machines.—(1) No person employed *(a)* to work *(b)* in premises to which this Act applies *(c)* shall work *(b)* there at any machine to which this section applies unless he has been fully instructed as to the dangers arising in connection with it and the precautions to be observed, and—

  (a) has received a sufficient training in work at the machine; or

  (b) is under adequate supervision by a person who has a thorough knowledge and experience of the machine.

(2) This section applies to such machines as may be prescribed by order *(d)* of the Minister *(e)*, being machines which in his opinion *(f)* are of such a dangerous character that persons ought not to work at them unless the foregoing requirements are complied with.

General note. As to civil liability, see the Introduction to this Act.
In *M'Cafferty v Brown* 1950 SC 300, it was held that the cognate provisions of s. 21 of the Factories Act 1937 (now s. 31 of the Factories Act 1961) imposed no obligation on the person employed.

(a) **Employed.** For definition, see s. 90(1), (4).

(b) **Work.** See note (a) to s. 3.

(c) **Premises to which this Act applies.** See ss. 1 to 3.

(d) **Order.** As to the making of orders, see s. 80. The Prescribed Dangerous Machines Order 1964 has been made under this section and is printed below.

(e) **Minister.** For definition, see s. 90(1).

THE PRESCRIBED DANGEROUS MACHINES ORDER 1964
(S.I. 1964 No. 971)

Dated 25 June 1964

The Minister of Labour by virtue of the powers conferred on him by section 19 of the Offices, Shops and Railway Premises Act 1963 (hereinafter in this Order referred to as "the Act") and of all other powers enabling him in that behalf, hereby makes the following Order:—

1.—(1) This Order may be cited as the Prescribed Dangerous Machines Order 1964 and shall come into operation on 1 August 1964.

(2) The Interpretation Act 1889 [Interpretation Act 1978] shall apply to the interpretation of this Order as it applies to the interpretation of an Act of Parlianemt.

2. The machines specified in the Schedule to this Order are hereby prescribed as being machines which in the opinion of the Minister of Labour are of such a dangerous character that persons ought not to work at them unless the requirements of section 19(1) of the Act are complied with.

SCHEDULE

Article 2

PART I

The following machines when worked with the aid of mechanical power—

1. Worm-type mincing machines.
2. Rotary knife bowl-type chopping-machines.
3. Dough brakers.
4. Dough mixers.
5. Food mixing machines when used with attachments for mincing, slicing, chipping or any other cutting operations, or for crumbling.
6. Pie and tart making machines.
7. Vegetable slicing machines.
8. Wrapping and packing machines.
9. Garment presses.
10. Opening or teasing machines used for upholstery or bedding work.
11. Corner staying machines.
12. Loose knife punching machines.
13. Wire stitching machines.
14. Machines of any type equipped with a circular saw blade.
15. Machines of any type equipped with a saw in the form of a continuous band or strip.
16. Planing machines, vertical spindle moulding machines and routing machines, being, in any case, machines used for cutting wood, wood products, fibre-board, plastic or similar material.

Part II

The following machines whether worked with the aid of mechanical power or not—
17. Circular knife slicing machines used for cutting bacon and other foods (whether similar to bacon or not).
18. Potato chipping machines.
19. Platen printing machines, including such machines when used for cutting and creasing.
20. Guillotine machines.

---

20. [*repealed*].

General note. This section, under which the Minister had power to make regulations, is repealed by S.I. 1974 No. 1943, reg. 2(a), Sch. 1, but by reg. 4(3) the Regulations set out below, made under the repealed power, are continued in force; the Regulations are printed as amended by S.I. 1974 No. 1943, reg. 3(3).

THE OFFICES, SHOPS AND RAILWAY PREMISES
(HOISTS AND LIFTS) REGULATIONS 1968
(S.I. 1968 No. 849, as amended by S.I. 1974 No. 1943, S.I. 1983 No. 1579
and S.I. 1992 No. 195)

Dated 27 May 1968, made by the Secretary of State under ss. 20, 80(5) and (6) of the Offices, Shops and Railway Premises Act 1963 and all other enabling powers.

Citation, commencment and interpretation
1.—(1) These Regulations may be cited as the Offices, Shops and Railway Premises (Hoists and Lifts) Regulations 1968 and shall come into operation on 28 May 1969.
(2) The Interpretation Act 1889 [Interpretation Act 1978] shall apply to the interpretation of these Regulations as it applies to the interpretation of an Act of Parliament.
(3) In these Regulations, unless the context otherwise requires, the following expressions have the meanings hereby assigned to them respectively, that is to say—
    "inspector" means an inspector appointed by a fire authority under section 52(2) of the Act or by the Health and Safety Executive or by a local authority under section 19 of the Health and Safety at Work etc. Act 1974
    "lift" includes a hoist but does not include any lifting machine or appliance unless it has a platform or cage the direction of movement of which is restricted by a guide or guides;
    "liftway" includes a hoistway;
    "prescribed" means prescribed by order of the Secretary of State; and
    "the Act" means the Offices, Shops and Railway Premises Act 1963 as amended by or under any other Act.

Application of Regulations
2.—(1) Except as provided in paragraph (2) of this regulation and subject to the provisions of regulation 3, these Regulations shall apply to *lifts* and *liftways* which are wholly or partly situate in office premises, shop premises and railway premises to which *the Act* applies, or which are wholly or partly situate in a part of a building which is used for the purposes of, but is not comprised in, premises to which *the Act* applies.
(2) Nothing in these Regulations shall apply to premises which are in a covered market place, being a covered market place to which section 51 (power to adapt Act in relation to covered markets) of *the Act* relates.

Exemptions and modifications

3.—(1) In the case of a continuous *lift*, regulations 7 to 9 shall not apply and in any such case regulations 6(1) shall have effect as if for the references to six months there were substituted references to twelve months.

(2) In the case of a *lift* not connected with mechanical power, regulations 7(2) and (3) and 9 shall not apply, and in any such case—

(a) regulation 6(1) shall have effect as if for the references to six months there were substituted references to twelve months; and

(b) any gates required to be fitted under regulation 7(1) shall be kept closed and fastened except when the cage or platform is at rest at the landing.

(3) In the case of any class or description of *lift* or *liftway* specified in the first column of the Schedule to these Regulations, the requirements of the provisions of the Regulations specified in the second column of the said Schedule and set opposite to that class or description shall not apply; subject however to the conditions and limitations (if any) set opposite thereto in the third column of the said Schedule.

Obligations under Regulations

4.—(1) In relation to matters within his or their control or within the control of his or their servants or agents, the duty to comply with these Regulations shall be—

(a) in the case of a *lift* or *liftway* situate in a building to which section 42 of *the Act* applies or in premises outside the building being premises occupied together with office or shop premises forming part of the building, upon the owner of the building;

(b) in the case of a *lift* or *liftway* situate in a building to which section 43 of *the Act* applies or in premises outside the building being premises occupied together with office or shop premises forming part of the building, upon the persons who between them own the building; and

(c) in the case of a *lift* or *liftway* situate in a set of fuel storage premises to which section 44 of *the Act* applies, upon the owner of that set of premises.

(2) Except as provided in the foregoing paragraph of this regulation, the duty to comply with these Regulations shall be upon the occupier of any premises to which *the Act* applies in connection with which the *lift* or *liftway* is used.

Construction and maintenance

5.   Every *lift* shall be of good mechanical construction, sound material and adequate strength, and shall be properly maintained.

Examinations and reports

6.—(1) Every *lift* shall be thoroughly examined by a competent person at least once in every period of six months and a record of every such thorough examination and of the results thereof, containing the particulars required by the Lifting Plant and Equipment (Records of Test and Examination etc.) Regulations 1992, shall within twenty-eight days be sent to the person having the duty under regulation 4 to comply with these Regulations as respects that *lift*: provided that where a *lift* to which these Regulations apply is so situate that it or any part of it is required to be thoroughly examined by virtue of section 22(2) of the Factories Act 1961, a thorough examination of that *lift* shall not be required on any occasion on which it would otherwise be required by the foregoing provisions of this paragraph if and to the extent to which a thorough examination of the *lift* or any part of it has been made within the period of six months then immediately preceding in accordance with the provisions of the said section 22(2) and a record of the thorough examination and of the results thereof has been made as required by the said section 22(2).

(2) The record of every thorough examination and of the results thereof made in pursuance of paragraph (1) of this regulation shall be preserved and the particulars in that record shall be kept readily available for inspection by any inspector for, in each case, two years after the date when the record is signed or otherwise authenticated.

(3) Where the examination shows that the *lift* cannot continue to be used with safety unless certain repairs are carried out immediately or within a specified time, the person

who authenticates the record shall within twenty-eight days of the completion of the examinaton also send a copy of the particulars contained in the record—

(a) to such one or more of the following as the case may require, that is to say, the local authority, the Health and Safety Executive having, in each case, the duty to enforce these Regulations in the premises in which the *lift* is situate or in connection with which the *lift* is used; and

(b) in the case of a *lift* or *liftway* situate in a building of which part consists of premises to which the Factories Act 1961 applies, to the Health and Safety Executive (except in cases where a copy of the particulars contained in the record is required to be sent to him by sub-paragraph *(a)* of this paragraph).

Enclosures and gates

7.—(1) Every *liftway* shall be efficiently protected by a substantial enclosure fitted with gates, and the enclosure shall be such as to prevent, when the gates are shut, any person falling down the way or coming into contact with any moving part of the *lift*.

(2) Any such gate shall, subject to regulation 3(1) and (2) and paragraph (3) of this Regulaton, be fitted with efficient interlocking or other devices to secure that the gate cannot be opened except when the cage or platform is at the landing and that the cage or platform cannot be moved away from the landing until the gate is closed.

(3) If in the case of a *lift* constructed or reconstructed before the date of the making of these Regulations, it is not reasonably practicable to fit it with such devices as are mentioned in the last foregoing paragraph, it shall be sufficient if the gate—

(a) is provided with such arrangements as will secure the objects of that paragraph so far as is reasonably practicable; and

(b) is kept closed and fastened except when the cage or platform is at rest at the landing.

(4) Every *lift* and every such enclosure as is mentioned in paragraph (1) of this regulation shall be so constructed as to prevent any part of any person or any goods carried in the *lift* being trapped between any part of the *lift* and any fixed structure or between the counterbalance weight and any other moving part of the *lift*.

Maximum working load

8. There shall be marked conspicuously on every *lift* the maximum working load which it can safely carry, and no load greater than that load shall be carried on any *lift*.

Lifts used for carrying persons

9.—(1) The following additional requirements shall apply to *lifts* used for carrying persons, whether together with goods or otherwise—

(a) efficient automatic devices shall be provided and maintained to prevent the cage or platform overrunning; and

(b) every cage shall on each side from which access is afforded to a landing be fitted with a gate, and in connection with every such gate efficient devices shall be provided to secure that, when persons or goods are in the cage, the cage cannot be raised or lowered unless the gate is closed, and will come to rest when the gate is opened.

(2) In the case of a *lift* constructed or reconstructed before the date of the making of these Regulations, in connection with which it is not reasonably practicable to provide such devices as are mentioned in sub-paragraph (b) of the foregoing paragraph, it shall be sufficient if—

(a) such arrangements are provided as will secure the objects of that paragraph so far as is reasonably practicable; and

(b) the gate is kept closed and fastened except when the cage is at rest or empty.

(3) In the case of a *lift* used as mentioned in paragraph (1) of this regulation, which was constructed or reconstructed after the date of the making of these Regulations, where the platform or cage is suspended by rope or chain, there shall be at least two ropes or chains separately connected with the platform or cage, each rope or chain and its attachments being capable of carrying the whole weight of the platform or cage and its maximum working load, and efficient devices shall be provided and maintained

which will support the platform or cage with its maximum working load in the event of a breakage of the ropes or chains or any of their attachments.

SCHEDULE

Regulation 3(3)

Class or description of lift or liftway	Requirements of the Regulations which shall not apply	Conditions or limitations (if any)
1. *Liftways* of pavement *lifts*, that is to say, *lifts* in the case of which the provision of a permanent enclosure at the top landing would obstruct a street or public place, or yard or other open space within premises to which *the Act* applies where persons are required to pass.	Regulations 7(1), in so far as it requires the *liftway* to be protected by an enclosure and gate at or above the top landing. Except in the case of a *lift* with more than one landing other than the top landing. Regulations 3(2)(b) and 7(2) and (3).	The *liftway* shall be securely covered or securely fenced at the top landing except when and where access is required for persons, goods or materials. Every gate shall be kept closed and fastened except when the cage or platform is at the landing.
2. Mobile *lifts* used in various positions for the stacking of goods or materials or for loading or unloading directly to or from vehicles, which have no fixed landings above the lowest landing.	Regulations 3(2)(b) and 7(1) to (3) and, when the maximum height of the platform above ground or floor level does not exceed 2 metres. Regulation 9(3).	The *lift* shall be so constructed that it is stable and its stability shall in all circumstances be maintained. Where the height of the platform of a *lift* used for carrying persons exceeds 2 metres above ground or floor level, the edges of the platform on which persons stand shall be protected to a height of at least 920 millimetres above the platform by suitable guard rails, lower rails and toe boards of adequate strength or by other equally effective means; any gate provided shall, unless equally effective means are provided, open inwards only towards the platform and be arranged so as automatically to return to the closed and fastened position; and the button, handle or other device by which the movement of the platform is controlled shall be on the platform and be such that the platform cannot be in motion

Class or description of *lift* or *liftway*	Requirements of the Regulations which shall not apply	Conditions or limitations (if any)
		unless the control device is being held or pressed by a person on the platform.
3. *Lifts* which are fixed in position and which are used for the stacking of goods or materials or for loading or unloading directly to or from vehicles, which have no fixed landings above the lowest landing and in the case of which the maximum height of the cage or platform above ground or floor level exceeds 2 metres.	Regulations 3(2)(b) and 7(1) to (3).	The *liftway* shall be protected at ground or floor level by an enclosure not less than 2.2 metres in height and fitted with a gate or gates in connection with which regulations 3(2)(b) and 7(2) and (3) shall apply, and if the *lift* is used for carrying persons it shall be provided with a cage.
4. Platform *lifts* which are fixed in position and in the case of which the maximum height of the platform above ground or floor level does not exceed 2 metres.	Regulations 3(2)(b), 7(1) to (3) and 9(3).	A gate or gates or other means shall be provided to prevent any person being endangered by the underside of the platform or by any fitting attached to it.
5. *Liftways* of *lifts* which are not used for carrying persons and into or from which goods or materials are not loaded or unloaded except at a height of not less than 840 millimetres above the level of the floor or ground where loading or unloading is performed.	Regulations 3(2)(b) and 7(2) and (3).	This exemption shall not apply to any gate unless there is a fixed enclosure not less than 840 millimetres in height below the bottom of the gate and reaching down to the level of the floor or ground; and every gate to which this exemption applies shall— (i) be fitted with an efficient device to secure that the cage or platform cannot be raised or lowered unless the gate is closed, and will come to rest when the gate is opened or, (ii) where it is not reasonably practicable to fit such a device be kept closed and fastened except when the cage or platform is at rest at the gate.

Class or description of *lift* or *liftway*	Requirements of the Regulations which shall not apply	Conditions or limitations (if any)
6. *Lifts* which are not connected with mechanical power and which are not used for carrying persons, and the enclosures of the *liftways* of such *lifts*.	Regulation 7(4).	
7. *Lifts* in the case of which the doors of the *liftway* are of solid construction and the interior surfaces of the said doors and of the *liftway* opposite to any side of the cage in which there is an opening are, throughout the height of travel of the cage, smooth and flush with each other save for any recess designed for working purposes and not more than 13 millimetres in depth, and hand grips not exceeding 26 millimetres in depth provided for closing doors and so constructed as to prevent trappings.	Regulations 9(1)(b) and (2).	
8. *Liftways* of *lifts* into or from which goods or materials are loaded or unloaded automatically and to the platform or cage of which there is no access for persons.	Regulation 7(1) in so far as it requires a gate at the openings in the enclosure where goods or materials are loaded or unloaded automatically.	Means shall be provided at the loading and unloading openings in the enclosure to prevent, so far as is reasonably practicable, any person falling down the *liftway* or comming into contact with any moving part of the *lift*.
9. *Liftways* of *lifts* which are not used for carrying persons and on which the goods or materials stacked on the platform or in the cage are loaded or unloaded with the top layer of the stack at landing level.	Regulations 3(2)(b) and 7(2) and (3).	This exemption shall not apply to any gate unless there is a fixed enclosure not less than 840 millimetres in height below the bottom of the gate and reaching down to the level of the floor or grounds, and unless any such gate can only be opened or remain open when the

Class or description of *lift* or *liftway*	Requirements of the Regulations which shall not apply	Conditions or limitations (if any)
		floor of the cage or platform is at the landing level or not more than 1.5 metres below that level; and when the gate is open the cage or platform shall not be capable of being moved more than 300 millimetres at one time and at a speed not greater than 0.12 metres per second; and provision shall be made to prevent any person being trapped by the top of the cage. The arrangements shall be such that when the gate is open the platform or cage cannot be in motion unless the button, handle, or other device by which the movement of the cage or platform is controlled is being held or pressed by a person close to the gate.
10. *Lifts* and *liftways* the landing and cage entrances of which are protected by lattice gates.	Regulations 7(1) and (4) in so far as they relate to the protection to be provided by the gates.	The gates when shut shall extend to the full height and width of the entrance opening and, except in the case of gates installed before the date of the coming into operation of these Regulations, shall have no openings exceeding 65 millimetres in width. Measures shall be taken to prevent the access of feet through the cage gate or the landing gate into the *liftway*, and to prevent the access of fingers through the landing gate to the interlocking mechanism and control devices in the cage or on the platform.
11. *Lifts* used for raising or lowering or tipping standard gauge or broader gauge railway rolling-stock.	Regulation 7(1) in so far as it requires the recognised entrances to the enclosure, being entrances through which the rolling-stock passes, to be fitted with gates; regulations 3(2)(b), 7(2) and (3), and 9(1)(b) and (2).	So far as is reasonably practicable, means shall be provided at such entrances to the enclosure to prevent any person from falling down the *liftway* or being struck by any moving part of the *lift*.

21., 22.   [*repealed*].

---

23.   Prohibition of heavy work.—(1) No person shall, in the course of his work in premises to which this Act applies *(a)*, be required to lift *(b)*, carry or move a load so heavy as to be likely to cause injury *(c)* to him.

(2) [*repealed*].

General note. This section is repealed by the Manual Handling Operations Regulations 1992, S.I. 1992 No. 2793, except insofar as the prohibition contained in it applies to any person specified in s. 90(4) of this Act.

See the cognate provisions of s. 72 of the Factories Act 1961.

(a) Premises to which this Act applies. See ss. 1 to 3.

(b) Required to lift. A person is not "employed to lift" (within s. 72 of the Factories Act 1961) a load so heavy as to be likely to cause injury to him if he lifts such a load by himself when he has been told to ask for help which was readily available (*Peat v NJ Muschamp & Co Ltd* (1969) 7 KIR 469, CA) but where lifting a heavy load is incidental to work which a person has been given to do, the employer may be in breach of s. 72 of the Factories Act 1961 if he does not give that person specific instructions to obtain assitance in the lifting (*Brown v Allied Ironfounders Ltd* [1974] 2 All ER 135, [1974] 1 WLR 527, HL).

(c) Likely to cause injury. The prohibition covers the continual lifting of an object which if lifted once would not fall within the prohibition (*Chessum v Lesney UK Sales Ltd* (17 November 1982, unreported).

24.–27.   [*repealed*].

Fire precautions

28.–41.   [*repealed*]. See now the Fire Precautions Act 1971.

Special provisions with respect to buildings whereof parts are office, etc., premises and with respect to certain contiguous fuel storage premises

42.   Provisions with respect to buildings in single ownership.—(1) A building *(a)* to which this section applies is one all parts of which are in the same ownership *(b)* and a part of which consists of premises to which this Act applies *(c)*, being premises held under a lease or an agreement for a lease or under a licence; and in this section a reference to a common part of a building to which this section applies shall be taken to refer to a part of the building that is used for the purposes of, but is not comprised in, a part of the building that consists of premises to which this Act applies.

(2) The following provisions shall have effect for securing the cleanliness *(d)* of common parts *(e)* of buildings *(a)* to which this section applies, that is to say:—

(a) every common part of a building to which this section applies, and all furniture, furnishings and fittings in such a part, shall be kept in a clean state;

(b) [*repealed*].

(3) The following provisions shall have effect for securing the illumination *(f)* of common parts *(e)* of buildings *(a)* to which this section applies, that is to say:—

(a) effective provision shall be made for securing and maintaining, in every such part of a common part of a building to which this section applies as the following, namely, a part in which persons are working or passing, suitable and sufficient lighting, whether natural or artificial;

(b) [*repealed*];

(c) all glazed windows and skylights used for the lighting of a part of a common part of a building to which this section applies in which the securing of lighting is required by this subsection to be provided for shall, so far as reasonably practicable *(g)*, be kept clean on both the inner and outer surfaces and free from obstruction;

(d) all apparatus installed in a common part of a building to which this section applies for producing artificial lighting in a part of that part in which the securing of lighting is required by this subsection to be provided for shall be properly maintained *(h)*,

but paragraph (c) above shall not affect the whitewashing or shading of windows or skylights for the purpose of mitigating heat or glare.

(4) Section 16(1) of this Act shall apply to floors, stairs, steps, passages and gangways comprised in, or constituting, a common part *(e)* of a building *(a)* to which this section applies as it applies to floors, stairs, steps, passages and gangways in premises to which this Act applies, section 16(2) of this Act shall apply to a staircase comprised in, or constituting, a common part of such a building as it applies to such a staircase as is mentioned in that subsection, and section 16(3) of this Act shall apply to an open side of such a staircase as is first mentioned in this subsection as it applies to an open side of such a staircase as is mentioned in the said subsection (2).

(5) In the event of a contravention *(i)*, in relation to a common part *(e)* of a building *(a)* to which this section applies, of subsection (2) or (3) of this section ... and in the event of a contravention, in relation to any thing constituting, or comprised in, any such common part, of section 16 of this Act, as applied by the last foregoing subsection, the owner *(b)* of the building shall be guilty of an offence *(j)*.

(6) For a contravention *(i)*, in relation to premises comprised in a building *(a)* to which this section applies, of section 9 of this Act (other than a contravention consisting in a failure to keep clean conveniences provided in pursuance of that section, not being conveniences provided for use jointly by the persons employed to work in the premises and by other persons), the owner *(b)* of the building shall be responsible instead of the occupier of the premises.

(7) For a contravention *(i)*, in relation to premises comprised in a building *(a)* to which this section applies, of section 10 of this Act (other than a

contravention consisting in a failure to provide means of cleaning or drying or a failure to keep clean and in orderly condition the place where facilities are provided in pursuance of that section, not being facilities provided for use jointly by the persons employed to work in the premises and by other persons) the owner *(b)* of the building shall be responsible instead of the occupier of the premises.

(8)–(16) [*repealed*].

(a) **Building.** See note *(f)* to s. 1.

(b) **Ownership.** For definition, see s. 90(1).

(c) **Premises to which this Act applies.** See ss. 1 to 3.

(d) **Cleanliness.** Compare s. 4.

(e) **Common part.** For definition, see sub-s. (1).

(f) **Illumination.** Compare s. 8.

(g) **Reasonably practicable.** See INTRODUCTORY NOTE 5.

(h) **Properly maintained.** See INTRODUCTORY NOTE 10.

(i) **Contravention.** A contravention of any provision includes a failure to comply with that provision (s. 90(1)).

(j) **Offence.** See ss. 63, 67.

---

43. Provisions with respect to buildings plurally owned.—(1) A building *(a)* to which this section applies is one of which different parts are owned *(b)* by different persons and of which a part consists of premises to which this Act applies *(c)*; and in this section a reference to a common part of a building to which this section applies shall be taken to refer to a part of the building that is used for the purposes of, but is not comprised in, a part of the building that consists of premises to which this Act applies.

(2) Subsections (2) and (3) of the last foregoing section shall, with the substitution, for references to buildings to which that section applies and to common parts *(d)* thereof, of references respectively to buildings to which this section applies and to common parts thereof, have effect for securing the cleanliness and illumination of common parts of buildings *(a)* to which this section applies as they have effect for securing the cleanliness and illumination of common parts of buildings to which that section applies; and in the event of a contravention *(e)*, in relation to a common part *(d)* of a building to which this section applies, of either of those subsections or of regulations under either of them, the owner *(b)* of the part (or, if there are more owners than one of the part, each of them) shall be guilty of an offence *(f)*.

(3) Section 16(1) of this Act shall apply to floors, stairs, steps, passages and gangways comprised in, or constituting, a common part *(d)* of a building *(a)* to which this section applies as it applies to floors, stairs, steps, passages and gangways in premises to which this Act applies, section 16(2) of this Act shall apply to a staircase comprised in, or constituting, a common part of such a building as it applies to such a staircase as is mentioned in that subsection, and

section 16(3) of this Act shall apply to an open side of such a staircase as is first-mentioned in this subsection as it applies to an open side of such a staircase as is mentioned in the said subsection (2); and in the event of a contravention *(e)*, in relation to any thing constituting, or comprised in, any common part, of section 16 of this Act as applied by this subsection, the owner *(b)* of the part (or if there are more owners than one of the part, each of them) shall be guilty of an offence *(f)*.

(4) For a contravention *(e)*, in relation to premises consisting of part of any such part of a building *(a)* to which this section applies as is owned *(b)* by one of the persons who between them own the building (being premises held under a lease or an agreement for a lease or under a licence), of section 9 of this Act (other than a contravention consisting in a failure to keep clean conveniences provided in pursuance of that section, not being conveniences provided for use jointly by the persons employed to work in the premises and by other persons), the first-mentioned person shall be responsible instead of the occupier of the premises.

(5) For a contravention *(e)*, in relation to premises consisting of part of any such part of a building *(a)* to which this section applies as is owned *(b)* by one of the persons who between them own the building (being premises held under a lease or an agreement for a lease or under a licence), of section 10 of this Act (other than a contravention consisting in a failure to provide means of cleaning or drying or a failure to keep clean and in orderly condition the place where facilities are provided in pursuance of that section, not being facilities provided for use jointly by the persons employed to work in the premises and by other persons) the first-mentioned person shall be responsible instead of the occupier of the premises.

(6)–(14) [*repealed*].

(a) **Building.** See note *(f)* to s. 1.

(b) **Owner.** For definition, see s. 90(1).

(c) **Premises to which this Act applies.** See ss. 1 to 3.

(d) **Common part.** For definition, see sub-s. (1).

(e) **Contravention.** A contravention of any provision includes a failure to comply with that provision (s. 90(1)).

(f) **Offence.** See ss. 63, 67.

---

44. Provisions with respect to contiguous fuel storage premises in single ownership. Where two sets or more of fuel storage premises *(a)* any of which is held under a lease or an agreement for a lease or under a licence are established on a parcel of land all parts of which are in the same ownership *(b)*, then—

   (a) for a contravention *(c)*, in relation to any of those sets of premises, of section 9 of this Act (other than a contravention consisting in a failure to keep clean conveniences provided in pursuance of that section, not being conveniences provided for use jointly by the persons employed to work in that set of premises and by other persons); and

(b) for a contravention *(c)*, in relation to any of those sets of premises, of section 10 of this Act (other than a contravention consisting in a failure to provide means of cleaning and drying or a failure to keep clean and in orderly condition the place where facilities are provided in pursuance of that section, not being facilities provided for use jointly by the persons employed to work in that set of premises and by other persons);

the owner *(b)* of that set of premises shall be responsible instead of the occupier thereof.

(a) **Fuel storage premises.** For definition, see s. 90(1).

(b) **Ownership.** For definition, see s. 90(1).

(c) **Contravention.** A contravention of any provision includes a failure to comply with that provision (s. 90(1)).

Exemptions

45. [*repealed*].

---

46. Power of authorities who enforce Act to grant exemptions from certain requirements thereof.—(1) The authority having power to enforce, with respect to any premises, the following provisions of this Act, namely, section 5(2) and sections 6 and 9, may—

(a) exempt the premises or any room therein from all or any of the requirements imposed by the said sections 5(2) and 6;
(b) exempt the premises from all or any of the requirements imposed by the said section 9,

if satisfied that, in the circumstances affecting the subject of the exemption, compliance with the requirements or requirement from which exemption is granted is not reasonably practicable *(a)*.

(2) The authority having power to enforce *(a)* section 10(1) of this Act with respect to any premises may, if satisfied that it it not reasonably practicable for running water to be supplied there or for running water so supplied to be heated, exempt the premises from so much of that subsection as requires the water supplied to be running water.

(3) An exemption under subsection (1) of this section of, or of a room in, any premises from a requirement of a provision of this Act may be granted for a period not exceeding two years, but may from time to time be extended for a further such period beyond the expiration of the period at the expiration of which it would otherwise expire if the authority having power to enforce that provision with respect to the premises are satisfied as mentioned in subsection (1) of this section and are further satisfied that the person who, if the exemption were not in force, would be responsible *(b)* for a contravention *(c)* in relation to the premises of that provision (being a contravention *(c)* consisting

in a failure to comply with that requirement) has not failed to do anything the doing of what might have rendered compliance with that requirement reasonably practicable *(a)*.

(4) An exemption under subsection (2) of this section may be granted without limit of time or for a specified period; but the grant of such an exemption for a specified period shall not preclude the grant of the like exemption for further periods.

(5) An exemption of, or of a room in, any premises from a requirement imposed by a provision of this Act shall not be granted or extended under this section—

(a) except upon application made to the authority having power to enforce with respect to the premises the provision imposing the requirement in such form as may be prescribed by order *(d)* made by the Minister *(e)*—
  (i) in a case where the grant of an exemption is sought, by the person who would be responsible *(c)* for a contravention *(c)* in relation to the premises of that provision (being a contravention *(c)* consisting in a failure to comply with that requirement);
  (ii) in a case where the extension of an exemption is sought, by the person who, if the exemption were not in force, would be responsible *(b)* as aforesaid;
(b) unless the application is accompanied by a certificate in such form as may be so prescribed, that the obligation to which the applicant is subject by virtue of subsection (6)(a) below has been complied with; and
(c) until the expiration of the period of fourteen days beginning *(f)* with the day next following that on which the application is made.

(6) In relation to an application for the grant or extension of an exemption under this section of, or of a room in, any premises, compliance by the applicant with the following requirements shall be requisite, namely,—

(a) he must, immediately before the application is made, post in the premises, in such a position, and in such characters, as to be easily seen and read by the persons employed *(g)* to work *(h)* in the premises, a notice—
  (i) stating that such an application is being made;
  (ii) specifying the requirement from which exemption or, as the case may be, further exemption, is being sought;
  (iii) specifying the period for which the grant or, as the case may be, the extension, is being sought (or if, where a grant of exemption is being sought under subsection (2) of this section, it be the case that the grant thereof without limit of time being sought, specifying that fact);
  (iv) specifying the name and address of the authority to whom the application is being made and notifying the persons aforesaid that written representations with respect to the application may be made by any of them to that authority before the expiration of the period of fourteen days beginning *(f)* with the day next following that on which the notice is posted in compliance with this paragraph;
(b) he must keep the said notice posted as aforesaid throughout the last-mentioned period,

and a person making an application under this section who fails to comply with an obligation to which he is, in relation to the application, subject by virtue of this subsection shall be guilty of an offence *(i)* and liable on summary conviction to a fine not exceeding level 1 on the standard scale.

(7) An exemption under this section of, or of a room in, any premises from a requirement imposed by a provision of this Act may, if the authority having power to enforce that provision with respect to the premises cease to be satisfied with respect to the matters with respect to which they were satisfied when the exemption was granted or, if the exemption has been extended under subsection (3) of this section, when it was extended, be withdrawn by that authority provided that three months' notice *(j)* of intention to withdraw it has been given *(k)* to the person who, if the exemption were not in force, would be responsible *(b)* for a contravention *(c)* in relation to the premises of that provision (being a contravention *(c)* consisting in a failure to comply with that requirement).

(8) Where an exemption of, or of a room in, any premises from a requirement imposed by a provision of this Act or an extension of such an exemption is granted under this section by an authority, a certificate of the grant or extension shall be sent by the authority to the person who, if the exemption were not in force, would be responsible *(b)* for a contravention *(c)* in relation to the premises of that provision (being a contravention) *(c)* consisting in a failure to comply with that requirement).

(9) A certificate such as is mentioned in the last foregoing subsection shall, so long as the exemption whose grant or extension is certified thereby continues in force, be kept posted in the premises to which the exemption relates in such a position as to be easily seen and read by the persons employed *(g)* to work *(h)* in the premises.

(10) Notice of the refusal by an authority to grant or extend an exemption under this section shall be given *(k)* by them to the applicant for the grant or extension and also (if it be the case that representations with respect to the application were duly made by the persons employed *(g)* to work *(h)* in the premises to which the application related or any of those persons), either individually to such of those persons as duly made representations or to a person appearing to the authority to be representative of such of those persons as duly made representations or to each of a number of persons who appear to be authority to be representative between them of such of those persons as duly made representations.

(11) A person who is aggrieved *(l)*—

   (a) by the refusal of an authority to grant or extend an exemption under this section of, or of a room in, any premises; or
   (b) by a notice of intention to withdraw such an exemption;

may, within twenty-one days *(m)* of the refusal or, as the case may be, service of the notice *(k)*, appeal *(n)*, if the premises are situate in England and Wales, to a magistrates' court *(o)* acting for the petty sessions area *(p)* in which they are situate, or, if they are situate in Scotland, to the sheriff within whose jurisdiction they are situate, and on any such appeal *(n)*—

   (i) in a case falling within paragraph (a) above, the court or sheriff, if satisfied with respect to the matters with respect to which the authority would have to have been satisfied as a condition of their granting or extending the exemption, may order *(q)* the authority to grant or extend it, in the case of an exemption under subsection (1) of this section, for such period not exceeding two years as may be specified in the order, and, in the case of an exemption under subsection (2) of this section, either without limit of time or for such period as may be so specified;

(ii) in a case falling within paragraph (b) above, the court or sheriff, if satisfied with respect to the matters with respect to which the authority were satisfied when the exemption was granted or, if it has been extended, when it was extended, may order *(q)* the authority to cancel the notice of intention to withdraw the exemption.

(12) [*repealed*].

(13) In relation to an application made under this section with respect to, or to a room in, premises which form part of a building to which section 42 or 43 of this Act applies, subsection (6) above shall have effect with the substitution, for the words in paragraph (a) "post in the premises", of the words "post in the premises or in a part of the building which for the purposes of the said section 42 or the said section 43 (as the case may be) is referred to as a common part of the building".

(14) [*repealed*].

(a) **Reasonably practicable.** See INTRODUCTORY NOTE 5, where the effect of these words on civil liability is discussed. Although the exempting authority would clearly not be bound by the cases there cited, it is submitted that those cases would become relevant on an appeal under sub-s. (11).

(b) **Persons who would be responsible.** The person responsible for a contravention of s. 5(2) or s. 6 would be the occupier of the premises, and the person responsible for a contravention of s. 9 or s. 10 would be the occupier of the premises or, in certain cases, the owner of the building or one of the persons who between them own the building; see s. 63 in conjunction with ss. 46(2), (7), 43(4), (5).

(c) **Contravention.** A contravention of any provision includes a failure to comply with that provision (s. 90(1)).

(d) **Order.** For the making of orders, see s. 80.

(e) **The Minister.** For definition, see s. 90(1).

(f) **Beginning.** In calculating the period the day from which it runs must be included; see *Hare v Gocher* [1962] 2 QB 641, [1962] 2 All ER 763.

(g) **Employed.** For definition, see s. 90(1), (4).

(h) **Work.** See note *(a)* to s. 3.

(i) **Offence.** For offences, see ss. 63, 67.

(j) **Three months' notice.** The period of three months is to be calculated exclusive of the day on which the notice was given and the day on which the exemption is withdrawn; see, in particular, *R v Turner* [1910] 1 KB 346, CCA, *Re Hector Whaling Ltd* [1936] Ch 208 and *Thompson v Stimpson* [1961] 1 QB 195, [1960] 3 All ER 500, CA.

(k) **Notice given; served.** See as to the service or giving of notices, the Health and Safety at Work etc. Act 1974, s. 46.

(l) **Person aggrieved.** See INTRODUCTORY NOTE 14.

(m) **Within 21 days.** It is a rule of general application that where a period of time from or after a specified event or date is prescribed by a statute or any instrument for the performance of any act, the day so specified is to be excluded from the computation of the period of time.

(n) Appeal. The appeal is by way of complaint for an order; see the Magistrates' Courts Rules 1981, S.I. 1981 No. 552, rule 34.

The dismissal of a complaint by justices is an order from which s. 72 provides an appeal to the Crown Court (*R v Recorder of Oxford, ex p Brasenose College* [1970] 1 QB 109, [1969] 3 All ER 428, DC). See also, as to suspension or rescission of the order on further complaint, the Magistrates' Courts Act 1980, s. 63.

(o) Magistrates' court. For definition, see s. 90(1).

(p) Petty sessions area. For definition, see s. 90(1).

(q) Order. Quaere whether disobedience to the order is punishable under the Magistrates' Courts Act 1980, s. 63(3).

Prohibition of levying of charges on employees for things done in compliance with Act

47. [*repealed*].

Notification of accidents

48. [*repealed*].

Information

49. Notification of fact of employment of persons.—(1) Before a person first begins, after the coming into operation of this subsection with respect to any office *(a)*, shop *(b)* or railway premises *(c)*, to employ *(d)* persons to work *(e)* therein, he shall serve *(f)* on the appropriate authority *(g)* two copies of a notice stating that persons will be employed *(d)* by him so to work *(e)* and containing such other (if any) information as may be prescribed by order *(h)* of the Minister *(i)*, being a notice in such form and of such size as may be so prescribed.

(2) [*repealed*].

(3) A person who fails to comply with an obligation to which he is subject by virtue of the foregoing subsections shall be guilty of an offence *(j)* and liable on summary conviction to a fine not exceeding level 1 on the standard scale.

(4) Proceedings for an offence under this section may be commenced at any time within twelve months *(k)* from the time when the offence was committed.

(5) In this section "apppropriate authority" has the same meaning as in the last foregoing section.

(a) Office premises. See s. 1(2), (5).

(b) Shop premises. See s. 1(3), (5).

(c) **Railway premises.** See s. 1(4), (5).

(d) **Employ; employing; employed.** See s. 90(1).

(e) **Work.** See note (a) to s. 3.

(f) **Serve . . . notice.** See the Health and Safety at Work etc. Act 1974, s. 46.

(g) **Appropriate authority.** By sub-s. (5), this has the same meaning as in s. 48(5).

(h) **Order.** As to the making of orders, see s. 80. The Notification of Employment of Persons Order 1964 has been made under this section and is printed below.

(i) **The Minister.** For definition, see s. 90(1).

(j) **Offence.** For offences, see ss. 63, 67, 86(1).

(k) **Within 12 months.** This is an exception to the provisions of the Magistrates' Courts Act 1980, s. 127(1), under which the time limit is six months. The day upon which the offence was committed is excluded from the period; see, in particular, *Goldsmiths' Co v West Metropolitan Rly Co* [1904] 1 KB 1, CA, and *Stewart v Chapman* [1951] 2 KB 792, [1951] 2 All ER 613.

THE NOTIFICATION OF EMPLOYMENT OF PERSONS ORDER 1964
(S.I. 1964 No. 533, as amended by S.I. 1992 No. 1811)

Dated 6 April 1964

The Minister of Labour by virtue of the powers conferred on him by section 49 of the Offices, Shops and Railway Premises Act 1963 (hereafter in this Order referred to as "the Act") and of all other powers enabling him in that behalf, hereby makes the following Order—

1.—(1) This Order may be cited as the Notification of Employment of Persons Order 1964 and shall come into operation on 1 May 1964.
(2) The Interpretation Act 1889 [Interpretation Act 1978] shall apply to the interpretation of this Order as it applies to the interpretation of an Act of Parliament.

2. In the case of railway premises and office premises, being office premises occupied by railway undertakers for the purposes of the railway undertaking carried on by them and situate in the immediate vicinity of the permanent way (not being office premises comprised in hotels)—
(a) the notice required by section 49(1) of the Act to be served on the appropriate authority by a person before first beginning after the coming into operation of that subsection to employ persons to work in any such premises shall be in the form set out in Parts I, III and IV of Schedule 1 to this Order and contain the information therein specified; and
(b) the notice required by section 49(2) of the Act to be served on the appropriate authority by a person who at the date of coming into force of that section with respect to any such premises is employing persons to work therein shall be in the form set out in Parts II, III and IV of the said Schedule 1 and contain the information therein specified.

3. In the case of office premises, other than office premises to which article 2 of this Order applies, and in the case of shop premises—
(a) the notice required by section 49(1) of the Act to be served on the appropriate authority by a person before first beginning after the coming into operation of that subsection to employ persons to work in any such premises shall be in the form set out in Parts I and III of Schedule 2 to this Order and contain the information therein specified; and

(b)   the notice required by section 49(2) of the Act to be served on the appropriate authority by a person who at the date of coming into force of that section with respect to any such premises is employing persons to work therein shall be in the form set out in Parts II and III of the said Schedule 2 and contain the information therein specified.

4.   [*revoked*].

5.   The period before the expiration of which a notice under section 49(2) of the Act is required by the said subsection to be served on the appropriate authority shall be the period of 3 months beginning with 1 May 1964.

SCHEDULE 1

Article 2
OSR. 7

NOTICE IN FORM PRESCRIBED BY THE MINISTER OF LABOUR, OF EMPLOYMENT OF PERSONS IN RAILWAY PREMISES OR CERTAIN OFFICE PREMISES OCCUPIED BY RAILWAY UNDERTAKINGS.

PART I

Notice is hereby given that on the .... *(insert date)*, the railway undertaking specified in Part III of this notice will begin to employ persons to work in the premises contained in the establishments shown in Part IV of this notice.

PART II

Notice is hereby given that the railway undertaking specified in Part III of this notice is employing persons to work in the premises contained in the establishments shown in Part IV of this notice.

PART III

Name of railway undertaking ....
Signature of person authorised to
   sign on behalf of the undertaking ....
Date ....

SCHEDULE 2

Article 3
OSR. 1

NOTICE IN FORM PRESCRIBED BY THE MINISTER OF LABOUR, OF EMPLOYMENT OF PERSONS IN OFFICE OR SHOP PREMISES

PART I

Notice is hereby given that on the .... *(insert date)*, the employer specified in Part II of this notice, will begin to employ persons to work in the premises described therein.

PART II

Notice is hereby given that the employer specified in Part III of this notice is employing persons to work in the premises described therein.

PART III

1. *(a)* Name of the employer ....
   (b) Trading name, if any ....
2. *(a)* Postal address of the premises ....
   ....
   (b) Telephone No. ....
3. Nature of business ....
4. How many persons are or will be employed by the employer in office or shop premises at the above address in the following types of workplace?
   (a) Office   ..   ..
   (b) Shop (retail)   ..   ..
   (c) Wholesale   department   or warehouse   ..   ..
   (d) Catering establishment open to the public   ..   ..
   (e) Staff canteen   ..   ..
   (f) Fuel storage depot   ..   ..
          TOTAL   ..   ..   ..   _____
   Of the TOTAL, how many are females?   ..   ..
5. How many of the total are or will be employed on floors *other* than the ground floor?   ..   ..
6. Of the total stated in reply to question 4, are any (or will any be) housed in separate buildings?   *(Answer Yes or No)* ....
7. Is the employer the owner of the building(s) (or part of the building(s)) containing the premises?   *(Answer Yes or No)* ....
8. If not, state the name and address of the owner(s) or person(s) to whom rent is paid   ..   ..
   ....
   Signature of employer or person authorised to sign on his behalf   ....Date ....

For official use

---

50. [*repealed*].

General note. This section was repealed by S.I. 1974 No. 1943, reg. 2(a), Sch. 1, but by reg. 4(3) the Regulations set out below, made under the repealed power, were continued in force. The Schedule of the Regulations below is not printed in this book.

These Regulations have now been revoked by the Health and Safety Information for Employees Regulations 1989.

THE INFORMATION FOR EMPLOYEES REGULATIONS 1965
(S.I. 1965 No. 307, as amended by S.I. 1981 No. 917, S.I. 1982 No. 827 and S.I. 1985 No. 2093)

Date 25th February 1965, made by the Minister of Labour under section 50 of the Offices, Shops and Railway Premises Act 1963 and all other enabling powers.

PART IV

Name of establishment containing premises to be registered on this Schedule (e.g., station, depot)	Postal address or location on line	Details of persons responsible for liaison with (a) H.M. Factory Inspectorate (b) the Fire Authority			Number of persons employed	Number of these (if any) working in		Greatest number of persons employed at any one time	Number of females in total figure in col. (6)
		Official position	Address (if different from (2))	Tele-phone number		Offices	Can-teens		
(1)	(2)	(3)	(4)	(5)	(6)	(7)	(8)	(9)	(10)

1.—*(1) These Regulations may be cited as the Information for Employees Regulations 1965 and shall come into operation on 1 June 1965.*

(2) The Interpretation Act 1889 [Interpretation Act 1978] shall apply to the interpretation of these Regulations as it applies to the interpretation of an Act of Parliament.

2. *These Regulations shall apply to all office premises, shop premises and railway premises to which the Act applies except premises which are in a covered market place being a covered market place to which section 51 (power to adapt Act in relation to covered markets) of the Act relates and in the following Regulations the expression "premises" shall be construed as meaning premises to which these Regulations apply.*

3. *The employer of persons employed to work in premises shall either—*

(a)   at all times at which persons are employed by him to work in the premises, keep posted therein in accordance with these Regulations a copy or copies of the abstract of the Act and the regulations thereunder (hereafter in these Regulations referred to as "the abstract"), being the abstract set out in the Schedule to these Regulations; or

(b)   give, in accordance with these Regulations, a copy of the book (hereafter in these Regulations referred to as "the explanatory book") entitled "Explanatory Book for Employees" (OSR. 9A), dated August 1964, prepared under the auspices of the Minister of Labour, to persons employed by him for more than four weeks on any occasion to work in the premises:

Provided that where, by reason of the circumstances of his work or of the position or positions in which the copy or copies of the abstract provided by his employer in accordance with these Regulations are kept posted in premises, any person employed for more than four weeks on any occasion to work in the premises cannot easily see and read a copy of the abstract, his employer shall give to him, in accordance with these Regulations, a copy of the explanatory book.

4. *Copies of the abstract kept posted in premises in accordance with the last foregoing Regulation—*

(a)   shall be posted in such numbers and characters and in such positions as to be easily seen and read by all the persons employed to work in the premises whose employment therein on any occasion has lasted for more than four weeks except persons so employed who, in accordance with these Regulations, have been given copies of the explanatory book; and

(b)   where posted in the open, shall be protected from the weather.

5. *Where an employer relies for compliance, either in whole or in part, with regulation 3 upon the giving to persons employed to work in premises (or certain of those persons) of copies of the explanatory book, it shall be the duty of the employer—*

(a)   to give (unless, in accordance with these Regulations, he has done so within the immediately preceding period of twelve months) to every such person a copy of that book not later than four weeks after any occasion on which, after the date on which these Regulations come into operation, he begins to be employed by that employer to work in premises;

(b)   to give a copy of that book to every such person who at the date on which these Regulations come into operation is employed by that employer to work in premises and whose employment therein has then lasted, or thereafter lasts for more than four weeks.

SCHEDULE

[The Schedule prescribes the abstract of the Act and Regulations, obtainable as Forms 9, 9A or 9B.]

Power to adapt Act in relation to covered markets

51.   [*repealed*].

Enforcement

52.   [*repealed*].

53.–58.   [*repealed*].

---

59.   Restriction of disclosure of information. If a person discloses (otherwise than in the performance of his duty or for the purposes of any legal proceedings, including arbitrations, or for the purposes of a report of any such proceedings as aforesaid) any information obtained by him in any premises entered by him in exercise of powers conferred by or by virtue of this Act, he shall be guilty of an offence . . . (*a*).

(*a*) *Offence.* For offences, see ss. 63, 67, 86(1).

60.–62.   [*repealed*].

Offences, penalties and legal proceedings

63.   Offences.—(1) In the event of a contravention (*a*), in relation to any premises to which this Act applies (*b*), of any such provisions of this Act as are mentioned in subsection (2) of this section or of regulations made under any such provisions, then—

   (a)   except in a case falling within either of the two following paragraphs, the occupier of the premises shall be guilty of an offence;
   (b)   in a case where the contravention (*a*) is one for which, by or by virtue of this Act, some other person or persons is or are made responsible as well as the occupier of the premises, that other person or those other persons and the occupier shall each be guilty of an offence;
   (c)   in a case where the contravention is one for which, by or by virtue of this Act, some other person or persons is or are made responsible instead of the occupier (*c*) of the premises, that other person or each of those other persons shall be guilty of an offence.

   (2) The provisions of this Act referred to in the foregoing subsection are sections 4, 5, 6(1) to (5), 7 to 12, 13(1), 14 to 19, 23 . . . 24, 46(9) and 48(1) and (2).

(3) A person who contravenes *(a)* a provision of regulations under section 20 or 50 of this Act shall be guilty of an offence.

(a) **Contravention; contravenes.** A contravention of a provision includes a failure to comply with that provision (s. 90(1)).

(b) **Premises to which this Act applies.** See ss. 1 to 3.

64.–66. [*repealed*].

---

67. Defence available to persons charged with offences. It shall be a defence *(a)* for a person charged with a contravention *(b)* of a provision of this Act or of regulations thereunder to prove that he used all due diligence *(c)* to secure compliance with that provision.

General note. The wording of this section makes it clear that it is only concerned with criminal liability and does not provide a defence to a civil action; cf. *Yelland v Powell Duffryn Associated Collieries Ltd* [1941] 1 KB 154, [1941] 1 All ER 278, CA; *Potts (or Riddell) v Reid* [1943] AC 1, [1942] 2 All ER 161, HL; and *Gallagher v Dorman, Long & Co Ltd* [1947] 2 All ER 38, CA.

(a) **Defence.** The burden of proof laid on the defendant is less onerous than that resting on the prosecutor as regards proving the offence, and may be discharged by satisfying the court of the probability of what the defendant is called on to prove; see *R v Carr-Briant* [1943] KB 607, [1943] 2 All ER 156, CCA, and *R v Dunbar* [1958] 1 QB 1, [1957] 2 All ER 737, CCA.

(b) **Contravention.** For definition, see s. 90(1).

(c) **All due diligence.** See INTRODUCTORY NOTE 7.

---

68. [*repealed*].

---

69. Removal or defacement of documents posted in pursuance of Act or regulations under it. If, without reasonable excuse, a person removes... a notice or other document which is for the time being posted or displayed in any premises in pursuance of a provision of this Act or of regulations thereunder, he shall be guilty of an offence and liable on summary conviction to a fine not exceeding level 1 on the standard scale.

70.–71.   [*repealed*].

---

72.   Appeal from orders made on complaint. A person aggrieved *(a)* by an order *(b)* made by a magistrates' court *(c)* on determining a complaint under this Act may appeal *(d)* therefrom to the Crown Court.

(a) *Person aggrieved.* See INTRODUCTORY NOTE 14.

(b) *Order.* This includes the dismissal of a complaint (*R v Recorder of Oxford, ex p Brasenose College* [1970] 1 QB 109, [1969] 3 All ER 428).

(c) *Magistrates' court.* For definition, see s. 90(1).

(d) *Appeal.* See as to appeals the Supreme Court Act 1981, s. 48.

---

73.   Power of county court and sheriff to modify agreements and apportion expenses.—(1) A person who, by reason of the terms of an agreement or lease relating to any premises, is prevented from therein carrying out or doing any structural or other alterations or other thing whose carrying out or doing is requisite in order to secure compliance with a provision of this Act or of regulations thereunder which is, or will become, applicable to the premises, . . . , may apply to the county court *(a)* within whose jurisdiction the premises are situate, and the court may make such an order setting aside or modifying any terms of the agreement or lease as the court considers just and equitable in the circumstances of the case *(b)*.

(2) Where the carrying out or doing in any premises of any structural or other alterations or other thing whose carrying out or doing is requisite as mentioned in the foregoing subsection involves a person having an interest in the premises in expense or in increased expense, and he alleges that the whole or part of the expense or, as the case may be, the increase ought to be borne by some other person having an interest in the premises, the first-mentioned person may apply to the county court *(a)* within whose jurisdiction the premises are situate, and the court, having regard to the terms of any agreement or lease relating to the premises, may by order give such directions with respect to the persons by whom the expense or increase is to be borne, and in what proportions it is to be borne by them and, if need be, for modification of the terms of any such agreement or lease so far as concerns rent payable in respect of the premises as the court considers just and equitable in the circumstances of the case *(b)*.

(3) In the application of this section to Scotland, for references to a county court there shall be substituted references to the sheriff.

(a) *Apply to the county court.* In *Horner v Franklin* [1905] 1 KB 479, CA and *Stuckey v Hooke* [1906] 2 KB 20, CA, it was held that the provisions of the Factory and Workshops Act 1901 similar to those of sub-s. (1) gave exclusive jurisdiction to the county court.

(b) Just and equitable. The terms of the lease or agreement are part of the circumstances of the case and, although not binding on the court, ought to be considered; see *Monk v Arnold* [1902] 1 KB 761; *Horner v Franklin*, above; *Stuckey v Hooke*, above.

Amendments of other Acts

74. Amendment of sections 123(1) and 124(1) of Factories Act 1961, and provisions consequential thereon.—(1) For the purposes of section 123(1) (application of Act to electrical stations) of the Factories Act 1961, office premises *(a)* to which this Act applies which are comprised in premises to which that subsection applies shall, notwithstanding that they are so comprised, be deemed not to form part of the premises.

(2)–(4) [*repealed*].

(a) Office premises. See s. 1(2), (5).

---

75. Amendment of section 125(1) of Factories Act 1961, and provisions consequential thereon.—(1) For the purposes of section 125(1) (docks, etc.) of the Factories Act 1961, office premises *(a)* to which this Act applies which are comprised in premises to which that subsection applies shall, notwithstanding that they are so comprised, be deemed not to form part of the premises.

(2) [*repealed*].

(3) The reference in the said section 125(1) to a warehouse in or for the purposes of which mechanical power is used, being a warehouse neither forming part of a factory nor belonging to the owners, trustees or conservators of a dock, wharf or quay, shall be construed as not including a building occupied by a wholesale dealer or merchant where goods are kept for sale wholesale *(b)* or a part of a building so occupied where goods are so kept.

(a) Office premises. See s. 1(2), (5).

(b) Buildings occupied by a wholesale dealer, etc. Such a building or part of a building constitutes "shop premises"; see s. 1(3)(a)(iii).

---

76. [*repealed*].

---

77. [*repealed*].

---

78.   Provision for securing exercise of local Act powers in conformity with this Act. A person required by or under a local Act to effect any alterations to, or to any apparatus or fittings in, a building *(a)* shall not be treated as having acted in contravention *(b)* of that enactment by reason of his failure to effect those alterations in so far as the failure is attributable to the fact that remedying it would involve a contravention *(b)* of this Act or regulations thereunder.

(*a*) **Building.** "Building" includes structure (s. 90(1)).

(*b*) **Contravention.** A contravention of a provision includes a failure to comply with the provision (s. 90(1)).

General provisions

79.   [*repealed*].

---

80.   Regulations and orders.—(1) Any regulations or orders made under this Act by the Minister *(a)* ... shall be made by statutory instrument *(b)*.

(2) A statutory instrument *(b)* containing regulations under this Act shall be subject to annulment *(c)* in pursuance of a resolution of either House of Parliament.

(3) Any power conferred by this Act to make regulations and any power conferred by or by virtue of this Act to make an order ... shall respectively include power to make different provisions in relation to different circumstances.

(4) Any power conferred by this act to prescribe standards or impose requirements shall include power to do so by reference to the approval of the Health and Safety Executive.

(5)–(6) [*repealed*].

(7) Any power conferred by or by virtue of this Act to make an order shall include power to vary or revoke the order by a subsequent order and the provisions of section 50 of the Health and Safety at Work etc. Act 1974 shall apply to any such power as they apply to a power to make regulations.

(8) [*repealed*].

(*a*) **The Minister.** For definition, see s. 90(1).

(*b*) **Contravention.** A contravention of a provision includes a failure to comply with the provision (s. 90(1)).

(*c*) **Annulment.** For provisions as to annulment, see the Statutory Instruments Act 1946, ss. 5(1) and 7(1); and see also the Laying of Documents before Parliament (Interpretation) Act 1948.

---

81. [*repealed*].

---

82. Expenses and receipts.—(1) There shall be defrayed out of moneys provided by Parliament—

(a) any expenses incurred by the Minister *(a)* in carrying this Act into effect;

(b) any increase attributable to this Act in the expenses of the Minister of Power which, by virtue of section 3(3) of the Ministry of Fuel and Power Act 1945, are defrayed out of moneys so provided;

(c) any increase attributable to this Act in the sums payable by way of General Grant, Rate Deficiency Grant or Exchequer Equalisation Grant under the enactments relating to local government in England and Wales or in Scotland.

(2) Any sums received under this Act by the Minister *(a)* shall be paid into the Exchequer.

(a) The Minister. For definition, see s. 90(1).

---

83. Application to the Crown.—(1) The following provisions of this Act, namely sections 4 to 19, 24, 27, . . . , 42 and 43 shall, in so far as they impose duties failure to comply with which might give rise to a liability in tort *(a)*, be binding upon the Crown, and accordingly, for the purposes of those provisions and regulations under any of them, persons in the service of the Crown shall be taken to be employed *(b)* if, apart from this subsection, they would not be so taken.

(2) Section 24(7) of this Act shall, in its application to premises occupied by the Crown, have effect with the substitution, for the reference to the authority having power to enforce compliance with the foregoing provisions of that section, of a reference to the Health and Safety Executive.

(3) [*repealed*].

(4) Section 46 of this Act shall, in the case of premises occupied *(c)* by the Crown, have effect as if, for any reference to an authority having power to enforce any provision of this Act, there were substituted a reference to the Health and Safety Executive and as if the words in subsection (3) from "and are further satisfied" onwards, and subsection (5) to (13), had been omitted . . .

(5) [*repealed*].

(6) The reference in subsection (1) of this section to a liability in tort shall be construed as not including such a liability towards a member of the armed forces of the Crown, and the reference in that subsection to persons in the service of the Crown shall be construed as not including any such member.

(7) In the application of this section to Scotland any reference to a liability in tort shall be construed as a reference to a liability in reparation arising from any wrongful or negligent act or omission.

(*a*) **Liability in tort.** By sub-s. (6), liability towards a member of the armed forces is excluded. With regard to visiting forces, see s. 84. As to liability in tort generally under this Act, see the LEGAL PRINCIPLES in the introductory section.

(*b*) **Employed.** For definition, see s. 90(1).

---

84.   Exclusion of application to visiting forces.—(1) This Act shall not operate to create, towards a member of the naval, military or air forces of a country to which this section applies, a liability in tort (*a*) against the Government of that country in respect of anything done or omitted by it or against another member of those forces in respect of anything done or omitted by him in the course of his duty.

(2) This section applies to India, Pakistan, Ghana, the Federation of Malaya, the Republic of Cyprus, Tanganyika, Zambia, Botswana, Lesotho, Singapore, Swaziland, Tonga, Bangladesh, Western Samoa, Nauru, the New Hebrides, Brunei, Maldives, Namibia, and any country designated for the purposes of any provision of the Visiting Forces Act 1952 by Order in Council under section 1(2) of that Act.

(2A) This Act shall not operate to create towards a member of a headquarters or organisation designated for the purposes of the International Headquarters and Defence Organisations Act 1964 (*b*) who is a member of the naval, military or air forces of any country a liability in tort against the headquarters or organisation in respect of anything done or omitted by it or against another member thereof in respect of anything done or omitted by him in the course of his duty.

(3) In the application of this section to Scotland the reference to a liability in tort shall be construed as a reference to a liability in reparation arising from any wrongful or negligent act or omission.

(*a*) **Liability in tort.** See the LEGAL PRINCIPLES in the introductory section.

(*b*) **Designated.** See the International Headquarters and Defence Organisations (Designation and Privileges) Order 1965, S.I. 1965 No. 1535.

---

85.   Exclusion of application to factories, to certain fish salerooms and to parts below ground of mines.—(1) ... , nothing in this Act shall apply to any premises which, for the purposes of the Factories Act 1961, form part of a factory (*a*).

(2) With the exception of section 75(3) of this Act, nothing in this Act shall apply to any premises which, not being office premises (*b*) are used for the sale of fish (*c*) by wholesale and constitute, or are comprised in, premises to which certain provisions of the Factories Act 1961 apply by virtue of sections 125(1) (docks, etc.) of that Act.

(3) Nothing in this Act shall apply to any part below ground of premises which, for the purposes of the Mines and Quarries Act 1954, are a mine (*d*).

(a) **Factory.** For definition, see s. 175 of the Factories Act 1961.

(b) **Office premises.** See s. 1(2), (5).

(c) **Fish.** For definition, see s. 90(1).

(d) **Mine.** For definition, see s. 180 of the Mines and Quarries Act 1954.

---

86.   Exclusion of application to premises occupied for transitory purposes.— (1) It shall be a defence *(a)* in any legal proceedings to recover damages and in any prosecution, in so far as the proceedings or prosecution are or is based on an allegation of a contravention *(b)* in relation to any premises, of a provision of this Act or regulations thereunder, to prove that at the time of the alleged contravention *(b)* the premises were occupied for a purpose that was accomplished before the expiration of a period beginning *(c)* with the day on which they were occupied for that purpose and of such of the following lengths as is applicable to the circumstances of the case, that is to say, six months if the premises consist of a movable structure, and six weeks *(d)* if not.

(2) The foregoing subsection shall not apply to a prosecution for an offence consisting in a failure to comply with an obligation imposed under section 49(1) of this Act to notify the appropriate authority *(e)* that persons would be employed *(f)* to work *(g)* in any premises; but in any such prosecution it shall be a defence to prove that the persons in question were employed to work in the premises while they were occupied as mentioned in the foregoing subsection.

(a) **Defence.** See note *(a)* to s. 67.

(b) **Contravention.** A contravention of a provision includes a failure to comply with that provision (s. 90(1)).

(c) **Beginning.** In calculating the periods of six months or six weeks, the day on which the premises were occupied is to be included; cf. *Hare v Gocher* [1962] 2 QB 641, [1962] 2 All ER 763.

(d) **Six weeks.** The definition of "week" in s. 90(1) applies only "unless the context otherwise requires"; here "six weeks" clearly means forty-two days.

(e) **Appropriate authority.** For definition, see s. 49(5).

(f) **Employed.** For definition, see s. 90(1).

(g) **Work.** See note *(a)* to s. 3.

Provisions with respect to Northern Ireland, Isles of Scilly and Inner and Middle Temples

87.   [*repealed*].

---

88.   Application to Isles of Scilly.—This Act shall apply to the Isles of Scilly as if those Isles were a county district and the Council of those Isles were the council of the district.

---

89.   [*repealed*].

Interpretation

90.   Interpretation.—(1) In this Act, unless the context otherwise requires, the following expressions have the meanings hereby assigned to them respectively, that is to say—

except in section 1(4) of this Act, "building" includes structure *(a)*;

"contravention" includes, in relation to a provision of this Act or of regulations thereunder, a failure to comply with the provision, and the expression "contravene" shall be construed accordingly;

"employed" means employed under a contract of service or apprenticeship (whether oral or in writing, express or implied) *(b)*;

"fish" includes molluscs and crustaceans;

"fuel storage premises" has the meaning assigned to it by section 1(3)(a) (v) of this Act *(c)*;

"magistrates' court" has the same meaning as in the Magistrates' Courts Act 1952 *(d)*;

"the Minister" means the Minister of Labour *(e)*;

"notice" means a notice in writing;

"office premises" has the meaning assigned to it by section 1(2) of this Act *(f)*;

"owner"—

(a)   as respects England and Wales, means the person for the time being receiving the backrent of the premises, building or part of a building in connection with which the word is used, whether on his own account or as agent or trustee for another person, or who would so receive the backrent if the premises, building or part were let at a backrent, and

(b)   as respects Scotland, means the person for the time entitled to receive or who would, if the same were let, be entitled to receive, the rents of the premises, building or part of a building in connection with which the word is used and includes as trustee, factor, tutor or curator, and in the case of public or municipal property, applies to the persons to whom the management thereof is entrusted,

and "owned" and "ownership" shall be construed accordingly *(g)*;

"petty sessions area" has the same meaning as in the Magistrates' Courts Act 1952 *(d)*;

"place of public entertainment" means—

(a)   any premises used mainly for public music and dancing in respect of which there is in force a licence granted under the Disorderly Houses Act 1751;

(b) any premises in respect of which there is in force a licence granted under section 1 of the Cinemas Act 1985;

(c) a place of public resort had or kept under the authority of letters patent from Her Majesty, Her heirs or successors, or predecessors, or a licence under the Theatres Act 1843, for the performance of stage plays as defined in that.

"police authority" has the same meaning as in the Police Pensions Act 1921 *(h)*;

"railway premises" has the meaning assigned to it by section 1(4) of this Act *(i)*;

"railway undertakers" means any persons authorised by an enactment or a provision of an order or scheme made under or confirmed by an Act to construct, work or carry on a railway;

"shop premises" has the meaning assigned to it by section 1(3) of this Act *(j)*;

"week" means the period between midnight on Saturday night and midnight on the succeeding Saturday night.

(2) [*repealed*].

(3) For the purposes of this Act—

(a) persons employed by railway undertakers *(k)* to do work the general control of the doing of which is exercised at railway premises, or at office premises occupied by the undertakers for the purposes of the railway undertaking carried on by them and situate in the immediate vicinity of the permanent way, shall be deemed to be employed to work in the premises at which the general control of the doing of their work is exercised notwithstanding that their work is in fact done elsewhere;

(b) neither railway premises nor such office premises as aforesaid shall be taken to be premises in the case of which persons are employed to work therin by reason only of the fact that persons employed by the undertakers who occupy the premises resort to the premises for the purpose only of discharging duties whose discharge is incidental to the work that they are primarily employed to do.

(4) For the purposes of this Act, any such person as follows shall be taken to be employed, namely—

(a) a person appointed under section 6 or 7 of the Registration Service Act 1953 who exercises and performs his powers and duties in premises provided and maintained by the council within whose area his district or sub-district is situate;

(b) [*repealed*];

(c) a member of a police force maintained by a police authority.

(5) The definition of a class of premises, rooms or persons for the purposes of any regulations or under this Act may be framed by reference to any circumstances whatever.

(6) Any reference in this Act to any other enactment shall, unless the context otherwise requires, be construed as a reference to that enactment as amended or extended by or under any subsequent enactment.

*(a) **Structure.*** In *Hobday v Nichols* [1944] 1 All ER 302 (where the meaning of "structure" in a bye-law under the Land Drainage Act 1930 was in issue), Humphreys J (with

whom the other members of the Court agreed) said: "Structure, as I understand it, is anything which is constructed; and it involves the notion of something which is put together, consisting of a number of different things which are so put together or built, constructed as to make one whole which is then called a structure". See also, in particular, *Mills and Rockleys Ltd v Leicester City Council* [1946] KB 315, [1946] 1 All ER 424; *Cardiff Rating Authority and Cardiff Assessment Committee v Guest Keen Baldwin's Iron and Steel Co Ltd* [1949] 1 KB 385, [1949] 1 All ER 27, CA and *BP Refinery (Kent) Ltd v Walker (Valuation Officer)* [1957] 2 QB 305, [1957] 1 All ER 700, CA.

(b) **Employed.** See also sub-ss. (3) and (4). Fiscal considerations have, in recent years, led to the styling as independent contractors of workmen who are, in reality, servants. For the considerations which apply to the correct characterisation of such persons see *Global Plant Ltd v Secretary of State for Health and Social Security* [1972] 1 QB 139, [1971] 3 All ER 385, and the authorities there referred to.

(c) **Fuel storage premises.** See also s. 1(3).

(d) **Magistrates' Courts Act 1952.** See the Magistrates' Courts Act 1980, ss. 148(1), 150(1).

(e) **Minister of Labour.** Now the Secretary of State for Employment (S.I. 1968 No. 729 and S.I. 1970 No. 1537).

(f) **Office premises.** See also s. 1(5).

(g) **Owner.** This definition, so far as it relates to England and Wales, may be compared with that contained in s. 176(1) of the Factories Act 1961 or in s. 343(1) of the Public Health Act 1936.

A "rackrent" is "a rent of the full value of the tenement, or near it" (Blackstone, in Comm. 43), and see *London Corpn v Cusack-Smith* [1955] AC 337, [1955] 1 All ER 302, HL. The date at which the question, whether premises are let at a rackrent, is to be investigated, is the date of the lease, and later changes of circumstance are irrelevant (*ibid.*, and see also *Borthwick-Norton v Collier* [1950] 2 KB 594, [1950] 2 All ER 204, CA). There is no statutory definition of "rackrent" in the Offices, Shops and Railway Premises Act 1963 (compare the Public Health Act 1936, s. 343(1)). The question, whether the tenant is paying the full, or nearly the full, economic rent of the premises is thus one of fact and degree in the circumstances of any particular case. If the lease contains covenants restricting the use of the premises, these must be taken into account (*Borthwick-Norton v Collier*, above) and the payment of a premium for the lease is usually conclusive that the rent received is not a rackrent (*Ex p Connolly to Sheridan and Russell* [1900] 1 IR 1, CA). Other factors which tend to indicate that the rent is not a rackrent are, for example, the surrender by the tenant of an existing lease of the premises at less than the current rent in consideration of the grant of the lease under examination, or the existence of a covenant by the tenant to do extensive repairs immediately upon the grant of the lease.

If premises are let to a tenant at a rackrent, then the landlord is plainly the "owner" within the definition under consideration. If premises are let to a tenant at less than a rackrent, the first limb of the definition does not apply, and the person who "would so receive the rackrent if the premises . . . were let at a rackrent" is the tenant, for he alone is entitled to make a new lease at a rackrent (*London Corpn v Cusack-Smith*, above, *per* Lord Oaksey (at 348, 306), *per* Lord Reid (at 358, 313), *per* Lord Tucker (at 366, 318) and *per* Lord Keith of Avonholm (at 367, 319)). If premises are both let and sublet at rackrents, the head-landlord is undoubtedly an "owner", and, according to some of the opinions expressed in *London Corpn v Cusack-Smith*, above, the intermediate tenant may also be an "owner" (see *ibid., per* Lord Porter (at 353–356, 307–310), *per* Lord Reid (at 358–359, 312–313) and *per* Lord Tucker (at 366, 318)). The opinions thus last expressed turned to some extent upon the presence of the phrase, "any owner", in s. 19(1) of the Town and Country Planning Act 1947, so that it does not necessarily follow from them that a similar construction would be placed upon the wording of the definition now under examination. If premises are let at a rackrent and sublet at less than a rackrent the head-landlord is the "owner"; if premises are let at less than a rackrent and sublet at a rackrent the intermediate tenant is the owner; and if premises are both let and sublet at less than rackrents the sub-tenant is the "owner".

(h) *Police Pensions Act 1921.* See now the Police Act 1964, s. 62, Sch. 8.

(i) *Railway premises.* See also s. 1(5).

(j) *Shop premises.* See *ibid.*, s. 1(5).

(k) *Railway undertakers.* For definition, see sub-s. (1).

Short title, commencement, extent and repeal

91. Short title, commencement, extent and repeal.—(1) This Act may be cited as the Offices, Shops and Railway Premises Act 1963.

(2) This Act shall come into operation on such day as the Minister (a) may by order (b) appoint, and different days may be appointed for the coming into operation of different provisions, of a particular provision in relation to premises of different classes (c) or of a particular provision for different purposes.

(3) This Act shall not extend to Nothern Ireland . . .

(4) The enactments specified in columns 1 and 2 of Schedule 2 to this Act are hereby repealed to the extent respectively specified in relation thereto in column 3 of that Schedule.

(a) *The Minister.* For definition, see s. 90(1).

(b) *Order.* As to the making of orders, see s. 80. The Offices, Shops and Railway Premises Act 1963 (Commencement No. 1) Order 1964 (S.I. 1964 No. 191), the Offices, Shops and Railway Premises Act 1963 (Commencement No. 2) Order 1964 (S.I. 1964 No. 1045) and the Offices, Shops and Railway Premises Act 1963 (Commencement No. 3) Order 1989 (S.I. 1989 No. 2312) have been made under this section.

(c) *Class of premises.* See s. 90(5).

SCHEDULES

SCHEDULE 1 [*repealed.*]

SCHEDULE 2

Section 91

ENACTMENTS REPEALED

Session and Chapter	Short Title	Extent of Repeal
26 Geo. 5 & 1 Edw. 8 c. 49	The Public Health Act 1936	In section 44(3), the words "to a shop to which the Shops Act 1934, applies, or". In section 45(4), the words "to a shop to which the Shops Act 1934, applies, or". Section 46(4). Section 92(3).
14 Geo. 6 c. 28	The Shops Act 1950.	Sections 37 to 39. In section 45, the words "or section thirty-seven". In section 69(1), the words "and section thirty-seven". In section 72, subsections (2) and (3), and in subsection (4), paragraph (b). In section 74(1), the definitions of "owner", "Public Health Acts" and "sanitary authority". In section 75, the last paragraph.
6 & 7 Eliz. 2 c. xxi.	The London County Council (General Powers) Act 1958.	Section 18.
8 & 9 Eliz. 2 c. 47.	The Offices Act 1960.	The whole Act.

PART 9

AGRICULTURE

SUMMARY

INTRODUCTION

The Agriculture (Poisonous Substances) Act 1952 and the Agriculture (Safety, Health and Welfare Provisions) Act 1956 empowered the appropriate Ministers to make regulations giving effect to the specific purposes of each Act and to appoint inspectors.

These powers, together with many other provisions of the Acts, were repealed as a consequence of the Health and Safety at Work etc. Act 1974.

The Agricultural legislation has been profoundly affected by the 1992 Regulations implementing the European Directives (see HISTORICAL INTRODUCTION).

Those Regulations made under the Agriculture (Safety, Health and Welfare Provisions) Act 1956 still in force are printed below.

THE AGRICULTURE (POISONOUS SUBSTANCES) ACT 1952

(15 & 16 Geo. 6 & 1 Eliz. 2, c. 60)

ARRANGEMENT OF SECTIONS

An Act to provide for the protection of employees against risks of poisoning by certain substances used in agriculture

[30 October 1952]

1.–5. [*repealed or otherwise spent*].

---

6. Provisions as to samples.—(1) An inspector appointed under the Health and Safety at Work etc. Act 1974 may take for analysis a sample of any substance or thing which in his opinion may be or contain a substance to which this Act applies, and which he finds on, or has reasonable cause to believe to be in transit to or from, such land or premises are mentioned in subsection (2) of section 3 of this Act.

(2) An inspector taking a sample under the preceding subsection with the intention of having it analysed shall, if practicable, forthwith after taking it give information of his intention to the employer *(a)* of any person when working as mentioned in subsection (1) of section 1 of this Act on the land or premises in question, and shall then and there divide the sample *(b)* into parts, each part to be marked, and sealed or fastened up, in such manner as its nature will permit, and shall—

(a) if required so to do by an employer so informed, deliver one part to him;

(b) retain one part for future comparison; and

(c) if the inspector thinks fit to have an analysis made, submit one part to an analyst approved by the Health and Safety Executive for the purposes of this Act.

(3) Where it is not practicable for the inspector to give information of his intention as mentioned in the last preceding subsection to an employer *(a)*, the inspector shall, if he intends to have the sample analysed and if he can ascertain the name and address of the employer, forward one part of the sample to him by registered post or otherwise, together with a notice informing him that he intends to have the sample analysed.

(4) A document purporting to be a certificate by an analyst approved by the Health and Safety Executive for the purposes of this Act as to the result of an analysis of a sample shall in proceedings under this Act be admissible as evidence *(c)* of the matters stated therein, but either party may require the person by whom the analysis was made to be called as a witness.

(5) In any proceedings under this Act in which the prosecutor intends to rely on evidence relating to a sample taken under this section, the summons shall not be made returnable less than fourteen days from the day on which it is served, and a copy of any certificate of analysis obtained on behalf of the prosecutor shall be served with the summons.

(6) In any proceedings under this Act in which the prosecutor relies on evidence relating to a sample taken under this section, the part of the sample retained by the inspector for future comparison shall be produced *(d)* at the hearing.

(7) The court before which any proceedings are taken under this Act may, if it thinks fit, and upon the request of either party shall, cause the part of any sample produced before the court under the last preceding subsection to be sent to the Government Chemist *(e)* who shall make an analysis, and transmit to the court a certificate of the result thereof, and the cost of the analysis shall be paid by the prosecutor or the defendant as the court may order.

If, in a case where an appeal is brought, no action has been taken under the preceding provisions of this subsection, those provisions shall apply also in relation to the court by which the appeal is heard.

(a) **Employer.** For definition, see s. 10(1).

(b) **Divide the sample.** See 18 *Halsbury's Laws* (4th Edn.) 1052 *et seq.*

The division must be such that each of the three parts may be sufficient for analysis; see *Lowery v Hallard* [1906] 1 KB 398 (a decision on s. 14 of the Sale of Food and Drugs Act 1875 (repealed)).

(c) **Evidence.** Compare ss. 15, 16 of the Road Traffic Offenders Act 1988. The effect of this subsection is to make the contents of the certificate admissible despite the hearsay rule. The subsection does not state that the certificate shall be "sufficient" evidence of its contents, but nonetheless it is conceived that its effect is the same, so that if the certificate is the only evidence tendered on the issue the court is bound to accept it (cf. *Preston v Fennell* [1951] 1 KB 16, [1950] 1 All ER 1099, decided on s. 81(1) of the Food and Drugs Act 1938 (repealed)). If evidence is called to rebut the certificate, the court must then weigh the whole evidence in arriving at a conclusion (cf. *Hewitt v Taylor* [1896] 1 QB 287; decided on s. 21 of the Sale of Food and Drugs Act 1875). Subsection (4) of the present Act is modified in its application to Scotland; see s. 11(4).

(d) **Produced.** See 18 *Halsbury's Laws* (4th edn.) 1295.

(e) **Government Chemist.** See 18 *Halsbury's Laws* (4th edn.) 1296.

---

7.   Application to the Crown. This Act and regulations thereunder shall bind the Crown, but regulations under this Act may provide for modifications or exceptions in the application of this Act or such regulations to, or in relation to, the Crown.

8., 9.   [*repealed*].

---

10.   Interpretation.—(1) In this Act the following expressions have the meanings hereby assigned to them respectively, that is to say—

"agriculture" *(a)* includes dairy-farming, the production of any consumable produce which is grown for sale or for consumption or other use for the purposes of a trade or business or of any other undertaking (whether carried on for profit or not), and the use of land as grazing, meadow or pasture land or orchard or osier land or woodland or for market gardens or nursery grounds;

"consumable produce" *(b)* means produce grown for consumption or for other use after severance from the land on which it is grown;

"worker" *(c)* means a person employed under a contract of service or apprenticeship, and "employer" and "employed" have corresponding meanings.

(2) Any references in this Act to a contravention of any provision shall include a reference to a failure to comply with that provision.

(a) **Agriculture.** This definition differs from that in the Agriculture Act 1947, s. 109 (3), and the Agricultural Holdings Act 1986, s. 96(1), but is identical with that in the Agriculture (Safety, Health and Welfare Provisions) Act 1956, s. 24(1), printed in this Part.

(b) **Consumable produce.** This definition is identical with that in the Agriculture (Safety, Health and Welfare Provisions) Act 1956, s. 24(1).

(c) **Worker . . . contract of service.** See note *(e)* to s. 24 of the Agriculture (Safety, Health and Welfare Provisions) Act 1956.

---

11.   Application to Scotland.—(1) The provisions of this section shall have effect for the purposes of the application of this Act to Scotland.

(2) Nothing in section three shall be construed as authorising an inspector to institute proceedings in any court in Scotland for an offence against this Act.

(3) Section five shall not apply, but—

(a) where a contravention of any provision of this Act or of regulations thereunder for which any person on conviction would be liable to a penalty under this Act was due to an act or default of any other person, then, whether proceedings are or are not taken against the first-mentioned person, that other person may be charged with and convicted of the contravention and shall be liable on conviction to the same punishment as might have been inflicted on the first mentioned person if he had been convicted of the contravention; and

(b) where a person who is charged with a contravention of any provision of this Act or of regulations thereunder proves to the satisfaction of the court that he has used all due diligence to secure that the provision in question was complied with, he shall be acquitted of the contravention.

(4) For the purposes of any proceedings under this Act a certificate which is admitted as evidence under subsection (4) of section six shall be sufficient evidence of the matters stated therein unless a party requires the person by whom the analysis in question was made to be called as a witness, and in the latter event any evidence given by that person as to the result of the analysis shall be sufficient evidence of that result.

(5) In the application of section six the expression "defendant" means accused; the expression "hearing" means trial; any reference to a summons shall be construed as a reference to a complaint; and for reference to the day on which a summons is served and to the day on which it is returnable there shall be substituted respectively references to the day on which a complaint is served and to the day on which the prosecution thereon proceeds to trial.

---

12.   Short title and extent.—(1) This Act may be cited as the Agriculture (Poisonous Substances) Act 1952.

(2) This Act shall not extend to Northern Ireland.

THE AGRICULTURE (SAFETY, HEALTH AND WELFARE PROVISIONS) ACT 1956

(4 & 5 Eliz. 2 c. 49)

ARRANGEMENT OF SECTIONS

An Act to provide for securing the safety, health and welfare of persons employed in agriculture and certain other occupations and the avoidance of accidents to children arising out of the use in connection with agriculture, of vehicles, machinery or implements; and for purposes connected with the matters of aforesaid. [5 July 1956]

Safety, health and welfare of employees

1. Regulations for securing safety and health of employees.—(1)–
(5) [*repealed*].

(6) A person who contravenes *(a)* any provision of regulations under this
section shall be guilty of an offence *(b)*.

(7) [*repealed*].

General note. The powers to make regulations under this section are repealed by S.I.
1975 No. 46, reg. 2, Sch. 1, but by reg. 5(3) regulations made under those powers are
continued in force. The Regulations are the Agriculture (Ladders) Regulations 1957
(S.I. 1957 No. 1385), the Agriculture (Power Takeoff) Regulations 1957 (S.I. 1957 No.
1386), the Agriculture (Circular Saws) Regulations 1959 (S.I. 1959 No. 427), the
Agriculture (Safeguarding of Workplaces) Regulations 1959 (S.I. 1959 No. 428), the
Agriculture (Stationary Machinery) Regulations 1959 (S.I. 1959 No. 1216), the Agricul-
ture (Threshers and Balers) Regulations 1960 (S.I. 1960 No. 1199), the Agriculture
(Field Machinery) Regulations 1962 (S.I. 1962 No. 1472) and the Agriculture (Tractor
Cabs) Regulations 1974 (S.I. 1974 No. 2034). The foregoing Regulations are printed
below and amended and revoked as noted thereto.

(a) ***Contravenes.*** A contravention of a provision includes a failure to comply with that
provision (s. 24(2)).

(b) ***Offence.*** With the repeal of s. 14 of this Act, "Punishment of offences", an office
under the Act is "an offence under . . . the existing statutory provisions, being an offence
for which no other penalty is specified", within the meaning of s. 33(3) of the Health
and Safety at Work etc. Act 1974 and falls, therefore, to be dealt with under that section.

---

2. [*repealed*].

3.   General provisions as to sanitary conveniences and washing facilities.—
(1) If it appears *(a)* to the Health and Safety Executive that an agriculture unit
(b) on which workers are employed *(c)* in agriculture *(d)* is without suitable and
sufficient sanitary conveniences *(e)* available for the use of workers so employed,
the Executive shall, by notice *(f)* to the appropriate person *(g)*, require him,
within such time as may be specified in the notice, to execute such works or take
such other steps for the purpose of providing the unit with suitable and
sufficient sanitary conveniences available for the use of workers employed
thereon in agriculture as may be specified in the notice.

(2) If it appears *(a)* to the Health and Safety Executive that an agriculture
unit *(b)* on which workers are employed *(c)* in agriculture *(d)* is without suitable
and sufficient washing facilities available for the use of workers so employed,
the Health and Safety Executive shall, be notice *(f)* to the appropriate person
(g), require him, within such time as may be specified in the notice, to execute
such works or take such other steps for the purpose of providing the unit with
suitable and sufficient washing facilities available for the use of workers
employed thereon in agriculture as may be specified in the notice.

(3) In considering, for the purposes of this section, whether an agriculture
unit *(b)* is or is not without suitable and sufficient sanitary conveniences

available for the use of workers employed on the unit in agriculture *(d)* or, as the case may be, is or is not without suitable and sufficient washing facilities for the use of workers, so employed, regard shall be had to the number and sex of the workers so employed, the location and duration of their work and all other relevant circumstances.

(4) A notice under this section requiring the execution of works involving the provision of fixed equipment *(h)* must specify the place where the works are to be executed.

(5) The Health and Safety Executive shall not serve a notice under this section requiring the execution of works involving the provision of fixed equipment unless it is satisfied *(i)* that special circumstances exist which render requisite the provision of such equipment, and no such notice shall be of any effect unless it states that . . . the Executive is so satisfied and what those circumstances are.

(6) For the purposes of this section the expression "appropriate person" means—

(a) in the case of a notice requiring the execution, on land comprised in an agricultural holding *(j)*, of works involving the provision of fixed equipment, the landlord of the holding;
(b) in any other case, the occupier of the unit to which the notice relates.

(7) A person aggrieved by a notice under this section requiring him to execute works involving the provision of fixed equipment may, within twenty-eight days from the service of the notice, appeal *(k)* to a magistrates' court on any of the following grounds which are appropriate to the circumstances of the case, namely—

(a) that the Health and Safety Executive has refused unreasonably to approve the execution of alternative works, or that the works required by the notice to be executed are otherwise unreasonable in character or extent, or are unnecessary;
(b) that it is unreasonable to require the execution of the works at the place specified in the notice;
(c) that the time within which the works are to be executed is not reasonable for the purpose,

and the court may make such order either confirming or quashing or varying the notice as it thinks fit.

(8) A person aggrieved by a decision *(l)* of a magistrates' court under this section may appeal to the Crown Court.

(9) Subject to the rights of appeal conferred by the foregoing provisions of this section and (where an appeal is brought in exercise of any such right) to any order made by the court on the appeal, a person upon whom a notice is served under this section who fails to comply with the requirements of the notice shall be guilty of an offence *(m)*:

Provided that, in any proceedings under this subsection for an offence consisting in a failure to comply with the requirements of a notice other than one to which subsection (7) of this section applies, it shall be open to the defendant to question the reasonableness of the requirements of the notice.

(10) [*repealed*].

General note. This section is to be repealed as from 1 January 1996 by the Workplace (Health, Safety and Welfare) Regulations 1992 for workplaces in existence on 31 December 1992. Those Regulations will apply to those workplaces from the former date. Workplaces coming into use after 31 December 1992 and modifications, extensions and conversions started after 31 December 1992 to existing workplaces must conform to those Regulations as soon as they come into use. By s. 25(3) this section is modified in its application to Scotland.

(*a*) ***Appears.*** Regard must be had to the matters specified in sub-s. (3) and, where fixed equipment is required, to the matters specified in sub-s. (5). Provided that those matters are taken into account, and that the Health and Safety Executive acts *bona fide* and *intra vires*, the courts will not enquire into the correctness of this decision to give a notice under the section; *Robinson v Sunderland Corpn* [1899] 1 QB 751, *per* Channel J at 756, 757; *Point of Ayr Collieries Ltd v Lloyd-George* [1943] 2 All ER 546, CA; *Re City of Plymouth (City Centre) Declaratory Order 1946, Robinson v Minister of Town and Country Planning* [1947] KB 702, [1947] 1 All ER 851, CA, *per* Somervell LJ at 721: 861, 862; *Thorneloe and Clarkson Ltd v Board of Trade* [1950] 2 All ER 245. See generally, 1 (2) *Halsbury's Laws* (4th edn.) 926 *et seq.*

(*b*) ***Agriculture unit.*** For definition, see s. 24(1).

(*c*) ***Workers are employed.*** For definition, see s. 24(1).

(*d*) ***Agriculture.*** For definition, see s. 24(1).

(*e*) ***Sanitary conveniences.*** For power to secure the maintenance and cleanliness of conveniences, see s. 5.

(*f*) ***Notice.*** The form and mode of service of notices are specified by s. 20; see also sub-ss. (4) and (5) of the present section.

(*g*) ***Appropriate person.*** For definition, see sub-s (6).

(*h*) ***Fixed equipment.*** For definition, see s. 24(1).

(*i*) ***Satisfied.*** See note (*a*).

(*j*) ***Agricultural holding.*** For definition, see s. 24(1).

(*k*) ***Appeal.*** The appeal is by way of complaint for an order; see r 34 of the Magistrates' Court Rules 1981, S.I. 1981 No. 552. The magistrates may therefore award costs as provided in s. 64 of the Magistrates' Courts Act 1980.

(*l*) ***Persons aggrieved by a decision.*** See INTRODUCTORY NOTE 14.

(*m*) ***Offence.*** See note (*b*) to s. 1.

---

4. [*repealed*].

---

5. Power of the Health and Safety Executive to secure maintenance and cleanliness of sanitary conveniences.—(1) It it appears to the Health and Safety Executive that a sanitary convenience (*a*) provided for the use of workers employed in agriculture (*b*) on an agricultural unit (*c*) (being a convenience provided on the unit or provided in pursuance of regulations (*d*) under the last foregoing section elsewhere) is not being properly maintained or is not being kept clean, they shall, by notice to the occupier of the unit (or, where the convenience is provided in pursuance of such regulations as aforesaid, to the person who provided it) require him, as the case may be, to take, within such time as may be specified in the notice, such steps for the purpose of securing the proper maintenance of the convenience as may be so specified or to cleanse the convenience forthwith.

(2) A person who fails to comply with the requirements of a notice under this section shall be guilty of an offence *(e)*:

Provided that, in any proceedings under this subsection for an offence consisting in a failure to comply with the requirements of a notice requiring the taking of steps for the purpose of securing the proper maintenance of a convenience, it shall be open to the defendant to question the reasonableness of the requirements of the notice.

General note. This section is to be repealed as from 1 January 1996 by the Workplace (Health, Safety and Welfare) Regulations 1992 for workplaces in existence on 31 December 1992. Those Regulations will apply to those workplaces from the former date. Workplaces coming into use after 31 December 1992 and modifications, extensions and conversions started after 31 December 1992 to existing workplaces must conform to those Regulations as soon as they come into use.

(a) **Sanitary convenience.** The Health and Safety Executive has power under s. 3(1) to require the provision of suitable and sufficient sanitary conveniences, on agricultural units, for workers in agriculture.

(b) **Workers employed in agriculture.** For definition, see s. 24(1).

(c) **Agricultural unit.** For definition, see s. 24(1).

(d) **Regulations.** No regulations under s. 4 (repealed) were made.

(e) **Offence.** See note *(b)* to s. 1.

_____

6. [*repealed*].

_____

Measures for avoiding accidents to children

7. Power to prohibit children from riding on or driving vehicles, machinery or implements used in agriculture.—(1), (2) [*repealed*].

(3) A person who causes *(a)* or permits a child, in contravention *(b)* of the provisions of regulations under this section *(c)*, to ride on or drive a vehicle or machine or, as the case may be, to ride on an agricultural implement, shall be guilty of an offence *(d)*.

General note. For the law relating to the employment of children, see 24 *Halsbury's Laws* (4th edn.) 867 *et seq.* to reg. 3 of the Agriculture (Ladders) Regulations 1957.

(a) **Causes.** See note *(a)* to reg. 3 of the Agriculture (Ladders) Regulations 1957.

(b) **Contravention.** A contravention of any provision includes a failure to comply with that provision (s. 24(2)).

(c) **Regulations under this section.** The power to make regulations under this section is repealed by S.I. 1975 No. 46, reg. 2, Sch. 1, but by reg. 5(3) regulations made under the

repealed power are continued in force: see the Agriculture (Avoidance of Accidents to Children) Regulations 1958, S.I. 1958 No. 366.

(d) *Offence.* See note (b) to s. 1.

Notification and investigation of accidents and diseases

8. [*repealed*].

---

9.   Inquest in case of death by accident.—(1) Where a coroner (a) holds an inquest (b) on the body of a person whose death may have been caused by an accident occurring in the course of agricultural (c) operations, the coroner shall adjourn the inquest unless an inspector (d) or some other person on behalf of the appropriate Minister (e) is present to watch the proceedings, and shall, at least four days before holding the adjourned inquest, give to an inspector notice of the time and place of holding the adjourned inquest:
   Provided that—

   (a)   the coroner, before the adjournment, may take evidence to identify the body and may order the interment (f) thereof; and
   (b)   if the inquest relates to the death of not more than one person, the coroner shall not be bound to adjourn the inquest in pursuance of this section if, not less than twenty-four hours before it is held, he informed an inspector of the time and place of the holding thereof.

   (2) Where evidence is given at any such inquest at which an inspector (d) is not present of any neglect as having caused or contributed to the accident, or of any defect in any building, structure, machinery, plant, equipment or appliance appearing to the coroner or jury (g) to require a remedy, the coroner shall give to an inspector notice (h) of the neglect or defect.

(a) *Coroner.* For the appointment and powers of coroners, see the Coroners Act 1988 and 9 *Halsbury's Laws* (4th edn.) 1009 *et seq.*

(b) *Inquest.* The holding of and procedure at coroners' inquests is governed by the Coroners Rules 1984, S.I. 1984 No. 552. By those Rules, where a coroner holds an inquest on the body of a person whose death may have been caused by an accident or disease notice of which is required to be given to an inspector or enforcing authority the coroner must adjourn the inquest unless the inspector or a representative of the enforcing authority is present to watch the proceedings. He must also, at least four days before holding the adjourned inquest, give the inspector or enforcing authority notice of the time and place of holding the adjourned inquest.

(c) *Agriculture.* For definition, see s. 24(1).

(d) *Inspector.* For definition, see s. 24(1).

(e) *Appropriate Minister.* For definition, see s. 24(1).

(f) *Interment.* A body must not be disposed of before a certificate of the registrar of births, deaths and marriages or an order of the coroner has been delivered to the person effecting the disposal; see the Births and Deaths Registration Act 1926, s. 1(1) and the

Births and Deaths Registration Act 1953, s. 43(1) and First Schedule, para. 2. As to registration, see the Registration of Births and Deaths Regulations 1987 (S.I. 1987 No. 2088).

(g) *Jury.* If a death was caused by an accident, poisoning or disease, notice of which must be given to a govenment department or to any inspector or other officer of a government department, a coroner cannot sit without a jury; see the Coroners Act 1988, s. 8.

(h) *Notice.* See the Health and Safety at Work etc. Act 1974, s. 46(1).

10.–14. [*repealed*].

Supplementary provisions

15. [*repealed*].

---

16. Defence available to persons charged with offences. It shall be a defence (a) for a person (b) charged with a contravention (c) of a provision of this Act or of regulations thereunder to prove (d) that he used all due diligence (e) to secure compliance with that provision.

General note. There is no similar provision in the Factories Act 1961, but an identical provision is to be found in s. 67 of the Offices, Shops and Railway Premises Act 1963.

(a) *Defence.* The section is concerned only with criminal liability and does not provide a defence to a civil action: *Yelland v Powell Duffryn Associated Collieries Ltd* [1941] 1 KB 154, [1941] 1 All ER, 278, CA; *Potts* (or *Riddell) v Reid* [1943] AC 1, [1942] 2 All ER 161, HL and *Gallagher v Dorman, Long & Co Ltd* [1947] 2 All ER 38, CA.

(b) *Person.* Unless the contrary intention appears, "person" includes any body of persons corporate or incorporate [Interpretation Act 1978, Sch. 1].

(c) *Contravention.* A contravention of any provision includes a failure to comply with that provision (s. 24(2)).

(d) *Prove.* The burden of proof laid on the defendant is less onerous than that resting on the prosecutor as regards proving the offence, and may be discharged by satisfying the court of the probability of what the defendant is called on to prove; see *R v Carr-Briant* [1943] KB 607, [1943] 2 All ER 156, CCA, and *R v Dunbar* [1958] 1 QB 1, [1957] 2 All ER 737, CCA.

(e) *Due diligence.* See INTRODUCTORY NOTE 7.

17.–21. [*repealed*].

---

22.   Application to the Crown. Sections one, two and six of this Act and regulations under any of those sections shall, in so far as they impose duties failure to comply with which might give rise to a liability in tort, be binding upon the Crown.

General note. The Crown is not amenable to criminal proceedings, but this section, together with the Crown Proceedings Act 1947, s. 2(2), makes the Crown civilly liable for breach of a duty imposed by ss. 1, 2 and 6 and by regulations under those sections, to the same extent as a private individual of full age and capacity. For proceedings against the Crown generally, see 8 *Halsbury's Laws* (4th edn.) 968 *et seq.*

---

23.   [*repealed*].

---

24.   Interpretation.—(1) In this Act, unless the context otherwise requires, the following expressions have the meanings hereby assigned to them respectively, that is to say—

"agriculture" includes dairy-farming, the production of any consumable produce which is grown for sale or for consumption or other use for the purposes of a trade or business or of any other undertaking (whether carried on for profit or not), and the use of land as grazing, meadow or pasture land or orchard or osier land or woodland or for market gardens or nursery grounds, and "agricultural" shall be construed accordingly *(a)*;

"agricultural holding" *(b)* "fixed equipment' *(c)* and "landlord" *(d)* have the same meanings as in the Agricultural Holdings Act 1986;

"agricultural unit" *(a)* means land which is occupied as a unit for agricultural purposes;

"consumable produce" means produce grown for consumption or for other use after severance from the land on which it is grown;

"inspector" means an inspector appointed by the Health and Safety Executive under section 19 of the Health and Safety at Work etc. Act 1974;

"worker" means a person employed under a contract of service *(e)* or apprenticeship and "employer" and "employed" have corresponding meanings;

"young person" means a person who is over compulsory school age for the purposes of the Education Act 1944, but has not attained the age of eighteen *(f)*.

(2) Any reference in this Act to a contravention of any provision shall include a reference to a failure to comply with that provision.

(3) [*repealed*].

(4) Any reference in this Act to any other enactment shall be construed as a reference to that enactment as amended by any subsequent enactment.

(a) *Agriculture; agricultural unit.* The definitions in this section are not identicial with those in s. 109(2), (3) of the Agriculture Act 1947, nor with those in s. 96(1) of the Agricultural Holdings Act 1986.

(b) Agricultural holding. This expression is defined in s. 1(1) of the Agricultural Holdings Act 1986. By that subsection "agricultural holding" means the aggregate of the land (whether agricultural land or not) comprised in a contract of tenancy which is a contract for an agricultural tenancy not being a contract under which the land is let to the tenant during his continuance in any office, appointment or employment held under the landlord.

(c) Fixed equipment. See s. 96(1) of the Agricultural Holdings Act 1986, which provides: "'fixed equipment' includes any building or structure affixed to land and any works on, in, over or under land, and also includes anything grown on land for a purpose other than use after severance from the land, consumption of the thing grown or of its produce or amenity, and any reference to fixed equipment on land shall be construed accordingly".

(d) Landlord. See s. 96(1) of the Agricultural Holdings Act 1986 which provides: "'landlord' means any person for the time being entitled to receive the rents and profits of any land".

(e) Worker ... contract of service. This definition of the term "worker" requires examination in two respects. In the first place, a "worker' must be in contractual relations with his employer (see *O'Sullivan v Thompson-Coon* (1973) 14 KIR 108, DC—relief worker supplied to farmer by agency held not to have contracted with farmer). In view of the statement in the Gowers Committee Report (Cmnd. 7664), para. 123, that "two-thirds of the country's agricultural undertakings consist of small units where a substantial part of the necessary labour is supplied by the farmer himself and his family" it is clearly of importance to decide in any given case whether a person working on a farm is working under an arrangement which is enforceable in law as a contract, or whether he is not. For there to be a contract there must be consideration moving from the employer (which need not be a money consideration) and possibly also an intention on each side to create legal relations, although this latter requirement is the subject of controversy. In the second place, the contract must be one of service, and not one for services (see *O'Sullivan v Thompson-Cook*, above). This is the distinction drawn, principally in the law of tort, between a servant and an independent contractor.

(f) Young person ... eighteen. Section 35 of the Education Act 1944 provides that a person shall be deemed to be over compulsory school age as soon as he has attained the age of fifteen years but, pursuant to the proviso to that section, the age has been raised to sixteen years with effect from 1 September 1972 (Raising of the School Leaving Age Order 1972, S.I. 1972 No. 444).

---

25. Application to Scotland. [*Not printed in this book. Note the amendments made to this section by S.I. 1975 No. 46 and S.I. 1977 No. 746*].

---

26. Short title and extent.—(1) This Act may be cited as the Agriculture (Safety, Health and Welfare Provisions) Act 1956.

(2) This Act shall not extend to Northern Ireland.

THE AGRICULTURE (AVOIDANCE OF ACCIDENTS TO CHILDREN) REGULATIONS 1958

(S.I. 1958 No. 366)

General note. A contravention of these Regulations is, by virtue of s. 7(3) of the Agriculture (Safety, Health and Welfare Provisions) Act 1956, an offence. These Regulations do not bind the Crown; see s. 22 of the Act.

Citation and commencement

1. These regulations, which may be cited as the Agriculture (Avoidance of Accidents to Children) Regulations 1958, shall apply to Great Britain *(a)* and shall come into operation on the 1st day of July 1958.

   (a) **Great Britain.** See INTRODUCTORY NOTE 4.

Interpretation

2.—(1) In these Regulations:—

   "child" means a child who has not attained the age at which his employment ceases to be prohibited *(a)*—

   (i) in England and Wales *(b)* under paragraph (a) of subsection (1) of section 18 of the Children and Young Persons Act 1933, or
   (ii) in Scotland under paragraph (a) of subsection (1) of section 28 of the Children and Young Persons (Scotland) Act 1937;

   "trailer" means any vehicle used as a trailer whether or not designed to be so used, but does not include any such vehicle drawn by an animal.

   (2) In these Regulations any reference to a tractor, machine, implement, *trailer* or other vehicle includes any drawbar, tow-bar or coupling which may be used for the purpose of towing or propelling.

   (3) The Interpretation Act 1889 [Interpretation Act 1978] applies to the interpretation of these Regulations as it applies to the interpretation of an Act of parliament.

   (a) **Age at which his employment ceases to be prohibited.** Under the Acts set out in sub-paras. (i) and (ii), as respectively amended by the Education (Miscellaneous Provisions) Act 1948, s. 11(1) and the First Schedule, Part II, and the Education (Scotland) Act 1949, s. 5 and the Schedule, Part II, the age is at present thirteen. A person attains a given age at the commencement of the relevant anniversary of his birth: Family Law Reform Act 1969, s. 9.

   (b) **England and Wales.** See INTRODUCTORY NOTE 4.

Prohibition on riding on vehicles and machines

3.—(1) Subject to paragraph (2) of this regulation no *child* shall ride on any of the following classes of vehicles or machines while such vehicles or machines are being used in the course of agricultural operations or are going to or from the site of such operations:—

(a) tractors;
(b) self-propelled agricultural machines;
(c) *trailers*;
(d) *trailers* into which any conveyor mechanism is built;
(e) machines mounted in whole or part on tractors or vehicles, or towed or propelled by tractors or vehicles;
(f) binders or mowers drawn by animals.

(2) The foregoing paragraph shall not apply as respects sub-paragraph (c) thereof in circumstances where the *child* rides—

(a) on the floor of the *trailer*; or
(b) on any load carried by the *trailer* provided that the *trailer* has four sides each of which is higher than the load.

Prohibition on driving vehicles and machines

4. No *child* shall drive any tractor, or self-propelled vehicles or machine while that tractor, vehicle or machine is being used in the course of agricultural operations or is going to or from the site of such operations.

Prohibition on riding on implements

5. No *child* shall ride on any of the following implements while they are being towed or propelled:—

(a) agricultural implements mounted in whole or in part on tractors or vehicles, or towed or propelled by tractors or vehicles;
(b) animal-drawn rollers.

THE AGRICULTURE (CIRCULAR SAWS) REGULATIONS 1959

(S.I. 1959 No. 427, as amended by S.I. 1976 No. 1247, S.I. 1981 No. 1414, S.I. 1989 No. 2311 and S.I. 1992 No. 2932)

General note. These Regulations give effect to the general provisions of s. 1 of the Agriculture (Safety, Health and Welfare Provisions) Act 1956. They may be compared with the Woodworking Machines Regulations 1974, which apply to factories and to certain other premises.

A contravention of the Regulations is, by s. 1(6) of the Act of 1956, an offence, and in so far as the Regulations impose duties failure to comply with which might give rise to a liability in tort, they are binding on the Crown; see s. 22 of the Act. If a circular saw, as defined by these Regulations, is also a stationary machine as defined by the Agriculture (Stationary Machinery) Regulations 1959 the latter Regulations also apply (*ibid.*, reg 2(3)).

Citation, extent and commencement
1. These Regulations, which may be cited as the Agriculture (Circular Saws) Regulations 1959 shall apply to Great Britain *(a)* and shall come into operation as follows:—

    (a) this regulation and regulations 2 and 6 shall come into operation on the date of the making of these Regulations;

    (b) regulation 3 (in its application to paragraph 3 of the First Schedule to these regulations), regulation 4 (in its application to paragraph 9 of that Schedule) and regulation 5 shall come into operation six months after the making of these Regulations; and

    (c) regulation 3 (except in its application to the said paragraph 3) and regulation 4 (in its application to paragraph 8 of the said First Schedule) shall come into operation twelve months after the making of these Regulations.

General note. In sub-para (b), the words from the beginning to "and" where it first occurs and sub-para (c) are revoked by the Provision and Use of Work Equipment Regulations 1992, S.I. 1992 No. 2932, as from 1 January 1993 except, insofar as it applies to work equipment first provided for use in the premises or undertaking before 1 January 1993, it is revoked as from 1 January 1997.

    (a) **Great Britain.** See INTRODUCTORY NOTE 4.

Interpretation
2.—(1) In these Regulations—

    "the Act" means the Agriculture (Safety, Health and Welfare Provisions) Act 1956;

"agriculture", "worker", "employer" and "employed" having the meanings respectively assigned to them, as respects England and Wales, by subsection (1) of section 24 of *the Act*, and, as respects Scotland, by that subsection as applied by subsection (10) of section 25 of the Act;

"circular saw" means a machine intended for sawing wood by means of a circular blade, exceeding 300 millimetres in diameter, in a fixed or portable bench or frame, but does not include a swing or other saw which is operated by movement towards the wood.

(2) The Interpretation Act 1889 [Interpretation Act 1978] applies to the interpretation of these Regulations as it applies to the interpretation of an Act of Parliament.

Obligations affecting employers only
3. Subject to the provisions of these Regulations the *employer* of a *worker employed* in *agriculture* shall not cause *(a)* or permit a *worker* so *employed*, in the course of his employment, to operate or assist at a *circular saw* unless the requirements contained in Part I of the First Schedule to these Regulations are complied with.

General note. This regulation is revoked by the Provision and Use of Work Equipment Regulations 1992, S.I. 1992 No. 2932, as from 1 January 1993 except, insofar as it applies to work equipment first provided for use in the premises or undertaking before 1 January 1993, it is revoked as from 1 January 1997.

(a) **Cause.** See note *(a)* to reg. 3 of the Agriculture (Ladders) Regulations 1957.

Obligations affecting workers only
4. Subject to the provisions of these Regulations a *worker employed* in *agriculture* who, in the course of his employment, operates a *circular saw* shall comply with the requirements contained in Part II of the First Schedule to these Regulations.

Obligations affecting both employers and workers
5.—(1) Subject to the provisions of these Regulations—

(a) the *employer* of a *worker employed* in *agriculture* shall not cause *(a)* or permit a *worker* so *employed*, in the course of his employment, to operate, and
(b) a *worker* so *employed* shall not, in the course of his employment, operate,

a *circular saw* unless the requirements contained in Part III of the First Schedule to these Regulations are complied with, or in contravention of paragraph 1 of the Second Schedule to these Regulations.

(2) Subject to the provisions of these Regulations—

(a) the *employer* of a *worker employed* in *agriculture* shall not cause *(a)* or permit a *worker* so *employed*, in the course of his employment, to operate or assist at, and
(b) a *worker* so *employed* shall not, in he course of his employment, operate or assist at,

a *circular saw* in contravention of paragraphs 2 and 3 of the Second Schedule to these Regulations.

General note. In para (1), the words from "unless" to "or" are revoked by the Provision and Use of Work Equipment Regulations 1992, S.I. 1992 No. 2932, as from

1 January 1993 except, insofar as it applies to work equipment first provided for use in the premises or undertaking before 1 January 1993, it is revoked as from 1 January 1997.

  (a) **Cause.** See note (a) to reg. 3 of the Agriculture (Ladders) Regulations 1957.

Certificates of Exemption
6.—(1) Notwithstanding anything in these Regulations, the Health and Safety Executive may grant certificates exempting (for such periods as may be specified therein and subject to such conditions, if any, as may be so specified) particular cases or particular persons from the operation of the provisions of these Regulations, and where any such conditions are imposed, an *employer* of a *worker employed* in *agriculture*, and a *worker* so *employed*, to whom any such certificate applies shall comply with those conditions.

  (2) [*revoked*].

SCHEDULE 1

Regulation 3

  General note. This Schedule is revoked by the Provision and Use of Work Equipment Regulations 1992, S.I. 1992 No. 2932, as from 1 January 1993 except, insofar as it applies to work equipment first provided for use in the premises or undertaking before 1 January 1993, it is revoked as from 1 January 1997.

PART I
REQUIREMENTS AFFECTING EMPLOYERS ONLY

  1.   Construction and maintenance—Every *circular saw* shall be substantially constructed and properly maintained (a).

  (a) **Properly maintained.** See INTRODUCTORY NOTE 10.

  2.   Lighting.—At every *circular saw* there shall be adequate natural or artificial light.

  3.   Defective saw blades.—No saw blade shall knowingly be used if—
  (a) it is cracked;
  (b) it has been repaired by brazing or welding;
  (c) it has two or more teeth missing;
  (d) while in motion its teeth come in contact with the bench table, whether by reason of warping, misalignment or otherwise.

  4.   Riving knives.—In a direct line behind the saw blade, and in the same vertical place there shall be a metal riving knife having a smooth surface. The knife shall be strong and rigid, its front edge extending upward and forward, and shall also conform with the following conditions, that is to say—
  (a) the distance between the front edge of the knife and the teeth of the saw blade shall not exceed 12 millimetres at the level of the top surface of the bench table;
  (b) the knife shall extend upward from the bench table for a distance of not less than half and not more than the full height of the saw blade above the bench table.

  5.   Top guards.—(1) The cutting edge of the saw blade above the bench table shall be guarded by a guard which shall—
  (a) be rigid, not less than 25 millimetres wide measured horizontally, and as close to the edge of the saw blade as is practicable in the circumstances of use; and
  (b) extend forward from above the riving knife at least as far as to a point that is directly over the point at which the cutting edge of the saw blade passes below the level of the upper surface of the bench table.
  (2) So much of the guard as extends beyond the top of the saw blade shall, so far as it is not parallel to the bench table, slope or curve in a downward direction only.

6.   Bottom guards.—(1) The part of the saw blade below the bench table shall be guarded by two plates of metal or other suitable material, one on each side of the blade.

(2) Such plates shall not be more than 150 millimetres apart and shall extend from the axis of the saw blade outward to a distance of not less than 50 millimetres beyond the edge of the saw blade:

Provided that this paragraph shall not apply if the *circular saw* is so constructed and maintained as to afford no less protection against coming in contact with the saw blade from below the bench table than would require to be afforded under this paragraph.

7.   Special provision for circular saws with swinging tables.—(1) The provisions of this paragraph apply to a *circular saw* constructed with a swinging table, being a saw designed solely for cross-cutting.

(2) The cutting edge of the saw blade above the level of its axis shall be guarded by a guard which shall—

(a)   be rigid, not less than 25 millimetres wide measured horizontally, and as close to the edge of the saw blade as is practicable in the circumstances of use; and

(b)   extend upward and forward from the level of its axis to the top of the saw blade and thence at least as far as to a point that is directly over the point at which the cutting edge of the saw blade passes below the level of its axis.

(3) So much of any such guard as extends beyond the top of the saw blade shall, so far as it is not horizontal, slope or curve in a downward direction only.

(4) The part of the saw blade below the level of its axis shall be guarded by two plates of metal or other suitable material, one on each side of the blade.

(5) Such plates shall not be more than 150 millimetres apart and shall extend from the axis of the saw blade outward to a distance of not less than 50 millimetres beyond the edge of the saw blade:

Provided that the last foregoing sub-paragraph and this sub-paragraph shall not apply if the *circular saw* is so constructed and maintained as to afford no less protection against coming in contact with the saw blade below the level of its axis than would require to be afforded under this subparagraph.

(6) Paragraphs 4, 5 and 6 of this Schedule shall not apply to a circular saw of the kind mentioned in sub-paragraph (1) of this paragraph.

PART II
REQUIREMENTS AFFECTING WORKERS ONLY

Regulation 4

8.   Use of safety appliances.—Without prejudice to subsection (1) of section 13 of *the Act (a)* (which makes it an offence for a *worker* wilfully to interfere with, or misuse, any equipment, appliance, facilities or other thing provided in pursuance of the Act or regulations thereunder) a *worker* shall keep in position and shall make full use of every riving knife, guard, facility and other thing provided, which satisfies the requirements of this Schedule:

Provided that nothing in this paragraph shall prevent a worker from carrying out adjustments to a *circular saw* (including any riving knife or guard), while the saw blade is not in motion.

(a) Section 13. This provision is repealed. See now the Health and Safety at Work etc. Act 1974, s. 8.

9.   Defective saws.—(1) If any *circular saw* which a *worker* is *employed* to operate is or becomes defective within the meaning of this paragraph, any *worker employed* to operate the saw, shall on discovering that it is defective, forthwith report the fact to his *employer*.

(2) A *circular saw* is defective within the meaning of this paragraph if—

(a)   the saw blade is cracked, or two or more teeth thereof are missing;

(b)   the teeth of the saw blade while in motion come in contact with the bench table;

(c)   any riving knife or guard (of the respective kinds required under Part I of this Schedule) which has been fitted to a *circular saw* is damaged or missing.

(3) Nothing in this paragraph shall absolve an *employer* from complying with the requirements contained in Part I of this Schedule.

General note. The requirements contained in this Part must be explained to a worker before he operates or assists at a circular saw; see Sch. 2, para. 3.

PART III

REQUIREMENTS AFFECTING BOTH EMPLOYERS AND WORKERS

Regulation 5

10.   Floors.—The floor or ground area used by a *worker* operating a *circular saw* shall be unobstructed and shall afford him a firm foothold.

11.   Push-sticks, etc.—At every *circular saw* which is fed by hand a suitable push-stick or push-block of wood shall be used, whenever risk of injury can be thereby reduced.

12.   Prohibition of adjustments while saw blade is in motion.—No adjustment shall, while the saw blade is in motion, be made to any part of a *circular saw* (including any riving knife or guard) other than to any device fitted to the saw for determining the rate of feed or the width, depth or angle at which he wood is to be cut.

General note. The requirements contained in this Part must be explained to a worker before he operates or assists at a circular saw; see Sch. 2, para. 3.

SCHEDULE 2

Regulation 5

OTHER PROVISIONS AFFECTING BOTH EMPLOYERS AND WORKERS

1.   Instruction and supervision.—(1) A *worker* who has never operated a *circular saw* shall not operate a *circular saw* unless its working or the working of one of similar type has been demonstrated to him by a person over the age of eighteen years having a thorough knowledge of the working of the saw to be operated or of the working of one of similar type.

(2) Without prejudice to the generality of the foregoing sub-paragraph, a *worker* who has attained school-leaving age but has not attained the age of eighteen years shall not operate a *circular saw* except under the supervision of a person who—

(a)   has attained the age of eighteen years; and

(b)   has a knowledge of the working of the *circular saw* to be operated.

2.   Minimum age.—A *worker* shall not operate or assist at a *circular saw* unless he has attained school-leaving age.

3.   Explanation of regulations.—A *worker* shall not operate or assist at a *circular saw* unless the requirements contained in Parts II and III of the First Schedule and the provisions of paragraph 1 of this Schedule have first been explained to him.

(a) *Attained the age.* See note (a) to reg. 2 of the Agriculture (Avoidance of Accidents to Children) Regulations 1958.

THE AGRICULTURE (FIELD MACHINERY) REGULATIONS 1962

(S.I. 1962 No. 1472, as amended by S.I. 1976 No. 1247, S.I. 1981 No. 1414, S.I. 1989 No. 2311 and S.I. 1992 No. 2932

General note. A contravention of these Regulations is, by s. 1(6) of the Agriculture (Safety, Health and Welfare Provisions) Act 1956, an offence. These Regulations, in so far as they impose duties failure to comply with which might give rise to a liability in tort, are binding on the Crown; see s. 22 of that Act.

These Regulations apply to any machine designed or adapted for use in agriculture other than a machine designed or adapted for stationary use only (*ibid.*, reg. 2(1) and Sch. 1, para. 1(1)). As to stationary machines, see the Agriculture (Circular Saws) Regulations 1959, Agriculture (Stationary Machinery) Regulations, 1959, and the Agriculture (Threshers and Balers) Regulations 1960.

Citation, extent and commencement

1. These Regulations, which may be cited as the Agriculture (Field Machinery) Regulations 1962, shall apply to Great Britain (*a*) and shall come into operation as follows—

(a) this regulation, and regulations 2 and 5, shall come into operation on the date of the making of these Regulations (*b*);

(b) regulation 3 (in its application to paragraphs 14 and 15 of Part II of schedule 1 to these Regulations, and to Parts III, IV and V thereof) shall come into operation three months after the making of these Regulations;

(c) regulation 3 (in its application to the remainder of the said Part II) as respects *field machines* which are new, and paragraph (1) of regulation 4 of these Regulations shall come into operation on the 1 July 1964;

(d) regulation 3 (in its application to the remainder of the said Part II as aforesaid) as respects *field machines* which are not new, and paragraph (2) of regulation 4 of these Regulations, shall, in relation to machines of the several classes mentioned in the first column of Schedule 2 to these Regulations, come into operation on the dates respectively applicable to each such class shown in the second column of that Schedule.

(*a*) **Great Britain.** See INTRODUCTORY NOTE 4.

(*b*) **Date . . . regulations.** That is, 13 July 1962.

Interpretation

2.—(1) In these Regulations—

"the Act" means the Agriculture (Safety, Health and Welfare Provisions) Act 1956;

2127

"agriculture", "agricultural unit" and (subject to paragraphs (2) to (5) of regulation 3 of these Regulations) "worker", "employer" and "employed" have the meanings respectively assigned to them, as respects England and Wales *(a)*, by subsection (1) of section 24 of *the Act*, and, as respects Scotland, by that subsection as applied by subsection (10) of section 25 of *the Act*;

"field machine" has the meaning assigned to it in Part I of Schedule 1 to these Regulations.

(2) For the purposes of these Regulations—

(a) a *worker* works at a *field machine* if—
    (i) he drives, operates or assists in the operation of the *field machine*; or
    (ii) he is present at the site where the *field machine*, or any other machine operated in conjunction with such *field machine*, is being used and performs any task which is necessarily incidental to such use, and
(b) a *field machine* is new if the first sale of it, since its manufacture, to a purchaser for use by him in agriculture occurs on or after the 1 July 1964.

(3) Expressions used in Parts II, III, IV, and V of Schedule 1 to these Regulations of which there are definitions in Part I thereof have the meanings thereby respectively assigned to them.

(4) The Interpretation Act 1889 [Interpretation Act 1978] applies to the interpretation of these Regulations as it applies to the interpretation of an Act of Parliament.

(a) **England and Wales.** See INTRODUCTORY NOTE 4.

Obligations affecting employers, workers and others
3.—(1) Subject to the provisions of these Regulations—

(a) the *employer* of a *worker employed* in *agriculture* shall not cause *(a)* or permit him, in the course of his employment, to work at a *field machine (b)* unless the requirements contained in Part II of Schedule 1 to these Regulations, applicable to such *worker* in respect of such machine, are complied with;
(b) every *worker employed* in *agriculture* shall comply with the requirements contained in Part III of the said Schedule 1, and his *employer* shall not cause *(a)* or permit him to contravene any such requirement;
(c) a *worker employed* in *agriculture* who, in the course of his employment, works at a *field machine (b)* shall comply with the requirements contained in Part IV of the said Schedule 1 applicable to such *worker* in respect of such machine; and
(d) no person shall contravene any requirement contained in Part V of the said Schedule 1:

Provided that sub-paragraph (d) of this paragraph shall apply to persons other than *workers* only in so far as failure to comply with the requirements of the said Part V would expose a *worker* to risk of injury.

(2) Where a *worker employed* in *agriculture* works at a *field machine (a)* elsewhere than on an *agricultural unit* of which his *employer* is the occupier, the *worker* shall, while so working, be deemed for the purposes of these Regulations to be in the employment of the occupier of the *agricultural unit* on which the *field machine* is being used, or (in cases where paragraph (3) of this regulation applies) of the agricultural contractor to whom the *field machine* belongs.

(3) Where a *worker employed* in *agriculture* works at a *field machine (a)* belonging to an agricultural contractor, the *worker* shall, while so working, be deemed for the purposes of these Regulations to be in the employment of the agricultural contractor.

(4) For the purposes of these Regulations a *field machine* belongs to an agricultural contractor if he is the owner thereof, or if he has hired or borrowed it from the owner.

(5) Where by virtue of paragraphs (2) or (3) of this regulation any person is deemed to be the *employer* of a *worker employed in agriculture*, paragraph (1) of this regulation, in its application to *employers*, shall not apply to any person other than the person so deemed as aforesaid.

(a) **Cause.** See note *(a)* to reg. 3 of the Agriculture (Ladders) Regulations 1957.

(b) **Work at a field machine.** See, as to working at a field machine, the provisions of reg. 2(2)(a).

Prohibition of sale and letting on hire of non-complying field machines
4.—(1) No person shall sell to a purchaser, for use in *agriculture* in Great Britain *(a)*, any *field machine* that does not comply with the requirements contained in Part II of Schedule 1 to these Regulations (other than paragraph 15(1) thereo):
Provided that this paragraph shall not apply in respect of a *field machine* that has been previously been sold to a purchaser for use by him in *agriculture.*

(2) No person shall let on hire for use in *agriculture* in Great Britain *(a)* any *field machine* that does not comply with any of the requirements contained in the said Part II.

(3) For the purposes of this regulation a *field machine* which is the subject of a hire purchase contract shall be deemed to be sold and not to be let on hire.

(a) **Great Britain.** See INTRODUCTORY NOTE 4.

Certificate of exemption
5.—(1) Notwithstanding anything in these Regulations, the Health and Safety Executive may grant certificates exempting (for such periods as may be specified therein and subject to such conditions, if any, as may be so specified) particular cases or particular persons from the operation of the provisions of these Regulations, and where any such conditions are imposed, the *employer* of a *worker employed* in *agriculture* (including any person deemed by these Regulations to be an *employer*), and a *worker* so *employed*, to whom any such certificate applies, shall comply with those conditions.

(2) [*revoked*].

SCHEDULE 1

Regulation 2(3)

PART I
INTERPRETATION

1.—(1) In this Schedule the following expressions have the meanings hereby respectively assigned to them, that is to say—

"field machine" means any machine designed or adapted for use in *agriculture* other than a machine so designed or adapted for stationary use only, and includes a *power driven* handtool and (subject to paragraphs 11 and 13 of this Schedule) a trailer, but does not include a self-propelled road vehicle which is designed primarily for the carriage of persons or of loads, or an aircraft;

"ground wheel" means, in relation to a *field machine*, any wheel thereof which revolves in contact with the ground;

"manual" means by hand, foot or other bodily means, and "manually" has a corresponding meaning;

"pedestrian controlled", in relation to a *field machine*, means a *field machine* which can be operated only by a person on foot;

"power driven" means driven by any form of power other than that derived from a *ground wheel*;

"prime mover" means every engine, motor, or other appliance which provides mechanical energy to a *field machine*;

"pulley" includes a roller on which a belt is carried;

"safety device" means any thing required under this Schedule to be provided for a *worker's* safety;

"trailer" means a vehicle (whether or not fitted with machinery) designed or adapted to be towed, being a vehicle primarily intended for the carriage of loads.

(2) References in this Schedule to a *worker* operating a *field machine* include (except where the context otherwise requires) references to a *worker* assisting in the operation thereof, and references to a *worker* (or to any part of a *worker*) coming in contact with any part of a *field machine* shall be construed as references to his coming in contact therewith, either directly or by means of his clothes.

PART II

REQUIREMENTS APPLICABLE TO EMPLOYERS

Regulations 3(1)(a)

Components of field machines

2.—(1) Subject to the provisions of this paragraph every component of a *field machine*, being a component to which this paragraph applies, shall—

   (a) if the component is driven by any *ground wheel* of the machine, be so situated or so guarded that any *worker* who operates the machine, while in the normal operating position applicable to such *worker*, is protected from coming in contact with such component;

   (b) if the component is *power driven*, be so situated or so guarded that any *worker*, working at the machine, is protected from coming in contact with such component.

(2) The components to which this paragraph applies are—

   (a) in the case of every *field machine*, any shafting, *pulley*, flywheel, gearing, sprocket, belt *(a)* chain *(a)* or as respects any fan (in addition to any of the foregoing components) any wing or blade thereof; and

   (b) in the case of a *field machine* designed to perform a function by means of reciprocal action, (in addition to the components mentioned in sub-paragraph (a) hereof) the reciprocating parts of such a machine if they are so situated in relation to any other part of the machine as to expose the *worker* to risk of injury:

Provided that this paragraph shall not apply to—

   (i) so much of any such component as functions in contact with the soil;

  (ii) any axle of a *ground wheel*, or any component forming part of the track gear of a track laying tractor;

 (iii) any smooth pulley *(a)* or smooth flywheel (a);

 (iv) any reciprocating knife; or

  (v) any shaft to which the Agriculture (Power Takeoff) Regulations 1957 apply,

and, as respects belts and chains, shall have effect subject to the two next following sub-paragraphs.

(3) As respects a belt or chain (other than a conveyor belt or chain for the movement of materials) it shall be sufficient compliance with this paragraph, so far as the requirements thereof are met by guarding, if the belt or chain is guarded at its run-on points *(a)* and, in the case of a *field machine* designed for operation by a *worker* while on the machine, at every place where such a *worker* would (but for this provision) be exposed to risk of injury by such belt or chain; but this modification of requirements shall not apply where a belt or chain has fastenings which expose a *worker* to risk of injury.

(4) As respects a conveyor belt or chain for the movement of materials it shall be sufficient compliance with this paragraph, so far as the requirements thereof are met by guarding, if the belt or chain is guarded at its run-on points; but, if a *worker* is required to handle anything on such a belt or chain, or to work so close to it as to be exposed to risk of injury, the requirements of this paragraph shall be met only if the side of the belt or chain is so guarded, at every place where a *worker* is required to handle anything on the belt or chain, that the worker is protected from coming in contact with such side.

(5) In this paragraph "belt" includes any flexible material used to transmit power from one *pulley* to another; "chain" means any chain composed of links of metal or other non-flexible material used to transmit power from one sprocket to another; "run-on point" means the on-running point of contact of a belt with a *pulley*, or of a chain with a sprocket; and "smooth *pulley*" and "smooth flywheel" mean respectively a *pulley* or flywheel which has a continuous, unbroken and smooth surface between the centre and the rim, and has no protuberance which exposes a *worker* to risk of injury.

(6) The mention of particular guarding requirements in the two next following paragraphs shall be without prejudice to the application of this paragraph to any *field machine* to which either of those paragraphs applies.

General note. Paragraph 2 is revoked by the Provision and Use of Work Equipment Regulations 1992, S.I. 1992 No. 2932, as from 1 January 1993 except, insofar as it applies to work equipment first provided for use in the premises or undertaking before 1 January 1993, it is revoked as from 1 January 1997.

(a) Belt, chain; run-on point; smooth pulley; smooth flywheel. For the definition of these expressions in this paragraph, see sub-para. (5).

Guarding of operative parts of certain field machines
3.—(1) This paragraph applies to any *power driven field machine* which has rotating knives, tines, flails, or other parts similar thereto (in this paragraph referred to as "the operative parts") operating in or near the ground:
Provided that this paragraph shall not apply to—
 (i) a cylinder mower, haymaking machine, hedge cutter, potato spinner, root gapper or thinner, or to
 (ii) any *pedestrian controlled field machine* whose operative parts rotate in a vertical or near vertical plane.
(2) Every *field machine* to which this paragraph applies shall be fitted with a guard which—
 (a) covers operative parts of the machine being as near to such parts as practicable; and
 (b) fulfils the other conditions respectively applicable to such a machine set forth in the two next following sub-paragraphs.
(3) When the operative parts of the *field machine* rotate in a vertical or near vertical plane the said guard shall cover each end of the rotating assembly as well as the top thereof, and shall extend downwards so as to be near the ground as practicable.
(4) Where the operative parts of the *field machine* rotate in a horizontal or near horizontal plane the said guard shall, unless it extends downwards below the plane of the rotating assembly so as to be as near the ground as practicable, extend at least 300 millimetres beyond the periphery of such parts.

General note. Paragraph 3 is revoked by the Provision and Use of Work Equipment Regulations 1992, S.I. 1992 No. 2932, as from 1 January 1993 except, insofar as it applies to work equipment first provided for use in the premises or undertaking before 1 January 1993, it is revoked as from 1 January 1997.

Guarding of specific field machines

4.—(1) As respects every *power driven* potato spinner the digging reel thereof shall be guarded with a horizontal guard rail surrounding such reel, such guard rail being not less than 300 millimetres, measured horizontally from the reel, and not less than 600 millimetres, nor more than 920 millimetres from the ground; and, where such a potato spinner has a receiving reel, that reel also shall be guarded in like manner.

For the purpose of any of the said measurements a potato spinner shall be assumed to be in the operating position.

(2) Every chain saw designed or adapted for operation by one person, shall, unless it has a guard between the handle and the saw which protects the operator's hand from slipping off the handle on to the saw, be fitted with a rigid safety bar which extends above and along the back of the saw from the end nearer to the operator for at least 230 millimetres.

(3) As respects every chain saw designed or adapted for operation by more than one person, being a saw which requires for its operation that one person shall be stationed at each end, the whole of the back of the saw shall be guarded by a rigid safety bar.

(4) Every rotary hedge cutter shall be so guarded as to protect every *worker* working at it while in the normal operating position from injury by material ejected by or from its cutting parts.

(5) As respects every pick-up baler the pick-up shall be fitted with a rigid guard rail *(b)* which affords an adequate handhold *(c)* and which—

(a) extends for the whole width of the pick-up;

(b) is placed in such a position that when pick-up is in the operating position the guard rail is not less than 460 millimetres nor more than 1.05 metres from the ground; and

(c) is not less than 300 millimetres in front of the foremost evolving part of the pick-up.

General note. Paragraph 4 is revoked by the Provision and Use of Work Equipment Regulations 1992, S.I. 1992 No. 2932, as from 1 January 1993 except, insofar as it applies to work equipment first provided for use in the premises or undertaking before 1 January 1993, it is revoked as from 1 January 1997.

Cutter bars

5.—(1) Where a *field machine* is fitted with a cutter bar (not being a cutter bar having a reel over the fingers which extends to at least 300 millimetres in front thereof), the points of the fingers shall except when the cutter bar is in use be at all times completely and securely covered by a rigid guard.

(2) Without prejudice to the generality of the foregoing exception a cutter bar shall be deemed to be in use if it is undergoing repair or adjustment, or is being transported from one part of an *agricultural unit* to another in the course of a single agricultural operation.

General note. Paragraph 5 is revoked by the Provision and Use of Work Equipment Regulations 1992, S.I. 1992 No. 2932, as from 1 January 1993 except, insofar as it applies to work equipment first provided for use in the premises or undertaking before 1 January 1993, it is revoked as from 1 January 1997.

Stopping devices

6.—(1) Every *prime mover* shall be fitted with a device by means of which the *prime mover* may be quickly be stopped.

(2) The purpose and method of operation of every such device shall be clearly indicated.

(3) Every such device shall be so constructed and maintained that—

(a) it does not depend on sustained *manual* pressure for its operation; and

(b) when it is set at the "off" or "stop" position the *prime mover* is incapable of being re-started unless the device is *manually* re-set.

(4) Every such device shall be readily accessible—

(a) in the case of a self-propelled *field machine*, to the driver thereof at the normal driving position;

(b) in the case of a *field machine* which is *pedestrian controlled*, to the *worker* operating it at the normal control position;

(c) in the case of a *field machine* having its own *prime mover*, being a machine which is both towed and manned, as respects that *prime mover*, to at least one *worker* operating the machine at the normal operating position applicable to such *worker*, provided that this requirement shall not apply where there is readily accessible to at least one such *worker* at the said position a device by means of which the power from that *prime mover* may quickly be disconnected.

(5) In the case of a *field machine* having its own *prime mover* being a machine which is towed but is not manned, the stopping device required by this paragraph shall be as near as practicable to that *prime mover*.

(6) Without prejudice to subparagraph (1) of this paragraph, every self-propelled *field machine* (other than a machine which is *pedestrian controlled*) shall be fitted with a device, readily accessible to the driver of the machine at the normal driving position, by means of which the power from the *prime mover* may quickly be disconnected.

(7) Where a *field machine* is fitted with a clutch (other than a clutch which on release automatically returns to the engaged position) effective means shall be provided to secure the clutch in the disengaged position so that it is incapable of being re-engaged unless it is *manually* operated.

General note. Paragraph 6 is revoked by the Provision and Use of Work Equipment Regulations 1992, S.I. 1992 No. 2932, as from 1 January 1993 except, insofar as it applies to work equipment first provided for use in the premises or undertaking before 1 January 1993, it is revoked as from 1 January 1997.

Differential locks

7. Every *manually* operated device fitted to a self-propelled *field machine*, the function of which is to lock the differential gear of the mutually opposite driving wheels of such a machine, shall be so designed, fitted and maintained that the position of the controlling mechanism clearly indicates to the driver of the machine whether or not such gear is locked.

Valves and cocks

8. At every *manually* operated cock or valve provided for operating or isolating any part of the hydraulic or pneumatic system embodied in a *field machine* there shall be an indicator clearly showing the effect of movement of the valve or cock in any direction.

Drawbar jacks

9.—(1) Every *field machine* having a drawbar, being a machine to which this paragraph applies, shall be fitted with a jack capable of raising and lowering the drawbar.

(2) Every such jack shall be so constructed, and so secured to the *field machine*, as to prevent the drawbar from falling when the jack is in use.

(3) No such jack shall be removed from a *field machine* to which it is fitted except where removal is necessary for the operation of the machine, for repair or for replacement.

(4) This paragraph applies to any *field machine* having a drawbar, being a machine which is mounted on two wheels—

(a) in the case of a *trailer*, if its unladen weight is more than 500 kilograms;

(b) in the case of any other *field machine*, if, when the machine is unladen, the downward force exerted by the drawbar at the point of hitch is more than 250 newtons:

Provided that this paragraph shall not apply to a *field machine* if the drawbar is of a type that is designed exclusively for attachment otherwise than by *manual* means.

(5) For the purposes of this paragraph the downward force exerted by a drawbar shall be calculated on the basis that the *field machine* is at rest on level ground and that the drawbar is at a height of 410 millimetres therefrom.

Prohibition of use of pointed hooks and spikes

10. No pointed hook or spike shall be used, or form part of any device, for the attachment of a bag or other container to a *field machine*.

Standing platforms

11.—(1) Every *field machine* (other than a *trailer*) on which a *worker* may be required to stand while the machine is being operated shall be fitted with a platform which complies with sub-paragraph (2) of this paragraph.

(2) The said platform shall afford the *worker* adequate and flat standing space and a firm foothold, and shall be fitted at each side with—

(a) toe-boards, which shall be at the edge of the platform or not more than 50 millimetres outside it, and shall extend not less than 75 millimetres above the platform; and

(b) guard rails which shall be not less than 920 millimetres nor more than 1.05 metres above the platform:

Provided that—

(i) no toe-board or guard rail need be fitted to the platform—

(a) if the *field machine* itself affords no less protection to a *worker* against falling from the platform than would be afforded if a toe-board or guard rail (as the case may be) were fitted to the platform;

(b) at places on the platform where it is necessary to permit the access of persons or the movement of materials;

(c) in the case of a platform not being more than 600 millimetres from the ground, at any side thereof from which a *worker* would, if he fell, fall clear of the machine or anything attached thereto, and

(ii) in the case of a drill having a rear platform, it shall be sufficient compliance with this sub-paragraph if there is—

(a) in front of the *worker* operating the drill a hand-rail which is within his reach from any part of the platform, or behind such *worker* a guard rail; and

(b) a toe-board at the leading edge of the platform.

(3) In the case of every *field machine* (including a *trailer*) having a *ground wheel* which protrudes through or is adjacent to a platform, being a platform on which a *worker* may be required to stand while the machine is being operated, each such *ground wheel* shall be so guarded as to protect the *worker's* legs and feet from coming in contact with such a wheel whenever the *worker* is on the platform.

(4) Every *trailer* on which a *worker* may be required to stand while it is being operated shall, whenever it is attached to a pick-up baler, be fitted with—

(a) a toe-board, which shall be not less than 100 millimetres high at the leading edge of the trailer, and shall extend the whole width thereof; or

(b) a triangular drawbar, of which the side nearest to the trailer shall be not less than the width thereof, and which shall be so constucted and maintained (b) that the area contained by its three sides affords firm support for the *worker's* feet.

(5) In this paragraph references to toe-boards include references to other fitments serving the like purpose no less effectively, and references to *trailers* include references to bale or other sledges.

Seats and footrests

12.—(1) Every *field machine* on which a *worker* may be required to be seated while the machine is being operated shall be fitted with—

(a) a seat of adequate strength, being fitted with a back-rest, or otherwise so shaped, as to protect the *worker* against slipping from the seat; and

(b) adequate and convenient footrests being so constructed and placed in position as to protect a *worker's* feet from slipping and from thereby coming in contact with any moving part of the machine, including its *ground wheels* and track gear.

(2) Whenever a *ground wheel* or track gear of a *field machine* is adjacent to a seat or footrest (whether or not the seat or footrest is part of that or of another *field machine*), a

guard shall be fitted which shall protect the legs and feet of a *worker* seated on the *field machine* from coming in contact with such *ground wheel* or track gear.

Mounting devices

13.—(1) Every *field machine* to which this paragraph applies shall be fitted with a mounting device which shall afford to a *worker* working at the machine a safe and convenient means of mounting, and dismounting from it.

(2) This paragraph applies to any *field machine* in relation to which the mounting distance from the ground in order to reach the position where the *worker* is required to work exceeds 550 millimetres; but does not apply to a *trailer*.

(3) In this paragraph "mounting device" means the combination of a mounting step, not more than 550 millimetres from the ground, with a suitable handhold, being together designed as a means of mounting, and dismounting from, the machine, whether or not such step and handhold are designed exclusively for such purpose.

Towing devices

14.—(1) Whenever a *field machine* is used for *towing*, or is itself *towed*, the *towing device* shall be so constructed, fitted and maintained *(a)* as to be secure for the purpose; and without prejudice to the generality of such requirement where such device includes a coupling pin it shall be firmly secured in position.

(2) In this paragraph "towing device" means everything which directly or indirectly serves as the means of connection of the *field machine* to that which is towed or (as the case may be) is used for *towing*, "towing" includes propelling and winching, and "towed" has a corresponding meaning.

(3) Nothing in this paragraph shall render unlawful the use of a safety breakaway hitch in connection with a machine any of whose parts operate directly in the soil, which any such part is so operating.

(a) **Maintained.** See INTRODUCTORY NOTE 10.

Maintenance

15.—(1) Every *field machine*, including every part thereof, shall be so maintained *(a)* as to be safe, in relation to the time when the machine is in use, for a *worker* to use it.

(2) Every *safety device* with which a *field machine* is provided shall be of adequate strength *(b)* and shall be properly secured in position and maintained *(a)*.

General note. Paragraph 15 is revoked by the Provision and Use of Work Equipment Regulations 1992, S.I. 1992 No. 2932, as from 1 January 1993 except, insofar as it applies to work equipment first provided for use in the premises or undertaking before 1 January 1993, it is revoked as from 1 January 1997.

(a) **Maintained.** See INTRODUCTORY NOTE 10.

(b) **Adequate strength.** See note *(c)* to paragraph 5 of the Schedule to the Agriculture (Safeguarding of Workplaces) Regulations 1959, printed in this Part.

PART III

REQUIREMENTS AS RESPECTS WHICH BOTH EMPLOYERS AND WORKERS ARE RESPONSIBLE

Regulation 3(1)(a) and (b)

16.—(1) A *worker* shall not ride on the drawbar or other linkage of a *field machine*, or of any machine towed or propelled by a *field machine*, while the *field machine* is engaged in towing or propelling.

(2) A *worker* shall not mount, or, except in an emergency, dismount from, a self-propelled *field machine* while it is engaged in towing or propelling.

General note. Paragraph 16 is revoked by the Provision and Use of Work Equipment Regulations 1992, S.I. 1992 No. 2932, as from 1 January 1993 except, insofar as it applies to work equipment first provided for use in the premises or undertaking before 1 January 1993, it is revoked as from 1 January 1997.

PART IV
REQUIREMENTS APPLICABLE TO WORKERS
Regulation 3(1)(c)

Use of safety appliances

17.—(1) Subject to the provisions of this paragraph, and without prejudice to subsection (1) of section 13 *(a)* of *the Act* (which makes it an offence for a worker wilfully to interfere with, or misuse, any equipment, appliance, facilities or other thing provided in pursuance of *the Act* or regulations thereunder), a *worker* shall keep in position and shall make full use of every *safety device* which satisfies the requirements of this Schedule:

Provided that if any part of a *field machine* required to be guarded is not in motion, the guard may be removed therefrom by a *worker* who has attained school-leaving age for so long only as is necessary—

(a) for the cleaning, repair or adjustment of such part while it is not in motion;

(b) for carrying out any essential adjustment to such part while it is in motion, being an adjustment which cannot otherwise be carried out.

(2) Nothing in the last foregoing sub-paragraph shall prevent a guard from being temporarily removed from a *prime mover* by a *worker* who has attained school-leaving age if its removal is necessary in order to start the *prime mover* by hand.

General note. Paragraph 17 is revoked by the Provision and Use of Work Equipment Regulations 1992, S.I. 1992 No. 2932, as from 1 January 1993 except, insofar as it applies to work equipment first provided for use in the premises or undertaking before 1 January 1993, it is revoked as from 1 January 1997.

(a) Section 13. This provision is repealed. See, now, the Health and Safety at Work etc. Act 1974, s. 8.

Damaged safety devices

18.—(1) If any *safety device* is or becomes damaged or defective, any *worker* employed to operate any *field machine* to which such a device has been fitted shall, on discovering that the device is damaged or defective, forthwith report the fact to his *employer*, or, in cases where for the purposes of these Regulations some other person is deemed to be his *employer*, to that person.

(2) Nothing in this paragraph shall absolve an *employer*, or a person deemed for the purposes of these Regulations to be an *employer*, from complying with the requirements contained in Part II of this Schedule.

General note. Paragraph 18 is revoked by the Provision and Use of Work Equipment Regulations 1992, S.I. 1992 No. 2932, as from 1 January 1993 except, insofar as it applies to work equipment first provided for use in the premises or undertaking before 1 January 1993, it is revoked as from 1 January 1997.

PART V
REQUIREMENTS APPLICABLE TO EMPLOYERS, WORKERS AND
OTHERS
Regulation 3(1)(d)

19.—(1) No person shall set a self-propelled *field machine* in motion over the ground except from the driving position thereof.

(2) No person shall, except in an emergency, leave the driving position of a self-propelled *field machine* while it is in motion over the ground.

(3) This paragraph, in its application to *field machines* which are remotely controlled, shall have effect as if for the references to the driving position there were substituted references to the place at which the remote controls are operated.

General note. Paragraph 19 is revoked by the Provision and Use of Work Equipment Regulations 1992, S.I. 1992 No. 2932, as from 1 January 1993 except, insofar as it applies to work equipment first provided for use in the premises or undertaking before 1 January 1993, it is revoked as from 1 January 1997.

SCHEDULE 2

Regulation 1(d)

Class of field machine	Date of coming into operation
Class I Bale sledges. Corn and seed drills (including combined corn and fertiliser drills). Farmyard manure spreaders. Lime and fertiliser distributors. Liquid manure distributors. Loaders and elevators, whether or not tractor mounted. Potato planters. Rotary cultivators and hoes. Seedling transplanters.	1 July 1964
Class II Binders. Combine harvesters, whether self-propelled or tractor drawn. Pea and bean harvesters. Pick-up balers. Windrowers.	1 January 1965.
Class III *Pedestrian controlled field machines.* *Power driven* handtools. Tractors.	1 January 1966.
Class IV Forage harvesters. Haulm pulverisers. Hedge cutters. Mowers. Potato elevator diggers. Potato harvesters. Potato spinners. Root gappers and thinners. Root harvesters, savers and toppers. Rotary cutters and slashers. Sprayers and dusters.	1 January 1967.
Class V *Field machines* not included in Classes I to IV of this Schedule.	1 January 1968.

THE AGRICULTURE (LADDERS) REGULATIONS 1957

(S.I. 1957 No. 1385, as amended by S.I. 1981 No. 1414)

General note. These Regulations give effect to the general provisions of s. 1 of the Agriculture (Safety, Health and Welfare Provisions) Act 1956, and in particular to the provisions of sub-s. (3)(f) thereof. A contravention of the Regulations is, by s. 1(6) of that Act, an offence. These Regulations are, in so far as they impose failure to comply with which might give rise to a liability in tort, binding upon the Crown; see *ibid.*, s. 22.

Citation, extent and commencement
1. These Regulations, which may be cited as the Agriculture (Ladders) Regulations 1957 shall apply to Great Britain *(a)* and shall come into operation three months after the making thereof.

(a) **Great Britain.** See INTRODUCTORY NOTE 4.

Interpretation
2.—(1) In these Regulations—
"agriculture", "agriculture unit", "worker", "employer" and "employed" have the meanings respectively assigned to them, as respects England and Wales *(a)* by subsection (1) of section 24 of the Agriculture (Safety, Health and Welfare Provisions) Act 1956 and, as respects, Scotland, by that subsection as applied by subsection (10) of section 25 of that Act;
"ladder" does not include a permanently fixed *ladder*, or a *ladder* made of rope or other non-rigid materal, but save as aforesaid includes every kind of *ladder* (including *steps* and a *trestle-ladder*), whether made of wood, metal or other material;
"rung" means the rail or tread, serving as a step, set into the stiles of a *ladder;*
"steps" means a *ladder* (other than a *trestle-ladder*) provided with a means of self-support;
"stile" means the side-rail of a *ladder* into which the *rungs* are fitted;
"tie-rod" means a metal rod, extending through both *stiles*, which is so secured as to prevent the *stiles* moving apart;
"trestle-ladder" means a *ladder* made of two frames hinged together at the top, both being fitted with *rungs*.

(2) The Interpretation Act 1889 [Interpretation Act 1978] applies to the interpretation of these Regulations as it applies to the interpretation of an Act of Parliament.

(a) *England and Wales.* See INTRODUCTORY NOTE 4.

Obligations on employer only
3.—(1) The *employer* of a *worker employed* in *agriculture* shall not cause *(a)* or permit to be used by any *worker* so *employed*, in the course of his employment, any *ladder* unless it is of good construction and sound material, and is properly maintained *(b)*.

(2) Without prejudice to the generality of the foregoing paragraph a *ladder* shall not be regarded as complying therewith if—

(a) where a *ladder* has wooden *stiles* or *rungs*, the grain thereof does not run lengthwise, or either *stile* ot any *rung* contains any defect to weaken it which reasonable examination would disclose;
(b) where a *ladder* has wooden *stiles*, any *rung* of the *ladder* is supported solely by nails or screws;
(c) where a *ladder* has wooden *rungs*, the *rungs* are not fixed into the *stiles* by rabbet, notch or mortise, and (unless *tie-rods* are fitted not more than 610 millimetes from each end of the *ladder* and not more than 2.44 metres apart throughout its length) are not through-tenoned and wedged in the *stiles*;
(d) in the case of *steps* or a *trestle-ladder*, it is not fitted with a device that is effective, in the circumstances in which it is used, in preventing the back support from spreading;
(e) (except in the case of a *trestle-ladder*) the distance between adjacent *rungs* exceeds 305 millimetres from centre to centre.

(a) **Cause.** In *McLeod (or Houston) v Buchanan* [1940] 2 All ER 179, at 187, HL, Lord Wright said: "To 'cause' . . . involves some express or positive mandate from the person 'causing' to the other person, or some authority from the former to the latter, arising in the circumstances of the case." See also, in particular, *Kirkheaton District Local Board v Ainely Sons & Co* [1892] 2 QB 274, CA; *Shave v Rosner* [1954] 2 QB 113, [1954] 2 All ER 280; *Lovelace v DPP* [1954] 3 All ER 481, [1954] 1 WLR 1468 and *Ellis v Smith* [1962] 3 All ER 954, [1962] 1 WLR 1486.

(b) **Good construction . . . maintained.** Compare the cognate provisions of s. 28(5) of the Factories Act 1961, and of reg. 31 of the Construction (Working Places) Regulations 1966. For "properly maintained" see INTRODUCTORY NOTE 10.

Obligations on both employer and worker
4.—(1) Subject to the provisions of this regulation the *employer* of a *worker* in *agriculture* shall not cause *(a)* or permit to be used by any *worker* so *employed*, in the course of his employment, and a *worker employed* in *agriculture* shall not, in the course of his employment, use any *ladder* if—

(a) it is not strong enough for the purposes and manner of its use;
(b) any *rung* is missing;
(c) it is not equally supported on each *stile*, is not securely placed or held in position;
(d) the top of the *ladder* does not extend above any point at which it is necessary for the *worker* to get on or off the *ladder*.

(2) Sub-paragraph (d) of paragraph (1) of this regulation shall not apply—

(a)   to *steps* and *trestle-ladders*; or

(b)   if there is available to the *worker*, apart from the *ladder* itself, some means of secure hand-hold.

(a) **Cause.** See note (a) to reg. 3.

Reporting by workers of defects

5.—(1)   If any *ladder*, with which a *worker employed* in *agriculture* is *employed* to work, develops a defect to which this regulation applies, any such *worker employed* to work with that *ladder* on discovering that defect, shall forthwith report it to his *employer.*

(2)   The defects to which this regulation applies re—

(a)   the absence of any *rung*;

(b)   the cracking or breaking of any wooden *stile* or *rung*; and

(c)   in the case of *steps* or a *trestle-ladder* the absence or breaking of any stop or cord with which such a *ladder* was designed to be operated.

(3)   Nothing in this regulation shall absolve an *employee* from compliance with regulation 3, or an *employer* or *worker* from compliance with regulation 4, of these Regulations.

THE AGRICULTURE
(POWER TAKE-OFF)
REGULATIONS 1957

(S.I. 1957 No. 1386, as amended by S.I. 1976 No. 1247, S.I. 1981 No. 1414 and S.I. 1991 No. 1913)

General note. These Regulations are revoked by the Provision and Use of Work Equipment Regulations 1992, S.I. 1992 No. 2932, as from 1 January 1993 except, insofar as they apply to work equipment first provided for use in the premises or undertaking before 1 January 1993, they are revoked as from 1 January 1997.

These Regulations give effect to the general provisions of s. 1 of the Agriculture (Safety, Health and Welfare Provisions) Act 1956. A contravention of the Regulations is, by s. 1(6) of the Act, an offence. These Regulations, in so far as they impose duties failure to comply with which might give rise to a liability in tort, are binding on the Crown; see s. 22 of the Act.

Citation, extent and commencement
1. These Regulations, which may be cited as the Agriculture (Power Take-off) Regulations 1957, shall apply to Great Britain *(a)* and shall come into operation as follows—

(a) regulation 3 hereof (which relates to the guarding of the power take-off of a tractor) shall come into operation on the 1st day of August, 1958:
Provided that in relation to any tractor that is not new on that data and is not designed by its manufacturer to have attached to it a shield of the kind referred to in that regulation, the said regulation shall not come into operation until the 1st day of August, 1959;

(b) regulation 4 hereof (which relates to the guarding of the power take-off shaft of other machinery) shall come into operation on the 1st day of February, 1959;
Provided that in relation to any machine that is not new on that date, the said regulation shall not come into operation until the 1st day of August, 1959; and

(c) the remainder of the regulations shall come into operation on the date on which they are made.

(a) **Great Britain.** See INTRODUCTORY NOTE 4.

Interpretation
2.—(1) In these Regulations—

"Agriculture", "agricultural unit", "worker", "employer" and "employed" have the meanings respectively assigned to them, as respects England and Wales *(a)* by subsection (1) of section 24 of the Agriculture (Safety, Health and Welfare Provisions) Act 1956, and, as respects Scotland, by that subsection as applied by subsection (10) of section 25 of that Act;

"power take-off" means the splined shaft of any tractor intended for transmitting power to any machine by means of the *power take-off shaft* of that machine;

"power take-off shaft" means, as respects any machine, its shaft (including any couplings and clutches up to the first fixed bearing of the machine) intended for attachment to the *power take-off* of any tractor.

(2) Any vehicle having a splined shaft intended for transmitting power to any machine by means of the *power take-off shaft* of that machine shall be deemed to be a tractor for the purposes of these Regulations.

(3) A tractor or machine is new for the purposes of these regulations if it has never been used since manufacture, or has only been used for test or demonstration.

(4) The Interpretation Act 1889 [Interpretation Act 1978] applies to the interpretation of these Regulations as it applies to the interpretation of an Act of Parliament.

(a) **England and Wales.** See INTRODUCTORY NOTE 4.

Guarding of power take-off
3.—(1) Subject to paragraph (3) of this regulation, the *employer* of a *worker employed* in *agriculture* shall not cause (a) or permit to be used on an *agricultural unit* on which such a *worker* is *employed*, and a *worker employed* in *agriculture* shall not use, any *tractor* having a *power take-off*, while the engine is in motion unless—

    (a) the *power take-off* is guarded by a shield so designed, and so attached to the tractor, that it protects a *worker* from coming in contact, from above or from either side, either directly of by means of his clothes, with the *power take-off* of that *tractor*, or

    (b) the *power take-off* is not in use, and is completely enclosed by a cover so attached to the tractor that contact with any part of the *power take-off* is impossible.

(2) Every shield and cover required by this regulation shall be substantially constructed of metal or other material, and shall be capable when attached to a tractor of supporting a weight of not less than 120 kilograms.

(3) Nothing in paragraph (1) of this regulation shall apply to a tractor of a type in respect of which EEC type-approval has been granted with regard to its *power take-off* and the protection of that *power take-off* in accordance with—

    (a) Council Directive 74/150/EEC relating to the type-approval of wheeled agricultural or forestry tractors, as amended by Council Directive 79/694/EEC, Council Directive 82/890/EEC, Council Directive 88/297/EEC and the Act concerning the conditions of accession of the Kingdom of Spain and the Portuguese Republic and the adjustments to the Treaties which forms part of the Treaty concerning the accession of the Kingdom of Spain and the Portuguese Republic to The European Economic Community and to the European Atomic Energy Community, signed at Lisbon and Madrid on 12th June 1985; and

    (b) Council Directive 86/297/EEC relating to the *power take-offs* of wheeled agricultural and forestry tractors and their protection.

General note. Subsection (3) was added by S.I. 1991 No. 1913.

(a) **Cause.** See note (a) to reg. 3 of the Agriculture (Ladders) Regulations 1957.

Guarding of power take-off shaft
4.—(1) Subject to the provisions of this regulation, the *employer* of a *worker employed* in *agriculture* shall not cause (a) or permit to be used on an *agricultural unit* on which such a *worker* is *employed*, and a *worker employed* in *agriculture* shall not use, any machine having a *power take-off shaft* unless—

(a)   the entire length of the shaft, whilst in motion, is wholly enclosed in a guard so designed, and so attached to the machine, that it protects a *worker* from coming in contact, either directly or by means of his clothes, with any part of the *power take-off shaft* of that machine, or
(b)   in the case of a machine which is not new on the coming into operation of this regulation, and in respect of which the distance between any part of its *power take-off shaft* and the ground does not exceed 600 millimetres, the entire length of the shaft, whilst in motion, is either wholly enclosed as aforesaid, or is partly enclosed in the manner described in paragraph (2) of this regulation.

(2) A *power take-off shaft* is partly enclosed for the purpose of sub-paragraph (b) of paragraph (1) of this regulation if the shaft is provided with a guard over its entire length on top and on both sides to a depth of at least 50 millimetres (measured at right angles to the shaft) below the lowest point of its circumference.

(3) Paragraph (1) of this regulation shall not apply to a machine that is so constructed and maintained as to afford no less protection against coming in contact with the *power take-off shaft* of the machine than would require to be afforded under the said paragraph (1):
Provided that where a machine is so constructed and maintained as to afford such measure of protection as aforesaid in respect of only a part of the *power take-off shaft* of the machine, the said paragraph (1) shall apply to that machine in respect of any part of the shaft as to which such protection is not so afforded.

(4) Every guard required by this regulation shall be substantially constructed, and shall be maintained (b) in good condition.

(a) **Cause.** See note (a) to reg. 3 of the Agriculture (Ladders) Regulations 1957.

(b) **Maintained.** See INTRODUCTORY NOTE 10.

Certificates of exemption
5.—(1) Notwithstanding anything in these Regulations, the Health and Safety Executive may grant certificates exempting (for such periods as may be speci-

fied therein and subject to such conditions, if any, as may be so specified) particular cases or particular persons from the operation of the provisions of these Regulations, and where any such conditions are imposed, an *employer* of a *worker employed* in *agriculture*, and a *worker* so *employed*, to whom any such certificate applies shall comply with those conditions.

THE AGRICULTURE (SAFEGUARDING OF WORKPLACES) REGULATIONS 1959

(S.I. 1959 No. 428 as amended by S.I. 1976 No. 1247 and S.I. 1981 No. 1414)

General note. These Regulations give effect to the general provisions of s. 1 of the Agriculture (Safety, Health and Welfare Provisions) Act 1956. A contravention of the Regulations is, by s. 1(6) of the Act, an offence. In so far as they impose duties failure to comply with which might give rise to a liability in tort, the Regulations are binding on the Crown; see s. 22 of the Act.

Citation, extent and commencement
1. These Regulations, which may be cited as the Agriculture (Safeguarding of Workplaces) Regulations 1959, shall apply to Great Britain *(a)* and shall come into operation on the 1st day of April, 1961.

(a) **Great Britain.** See INTRODUCTORY NOTE 4.

Interpretation
2.—(1) In these Regulations—

"the Act" means the Agriculture (Safety, Health and Welfare Provisions) Act 1956; and

"agriculture", "agricultural unit", "workers", "employer" and "employed" have meanings respectively assigned to them, as respects England and Wales *(a)*, by subsection (1) of section 24 of the Act, and, as respects Scotland, by that subsection as applied by subsection (10) of section 25 of the Act.

(2) Expressions used in Parts II and III of the Schedule to these Regulations of which there are definitions in Part I thereof have the meanings thereby respectively assigned to them.

(3) The Interpretation Act 1889 [Interpretation Act 1978] applies to the interpretation of these Regulations as it applies to the interpretation of an Act of Parliament.

(a) **England and Wales.** See INTRODUCTORY NOTE 4.

Obligations applicable to employers and occupiers
3.—(1) Subject to the provisions of these Regulations—

(a) the *employer* of a *worker employed* in *agriculture* to work on an *agricultural unit* of which the *employer* is the occupier, and

(b) the occupier of an *agricultural unit* on which a *worker employed* in *agriculture* is employed to work by an *employer* other than the occupier of that unit,

shall not cause *(a)* or permit a *worker* so *employed*, in the course of his employment, to work at or to use any place on that unit unless the requirements applicable to such a place contained in Part II of the Schedule to these Regulations are complied with.

(2) This regulation shall not apply in respect of a *worker* while working on the construction, alteration or maintenance of a building *(b)*.

(a) **Cause.** See note *(a)* to reg. 3 of the Agriculture (Ladders) Regulations 1957, printed in this Part.

(b) **Construction, etc. of a building.** These terms have been judicially interpreted as they occur in s. 176 of the Factories Act 1961; for this interpretation, see the notes thereto.

Obligations applicable to workers
4.—(1) Subject to the provisions of these Regulations a *worker employed* in *agriculture* to work on an *agricultural unit* shall comply with the requirements contained in Part III of the Schedule to these Regulations.

(2) This regulation shall not apply in respect of a *worker* while working on the construction, alteration or maintenance of a building *(a)*.

(a) **Construction, etc. of a building.** See note *(b)* to reg. 3.

Certificate of exemption
5.—(1) Notwithstanding anything in these Regulations, the Health and Safety Executive may grant certificates exempting (for such periods as may be specified therein and subject to such conditions, if any, as may be so specified) particular cases or particular persons from the operation of the provisions of these Regulations, and where any such conditions are imposed, the *employer* of a *worker employed* in *agriculture*, and a *worker* so *employed*, to whom any such certificate applies shall comply with these conditions.

(2) [*revoked*].

SCHEDULE

PART I

Regulation 2(2)

Interpretation
In this Schedule—

"cover" includes a grid which affords a worker no less protection against falling than would be afforded by a cover other than a grid;

"floor" means any structural surface within a building, or forming part of a building, on which a *worker* has to work, or over or across which he has to pass in connection with his work, but does not include any part of a *stairway*;

"stairway" means a permanent staircase or a permanently fixed ladder being a staircase or ladder which is either within a building or gives access to a building or to a part of a building; and

"step" means, in relation to any *stairway*, any tread or rung thereof.

PART II
REQUIREMENTS APPLICABLE TO EMPLOYERS (OR, IN CERTAIN CASES, TO OCCUPIERS)
Regulation 3

1. General. Every *stairway* and every *floor* shall be as safe as is reasonably practicable *(a)* for the purposes for which it is used.

(a) Reasonably practicable. See INTRODUCTORY NOTE 5.

2. Construction and maintenance of stairways.—(1) No *step* of a *stairway* shall depend for its support on being secured solely by nails, screws or other similar fixing: Provided that nothing in this sub-paragraph shall prevent the *steps* of a *stairway* from being supported by brackets or bearers which are secured in such a manner.

(2) No *stairway* shall have any *step* missing or any defect likely to weaken the *stairway* which reasonable examination would disclose.

3. Handrails for certain stairways.—(1) Subject to the provisions of this paragraph every *stairway* shall be fitted with a handrail *(a)* or handrails.

(2) If a *stairway* has an open side the handrail shall be on that side; if the *stairway* has two open sides there shall be a handrail on each side; if there is no open side the handrail may be on either side.

(3) Every handrail fitted in accordance with the foregoing provisions of this paragraph—

(a) shall be of wood, metal or other suitable material, and shall be smooth and rigid;
(b) shall be of adequate strength and shall be securely fixed in position; and
(c) shall extend the whole length of the *stairway*:
    Provided that if it is impossible for a handrail to extend the whole length of the *stairway* without obstructing access thereto the handrail need not extend so as to obstruct access to the *stairway*.

(4) This paragraph shall not apply to a *stairway*—
(a) which extends less than 920 millimetres measured vertically from the ground, or floor level, on which the bottom of the stairway rests; or
(b) to which paragraph 4 of this Schedule applies.

(a) Handrail. A handrail is quite different from a guardrail. A guardrail is one of such a character as will provide a physical barrier against a person falling over the side which is guarded. A handrail is a rail which can be gripped by the hand; it need not necessarily act as a physical barrier; it need only be such a rail as to enable any person, by gripping it, to steady himself against falling (*Corn v Weir's Glass (Hanley) Ltd* [1960] 2 All ER 300, [1960] 1 WLR 577, CA, so interpreting the cognate provisions of reg. 27 of the Building (Safety, Health and Welfare) Regulations 1948 (now spent)).

4. Special provision for steep stairways.—(1) This paragraph applies to a *stairway* which is at an angle of 30 degrees or less from the vertical.

(2) Every *stairway* to which this paragraph applies shall be provided with a secure handhold *(a)* for use by a *worker* at the highest point at which he has to get on or off the

stairway; whether by extension of at least one stile for not less than 920 millimetres above such point or by some other means.

(a) Handhold. The mere fact that a person falls from a stairway does not demonstrate the absence of a secure handhold (*Wigley v British Vinegars Ltd* [1964] AC 307, [1962] 3 All ER 161, HL, a case upon what is now s. 29(2) of the Factories Act 1961).

5.   Apertures in floors and walls, and edges of floors.—(1) Subject to the provisions of this paragraph, every aperture in a *floor (a)*, being an aperture through which a *worker* is liable to fall more than 1.5 metres, shall be guarded by—

(a) a *cover*; or

(b) a fence not less than 920 millimetres high; or

(c) a guard rail *(b)* not less than 920 millimetres nor more than 1.05 metres above the level of the floor.

(2) Subject to the provisions of this paragraph, every edge of a *floor*, being an edge of a *floor* from which a *worker* is liable to fall more than 1.5 metres, shall be guarded by—

(a) a fence not less than 920 millimetres high; or

(b) a guard rail *(b)* not less than 920 millimetres nor more than 1.05 metres above the level of the *floor*.

Provided that this sub-paragraph shall not apply where a *floor* terminates at an aperture in a wall.

(3) Subject to the provisions of this paragraph, every aperture in a wall in a building, being an aperture through which a *worker* is liable to fall more than 1.5 metres, shall be guarded by—

(a) a door or fence not less than 920 millimetres high; or

(b) a guard rail *(b)* not less than 920 millimetres nor more than 1.05 metres above the level of the *floor*.

Provided that this sub-paragraph shall not apply if—

(i) the height of the aperture from top to bottom does not exceed 1.2 metres; or

(ii) the bottom of the aperture is more than 600 millimetres above the *floor*.

(4) Every *cover*, door, fence or guard rail *(b)* fitted in accordance with the foregoing provisions of this paragraph shall be of adequate strength *(c)*; shall (except as provided by sub-paragraph (6) of this paragraph) be securely fixed in position, or, in the case of any door, shall be kept shut; and shall be properly maintained *(d)*.

(5) Every guard rail *(b)* shall be so fitted that it is not outside a line plumb with the edge of the aperture or of the *floor* to be guarded:

Provided that a guard rail may be fitted not more than 250 millimetres outside such a line if there is also fitted within a distance of 250 millimetres an intermediate rail which is not less than 460 millimetres nor more than 530 millimetres above the level of the floor.

(6) No *cover* or door fitted in accordance with the foregoing provisions of this paragraph shall be opened or removed, and no fence or guard rail *(b)* so fitted shall be removed—

(a) except for the time and to the extent necessary for the access of persons or the movement of materials; and

(b) unless there is a secure handhold *(e)* available for use when the *cover*, fence or guard rail is not in position, or, as the case may be, the door is open (so, however, that a handhold shall not be necessary where the cover consists of a self-closing trap door).

(7) This paragraph shall not apply to an aperture, or to an edge of a *floor*, used as access to a stairway.

(a) Aperture in a floor. See the cognate provisions of s. 28(4) of the Factories Act 1961 and note *(a)* thereto.

(b) Guard rail. See note *(a)* to paragraph 3.

(c) Adequate strength. Whether plant or equipment is of adequate strength must be judged with regard to the use to which it is being put at the relevant time; *Milne v C F Wilson & Co (1932) Ltd* 1960 SLT 162; *Ball v Richard Thomas & Baldwins Ltd* [1968] 1 All ER 389, [1968] 1 WLR 192, CA.

(d) **Properly maintained.** See INTRODUCTORY NOTE 10.

(e) **Handhold.** See note *(a)* to paragraph 4.

6. Grain pits, stokeholds and furnace pits.—(1) Every grain pit, stokehold or furnace pit into which a *worker* is liable to fall more than 1.5 metres shall be guarded by—

(a) a *cover*; or

(b) a fence not less than 920 millimetres; or

(c) a guard rail *(a)* not less than 920 millimetres nor more than 1.05 metres above the level of the ground.

(2) Every *cover*, fence or guard rail *(a)* fitted in accordance with the foregoing provisions of this paragraph shall be of adequate strength *(b)*; shall (except as provided by sub-paragraph (4) of this paragraph) be securely fixed in position; and shall be properly maintained *(c)*.

(3) Every guard rail *(a)* shall be so fitted that it is not outside a line plumb with the edge of the grain pit, stokehold or furnace pit to be guarded.

(4) No *cover*, fence, or guard rail *(a)* shall be opened or removed except for the time and to the extent necessary for the access of persons or the movement of materials.

(a) **Guard rail.** See note *(a)* to paragraph 3.

(b) **Adequate strength.** See note *(c)* to paragraph 5.

(c) **Properly maintained.** See INTRODUCTORY NOTE 10.

PART III
REQUIREMENTS APPLICABLE TO WORKERS
Regulation 4

7. Non-removal of safety appliances. Without prejudice to subsection (1) of section 13 of *the Act (a)* (which makes it an offence for a *worker* wilfully to interfere with, or misuse, any equipment, appliance, facilities or other thing provided in pursuance of the Act or regulations, thereunder) a *worker* shall not open or remove any *cover* or door, fence or guard rail *(b)*, except as permitted under Part II of this Schedule.

(a) **Section 13.** This provision is repealed. See, now, the Health and Safety at Work etc. Act 1974, s. 8.

(b) **Guard rail.** See note *(b)* to para. 5.

8. Reporting of defects.—(1) Subject to the provisions of this paragraph if—

(a) any *step* of a *stairway*, or

(b) any handrail, *cover*, fence or guard rail *(a)* (of the respective kinds required under Part II of this Schedule) which has been fitted to anything which has to be guarded in accordance with Part II of this Schedule,

is or becomes defective within the meaning of this paragraph, any *worker* who has to use that *stairway*, or (as the case may be) has to work where such *cover*, fence or guard rail is fitted, shall on discovering that it is defective, forthwith report the fact to his *employer*.

(2) A *step* of a *stairway* is defective within the meaning of this paragraph if it is missing or broken.

(3) A handrail, *cover*, fence or guard rail *(a)* is defective within the meaning of this paragraph if it is broken.

(4) This paragraph shall not apply to a *worker* whose *employer* is not the occupier of the *agricultural unit* on which the *worker* is *employed* to work.

(5) Nothing in this paragraph shall absolve an *employer* from complying with the requirements contained in Part II of this Schedule.

(a) **Guard rail.** See note *(b)* to paragraph 5.

THE AGRICULTURE (STATIONARY MACHINERY) REGULATIONS 1959

(S.I. 1959 No. 1216, as amended by S.I. 1976 No. 1247,
S.I. 1981 No. 1414 and S.I. 1989 No. 2311)

General note. These Regulations are revoked by the Provision and Use of Work Equipment Regulations 1992, S.I. 1992 No. 2932, as from 1 January 1993 except, insofar as they apply to work equipment first provided for use in the premises or undertaking before 1 January 1993, they are revoked as from 1 January 1997.

A contravention of these Regulations is, by s. 1(6) of the Agriculture (Safety, Health and Welfare Provisions) Act 1956, an offence. These Regulations, in so far as they impose duties failure to comply with which might give rise to a liability in tort, are binding upon the Crown; see s. 22 of that Act.

Citation, extent and commencement

1. These Regulaions, which may be cited as the Agriculture (Stationary Machinery) Regulations 1959, shall apply to Great Britain *(a)* and shall come into operation as follows—

(a) this regulation and regulations 2 and 5 shall come into operation on the date of the making of these Regulations *(b)*;

(b) regulation 3 (in its application to sub-paragraph (1) of paragraph 4 and to paragraphs 6 to 8 of the Schedule to these Regulations, and regulation 4, shall come into operation one year after the making of these Regulations; and

(c) regulation 3 (except in its application as aforesaid) shall come into operation two years after the making of these Regulations.

(a) **Great Britain.** See INTRODUCTORY NOTE 4.

(b) **The date . . . regulations.** That is, 14 July 1959.

Interpretation

2.—(1) In these Regulations—

"the Act" means the Agriculture (Safety, Health and Welfare Provisions) Act 1956;

"agriculture", "worker", "employer" and "employed" have the meanings respectively assigned to them, as respects England and Wales *(a)*, by subsection (1) of section 24 of *the Act*, and, as respects Scotland, by that subsection as applied by subsection (10) of section 25 of the Act;

"stationary machine" has the meaning assigned to it in Part I of the Schedule to these Regulations.

(2) Expressions used in Parts II and III of the Schedule to these Regulations of which there are definitions in Part I thereof have the meanings thereby respectively assigned to them.

(3) The provisions of these Regulations shall apply, in addition to the provisions of the Agriculture (Circular Saws) Regulations 1959, to any *stationary machine* that is a circular saw as therein defined.

(4) The Interpretation Act 1889 [Interpretation Act 1978] applies to the interpretation of these Regulations as it applies to the interpretation of an Act of Parliament.

(*a*) *England and Wales.* See INTRODUCTORY NOTE 4.

Obligations affecting employers
3. Subject to the provisions of these Regulations the *employer* of a *worker* in *agriculture* shall not cause (*a*) or permit a *worker* so *employed*, in the course of his employment, to work at a *stationary machine* unless the requirements contained in Part II of the Schedule to these Regulations are complied with.

(*a*) *Cause.* See note (*a*) to reg. 3 of the Agriculture (Ladders) Regulations 1957.

Obligations affecting workers
4. Subject to the provisions of these Regulations a *worker employed* in *agriculture* who, in the course of his employment, works at a *stationary machine* shall comply with the requirements contained in Part III of the Schedule to these Regulations.

Certificates of Exemption
5.—(1) Notwithstanding anything in these Regulations, the Health and Safety Executive may grant certificates exempting (for such periods as may be specified therein and subject to such conditions, if any, as may be so specified) particular cases or particular persons from the operation of the provisions of these Regulations, and where any such conditions are imposed, an *employer* or *workers* employed in *agriculture*, and a *worker* or *employer*, to whom any such certificate applies shall comply with those conditions.

(2) [*revoked*].

SCHEDULE

Regulation 2(2)

PART I
INTERPRETATION

1.—(1) In this Schedule—
"belt" includes any flexible material used to transmit power from one pulley to another;
"primary driving belt" means a *belt* for transmitting power from the driving pulley to a *prime mover* to any *stationary machine* (other than a *prime mover*);
"prime mover" means any internal combustion engine or electric motor, whether or not any such engine or motor is designed for stationary use only;
"run-on point" means the on-running point of contact of a *belt* with a pulley, or of a chain with a sprocket;

"shafting" means a shaft or system of shafts (including any couplings and clutches) used for transmitting power;

"stationary machine" means any machine (together with any transmission machinery used therewith) designed or adapted for stationary use *(a)* only, and includes any *prime mover* which is so designed or adapted, but does not include a thresher, huller, baler or trusser *(b)*;

"striking gear" means a device by which a *belt* while in motion can be moved from a fast to a loose pulley, and *vice versa;*

(2) References in this Schedule to a *worker* coming in contact with any part of a *stationary machine*, or *prime mover* that is not a *stationary machine*, shall be construed as references to his coming in contact therewith either directly or by means of his clothes.

(a) **Stationary use.** Machinery which is not designed or adapted for stationary use only may be governed by the provisions of the Agriculture (Threshers and Balers) Regulations 1960 or the Agriculture (Field Machinery) Regulations 1962.

(b) **Thresher . . . trusser.** Such machines, if stationary, are governed by the Agriculture (Threshers and Balers) Regulations 1960; if mobile, they are governed by the Agriculture (Field Machinery) Regulations 1962.

PART II
REQUIREMENTS APPLICABLE TO EMPLOYERS
Regulation 3

Components of stationary machinery
2.—(1) Subject to the provisions of this paragraph every component of a *stationary machine*, being a component to which this paragraph applies, shall be so situated or so guarded as to protect a *worker* from coming in contact therewith.

(2) Without prejudice to the generality of the foregoing sub-paragraph a component, and any part of a component, shall be deemed to be so situated as aforesaid if it is more than 2 metres from every floor, platform staircase, fixed ladder or other place to which a *worker* has access in the course of his employment.

(3) The components of a *stationary machine* to which this paragraph applies are any *shafting*, pulley, flywheel, gearing, sprocket, chain, *belt*, or, as respects any fan, (in addition to any of the foregoing components) any wing or blade thereof:

Provided that this paragraph shall not only apply to a shaft to which the Agriculture (Power Take-off) Regulations 1957 apply, and shall only apply to a *primary driving belt* if the *prime mover* and the *stationary machine* which it drives by means of such belt are both permanently fixed installations.

(4) Nothing in this paragraph shall require the guarding, elsewhere than at the *run-on points*, of any chain or *belt* moving at less than 0.15 metres per second, or of any conveyor chain or *belt* for the movement of materials.

Primary driving belts
3.—(1) Whenever power is transmitted by means of a *primary driving belt* from a *prime mover* to a *stationary machine* (other than a *prime mover*) every *run-on-point* both on the *prime mover* and on the *stationary machine* shall be so situated or so guarded as to protect a *worker* from coming in contact therewith.

(2) Without prejudice to the generality of the foregoing sub-paragraph a *run-on point* shall be deemed to be so situated as aforesaid if it is more than 2 metres from every floor, platform, staircase, fixed ladder or other place to which a *worker* has access in the course of his employment.

Guarding of certain feeding inlets and discharge outlets
4.—(1) The feeding inlet and discharge outlet stationary grain auger, and of every power-driven *stationary machine* which grinds, crushes, bruises or pulverises grain, shall be so guarded as to protect a *worker* from coming in contact with any moving part of the auger or with any internal moving part of any such machine.

(2) The feeding inlet and discharge outlet of every power-driven *stationary machine*, which cuts or pulps roots, chops hay or straw, or grinds, breaks, mixes or pulverises feeding stuffs (other than grain) shall be so guarded as to protect a *worker*, in the normal operating position, from coming into contact with any internal moving part of any such machine.

(3) The requirements contained in this paragraph shall be in addition to and not in derogation of the requirements contained in paragraph 2 of this Schedule.

Means to be provided for quickly stopping machinery

General provisions

5.—(1) Every *prime mover* from which power is transmitted to a *stationary machine* (other than a *prime mover*) shall be provided with a readily accessible device (whether or not a switch) by means of which the *prime mover* may quickly be stopped.

(2) Such device shall be situated on or near the *prime mover* unless the *prime mover*—

(a) is more than 2 metres from every floor, platform, staircase, fixed ladder or other place to which a *worker* has access in the course of this employment, or

(b) is otherwise so situated as to protect a *worker* from coming in contact therewith.

(3) Every *stationary machine* (other than a *prime mover*) shall be fitted with a loose pulley and *striking gear*, or with a clutch or other device, readily accessible to the operator of the machine, by means of which the power transmitted from the *prime mover* may quickly be disconnected:

Provided that this sub-paragraph shall not apply if the *prime mover* may be stopped by a device readily accessible to the operator of the machine.

(4) Notwithstanding anything in the last foregoing sub-paragraph, the means of disconnecting the power to any *stationary machine* at which a *worker* dresses or handles agricultural produce on or near any moving part of such machine, shall be within reach of every such *worker* (or, if at any time such machine there is more than one such *worker* within reach of one of them) from his working position.

(5) Where any such *stationary machine* as is mentioned in sub-paragraph (4) of this paragraph has two or more stages the provisions of sub-paragraphs (3) and (4) of this paragraph shall apply in relation to each stage thereof at which a *worker* is *employed* to work.

(6) Every device for stopping a *prime mover* in accordance with sub-paragraph (1) of this paragraph, and every device for disconnecting the power to a *stationary machine* (other than a *prime mover*) in accordance with sub-paragraph (3) of this paragraph, shall be so constructed and maintained that the power cannot be reconnected by vibration.

Special provisions for switches

(7) At every switch controlling a *prime mover* it shall be clearly indicated how the *prime mover* may be stopped.

(8) At every switch controlling a *prime mover* it shall be clearly indicated which *prime mover* the switch controls:

Provided that this sub-paragraph shall not apply where any such switch is mounted on the *prime mover* which it controls, or on a *stationary machine* (other than a *prime mover*) of which a *prime mover* is an integral part.

(9) Where a *prime mover*, or a *stationary machine* (other than a *prime mover*) of which a *prime mover* is an integral part, is controlled by two or more manually operated switches they shall be connected in such manner that if the power is disconnected at any one such switch it shall be incapable of being reconnected unless that switch is subsequently manually operated.

In this sub-paragraph "manually operated" means operated by hand, foot or other bodily means.

Maintenance of belts

6. Every *belt* (including a *primary driving* belt) together with its fastenings, which is used in connection with a *stationary machine*, shall be properly maintained *(a)*, and no such *belt* shall rest or ride directly on a revolving shaft.

Lighting

7. At every *stationary machine,* and at every *prime mover* used therewith, there shall be adequate natural or artificial light.

Guard

8. Every guard required by this Schedule shall be of adequate strength and shall be properly maintained *(a).*

*(a) **Adequate strength; properly maintained.*** See notes *(c)* and *(d)* to paragraph 5 of the Schedule to the Agriculture (Safeguarding of Workplaces) Regulations 1959.

PART III
REQUIREMENTS APPLICABLE TO WORKERS

Regulation 4

Use of safety apliances

9.—(1) Without prejudice to subsection (1) of section 13 of *the Act (a)* (which makes it an offence for a *worker* wilfully to interfere with or misuse, any equipment, appliances, facilities or other thing provided in pursuance of *the Act* or regulations thereunder) a *worker* shall keep in position and shall make full use of every guard, facility and other thing provided, which satisfies the requirements of this Schedule:

Provided that a guard may be removed from a *stationary machine,* or from a *prime mover* that is not a *stationary machine,* by a *worker* who has attained [school-leaving age].

    (a) while the machine or *prime mover* is not in motion for so long only as is necessary for cleaning, repair or adjustment; or

    (b) while the machine or *prime mover* is in motion for so long as is necessary for carrying out any essential adjustment, being an adjustment which cannot be carried out unless the machine or *prime mover* is in motion.

(2) Nothing in the last foregoing subparagraph shall prevent a guard from being temporarily removed from a *prime mover* by a *worker* who has attained [school-leaving age] if its removal is necessary in order to start the *prime mover* by hand.

*(a) **Section 13.*** Repealed. See the Health and Safety at Work etc. Act 1974, s. 8.

Damages guards

10.—(1) If any guard required under Part II of this Schedule which has been fitted to a *stationary machine,* of any component thereof, or to a *prime mover* that is not a *stationary machine,* or any component thereof, is or becomes damaged, any *worker employed to operate that machine or prime mover* shall, on discovering that it is damaged, forthwith report the fact to this *employer.*

(2) Nothing in this paragraph shall absolve an *employer* from complying with the requirements contained in Part II of this Schedule.

THE AGRICULTURE (THRESHERS AND BALERS) REGULATIONS 1960

(S.I. 1960 No. 1199, as amended by S.I. 1976 No. 1247, S.I. 1981 No. 1414, S.I. 1989 No. 2311 and S.I. 1992 No. 2932

General note. A contravention of these Regulations is, by s. 1(6) of the Agriculture (Safety, Health and Welfare Provisions) Act 1956, an offence. These Regulations, in so far as they impose duties failure to comply with which might give rise to a liability in tort, are binding on the Crown; see s. 22, of that Act. In the case of some of the machines governed by these Regulations protection was formerly afforded by the Threshing Machines Act 1878 and the Chaff-Cutting Machines (Accidents) Act 1897. Many of the provisions of the Schedule are overtaken by the Provisional Use of Work Equipment Regulations, S.I. 1992 No. 2932.

Citation, extent and commencement
1.   These Regulations, which may be cited as the Agriculture (Threshers and Balers) Regulations 1960, shall apply to Great Britain *(a)* and shall come into operation on the 1st day of August, 1961.

(*a*) **Great Britain.** See INTRODUCTORY NOTE 4.

Interpretation
2.—(1) In these Regulations—
   "the Act" means the Agriculture (Safety, Health and Welfare Provisions) Act 1956;
   "agriculture", "agricultural unit" and (subject to regulation 6 of the Regulations) "worker", "employer" and "employed" have the meanings respectively assigned to them, as respects England and Wales *(a)*, by subsection (1) of section 24 of *the Act*, and, as respects Scotland, by that subsection as applied by subsection (10) of section 25 of *the Act*;
   "thresher" and "baler" have the meanings respectively assigned to them in Part I of the Schedule to these Regulations.

   (2) For the purposes of these Regulations a *worker* works at a *thresher* or *baler* if—
   (a) he operates or assists in the operation of the *thresher* or *baler*;
   (b) he is present at the site where threshing or baling is being carried out and performs any task which is necessarily incidental thereto.

   (3) Expressions used in Parts II, III, and IV of the Schedule to these Regulations of which there are definitions in Part I thereof have the meanings thereby respectively assigned to them.

   (4) The Interpretation Act 1889 [Interpretation Act 1978] applies to the interpretation of these Regulations as it applies to the interpretation of an Act of Parliament.

(a) **England and Wales.** See INTRODUCTORY NOTE 4.

Obligations affecting employers

3.—(1) Subject to the provisions of these Regulations the *employer* of a *worker employed* in *agriculture* shall not cause *(a)* or permit a *worker* so *employed*, in the course of his employment, to work at a *thresher* or *baler* unless the requirements contained in Part II of the Schedule of these Regulations are complied with.

(a) **Cause.** See not *(a)* to reg. 3 of the Agriculture (Ladders) Regulations 1957.

Obligations affecting employers and workers

4.   Subject to the provisions of these Regulations—

   (a)   the *employer* of a *worker employed* in *agriculture* shall not cause *(a)* or permit a *worker* so *employed*, in the course of his employment, to work at, and
   (b)   a *worker* or *employed* shall not, in the course of his employment work at,

a *thresher* or *baler* unless the requirements contained in Part III of the Schedule to these Regulations are complied with.

(a) **Cause.** See note *(a)* to reg. 3 of the Agriculture (Ladders) Regulations 1957.

Obligations affecting workers

5.   Subject to the provisions of these Regulations a *worker employed* in *agriculture* who, in the course of his employment, works at a *thresher* or *baler* shall comply with the requirements contained in Part IV of the Schedule to these Regulations.

Persons deemed to be employers

6.—(1) Where a *worker employed* in *agriculture* works at a *thresher* or *baler* elsewhere than in an *agricultural unit* of which his *employer* is the occupier, the *worker* shall, while so working, be deemed for the purposes of these Regulations to be in the employment of the occupier of the *agricultural unit* on which the threshing or baling is being carried out, or (in cases where paragraph (2) of this regulation applies) of the agricultural contractor to whom the *thresher* or *baler* belongs.

(2) Where a *worker employed* in *agriculture* works at a *thresher* or *baler* belonging to an agricultural contractor, the *worker* shall, while so working, be deemed for the purposes of these Regulations to be in the employment of the agricultural contractor.

(3) For the purposes of these Regulations a *thresher* or *baler* belongs to an agricultural contractor if—

   (a)   he is the owner thereof; or
   (b)   he has hired or borrowed it from the owner.

(4) Where by virtue of paragraphs (1) or (2) of this regulation any person is deemed to be the *employer* of a *worker employed* in *agriculture*, regulations 3 and 4 of these Regulations, except in their application to *workers*, shall not apply to any person other than the person so deemed as aforesaid.

Certificates of Exemption
7.—(1) Notwithstanding anything in these Regulations, the Health and Safety Executive may grant certificates exempting (for such periods as may be specified therein and subject to such conditions, if any, as may be so specified) particular cases or particular persons from the operation of the provisions of these Regulations, and where any such conditions are imposed, the *employer* of a *worker employed* in *agriculture* (including any person deemed by these Regulations to be an *employer*), and a *worker* so *employed*, to whom any such certificate applies, shall comply with those conditions.

(2) [*revoked*].

SCHEDULE 1

Regulation 2(3)

PART I
INTERPRETATION

1.—(1) In this Schedule—
"baler" means a *stationary machine (a)* used for baling or trussing straw or fodder, and includes a trusser;
"belt" includes any flexible material used to transmit power from one pulley to another;
"deck" means any platform (other than any temporary extension thereof) of a *thresher* designed for a worker to stand on while working at the *thresher*;
"primary driving belt" means a *belt* for transmitting power from the driving pulley of a *prime mover* to a *thresher* or *baler*;
"prime mover" means every engine, motor or other appliance which provides mechanical energy to a *thresher* or *baler*;
"run-on point" means the on-running point of contact of a *belt* with a pulley, or of a chain with a sprocket;
"shafting" means a shaft or system of shafts (including any couplings and clutches) used for transmitting power;
"stationary machine" means any machine (together with any *prime mover* forming an integral part thereof and any transmission machinery used therewith) designed, or permanently converted, for stationary use only;
"thresher" means a *stationary machine (a)* used for threshing grain or seed, and includes a huller but does not include a pea-viner.
(2) References in this Schedule to a *worker* coming in contact with any part of a *thresher* or *baler* (or in relation to a *primary driving belt*, with any *run-on point*), shall be construed as references to his coming in contact therewith either directly or by means of his clothes.

(a) **Stationary machine.** Mobile machines are governed by the Agriculture (Field Machinery) Regulations 1962.

PART II
REQUIREMENTS APPLICABLE TO EMPLOYERS

Regulation 3

Threshers

Guarding of drum feeding mouth
2.—(1) Subject to the provisions of this paragraph the drum feeding mouth of every *thresher* shall, whenever produce is being fed to the drum, be so guarded as to protect a *worker* from coming in contact with the drum:
Provided that nothing in this sub-paragraph shall require the feeding mouth to be guarded in a manner that would render it impracticable for produce to be fed to the drum.

(2) Without prejudice to the generality of the foregoing sub-paragraph, the requirements thereof shall be deemed to be complied with if a *thresher* is fitted with a shelf-feeder which affords a *worker* no less protection against coming in contact with the drum than if the drum feeding mouth were guarded in accordance with that sub-paragraph.

General note. This paragraph is revoked by the Provision and Use of Work Equipment Regulations 1992, S.I. 1992 No. 2932, as from 1 January 1993 except, insofar as it applies to work equipment first provided for use in the premises or undertaking before 1 January 1993, it is revoked as from 1 January 1997.

Fitting of cover over drum feeding mouth
   3.—(1) If while the drum of a *thresher* is rotating produce is not being fed to the drum, the drum feeding mouth shall be so covered as to render it impossible for a *worker* to come in contact with the drum.
   (2) A cover required in accordance with the foregoing sub-paragraph shall, for the purposes of this Schedule, be treated as a guard.

General note. This paragraph is revoked by the Provision and Use of Work Equipment Regulations 1992, S.I. 1992 No. 2932, as from 1 January 1993 except, insofar as it applies to work equipment first provided for use in the premises or undertaking before 1 January 1993, it is revoked as from 1 January 1997.

Decks
   4.—(1) The *deck* of every *thresher* from which a *worker* is liable to fall more than 1.5 metres shall be fitted with a guard (being a guard which complies with sub-paragraph (2) of this paragraph)—
      (a) at each end of the *deck*; and
      (b) at the side of the *deck* not being used for the movement of produce:
   Provided that one gap of not more than 600 millimetres may be left in the guard for access to the *deck* by a *worker.*
   (2) The said guard—
      (a) shall consist of a guard rail, rope, chain or fence;
      (b) shall be not less than 920 millimetres nor more than 1.2 metres above the *deck*; and
      (c) shall be supported by uprights not more than 2.4 metres apart.
   (3) The foregoing sub-paragraphs shall not apply to any floor to which the Agriculture (Safeguarding of Workplaces) Regulations 1959 apply.

Prohibition of use of pointed hooks and spikes
   5. No pointed hook or spike shall be used, or form part of any device, for the attachment of a sack or bag to a *thresher.*

Balers and trussers

Guarding of dangerous parts of balers and trussers
   6.—(1) Every *baler* shall at both sides be fitted with a guard so situated as to protect a *worker* from coming in contact with the ram.
   (2) Every trusser shall be fitted with a guard so situated as to protect a *worker* from coming in contact with the discharge arms.

General note. This paragraph is revoked by the Provision and Use of Work Equipment Regulations 1992, S.I. 1992 No. 2932, as from 1 January 1993 except, insofar as it applies to work equipment first provided for use in the premises or undertaking before 1 January 1993, it is revoked as from 1 January 1997.

Threshers and balers

Construction and maintenance
   7. Every *thresher* and every *baler* shall be of sound construction and properly maintained *(a).*

General note. This paragraph is revoked by the Provision and Use of Work Equipment Regulations 1992, S.I. 1992 No. 2932, as from 1 January 1993 except, insofar as it applies to work equipment first provided for use in the premises or undertaking before 1 January 1993, it is revoked as from 1 January 1997.

(a) *Properly maintained.* See INTRODUCTORY NOTE 10.

Components of threshers and balers

8.—(1) Subject to the provisions of this paragraph every component of a *thresher,* and every component of a *baler,* being a component to which this paragraph applies, shall be so situated or so guarded as to protect a *worker* from coming in contact therewith.

(2) Without prejudice to the generality of the foregoing sub-paragraph, where a *thresher* or *baler* is permanently fixed in one position, a component, and any part of a component, shall be deemed to be so situated as aforesaid if it is more than 2 metres from every floor, platform, staircase, fixed ladder or other place to which a *worker* has access in the course of his employment.

(3) The components to which this paragraph applies are any *shafting,* pulley, fly-wheel, gearing, crank, sprocket, *belt* or *chain*:

Provided that this paragraph shall not apply to shafts to which the Agriculture (Power Take-off) Regulations 1957 apply, and, as respects *belts* and chains, shall have effect subject to the next following sub-paragraph.

(4) In the case of—

(a) a *primary driving belt* in respect of which the *prime mover* and *thresher* or *baler* are not permanently fixed in relation to each other; and

(b) any *belt* or chain connecting a *thresher* and a *baler* which are not so fixed as aforesaid,

the provisions of sub-paragraph (1) of this paragraph shall apply only in relation to the *run-on points.*

General note. This paragraph is revoked by the Provision and Use of Work Equipment Regulations 1992, S.I. 1992 No. 2932, as from 1 January 1993 except, insofar as it applies to work equipment first provided for use in the premises or undertaking before 1 January 1993, it is revoked as from 1 January 1997.

Means of quickly stopping machinery

9.—(1) Means shall be provided, in accordance with the following provisions of this paragraph, of quickly stopping every *thresher* and *baler,* that is to say, either—

(a) the *prime mover* shall be fitted with a readily accessible device (whether or not a switch) by means of which the *prime mover* may quickly be stopped; or

(b) the *thresher* or *baler* shall be fitted with such a device by means of which it may be immediately disconnected from its *prime mover.*

(2) Every such device as is mentioned in the foregoing sub-paragraph shall be so constructed and maintained that the power cannot be reconnected to the *thresher* or *baler* unless the device is manually operated.

(3) Where a *prime mover,* whether or not forming an integral part of a *baler* or *thresher,* is controlled by two or more manually operated switches, they shall be connected in such a manner that if the power is disconnected at any one such switch, it shall be incapable of being reconnected unless that switch is subsequently manually operated.

(4) In the last two foregoing subparagraphs "manually operated" means operated by hand, foot or other bodily means.

General note. This paragraph is revoked by the Provision and Use of Work Equipment Regulations 1992, S.I. 1992 No. 2932, as from 1 January 1993 except, insofar as it applies to work equipment first provided for use in the premises or undertaking before 1 January 1993, it is revoked as from 1 January 1997.

Belts

10.—(1) Every *belt* (including a *primary driving belt*) together with its fastenings which is used in connection with a *thresher* or *baler* shall be properly maintained *(a).*

(2) No such *belt* shall rest or ride directly on a revolving shaft.

(3) No fastening on a *primary driving belt* shall be such as to constitute a danger to a *worker.*

General note. This paragraph is revoked by the Provision and Use of Work Equipment Regulations 1992, S.I. 1992 No. 2932, as from 1 January 1993 except, insofar as it applies to work equipment first provided for use in the premises or undertaking before 1 January 1993, it is revoked as from 1 January 1997.

(*a*) **Properly maintained.** See INTRODUCTORY NOTE 10.

Lighting
11. At every *thresher* and every *baler*, and at every *prime mover* used therewith, there shall be adequate natural or artificial light.

General note. This paragraph is revoked by the Provision and Use of Work Equipment Regulations 1992, S.I. 1992 No. 2932, as from 1 January 1993 except, insofar as it applies to work equipment first provided for use in the premises or undertaking before 1 January 1993, it is revoked as from 1 January 1997.

Guards
12. Every guard required by this Schedule shall be of adequate strength (*a*) and shall be properly maintained (*b*).

General note. This paragraph is revoked by the Provision and Use of Work Equipment Regulations 1992, S.I. 1992 No. 2932, as from 1 January 1993 except, insofar as it applies to work equipment first provided for use in the premises or undertaking before 1 January 1993, it is revoked as from 1 January 1997.

(*a*) **Adequate strength.** See note (*c*) to paragraph 5 of the Schedule of the Agriculture (Safeguarding of Workplaces) Regulations 1959.

(*b*) **Properly maintained.** See INTRODUCTORY NOTE 10.

PART III
REQUIREMENTS APPLICABLE TO EMPLOYERS AND WORKERS
Regulation 4

Threshers

Prohibited standing places for workers
13. A *worker* shall not, while the drum of a *thresher* is rotating, stand on any platform, or other surface, which slopes down directly into the drum feeding mouth of the *thresher.*

Minimum age for feeding into drum feeding mouth
14. A *worker* shall not feed produce into the drum feeding mouth of a *thresher* unless he has attained the age of 18 years.

Balers

Prohibition of being on baler during operation
15. A *worker* shall not be on top of a *baler* while it is being operated.

PART IV
REQUIREMENTS APPLICABLE TO WORKERS
Regulation 5

Threshers and balers

Use of safety appliances
16.—(1) Subject to the provisions of this paragraph, and without prejudice to subsection (1) of section 13 of *the Act* (*a*) (which makes it an offence for a *worker* wilfully to

interfere with, or misuse, any equipment, appliance, facilities or other thing provided in pursuance of *the Act* or regulations thereunder), a *worker* shall keep in position and shall make full use of every guard, facility and other thing provided, which satisfies the requirements of this Schedule:

Provided that a guard may be removed from a *thresher* or *baler* (and from a *primary driving belt*) by a *worker* who has attained school-leaving age—

   (a) while the *thresher* or *baler* is not in use for so long only as is necessary for repair or adjustment; or

   (b) while the *thresher* or *baler* is in use for so long as is necessary for carrying out any essential adjustment, being an adjustment which cannot be carried out unless the *thresher* or *baler* is in use.

(2) The foregoing sub-paragraph shall not apply in respect of any period while a *thresher* or *boiler* is disconnected from its *prime mover*.

General note. This paragraph is revoked by the Provision and Use of Work Equipment Regulations 1992, S.I. 1992 No. 2932, as from 1 January 1993 except, insofar as it applies to work equipment first provided for use in the premises or undertaking before 1 January 1993, it is revoked as from 1 January 1997.

   (a) **Section 13.** Repealed. See now the Health and Safety at Work etc. Act 1974, s. 8.

Damaged guards

17.—(1) If any guard required under Part II of this Schedule is or becomes damaged, any *worker employed* to work at any *thresher* or *baler* to which such a guard has been fitted shall, on discovering that the guard is damaged, forthwith report the fact to his *employer*, or, in cases where for the purposes of these Regulations some other person is deemed to be his *employer*, to that person.

(2) Nothing in this paragraph shall absolve an *employer*, or a person deemed for the purposes of these Regulations to be an *employer*, from complying with the requirements contained in Part II of this Schedule.

General note. This paragraph is revoked by the Provision and Use of Work Equipment Regulations 1992, S.I. 1992 No. 2932, as from 1 January 1993 except, insofar as it applies to work equipment first provided for use in the premises or undertaking before 1 January 1993, it is revoked as from 1 January 1997.

THE AGRICULTURE
(TRACTOR CABS)
REGULATIONS 1974

(S.I. 1974 No. 2034 as amended by S.I. 1976 No. 1247, S.I. 1981 No. 1414,
S.I. 1984 No. 605 and S.I. 1990 No. 1075)

General note. A contravention of these Regulations is, by s. 1(6) of the Agriculture
(Safety, Health and Welfare Provisions) Act 1956, an offence. These Regulations, in so
far as they impose duties, failure to comply with which might give rise to a liability in tort,
are binding on the Crown; see s. 22 of that Act.

Citation, extent and commencement
1. These Regulations, which may be cited as the Agriculture (Tractor Cabs)
Regulations 1974, shall apply to Great Britain *(a)* and shall come into operation
on the date *(b)* on which they are made.

(a) **Great Britain.** See INTRODUCTORY NOTE 4.

(b) **Date . . . made.** That is to say, 5 December 1974.

Interpretation
2.—(1) In these Regulations, unless the context otherwise requires—

"agriculture", "worker", "employer" and "employed" have the meanings respectively assigned to them, as respects England and Wales, by subsection (1) of section 24 of the Agriculture (Safety, Health, and Welfare
Provisions) Act 1956, and, as respects Scotland, by that subsection as applied
by subsection (10) of section 25 of that Act;
"approval mark" means one of the two marks, incorporating a crown
inside a triangle, illustrated in paragraph 1 of Part I of the Schedule to these
Regulations, and "appropriate approval mark" means—

(a) in relation to a *safety cab* fitted to a tractor which is or has been new on or
after 1 June 1976, or in relation to a *safety cab* which itself is or has been
new on or after 1 September 1977, the mark illustrated in sub-paragraph
(1) of that paragraph;
(b) in relation to any other *safety cab*, either approval mark;

"approved", in relation to a *safety cab*, means approved in accordance with
regulation 3 for use with a *tractor* and any *safety cab* which is marked with a
component type-approval mark in accordance with—

(a) Council Directive 77/536/EEC relating to the roll-over protection structures of wheeled agricultural or forestry *tractors*, as amended by Council
Directive 87/354/EEC;
(b) Council Directive 79/622/EEC relating to the static testing of the

2162

roll-over protection structures of wheeled agricultural or forestry tractors, as amended by Council Directive 87/354/EEC and as adapted to technical progress by Commission Directives 82/953/EEC and 88/413/EEC;

(c) Council Directive 86/298/EEC relating to the rear-mounted roll-over protection structures of narrow-track wheeled agricultural and forestry tractors; or

(d) Council Directive 87/402/EEC relating to the roll-over protection structures mounted in front of the driver's seat on narrow-track wheeled agricultural and forestry *tractors*,

shall be deemed to be approved and correctly marked with the appropriate *approval mark* and supplementary marks in accordance with that regulation if it is fitted to and for use with a *tractor* of the type to which it was attached when tested pursuant to the relevant Directive specified above, and the driver-perceived noise level is within either of the limits specified in Article 2.1 of Council Directive 77/311/EEC (relating to the driver-perceived noise level of wheeled agricultural or forestry tractors) when measured in accordance with the relevant Annex to that Directive;

"building" includes any underground premises;

"the Executive" means the Health and Safety Executive;

"marked" means marked in the manner described in Part II of the Schedule to these Regulations;

"new" means not previously sold to any purchaser for use by him in *agriculture*;

"safety cab" means a rigid framework or cab designed to protect the driver of a *tractor* to which it is fitted from being crushed if the *tractor* overturns, and includes a safety frame;

"supplementary marks" means the marks described in paragraph 2 of Part I of the Schedule to these Regulations;

"tractor" means a wheeled *tractor* weighing 560 kilograms or more when assembled in the lightest form commercially available, without water, fuel or lubricating oil, but does not include a half-tracked vehicle or a steam traction engine.

(2) For the purposes of these Regulations a *tractor* or a *safety cab* which is made the subject of a contract for hire purchase shall be deemed to be sold, and not let on hire.

(3) A *tractor* is properly fitted with a *safety cab* for the purposes of these Regulations if the *safety cab* is—

(a) so maintained and so fitted to the *tractor* as to afford the protection (including protection from noise) for which it is designed, and

(b) equipped with an efficient automatic wiper for any windscreen it may have.

(4) Where the first sale, letting on hire or loan of a *tractor* for use in *agriculture* by the purchaser, hirer or borrower, as the case may be occurred before 1 September 1970, regulations 4(c) and 5 of these Regulations shall not apply to that tractor until 1 September 1977.

(5) The Interpretation Act 1889 [Interpretation Act 1978] shall apply to the interpretation of these Regulations as it applies to the interpretation of an Act of Parliament, and as if these Regulations and the regulations hereby revoked were Acts of Parliament.

Approved safety cabs

3.—(1) Subject to the following provisions of this regulation, the *Executive* may approve a *safety cab* of which model for use with a *tractor* of any description by issuing a certificate of approval to the manufacturer of the *safety cab* approving the use of *safety cabs* of that model when fitted to *tractors* of that description.

(2) Before issuing a certificate of approval *the Executive* shall be satisfied that *safety cabs* of the model to which it relates would be capable of satisfying the requirements relating to protective cabs set out in Council Directive 77/536/EEC (as amended by Council Directive 87/354/EEC), Council Directive 79/622/EEC (as amended by Council Directive 87/354/EEC and as adapted to technical progress by Commission Directives 82/953/EEC and 88/413/EEC), Council Directive 86/298/EEC or Council Directive 87/402/EEC when fitted to *tractors* of descriptions specified in the certificate.

(3) In the case of a certificate of approval issued on or after 14 June 1990 the Executive shall further be satisfied before issuing the certificate, that the noise levels inside *safety cabs* of the model to which it relates, when fitted to *tractors* of descriptions specified in the certificate, would within either of the limits specified in Article 2.1 of Council Directive 77/311/EEC is measured in accordance with the relevant Annex to that Directive.

(4) Where a certificate of approval is issued for any model of *safety cab* in respect of which *the Executive* has been satisfied as to the matters specified in paragraph (3) above, the fact shall be stated in the certificate.

(5) While a *safety cab* is fitted to a *tractor* which is or has been *new* on or after 1 June 1976, or where a *safety cab* itself is or has been *new* on or after 1 September 1977, it shall not be an *approved safety cab* for the purpose of these Regulations unless *the Executive* has been satisfied as to the matters specified in paragraph (3) above (appertaining at the time the certificate of approval was issued) in relation to *safety cabs* of that model, and the fact is stated in the certificate of approval.

(6) A certificate of approval may prescribe specifications for the construction of *safety cabs* of the model to which it relates, and unless a *safety cab* is constructed in accordance with any specifications so prescribed it shall not be a *safety cab* of that model.

(7) Such specifications may be prescribed by reference to documents other than the certificate of approval, by reference to specimens of *safety cabs* or materials, and in any other manner.

(8) An *approved safety cab* shall cease to be *approved* if it is materially changed as a result of damage, alteration, neglect or any other cause.

(9) *The Executive* may at any time by notice in writing to the manufacturer, given not less than one month before it is due to take effect, amend or revoke a certificate of approval.

(10) It shall be a condition of every certificate of approval that the manufacturer to whom it is issued—

(a) shall cause every *safety cab* approved under the certificate to be marked with the correct *approval mark* and *supplementary marks* before it is sold or let on hire; and

(b) shall on request, at any resaonable time before sale, whether during or after manufacture,

(i) make available for inspection by or on behalf of *the Executive* any *safety cab* manufactured by him;

(ii) submit to such tests as *the Executive* may require any *safety cab* which purports to be or is intended to be *approved* under the certificate.

(11) *The Executive* shall not require a *safety cab* to be tested under paragraph (10) above unless in their opinion there is reason to believe either that the *safety cab* is not a *safety cab* of the model to which the certificate relates or that it is not capable of satisfying the construction and testing requirements of Council Directive 77/536/EEC (as amended by Council Directive 87/354/EEC), Council Directive 79/622/EEC (as amended by Council Directive 87/354/EEC and as adapted to technical progress by Commission Directives 82/953/EEC and 88/413/EEC), Council Directive 86/298/EEC or Council Directive 87/402/EEC.

(12) Where a manufacturer fails to comply with a condition of a certificate imposed on him by paragraph (10) above, *the Executive* may by notice given to him in writing revoke the certificate forthwith.

(13) Amendment or revocation of a certificate of approval shall not affect any *approved safety cab* sold before the amendment or revocation takes effect.

3A.   [*revoked*].

Sale and hire of tractors and safety cabs
4.   No person shall—

(a) sell a *new tractor*, or let it on hire *(a)*, to a person for use by him in *agriculture* in Great Britain *(b)*, unless it is properly fitted *(c)* with a *safety cab* which is—
   (i) *approved* for use with that tractor,
   (ii) marked with the *appropriate approval mark*, and
   (iii) marked with *supplementary marks* which relate to that *approval mark* and which include the name of the make, and the name or number of the model of that *tractor*;
(b) sell a *new safety cab*, or let it on hire *(a)* for use in *agriculture* in Great Britain, unless it is—
   (i) *approved*, and
   (ii) marked with the *appropriate approval mark* and *supplementary marks*;
(c) let a *tractor* on hire for use in *agriculture* in Great Britain, unless it is properly fitted *(c)* with a *safety cab* marked with the *appropriate approval mark*.

(a) **Let on hire.** See reg. 2(2).

(b) **Great Britain.** See INTRODUCTORY NOTE 4.

(c) **Properly fitted.** See reg. 2(3).

Obligations on employers, workers and others
5.—(1) The *employer* of a *worker employed* in *agriculture* shall ensure—

(a) that *every tractor* driven by that *worker* in the course of his employment is properly fitted *(a)* with a *safety cab* marked with the *appropriate approval mark,* and

(b)   so far as it is reasonably practicable *(b)* for him to do so, that every *safety cab* fitted to a *tractor* so driven by that *worker* is *approved* for use with that *tractor.*

(2)   No *worker employed* in *agriculture* shall drive a *tractor* in the course of his *employment,* and no person shall cause *(c)* or permit him to do so, unless it is properly fitted *(a)* with a *safety cab* marked with the *approval mark.*

(3)   No *worker employed* in *agriculture* shall drive a *tractor* in the course of his *employment* if it is fitted with a *safety cab* which he knows is not approved for use with that *tractor,* and no person shall cause *(c)* or permit such a *worker* to drive a *tractor* in the course of his *employment* if it is fitted with a *safety cab* which the person knows is not *approved* for the use with that *tractor.*

(4)   Nothing in this regulation shall apply to a *tractor—*

(a)   while it is being used for the purpose of carrying out an agricultural operation in a hop-garden, hop-yard or orchard, where it is not reasonably practicable *(b)* to use the *tractor* for the purpose if it is fitted with a *safety cab approved* for use with that *tractor;*

(b)   while it is being driven to or from a hop-garden, hop-yard or orchard for the purpose of or after being used there without an *approved safety cab* in compliance with sub-paragraph *(a)* above;

(c)   while it is being used inside, or in close proximity to, a *building* for the purpose of carrying out an agricultural operation involving its use inside that *building,* where it is not reasonably practicable by reason of the height, shape or construction of the *building* to use the *tractor* for the purpose if it is fitted with a *safety* cab *approved* for the use with that *tractor,* or

(d)   while it is being driven to or from any *building* for the purpose of or after being used there without an *approved safety cab* in compliance with sub-paragraph (c) above, unless the *tractor* is at the same time engaged in, or being driven from or to the site of, any agricultural operation for which such a *safety cab* is required by this regulation.

(a) Properly fitted. See reg. 2(3).

(b) Reasonably practicable. See INTRODUCTORY NOTE 5.

(c) Cause. See note *(a)* to reg. 3 of the Agriculture (Ladders) Regulations 1957.

Obligation on workers to report overturning or damage
6.   Every *worker employed* in *agriculture* to drive or maintain a *tractor* fitted with a *safety cab* marked with the *approval mark* shall forthwith report to his *employer—*

(a)   any occasion where the *tractor* overturns;

(b)   any damage caused to the *safety cab* or to fittings which secure it to the *tractor;* or

(c)   any defect in the windscreen wiper if one is fitted.

Restrictions on marking of safety cabs
7.—(1)   No person other than the manufacturer of a *safety cab* shall, without the consent of *the Executive* in writing, apply *(a)* to it any mark calculated to suggest—

(a) that the *safety cab* is *approved,* or

(b) that the *safety cab* is *approved* for use with a *tractor* of a specified description, or

(c) that the *safety cab* has been *approved* as being of a particular standard, whether the *safety cab* is so approved or not.

(2) Subject to the provisions of paragraph (3) below, no person shall apply *(a)* to a *safety cab* any mark calculated falsely to suggest—

(a) that the *safety cab* is *approved*; or

(b) that the *safety cab* is *approved* for use with a *tractor* of a specified description; or

(c) that the *safety cab* has been *approved* as being of a particular standard.

(3) The application *(a)* of a mark to a *safety cab* by its manufacturer before the time when it is first sold or let on hire *(b)* shall not give rise to a contravention of paragraph (2) above unless the mark remains on the *safety cab* until that time, in which case the manufacturer shall be deemed for the purposes of that paragraph to have applied the mark to the *safety cab* at that time.

(4) No person other than the manufacturer of a *safety cab* shall, without the consent of *the Executive* in writing, alter, remove, obliterate or deface any mark on that *safety cab* which is, or which purports to be, a mark required by these Regulations.

(5) For the purpose of this regulation a person applies a mark to a *safety cab* if he affixes or annexes it to, or in any manner marks it on or incorporates it with, the *safety cab*.

(a) **Apply.** See para. 5.

(b) **Let on hire.** See reg. 2(2).

Certificates of exemption
8.—(1) Notwithstanding anything in these Regulations, *the Executive* may grant certificated exemption, for such periods and subject to such conditions, if any, as may be specified therein, particular cases or particular persons from the operation of all or any of the provisions of these Regulations.

(2) Any breach of a condition imposed by such a certificate of exemption shall, while it continues, render the certificate void in relation to any *tractor* or *safety cab* affected by the breach.

Regulations revoked
9. The Agriculture (Tractor Cabs) Regulations 1967 and the Agriculture (Tractor Cabs) (Amendment) Regulations 1973 are hereby revoked.

Savings
10. Nothing in the Agriculture (Tractor Cabs) (Amendment) Regulations 1990 ("the 1990 Regulations") shall affect the validity of any certificate of approval issued in accordance with regulation 3 of these Regulations before the coming into force of the 1990 Regulations.

SCHEDULE

PART I
MARKS ON SAFETY CABS

1.—(1) Where the Executive has been satisfied, before issuing a certificate of approval (whether issued before or on or after 1 September 1977), that the noise levels inside *safety cabs* of the model to which it relates, when fitted to *tractors* of descriptions specified in the certificate, would be within either of the limits specified in Article 2.1 of Council Directive 77/311/EEC if measured in accordance with the relevant Annex to that Directive, the *approval mark* on the *approved safety cab* of that model shall be the following symbol:

(2) In any other case the *approval mark* on an *approved safety cab* shall be the following symbol:

2. The *supplementary marks* on a *safety cab* shall be—
(a) the name of the make, and the name or number of the model, of every *tractor* for use with which the *safety cab* is *approved* at the time of marking, and
(b) the serial number of the cab.

PART II
MANNER IN WHICH SAFETY CABS ARE TO BE MARKED

Safety cabs shall be marked in the following manner—
 (a) Every mark required by these Regulations shall be on the main structure of the *safety cab.*
 (b) Every such mark shall be clear, legible and permanent, and in a prominent and easily accessible position.
 (c) The name of the make or model of a *tractor* may be represented by a recognisable abbreviation of that name.
 (d) Where a model of *tractor* is referred to, it shall be described in such a way as not to include any *tractor* for use with which the *safety cab* is not *approved.*
 (e) *Supplementary marks* relating to the same *approval mark* shall be as near as is reasonably practicable to the *approval mark* and to each other.
 (f) Where there is more than one *approval mark* on a *safety cab* the *supplementary marks* relating to each shall be separate and clearly distinguishable from those relating to the other.

PART 10
OFFSHORE AND DIVING

SUMMARY

SUMMARY

THE MINERAL WORKINGS (OFFSHORE INSTALLATIONS) ACT 1971

(1971 c. 61)

General note. References to the Secretary of State shall be construed as references to the Health and Safety Executive by virtue of the Offshore Safety (Repeals and Modifications) Regulations 1993, S.I. 1993 No. 1823. The transfer of responsibility from the Department of Energy to the HSE was one of the recommendations of the Cullen Report (Cmd. 1310, 1990) on the Piper Alpha disaster of 6 July 1988.

ARRANGEMENT OF SECTIONS

An Act to provide for the safety, health and welfare of persons on installations concerned with the underwater exploitation and exploration of mineral resources in the waters in or surrounding the United Kingdom, and generally for the safety of such installations and the prevention of accidents on or near them.

[27 July 1971]

BE IT ENACTED by the Queen's most Excellent Majesty, by and with the advice and consent of the Lords Spiritual and Temporal, and Commons, in this present Parliament assembled, and by the authority of the same, as follows:

1. Application of Act.—(1) This Act shall apply to any activity mentioned in subsection (2) below which is carried on from by means of or on an installation which is maintained in the water, or on the foreshore or other land intermittently covered with water, and is not connected with dry land by a permanent structure providing access at all times and for all purposes.

(2) The activities referred to in subsection (1) above are—

(a) the exploitation or exploration of mineral resources in or under the shore or bed of *controlled waters*;

(b) the storage of gas in or under the shore or bed of *controlled waters* or the recovery of gas so stored;

(c) the conveyance of things by means of a pipe, or system of pipes, constructed or placed on, in or under the shore or bed of *controlled waters*; and

(d) the provision of accommodation for persons who work on or from an installation which is or has been maintained, or is intended to be esablished, for the carrying on of an activity falling within paragraph (a), (b) or (c) above or this paragraph.

(3) Her Majesty may by Order in Council provide that, in such cases and subject to such exceptions and modifications as may be *prescribed* by the Order, this Act shall have effect as if—

(a) any reference to *controlled waters* included a reference to waters in any area specified under section 22(5) of the Oil and Gas (Enterprise) Act 1982; and

(b) in relation to installations which are or have been maintained, or are intended to be established, in *controlled waters*, any reference in subsection (2) above to *controlled waters* included a reference to waters in a *foreign sector of the continental shelf* which are adjacent to such waters.

(4) In this Act—

"controlled waters" means—

(a) tidal waters and parts of the sea in or adjacent to the United Kingdom *(a)* up to the seaward limits of territorial waters;

(b) waters in any area designated under section 1(7) of the Continental Shelf Act 1964; and

(c) such inland waters as may for the time being be specified for the purposes of this paragraph by Order in Council;

"foreign sector of the continental shelf" means an area within which rights are exercisable with respect to the sea bed and subsoil and their natrual resources by a country or territory outside the United Kingdom.

"offshore installation" means any installation which is or has been maintained, or is intended to be established, for the carrying on or any activity to which this Act applies.

(5) In this section—

"exploration" means exploration with a view to exploration;

"inland waters" means waters within the United Kingdom other than tidal waters and parts of the sea;

"installation" includes—

(a) any floating structure or device maintained on a station by whatever means; and

(b) in such cases and subject to such exeptions as may be *prescribed* by Order in Council, any apparatus or works which are by virtue of section 33 of the Petroleum and Submarine Pipe-lines Act 1975 to be treated as associated with a pipe or system of pipes for the purposes of Part III of that Act,

but, subject to paragraph (b) above, does not include any part of a pipe-line within the meaning of that section;

"modifications" includes additions, omissions and alterations.

(6) The fact that an installation has been maintained for the carrying on of an activity falling within subsection (2) above shall be disregarded for the purposes of this section if, since it was so maintained, the installation—

    (a) has been outside *controlled waters* or, where it was so maintained in a part of a *foreign sector of the continental shelf* adjacent to those waters, the area consisting of those waters and that part; or

    (b) has been maintained for the carrying on of an activity not falling within that subsection.

(7) Orders in Council made under this section may be varied or revoked by a subsequent Order so made; and any statutory instrument containing an Order under subsection (3) above shall be subject to annulment in pursuance of a resolution of either House of Parliament.

    (a) **United Kingdom.** See INTRODUCTORY NOTE 4.

––––––––––––––––––

2. [*repealed*].

––––––––––––––––––

3. **Construction and survey regulations for** *offshore installations.*—(1)– (3) [*repealed*].

(4) It shall be the duty of the *owner* of the *offshore installation,* and of the *installation manager* and of every person who, in relation to the installation, is a concession owner, to ensure that the provisions of regulations under this section are complied with, and, if regulations under this section are contravened in any respect in relation to an *offshore installation* when it is within *controlled waters,* the *owner* of the *offshore installation,* the *installation manager* and every person who, in relation to the installation, is a concession owner shall each be guilty of an offence under this section and shall be liable—

    (a) on summary conviction to a fine not exceeding the *prescribed* sum,

    (b) on conviction on indictment to imprisonment for a term not exceding two years, or to a fine, or both.

––––––––––––––––––

4. **Masters of** *offshore installations.*—(1) Every *offshore installation,* so long as it is in *controlled waters,* shall be under the charge of a person appointed to be or act as manager of the installation, and the *owner* of the installation shall appoint to be *installation manager*—

    (a) a person who, to the best of the knowledge and belief of the *owner,* has the skills and competence suitable for the appointment, and

    (b) another or others to act where necessary in place of the *installation manager,*

and shall inform the Secretary of State of any appointment under this subsection by giving notice in the *prescribed* form and containing the *prescribed* particulars.

(2) [*repealed*].

(3) The *owner* may, under subsection (1)(a) above, appoint two or more persons to be managers in rotation, and the persons appointed under subsection (1)(b) above shall act where necessary in place of any of them.

(4) If at any time the *owner* is satisfied that an *installation manager* appointed in pursuance of subsection (1) above does not have the requisite skills and competence, he shall terminate the appointment as soon as practicable, and shall give the Secretary of State notice in the *prescribed* form of the action taken by him.

(5) It shall be the duty of the *owner*, in order to ensure that an *installation manager* appointed under subsection (1)(a) above is on the installation when it is manned, from time to time place a person so appointed on the installation, and to ensure that he remains there until relieved, or so long as it is manned.

(6) If the *owner* fails to comply, or to ensure compliance with the provisions of this section, he shall be guilty of an offence under this section, and liable on summary conviction to a fine not exceeding level 5 on the standard scale.

(7) The operation of this section may be excluded in whole or in part in relation to any particular installation by directions of the Secretary of State given in such manner and to such persons as he thinks appropriate.

(8) In this Act references to the manager of an *offshore installation* or to an *installation manager* are to be taken, except in so far as the context otherwise requires, as references to the person for the time being in charge of the installation and appointed as required by paragraph (a) or (b) of subsection (1) above.

General note. References to the Secretary of State shall be construed as references to the Health and Safety Executive by virtue of the Offshore Safety (Repeals and Modifications) Regulations 1993, S.I. 1993 No. 1823.

---

5. Masters of *offshore installations, further provisions.*—(1) The manager of an *offshore installation* shall not be absent from the installation at any time when it is manned, except in case of sudden sickness or other cause beyond his control, or for other sufficient reason, and a person failing to comply with this subsection shall be guilty of an offence under this section, and liable on summary conviction to a fine not exceeding level 5 on the standard scale.

(2) Except as otherwise provided by this Act, the manager of an *offshore installation* shall have in relation to its general responsibility for matters affecting safety, health or welfare or, where connected with safety, health or welfare, the maintenance of order and discipline, and for the disharge of that responsibility shall exercise authority over all persons in or about the installation:
Provided that this subsection shall not extend to any matters for which another person is responsible as master, captain or person in charge or any vessel, aircraft or hovercraft.

(3) If a person subject to the authority of the manager of an *offshore installation* wilfully disobeys a lawful command given him by the manager in exercise

of that authority, he shall be liable on summary conviction to a fine not exceeding level 3 on the standard scale.

(4) The manager of an *offshore installation* shall not permit the installation to be used in any manner, or permit any operation to be carried out on or from the installation, if the seaworthiness or stability of the installation is likely to be endangered by its use in that manner, or by the carrying out of that operation or by its being carried out in the manner proposed, and it shall be the duty of the *owner* of the installation to ensure that the provisions of this subsection are complied with by the *installation manager*.

If an *installation manager* or *owner* fails to comply, or ensure compliance, with this subsection he shall be guilty of an offence under this section, and liable—

(a) on summary conviction, to a fine not exceeding £1,000,
(b) on conviction on indictment to imprisonment for a term not exceeding two years, or to a fine, or both.

(5) Where at an *offshore installation* there is an emergency or apprehended emergency endangering the seaworthiness or stability of the installation or otherwise involving a risk of death or serious personal injury, the *installation manager* may take or require to be taken any such measures as are necessary or expedient to meet or avoid the emergency; and no regulation or condition having effect by virtue of this Act shall apply to prohibit or restrict the taking of any such measures by virtue of this subsection.

(6) If the *installation manager* has reasonable cause (a) to believe that it is necessary or expedient for the purpose of securing the safety of an *offshore installation* or persons in or about it, or maintaining order and discipline among those persons, the *installation manager* may cause any of those persons to be put ashore in the United Kingdom; and where any of those persons has done or is about to do any act endangering or likely to endanger the safety of the installation or persons in or about it or the maintenance of order and discipline among those persons, or the *installation manager* with reasonable cause (a) suspects him of having done or being about to do any such act, the *installation manager* may take or cause to be taken such other reasonable measures against him, by restraint of his person or otherwise, as the *installation manager* thinks necessary or expedient:

Provided that this subsection shall not extend to any matters for which another person is responsible as master, captain or person in charge of any vessel, aircraft or hovercraft.

(7) A person shall not be kept under restraint by virtue of subsection (6) above for longer than twenty-four hours unless—

(a) the intention is that he shall be put ashore in the United Kingdom in accordance with that subsection at the earliest opportunity; and
(b) within those twenty-four hours or as soon as practicable afterwards notice of his being kept under restraint and of the reason for it is sent to the *prescribed* authority in the United Kingdom.

(8) The manager of an *offshore installation* shall notify the *owner* as soon as practicable of any event which occurs at the installation and which the *owner* is

by any regulation or condition having effect by virtue of this Act required to notify to the Secretary of State or the Executive.

If a person fails to comply with the provisions of this subsection he shall be guilty of an offence under this section, and liable on summary conviction to a fine not exceeding level 3 on the standard scale.

(9) The operation of this section may be excluded in whole or in part in relation to any class or description of installation by regulations under this Act, or in relation to any particular installation by directions of the Secretary of State given in such manner and to such persons as he thinks appropriate.

General note. References to the Secretary of State in subsection (9) shall be construed as references to the Health and Safety Executive by virtue of the Offshore Safety (Repeals and Modifications) Regulations 1993, S.I. 1993 No. 1823.

(a) Reasonable cause to believe. There must also be actual belief: *R v Banks* [1916] 2 KB 621, CCA; *R v Harrison* [1938] 3 All ER 134, CCA.

---

6. [*repealed*].

---

7. Regulations: general provisions.—(1), (2) [*repealed*].

(3) The punishment for an offence created by regulations under this Act shall be—

(a) on summary conviction a fine not exceeding £400,
(b) on conviction on indictment imprisonment for a term not exceeding two years, or a fine, or both,

but without prejudice to any further restriction on the punishments which can be awarded contained in the regulations, and without prejudice to the exclusion of proceedings on indictment by the regulations.

(4) The operation of any regulations made under this Act may be excluded in whole or in part in relation to any particular installation by directions of the Secretary of State given in such manner and to such persons as he thinks appropriate.

(5) Any exemption or exclusion by directions of the Secretary of State under this Act, may be made subject to the imposition of conditions specified by the directions.

(6) Where in pursuance of this section a person is exempted or excluded from the requirements of any provision of this Act, or of regulations under this Act, but subject to a condition, and the condition is not observed, the exemption or exclusion shall not have effect, and proceedings may be brought in respect of any breach of duty as if the exemption or exclusion had not had effect.

(7), (8) [*repealed*].

General note. References to the Secretary of State shall be construed as references to the Health and Safety Executive by virtue of the Offshore Safety (Repeals and Modifications) Regulations 1993, S.I. 1993 No. 1823.

---

8. [*repealed*].

---

9.   Offences: general provisions.—(1) Where an *offence under this Act* which has been committed by a body corporate is proved to have been committed with the consent or connivance *(a)* of, or to be attributable to any neglect on the part of, a director, manager *(b)* secretary or other similar officer *(c)* of the body corporate, or any person who was purporting to act in any such capacity, he, as well as the body corporate, shall be guilty of that offence and shall be liable to be proceeded against and punished accordingly.

In this subsection "director", in relation to a body corporate established by or under any enactment for the purpose of carrying on under public ownership any industry or part of an industry or undertaking, being a body corporate whose affairs are managed by its members, means a member of that body corporate.

(2) In proceedings for an *offence under this Act* an averment in any process of the fact that anything was done or situated within *controlled waters* shall, until the contrary is proved, be sufficient evidence of that fact as stated in the averment.

(3) In proceedings for an offence under section 3, section 4 or section 5 of this Act, it shall be a defence for the accused to prove—

(a)   that he has used all due diligence to enforce the execution of this Act, and of any relevant regulation made under this Act, and

(b)   that any relevant contravention was committed without his consent, connivance or wilful default.

(4) Proceedings for any *offence under this Act* may be taken, and the offence may for all incidental purposes be treated as having been committed, in any place in the United Kingdom.

(5) [*repealed*].

(a) **Connivance.** See INTRODUCTORY NOTE 6.

(b) **Manager.** See *R v Boal (Francis)* [1992] QB 591, [1992] 3 All ER 177, CA, a case on the almost identical wording of s. 23(1) of the Fire Precautions Act, in which it was held that only those responsible for deciding corporate policy and strategy were "managers".

(c) **Similar officer.** The Director of Roads of a Regional Council is such an officer: *Armour v Skeen* [1977] IRLR 310.

---

10.   [*repealed*].

---

11.   Civil liability for breach of statutory duty.—(1) This section has effect as respects—

    (a) a duty imposed on any person by any provision of this Act, or

    (b) a duty imposed on any person by any provision of regulations made under this Act which expressly applies the provisions of this section.

(2) Breach of any such duty shall be actionable so far, and only so far, as it causes personal injury *(a)*, and references in section 1 of the Fatal Accidents Act 1846, as it applies in England and Wales, and in Northern Ireland, to a wrongful act, neglect or default shall include references to any breach of a duty which is so actionable.

(3) Subsection (2) above is without prejudice to any action which lies apart from the provisions of this Act.

(4) Neither section 9(3) of this Act, nor any defences afforded by regulations made in pursuance of section 7(2)(b) of this Act, shall afford a defence in any civil proceedings, whether brought by virtue of this section or not.

(5) So far as the provisions of this section impose a liability on a concession owner, those provisions and the other provisions of this Act to which they relate shall bind the Crown, and accordingly, for the purposes of those provisions, and of any regulations or conditions having effect under any of those provisions, persons in the service of the Crown shall be taken to be employed whether or not they would be so taken apart from this subsection:

Provided that this subsection shall not give any right of action to a person as being a member of the armed forces of the Crown.

(6) Nothing in the last preceding subsection shall authorise proceedings to be brought against Her Majesty in her private capacity, and this subsection shall be construed as if section 38(3) of the Crown Proceedings Act 1947 (interpretation of references in that Act to Her Majesty in her private capacity) were contained in this Act.

(7) In this section "personal injury" *(a)* includes any disease and any impairment of a person's physical or mental condition and includes any fatal injury.

    (a) Causes personal injury. See note *(e)* to s. 47(1) of the Health and Safety at Work etc. Act 1974.

---

12.   Interpretation.—(1) In this Act, unless the context otherwise requires—

    "controlled waters" has the meaning given by section 1(4) of this Act.

    "designated area" has the same meaning as in the Continental Shelf Act 1964.

    "foreign sector of the continental shelf" has the meaning given by section 1(4) of this Act.

"installation manager" has the meaning given by section 4(8) of this Act,
"offence under this Act" includes an offence under regulations made under this Act,
"offshore installation" has the meaning given by section 1(4) of this Act,
"owner", in relation to an *offshore installation*, means the person who has registered the installation pursuant to regulations under section 2 of this Act or, if there is no such person, the person for the time being having the management of the installation, or of its main structure,
"prescribed" means prescribed by regulations under this Act,

(2) A person who has the right to exploit or explore mineral resources in any area, or to store gas in any area and to recover gas so stored, shall be a concession owner for the purposes of this Act in relation to any *offshore installation* at any time if, at that time, there is carried on from, by means of or on the installation any of the following activities, namely—

(a) the exploitation or exploration of mineral resources, or the storage or recovery of gas, in the exercise of that right;

(b) the conveyance in that area by means of a pipe or system of pipes, of minerals gotten, or gas being stored or recovered, in the exercise of that right; and

(c) the provision of accommodation for persons who work on or from an installation which is or has been maintained, or is intended to be established, for the carrying on of an activity falling within paragraph (a) or (b) above or this paragraph.

(3) The fact that an installation has been maintained for the carrying on of an activity falling within subsection (2) above shall be disregarded for the purposes of paragraph (c) of that subsection if, since it was so maintained, the installation—

(a) has been outside *controlled waters* or, where it was so maintained in a part of a *foreign sector of the continental shelf* adjacent to those waters, the area consisting of those waters and that part; or

(b) has been maintained for the carrying on of an activity not falling within that subsection.)

(4) It is hereby declared that, notwithstanding that this Act may affect individuals or bodies corporate outside the United Kingdom, it applies to any individual whether or not he is a British subject, and to any body corporate whether or not incorporated under the law of any part of the United Kingdom.

(5) Any reference in this Act to a contravention of a provision of this Act or of regulations made under this Act includes a reference to a failure to comply with such a provision.

(6) Any reference in this Act to any enactment or Act of Parliament includes a reference to an enactment or Act of the Parliament of Northern Ireland.

(7) Except where the context otherwise requires, any references in this Act to any enactment shall be construed as a reference to that enactment as amended, extended or applied by or under any other enactment.

---

13. Financial provisions.—(1) There shall be paid out of money provided by Parliament—

(a) any expenses incurred by the Secretary of State under this Act, and

(b) any increase in money so payable under any other Act which is an increase attributable to this Act.

(2) Any receipts of the Secretary of State under this Act shall be paid into the Consolidated Fund.

---

14.   Short title, commencement and saving.—(1) This Act may be cited as the Mineral Workings (Offshore Installations) Act 1971.

(2) This Act shall come into force on such dates as the Secretary of State may by order in a statutory instrument appoint, and an order under this subsection may appoint different date for different provisions of this Act, or for different purposes.

(3) [*repealed*].

SCHEDULE

[*repealed*].

THE OFFSHORE INSTALLATIONS (REGISTRATION) REGULATIONS 1972

(S.I. 1972 No. 702, as amended by S.I. 1991 No. 679)

General note. References to the Secretary of State shall be construed as references to the Health and Safety Executive by virtue of the Offshore Safety (Repeals and Modifications) Regulations 1993, S.I. 1993 No. 1823. The transfer of responsibility from the Department of Energy to the HSE was one of the recommendations of the Cullen Report (Cmd. 1310, 1990) on the Piper Alpha disaster of 6 July 1988.

Citation, commencement and interpretation

1. These Regulations may be cited as the Offshore Installations (Registration) Regulations 1972 and shall come into operation on 1 June 1972.

2. (1) For the purposes of these Regulations—

"mobile installation" means an offshore installation which can be moved from place to place without major dismantling or modification, whether or not it has its own motive power; and "fixed installation" means an offshore installation which is not a *mobile installation.*

(2) Nothing in these Regulations shall apply to dredging installations which are registered as vessels (whether in the United Kingdom or elsewhere).

(3) References in these Regulations to an offshore installation shall by virtue of section 12(2) of *the Act* include references to a part of an offshore installation capable of being manned by one or more persons only where the part does not form or is not intended to form part of an installation already registered under these Regulations.

(4) References in these Regulations to the relevant waters are references to the waters to which *the Act* applies.

(5) The Interpretation Act 1889 [Interpretation Act 1978] shall apply to the interpretation of these Regulations as it applies to the interpretation of an Act of Parliament.

Register and fees relating to offshore installations

3.—(1) A Register of Offshore Installations shall be maintained at the offices of the Health and Safety Executive and applications for the registration or reregistration of offshore installations, for the amendment of entries in the Register and for the issue or amendment of certificates of registration and notifications required by any provision of these Regulations to be given to the Secretary of State shall be addressed to him at those offices.

(2) Where application is duly made to register an offshore installation, the Secretary of State shall cause particulars of the installation to be entered in the

Register and two copies of a certificate of registration to be issued; and when application is duly made to reregister an installation he shall cause it to be reregistered and two copies of a fresh certificate of registration to be issued accordingly:

Provided that the Secretary of State may decline to cause an installation to be registered or reregistered if it appears to him—

(a) that the person or persons applying are not in a position to discharge the duties imposed on the owner by or under *the Act*, or

(b) that the name or other designation submitted for registration is likely to be confused with that of any other installation already registered under these Regulations.

(3) Such amendments to the Register and to certificates of registration shall be made as the Secretary of State may from time to time consider necessary.

(4) The [Health and Safety Executive] may from time to time issue forms for use in connection with applications and the furnishing of information under these Regulations.

(5) There shall be payable in respect of an application to register or reregister an offshore installation under these Regulations or for the issue of a further copy of a certificate of registration the relevant fee specified in the Schedule hereto.

Duty to secure registration of offshore installations

4. On or after 30 June 1972—

(a) no *fixed installation* shall be established in the relevant waters,

(b) no *mobile installation* shall be brought into those waters with a view to its being stationed there, and

(c) no fixed or *mobile installation* shall be maintained in those waters, unless it is registered pursuant to these Regulations:

Provided that the Secretary of State may grant exemption from the application of this Regulation until 31 August 1972 in relation to any installation if application to register it was made before 30 June 1972.

5.—(1) An application for the first registration of an offshore installation shall include the following particulars—

(a) the name and address of the person or persons seeking to register it;

(b) where no address furnished pursuant to head (a) is an address in the United Kingdom, and address in the United Kingdom to which communications for the owner may be sent;

(c) a name or other designation for the installation;

(d) particulars of any other registration of the installation (whether as a vessel or otherwise and whether in the United Kingdom or elsewhere);

(e) an indication of the nature and the function or proposed function of the installation;

(f) an indication whether the installation is a mobile or a *fixed installation* and, in the case of a *mobile installation*, whether it has its own motive power;

(g) if the application relates to a part of an installation, particulars of any major additions expected to be made;

(h) an indication of the location at which the installation is stationed or intended to be stationed in the relevant waters;

(i) an indication of the period for which it is expected the installation will be stationed at the location mentioned pursuant to head (h); and

(j) in the case of a *mobile installation*, its tonnage.

(2) An application to reregister an offshore installation shall include sufficient information to identify the installation and particulars of the respects (if any) in which any particulars previously supplied about that installation are no longer correct.

Obligation to notify the Secretary of State of changed particulars

6.—(1) The owner of an offshore installation shall notify the Secretary of State forthwith—

(a) if the installation is converted from a *mobile installation* to a *fixed installation*, or vice versa;

(b) if the installation is dismantled, abandoned or destroyed;

(c) if the installation is combined with another installation or is divided so as to constitute two separate installations;

(d) in the case of an installation not on station in the relevant waters at the date of registration, of its arrival on station there;

(e) if the installation is removed to a new station in the relevant waters or removed to a place outside those waters;

(f) if the person or any of the persons in whose name the installation is registered cease to be in a position to discharge the duties imposed on the owner by or under *the Act*;

(g) if any other person or persons acquire rights enabling him or them to discharge or join in the discharge of the duties imposed on the owner by or under *the Act*; or

(h) if any error is discovered in any information furnished to the Secretary of State pursuant to these Regulations or if any other event occurs which makes the information so furnished incorrect in any material respect.

(2) Any notification made pursuant to paragraph (1) shall include sufficient information for the registered particulars to be amended where appropriate.

Cancellation and expiration of registration

7. The Secretary of State may cancel the registration of an installation if he learns that it has been dismantled, abandoned, destroyed or combined with another installation, or if it appears to him that any person or persons in whose name the installation is registered are no longer in a position to discharge the duties imposed on the owner by or under *the Act* or that any other person or persons have acquired rights enabling him or them to discharge or join in the discharge of those duties.

8. Unless previously cancelled, registration under these Regulations shall remain effective for a period of 25 years in the case of a *fixed installation* and for a period of 10 years in the case of a *mobile installation*.

Display of information

9.   One copy of the current certificate of registration issued under these Regulations shall be kept posted on board the offshore installation to which it relates in such a position that it can be conveniently read.

10.—(1) Save where the nature of the structure makes it impracticable, an offshore installation registered in accordance with these Regulations shall display its registered name or other designation in such a manner as to make the installation readily identifiable on approach by sea or air.

(2) No offshore installation shall display any name, letters or figures likely to be confused with a registered name or other designation.

Offences and penalties

11.—(1) A contravention of regulation 4 shall be an offence for which the owner of the relevant installation and the concession owner shall each be liable on summary conviction to a fine not exceeding £200.

(2) A contravention of any requirement of regulation 6, 9 or 10 of these Regulations shall be an offence for which the owner of the relevant installation shall be liable on summary conviction to a fine not exceeding £200.

(3) A contravention of any requirement of regulation 4, 9 or 10 of these Regulations shall be an offence for which the installation manager in charge of the relevant installation at the time of the contravention shall be liable on summary conviction to a fine not exceeding £100.

(4) A person who wilfully makes or signs a false statement for the purposes of these Regulations shall (without prejudice to any other penalty) be liable on summary conviction to a fine not exceeding £200.

(5) It shall be a defence in any proceedings for an offence under paragraphs (1) to (3) of this regulation for the person charged to prove—

(a) that he exercised all due diligence to prevent the commission of the offence; and
(b) that the relevant contravention was committed without his consent, connivance or wilful default.

SCHEDULE

FEES

	£
On application for the first registration of an offshore installation ..	£100
On application for reregistration following the expiration or cancellation of a previous registration	£500
On application for a further copy of a certificate of registration	£2

THE OFFSHORE INSTALLATIONS (MANAGERS) REGULATIONS 1972

(S.I. 1972 No. 703, as amended by S.I. 1991 No. 679)

General note. References to the Secretary of State shall be construed as references to the Health and Safety Executive by virtue of the Offshore Safety (Repeals and Modifications) Regulations 1993, S.I. 1993 No. 1823. The transfer of responsibility from the Department of Energy to the HSE was one of the recommendations of the Cullen Report (Cmd. 1310, 1990) on the Piper Alpha disaster of 6 July 1988.

Citation, commencement and interpretation

1.—(1) These Regulations may be cited as the Offshore Installations (Managers) Regulations 1972 and shall come into operation on 31 August 1972.

(2) The Interpretation Act 1889 [Interpretation Act 1978] shall apply to the interpretation of these Regulations as it applies to the interpretation of an Act of Parliament.

Notice of appointment and termination of appointment

2.—(1) The notice which under section 4(1) of *the Act* the owner of an installation is required to give to the Secretary of State regarding the appointment of an installation manager or of a person to act where necessary in place of the manager shall be given in writing in the form set out in Schedule 1 hereto and the particulars to be contained in the notice shall be the particulars required to complete that form in relation to the appointment.

(2) The notice which under subsection (4) of section 4 of the Act the owner of an installation is required to give to the Secretary of State as respects the termination of an appointment under that subsection shall be given in writing in the form set out in Schedule 2 hereto.

(3) The notices referred to in paragraphs (1) and (2) above shall be addressed to the Secretary of State at the offices of the Health and Safety Executive.

3.—(1) The installation manager for the time being in charge of an off-shore installation shall ensure that a notice of his appointment is kept posted on board the installation in such a position that it can be conveniently read.

(2) In the event of a failure to comply with this Regulation the installation manager shall be liable on summary conviction to a fine not exceeding £50.

Notice of restraint

4. The authority to whom notice shall be given pursuant to section 5(7) of the Act of the fact that a person has been kept under restraint and of the reasons for it shall be the Health and Safety Executive.

Exclusions from the obligations of sections 4 and 5 of the Act

5.   Sections 4 and 5 of the Act shall have no operation in relation to installations registered as vessels (whether so registered in the United Kingdom or
elsewhere) which are dredging installations or which are in transit to or from a
station, or in relation to installations which are unmanned.

SCHEDULE 1

FORM OF NOTIFICATION OF APPOINTMENT OF AN INSTALLATION MANAGER
MINERAL WORKINGS (OFFSHORE INSTALLATIONS) ACT 1971
Notice of Appointment Under Section 4(1)

NOTE: For convenience of notification and recording, this form should be completed
in respect of one appointee only. If it is desired to notify particulars of other appointments in respect of the same offshore installation, separate forms should be used for
each appointment, but information need not be duplicated.

Notice is hereby given that (^{1})

....was on (^{2}) ....

appointed

   *to be manager

   *to be a person to act where necessary in place of the manager of offshore installation

(^{3}) ....

pursuant to the requirements of section 4(1) of the Mineral Workings (Offshore

Installations) Act 1971.

†The appointee succeeds (^{4})..

whose appointee succeeds (^{4}) ....

whose appointment* [ceases]* [ceased] on (^{2})..

The appointee is aged and the qualifications, skills and experience which are considered to make him a suitable person for the appointment are as follows:—(^{5})

....

....

....

†The appointee is one of two or more persons appointed to act as manager and the

general nature of the rotation arrangement and the manner in which it is determined

who is in charge when more than one is appointed are as follows:—(^{5})

....

....

....

†The appointee is one of two or more persons appointed to act in place of the manager(s) and the arrangement whereby it is determined whether this appointee or another acts in place of the manager(s) is as follows:—(^{5})

....

....

....

Dated... signed ....

on behalf of (^{6}) ....status of signatory(^{7})................................

        (*)Delete as appropriate   (†)Delete if inappropriate.

(^{1}) Insert name of appointee.
(^{2}) Insert date.
(^{3}) Insert registered name or other designation of the installation or if no name or other designation has yet been registered under the Act other particulars sufficient to identify the installation.
(^{4}) Give name of superseded appointee.
(^{5}) Give brief particulars.
(^{6}) Give name of installation owner.
(^{7}) E.g. director or secretary of a body corporate.

SCHEDULE 2

FORM OF NOTIFICATION OF STATUTORY TERMINATION OF AN APPOINTMENT PURSUANT OF
SECTION 4(4) OF THE MINERAL WORKINGS (OFFSHORE INSTALLATIONS) ACT 1971

MINERAL WORKINGS (OFFSHORE INSTALLATIONS) ACT 1971

Notice of Termination of Appointment Under Section 4(4)

   Notice is hereby given that the appointment

of(^{1}) .... made on(^{2}) ....

under section 4(1) of the Mineral Workings (Offshore Installations) Act

1971 in relation to the offshore installation(^{3})..

was on(^{4}) .... terminated with effect from (^{5})

pursuant to the requirements of section 4(4) of the Act.

Dated... signed..

on behalf of(^{6}) ....status of signatory(^{7}) ....

(^{1}) Insert name of appointee.
(^{2}) Insert date of appointment.
(^{3}) Insert registered name or other designation of the installation or if no name or other designation has yet been registered under the Act other particulars sufficient to identify the installation.
(^{4}) Insert date of termination.
(^{5}) Insert relevant date.
(^{6}) Give name of installation owner.
(^{7}) E.g. director or secretary of a body corporate.

THE OFFSHORE INSTALLATIONS (INSPECTORS AND CASUALTIES) REGULATIONS 1973

(S.I. 1973 No. 1842, as amended by S.I. 1991 No. 679)

General note. References to the Secretary of State shall be construed as references to the Health and Safety Executive by virtue of the Offshore Safety (Repeals and Modifications) Regulations 1993, S.I. 1993 No. 1823. The transfer of responsibility from the Department of Energy to the HSE was one of the recommendations of the Cullen Report (Cmd. 1310, 1990) on the Piper Alpha disaster of 6 July 1988.

1. Citation, commencement and interpretation.—(1) These Regulations may be cited as the Offshore Installations (Inspectors and Casualties) Regulations 1973 and shall come into operation on 1 December 1973.

(2) In these Regulations unless the context otherwise requires—

"casualty" means a casualty or other accident involving loss of life or danger to life suffered by a person—

(a) employed on, on or working from an *offshore installation*; or
(b) on or working from an attendant *vessel*, in the course of any operation undertaken on or in connection with an *offshore installation*;

"disease" includes any ailment or adverse condition, whether of body or mind;

"equipment" means any plant, machinery, apparatus or system used, formerly used or intended to be used (whether on or from an *offshore installation* or on or from an attendant *vessel*) in the assembly, reconstruction, repair, dismantlement, operation, movement or inspection of an *offshore installation* or the inspection of the sea bed under or near an *offshore installation*;

"inspector" means a person appointed as an inspector under section 6(4) of *the Act*;

"manager" includes, where no manager is appointed pursuant to section 4 of *the Act*, any person made responsible by the owner for safety, health and welfare on board an *offshore installation*;

"offshore installation" includes any part of an offshore installation whether or not capable of being manned by one or more persons; and

"vessel" includes an aircraft, a hovercraft and any floating structure other than an *offshore installation*.

(3) The Interpretation Act 1889 [Interpretation Act 1978] shall apply to the interpretation of these Regulations as it applies to the interpretation of an Act of Parliament.

PART I
INSPECTION OF OFFSHORE INSTALLATIONS

Functions and powers of inspectors

2.—(1) For the purpose of ensuring that the provisions of *the Act* and of regulations thereunder are complied with, of investigating a *casualty* and generally assisting the Secretary of State in the execution of *the Act*, an *inspector*, at any time—

(a) may board an *offshore installation* and obtain access to all parts of it;

(b) may inspect an *offshore installation* and any *equipment*;

(c) may inspect the sea bed and subsoil under or near an *offshore installation*;

(d) may inspect and take copies from any certificate of insurance issued under regulations made under paragraph 4(2)(b) or (3) of the Schedule to *the Act* or any copy thereof so required to be maintained on an *offshore installation,* from any installation logbook or other record required to be maintained under regulations made under paragraph 11 of that Schedule or from any other document relating to the operation or safety of an *offshore installation* or of any *equipment*;

(e) may test any *equipment*;

(f) where a *casualty* has occurred or is apprehended, may dismantle any *equipment* or test to destruction or take possession of any *equipment*;

(g) may require the owner or *manager* or any person on board or near to an *offshore installation* to do or to refrain from doing any act as appears to the *inspector* to be necessary or expedient for the purpose of averting a *casualty* (whether the danger is immediate or not), or minimising the consequences of a *casualty*.

(2) An *inspector* shall permit the owner or *manager* or any person nominated by the owner or *manager* to be present when any inspection, test or dismantlement is carried out under this regulation.

(3) A requirement under paragraph (1)(g) above shall cease to have effect at the expiration of 3 days after the date on which it is given, unless the Secretary of State by notice given to the owner of the *offshore installation* extends its operation (with or without variation) for a further period or periods:

Provided that, before giving notice extending the operation of the requirement, the Secretary of State shall consult with the owner of the installation and shall consider any representations made by him.

3.—(1) In connection with any of his functions under regulation 2 an *inspector*—

(a) may make such requirements of any person (including the owner and *manager* of the installation) as appear to the *inspector* to be required for the performance of those functions whether by himself or any other person acting at the direction of the Secretary of State:

Provided that before making a requirement in connection with any of paragraphs (1)(e), (f) or (g) of that Regulation, the *inspector* shall consult with the owner or *manager* with a view to maintaining safety and to minimising interference with the operation of the installation;

(b)   may require any person to produce to the *inspector* any article to which this regulation applies and which is in his possession or custody;

(c)   may make notes, take measurements, make drawings and take photographs of an *offshore installation* and of any article to which this regulation applies;

(d)   may require the owner or *manager* of the installation to furnish to him any article to which this regulation applies (other than a document) or, in the case of any article on any *vessel*, may so require the master, captain or person in charge of the *vessel*;

(e)   may require the owner or *manager* of an *offshore installation* or any person employed on or in connection with the installation or *equipment* to carry out or to assist in carrying out any inspection, test or dismantlement of the *offshore installation* or of any *equipment*;

(f)   may require the owner or *manager* of an *offshore installation* or the concession owner concerned to assist him in carrying out an inspection of the sea bed or subsoil under or near the installation; and

(g)   may require the owner or *manager* to provide at any reasonable time conveyance to or from the installation of the *inspector*, any other person acting at the direction of the Secretary of State, any *equipment* required by the *inspector* for testing and any article of which he has taken possession pursuant to these Regulations.

(2)   This regulation applies to articles of the following descriptions, that is to say, any *equipment* or part thereof, a specimen of any material or substance (including a natural substance) on or near an *offshore installation* and any document of a description referred to in regulation 2(1)(d).

4.—(1)   An *inspector* may require an owner or a *manager* of an *offshore installation* or any other person to furnish to him or to a person acting at the direction of the Secretary of State such information as he may reasonably demand in exercise of the *inspector*'s functions under regulation 2.

(2)   Information required to be furnished under paragraph (1) may, and if so required by the *inspector* shall, be furnished in writing, and if furnished orally may be so furnished in the presence of any person whom the person furnishing the information reasonably desires to be present and, if practicable and that person so wishes, in the presence of the *manager* of the installation.

5.   Duties of owners of *offshore installations* and others.—(1)   The owner or *manager* of an *offshore installation* shall provide an *inspector* and any other person acting at the direction of the Secretary of State with reasonable accommodation and means of subsistence while on board an *offshore installation* for the purposes of these Regulations.

(2)   The owner or *manager* of an *offshore installation* and any other person, in relation to any *offshore installation* in any area in respect of which he is the concession owner, shall afford generally or so cause to be afforded to an *inspector* and any other person acting at the direction of the Secretary of State all such facilities and assistance (including the carrying out of any procedures by way of demonstration) as an *inspector* or such other person may reasonably require in performing the functions of an *inspector* under these Regulations; and an *inspector* or such other person may require accordingly.

6.   Disclosure of information. A person acting at the direction of the Secretary of State (not being a person holding office under Her Majesty) shall not disclose to any other person any information obtained or received by him while acting at such direction—

(a)   by virtue of these Regulations other than regulation 4(1), without the consent of the owner; or

(b)   by virtue of regulation 4(1), without the consent of the person who furnished the information; or

(c)   under any provision of these Regulations, without the consent of the Secretary of State.

Offences under Part I

7.—(1) Any person—

(a)   who fails to comply with any requirement made of him under this Part of these Regulations; or

(b)   who obstructs any other person in the performance of his functions, powers or duties under, or in complying with any requirement made of that person under, this Part of these Regulations; or

(c)   who, without permission granted by an *inspector* or other person acting at the direction of the Secretary of State, removes, conceals or tampers with any article of which possession has been taken by an *inspector* or such a person,

shall be guilty of an offence.

(2) An owner or *manager* who fails to provide accommodation and means of subsistence pursuant to regulation 5(1) shall be guilty of an offence.

(3) An owner, *manager* or concession owner who fails to afford or cause to be afforded facilities and assistance pursuant to regulation 5(2) shall be guilty of an offence.

(4) A person acting at the direction of the Secretary of State who discloses any information in contravention of regulation 6 shall be guilty of an offence.

8.—(1) It shall be a defence to a charge—

(a)   under regulation 7(1)(a) relating to failure to comply with a requirement made under regulation 5(2); or

(b)   under regulation 7(3) relating to failure to afford facilities or assistance under regulation 5(2),

to show that the person charged, being the *manager* of the *offshore installation* to which the charge relates, was acting, in respect of the facts alleged, under and in accordance with the provisions of subsections (4) or (6) of section 5 of *the Act* (which confers powers on the *manager* of an *offshore installation*).

(2) The fine which may be imposed under regulation 7(2) shall not exceed £100 and proceedings on indictment thereunder shall be excluded.

(3) The variation or revocation of any requirement given or made under any provision of these Regulations shall not affect liability for any offence committed before the variation or revocation takes effect.

PART II

CASUALTIES

Reports of casualties

9. Where a *casualty* has occurred, the *manager* of the *offshore installation* on or near to which it occurred—

   (a) shall, in the most expeditious manner practicable, immediately inform the owner of the installation of its occurrence with brief particulars of the *casualty*, including the position of the installation, the time of the *casualty* and the identity of any person killed, lost or seriously injured;

   (b) shall sign an entry in the installation logbook maintained on the installation in accordance with regulations made under paragraph 11 of the Schedule to *the Act* containing particulars of the matters specified in the Schedule to these Regulations; and

   (c) shall, as soon as practicable and in any event within 3 days after the occurrence of the *casualty*, deliver to the installation owner particulars in writing of the matters specified in the Schedule to these Regulations.

10.   An owner of an installation—

   (a) upon being informed of the occurrence of a *casualty* shall, in the most expeditious manner practicable give to the Health and Safety Executive all information relating to it in his possession; and

   (b) as soon as practicable and in any event within 3 days after receipt by him of written particulars pursuant to regulation 9(c), shall deliver to the Health and Safety Executive a copy of those particulars together with—

     (i) the name or other designation of the *offshore installation*;

     (ii) the owner's name and address; and

     (iii) the name and address of the *manager* of the installation at the time of the *casualty*; and

   (c) so soon as it comes to his knowledge that any person injured in a *casualty* has died, give notice of the death to the Health and Safety Executive notwithstanding, if such be the case, that he is required to send a return of the death to the Registrar General of Shipping and Seamen.

11.   Disturbance of site of *casualty*. No person shall disturb the place where a *casualty* has occurred or tamper with anything thereat before—

   (a) the expiration of 3 clear days after the owner of the installation has, pursuant to regulation 10(a), given to the Health and Safety Executive information relating to the *casualty*, or

   (b) an *inspector* has concluded an investigation of the *casualty*;

whichever first occurs:

Provided that nothing in this regulation shall prohibit the doing of anything by or with the consent of an *inspector*.

12.   Returns of injuries, etc.—(1) The owner of an *offshore installation* shall make a return of every accident, injury or *disease* (other than an injury required to be notified under regulation 9) suffered by any person on or working from the installation and by any person on or working from an attendant *vessel* who is injured in the course of any operation undertaken on or in connection with the installation by reason of which such person is disabled from work for a continuous period of 3 days.

(2) A return under this regulation—

(a) shall relate to a period of 3 months ending on the last day of March, June, September or December excluding therefrom any period during which there is no obligation to maintain an installation logbook under regulations made under paragraph 11 of the Schedule to *the Act*;
(b) shall be made to the Health and Safety Executive within 10 days after the end of the period to which it relates; and
(c) shall contain particulars of the following—
  (i) the name or other designation of the *offshore installation*;
  (ii) the name and address of the owner of the installation;
  (iii) the name of each person injured or suffering from a *disease* and the name and address of his employer; and
  (iv) the date and time of any injury and the date when the symptoms of any *disease* were first observed,

together with a reference to any relevant entry in an installation logbook and brief particulars of the accident or of the injury or *disease*.

13.   Special reports of casualties. Where a *casualty* occurs, the Secretary of State may, at any time, direct an *inspector* to make a special report with respect thereto, and the Secretary of State may cause any such report to be made public at such time and in such manner as he thinks fit.

14.   Offences under Part II.—(1) Any person who fails to comply with an obligation imposed on him under regulations 9, 10, 11 or 12 shall be guilty of an offence.

(2) In any proceedings taken in respect of a contravention of regulation 11, it shall be a defence to show—

(a) that the doing of the act in question was necessary for securing the safety of the *offshore installation* or of any person on it or near it; or
(b) that the doing of the act in question was necessary to secure that the normal movement or operation of the *offshore installation* or the normal operation of any *equipment* on it should not be unreasonably impeded: Provided that—
  (i) an investigation by an *inspector* was not thereby prejudiced; and
  (ii) the installation *manager* or the installation owner had informed the Health and Safety Executive or an *inspector* at least 24 hours before the doing of the act that the act was to be done; and

   (iii) an adequate plan or other record made by some responsible
        person is produced showing any part of the installation and any
        article affected by the doing of the act in the state in which it was
        immediately before the doing of the act.

THE SCHEDULE

Regulations 9, 10

Particulars of casualty on or near to an Offshore Installation

1. The date and time of the *casualty*.
2. The place where, or the position of the *offshore installation* when, the *casualty* occurred.
3. The place on the installation or elsewhere where the *casualty* occurred.
4. A description of the *casualty*, including any operation being carried out, and any *equipment* being used.
5. A description of any damage sustained by the *offshore installation*, any *equipment* or any *vessel* and the name and port or place of registry of any *vessel* involved.
6. The name of any person killed, lost or seriously injured in the *casualty* and the name and address of his employer and a description of any injury, including an injury resulting in death.
7. The name and address of any witness to the *casualty* and the name and address of his employer.

THE OFFSHORE INSTALLATIONS (CONSTRUCTION AND SURVEY) REGULATIONS 1974

(S.I. 1974 No. 289)

General note. It is to be borne in mind that the Workplace (Health, Safety and Welfare) Regulations, S.I. 1992 No. 3004, do not apply to a workplace where the only activities being undertaken are the exploration for or extraction of mineral resources.

References to the Secretary of State shall be construed as references to the Health and Safety Executive by virtue of the Offshore Safety (Repeals and Modifications) Regulations 1993, S.I. 1993 No. 1823.

The transfer of responsibility from the Department of Energy to the HSE was one of the recommendations of the Cullen Report (Cmd. 1310, 1990) on the Piper Alpha disaster of 6 July 1988.

Citation, commencement and interpretation
1. These Regulations may be cited as the Offshore Installations (Construction and Survey) Regulations 1974 and shall come into operation on 1 May 1974.

2.—(1) In these Regulations and in the Schedules hereto, unless the context otherwise requires—

"Certificate of Fitness" means a certificate issued by a *Certifying Authority* under regulation 9;

"Certifying Authority" means the Secretary of State or any person, committee, society or other body of persons appointed by the Secretary of State pursuant to regulation 4;

"environmental factors" mean the matters referred to in Part II of Schedule 2;

"equipment" means any plant, machinery, apparatus or system attached to or forming part of an offshore installation;

"fixed installation" means an offshore installation which is not a *mobile installation*;

"mobile installation" means an offshore installation which can be moved from place to place without major dismantling or modification, whether or not it has its own motive power;

"operations manual" means written particulars provided by the owner of an offshore installation for the information, guidance and instruction of the manager thereof in securing, in the case of a *fixed installation*, the safety of the installation when established at a station and, in the case of a *mobile installation*, the safety, *seaworthiness* and stability of the installation when moving to or from, or being located on, or removed from, or maintained at, a station;

"primary structure" means all structural components of an offshore installation, the failure of which would seriously endanger the safety of the installation;

"relevant waters" means waters to which *the Act* applies;

"seaworthiness" means the capacity of a *mobile installation* to withstand, while floating, all relevant *environmental factors*;

"survey" means an examination conducted by a *surveyor* of an offshore installation or any part thereof or of any *equipment*, including the scrutiny of any document relevant thereto, and the conducting of any tests which a *surveyor* considers necessary in order to assess the integrity or safety of any item and whether any requirement of these Regulations has been complied with; and

"surveyor" means a surveyor appointed by a *Certifying Authority*.

(2) Nothing in these Regulations shall apply to an offshore installation which is a dredging installation and which is registered as a vessel (whether so registered in the United Kingdom or elsewhere) or to an offshore installation which can be navigated or operated when wholly submerged in water.

(3) The Interpretation Act 1889 shall apply to the interpretation of these Regulations as it applies to the interpretation of an Act of Parliament.

Certification of offshore installations
3.—(1) On or after 31 August 1975:—

(a) no *fixed installation* shall be established in the *relevant waters*;
(b) no *mobile installation* shall be brought into those waters with a view to its being stationed there; and
(c) no fixed or *mobile installation* shall be maintained in those waters,

unless there is in force in respect thereof a valid *Certificate of Fitness.*

(2) On or after the date specified in paragraph (1), no *mobile installation* shall be moved to a station in the *relevant waters* unless prior to moving the owner of the installation has obtained from a competent person a report on the *environmental factors* at that station and the owner has reasonable grounds for believing that the installation is capable of withstanding those factors.

4.   The Secretary of State may appoint any person, committee, society or other body of persons to cause *surveys* and assessments to be made pursuant to these Regulations and to certify offshore installations as fit for any of the purposes specified in these Regulations.

5.—(1) An application for a *Certificate of Fitness* in respect of an offshore installation, or for a renewal thereof, shall—

(a) be made by or on behalf of the owner of that installation;
(b) be made to a *Certifying Authority* in the form specified in Part I of Schedule 1 duly completed and signed;
(c) be accompanied by such information as may be necessary to enable the fees to be calculated in accordance with regulation 13;
(d) be accompanied by sufficient plans, drawings, specifications, reports and other documents and information to enable the *Certifying Authority* to ascertain whether the requirements specified in Schedule 2, or such of the same as are applicable to the installation and its *equipment*, have been complied with; and
(e) be accompanied by the *operations manual* relating to the installation:

Provided that it shall be permissible to submit any document referred to in paragraphs (d) and (e) at any date prior to the grant of the *Certificate of Fitness.*

(2) If upon receipt of an application for a *Certificate of Fitness* in respect of an offshore installation, or for a renewal thereof, the *Certifying Authority* shall be of opinion that the application and the supporting documents and information comply with the requirements of paragraph (1), the Authority shall—

(a) cause to be carried out, or ensure that there has already been carried out, by a competent person, an independent assessment of the design and method of construction of the installation to ascertain whether the requirements specified in Schedule 2 hereto, or such of the same as are applicable to the installation and its *equipment,* have been complied with, and an independent assessment of the provisions of the *operations manual* to ascertain whether the information, guidance and instructions contained therein are adequate and appropriate in relation to the installation; and

(b) cause to be carried out a major *survey* of the installation and its *equipment* in accordance with regulation 8(1) in order to ascertain whether the installation conforms to the design and method of construction referred to in sub-paragraph (a) and whether the requirements specified in Schedule 2, or such of the same as are applicable to the installation and its *equipment,* have been complied with.

Surveys of offshore installations
6.—(1) A *Certifying Authority* shall appoint, from among persons appearing to the Authority to be suitably qualified, *surveyors* whose duty it shall be to conduct the *surveys* required by these Regulations.

(2) In carrying out any such *survey,* a *surveyor* shall be accorded all necessary facilities therefor by the owner and manager of the installation concerned, and the installation and any of its *equipment* shall be submitted to such tests as may in the opinion of the *surveyor* be necessary to ascertain whether the requirements specified in Schedule 2, or such of the same as are applicable, have been complied with.

(3) On completing a *survey,* a *surveyor* shall make a declaration to the *Certifying Authority* giving the date of completion of his *survey,* the results thereof and his findings as to whether the installation complies with the requirements of Schedule 2, or such of the same as may be applicable, on a form specified by the Authority for that purpose, which form shall remain in the Authority's custody.

7.—(1) If at any time while an application for a *Certificate of Fitness* is being considered by a *Certifying Authority* or while a *Certificate of Fitness* is in force any alteration should be made to any plan, drawing, specification or other document (apart from an *operations manual*), a copy of which was previously submitted pursuant to these Regulations, the owner of the installation concerned shall forthwith upon such alteration send particulars thereof to the *Certifying Authority* which is considering the application or which issued the certificate in force of both those Authorities (as the case may be).

(2) No alteration shall be made to the provisions of any *operations manual*, which has previously been submitted to a *Certifying Authority*, without the consent of that Authority.

(3) If at any time while an application for a *Certificate of Fitness* is being considered by a *Certifying Authority* or while a *Certificate of Fitness* is in force there occurs in respect of the offshore installation to which the application or certificate (as the case may be) relates any of the following events:—

(a) it is damaged, or is suspected of having been damaged, in a manner likely to impair the safety, strength, stability and, in the case of a *mobile installation*, *seaworthiness* of the installation; or

(b) it demonstrates signs of deterioration in its structure to an extent likely to impair the safety, strength, stability and, in the case of a *mobile installation*, *seaworthiness* of the installation; or

(c) its *equipment* is subjected to any alteration, repair or replacement; the owner of the installation shall forthwith notify in writing the *Certifying Authority* which is considering the application or which issued the certificate in force or both those Authorities (as the case may be) of the occurrence of that event, giving whatever particulars may be required to enable the Authority concerned to determine whether or not an additional *survey* should be carried out.

(4) No repair, replacement, alteration or dismantlement shall be carried out in respect of any offshore installation at any time while a *Certificate of Fitness* is in force in respect of that installation unless the procedures specified in sub-paragraphs (a), (b) and (c) of paragraph 1 of Part VII of Schedule 2 are observed in respect thereof, the references in those sub-paragraphs to "the *Certifying Authority*" being taken to refer to the *Certifying Authority* which issued the before-mentioned *Certificate of Fitness* and the reference therein to "such work" being taken to refer to such repair, replacement, alteration or dismantlement (as the case may be).

8.—(1) In respect of every offshore installation in relation to which there is no *Certificate of Fitness* in force or in respect of which a *Certificate of Fitness* is in force and a renewal thereof is sought, there shall be carried out a *survey* (herein referred to as a "major survey") which shall include a thorough examination of the installation and its *equipment* in order to ascertain the matters specified in regulation 5(2)(b):

Provided that a *Certifying Authority* may accept as part of a major survey the results of a *survey* carried out otherwise than under these Regulations if satisfied that the results so obtained are equivalent to those which would have been obtained in the course of a major survey:

Provided further that at any time after the installation has been subjected to a major survey a *Certifying Authority* may accept, instead of a subsequent major survey, a series of continuous surveys conducted in rotation in conjunction with the annual surveys required under paragraph (2) if satisfied that the results so obtained are equivalent to those which would have been obtained in the course of a major survey.

(2) (a) In respect of every installation to which a *Certificate of Fitness* is in force, there shall be carried out on behalf of the *Certifying Authority* which issued that certificate surveys (hereinafter referred to as "annual surveys") of a selection of the members, joints and areas of the *primary structure* of the installation, the parts of the installation referred to in Part V of Schedule 2 and its *equipment,* the selection being sufficient in number, disposition or extent (as the case may be) to provide reasonable evidence as to whether the installation and its *equipment* continue to comply with the requirements of Schedule 2, or such of the same as may be applicable.

(b) The first annual survey shall be carried out within not less than 9 nor more than 18 months after the date of issue of the *Certificate of Fitness* and thereafter similar surveys shall be carried out within not less than 9 nor more than 15 months of each anniversary of the date of issue of the certificate during the period in which it is in force.

(3) Upon receipt of notification pursuant to regulation 7(3) of the occurrence in respect of an installation of any of the events specified therein, or if the *Certifying Authority* otherwise has reason to believe that any such event has occurred, the *Certifying Authority* may cause such additional *survey* of the installation and its *equipment* to be carried out as the Authority thinks fit to ascertain, in the case of an installation in respect of which an application for a certificate is being considered, whether any changes have been made or taken place sufficient to render no longer accurate the data which accompanied the application and, in the case of an installation in respect of which a *Certificate of Fitness* is in force, whether the installation and its *equipment* continue to comply with the requirements of Schedule 2, or such of the same as may be applicable.

Certificates of Fitness

9.—(1) After considering all documents and other information submitted in pursuance of regulation 5(1) and all declarations of *survey* and the results of all assessments carried out in pursuance of regulation 5(2) the *Certifying Authority* may, if the Authority is satisfied that it is proper to do so, issue a *Certificate of Fitness* in accordance with these Regulations certifying that the offshore installation concerned is fit to be established or stationed (according to whether it is respectively a fixed or a *mobile installation*) and maintained in the *relevant waters.*

(2) A *Certificate of Fitness* shall be in the form set out in Part II of Schedule 1 and may contain whatever limitations the *Certifying Authority* considers it appropriate to specify as respects the movement, location and operation of the installation to which it relates having regard to the design of the installation, the method of its construction, the materials employed in its construction and the *environmental factors.* The *Certifying Authority* shall issue two copies of the *Certificate of Fitness* to the owner of the installation.

(3) One copy of the current *Certificate of Fitness* shall be kept posted on board the installation to which it relates in such a position that it can be conveniently read, save for occasions when in pursuance of these Regulations any amendment or endorsement required to be made thereto is being effected.

(4) The *Certifying Authority* may amend any *Certificate of Fitness* by recording on the copy of the certificate referred to in paragraph (3) any changes which have occurred since it was issued, and a record of any *survey* made in pursuance

of regulation 8(2) or (3) in connection with the installation to which the certificate relates shall be endorsed thereon on behalf of the *Certifying Authority* by the *surveyor* who carried it out. The *surveyor* shall also furnish the owner of the installation with a copy of the endorsement made by him.

10.—(1) If, after considering the matters referred to in regulation 9(1), the *Certifying Authority* is not satisfied that a *Certificate of Fitness* may properly be issued, the Authority shall send a notification in writing to that effect to the owner of the offshore installation concerned giving the reasons for the conclusion, and shall at the same time send a copy of that notification to the Secretary of State.

(2) If, after considering any declaration of *survey* carried out in pursuance of regulation 8(2) or (3), or particulars of any alteration to a document submitted in pursuance of regulation 7(1), the *Certifying Authority* is of opinion that the installation is not, or is no longer, fit to be maintained in the *relevant waters* or in any part thereof to which it may be limited by the terms of the *Certificate of Fitness* issued in respect of it, the Authority shall send a notification in writing to that effect to the owner of the offshore installation concerned giving the reasons for forming that opinion, and shall at the same time send a copy of that notification to the Secretary of State.

11.—(1) Subject to paragraph (2), the Secretary of State may terminate a *Certificate of Fitness* if he is satisfied that—

(a) information supplied in connection with the application therefor was incorrect in a material particular; or

(b) the installation to which it relates is not, or is no longer, fit to be maintained in the *relevant waters* or in any part of such waters to which it may be limited by the terms thereof; or

(c) there has been a failure to observe any limitation contained therein respecting the movement, location or operation of the installation; or

(d) the installation to which it relates has been moved to a station contrary to the provisions of regulation 3(2); or

(e) there has been a failure to comply with any regulation; or

(f) it has been superseded by a new *Certificate of Fitness,* or by an exemption made by the Secretary of State, issued in respect of the same installation; or

(g) the installation has in the opinion of the Secretary of State changed in character to such an extent that the issue of a new *Certificate of Fitness* is desirable.

(2) Before a *Certificate of Fitness* is terminated in accordance with paragraph (1), both the owner of the installation to which it relates, and the *Certifying Authority* which issued the certificate, shall be given notification in writing of the reasons for such termination, and the date on which it is to take effect, which shall not be less than 30 days after the date of issue of the said notification.

(3) A *Certificate of Fitness* shall be valid for such period as the *Certifying Authority* may specify, not exceeding 5 years from the date of completion of the last major *survey* carried out pursuant to regulation 8(1) or of the last equivalent *survey* carried out in accordance with the second proviso to that regulation, unless it is previously terminated by the Secretary of State in accordance with paragraph (1). The date of expiration shall be recorded on the certificate by the *Certifying Authority.*

Exemptions

12.—(1) The Secretary of State may exempt any offshore installation or part of an offshore installation from all or any of the provisions of these Regulations and any such exemption may be made subject to any conditions which the Secretary of State sees fit to impose.

(2) Where an installation or part of an installation has been exempted in accordance with paragraph (1) but subject to a condition and the condition is not observed, the exemption shall not have effect and proceedings may be brought in respect of any breach of duty as if the exemption had not been made.

(3) When an installation or part of an installation has been exempted in accordance with paragraph (1), the *Certifying Authority* shall endorse a note of such exemption and of any conditions to which it is made subject on the *Certificate of Fitness* (if any) relating to that installation issued in accordance with regulation 9.

Fees

13.—(1) There shall be payable in respect of the services provided in accordance with these Regulations the fees specified in Schedule 3:

Provided that if the Secretary of State is satisfied that the cost of work required to be performed in a particular case exceeds the maximum sum payable in accordance with the provisions of Schedule 3 he may, at his discretion, authorise such higher sum as, in all the circumstances, he considers proper.

(2) On the making of an application for a *Certificate of Fitness* under regulation 5, a sum not exceeding 5 per cent. of the maximum fee specified in paragraph 1 of Schedule 3 shall be payable to the *Certifying Authority* which may require that the balance of the fees and expenses due shall be payable at any time before giving its decision regarding the application.

Offences

14. A person who wilfully falsifies or uses a false document or who supplies or uses information or makes any statement which he knows to be false in a material particular for the purposes of these Regulations shall be guilty of an offence.

SCHEDULE 1

Regulation 5(1)

PART I
FORM OF APPLICATION FOR A CERTIFICATE OF FITNESS

MINERAL WORKINGS (OFFSHORE INSTALLATIONS) ACT 1971

THE OFFSHORE INSTALLATIONS (CONSTRUCTION AND SURVEY)
REGULATIONS 1974

1. Name or other designation of the installation([1])

2. Name(s) and address(es) of the owner(s) of the installation ....

....

3. Address of owner(s) in the United Kingdom for the service of notices

....

4. Particulars of registration of the installation([1]):

   (a) Date of issue of the certificate ....

   (b) Certificate number ....

5. Particulars of any previous Certificates of Fitness issued in respect of the installation:

   (a) Date of issue of the certificate(s) ....

   (b) Certificate number(s) ....

   (c) Certifying Authority(ies) ....

   ....

6. Particulars of any other certificates which may be of relevance([2]).....................

   ....

7. Present location of the installation and intended location (if different) ([3])

   ....

8. Name(s), address(es) and qualifications of the designer(s) of the installation

   ....

   ....

9. Name(s), address(es) and qualifications of the person(s) under whom construction of the installation was (or is being) supervised..

   ....

10. Brief details of the documents lodged in support of the application([4])

    ....

    ....

11. Current construction cost of installation([5]) ....

I/We being the above-named owner(s) of the above-described offshore installation, hereby make application for a Certificate of Fitness to be issued for that installation in accordance with the provisions of the said Act and Regulations, and I/we hereby declare that the information given in this application and in any documents lodged herewith is correct.

Dated ....19...........................   Signed
                                                   on behalf of ([6]) ....
                                                   status of signatory([7]).........

NOTES

(1) Pursuant to the Offshore Installations (Registration) Regulations 1972.
(2) E.g. insurance and (in the case of vessels) merchant shipping certificates.
(3) Where appropriate, give name of dock, yard or harbour or (if at sea) geographical co-ordinates and licence block number (if any).
(4) Pursuant to regulation 5(1)(c), (d) and (e) of the Offshore Installations (Construction and Survey) Regulations 1974.

(5) This may be required to determine the amount of the fee pursuant to Regulation 13 of the said Regulations.

(6) Give the name(s) of the owner(s).

(7) E.g. director or secretary of a body corporate.

PART II
FORM OF CERTIFICATE OF FITNESS

Regulation 9(2)

UNITED KINGDOM OF GREAT BRITAIN AND NORTHERN IRELAND
CERTIFICATE OF FITNESS OF OFFSHORE INSTALLATION

Certificate Number ....

Name or other designation of the offshore installation ....

Description of installation ....

Name(s) of owner(s) ....

THIS IS TO CERTIFY pursuant to regulation 9(1) of the Offshore Installations (Construction and Survey) Regulations 1974 that the above-described offshore installation is fit to be * established/stationed and maintained in waters to which the Mineral Workings (Offshore Installations) Act 1971 applies,† subject to the following limitations:

This Certificate remains valid subject to annual and additional surveys in accordance with the Regulations until ...... unless previously terminated by the Secretary of State.

Issued at ....on ....19 ....

Signed...............................

Designation..........................

on behalf of.........................

A Certifying Authority

Appointed pursuant to the

Regulations.

*delete whichever is inapplicable
†delete if inapplicable

SCHEDULE 2

PART I
INTERPRETATION

In this Schedule—

"non-slip surface" means a surface designed to prevent or reduce slipping;

"recognised" in relation to a standard practice (including a code of practice) or specification means recognised by the *Certifying Authority* in the particular instance; and

"suitable" in relation to a material or an article means that the properties and characteristics of the material or article are such that it can safely be used for the purpose described.

PART II
ENVIRONMENTAL CONSIDERATIONS

1.   Every offshore installation shall be capable of withstanding any combination of—
(a)   meteorological and oceanological conditions; and
(b)   properties and configuration of the sea bed and subsoil,
to which the installation may foreseeably be subjected at the place at which it is, or is intended to be, located, as assessed in accordance with paragraphs 2 and 3.

2.   An assessment of the matters referred to in paragraph 1 shall be made by a competent person and (to such extent as may be relevant to the installation concerned) shall take into consideration—
(a)   the water depth, the tidal range and the height of wind-induced and pressure-induced wave surges;
(b)   the frequency and direction of winds and their respective speeds, averaging periods and heights above the surface of the sea;
(c)   the heights, directions and periods of waves, the probability of their occurrence and the effect of currents, sea bed topography and other factors likely to modify their characteristics;
(d)   the direction, speed and duration of tidal and other currents;
(e)   characteristics of the sea bed which may affect the foundations of the installation;
(f)   air and sea temperature extremes;
(g)   the extent to which marine growth may form on the submerged sections of the installation; and
(h)   the extent to which snow and ice may accumulate on or against the installation.

3.   In assessing the matters referred to in paragraph 2—
(a)   the minimum values to be ascribed by the competent person shall not be less than those likely to be exceeded on average once only in any period of 50 years; and
(b)   full account shall be taken of the records, predictions and other information available from the Institute of Oceanographic Science, the Meteorological Office of the Ministry of Defence or from any other body of comparable status fulfilling substantially the same functions or any of them.

PART III
FOUNDATIONS

1.   Those parts of an offshore installation which either from time to time or at all times are, or are intended to be, in direct contact with, and transmitting loads to, the sea bed and subsoil shall be capable of maintaining the integrity of the *primary structure* of the installation and of the sea bed and subsoil and generally of supporting the installation and maintaining it in a safe and stable condition.

2.   An assessment of the matters referred to in paragraph 1 shall be made by a competent person and shall include an investigation of the site or intended site of the installation concerned in order to ascertain and take into consideration—
(a)   the configuration of the sea bed and subsoil;
(b)   the properties and condition of the sea bed and subsoil;
(c)   the presence of any man-made hazards or obstructions; and
(d)   all other factors likely to affect the stability of the sea bed and subsoil,
at that site, such investigation to comply, so far as possible under marine conditions, with a recognised code of practice.

PART IV
PRIMARY STRUCTURE

1. *Forces*
Every offshore installation shall be capable of withstanding any foreseeable combination of forces arising from—
(a) the weight of the installation, including all *equipment* and stores thereon;
(b) the buoyancy of any structural element which may be, or may become, submerged in water;
(c) the process of moving the installation or any part thereof from place to place;
(d) the operation of maintaining the installation in any desired position;
(e) the *environmental factors*;
(f) the inertia of structural and other masses when the installation is constrained to move under the influence of the forces exerted by the *environmental factors*;
(g) the operation of *equipment* and all functional activity associated with the installation;
(h) ships berthing and departing, aircraft landing and taking off, and any other operations associated with the transfer of persons, stores and *equipment*;
(i) the fabrication, assembly, erection, alteration and dismantlement of the installation; and
(j) (in the case of a *mobile installation*) changes of trim or during transition between the floating and sea bed and subsoil supported modes, or a combination of the two,
together with any impact or impulse forces developed in consequence of the sudden application of all or any of the above-mentioned forces.

2. *Design criteria*
In respect of every offshore installation—
(a) stresses (including stresses caused by the forces referred to in paragraph 1) shall be calculated either by means of a mathematical analysis of the *primary structure* of the installation appropriate to that structure and approved by the *Certifying Authority* or by means of established rules for design approved by the *Certifying Authority*;
(b) factors of safety and maximum working stresses shall be in accordance with the recommendations contained in codes of practice and other recognised standards appropriate to the material concerned and the conditions under which the material is to be used;
(c) the design of joints and other structural details shall be such as to minimise stress concentrations;
(d) the calculated fatigue life of the *primary structure* shall be capable of being demonstrated to the reasonable satisfaction of the *Certifying Authority* as exceeding the period for which a Certificate of Fitness may be granted;
(e) the frequency at which the installation or any of its structural components naturally vibrate shall not be so approximate to the frequency of any foreseeable external force as to cause abnormal displacement; and
(f) deflections in structural components shall not be such as to affect the safety of the installation.

3. *Stability*
(a) Every *mobile installation* shall be constructed so that—
(i) under any combination of forces envisaged in paragraph 1 the forces of weight and buoyancy shall operate to induce the installation to maintain, or return to, an upright position;
(ii) any part thereof intended to remain buoyant on immersion in water and being of sufficient magnitude shall be subdivided into watertight compartments by means of watertight decks, bulkheads or other internal structures

strong enough to withstand any hydrostatic pressures to which that part may foreseeably be subjected; and

(iii) in any conditions permitting operations to be carried on it will remain afloat and stable notwithstanding the flooding of any one watertight compartment.

(b) Every *fixed installation* and every *mobile installation* designed to be supported from time to time by the sea bed and subsoil shall—

(i) be capable of withstanding the sliding forces and the overturning moments to which it may foreseeably be subjected without loss of positive bearing on any part of the foundation of the installation; and

(ii) impose on the foundation only such loads as may safely be supported by the sea bed and subsoil, and without causing settlement likely to endanger the integrity and stability of the installation.

PART V
SECONDARY STRUCTURE AND FITTINGS

1. *Superstructure*

The superstructure of every offshore installation shall be capable of withstanding all forces to which it may foreseeably be subjected and, in particular—

(a) deck houses and other structures on decks which may be swept by waves shall be constructed in accordance with recognised requirements;

(b) every external part of the installation which is not designed to resist wave impact shall be positioned so as to maintain at all times a clearance above the highest wave crest which may reasonably be anticipated; and

(c) every deck shall be capable of carrying all concentrations of loads to which it may foreseeably be subjected.

2. *Helicopter landing area*

Every helicopter landing area forming part of an offshore installation shall—

(a) be located in a position readily accessible to and from the living accommodation of the installation or any other area of the installation likely to be regularly manned;

(b) be large enough, and have sufficient clear approach and departure paths, to enable any helicopter intended to use the landing area safely to land thereon and to take off therefrom in any wind and weather conditions permitting helicopter operation;

(c) be strong enough to withstand any landing by any helicopter intended to be used;

(d) be provided with a non-slip surface for landing, constructed so that rainwater and fuel spills shall not collect thereon or fall therefrom on to other parts of the installation;

(e) be provided with suitable tie-down points;

(f) be provided with markings and lighting sufficient to enable easy identification of the landing area by day or night and have any obstructions thereon clearly marked and illuminated; and

(g) be equipped with suitable safety nets along the sides thereof over which persons might fall.

3. *Bollards*

Every bollard and towing bitt forming part of or attached to an offshore installation shall—

(a) be of a pattern suitable for its intended use;

(b) possess a working strength not less than the breaking strength of the strongest rope or cable intended to be used thereon;

(c) be secured to suitable strong points;

(d) be positioned so as to have a clear lead to associated fairleads and winches; and

(e) possess, together with such fairleads, working surfaces of suitable radii.

4. *Openings*

On every offshore installation—

(a) every opening affording persons access to or egress from any part of the installation intended to become buoyant on immersion in water, and every opening in
a bulkhead (being a bulkhead intended to effect a watertight partition between
compartments of the installation) shall be fitted with an efficient watertight door
or hatch of suitable material and attached permanently and strongly to the
bulkhead, deck or other structure in which the opening is located;

(b) the surrounds of every such opening shall be framed and stiffened so as to make
their strength equal to that of the unpierced bulkhead, deck or other structure in
which the opening is located;

(c) every door intended to be watertight shall be fitted with a surrounding gasket and
equipped so as to be capable of being efficiently secured from either side;

(d) the sill height of every door intended to be watertight and the coaming height of
every hatch located in an open deck shall accord with recognised practice;

(e) every discharge port in a compartment intended to be watertight shall be fitted
with an automatically acting non-return valve and with either a second such valve
or a device whereby the port may be closed from a position outside and above the
compartment;

(f) every inlet port shall be fitted with a device whereby it may be closed from a
position which is readily accessible at all times;

(g) pipes and ducts led through a watertight compartment shall be constructed so as
to maintain the watertight integrity of the compartment; and

(h) every other aperture in a compartment intended to be watertight and capable of
being flooded on immersion in water shall be provided with a means of closure
which will enable such aperture to be watertight.

5. *Fendering*

(a) Every system of fendering forming part of or attached to an offshore installation
shall be capable of resisting and absorbing all forces to which it may foreseeably
be subjected in such a manner that the *primary structure* of the installation is not
thereby damaged.

(b) All such fenders shall be securely attached to the installation and extend in the
vertical plane a distance sufficient to avoid possible hazard to vessels alongside
the installation at any state of tide.

6. *Living accommodation*

Every offshore installation shall be provided with accommodation—

(a) placed and constructed so as to afford persons on the installation protection
from weather, fire, noise and vibration;

(b) sufficient in area to meet the needs of the maximum number of persons likely to
be on board the installation at any one time; and

(c) containing facilities and *equipment* for that number of persons as respects sleeping, food and water storage, food preparation and consumption, sanitary and
recreational requirements.

7. *Decks, stairways, etc.*

Every deck, passageway, walkway, stairway and ladder forming part of or attached to an
offshore installation shall incorporate—

(a) non-slip surfaces where practicable;

(b) protection of any exposed parts and openings, with the provision of suitable
guard rails and toe-boards or similar devices;

(c) as respects ladders, suitable safety caging or rest platforms; and

(d) features affording protection against fire, including the isolation of areas by
means of fire-resisting bulkheads and fire doors capable of being opened from
either side.

8.   *Escape routes—*

On every offshore installation

(a)   every general area which is likely to be regularly manned shall have at least two separate escape routes situated as far apart as practicable and leading to abandonment stations situated either on the helicopter deck, or on the survival craft embarkation deck, or at sea-level, or at any combination of those locations;

(b)   every such escape route and abandonment station shall be readily accessible and unobstructed;

(c)   means of escape leading to an upper level shall, wherever practicable, be provided in the form of ramps or stairways and means of escape leading to a lower level shall, wherever practicable, be provided in the form of ramps, stairways or chutes;

(d)   personnel landings shall be provided for ensuring safe embarkation at sea-level; and

(e)   every boat landing shall incorporate non-slip surfaces and suitable guard rails.

PART VI
MATERIALS

1.   Every part of an offshore installation shall be composed of material which is suitable having regard to the nature of the forces and the *environmental factors* to which that part may foreseeably be subjected. All such material, so far as consistent with its function, shall be incombustible.

2.   Any material not entirely protected against corrosion and forming part of an offshore installation shall be of sufficient mass to allow for losses which may arise from corrosion.

3.   Without limiting the generality of the foregoing—

(a)   steel employed as structural material shall be selected from suitable grades of mild or higher tensile steels which conform to a recognised standard;

(b)   welding material employed as structural material shall be compatible with the material joined, shall be selected in accordance with a recognised code of practice for welding operations and shall comply with a recognised standard;

(c)   concrete employed as structural material shall consist of materials selected in accordance with a recognised code of practice relating to structures used in a marine environment and shall comply with a recognised standard;

(d)   aluminium alloys employed as structural material shall be selected from alloys which conform to a standard recognised for marine use; and

(e)   all other structural material shall be suitable for use in a marine environment.

PART VII
CONSTRUCTION

1.   In respect of any work relating to the fabrication or assembly of an offshore installation taking place at any time while an application for a Certificate of Fitness is being considered by a *Certifying Authority*—

(a)   such work shall be carried out in accordance with drawings, specifications and other documents approved or recognised by the *Certifying Authority* and complying with the requirements of these Regulations;

(b)   only those materials described in documents approved or recognised by the *Certifying Authority* shall be incorporated in the structure of the installation; and

(c)   except where the documents approved or recognised by the *Certifying Authority* otherwise provide, workmanship and methods of construction shall be, and shall be inspected, in accordance with recognised standards and codes of practice and, without limitation to the generality of the

(i) all welding shall be in accordance with a recognised standard or code of practice and performed by suitably qualified persons; and

(ii) concrete shall be prepared and placed in accordance with a recognised standard or code of practice appropriate for a marine environment, by suitably experienced persons and under the direction of a competent person experienced in marine concrete construction work.

2. In respect of any work relating to the fabrication or assembly of an offshore installation taking place otherwise than as mentioned in paragraph 1, suitable evidence, whether by means of records, tests or otherwise, that such work has been carried out to a standard comparable with the requirements of paragraph 1, shall be produced to the satisfaction of the *Certifying Authority*.

PART VIII
EQUIPMENT

General requirements

1. Every item of *equipment*—
(a) shall comply with a recognised standard or specification;
(b) shall be suitable for its intended purpose and incorporate efficient control apparatus, guards, shields and other means of protecting personnel;
(c) shall be located to ensure safe operation and, if located in an area within which danger of fire or explosion from ignition of gas, vapour or volatile liquid exists or is likely to exist, shall be suitable for use in that area;
(d) shall be provided with a safe means of access;
(e) if capable of causing noise or vibration which is, or is likely to be, injurious to health, shall be suitably insulated; and
(f) shall be so installed and disposed, both individually and in relation to other items of *equipment* of the installation, as to reduce to a minimum any potential danger to the installation and its personnel.

Specific requirements

2. *Ballasting*
Where necessary to permit operations to be carried on safely, every *mobile installation* shall be provided with ballast tanks whose number, location and sub-division, together with their associated *equipment*, shall be capable of trimming the installation efficiently.

3. *Bilge pumping*
(a) Every offshore installation shall be provided with a means of pumping bilges and of draining all compartments and sections intended to be watertight, other than those containing liquids connected to a separate pumping and drainage system.
(b) The capacity and arrangement of the pumping and drainage apparatus shall be in accordance with recognised practice.

4. *Dynamic positioning*
Where an offshore installation is equipped with a dynamic positioning system such system shall be capable of maintaining the installation in position and on correct heading in all conditions permitting operations to be carried on.

5. *Mooring*
(a) Where an offshore installation is equipped with a mooring system such system shall be capable of enabling the installation to be securely moored in all conditions permitting operations to be carried on.

(b) The mooring system shall incorporate suitable anchors, chain cables and wire ropes, with suitable windlasses and winches which shall be securely attached to the structure of the installation.

(c) It shall not be necessary for the whole of the mooring system to be contained on or within the installation.

(d) No anchor or chain cable shall be incorporated which has not been tested and marked in the manner specified in the Anchors and Chain Cables Act 1899 or in any rules made under section 1(1) of the Anchors and Chain Cables Act 1967 or in accordance with any recognised practice.

6.   *Platform elevation and descent*

Where an offshore installation is equipped with a system for raising and lowering the platform thereof that *equipment* shall—

(a) have a lifting capacity exceeding the maximum gravity load;

(b) be of a capacity sufficient to support the platform in an elevated position in the event of failure of any part of the mechanism; and

(c) be fitted with—

   (i)   means of keeping free from ice those parts essential to the proper functioning of the *equipment*; and

   (ii) devices for recording at all times the load borne by the *equipment*.

7.   *Ventilation, heating and cooling*

(a) Every offshore installation shall be provided with ventilation, heating and cooling systems capable of maintaining a temperate and non-injurious atmosphere in all areas to be used for living accommodation and all other enclosed areas likely to be manned.

(b) In any area on the installation where flammable or noxious gases may occur, a separate and suitable ventilation system shall be provided capable of removing therefrom any such gases in a manner avoiding contamination of other areas of the installation by those gases.

8.   *Lighting*

Every offshore installation shall be provided throughout with lighting capable of supplying illumination sufficient to ensure safety of the persons thereon and arranged so as to ensure that operational control areas, escape routes and embarkation areas remain illuminated in both normal and emergency conditions.

9.   *Emergency power supply*

On every offshore installation, additional to and independent of the main source of electrical power, *equipment* shall be provided capable of providing during an emergency a sufficient supply of electricity to those services required to ensure the safety of the installation and of persons thereon.

SCHEDULE 3

Regulation 13

FEES

1.   *Surveys*

(a) For the carrying out pursuant to regulation 8 of a survey there shall be payable to the Certifying Authority a sum equal to the cost of the work performed, subject to a maximum sum determined in accordance with the following Table:

TABLE

Type of Survey	Maximum Fee	
	Current Construction Cost	Maximum Fee per £1million of Current Construction Cost or part thereof
Major survey, pursuant to regulation 8(1), of an installation in respect of which no Certificate of Fitness is in force	For the first £1million For the next £5million For the next £5million For the next £5million Thereafter	2.5% of current construction cost 0.7% ” ” ” ” 0.5% ” ” ” ” 0.3% ” ” ” ” 0.2% ” ” ” ”
Major survey, pursuant to regulation 8(1), of an installation in respect of which a Certificate of Fitness is in force and a renewal thereof is sought	Two thirds of the fee calculated on the above-mentioned scale	
Annual survey pursuant to regulation 8(2)	One tenth of the fee calculated on the above-mentioned scale	
Additional survey pursuant to regulation 8(3)	Two thirds of the fee calculated on the above-mentioned scale	

(b) For the purpose of paragraph (a) the current construction cost of an offshore installation shall be the cost at the time of the survey, of designing, constructing and testing a similar installation and installing its equipment in the United Kingdom, as agreed between the owner of the installation and the Certifying Authority or, in the event of disagreement, as determined by the Secretary of State.

(c) In addition to the fee payable in accordance with paragraph (a), there shall also be payable a sum equal to the cost of travelling and subsistence expenses reasonably incurred by the surveyor.

2. *Certificates of Fitness*

(a) For the issue pursuant to regulation 9 of a Certificate of Fitness (in duplicate) there shall be payable to the Certifying Authority the fee of £10.

(b) For the issue of each additional copy of a Certificate of Fitness there shall be payable to the Certifying Authority the fee of £2.

OFFSHORE INSTALLATIONS (OPERATIONAL SAFETY, HEALTH AND WELFARE) REGULATIONS 1976

(S.I. 1976 No. 1019, as amended by S.I. 1984 No. 419, S.I. 1989 No. 1672 and S.I. 1992 No. 2932)

PART I
PRELIMINARY

General note. It is to be borne in mind that the Workplace (Health, Safety and Welfare) Regulations (S.I. 1992 No. 3004) do not apply to a workplace where the only activities being undertaken are the exploration for or extraction of mineral resources.

It has been held that the purpose of these Regulations is to protect employees not only while they are working but also at all times when they are at or near the installation; hence the employer is vicariously liable for a foreman who endangered the safety of a fellow employee and it was irrelevant that the foreman was acting outside the scope of his employment (*Macmillan v Wimpey Offshore Engineers and Constructors Ltd* 1991 SLT 515).

Reference to the Secretary of State shall be construed as references to the Health and Safety Executive by virtue of the Offshore Safety (Repeals and Modifications) Regulations 1993, S.I. 1993, No. 1823. The transfer of responsibility from the Department of Energy to the HSE was one of the recommendations of the Cullen Report (Cmd. 1310, 1990) on the Piper Alpha disaster of 6 July 1988.

1. Citation, commencement, interpretation and application.—(1) These Regulations may be cited as the Offshore Installations (Operational Safety, Health and Welfare) Regulations 1976 and shall come into operation on 15 November 1976.

(2) In these Regulations—

"electrical equipment" means, in relation to an offshore installation, any part of the equipment of the installation designed for the generation, conversion, storage, transmission, transforming or utilisation of electricity;

"employee" means an individual who has entered into or works under a contract of service or apprenticeship with an employer whether such contract is express or implied, oral or in writing;

"fixed installation" means an offshore installation which is not a *mobile installation*;

"hazardous area" has the meaning given by regulation 2(1) below;

"helicopter landing officer" has the meaning given by regulation 21 below;

"inspector" means a person appointed under section 6(4) of the *Act*;

"installation manager" includes, where no manager is appointed pursuant to section 4 of the *Act*, any person made responsible by the owner for safety, health and welfare on an offshore installation;

"lifting appliance" means any lifting machine or appliance used for the purpose of moving or suspending goods or materials;

"lifting gear" includes hooks, slings and all means of attaching such gear to a load;

"mechanical equipment" means, in relation to an offshore installation, any part of the equipment of the installation designed for the generation, conversion, storage, transmission or utilisation of mechanical energy which is not *electrical equipment*;

"medical stores" has the meaning given by regulation 27(6) below;

"medically trained person" has the meaning given by regulation 31(2) below;

"mobile installation" means an offshore installation which can be moved from place to place without major dismantling or modification, whether or not it has its own motive power;

"radiotelephone operator" has the meaning given by regulation 18(2) below;

"responsible person" means, in relation to any structure, equipment, operation or substance, the relevant competent person appointed under regulation 30(1) below to be responsible for the particular activity or thing;

"sick bay" has the meaning given by regulation 27(1) below;

"work permit" has the meaning given by regulation 3(3) below.

(3) The Interpretation Act 1889 shall apply to the interpretation of these Regulations as it applies to the interpretation of an Act of Parliament.

(4) These Regulations shall apply to any offshore installaton, not being a dredging installation registered (whether in the United Kingdom or elsewhere) as a vessel, which is maintained in controlled waters for the carrying on of any activity to which the *Act* applies.

General note. The definitions "medical stores", "medically trained person" and "sick bay" are revoked except insofar as they apply to any offshore installation maintained in tidal waters and parts of the sea in or adjacent to Northern Ireland up to the seaward limits of territorial waters.

PART II
SAFETY

2. Hazardous areas.—(1) There shall be included in the written particulars comprised in the operations manual relating to any offshore installation submitted to a certifying authority under regulation 5(1) of the Offshore Installations (Construction and Survey) Regulations 1974 drawings of the installation clearly and accurately showing any part of the installation in which there is likely to be danger of fire or explosion from the ignition of gas, vapour or volatile liquid (in these Regulations referred to as a "hazardous area").

(2) The door or hatch for any opening giving access to a *hazardous area* shall bear on the outside the words "HAZARDOUS AREA" in red capital letters at least 50 millimetres high.

3. Work permits.—(1) No welding or flame cutting or any other work involving or giving rise to a source of ignition, nor any work on *electrical equipment*, nor any work at a place where there is inadequate ventilation for diluting and dispelling injurious or flammable fumes, vapours or gases likely to be given off or for providing a sufficiency of oxygen, shall be carried on by any person on any offshore installation otherwise than in accordance with the written instruction of the *installation manager* given to a *responsible person*, which instruction shall state the nature of the work, the period during which the work may take place and any precautions to be taken to avoid endangering the safety of the installation and persons thereon.

(2) On receipt of the written instruction the *responsible person* shall take all practicable steps to ensure the safety of the installation and persons thereon.

(3) The *responsible person* shall give to the person in charge of the work an authority in writing (in these Regulations referred to as "a work permit") which shall be signed by the *responsible person* and shall specify the work to be carried out, the precautions which have been taken to ensure that the work is carried out safely, any particular to be followed or particular equipment to be used or worn, the period for which the permit is to continue in force and the name of the person to whom it is issued.

(4) It shall be the duty of the person to whom any *work permit* has been issued, on the work to which it relates being completed or ceasing to be carried on by him:—

(a)   to sign thereon a declaration that the work which he has carried out has been properly performed and either completed or ceased to be carried on and that the equipment affected by the work has been left in a safe condition; and

(b)   to deliver the *work permit* to a *responsible person*.

(5) On receipt of the *work permit* the *responsible person* shall check and satisfy himself that the work to which it relates has been properly performed and that any affected equipment has been left in a safe condition.

(6) When satisfied that the work required by the written instruction of the *installation manager* has been properly completed, the *responsible person* shall check that any tools or apparatus required in connection with that work have been removed and shall, when safe so to do, remove any thing temporarily required for safety while that work was in progress. When the *responsible person* has checked and satisfied himself that normal operations may be safely resumed he shall deliver to the *installation manager*—

(a)   all *work permits* relating to the work required by the manager's written instruction;

(b)   the written instruction; and

(c)   a certificate signed by the *responsible person* that—

(i)   the required work has been properly completed;

(ii)   all tools and apparatus and any thing temporarily required for safety have been removed; and

(iii)   normal operations may be safely resumed.

(7) The *installation manager* shall ensure that a record of the issue and return of *work permits* shall be preserved and kept in a safe place on the installation or at such other place as an *inspector* may approve for a period of at least one year from the date of issue.

(8) The issue of a *work permit* shall not affect any obligation of any person subsisting by virtue of these Regulations or otherwise.

4.   Dangerous substances.—(1) No radioactive, corrosive, toxic or explosive substance or any substance which is stored or used at a pressure greater than atmospheric pressure, shall be kept by any person on an offshore installation except in suitable receptacles clearly marked with the contents at a place as far as reasonably practicable from any *hazardous area* and any living accommodation.

(2) No flammable substance shall be so kept except in such receptacles at a place as far as reasonably practicable from any other *hazardous area* and any living accommodation.

(3) Every place at which for the time being any substance mentioned in paragraph (1) or (2) above is kept shall be in the charge of a *responsible person.*

(4) Without prejudice to regulation 2(2) above, any door or hatch giving access to any place at which for the time being any such substance as is mentioned in paragraph (1) or (2) above is kept, shall bear on the outside the word "DANGER" in red capital letters at least 50 millimetres high with an adequate description or indication of the substance in question.

(5) No such substance as is mentioned in paragraph (1) or (2) above shall be used by any person on any offshore installation unless all reasonably practicable precautions have been taken against any danger to which any person on the installation may be exposed by the use of the substance.

(6) There shall be accurately shown on the drawings of the installation in the operations manual referred to in regulation 2(1) above any part of the installation in which are stored any of the substances mentioned in paragraph (1) or (2) above.

5.   General maintenance.—(1) All parts of every offshore installation and its equipment shall be so maintained (*a*) as to ensure the safety of the installation and the safety and health of the persons thereon.

(2) There shall be at all times in force in respect of all parts of every offshore installation and its equipment a scheme providing for their systematic examination, maintenance and, where appropriate, testing.

(3) Save as provided in regulations 6(2) and 25(2) below, all maintenance, examination and testing of any part of an offshore installation and its equipment shall be carried out by, or under the supervision of, a *responsible person.*

(4) Where any examination or test shows that any equipment cannot be safely used until repaired, the person who made the examination or test shall immediately report the fact in writing to the *installation manager* who shall read and sign the report and enter the report in the installation's logbook and such equipment shall not be used by any person until repaired and found satisfactory by a *responsible person.*

(5) Subject to paragraph (6) below and regulation 6(1) below, any scheme under paragraph (2) above shall specify the intervals (which may be different for different parts of the installation and its equipment) within which all parts

of the installation and its equipment are to be examined and, where necessary, tested, and the nature of the examination and testing to be carried out on each occasion.

(6) Any equipment of an offshore installation of a kind specified in column 1 of Parts I and II of Schedule 1 to these Regulations shall be examined and, where necessary, tested at the time or at intervals not exceeding the intervals specified with respect to that kind of equipment in column 2 of that Schedule.

(7) The scheme for each offshore installation under paragraph (2) above or copies thereof and a record of every examination and test of any part of the installation and its equipment made pursuant to the scheme or under paragraph (5) above shall be preserved and kept in a safe place on the installation, or such other place as may be approved by an *inspector,* for a period of at least two years and each record shall be read and signed by the person by whom or under whose supervision the examination and test was carried out and shall specify:—

> (i)   the part of the installation and its equipment to which the record relates;
> (ii) the nature of the examination and test, and the time or intervals at which it was due to be carried out; and
> (iii) any defect revealed by the examination and test and the action taken to remedy it.

(a) *"Maintained".* In the context of reg. 5, maintained has been held simply to mean "kept", so that a failure to clean slurry from a deck amounted to a breach (*Breslin v Britoil plc* [1992] SLT 414n).

6.   Independent examination of lifting appliances and gear.—(1) Without prejudice to the generality of regulation 5 above, every *lifting appliance* and every piece of *lifting gear* shall be thoroughly examined and, where necessary, tested—

> (a) before it is used for the first time; or
> (b) having already been used, if and whenever subsequently substantially altered or repaired, before it is again used; and
> (c) at the times and intervals set out in Part III of Schedule 1 to these Regulations.

(2) Such examination and testing shall be carried out by a competent person who is neither the owner of the installation nor his *employee.*

(3) The record of every examination and test of such appliances and gear shall be in the form set out in Part IV of Schedule 1 to these Regulations or in a form substantially to the same effect. Each record shall be signed by the person who carried out the examination or test and a copy thereof shall be delivered or sent to the owner within 14 days of the examination and the owner shall ensure that such copy is preserved in a safe place on the installation, or at such other place as an *inspector* may approve, until such time as the copy of the next record relating to all appliances and gear referred to in such copy has been received by him.

(4) Whenever any examination shows that any appliance or piece of gear cannot be safely used until repaired written notice of such condition shall be

given to the *installation manager* forthwith by the person who made the examination or test and a copy of the record required by paragraph (3) above shall be sent by such person to the Secretary of State within 7 days of the examination or test.

7. Written instructions.—(1) There shall be provided in respect of every offshore installation by the owner of the installation written instructions specifying practices to be observed to ensure the safety of the installation and the safe use of the equipment thereon.

(2) Any written instructions provided under paragraph (1) above shall include provisions relating to the matters specified in Schedule 2 to these Regulations.

(3) The owner of an offshore installation shall, upon demand, furnish to the Secretary of State a copy of the written instructions provided in respect of the installation under paragraph (1) above.

(4) If the Secretary of State is of the opinion that any written instructions provided in respect of an offshore installation under paragraph (1) above do not make sufficient provision to ensure the safe use of the equipment of the installation and safety in carrying out all operations on the installation, he may serve on the owner of the installation a notice in writing stating that he is of that opinion and specifying the matter for which, in his opinion, provision or, as the case may be, different provision ought to be made and the nature of the provision that, in his opinion, ought to be made, and the owner of the installation shall, before the expiration of such period beginning with the date of service of the notice as may be specified thereon, amend the written instructions accordingly.

(5) A notice for the purpose of paragraph (4) above shall be sufficiently served on the owner of an offshore installation by addressing it to him and delivering it to him or sending it by post addressed to him at the last address in the United Kingdom notified for the purposes of regulation 5(1)(a) or (b) of the Offshore Installations (Registration) Regulations 1972.

(6) It shall be the duty of every *installation manager* to ensure that the activities of any person engaged in any operation or work on, from or in connection with an offshore installation are carried out in accordance with the written instructions provided in respect of the installation under paragraph (1) above and that the relevant part of the written instructions is brought to the attention of every such person.

8. Movement of offshore installations. At a time when an offshore installation is in course of being raised or lowered or dismantled no person who is not essential to the operation shall be thereon and no person who is thereon shall be thereon without the written consent of the *installation manager*.

9. Safety of equipment. All equipment necessary for the carrying out of any operations on an offshore installation in accordance with the written instructions provided in respect of the installation under regulation 7(1) above shall be provided on the installation.

10. Construction etc. of equipment—general. All equipment of an offshore installation shall be of good construction, sound material, adequate strength and free from patent defect and suitable for any purpose for which it is used.

General note. This regulation is revoked by the Provision and Use of Work Equipment Regulations 1992, S.I. 1992 No. 2932, as from 1 January 1993 except, insofar as it applies to work equipment first provided for use in the premises or undertaking before 1 January 1993, it is revoked as from 1 January 1997.

11. Construction etc of *electrical equipment*. All *electrical equipment* shall be sufficient in size and power for the work for which it is to be used and so constructed, installed, protected, worked and maintained as to prevent danger so far as practical.

12. Dangerous machinery and apparatus.—(1) Every dangerous part of any machinery or apparatus shall so far as is practicable be effectively guarded.

(2) For the purpose of this regulation "effectively guarded" means provided with—

    (a) in the case of any moving dangerous part—
        (i) an enclosure with movable parts which incorporate such safety devices as will prevent the dangerous part from moving until it is enclosed in such a way as to prevent any person or his clothing from coming into contact with that part and prevent any movable part of the enclosure from moving unless, by cutting off the power or otherwise, risk of injury from the dangerous part is prevented; or
        (ii) a fixed enclosure, adequately secured in such a position as to prevent any person or his clothing from coming into contact with the dangerous part; and
    (b) in the case of any other dangerous part such a fixed enclosure.

(3) All guards and safety devices provided for moving dangerous parts of machinery or apparatus shall be constantly maintained and kept in position while the parts for which they are provided are moving except when such parts are necessarily exposed for an examination, adjustment or lubrication which it is necessary to carry out while they are moving and all practicable arrangements are made to reduce to a minimum the risk of injury to all persons at risk.

(4) Where it is necessary, in accordance with paragraph (3) above, to remove or render inoperative safety guards or devices in order to perform an examination, adjustment or lubrication no person other than a *responsible person* shall perform that operation and there shall be another person instructed in the steps to be taken in case of emergency who shall be immediately available within sight or hearing of the *responsible person* performing the operation.

General note. This regulation is revoked by the Provision and Use of Work Equipment Regulations 1992, S.I. 1992 No. 2932, as from 1 January 1993 except, insofar as it applies to work equipment first provided for use in the premises or undertaking before 1 January 1993, it is revoked as from 1 January 1997.

13. Marketing of lifting applicances and gear.—(1) Every *lifting appliance* or piece of *lifting gear* used as or forming part of the equipment of an offshore installation shall be plainly marked with its safe working load or loads as shown on the latest record of thorough examination required under regulation 6(3) and no *lifting appliance* or piece of *lifting gear* shall be used by any person for any load exceeding the safe working load marked thereon.

(2) In the case of a multiple sling, the safe working load at different angles of the legs shall be marked in the manner described in Schedule 3 to these Regulations.

14. General Safety. At all times all reasonably practicable steps shall be taken to ensure the safety of persons at all places on the installation including the provision of safe means of access to and egress from any such place and in particular, but without prejudice to the generality of the foregoing:—

(a) all scaffolding on the installation shall be so secured as to prevent accidental displacement;

(b) every ladder shall be so fixed that the stiles or sides of the ladder are evenly supported or suspended and so secured as to prevent slipping;

(c) every working platform shall be not less than 65 centimetres wide and shall be securely fastened to ledgers, standards or uprights or its movement prevented by other means and any working platform or walkway from which a person will be liable to fall a distance of more than 2 metres or into the sea shall where practicable be provided with a toe-board not less than 15 centimetres high and suitable guard rails of adequate strength comprising at least three courses so arranged that the lowest rail is not more than 76 centimetres above the toe-board and the highest rail is not less than 1 metre above the platform or walkway and the openings between the rails are not more than 40 centimetres;

(d) where any person is to work at any place on the installation from which he will be liable to fall into the sea or a distance of more than 2 metres and where it is not practicable to comply with paragraph (c) above, safety nets or safety sheets of suitable design and construction shall, if practicable, be so provided in such positions as to prevent, without causing any undue injury to any such person, that person so falling;

(e) where any person is to work at any place on the installation from which he will be liable to fall into the sea or a distance of more than 2 metres and it is not practicable to ensure his safety by the provision of fencing or safety nets or sheets, there shall be provided for that person, and that person shall use, a suitable safety belt which, together with its lines, fittings and anchorages, is so designed and constructed as to prevent serious injury to that person in the event of his falling; and

(f) where any person in getting to or from the place at which he is to work will be liable to fall into the sea and it is not practicable to ensure his safety by the provision of the means described in sub-paragraph (d) or (e) above, there shall be provided for that person and that person shall wear, a suitable life-jacket.

15. Drilling and production. The provisions of Schedule 4 to these Regulations for securing the safety of offshore installations, their equipment and persons on them during drilling and production operations shall have effect.

16.   Personal safety equipment.—(1) There shall be provided on every off-shore installation:—

(a) a suitable safety helmet for every person on the installation:

(b) sufficient suitable protective clothing and equipment, including eye protectors, ear protectors, welding masks or goggles, welding aprons, breathing apparatus for use in toxic or oxygen deficient atmospheres, gloves, overalls, safety boots or shoes for all persons engaged in oper-ations where they are exposed to risk of injury or disease.

(2) All helmets, clothing and equipment provided under paragraph (1) above shall be kept in good repair and in clean condition.

(3) Any person on an offshore installation for whom a helmet or any clothing or equipment has been provided under paragraph (1) and paragraph (2) above shall use it, where needed or when required by a *responsible person*.

17.   *Electrical equipment.*—(1) No unaccompanied person shall do any work or carry out any examination and test under these Regulations on any *electrical equipment* of an offshore installation for which a *work permit* is required and, where any persons do any such work, one of them shall be a *responsible person*.

(2) No person shall take onto, or use on, an offshore installation any apparatus designed for the generation, conversion, storage, transmission, transforming or utilisation of electricity which is not to be used as, or form part of, the equipment of the installation except with the written permission of the *installation manager*.

18.   Signalling equipment.—(1) Subject to paragraph (5) below, there shall be provided on every offshore installation such signalling equipment as will enable effective communication by radiotelephone, on appropriate channels, to be maintained between the installation and radio stations in the United Kingdom and between it and vessels, helicopters and other offshore instal-lations.

(2) Any equipment provided under paragraph (1) above shall be installed in a separate building or room and provided with adequate facilities for the use of the operator of the equipment (in these Regulations referred to as "the radiotelephone operator").

(3) No building or room in which any equipment provided under para-graph (1) above is installed shall be in a *hazardous area* and any such building or room shall be so situated as to enable the *radiotelephone operator* when in the radiotelepone operating position either to have any helicopter landing in full view or to speak to the *helicopter landing officer* when that person is in a position at which he has the area in full view.

(4) An instruction card giving a clear summary of the radiotelephone dis-tress, emergency and safety procedures shall be displayed in full view of the radiotelephone operating position.

(5) Paragraph (1) above shall not apply in relation to any offshore instal-lation which is not normally manned but, at any time when such an installation is manned, such signalling equipment shall be provided on it as will enable

effective communication by radio to be maintained either between the installation and radio stations in the United Kingdom or between it and any other offshore installation which is provided with such equipment as is mentioned in paragraph (1) above.

PART II

SAFETY

19.   *Radiotelephone operators.*   There shall be present on every offshore installation at any time when it is manned at least one person fully trained to be the *radiotelephone operator* who is the holder of a certificate of competence valid with respect to the equipment provided on the installation under regulation 18(1) above issued by the Secretary of State under section 7(1) of the Wireless Telegraphy Act 1949.

20.   Operational Information.—(1) There shall be provided on every offshore installation suitable means for ascertaining at any time—

(a)   the wind speed and direction;
(b)   the air temperature; and
(c)   the barometric pressure.

(2)   There shall be provided on every *mobile installation* suitable means for ascertaining at any time—

(a)   the roll, pitch, heave, yaw and heading of the installation; and
(b)   the sea state.

(3)   There shall be at all times in force in respect of every offshore installation a scheme providing for the systematic ascertainment and recording of—

(a)   the matters mentioned in paragraph (1) above and, in the case of a *mobile installation,* paragraph (2) above, and
(b)   the visibility and the cloud base and cover.

21.   *Helicopter landing officer.*   There shall be present on every offshore installation at any time when it is manned a competent person appointed by the *installation manager* to be responsible for the control of helicopter operations in relation to the installation (in these Regulations referred to as "the helicopter landing officer"), and the manager shall secure that all persons engaged in all such helicopter operations or who are in or near any helicopter landing area are under the immediate and effective control of the helicopter landing officer.

22.   Helicopter operations.—(1) No helicopter shall land on a manned offshore installation without radio communication having been established between the helicopter and the installation since prior to the time when the helicopter became airborne.

(2)   No helicopter shall take off from a manned offshore installation without radio communication having been established between the helicopter and the installation.

(3) Where radio communication has been established between an airborne helicopter and a manned offshore installation, the *radiotelephone operator* of the installation shall continuously listen for signals by radio from the person in charge of the helicopter until it ceases to be airborne.

(4) Where radio communication has been established between a helicopter and a manned offshore installation and the person in charge of the helicopter has been given permission by the *installation manager* to land on the installation, the *installation manager* shall, if requested by the person in charge of the helicopter, furnish him with particulars of the matters relating to the installation mentioned in paragraphs (1) and (3) *(b)* of regulation 20 above and, in the case of a *mobile installation*, paragraph (2) of that regulation for a period of 10 minutes before any time specified by that person as the estimated time of arrival of the helicopter over the installation.

(5) The manager of a manned offshore installation shall, if requested by the person in charge of a helicopter on the installation, furnish him with such particulars as are referred to in paragraph (4) above for a period of 10 minutes before any time specified by that person as the anticipated time of departure of the helicopter from the installation.

(6) No helicopter shall land on or take off from an unmanned offshore installation without radio communication having been established between the helicopter and the nearest manned installation.

(7) There shall be provided on every offshore installation all equipment needed for use in connection with helicopter operations including—

    (a) chocks and tie-down ropes;
    (b) scales for baggage weighing;
    (c) a suitable power source for starting helicopters, and
    (d) equipment for clearing the helicopter landing area of snow and ice.

(8) There shall also provided on every offshore installation and stored in the immediate vicinity of the helicopter landing area in a secure container of suitable construction all equipment needed for use in the event of an accident involving a helicopter including—

    (a) an aircraft type axe;
    (b) a large axe;
    (c) a heavy duty hacksaw with blade;
    (d) two spare hacksaw blades;
    (e) a grab hook;
    (f) a quick release knife;
    (g) a crowbar; and
    (h) a pair of 24 inch bolt croppers.

(9) There shall be provided on any offshore installation which is normally manned and is stationed more than 50 nautical miles from any land—

    (a) a sufficient quantity of fuel for helicopters to enable a helicopter to be flown from the installation to a suitable landing place on land; and
    (b) safe and efficient equipment for refuelling a helicopter on the helicopter landing area, and for establishing the quality of any fuel provided for helicopters.

(10) It shall be the duty of the *helicopter landing officer* to report to the *installation manager* any shortage in, replacements necessary for, or repairs

required to the equipment required by paragraph (7), (8) and (9) of this regulation.

23.   Helicopter movements.—(1) It shall be the duty of the *helicopter landing officer* of an offshore installation to ensure, before any helicopter lands on or takes off from the installation, that—

(a)   the helicopter landing area is clear of obstructions, including—
  (i)   any ice, snow, heavy spray or seas on deck;
  (ii)   loose tools, machinery or other articles; and
  (iii)   oil, gas or other flammable substance;
(b)   any cranes in the immediate vicinity of the helicopter landing area have ceased to operate;
(c)   no persons other than persons whose presence is necessary for safe helicopter operations are in the vicinity of the helicopter landing area;
(d)   the fire-fighting equipment for the helicopter landing area is manned by adequately trained persons;
(e)   any vessel standing by to render assistance to the installation has been informed that helicopter operations are to take place; and
(f)   any safety nets on or around the helicopter landing area are properly secured and in good condition.

(2)   Whenever a helicopter is stationary on board an offshore installation with its rotors turning, no person shall, except in case of emergency, enter upon or move about the helicopter landing area otherwise than in front of the helicopter, within view of the person in charge of it and at a safe distance from its engine exhausts and tail rotor.

24.   Vessels, aircraft and hovercraft. The master, captain or person in charge of any vessel, aircraft or hovercraft shall not cause or permit the vessel, aircraft or hovercraft to be moored to or landed on, or cause or permit any person to alight on, any offshore installation except with the permission of the *installation manager.*

PART III

HEALTH

25.   Drinking water.—(1) There shall be provided and maintained on every offshore installation, at suitable points clearly marked "Drinking Water" conveniently accessible to all persons on the installation, an adequate supply of clean wholesome drinking water.

(2)   Any supply of drinking water on an offshore installation shall be tested for purity by a competent person at intervals not exceeding 3 months.

26.   Provisions. All provisions for consumption by persons on an offshore installation shall be fit for human consumption, palatable and of good quality.

27.   *Sick bay.*—(1) There shall be provided and maintained in good order and in clean condition on every offshore installation a room in a position conveniently accessible to all persons on the installation suitable for the medical treatment and care of sick and injured persons (in these Regulations referred to as the "sick bay").

(2) Every *sick bay* shall be properly constructed and provided with interior surfaces which may easily be kept clean.

(3) Any door or hatch for any opening giving access to a *sick bay* shall bear on the outside the words "SICK BAY" in red capital letters at least 50 millimetres high.

(4) Except on a *fixed installation* on which less than 20 persons are ordinarily employed, no *sick bay* shall be used for any purpose other than the medical treatment and care of sick or injured persons.

(5) There shall be provided in, or in suitable accommodation in the immediate vicinity of, every *sick bay* a bath and in the immediate vicinity of the *sick bay* a water closet. There shall be provided and maintained at all times a supply of sufficient hot and cold water for that bath and of cold water for that water closet.

(6) Every *sick bay* shall be provided with the quantities of the equipment, medicines, sundries, instruments, appliances, dressing and first aid kits (in these Regulations referred to as "medical stores") required by paragraph (9) below and Schedule 5 to these Regulations. The medical stores shall be packaged, labelled and stored and be of the required quality in compliance with any provision of that Schedule. All medicines shall be clearly marked with the description given in the British Pharmacopeia ("BP"), the British Pharmaceutical Codex ("BPC") or the British National Formulary ("BNF").

(7) The medicines specified in Part II (Medicines) of that Schedule in any *sick bay* shall be kept in a secure locked container, the keys for which shall at all times be in the possession of the *installation manager* or a *medically trained person* appointed by him for that purpose, and which shall not be opened by any person except under the authority of the *installation manager* or a person so appointed. The medicines specified in Head 1 of that Part and forming part of the *medical stores* may be administered by a *medically trained person* and those in Head 2 of that Part only by, or in accordance with the directions of, a qualified medical practioner.

(8) A legible copy of the instructions and requirements set out in the said Part II (Medicines), together with the recommendations therein, shall at all times be displayed conveniently and prominently in every *sick bay*.

(9) There shall be at least one first aid kit immediately to hand at all times for each *medically trained person* required by regulation 31 below.

General note. This regulation is revoked except insofar as it applies to any offshore installation maintained in tidal waters and parts of the sea in or adjacent to Northern Ireland up to the seaward limits of territorial waters.

PART IV
WELFARE

28. Young Persons. No person under the age of 18 years shall be employed on any offshore installation.

29.   Hours of work. It shall be the duty of every *installation manager* to ensure that an accurate record is maintained on the installation of the number of hours worked by each person on the installation.

PART V
MANAGEMENT

30.   Operational staff.—(1) There shall be provided on every offshore installation a sufficient number of competent persons appointed by the *installation manager* to be responsible for the control and safety of:—

   (a) the structure of the installation;
   (b) the *electrical equipment* of the installation;
   (c) the *mechanical equipment* of the installation;
   (d) *lifting appliances* and *lifting gear*;
   (e) drilling operations;
   (f) production operations;
   (g) the handling and storage of acids, caustic alkalis, explosives, radioactive and other dangerous substances; and
   (h) any other unusual or dangerous operation,

and the *installation manager* shall ensure that a list of all such persons on the installation is maintained on the installation at a place where it can be conveniently read by persons on the installation.

(2) Every person who uses any equipment (other than domestic equipment) or who is engaged in carrying out any operation (other than an operation of a domestic nature) on or near an offshore installation shall either—

   (i) have experience of and be competent to use that equipment or have experience of and be competent to be engaged in that operation; or
   (ii) work under the close supervision of a person who has experience of and is competent to use that equipment or who has experience of and is competent to be engaged in that operation as the case may be.

31.   Medical staff.—(1) On every offshore installation which is normally manned there shall be at least one *medically trained person* and, whenever there are 40 or more persons thereon, at least two of them shall be *medically trained persons.*

(2) In this Regulation "medically trained person" means a person who—

   (a) is either—
     (i) a registered nurse or an enrolled nurse within the meaning of the Nurses Act 1957 or the Nurses (Scotland) Act 1951; or
     (ii) the holder of a certificate of competency issued within the previous three years by the St. John Ambulance Association of the Order of St. John, the St. Andrew's Ambulance Association or the British Red Cross Society; and
   (b) has received adequate training in the use of the mechanical artificial respiration equipment provided under Part V (Instruments and Appliances) of Schedule 5 to these Regulations.

General note. This regulation is revoked except insofar as it applies to any offshore installation maintained in tidal waters and parts of the sea in or adjacent to Northern Ireland up to the seaward limits of territorial waters.

PART VI
GENERAL DUTIES

Civil liability and offences

32.   Duties of persons.—(1) It shall be the duty of the *installation manager*, and of the owner of the installation and of the concession owner, to ensure that the provisions of these Regulations are complied with in respect of any offshore installation.

(2) It shall be the duty of the employer of an *employee* employed by him for work on or near an offshore installation to ensure that the *employee* complies with any provision of these Regulations imposing a duty on him or expressly prohibiting him from doing a specified act.

(3) It shall be the duty of every person while on or near an offshore installation—

(a)   not to do anything likely to endanger the safety or health of himself or other persons on or near the installation or to render unsafe any equipment used on or near it;

(b)   to co-operate with his employer, if employed, and any other person on whom a duty or requirement is imposed by these Regulations so far as is necessary to enable that duty or requirement to be performed or complied with; and

(c)   to report immediately to the appropriate *responsible person* or, if no such person be appointed or, if appointed, unavailable, to the *installation manager* any defect in any equipment which appears to him likely to endanger the safety, health or welfare of persons on or near the installation or the safety of the installation and any equipment used with it.

(4) It shall be the duty of any person in charge of a helicopter to ensure that the provisions of regulation 22(1), (2) and (6) above are complied with in respect of that helicopter.

(5) Where in any case a person has reasonable grounds for believing that any provision of regulation 3(1) above has not been complied with it shall be the duty of that person to report the circumstances to the *installation manager*.

(6) It shall be the duty of the owner of an offshore installation to ensure that at least one copy of these Regulations is provided on the installation and it shall be the duty of the *installation manager* to ensure that all relevant provisions of these Regulations are brought to the attention of every person on the installation.

(7) It shall be the duty of the manager of an offshore installation to ensure that a notice stating the address of the office of an *inspector* is kept posted in a conspicuous place on the installation.

Civil liability and offences

33.   Civil liability. The provisions of section 11 of the Act (which makes provision for civil liability for breach of statutory duty) shall apply to the duties imposed on any person by these Regulations.

34.   Offences.—(1) In the event of any contravention of any of these Regulations on, or in connection with, or in relation to, an offshore installation, the *installation manager*, the concession owner and the owner of the installation shall each be guilty of an offence.

(2) In the event of any contravention by any other person of any of these Regulations which expressly imposes any duty upon him or expressly prohibits him from doing a specified act, that person shall also be guilty of an offence.

(3) If any person enters any information knowing it to be false in any record or other document required to be provided or maintained under these Regulations or knowingly falsifies any such record or document or uses any such record or document for the purposes of these Regulations knowing it to be false in a material particular, that person shall be guilty of an offence.

(4) It shall be a defence in any proceedings for an offence under paragraphs (1) or (2) above for the accused to prove—

(a) that he exercised all due diligence to prevent the commission of the offence; and

(b) that the relevant contravention was committed without his consent, connivance or wilful default.

SCHEDULE 1

Regulations 5(6) and 6(1) and (3)

EXAMINATION AND TESTING OF EQUIPMENT

PART I

INTERVALS FOR EXAMINATION OF CERTAIN EQUIPMENT

(1)	(2)
Equipment	*Intervals for examination*
Those parts of *lifting appliance* wire-lines which are liable to suffer wear or other deterioration	Intervals of 7 days

PART II

TIME OR INTERVALS FOR EXAMINATION AND TESTING OF CERTAIN EQUIPMENT

Equipment	*Time or intervals for examination and testing*
Portable gas detection systems	Intervals of 28 days and immediately before use
Lifting appliance safety load indicators and alarms	Intervals of 7 days
Radiotelephone equipment	For correct operation—daily Thorough examination—intervals of 12 months

PART III
TIME OR INTERVALS FOR THOROUGH EXAMINATION AND TESTING OF CERTAIN EQUIPMENT

Equipment	Time or intervals for examination
Lifting appliances and *lifting gear*	Immediately before being put into use after installation, re-installation or substantial alteration or repair and subject thereto, intervals of 6 months
	Time or intervals for testing
Lifting appliances and *lifting gear*	Immediately before being put into use after installation re-installation or substantial alteration or repair

PART IV
FORM OF RECORD OR THOROUGH EXAMINATION OF LIFTING APPLIANCE OR LIFTING GEAR

Name and address of installation owner: Name or designation of offshore installation:

1. Description and distinguishing mark or number of *lifting appliance* or lifing gear

2. Maker and date of make

3. Date of last record of examination (if seen)
Name of person who conducted last examination, and of his employer

4. Date first put into use (if known)

5. Parts not accessible for thorough examination

6. Parts that require opening up at the next examination

7. Particulars of defects and remedy:
particulars of any defect found in the *lifting appliance* or *lifting gear* which affects the safety of the appliance and the repairs (if any) required, either:
 (i) immediately, or
(ii) within a specified time (which must be stated),
to enable the *lifting appliance* or lifting gear to continue to be used with safety *(if no such repairs are required the word "NONE" is to be entered)*

8. Safe Working Load subject to the repairs, renewals and alterations (if any) specified above

In the case of a crane with a variable operating radius, including a crane with derricking jib, the safe working load at various radii of the jib, trolley, or crab is to be stated

I hereby certify that on .... (date) the item described in this report was thoroughly examined, so far as accessible, and the above particulars are correct.

Signature of person
conducting examination ....

Counter-signature on
behalf of employer ....

Name of person ....
conducting examination ....

Name of employer ....

Date

Date

Continuation sheet (please number items as above)
Details of component test certificates seen by person conducting examination.

SCHEDULE 2

Regulation 7(2)

MATTERS TO BE PROVIDED FOR IN WRITTEN INSTRUCTIONS

Drilling production procedures
1. (a) Drilling operations on multiwell platforms.
   (b) Workover operations.
   (c) Installation of blowout preventers.
   (d) Operations on wellhead.
   (e) Venting of gas.
   (f) Venting of oil.
   (g) Formation testing.
   (h) Swabbing.
   (i) Plugging and abandonment.
   (j) Smoking and use of naked lights.
   (k) Detection of and protection from sour gases.
   (l) Transportation, storage, handling and use, including action to be taken in emergency, of—
       (i) acids and other dangerous chemicals,
       (ii) explosives,
       (iii) radioactive substances,
       (iv) flammable materials, including flammable waste, and
       (v) other dangerous materials.

Electrical procedures
2. (a) Access by persons.
   (b) Additions or alterations to the electrical supply system.
   (c) Precautions to be taken before and during the operation and maintenance of *electrical equipment.*
   (d) Use of portable insulating stands, screens and protective clothing.
   (e) Special precautions to be taken when working near bare conductors.
   (f) Use of portable equipment using electrical power.
   (g) Treatment of persons suffering from electrical shock.

Mechanical equipment procedures
3. (a) General operation of *mechanical equipment.*
   (b) Operation of *lifting appliances, lifting gear*, including use of slings, chains, wire ropes and other lifting tackle.
   (c) Handling and use of compressed air.
   (d) Handling and storage of loose tools.
   (e) Limitations on, and precautions during, welding and cutting.
   (f) Limitations on, and precautions during, operations involving cutting into live lines and the use of mechanical seal plugs.
   (g) Inspection or maintenance of dangerous machinery or apparatus when it is necessary to remove or render inoperative guards and other safety devices.

Personal procedures
4. (a) Liaison with medical practitioners.
    (b) Arrangements for general medical advice and for medical treatment in the event of injury or disease.
    (c) General arrangements for safety of persons.
    (d) Personal hygiene for kitchen staff and cleanliness of food rooms and kitchen.
    (e) House-keeping and disposal of waste materials.
    (f) Use of protective clothing and personal safety equipment.
    (g) Working in exposed positions.
    (h) Transfer of persons to and from vessels, aircraft and hovercraft.

Procedures to secure safety of the installation
5. (a) Communication with radio stations on land and attendant vessels.
    (b) Obtaining meteorological information.
    (c) Movement of the installation to and from station.
    (d) Mooring of the installation.
    (e) Monitoring sea-bed conditions.
    (f) Jacking up and down or ballasting and de-ballasting.
    (g) Monitoring accretions to the installation including marine growth, snow and ice.
    (h) Keeping of records affecting safety of the installation.
    (i) Procedures relating to movement of vessels, aircraft and hovercraft attending the installation.
    (j) Transfer of equipment to and from vessels, aircraft and hovercraft.
    (k) Refuelling of helicopters on the installation.

Paragraph 4, sub-paras. (a) and (b) revoked for certain purposes by S.I. 1989 No. 1672 reg. 2, Schedule.

SCHEDULE 3

Regulation 13(2)

MARKING OF SAFE LOADS ON MULTIPLE SLINGS

Every multiple sling shall carry a mark in one of the forms below:

| SWL x tonnes
$0°$ –$90°$ | or | SWL x t
$0°$ –$90°$ |

where x is the safe working load ("SWL") in metric tonnes for any angle between the relevant sling legs ("the included angle") up to a limit of $90°$.

For the purpose of this Schedule the included angle means—
    (a) in the case of 2-leg slings, the angle between the legs;
    (b) in the case of 3-leg slings, the angle between any two adjacent legs; and
    (c) in the case of 4-leg slings, the angle between any two diagonally opposite legs.

SCHEDULE 4

Regulation 15

PROVISIONS RELATING TO DRILLING AND PRODUCTION

1.   The provisions of paragraphs 2 to 6 below shall have effect in relation to every offshore installation on which drilling operations are carried on.

Blowout preventers, controls and accumulators
2.—(1) One set of controls for the blowout preventers shall be installed near to the driller's stand and another set of such controls for use in case of emergency shall be installed at a safe distance from the drilling rig.

(2) Every accumulator shall be capable of maintaining a pressure capacity reserve at all times to provide for one operation of every set of hydraulic preventers and every pump and accumulator shall be capable of maintaining adequate accumulator pressure for repeated operations.

Stabbing boards and associated equipment

3. The safety devices incorporated in every stabbing board and its attachments and actuating hoist shall be adequate to support the platform when fully manned and where a hook is used for raising and lowering a stabbing board, it shall be either clamped or provided with an effective safety latch to prevent accidental disengagement.

Elevators

4. Every hook used for hoisting drill pipe, casing or tubing shall be provided with an efficient latch or other device capable of preventing the elevator links or other equipment becoming detached from the hook.

Travelling block

5. An effective automatic contrivance shall be provided for use with every derrick hoisting equipment to prevent running the travelling block into the crown block.

Blowout detection

6. There shall be installed efficient equipment to warm the driller of loss of circulation or an incipient blowout, and the equipment shall give visual and audible warning of danger at the driller's stand.

Hydrogen sulphide

7. Where hydrogen sulphide is or may be present—
(a) efficient means shall be provided and used on every offshore installation for detecting its presence and measuring its concentration on the installation; and
(b) a sufficient number of sets of suitable breathing apparatus shall be provided at readily accessible places on the installation.

PART II
PROVISIONS RELATING TO PRODUCTION

8. The provisions of paragraph 9 to 11 below shall have effect in relation to every offshore installation on which production operations are carried on.

Control devices

9. All completed wells shall be fitted with such control devices as are necessary to ensure compliance with the requirements of Model Clause 16 of Schedule 4 to the Petroleum (Production) Regulations 1966, as amended by section 17(1) of, and paragraph 7 of Part I of Schedule 2 to, the Petroleum and Submarine Pipe-lines Act 1975.

Gas flare systems

10. All gas flare systems shall be so constructed that no flammable solid matter may pass through them, and shall be equipped with an efficient liquid scrubber to remove all liquid possible.

Hydrogen sulphide

11.   Where hydrogen sulphide is or may be present the provisions of paragraph 7 of Part I of this Schedule shall apply.

SCHEDULE 5

Regulation 27(6), (7), (8)

MEDICAL STORES FOR SICK BAYS

PART I

EQUIPMENT

(a)   A sink with smooth impervious internal surfaces having a constant supply of hot and cold water.

(b)   A suitable working surface with a smooth impervious top.

(c)   A means of sterilising instruments.

(d)   Suitable storage for drugs, dressings and equipment.

(e)   A bed or couch approachable from both sides.

(f)   Sufficient suitable stretchers, including at least one suitable for winching a sick or injured person into a helicopter or vessel and at least one collapsible and suitable for use in confined spaces.

(g)   Sufficient blankets.

(h)   A footbath, or a basin or bowl suitable for use as a footbath.

General note.   Revoked for certain purposes by S.I. 1989 No. 1672, reg. 2, Schedule.

PART II
MEDICINES

Head 1—Medicines which may be administered by medically trained persons

Name of medicine	Recommended for the following conditions	Special labelling instructions	Special packaging and storage requirements	Quantities for installations carrying:	
				Up to 40 persons	Over 40 persons
Aluminium hydroxide tablets BP 500 mgm	Indigestion	Chew before swallowing	Keep in cool place	300	500
Soluble Asprin and Codeine tablets BP 300 mgm	Minor pains		Foil strip packed	300	500
Benzocaine compound ointment BPC	Piles		To be carried in 25 g containers	100 g	100 g
Benzoic acid compound ointment BPC	Skin infections		To be carried in 25 g containers	100 g	200 g
Benzoin compound tincture BPC	Relief of catarrh			100 ml	200 ml
Bezyl benzoate application BP	Scabies	For external use only		500 ml	1 litre
Calamine lotion BP	Irritating rashes	For external use only—shake bottle	To be carried in green or amber vertically ribbed bottles	1 litre	2 litres
Cetrimide cream BPC	Application to open wounds before dressing		To be carried in 5 g tubes	30 g	50 g

Name of medicine	Recommended for the following conditions	Special labelling instructions	Special packaging and storage requirements	Quantities for installations carrying:	
				Up to 40 persons	Over 40 persons
Cetrimide solution, strong BPC	Cleansing open wounds	Dilute before use in the proportion of 1:40 (w/v) with freshly boiled water. *Caution*—the diluted solution must not be used later than 1 week after preparation		100 ml	200 ml
Chloramphenicol eye ointment BPC 1%	Eye infections	*Caution*—do not use later than 1 month after opening container (Date of opening ....)	To be carried in 4 g tubes	16 g	16 g
Clove oil BP	Toothache	Do *not* apply to gums		30 ml	30 ml
Co-trimoxazole tablets BP	Urinary tract infections			100	100
Diphenoxylate hydrochloride tablets 2.5 mgm with atrophine sulphate 25 mcgm	Diarrhoea			50	100
Ear drops containing in each ml neomycin sulphate 3,400 units Polymyxin B sulphate 10,000 units and hydrocortisone 10 mg	Infections of the outer ear		To be carried in 5 ml dropper container	20 ml	40 ml
Hydrocortisone cream BPC (0.1%)	Irritating rashes	Do not use after expiry date	To be carried in 15 g tubes	75 g	150 g
Hyoscine hydrobromide tablets BP 0.3 mg	Seasickness	May cause drowsiness	Keep in cool place	50	100

Name of medicine	Recommended for the following conditions	Special labelling instructions	Special packaging and storage requirements	Quantities for installations carrying: Up to 40 persons	Quantities for installations carrying: Over 40 persons
Ipecacuanha and morphine mixture BPC	Relief of cough			2 litres	4 litres
Kaolin and morphine mixture BPC	Diarrhoea	Shake bottle before use		1 litre	2 litres
Kaolin poultice BP	Skin and muscle inflamation		To be carried in 200 g sealed tins	400 g	800 g
Magnesium trisilicate compound powder BPC	Indigestion			500 g	1 kg
Methyl salicylate liniment BPC	Rheumatic pains	For external use only	To be carried in green or amber vertically ribbed bottles	300 ml	500 ml
Mouthwash solution—Tablets BPC	Mouthwash or gargle	Dissolve one tablet in 250 ml warm water	To be stored in amber glass bottles with lined screw caps or in plastic cans or in foil strip. To be stored away from light	250	250
Nitrazepam tablets BP 5 mg	Sleeping tablets			20	30
Opiate squill linctus (Gee's linctus)	Relief of cough			1 litre	2 litres

Name of medicine	Recommended for the following conditions	Special labelling instructions	Special packaging and storage requirements	Quantities for installations carrying:	
				Up to 40 persons	Over 40 persons
Paracetamol tablets BP 500 mg	Relief of minor pains		To be stored in airtight containers. Protect from light	300	500
Senna tablets BP	Laxative			100	100
Sodium bicarbonate BP	(a) Antacid for indigestion (with water in 5% solution)			500 g	500 g
	(b) Irrigating acid burns (with warm water in 1% solution)				
Sulphacetamide eye drops BPC 10% (Antiseptic eye drops)	Eye infection	Do not use later than 1 month after opening container Date of opening	To be carried in 10 ml dropper containers Protect from light	40 ml	60 ml
Surgical spirit BPC	Disinfectant rub		To be stored in vertically ribbed bottles	300 ml	500 ml
Vitamin C tablets BP 25 mg			To be stored away from light. Avoid contact with metal	200	400

Name of medicine	Recommended for the following conditions	Special labelling instructions	Special packaging and storage requirements	Quantities for installations carrying:	
				Up to 40 persons	Over 40 persons
Water for injections BP			To be carried in 2 ml ampoules	100 ml	200 ml
White soft paraffin BP	Protective ointment			200 g	200 g
Zinc ointment BP	Soothing ointment			100 g	200 g
Zinc, starch and talc dusting powder BPC	As talcum powder			100 g	200 g
Zinc undecenoate dusting powder BPC	Athlete's foot			300 g	400 g

General note. Revoked for certain purposes by S.I. 1989 No. 1672, reg. 2, Schedule.

PART II

Head 2—Medicines which may be administered only by, or on advice from, a qualified medical practitioner

Name of medicine	Recommended for the following conditions	Special labelling instructions	Special packaging and storage requirements	Quantities for installations carrying:	
				Up to 40 persons	Over 40 persons
Amethocaine eye drops BPC 0.5% (Anaesthetic eye drops)	Eye infections	Do not use later than 1 month after first opening the container. Do not allow dropper to touch eyelids. Ensure solution falls directly on eyeball. Cover eye with protective eyeshade immediately after application	To be in single dose containers Protect from light	10 doses	10 doses
Ampicillin capsules BP 250 mgm	Infections			50	100
Diazepam injection 13 BNF 10 mg in 2 ml	Sedative			5	10
Diazepam tablets BP 5 mg	Sedative			50	100
Glyceryl trinitrate tablets BP 0.5 mg	Heart pain	Allow tablets to dissolve under tongue Date of manufacture	Renew stocks 2 years from date of manufacture	100	100

Name of medicine	Recommended for the following conditions	Special labelling instructions	Special packaging and storage requirements	Quantities for installations carrying: Up to 40 persons	Over 40 persons
Hydrocortisone sodium phosphate injection BPC 100 mg in 1 ml	Treatment of anaphylactic shock	Do not use after expiry date		10	20
Morphine sulphate injections BP 15 mg in 1 ml ampoules	Relief of severe pain			24 ampoules	42 ampoules
Penicillin V capsules BP or tablets BP 250 mg	Infections			100	100
Pethidine injections BP 100 mg in 2 ml ampoules	Relief of severe pain			25 ampoules	50 ampoules
Pethidine tablets BP 25 mg	Relief of severe pain			50	100
Fortified Procaine penicillin injection BP	Infections	Do not use later than 24 hours after adding water or after expiry date given on label. Label to state volume of sterile water to be used	Keep in cool dry place	26 vials	26 vials
Promethazine hydrochloride tablets BP 10 mg	Allergies	May cause drowsiness		100	100
Tetracycline tablets BP 250 mg	Infections	Do not use after expiry date		50	100

General note. Revoked for certain purposes by S.I. 1989 No. 1672, reg. 2, Schedule.

PART III
DRESSINGS

Article	Requirements as to packaging and labelling	Quantities for installations carrying:	
		up to 40 persons	over 40 persons
Bandages:			
crepe, 7.5 cm × 4.5 m, stretched	Each bandage to be individually wrapped and labelled; measurements to be stated on label	6	6
elastic adhesive, 7.5 cm × 4 m	Each bandage to be in an individual sealed container	3	3
triangular, approx. 90 cm side × 127 cm base	Each bandage to be individually wrapped and labelled; measurements to be stated on label	5	10
tube gauze, seamless, of suitable size for finger dressings, length 20 m, with applicator	To be carried in a box, rolled on a core	1 roll	2 rolls
open wove bandages:	Each bandage to be individually wrapped and labelled; measurements to be stated on label		
5 cm × 5 m		10	20
7.5 cm × 5 m	ditto	20	30
Cotton wool; absorbent:	To be carried sertilised and rolled. The packets to be labelled with the words "Sterilised Cotton Wool"		
15 g		15 packets	30 packets
25 g	To be carried rolled. The packets to be labelled with the words "Cotton Wool"	15 packets	30 packets
100 g	ditto	2 packets	4 packets
Dressings:			
burn and wound—individual	Paraffin gauze dressing BPC. Packaging and labelling to conform to the specification given in Part IV of Schedule 2 to the Merchant Shipping (Medical Scales) Regulations 1974[1]	3 containers	5 containers
burn and wound—continuous strip 19 cm × 5 m	Each dressing to be carried in a hermetically sealed container and to be labelled with an additional label as follows: "This dressing is for use in cases of extensive burns."	2 containers	4 containers

Article	Requirements as to packaging and labelling	Quantities for installations carrying:	
		up to 40 persons	over 40 persons
closures, skin adhesive, length 5 cm approx. Standard No. 13 BPC	To be carried in tins with the dressings individually sealed in transparent envelopes	100 closures	100 closures
	Container to bear an additional label as follows: "Small plain wound dressing. Directions. Open by pulling tab. Avoid touching wound and when opening the dressing do not finger the face of the sterilised pad. Place pad over the wound, retain hold of short end of bandage, wind remainder firmly and tie a knot."	5	10
Standard No. 14 BPC	Container to bear an additional label as follows: "Medium plain wound dressing. Directions. Open by pulling tab. Avoid touching wound and when opening the dressing do not finger the face of the sterilised pad. Place pad over wound, retain hold of short end of bandage, wind remainder firmly and tie in a knot."	5	10
Standard No. 15 BPC	Container to bear an additional label as follows: "Large plain wound dressing. Directions. Open by pulling tab. Avoid touching wound and when opening the dressing do not finger the face of the sterilised pad. Place pad over wound, retain hold of short end of bandage, wind remainder firmly and tie in a knot."	5	10
elastic adhesive dressing strip, medicated, BPC, 6 cm × 1 m	To be carried in a packet.	2 packets	4 packets
Absorbent gauze BPC, 90 cm × 30 cm	To be carried in packets bearing an additional label with the words "Absorbent Gauze BPC sterilised"; measurements to be stated on label	10 packets	20 packets
Gauze pads BPC 7.5 cm × 7.5 cm	To be carried in packets of 5, sterilised and labelled	10 packets	20 packets

Article	Requirements as to packaging and labelling	Quantities for installations carrying:	
		up to 40 persons	over 40 persons
Absorbent ribbon gauze BPC 2.5 cm × 5 m	To be carried in a packet bearing an additional label with the words "Absorbent Ribbon Gauze BPC sterilised"; measurements to be stated on label	1 roll	1 roll
Absorbent lint BPC: 15 cm × 30 cm	To be carried in packets bearing an additional label with the words "Absorbent Lint BPC sterilised"; measurements to be stated on label	10 packets	20 packets
30 cm × 30 cm	ditto	10 packets	20 packets
Zinc oxide plaster BPC: 2.5 cm × 5 m	To be carried on a spool	1 spool	2 spools
7.5 cm × 5 m	To be carried on a spool	1 spool	2 spools

[1] S.I. 1974 No. 1193 (1974, II, p. 4517).

General note. Revoked for certain purposes by S.I. 1989 No. 1672, reg. 2, Schedule.

PART IV
SUNDRIES

Article	Special Requirements	Quantities for installations carrying:	
		up to 40 persons	over 40 persons
Antiseptic	To conform to the specification of Antiseptics given in Part II of Schedule 2 to the Merchant Shipping (Medical Scales) Regulations 1974	500 ml	1 litre
Bedpan	To be of good quality stainless steel or plastic	1	1
Book: Ship Captain's Medical Guide. 20th Edition, with all amendments published before the date of making these Regulations		1	1
Cervical collar	To consist of sponge rubber 6.5 cm × 37 cm, enclosed in a length of tube gauze or surgical tubular neck dressing	1	1
Disinfectant	To conform to the specification of disinfectants given in Part I of Schedule 2 to the Merchant Shipping (Medical Scales) Regulations 1974	5 litres	10 litres
Eye baths	To be of glass, porcelain or a plastic which is unaffected by immersion in boiling water for at least five minutes	2	2
Eye shades		5	5
Finger stalls, protective	Assorted sizes, with tapes	5	10
Glass, medicine	Graduated, glass or plastic, British Standard 3221	2	2

Article	Special Requirements	Quantities for installations carrying: up to 40 persons	Quantities for installations carrying: over 40 persons
Gloves, surgical	Rubber or plastic, size 8	2 pairs	2 pairs
Hotwater bottles	Approximately 20 cm × 30 cm, rubber, with covers	2	2
Lotion bowl	To be of good quality stainless steel or plastic, minimum size 200 mm × 90 mm, lettered "Medical"	1	1
Measure: dispensary 50 ml	Conical, graduated (5 to 50 ml) British Standard 1922/69	1	2
5 ml plastic measuring spoons	British Standard 3221 Part 4	2	2
Methylated spirit (mineralised)	Label to be marked "Not to be taken"	500 ml	1 litre
Safety pins	Rustless, 5 cm	50	50
Waterproof sheeting	Rubber or plastic 1 metre × 2 metres. To be rolled on a wooden core, surface to be smooth and non-adhesive.	12	12

General note. Paragraphs 4(a) and (b) are revoked except insofar as they apply to any offshore installation maintained in tidal waters and parts of the sea in or adjacent to Northern Ireland up to the seaward limits of territorial waters.

PART V
INSTRUMENTS AND APPLIANCES

Article	Special requirements	Quantities for installations carrying:	
		up to 40 persons	over 40 persons
Canvas roll for instruments	For use as a container for the ring saw, forceps (epilation and Spencer Wells') scissors and thermometers (clinical and low reading)	1	1
Forceps:			
epilation, with oblique ends for removal of splinters	To be of rustless and stainless steel throughout	1 pair	1 pair
Spencer Wells' 5 in. (12.5 cm)	ditto	2 pairs	2 pairs
Artificial Respirator, mechanical		1	1
Resuscitator (mouth to mouth) short oral airway with non-return valve, Brook Airway type	To be portable, with an adequate supply of oxygen	2	2
Ring saw			
Scalpel, with straight detachable blade, size 23	To be made of carbon or stainless steel throughout and to be carried in a metal, wooden or plastic box, with six spare blades	1 set	1 set
Scissors, 7 in. (18 cm)	One blade sharp-pointed and the other round. To be of rustless and stainless steel	1 pair	1 pair
Sphygmomanometer		1	1
Splints, common		1 set	1 set
Stethoscope		1	1
Suspensory bandages with under straps:			
medium		2	4
large		2	4

Article	Special Requirements	Quantities for installations carrying:	
		up to 40 persons	over 40 persons
Syringes, hypodermic, sterile, disposable, Luer fitting	2 ml syringes with 21 SWG × 4 cm needles	10	20
ditto	5 ml syringes with 21 SWG × 4 cm needles	5	10
Thermometers: clinical	To conform to British Standard 691. To be carried in a metal or plastic protective case with an explanatory slip on use	2	2
low reading	To be carried in a metal or plastic protective case with an explanatory slip on use	2	2
Tongue depressors	To be made of wood	50	50

PART VI
FIRST AID KITS

Specification of every kit

Article	Special requirements	Quantities in each kit
Bandage, triangular BPC, approx. 90 cm side × 127 cm base	Each bandage to be individually wrapped and labelled, measurements to be stated on label	8
Cotton Wool, absorbent 100 g	To be carried rolled. The packets to be labelled with the words "Cotton Wool"	2 packets
Dressings:		
Standard No. 13 BPC	Container to bear an additional label as follows: "Small plain wound dressing. Directions. Open by pulling tab. Avoid touching wound and when opening the dressing do not finger the face of the sterilised pad. Place pad over wound, retain hold of short end of bandage, wind remainder firmly and tie in a knot."	4
Standard No. 14 BPC	Container to bear an additional label as folows: "Medium plain wound dressing. Directions. Open by pulling tab. Avoid touching wound and when opening dressing do not finger the face of the sterilised pad. Place pad over wound, retain hold of short end of bandage, wind remainder firmly and tie in a knot."	2
Standard No. 15 BPC	Container to bear an additional label as follows: "Large plain wound dressing. Directions. Open by pulling tab. Aviod touching wound and when opening the dressing do not finger the face of the sterilised pad. Place pad over wound, retain hold of short end of bandage, wind remainder firmly and tie in a knot."	1

Article	Special requirements	Quantities in each kit
Absorbent ribbon gauze BPC, 2.5 cm × 5 m	To be carried in packet bearing an additional label with the words "Absorbent Ribbon Gauze BPC sterilised"; measurements to be stated on label	1 roll
Resuscitator (mouth to mouth) short oral airway with non-return valve, Brook Airway type		1
Safety pins	Rustless, 5 cm, on a card	6
Scissors, 7 in. (18 cm)	One blade sharp-pointed and the other round. To be of rustless and stainless steel	1 pair
Splints, inflatable:		
arm		1 set
leg		1 set
Waterproof bag or case	To be of sufficient size to contain the articles required for the First Aid Kit	1

General note. This Schedule is revoked except insofar as it applies to any offshore installation maintained in tidal waters and parts of the sea in or adjacent to Northern Ireland up to the seaward limits of territorial waters.

THE OFFSHORE INSTALLATIONS (EMERGENCY PROCEDURES) REGULATIONS 1976

(S.I. 1976 No. 1542, as amended by S.I. 1984 No. 419)

General note. References to the Secretary of State shall be construed as references to the Health and Safety Executive by virtue of the Offshore Safety (Repeals and Modifications) Regulations 1993, S.I. 1993 No. 1823. The transfer of responsibility from the Department of Energy to the HSE was one of the recommendations of the Cullen Report (Cmd. 1310, 1990) on the Piper Alpha disaster of 6 July 1988.

1. Citation and commencement. These Regulations may be cited as the Offshore Installations (Emergency Procedures) Regulations 1976 and (with the exception of regulations 4 and 5 which shall come into operation on 1 February 1977) shall come into operation on 18 October 1976.

2. Interpretation.—(1) In these Regulations—

"emergency" includes an apprehended emergency;

"emergency equipment" means any equipment of an offshore installation provided for use in an emergency;

"emergency procedure manual" has the meaning given by regulation 4(1) below;

"emergency station" has the meaning given by regulation 6(1) below;

"fixed offshore installation" means an offshore installation which is not a *mobile offshore installation*;

"installation manager" includes, where no manager is appointed pursuant to section 4 of the Act, any person made responsible by the owner for safety, health and welfare on any offshore installation;

"mobile offshore installation" means an offshore installation which can be moved from place to place without major dismantling or modification, whether or not it has its own motive power;

"muster list" has the meaning given by regulation 6(1) below; and

"stand-by vessel" has the meaning given by regulation 10(1) below.

(2) The Interpretation Act 1889 shall apply to the interpretation of these regulations as it applies to the interpretation of an Act of Parliament.

3. Application. These Regulations shall apply to any offshore installation, not being a dredging installation registered (whether in the United Kingdom or elsewhere) as a vessel, which is maintained in controlled waters for the carrying on of any activity to which *the Act* applies.

4. *Emergency procedure manual.*—(1) There shall be provided in respect of every offshore installation which is normally manned a book (in these Regulations referred to as the "emergency procedure manual") specifying the action to be taken in the event of an emergency on or near the installation and, in particular, in the following cases—

   (a) a fire or explosion;
   (b) a blow-out of a well;
   (c) a leak or spillage of any oil or gas;
   (d) a storm or severe weather conditions affecting the stability of the installation;
   (e) a movement of the sea bed affecting the stability of the installation;
   (f) a failure of the structure of the installation;
   (g) a failure of the equipment of the installation affecting the safety of persons;
   (h) a failure of the means for keeping the installation on station;
   (i) a collision involving the installation;
   (j) an accident involving a helicopter;
   (k) a person falling from the installation; and
   (l) a death, a serious injury or illness.

(2) There shall also be specified in the *emergency procedure manual*—

   (a) a code of signals suitable for transmission by means of a general alarm system for signifying the occurrence of specific emergencies and the action to be taken in respect of any of them, and instructions for the transmission of any of those signals by those means;
   (b) instructions for the operation of the *emergency equipment*;
   (c) instructions for rendering safe any work being carried on or any equipment being used on or near the installation in the event of an emergency;
   (d) instructions for evacuating all persons on or near the installation therefrom; and
   (e) the places on the installation at which plans showing the location of the *emergency equipment* are to be provided.

(3) The *emergency procedure manual* shall contain particulars of—

   (a) the emergency services arranged for divers diving near the installation as reqiured by regulation 20 of the Offshore Installations (Diving Operations) Regulations 1974 (which regulation requires the employers of divers to arrange rescue services for divers carrying on diving operations in connection with offshore installations);
   (b) the action to be taken by the *stand-by vessel* for the transmission of emergency signals, the recovery of persons in the sea and the evacuation of persons from the installation;
   (c) any action arranged by the owner of the installation to be taken by any person on land or another installation for providing assistance; and
   (d) any available search and rescue services.

(4) The *emergency procedure manual* shall contain the names and addresses of any public or local authorities to which any particular emergency is to be reported and specify the method of and the time for making the report.

(5) A copy of the *emergency procedure manual* in English (together with translations thereof in such other languages as are appropriate) shall be made available at a suitable and readily accessible place on the installation.

(6) The owner of an offshore installation which is normally manned shall, upon demand, furnish to the Secretary of State a copy of its *emergency procedure manual.*

(7) If the Secretary of State is of the opinion that the *emergency procedure manual* does not make sufficient provision for securing safety in the use of *emergency equipment* and the taking of action in the event of an emergency on or near the installation, he may serve on the owner of the installation a notice in writing stating that he is of that opinion and specifying the matter for which, in his opinion, provision or, as the case may be different provision ought to be made and the nature of the provision that, in his opinion, ought to be made, and the owner of the installation shall, before the expiration of such period beginning with the date of service of the notice as may be specified therein, amend the *emergency procedure manual* accordingly.

(8) A notice for the purpose of paragraph (7) above shall be sufficiently served on the owner of an offshore installation by addressing it to him and delivering it to him or sending it by post addressed to him at the last address in the United Kingdom notified for the purposes of regulation 5(1)(a) or (b) of the Offshore Installations (Registration) Regulations 1972 (which Regulation relates to applications for the first registration of offshore installations).

5. Instruction notices. In any space on an offshore installation in respect of which there is a provision in the *emergency procedure manual* that particular action be taken in an emergency there shall be displayed a notice specifying that provision. The notice shall be in clear and permanent lettering in English and such other languages as are appropriate and shall be displayed in such a position that it can be easily read.

6. *Muster list.*—(1) There shall be provided in respect of every offshore installation when it is manned by 5 or more persons a list (in these Regulations referred to as the "muster list") showing in respect of every person on the installation the station to which each person shall go in the event of an emergency (in these Regulations referred to as the "emergency station") and any duties to be carried out in an emergency which are assigned to particular persons.

(2) The *muster list* shall set out the person appointed to be in charge of each *emergency station* and the persons to whom duties are assigned in connection with the following matters—

  (a) the closing of wells;
  (b) the closing of pipes carrying hydrocarbons or other flammable substances and the associated valves and vents;
  (c) the closing of fire doors and ventilators;
  (d) the closing of watertight doors;
  (e) the stopping of machinery;
  (f) the extinction of fire;
  (g) the equipping of survival craft and liferafts and making them ready for use;
  (h) the launching of survival craft and liferafts; and
  (i) the securing of the safety of visitors to the installation.

(3) Copies of the *muster list* shall be displayed in English and all appropriate languages in such positions that they may easily be read in all accommodation areas and at each *emergency station* copies of the parts of the *muster list* relevant to the particular station shall be similarly displayed.

7.   Musters.—(1) On every offshore installation which is normally manned, musters shall take place so as to ensure that the persons on the installation are practised in the duties set out as assigned to them in the *muster list* at least once every 28 days, and, in the case of a mobile installation, immediately on arrival at, or immediately before departure from, a station.

(2) Every person on the installation shall be made aware of the signal for summoning all persons to their *emergency stations* and be instructed that, on the signal being given on the general alarm system, he is required to go to his *emergency station*.

(3) Every person on the installation not in charge of an *emergency station* shall be instructed that, on arrival at his *emergency station*, he is required to report to the person in charge of the station.

(4) Every person in charge of an *emergency station* shall be instructed that his duties as such a person include—

(a) establishing the whereabouts of every person required to go to the station;

(b) requiring every person arriving at the station to state what duties are set out as assigned to him in the *muster list*; and

(c) reporting to the manager as to the whereabouts of every person required to go to the station and as to the knowledge of their duties of persons arriving at the station.

8.   Drills.—(1) There shall be held at intervals not exceeding 12 days on every offshore installation which is normally manned a drill whereby—

(a) each person on the installation to whom duties have been assigned in the event of emergency involving the use, handling or operation of *emergency equipment* is instructed in the correct use, handling or operation of that equipment; and

(b) all *emergency equipment* used in the drill is examined, cleaned and, where appropriate, recharged or replaced and all portable equipment so used is returned to the place where it is ordinarily kept.

(2) At intervals not exceeding 8 weeks there shall be held on every offshore installation which is normally manned and is equipped with totally enclosed motor propelled survival craft a drill in relation to the loading, swinging out and, if reasonably practicable, lowering over the water of all such craft.

9.   Records. Without prejudice to anything contained in regulation 3(2) of the Offshore Installations (Logbooks and Registration of Death) Regulations 1972 (which Regulation relates to entries made in installation logbooks) an entry shall be made in the installation logbook maintained on any offshore installation under regulation 2(1) of those Regulations of every muster and every drill held on the installation under regulations 7 and 8 above respectively.

10. Stand-by services.—(1) There shall be present within 5 nautical miles of every offshore installation when it is manned a vessel (in these Regulations referred to as the "*stand-by vessel*") ready to give assistance in the event of an emergency on or near the installation and—

(a) which is capable of accommodating safely on board all persons who may be on the installation at any time; and

(b) which is equipped to provide first aid treatment for all such persons.

(2) Means for radio communication on appropriate wavelengths between every installation and its *stand-by vessel* shall be provided for at all times by suitable and effective equipment. Alternative means of communication shall also be provided on every installation and its *stand-by vessel*.

11. Duties of persons. In respect of any offshore installation it shall be the duty of—

(a) the owner of the installation and the concession owner to ensure that these Regulations are complied with;

(b) the *installation manager* to ensure that—

(i) regulations 6 to 9 above are complied with;

(ii) every person subject to his authority is made aware of those provisions of the *emergency procedure manual* and of these Regulations which are relevant to him; and

(iii) subject to section 5(5) of *the Act*, the appropriate measures specified in the *emergency procedure manual* are taken in the event of an emergency on or near the installation; and

(c) every person on the installation to acquaint himself with his *emergency station* and any duties assigned to him in the event of an emergency.

12. Civil liability. The provisions of section 11 of *the Act* (which makes provision for civil liability for breach of statutory duty) shall apply to the duties imposed on any person by these Regulations.

13. Offences.—(1) In the event of any contravention of any of these Regulations in or in connection with, or in relation to, an offshore installation, the *installation manager*, the concession owner and the owner of the installation shall each be guilty of an offence.

(2) In the event of any contravention by any person of regulation 11(c) above, that person shall also be guilty of an offence.

(3) If any person enters any information knowing it to be false in any record or any other document required to be provided or maintained under these Regulations or knowingly falsifies any such record or document or uses any such record or document for the purposes of these Regulations knowing it to be false in a material particular, that person shall be guilty of an offence.

(4) It shall be a defence in any proceedings for an offence under paragraphs (1) and (2) above for the accused to prove—

   (a) that he exercised all due diligence to prevent the commission of the offence; and

   (b) that the relevant contravention was committed without his consent, connivance or wilful default.

THE OFFSHORE INSTALLATIONS (LIFE-SAVING APPLIANCES) REGULATIONS 1977

(S.I. 1977 No. 486, as amended by S.I. 1984 No. 419, S.I. 1989 No. 1672, S.I. 1989 No. 1940 and S.I. 1990 No. 707)

General note. References to the Secretary of State shall be construed as references to the Health and Safety Executive by virtue of the Offshore Safety (Repeals and Modifications) Regulations 1993, S.I. 1993 No. 1823. The transfer of responsibility from the Department of Energy to the HSE was one of the recommendations of the Cullen Report (Cmd. 1310, 1990) on the Piper Alpha disaster of 6 July 1988.

Whereas the Secretary of State has consulted pursuant to section 7(1) of the Mineral Workings (Offshore Installations) Act 1971 (hereinafter referred to as "the Act") with organisations in the United Kingdom appearing to him to be representative of those persons who will be affected by the following Regulations:

Now, therefore, the Secretary of State, in exercise of his powers under sections 6 and 7 of, and paragraphs 1(1), 4(1), 7, 8(2), 11, 12, 13 and 14 of the Schedule to, *the Act*, as extended and amended by section 44 of the Petroleum and Submarine Pipe-lines Act 1975, and of all other powers enabling him in that behalf, hereby makes the following Regulations:—

1. Citation and commencement. These Regulations may be cited as the Offshore Installations (Life-saving Appliances) Regulations 1977 and shall come into operation on 1 June 1977.

2. Interpretation.—(1) In these Regulations—

"appropriate languages", in relation to any information to be displayed under these Regulations, means English and such other languages as are necessary to enable the information to be understood by all persons on the installation who may need to refer to it.

"fixed offshore installation" means an offshore installation which is not a *mobile offshore installation*;

"inspector" means a person appointed as an inspector under section 6(4) of *the Act*;

"installation manager" includes, where no manager of an offshore installation is appointed pursuant to section 4 of *the Act*, any person made responsible by the owner for safety, health and welfare on the installation;

"life-saving appliance" means any equipment required to be provided under these Regulations;

"mobile offshore installation" means an offshore installation which can be moved from place to place without major dismantling or modification, whether or not it has its own motive power;

"normally manned offshore installation" means an offshore installation on which persons are normally present;

2289

"totally enclosed motor propelled survival craft" means a motor propelled survival craft of rigid construction specially designed and constructed for carrying persons safely through fire on water.

(2) The Interpretation Act 1889 shall apply to the interpretation of these Regulations as it applies to the interpretation of an Act of Parliament.

3.   Application.   These Regulations shall apply to any offshore installation, not being a dredging installation registered (whether in the United Kingdom or elsewhere) as a vessel, which is maintained in controlled waters for the carrying on of any activity to which *the Act* applies.

4.   *Life-saving appliances—general.*—(1) Every survival craft, life raft, life buoy and life jacket with which an offshore installation is provided shall—

(a)   be of a type for the time being approved by the Secretary of State for offshore installations of a class or description which includes that installation;

(b)   be properly constructed of suitable materials having regard to its life-saving function and the circumstances in which it may be used or kept ready for use; and

(c)   be of such colour as will make it conspicuous when in use.

(2) All *life-saving appliances* shall be available for immediate use and shall, where necessary, be protected from damage.

5.   Survival craft and life rafts.—(1) Every *normally manned offshore installation* shall be provided with—

(a)   *totally enclosed motor propelled survival craft* having, in the aggregate, sufficient capacity to accommodate safely on board all persons on the installation; and

(b)   either—

(i)   additional *totally enclosed motor propelled survival craft* having, in the aggregate, together with the survival craft provided under sub-paragraph (a) above, sufficient capacity to accommodate safely on board 1½ times the number of persons on the installation; or

(ii)   additional survival craft or life rafts having, in the aggregate, together with the survival craft provided under sub-paragraph (a) above, sufficient capacity to accommodate safely on board twice the number of persons on the installation.

(2) There shall be provided in respect of every *totally enclosed motor propelled survival craft* provided under paragraph (1) above devices whereby the craft may be—

(a)   lowered into the water by one person on the craft; and

(b)   when closed down, disengaged from its launching apparatus by one person inside the craft.

(3) There shall be displayed inside every *totally enclosed motor propelled survival craft* clear instructions in *appropriate languages* for disengaging the craft from its launching apparatus and for operating the craft.

(4) The survival craft or life rafts provided under paragraph (1) above shall be suitably positioned having regard to the number of persons likely to be present in different parts of the installation.

(5) All apparatus for launching a survival craft or life raft shall be of such strength that the craft or raft can be safely lowered into the water when loaded with its full complement of persons and equipment and so arranged that the craft or raft can be so lowered without risk of obstruction.

(6) There shall be displayed near all apparatus for launching a survival craft or life raft clear instructions in *appropriate languages* for operating the apparatus.

(7) Every survival craft and life raft (other than an inflatable life raft) provided under paragraph (1) above shall be clearly and permanently marked with the name or other designation of the installation.

(8) Every survival craft and life raft so provided shall be equipped with—

(a) a waterproof electric hand lamp suitable for signalling;
(b) a sufficient supply of clean wholesome drinking water having regard to the number of persons that the survival craft is intended to accommodate, safely kept in suitable containers;
(c) a suitable first-aid outfit having regard to the number of persons the survival craft is intended to accommodate.

(9) Every *totally enclosed motor propelled survival craft* so provided shall be provided with a radio of a type for the time being approved by the Secretary of State capable of transmitting and receiving on 2182 kHz or VHF Channel 16.

(10) Every offshore installation provided with motor propelled survival craft shall also be provided with a suitable set of tools and spare parts for repairing each type of engine installed in those craft.

(11) Each set of tools and spare parts provided under paragraph (10) above shall be kept in a secure container of substantial construction bearing on the outside, in clear and permanent capital letters, the words "EMERGENCY REPAIR KIT—FOR USE ONLY IN THE REPAIR OF SURVIVAL CRAFT ENGINES".

6. Life buoys.—(1) Life buoys shall be provided on every offshore installation in such numbers and stowed in such places that at least one is readily accessible from any part of a deck of the installation from which a person is liable to fall into the water.

(2) Every life buoy so provided shall be stowed so that it can be readily cast loose.

(3) Every life buoy so provided shall be marked in clear and permanent capital letters with the name or other designation of the installation.

(4) Every life buoy so provided shall have attached to it a self-igniting buoyant light lit by an electric battery and inextinguishable in water.

7. Life jackets.—(1) Every offshore installation shall be provided with at least as many life jackets as 1½ times the number of persons on the installation.

(2) Every life jacket so provided shall, except when worn, be stowed at a suitable place on the installation and be readily available for use at all times.

(3) A conspicuous indication that life jackets are kept in the vicinity shall be displayed at each place where life jackets are stowed under paragraph (2) above.

8.   Means of escape.—(1) Every offshore installation shall be provided with suitable and sufficient means for persons to descend from the installation to the water in an emergency in addition to any *life-saving appliances* provided under Regulation 5 above.

(2) Any appliance used in the means so provided which does not form part of the installation shall be stowed so as to be readily available and so designed and constructed as to be capable of withstanding wind and waves when in use.

9.   Alarm and public address system.—(1) On every *normally manned offshore installation* there shall be provided—

   (a)   a general alarm system capable of raising the alarm by signals audible at every part of the installation where aural communication is practicable; and

   (b)   a public address system capable of being heard distinctly at all parts of the installation where persons are frequently present and aural communication is practicable.

(2) Each of the systems provided under paragraph (1) above shall also be capable of—

   (a)   providing a conspicuous visible warning in every part of the installation—

      (i)   in the case of the general alarm system, where aural communication is not practicable, and

      (ii)   in the case of the public address system, where persons are frequently present and aural communication is not practicable; and

(3) Each of the systems so provided above shall be supplied by two sources of electric power which shall be independent of each other and of which one shall be so designed as to be available in any emergency.

(4) There shall be displayed at or near to each place for operating either of the systems so provided clear instructions in *appropriate languages* for operating it.

10.   *Life-saving appliance plans.*—(1) There shall be kept on every offshore installation or at such other place as may be approved by an *inspector* a plan showing the position of all *life-saving appliances* (except life jackets issued to particular persons) on the installation.

(2) Copies of or extracts from the plan with such explanation in the *appropriate languages* as may be necessary shall be so displayed as to enable a person in any living accommodation or working space on an offshore installation readily to ascertain the position of all *life-saving appliances* in the vicinity.

11.   Examination of *life-saving appliances.*—(1) On or after 1 June 1978 no person shall be present on any offshore installation unless the *life-saving* *appliances* and the plans required to be kept or displayed under regulation 10 above on that installation have been examined by a person acting at the direction of the Secretary of State since these Regulations came into operation and in any case within the preceding 2 years.

(2) A copy of any certificate issued by the Secretary of State as to the result of any such examination shall be kept on the installation or at such other place as the *inspector* may approve and be open to inspection by any person on or (as the case may be) about to visit the installation.

(3) There shall be furnished to the Secretary of State within 7 days of any replacement of a *life-saving appliance* on an offshore installation by a *life-saving appliance* of a different type full particulars in writing of that replacement.

(4) The owner of any offshore installation in respect of which an examination is carried out under paragraph (1) above shall pay to the Secretary of State on demand a fee for the examination calculated in accordance with the provisions of the Schedule to these Regulations.

12.   Copies of Regulations. A copy of these Regulations shall be kept on every *normally manned offshore installation* and be open to inspection by any person on the installation.

13.   Duties of persons. It shall be the duty of the owner of an offshore installation and of the *installation manager* and of the concession owner to ensure that these Regulations (except regulation 11(4) above) are complied with.

14.   Civil liability. The provisions of section 11 of *the Act* (which makes provision for civil liability for breach of statutory duty) shall apply to the duties imposed on any person by these Regulations.

15.   Offences.—(1) In the event of any contravention of any of these Regulations (except regulation 11(4) above) in or in connection with, or in relation to, an offshore installation, the *installation manager*, the concession owner and the owner of the installation shall each be guilty of an offence.

(2) If any person enters any information knowing it to be false in any document issued under these Regulations or knowingly falsifies any such document or uses any such document for the purposes of these Regulations knowing it to be false, that person shall be guilty of an offence.

(3) It shall be a defence in any proceedings for an offence under paragraph (1) above for the accused to prove—

(a) that he exercised all due diligence to prevent the commission of the offence; and

(b) that the relevant contravention was committed without his consent, connivance or wilful default.

Regulation 11(4)

EXAMINATION FEES

The fee payable for an examination carried out in respect of any offshore installation under regulation 11(1) shall be—

(a) a sum based on the time spent by the person carrying out the examination on carrying it out and in travelling to and from the installation calculated in accordance with the table below.

TABLE

Time spent	Rate per hour or part thereof
On any day except a Saturday, Sunday or public holiday—	
between 8 a.m. and 6 p.m.	£37.00
before 8 a.m. or after 6 p.m.	£55.00
On a Saturday	£55.00
On a Sunday or public holiday	£74.00

and

(b) a sum equal to the cost of travelling and subsistence expenses reasonably incurred by the person carrying out the examination.

THE OFFSHORE INSTALLATIONS (FIRE-FIGHTING EQUIPMENT) REGULATIONS 1978

(S.I. 1978 No. 611, as amended by S.I. 1984 No. 419 and S.I. 1990 No. 707)

General note. References to the Secretary of State shall be construed as references to the Health and Safety Executive by virtue of the Offshore Safety (Repeals and Modifications) Regulations 1993, S.I. 1993 No. 1823. The transfer of responsibility from the Department of Energy to the HSE was one of the recommendations of the Cullen Report (Cmd. 1310, 1990) on the Piper Alpha disaster of 6 July 1988.

1. Citation and commencement. These Regulations may be cited as the Offshore Installations (Fire-fighting Equipment) Regulations 1978 and shall come into operation on 1 April 1979.

2. Interpretation—(1) In these Regulations—

"accommodation space" means any room used for eating, sleeping, cooking or recreation, or as an office, sick bay, laundry room or locker room, any corridor giving access to any of these rooms, and any storeroom in the vicinity of any of these rooms;

"appropriate languages" in relation to any information to be displayed under these Regulations, means English and such other languages as are necessary to enable the information to be understood by all persons on the installation who may need to refer to it;

"ashore" means on land in the United Kingdom;

"the control point" has the meaning assigned to it by regulation 5(2) below;

"fire-fighting equipment" means any equipment required under regulations 5 to 17 below and any other equipment for the purpose of detecting or indicating the presence of, preventing the spread of, or extinguishing, a fire, or of detecting or indicating the presence of, or measuring, an accumulation of flammable gas;

"fixed offshore installation" means an offshore installation which is not a *mobile offshore installation*;

"inspector" means a person appointed under section 6(4) of *the Act*;

"installation manager" includes, where no manager of an offshore installation is appointed pursuant to section 4 of *the Act*, any person made responsible by the owner for safety, health and welfare on an offshore installation;

"mobile offshore installation" means an offshore installation which can be moved from place to place without major dismantling or modification, whether or not it has its own motive power;

"normally manned offshore installation" means an offshore installation on which persons are normally present;

"working space" means any workshop, engine room or generator room, and any space containing equipment in which petroleum or any other flammable substance is stored, conveyed, processed or consumed.

(2) The Interpretation Act 1889 shall apply to the interpretation of these Regulations as it applies to the interpretation of an Act of Parliament.

3.   Application. These Regulations shall apply to any offshore installation, not being a dredging installation registered (whether in the United Kingdom or elsewhere) as a vessel, which is maintained in controlled waters for the carrying on of any activity to which *the Act* applies.

4.   *Fire-fighting equipment*—general.—(1) Any *fire-fighting equipment* which is provided on an offshore installation shall be of a type for the time being approved by the Secretary of State for offshore installations of a class or description which includes that installation.

(2) All *fire-fighting equipment* shall be kept available for immediate use and shall, where necessary, be protected from damage.

5.   Automatic fire detection systems.—(1) Every offshore installation shall be provided with an automatic fire detection system.

(2) The system provided under paragraph (1) above on a *normally manned offshore installation* shall be capable of—

(a) indicating both audibly and visibly the presence of a fire in any *working space* on the installation not protected by the automatic sprinkler system provided under regulation 12 below—
  (i)   at a place (hereafter in these Regulations referred to as "*the control point*") at which the public address system provided on the installation may be operated; and
  (ii) at another place on the installation where someone is present at all times when *the control point* is unmanned; and
(b) indicating the location of any such fire at *the control point.*

(3) The system provided under paragraph (1) above on an installation which is not normally manned shall be capable of indicating both audibly and visibly the presence of a fire in any *working space* on the installation at a place which is continuously manned either on another installation or *ashore.*

6.   Flammable gas detection and measuring equipment.—(1) Every offshore installation shall be provided with an automatic flammable gas detection system capable of monitoring continuously every part of the installation in which flammable gas may accidentally accumulate.

(2) The system provided under paragraph (1) above on a *normally manned offshore installation* shall be capable of—

(a) indicating both audibly and visibly the presence of an accumulation of flammable gas in any part of the installation which is monitored by the system—
  (i)   at *the control point* on the installation; and
  (ii) at another place on the installation where someone is present at all times when *the control point* is manned; and

(b) indicating the location of any such accumulation at *the control point.*

(3) The system provided under paragraph (1) above on an installation which is not normally manned shall be capable of indicating both audibly and visibly the presence of an accumulation of flammable gas in any part of the installation which is monitored by the system at a place which is continuously manned either on another installation or *ashore.*

(4) Whenever an offshore installation is manned it shall be provided with two portable devices capable of measuring accurately an accumulation of flammable gas.

7. Fire alarm systems. Every *normally manned offshore installation* shall be provided with a manually actuated fire alarm system by means of which—

(a) the presence of a fire in any part of the installation can be indicated both audibly and visibly by a person in or near that part—
  (i) at *the control point* on the installation; and
  (ii) at another place on the installation where someone is present at all times when *the control point* is unmanned; and
(b) the location of any such fire can be indicated by such a person at *the control point.*

8. Remote control safety equipment.—(1) Every offshore installation shall be provided with equipment for each of the following purposes—

(a) stopping any ventilator fan;
(b) closing any ventilator;
(c) stopping any pump used to discharge fuel for prime movers, boilers or other fired processes on the installation; and from any pressure vessel or storage tank;
(d) preventing the escape of fuel from prime movers, boilers or other fired processes on the installation.

(2) Any equipment provided under paragraph (1) above shall be capable of operation from a position which is outside the relevant room and which will not be made inaccessible by a fire within the relevant room.

(3) In the foregoing paragraph "the relevant room" means, in relation to equipment provided in respect of a fan or ventilator, the space or room it ventilates, and in relation to equipment provided in respect of a pump, vessel or tank, the space or room in which the pump, vessel or tank is situated.

9. Fire mains.—(1) Every *normally manned offshore installation* shall be provided with a water main by means of which water can be supplied to any part of the installation.

(2) The main provided under paragraph (1) above shall be—

(a) connected to at least two pumps situated in different parts of the installation; and
(b) capable, when supplied by any pump, of maintaining a supply of water to any part of the installation at a pressure sufficient for fire-fighting by means of hand-held hoses.

(3) The pumps which are connected to the main provided under paragraph (1) above—

   (a) shall be so arranged that the pumps in any one part of the installation are connected to a source of power which is remote from the sources of power to which the pumps in other parts of the installation are connected; and

   (b) shall each be capable, once actuated, of operating automatically for 12 hours.

10.   Hydrants and fire hoses.—(1) Every *normally manned offshore installation* shall be provided with hydrants, which shall be connected to the main provided under Regulation 9 above, and fire hoses, one of which shall be kept next to each hydrant.

   (2) Nozzles capable of producing a water jet, water spray and water fog shall be provided, and one shall be fitted to or kept next to each fire hose.

   (3) The positions of the hydrants and the lengths of the fire hoses kept next to them shall be such that two hoses attached to separate hydrants may be promptly brought to bear upon a fire in any part of the installation.

11.   Water deluge system and water monitors.—(1) Every *normally manned offshore installation* shall be provided with a water deluge system or water monitors (or both) by means of which any part of the installation containing equipment used for storing, conveying, or processing petroleum (other than petroleum intended as fuel for prime movers, boilers or other fired processes on the installation) can be protected in the event of a fire.

   (2) If a deluge system is provided under paragraph (1) above, it shall be connected to a water main, and if water monitors are provided a main shall be provided which is so arranged that any monitor may readily be connected to it.

   (3) Any main to which a deluge system is connected or to which water monitors may be connected shall be—

   (a) connected to at least two pumps; and

   (b) capable, when supplied by either pump if only two are connected or by any two pumps if more than two are connected, of maintaining a supply of water at a pressure sufficient to enable the system or the monitors (as the case may be) to operate efficiently.

(4) The pumps which are connected to a main to which a deluge system is connected or to which water monitors may be connected—

   (a) shall be so arranged that, where only two pumps are connected, one pump, or, where more than two pumps are connected, two pumps and their sources of power shall be remote from any part of the installation containing equipment of the kind described in paragraph (1) above; and

   (b) shall each be capable, once actuated, of operating automatically for 12 hours.

12.   Automatic sprinkler systems.—(1) Every *normally manned offshore installation* shall be provided with an automatic sprinkler system capable of—

(a) detecting the presence of a fire in any *accommodation space*;

(b) operating automatically to protect any such space in which a fire is present;

(c) indicating both audibly and visibly that a sprinkler has come into operation—

    (i) at *the control point* on the installation; and

    (ii) at another place on the installation where someone is present at all times when *the control point* is unmanned; and

(d) indicating the location of any sprinkler which has come into operation at *the control point*.

(2) The system provided under paragraph (1) above shall be connected to a water main which is—

(a) connected to a pump which is—

    (i) remote from any *accommodation space*;

    (ii) connected to a source of power which is remote from any *accommodation space*; and

    (iii) capable, once actuated, of operating automatically for 4 hours; and

(b) capable when supplied by that pump, of maintaining a supply of water to the system at a pressure sufficient to enable it to operate efficiently.

13. Fixed fire extinguishing systems. *The control point* on an offshore installation and every space on an offshore installation which contains—

(a) internal combustion machinery having in aggregate a power of 750 kw or more;

(b) an oil or gas-fired boiler, heater or incinerator having a thermal rating of 75 kw or more; or

(c) any equipment through which fuel for prime movers, boilers or other fired processes on the installation is pumped at a pressure in excess of 10 kg/cm^2,

shall be provided with a fixed fire extinguishing system.

14. Fire extinguishers.—(1) Fire extinguishers shall be provided on every offshore installation in such numbers and in such places that at least one extinguisher is readily accessible from any part of the installation.

(2) Each extinguisher provided under paragraph (1) above shall be of a type suitable for use in fighting a fire of the kind which is most likely to occur in the part of the installation in which it is placed.

15. Helicopter landing area equipment.—(1) Every offshore installation shall be provided with—

(a) one or more dry powder fire extinguishers having in aggregate a capacity of not less than 45 kg; and

(b) either—

    (i) one or more carbon dioxide fire extinguishers with applicators having in aggregate a capacity of not less than 18 kg; or

    (ii) one or more halogenated hydro-carbon fire extinguishers with applicators having in aggregate a capacity of not less than 12 kg.

(2) The fire extinguishers provided under paragraph (1) above shall be kept at places which are readily accessible from the helicopter landing area.

(3) Every offshore installation which is normally manned shall be provided with—

(a) a low expansion foam application system capable of discharging foam solution onto the landing area at a rate of not less than 6 litres per minute per square metre of the prescribed area; and

(b) sufficient foam compound to enable the rate prescribed in sub-paragraph (a) above to be continuously maintained for a period of not less than five minutes.

(4) In this regulation, "the prescribed area" means an area equal in size to $0.75(L)^2$ where L is the overall length of the longest helicopter which the landing area is designed to accommodate, measured along its rotors in a fore and aft line.

16. Fireman's equipment.—(1) Every *normally manned offshore installation* shall be provided with four sets of fireman's equipment and every offshore installation which is not normally manned shall be provided with two sets of such equipment.

(2) Each set of equipment provided under paragraph (1) above shall comprise the following—

(a) a protective outfit, including gloves, boots, a face mask or hood and a helmet;

(b) a self-contained breathing apparatus;

(c) a portable battery-operated safety lamp capable of functioning efficiently for a period of not less than 3 hours;

(d) a fireman's axe; and

(e) a safety harness and lifeline.

(3) The sets of equipment provided under paragraph (1) above shall be kept in pairs, and one pair shall be kept at a place which is readily accessible from the helicopter landing area.

17. Fire blankets.—(1) Every offshore installation which has a galley shall be provided with a fire blanket.

(2) Every blanket provided under paragraph (1) above shall be kept at a place which is readily accessible to anyone in the galley in a container which is marked with clear instructions in *accommodation space* for the use of the blanket.

18. Operating instructions. Clear instructions in *accommodation space* for operating the equipment which is provided on an offshore installation under regulations 5 to 8 and 11 to 15 above, and any breathing apparatus which is provided under regulation 16 above, shall be displayed on the equipment if it is portable or if it is not portable on it or at or near to each place for operating it.

19. *Fire-fighting equipment* plans.—(1) There shall be kept on every offshore installation or at such other place as may be approved by an *inspector* a plan showing the position of all the *fire-fighting equipment* which is provided on the installation.

(2) Copies of or extracts from the plan with such explanation in the *accommodation space* as may be necessary shall be so displayed as to enable a person in any accommodation or *working space* on an offshore installation readily to ascertain the position of all the *fire-fighting equipment* in the vicinity.

20. Examination of *fire-fighting equipment*.—(1) On or after 1 April 1980 no person shall be present on any offshore installation unless the *fire-fighting equipment* and the plans required to be kept or displayed under regulation 19 above on that installation have been examined by a person acting at the direction of the Secretary of State since these Regulations came into operation and in any case within the preceding 2 years.

(2) A copy of any certificate issued by the Secretary of State as to the result of any such examination shall be kept on the installation or at such other place as the *inspector* may approve and shall be open to inspection by any person on or (as the case may be) about to visit the installation.

(3) There shall be furnished to the Secretary of State within 7 days of any replacement of any *fire-fighting equipment* on an offshore installation by *fire-fighting equipment* of a different type full particulars in writing of that replacement.

(4) The owner of any offshore installation in respect of which an examination has been carried out under paragraph (1) above shall pay to the Secretary of State on demand a fee for that examination calculated in accordance with the provisions of the Schedule to these Regulations.

21. Copies of Regulations. A copy of these Regulations shall be kept on every *normally manned offshore installation* and shall be open to inspection by any person on the installation.

22. Duties of persons. It shall be the duty of the owner of an offshore installation and of the *installation manager* and of the concession owner to ensure that these Regulations (except Regulation 20(4) above) are complied with.

23. Civil liability. The provisions of section 11 of *the Act* (which makes provision for civil liability for breach of statutory duty) shall apply to the duties imposed on any person by these Regulations.

24. Offences.—(1) In the event of any contravention of any of these Regulations (except regulation 20(4) above) on, or in connection with, or in relation to, an offshore installation, the *installation manager*, the concession owner and the owner of the installation shall each be guilty of an offence.

(2) If any person enters any information which he knows to be false in any document issued under these Regulations or knowingly falsifies any such

document or uses any such document for the purposes of these Regulations knowing it to be false, that person shall be guilty of an offence.

(3) It shall be a defence in any proceedings for an offence under paragraph (1) above for the accused to prove—

(a) that he exercised all due diligence to prevent the commission of the offence; and

(b) that the relevant contravention was committed without his consent, connivance or wilful default.

SCHEDULE

Regulation 20 (4)

EXAMINATION FEES

The fee payable for an examination carried out in respect of any offshore installation under regulation 20(1) shall be—

(a) a sum based on the time spent by the person carrying out the examination in carrying it out and in travelling to and from the installation calculated in accordance with the table below:

TABLE

Time spent	Rate per hour or part thereof
On any day except a Saturday, Sunday or public holiday—	
between 8 a.m. and 6 p.m.	£37.00
before 8 a.m. or after 6 p.m.	£55.50
On a Saturday	£55.50
On a Sunday or public holiday	£74.00

and

(b) a sum equal to the cost of travelling and subsistence expenses reasonably incurred by the person carrying out the examination.

THE OFFSHORE INSTALLATIONS (WELL CONTROL) REGULATIONS 1980

(S.I. 1980 No. 1759, as amended by S.I. 1991 No. 308)

General note. References to the Secretary of State shall be construed as references to the Health and Safety Executive by virtue of the Offshore Safety (Repeals and Modifications) Regulations 1993, S.I. 1993 No. 1823. The transfer of responsibility from the Department of Energy to the HSE was one of the recommendations of the Cullen Report (Cmd. 1310, 1990) on the Piper Alpha disaster of 6 July 1988.

1. Citation, commencement and interpretation.—(1) These Regulations may be cited as the Offshore Installations (Well Control) Regulations 1980 and shall come into force on 1 January 1981.

(2) In these Regulations—

"installation manager" includes, when no manager of an offshore installation is appointed pursuant to section 4 of the Mineral Workings (Offshore Installations) Act 1971, any person made responsible by the owner of the installation for safety, health and welfare on the installation;

"responsible person", in relation to an offshore installation, means a competent person appointed by the *installation manager* to be responsible for the control and safety of drilling operations or production operations under regulation 30(1) of the Offshore Installations (Operational Safety, Health and Welfare) Regulations 1976.

2. Well control operations.—(1) No drilling operations or work over operations on a well controlled by the hydrostatic pressure of the wellbore fluid and for which no flow control device is installed except blowout prevention equipment shall be carried on on an offshore installation unless they are carried on by persons in the immediate charge of a person (hereafter in this Regulation referred to as "the driller") appointed for that purpose by a *responsible person* and who is himself acting under the general supervision of a person (hereafter in this regulation referred to as "the drilling supervisor") appointed for that purpose by a *responsible person.*

(2) No person shall be appointed or shall act as a driller or a drilling supervisor unless he is the holder of a certificate granted within the preceding two years by the Secretary of State on the recommendation of the Offshore Petroleum Industry Training Board or its successor, the Offshore Petroleum Industry Training Organisation Limited, that he has an adequate knowledge of well control techniques including, in the case of a drilling supervisor, those relating to the safe resumption of normal working.

(3) [*revoked*].

(4) It shall be the duty of the employer of an employee employed by him for such operations on an offshore installation as are mentioned in paragraph (1)

above to ensure that the employee complies with the provisions of paragraph (2) above so far as they prohibit him from acting as a driller or a drilling supervisor unless he is the holder of a specified certificate.

3.   Offences.—(1) In the event of a contravention of regulation 2 above on an offshore installation, the *installation manager*, the concession owner and the installation owner shall each be guilty of an offence.

(2) In the event of any contravention by any other person of regulation 2(2) or (4) above, that person shall also be guilty of an offence.

(3) Any person who, with intent to deceive, forges or uses such a certificate as is mentioned in regulation 2(2) above or makes or has in his possession a document so closely resembling any such certificate as to be calculated to deceive shall be guilty of an offence.

(4) It shall be a defence in any proceedings for an offence under paragraph (1) above for the accused to prove—

(a) that he exercised all due diligence to prevent the commission of the offence; and

(b) that the relevant contravention was committed without his consent, connivance or wilful default.

THE OFFSHORE INSTALLATIONS (SAFETY REPRESENTATIVES AND SAFETY COMMITTEES) REGULATIONS 1989

(S.I. 1989 No. 971, as amended by S.I. 1992 No. 2885)

General note. These Regulations are to be compared with the Safety Representatives and Safety Committees Regulations, S.I. 1977 No. 500, amended by S.I. 1992 No. 2051 which apply onshore and are set out in Part 2 of this book. One significant difference is that under these Regulations safety representatives are elected by the workforce whereas under the "onshore" Regulations safety representatives may only be appointed if there is a recognised union, and it is left to the union as to the method of selection. These Regulations therefore, unlike the "onshore" Regulations, do not contain the discrepancy with the European Framework Directive 89/391 which requires safety representatives for workers, whether or not a union is recognised.

The position of safety representatives and committees is fortified by the Offshore Safety (Protection of Victimisation) Act 1992.

References to the Secretary of State shall be construed as references to the Health and Safety Executive by virtue of the Offshore Safety (Repeals and Modifications) Regulations 1993, S.I. 1993 No. 1823. The transfer of responsibility from the Department of Energy to the HSE was one of the recommendations of the Cullen Report (Cmd. 1310, 1990) on the Piper Alpha disaster of 6 July 1988.

Whereas the Secretary of State has consulted pursuant to section 7(1) of the Mineral Workings (Offshore Installations) Act 1971 (hereinafter referred to as "the 1971 Act") with organisations in the United Kingdom appearing to him to be representative of those persons who will be affected by the following Regulations;

Now, therefore, the Secretary of State, in exercise of his powers under sections 6 and 7 of, and paragraphs 1 and 6 of the Schedule to, *the 1971 Act*, and of all other powers enabling him in that behalf, hereby makes the following Regulations:

PRELIMINARY

1. Citation and commencement. These Regulations may be cited as the Offshore Installations (Safety Representatives and Safety Committees) Regulations 1989 and shall come into force on 18 September 1989.

2. Interpretation. In these Regulations—

"the 1974 Act" means the Health and Safety at Work etc. Act 1974;

"appropriate languages" in relation to any information to be displayed on the installation under these Regulations means English and such other languages as are necessary to enable the information to be understood by all persons on the installation who may need to refer to it;

"elected" includes being declared the safety representative for a constituency under regulation 12 below by virtue of being the only candidate duly nominated for that position;

"employed" means employed or engaged under a contract of service or for services and related expressions shall be construed accordingly;

"installation logbook" means a logbook which is required to be maintained under regulation 2 of the Offshore Installations (Logbooks and Registration of Death) Regulations 1972;

"installation manager" includes, where no manager is appointed pursuant to section 4 of *the 1971 Act*, any person made responsible by the installation owner for safety, health and welfare on board an offshore installation;

"occupational health and safety" means the health and safety of the workforce while on or working from an installation and while boarding or leaving it;

"the prescribed period" means the period of five weeks or such shorter period as is reasonably practicable to make representations, or nominations, or to vote as the case may be;

"a week" means any period of seven days;

"workforce" includes every person who is for the time being working on or from an offshore installation under a contract of service or a contract for services, other than the *installation manager*, a body corporate or an unincorporated body of persons.

3. Application. These Regulations shall apply to an offshore installation, not being a dredging installation registered in the United Kingdom or elsewhere, which—

(a) is maintained on a working station in controlled waters for the carrying on of an activity to which *the 1971 Act* applies, and

(b) is normally manned.

Election of Safety Representatives etc.

4. Safety representatives. The *workforce* shall be entitled to nominate and elect safety representatives in accordance with the following provisions of these Regulations.

5. Constituencies. (1) The *installation manager* shall establish and thereafter, in consultation with any safety committee established in accordance with regulation 19 below, maintain for the purposes of these Regulations a system of constituencies, which shall be established by reference to one or more of the following factors—

(a) the areas of the offshore installation,

(b) the activities undertaken on or from the installation,

(c) the employers of members of the *workforce*, and

(d) other objective criteria which appear to the *installation manager* to be appropriate to the circumstances of the installation.

(2) The system of constituencies shall be such that—

(a) there shall be at least two constituencies;

(b) every member of the *workforce* can be assigned to a constituency; and

(c) the number of persons who may at any time be assigned to a constituency shall not exceed forty and shall be no fewer than three.

(3) In determining the number of persons to be assigned to a constituency the *installation manager* shall have regard, in particular, to the nature of the work undertaken by the members of the constituency and the hazards related thereto.

(4) The *installation manager* shall signify the establishment or modification of a constituency by ensuring the posting in *appropriate languages* at suitable places on the installation so that they can easily be read by all the members of the *workforce* of—

(a) particulars of the establishment or modification of the constituency; and
(b) subject to paragraph (7) below, notice that the *installation manager* will consider any representations with regard to such particulars as may be made to him within the *prescribed period* commencing with the date of their posting in accordance with paragraph (5) below.

(5) Subject to paragraph (7) below, representations may be made by any member of the *workforce* and, if the constituency is intended to be comprised exclusively of persons *employed* by the same employer, that employer.

(6) If any representations are made to him in accordance with paragraph (4)(b) above, the *installation manager* shall forthwith consider them, and if he considers that they necessitate amendment of the particulars referred to in paragraph (4)(a) above he shall ensure that amended particulars in *appropriate languages* are posted at suitable places as prescribed in paragraph (4) above.

(7) Where an *installation manager* proposes to establish a constituency and there is in existence on the installation a safety committee established under regulation 19 below, paragraphs (4)(b), (5) and (6) above shall not apply but the *installation manager* shall consult the safety committee and if the constituency is intended to be comprised exclusively of persons *employed* by the same employer, that employer.

6. Membership of constituency.—(1) The *installation manager* shall as soon as practicable ensure that every member of the *workforce* is assigned to a constituency established under regulation 5 above.

(2) The *installation manager* shall subsequently ensure that each new member is assigned to a constituency and informed in writing of the constituency to which he has been assigned and of the name of the safety representative of that constituency and the safety representative shall be informed in writing of the name of any new member of the *workforce* assigned to his constituency.

(3) Paragraphs (1) and (2) above shall not apply to any member of the *workforce* who at no time while on the offshore installation is expected to remain thereon for any period longer than forty-eight hours.

7. Elections. Subject to regulation 15 below, the members of the *workforce* assigned to a constituency may elect one safety representative in accordance with the provisions of regulations 8 to 13 below.

8. Nominations. As soon as practicable after—

(a) the establishment or modification of a constituency, or

(b) the expiry of a period of two years since the safety representative was last *elected*, or

(c) a person's ceasing to be the safety representative in accordance with paragraph (b), (c) or (d) of regulation 14 below,

the *installation manager* shall ensure that a notice in *appropriate languages* is posted at suitable places as prescribed in regulation 5(4) above and that an election is to take place in relation to the constituency in question, with details of the members of that constituency; and he shall invite the nomination of candidates for election to be made to him during the *prescribed period* commencing with the date of posting of the notice.

9.   Candidates. (1) A person shall be eligible to be a candidate for election as the safety representative for a constituency if the *installation manager* is satisfied that he is a member of that constituency, that he is willing to stand as a candidate for the constituency, that he has been nominated by a second member of the constituency, and that his nomination has been seconded by a third member.

(2) The *installation manager* shall provide every person who is eligible to be a candidate with reasonable facilities to enable him to promote his election campaign.

10.   List of candidates. After the expiry of the period allowed for nominations under regulation 8 above and within one *week* from that date, the *installation manager* shall ensure that there is displayed in *appropriate languages* at suitable places as prescribed in regulation 5(4) above—

(a) a list of duly nominated candidates; or

(b) if no candidate has been duly nominated, notice of the existence of a vacancy.

11.   Secret ballot.—(1) If in any constituency more than one candidate is duly nominated, the *installation manager* shall, throughout the *prescribed period* commencing with the expiry of the one *week* period specified in regulation 10 above, conduct a secret ballot in which each member of that constituency shall be entitled to vote for one candidate in the constituency.

(2) If the Secretary of State receives a claim in writing from a member of the *workforce* that a ballot held for the purposes of paragraph (1) above does not comply with the requirements of that paragraph or has not been conducted fairly, he may, if he is satisfied that the claim is justified, declare the ballot to be a nullity and direct the *installation manager* or the installation owner to conduct a further ballot in accordance with such requirements as the Secretary of State may specify.

(3) The *installation manager* or the installation owner shall comply with any directions given by the Secretary of State under paragraph (2) above.

12.   Results. The *installation manager* shall—

(a)   ensure that within one *week* from the expiry of the election period prescribed in regulation 11(1) above or specified under regulation 11(2) above a notice in *appropriate languages* is posted at suitable places as prescribed in regulation 5(4) above certifying the result of the ballot or, in the case of a constituency for which only one candidate has been duly nominated, declaring that candidate to be the safety representative for that constituency; and

(b)   as soon as is practicable thereafter issue to every person *elected* to be a safety representative a document signed and dated by him which certifies the date on which the person was *elected*, the name of the person's employer (if any), the name or other designation of the offshore installation and a description which is sufficient to identify the constituency he represents.

13.   No candidate. If in any constituency no candidate has been nominated in accordance with regulation 9 above and no safety representative holds that position by virtue of regulation 15 below—

(a)   the *installation manager* shall, until a candidate has been so nominated or a safety representative holds that position under the said regulation 15, keep and update at monthly intervals a list of members for the time being of the constituency and the latest copy of the list shall be posted at suitable places as prescribed in regulation 5(4) above on the installation; and

(b)   the *installation manager* shall record those facts in the *installation logbook*, and if an eligible candidate is subsequently nominated in accordance with regulation 9 above the *installation manager* shall arrange for an election to be held for the constituency, in accordance with the foregoing provisions of these Regulations concerning elections.

14.   Cessation of representation. A person shall cease to be a safety representative for the purposes of these Regulations—

(a)   on the election of another representative for his constituency in accordance with regulations 8 to 13 above, or

(b)   if he resigns, or

(c)   if his employment is terminated, or

(d)   if he has been absent from the installation for which he is a safety representative for a continuous period of twelve *weeks*.

15.   Safety representatives for single employer constituencies.—(1) Where a person has not more than two years previously been *elected* in accordance with the foregoing provisions of these Regulations as a safety representative on an offshore installation for a constituency, the members of which were exclusively the employees of his present employer, he may, subject to paragraphs (2) and (3) below, continue to hold that position without re-election as a safety representative for a constituency, the members of which are exclusively employees of his present employer, on any other offshore installation on which he is subsequently a member of the *workforce*.

(2) Subject to paragraph (3) below, no person shall hold a position as a safety representative for a constituency under paragraph (1) above if the constituency is already represented by a safety representative.

(3) No person shall hold a position as a safety representative under paragraph (1) above on more than one offshore installation at any time unless the installations are for the time being normally linked by a bridge.

16.   Functions of safety representatives.   Each safety representative shall have the following functions—

(a)   to investigate potential hazards and dangerous occurrences and to examine the causes of accidents where the interests of the members of his constituency might be involved or those of any other member of the *workforce* when that person's safety representative is not available or there is no safety representative for that person's constituency;

(b)   to investigate complaints by any member of his constituency relating to the *occupational health and safety* of any member of the *workforce* and to investigate complaints by any other member of the *workforce* when that person's safety representative is not available or there is no safety representative for that person's constituency;

(c)   to make representations to the *installation manager* and, where appropriate, to every employer on matters arising out of paragraph (a) or (b) above;

(d)   to make representations to the *installation manager* and, where appropriate, to every employer on general matters affecting the *occupational health and safety* of members of the *workforce*;

(e)   to attend meetings of the safety committee established under regulation 19 and 20 below;

(f)   to represent his constituency members in consultations on the offshore installation with Inspectors appointed under section 6(4) of 1971 Act; and

(g)   to consult members of his constituency either individually or, so far as is reasonably practicable, collectively on any matters arising out of the foregoing provisions of this regulation and the provisions set out in regulation 22 below, as appropriate,

but no function conferred on a safety representative by this regulation shall be construed as imposing a duty on him.

17.   Powers of safety representatives.—(1) To enable him to fulfil his functions under regulation 16 above, a safety representative may exercise the powers set out in paragraphs (2), (3), (4)(b) and (5) of this regulation and he may seek advice and guidance whether from persons on the offshore installation or elsewhere on any matter arising out of regulation 16 above and regulation 22 below, as appropriate.

(2) A safety representative may inspect any part of the offshore installation or its equipment if—

(a)   he has given the *installation manager* and, if his employer is not the installation owner, his employer, reasonable notice in writing of his intention to do so, and

(b) he has not inspected that part of the installation or its equipment in the previous three months,

and he may carry out more frequent inspections by agreement with the *installation manager* and, if his employer is not the installation owner, his employer.

(3) If—

(a) there has been a notifiable incident, and
(b) it is safe for an inspection to be carried out, and
(c) the interests of the members of his constituency might be involved,

a safety representative may inspect the part of the installation or the equipment concerned and, so far as is necessary for the purpose of determining the cause, he may inspect any other part of the installation or its equipment: provided that the safety representative shall first notify of his intention to carry out the inspection—

(i) the *installation manager*; and
(ii) where his employer is not the installation owner and it is reasonably practicable to notify him, his employer.

(4) Where two or more safety representatives consider there is an imminent risk of serious personal injury arising from an activity carried out on the installation—

(a) they shall make representations to the *installation manager* who shall prepare and send a report in writing on the matter to an inspector appointed under section 6(4) of *the 1971 Act* as soon as is reasonably practicable; and
(b) a safety representative may make a report in writing by the fastest practicable means to an inspector appointed under section 19 of that Act.

(5) A safety representative may receive information given under section 28(8) of *the 1974 Act* by an inspector appointed under section 19 of that Act.

(6) In this regulation, "notifiable incident" means any casualty, accident, injury or disease which is required to be notified by the installation owner or the *installation manager* under regulation 9 or 12 of the Offshore Installations (Inspectors and Casualties) Regulations 1973.

18. Documents. A safety representative shall subject to regulation 18A(2)(a) below be entitled to see and be supplied, by or on behalf of the *installation manager*, with copies of any document relating to the *occupational health and safety* at work of the workforce which is required by any statutory provision to be kept on the offshore installation, except a document consisting of or relating to any health record of an identifiable individual or a safety case or revision to which regulation 18A below applies.

18A.—(1) A safety representative shall be entitled—

(a) to be supplied, by or on behalf of the installation manager, with a written summary of the main features of a safety case or revision thereof relating to the offshore installation and prepared pursuant to the Offshore

Installations (Safety Case) Regulations 1992, such summary to include any particulars concerning remedial work and the time by which it will be done;

(b) to see a copy of that safety case or revision;

(c) to be supplied, by or on behalf of the installation manager, with copies of such parts of that safety case or revision thereof as the safety representative needs for the purpose of performing any of his functions in circumstances where his entitlement under sub-pararaphs (a) and (b) is insufficient for that purpose.

(2) The references in—

(a) regulation 18 to seeing a document, where the statutory provision concerned allows the information in the document to be kept on film or in electronic form and it is so kept;

(b) regulation l8A(1)(a) to seeing a safety case or revision, where the information in it is kept on film or in electronic form on the installation,

are references to having appropriate facilities to enable him to read that information.

SAFETY COMMITTEES

19. Safety committee—establishment. The owner of an offshore installation for which one or more safety representatives have been *elected* or hold that position by virtue of regulation 15 above shall establish a safety committee.

20. Membership of safety committee. (1) The safety committee shall include the *installation manager* as chairman, one further person who may be appointed by the installation owner or the *installation manager,* all the safety representatives, and such other persons as the safety committee may co-opt by the unanimous vote of the members of the committee present and voting on the co-option.

(2) A person co-opted to the safety committee under paragraph (1) above shall not be entitled to vote on the co-options of another to the committee.

21. Safety committee—meetings. (1) The first meeting of a safety committee shall be called by the chairman within six *weeks* of the date of its establishment, and thereafter the chairman shall call a meeting at least once in every three months.

(2) In calling a meeting, the chairman shall endeavour to appoint a date on which the members can attend.

(3) A safety representative may nominate a member of his constituency to attend meetings as a member in his stead when he is unable to attend.

(4) The quorum for a meeting of a safety committee shall be the chairman and such number of safety representatives or persons nominated under paragraph (3) above as represent a third (rounded up to a whole number) of the number of safety representatives holding office at the date the meeting is called.

22.   Safety committee functions.—(1) A safety committee shall have the following functions in relation to the offshore installation which it serves—

(a)   without prejudice to the performance of any obligation imposed on the *installation manager* or any other person by or under any enactment, to keep under review the measures taken to ensure the *occupational health and safety* of the *workforce;*

(b)   to keep under review, and to make recommendations to the *installation manager* with regard to, the system of the constituencies so as to ensure adequate representation of the *workforce* on health and safety matters;

(c)   to keep under review the arrangements for the training of safety representatives in accordance with regulation 27 below and to make representations to the employers as appropriate;

(d)   without prejudice to the requirements of regulation 21(1) above, to keep under review the frequency of safety committee meetings, the circumstances under which they may be called and to make representations to the *installation manager* as appropriate;

(e)   to consider representations from any member of the safety committee on any matter affecting the *occupational health and safety* of the *workforce* and make recommendations to the *installation manager* as appropriate;

(f)   to consider the causes of accidents, dangerous occurrences and cases of occupational ill health and make recommendations to the *installation manager* as appropriate;

(g)   to consider any document relating to the *occupational health and safety* of the *workforce* which is required by any statutory provision to be kept on the offshore installation, except any document consisting of or relating to any health record of an identifiable individual;

(h)   to prepare and maintain a record of its business a copy of which shall be kept on the installation for one year from the date of the meeting and as soon as practicable after each meeting send the record of that meeting to the installation owner who shall keep it at a place onshore in the United Kingdom until the sixth anniversary of the expiry of the year to which the record relates,

but no function given to a safety committee by this regulation shall be construed as imposing a duty on it.

(2) A safety committee shall seek to advance co-operation on matters affecting *occupational health and safety* between all parties on the installation which the committee serves and to that end shall seek to promote and develop measures to ensure the *occupational health and safety* of the *workforce.*

INSTALLATION OWNERS, INSTALLATION MANAGERS AND EMPLOYERS

23.   Duties of installation owners and *installation managers.* In respect of every offshore installation served by a safety committee it shall be the duty of the installation owner and of the *installation manager—*

(a)   to facilitate the exercise by the committee of its functions and by the safety representatives of their functions and powers in respect of the installation under these Regulations, and for that purpose to make available the necessary accommodation, facilities for communication and office equipment supplies; and

(b) to consult safety representatives with a view to the making and maintenance of arrangements which will enable them and the *workforce* to
co-operate effectively in promoting and developing measures to ensure
the health and safety of persons working on or from the installation, and
in checking the effectiveness of such arrangements.

(c) without prejudice to paragraph (b) above, to consult safety representatives on the preparation of a safety case relating to the installation under
the Offshore Installations (Safety Case) Regulations 1992.

24.   Information.—(1) It shall be the duty of the installation owner, the
installation manager and any employer of the *workforce* each to make available to
safety representatives the information relating to *occupational health and safety*
within his knowledge as may be necessary to enable the safety representatives to
fulfil their functions except—

(a) any information the disclosure of which would be against the interests of
national security, or

(b) any information relating specifically to an individual, unless he has
consented to its being disclosed, or

(c) any information relating specifically to an individual, unless he has
consented to its being disclosed, or

(d) any information the disclosure of which would, for reasons other than its
effect on *occupational health and safety*, cause substantial injury to the
undertaking of any of the parties on whom the duty is imposed or, where
the information has been supplied to any of the parties by some other
person, to the undertaking of that other person, or

(e) any information obtained by the employer for the purpose of bringing,
prosecuting or defending any legal proceedings.

25.   Documents etc.—(1) It shall be the duty of the installation owner, *installation manager,* and any employer of members of the *workforce* on the offshore
installation, to make available to safety representatives and safety committees
any documents which safety representatives and safety committees are entitled
to see under regulation 18 or 18A and to provide the facilities to which a safety
representative is entitled under those regulations.

(2) It shall be the duty of the installation owner to ensure that at least one
copy of these Regulations is readily available on the installation for inspection
by the *workforce.*

26.   Time off.—(1) It shall be the duty of the employer of a safety representative to permit him to take such time off from his work on the offshore
installation without loss of pay during his working hours as is necessary—

(a) for the purpose of performing his functions as a safety representative,
and

(b) to undertake training in accordance with regulation 27 below.

(2) Where a safety representative is permitted to take time off in accordance
with paragraph (1) above, his employer shall pay him—

    (a) where the safety representative's remuneration for the work he would ordinarily have been doing during that time does not vary with the amount of work done, as if he had worked at that work for the whole of that time;

    (b) where the safety representative's remuneration for that work varies with the amount of work done, an amount calculated by reference to the average hourly earnings for that work (ascertained in accordance with paragraph (3) below).

    (3) The average hourly earnings referred to in paragraph 2(b) above are the average hourly earnings of the safety representative concerned or, if no fair estimate can be made of those earnings, the average hourly earnings for work of that description of persons in comparable employment with the same employer or, if there are no such persons, a figure of average hourly earnings which is reasonable in the circumstances.

    (4) Any payment to a safety representative by an employer in respect of a period of time off—

    (a) if it is a payment under any contractual obligation, shall go towards discharging the employer's liability in respect of the same period under paragraph (2) above;

    (b) if it is a payment under paragraph (2) above, shall go towards discharging any liability of the employer to pay contractual remuneration in respect of the same period.

27. Training. It shall be the duty of the employer of a safety representative to ensure that he is provided with such training in aspects of the functions of a safety representative as may be reasonable in all the circumstances and the employer shall meet any reasonable costs associated with such training including travel and subsistence costs.

MISCELLANEOUS

28. Offences.—(1) If an installation owner, *installation manager* or employer fails to comply with an obligation imposed upon him by these Regulations he shall be guilty of an offence.

    (2) In proceedings for an offence under this regulation, it shall be a defence for the person charged to prove—

    (a) that he exercised all due diligence to prevent the commission of the offence; and

    (b) that the relevant failure to comply was committed without his consent, connivance or wilful default.

29. Exercise of functions. No requirement imposed or power conferred upon any person by these Regulations shall be construed as requiring or empowering that person to disregard any requirement imposed upon him by or under any enactment.

THE OFFSHORE INSTALLATIONS (EMERGENCY PIPE-LINE VALVE) REGULATIONS 1989

(S.I. 1989 No. 1029)

Whereas the Secretary of State has consulted pursuant to section 7(1) the Mineral Workings (Offshore Installations) Act 1971 (hereinafter referred to as "the 1971 Act") and section 32(1) of the Petroleum and Submarine Pipe-lines Act 1975 (hereinafter referred to as "the 1975 Act") with organisations in the United Kingdom appearing to him to be representative of those persons who will be affected by the following Regulations;

Now, therefore, the Secretary of State, in exercise of his powers under sections 6, 7 and 11 of, and paragraphs 1(1), 3 and 7 of the Schedule to, *the 1971 Act* and section 26 of *the 1975 Act*, and of all other powers enabling him in that behalf, hereby makes the following Regulations:—

1. Citation and commencement. These Regulations may be cited as the Offshore Installations (Emergency Pipe-line Valve) Regulations 1989 and shall come into force on 12 July 1989.

2. Interpretation. In these Regulations—

"associated installation" means, in relation to a riser or valve, the offshore installation served by it;

"controlled waters" means controlled waters within the meaning of section 1(4) of *the 1971 Act*;

"emergency shut-down system" means the system comprising mechanical, electrical, electronic, pneumatic, hydraulic or other arrangements by which the plant and equipment on an offshore installation are automatically shut down in the event of an emergency;

"emergency shut-down valve" means a valve fitted for the purposes of regulation 5 below;

"fixed installation" means an offshore installation which is not a floating installation;

"floating installation" means an offshore installation which is supported by its buoyancy in the water;

"installation manager" means the manager of an *associated installation*;

"manager" includes, where no manager of an *associated installation* is appointed pursuant to section 4 of *the 1971 Act*, any person made responsible by the owner for safety, health and welfare on the installation;

"offshore installation" means any offshore installation for the purposes of *the 1971 Act* which is maintained in *controlled waters* for the carrying on of any activity to which *the 1971 Act* applies other than an offshore installation which is—

(a)   entirely below sea-level at all states of the tide;

(b)   used exclusively for flaring; or

(c)   not normally manned and used exclusively for the loading of substances into vessels or for their reception and storage prior to such loading;

"owner", in relation to a pipe-line in respect of which no person has been designated as its owner in pursuance of section 33(3) of *the 1975 Act,* means the person in whom the pipe-line is vested;

"pipe-line" means a pipe or system of pipes which is connected by means of a riser to an offshore installation and which is used for the purpose of conveying any substance which is flammable or toxic not being a pipe-line with a nominal internal diameter of less than 40 millimetres;

"quick-disconnect fittings" means fittings on a riser serving a *floating installation* which are designed to allow the flexible part of the riser to be disconnected quickly from the installation;

"riser" means that section of a *pipe-line* which connects an *offshore installation* to a section of the *pipe-line* which lies in, or in close proximity to, the sea-bed and extends outwards from the installation.

3.   Application. These Regulations shall apply—

(a)   in respect of *pipe-lines* constructed in pursuance of a works authorisation granted for the purposes of section 20 of *the 1975 Act* after the coming into force of these Regulations, from the construction of the *pipe-line;* and

(b)   in respect of other *pipe-lines,* on and after 31 December 1990.

4.   Prohibition on use of *pipe-lines.* No *pipe-line* shall be used unless it complies with the provisions of regulations 5, 6 and 8 below.

5.   Incorporation of *emergency shut-down valves.*—(1) There shall be incorporated in every *riser,* and thereafter maintained in good working condition, a valve which shall be capable of blocking the flow of substances within the *pipe-line* at the point at which it is incorporated.

(2) The valve shall be held open by an electrical, hydraulic or other signal to the mechanism for actuating the valve on the failure of which signal the valve shall automatically close.

(3) The valve shall also be capable of being closed—

(a)   by a person positioned by it; and

(b)   automatically by the operation of the *associated installation*'s *emergency shut-down system.*

(4) If the *pipe-line* of which the *riser* forms part is designed to allow for the passage of equipment for testing, inspecting or maintaining the *pipe-line,* the valve shall also be designed to allow for such passage.

(5) The valve and its actuating mechanism shall so far as reasonably practicable be protected from damage arising from fire, explosion or impact.

6.   Location of *emergency shut-down valves.*—(1) Every *emergency shut-down valve* shall be located in a position in which it can be safely and fully inspected, maintained and tested.

(2) In the case of a *riser* which serves a *fixed installation*, the *emergency shut-down valve* shall, so far as this is consistent with paragraph (1) above, be located—

(a) if part of the *riser* is located within a water-filled encasement, above the highest possible level of the water in the encasement;

(b) if part of the *riser* is located within an air-filled encasement, in that part; and

(c) in any other case, above the level on the *riser* of the highest wave crest which may reasonably be anticipated.

(3) In the case of a *riser* which serves a *floating installation*, the *emergency shut-down valve* shall, so far as this is consistent with paragraph (1) above, be located—

(a) if part of the *riser* is held under tension from the *associated installation*, as near as practicable to the flexible pipe which links that part with the part of the *riser* which is on the installation; and

(b) in any other case, above both the level on the *riser* of the highest wave crest which may reasonably be anticipated and any *quick-disconnect fittings*.

(4) Subject to paragraphs (1) to (3) above, every *emergency shut-down valve* shall be located so that the distance along the *riser* between the valve and the base of the *riser* is as short as reasonably practicable.

7. Operation and use of *emergency shut-down valves*.—(1) After an *emergency shut-down valve* has operated so as to block the flow of substances within the *pipe-line*—

(a) the *installation manager* shall ensure that the *manager* of every other *offshore installation* to which the *pipe-line* is connected and the person for the time being entitled to operate the *pipe-line* are notified; and

(b) the valve shall not be re-opened so as to permit the flow of such substances unless the reason for the operation of the valve has been established to the satisfaction of the *installation manager* and he has authorised the re-opening of the valve.

(2) Before giving his authority for the purpose of paragraph (1)(b) above, the *installation manager* shall ensure that the *manager* of every other *offshore installation* to which the *pipe-line* in question is connected and the person for the time being entitled to operate the *pipe-line* have been consulted.

(3) An emergency shut-down shall be used only to block the flow of substances through the *pipe-line* into which it is fitted and shall not be used to adjust that flow.

8. Inspection and testing.—(1) There shall be carried out in respect of every *emergency shut-down valve*—

(a) at intervals not exceeding 3 months, an inspection of the valve and of the mechanism for actuating it for the purpose of identifying any external leak, external damage or external corrosion;

(b) at intervals not exceeding 6 months, a testing which shall include the partial closing of the valve, and its re-opening, by a person positioned by it; and

(c) not less than 2 months or more than 4 months after every testing for the purposes of sub-paragraph (b) above, a testing which shall include the full closing and re-opening of the valve by the activation of the *associated installation*'s *emergency shut-down system*.

(2) The period within which the first inspection and testing for the purposes of sub-paragraphs (a) and (b) of paragraph (1) above is to be carried out in respect of an *emergency shut-down valve* shall commence with the date on which these Regulations first apply to the *pipe-line* in question.

(3) A record of each inspection or testing carried out for the purposes of paragraph (1) above shall be made and this shall state in relation to the inspection or testing—

(a) the identity of the *emergency shut-down valve* and the *pipe-line*;

(b) the names of the owner of the *pipe-line*, the owner of the *associated installation* and the *manager* of that installation;

(c) the date on which it was carried out;

(d) the name, qualifications and employer (if any) of every person engaged in carrying it out;

(e) particulars of the procedures and any equipment used to carry it out; and

(f) any damage or defect revealed and the action taken or proposed to be taken to remedy it.

(4) Every record made in accordance with paragraph (3) above shall be preserved together with any document produced in the course of the inspection or testing in question and a copy of the record and documents shall be kept—

(a) for a period of 2 years from the inspection or testing, on the *associated installation*; and

(b) for a period of 5 years from the inspection or testing, at a principal place of business in the United Kingdom of the owner of the *pipe-line* in question.

(5) For the purposes of paragraph (4) above "document" has the same meaning as in Part I of the Civil Evidence Act 1968.

9. Duties of persons.—(1) It shall be the duty of the owner of an *associated installation* and the *installation manager* to afford, or cause to be afforded, to the owner of the *pipe-line* in question and the person for the time being entitled to operate it such facilities and assistance as they may reasonably require for the purpose of securing that regulations 4 to 6, 7(3) and 8 above are complied with.

(2) It shall be the duty of—

(a) the owner of the *pipe-line* to ensure that regulation 4 above is complied with;

(b) the owner of the *pipe-line*, the owner of the *associated installation* and the concession owner to ensure that regulations 5, 6 and 7(3) above are complied with;

(c) the *installation manager* to ensure that regulation 7(1) and (2) above is complied with; and

(d) the owner of the *pipe-line*, the owner of the *associated installation*, the concession owner and the *installation manager* to ensure that regulation 8 above is complied with.

(3) It shall be the duty of every person while on or near an *associated installation—*

(a) not to contravene the provisions of regulation 7(1)(b) above; and

(b) to co-operate with any other person on whom a duty is imposed by these Regulations so far as is necessary to enable that duty to be performed.

10.   Amendment of the Submarine Pipe-lines Safety Regulations 1982.— Regulation 6 of the Submarine Pipe-lines Safety Regulations 1982 shall be amended by the addition at the end of paragraph (2)(a) of the words—

"or, if different, any *emergency shut-down valve* incorporated in the *pipe-line* for the purposes of regulation 5 of the Offshore Installations (Emergency Pipe-line Valve) Regulations 1989.".

11.   Civil liability. The provisions of section 11 of *the 1971 Act* (which makes provision for civil liability for breach of statutory duty) shall apply to the duties imposed on any person by these Regulations.

12.   Offences.—(1) In the event of a contravention of regulation 9 above, the person contravening the regulation shall be guilty of an offence.

(2) In any proceedings for an offence under this regulation it shall be a defence for the person charged to prove:—

(a) that he exercised all due diligence to prevent the commission of the offence; and

(b) that the relevant contravention was committed without his consent, connivance or wilful default.

THE OFFSHORE INSTALLATIONS AND PIPELINE WORKS (FIRST-AID) REGULATIONS 1989

(S.I. 1989 No. 1671)

General note. References to the Secretary of State shall be construed as references to the Health and Safety Executive by virtue of the Offshore Safety (Repeals and Modifications) Regulations 1993, S.I. 1993 No. 1823. The transfer of responsibility from the Department of Energy to the HSE was one of the recommendations of the Cullen Report (Cmd. 1310, 1990) on the Piper Alpha disaster of 6 July 1988.

1. Citation and commencement. These Regulations may be cited as the Offshore Installations and Pipeline Works (First-Aid) Regulations 1989 and, subject to the provisions of regulation 5(2)(b) below, shall come into force on 13 September 1990.

2. Interpretation. In these Regulations, unless the context otherwise requires—

"the 1971 Act" means the Mineral Workings (Offshore Installations) Act 1971,

"the 1974 Act" means the Health and Safety at Work etc. Act 1974;

"the 1989 Order" means the Health and Safety at Work etc. Act 1974 (Application outside Great Britain) Order 1989,

"first-aid" means—

(a) in cases where a person will need help from a medical practitioner or nurse, treatment for the purpose of preserving life and minimising the consequences of injury and illness until the appropriate help is obtained; and

(b) treatment of minor injuries or illnesses which would otherwise receive no treatment or which do not need treatment by a medical practitioner or nurse (in this sub-paragraph "treatment" includes redressing and other follow-up treatment);

"offshore installation" means an offshore installation within the meaning of *the 1971 Act* which is within—

(a) tidal waters and parts of the sea in or adjacent to Great Britain up to the seaward limit of territorial waters;

(b) waters in any area designated under section 1(7) of the Continental Shelf Act 1964;

(c) inland waters within Great Britain;

"person in control" means—

(a) in relation to an *offshore installation*—

(i) the installation manager, or where no such manager has been appointed, the person made responsible by the owner for health and safety on the installation,

2321

      (ii) the owner, and

      (iii) every person who, in relation to the installation, is a concession owner, all as defined in section 12 of *the 1971 Act*;

  (b) in relation to pipeline works, the owner of the pipeline or the proposed owner of the proposed pipeline as both are defined in section 33(3) of the Petroleum and Submarine Pipe-lines Act 1975 or, if no person has been designated as the owner of the pipeline or proposed owner of the proposed pipeline in pursuance of the said section 33(3), the person in whom the pipeline is vested or the person for whom it is to be constructed;

  (c) in relation to any activity in connection with an *offshore installation*—

      (i) the owner of the installation as defined in section 12 of *the 1971 Act*, and

      (ii) the employer of persons engaged in that activity;

"pipeline" means any pipeline or part of a pipeline in relation to which sections 1 to 59 and 80 to 82 of *the 1974 Act* are applied by article 5 of *the 1989 Order* and any pipeline or part of a pipeline which is connected to it or to an *offshore installation* and which is in, under or over inland waters within Great Britain or tidal waters and parts of the sea in or adjacent to Great Britain;

"pipeline works" means any of the works mentioned in sub-paragraphs (a) to (d) of the definition of pipeline works in article 5 of *the 1989 Order* which relate to a pipeline within the meaning of these Regulations;

"sick bay" means a room for the medical treatment and care of sick and injured persons.

3. Application of Regulations. These Regulations apply to or in relation to premises and activities—

  (a) in Great Britain which are or are connected with *offshore installations* or *pipeline works*, and

  (b) outside Great Britain in circumstances in which sections 1 to 59 and 80 to 82 of *the 1974 Act* apply by virtue of articles 4 and 5 of *the 1989 Order*.

4. Extension of meaning of "work" and "at work". For the purposes of these Regulations and of Part I of *the 1974 Act*, the meaning of "work" and "at work" shall be extended, in relation to the provision of *first-aid* and other medical assistance, the provision of advice in connection with health, and the provision of information in connection with all the foregoing, so that all persons employed or self-employed are treated as being at work whether or not they are on duty, if they are on—

  (a) an *offshore installation*;

  (b) a vessel engaged in *pipeline works*; or

  (c) a vessel from which any of the following activities in connection with an *offshore installation* are being carried on, that is to say construction, reconstruction, alteration, repair, maintenance, cleaning, demolition, dismantling and any activity immediately preparatory thereto.

5. Duty of *person in control*.—(1) The *person in control* of an *offshore installation*, *pipeline works* or any of the following activities in connection with an *offshore* *installation* carried on from a vessel, that is to say construction, reconstruction, alteration, repair, maintenance, cleaning, demolition, dismantling and any activity immediately preparatory thereto, shall—

  (a) provide, or ensure that there are provided, such equipment, facilities and medications and such number of suitable persons as are adequate and appropriate in the circumstances for rendering *first-aid* to, and treating in accordance with the directions of a registered medical practitioner (who may or may not be present) persons who are injured or become ill while at work;

  (b) provide, or ensure that there is provided, such number of suitable persons as is adequate and appropriate in the circumstances for giving simple advice in connection with the health of persons at work;

  (c) make, or ensure that there are made, such arrangements as will enable—

    (i) the work of the suitable persons referred to in sub-paragraphs (a) and (b) of this paragraph to be supervised by one or more suitably qualified registered medical practitioners, and

    (ii) the advice or presence, as appropriate, of a suitably qualified registered medical practitioner to be obtained when needed;

  (d) ensure that persons at work are informed of the provisions and arrangements that have been made under sub-paragraphs (a), (b) and (c) of this paragraph, in particular, but without prejudice to the generality of the foregoing, as to the location of equipment, facilities, medications and personnel.

  (2) (a) For the purposes of paragraph (1)(a) and (b) of this regulation, a person shall not be suitable unless he has undergone such training, or further training, and has obtained such qualifications, or further qualifications, as the Secretary of State may approve for the time being in respect of the relevant case or class of case.

  (b) Sub-paragraph (a) of this paragraph shall not apply until 13 September 1992 to a person who has been employed as a medically trained person on an *offshore installation* (including any time spent away from such installation on leave or training courses) throughout the two years immediately preceding the coming into force of these Regulations.

  (c) For the purposes of sub-paragraph (b) of this paragraph a "medically trained person" is a person who—

    (i) is either a registered nurse or the holder of a certificate of competency issued within the previous three years by the St John Ambulance Association of the Order of St John, the St Andrew's Ambulance Association or the British Red Cross Society, and

    (ii) has received some adequate training in the use of mechanical artificial respiration equipment.

  (3) Nothing in this regulation shall require alteration of the siting or construction of a *sick bay* which at the date of the coming into force of these Regulations exists either on an *offshore installation* in respect of which there is a valid Certificate of Fitness issued under the Offshore Installations (Construction and Survey) Regulations 1974, or on a vessel if—

  (a) the *sick bay* is provided with interior surfaces which may easily be kept clean; and

  (b) there is provided—

    (i) in the *sick bay* or in suitable accommodation in its immediate vicinity a bath accessible from three sides,

    (ii) in suitable accommodation in the immediate vicinity of the *sick bay*, a water-closet and a hand wash-basin, and

    (iii) a supply of sufficient hot and cold water for the bath and hand wash-basin and of sufficient cold water for the water-closet.

6. Defence in proceedings for contravening these Regulations. In any proceedings for an offence of contravening these Regulations it shall be a defence for any person to prove that he took all reasonable precautions and exercised all due diligence to avoid the commission of that offence.

7. Power to grant exemptions.—(1) Subject to paragraph (2) of this regulation, the Secretary of State may, by a certificate in writing, exempt any person, class of persons, *offshore installation*, class of *offshore installations*, *pipeline works*, class of *pipeline works*, activity or class of activity from all or any of the requirements of these Regulations, and any such exemption may be granted subject to conditions and to limit of time and may be revoked by a certificate in writing at any time.

    (2) The Secretary of State shall not grant any such exemption unless, having regard to the circumstances of the case, and in particular to—

    (a) the conditions, if any, which he proposes to attach to the exemption; and

    (b) any other requirements imposed by or under any enactment which apply to the case, he is satisfied that the health, safety and welfare of persons at work will not be prejudiced in consequence of it.

8. Amendment of the Health and Safety (First-Aid) Regulations 1981. Regulation 7 of the Health and Safety (First-Aid) Regulations shall be amended as follows—

    (a) for paragraph (c) substitute the following paragraph—
        "where the Merchant Shipping (Medical Stores) Regulations 1986 apply;";

    (b) after paragraph (f) add the following paragraph—
        "where the Offshore Installations and Pipeline Works (First-Aid) Regulations 1989 apply.".

THE OFFSHORE SAFETY ACT 1992

(1992 c. 15)

General note. This Act is part of the legislative response to the Cullen Report (Cmd 1310, 1990) on the Piper Alpha disaster on 6 July 1988. The Act prepares the ground for further Regulations to establish a new objective oriented framework for the offshore oil and gas industry in line with the Health and Safety at Work etc. Act 1974.

ARRANGEMENT OF SECTIONS

An Act to extend the application of Part I of the Health and Safety at Work etc. Act 1974; to increase the penalties for certain offences under that Part; to confer powers for preserving the security of supplies of petroleum products; and for connected purposes.

[6th March 1992]

Be it enacted by the Queen's most Excellent Majesty, by and with the advice and consent of the Lords Spiritual and Temporal, and Commons, in this present Parliament assembled, and by the authority of the same, as follows—

1. Application of Part I of 1974 Act for offshore purposes.—(1) The *general purposes* of *Part I of the Health and Safety at Work etc. Act 1974* ("the 1974 Act") shall include—

(a) securing the safety, health and welfare of persons on *offshore installations* or engaged on pipe-line works;

(b) securing the safety of such installations and preventing accidents on or near them;

(c) securing the proper construction and safe operation of pipe-lines and preventing damage to them; and

(d) securing the safe dismantling, removal and disposal of offshore installations and pipe-lines;

2325

and that Part shall have effect as if the provisions mentioned in subsection (3) below were existing statutory provisions within the meaning of that Part and, in the case of the enactments there mentioned, were specified in the third column of Schedule 1 to that Act.

(2) Without prejudice to the generality of *subsection (1) of section 15* of the 1974 Act (health and safety regulations), regulations under that section may—

(a) repeal or modify any of the provisions mentioned in subsection (3) below; and

(b) make any provision which, but for any such repeal or modification, could be made by regulations or orders made under any enactment there mentioned.

(3) The provisions referred to in subsections (1) and (2) above are—

(a) the *Mineral Workings (Offshore Installations) Act 1971*;

(b) *sections 26, 27 and 32* (safety, inspectors and regulations) of the *Petroleum and Submarine Pipe-lines Act 1975*;

(c) in the *Petroleum Act 1987, section 11(2)(a)* (regulations) so far as relating to safety requirements and *sections 21 to 24* (safety zones); and

(d) the provisions of any regulations or orders made or having effect under any enactment mentioned in the foregoing paragraphs.

(4) In this section—

"offshore installation" means any installation which is an offshore installation within the *meaning of the Mineral Workings (Offshore Installations) Act 1971*, or is to be taken to be an installation for the purposes of *sections 21 to 23 of* the *Petroleum Act 1987*;

"pipe-line" and "pipe-line works" have the same meanings as in *section 26(1) of the Petroleum and Submarine Pipe-lines Act 1975*.

(5) The provisions mentioned in subsection (3) above and the definitions in subsection (4) above shall have effect as if any reference in—

(a) *section 1(4) of the Mineral Workings (Offshore Installations) Act 1971*;

(b) *section 20(2) of the Petroleum and Submarine Pipe-lines Act 1975*; or

(c) *section 16(1) or 21(7) of the Petroleum Act 1987,*

to tidal waters and parts of the sea in or adjacent to the *United Kingdom*, or to the *territorial sea* adjacent to the *United Kingdom*, were a reference to tidal waters and parts of the sea in or adjacent to *Great Britain*, or to the territorial sea adjacent to *Great Britain*.

----

2. Application of Part I for other purposes.—(1) The *general purposes of Part I of the 1974 Act* shall include—

(a) securing the proper construction and safe operation of pipe-lines and preventing damage to them;

(b) securing that, in the event of the accidental escape or ignition of anything in a pipe-line, immediate notice of the event is given to persons who will or may have to discharge duties or take steps in consequence of the happening of the event; and

   (c) protecting the public from *personal injury*, fire, explosions and other dangers arising from the transmission, distribution, supply or use of gas,

and that Part shall have effect as if the provisions mentioned in subsection (3) below were existing statutory provisions within the meaning of that Part and, in the case of the enactments there mentioned, were specified in the third column of Schedule 1 to that Act.

   (2) Without prejudice to the generality of subsection (1) of section 15 of the 1974 Act (health and safety regulations), regulations under that section may—

   (a) repeal or modify any of the provisions mentioned in subsection (3) below; and

   (b) make any provision which, but for any such repeal or modification, could be made by regulations made under any enactment mentioned in paragraph (b) of that subsection.

   (3) The provisions referred to in subsections (1) and (2) above are—

   (a) sections 27 to 32 and 37 (avoidance of damage to pipe-lines and notification of accidents etc.) of the Pipe-lines Act 1962;

   (b) in the Gas Act 1986, section 16 (standards of quality) so far as relating to standards affecting safety and section 47(3) and (4) (provision which may be made by regulations) so far as relating to regulations under section 16 so far as so relating; and

   (c) the provisions of any regulations made or having effect under any enactment mentioned in paragraph (b) above.

   (4) In this section—

   "gas" means any substance which is or (if it were in a gaseous state) would be gas within the meaning of Part I of the Gas Act 1986;

   "pipe-line" has the same meaning as in the Pipe-lines Act 1962.

---

3. Provisions consequential on sections 1 and 2.—(1) In consequence of the provision made or authorised to be made by section 1 above, the following shall cease to have effect, namely—

   (a) section 1(4) of the Continental Shelf Act 1964 (model clauses to include provision for the safety, health and welfare of persons employed on offshore operations);

   (b) section 84(5) of the 1974 Act (inspectors not to institute proceedings for offences under Part I committed outside Great Britain);

   (c) in the Petroleum and Submarine Pipe-lines Act 1975, section 28(2)(b) (notices with respect to unsafe works) and, so far as relating to proceedings for offences created by regulations under section 26 or 27, section 29(2) (institution of proceedings);

   (d) in the Oil and Gas (Enterprise) Act 1982, section 27(3) (prosecutions) so far as relating to prosecutions for offences under the Mineral Workings (Offshore Installations) Act 1971 or section 23 of the Petroleum Act 1987; and

   (e) in the Petroleum (Production) (Seaward Areas) Regulations 1988, clause 26 of the model clauses set out in Schedule 4 and clause 11 of the model clauses set out in Schedule 5.

(2) Also in consequence of that provision—

(a) any incorporation in a licence of a model clause specified in Schedule 1 to this Act shall cease to have effect;

(b) any functions of the Secretary of State under a licence, or under section 2 of the Petroleum (Production) Act 1934, may be exercised without regard to safety considerations; and

(c) nothing done in the exercise of any such functions shall prejudice or affect the operation of the relevant statutory provisions within the meaning of Part I of the 1974 Act or any requirements imposed under those provisions.

(3) In consequence of the provision made by section 2 above, in the Gas Act 1986—

(a) section 18(1) (safety regulations) shall cease to have effect;

(b) section 47(5) (restriction on institution of proceedings) shall cease to have effect so far as relating to proceedings for offences created by regulations made or having effect under section 16 so far as relating to standards affecting safety;

(c) in sub-paragraph (2) of paragraph 6 of Schedule 8 (saving), for the words "the general purpose mentioned in section 18(1) of this Act" there shall be substituted the words "the general purpose of protecting the public from personal injury, fire, explosions and other dangers arising from the transmission or distribution of gas through pipes, or from the use of gas supplied through pipes"; and

(d) after that sub-paragraph there shall be inserted the following sub-paragraph—

"(2A) In sub-paragraph (2) above 'gas' has the same meaning as in Part I of this Act."

(4) In this "licence" means a licence granted under section 2 of the Petroleum (Production) Act 1934, whether before or after the commencement of this section.

---

4. Increased penalties under Part I.—(1) In subsection (6) of section 15 of the 1974 Act (health and safety regulations), after paragraph (d) there shall be inserted the following paragraph—

"(e) in the case of regulations made for any purpose mentioned in section 1(1) of the Offshore Safety Act 1992, may provide that any offence consisting of a contravention of the regulations, or of any requirement or prohibition imposed by or under them, shall be punishable on conviction on indictment by imprisonment for a term not exceeding two years, or a fine, or both.".

(2) After subsection (1) of section 33 of that Act (offences under Part I) there shall be inserted the following subsection—

"(1A) Subject to any provision made by virtue of section 15(6)(d), a person guilty of an offence under subsection (1)(a) above consisting of failing to discharge a duty to which he is subject by virtue of sections 2 to 6 shall be liable—

(a) on summary conviction, to a fine not exceeding £20,000;

(b) on conviction on indictment, to a fine.''.

(3) After subsection (2) of that section there shall be inserted the following subsection—

''(2A) A person guilty of an offence under subsection (1)(g) or (o) above shall be liable—

(a) on summary conviction, to imprisonment for a term not exceeding six months, or a fine not exceeding £20,000, or both;

(b) on conviction on indictment, to imprisonment for a term not exceeding two years, or a fine, or both.''.

(4) In subsection (3) of that section—

(a) after the words ''section 15(6)(d)'' there shall be inserted the words ''or (e)''; and

(b) for the words ''an offence under any paragraph of subsection (1) above not mentioned in the preceding subsection, or of an offence under subsection (1)(e) above not falling within the preceding subsection'' there shall be substituted the words ''an offence under subsection (1) above not falling within subsection (1A), (2) or (2A) above''.

(5) Subsections (4)(d) and (5) of that section shall cease to have effect.

(6) This section does not affect the punishment for any offence committed before the commencement of this section.

———————

5. Directions for preserving security of petroleum and petroleum products.—(1) The *Secretary of State* may, after *consultation* with the *Health and Safety Executive* and with a person to whom this section applies, give to that person such directions of a general character as *appear* to the Secretary of State to be requisite or expedient for the purpose of preserving the security of any *offshore installation, onshore terminal* or *oil refinery.*

(2) If it appears to the Secretary of State to be requisite or expedient to do so for the purpose mentioned in subsection (1) above, he may, after consultation with the Health and Safety Executive and with a person to whom this section applies, give to that person a direction requiring him (according to the circumstances of the case) to do, or not to do, a particular thing specified in this direction.

(3) A person to whom this section applies shall give effect to any direction given to him by the Secretary of State under this section notwithstanding any other duty imposed on him by or under any exactment.

(4) The Secretary of State shall *lay before each House of Parliament* a copy of every direction given under this section unless he is of the opinion that disclosure of the direction is against the *interests of national security* or the commercial interests of any person.

(5) A person shall not disclose, or be required by virtue of any enactment or otherwise to disclose, anything done by virtue of this section if the Secretary of State has notified him that the Secretary of State is of the opinion that disclos-

ure of that thing is against the interest of national security or the commercial interests of some other person.

(6) This section applies to any person who is the operator of an offshore installation, onshore terminal or oil refinery.

(7) In this section—

"offshore installation" has the same meaning as in section 1 above;
"oil refinery" includes an installation for processing petroleum products;
"onshore terminal" means an onshore terminal which receives petroleum directly or indirectly from an offshore installation;
"petroleum" has the same meaning as in the Petroleum (Production) Act 1934;
"petroleum products" has the same meaning as in the Energy Act 1976.

---

6.   Corresponding provisions for Northern Ireland 1974 c. 28. An Order in Council under paragraph 1(1)(b) of Schedule 1 to the Northern Ireland Act 1974 (legislation for Northern Ireland in the interim period) which contains a statement that it is only made for purposes corresponding to the purposes of this Act—

(a) shall not be subject to paragraph 1(4) and (5) of that Schedule; but
(b) shall be subject to annulment in pursuance of a resolution of either House of Parliament.

---

7.   Short title, repeals, commencement and extent.—(1) This Act may be cited as the Offshore Safety Act 1992.

(2) The enactments mentioned in Schedule 2 to this Act are hereby repealed to the extent specified in the third column of that Schedule.

(3) The following provisions of this Act, namely—

(a) section 2(3)(b) and (c);
(b) section 3(1)(a) and (e), (2) and (3)(b); and
(c) subsection (2) above so far as relating to the repeal in the Continental Shelf Act 1964 and the second repeal in the Gas Act 1986,

shall not come into force until such day as the Secretary of State may by order made by statutory instrument appoint, and different days may be appointed for different provisions or for different purposes.

(4) This Act, except section 6 above, does not extend to Northern Ireland.

SCHEDULE 1

Section 3(2)

MODEL CLAUSES REFERRED TO IN SECTION 3(2)

Petroleum (Production) Regulations 1935

The clause entitled "Health and safety of workers and employees" in the model clauses set out in Part I of Schedule 2 to the Petroleum (Production) Regulation 1935.

Petroleum and Submarine Pipe-lines Act 1975

Clause 24 of the model clauses set out in Part II of Schedule 2 to the Petroleum and Submarine Pipe-lines Act 1975 (Schedule 4 to the Petroleum (Production) Regulations 1966 as amended).

Clause 24 of the model clauses set out in Part II of Schedule 3 to that Act (Schedule 3 to those Regulations as amended).

Petroleum (Production) Regulations 1976

Clause 24 of the model clauses set out in Schedule 4 to the Petroleum (Production) Regulations 1976.

Clause 24 of the model clauses set out in Schedule 5 to those Regulations.

Petroleum (Production) Regulations 1982

Clause 24 of the model clauses set out in Schedule 4 to the Petroleum (Production) Regulations 1982.

Clause 23 of the model clauses set out in Schedule 5 to those Regulations.

Clause 11 of the model clauses set out in Schedule 7 to those Regulations.

Petroleum (Production) (Landward Areas) Regulations 1984

Clause 15 of the model clauses set out in Schedule 3 to the Petroleum (Production) (Landward Area) Regulations 1984.

Clause 21 of the model clauses set out in Schedule 4 to those Regulations.

Clause 22 of the model clauses set out in Schedule 5 to those Regulations.

Petroleum (Production) (Seaward Areas) Regulations 1988

Clause 26 of the model clauses set out in Schedule 4 to the Petroleum (Production) (Seaward Areas) Regulations 1988.

Clause 11 of the model clauses set out in Schedule 5 to those Regulations.

SCHEDULE 2

Section 7(2)

REPEALS

Chapter	Short title	Extent of repeal
1964 c. 29.	The Continental Shelf Act 1964.	Section 1(4).
1974 c. 37.	The Health and Safety at Work etc. Act 1974.	In section 33, subsections (4)(d) and (5). Section 84(5).
1975 c. 74.	The Petroleum and Submarine Pipe-lines Act 1975	Section 28(2)(b). Section 29(2), so far as relating to proceedings for offences created by regulations under section 26 or 27 of that Act.
1982 c. 23.	The Oil and Gas (Enterprises) Act 1982.	Section 27(3), so far as relating to prosecutions for offences under the Mineral Workings (Offshore Installations) Act 1971 or section 23 of the Petroleum Act 1987.
1986 c. 44.	The Gas Act 1986.	Section 18(1). Section 47(5), so far as relating to proceedings for offences created by regulations made or having effect under section 16 of that Act so far as relating to standards affecting safety.

THE OFFSHORE SAFETY (PROTECTION AGAINST VICTIMISATION) ACT 1992

General note. This Act was also introduced as part of the legislative response to the recommendations contained in the Cullen Report (Cmd. 1310, 1990) on the Piper Alpha disaster of 6 July 1988. It is intended to protect against victimisation of safety representatives and safety committees for carrying out their functions by extending to them remedies for unfair dismissal and discrimination hitherto unavailable.

An Act to protect employees working on offshore installations against victimisation when acting as safety representatives or members of safety committees.   [16 March 1992]

Be it enacted by the Queen's most Excellent Majesty, by and with the advice and consent of the Lords Spiritual and Temporal, and Commons, in this present Parliament assembled, and by the authority of the same, as follows—

1. Protection against victimisation.—(1) In relation to an offshore employee, the Employment Protection (Consolidation) Act 1978 and the Trade Union and Labour Relations (Consolidation) Act 1992 shall each have effect as if—

    (a) the purposes specified in section 146(1) of the 1992 Act (action short of dismissal on grounds related to union membership or activities) included preventing or deterring him from carrying out any relevant functions, or penalising him for doing so; and

    (b) the reasons specified in section 152(1) of the 1992 Act (dismissal on grounds related to union membership or activities) included the reason that he had carried out, or proposed to carry out, any such functions.

(2) In this section—

    "offshore employee" means an employee (within the meaning of the 1978 Act) who is or was employed on an offshore installation;

    "offshore installation" means any installation which is an offshore installation within the meaning of the Mineral Workings (Offshore Installations) Act 1971, or is to be taken to be an installation for the purposes of sections 21 to 23 of the Petroleum Act 1987;

    "relevant functions", in relation to an offshore employee, means any functions conferred on him, as a safety representative or as a member of a safety committee—

    (a) by the Offshore Installations (Safety Representatives and Safety Committees) Regulations 1989; or

    (b) by any corresponding regulations made under Part I of the Health and Safety at Work etc. Act 1974.

(3) In relation to any time before the commencement of the 1992 Act, subsection (1) above shall have effect as if—

(a) the reference to that Act were omitted; and
(b) the references to sections 146(1) and 152(1) of that Act were references
     to *sections 23(1) and 58(1)* respectively of the 1978 Act.

2.   Short title and extent.—(1) This Act may be cited as the Offshore Safety
(Protection Against Victimisation) Act 1992.

(2) This Act does not extend to Northern Ireland.

THE OFFSHORE INSTALLATIONS (SAFETY CASE) REGULATIONS 1992

(S.I. 1992 No. 2885)

General note. These Regulations put into effect a central recommendation of the Cullen Report (Cmd. 1310, 1990) on the Piper Alpha disaster on 6 July 1988. It is entirely consistent with the thrust of the Framework Directive 89/391 in that a full assessment of the installation is required from a safety point of view ("the safety case").

ARRANGEMENT OF REGULATIONS

The Secretary of State, in exercise of the powers conferred on her by sections 15(1), (2), (3)(a), (4)(a), (5)(b), (6)(b), and 82(3)(a) of, and paragraphs

1(1)(c) and (2), 8(1), 9, 14, 15(1) and 16 of Schedule 3 to, the Health and Safety at Work etc. Act 1974 ("the 1974 Act") and section 1(2) of the Offshore Safety Act 1992 and of all other powers enabling her in that behalf and for the purpose of giving effect without modifications to proposals submitted to her by the Health and Safety Commission under section 11(2)(d) of the 1974 Act after the carrying out by the said Commission of consultations in accordance with section 50(3) of that Act, hereby makes the following Regulations:

1.   Citation and commencement. These Regulations may be cited as the Offshore Installations (Safety Case) Regulations 1992 and shall come into force on 31 May 1993, except regulation 11 which shall come into force on 30 November 1995.

2.   Interpretation.—(1) In these Regulations, unless the context otherwise requires—

"the 1971 Act" means the Mineral Workings (Offshore Installations) Act 1971;
"the 1989 Order" means the Health and Safety at Work etc. Act 1974 (Application Outside Great Britain) Order 1989;
"approves" means approves in writing;
"the Executive" means the Health and Safety Executive;
"combined operation" means an activity referred to in paragraph (7);
"concession owner" in relation to a fixed installation means a concession owner within the meaning of section 12(2) of the 1971 Act as if "or is to be" appeared after "there is" in the subsection;
"construction activity" in relation to an installation means—

(a)   the construction of the installation at the place where it is to be operated;
(b)   the dismantling or demolition of the installation at the place where it was operated; or
(c)   any activity on or in connection with the installation which involves the use of a heavy lift vessel;

"decommissioning" in relation to an installation means taking the installation or any plant thereon out of use with a view to the abandonment of the installation, and "decommissioned' ' shall be construed accordingly;
"diving bell" means a diving bell within the meaning of regulation 2 of the Diving Operations at Work Regulations 1981;
"fixed installation" means an installation other than a mobile installation;
"heavy lift vessel" means a vessel whose primary function is to—

(a)   lift an installation or part thereof, or
(b)   lift plant onto or off an installation;

"installation" means an offshore installation within the meaning of section 1 of the 1971 Act as if in the definition of "controlled waters" in section 1(4) of that Act the reference to the United Kingdom were a reference to Great Britain;
"major accident" means—

(a) a fire, explosion or the release of a dangerous substance involving death or serious personal injury to persons on the installation or engaged in an activity on or in connection with it;

(b) any event involving major damage to the structure of the installation or plant affixed thereto or any loss in the stability of the installation;

(c) the collision of a helicopter with the installation;

(d) the failure of life support systems for diving operations in connection with the installation, the detachment of a diving bell used for such operations or the trapping of a diver in a diving bell or other sub-sea chamber used for such operations; or

(e) any other event arising from a work activity involving death or serious personal injury to five or more persons on the installation or engaged in an activity in connection with it;

"mobile installation" means an installation (other than a floating production platform) which can be moved from place to place without major dismantling or modification, whether or not is has its own motive power;

"notified" means notified in writing, and related expressions shall be construed accordingly;

"operator" in relation to—

(a) a fixed installation means the person appointed by a concession owner to execute any function of organising or supervising any operation to be carried out by such installation or, where no such person has been appointed, the concession owner;

(b) a mobile installation means the person for whom the owner has agreed to carry out the operation concerned or, where there is no such agreement, the owner;

"owner" in relation to—

(a) a mobile installation means the person who has registered the installation pursuant to regulations under section 2 of the 1971 Act or, if there is no such person, the person for the time being having the management of the installation, or of its main structure;

(b) a pipe-line means an owner within the meaning of section 33(3) of the Petroleum and Submarine Pipe-Lines Act 1975;

"pipe-line" has the same meaning as in section 26(1) of the Petroleum and Submarine Pipe-Lines Act 1975;

"quantitative risk assessment" means the identification of hazards and the evaluation of the extent of risk arising therefrom incorporating calculations based upon the frequency and magnitude of hazardous events;

"relevant statutory provisions" means those relevant statutory provisions which apply to or in relation to installations or activities on or in connection with them;

"relevant waters" means—

(a) tidal waters and parts of the sea in or adjacent to Great Britain up to the seaward limits of territorial waters, and

(b) any area designed by order under section 1(7) of the Continental Shelf Act 1964;

"safety case" shall be construed in accordance with paragraph (2);

"stand-by vessel" has the same meaning as in regulation 10 of the Offshore Installations (Emergency Procedures) Regulations 1976;

(2) Any reference in these Regulations to a safety case is, subject to regulation 8(3), a reference to a document containing the particulars specified in regulation 8 and the Schedule referred to in the provision pursuant to which the safety case is prepared; and a safety case may contain such particulars by reference to the same particulars in an earlier safety case relating to the same installation and sent to the Executive pursuant to these Regulations.

(3) Any provision of these Regulations requiring particulars to be included in a safety case which are also required to be included by virtue of a more general provision of the Regulations is without prejudice to the generality of the more general provision.

(4) Any reference in these Regulations to the Executive accepting a safety case or revision is a reference to the Executive notifying the person who sent the safety case or revision to the Executive that it is satisfied with the case for health and safety made out in the safety case or in the revision, as appropriate.

(5) Any reference in these Regulations to operating an installation is a reference to carrying out from, by means of or on the installation an activity mentioned in section 1(2) of the 1971 Act.

(6) Any reference in these Regulations to the commencement of drilling a well includes a reference to the recommencement of drilling after the well has been completed, suspended, or abandoned by plugging at the sea-bed.

(7) For the purposes of these Regulations two or more installations shall be treated as engaged in a combined operation with each other if an activity carried out from, by means of or on one of the installations—

(a) is carried out temporarily for a purpose related to the other installation or installations; and
(b) could affect the health or safety of persons on any of the installations or of persons engaged in an activity in connection with any of the installations.

(8) Any reference in these Regulations to an activity in connection with an installation is a reference to any activity in connection with an offshore installation specified in article 4(1)(b) of the 1989 Order.

(9) Where an operator or owner of an installation is succeeded by a new operator or owner, anything done in compliance with these Regulations by the operator or owner in relation to the installation shall, for the purposes of these Regulations, be treated as having been done by his successor.

(10) Unless the context otherwise requires, any reference in these Regulations to—

(a) a numbered regulation or Schedule is a reference to the regulation or Schedule in these Regulations so numbered;
(b) a numbered paragraph is a reference to the paragraph so numbered in the regulation or Schedule in which the reference appears.

3. Application. These Regulations shall apply—

(a) in Great Britain, and
(b) to and in relation to installations and activities outside Great Britain to which sections 1 to 59 and 80 to 82 of the Health and Safety at Work etc. Act 1974 apply by virtue of article 4(1) and (2)(b) of the 1989 Order.

4. Safety cases for fixed installations.—(1) The operator of a fixed installation which is to be established shall—

    (a) prepare a safety case containing the particulars specified in regulation 8
        and Schedule 1; and

    (b) send the safety case to the Executive,

at such time before completion of the design of the installation as will enable
him to take account in the design of any matters relating to health and safety
raised by the Executive within 3 months of that time.

    (2) The operator of a fixed installation shall ensure that it is not operated
unless—

    (a) he has prepared a safety case containing the particulars specified in
        regulation 8 and Schedule 2;

    (b) he has sent the safety case to the Executive at least 6 months before
        commencing the operation; and

    (c) the Executive has accepted the safety case.

    (3) For the purposes of paragraph (2) the operation of an installation shall
be treated as commenced—

    (a) on the commencement of the first well drilling operation from the
        installation which may involve the release of hydrocarbons from
        beneath the sea-bed; or

    (b) when hydrocarbons are brought onto the installation for the frist time
        through a pipe-line or well,

whichever is earlier.

    (4) A safety case prepared pursuant to paragraph (2) may be prepared in
relation to more than one fixed installation where the Executive so approves,
and where a safety case is to be so prepared in relation to installations with
different operators is shall be sufficient compliance with paragraph (2)(a) and
(b) if the operators prepare and agree the safety case containing the particulars
referred to in that paragraph and one of them sends it to the Executive in
accordance with paragraph (2)(b).

5. Safety case for mobile installations. The owner of a mobile installation
shall ensure that the installation is not moved in relevant waters with a view to its
being operated there unless—

    (a) he has prepared a safety case containing the particulars specified in
        regulation 8 and Schedule 3;

    (b) he has sent the safety case to the Executive at least 3 months before the
        movement of the installation in those waters with a view to its being
        operated there; and

    (c) the Executive has accepted the safety case.

6. Safety case for combined operations.—(1) In preparing a safety case for
an installation pursuance to regulation 4(2) or 5 or a revision thereof pursuant
to regulation 9 account need not be taken of the fact that the installation is or is
to be engaged in a combined operation with another installation.

    (2) The operator of a fixed installation shall ensure that the installation is
not engaged in a combined operation with a mobile installation, and the owner

of a mobile installation shall ensure that the installation is not engaged in a combined operation with a fixed or mobile installation unless—

    (a) the operators of the installations so engaged and the owner of every mobile installation so engaged have prepared and (unless they are the same person) agreed a safety case containing the particulars specified in Schedule 4;

    (b) the safety case has been sent by an operator to the Executive—

        (i) in a case where a mobile installation is to carry out an operation on a well connected to a fixed installation (other than a well which is beneath or immediately adjacent to the installation), at least 4 weeks,

       (ii) in any other case 6 weeks,

       before the combined operation is commenced, and

    (c) the Executive has accepted the safety case.

7. Safety case for abandonment of fixed installations. The operator of a fixed installation shall ensure that the installation is not decommissioned unless—

    (a) he has prepared a safety case containing the particulars specified in regulation 8 and Schedule 5;

    (b) he has sent the safety case to the Executive at least 6 months before the commencement of the decommissioning; and

    (c) the Executive has accepted the safety case.

8. Management of health and safety and control of major accident hazards.—
(1) An operator or owner who prepares a safety case pursuant to these Regulations (in this regulation referred to as "the duty holder") shall, subject to paragraphs (2) and (3), include in the safety case sufficient particulars to demonstrate that—

    (a) his management system is adequate to ensure that the relevant statutory provisions will (in respect of matters within his control) be complied with in relation to the installation and any activity on or in connection with it;

    (b) he has established adequate arrangements for audit and for the making of reports thereof;

    (c) all hazards with the potential to cause a major accident have been identified; and

    (d) risks have been evaluated and measures have been, or will be, taken to reduce the risks to persons affected by those hazards to the lowest level that is reasonably practicable.

(2) Paragraph (1) shall only require the particulars in the safety case to demonstrate the matters referred to in that paragraph to the extent that it is reasonable to expect the duty holder to address them at the time of sending the safety case of the Executive.

(3) Without prejudice to paragraphs 2 and 3 of Schedule 4, this regulation shall not apply to a safety case prepared pursuant to regulation 6(2).

(4) In this regulation—

(a) "audit" means systematic assessment of the adequacy of the management system or achieve the purpose referred to in paragraph (1)(a) carried out by persons who are sufficiently independent of the system (but who may be employed by the duty holder) to ensure that such assessment is objective;

(b) "management system" means the organisation and arrangements established by the duty holder for managing his undertaking.

9. Revision of safety cases.—(1) An operator or owner who has prepared a safety case pursuant to these Regulations shall revise its contents as often as may be appropriate; but nothing in this paragraph shall require the revision to be sent to the Executive.

(2) Where a revision to be made under paragraph (1) (other than a revision to a safety case prepared pursuant to regulation 4(1)) will render the safety case materially different from the last version sent to the Executive pursuant to these Regulations, the revision shall not be made unless—

(a) the safety case incorporating the proposed revision has been sent to the Executive at least 3 months before the revision is to be made; and

(b) the Executive has accepted the revision,

and for the purposes of this paragraph in determining whether a revision will render the safety case materially different from the version referred to above, regard shall be had to the cumulative effect of that revision and any previous revisions made under paragraph (1) but not subject to this paragraph.

(3) Where the revision—

(a) relates to the drilling of a well or the carrying out of any other operation on a well the period referred to in paragraph (2)(a) shall be 21 days,

(b) is of a safety case prepared pursuant to regulation 6(2) and does not relate to the matters referred to in sub-paragraph (a), the period referred to in paragraph (2)(a) shall be 6 weeks,

instead of 3 months.

(4) Where an operator or owner has prepared a safety case in respect of an installation in accordance with regulation 4(2) or 5 or made a revision thereof in accordance with this paragraph, no person shall operate the installation beyond a period of 3 years from the date on which the last safety case or revision was accepted by the Executive unless during that period—

(a) the operator or owner who prepared the safety case or revision has revised the safety case and sent the revision to the Executive at least 3 months before that period has expired; and

(b) the Executive has accepted the revision.

10. Duty to conform with safety case.—(1) Where—

(a) an operator or owner has prepared a safety case pursuant to these Regulations (except regulation 4(1)) or made a revision thereof pursuant to regulation 9,

(b) the safety case or revision describes any health or safety procedures or arrangements to be followed, and

    (c) the Executive has accepted the safety case under the regulation concerned or in the case of a revision subject to regulation 9(2) or (4) has accepted it under that regulation,

he shall ensure that those procedures and arrangements are followed.

    (2) In criminal proceedings for a contravention of paragraph (1) it shall be a defence for the accused to prove that—

    (a) in the particular circumstances of the case it was not in the best interests of the health and safety of persons to follow the procedures or arrangements concerned and there was insufficient time to revise the safety case pursuant to regulation 9, or

    (b) the commission of the offence was due to the contravention by another person of regulation 14 and the accused had taken all reasonable precautions and exercised all due diligence to ensure that the procedures or arrangements were followed.

11.   Notification of well operations.—(1) The operator of a fixed installation shall ensure that the drilling of a well from the installation is not commenced unless at least 21 days before its commencement he has sent to the Executive a notification containing the particulars specified in Schedule 6.

    (2) The operator of a mobile installation shall ensure that the carrying out of any operation in relation to a well or proposed well from the installation (including the drilling of a well) is not commenced unless at least 21 days before its commencement he has sent to the Executive a notification containing the particulars specified in Schedule 6.

    (3) Paragraphs (1) and (2) shall not apply where the drilling or operation is commenced before 21 December 1995.

    (4) Where there is a material change in any of the particulars notified pursuant to paragraph (1) or (2), the operator of the installation concerned shall notify the Executive of that change as soon as is practicable thereafter.

12.   Notification of construction activities.—(1) The operator of an installation shall ensure that the carrying out of any construction activity is not commenced unless at least 28 days before its commencement he has sent to the Executive a notification containing the particulars specified in Schedule 7.

    (2) Paragraph (1) shall not apply where the construction activity is commenced before 28 June 1993.

13.   Transitional provisions.—(1) Where a relevant activity is taking place on 31 May 1993 or it takes place within 6 months after that date, it shall be sufficient compliance with regulation 4(2), 5, 6 or 7 if—

    (a) the safety case referred to in that regulation is sent to the Executive within 6 months after that date, and

    (b) the Executive accepts the safety case within 30 months after that date ("the transitional period").

    (2) The absence of acceptance by the Executive of a safety case prepared pursuant to regulation 4(2), 5, 6 or 7 shall not prevent the carrying on of a relevant activity during the transitional period.

(3) Regulation 6(2) shall not apply if the engagement of the installation in the combined operation ceases and is not re-commenced during the transitional period.

(4) Where, on 31 May 1993, a mobile installation is being operated in relevant waters or is being maintained on a station in relevant waters with a view to its being operated there, the installation shall, for the purposes of regulation 5, be treated as being moved on that date in relevant waters with a view to its being operated there; and the preceding provisions of this regulation shall apply accordingly.

(5) In this regulation "relevant activity" in relation to any provision means the activity prohibited by that provision.

14.   Co-operation.—(1) Every person to whom this regulation applies shall co-operate with the operator and owner of an installation (in this regulation referred to as the first-mentioned installation) and with the operator and owner of an installation engaged in a combined operation with it, so far as is necessary to enable them to comply with the provisions of these Regulations.

(2) This regulation applies to—

(a)   the operator of the first-mentioned installation insofar as paragraph (1) requires him to co-operate with the owner of that installation and with the operator and owner of an installation engaged in a combined operation with it;

(b)   the owner of the first-mentioned installation insofar as paragraph (1) requires him to co-operate with the operator of that installation and with the operator and owner of an installation engaged in a combined operation with it;

(c)   any other employer of persons and a self-employed person carrying out an activity on the first-mentioned installation or in connection with it;

(d)   the operator and owner of an installation connected by a pipe-line to the first-mentioned installation;

(e)   the person in control of a stand-by vessel for the first-mentioned installation;

(f)   the persons in control of a heavy lift vessel used in relation to the first-mentioned installation; and

(g)   the owner of a pipe-line connected to the first-mentioned installation.

15.   Keeping of documents.—(1) An operator or owner who prepares a safety case pursuant to these Regulations shall—

(a)   ensure that when the safety case is sent to the Executive it is notified of an address in Great Britain for the purposes of sub-paragraph (b), (c) and (g) below;

(b)   keep a copy of the safety case and any revision thereof at the address referred to in sub-paragraph (a) above and on the installation to which the safety case relates;

(c)   keep a copy of each audit report at that address;

(d)   ensure that in respect of each audit report a written statement is made recording—

(i)   the main findings of the report;

    (ii) the recommendations in the report;
    (iii) the action proposed to implement those recommendations includ-
        ing the timescales involved;
  (e) keep a copy of that statement on the installation to which it relates;
  (f) ensure that a record is made of any action taken in consequence of an
     audit report; and
  (g) keep a copy of that record at the address referred to in sub-paragraph
     (a) above and on the installation to which it relates.

(2) The copy of the audit report, record and written statement referred to in paragraph (1) shall be kept for a period of 3 years after it has been made, and the copy of the safety case and revision referred to in that paragraph shall be kept for so long as it is current.

(3) It shall be sufficient compliance with paragraph (1)(b), (c), (e) and (g) for the information in the documents referred to in those sub-paragraphs to be kept at the place referred to therein on film or by electronic means provided that the information is capable of being reproduced as a written copy at that place and it is secure from loss or unauthorised intereference.

(4) In this regulation "audit report" means a report made pursuant to the arrangements referred to in regulation 8(1)(b).

16. Amendments of the Offshore Installations (Safety Representatives and Safety Committees) Regulations 1989. The provisions of Schedule 8 shall have effect.

17. Exemptions.—(1) Subject to paragraph (2), the Executive may, by a certificate in writing, exempt any person, installation or class of persons or installations from any requirement or prohibition imposed by these Regu-lations and any such exemption may be granted subject to conditions and with or without limit of time and may be revoked by a certificate in writing at any time.

(2) Without prejudice to the generality of paragraph (1), where any require-ment or prohibition in these Regulations makes reference to—

  (a) either a time or period for sending a safety case or notification to the
     Executive, the Executive may, subject to paragraph (3) and in the
     particular case, specify a later time or shorten the period,
  (b) a period beyond which something shall not be done, the Executive may,
     subject to paragraph (3) and in the particular case, lengthen the period,

and the exercise of such a power shall have effect as an exemption granted by the Executive subject to the condition that the requirement or prohibition is observed with the later time or shorter or longer period substituted for that referred to in it.

(3) The Executive shall not grant any such exemption unless, having regard to the circumstances of the case, and in particular to—

  (a) the conditions, if any, which it proposes to attach to the exemption; and
  (b) any other requirements imposed by or under any enactment which
     apply to the case,

it is satisfied that the health and safety of persons who are likely to be affected by the exemption will not be prejudiced in consequence of it.

SCHEDULE 1

Regulation 4(1)

PARTICULARS TO BE INCLUDED IN A SAFETY CASE FOR THE DESIGN OF A FIXED INSTALLATION

1. The name and address of the operator of the installation.
2. A general description of the means by which the management system of the operator, referred to in regulation 8, will ensure that the structure and plant of the installation will be designed, selected, constructed and commissioned in a way which will reduce risks to health and safety to the lowest level that is reasonably practicable.
3. A description, with scale diagrams, of—
   (a) the main and secondary structure of the installation;
   (b) its plant;
   (c) the layout and configuration of its plant;
   (d) the connections to be made to any pipe-line or installation; and
   (e) any wells to be connected to the installation.
4. A scale plan of the intended location of the installation and of anything to be connected to it, and particulars of—
   (a) the meteorological and oceanographic conditions to which the installation may foreseeably be subjected; and
   (b) the properties of the sea-bed and subsoil at its location.
5. Particulars of the types of operation, and activities in connection with an operation, which the installation is to be capable of performing.
6. The maximum number of persons—
   (a) expected to be on the installation at any time; and
   (b) for whom accommodation is to be provided.
7. Particulars of the plant and arrangements for the control of operations on a well, including those—
   (a) to control the pressure in a well;
   (b) to prevent the uncontrolled release of hazardous substances; and
   (c) to minimise the effects of damage to sub-sea equipment by drilling equipment.
8. A description of any pipe-line with the potential to cause a major accident, including—
   (a) the fluid which it conveys;
   (b) its dimensions and layout;
   (c) its contained volume at declared maximum allowable operating pressure; and
   (d) any apparatus and works intended to secure safety.
9. Particulars of plant and arrangements for—
   (a) the detection of the presence of toxic or flammable gas; and
   (b) the detection, prevention or mitigation of fires.
10. A description of the arrangements to be made for protecting persons on the installation from hazards of explosion, fire, heat, smoke, toxic gas or fumes during any period while they may need to remain on the installation following an incident which is beyond immediate control and for enabling such persons to be evacuated from the installation where necessary, including the provision for—
    (a) temporary refuge;
    (b) routes from locations where persons may be present to temporary refuge and for egress therefrom to points from where the installation may be evacuated;
    (c) means of evacuation at those points; and
    (d) facilities within temporary refuge for the monitoring and control of the incident and for organising evacuation.
11. A statement of performance standards which have been established in relation to the arrangements referred to in paragraph 10 (including performance standards

which have been established for structures and plant provided pursuant to such arrangements), and a statement of the minimum period for which the arrangements as a whole are intended to be effective following an incident referred to in that paragraph.

12.   A demonstration, by reference to the results of suitable and sufficient quantitative risk assessment, that the measures taken or to be taken in relation to the hazards referred to in paragraph 10, including the arrangements mentioned in that paragraph, will reduce risks to the health and safety of persons to the lowest level that is reasonably practicable.

13.   Particulars of the intended methods of design and construction, and of the principal codes of practices to be observed in relation to them.

14.   A description of—

(a)   the principal features of the design of the installation, and the arrangements and procedures for its completion; and

(b)   the arrangements and procedures for the construction and commissioning of the installation,

which are intended to ensure that risks from a major accident will be at the lowest level that is reasonably practicable.

SCHEDULE 2

Regulation 4(2)

PARTICULARS TO BE INCLUDED IN A SAFETY CASE FOR THE OPERATION OF A FIXED INSTALLATION

1.   The name and address of the operator of the installation.

2.   A description, with scale diagrams, of

(a)   the main and secondary structure of the installation and its materials;

(b)   its plant;

(c)   the layout and configuration of its plant;

(d)   the connections to be made to any pipe-line or installation; and

(e)   any wells to be connected to the installation.

3.   A scale plan of the location of the installation and of anything connected to it, and particulars of—

(a)   the meterological and oceanographic conditions to which the installation may foreseeably be subjected; and

(b)   the properties of the sea-bed and subsoil at its location.

4.   Particulars of the types of operation, and activities in connection with an operation, which the installation is capable of performing.

5.   The maximum number of persons—

(a)   expected to be on the installation at any time; and

(b)   for whom accommodation is to be provided.

6.   Particulars of the plant and arrangements for the control of operations on a well, including those—

(a)   to control the pressure in a well;

(b)   to prevent the uncontrolled release of hazardous substances; and

(c)   to minimise the effects of damage to sub-sea equipment by drilling equipment.

7.   A description of any pipe-line with the potential to cause a major accident, including—

(a)   the fluid which it conveys;

(b)   its dimensions and layout;

(c)   its contained volume at declared maximum allowable operating pressure; and

(d)   any apparatus and works intended to secure safety.

8.   Particulars of plant and arrangements for—

(a)   the detection of the presence of toxic or flammable gas; and

(b)   the detection, prevention or mitigation of fires.

9.   A description of the arrangements made or to be made for protecting persons on the installation from hazards of explosion, fire, heat, smoke, toxic gas or fumes during

any period while they may need to remain on the installation following an incident which is beyond immediate control and for enabling such persons to be evacuated from the installation where necessary, including the provision for—

    (a) temporary refuge;

    (b) routes from locations where persons may be present to temporary refuge and for egress therefrom to points from where the installation may be evacuated;

    (c) means of evacuation at those points;

    (d) facilities within temporary refuge for the monitoring and control of the incident and for organising evacuation.

10.   A statement of performance standards which have been established in relation to the arrangements referred to in paragraph 9 (including performance standards which have been established for structures and plant provided pursuant to such arrangements), and a statement of the minimum period for which the arrangements as a whole are intended to be effective following an incident referred to in that paragraph.

11.   A demonstration, by reference to the results of suitable and sufficient quantitative risk assessment, that the measures taken or to be taken in relation to the hazards referred to in paragraph 9, including the arrangements mentioned in that paragraph, will reduce risks to the health and safety of persons to the lowest level that is reasonably practicable.

12.   Particulars of the main requirements in the specification for the design of the installation and its plant, including any limits for safe operation or use specified therein.

13.   Sufficient particulars to demonstrate that the design of the installation, its plant and the pipe-lines connected to it is such that the risks from a major accident are at the lowest level that is reasonably practicable.

14.   Particulars concerning any remedial work to be carried out to the installation or the plant referred to in the preceding paragraphs, and the time by which it will be done.

SCHEDULE 3

Regulation 5

PARTICULARS TO BE INCLUDED IN A SAFETY CASE FOR A MOBILE INSTALLATION

1.   The name of the owner of the installation.

2.   A description, with scale diagrams, of:

    (a) the main and secondary structure of the installation and its materials;

    (b) its plant; and

    (c) the layout and configuaration of its plant.

3.   Particulars of the types of operation, and activities in connection with an operation, which the installation is capable of performing.

4.   The maximum number of persons—

    (a) expected to be on the installation at any time; and

    (b) for whom accommodation is to be provided.

5.   Particulars of the plant and arrangements for the control of operations on a well, including those—

    (a) to control the pressure in a well;

    (b) to prevent the uncontrolled release of hazardous substances; and

    (c) to minimise the effects of damage to sub-sea equipment by drilling equipment.

6.   Particulars of plant and arrangements for—

    (a) the detection of the presence of toxic or flammable gas; and

    (b) the detection, prevention or mitigation of fires.

7.   A description of the arrangements made or to be made for protecting persons on the installation from hazards of explosion, fire, heat, smoke, toxic gas or fumes during any period while they may need to remain on the installation following an incident which is beyond immediate control and for enabling such persons to be evacuated from the installation where necessary, including the provision for—

(a) temporary refuge;
(b) routes from locations where persons may be present to temporary refuge and for egress therefrom to points from where the installation may be evacuated;
(c) means of evacuation at those points;
(d) facilities within temporary refuge for the monitoring and control of the incident and for organising evacuation.

8.   A statement of performance standards which have been established in relation to the arrangements referred to in paragraph 7 (including performance standards which have been established for structures and plant provided pursuant to such arrangements), and a statement of the minimum period for which the arrangements as a whole are intended to be effective following an incident referred to in that paragraph.

9.   A demonstration, by reference to the results of suitable and sufficient quantitative risk assessment, that the measures taken or to be taken in relation to the hazards referred to in paragraph 7, including the arrangements mentioned in that paragraph, will reduce risks to the health and safety of persons to the lowest level that is reasonably practicable.

10.   Particulars of the main requirements in the specification for the design of the installation and its plant, including any limits for safe operation and use specified therein.

11.   Particulars of—
(a) the limits of the environmental conditions beyond which the installation cannot safely be stationed or operated;
(b) the properties of the sea bed and subsoil which are necessary for the safe stationing and operation of the installation; and
(c) the locations in which the installation may be stationed and operated safely.

12.   Sufficient particulars to demonstrate that the design of the installation and its plant is such that the risks from a major accident are at the lowest level there is reasonably practicable.

13.   Particulars concerning any remedial work to be carried out to the installation or the plant referred to in the preceding paragraphs, and the time by which it will be done.

SCHEDULE 4

Regulation 6(2)

PARTICULARS TO BE INCLUDED IN A SAFETY CASE FOR COMBINED OPERATIONS

1.   The names and addresses of the operators and owners preparing the safety case.

2.   Particulars which, were it not for regulation 6(1), would be contained in the safety cases prepared for the installations pursuant to regulation 4(2) or 5 or in a revision thereof pursuant to regulation 9.

3.   Sufficient particulars to demonstrate that the management systems referred to in those safety cases pursuant to regulation 8 will be co-ordinated so as to reduce the risks from a major accident to the lowest level that is reasonable practicable.

4.   Particulars of any plant installed solely for the purpose of permitting the installations to engage in the combined operation.

5.   A demonstration that any limits for the safe operation or use of plant which are contained in the specifications for the design of the installations or their plant will not be exceeded while the installations are engaged in the combined operation.

6.   A programme of work for the combined operation.

7.   The date when the installations will cease to be engaged in the combined operation.

SCHEDULE 5

Regulation 7

PARTICULARS TO BE INCLUDED IN A SAFETY CASE FOR THE ABANDONMENT OF A FIXED INSTALLATION

1.   The name and address of the operator of the installation.
2.   A description, with scale diagrams, of—
(a)   the main and secondary structure of the installation and its materials;
(b)   its plant;
(c)   the layout and configuration of its plant;
(d)   the connections made to any pipe-line or installation; and
(e)   any wells connected to the installation.
3.   A scale plan of the location of the installation and of anything connected to it, and particulars of—
(a)   the meteorological and oceanographic conditions to which the installation may foreseeably be subjected; and
(b)   the properties of the sea-bed and subsoil at its location.
4.   Particulars of the operations which were being carried out, including activities on and in connection with the installation relating to each operation.
5.   The maximum number of persons at work on the installation during decommissioning.
6.   Particulars of the plant and arrangements for the control of the operations on a well, including those—
(a)   to control the pressure in a well;
(b)   to prevent the uncontrolled release of hazardous substances; and
(c)   to minimise the effects of damage to sub-sea equipment by drilling equipment.
7.   A description of any pipe-line with the potential to cause a major accident, including—
(a)   the fluid which it conveys;
(b)   its dimensions and layout;
(c)   its contained volume at declared maximum allowable operating pressure; and
(d)   any apparatus and works intended to secure safety.
8.   Particulars of plant and arrangements for—
(a)   the detection of the presence of toxic or flammable gas;
(b)   the detection, prevention or mitigation of fires; and
(c)   the protection of persons from their consequences.
9.   Particulars of escape routes, embarkation points and means of evacuation to enable the full and safe evacuation and rescue of persons to take place in an emergency.
10.   Sufficient particulars to demonstrate that the proposed arrangements, methods and procedures for—
(a)   dealing, by way of abandonment or otherwise, with any wells to which the installation is connected;
(b)   decommissioning the installation and connected pipe-lines; and
(c)   demolishing or dismantling the installation and connected pipe-lines,
take adequate account of the design and method of construction of the installation and its plant, and reduce risks from a major accident to the lowest level that is reasonably practicable.

SCHEDULE 6

Regulation 11

PARTICULARS TO BE INCLUDED IN NOTIFICATION OF WELL OPERATIONS

1.   The name and address of the operator of the installation.
2.   Particulars of the fluids to be used to control the pressure of the well.

3.   Particulars of any plant, not described in the current safety case for the installation, which is to be used in connection with the operations on the well.

4.   Particulars to the type of well, its number, and slot number, and the name of any field development of which it may be part.

5.   Particulars, with scale diagrams, of—
(a) the location of the top of the well;
(b) the directional path of the well-bore;
(c) its terminal depth and location; and
(d) its position, and that of nearby wells, relative to each other.

6.   A description of the operations on the well or, in the case of a fixed installation, of the operations involved in the drilling of the well, and a programme of works which includes—
(a) the dates on which the operations are expected to commence and finish; and
(b) the intended operational state of the well at the end of the operations.

7.   A description of—
(a) any activities on or in connection with the installation, during operations on the well described pursuant to paragraph 6, which will involve any hazards with the potential to cause a major accident;
(b) such hazards.

8.   In the case of a well which is to be drilled—
(a) particulars of the geological strata and formations, and of fluids within them, through which it will pass, and of any hazards with the potential to cause a major accident which they may contain;
(b) the procedures for effectively monitoring the direction of the well-bore, and for minimising the likelihood and effects of intersecting nearby wells; and
(c) a description of the design of the well, including the limits on its safe operation and use.

9.   In the case of an existing well—
(a) a diagram of the well;
(b) a summary of earlier operation in relation to it;
(c) the purposes for which it has been used;
(d) its current operational state;
(e) its state of repair;
(f) the physical conditions within it; and
(g) its production capacity.

10.   Where operations in relation to a well are to be carried out from a mobile installation, particulars of—
(a) the meteorological and oceanographic conditions to which the installation may foreseeably be subjected;
(b) the depth of water; and
(c) the properties of the sea-bed and subsoil,
at the location at which the operations will be carried out.

11.   Where operations in relation to a well are to be carried out from a mobile installation, sufficient particulars to demonstrate that the arrangements and procedures of the operator and owner of the installation for managing the operations are co-ordinated to reduce risks from a major accident to the lowest level that is reasonably practicable.

SCHEDULE 7

Regulation 12

PARTICULARS TO BE INCLUDED IN NOTIFICATION OF CONSTRUCTION ACTIVITIES

1.   The name and address of the operator of the installation.
2.   The location at which the construction activity is to take place.
3.   The name of any installation or heavy lift vessel to be involved in the construction activity (including one providing accommodation for persons engaged in the activity).

4.   The dates on which the construction activity is expected to commence and finish.

5.   A description of the nature of the construction activity and of the hazards with the potential to cause a major accident which it involves.

6.   Particulars of the proposed programme of work.

7.   The name of an individual who will be able to make arrangements to facilitate any inspection by an inspector of the construction activity, and details of how that person can be contacted.

SCHEDULE 8

Regulation 16

AMENDMENTS TO THE OFFSHORE INSTALLATIONS (SAFETY REPRESENTATIVES
AND SAFETY COMMITTEES) REGULATIONS 1989

THE DIVING OPERATIONS AT WORK REGULATIONS 1981

(S.I. 1981 No. 399, as amended by S.I. 1990 No. 996 and S.I. 1992 No. 608)

ARRANGEMENT OF REGULATIONS

Now, therefore, the Secretary of State in exercise of the powers conferred on him by sections 15(1), (3) (a) and (b), (4) (a), (5) (b) and (9) and 80(1), (2) (b) and (c) and (4) and 82(3) (a) of, and paragraphs 1(1) (a) and (c), (2), 4(1) and (2), 7, 8(1) and (2), 9, 10, 11, 14, 15(1) and (2), 16, 20 and 21(a), (b) and (c) of Schedule 3 to the 1974 Act [the Health and Safety at Work etc. Act 1974] and of all other powers enabling him in that behalf and so as to give effect without modification to the said proposals of the Commission and to the said revocation and modification of Regulations, hereby makes the following Regulations—

1. Citation and commencement. These Regulations may be cited as the Diving Operations at Work Regulations 1981 and shall come into operation on 1 July 1981.

General note. These Regulations revoke the Diving Operations Special Regulations 1960 and the Offshore Installations (Diving Operations) Regulations 1974. The Submarine Pipe-lines (Diving Operations) Regulations 1976 were revoked by S.I. 1993 No. 1823. They apply to diving operations in which the divers are at work either (i) in Great Britain or (ii) outside Great Britain in circumstances covered by the Health and Safety at Work etc. Act 1974 (Application outside Great Britain) Order 1989. They also apply where a surface compression chamber is being used in connection with a diving operation or the testing of equipment for use in a diving operation.

A guidance booklet "A Guide to the Diving Operations at Work Regulations 1981" is published by the Health and Safety Executive.

2. Interpretation.—(1) In these Regulations, unless the context otherwise requires—

"the 1989 Order" means the Health and Safety at Work etc. Act 1974 (Application outside Great Britain) Order 1989;

"breathing mixture" means air or any other mixture of gases which is fit for breathing;

"concession owner" means a person who is a concession owner for the purposes of the Mineral Workings (Offshore Installations) Act 1971 in accordance with section 12(2) of that Act;

"diver" shall be construed in accordance with paragraph (2)(b);

"diver's log book" means the diver's log book described in regulation 7(3)(a);

"diving bell" means any compression chamber which is capable of being manned and is used or designed for use under the surface of water in supporting human life being a chamber in which any occupant is or may be subjected to a pressure of more than 300 millibars above atmospheric pressure during normal operation; and "bell diving" shall be construed accordingly;

"diving contractor" has the meaning assigned by regulation (5)4;

"diving operation" shall be construed in accordance with paragraph (2)(a) and (c);

"diving rules" means required by regulation 5(1)(b);

"diving supervisor" means in relation to any *diving operation*, the competent person referred to in regulation 6 who has been appointed in relation to that operation by the *diving contractor*;

"emergency" means an emergency affecting or likely to affect the health or safety of a *diver* engaged in a *diving operation*;

"first-aid" means—

(a) in cases where a person will need help from a medical practitioner or nurse, treatment for the purpose of preserving life and minimising the consequences of injury and illness until the appropriate help is obtained, and

(b) treatment of minor injures and illness which would otherwise receive no treatment or which do not need treatment by a medical practitioner or nurse, and in this sub-paragraph "treatment" includes redressing and other follow-up treatment;

"offshore installation" has the meaning assigned by the 1989 Order *(a)*;

"pipe-line" and "pipe-line works" have the meanings assigned to "pipe-line" and "pipe-line works" respectively by the 1989 Order;

"self-contained" in relation to any diving plant and equipment, means diving plant and equipment in which the supply of *breathing mixture* is carried by the *diver* independently of any other source.

(2) For the purposes of these Regulations—

(a) a *diver* shall be deemed to be engaged in a *diving operation* from the time when he commences to prepare to dive until—

  (i) if he entered the water he has left it and returned to a place from which the *diving operations* are being carried on, and
  (ii) he is no longer subject to raised pressure, and
  (iii) it may reasonably be anticipated that he will not need therapeutic recompression,

except that heads (ii) and (iii) shall not apply when for the purposes of receiving medical treatment he has been transferred to a hospital or other place which is not under the control of the *diving contractor* or *the diving supervisor*;

(b) a person shall be deemed not to be a *diver* if he—

  (i) is in a submersible chamber or craft or in a pressure resistant diving suit, and is not exposed to a pressure exceeding 300 millibars above atmospheric pressure during normal operation, or
  (ii) uses no underwater breathing apparatus or uses only snorkel type apparatus, or
  (iii) is taking part in the *diving operation* in a capacity other than as an employee *(b)* or self-employed person *(b)* or
  (iv) is on duty as a member of the armed forces of the Crown or visiting forces and is engaged in operations or operational training;

(c) a person who is engaged in any activity as a *diving supervisor*, or as a member of a diving team or in connection with the recompression or decompression of a *diver* engaged in a *diving operation* shall be deemed to be engaged in a *diving operation*.

(3) In these Regulations, unless the context otherwise requires, a reference to—

(a) a numbered regulation or Schedule is a reference to the regulation of, or Schedule to, these Regulations bearing that number;
(b) a number paragraph is a reference to the paragraph bearing that number in the regulation in which the reference appears.

(a) See the general note to reg. 1.

(b) *Employee; self-employed person.* For definitions, see the Health and Safety at Work etc. Act 1974, s. 52(1) and the Interpretation Act 1978, s. 11.

3. Application of these Regulations.—(1) Subject to paragraph (2) and regulation 5C(1), these Regulations shall apply to and in relation to all *diving operations* in which any *diver* taking part is at work as an employee or a self-employed person within the meaning of section 53 of the Health and Safety at Work etc. Act 1974, being *diving operations* either—

    (a) in Great Britain *(a)*, or

    (b) outside Great Britain in circumstances in which sections 1 to 59 of that Act apply by virtue of the 1989 Order *(b)*.

    (2) These Regulations shall apply to a *diving operation* only if at least one of the persons going under water is a *diver* for the purposes of the Regulations.

    (3) Where a person is exposed to a pressure greater than 300 millibars above atmospheric pressure in a surface compression chamber in connection with—

    (a) any *diving operation*, or

    (b) the testing or evaluation of any plant or equipment designed for use in *diving operations*,

then these Regulations shall apply to, and in relation to, him as if he were a *diver* engaged in a *diving operation* except—

    (i) regulations 7(1)(a), 8(2), (3) and (4), 10, 12(1)(b), (f), (g), (i) and (j), and

    (ii) regulations 7(1)(b) and 10A where the person is not exposed to a pressure greater than 5,000 millibars above atmospheric pressure,

but this paragraph shall not apply to a diver engaged in a diving operation or to a person to whom regulation 2(2)(b)(iv) applies.

    (a) **Great Britain.** For definition, see INTRODUCTORY NOTE 4.

    (b) See note *(a)* to reg. 2.

4. Duty to ensure compliance with these Regulations.—(1) In addition to any specific duty placed on him by these Regulations—

    (a) every *diving contractor* and every person who to any extent is responsible for, has control over or is engaged in a *diving operation*, and

    (b) in the case of—

        (i) an *offshore installation*, the owner,

        (ii) a proposed *offshore installation*, the *concession owner*,

        (iii) a *pipe-line*, the owner,

        (iv) a proposed *pipe-line*, the person who will be the owner when it is laid,

shall ensure so far as is reasonably practicable *(a)*—

    (c) that these Regulations are complied with, and

    (d) that they are complied with in such a way that persons involved are not exposed to risks to their health or safety.

    (2) (a) An employer *(b)* shall not permit any employee *(b)* of his to take part in a *diving operation* as a *diver* unless there is a *diving contractor* for that operation.

    (b) A person employed under a contract for services or who would be diving on his own account shall not take part in a *diving operation* as a *diver* unless there is a *diving contractor* for that operation.

(a) **Reasonably practicable.** See INTRODUCTORY NOTE 5.

(b) **Employer; employee.** For definitions, see note (b) to reg. 2.

5.   Diving contractors.—(1) Every *diving contractor* shall in respect of each *diving operation*—

(a)   appoint one or more *diving supervisors (a)* in accordance with paragraph (3) to be in immediate control of the operation;

(b)   issue *diving rules* in accordance with regulation 9 and Schedule 1 for regulation the conduct of all persons engaged in the *diving operation*;

(c)   provide a diving operations log book, which is to be maintained in accordance with regulation 6, and shall keep it for at least two years after the date of the last entry in it;

(d)   ensure that all plant and equipment, including any plant and equipment required by regulation 12, which is necessary for the safe conduct of the *diving operation* is available for immediate use;

(e)   not permit the use of compressed natural air as the *breathing mixture* in any *diving operation* at a depth exceeding 50 metres except where the use is for therapeutic purposes;

(f)   provide the equipment, facilities, medications and personnel referred to in regulation 13A(1);

(g)   ensure that persons engaged in the diving operation are informed of the nature of the arrangements that have been made in connection with the provision of first-aid, which information shall include details of—

(i)   the location of first-aid equipment, facilities, medications and personnel, and

(ii) any standing instructions from a registered medical practitioner (who may or may not be present) in respect of the management and handling of persons who are injured or become ill while engaged in a diving operation.

(2)   Every *diving contractor* shall so far as is reasonably practicable (b) ensure that—

(a)   each *diving operation* is carried out from a suitable and safe place with the consent of any person having control of that place;

(b)   emergency services are available including in particular in the case of diving—

(i)   using saturation techniques, or

(ii) at a depth exceeding 50 metres,

facilities for transferring the *divers* safety under a suitable pressure to a place where treatment can be given safely under pressure;

(c)   there are effective means of communications between the place at which operations are being or are to be carried out and—

(i)   persons having control of that place, and

(ii) the emergency services.

In this paragraph, "saturation techniques" means procedures by means of which a *diver* avoids repeated decompressions to atmospheric pressure by being continuously subjected to an ambient pressure greater than atmospheric pressure so that his body tissues and blood become saturated with the inert element of the breathing mixture.

(3) (a)   Each *diving supervisor* shall be appointed in writing and where two or more *diving supervisors* are appointed in respect of any *diving operation*,

the *diving contractor shall specify which part or parts of the diving operation* each is to supervise at any one time; except that the *diving contractor* may permit two duly appointed supervisors to arrange between themselves the time at which one is to take over from the other.

(b)   A person shall not be appointed to be a *diving supervisor* unless—

   (i)   he is a competent person with adequate knowledge and experience of the diving techniques to be used in the *diving operation* for which he is appointed, and either—

  (ii)   he has qualified as a *diver*, in respect of the diving techniques to be used, under these Regulations or under any of the Regulations *(c)* revoked or modified by regulation 16 of these Regulations or under the Submarine Pipe-lines (Diving Operations) Regulations 1976, or

 (iii)   during the period of two years immediately preceding the coming into operation *(d)* of these Regulations he acted as a *diving supervisor* of a *diving operation* in which the same diving techniques were used,

except that heads (ii) and (iii) shall not apply where the *diving operation* is to be carried on in water which is not more than 1.5 metres deep.

(4) For the purposes of these Regulations, "diving contractor" in relation to any *diving operation* means—

(a)   in any case where any of the *divers* taking part are employees *(e)*—

   (i)   their employer, or

  (ii)   if there is more than one employer, such one of them as those employers may appoint in writing;

(b)   if there is no *diving contractor* by virtue of the preceding sub-paragraph and the operation is carried on—

   (i)   from or in connection with an *offshore installation*, the manager of the installation appointed pursuant to section 4 of the Mineral Workings (Offshore Installations) Act 1971 or where no such manager has been appointed, the person made responsible by the owner for health and safety on the installation,

  (ii)   in connection with a proposed *offshore installation*, the *concession owner*,

 (iii)   in connection with a *pipe-line*, the owner of the *pipe-line*,

 (iv)   in connection with a proposed *pipe-line*, the person who will be the owner of the *pipe-line* when it is laid;

(c)   if there is no *diving contractor* by virtue of either of the preceding sub-paragraphs, any *diver* employed under a contract for services or diving on his own account and if there is more than one such person, such one of the them as they may appoint in writing.

In this paragraph—

"in connection with an *offshore installation*" and "in connection with a proposed *offshore installation*" does not include any *pipe-line works*;

"in connection with a *pipe-line*" and "in connection with a proposed *pipe-line*" means in connection with that part of it with which the *diving operation* is concerned and includes *pipe-line works*; and "the owner" means the owner of that part.

(a) **Diving supervisor.** For the duties of a diving supervisor, see reg. 6.

(b) **Reasonably practicable.** See INTRODUCTORY NOTE 5.

(c) **Regulations.** That is to say, the Diving Operations Regulations 1960, the Offshore Installations (Diving Operations) Regulations 1974 and the Merchant Shipping (Diving Operations) Regulations 1975.

(d) **Coming into operation.** The Regulations came into operation on 1 July 1981 (reg. 1).

(e) **Employee.** For definition, see note *(b)* to reg. 2.

5A. Registration of diving contractors.—(1) No person shall act as a *diving contractor* unless he is registered in accordance with this regulation.

(2) A person shall be registered in accordance with this regulation if—

(a) he has given written notice to the Executive including the information listed in Schedule 1A; and

(b) the Executive has issued an acknowledgement under paragraph (4); and

(c) the registration has not expired in accordance with paragraph (5) or (7).

(3) The Executive may approve a form of notice for the purposes of paragraph (2), and where it does so any such notice shall be in the form for the time being so approved.

(4) The Executive shall serve written acknowledgement on each *diving contractor* who has given written notice under paragraph (2)(a) and such acknowledgement shall include the date it is issued and the date on which registration will expire.

(5) Subject to paragraph (7), registration shall expire 12 months after the later of—

(a) the date the acknowledgement under paragraph (4) is issued; or

(b) where notice under paragraph (2)(a) has been received by the Executive no more than one month before the expiry of an existing registration under this regulation of the same *diving contractor*, the date of expiry of the existing registration.

(6) Any person who is registered in accordance with this regulation shall give further written notice to the Executive of any change in the information required by paragraph (2)(a) forthwith after such change or at such later time as the Executive may approve in any case or class of case.

(7) For the purposes of this regulation the Executive may on or before 17 June 1993 approve registration in any case or class of cases for a period longer than 12 months and the registration so approved shall expire at the end of that period.

5B. Only registered diving contractors to be used. No person shall enter into a contract whereby any other person acts as a *diving contractor* unless he is satisfied that such other person is registered in accordance with regulation 5A.

5C. Notification of projects involving diving operations.—(1) This regulation shall apply to and in relation to *diving operations* mentioned in regulation

3(1)(b) being *diving operations* outside Great Britain in circumstances in which sections 1 to 59 of the Health and Safety at Work etc. Act 1974 apply by virtue of article 4, other than article 4(2)(a), and article 5 of *the 1989* Order.

(2) Every person who enters into a contract whereby any other person acts as a *diving contractor* shall notify the enforcing authority of each project in which that other person acts as such.

(3) Notification under this regulation shall include the information listed in Schedule 1B.

(4) Subject to paragraph (6), notification of any project under this regulation shall be given not less than 21 days before *diving operations* which comprise or form part of that project commence.

(5) Subject to paragraph (6), notification under this regulation shall be in writing.

(6) Where it is not reasonable to expect notification under this regulation as required by paragraphs (4) and (5), then—

  (a) notification shall be given forthwith after any information required by paragraph (3) becomes available to the person required by paragraph (2) to notify the enforcing authority;
  (b) notification shall include such of the information required by paragraph (3) as is available to the person required by paragraph (2) to notify the enforcing authority and has not been included in a previous notification in respect of the same project; and
  (c) notification shall be given by the fastest means available but, where that means is not in writing, shall also be confirmed in writing without delay.

(7) The Executive may approve a form of notification under this regulation and where it does so any such notification shall, subject to paragraph (6), be in the form for the time being so approved.

6. The diving supervisor.—(1) Every *diving supervisor* shall, so far as is reasonably practicable *(a)* ensure that each *diving operation* for which he is appointed is carried out in accordance with the *diving rules* and under his immediate control.

(2) In relation to each *diving operation* the *diving supervisor* shall—

  (a) ensure that plant and equipment is not used unless regulation 13(1)(c) and (d) has been complied with;
  (b) comply with regulation 9(4);
  (c) enter in the diving operations log book provided under regulation 5(1)(c) an accurate record of the matters specified in Schedule 2 and shall sign the entries daily during the course of the *diving operation*;
  (d) countersign the entries relating to the *diving operation* in the diver's log book *(b)* of each *diver* who took part in that operation.

(3) A person shall not dive while he is the *diving supervisor* for the time being in charge of a *diving operation* or any part of it.

(a) **Reasonably practicable.** See INTRODUCTORY NOTE 5.

(b) **Diver's log book.** See reg. 7(3)(a).

7.   Divers.—(1) A person shall not take part in any *diving operation* as a *diver* unless he—

(a)   has a valid certificate of training issued under regulation 10, and

(b)   has a valid certificate of diving *first-aid* issued under regulation 10A or is a suitable person for the purposes of regulation 13A(1), and

(c)   has a valid certificate of medical fitness to dive issued under regulation 11, and

(d)   is competent to carry out safely the work which he is called upon to perform in that operation,

but sub-paragraphs (a) and (b) above shall not apply to a person taking part in a diving operation as part of training which if successfully completed would lead to the issue of a certificate such as is mentioned in either of those sub-paragraphs, and sub-paragraphs (b) and (c) above shall not apply to a person who enters a compression chamber in order to provide treatment in an emergency.

(2) Every *diver* engaged in a *diving operation* shall inform the *diving supervisor* appointed in respect of that operation if he is unfit or if there is any other reason why he should not go or remain under water or in a compression chamber as the case may be.

(3) (a) Every diver engaged in a *diving operation* shall maintain a personal log book (*"diver's log book"*) in which he shall enter his name and which shall contain his signature and a photograph which is a reasonable likeness of him.

(b) On every day on which he takes part in a *diving operation* a *diver* shall record in his log book the matters set out in Schedule 3, and he shall sign each entry and it shall be contersigned by the *diving supervisor*.

(4) Every *diver* shall present his diver's log book to the doctor examintion him for the purposes of regulation 11.

(5) Every *diver* shall retain his driver's log book for at least two years from the date of the last entry in it.

8.   Diving team.—(1) At all times when any *diving operation* is, or is about to be, carried out there shall be present a sufficient number of divers, personnel referred to in regulation 13A(1) and other competent persons ("the diving team") necessary to—

(a)   ensure that so far as is reasonably practicable the operation can be undertaking safely;

(b)   operate plant, equipment or other facilities necessary for the safe conduct of the operation;

(c)   render first-aid to, and treat in accordance with the directions of a registered medical practitioner (who may or may not be present), persons who are injured or become ill while engaged in a *diving operation*.

(2) Subject to paragraphs (4) and (5), in addition to the *diver* or *divers* who will be diving in a *diving operation*—

(a)   there shall be another *diver* ("the standby diver") who shall—

(i) where a *diving bell* is being used, descend in the bell to the depth from which work is to be carried out and shall remain in the bell to monitor the *diver* or *divers* who leave it and be in immediate readiness to render assistance to them.

    (ii) in all other cases, be in immediate readiness to dive except that two *divers* in the water at the same time who are near enough to be able to communicate with and to render assistance to each other in an emergency may each be regarded as the standby *diver* for the other;

(b) in the following cases there shall be an extra *diver* on the surface in addition to the standby *diver*:—

    (i) where diving stops are required for the purpose of routine decompression,

    (ii) where the diving will be at a depth of 30 metres or more,

    (iii) where there is a special hazard and in particular where a *diver* will be endangered in a current or where there is a risk of a *diver* being trapped or his equipment entangled.

(3) The standby *diver* and any *diver* required by paragraph (2)(b) shall be in addition to—

(a) any members of the team *(b)* required to attend or work any plant, equipment or other facilities;

(b) the *diving supervisor,*

except that the standby *diver (c)* and the extra *diver* required by paragraph (2)(b) may perform other duties in the diving team *(b)* where to do so would not prejudice the safety of any person in the water if he is called upon to dive.

(4) Paragraph (2) shall not prevent the standby *diver (c)* or any *diver* required by paragraph (2)(b) from going to the assistance of any other *diver* in an *emergency.*

(5) Paragraph (2) shall not apply where the *diving operation* is to be carried on in water which is not more than 1.5 metres deep.

(a) **Reasonably practicable.** See INTRODUCTORY NOTE 5.

(b) **Team.** See para. (1).

(c) **Standby diver.** See para. (2)(a)(i).

9.   Diving rules.—(1) The *diving rules* required by regulation 5(1)(b) shall include provisions for securing the health and safety of persons engaged in the *diving operation* and in particular shall—

(a) make provision relating to such of the matters specified in Schedule 1 as are relevant to the *diving operation* to be undertaken;

(b) require the use of such of the plant and equipment specified in regulation 12 as is relevant to the *diving operation* to be undertaken.

(2) The *diving contractor* shall, if an inspector appointed pursuant to section 19 of the Health and Safety at Work etc. Act 1974 so requires, supply the inspector with a copy of the *diving rules* issued by him for any *diving operation* or intended operation or such part of those rules as the inspector may require.

(3) The *diving contractor* shall supply the *diving supervisor* with a copy of the *diving rules.*

(4) The *diving supervisor* shall make available to each member of the diving team *(a)* a copy of the part of the *diving rules* relevant to that member.

(*a*) **Diving team.** See reg. 8(1).

10.   Qualification of divers.—(1) The certificate of training required by regulation 7(1)(a) shall be valid only if—

(a) it has been issued by the Health and Safety Executive (*a*) or by a person or body of persons approved by the Executive for the purposes of this sub-paragraph, and

(b) it states—

    (i) the name of the individual to whom it relates ("the diver"),

    (ii) the category or categories of diving to which it relates,

    (iii) that the person or body issuing the certificate is satisfied that the diver has attained a satisfactory standard of competence (whether by training, experience or a combination of both) in the matters specified in Schedule 4 which are relevant to the category or categories of diving to which the certificate relates, except that where the person or body is not satisfied on all such matters, but nevertheless considers it appropriate to issue a certificate subject to restrictions within a category of diving, those restrictions shall be stated in the certificate;

(c) it has not ceased, in accordance with paragraph (2), to be valid.

(2) If—

(a) the person or body which issued a certificate declares it to be no longer valid, or

(b) the Executive declares a certificate to be no longer valid, whether or not the certificate was issued by the Executive,

then that certificate shall cease to be a valid certificate for the purposes of paragraph (1).

(3) The certificate of training shall be kept in the diver's log book (*b*).

(4) [*revoked*].

(5) Without prejudice to the generality of paragraph (1)(a), where a person or body approved for the purposes of this regulation or the Executive

(a) refuses to issue a certificate of training, or

(b) declares a certificate of training it has issued to be no longer valid,

the Executive, upon application being made to it by the person aggrieved, within 28 days of his being notified of the refusal or declaration as the case may be, shall review that decision and if it is satisfied that it should be reversed or altered shall in either case issue a certificate of training.

(*a*) **Health and Safety Executive.** For the functions of this body, see the Health and Safety at Work etc. Act 1974, and in particular s. 11 thereof.

(*b*) **Diver's log book.** See reg. 7(3)(a).

10A.   Certificate of diving first-aid.—(1) The certificate of diving *first-aid* required by regulation 7(1)(b) shall be valid only if—

(a) it has been issued by the Health and Safety Executive or by a person or body of persons approved by the Executive for the purpose of this sub-paragraph;

(b) the date mentioned in sub-paragraph (c)(iv) below has not passed;

(c) it states—

    (i) the name of the individual to whom it relates *("the diver"),*

    (ii) the category or categories of diving to which it relates,

    (iii) that the person or body issuing the certificate is satisfied that the diver has attained a satisfactory standard of competence in *first-aid* appropriate to the category or categories of diving to which it relates,

    (iv) the date on which it will cease to be valid unless further training is undertaken and an appropriate endorsement thereon obtained from the Executive or a person or body of persons approved by the Executive for the purposes of this provision; and

(d) it has not ceased, in accordance with paragraph (2), to be valid.

(2) If—

(a) the person or body which issued a certificate declares it to be no longer valid, or

(b) the Executive declares a certificate to be no longer valid, whether or not the certificate was issued by the Executive,

then that certificate shall cease to be a valid certificate for the purposes of paragraph (1).

(3) The certificate of diving *first-aid* shall be kept in the diver's log book.

(4) Without prejudice to the generality of paragraph (1)(a), where a person or body approved for the purposes of that paragraph or the Executive—

(a) refuses to issue a certificate of diving *first-aid* relating to the category or categories of diving requested by the *diver*;

(b) refuses to endorse a certificate of diving *first-aid* already issued; or

(c) declares a certificate of diving *first-aid* it has issued to be no longer valid,

the Executive, upon application being made to it by the person aggrieved, within 28 days of his being notified of the refusal or declaration, shall review the decision and if it is satisfied that it should be reversed or altered issue, re-issue or endorse the certificate.

11. Certificate of medical fitness to dive.—(1) The certificate of medical fitness to dive required by regulation 7(1)(c) shall be valid in respect of a particular *diving operation* only if—

(a) it has been issued by an approved doctor *(a)* or by the Health and Safety Executive *(b)* in accordance with the following provisions of this regulation;

(b) the diving undertaken does not contravene any limitation contained in the certificate pursuant to paragraph (3)(a)(v);

(c) the period mentioned in paragraph (3)(a)(vi) has not expired.

(2) A certificate of medical fitness shall only be issued for the purposes of paragraph (1) after the person concerned has undergone an examination carried out by an approved doctor *(a)* in such manner and including such tests as the Executive may require either generally or for that case or class of case.

(3) The certificate of medical fitness to dive shall—

(a) state—
   (i) the name of the person to whom it relates,
   (ii) the date of the medical examination,
   (iii) the date of any X-ray taken for the purposes of that examination,
   (iv) that the person is considered fit to dive,
   (v) any limitation on the diving or compression for which the person is considered fit,
   (vi) the period not exceeding 12 months for which the person is considered fit,
   (vii) the name, address and telephone number of the approved doctor *(a)* issuing the certificate;
(b) be signed by the doctor issuing it, or on behalf of the Executive as the case may be.

(4) The certificate of medical fitness shall be entered in the diver's log book *(c)*; and the entry shall be in such form as the Executive may approve.

(5) If an approved doctor *(a)* decides, after examination, that a person is unfit to dive, he shall enter this fact in the diver's log book *(c)* together with the information required by paragraph (3)(a)(i)–(ii) and (vii) and shall sign the entry.

(6) An employment medical adviser *(d)* may on medical grounds revoke a certificate of medical fitness after, where reasonably practicable, consulting the doctor who issued that certificate.

Without prejudice to the generality of paragraph (1)(a), where an approved doctor *(a)* decides—

(a) that a person is unfit to dive, or
(b) that a person is fit to dive subject to limitations,

the Executive, upon application being made to it by that person within 28 days of the decision, shall review the decision and if it is satisfied that it should be reversed or altered shall issue a certificate of fitness to dive subject to such limitations, if any, as it considers appropriate.

(8) In this regulation, "an approved doctor" means a medical practitioner approved for the time being by an employment medical adviser *(d)* for such purposes of these Regulations as he may specify in the instrument of approval; and "employment medical adviser" means a person appointed under Part II of the Health and Safety at Work etc. Act 1974 to be such an adviser and who is authorised by the Executive to give approvals under this paragraph or to make revocations under paragraph (6) as the case may be.

(a) Approved doctor. See para. (8).

(b) Health and Safety Executive. See note *(a)* to reg. 10.

(c) Diver's log book. See reg. 7(3)(a).

(d) Employment Medical Adviser. See para. 8.

12. Plant and equipment.—(1) The plant and equipment mentioned in regulation 5(1)(d) shall—

(a) include a means of supply a *breathing mixture* (including a reserve supply for immediate use in the event of an *emergency* or for therapeutic recompression or decompression)—
   (i) suitable in content and temperature and of adequate pressure, and
   (ii) at an adequate rate,
to sustain prolonged vigorous physical exertion at the ambient pressure for the duration of the *diving operations*;

(b) include a lifeline for each *diver* except—
   (i) where the nature of the *diving operations* renders a lifeline unsuitable and an alternative system for ensuring the *diver's* safety is used, or
   (ii) in a case where two *divers* are at a depth not exceeding 30 metres and each is acting as standby diver *(a)* for the other and one of them is connected to the surface by a lifeline;
and in this sub-paragraph "lifeline" means a rope, gas hose, communication cable or any combination thereof which is adequate in strength and suitable for recovering and lifting the *diver* and his equipment from the water;

(c) enable each *diver* to communicate wth the *diving supervisor* except—
   (i) where paragraph (1)(b)(i) applies,
   (ii) where paragraph (1)(b)(ii) applies in which case one of the *divers* shall be able to communicate with the *supervisor*,
and in a case where a *diving bell* is being used enable the *diver* who leaves the bell to communicate with the *diver* remaining in it;

(d) in addition to the means of communication required by sub-paragraph (c) above, include where reasonably practicable *(b)* a system enabling oral communication to be made between each *diver* and the *diving supervisor*;

(e) include such plant and equipment as may be necessary to ensure that *divers* may safely enter and leave the water;

(f) in the case of any of the following *diving operations*, include a surface compression chamber with all necessary ancillary equipment; and the chamber and equipment shall comply with Schedule 5—
   (i) at a depth in excess of 50 metres,
   (ii) at a depth exceeding 10 but not exceeding 50 metres where the routine decompression time exceeds 20 minutes,
   (iii) at a depth exceeding 10 but not exceeding 50 metres where the routine decompression time is 20 minutes or less and effective arrangements have not been made for the rapid conveyance of any *diver* requiring therapeutic recompression for the location of the *diving operations* to a suitable two-compartment chamber,
   (iv) from or in connection with an *offshore installation*, a proposed *offshore installation*, a proposed *offshore installation* or *pipe-line works*;

(g) for a *diving operation* at a depth exceeding 50 metres include a *diving bell* which shall have all necessary ancillary equipment and shall comply with the requirements of Schedule 6;

(h) include such plant and equipment, if any, as may be necessary to ensure that each *diver's* body temperature is kept within safe limits and in all cases where the *diving operation* is—
   (i) at a depth exceeding 50 metres there shall be a means of heating the *diver*, and

  (ii) at a depth exceeding 150 metres there shall also be a means of heating the *diver's breathing mixture*;
 (i) where a *diving operation* is to be carried on during the hours of darkness include—
  (i) a lamp or other device attached to the *diver* to indicate his position when he is on the surface, and
  (ii) such plant and equipment as may be necessary to illuminate adequately the place on the surface from which the diving is being carried on, except where the nature of the *diving operations* render such illumination undersirable;
 (j) include depth measuring devices which where reasonably practicable shall be suitable for surface monitoring.

(2) Where a person is deemed to be engaged in a *diving operation* by virtue of regulation 3(3), the surface compression chamber and its ancillary equipment shall comply with Schedule 5.

(3) Where any vessel, hovercraft, floating structure or *offshore installation* is used in a *diving operation* there shall be means of securing that it is—

 (a) at anchor or aground, or
 (b) made fast to the shore, to a fixed structure or to an *offshore installation* which is in a fixed position, or
 (c) maintained in a position using its propulsion system or a dynamic positioning system with adequate precautions to secure the safety of the *diver* from these systems and the flow of water created.

(4) All plant and equipment used in a *diving operation* shall—

 (a) be properly designed, of adequate strength and of good construction from sound and suitable material *(c)*;
 (b) be suitable for the conditions in which it is intended to be used;
 (c) where its safe use depends on the depth or pressure at which it is used, be marked with its safe working pressure or the maximum depth at which it may be used;
 (d) at whatever temperature it is to be used, be adequately protected against malfunctioning at that temperature.

(5) Each gas cylinder used in a *diving operation* shall be legibly marked with the name and the chemical formula of its contents.

  (a) Standby diver. See reg. 8(2)(a).

  (b) Reasonably practicable. See INTRODUCTORY NOTE 5.

  (c) Of adequate strength. See the analogous provisions of the Factories Act 1961, s. 22 and see also INTRODUCTORY NOTE 11.

13. Maintenance, examination and testing of plant and equipment.—
(1) The plant and equipment specified in regulation 12(1), (2) and (5) shall not be used in any *diving operation* unless—

 (a) it is maintained *(a)* in a condition which will ensure so far as is reasonably practicable *(b)* that it is safe while it is being used;
 (b) the register maintained under paragraph (4) contains—
  (i) a certificate by a competent person that it complies with regulation 12(4), and

    (ii) in the case of a surface compression chamber or a *diving bell*, sufficient information, including information relating to the materials used in its construction, to enable it to be safely used, repaired or altered;

(c) there is in force a certificate issued under paragraph (2) by a competent person that it has been examined and tested and that it may be safely used;

(d) it has been examined by a competent person within the six hours immediately before the *diving operation* commenced.

(2) The certificate referred to in paragraph (1)(c) shall—

(a) state—
    (i) the plant and equipment to which it relates,
    (ii) that the competent person has examined it,
    (iii) that it has been tested by him or under his close supervision,
    (iv) the pressure, depth or other conditions under which it can be safely used, and
    (v) the period during which it can be safely used which shall not exceed six months;

(b) cease to be valid—
    (i) when any repair or alteration has to be made to the plant or equipment which affects its safe working,
    (ii) on the expiration of six months or such shorter period as may be certified under sub-paragraph (b)(v) above.

(3) For the purposes of paragraph (2)(a)(iii) the competent person need not cause a pressure leak test or an internal pressure test to be repeated—

(a) in the case of a surface compression chamber or a *diving bell*—
    (i) if a pressure leak test to a safe working pressure has been carried out and certified within the previous two years, or as the case may be,
    (ii) if an internal pressure test has been carried out and certified within the previous five years;

(b) in the case of a seamless gas cylinder not taken under water if either a pressure leak test to a safe working pressure or an internal pressure test has been carried out and certified within the previous five years;

(c) in the case of any other item or plant or equipment which will be subjected to an internal pressure in excess of 500 millibars above external pressure, if either a pressure leak test to a safe working pressure or, an internal pressure test has been carried out and certified within the previous two years.

(4) The *diving contractor* shall—

(a) enter in, attach to or insert into a register kept for the purpose, the certificates and information required by paragraph (1)(b) and (c);

(b) retain each such register—
    (i) in the case of a register containing certificates relating to any surface compression chamber or *diving bell* or seamless gas cylinder not taken under water, for at least five years from the date of the last such certificate,
    (ii) in any other case, for at least two years from the date of the last certificate it contains.

(a) **Maintained.** See INTRODUCTORY NOTE 10.

(b) **Reasonably practicable.** See INTRODUCTORY NOTE 5.

13A.   Equipment, facilities, medications and personnel.—(1) The equipment, facilities, medications and personnel mentioned in regulations 5(1)(f) and 8(1) shall be such equipment, facilities, medications and number of suitable persons (being at least one in the case of mixed gas or *bell diving*) as are adequate and appropriate in the circumstances for rendering first-aid to, and treating in accordance with the directions of a registered medical practitioner (who may or may not be present), persons who are injured or become ill while engaged in a diving operation.

(2)   For the purposes of paragraph (1), a person shall not be suitable unless he—

(a)   has a valid certificate of medical fitness to dive issued under regulation 11, and

(b)   has undergone such training, if any, or futher training, and has obtained such qualifications or further qualifications as the Health and Safety Executive may from time to time approve in respect of that case or class of case, and

(c)   maintains a *diver's log book* whether or not he is a diver.

14.   Exemption certificates.—(1)   Subject to paragraph (2), the Health and Safety Executive *(a)* may, by a certificate in writing, exempt any person or class of persons, any *diving operation* or class of *diving operations* and any plant and equipment or class of plant and equipment from any requirement or prohibition imposed by any provision of these Regulations, and any such exemption may be granted subject to conditions and to a limit of time and may be revoked at any time.

(2)   The Executive shall not grant any such exemption unless, having regard to the circumstances of the case, and in particular to—

(a)   the conditions, if any, which it proposes to attach to the exemption, and

(b)   any other requirements imposed by or under any enactment which apply to the case,

it is satisfied that the health and safety of persons who are likely to be affected by the exemption will not be prejudiced in consequence of it.

(a) **The Health and Safety Executive.** See note *(a)* to reg. 10.

15.   Transitional provisions.—(1) It shall be a sufficient compliance with regulation 10 if instead of the certificate of training the diver's log book *(a)* includes a certificate issued by the *diving contractor* during the first six months immediately after the coming into operation of these Regulations that he is satisfied that the *diver's* experience during the two years immediately preceding the issue of the certificate is such that he is competent to take part in *diving operations* of the category stated in the certificate; in this paragraph "the diving contractor" means the first relevant *diving contractor* after these Regulations come into operation.

(2) The Health and Safety Executive *(b)* may revoke a certificate issued under paragraph (1) at any time if, after making such enquiries as it considers necessary, it considers that in all the circumstances of the case it is appropriate to do so.

(3) A certificate of medical fitness issued under any of the Regulations revoked or modified by regulation 16 of these Regulations or under the Submarine Pipe-lines (Diving Operations) Regulations 1976 shall have effect for the purposes of these Regulations as if it had been issued under regulation 11(1) of these Regulations as the case may be.

(a) **Diver's log book.** See reg. 7(3)(a).

(b) **The Health and Safety Executive.** See note *(a)* to reg. 10.

16. Revocations and modification.—(1) The Diving Operations Special Regulations 1960, and the Offshore Installations (Diving Operations) Regulations 1974 are hereby revoked.

(2) For regulation 2(1) of the Merchant Shipping (Diving Operations) Regulations 1975 there shall be subsituted the following paragraph—

"(1) These Regulations shall apply to all diving operations (other than diving operations to which the Diving Operations at Work Regulations 1981 apply) carried on from, on, in or near any submersible or supporting apparatus to which Part IV of the Act applies, being diving operations carried on in the course of or in connection with any trade or business (not including archaeology or non-commercial research) other than a school for the training of divers.".

SCHEDULE 1

Regulations 5(1)(b) and 9

MATTERS IN RESPECT OF WHICH PROVISION IS TO BE MADE IN DIVING RULES

Planning
1. *Consideration of—*
(a) meteorological conditions, including forecasted conditions;
(b) tidal information including local tide tables and indications of speed of current to be expected;
(c) proposed shipping movements;
(d) air and water temperatures;
(e) underwater hazards of the diving site, including any culverts, penstocks, sluice valves or areas where differences in hydrostatic pressure may endanger the *diver*;
(f) depth and type of operation;
(g) suitability of plant and equipment;
(h) availability and qualifications of personnel;
(i) the effect on a *diver* of changes of air pressure if he flies after diving;
(j) the activities of any person who will be diving in connection with the *diving operation* whether or not he is a *diver* for the purposes of these Regulations.

Preparations
2. (a) Consultation with persons having any control over or information related to the safety of any *diving operations*; and in particular persons having control of

lifting appliances or having control of or information about shipping movements;
- (b) selection of the *breathing* apparatus and *mixtures*;
- (c) check of plant and equipment;
- (d) allocation of personnel;
- (e) personal fitness of *divers* for underwater operations;
- (f) precautions against cold in and out of the water;
- (g) signalling procedures;
- (h) precautions against underwater hazards of the diving site.

Procedures during diving

3. (a) Responsibilities of *diving supervisor, divers* and surface support;
- (b) use of all types of personal diving equipment;
- (c) supply of gas and gas mixture, including maximum and mimimum partial pressure of gases;
- (d) operations direct from an installation, work site or craft;
- (e) operations in relation to diving bell;
- (f) working in different locations;
- (g) operations and use of equipment under water;
- (h) limits on depth and time under water;
- (i) descent, ascent and recovery of *divers*;
- (j) descent, ascent and recovery of *diving bell*;
- (k) diving tables for use in decompression procedures for both single and repetitive diving and in therapeutic decompression procedures; and for inland waters the need to take account of the effect on pressure of the altitudes at which the diving takes place;
- (l) control in changing conditions;
- (m) time for which *divers* are to remain in vicinity of the surface compression chamber;
- (n) maintenance of log books.

Emergency procedure

4. (a) Emergency signalling;
- (b) emergency assistance under water and on the surface;
- (c) therapeutic recompression and decompression and the availability of chambers for that purpose;
- (d) first aid;
- (e) medical assistance;
- (f) calling assistance from emergency services including advance liaison with those services where appropriate;
- (g) precautions in the event of evacuation of the installation, work site, vessel, hovercraft or floating structure;
- (h) provision of emergency electrical supplies.

SCHEDULE 1A

Regulation 5A

PARTICULARS OF DIVING CONTRACTORS

1. The *diving contractor's* name and the address where notices may be served on him.

2. A telephone number where the *diving contractor* may be contacted.

3. Any location where the *diving contractor* knows or expects he will undertake *diving operations* in the next year.

4. Whether the *diving contractor* will undertake *diving operations*—
(a) at any premises or in relation to any activities mentioned in article 4, other than article 4(2)(a), or article 5 of the 1989 Order; or
(b) at premises and in circumstances other than those mentioned in sub-paragraph (a); or
(c) both.
5. The nature of the work likely to be done during intended *diving operations.*
6. The level of competence likely to be required of divers (expressed by reference to the relevant Parts of Schedule 4).

SCHEDULE 1B

Regulation 5C

PARTICULARS OF DIVING PROJECTS

1. The *diving contractor's* name and address where notices may be served on him.
2. A telephone number where the *diving contractor* may be contacted.
3. The date or dates the *diving operation* or operations will start.
4. The number of days on which it is expected *diving operations* will take place.
5. The location or locations where diving will take place, including, in particular any offshore installation or pipeline in respect of or in connection with which diving will take place.
6. The total number of persons who will or are expected to comprise the *diving team.*
7. Whether the breathing mixture will be air or the *diving* will use saturation techniques.
8. The name or other sufficient identification of each diving support vessel, barge, installation or other place from which divers are intended to be deployed, and the method of maintaining its position at the location where diving will take place.
9. A description of the nature and purpose of the *diving operation* or operations sufficient to show what risks are involved.
10. The name of an individual who is able to make arrangements to facilitate any inspection and a telephone number where that individual may be contacted.

SCHEDULE 2

Regulation 6

MATTERS TO BE ENTERED IN THE DIVING OPERATIONS LOG BOOK

The following matters shall be entered in the diving operations log book in respect of each *diving operation*—
(a) the name of the *diving contractor;*
(b) the dates on which and the period during which the *diving operation* was carried on;
(c) the name or other designation of the craft or *offshore installation* or work site in connection with which the *diving operation* was carried on and the location of that craft or *offshore installation* or work site;
(d) the name of the *diving supervisor* and the period for which he is acting in that capacity in respect of that *diving operation;*
(e) the names of the other persons engaged in the *diving operation* including those operating any diving plant or equipment and their respective duties;
(f) the arrangements for emergency support;
(g) the procedures followed in the course of the *diving operation* including details of the decompression schedule used;

(h)   the maximum depth reached in the course of the operation for each *diver*;

(i)   for each *diver*, in respect of each dive he makes, the time he leaves the surface, his bottom time (that is the period from the time he leaves the surface until he starts to ascend) and the time he reaches the surface;

(j)   the type of *breathing* apparatus and *mixture* used;

(k)   the nature of the *diving operation*;

(l)   any decompression sickness, other illness, discomfort or injury suffered by any of the *divers*;

(m)   particulars of any *emergency* which occurred during the *diving operation* and any action taken;

(n)   any defects that are discovered in any plant or equipment used in the *diving operations*;

(o)   particulars of any environmental factors affecting the *diving operation*;

(p)   any other factors relevant to the safety or health of the persons engaged in the operation.

SCHEDULE 3

Regulation 7

MATTERS TO BE ENTERED IN THE DIVER'S LOG BOOK

The following matters shall be entered in the diver's log book in respect of each *diving operation* in which he take part—

(a)   the name and address of the *diving contractor*;

(b)   the date;

(c)   the name or other designation and the location of the *offshore installation*, work site, craft or harbour from which the *diving operation* was carried on;

(d)   the name of the *diving supervisor*;

(e)   the maximum depth reached on each occasion;

(f)   the time he left the surface, his bottom time and the time he reached the surface on each occasion;

(g)   where the dive includes time spent in a compression chamber, details of any time spent outside the chamber at a different pressure;

(h)   the type of *breathing* apparatus and *mixture* used by him;

(i)   any work done by him on each occasion and the equipment (including tools) used by him in that work;

(j)   any decompression schedules followed by him on each occasion;

(k)   any decompression sickness or other illness, discomfort or injury suffered by him;

(l)   any other factor relevant to his safety or health.

SCHEDULE 4

Regulation 10(1)(b)(iii)

MATTERS IN RESPECT OF WHICH A DIVER HAS TO ATTAIN A SATISFACTORY STANDARD OF COMPETENCE

PART I

BASIC AIR DIVING

1. The theory of air diving.

2. Use of *self-contained* and surface supplied diving equipment.

3. Diving safely and competently in various conditions not exceeding 50 metres in depth, including the safe use of hand tools and hand held power tools and equipment.

4. Use of diver communication systems appropriate to air diving.

5. Emergency procedures for air diving.

6. Surface compression chamber operation, therapeutic recompression, decompression and the decompression tables appropriate to air diving.

7. [*revoked*].

8. Relevant legislation and guidance.

PART II
MIXED GAS OR BELL DIVING

1. All the matters specified in Part I of this Schedule.

2. The theory of mixed gas and *bell diving*.

3. Glass and gas systems.

4. Diving safely and competently to representative depths exceeding 50 metres from a *diving bell*.

5. Use of diver communication systems appropriate to mixed gas and *bell diving*.

6. Diving bell operation, transferring to surface compression chamber, recompression on mixed gas and decompression and decompression tables appropriate to mixed gas diving.

7. Emergency procedure for mixed gas and *bell diving*.

8. [*revoked*].

9. Legislation and guidance relevant to mixed gas diving not covered under paragraph 8 of Part I of this Schedule.

PART III
AIR DIVING WHERE NO SURFACE COMPRESSION CHAMBER IS REQUIRED ON SITE

1. The theory of air diving.

2. Use of surface-supplied diving equipment.

3. Use of *self-contained* diving equipment.

4. Diving safely and competently in various conditions.

5. Use of diver communication systems appropriate to air diving.

6. Emergency procedures for air diving.

7. Therapeutic recompression, decompression and the decompression tables appropriate to air diving.

8. [*revoked*].

9. Relevant legislation and guidance.

PART IV
AIR DIVING WITH SELF-CONTAINED EQUIPMENT WHERE NO SURFACE COMPRESSION CHAMBER IS REQUIRED ON SITE

All matters specified in Part III except the use of surface-supplied diving equipment.

SCHEDULE 5
Regulation 12(1)(f)

SURFACE COMPRESSION CHAMBERS

A surface compression chamber shall—

    (a) have at least two compartments with doors each of which acts as a pressure seal and can be opened from either side ("a two-compartment chamber"); or alternatively a single compartment chamber may be used where—

        (i) the *divers* do not go to a depth exceeding 50 metres, and

(ii) the *diving operations* are not carried on from or in connection with an *offshore installation* or *pipe-line works,* and

(iii) facilities are provided for transferring persons under pressure from that chamber to a two-compartment chamber within four hours;

(b) in the case of a two-compartment chamber, have sufficient space in at least one of its compartments to enable two adults to lie down inside the chamber without difficulty and if the chamber is to be used in circumstances in which a person is intended to remain inside under pressure for a continuous period of 12 hours or more, excluding any therapeutic decompression, it shall have a minimum internal diameter of two metres, except that in the case of equipment taken into use for the first time before 1 July 1982 the minimum internal diameter shall be 1.75 metres;

(c) where a *diving bell* is used, be capable of allowing a person to transfer under pressure from the bell to the surface compression chamber and vice versa;

(d) provide a suitable environment and suitable facilities for the persons who are to use it, having regard to the kind of operation in connection with which it is used and the period during which the pressure is raised;

(e) be so designed as to minimise the risk of fire;

(f) have a lock through which food and medical supplies may be passed into the chamber while its occupants remain under pressure;

(g) be equipped with such valves, gauges and other fittings (which are to be made of suitable materials and so designed as to minimise the noise inside the chamber during rapid pressurisation) as are necessary to control and indicate the internal pressures of each compartment from outside the chamber;

(h) be fitted with adequate equipment, including reserve facilities, for supplying and maintaining the appropriate *breathing mixture* to persons inside it;

(i) be equipped with a two-way oral communication system;

(j) be fitted with equipment for heating and lighting the chamber and adequate sanitary facilities.

SCHEDULE 6

Regulation 12(1)(g)

DIVING BELLS

A *diving bell* shall—

(a) be equipped with means by which each *diver* using the bell is able to enter and leave it without difficulty;

(b) be capable of allowing a person to transfer under pressure from it to a surface compression chamber and vice versa;

(c) be equipped with doors which act as pressure seals and which may be opened from either side;

(d) be equipped with such valves, gauges and other fittings (which are to be made of suitable materials) as are necessary to control and indicate the pressure within the bell as to indicate to those inside the bell and to the *diving supervisor* the external pressure on the bell;

(e) be fitted with adequate equipment including reserve facilities for supplying the appropriate *breathing mixture* to persons occupying or working from the bell;

(f) be equipped with a two-way oral communication system which enables contact to be maintained both with persons at the place from which the *diving operation* is carried on and with *divers* while they are outside the bell;

(g) be fitted with equipment for lighting and heating the bell;

(h) without prejudice to the generality of regulation 13A(1), contain adequate *first-aid* equipment and facilities and be fitted with lifting equipment sufficient to enable an unconscious or injured *diver* to be hoisted into the bell by a person inside;

(i) be provided with means by which, in the event of any *emergency*, it can be rapidly located by through water signals from the stricken bell and the lives of trapped persons can be sustained for at least 24 hours or, where that is not practicable, sustained for as long as is practicable;

(j) be used in association with lifting gear which enables the chamber to be lowered to the depth from which the *diving operations* are to be carried on, maintained in its position and raised, in each case without excessive lateral, vertical or rotational movement taking place; and

(k) be provided with a means by which, in the event of failure of the main lifting gear, the chamber can be returned to the surface; if those means involve the shedding of weights, they shall be capable of being shed from the bell by a person inside it and a means shall be incorporated to prevent their accidental shedding.

CERTIFICATE OF EXEMPTION No. DOW/1/81
(GENERAL)

The Health and Safety Executive in exercise of the powers conferred on it by regulation 14 of the Diving Operations at Work Regulations 1981 and being satisfied that the health and safety of persons who are likely to be affected by the exemption will not be prejudiced in consequence of it HEREBY EXEMPT diving operations—

(a) which are primarily for the purposes of archaeology, and

(b) in which no person at work dives at a greater depth than 50 metres or his routine decompression time exceeds 20 minutes,

from regulations 4, 5, 6, 7(1)(a), 7(2), 7(3)(b), 8, 9, 10, 12 and 13 of, and Schedules 1 to 6 to, the Diving Operations at Work Regulations 1981 SUBJECT TO the following conditions in relation to each such diving operation—

1. That every person diving at work and his employer, if any, ensures so that as is reasonably practicable that—

(a) the plant and equipment which he will use—

   (i) include a means of supplying a breathing mixture (including a reserve supply for immediate use in the event of an emergency or for therapeutic recompression or decompression) suitable in content and temperature and of adequate pressure, and at an adequate rate, to sustain prolonged vigorous physical exertion at the ambient pressure for the duration of the diving operation;

  (ii) is properly designed, of adequate strength and of good construction from sound and suitable material;

 (iii) is suitable for the condition in which it is intended to be used;

 (iv) where its safe use depends on the depth or pressure at which it is used, is marked with its safe working pressure or the maximum depth at which it may be used;

  (v) at whatever temperature it is to be used, is adequately protected against malfunctioning at that temperature;

(b) each gas cylinder he will use is legibly marked "breathing air".

2. That every person diving at work—

(a) is trained and competent to operate the plant and equipment he will use;

(b) ensures that the plant and equipment he will use is inspected by a competent person within the six hours immediately before he dives and ensures so far as is reasonably practicable that it is maintained in a safe condition whilst it is being used.

3. That every person diving at work ensures so far as is reasonably practicable that—

(a) the diving operation is carried on in accordance with a code of safe diving practice;

(b) there is a person on the surface in immediate control of the operation;

(c) there is another person available to render assistance in an emergency, that other person being either on the surface in immediate readiness to dive or in the water in a position to render assistance.

4. That every person diving at work enters the following particulars in the log book required by regulation 7(3)(a) of the Regulations—

(a) the date;

(b) the name or other designation and the location of the work site;

(c) the maximum depth reached on each occasion;

(d) the time he left the surface, his bottom time and the time he reached the surface on each occasion;

(e) the type of breathing apparatus used by him;

(f) any work done by him on each occasion and the equipment (including tools) used by him in that work;

(g) any decompression schedules followed by him on each occasion;

(h) any decompression sickness or other illness, discomfort or injury suffered by him;

(i) any other factors relevant to his safety or health.

CERTIFICATE OF EXEMPTION No. DOW/2/81
(GENERAL)

The Health and Safety Executive in exercise of the powers conferred on it by regulation 14 of the Diving Operations at Work Regulations 1981 and being satisfied that the health and safety of persons who are likely to be affected by the exemption will not be prejudiced in consequence of it HEREBY EXEMPT diving operations—

(a) which are primarily for the purposes of journalism, and

(b) in which no person at work dives at a greater depth than 50 metres or his routine decompression time exceeds 20 minutes,

from regulations 4, 5, 6, 7(1)(a), 7(2), 7(3)(b), 8, 9, 10, 12 and 13 of, and Schedules 1 to 6 to, the Diving Operations at Work Regulations 1981 SUBJECT TO the following conditions in relation to each such diving operation—

1. That every person diving at work and his employer, if any, ensures so far as is reasonably practicable that—

(a) the plant and equipment which he will use—

(i) include a means of supplying a breathing mixture (including a reserve supply for immediate use in the event of an emergency or for therapeutic recompression or decompression) suitable in content and temperature and of adequate pressure, and at an adequate rate, to sustain prolonged vigorous physical exertion at the ambient pressure for the duration of the diving operation;

(ii) is properly designed, of adequate strength and of good construction from sound and suitable material;

(iii) is suitable for the conditions in which it is intended to be used;

(iv) where its safe use depends on the depth or pressure at which it is used, is marked with its safe working pressure or the maximum depth at which it may be used;

(v)   at whatever temperature it is to be used, is adequately protected against malfunctioning at that temperature;

(b) each gas cylinder he will use is legibly marked "breathing air".

2. That every person diving at work—

(a) is trained and competent to operate the plant and equipment he will use;

(b) ensures that the plant and equipment he will use is inspected by a competent person within the six hours immediately before he dives and ensures so far as is reasonably practicable that it is maintained in a safe condition whilst it is being used.

3. That every person diving at work ensures so far as is reasonably practicable that—

(a) the diving operation is carried on in accordance with a code of safe diving practice;

(b) there is a person on the surface in immediate control of the operation;

(c) there is another person available to render assistance in an emergency, that other person being either on the surface in immediate readiness to dive or in the water in a position to render assistance.

4. That every person diving at work enters the following particulars in the log book required by regulation 7(3)(a) of the Regulations—

(a) the date;

(b) the name or other designation and the location of the work site;

(c) the maximum depth reached on each occasion;

(d) the time he left the surface, his bottom time and the time he reached the surface on each occasion;

(e) the type of breathing apparatus used by him;

(f) any work done by him on each occasion and the equipment (including tools) used by him in that work;

(g) any decompression schedules followed by him on each occasion;

(h) any decompression sickness or other illness, discomfort or injury suffered by him;

(i) any other factors relevant to his safety or health.

CERTIFICATE OF EXEMPTION No. DOW/4/81
(GENERAL)

The Health and Safety Executive in exercise of the powers conferred on it by regulation 14 of the Diving Operations at Work Regulations 1981 and being satisfied that the health and safety of persons who are likely to be affected by the exemption will not be prejudiced in consequence of it HEREBY EXEMPT diving operations—

(a) which are solely in connection with the training of amateur divers, and

(b) in which no person at work dives at a greater depth than 50 metres or his routine decompression time exceeds 20 minutes,

from regulations 4, 5, 6, 7(2), 7(3)(b), 8, 9, 12 and 13 of, and Schedules 1, 2, 3, 5 and 6, to the Regulations subject to the following conditions in relation to each such diving operation—

1. That every person diving at work and his employer, if any, ensures so far as is reasonably practical that—

(a) the plant and equipment he will use—

(i) include a means of supplying a breathing mixture (including a reserve supply for immediate use in the event of an emergency or for therapeutic recompression or decompression) suitable in content and temperature and of adequate pressure, and at an adequate rate, to sustain prolonged vigorous physical exertion at the ambient pressure for the duration of the diving operation;

(ii) is properly designed, of adequate strength and of good construction from sound and suitable material;

(iii) is suitable for the conditions in which is is intended to be used;

(iv) where its safe use depends on the depth or pressure at which it is used, is marked with its safe working pressure or the maximum depth at which it may be used;

(v) at whatever temperature it is to be used, is adequately protected against malfunctioning at that temperature;

(b) each gas cylinder he will use is legibly marked "breathing air".

2. That every person diving at work—

(a) is trained and competent to operate the plant and equipment he will use;

(b) ensures that the plant and equipment he will use is inspected by a competent person within the six hours immediately before he dives and ensures so far as is reasonably practicable that it is maintained in a safe condition whilst it is being used.

3. That every person diving at work ensures so far as is reasonably practicable—
(a) the diving operation is carried on in accordance with a code of safe diving practice;
(b) when he is diving other than in a swimming pool or training tank there is a person on the surface in immediate control of the operation;
(c) there is another person available to render assistance in an emergency, that other person being either on the surface in immediate readiness to dive or in the water in a position to render assistance.

4. That every person diving at work enters the following particulars of every operation in his personal log book required by regulation 7(3)(a) and in an operations record book—

Personal Log Book
(a) Name and place at which the operation is carried on;
(b) Date and period during which the operation was carried out;
(c) Details of each dive, including depth and time;
(d) Particulars of any emergency and action taken;
(e) Signature of diver at work.

Operations Record Book
(f) Name and place at which the operation was carried on;
(g) Date and period during which the operation was carried on;
(h) Names of persons giving and details of each individual's dive including time and depth;
(i) Particulars of any emergency and action taken;
(j) Signature of diver at work.

INDEX

NOTES

NOTES

OLD EDITION
see 3rd ed.
with JVosper

¡ WARNING !
OUT OF DATE
PUBLICATION
Use at own Risk!